Operation World is a tremendously useful resource that I use personally, with my family and in my ministry. No Christian family, local church library, Christian leader should be without this vision building, prayer enhancing, information packed tool.

Rev Dr Geoff Tunnicliffe, CEO/Secretary General, World Evangelical Alliance

For years I have used *Operation World* to pray for people in every tongue, tribe and nation. *Operation World* is a time-honored and well-tested global manual of prayer which will provide for you everything you need to bring the nations of the world before the throne of God. It will expand your heart, vision and passion for the peoples of the world and God's deep desire to reach those in the darkest corners with His help and hope.

Joni Eareckson Tada, Author & Speaker

Operation World is one of the most important Christian books in the world because it mobilises the church to reliably informed intercession. As a long-haired student I kept a previous edition by my bedside and prayed through almost every nation. Today, I recommend *Operation World* wherever I go. Jason Mandryk and his team have done the Body of Christ a great service through years of research, analysis and impressive attention to detail. Just as Generals need military intelligence and doctors check the pulse, so pastors, missionaries and intercessors will want this latest edition of *Operation World* on their bookshelves. Or better still beside their beds.

Pete Greig, International Director, 24-7 Prayer and Director of Prayer, Alpha International

I have been involved with this book for over 35 years as a part of my spiritual DNA. A few words come to mind, first of all 'information': a wealth of information. Secondly, 'vision': this book is going to help you increase your vision for the people of the world and for how God is working across the world. Third, 'prayer': it's going to help you in your ministry of prayer. A lot of people have told me how this book has completely changed their viewpoint and their way of life through prayer. This is probably one of the most important missionary tools in the entire history of missions.

George Verwer, Founder, Operation Mobilization and World Missions Advocate

Only in heaven will be known the effect that prayer has had in speeding the work of world evangelisation. We may discover that it was the most powerful force exerted by the church in making a difference in this world. But to pray powerfully we must be informed. Throughout modern missions, innovative Christians have found ways to inform people praying for the world. Few have been as effective and useful as *Operation World*. I am so happy that a new edition is being released.

Ajith Fernando, National Director, Youth for Christ, Sri Lanka

Outside of the Bible, no book has had a greater practical impact on my personal prayer life than *Operation World*. God has used this book to open my eyes and the eyes of the church I pastor to the needs of the world and the greatness of the God who desires to make His glory known in the world. I eagerly welcome this new edition and wholeheartedly recommend it.

David Platt, Senior Pastor, The Church at Brook Hills, USA and Author of *Radical: Taking Back Your Faith from the American Dream*

Operation World has been one of the greatest tools for prayer mobilization for our world ever since it was first published. The scope and thoroughness of the research done by Jason Mandryk and his colleagues is truly commendable.

Dr Joseph D'souza, President, Dalit Freedom Network

In the world of missions, I know of nothing more significant than *Operation World*, when it comes to learning about the need, opportunity and prayer points for world evangelism. Here is your bridge to walk into every continent, nation, community and touch them with your prayers and commitment. In my 44 years of involvement in world missions, the information from *Operation World* gave me understanding and motivation to pray and do what I could to fulfill the desire of God's heart to reach the untold millions. Next to your Bible, *Operation World* will be the most important book you will own. Go nowhere without it. Pray daily sharing the burden of our Lord.

Dr K P Yohannan, International Director, Gospel For Asia

Operation World is incendiary. The information is solid and engaging. But what may surprise you is the sense of anticipation that God really is advancing and fulfilling His purposes in every people and place. That spark of hope makes it easy to escape the boredom of your own concerns and pray with sincerity and clarity for distant lands and peoples. It's like building a fire with wood already soaked in gasoline.

Steve Hawthorne, Co-Editor, *Perspectives on the World Christian Movement*

In six passages, the scriptures are clear: Christ won't come back until all nations (ethnic groups) are reached. If you cherish Christ and his return, get to know the nations and focus your prayer and efforts on redeeming them for His kingdom. The best way to begin this process is through *Operation World*!

Bob Sjogren, President, UnveilinGLORY

Operation World continues to be the most informative, visionary prayer guide to missions throughout the world today. It helps believers everywhere to expand their vision and pray knowledgeably about the critical needs in every country. It is making a tremendous contribution to the fulfillment of the Great Commission.

Paul Eshleman, Vice President, Campus Crusade for Christ International and Director, Finishing the Task Network

I am honored to commend *Operation World* to all Christians everywhere, who believe we must pray for the harvest! Each week we hold a global prayer time focusing on a nation of the world. We therefore pray through the world every 4 years. *Operation World* is our text, bringing clarity to our prayers, and vision for the task to take the gospel to all nations!

Lon Allison, D Min, Executive Director, Billy Graham Center, Wheaton College, USA

In my opinion, *Operation World* is the premier publication available for reliable statistics. Without fail, I have my students refer to this invaluable resource as they prepare their country profiles.

Phil Parshall, SIM-USA Missionary at Large and Author

With its international network of ministries operating in every continent, Langham Partnership International has found *Operation World* to be an invaluable source of background information on every country we work in - and many where we don't yet but hope to as God opens doors in the future. It has provided an objective platform of information that combines well with our own experiential perceptions in the task of strategic planning. We eagerly look forward to accessing the information in this updated version.

Christopher J H Wright, International Director, Langham Partnership International and Author of *The Mission of God*

The day after I became a Christian in the 1980s, the friend who led me to Christ took me to a bookstore and bought two books for me - The Bible and *Operation World*. The Scriptures helped me gain God's heart for the nations, and *Operation World* helped focus my life on where and how I could strategically serve Him. Later we founded a ministry and have produced a number of books profiling Asia's unreached people groups. The Body of Christ owes much to Jason and his team for their hard work. I am glad to endorse *Operation World* to all believers who are interested in seeing the Great Commission completed and the Name of Jesus glorified throughout the earth.

Paul Hattaway, Author of *The Heavenly Man* and *Operation China* and Director, Asia Harvest

Operation World changed our lives! In 1999, my wife and I began praying for a country each night in *Operation World*. God opened our hearts wide for lost people especially in the Middle East. Every night as we would read about Iran, Israel and other nations, our hearts were gripped with the need to reach these countries for Christ. Within two years, God called us to leave senior pastoring a local church in the Colorado Springs area and to go to the very places that we had been praying for! So as you pray through *Operation World*, just remember, God may radically change your world to reach His world.

Tom and JoAnn Doyle, e3 Partners, Middle East-Central Asia

The greatest contribution to effective intercession for the nations ever published is *Operation World*. This comprehensive guide is the first source our ministry goes to in gathering information for practical, focused, intercessory prayer for what God is doing globally. There is simply nothing comparable. To pray through this fact-filled guide annually is to become a true missionary of prayer to the nations of the world!

Dr Dick Eastman, International President, Every Home for Christ

For many years, Voice of the Martyrs has relied on *Operation World's* meticulously researched information in our efforts to help persecuted believers and motivate Christians in America to pray. In our ministry, we are constantly urging our readers to pray, because we know the power of prayer.

Operation World provides detailed, first-rate information that is not readily available elsewhere. This information is invaluable for understanding the circumstances of Christians around the world and for praying in a more focused manner for specific situations. I am grateful for people who pray for the nations. It is my privilege to recommend the 2010 edition of *Operation World*. I hope it will encourage you to continue praying for God's work around the world.

Tom White, Executive Director, Voice of the Martyrs

Operation World has remained a veritable source of mission information about the status of the remaining task and a tool that brings together in one volume detailed update that inspires passion for the unreached and stirs up hearts to intercede. There are also illustrations and stories which proffer transferable strategies and techniques for engaging the task as well as highlight strategic networking patterns. The previous editions have been both mission handbook and missiological compass which had contributed immensely in advancing the cause of missions especially in the global south. I am very much expectant about greater impact from this current edition and therefore strongly recommend it to the seriously minded mission community.

Reuben Ezemadu, International Director, Christian Missionary Foundation (CMF) and Continental Coordinator, Movement for African National Initiatives

Operation World, since its inception, has been a great gift to God's global church. It offers a clear concise update on the state of each country in the world with some helpful prayer points. It is a wonderful resource which has been widely used among university students around the world and has been a great means of increasing their global awareness. I use it myself. It is an invaluable resource. It is one of the best resources I know to enable pastors and Christian leaders to help those in their care to become better informed and, as a result, engaged in contributing to taking the gospel to the ends of the earth by praying, supporting or going.

Lindsay Brown, International Director, Lausanne Committee for World Evangelization

I am delighted to commend the new edition of *Operation World* after much work by the totally dedicated Jason Mandryk and his hard-working team with newer insights, fresh facts and up-to-date information of the world to fuel prayer and plan the way forward in missions. I associate my own zeal for world prayer and missional growth to my involvement with the *Operation World* project since the early '80s. *OW* has became a very special most used effective authentic encyclopedic referring tool for even the newly born first-generation churches to become World Christians. *OW* has conscientized, prompted all missional followers of Christ, drawing them out of parochialism to envision the world with a new passion and strategy to communicate the Gospel to the globalised lost world to follow Christ. *OW* birthed many mission movements by its passionate appeal and correct information. I warmly appreciate and recommend this new *Operation World* to move us forward with the Gospel afresh across the globe more than ever. May you be a changed person after using the new *OW* to proclaim the Good News of the Savior, the Lord Jesus Christ.

Dr K Rajendran, General Secretary, India Missions Association and Chairman, World Evangelical Alliance Mission Commission.

No other tool has impacted WEC as a mission agency more than *Operation World*. The data has guided our strategies and new advances and the prayers stimulated by this resource have been God's tool to bring transformation into lives and people groups. God has truly used *Operation World* to shape us as a mission and to change the world.

Louis Sutton, International Director-elect, WEC International

Few documents combine the awesome effect of touching individuals, movements and nations. *Operation World* has also changed the way the Church in Africa, especially IFES students, prays for the world and its people. By facilitating global intercession *Operation World* has contributed immensely in provoking a global vision for the world-wide Church. This all-important fuel-for-prayer document has no doubt helped many, including my family and I, to pray for the world in an informed and innovative manner. Do not miss the opportunity to change the world through transformational prayer - *OW* provides an excellent road-map.

Rev Gideon Para-Mallam, Regional Secretary, IFES and International Deputy Director for English and Portuguese Speaking Africa, Lausanne Committee for World Evangelization

For decades, *Operation World* has been the most significant book in the global missions movement. This edition continues that unparalleled tradition. Read this volume with an open heart. You will learn spiritual intelligence on what God is doing around the globe. More than that, however, pray through this book. You will be a partner with the Lord in advancing his kingdom against all the powers of darkness.

Stan Guthrie, Editor at Large, *Christianity Today* and Author of *Missions in the Third Millennium* and *All That Jesus Asks*

Operation World grabs your heart and brings you to your knees on behalf of a world in need of Jesus. Meticulously researched, it represents one of the finest resources anywhere for those engaged in the Great Commission. Next to my Bible, it's one of the first tools I reach for in mobilizing believers for mission - whether in Bulawayo or Boise. Let it expand your world...and inspire you to touch the nations!

Dr Dean Carlson, Vice-President of Global Ministries, OC International and Global Advocate, Movement for African National Initiatives

I personally welcome the 2010 edition of *Operation World*. Since the time the first edition of this book was printed, the world has been different, because it was possible for us to know where the need for the gospel was and gave us a detailed picture of unreached nations and peoples. The Spanish version was obligatory reading for all those who were interested in mission. Hundreds were called to the mission field by reading its pages and we hope it will continue happening with this new edition.

David Ruiz, Associate Director, World Evangelical Alliance Mission Commission

As a producer of reference works on global Christianity that usually are destined for library collections, I greatly anticipate the arrival of a new edition of *Operation World*. It provides an affordable, compact, and portable guide to the world while maintaining high standards for research and carefully-crafted analysis as a backdrop for prayer. Enthusiastically recommended!

Todd M Johnson, Center for the Study of Global Christianity, Gordon-Conwell Theological Seminary

Operation World is a powerful prayer-guide-and-encyclopedia-in-one that helps believers to pray strategically and effectively for the nations. Knowledgeable, strategic prayers are like laser-guided missiles that first pass the throne of God, and eventually hit their mark. This resource is the GPS that helps us know how to specifically direct our prayers. *OW* is for people who are not content with simple 'bless the nations' prayers. It provides helpful information so believers can pray strategically for key issues and concerns of a nation.

Dave Flynn, National Director, Perspectives Study Program

Operation World is an 'out of the stands and onto the playing field' kind of book. Other than Scripture, *Operation World* has the potential to have the greatest impact on the life of a believer of any book ever published. It uniquely reveals the heart-throb of God for the world and His unfolding drama of redeeming followers of Jesus from every tribe, tongue, nation and people. Be prepared for a radical transformation in how you view the world and your Christian life!

Daniel Scribner, Director, Joshua Project

This longstanding and trusted resource cuts through the fog to provide an up-to-date snap-shot of what in the world God is doing among the peoples. *Operation World* will become one of your most valuable books for understanding the nations and how to pray for them! Get it, but don't shelve it. Use it!

J D Payne, National Missionary, North American Mission Board and Associate Professor of Church Planting and Evangelism, Southern Baptist Theological Seminary

Operation World

Seventh Edition

Operation World

Seventh Edition

Jason Mandryk

WEC International

Biblica Publishing
We welcome your questions and comments.

USA   1820 Jet Stream Drive, Colorado Springs, CO 80921
www.Biblica.com

Operation World
Hardcover edition: **ISBN: 978-1-85078-861-4**
Paperback edition: **ISBN: 978-1-85078-862-1**

12 11   / 6 5 4 3

Published in 2010 by Biblica Publishing

A catalog record for this book is available through the Library of Congress.

1st edition	Dorothea Mission	1974
2nd edition	STL	1978
	revised	1979
3rd edition	STL	1980
4th edition	STL & WEC International	1986
	reprinted 1986, 1987, 1990 (twice)	
5th edition	OM Publishing	1993
	reprinted with corrections 1995	
	reprinted 1997, 1998, 2000	
6th edition	Authentic Lifestyle	2001
	updated and revised 2005	
	reprinted 2008, 2009	
7th edition	Biblica Publishing	2010
	reprinted 2011 (twice)	

Cover design by projectluz.com
Interior design by Samantha Redwood
Printed in the United States of America

A Note from Patrick Johnstone

The achievement of Jason and his team in completing this edition of *Operation World* should not be underestimated! Praise God that this edition is now complete.

Jason and I completed the last re-write in 2001. Publication was three days before the world-changing impact of 9/11. The book was immediately out of date, though many of the subsequent events were already hinted at in the completed text.

Some have commented to me, "How can you give away your 'baby'?" My quick response is, "Very easily!" *Operation World* has been part of my life since I was a young missionary of 26, and I grew with the book. Yet I am convinced of the biblical ministry model of timely handover of leadership and responsibility, but finding a successor had to be something God brought about. I believed that Jason Mandryk was the right person able to take on this challenge. He had the harder task to pick up a matured ministry and produce a new edition that maintained both past achievements and improved on them. I trust that readers concur that the quality, accuracy and appositeness of each prayer point or observation bears this out. I knew that I was committing Jason to years of effort that demanded a high degree of dedication, loneliness, frustration and spiritual battles. Every edition has had its death points so that completion looks an impossible dream. Jason has had these in good measure.

My own contribution to this volume has been limited to prayer, preparing improvements in measuring the world's evangelicals and responses to questions from Jason and the team. It is no longer "my" book! Operation World is more than a prayer manual; its database is unique and contains over 50 years of statistics relating to world evangelization, but we have never before used this to explain the trends they reveal. A year after publication of this edition of *Operation World* I aim to publish an illustrated book in print and electronic format, *The Future of the World-wide Church, Possibilities for 21st Century Ministry*, which is intended to do this.

This English edition is not the only one we expect to see published. Past editions have been published in German, Korean, Portuguese, Spanish, French, etc, and more recently in Chinese and other languages. This delights me because they have been a contributing factor to the emergence of a worldwide missions force as Christians pored over the global information and turned this into prayer and vision for going out in obedience to the Great Commission. I believe this edition will contribute even more to this healthy globalization.

May our world be significantly impacted and changed as fruit of this labour.

Patrick Johnstone
WEC International
England
August 2010

Contents

The World and its Regions

Countries

Operation World

Contents

Notes:

1. Territories without permanent inhabitants have not been listed, including Antarctica.

2. States under the occupation or jurisdiction of other states are included under the latter. For instance, the Western Sahara is under Morocco; Tibet is under China; Kosovo is under Serbia. This is to represent the de facto situation and is not an expression of a political opinion.

Appendices

Acknowledgements

When I accepted the mantle of *Operation World* from Patrick Johnstone, I did so with a mixture of soberness and exhilaration, of anticipation and foreboding. Had I known the trials and tribulations about to ensue, I would have thought and prayed a lot longer before accepting! It has been an exercise in patience, in faith and often in desperation. It has been the locus wherein the Spirit of God stretched, grew and indeed humbled me. Yet these past few years have also been a great blessing. To daily encounter reports and stories of God at work among the nations and to meet so many saints who live and work for His glory and the completion of the Great Commission is truly a rare privilege for which I thank God.

I cannot "sign off" on this project without acknowledging the long-term love and prayers of my family, especially my parents, as well as my two home churches, Trinity Baptist Church in Winnipeg and the King's Church in Amersham. Their encouragement and the gracious generosity of a handful of long-term supporters have enabled me to be here.

But this work has been, almost from the outset, a team effort. To recount every person in each country who assisted us in one way or another would require another book in itself. This list must be limited to a small proportion of all who had a hand in the process. We must begin with all those who volunteered their time and efforts in the last five years by coming here to Bulstrode to work with us on site. These precious friends are:

Peter Yardley *England*	Since the early 1990s
Laura Worku *England*	Jan 2005–July 2006
Jasmine Jaffarian *USA*	June 2005–Aug 2005
Aaron Talbot *Canada*	Nov 2005–Oct 2006
Dave Bock *Canada*	April 2006
Anjali Sethi *Canada*	June 2006–May 2007, Aug 2009
Eunike Wetzel *Germany*	Sept 2006–Oct 2006
Isaque Hattu *Brazil*	March 2007
Matias Vallve & Susan Fischer *Chile*	Nov 2007–Feb 2008
Joy Lee *USA*	Dec 2007–Feb 2008
Daniel & Arnelle Helbling *USA*	April 2008–Oct 2008
Ann-Kathrin Bauer *Germany*	May 2008–Aug 2008
Elisama Lopes *Brazil*	May 2008–Aug 2008
Sammy Chan *Hong Kong*	July 2008
Miriam Soares de Almeida *Brazil*	Aug 2008–Oct 2008
Janete Lacerda *Brazil*	Oct 2008–Dec 2008
Julia Lee *Canada*	Jan 2009, Jan 2010
John Bardsley *Australia*	Feb 2009–July 2009
Nkosana Phiri *England*	Feb 2009–Dec 2009
Kannan Rajendran *India*	Nov 2009–Jan 2010

Those who have stayed the course and are with us as we complete this project come from a wide array of backgrounds, which has in itself made the Operation World team stronger and more balanced. As with the above list, all have contributed to varying degrees and in different ways, but all have been an integral part of the team, and God knows the value of their sacrificial labour. We are not just colleagues and brothers and sisters in Christ, but dear friends as well! Praise God for how He has worked in our midst, especially in the last few months of preparation. These include:

Jason Mandryk *Canada*	1995–present
Fiona Fraser *Scotland*	Nov 2005–present
Jenny Lo *USA*	Aug 2006–May 2007, Aug 2008–Aug 2010
(With gracious husband, **Abe Lo,** *and team mascot,* **Isaac Lo***)*	
Lisa Wyckoff *USA*	Nov 2007–present
Shin-seon Jeong *South Korea*	April 2008–June 2008, Dec 2009–present
Molly Wall *USA*	Jan 2009–present
Margaret Bardsley *Australia*	Feb 2009–present
Tony Woodward *England*	May 2009–present
Michael & Dawna Jaffarian *USA*	Oct 2009–present
David Phillips *England*	Feb 2010–present

Finally, several others must be mentioned for their specific roles in supporting the completion of this edition. Sincere thanks must be extended:

To the **WEC UK team** for providing leadership and spiritual covering to us, even amid transition for them.

To the **WEC International Office** for the fellowship, encouragement and direction offered out of love and affinity.

To the **Bulstrode community** for being gracious hosts to the Operation World offices and to many of the team members, and for bearing with us (and me!) even when we had to place more focus on our own project than on the wider fellowship.

To our agent, **Pieter Kwant**, for continuing to do such excellent work not merely in making our "product" successful but also in sharing our vision for the glory of God to be proclaimed among the nations.

To our **friends and partners at GMI** who once again furnished us with great skills and talents in the production of our maps, the electronic version of *Operation World* and the website.

To **Maurice Manktelow** for once again and in his spare time patiently coaching me through the steep learning curve of database development and for always finding time to bail us out of a fix when the skills required to achieve our needs were beyond me. Thanks also to **Chris Maynard** for his help extrapolating data for the graphs and charts.

To **our publishers** past and present. We enjoyed a long and close relationship with **Authentic UK**, but we are excited about the dynamism and shared vision of the **Biblica** team, with whom we have forged good bonds in a short period of time.

To our designers, **Paul Lewis** and **Samantha Redwood**, whose brilliant work freshened up the book while retaining the core elements that make it what it is, and to **Dana Bromley**, **Margaret Antill**, **J Robert Parks**, **Pamela Murray** and an array of volunteers for pouring their copyediting and proofing expertise into this lengthy manuscript.

As this years-long project comes to a conclusion, we have experienced a gamut of emotions!

Gratefulness to our Lord for His grace, enabling and guiding in the book's compilation, and His patience with us in all our human weakness.

Thankfulness to all past and present servants of the Lord whose contributions helped make *Operation World* the prayer and mobilization tool it has become. More than ever, *Operation World* is a global collaborative project due to the thousands of people who have contributed to this edition.

Relief that we completed such a massive project with its global and eternal implications. At times, it seemed impossible.

Expectation that God will use this edition to inform and inspire prayer for millions, mobilizing His Church to complete the Great Commission and hasten the return of the Lord Jesus.

Jason Mandryk
Bulstrode
United Kingdom
August 2010

A Brief History
Seventh Edition

A book such as this cannot be produced by one person alone, nor has it been. *Operation World,* as it is now known, was pioneered by and became almost synonymous with **Patrick Johnstone**. With Patrick moving on from the leadership role and handing the reins to me, I feel both honoured and inadequate to meet the high standards of spirituality and excellence in research that he has set. Here are a few of the many people, resources and events that shaped *Operation World* to become what it is today.

1792 **William Carey**'s vision for a lost world led to his writing the book *An Enquiry into the Obligation of Christians to Use Means for the Conversion of the Heathens.* This was the first global survey ever printed. His life and writing have inspired us all.

1900 **Dr Andrew Murray**, that great man of God in South Africa, challenged a sleeping Church in his book, *The Key to the Missionary Problem*, to hold **Weeks of Prayer for the World.**

1943 **Hans von Staden** was called of God to minister in the rapidly developing urban slums of Southern Africa. The **Dorothea Mission**, under his leadership, developed with a passion for evangelism and a strong emphasis on prayer, faith and vision for world evangelization. This became Patrick's heritage when he joined the work in 1962.

1962 **Weeks of Prayer for the World** began, and over the years probably 100 or so of these were held in Africa and Europe. It was Patrick's early involvement in these that impelled him to make maps and gather information that ordinary African Christians could understand and turn into intercession.

1964 The first *Operation World* was proposed by Hans von Staden, who also suggested the title. A little booklet, it covered 30 countries with basic information and some prayer items for use in the Weeks of Prayer.

1968 **Jill Amsden** married Patrick, joining their lives and ministries. Together they had three children. Jill ultimately became the author of the children's equivalent of *Operation World*, entitled *You Can Change the World*. She wrote this while ill with cancer, and completed the text of that remarkable book just before she died in 1992. **Daphne Spraggett** prepared the book for print and then wrote a second volume. Daphne then re-worked both books to produce a new combined volume entitled *Window on the World*. This in turn was the inspiration for the *Children's Prayer Atlas*, a project in progress from the Operation World (OW) team.

1974 The first globally-focused *Operation World*. When Patrick was challenged in 1970 to re-write it, he rashly said that any future edition would need to cover the world, not understanding then the enormity of the task! The work began, using odd moments in a busy itinerant ministry of team evangelism and Bible translation in Zimbabwe (then Rhodesia). His office was the back of a van or church vestries in towns and cities of that land. Two cardboard boxes served as filing cabinets. Major problems included the lack of any good missiological libraries and increasing postal isolation from the outside world due to sanctions imposed on Rhodesia. This limited edition was printed by the Dorothea Mission Press.

1975 **Dr Ralph Winter** arranged for its re-publication by the William Carey Library under the title *World Handbook for the World Christian*. This was a courageous step, for other well-known publishers turned it down as "unmarketable" – now to their expressed regret. We reckon that, in all six editions and in over 12 languages, over 2 million copies had been printed by 2005.

1976 **George Verwer** of **Operation Mobilisation** became involved. He pressed for a new edition, which was completed in 1978. This was the first edition published by **STL** (now **Biblica**). George has ever since remained *Operation World*'s greatest supporter and promoter.

1978 **Other language editions of** *Operation World* developed out of the 1978 edition. *Operation World* has been translated into 15 languages. Of these, multiple editions were published in German, French, Spanish, Portuguese and Korean. These versions have played a significant role in the burgeoning missions movement in the non-English-speaking world.

1979 **WEC International.** Patrick and Jill were released by the Dorothea Mission and commenced their ministry as International Directors for Research in WEC, a large pioneer church-planting mission with workers from all continents. These were times of restructuring and of rapid change, growth and advances into pioneer areas. It was in this context that the 1986 and 1993 editions of *Operation World* were written. During this time, the WEC International Research Office was developed, with its large holdings of global information, maps, databases and tools for envisioning the Church.

1994 I met Patrick for the first time as a graduate student at Providence Theological Seminary, where I learned much under the tutelage of my then academic mentor, **Dr Jonathan Bonk**. Dr Bonk's influence shaped me profoundly and prepared me for the work to which God called me after I attended a presentation by Patrick on the state of world evangelism. Patrick's rapid-fire use of overhead transparency maps, charts and other graphics, his global, organic view of the Church and his astonishing knowledge of the harvest field and harvest force were the catalysts God used to call me to Operation World.

1995 **Robyn Erwin** married Patrick and has stood with him in all the demands of public ministry since then.

1995 I joined WEC as a short-term worker for two years to work with Patrick. I did not know those two years would become 15 – and counting.

2001 The **Sixth Edition** was completed with the help of a capable and committed team. This edition saw more copies printed and a greater distribution of the electronic version than ever before. It also saw the launch of an Operation World website.

2002 I began a sabbatical period on the OM ship, **MV Doulos**. It was a brilliant experience that combined the learning and ministry skills I had acquired through *Operation World* with a stretching and growing time of public ministry in 30 countries.

2004 On my return to England, Patrick handed over the leadership of the Operation World team to me. This was a huge act of trust on his part and a huge leap of faith on mine. The "team" at that time consisted of only me – all others had moved on to other ministries or to glory.

2005 **A revised edition of the 2001 edition** was published. This incorporated changes in the post-9/11 world and the upheavals that shook many nations in those intervening years.

2005 Another Operation World team member arrived, Laura Bedford (now Laura Worku), with whom I had worked on the MV *Doulos*. This was the beginning of a new team.

2006 Work began in earnest to produce a new edition of *Operation World*. Team members came and went – and often came back again! But the Lord was faithful to bring the right personalities with the right gifts and skills at the right times.

2010 August. Completion of the **seventh edition of Operation World** is an occasion of rejoicing and thankfulness. As we send this book out for publication, we pray fervently that the Lord Jesus Christ might be glorified, the Church mobilized and world evangelization furthered. To Him alone be the praise, glory and victory in the spiritual battles ahead of us.

Operation World

The Ethos of *Operation World*

A number of fundamental assumptions have been made in compiling this book. We realize that we will never satisfy all readers, but we trust that we have been sensitive to other theological and political points of view beyond our own. The people directly involved in the composition of this volume represent over 10 nationalities, 3 generations and 20 denominations. Even this is only a tiny proportion of the vast diversity in the body of Christ. Our own perspectives inevitably influence the selection of material and opinions expressed, and for these we must accept responsibility.

All views here expressed are our own and not necessarily those of the publishers or of any organization mentioned in this book. We cherish constructive advice for future revisions and always endeavour to engage in fruitful dialogue with our critics. A number of these have eventually become some of our more helpful correspondents! We made the following decisions:

Readership. We are writing for Bible-believing Christians who want to obey the last great command of the Lord Jesus by evangelizing the world and completing the Great Commission. This means primarily – but not exclusively – evangelical Christians (which broadly means Protestant, Independent and Anglican Christians), though we realize there are many outside these categories who use *Operation World*. We trust that we have been sensitive enough to enable this book to be used more widely, yet without compromising our own theological position.

Theology. As evangelical believers, we attempt to take a central position in more controversial issues that perplex evangelicals, such as church government, baptism, the sovereignty of God, the work of the Holy Spirit and social involvement. The perceptive reader will, no doubt, see an unintended bias that reflects the author's own views. In a broader sense, *Operation World* closely associates its outlook with that of the Lausanne Covenant, not just in theology but also in framing our understanding of the nature and scope of the Great Commission.

Politics. We, the Operation World team, are predominantly white Westerners (although decreasingly so!) and, as such, cannot divorce ourselves completely from the societies and cultures from which we have emerged. We have, however, sought as far as possible to write about each country by balancing the local perspective with the broader, global perspective. This means we have, at times, spoken to the endemic wrongs of a specific nation or Church. Our desire is that this book be of global value. What might have seemed to us prophetic forthtelling regarding a nation's ills might come across as insensitive judgementalism. Our aim here was for balance, but we have no doubt fallen short in a number of instances.

Time validity. With the accelerating rate of change in the world, the idea of "up-to-the-minute" statistics is a specious myth! Any statistic seen in print or on the web is almost certainly "out of date" before you even read it. Nevertheless, the purpose of *Operation World* is to trace the work of God through the years and decades. The prayer points are framed in such a way as to not be invalidated, for example, by an election, a natural disaster or any other temporal change in a nation; they are long-term issues that usually take decades of sustained intercession to see significant changes. That said, there is nothing we would like more than to see the entire book invalidated by God miraculously answering every prayer in this volume.

An emphasis on the Church. Early editions were rightly criticized for overemphasizing mission agencies and the contribution of missionaries. We sought to rectify this, but it is important to realize that these agencies are often the best communicators of prayer information, hence the system of highlighting the initials of mission agencies whose addresses are given in Appendix 3. In these later editions, we centre our information on the body of Christ in each country. Thankfully, our list of thousands of correspondents and contacts is composed of an increasingly equal and effective balance between national Christian leaders and expatriate Christian workers.

The selection of agencies mentioned is not intended to be a mark of validation or rejection. We have drawn attention to some having international and interdenominational interest to a wide spectrum of English-speaking readers. The electronic version holds a much greater wealth of agency information. A number of influential agencies – especially in certain countries – asked not to be mentioned by name; we have respected this on every such occasion. For others, our efforts to establish mutually-helpful exchanges met with bounced e-mails or even silence.

To finance and resource this massive project is itself an act of faith. Many people envision some multimillion-dollar sprawling campus with underground bunkers of supercomputers, hyper-qualified, high-flying technical experts and an army of data-entry drones! In truth, as with most research projects and many strategic Great Commission endeavours, we operate with old, often outdated gear in whatever donated or subsidized office space we are allocated. Every person working on the Operation World team is a volunteer or a missionary – sent and supported to this strategic work as his or her field of service. Each of us must trust and call out to God to provide for our financial needs. Very few of us trained specifically for mission research. All royalties from *Operation World* books and other resources sold go into a trust fund used to cover the ministry and production costs of future editions. This is one of several reasons the entirety of *Operation World* is not made available for free on the Internet.

The burden for prayer. Our longing is for this book to be seen as a tool for prayer. The spiritual tone and vision that express the heart and priorities of our heavenly Father is in the forefront. All other issues *must* be secondary. Borrowing liberally from the 2001 edition of *Operation World,* the ethos of prayer is best reflected in the following paragraphs:

The book in your hands weighs less than one kilogram, yet if all the desires, requests and goals expressed in it were to be implemented it would radically change the nations of this world. Wars would be ended, ethnic hatreds tamed, politicians become honest, economic justice achieved, poverty eliminated, ecological degradation ended and disease halted. The Church of the Lord Jesus Christ would be provided with godly leaders, it would be renewed, revived, united in vision, mobilized for mission and readied for the return of its Head. Jesus would return with the world evangelized and the Church complete! That is the wish. How much of the earthly and how quickly the eternal agendas would be achieved depends heavily on one activity – prayer in the name of Jesus to a loving, sovereign Father.

It is a mystery that our loving Father has somehow limited His omnipotence to partner with His redeemed people so that His actions in the world are inextricably linked with our prayers. The following pages give something of the needs and challenges of our needy, sin-sick, doomed world. The nations are there for the asking. God is calling you and me into the ministry of intercession for them.

We have plenty of opposition in the heavenlies and from human powers and persecutors. The enemy will seek to frighten us with these and dangle allurements to distract us from the vision of a heavenly, eternal Kingdom filled with people from every race, tribe, people and tongue. Yet Jesus offers us a share in His reign. At times, we may look up to Him in agony, but we must see our true position – looking down with Him, exercising the authority bequeathed by Him in the Great Commission He has given to every Christian. May we become intercessors with a world vision that prays Satan-defeating, Kingdom-taking, people-reaching, captive-releasing, revival-giving, Christ-glorifying prayers.

Prayer changes not only people, situations and even the course of history, but it also changes those who pray! It is dangerous for the enemy and also "dangerous" for you. There is a price to pay for standing in the gap between fallen humanity and a righteous God. That price may mean becoming an answer to your own prayers by giving your own time and finances – or even by going out as a witness in your Jerusalem (where you now live), your Judea (your own country), your Samaria (the other ethnic groups in your own country) or even to the ends of the earth. Our prayer is that many will give their whole lives for this most noble of causes – to obey Jesus' last command in making disciples of all nations and so ready the Church and the world for the grand climax of His glorious return.

Operation World

Prayer and the Nations

The countless prayers this book will inspire serve no purpose in and of themselves. Prayer is not a self-validating exercise; in a world where there is no loving, sovereign God, prayer would be weakness at best and folly at worst. No, each and every prayer is a tiny piece of a great cosmic puzzle, which when fitted together will allow for the completion of the grand picture of the Almighty Lord's plan for humanity and the universe. We do not merely pray *about* the many points featured herein, we pray *toward* something, and that something is magnificent – the fulfilment of the Father's purposes and His Kingdom come.

In keeping with all we see of God's character and commands, we long for poverty to end, for justice toward the oppressed, for the blind to see and the lame to walk, for widows and orphans to be looked after, for those in chains to be set at liberty, for the earth to be rightly stewarded, for wars to cease, for those at enmity with each other to be reconciled and for those who are lost to be found by Jesus and the salvation He brings. Many believers (and many who are not) work faithfully to see these things come to pass.

In the end, such a vision will never completely come to pass without Jesus returning to assume the Kingship of this world. It is *this* that is the ultimate purpose of the Great Commission; even the evangelization of the entire world is not an end in itself. Our mission is to see vibrant, growing, mature churches planted and multiplied among every people, and so fulfil our Lord's mandate. But this is only the preparation and completion of the Bride; her Heavenly Bridegroom awaits her readiness. Too often we immerse ourselves in the task but lose sight of its ultimate purpose – the glory of God.

> Here lies the supreme missionary motivation. It is neither obedience to the Great Commission, nor compassion for the lost, nor excitement over the gospel, but zeal (even "jealousy") for the honour of Christ's name ... no incentive is stronger than the longing that Christ should be given the honour that is due to His Name. (John Stott)

It is a wonder and a mystery that God allows His glory to be placed in our hands – being such frail, foolish, unfaithful creatures as we are. Our track record as stewards of His reputation is poor, from Israel through the early Church to today. Despite this, He entrusts the fulfilment of His plans and purposes to us. But He has not left us as orphans. He has left us with assurances. In Matthew 28:18-20, Jesus tells His disciples, "All authority in heaven and on earth has been given to me". Then He states, "I am with you always, to the end of the age" (ESV). These promises are profound bookends to Matthew's Great Commission! In Revelation 2:26-27, to those who hold fast and endure until the end, Jesus subsequently promises, "to him ... I will give authority over the nations". More staggering is the affirmation that "he will rule them ... *even as I myself have received authority from my Father*" (ESV, emphasis added). The same authority Jesus received from the Father – *all* authority in heaven and on earth – has been promised to those who endure!

In light of this, prayer takes on a whole new dimension. As Martin Luther observed, "Prayer is not overcoming God's reluctance, but laying hold of His willingness". Even non-believers recognize this reality; Mahatma Gandhi said, "Prayer is not an old woman's idle amusement. Properly understood and applied, it is the most potent instrument of action".

Prayer is indeed potent, and it has many facets. Prayer – especially sustained intercession for the unreached peoples of this world who do not yet know Jesus – is action:

Prayer is an act of faith. Faith even the size of a mustard seed can move mountains, but many of us prefer the less spectacular but safer results that come from operating in our own strength. Again, in a godless universe, the idea of prayer for the evangelization of the world is beyond absurd. Do we really believe that our prayers to an invisible God can and will change the hard hearts of tyrants, break down oppressive social and religious systems, and deliver fullness of life to those who suffer in abject hopelessness? FB Meyer wrote, "You do not test the resources of God until you attempt the impossible".

Prayer is an act of obedience. Our Lord instructs us to pray; as His servants, this should be the end of the matter! God commands His anointed ones to "Ask of me and I will surely give the nations as your inheritance" (Ps 2:8, NASB). Psalm 2 echoes through the life of Jesus, in the book of Acts (4:24-31) and in Revelation (2:26-27). Israel's last great judge, Samuel, tells his people, "Moreover, as for me, far be it from me that I should sin against the Lord by ceasing to pray for you" (1 Sam 12:23, ESV). The apostle Paul instructs churches he planted to "pray without ceasing" and to "pray at all times" (1 Thess 5:17 and Eph 6:18, NASB). Praying for the nations can have significant personal consequences as well – for countless missionaries, their first step on the path toward Christian service began with prayer and resulted in their obedient response to God calling them to be answers to their own prayers.

Prayer is an act of worship. The imitation and adoration of Christ must necessarily include prayer, for His own life exemplified prayer. What is more, when we pray, we are recognizing the sovereignty of God as well as acknowledging our own helplessness. We put Him back on the throne of our own lives and of the world. Psalms 67 and 96 are resounding examples of the intricately bound nature of prayer, worship and mission. The temple – the locus of the presence of God on earth and the centre of worship for the nation of Israel – was set out to be a house of prayer for all nations (Is 56:7-8).

Prayer is an act of warfare. When we seek to rescue unreached peoples and lost souls from the grip of the evil one, we must expect violent opposition in the heavenlies. The gates of hell will not prevail against the Church, but they must be stormed; they will not open of their own accord. It is no accident that the passage of the armour of God in Ephesians 6 ends with the exhortation to be "praying at all times in the Spirit, with all prayer and supplication" (Eph 6:18, ESV). Warfare has casualties, but we are not mere collateral damage. God is in control, yet at times He allows His people the honour of suffering the consequences of this war.

Prayer is an act of sacrifice. As noted above, our choice to stand in the gap can have heavy consequences. But beyond the spiritual price that intercessors often pay, the simple choice to pray usually happens to the exclusion of something else in our lives. Often that something else is frivolous, but at times prayer must come at the expense of important things, such as our own work, our sleep or our time with loved ones. Busyness is an especially modern affliction, yet even 500 years ago Luther understood this principle: "I have so much business, I cannot get on with-out spending three hours daily in prayer". Jesus retreated from perfectly legitimate ministry activities to seek intimacy with the Father. How can we do less?

Prayer is an act of labour. Prayer is hard work! Anyone who has persevered in early morning or late night hours, in all-night vigils, even in seemingly interminable midweek prayer meetings knows the difficulty of sustaining a life of prayer. It does not come naturally to us as creatures of flesh and blood. As stated by Oswald Chambers, "Prayer does not fit us for the greater work; prayer *is* the greater work".

Prayer is an act of love. It is true that our love for unsaved family members, for non-Christian friends, for unreached peoples can drive us to prayer. But ultimately, prayer is the domain of God, and it is impossible to be passionate about prayer if you are not already passionate for Him. Our engagement in faithful, overcoming intercession for the salvation of all peoples and the redemption of the world can be sustained only by a deep and unshakeable love for our Lord. After all, it is for His glory that we long to see the world changed through prayer.

It is this longing for God's glory and for the return of Jesus as King that drives our prayers. We resonate with the words of Revelation 22:17-20, "The Spirit and the Bride say, 'Come.' And let the one who hears say, 'Come.' ... Amen! Come, Lord Jesus" (ESV).

Operation World

How to Use *Operation World*

This book is written for two main purposes:

To inform for prayer. The layout of this book is in the form of a prayer diary, with praise points and prayer requests assigned for each day of the year.

To mobilize for ministry. Information and relevant statistics are given to channel ministry to the least reached and most needy parts and peoples of our world. For many Christians, this book is their only source of global prayer information. Earlier editions became an essential resource for the growing missions movement around the world – in a particular way this has been true of the non-English editions. Every year more people discover *Operation World,* even as more editions are produced in other languages.

To enhance its usefulness, we offer some suggestions that may help you use this book appropriately and effectively.

For Use in Your Home, Church or School

In private

1 **Pray through the book using the running calendar,** perhaps taking only one or two items the Holy Spirit lays on your heart. Why not mark items covered in prayer and later make note of God's answers? Those of special, strategic significance are indicated by an outline around the blue number.

2 **Keep the book near your television, radio, newspaper or computer.** When news comes of major events in a far-off land, find out the spiritual dimensions and turn secular news into spiritual dynamite.

3 **Use it together with prayer letters, mission magazines and websites.** The wider context is missing from these valuable resources. This book will give depth and perspective.

In the family

4 **Read a small section at family time** (devotions, meals, while travelling), and pray for the country of the day. The children's versions (*You Can Change the World* 1 and 2, *Window on the World* and the forthcoming *Children's Prayer Atlas*) are beautifully designed as family prayer resources.

5 **Use the book as a source of informative fun and quiz games.** This is a favourite activity of the OW team; perhaps we need to get out more!

In your church

Missions and prayer for the world should be at the heart of every fellowship. *Operation World* can help stimulate this within a group through its praise and prayer points.

6 **Church services.** Use prayer items during the intercessory period of worship services.

7 **Prayer meetings** should be the spiritual engine room for the global missionary force; in this we agree with William Carey! Wise use of the information in this book can stimulate more informed prayer for the world and for your own church's missionaries and mission programmes.

8 **Church bulletins and magazines.** Use quotes from relevant sections of the book in your church publications to spark interest and stimulate prayer. Please quote the source! To inform and stimulate prayer, OW also produces other resources designed for small groups, large congregations and huge conferences. These include, but are not limited to, maps, prayer cards, podcasts, videos and presentation materials. Please refer to the last pages of this book, which tell how you may obtain these.

In teaching on missions

9 **Many Bible schools** make praying through *Operation World* a core component of their courses. Instructors use it to teach on missions – many Christians have been led into specific missionary service as a result. The present author can be included among this number (thank you, Dr Bonk!).

For Use in Christian Research

Operation World contains only a minute proportion of the vast amount of news items, articles, reports, correspondence and statistics assembled during its production. Those seeking a greater degree of information can contact our ministry to ask about gaining access to these resources. Some are available in the electronic version, which includes the following:

1 **Electronic search tools** to more quickly and easily locate and bring together linked information for exporting and printing.

2 **Access to the databases** from which our statistics and sources for this book were selected, including:

a) **The world's denominations.** Data on the number of congregations, memberships, affiliated Christians and, where known, attendances for 7,357 specific denominations, and records referring to a total of 38,102 denominations covering 1960-2010. Every figure is either sourced or shown as estimated or derived.

b) **The religions of the world** between 1900 and 2025 (projected), showing the astonishing changes in religious affiliation over that period for every country.

c) **The mission agencies and missionaries of the world** and statistics gathered by field and/or region (where information may be sensitive) covering 1980-2010. Contact information and select worker statistics for 3,210 mission agencies, representing over 80,000 teams and locations.

d) **Country information** with a wider range of categories than we could use in the book.

e) **Assorted spreadsheets, reports, lists and charts** used to prepare material for this book. Much is very interesting and useful but has no place appearing in a populist, single-volume book!

3 **Graphics and maps** used in *Operation World* but with full colour added. In this book, only two of the four possible country-specific charts were included; the electronic version should contain all four for each country.

For Use in Prayer Days, Conferences, Concerts of Prayer, Prayer Journeys and Other Prayer Venues

Operation World's original purpose was to provide fuel for prayer conferences for the world. Here are a few guidelines for prayer-session leaders.

1 **Be brief.** The people are gathered to *pray*, not to be impressed by the amount of information presented. Ideally, less than one-third of the time should be set aside for reporting on the need.

2 **Be personal.** We deliberately refrain from mentioning individuals, but rather give the overall situation in a country. Personal information on individual workers and specific situations connected to those praying will yield greater personal interest and investment in the prayer time.

3 **Be selective.** Too many facts will not be retained unless they are written down; better to carefully select just a few items for prayer that will burden believers long after the meeting.

4 **Be careful with statistics.** Too many figures make any report very dull! This is why the statistical sections are in a smaller type. Choose only those statistics that specifically apply to the prayer items you mention. The many figures are given so that you may have the resources you might need.

5 **Be dependent on the leading of the Holy Spirit.** The burdens imparted by the Holy Spirit inspire others to pray in the Spirit and move them into God's will for their lives. This could mean commitment to intercession, financial giving or going to a particular area or people for which prayer has been made.

Explanation of Statistics and Abbreviations

The purpose of this book is to inform and inspire God's people to prayer and action in order to change the world. Statistics are an essential element of this, giving a solid factual basis for all that follows. These carefully researched figures are the spine of *Operation World*, giving strength and support to the prayer points that flesh out the book. We believe that careful observation and fact-finding, done with discernment and trust in God, is entirely scriptural. Some wrongly associate statistical research with God's anger against Israel and judgement of King David's census in 2 Samuel 24. Yet God also permitted, favoured and even instructed the gathering and use of meticulous statistics and careful enumeration by Moses, Joshua, the Chronicler, Ezra, Ezekiel, Luke, John and others in Scripture.

This book's description of each region and country is divided into two parts:

1 **Statistical and background information** in two-column format.

2 **Specific items for praise and prayer.**

The statistics are included as background to the prayer information, hence the difference in type size and font on a tinted background.

A brief explanation of their significance is given below. A more detailed explanation of the sources and how these figures were handled is given in Appendix 6 Operation World Database and Appendix 7 Statistical Sources.

The availability, consistency and accuracy of secular, religious and Christian statistics vary enormously from country to country, denomination to denomination, mission agency to mission agency. Some groups do not even keep statistics. The inadequacy of many sources, varied dates of publication, the refusal to divulge information (usually for security reasons) as well as the sheer time frame over which *Operation World* is compiled make for an inevitable margin of error. Add to this our own human limitations, and we plead for the reader's sympathy. Should any errors or discrepancies be discovered – almost an inevitability despite rigorous checking and proofing – please submit suggestions or corrections via the Operation World website [www.operationworld.org]. We welcome input and dialogue; the entire premise of the ministry is collaborative, relying heavily upon literally thousands of contacts and correspondents scattered around the globe.

We pray these statistics present a reasonably balanced account of what God is doing in our world and of the challenges facing us as we press on to complete the Great Commission. Apart from Operation World, only the World Christian Database/World Religions Database shares our folly in attempting so massive a task as compiling a comprehensive body of data relating to the world's religions, denominations and churches and to the progress of the Great Commission.

Below are explanations of how each category of statistics is handled in the order and format used throughout the book.

Our statistical base date is June 2010. Most of the statistics used are compiled from data gathered between 2005 and 2010. The textual information is valid for July 2010.

* * *

Geography 🌍

Area Given in square kilometres. The area does not imply approval or disapproval of the political status quo of disputed territories, but is a reflection of the actual situation in May 2010. Included in this category are places such as Western Sahara (included under Morocco), Kashmir (various parts of which are claimed by Pakistan, India and China), Georgia (with its breakaway republics) and others.

Population Figures given are for 2010, 2020 and 2030. These figures are exact quotes of estimates from the 2008 UN population database. *Operation World* uses the UN medium population growth trajectory for future dates. We recognize that for some countries, the 2010 population figure may not agree with national government sources. For the sake of consistency, the UN figures are used for all country population statistics. Average annual growth rates are given in the second column, and population density in people/sq km in the third column and rounded to the nearest whole number.

Capitals and Other Cities City populations were generally taken from the WCD. In the large majority of cases, these figures represent conurbations, though at times city proper populations were more representative. Outside of municipal areas, migrant settlements and massive urban sprawl can render such estimates difficult due to their highly derivative or unreliable nature. Most world-class cities are mentioned by name, that is, those with a population exceeding 1 million.

Urbanites (Urban population) This is taken from the UN Human Development Report (2009). For countries without UN data available, figures come from the WCD.

Pop under 15 yrs These figures are exact quotes of estimates from the UN World Health Organization.

Life expectancy These figures are taken from the UN Human Development Report (2009).

Peoples 👪

Ethnic diversity is shown in a manner considered the most helpful for the reader. The figures for peoples were largely derived from the Joshua Project list, with adjustments where necessary or where more current or more accurate data was available.

Groupings of peoples are given in larger type as a percentage of the country's total population. The exception is when the percentage in question is very small. The decision was taken to generate these figures as percentages rather than as absolute numbers. This

is more helpful for comparative purposes, and assuming a relatively consistent population growth, gives the figures much greater longevity. When a number is given in parentheses immediately following a people name, that number refers to the subgroups that make up that people. For example, Fulani(4) indicates that there are four Fulani peoples found in that country.

Smaller peoples are not mentioned by name unless there is a particular challenge or point of wider interest to note. The cut-off point for specific mention of a people in this section was generally held to be 1% of the total population.

Refugees and temporarily resident communities are often listed but not always included in national percentages. Each country is handled on a case-by-case scenario.

Language/Literacy Figures quoted are from the UN Gender Info Database. Because functional literacy may be much lower than the official figure quoted, an estimate is sometimes also given.

Official languages Those languages known to be recognized as such in June 2010.

All languages and **Indigenous languages** These figures are extracted from the SIL Ethnologue database.

Languages with Scriptures This data is also from SIL. The number of languages in which there is a full Bible (Bi), or only a New Testament (NT), or just portions (por) is given. The number of active language translation projects is indicated by work/s in progress (w.i.p.). Further information on translation needs is often given in the Challenges for Prayer.

Economy 📈

HDI Rank (Human Development Index Ranking) is a composite of data reflecting measures of life expectancy at birth, literacy, education and standard of living. We have figures for 182 countries, taken from the 2009 UN Human Development Report, where each country is ranked according to its assigned HDI.

Public debt represents the total public debt in a country's home currency and is given as a percentage of the Gross Domestic Product (GDP). This gives a rough guide to the health of the economy – a high percentage of over 100% is most unhealthy. Figures taken from the CIA World Factbook (2008).

Income/person is the gross domestic product (GDP) in US dollars divided by the population. This is also given as a percentage of the US figure to give a rough indication of living standards. This is not, however, an indication of purchasing power within the country, which reduces the disparities. GDP per capita figures are from the International Monetary Fund (IMF).

Politics 🗙

The brief comments are intended to be a most basic introduction for the purpose of background summary. It is not intended to be a full political assessment. Hopefully, it is not too biased by the author's own viewpoint.

Religion 👣

Religions Table
Religions are listed in order of their percentage (Pop %) of the national population, obtained from many sources. The absolute number (Population) is derived from this percentage and the total population. The growth rate (Ann Gr) given is for the period 2005-2010.

Christian (MegaBloc) Tables
Six ecclesiological MegaBlocs of Christians (and two extra blocs) are used:

Protestant	P
Independent/Indigenous	I
Anglican	A
Catholic	C
Orthodox	O
Marginal	M
Unaffiliated	U
Doubly affiliated	

The letter after the MegaBloc is important and is used frequently as an abbreviation in the text and tables.

Use of computer databases to derive the denominational tables, ease of layout and reading and the decision to keep a close association of the P,I,A MegaBlocs made it preferable to list them in the order given above, irrespective of size. See Appendix 6 for an explanation of why we use a broad definition of "Christian", including several groups that many believers may not regard as "Christian".

The percentage of Christians (Pop %) represents the total number of the total population who are claimed to be Christian, either by the individuals themselves in a government census or by the churches to which they are affiliated. When significant differences occur between these two, we have attempted to reconcile by various means and publish a figure that is as close to the real situation as we understand it.

Where the official or estimated percentage is higher than that claimed by the churches, an unaffiliated percentage and total is added under

the six main MegaBloc statistics to reconcile the two.

Double affiliation can seriously distort totals. Where this is known to be a factor, a subtraction total is also appended to the MegaBloc table to allow for those who have changed religion or denomination, but are counted by both. This subtraction total is also appended to the list of denominations that follows the MegaBloc table.

Disaffiliation occurs when churches – mostly large established state churches – continue to publish high figures, while many within that total have ceased any association with that church, and usually with organized Christianity in general.

Church attendance is used only by a few denominations as a means of tracking their growth. The inconsistency of results, and the paucity of countries with such figures, forced us to abandon this as a consistent practice, but it remains helpful as a guideline for those groups that do utilize such a means. Any such figures are entered into the database, which is in the digital version of *Operation World*.

Growth rates (Ann Gr) are given and represent average annual growth between 2005 and 2010.

The denominational listings (Churches) contain a representative selection of the larger denominations with:

The number of Congregations (Congs), with widely differing denominational conceptions as to what constitutes a congregation.

Adult baptized or confirmed Members. This refers to those old enough to have made a deliberate decision to become a confirmed member of a congregation, and often refers only to those on the rolls of church membership.

The Affiliates figure represents the whole Christian community or inclusive membership, which includes children, non-member adherents and other participants in the faith community.

We have sought to cross-calculate a derivation for all three figures when only one or two are provided so that meaningful comparisons and totals can be made. We have also had to make projections to 2010 for denominations where recent statistics were not available. See a more detailed explanation in Appendix 6, and further details in the digital version of *Operation World*.

TransBloc Movement Table
Evangelical percentages for 1960-2010 are carefully derived according to the methodology described in Appendix 6. The greatest degree of accuracy is for denominations where evangeli-

cals are necessarily 0% or 100% of the denomination by virtue of its articles of faith. Accuracy is reduced and assessment more subjective in lands where there are large state or traditional churches to which a majority of the population belong and where there is not a clearly established evangelical movement within that church. The denominational tables in the digital version give the assigned estimates. These evangelical percentages are the unique contribution of *Operation World* to the global body of knowledge regarding the Christian faith.

Renewalist movements, in concept, encompass all followers of both the Pentecostal and charismatic/neocharismatic renewal movements in the Holy Spirit, across all denominations in which they are found.

Charismatic percentages for 1990-2010 are derived as described in Appendix 6. Adequately accurate assessments of the denominational breakdown of charismatics before 1990 are not obtainable.

Pentecostals are defined by denominational type and are exclusively within the Protestant and Independent MegaBlocs. All Pentecostals are, by definition, both charismatic and evangelical and therefore a subset of both. This is indicated by indentation in the table.

The inter-relatedness of these three TransBloc movements is complex but has to be faced, because it represents the real world in which we live. Evangelicals and charismatics are found in at least five of the six MegaBlocs in varying proportions. There are Christians who are both evangelical and charismatic, evangelicals who are not charismatic, charismatics who are not evangelical and there are Christians who are neither charismatic nor evangelical. Pentecostals are both evangelical and charismatic by definition. But there are also evangelical charismatics who are not Pentecostal. This is the most common difficulty readers have with *Operation World* information; failure to appreciate this complex issue often leads to many misunderstandings of the dynamics of the Church.

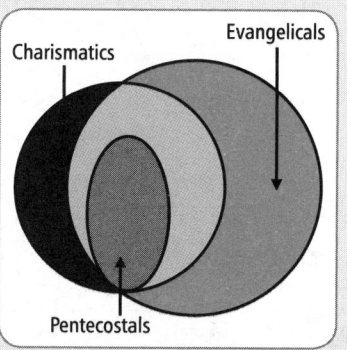

Missionary statistics

Despite momentous efforts on the part of the Operation World team to gather statistics on missionaries serving around the world, a number of factors have conspired to prevent meaningful data being published.

The dizzying complexity of attempting to categorize those who serve God in the Great Commission. There are almost as many definitions of the word "missionary" as there are organizations sending them out! Long-term, short-term, mission-tripper, cross-cultural, near-cultural, non-residential, transnational, tentmaker, student, business-as-mission, NGO, salaried employee of a Christian agency, evangelist, pastor . . . a myriad of issues blur what used to be a straightforward matter. Different understandings of the term "missionary" in different emerging Majority World sending countries complicate the picture as well.

The post-9/11 world is one of international terrorism, religious fundamentalism, violence, abduction, kidnapping and hostage taking. Christian foreign workers are particularly vulnerable and obvious targets for all of the above. As a result, almost all mission organizations are very cautious about sharing data regarding their field workers.

It is therefore no longer possible to produce reliable figures of the number of missionaries serving in a country. Any such attempts would rely heavily on broad estimations and statistics more than 10 years old. In the last 10 years, radical changes have been afoot in terms of which countries have grown in mission sending and in terms of what these thousands of different groups conceive a missionary to be.

We have made substantial efforts to publish reliable data on the number of missionaries serving with specific agencies and the number of missionaries from specific countries. In these cases, the cooperation of the agencies themselves and the presence of national-level umbrella networks of Protestant, Independent and Anglican mission organizations have been varied. It has been on occasion discouraging and even shocking to discover within many agencies and countries the lack of effort to understand the numbers and locations of their own missionaries.

[Organizational abbreviations in bold type in the text are the 115 associations or networks and 112 agencies for which we give contact addresses and worker information in Appendix 3. A larger list of agencies with addresses is available in the digital version of *Operation World*. Other abbreviations used in the text are listed in Appendix 4.]

Explanation of Statistics and Abbreviations

Charts and Graphs

These charts and graphs tell fascinating stories of growth and of decline in the world's religions and in TransBloc movements. We have added two new kinds of charts to this edition. The MegaBloc Pie Chart demonstrates the proportion of the overall Christian population broken down by the respective MegaBlocs. The Annual Growth Rates Chart compares the average annual growth rates for 2005-2010 for the various groups represented. Every country will contain percent growth rates for total population, Christians, evangelicals and one other religious group. Unfortunately, space prohibits fuller explanations of the underlying trends.

Religions Graph

This graph shows the growth or decline of religions over the 20th Century and extrapolates to 2025.

Non-Christian religions and ideologies are shown from the top downward.

Major Christian traditions are shown from the bottom upward. Where the number of Christians is very small, only the total Christian population is indicated by X. Sometimes a combination of the smaller MegaBlocs is represented by an X alongside individual larger MegaBlocs.

Non-Christian religions that are too small in percentage to be of significance are left as white space at the very top of the chart. Please refer to the accompanying statistics for that country to identify them.

The letter on the graph will help identify the religion without referring constantly to this key. It is usually the first letter of the religion listed under the Religion section. Only the larger religions are included for each country. See the sample graph below.

The right-hand vertical scale allows the proportion of the major religious groups to be seen in comparison with each other, and as a percentage of the country's total population.

Abbreviations of non-Christian religious groupings are shown below. (Christian Mega-Bloc abbreviations explained on pxxx).

Buddhist	B
Chinese	Ch
Ethnoreligionist	E
Hindu	H
Jewish	J
Muslim	M
Non-religious	N
Christian marginal sects	S
Other, combined groups	Z

Note. Religions Graph only, M indicates Muslim rather than Marginal Christian, here represented by S.

TransBloc Movement Graph

The growth of evangelicals (Evang) is always given (not members, so as to compare percentages with other religions). Usually, the estimated growth of charismatics (Char) from 1990-2010 is given.

Likewise, the growth of Pentecostals (Pente) – who are by definition both evangelical and charismatic - is also given when their numbers warrant.

The time scale is different from the religions graph and covers only 1960-2010, the period of the most dramatic change in history for these TransBloc movements.

The percentage of the population indicated varies according to countries. Note carefully the scale on the right-hand side before making comparisons. See the sample graph below.

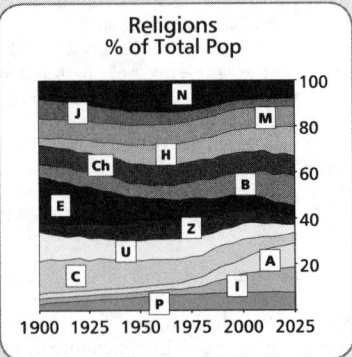

Religions
% of Total Pop

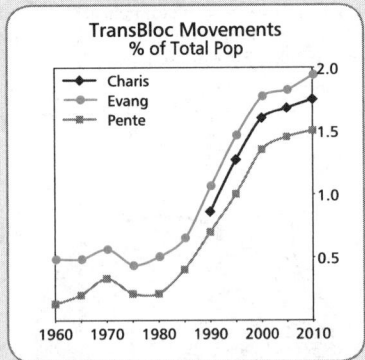

TransBloc Movements
% of Total Pop

Key to the figures:
The time scale on the bottom line is 1900-2025.

2010 is the year for which the statistics in this book are valid. 2010-2025 represents projections through that period.

MegaBloc Pie Chart

The data for this chart is taken from 2010. Each wedge and the associated percentage figure refer to a MegaBloc's proportion of the country's total number of Christians, not the country's overall population. The colour scheme is designed to communicate the Mega-Blocs where evangelicals are most likely to figure.

The order of the wedges is always the same, regardless of size: P, I, A, C, O, M, U. But, when MegaBlocs represent less than 1% of the Christian population, they are pulled out of their normal sequence and bundled into an "extra Christians" category, represented here by an X.

Some countries have significant numbers of doubly affiliated Christians. These negative percentages are of course impossible to visually represent in a pie chart. Therefore, we have proportionately decreased all MegaBlocs in such countries so as to reduce the numbers to total up to 100% of all Christians (rather than, for example, totalling up to 110% of all Christians with -10% doubly affiliated).

Annual Growth Rates Chart

This data refers to average annual growth rates (AGR) for 2005-2010. Every country will contain percent growth rates for Total Population, Christians and Evangelicals. Every country will also contain percent growth rates for one other group, either the largest religion or the second largest when Christianity is the largest.

This chart compares the vitality of growth of the respective groups; it has nothing to do with the sizes of the populations. It is particularly helpful for countries where Christians are a very small or a very large proportion of the country's population, and where one or two groups are growing or declining at a markedly different rate from the total population. The right axis is adjusted to an appropriate scale for each country; in some cases, this may include negative growth rates.

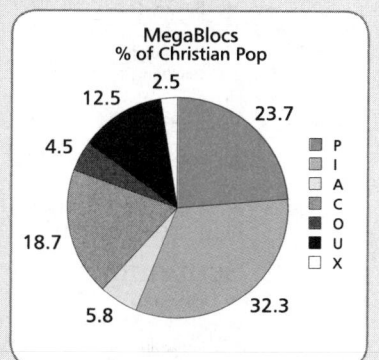

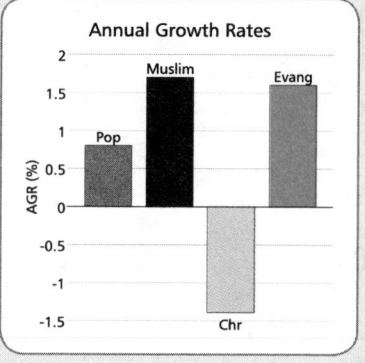

Prayer Calendar

January

1 *The World*
2
3
4
5
6
7
8
9
10
11
12 *Africa*
13
14
15
16
17
18
19 *The Americas*
20
21
22
23
24
25 *Asia*
26
27
28
29
30
31

February

1 *Europe*
2
3
4
5
6 *Pacific*
7
8
9 Afghanistan
10
11 Albania
12 Algeria
13
14 American Samoa, Andorra
15 Angola
16
17 Anguilla, Antigua & Barbuda
18 Argentina
19
20 Armenia
21
22 Aruba
23 Australia
24
25 Austria
26
27 Azerbaijan
28 Bahamas, Bahrain

March

1 Bangladesh
2
3
4 Barbados
5 Belarus
6 Belgium
7
8 Belize, Bermuda
9 Benin
10 Bhutan
11 Bolivia
12
13 Bosnia
14 Botswana
15 Brazil
16
17
18
19 BIOT, British Virgin Is, Brunei
20 Bulgaria
21 Burkina Faso
22
23 Burundi
24 Cambodia
25
26 Cameroon
27
28 Canada
29
30 Cape Verde Is, Cayman Is
31 Central African Republic

July

1 (India)
2
3
4
5 Indonesia
6
7
8
9
10
11
12
13
14 Iran
15
16
17 Iraq
18
19 Ireland
20 Israel
21
22 Italy
23
24 Jamaica
25 Japan
26
27
28 Jordan
29
30 Kazakhstan
31

August

1 Kenya, Kiribati
2
3 Korea, North
4
5 Korea, South
6
7 Kuwait
8 Kyrgyzstan
9 Laos
10 Latvia
11 Lebanon
12 Lesotho
13 Liberia
14
15 Libya
16 Liechtenstein, Luxembourg
17 Lithuania
18 Macedonia
19 Madagascar
20 Malawi
21 Malaysia
22
23 Maldives
24 Mali
25
26 Malta, Martinique
27 Mauritania
28 Mauritius, Mayotte
29 Mexico
30
31

September

1 Micronesia
2 Moldova, Monaco
3 Mongolia
4 Montenegro, Montserrat
5 Morocco
6
7 Mozambique
8
9 Myanmar
10
11 Namibia, Nauru
12 Nepal
13
14 Netherlands, Neth Antilles
15 New Caledonia
16 New Zealand
17 Nicaragua
18 Niger
19
20 Nigeria
21
22
23 Norway
24 Oman
25 Pakistan
26
27
28
29 Palestine, Panama
30 Papua New Guinea

Operation World

April

1 (Central African Republic)
2 Chad
3
4 Chile
5 China, PRC
6
7
8
9
10
11
12
13
14
15
16
17
18
19
20 China, Hong Kong
21 China, Macau
22 China, Taiwan
23
24 Colombia
25
26 Comoro Islands
27 Congo-DRC
28
29 Congo
30 Cook Islands

May

1 Costa Rica
2 Côte d'Ivoire
3
4 Croatia
5 Cuba
6 Cyprus
7 Czech Republic
8 Denmark
9 Djibouti
10 Dominica, Dominican Republic
11 Ecuador
12 Egypt
13
14 El Salvador
15 Equatorial Guinea
16 Eritrea
17
18 Estonia
19 Ethiopia
20
21 Faeroe Is, Falkland Is
22 Fiji
23 Finland
24 France
25
26 Fr Guiana, Fr Polynesia
27 Gabon
28 Gambia, The
29 Georgia
30 Germany
31

June

1 (Germany)
2 Ghana
3
4 Gibraltar, Greece
5
6 Greenland, Grenada
7 Guadeloupe, Guam
8 Guatemala
9 Guinea
10
11 Guinea-Bissau
12 Guyana
13 Haiti
14
15 Holy See
16 Honduras
17 Hungary
18 Iceland
19 India
20
21
22
23
24
25
26
27
28
29
30

October

1 Paraguay
2 Peru
3 Philippines
4
5
6 Poland
7 Portugal
8 Puerto Rico
9 Qatar, Réunion
10 Romania
11
12 Russia
13
14
15
16
17 Rwanda
18 Samoa, San Marino, São Tomé & Príncipe
19 Saudi Arabia
20
21 Senegal, Seychelles
22
23 Serbia
24 Sierra Leone
25 Singapore
26 Slovakia
27 Slovenia
28 Solomon Islands
29 Somalia
30
31 South Africa

November

1 (South Africa)
2 Spain
3
4 Sri Lanka
5
6 St Barthélemy, St Helena, St Kitts & Nevis, St Lucia
7 St Martin, St Pierre & Miquelon, St Vincent
8 Sudan
9
10
11 Suriname, Swaziland
12 Sweden
13 Switzerland
14 Syria
15 Tajikistan
16 Tanzania
17
18 Thailand
19
20 Timor Leste
21 Togo
22 Tonga, Trinidad & Tobago
23 Tunisia
24 Turkey
25
26
27 Turkmenistan
28 Turks & Caicos Is, Tuvalu
29 Uganda
30

December

1 Ukraine
2
3 United Arab Emirates
4 United Kingdom
5
6
7 United States of America
8
9
10
11
12 Uruguay
13 Uzbekistan
14
15 Vanuatu
16 Venezuela
17
18 Vietnam
19
20 Virg Is (USA), Wallis & Futuna Is
21 Yemen
22
23 Zambia
24 Zimbabwe
25
26 Global Facts & Figures (App 1)
27 Prayer Networks (App 2)
28 Mission Organizations (App 3)
29 World Leaders
30 *Operation World*
31 The Lord's Return

Prayer Calendar

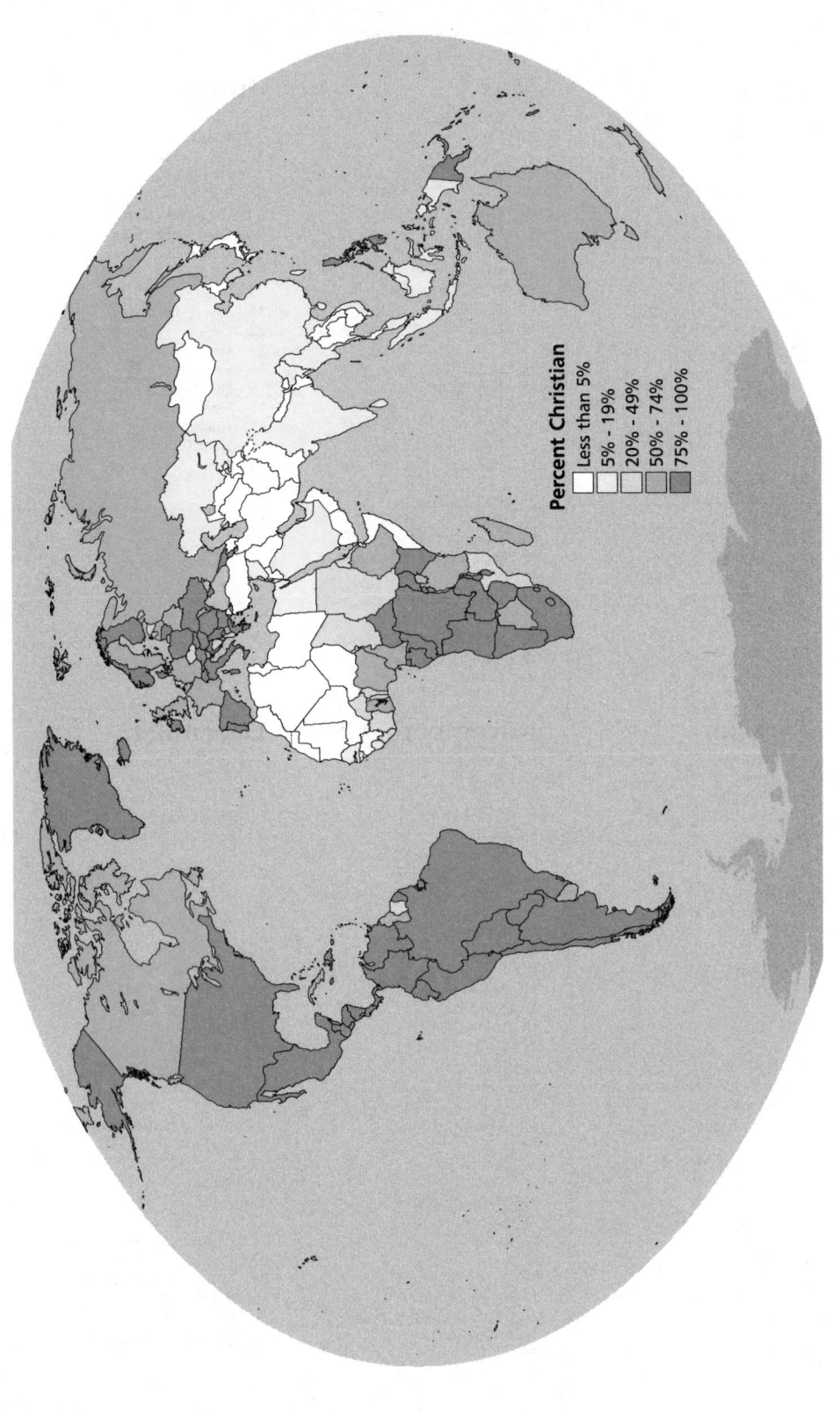

Percent Christian

Less than 5%
5% - 19%
20% - 49%
50% - 74%
75% - 100%

The World

The world's six continents – as defined by the United Nations. In this book, we follow this classification with a couple of exceptions: Cyprus is included in Europe, and the Caribbean region is separated from Latin America to become a sub-continent within the Americas.

Geography 🌍

Area 134,940,000 sq km. Antarctica, with 14 million sq km, is not included.

Population (in millions)		Ann Gr	Density
1950	2,529	1.1%	19/sq km
1955	2,763	1.9%	20/sq km
1960	3,023	1.9%	22/sq km
1965	3,332	2.0%	25/sq km
1970	3,686	2.1%	27/sq km
1975	4,061	2.0%	30/sq km
1980	4,438	1.9%	33/sq km
1985	4,846	1.8%	36/sq km
1990	5,290	1.8%	39/sq km
1995	5,713	1.6%	42/sq km
2000	6,115	1.4%	45/sq km
2005	6,512	1.3%	48/sq km
2010	6,908	1.2%	51/sq km
2015	7,302	1.1%	54/sq km
2020	7,675	1.0%	57/sq km
2025	8,012	0.9%	59/sq km
2030	8,309	0.7%	62/sq km

The world's population nearly doubled between 1970 and 2010. Global population growth rates peaked around 1970 and have steadily declined since then – the main contribution to this decline is smaller family size.

Cities There are 487 cities of over 1 million inhabitants, and 21 of over 10 million. **Urbanites** 51%. The urban population reached over 50% for the first time in history in 2009.

City Proper		Urban Agglomeration	
Shanghai	13.8m	Tokyo	36.7m
Mumbai	13.8m	Delhi	22.2m
Karachi	13.0m	São Paulo	20.3m
Delhi	12.6m	Mumbai	20.0m
Istanbul	11.4m	Mexico City	19.5m
São Paulo	11.0m	New York-Newark	19.4m
Moscow	10.5m	Shanghai	16.6m
Seoul	10.5m	Kolkata	15.6m
Beijing	10.1m	Dhaka	14.6m
Mexico City	8.8m	Karachi	13.1m

Note the difference in population between City Proper and Urban Agglomeration (source: UN).

Peoples 👪

The Joshua Project lists 16,350 distinct peoples; the World Christian Database lists 13,674 peoples. Both of these are based on an understanding of groups on an ethnolinguistic basis, transnational peoples being counted multiple times. We have generally used the former for both figures and taxonomy, with adjustments where more appropriate or recent data has come to light.

Languages The ministry envisaged helps define the boundary between a language and a dialect. The total numbers, therefore, vary.

> Ethnologue (2009 figures): 6,909 languages.
> The World Christian Encyclopedia: 13,511 languages and 30,000 dialects.
> Global Recordings Network estimates over 10,000 spoken languages and dialects.

Largest languages (First language speakers) Chinese 1,213 million; Spanish 329mill; English 328m; Arabic 221m; Hindi 182m; Bengali 181m; Portuguese 178m; Russian 144m; Japanese 122m; German 90m.

Languages with 0.00% Christian (Minimum 1 million speakers, fewer than 1 Christian per 10,000) East Uyghur 8.8m; Luri 5.4m; South Baloch 4.4m; Mazadarani 3.8m; Kedah Malay 2.9m; West Baloch 2.5m; East Baloch 2.3m; Aimaq 1.7m; Bedauye 1.6m; Chechen 1.4m; Dimli 1.3m; Manga 1.2m; Chittagong Asho 1.2m; Bele For 1.1m; Djamb 1.0m.

Official languages Populations in countries with: English 2,009m; Chinese 1,535m; Standard Hindi 1,214m; Spanish 412m; Arabic 351m; Portuguese 249m; French 242m; Indonesian 233m; Urdu 185m; Russian 175m; Bengali 164m; Japanese 125m. Not all in these countries speak the official language.

Languages with Scriptures (WBT translation stats) 457 Bi 1,202 NT 953 por; 2,582 total.

> Languages spoken in the world: 6,909.
> Number of active language programmes: 1,363.
> Languages that may need Scripture translation: 2,252.
> Languages with adequate Scriptures: 662.
> Population of people groups waiting for work to begin: 200m.

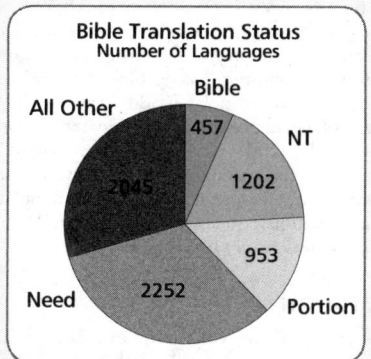

Bible Translation Status
Number of Languages

All Other

Bible 457

NT 1202

Portion 953

Need 2252

2045

Economy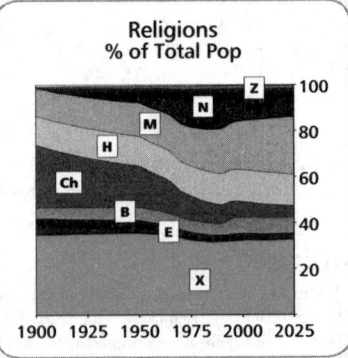

With the onset of globalization and the upward financial surge of a number of Majority World countries (China, India, Brazil, UAE and other Gulf microstates, several Southeast Asian countries), the gap between established economies and those that are emerging is lessening. At the same time, the poorest countries are being left behind due to a number of causes – lack of resources, lack of infrastructure, crippling debt, endemic corruption, high birth rates, unemployment, the economic effects of disease, ecological degradation and vulnerability to natural disasters. In many countries, remittances sent home by economic migrants abroad are a huge chunk of the GDP. With increased human mobility and ever-greater globalization, the ripple effect of any economic crash can affect an entire region or indeed the whole world, as did the financial crisis of 2008-2010. Increased levels of consumption, especially when adopted by the billions of people in Asia, may push the already-stretched resources of the world over the brink. The world must be weaned off its reliance upon fossil fuels and extraction economies (mining, logging, fishing, others), and more sustainable alternatives must be developed, especially as massive new economies in the Majority World push hard to catch up to the West. Other global economic issues that must be addressed: black market economies, especially in human and drug trafficking; financial controls over irresponsible banking and investment companies; overburdened pension schemes in developed countries; further relief of public debt in lower income countries and further economic development in poorer regions (which also profoundly affects issues of immigration).

Politics

The collapse of European Communism and the end of the Cold War in 1989-91 radically changed global politics. Now, countries tend to be driven much more by economics than by political ideology. The influence of religious and ethnic sensitivities has also increased. Coalescing continental groupings of nations into political allies and economic trading blocs has created a much more multi-polar world than the dualist nature of global politics that dominated the latter part of the 20th Century. Various forms of democracy and market economics have become much more widespread, yet the shape these take in many nations scarcely resembles what Western traditionalists would have envisioned.

Religion

The 20th Century was a time of dramatic shifts in religious profession. In light of the ever-broader values – including secularism, pluralism and liberalism – that globalization imposes onto the world, many regions, countries and ethnic groups react by reasserting a more traditional or fundamental expression of their faith. This goes for much of the Muslim world, the Hindu world, many contexts of traditional ethnic religions and even Christianity. Persecution remains, with some countries and areas seeing intensified levels and others seeing decreased levels. The Pew Religious Forum lists 43 countries with high or very high government restrictions on religious freedom and 36 with moderate restrictions. The Open Doors World Watch List of the 50 nations with the highest levels of persecution of Christians includes 39 predominantly Muslim countries, 6 Secular/Communist/Marxist states, 4 Buddhist countries and 1 Hindu country.

Religions	Pop %	Population	Ann Gr*
Christian	32.29	2,229,951,315	1.2%
Muslim	22.90	1,581,765,792	1.9%
Hindu	13.88	958,695,903	1.2%
Non-religious	13.58	937,904,918	0.7%
Buddhist	6.92	478,164,008	1.3%
Chinese	5.94	409,917,596	0.0%
Ethnoreligionist	3.00	206,942,003	0.6%
Other	0.85	58,613,020	0.8%
Sikh	0.35	23,990,543	1.4%
Jew	0.21	14,523,554	0.3%
Baha'i	0.09	6,181,049	0.9%

*Only religions with a growth rate of over 1.2% are increasing faster than the world's population.

This table shows the breakdown of the world's countries by continent and the predominant religion. For example, 33 African countries are predominantly Christian.

Religions	Af	As	Eu	Am	Pa	World
Christian	33	5	43	53	25	159
Muslim	22	27	2	0	1	52
Buddhist/Ch	0	13	0	0	1	14
Non-religious	0	2	2	0	0	4
Hindu	0	2	0	0	0	2
Ethnoreligionist	1	0	0	0	0	1
Jewish	0	1	0	0	0	1
Total	**56**	**50**	**47**	**53**	**27**	**233**

**Religions
% of Total Pop**

Christians	Pop %	Affiliates	Ann Gr
Protestant	7.19	496,978,493	1.8%
Independent	3.73	257,390,482	2.6%
Anglican	1.18	81,565,557	1.6%
Catholic	15.77	1,089,734,865	0.6%
Orthodox	3.52	243,133,169	0.2%
Marginal	0.66	45,295,532	1.9%
Unaffiliated	1.90	131,063,056	1.3%
Doubly Affiliated (2)	*-1.61*	*-111,267,574*	*0.0%*

TransBloc	Pop %	Population	Ann Gr
Evangelicals			
Evangelicals	7.90	545,886,818	2.6%
Renewalists			
Charismatics	6.17	426,097,092	3.4%
Pentecostals	2.57	178,082,864	2.6%

Orthodox and Catholics are declining as a percentage of the world's population, but Protestants and Anglicans are slowly growing (mainly because of growth in the non-Western world). The Marginal MegaBloc (mainly JWs and Mormons) grew substantially from under 1 million followers in 1900 to 45 million in 2000. Growth of newer "post-denominational" churches and networks has characterized the past generation with a bewildering variety of expressions of Christian belief and practice. This Independent MegaBloc grew from 7 million in 1900 to well over 250 million in 2010. Many are independent evangelical, Pentecostal and charismatic denominations and networks.

The following diagram illustrates this change over the 20th Century and projection to 2025, assuming present trends continue.

The most dynamic growth in Christianity is within movements that transcend the Christian MegaBlocs and within component denominations and networks.

Evangelicals emerged as a dynamic force after the revivals of the 18th and 19th Centuries and were used of God in the great expansion of Christianity in the 19th and 20th Centuries. The startling growth of non-Western (AfAsLA) evangelicals in the latter half of the 20th and early part of the 21st Centuries is evident.

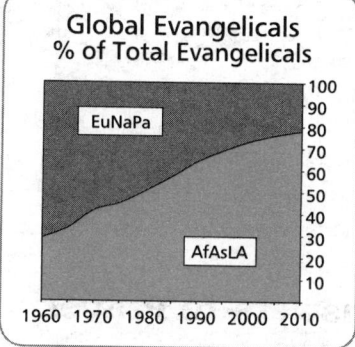

Global Evangelicals
% of Total Evangelicals

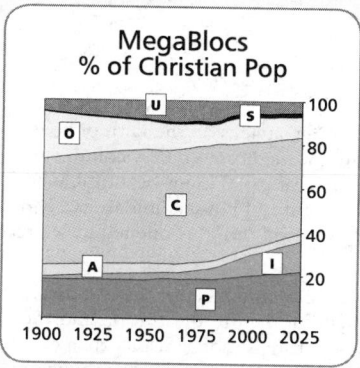

MegaBlocs
% of Christian Pop

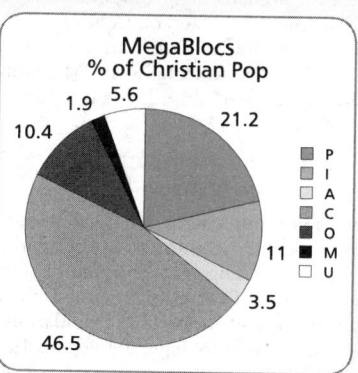

MegaBlocs
% of Christian Pop

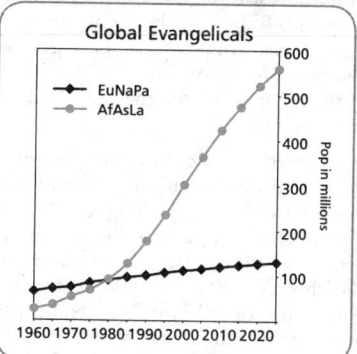

Global Evangelicals

Pentecostals sprang out of early 20th Century revivals. Their growth is spectacular – from virtually no Pentecostals in 1900 to over 177 million in 2010. Pentecostals are by definition evangelical. They are also by definition a subset of charismatics, usually First Wave charismatics.

Charismatics began to multiply within nearly all MegaBlocs and denominations, but primarily emerged from mainline confessions throughout the 1950s and 1960s (Second Wave). Subsequently, other charismatics from a broader array of backgrounds formed their own new networks and structures (Third Wave). The latter comprises a large segment of the Independent MegaBloc. All charismatics (including historic Pentecostal denominations, individuals within non-charismatic denominations and those in post-denominational networks) have grown from less than a million in 1900 to around 425 million in 2010.

This diagram shows the growth of these movements over the past 50 years.

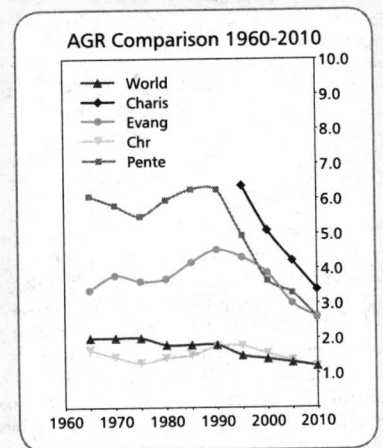

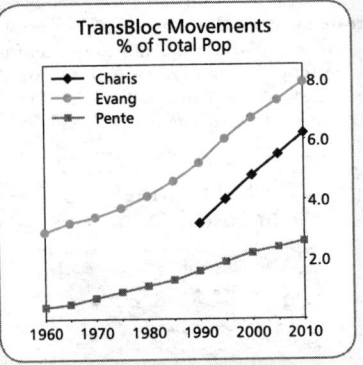

Note that all Pentecostals are both evangelical and charismatic and are P or I. Most evangelicals are P, I or A, and smaller numbers are C or O. Most charismatics in P, I or A are evangelicals; much less so among C.

Answers to Prayer

God remains sovereign in our world today, now as ever. Yet, attacks on the faith of believers are widespread. Today's media zoom their cameras in on and dedicate endless column inches to wars, disasters, famines, scandals, tragedies and every form of evil. Things beautiful, wholesome and good, however, are less photogenic, so the works of God and His servants are rarely noticed. Like the disciples on the road to Emmaus (Luke 24), we need our eyes opened to see reality – God among us.

Here on earth, we see through a glass dimly (1 Cor 13:12) – much better that we dwell on this picture: a countless multitude from every people, standing before the throne and the Lamb, celebrating and praising God (Rev 7:9-10). Today, this picture is more a reality than ever before – it has been a most remarkable generation in Church history. Patrick Johnstone, when queried in 1979 about the most difficult places for gospel breakthrough, named Mongolia and Albania. Today, there are at least 40,000 Mongolian believers. Albania is open and churches are growing. Who among us, 30 years ago, could have envisioned over 100 million Chinese Christians, massive people movements in Iran, Algeria and Sudan, breakthroughs in Mozambique, Cambodia and Nepal, and the beginnings of freedom for hundreds of millions of oppressed in India? Only God!

So here, as in subsequent sections of this book, we begin with answers to prayer – especially those from the past decade – with all gratitude and praise to our sovereign Lord.

① The unprecedented harvest of new believers continues across Africa, Asia and Latin America, in contrast to the relative stagnation or decline in the rest of the world. The tables below reveal a remarkable story of a growing, spreading and diversifying Church. The table of statistics shows the relative change of the world's population for each of the MegaBlocs. Christianity has slightly declined as a percentage of the world's population since 1900 – only the Protestant, Independent and Marginal MegaBlocs have defied this trend to gain a proportion of the world's population.

Change in MegaBlocs as a Percentage of World Population					Percentage of World's Christians in AfAsLA by MegaBloc			
	1900	1960	2010	2025		1900	1960	2010	2025

	1900	1960	2010	2025		1900	1960	2010	2025
P	6.2	6.5	7.2	7.6	P	5.4	17.7	66.7	73.7
I	0.4	1.0	3.7	4.8	I	2.4	56.8	87.8	90.1
A	1.9	1.4	1.2	1.3	A	4.0	9.8	62.8	72.9
C	16.8	18.4	15.8	15.0	C	26.8	47.5	69.3	72.9
O	7.6	4.2	3.5	3.1	O	9.2	20.5	24.4	28.9
M	0.2	0.3	0.7	0.7	M	6.5	23.0	62.9	67.1
U	1.7	3.4	1.9	1.7	U	6.4	28.7	43.3	43.6
2	-0.1	-0.4	-1.6	-1.6	All Christians	16.7	35.3	63.2	69.1
Total	34.7	34.8	32.3	32.6					

a) Christianity re-affirmed as a global religion. The concept of Christianity as a European "white-man's religion" is demonstrably a myth. Though sometimes small in number, all but concealed, or mostly members of a minority people group, there are now Christians living and fellowshipping in every country on earth. World mission, globalization and high migration rates have dispersed the Church into every corner of the world, both to previously unevangelized areas and back to traditionally Christian regions where the Church is in sharp decline.

b) The astonishing shift of Christianity's centre of gravity to the Majority World. The tables reveal that, though Christianity's percentage in the world population has changed little, the proportions between the Majority World and the West/North have changed dramatically. This is praiseworthy, as hundreds of millions heard the good news for the first time in the past century. It is also an indication that the missionary efforts of the past 200 years have borne incredible fruit, though at times it was slow in coming. Years and generations of prayer and faithful service to the unevangelized world by both missionaries and indigenous Christians have not been in vain.

c) The strength and growth of the Church in lands that now have, or have had in the past, severe persecution. Some examples of places where both persecution and Church growth are prominent include China, India, Sudan, Ethiopia, Vietnam, Iran and Myanmar, to name but a few.

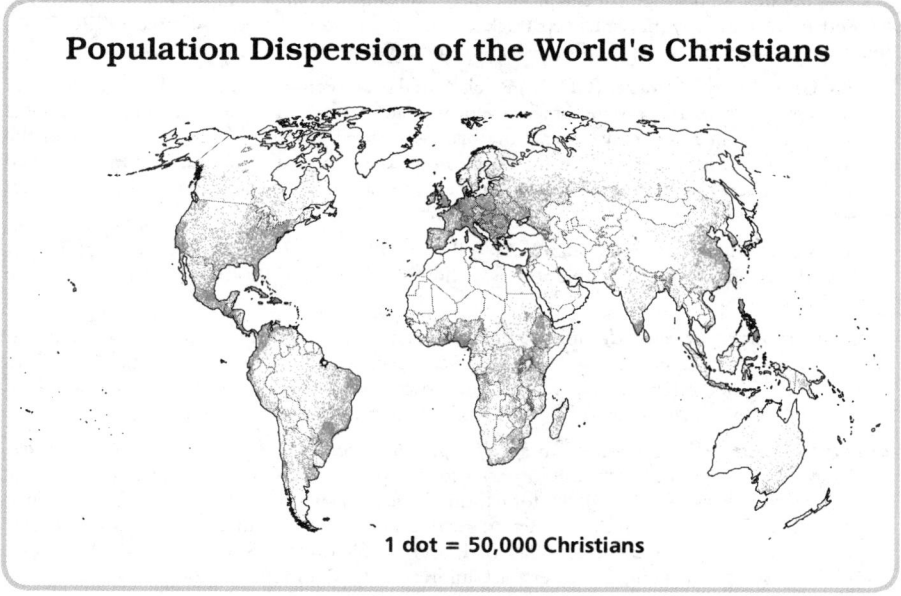

Population Dispersion of the World's Christians

1 dot = 50,000 Christians

2 **Evangelical Christianity grew at a rate faster than any other world religion or global religious movement.** The post-WWII surge of evangelical missions was an astonishing success story, but most of the subsequent growth came from a new generation of indigenous evangelical movements around the world. Evangelicals numbered 89 million (2.9%) in 1960, but by 2010 they were 546 million (7.9%). The growth rate peaked around 1990 at 4.5%. With population growth rates for the world generally in decline, it is almost inevitable that all other rates will see a relative decline as well. Without an amazing outpouring of the Holy Spirit, such growth cannot be sustained.

3 **Renewal movements have grown at an unforeseen rate** – from the birth of the Pentecostal movement at the beginning of the 20th Century, to the first stirrings of charismatic renewal in the 1950s and 1960s, to the Third Wave in the latter part of the 20th Century, and finally to the 21st Century and what many believe is a new (and possibly final) global outpouring of the Holy Spirit that exceeds them all. Pentecostals grew from 12 million in 1960 to 178 million in 2010; charismatics from 167 million in 1990 to 426 million in 2010. The charismatic renewal has touched many parts of the Church, in thousands of denominations, in nearly every country. Despite imperfections (sinful humans are involved, after all), charismatic renewal has revitalized the faith of approaching half a billion people in an era where opposition and temptation come from myriad quarters.

4 **The gospel took root within hundreds of the world's least reached peoples.** In many cases, peoples with no known believers ten or twenty years ago now have churches within them, some of them thriving, growing churches now involved themselves in the Great Commission! The 1990s saw the most concerted attempt to analyze the need of the world – a process in which *Operation World* itself played a part. And 1995 saw the beginning of the Joshua Project List (JPL), originally a list of 1,583 of the world's least reached peoples. While this is expanded to now include all peoples in the world (16,350), the original list served as a catalyst for the Church to pray for, adopt and engage with every one of these least reached peoples. It also inspired national-level research in many countries where the 1,583 were found; this missiological and people group research by Majority World Christians has been a major step toward completion of the Great Commission. Much pioneering work remains, but praise God for miraculous opening of doors and receptivity to the gospel in new places – some once considered all but impossible to reach.

5 **Prayer movements and networks multiplied and grew** as God's people joined together to pray on an unprecedented scale and with greater focus and breadth. Movements on local, national and international levels are praying for communities, nations, peoples and thematic issues as well. Sustained, informed, impassioned intercession is occurring as never before and throughout the globe. There are simply too many grassroots movements to list and more than anyone can keep track of, but International Prayer Connect (IPC) links hundreds of prayer networks and ministries to focus prayer on common global concerns.

a) ***The Global Day of Prayer*** (GDOP) is celebrated every Pentecost Sunday. It originated over 10 years ago from a city-wide prayer event in Cape Town. It is an African-initiated, annual call to repentance and prayer that now brings together believers in every country in the world to focus locally and globally on pleading with the Lord for our communities and nations. Tens, if not hundreds, of millions of Christians have participated in these meetings over the years.

b) ***Grassroots prayer networks,*** such as 24/7 Prayer and IHOP (International House of Prayer), draw thousands of young people into a worldwide, unbroken stream of prayer and worship to God.

c) ***Days of prayer for countries and nations.*** Dozens of countries dedicate one day each year to pray for their nation. These days are observed nationally, but concerned believers from around the globe often participate from their own locales as well. Some are specifically held to mobilize prayer from abroad for less reached nations.

d) ***Days or networks of prayer for specific peoples, vulnerable groups or special issues.*** Believers in any country can join in prayer for the persecuted Church (International Day of Prayer for the Persecuted Church), for Muslims (the 30-Days Prayer Network), for unreached peoples or regions (Global Prayer Digest, Praying Through the Arabian Peninsula, others), for groups and areas of great need (Call to Prayer for Victims of Sex Trade Trafficking, Viva Network World Weekend of Prayer for Children at Risk) and many more.

For a more extensive (but far from comprehensive) list of prayer networks and ministries, see Appendix 2 Further Prayer Information on p923.

6 **Aid, development and charity work across the globe** escalated through the 1980s and 1990s and continue in this decade. The civil sector (NGOs) is now the eighth-largest economy in the world, worth over $1 trillion per year globally. Praise God that, more than before, the needs of the most vulnerable and needy are being addressed. Also give thanks for:

a) *A more holistic understanding of evangelical mission* within the Church. Ministry that cares for orphans and widows, uplifts the poor, brings liberty to the oppressed and sets captives free reflects the heart of God, the values of the Scriptures and the role of the Church. Caring for the downtrodden and vulnerable and demonstrating practically Christ's love are increasingly – and rightly – the focused activities of evangelical ministry. At many times, evangelicals in particular have lacked a healthy balance of spiritual ministry and practical ministry (as if the purposes of God could be so easily compartmentalized!). Give thanks for the Church's increasing understanding that Christ's Kingdom can and must transform every aspect of life and community.

b) *Doors to many places and peoples previously closed are open* to aid workers, educators, technical tradesmen and virtually any other occupation. Believers have opportunities to enter countries and serve with NGOs, to see redemptive changes occur in communities, to collaborate with other altruistic-minded people and organizations. Just as significant are the opportunities to present an excellent witness for God's transforming love through practical assistance to those in need.

Pray that this global trend might continue to pave roads for the spread of the gospel to those among whom Christians wish to serve, to non-Christians labouring alongside Jesus' followers and to community and government leaders who are themselves potentially great change-makers for the Kingdom of God.

7 **The globalization of the Great Commission movement** has profoundly changed the face of mission. Since the late 1970s, there has been a surge of interest and involvement in missions from the Majority World. Mission sending has recently gained or maintained momentum in countries such as Ethiopia, Nigeria, Brazil, Philippines, South Korea and others. Involvement by the more traditional sending regions of North America, Europe and the Pacific has stayed level at best and often declined. The world missions force is more multicultural and multinational than ever before. It faces challenges – and solutions – distinct to the 21st Century. For a listing of the world's missionaries sent by country, see Appendix 3 Further Mission Information on p930.

a) *The Majority World Church as the dominant force in mission sending.* The USA remains the largest sending nation of foreign missionaries, but South Korea has replaced the UK as the second largest. India's missionary movement flourishes even as the foreign missionary presence within India dries up. India trails the USA in total workers; although the vast majority of India's missionaries serve within India, many work in a cross-cultural environment. According to some reliable sources, China's population of missionaries (those who go and are sent out as such from their churches) exceeds even the USA, although the large majority remain within China itself. Mission from the Majority World is shaped by several factors:

i *The increasing number of national sending agencies and associations.* This is especially true among newer Churches who send workers from the first or second generation of believers. Central and East Asia as well as Eastern Europe are encouraging examples of this in the past decade. Growing numbers of countries are forming sending structures to facilitate sending workers from their nations to the world. Most countries with sizeable evangelical populations have mission associations that connect and resource mission structures within the country.

ii *Partnerships between Global North and South workers and agencies.* The North is learning to work as equals with or even serve under the leadership of those from the Global South. International agencies increasingly see their new recruits come from countries in the Majority World.

iii *The emergence of distinctive mission movements and visions for reaching the unreached.* God has long placed on the hearts of believers around the world desires and plans for reaching the nations. Some have been pursued across many decades – the Back to Jerusalem vision among the Han Chinese aims to retrace the historic Silk Road trade routes between Asia and the Mediterranean, with 100,000 Chinese church-planting evangelists sharing Jesus along the way. Other visions have been birthed more recently, such as Nigeria's Vision 5015 to send 50,000 workers in 15 years with the gospel across the north of Africa, also toward Jerusalem. Latin American movements send workers to North Africa, the Middle East and Europe. Pacific Islanders, building on the Deep Sea Canoe vision, send workers to other indigenous peoples.

b) New methods of sending workers to the least reached are being explored. Modern Protestant mission has, for the past two centuries, been propelled with great success by the mission agency structure, even despite its failures and limitations. This model will continue to provide an excellent means of sending and supporting the world's mission force among the nations. But in some cases, changes in global politics and economics necessitate developing new models and paradigms of mission work. Some of these are highly successful, others are not, while others wait with birth pangs.

i *Affinity partnering networks have formed across agencies* for shared vision and focus. This focus might apply to a people, a region or a religious bloc. Such networks provide partnership, shared resources, research initiatives and, in some cases, umbrella groups serving pioneer workers from all agencies reaching the target peoples. Most of these operate in sensitive, creative-access contexts, so listing them by name would be unhelpful to their cause.

ii *Relief and development work by mission agencies allows* many believers, passionate about social causes and the gospel, to serve abroad. World Vision, World Relief, Tearfund and MedAir are just a few familiar names among hundreds, if not thousands, of such agencies. Others, however, serve Christ but work through secular international NGOs such as the UN, *Médecins Sans Frontières*, Oxfam, CARE International and others.

iii *Experts in business, industry, education or other fields* serve as lay workers around the world. Outstanding opportunities for such exist, in many cases, among the least reached. While some serve through agencies, others go on their own or with loose connections to networks. For many professionals with a passion for the Great Commission, it makes no sense to re-train to work, for example, as a pastor or evangelist, when open doors and natural peer networks already exist for lawyers, engineers, architects and entrepreneurs.

iv *Believers living in diaspora are increasingly a strong mission force.* Filipinos, South Koreans, Chinese, South Asians and Nigerians in particular see opportunities for such Kingdom service. When such diasporas lock into the power of these millions of potential tentmakers, the awakening of intentional missional living will reap an abundant harvest in their host countries.

There are strengths and weaknesses involved in each method, and finding new ways forward is never tidy. Pray that devoted followers of Christ might, with passion, urgency, wisdom and discernment, seize available opportunities to more effectively reach the world's least reached.

c) Areas of crisis and tension draw increased attention to fields of great need. Consider:

i *The heightened awareness, globally, of the size, complexity and evangelistic challenges of the Muslim world* – largely through events of 9/11 – birthed in many believers a burden for Muslims. In the past 20 years, more Muslims than ever before have come to Christ, more workers serve in Muslim heartlands, more agencies focus on these regions and more sustained intercession is given for these peoples precious to God. There are the beginnings of what may well become a flood of Muslims discovering Jesus, demonstrating His Lordship over all peoples.

ii *Political crises in Buddhist strongholds such as Tibet, Thailand and Cambodia similarly caused increased interest in the Buddhist world,* long a tough mission challenge with little progress. Mongolia, Cambodia and Vietnam, all strongly influenced by Buddhism, now see unprecedented Christian growth. A trickle of first fruits is also occurring among Tibetan peoples. May the rest of the Buddhist world soon experience the same.

iii *The upheaval in the Hindu world* has likewise drawn greater attention to this large swathe of the human population. Civil war and continued turmoil in Nepal, unrest, religious violence and persecution in certain parts of India and the continued plight of the Dalits/Untouchables have all attracted prayer, mobilization and ministry on a great scale. This, in turn, has yielded incredible growth in the Church in Nepal and India. Pray, however, for an awakening of focus and a harvest force to work among higher caste and middle class Hindus.

8 **Collaboration of the Church on a global level** now shapes the prospects for finishing the Great Commission task. Praise God for:

a) Events drawing mission-minded groups together. Several commemorative events held in 2010 – all reflecting on 100 years of Protestant missions, from the 1910 World Missionary Conference to the present – brought the worldwide Church together to celebrate God's work in the past century and to look toward completing the task of world evangelization together. Most notable for evangelicals may be the Third Lausanne Congress on World Evangelization (**LCWE**). Even the preparatory meetings and exercises for these events have created a great spirit of unity and purpose for those involved.

b) Shared focus and vision. Global movements significantly shaped the course of world mission in the past generation. In addition to the GDOP and **LCWE** mentioned above, a handful of movements gathered Christian leaders to collaborate in ministry efforts.

i *The Lausanne Congress for World Evangelization* launched in 1974, with Billy Graham as its driving force. No other meeting – not since Acts 15 – has had as far-reaching and monumental an impact on world mission as the **LCWE**. The two key results of this gathering are the Lausanne Covenant (the evangelical manifesto and statement of faith) and the emergence of "people group" thinking – an area previously unheard of or ignored. Lausanne, along with the World Evangelical Alliance (**WEA**), are the key fellowships linking together the world's evangelicals.

ii *The AD2000 and Beyond Movement,* launched in 1989, proved to be the most global, focused movement for world evangelization in the Church's history. Events such as the Global Consultations on World Evangelism in 1995 (Seoul) and 1997 (Pretoria) were essential for setting the tone for global mission in the following years. Its ministry ended in January 2001, according to its charter, but the effects continue to impact the 21st Century.

iii *The Ethne Movement* followed from a series of consultations and conferences carrying parts of the AD2000 Movement beyond the year 2000. The specific and only focus of this movement remains collaborating across countries and regions to reach the world's remaining unreached peoples.

iv *Other movements have emerged* to connect ministries and churches, to mobilize and inspire and to focus attention on specific challenges while maintaining a global scope. Some key examples: Transform World with its focus on the 4/14 Window (reaching children between the ages of 4 and 14), Call2All, Finishing the Task, the Billion Soul Coalition and many others.

c) Shared ministry and resources. It is difficult to measure the impact of multiple means of ministry to non-believers – personal witness, literature, Scripture translation, Christian audio resources, TV, the Internet and the many other tools God uses. But the cumulative effects of multiple layers of ministry greatly increase the likelihood of non-Christians hearing the gospel and the possibility of response.

i *Scripture availability and translation.* Through the combined ministries of the Bible Societies and Bible translation agencies, 95% of the world's population has access to Scripture in a language they can understand, though not always in a heart language. The remaining 5% represents over 300 million people. Vision 2025 aims to see a Bible translation programme started in every language that needs one by the year 2025 – since 1999, new translation programmes for 617 languages have started for communities with no known Scriptures. This equals 82% of the 750 programmes known to Wycliffe started by all organizations during this same time. The Epic Partnership unites **WBT** (Bible translation), **YWAM** (training young people for evangelism), **CCCI** (audio/visual resources and national partnerships) and **IMB** (church planting strategies) to reach the estimated four billion people who learn primarily through the spoken rather than the written word.

ii *Audio resources.* The 10K Challenge is an initiative to see in this generation a recording work started in 4,400 more heart languages. This will bring the total number of languages in which **GRN** has made recordings up to the 10,000 mark. The World by Radio consortium of Christian broadcasting agencies committed to provide Christian radio programming for every person on earth in a language they could understand.

iii *The JESUS film* has had several billion individual viewings worldwide since 1979, through the work of more than 1,500 Christian agencies. This has yielded over 200 million responses. Available in over 1,000 languages, well over 99% of the world's population should be able to view the film in a language they know.

iv Media ministries are ever more crucial in the 21st Century as electronic and digital media come to dominate the world of communication. Christian satellite TV (especially in the Middle East and West Asia), **EHC**, FCBH, digital audio Bibles and more could be added to these multiple layers of global gospel coverage.

v The Internet as a tool for evangelism, discipleship, fellowship, worship and training is limited only by the creativity and commitment of Christians. The possibilities are endless. This tool, probably more than any other, will shape the nature of the Church and mission as the 21st Century unfolds. Paired inexorably with this is the phenomenal spread of mobile phones and their potential for evangelism and ministry.

vi Research organizations and networks. Previously conducted by but a handful of individuals or agency offices, global collaboration among these entities is increasing. National and global-level research groups help piece together the status of global Christianity and world evangelization; they present findings and, in doing so, shape mission strategy, mobilize workers and fuel prayer. Praise God for a spirit of collegiality in this essential work. Pray for more believers with the right skills and giftings who are willing and eager to be involved.

The sobering fact is that, even with all this activity, probably 24–27% of the world's population have not had the good news presented to them in a way they could appreciate and meaningfully respond to.

Global Hot Spots

Listed here are some of the critical international hot spots most likely to cause turmoil, conflict, suffering or even war in the coming years. These need to be covered in prayer. Please see the individual regions and countries for more details; there are too many to develop a more comprehensive list.

1 **The future of Jerusalem.** The world's holiest city is probably also its most volatile flashpoint. Conflict between Israelis and Palestinians has resisted major international efforts to resolve it. The fundamental and seemingly irreconcilable differences between most Israelis and Arabs mean that any outbreak of serious conflict can easily embroil neighbouring countries – especially Lebanon and Syria. Many feel that such a war is almost inevitable. Pray for the peace of Jerusalem.

2 **The Korean Peninsula** is shared between an untenable, failing dictatorship and an affluent but nervous democracy. If or when reunification comes, the main questions are whether it will happen peacefully and at what cost rebuilding the North will occur. War would be disastrous for both sides.

3 **Somalia** is a textbook example of a failed state; it is a broken land populated by warlords, pirates, an uprooted and exiled shambles of a government and a number of aggressive Islamist groups. The upheaval has spilled into the Horn of Africa and significantly affected marine traffic in the busy shipping lanes along its coast.

4 **Central Africa,** while not the cauldron of anarchy it was in the 1990s, retains much of the upheaval and unrest of those dark times. Eastern DRC and northwest Uganda in particular still suffer from the predations of lawless militias.

5 **Afghanistan and Pakistan** remain vulnerable to religious extremism. While the former has been stabilized significantly by heavy foreign military presence, religious terrorism and violence have gripped Pakistan in the past decade. The porous mountain borders between the two countries offer the ideal location for the Taliban to persist with their radical Islamist agenda. Both remain among the world's most unstable and dangerous nations.

6 **China's growing self-confidence and assertiveness** seem less of a threat externally as it seeks to engage the world as a financial, rather than a military, power. However, its increasing global strength is not without its opponents – and victims. There are also increasing tensions with the Uyghur and Tibetan minorities, the looming demographic and economic fallout of a rapidly aging population resulting from the One Child Policy and the massive gender gap with a shortfall of millions of females. All have serious consequences.

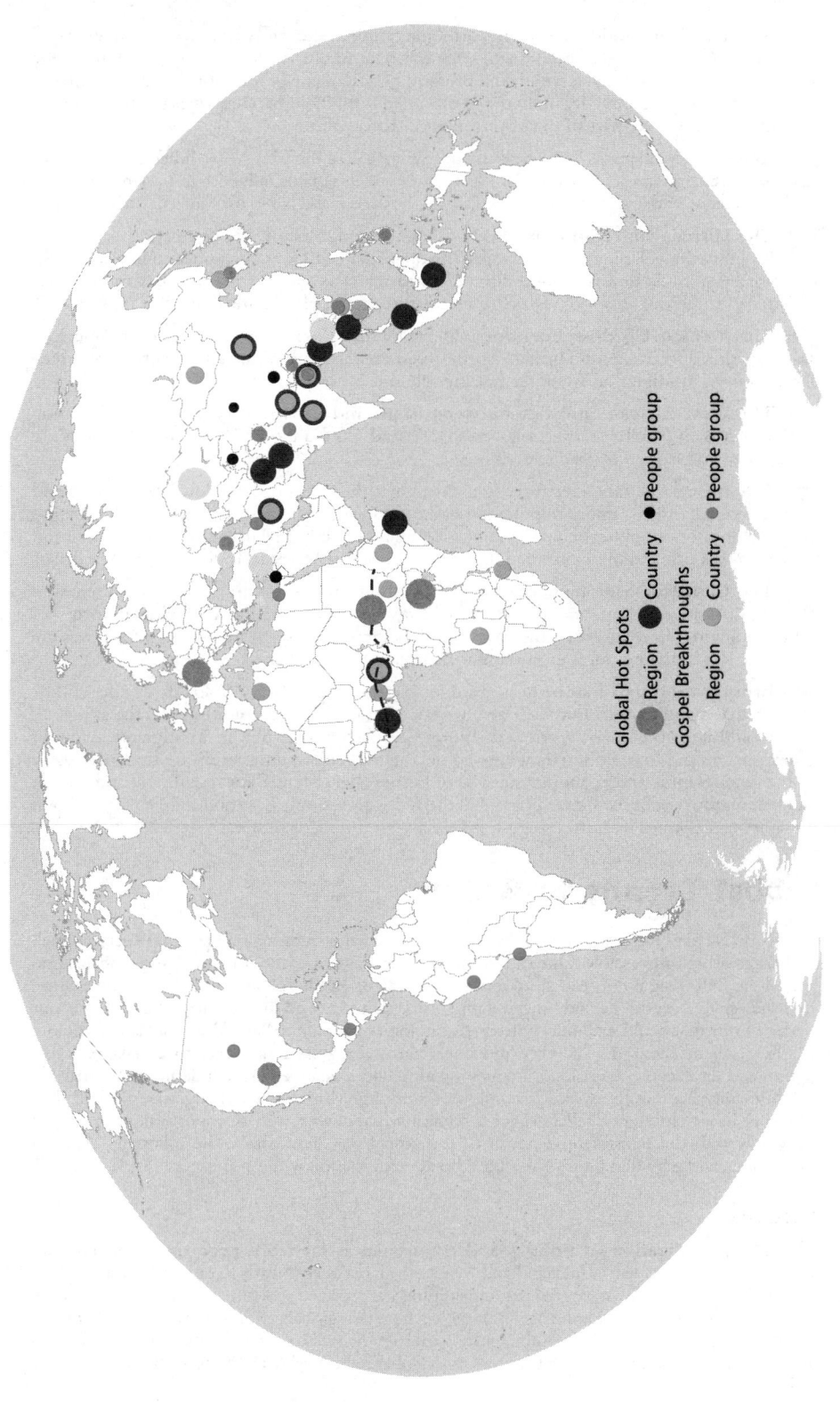

Global Hot Spots
● Region ● Country ● People group

Gospel Breakthroughs
● Region ● Country ● People group

7 **Sudan's deep divide** between north and south is currently spanned by an awkward truce after decades of conflict and civil war. The results of the 2011 referendum in the south regarding independence will bring profound consequences. Additionally, Darfur remains an unresolved tragedy. Literally millions are uprooted from these two regions, victims of Arabist, Islamist agendas on the part of the government in Khartoum.

8 **Iran** is a regional power unto itself and the Shi'ite half of the West Asia/Middle East region. Its unbending stance on developing nuclear power and its notable influence in Iraq may put it on a collision course with other nations, particularly in the West. It also has its own internal stability issues.

9 **The Himalayan region** simmers with tension and division. The competing claims over Kashmir, the volatile nature of Nepal, the oppression of Tibet, the upheaval in Bangladesh and Northeast India and the opposition of India and Pakistan on many issues make this a potentially dangerous area – especially since the three main players are all nuclear powers.

10 **The Mexico–US drug corridor** is an area where the hedonistic excesses of American appetites effectively fund brutal wars between various drug cartels and government forces. Tensions from immigration issues further fuel the fire.

11 **The West African fault line between Islam and Christianity** has seen clashes, mob violence and civil war, especially in Nigeria and Côte d'Ivoire. Religious differences are exacerbated and fuelled by ethnic divisions.

12 **A Southeast Asian corridor,** from Myanmar through Thailand down to Malaysia and Indonesia, offers a range of potential flashpoints – the Burmese military junta's brutality, the widening socio-political chasm and possible military coup in Thailand, the Muslim unrest in Thailand's south and the continued threat of Islamism in Malaysia, Indonesia and Mindanao.

13 **The Caucasus** has long been a hotbed of ethnic violence, with the overlay of renewed Russian imperialism and deep religious divides. More radical and violent forms of Islam are beginning to assert themselves, and secessionist regions in the Russian Caucasus are displaying increasing boldness in pushing for autonomy.

14 **Immigration** into Europe is an unstoppable tide of humanity from Africa, the Middle East, Asia and Eastern Europe. The plunging birthrates in EU countries and the affluence, stability and generous social services in Europe are factors that pull in immigrants, many of whom are coming from countries where conflict rages. While immigration is utterly necessary for the demographic and economic survival of Europe, the potential for resentment and violent backlash on the part of the native peoples of the EU is also strong. Postmodern secularism, Islam and Christianity must learn to co-exist or face a very turbulent future.

Global Trends to Watch

The world is changing at an ever-increasing rate, sometimes so dizzyingly fast that keeping track of changes is nigh impossible. One cannot discuss world issues without mentioning globalization – all of the following points touch upon it in one way or another. The confluence of the following issues spells a crucial period for humanity – one that may end in unmitigated disaster for our species or one that could spell new systems, technologies and values that address the dangers before us. The crises in economic inequity and uncertainty, energy systems, terrorism, massive immigration and displacement, ecological contamination and climate change all demonstrate that the way humanity handles the world is simply not working. Monumental changes are needed. The following issues represent challenges for a biblical worldview as well as opportunities to impact the world with the transforming power of the gospel of Christ. Bathe the following crises in intercession, and pray that God's will might be done in the following realms:

Social

1 **The globalization of politics and economics is far from accomplished.** The vast differences between Somaliland and Switzerland, between North Korea and New Zealand indicate this clearly. Many states, regions and cultures have reacted – at times, violently – against the unwelcome and fear-inducing intrusion of the changes that globalization brings. Yet, the shrinking of the world generates a global youth culture, a globally networked world economy, a global news and media industry and, one might dare to say, a globalized evangelical Church culture.

2 **International terrorism came to the fore** in 2001 with the 9/11 tragedy and subsequent attacks in Madrid, London, Moscow, Bali, Iraq, Pakistan, Mumbai and elsewhere. Most, but not all, are driven by radical Islamist groups against what they perceive to be wicked worldly powers. Increasingly available firearms, easy access to the knowledge and means of bomb-making and the willingness of many terrorists to maximize damage by committing suicide all create the potential for very destructive attacks. In the past decade, a vast amount of money, manpower and expertise have been spent on intelligence, surveillance, prevention and proactive actions against terrorist groups. These have had notable implications for international travel, trade and diplomacy, shaping profoundly the foreign and domestic policies of many nations, particularly the USA.

3 **The insidious power of international crime empires.** Globalization probably benefits the wicked and corrupt as much as, if not more than, those with good intentions. Some of these are the US mafia, the Colombian drug cartels, Chinese Triads, Japanese yakuza, Jamaican yardies, Russian Bratva, the Calabrian 'Ndrangheta, Sicilian Cosa Nostra, Neapolitan Camorra and many others.

a) *Drug networks* link the largest growers (Andean republics, Central Asia, the Golden Triangle of Southeast Asia) with the largest users (the West, China, India).

b) *Smuggling of contraband* ranges from cigarettes and alcohol, to antiques and art, to live animals and weapons and firearms.

c) *Money laundering* on a massive scale.

d) *Control and extortion of politicians and business and industry leaders* as well as their influence over entire economies.

4 **Human trafficking** is now the main activity of traffickers, replacing drugs and firearms, and is one of the great blights of our time. Today, approaching 30 million people live in what amounts to slavery. This industry generates $32 billion annually. The vast majority of the 800,000 who are smuggled across international borders each year are either deceived or coerced; 80% of them are women or children, and 70% of the women are trafficked for sexual exploitation. Around 1.2 million children are used by the global commercial sex trade. Only a tiny fraction of traffickers – who are women almost as frequently as men – are ever brought to justice.

5 **Threats to human health,** including disease. HIV/AIDS has been the high profile disease of the past 20 years, but treatments, increasing awareness and changing behaviour patterns see infection rates declining. Cancer continues to take many lives all over the world. New, resistant strains of old diseases, such as malaria and tuberculosis, are spreading. HIV, SARS and H5N1 are examples of recent pandemics; fears abound of new ones, more virulent and deadly. Less glamorously, diseases associated with malnutrition, poverty, unclean water supplies and lack of sanitation are even greater threats to children – pneumonia, diarrhoea, TB and others. Included in this is malaria, which kills as many people globally as AIDS and has a similarly devastating effect on economies. Air and water pollution probably contribute to as many deaths annually as all of these diseases combined.

6 **Technological developments** have taken modern civilization in unanticipated directions. There are no flying cars, moon colonies or teleportation devices (yet!), but technology has advanced in a number of areas at a rate no one could have conceived. In all of these areas are great potential benefits and risks as well as the human ability to exploit them for good or for evil.

a) *Communications technology* that connects machines, people and communities. The digital revolution continues to push forward. The ubiquity of the Internet and the rapid global exchange of information radically alter the way the world works – financially, politically and socially. Cyber warfare, therefore, is an area of quickly increasing interest and growth.

b) *Developments in computing* and mobile phone technologies continue at a dizzying rate. Ever-smaller components with ever-greater processing power, robotics, cloud programming, artificial intelligence and virtual reality may all profoundly impact the future of every area of our lives. One risk for ministry is the reduced amount of personal, face-to-face contact that may occur for humans in the future, but the above two trends also point toward the possibility of seeing the gospel reach every last corner of human population via new media.

c) *Medical technology* is likewise pressing forward – especially into new areas such as genetics (particularly in mapping the genome of humans, animals and plants) and stem cell and cloning research.

d) *Energy research* is possibly the highest profile and most globally important area needing technological progress. Fossil fuels are highly polluting, nuclear power dangerous and alternative energies – such as bio-fuels, solar, wind and wave – are as yet inefficient and inadequate. More than ever before, finding efficient, safe, non-polluting, renewable energy sources is attracting greater research and investment. A breakthrough in energy technology would transform the world's economy and ecology.

e) Nanotechnology has profound implications in almost every area of human activity – medicine, computing, engineering and communications to name a few.

Demographic

7 **Demographic contrasts.** Even though population growth is slowing in every area of the world, there are vast gaps in fertility rates around the globe. Populations continue to increase rapidly in Yemen, Afghanistan-Pakistan and much of West, Central and Eastern Africa. Much of Europe and parts of East Asia and southern Africa have sub-replacement fertility and face either terminal demographic decline or the necessity of large-scale immigration for civilization's survival. Rising ages of life expectancy, lower mortality rates and smaller families are good things, but the rapid aging of the human population will introduce altogether new challenges in the future. Massive immigration from more youthful, poor countries to more affluent – and aged – ones is one effect; care for rapidly increasing numbers of the elderly is another.

8 **Urbanization.** The past 50 years have seen great levels of sustained global urbanization – hundreds of millions of people moving from rural areas to cities. The population of the world living in urban contexts rose from 13% in 1900 to 29% in 1950, to break the 50% threshold in 2009. By 2030, it is estimated that 60% will live in cities, and 70% by 2050. With the impossibility of developing infrastructure as quickly as urban population growth (especially in poorer countries), many of those newly arrived in cities are forced to live in slums and shantytowns on the outskirts. These cities are at the centre of the world's economies – the world's largest 25 cities account for more than 50% of all wealth, and most likely for much of its vice as well. Increasingly, urban megaregions (such as Hong Kong-Shenzen-Guanzhou, Greater Tokyo, Rio de Janeiro-São Paulo and the Washington-NYC-Boston conurbations) present entirely new challenges for the future with massive urban sprawl, vast inequalities and vast hunger for resources. In many countries, urbanites have immensely greater opportunities to improve their quality of life. Cities, with their dense overlay of many value and belief systems, often break down previously held barriers regarding class, race and religion and allow for much greater social and economic mobility. They will necessarily be at the heart of future mission strategy.

9 **International migrations.** There are now 200-250 million people living outside the land of their birth. Greater levels of migration are fuelled by: increasing gaps, internationally, in quality of life; population growth (and decline); climate change and ecological ruin; financial, educational and social opportunities; and upheaval, conflict and persecution. Large-scale migrations into Western Europe, North America, South Africa, Siberia, Australia and other places will continue to increase regardless of what barriers are raised or laws passed – such epic scales of the global movement of humanity cannot be stopped by legislation. But violent xenophobia has been an increasingly common reaction. The "threat" of immigration could also be a great opportunity for Christian ministry – many migrants come from less-evangelized lands, and many others come as vibrant, witnessing Christians.

10 **The treatment of women** continues to be a scandal in much of the world. In many of the poorer parts of the world, women carry the burden of the workload as well as raise the family, despite having a significantly lower social and economic status and fewer rights and recognitions than men. Violence against women persists in just about every country in the world. The large majority of women who endure abuse or rape never report it and so suffer alone. In conflict areas, women suffer greater deprivation and risk than men: assault, abuse, abduction and rape statistics in places such as Rwanda, Liberia, the Balkans and Cuidad Juárez during their times of conflict have borne this out. Many millions of girls are denied primary education for cultural, religious or economic reasons. Worse yet, culturally established sexism has led to around 30 million cases of selective abortion of females or female infanticide, predominantly in India and China. This in turn fuels the growth of trafficking and abducting women – and girls – as brides or sex slaves.

11 **Language extinctions.** Globalization threatens the world's rich language – and therefore cultural – diversity. Eight languages are spoken by more than 100 million people each.

These eight total up to 2.9 billion mother tongue speakers (42% of human population), not to mention hundreds of millions or billions more who have learned them.

a) Advances in communications technology (such as the Internet and digital technology) have placed great power into the hands of a very few languages, English predominant among them. This has great implications in economics, politics and science. Having a handful of global mega-languages, which aids in international communication, is also a cultural juggernaut that crushes many smaller cultures. Technological developments have greatly aided communications in a few languages, but translation technology is not yet advanced enough to significantly benefit the many smaller languages.

b) Languages are dying out. About 472 languages are regarded as nearly extinct; 133 have fewer than 10 speakers, and 1,520 have fewer than 1,000 speakers. Estimates are that at least half of the 6,909 languages may be extinct in 2100. Only 39 languages are used as teaching languages in the world's universities. The efforts of Bible translators together with literacy workers are significant in preserving languages, restoring pride in cultures and allowing the gospel to be effectively communicated and to flourish in the heart language and culture of a people.

c) Multilingualism is practiced by the majority of the world's population – some estimate up to 75%. One further redemptive role the world's mega-languages can serve is to function as gateway languages to bring vitality and resources into the heart languages of multi-language speakers. Developing evangelism and discipleship tools, hymnody and theology into these heart languages can effectively further Kingdom advance.

Environmental

12 **Water will be among the world's most crucial issues** in the future. Given that sufficient fresh water exists globally to sustain humanity (even if the locations of water sources and human population do not match up well), the salient issues on a global level are more about ethics, equity, distribution and consumption.

a) Access to clean water. Already, around one in six people lacks access to safe drinking water; by 2025, it is estimated that three billion will lack access to fresh water. Additionally, nearly one in three lacks access to adequate sanitation, and this in turn contributes greatly to disease, malnutrition and mortality, especially among children.

b) Current wastefulness. The developed world uses more than 30 times more water per person than the developing world. And the vast bulk of water waste is through inefficient agricultural systems, which account for 70% of humanity's use of fresh water. Even diets (such as high consumption of red meat) that require much more water are a source of inequitable water use; the aspirations of most of the world to Western lifestyles, consumption levels and industrial output will generate even more waste and place even greater stresses on water supplies.

c) Future societal and demographic changes. The large majority of future population growth will be in areas where safe water is in short supply. This, combined with ever greater industrialization (greater demands for water) and urbanization (population moving further from clean water sources), means that demands on water supplies will be even more intense in the future.

d) Over-exploitation of limited water resources is poised to become a serious problem in the USA, Australia, southern Europe, South Asia, China and much of Africa. Aquifers are over-tapped and rivers are running dry. Water-rich countries such as Canada and Russia are moving to secure their own vast supplies of fresh water. Tension and even conflict already exist over:

i *The Amu Darya/Oxus of Central Asia.*

ii *The Tigris-Euphrates* (Turkey, Syria, Iraq, Iran).

iii *The Jordan* (Israel, Syria, Jordan).

iv *The Nile* (Egypt, Sudan, Ethiopia).

v *The nations to the north and south of the Sahara Desert.*

These factors combined spell out the inevitability of increasing tensions over limited water supplies, of greater pressure to reduce waste and make desalinization more efficient and of the drive behind massive levels of migration.

13 **Demands for other natural resources,** when combined with population growth and increasing levels of consumption, are at the core of what will make or break human civilization's progress in the 21st Century.

a) Energy consumption is still vastly dominated by non-renewable resources such as fossil fuels. Until greener and more renewable sources can be developed to a level that makes them feasible alternatives, nuclear power might be the only other alternative.

b) Food production is another area where great changes are afoot. Genetically modified crops, the environmental impact of current agricultural systems and current trends in global dietary patterns all raise serious economic, environmental and ethical questions – from organic foods to raising cattle to fishing. The existence of food is not a problem for the world's masses; at the heart of most problems are the amount of waste and the cost and difficulty of production and distribution. Growing crops for fuel, rather than food, intensifies these troubles.

c) Other natural resources are also being rapidly depleted. Some resources, such as old-growth hardwood trees, can be renewed, though not nearly at the speed demanded by consumption. Others, such as minerals, are non-renewable, yet they are being extracted and used at increasing rates.

14 **Climate change** is now generally accepted as having a human causal component. Population growth, rapid industrialization and increasing consumption have an undeniable environmental/ecological impact. The negative implications of possible global warming are: desertification, soil exhaustion, greater frequency of natural disasters such as flooding and drought, water table salinization, flooding in low-lying coastal systems, massive loss of habitat for millions of species and unprecedented human migration. The staggering scale of waste and pollution – from plastics to pesticides and hormones and more – affects our water systems, our climate and even our biology. Despite the fact that humans still know little about these complex dynamics, green ethics have almost become a religion in themselves, the adherence to which is demanded in much of the developed world. However, it has also fostered in the Church the rightful and necessary development of a theology of Creation stewardship and compelled Christians to reconsider how biblical our lifestyles are.

The Church Worldwide

The Church is the primary locus for the work of God in bringing the good news of Jesus Christ to those who have not heard or believed. It is God's chosen means for carrying out the Great Commission and completing His purposes for humanity (Rev 5:9-10, 7:9-10). It is also the venue for the work of the Holy Spirit among God's people – for sanctifying, for discipling, for attaining maturity to the measure of the stature of the fullness of Christ (Eph 4:13, 5:17).

The Church on earth is only an imperfect manifestation of the one, true and invisible Church of the Lord Jesus Christ. On earth, it is driven by conflict, by deep and fundamental disagreements on theological outlook, by cultural differences, by personal rivalries and by the sheer scope of how it tries (or fails to try) to work out its understanding of the gospel in its local context. Yet, all those who belong to Jesus together comprise the indivisible body of Christ, with Him as the head over us all (Eph 1:22-23). Jesus prayed for our unity (John 17:23) and promised that the gates of hell would not prevail against the Church (Matt 16:18). The Holy Spirit works in countless ways and places through the breadth of all those who call upon the name of the Lord. Here are some of the key issues where prayer for the global Church is warranted:

1 **Maintaining a clear witness to the uniqueness of Christ** in the midst of growing religious pluralism and post-modernity. Even among Christians, a creeping universalism can be observed as gaining ground. The convictions of believers regarding the uniqueness of Jesus, and His claim to be the only way to the Father, are being challenged from within and without the Church. In a world where relativism dominates, Christians will increasingly be criticized for being "intolerant" and for holding to their exclusive truth claims regarding Jesus. Relativism, subjectivism and existentialism that deny the existence and primacy of objective reality are a threat to the authority of Scripture and the truth of the gospel.

2 **Sustaining the centrality of the Scriptures** in today's world, when many Christians and even evangelicals, especially in the West, are becoming uncertain in their convictions or compromised on the authority and inerrancy of the Word of God. Believers' thoughts, values and worldviews are often shaped more by the prevailing culture, philosophies, superstitions and religions of the society around them than by the Bible. This undermines and contaminates Christians' faith, it robs them of spiritual power, assurance and joy and it sidetracks believers into focusing on secondary or irrelevant issues. There are several areas where the Church is divided on the right way to live and serve:

*a) **Issues of culture and compromise with the world.*** Where contextualization ends and syncretism begins is hard to discern. This is as much a challenge for hi-tech, postmodern secular Western contexts as it is for more primitive subsistence cultures where the spirit world is a profound part of everyday life.

*b) **Prosperity theology,*** which can range from a healthy recognition that God wishes to bless His people to a thinly veiled avarice that uses the Lord as a mere vehicle for personal enrichment. This is no longer confined to a few slick American televangelists; it is a central issue for the Church to address on every continent. No one can serve God and mammon; may every church, every leader and every believer understand this.

*c) **Gender and sexuality.*** The appropriate role of women in the Church is one area of differing convictions. The issue of homosexuality, its nature and its practice, will possibly be one of the most divisive issues among Christians in coming years, even in cultures that have traditionally been very conservative regarding sexuality and gender roles.

③ The effective functioning of local congregations. Each should be an organic entity, a community where all members participate in body life. Each believer has gifts to contribute to the up-building of the whole, yet rarely do congregations function in this way. Mobilizing the laity remains a great challenge for most churches. All kinds of new forms of church life are being attempted. For evangelicals, everything is being tried – from a return to liturgical forms to restorationist movements to trendy modernistic styles to radically new expressions. Pray that each unique congregation might serve to build up believers, draw in the unchurched and glorify Christ. Pray for wisdom for church leaders to know how to best achieve this for their congregation, whatever its context. When the Church fails in this duty, nominalism becomes widespread.

④ Leadership development is the crucial bottleneck to Church growth. There is a worldwide lack of men and women truly called of God and deeply taught in the Scriptures to lead the churches, people willing to suffer the burdens and responsibilities of leadership for the sake of the Saviour who redeemed them; in many contexts this means deprivation, scorn and even risk of death. Those who accurately and effectively expound the Scriptures are few, especially in areas where the churches are growing rapidly. New methods and means of multiplying well-trained, godly, effective leaders must be developed; traditional methods alone will not suffice to produce the number and quality required to meet the need. Ministers who are seminary graduates are often the least likely to have a biblical worldview. Pastors, ministers and elders all need constant upholding in prayer.

⑤ Discipleship is regarded by many Christian leaders as the greatest challenge facing the Church today. In regions such as Africa, Latin America and parts of Asia, where the Church has grown remarkably fast, there are literally millions of new believers who need to learn the Word and the Christian walk. Shaping their worldview and lifestyle biblically will form growing, mature followers of Christ; failing to do so will cause many to fall away into unbelief, false teaching or spiritual lukewarmness. While this is an urgent crisis in places where the Church is rapidly increasing, it is no less important in areas with a long Church history. There is, as ever, a genuine need for effective Bible study and teaching in Christians' heart languages, genuine fellowship and a commitment to involvement in ministry.

⑥ An outward emphasis that remains focused on outreach, evangelism, mission and community engagement is essential for healthy churches. Where believers are a small and despised minority, or in countries where there is widespread decline in commitment to the Lord, Christians are often intimidated, fearful or just apathetic. Both the Bible and history demonstrate clearly that witnessing churches are growing churches, and the Lord of the Harvest promises that His Word will not go forth in vain. Pray for all Christians to become vibrant witnesses for the Lord.

⑦ A holistic ethos that sees the Church engage society on all levels. The transformation that the invisible Kingdom brings should not be locked within the four walls of a church. Both congregations and missions are recognizing that the gospel can change not only individual lives, but entire communities and societies as well. Many initiatives and streams pray, mobilize and work to see the power and love of Christ made real in the following areas: the Church, family, education, government and law, media and communication, the arts and entertainment, business and finance.

⑧ Young people. In this modern age, many drift away from the Church and into the passions of youth (or often, the apathy of youth!), even after a Christian upbringing. There are a host of theories and explanations as to why the younger generation is leaving the Church in droves. This dynamic plays itself out much more widely than just in the post-Christian West. The temptations of the world are more accessible than ever, and the pressures they place on believing young people are intense. Every new generation needs to be evangelized afresh.

9 **The vitality of Christians' spiritual life** – privately and corporately – is a subject always worthy of prayer. Whether it is referred to as renewal, revival, awakening or transformation, what matters is the need for the Holy Spirit to be active in the individual and corporate spiritual life of the Church. Any group that obeys the Word of God and welcomes the Spirit of God will inevitably see the power and love of God made real to them and through them. However, the longing for the move of God's Spirit has also led to an unhealthy chasing after signs, the emphasis on spiritual power rather than godly character and the cheap commodification of the Holy Spirit rather than a humble submission to the Third Person of the Godhead.

10 **The rise in levels of persecution – especially for Christians.** The end of the European colonial era, the end of Christianity's status as state religion in most of the West and the resurgence of religious sentiment globally, especially fundamentalism, all mean that Christians generally no longer operate from a position of power or privilege. Christians are subject to persecution in much of the world. Evangelicals are subject to even more due to their proselytism and commitment to the uniqueness of Christ. The presence of persecution and hardship in the life of the Church appears to be normative in Scripture; contexts where persecution does not exist at all should be as much cause for concern as places where it is intense.

a) The main offenders:

   i *Muslim countries and regions* – the rise of extreme Islamist interpretations of the Muslim faith and the association of Christianity with "the Great Satan" have made Christians vulnerable to heightened religious violence coming from radicalized Muslims. The increasing application of shari'a law creates a climate where harsh persecution can easily occur. In a handful of countries, the courts may sentence a national to death for becoming a Christian; imprisonment awaits in several other nations. Beyond the government stance on such apostasy from Islam, community leaders and family members pressure new believers to revert to Islam and, occasionally, will murder those who will not.

   ii *Marxist/Communist states* continue to make life very difficult for Christians – this is especially true in North Korea, where profession of faith leads to imprisonment and death, and in Laos, Vietnam, China and Cuba, where unregistered Christians have suffered severely.

   iii *Hindutva* philosophy in India and radicalization of some Hindus in Nepal have led to heightened pressure and acts of terror against Christians in parts of these countries.

   iv *Buddhists* have persecuted and maltreated Christians in Myanmar, Sri Lanka and Bhutan.

   v *Christian governments,* or government structures that endorse only one form of Christianity, have often been among the harshest persecutors of evangelicals. Examples of such instances include Eritrea, Belarus, southern Mexico and Russia.

   vi *Secular governments* – most notably in Western Europe – in their attempts to safeguard against dangerous sects and to further erase religion from public life have passed laws that make life difficult for believers to publicly practice their faith. Pluralism in such contexts apparently requires tolerance of every lifestyle and value system – except for biblical Christianity.

b) Christians' concern for the persecuted Church is growing. There are several networks and ministries mobilizing prayer for and support of Christians suffering: Voice of the Martyrs, Open Doors, Release International, Christian Solidarity Worldwide, International Justice Mission, Barnabas Fund, Christian Freedom International, International Christian Concern, WEA Religious Liberties Commission and many others. The annual International Day of Prayer for the Persecuted Church is coordinated globally by WEA. Open Doors maintains a persecution index for the world's nations, updated once a year.

The Great Commission

Jesus founded a missionary team – the apostles – and called others to assist in the mission. The Church was the result, through which He calls others to continue the task. Therefore, the Church is in essence a missionary agency in its origin, life and continued growth and not a static institution in society. The whole Church must be involved, interceding for God's world, recognizing and sending out those members specifically called and supporting them in every way. In this, all Christians can be united in reaching the world for Christ.

1 **Missionary vision in the Church.** An Acts 1:8 strategy is needed for every church and denomination. Amazing results have been achieved by a dedicated few. How speedily the world would be evangelized if all believers and every congregation obeyed the commands of Jesus in Acts 1 and believed His promises of enablement through the Holy Spirit! Pray for the awakening and growth of missionary concern. Ask for the Church to pray, give and go to the harvest fields, and request of the Lord the following:

a) *The speediest possible completion of the goals given in the Great Commission* by the Lord Jesus to His Church. Until the gospel of the Kingdom is indeed preached in all the world for a witness to all *ethne*, the end cannot come (Matt 24:14).

b) *All churches to make obedience to the Great Commission their primary ministry objective.* Biblically, this goes beyond mere evangelism to include the imperative of discipleship ("make disciples of all nations . . . teaching them to observe all that I have commanded you" Matt 28:19-20 ESV). Only through the mobilized resources of the whole Church will we be able to bring the task to conclusion, or closure, in our generation.

c) *All leadership training institutions and programmes* to ensure that the centrality of mission to the purpose of the Church is a fundamental and essential core component of every course. To a large degree, failure to do this has caused centuries of neglect and marginalization of world evangelization in churches and agencies.

d) *The multiplication of missionary prayer movements,* the component of the Great Commission in which every Christian can actively participate. This must involve strategic intercession for mission workers, for specific teams and projects, for unevangelized peoples and for spiritual warfare to open the way for the gospel to bear much fruit among those the enemy wishes to isolate from the good news.

e) *The adoption of unreached peoples* by mission agencies, churches, Christian groups, prayer circles and individuals. Such adoption can be expressed through prayer and intercession, through advocacy and raising awareness and through the support of those working among said peoples.

2 **Mission agencies.** Protestant and Independent missionary-sending and support agencies have multiplied over the past two centuries; this is a worldwide phenomenon of great significance. Pray for:

a) *Effective strategies to evangelize each people group or society,* based on a detailed understanding of their beliefs and way of life, a clear understanding of God's purpose both for life and salvation and an understanding of the ultimate goal of making disciples. Without adequate preparation and understanding, enthusiasm and resources can be wasted with results that dishonour Christ.

b) *Adaptability* in a rapidly changing world. Missions are aiming at a fast moving and changing target. The lifestyles and conditions of the world's peoples change rapidly due to economics, ecology, urbanization, culture shifts, information technology and complex patterns of migration. Religious fundamentalism is resurgent, and many nations seek to exert their authority by controlling or eliminating the Church. Mission agencies must be constantly alert to field contexts and be flexible enough in structure and strategies to seize opportunities when they arise.

c) *Leadership* in mission agencies. Leaders need great wisdom in setting clear objectives, guidance in selecting and placing workers, ability in giving pastoral care, and skills in maintaining good relationships with secular authorities, other missions and national Churches.

d) *Relationships with national Churches.* Most missionary work is now done in contexts where indigenous Christians exist, gather and even minister in their own evangelistic capacity. Expatriate Christians must learn to serve in harmony with the local church where it exists, as each acts in humility and grace toward the other. Tensions and misunderstandings can occur and cultures can vary greatly, but each needs the other to see the task fulfilled.

e) *Effective cooperation among missionary agencies* honours God by eliminating unnecessary duplication and unbiblical competition between agencies and denominations. Too often, the theological fragmentation and ethnocentrism that plagues sending churches are exported into foreign contexts, where such histories and issues are largely irrelevant. This is a poor testimony and presents a confusing message.

f) ***The formation of networks*** and collaborative strategies is crucial in areas where missions must operate in a circumspect manner. When a host of agencies work separately in areas wary of or opposed to Christian mission, they can soon appear as an external threat. Networks that provide overall strategy and broker the work of many agencies and churches on a field can be highly effective for Kingdom advance. Within such larger frameworks, the different nationalities and agencies can understand and apply their unique strengths and giftings for the benefit of the overall mission effort and the national Church.

3 **Missionaries.** The harsh realities of spiritual labour soon dispel the imagined glamour of pioneer missionary work. Both the missionaries and the churches that send them need to have realistic expectations, adequate support on every level and unflinching devotion to the task. Pray for:

a) ***Vital, supportive home fellowships of believers*** who are willing to pray the missionary out to the field and keep him or her there through the years of greatest effectiveness. This is difficult to maintain with rapid changes and turnovers in membership and in the pastoral team in most congregations. Congregations must see themselves as local launching pads for the essential task of global mission, rather than as local institutions where foreign ministry is an optional add-on.

b) ***The supply of their financial needs.*** Mission is too often regarded by churches as a charitable extra – if there are sufficient funds left over from the local essentials. Many missionaries live sacrificially for Christ, in harsh and demanding contexts, with simple lifestyles and neither present nor future guarantees of income or security. This is especially the case for those from newer sending nations where churches do not yet appreciate the importance of financial support for mission. Missionary lifestyles also need to be sensitive to the living standards of the contexts in which they work.

c) ***Adequate preparation for missionary work.*** This is arduous and long – theological training, ministry experience, language learning and adaptation to a new land may take years before an effective ministry can be exercised. Those years can be traumatic and discouraging. The significant number of missionaries who fail to return for a second term of service is indicative of possible deficiencies in selection, preparation, structure and pastoral care. With the increased amateurization of mission, training and preparation are increasingly compromised for the sake of getting people "on the ground" as soon as possible. But it is more training – and not less – that will see healthy, growing, culturally appropriate churches planted in cross-cultural situations.

d) ***Cultural adjustment.*** Many prospective missionaries cannot make the adjustment to new foods, lifestyles, languages, value systems and attitudes. Some return home disillusioned and with a sense of failure; others react wrongly on the field and hinder fellowship and witness; yet others go too far in their adaptation and compromise their health and sometimes their faith. Wisdom is precious in such situations, as is an authentic biblical love for the people and culture where the work is occurring.

e) ***Spiritual vitality and a rich devotional life.*** In the role of spiritual leadership, as a living testimony to the efficacy of the gospel, often in isolation from other believers and as an ambassador of God's Kingdom in dark places, a missionary cannot afford to exist with a tepid spiritual life.

f) ***Protection from Satan's attacks.*** The powers of darkness are real. In many areas, Satan's kingdom has never before been challenged. Missionaries must be more vigilant on the field than in home situations. They need to be able to discern between cultural differences and spiritual opposition, but the spiritual authority to resist evil attacks is even more vital. These can come through many means, including physical health and disease, attacks upon the mind and attitude, in relationships and in physical threats such as violent attacks and hostage taking.

g) ***Family life.*** For singles, the missionary call may mean foregoing marriage for the sake of the gospel – loneliness can be a heavy burden to bear. Yet, singleness on the field can also bring rapid language and culture acquisition and flexibility of lifestyle and ministry. For others, family life may be made difficult by living conditions, inadequate amenities or lack of finance; long separations, many visitors and excessive workloads may disrupt it. Missionaries' children may be separated from their parents for long periods because of education; children's educational needs bring to an end the field ministry of countless missionary families. But family life can be a real asset for integrating into the target community as well as a great opportunity to demonstrate the gospel through family relationships.

h) *Calling and commitment.* The assurance that God has guided one to a particular ministry is often the only anchor to retain workers in difficult situations, misunderstandings, broken relationships and "impossible" crises. Pray that none may leave a place of calling for a negative or superficial reason, but only because of a positive leading from God.

i) *Built-in obsolescence.* Missionary presence on a field could end suddenly for a host of reasons; when expatriate workers make themselves irreplaceable this can spell disaster for the health of fledgling churches and movements. Success should be understood as having been achieved when the missionaries are no longer needed for the role for which they came. The ideal goal of all missionaries should be to train their own replacements from among local believers.

j) *Re-entry* – temporary or long-term – which can be traumatic. Returning missionaries need adequate debriefing, preparation for reverse culture shock and the continued support of God's people; these help establish an effective rapport with churches at home, build a fruitful ministry on the home end and prepare for a return to the field.

The Unfinished Task – Religious Systems

The 20th Century was one in which secularism seemed destined to triumph, yet the world has seen a resurgence in religious sentiment and commitment in every region and in almost every religion. Religion plays a profound role in most societies; the few societies where it does not seem lodged in a pattern of demographic decline and/or large-scale immigration of religious populations.

1 **The revitalization of the world religions.** Contrary to the expectations of the secular agenda, religion has not faded into an irrelevant historical footnote. Perhaps as a reaction against globalization, perhaps as a reaction against secular arrogance and emptiness, perhaps as a demonstration of the deeply spiritual nature of humanity, religion is alive and well in the 21st Century.

2 **The rise of fundamentalism** in the majority of the world's faith systems. Most people would associate the term "fundamentalist" with Muslim terrorists or strident Christian conservatives, but today some groups of Hindus, Buddhists, Jews, ethnoreligionists and, increasingly, atheists fit such a term quite adequately. Recently, secularism as a social construct and atheism as a belief system in the West have, in some circles, become particularly aggressive and assertive, seeking to eradicate religion from the public sphere and humiliate those of religious – or at least Christian – persuasion.

3 **The unfolding of future global faith.** Cultural influence, proselytism and birthrates would indicate that global religious dominance will be contested by three main forces – Christianity, Islam and non-religion. All other faiths are limited to a specific region and/or are not growing. Non-religious people tend to have the lowest birthrates, but the trend toward secularization in many parts of the world has sustained and even swelled their numbers. Proportionately, few convert to Islam, but high birthrates and low apostasy rates have propelled Islam to 22.9% of the human population. Christianity has declined slightly from 34.5% in 1900 to 32.3% in 2010. The precipitous decline of the past 30 years in Europe has been offset by growth in Asia and Africa. Where it does occur, Christian growth has been from both conversion and natural birthrates.

4 **Christianity** has become the most global of religions. There is no country without a Christian witness or fellowship of indigenous believers (although in a very few cases, they must remain secretive). There are 14 countries with a resident Christian population of less than 1%, and a further 23 with less than 5%. Much has been covered in the section on the Church in the previous pages.

a) **Nominalism** is a major issue, and not just in the West. In many Christianized countries, most of the population need to be re-evangelized; living in the afterglow of a Christian heritage does not confer eternal salvation. Many traditionally Christian populations know nothing of a personal faith, true repentance from sin and working out their salvation in relationship with the living God. Many others rely on good works to earn salvation rather than trusting in and living out of God's free gift of grace. The majority of those who identify themselves as Christian do not actively practice their faith.

b) **Christo-pagans**, while statistically counted as Christians, are practicing occultists, shamanists, fetishists and others under a veneer of Christianity. This is particularly prevalent in Latin America among the Amerindians and Mestizo. It is also widespread in Africa, where many indigenous groups are more influenced by ethnic religions than by the gospel. Europe and Asia, too, have millions of professing Christians who are just as syncretistic. Evangelizing such people and making them into disciples of the Lord Jesus are just as necessary as winning those of other religions, but the strategy required to do so effectively needs to be radically different.

c) **"Christian" cults and marginal groups.** There are millions who define their own church or group as the sole possessors of Truth – some such are the Mormons, Jehovah's Witnesses and many smaller groups. Although the Bible is present and Jesus highly regarded, they add to or take away from the Words of Life. They need to be freed from the teachings that ensnare them.

5 **Muslims** live largely in the great arc of territory stretching from West Africa through the Middle East, Central Asia, to Indonesia. Their growth in the past 100 years has been rapid – from 12.3% in 1900 to 22.9% in 2010. Most numerical growth is through higher birth rates. Conversion growth is greatest in West Africa, Indonesia and the USA. In the past decade, Islam itself has been shaken significantly by internal crises. Pray for:

a) **The eyes and hearts of Muslim individuals and families to be opened** to the person of the Lord Jesus Christ. The essential framework of Islamic belief contradicts fundamental biblical truths about the nature and person of Jesus. This, combined with the traditionally hostile history between Christianity and Islam, means that barriers to faith are so numerous that a deep working of the Holy Spirit is required, often through supernatural revelations or miracles.

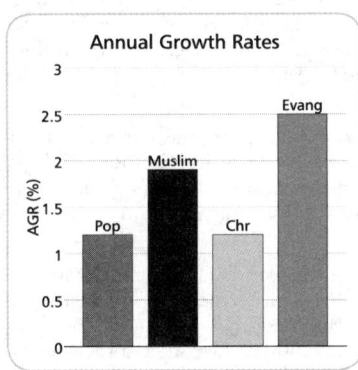

Annual Growth Rates

b) **The opening up of the Muslim world on a macro level.** Recently, major cracks have been appearing in the Islamic world; it is not the monolithic entity many claim it to be. The murderous extremes and terror tactics of radical Islamism horrify the world, including many moderate, peace-loving Muslims. Divisions and factions within Islam see extremists turn their guns and bombs upon one another. The reaction is often disillusion and disgust. There are growing numbers of ex-Muslims, people who leave Islam mostly for atheism, agnosticism or Christianity. Many anticipate a coming harvest of millions into the Kingdom of God from among the Muslim world.

c) **Muslim background believers in Christ,** whose numbers are beginning to multiply much more quickly. The few isolated pockets of such growth are becoming wider regions, such that, in most of the Muslim world, movements of people to Jesus are occurring. There are, however, a few exceptions: much of North Africa, Somalia, the Levant, Turkey, Pakistan and North India and among the Malay peoples of Southeast Asia. Believers from Muslim backgrounds often face severe pressures and even death, even in countries where this trickle of salvations is now a rushing stream.

d) **Christian ministries to Muslims.** The past 20 years have seen a rapid (and overdue) increase of outreach to Muslims. Geography, culture, ignorance, inexperience, prejudice and fear have all contributed to limit outreach to the Islamic world. Sensitive and sensible ministry proves that Muslims can be very responsive to the good news. Exact numbers are impossible to obtain, but only a mere estimated 10% of foreign missionaries work among Muslims – although Muslims consist of around 37% of all non-Christians in the world. Pray for more to be called, equipped and led into fruitful ministry to Muslims.

6 **The non-religious, or secular, bloc** has shown the most massive growth in the past century, from a tiny 0.2% of the world's population in 1900, peaking in 1980, but in 2010 representing 13.6% – mainly Europeans and Chinese. The collapse of European Communism (and the continued weakening of Communism everywhere) sees a notable rise in religious populations in these lands, but likewise countless millions of Christians are non-religious in everything but name. Christians have generally proven singularly ineffective in communicating the gospel to secular, postmodern culture. But secularism is very effective at undermining Christianity – at least where the Christian faith has been lightly held. Pray that effective ways might be found to guard against and reach out to this "faith". Pray that the ultimate emptiness of this worldview might be exposed and the tide of secular materialism reversed.

7 **Hinduism** has made notable missionary inroads in the West through the wide acceptance of transcendental meditation, yoga, New Age thinking, sects such as Hare Krishna, and Indian gurus. It has also become more militant and repressive of Christians in its heartlands of India and Nepal, reacting against the evangelism and growth of the Church.

a) The Indian sub-continent has the largest concentration and variety of least-reached peoples and people groups on earth. The gospel has spread most to the poor and marginalized, while the main body of caste Hindus remains unevangelized.

b) Reaching out to caste Hindus and the burgeoning middle class of India is a great need. Pray for Indian Christians and others to be called and enabled to reach them. Christians are generally regarded as both coming from the lowest castes and preying upon the same, and effective witness to other strata of Hindu society will require a new approach than what has been effective at reaching Dalits and tribals.

c) Contextualized, culturally appropriate patterns of Christian life, worship and community are needed. Pray for the Holy Spirit to bring the light of the gospel to influential Hindus.

8 **Buddhism** is the state religion of four nations in Asia, the majority in a further three and a significant minority in yet another nine. The majority of this total is actually a mixture of Buddhism with Chinese religions, Daoism, Confucianism and Shinto. The various religious systems are so intermingled that a clear differentiation is hard to make. If observers of all these religions are added together, the total virtually doubles the population of the Buddhist world. There are also new religions that are offshoots of Buddhism – Cao Dai in Vietnam, Falun Gong in China, Sokka Gokkai in Japan. Buddhism has actually enjoyed a measure of resurgence in East and Southeast Asia in the post-Communist era. The Dalai Lama of Tibet has popularized Buddhism in the West. The proportion of Buddhists who have come to Christ is minute – two radically different worldviews make effectively communicating the gospel a difficult and pains-taking task. Pray for a breakthrough in the Buddhist world; thus far, the only major movements to Christ have been in places where Communism or foreign oppression first shattered the grip of Buddhism.

9 **Ethnic religions and animism** actually see a resurgence throughout much of the world. In traditional cultures, such religions might be in relative decline, but they continue to deeply influence and underlie the four major world religions that have supplanted them. Many followers of world religions remain, in practice, shamanists, idolaters, spiritists, ancestor worshippers, fetishists, wiccan and others. In the Western world, widespread fascination with the occult, mysticism and new religious movements is an indication of the fierceness of the spiritual conflict in which we are engaged.

10 **Sikhism,** originating in northwest India, is one of the more recent world religions. Many Sikhs have migrated to other countries – Canada, East Africa, the UK, Southeast Asia. Few Christians have ever sought to understand their religion to find ways of sharing the gospel. Christians from a Sikh background remain relatively few, but this is beginning to change as believers start to reach out to Sikhs both in India and in the Sikh diaspora.

11 **Jews** are declining in number in most countries – through low birthrates, secularization, conver-sions to Christ and emigration to Israel. Nearly 37% of all Jews now live in Israel. Of the world's 14.8 million Jews, some estimate that there may be about 150,000 Messianic Jews, the majority in the USA. That Jews should find salvation in Messiah Yeshua remains a key concern for Christians.

12 **Numerous other religious groups** remain challenges for Christian witness – Baha'i, Jains, Parsees. Very few Jains or Parsees have ever come to faith in Christ.

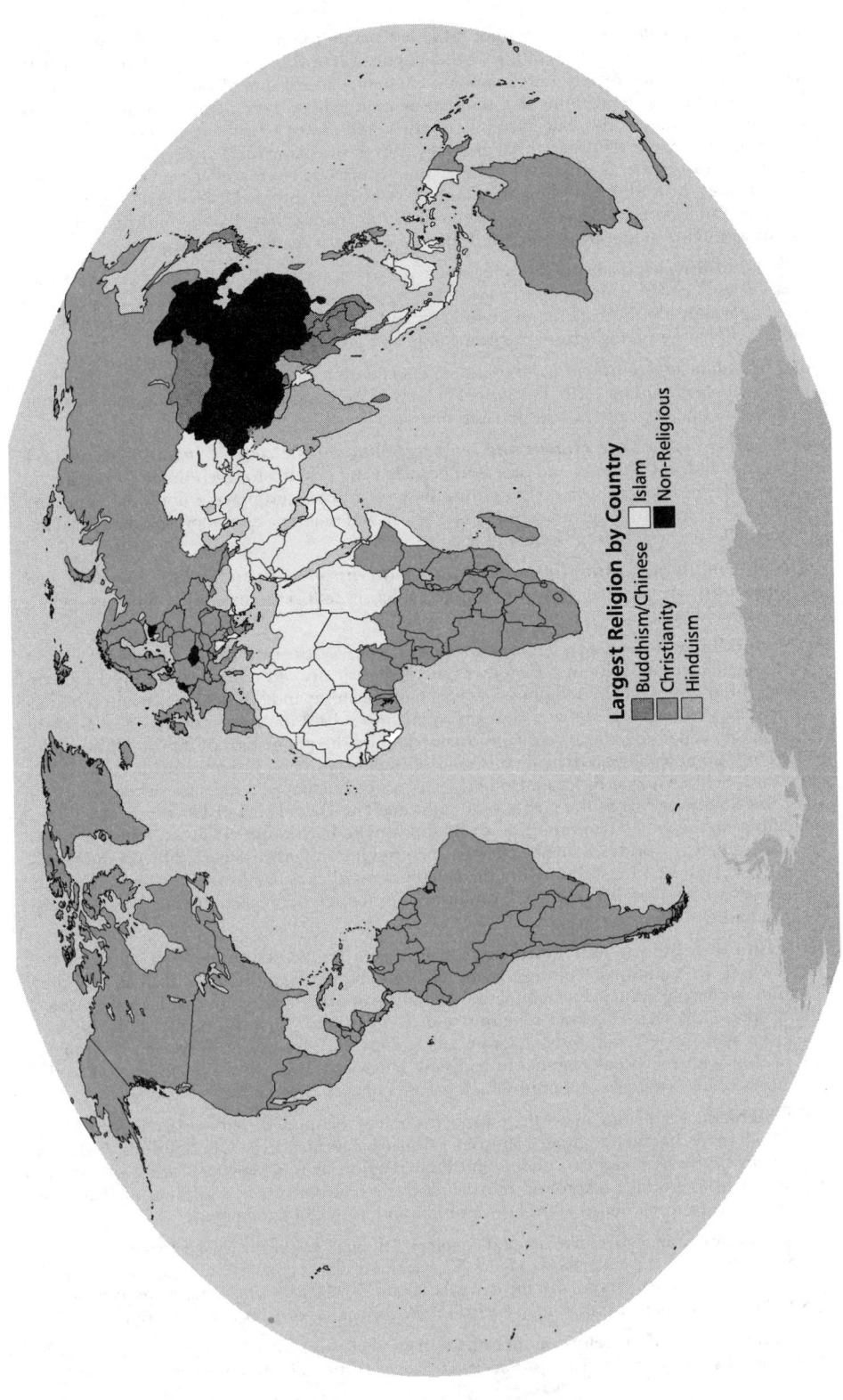

Largest Religion by Country

Buddhism/Chinese
Christianity
Hinduism
Islam
Non-Religious

The Unfinished Task – The World's Peoples

It was only during the 1990s – nearly 2,000 years after Jesus' command to disciple all peoples – that a reasonably complete listing of the world's peoples and languages was developed. Now we have a rather clear and increasingly detailed picture, courtesy of painstaking research done by various key groups with such a global vision. The SIL Ethnologue, the Joshua Project List, the *World Christian Encyclopedia* and a handful of other resources are at the heart of this information, which is both fuel for prayer and data for mission strategy.

Here is a summary of our present assessment of least reached peoples. Of the world's 16,350 peoples in the Joshua Project List (10,340 if country boundaries are ignored), 6,645 are counted in the Least Reached/Unreached category – 40.6% of all peoples. The total population of individuals from unreached peoples is 2.84 billion, or 41.1% of humanity. It is important to remember that there can be Christian individuals within an unreached people as well as unreached individuals within Christianized peoples. The vast majority of the unreached originate from the 10/40 Window area and fall into 11 major Affinity Blocs. Their affinities include culture, language use, geography, history and others. See the map on p26. The table below shows the number of peoples and their populations (in millions).

Affinity Bloc	Peoples			Population		
	Total	Unreached	% Unreached	Total(m)	Unreached(m)	% Unreached
Arab World	573	369	64.4	332.1	225.5	67.9
East Asian	454	197	43.4	1,518.4	305.6	20.1
Horn of Africa	160	60	37.5	104.3	23.7	22.7
Iranian–Median	273	250	91.6	154.3	153.4	99.4
Jews	181	176	97.2	14.8	14.4	97.3
Malay	1,018	278	27.3	358.6	181.5	50.6
South Asian*	3,718	3,293	88.6	1,553.9	1,420.2	91.4
Southeast Asian	615	452	73.5	226.6	135.1	59.6
Sub-Saharan	2,994	570	19.0	693.8	133.2	19.2
Tibetan–Himalayan	770	429	55.7	95.8	67.4	70.4
Turkic	311	254	81.7	170.7	166.7	97.7
Rest of world	5,283	320	6.1	1,685.0	13.0	0.8

*South Asian Affinity Bloc includes sub-groups determined by caste.

Within these Affinity Blocs are the more closely related 251 People Clusters. They can range from 3 peoples to 1,137 peoples and from 67,000 to 1.2 billion. Many of these are mentioned later in the book.

Affinity Bloc	Clusters	Largest People Clusters
Arab World	19	Egyptian, Levant Arab, Maghreb Arab, Arabian Arab, Sudanese Arab
East Asian	7	Chinese, Japanese, Korean, Hui, Manchu, Mongolian
Horn of Africa	6	Ethiopian, Oromo, Somali, Omotic
Iranian–Median	10	Persian, Pashtun, Kurd, Baloch, Tajik
Jews	1	
Malay	33	Jawa, Central Filipino, Sunda-Betawi, Malay, Malagasy, Madurese, Bugi-Makassar
South Asian	27	Hindi, Bengali, Urdu Muslim, Rajasthani, Jat, Telugu, Marathi-Konkani, Tamil
Southeast Asian	15	Vietnamese, Thai, Mon-Khmer, Zhuang, Miao/Hmong, Tai
Sub-Saharan	54	Central Lakes Bantu, Yoruba, Guinean, Hausa, Fulani, Gur, Benue, Nilotic
Tibetan–Himalayan	14	Burmese, West China/Lolo, Tibetan, South Himalayan, Kuki-China-Naga
Turkic	9	Turk, Azerbaijani, Uzbek, Uyghur, Kazakh, Ural-Siberian, Turkmen, Kyrgyz
Rest of world	56	

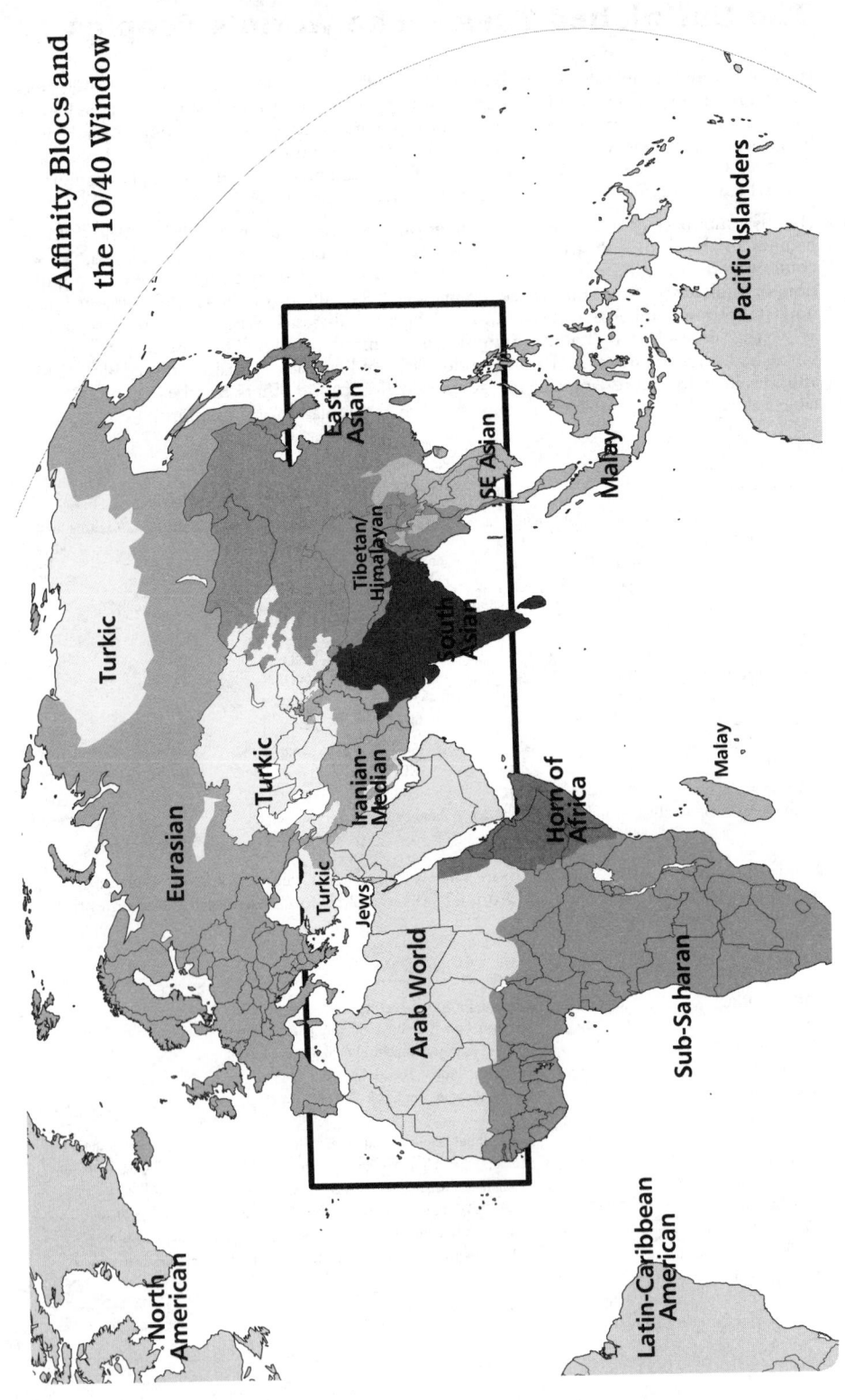

Affinity Blocs and the 10/40 Window

Pacific Islanders

East Asian

SE Asian

Malay

Turkic

Tibetan/Himalayan

South Asian

Iranian-Median

Eurasian

Turkic

Turkic

Jews

Horn of Africa

Malay

Arab World

Sub-Saharan

North American

Latin-Caribbean American

The Unfinished Task – Challenges for Prayer

1 **The majority of the least reached** are last to hear the gospel precisely because they are the most isolated from witnessing Christians and the most difficult to reach. This is due to a combination of geographic, linguistic, political, religious, social and spiritual barriers. In order to hear, they will generally need cross-cultural gospel input from workers called of God, at least until there is an established Church among their people. Pray that they may have a revelation of the grace and power of God for effective, growing churches to be planted.

2 **Few of the 6,645 least reached peoples have no known Christians** among them, but Christians generally constitute a very small minority – on average 0.4% of the population. In coming to Christ, and especially in trying to reach their own people, they face many pressures and even persecution. Pray that these Christians may know the sustaining grace of God and power of the Holy Spirit as they endeavour to evangelize their own people.

3 **There are many very small groups by population size** – 574 have less than 100 people, 3,040 have less than 1,000 people and 7,930 have less than 10,000 people. For many, information is inadequate to understand their needs, their culture and the urgency of outreach to them. This highlights the need for good national and international research teams to find out the needs so the Church may be activated to bring them the good news.

4 **Churches around the world need to gain a vision for unreached peoples.** Peoples – or *ethne* in NT Greek – are the fundamental units in God's plan for the redemption of all humanity; this is a non-negotiable biblical reality. Sadly, in the post-AD 2000 world, many have moved on to other, more "trendy" ways of regarding the world's need, each of which is helpful and important, but without the primacy of the biblical concept of *ethne*.

5 **There must be disciples made from every people on earth,** made clear throughout the Old Testament, the Gospels and Revelation. This implies the need for a body of believers in every people and, more, a Church that impacts every part of that people. This goal is the essence of the Great Commission and the crux of God's purposes for humanity. It is also linked to the coming again of the Lord Jesus for His Church. Pray that the Church may passionately pursue this goal to conclusion and then be the generation that brings back the King!

Scripture on the Great Commission

The Lord Jesus Christ gave His Church clear instructions after His resurrection and before He was taken up to heaven (all verses below are taken from the ESV):

The evangelistic challenges. Mark 16:15: "Go into all the world and proclaim the gospel to the whole creation." Luke 24:47: "...that repentance and forgiveness of sins should be proclaimed in his name to all nations, beginning from Jerusalem".

The discipling challenge. Matthew 28:19-20: "Go therefore and make disciples of all nations, baptizing them in the name of the Father and of the Son and of the Holy Spirit, teaching them to observe all that I have commanded you."

The missiological challenge. John 17:18: "As you sent me into the world, so I have sent them into the world." John 20:21: "As the Father has sent me, even so I am sending you."

The global challenge. Acts 1:8: "You will be my witnesses in Jerusalem and in all Judea and Samaria, and to the end of the earth."

This encompasses the task before us; it is vast in scope. John P Jones wrote in 1912, "This enterprise is not only the greatest that the world has ever known; it is also the most difficult of achievement." Yet, we believe that the Great Commission is not merely an ideal to aspire toward, but an achievable command given by the Lord. In each of the passages referenced above, the commissioning of the Church was accompanied by assurances of God's power and authority and the very real presence of the Holy Spirit. The scale of the task before us is matched only by the greatness of the God who promises to accompany and empower us.

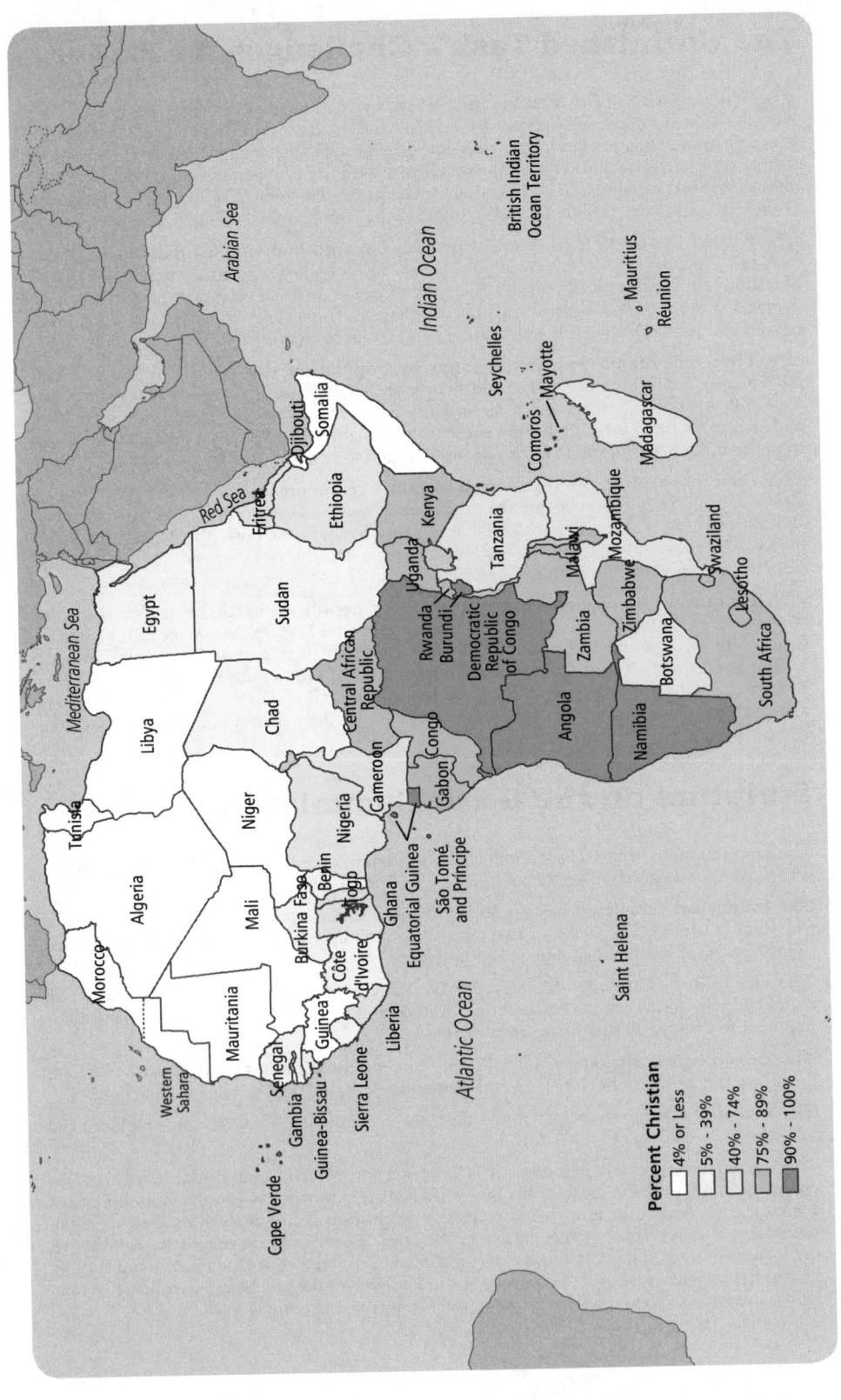

Percent Christian

- 4% or Less
- 5% - 39%
- 40% - 74%
- 75% - 89%
- 90% - 100%

Country	2010 Pop (mill)	Main Rel	Chr	Evang	Non-Chr	Unev	All	UP	Chr
				(% of total pop)			(# of peoples)		
Algeria	35.42	M	0.3	0.2	99.7	66.0	41	35	5
Angola	18.99	X	94.1	22.5	5.9	1.3	60	2	45
Benin	9.21	XEM	39.9	8.3	60.1	25.5	69	13	17
Botswana	1.98	XE	65.6	8.07	34.4	5.4	51	1	27
Burkina Faso	16.29	MEX	20.7	8.9	79.3	37.1	79	28	4
Burundi	8.52	X	90.5	27.04	9.5	1.1	12	3	8
Cameroon	19.96	XME	53.8	9.0	46.2	17.9	290	16	205
Cape Verde Islands	0.51	X	94.6	6.6	5.4	0.5	7	0	7
Central African Republic	4.51	XM	76.4	32.3	23.6	17.1	87	7	58
Chad	11.51	MX	38.5	10.1	61.5	50.2	141	72	39
Comoros	0.69	M	0.9	0.2	99.1	66.8	12	8	3
Congo-DRC	67.83	X	92.2	18.7	7.9	1.3	239	4	222
Congo, Republic of	3.76	X	89.7	15.9	10.3	1.2	77	3	71
Cote d'Ivoire	21.57	MXE	33.6	10.5	66.4	26.9	106	34	37
Djibouti	0.88	M	1.8	0.1	98.3	61.1	11	6	5
Egypt	84.47	MX	12.8	3.9	87.2	32.2	39	23	8
Equatorial Guinea	0.69	X	90.0	4.4	10.0	1.5	22	2	20
Eritrea	5.22	MX	47.3	2.1	52.7	30.5	19	9	3
Ethiopia	84.98	XM	60.7	19.6	39.3	17.5	116	20	30
Gabon	1.50	XM	79.4	12.7	20.7	2.2	49	4	43
Gambia, The	1.75	M	4.5	0.8	95.5	61.2	32	14	7
Ghana	24.33	XME	63.4	24.2	36.6	12.6	109	20	49
Guinea	10.32	M	4.5	0.7	95.5	64.2	47	29	5
Guinea-Bissau	1.65	MEX	10.9	1.6	89.1	57.6	32	14	4
Kenya	40.86	X	82.7	48.9	17.3	6.2	115	35	49
Lesotho	2.08	X	89.3	12.1	10.7	0.7	13	1	11
Liberia	4.10	EXM	41.4	14.6	58.6	27.8	40	4	24
Libya	6.55	M	2.6	0.3	97.4	59.8	40	28	9
Madagascar	20.15	XM	53.5	11.5	46.5	21.0	50	9	10
Malawi	15.69	XM	76.0	19.6	24.0	4.7	33	4	21
Mali	13.32	M	2.6	0.7	97.4	62.6	62	37	2
Mauritania	3.37	M	0.3	0.1	99.8	75.5	19	14	3
Mauritius	1.29	HXM	32.7	10.1	67.3	27.5	17	5	4
Mayotte	0.20	M	1.6	0.1	98.4	74.5	11	8	2
Morocco	32.78	M	0.1	<0.1	99.9	69.6	30	24	5
Mozambique	23.41	XEM	46.5	11.1	53.5	13.0	62	8	16
Namibia	2.21	X	91.4	12.2	8.6	3.8	35	2	25
Niger	15.89	M	0.3	0.1	99.7	62.6	37	28	4
Nigeria	158.26	XM	51.3	30.8	48.7	21.5	522	67	175
Réunion	0.84	X	87.0	5.9	13.0	3.2	16	4	10
Rwanda	10.28	X	89.1	26.9	10.9	1.3	13	3	9
Saint Helena	<0.01	X	94.7	8.8	5.3	0.6	3	0	3
São Tomé & Príncipe	0.17	X	87.6	4.3	12.5	0.5	7	0	7
Senegal	12.86	M	6.4	0.2	93.6	58.2	57	27	7
Seychelles	0.08	X	96.1	5.9	3.9	0.9	10	3	7
Sierra Leone	5.84	MEX	13.2	3.9	86.9	43.8	31	12	5
Somalia	9.36	M	0.3	0.1	99.7	65.9	22	17	5
South Africa	50.49	XE	75.2	21.1	24.8	2.2	62	5	41
Sudan	43.19	MXE	26.1	14.7	73.9	50.7	246	138	42
Swaziland	1.20	XE	84.7	25.1	15.3	1.0	12	1	10
Tanzania	45.04	XME	54.1	17.9	45.9	16.3	160	33	72
Togo	6.78	XEM	45.4	10.7	54.6	22.1	56	6	20
Tunisia	10.37	M	0.2	<0.1	99.8	65.9	23	15	7
Uganda	33.80	XM	84.7	37.0	15.3	1.4	66	6	53
Zambia	13.26	XE	87.0	25.7	13.1	2.3	82	5	51
Zimbabwe	12.64	XE	78.0	30.9	22.0	1.9	44	3	30
TOTAL	1,033		48.8	17.2	51.5	24.7	3,743	919	1,661

Africa

Geography 🌍

Area 30,244,000 sq km; 20.3% of the world's surface area. Of this, 20.6 million sq km are in countries south of the Sahara, and 9.68 million in the nations of North Africa.

Comments on countries included in the map, table and text:

All countries included – 57.
Western Sahara is included with Morocco because Morocco occupies the territory.
The Spanish enclaves of Ceuta and Melilla on Morocco's north coast are included in Spain.
The following small island countries and territories around Africa are included under Africa: Cape Verde, Comoros, St Helena, Mauritius, Mayotte, Réunion, São Tomé and Príncipe, Seychelles, British Indian Ocean Territory.
Somalia still includes Somaliland and Puntland, despite their de facto autonomous existence.

Population		Ann Gr	Density
2010	1,033,042,510	2.3%	34/sq km
2020	1,276,369,389	2.1%	42/sq km
2030	1,524,187,297	1.7%	50/sq km

Africa has 15% of the world's population.

Cities There are 52 cities in Africa of over 1 million, 2 of which are over 10m; if conurbations were measured to include outlying slums and shantytowns, this number would increase. **Urbanites** 40%. **Pop under 15 yrs** 41.2%. **Life expectancy** 54.9 years.

Peoples 👪

Nearly 2,500 ethnic groups.

Sub-Saharan African 67.1%. 2,111 peoples. The 53 people clusters can be grouped into three major blocs – West African, Sudanic and Bantu. Among the largest clusters:

Central-Lakes Bantu 5.3%. 67 peoples.
Guinean 3.5%. 119 peoples.
Yoruba 3.5%. 19 peoples.
Hausa 3.3%. 4 peoples.
Fulani 3.2%. 18 peoples.
Gur 3.0%. 113 peoples.
Benue 3.0%. 301 peoples.
Nilotic 2.8%. 90 peoples.
Nguni Bantu 2.6%. 8 peoples.
Igbo 2.6%. 10 peoples.
Makua-Yao Bantu 2.4%. 27 peoples.
Central-South Bantu 2.3%. 97 peoples.
Central-Congo Bantu 2.2%. 120 peoples.
Central-Tanzania Bantu 2.2%. 49 peoples.
Remnants of the pre-negroid peoples:
Khoisan (San) in Southern Africa (1.9 million).

Pygmies in the rainforests of Central Africa (740,000).

Arab 19.5%. 137 peoples. Mostly in North Africa; some in the Sahel and on the East African coast. Many mutually unintelligible dialects spoken.
Arab(8) 9.9%. Mostly made up of Maghreb (5.5%) and Sudan (2.6%) Arabs.
Egyptian 7.2%. Arab, but includes assimilated older indigenous ethnicities such as the Copts.
Berber(5) 1.8%. The indigenous peoples of North Africa, most found in the Maghreb and Sahara. Increasingly assimilated with Arab ethnicities.
Bedouin(2) 0.4%.
Tuareg(7) 0.2%.
Horn of Africa-Cushitic 10.0%. 105 peoples. Ethiopian 3.8%, 21 peoples. Oromo 2.9%, 19 peoples. Somali 1.4%, 9 peoples. Omotic 1.3%, 51 peoples.
Malay 1.9%. 37 peoples. Almost entirely Malagasy cluster.
White Caucasian 0.8%. Mostly in South Africa, but expatriate minorities in most lands.
South Asian 0.6%. 24 peoples. Majority are in Mauritius and KwaZulu-Natal; small minorities in many other countries.
Other 0.1%.

Literacy 61%. All languages 2,110; 30.5% of the world's total. The continued use of European languages in education is at the expense of local languages. In only 6 nations is an African language officially used as the main means of conducting the nation's business. **Languages with Scriptures** 173Bi 335NT 223por (figures from UBS). There is work in progress in 693 languages and a definite need for translators in 225 more. This latter number could rise as high as 926 after careful field research. Africa is one of the greatest remaining challenges for Bible translation, with existing openings for missionary translators.

Economy 📈

In the 50 years since a wave of independence ended colonial control over most of Africa, the economic conditions of the continent have largely worsened; a few have seen progress. Africa retains vast wealth of natural resources. There is a large diaspora still concerned for the land of its roots – those outside Africa, but having African roots or descent, are approaching 150 million in population. Promising signs are on the horizon, such as increasing foreign investment and economic diversification, but others claim this is largely foreign economic exploitation rather than investment. A population swell is about to produce Africa's largest ever population of working age. But many struggles still exist, and some key causes are:

Population growth. Africa's population growth rate is the world's highest by far (2.3%/year compared to the global rate of 1.2%/year). It is, however, slowing rapidly through reduced birthrates, emigration and the effects of disease.

Unsustainable demands on the land, a consequence of rapid population growth. Of all continents, Africa's soil is the most depleted of nutrients. Overgrazing and deforestation wrought great damage to local ecosystems and sped up desertification. Climate change accelerates the frequency of food crises; drought, flooding and unpredictable weather make farming almost untenable in many areas. Most Africans are subsistence farmers or keepers of livestock, but population growth has forced millions to subdivide their land into ever-tinier plots, a frequent cause of strife and even violence and war.

Low investment in agriculture and in development of viable methods of food production, distribution and sale. Fertilizer and improved strains of seeds are used only in a few areas where commercial farming is successful; most do not have access to such boons and, as a result, 80% of Africa's farmland is severely degraded. Food aid often distorts local marketing and diet patterns. Forty years ago, Africa was a net food exporter; today it is dependent on imports and food aid.

Foreign debt, the reduction of which has been an area of real progress, remains a shackle on African growth. Many countries spend more on debt servicing than on health and education. Several initiatives resulted in the World Bank forgiving the debts of around 20 of Africa's most heavily indebted countries – many billions of dollars of debt. The intended re-allocation of these forgiven debt payments into economic development, education and health care will make such actions doubly effective.

The complex dynamics of foreign aid and investment. Many, including many within Africa, believe that too much aid is flowing into Africa – hundreds of billions of dollars in aid – and that most of it is poorly handled. Increasingly, there is a call for investment and trade to uplift the continent rather than aid, which inhibits healthy growth and keeps Africa dependent on such handouts. China is now Africa's largest economic partner and has already had a huge impact; China's hunger for resources has created much trade, but it has also increased tension and resentment at how it does business.

The lack of infrastructure, essential for development, and the inability to maintain what infrastructure does exist – in energy and power, in transportation, in communications and in managing water resources. In these areas, Africa lags desperately behind even other poor regions of the world.

The lack of an educated middle class/business class undermined economic growth right from the early years of independence, although this is changing today. The illiteracy rate is 40%. There is a monstrous gap between the few rich and the multitudinous poor. Brain drain continues to see up to 20,000 university-educated professionals emigrate each year, a huge loss when low literacy and reduced life expectancy make such people all the more vital to retain.

Corruption and graft by rulers and officials who enrich themselves or their ethnic group. Some estimate that 25% of Africa's combined national income is lost through corruption – amounting to $150 billion per year. Some political leaders (and some rebel leaders as well) have built personal fortunes amounting to billions of dollars.

Disease – the high prevalence of malaria, AIDS and other diseases such as tuberculosis and sleeping sickness. Malaria kills about twice as many people as AIDS and TB combined. The effects of widespread illnesses and shortened lifespans on education, family stability and economic output are devastating. Whole economies are crippled as a result. The lack of clean water is not a disease in itself, but it contributes hugely to the spread of disease and to malnutrition.

Military conflict currently afflicts 15 African countries. Most of the world's active wars in the last 20 years have been in Africa. Millions have been internally displaced or made refugees. The destruction and upheaval of wars, coups and strife might contribute more to suffering than any other problems Africa endures.

Of the 33 lowest-ranking nations on the UN Human Development Index, 32 are in Africa. **Income/person** $1,574 (3% of USA).

Politics ✗

Sub-Saharan Africa's isolation from the rest of the world ended in the "Scramble for Africa" by the European colonial powers in the 19th Century. A century of colonial rule brought a measure of peace, education, improvement in living standards and some economic development. One negative effect was the legacy of inappropriate colonial borders, which cut through African ethnic, economic and political networks and has subsequently been the cause of much pain, tension and war. Between 1957 and 1994, all states in continental Africa became independent. Major, current political issues in Africa feature:

Political progress. Multiparty politics and democracy appear to be taking hold in many parts of the continent – a desired result from the Western perspective, but a debatable one from an African view. From 1960 to 1990, just one sub-Saharan African political leader was voted out of office and then willingly stepped out. From 1990 to 2004, there were more than a dozen. Only a handful of states have not had a multi-party election in the last 10 years. Voting turnouts are higher, and greater numbers of women are involved in politics. Even so, many leaders are effectively elected-rulers-for-life. In many cases, kleptocracy, poor economic policies, tribal favouritism and general ineptitude often mire their countries even deeper into the grip of poverty. The concept of the failed state applies to a number of African countries.

Pan-African governance and international relations – notoriously ineffective and self-serving in the past but increasingly helpful today. The African Union established much improved Africa-wide development plans (NEPAD) as well as more pro-active policing and peacekeeping strategies. Peer reviews of member states' democratic processes, and observation of human rights, are beginning to have an effect and to engender more accountability and more effective democracies; African leaders have traditionally been very reticent to criticize one another.

Foreign interest, involvement and investment, which have significantly changed, hopefully offer more possibilities for the future than did the exploitation of the colonial past. During the Cold War, Africa was yet another playing field in the global contest for ideological dominance. Now, post-Cold War Africa sees a number of power blocs – including China, the EU, the US and even the Arab World – competing for resources, trade and investment opportunities.

The artificial, colonially drawn frontiers that have defined African countries for 50 years are under threat. Secessionist movements and wars have afflicted Sudan, Somalia, Ethiopia and Eritrea, DRC and, to a degree, Angola and Côte d'Ivoire. Altering boundaries to reflect de facto realities may benefit Africa in the long term, but it will introduce great tension and conflict before all issues are resolved.

"Ethnic cleansing" has caused tragic bloodshed, tides of refugees and even armies with many child-soldiers in Rwanda, Burundi, DRC, Liberia, Sierra Leone, Sudan, Uganda and South Africa (with refugees). The nine-nation Great Lakes War in Central Africa, which followed the Rwanda genocide, still simmers in some capacity and will continue to as long as the countries of that region fail to address the war and its causes in a decisive manner.

Violent Islamist movements deeply affect the continent, from Algeria in the north to South Africa. Jihadist groups in North Africa, Islamist radicals in Somalia and northeast Kenya, massacres of Christians in northern Nigeria and concerted government-endorsed attacks against Christians in Sudan are just some of the consequences of these movements.

Religion

Religion is vitally important in Africa – it is more significant than nationality or ethnicity in how Africans identify themselves. Religious freedom has increased over much of Africa in recent decades, but there are restrictions in North Africa and in some other Muslim-majority countries. Persecution of varying intensity is present in a number of nations: Morocco, Mauritania, Algeria, Tunisia, Libya, Egypt, Sudan, Somalia, Djibouti, Eritrea, Nigeria, Tanzania and Comoros. The intensity of the threat to Christians in Somalia, Eritrea and northern Nigeria is particularly terrible.

Religions	Pop %	Population	Ann Gr
Christian	48.77	503,742,508	2.6%
Muslim	41.47	428,349,774	2.4%
Ethnoreligionist	8.32	85,963,109	0.2%
Non-religious	1.02	10,555,845	3.6%
Hindu	0.21	2,201,029	1.5%
Baha'i	0.16	1,702,239	2.0%
Other	0.02	197,920	2.9%
Jewish	0.01	88,032	-1.4%
Sikh	<0.01	36,730	0.5%
Buddhist	<0.01	35,931	1.4%
Chinese	<0.01	33,481	3.4%

Christians	Pop %	Affiliates	Ann Gr
Protestant	14.53	150,105,310	3.2%
Independent	9.63	99,447,070	2.6%
Anglican	4.77	49,273,112	3.1%
Catholic	15.95	164,794,368	2.5%
Orthodox	4.50	46,462,739	1.9%
Marginal	0.52	5,398,146	3.7%
Unaffiliated	2.11	21,799,177	1.3%
Doubly affiliated	*-2.87*	*-29,629,227*	*2.7%*

TransBloc	Pop %	Population	Ann Gr
Evangelicals			
Evangelicals	17.7	182,442,247	3.6%
Renewalists			
Charismatics	13.7	141,357,535	4.2%
Pentecostals	5.8	59,803,540	3.6%

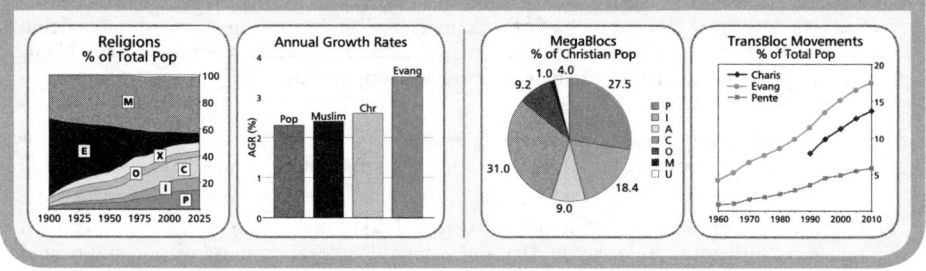

Answers to Prayer

1 **Christianity has grown** to become the religion of almost half of Africa's population, and nearly two-thirds of sub-Saharan Africa. From 1900 to 2010, Christian numbers grew from 9.1% of the population to 48.8%, and from 7.5 million to 504 million.

2 **Evangelical growth has been even more spectacular.** In 1900, evangelicals numbered 1.6 million (1.5%), but in 2010, they were 182 million (17.7%). This is nearly as much as all evangelicals in the Americas combined and is the largest evangelical population of any continent. African evangelicals are also increasing at a faster rate than any other continent.

3 **Third Wave Pentecostal groups,** strongly evangelical, have become a major element in the African Church. They are strong on the Scriptures and outreach, expectant of miracles, fervent in prayer and courageous against the powers of darkness. The Redeemed Christian Church and Deeper Life Bible Church were both started in Nigeria and have planted churches in dozens of countries. Groups such as the Church of Pentecost (Ghana), the Zimbabwe Assemblies of God, and others in Kenya, Tanzania, Côte d'Ivoire and elsewhere continue to grow and plant new churches.

4 **A number of countries experienced significant growth** in the Church – either large-scale church growth or breakthrough among previously unevangelized peoples. These include Ethiopia, Sudan, Benin, Nigeria, Algeria, Mozambique and Angola, just to name a few.

5 **Prayer movements** have a remarkable impact in Africa. The Global Day of Prayer originated in Cape Town through Transformation Africa and now involves tens, if not hundreds, of millions of Christians each year. The all-night prayer meetings of the Redeemed Christian Church in Nigeria – called the Holy Ghost Services – attract an average of 500,000, but this is merely the most well known of many such meetings. The familiarity of Africans with the reality of spiritual warfare, and their willingness to faithfully put in many hours of intercession, are possibly the most significant factors in the remarkable church growth on this continent.

6 **The impact of the gospel on the educated.** The ministries of SU, **IFES** and others among students have been remarkable; through these and the ministries of churches and agencies, a large proportion of Africa's professionals and leaders in Anglophone and Francophone countries are committed Christians. Their influence is becoming decisive in addressing corruption and social evils and in affecting the power structures of society; the fruit of this can be seen in the positive changes all over Africa in the last decade. Pray for this to continue!

7 **The mission force** of African agencies and missionaries continues to grow and diversify. Lacking the established infrastructures and financial resources of the West, Africans find creative new ways to train and send church planters. Specific areas of praise:

a) Mobilizing. Key to the whole African mission endeavour is the work of **MANI** (Movement for African National Initiatives), a pan-African mission mobilizing and networking movement. Vision 5015 is the ambitious plan to raise up 50,000 Nigerian missionaries in the next 15 years. Several other nations have similar long-term mobilizing plans for raising up missionaries and reaching the unreached in their own countries.

b) Research. A number of more specific research initiatives – usually on the national or regional level – are assisting greatly in identifying the task remaining and offering insight on strategy and methodology.

c) **Reaching Muslims.** The vast bulk of Africa's unreached are Muslim, many of them practicing an African brand of folk Islam. As demonstrated in West Africa, East Africa and elsewhere, sub-Saharan Africans can be extremely effective at winning Muslims to Jesus and are doing so to greater effect than ever.

d) **Holistic ministry.** African churches and missions are becoming savvy about the great effectiveness of combining prayer, compassionate ministry, development work and church planting.

e) **Bible Translation.** Increasing numbers of Africans lead translation programmes in their own languages. Numerous seminaries in Africa now provide education in translation and related studies so the African Church can address the enormous translation challenges it faces.

Africa's Hot Spots

The following warrant sustained intercession:

1 **Central Africa,** where ethnic and international conflicts have brutalized the populations. Tensions between the Hutu and Tutsi peoples in Rwanda and Burundi led to civil wars and periodic genocidal massacres over the past five decades. The Rwanda genocide of 1994 triggered a chain reaction of war and waves of refugees, affecting surrounding countries. The Second Congo War of 1998-2003 embroiled DRC, Namibia, Zimbabwe, Angola, Chad, Uganda, Rwanda and Burundi in a confused and bloody conflict that involved irregular militia groups as much as national armed forces – and had no real decisive winners, only losers. Eastern Congo in particular has been devastated, and the simmering of disgruntled militias and ethnicities poses a continued threat there. The heterodox and occultic Lord's Resistance Army also plagues the population of Uganda as well as southern Sudan and northeast DRC with raids, murder, mutilation, abduction and enslavement. Pray for righteous leaders – locally, nationally and internationally – who will act with justice and decisiveness to prevent war and conflict. Pray also that the lives of those devastated by loss and destruction might be rebuilt from the ashes.

2 **East Africa** remains a place of instability and regional violence, despite the settling of the Ethiopia-Eritrea war of 1998-2000 into an uneasy, arbitrated truce.

a) **Somalia's descent into anarchy** seems to have plumbed new depths. A combination of deep poverty, lack of resources, famine, historical colonial influences and the deeply clan-based societal structure creates a dangerous cocktail. Hard-line Islamist groups vie against the Ethiopian-backed Transitional Federal Government, taking and retaking each other's strongholds. This situation allowed foreign fishing fleets to plunder the fish stocks off the Somali coast, which in turn generated an armed response by Somalis and the flourishing of piracy. Small Somali boats and armed crews seize vulnerable foreign vessels by force and demand a ransom – such activity is the highest earner of foreign exchange in some parts of Somalia.

b) **Kenya suffered unexpected violence** in 2007-2008 after a disputed election. What began as political protests against electoral fraud, and was tied to land ownership issues, soon descended into ethnic violence, and much destruction of property and life ensued. Finally, a coalition government was brokered, but the events demonstrate that even stable democratic countries are never far from conflict.

3 **Sudan's civil strife** has been the norm for decades. It became somewhat of an international pariah due to the persistent violence and oppression endorsed by the regime. Pray for peace.

a) **The north-south tensions** have plunged the country into outright civil war for 38 of the last 55 years. These are intensified by the racial and religious divide between north and south, the Arabization agenda of the regime, with its Islamic jihad overtones, as well as the oil wealth in the south.

b) **Darfur,** despite being overwhelmingly Muslim in composition, has also been subject to horrific oppression by the government-sponsored Janjawid militia. These troubles have in turn spilled into Chad and, to a lesser degree, Central African Republic, affecting millions in both countries.

4 **Nigeria and the Sahel,** through which runs the north-south fault line between Muslim and Christian majority areas. The sporadic outbreaks of violence in Nigeria escalated into more frequent and intense pogroms against Christians by increasingly bloodthirsty fundamentalist Muslim groups (often importing fighters from farther afield). Christian response has been largely peaceful, but not always. Besides the religious fault line, the conflict also touches upon tensions over land between southern settled farmers and northern pastoralists. Côte d'Ivoire, Ghana and other West African nations face similar tensions. Should something as terrible as north-south civil war in Nigeria break out, the likelihood is high of meltdown in much of the rest of West Africa. Pray for those orchestrating violence to be foiled and for those on both sides who love peace to prevail through wisdom, discipline and graciousness. Pray also for Christians to continue evangelizing the region's Muslims with love and without fear.

5 **Southern Africa** is not free from tensions and potential troubles, either. The well-documented abuses by the government in Zimbabwe, the crippling effect of HIV/AIDS, the general lack of good governance and the growing uncertainty over South Africa's stability add up to a need for heartfelt prayer. The escalating racial tensions in South Africa and the cruel violence against foreign refugees (mostly fleeing Zimbabwe) point to an underlying reality that the future health of the "rainbow nation" is under more threat than ever.

Trends to Watch

A few of the major international trends are given for prayerful attention. See individual countries for more specific details.

1 **Africa's continuing struggle with poverty** has taken on some new dynamics, but is no less urgent. As explained in the economic section, the causes are many and complex. For a region with many natural resources and a vast, young workforce, the situation should not be as bad as it is. This is partly due to internal, local causes and in part to exploitation and unfair trade practices imposed from abroad. Areas where prayer and action are warranted:

a) Reducing local causes of poverty, particularly corruption, would reinject many billions of dollars back into the grassroots economy. Were greater economic accountability imposed and budgets actually spent on developing trade and production, many could be lifted out of poverty. Were wars and conflicts ended, infrastructure developed and education and health improved, a massive difference could be made.

b) Appropriate aid and development programmes. Short-term fixes without long-term plans, the distortion of economies and the creation of dependency must all be addressed. Aid that fails to generate local jobs and production, that empowers agencies rather than the people and that can be abused or siphoned away from those for whom it is intended must be ended. Much of the development business is poorly organized and fragmented, and any such work must be done from a servant mentality – neo-colonial, manipulative uses of assistance will only further perpetuate the problems.

c) Fairer investments and trade agreements with foreign countries. Africans are calling for more trade, not more aid, but it must be on terms that do not unduly favour richer nations. Fair prices for African produce must be offered. Dumping unwanted and inappropriate foodstuffs and medicines as aid can create more problems than it solves, as can flooding the vulnerable African market with cheap foreign-produced items, such as Chinese textiles.

2 **Disease still looms** as a deathly spectre over Africa. A higher proportion of infants, children and adults are lost to disease in Africa than anywhere else. Tens of billions of dollars in productivity are lost each year to the effects of disease upon the working population. Of specific concern are:

a) HIV/AIDS. Although no longer at its peak infection rate, HIV still afflicts nearly 23 million people in sub-Saharan Africa alone. In some areas, up to one-third of the adult population were infected. This region accounts for 68% of new infections among adults, 91% among children and 72% of AIDS-related deaths. Life expectancy fell by half in parts of southern Africa. A staggering 14.2 million children have lost one or both parents to AIDS. Entire communities and economies have been decimated. NGOs, including many Christian ones, have done much good work in education, prevention, treatment and care for those at risk or already suffering. Still, the Church needs to rise up, break the stigma associated with AIDS and minister life and truth to Africa. Ample opportunity exists to eradicate this plague within one generation; a UN report states that if HIV still infects millions of Africans by 2025, it will not be because there was no choice, but because of a lack of political will. Pray for wise and firm decision making; pray as well for the changing of sinful behavioural patterns that allow for AIDS to persist and spread.

b) *Malaria*, though a much less "glamorous" disease than AIDS, is even more destructive to Africa's health and welfare. Malaria kills a child on average every 30 seconds; this is more than twice as many as HIV/AIDS claims and just as debilitating to the population's strength and wellbeing. More than $12 billion in output is lost each year. The cost of widespread prevention (largely through mosquito nets) is a mere fraction of that amount, yet less than 5% of Africa's children sleep under nets. Treatment-resistant strains of malaria are emerging, making prevention all the more vital. Pray for greater attention to be paid to this disease that steals, kills and destroys, and for greater action mobilized to eradicate it.

3 **African democratic institutions remain vulnerable,** but are strengthening with time. Authoritarian, autocratic leadership that suppresses opposition and robs from its own people still exists, but in many parts of the continent, there are signs of it being replaced by more responsible governments. Pray for more Christian politicians who are undefiled by corruption and resolute in transparency and righteousness. Sub-Saharan Africa is majority Christian – surely its elected officials should likewise be. Some Christian leaders have lost credibility in the past decade, but others have maintained a good testimony. The increased involvement of women in politics, both grassroots and leadership, should help to point the way forward to more egalitarian and accountable political structures. Pray that a revolution in African power structures might occur as communication and information technologies spread, empowering local movements to keep leaders accountable.

4 **Emigration, displacement and human trafficking** are issues that profoundly affect Africa and, by extension, the rest of the world. Almost all of Africa's countries face these problems. Conflict and poverty have driven tens of millions out of their traditional home areas and, while many seek a better life abroad, the large majority remain displaced within Africa. Often, out of a desire to get a family foothold in a wealthier country, young people – especially women – and even children are sent abroad and into highly vulnerable situations. Getting oneself into Europe by any means necessary is regarded as the pathway to a better life; wicked men profit from this desperation, and many lives and families are ruined by the pursuit of such far-off dreams. Pray for justice and righteousness on a global level that will remove the need for such risky endeavours.

5 **The Muslim-Christian fault line** stretches from Senegal across the Sahel to Ethiopia and along Africa's Indian Ocean seaboard. The potential for widened conflagrations and confrontations is high because of increasingly aggressive Islamist movements and because of African Christian evangelism gaining converts from within Muslim communities. This has been a major factor contributing to war or mass violence in Sudan, Nigeria and Côte d'Ivoire, but another nine nations are at risk.

6 **The continued power of African traditional religions.** The low percentage of followers of pre-Christian ethnic religions is not a true reflection of reality. Underlying both Muslim and Christian religious profession is a value system steeped in the old ways – fetishism, ancestor worship, idolatry and others. Personal, tribal and national crises reveal this. The terrible events in Africa that have so impacted many nations in recent years cannot be understood without realizing this factor. Pray for the powers of darkness to be bound in Jesus' name, and pray that Christian leaders and churches may challenge these powers and not succumb to them.

The Church in Africa

African Christianity has established itself as a truly potent force, both on the continent and even on a global level. The colonial past is fading and a new level of confidence, dynamism, vision and maturity is evident. In many countries, the Church has established itself as the only effective social organization that can bring reconciliation among ethnic groups and cope with the many economic, health and education challenges in collapsing societies. Challenges the Church must address:

1 **Discipleship** is rightly being addressed as Africa's greatest challenge. The growth of Christianity has been sensational, but the follow-up has traditionally been lacking. Non-Christian customs and worldviews permeate the Church. Syncretism is a major problem in many areas. Thorough repentance and renunciation of sin and the works of darkness are often lacking, and many Christians are not free from the influence of witchcraft and evil spirits. Churches and ministries throughout Africa now place a high priority on discipleship. This will shape more Christ-like character and promote a biblical worldview among church-goers.

2 **Africa's role in the global Church** is more important than ever. Its contribution to revitalizing the flagging churches in Europe is crucial. Even more crucial is its role in defending biblical faith and traditional reading of the Scriptures against the creeping relativism and liberalism that besets much of the Church in the West. This is of particular import as Africa sits on the frontline of the work of evangelizing the Muslim world; the flagging vigour and insipid moral stance of many Western denominations will have little impact – or even counterproductive impact – on the Islamic world.

3 **Pray for unity in such great diversity.** There are over 15,000 denominations, church clusters and networks in Africa. Countless independent congregations exist with no overarching accountability or relationships. Pray:

a) *That leaders might place their agendas at the foot of the cross.* The desire for influence and power, the ethnocentric bias that lies behind many splits, the personal pride and carnality behind many divisions in churches and ministries – all must be crucified with Christ.

b) *For pan–African* bodies such as the **AEA** (Association of Evangelicals of Africa). The role of the **AEA** is strategic in linking national evangelical denominations in fellowship, in stimulating vision and in promoting leadership training, culturally relevant biblical theology and social action. The **AEA** is present in 33 countries, with 34 parachurch associate members. It represents over 70 million African evangelicals.

4 **Leadership training is recognized as the critical bottleneck.** Leaders are in short supply at every level – for village congregations, for the urban educated, for theological training, for missionary endeavour and for national-level leadership. Pray for:

a) *The serious consideration of what kind of training* is most appropriate for Africans. This includes teaching and communication methods, curriculum and content, length of courses and modules. Too much foreign structure and content has been imposed; Africans must develop training that works for Africans and deals with the Afrocentric issues facing the Church.

b) *Theological institutions.* These have multiplied for students at primary, secondary and post-secondary levels. ACTEA, Africa's primary accreditation body, lists in its directory over 150 theological colleges and programmes. There are only two post-graduate level institutions, both in Nairobi. Countries with the most accredited programmes: Nigeria (24), Kenya (21), Ethiopia (14) and South Africa (11). The high incidence of such institutions in Anglophone Africa is offset by the paucity of the same in Francophone and Portuguese-speaking Africa.

c) *Selection of students.* Discernment is needed to know those anointed by the Spirit for future leadership and those applying out of a baser motive for prestige, potential employment, desire for education or others.

d) *Funds.* The poverty of the Church and lack of understanding among potential donors hamper the development of Bible training institutions. The financial needs are endless. Generosity from the African and the global Church is required for such vital ministry to continue.

e) *TEE programmes, modular training and training-in-service* are all key for training both lay leadership and the many overworked and bivocational pastors. Several hundred TEE programmes now operate in Africa, accounting for over 100,000 students. Despite past obstacles, TEE is establishing itself as an effective alternative for theological training.

f) *African theologians,* who are now emerging as global theological leaders. A truly indigenous evangelical African theology was slow to develop but is now making great strides. A clear stand by African theologians to expound the universal and unchangeable truths of Scripture in the African context is needed, which will also counteract error, African misconceptions of the gospel and the very real powers of darkness. One such example is the *African Bible Commentary*, a one-volume commentary on the whole Bible written exclusively by Africans.

5 **The development of a missions vision in the Church.** Africa is becoming a formidable missionary-sending region. Praise God for the rapid growth and spread of African missions, essential for finishing the task in Africa itself. Pray for:

a) ***The poverty mentality to be overcome.*** Western colonial influence, and then some patronizing attitudes by foreign missions, have subverted the continent and created a mindset of dependence. Too many Africans immediately look to Western (or increasingly Asian) sponsorship to meet every need.

b) ***Funds to be made available to train and send out missionaries.*** The wherewithal to send workers exists in Africa, but only if churches see missionary sending and support as non-negotiable and then give sacrificially.

c) ***Congregations to see missions as fundamental*** to the gospel itself and the task of every believer. Participation in the Great Commission beyond the immediate context has largely been ignored in most African churches.

d) ***Effective cross-cultural training for missions.*** There is still a shortfall of innovative training mechanisms to produce the necessary results. Some have been set up and are growing in different parts of Africa – such as in West Africa through the Nigerian **CAPRO** and **CMF**, in East Africa through the Africa Inland Church, in South Africa through various agencies.

e) ***Christian research*** – it has come a great distance, but more needs to be done. Beyond identifying and enumerating unevangelized peoples, strategy and methodology must be developed in mobilizing workers and effectively reaching the unreached.

6 **Cross-cultural missions.** The missionary force is increasingly African and multi-continental, and less Western. Much sensitivity and humility is required for effective ministry that reaches the unevangelized and defers to the maturity and vision of the growing African Church. The need for missionaries continues to be greater than the supply of those with the gifting and vision for:

a) ***Partnership.*** Honour must be given to the huge impact of dedicated missionaries in the past, who achieved so much despite the frequent neglect or even opposition of colonial rulers. But today's realities mean that ministry in Africa can largely be led by Africans, supported by expatriates. Pray for unity and fellowship that transcend all social and cultural barriers within mission agencies, among agencies themselves and between the indigenous churches and agencies.

b) ***Pioneer areas.*** These still abound; see below. A high degree of commitment and sacrifice will be required to reach present pioneer areas where conditions are sometimes very hard. In some cases missionaries will need to learn two to four languages before they can reach the least-reached.

c) ***Church support personnel*** for teaching, youth work and other areas are needed as never before – all areas in which African workers could do better, were enough willing and able. For expatriates to minister under African leadership and as part of the Church in Africa is essential.

d) ***Specialists*** for Bible translation, theological education and media ministries (audio materials, radio, television, the Internet and Bible-storying).

e) ***Holistic ministry,*** which is in ever-growing demand. Needs in areas such as counseling, working with children at risk, education, health care, agriculture, business development and many others neglected by governments can be met by Christian organizations, providing a beautiful testimony to the transforming power of the gospel. Pray for a balance where all the needs of the whole person – spiritual, physical and relational – can be met.

f) ***Mission sending from Africa is ready for the next phase.*** The 2011 **MANI** Consultation will assess the state of the African Church, build the long-term sustainability of mission sending and begin a resource mobilization process. This is essential for a continent with many willing to work but lacking the training and material resources to do mission the way Westerners and East Asians have traditionally done.

The Unreached of Africa

Africa has 13 of the world's 20 least-evangelized countries by percentage. There are many clusters of unreached peoples in Africa. The vast majority are Muslim of varying degrees of commitment and orthodoxy. Reaching them will be a great challenge in terms of spiritual opposition, cultural learning and effective mission strategies.

1 **The Arabs of North Africa.** Arriving from the Arabian peninsula in the early years of Islam, the Arabs conquered the Maghreb and imposed Islam upon the population. There has been little by way of outreach to them until recent years – and even less by way of response. They number nearly 210 million from Mauritania across to Egypt.

2 **The Imazighen, or Berber.** North Africa's original inhabitants; they were conquered by Rome, many becoming Christian, then conquered by Arab Muslims in the 8th Century and assimilated into Islam. There are 18 million Imazighen in 76 distinct sub-groups living in 17 countries. Major groups include the Kabyle (3.3m), Riff (2.6m), Shilha (8.7m) and Shawiya (1.9m). Only among the Kabyle has there been a significant turning to Christ. Less than 0.4% might be considered Christian. Several partnerships of agencies concerned for them exist.

3 **The Tamacheq (Tuareg)** are related to the Berber, but have a unique culture and live in the central Sahara Desert. They number 2.5 million in seven countries and comprise 16 sub-groups. Believers among them are increasing, but only in Niger and Mali are there established groups. A number of agencies have formed a partnership for their evangelization.

4 **The peoples of the West Africa coastal nations,** including the Wolof, Malinke, Jula and Susu clusters. Totalling 17.2 million people, they include 114 peoples speaking 75 languages and dialects. The largest peoples are the Wolof of Senegal (4.6m), Maninke of Guinea (2.4m), Maninka of Côte d'Ivoire (1.9m), Mandinka of Senegal and Gambia (1.4m) and Susu of Guinea (1.1m). They remain largely unevangelized, even though there are a number of Christian workers and African churches among neighbouring peoples.

5 **The interior peoples of West Africa.** These consist of the Kanuri, Bambara, Songhai, Soninke people clusters, adding up to 78 peoples with 31 languages and 22.3 million people. Largest among them are the Yerwa Kanuri of Nigeria (5.5m), the Zarma of Niger (4.5m), the Bambara of Mali and Côte d'Ivoire (3.1m, 1.0m), the Songhai-Koryaboro of Mali and Niger (1.6m) and the Soninke of Mali (1.0m). Of these, only the Bambara (5.0%) and Koryaboro (0.4%) have a notable Christian population. Many smaller peoples have no known believers.

6 **The Fulbe** (Pulaar, Fulani) number 31.9 million in 50 or so distinct ethnic groups speaking related dialects. They have spread from Senegal to become a major component of nearly every country of the Sahel as far east as Sudan. They are the largest nomadic-culture people in the world. More than half now live settled lifestyles and are more strongly Muslim than their nomadic or semi-nomadic brethren. Planting churches among them has been hard and slow with small breakthroughs in Benin, Nigeria and Chad. The Fulbe represent one of the major challenges for missions in Africa today. There are dozens of agencies with some outreach or ministry to the Fulbe, and several partnerships have been formed specifically to synergize ministry among them.

7 **The Hausa** are dominant in Niger and northern Nigeria, but live in 20 countries in total and number 32.4 million. Hausa has become the major language for much of Nigeria, Niger and beyond. Many resources exist in Hausa – the Bible, the JESUS film, radio broadcasting – and much ministry is done in Hausa, but few have turned to Christ from Islam. Response is greatest among the Maguzawa section of the Hausa. Evangelization of the Hausa remains a major challenge to the Church.

8 **The peoples of Sudan, Chad, the CAR and Egypt.** These include the Nubian cluster (30 peoples, 3.0m), the Ouaddai-Fur (38 peoples, 3.2m) and smaller Guera-Naba cluster (6 peoples, 0.5m). Among the Nubians, only the Dongolawi number over 500,000 (0.9m in Egypt, with only 0.1% Christian). Among the Ouaddai-Fur, only the Fur (0.9m) and Masalit (0.4m) are this populous, and they have few, if any, Christians. The Fur and Masalit are among the peoples who have tragically suffered in the Darfur crisis at the hands of other Muslims. The Nubians of the Nile River valley were for a long time Christian, but were forcibly Islamized in the 17th Century.

9 **The Horn of Africa-Cushitic peoples.** There are 101 million in 160 ethnic groups living mainly in Sudan, Eritrea, Ethiopia and Somalia. They are represented in six people clusters – Afar, Beja, Ethiopian (often referred to as "Semitic"), Omotic, Oromo and Somali. A number of peoples are Christian. The great challenge remains to reach the Somali (15.7m), Beja (3.2m) and Afar (2.3m). Many Christian agencies are burdened to bring the gospel to them and see a harvest; there have been many attempts, but the risk and the cost are great. It is effectively impossible for outsiders to do mission work among the Somali and Afar clusters in their home countries, but there is a sizeable Somali diaspora in Africa and beyond.

10 The Swahili-speaking Bantu peoples of Africa's east coast, concentrated in Tanzania, Kenya, Mozambique, Madagascar and Comoros. Almost all are Muslim. Major groupings: Swahili (1.5m, mostly in Zanzibar), Comorian (0.9m), Zaramo (0.8m), Shirazi (0.7m). They are stoutly Muslim and traditionally resistant to Christian outreach.

11 A number of Chadic, Nilotic and Nuba mountain peoples are thoroughly unreached, even though they are from clusters with significant Christian populations and are related to highly Christianized peoples. Among Africa's least reached are 44 Chadic peoples, 15 Nilotic peoples and 26 Nuba Mountain peoples. They live primarily in Sudan, Chad, Cameroon and Nigeria.

12 East Asian peoples – numbering 5.7 million in 24 peoples. They are mostly present in Africa due to British colonial transplanting. They remain largely isolated from indigenous Christians and have hardly been touched at all by cross-cultural mission work.

Major Great Commission Challenges

1 Islam is the major challenge for Christianity today – both the 182 million Muslims north of the Sahara and the 246 million in sub-Saharan Africa. The "race" to win peoples to Christ from the traditional religions in West Africa and across the Sahel has largely been lost; most have been Islamized, even if only superficially. More recently, Muslim missionary efforts have extended to nearly every country in Africa, and in many places, especially in Central Africa, they are very successful. The use of oil-funded education, aid projects and grants, and a well-orchestrated drive to give Islam a role in Africa's political life, have had some success. African Christians as well as mission agencies need to make Muslims a priority for demonstrations of the love of Christ, and culturally sensitive approaches must be developed for planting churches among them.

2 Nations with the smallest number of evangelicals. These are priority countries with less than 1% evangelicals: Morocco, Algeria, Tunisia, Libya, Mauritania, Senegal, Gambia, Mali, Guinea, Niger, Djibouti, Somalia, Mayotte and Comoros. They fall into four main groups – North Africa, West Africa, Horn of Africa and the Indian Ocean Islands.

3 Cities. Africa's urban population has rapidly risen from 130 million in 1990 up to 390 million in 2010. It is the world's most rapidly urbanizing continent. Lack of economic development and poor infrastructure mean that it is the slums, shantytowns and informal settlements that have mushroomed. These cities have become focal points for dire poverty, squalor, crime, prostitution, disease and misery. New ways must be found to impact these cities for God and plant churches that will transform urban areas.

The Americas

The Americas represent two continents and 53 countries and territories. The constituent states of the "New World" have much in common, especially regionally, but great diversity exists as well.

The indigenous Amerindian inhabitants were wrongly called "Indians" by the Europeans, who accidentally stumbled upon their continents in 1492. They ranged from the Inuit of the Arctic polar region to the Fuegians on the tip of South America, in hundreds of distinct ethnicities and languages.

European colonization generated an extraordinary history – the theft, plunder and subjugation of the Americas by adventurers, explorers and settlers from Europe, aided by the devastating and deadly effect of European diseases upon the indigenous population. The manner in which native peoples were exterminated, subjugated or oppressed remains a shadow that hangs over the New World to this day.

The tragic history of the use of African slave labour in most of the warmer countries has likewise left a legacy of hurt which continues to profoundly shape the dynamics of race relations in the Americas.

The end of colonial rule occurred within a common time frame – largely between 1776 and 1830 for most countries. The development of government and legislation during this era means that most states have similar democratic political structures.

There is a commonality of language. Four main colonial tongues – English, Spanish, Portuguese and French – account for the vast majority of communication today. Indigenous languages may be experiencing a revival in some areas, but the numbers of those who speak them, especially as a primary language, is a small minority for all but a few countries.

Trade patterns and economic free trade zones are developing rapidly and drawing together these nations with increasingly strong ties. This is true for North America (NAFTA), the Caribbean (CARICOM) and South America (Mercosur and CAN).

Other factors link the Americas intimately together: the migration of peoples from south to north largely for economic purposes and the extensive impact and influence of drug trafficking.

The statistics for the Caribbean, Latin America and North America are handled separately, but the analysis and prayer points are presented together.

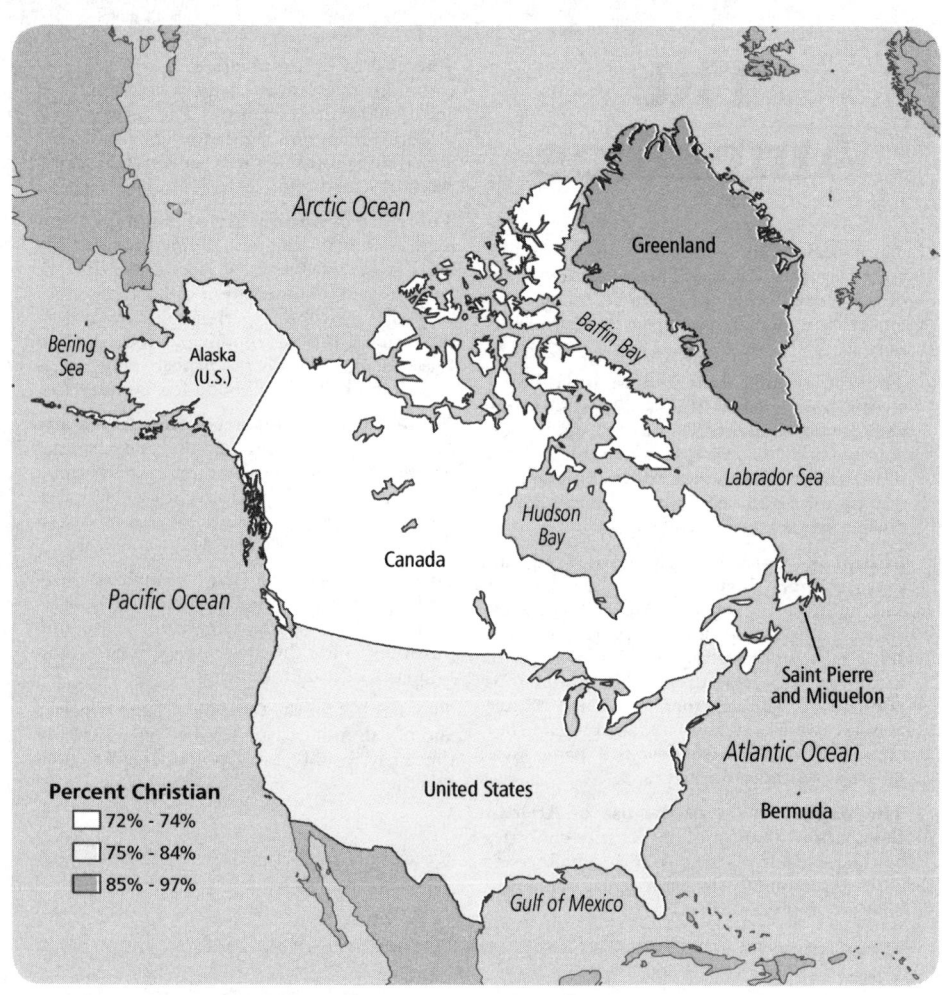

Country	2010 Pop (mill)	Main Rel	Chr	Evang (% of total pop)	Non-Chr	Unev	All (# of peoples)	UP	Chr
Bermuda	0.06	X	90.5	24.3	9.5	1.0	9	1	7
Canada	33.89	XN	72.1	7.7	27.9	3.3	156	16	132
Greenland	0.06	X	96.6	4.7	3.4	0.7	5	0	5
St Pierre & Miquelon	0.01	X	96.9	<0.1	3.1	0.5	3	0	3
USA	317.64	XN	77.6	28.9	22.4	1.7	363	59	254
TOTAL	351.66		77.1	26.8	22.9	1.8	536	76	401

North America

Geography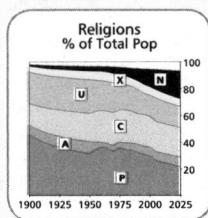

Area 21,779,847 sq km. Nearly 16% of the world's land surface. North America contains three of the 13 largest countries of the world: Canada (2nd largest), USA (4th) and Greenland (13th). Mexico, while geographically in North America, is included for cultural, linguistic and demographic reasons with Latin America.

Population		Ann Gr	Density
2010	351,659,164	1.0%	16/sq km
2020	383,383,802	0.8%	18/sq km
2030	410,203,679	0.6%	19/sq km

In 2010, this represented 5.1% of the world's population.

Cities There are 49 cities of over 1 million people, 2 of which are over 10m. **Urbanites** 82%. **Pop under 15 yrs** 20.6%. **Life expectancy** 79.2 years.

Peoples

European origin 66.4%. Communities from every ethnic group in Europe have settled in the Americas. Largest: Anglo–Celt, French, Slav, Germanic, Italian, Portuguese.
Latin American–Hispanic 12.2%. Most are from Mexico, Central America and the Caribbean. Rapidly increasing.
African–American 11.5%. Almost entirely urban. Most are descendants of slaves imported from Africa between the 17th and 19th Centuries. They are a majority in Bermuda.
East Asian 2.0%. Chinese 1.0%; Korean 0.7%.
Jews 1.8%.
Arab World 1.5%. 11 peoples. Levant Arabs largest.
Native Americans 1.3%. Only in Greenland are they a majority; elsewhere, often a marginalized underclass alongside a large majority that overran their continent.
South Asian 1.1%.
Other 2.2%. Southeast Asian 0.7%; Malay peoples 0.5%; African 0.4%; Iranian–Median 0.2%; Pacific Islanders 0.2%.

Literacy 99%. **All languages** 443. English is the major language of communication except for French in Quebec, Canada and in St Pierre & Miquelon; Danish in Greenland. Spanish is of increasing importance, especially in southern USA. **Languages with Scriptures** (of indigenous North American languages) 9Bi 31NT 48por 27w.i.p.

Economy

The world's wealthiest continent; the US economy is a barometer and pacesetter for the rest of the world and remains the largest. North America is still the engine for much of the world's economic growth and with some of the world's highest living standards. But its overall influence is proportionately less than in the 20th Century as new economic powers elsewhere rise to prominence.

Income/person $47,207 (100% of USA).

Politics

The USA was the world's sole superpower of the 1990s and 2000s after emerging triumphant from the Cold War. It used (and abused) this position to further its foreign and economic policies. Today's new multi-polar context of world powers changes North America's perceived and expected role.

The economic and political strengths of the USA have the potential to overwhelm its neighbours, which encourages a mix of cautious cooperation and defensive nationalism on the part of the latter.

Religion

The continent with the least religious discrimination.

Religions	Pop %	Population	Ann Gr
Christian	77.09	271,097,376	0.5%
Non-religious	16.75	58,886,075	3.2%
Muslim	1.75	6,160,353	2.3%
Jew	1.60	5,613,878	-0.7%
Other	0.77	2,700,009	5.7%
Buddhist	0.76	2,659,829	2.9%
Hindu	0.48	1,672,990	2.2%
Ethnoreligionist	0.45	1,598,675	2.4%
Sikh	0.17	590,885	3.4%
Baha'i	0.11	383,851	-3.4%
Chinese	0.08	295,242	1.9%

Christians	Pop %	Affiliates	Ann Gr
Protestant	25.78	90,669,459	0.0%
Independent	7.12	25,032,587	1.5%
Anglican	0.80	2,803,292	0.1%
Catholic	23.01	80,900,164	0.8%
Orthodox	1.80	6,332,898	0.9%
Marginal	3.45	12,133,849	0.5%
Unaffiliated	17.30	60,700,884	0.3%
Doubly affiliated	*-2.12*	*-7,450,000*	*0.7%*

TransBloc	Pop %	Population	Ann Gr
Evangelicals			
Evangelicals	26.84	94,384,693	0.68%
Renewalists			
Charismatics	18.47	64,945,181	2.31%
Pentecostals	6.29	22,125,247	1.06%

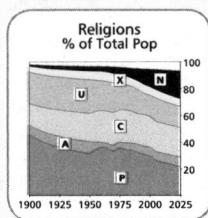

Religions % of Total Pop

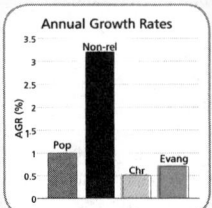

Annual Growth Rates

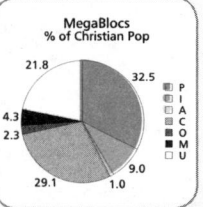

MegaBlocs % of Christian Pop

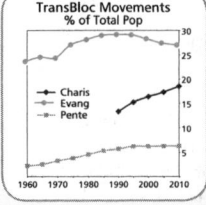

TransBloc Movements % of Total Pop

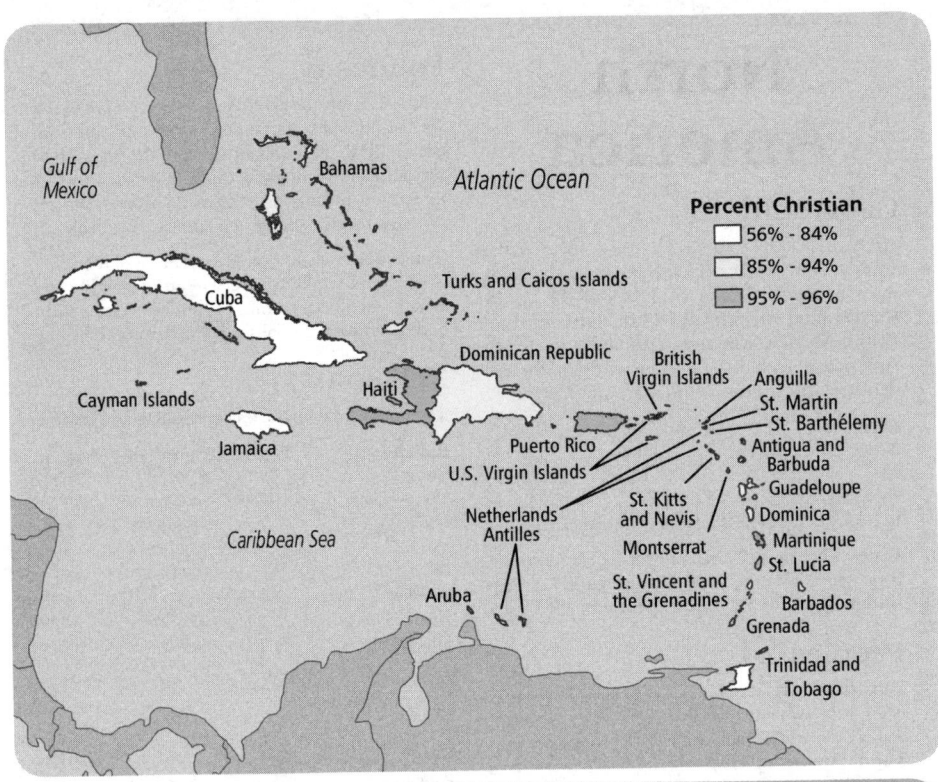

Country	2010 Pop (mill)	Main Rel	Chr	Evang	Non-Chr	Unev	All	UP	Chr
				(% of total pop)			(# of peoples)		
Anguilla	0.02	X	90.0	17.2	10.0	0.7	6	0	5
Antigua and Barbuda	0.09	X	92.9	19.9	7.5	0.6	6	0	5
Aruba	0.11	X	92.9	7.6	7.1	0.9	8	2	5
Bahamas, The	0.35	X	94.7	35.9	5.4	0.6	10	1	9
Barbados	0.26	X	94.9	34.2	5.1	1.2	11	2	7
British Virgin Islands	0.02	X	84.9	27.3	15.1	0.8	7	0	5
Cayman Islands	0.06	XE	77.1	21.3	22.9	2.3	11	1	9
Cuba	11.20	XNE	56.5	8.8	43.5	0.9	14	2	10
Dominica	0.07	X	91.8	16.8	8.3	0.6	11	0	8
Dominican Republic	10.23	X	94.4	9.1	5.7	0.5	18	2	13
Grenada	0.10	X	93.7	19.6	6.3	0.5	7	0	7
Guadeloupe	0.47	X	94.1	4.3	5.9	0.6	8	0	7
Haiti	10.19	X	95.1	16.0	4.9	0.5	9	1	6
Jamaica	2.73	XE	82.9	28.0	17.1	1.0	11	1	8
Martinique	0.41	X	95.8	6.1	4.2	0.6	9	0	7
Montserrat	0.01	X	95.3	23.4	4.7	0.5	6	0	5
Netherlands Antilles	0.20	X	91.6	7.7	8.4	1.1	15	3	11
Puerto Rico	4.00	X	95.3	25.2	4.7	0.6	15	1	12
St Barthélemy	0.01	XN	61.0	2.3	39.0	<0.1	n/a	n/a	n/a
St Kitts & Nevis	0.05	X	93.0	21.8	7.1	0.6	5	0	4
St Lucia	0.17	X	95.1	14.6	4.9	1.4	6	0	5
St Martin	0.04	XN	83.9	2.5	16.2	<0.1	n/a	n/a	n/a
St Vincent	0.11	X	90.1	39.1	9.9	1.3	11	0	9
Trinidad & Tobago	1.34	XH	65.6	20.2	34.4	8.8	15	2	12
Turks & Caicos	0.03	X	90.4	32.4	9.7	0.9	11	1	9
US Virgin Islands	0.11	X	95.0	23.8	5.1	0.6	11	1	9
TOTAL	42.36		82.9	14.3	17.1	0.6	235	19	183

Caribbean

Geography

Area 245,000 sq km. Comprising 26 sovereign states, overseas departments and dependencies.

Population		Ann Gr	Density
2010	42,311,877	0.8%	173/sq km
2020	45,469,888	0.7%	186/sq km
2030	47,922,134	0.5%	196/sq km

The Caribbean has 0.6% of the world's population.

Cities There are 4 cities of over 1 million people. **Urbanites** 67%. **Pop under 15 yrs** 28.5%. **Life expectancy** 71.9 yrs.

Peoples

Much of the language, culture and ethnicity have been determined by the respective colonizing powers in each island, and by the groups (including slaves and indentured labourers) they brought over to settle them. 73 peoples.

Latin-Caribbean Americans 86.6%. 19 peoples.
    Hispanic 33.2%. Dominated by Cubans, Puerto Ricans.
    Francophone African-Caribbean 26.9%. Mostly in Haiti, also Guadeloupe and Martinique.
    African-American Hispanic 21.4%. Dominican Republic, also Puerto Rico.
African-Caribbean peoples 10.1%. 17 peoples. Largest in Jamaica, Tobago, Barbados, Bahamas.
South Asians 1.6%. Forming a majority in Trinidad and a significant minority on a few other islands.
Other 1.7%. Europeans, Anglo-Americans, Arabs, East Asians.
Literacy 82%. **All languages** 47. **Languages with Scriptures** (of indigenous Caribbean languages) 2Bi 2NT 7w.i.p.

Economy

Upon European colonization, became dominated by plantation economies. Upon independence, continued to be dominated by export economies, many islands often dominated by a single type of crop or resource and dependent on Europe or North America's need for that export. Currently, most islands depend heavily upon the still-growing tourist sector. This brings much money, but has many negative effects. Offshore finance, and the ethics thereof, has become an issue on a few islands.

Income/person $6,082 (13% of USA).

Politics

Barring Cuba, democratic government is in place, generally reflecting the political systems of islands' respective colonizers.

Religion

Again, religious faith tends to reflect largely whichever European power controlled each island. Additionally, some local influences are significant – Rastafarianism in Jamaica and elsewhere, *Santería* in Cuba, voodoo in Haiti and others.

Religions	Pop %	Population	Ann Gr
Christian	82.90	35,117,154	1.0%
Non-religious	8.87	3,758,393	-0.5%
Ethnoreligionist	6.77	2,865,899	0.9%
Hindu	0.81	341,249	0.2%
Muslim	0.28	118,008	1.4%
Other	0.13	53,739	1.8%
Baha'i	0.11	47,013	1.2%
Chinese	0.06	26,194	0.3%
Jew	0.03	11,225	0.5%
Buddhist	0.03	10,887	-1.8%
Sikh	0.02	9,675	-0.4%

Christians	Pop %	Affiliates	Ann Gr
Protestant	13.23	5,605,036	2.0%
Independent	3.98	1,684,778	2.9%
Anglican	1.35	569,925	0.0%
Catholic	59.78	25,324,060	0.6%
Orthodox	0.06	24,358	1.6%
Marginal	1.46	620,530	1.9%
Unaffiliated	6.86	2,904,366	0.8%
Doubly affiliated	*-3.78*	*-1,602,762*	*-1.1%*

TransBloc	Pop %	Population	Ann Gr
Evangelicals			
Evangelicals	14.30	6,058,290	2.4%
Renewalists			
Charismatics	12.06	5,107,607	3.2%
Pentecostals	6.70	2,838,380	2.7%

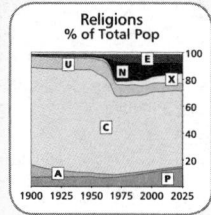

Religions % of Total Pop

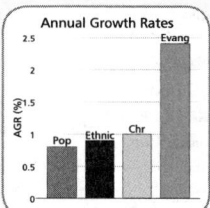

Annual Growth Rates

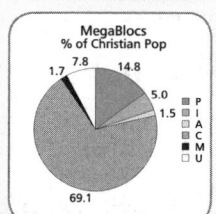

MegaBlocs % of Christian Pop

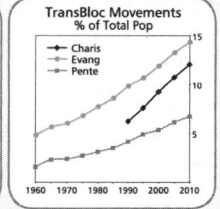

TransBloc Movements % of Total Pop

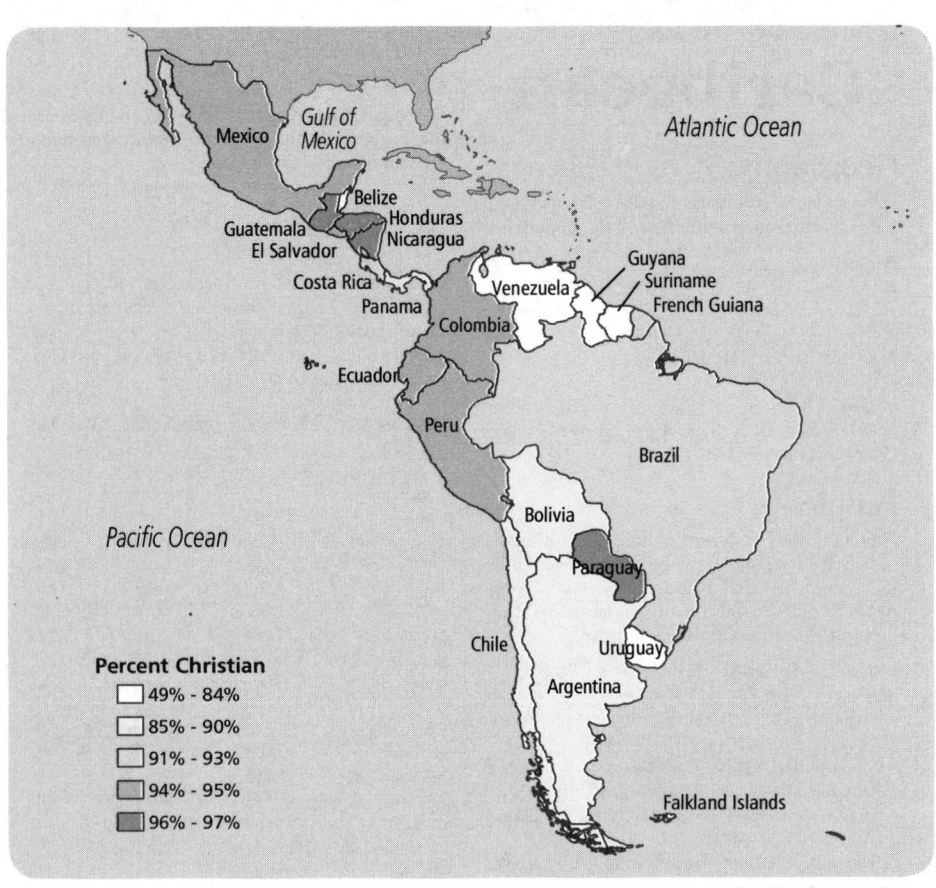

Percent Christian
- 49% - 84%
- 85% - 90%
- 91% - 93%
- 94% - 95%
- 96% - 97%

Country	2010 Pop (mill)	Main Rel	Chr	Evang	Non-Chr	Unev	All	UP	Chr
				(% of total pop)			(# of peoples)		
Argentina	40.67	X	90.6	9.1	9.4	1.1	60	1	50
Belize	0.31	X	83.9	18.8	16.1	2.1	14	1	10
Bolivia	10.03	X	91.0	16.2	9.0	0.7	43	1	33
Brazil	195.42	X	91.4	26.3	8.6	0.6	289	58	116
Chile	17.13	XN	87.2	18.4	12.8	0.8	26	2	23
Colombia	46.30	X	94.4	7.5	5.6	0.8	92	4	61
Costa Rica	4.64	X	93.9	14.8	6.1	0.6	21	1	19
Ecuador	13.77	X	94.5	8.5	5.6	1.0	31	2	20
El Salvador	6.19	X	94.6	31.7	5.4	0.6	13	2	9
Falkland Islands	<0.01	XN	65.2	10.8	34.8	0.7	5	0	5
French Guiana	0.23	X	91.3	4.5	8.8	2.0	25	1	17
Guatemala	14.38	X	96.1	24.4	3.9	0.5	60	1	57
Guyana	0.76	XH	52.7	19.8	47.3	18.5	22	2	15
Honduras	7.62	X	96.6	23.0	3.4	0.6	24	3	19
Mexico	110.65	X	95.0	8.3	5.0	0.6	317	14	303
Nicaragua	5.82	X	97.7	29.8	2.3	0.6	18	1	14
Panama	3.51	X	90.5	19.3	9.5	0.9	32	1	23
Paraguay	6.46	X	96.3	6.1	3.7	0.6	39	1	32
Peru	29.50	X	95.5	11.6	4.6	0.7	104	5	69
Suriname	0.52	XHM	49.6	13.8	50.4	17.3	26	1	16
Uruguay	3.37	XN	64.7	6.2	35.3	1.7	30	1	28
Venezuela	29.04	XN	84.5	10.8	15.5	1.0	65	2	44
TOTAL	546.34		92.2	16.7	7.8	0.7	1356	105	983

Latin America

Geography 🌍

Area 20,286,362 sq km. Comprising 22 countries; 15% of the world's land area. Can be divided into three almost equal areas in terms of population and land area: Central America, Spanish South America and Brazil.

Population		Ann Gr	Density
2010	546,336,631	1.2%	27/sq km
2020	600,072,795	0.9%	30/sq km
2030	641,936,651	0.6%	32/sq km

Latin America has 10.1% of the world's population.

Cities There are 61 cities of over 1 million people. Mexico City and São Paulo are two of the world's largest cities. **Urbanites** 80%. **Pop under 15 yrs** 29.7%. **Life expectancy** 73.5 years.

Peoples 👪

Racial intermingling is such that a breakdown of ethnic groups is only approximate. Though there is generally more class consciousness than colour consciousness, there are wide differences in ethnic composition among the countries. 951 peoples, mostly made up of small Amerindian tribes.

Latin Americans 96.5%. 874 peoples.
  Hispanic 49.4%. 21 peoples.
  Brazilian 33.6%. Mixed race, Mestiço and whites.
  Quechua 2.9%. 46 peoples in Peru and Ecuador.
  South American Indigenous 2.8%. 287 small peoples scattered throughout South America.
  Maya 1.4%. 52 peoples in Guatemala and Mexico.
  Amazon 1.3%. 92 peoples in Amazon basin, mostly Brazil, also Venezuela, Colombia, Peru.
  Guarani 1.3%. 42 peoples concentrated in southwest Brazil, Paraguay, Northern Argentina.
  Others 3.8%. Includes Aymara(4); Aztec(39); Mixe(12); Mixteco(60); Otomi(11); Zapoteco(101).
European origin peoples 1.7%. Italian 0.6%; Spanish 0.4%; Germanic 0.2%; Portuguese 0.2%.
Others 1.8%. Arab 0.5%; East Asian 0.5%; South Asian 0.3%; African-American 0.2%; Anglo-American 0.2%.

Literacy 90%. **All languages** 503. **Languages with Scriptures** (of indigenous South and Central American languages) 32Bi 291NT 130por 276w.i.p.

Economy 📈

Rapid development since the 1980s as democracy and free market economics took root, trade barriers were lowered and regional communications, trade and transport improved. Further growth is mitigated by undeveloped infrastructures, latent corruption, vested interests, communications and the massive gap between rich and poor. The formation of a single trade bloc encompassing all of South America will be a major step forward. Most economies are heavily dependent on the export of natural resources – minerals, products of the Amazon, oil, beef and others. The humble coca leaf, and its illegal byproduct cocaine, profoundly shapes the legal and illegal economies of many states within and beyond South America itself.

Income/person $7,716 (16% of USA).

Politics ⚔️

The end of the Cold War and the eclipse of Communism reinforced throughout Latin America the trend toward a more democratic government, but generally to the left of the political spectrum. In several countries, commitment to an accountable democracy has been low with authoritarian tendencies still evident, but the era of military strongmen in government is all but over.

Religion 🛐

In 1900, almost the entire Spanish and Portuguese-speaking population was considered Catholic, although much of it had syncretistic influences from pre-Columbian ethnic religions. The changes since then have been dramatic – from a narrow traditionalism, with strong opposition to Protestant missionary activity, to freedom of religion and the continued rapid rise of evangelicals. Secularism and spiritism have also grown significantly in the last 20–30 years. The Catholic Church has responded in an attempt to check its losses and regain the initiative and hearts of the people.

Religions	Pop %	Population	Ann Gr
Christian	92.14	503,374,334	1.1%
Non-religious	4.15	22,691,352	1.4%
Ethnoreligionist	2.74	14,978,421	1.3%
Other	0.24	1,472,668	3.0%
Muslim	0.23	1,278,868	2.8%
Buddhist	0.15	813,190	1.9%
Baha'i	0.14	742,766	3.6%
Jew	0.11	591,103	4.4%
Hindu	0.07	391,386	0.0%
Chinese	0.03	185,542	1.6%

Christians	Pop %	Affiliates	Ann Gr
Protestant	11.24	61,422,738	2.5%
Independent	7.52	41,110,321	3.0%
Anglican	0.07	371,615	1.5%
Catholic	77.35	422,610,023	0.2%
Orthodox	0.09	516,301	0.6%

Marginal	2.11	11,540,870	2.6%
Unaffiliated	1.81	9,907,879	4.6%
Doubly affiliated	*-8.08*	*-44,149,570*	*-2.5%*

Evangelicals have grown rapidly, but not as fast as some have claimed (largely exuberant Pentecostal over-reporting).

TransBloc	Pop %	Population	Ann Gr
Evangelicals			
Evangelicals	16.73	91,423,319	2.6%
Renewalists			
Charismatics	20.16	110,154,594	2.9%
Pentecostals	12.03	65,717,792	2.5%

Religions % of Total Pop

Annual Growth Rates

MegaBlocs % of Christian Pop

TransBloc Movements % of Total Pop

Answers to Prayer in the Americas

1 **Political stability** and a steady shift toward democratic structures, and away from the military regimes of the past, are profound blessings. The end of the Cold War, which made Latin America a contested area between the USA and USSR, and the leftward swing of national politics have been crucial in the early formation of government by and for the people.

2 **The Catholic Church is experiencing significant new vitality,** through new readings of Scripture, through higher profile evangelical teaching outside of Catholicism, through the Alpha Course and through the more charismatic faith of Hispanic and Latin American Catholics. Much of this is a reaction to the dynamic growth of evangelicals, especially in South America. Millions have been impacted by personal encounters with the Lord Jesus. Many have become fervent evangelical believers, both within the Catholic Church and, increasingly, outside it.

3 **The positive spiritual impact of North America,** and especially the USA, on the world. Praise God for:

a) Great evangelists and missionary statesmen who touched the world (Finney, Moody, Billy Graham and others).

b) The immeasurable effects of writers, speakers, pastors and trainers on the global body of Christ, through training, teaching, discipling and empowering.

c) Unstinting generosity in giving financially to good causes – especially mission advances.

Pray that godly North Americans might continue to engage with the needs of the world in a humble, passionate and informed way. Hollywood's portrayal of American life is a perversion of the values that made the USA a great nation.

4 **The growth of evangelicals in Latin America** in the last century, especially the last generation, is spectacular. In 1900, evangelicals numbered about 700,000, or 1% of the population (only about 200,000 of these being in Spanish and Portuguese-speaking countries). By 2010, they reached 91 million, or 16.8% of the population. Most of this growth was fuelled by the steady, faithful proclamation and witness of tens of thousands of laymen and pastors planting small churches out of a passion for the gospel. The New World is home to over 35% of the world's evangelicals.

5 **Pentecostals** demonstrate the greatest vigour and are now the largest component of evangelicals in Latin America with over 66 million affiliates and 12.1% of the population. The Americas represent 50% of the world's Pentecostals, despite having less than 14% of the world's population. Their greatest success is among the poor. Growth is weakened by multiple splits, inadequate discipling of converts and often exaggerated claims of growth.

6 **Praise God for the divinely ordered convergence in Latin America** of spiritual, economic and social conditions that allows evangelicals to have a great impact. They now wield notable influence in many nations where they were previously marginalized as dangerous sects. Today, political, police and civic leaders court evangelicals, not just for the formidable numbers of votes to be won, but also for the transforming effect that evangelical ministries offer to society. Often, Christian ministries are the only effective solution to otherwise intractable troubles. Numerical growth continues, but evangelicals have also notably grown in stature and maturity.

7 **People movements are growing among the Amerindians,** who have long been resistant or indifferent to the gospel. Church growth is occurring among Quechua and Aymara churches in the Andes, Mayan peoples in Central America and, increasingly, native peoples in North America. Also notable is the increasing indigenization of the gospel, centuries after it should have originally happened!

8 **The Bible translation achievements** of **WBT**, SIL and UBS are remarkable. The pioneer work of **WBT** and SIL in providing NTs in indigenous languages has sparked ingatherings of peoples into churches across the Americas. Among hundreds of primarily oral languages, audio translations are underway, as are productions of new modern translations and children's versions of the Bible story.

9 **Missions vision has rapidly grown and matured** in Latin America. The 1987 COMIBAM conference in São Paulo, Brazil, generated continent-wide interest and sparked numerous initiatives to reach the unreached. At that time, there were around 60 agencies with 1,600 missionaries. Today, there are over 400 agencies representing more than 10,000 missionaries! An increasing proportion serve outside Latin America and in the unevangelized world. Major sending nations are Brazil, Mexico, Argentina and Peru, but missionary sending structures are developing in most lands. Quite apart from this are the thousands who serve God abroad as economic migrants or deliberate tentmakers.

10 **The impact of the media** is significant all over the New World. Widespread use by Christians of local, national and international radio and television networks as well as the Internet has a massive influence. The influence of the medium of television – for both spreading the good news and for proliferating ungodly values – cannot be understated. The multiplication of local television and radio stations and broadcasts as well as countless thousands of Christian and evangelistic websites, mobile phone applications and other digital tools further widen the opportunities for proclamation of the gospel.

Hot Spots of the Americas

1 **Illegal drugs, particularly cocaine,** cause untold suffering and upheaval. They have wrought havoc in the countries producing the coca leaf as a crop (Colombia, Bolivia, Ecuador, Peru, others), to the countries used for trans-shipment (Central America and Caribbean, but mostly Mexico), to the consumers (primarily the US), but in fact all countries. Addictions, broken lives, violence, crime and corruption, greed, and overwrought judicial, law enforcement and prison systems are all results of this systemic sin. Criminal cartels and leftist guerrillas are funded while legitimate governments are seemingly powerless to stop the billions of dollars enriching wicked men. Gangs involved in trafficking wield more power than the government in some areas. Quite apart from cocaine, new forms of synthetic drugs are more easily produced and harder to detect, but just as dangerous. Current strategies to end the drug trade are not effective at reducing production, demand or dealers. Pray for effective and viable policies to combat this evil, and pray that God might move in such a way as to end the seemingly insatiable appetite that fuels the whole evil structure.

2 **Widespread human need exists,** even in these relatively stable and affluent continents. Economic poverty is the most obvious, having been a defining factor for decades in the political and even theological developments in Latin America. But lack of education and literacy, health issues, lack of clean water and sanitation, and persistent urban violence and crime all continue to plague much of the region. The Caribbean has the highest murder rate of any region in the world. While democratic government continues to take root, in many countries it is a fledgling and needs both integrity by leaders and committed endurance by the population.

3 **Environmental degradation and exploitation** will have a direct and tragic impact on Amerindian peoples and indirectly on the entire world. The disappearing Amazon rainforest is only the most prominent of such issues; the Central American forests and overuse of US aquifers are other serious issues. Short-term greed is doing long-term or even permanent damage. Unsustainable consumption and industrial pollution exacerbate the problem. Biblical stewardship of natural resources is a theological imperative.

4 **The resurgence of indigenous peoples** – and their fight for recognition, greater autonomy and self-determination. From Arctic to tropics to Antarctic, natives were routinely exterminated, subjugated and swindled out of their lands and rights. In many regions this struggle took on violent overtones – Guatemala, Peru, Mexico – while in others it has been chiefly legal and political. Such trends also foster growth in the pre-Christian religions and superstitions once held by these peoples. Additionally, the legacy and progeny of the 11 million African slaves brought to the New World are issues that likewise demand repentance, reparation and reconciliation from the European colonizers. It was chiefly Christians who fought to end the slave trade and evangelize the native peoples of the Americas; it should be Christians who lead the way in walking out the path of full reconciliation.

5 **Countries facing an uncertain, possibly traumatic future:**

a) ***Cuba,*** after the 2009 resignation of Fidel Castro as president, still needs to recover from over five decades of Marxism and economic isolation.

b) ***Venezuela,*** with its oil wealth and belligerent leftist leader, vies for political leadership of all of South America. Territorial claims against Colombia and Guyana could trigger future clashes.

c) ***Haiti,*** where the devastation of the 2010 earthquake piled onto the extant poverty, human suffering, dictatorships and bad government.

d) ***Guyana,*** with unresolved ethnic tensions, unstable government and looming claims upon its territory by larger nations.

Trends to Watch

1 **Economic changes are sounding for the Americas in the 21st Century.** The Andean Community of Nations (CAN), CARICOM (Caribbean Single Market and Economy Treaty), MERCOSUR (Argentina, Brazil, Paraguay and Uruguay) and NAFTA (North American Free Trade Agreement) oversee the spread of shared markets and free trade arrangements. In the future, this may grow to encompass the entire New World. The emergence of Brazil as a world economic power, the proportionate decline of the USA as the same and the increased investment and involvement of China are all significant factors. Pray that economic policies might be determined with moral rightness and courage – not moved by selfish, vested interests of ethnicity, economic power structures or big business. Pray that the results may also benefit the poor and the marginalized, improve the quality of life and human rights and address vital ecological concerns.

2 **A healthier but still idiosyncratic approach to democracy** is growing in most countries. The majority of Latin Americans polled seem to favour governments with autocratic and populist strains, but they despise military dictatorships. The assumption that market capitalism is the only economic way forward empowers neo-liberal parties and economics. Democracy, once seen to empower only the elite, is increasingly being levelled – as the elections of Morales in Bolivia and Lula in Brazil indicate. However, corruption is still endemic to some nations, and political stability and healthy multiparty systems remain difficult to achieve, especially for poorer or smaller countries and those with weaker democratic traditions.

3 **A massive movement of peoples** – unprecedented since the discovery and colonization of the New World – is changing the face of many nations. North America is a land full of immigrants of every imaginable background, with Hispanics in particular increasing rapidly. The Caribbean routinely suffers a huge loss of its most gifted and well educated (including Christian leaders), with negative social and economic consequences. Internal migration in Brazil from the poor northeastern states to the burgeoning Amazon, and migration from poorer regions of Central America to wealthier areas, only partially complete the picture. Chinese and Arab peoples continue to immigrate to the Americas in large numbers.

4 **The rise of anti-Christian secularism and aggressive atheism** that seeks to marginalize the Church through control of the media and legislation. The increasing imposition of secularism upon civic, academic and political life, and the growing stridence of atheist apologists, disguise a specific disdain or even hatred for Christianity. The watchword of tolerance is exercised through multiculturalism and pluralism, but not extended to those who wish to practice their Christian faith in the public sphere.

The Church in the Americas

1 **The influence of the Church is simultaneously waning and waxing.** The religious forms once dominant in the Americas – Catholicism in Latin America and former French areas, mainline Protestantism in North America and much of the Caribbean – see a marked decline in their relative influence. Secularism, the growing presence of other world religions and the increasing personalization and subjectivization of spirituality all gravitate against classical Christian orthodoxy. Simultaneously, evangelicals and charismatics continue to grow – although not as fast as they once did – and play a greater role in both public life and social transformation.

2 **The Roman Catholic Church** has passed through 50 years of tumultuous change, in part spurred by the growth of evangelicals. The traditional monolithic structure that once dominated most of the continent has gone forever. Even South America, the world's most Catholic continent has gone from 92% Catholic in 1960 to 77% in 2010. Many regret the misused four centuries of monopoly that bred complacency, condoned syncretism and, more recently, endorsed the now largely discredited liberation theology. In recent years, an emphasis on Bible reading, the charismatic movement and efforts to make Catholicism more accessible to the masses have slowed its decline. Various powerful movements are discernible:

a) The charismatic movement. As many as half of Hispanic and Latin American Catholics gravitate toward charismatic expressions. The more egalitarian nature of this movement and the balance between adoration and activism give it a vitality lacking in much of the Catholic Church globally.

b) Traditional Catholicism. As a result of the conservativism of the last two popes, traditional Catholicism has re-emerged as a strong force and is leading to a further cooling of relationships with evangelicals. Pray for Catholics to come to a personal faith in Christ. Millions still strive to earn their entrance into heaven and gain temporal blessings by their pilgrimages, works and ceremonies.

c) Folk Catholicism is still the prevalent expression of spirituality for most Catholics. Heavily syncretized with pre-Columbian religious influences, this is a faith of saints, fiestas and hoped-for miracles, an escapist expression rather than one that engages the sources of the suffering from which its practitioners seek relief.

3 **Maturity in the churches is a great need.** Growth is undeniable in terms of numbers, finances and influence, but sanctification and maturity are often lacking. Churches that grow spectacularly often decline in the same manner. Pentecostals and charismatics demonstrate admirable evangelistic zeal and impact the poorer classes, but they have at times been weak in discipleship, interchurch fellowship and statistical and financial integrity. Of special importance:

a) Moral purity and sanctification that yield Christ-like character and holy lives and living for all to see. The prevalence of immorality and godlessness – in handling of personal finance, in sexuality, in family life, just to name a few – in countries with large evangelical populations and Christian majorities is an affront to God.

b) Discipleship and spiritual development. There is often a lack of commitment to this painstaking process of intangible growth, as well as a lack of the methods and structures to do so. Those congregations offering a high-energy show can be weak in the long, slow effort of discipleship.

c) *Consumeristic attitudes toward church,* where people attend based on what they can receive and therefore change churches frequently according to taste and mood. Such shallow attitudes undermine congregational health as well as personal Christian growth.

d) *Theological depth and biblical understanding* of the Word of God are lacking. Few churches place solid grounding in God's Word as a priority. Sermons can be Christian self-help messages rather than plumbing the depths of Scripture. As atheism and other religions assert their claims, believers must be equipped to retain confidence in the claims of Christ and to respond effectively to competing worldviews.

e) *Prayerfulness must be cultivated once more* in evangelical circles. The greatest periods of revival and growth routinely come on the back of prayer movements. The prayer meeting is disappearing as a normative expression of church life. Thank God that new prayer movements are rising up; pray that they might be rooted in congregational life rather than being parachurch alternatives to it.

f) *Evangelism is an alien activity to most evangelicals.* The passion for lost souls and the willingness to proclaim, to witness and to live out the good news must be reclaimed. Confidence in the universal truth and life-changing power of the gospel must be recaptured.

4 **Issues within evangelicalism in the 21st Century.** Pray about these issues:

a) *A reigniting of the flame of the Spirit* to bring back revival and growth. While still increasing, evangelicals are growing at less than half the rate of 25 years ago. This can partly be explained by slowing overall population growth rates and by overall sociological/demographic principles. But genuine biblical revival is too rare and is often replaced with glitzy showmanship, and what church growth does occur tends to be transfer growth from other churches.

b) *Evangelical nominalism,* a threat to every region of the Americas. The disconnect between notional assent to the claims of Jesus and living them out blunts the Church's cutting edge and creates a distaste for Christian hypocrisy among non-believers. Nowhere is this more apparent than in the US, where there is a gap of over 22 million between those who identify themselves as evangelical and those even remotely connected to church life. Pray for the integration of these millions into active and meaningful involvement.

c) *Prosperity theology* – a baptized acquisitiveness that can justify selfishness and focus on things of this world. It can turn God into a heavenly sugar-daddy who exists to bless us rather than a loving Father who wants engagement in every area of our lives. It syncretizes the gospel with materialism and stunts the potential growth of the Christian.

d) *Training for present and future leaders.* The majority of Latin and Caribbean evangelical congregations are led by pastors with little or no formal theological training. Many of those who do have a degree get it from sub-standard, unaccredited institutions. Lay leaders get even less by way of equipping. Pray for means by which biblically sound and culturally appropriate training can occur, from introductory-level modular training to doctoral-level education.

e) *Leadership patterns* that perpetuate the authority of one anointed leader-figure rather than promoting the life of the whole body of Christ. This gives great influence to father-figure pastors who function more as CEOs than shepherds. It excuses the laity from full participation in their biblical responsibilities, creating a performer/observer dynamic. It also often alienates and frustrates younger emerging leaders, whose development is held back by those refusing to loosen their grip and share responsibility and power.

f) *The full enculturation of the gospel into minority churches* for both indigenous and immigrant peoples. Appealing to the lowest common denominator in churches or defaulting to the prevalent expression of church is a great threat to the indigeneity and effectiveness of Christianity in each unique culture. Pray that believers and missionaries among these peoples might have the wisdom to see culturally appropriate expressions of God's Kingdom planted and growing in each distinct people.

5 **External concerns** that Christians in the Americas face include:

a) *The wise handling of social influence and political power by evangelicals.* This is an old tune in North America, but a new one in Latin America. There is increased awareness among evangelicals of their cultural, economic and political clout. Such power can divert believers from evangelism or stifle the Church's prophetic voice in a society in need of moral absolutes and ethical standards. The lure of such power often entices evangelicals to seek political power and brings discredit to the cause of Christ. Evangelicals are increasingly being voted into the highest offices of their respective countries.

b) **Willingness to confront social and economic injustices** in a biblical way. Social justice is one crucial benchmark of evangelical effectiveness in the 21st Century. The potential role of Christians in societal transformation is limitless, but addressing needs positively must accompany recognition of previous failures – including slavery, genocide and Christianization done with cruelty and insensitivity. A humble approach to reconciliation and reparation for sins of the past will empower believers to minister into the present day. There are countless contexts where the forgiveness of God, the discipline of a biblical lifestyle and the support of the body of Christ can have a massive redemptive effect.

c) **The challenge of false teachings.** These are expressed in many ways. In every case, training in apologetics and grounding in the Word for both pastors and believers are crucial to guarding against deception.

i *Pluralism and secularism* teach that Jesus is only one option among many. The uniqueness of Christ and the universal validity of the gospel must be instilled at every level of Christian life and worship.

ii *New Age teaching,* the occult and personalized (but unbiblical) spirituality. These can appear harmless but nevertheless contain dangerous deceptions. The trend among young people to accept the legitimacy of magic, sorcery and witchcraft due to popular culture is a concern.

iii *Syncretized Christianity* that compromises the biblical message with whatever prevalent values and trends occur in local contexts, whether materialism, hedonism, spiritism or animism.

iv *Spiritism* in its many forms is resurging. It is especially present in Brazil (Afro-spiritism such as *Candomble, Umbanda* and others), in Cuba (*Santería*) and in Haiti (voodoo), but exists throughout the Americas.

v *Marginal Christian cults.* Both Jehovah's Witnesses and the Mormons continue to grow and spread.

6 **The evangelical missions movement** has had an enormous impact on the world – firstly from North America and now increasingly from Latin America. Caribbean missions vision is still young but is now increasing. The maturing, evangelical, Latin American missions movement has expanded and organized greatly since the 1980s. Pray for:

a) **Congregations to learn the privileges and responsibilities** of being part of the Great Commission and of supporting cross-cultural outreach within their own lands and abroad.

b) **Financial support of workers, the lack of which is a major limitation.** The failure of congregations to understand the need to support their workers will limit the potentially incredible harvest force from Latin America.

c) **Alternate sending patterns** to the methods traditionally adopted by Western European and North American churches. Tentmaking and mission-oriented communities on the field are possibly more feasible alternatives.

d) **The development of viable and locally applicable sending structures** and training programmes that result in fruitful long-term missions involvement. The time and expense of theological training, of learning English and a field language, as well as slow or negligible church growth in unreached fields, can cause possible supporters to baulk.

The Unfinished Task in the Americas

Despite the large Christian presence and much evangelical activity, major challenges remain:

1 **Upper and upper-middle classes.** These tend to be less evangelical, often wearing their liberal Protestant or Catholic sensibilities quite lightly. In many cases, even these are intellectually atheist or Marxist but make a show of religion as a social networking mechanism. Specific strategies are needed to reach these influential classes.

2 **The urban poor.** In North America, they usually live in the decaying hearts of major cities; in Latin America, they live in huge slums that ring or even permeate the major cities. Churches have a great role to play and are well positioned to do so. Pray for the light of Jesus to shine through Christian ministry, effecting urban renewal with a reduction in crime, violence and substance abuse and a growth in education, employment and, most importantly, the winning of lives into the Kingdom.

3 **Whole regions of some countries** are far less evangelized than the rest of the country, such as Quebec Province in Canada, the northeastern states and Amazonia in Brazil, some of Mexico's states as well as entire nations such as French Guyana.

4 **Students in the universities.** In North America, this means an opportunity to reach out to students from nearly every nation on earth, many from unevangelized backgrounds. Throughout the Americas, it is a chance to reach nationals for Jesus and to disciple young believers into Christian leaders. **CCCI** and Navigators have extensive ministries to campuses, and **IFES** has well-established work in the majority of countries, with younger movements in others. Pray for all agencies concentrating on this strategic sector of the community. A clear, radiant, evangelical student witness in every university is a key target for prayer.

5 **Amerindian peoples.** Their populations range from less than 1% (Brazil, Argentina, North America), to nearly 50% (Peru 45%, Guatemala 40%), to higher (Bolivia 55%). In most of the smaller tribes there are Bible translation and church-planting ministries. However, among some tribes in Colombia, Venezuela and parts of Brazil and Mexico, various factors prevent the effective establishment of an ongoing work. These include historic resentment toward centuries of maltreatment, geographic inaccessibility, government restrictions, anti-Christian anthropologists and the terrorization of local peoples by narcotics gangs and economic exploiters. The total population of unreached is relatively small, probably not exceeding one million, but the number of tribes is many. Amerindian leaders actively use the international media to expose their plight and to gain recognition of their cultural, political and land-ownership rights. Pray for justice where they have been denied such. Pray for Christians wishing to reach them to be trained in missiology and anthropology so as to be more sensitive and astute in how best to express the good news to them.

6 **Immigrant communities** from all over the world. Nearly every significant culture has a migrant community in the Americas. For special mention:

a) Chinese – over four million all over the Americas. The one million in Latin America are less reached. Their numbers are being augmented by immigrants, especially from Mainland China. The latter need specialized ministry in order to reach them.

b) Japanese – around three million with communities in Brazil (1.4m), USA (1.2m) and Peru.

c) Muslims – mainly Arabs in Latin America, but increasing in numbers throughout the Americas via immigration from the Middle East. There are also South Asian Muslims in the Anglophone countries and Javanese Muslims in Suriname. Brazil is especially seeing Muslim growth. Events of the 21st Century have brought focus on these peoples and increased outreach to them. Many Arabs in Latin America are Christian and could be instrumental in reaching Muslims or enabling Latin Americans to do so.

7 **The Jews** of the southern part of Latin America – one of the least-evangelized major concentrations of their people in the world.

8 **The Romani (Gypsies)** – present, but usually unrecognized and often undetected in most Latin American countries, and numbering over one million. They often remain deliberately incognito in order to avoid marginalization in society, but they have notable needs in terms of education and health, and especially need to be reached with the gospel.

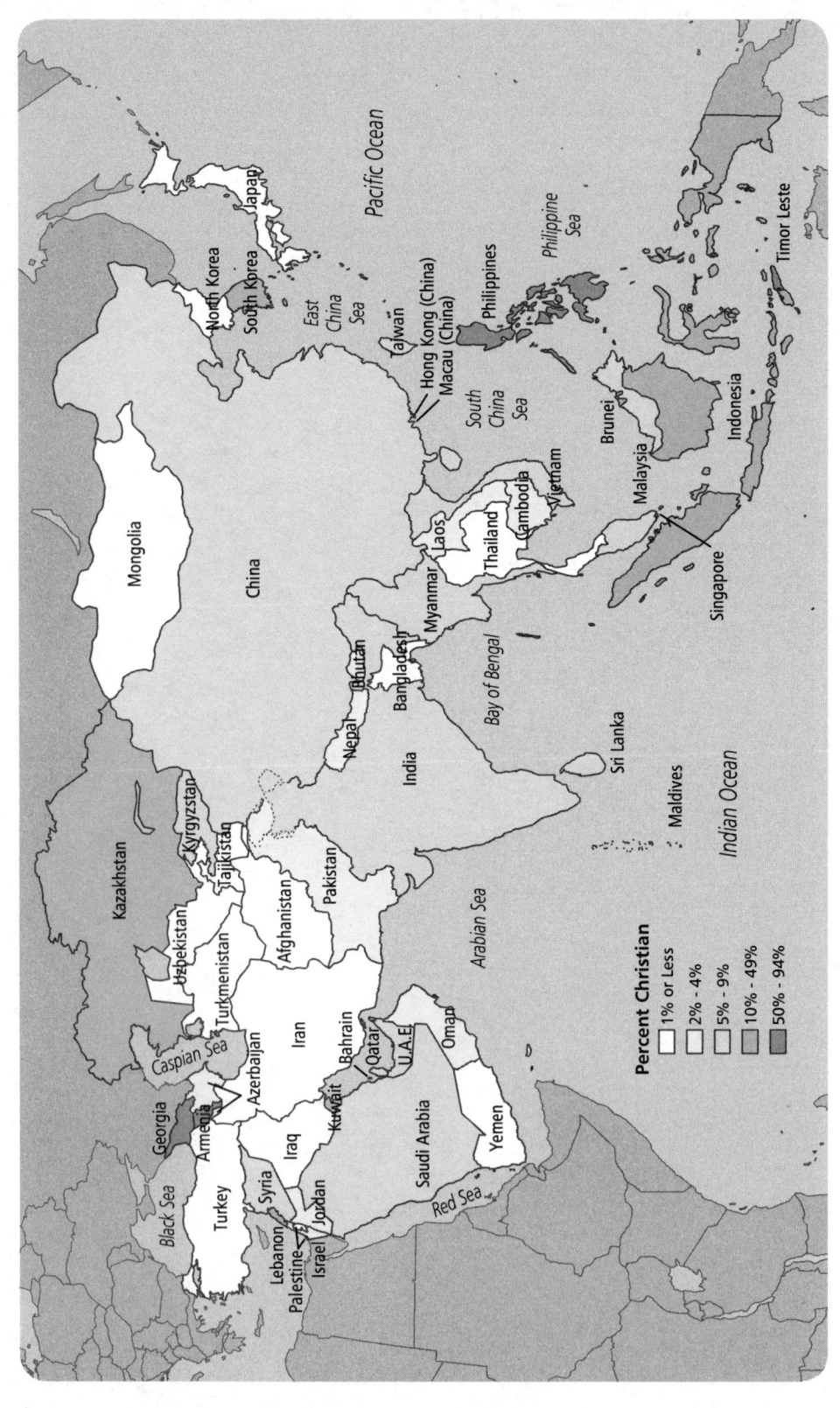

Percent Christian

- 1% or Less
- 2% - 4%
- 5% - 9%
- 10% - 49%
- 50% - 94%

Country	2010 Pop (mill)	Main Rel	Chr	Evang (% of total pop)	Non-Chr	Unev	All (# of peoples)	UP	Chr
Afghanistan	29.12	M	<0.1	<0.1	100.0	78.5	76	71	4
Armenia	3.09	X	94.4	8.7	5.6	2.5	26	9	15
Azerbaijan	8.93	M	2.7	0.2	97.3	65.5	40	25	13
Bahrain	0.81	M	9.8	2.9	90.2	47.5	16	6	5
Bangladesh	164.43	M	0.7	0.4	99.3	54.2	400	353	13
Bhutan	0.71	BH	2.1	1.8	97.9	78.4	35	32	1
Brunei	0.41	MX	11.4	6.1	88.6	51.8	26	8	3
Cambodia	15.05	B	3.1	1.6	96.9	48.8	42	30	5
China, Hong Kong	7.07	ChNX	12.4	6.1	87.6	18.4	11	4	2
China, Macau	0.55	ChBN	5.4	1.7	94.7	26.3	12	4	6
China, PRC	1,330.58	NChB	7.9	5.7	92.1	35.5	516	427	19
China, Taiwan	23.56	ChB	5.8	2.8	94.2	36.0	41	13	24
Georgia	4.22	XM	78.7	1.6	21.3	6.2	36	13	21
India	1,214.46	HM	6.3	2.2	93.7	45.0	2533	2223	115
Indonesia	232.52	MX	15.9	5.6	84.2	41.6	783	200	367
Iran	75.08	M	0.5	0.2	99.5	66.0	103	93	7
Iraq	31.47	M	1.6	0.2	98.4	60.6	33	20	10
Israel	7.29	JM	2.0	0.4	98.0	52.4	53	40	8
Japan	127.00	BZ	1.5	0.5	98.5	29.9	34	23	4
Jordan	6.47	M	2.2	0.3	97.8	56.9	21	14	5
Kazakhstan	15.75	MNX	12.2	0.7	87.9	37.7	76	41	30
Korea, North	23.99	NEZ	1.5	1.0	98.5	59.6	7	4	2
Korea, South	48.50	NXB	31.0	16.8	70.0	1.5	11	0	5
Kuwait	3.05	MX	13.8	1.5	86.2	45.7	29	11	7
Kyrgyzstan	5.55	M	5.3	0.7	94.7	55.3	47	27	16
Laos	6.44	BE	3.4	2.6	96.6	56.2	147	134	0
Lebanon	4.25	MX	32.0	0.5	68.0	11.7	23	8	11
Malaysia	27.91	MCh	9.4	4.3	90.6	44.1	182	56	33
Maldives	0.31	M	0.2	0.1	99.8	79.6	10	5	2
Mongolia	2.70	BEN	1.7	1.2	98.3	59.9	20	17	1
Myanmar	50.50	B	9.0	5.0	91.0	41.1	142	51	43
Nepal	29.85	HB	2.9	2.8	97.1	59.5	351	325	6
Oman	2.91	M	2.8	0.8	97.2	55.4	35	25	5
Pakistan	184.75	M	2.5	0.6	97.6	57.1	389	374	7
Palestine	4.41	M	1.6	0.1	98.4	48.5	20	8	11
Philippines	93.62	X	92.3	12.4	7.8	6.3	186	19	58
Qatar	1.51	M	5.9	1.0	94.1	50.1	23	7	6
Saudi Arabia	26.25	M	5.4	0.3	94.6	60.1	41	24	7
Singapore	4.84	BNXM	16.0	7.8	84.0	25.7	51	21	10
Sri Lanka	20.41	BH	8.4	1.2	91.6	39.3	76	64	9
Syria	22.51	M	6.3	0.1	93.7	45.7	34	16	13
Tajikistan	7.07	M	1.0	0.1	99.0	59.0	46	27	16
Thailand	68.14	B	1.1	0.5	98.9	44.8	113	75	7
Timor Leste	1.17	XE	87.4	2.3	12.6	6.5	23	0	18
Turkey	75.71	M	0.2	<0.1	99.8	51.6	60	38	18
Turkmenistan	5.18	M	1.8	<0.1	98.2	68.0	42	22	16
United Arab Emirates	4.71	MH	8.6	1.3	91.5	44.1	43	26	7
Uzbekistan	27.79	MN	0.8	0.3	99.3	56.7	67	37	21
Vietnam	89.03	BN	9.4	1.8	90.6	31.1	113	63	7
Yemen	24.26	M	0.1	<0.1	99.9	65.4	28	17	7
TOTAL	4,165.86		8.8	3.5	91.2	41.7	7272	5150	1046

Asia

Geography 🌏

Area 31,829,200 sq km. Approximately 23.5% of the world's surface area. Russia east of the Ural Mountains is geographically part of Asia, but here all of the Russian Federation is included with Europe. Included here are the Trans-Caucasus states (Armenia, Azerbaijan and Georgia) as well as the West Asian/Middle Eastern countries. Includes amazing geographic and ecological diversity – tropical rain forest, desert, alluvial plains, hills and the world's highest mountain range.

Population		Ann Gr	Density
2010	4,166,741,314	1.1%	131/sq km
2020	4,596,255,892	0.9%	144/sq km
2030	4,916,700,792	0.6%	154/sq km

60.3% of the world's population live in Asia.

Cities There are 254 cities of over 1 million people, 11 of which are over 10m. 28 of the world's 50 largest cities are in Asia, including the largest, Tokyo/Yokohama (with approximately 37 million people). **Urbanites** 43%. **Pop under 15 yrs** 27.8%. **Life expectancy** 69.1 yrs.

Peoples 👪

There are around 4,860 ethno-linguistic peoples in Asia's nations. These are grouped into 28 of the world's 71 ethno-linguistic families. These can be further grouped in 8 major Affinity Blocs of peoples that contain over 80% of the world's least reached peoples.

South Asian 37.0%. 2,363 peoples. Hindi 11.0%; Bengali 8.2%; Urdu Muslim 2.6%; Rajasthani 1.7%; Jat 1.6%; Telugu 1.6%; Marathi-Konkani 1.5%; Tamil 1.5%; Gujarati 1.2%; Malayali 0.9%; Kannada 0.9%; Punjabi 0.8%.
East Asian 36.3%. 121 peoples. Chinese 30.3%; Japanese 3.2%; Korean 1.8%; Chinese-Hui 0.5%.
Malay 8.1%. 804 peoples. Jawa 2.2%; Central Filipino 1.9%; Sunda-Betawi 0.9%; Malay 0.6%.
Southeast Asian 5.4%. 382 peoples. Vietnamese 1.9%; Thai 1.4%; Mon-Khmer 0.6%; Zhuang 0.5%.
Turkic 3.7%. 56 peoples. Turkish 1.3%; Azerbaijani 0.7%; Uzbek 0.7%.
Iranian–Median 3.6%. 108 peoples. Pashtun 1.2%; Persian 1.2%; Kurd 0.7%.
Arab World 2.8%. 46 peoples. Levant Arab 1.4%; Arab Peninsula 0.7%.
Tibetan/Himalayan 2.3%. 600 peoples. Burmese 0.8%; West China/Yi 0.5%.
Eurasian 0.5%. 75 peoples.

Literacy 77%. **All languages** About 2,322 distinct languages; 33.6% of the world's languages. **Languages with Scriptures** 161Bi 270NT 220por 418w.i.p. 879 languages have a definite or likely need for further translation work.

Economy 📈

Vast extremes of wealth exist in Asia, from the world's richest individuals and families to arguably the most destitute. Asia includes some of the most technologically advanced countries as well as those with some of the most primitive living conditions and subsistence economies. In the Middle East, Arabian Peninsula, Caspian Sea and Brunei, oil has transformed many countries from sleepy backwaters to fabulously wealthy oil states. Several other countries (such as Japan, Singapore, South Korea and parts of China and Taiwan) are economically advanced due to a highly educated and motivated workforce and post-industrial market economies. Some still struggle to shake off the effects of the disintegration of global Communism and the Soviet Union – Central Asia in particular, the Caucasus states, Mongolia and North Korea. Others still depend to varying degrees on raw materials and/or cheap labour in efforts to race ahead economically (much of South and Southeast Asia). Economic growth in China and India has seen hundreds of millions of people lifted from poverty in the last generation. India's great technological strides forward and China's powerful financial growth will serve to make them two of the 21st Century's economic superpowers. Endemic corruption in many nations, ageing populations (Japan, China, South Korea, Singapore), possible future tensions over water supplies and use, and dropping reserves of oil are some of the major challenges to be faced.

Income/person $4,056 (9% of USA).

Politics 🗙

Home of the majority of the world's most ancient civilizations, and the full gamut of political expression – democracy, republic, monarchy, totalitarian regime, militocracy, theocracy and just about everything else. For the last five centuries, European nations and those around the Atlantic Ocean were the centre of gravity of world politics. In the 21st Century, that centre has moved decisively to the newly powerful, vigorous nations of Asia and the Pacific. In 1900, all but five Asian nations were under Western control; by 2000, there were none. The Cold War between two European ideologies was often contested in violent ways in Asia; 16 countries were at one point, or currently are, under Communist control. Ten Asian nations have, at least in name, hereditary rulers. Seemingly more prone to authoritarian rule, many of Asia's democracies have a very different nature from what is regarded as democracy in the West. Asia has four nuclear powers with others aspiring to join them. It is the continent with the highest number of military conflicts in the last 50 years, and is host to the majority of the world's most sensitive flash points.

Religion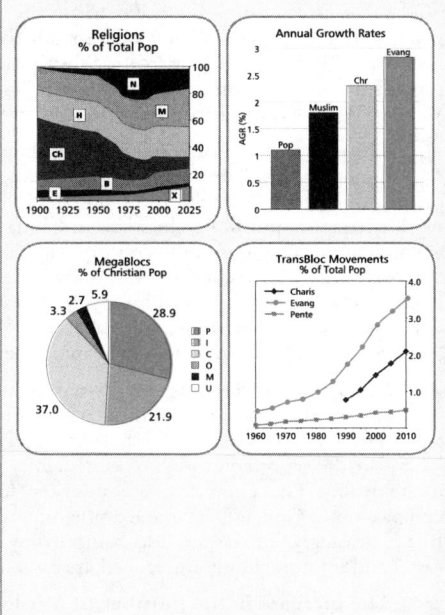

The role of religion in society, politics and national identity has grown in the last 20 years. Of all continents, persecution is most intense and lack of religious freedom most widespread in Asia, yet Christian growth is also most prominent here. Amazing religious diversity as well as great differences in both religious tolerance and the role religion plays in societies can be found in Asia; from diverse multi-religious societies such as India to virtually mono-religious nations such as Yemen, from secularism or even state-endorsed atheism as in North Korea to virtual theocracies like Iran and Saudi Arabia. Asia is the only continent where Christianity is not the largest religion. It is home of the three other major world religions apart from Christianity – Islam, Hinduism and Buddhism. It is also the heartland of other significant religions – Sikhism, Jainism, Daoism, Confucianism, Baha'i, Judaism – and apart from the latter, contains the greatest concentration of the adherents of all of these groups. Therefore, Asia remains by far the most significant challenge for world evangelization.

Christians	Pop %	Affiliates	Ann Gr
Protestant	2.74%	114,328,696	2.4%
Independent	2.01%	83,659,098	3.0%
Anglican	0.02%	1,004,698	1.6%
Catholic	3.42%	142,312,320	1.8%
Orthodox	0.29%	12,235,698	-0.4%
Marginal	0.26%	10,925,593	2.3%
Unaffiliated	0.53%	22,121,339	4.6%
Doubly affiliated	*-0.44%*	*-18,357,169*	*1.9%*

Only four Asian countries have a Christian majority – Armenia, Georgia, the Philippines and Timor Leste.

TransBloc	Pop %	Population	Ann Gr
Evangelicals			
Evangelicals	3.53	146,854,085	3.0%
Renewalists			
Charismatics	2.09	87,151,696	4.2%
Pentecostals	0.48	20,070,052	2.0%

Religions	Pop %	Population	Ann Gr
Muslim	26.42	1,100,825,428	1.8%
Hindu	22.86	952,505,521	1.2%
Non-religious	16.28	678,246,617	0.3%
Buddhist	11.32	471,469,326	1.2%
Chinese	9.82	409,233,744	0.0%
Christian	8.84	368,075,984	2.3%
Ethnoreligionist	2.42	100,639,972	0.8%
Other	1.27	52,931,215	0.5%
Sikh	0.55	22,812,972	1.3%
Jew	0.14	5,973,911	1.5%
Baha'i	0.08	3,146,901	0.4%

Answers to Prayer

1 **Church growth in Asia continues to be remarkable;** for its sheer scale, for its unprecedented occurrence in previously unevangelized nations and regions and, in many areas, for how long it has been sustained. Some of the greatest growth in the past decade or two has been in China, India, Nepal, Iran, Bangladesh, Cambodia, Vietnam and, although unverifiable, North Korea.

a) All Christians have increased from 22 million (2.3%) in 1900 to nearly 370 million (8.8%) in 2010.

b) Protestant, Independent and Anglican Christians increased from under 3 million (0.3%) in 1900 to nearly 200 million (4.9%) in 2010.

c) Catholic growth was slower, but still significant – from 11.1 million (1.2%) to 142 million (3.4%) over the same period.

d) Evangelicals in Asia, nearly 150 million, now number more than those on any other continent apart from Africa. It is also the continent with the second-fastest growing evangelical population; if measured only by conversion rate (and not including biological growth), Asia has the fastest growing evangelical population by a significant margin – 33% faster than any other region.

2 **Lands previously cut off from overt Christian ministry** are now home to dynamic, growing churches and unprecedented numbers of believers. This started with China in earlier decades, then moved to the former Soviet countries in Central Asia, the Caucasus Republics and Mongolia in the 1990s, and most recently in a number of Southeast Asian countries. Even in the heart of the Muslim world, thriving ministry to Christian populations (and other expatriate, non-Muslim peoples) is happening. Only in Saudi Arabia and Maldives are there no public-meeting Christian congregations; even in these countries (and many others), there are numbers of believers meeting together privately or in secret.

3 **Many previously unevangelized peoples** are experiencing spiritual first fruits and in some cases breakthrough. There are too many to list, but some of the more prominent peoples to experience such include Shaikh (Bengali), Vietnamese, Burmese, Pashtun, Persian, Iraqi Arab, Bhil, Gond, Khmer, Kazakh, Kurd and Kyrgyz. Additionally, significant Christian growth has occurred in several clusters of smaller peoples, such as in the region of North Vietnam-Laos-Myanmar-Yunnan Province in China and in Western China-Nepal.

4 **China is in the midst of amazing changes.** Beyond the economic shift that has lifted hundreds of millions out of poverty, beyond the positive changes that the further opening of the country has brought, the Church in China is signalling a massive change in this, the world's largest population. Christians in China now almost certainly exceed 100 million. They are present in all regions of the country and come from all walks of life. They love their country and have ambitious visions to see it transformed by the power of the gospel. The government, traditionally a ruthless persecutor of the Church, now recognizes the positive social impact Christians can make and increasingly accepts the reality that the Church in China is there to stay – and will play a major role in shaping the country's future.

5 **India is experiencing its own extraordinary harvest.** Much of this is happening among the Dalits, the Untouchables outside of the caste system. Due to continuing persecution, social mores and the systemic discrimination that occurs against those who become Christian, the reported growth of Christianity is very modest compared to what is more likely to be reality. The compassionate ministry to Dalits and Tribal peoples demonstrates the compassion of God and generates a phenomenal response that ministries cannot keep up with. But increasingly, inroads are also being made into the fast-growing middle classes, the upper castes and into previously unreached areas such as Uttar Pradesh and Bihar.

6 **The increase in the number of Muslim Background Believers** (MBBs). The hatred and violence of Islamist extremists most likely contribute to many Muslims' disillusion and greater openness to the gospel. While there are pockets of particularly momentous change, the inflow of Muslims into the Kingdom of God is indeed happening through much of the Muslim world, albeit under the radar and on a modest level in many areas. Dreams and visions from the Lord, combined with encounters with Scripture and demonstrations of God's love, play a large role in many of these testimonies. Other major factors include specific and sustained intercession for the Muslim world, increased efforts to reach them, more sensitive cultural approaches and the widespread use of media – satellite television programmes, radio and film/video. The impact of the Internet in communicating the gospel, leading Muslims to faith in Jesus and discipling new believers cannot be overstated.

7 **The indigenization of Christian ministry and leadership in Asia.** The recent growth of the Church has largely been through the work of national workers, local evangelists and ordinary believers. These churches are, more than ever, Asian in structure, style and leadership – taking forms relevant for those they are trying to reach. Beyond the continent itself, Asian Christian leadership is assuming a much greater role in the global body of Christ. This includes countries such as South Korea, China and India but also places such as Sri Lanka, the Philippines and Indonesia.

8 **The emergence of a mature, international missionary involvement.** The growth of commitment and involvement in cross-cultural outreach in India is praiseworthy. South Korea, the Philippines and the Chinese diaspora are major components of the world's missionary outreach. The Back to Jerusalem vision in China and the vision to mobilize the Filipino emigrant workforce could be the two most significant dynamics for world mission in the 21st Century. Yet humility, cultural sensitivity and genuine willingness to work together across denominations, nationalities and ethnicities are all needed for Asian mission work as much as for anywhere else.

9 **Increased stability in several areas** that were previously volatile or at war. The lot of the Afghan people has seen notable improvement since 2001, as has that of the Kurds, especially in Iraq. Indonesia and Pakistan have stabilized somewhat, and China has managed its incredible growth without provoking further tension or conflict with its neighbours.

Hot Spots of Asia

Listed below is a selection of the flash points in Asia that could have an effect – regionally and globally – on the political, economic, demographic and military spheres. They could also have profound influence on the efforts to evangelize the regions in question – the challenge lies before both local and national political leaders as well as the Church.

1 **The unresolved conflict between Israel and the Palestinians.** All international efforts to broker a viable peace deal have ultimately failed. There are deep differences between the claimants – on the land and on Jerusalem itself – with hawkish elements in both groups. While Israel continues to settle its people on occupied land and while Muslim nations refuse to recognize Israel's rights of existence and sovereignty, a peaceful resolution is highly unlikely. Factoring in antagonistic external players, without heavenly intervention, future war seems almost inevitable – the nations involved are all preparing for this possibility. Desperation, hatred and the fearsome arsenals of weapons would generate a terrifying toll on the region. Pray for all parties involved in the confrontation and for world leaders attempting to defuse the situation.

2 **China's re-emergence as a global superpower** is possibly the major global political and economic factor in the first decades of the 21st Century. China is growing more assertive in international diplomacy and political engagement. The pragmatic marriage of centralized state control with an increasingly capitalist economy has achieved stupendous financial growth. But such growth, fuelled by massive consumption of resources, cannot be sustained indefinitely; what happens when the bubble bursts will have a global impact. The major demographic shift to an aged population (as a result of the one-child policy) will place great burdens on those of working age. The huge gender gap – in many areas, a shortfall of 20-30% from equal gender balance – has further serious implications for long-term societal stability. The quasi-colonization by ethnic Han of China's hinterlands (Inner Mongolia, Xinjiang, Qinghai, Tibet, Yunnan) and accelerating immigration to under-populated and under-developed Russian Siberia are all potentially calamitous to the indigenous populations.

3 **The Himalayas region simmers with tension.** The conflict over Kashmir is the most intractable of problems, with Pakistan and India (and China) holding conflicting claims over territory. The Kashmir dispute has profoundly shaped Pakistan's domestic and foreign policies, has provoked an arms race between Pakistan and India and has already resulted in four wars. China and India are in dispute over territorial claims not just in Kashmir but also in Arunachal Pradesh and Ladakh. Strife also exists over India's hosting of the Tibetan government-in-exile and in Tibet itself. Add to this the Nepal Civil War of 1996-2006 (and continuing tensions), and you have a region filled with potential flashpoints.

4 **Unrest in Southeast Asia** is due to a combination of political and religious factors. The fault line in Thailand's political impasse seems unbridgeable and may point to more intense civil strife – or even war – in the future; Muslim unrest in the south of the country adds to the pressure. While Indonesia has stabilized somewhat, threats remain to its integrity even as rumblings of deeper discontent in Malaysia can be heard. This arises from the complex interplay of weak democratic government, vested interests, rising Islamic extremism and ethnic resentments.

5 **The deep mistrust between the Persian Shi'a Muslim and the Arab Sunni Muslim worlds.** The seven-year Iran-Iraq War in the 1980s, and the conflict and manoeuvering after the Second Gulf War (2003ff), were new chapters in the centuries-old conflict. Iran's nuclear developments and increasing regional assertiveness – especially via the Shi'as in Iraq – significantly affect this religious and political fault line.

6 **The Golden Triangle** (parts of Myanmar, Thailand, Laos, Vietnam and Yunnan), already notorious for insurgency, lawlessness, drug production and trafficking, has now added human trafficking to its list of evils.

7 **The Korean Peninsula** has remained one of the world's most dangerous flash points since the Korean War ceasefire of 1953. As North Korea gets ever more desperate to maintain an untenable system, the chance of collapse, crisis or even war increases. The deaths of millions by starvation and the North's nuclear ambitions make this a weighty and urgent issue. Pray for an end to the sufferings of North Koreans and for a wisely managed eventual reunification of Korea.

8 **Afghanistan's troubles are not yet over.** It still sits under foreign military presence and a flawed and fledgling political system. The Taliban violently oppose both the former and the latter, and their influence is still significant in several regions of Afghanistan and Pakistan. Afghanistan has known only war for so many decades, yet stability is being established – and the good news is carefully, subtly being shared and demonstrated.

9 **Yemen is a tinderbox of trouble.** Rapid population growth (the population doubles every 21 years!), endemic poverty, a turbulent and clannish society, growing Islamist extremism and violence against foreign powers all point to a looming ignition point.

Trends to Watch

Globalization and modernization are bringing huge changes to billions of peoples. Listed here are some of the major trends. These will profoundly shape the futures of governments and entire populations, impact Christian theology, ministry strategy and deployment of workers and will change the responsiveness of whole populations to the gospel.

1 **Unprecedented levels of migration, globalization and mobility** change the composition of entire countries. These are occurring in many regions and in different ways:

a) The oil-rich states of the Middle East receive millions of economic migrants from poorer regions of Asia – other Arab nations, South Asia and Southeast Asia. Populations in countries such as the UAE, Qatar and Bahrain are mostly expatriates.

b) Southeast and South Asia have millions of relocated people. Some reside long-term due to conditions in their homelands, many simply look for work where they can find it and others are trafficked against their will to work in industrial sweatshops or brothels. In the latter cases, organized crime rings are the greatest beneficiaries of such wicked structures of sin.

c) Human exports as economic policy. For countries such as the Philippines, Bangladesh, Nepal, China, India, Pakistan, Myanmar, Thailand, Vietnam and Indonesia, remittances from money earned abroad and sent back to families have become a major earner of foreign exchange, in some cases one of the largest sectors of national income.

d) Urbanization is occurring in Asia more quickly than anywhere in the world, apart from Africa. Literally hundreds of millions of people are moving from traditional rural areas (and lifestyles) into urban areas (usually slums), looking for work and a new life. Such people are often vulnerable to exploitation, loneliness and desperation.

2 **Demographic shifts** will have massive implications for Asia's future. The rapidly rising life expectancies and reduced birth rates of the populations of China, Japan and South Korea will place great burdens on the next generation. The gender gap is caused by selective abortion and infanticide in East and South Asia; these have created a deficit of tens of millions of girls, giving rise to prostitution, sex trafficking, wife-buying and abduction. Then there are the burgeoning populations in most of the Arab world, particularly Yemen and Palestine (also the poorest Arab countries) as well as Afghanistan, Pakistan and many Southeast Asian countries. Over the next 50 years, all of these dynamics combined will generate incredible pressures on nation-states and fuel large-scale migration and unrest.

3 **The supply of safe water,** increasingly in demand but in ever-scarcer supply, is an international issue that will only become more hotly contested. Climate change will also have an unpredictable effect on water supply, dramatically affecting the most vulnerable areas; it will affect agriculture, sanitation and the health of millions. Preventable water-related issues cause a high proportion of child mortality. There are genuine possibilities of huge numbers of refugees and even war as a result of water scarcity. Greater tensions will most likely concern the Jordan River (Arabs and Israelis), the Tigris/Euphrates Rivers (Turkey, Syria, Iraq), the Amu Darya/Syr Daria/Aral Sea (Central Asia), the Indus/Ganges/Brahmaputra Rivers (South Asia) and the Mekong River (China and Southeast Asia).

4 **Trafficking is a major means of illegal and illicit income.** Drug trafficking remains the most well known and violent of these trades. There are two main hubs of heroin production: Afghanistan and the Golden Triangle. Human trafficking, usually for manual labour or the sex trade, has accelerated rapidly in the last few years. It particularly affects the poorer countries, where women are sold or enter into indentured slavery and are forced to pay off debt through prostitution. But it also affects wealthier countries; places such as Japan, parts of China, Thailand, India and many Arab countries traffic in girls from abroad to populate brothels. International trade in illegally logged hardwoods and endangered species has also soared due to demand from East Asia's growing financial elite. The wealthy and criminal networks prosper as a result; the rural poor invariably suffer.

5 **Intractable divisions within and between nations** threaten stability and peace in many places. Some of these are international in nature: India-Pakistan, North and South Korea, Israel-Palestine-Lebanon are examples. Others involve active secessionist or rebel movements within nations: India (Kashmir), China (Tibet and Xinjiang), Myanmar, Thailand, Sri Lanka, Georgia and the Philippines. Furthermore, political and political-religious divides in several other states might be resolved peacefully or they could result in civil conflict or war: Thailand, Nepal, Iran, Pakistan, Afghanistan, Yemen, Indonesia, Malaysia and Central Asia. In a number of these cases, such tensions have recently been played out at great human cost. There remain restive minorities – ethnic, religious and political – in many of these states and in others as well.

6 **Asia's economic growth** continues to be phenomenal, but much of it is also either unsustainable or fragile. This ranges from oil-rich states with limited reserves, to dwindling natural resources (Southeast Asian rainforests and Central Asian cotton fields), to nations heavily reliant on investments/finance and exports (effectively, all of East Asia). Such growth is also uneven, in many cases fabulously enriching a small minority while leaving the majority still mired in poverty. While there is great potential to create wealth and economically empower hundreds of millions more, there is also the equal possibility of greater corruption and of financial crashes that reverberate throughout the globe, with severe consequences. Pray for growth based on sustainable models and for the multiplication of wealth that is equitable and just for all.

7 **Ecological disasters loom on the horizon,** largely because of rapid industrialization, unsustainable growth in energy consumption and pollution. There is a litany of tragedies for Asia: drying of the Aral Sea in Central Asia, leaving a poisonous desert; desertification in China and Mongolia; rapid destruction of tropical forests in Southeast Asia and Indonesia; the threatened future of coral reefs and the whole of the Maldives due to global warming; increasingly frequent flooding of much of Bangladesh's and some of India's land areas; the monumental environmental troubles in China resulting from massive energy projects and rapid industrialization and the accelerating increase in pollution (much of it as a result of greater personal consumption such as automobile use). While it is hard to deny Asia the right to advance its economies as the West took liberty to do, the sheer scale of the continent and the speed at which it is happening threaten to overwhelm the environment with globally disastrous consequences.

8 **The resurgence of non-Christian world religions** increasingly influences politics, restricts religious freedom, heightens inter-ethnic divisions and affects Christian outreach and strategy.

a) Islam is a faith undergoing several crises. It remains robust and growing at its fringes in Africa, Europe and parts of Asia, while closer to home, cracks in the facade reveal deeper fault lines within the faith. The accelerated growth of radical Islamist movements generates terror and violence in many countries in Asia, from Turkey to Indonesia, from Yemen to Northwest China. Yet many other Muslims in Asia are increasingly tolerant and retain their Islamic identity in a more globalized and modern world. Also rapidly increasing are those who leave their faith behind – either retaining the merest facade of Muslim cultural identity or abandoning Islam altogether – for non-religion or often for Christianity. Pressure grows to implement shari'a law in many Middle Eastern nations. There are strong movements to achieve the same in Malaysia and Indonesia, despite their large non-Muslim populations. The level of persecution against Christians has markedly increased. There are 26 Asian countries with a Muslim majority.

b) ***Extreme Hindu groups*** have faced setbacks in India's last two national elections, but remain very influential, especially in particular states such as Orissa, Gujarat, Madhya Pradesh, Chhattisgarh and others. They also wield notable influence in Nepal. India's already complex social fabric is threatened by Hinduist attacks on Muslims and Christians, by forced "conversions" of Dalits and Tribals and by Muslim attacks on Hindus. Outspoken and frequently violent opposition to Christian proselytism is not uncommon. Evangelistic endeavours in both countries are under pressure.

c) ***Buddhists*** are reacting to effective Christian ministry in Sri Lanka, Myanmar and among Tibetan peoples. Korean Buddhism is experiencing rapid growth whilst earlier Christian growth has plateaued. Buddhism, together with underlying ethnic religions (Daoism, Shintoism, Shamanism, others), is the majority religion of 13 Asian countries and is strong in those still under Communist rule.

d) ***Asia's indigenous ethnic religions*** have regained influence – Shintoism in Japan, Daoism and Confucianism in Chinese countries, shamanism in Mongolia and others.

e) ***Extreme Orthodox Judaism*** wields a disproportionately large political influence on Israel, a factor further complicating any efforts made for peace.

9 **The resilience of totalitarianism.** The extreme repression of the North Korean Communist regime – and the persistence of authoritarian central regimes in Vietnam, Laos, China, Myanmar, Turkmenistan, Saudi Arabia and others – could lead to unexpected and sudden events that reverberate around the world. Only about five or six Asian countries have genuine, deep-rooted cultures of democratic freedom. Democracy is fragile in Thailand, Indonesia, Philippines and Malaysia and is only in its infancy in places such as Iraq and Afghanistan. In Central Asia, the fledgling democracies are often a sham, and Russia has moved to reassert its authority over the region. In many countries, a semblance of democracy is trumped by older and deeper authority and governance structures, and for most of these, such an arrangement is eminently workable.

10 **The revolution in information technology** cannot but deeply affect Asia. Some countries will benefit from the large and well-educated workforce that specializes in IT – India and China are foremost among these. East Asia leads the world in technological innovation on many levels. But a more profound effect will be from rapidly spreading information and global awareness in previously isolated nations. Just as swift will be authoritarian states moving to suppress such information and monitor their populations. Awareness and knowledge of oppression, injustice and corruption will spread more than ever before – and hopefully elicit a righteous response from the global community. Even more significantly, the good news of Jesus Christ is reaching via satellite television and Internet into homes and communities that would otherwise be unreached and unreachable by traditional means.

11 **The severity of the AIDS pandemic** is intensifying in certain regions. Two major infection points are Mumbai, India, and Bangkok, Thailand, where the flourishing sex industry helps spread the scourge to poorer, surrounding lands. India has more cases of HIV than any other nation. More recently, relaxed morals and greater mobility in China make it a region where the disease has spread rapidly. Many are concerned that cultural mores, stigma and lack of decisive action allow the issue to be swept under the proverbial carpet, rather than determinedly eradicated.

12 **The reassertion of Russian authority in its former sphere of influence.** Already, countries such as Georgia and Kyrgyzstan feel the power of Russian foreign policy. While Moscow may never rule outright as it did in the USSR, the more aggressive Russian stance in Central Asia and the Caucasus may profoundly affect regional politics and extend beyond these countries into Iran, Turkey, Afghanistan and even China.

The Church in Asia

1 The Middle East/West Asia.

a) *The region that witnessed the birth of the Church* now sees its rapid decline. Large-scale and sustained emigration after centuries of tenacity has denuded the Middle East of the bulk of its Christian communities. For it to have endured this long, despite discrimination and persecution, is remarkable. Now, the rising influence of Muslim extremists increases the pressure to marginalize and eliminate any Christian presence in the region. Orthodox Jewish pressures on Messianic Jews are also acute. Pray that the ancient Orthodox and Catholic communities might come to new life and vigour to become effective witnesses.

b) *Protestant denominations* are few and small, and many struggle with nominalism. They likewise face pressure and persecution, although in a number of countries they are growing. Interdenominational relationships have not always been smooth and gracious. Pray for unity, strength and revitalization.

c) *Believers from a Muslim background* (BMB/MBB) are growing in number in almost every context and on an unprecedented scale. This is happening in trickles (in places such as the Arabian Peninsula) and in torrents (Iran, Iraq). Pray for:

  i *All who have come to Christ from such backgrounds.* They have specific spiritual, social and personal needs that are different from Christians of other backgrounds. Pressures on them are usually acute – from relatives, employers and authorities – and can range from ostracism to martyrdom. For many, emigration is the only way out of impossible situations. Pray for courage in the face of opposition and for faithfulness in all situations.

  ii *The witness of believers.* There is great potential to communicate the gospel through the testimony of believers' lifestyles, through their work habits, through their marriages and through family relationships. Christian homes can demonstrate profoundly the power and love of Christ. Pray for those who have come out of a Muslim background to witness with both wisdom and fearlessness.

  iii *Networking for Muslim-background believers.* It is easy for them to slip into isolation and discouragement. Pray for the development of networks that will afford opportunities for fellowship with those of similar background. Pray for such believers to be discipled appropriately, and to find both employment and marriage partners – neither of which is easy for Muslim-background believers still living in Islamic contexts.

d) *Trained leadership for the churches* remains a challenge. There are few in training and few institutions in the Middle East that can provide it. Many of those who study in the West find good ministry opportunities there, so few return home. Training structures for the underground and MBB churches also need to be developed further to meet the demands of these burgeoning groups.

e) *Missions vision is growing.* Increasing numbers of Middle Eastern Christians are capturing a burden to reach out to Muslims, especially in lands closed to normal mission work – in North Africa, the Arabian Peninsula and others.

f) *The impact of Christian satellite TV and the Internet* has been momentous, greater than in any other region of the world. It has been highly effective at sharing the good news in restricted access nations, at offering sound defence of the gospel in the face of Muslim accusations and at offering solid discipleship to believers.

2 Central Asia.

a) *Indigenous evangelical Christians have multiplied* to number tens of thousands in Azerbaijan, Kyrgyzstan, Kazakhstan, Uzbekistan and even Turkey, but in all of these places they face pressures from many sides – the government, Islamist groups, the Orthodox hierarchy and family members/society at large. The perception of evangelicalism as being foreign is one reason for such trouble; the hard line taken by many governments against religious extremism has unintended consequences for Christian groups. Pray for the rooting of the Christian faith in Central Asian cultural forms, for continued growth, for the positive witness of believers and for the further development of mature indigenous leadership. Pray also for Russian, Ukrainian, German, Korean and other expatriate believers who still comprise a majority of evangelicals in these lands.

b) Pressures on Christians are more severe in Uzbekistan, Tajikistan and especially Turkmenistan. Foreign workers have been expelled from these countries, congregations scattered and church leaders imprisoned. Pray that the remnant might stand strong and even grow amid these tribulations. In Afghanistan, despite the defeat of the Taliban as a military force, indigenous believers face great risks and must be very cautious in meeting together.

c) Multi-national partnerships of expatriate believers exist for each of these nations. They have raised up intercession, mobilized mission, fostered cooperation and encouraged local believers. Pray that their continued carrying of these burdens might bring forth greater harvest in these needy regions.

③ South Asia.

a) Decline and nominalism go hand in hand in several areas. For decades, the Christian population in Sri Lanka has steadily reduced as a percentage of the national total. The same problem exists among the established, traditional churches of India and Pakistan. Emigration and a lack of evangelistic vision contribute significantly to this. Pray for a reversal to this trend.

b) Growth is definitely occurring, predominantly among Tribal groups, Dalits and the lowest castes. In fact, the response to the gospel is such that churches are unable to keep up with the demands of those expressing interest in or commitment to the Lord. It is likewise nearly impossible to enumerate all that is occurring, especially in India, because of the sheer scale of what transpires there, the lack of structure to much of the ministry and the socio-religious climate that keeps many within their traditional religious frameworks, even after meeting Jesus.

c) Persecution remains present in all countries of South Asia, although location, social context and time frame all factor into the intensity thereof. Christians are on the receiving end of persecution – mostly from Hindus in India and Nepal, from Muslims in Pakistan, Bangladesh and the Maldives and even from Buddhists in Sri Lanka. Some of this is unavoidable, as responses of resentment and fear of church growth. But some result from lack of sensitivity and wisdom by Christians ministering into these situations. Pray that evangelists, church planters and missionaries might share the gospel with love and boldness, but also with humility and wisdom.

d) Missions vision. The vast majority of Kingdom increase in this region is through the faithful witness of indigenous believers sharing the good news village by village and town by town. But the gospel has rarely jumped across ethno-linguistic or caste boundaries. This is changing as the South Asian Church increasingly commits to reach the least reached groups in its region – of which there are literally thousands. Predominantly in India but also in Nepal, Pakistan and elsewhere, ministries specifically seek to communicate, in a focused manner, the life-giving gospel to these unevangelized groups. This will take great patience and faith, since new languages, new cultures and new methods of ministry must be learned – with no guarantee of immediate response – but already, India has more national missionaries than any other nation. May other South Asian countries catch the same vision.

④ Southeast Asia.

a) Church impact is very uneven in this region, but includes a number of areas where minorities are remarkably responsive to the gospel. Large ethnic minority churches thrive in Myanmar, Vietnam, Thailand, Indonesia and Malaysia, while the majority populations remain rooted in Buddhism or Islam. Pray for these groups to continue to grow in the Lord and transmit the gospel to neighbouring peoples. The Philippines and Timor Leste are two of Asia's four majority Christian countries.

b) Exciting growth has occurred, especially in areas previously closed or hostile to the good news. The Church is growing to unprecedented levels in Vietnam, Cambodia, Laos and even in some areas of Indonesia. But the breakthrough is yet to come, especially among the namesake peoples of several nations: the Thai of Thailand, the Burmese of Burma/Myanmar, the Malays of Malaysia and the Lao of Laos.

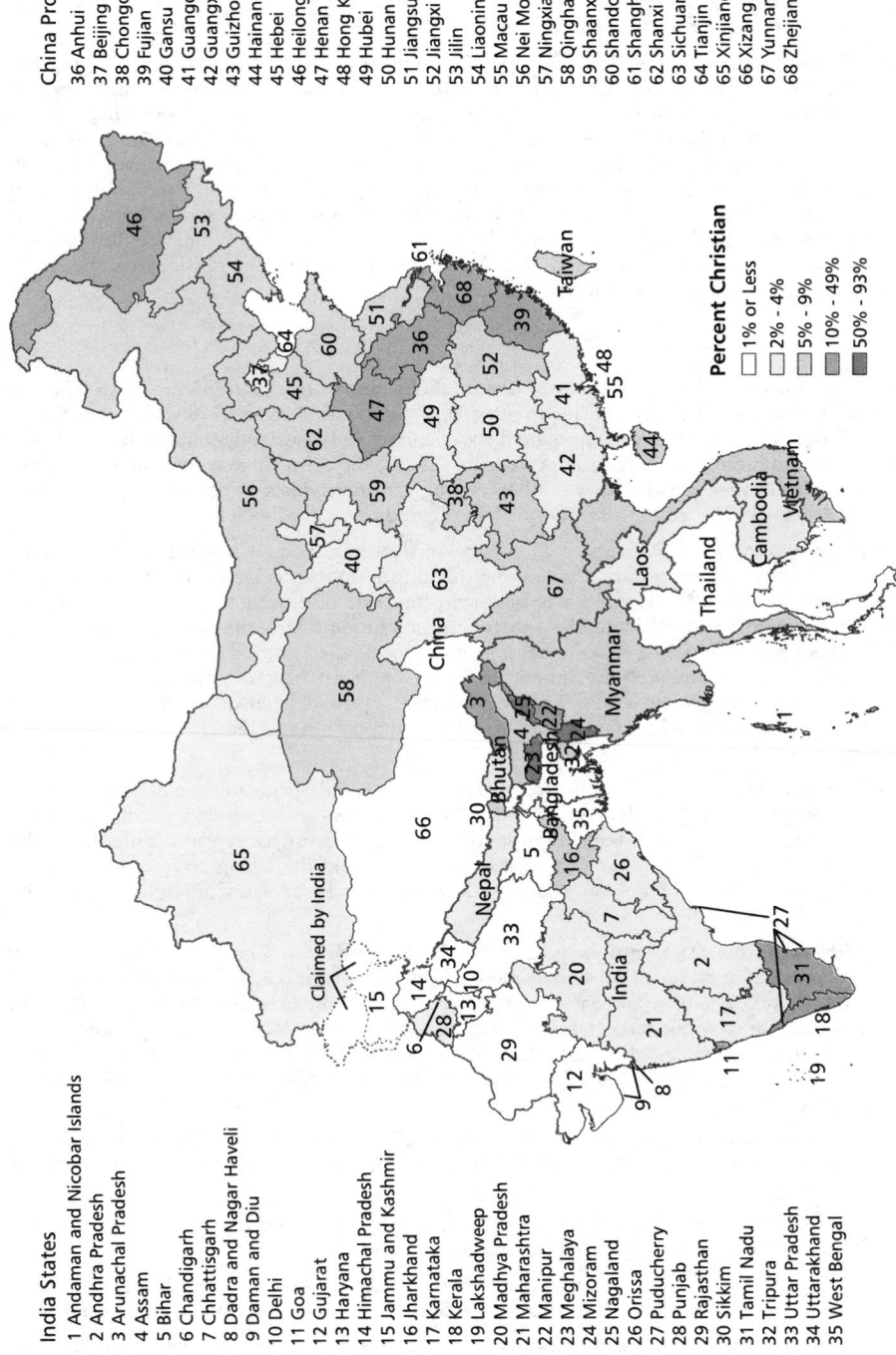

India States

1 Andaman and Nicobar Islands
2 Andhra Pradesh
3 Arunachal Pradesh
4 Assam
5 Bihar
6 Chandigarh
7 Chhattisgarh
8 Dadra and Nagar Haveli
9 Daman and Diu
10 Delhi
11 Goa
12 Gujarat
13 Haryana
14 Himachal Pradesh
15 Jammu and Kashmir
16 Jharkhand
17 Karnataka
18 Kerala
19 Lakshadweep
20 Madhya Pradesh
21 Maharashtra
22 Manipur
23 Meghalaya
24 Mizoram
25 Nagaland
26 Orissa
27 Puducherry
28 Punjab
29 Rajasthan
30 Sikkim
31 Tamil Nadu
32 Tripura
33 Uttar Pradesh
34 Uttarakhand
35 West Bengal

China Provinces

36 Anhui
37 Beijing
38 Chongqing
39 Fujian
40 Gansu
41 Guangdong
42 Guangxi
43 Guizhou
44 Hainan
45 Hebei
46 Heilongjiang
47 Henan
48 Hong Kong
49 Hubei
50 Hunan
51 Jiangsu
52 Jiangxi
53 Jilin
54 Liaoning
55 Macau
56 Nei Mongol
57 Ningxia
58 Qinghai
59 Shaanxi
60 Shandong
61 Shanghai
62 Shanxi
63 Sichuan
64 Tianjin
65 Xinjiang
66 Xizang
67 Yunnan
68 Zhejiang

Percent Christian

1% or Less
2% - 4%
5% - 9%
10% - 49%
50% - 93%

Taiwan

China

Nepal

Bhutan

Bangladesh

Myanmar

Laos

Thailand

Cambodia

Vietnam

India

Claimed by India

c) *Persecution* still occurs, and in some areas, quite intensely. The Laos and Myanmar governments are particularly hostile to Christians, and in Vietnam, the Church is growing amid notable pressure. While there is more freedom due to large Christian populations in Malaysia and Indonesia, the influence of more hard line and less tolerant Islamic groups makes life increasingly difficult for the Church generally, and more specifically for Christians from a traditionally Muslim-peoples background. Pray that the Church might stand strong in the face of opposition and fearlessly spread the light of the gospel even to its enemies.

d) *Missions vision.* In much of Southeast Asia, missions vision is limited to impacting the unreached majorities in each respective country. The sizeable Christian minorities in Singapore and Malaysia have an outstanding mission-sending record. But something special is happening in the Philippines, and to a lesser degree, in Indonesia. There are millions of economic migrants who live and work abroad as part of the Filipino diaspora. They are increasingly gaining a vision to use their presence throughout the world as an opportunity to shine the light of Jesus – even into the most difficult countries, such as those in the Arabian Peninsula and the Middle East. As their home churches back in the Philippines begin to see themselves as sending churches for these newly realized tentmaking missionaries, the Kingdom impact on the world will be massive.

5 **East Asia.**

a) *The Church in East Asia is one of remarkably contrasting situations.* In South Korea, it is a large and influential minority, an integral part of South Korean society. In North Korea, it is an underground movement hunted down and reviled by the autocratic regime. In Japan, it is insignificant in size but respected. In Taiwan, the Church is larger but still a small minority. In mainland China it is a burgeoning and increasingly important minority, while in Mongolia it is a rather new, but quickly growing element of society.

b) *Persecution* remains particularly intense in North Korea, where Christians are targeted for extra misery and oppression from among this already-longsuffering people. The number of martyrs in North Korea will never be known this side of heaven, but countless thousands have suffered and died as a result of their faith in Jesus. In China, the intense persecution of decades past is subsiding in some regions but remains the same in others; it appears to no longer be a nationwide government policy to oppress Christians, but at the local level persecution can remain severe. Even in the more open societies of Japan, Mongolia, and South Korea, active witnessing Christians can face opposition and strong pressure to conform to societal norms.

c) *New challenges* emerge for churches that are now multiple-generations old. With the rapid increase in material wealth in much of East Asia, Christians are presented with the challenges of materialism, affluence and the prosperity gospel – success has replaced suffering as the marker of a faithful believer. Nominalism, hedonism and the falling away of the younger generation into worldliness are relatively new issues the East Asian Church faces, issues the West has dealt with for some time.

d) *Missions vision.* The missionary legacy of the South Korean Church is outstanding for a nation its size. It produces the second-most foreign missionaries of any country in the world; a high proportion of these are sent as long-term and highly trained workers to the unevangelized world. In China, while foreign mission sending is still very modest, the looming impact of the Back to Jerusalem vision could be historically unprecedented; as many as 100,000 church-planting evangelists have spread throughout Asia and the Middle East. Yet several key issues for prayer remain:

   i *Cultural sensitivity* as well as recognizing the need for a contextualized gospel that does not assume the homogeneity of the sending culture and allows indigenous expressions of the Church to flourish.

   ii *Maturity in missions* and willingness to learn from mistakes of the past – and to not repeat them – for example in paternalism and use of funds.

   iii *Partnerships with Western, Latino and African missionaries to be mutually beneficial* whether serving together in international agencies or through interagency cooperation on fields.

   iv *Retention of Asian missionaries* who serve cross-culturally. Missionary attrition and the personal costs of ministering in the heart of the unevangelized world must all be addressed, including dealing with culture shock and culture acquisition. The provision of good member care is an essential element for the continued strength and health of mission sending from East Asia.

The Unfinished Task in Asia

1 **While we praise God for great strides** in the evangelization of Asia, the remaining challenge is awesome. Asians comprise:

a) Over 81% of the 4.7 billion non-Christians in the world.

b) 85.4% of World A – unevangelized individuals. Asian countries represent 9 of the world's 10 largest unevangelized populations.

c) The three largest non–Christian religions in the world are rooted in Asia; they are also the most challenging for Christians. In Asia, there are 1.1 billion Muslims, 950 million Hindus and 470-920 million Buddhists (the higher figure if the Chinese, Japanese and other intermingled ethnic religions are included).

d) There are also 680 million Asians with no formal religious affiliation who present a unique challenge in their own right.

2 **Of the 37 countries of the world that are less than 10% Christian,** 32 are in Asia. Of the 14 countries that are less than 2% Christian, 12 are in Asia.

3 **The least reached peoples on earth** are predominantly Asian. The Joshua Project lists 16,350 ethno-linguistic peoples. Of the 6,648 least reached peoples on this list, 5,150 are in Asia.

4 **The unreached peoples of Asia** can be grouped by Affinity Blocs of language, race, culture, geography and history. The salient needs of these blocs are briefly outlined here. (See map on p26.)

a) The Arab World. Population in Asia: 112 million with 166 peoples. The majority of the 12 Arab countries have either shrinking churches due to emigration or small Christian populations with little visible presence. Points for prayer:

  i *Arab believers* need courage to use opportunities to witness and to trust God that Muslims can be saved and become committed believers. The increasing radicalization of Islam in this region can create a climate of oppression that prevents open witness.

  ii *The Internet* is probably the most exciting medium where ministry is having an astounding effect. Opportunities for evangelism, apologetics, Bible study, discipleship, worship and fellowship are countless, and the gospel impact in the Arab world through the Internet is truly amazing.

  iii *Satellite television programmes,* broadcast daily, are watched by millions of Arabic-speaking Muslims. In many countries, nearly every home owns a satellite dish. As with the Internet, this technology defies boundaries and borders and is bearing unprecedented fruit.

  iv *Radio broadcasts* also reach into this region from abroad. Many listen and then receive tactful follow-up ministry.

  v *Christian films,* including the JESUS film, *The Passion of the Christ* and others, yield remarkable responses.

  vi *There are many opportunities for Christian expatriates* to serve in Arab lands and live for Jesus. These range from the humble but profound influence of Asian domestic workers all the way up to more socially elite roles such as diplomats, businessmen, academics and doctors.

b) The Iranian–Median bloc. Population in Asia: 146 million; 213 peoples. Major people clusters: Persian (46m); Pashtun (48m); Kurds (28m); Baloch (10m). These include some of the least evangelized peoples on earth. Major opportunities for witness:

  i *Expatriate Christians* serving in these lands – openings are few, but they do exist.

  ii *Millions have been uprooted* because of war, oppression and poverty. Christians and churches have been planted among many of these who have found their way into another nation.

iii Media ministries. Persian peoples are seeing the same kinds of phenomenal responses to Christian radio and satellite television broadcasts, Internet ministry and Christian literature. But the other people clusters have few materials translated into their languages, few opportunities to interact with those materials – and few responses.

c) **South Asians** are the largest of these eight blocs with 1.5 billion individuals, nearly 800 ethno–linguistic peoples and 3,400 ethno–cultural groups that incorporate ethnicity, language and caste. There are three major components – the Indo–Aryans, Dravidians and Tribals. While there have been significant turnings to Christ among a number of groups, most such responses are from those outside the caste system (Tribals and Dalits) or from the lowest of the castes. The upper castes, the ruling and the middle classes remain largely unreached. Reaching them is a completely different challenge requiring a different approach.

d) **The Turkic bloc** stretches from southeast Europe to northeast Siberia across most of Central Asia. Population in Asia: 149 million with 209 peoples. Most Turkic peoples were under Communist rule for much of the 20th Century, but spiritual responsiveness in Central Asia and the Caucasus since the end of the Soviet Union dwarfs what has happened in Turkey itself. Major opportunities for witness:

i *Opportunities for expatriate Christian witness* are limited and must be carried out with great sensitivity and wisdom. There are many openings in a tentmaking capacity; several hundred, if not thousands, serve in this way already.

ii *Indigenous believers* have rapidly increased among the Turkic peoples (possibly over 60,000 in 2010), but from a baseline of nearly zero just a couple of decades ago, such totals are relatively modest. Among each of the Kyrgyz, Kazakh, Uzbek and Azerbaijani (especially in Iran) peoples, believers now number over 10,000. Yet the total number of evangelicals amounts only to around 0.04% of the Turkic population in Asia.

iii *Media input* has increased through Bible translation (IBT, UBS, others), literature, radio, satellite television (especially for Turks, Azeris and Central Asian peoples who understand Russian), the JESUS film and Christian materials on the Internet.

e) **The East Asian bloc.** Population in Asia: 1.5 billion. Major people clusters in Asia: Han Chinese (1.2billion); Japanese (127m); Korean (74m). There is now a large dynamic Christian presence among the Koreans and most Mainland and Overseas Chinese communities. The challenges remaining are the much less responsive Japanese, the Chinese Muslim Hui, the Manchu and the Chinese majority in Taiwan.

f) **The Tibetan/Himalayan bloc** of the Himalayas, Central Asia, northeast India, Myanmar and China. Population in Asia: 93 million in 762 peoples. Major people clusters: Burmese (32m); West China/Yi (21m); South Himalaya (7.2m); Tibetan (7.1m); Kuki-Chin-Naga (6.3m); Garo-Tripuri (4.9m) and Karen (4.8m). Many peoples in northeast India, Myanmar and Yunnan province in China have become Christian. The major challenges are:

i *The strongly Buddhist Tibetans,* most living in Chinese Tibet, Bhutan and north Nepal. Believers are numbered in hundreds only. Ministry opportunities are limited, but workers are nevertheless needed to witness to them.

ii *The West China/Yi peoples,* mostly found in Sichuan, Yunnan and Tibet. They predominantly remain practitioners of traditional ethnic religions, and their response to Christian witness (where it has occurred at all) is widely mixed.

iii *The South Himalayan peoples,* largely in India and Nepal and overwhelmingly Hindu and Buddhist in confession. The large majority are unreached.

iv *The long-resistant Burmese* have heard the gospel for two centuries. Few have turned from Buddhism to Christ, but the number of believers is beginning to increase. Many of the Tribal peoples (especially Chin, Karen and Kachin) have responded in much greater numbers.

g) **The Southeast Asian bloc.** Population in Asia: 216 million in 539 peoples. Major people clusters: Vietnamese (75m); Thai (54.6m); Mon-Khmer (25m); Zhuang (18.8m); Miao/Hmong (10.7m). Most are Buddhist or animist. Responses to the gospel are varied. Some groups have many Christians, such as among the Hmong/Montagnard peoples of Vietnam, the Khasi of India and the Wa of Myanmar and China. Also, a rapidly growing number of Christians are among the Vietnamese. The special challenges are for:

i *The Thai.* Nearly 200 years of freedom to proclaim the gospel has resulted in low response, weak churches and unchallenged, entrenched spiritism and Buddhism. The percent of ethnic Thai who follow Jesus has remained stagnant for some time.

ii *The many Tai, Yao-Mien and Miao/Hmong peoples* of China and Southeast Asia. In only a handful of the hundreds of peoples are there viable, growing churches.

iii *The Laotians.* The authoritarian regime has been particularly harsh in repressing Christians – most of whom are minority peoples and relatively few ethnic Lao.

h) *The Malay peoples.* The Malay family of peoples extends westward to Madagascar in Africa and to Polynesia in the Pacific. Population in Asia: 326 million in 910 peoples. Major clusters: Jawa (87.6m); Central Filipino (77.0m); Sunda-Betawi of Java (35.2m); Malay (23.9m); Madura (14.7m). The more outlying Filipinos, Pacific Islanders, eastern Indonesian peoples and the Malagasy are largely Christian, but the heartlands of Indonesia and Malaysia are largely Muslim. Christians are very few in most peoples. Of special challenge are:

i *Sumatra, Indonesia* – one of the world's largest islands with around 48 million people and a large Christian population only among the Batak and Nias peoples. The Aceh, Gorontalo, Lampung, Melayu, Minangkabau, Musi, Ogan and Pasemah clusters are largely Muslim and barely touched by the gospel.

ii *Java,* with 140 million people, is the most populous island in the world, but it has a significant Christian community only in cosmopolitan Jakarta and among certain sections of the Jawa. The Sunda and Madura peoples remain unreached and largely resistant to Christian ministry.

iii *The Malay* of Malaysia, Indonesia, Thailand and Singapore number 24 million and remain resolutely Muslim despite large Christian minorities in their midst.

iv *The Muslim peoples cluster of Mindanao, Sulawesi and the Moluccas.* They are among the most ardently Muslim peoples in the world, living alongside Christian populations from the same people clusters and at times engaged in brutal violence against them. They include the following clusters: Bugi–Makassar (9.7m, 28 peoples); Filipino Muslim (4.7m, 15 peoples); Toraja (1.6m, 20 peoples); Tukangbesi (1.0m, 18 peoples) and Gorontalo (1.0m, 5 peoples).

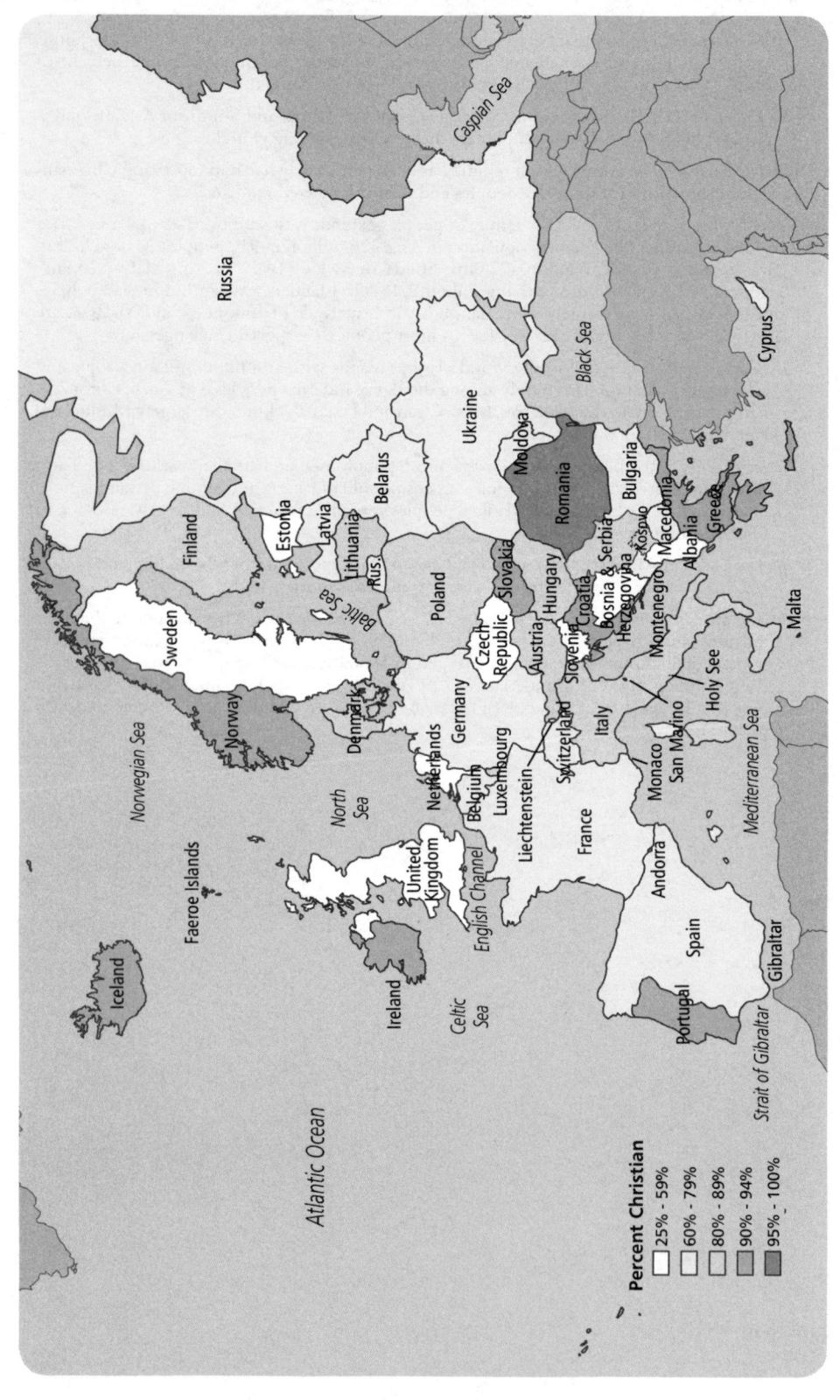

Country	2010 Pop (mill)	Main Rel	Chr	Evang (% of total pop)	Non-Chr	Unev	All (# of peoples)	UP	Chr
Albania	3.17	MX	30.5	0.5	69.5	22.1	13	2	8
Andorra	0.09	X	90.8	0.4	9.2	1.6	11	3	8
Austria	8.39	XN	82.6	0.5	17.4	3.0	47	7	36
Belarus	9.59	XN	70.5	1.3	29.5	1.0	28	5	17
Belgium	10.70	XN	62.7	1.2	37.3	2.9	38	10	21
Bosnia	3.76	MX	41.0	0.1	59.0	27.9	20	4	14
Bulgaria	7.50	XM	79.9	1.9	20.1	5.7	34	8	25
Croatia	4.41	X	92.0	0.4	8.0	1.4	32	3	27
Cyprus	0.88	XM	72.4	0.8	27.6	11.8	19	3	14
Czech Republic	10.41	NX	25.9	0.7	74.1	0.9	39	5	30
Denmark	5.48	X	85.3	3.5	14.7	2.8	32	8	21
Estonia	1.34	NX	45.3	4.9	54.7	1.7	37	6	25
Faeroe Islands	0.05	X	90.6	28.8	9.4	0.5	5	0	5
Finland	5.35	XN	83.8	12.1	16.3	1.0	35	7	24
France	62.64	XNM	61.1	1.0	38.9	5.2	101	33	56
Germany	82.06	XN	64.3	2.1	35.8	2.9	82	19	55
Gibraltar	0.03	X	84.8	2.9	15.2	4.8	7	2	4
Greece	11.18	X	91.5	0.4	8.5	2.2	46	10	32
Holy See	<0.01	X	100.0	2.5	0.0	0.0	2	0	2
Hungary	9.97	XN	88.0	2.8	12.0	1.2	23	2	20
Iceland	0.33	X	90.6	3.8	9.4	0.6	11	1	10
Ireland	4.59	X	91.7	1.6	8.3	1.0	24	3	19
Italy	60.10	XN	82.4	1.1	17.6	1.8	63	11	49
Latvia	2.24	XN	60.0	7.0	40.0	1.1	34	7	25
Liechtenstein	0.04	XN	79.2	0.5	20.8	3.9	8	1	7
Lithuania	3.26	XN	85.4	1.1	14.6	0.8	24	7	16
Luxembourg	0.49	XN	81.6	0.5	18.4	1.2	19	1	16
Macedonia	2.04	XM	65.5	0.2	34.5	10.5	25	6	17
Malta	0.41	X	96.8	1.3	3.2	0.5	11	2	9
Moldova	3.58	XN	73.4	3.7	26.6	1.4	31	8	21
Monaco	0.03	XN	84.8	1.2	15.2	1.5	15	1	13
Montenegro	0.63	XM	77.1	0.1	23.0	7.5	24	2	20
Netherlands	16.65	XN	46.6	4.3	53.5	4.0	60	12	36
Norway	4.86	X	91.1	8.4	8.9	2.6	56	14	36
Poland	38.04	XN	89.6	0.3	10.4	0.6	24	3	21
Portugal	10.73	X	91.4	3.0	5.6	0.8	31	4	24
Romania	21.19	X	97.0	5.4	3.0	0.4	29	6	22
Russia	140.37	XNM	66.9	1.2	33.1	7.9	163	77	57
San Marino	0.03	XN	88.8	<0.1	11.2	0.6	4	0	4
Serbia	7.77	XM	80.4	0.6	19.6	2.9	33	6	26
Slovakia	5.41	X	93.3	1.2	6.7	0.8	20	1	18
Slovenia	2.02	XN	54.2	0.1	45.8	1.5	19	1	17
Spain	45.45	XN	77.1	1.0	22.9	1.6	53	6	42
Sweden	9.29	XN	57.2	6.9	42.8	2.4	63	8	49
Switzerland	7.59	XN	75.8	4.4	24.2	2.6	40	7	29
Ukraine	45.43	XN	79.0	3.8	21.0	2.2	66	22	36
United Kingdom	62.13	XN	59.7	8.8	40.3	3.0	104	28	64
TOTAL	731.69		71.3	2.5	28.7	3.8	1705	382	1147

Europe

This includes all the countries of Europe and the entire Russian Federation (including all of Siberia, which is technically in Asia).

Geography 🌍

Area 22,978,500 sq km of which 74% is in the Russian Federation. This is 17% of the earth's surface.

Population		Ann Gr	Density
2010	732,758,546	0.1%	32/sq km
2020	732,951,550	0.0%	32/sq km
2030	723,373,060	-0.2%	31/sq km

Europe has 10.6% of the world's population. In 1900, the proportion was 25%.

Cities There are 61 cities of over 1 million people, 2 of which are over 10m. **Urbanites** 73%. **Pop under 15 yrs** 15.6%. **Life expectancy** 75.6 years.

Peoples 👪

Europe's ethnic diversity and long history of conflicts ultimately moulded much of the political framework of the nations of today. Major groupings of peoples:

Slavic 33.6%. Eastern Slav 23.7%; Western Slav 7.2%; Southern Slav 3.8%. 22 peoples, majority in 12 nations.
Germanic 15.4%. 23 peoples, majority in 6 central European countries.
Anglo–Celts 8.4%. 15 peoples, majority in UK and Ireland.
Italian 8.1%. 19 peoples.
French 7.2%. 14 peoples.
Spanish 5.4%. 9 peoples.
Romanian 3.1%. 5 peoples.
Scandinavian 2.6%. 6 peoples, majority in 5 countries.
Hungarian 1.6%.
Portuguese 1.6%.
Greek 1.6%. 5 peoples.
Finno–Ugric 1.3%. Northern Europe and Russian Arctic. 33 peoples.
Other European 4.0%. Including Albanian, Caucasus, Baltic, Basque, Armenian and other people clusters.
Non-European peoples 6.1%. 261 peoples. Including Turkic peoples (many in Russia) 2.2%; South Asian (including Romani/Gypsy) 1.2%; Arab World 1.0%, and every other Affinity Bloc.

Literacy 99%. **Indigenous languages** 269, 3.9% of the world's total. **Languages with Scriptures** 63Bi 31NT 61por 23w.i.p. There are 73 languages with translation needs.

Economy 📈

From 1500-1940, the world's dominant trading and industrial region. The destruction of two world wars in the 20th Century crippled development across the continent. In the east, Marxist economics miserably failed to achieve the Utopia it promised, but left behind polluted ecologies, rusting infrastructures and a damaged work ethic. In the west, progress continued – though hampered to a degree by some trade and industry restrictions and generous union and welfare arrangements – but was bolstered significantly by the growing clout of economic collaboration and union. The last decade was highlighted by the expansion of the EU to 27 states and 3 candidate countries in 2010, by the continued struggle of much of Eastern Europe to reduce the economic gap between themselves and the west and by the significant impact of the 2008-2009 financial crisis on many countries in Europe. The combined impact of affluence and a rapidly falling birthrate make Western Europe a magnet for millions from more impoverished lands of Eastern Europe, Africa and Asia.

Income/person $29,462 (62% of USA).

Politics ⚔

From the French Revolution in 1789 until the tearing down of the Berlin Wall in 1989, European political ideologies have had worldwide dominance. Humanism, secularism, socialism, Marxism, fascism, Nazism and amoral capitalism have all contributed to such evils as global wars, colonialism and oppression. To the surprise of many secular Europeans, religion and ethnocentrism remain important and major causes for political confrontations, but faith groups are also crucial to much of the social welfare work that occurs. Europe is enjoying a period of unprecedented peace, but tensions within and among European states as well as the growing issue of immigration continue to require watchfulness and wisdom.

Religion 🙏

After the Muslim invasions of the 8th Century, Christianity was suppressed or wiped out in the lands of the Middle East where the early Church first took root. For nearly 1,000 years, Europe was the last bastion of Christendom. The encircling Muslim lands – and Turkey's occupation of southeast Europe – effectively prevented any missionary outreach to Africa and Asia. The emergence of Europe as a colonial power in the 15th Century and the theological impetus of the Reformation in the 16th Century provided the platform for the Church to become a force for world evangelization. The last 250 years have been years of worldwide advance for the gospel but, conversely, decline in Europe. However, in many countries that have seen secularism and anti-religious social policies have their sway, an upswing of spirituality is also occurring.

Religions	Pop %	Population	Ann Gr
Christian	71.34	522,017,165	-0.3%
Non-religious	21.45	156,917,869	1.1%
Muslim	6.07	44,381,426	1.7%
Buddhist	0.35	2,539,523	1.9%
Jew	0.29	2,126,325	-1.3%
Other	0.19	1,403,686	1.4%
Hindu	0.14	1,054,915	2.3%
Ethnoreligionist	0.08	579,375	-0.4%
Sikh	0.07	498,474	2.1%
Baha'i	0.01	101,002	0.2%
Chinese	0.01	68,197	1.0%

The rise of secularism was temporarily slowed by the collapse of Communism, but as greater freedom of religious belief becomes commonplace, a practical atheism or fuzzy spirituality has become the predominant belief system among Europeans, with numbers far higher than the non-religious figures above would indicate.

Christians	Pop %	Affiliates	Ann Gr
Protestant	9.11	66,680,808	-0.1%
Independent	0.75	5,492,468	1.0%
Anglican	3.12	22,835,894	-0.8%
Catholic	33.51	245,192,242	-0.5%
Orthodox	24.14	176,662,319	-0.2%
Marginal	0.54	3,918,130	0.4%

	Pop %	Population	Ann Gr
Unaffiliated	1.37	10,051,449	-1.1%
Doubly affiliated	*-1.22*	*-8,934,950*	*1.3%*

The rate of decline of Christians is accelerating. Many of the Christians in the percentages above have no meaningful involvement with Church life. Regular church-goers would probably be under 10% of Europe's population.

TransBloc	Pop %	Population	Ann Gr
Evangelicals			
Evangelicals	2.50	18,342,106	1.1%
Renewalists			
Charismatics	1.81	13,156,939	2.1%
Pentecostals	0.81	5,930,096	2.1%

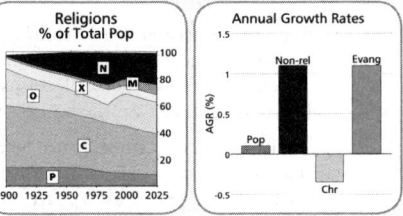

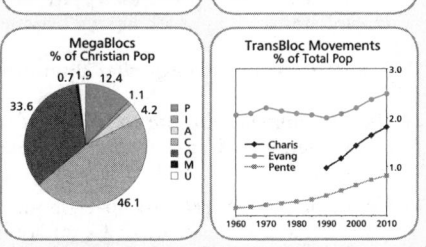

Answers to Prayer

1 **Europe has enjoyed a relatively stable two decades** – at least by its own tumultuous standards – almost unprecedented in its history. Most nations and peoples enjoy liberty and self-determination on a level not known for many generations. This stability has also assisted in the development of sophisticated and advanced economies that are more suited for the 21st Century than is true for most parts of the world.

2 **Religious freedom** in the former Communist world means the opportunity for Christians to practice their faith publicly and to enjoy fellowship and collaboration with their brethren from elsewhere in Europe and the world. It sees new expressions of Christian faith emerging in Central and Eastern Europe that engage the spiritual, social, relational and economic needs of many who feel lost in the vacuum of power and philosophy left by former Communist regimes.

3 **Positive and encouraging developments in the Church:**

a) *Evangelicals are growing in strength, confidence and a sense of identity* in most countries. This is demonstrated by the increase in an evangelical presence in mainline churches, which are otherwise declining, in the stability of conservative denominations and in the arrival of dynamic new evangelical and charismatic fellowships and networks onto the Church scene. All of this is modest compared to great gains in Asia and Africa but is light in an otherwise bleak European religious landscape.

b) *The impact of evangelical and charismatic movements* within the mainline confessions. The Church of England is significantly touched by renewal, by evangelical activism and especially by discipleship courses – the Alpha Course and Fresh Expressions being two of the most notable of these. Charismatic movements within Catholicism also touch many lives in Europe and beyond.

c) The emergence of patterns of church, worship, mission and social action which reflect spiritual authenticity, holism, social engagement, postmodernity and multiculturalism. These are especially strong among, but not limited to, young people.

d) The proliferation of new prayer movements such as 24/7 Prayer, the Global Day of Prayer, March for Jesus, boiler rooms, sustained prayer for the Muslim world during Ramadan as well as many national and local initiatives. Together, these mobilize unprecedented numbers of believers into corporate prayer.

e) The emergence of pan-European ministry, such as the European Evangelical Alliance (including initiatives like Mission-Net with its large European conferences), Hope for Europe, and Pro-Christ.

f) A growing ecumenism of the faithful that accepts theological and ecclesiological differences and recognizes the need for spiritual unity and cooperation in the face of increasing marginalization. Believers join across confessional, national and ethnic boundaries to maximize social, political and civic impact on the world's most secular continent.

g) The positive impact of immigrant believers in European countries. Their presence and growth has offered new spiritual passion and confidence in the gospel that many flagging European churches need. They have also demonstrated that Christianity is a global and dynamic force, and not a relic of a bygone era.

4 Socio-cultural trends that open doors for Christian witness:

a) Disillusionment with the emptiness of enforced secularism and hyper-modernity leads to a new interest in spirituality and the metaphysical. Presented rightly, Jesus is of great appeal to such seekers.

b) Upheaval and uncertainty in economics and politics, civic disintegration, violence and crime likewise cause many to ask questions about morals and meaning.

c) Militant atheism with strong anti-Christian, anti-religious rhetoric in some parts of the EU is strident and ugly enough in character to cause many to reconsider questions of faith and God.

d) The influx of non-Christian religions into Europe raises the issue of the religious identity of Europe as a civilization, both in history and for the future.

e) Christian immigration has brought the presence of dynamic and lively congregations into nearly every part of Europe. African, Caribbean, Latin American and Asian churches are bringing a new and much-needed confidence to the Church scene, reminding all that Christianity is a truly global faith.

5 **The edges of Europe – North Africa, the Middle East and Turkey** – are much more accessible through changes in travel, communication, trade and culture. These provide more opportunities for immigrants to gain access into Europe (where they ostensibly might encounter believers), and more so for active Christians to visit these places for tourism, study and business.

6 **The impact of media for Christian witness.** Radio and television had a powerful impact in post-Communist Eastern Europe. Today, digital and social media allow greater connectivity for Christians, greater potential audiences for Christian content and greater venues for actual interaction between believers and those interested to know more. Many decisions for Christ are made online, much discipleship and fellowship as well.

Hot Spots of Europe

Geopolitical peace and stability are neither universal nor assumed. The following issues warrant prayer:

1 **Russia has re-asserted its power** in recent years with growing confidence. It has reeled back into its sphere of influence several of the regions and countries that appeared to be drifting away, and has acted with its old ruthlessness toward restive and problematic peoples and nations. The previous 10-20 years witnessed a power vacuum left by departing Soviets which was filled by oligarchs, mafia and corrupt politicians – who massively enriched themselves and left a disillusioned and impoverished majority reminiscing after the stabilities and certainties of the old Communist regime. Despite declining populations and unresolved tensions, Russia remains a huge player in both the European and the global scenes. Pray for a government that is effective and uncorrupted, bringing economic betterment for its entire population and allowing greater human rights and freedoms.

2 **The Caucasus** remains a centre of unresolved tensions – with its ethnic and religious diversity, history of war and repression, and straddling the oil-rich but politically sensitive region, where many major powers (Russia, Turkey, Iran, the West) have conflicting areas of concern. In all likelihood, decades of unrest lie ahead. Its peoples represent one of the most difficult challenges for evangelization, with many ethnic groups still totally unreached.

3 **Restive ethnic enclaves within nations** remain potentially threatening to stability. These include Kosovo, the Basque and Catalonian regions in Spain, Northern Ireland, Trans-Dniester in Moldova, Abkhazia, South Ossetia, Northern Cyprus, the large Hungarian and Albanian minorities in several Central European and Balkan countries and, more recently, the large Muslim minority in France.

Trends to Watch

1 **Massive cultural shifts are occurring right across the continent** as Europe finally reaps the harvest sown from the Enlightenment through WWI up to today. Christianity was effectively replaced by humanist philosophies and nationalism. Europe can be regarded not only as postmodern, but also post-rational and certainly post-Christian. It is no accident that the regions of the world where relativism, individualism and existentialism reign supreme are also spiritually the bleakest. This has had several debilitating effects:

a) *Cynicism is now apparently the "-ism" of choice,* as the younger generation increasingly disengages from traditional civic responsibilities, such as politics and community service, and feels alienated from older generations. The elevation of the individual and instant gratification spur on hedonistic, nihilistic lifestyles that often end in dysfunction, emptiness, loneliness and despair.

b) *Moral uncertainty.* With transcendent authority undermined (and the authority of the Bible dismissed long ago), right and wrong are determined by consensual bureaucracy or individual inclination, leading to a morass of relativism.

c) *Societal disintegration.* Traditional values regarding the family, childbirth, marriage, sexuality, sanctity of life and community are being dismantled not just culturally, but also legally. These have severe repercussions in the areas of demographic decline, future economic burdens and psychological and social health. As traditional foundations of healthy societies are deconstructed in Europe, some suggest the term "sociocide", self-aware civilizational suicide, as an adequate description.

Pray that Europe's sophisticated societies might turn back from the brink, affirming and working out together the Judeo-Christian values that so profoundly shaped them and gave them the freedoms they now misplace.

2 **Freedom of public religious expression continues to erode,** largely due to insistent secularism. It is acceptable to have religious faith – as long as it remains a thoroughly private affair that is not inflicted upon the secular public. This manifests itself through:

a) *Prevalent secular values,* which regard Christian absolutes with intolerance. Practicing Christians are marginalized and caricatured in the media and popular culture. There is a growing acceptance of contempt for organized religion and the failure to recognize any positive or redemptive element therein. Christians, and evangelicals in particular, make soft targets for those who hate religion and insist on sidelining it from the public sphere.

b) *National governments and the EU* press on with legislation that attempts to safeguard freedoms and human rights, but in doing so virtually shackles the public practice of biblical faith. In a number of countries, a conciliatory approach to handling Islam, other faiths and even atheism is not equally extended to Christianity. Some regard this as a byproduct of pluralism; others see anti-Christian conspiracies. Historically, the less than stellar track record of most state churches regarding conflict, political meddling and moral purity, plus the effective withdrawal from the fray of Pietists and Anabaptists, places Christianity on a weak footing regarding its right to speak into nation-building in secular Europe.

c) **The Orthodox Church,** which in many countries of central and eastern Europe has equated national identity with specific religious affiliation. Minority religious groups are often discriminated against, harassed and subject to misleading propaganda. The Orthodox establishment's collusion with national governments to maintain religious hegemony often intensifies the difficulties evangelicals face in attempting to worship and minister.

Pray that believers might proclaim the good news regardless of the cost. Networks that represent the Church – such as the European Evangelical Alliance – need to negotiate the shifting currents of laws and culture with the shrewdness of serpents, while remaining as innocent as doves in living out pure and blameless lives that glorify Jesus and compel others to do the same.

3 **Political integration carries on** as the EU expands its borders and passes legislation to be applied from the Black Sea to the North Atlantic. Laws that influence the daily lives of hundreds of millions are being passed in Brussels. There is great potential strength in consistent laws and economic integration across the EU, but the removal of national sovereignty and civic and political authority from its member states carries inherent dangers. Pray that the EU might act with wisdom and insight that ensures the long-term stability of its member states while caring for vulnerable populations in Europe and around the world.

4 **Ethnic tensions and nationalism,** intensifying in some places, are increasingly relevant in others. Many countries live simultaneously with broad ethnic diversity and multiculturalism while also struggling with endemic racism. Beyond regional challenges of long-held ethnic hostilities and restive minority populations, tensions regarding increased immigration have increased as well. This applies to both people movements within Europe as well as immigration from other continents.

5 **Immigrants continue to flow into Europe,** both legally and illegally. Europe's ageing population and low fertility rates make immigration an economic necessity, but it is still feared and opposed by many. By extension, multiculturalism and pluralism are inevitably if not already ensconced. The population of immigrants from outside Europe probably now exceeds 30 million. Immigration accounts for the vast bulk of the continent's population growth, and literally millions more seek merely to get entry to Europe by any means in order to benefit from the generous social safety nets available. This can be seen as a threat to traditional European identity; it can also be regarded as an opportunity for the gospel as many come from countries where Christian witness is restricted. Pray for the Church to seize this opportunity for witness to the unevangelized.

6 **Criminal exploitation of immigration** was inevitable due to the sheer numbers involved and their great desire to gain entry into Europe. Many pay exorbitant sums for the services of traffickers; others try to sneak in by countless different methods. Hundreds of thousands are illegally trafficked against their will into the EU, most of them women to be used in the sex trade. The majority of these come from Eastern Europe, but in fact women and children from every region of the world are enslaved into prostitution. Others are forced to work in inhuman conditions for low wages, while still others are forced to marry against their will to secure legal access for their bogus spouses. Pray for governments, faith groups and communities to band together to end these evils and see justice done for the victims.

7 **The growth of Islam** through immigration and a higher birth rate is such that Islam has become the second religion of Europe. It is the largest religion in Albania, Bosnia and of other potential nations – Kosovo as well as several republics in the Russian Federation. Integration and extremism remain serious but unresolved issues. But higher birthrates, the continued immigration of Muslims, savvy lobbying for concessions to Muslim sensibilities and a fundamental inability to exist as a placid minority mean the rise of Islam's influence in Europe. Some Muslims seek to assimilate into a multicultural Europe on their own terms; others intend to dominate Europe's future and impose shari'a law. Alarm and fear characterize the response of many, including Christians. Yet Muslims form a possible bulwark against further secularization and atheism. Most are deeply moral people, and many are not far from the Kingdom of God. Pray that Christians might cooperate with our fellow monotheists when appropriate and extend the love of Jesus and power of the gospel at all times.

8 **Demographic realities make a return of religious faith** almost inevitable. Sub-replacement fertility among the atheist and secular elites is contrasted heavily with higher birth rates among those of religious faith. Add to this the highly religious character of most immigrant populations and, despite its own best efforts, 21st Century Europe will likely become more religious in character – unless it can subvert the majority of its current religionists and its future immigrants to buy into the secularist mindset. Europe's future looks to be a pluralistic one – not secular, not Christian, not Muslim, but an uneasy coexistence of the three.

The Church in Europe

1 **Massive decline in church attendance** and participation in religious life, with a lesser but still pronounced decline in religious self-identification, characterized the last generation in Europe. These trends began with the Enlightenment and peaked in the 20th Century with liberal church doctrine, the prevalence of secularism and a loss of confidence in the gospel.

2 **Most of the world's ecclesiastical leaders** are still based in Europe and hail from Europe. Catholics, Orthodox, Anglicans, Lutherans, Reformed Churches and many others still look to Europe for spiritual leadership. The Christian world remains profoundly influenced from Europe – ironic in that it is by far the most secular and least religious continent.

3 **Catholicism has been rocked by sex abuse scandals,** even more than by the Vatican's inflexible stance on contraception, the ordination of women and the obligatory celibacy of Roman Catholic priests. The inadequate and long-delayed response of the Vatican – and the apparent cover-ups – yield outrage and anger, disillusionment and disgust. Now the increasing antipathy toward Catholicism and, by extension, to all organized religion, heralds yet another sad chapter in the decline of faith as a redemptive force in European life. Catholicism is now fighting a rear-guard action, willing to accept significant numerical losses in order to preserve the integrity of its teaching. Pray that these tragic abuses might catalyze deep changes in Catholicism, bringing redemption to many.

4 **Moral confusion in the Protestant churches** is an outworking of the liberal theology that dominated theological thinking in all of Western Europe for most of the 19th and 20th Centuries. Mainline Protestant denominations were – and still are – spiritually crippled by the resulting loss of confidence in the Scriptures and in the uniqueness of the gospel. Evangelicals have done better, but still need to develop a mature theology that addresses the whole range of moral issues – relativism, human rights, gender issues, sexuality and the sanctity of life, to name a few – with authority, relevance and from a strong biblical basis. Biblical illiteracy is shockingly common considering the high levels of education and historic influence of Scripture in European society.

5 **A new generation of leaders must be raised up and trained.** This need has reached crisis proportions in much of the Catholic, Orthodox and mainline Protestant denominations. The rapid ageing of the faithful, the lack of young people and the shift in culture mean that, in most countries, very few are entering the priesthood. Leadership is much younger in the evangelical, Pentecostal and charismatic movements; the need, however, remains urgent – committed, culturally aware and biblically sound leaders who can pastor, teach, evangelize, speak prophetically into Church and society and plant churches in places where there are none. Bible colleges, seminaries, TEE courses, discipleship schools and other training programmes face a challenging task in producing such leadership.

6 **Emerging church movements have flourished** over the past decades, resulting in thousands of fellowships among younger people. Such movements are becoming more mature; they often operate from a missional platform and assist the traditional churches in reaching out to the younger generation more effectively. These dynamic networks often align more along the lines of subculture than of ethnicity or nationality; charismatic practices, worship music, creative prayer, a communal ethos and grassroots social engagement are their hallmarks. Pray for them to capture the right balance of wisdom, passion and biblical understanding. Pray that they might have a renewing and redemptive impact on the Church and society respectively.

7 **Evangelical churches face many challenges and opportunities.** Wrestle in prayer with the following points:

a) *The traditional roots of evangelicals in Europe* are in the Pietist, Puritan, Anabaptist and Free Churches, inheriting a tendency toward quietism and withdrawal from engagement with society. There has also been a prevalent inferiority complex and lack of confidence among evangelicals in many European countries, both East and West. Thank God that this is changing – evangelicals are more self-aware, more adaptive, better organized and interconnected and more prepared to stand up for themselves and for what they believe is right in societies that threaten to marginalize them and perpetrate injustice.

b) *Europe's spinning moral compass and crumbling societies* offer opportunities for evangelicals to have a powerful redemptive influence and to restore spiritual and ethical standards. These can be achieved by an active holism that engages with humility and passion the many needs in Europe today – community building, ecological responsibility, political involvement, economic and social justice, combating the structures of sin and so forth.

c) *Society regards the universal and spiritual claims of evangelicals with cynicism* and anticipates hypocrisy and failure. There is therefore a great need for holiness, humility, transparency, community, authenticity and intergenerational, interracial harmony. Should Christians successfully demonstrate these, they will discover great responsiveness and authority from many quarters – and probably greater persecution from others.

d) *Healthier relationships with Catholic and Orthodox Churches* throughout Europe must be cultivated. This is not merely to open doors for evangelicals to freely, but sensitively, function in the traditional strongholds of these confessions, but also to form a Christian bloc that stands together for biblical righteousness and faith and against the further secularization and Islamization of the continent.

e) *Spiritual warfare and the need to engage in it* must be recognized in the Church – Europe's great academic legacy and cultural sophistication can undermine the recognition that the struggle is not against flesh and blood.

8 **Immigration is a boon and a wake up call for the Church.** The unevangelized are being brought to its doorstep, but more importantly, Christian migrants are swelling the ranks of the faithful. This is true for Catholic, Protestant and Independent Christian groups.

a) *The influx of Christian migrants* from Africa, Asia, Latin America and the Caribbean provides a much-needed impetus to church life. Some claim that almost 50% of the EU's migrants are church members. The sheer numerical presence of Christians as a result of immigration has shored up a flagging Church.

b) *Christian immigrants' spiritual vibrancy, evangelistic passion and confidence in the gospel* are making an impact on religious life in Europe. Many Christian migrants come from nations where persecution is common and where other religions are the majority. Their bold witness and unswerving faith is much needed in the West. Praise God for such faith; pray that it might yield fruit and rub off onto the indigenous Christians of Europe.

c) *Cross-cultural mission to Europe is changing and growing:*

  i *Until now, immigrant churches* focused almost solely on evangelizing their own nationality or closely related ethnicities. But this is changing. More and more, there is a vision to reach out cross-culturally to their host nations. Pray for this vision to grow, and for wisdom in transplanting the Christian faith from Majority World cultures onto European soil.

  ii *Intentional missionary service from overseas to Europe* was once dominated by the US. This has been reduced, but new waves of African, Latin American and Asian missionaries are coming and serving in many ways. Pray for adequate preparation, for realistic expectations and for effective outreach that remains focused on its goal. It is easy to get sidetracked into ministering in responsive immigrant churches rather than continuing to till the hard soil of the spiritually needy European communities.

d) *Effective collaboration and partnership* between immigrant and indigenous churches in Europe are essential and hold immense promise and power. These can give grounding, training and resources to the newer churches and offer energy, spiritual vitality and links to burgeoning communities that the older churches need. Together, churches can offer a shining example of Christ's reconciling power. Immigrant churches are undeniably vital to Europe's future. Pray for God to raise up men and women who will pioneer this bridging of different cultures and backgrounds into one unified body that will glorify Jesus and win Europe back to the gospel.

The Unfinished Task in Europe

1 **Great swathes of Central and Western Europe are truly post-Christian** – where committed Christian remnants are small in number, low in confidence and marginalized. The battle against secularization and social irrelevance has been lost. What faith remains is confined to private belief. These regions are some of the most devoid of spiritual life in the world and urgently need to be re-evangelized.

2 **The heartlands of Protestantism** are now some of the most irreligious and secular on the entire continent. They include parts of Germany, Sweden and Denmark, the Low Countries, England, Wales and Scotland, France and the Czech Republic. Many of these areas have had little meaningful exposure to biblical Christianity for several generations. It is a sober indictment that such a great heritage of biblical Christianity has given way to pervasive godlessness.

3 **Many European countries and peoples** possess a strong and ancient Christian tradition, but very few evangelicals. These include Orthodox and Catholic heartlands such as Serbia, Poland, Montenegro, Macedonia, the Czech Republic, Austria, Greece, the Basque region, Belarus, Georgia, Russia and more. In 17 nations in Europe, evangelicals make up less than 1% of the population. And of these, five have a percentage of less than 0.25%. Pray for the planting of many vibrant, witnessing groups of believers in these lands.

4 **The younger generation** represents a new challenge; many have grown up in a context devoid of Christian witness or explicitly Christian values. Such beliefs are not seen as relevant or important for most people under age 25. Spirituality is in vogue, but this tends to incorporate New Age, esoterism, eastern religions or the occult and rarely translates into participation in church life. Yet the door remains open to a culturally and generationally relevant expression of the gospel; Christian movements that resonate with young people have emerged in the last decade and resulted in thousands of groups of believers meeting together, but much remains to be done.

5 **Unreached peoples.** Over 400 peoples live within Europe's countries; nearly 250 of them can be regarded as only partially evangelized at best and often are completely unevangelized. Of these, the majority are immigrant or refugee peoples for whom specialized outreach is needed, including:

a) *Muslim ethnic groups* from the Middle East, North Africa, sub-Saharan Africa and the Balkans (including Bosniaks, Albanians and Turks).

b) *The Jewish remnant* – reduced in many countries to a mere fragment of their former numbers during the Holocaust and through emigration to Israel, but still needing to be brought to the Messiah.

c) *The many ethnic minorities of the Russian Federation* – in the Caucasus, Siberia, the Urals and the Arctic.

d) *The Chinese,* who number over one million in Europe – a number climbing steadily, and almost doubled if Siberia and the Russian Far East are included. While in several parts of the UK and Germany there are thriving congregations, in most of Europe they are unreached.

e) *Asians from South and Southeast Asia*, especially in Western Europe, who are from unevangelized peoples in their home countries and who remain equally isolated from Christians in their host nations.

Pray also for the formation of missional networks that seek to effectively witness to these groups – the Evangelical Alliances of Europe and Ethne Europe are two such examples. It is possible that there are more non-Europeans engaged in reaching the continent's unreached than Europeans; pray that European believers would gain a greater burden for the lost on their own doorstep.

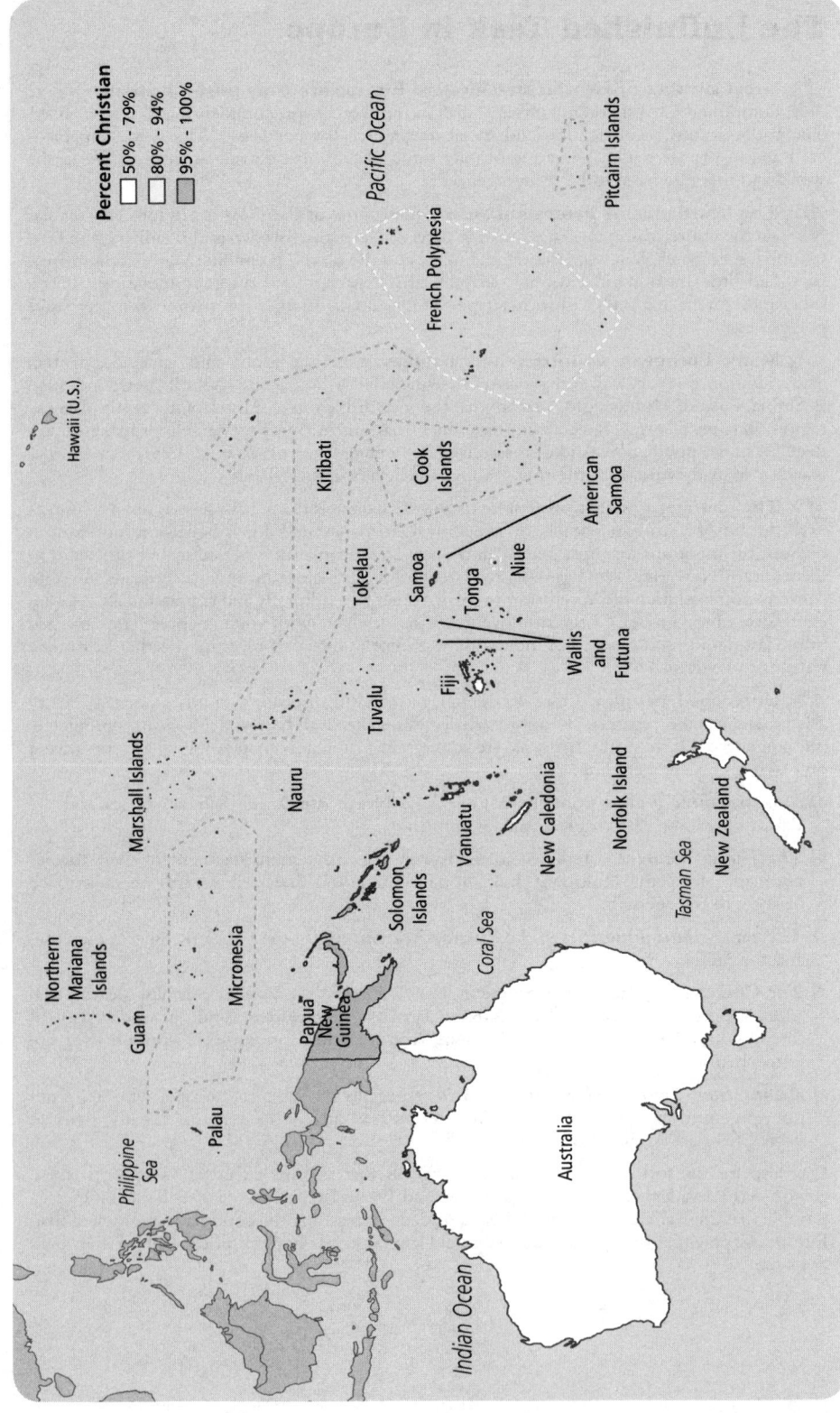

Percent Christian

- 50% - 79%
- 80% - 94%
- 95% - 100%

Country	2010 Pop (mill)	Main Rel	Chr	Evang (% of total pop)	Non-Chr	Unev	All (# of peoples)	UP	Chr
American Samoa	0.07	X	95.1	21.3	4.9	0.6	10	1	9
Australia	21.51	XN	69.5	14.5	30.5	2.9	142	10	92
Christmas Island	<0.01	BMXCh	18.2	3.0	81.8	n/a	n/a	n/a	n/a
Cocos (Keeling) Islands	<0.01	MX	19.4	1.3	80.6	n/a	n/a	n/a	n/a
Cook Islands	0.02	X	96.2	12.6	3.8	0.4	9	0	9
Micronesia (FSM)	0.11	X	96.6	24.3	3.4	0.8	24	1	22
Fiji	0.85	XH	65.0	25.2	35.0	14.5	35	4	26
French Polynesia	0.27	X	92.2	7.2	7.8	0.5	16	0	14
Guam	0.18	X	96.7	14.2	3.3	1.2	13	1	10
Kiribati	0.10	X	98.5	7.2	1.5	0.5	7	0	6
Marshall Islands	0.06	X	97.1	44.5	2.9	0.5	7	1	5
Nauru	0.01	X	91.5	12.1	8.5	3.6	9	0	8
New Caledonia	0.25	XN	80.6	7.0	19.4	1.5	47	0	45
New Zealand	4.30	XN	53.2	18.2	46.8	2.1	62	5	45
Niue	<0.01	X	94.9	8.0	5.1	0.6	5	0	3
Norfolk Island	<0.01	XN	68.6	22.7	31.4	n/a	n/a	n/a	n/a
Northern Mariana Islands	0.09	X	85.2	12.7	14.8	1.2	12	0	10
Palau	0.02	X	95.9	23.9	4.1	0.5	7	0	7
Papua New Guinea	6.89	X	95.8	25.7	4.2	1.4	879	3	747
Pitcairn Islands	<0.01	X	100.0	n/a	0.0	0.0	n/a	n/a	n/a
Samoa	0.18	X	96.6	18.0	3.4	0.5	8	0	8
Solomon Islands	0.54	X	95.8	33.3	4.2	0.5	71	0	70
Tokelau Islands	<0.01	X	100.0	3.4	0.0	0.5	n/a	n/a	n/a
Tonga	0.10	X	95.8	15.5	4.2	0.5	10	0	9
Tuvalu	0.01	X	97.7	17.8	2.3	0.5	6	0	6
Vanuatu	0.25	X	94.1	45.9	5.9	1.2	112	0	102
Wallis & Futuna Islands	0.02	X	99.0	0.9	1.0	0.5	4	0	4
TOTAL	35.84		74.0	17.8	26.0	2.6	1495	26	1257

Pacific

Geography 🌐

Area 8,515,800 sq km constituting 6.3% of the world's land surface. There are 25,000 islands scattered over 88 million sq km of ocean; this is larger than the combined areas of Africa, Asia and Europe. It comprises one continent (Australia), two large land masses (New Zealand and Papua New Guinea [PNG]) and 26 smaller island states and territories. The smallest territories are grouped with related states in the country section: Christmas Is, Cocos Is, Norfolk Is with Australia; Johnston Is, Midway Is, Wake Is with Guam; Niue, Pitcairn Is and Tokelau with Cook Islands.

Population		Ann Gr	Density
2010	35,838,336	1.3%	4/sq km
2020	40,329,252	1.1%	4/sq km
2030	44,571,610	1.0%	5/sq km

The Pacific has 0.5% of the world's population.

Cities There are 6 cities of over 1 million people – 5 in Australia, 1 in New Zealand. **Urbanites** 70%. **Pop under 15 yrs** 21.3%. **Life expectancy** 76.3 years.

Peoples 👪

1,294 ethnolinguistic peoples, two-thirds of which are found on PNG. European-descended peoples in Australia and New Zealand dominate both the population and the overall demographic trends of the Pacific. If calculated without these groups, the Pacific region would be constituted of 77% Pacific Islanders and 20% Asians.

European 63.8%. 45 peoples. The majority in Australia and New Zealand, where most are of British descent but increasingly diverse in origin. Large French minority in New Caledonia.

Pacific Islanders 28.2%. 1,201 peoples.

New Guinean 17.4%. 870 peoples. PNG contains the highest concentration of ethnicities and languages in the world. These and the following three clusters make up the majority of the Melanesian ("black islands") peoples.

Aborigine 1.6%. Native peoples of Australia. 74 peoples.

Fijian 1.2%. 12 peoples.

Solomons 1.2%. 58 peoples.

Polynesian 4.3% (Polynesia means "many islands"). 33 peoples. The majority of indigenous inhabitants of New Zealand and islands of the central Pacific. Polynesians are one of the most remarkable seafaring races in the world.

Micronesian 1.2% (Micronesia means "small islands"). 24 peoples. The majority in island groups on, or north of, the equator.

Asian 7.6%. 44 peoples. South Asian majority in Fiji, and smaller communities in Australia and New Zealand.

Chinese communities expanding in many territories throughout the region. Filipino, Vietnamese, Arab, Persian, Korean also increasing, especially in Australia and New Zealand.

Other 0.4%.

Literacy 90%. **All languages** 1,250 being 18.1% of world's total. **Languages with Scriptures** 37Bi 252NT 185por 265w.i.p. There are 414 languages in which Bible translation work may still be needed, most of these languages spoken by a very small number of people.

Economy 📊

Australia and New Zealand are "first world" countries with some of the world's highest standards of living, but within both are great and increasing divides of wealth and poverty. All other states are significantly less affluent. Small populations, constant emigration of many of the brightest and best people, limited resources and vast distances between island states hold back development of most islands. Most Pacific cultures have traditionally existed on subsistence economies. Now, Pacific Rim nations have the greatest influence – in competition with Australia/NZ, the EU and the USA – for the natural resources, the geographic space (military bases, satellites/telecommunications, fishing rights) and the tiny islands' votes in the decision making of world governing bodies.

Income/person $32,457 (68% of USA), but this figure is skewed by the stronger economies of Australia and NZ compared to the rest of the region.

Politics ☒

Most islands are independent or self-governed, with a few exceptions. Good governance is an issue as traditional forms of leadership are replaced by quasi-democratic governments. In some cases, intervention and oversight of Australia and New Zealand have been welcomed and beneficial (PNG, Bougainville, Solomon Islands), but others have rejected such overtures (Fiji). China, Japan and Taiwan are increasingly influential politically due to higher economic investments. Many of the younger generation are frustrated with and resentful of foreign economic and political control, and they see the older generation as having sold out to these corrupting influences. There is growing interest in developing regional cooperation to protect the island economies and cultures from abuse by Pacific Rim nations.

Religion 🏝

Commitment to participation in church life has been eroded by secularism, nominalism and changing patterns of Christian expression. Australia and NZ have low fertility rates among their primarily Christian peoples, which accounts for part of the relative decline. The rest of the Pacific, with the exception of Fiji, has a large Christian majority with higher fertility rates.

Mormonism grew rapidly among Polynesians in the 20th Century exposing the inadequate discipling of the Churches.

Religions	Pop %	Population	Ann Gr
Christian	74.02	26,526,812	0.9%
Non-religious	19.11	6,848,764	2.2%
Muslim	1.82	651,939	4.2%
Buddhist	1.77	635,322	5.0%
Hindu	1.48	528,806	2.1%
Ethnoreligionist	0.88	316,552	2.8%
Jew	0.33	119,081	1.7%
Chinese	0.21	75,197	1.1%
Baha'i	0.16	57,277	2.1%
Sikh	0.11	39,375	4.1%
Other	0.11	39,213	5.5%

Christians	Pop %	Affiliates	Ann Gr
Protestant	22.79	8,166,446	0.8%
Independent	2.69	964,160	3.0%
Anglican	13.13	4,707,021	-0.3%
Catholic	24.00	8,601,688	0.8%
Orthodox	2.51	898,856	1.5%
Marginal	2.12	758,414	1.5%
Unaffiliated	9.90	3,577,962	0.2%
Doubly affiliated	*-3.19*	*-1,143,896*	*-4.5%*

TransBloc	Pop %	Population	Ann Gr
Evangelicals			
Evangelicals	17.81	6,382,078	1.66%
Renewalists			
Charismatics	11.76	4,213,545	3.15%
Pentecostals	4.46	1,597,757	3.04%

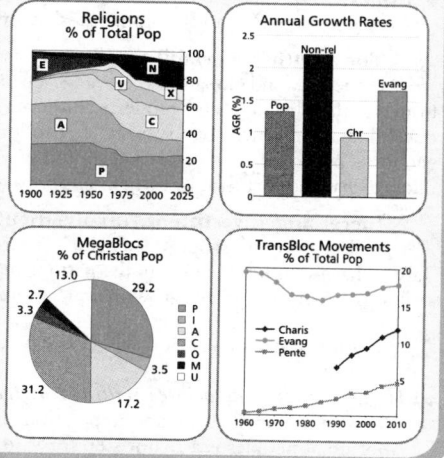

Answers to Prayer

1 **The strength of Christianity in the Pacific.** The Pacific was one of the first areas to be evangelized in the modern Protestant missionary era. By the end of the 19th Century, most of the Pacific region had become Christian through the sacrificial labours of early LMS, Methodist, Anglican and Pacific Islander missionaries. Missionary casualties were high through disease, violent death and cannibalism, but great people movements brought whole peoples and islands to Christianity.

2 **Renewal of the Pacific Islands vision for mission and prayer.** The South Pacific Prayer Assembly and Deep Sea Canoe Movement are recapturing this great 19th Century heritage. In recent years, New Zealand has had a good record in sending out missionaries. Other nations such as Fiji and PNG are seeing more significant sending movements occur.

Hot Spots in the Pacific

1 **Unrest and violence** have occurred in several locations for ethnic, economic, political and socio-cultural reasons. Fiji – with its split between indigenous Fijians and the large ethnic Indian population and its history of coups – remains the most obvious example. But Bougainville, other parts of PNG and the Solomon Islands have seen upheaval in the not too distant past. Tribalized culture, limited resources and some resentment against the influence of Western and Asian powers mean that a number of islands could witness similar kinds of upheaval in the near future.

2 **The younger generation** in many Pacific Island nations feel disenfranchised and betrayed by their forebears. They often have little opportunity for meaningful employment or education. Emigration, restlessness, frustration, mischief and even organized crime are the result. In some countries, those under age 25 comprise up to 40% of the population.

Trends to Watch

1 **A large-scale demographic shift** is occurring across the region. Migration is happening on an unprecedented scale. Many Pacific Island ethnicities have a larger population in diaspora than in their traditional homeland. The main contributing factors are:

a) *Demographic.* As Australia and New Zealand deal with ageing populations and low fertility rates (at least among the majority Caucasian population), the Pacific Islands have high fertility rates and a burgeoning young population.

b) *Economic.* Vast disparity between the haves and have-nots, lack of opportunity in the Pacific Islands and the need to fill current and future employment gaps in wealthy nations (especially Australia/New Zealand) pull many Islanders away from their traditional homelands.

2 **The health and viability of many isolated island communities** are threatened by modernity and globalization, large-scale unemployment, heavy dependence on aid, isolation from health, education and modern consumer goods as well as prohibitive costs of inter-island travel. The replacement of a subsistence economy, driven by agriculture and fishing, with a cash economy pushes many men abroad to find work, generates a brain (and muscle) drain and introduces a changed diet that, in turn, intensifies already existing health issues.

3 **Increasing investment, involvement and immigration** from Pacific Rim nations will profoundly shape the Pacific's future. China in particular but also Japan, Korea and Taiwan have significant stakes in the natural, material and human resources of the Pacific islands, stakes that will most likely grow in scale and influence.

4 **Ethnic harmony** is and will continue to be a major issue:

a) *Historic wrongs associated with the arrival of Europeans are being faced.* Apologies and efforts at reconciliation and reparation are occurring; Australia's formal apology to its Aboriginal peoples is a major step forward. Christians must be in the forefront in doing all possible to achieve fair reconciliations and to honour cultural distinctives.

b) *Relations among various groups can be tense and uncertain.* Flashpoints in Australia and Fiji reveal cultural and religious gulfs between the newer immigrant communities and the majority and indigenes. Relations among various Pacific Island ethnicities have not necessarily been traditionally harmonious, as the bloody pre-Christian history of the region illustrates.

The Church in the Pacific

1 **The shape of Christianity in the Pacific** is rapidly and radically changing. There are several contributing factors:

a) *Secularism and multiculturalism* are rising; these undermine the strong Christian heritage of these nations and relegate Christianity to a mere place at the table of competing belief systems. The arrival of a more assertive atheism, Mormonism, Islamism, Baha'i-ism and Buddhism all rattle the religious status quo. Confidence in the veracity of the gospel cannot help but be threatened.

b) *The decline of traditional forms of Christianity.* The denominations that had such a great impact in the Pacific Islands and the traditionally strong denominations in Australia and New Zealand are suffering in numbers and in vitality. Pentecostal and charismatic groups are mostly growing in their stead.

c) *The decaying interest to participate in organized Christianity.* There is a prevalent indifference to spiritual things among the majority of unbelievers, and the Church is increasingly a marginal concern for the younger generation of Kiwis and Aussies, even for those who believe in and follow Jesus. Rather than inviting radical change, most churches seek to maintain a level of satisfaction among their middle class and middle-aged constituency, by whom they are currently steered.

d) *The rapidly changing ethnic and age composition of the Church.* Immigration brings many young Pacific Islanders and other migrants into churches of the two dominant nations of the region. These changes have vast implications not just for the future of Christianity, but also for the future of these countries. The Church must retool itself in order to integrate and meet the needs of this growing component of the body of Christ. This will impact generational focus, church finance, church culture, worship and fellowship patterns, leadership styles and many other issues as well.

2 **Disciple-making is the key to the Pacific,** a region that remains majority Christian. It was critical to past failings and will be crucial to future challenges. The inability to move beyond Christianization, and into making mature believers, is a large part of the Church's decline in Australia and New Zealand and the reason for the vulnerability of the Church in the Pacific Islands. Pray for a mentality in the Church that places priority and focus rightly on shaping disciples.

3 **The disparity in culture, class and income** between most churches in New Zealand and Australia and most immigrant peoples is a barrier to effective ministry. If churches want to be relevant and have an impact on these burgeoning populations and on the future of the Pacific region, they must step out of their comfort zones and learn to minister cross-culturally and in contexts of economic need. For social and economic justice to truly be rooted in Pacific society, the Church must be at the heart of the process.

4 **The need to revive a vision for evangelical cooperation and mission.** Vast geographical distances and the lack of unity and shared identity – especially between the many Pacific islands and the dominant Australia/New Zealand – are challenges. Yet determination still exists to foster unity and prophetic vision: The Evangelical Fellowship of the South Pacific, the Deep Sea Canoe Movement and, perhaps most notably, the South Pacific Prayer Assembly serve to see God move in new and effective ways in the Pacific.

5 **The Church has thus far failed to meet the mission challenge** on its own soil. The mission opportunities afforded by immigration and a multicultural society – and the need to train church and mission leaders in effective evangelism, church planting and discipleship skills – remain largely unaddressed. Pray for an awakening in the Church and in training infrastructures that can meet the growing challenge.

6 **The rapid growth of Mormonism in Polynesia,** winning many nominal Protestants, is a rebuke to the traditional churches. Polynesia is rapidly becoming Mormon – especially Tonga and American Samoa, which are over 20% Mormon, and Samoa and French Polynesia, which are over 10% Mormon.

7 **Completing the task of world evangelization in the Pacific.**

a) There are very few unevangelized tribal peoples; some exist in New Guinea's interior. Many more are only superficially evangelized and need more thorough ministry.

b) The few evangelical believers in parts of New Caledonia, French Polynesia and on many of the nominally Christian island groups. Some areas need to be re-evangelized.

c) The Indians of Fiji are the largest unreached people in the Pacific. Pray for effective evangelization of these Muslims and Hindus.

d) The Chinese are increasing through immigration. In some islands, this is for trade or low-paid labour; in Australia and New Zealand, it is as professionals and students. Many remain unevangelized, despite notable responsiveness to appropriate outreach.

e) International students are more concentrated in Australia and New Zealand than in just about anywhere else in the world. They are often very open to the gospel. Churches need to acquire a vision for this highly strategic group of future leaders in their homelands, which are usually very restrictive in terms of access for Christian mission.

f) Other immigrant groups, especially to Australia and New Zealand. This includes Arabs, Iranians, Malays and Indonesians, Europeans, Somalis as well as East and Southeast Asian peoples. In most cases, they will have greater opportunity for exposure to the good news in their new lands than in their countries of origin.

g) Translation of Scripture. There remain hundreds of languages without the Bible. Many of them may need translators.

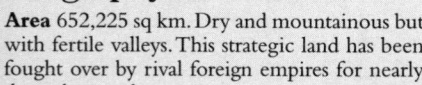

Afghanistan

Islamic Republic of Afghanistan

Asia

Geography

Area 652,225 sq km. Dry and mountainous but with fertile valleys. This strategic land has been fought over by rival foreign empires for nearly three thousand years.

Population		Ann Gr	Density
2010	29,117,489	3.51%	45/sq km
2020	39,584,751	2.94%	61/sq km
2030	50,648,930	2.41%	78/sq km

No comprehensive census or careful ethnic survey has been made for decades; a census is planned for 2010. Due to years of conflict, Afghan refugees are approximately 2 million in Iran, 2 million in Pakistan and smaller numbers around the world. As many as 4.5 million have returned to Afghanistan since 2001.

Capital Kabul 3,731,312. The civil war extensively damaged the capital and many villages. Significant reconstruction has been done in the capital. **Other cities** Kandahar 475,000; Mazar-e-Sharif 336,000. **Urbanites** 24.8%. **Pop under 15 yrs** 46%. **Life expectancy** 43.6 yrs.

Peoples

Iranian–Median 76.2%. 31 peoples. Largest: Pashtun (Pathan) 42.7%; Tajik 26.2%; Aimaq(6) 5.0%; Baloch 1.2%.
Turkic 21.5%. 9 peoples. Hazara 12.9%; Uzbek 6.4%; Turkmen 2.1%.
South Asian 2.1%. 28 peoples, all smaller in numbers. Brahui 0.8%.
Other 0.2%.
These numbers do not include the large number of military personnel nor the expatriate NGO workers in the country.
Literacy 28.1% (around 15% for women).
Official languages Pashtu (used by 50% of population), Dari (Afghan Persian, used by 70%). **All languages** 41. **Indigenous languages** 38. **Languages with Scriptures** 1Bi 1NT 7por.

Economy

Shattered by decades of war. The countryside was bombed and still contains over 1 million landmines and other undetonated ordnances. The ongoing conflict destroyed much of the infrastructure, including housing and irrigation; rebuilding infrastructure and developing public sector buildings are focal points of redevelopment. Extensive gas and mineral deposits offer potentially lucrative exports. Investment of extensive foreign aid and millions of former refugees returning have generated an influx of funds and entrepreneurial initiative. The conflict with armed opposition groups, including the Taliban, continues to stunt recovery and growth. Despite efforts to eradicate its cultivation, as much as one-third of the nation's GDP has come from the production of opium, although this is decreasing.
HDI Rank 181st/182. **Public debt** 76% of GDP.
Income/person $416 (1% of USA).

Politics

The monarchy was overthrown in 1973. The republican government ended in a Marxist coup in 1978. Then followed an invasion by the USSR. Ten years of war ensued, culminating in the withdrawal of the Soviet forces in 1988–89. Civil war among ethnic, political and religious factions continued, with enormous damage and large numbers of casualties. The extreme Islamist (mainly) Pashtun Taliban gained control of over 90% of the country by 2001. The post-9/11 invasion by US-led forces allied with anti-Taliban Afghan factions has attempted to oust Al Qaeda and the Taliban. A new democratic government structure and a new constitution were established 2002–2004. Despite the increasing presence of NATO troops, the Taliban continue to operate and resist the foreign military presence. The re-election of the president in 2009 was widely recognized as tainted; Afghanistan still struggles with corruption.

Religion

The Taliban's takeover of the country imposed a deviant expression of strict Wahhabist Islam, particularly devastating for the lot of women in society. Since the entry of foreign military forces and the establishment of the Loya Jirga, the acceptable interpretations of Islam have been less strict, and while there is limited freedom to practice other religions (such as Shi'a Islam, Sikhism and Hinduism), there appears to be no freedom to propagate another faith or to convert from Islam. Shi'a Muslims are 20% of the population.

Religions	Pop %	Population	Ann Gr
Muslim	99.85	29,074,395	3.5%
Non-religious	0.07	20,382	15.8%
Christian	0.05	<15,000	14.6%
Hindu	0.01	<3,000	3.5%
Other	0.01	<3,000	-9.9%
Sikh	0.01	<2,500	1.1%

The "high" number of Christians is due to the increased population of resident foreigners. Foreign military have not been counted.

Answers to Prayer

1 **The ousting of the Taliban** from power by the alliance of US-led Western troops and Afghan warlords opposed to the Taliban has come at a great cost. Following the overthrow of the Taliban, the Afghan people, particularly women, have gained new freedoms and opportunities. These still occur largely within and are limited by the framework of traditional Afghan culture.

2 **The increase of Afghan believers** is impossible to document, yet undeniable. At least several hundred Afghans now follow Christ, when 20 years ago perhaps a few dozen were believers.

3 **Christian media** have been developed in many formats – audio/MP3, mobile phone memory, radio, video, literature and the Internet – for evangelism and discipleship. This is an area of real growth and excitement.

Challenges for Prayer

1 **The present political situation** – a foreign military working with a national government that is trying to be both progressive and conservative – is far from ideal, but it is an improvement from the tyranny of the Taliban. The Taliban imposed a harsh brand of Islam on the nation and continue to be a threat to national stability and security. The power of the warlords and tribal leaders is greater than that of the government forces or the US military; currently, most of them side with the NATO/Loya Jirga entente. Pray that the Afghan government might serve and govern with humility and wisdom. Pray that the people of Afghanistan may experience genuine freedom and an improved quality of life. Pray also that attempts by insurgents and warlords to destabilize the country might be thwarted and that a settlement might be negotiated.

2 **The upheaval of the last 30 years** reduced the country to ruin and destitution. The Soviets (1979-89), the Mujahedeen (1992-96) and the Taliban (1996-2001) all perpetuated different problems and failed to build up the nation. Over one million died and an estimated four million children were orphaned. Though the country still suffers from conflict, progress has been made in those areas where there is peace. The suffering takes many forms; Afghans perceive poverty and lack of security to be the greatest problems. Pray for practical, timely and sustainable solutions to each of these:

a) *Continued threat of violence.* The Taliban are very active and often operate from civilian buildings or in civilian guise. Hundreds of thousands of land mines and other undetonated ordnance still litter the country.

b) *Health risks.* Afghanistan is the world's most dangerous place for a child to be born. Infant mortality rate is among the world's highest. Many causes of death are preventable (diarrhoea, cholera, dysentery and pneumonia), but lack of health care and clean water (78% do not have regular access to clean water) causes many deaths. Refusal to allow women to receive medical care from men causes high maternal mortality rates.

c) *The disabled.* There are an estimated one million people suffering with disabilities, mostly with damaged or destroyed limbs as a result of war. In remote areas, many are still being injured by landmines. This is one of the world's highest proportions of disabled people, in a nation with little provision for their care or rehabilitation.

d) Poverty and living standards. Most Afghans live in poverty. There is little employment. Many who fight for the Taliban do so largely to collect the wage offered. Some 80% of the population seek to exist by subsistence farming, but access to water is a problem, especially since almost all irrigation was destroyed by war. Fewer than 15% of homes have access to electricity. Yet employment opportunities are increasing, and the economy is improving in the stable areas.

e) Drugs are a scourge on the nation, and indeed the world, as Afghanistan grows 90% of the world's opium-producing poppies.

> i *Poppy cultivation* has long been the main internal source of income, peaking at one-third of the GDP (a proportion now greatly reduced due to the massive influx of aid). This lucrative harvest heavily financed the Taliban. Failure to find a sustainable alternative crop drives impoverished farmers to continue, despite its prohibition in Islam. Pray for the success and feasibility of alternative agricultural projects.
>
> ii *Heroin and opium addicts* abound in Afghanistan (up to one million drug users) and globally. Every year, more Westerners and Russians die from heroin and opium overdoses than there were fatalities during all the years of Soviet and then NATO occupation.

3 **Recovery and rebuilding** are occurring in many sectors of society. Among nationals, there is a real mix of optimism and pessimism as to whether genuine improvements can be made. Pray for the following issues:

a) Billions of dollars in foreign aid are being poured into the country – especially by the NATO countries, China and India. Over 1,500 NGOs are registered – only 350 of them are foreign. Inefficiency and corruption are very real threats, but the recent implementation of tighter government regulations has forced NGOs to be transparent and efficient with their funds and activities.

b) A new generation of Afghans with a different attitude. Sixty percent of Afghans are under the age of 20 and have known nothing but war; they long for opportunities in education and employment and some freedom of choice. Up to 4.5 million Afghans have returned after fleeing the country when it was under Taliban control. Many of them bring financial resources, international connections and an entrepreneurial spirit to help establish new businesses.

c) National security. Establishing well-trained, disciplined, Afghan-national military and police forces is vital. These institutions must build a reserve of trust with the people, but are themselves prone to corruption and infiltration by Taliban sympathizers.

d) Physical infrastructure was devastated by nearly 30 years of war. The reconstruction of roads, medical facilities, schools and other public service buildings is crucial for the nation's future.

e) Human development is equally vital. The infant mortality rate, although very high, is dropping rapidly as health services improve. A record number of children are enrolled in school. Micro-enterprise initiatives are giving many opportunities to start small businesses, earn a respectable living and provide for others.

f) Christian involvement in aid and development. Since 1966, a number of Christian relief and development agencies have ministered to the blind, maimed, sick, deprived, illiterate and needy, in the name and Spirit of the Lord Jesus. Many Christians – most of them in humanitarian capacities – work to serve the people of Afghanistan. Practical demonstrations of Christian care and love impress many Afghans, breaking down prejudices and preparing hearts for the gospel. In addition to the tragedies of lives lost, enforced reductions of personnel and even withdrawal of entire organizations from the country caused a great loss of many effective workers. Pray for both courage in the face of adversity and wisdom to know how best to demonstrate Christ's love to the Afghan people.

4 **Afghanistan is one of the least reached countries in the world.** There are 48,000 mosques but not a single church building. Pray for the 70 unreached peoples of this land, especially for the following groups:

a) Pashtuns. They number over 40% of the Afghan population and are politically dominant. Pashtun on both sides of the Afghanistan-Pakistan border comprise what has been called the largest Muslim tribal society in the world – as many as 46 million people in over 30 major sub-tribes. Christians among them remain few, though urban, educated Pashtuns in exile have shown some response. Pray that multitudes might be released from fear, prejudice, the strongholds of Islam and pride in *pashtunwali* (their tribal code of honour); there is evidence of an intense spiritual battle for breakthrough among this people.

b) Tajiks in the northeast. Speaking Dari (a form of Persian), they are closely related to the Pashtuns. Some Tajik groups were among the last people to resist the Taliban, yet they remain over 99% Muslim. Pray for their spiritual freedom.

c) Hazaras, Shi'a Muslims of Mongol descent. Being a Shi'a group, they have been severely persecuted through the years and were even massacred by the Sunni Taliban. They have demonstrated greater openness to the gospel in recent years.

d) Uzbeks and Turkmen of the north have shown encouraging responsiveness as refugees in other lands, but as in their namesake countries, only a tiny proportion are believers.

e) The six Aimaq tribes of the west, of nomadic background, and the Baloch and Brahui of the south. There are very few if any believers from these isolated groups.

f) The nine Nuristani tribal groups in the mountains north and east of Kabul. They speak five languages and 16 dialects; many of these are mutually unintelligible.

g) The five Ismaili Muslim Pamir people groups and the Kyrgyz living in the far northeast of Afghanistan, along the high Pamir Mountain range. These people groups are isolated in small valleys, far from good roads. Ismaili Muslims tend to be more open to the good news, and a small community of believers was birthed some years ago. Praise God for good distribution of gospel audio materials among the Kyrgyz.

h) The numerous Dardic people groups near the volatile border region with Pakistan. The largest of these is the Pashai, numbering in the hundreds of thousands of people.

i) The nomadic Gujar and Jugi/Kuchi/Ghorbat people groups.

5 **The Church in Afghanistan** remains almost entirely underground, despite a slight improvement in the situation since the fall of the Taliban. Expat believers, who have increased greatly in number, must be very circumspect in their faith and witness. Pray for:

a) Afghan believers. Their numbers are increasing, as are the resources available to help disciple them. There are probably several thousand indigenous Christians; no exact number is known. They can never meet publicly, and even their secret meetings must change times and locations to avoid detection. In rural areas, they often believe as family groups, even as extended families. Also multiplying are small groups of Afghan believers in South Asia, Europe and North America. Pray for the protection of these precious believers, and for the clarity and consistency of their witness.

b) Afghans being reached by the gospel. Most are devoutly Muslim, but many, uncomfortable with terrorist actions in Islam's name, are interested in discovering more about Jesus Christ. The long-term presence of Christians working in aid, development and business, the return of former refugees who encountered the gospel while abroad, the presence of Christian radio as well as dreams and visions of Jesus have all moved mountains. The greatest difficulty is that of identity – many cannot see how to be both Afghan and openly Christian, especially when no such recognition is offered within the wider Afghan society. Pray that an expression of faith will emerge that allows them to be truly Afghan while truly following Jesus.

c) Safety and perseverance for believers as severe repercussions and persecution loom. The inevitable discovery of spiritual movements among believers from a Muslim background received high profile media coverage in Afghanistan and promises of harsh penalties – even death – from both family members and the authorities. Pray that no attacks of the enemies of the gospel might discourage or destroy the Church, but that in the crucible of suffering, the body of Christ might mature and even grow.

6 **The status of women** especially warrants prayer. They were effectively banned from public life by the Taliban. Widows endure particularly harsh plights, and depression and suicide are common. Worse, they have a life expectancy of only 44 years, with one of the highest maternal mortality rates in the world. Female literacy is under 20%, over one-half of Afghan brides are under age 16, only 5% attend secondary school and one-third are subjected to violence. Many still suffer the traumas of years of war and of pressures such times brought upon women in Afghan society. Although employment and social engagement can be very sensitive issues, younger girls are increasingly attending school; one-third of primary students are girls. Special radio programmes minister to women by communicating from the Bible the love and value that God holds for them. Pray for the disenfranchised women of Afghanistan, that they might receive justice, opportunity and freedom from fear and oppression, but especially that they might find Christ amid their suffering.

7 The need for the Scriptures. After decades of work, the whole Dari Bible is finally available (UBS); around 70% can understand this language. The NT in Pashto is available – albeit in a Pakistani and not an Afghan dialect and therefore not entirely understood. Work on an Afghan Pashto NT is underway. A full Bible translation does not exist in any indigenous minority language; pray that these might come to fruition. Praise God for translation progress in Hazaragi (Gospel of Luke), Kyrgyz (audio NT), Southern Uzbek (Genesis, Exodus and Matthew, with the full NT by 2012) and eight other languages either ongoing or beginning translation work. Pray also for the entry and distribution of God's Word into this closed land; the government, the Taliban and even NATO forces and NGO groups oppose it.

8 Media is a strategic and indeed essential ministry. Pray that all appropriate methods of witness may be used in the most effective manner.

a) *Literature.* Culturally appropriate discipleship courses and other training materials are being developed in the major languages of Afghanistan, in addition to many other types of evangelistic materials. These have been effective in reaching Afghans in exile and at home. Pray for those involved in producing, distributing and studying these materials.

b) *Audio resources.* A set of 45 Scripture stories has been produced in Hazaragi, which can be an effective template for other languages. **GRN** made audio recordings in 65 languages and dialects; many need transmission into modern formats. Worship music on CD in Afghan styles and languages is now available. Several organizations have collaborated to make portable pre-recorded audio players – one evangelistic, one of the NT in Dari and one for discipleship. Pray for their widespread distribution throughout the country.

c) *Radio* is a strategic way to proclaim the good news, since the majority of Afghans still listen to shortwave radio. FEBA, IBRA, and **GFA** Radio broadcast in the major languages of the country. Pray for the provision of and support for more Dari- and Pashto-speaking Christians to prepare programmes and answer mail. A handful of ministries have combined to develop many materials for radio and other media. "The Church in the Home" and other programmes have been especially helpful for national believers. Pray also for programming to commence in other languages.

d) *The JESUS film* is available in Baluchi, Brahui, Dari, Hazaragi, Pashto, Tajik and Southern Uzbek. Pray for its widespread use.

e) *TV,* a rapidly expanding medium. Pars, part of the **SAT-7** family, is growing fast and offers Christian programming in Farsi, the language of Iran closely related to Dari. A Dari programme is being developed.

f) *Christian websites* have been very effective in reaching the global Afghan diaspora. Sites such as RadioAfghan.com, Sound of Life (sadayezindagi.com), The Voice of Christ (afghantv.com), afghanbibles.com and afghanbibles.org make available literally thousands of audio files and documents for download in several Afghan languages, developed for the evangelization and discipleship of Afghan peoples.

g) *Video resources.* Culturally appropriate videos are being developed that present narrative Scripture portions as stories about the main Bible characters. These will be available in Southern Uzbek in 2010 and other languages in coming years, starting with Dari.

h) *Mobile phones.* One of the fastest ways through which Scripture may be spread is sharing audio and audio-text Scripture files via mobile phone. This makes the mobile phone potentially the best evangelistic tool in the country!

Albania
Republic of Albania
Europe

Geography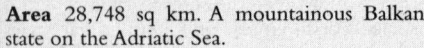

Area 28,748 sq km. A mountainous Balkan state on the Adriatic Sea.

Population		Ann Gr	Density
2010	3,169,087	0.37%	110/sq km
2020	3,337,789	0.50%	116/sq km
2030	3,416,490	0.12%	119/sq km

Capital Tirana 444,000. Unofficially the population is closer to 1 million. **Urbanites** 48%. **Pop under 15 yrs** 24%. **Life expectancy** 76.5 yrs.

Peoples

Albanian 91.2%. Tosk in south 62.8%; Gheg in north 19.0%; Aromanian/Vlach 9.5%.
Other 9.8%. Greek 3.2%; Romani (Gypsy) more than 2.7%; Serb 1.2%; Macedonian 1.1%.
Literacy 98.7%. **Official language** Albanian. **All languages** 7. **Languages with Scriptures** 4Bi 2NT 3por.

Economy

Emerged from a Communist (but effectively medieval) economy in the 1990s, but remains one of Europe's two poorest nations. While there is marked improvement, poor infrastructure, corruption and high emigration rates hamper further growth.
HDI Rank 70th/182. **Public debt** 51.9% of GDP. **Income/person** $4,090 (9% of USA).

Politics

The Communist regime, imposed on the country in 1944, crumbled in 1991, a few years after the death of dictator Enver Hoxha. Since then, multiparty elections have generally been peaceful and closely contested, the most recent being in 2009. The sensitive concept of "Greater Albania" and Kosovo's self-declared independence are important issues.

Religion

No religion was allowed to exist in Communist Albania from 1967. The ban was lifted in 1990, but no legal provision for religious freedom was made until 1998. Since then, Albania enjoys total religious freedom, cherished by many. The majority of Albanians are very nominal, but some traditional religious groups have had a tendency to resent and oppose the proselytism and activities of both evangelicals and marginal cults.

Religions	Pop %	Population	Ann Gr
Muslim	62.40	1,977,510	2.0%
Christian	30.47	965,621	-0.5%
Non-religious	6.98	221,202	-7.5%
Baha'i	0.14	4,437	1.9%
Jewish	0.01	317	0.4%

Christians Denoms		Pop %	Affiliates	Ann Gr
Protestant	12	0.31	10,000	6.5%
Independent	16	0.41	13,000	2.6%
Catholic	2	13.12	416,000	-2.5%
Orthodox	4	17.00	539,000	1.2%
Marginal	2	0.42	13,000	3.6%
Doubly affiliated		-0.79	-25,000	2.6%

Churches	MegaBloc	Congs	Members	Affiliates
Orthodox Church	O	330	317,365	530,000
Catholic Church	C	47	187,273	412,000
Jehovah's Witnesses	M	82	2,556	11,500
Byzantine Catholic	C	12	1,875	3,750
Char/Pente groups	I	60	1,882	3,200
Foursquare Gospel	P	12	1,000	2,100
Word of Life	I	12	1,379	2,000
Latter-day Saints (Mormon)	M	10	1,605	1,950
New Apostolic Church	I	12	1,084	1,800
Assemblies of God	P	12	400	1,550
Christ Groups (EHC)	I	27	900	1,350
Baptist churches	P	8	500	1,000
Christian Brethren	P	15	500	700
Other denominations[17]		96	10,789	17,744
Doubly affiliated				-25,000
Total Christians[36]		**735**	**529,108**	**965,644**

TransBloc	Pop %	Population	Ann Gr
Evangelicals			
Evangelicals	0.5	14,466	4.6%
Renewalists			
Charismatics	0.4	12,891	4.4%
Pentecostals	0.2	6,596	5.2%

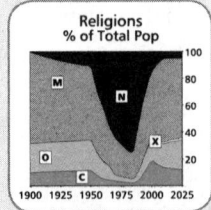

Religions
% of Total Pop

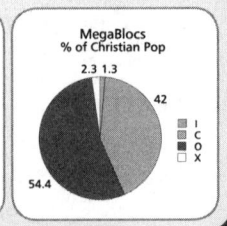

MegaBlocs
% of Christian Pop

Answers to Prayer

1 **Thank God for His work in this land** that, for years, was resolutely closed to the gospel. Many credit concentrated prayer and intercession as major factors in seeing Albania opened for ministry. Much good work has been done since then.

2 **The Albanian Church is maturing** from the infancy stages of the 1990s into a wide-ranging community of believers with greater indigenous leadership, nationwide organizational structures and a more holistic vision for discipleship and evangelism. All these have been achieved in a climate of politico-economic instability and antipathy toward non-traditional confessions.

3 **The number of evangelicals has grown** in just a few years from nearly zero to several thousand. While not a huge proportion of the population, indications are that many more, while uncommitted to local fellowships, certainly identify with evangelical beliefs.

Challenges for Prayer

1 **Albania has a long road ahead to recover** completely from the devastation of atheistic Communism. Economically, morally and, in particular, spiritually, there remains much to be done to build a healthy and productive society. The anarchy, chaos and corruption of the 1990s and 2000s are outworkings of the nation's grim past, but there is praiseworthy progress of late. Pray that Albania's government and business cultures might be positively impacted by the influence of believers. Biblical ethics in these contexts can be in short supply.

2 **The religious climate is very hazy.** Albanians' pragmatic and tolerant approach ("if it works, use it") to religion contributes to this. Pray that wider-Balkan religious tensions will not begin to grow here; the three main confessions (Muslim, Orthodox, Catholic) are often uncomfortable with more recent groups. The statistical figures for religions and denominations are only a guideline, since there are no reliable sources and the large majority of affiliates are very nominal in their practice.

3 **Islam is the largest religion in Albania** (some say up to 70% Muslim), but this normally extends to an inherited cultural affiliation and little more. Moderate Sunni and the Bektashi Sufi sect are the largest groups. Despite widespread Islamization efforts from abroad spending many millions of dollars, most Albanians resist religious entrenchment. Superstition and folk Islam prosper. Pray for Albanian Muslims to encounter the living Christ.

4 **Evangelicals are in a transition phase.** The frenetic activity of the 1990s has been replaced with more strategic ministry and consolidation. There are fewer long-term missionaries now than in the initial rush after the country opened; more committed workers are needed. National leadership is developing and growing, but had to start from a baseline of almost zero. Scattergun evangelism is being replaced by a more focused and strategic approach. More than 160 evangelical congregations are connected and represented by the Albanian Evangelical Alliance (VUSH). Pray for the following ministries:

a) Leadership training is the most vital need for prayer due to the Church's rapid growth in the last two decades, to widespread biblical ignorance and to a previous desperate lack of biblical leadership models. At least six groups run training institutes – Albanian Bible Institute, The Centre for Christian Leadership, Evangelical Theological College (**AoG**), **YWAM**, Christ for the Nations (Nehemiah) and Southeastern Europe Theological Seminary. There are several other training programmes as well as deliberate mentoring of promising Albanian leaders in less-academic settings. TEE, with BILD International, is also a useful tool due to prevalent poverty and the poor infrastructure.

b) Evangelism and church planting. There are still many towns and villages without an evangelical presence, and where there is one, signs of second-generation spiritual lapses are already apparent. Pray for the good news to continue to spread. The Albanian Church Planters Mission was formed to prepare evangelists for this express purpose. Pray also that resulting churches and Christians might reflect the Lord Jesus Christ in an Albanian context.

c) **Holistic mission** is possibly the defining ministry of the young Albanian Church. Almost all mission agencies and national ministries combine practical and much-needed assistance with sharing the gospel. Help ministries abound, designed to assist the poor and suffering and to provide employment opportunities for Christians. Pray for a profound impact from this love in action. Albanian believers are now being equipped to have a holistic gospel impact on their society as well. This will potentially affect fields as diverse as medicine, politics, law, business, parenting, et al. Pray that such efforts might bear fruit that matures and expands the Church and transforms the country.

d) **Missionaries from Albania.** Praise God that Albania's young Church is committed to its part in fulfilling the Great Commission. Numerous churches and organizations are sending Albanian workers to other lands. Albania's historical legacy of Islam and Communism has equipped many Albanians to make excellent missionaries to the unevangelized world. Pray that this movement would grow and that the Albanian Church itself would strive to support their workers in every way.

5 **Evangelical mission agencies** have a vital role to play, particularly by serving the Albanian Church through training, resource development and holistic mission. The Albania Encouragement Project networks over 60 agencies covering every type of ministry. Pray for unity among the diverse groups, and pray for a spirit of humility and partnership as they work with the national Church to see genuine transformation.

6 **The least-reached minorities:**

a) **The Bektashi,** a Sufi dervish movement, is deemed heretical by the Sunni majority because its beliefs are more influenced by folk religion and the occult. As many as 600,000 Albanians are associated with this movement. Some have become evangelical believers.

b) **The Vlach** (related to the Romani Gypsy) are looked down upon by many. Most are culturally Orthodox. A few groups work among them and are seeing some fruit.

c) **The Gorani, Golloborda and Cham** are culturally Muslim. They are quite isolated, but there is some ministry among them via short-term teams.

d) **The Rufai.** Another mystic group, similar to the Bektashis but independent from them, is the dervish sect called the Rufai or Rif'ai (howling dervishes).

7 **The Albanian diaspora.** Over half of all Albanians live outside Albania. Their spiritual need is now greater than that of Albania itself. Pray for these:

a) **Kosovar Albanians** are 98% Muslim, with about 1,000 evangelicals in 12 congregations in Kosovo. The upheaval involving Serbia and NATO opened doors for evangelism and ministry.

b) **Albanians living in Macedonia (600,000 to 700,000) and Montenegro (40,000).** Almost all are Muslim, with very little Christian outreach to them.

c) **Albanians further afield.** Indigenous Albanian populations have long been in Italy and Greece, but now their numbers have swelled: Greece (500,000), Italy (450,000) and Germany, as well as Switzerland, Netherlands and the UK, with over 100,000 each. New York City alone may have over 100,000 Albanians, and large populations can be found in Boston and Detroit also.

d) **Criminal activities seem sadly widespread among some segments of the diaspora.** Most heinous of these is illegal trafficking of people, primarily for prostitution, but other trafficking includes that of drugs and arms.

8 **Christian help ministries:**

a) **Scripture translation.** There are three complete translations of the Bible in Albanian; one literal, one paraphrased and one Catholic. The NT was recently retranslated into modern Albanian in a collaborative project of Orthodox, Catholics and Protestants; a new OT translation is underway in the same project. Pray for accuracy, timely completion and for widespread use of the Scriptures.

b) **Religious literature** from many faiths flooded the country upon the fall of Communism. **EHC** blanketed the country with Christian literature twice. Christian books are published by Vernon, *Karte e Pende* and *Shigjeta* as well as by several missions, but there are very few

Christian bookstores. Pray for translation of useful Christian books and literature and for their impact.

c) ***Christian radio*** is an area of great growth. **TWR**, Albanian partners Gospel Waves and Radio 7 produce and broadcast non-stop on shortwave and FM via several transmitters and stations. They are hoping to expand their broadcast reach into Kosovo as well. Words of Hope is also producing and broadcasting radio programmes in Albania. Pray for wider coverage so that people in more isolated areas may also be blessed.

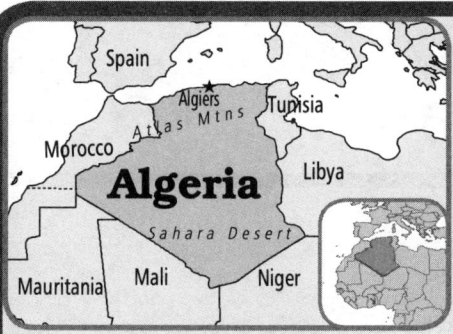

Algeria
Democratic and Popular Republic of Algeria
Africa

Geography

Area 2,381,741 sq km. Agriculture is possible on the Mediterranean coast, in the Atlas Mountains and at oases; 80% is desert.

Population	Ann Gr	Density
2010	35,422,589	1.52%	15/sq km
2020	40,630,046	1.30%	17/sq km
2030	44,726,253	0.85%	19/sq km

Over 90% live north of the Atlas Mountains. About 500,000 are nomadic or semi-nomadic in the Sahara. A further 4 million ethnic Algerians live in Europe. **Capital** Algiers 2,799,667. **Other major cities** Oran 767,000; Constantine 630,000. **Urbanites** 66.5%. **Pop under 15 yrs** 27%. **Life expectancy** 72.2 yrs.

Peoples

Maghreb Arabs 69.9%. Many are Arabized Berber. **Berber** 22.8%. 14 groups, including Kabyle 9.4%; Shawiya 5.3%; Imazighen 3.8%; Rif/Northern Shilha 2.0%. **Bedouin** 6.0%. 8 groups. Tajakant 4.0%. **Other Arabs** 1.0%. **Other** 0.3%. Asian, European, sub-Saharan African. **Literacy** 69.8%. **Official languages** Arabic and Berber. French and English are widely used, and 25% speak one of the Berber languages. **All languages** 22. **Indigenous languages** 18. **Languages with Scriptures** 2Bi 1NT 7por.

Economy

A fast-growing economy due to oil/gas reserves and rapid nationalization of related industry. Most oil wealth does not reach the ordinary citizen. Foreign debt repayment is ahead of schedule, but the financial structures of the country are generally poor and unemployment is high. **HDI Rank** 104th/182. **Public debt** 8.4% of GDP. **Income/person** $4,588 (10% of USA).

Politics

French colony for 132 years. Independence in 1962 after a bitter war of liberation. A one-party socialist regime backed by the army held power for over 25 years. Economic failure and political abuses of power provoked widespread agitation for change. Islamists won the 1992 elections but the army intervened. An ensuing civil war caused more than 100,000 deaths. The current president's attempts at forging peace via the Charter for Peace and National Reconciliation meet with broad national approval, but the government appears to be accommodating militant Islamist groups to a dangerous degree, and this appeasement approach may prove disastrous in the long-run.

Religion

Freedom of religion is dwindling since legal changes in 2006, and persecution has been intensifying since 2008. Islamist groups are increasingly intolerant of other expressions of faith. Catholics and the Protestant Church of Algeria are the only Christian bodies officially recognized. Muslim fundamentalists are strongly agitating for the institution of Islamic shari'a law.

Religions	Pop %	Population	Ann Gr
Muslim	97.29	34,462,637	1.4%
Non-religious	2.40	850,142	5.3%
Christian	0.28	99,183	7.5%
Chinese	0.02	7,085	1.5%
Baha'i	0.01	3,542	1.5%

Christians Denoms		Pop %	Affiliates	Ann Gr
Protestant	8	0.03	10,000	12.2%
Independent	3	0.24	86,000	7.5%
Catholic	1	0.01	3,000	0.0%
Orthodox	4	<0.01	1,000	-1.8%
Marginal	1	<0.01	100	0.0%

Churches	MegaBloc	Congs	Members	Affiliates
Indigenous MBB groups	I	64	25,455	84,000
Protestant Ch of Algeria	P	32	2,500	4,175
Catholic Church	C	16	1,875	3,000
Assemblies of God	P	18	1,667	2,500
Orthodox groups	O	10	1,115	1,450
Other denominations[9]		25	2,033	4,508
Total Christians[17]		**165**	**34,645**	**99,633**

TransBloc	Pop %	Population	Ann Gr
Evangelicals			
Evangelicals	0.2	84,081	8.1%
Renewalists			
Charismatics	0.1	30,296	9.1%
Pentecostals	<0.1	2,500	38.0%

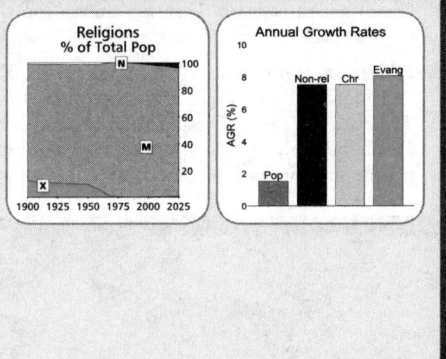

Answers to Prayer

1 **The growth of the Algerian Church** over the past decade is an answer to prayer. A long road of tearful sowing by a tenacious succession of missionaries and intercessors is bearing beautiful fruit – while impossible to assess accurately, some believe that the number of believers far exceeds 100,000. The large majority are Kabyle Berber in background, but faith is growing among Arabs and almost every other people as well. New fellowships are popping up all over the country. This is in part due to the commitment of Berber believers to move into unreached, Arab areas in order to sow the seeds of the good news.

2 **The Church is a very indigenous, truly Algerian expression of faith.** Scriptures and study materials, worship styles and, increasingly, training and leadership are all expressed in culturally relevant ways. The resources available to believers in their own languages and forms, once scarce, are multiplying.

3 **Unity among Berber, Arab and foreign Christians** stands in glorious contrast to the legacy of animosity among these ethnic groups so prevalent for centuries outside of faith in Christ.

Challenges for Prayer

1 **Algeria has suffered deeply** in the past. From French colonial exploitation to the war of liberation to the more recent brutal civil war that cost over 100,000 lives, its people are familiar with violence and loss. Pray for the following issues:

a) The spiritual and psychological legacies of a land fraught with bloodshed. Fear of murderous attacks by terror groups has lessened, but the violence has never ended. Many people are war-weary and wish for the upheaval to end, but that seems a distant dream.

b) Democracy is enshrined in the constitution but struggles elsewhere to hang on. A single-party state more or less remains, and the freedoms promised on paper rarely materialize.

c) Human rights abuses are widespread. Change to some laws opened the door for further abuse. The Charter for Peace and National Reconciliation is more lenient to the perpetrators of civil war crimes than to the victims; few will be brought to account for the terrible crimes committed (by both terrorist groups and state security forces), and the media will be subject to greater state control. Most vulnerable are non-Muslims.

2 **Islam in Algeria is volatile and deeply polarized** between secularists – who espouse a more liberal Islam and a Western view of progress – and Islamists, who want to submit all of society to shari'a principles. Since 1992, fundamentalists led by the Islamic Armed Group (GIA) have waged a bloody war of terror – with the state, the media and foreigners as targets. There is once again a strong push to re-enter the political sphere as

Islamists gain ground in popularity. Meanwhile, they are moving at the grassroots level by gaining control of schools and mosques, and intimidating or even murdering imams who oppose them. Pray that God might use Islamists to draw many more into discovering Christ, as He has done elsewhere. Pray for powerful conversions to Jesus among Islamist leaders in Algeria.

3 **The Berber peoples** comprise 23% of the population, although the dominant Arabs may be largely an ancient admixture of Arab and Berber. Domination by Arab language and culture spawns Berber nationalism, a significant force as they seek to reaffirm their identity and return to their cultural roots. Their forebears were once Christian, and now many thousands have turned to Christ among the Kabyle, some through supernatural revelations of the Lord Jesus, but mainly through personal evangelism.

a) *Praise God for the continued growth of this people movement to Christ.* Pray that it may continue to spread and to deepen. Reprisals are beginning to occur against the young and growing Church.

b) *Pray for reconciliation efforts* by the president and government. Legislation for a greater recognition of Berber language and culture will go a long way in bridging the divide between these two intransigent groups. Some Berbers identify themselves with Christianity and the West more out of spite toward "Arabic" Islam than out of love for Jesus.

4 **Persecution of Christians is intensifying** as a reaction to unprecedented church growth; the future of the Church in Algeria hangs in the balance. Legislation passed has made proselytism a criminal offence. A law forbidding the "practice of non-Muslim worship" outside of pre-approved buildings was cleverly followed by a spate of church closings. Believers face threats and intimidation by family, friends, employers, Muslim extremists and now the government. The Algerian Church has grown due to bold witness and evangelism. Pray that they will respond to these pressures with faith and perseverance.

5 **The Algerian Church faces many other challenges** outside of persecution. Pray for the following issues:

a) *Unity* between the few Christian associations with a public presence. Officially this constitutes the Catholics and the Protestant Church of Algeria (EPA). The Assemblies of God also formed a new association. There is some disagreement between Christian groups on the best way to share the good news in this heavily Muslim nation.

b) *The establishment of strong indigenous groups and church leaders.* The rapid growth and sensitive context makes leadership development a constant challenge. TEE is developing quickly in order to help raise up a new generation of leaders. Resources are increasingly available in many new media formats, allowing discipleship and training to occur anywhere. There are also three theological schools in the country.

c) *A strengthening of Christian families.* Religious and social pressures usually force Christian girls to hide their faith and marry Muslims. Pray for the few Christian couples, for their strength and endurance, and that they may minister to the Church.

d) *Unemployment among Christians from a Muslim background* is as high as 90%. This creates financial burdens for churches, the inability to support pastors and many temptations and complications for those seeking to follow Jesus. Pray for micro-enterprise schemes that create jobs for believers, such as the House of Hope and the EPA programmes.

6 **The unreached** comprise virtually the whole nation.

a) *The growing cities* – the educated elite, the middle class and the teeming slums. Algeria rapidly urbanized as people fled into the cities to escape the violence of civil war.

b) *Young people* are frustrated and disillusioned. Many attempt to move to Europe (often illegally) in search of more freedom and a better life. Those under age 30 make up 65-70% of the population, and this generation comprises the large majority of the Christians in Algeria.

c) *The Berber peoples* of the Atlas Mountains. Apart from the Kabyles, the other 13 groups are among Africa's least evangelized. But there is now a Christian witness in the midst of all these, and possibly groups of believers as well.

d) *The Tuareg and Bedouin peoples.* Only a handful of believers were known just a few years ago. They are now rapidly responding to the gospel. Creative strategies will be required to effectively reach those who maintain the traditional nomadic lifestyle.

e) *The Mzab oasis towns in the Sahara.* Even these tight-knit and deeply religious communities are being reached by Algerian believers; a very small but growing number have come to Christ.

7 **Pray for the active mission force.** Pray that God would raise up more workers to help strengthen the local church. Work is under way in many areas. Especially pray for these:

a) *Relief work* remains very much an urgent priority, but one that requires sensitivity.

b) *Christian music.* Much is being written in Kabyle, less so in other languages. Pray for increased production quality and wider dissemination of this valuable tool for witness and discipleship.

c) *Work among the children of Christians.* There is no ministry specifically geared for children. Pray for strong discipleship of Christian children at home; at school they are bombarded with Quranic teaching.

d) *The leadership of the Algerian Church in Europe,* and for missionary calls to their home-land. There are over 3,000 Algerian Christians in Europe, many of whom fled the violence or persecution back home. Pray for many to be raised up as apostles to their own people.

8 **Algerians in Europe** exceed four million; many are there illegally. They are more accessible to the gospel in Europe, but also to Islamic preaching. Pray for the network of agencies and churches seeking to reach them (**AWM, WEC,** Avant and others). Pray for discipling of individuals and planting of Arabic- and Berber-speaking congregations that can then be channels for the gospel to their homeland.

9 **Bible translation and distribution** are fraught with obstacles and restrictions. Translation work is proceeding in a few Berber languages and in Algerian Arabic, a language spoken by up to 25 million people; most do not understand Standard Arabic. Pray for rapid completion of these projects and for the transfer of these resources into safer and less conspicuous media. The government ban on importing Bibles is a major obstacle to the discipleship and maturation of the Church; pray that the rapidly growing community of believers might have adequate access to Scripture.

10 **Christian media** are vital in this internally restrictive situation. Pray for:

a) *Radio.* Both **AWM** and Avant have a comprehensive strategy of preparing radio programmes, evangelistic and discipleship literature and follow-up programmes (radio, satellite TV, personal counselling, magazines and BCCs). Arabic, Kabyle and other languages have broadcasts mostly through **TWR** and **HCJB**; pray for more broadcasting hours. Several thousand are reported as having found faith via this medium.

b) *Audio-visual.* The JESUS film on video has had a wide impact in Kabyle and in Arabic; it is available in seven other languages. The More Than Dreams DVD is also being used effectively.

c) *Satellite TV* is the medium of greatest fruitfulness and even greater potential. About 85% of homes have satellite dishes and thereby full access to the good news. About 20 channels are reaching Muslims, and CBN, Life TV and CNA develop programmes specifically for Maghreb peoples. Pray for even better use of this powerful means of witnessing, teaching and encouraging.

d) *Use of portable media.* Music, Scripture, teaching and training series, testimonies and even discipling chat rooms are all available on the Internet, DVD, CD and on handheld electronic devices. Praise God for the increase of these resources and their unstoppable accessibility; pray for their wider distribution.

Samoa

South Pacific Ocean

Pago Pago

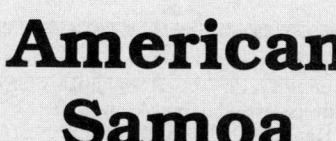

American Samoa

Territory of
American Samoa

Pacific

Geography

Area 199 sq km. Archipelago in the Polynesian Pacific.

Population		Ann Gr	Density
2010	68,505	1.76%	344/sq km
2020	79,811	1.49%	401/sq km
2030	91,468	1.27%	460/sq km

There are as many Samoans in diaspora (USA, especially Hawaii) as in America Samoa.
Capital Pago Pago 61,100. **Urbanites** 93%.
Pop under 15 yrs old 36%. **Life expectancy** 76.2 yrs.

Peoples

Polynesian 92.9%. Samoan 60,000; Tongan 2,500.
Asian 2.9%. Korean, Chinese, Filipino.
Caucasian 1.2%. Americans.
Mixed and other 3%. Mixed race.
Literacy 99.4%. **Official languages** Samoan, English. **All languages** 6. **Indigenous languages** 2. **Languages with Scriptures** 3Bi.

Economy

A largely traditional Polynesian economy. Tuna fishing and canning dominate the economy. Its remoteness and devastating hurricanes limit economic development. Remittances sent by Samoans abroad also contribute to the economy.
Income/person $9,040 (19.8% of mainland USA).

Politics

US unincorporated territory since 1900, bestowing all rights of US citizens except ability to vote in US elections.

Religion

Complete freedom of religion.

Religions	Pop %	Population	Ann Gr
Christian	95.10	65,148	1.7%
Non-religious	2.50	1,713	3.5%
Baha'i	1.50	1,028	2.2%
Buddhist	0.77	527	3.7%
Chinese	0.13	89	3.4%

Christians Denoms		Pop %	Affiliates	Ann Gr
Protestant	12	56.75	39,000	1.4%
Independent	6	3.81	3,000	1.9%
Anglican	1	0.25	<500	-1.1%
Catholic	1	18.98	13,000	1.6%
Marginal	5	24.67	17,000	1.9%
Doubly affiliated		*-9.34*	*-6,000*	*0.0%*

Churches	MegaBloc	Congs	Members	Affiliates
Congregational Chr Ch	P	40	11,976	20,000
Latter-day Saints (Mormon)	M	37	7,800	15,300
Catholic Church	C	8	5,200	13,000
Assemblies of God	P	30	5,921	9,000
Methodist Church	P	14	3,217	4,600
Seventh-day Adventist	P	7	1,900	3,800
Jehovah's Witnesses	M	3	278	750
Samoan Full Gospel Ch	I	2	260	473
Baptist Churches	P	7	185	370
Other denominations[16]		54	2,471	4,265
Doubly affiliated				*-6,400*
Total Christians[25]		**202**	**39,208**	**65,158**

TransBloc	Pop %	Population	Ann Gr
Evangelicals			
Evangelicals	21.3	14,597	1.8%
Renewalists			
Charismatics	17.5	11,989	2.2%
Pentecostals	15.1	10,373	1.6%

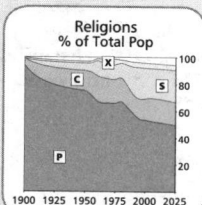

Religions
% of Total Pop

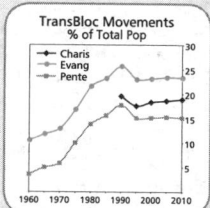

TransBloc Movements
% of Total Pop

Challenges for Prayer

1 **American Samoa enjoys a higher economic status than Samoa to its west,** but suffers the concomitant materialism. Pray that the indigenous people (and their relatives in diaspora) may find their destiny in wholehearted commitment to the Lord Jesus Christ.

2 **Praise God for the evangelical ministries and churches** making an impact for the Lord. Evangelical groups, especially Assemblies of God, have grown rapidly. There is also a **YWAM** base in the islands.

3 **Remarkable growth among cults** (especially Mormons) exposes the nominalism, too-long entrenched, in the mainline churches. Pray for awakening and renewal in these rapidly declining churches.

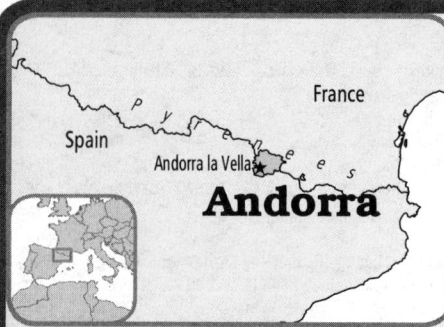

France
Spain
Andorra la Vella
Andorra

Andorra

Principality of Andorra

Europe

Geography

Area 468 sq km. In the heart of the Pyrenees Mountains, between France and Spain.

Population		Ann Gr	Density
2010	86,685	1.68%	185/sq km
2020	100,129	1.38%	214/sq km
2030	113,066	1.18%	242/sq km

Most growth is through immigration.
Capital Andorra la Vella 25,100. **Urbanites** 88.0%. **Pop under 15 yrs** 15%. **Life expectancy** 83.6 yrs.

Peoples

European 97.8%. Andorran 35.6%; Spanish 37.7%; Portuguese 11.4%; French 6.5%.
Other 2.2%.
Literacy near 100%. **Official language** Catalan. **All languages** 5. **Indigenous languages** 3. **Languages with Scriptures** 3Bi.

Economy

A tax haven for goods and banking. Surrounded by EU but not part of it. Wealthy, primarily through tourism (10 million visitors annually, accounting for 80% of GDP) but also through duty-free sales and import/export.
HDI Rank 28th/182. **Public debt** 8.6% of GDP.
Income/person $38,589 (84.6% of USA).

Politics

Self-governing co-principality since 1278; nominally ruled by the French president and the Spanish bishop of Urgel. Since 1993, Andorra has had its own constitution, judiciary and foreign policy.

Religion

Official freedom of religion since 1993. The Catholic Church remains the established church.

Religions	Pop %	Population	Ann Gr
Christian	90.78	78,693	1.4%
Non-religious	5.90	5,114	3.1%
Muslim	2.30	1,994	10.8%
Hindu	0.60	520	3.5%
Jewish	0.30	260	0.4%
Baha'i	0.12	104	1.7%

Christians Denoms		Pop %	Affiliates	Ann Gr
Protestant	3	0.22	<1,000	7.2%
Independent	1	0.10	<1,000	2.4%
Anglican	1	0.12	<1,000	10.8%
Catholic	1	89.06	77,000	1.5%
Marginal	2	0.53	<1,000	4.2%
Unaffiliated		0.80	1,000	0.0%

Churches	MegaBloc	Congs	Members	Affiliates
Catholic Church	C	8	61,760	77,200
Pentecostal groups	P	2	100	150
Christian Community	I	1	69	90
Christian Brethren	P	1	30	45
Other denominations[3]		17	380	562
Total Christians[8]		**29**	**62,339**	**78,047**

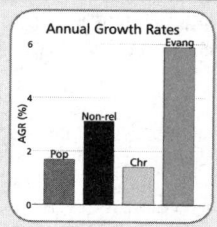

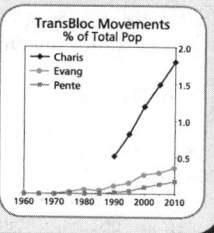

TransBloc	Pop %	Population	Ann Gr
Evangelicals			
Evangelicals	0.4	310	5.9%
Renewalists			
Charismatics	1.8	1,562	5.6%
Pentecostals	0.2	150	8.4%

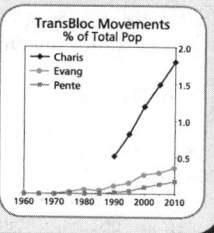

A

Challenges for Prayer

1 **Materialism holds Andorra in a tight grip.** Formerly a smugglers' refuge, Andorra now attracts well-heeled tourists, financiers and those taking advantage of duty-free goods. Pray that empty materialism would be seen as the ultimately unfulfilling falsehood that it is.

2 **Ninety percent of Andorrans are affiliated with the Catholic Church,** but true spirituality is thin on the ground, and the Church is on the defensive. Many consult mediums, seers and astrologers for guidance and advice, usually at a significant financial cost. Few seek guidance from Catholic priests. Ask God to reinvigorate the Christian spiritual life of Andorra by the Holy Spirit and to expose and disarm the power of the occult.

3 **Biblical Christianity struggles to retain a foothold.** Catholicism has lost much of its zeal, and the handful of other congregations where evangelicals worship grow very slowly. Praise God for committed expatriate believers and for the few indigenous Andorran believers. Pray that all faithful disciples of Christ might have the passion and discernment that will enable them to effectively share their faith.

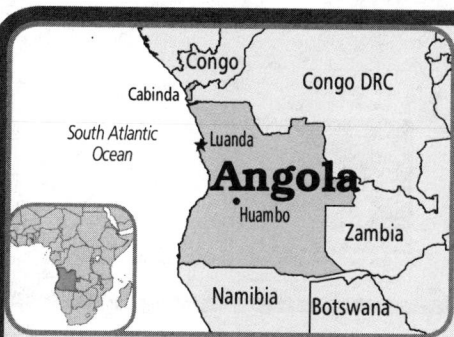

Angola

Republic of Angola

Africa

Geography 🌍

Area 1,246,700 sq km. Large coastal state on the South Atlantic coast. Cabinda is an oil-rich coastal enclave to the north of the Congo River.

Population	Ann Gr	Density
2010	18,992,707	2.71%	15/sq km
2020	24,507,000	2.47%	20/sq km
2030	30,415,585	2.08%	24/sq km

All population figures are estimates. Due to continual conflict, there has been no census since 1973.

Capital Luanda 4,772,334. **Other major city** Huambo 1.0 million. **Urbanites** 58.5%. **Pop under 15 yrs** 45%. **Life expectancy** 46.5 yrs.

Peoples 👪

Bantu 97.6%. 41 peoples, Largest: Ovimbundu 25.5%; Mbundu 22.9%; Kongo(3) 12.9%; Chokwe 5.0%; Luvale 8.1%; Nyaneka 3.7%; Kwanyama 3.3%; Luchazi 2.2%; Lunda(2) 2.0%; Nyemba 1.6%; Mbwela 1.3%; Nkhumbi 1.2%.
Khoisan 0.6%. 9 peoples.
Other 1.8%. Mixed race 1.2%; Westerners 0.6%.
Literacy 66.8%. **Official language** Portuguese.
All languages 41. **Languages with Scriptures** 12Bi 5NT 13por 3w.i.p.

Economy 📈

Widespread poverty despite having some of the world's richest natural resources. Enormous untapped potential – huge oil reserves, diamonds, minerals and good agricultural land. Great oil and diamond wealth (Angola is the largest oil exporter in sub-Saharan Africa), but with little trickle-down benefit to the millions of destitute. The nation's infrastructure was devastated by war, but is rebuilding rapidly.

A

HDI Rank 143rd/182. **Public debt** 15.5% of GDP. **Income/person** $5,054 (11% of USA).

Politics

A Portuguese colony for 450 years. The formerly Marxist-oriented MPLA gained control of the government in 1975 via a coup orchestrated in Lisbon that ended colonial rule. It was then propped up with Cuban military assistance. The UNITA nationalist movement, initially supported by the West and by South Africa, waged a civil war against the MPLA. These years of conflict saw millions internally displaced, 900,000 die prematurely, and the nation laid to waste. After the negotiated peace deal in 1990, while theoretically under UN protection, even larger numbers died. Further fighting broke out in 1998, the rebel leader was killed in 2002; UNITA is now active more as an opposition political party than as a rebel group. Parliamentary elections, which also determined the President, were held in 2008. Separatist agitation persists in the enclave of Cabinda.

Religion

The first president, a Marxist, vowed to eradicate Christianity within 20 years (and obviously failed!). Many believers suffered during this time. Since the conflict ended, religious freedom has been prevalent, but the government is moving to attempt to control the growth of new indigenous and often syncretized religious groups.

Religions	Pop %	Population	AnnGr.
Christian	94.09	17,870,238	3.0%
Ethnoreligionist	4.00	759,708	-5.3%
Muslim	1.10	208,920	78.2%
Non-religious	0.80	151,942	-0.8%
Baha'i	0.01	1,899	2.7%

Christians Denoms		Pop %	Affiliates	Ann Gr
Protestant	80	26.55	5,043,000	4.1%
Independent	700	2.73	519,000	2.5%
Anglican	2	0.63	120,000	2.7%
Catholic	1	64.24	12,200,000	3.4%
Marginal	2	1.53	291,000	4.8%
Unaffiliated		3.10	589,000	-8.9%
Doubly affiliated		*-4.65*	*-883,000*	*0.0%*

Churches	MegaBloc	Congs	Members	Affiliates
Catholic Church	C	349	6,971,429	12,200,000
Assemblies of God	P	259	570,571	1,900,000
Evang Congreg Ch	P	2,943	382,609	880,000
Seventh-day Adventist	P	1,228	350,000	595,000
Christian Brethren	P	1,689	202,703	450,000
Evang Baptist Ch	P	411	123,404	290,000
Jehovah's Witnesses	M	711	72,500	290,000
Church of God	P	583	105,000	241,500
Ev Ch of SW Angola	P	743	59,406	180,000
African Apostolic Ch	I	867	52,000	130,000
Anglican Church	A	400	60,000	120,000
Evang Reformed Ch	P	640	48,000	120,000
Baptist Convention	P	688	55,000	110,000
Other denominations[770]		2,668	327,637	666,290
Doubly affiliated				*-883,200*
Total Christians[785]		**14,179**	**9,380,259**	**17,289,590**

TransBloc	Pop %	Population	Ann Gr
Evangelicals			
Evangelicals	22.5	4,277,143	4.4%
Renewalists			
Charismatics	25.3	4,797,455	6.3%
Pentecostals	12.4	2,349,840	5.0%

Religions % of Total Pop

TransBloc Movements % of Total Pop
- Charis
- Evang
- Pente

Answers to Prayer

1   **The consolidation of peace** appears to be happening, since the conflict ended and most of the displaced millions have returned home. Reconciliation movements are gaining steam (with the Church at the forefront), and rebuilding the country is an achievable goal, given the country's natural resources. There are 20 universities today, where there were at most five when the war ended. Roads have improved so much that journeys which previously took two to three days now take a few hours.

2   **The remarkable growth of biblical Christianity** amid war and poverty. Evangelicals quadrupled from 1990 to 2010, despite the extremely difficult conditions.

Challenges for Prayer

1 **Forty years of almost constant war** (1962-2002) have devastated Angola. Innocent civilians suffered the most – 90% of the casualties were civilians, millions were uprooted, their homes and churches destroyed and hunger was used as a bargaining chip in the power play for aid. One in 350 Angolans is a victim of landmines, 70-90% of the population live in poverty, and the length of roads destroyed or damaged amounts to nearly twice the circumference of the planet. Greater than the physical damage are the psychological, social and spiritual wounds, which will require years to overcome. Pray for:

a) *Those seeking to alleviate physical suffering* by clearing landmines and rebuilding infrastructure, homes, hospitals, schools and churches. The six million landmines are being cleared – but over 80,000 people have already been crippled by them. Early signs of progress are promising. Many agencies are involved, including WVI, Tearfund and several consortiums of churches and agencies such as Church Action in Angola.

b) *Healing of the invisible wounds.* Reconciliation is a painstaking process, and the sheer number of those hurting means that more counselling and training are long-term needs.

2 **Luanda and other major cities** attracted the displaced but had no capacity to shelter them properly, so squalid squatter camps rapidly sprung up. A large proportion of the rural population fled to urban areas due to food shortages and lack of security. The government is accused of failing to care for these unwilling refugees. There are large numbers of orphaned and abandoned children; many are falsely accused of witchcraft by relatives as a pretext for getting rid of them. Others are forced or sold into prostitution to feed themselves. Pray for those working with the urban poor and the children at risk.

3 **The Church, despite great growth, has not emerged unscathed** from decades of conflict. Much prayer is needed, specifically for:

a) *Forgiveness and love in action.* The Church must be at the forefront of activities aimed to overcome the longstanding tribal loyalties and partisan politics. Such forgiveness must include many who perpetrated crimes against Christians and Christians who compromised under pressure.

b) *The right relationship between Church and state.* Religious freedom is a blessing, but Angola has a reputation for having dangerous syncretistic cults that mix elements of Christianity with animistic tribal religions. The government attempts to encourage the work of established and reputable denominations, while limiting the effects of the cults.

c) *Christ-like, holy living by followers of the Lord Jesus* that commends the gospel to unbelievers and passionately reaches out to their disillusioned, apathetic neighbours – non-practising Christians number in the millions.

d) *Unity in the gospel.* There is much new growth among Independent congregations and groups unaffiliated with any larger body, but too much work is done in isolation and without partnership. The Angola Evangelical Alliance links 11 denominations and two parachurch organizations for coordinated action. The Council of Christian Churches in Angola (WCC) also draws Christian groups together.

4 **The challenge to biblical faith is great.** Explosive growth is worthless if the Church is permeated with false beliefs and ignorance of the Bible. Witchcraft and animistic practices continue to infiltrate and pollute many churches and lives. Islam's assertiveness, simple message and financial backing cause it to grow. Those who claim to follow Christ need to be taught what such a claim truly means.

5 **Christian leadership is still the most critical challenge** before the Church. Only a fraction of congregations have trained pastors. This shortage results in division, petty legalism, compromise and condoned sin, including elements of witchcraft. The increase in Bible schools and seminaries is still not keeping pace with the needs. Around 25 Bible schools and two seminaries exist (interdenominational [**SIM**, **AME**, **AIM**], Assemblies of God, Baptist, Methodist, Lutheran, Catholic). Among evangelicals, the Superior Institute for Evangelical Theology of Lubango is the largest and is well respected. Just as vital are the practical discipleship/training programmes, such as those run by **YWAM** and the many Brazilian-originated ministries. TEE and mobile-education programmes, such as Africa's Hope (**AoG**), SEAN (UK) and BTCP, are all the more important given the scope of the task and the prevailing poverty. Pray for provision of funds, buildings, libraries and, above all, godly teachers; pray also for effective spiritual growth and ministry of those trained.

6 **Young people and children.** Their numbers dominate Angola's population, despite the huge odds stacked against them. In 2006, the mortality rate for children under age five was 26%, and 45% of that same group suffered chronic malnutrition. The legacy of Marxism and war is a generation burdened with many scars and deprived of educational opportunity and physical security. Most of Angola's Christians are under age 25; ministry focused on them must occur for the sake of the Church's future. Pray for:

a) Primary and secondary schools to be rebuilt, well staffed and full. This generation is the first in a long time to know peace; pray that solid education might bring hope for the future.

b) Ministry to students. Pray for the impact of Scripture Union, **CEF**, **IFES** and other such groups in schools once hostile to Christianity.

c) Churches to increase their vision for evangelizing and discipling children and young people. **OM**, **YWAM**, **AIM** and the Brethren are just a few of many working in this capacity.

7 **The foreign missionary presence** was a good testimony during the years of suffering. The nature of their ministries will most likely shift from aid/relief to development, and from evangelism to discipleship and training. The nation's crippled infrastructure and young Church will need generous and loving partnerships between foreign agencies and Angolan ministries to lead the way forward. Mission agencies include **YWAM**, REMAR, Brazilian Baptists, **OM**, **MAF**, **BCB**, Christ Community Church. Pray for the following aspects of ministry:

a) Humanitarian ministries, such as WVI, Samaritan's Purse and most of the traditional sending agencies, focus on primary health care, education, vocational training and disease prevention as well as provision of the supplies needed to continue such programmes.

b) Support ministries such as **MAF** are strategic, given the disastrous state of the transport infrastructure.

c) "Traditional" mission agencies find themselves surrounded by need and requiring wisdom and resources. Most missions work holistically, ministering to both physical and spiritual needs of Angolans. There are many and diverse ways to serve in God's Kingdom here; pray for more workers.

8 Media and support ministries:

a) The Bible Society is developing Scriptures in nine languages and new translations in Chokwe, Kikongo, Kimbundu, Luchazi and Umbundu. Scripture is needed in 12 languages. A great demand for Bibles persists, but deep poverty limits sales. The Gideons actively distribute Bibles.

b) Christian literature is scarce, and little is available in Portuguese and even less in indigenous languages. Low literacy rates hamper the usefulness of printed matter; pray for programmes that will enable many Angolans to read the Word of Life. There is a tremendous hunger for good Christian literature, but it is usually quite expensive for most Angolans. There are now around 20 evangelical libraries slowly adding materials, first in Luanda and now in some other provinces.

c) GRN has recordings in 30 languages and dialects. These audio resources are crucial in an oral and low-literacy nation such as Angola.

d) Radio broadcasts, through **TWR**, reach the land in 10 indigenous languages and in Portuguese. Pray for more programmes for these languages and a wider listening audience.

e) The JESUS film is available in at least Portuguese, Kongo, Kwangali and Kwanyama, but 40 more languages need translation. Pray for completion and effective use of these.

British Virgin Islands

Anguilla

Caribbean Sea

St. Martin — The Valley

St. Barthelémy

Saba (Neth. Antilles)

Anguilla
British Dependency of Anguilla
Caribbean

Geography 🌍

Area 91 sq km. The most northerly of the Leeward Islands.

Population		Ann Gr	Density
2010	15,465	2.50%	170/sq km
2020	17,811	1.17%	196/sq km
2030	18,881	0.50%	207/sq km

Capital The Valley 1,700. **Urbanites** 100%. **Pop under 15 yrs** 28%. **Life expectancy** 77.3 yrs.

Peoples 👪

African Caribbean 90.1%.
Mixed race 4.7%.
Euro-American 3.7%.
Other 1.5%.
Nearly 30% of the population are non-Anguillan, triple the number of 20 years ago.
Literacy 95%. **Languages** English, English Creole. **All languages** 3. **Indigenous languages** 2. **Languages with Scriptures** 1Bi.

Economy 📈

Tourism is effectively the island's only industry. **Income/person** $7,500 (20.3% of USA).

Politics 🗡

A British dependent territory. There is representative internal self-government.

Religion ⛪

Complete freedom of religion.

Religions	Pop %	Population	Ann Gr
Christian	89.99	13,917	2.4%
Ethnoreligionist	4.30	665	4.0%
Non-religious	3.45	534	2.3%
Baha'i	1.12	173	3.3%
Muslim	0.80	124	5.9%
Hindu	0.34	53	8.2%

Christians Denoms		Pop %	Affiliates	Ann Gr
Protestant	9	45.20	7,000	3.5%
Anglican	1	29.74	5,000	2.8%
Catholic	1	5.50	1,000	2.5%
Marginal	1	1.10	<1,000	1.9%
Unaffiliated		8.50	1,000	-12.9%

Churches	MegaBloc	Congs	Members	Affiliates
Anglican Church	A	8	1,840	4,600
Methodist Church	P	4	2,000	4,000
Baptist Church	P	3	283	850
Catholic Church	C	2	340	850
Seventh-day Adventist	P	3	400	800
Ch of God of Prophecy	P	2	300	600
Other denominations[6]		8	386	910
Total Christians[12]		**30**	**5,549**	**12,610**

TransBloc	Pop %	Population	Ann Gr
Evangelicals			
Evangelicals	17.2	2,662	4.0%
Renewalists			
Charismatics	11.1	1,709	4.9%
Pentecostals	5.2	810	5.5%

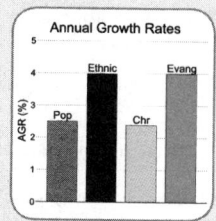

Annual Growth Rates

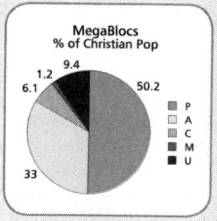

MegaBlocs % of Christian Pop

Challenges for Prayer

1 **Anguilla is a remnant of a bygone era** as a little colonial outpost. Pray that this small island and its churches may not be bypassed by the Holy Spirit. Pray that religious traditions might be infused with real spiritual life.

2 **The quiet nature of Anguilla** could be significantly changed by even small numbers of immigrants; increased tourist traffic and resort size present challenges. Pray for spiritual strength in the midst of change.

3 **Interdenominational cooperation** needs further improvement despite the island's small size. Pray that Christ's followers may function effectively as a united body.

A

Antigua and Barbuda

State of Antigua and Barbuda

Caribbean

Geography

Area 442 sq km. Three islands; Antigua is volcanic, Barbuda coralline.

Population		Ann Gr	Density
2010	88,550	1.17%	200/sq km
2020	97,436	0.90%	220/sq km
2030	104,749	0.66%	237/sq km

Capital St. John's 26,800. **Urbanites** 30.3%. **Pop under 15 yrs** 28%. **Life expectancy** 72.2 yrs.

Peoples

African Caribbean 83.8%.
Euro-American 15.8%. US Americans, British.
Other 0.3%. South Asian.
Literacy 85.8%. **Languages** English, English Creole. **All languages** 4. **Indigenous languages** 2. **Languages with Scriptures** 1Bi 1por 1w.i.p.

Economy

Officially, tourism is the mainstay. Questionable activities also play a major part in the informal economy, but the government works to control and remove these elements.
HDI Rank 47th/182. **Public debt** 19.1% of GDP. **Income/person** $14,556 (31% of USA).

Politics

British colony for 349 years; independence in 1981 as a constitutional monarchy.

Religion

Complete freedom of religion.

Religion	Pop %	Population	Ann Gr
Christian	92.51	81,918	1.0%
Ethnoreligionist	3.70	3,276	2.3%
Non-religious	2.10	1,860	5.5%
Baha'i	0.99	877	1.8%
Muslim	0.60	531	4.9%
Hindu	0.10	89	3.3%

Christians	Denoms	Pop %	Affiliates	Ann Gr
Protestant	22	33.81	30,000	1.9%
Independent	6	1.47	1,000	2.5%
Anglican	1	33.88	30,000	-0.3%
Catholic	1	9.37	8,000	0.2%
Marginal	2	1.37	1,000	0.7%
Unaffiliated		12.60	11,000	1.9%

Churches	MegaBloc	Congs	Members	Affiliates
Anglican Church	A	11	13,514	30,000
Catholic Church	C	6	5,461	8,300
Moravian Church	P	9	3,000	6,000
Methodist Church	P	7	2,900	5,800
Pentecostal churches	P	11	2,273	5,000
Seventh-day Adventist	P	3	870	3,480
Wesleyan Church	P	12	1,856	3,100
Ch of the Nazarene	P	6	780	1,131
Jehovah's Witnesses	M	5	432	1,080
Baptist Church	P	4	580	969
Other denominations[19]		51	3,166	5,893
Total Christians[32]		**125**	**34,832**	**70,753**

TransBloc	Pop %	Population	Ann Gr
Evangelicals			
Evangelicals	19.9	17,595	3.2%
Renewalists			
Charismatics	13.9	12,327	4.4%
Pentecostals	8.3	7,318	5.5%

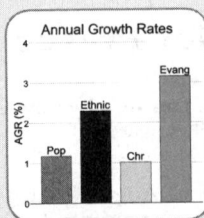

Annual Growth Rates

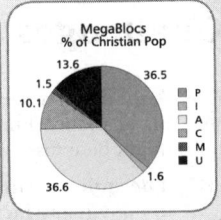

MegaBlocs % of Christian Pop

Challenges for Prayer

1 **Antiguans are almost all Christian by background,** including many evangelicals, but complacency prevails in the face of serious moral and spiritual challenges. Pray for revival that galvanizes Christians to prayer, and for involvement that impacts their society.

2 **Strongholds of sin remain entrenched** – money laundering, drug dealing, violence, gambling and others. The recent arrest in the USA of a major investor in Antigua is wreaking some havoc in the economic and political spheres. Pray that righteous authorities and the prayers of the saints may break down these structures of sin; pray for wisdom and discernment for the government in handling these difficult issues.

3 **Unity among the churches is essential.** Pray for effective cooperation between the constituent congregations and agencies of the United Evangelical Association.

4 **Two local Christian radio stations.** Pray that Abundant Life Radio and Caribbean Radio Lighthouse might be powerful influences for the Kingdom.

Argentina
Argentine Republic
Latin America

Geography

Area 2,780,092 sq km. Latin America's second-largest country, with a great range of climate, rainfall and topography. The 16,300 sq km Islas Malvinas (Falkland Islands) are claimed by Argentina but remain under British rule. There is one federal district and 23 provinces.

Population		Ann Gr	Density
2010	40,665,732	0.98%	15/sq km
2020	44,304,105	0.81%	16/sq km
2030	47,255,305	0.59%	17/sq km

Capital Buenos Aires City 13,074,389. **Other major cities** Cordoba 1.5 million; Rosario 1.2mill. **Urbanites** 92.4%. **Pop under 15 yrs** 25%. **Life expectancy** 75.2 yrs.

Peoples

Hispanic 79.1%. White Argentinean 72.1%; Mestizo/Criolloa 4.4%; Uruguayan 1.8%; other Latino nationalities. There are possibly as many as 1 million illegal immigrants from other Latin American countries.

European 9.8%. 22 groups. Italian 4.7%; Galician 1.7%; Spanish 1.3%.
Amerindian 7.1%. 26 peoples. Guarani(3) 2.5%; Quechua(3) 3.6%.
Middle Eastern 3.3%. Lebanese, Syrian and Palestinian Arabs 2.7%; Jews 0.5%.
Asian 0.7%. Chinese, Romani, others.
Literacy 97.2%. **Official language** Spanish. **All languages** 40. **Indigenous languages** 25. **Languages with Scriptures** 8Bi 7NT 7por 3w.i.p.

Economy

Abundant natural resources and a highly educated workforce. Agricultural products, particularly beef, soybeans, wheat and corn are economic mainstays. Inept governments took the nation from one of the world's richest in 1900 to almost total economic meltdown. The military junta of the 1970s and the subsequent governments could not break Argentina out of the downward economic spiral, which decimated the formerly strong middle class and deepened the gap between rich and poor. A strong recovery has occurred since 2001, but has not sufficiently reduced poverty and unemployment. Economic growth and inflation are high.
HDI Rank 49th/182. **Public debt** 48.6% of GDP. **Income/person** $8,171 (17% of USA).

Politics

Independent from Spain in 1816. Peronist alienation of too many segments of society, inflation and leftist urban terrorism provoked the 1976 military takeover. Incompetence, a failed war over the Falklands and harsh treatment of its own population's rights led to restoration of democratic rule in 1983. Commitment to democracy and openness helped put to rest the ghosts of the past. The continuity of democracy during the tenure of successive Presidents Kirchner then Fernandez (husband and wife) has aided stability.

Religion

Roman Catholicism has traditionally been conservative here and generally enjoyed good relations with government especially the military regimes. More recently, tensions have increased between the state and the Catholic Church, with increasing freedom for and recognition of religious minorities. Evangelicals enjoy respect and freedom.

Religions	Pop %	Population	Ann Gr
Christian	89.28	36,306,366	0.7%
Non-religious	8.68	3,529,786	4.5%
Muslim	0.75	304,993	3.0%
Other	0.55	223,662	2.1%
Jewish	0.51	207,395	-0.5%
Animist	0.12	48,799	-2.1%
Buddhist	0.07	28,466	4.1%
Baha'i	0.03	12,200	1.0%
Hindu	0.01	4,067	1.0%

Christians Denoms	Pop %	Affiliates	Ann Gr
Protestant	100	6.32	2,571,000	2.1%
Independent	75	5.52	2,244,000	2.8%
Anglican	1	0.05	22,000	1.5%
Catholic	1	86.98	35,370,000	0.5%
Orthodox	9	0.43	174,000	0.9%
Marginal	7	1.87	761,000	2.7%
Doubly affiliated		-11.89	-4,837,000	0.0%

Churches	MegaBloc	Congs	Members	Affiliates
Catholic Church	C	6,250	24,758,621	35,370,000
Nat Union AoG (USA)	P	1,058	165,000	850,000
Assemblies of God	P	1,135	303,030	500,000
Latter-day Saints	M	1,266	202,500	405,000
Vision de Futuro	I	595	166,667	300,000
Jehovah's Witnesses	M	1,880	126,364	278,000
New Apostolic Church	I	481	125,000	250,000
Baptist Convention	P	897	105,000	168,000
Christian Brethren	P	2,114	93,000	158,100
Seventh-day Adventist	P	448	103,000	133,900
New Test Miss Union	P	85	59,000	118,000
Chr Pent Ch of God	I	493	46,818	103,000
Ev Pente Ch of Chile	I	38	45,000	76,500
Ch of God Association	I	617	27,143	76,000
Ch of the Lord Mission	I	230	29,000	72,500
Foursquare Gospel Ch	P	605	29,279	65,000
Ev Meth Ch of Arg	P	444	40,000	60,000
United Evang Ch (Toba)	I	270	27,000	59,400
Ch of God (Cleveland)	P	393	27,000	58,000
Other denominations[175]		11,106	973,383	1,728,682
Doubly affiliated Pentecostals				-386,500
Doubly affiliated				-4,450,500
Total Christians[194]		**30,317**	**27,443,805**	**36,306,582**

TransBloc	Pop %	Population	Ann Gr
Evangelicals			
Evangelicals	9.1	3,710,570	2.1%
Renewalists			
Charismatics	17.4	7,063,805	3.3%
Pentecostals	7.1	2,892,630	2.4%

Missionaries from Argentina
P,I,A 494 (350 long-term) in 58 agencies: to Europe 158, Argentina 50, elsewhere in South America 65, Africa 52.

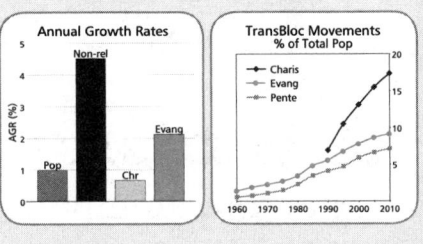

Answers to Prayer

1 **Renewal, large-scale evangelism and sustained intercession** since 1983 have deeply affected the nation and touched the world through Argentinean evangelists, teachers, missionaries and leaders.

2 **The succession of crises** – the military dictatorship, the disappearances of dissidents, the failed Falklands/Malvinas war in 1982 and massive economic disaster in 1999-2002 – led the nation into spiritual hunger, drawing them back to God and galvanizing their commitment to justice and democracy.

3 **Prison ministry continues to transform the nation's jails.** Revival began in Olmos high-security prison, with half of its 3,000 inmates now believers, and spread to 200 other institutions. An estimated 25% of prisoners are Christian; one prison, Cristo la Única Esperanza, is the only completely evangelical prison in Latin America. Around 250 pastors work in prisons.

Challenges for Prayer

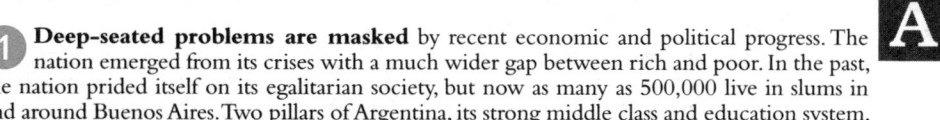

1. **Deep-seated problems are masked** by recent economic and political progress. The nation emerged from its crises with a much wider gap between rich and poor. In the past, the nation prided itself on its egalitarian society, but now as many as 500,000 live in slums in and around Buenos Aires. Two pillars of Argentina, its strong middle class and education system, are under threat. Pray for the country's decision makers to focus beyond mere economic growth to assisting the most needy and building a solid foundation for the future.

2. **Spiritual hunger led to growth.** Evangelical numbers, under one million in 1980, reached 3.7 million by 2010. It is no coincidence that this growth was simultaneous to some of Argentina's most troubled times. Pray that the Spirit will continue to draw many to himself and to do a deep work in believers. But spiritual openness is also seeing many drawn into cults, including Umbanda occultism from Brazil as well as to churches with some questionable teachings.

3. **Behind Argentina's sophistication and postmodern façade** lie intense spiritual struggles for souls. The low-key but widespread influence of the occult (Western and Latin expressions), one of the world's highest Mormon populations and the growing Muslim population all vie for souls with postmodern agnosticism, hedonistic lifestyles and Christianity. Spiritism's hidden currents strongly influence far more people than will openly identify with such groups. Past battles were won through intercession; pray for protection and continued spiritual health for all in the forefront of the battle.

4. **Unity of believers is essential to growth and revival.** Locally, Councils of Pastors meet for prayer in key cities, and, slowly, trust is being built and cooperative ministry enhanced. On a national level, the National Evangelical Alliance (ACIERA) draws together leaders from across the evangelical spectrum. Pray that leaders may hear what the Spirit is saying to the Church today and act together in faith.

5. **Church leadership remains a critical bottleneck** in further growth. Leaders who train, disciple and release other leaders into ministry and who minister in the Word and the Spirit are always needed. Pray for those involved in training through seminaries, Bible schools and TEE; there are literally hundreds across the country. Pray also for students who are hindered by lack of finance, facilities or time.

6. **Amerindians from the Chaco** have long been a marginalized and exploited minority, their cultures ravaged by the majority. Only in 1996 did the peoples of the Chaco region gain official title to their lands. Many of these groups' beliefs are a highly syncretized blend of Catholicism and animism. Chaco peoples have become believers through the work of **CMS** (Wichi, Toba, Chorote, Chiriguano), Mennonites, **BMS** and Argentinean Baptists (Wichi) and through **WV** (Guarani). Pray for maturing of the indigenous Church, and for both expatriates and mainstream Argentineans to be sensitive to this. Pray also for ongoing translation programmes in indigenous languages (SIL/LETRA, UBS, **CMS**).

7. **Specific sections of the population** with ministry and outreach needs are numerous:

a) *The estimated 200,000-strong Jewish community,* mostly in Buenos Aires, is one of the world's largest. They are highly secularized and prosperous, and their identity is being diluted as many marry outside the faith. Chosen People Ministries and ten other agencies minister to Jews. There are several Messianic assemblies in Buenos Aires.

b) *The sophisticated upper class,* who have been harder to reach with the gospel.

c) *The urban poor.* This group has grown in size and includes up to 500,000 slum dwellers, homeless people and thousands of street kids. Local churches are increasing their focus in this area, but significantly more needs to be done on every level – spiritual, social and economic. Buenos Aires is one of the world's largest urban areas; many of those who live there do so in poverty and with virtually no meaningful engagement with the gospel.

d) *University students,* many living below the poverty line, number 1.2 million just in state universities alone, over half being in Buenos Aires. There are few students who actively witness. Pray for ABUA(**IFES**) and **CCCI** – they have over 20 groups and more than 60 workers.

e) Quechua and Aymara from Argentina, Chile and Bolivia flocked to Buenos Aires, where they have become a labouring under-class. They have a small evangelical minority, but are mostly syncretized Catholics or animists.

f) South American immigrants from the five neighbouring countries number up to three million; perhaps half of them are illegal and work in low-level jobs. There are reportedly 1.8 million from Bolivia and 1.5 million from Paraguay. Some bring their Christian faith with them; more import their syncretistic and animistic beliefs.

g) East Asian immigrants. Chinese (around 70,000) and the smaller Korean, Japanese and Vietnamese communities are growing. **CMA** is one of a few agencies reaching these.

8 **The missionary vision of the national Church** is growing and maturing – and it possesses great potential to make Argentina a major sending nation. A number of Argentineans are internationally respected mission leaders. *La Red Misiones Mundiales* (part of **COMIBAM**) has played a major interdenominational role in networking agencies, training centres and churches as well as stimulating and facilitating the vision for missions. The *Centro de Entrenamiento* and RAIM have been doing excellent work in mission mobilization. The Argentinean missions movement has set ambitious goals in terms of mobilizing churches, generating finance and sending workers. Pray that pastors and churches may gain a vision for the unreached peoples of the world.

9 **Expatriate mission agencies have a continuing role** in Bible teaching, mobilizing for mission, reaching minority groups and developing holistic ministries through partnership with national agencies and churches. Pray that expatriate Christian workers might partner well with the strong national Church to see society fully reached and touched by the gospel.

10 **Media ministries for prayer:**

a) Literature. **EHC**, involved in house-by-house distribution since 1958, has covered the country twice. UBS oversees the distribution of literally millions of gospel portions, NTs and Bibles every year.

b) GRN. Recordings are available and have been distributed in 17 indigenous languages and in most immigrant/foreign languages.

c) Radio and television. Christians broadcast all across the country on FM radio stations. Both **TWR** and **HCJB** broadcast by satellite, shortwave and FM with coverage for much of the day. Indigenous languages enjoy over 100 hours per week, though no radio programmes in Guarani exist. Television is a growing medium with Christian programmes and stations increasing.

d) Other media. Pray for the Pastor's Council in Buenos Aires which has ambitious strategies to evangelize that megacity. The JESUS film, seen by a large proportion of the population, is available in seven indigenous languages. The Internet is used widely, with its great wealth of resources available in Spanish.

Armenia
Republic of Armenia
Asia

Geography

Area 29,800 sq km. Landlocked, mountainous Caucasus state. Nagorno-Karabakh, a 4,400 sq km enclave in Azerbaijan populated by Armenians, is controlled by Armenia along with a corridor of land connecting it to the rest of Armenia.

Population		Ann Gr	Density
2010	3,090,379	0.17%	104/sq km
2020	3,175,114	0.23%	107/sq km
2030	3,169,803	-0.07%	106/sq km

Capital Yerevan 1,111,664. **Urbanites** 63.7%. **Pop under 15 yrs** 20%. **Life expectancy** 73.6 yrs.

Peoples

Armenians 97.8%. A Caucasian people.
Other 2.2%. Azerbaijani, Kurd, Russian, Ukrainian, others.
Literacy 99.4%. **Official language** Armenian. **All languages** 12. **Indigenous languages** 7. **Languages with Scriptures** 3Bi 2NT 2por.

Economy

Economic prospects were hampered by a devastating earthquake in 1988, by the legacy of Soviet-era infrastructure and by an economic blockade imposed by Azerbaijan and Turkey. Economic reforms in the mid-1990s, remittances from the large Armenian diaspora and increasing direct foreign investment spell forward progress. Agriculture, refining and processing metals and, increasingly, tourism are important. Underemployment and poverty remain widespread.
HDI Rank 84th/182. **Public debt** 92.5% of GDP. **Income/person** $3,685 (8% of USA).

Politics

Rarely in its 2,500-year history has Armenia been independent. This country has been a victim of its location as a strategic buffer between the Byzantine/Turkish, Russian/USSR and Persian empires. The conflict with Azerbaijan over the status of the ethnic Armenian enclave Nagorno-Karabakh, tensions with Turkey over the border (closed since 1993) and Turkey's failure to recognize the genocide of 1915-1917 all dominate the political life of the country. An armed cease-fire since 1994 has left the country in an uncomfortable limbo that seems impossible to resolve, despite talks intensifying over the last few years. Its position between two potentially hostile neighbours results in close diplomatic ties with Russia. The government is relatively stable and democratic, but some see the 2008 elections – won by the incumbent government – as deeply flawed.

Religion

Religious freedom followed the collapse of communism. An intimate link between the government and the Armenian Apostolic Church continues, with some minor discrimination against other religious expressions.

Religions	Pop %	Population	Ann Gr
Christian	94.43	2,918,245	-0.3%
Non-religious	3.73	115,271	17.6%
Muslim	1.80	55,627	-0.9%
Baha'i	0.03	927	0.2%
Jewish	0.01	309	0.2%

Christians Denoms		Pop %	Affiliates	Ann Gr
Protestant	10	0.93	29,000	4.6%
Independent	13	1.40	43,000	3.7%
Catholic	1	7.28	225,000	-0.2%
Orthodox	8	84.65	2,616,000	-0.4%
Marginal	2	0.98	30,000	6.1%
Doubly affiliated		*-0.81*	*-25,000*	*0.0%*

Churches	MegaBloc	Congs	Members	Affiliates
Armenian Apostolic	O	175	1,417,582	2,580,000
Catholic Church	C	27	134,731	225,000
Pentecostal chs	I	350	14,000	35,000
Jehovah's Witnesses	M	88	11,300	28,250
Russian Orthodox	O	3	8,625	17,250
Armenian Evangelical	P	18	6,471	11,000
Ancient Ch of the East	O	9	4,688	7,500
Baptist Church	P	125	3,500	7,000
Charismatic groups	I	16	3,300	5,280
Other denominations[17]		137	15,951	27,215
Doubly affiliated				*-25,000*
Total Christians[34]		**948**	**1,620,148**	**2,918,495**

TransBloc	Pop %	Population	Ann Gr
Evangelicals			
Evangelicals	8.7	268,186	1.43%
Renewalists			
Charismatics	5.8	179,630	3.1%
Pentecostals	1.3	41,660	3.7%

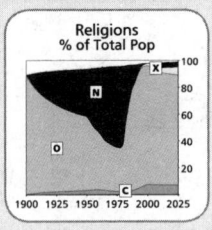

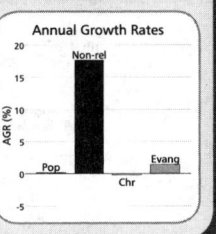

Answers to Prayer

1 **Praise God for the survival of the Armenian Church** through the centuries, despite frequent harsh oppression, and for the growth in numbers of committed believers in the last two decades.

2 **The increasingly committed faith among the Armenian diaspora** is resulting in church growth not only among those abroad but also in Armenia itself, as diaspora Christians focus ministry and prayer on the land of their fathers.

Challenges for Prayer

1 **Good relations with neighbours are key to Armenia's future.** The political and economic scenes are deeply affected by this issue. Centuries of bitter conflict, oppression and massacres left a legacy of hatred and mistrust of these nations. From 1915-17, the Turks killed up to 1.5 million Armenians in what many regard as an unrecognized genocide. Much has been made of Turkey's refusal to accept responsibility. However, small but significant progress between the two nations has been achieved in recent years; a timetable is set to normalize diplomatic relations between them and to open their shared border once again. Pray that Armenians would be able to forgive, and pray for the establishment of trade, trust and cooperation between Armenia, Turkey and Azerbaijan.

2 **The control of Nagorno-Karabakh,** now functionally independent, is unresolved and a millstone around the necks of all involved. Refugees on both sides of the conflict (250,000 Armenians from Azerbaijan, and 530,000 Azeris from Armenia and western Azerbaijan) are still displaced. Although the armed cease-fire has held, all diplomatic solutions have failed. Both nations refuse to back down, and Nagorno-Karabakh itself refuses to accept any resolution into which it does not have direct input. Pray for an answer that is acceptable to all and that allows each group to move forward.

3 **Armenia was the world's first Christian nation** and enjoys a great spiritual legacy of more than 1,700 years of Christianity. Pray that Armenian Christians might become sources of light and blessing to the surrounding region; few peoples here have a significant indigenous church. Armenian Christians are only now realizing the blessing of their Christian heritage and the mission responsibility that lies with it. Pray that this movement may grow.

4 **The Armenian Apostolic Church has long been a cultural refuge** in times of persecution, but the very traditional nature of the Church, which is key to Armenian self-identity, also keeps them from discovering the living Christ. It often inoculates Armenians against the message shared by other Christian groups. Pray for:

a) *Unity and cooperation within the Church.* There are two main groups, tracing back nearly 1,000 years, which use different dialects. Pray that these two (Eastern and Western) will find common ground and the ability to work together for the purposes of God.

b) *Deep spiritual regeneration of the Church* and for godly leaders. This Church will almost certainly remain the dominant religious force in Armenian life. Therefore, pray that there would be a radical transformation therein that sees Christ glorified and many saved.

c) ***An appreciation of, and fellowship with, the smaller denominations in Armenia.*** Though this is improving, significant suspicion and occasional hostility toward non-Orthodox groups remain.

5 **The Armenian Church-Loving Brotherhood,** an evangelical-oriented movement within the Apostolic Church, was formally founded in 1895. Its main emphases are Bible study groups, personal witness, publishing and distribution of evangelical literature and Bibles, and work among the poor and needy, especially orphans. There are a couple of hundred workers in the movement, with thousands of people associated with it, particularly younger people. Pray for this movement and its influence for good on the nation.

6 **The growth of evangelicals since independence** has largely been through the Brotherhood and the many Pentecostal/charismatic groups popping up (in a very-difficult-to-document manner). Baptists and the Armenian Evangelical Church have grown, but not as rapidly. Pray for growth and maturity of all these groups and for unity to take precedence over short-term growth.

7 **Training for leaders and laity is lacking,** but is being addressed. The one small Pentecostal Bible school in Yerevan has been joined by a Baptist theological college and a new theological academy through the Armenian Missionary Association of America. AIMS conducts valuable leadership training seminars. Armenian Christian workers are strategically located to bless surrounding nations, since Armenia is an island of Christianity in a sea of Islam.

8 **Evangelical Christianity has thrived among the Armenian diaspora** of up to eight million, with many congregations in the Middle East, North America and elsewhere. Most Armenians retain close links with their homeland even after many generations away. Since 1988, a host of Armenian churches and ministries have given generously and invested in reaching their homeland, with remarkable results. Pray for the world to be blessed through this global people.

9 **Christian help ministries.** Pray for:

a) ***Relief work.*** The legacy of the communist era includes economic depression, widespread poverty and unemployment. These heighten the value of a number of ministries (Tearfund, Elam Ministries, Love Armenia) that focus on enabling Armenians to provide for themselves economically, especially believers.

b) ***Youth camps*** in the summer provide an excellent opportunity to communicate the reality and power of the gospel to young people. Thousands each year are reached and discipled through the ministry of AMAA, which runs such camps in Armenia and several other nations.

c) ***Student witness is fruitful.*** CSUA(**IFES**) has groups in eight universities and colleges; others work among students, especially through summer camps (SU, Baptists). Pray for openness within students as well as permission from campus and government authorities to minister.

d) ***Bible distribution.*** Bible reading is very rare in this culturally Christian nation, but a modern Armenian version of the NT has recently been released, which may help change this. A modern-language OT is in progress. The Bible Society has an established ministry with a well-used Bible Centre in Yerevan and is reaching into schools. **EHC** focuses on literature distribution, often to mixed reception.

e) ***The JESUS film*** is widely used in four languages.

f) ***Christian Radio.*** **TWR** in Albania broadcasts in Kurmanji and Armenian. **TWR** also broadcasts from Armenia to nine Central Asian and Middle Eastern countries – 60 of the least-reached mega-peoples are within range of the station.

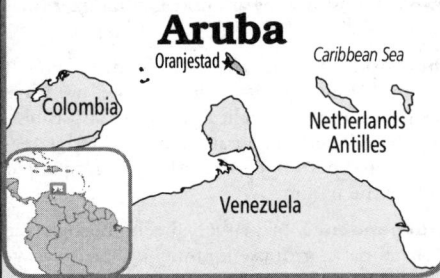

Aruba

Oranjestad ✈ Caribbean Sea

Colombia

Netherlands Antilles

Venezuela

Aruba

Caribbean

Geography

Area 193 sq km. An island 28 km north of Venezuela. Dry and sandy with no fresh water and few natural resources.

Population		Ann Gr	Density
2010	107,380	1.23%	556/sq km
2020	110,721	0.28%	574/sq km
2030	112,460	0.09%	583/sq km

Capital Oranjestad 33,200. **Urbanites** 46.9%. **Pop under 15 yrs** 19%. **Life expectancy** 79.4 yrs.

Peoples

Antillean 80.0%. Antillean Creole (Papiamento speakers) 82,700.
Other 20.0%. Spanish-speaking (Latin American) 11,870; Dutch 3,800.
Literacy 97.3%. **Official language** Dutch, Papiamento (a Creole of Spanish, Portuguese, Dutch, English, Indian and African languages). **All languages** 5. **Indigenous languages** 3. **Languages with Scriptures** 3Bi.

Economy

Heavily dependent on tourism. Other industries make minor contributions to the economy. **Public debt** 14.4% of GDP. **Income/person** $31,676 (69.5% of USA).

Politics

Aruba withdrew from Netherlands Antilles in 1986. It is now a self-governing part of Kingdom of the Netherlands.

Religion

Full religious freedom.

Religions	Pop %	Population	Ann Gr
Christian	92.93	99,788	1.1%
Non-religious	5.00	5,369	3.4%
Ethnoreligionist	1.20	1,289	3.0%
Muslim	0.36	387	3.6%
Chinese	0.14	150	-0.2%
Baha'i	0.13	140	1.2%
Buddhist	0.12	129	1.2%
Jewish	0.12	129	-0.4%

Christians	Denoms	Pop %	Affiliates	Ann Gr
Protestant	17	7.78	8,000	2.2%
Independent	12	2.33	2,000	2.6%
Anglican	1	0.79	1,000	1.2%
Catholic	1	74.50	80,000	0.5%
Marginal	2	2.21	2,000	1.6%
Unaffiliated		5.30	6,000	8.5%

Churches	MegaBloc	Congs	Members	Affiliates
Catholic Church	C	44	16,000	80,000
Jehovah's Witnesses	M	12	780	1,950
Evangelical Church	P	11	1,108	1,850
Assemblies of God	P	7	650	1,625
Dutch Reformed Ch	P	5	749	1,250
Anglican Church	A	1	255	850
Methodist Church	P	3	330	825
Pentecostal churches	I	11	400	800
Seventh-day Adventist	P	6	460	736
Baptist Church	P	4	440	735
Other denominations[20]		22	1,955	3,458
Total Christians[33]		**126**	**23,127**	**94,079**

TransBloc	Pop %	Population	Ann Gr
Evangelicals			
Evangelicals	7.6	8,153	2.8%
Renewalists			
Charismatics	6.8	7,287	8.8%
Pentecostals	2.5	2,675	3.1%

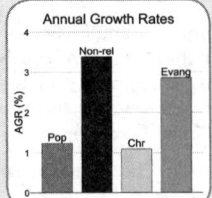

Annual Growth Rates

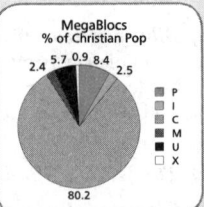

MegaBlocs % of Christian Pop

Challenges for Prayer

1 **The evangelical presence has grown,** predominantly due to the more recent arrivals. Large numbers have immigrated from Latin America, the Caribbean and Asia, but evangelical growth is not even. There are several English-speaking churches and many congregations using Papiamento. Pray for a greater impact on the Asian immigrant population.

2 **Unity among believers** is a key issue for the diverse churches in Aruba. Division can undermine any numerical growth of believers. The greatest threat to this unity is the importation of alien theology, church culture and preaching style common among the televangelists and prosperity preachers seen on foreign Christian TV. Praise God for increased fellowship and cooperation among pastors, enabling evangelicals to present a united front and impact society on issues such as homosexual marriage legislation, teen drug addiction and the high rate of illegitimate births (about 50%).

3 **Media.** There are three Christian radio stations on Aruba: Radio Victoria (originally **TEAM**) and two others broadcast to Aruba and the Venezuelan coast. **TWR** broadcasts to Bonaire on its FM station and internationally through shortwave and the Internet. The gospel is also proclaimed on programmes that appear on secular radio and TV. Pray for the enduring fruitfulness of these strategic ministries.

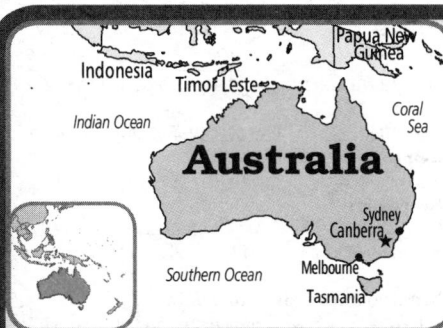

Australia
Commonwealth of Australia
Pacific

Geography

Area 7,682,300 sq km. This island continent is the world's driest, but better watered in the east, southeast and southwest coastal regions, where most live in highly concentrated urban areas. There are three permanently inhabited dependent territories: Norfolk Island (35 sq km; 2,037 pop), Christmas Is. (135 sq km; 1,408 pop), Cocos Is. (14 sq km; 591 pop).

Population		Ann Gr	Density
2010	21,507,384	1.07%	3/sq km
2020	23,669,589	0.93%	3/sq km
2030	25,650,046	0.76%	3/sq km

Capital Canberra 387,000. **Other major cities** Sydney 4.4 million; Melbourne 3.9mill; Brisbane 2.0m; Perth 1.6m; Adelaide 1.2m. **Urbanites** 89.1%. **Pop under 15 yrs** 19%. **Life expectancy** 81.4 yrs.

Peoples

28% of Australians were born overseas, increasingly from non-Western backgrounds. The new category of "Australian" on the recent census has not proved helpful to understanding ethnicity.

Anglo–Australian 67.9%. Predominantly British and Irish roots.

European 16.6%. Migrants from nearly every ethnic group in Europe. Many would be of first- and second-generation European ethnic background, but regard themselves as Australian. Italian 1.9%; Greek 1.6%.

Asian 6.9%. Chinese 3.4%; Vietnamese 1.2%; Filipino 1.0%; Indian 1.0%.

Australian Aborigine 2.6%. Total 550,000; increased due to acceptance of a broader definition of the term Aboriginal from the 1990s onward. Less than one-third can speak one of the more than 100 remaining indigenous languages. In 1780, there were 300,000 speaking 260 languages.

Middle Eastern/West Asian 2.4%. Arabic-speaking 1.2%; Jews 0.5%; Iranians 0.4%; Turks 0.3%.

Anglo–New Zealander 1.8%.

Other 1.8%. Pacific Islander, Latin American, African.

Literacy 99%. **Official language** English. 20% of the population use English as a second language. **All languages** 207. **Indigenous languages** 161. **Languages with Scriptures** 1Bi 11NT 37por 13w.i.p.

Economy

Advanced market economy balanced between services, mining and agricultural exports, industry and tourism. Increasing economic links with East Asia. A high standard of living in a liberal economy with a very strong middle class, but poverty has increased, especially since 2000. The fragile ecology is constantly under threat – the severe drought has decimated agriculture, and bush fires cost many lives and millions of dollars in damage.

HDI Rank 2nd/182. **Public debt** 14.7% of GDP. **Income/person** $46,824 (103% of USA).

Politics

A federal, parliamentary democracy formed in 1901 with six states and two federal territories. The British monarch is the constitutional head of state, represented by a governor general. While a referendum in 1999 narrowly upheld the desire to remain a parliamentary monarchy, those with republican aims continue to push for this goal.

Religion

A secular state with freedom of religion. The increase of those claiming no religion, and the arrival of many non-Christian immigrants, make Australia a much more pluralistic society.

Religions	Pop %	Population	Ann Gr
Christian	69.50	14,947,632	0.5%
Non-religious	23.23	4,996,165	1.9%
Buddhist	2.60	559,192	5.5%
Muslim	2.50	537,685	4.7%
Hindu	0.95	204,320	4.6%
Jewish	0.52	111,838	1.9%
Ethnoreligionist	0.27	58,070	1.8%
Chinese	0.27	58,070	1.1%
Sikh	0.10	21,507	3.2%
Baha'i	0.06	12,904	1.1%

Christians	Denoms	Pop %	Affiliates	Ann Gr
Protestant	129	11.34	2,440,000	0.1%
Independent	46	1.21	260,000	3.3%
Anglican	1	17.62	3,790,000	-0.3%
Catholic	1	25.03	5,383,000	0.5%
Orthodox	38	4.10	882,000	1.4%
Marginal	45	1.28	276,000	1.0%
Unaffiliated		11.20	2,409,000	-1.6%
Doubly affiliated		-2.28	-490,000	0.0%

Churches	MegaBloc	Congs	Members	Affiliates
Catholic Church	C	1,425	3,764,336	5,383,000
Anglican Church	A	3,300	681,655	3,790,000
Uniting Church	P	2,750	159,750	1,278,000
Greek Orthodox	O	270	344,056	492,000
Baptist Union	P	950	61,000	325,000
Assemblies of God	P	1,120	96,847	215,000
Jehovah's Witnesses	M	803	66,484	121,000
Latter-day Saints	M	290	83,042	118,750
Russian Orthodox	O	24	51,513	78,300
Presbyterian Ch of Aus	P	775	35,100	70,200
Lutheran Church	P	500	25,185	68,000
Churches of Christ	P	390	34,919	64,600
Seventh-day Adventist	P	411	54,500	64,000
Coptic Orthodox	O	20	43,357	62,000
Salvation Army	P	388	20,200	47,000
Chr Brethren (Open)	P	320	20,800	46,176
Other denominations[242]		4,229	422,801	808,174
Doubly affiliated				-490,000
Total Christians[260]		**17,965**	**5,965,545**	**12,541,200**

TransBloc	Pop %	Population	Ann Gr
Evangelicals			
Evangelicals	14.4	3,106,949	1.1%
Renewalists			
Charismatics	9.7	2,082,584	2.9%
Pentecostals	1.6	353,224	3.2%

Missionaries from Australia
P,I,A 3,756 (3,193 long-term, 563 short-term), with numbers declining since 2000. In about 90 agencies, 13 with more than 50 missionaries each.

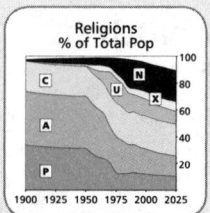

Religions % of Total Pop

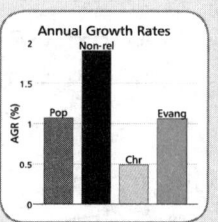

Annual Growth Rates

Answers to Prayer

1 **Australia's Christians, particularly evangelicals,** are facing the challenges of a post-Christian and multicultural nation with faith, dynamism and considered strategies. Recognizing social change and relative Christian decline, small but growing numbers of ministries and congregations are adapting to become more dynamic in reaching out to the majority population and to become more strategic and missiologically astute in reaching the immigrant minorities, who often come from other faith backgrounds. There is a long way to go, but a transition is becoming visible in Australian Christianity.

2 **The political leaders of Australia,** from recent prime ministers down to many parliamentarians and cabinet members, are profoundly influenced by their belief in Christianity. Increasing secularization is taking a firmer grip on society generally, although a relatively strong Christian representation in politics remains a positive influence in protecting the long-established, biblically based values that shaped law and public life over many generations in Australia. A Christian ethic also aided in issuing a formal apology for the mistreatment of aboriginals.

Challenges for Prayer

1 **Australia is undergoing many changes,** all of which place greater strains and tensions on the nation. Some examples for prayer are:

a) Increasing pluralism and aggressive secularization have taken greater hold of Australia's public life. A traditionally Christian country, Australia is now characterized more by its diversity of religions under a secular rubric, with increasingly secular laws – especially regarding issues of sexuality, religion and the sanctity of life. Pray that Christian values might not be driven into the margins, but that believers might engage secular society in a productive and relevant manner.

b) Sustained immigration has created a multicultural country – at least in the larger cities – and introduced fast-growing religious and ethnic minorities, with all the attending tensions. These changes enrich the nation in many ways, but they also place clear challenges before those wishing to retain its Christian and/or Anglo-Saxon heritage.

c) Australia's role as regional peacekeeper and stable democracy is a blessing to many Pacific and Asian countries (Timor, Bougainville, Solomon Islands, others). Thank God for the wherewithal and willpower to save lives abroad, and pray that this role would bond Australians together and establish stability overseas. Attitudes toward refugees and asylum seekers are strained by the constant inflow of people.

d) The precarious ecology is overexploited, in urban settings as much as in rural ones. Australia's ecology is possibly the most fragile of any continent, and with the years-long drought and increasing use of land and water, serious ramifications for the future must be addressed. It may be that the land itself fails, even if Australian society succeeds. Government and grassroots efforts to preserve Australia's environment are, however, admirable in their scope and commitment. Pray for wisdom in conservation and stewardship.

2 **The Church in Australia faces a mighty challenge** – to remain relevant. While over two-thirds of Australians identify themselves in some way as Christian, only 10% regularly attend church, and increasing numbers have negative attitudes toward the Church's perceived intolerance and authoritarianism. Secularism is not so much the dominant ideology as is an individualized, New Age, pick-and-choose spirituality with no accountability. Almost all mainline churches face stagnation or decline, and growth even among evangelicals has slowed. Pray for reformation and revival of the Church, and for this to impact every sphere of society.

3 **Evangelicals are a dynamic and diverse entity.** They are strong in the Sydney Anglican diocese and a growing minority in the Melbourne diocese. Some mainline churches have evangelical majorities; all have at least significant and active minorities. The greatest growth is among Pentecostal/charismatic groups – put together, they would constitute Australia's third-largest denomination. Some of this is transfer growth from other churches, but much is also from conversion growth. Pray for the following issues:

a) Mainline churches are in varying degrees of polarization over issues such as ordination of women, homosexuality and traditional church structures, all leading to further division.

b) Christian holistic ministry – such as ministry to the disabled, to addicts, to the poor and homeless – is an area of great opportunity, since the state cannot meet all the needs and increasingly leaves such activities to charities. But increasing government legislation and controls in these areas create many hurdles that must be overcome.

c) The ideological debate with secular materialists may be the greatest battle facing the Church. Issues of human origin, human sexuality and the existence of God are hot topics for debate. Pray that evangelicals communicate the truth in love; pray for a bold witness to the uniqueness of Jesus that comes through with humility and compassion.

4 **The missions vision in Australian churches is mixed.** Australia actually has a very good missionary-sending ratio as a nation, but much of the burden is being carried by a small minority of churches. The vision for world evangelization must be imparted to pastors during their theological training. Mission-awareness courses such as Perspectives on the World Christian Movement (USCWM) and Kairos are helping to shift the mentality regarding mission. Training programmes are also getting a makeover, from solely academic study to more hands-on and engaging training (Sydney Missionary and Bible College, Worldview, Vose

Seminary, Australian College of Ministries). Australian missionaries at home and abroad are often at the forefront of creative and missiologically astute methods of reaching the un-evangelized; pray that this contribution might be multiplied.

5 **Less-reached peoples are found in increasing numbers and diversity.** Pray for those local churches with active ministries to such cultural communities, and for the work of local congregations and mission agencies seeking to share Christ with them. Despite Australia being an evangelistically open country, many of these immigrants face issues of religious freedom and persecution for becoming Christians and even for considering such a decision.

a) *Many people in working-class urban areas* – and in some isolated mining and farming communities in the vast interior, northwest and north – have had no vital biblical witness. A number of ministries reach out to these tiny and scattered communities.

b) *Muslims* – more than 500,000 from over 70 nationalities with 160,000-200,000 living in the Sydney area (dominated by Lebanese and Turks) and nearly 100,000 in the Melbourne area. The Muslim population has increased nearly 200-fold since 1947, and there are now over 100 active mosques and prayer centres.

c) *Chinese.* Up to 500,000 people living in Australia are of Chinese ethnic background. About 20% of the Chinese are professing Christians; others are secular or adhere to the various Chinese traditional religions. There are over 200 Chinese evangelical congregations in Australia, more than 100 in Sydney alone. Australia's largest Presbyterian church is Chinese. Some of the most lively student groups in universities are of the Overseas Christian Fellow-ships, and these are predominantly Chinese. Pray for the complete evangelization of the Buddhists and non-Christians among them.

d) *Vietnamese* – as many as 260,000. This number includes the flow of refugees and immigrants since the Vietnam War as well as their children. A minority are Christian, but the second generation faces the challenge of finding their faith somewhere between two cultures.

e) *The diverse peoples from the Balkans and Eastern Europe.* Most still retain the use of their mother tongue: Croatian, Macedonian, Serbian, Bosnian and Albanian as well as Polish, Russian and Ukrainian. They come from some of Europe's least evangelized countries, and there are very few evangelical believers among them.

f) *Jews* number over 100,000; those of part-Jewish heritage number even more. Melbourne and Sydney have the highest concentrations of Jews. Celebrate Messiah Australia has a fruitful ministry among Melbourne's growing Jewish community, where there are many recent immigrants from Russia. CWI has a witness in Sydney. **JFJ** and CPM also work among Jews in Australia.

g) *Southern Europeans.* Many use their original mother tongues; however, many second- and third-generation settlers have assimilated into English-speaking Australian society and are now estranged from their cultural roots, feeling out of place in their traditional denominations. Pentecostal Churches and Jehovah's Witnesses are the most successful in reaching them. Major groups are Italian, Greek, Maltese and Spanish. Melbourne is the second-largest Greek-speaking city in the world. These represent minorities that, if evangelized and motivated, could make an impact for God in their native lands.

6 **The 550,000 indigenous Aborigines** have been demoralized in their contacts with Western culture and greed; they are frustrated about their lack of control over their lands and their heritage. Recognition of the land rights of first Australians is a major political issue. Reconciliation between black and white Australians made a significant step forward with the prime minister's apology, along with National "Sorry" Day. Some Aborigines have adapted to the immigrant and majority cultures, but many are marginalized. Some retreated into the more inaccessible and inhospitable parts of the country, while others moved into larger towns and cities. Insensitivities at times and even cruelties by whites are to a degree offset by the loving contribution of many missionaries to the Aborigines over the years. Widespread abuse occurring within some Christian communities is also mitigated by the influence of some excellent, out-spoken Aboriginal leaders who are catalyzing positive changes.

a) *Most Aborigines are Christian,* the result of considerable missionary effort in the past. But nominalism, a cultural disconnect from "Western religion", poverty and often substance abuse stunt the spiritual growth of these unique peoples. Church leaders are trying to combine

Christian values with Aboriginal culture in the best possible way for both worship and for outreach. In a number of areas, especially in the north and west of the country, there are strong congregations with effective outreach.

b) Pray for the Aboriginal Evangelical Fellowship, a key coordinating body of Aboriginal Christians, as it encourages leadership development through its training college, outreach and church planting in every Aboriginal community. Pray that believers may boldly proclaim the liberating power of the gospel in the face of hostility from political activists.

c) Pray for the nearly 500 missionaries in 26 denominational and interdenominational agencies working among these people (such as the Australian Indigenous Ministries, Australian Churches of Christ Indigenous Mission, United Aborigine Mission, **CMS**, MAF, World Outreach and Baptists). Two Aboriginals have been elected to the Sydney Anglican Synod.

d) Bible translation is in progress in 13 of these small language groups; 28 languages have Scripture portions, 12 have the entire NT. Up to 20 still need translation. The entire Bible now exists in Kriol, the most widespread Aboriginal language – a job requiring 30 years and 100 linguists!

e) GRN recordings in several languages are vital contributions to the task because of the great linguistic variety and the lower functional literacy among the Aborigines.

7 **Student ministry** is one area needing greater attention. Witness to the nearly 600,000 students in 40 universities and many more colleges has had some impact, but not nearly as much as potential would allow. AFES(**IFES**) is on almost every campus (with 53 groups and nearly 100 workers/volunteers), Student Life (**CCCI**) is on over 20 and Navigators on 5. A notable trend is that foreign students are proving more responsive to outreach than Australians. Praise God for this open door, but pray that Australians might also be reached during this crucial phase of their lives. Pray for a greater evangelistic zeal, a larger harvest for the Kingdom and an increased flow of missionaries from these groups to the world.

8 **Young people and children.** With a drastic drop in Sunday school attendance, alternative methods must be found to reach the younger generation. Christian school systems are growing rapidly. The Inter-Schools Christian Fellowship (SU) has a valuable ministry in secondary schools. In every state except South Australia, religious instruction is conducted in schools by volunteers from churches, but this is increasingly one voice among competing religions (Islam and Baha'i, especially). Many groups – such as **YFC**, the Crusader Movement, God Squad and others – seek to evangelize young people. The innovative Fusion International developed a well-researched and culturally relevant range of ministries to youth, kids and families, and is based in 25 centres with over 200 full-time workers across the country. A non-religious chaplaincy/counsellor role is filled by committed believers in hundreds of schools, many of them through SU. Pray for their faith to help them offer caring support and wise advice to students dealing with many personal and social issues.

9 **Pray for Christian media:**

a) Radio. Opportunities abound for Christian radio, since local and national stations are legally obliged to allocate broadcast time to religious content. Vision Radio, a ministry of UCB, met this challenge beginning in 1999 and now provides Christian programming to over 350 stations nationally. There are 32 full-time Christian FM stations. Pray for meaningful contact with mainstream Australians. A new **HCJB** transmitter in Western Australia has the potential to broadcast to 60% of the world's population.

b) Literature. There are 126 stores in the Christian Booksellers Association (15 of **CLC**). Pray for a punchy new style of literature with which to impact the younger generation. Evangelistic and teaching materials produced by The Bible Society, ACTS International and World Home Bible League are especially worthy of prayer support.

c) Visual media. Create International, based in Perth, produces Christian and mission-oriented material of high quality and impact.

d) The Internet is an area of outreach with great potential. Some churches are learning to use the web to strategically and effectively reach their communities, but much more can be done. There are considerable training opportunities for churches and ministries to learn new outreach opportunities that come with the digital age.

Christmas Island

Territory of Christmas Island

Geography

Area 135 sq km. 2,360 km northwest of Perth.

Population		Ann Gr	Density
2010	1,600	1.30%	12/sq km
2020	1,800	1.39%	13/sq km
2030	2,150	1.46%	16/sq km

Peoples

Chinese 70%. **European** 20%. **Malay** 10%.
Official language English, but Chinese is more widely spoken.

Economy

Phosphate mining (which closes and re-opens frequently); commercial spaceport construction planned.

Politics

Non-self-governing dependent territory of Australia.

Religion

Religions	Pop %	Population	Ann Gr
Buddhist	36.00	576	1.9%
Muslim	25.00	400	1.7%
Christian	18.19	291	1.4%
Chinese	15.00	240	0.0%
Non-religious	5.81	93	-0.7%

Cocos (Keeling) Islands

Territory of Cocos (Keeling) Islands

Geography

Area 14 sq km. Two atolls and 27 coral islands halfway between Australia and Sri Lanka.

Population		Ann Gr	Density
2010	670	0.92%	48/sq km
2020	720	0.57%	51/sq km
2030	760	0.53%	54/sq km

Peoples

Malay 72%. **European** 24%. **Chinese** 4%.
Languages Malay, English.

Economy

Coconut plantation is the sole crop; some small income from tourism. Dependent on assistance and food supplies from Australia.

Politics

Non-self-governing dependent territory of Australia.

Religion

Religions	Pop %	Population	Ann Gr
Muslim	71.40	478	1.0%
Christian	19.40	130	0.0%
Non-religious	6.30	42	3.7%
Chinese	2.90	19	0.2%

Norfolk Island

Territory of Norfolk Island

Geography 🌏

Area 14 sq km. One main and two smaller islands. 1,500 km east of Australia.

Population		Ann Gr	Density
2010	2,234	0.74%	64/sq km
2020	2,405	0.74%	69/sq km
2030	2,589	0.74%	74/sq km

Pop under 15 yrs 14%.

Peoples 👥

Anglo-Celtic 95%. **Pacific Islanders** 5%. Many are descendants of Pitcairn mutineers.
Languages English.

Economy 📈

Self-sufficient in agriculture; tourism is the main earner.

Politics ☒

Self-governing dependent territory of Australia.

Religion ⛪

Religions	Pop %	Population	Ann Gr
Christian	68.60	1,533	0.5%
Non-religious	31.40	701	1.3%

Challenges for Prayer

1 **The isolation of the islands and their limited resources** make Christian ministry difficult. Isolation also makes their communities' very existence somewhat precarious – depending on assistance from Australia, potential disaster from violent weather and a great distance from immediate help. Pray for God to move among the existing churches to foster renewal and awakening, and for believers to reach out effectively to others, particularly to the Malays of Cocos Island and the Chinese of Christmas Island.

Population		Ann Gr	Density
2010	8,387,491	0.37%	100/sq km
2020	8,539,439	0.17%	102/sq km
2030	8,636,780	0.08%	103/sq km

Capital Vienna 1,705,594. **Urbanites** 67.6%. **Pop under 15 yrs** 15%. **Life expectancy** 79.9 yrs.

Austria

Republic of Austria

Europe

Geography 🌏

Area 83,855 sq km. Landlocked. The Alps in the south and west; flat plains along the Danube River in the east.

Peoples 👥

Germanic 91.1%. Austrian 84.4%; Swiss German 3.4%; German 3.2%.
Balkan 3.1%. Bosniak 0.9%; Croat 0.7%; Slovene 0.4%.
Other European 1.7%. Polish 0.5%.
Other 4.1%. Turkish 0.9%; Chinese 0.4%; Afghan 0.4%; Kurd 0.3%.

A large number of undocumented foreigners are also resident in Austria.
Literacy 99.0%. **Official language** German. **All languages** 20. **Indigenous languages** 9. **Languages with Scriptures** 5Bi 1NT 2por 1w.i.p.

Economy 📈

Mixed economy with strong tourist, commercial, agricultural and industrial sectors. Many trade and commercial links with Central European economies, especially Germany. Over 10% of the workforce is foreign.

HDI Rank 14th/182. **Public debt** 62.6% of GDP. **Income/person** $50,039 (105% of USA).

Politics

The heart of the former Austro-Hungarian Empire until 1918. A multiparty democratic republic and a member of the EU. A neutral buffer state between West and East from 1955 to 1990 with permanent neutrality its continuing official policy. Currently ruled by a centre-left party, but far-right anti-immigration parties remain influential.

Religion

Relationship between the state and the Catholic/Reformed Churches is defined by the constitution. Legislation in 1998 enabled evangelical groups (among others) to receive state recognition as religious "entities"; however, the status given falls short of that afforded religious groups, rendering associated benefits unattainable at present.

Religions	Pop %	Population	Ann Gr
Christian	82.57	6,925,551	-0.4%
Non-religious	11.48	962,884	5.7%
Muslim	5.50	461,312	3.1%
Buddhist	0.20	16,775	5.0%
Jewish	0.10	8,387	0.4%
Other	0.06	5,032	4.1%
Hindu	0.04	3,355	0.4%
Chinese	0.03	2,516	8.9%
Baha'i	0.01	839	0.4%
Sikh	0.01	839	0.4%

Christians Denoms		Pop %	Affiliates	Ann Gr
Protestant	45	4.32	363,000	0.2%
Independent	11	0.21	17,000	-3.2%
Anglican	1	0.04	3,000	0.3%
Catholic	1	64.50	5,410,000	-1.2%
Orthodox	11	2.37	199,000	1.3%
Marginal	17	0.57	48,000	-0.1%
Unaffiliated		10.56	886,000	4.4%

Churches	MegaBloc	Congs	Members	Affiliates
Catholic Church	C	2,633	3,606,667	5,410,000
Lutheran Church	P	163	160,100	320,200
Other Orthodox	O	25	131,293	193,000
Jehovah's Witnesses	M	293	21,667	39,000
Old Catholic Church	I	12	5,500	11,000
Prot Reformed Ch in A	P	10	6,500	10,400
Free Chr Chs (AoG)	P	69	3,546	7,500
Romanian Pente groups	P	31	3,095	6,500
Seventh-day Adventist	P	69	3,800	5,000
Latter-day Saints (Mormon)	M	9	3,037	4,100
Evang Free Ch (BEG)	P	46	1,500	2,500
Federation of Baptist Chs	P	22	1,413	2,050
Other denominations[46]		271	16,036	29,082
Total Christians[86]		**3,653**	**3,964,154**	**6,040,332**

TransBloc	Pop %	Population	Ann Gr
Evangelicals			
Evangelicals	0.5	40,524	2.1%
Renewalists			
Charismatics	0.5	43,041	3.4%
Pentecostals	0.2	17,695	6.9%

Missionaries from Austria

P,I,A 90 (82 long-term, 8 short-term); 81 cross-cultural, 71 international.

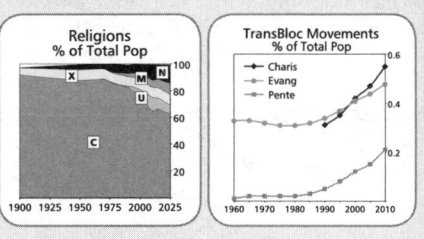

Religions % of Total Pop

TransBloc Movements % of Total Pop — Charis, Evang, Pente

Challenges for Prayer

1 **Austria, a nation of culture, music, art and beautiful scenery,** lies for the most part spiritually empty. While 84% of Austrians believe in God (high for Europe), few have met Jesus personally. Rates of suicide, abortion and alcoholism indicate the great need for spiritual foundations. Pray for the shell of religion in this nation to be filled by the living presence of Christ.

2 **Austria's longstanding Catholic culture is in serious decline.** Record numbers leave the Church each year. Annual membership loss accelerated through the 1990s and 2000s to around 1% per year, a trend showing no sign of changing. The church tax (1% taxable income) and prominent sex scandals among the clergy both contribute to breaks from the church. Seeking God outside the confines of Catholicism is little understood at present. Pray fervently for the growing renewal movement in the Catholic Church.

3 **The Lutheran and Reformed Churches have been in decline** for decades. A year which passes without numerical decrease is seen as a victory. Formalism and tradition have little attraction for the younger generation. There are a number of Bible-believing pastors, but nominalism is as common as in the Catholic Church. Pray for ABCÖ and PGB, two groups of evangelical pastors and lay leaders seeking to deepen spiritual life and combat theological liberalism within the Lutheran Church. Pray too for a move of the Spirit of God that makes these churches a force for the evangelization of the land.

4 **Almost all church growth occurs within evangelical/charismatic churches.** Pentecostal churches nearly doubled between 2000 and 2010. Even so, all evangelicals number only 0.5% of the population. Pray for further multiplication of congregations where the Lord Jesus Christ is proclaimed and honoured. Pray also for the efforts of the *Runde Tisch* (WdV) working across all Christian blocs, as well as the Evangelical Alliance (ÖEA) and the Fellowship of Evangelical Congregations in Austria (ARGEGÖ). Their work is vital in bringing cooperation and partnership to the diverse Christian framework.

5 **Pastors for the multiplying congregations are a great need.** Locating leaders, training them capably, then supporting them adequately is a challenge. BAO (Bible Training on Location), a decentralized programme of non-formal courses based in Vienna, has over 500 students receiving training and is seeking to expand further in Austria. The Evangelical Academy (EVAK) operates a Bible college in three locations. Pray for these as well as the Evangelical Education for Austria (EBÖ) and other training programmes. Pray for God to raise up men and women with passion for the Kingdom, for holiness and for people to be won.

6 **Austria needs more full-time workers.** It is possible that more Austrians are serving God outside Austria than inside it. Major foreign agencies: **OM**, International Teams, **WV**, **DMG**, **CEF**, *Missionhaus Bibelschule*. The majority of evangelical churches were planted through the ministry of these Kingdom workers and are often still dependent on their leadership. A traditionally slow and difficult field, Austria is showing signs of accelerating response to the gospel. Pray for the Lord of the harvest to send more workers, both Austrians and foreign missionaries, to this needy field.

7 **Less-reached sections** of the population:

a) *Provinces.* Lower Austria and Burgenland in the east, Styria in the southeast and Voralberg and Tyrol in the west have fewer evangelicals.

b) *Rural areas.* People living away from the cities have little chance to encounter the gospel. Most do not have an evangelical group in their midst. Pray for believers to reach out to these neglected areas.

c) *Cults and sects.* The aggressive activities of New Age movements, Eastern religions, Jehovah's Witnesses (more numerous than evangelicals), Mormons and the New Apostolic Church have gained thousands of followers. The Dalai Lama conducted a rite wherein he released 722 spirits to make Austria the bridgehead of Buddhism for Western Europe. Pray both for the nullification of these efforts and for the release of those ensnared in false beliefs.

8 **Foreign migrants and refugees** have flooded into Austria since WWII – fleeing Communism up until 1990, then the Balkan strife, and now increasingly hailing from Asia. Pray that Austrian believers may demonstrate compassion to these strangers in their midst as the Bible commands. The gospel is being shared through Bible Society material and ministries such as Oasis Christian Centre. Pray for fruitfulness.

a) *The six ethnic groups of the former Yugoslavia.* There are several evangelical congregations, but these peoples are some of the least reached of Europe.

b) *Muslim Turks, Afghans, Kurds, Pakistanis.* Unabated immigration, high birthrates and poor integration stoke the fires of xenophobia from the far right.

9 **Young people are more open to the gospel** than the previous generation, but churches are poorly equipped for effective youth ministry. Pray for the necessary training for the churches and for a spiritual harvest amongst the youth.

a) *Witness among the 250,000 students* is one of the most fruitful in the land today. The majority are in Vienna, which also hosts many thousands of international students. The seven universities all have active ministry in them. Pray for the ministries of ÖSM(**IFES**), **CCCI** and Navigators on the campuses of Austria. Both **CEF** and SU have ministries focusing on school-age children.

b) Growing prayer movements among teenagers led to the formation of an Austrian Prayer Congress (APC) of over 1,000 meeting biannually. SU started a prayer movement within schools equipping and encouraging students to pray for peers and teachers. Pray for these efforts and others such as JAM among older youth in Vienna, and ABÖJ among younger youth country-wide.

10 Media ministries for prayer:

a) Literature ministries. Scripture distribution by The Bible Society and the literature ministries of Austrian Bible Mission, *Christliche Bücherzentrale* (CBZ) and **CLC** all need prayer. The Bible is widely available to all.

b) Radio and TV. Plentiful programmes are broadcast by radio and on satellite in English and German, though good German-language programming is not accessible in large areas of Austria. Material in German on the Internet abounds. Most expatriate languages have Christian radio broadcasts, though again accessibility is limited.

Azerbaijan
Republic of Azerbaijan
Asia

Geography

Area 86,600 sq km. Caucasian republic on the Caspian Sea, including a 5,632 sq km enclave, Nakhichevan, between Armenia and Iran, and the disputed 4,400 sq km region of Nagorno-Karabakh.

Population		Ann Gr	Density
2010	8,933,928	1.11%	103/sq km
2020	9,837,837	0.86%	114/sq km
2030	10,322,946	0.38%	119/sq km

Capital Baku 1,972,113. **Urbanites** 52.2%. **Pop under 15 yrs** 24%. **Life expectancy** 70 yrs.

Peoples

Turkic 86.8%. Azeri 86.1%; Tatar 0.3%; Turk 0.2%. More than 15 mill. Azeris live abroad, mostly in Iran.
Eurasian 4.4%. Russian 1.9%; Armenian 1.8%; Ukrainian 0.4%. In decline through emigration. Almost all Armenians are in the enclave of Nagorno-Karabakh.
Caucasus 3.7%. Lezgi 2.3%; Avar 0.6%; Georgian 0.2%; Tsakhur 0.2%.

Iranian-Median 5.0%. Talysh 4.0%; Tat 0.7%; Kurds 0.3%.
Others 0.1%. Jews, Assyrian.
Literacy 98.8%. **Official language** Azerbaijani (with 20 dialects). **All languages** 34. **Indigenous languages** 16. **Languages with Scriptures** 2Bi 2NT 7por.

Economy

Booming oil-dominated economy with reserves under the Caspian Sea. Baku was the world's original oil-boom city over a century ago. The glut of oil money enriches an elite few, while 40% of the population live in poverty. The government is proud of having reduced this number significantly in the last few years. A post-Communist market economy is marred by widespread corruption, bureaucracy, a declining agricultural sector and the draining effect of the long-term standoff with Armenia over Nagorno-Karabakh.
HDI Rank 86th/182. **Public debt** 4.1% of GDP. **Income/person** $5,349 (11% of USA).

Politics

A long history of subjugation by Arabs, Mongols, Persians, Turks and Russians. Independent in 1991 from the USSR. A difficult first decade was beset by internal coups and war with Armenia over the enclave of Nagorno-Karabakh in West Azerbaijan. Nearly 1 million Azeris were displaced by this conflict. The president, re-elected in a shady election, is the son of the previous president. They have overseen a political shift away from Russia toward Turkey and the West.

Religion

Official religious freedom is tempered by reactions against "foreign" religions and fears of Islamist extremism. Christian work is increasingly opposed, especially through obstruction and intimidation, if not outright persecution. Most Muslims are Shi'a (80%), a trait shared with neighbouring Iran.

Religions	Pop %	Population	Ann Gr
Muslim	87.58	7,824,334	1.4%
Non-religious	9.55	853,190	-0.7%
Christian	2.74	244,790	-0.3%
Jewish	0.11	9,827	-2.2%
Baha'i	0.02	1,787	1.1%

Christians Denoms		Pop %	Affiliates	Ann Gr
Protestant	8	0.11	10,000	4.8%
Independent	10	0.07	6,000	3.7%
Catholic	1	<0.01	<500	8.2%
Orthodox	3	2.55	228,000	-0.7%
Marginal	1	0.01	1,000	3.4%

Churches	MegaBloc	Congs	Members	Affiliates
Armenian Apos Ch	O	8	67,582	123,000
Russian Orthodox Ch	O	8	62,338	96,000
Georgian Orth Ch	O	3	5,090	8,500
Baptist Church	P	40	4,000	6,160
Word of Life	I	4	1,250	1,875

Jehovah's Witnesses	M	6	700	1,190
Seventh-day Adventist	P	6	700	910
Indep Pentecostals	P	11	512	850
Other denominations[15]		37	4,382	6,694
Total Christians[23]		**123**	**146,554**	**245,179**

TransBloc	Pop %	Population	Ann Gr
Evangelicals			
Evangelicals	0.2	18,517	3.7%
Renewalists			
Charismatics	0.1	10,065	2.8%
Pentecostals	<0.1	4,370	4.0%

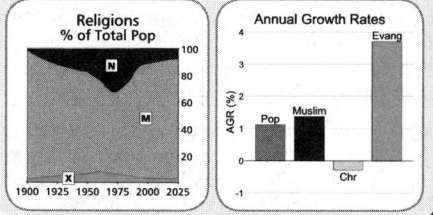

Answers to Prayer

1 **An Azeri Church has emerged,** although not without trials. A reasonable estimate places the number of Azeri Christians in the country at 6,000; a more verifiable total would be 3,000. Either one marks solid growth since 1991 – when there were a mere 40 Christians. Azeri Christian music, literature, poetry and other expressions of worship and culture are beginning to flourish. The number of ethnic Azeris in Iran who follow Christ is much higher.

Challenges for Prayer

1 **Azerbaijan remains a politically volatile nation.** The conflict with Armenia remains unresolved, with both sides manipulating the suffering of many for their own advantage. Regional tensions – involving Russia and its southern republics, Turkey, Georgia, Iran and with NATO – complicate matters further. Azerbaijani military spending is at an all-time high, and no long-term solution to any problem has been found, with most players being intransigent on key issues. Pray for stability and a genuine will to make peace in and around Azerbaijan.

2 **The economic boom** associated with oil will not last long, and is predicted to dry up before 2025. The bonanza sees Baku blossom with wealthy elite and luxury goods. Outside of the capital, little effect is observable. Promised economic reforms have lagged, but it is vital that the current wealth is invested heavily into long-term infrastructure and into developing other sources of income.

3 **Christianity retains an unhealthy association** with Russian imperialism, Armenian enmity and Western neo-colonialism. The openness and freedoms immediately following independence have dwindled somewhat, in terms of religion, media and human rights. The state feels threatened by many forces, internal and external. Pray for increased commitment to fundamental freedoms and for disassociation of the gospel message from foreign cultures.

4 **Azerbaijani believers continue to increase** in number, although most Christians (at least in name) are still of foreign ethnicities. The majority of believers are in Baku, where there are many Azeri-led and Azeri-language congregations. Pray for the maturing of upcoming Azeri leaders and for good fellowship among believers. Cooperation and discipleship/training ministries are key needs. There are a handful of small Bible schools in Baku, most under threat of closure. Unregistered house church networks are spreading. They possess a vision to reach every town and village in the nation. Pray for a strong Church with an effective witness to non-Christians.

5 **The Church faces intensifying opposition,** even as it grows. Many churches find intimidation, surveillance and obstructionist tactics increasingly common. Despite these, there is relative freedom to share the gospel sensitively – many Azeris are Muslim out of cultural affiliation rather than deliberate choice. Pray that Christian witness to the majority Muslim population may be with humility, wisdom and love.

6 **Draconian registration laws** enacted in 2010 make life difficult not just for most Christian groups, but also for other faiths, including Muslims. The government seeks to regulate and restrict religious practice, which it evidently sees as a threat. There are now harsh legal restrictions against religious groups who teach children or who produce literature, against the involvement of foreigners for religious purposes and against developing property for worship purposes. Congregations can legally function only at the location where they are registered, and the registration process is highly obstructive and subject to extortion and manipulation by unscrupulous officials.

7 **Nagorno-Karabakh** is an almost entirely Armenian enclave existing as a de facto separate state within Azerbaijan's borders, using Armenian money, licence plates and such. Escalating tensions began in 1987 and culminated in a war in 1990 with Nagorno-Karabakh's declaration of independence. A corridor between the enclave and Armenia exists, across which soldiers from both sides eye each other daily. Pray for:

a) Conflict to be avoided. Many fear an impending reawakening of hostilities as Azeri military spending and its ambitions peak. No one has committed to finding a political solution. Pray for the deliberate choice of all leaders to find a workable and peaceful solution.

b) The proclamation of the gospel. Orthodox churches have re-established, but there is little known non-Orthodox, evangelical witness, despite relative freedom to establish such. Pray for the good news to be made known, and for a renewal within the Orthodox Church, which is so deeply tied to Armenian identity.

8 **Expatriate Christians** must minister with discretion, since open proselytism is forbidden. But there are ample opportunities to demonstrate Christ's love to Azerbaijanis, especially via tentmaking and development work. The Azeri Church is open for foreign believers to partner with them in ministry. Pray for an increase of new Kingdom workers there and for their fruitfulness.

9 **The unreached:**

a) Most Azerbaijani towns and villages have never been evangelized.

b) The poor and displaced. Employment opportunities (outside of the fortunate few in the oil industry), clean water supplies and long-term solutions related to the 800,000 displaced are all needs. There are many untapped ways of showing Christian compassion to them.

c) The Caucasus peoples are mostly Muslim and unevangelized. The only exceptions are Georgians and Udi, who are traditionally Orthodox. Pray for the Lezgi, Avar, Tsakhur, Kryz and Buduq peoples, the most populous of these peoples.

d) The Indo-Iranian-speaking minorities of Talysh, Tat and Kurds are unreached.

10 **Christian help ministries.** Pray for the impact of:

a) Christian literature. There is a quickly growing collection of Christian books in Azeri (more than 100, with another 20-30 in progress), the majority of them published unofficially. Pray for this vital and strategic work. There are a couple of Christian bookstores in Baku.

b) Bible translation. The Azeri Bible is available in both North and South Azeri, and the NT in audio format for North Azeri. Translation needs are most keenly felt among the minority Caucasus languages.

c) Christian radio/audio. There is a notable lack of radio programmes in Azeri. This is a matter for prayer, both for programme development and for stations from which to broadcast.

Christian audio programmes on cassette/CD are available in 12 languages through **GRN**. Increasing numbers of worship songs are being written and released in Azeri musical genres and language.

d) The JESUS film is available in Avar, North Azeri, Kurmanji, Lezgi, Russian and Talysh.

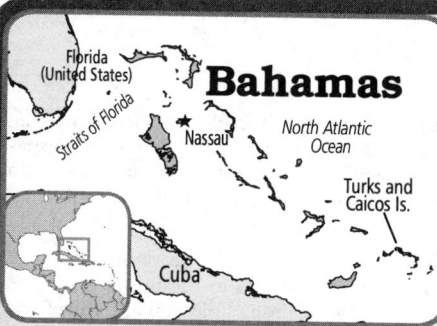

Bahamas

North Atlantic Ocean

Nassau

Turks and Caicos Is.

Florida (United States)

Straits of Florida

Cuba

Bahamas
Commonwealth of the Bahamas
Caribbean

Geography

Area 14,000 sq km. An archipelago of 700 coral islands between Florida and Cuba. Forty are inhabited.

Population		Ann Gr	Density
2010	345,736	1.21%	25/sq km
2020	384,329	1.01%	28/sq km
2030	417,513	0.76%	30/sq km

Capital Nassau 251,000. **Urbanites** 84.1%. **Pop under 15 yrs** 26%. **Life expectancy** 73.2 yrs.

Peoples

African Caribbean 79.0%. Bahamian 24%; Haitian 7.9%; Jamaican 1.6%.
European 10.7%.
Other 0.8%.
Literacy 95.5%. **Official language** English. **All languages** 4. **Indigenous languages** 2. **Languages with Scriptures** 1Bi.

Economy

Heavily dependent on tourism (80% from USA) and tourism-driven development. Banking is also important; Bahamas functions as a tax haven for many.
HDI Rank 52nd/182. **Public debt** 6.94% of GDP. **Income/person** $22,359 (47% of USA).

Politics

Independent from Britain in 1973 as a parliamentary monarchy. A stable democracy since 1992.

Religion

Complete freedom of religion.

Religions	Pop %	Population	Ann Gr
Christian	94.65	327,239	1.1%
Non-religious	3.50	12,101	2.1%
Ethnoreligionist	1.05	3,630	4.4%
Baha'i	0.45	1,556	3.6%
Jewish	0.30	1,037	16.3%
Chinese	0.05	173	-2.4%

Christians	Denoms	Pop %	Affiliates	Ann Gr
Protestant	30	61.38	212,000	1.3%
Independent	37	9.14	32,000	3.8%
Anglican	1	13.68	47,000	0.3%
Catholic	1	14.38	50,000	0.3%
Orthodox	1	0.16	1,000	0.8%
Marginal	4	1.87	6,000	2.6%
Unaffiliated		2.14	7,000	-8.6%
Doubly affiliated		*-8.10*	*-28,000*	*0.0%*

Churches	MegaBloc	Congs	Members	Affiliates
Baptist Union	P	292	70,659	118,000
Catholic Church	C	107	28,400	49,700
Anglican Church	A	110	19,874	47,300
Seventh-day Adventist	P	50	13,500	16,200
Assemblies of God	P	41	3,649	13,500
Ch of God (Cleveland)	P	108	6,400	12,800
Other denominations[68]		567	44,468	90,328
Doubly affiliated				*-28,000*
Total Christians[74]		**1,275**	**186,950**	**319,828**

TransBloc	Pop %	Population	Ann Gr
Evangelicals			
Evangelicals	35.9	124,174	2.5%
Renewalists			
Charismatics	16.1	55,729	5.4%
Pentecostals	13.0	44,800	3.3%

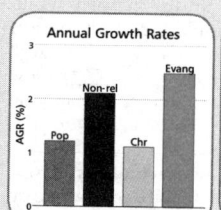

Annual Growth Rates

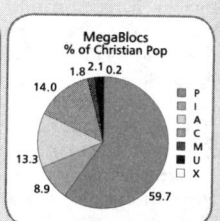

MegaBlocs % of Christian Pop

Answers to Prayer

B

1. **Thank God for the strong Christian legacy** and the public faith of many political leaders. Pray for the unifying work of the Bahamas Christian Council, which represents the majority of churches in the islands, and for the increasing influence of the National Day of Prayer.

Challenges for Prayer

1. **Materialism,** stimulated mostly by tourism, deeply affects all levels of society. Lowering standards of morality see a rise in births out of wedlock, drug use and violent crime (especially armed robbery). The staggering wealth of foreign residents and tax shelters display a different world from the average Bahamian, not to mention the even poorer Haitian immigrants. Pray for social righteousness and a government that works to serve all strata of society.

2. **Christian commitment is low** and nominalism widespread, despite nearly all Bahamians claiming to be Christian. Few are willing to commit themselves to the Lord's work, and many congregations are without adequate pastoral care. Most households own a Bible; few actively read it. Pray for revival and for a missionary vision among believers.

3. **The younger generation** is increasingly out of touch with and alienated from traditional church culture. Specific efforts to reach, disciple and integrate them into the larger body of Christ are needed.

4. **There is a growing Haitian Diaspora** who are resented by Bahamians. Pray for God to enable the Bahamian Church to minister meaningfully to this needy group in their midst.

Bahrain

The State of Bahrain

Asia

Geography

Area 691 sq km. A group of one larger and 32 smaller barren islands in the Arabian Gulf, between the Qatar peninsula and Saudi Arabian mainland – linked to the latter by a causeway.

Population		Ann Gr	Density
2010	807,131	2.10%	1,168/sq km
2020	953,213	1.57%	1,379/sq km
2030	1,085,431	1.24%	1,571/sq km

Capital Manama 167,000. **Urbanites** 88.6%. **Pop under 15 yrs** 26%. **Life expectancy** 75.6 yrs.

Peoples

Arab 50%. Bahraini 40%; Other Arab (Saudi, Palestinian, Egyptian, others) 10%.
Iranian 15%. Farsi, Kurds, others.
Bahraini Farsi 10%.
South Asian 15%. Indian (Malayli, Tamil, Telugu, others) 10%; Pakistani 5%.
East Asian 7%. Filipino, Korean, Chinese.
European 1.5%. UK 1%; US citizens; others.
Other 1.5%.
Literacy 87.7%. **Official language** Arabic. **All languages** 12. **Indigenous languages** 3. **Languages with Scriptures** 2Bi.

Economy

First to produce oil in the Gulf, will also be the first to run out. Diversification efforts, including moving away from solely an industry-based economy to focus on finance/business (freest economy in the Middle East) and increasingly IT, healthcare and education. Unemployment and poverty are very real issues that will become more challenging as Bahrain faces up to its dwindling oil and water supplies. About half the labour force is foreign.
HDI Rank 39th/182. **Public debt** 28.7% of GDP. **Income/person** $27,248 (57% of USA).

Politics

British Protectorate until 1971. Absolute rule by an Emir between 1975 and 2001. Now a constitutional monarchy with two levels of parliament, the lower one elected. The ruling family (holding kingship and almost all important posts) is Sunni, but two-thirds of the indigenous population is Shi'a. With an increasingly active parliament, long-running tensions between the two groups are beginning to subtly change the political dynamics of the nation.

Religion

Islam is the official religion, and almost all Bahrainis are Muslims. Proselytizing Muslims is illegal. Expatriate Christians are very free to worship together in churches; practitioners of other faiths are free to do the same. With limited compounds, though, dozens of congregations must share the same building.

Religions	Pop %	Population	Ann Gr
Muslim	83.23	671,775	2.0%
Christian	9.81	79,180	2.4%
Hindu	6.00	48,428	5.5%
Non-religious	0.50	4,036	-12.8%
Baha'i	0.21	1,695	3.1%
Other	0.10	807	2.1%
Jewish	0.08	646	24.2%
Buddhist	0.05	404	6.8%
Ethnoreligionist	0.02	161	2.1%

Christians Denoms		Pop %	Affiliates	Ann Gr
Protestant	21	1.16	9,000	2.8%
Independent	56	2.02	16,000	3.1%

Anglican	1	0.37	3,000	0.0%
Catholic	4	5.83	47,000	2.2%
Orthodox	2	0.30	2,000	0.6%
Marginal	2	0.02	200	6.4%
Unaffiliated		0.10	1,000	0.0%

Churches	MegaBloc	Congs	Members	Affiliates
Catholic Church	C	6	11,125	44,500
South Asian churches	I	35	4,200	8,820
Church of South India	P	1	2,778	5,000
Filipino churches	I	14	2,100	3,780
Anglican Church	A	3	1,796	3,000
Melkite Greek Cath Ch	C	2	850	2,550
Coptic Orthodox Ch	O	1	800	2,000
Other denominations[41]		58	4,776	8,733
Total Christians[86]		**120**	**28,425**	**78,383**

TransBloc	Pop %	Population	Ann Gr
Evangelicals			
Evangelicals	2.9	23,579	3.3%
Renewalists			
Charismatics	2.5	20,261	6.8%
Pentecostals	0.7	5,710	7.2%

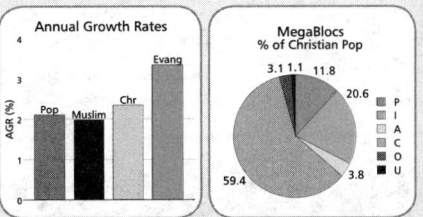

Annual Growth Rates

MegaBlocs % of Christian Pop

Challenges for Prayer

1 **Bahrain enjoys greater freedoms** than almost all Gulf countries and therefore is spiritually strategic. With greater freedoms, the accompanying vices are becoming problems. Many Saudis and Kuwaitis visit here to enjoy the more relaxed environment. Pray for them to meet Christians and encounter the gospel. Pray for the king as he leads the nation forward.

2 **Christian ministry** in Bahrain has good foundations. For over a century, the American Mission Hospital has been well known and highly regarded. Pray that this may continue and that there may be fruit from the tactful witness of believers.

3 **Praise God for the local believers.** Some are integrated into the various churches; others are in more informal networks. Pray for spiritual growth and especially for unity and cooperation among these groups, as a testimony to their fellow Arabs.

4 **Among the large expatriate community** (predominantly from South and East Asia and the Middle East, but also the West and Africa), a considerable number of active Christians meet formally and informally. Pray that expat believers might have courage and wisdom to share their faith outside their cultural group as well as a sense of God's purpose in bringing them to Bahrain. One area of great potential is in education. The internationalization of education opens many opportunities, since locals prize good education and much schooling is in English. Pray for believing teachers who will be witnesses in their jobs.

5 **The labour force** is 59% foreign, drawn from more than 50 nations. Most are on temporary contracts and often must endure poor treatment, poor pay and unrealistic expectations from back home. Pray that Christians within these national groups may win people for Christ. The less evangelized of these expatriate communities are Iranians, Sri Lankans and Hindus and Muslims from India and Pakistan. Nearly half the congregations and house groups are from south India.

6 Media ministries:

a) Internet. High-speed connection is widely available, giving access to all kinds of Christian resources. Chat rooms are especially popular, since seekers can inquire about Jesus anonymously.

b) Christian TV and radio. A number of satellite broadcasts to the Gulf are watched in Bahrain. DVDs of all kinds are also available. Gospel radio is broadcast on medium and shortwave as well as on the Internet.

c) Christian literature. The Christian bookstores in Manama continue to bless locals and expats, but they also struggle. The Bible Society works to provide Scriptures in Arabic as well as in the many languages of the temporary workers.

Bangladesh
People's Republic of Bangladesh
Asia

Geography

Area 143,998 sq km. Occupying the delta and floodplains of the Ganges and Brahmaputra Rivers, with high rainfall and frequent flooding.

Population		Ann Gr	Density
2010	164,425,491	1.43%	1,142/sq km
2020	185,552,357	1.15%	1,289/sq km
2030	203,214,204	0.83%	1,411/sq km

Capital Dhaka 14,648,354. **Other major cities** Chittagong 5.0 million; Khulna 1.7mill. **Urbanites** 28%. **Pop under 15 yrs** 32%. **Life expectancy** 65.7 yrs.

Peoples

All ethnic groups/cultures/castes: 399. Muslims and Hindus have distinct cultures and dialects.
Bengali 94.3%. 136 peoples. Shaikh 85.6%; Namasudra 2.1%; Kayastha 1.2%; Rajbansi 1.0%.
Urdu Muslims 2.0%. 35 peoples. Ansari 0.8%; Sayyid 0.7%; Bihari Muslim 0.2%.
Other South Asian 2.6%. 180 peoples, including

from the following people clusters: Hindi(65 peoples); Munda–Santal(10); Oriya(23); Punjab(19); Rajastan(16); Tamil.
Other 1.1%. Including 46 Tibetan/Himalayan peoples, other Asians, Westerners.
Literacy 41.1%. **Official language** Bangla; English also used. **All languages** 46. **Languages with Scriptures** 14Bi 7NT 8por.

Economy

Among the world's poorest nations, suffering from gross over-population and periodic natural disasters (such as devastating floods and cyclones) with enormous loss of life and property. Poverty is endemic and seems impossible to overcome, but some progress is being made. Major sources of income are agriculture, textiles, clothing, jute and funds sent home from Bangladeshis working abroad. Nearly half the population lives on less than $1/day.
HDI Rank 146th/182. **Public debt** 39% of GDP. **Income/person** $521 (1% of USA).

Politics

Part of Pakistan for 24 years. Independence in 1971 after a bitter civil war; political instability thereafter with assassinations, 18 military coups and a nine-year military dictatorship which ended in 1991. One of the Islamic world's only democracies is rendered ineffective by unrest and personal animosity between two women who have led the two main political parties. Military and Islamist groups remain influential and ready to pick up the pieces should the state fail. Often rated among the world's most corrupt nations.

Religion

A secular state 1971–88. Islam became the state religion in 1988. Officially there is religious freedom, but this is being steadily eroded by Islamist pressure and a legal system lacking safeguards for ethnic or religious minorities. Islamists are a strong and growing minority.

Religions	Pop %	Population	Ann Gr
Muslim	89.01	146,355,130	1.5%
Hindu	9.10	14,962,720	0.4%
Christian	0.66	1,085,208	3.1%
Buddhist	0.60	986,553	1.4%
Ethnoreligionist	0.49	805,685	0.2%
Non-religious	0.11	180,868	3.4%
Sikh	0.02	32,885	1.4%
Baha'i	0.01	16,443	1.4%

Christians Denoms		Pop %	Affiliates	Ann Gr
Protestant	28	0.21	347,000	3.4%
Independent	23	0.26	435,000	3.7%
Catholic	1	0.19	311,000	1.9%

Included are tens of thousands of Jesus-followers who have not left their culturally Muslim identities.

Churches	MegaBloc	Congs	Members	Affiliates
Catholic Church	C	85	170,879	311,000
Muslim followers of Jesus	I	330	33,000	132,000
Talitha Koumi	I	919	45,935	71,200
Church of the Nazarene	P	800	25,568	45,000
Bangladesh Bapt Sangha	P	335	18,000	39,000
Seventh-day Adventist	P	137	28,800	38,880
Free Christian Churches	P	321	18,300	38,500
All One in Christ Fell	I	168	13,400	33,500
Bangladesh Bapt Ch Fell	P	400	13,156	32,100
Other Independent	I	102	10,200	30,600
Garo Baptist Union	P	148	11,718	26,600
Methodist Church	P	319	18,500	24,605

Tribal Baptist Ch	I	256	20,500	24,600
New Apostolic Church	I	57	11,400	22,800
Assemblies of God	P	108	7,483	22,000
New Covenant Church	I	57	6,821	19,100
Church of Bangladesh	P	67	6,084	17,400
Free Bapt Chs (New Life)	I	186	4,655	15,500
Evang Christian Ch	I	46	6,025	14,700
Believers Church	P	150	8,000	14,000
Other denominations[29]		1,096	62,144	112,577
Total Christians[54]		6,087	540,568	1,085,699

TransBloc	Pop%	Population	Ann Gr
Evangelicals			
Evangelicals	0.4	633,467	3.6%
Renewalists			
Charismatics	0.2	338,660	3.9%
Pentecostals	<0.1	36,948	5.1%

Missionaries from Bangladesh

P,I,A about 500, most not cross-cultural.

Annual Growth Rates

TransBloc Movements % of Total Pop

Answers to Prayer

1 **Progress in the fight against poverty** has been made. The thousands of NGOs operating contributed immeasurably to this. Bangladesh is now the furthest along of all South Asian nations toward meeting the UN Millennium Development Goals for 2015 (focused on poverty reduction, education, etc). Micro-credit has been the flagship strategy for this progress.

2 **Encouraging growth among believers** both inside and outside conventional church structures. Churches are increasing, especially indigenous denominations, but numbers of Christ-followers who remain in the traditional structures of their faith background are also growing.

Challenges for Prayer

1 **The cycle of poverty** will perpetuate itself until fundamental changes occur. Pray for long-term, penetrating transformation in the following areas of desperate need:

a) *The economy is sorely underdeveloped.* Bangladesh has little infrastructure, very few natural resources, and therefore affords few ways of making an income. Most people work in agriculture or textiles for scandalously low wages. The majority of Bangladeshis live in gripping poverty, with a very small wealthy minority.

b) *A solid social foundation* for progress is lacking. Education levels are low (but improving), and overpopulation creates problems in a nation already wanting in land, resources and employment opportunities. Women have been the backbone of micro-credit success (80% of households participate in benefits from micro-credit), yet often suffer undignified and inequitable treatment.

c) *A frightening vulnerability* to changes in climate and economy. With such widespread poverty, a large proportion of income is spent on food. Significant rises in food prices have a devastating effect, but not as devastating as the effect of flooding from swollen rivers and monsoons. With alarming regularity, the nation is made to endure tragic loss of life and property.

B

2 **The political situation** offers little hope for significant change and seems a venue for feuding between two very wealthy clans rather than a means to improving the lot of the poor majority. Many see Bangladeshi democracy as merely lip service to Western ideals in order to secure aid. Corruption is endemic and deeply rooted. Pray for governance that is just, transparent and effective at assisting those in need while thwarting those seeking to gain at the expense of the nation.

3 **Religious discrimination** and tension is rising. Islamists, while a small minority, exert increasing pressure for governance by shari'a principles. Minority groups, even Muslim ones, find themselves vulnerable. Christians, Buddhists and especially Hindus suffer as persecution intensifies, occasionally to the point of destruction of property and sometimes even death. Forced reconversion to Islam is an increasing threat. Since independence, the percent of the population comprising minority sections of society has been reduced to half. Pray for binding of the powers of darkness operating in religious, social and ethnic realms. Pray also that the constitutional freedom allowing all to practise and propagate their own religions might be maintained.

4 **The churches have been growing faster** than the population rate for the last 50 years. Pray specifically for:

a) *The people-movement tribal churches.* Significant church growth (greater than 10% evangelical) has occurred among the following peoples: Santal, Munda, Khasi, Garo, Maramei, Ralte, Mizo, Poi. Another 18 groups have more than 5% evangelicals and multiplying churches. Pray that these churches may become strong and full of vision for mission.

b) *The churches among sections of the Hindu population.* The majority of indigenous believers have traditionally been from a Hindu background, and usually from the less populous and lower caste peoples. The ill-treatment of Hindus in Bangladesh has made them more amenable to the gospel.

c) *Believers from a Muslim background.* There are tens of thousands who now call on Jesus as Lord, but a wider breakthrough awaits. Some have found Christ through highly contextualized "Jesus mosques", others through relational networks, even visions and dreams. Pray for these fledgling movements with such staggering potential to grow, spread and mature.

5 **The Church has many needs,** the greatest of which is spiritual awakening. Pray that the Holy Spirit will move in these areas:

a) *Nominal Christianity.* Early people movements brought thousands from marginalized sections of society into the Church. Poverty, illiteracy and lack of trained, godly leadership led to shallowness and nominalism.

b) *Unity.* Imported and indigenous divisions hinder the Church's witness to other faiths and make it easier to legislate against and intimidate Christians. Pray for the National Christian Fellowship of Bangladesh as it encourages evangelical unity and cooperative action in evangelism, teaching and aid programmes.

c) *Outreach.* After years of little interest, there is growing involvement in reaching out to others with the gospel. This marks a major transition in the national Church.

d) *Finance.* Christians generally come from lower classes and castes, which, together with their minority faith, limits employment opportunities. This can create a situation of perpetual dependency on foreign aid. National Christian workers are sometimes drawn by the much-needed salary more than the desire to serve. Pray for means by which believers and churches may be self-sustaining.

6 **Leadership for the churches** is much needed. Many pastors minister while holding down full-time jobs. A lack of resources limits the number of not only full-time ministers, but also full-time theological students. Pray for creative and responsible methods of offering relevant instruction. Spiritually mature lay leaders are also in short supply; pray for both renewal and training opportunities.

a) Key interdenominational residential schools are the College of Christian Theology Bangladesh and the Christian Discipleship Centre. Both also run TEE and short-term programmes which are of great strategic importance.

b) Denominational Bible schools and seminaries are also important in Bangladesh, run by **AoG**, **GFA**, **ABWE**, Free Baptist, Anglican, Adventist, Lutheran and Church of Bangladesh.

c) Indigenous Bible schools offer training in local community outreach, tailored to the needs of culturally Muslim followers of Jesus.

7 **There are over 20,000 registered NGOs** which have multiplied to meet the land's endless social needs. Indigenous secular NGOs such as the Grameen Bank significantly improved the lives of millions of the poor. The Bangladesh Rehabilitation Assistance Committee (BRAC) is the world's largest NGO (2009), a status accompanied by both large-scale success in development work and growing criticism as a "second government" with too little accountability. Christian NGOs have administered aid since independence and, during the nation's frequent natural calamities, have demonstrated generosity and impartiality. HEED Bangladesh (Health, Education & Economic Development), WVI, World Concern and others seek to uphold Christian values and prepare the way for local church and mission involvement. Tearfund seconds workers and helps in funding projects and in research.

8 **Bengali people** are by far the largest unreached people in the world, numbering around 240 million globally. The majority live in Bangladesh and India, but large communities live in Britain, the USA and elsewhere. It was to the Bengali that William Carey went as a missionary. Although they revere Carey's memory, the great breakthrough has still not come after 200 years. There are signs of the trickle becoming a flood, however. Pray specifically for:

a) Muslims, who number over 140 million in Bangladesh alone. The Bengali are claimed as Islam's greatest missionary success. But the majority follow "folk" Islam – a blend of Sufi-influenced Islam, indigenous culture and Hinduism. Pray for:

i Openness to the gospel – the vast majority have never heard the true gospel.

ii More workers – given their population, the numbers committed to reaching them are pitifully few (perhaps only four Protestant missionaries for every one million Bengalis). Pray for a surge in Kingdom workers committed to the evangelization of Bengalis.

iii Those who have responded – many have remained in their cultural/religious context while committing their lives to Jesus. Pray for the nurturing of these followers; pray for leaders who model biblical values and lifestyles, for God-honouring worship patterns and for cultural relevance without compromise of biblical faith. They often face social and family pressure to renounce Christ and opposition from some Islamic leaders. Pray that new believers may experience dependence on God in poverty, firmness under persecution, evangelistic vision and unity with other established Christian communities from differing cultural backgrounds.

b) Hindus, who feel increasingly vulnerable as a religious minority – there have been many incidents of violence and persecution against them. Pray for this hardship to spark openness to Jesus. Some followers of Jesus remain within the Hindu context and do not link with "foreign" Christian bodies. There are 228 Hindu people groups and/or castes, of which 204 are classified as least-reached/unreached. Only among 14 groups has there been any significant response. The upper castes have remained resistant to the gospel.

9 **The tribal peoples'** very existence is threatened as the Bengali population explosion pushes further into traditional tribal lands. Several peoples of the Chittagong Hill Tracts suffer from this slow squeeze; their lands and even their culture are under threat as Islamization accompanies Bengalization. Pray for a just settlement – the granting of limited autonomy to the region has not improved the situation much. Pray also for Christian agencies seeking to bring tribal peoples to Christ (Global Interaction, **ABWE**, **BMS**, **GFA**, **IMB**, Presbyterians and Lutherans). Some groups are almost entirely unreached while others have large Christian populations.

10 **Other unreached groups:**

a) Bihari Muslims (Urdu-speaking) are unwanted by Pakistan and stigmatized as traitors in Bangladesh for their role in the 1971 war. Most still live in dozens of former refugee camps.

Pray for reconciliation with the Bengali people. Pray for a development plan for them, for Christian workers and for openness to the gospel.

b) Rohingya Muslims. As many as 250,000 of them have fled persecution from the Buddhist Myanmar government. Huddled into refugee camps, facing starvation and often subject to forced repatriation or maltreatment, they have never been evangelized. Pray for those seeking openings to reach them.

11 **Mission agencies** have played a valuable role with their social uplift programmes, hence their emphasis on institutions and aid. Pray for the following:

a) Evangelism and church planting. This core aspect is still not occurring on a level that will see the entire nation reached. Blatant proselytism is not tolerated, but relational evangelism is effective. Increasingly strict limitations have been placed on missionaries; some believe expatriate mission work may eventually be squeezed out altogether, especially if Islamists have their way.

b) Development/aid, another area of rightful focus and one which bears good fruit. **ABWE**, **AoG**, **ELCA**, Mennonite Central Committee, The Leprosy Mission, Interserve, **SIM**, **OM** and **YWAM** are just a few of the many ministries providing much needed assistance for the millions who suffer whilst building good relationships with local governments.

c) At risk people. Child labourers and sex workers are forced into involuntary servitude in tragically high numbers (hundreds of thousands and millions, respectively). Gripping poverty and rampant corruption contribute to these structures of sin and create a living hell with no easy way out. Agencies such as **CMS**, Salvation Army, Habitat for Humanity, Compassion, and Tearfund minister into these situations.

d) Business ventures started and run by Christians provide another avenue for serving those in need. Entrepreneurs and investors are currently welcomed by this country.

12 **Scripture is in great demand** despite legal complications involving the use of Koranic language in the Bible and attempts to "protect" Muslims from Christian Scriptures. Pray for:

a) Literature distribution. The Bible Society and its extensive ministry of Scripture production distributes around one million Bibles, NTs and Scripture portions each year. **EHC** has distributed over nine million tracts door-to-door and provided over 200,000 BCC courses to seekers.

b) Literacy issues. The availability of the Bible in the Muslim Bengali dialect avails little when over 50% of the population suffers from literacy problems. Pray for effective programmes that will combine literacy training with Scripture. Pray for initiatives in sharing the Bible orally, through story telling and other means.

c) The translation of the Bible into tribal languages. At least five and possibly more translations are needed; work is in progress in some of these.

13 **Other Christian media** are important when so much of the population is illiterate. Pray for effective outreach through:

a) Radio. Christian broadcasters (mostly **TWR**, **GFA**, FEBA, Adventists) transmit over 500 hours per week over shortwave in Bengali, Burmese, English, Hindi and a host of other tribal languages. Pray especially for the production of suitable and sufficient programmes for the non-Christian majority.

b) The JESUS film, used among Hindus and Muslims with good response. It is completed in Bangla, Sylheti, Assamese and 15 other languages. Pray for the spiritual growth of new believers coming to Christ through the JESUS film.

c) Audio ministry. **GRN** has a staggering 91 languages and dialects with audio resources. The HELP (Health, Education and Leadership Programme) audio series prepares young people to serve God and their country.

St. Vincent & the Grenadines
North Atlantic Ocean
Bridgetown
Caribbean Sea
Barbados
Grenada

Barbados

Caribbean

Geography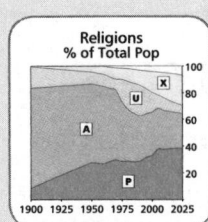

Area 430 sq km. The most easterly of the Windward Islands.

Population		Ann Gr	Density
2010	256,552	0.26%	597/sq km
2020	261,687	0.16%	609/sq km
2030	260,485	-0.12%	606/sq km

Capital Bridgetown 114,000. **Urbanites** 40.8%.
Pop under 15 yrs 17%. **Life expectancy** 77 yrs.

Peoples

African Caribbean 92.2%.
Mixed 2.8%.
European-origin 2.4%.
Other 2.6%. South Asian, Chinese.
Literacy 99.7%. **Official language** English.
Bajan is a distinctive Barbadian dialect of English.
All languages 3. **Indigenous languages** 2.
Languages with Scriptures 1Bi.

Economy

One of the most prosperous and successful island states of the Caribbean, with an increasingly diverse economy based on tourism, sugar, light industry and off-shore banking.
HDI Rank 37th/182. **Income/person** $13,314 (28% of USA).

Politics

Parliamentary government since 1647. Independent from Britain in 1966. Stable democratic rule since then.

Religion

Complete freedom of religion.

Religions	Pop %	Population	Ann Gr
Christian	94.94	243,570	0.2%
Non-religious	2.15	5,516	1.7%
Muslim	0.90	2,309	1.9%
Other	0.80	2,052	4.5%
Baha'i	0.75	1,924	1.7%
Hindu	0.40	1,026	1.8%
Buddhist	0.04	103	0.3%
Ethnoreligionist	0.02	51	15.2%

Christians	Denoms	Pop %	Affiliates	Ann Gr
Protestant	30	41.01	105,000	0.6%
Independent	12	11.76	30,000	3.8%
Anglican	1	31.96	82,000	-0.5%
Catholic	1	4.29	11,000	0.3%
Orthodox	3	0.74	2,000	0.5%
Marginal	5	3.73	10,000	2.2%
Unaffiliated		10.40	27,000	0.0%
Doubly affiliated		*-8.97*	*-23,000*	*0.0%*

Churches	MegaBloc	Congs	Members	Affiliates
Anglican Church	A	43	22,162	82,000
Seventh-day Adventist	P	57	18,500	26,085
Methodist Church	P	32	4,805	16,000
Pente Assem of W Indies	P	23	8,000	14,000
NT Ch of God (Clev)	P	44	4,500	12,500
Other indigenous Pente	I	64	5,150	12,000
Spiritual Baptists	I	60	6,000	12,000
Catholic Church	C	6	6,707	11,000
Jehovah's Witnesses	M	31	3,193	7,982
Ch of the Nazarene	P	33	3,700	5,957
Wesleyan Holiness Ch	P	37	2,800	5,600
Other denominations[38]		154	16,210	34,742
Doubly affilliated				*-23,000*
Total Christians[52]		**584**	**101,727**	**216,866**

TransBloc	Pop %	Population	Ann Gr
Evangelicals			
Evangelicals	34.2	87,614	0.8%
Renewalists			
Charismatics	23.9	61,405	1.3%
Pentecostals	16.1	41,360	0.6%

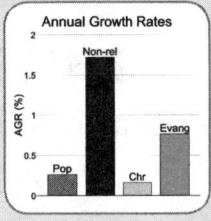

Religions % of Total Pop

Annual Growth Rates

Challenges for Prayer

1 **The legacy of slavery** must be completely routed. Toward this end, a ceremony initiated by Christians was conducted in 1998 to great effect. In 1999 there was a national act of repentance during the anniversary of independence celebrations. This island, with the oldest Anglican theological college in the Western Hemisphere, also saw Anglican parishes endorse and prosper from slavery. This, too, has seen an act of public repentance. Pray that, through these acts and the extension of forgiveness, any remaining scars might be removed forever.

2 **Since settlement in 1627, Barbados has been Christian.** But despite overwhelming religious profession and a large number of evangelicals, real commitment to the lordship of Jesus is the exception rather than the rule. Materialism, spreading theological liberalism, decreasing church attendance, increased violence and crime are all symptoms of spiritual decline. Pray for the Spirit's renewal and for the Church in Barbados to reawaken.

3 **The Church needs God's intervention.** While unity is growing, there is still some mistrust among denominational leaders, particularly between the established denominations and the many fast-growing independent churches and congregations. Pray for a genuine commitment to fellowship and prayer by those in Christian ministry. Pray for the Barbados Evangelical Association and Barbados Christian Council, which seek to provide the platform for this.

4 **External challenges to the gospel** are evident – increased activity in and acceptance of the occult as well as intensified efforts by Muslims and Mormons to win those disillusioned with what they see of traditional Christianity. Pray for the confounding of these efforts and for true Christians to powerfully demonstrate God's love and truth.

5 **Young people** desperately need spiritual guidance. The culture of immorality is pervasive, and even church-going teens are subject to its temptations. Illegitimate births and cohabitation are widespread. Pray that churches may offer effective programmes for children and youth, while demonstrating positive holiness. Pray also for the ministries of **CEF**, IS/ISUF(**IFES**), **YFC**, **YWAM** and others, whose potential impact among children and young people is massive.

Population		Ann Gr	Density
2010	9,587,940	-0.47%	46/sq km
2020	9,112,495	-0.52%	44/sq km
2030	8,563,882	-0.66%	41/sq km

Capital Minsk 1,852,223. **Urbanites** 74.3%. **Pop under 15 yrs** 15%. **Life expectancy** 69 yrs.

Peoples

Slavic 97.9%. Belarusian 77.6%; Russian 13.2%; Polish 4.2%; Ukrainian 2.9%.
All other peoples 2.1%. 22 groups, mostly from the former USSR.
Literacy 99.6%. **Official languages** Belarusian and Russian; the latter is more widely used. **All languages** 11. **Indigenous languages** 2. **Languages with Scriptures** 1Bi 1NT 1por.

Economy

Little decentralization since the Soviet era; almost 80% of industry remains in state hands, with significant renationalization since 2005. Market reform and privatization are moving at a snail's pace. Traditionally strong industrial and agricultural bases. Heavily dependent on trade with its closest ally, Russia. Still impacted by economic and health consequences of the 1986 Chernobyl nuclear disaster.

Belarus

Republic of Belarus

Europe

Geography

Area 207,600 sq km. Landlocked; fertile agricultural land with extensive forests on the North European plains. Surrounded by Russia, Ukraine, Poland, Lithuania and Latvia. Smallest of the three Slavic nations of the former USSR.

Catholic	2	10.44	1,001,000	-0.7%
Orthodox	8	57.83	5,544,000	0.6%
Marginal	1	0.09	8,000	-0.4%

HDI Rank 68th/182. **Public debt** 1.4% of GDP. **Income/person** $6,235 (13% of USA).

Politics 🔲

Often called "Europe's last dictatorship", Belarus is a republic in name only. Its centuries-long domination by Russia continues into the post-Soviet era. The political turmoil of the 1990s drove it into even closer ties with its eastern neighbour. Political leadership still clings to the autocratic Communist past and has proved intransigent to Western diplomatic overtures.

Religion ♿

There is very little religious freedom despite its guarantee in the constitution. A law passed in 2002 makes non-registration of religious congregations illegal, and registration is a tedious, expensive and occasionally impossible process. Protestants in particular have seen the government's stance go from antipathy to outright hostility.

Religions	Pop %	Population	Ann Gr
Christian	70.53	6,762,374	0.4%
Non-religious	28.14	2,698,046	-2.6%
Muslim	0.61	58,486	1.6%
Jewish	0.51	48,898	-0.9%
Other	0.11	10,547	1.5%
Baha'i	0.10	9,588	-0.5%

Christians Denoms	Pop %	Affiliates	Ann Gr
Protestant	24	1.36	131,000	3.0%
Independent	3	0.81	77,000	-1.0%

Churches	MegaBloc	Congs	Members	Affiliates
Belarus Orthodox Ch	O	1,400	3,828,671	5,475,000
Catholic Church	C	400	795,600	994,500
Pentecostal Union	P	480	36,500	73,000
Autocephalic Orth Ch	O	56	36,250	58,000
Old Believers	I	30	29,870	46,000
Fringe Orthodox groups	I	22	19,156	29,500
Pente, unregistered	P	54	9,000	18,000
Evang Chr Baptist Un	P	325	15,000	16,700
Jehovah's Witnesses	M	48	2,447	8,150
Seventh-day Adventist	P	81	5,750	6,500
Uniate Catholic	C	24	3,892	6,500
Other denominations[27]		190	16,126	30,816
Total Christians[38]		**3,110**	**4,798,262**	**6,762,666**

TransBloc	Pop %	Population	Ann Gr
Evangelicals			
Evangelicals	1.3	122,576	3.0%
Renewalists			
Charismatics	1.2	111,453	3.1%
Pentecostals	1.0	94,881	3.6%

Religions % of Total Pop

Annual Growth Rates

Answers to Prayer

1 **The believing Church in Belarus is growing,** even as Belarus's overall population slides downward. Much of the growth occurs in the context of persecution and state hostility, and often believers must meet in difficult circumstances. But the Church is definitely increasing in numbers, in maturity and in confidence.

Challenges for Prayer

1 **Belarus stumbled into an unexpected independence,** yet it remains, in political structure and operation, a virtual throwback to the Communist era. Elections are largely a sham, and the nation remains firmly in Moscow's sphere of influence. The prospects of a grassroots democratic revolution seem very slim. But growing numbers are opposed to the regime and vocally in favour of increased freedoms; change came unexpectedly and quickly to the USSR in 1991 and more recently to Ukraine and Georgia. Pray for hope, justice and a brighter future for the people of Belarus.

2 **The cultural and political dominance by Russia and Poland** lasted for many centuries. Belarus itself lacks, to some degree, its own identity. Pray for a truly indigenous expression of Belarusian Christianity to develop and then spread using all methods: church services, theological education, literature, broadcasting.

3 **The Chernobyl catastrophe in 1986** occurred in the Ukraine, but affected Belarus most severely. Subsequent environmental and human devastation is significant, with 20% of the nation's land area affected, two million people uprooted and several thousand dead or dying from radiation-induced cancer. The government views "radiophobia" as the biggest problem now, since it prevents effective resettlement and recultivation of the affected area. Many charities were set up to care for those affected, particularly orphans and children born with health issues. Pray for wisdom for those overseeing resettlement, help for those already affected and hope for those who still live in uncertainty as a result of the disaster.

4 **Orthodoxy and Catholicism enjoy privileged status** as historic Slavic religious entities, but even these face limitations. Other denominations face opposition from the establishment.

a) The acceptance of Russian Orthodoxy by the state is in keeping with a traditional Slavic identity, and Orthodoxy remains largely a ritualistic entity for the purposes of baptising, marrying and burying. Renewal and reformation within the ancient confessions could potentially impact millions; pray for such to occur.

b) Religious movements face increasing pressure from government officials. These include Orthodox expressions that do not submit to the state-approved Moscow patriarchate (such as Old Believers, autocephalous and splinter Orthodox groups), Uniate Catholics, Protestants and groups such as Hare Krishna, Buddhists and pre-Christian pagans.

5 **Evangelical Christians are increasing** despite concerted opposition and intensifying persecution. The state steadfastly maintains laws that forbid meeting in homes for worship, forming congregations of less than 20 people, opening religious schools, ministering outside of the home city, and importing and distributing non-state-approved literature. All religious activity must receive state permission. All congregations are required to register; obstructionism in the registration process prevents many churches from meeting or growing. The inability to buy or rent property for worship is the biggest problem for evangelicals. Pray for:

a) Patient, overcoming faith for believers to withstand such difficulties. Evidence suggests that evangelicals are persisting, growing and finding ways to deal with these challenges.

b) Those in government who harass and persecute God's Church, that they might (hopefully through believers) discover the truth of the gospel and the love of Christ.

c) Unity among the various evangelical groups – different denominations, registered and unregistered churches. Pray for greater cooperation to replace mistrust in many denominations.

d) The emergence of a truly Belarusian evangelicalism, one that is culturally relevant and reflective of national character, one that allows for worship and ministry from an indigenous foundation. Evangelicals are usually perceived as agents of the West.

e) Training of new leaders. As the Church grows, the new post-Communist generation needs to be discipled and shaped according to biblical values. This must be done amid repressive laws that restrict meeting, training and education.

6 **Foreign missionary presence** is slowly being squeezed out by refusing visas for foreign religious workers; Catholic missionaries have been the most frequent victims of this approach. Even Slavs from neighbouring countries who have been specifically invited by churches to teach are often refused permission. Pray for divine openings and opportunities for those God is calling into Belarus; pray also that the national Church would be specially enabled to evangelize, disciple and minister without the partnership of many foreign Christian workers.

7 **The less-evangelized.** There are some significant non-Christian minorities:

a) Jews. As many as 70,000 Jews live in Belarus, mostly in Minsk, but their numbers are declining. There is a Messianic Jewish group in Minsk, but the majority still need to be reached.

b) Muslims. Smaller groups of Muslims are immigrating from elsewhere in the former USSR, adding to the Tatar population, resident since the 15th Century. Very few Muslims have had a chance to encounter the good news.

8 Christian help ministries for prayer:

a) The Bible Society (UBS) finds a widespread desire for the Bible and Children's Bibles in both official languages. A Belarusian Bible completed in 2009, in collaboration with the Orthodox Church, is very popular.

b) Christian literature needs to be made more available. **CLC** has 16 outlets (three full-time), but more solid, evangelistic and teaching materials need to be translated into Belarusian and then distributed throughout the country.

c) **TWR** has a local base for programme production. It also broadcasts into the country in both major languages. **FEBC** and **HCJB** shortwave broadcasts are also available in Russian. Alpha Radio and BTMR (Baptist) broadcast locally as well.

Belgium

Kingdom of Belgium

Europe

Geography

Area 30,528 sq km. One of the Low Countries; often called "The Crossroads of Western Europe".

Population		Ann Gr	Density
2010	10,697,588	0.54%	351/sq km
2020	11,048,254	0.31%	362/sq km
2030	11,302,616	0.20%	370/sq km

Europe's second-most-densely populated country – after the Netherlands.
Capital Brussels 1,904,133. Capital of the EU and headquarters of NATO. **Other major cities** Antwerp 965,000; Gent 237,000. **Urbanites** 97.4%. **Pop under 15 yrs** 17%. **Life expectancy** 79.5 yrs.

Peoples

European 93.2%.
  Flemish 54.4%. Language mutually intelligible with Dutch; mainly in north and west.
  Walloon 31.1%. French-speaking; mainly in south and east.
  Other European 7.7%. Italian 2.6%; French 1.1%; Dutch 1.0%; German 0.9%.
  Foreign 6.8%. Arabic-speaking (mainly North African)

2.7%; Turk 0.5%; Jews 0.4%. Also large numbers of Sub-Saharan Africans and Latin Americans.
Literacy 99%. **Official languages** Flemish, French and German. **All languages** 29. **Indigenous languages** 10. **Languages with Scriptures** 4Bi 2por.

Economy

Strong economy based on advantageous geographical position, highly skilled workforce, good infrastructure and the presence of many international organizations.
HDI Rank 14th/182. **Public debt** 89.6% of GDP. **Income/person** $47,289 (100% of USA).

Politics

Became a nation in 1830 as a constitutional monarchy. Deeply divided along linguistic lines. Fully federal constitution since 1993 to reduce tensions between Walloons and Flemings and to stave off possible national fragmentation. Effective national government has been in a state of paralysis for years due to intransigent parties in a succession of failed coalition governments. Distrust, weariness and apathy characterize Belgians' attitudes toward the federal government. Regional governments are much more effective and trusted due to the lack of language differences. Liberal social policies consistently pursued to a degree only matched by the Netherlands.

Religion

Full freedom of religion. Most groups have official status with the government (Protestants through various alliances and networks), but a media bias persists against evangelicals. Religion is largely irrelevant for a large majority of Belgians.

Religion	Pop %	Population	Ann Gr
Christian	62.72	6,709,527	-0.5%
Non-religious	32.05	3,428,577	2.3%
Muslim	4.40	470,694	3.0%
Jewish	0.43	46,000	1.0%
Buddhist	0.30	32,093	2.7%
Hindu	0.05	5,349	5.1%

B

Sikh		0.03	3,209	9.0%
Other		0.02	2,140	0.5%

Christians	Denoms	Pop %	Affiliates	Ann Gr
Protestant	54	1.01	108,000	1.1%
Independent	18	0.24	26,000	4.0%
Anglican	1	0.10	11,000	0.6%
Catholic	3	47.69	5,101,000	-2.1%
Orthodox	8	0.65	70,000	1.3%
Marginal	15	0.55	59,000	-0.8%
Unaffiliated		12.50	1,335,000	7.0%

Churches	MegaBloc	Congs	Members	Affiliates
Catholic Church	C	3,940	5,530,303	7,300,000
Jehovah's Witnesses	M	350	23,750	47,500
United Prot Ch of B	P	108	22,384	38,500
Russian Orthodox	O	18	4,667	28,000
Greek Orthodox	O	10	19,708	27,000
Union of Pente (VVP)	P	99	6,200	12,400
Anglican Church	A	13	3,333	11,100
Free Evangelical Chs	P	73	6,000	10,500
Latter-day Saints (Mormon)	M	19	4,833	6,380
Ch of God (Cleveland)	P	37	4,793	5,800
German-speaking Ev Ch	P	5	2,930	4,893
Baptist Churches	P	52	3,000	4,800
Other denominations[79]		572	41,177	77,834
Disaffiliated Catholics				-2,200,000
Total Christians[99]		**5,297**	**4,006,411**	**5,374,707**

The Belgian denominational context is complex, with separate associations for the different regions of the country, along with overlapping alliances, networks, federations and synods connecting together in different ways. Excellent research has been done on church life, but uses ecclesiological terminology differently from *OW*; reconciling such research is never straightforward.

TransBloc	Pop %	Population	Ann Gr
Evangelicals			
Evangelicals	1.2	132,569	2.5%
Renewalists			
Charismatics	0.9	94,210	1.4%
Pentecostals	0.3	30,570	4.0%

Religions % of Total Pop

Annual Growth Rates

Answers to Prayer

1 **The growth of evangelical believers** has been sustained over many years. While only at a modest 1.2% of the population, evangelical faith in Belgium has never been stronger. While growth is most prominent among Pentecostals, the more conservative churches in Flanders and Wallonia see an increase through determined church planting and relational witness.

2 **The presence of many immigrant believers** has also given impetus to the increase of faith. About half of all evangelicals in Belgium are foreigners, significant numbers of whom came to faith while in Belgium. Most praiseworthy is the very deliberate self-identification as "international churches" rather than "immigrant churches" – reflecting their multicultural nature and intention to reach out to Belgians and other Europeans.

3 **Unity and cooperation** among the many Protestant and evangelical groups – with the government as well as toward each other – have made great strides in the last decade. What was once a major flaw in Belgian evangelicalism, i.e., lack of unity, can now arguably be seen as a major strength.

4 **The government extended an apology to the people of Congo** in 2002 for its role in the 1961 assassination of the Congo's first prime minister. Albeit a small step among many needed for full reconciliation and reparation, it was the first time a European nation publically acknowledged and apologized for such an abuse of colonial power.

Challenges for Prayer

1 **Belgium is a deeply divided nation.** For 2,000 years, its territory has straddled the cultural divide between the Latin/Romance and Germanic worlds. Walloon-Flemish rivalry and resentments colour the use of language, the economy, politics, religious life and worldviews of both communities. The growing immigrant population adds a third angle to this dynamic. An eventual breakup of Belgium is within the realm of possibility; this defining issue has paralyzed political progress. Pray that national leaders at every level may have wisdom regarding this complex challenge. Pray that the Church might be a profound example of unity to the wider society, and that real reconciliation and peace might be shaped in Belgium.

2 **Belgium has witnessed, for centuries, blood spilled** on their land by other European powers, irrevocably wounding Belgian character and identity. The Protestant community is only in the last few decades recovering from the destruction of its 600 congregations by the Spanish Inquisition in the 16th Century. Pray that the defilement of past violence might be removed by Christ's own blood, and pray that true healing of past damages and fear might occur.

3 **Catholicism is in rapid decline.** Atheists and the non-religious now number 31%. Only 48% saw themselves as Catholic in 2010. Nominalism is pervasive; nationally, only 7% attend mass, and as low as 1% in some parts of Flanders and less than 0.5% in some Walloon cities. The Church faces five major crises – declining commitment, waning influence, a severe lack of students in seminaries, mass defections and, most of all, the pedophilia scandals that have destroyed Catholicism's reputation. The number of priests today is less than half that of 1960; their average age is over 65. The charismatic movement brought some new life but remains quite small. Pray for revival in this materially prosperous but spiritually poor land.

4 **Rapid secularization** has allowed the introduction of several very liberal laws that are an affront to a biblical understanding of the sanctity of life, sexuality and marriage. These both reflect and encourage an erosion of the moral foundations of society, coinciding with widespread recreational drug use, sexual immorality and occult and New Age activities. Pray for all false and erroneous beliefs to be exposed as such before the light of God's revelation.

5 **Protestantism has had mixed fortunes** – over the last 40 years, evangelicalism grew while mainline Protestantism declined. The growth of evangelical, and especially Pentecostal, groups as well as the evangelical wing of the largely liberal United Protestant Church (EPUB) has offset the decline in the mainline Protestantism. For prayer:

a) *The national body ARPEE/CACPE* has, since 2003, represented before the government the various Protestant and evangelical denominations, giving them a unified voice in society, legal legitimacy (to avoid the "sect/cult" label) and equal access to government subsidies.

b) *The strengthening of fellowship and ministry links* among denominations. The *Evangelische Alliantie* was formed in Flanders in 1980, the Fédération Evangélique in Wallonia in 1989. They formed in 1998 a national evangelical synod. Together with EPUB, they represent most Protestants and evangelicals before the government under the ARPEE/CACPE.

6 **The Bible has been reintroduced to Belgian society** after many centuries of being discouraged, even banned, by the Catholic Church before 1960. UBS unveiled a new translation of the Bible in 2004, leading to a year-long promotional tour in 2006. A Bible multimedia exhibit, Expo Biblia, united the Flemish and French Bible Societies in efforts to reintroduce to Belgians the history and stories of the Bible. BEM also has portable multimedia Bible exhibits open to the public in French- and Flemish-speaking regions. Pray that the Word of God might take root deeply within the fabric of Belgian society.

7 **Leadership in the churches is a challenge.** The lack of Belgian, and especially Flemish, Christian workers and pastors is crippling indigeneity and growth. There are very few full-time pastors; most are bivocational. This in turn undermines first-generation believers (the majority of indigenous Belgian evangelicals), since they need solid discipleship in post-Christian Belgium. Immigrant churches, through their tithing, have shown that it is possible to support a full-time pastor, even with a small congregation. Pray, in this light, for the ongoing work of well-established Belgian Bible training institutions.

8 **Specific, focused ministry** is vital in a nation lacking moral absolutes and with churches lacking the leadership necessary to mentor and guide. Pray specifically for:

a) *Francophone children's ministry.* *Objectif 4-14*, created in 2007, emphasizes children's ministries to evangelical Francophone churches. Results were so positive that ongoing collaboration, resource development, Internet outreach and, in a few cases, new church plants continue today. **CEF, BEM, AI**, OAC and **AoG**, among others, serve children in Belgium.

b) *Prayer movements.* Stemming from the Flemish Evangelical Alliance, organic prayer movements such as *Kniel/Breeze* draw youth together to regularly pray and talk about God through websites, online forums and chats, local meetings and workshops. One movement, started (in 2005) and led by youth, now claims over 175 groups. Pray4Belgium is a website mobilizing prayer and connecting different Belgian prayer ministries.

c) **Mobilization for mission. OM** provides ongoing opportunities through Teens In Mission for Belgian youth to participate in mission and outreach. Missions Day conferences are generally held annually, hosted by **WBT**, **SIM**, Awake Ministries International, Eden Project and other related ministries. Pray for many young people to devote themselves to service among the Belgian peoples and even throughout the world.

9 **Specific outreach challenges:**

a) **Spiritually, Belgium is one of the most needy countries** in Europe, with great spiritual apathy and faith largely banished from the public sphere.

b) **The areas of greatest need** – the smaller towns and villages in the Flemish-speaking areas and the Francophone Ardennes region (Liège, Namur and Luxembourg).

c) **Brussels is a strategic city.** The capital region's population is over 1.1 million. It is 32% foreign, 8% evangelical and close to 13% Muslim (largely Moroccan and Turk) – with over 45 nationalities of 1,000 people or more. It ranges from increasing numbers of impoverished neighbourhoods to growing communities of affluent young professionals, from the often-isolated and marginalized immigrant groups to the powerful Eurocratic community. Pray for the various church and mission programmes reaching out to the diverse facets of Brussels' society – Serve the City (Christian Associates), BEM, **IMB** and **AoG** are but a few of many.

d) **Antwerp now has over 100 evangelical congregations** (up from 10 in 1970), but 80% are non-Flemish. The unity and cooperation between these churches is commendable. A number of local and international ministries are reaching out to the large Moroccan community. The majority of Belgium's Orthodox Jewish population live in Antwerp with little or no outreach to them.

e) **Muslim peoples** (North Africans, Turks, Kurds) have increased through legal and illegal immigration – the majority living in poorer urban areas. Muslims are the second-largest religious population, and there are now 380 mosques in Belgium. There is some outreach, with a handful of Arabic-speaking congregations, two Kurdish and one Turkish fellowship of believers, but many more workers are needed.

f) **Asian communities. OMF** reports nine Chinese churches in Belgium, and the **AoG** has one couple working among the Chinese. BEM has a Japanese couple working within the Japanese community and have planted a Japanese church. A number of other Asian communities (Korean, Vietnamese, Sri Lankan, Iranian, Filipino) have at least one church each.

g) **The Eastern European population** is rapidly growing – Polish, Russians, Bulgarians, Kosovars, Romanians and others. Only the Romanians have a significant number of evangelical congregations; the Polish and Kosovars have none. There is little or no outreach to these peoples.

h) **The student population** of over 250,000 students, in 17 universities and numerous colleges, is a major challenge. **IFES** has a ministry in seven Flemish universities (Ichthus with 150 students involved) and in several French universities (GBU). The small work grows very slowly, despite the large number of students. **OM**, **AoG**, **YWAM** and others have active student ministries, often through coffee houses, Bible studies or conferences.

i) **The missions vision of immigrant churches** is beginning to develop. The great outreach potential in these churches is as yet unrealized. Reaching out effectively to native Belgians is a step beyond the evangelism they already do among their own immigrant populations, but they are starting to be effective at planting churches among other immigrant populations.

10 **Christian media and support ministries** – pray for their effective use:

a) **Christian literature** is produced by **EHC**, SU, Biblical Literature in French (BLF), **OM**, BEM, **YWAM** and **AoG**. BLF has a large printing press and has published over 500 titles.

b) **Christian bookstores** number 18 (10 in French, 8 in Dutch) – BEM with 7.

c) **Electronic media.** A total of 5.5 hours of TV annually and 5.5 hours of radio weekly are produced by the evangelical ERTS for national Flemish TV and radio channels. Increasingly, churches and ministries utilize the Internet for outreach and discipleship, with specific focus on youth and children's sites. There are number of full-time evangelical Internet radio stations operating in Belgium.

d) **Christian political initiatives** such as *C'Axent, Chrétiens Démocrates Francophones* and VCD serve the political arena through election and support of politicians with Christian values.

B

e) **Innovative outreach** is increasing to the often-overlooked segments of society. Such outreach includes Bible exhibits on river barges (BEM), ministry to seafaring crews from around the world docking at Belgian ports (Open Air Campaigners), outreach to bars (**YWAM**), Christian centres for marriage and family counselling and for women in crisis and a Mennonite Centre for family/community reconciliation. Serve the City is impacting a number of Belgian cities by combining practical service with sharing the gospel.

Belize
Latin America

Geography 🌍

Area 22,965 sq km. A Caribbean coastal enclave bordering Guatemala and Mexico. It has the world's second-largest coral barrier reef.

Population		Ann Gr	Density
2010	312,928	2.08%	14/sq km
2020	374,549	1.72%	16/sq km
2030	429,814	1.27%	19/sq km

Central America's most sparsely populated country. **Capital** Belmopan 20,300. **Other major city** Belize City 66,800. **Urbanites** 52.7%. **Pop under 15 yrs** 35%. **Life expectancy** 76 yrs.

Peoples 👪

Most of the population is of mixed descent.
Mestizo/Ladino 46.7%. Predominantly Guatemalan and Honduran backgrounds.
Belize Creole 25.0%. Mainly English-Creole speaking. Politically dominant.
Amerindian 10.6%. Mayans, 3 main languages: Ketchi, Mopan and Yucatec. The indigenous peoples of Belize.
Garifuna (Black Carib) 6.0%. Descendants of African slaves and Arawakans forcibly relocated from the Caribbean.

Europeans 4.9%. Mainly German Mennonites and British.
Other 6.8%. East Indian 3.0%; Chinese 2.7%.
Literacy 76.9%. **Official language** English. Spanish spoken by the majority of the population.
All languages 12. **Indigenous languages** 8. **Languages with Scriptures** 6Bi 1NT 2por 1w.i.p.

Economy 📈

Solid economic growth is offset by a large trade deficit and foreign debt. Main sources of income are ecotourism (40% of the country is national parks and reserves) and marine and agricultural products. The slow death of the coral reef portends the same for the tourist industry. Discovery of oil in the pristine jungles and wetlands will set industrialists and environmentalists at odds. Most jobs are manual labour, and with the highest cost of living in Central America; poverty is widespread.
HDI Rank 93rd/182. **Public debt** 67.8% of GDP. **Income/person** $4,241 (9% of USA).

Politics ☒

Formerly British Honduras; independent from Britain in 1981 as a stable parliamentary democracy, and member of the Association of Caribbean States and the Caribbean Community.

Religion ✝

A secular state with freedom of religion.

Religions	Pop %	Population	Ann Gr
Christian	83.94	262,672	1.9%
Non-religious	7.80	24,408	3.7%
Baha'i	2.95	9,231	2.4%
Hindu	2.30	7,197	2.1%
Jewish	1.04	3,254	1.7%
Ethnoreligionist	0.96	3,004	1.3%
Muslim	0.65	2,034	3.7%
Buddhist	0.36	1,127	2.7%

Christians Denoms	Denoms	Pop %	Affiliates	Ann Gr
Protestant	32	33.92	106,000	4.2%
Independent	29	3.16	10,000	6.9%
Anglican	1	3.26	10,000	-2.4%
Catholic	1	50.33	158,000	1.8%
Marginal	2	3.17	10,000	5.4%
Unaffiliated		3.63	11,500	5.3%
Doubly affiliated		*-13.53*	*-42,000*	*0.0%*

Ch of God (Cleveland)	P	30	2,040	3,468
Pentecostal Ch of God	P	56	1,525	3,050
Other denominations[22]		188	9,199	15,676
Doubly affiliated Pentecostals				*-10,000*
Doubly affiliated				*-32,340*
Total Christians[65]		**911**	**163,712**	**251,317**

Churches	MegaBloc	Congs	Members	Affiliates
Catholic Church	C	65	85,135	157,500
Seventh-day Adventist	P	174	33,000	46,000
Assemblies of God	P	65	2,800	16,000
Anglican Church	A	22	5,829	10,200
Mennonite Churches	P	18	3,800	7,600
Jehovah's Witnesses	M	40	2,010	5,025
Latter-day Saints (Mormon)	M	24	2,934	4,900
Methodist Church	P	9	3,139	4,300
Ch of the Nazarene	P	38	2,850	4,132
Baptist Association	P	60	2,180	4,077
Ch of God in Christ	I	32	2,370	4,029
Independent churches	I	45	1,818	4,000
United Pentecostal Ch	P	45	3,083	3,700

TransBloc	Pop %	Population	Ann Gr
Evangelicals			
Evangelicals	18.8	58,782	4.8%
Renewalists			
Charismatics	13.1	41,112	6.3%
Pentecostals	7.6	23,757	7.2%

Religions % of Total Pop

MegaBlocs % of Christian Pop

Challenges for Prayer

1. **Belizeans are largely professing Christians, but syncretism is common.** The Spanish-speaking immigrants with their superstitions, the Mayans with their underlying paganism and the Garifuna with their black magic all need a culturally relevant and sensitive presentation of the true gospel.

2. **Evangelicals have steadily grown** from 4.6% in 1960 to 19% in 2010. Challenges to be tackled:

a) *Widespread legalism* in churches, where appearances and knowledge hold sway over true spiritual transformation. Pray for revival and a holy dissatisfaction with the spiritual status quo.

b) *Pastors are stretched,* with 70% of pastors forced to work bivocationally. They recognize a great need for training – but distance and cost prohibit centralized, formal training programmes.

c) *Belize is an "over-evangelized" nation* with few true disciples and little fruit. A high proportion of Christians are claimed by multiple denominations, but only 10% of the population actually attend regularly – indicating that nominalism is a problem, even among evangelicals.

d) *Unity is an uphill battle* against significant cultural and denominational diversity. Barriers among churches are formidable and persistent. Pray for initiatives that will break down these walls and draw together Hispanic, English, German and Mayan-speaking believers.

e) *The less-reached peoples* need clearer and more culturally appropriate ministry. These include the Garifuna, Mayans, Indians (almost entirely Hindu or Muslim) and Chinese.

3. **Many missions, especially short-term, have saturated this small nation.** Much has been positive, particularly in the areas of medicine/health care (especially in the remote and poorer areas), literacy and training. But the never-ending presence of mission-trippers creates dependency, which actually undermines the national Church. Pray for fruitful partnerships that empower and require true sacrifice by all for Kingdom purposes.

4. **HIV/AIDS is a serious threat.** The 2.4% (and rising) infection rate is the highest in Central America. He Intends Victory and Lighthouse Christian Radio both serve to educate, prevent and minister on this issue and to those who suffer.

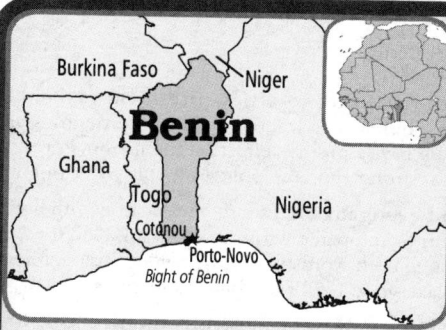

Burkina Faso
Niger
Benin
Ghana
Togo
Cotonou
Nigeria
Porto-Novo
Bight of Benin

Benin
Republic of Benin
Africa

Geography

Area 112,622 sq km. A long, narrow country wedged between Nigeria and Togo.

Population		Ann Gr	Density
2010	9,211,741	3.20%	82/sq km
2020	12,176,895	2.72%	108/sq km
2030	15,398,946	2.27%	137/sq km

Capital Porto-Novo 287,000. **Other major cities** Cotonou 844,000, Parakou 292,000. **Urbanites** 42%. **Pop under 15 yrs** 43%. **Life expectancy** 61 yrs.

Peoples

More than 60 ethnic groups, mostly in the south. **Guinean** 59.5%. Fon 19.0%; Aja 8.6%; Gun 6.3%; Ayizo-Gbe 4.6%; Toli-Gbe 2.5%; Weme-Gbe 2.4%; Saxwe-Gbe 2.2%.
Gur 17.4%. Bariba 7.2%; Ditammari 1.7%; Kpila 1.4%.
Yoruba(12) 13.1%.
Fulani(2) 4.8%.
Others 5.2%. Mande(3) 1.4%; Songhai(3) 1.0%. Various Africans, French, Lebanese.
Increasing undocumented numbers of Burkinabé and Togolese are present.
Literacy 33.6%. **Official language** French. Trade languages, Fon in south, Dendi in north. **All languages** 56. **Indigenous languages** 54. **Languages with Scriptures** 7Bi 11NT 12por 15w.i.p.

Economy

Agriculture is key to the economy, with cotton accounting for nearly half of the GDP. Its neighbour Nigeria dominates trade with Benin, in both official and "informal" capacities. A shift from Marxist policies to a free-market economy has borne fruit, but Benin remains one of the world's poorest countries.
HDI Rank 161st/182. **Public debt** 56.5% of GDP. **Income/person** $828 (2% of USA).

Politics

Independent from France in 1960. After seven coups and one Marxist regime, a democracy was formed in 1991. The government has since remained stable and witnessed a smooth transition via elections from the previous president to its current one.

Religion

Complete religious freedom. All religions are free to practice and propagate their faith.

Religions	Pop %	Population	Ann Gr
Christian	39.89	3,674,563	3.8%
Ethnoreligionist	35.95	3,311,621	1.6%
Muslim	23.50	2,164,759	4.9%
Baha'i	0.30	27,635	7.0%
Non-religious	0.27	24,872	4.8%
Other	0.09	8,291	5.7%

Widespread syncretism among Muslims and Christians means ethnic religions could have an influence on up to 80% of Beninese.

Christians	Denoms	Pop %	Affiliates	Ann Gr
Protestant	95	5.92	545,000	3.5%
Independent	315	4.98	459,000	3.6%
Catholic	1	21.49	1,980,000	3.8%
Marginal	2	4.80	442,000	2.7%
Unaffiliated		2.70	249,000	3.3%

Churches	MegaBloc	Congs	Members	Affiliates
Catholic Church	C	220	1,106,145	1,980,000
Christianisme Celeste	M	1,025	205,000	410,000
Assemblies of God	P	1,050	161,765	275,000
Prot Methodist Ch	P	400	80,000	136,000
Apostolic Church	I	629	44,000	88,000
Church of Pentecost	I	273	20,591	45,300
Born Again Believers Un	I	490	19,600	44,100
Cherubim and Seraphim	I	667	20,000	40,000
Pentecostal Faith Ch	I	303	15,150	37,118
UEEB	P	449	9,100	32,918
Jehovah's Witnesses	M	198	8,900	31,773
Un Bapt of Prot Chs of B	P	140	10,500	21,000
Assem, Disciples of Christ	I	145	7,830	18,792
Baptist Church	P	320	5,345	17,800
African Revival Ch	I	105	6,720	16,128
Universal Evang Ch	I	116	5,800	13,920
Other denominations[397]		2,030	106,957	217,653
Total Christians[413]		**8,560**	**1,833,403**	**3,425,502**

TransBloc	Pop %	Population	Ann Gr
Evangelicals			
Evangelicals	8.3	767,515	4.3%
Renewalists			
Charismatics	14.8	1,358,958	3.7%
Pentecostals	6.3	581,938	3.6%

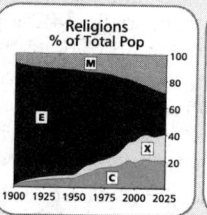

Religions
% of Total Pop

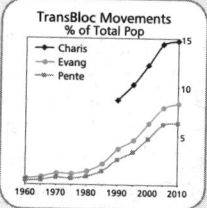

TransBloc Movements
% of Total Pop

Answers to Prayer

1 **The fair elections and recent peaceful transition to a new president** cannot be taken for granted in this troubled region. The current leader's solid background as an economist and his open faith as a Christian should have a positive effect on the nation. Pray for courage, integrity and protection for him, and for strong and wise policies by his government.

2 **There is great freedom to minister and evangelize** in Benin – interaction with both animist and Islamic people groups can occur in an open environment. Thank God for the many opportunities to share the good news through both word and deed. Pray for this openness to continue and for churches and missions to make good use of it while it still exists.

3 **Church growth** continues across the country. **AoG** churches in the north and south, **SIM**-related UEEB churches (*Union des Eglises Evangéliques du Bénin*) in the north and **IMB** in the south all see sustained growth. But these are outstripped by a host of younger, African-originated churches that have emerged in the last 25 years. Evangelicals have grown from 50,000 in 1980 to 770,000 in 2010. **DAWN** and ARCEB (Action for Research and Growth of the Church in Benin) oversaw a study engendering the goal to plant 20,000 congregations by 2020. Pray for endurance that sees every region reached and churches planted among every people in Benin.

Challenges for Prayer

1 **Economic advancement and endemic corruption.** Genuine efforts to uplift the economy too often fail because of corruption; as a result, Benin remains one of the world's 20 least-developed countries. Up to 70% of the skilled workforce must subsist by taking manual or menial-labour jobs. Pray that those in positions to enrich themselves at the nation's cost might instead be honest and self-sacrificing workers and leaders.

2 **Structures of sin** such as people-smuggling and the black market (*fayawo*) are highly influential. Some 75% of economic activity is underground. This is deeply tied to Nigerian interests and makes Benin very vulnerable financially. Allegedly, tens of thousands of children are smuggled from Benin each year to work as child labourers, mostly to their eastern neighbours. They are often maltreated and abused. Pray for justice and righteousness to take root in Benin and for Nigeria's influence to become a more positive and godly one.

3 **Less-reached peoples.** Most peoples are still considered unreached – only a handful of smaller peoples have a Christian (Catholic) majority. Benin has Africa's highest percentage of followers of traditional religions and is probably the least evangelized non-Muslim country in Africa. For specific prayer:

a) **The Fon** are the most numerous people in Benin. It was from Fon animism that voodoo developed. The Fon have a significant Christian population, but many are nominal and voodoo still permeates their lives. Outreach by several Western and African missions birthed a large number of churches, as growth and responsiveness are found in equal measure. Pray for more Fon Christian leaders, and for believers untainted by animistic influences.

b) **The Gbe** include 19 southern peoples from the Kwa/Guinean grouping, forming a patchwork of unreached and unevangelized peoples – accounting for 59.5% of Benin's population. Among most of these peoples, indigenous evangelical churches are few, but growth is occurring.

c) **The Ede Nago** are located on the southeastern border with Nigeria, in the region of Ketou. Until recently, they had little real exposure to the gospel and have no Scripture in their tongue. Related to them are the Idacca who live in south central Benin and are over 90% animist. There are now teams working among them.

d) **Muslim peoples.** Most reside in the less evangelized far northern part of the country. They include the Dendi, Zerma, Hausa, Foodo and Kotokoli. Only the Zerma and Hausa have the whole Bible, and neither is more than 1% evangelical. Pray for teams to reach them – **SIM**, **AoG** and **IMB** all target specific peoples.

e) **The Fulbe (Fula)** peoples of the far north have experienced a real breakthrough, with several thousand coming to Christ through Western (**SIM**, **AoG**) and indigenous ministries. There is a Bible school and a growing number of radio programmes for the Fula, and their receptivity to the gospel continues.

f) ***The 1.3 million urbanites*** of the two capitals. Rapid urbanization brings many from unevangelized peoples into the cities, including a quickly growing Muslim population. Teams are needed to specifically reach these groups in their new urban context; pray for awareness of the cultural differences among peoples and how best to reach each one. Nigerian missions and a number of Benin-originated churches are doing urban evangelism in several cities.

B

4 **Animism is a powerful force** in Benin. Although Christianity is poised to numerically overtake ethnic religions in the near future, far too many Christians have a syncretized, compromised faith that sees them in church on Sunday and consulting the witch doctor during the week. Pray for a revival that purifies the Church and sees Christians honouring God alone. Pray also for many witch doctors to experience the power of Jesus and turn to Him.

5 **The Church in Benin** is desperate for discipleship. There is a shortfall of trained pastors able to meet the needs of the growing Christian population, nor are there enough new leaders being produced. Developing well-trained, biblically literate and holy-living leaders and disciples will enable the shift from syncretized Church to sanctified bride.

6 **Training institutes** are crucial to forming a strong Church. Pray for teachers and students at AoG Bible Institute, UEEB's six Bible schools and one Bible college, Benin Bible Institute (Mennonite), Bible Training Center (Church of Christ), Christ's Power Ministries training centre, several other schools and hundreds more in TEE programmes. These vital schools need general staff and lecturers as well as bursaries and scholarships for students, who are usually impoverished.

7 **Pray for missions.** Outreach to central and northern Benin is only 60 years old. The largest groups: **CMF, SIM, WBT, CEF, YWAM**. Because so many are unevangelized and responsiveness is high, more workers are absolutely vital. Other West Africans can play a huge part in this need. The UEEB operates the only evangelical mission hospital in the north; **SIM** partners with UEEB leadership in this endeavour. Holistic ministry (such as village health ministries and rural development) brings remarkable response – pray for more groups that will combine development, education and healthcare with gospel proclamation.

8 **Young people** are a vital element of the Church, especially with Benin's population burgeoning with youth. Responsiveness is high, but ministry aimed specifically at youth seems to be less of a priority than in the past. Pray for more outreach via youth centres, camps and student groups. Praise the Lord for the ministry of GBEEB(**IFES**) workers to students.

9 **Bible translation remains a pressing need.** Nearly half of Benin's languages are without a Bible or even a NT. **SIM** translation teams are working in four languages, and SIL in eight. Pray for the inter-mission linguistic centre, which facilitates translation work by providing technology and resources. There is also a great need for other literature to be translated and printed: TEE materials, Bible commentaries and many others. Pray that this might help the Church become more biblically literate.

10 **Media opportunities** are highly strategic in an oral society with literacy rates of only 40%. Pray for:

a) ***The effective use of audio recordings*** in evangelism and teaching. **GRN** produced recordings in 46 languages, some of which are spoken by the least evangelized groups in Benin. Cassettes, CDs and MP3 playing devices are all very useful.

b) ***The Lord recently raised up many new partnerships*** between the JESUS film and churches in Benin. Pray for these to impact Benin's peoples with lasting evangelism and discipleship. The film has been translated into nine languages, with one more in progress.

c) ***Radio.*** **SIM**/UEEB broadcasts in 14 languages over 21 FM stations, accounting for many hours a week of programming. **TWR** now broadcasts on AM bandwidth from its new transmitter in Benin. This will potentially reach 112 million West Africans with the gospel. There are many other local stations with Christian content, both in Benin and in Nigeria.

d) ***Television.*** Christian television broadcasts from Nigeria can be seen in most of Benin. Pray for effective programmes relevant to people in Benin and for sound biblical material that impacts many.

Bermuda

Hamilton

North Atlantic Ocean

Bermuda
Colony of Bermuda Islands
North America

Geography

Area 54 sq km. About 200 small islands in the North Atlantic. The world's most northerly coral reefs and the third most-densely populated country.

Population		Ann Gr	Density
2010	64,995	0.25%	1,204/sq km
2020	65,846	0.11%	1,219/sq km
2030	65,873	-0.04%	1,220/sq km

Capital Hamilton 11,600. **Urbanites** 100%. **Pop under 15 yrs** 18%. **Life expectancy** 77.9 yrs.

Peoples

About 29% of the population are foreign-born.
African Caribbean 55%. From many Caribbean nations.
Other 45%. Mainly from UK, USA, Canada, Portugal.
Literacy 98%. **Official language** English.
All languages 2. **Indigenous languages** 1.
Languages with Scriptures 1Bi.

Economy

Its superb climate and geographical position make it a tourist paradise and a lucrative tax haven for many offshore companies.
Public debt 2.2% of GDP. **Income/person** $90,015 (197% of USA).

Politics

A dependent territory of the UK. A stable self-governing parliamentary democracy, but the largest government apparatus per citizen in the world.

Religion

Freedom of religion.

Religions	Pop %	Population	Ann Gr
Christian	90.54	58,846	0.2%
Non-religious	6.70	4,355	1.2%
Ethnoreligionist	2.10	1,365	0.3%
Baha'i	0.60	390	4.0%
Buddhist	0.04	26	0.3%
Jewish	0.02	13	0.3%

Christians Denoms		Pop %	Affiliates	Ann Gr
Protestant	26	36.02	23,000	0.5%
Independent	3	10.00	6,000	-0.1%
Anglican	1	18.46	12,000	-1.6%
Catholic	1	14.62	10,000	0.5%
Orthodox	1	0.08	<100	1.9%
Marginal	4	2.15	1,000	0.9%
Unaffiliated		9.21	6,000	3.7%

Churches	MegaBloc	Congs	Members	Affiliates
Anglican Church	A	15	2,400	12,000
Catholic Church	C	6	7,308	9,500
Seventh-day Adventist	P	10	3,800	5,586
African Meth Epis Ch	I	10	2,120	5,300
Methodist Church	P	8	832	2,770
Salvation Army	P	6	1,456	2,330
NT Ch of God (Cleveland)	P	5	1,000	1,500
Ch of God (Anderson)	P	3	609	1,400
Baptist Church	P	3	350	1,060
Christian Brethren	P	7	530	880
Other denominations[26]		84	5,563	10,535
Total Christians[36]		**157**	**25,968**	**52,861**

TransBloc	Pop %	Population	Ann Gr
Evangelicals			
Evangelicals	24.3	15,789	0.6%
Renewalists			
Charismatics	17.6	11,453	1.7%
Pentecostals	4.7	3,080	1.5%

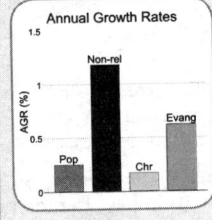

Annual Growth Rates

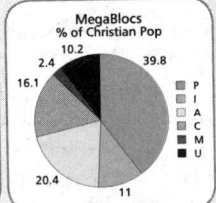

MegaBlocs % of Christian Pop

Challenges for Prayer

1 **The world's wealthiest Black majority territory still faces challenges.** The disparity of wealth and the aging population will test the practical righteousness of the churches as will the influx of immigrants from poorer Caribbean nations. Gang-related violence has rapidly escalated in recent years. Pray for a godly response to these issues.

2 **Bermuda is an earthly paradise,** and Christianity is a strong part of its heritage. Sadly, the appearance of religion takes priority over genuine spirituality. Pray for revival that brings lifestyles in line with biblical knowledge.

3 **The Church's impact is blunted** by a failure to work together as much as is possible. However, United for Change – a large fellowship of pastors representing most evangelical churches – has recently formed to make prayer the overall priority among believers and to bring a united voice to the community on moral issues. Pray for genuine unity and collaboration for effective ministry in Bermuda and beyond.

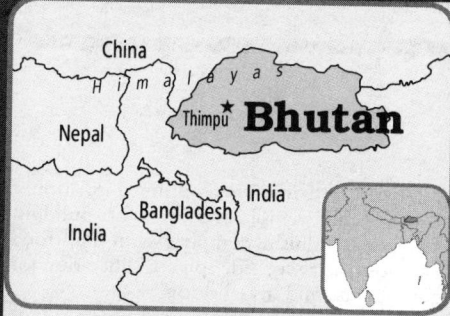

South Himalayan 15.7%. Lepcha 10.6%; Gurung 4.4%.
Tibetan 6.5%. Dzala 2.8%; Lakha 1.4%; Tseku 1.0%.
South Asian 27.5%. Pahari Nepali 17.7%; Assamese 3.8%; Walang 3.0%; Santali 2.4%.
Literacy 47%. **Official language** Dzongkha. Nepali is also widely used. **All languages** 35. **Indigenous languages** 25. **Languages with Scriptures** 4Bi 2NT 6por.

Economy

Undeveloped subsistence economy. Rising unemployment from lack of economic development. Infrastructure development is very difficult due to isolation and topography. Tourist numbers are strictly controlled. Around 23% live in poverty, but Bhutan is rated one of the world's happiest countries.
HDI Rank 132nd/182. **Public debt** 65% of GDP. **Income/person** $2,114 (4% of USA).

Politics

Autocratic and benign Buddhist monarchy with a docile parliament; a slow democratization is taking place. India plays a major role in its external affairs. The government fiercely protects its own sovereignty. Large-scale Nepali immigration over the past century and agitation for more democracy have provoked severe measures against non-Bhutanese peoples since 1985, culminating in what effectively amounted to ethnic cleansing of Nepalis.

Religion

The state religion is Vajrayana Buddhism – Lamaistic Buddhism influenced by Bon (pre-Buddhist animism). Other religions are barely tolerated foreign intrusions. Proselytism and incitement to convert are illegal. Church buildings are not allowed, and Christians are not privy to many of the state benefits available to Buddhists, such as free education.

Bhutan

Kingdom of Bhutan – Druk Yul

Asia

Geography

Area 47,000 sq km. A small kingdom in the eastern Himalaya Mountains.

Population		Ann Gr	Density
2010	708,484	1.74%	15/sq km
2020	819,781	1.27%	17/sq km
2030	902,168	0.85%	19/sq km

The above are government figures. Other sources claim much higher numbers.
Capital Thimpu 93,000. **Urbanites** 36.8%. **Pop under 15 yrs** 31%. **Life expectancy** 65.7 yrs.

Peoples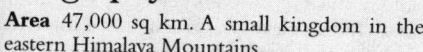

There are significant differences over the size of the population of ethnic Nepalis, many of whom were driven out of Bhutan from 1989 onward.
Tibetan/Himalayan 72.5%.
  Bhutanese 50.0%. Tshangla/Sharchop 17.8%; Dzongkha 14.0%; Kheng 7.4%; Matpa 3.7%; Bumthangpa 2.0%; Kurteop 1.9%; Nyenpa 1.9%.

Religions	Pop %	Population	Ann Gr
Buddhist	74.56	528,246	1.8%
Hindu	22.43	158,913	1.5%
Christian	2.11	14,949	3.6%
Muslim	0.50	3,542	1.7%
Ethnoreligionist	0.40	2,834	-0.6%

TransBloc	Pop %	Population	Ann Gr
Evangelicals			
Evangelicals	1.8	12,983	3.1%
Renewalists			
Charismatics	1.1	7,836	2.8%
Pentecostals	0.1	440	3.1%

Christians Denoms		Pop %	Affiliates	Ann Gr
Protestant	6	0.67	5,000	2.0%
Independent	9	1.24	9,000	3.8%
Catholic	1	0.20	1,000	7.0%

Churches	MegaBloc	Congs	Members	Affiliates
Indigenous house chs	I	26	2,597	4,000
Believers Church	P	25	2,250	3,000
Indian Evang Team	I	13	1,000	2,000
Catholic Church	C	1	1,053	1,400
Other denominations[12]		79	2,491	4,490
Total Christians[16]		**144**	**9,391**	**14,890**

Religions % of Total Pop

TransBloc Movements % of Total Pop

Challenges for prayer

1 **Bhutan is one of the world's least evangelized nations.** The continued isolationist policies of the government combined with the highly significant role of the Buddhist monarchy further reinforce the hold of tantric Vajrayana Buddhism, complete with the strong occultic/demonic influence of pre-Buddhist Bon animism. Pray for true spiritual liberation for this land of the Dragon (Druk Yul). Pray for King Wangchuk and his salvation.

2 **The Tibetan/Himalayan peoples** comprise the majority population, with the Bhutanese people cluster numbering 50% of the population. They are strongly Buddhist, and Christians among them number only a few hundred. These scattered believers are limited to small fellowships at best; most have faced varying degrees of persecution or social ostracism. Among the five largest peoples (Dzongkha, Tshangla, Lepcha, Kheng, Gurung), only the Lepcha have any significant Christian population. Pray for the emergence of a vital witnessing fellowship in every ethnic group of the Bhutanese.

3 **The Nepali population** has suffered what amounts to ethnic cleansing since 1990. The Buddhist Bhutanese majority has suppressed Nepali culture and language and even allowed violence against people and property in the course of expelling up to 150,000 Nepali Bhutanese. The vast majority of these huddle in meagre UN refugee camps in southeast Nepal, though some emigrate to Western nations. In these camps, several dozen informal Christian fellowships have formed among those who have found faith, and the number of believers is growing. Pray that the compassion of Jesus might be demonstrated to these displaced people.

4 **Bhutan was effectively closed to all Christian witness** until 1965. This was followed by 25 years of slight relaxation, during which Indian and other expatriate NGOs were able to witness. Since 1990, restrictions have increased. The spread of Christian witness and the potentially "destabilizing" effects on society of proselytism and Western-style democracy are the pretexts for harsh treatment of Christians. Pray for the growth of the Church in this land.

5 **Christians are denied religious freedom** and are persecuted in various ways. Church buildings are forbidden in all but a very few cases; most fellowships must meet in homes. Bhutanese who become Christian face the loss of their citizenship, of other benefits – such as free education, health care, employment – and of access to electricity and water. In some instances, harassment and beatings occur. Despite these, groups of believers are forming and increasingly spreading across the breadth of the country.

6 **Foreign Christians** have made an impact in two ways:

a) Mission agencies were allowed to be involved in health, agriculture and education programmes, but these are increasingly winding down to nothing. A few small aid projects continue. Visas are difficult to obtain. Pray that God will once again open doors for Christian ministries to sensitively bring the love of Christ into Bhutan. **GFA** has a Bible college in the capital city of Thimpu.

b) Border ministries. Indian believers in particular, but also Nepalis and others, are active in evangelism and literature distribution among Bhutanese. Many Christians in Bhutan have come to the Lord by these means. Pray that Bhutanese as well as Bhutanese students in India and around the world may hear the gospel and respond positively.

7 **Media ministries** are particularly helpful when witness within the country must be done cautiously. Pray for:

a) Scripture translation and distribution. The NT has been translated in Dzongha, the national language. The majority of indigenous languages have no Scriptures whatsoever. Pray for the effective spread of Christian materials in the country and at the borders (**GFA**, **EHC**).

b) Audio materials. **GRN** has produced Scripture or Christian recordings in 10 languages.

c) Other media. Shortwave radio is available in some languages of Bhutan. **GFA** locally broadcasts a programme in the indigenous Dzongkha language. The JESUS film is used in and around Bhutan in five languages.

Bolivia
Republic of Bolivia
Latin America

Geography

Area 1,099,000 sq km. Landlocked Andean state. High plateau in southwest, tropical lowlands in north and east. One of only two landlocked republics in the Americas.

Population		Ann Gr	Density
2010	10,030,832	1.78%	9/sq km
2020	11,637,914	1.40%	11/sq km
2030	13,034,153	1.05%	12/sq km

Capital La Paz (administrative) 1,673,401; Sucre (legal) 288,000. **Other major city** Santa Cruz 1.7 million. **Urbanites** 66.5%. **Pop under 15 yrs** 36%. **Life expectancy** 65.4 yrs.

Peoples

Mestizo 43.7%. Mixed race, Spanish-speaking, predominantly urban. Includes Mestizo, whites and Afro-Bolivians.

Amerindian 53.6%.
   Highland peoples 49.8%. Quechua(2) 27.3%; Aymara(2) 22.5%.
   Lowland peoples 3.8%. About 27 groups. Up to 10 more have recently become extinct. Major groups are Chiquitano 1.7%; Guarani(5) 1.4%.

Other 2.7%. German 2.0%. 10 other European and Asian groups.

Literacy 86.5%; functional literacy nearer to 50%. **Official languages** Spanish, Aymara, Quechua. **All languages** 41. **Indigenous languages** 37. **Languages with Scriptures** 5Bi 18NT 21por 6w.i.p.

Economy

Once South America's richest area, but corrupt, unstable governments, the fall in silver, tin and cotton prices on international markets and a poor infrastructure render it the continent's poorest nation. Devastating floods in 2007 pressed matters further. Discoveries of huge natural gas deposits, which were nationalized, are the engine of current economic growth. These deposits strongly link Bolivia to Brazil economically. Reducing poverty and unemployment are primary governmental goals. Honest agriculture is often undermined by coca growing.

HDI Rank 113th/182. **Public debt** 45.2% of GDP. **Income/person** $1,656 (3% of USA).

Politics

Independence from Spain in 1825 after a long war for freedom. Over 200 successful coups or revolutions have held back meaningful progress. Since 1985, democratic governments have stabilized the country; improvements are tangible. Since the 1990s, the rights of underprivileged indigenous peoples and of the poorest Bolivians have been increasingly recognized. President Morales was elected in 2006 with an absolute majority and re-elected in 2009 with a two-thirds majority – rare in Bolivian politics. Four (gas-rich) regions out of nine strongly voted for autonomy in 2006, raising the stakes on issues of presidential powers and regional autonomy and generating significant unrest. The leftist leanings of former coca-grower President Morales see Venezuela and Cuba emerge as close allies.

Religion

The Catholic Church retains State Church status, but rapid growth of non-Catholic religious bodies threatens this. Issues of religious freedom and relation of Church and state must be resolved. The government actively encourages a revival of indigenous religious traditions. Most of the population have been baptized Catholic but are practicing animists or Christo-pagans, so statistics here must be interpreted in this light. The majority of Quechua and Aymara are in this category.

Religions	Pop %	Population	Ann Gr
Christian	90.97	9,125,205	1.6%
Non-religious	3.74	375,160	3.6%
Ethnoreligionist	3.10	310,961	4.6%
Baha'i	1.90	190,589	2.9%
Chinese	0.20	20,062	1.8%
Buddhist	0.05	5,016	1.8%
Jewish	0.03	3,009	10.4%
Muslim	0.01	1,003	1.8%

Christians Denoms	Pop %	Affiliates	Ann Gr
Protestant	68	12.86	1,290,000	3.8%
Independent	61	4.64	466,000	5.4%
Anglican	1	0.01	2,000	2.9%

Catholic	1	77.56	7,780,000	0.9%
Orthodox	1	0.04	4,000	1.0%
Marginal	2	2.33	233,000	3.6%
Doubly affiliated		-6.48	-650,000	0.0%

Churches	MegaBloc	Congs	Members	Affiliates
Catholic Church	C	900	4,523,256	7,780,000
Seventh-day Adventist	P	368	132,353	225,000
Assem of God of Bol	P	1,550	96,500	193,000
Latter-day Saints (Mormon)	M	411	93,750	180,000
Evang Christian Union	P	1,977	85,000	170,000
Bolivian Assem of God	I	783	36,000	80,000
Baptist Union	P	291	33,742	55,000
Jehovah's Witnesses	M	293	20,500	53,300
Ekklesia Bolivia	I	8	24,000	48,000
Friends Nat Evang Ch	P	414	19,872	31,000
Holiness Church	P	429	15,000	30,000
Reformed Ch of God	I	240	18,000	28,800
Evang Friends Int	P	212	17,000	27,200
Christian Brethren	P	457	13,700	25,345
Bolivian Chr Mission	I	158	12,600	25,200
Bol Evang Ch of God	P	400	20,000	25,000
Other denominations[118]		5,074	296,959	798,931
Doubly affiliated				-650,000
Total Christians[134]		**13,965**	**5,458,232**	**9,125,776**

TransBloc	Pop %	Population	Ann Gr
Evangelicals			
Evangelicals	16.2	1,628,371	4.6%
Renewalists			
Charismatics	13.1	1,312,505	5.8%
Pentecostals	7.9	787,735	5.2%

Missionaries from Bolivia
P,I,A 129 (71 long-term) in 24 agencies: to Bolivia 53, Middle East 13, Europe 13.

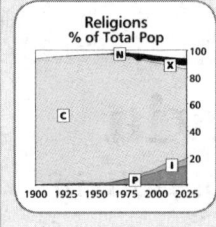

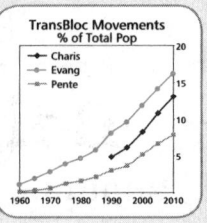

Answers to Prayer

1 **The 50-year responsiveness** of many sections of the population continues in the new millennium, with evangelicals doubling in percentage since 1990 and increasing 43-fold in number since 1960.

2 **Aymara and Quechua** peoples, who date back to pre-Inca times, have both experienced major church growth in their midst, and spiritual responsiveness seems to be increasing.

3 **Both the churches and the state take the challenge of poverty seriously.** The resources to tackle this issue exist, but until now, the willpower and wisdom were lacking.

Challenges for Prayer

1 **The political context** of Bolivia changed significantly in the last 10 years. A socialist president with strong agendas, a shift to the political left regionally, claims for ocean access (through Chilean territory) and a push for autonomy by some regions of Bolivia all unsettle the status quo. Attempted constitutional amendments and rich gas deposits intensify tensions between the white elite, highland Quechua and Aymara of the west, and the mestizo and Indian peoples in the gas-rich east. Pray for peace within and around Bolivia. Pray also for wise governance that will bring justice for the poorest Bolivians and the mistreated indigenous peoples, while strengthening the economy for the benefit of all.

2 **Poverty, economics and the coca leaf are inextricably linked.** Around 70% of the population are mired in poverty, half of those in abject poverty. Growing coca is much more profitable than growing other agricultural products, and many of Bolivia's population are farmers. The president advocates growing the leaf for traditional purposes, but it is impossible to control how all of the coca-leaf harvest is processed. Pray that individuals, both those in power and those in poverty, would have the courage to reject temptation and to make good decisions.

3 **The spiritual grip of the enemy remains strong** after centuries of entrenched paganism, and continues its hold on the Church. Christians now recognize that spiritual warfare is essential to consolidate what breakthroughs have been achieved. Pray that the Church will wake up to the enemy's deep-seated influence, bind the strong man and pray in transformation and harvest.

4 **The Catholic Church is confronted by multiple crises.** Its long-held political supremacy is rapidly declining as is its share of Bolivia's population. Large losses to faith groups provoke local discrimination and pressure against non-Catholics. It has failed to develop an indigenous clergy and to challenge the rampant paganism within the majority it claims to shepherd. Pray that the millions of nominal and Christo-pagan Catholics might come to a living faith in Christ.

5 **Evangelical Christians are growing** in number and in influence, but face many challenges. Low literacy levels, lack of biblical knowledge and limited discipleship opportunities give rise to theological error and moral failure. There is a great need to raise the standard of discipleship. The Association of Evangelicals (ANDEB), a major fellowship link for churches, is committed to widespread prayer and unity. Pray for these to be achieved and for believers to increase both in quantity and quality. Some other evangelical goals are:

a) *For Bolivia to become at least 30% evangelical.* While growth is impressive, this goal is still some way off from being achieved.

b) *Increased mission sending.* Bolivia's sending has increased significantly, but there is still scope for further growth, especially into cross-cultural missions.

c) *Social engagement.* Evangelicals must be at the core of Bolivia's battle against poverty, injustice and vice by demonstrating radical Kingdom values.

6 **Leadership training is a desperate need** recognized by all – precipitated by rapid church growth in past decades. Only a tiny fraction of pastors have formal theological training. There are over 30 Protestant seminaries and Bible schools as well as a variety of TEE institutes, BCCs and in-service training programmes; all of the above will not suffice to meet the need unless the Spirit actively calls, raises up and sanctifies thousands of new leaders. Pray for this.

7 **The less-reached:**

a) *The upper classes* have long held exclusive control of the reins of power, and the gap between rich and poor is widening. Although a number in this class have come to faith, evangelicalism remains largely the domain of the poor. Ekklesia Church is one denomination impacting this group; some of the newer charismatic churches also see response.

b) *Rural villages.* A high proportion of Quechua, Aymara and lowland peoples live in hard-to-access mountain or forest regions. Those who have been reached at all are almost always under-resourced in terms of teaching, discipleship and Christian resources.

c) New urban populations. Many migrants have drifted to the cities looking for work. They are often rootless, vulnerable and usually menial labourers working for a pittance; the majority are Quechua or Aymara.

d) The more than 300,000 tertiary students in the 59 universities and colleges face difficult prospects, are often disillusioned with traditional values and are confronted by post-Christian value systems. CCU(**IFES**) and **CCCI** have dozens of workers and hundreds of students, but the large majority of campuses and students remain untouched.

e) Young people are rarely specifically ministered to, yet over 67% of the population are under age 30. Widespread unemployment, urban violence and easy availability of drugs make reaching and discipling them all the more vital. Pray for SU and many others seeking to reach and disciple the youth, but most important, pray that local congregations would understand the great importance and potential in reaching youth.

f) Children. Up to 75% of Bolivia's children are raised in a context of poverty; chronic malnutrition is all too common. Perhaps 100,000 are homeless or street kids – almost all the boys have used drugs, and many of the girls have experienced sexual abuse. Pray for the development of children's ministries and for churches to see the importance of these.

8 **Lowland tribes** have been largely evangelized through great sacrifice and with considerable success. Praise the Lord for the work of **NTM**, **SIM**, **WGM**, UWM, South American Mission and others. Their ministries have been strongly attacked by anti-Christian anthropologists and commercial exploiters of these lands as "genocidal", but these claims prove spurious in the face of real exploiters. Pray for maturity in indigenous leaders, integration of these believers into Bolivian life, sound conversion of the second generation of Christians and development of a healthy indigenous Christianity as part of their culture.

9 **Foreign missions.** Early missionaries struggled long against hostility, persecution and harsh living conditions before the harvest ripened. The contribution of AEM (now **SIM**) was unique in pioneering most of the major gospel advances and ministries in the country. Foreign ministry must now focus on developing leaders (especially among the Quechua and Aymara), reaching and discipling young people and developing holistic ministries. Major missions include **SIM**, **NTM**, **YWAM**, **WGM**, SAM(USA), **AM**. Korean missionaries were instrumental in founding two of the three Christian universities.

10 **Bible translation and distribution.** The Bible Society has been and remains instrumental in all aspects of this vital ministry. Over one million NTs have been distributed in schools. The Aymara and Quechua Bibles are in great demand, but without effective literacy programmes, their impact is blunted. Nearly every Amerindian language that warrants translation work has received it; SIL, The Bible Society and the Catholics have been instrumental in this. Pray for a powerful impact of God's Word on all groups in Bolivia.

11 **Christian media:**

a) TV and radio have a massive role to play, since a radio is a vital possession to every family. Listenership of local radio stations is increasing. There are now 11 local evangelical stations, including Ekklesia, *Musoj Chaski* radio in Quechua (launched by **NTM**, **SIM**, Pioneers) and others. International stations (**HCJB**, **TWR**, others) broadcast daily in Spanish, and **HCJB** especially in Quechua and Aymara. Pray for this vital medium in a country where all other media are restricted in impact by illiteracy, poverty and isolation.

b) Christian literature in Aymara and Quechua, especially tracts, teaching materials and books, is in short supply. **SIM** has a significant ministry in this area. There are 13 Christian bookstores.

c) The JESUS film, widely used with considerable impact in Spanish, Aymara and Quechua, has been seen by a high proportion of the population.

Croatia

Serbia

Bosnia-Herzegovina ★Sarajevo

Adriatic Sea

Montenegro

Bosnia

Bosnia and Herzegovina

Europe

Geography

Area 51,129 sq km. Mountainous Balkan state bracketed by Serbia, Montenegro and Croatia.

Population		Ann Gr	Density
2010	3,759,633	-0.11%	74/sq km
2020	3,676,677	-0.27%	72/sq km
2030	3,519,821	-0.49%	69/sq km

The 1992-1995 civil war displaced 1.8 million people. Many have returned, but only a minority to their old homes, effectively entrenching ethnic partitions.
Capital Sarajevo 396,000. **Urbanites** 48.6%.
Pop under 15 yrs 15%. **Life expectancy** 75.1 yrs.

Peoples

Massive shifts in population from 1991-2002. Resettlement rate has plummeted since 2005.
Slavic 94%. Nearly all speaking Serbo-Croatian, with some dialect differences between the major groups.
  Bosniak 48.4%. Mainly in central and northwest Bosnia.
  Serb 29.3%. Mainly in the "Republic of Srpska" in north and east Bosnia.
  Croat 16.6%. Mainly in southwest and on the north border.
Other 5.8%. Romani 2.2%; several European groups, Turks, Arabs, Jews.
Literacy 94.6%. **Official language** Bosnian.
All languages 8. **Indigenous languages** 4.
Languages with Scriptures 3Bi 1NT 1por.

Economy

The war of the early 1990s devastated Bosnia and shattered its fragile agrarian infrastructure. Massive population movements, wholesale destruction and disruption of communications sank the economy further. Foreign aid is still important as is rebuilding the infrastructure; tourism is growing in importance. Seemingly, the only issue the different communities agree upon is to aspire to the financial windfall of EU membership.
HDI Rank 76th/182. **Unemployment** 43%.
Public debt 40% of GDP. **Income/person** $4,625 (10% of USA).

Politics

Bosnia separated from Serbia in AD 960 and, during the 500-year Turkish occupation, many Bosnians became Muslim. WWII saw hundreds of thousands of Serbs exterminated by Croat and Bosniak Nazi collaborators. The breakup of Yugoslavia led to a Croat-Muslim alliance in support of independence in March 1992, which was swiftly and militarily contested by the Serb minority. The three-sided war among Serbians, Croatians and Bosnians caused immense damage, loss of life, displacement of millions and wartime atrocities (most notably by Serbs upon Bosniaks). The war ended in 1995 with no winner and the nation partitioned between the Serb Republic and the Croat-Muslim Federation. Real power lies with NATO and international agencies, trying to orchestrate a transition to a feasible post-war arrangement.

Religion

Ethno-nationalistic religious confessions replaced communism as the prevailing ideology. The very few who identify with other faith groups are almost considered traitorous. The long history of ethno-religious hostility can also feed religious extremism.

Religions	Pop %	Population	Ann Gr
Muslim	54.16	2,036,217	0.0%
Christian	40.98	1,540,698	-0.2%
Non-religious	4.85	182,342	-0.3%
Jewish	0.01	376	-0.1%

Christians Denoms		Pop %	Affiliates	Ann Gr
Protestant	6	0.07	3,000	1.6%
Independent	7	0.03	1,000	1.0%
Catholic	1	12.58	473,000	0.4%
Orthodox	1	28.19	1,060,000	-0.5%
Marginal	1	0.07	2,000	4.6%
Unaffiliated		0.07	2,000	14.9%

Churches	MegaBloc	Congs	Members	Affiliates
Serbian Orthodox Ch	O	290	731,034	1,060,000
Catholic Church	C	275	326,207	473,000
Jehovah's Witnesses	M	32	1,623	2,500
Evangelical Ch (Pente)	P	15	350	850
Seventh-day Adventist	P	22	455	700
Baptist Church	P	12	360	540
Other denominations[10]		15	921	1,487
Total Christians[16]		**661**	**1,060,950**	**1,539,077**

TransBloc	Pop %	Population	Ann Gr
Evangelicals			
Evangelicals	0.1	2,207	2.1%
Renewalists			
Charismatics	0.1	2,230	1.7%
Pentecostals	<0.1	875	2.5%

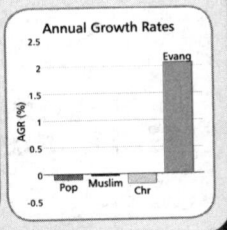

Challenges for Prayer

1   **The tragedy of 1992–1995** was only the latest in a long cycle of violence plaguing this region. Irreconcilable animosity has burdened Bosnia with two separate mini-states and a presidency rotating among the three main factions, an inefficient and expensive situation that drains up to 50% of the GDP. Few of the displaced have resettled in their original homes, preferring to huddle together along sectarian lines. Although buildings and roads are being restored, deep communal wounds remain. Appropriate justice for war criminals still at large and fair solutions for all must be obtained. True reconciliation and unity will occur only by a powerful intervention from the Great Reconciler.

2   **The post-war socio-economic situation is troubled,** and recovery is slow. A poor country even before the strife, Bosnia still struggles with poverty. Only organized crime syndicates do well for themselves; these groups must be shut down if Bosnia hopes to join the EU with all the accompanying financial rewards. Young people in particular are pessimistic – more than 60% want to leave the country; the brain and youth drains further sap Bosnia's potential. Pray for economic transformation, and for a new generation of Bosnians to lead their nation into a bright future rather than flee a sinking ship.

3   **Religious communities are as entrenched as ever** and deeply divided along ethnic lines. Orthodoxy has been subverted by Serb nationalism, and Catholicism by Croat nationalism. Militant Wahhabism from the Middle East (that has bankrolled the rapid rebuilding of mosques, many illegally) is replacing the previously European, Sufi-influenced moderate Islam of Bosnia. A precious few are building bridges across religious divides. All groups view Protestants and Independents suspiciously. Pray for the Spirit to move powerfully among all Churches and for Christians to recognize that their citizenship lies first in Heaven.

4   **Evangelical believers have increased significantly** but still represent only a miniscule proportion of the population. From three congregations in 1991, there are now about 35. Only evangelicals are effectively bridging the ethnic fault lines. Baptists and Pentecostals predominate, but several other smaller churches are also at work. Baptists run a seminary in Sarajevo, and both Pentecostals and Baptists have Bible schools. An Evangelical Alliance has been founded for Bosnia. Pray for believers and their witness in this divided land. Bosnia is not a spiritually receptive place; pray that many hearts might open to the gospel.

5   **The unreached:**

a) Bosniak Muslims are possibly the least evangelized people in Europe. From a mere handful, the number of believers in Jesus has grown to over 500. Islamic mission activities may cause them to be even harder to reach.

b) The Orthodox Serbs. Having endured under Islamic rule for 500 years, they now find themselves international pariahs. Pray that bitterness and disillusionment might be healed; pray also that the faith for which they suffered so long might come alive and transform this people.

c) The largely Muslim Romani (Gypsy) and the wholly Muslim Turks are contrasting pictures. Among the Turks, there is almost no ministry or response. The Romani are one of the poorest and most despised groups, but also one of the most responsive to the gospel.

d) Student ministry. Among 30,000 tertiary students (the majority in Sarajevo), there are fewer than 40 believers. **IFES** now works among these students, as does **CCCI**; pray for lasting fruit.

6 **Expatriate Christian input** is definitely needed for believers in Bosnia to have a greater impact, and there are many ways to impact the nation. Pray that those engaged in leadership development, aid, rehabilitation, outreach and church planting ministries might fully identify with the people, and that through these a harvest may be won. Pray for effective networking among expatriates. The largest agencies: Pioneers, **OM**, Novi Most International and TE.

7 **Creative means of sharing Christ's love** are both necessary and effective. Among them are the Alpha Course, house construction and repairs, ESL and German-language acquisition, handicrafts, coffee bars, sports and camps, youth ministries and, most strategically, prayer and intercession – the foundation for all other ministry.

8 **Christian media ministries** for prayer:

a) The Federation of Bosnia and Herzegovina Bible Society was formed in 1999 as a cooperative effort for Scripture and literature publication. The Bible Society is translating the entire Bible into Bosnian.

b) TWR broadcasts in Serbian (6.5 hours/week), Croatian (4.5 hours/week) and Bosnian (2.5 hours/week). More Christian radio is clearly needed in the major languages.

c) The JESUS film is available in Serbian, Bosnian, Croatian and Romani.

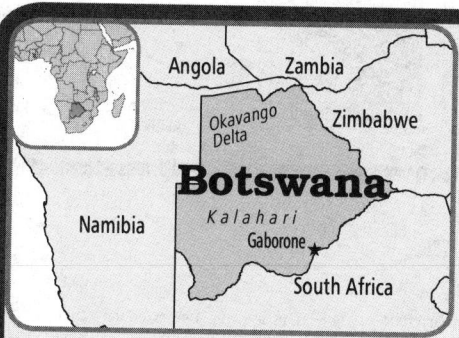

Tswana 69.1%. Eight major tribes, most living along the southeastern border with South Africa.

Other 26.3%. Kalanga 10.1%; Ndebele 3.3%; Shona 2.4%; Kgalagadi 2.3%; Herero 1.2%; Mbukushu 1.1%; Yeyi 1.1%.

San (Bushmen) 2.8%. Fourteen groups, with over 30 dialects.

Other 1.8%. Zimbabwean, Angolan, South African, Asian, British.

Literacy 78.9%. **Official languages** English, Setswana. **All languages** 40. **Indigenous languages** 29. **Languages with Scriptures** 7Bi 5NT 7por 2w.i.p.

Botswana

Republic of Botswana

Africa

Geography 🌍

Area 581,730 sq km. The Kalahari Desert covers 80% of the country. Dry and prone to severe droughts.

Population		Ann Gr	Density
2010	1,977,569	1.46%	3/sq km
2020	2,227,418	1.13%	4/sq km
2030	2,434,182	0.82%	4/sq km

Capital Gaborone 201,000. **Urbanites** 61.1%. **Pop under 15 yrs** 33%. Life expectancy 53.4 yrs.

Peoples 👪

Bantu 95.4%.

Economy 📈

Benign neglect in colonial times. Rapid development since independence through export of diamonds, copper, nickel, gold and beef. Tourism is a burgeoning element of the economy. Earnings have been wisely used to develop the country; leaders have been notably corruption-free. The most stable and sustained growth in Africa over the last 20 years.

HDI Rank 125th/182. **Public debt** 5.9% of GDP. **Income/person** $7,554 (16% of USA).

Politics ⚔

Independence from Britain in 1966. Has a stable, multiparty democracy, a rarity in Africa.

Religion ⛪

Complete freedom of religion. After over 150 years of having the gospel, the old tribal worldviews and beliefs remain strong and often spiritually unchallenged.

Religions	Pop %	Population	Ann Gr
Christian	65.56	1,296,494	1.6%
Ethnoreligionist	32.60	644,687	1.1%
Baha'i	0.83	16,414	2.2%
Muslim	0.45	8,899	3.9%
Hindu	0.24	4,746	3.2%
Non-religious	0.15	2,966	1.5%
Chinese	0.10	1,978	60.8%
Buddhist	0.05	989	6.1%
Sikh	0.01	198	1.5%
Jewish	0.01	198	1.5%

It is impossible to neatly categorize the religious sentiments and views of the peoples in Botswana. Many adhere to both Christian and animist views.

Christians Denoms		Pop %	Affiliates	Ann Gr
Protestant	52	11.22	222,000	0.7%
Independent	157	31.70	627,000	0.4%
Anglican	1	0.61	12,000	1.4%
Catholic	1	3.99	79,000	-1.0%
Orthodox	1	<0.01	<1,000	0.0%
Marginal	4	0.66	13,000	0.7%
Unaffiliated		17.38	344,000	4.0%

Churches	MegaBloc	Congs	Members	Affiliates
Catholic Church	C	98	45,930	79,000
Zion Christian Ch	I	18	31,500	63,000
Spiritual Healing Ch	I	71	28,500	57,000
St. Engenas Zion Chr Ch	I	30	20,800	41,600
Assemblies of God in B	P	78	15,200	31,160
Seventh-day Adventist	P	90	25,250	30,300

United Cong Ch of S Afr	P	26	8,709	29,000
St. Johns Apos Faith	I	413	8,251	25,000
Holy Full Gospel Apos Ch	I	19	9,700	24,250
Evang Luth Ch in B	P	64	15,986	23,500
Methodist Church	P	62	5,500	14,850
Anglican Ch of B	A	107	3,634	12,100
Apostolic Faith Mission	P	21	5,330	10,660
Full Gospel CoG in S Afr	P	224	4,700	9,400
Evang Luth Ch of S Afr	P	21	3,182	9,100
Deeper Life Bible Ch	I	4	316	600
Other denominations[200]		2,821	232,722	492,430
Total Christians[216]		**4,167**	**465,210**	**952,950**

Many Christians in Botswana hold denominations loosely and move freely between churches on a frequent basis.

TransBloc	Pop %	Population	Ann Gr
Evangelicals			
Evangelicals	8.1	159,689	1.2%
Renewalists			
Charismatics	33.9	670,746	0.6%
Pentecostals	5.6	111,454	1.3%

Religions % of Total Pop

TransBloc Movements % of Total Pop

Answers to Prayer

1 **Botswana is a rare African state** – economic growth is steady, corruption rare and a multiparty democracy the norm. Praise God for the stability that enables the government to build up the nation's infrastructure. Give thanks also for religious freedom and openness, allowing many agencies to establish work here, from evangelism and church planting to more social and holistic ministries. Vision 2016 is a government-initiated set of long-term goals regarding health, economy and society, which line up very naturally with biblical principles.

Challenges for Prayer

1 **The Tswana were the first Bantu people** in Africa to respond to the gospel; several tribes turned to God in the 19th Century through the LMS from England. Other missions followed. Today, the majority of Tswana are Christian in name. Sadly, there is widespread immorality, drunkenness and a breakdown of the traditional family structure, including a high proportion of illegitimate children. Other less numerous groups resent the Tswana's socio-political influence in Botswana. Pray for a reversal of the moral decline and for renewal among the Tswana.

2 **AIDS has devastated the country.** Botswana has the world's second-highest prevalence of AIDS after Swaziland. The disease, spread mostly by sexual promiscuity, has stolen 28 years from the nation's life expectancy and created a situation so dire that a recent president stated, "We are threatened with extinction." Over 100,000 AIDS orphans exist in the country, a staggering number for such a small population. Pray for the following:

a) *The government* has fast-tracked a programme that makes anti-retroviral drugs available through the public sector, drugs that will keep many alive. Pray that the government might have wisdom to know and do what is right. Pray that people will make use of these services in a way that effectively prolongs their lives.

b) *The many ministries* working with AIDS victims and orphans. There are countless opportunities to demonstrate Christian love in this context. Pray for compassionate ministry to those who suffer and for effective preventative work among those not yet infected, particularly youth abstinence programmes.

c) *Individual congregations.* Not a single church exists whose membership is unaffected by AIDS. Pray for the ending of any stigma toward sufferers and for congregations to work together for mutual support and prevention.

3 **Most mainline Protestant churches** were established by Western missions in generations past, but now are generally in decline. Some suggest that the mainline churches' struggles today are a legacy from the early missionaries' failure to contextualize the gospel to local culture; this has resulted in pervasive nominalism. Both local congregations and denominational structures are affected. Pray for revival among these historic churches.

4 **The more-recently established Pentecostal churches** grew rapidly in terms of both the number and size of congregations, but this growth has slowed of late. Some comment that these churches are among the few that have enabled significant lifestyle-change among their members. Pray for the impact of these churches on both spiritual and compassionate ministries.

5 **African Initiated Churches** (Spiritual Churches or AIC) are the largest religious grouping in the country. They are made of several large and also hundreds of small denominations. There is a great deal of diversity among them, ranging from biblically orthodox groups to marginal fringe groups. Most of these Churches stress the healing power of God. Of all the churches, they are most clearly engaged in the struggles of culture and faith, which have led some into syncretistic practices. Since there are no paid pastors, many are led by those with little education or theological training. A few have taken college-level theological courses; some have studied at a more basic level. Several groups run basic theological courses specifically geared to help these leaders. Mennonite Ministries Botswana has worked for 30 years with AICs through Bible education. Pray for African Indigenous Churches to use their strengths to reach out to others with the gospel of Jesus.

6 **Networking between churches and ministries** is a strong point in Botswana. The Evangelical Fellowship of Botswana, the Botswana Council of Churches and the Organization of African Initiated Churches (OAIC) work together on a variety of joint projects. Joining Hands (a missions network) draws together many for initiatives such as MANI and the Micah Challenge to enable better networking. Pray that this cooperation and unity might yield greater fruitfulness in ministry.

7 **Less-reached peoples:**

a) *The Kalanga* live under the cultural dominance of the Tswana. While mission churches have not penetrated the Kalanga areas, many AIC and Pentecostal churches are involved with these people. Most can speak Setswana, but the Bible is now available in Kalanga (Lutheran Bible Translators). There are very few other written resources in Kalanga. Pray for this people and the impact of the gospel among them.

b) *The Yeyi* (20,000) of the Okavango Delta have had little exposure to a living Christianity, and that only through the Tswana language. The efforts of Love Botswana Outreach, Word to Africa and Calvary Ministries are now seeing response.

c) *The Nambya* (15,000) of the northeast are more numerous and better evangelized in neighbouring Zimbabwe, but are still the third-largest group in Botswana with less than 2% evangelicals.

d) *The San* have suffered the almost complete destruction of their desert-adapted way of life, due to the development of ranching, mining and tourism. There are no longer any purely nomadic San – all are resettled in poverty on the fringes of towns and villages. Response is slow, but several thousand San may now be Christian in about 20 congregations through the efforts of a dozen agencies (**SIM**, Reaching the Unreached, Calvary Ministries, Xanagas Mission, Word to Africa, Lutherans and others). Pray that these agencies may be able to help the San adapt to modernity, yet retain their cultural heritage and, above all, find their true identity in Christ.

e) ***The Mbukushu and Herero peoples*** fled the Okavango Delta due to the civil war and violence spilling out of Angola. A number of congregations have been established among them only recently. Pray for these young churches to flourish and grow.

8 **Ministry to young people** is particularly strategic, given the low life expectancy, high rates of teen pregnancy and the widespread impact of AIDS. The Open Baptists, SU, YFC and IFES are a few of the main groups focusing on spiritual ministry, life training, AIDS prevention and discipleship.

9 **Christian media** and support ministries for prayer:

a) ***The Bible Society*** oversees the translation programme, and Wycliffe works on many of the projects. Pray for wisdom in choice of minority languages for translation projects, the most challenging being the many small San languages. In many of Botswana's languages, quality Christian literature is scarce and expensive.

b) ***Radio broadcasts and Christian TV*** are areas in need of growth. **TWR** broadcasts several hours a week in English on shortwave. Love Botswana Studio 7 produces programming for youth (Reach4Life) airing on the two major national stations. They are establishing local Christian radio and TV once licences are granted. Indigenous languages of Botswana will be targeted.

c) ***GRN*** has available recordings in 29 languages, including many San dialects.

d) ***The JESUS film*** is available in six languages: Tswana, Mbukushu, Herero, Kalanga, Afrikaans and Yeye. Production is underway in other languages.

e) ***The Flying Mission*** serves the cause of Christ through aviation as well as HIV/AIDS work. They have six planes and 22 staff.

Population		Ann Gr	Density
2010	195,423,252	0.99%	23/sq km
2020	209,051,123	0.60%	25/sq km
2030	217,146,118	0.31%	26/sq km

Capital Brasilia 3,904,918. **Other major cities** São Paulo 20.3 million; Rio de Janeiro 12.0mill; Belo Horizonte 5.9m; Porto Alegre 4.1m; Salvador 3.9m; Recife 3.9m; Fortaleza 3.7m; Curitiba 3.5m; 12 other cities with populations over 1m. **Urbanites** 86.5%. **Pop under 15 yrs** 26%. **Life expectancy** 72.2 yrs.

Peoples

Brazil is a melting pot of nations, with much intermarriage and blending of the many immigrant ethnicities. Most Brazilians have at least some mixed ethnic heritage.

European 50.2%. Including the world's largest diaspora populations of Portuguese, Italian and Spanish, and the second largest of Germans.

Mixed race 38.0%. Mestizo and Mulatto.

African 6.4%. Descendants of slaves brought from West Africa and Angola.

Asian 5.6%. Arab 4.0%; Japanese 0.7% (the world's largest Japanese population outside Japan); Jews; Chinese.

Amerindian 0.41%. 275 indigenous tribal groups speaking 185 different languages. Detribalized Amerindian 0.34%. Only 700,000 tribal people remain, threatened by

Brazil
Federated Republic of Brazil
Latin America

Geography

Area 8,511,965 sq km. One-half of the land surface and population of South America. The world's fifth largest country in both area and population.

encroachment of new settlers, loss of land, disease and detribalization.

Literacy 88.6%. **Official language** Portuguese. **All languages** 193. **Indigenous languages** 181. **Languages with Scriptures** 6Bi 52NT 72por 80w.i.p.

Economy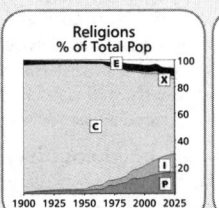

Vast natural resources combine with a huge labour force to create an emerging economic superpower, especially in agriculture. Sustained strong growth has pushed the crises of the 1980s behind and has stabilized the economy. One great challenge will be to increase agricultural space without traumatizing the precious Amazon and Pantanal ecosystems – stewardship versus exploitation. There is a vast gap between rich and poor, but this is improving significantly.

HDI Rank 75th/182. **Public debt** 38.8% of GDP. **Income/person** $8,295 (17% of USA). **Unemployment** 10%.

Politics

Independent from Portugal in 1822 as a kingdom, it became a federal republic in 1889. Authoritarian military rule between 1964 and 1985 left a legacy of social inequality, bureaucratic inefficiency and state ownership of large parts of the economy. Multiparty democracy restored in 1985. The left-leaning government has been ambitious in reducing poverty and reforming social, fiscal and political policies. A strong anti-corruption stance has had notable effect, not least upon the party itself.

Religion

Freedom of religion and separation of church and state. There is still a residual bias to Catholicism in government circles, but this is rapidly decreasing as the influence of the *evangélicos* grows.

Religions	Pop %	Population	Ann Gr
Christian	91.40	178,616,852	1.1%
Ethnoreligionist	5.40	10,552,856	1.8%
Non-religious	2.24	4,377,481	-5.3%
Other	0.30	586,270	3.9%
Muslim	0.29	566,727	4.0%
Buddhist	0.26	508,100	1.8%
Jewish	0.06	117,254	1.0%
Chinese	0.02	39,085	1.0%
Baha'i	0.02	39,085	1.0%
Hindu	0.01	19,542	1.0%

Christians	Denoms	Pop %	Affiliates	Ann Gr
Protestant	150	16.34	31,932,000	1.7%
Independent	324	12.42	24,271,000	2.3%
Anglican	3	0.07	135,000	1.8%
Catholic	1	72.79	142,250,000	-0.4%
Orthodox	15	0.09	179,000	0.0%
Marginal	57	1.54	3,005,000	3.0%
Doubly affiliated		*-11.85*	*-23,160,000*	*0.0%*

Churches	MegaBloc	Congs	Members	Affiliates
Catholic Church	C	9,250	103,832,117	142,250,000
Assemblies of God	P	116,000	15,676,692	20,850,000
Univ Ch, Kingdom of God	I	5,875	3,525,000	7,050,000
God Is Love	I	4,300	2,155,689	3,600,000
Foursquare Gospel Ch	P	8,600	1,905,325	3,220,000
Reborn in Christ	I	1,917	958,333	2,300,000
Seventh-day Adventist	P	6,030	1,560,000	1,950,000
Brazil for Christ	I	4,600	1,159,880	1,937,000
Christian Congregation	I	4,700	945,500	1,891,000
Jehovah's Witnesses	M	10,543	738,000	1,719,540
Baptist Convention	P	6,950	900,000	1,560,000
Latter-day Saints (Mormon)	M	1,975	770,073	1,055,000
Cornerstone Gospel	I	779	428,571	900,000
Maranatha Christian	I	6,000	300,000	750,000
Sara Nossa Terra	I	833	416,667	750,000
Lutheran Confession	P	2,700	484,615	693,000
Catholic Apos Ch of B	I	350	305,556	550,000
Presbyterian Church	P	2,280	311,377	520,000
Nat Baptist Convention	I	3,600	306,369	481,000
Grace of God Int Ch	I	2,000	168,539	450,000
Adventist Ch of Promise	I	558	195,455	430,000
Restoration Church	I	860	215,000	430,000
Evang Cong Chr Ch	P	2,775	222,000	399,600
Methodist Church	P	3,340	167,000	278,890
Evang Luth Ch of B	P	2,100	138,323	231,000
Pente Ch of Christ	P	582	58,214	163,000
ABWE	P	1,943	68,000	136,000
Other denominations[523]		30,088	2,466,149	5,225,901
Doubly affiliated Pentecostals				*-5,680,000*
Doubly affiliated				*-17,480,000*

Total Christians[550] 241,528 140,378,444 178,616,000

Note: Catholics and many Pentecostal groups claim high numbers. These have been kept as stated by the denominations themselves in most cases, but two large, doubly counted categories have been introduced to compensate for the impossibly high figures. Numbers given here are therefore substantially higher for these groups than those given in the 2001 edition of *Operation World*.

TransBloc	Pop %	Population	Ann Gr
Evangelicals			
Evangelicals	26.3	51,334,091	1.7%
Renewalists			
Charismatics	31.2	60,889,473	1.9%
Pentecostals	20.9	40,772,374	1.7%

Missionaries from Brazil

P,I,A 3,438 (1,976 long-term) in 115 agencies: in Brazil 744, elsewhere in South America 879, Africa 488, Europe 389.

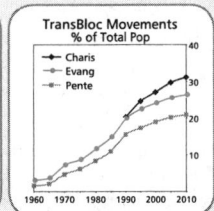

Answers to Prayer

B

1 **The sustained increase of** *evangélicos* (from 2 million in 1960 to 51.3 million in 2010) makes Brazil one of the largest evangelical populations in the world. While not without controversy, their steady forward march is changing the makeup of Brazil's population and orientation.

2 **The Brazilian missionary movement** has likewise grown and matured in just one generation, to the point where, in 2010, they sent just under 2,000 Protestant, Independent and Anglican missionaries – the 14th largest number sent by any nation. These missionaries are wedding Latin American passion and dynamism to their increasing experience and cross-cultural awareness on the field.

3 **Prayer movements and meetings** are a strength of Brazilian Christianity. Huge gatherings, sustained intercession networks (such as the women's prayer network in Goiania, which brought about much change there) and the spiritually oriented Brazilian mentality combine to make this a nation with many prayer warriors.

4 **Large-scale events celebrating Jesus** – such as the Global Day of Prayer, the March for Jesus, the National Council of Indigenous Pastors and Leaders and other such rallies – are recording unprecedented numbers. These proclaim Christ to the nation, but they also build a much greater sense of unity within the striking breadth of Christian expression in Brazil. Less numerous but just as significant was the Meeting of Indigenous Amazonian People which drew together 47 ethnic groups for reconciliation, fellowship, training and commitment to evangelize the rest of the region.

Challenges for Prayer

1 **The nation and government** have made great strides but still face massive challenges. Pray about the following:

a) **Endemic corruption and cronyism** have been addressed aggressively, and idolatrous structures are crumbling. These have come at some cost, but they are moves in the right direction, bringing political accountability and economic transparency, establishing justice and enabling economic opportunity. Pray that future governments would not shirk from the painful but necessary process of excising all that is putrid and corrupt.

b) **Poverty still affects tens of millions.** Admirable reforms and progress are being achieved, but a significant proportion of dwellers in large cities still live in poverty-stricken, crime-ridden favelas, and the education and health care sectors are in serious need of improvement. The poor, especially street children and indigenous peoples, often suffer terrible discrimination and exploitation. Debt slavery affects up to 250,000 people (the official number is 25,000), especially in the Amazon.

c) **Crime is a serious problem.** Brazil is the world's second-highest consumer of illicit drugs and has the world's highest rate of firearm homicides. Nearly 150 people a day were murdered in Brazil in the years between 2000 and 2010. The police response has been brutally heavy-handed and rife with corruption, and the nation's prisons are notoriously overcrowded and violent. Unprecedented breakthrough, spiritual and social, is needed to turn this around.

d) **Racial differences** may not seem an issue in the ethnic melting pot of Brazil, but statistics bear out a different view of Brazil's complex racial context. While blacks/morenos are 40% of the population, they only account for 3% of college graduates and form the majority of Brazil's poor. Although nearly half have African ancestry, less than 7% openly claim it on the census. This is, however, more a case of social rather than racial discrimination.

2 **Brazil is a spiritually open country,** for good and for ill, and is probably more Spiritist than Catholic in underlying worldview. Although "non-religion" is actually the fastest-growing faith group, few of that category would be hardcore atheists. Most follow Afro-Brazilian cults (such as *Candomblé, Macumba, Umbanda*) derived from African animism and witchcraft, but "high Spiritism" (Kardecism) is more popular among whites. Only 1.3% identified themselves solely as Spiritist in the census, but around 10 million practice, and even one-third or more Brazilians visit Spiritist priests or guides; many quite happily practice Catholicism and Spiritism together. The ecstatic experiences, flexible practices and emotional mysticism give it great appeal to the Brazilian mindset. Pray for all spiritual falsehoods to be exposed as such and for Christ alone to be exalted as Lord in Brazil; pray for those in actual spiritual bondage to be delivered through Jesus.

3 **Catholics in Brazil** number more than in any other country, but the Church itself remains in crisis. The defection rate has slowed, but it continues to lose members to evangelicals, to Spiritists and to non-religion. By 2025, Catholicism could be a minority religion, having held 95% of the population in 1950. Around 70% of ex-Catholics are now evangelicals. Even within Catholicism, only a small minority remain traditionally Catholic and faithful in practice; many others are influenced by Spiritism, nominalism or the charismatic renewal. The grassroots "Base Community" movement, the engine room of liberation theology, has lost much of its drive, but nearly one million "Bible circles" persist, hosting studies of Scripture. Pray that the Bible and its truths may mould the lives of Catholics. Other points for prayer:

a) *A desperate shortage of priests.* Of the current 18,000, many are foreigners. Another 100,000 are needed to meet all the needs; currently there is one priest for every 6,300 Catholics.

b) *Increasing loggerheads with the government* as the Church loses its preferred status and influence in areas such as contraception, abortion, homosexuality and transgender issues.

c) *The charismatic movement* grows in strength, numbers and maturity; over 15 million are a part of this.

d) *The successes of evangelical denominations* have stimulated a more people-friendly, contemporary worship and ministry and a greater growth of evangelical Catholics, as well as an increase in traditional mass attendance.

4 **The emergence of evangelicals** in Brazil has been dramatic. Yet despite the growth – from 2.9% in 1960 to 26.3% in 2010 – there are many prayer needs:

a) *Numerical rather than spiritual growth is the emphasis* of too many groups, to the point of dishonest inflation of numbers and disregard for discipleship. As a result, churches have "multiplied", but congregations are filled with immature, unfed spiritual infants whose faith is overly based on emotionalism, petty legalism and the personality of leaders. Such zeal without maturity leads to spiritual error, nominalism, widespread church-hopping without commitment to a particular church and large-scale backsliding.

b) *Prosperity theology* has shaped much of Pentecostalism in Brazil, with those on top of the pyramid enjoying celebrity status and lifestyles – as well as financial scandals – while millions of poor hold out for a miracle of healing or financial blessing. Pray for a right balance between expectation of blessing and daily sanctification.

c) *Leadership models are sorely lacking,* as witnessed by the scandals and moral failures of some high-profile leaders characterized more by their wealth, power and lack of accountability than their humility and faithfulness. The celebrity bishop model is unsustainable, and there needs to be new ways of shaping and growing leaders who will be well suited for bringing discipleship and societal impact to Brazil's evangelicals.

d) *Effective appropriate training* is a key to addressing the above issues. Rapid growth, especially among Pentecostals, has generated a dearth of trained leaders. With over 200,000 evangelical congregations, traditional education models are inadequate to meet the need. Many are making pastoral training a top priority now; Baptists, Presbyterians and Foursquare are examples of such groups developing new seminaries, TEE programmes and in-service training opportunities. AoG has over 17,000 students on 420 extension campuses, but even this is not enough to meet the need. Pray for wise and creative solutions to this challenge.

e) *Unity.* Evangelical denominations have mushroomed in the last 20 years as new groups form with almost every theological disagreement or inter-personal conflict. There could be over 4,000 distinct evangelical groups. The success mentality based on numbers and income can induce rivalry and jealousy. Pray for the Evangelical Association of Brazil to be a means of fostering lasting unity, fellowship and prayerful cooperation.

5 **Evangelical impact on society** has until now been negligible. But with rapid growth comes increased power and responsibility. Pray for:

a) **Socio-political influence.** No longer a tiny, marginalized group, evangelicals now hold nearly as much clout as the Catholic Church. Churches are beginning to wield this strategically, both as a voting bloc and in lobbying the government on various issues. Pray for assertive holiness that is combined with gracious humility in presenting the face of the Church to the nation.

b) **Transformational ministry** is greatly needed in a nation ravaged by inequality, injustice, crime, immorality and HIV/AIDS. While mainline churches have a long association with compassionate works, evangelicals have done far too little to effect transformation. Only 12% of churches have any kind of social programme, and most of those are very limited in scope. Once evangelicals address these challenges on a massive scale, then they can consider themselves to truly be "good news people".

6 **Brazil has become a leading mission-sending nation** with great emphasis on the unevangelized and on church planting. Brazillians' faith, enthusiasm, adaptability and talents (football, music, dancing) open many doors, but poor preparation and support can undermine all these. Pray for:

a) **More who will go to the field** and more churches who will send them. While just under 2,000 is a formidable number of missionaries sent, given the mass of Brazil's evangelicals, the sending ratio is actually very poor. The large majority of congregations have no involvement in missions, and the explosive growth of missions in the 1980s and 1990s may not be characteristic of 2000-2020. There is still great and untapped potential!

b) **Mobilization and facilitation.** *Associação de Missões Transculturais Brasileiras* (AMTB) mobilizes churches into mission and serves as a resource and linking network for 35 of the largest Brazilian cross-cultural mission agencies. *Associação de Conselhos Missionários de Igrejas* (ACMI) aims to help local churches set up viable missions structures, programmes and channelling mechanisms.

c) **Missionaries sent from Brazil.** Pray for their recruitment, their effective training and preparation for the field and their long-term survival and fruitfulness in cross-cultural situations. More and better training programmes are improving the level of adequate preparation that was previously lacking for many workers. Unrealistic expectations and traditionally poor levels of pastoral support are also being addressed.

d) **Sending churches to increase their long-term commitment** to pray for, send and support missionaries. Prayer support is often very strong, but at times promised financial support never arrives. Attrition from Brazilian missions has been disproportionately high in the past, and better support from the home end is an integral part of the solution to this.

7 **The challenge of the less-reached regions.** Brazil's evangelical population is very unevenly distributed; the northeast and south in particular lack an evangelical presence.

a) **The squalid favelas.** These slums are a highly visible blight in every major city – nearly 20% of Brazil's population and up to one-third of Rio de Janeiro and São Paulo's populations live in slums (there are now 600 *favelas* in Rio alone). They were swelled initially by rural-urban migration and more recently by downwardly mobile middle classes. Criminal ganglords often preside over a web of extortion, drugs, violence, prostitution and disease, but the police's heavy-handed and frequently corrupt approach often makes them as much a part of the problem as the solution. However, the desperation has also brought responsiveness to the outreach directed there, often by Pentecostals who have come from the same background as those they are attempting to reach.

b) **The poor and underdeveloped northeast** has Brazil's lowest percentage of evangelicals, in particular Piauí and Ceará. The poor Sertão hinterlands contain hundreds of municipalities that are less than 5% evangelical. There is a great exodus of the poor to the Amazon and the cities of the northeast. Pray for a wise ministry approach that weds church planting with relief and development through an effective Brazilian and expatriate missionary presence.

c) **The Amazon basin,** larger than the whole of non-Russian Europe, is of huge global importance because of its oxygen-generating forests and biodiversity. The challenges for outreach are the pioneer settlements springing up along new roads through the forests and the 36,000 yet-unchurched river communities accessible only by boat. **UFM**, **AoG**, Baptists, **YWAM** and many others are involved with **MAF** support in some areas. Church planting is made difficult by the relative poverty, the migration of church members to cities and geographical isolation. There are around 180 missionary boats linked with the local churches, but the unchurched are those located farther away from the major rivers.

d) *The cities.* Although they have many churches, cities also contain ethnic minorities and the nation's elite, which have been far less impacted by the gospel. Pray that the Church may find effective means to break through into these groups.

8 **Immigrant peoples.** Pray for a greater missionary burden by the Brazilian Church for these peoples and for effective outreach and church planting among them.

a) *The 1.5 million Japanese* – the largest Japanese community outside of Japan. Approximately 60% of Japanese Brazilians claim to be Catholic, but ancestor worship, Shintoism and Buddhism also tend to be part of their practice. There are a growing number of evangelical churches among Japanese-Brazilians, including the Japan Holiness Church (**OMS**), **AoG**, Free Methodists and Lutherans. Over 300,000 Japanese-Brazilians have moved to Japan, where they face discrimination. Pray for a strengthened witness to Japanese-Brazilians.

b) *Over 200,000 ethnic Chinese* now live in Brazil, largely in the São Paulo area. Most are Buddhist or Daoist; 4% are evangelical. **IMB** missionaries are planning outreach to them, and LifeWay Christian Resources plans to distribute a modern Chinese translation of the New Testament there.

c) *Jews,* who have been settling here since the earliest colonial days and number up to 150,000. There are few Christians among them and very limited, if any, specific outreach.

d) *Muslims,* consisting of mostly Arabs and a few thousand Turks. Although there may be over a million Brazilians with some Arab blood, many are Catholic. Islam is growing, via immigration, childbirth and some conversions, but Christians are increasingly reaching out.

9 **The indigenous Amerindians** have endured centuries of prejudice, oppression, massacre and exploitation, which continue to this day by encroaching woodcutters, gold prospectors and ranchers. Their unique cultures are disintegrating through despair, disease, substance abuse and suicide. Six million indigenous people in AD 1500 now number a mere 700,000, with many reduced to small bands in inaccessible areas. The large majority of these tribal groups now number less than 1,000 people. Fully 70% of Brazil's unevangelized peoples live in the Amazon basin. Pray for:

a) *A change in attitude of Brazilians* to see these peoples as national treasures rather than as nuisances who slow the rapid but shortsighted development in the Amazon and Pantanal. Government laws and policies are in place to prevent the exploitation of people and land, but they have not been effectively implemented.

b) *A balanced approach to protection* that actually helps the Amerindians. Their isolation has yielded their immune systems highly vulnerable to outside diseases. But occasionally, those (self-)appointed to "protect" them instead perpetuate their misery by enforcing their isolation and preventing them from choosing their own appropriate development and integration into the wider world.

c) *The growth of Christian networks among these peoples.* CONPLEI (National Council of Evangelical Indigenous Pastors and Leaders) is a rapidly expanding indigenous, evangelical movement for tribal groups. CONPLEI gatherings host over 1,000 Amerindian evangelical leaders from around 50 tribal groups.

d) *Christian agencies ministering to them,* in 25 agencies with over 1,000 workers. The large majority are now Brazilian, with greater freedom and access for outreach. Pray for the work of **NTM**, with 500 staff and missionaries working in 36 tribes (and hoping to reach another 9), SIL in over 30 languages, **WEC** (*Projeto Amanajé*) in 13 groups, **UFM** in 7 groups, **YWAM**, **CMS** and many Brazilian agencies. Pray that the gospel might be shared in ways that honour and preserve the culture while elevating Christ. There are 103 tribal groups with no missionary presence.

e) *Bible translation and Scripture use* – SIL and ALEM (from Brazil) are pouring effort, time and personnel into this ministry which includes literacy, intercultural education and the preservation of oral traditions. There are projects in 45 languages, but a further 10 languages need Scripture translation, and many language groups need Scripture-use projects.

*f) **Urbanized and detribalized Amerindians*** are a new missiological challenge. Increasingly, many groups migrate into cities, where they experience great cultural disorientation and exploitation. Without necessary labour or language abilities, they gravitate toward menial labour, destitute slums and, too often, crime.

*g) **The Yanomami*** (12,000 pop in Brazil) straddle the Brazil-Venezuela border. Their land has been invaded, despoiled and poisoned by over 1,000 illegal gold miners. Over 2,000 Yanomami have been killed in clashes with settlers. Disease, deforestation and further mining seriously threaten the existence of this shamanistic people. **NTM, UFM** and **YWAM** work with them.

*h) **The Guarani*** – on the Paraguay border, numbering 34,000 – have been so thoroughly robbed of their ancestral lands that they are rapidly dying out through a wave of suicides, diseases and malnutrition/infant mortality. Many missionary groups from several denominations work among them.

*i) **The Kaiwa*** on the Paraguay border number more than 35,000 and struggle with similar issues as the Guarani. An oral evangelism approach is being taken to reach them.

10 **The younger generation** is fairly large (26.8% of the population) and very much in need. There is a serious shortfall of ministry directed toward children and young people; churches are only now tailoring ministry to their unique evangelistic and discipleship needs. If these are not met, all the gains of this generation could be lost in the next. Pray for:

*a) **Children at risk.*** Remember before the Lord:

   i The 8 million children at risk. Pray for the many churches and agencies with orphanages, homes of refuge and ministries of rehabilitation and training (**YWAM, UFM, WH, WEC, AM, CEF** and APEC, a Brazilian group).

   ii The many threats to such children's lives: drug abuse, prostitution and particularly murder, either in gang violence or by police death squads (2,000 murders every year).

   iii The 7 million child labourers.

   iv The 600,000 girls involved in prostitution.

   v The need for Christians not only to minister to the needy but also to tackle the causes of these issues.

*b) **University students*** face many pressures, from educational to moral to financial. There are nearly 2 million tertiary students in Brazil. Pray for more workers to minister to them. There are many dynamic Brazilian-originated ministries for students and youth. Most are connected with specific churches or denominations, but others, such as Tribal Generation, work across all such boundaries. US-originated ministries such as ABUB(**IFES**), **CCCI** and Navigators are also active in helping students come to the Lord, building them up in the Word and encouraging missionary vision. ABUB has a significant publishing organization.

11 **The role of missionaries has changed** over the years as Brazil's evangelicals have grown and matured. Expatriate workers are most needed in training leaders, preparing Brazilian missionaries, helping locals establish holistic ministries and pioneering work in the Amazon region. Missions with the largest number of workers: **BMM, NTM, CC, ABWE, YWAM**, PCKH(Korea), Brazil Gospel Fellowship, **CW, WEC**, Project Amazon. Pray that the foreign missionary force would be deployed in a strategic manner most beneficial to the Brazilian Church and mission movement.

12 **Christian literature and media.**

*a) **Scriptures.*** A large proportion of evangelicals read the Bible daily. The Bible Society alone sells/distributes over 5 million Bibles per year; the Gideons distribute 6.7 million NTs per year. Through these and other groups, up to 300 million Scripture portions and pieces of Christian literature are distributed each year.

*b) **Christian books.*** Brazil's most widely sold books are about magic, the occult and psychographed (dictated by the dead) books. Evangelicals are not avid consumers of Christian books, despite there being many Christian publishing houses. Pray for more Christian books that will resonate with the Brazilian mentality to both disciple Christians and challenge non-Christians.

c) *The JESUS film* is available in 25 languages, including 22 Amerindian languages.

d) *Radio and TV* are booming areas of ministry. There are countless radio programmes. Many larger churches have their own TV stations, either local or national. These transmit good content but also the bad aspects of "show-biz Christianity". Internationally, **TWR**, **HCJB** and others beam over 1,000 hours across FM, AM and shortwave each week.

e) *Audio resources.* **GRN** has prepared tapes in 90 indigenous languages, many of which are the only Christian material for that whole language. **WBT**, UBS, FCBH and others are part of the resource development.

f) *Internet.* The tech-savvy younger generation connect with each other, watch or hear sermons online and access Bible study, discipleship and prayer materials on the myriad websites run by churches or para-church ministries. This is an increasingly vital part of effective young people's ministry in particular.

Indian Ocean

British Indian Ocean Territory

Diego Garcia

British Indian Ocean Territory

Geography

Area 153 sq km. Mainly the Chagos Archipelago in the central Indian Ocean. 55 islands across 54,000 sq km of ocean.

Population		Ann Gr	Density
2010	2,000	0.00%	333/sq km
2020	2,000	0.00%	333/sq km
2030	2,000	0.00%	333/sq km

At present, approximately 4,000 US and UK military personnel as well as civilian private contractors (mostly from Mauritius and Philippines).

Politics

The original islanders were removed to Mauritius to make way for opening the island of Diego Garcia as a strategic US/UK military base. Financial compensation was paid to both Mauritius and the Chagossians. Resettlement back to Diego Garcia is complicated due to the US's exclusive military lease of the island from the UK government, which administers the territory. Although the UK High Court granted the islanders the right of return in 2006, in 2008 the UK government appealed this decision and the UK House of Lords upheld the appeal. Islanders still cannot return to their traditional homelands.

See under Mauritius.

B

British Virgin Islands

Caribbean Sea

Road Town

U.S. Virgin Islands

British Virgin Islands

Colony of British Virgin Islands

Caribbean

Geography

Area 153 sq km. An archipelago of 60 coralline and volcanic islands, of which 15 are inhabited. The most northeastern of the Leeward Islands.

Population		Ann Gr	Density
2010	23,276	1.12%	152/sq km
2020	25,290	0.76%	165/sq km
2030	26,888	0.56%	176/sq km

Capital Road Town 9,600. **Urbanites** 41.0%. **Pop under 15 yrs** 26%. **Life expectancy** 78.9 yrs.

Peoples

A high percentage of the population are foreign-born.
African Caribbean 88.8%.
Euro–American 6.9%.
Other 4.3%. East Indian 3.1%.
Literacy 97.8 %. **Official language** English. **All languages** 2. **Languages with Scriptures** 1Bi.

Economy

Tourism and offshore finance dominate the economy. Over 550,000 companies are registered here, with all the consequent implications of being a tax haven.
Income/person $38,500 (84% of USA).

Politics

A dependent territory of the UK, with internal democratic government.

Religion

There is freedom of religion.

Religion	Population %	Affiliates	Ann Gr
Christian	84.93	19,768	1.0%
Other	7.29	1,697	0.4%
Non-religious	5.30	1,234	3.6%
Muslim	0.88	205	2.1%
Baha'i	0.85	198	0.0%
Hindu	0.75	175	2.5%

Christians	Denoms	Pop %	Affiliates	Ann Gr
Protestant	11	50.72	12,000	1.5%
Independent	5	1.72	400	5.9%
Anglican	1	13.49	3,000	0.9%
Catholic	1	3.52	1,000	0.8%
Marginal	3	3.65	1,000	2.7%
Unaffiliated		11.80	3,000	0.0%

Churches	MegaBloc	Congs	Members	Affiliates
Methodist Church	P	6	2,865	5,500
Anglican Church	A	5	1,036	3,140
Seventh-day Adventist	P	7	1,500	2,145
Ch of the Nazarene	P	17	750	1,500
Catholic Church	C	4	328	820
Baptist Church	P	3	272	680
Ch of God (Holiness)	P	4	272	680
Jehovah's Witnesses	M	3	248	670
NT Church of God	P	3	201	670
Other denominations[12]		13	618	1,210
Total Christians[21]		**65**	**8,090**	**17,015**

TransBloc	Pop %	Population	Ann Gr
Evangelicals			
Evangelicals	27.3	6,354	2.5%
Renewalists			
Charismatics	9.6	2,229	3.9%
Pentecostals	5.6	1,310	3.6%

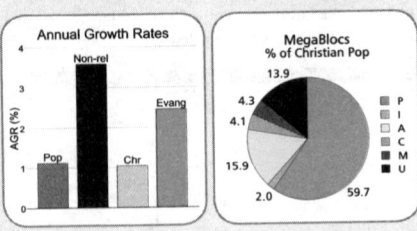

Annual Growth Rates

MegaBlocs % of Christian Pop

Challenges for Prayer

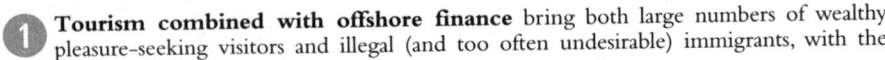

1 **Tourism combined with offshore finance** bring both large numbers of wealthy pleasure–seeking visitors and illegal (and too often undesirable) immigrants, with the inevitable moral impact on island life. Pray for local Christians and for their witness to both tourists and immigrants.

② **This "Paradise" is one of the most beautiful in the world,** yet vice has a strong grip. Most of the population profess Christianity, and church attendance is high, but the fruit of faith is not in evidence. Pray for Christian lifestyles to be in accordance with confession.

③ **The motto of the Virgin Islands** is "Where there's no vision, the people will perish." Pray that local Christians might recover a powerful vision for the lost in their own islands and abroad.

B

Brunei

State of Brunei Darussalam

Asia

Geography 🌐

Area 5,765 sq km. Two small enclaves on the island of Borneo, separated by the East Malaysian state of Sarawak. Tropical, 70% forest, with heavy rainfall.

Population		Ann Gr	Density
2010	407,045	1.92%	71/sq km
2020	478,259	1.54%	83/sq km
2030	546,651	1.27%	95/sq km

Capital Bandar Seri Begawan 22,700. **Urbanites** 75.7%. **Pop under 15 yrs** 27%. **Life expectancy** 77 yrs.

Peoples 👪

Malay 69.6%. Dominant in government and civil service. Tribal peoples have been absorbed into the Malay population: Brunei Malay 43.9%; Dusun 6.2%; Tutong/Bisayan 4.9%; Tutung 4.3%; Bajau 2.8%. Non-Islamized Tribal peoples: Iban 5.6%; Dayak 0.9%; Kayan 0.5%.
Chinese 15.6%. Most are non-citizen residents. Commercial focus, but gradually declining through emigration.
Other 14.8%. Mostly immigrant workers. Filipino 7.9%; Indonesian 2.3%; British 1.7%; Indo-Pakistani 1.2%.
Literacy 92.7%. **Official languages** Malay, English. **All languages** 17. **Indigenous languages** 15. **Languages with Scriptures** 9Bi.

Economy 📈

One of the richest states in Asia, with free education and health care, no income tax for most and heavily subsidized housing, fuel and staple food. Hydrocarbons account for 90% of exports, but proven deposits could be exhausted as early as 2020. Recent disasters in investment and a need for economic diversification have spurred eco-tourism and a push for self-sufficiency in rice growing.
HDI Rank 30th/182. **Public Debt** 11% of GDP.
Income/person $37,053 (78% of USA).

Politics ✖

Refused to join the Malaysian Federation in 1963. A Protectorate of Britain until full independence in 1983. The Sultan rules as an absolute monarch, maintaining the tradition of a Muslim monarchy that dates back to the 15th Century. A legislative council is appointed by the Sultan.

Religion 🙏

Islam is the state religion. Constitutional guarantees for the free practice of other religions are not always adhered to.

Religions	Pop %	Population	Ann Gr
Muslim	65.31	265,841	2.2%
Christian	11.39	46,362	1.4%
Buddhist	8.90	36,227	1.6%
Ethnoreligionist	6.60	26,865	1.3%
Chinese	5.30	21,573	1.2%
Non-religious	1.50	6,106	3.3%
Hindu	0.73	2,971	1.4%
Baha'i	0.24	977	0.3%
Other	0.03	122	10.5%

Christians Denoms		Pop %	Affiliates	Ann Gr
Protestant	8	2.33	9,000	1.9%
Independent	10	2.70	11,000	4.2%
Anglican	1	1.01	4,000	-0.5%
Catholic	1	5.16	21,000	0.0%
Marginal	1	0.06	<300	7.5%
Unaffiliated		0.08	<500	0.0%

Churches	MegaBloc	Congs	Members	Affiliates
Catholic Church	C	3	11,732	21,000
Tribal churches	I	21	2,550	5,100

Borneo Evangelical Ch	P	7	2,045	4,500
Anglican Church	A	3	400	4,100
Brunei Chr Fellowship	I	2	1,225	2,450
Bethel Chapel	P	2	495	1,040
Christian Brethren	P	2	425	765
Other denominations[11]		32	3,358	6,855
Total Christians[21]		**72**	**22,230**	**45,810**

TransBloc	Pop %	Population	Ann Gr
Evangelicals			
Evangelicals	6.1	24,677	2.4%
Renewalists			
Charismatics	3.4	13,900	4.2%
Pentecostals	0.5	2,130	3.4%

Religions % of Total Pop

MegaBlocs % of Christian Pop

Challenges for Prayer

1 Islam dominates life in Brunei, with a brand that is conservative but not radical. Islamization by financial and career inducements as well as by general pressure to convert and conform has yielded a slow but steady trickle of converts from among the tribal and Chinese minorities. Despite constitutionally guaranteed religious freedom, it is illegal to proselytize and illegal for a Muslim to convert to another religion. Other religions are often infiltrated by government agents for monitoring purposes. Pray for an atmosphere of religious freedom and spiritual openness and for the observance of the constitutional right for other religions to be practiced.

2 The Sultan is alleged to be the world's second wealthiest royal. The Sultan is reluctant to diversify the economy and liberalize government structures, believing that external influences might destabilize the country. Yet, he has established a world-class university and is working toward a smooth handover to the crown prince. Pray for conversions to Christ in the large royal family; the Sultan has shown evidence of becoming increasingly spiritual. Pray also that in following him, the Sultan's subjects might seek after spiritual truth and in doing so find Jesus.

3 The Christian Church exists under very difficult conditions. Evangelism is illegal, and although the number of Christians grows, no new registrations for churches are forthcoming. No foreign Christian workers are permitted – visiting ministers must arrive unannounced and in secret. Importing Bibles and Christian literature is illegal for ministry purposes, but not for personal purposes. Religious instruction in all schools, including the six Christian schools, is on Islam alone. Pray for:

a) *Perseverance, boldness and unity.* Their harsh treatment has drawn together most of the churches and birthed a holy determination among many. Pray for Christians to stand strong in the face of persecution.

b) *Christian leadership* that is schooled in the Word, anointed by the Spirit and able to build up all believers. Almost every Bible study and underground church is run by an untrained layperson.

c) *Numerical growth despite restrictions.* Most of those converted are local tribal peoples and Chinese; pray for new believers from among all ethnic groups and segments of society.

4 The effective evangelism of Brunei is a target set by several mission groups and by churches in neighbouring countries. This burden has increased intercession and planning. Pray for creative and powerful means of bringing the good news to those in Brunei. Pray for an opening for Kingdom workers to minister inside the nation.

5 The unreached.

a) *The Malay majority* are Muslim with a handful of Christians, none daring to publicly make his or her faith known. There is little reason for people to change their spiritual status quo; pray for the Spirit to move in the hearts of Malays.

b) **The Chinese** lack security and are still regarded as foreigners, even if born in Brunei. Most still follow the traditional religions of China or are secular. Less than 20% are Christian and, of those, many do not pursue the Christian life. Chinese Christian businessmen from Brunei and from abroad have significant potential to impact Brunei economically and spiritually.

c) **Tribal peoples** have either converted to Islam and then been absorbed into the mainstream of national life, or they have remained isolated in jungle villages. Pray for those still in villages; there is a fairly strong Church and witness to them.

d) **The expatriate workforce** will inevitably grow. The largest groups are Muslim Bangladeshis and Indonesians, Hindu Indians and Nepalis (the latter making up much of the Brunei army), Buddhist Thai and Catholic Filipinos. The presence of many Filipino believers holds great potential for reaching the majority unreached (Brunei Malays).

Bulgaria

Republic of Bulgaria

Europe

Geography

Area 110,912 sq km. Balkan state adjoining Turkey, Greece, Macedonia, Serbia and Romania.

Population		Ann Gr	Density
2010	7,497,282	-0.63%	68/sq km
2020	7,017,086	-0.69%	63/sq km
2030	6,468,602	-0.85%	58/sq km

Capital Sofia 1,196,287. **Urbanites** 71.7%. **Pop under 15 yrs** 13%. **Life expectancy** 73.1 yrs.

Peoples

Slavic 85.0%. Bulgarian 82.0%; Macedonian 2.7%; Russian 0.2%.
Turkic 9.4%. Turks 8.2%; Millet 1.2%.
Gypsy 4.7%. Four groups speaking Romani, Turkish or Bulgarian.
Other 0.9%. Albanian 0.2%; Armenian 0.1%.
Literacy 98.2%. **Official language** Bulgarian. **All languages** 16. **Indigenous languages** 12. **Languages with Scriptures** 3Bi 5NT 6por.

Economy

Rapid industrialization under Communist rule; minerals and manufacturing are important. Essential economic reforms begun in 1997 stabilized the economy. Mass privatization and foreign investment in real estate, tourism, IT and communication changed the Bulgarian economy and labour market. High unemployment in rural areas led to over 200,000 emigrating to seek jobs. Reforms in education, healthcare and regional development are the greatest challenges. Poor public administration, corruption and strong organized crime networks obstruct progress.

HDI Rank 61st/182. **Public debt** 14% of GDP. **Income/person** $6,561 (14% of USA).

Politics

A nation since the 5th Century, but rarely independent. Ruled by the Ottoman Empire 1396-1878; severe Communist rule 1947-1989; multiparty democracy instituted in 1990. Entry into the EU – finalized in 2007 – drove the liberalization of the nation's politics and economy.

Religion

Orthodoxy was the state religion until 1945 and is currently recognized as the "traditional" religion of Bulgaria. The Communists persecuted Christians and manipulated denominational leadership until 1989. Religious freedom is still not truly realized, although the situation has improved greatly since the 1990s.

Religions	Pop %	Population	Ann Gr
Christian	79.91	5,991,078	-0.7%
Muslim	12.10	907,171	-0.4%
Non-religious	7.94	595,284	-0.2%
Jewish	0.04	2,999	-0.6%
Baha'i	0.01	750	-0.6%

Christians Denoms		Pop %	Affiliates	Ann Gr
Protestant	29	1.70	127,000	0.7%
Independent	15	0.58	44,000	2.5%
Catholic	1	0.99	74,000	0.0%
Orthodox	4	78.56	5,890,000	-0.7%
Marginal	4	0.15	11,000	4.7%
Doubly affiliated		-2.07	-156,000	0.0%

Churches	MegaBloc	Congs	Members	Affiliates
Bulgarian Orthodox	O	3,509	4,000,000	5,400,000
Orth Ch of Bulgaria	O	299	340,741	460,000
Catholic Church	C	55	54,815	74,000
Pentecostal Union	P	571	37,762	54,000
Church of God(3)	P	410	22,754	38,000
Church of God Union	I	177	22,155	37,000
Armenian Orthodox	O	10	13,139	18,000
Seventh-day Adventist	P	120	8,400	11,340
Baptist Union	P	83	5,000	7,500
Other denominations[42]		463	25,633	35,799
Doubly affiliated				-145,000
Total Christians[54]		**5,697**	**4,530,899**	**5,990,639**

TransBloc	Pop %	Population	Ann Gr
Evangelicals			
Evangelicals	1.9	145,536	0.7%
Renewalists			
Charismatics	1.8	136,182	1.0%
Pentecostals	1.7	126,234	1.0%

Religions % of Total Pop

Annual Growth Rates

Answers to Prayer

1 **Bulgaria's transformation** from harsh spiritual repressiveness in the 1980s to relative openness and freedom today. Evangelicals face periodic opposition at the local level, but Bulgaria's move towards EU membership had an opening effect in the religious sphere also. There is a definite sense of progress in inter-church relations, though further progress is needed.

2 **Significant growth of evangelical and charismatic believers.** Evangelicals went from 0.4% of the population in 1980 to close to 2% today. Growth was significant in the 1990s and, with overall population decline, even maintaining the plateaued numbers since 2000 can be seen as progress.

Challenges for Prayer

1 **Bulgaria's troubled past** is not yet completely behind. Corruption and powerful organized crime syndicates persist. Poverty is widespread, as are divorce and abortion – there are more abortions than live births. Many of the youngest and brightest emigrate seeking jobs and money. Pray that wholeness will come to this nation as only the transforming gospel can bring.

2 **The Orthodox Church** needs renewal and new life. A bitter schism weakened and undermined the Church, stemming from the collusion of Orthodox leaders with the former Communist regime. Disunity persists, even at the local level. Orthodoxy is still largely equated to a Bulgarian identity, but this is changing as other religious groups take root and grow. Pray for a genuine move of the Holy Spirit that brings reconciliation of rifts and a full realization of Orthodoxy's spiritual richness.

3 **Evangelicals have grown, matured and unified** in response to challenges and opposition of the past two decades. Pray for:

a) *The Evangelical Alliance* (BEA). Its work of drawing diverse churches together to act and speak with a common voice is crucial to further growth.

b) *The Bulgarian body of Christ* is capable of making an immense positive impact on this country where racial tensions abound and where hope for the future is rare. True unity amongst believers of different ethnic and denominational backgrounds could be a powerful testimony.

c) *Sofia, the capital* and Bulgaria's only large city, has many churches, but more are needed. Pray for the nation's centre of influence to be saturated with the gospel. Meanwhile, 2,500 villages are without any evangelical church. Pray that the peoples of the rural areas would not be neglected; their spiritual need is great.

4 **Consolidating church growth** is a priority. Pray for:

a) *Training of church leadership.* Residential, TEE and informal training courses (such as EQUIP and the Global Leadership Summit) are multiplying – all necessary to prepare more leaders for growing churches. Pray especially for the interdenominational Evangelical Theological Institute, a cooperative effort formed through the merger of four different schools. Pray for the staff and students, and for provision of financial and academic resources necessary to provide a solid biblical foundation for ministry.

b) *Discernment of doctrinal error.* Every modern heresy and cult seems to have targeted this country – Mormons, Jehovah's Witnesses, extreme "prosperity" teachings and other Christian and eastern cults are very active, sending many missionaries. Pray for wise leaders and a biblically knowledgeable Church to discern false doctrine.

c) *New indigenous agencies* have sprung up, many characterized by creativity and activism. They aim to reach children, prisoners, and ethnic minorities and to provide literature, Bibles, and Christian teaching in schools and camps. The need for wise coordination and adequate funding mechanisms is urgent.

d) *Country-wide vision.* Pray for the influence and use of the BEA and others in setting – and achieving, by God's grace – ambitious goals for the effective evangelization of the country.

5 **Cross-cultural missions are increasing.** Bulgarians serve in Turkey, India, Zimbabwe and throughout Europe. Increasing numbers go with short-term teams to neighbouring countries. Pray for greater vision for the world in Bulgarian churches. Pray for greater awareness and cultural sensitivity among Christians toward ethnic minorities in Bulgaria.

6 **Islam's legacy** here dates to the Ottoman era, but most Bulgarian Muslims practice folk magic and are largely unaware of many Islamic teachings. Muslim missionaries (who outnumber Christian ones), teachers and funds pour into the country to teach Bulgarian Muslims a purer Islam and to push for greater Islamic influence. Pray that Bulgaria's 900,000 Muslims would discover Jesus as the true light and Lamb of God.

7 **Ethnic minorities suffered** severely at times at the hands of the Bulgarian majority. Bulgaria's straddling of a Balkan, Slavic and Turkish cultural fault line has generated trouble for centuries. Considerable discrimination continues, and both Turks and Gypsies have formed political parties to press for their rights. Pray specifically for:

a) *The Rumelian Turks* in the east who deeply resent the attempts of the Communist regime to forcibly Bulgarize them in the 1980s. Their language, religion and culture are now fully recognized. Barely 150 evangelical believers are known among them. Specific long-term church planting ministry is a recent development. Pray for the trickle of conversions to become a flood.

b) *The Millet,* an oppressed Turkish-speaking Gypsy minority, experienced a people movement to Christ among them during the 1990s. Of the up to 15,000 believers, as many as 80% were women and children, most coming to faith by way of dreams, visions and healings. This group of believers has since shrunk to less than half that number. Pray for the conversion of men also, largely unemployed and bound by alcohol. Pray too for Christians with knowledge of Turkish who seek to disciple these groups of largely leaderless believers (Ichthus Fellowship and Bulgarian national groups).

c) *The Romani,* with widespread illiteracy, are generally despised and at the bottom of the social order. The Orthodox/Muslim ratio among them is about 60/40. Many are deeply involved in the occult, crime and gambling, but major church growth has occurred amidst them as well – more than 20,000 have turned to the Lord, mainly through the Pentecostals, Baptists and the Church of God. The Romani NT and Romani-language radio ministry are valuable.

d) *Bulgarian-speaking Muslims in the south* have an identity crisis – rejected both by Bulgarians (religion) and Turks (language); a specific ministry is needed to reach them. Only a handful of congregations exist among them, but Bulgarian workers have increased focused prayer and church planting work among this group in recent years.

8 **Foreign missions** have traditionally found Bulgaria a tricky place in which to minister, yet missionaries and tentmakers who will learn the culture and language are still needed and can play a valuable role. Pray for:

a) *More workers for the field.* There are increasingly open doors and opportunities to serve the Church in Bulgaria through training, teaching and serving. Partnering with nationals to reach the unreached minorities is also a need.

b) *Missions and money.* A sudden and disproportional injection of foreign funds in the 1990s created dependent churches and a negative bias against evangelicals who "buy" converts. A focus on humanitarian work further painted evangelicals with the brush that the gospel is only for the poor and illiterate. Every infusion of money is both extremely useful and potentially damaging. Pray for great wisdom in the use of funds, and against overdependence upon such resources.

9 **Ministry to young people** is crucial. The current generation differs greatly from their Communist-era parents. There are some excellent developments in this ministry area but more are needed. **CCCI** is active. **IFES** has established student groups in 10 cities, but needs prayer to reach more unbelieving students effectively.

10 **Christian media ministries.** Difficult conditions for evangelism in the 1990s invited a more creative and savvy approach. Bulgaria's use of media for spreading the gospel is praiseworthy. From tracts to glossy magazines to Internet and television, it is estimated most Bulgarians are exposed to the gospel through mass media. The same media further serves the Church by keeping it informed of both domestic and international issues, with the Internet in particular increasing resource availability (sermons, music, articles, etc).

11 **Pray for lasting fruit** from:

a) *Literature.* Every large city has at least one Christian bookstore (**CLC**, Veren Publishers, others), and most larger churches have books for sale. Pray for viability amidst the prevailing poverty. **EHC**, SGM and the Bible League have plans for a nation-wide literature distribution campaign. Effective cooperation between foreign and national literature agencies is needed. Several indigenous Christian publishers have emerged, but struggle financially to produce and sell copies.

b) *Bible translation and distribution.* One Orthodox and three Protestant revisions of the Bulgarian Bible have been published in recent years, the latest edition completed in 2010. A children's Bible, "My First Bible", aims to reach schools and young students. The Bible League and Bulgarian Bible Society focus on Scripture distribution. Pray also for the Scripture that is already available in minority languages; low literacy is a challenge which limits its use and effectiveness.

c) *Christian radio and TV.* Studio 865 (national partner of **TWR**) has a studio producing TV and radio programmes in Bulgarian and Romani. Discipleship courses are vital to nurturing the many new believers. Shalom TV produces programmes with Christian and Bulgarian folklore content.

d) *Other Christian media.* The JESUS film is available in Bulgarian, Romani, Romanian and Turkish. It was very effective as part of an interdenominational nationwide campaign which also used the children's version of the film and the *Book of Hope*.

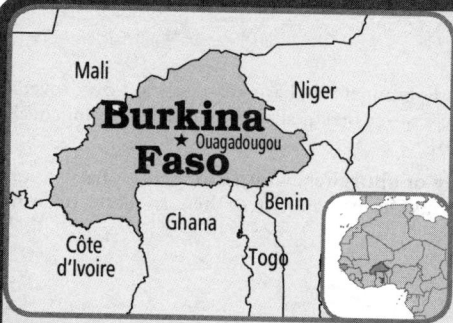

Mali

Niger

Burkina Faso
★ Ouagadougou

Benin

Ghana

Côte
d'Ivoire

Togo

Burkina Faso

Africa

Geography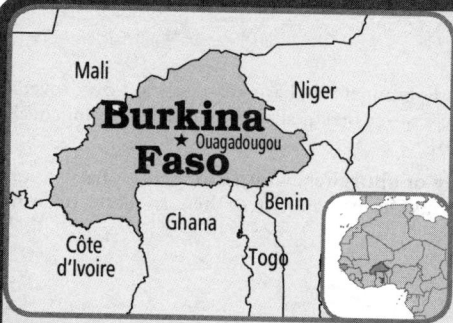

Area 274,200 sq km. A landlocked country of the Sahel. Prone to drought and famine.

Population		Ann Gr	Density
2010	16,286,706	3.45%	59/sq km
2020	21,871,161	2.84%	80/sq km
2030	27,939,915	2.38%	102/sq km

Over 3 million Burkinabé (people of Burkina Faso) have migrated to other lands: 80% to Côte d'Ivoire, others to Niger, Mali, Gabon and France.

Capital Ouagadougou 1,907,951. **Urbanites** 20.4%. **Pop under 15 yrs** 46%. **Life expectancy** 52.7 yrs.

Peoples

Over 78 distinct ethno-linguistic people groups.
Gur (45 peoples) 77.0%. Mossi 50.4%; Gurma 5.4%; Lobi 3.1%; Bwama(3) 2.4%; Nuna(2) 1.7%; Senufo(3) 1.4%; Lyele 1.4%; Kurumfe 1.3%; Birifor 1.1%; Kasem 1.1%.
Fulani 7.8%. 4 peoples. Gurmanche 5.8%; Jelgooji 1.9%.
Mande 5.7%. Bissa 3.0%; Northwester Samo 1.0%.
Malinke–Jula 4.6%. 3 peoples. Bobo Madare 2.6%; Jula/Dioula 1.8%.
Malinke 2.5%. 7 peoples. Marka 1.4%.
Other African 2.1%. Songhai 1.1%.
Non-Africans 0.3%. Arabs, Westerners.
Literacy 23.6%. **Official language** French, spoken by a minority of the population. Trade languages Moore (the Mossi language), Jula in south and west. **All languages** 70. **Indigenous languages** 68. **Languages with Scriptures** 7Bi 16NT 28por 28w.i.p.

Economy

One of the world's poorest countries. About 90% of the population rely on subsistence agriculture, which is vulnerable to drought; cotton is the main cash crop. There is some potential for gold and other mineral resources to be exploited. High national debt, low levels of education (especially for girls) and a negative impact from the strife in neighbouring Côte d'Ivoire.
HDI Rank 177th/182. **Public debt** 39% of GDP. **Income/person** $578 (1% of USA).

Politics

Independent of France in 1960. Six coups since 1966. A military coup in 1987 ousted the then-leftist government. The leader of this coup has since been elected three times with a large majority of the vote. While retaining tight control over the military and the political power structures (in the name of stability), he has also introduced multiparty democracy.

Religion

Religions	Pop %	Population	Ann Gr
Muslim	52.20	8,501,661	3.9%
Ethnoreligionist	26.44	4,306,205	2.2%
Christian	20.69	3,369,719	3.9%
Non-religious	0.65	105,864	5.1%
Baha'i	0.02	3,257	3.5%

Christians Denoms		Pop %	Affiliates	Ann Gr
Protestant	14	8.50	1,384,000	3.9%
Independent	62	0.66	108,000	5.1%
Catholic	1	11.50	1,873,000	3.9%
Marginal	1	0.03	4,000	2.7%

Churches	MegaBloc	Congs	Members	Affiliates
Catholic Church	C	2,420	1,088,953	1,873,000
Assemblies of God	P	7,100	611,732	1,095,000
CMA	P	800	28,200	90,800
Evang Ch Assoc	P	743	25,926	70,000
Reformed Church	P	60	10,825	32,800
Apostolic Church	P	160	12,500	26,250
Apostolic Mission Ch	P	125	8,000	20,300
Centre Int d'Evang	I	105	8,400	18,500
Evang Pente Assoc	P	187	4,118	14,700
Protestant Evang Ch	P	106	3,500	12,000
Baptist Convention	P	62	6,100	10,000
Other denominations[67]		662	46,109	105,621
Total Christians[78]		**12,530**	**1,854,363**	**3,368,971**

TransBloc	Pop %	Population	Ann Gr
Evangelicals			
Evangelicals	8.9	1,441,771	4.1%
Renewalists			
Charismatics	8.4	1,374,516	4.6%
Pentecostals	7.2	1,173,072	4.4%

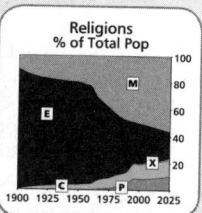

Religions
% of Total Pop

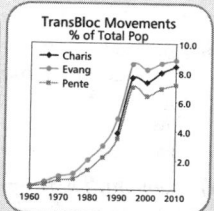

TransBloc Movements
% of Total Pop

Answers to Prayer

1 **The increase of Christianity,** particularly evangelicals, has been sustained over several decades. The growth of the early 1990s may never be equalled. Nonetheless, evangelicals grew from 10,000 in 1960 to 1.44 million in 2010.

2 **Give praise for the vibrant AoG family of churches,** with a strong missionary vision and claims of over one million affiliates. A significant minority of these are converts from Muslim backgrounds.

Challenges for Prayer

1 **As a landlocked, resource-poor, underdeveloped country,** Burkina Faso naturally struggles with poverty. There is little likelihood of immediate or rapid improvement of the situation, and both the economic reality and the poverty mentality that grip the land must be dealt with. Pray for:

a) *Aid, development, microfinance and microenterprise projects* that will actually lift the people out of poverty rather than create further dependence. Pray against corruption in the government and the aid industry that siphons resources away from the people most in need of it; pray for creative solutions to this longstanding problem.

b) *The many Burkinabé* who emigrate for work. An estimated three million Burkinabé worked in Côte d'Ivoire before violence broke out there in 2002. Large numbers fled back to Burkina Faso, but are now returning to Côte d'Ivoire. As many as 70% of these emigrés convert to Islam while away from home. Burkina churches are taking up the challenge by sending pastors and missionaries to reach these Burkinabé abroad, especially **AoG**, **CMA** and **WEC**, but more are needed.

c) *Rapid urbanization* continues as subsistence agriculture and traditional rural life prove inadequate to support families or to keep young people occupied. Rural churches now set up branches in the capital to maintain contact with their students and educated members; this also strengthens the church in the home territory.

2 **The spirit world is very real in Burkina Faso,** where, as the saying goes, the population is "50% Muslim, 20% Christian and 100% animist". The power of the occult has yet to be decisively challenged and broken in many peoples of Burkina Faso. Few countries in West Africa are more dominated by idolatry, fetishism and secret societies. Even in churches, occult power is wielded, hampering and polluting the message of Christ. The most strongly animist groups include the Lobi, Birifor and Dogosi peoples (**WEC**), Dagara (Canadian Pentecostals, **AoG**, **WEC**), Senufo and Bobo (**CMA**), Lyele (**IMB**), Karaboro and several smaller groups. Almost all live in the west and southwest of the country. Pray that the power of the risen Christ might be demonstrated for the saving of many.

3 **The evangelical churches** find themselves stretched by the growth of recent years. Failure to consolidate this growth has in some areas resulted in backsliding and losses to Islam. There are many needs:

a) *The crisis of leadership,* generated by the rapid multiplication of churches since the early 1990s. Pray for Bible schools run by the major churches and missions in local languages and in French (**SIM**, **CMA**, **AoG**, **WEC** and Pentecostals), and pray for independent faculties such as the *Institut Biblique Supérieur, Institut Biblique du Sahel* and *Institut Logos*. Pray for development of sustainable training programmes that suit the needs of churches and national believers.

b) *Pray for church leaders* at this vital time. Church growth has also created the great challenge of discipling many new believers. Pray for mature, godly wives for these pastors and evangelists who often struggle to find an appropriate helpmate. Pray for Christian leaders able to stand firm against idolatrous practices and against the pressures of living in a society that is predominantly Muslim, animist and tribally hierarchical.

c) *Economic hardship* is widespread in the Church, as in the rest of the nation. Pray that national believers may overcome a "poverty and dependence mentality". Pray for sacrificial servant leadership, for microenterprise and international partnership projects and for corporate economic righteousness to be practiced by all Christians.

d) ***The growing AIDS crisis*** is being addressed by both government and Christian initiatives, but the challenge remains great. Estimates of the HIV rate range from 1.6% to over 10% of the adult population. Awareness, prevention and care are all being taken up by churches and missions.

4 **The challenge of unity.** In the past, denominationalism kept Christians divided, but there is definite progress in this area. Churches are increasingly cooperating with each other, as are mission organizations. This is occurring especially through pastors' fraternal connections on the local level. But several schisms and splits out of the large **AoG** demonstrate that unity is still some way off. Pray that the Holy Spirit might convict the hearts of believers and build unity among them for the greater glory of God.

5 **Pray for the unreached.** Despite church growth, increased evangelism and mission and continued responsiveness, 27 unreached peoples remain without an effective witness; 17 of these are Muslim. Most unevangelized lie within the area of witness of several existing mission projects. Churches and missions working in areas with unreached people often tend to favour more responsive or closely related peoples. Pray for the recruitment and deployment of pioneer workers from Africa and the world to evangelize the unreached. Specific challenges include:

a) ***Muslims,*** who are stronger in the north but continue to grow in nearly every ethnic group. Only a fraction of the missionary force in Burkina is specifically committed to ministering among Muslims.

   i *Groups include* the urbanized Soninke, rural Tuareg (**WH, AoG**), the Kurumba (**AoG**) and Songhai (**WH**), all in the north; Bolon in the northwest; the Jula (**CMF**) and the Bobo Madare (targetted by **CAPRO**) in the west.

   ii *Pray also for the partly nomadic Fulbe,* who are a strategic people strung across Central and West Africa. They are responding to the gospel as never before through the witness of several groups: **SIM, AoG, WEC, WH,** WOI. Converts often face persecution and exclusion from their own people; pray for large enough groups of believers to form in order to overcome the stigma of following Jesus. Pray for the national-level conferences for Fulani believers, holistic church planting efforts, Fulani literacy centres, radio broadcasts, a chronological storying discipleship programme and the plans for a Fulani-language Bible school and missionary training centre.

b) ***Unreached non–Muslim peoples.*** Most of these groups are being steadily Islamized, and time is running out before they are inoculated against the gospel by Muslims. They include the Dogose, the Senufo and sub-groups such as the Karaboro (**CMA**, Mennonites) and the numerous groups related to the Lobi (**WEC**). They are concentrated in the west and southwest.

6 **Missionaries** working in Burkina Faso have a vital role in this land with so many physical and spiritual needs. The work is hard and victories long in coming. But receptivity is high, and missionaries are welcome. Major missions working in the country are **WBT, SIM, CMA,** Mennonites, **AoG, IMB,** Apostolic Church, **WEC,** Lutherans, **CAPRO** and Deeper Life. Pray for their protection and encouragement. Missionary reinforcements are needed in a wide range of ministries.

7 **VIMAB (the Burkinabé AoG)** is becoming a success story of indigenous missions. More than 150 couples serve as missionaries in home and foreign missions. Despite the fact that 25% of VIMAB churches are involved in missions support, most of these missionaries will face hardship and poverty on the field. Thus far, most of their work is among the more evangelized Mossi. Pray that these dynamic churches might truly catch a vision to reach the unreached peoples among them and in neighbouring nations. Pray for their growth as a mission-sending body, and pray for the sacrificial ministry of both the missionaries and their supporters.

8 **The Church in general does not yet have a strong missions vision,** in part due to issues of poverty and a dependence mentality. CAPRO, World Outreach, **SIM** (through the Sahel Missiological Institute) and others work to mobilize churches and provide cross-cultural training to those called. Pray that the Lord might stir a strong grassroots movement that places missions at the top of church agendas.

9 **Christian aid and relief** are largely coordinated by the Federation of Evangelical Churches and others, such as CREDO/Tearfund and Compassion. Much has been done to alleviate suffering and to stave off future disasters. Literacy centres enable a better future for many. Both mission and Christian leaders need wisdom in the area of administration – especially in such a poor country with so many infrastructure needs and with the temptations in handling large amounts of aid and money. The long-term presence of aid workers lends much credibility to the Christian cause and creates in people the willingness to listen. Pray for the hearts of both Muslims and fetishists to be opened to God's Word.

10 **Young people** – many will move to urban centres for a better education and to search for employment. This breaks down the traditional village and family structures. Street kids are increasingly common. Pray for:

a) *Student ministry.* SU works in high schools, **CCCI** is growing and GBUAF(**IFES**) is in high schools and the Ouagadougou University. The latter has 18 university groups serving 600 students, and 150 high school groups serving 2,000 students.

b) *Educational ministry.* Education is at a premium in Burkina Faso, giving many opportunities to teach French and English classes and to utilize the many translations of Scripture as literacy tools. Reading rooms are a popular and effective ministry in assisting and reaching out to youth.

11 **Bible translation** is a ministry of major significance, with three key bodies involved – UBS, ANTBA (a national translation and literacy agency) and SIL. Only five languages of any notable population have the whole Bible – Moore(Mossi), Bambara, Bobo Madare (in 2004), Gourmanchema (Gurma, in 2008) and Jula (2008). **WBT** has six workers committed, and five other missions (including **WEC** and the Mennonites) are involved in translation work. There are currently 28 active Bible translation projects with a need for 12 more. Present and future translators need prayer in order to complete this immense task; several of these languages have no written form, so for each, one must first be developed. Literacy programmes are also essential for many areas so that Burkinabé may read the new translations – ANTBA is doing extensive work in this area.

12 **Media ministries** – high levels of illiteracy and poverty and the limited availability of literature in local languages enhance the importance of other media.

a) *Radio* is used to broadcast the gospel in many languages and into many remote areas. *Radio Evangile Développement* was one of the first, but now there are many indigenously run Christian radio stations, especially in the west and southwest.

b) *Audio materials* for evangelism and teaching have not been adequately used, yet they are vital for ministry. **GRN** has made recordings in 73 languages and dialects, including over 20 "tailender" languages that previously had no translated Scriptures. Pray for the wise distribution of solar and crank-wound players such as the Saber, Proclaimer and MegaVoice.

c) *The JESUS film* is proving a key pioneer evangelistic tool in Bambara/Jula and is available in 15 Burkinabé languages.

Burundi

Republic of Burundi

Africa

Geography 🌍

Area 27,834 sq km. A mountainous, fertile country on the northeast shore of Lake Tanganyika, south of its "twin" Rwanda.

Population		Ann Gr	Density
2010	8,518,862	2.92%	306/sq km
2020	10,318,041	1.85%	371/sq km
2030	11,936,405	1.35%	429/sq km

The 2nd highest population density in Africa.
Capital Bujumbura 480,000. **Urbanites** 11%.
Pop under 15 yrs 38%. **Life expectancy** 50.1 yrs.

Peoples 👪

Kirundi-speaking 98.2%. Considerable inter-ethnic mixing.
  Hutu 83.6% (estimate).
  Tutsi 13.6% (estimate).
  Twa Pygmies 1%. Neglected by other groups.
Other African 1.6%. Congolese/Lingala 1.5%.
Other 0.2%. South Asian, European, Arab.
Literacy 58%. **Official languages** Kirundi, French. All speak Kirundi. English use widespread.
All languages 4. **Indigenous languages** 3. **Languages with Scriptures** 3Bi.

Economy 🗺️

Landlocked and overcoming decades of conflict, Burundi is highly in debt and heavily dependent on outside aid despite recent political and economic stability. Tea and coffee exports are subject to weather and market fluctuations, and mineral resources are largely unexploited. Soil erosion is a serious problem due to "overcrowding" in a high density and highly agrarian society. It remains one of the world's poorest nations with 70–80% living below the poverty line.
HDI Rank 174th/182. **Public debt** 156% of GDP. **Income/person** $138 (<0.5% of USA).

Politics ⚔️

For 400 years, Tutsi lordship over the Hutu majority dominated the political life of Burundi. After the country's independence from Belgium in 1962, the Tutsi constitutional monarchy was replaced by a military regime in 1966. Tutsi-dominated governments and military regimes since then have managed to retain Tutsi control of the army, commerce and education. The human rights record of the government has been appalling – Hutu attempts to gain power were followed by pogroms in 1972, 1988 and 1993-95. Since a peace accord in 2000, conflict has been reduced and almost removed altogether. Signs of encouraging progress include a new constitution safeguarding interests of minority groups, peaceful democratic elections in both 2005 and 2010 with a Hutu president, and an army more representative of the population.

Religion 🙏

Freedom of religion.

Religions	Pop %	Population	Ann Gr
Christian	90.46	7,704,984	3.1%
Muslim	5.50	468,537	5.2%
Ethnoreligionist	3.80	323,717	0.9%
Non-religious	0.09	7,667	5.4%
Baha'i	0.08	6,815	2.9%
Other	0.07	5,963	2.9%

Christians	Denoms	Pop %	Affiliates	Ann Gr
Protestant	27	9.89	842,000	5.2%
Independent	26	10.59	902,000	3.2%
Anglican	1	8.49	724,000	3.8%
Catholic	1	60.92	5,190,000	2.6%
Orthodox	1	0.02	2,000	0.0%
Marginal	1	0.19	16,000	12.2%
Unaffiliated		1.3	110,000	-13.4
Doubly affiliated		-1.35	-115,000	0.0%

Churches	MegaBloc	Congs	Members	Affiliates
Catholic Church	C	130	2,965,714	5,190,000
Anglican Church	A	8,203	246,088	723,500
Church of Pentecost	I	3,646	382,778	689,000
Seventh-day Adventist	P	250	121,200	220,584
Pente Evang Fell of Afr	P	465	89,000	165,000
Eglise Vivante	I	45	47,500	95,000
Methodist Ch Union	P	500	50,000	86,500
Christian Brethren	P	95	25,000	70,000
Evang Episcopal Ch	P	210	32,500	65,000
Union of Baptist Chs	P	95	32,418	59,000
Foursquare Gospel	P	354	20,700	41,400
Friends (Quakers)	P	74	17,000	34,000
United Methodist Ch	P	75	15,000	34,000
Other denominations[43]		1,492	120,813	236,000
Doubly affiliated				-115,000
Total Christians[56]		**15,634**	**4,165,711**	**7,593,984**

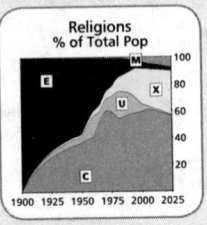
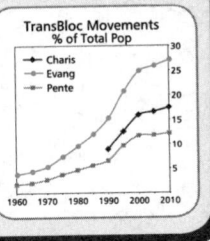
Answers to Prayer

1 **Praise God for stability,** manifested through the signing of a peace accord by every rebel group, a new constitution and an elected government that represents both Hutu and Tutsi. After the horrors of this region of Africa in the 1990s, Burundi has made significant progress. Over 450,000 people once uprooted have now returned home. Most refugee camps have closed or are closing, and some IDP camps have become permanent. The current president is a professing born-again Christian.

2 **Praise for sustained evangelical growth,** although this now has slowed compared to the tumultuous 1990s. Nearly all Protestant and Anglican churches have seen significant growth, even during the periods of war. Many realize that nominal, shallow Christianity is inadequate to change lives and overcome the deep-seated tensions among ethnic groups. A number of groups in Burundi distinguish themselves by their admirably holistic approach to ministry.

Challenges for Prayer

1 **The socio-political situation** is one of cautious hope. There have been many encouragements, but threats to the fragile new peace remain. The final rebel group, the FNL, signed the peace accord only in 2008. Pray for these key issues:

a) **Decades-old enmity between Tutsi and Hutu** that boiled into a violent eruption claiming 300,000 lives in the 1990s has simmered down with the peace accord and representational government. The systematic humiliation of Hutus has all but ceased, leading to a more peaceful co-existence. There is widespread intermarriage between these groups. Pray for genuine respect and cooperation as these two peoples build Burundi's future together.

b) **The president** is a former leader of a rebel Hutu group. He is a believer and has actively sought the counsel of Church leaders on several issues. His relative political inexperience, his past as a rebel fighter and Satan's desire to tear down Christian leaders each pose a danger; pray for moral integrity, wise advisors and spiritual grace to do the right things in the right way.

c) **The surplus of firearms** from decades of conflict contributes to the sudden rise of violent crime, especially armed robbery. With widespread poverty and no proper disarmament programme, such an occurrence was almost inevitable. Pray for the effectiveness of disarmament and gun amnesty programmes, many of which are run by church bodies; pray for people to hand in their weapons and pursue peace rather than lawlessness.

d) **Widespread corruption** persists, with bribery all but requisite for transactions of almost any nature. A 2008 survey ranked Burundi among the top states where corruption is worsening. The anti-corruption body has failed in its efforts to bring improvement. Pray for the lasting change only the gospel can bring.

2 **True peace and reconciliation** is something to work toward. Revival in the 1950s brought blessing and great church growth, but a generation later the land is physically, morally and spiritually devastated. Most Burundians recognize the Church as the only institution in the land able to bring true reconciliation and peace; this in turn can be achieved only through God's intervention. Pray that the spirits of enmity and vengeance may be bound by the power of Christ. Pray for the peace-building work of groups such as the National Council of Churches and its constituent members, of World Vision and World Relief, Tearfund, African Enterprise, the Alpha Course and many others.

③ Leadership for the churches is in short supply; violence caused the closure of Bible schools which in turn cut off the supply of trained leaders. Now, schools are being re-established and new ones opened, but poverty holds back many prospective students from enrolling. Ask the Lord for financial provision for those who wish to equip themselves for the Lord's service. Pray also for the following, all vital in meeting the urgent need for Christian leaders:

a) *Bible schools and theological colleges.* These include the Mweya Theological Institute (Free Methodists and **WGM**), a Pentecostal Bible school, the Matana Institute (Anglican-MAM) and Partners Trust International.

b) *Christian universities,* a new development in Burundi. Most notable are Hope Africa University (Free Methodists) and the University of Light (Anglican). These seek to provide higher education with a biblical worldview, shaping the future leaders of the nation.

c) *Modular training and TEE.* Both Great Lakes Outreach and Great Lakes Leadership Training (Friends) offer the former, while several groups, including Mweya, **CMS** and the **LM** offer TEE programmes. Emmaus, a Brethren ministry, runs BCCs not just in Burundi but throughout the region.

④ Peoples and groups of greater spiritual need include:

a) *The Twa* (Pygmy) who are relatively well evangelized. About 8% are Christian. Their social marginalization and outright oppression is severe, and their education, health and economic status grim.

b) *The Burundian refugee population,* Africa's largest in the 1990s, who live mostly in Tanzania. In 1972 about 200,000 fled to Tanzania where they have been ever since, a number that more than doubled in 1994. Over 12% of all Burundians were displaced by the genocide, many for more than five years. The camps are hotbeds of disease, abuse and resentment. Ministry to this group is difficult to sustain, but absolutely vital.

c) *Returning refugees and IDPs* are a mixed group – some are eager to return, some cautious, some forced against their will to leave their temporary host country. They number more than 300,000 and represent one of the biggest challenges to the nation and the Church. They often lack even basic services (health, education, even shelter) and land. The problem with the lack of land is intensified by returners claiming their old property. Life in camps made them dependent on handouts and lacking in initiative, traits that will spell disappointment and worse in poverty-stricken Burundi. The Anglicans, Lutherans, Tearfund, **FIDA** and REMA (a local NGO) are just a few of many organizations focusing on this area of great need.

d) *The Muslim community* has grown dramatically in recent years due to political manipulation by a former party chairman, external investment in Islamization, and the blamelessness of Muslims in the 1993 genocide. Unsubstantiated claims place Islam at 12% of the population. While this is unlikely, the rapid growth of Islam shows no signs of slowing. Most Christians and churches have little idea how to effectively minister to Muslims; pray for outreach training and for Christians to gain a heart for their Muslim neighbours and countrymen.

⑤ Young people and children suffered the brunt of the violence, upheaval and poverty of the last decades. Lift these issues up in prayer:

a) *The physical needs of children.* Around 560,000 children have lost at least one parent, 45% of children under five are undernourished and many thousands suffer from malaria and AIDS. Violence against children is common. Only half of children attend school; but praise God for debt relief, which allows the government to offer free primary education to all children. This should raise enrolment significantly. Pray for the many ministries and NGOs that focus on caring for children and providing them with life opportunities.

*b) **Specific ministry to children*** has been almost non-existent, but some agencies are beginning to focus on this issue. **CEF**, SU, the Anglicans, and New Generation (a local NGO) are examples of such.

*c) **Student and youth ministry***. SU continues to have an effective ministry, especially in the area of evangelism. Seven growing GBU(**IFES**) groups now focus on evangelism and training leaders. **YFC** and the Alpha Course also have specific ministry to young people, the former developing Homes of Hope, where orphans from different ethnicities are raised together in a Christian setting.

6 **There is a genuine need for expatriate Christian workers.** Between 1970 and 1985, nearly all missionaries were expelled by the regime of that time; few returned thereafter due to ongoing instability. Many are needed to work with national leaders in areas of discipleship, theological education, reconciliation and trauma counselling, literacy and education and holistic development. Now, numbers of workers are increasing, but the large majority of these focus on Bujumbura, the capital. Pray for more workers for the neglected rural areas and for ministry that empowers Burundi believers rather than creates dependency. Pray for the calling of the right missionary personnel and their effectiveness, for godly modelling and good relationships with national believers.

7 **Christian media** – specific prayer targets:

*a) **Bibles and Christian literature*** – there remains a great shortfall. Prayer for millions more Bibles and Christian books would not be amiss. The African Pastors' Fellowship, Anglican Church and Langham Partnership are collaborating to foster writing and publishing books in Kirundi, especially for pastors. Several other Christian literature ministries exist as well.

*b) **Literacy programmes*** – the adult literacy rate is 58%, but the functional rate is lower. This situation is steadily improving because of free primary education and increasing numbers of churches and NGOs with literacy programmes.

*c) **Radio*** – **TWR** and IBRA combine to broadcast over 170 hours per week, but less than 10 hours are in Kirundi. Voice of Hope Radio is a Burundian Christian FM station reaching from Bujumbura out to Burundi and neighbouring countries. Pray for life to be imparted through these broadcasts.

*d) **Audio*** – **GRN** has audio resources in Kirundi and African French. FCBH completed the Kirundi audio NT, and has seen over 115 listening groups established.

*e) **TV and video*** – A French African Christian programme, *Le Club 700*, is on national television every week. The JESUS film has been viewed by most Burundians. Heritage Television provides daily Christian programming. Pray for lasting impact.

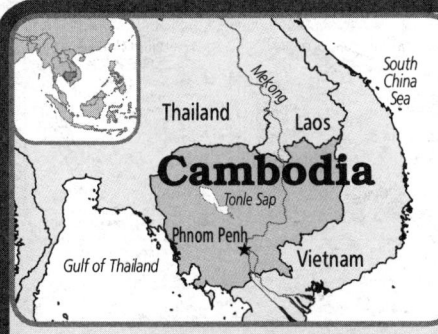

Cambodia

Kingdom of Cambodia

Asia

Geography

Area 181,035 sq km. Fertile, forest-covered state of southwest Indo-China on the Mekong River.

Population		Ann Gr	Density
2010	15,053,112	1.66%	83/sq km
2020	17,706,611	1.60%	98/sq km
2030	20,100,161	1.16%	111/sq km

Capital Phnom Penh 1,962,498. **Urbanites** 22.8%. **Pop under 15 yrs** 33%. **Life expectancy** 60.6 yrs.

Peoples

Mon-Khmer 87.9%. 19 peoples. Khmer 86.9%; Tribal groups 1.0%.
Other Southeast Asian 7.7%. Vietnamese 4.2%; Cham(4) 2.4%; Lao 0.6%.
Chinese 4.1%. Six language groups.
Other 0.3%. Various Western and South Asian groups.
Literacy 73.6%. **Official language** Khmer. **All languages** 25. **Indigenous languages** 23. **Languages with Scriptures** 3Bi 3NT 3por.

Economy

One of the world's poorest countries and heavily dependent on foreign aid. Years of war and genocide followed by venal and corrupt governments have hindered development and kept most of the population poor; 38% live below the poverty line. Significant progress is being made in economic development, but the rural poor are being left behind. Agriculture, garments and tourism are the biggest earners, with offshore oil/gas deposits promising future income. Illegal logging and the sex trade enriches a small number of wicked men, but causes suffering to many.
HDI Rank 137th/182. **Public debt** 63% of GDP. **Income/person** $823 (2% of USA).

Politics

A ceremonial monarchy. Powerful kingdoms from 1st to 14th Centuries. Thereafter for 500 years, a pawn in regional and global conflicts with Thai, Vietnamese, French, Japanese and US invasion, occupation or aggression. A tragic victim of the Vietnam War (1970–75), then of the extreme Marxist Khmer Rouge from 1975, when it endured one of the most savage slaughters in the 20th Century. Almost all former military personnel, civil servants, doctors, educated people and wealthy people and their families were killed, and the nation was turned into a vast labour camp. The Vietnamese army ousted the Khmer Rouge in 1979, but civil war among four contending armies raged with superpower support until 1991. Internationally-initiated democracy arrived in 1993. Since then, the same prime minister has remained in power as elected leader. Corruption is rife and profoundly affects political life.

Religion

Buddhism has been the national religion since the 15th Century. The Khmer Rouge sought to eradicate all religion; 90% of Buddhist monks and most Christians perished. Since 1979 there have been periods of more tolerance, and since 1990 Christians have been allowed to worship openly, but a few limitations on mission activity have been legislated as well.

Religions	Pop %	Population	Ann Gr
Buddhist	83.34	12,545,264	1.2%
Ethnoreligionist	4.80	722,549	2.5%
Christian	3.13	471,162	8.4%
Non-religious	2.97	447,077	2.7%
Chinese	2.85	429,014	4.4%
Muslim	2.30	346,222	3.5%
Other	0.26	39,138	1.7%
Hindu	0.22	33,117	5.8%
Baha'i	0.13	19,569	3.3%

Christians	Denoms	Pop %	Affiliates	Ann Gr
Protestant	29	1.46	220,000	9.2%
Independent	9	0.25	38,000	4.3%
Anglican	1	<0.01	<1,000	4.4%
Catholic	1	0.16	23,000	2.2%
Marginal	2	0.06	9,000	2.3%
Unaffiliated		1.20	181,000	8.0%

Churches	MegaBloc	Congs	Members	Affiliates
Foursquare Gospel Ch	P	818	61,364	135,000
Catholic Church	C	21	12,316	23,400
River of Life	I	340	8,533	12,800
Assemblies of God	P	40	2,229	10,700
Methodist Church	P	365	4,800	9,600
Cambodia Baptist Conv	P	175	6,095	8,600
Cambodia for Christ	I	72	5,000	8,000
Latter-day Saints (Mormon)	M	23	3,077	8,000

Khmer Evangelical Ch	P	182	2,150	7,950
Seventh-day Adventist	P	8	3,700	7,400
Harvest-time Ministries	I	152	3,804	6,200
New Life Fellowship	I	60	1,400	3,500
Other denominations[25]		453	27,975	50,239
Total Christians[42]		**2,709**	**142,443**	**291,389**

TransBloc	Pop %	Population	Ann Gr
Evangelicals			
Evangelicals	1.6	240,196	8.8%
Renewalists			
Charismatics	1.3	195,426	10.3%
Pentecostals	1.0	150,079	12.5%

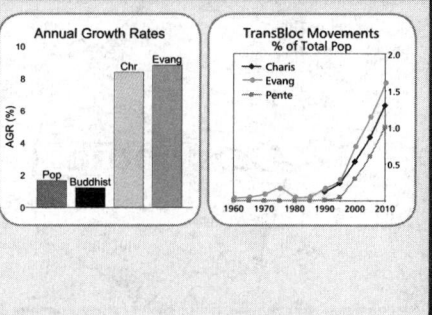

Answers to Prayer

1 **An open door for ministry remains,** although some limitations are in place. The great suffering of Cambodians in the past has been transformed into great responsiveness to the gospel as many and diverse ministries see sustained fruit.

2 **Unprecedented – and unexpected – church growth** over the last 20 years. From only a few thousand Christians surviving into the 1990s (0.07% evangelical in 1985), believers may now top 3.5% of the population. This growth is almost entirely through church multiplication, and done by indigenous church planters and evangelists.

Challenges for Prayer

1 **The scars of the terrible genocide of 1975-79 remain evident.** Nearly two million were killed, over 60,000 lost life or limb to landmines and most of the population over age 30 need deep healing from the trauma of their losses and suffering. Pray for:

a) Justice to be seen to be done regarding those who perpetrated the crimes. International tribunals face difficulty in bringing the Cambodian government/judiciary on board with the justice process, and the culture of corruption and impunity still holds sway. The beginning of Khmer Rouge trials should assist in this process.

b) Healing for the deep psychological wounds. Many cope with the trauma through detachment and suppression of trauma, some by inflicting pain on others. Pray that counselling and the Holy Spirit might bring true restoration.

c) A government that seeks the good of all, and is worthy of the trust of the people. Violence, manipulation, graft and selfishness hitherto have been the rule. The situation is so ingrained and endemic on every level that it must be torn out by the roots.

2 **Spiritual darkness persists in Cambodia** and must be lifted by prayer. That darkness is seen in the ubiquitous spirit shrines, Buddhism's opposition to any ideological rival and a general moral collapse. Structures of sin are prevalent throughout, and the people of Cambodia are made to suffer by the enemy of souls. Pray for the light of the gospel to so shine that the structures of society as well as of individuals may be decisively changed. Beyond the gripping poverty are the following:

a) Land grabbing. Unscrupulous officials (who pocket the income) have sold huge swathes of Cambodia's land to rapacious foreign developers and speculators, with locals driven out and evicted from their homes to make way for hotels and resorts. Cambodia is being sold/stolen from under the feet of its own people.

b) Children at risk. The genocide of the 1970s and 1980s created a very young nation where 60% of the population are 24 years old or younger. But many of this generation are sadly exploited by others. Pray for deliverance and salvation for these:

i *Child labourers.* Poverty forces over 1.5 million children under age 15 to work to survive and supplement their family's meagre income, often at the price of their education, their health or even their lives.

ii *Sex trade victims* number up to 100,000. A recent study estimated 20% of tourists to Cambodia made use of the sex trade, often with the young or underage. Yet even this is a small amount compared to the widespread use of prostitutes by Cambodian men. That factor combined with others, gives the nation one of the highest rates of HIV in Asia. Many poor parents sell their own children to traffickers for as little as $10. The Vietnamese ethnic minority is especially targeted by traffickers, being both light-skinned and detested by most Khmer. The much-publicized rescues of these girls, as young as age six, are only the beginning of a long process of healing and equipping for a life after the sex trade.

iii *Homeless children and orphans.* Family structures shattered by the Khmer Rouge and subsequent poverty caused high numbers of street kids and unwanted children. Many Christian ministries see a high response to Jesus' love among these precious souls. At one point, orphanages were booming, but as the population stabilizes, drop-in centres and increased ministry to extended families are becoming more appropriate.

c) **Drug trafficking and abuse** have increased greatly in the last 15 years. Addictive drugs hold sway over many locals, while crime lords profit from the suffering.

3 **The Cambodian Church has survived** against all odds. Beginning in 1923, **CMA** missionaries laboured for 47 years before breakthrough began. Then the Church was nearly extinguished during the slaughter of the 1970s; 90% of Christians died or fled to Thai refugee camps – where a great harvest was reaped for the Kingdom. During the 1990s, churches spread to all 19 provinces. Pray for:

a) **Continued freedom of religion.** The constitution guarantees it, but the government has re-affirmed the ban on door-to-door evangelism and on public distribution of tracts. The use of financial inducements for purposes of conversion by some religious groups has forced responsible Christian groups to reconsider their methods and avoid such negative associations. Pray for continued freedom to wisely and appropriately spread the good news.

b) **Freedom and deliverance** from past sin, hatred, suffering and abuse through the blood of Jesus. Deep healing is required for many who suffered acute trauma. Many of the former Khmer Rouge have become believers; receiving God's forgiveness for past crimes is essential.

c) **Children and young people** to be effectively discipled in the churches and shown how to live in healthy family structures; few are equipped for this. But this generation must begin to lead the Cambodian Church now.

d) **Future growth and vision.** Mission Kampuchea 2021 is a shared vision by the national Churches to see a church in every village and people group in Cambodia by 2021. Currently, an estimated 11,000 villages are without a church.

4 **Mature leadership for the churches** is the greatest challenge. The loss of so many educated people in the Khmer Rouge slaughter, combined with the dysfunctional society, pushed many new Christians quickly into leadership before they were ready. Pray for:

a) **The Bible schools** – Phnom Penh Bible School, Cambodia For Christ (CFC) Ministry Training College, **AoG** and Methodists are just a few among several Bible schools. Residential, full-time academic programmes can be a difficult model to successfully translate into the Cambodian context of life and ministry.

b) **Existing pastors.** Their lack of training, their need to provide for themselves and the overwhelming practical needs of the faithful are huge challenges. Numerous leadership training courses are available that offer on-the-job development for Christian leaders. Pray for wisdom, holiness, power in the Spirit and ways to build up their fledgling congregations spiritually, relationally and economically.

c) **Unity.** That any religious group can register directly with the Ministry of Religion, plus the existence of 13 Protestant umbrella groups, indicate the fragmentation of this rather small national Church. Divisiveness has been a problem in the short history of the Church here. The Evangelical Fellowship of Cambodia represents about 80% of the Christian community; it is increasingly able to cooperate with other notable networks, such as the Cambodian

Christian Evangelical Alliance, Cambodian Christian Federation and the Cambodian Baptist Convention. Pray for a greater sense of unity and for more partnerships that are effective.

5 **Foreign Christian workers** can contribute in many ways to the myriad challenges facing the Cambodian Church. Pray for more long-term expatriate workers who learn the language, identify with the culture and serve for the long haul. Ministries can easily fall into the trap of "short-termism" and burdensome mission trips. Training and discipling the burgeoning Cambodian Church to finish the task are just as vital as the essential humanitarian work being done, and much pioneer evangelism remains unfinished. There is great freedom for ministry when it is done in a culturally appropriate and sensitive manner.

6 **Christian ministry to physical needs** is a major concern.

a) The social needs are enormous. The murder of most of those with skills or an education makes expatriate input essential. Rehabilitation, orphanages, reconstruction, health care, projects for agriculture, fisheries, water management and education are all ministries where Christians have significant input. Pray for:

   i *The dozens of Christian NGOs* both large and small (ICFG, CORD, World Relief, **FH**, **WEC, OMF, CMA**, WVI, **AoG, YWAM, AOI**, Mennonites and many others).

   ii *Effective cooperation among Christian agencies*. A fine example of foreign agencies working together is International Cooperation Cambodia, constituting SAO, SIL, Interact, World Concern and Danmission.

b) The complex issues of poverty, foreign aid and dependency. An honest desire to alleviate suffering can cause as many problems as it solves. Overlapping with evangelism, it can also generate both the "rice Christian" phenomenon and resentment from the Buddhist majority over underhanded proselytism tactics. Pray for wisdom and sensitivity for Christians ministering to physical needs.

7 **Pray for the less-reached.** The window of opportunity that now sees many enter the Kingdom may not stay open for much longer; the opportunities must be urgently seized. Pray for:

a) The Buddhist majority. Buddhism has lost some of its monopolistic grip on the people, but reactionary forces are moving against the clearly noticeable growth of the Church.

b) The Cham, almost entirely Muslim. The majority practice folk Islam, which incorporates animistic practices into more orthodox Islamic practices; within this is a strong strain of Fojihed Islam, which is rife with pre-Islamic magic and superstitions. There are a few Christians; pray for them to be gathered into fellowship together. Khmer Christians have not yet met this evangelistic challenge; pray also for wisdom for those already reaching out to the Cham.

c) The tribal peoples. Only among the Mnong, Jarai, Krueng and Stieng have significant numbers come to Christ. A further 18 Southeast Asian peoples can be considered unevangelized; pray for loving and appropriate witness to these peoples.

d) The six Chinese language groups constitute nearly 600,000 people who have largely assimilated into Cambodian society, but who are mostly unreached. Pray for Chinese believers from abroad to come as apostles to these people.

8 **Christian ministries** have diversified in recent years. Pray specifically for:

a) Literature. **CMA** has translated a range of materials, especially for church planting training. The Bible Society and others provide Khmer Bibles, NTs and Scripture portions. A new Khmer Bible was completed in 1998. Lifewords tracts and literature are widely appreciated.

b) Fount of Wisdom is a joint effort of **CMA**, EFC, **AoG** and **OMF** that trains Cambodian Christian writers, encourages production of indigenous materials for the Church and translates useful Christian literature from other languages. Pray for its positive impact on the Church and on the nation.

c) The JESUS film is being used in Khmer, Chinese, Vietnamese and other tongues. Father's Hope is another film being used by The Book of Hope team to reach out to Cambodians.

d) *Audio and video resources.* **GRN** provides audio resources in 18 languages. God's Story and Megavoice both have material in Khmer.

e) *Christian radio.* Over 300 hours per week, many in Khmer and on FM, can be heard. **FEBC** broadcasts 115 hours per week on local FM radio with notable response. **TWR**, **GFA**, World Harvest Radio and Lutheran Hour also broadcast in Khmer or various minority languages.

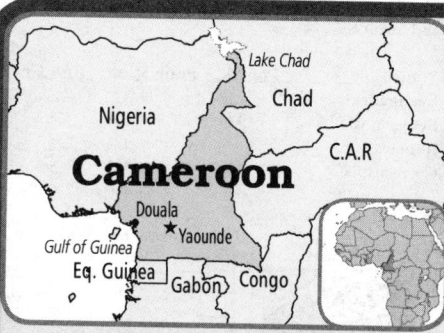

Cameroon
Republic of Cameroon
Africa

Geography

Area 475,442 sq km. On the continental "hinge" between West and Central Africa. Semi-arid in the north, grasslands in the centre, rainforest in the south.

Population		Ann Gr	Density
2010	19,958,351	2.29%	43/sq km
2020	24,348,543	1.89%	52/sq km
2030	28,601,794	1.56%	61/sq km

Capital Yaounde 1,800,762. **Other major city** Douala 2.1 million. **Urbanites** 58.4%. **Pop under 15 yrs** 41%. **Life expectancy** 50.9 yrs.

Peoples

About 286 peoples, with many more sub-groups and dialects. One of Africa's most ethnically and linguistically complex countries. Only the larger are mentioned here.

Grassfields Bantu 26.5%. Also called Cameroon-Bamikele Bantu. 60 peoples. Bamileke(10) 11.9%; Bamun 2.3%; Kom 1.2%; Nso 1.2; Widikum 1.0%.

Northwest Bantu 24.7%. Includes Central Congo Bantu. 53 peoples. Ewondo 7.7%; Bulu Fang 5.1%; Bassa 2.5%; Duala 1.0%.

Chadic 9.7%. 58 peoples. Mafa 1.5%; Masa 1.1%.

Fulani 9.4%. 3 peoples.

Other Benue-Congo 8.7%. 61 peoples. Bete 4.7%.

Adamawa-Ubangi 5.5%. 33 peoples. Gbaya 1.4%; Tupuri 1.1%.

Other African 13.3%. Cameroonian Creole 5.8%; detribalized Cameroonian 5.7%; Hausa 1.4%.

Others 2.2%. Arab 0.9%; Western, Asian.

Literacy 67.9%. **Official languages** French, English. **All languages** 279. **Languages with Scriptures** 20Bi 46NT 68por 93w.i.p.

Economy

Largely based on agriculture and oil exports, both of which Cameroon has in abundance. Great potential for development with ample rain and minerals. Development is hampered by decline in world prices for coffee and cocoa and by an overvalued currency. The majority are employed in agriculture. Unemployment is high, despite a top-heavy civil service employing many. High debt levels have been reduced through debt-relief servicing in exchange for suggested economic restructuring. One of Africa's highest literacy rates, and one of the world's highest corruption rates.

HDI Rank 153rd/182. **Public debt** 13.5% of GDP. **Income/person** $1,224 (3% of USA).

Politics

A German colony between 1884 and 1919, then divided between Britain and France. Independence from France in 1960, and union with English-speaking West Cameroon in 1961 as a bilingual, one-party republic. Popular pressure forced the president (who retains strong unilateral powers) to accede to multiparty elections in 1992, which, along with the 1997 elections, were boycotted by opposition groups. Having won elections in 2004, he also won a constitutional amendment allowing him to run again in 2011. International and opposition groups claim government suppression of opposition. Cameroon is a member of the British Commonwealth and *La Francophonie* and is closely allied to France, including on issues of foreign policy. Simmering tensions between Anglophone and Francophone regions could spell trouble for the future.

Religion

Secular state that guarantees religious freedom. Islam is strong in the north, especially among the Fulbe, and interfaith tensions have increased over recent decades, especially with the increased profile of more radical Islamism.

Religions	Pop %	Population	Ann Gr
Christian	53.80	10,737,593	2.4%
Muslim	26.00	5,189,171	2.7%
Ethnoreligionist	18.99	3,790,091	1.4%

Non-religious	0.90	179,625	4.7%
Baha'i	0.25	49,896	3.1%
Other	0.06	11,975	6.1%

Christians	Denoms	Pop %	Affiliates	Ann Gr
Protestant	38	19.10	3,813,000	2.7%
Independent	88	4.18	834,000	5.4%
Catholic	1	23.42	4,675,000	1.8%
Orthodox	1	0.01	1,000	0.0%
Marginal	7	0.39	78,000	2.4%
Unaffiliated		6.70	1,337,000	-0.4%

Churches	MegaBloc	Congs	Members	Affiliates
Catholic Church	C	5,599	2,799,401	4,675,000
Evang Ch of Cam	P	770	784,431	1,310,000
Presby Ch of Cam	P	3,688	398,305	705,000
Presby Ch in Cam	P	1,825	191,617	320,000
Evang Lutheran Ch	P	528	142,515	238,000
Cameroon Bapt Conv	P	1,031	103,125	165,000
Seventh-day Adventist	P	850	112,000	161,000
Presby Orthodox Ch	I	1,725	86,228	144,000
Lutheran Brethren Ch	P	1,050	85,030	142,000
Full Gospel Mission	P	850	69,000	138,000
Chr Miss Fell Int	I	1,425	57,000	96,900
Baptist Pentecostal Ch	P	288	57,665	96,300

Union of Baptist Chs	P	376	48,050	96,000
Union of Ev Chs of Cam	P	310	37,200	93,000
Apostolic Church	P	760	50,000	75,000
Jehovah's Witnesses	M	550	35,000	67,000
Other denominations[118]		6,300	396,941	878,197
Total Christians[134]		**27,925**	**5,453,508**	**9,400,397**

Many of these statistics are estimates; few denominations keep records.

TransBloc	Pop %	Population	Ann Gr
Evangelicals			
Evangelicals	9.0	1,804,104	4.3%
Renewalists			
Charismatics	6.5	1,294,403	5.8%
Pentecostals	3.9	768,440	6.6%

Religions % of Total Pop

TransBloc Movements % of Total Pop

Answers to Prayer

1 **The growth of evangelicals** continued post-2000 despite the decrease in high-profile campaigns. Most of the recent growth is through localized church planting, particularly among newer Pentecostal denominations.

2 **Many significant leaders** – professional, military, police and political – have been converted, giving hope for changing a society infamous for corruption. There is an increasing influence of the gospel in parliament, including regular prayer meetings when parliament is in session.

3 **Media use for evangelism has increased,** building on the legalization in 2000 of Christian private radio and TV broadcasting. There has been notable impact through Bible translation and literature distribution as well as through electronic media.

Challenges for Prayer

1 **Cameroon faces internal forces** that could disable the nation. Cameroon is blessed with material resources, relative stability and diversity; these all have their costs and risks.

a) *Widespread and deeply entrenched corruption,* for decades, has crippled Cameroon's economic and political progress. This blight runs deep in government administration, the police, the legal system and business. Anti-corruption initiatives (done at the behest of the international bodies that hand out loans and forgive interest on debts) have made some progress, but a deeper change of attitudes must occur. Pray that those stealing from the nation would be caught and stopped; pray also for a change in people's lax attitude toward and acceptance of corruption.

b) *Deep divisions* of language, politics and faith are all potential flashpoints of tension and violence. Cameroon is divided between French and English regions, between Christian, Muslim and traditional religions, between government cronies and increasingly frustrated opposition. Pray for God to raise up reconcilers and peacemakers in this divided land.

c) Integrity in leadership will make a difference if even just a few key people speak, act and live with integrity. Pray for leaders who will be examples of righteousness and transparency rather than perpetuators of the status quo.

2 **The spiritual poverty of the churches** is the country's greatest tragedy. Nominal Christianity is a bigger problem in Cameroon than in most of Africa. The early pioneer work of Catholics, Presbyterians, Lutherans and Baptists was damaged by compromise and the arrival of liberation theology. Tribalism, pagan practices, alcoholism and low moral standards are endemic. Most in these churches (Council of Protestant Churches of Cameroon) have little concern for the unreached of the north, and they are only now starting to have a prophetic voice to address the major ills of society. Pray for deep repentance, lasting deliverance and true revival, and pray for a restoration of Bible reading, preaching and holiness among Christians.

3 **Evangelicals, especially Pentecostals, have grown rapidly** in the last 20 years, having had a late start due to the hostility of older denominations. A number of these groups have been started by other African evangelists – in particular Nigerians – rather than by Westerners. Pray for:

a) Greater spiritual unity and cooperation between charismatic and non-charismatic groups. Many older denominations see these younger churches as divisive, fragmented upstarts with poor theology and an unhealthy fixation on signs, wonders and money.

b) More effective discipling in the churches. The growth of recent years and the focus on numbers of converts rather than on quality of disciples have caused a lack of trained leaders and spiritual growth. Pray for the formation of a genuinely evangelical association of churches in Cameroon that will assist with this challenge.

c) Pastors and leaders of great integrity and spirituality. Many of these churches lack accountability structures, and their leaders are often accused of being charlatans seeking wealth by manipulating the faithful. Pray that those with pure motives and hearts may see their churches grow, while the wolves in sheep's clothing may be exposed as fakes.

d) Biblical engagement across all spheres of society. The newer churches deliberately avoid being involved in issues of politics, justice, education etc., concentrating solely on spiritual and material blessings for their members. Pray for the maturation of these groups such that they might have a holistic vision and profound impact on the nation.

4 **Leadership and discipleship training** in the churches are urgent needs, as Cameroon's churches struggle with shallow and biblically illiterate Christianity. Today's spiritual mess has its roots in a failure in theological training. Pray for:

a) Godly leaders, well trained in the Scriptures. Some church leadership is more noted for pride, power struggles, disunity, moral failure and misuse of funds than for holy living. Pray for the provision of born-again, godly staff for the nearly 20 denominational and interdenominational theological schools in Cameroon. Pray also for a spiritual revolution in these theological faculties and seminaries that will bring new life and biblical standards to churches so long deprived.

b) Pray for lay training programmes that will introduce the Bible to Christians. For many, the pastor's sermon is the extent of their interaction with Scripture. There are increasing numbers of modular-training programmes, aimed at poorer, bi-vocational pastors and church members. Pray also for the two Christian universities that aim to provide quality academic education within the framework of a Christian worldview.

5 **The growing missions vision** and networking are bearing fruit:

a) Greater evangelical cooperation to reach the unconverted. Specific initiatives:

i *Christian Missionary Fellowship International* (CMFI) is a Cameroonian mission with remarkable ministries in prayer, missions and publishing, all having a global impact.

ii *Cameroon for Christ,* launched in 1996, involves many denominations and churches in research and evangelism of the 2,400 villages of the north.

iii *Mission BINAM* is a network targeting the idol worshippers of West Cameroon – especially the Bamiléké. It remains very active in evangelism and works with Inserv and GMI to train researchers for church and mission needs in Cameroon.

b) The growing involvement of Cameroonians in cross-cultural missions. Dozens of indigenous denominations and churches send missionaries to the north and to neighbouring lands. CMFI has sent and supports dozens of missionaries in 60 countries. **CCCI** and the Full Gospel Mission send Cameroonians abroad as missionaries, and the Baptist Seminary has a training track for Cameroonian students in Bible translation.

6 **Young people** are increasingly restive, frustrated by the unchanging political status quo, the high unemployment and the endemic cheating, bribery and favouritism in the education system. Many turn to crime and prostitution, and violent demonstrations are occurring in a country that has never before dealt with such disruptions. Pray for:

a) Effective Christian discipling in churches and by youth and children's agencies. Little is available. Lutheran Hour Ministries (LHM) develops Bible study programmes and BCCs for young people. Also, LHM and others run Christian camps and retreats for young people's discipleship.

b) Student ministry in schools and universities. YFC is a major ministry among young people, especially in the south. GBEEC(**IFES**) has a group in each university as well as high school groups in about 80 towns. **CCCI** sees particular fruit with the military and the military academy. **AoG**, SU, Academy Campus Forum and Campus Jubilee also have active student work. There are 460,000 secondary schools and 1.3 million tertiary students in the country. Christian groups in the north find themselves under increasing pressure from Muslims.

7 **Less-reached peoples.** A national survey in this complex nation is an urgent need; training and some research are underway. The Joshua Project lists 15 peoples as unreached. The major challenges:

a) Muslims – a majority in 59 peoples. These peoples comprise 23% of Cameroon's population and are almost all from the Chadic and Adamawa-Ubangi people clusters. The Gospel Fellowship Association works among almost all of the following groups:

i   *The Fulbe* have long been the proud rulers of the area. Christians among them have grown from the 10 known in 1991, but they are still few. Several agencies have ministry among them (Pioneers, Baptist, Lutheran Brethren, Gospel Fellowship Association).

ii *The Hausa, Kanuri, Kotoko and Fali.* There are few believers among these groups.

iii *The Shuwa Arabs* are nomadic, moving between Chad and Cameroon. Only one or two believers are known, and only one agency is known to be trying to plant churches.

b) The many peoples of the Mandara Mountains, 30% Muslim but mostly fetishist. Some church-planting agencies see the beginnings of breakthroughs.

c) The northern plains peoples – Giziga, Dii, Dowayayo and Mefele – among whom several missionaries and churches are at work. They are predominantly animist in their practices, but Islam has made notable inroads in recent years, polarizing these groups internally.

d) The Baka/Pygmies in the southeastern forests have long been neglected, but increasingly they are the focus of Christian ministry by Baka and cross-cultural workers (Anglican Frontier Missions, WorldTeam, SIL, CMFI). Bible translation is a significant need. Spiritual warfare among this highly animist and spiritual people is a key to seeing fruitfulness and growth.

8 **The missionary force** – the largest groups are **YWAM**, Norwegian Lutheran Mission, **CCCI**, **CEF**, LBT, North American Baptist Conference and Gospel Fellowship Association. Korean agencies represent many additional workers. Pioneer missionaries are especially needed for Bible translation ministry and to reach Muslim and northern animist peoples. Evangelical missionaries could help bring new life and vigour to the more nominal churches – but this requires skill and gifting of a high order.

9 **Bible translation** for Cameroon's 278 languages is an overwhelming task. The lack of indigenous, heart-language Scriptures is one of the contributory causes of spiritual poverty in the churches. Only 10 languages have a complete Bible, and fewer than 100 have any Scripture portion at all. Pray for:

a) Existing translation and literacy projects. Thirteen NT translations were completed from 2003 to 2009. CABTAL (Cameroon Association for Bible Translation and Literacy), SIL and several other agencies have invested much in these. Cameroon is SIL's largest African involvement. The faithful work of Bible translation is bearing fruit in church life. Literacy projects are just as vital as translation projects, since 40% of the population is still functionally illiterate. This is an area of great potential convergence of Christian agencies, government bodies and NGOs.

b) *Surveys are needed* to identify the translation needs of all Cameroon's languages; at least 59 are already identified as warranting a Bible translation project.

c) *The indigenous Cameroon Association for Bible Translation and Literacy* (CABTAL) networks with **WBT** and is committed to 28 translation projects, a number set to increase rapidly.

d) *The calling of more indigenous and expatriate workers* for translation, literacy and support work. LBT has 18 workers committed to translation. CABTAL and SIL help to mobilize the indigenous Church to get involved with the needs of Bible translation.

C

10 **Support ministries** for which intercession is needed:

a) *Christian literature* is a major need as well as opportunity. CMFI runs a publishing house that has already printed three million books and more than 10 million tracts. More literature workers, both expatriate and national, are needed for writing, publishing and distributing French, English and local-language materials. Ministries such as **EHC**, The Gideons and Book of Hope distribute hundreds of thousands of pieces of Christian literature each year as well as interact personally with the recipients.

b) *Christian radio programmes* and stations are an area of growth, especially in the Anglophone West. Many denominational groups are now taking advantage of this media platform. There are also many private Christian radio stations in English and French – *Radio Bonne Nouvelle* started in 2000 and has a network of five stations nationally. *Sawtu Linjilla* – a studio run by Lutherans and other churches and missions in Cameroon, Chad and CAR – produces French and Fulani radio programmes, cassettes and audio-visual materials. The aim is pre-evangelism among the northern Cameroon peoples who use Fulani as a trade language. More Christian radio and television stations and programmes are needed. **GRN** has Christian audio resources in literally hundreds of dialects.

c) *Visual media.* The JESUS film is a major evangelistic tool, resulting in thousands of converts and many churches planted. It is a praiseworthy tool in collaborative ministry among different agencies. The majority of the population have seen it at least once. It is available in over 30 languages, 20 of which are unique to Cameroon, with several more now in production. Pray for effective follow-up with the many people who indicate commitment upon seeing the film and the spiritual challenge given after. A number of Christian television stations are beginning to appear in Cameroon – pray that they might be a blessing for reaching the unreached and building up the body of Christ.

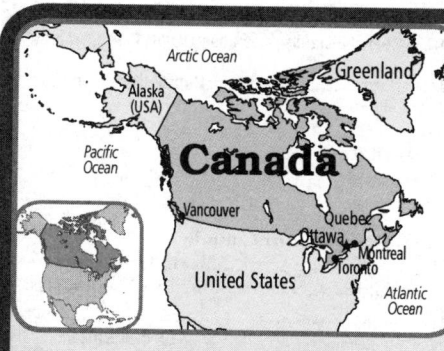

Canada

North America

Geography 🌎

Area 9,970,610 sq km. The world's second-largest country. Wide diversity of mountains, prairie grasslands and forests, but much is sparsely populated wilderness and arctic tundra.

Population		Ann Gr	Density
2010	33,889,747	0.96%	3/sq km
2020	37,101,286	0.89%	4/sq km
2030	40,095,665	0.73%	4/sq km

Capital Ottawa 1,182,230. **Other major cities** Toronto 5.5 million; Montreal 3.8mill; Vancouver 2.2m. **Urbanites** 80.6%. **Pop under 15 yrs** 17%. **Life expectancy** 80.6 yrs.

Peoples 👪

Canada is a mosaic of indigenous and immigrant nations and peoples, many of whom have retained much of their original culture. The high degree of cultural mixing makes classifications only approximate.

European origin 80.0%.

British 36%. English 21%; Scottish 15.2%. Majority in east, centre and west.

French 15.8%. Majority in Quebec. Although Canada is federally bilingual, with equal rights for both federal languages, there is a considerable separatist contingent among Francophones.

Mixed origins 14.5%.

Other European 13.7%. Germanic(6) 3.8%; Slavic(11) 3.1%; Italian 2.2%. Representing every nation in Europe. Includes many Germans, Italians, Ukrainians.

Asian 11.7%. Chinese 3.2%; South Asian(9) 3.1%; Filipino 0.8%; Arab(6) 1.1%; Jewish 1.1%.

Indigenous 2.9%. Native Canadian and Métis (mixed race), 75 languages.

African Caribbean 1.6%.

Latin American 1.5%.

African 1.1%.

Other 1.2%. US citizens, others.

Literacy 99%. **Official Languages** English, French. **All languages** 169. **Indigenous languages** 86 (several are nearly extinct). **Languages with Scriptures** 4Bi 10NT 7por 9w.i.p.

Economy

One of the world's leading industrial nations, but with the lowest public debt of G8 nations and one of the few developed countries to export energy. Canada's abundant natural resources, including minerals and water, point to a strong economic future. Canada's claim on the disputed but potentially lucrative Arctic region may shape much of the country's economic future. The service industry dominates employment. About 70% of Canada's trade is with the USA.

HDI Rank 4th/182. **Public debt** 63.8% of GDP. **Income/person** $45,085 (95% of USA).

Politics

A constitutional monarchy with multiparty parliamentary democracy. Ceased to be a British colony in 1867 when it became the Dominion of Canada. Polarization between Francophone Quebec and the other Anglophone provinces tends to peak at certain times and offers the largest threat to national unity. Large swathes of Canada's land area have been and are being restored to the First Nations peoples. Part of the G8 and G20 groups of nations.

Religion

Freedom of religion, but rapid secularization and pluralization are taking place at every level, inexorably changing the relationship between society and religion.

Religions	Pop %	Population	Ann Gr
Christian	72.07	24,424,341	0.4%
Non-religious	19.09	6,469,553	2.1%
Muslim	2.90	982,803	4.9%
Buddhist	1.10	372,787	4.0%
Jewish	1.10	372,787	1.0%
Hindu	1.00	338,897	3.1%
Sikh	0.90	305,008	3.4%
Other	0.75	254,173	2.4%
Chinese	0.59	199,950	2.4%
Ethnoreligionist	0.40	135,559	2.6%
Baha'i	0.10	33,890	1.0%

Christians	Denoms	Pop %	Affiliates	Ann Gr
Protestant	120	9.50	3,220,000	-0.5%
Independent	75	0.64	217,000	2.5%
Anglican	2	1.87	633,000	-0.3%
Catholic	5	40.09	13,587,000	0.8%
Orthodox	31	3.03	1,026,000	1.5%
Marginal	53	1.64	555,000	0.1%
Unaffiliated		15.30	5,185,000	-1.0%

Churches	MegaBloc	Congs	Members	Affiliates
Catholic Church	C	5,485	8,756,579	13,310,000
United Ch of Canada	P	3,290	562,162	1,248,000
Anglican Church	A	2,890	316,500	633,000
Greek Orthodox Ch	O	80	234,756	385,000
Pente Assemblies of C	P	1,115	166,883	257,000
Jehovah's Witnesses	M	1,320	111,100	209,979
Canadian Baptist Min	P	1,008	120,000	204,000
Antiochan Orthodox	O	19	124,138	180,000
Presbyterian Ch in C	P	852	104,790	175,000
Latter-day Saints (Mormon)	M	481	79,091	174,000
Evang Lutheran Ch	P	594	118,705	165,000
CMA	P	440	65,330	152,220
Ukrainian Catholic	C	99	74,251	124,000
Maronite Catholic Ch	C	18	36,000	108,000
Ukrainian Orth Ch of C	O	270	35,167	105,500
Fell of Evang Bapt Chs	P	503	58,100	87,150
Armenian Apostolic Ch	O	15	55,195	85,000
Lutheran Ch, Canada	P	324	53,556	72,300
Salvation Army	P	330	21,471	71,500
Christian Reformed Ch	P	246	46,689	70,500
Seventh-day Adventist	P	347	46,150	59,995
Coptic Orthodox Ch	O	25	37,179	58,000
Christian Brethren	P	395	27,665	46,200
Other denominations[262]		8,752	657,876	1,262,467

Total Christians[286]		28,898	11,909,333	19,243,811

TransBloc	Pop %	Population	Ann Gr
Evangelicals			
Evangelicals	7.7	2,601,683	0.8%
Renewalists			
Charismatics	6.4	2,167,256	1.6%
Pentecostals	1.3	439,404	1.3%

Missionaries from Canada

P,I,A 5,200 long-term: 2,500 in Canada. International: 122 agencies sending to 122 countries.

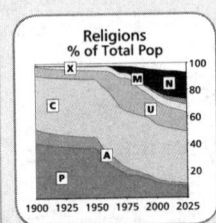

Religions % of Total Pop

Annual Growth Rates

Answers to Prayer

1 **The strong legacy of parliamentary democracy** has been influenced and shaped by Christian faith across all major parties. The proportion of elected members of parliament who are committed Christians is much higher than the average population.

Challenges for Prayer

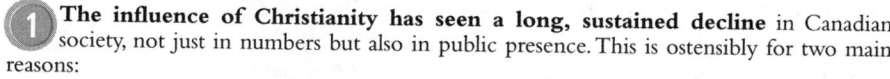

1 **The influence of Christianity has seen a long, sustained decline** in Canadian society, not just in numbers but also in public presence. This is ostensibly for two main reasons:

a) Increased and deliberate pluralization and secularization. The non-religious population has made the greatest gains in recent years, but other religions are also growing rapidly through immigration and high birthrates. As with several other Western nations, biblical Christianity faces significant antipathy from the media and popular culture.

b) A failure of relevance, morals, and theological and spiritual dynamism in the Church. Protestants and Anglicans together numbered 45% in 1950, but are now only 11%. In each denomination, the degree of theological liberalization – especially in the mainline United Church and in Anglicanism – has generally coincided with the rate of decline. On the positive side, this fading of Christendom has trimmed the "deadwood" from churches, but it still reflects a sad decline in the influence of the gospel in Canada. Pray for a much-needed revival, starting in the Church and radiating outward.

2 **Catholicism** is by far the largest religious influence in the country. Although Quebec in particular has a strong Catholic heritage, Catholicism is in fact strong throughout the country. It is growing as a proportion of the population and accounts for the largest number of incoming immigrants, a notable issue in a country built on the back of immigration. It is multicultural and thriving in the urban environment. There is a real vibrancy in Catholicism (apart from in Quebec itself) and charismatic renewal has been a significant part of this – two prominent ministries in this framework are Catholic Christian Outreach and National Evangelization Teams. Pray for this movement to grow and interface well with other expressions of living Christian faith in Canada.

3 **Evangelical witness** has not fared much better than Protestantism in recent decades.

a) Evangelicals represented 25% of the population in 1900, but less than 8% today. Surveys and studies disagree on whether this is now rising, stagnant or still in decline. While some evangelical and charismatic groups continue to grow, the decline of the historic denominations more than offsets this growth.

b) The new landscape of Canada offers significant challenges for evangelicals. The terms "born-again" and "evangelical" tend to carry negative weight, and there is a great gap in the public perception of "spirituality" as opposed to "religion". Overcoming the suspicion and dismissiveness of an unbelieving public and a hostile media will require humility, patience, wisdom and love.

c) The remarkable diversity of evangelicals reflects Canadian society in general. They are not only in mainline denominations and conservative Protestant groups, but they are increasingly from new, independent churches and emergent expressions as well. Evangelicals are racially, culturally and linguistically varied and include many immigrant communities. Pray for this diversity – and the unity found therein – to become both a strength for and testimony by evangelicals to the truth and power of the gospel.

d) Canadian evangelicals work together more effectively now than in earlier years, but they are still fragmented, again reflective of the cultural mosaic of Canadian society in general. Pray for the work of the Evangelical Fellowship of Canada, which seeks to draw together and represent evangelicals from all backgrounds.

4 **The large number of Bible institutes,** colleges, universities and theological seminaries – committed to a biblical view of Scripture – are fulfilling a major role in strengthening evangelical witness. These are spread across Canada. Some are experiencing renewal and growth. Some are struggling with enrolment and support. Pray for the students and their teachers, that missions may be a central aspect of their education.

5 **Quebec is a unique region** that has experienced in one or two generations the secularization and modernization that took France centuries to accomplish. While mostly French in language and culture, it is increasingly multicultural, with an Anglophone minority and growing immigrant communities. Pray for:

a) *Political currents* that swirl around the issue of separation from Canada. Although such sentiment has waned of late, it is never far from becoming prominent. Pray that Quebec might make a valuable contribution to the redemptive history of Canada.

b) *The Catholic Church* dominates Quebecois identity and culture (more than 80% self-identify as Catholic), but not attendance. Quebec's church attendance rate is Canada's lowest. There is a demonstrably low commitment to community activities; in particular, church and faith are highly personal and privatized.

c) *Evangelicals in Quebec.* Protestants are decidedly low in number and evangelical churches regarded as nearly cults. While Protestants are very mixed among French, English and immigrant cultures, there are also a significant number of practicing Catholics with evangelical beliefs. Pray for unity, fellowship and even collaboration.

d) *Church planting* needs to occur in much greater measure. To bring Quebec up to par with the rest of Canada in the numbers of evangelical congregations, 3,000 more churches must be planted.

e) *Ministry vision to Quebec and beyond.* Christian Direction/Urbanus partners with all denominations in the vision to have a spiritual impact on the whole Francophone world, starting in Quebec. French-Canadian evangelicals usually feel more affinity with other Francophone evangelicals globally than with Anglophone Canadian evangelicals.

6 **Canadian indigenous peoples** are largely Christian in name, but nominalism is a challenge for them as for the majority population. However, Pentecostal/charismatic churches are proportionately stronger among indigenous peoples than in any other demographic group in Canada. There are 600 reserves in Canada for First Nations peoples, all quite small in population.

a) *The shameful treatment of indigenous peoples* in the past by those of European descent must be overcome. Both the government and the Church, dominated by European-background Canadians, were guilty of political, religious, cultural and even sexual abuses. These past sins make for a history of abuse that is impossible to move past without repentance and forgiveness. Pray for the Truth and Reconciliation Commission initiated in June 2010.

b) *Pray for the growth of strong, well-led churches* that reflect First Nations culture and can reproduce others of the same quality. Especially pray for the development of indigenous leadership. There are many encouraging signs of growth and renewal in the native evangelical community, where a contextualized Church is only just beginning to flourish.

c) *Pray for missions that seek to evangelize* and plant churches, often in the inhospitable northern parts of the country. Denominational (Native Evangelical Fellowship of Canada, PAOC), mission-based (Interact, NAIM) and interagency (Inter-Mission Cooperative Outreach) ministries are dedicated to this. Indigenous missions movements to evangelize their own are also developing.

d) *Bible translation or revision* is still needed. There are 27 native languages with no Scripture, although many of these languages are declining rapidly or are all but extinct. Six languages have had the NT completed in the last 10 years and another six works are in progress. Pray for translators with Canadian Bible Society and SIL. Also, an increasing number of Christian radio and TV programmes are aimed at First Nations peoples.

e) *The hundreds of thousands of First Nations people* living outside reservations are neglected and spiritually needy, especially in cities such as Toronto, Winnipeg, Edmonton and Regina, where poverty and substance abuse continue to afflict them. Some outstanding ministries toward these peoples exist, but evangelicals generally have been slow to take up this challenge that sits right on their doorstep.

7 **The Inuit** (Eskimo) in the Arctic are mostly Anglican in name, but the worst of Western civilization has greatly altered and harmed the Inuit way of life, through ecological changes, residential schools and substance abuse. Greater autonomy for the Inuit and the recently created region of Nunavut offer significant hope for positive changes. Revivals and spiritual awakenings are well documented among the Inuit. In these isolated northern towns, it is helpful that, often, the Church is still the centre of the community. Pray for these revivals to continue and grow and to transform Inuit communities with the power of the gospel.

8 **A nation of immigrants,** having deliberately pursued a policy of immigration, Canada has the world's highest rate of immigration and receives large numbers of refugees. Nearly 75% of immigrants live in the country's three largest cities, and 95% in urban areas generally. Outreach and evangelization can be difficult in a context that deliberately embraces multi-cultural pluralism. Especially significant are:

a) The Chinese (1.4 million) population has grown rapidly since the 1980s, with a steady influx of immigrants. There are nearly 400 congregations among them, mostly in Toronto and then Vancouver. Church growth is encouraging, but challenges exist regarding second-generation withdrawal from the Church and assimilation of Chinese Christians into the broader Christian fellowship.

b) South Asians (numbering just over one million). They include Hindus, Sikhs and Muslims, and form the biggest bloc of unreached peoples in the country. Vancouver is the world's second-largest Sikh community.

c) Muslim peoples have been mostly of Arabic background, but increasing numbers of Afghans, Kurds, Somalis, Sudanese, East Africans and Southeast Asian Muslims can now be found. Very little specific outreach to them has been undertaken. Most of the few believers are Lebanese or Palestinian.

9 **Missionary vision** was once very strong but has steadily declined over the last 20 years. Support of national missionaries and relief and development programmes, however, has remained steady. Areas for prayer:

a) Overseas ministry. Canada once enjoyed a pride of place in sending aid and peacekeeping forces and in having a strong missionary-sending tradition. The latter of the three has decreased markedly. Pray for increased involvement by churches and individuals in the evangelization of the unreached around the world.

b) The great influx of immigrants creates sizeable unevangelized communities in Canada's cities. Reaching the scores of unreached ethnicities can happen within a stone's throw of most urban churches. Pray for a passion to reach out to these peoples whom God has placed on the doorsteps of evangelical congregations.

c) Missionary concern from within the many growing, ethnic-minority churches. Such a vision is vital for Canada and could be strategic for the evangelization of their lands of origin.

d) Nationwide missionary mobilizing. Pray for the unifying and strategic work of the Task Force for Global Mission of the Evangelical Fellowship of Canada. Pray also for Missionfest, a mobilizing conference held in several cities every year to raise awareness and stimulate missions vision.

10 **Specialized ministries for prayer:**

a) Christian media. There are a number of widely appreciated religious programmes and stations, particularly Vision TV, Crossroads and "It's a New Day". US Christian programmes continue to exercise notable influence over Canadian churches as well.

b) Student ministries in the nearly 300 colleges and universities, serving 1.1 million tertiary students. These give wide exposure to sections of the campus community. There are three movements linked with **IFES** (IVCF-English, GBU-French, Ambassadors for Christ-Chinese) who have groups in over 60 universities. There are also extensive ministries linked with Navigators and **CCCI**. **YFC** and OAC have good ministries in high schools. Pray that these and other ministries may make a deep and lasting impact.

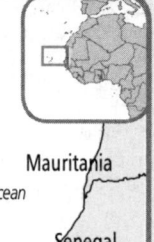

Cape Verde Islands

North Atlantic Ocean

Mauritania

Praia

Senegal

Cape Verde Islands

Republic of Cape Verde

Africa

Geography

Area 4,033 sq km. Fifteen dry, barren islands 600 km off the west coast of Africa.

Population		Ann Gr	Density
2010	512,582	1.43%	127/sq km
2020	583,509	1.26%	145/sq km
2030	644,903	0.91%	160/sq km

Capital Praia 128,000. **Urbanites** 61.1%. **Pop under 15 yrs** 36%. **Life expectancy** 71.1 yrs.

Peoples

Caboverdian Creole (mixed race) 72.8%.
African 25.3%. Fula and Balanta from Guinea-Bissau.
European 1.9%. Mostly of Portuguese background.
Literacy 81.2%. **Official language** Portuguese. **Trade language** Portuguese Creole. **All languages** 2. **Languages with Scriptures** 1Bi 1NT 1por 1w.i.p.

Economy

Arid land means 80% of food must be imported. Heavily dependent on aid and remittances from Caboverdian migrants. Unexploited tourist and fishing potential.
HDI Rank 121st/182. **Public debt** 55% of GDP.
Income/person $3,464 (7% of USA). **Unemployment** 21.1%.

Politics

Independent of Portugal in 1975 as a one-party socialist republic. A revised constitution in 1990 led to multiparty elections and a peaceful change of government.

Religion

The privileged position of the Catholic Church ended in 1975. A secular state with freedom of religion.

Religions	Pop %	Population	Ann Gr
Christian	94.56	484,698	1.3%
Muslim	3.10	15,890	4.3%
Non-religious	1.17	5,997	2.1%
Ethnoreligionist	1.04	5,331	0.7%
Baha'i	0.12	615	3.2%
Jewish	0.01	51	1.4%

Christians Denoms		Pop %	Affiliates	Ann Gr
Protestant	4	6.44	33,000	3.9%
Independent	6	4.28	22,000	5.5%
Catholic	1	89.35	458,000	1.2%
Marginal	2	2.69	14,000	3.5%
Unaffiliated		2.10	11,000	-3.3%
Doubly affiliated		*-10.30*	*-53,000*	*0.0%*

Churches	MegaBloc	Congs	Members	Affiliates
Catholic Church	C	82	215,023	458,000
Ch of the Nazarene	P	52	5,700	15,960
Seventh-day Adventist	P	30	5,700	15,600
New Apostolic Church	I	28	4,250	10,200
God Is Love Pente Ch	I	15	2,920	7,300
Latter-day Saints (Mormon)	M	36	5,259	7,100
Jehovah's Witnesses	M	28	1,675	6,700
Univ Ch, Kingdom of God	I	30	2,267	3,400
Other denominations[5]		20	921	2,500
Doubly affiliated				*-52,800*
Total Christians[13]		**321**	**243,715**	**473,960**

TransBloc	Pop %	Population	Ann Gr
Evangelicals			
Evangelicals	6.6	33,840	4.5%
Renewalists			
Charismatics	5.6	28,788	5.8%
Pentecostals	2.5	12,870	5.9%

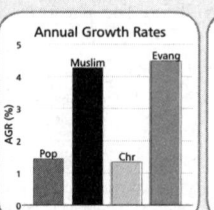

Annual Growth Rates

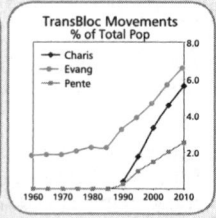

TransBloc Movements
% of Total Pop

Challenges for Prayer

1 **Economic and ecological problems** must be wisely addressed. Scant resources were poorly managed in the past, intensifying Cape Verde's poverty. Pray for government leaders who will make good decisions and develop the economy for the betterment of the whole nation.

2 **Most Caboverdians are Catholic in name,** but in practice are more influenced by superstitions and African fetishism. Christian literature is lacking in Creole, and most people have only a rudimentary grasp of Portuguese.

3 **Newer religious groups are growing rapidly.** This includes evangelicals, but also marginal groups. The Nazarenes have the longest Protestant presence. More recent arrivals feature Pentecostals from Brazil and the USA. Pray that more indigenous leaders and pastors may be trained for these growing groups. Pray that believers might mature and increase despite poverty and geographic isolation.

4 **There are 490,000 Caboverdians living in migrant communities;** the largest are in New England, USA (266,000), Portugal (80,000), Angola (46,000), Senegal and France. Their remittances are vital to those living in Cape Verde. Pray that many in these communities may become true disciples of Jesus and be spiritual and economic blessings to their homeland.

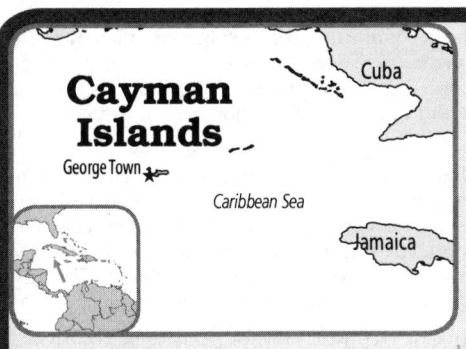

Cayman Islands

Honduran, Cuban, Nicaraguan.
Other 2.3%. Jews, various Asian groups.
Literacy 98%. **Official language** English. **All languages** 3. **Indigenous languages** 1. **Languages with Scriptures** 1Bi.

Economy

The most affluent Caribbean economy by a safe margin. The wealth of the territory is derived from banking, tourism, insurance and indirect taxation.
Public debt 13% of GDP. **Income/person** $28,648 (63% of USA).

Politics

A British dependent territory with representative government.

Cayman Islands

Caribbean

Geography

Area 264 sq km. Three coral islands south of Cuba.

Population		Ann Gr	Density
2010	56,628	1.49%	214/sq km
2020	61,463	0.75%	233/sq km
2030	64,991	0.49%	246/sq km

Capital George Town 32,000. **Urbanites** 100%. **Pop under 15 yrs** 17%. **Life expectancy** 79.9 yrs.

Peoples

Residents come from more than 100 nations, over half being foreign-born.
African Caribbean 69.7%.
Caucasian 18.3%. American, British, Canadian.
Latin American/Hispanic 9.7%. Mainly

Religion

Religions	Pop %	Population	Ann Gr
Christian	77.11	43,666	1.4%
Ethnoreligionist	13.00	7,362	0.7%
Non-religious	6.80	3,851	3.7%
Jewish	1.70	963	1.5%
Baha'i	0.90	510	1.7%
Hindu	0.28	159	2.2%
Muslim	0.21	119	2.5%

Christians	Denoms	Pop %	Affiliates	Ann Gr
Protestant	19	45.15	26,000	1.8%
Independent	11	8.09	5,000	2.4%
Anglican	1	1.06	1,000	1.8%
Catholic	1	7.24	4,000	0.3%
Marginal	4	1.38	1,000	2.8%
Unaffiliated		14.20	8,000	-2.3%

Churches	MegaBloc	Congs	Members	Affiliates
United Church	P	13	9,868	15,000
Seventh-day Adventist	P	11	2,800	4,200

					TransBloc	Pop %	Population	Ann Gr
Catholic Church	C	2	1,640	4,100	**Evangelicals**			
Baptist Church	P	5	486	1,350	Evangelicals	21.3	12,057	2.2%
United Apos Faith Ch	P	5	475	950	**Renewalists**			
Ch of God Holiness	P	5	588	940	Charismatics	11.1	6,275	2.0%
United Pentecostal Ch	P	7	425	850	Pentecostals	2.6	1,485	1.2%
Anglican Church	A	3	300	600				
Jehovah's Witnesses	M	3	234	550				
Bible Baptist Church	P	7	370	520				
Baptist Convention	P	2	250	380				
Other denominations[25]		34	2,968	6,185				
Total Christians[36]		**97**	**20,404**	**35,625**				

Annual Growth Rates (AGR %): Pop, Ethnic, Chr, Evang

MegaBlocs % of Christian Pop: 58.6, 18.4, 1.8, 9.4, 1.4, 10.5 — P, I, A, C, M, U

Challenges for Prayer

1 **The Islands' reputation as an offshore banking and tax haven,** vulnerable to money laundering operations, has been vigorously addressed by changes in the laws and regulations of the 600 banks here. There are over 70,000 registered companies, and banking assets rest at over $600 billion. Pray that the wealth of the islands may be used to extend God's Kingdom.

2 **Christianity is numerically strong.** There are more than 90 churches, many of them evangelical. With one church for approximately every 500 people, Christian faith and values should (and do) have a significant influence on society – pray that this might continue to be the case amid the materialism and hedonism. The nation's flag bears part of Psalm 24, "He hath founded it upon the seas". The new constitution includes recognition of the Christian heritage of the Cayman Islands. Pray that God's sovereign power would be acknowledged.

3 **Well over a million tourists** visit the islands each year. Pray for many to be confronted by the claims of Christ while in pursuit of pleasure.

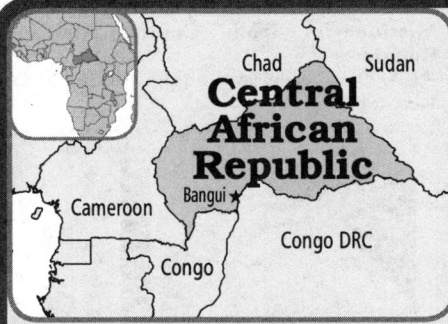

Chad
Sudan

**Central
African
Republic**

Cameroon
Bangui ★

Congo DRC

Congo

Central
African
Republic

République
Centrafricaine

Africa

Geography

Area 622,436 sq km. A landlocked state in Africa's geographical centre. Variation from tropical forest in the southwest to semi–desert in the northeast.

Population		Ann Gr	Density
2010	4,505,945	1.90%	7/sq km
2020	5,340,353	1.62%	9/sq km
2030	6,149,625	1.36%	10/sq km

Capital Bangui 718,000. **Urbanites** 38.9%. **Pop under 15 yrs** 41%. **Life expectancy** 46.7 yrs.

Peoples

About 80 ethnic groups.
Adamawa–Ubangi 78.7%. About 35 ethnic groupings. Largest: Gbaya(5) 27.8%; Banda(7) 21.9%; Mandja 9.5%; Mboum 6.0%; Yakoma 5.5%; Bokoto 3.6%.
Sudanic 6.2%. 12 groups on the northern border. Zande 3.0%; Banda-Dukpu 2.7%.
Bantu 3.0%. 10 groups in the southwest.
Fulbe 3.6%. Bagirmi Fulbe 2.4%; Mbororo 1.0%.
Sara–Bagirmi 4.9%. Kaba 2.0%; 10 others groups.
Arab 2.8%. Nomadic Shuwa Arabs 2.2%.
Pygmy 0.3%. Five groups mainly in the southwest forests.
Other 0.5%. Caucasians and groups dispersed from neighbouring countries.
Literacy 48.6%. **Official languages** French and Sango (trade language used by most of the population). **All languages** 82. **Indigenous languages** 71. **Languages with Scriptures** 5Bi 8NT 10por 9w.i.p.

Economy

Rich in natural and mineral resources, but underdeveloped infrastructure and landlocked status limit income. Diamonds account for 55% of exports. Conflict in neighbouring countries and within the Central African Republic (CAR) has undermined any potential to exploit the nation's resources. Farmers account for most of the working population. Health facilities are limited. There is a massive economic gulf between the richer capital and the poor hinterlands.
HDI Rank 179th/182. **Public debt** 96% of GDP. **Income/person** $459 (1% of USA).

Politics

Independent in 1960, the nation has thus far not fully utilized her freedom. Periods of democracy have been interspersed with military regimes and Bokassa's bizarre "Empire", 1976-79. The current president came to power through a coup in 2003 and was then fairly elected in 2005. Constant rebellions and military coups slow progress. Already-poor infrastructure is further damaged by frequent conflict; rebel groups constantly appear, and upheavals in surrounding countries make the rebuilding task a difficult one for a government already beset by the traditional challenges of tribalism, nepotism and corruption. The many rebel factions in the north are being monitored through the UN presence but the east is unstable due to the presence of the LRA which has spilled over from Uganda and Sudan.

Religion

Freedom of religion.

Religions	Pop %	Population	Ann Gr
Christian	76.37	3,441,190	1.9%
Muslim	13.80	621,820	3.9%
Ethnoreligionist	8.60	387,511	-0.7%
Non-religious	0.92	41,455	2.1%
Baha'i	0.31	13,968	1.3%

Christians Denoms		Pop %	Affiliates	Ann Gr
Protestant	20	25.11	1,131,000	2.1%
Independent	50	11.56	521,000	2.6%
Catholic	1	19.64	885,000	2.2%
Marginal	2	0.43	20,000	5.1%
Unaffiliated		19.63	885,000	-1.1%

Churches	MegaBloc	Congs	Members	Affiliates
Catholic Church	C	3,598	514,535	885,000
Grace Brethren	P	1,150	230,000	434,700
Elim Evangelical Chs	P	500	140,000	238,000
Evang Baptist Ch (OM)	P	965	68,500	129,465
AEBEC (ex BMM)	I	310	62,000	111,600
Co-op Ev Centrafricaine	I	380	50,500	101,000
Frat Un of Baptist Chs	P	138	46,500	88,350
UFEB (ex BMM)	I	179	43,000	81,700

AEAC Apostolique	P	646	42,000	69,300
Other independent chs	I	330	33,000	66,000
Evang Lutheran Ch	P	179	21,484	55,000
Churches of Christ	P	147	14,706	25,000
Evang Chs of the East	P	613	18,400	23,920
Un of Evang Baptist	I	106	17,000	23,800
Other denominations[42]		1,420	128,053	224,199
Total Christians[73]		**10,661**	**1,423,194**	**2,557,034**

TransBloc	Pop %	Population	Ann Gr
Evangelicals			
Evangelicals	32.3	1,453,346	2.3%
Renewalists			
Charismatics	15.6	701,921	3.5%
Pentecostals	12.9	581,328	3.2%

Missionaries from Central African Republic

P,I,A 99 in 7 agencies: most in CAR, Sudan 2, Rep of Congo 1.

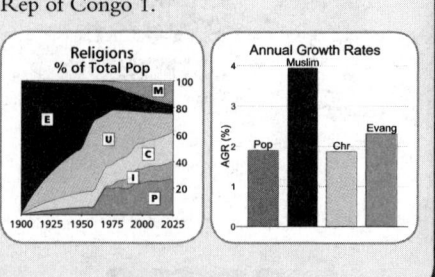

C

Answers to Prayer

1 **Solid foundations are laid** for developing a national-level strategy for mission and evangelism that spans denominational and organizational lines. The potential for massive church growth and consolidation exists; there is a growing interest among the churches for evangelism to unreached people groups.

2 **Praise God that the national Church is emerging** as a vehicle for witness and service. National missionaries and agencies are on the increase, and indigenous-led ministries are springing up. Bible translation work in mother tongues and literacy in the churches are progressing as well.

Challenges for Prayer

1 **The physical human needs** of CAR are immense. The seemingly endless series of coups and counter-coups devastated the economy and infrastructure. Pray for the following needs:

a) *Peace and stability,* particularly in the north and east. Constant uprisings and banditry grind down the already poor and blight the government's efforts to restore the infrastructure. Anarchy continues to reign in the north of the country, and hundreds of thousands have fled their homes in the past few years. Pray that banditry and chaos might not prevail and that a strong and just central government can establish peace throughout the country.

b) *The economy.* The nation, although blessed with vast mineral resources, is weak economically. Pray that the government might bring to bear a wise hand in increasing wealth that enriches the entire nation and not just a privileged few.

c) *Unemployment.* Pray for the emergence of employment opportunities for the many without work. Pray for the emergence of Christian businessmen who will be agents of transformation in the economic and spiritual spheres.

d) *Health.* CAR is another nation increasingly devastated by AIDS; HIV rates peaked at 15% of the adult population infected, although now reduced to 6%. Life expectancy is dropping year by year. Pray for programmes and ministries to combat not only HIV/AIDS but also diseases that come about from malnourishment, lack of clean water, faulty hygiene and poverty.

2 **Widespread evangelism,** especially in the 1960s and 1970s, yielded massive numbers of converts but a shortage of disciples. This has slowed the momentum of growth and is evident in the following challenges needing prayer.

a) *Widespread nominalism and syncretism.* The huge numbers of unaffiliated Christians reflect this, and even within most churches there is little depth of commitment and limited grasp and application of the truths of Scripture. Animistic religions may be decreasing on the surface, but their influence is still strong.

b) Denominational rifts hold back cooperative efforts. Pray against the root causes. A failure on the part of leaders to demonstrate Christ-like humility and graciousness in their walk and ministry not only stunts their own fruitfulness but passes on their flaws to their congregations. Breakdowns between church leaders and missionaries have on occasion caused heartache, multiplied splits and isolated ministries from one another. Pray for healing of past wounds and for a deeper appreciation and level of trust among God's servants, both national and expatriate.

c) The failure to make discipleship a top priority also means that high moral standards and honesty are frequently lacking in the churches. Pray that increased emphasis on disciple-making might yield Christians of high moral fibre.

3 **The unity of the Church** continues to be a fundamental need. Progress is being made within the Protestant framework, but bringing in the new and diverse Independent/AIC groups is essential. Pray for:

a) The AEC (Alliance des Evangéliques en Centrafrique) and the newly reconstituted National Committee on Evangelism and Missions (CONEM) as they work to bring healing and restoration in place of fragmentation and division.

b) Cooperative research of the harvest force and harvest field in CAR. AMI, FATEB, ACATBA/SIL and others make significant contributions in this area. Pray for resources to publish findings and for the evangelical community to be enthusiastic about its usefulness in evangelism, discipleship and church planting.

4 **Leadership development** is increasingly important, but not all denominations truly make it a priority. Much is happening, but it is only a fraction of what needs to be accomplished to train pastors and disciple believers. Pray for the following:

a) About 15 Bible schools – lack of staff, students, funds and resources means that some are Bible schools only in name. Foreign-developed curriculum and emphasis on paper qualification hamper the ability to train pastors equipped to deal with CAR's unique challenges. Pray for a release of funds; many are eager to study and only a lack of resources holds them back.

b) The Bangui Evangelical Graduate School of Theology (FATEB). This was the first evangelical theological seminary for French-speaking Africa. There are many qualified candidates seeking scholarships; pray for financial provision for students, staff and the school itself. Pray also for this institution and its spiritual impact throughout Africa. Grace Brethren, Baptist Mid-Mission and UFEB all have seminaries.

c) TEE has great potential, but poor infrastructure (roads, mail and such) limits its impact. Pray for creative solutions that will provide theological education to those seeking to go deeper in their study.

d) Women in ministry, a long-neglected area, now receives the attention it deserves. Christian Women's Union, Women's Aglow and PAFEC are all making inroads into releasing more women into ministry.

5 **Young people and children.** Almost half of the population are under the age of 15. A wide-ranging vision for this ministry is crucial, but too few churches have the vision, structures and workers to disciple the upcoming generation. Faithful teachers who will mentor the younger generation are needed. Pray for:

a) Children's ministry. CEF, SU, Adonai Heritage and others vitally impact kids. There is freedom to minister in schools; pray that this will be fully utilized. Other faiths actively entice young people via scholarships and grants as well as the temptations of magic.

b) Secondary students are responsive to the *Gospel of Hope* as the economic and political upheavals seem to offer only despair and disillusionment. Pray for the activities of UJC(**IFES**), *Jeunesse en Action* and **YWAM**; these ministries are present in almost every secondary and tertiary institution in the country.

c) The establishment of primary schools, in this case, church-run schools, is a transformational ministry that is much needed, yet much neglected. Pray that such schools might reflect and instill a Christian character as well as preparing young people for the challenges of their future.

6 **Bible translation.** Only two indigenous languages have a fully translated Bible: Sango and Zande. Pray for effective use of the newly revised Sango NT. Bible translation is in progress in seven other languages. Pray for the work of The Bible Society, **BMM** and SIL with its partner *Association Centrafricaine pour la Traduction de la Bible et l'Alphabétisation* (ACATBA). ACATBA also runs literacy and community development projects. Pray that through Bible translation, literature and song, churches might be instrumental in preserving, rather than extinguishing, each of these unique tongues and their related cultures.

C **7** **The less-reached.** The CAR was one of the world's most evangelized nations (at least on a superficial level), but the upheavals here and in Chad and Sudan have spelled backward progress in several regions.

a) *The northern lobe* is increasingly volatile and dangerous with churches and missions looted and burned. Pray specifically for the Runga (90% Muslim, 26,000), Sara Kaba (50% Animist, 17,000) and the Gula/Kara (65% Muslim, 16,000). AMI, **BMM**, *Eglise Coopération Evangélique* and the Apostolic Church work among these groups, and there is some breakthrough among the Kara. Pray also for the groups filtering in from neighbouring countries.

b) *Muslims* are increasing numerically on a modest level, but are seeing massive growth in influence and visibility, especially in cities. They have a disproportionately large control over trade and business, including imports and exports. Relatively little outreach is directed specifically at them, and few Christians feel equipped for this. Pray specifically for:

i *The influential urban Muslims* (Arab, Hausa) and the nomadic Shuwa Arabs and Fulbe/ Fulani. The Mbororo are the major Fulani subgroup in CAR. GBIM, *Nations en Marche* and others are working among them.

ii *The increasing Muslim minorities* among Christianized peoples. Sudanese influence and Libyan and Saudi money in the form of free education and medical care draw many nominal Christians into Islam.

iii *Converts from Islam to Jesus* are very influential within their community. Pray for these believers – their potential impact is great.

c) *The forest areas.* The need is great for adequate research, but there are pockets of unreached among the Bayaka (Pygmy) and other smaller-numbering peoples. Officially, there are 13,000 Bayaka, but some believe they may number several times more. They speak six languages. At least 10 agencies work with them in various ways.

8 **Mission agencies** play an important role in education, health and work with children at risk as well as in planting churches, translating the Scriptures and other areas. The largest are **BMM**, Grace Brethren, InterAct, **ELCA**, **RG**. Pray now for greater partnerships between the emerging national mission movements and foreign missions. Both have great talents and gifts to bring to a partnership.

a) *Mission vision and interest* in unevangelized peoples are growing in CAR and spreading to neighbouring countries. Adonai Missions runs a Bible school in Bangui with an emphasis on cross-cultural missions. *Nations en Marche* founded a polytechnic school for missionary training and a newly opened Bayaka Bible training school in the forest. These two ministries plus *Mission d'Evangelisation Pour le Salut du Monde* and others contribute to sending missionaries. Pray that all denominations will send students to be trained as missionaries and that those so trained will not be tempted to become city pastors.

b) *Church planting movements.* Church Planting Institute (CPI) and PIEVCA encourage church planting movements and local church initiatives all across the sub-region. A stronger emphasis on training indigenous church planters now bears great fruit. Pray for greater involvement by denominational leaders.

9 **Christian media and help ministries:**

a) *Christian Radio.* With several new Christian radio stations – *Voix de la Grâce*/Radio ESCA (Grace Brethren), *Radio Evangile Néhémie* (*Ambassade Chrétienne*), *Radio Notre Dame* (Catholic) and ICDI community radio (**HCJB**) – the gospel is going out to potentially millions every week. Several languages are broadcast several hours a day. Pray for proper coordination of Christian radio programmes and training of administrators to ensure effective ministry.

b) *Christian literature* is increasing. More than five new literature depots in the country make material available to more than 30% of the population each year. Pray for ACATBA, a national literacy programme, for World Missionary Press, and for oral evangelism work by local groups such as Evangelists without Borders.

c) *The JESUS film* has been widely shown in French, Sango, Gbaya (NW), Fulfulde and Zande. Pray for **CCCI** to achieve further progress; pray also for translators for other languages.

d) *GRN* has recordings available in 31 languages and counting. Audio resources (cassette, CD, digital players) are treasured in this poor country with widespread illiteracy; pray for wider distribution of these materials.

e) *The business, academic and professional elite.* Pray for progress in evangelism among these influential groups. Haggai Institute, Operation Africa and others are reaching out to them.

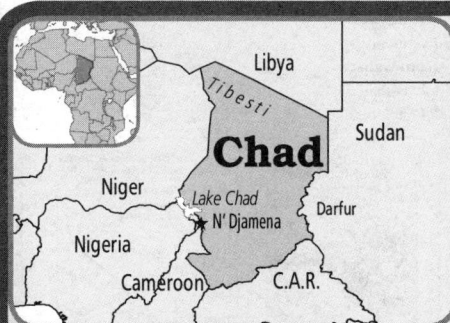

Chad

Republic of Chad

Africa

Geography

Area 1,284,000 sq km. Desert in the north, dry grassland in centre, thick bush in the south. The sea is 1,000 km distant.

Population		Ann Gr	Density
2010	11,506,130	2.81%	9/sq km
2020	14,897,328	2.57%	12/sq km
2030	19,017,747	2.38%	15/sq km

Capital N'djamena 828,717. **Urbanites** 27.6%. **Pop under 15 yrs** 46%. **Life expectancy** 48.6 yrs.

Peoples

Complex mix of 150 or more peoples.
Sara-Bagirmi 23.8%. 17 peoples: Sara Ngambai 10.1%; Sara Majingai-Ngama 3.0%; Goulai 2.6%; Sara Mbai 1.4%; Mango 1.1%; Bediondo Mbai 1.0%; Gor 1.0%; Kabba–Laka 1.0%; Bagirmi 0.7%.
Chadic 17.9%. 51 peoples in the southwest. Banana/Musey/Massa 2.8%; Marba 2.0%; Masana 1.7%.
Kanuri-Saharan 14.1%. Eight peoples in the north: Kanembu 6.3%; Tubu/Daza 3.6%; Kanuri 1.5%; Zaghawa 1.2%.
Ouaddai-Fur 12.7%. 21 peoples in the east: Maba

3.4%; Masalit 1.9%; Tama 1.0%; Daju 1.0%.
Adamawa-Ubangi 7.3%. 21 peoples in the southwest. Mundang 2.6%; Tupuri 1.5%.
Guera-Naba 4.4%. Six peoples in and around central mountains: Bilala 2.2%; Naba 1.2%.
Fulbe 2.9%. Three peoples. Adamawa 2.1%.
Other Sub-Saharan African 2.4%. Hausa 1.6%.
Arab 14.5%. Six peoples, mostly nomadic Shuwa (Baggara) Arabs.
Other 0.1%. Western.
Literacy 53.7% One of the lowest literacy levels in the world. **Official languages** French (only spoken by the educated), Arabic (perhaps 30% of Arabic speakers are fluent). **All languages** 133. **Indigenous languages** 131. **Languages with Scriptures** 10Bi 22NT 25por.

Economy

An agricultural economy where 80% engage in subsistence farming and raising livestock. Lack of rainfall, severe droughts, distance from the sea, post-independence civil wars and poor infrastructure hinder any economic progress. Physical infrastructure, especially the road system, has seen a boost in recent years. Some mineral wealth, significant oil deposits. The extraction of these is notably boosting the economy, but corruption is rife, and misspending threatens to nullify some of the benefit; a large share of the revenue is spent on military hardware. 80% live below the poverty line. **HDI Rank** 175th/182. **Public debt** 54.5% of GDP. **Income/person** $863 (2% of USA).

Politics

Independent from France in 1960. Since then, violence, insurgencies and coups have characterized Chad's politics, with interventions by Libya, France and others. The government is dominated by one tribe, the Zaghawa. It pays lip service to democracy and manipulated the democratic machinery to alter the constitution to keep its man in power. Numerous Chadian rebel groups often cause problems for the government. The conflict in neighbouring Darfur spilled over into Chad – including 400,000 refugees at its peak. This swelled the population but also brought in aid money being spent in and around refugee camps.

Religion

A secular state with freedom of religion. Muslims are dominant in government, trade and the army, though barely a majority in the country.

Religions	Pop %	Population	Ann Gr
Muslim	52.84	6,079,839	3.3%
Christian	38.46	4,425,258	3.2%
Ethnoreligionist	7.70	885,972	-0.4%
Baha'i	0.80	92,049	2.8%
Other	0.10	11,506	2.8%
Non-religious	0.10	11,506	-32.2%

Christians	Denoms	Pop %	Affiliates	Ann Gr
Protestant	30	9.25	1,065,000	2.9%
Independent	27	1.17	135,000	5.4%
Catholic	1	21.29	2,450,000	3.1%
Marginal	1	0.02	2,000	1.3%
Unaffiliated		6.72	733,000	1.1%

Churches	MegaBloc	Congs	Members	Affiliates
Catholic Church	C	564	1,296,296	2,450,000
Evang Ch of Tchad (EET)	P	1,785	350,000	450,000
Christian Assem (ACT)	P	1,030	153,333	230,000
Baptist Church	P	306	45,939	151,600
Lutheran Brethren Ch	P	714	25,000	102,667

Grace Brethren (EEF)	P	300	19,000	45,000
Evang Ch of Chr (ECWA)	I	145	9,700	24,250
Ch of the Brethren	P	83	5,000	15,000
Deeper Life Bible Ch	I	50	6,000	15,000
ECET	P	32	4,800	12,000
Evangelical Assemblies	P	32	4,800	12,000
Seventh-day Adventist	P	49	3,700	8,000
Chadienne Evang Ch	I	155	3,100	7,750
Ch of God (Cleveland)	P	172	8,600	3,130
Apostolic Church	P	60	1,200	3,000
Baptist Church (IMB)	P	28	1,800	2,700
Other denominations[43]		517	47,727	119,692
Total Christians[59]		**6,022**	**1,985,995**	**3,651,789**

TransBloc	Pop %	Population	Ann Gr
Evangelicals			
Evangelicals	10.1	1,161,358	3.2%
Renewalists			
Charismatics	2.3	268,223	4.5%
Pentecostals	0.3	36,876	9.3%

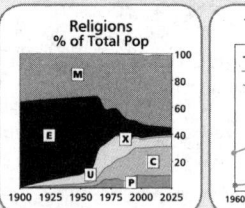

Religions % of Total Pop

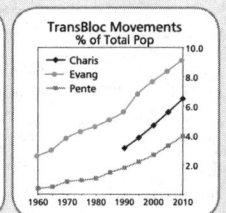

TransBloc Movements % of Total Pop

Answers to Prayer

1 **Praise God for continued religious freedom** and for the welcome to missionaries. Chad is one of very few Muslim-majority countries where Christian workers will find such openness and access and where the government is truly secular in its operations.

2 **The number of Muslims seeking to know more of Christ continues to grow.** Groups of believers from Muslim backgrounds are slowly beginning to multiply. The development of culturally helpful resources such as chronological Bible storying and Chadian Arabic Christian radio makes a huge difference.

3 **Many unreached peoples are being reached for the first time.** Labour by both indigenous and expatriate missions has seen the identification of Chad's least evangelized (97 people groups), and is yielding concentrated prayer and outreach to them.

4 **The tragic upheaval in Darfur** has brought many into contact with the gospel that otherwise may never have heard. Their persecution by other Muslims (such as the *janjawid* militias) has disillusioned many with Islam and has made some open to the loving ministry and witness of Christians.

Challenges for Prayer

1 **The need for a stable and just government** is as urgent as ever. The current regime is noted for violence, corruption (Chad frequently picks up the dubious honour of being the world's most corrupt nation) and tribalism, heavily favouring the Zaghawa. The complex patchwork of tribes, and the ethnic and religious fault lines between north and south, make stability hard to attain. The constant threat from bandits and rebel groups – from within Chad and from Darfur – further destabilizes the situation and hinders both socio-economic progress and Christian ministry. Pray for a government that is representative of both north and south, honest and committed to the betterment of all of its citizens.

2 **Freedom of religion** is a precious reality. The otherwise flawed regime at least attempts to preserve this, but it faces rebel threats that are often strongly Islamist and sponsored by foreign, hard line Islamic groups and nations. The south, previously victim of marginalization, is increasingly courted as a counterbalance to this threat. Pray that, while current freedoms still exist, Christians might fully utilize the opportunities.

3 **The ascendancy of Islam** has increased in the last three decades. Its numerical, financial and social advantages are used to consolidate its dominant position, and animist peoples are being steadily Islamized. Increasing numbers of Muslim northerners are found in the south, with mosques and Muslim schools built in predominantly Christian areas to serve them. Pray for:

a) *The overcoming of many emotional, cultural and historical barriers* to southerners witnessing to Muslims. Most Christians are ill-equipped and somewhat ill-disposed when it comes to sharing the gospel with Muslims, since they are used to operating in tribal languages and ministering to animist peoples. Many resent and fear the economic impact and influence of northern Muslim traders and the environmental impact of northern Muslim herdsmen and their herds.

b) *Agencies and denominations* that have a vision for Muslim outreach. Other, usually more urgent, issues tend to be higher on the agendas of national churches. But the long-term strategic importance of equipping the Church to withstand Islamization and to reach out to Muslims cannot be overstated. Mobilization and training in how to sensitively and effectively reach Muslims are clear needs; pray for Christians to be burdened for the salvation of their Muslim countrymen.

4 **The Church needs uplifting in prayer,** especially regarding the following issues:

a) *African traditional religions* are resurgent in the country, partly as an attempt to return to African roots. Tribal initiation rites are becoming a divisive issue for Christians. Pray also for liberation from all bondages by a deep working of the Holy Spirit in every congregation.

b) *The deception of the sects and secret societies.* Groups such as Rosicrucians, Masons and other specifically African quasi-Christian groups seek to lead Chadians astray. Pray for solid teaching that will enable Christians to discern between truth and lies.

c) *Nominalism* is a challenge, even in Chad. Good discipleship and teaching are the antidote to this.

d) *Tribalism and petty legalisms* cripple many congregations. Tribal rivalries and resentments (especially south-north) prevent Christian witness.

e) *Unity.* While most Protestant and Independent groups are evangelical, unity within and among denominations is under strain. Pray for the EEMET (Evangelical Alliance) and the Pentecostal Alliance as both attempt to unite Christians.

f) *Vision for outreach.* Ambitious, countrywide goals have dissipated, and some initiatives that had notable impact in the past have faded almost to nothing. Churches need to gain a passion for ministry that includes praying and giving as well as outreach.

Pray for God to raise up catalysts who will spur Chad's Christians to greater depths of faith and a greater commitment to the unevangelized.

5 **Training of leaders** remains a major challenge. Poverty, instability, violence, poor communication and lack of both financial wherewithal and management hinder training of pastors and evangelists. Pray for the Shalom Evangelical School of Theology in N'Djamena (ESTES), the Apostolic Bible School ESDRAS, CoG Bible Institute and several Christian Assemblies (ACT) schools. The Bible Training Centre (CFBP/RE) focuses on developing lay leaders and those who lack the education or time for formal theological training. Full-time biblical studies are a huge commitment when finances are miniscule and encouragement from local churches is low.

6 **The least-evangelized.** There are more unreached peoples in Chad than in any other African country. A number of agencies, cooperating admirably, are making progress with previously unreached peoples. The major people-cluster challenges:

a) *The Saharan peoples* (all Sunni Muslims) are politically dominant. They live predominantly in the northern deserts, Tibesti Mountains, northern shores of Lake Chad and the larger towns. Efforts by **TEAM** and one or two others to reach them are still in the early stages of progress. Only a handful of Christians are known in these groups, who are among Africa's least evangelized.

b) *The Guera-Naba* cluster live between N'Djamena and the Guera Mountains and are almost entirely Muslim. They include the Bilala, Kuka and Medogo – collectively known to some as the Lisi. There are some agencies beginning work among them.

c) *The 21 smaller people groups* from the Chadic cluster. They are concentrated in the Guera Mountains. Rapid Islamization is occurring (although they also retain much of their animism). The Evangelical Assemblies (AET) are the main church in this area. Some peoples related to these 21 groups are solidly Christian, and they have a force of 40-plus village evangelists and local missionaries. **WBT** is involved in several translation projects among these peoples.

d) *The Ouaddai-Fur* peoples are Muslim and live in the eastern provinces bordering Sudan. They are a major challenge – variety of languages, harsh living conditions, lack of roads, violence and upheaval from Darfur. This is one of the least evangelized areas of Africa. French-Swiss AMI and **WEC** pioneered this area, but only among the Maba and Masalit has work been established with a few small groups of Muslim Background Believers. None of these 19 peoples have been properly reached with the gospel.

e) *The Sara-Bagirmi.* The Barma (linguistically closely related to the Bilala) were pioneered by **WEC**, the Lutheran Brethren and **AIM**, but there are only a handful of known believers. To their east, along the Chari River, live a medley of smaller people groups; some have been pioneer evangelized by EET-**AIM**, but much work remains to be done.

f) *The Shuwa Arabs.* Some are urbanized, some rural and some nomadic or semi-nomadic. They are influential in Chad; theirs is the main language of communication in the country. Little outreach is directed specifically toward them; **WEC** is attempting to make some beginnings.

g) *The Adamawa Fulbe and the nomadic Mbororo Fulbe* are responding to the gospel in the south, but much more needs to be done.

h) *N'Djamena,* the only city in the country and the nation's focal point. The city and outlying areas account for around one million people. Most of Chad's ethnic groups can be found – and evangelized – here. There are a host of congregations in N'Djamena, most focusing on their own ethnicity. There are also several French-language, multi-ethnic churches. AMI has a work among street children, and the **IMB** and others have a well-regarded study and culture centre that serves as a platform for a variety of ministries. Pray for missionaries working in N'Djamena and for others to be called. Pray also for the thousands of Christians in N'Djamena – for their effective witness and for the calling of some to cross-cultural outreach.

i) *Refugees from Darfur* number up to 250,000. Most are from the Ouaddai-Fur peoples, many of whom are disillusioned with Islam. Their situation will likely persist for some years to come and presents an unprecedented opportunity for many to know Christ.

7 **Ministry to young people.** Only larger urban churches have much ministry specifically for young people. Many Christian students are affiliated with *Union des Jeunes Chrétiens* (UJC/**IFES**), which has groups in two universities and 60 high schools. UJC has been used to pioneer student movements in many other Francophone African countries. **CCCI** is very active in Chad, as are SU, the Navigators and independent evangelists, ministering to both young people and students. The great need is for suitable literature, disciplers and trainers of leaders.

8 **Missionary work** continues despite the upheavals of the last three decades. Great needs remain for missions to continue and grow in the areas of church planting, evangelism, Bible translation, Bible teaching, leadership development and holistic ministry that will uplift and enable the national Church. Pray for missionaries with a pioneer spirit, perseverance in language and culture acquisition, and endurance to minister in hard places.

a) Foreign missions. The main groups work together under the EET Church in an organization called COCOAM. Present member missions: **TEAM**, **WEC**, AMI, Vision Africa, **AIM**, MEDAF. Other missions include **WBT**, Frontiers, **MAF** (with two planes), EMET and **IMB**. Numbers of workers have declined in almost every agency; pray that this may be offset by the emergence of Chadian workers meeting the needs rather than those needs going unaddressed. There are many needs and opportunities: Bible translation, radio, HIV/AIDS education, leadership training, preaching, administration, evangelism, community health education, women's ministry and a vernacular Bible school, just to name a few.

b) Indigenous missions. A small but growing number of Chadian missionaries are involved in pioneer church planting and Bible translation. The *Centre de Formation Missionnaire* (CFM) exists to prepare Chadians for cross-cultural mission. Pray for such centres to increase; pray for the students' provision and training. SMEET is the national mission agency that is part of the EET. **YWAM** has a training centre for Chadians wishing to become missionaries. There is encouraging vision in Chad's churches to send out workers; the greatest challenge is for these missionaries to remain focused on cross-cultural mission rather than to become pastors of groups of Christians from southern Chad.

9 **Christian specialized ministries:**

a) Bible translation and literacy programmes. Pray for rapid progress and for Chadian believers called to these ministries. The Chadian organization ATALTRAB (**WBT**) is assuming a greater share of the remaining work as well as giving literacy training to Christian peoples who have Bibles but do not use them (many Christians are illiterate). There are 22 Scripture translation projects currently active. The whole Bible is available in only 12 of Chad's 120-plus languages. The NT in Chadian Arabic (Chad's most widely used language) is nearing completion, and OT work is well underway. Pray for the ministry of the large **WBT** team, The Bible Society (particularly distribution) and for the key contributions of **WEC**, **AIM**, **TEAM** and others.

b) The JESUS film, widely used in Arabic, is also available in 11 other languages. The Chadian Arabic version is well received.

c) GRN has prepared Christian audio resources in 104 languages and dialects, working from a base in Northern Cameroon. Many more recordings and languages are planned. Audio Scripture Ministries, Faith Comes By Hearing and Megavoice also contribute to this vital work, made all the more strategic by the oral culture and low literacy rates. Pray that these recordings may be widely and effectively used.

d) Storying. The transmission of biblical truth through the development of series of stories (and occasionally songs or poems) is culturally appropriate and being greeted with great enthusiasm by several peoples and language groups.

e) Radio is the medium of choice in Chad. Local Christian radio – run entirely by nationals – is very well received in the capital. Pray for an expansion into other locations. Pray for more materials and contributors, especially for programmes in the languages of the unreached. Pray also for finances; at this early stage, the projects run on the tiniest of budgets. TV beamed from abroad may become the primary medium of the future, but as of now, radio still retains primacy.

f) Medical ministry is vital in Chad – both a huge opportunity and a challenge. From primary healthcare for the poor and refugees, to raising awareness and care related to HIV/AIDS, to Christian-run hospitals, the opportunities to be a blessing and a witness to the peoples of Chad, although very difficult, must be taken up, both by expat and by national believers.

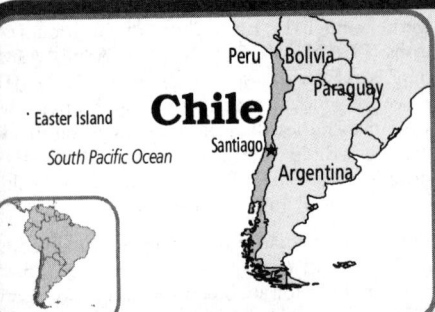

Chile

Peru, Bolivia, Paraguay, Easter Island, South Pacific Ocean, Santiago, Argentina

Chile

Republic of Chile

Latin America

Geography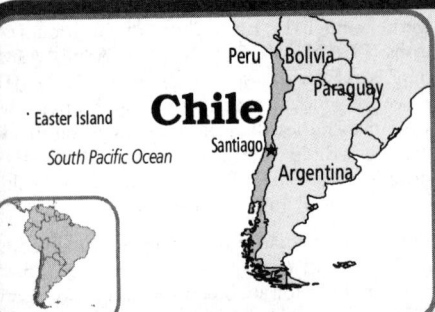

Area 756,626 sq km. A 4,200-km-long country wedged between the mountains of the Andes and the Pacific Ocean and averaging only 150 km in width. Also Easter Island/Rapa Nui in the Central Pacific. Great extremes from the hot, northern Atacama Desert to the Antarctic tundra in the south.

Population		Ann Gr	Density
2010	17,134,708	1.01%	23/sq km
2020	18,639,010	0.78%	25/sq km
2030	19,779,004	0.53%	26/sq km

About 40% of the population live near the capital, and 85% overall in the temperate central provinces.
Capital Santiago 5,951,554. **Other major city** Concepción 1.0million. **Urbanites** 89%. **Pop under 15 yrs** 23%. **Life expectancy** 78.5 yrs.

Peoples

A relatively homogeneous society.
Hispanic 95.9%. Chilean Hispanic 94.7% (estimated 51.9% white Hispanic, 42.8% Mestizo); other Latin American 1.2%.
Amerindian 3.2%. 7 peoples. Mapuche (Auracan) 1.8%; Huilliche 1.0%; Aymara 0.3%.
Other 0.9%. European, Asian, Middle Eastern.
Literacy 95.7%. **Official language** Spanish (but Mapudungun increasingly recognized). **All languages** 16. **Indigenous languages** 9. **Languages with Scriptures** 2Bi 1NT 2por 1w.i.p.

Economy

Mining and mineral exports are the most important economic activities; to a degree, the Chilean economy rises and falls on international copper prices. One of the more developed Latin American economies, with solid sectors in industry, agriculture and service. Has been boosted by an economic mini-boom after several years of a dragging economy. Poverty still widespread.
HDI Rank 44th/182. **Public debt** 5.2% of GDP. **Income/person** $10,117 (21% of USA).

Politics

Republic independent from Spain in 1810. The socialist government elected in 1970 was ousted in a bloody military coup in 1973. The controversial Pinochet regime imposed political conformity and economic change with many cases of human rights abuses. This painful legacy still affects the country deeply. The referendum and electoral defeats in 1988/89 opened the way for a democratic government.

Religion

The Catholic Church was disestablished in 1925 but still has a strong influence on society. There is liberty of faith and worship for all religions, by law and in practice.

Religions	Pop %	Population	Ann Gr
Christian	87.23	14,946,606	0.8%
Non-religious	10.48	1,795,717	1.0%
Ethnoreligionist	0.85	145,645	0.8%
Jewish	0.80	137,078	43.1%
Baha'i	0.40	68,539	28.5%
Muslim	0.20	34,269	-6.9%
Buddhist	0.04	6,854	-6.9%

Christians	Denoms	Pop %	Affiliates	Ann Gr
Protestant	51	11.69	2,003,000	1.7%
Independent	276	9.24	1,583,000	3.9%
Anglican	1	0.12	21,000	4.0%
Catholic	1	62.15	10,650,000	-0.7%
Orthodox	5	0.07	12,000	-2.4%
Marginal	2	4.12	706,000	1.1%
Unaffiliated		4.80	822,000	10.0%
Doubly affiliated		*-4.96*	*-850,000*	*0.0%*

Churches	MegaBloc	Congs	Members	Affiliates
Catholic Church	C	850	6,377,246	10,650,000
Pente Methodist Ch	P	2,649	423,810	890,000
Evang Pente Ch of C	I	2,563	435,664	623,000
Latter-day Saints (Mormon)	M	757	335,329	560,000
Evang Pente Meth Ch	P	1,722	137,762	197,000
Pentecostal Ch of Chile	P	459	137,762	197,000
Jehovah's Witnesses	M	750	75,000	146,250
Seventh-day Adventist	P	567	119,130	137,000
Voice in the Desert	I	932	55,909	123,000
United Meth Pent Ch	P	423	84,615	121,000
Evang Army of Chile	I	400	56,000	72,800
CMA	P	199	18,100	70,000
Baptist Convention	P	262	27,500	64,000
Other denominations[322]		11,472	1,130,975	1,923,272
Doubly affiliated Pentecostals				*-800,000*
Doubly affiliated				*-850,000*

| Total Christians[336] | | 24,005 | 9,414,802 | 14,124,322 |

Estimates for Pentecostals vary widely, reliable statistics are not kept by these groups.

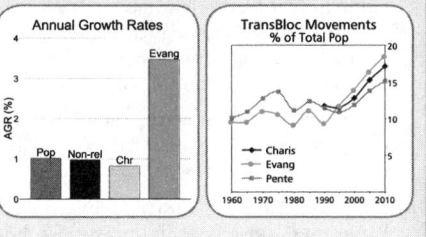

TransBloc	Pop %	Population	Ann Gr
Evangelicals			
Evangelicals	18.4	3,157,647	3.5%
Renewalists			
Charismatics	17.1	2,936,101	3.4%
Pentecostals	15.1	2,592,093	2.9%

Missionaries from Chile

P,I,A 198 (149 long-term) in 25 agencies: to Chile 35, elsewhere in South America 63, Europe 34.

Answers to Prayer

1 **Progress from dictatorship to democracy** and its social and economic stability place Chile in a rarified state for a Latin American country. People-power helped oust the military in 1988 and recently catalyzed action on social reforms, especially in the areas of education and poverty.

2 **The growth of evangelicals** in the last 40 years brings their number to 18% of the population. This growth is unique; a Pentecostal revival in 1909 within the Methodist Church gave birth to a dynamic, indigenous Pentecostal movement with evangelistic zeal. Growth is still occurring across almost all denominations with an evangelical presence. Recent emphases by the many Pentecostal denominations on ministering to the poor and cooperating together are both signs of a maturing movement.

Challenges for Prayer

1 **Chile must move on** from its scarred past and the pains of Pinochet's legacy – including a bloody coup, severe repression, more than 3,000 murdered and many times that number abused. Democratic structures have grown strong, but much progress is still needed for a fair, just and prosperous Chile to emerge. Forgiveness and grace are essential for this to happen.

2 **Social changes in Chile** reflect the shifts in life and belief in this traditionally conservative nation. Liberalization yields both positive and negative effects. Divorce was only recently legalized; before that, the number of marriages performed dropped by 45%, and 60% of children were born out of wedlock. One out of seven Chilean women is a mother by the age of 14. Crime, drug abuse and materialism are all on the rise. Many are disaffiliating themselves from traditional religious structures, with large numbers leaving both Catholicism and Pentecostalism. Pray that the positive aspects of traditional social structures would be affirmed and strengthened.

3 **The Roman Catholic Church** has recently declined in many ways:

a) *Identification tied to the former regime* and the past. In the past, both the dictatorship and the more powerful classes favoured Catholicism, and the Church did not do enough to assist the poor or to oppose injustice.

b) *Loss of political and social influence,* now that there is equality of all religions before the law. Liberalizing social forces see issues such as divorce, cohabitation and birth control increasingly commonplace.

c) *The perception of irrelevance.* The more dynamic and fast-moving evangelical groups have seized initiative with programmes and ministry for and on behalf of the poor. The same can be said of the upper classes, drawn to the success mentality of Pentecostals.

d) *Major losses in affiliates.* The explosive growth of Pentecostalism and the equally rapid increase of non-religious (or non-affiliated) sentiments have seen Catholicism decrease in just 20 years, from 82% of Chile's population to 62%. The majority of those remaining in the

Church treat Catholicism as a traditional identity rather than a deliberate life of faith. Only 12-13% of Catholics regularly attend mass. Pray that Catholics may adapt to a new era. Pray for Bible reading and reform to take place on a much deeper level, so that many might find their faith renewed and discover the living Jesus.

4 **Evangelicals face unprecedented opportunities as well as challenges.** They are poised to exercise a pivotal role in Chilean society. The danger remains that goodwill and respect may be eroded by failures and squandered opportunities. Pray about these key issues:

a) Fragmentation and unity. Chile holds the dubious honour of having the most divisive Pentecostal movement in the world. Churches and denominations split with alarming regularity, with already over 1,200 separate groups. The culture of division must be overcome by a solid commitment to unity – and this can only be achieved through humility, graciousness and repentance. Major unity meetings among the main Pentecostal groups from 2008 onward might point toward future progress in this area.

b) Nominalism and traditionalism. Long-term growth and consolidation have generated a more formal Pentecostalism that is often without spiritual gifts and true revival. Pentecostal nominalism is rife – less than half attend church weekly, and one-third do not attend regularly at all. Outdated leadership models and ministry patterns only enlarge the problem. Pray for a new Pentecost and revival amid these thousands of churches.

c) Poor leadership development manifests itself through inadequate training, lazy theology, legalism and replacement of solid biblical exegesis with personal opinions and visions. Pray for TEE (SEAN, FLET) programmes and the various theological institutions addressing this widespread need, such as the National Bible Institute of Chile, with 1,000 students in the capital and throughout the regions. Interest in training for pastors and laity is thankfully increasing.

d) Isolationism. Of the 18.4% of the population that are evangelical, almost 90% belong to indigenous groups that have reached many, but they do not work together locally and have no links with the global Church. This leaves the door open to theological error and abuse, and it stunts the potential for mission and ministry.

5 **The upper strata of society** have traditionally avoided evangelicalism, but this is changing. There is a notable shift toward identifying with non-Catholic Christianity. This is particularly true for denominations originating from outside Chile. Baptist groups, **CMA**, Anglicans (**CMS**), **AoG, CoN, SIM** and others have made some progress in planting churches among them. Pray for this group to experience the life-changing gospel in a dramatic way and for their influence to affect the nation for God's purposes.

6 **The poor** have, historically, been the recruiting ground for Pentecostals, consistent with global patterns. Ministry to them has been almost exclusively spiritual, but recently holistic ministry has grown, with greater focus on education, training and material assistance. Pray that the massive gap between the rich and poor in Chile might be addressed – by government, by churches and by missions.

7 **The Chilean Church lacks missions vision.** Its contribution for its size is very small, with little concern for world evangelization. The country's geographical and spiritual isolation and political upheaval all contribute to this deficiency. By setting up missions' training programmes, **COMIBAM** and locally based mission agencies (**OM, YWAM, CMA**, CENCAMI, **SIM, WBT** and others) have influenced the Latin American missions movement and stimulated some interest in missions.

8 **Foreign missions in Chile.** The major agencies are: **YWAM, ABWE, CC/CC, CB/** CMML, **AoG**, CC(USA), **MTW.** The major tasks by which missionaries can serve the Chilean Church are in teaching, developing leadership, building up holistic programmes and encouraging a missions vision. Pioneer work is limited to some people groups listed below and among the richest and poorest of society. Pray for a significant and lasting impact by these workers on Chile.

9 **Less-reached peoples.** Ethnic minorities, both indigenous and immigrant, find life in Chile to be difficult and are often faced with prejudice.

a) The Mapuche (speaking Mapudungun) are by far the largest and most independent of Chile's indigenous peoples. A strong nationalist movement is agitating successfully for improved land rights and cultural recognition. About 70% are nominally Catholic, but the old animistic religion is still the most influential spiritual force, along with their traditional religious shamans. The Anglican Church has a solid work among the Mapuche, with about 4,000 Christians. **CMA, AoG, MTW** and others have initiated work among them; **SIM** is developing Mapudungun TEE programmes. The Pentecostals have won many Mapuche migrants in the cities. The Mapudungun NT was completed in 1997.

b) Rapa Nui (Easter Islanders) are a largely Polynesian people. Most now live on the mainland, even as ethnic Chileans become the majority in their home islands. Their society is being overrun, they are losing their culture and language and the influence of many outside forces (tourism, film industry, AIDS and alcohol) are taking their toll. Most are nominally Catholic, but there are now four congregations of evangelicals and some missionaries working among them. The Rapa Nui NT was just recently completed.

c) Other Latin Americans. Chile's stability has attracted hundreds of thousands of Peruvians, Ecuadorians and Bolivians; they come as illegal migrants, and all face discrimination and injustice.

d) The Jews of Santiago can be regarded as an unevangelized people.

e) The Romani (Gypsies) are neglected by Christians and by society in general. The SdA have three churches with about 400 affiliates among them. The Chilean Romani NT was completed in 2005.

f) Palestinian immigrants have recently been arriving in large numbers. Santiago has over 70,000 Christian Palestinians (mostly Orthodox and Catholic), the largest concentration in the world outside of Palestine.

10 **Student witness** needs strengthening in the 54 universities and colleges and among the 500,000 students. There are now 25 GBU(**IFES**) groups, up from 14 in 2000. **CCCI** (16 full-time workers) has some impact in secondary schools and some universities. But Chile's evangelicals need to focus much more on reaching and discipling young people. Systemic inequalities and underinvestment in education prompted massive student demonstrations in 2006, which in turn forced government reforms. Pray for students to find their identity in Christ and not in the many other alternatives they face.

11 **Christian media:**

a) Literature is a useful but under-utilized evangelistic and teaching tool in a non-literary culture. **CLC** is the only major book distributor in the country; pray for its 35 national workers, seven bookstores and large wholesale distribution network.

b) Christian radio and TV programmes are widely available, with more than 60 Christian radio stations. Radio's influence on the spread of the gospel in Chile is massive. The first national evangelical TV channel started in 2008; pray that TV and the Internet would be used to grow and build the Church and to reach non-believers.

Han 0.4%; Min Zhong Han 0.2%; Puxian Han 0.2%; Subei 0.2%; Min Bei Han 0.2%; Pinghua Han 0.2%.
Chinese–Hui 1.3%. 4 peoples. Hui 1.0%; Huizhou 0.4%.
Manchu 1.0%.
Mongolian 0.7%. 19 peoples. Mongol 0.5%.
Other East Asian 0.3%. Korean, Japanese, Taiwanese.
Southeast Asian 3.3%. 167 peoples in southern provinces.
Zhuang 1.2%. 24 peoples. Central Hongshuihe 0.2%; Eastern Hongshuihe 0.2%.
Miao/Hmong 0.7%. 47 peoples.
Tai 0.5%. 28 peoples. Southern Dong 0.2%.
Yao–Mien 0.4%. 29 peoples.
Bouyei 0.2%. 5 peoples.
Other Southeast Asian 0.3%. Li, Mon-Khmer, Shan, Vietnamese people clusters.
Tibetan/Himalayan 2.5%. 238 peoples in western and southwestern provinces.
Nosu 0.2%. 7 peoples.
Tibetan 0.5%. 65 peoples.
West China/Yi 1.6%. 137 peoples. Tujia 0.7%; Bai 0.2%.
Other Tibetan/Himalayan 0.2%.
Turkic 1.0%. 26 peoples in northwest. Uyghur 0.8%.
Other 0.1%. Western, Iranian-Median, Malay peoples, African, Arab, Jews.
Literacy 91%. **Official language** Putonghua (Mandarin Chinese); local languages in the five Autonomous Regions. 15 regional mega-languages. There are an estimated 600 different spoken Han dialects, but one written language common to all. **All languages** 296. **Languages with Scriptures** 24Bi 16NT 27por.

China

People's Republic of China

Asia

(See p252 for Hong Kong, p256 for Macau, and p258 for Taiwan.)

Geography

Area 9,573,000 sq km. The fourth-largest state in the world, also containing the highest mountains and plateaus in the world. The climate and geography are extremely diverse, ranging from tropical in the south to sub-arctic in the north, from a highly industrialized and modern eastern seaboard to sparsely populated western deserts and mountain ranges. Hong Kong and Macau are integral parts of China, though their statistics are not included here; Taiwan's status is debated. These three are handled separately.

Population		Ann Gr	Density
2010	1,330,584,783	0.63%	139/sq km
2020	1,406,717,659	0.50%	147/sq km
2030	1,437,790,295	0.13%	150/sq km

Capital Beijing (Peking) 12,385,263. **Other major cities** Shanghai 16.6 million; Chongqing 9.4mill; Tianjin 7.9m. 111 cities or conurbations of over 1m inhabitants (included by province below). **Urbanites** 44.9% (unofficially considerably higher). **Pop under 15 yrs** 20%. **Life expectancy** 72.9 yrs.

Peoples

There are close to 500 indigenous, distinct ethnic groups, but 55 "nationalities" officially recognized for administrative convenience. Over many centuries of regional domination, the Han peoples have assimilated dozens, if not hundreds, of other ethnicities.
East Asian 93.1%. 73 peoples.
Chinese 89.8%. 41 peoples. Mandarin Han 60.1%; Wu Han 6.7%; Cantonese Han 4.8%; Jin Han 4.5%; Gan Han %; Xiang Han 2.8%; Min Nan Han 2.6%; Hakka 2.6%; Min Dong Han 0.7%; Hainanese Han 0.4%; Dan

Economy

The application of Maoist/Marxist economics from 1948 onward was a disaster, most pronounced during the Great Leap Forward and then the Cultural Revolution. Since 1978, pragmatists have exerted increasing influence on economic policy – reflected in the degree of liberalization applied to agriculture but even more so to industry and business. The result is "Chinese socialism", a form of socialized market economy. The last three decades of centrally managed change and growth have greatly raised China's living standards. The greatest growth has been in the coastal region and a few larger inland cities. After two centuries of eclipse, the nation's economic might is once again global, with China now the world's second-largest economy. It is also the world's largest holder of foreign exchange reserves; its role in global finance will be profound, and its economic policies will shape the world in the 21st Century. Quite apart from the tensions between centralized control and privatization, managing growth into the future will face monumental challenges. The huge amounts of natural resources required to maintain – never mind expand – such a massive economy have forced China to increasingly engage with other resource-rich nations, especially in the developing Global South. Impending crises loom in the areas of environmental degradation, healthcare, pensions, privacy, property ownership and unsustainable growth and consumption. Corruption, scandal, unethical business practices and illegal economic activity (such as human and drug trafficking) sadly abound, and China's human rights record abroad does it no favours. Massive urbanization and soaring social problems such as internal migration, family breakdown, suicide, divorce and unbalanced male-female ratios all add fuel to the potential fire. Nevertheless, managing the stability of a country of over 1.3 billion and lifting an unprecedented number of people out of poverty are themselves remarkable and unparalleled achievements.

HDI Rank 92nd/182. **Public debt** 15.6% of GDP. **Income/person** $3,259 (7% of USA).

Politics 🗡

This great and ancient nation has regained its place of importance in the world after nearly two centuries of decline and humiliation at the hands of Western powers and Japan. After the final conquest of mainland China in 1949, the Communist Party remoulded the nation along Marxist lines. The Cultural Revolution (1966-76) was the culmination of Mao Zedong's policy and caused great suffering. It is estimated that 20 million Chinese lost their lives during that time. Mao's death in 1976 was followed by a more pragmatic leadership under Deng Xiaoping. He initiated a series of carefully controlled economic, political and cultural reforms, but the crushing of the 1989 student protest in Tiananmen Square in Beijing and the collapse of Communism in Europe and the USSR left China diplomatically isolated. It responded by reverting to ideological rigidity and by increasing crackdowns on political, ethnic and religious dissent. From the 1990s onward, other extensive reforms have occurred, but still with tight state control over most sectors of life and society. Repression of minorities and dissidents, systemic violations of the rights to privacy and expression and a harsh penal code continue to plague China's political profile. China faces notable political challenges at home and abroad, with current ethnic and diplomatic tensions (Uyghurs, Tibetans, Taiwanese) as well as inevitable pressures and expectations as it emerges into the role of a world superpower. The social ills facing China are many, but an emerging civil sector, including both private and government-owned aid and development groups, will go a long way toward assisting the struggles.

Religion 🔥

Suppression and strict administrative control of religious groups characterize the years under the Communist regime; the government continues to strictly control the five officially recognized religious groups (Buddhism, Daoism, Islam, Protestant, Catholic) through a state-monitored patriotic association for each – including the Three-Self Patriotic Movement (TSPM) among Protestants and the Catholic Patriotic Association (CPA) among Catholics. During the Cultural Revolution, even these acquiescent structures were banned and all religious activity was forced underground, giving birth to the house church movement. In 1978, restrictions were eased and the TSPM and CPA resurrected as a means of regaining governmental influence over religious expression. By this point, however, the momentum of growth among unregistered churches was too strong to rein in; further persecution seemed to only encourage further growth, despite horrendous cruelties inflicted on many thousands of church leaders. More Christians are detained in China than in any other country, but many regard the persecution of house churches as an issue of political control rather than of religious freedom. The 21st Century sees signs of relative easing of persecution and pressure on most religious groups. Some say with cautious optimism that this is the beginning of real openness by the Party to grant true religious freedom and to utilize religious faith as a means to combat corruption, instill positive morals and cope with China's increasingly materialistic society, which is emerging with little by way of moral framework. The state recently recognized that there are over 300 million religious believers and over 50 million Christians in unregistered church networks. The traditional beliefs of the Chinese and many minorities are a blend of folk religions, Daoism and Buddhism. Buddhists are of three major strands: Mahayana and Theravada Buddhism, among Chinese and southern peoples such as Dai, Zhuang and others, and Lamaistic Buddhism among Tibetan and Mongolian peoples of the west and north. Islam is dominant in Xinjiang and Ningxia and is the major religion of the Hui, Uyghur, Dongxiang and other Turkic peoples. There are no confirmed numbers for religious/Christian data apart from the state-controlled structures of the TSPM and CPA; all others are estimates.

Religions	Pop %	Population	Ann Gr
Non-religious	44.36	590,247,410	0.2%
Chinese	28.50	379,216,663	-0.1%
Buddhist	12.50	166,323,098	2.5%
Christian	7.92	105,382,315	2.7%
Ethnoreligionist	4.55	60,541,608	1.1%
Muslim	1.87	24,881,935	0.3%
Other	0.30	3,991,754	4.4%

The historic hostility of the government toward any religious expression, and the fact that normative practice of religion has been private/secret, mean that exact statistics for religions do not exist. These are estimates based on government information and the work of China-focused researchers.

Christians	Denoms	Pop %	Affiliates	Ann Gr
Protestant	1	2.24	29,846,000	2.2%
Independent	680	4.12	54,833,000	3.0%
Catholic	2	1.60	21,295,000	2.7%
Orthodox	2	<0.01	17,000	5.5%
Marginal	21	0.23	3,053,000	3.7%
Doubly affiliated		-0.27	-3,600,000	0.0%

Churches	MegaBloc	Congs	Members	Affiliates
House Church Networks	I	997,333	34,906,667	52,360,000
TSPM/CCC	P	60,910	21,318,571	29,846,000
Roman Catholic Ch	C	36,821	9,573,427	13,690,000
Cath Patriotic Assoc	C	6,560	5,805,344	7,605,000
Ethnic minority chs	I	10,991	1,648,667	2,473,000
Orthodox Ch of China	O	94	9,444	17,000
Other denominations[25]		6,365	1,907,950	3,052,550
Doubly affiliated				-3,600,000
Total Christians[706]	**1,119,074**	**75,170,070**	**105,443,550**	

Official statistics exist only for the TSPM and CPA (who deliberately underreport and do not count children or unbaptized non-members). Estimates given by various official and house-church network leaders are used here. As the government becomes more accepting and transparent regarding the existence and scale of the unregistered house church networks, a number of China-watchers who attempt to enumerate Christians find their respective estimates growing increasingly closer to one another.

TransBloc	Pop %	Population	Ann Gr
Evangelicals			
Evangelicals	5.7	75,399,270	2.9%
Renewalists			
Charismatics	2.1	28,240,180	4.5%

Missionaries from China
P,I,A 120,000 long-term: 118,000 in China, 20,000 cross-cultural.

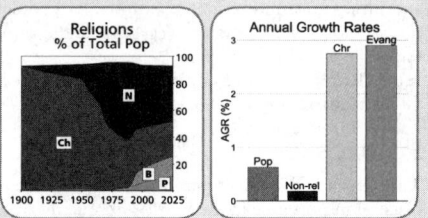

Religions % of Total Pop

Annual Growth Rates

Answers to Prayer

1 **The survival and growth of the Church** in China are two of the decisive events of our generation. The staggering recent growth of the Chinese Church has no parallel in history – from 2.7 million evangelicals in 1975 to over 75 million in 2010. Much growth is among the majority Han Chinese, with some growth among minority groups. A few groups with no known believers among them in the late 1990s now have networks of growing house churches.

2 **The faith and commitment of Christians** under what may have been the harshest and most widespread persecution of the Church in all history. Persecution and suffering refined the Church and shaped it to withstand successive waves of repression and government efforts to weaken or destroy it. God, powerfully working through the unwitting atheist rulers of China, cleared spiritual roadblocks for the advancement of Christianity through Mao Zedong; freed up the economy and gave more freedom to Christians through Deng; and, through Hu Jintao, God guided China to new levels of interconnectedness with the rest of the world, strengthening the link between the Chinese Church and the worldwide body of Christ.

3 **Christians are now found in every stratum of Chinese society.** The emergence of vibrant urban professional churches – a third expression of faith distinct from the official churches and traditionally rural house churches – marks a turning point for Christianity in China. Tragedies such as the Tiananmen Square (1989) massacre and the handling of the SARS epidemic (2002) spurred many to seek answers to difficult life questions. Corruption within the government and society has further disillusioned people. One result of such ideological disillusionment – together with rising distaste for crass materialism – has been a significant turning to God for the first time among urban professionals and rural and minority populations.

4 **Christians are engaging in social causes** and impacting the lives of millions. With social programmes once provided solely by the government but now often absent in a privatizing economy, the Church offers a platform to address these needs. Some faith groups form NGOs or serve communities in a less structured manner. The gospel confers strength in Jesus to face life's challenges and to demonstrate love for others in Christ-like service.

5 **The government's changing attitude and approach toward the Church,** particularly the unregistered Church. While substantial opposition and persecution remain, the Chinese government now, for the first time, recognizes the size of the unregistered Church as being at least 50 million and is making overtures toward its leaders. The Church is of such size and influence that it can no longer be ignored or denied; furthermore, the state is recognizing faith-based organizations' potential for addressing social ills.

6 **Welcome changes in government and society** in the last decade include another peaceful transition of power (this time to Hu Jintao), a series of fruitful economic reforms, pursuit of a socio-economically ideal "harmonious society", intensified opposition to corruption and graft in politics and a shift toward more transparency – as evidenced in the proactive handling of H1N1 after the ill-advised response to SARS. Perhaps most significantly, China's civil sector is being allowed to flourish and may usher in a new social conscience that rises from the people rather than being imposed upon them.

7 **There is a growing unity within the Church** – particularly among urban professional churches – strengthened through the joint response of state churches and underground congregations to the devastating 2008 Sichuan and 2010 Qijang earthquakes. The love and compassion extended by Christian relief workers were visible to many, including the government. This opportunity to serve together marked a turning point in modern Chinese Church history, a new era for both the Church's fundamental unity and its role within 21st Century China.

8 **Missions vision in the Church** – to unreached minorities within China and unevangelized nations beyond – is flourishing.

9 **Praise God for the growth of Christian media** as a means of spreading the gospel, the Word of God and Christian teaching. The fruitfulness of Christian radio and the remarkable faith of those who had broadcast into China for years with little visible evidence of a response are now plain to see. The Internet is also creating extraordinary new openings for sharing the gospel, for discipling and for communicating with believers and seekers. Perhaps most astonishing is the emergence of Christian publishing within China; although challenges remain in terms of quantities and distribution, Bibles and Christian book titles are being produced in impressive quantities.

Challenges for Prayer

General

1 **The window of opportunity for spiritual receptivity** might not be open indefinitely. China today faces materialism – with increasing wealth, the debilitating effects of spreading corruption, moral decline and the growing social and economic impact of the one-child policy. All of these may profoundly affect the spiritual openness of the nation and the Church itself. Pray that the Refiner's fire might keep burning and that the Church's spiritual cutting edge – honed in the midst of persecution – might not be blunted.

2 **China's rising role on the world stage** – demonstrated powerfully through the 2008 Olympics – is shaping what some call the "Chinese Century". China now holds astounding influence on world economics and politics, particularly throughout the Global South. Countless billions of dollars have been invested in Asia, Africa and Latin America to develop trade and goodwill and to exert influence. Yet, China itself remains politically oppressive and is wracked with corruption. Pray for God's Sovereign hand at work in and through the Chinese government; pray that all forms of wickedness may be opposed, that kindness be shown to the oppressed and that justice and prosperity for all be the goals of China's economic and foreign policies.

3 **China remains officially atheist,** and Communist Party members number well over 70 million. But the Christian population has eclipsed this number (it is also far outstripped by Chinese Buddhists). Increasing numbers of Party members are believers. Pray that the atheism promoted for so long – and now so assiduously propagated in the education system – will finally be revealed as hollow and deceptive lies. Pray also that all followers of Christ working in state structures might walk faultlessly and be a redemptive force within the government.

4 **Opposing forces at work in Chinese society** are creating tensions that demand urgent attention and foresight. The reformed central government struggles to maintain control over state authorities and trusts economic growth to solve most of the country's problems. But China's sheer size, its financial boom and the lack of freedom of information conspire to multiply injustices, expand the gap between rich and poor and defeat the egalitarian purposes of socialism. The following points of mounting pressure bear mention:

a) *Freedom of information.* The government vainly tries to control the flow of and exposure to information, while also promoting Internet use. But a bored and disillusioned new generation that hankers after freedom is not only finding creative ways to access information, but many are also developing potentially dangerous hacking skills in the process.

b) *Political and economic reforms.* Resistance to substantial political change is irreconcilable with the juggernaut of capitalism (and its results: crass materialism and personal greed). Issues surrounding property ownership, banking, the widening gap between rich and poor, private versus state-provided social services – to name just a few – beset policy-makers and must be addressed.

c) *Corruption and scandal.* Embezzlement, graft and widespread deception plague both government and business. China tops the list of countries willing to pay bribes in business, and rampant cheating and fraud tarnish academia. China's record on containing corruption has regressed, while other countries have made progress or remained the same in this area.

d) *Urbanization.* China now hosts the most massive human migration in history. In just a couple of generations, hundreds of millions of rural dwellers have relocated to China's urban centres, drastically changing the nation's demographics. Many millions simply cannot make a living farming, and urbanites earn 350% more than rural-area workers. Such rapid migration to urban areas leaves families lacking basic social services and educational opportunities, and creates problems such as overcrowding and unemployment.

e) *Ethnic unrest.* Internal strife remains at the forefront of both national and international attention, as conflict within Tibet and Xianjiang persists. Ultimately, reconciliation and the hope of peace lie only in the power of the gospel.

Coming change is inevitable and will be massive; pray that it might be well managed, peaceful and ultimately of spiritual benefit to China.

5 **Challenges of population growth** afflict Chinese with sobering troubles both now and even more acutely in the future. Although restrictions and their implementation are loosening, effects of the grievous "one-child policy" on society continue to be severe. The Chinese perform in excess of 13 million abortions per year, now a widely accepted form of birth control, particularly sex-specific (female) abortions. Many infants, if not aborted, are abandoned or kidnapped and trafficked. Some children who are raised without siblings are unduly pampered, potentially creating a sub-culture of self-absorption and indulgence. Further complications include

a) *Gender imbalance.* The rising generation will pay perhaps the heaviest cost related to the one-child policy, with studies predicting 20-30 million men left single by the year 2020. In some areas, young men outnumber young women by 30-40%; rape, abductions, female slavery, incest, prostitution, widespread homosexuality and the rapid spread of AIDS could be the results.

b) *Work force.* Coming decades will see a significant decrease in young workers for certain sectors of industry and the military in particular.

c) *Care for the elderly.* With fewer children available to care for aging parents, and with changes in pensions provided by the state, the need for elder care in the coming generation will present a burden on Chinese society. Many elders are, as with young children, abandoned and left without sufficient care.

Pray for wise policies to be implemented that will stabilize the population.

6 **Social and health needs** in China overwhelm the available resources. Pray that Christians in the caring and social professions find many openings to serve the suffering and to show and speak to them about the love of Jesus. Pray also for Christian lawyers who attempt to stand for justice on behalf of those unable to do so themselves. Pray specifically for:

a) *Those with disease and ill health.* Millions suffer with tuberculosis, diabetes is on a rapid rise and hundreds of thousands are HIV positive. Since the government changed its attitude on reporting infection rates, Christians now have more opportunities than ever to care for HIV patients and others suffering from debilitating and terminal diseases. Drug-use rates are rapidly increasing – now over one million users, two-thirds of whom are under age 35. Smoking is a ticking time bomb – 350 million smokers consume over two trillion cigarettes a year.

b) *The disabled.* Around 83 million disabled, or one-fifth of the world's total, live in China. Yearly, over 1.2 million are born with defects, and the number is rising. The medical profession is ill-equipped to offer sufficient help to the 40 million affected by mental illness. Praise God that China's hosting of the Paralympics in 2008 brought improvements in public perception and in quality of life and treatment for the disabled.

c) *The vulnerable and helpless.* Those most open to abuse and oppression remain women, orphans (three million in orphanages), refugees (especially from North Korea) and the millions living in poverty. Pray that true justice be administered, that rescue be granted to those in imminent danger and that mercy and compassion be shown to these through Christ's followers.

d) *The depressed and hopeless.* China now has the highest number of suicides in the world at nearly 300,000 per year, a majority of whom are women. Mental health issues are possibly the most urgent social need in China. Divorce rates are skyrocketing (1.5 million/year). Family and community life are deeply changed. Pray for family stability and well-being. Pray for many Christians to get involved in drug rehabilitation, marital counselling and suicide prevention.

e) *The overlooked.* Many suffer indignity and oppression unseen by most – the elderly without care, victims of natural disasters struggling to rebuild, migrants making their way in over-crowded enclaves of Chinese megacities, minority communities and those in the harsh penal system. Jesus sees and remembers them all; pray that the Church might also.

7 **China faces environmental disasters** on many fronts; possibly her heaviest burdens directly resulting from great economic achievements. Pollution of China's water sources has surpassed crisis level, and the combined effects of land, air and water pollution result in hundreds of thousands of deaths per year – to say nothing of the numbers born with defects or suffering environmentally-related illness. Chemical pollutants from agricultural and industrial waste continue to render Chinese cities and rural areas, as well as neighbouring countries, rife with dangers. Desertification of the northern provinces, combined with population growth, will affect millions in coming years. China has recently taken unprecedented steps toward addressing environmental concerns, though falling short of substantial progress. Pray for a government courageous and trusted enough to make the difficult decisions required for the long-term well-being of the nation.

The Church in China

1 **God has protected and grown the Church in China** on a scale unforeseen by anyone a few decades ago. Persecution designed to destroy the Church served instead to purify her through suffering and the power of the Holy Spirit, who inspired fervent prayer and zealous evangelism. By the 1980s, vast networks and communities of these believers met in house churches designed to withstand the harsh treatment meted out by the state. Through radio ministries, greater numbers of Christian workers in China and believers devoted to outreach, the Church saw great growth across the late 20th Century and into the new millennium. Pray for:

a) *The Three-Self Patriotic Movement and the China Christian Council (TSPM/CCC),* which together form the only state-recognized Protestant Church within China. Significant privileges of position include the ability to legally print and distribute Christian materials as well as to register and build church buildings. Limitations have long affected teaching, outreach and discipleship as well as the ability to grow at pace with the desires and needs of some congregations. Pray for:

   i *Increased printing and distribution of Bibles and Christian materials.* The value of such resources to both the TSPM and indeed all Christians in China is inestimable. The need and demand for such materials are enormous.

   ii *The neutralization of all attempts to impose unbiblical doctrines* on churches, to limit outreach and to forcibly restrict the life and ministry of the Church. Pray for revival and renewal to purify the TSPM and its associated churches. In the past, certain doctrines and practices were imposed on the TSPM as a state church of an atheistic regime, which greatly blunted its potential impact.

iii Future growth, under wise leadership, unhindered by limitations on resources. The TSPM/CCC has experienced consistently notable growth since its reconstitution in 1978. Pray for TSPM/CCC leaders and congregations to continue growing in their faith and sharing Christ with an increasingly interested Chinese population.

b) ***The traditional house-church networks*** have been for many decades the dynamic core of the Chinese Church. Being unregistered, they are therefore illegal and liable to great pressure by the government. Intense persecution forced these churches to adopt indigenous patterns and to focus on prayer, revival, simple living and a Christocentric theology. Their zealous outreach and passionate mission vision resulted in its world-changing growth and influence. Pray for:

i Relations between traditional house-church networks and the government. Long suffering underground with the label "sect" or "cult", the large majority of these networks decided not to pursue registration. This decision invites further pressure and persecution from the state. Most house church Christians are patriotic Chinese, but whose loyalty is first to God.

ii Adaptations that must occur due to vast migration of Chinese from rural to urban areas. Congregations and networks have been destabilized and disrupted as individuals and families shift locations, leaving some countryside groups leaderless and many migrants without church groups. Pray that the legacy of fervency, missions vision, commitment to God's Word and the power of the Holy Spirit will continue to define this movement as it undergoes such fundamental change.

iii Protection from heretical sects and doctrinally extremist groups. The lack of Bible knowledge and a paucity of leadership open the way for many exotic messianic, syncretistic and divisive groups. Some of these have spread over much of China, such as the aggressive and heretical Eastern Lightning cult. Pray that these groups' growth might be foiled by the proclamation of God's truth through biblical teaching, radio and literature.

iv Ongoing evangelistic outreach. Witnessing Christians and itinerant preachers have spread far and wide, despite often violent opposition from authorities. But many provinces, districts and towns are still unreached. Pray that Christians may continue to be bold for Jesus and implement their missionary strategy for reaching China.

c) ***Other house church networks,*** though smaller and often less organized than traditional ones, still represent substantial segments of the Chinese Church. Many of these are among indigenous minority groups formed because of radio broadcasts and related ministries. More recently, churches are emerging within the workplace, such as those within factories or offices owned or managed by Christians.

d) ***The urban professional Church*** has truly changed the face of Chinese Christianity in the last ten years. Many younger professionals, students and professors encountered Jesus while studying abroad, through campus Bible study groups or other forms of outreach, and returned to China eager to engage urban society with their newfound faith. These well-educated and energetic believers are strategically placed to impact the future of China, which will belong to those of influence within government, business, media, academia, the legal profession and the emerging civil sector. The growing Christian movement within these sectors relates to the government differently from any other Christian group. Pray for:

i This amazing work of God to continue as He draws many more unto Himself.

ii Leaders who are currently overstretched, balancing needs of families and the demands of careers with ministry and leadership in churches.

iii New models of ministry and church that will reach China's changing demographic.

iv Legal status that allows these churches to engage in social welfare work; many desire to bless their communities in such a way.

e) ***The Catholic Church*** was divided when the government set up the Catholic Patriotic Association in 1957 with its own structure and hierarchy independent of the Vatican. The majority of Catholics went "underground", with their own bishops and illegal seminaries. Catholics loyal to the Vatican suffered severe persecution because of their commitment to a foreign leader. There have been decades of rapprochement between the two Catholic groups, and the Pope now encourages them to take steps toward reconciliation. Catholic Christians make up around one-fifth of the Chinese Church; many Catholics are charismatic and ardent in their faith.

2 **Relationships among the various expressions of the Chinese Church** are at last strengthening, after decades of strain ranging from passively avoidant to intentionally acrimonious. As they are able, government-recognized churches in recent years assist the unregistered churches by providing them support and resources. Even more significantly, TSPM/CCC churches and house churches came together in the aftermath of the 2008 Sichuan earthquake, ministering jointly to communities and families in need. Pray for continued collaboration, understanding and unity as new generations of leaders forge relationships across historic dividing lines. Pray for genuine reconciliation at the foot of the Cross.

3 **Specific challenges facing the Chinese Church:**

a) ***Questions of moral and ethical conduct*** present themselves daily to Chinese Christians, who often lack access to a Bible and adequate biblical guidance, teaching and counsel for answers to difficult issues. While there is a core of seasoned and faithful men and women – mature, wise Christian leaders and elders offering sound counsel and stability for the churches – their numbers are far too few. Pray for continued guidance from the Holy Spirit, particularly in relation to the following:

i *Problems within marriages and families.* The generation of house church leaders absent from their families (either in and out of prison or gone for extended periods of itinerant ministry) yields, as a by-product, a number of their children leaving the ministry or even leaving the faith. In urban settings, the twin pressures of gainful employment and pastoring leave marriages and family relationships strained and in many cases broken. The increasing acceptance of extra-marital sexual relationships as a cultural norm further complicates matters. Pray that leaders find ways to model family relationships that honour God. Pray that wise counsel might be provided for struggling families and individuals, and pray that Chinese Christians might demonstrate the power of the gospel through transformed relationships with spouses, children and parents.

ii *Financial temptations.* Economic progress creates a new set of pressures on Christians, ranging from the desire for personal or church wealth to decisions regarding the stewardship of that wealth. Growing materialism coupled with excessive corruption are cultural norms. Pray for Christians to seek guidance from Scripture as they develop principles and guidelines for living in the world while still faithful to God.

b) ***Relations between Church and government*** are improving incrementally, but nearing a crucial decision point. Religious policies might be passed that allow for equality in registration of all religious groups, without requiring governmental control. Pray for a resolution that will best empower the Church to flourish, grow and bless the peoples of China and beyond.

c) ***Persecution*** remains a present reality. This is a measure of the government's fears of such a large movement they do not control and of the majority of the Church operating outside the government-sanctioned church bodies. Since 1996, persecution has increased against house churches unwilling to register with the TSPM/CCC. Arrests, heavy fines, forced closures and destruction of church buildings are increasing in some key areas; the state says this is because house churches are illegal and a potential political threat, not because they are Christian. But this does nothing to lessen the suffering endured by its victims.

d) ***Churches need godly leaders*** to teach and guide families and individuals in their community.

i *Some TSPM groups report one trained leader for every seven thousand believers* and even up to forty thousand in some areas – a shocking scale of need for trained leadership. Pray for formal training structures for the Three Self churches and for God to enable all who must lead, no matter what their circumstances.

ii *Younger leaders increasingly face pressures* from family and society to pursue financially lucrative career paths instead of a life of ministry. Balancing obedience to God's calling with honouring family and elders becomes a soul-rending process.

iii *Women constitute nearly 75 percent of the Church.* This leaves leadership, outreach and care for church members mostly in the hands of women. Pray for their strength and wisdom to manage many responsibilities. Pray also for more effective outreach among men and that both men and women might jointly serve the Church.

e) Bible-based training and discipleship remain crisis-level needs for all arms of the Church.

i *Seminaries* remain too few in number and small in size to meet the needs of a growing Church, with only 18 official seminaries graduating fewer than 1,000 students per year. Pray for those evangelical professors providing biblical teaching despite the prevailing liberal theology and textbooks. Pray that practical holiness might be central in the lives of faculty and students alike.

ii *Bible training centres and other informal training programmes* are rapidly springing up across China to equip the hundreds of thousands of lay leaders. Pray for an adequate supply of Bibles flowing to and through these programmes and for sound teaching and learning materials.

iii *A truly Chinese expression of biblical faith* is essential to move the Church forward into future generations. Pray that as changes come, theology, worship and community will enhance the God-given uniqueness of Chinese culture, while at the same time avoiding an unhealthy nationalism or ethnocentrism.

f) The predations of aggressive cults spread false teachings, rob the Church of many members and lead to confusion and misperceptions of biblical Christianity for many. Some of these cults verge on Christian teaching; others peddle outright deception. They often target churches to recruit new members. Christians (and leaders in particular) must be equipped to know the Truth so as to discern the lies proliferating among these groups.

4 **Increased contact and communication** with evangelical Christians around the world prove an enormous blessing at times and a formidable obstacle at others. Current partnership models range from sensationally misleading to humbly low key, from respectful to confrontational and from mutually honouring to exploitative. Finance and resource provisions are major components for good and for ill. Pray for wisdom, sensitivity and love to govern official partnerships and informal working relationships, and specifically for productive interaction with the urban Church.

5 **Missions vision is multiplying,** and increasing numbers of Chinese feel called to go forth. Some house church networks have long cherished and supported missions outreach to other provinces and to ethnic minorities. The Back to Jerusalem vision aims to send up to 100,000 missionaries from China throughout the unevangelized world. Some anticipate China may become the greatest sending nation in the 21st Century! Pray for quality preparation and training – facilitated in part by servant-hearted expatriate Christians – to equip Chinese churches for a task with which they are largely unfamiliar. Thousands of Chinese are already seeking to learn new languages and cultures and to live among other peoples in culturally acceptable ways. Inevitably, they will include trained ministers, business-savvy tentmakers, labourers, students and even "barefoot" missionaries with little but their radical faith in Jesus. Developing strategy, member care and partnerships with other nationalities in mission will all present significant challenges.

The Less Evangelized

About 8% of China's population today are Christian, but their distribution is quite uneven. In this section are given some of the nationally significant but less evangelized sections of the population.

1 **The "lost generation"** – the millions mobilized during the Cultural Revolution. They were exploited by warped ideology and robbed of their youth, their education and their chance for betterment during those years of madness. As parents, they now coddle and spoil their children to ensure the opportunities they themselves were denied. A chasm in life experience separates parent from child. Pray that they might find hope and peace in Christ.

2 **The Chinese military** is considered the largest in the world, including the armed forces (PLA) and the armed police (PAP). Combined, there are over four million in uniform, but very few Christians among them.

3 **The 500 million-plus captives of hollow and deceptive philosophies** found in ancient practices such as Daoism, Buddhism and Confucianism and in the newer Falun

Gong movement. These traditions are experiencing growth – with Confucian teachings especially being promoted and Buddhism rapidly growing. Young people are not so attracted, but many professionals and older generations seek such grounding and transcendent meaning. Pray that they might turn their hearts toward Truth and the freedom only the gospel can give.

4 **Children and young people** under age 15 number nearly 300 million. They face different pressures from the previous generation's hardships. Modernization, both in rural and urban areas, has come with drastic increases in juvenile crime and sexual permissiveness. One of the great needs of China today is for adults to intentionally invest in the discipleship and training of children and youth. Pray for:

a) Training within homes. When parents are active in the Church and maintain careers, there is often little time for attention to children. Pray for strength, endurance and ability for parents, extended families and community members to invest time into families and households, the most enduring social structure and the future of the Chinese Church.

b) Training within churches. Some TSPM/CCC churches have Sunday schools and youth programmes, but many churches lack adults who are able to invest in this crucial work. Effective, God-honouring resources and access to the Bible are important, but not always available.

c) Christian educators and schools. Atheism remains the underlying philosophy of Chinese education, itself a crucial tool for shaping this generation's worldview. Pray for sound Bible teaching in churches and homes that enables students to discern truth from false teachings. In urban settings, the desire for elite, private schools is on the rise. Pray for Christians who will seize the opportunity to found excellent educational institutions attractive to Chinese families seeking such.

5 **University students** are at the core of much recent church growth. Now numbering over 20 million (a 17 million increase since 2000!), these students are set to continue this key role in growth and maturity of the Chinese Church. Pray for:

a) Christians among them to be built up in their faith and to be fervent witnesses. Universities increasingly offer religious study programmes, even Christian study programmes. Still, the influence of atheism pervades higher education, where diverse ideologies compete for the minds of youth. Pray for excellent Christian academicians from around the world who will teach in these programmes and mentor students through their university years.

b) The establishment of Bible study groups on every one of the 2,000 campuses throughout China – such groups are increasing in number. Pray also for outreach efforts near campuses through cafés where students can find Bibles and mingle with Christians.

c) Those who study abroad. Well over 100,000 Chinese go overseas annually for study, but only about 25% of those return. Most go to Japan, Hong Kong, USA, Europe or Australia. US universities in particular see great increases in Chinese undergraduate and graduate students. Among them is an unprecedented openness, and a good proportion have come to the Lord. Pray for Christians in these countries to take advantage of opportunities to welcome and witness to Chinese students. Pray also for Chinese who return home as Christians to link well with their local faith communities – usually amid vastly different situations from those where they met Jesus.

6 **Muslims** officially number 20 million, but are almost certainly significantly more. Almost all are linked entirely to specific ethnic groups – the indigenous Uyghur, Kazak, Uzbek, Kyrgyz, Tajik, Tatar of Xinjiang, Salar of Qinghai, Dongxiang of Gansu and the Hui of Ningxia and elsewhere in China. Islam is an official religion in China but also a sensitive issue due to a history of Hui and Uyghur revolts and unrest. Few Christians in China live and work among the Muslim peoples, and while outreach by both foreign groups and Chinese Christians is increasing, such workers need adequate preparation and culturally sensitive approaches. Pray for the evangelization of these often isolated and even oppressed peoples, and for the calling of committed workers to them.

7 **Ethnic minorities** – non-Chinese peoples comprise 10.1% of the population, 135 million people in 474 distinct ethno-linguistic groups. Pray for:

a) Global concern for the evangelization of these numerous unreached peoples. Pray that a doorway to many peoples, still inaccessible to outsiders, might be opened or re-opened in cases where it has been closed in recent years.

% Christian	# of Peoples	% of PRC Total Pop
>50%	18 peoples	0.17
10-50%	20 peoples	0.29
5-10%	18 peoples	0.53
2-5%	26 peoples	0.35
1-2%	17 peoples	0.25
0.5-1%	35 peoples	1.26
0.1-0.5%	93 peoples	4.21
<0.1%	30 peoples	2.64
0.0%	217 peoples	0.35

12 indigenous peoples are over 50% Christian. Of these, only A-Hmao and Gha-Mu (both Miao peoples), Eastern Lipo and Lahu (both Yi peoples) and Lisu number over 100,000. 375 peoples are less than 1% Christian, totalling 8.46% of the population.

b) Greater involvement of Chinese Christians – both minorities and Han – in reaching them. In almost every case, great sensitivity and humility will be needed, especially by the dominant Han Chinese, in whatever missiological approach is taken.

c) The planting and growth of indigenous churches and discipling of leaders. Pray for those who will labour to make God's Word available in every heart language so that each indigenous Church will have direct access to the only basis for faith and godly living.

d) For greater gospel access to least evangelized groups. In many cases, geographic and cultural isolation are major factors; in others, spiritual resistance to the gospel is an influence. Some of the most strategic groups are restive minorities (such as Tibetans and Uyghurs) among whom violent protests or riots prompt harsh government crackdowns, making access extremely difficult.

e) Broadcast media. For a long time, radio programmes (**FEBC** and **TWR**) were the only effective means of sharing the Christian message with many of these groups. For some, this remains the case. Pray for the right content to be broadcast to the peoples who most need it.

8 **The Chinese diaspora,** present in nearly every nation in the world and numbering as many as 40 million. In many countries they are a very strong Christian community, but in others they remain unevangelized. Emigration from China has occurred for centuries; changes occurring in China today witnesses new populations moving to new areas. Sparsely populated Russian Siberia is one possible destination of potentially millions of Chinese. The Arab Gulf states employ countless Chinese labourers. And new Chinese-sponsored economic activities in Africa and Latin America bring many to these lands; in Africa alone are an estimated 750,000 Chinese labourers and business people.

Supportive Ministries

1 **Foreign Christians** are not welcome in China as missionaries. Yet, the ideological oppression of the Cultural Revolution is all but gone, and China's global interests, exchanges and relations make it possible for many Christians – both foreign-born Chinese and other expatriates – to contribute to Chinese society. There are perhaps two million foreigners now living in China from North America, Europe and other parts of Asia, with South Korea and Hong Kong sending many to mainland China. Recent years have seen increases in students from Africa as well.

a) Christians serve China in a variety of ways. Pray for:

i *Foreign experts and businessmen.* China appealed in recent years for 150,000 foreign experts to come serve in fields such as biotechnology, energy, agriculture, IT and especially finance. Additionally, foreigners are sought for English, Japanese and other language instruction as well as for university positions across many disciplines. Pray for many Christians to consider responding to this unprecedented appeal to work in China, to serve well and to impart their faith while on the job.

ii *Students* – usually for language or cultural studies in various universities. Recent years saw over 75,000 students (up from 10,000 in 2000) from over 175 countries studying in China, with South Korea, Japan, USA, Vietnam and Indonesia sending the most students. Pray for Christians among them to be used of God to share Christ with those who are genuinely seeking the Lord.

iii *Community development workers.* While over 150 foreign agencies assist China's development, the ability to found and run a private (not governmentally affiliated) NGO has sharply decreased in the last decade; in recent years, some NGO workers have lost their visas. Local NGOs have better success, though the greatest success comes from starting a business (a school, for example) while also providing needed social services. Development work is essential, especially among remote minority groups, rural populations, migrants in urban settings and other vulnerable groups within society. Opportunity also exists to help the Chinese Church serve communities in the wake of natural or human disaster. Pray for compassion and creativity for foreign Christians eager to assist in meeting these needs in Christ's name.

iv *Foreign tourists.* Over 22 million foreigners visited China in 2009 and spent around $29 billion USD. Many Christians were among them. Pray for their ministry of bringing literature, aid, comfort and, in some cases, teaching. Pray for safety for them and the items they bring with them; pray also for tact and wisdom in their contacts and for respect for the culture and peoples of China.

v *Chinese family members who visit their ancestral homes.* These have flocked to China in their millions. Christians among them have sometimes seen astonishing spiritual responsiveness when staying with relatives in China.

b) *Opportunities and freedom* to serve the Chinese in helpful ways will almost certainly increase in the future. Discerning groups will need to be as wise as serpents and as innocent as doves. Pray for:

i *Well-equipped workers from around the world.* Few Western workers, in particular, are able to speak Chinese fluently. Pray for an increase in Christian service in China, and for humility and a depth of language and culture learning that makes witness to Christ more effective at every level.

ii *Perseverance in times of challenge.* Leading up to the 2008 Olympic Games, the government increased pressure on foreign Christians, deporting workers and denying visas, accusing them of illegal religious activities. While persecution varies across regions and across the years, pray that the desire for development may overcome ideological fears and keep the door open for Christian input.

2 **Provision of Chinese Bibles remains inadequate,** despite a praiseworthy increase in the number of copies now available. The famine of the Scriptures is most acute for house churches, particularly in rural areas where the Church has grown with tremendous rapidity. The situation surrounding Bible printing, distribution and sales is complex, with a variety of factors contributing to the shortfall. Pray for:

a) *Equitable Bible distribution across all arms of the Chinese Church.* Amity Printing Company – a joint venture with UBS – printed its 50 millionth Bible in late 2007; it now has capacity to print upward of 10 million Bibles annually! However, the portion of these that remains in China (approximately 80%) goes to official points of distribution for sale through TSPM and CPA congregations; Bibles are not generally available for sale in bookstores. While some unofficial churches are increasingly able to buy affordable Bibles from the official churches, this monopoly on distribution and sales contributes to a shortage of Scripture availability across the Chinese Church. Pray for creativity in providing Bibles to a rapidly growing and diversifying Church.

b) *Ready availability of God's Word to all who seek it.* Affordable Bibles have largely met the demand among urban Christians. Yet astoundingly, millions of Christians in China remain without access to a Bible, sometimes sharing one copy among 10 or even 100 church members, particularly in rural areas. House churches have commenced their own Bible printing presses and offer free or low cost Bibles to those outside major cities, having provided over six million since 2000. Millions of additional Bibles and NTs are estimated to have been brought in by visitors. Importation of Bibles is legal, but it is prevented for largely economic reasons. Pray that this flow might increase and that all Christians might have access to a copy of the Scriptures. Pray that Bibles might be distributed throughout the country to all who seek God's Word.

③ Christian print materials. There is a seemingly insatiable demand for Bibles and Christian literature for purposes of outreach and equipping the Church. These include hymn books, teaching materials, biographies, tracts, apologetic materials to explain the gospel to students and intellectuals, Christian-living magazines and more. Pray for:

a) *Bible translation.* Around half a million Bibles have been printed across eight minority languages in the last thirty years, including a Braille version. Still, most minority groups do not have their own written languages, let alone translated Scriptures. Pray for this vital work, necessary for the health and indigenous development of the Church among every people.

b) *Scripture portions and adaptations.* In addition to full Bibles, Scripture portions are available in some languages and are increasingly used for outreach. A downloadable version of the Bible is planned for youth, enabling rapid distribution and use on MP3 players.

c) *Christian publishing.* Remarkably, around 900 Christian titles are now legally published and available within China, most by commercial or university presses and some by Amity Printing Company. A widening range of literature is published in Hong Kong with millions of copies sent to the mainland. Many agencies are involved in this ministry, including Christian Communications Ltd. (**CCL**), **OMF**, Asia Harvest, Antioch Mission–Chinese Church Support Ministries, **AOI**, **OD**, denominational bodies and many others. Pray for all aspects of publication and distribution.

d) *Bookstores.* There may be upward of 400 small Christian bookshops now operating legally in China, double the number of just five years earlier! Praise God for the drastic change in Christian literature availability, and pray for excellent books that may be used by the Spirit to powerfully change hearts and minds to the likeness of Christ.

e) *Scholarly literature.* With many professionals and academicians interested in Christianity and beginning to follow Jesus, suitable books for intellectuals are a great need.

   i *Apologetics material.* **OMF** has an extensive ministry here, having printed quality apologetic literature, which is very popular among this group. Academically rigorous exploration of questions or topics raised by a Marxist or atheistic worldview is important.

   ii *Magazines and periodicals.* A Chinese-language magazine, Overseas Campus, has been effective in reaching many mainland Chinese studying in North America and Europe.

   iii *Higher-education materials.* Pray for continued and increased production of quality materials used to train those seeking knowledge of Scripture, at universities and seminaries in particular, and for those with questions not always answered by mainstream Christian literature.

④ Christian radio broadcasting has long been and remains among the most potent media for evangelism and Christian teaching in China. Praise God that prior restrictions are now lifted. Many hundreds of hours of broadcasting in Putonghua and other Han Chinese dialects, as well as in minority languages, are beamed in from a range of Christian stations. Pray for lasting impact.

a) *The Radio Bible Project* – a collaborative effort of Faith Comes By Hearing, Biblica and **TWR** – has reached tens of millions with the Word of God in Putonghua since their first broadcast in 2004.

b) *Shortwave broadcasts.* **TWR** also reaches out to speakers of Amdo Tibetan, Hui, Nosu Yi and Uyghur, with five hours broadcast per week. **FEBC** also reaches ethnic minorities (Mongol, Tibetan, Uyghur, others). Programmes can often be broadcast only once a week in one- to two-hour time slots. Pray for available and eager listeners during select broadcast times.

c) *Massive numbers of responses to broadcasts* over the years forced radio ministries into broader work and more collaborative partnerships, combining an online presence, print media and CD/DVD distribution. **TWR** offers Church Radio Kits to fellowships that form around broadcasts, as well as "Seminary On The Air" training for those living in remote locations. **FEBC** receives an average of 2,000 hits per day on its website from listeners and enquirers. Pray for follow-up with all correspondents.

5 **Other electronic media** ministries play key roles in reaching hundreds of millions, many of whom have negligible interaction with Christians or churches. Pray for:

a) Visual resources within China which have increased, with Christian TV programmes broadcast via cable and satellite. DVDs for evangelism and training are more readily available through groups such as **OMF** and CCL. The JESUS film is also available in 43 languages within China.

b) New audio tools providing greater inroads for the gospel to often-overlooked groups. Scripture, music, poetry and other programming can be spread via MP3, Internet broadcasting and cassette tapes/CDs. Remote groups, often isolated and with lower literacy rates, can often be reached with portable, digital audio Bibles from MegaVoice and **TWR**. **GRN** has produced gospel messages in an astounding 330 languages and dialects. Pray for the Word of God to go forth through each of these channels and to bear fruit.

c) Internet use in China, which has exploded across the last decade. Many evangelistic and discipleship opportunities have been seized by Chinese Christians and foreign groups alike, but the potential for more remains. Some churches have websites; other groups post information about Jesus and Christianity, both commonly searched. Bible study and devotional materials are available for download. Online forums for discussion allow good opportunity for believers and non-believers to interact over important questions and topics. Pray for the continued use of the Internet in spreading the good news and nurturing the body of Christ.

Provinces of China

Nearly all of China's provinces are large enough in size and population to serve as countries in their own right. If taken individually, 11 of them would be among the 25 most populous countries in the world. Specific prayer is warranted. Bear in mind the following:

1 **Peoples classification** is a complex issue, made so by two mutually incompatible ways of regarding ethnicity:

a) Government census figures for 55 official "nationalities" by province. These are usually represented as percentages of a province's present population.

b) Ethnolinguistic people groups as reported by the Joshua Project list, Operation China and other similar approaches. These treatments include over 500 ethno-linguistic groups of China and are usually grouped by affinity bloc and people cluster. Since almost all minority populations of any size are present in multiple provinces but not enumerated as such in any reliable data sources, all inclusion of minority population percentages by province are estimates.

2 **Religions.** In a country often hostile to overt expressions of religion and not given to counting its population along religious lines, it is impossible to precisely measure where, in what manner and how much atheism, agnosticism, Confucianism, Daoism and Buddhism mix and overlap. Christianity, Islam and Lamaistic Buddhism are given estimated percentages.

3 **Christians.** The counting of Christians in China can be clouded by those who prefer publishing lower numbers (TSPM and government) and those who prefer larger numbers (some Christian agencies). Recently, state officials published statements on the numbers of Christians that are very close to what Christian researchers are claiming, an encouraging sign. We have broken down Christianity by provinces, using an array of sources to adjust each province's Christian numbers, and we believe this reflects as accurate a picture as can be currently obtained.

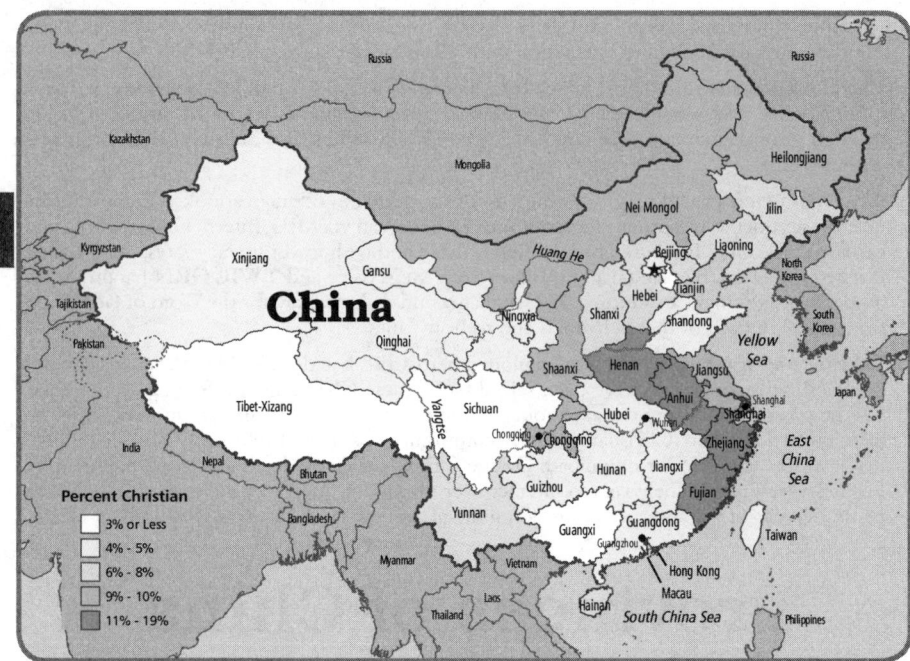

China

Percent Christian
- 3% or Less
- 4% - 5%
- 6% - 8%
- 9% - 10%
- 11% - 19%

Anhui Province

Geography

Area 139,900 sq km. One of the poorest provinces. Central China.
Population 62,933,000; 450 people/sq km.

Capital Hefei 2.4m. **Other major cities** Suzhou 2.1m; Huzhou 1.3m.

Peoples

Han Chinese 99.3%. Hui 0.6%. Other 0.1%.
Main languages Putonghua, Huizhou.

Religion

Muslim 0.6%. Christian 16.2%: House churches 10.2%, TSPM 4.9%, all Catholics 1.1%.

1 **Anhui lags behind China** in most areas of development, especially economically. There is great economic disparity between rural and urban areas; farmers face especially difficult livelihoods. Failed Maoist policies, poor administration and corruption, combined with famine and frequent floods, bring desperation and disillusionment. These have led many to turn to Christ. As a result, Anhui enjoys one of China's highest proportions of Christians, 16.2%, and its second-largest number of Christians (after Henan). Pray for just governance and wise development that will uplift the millions of impoverished in Anhui; pray that Christians might be an integral part of blessing the poor.

2 **Christian growth has been amazing** and sustained over several decades. From 50,000 Protestants in 1949, there are now possibly over nine million TSPM and house church Christians – counting proves too difficult due to the speed of the growth! Two of China's largest house-church networks started in the northwest of the province.

3 **Existing house–church networks face internal struggles.** Large networks are fracturing and cooperation is lacking among networks, often because of very minor theological differences or issues of control. The sheer number of believers forms a Christian culture, which in turn isolates many churches and Christians from unbelievers. Churches and leaders are at times so beset by internal politics that spiritual development and evangelism get relegated to a lesser status. Pray for unity among Christians, leaders and networks, and pray that discipleship and evangelism can once again assume primacy in churches.

4 **Training is a serious challenge** in such a fast-multiplying Church. The TSPM alone has nearly 5,000 meeting points, but less than 100 ordained pastors. Seminaries and other formal, theological education structures are desperately needed. Informal discipleship and training are needed even more. This is needed for both leadership development within the Church and for discipleship of all believers – many only have a very rudimentary understanding of their faith. Lack of a good biblical foundation makes churches highly vulnerable to the predations of cults and to unsound teaching within the Church. Extreme teachings regarding material possessions and wealth are increasingly prevalent.

5 **Persecution of unregistered churches** is notable in Anhui, more so than in most provinces. Many church leaders have been imprisoned and many ministries shut down, yet churches are not cowed and outreach continues. Pray for continued faithfulness in the face of persecution.

C

Beijing Municipality

Geography 🌍
Area 16,800 sq km. The nation's capital.
Population 16,284,000; 970 people/sq km. 25% are work-seeking migrants from other parts of China.

Peoples 👪
Han Chinese 95.0%, most speaking Putonghua. Hui 1.6%. Manchu 1.5%. Mongolian 0.2%. Expat population up to 1.7%.

Religion 🙏
Muslim 1.7%. Christian 4.5%: House churches 2.9%, TSPM 0.6%, all Catholics 1.0%.

1 **China is ruled from Beijing.** Pray for the nation's leaders to seek the good of the people and eschew self-interest, to have a sense for humanity amid the large-scale issues and to have the courage and wisdom to make the right, essential economic and political decisions that will impact billions.

2 **At the seat of China's power,** Party officials try to keep tight control of Christian activity by being particularly harsh toward unofficial ministries. TSPM churches are increasing and fall far short of having enough buildings to meet the spiritual interest. Ironically, this forces many of Beijing's Christians and seekers into the very unregistered networks the state attempts to suppress, which in turn has forced officials to assume a more open stance. Youth, students and business people are especially responsive, and innovative ministry is particularly effective among them. Pray for further cooperation between TSPM churches and house churches and for a government stance that allows both to continue to prosper.

3 **Beijing's influence and wealth** draw millions of people. At least three million from poorer rural backgrounds have migrated to Beijing; many recent converts come from this group. In contrast, the city also draws people from cosmopolitan business and academic communities from throughout China and, indeed, the entire world. Churches among them are also quietly growing; pray for this to continue.

Chongqing Municipality

Geography 🌍
Area Approximately 82,000 sq km. China's westernmost and newest municipality carved out of the eastern fifth of Sichuan Province.
Population 28,922,000; 352 people/sq km.
Major cities Chongqing 9.4m; Wanxian 2.2m.

Peoples 👪
Han Chinese 98.3%. Other 1.7%. Hui, Tujia, Miao.
Main languages Southwest Mandarin dialect. Also Min Nan, Wu, Xiang, Hakka.

Religion 🙏
Chinese traditional. Some Muslims. Christian 9.8%: House churches 5.8%, TSPM 1.5%, all Catholics 2.5%.

1 **Chongqing is the industrial and trade hub** for west and southwest China on the Yangtze River. Billions of yuan have flowed up the river to develop the city and municipality at a breathtaking pace and on a staggering scale. The population has likewise increased; Chongqing was the planet's fastest-growing urban area for the first decade of the 21st Century. Corruption and gangsterism inevitably followed. Pray for this incredible development to be managed with political fairness, financial transparency, environmental responsibility and for the long-term benefit of the tens of millions in the region.

C

2 **The massive Three Gorges Dam project** displaced up to 1.4 million people. Compensation for this enforced relocation was usually inadequate and/or stolen by corrupt officials. Many have chosen to move to Chongqing or Fuling. Pray for hearts opened to the gospel because of this traumatic change.

3 **Church growth in Chongqing** is steady, solid and significantly faster than even the rapid population growth of this booming region. In the last 10 years, it has enjoyed a notable boost in the Christian population, from conversions and migration. Pray for continued increases of Christian outreach and presence in this strategic but spiritually needy city; leaders and stable, mature believers will be desperately needed for a city in flux and for a fast-multiplying Church.

Fujian Province

Peoples ♟♟♟

Han Chinese 97.2%, speaking 8 Min languages; largest are Putian/Xinghua Fuzhou, Hoklo/Hokkien, Teochew, Hakka. Minorities 2.8%. She, Hui, Austronesian peoples(3).

Geography 🌐

Area 123,100 sq km on the coast facing Taiwan. **Population** 34,300,000; 278 people/sq km. **Capital** Fuzhou 2.8m. **Other cities** Xiamen 2.2m; Putian 1.1m; Quanzhou 1.1m.

Religion 📖

Buddhism and Daoism strong. Muslim 0.1%. Christian 14.8%: House churches 4.5%, TSPM 5.0%, all Catholics 5.3%.

---

1 **Fujian was one of China's first provinces to receive the gospel.** The first Protestant missionaries arrived in the early 19th Century. Over the decades, there has been much growth among TSPM and house churches and Catholics. The Assembly Halls (Watchman Nee) and the True Jesus Church are also strong, although regarded by many as aberrational in their teachings (especially the latter group). The provincial government here seems at times increasingly tolerant and open to the activity of unregistered Christian groups, but then at other times it cracks down on them. Praise God for what growth and freedom do exist; pray for the right steps that will release the Church into powerful witness and ministry in Fujian.

2 **Fujian's connection with Taiwan is ancient and profound.** Around 80% of Taiwan's population can trace their roots back to Fujian province. The Chinese diaspora in Southeast Asia and even globally is heavily weighted toward peoples from Fujian – Hokkien, Teochew, Hakka and others. Business, family and traditional connections between Taiwan and Fujian enable much potential ministry. But these links are also at the root of the revival of Buddhism and Daoism in the area, as Taiwanese seek to restore or build temples and shrines in their ancestral areas. Over 20,000 have been restored or built without legal permission. Pray that the connections between Fujian and overseas Chinese might serve to extend the gospel.

3 **Pray for the unreached in two significant groups:**

a) *The 400,000 She* (700,000 nationally) are a Hmong people related to the Miao, who had until recently been largely unevangelized. Most She are assimilated into Han or Hakka culture and are largely Daoist, with ancestral worship practices. But thousands in recent years have become believers; pray for this fledgling Church to grow in healthy ways.

b) *The 4,000 Ami, Bunun and Paiwan* are Austronesian groups, together called Gaoshan in China. They are related to the mountain peoples of Taiwan, where most became Christian.

Their mainland relatives have no known witness among them, and Christian resources in their languages (Bibles, the JESUS film and such), which are available to them in Taiwan, are not available in the mainland.

c) **Immigrants to Fujian from other areas of China,** attracted by Fujian's prosperity, are looking for work. In Xiamen, as much as 70% of the population are from other regions. In most cases, they will have come from parts of China that are significantly less blessed with the gospel; pray that the vibrant Church here might reach out with boldness and love to these economic migrants.

Gansu
Province

Geography 🌐

Area 366,500 sq km. Large northwestern province on the edge of the Gobi Desert. One of China's poorest and least-developed provinces. **Population** 26,841,590; 73 people/sq km. **Capital** Lanzhou 2.3m. **Other major city** Tianshui 1.3m.

Peoples 👪

Han Chinese and other migrants 90.2%. Hui 5.2%. Mongolian 2.4%. Mostly Dongxiang, also Bonan and Enger Yugur. Tibetan 2.2%. Rongmahbrogpa Amdo 0.6%, Jone, Baima, Boyu, Zhugqu, Saragh Yugur.

Religion 🙏

Muslim 6.2%, mainly Hui, Dongxiang. Lamaistic Buddhism 1.8%. Christian 4.9%: House churches 2.8%, TSPM 1.4%, all Catholics 0.6%.

1 **The Christian population is relatively small,** but is accelerating in growth. The area was pioneered by CIM (**OMF**), **CMA** and **AoG**, with very modest response. Increasing numbers are coming to Christ, especially the result of compassionate ministry by Christians to the sick and needy and of faithful witness by lay preachers. Areas of weakness include too few leaders with training and the rise of a number of marginal sects. **FEBC** radio broadcasts have led many to Christ in Gansu villages.

2 **The least evangelized:**

a) **The Dongxiang and Bonan** are of mixed Mongolian background and are strongly Muslim. No one has ever sought to evangelize these isolated peoples – probably China's least evangelized. There are a few dozen believers in each group. The Enger Yugur are related and have at least several dozen believers.

b) **The Muslim Hui** are numerous in the cities; the city of Linxia has only a handful of believers. Despite little outreach, there are a growing number of Hui believers scattered across China and a few small groups of believers. The Hui Bible was translated in 2009 and the NT is now in distribution.

c) **Tibetan peoples** are largely Lamaistic Buddhists and number 600,000. There is one Tibetan church. Four Tibetan peoples are indigenous to Gansu – the Jone and Saragh Yugur have small numbers of believers, but the Zhugqu and Boyu have none.

Guangdong Province

Geography 🌐

Area 197,100 sq km. On southeast coast. Both Hong Kong and Macau were British and Portuguese colonial enclaves of Guangdong and, though now under Chinese rule, remain Special Administrative Zones with their own autonomy. **Population** 96,376,000; 488 people/sq km. A "floating population" of seasonal migrant labourers swells the population by 15 to 30 million.

Capital Guangzhou (Canton) 8.9m. **Other major cities** Shenzhen 9.0m; Dongguan 5.3m; Foshan 5.0m; Shantou 3.5m; Zhongshan 2.2m; Huizhou 1.4m; Zhuhai 1.3m; Jiangmen 1.1m.

Peoples 👪

Han Chinese 98.0%. Predominantly Cantonese and, in northeast, Hakka; also Teochew. Ethnic minorities 2.0%. Yao(2), Zhuang, She.

Religion 🙏

Predominantly secularism and traditional Chinese religions. Christian 4.5%: House churches 2.9%, TSPM 0.8%, all Catholics 0.8%.

1 **Guangdong was the first province evangelized by Protestants.** Robert Morrison arrived in Macau in 1807. British seizure of Hong Kong and Western opium wars against China soured Guangdong's people to the gospel for many years. Christianity is still widely perceived as a foreign imposition; the province's Christian percentage is less than half the national level; most adhere to a blend of traditional Chinese superstitions and modern materialism. Pray for an increased openness to the gospel.

2 **This province has been economically booming for decades,** and its people have a long tradition of being traders and entrepreneurs. Shenzen, its primary port, grew from a small fishing village to a metropolitan area of over 12 million people in the span of 25 years! Migrant labour traditionally fuelled Guangdong's growth and wealth, with up to 30 million people from elsewhere working seasonally in the province. But with the rise of the economy in other parts of China, Guangdong's factories are now short of workers. Rapid increases in trade and wealth, the high proportion of migrants, famously crooked local officials and historically powerful organized crime groups create an environment ripe for corruption, exploitation, crime, sexual immorality and drug abuse – all of which have rates higher here than nationally. Pray that such moral declension might be addressed; pray that the Holy Spirit would work in individuals and society for God-pleasing change.

3 **The Biao Mien Yao and Zaomin Yao** in the northern mountains are largely unevangelized as are the Shaozhou Han; Christians among these comprise 1% or less.

4 **Cantonese, Hakka and Teochew** are major components of the Overseas Chinese in SE Asia and other continents. The Overseas Chinese are some of the wealthiest peoples of the world and have often proved very receptive to the gospel. Pray for an increased and continued harvest among them and that they might in turn be a blessing to Guangdong, their province of origin.

Guangxi Zhuang Autonomous Region

Geography

Area 220,400 sq km. The southernmost mainland coastal state, adjoining Vietnam. Subtropical. The home area of China's largest ethnic minority, the Zhuang, and the province therefore given a higher, though nominal, degree of autonomy.
Population 48,605,300; 220 people/sq km.
Capital Nanning 2.1m. **Other major city** Liuzhou 1.4m.

Peoples 👤👤👤

Han Chinese 60.3%. Mainly Putonghua, Hakka, Cantonese, Pinghua and Pingdi.
Ethnic minorities 39.7%.

> **Zhuang** 35.5%. 17 peoples. Northern Zhuang(7) 12.8m; Southern Zhuang(10) 4.2m; Tho 160,000; Nung 125,000.
> **Yao-Mien** 3.1%. Iu Mien(3) 1.3m; Biao Mien(2) 80,000; Nunu 63,000.
> **Tai** 0.9%. Mulao 225,000; Maonan 66,500; E 41,000.
> **Others** 0.2%. Jing (Vietnamese); Palyu (Mon-Khmer); Gelao (Miao/Hmong).

Religion

Mainly Chinese religions and animism among the minorities. Christian 2.0%: House churches 1.2%, TSPM 0.4%, all Catholics 0.4%.

C

1 **Guangxi is one of China's least-developed and most-remote provinces,** with one of the largest ethnic-minority populations. The isolated and mountainous terrain hampers development; the porous border with Vietnam and prevalent poverty put it at high risk of drug and human trafficking. Pray for development that is healthy for society, will oppose social evils and will not exploit minority populations.

2 **The area is also one of China's least evangelized** – some reckon Guangxi is as much as 90% unevangelized. Difficult terrain and poor transportation keep many villages isolated from the truth, and the government restricts the number of meeting points. Pray that Christians might carry the light of the gospel even to the darkest and most remote corners of the region. Praise God for rapid growth among the Han-majority house churches in recent years.

3 **The Zhuang people** are China's largest ethnic-minority population. They number around 17 million and are comprised of 17 sub-groups. Less than 1% are Christian. Most follow traditional animist beliefs, often combined with ancestor worship, Buddhism and Daoism. Younger generations are more likely to be urbanites, atheists and struggling to retain their cultural distinctiveness. Yet they are somewhat responsive to the gospel. **FEBC** radio programmes and the JESUS film in the largest of their dialects have helped in this, and the NT translation in progress will go a long way toward their evangelization and their cultural preservation.

4 **The numerous other minorities** include the Iu Mien peoples who number about 1.3 million, but are much less than 1% Christian; a few years ago there were hardly any known believers among them. Among the Biao Mien, Nunu, Mulao, E, Palyu and Gelao are very few or even no known believers and virtually no specific ministry. Pray for the evangelization of every people in Guangxi. Bible translation for most peoples has yet to begin.

Guizhou Province

Geography

Area 174,000 sq km. Mountainous, southern inland province. Poor and underdeveloped.
Population 38,697,000; 222 people/sq km.
Capital Guiyang 2.2m. **Other major city** Liupanshui 1.3m.

Peoples 👤👤👤

Han Chinese 63.7%.
Ethnic minorities 36.3%. 55% of the province's land is designated as autonomous regions for minorities.
Hui 0.4%.
Miao/Hmong 20.5%. 41 peoples. Largest, Miao-related: Hmu(3) 3.0m; Miao(21) 1.6m; A-Hmao 426,000; Hmong(7) 295,000; Gha-Mu 140,000; Ge 132,000; Ga Mong 69,000. Yao-related: Baheng(2) 50,000; Baonuo 25,000.
Tai 12.3%. 13 peoples. Largest: Bouyei 3.5m; Dong(2) 3.4m; Shui 520,000; Yanghuang 63,000; Mulao Jia 39,000.

Sino–Tibetan 3.1%. 10 peoples. Largest: Shuixi Nosu 260,000; Nanjingren 157,000.	0.5%. Christian 5.8% (mainly among Miao and minorities): House churches 3.2%, TSPM 1.8%, all Catholics 0.8%.

Religion

Buddhism mixed with polytheism and animism is strong among ethnic minorities. Muslim

C

1 **Praise God for the continued growth of the Church;** more areas and peoples than ever have been impacted by the good news. Two Miao peoples, A-Hmao and Gha-Mu, are majority Christian, and many Yi peoples have large Christian minorities (Guopu 20%, Lagou 35%, Wusa Nasu 30%, Tushu 10%). Most of these Christians are in the northwest. The 10,000 Christians of 1949 have grown to around 2.2 million in 2010. A number of peoples that had no believers now have small but growing churches among them.

2 **The challenge of the unreached also continues to be great.** Spiritual breakthrough in a few ethnic groups obscures the fact that most peoples remain unreached. Pray for:

a) *The 21 Miao peoples* – three have small Christian minorities, but 11 have no known believers.

b) *Many of the peoples indigenous to Guizhou* with no Christians whatsoever, including the four Yao peoples. The three million-plus Bouyei are only about 0.5% Christian and remain over 70% unevangelized. Most Hmong groups, as well as the Hmu and Shui, are very populous peoples but with only small numbers of believers. Pray for local and outside Christians to reach out to these.

Hainan Province

Geography

Area 34,300 sq km. A tropical island facing Vietnam. China's southernmost and smallest province, but its largest Special Economic Zone and tourist haven.
Population 8,611,000; 251 people/sq km.
Capital Haikou 1.6 mill.

Peoples

Han Chinese 74%. Mainly Hainanese, some Hakka; 10,000 from Indonesia. Tai 24.5%. Li(5) 1.25m; Lingao 730,000; Cun 89,000. Other 1.5%. Miao 60,000; Zhuang 50,000; Utsul (Cham) 8,000.

Religion

Mixture of polytheism, Buddhism, Daoism and ancestor worship among indigenous peoples. Christian 6.4%: House churches 4.9%, TSPM 1.3%, all Catholics 0.1%.

1 **Hainan's subtropical climate and pristine environment** have turned it into a booming economy focused on tourism. This is rapidly transforming a formerly sleepy island, attracting many well-heeled mainlanders, but also raising costs to beyond what many locals can afford. This bubble has already burst once. Pray against Hainan becoming an island of hedonism and iniquity for the super-wealthy; pray also that the opening up of the island might bring a greater degree of freedom to evangelize this once-frontier area.

2 **The Church in Hainan** grew considerably in recent decades, but not without difficulty. There have been significant divisions between TSPM and house churches as well as among Christian leaders. Likewise, researchers cannot seem to agree on the number of actual Christians in the island (OW's number is at the high end of estimates in this case). Pray for Christian unity to prevail and for the Church to be a profound witness to the power and authority of Christ.

3 **The five Li peoples** make up the largest indigenous group and have a history of rebellion against Chinese rule. Pray that they may openly receive the King of kings – only 2,000 have done so. Among the related Lingao, there are 3,000 Christians, and the Cun have 900. There is nothing of God's Word and no known Scripture recordings or the JESUS film in any of the seven languages or dialects; the only exceptions to this are the Gospel of Luke and the JESUS film in Lingao. Pray that these peoples may be reached.

Hebei Province

Geography 🌐

Area 202,700 sq km. Northeast China, almost surrounding Beijing and Tianjin.
Population 71,049,000; 350 people/sq km.
Capital Shijiazhuang 2.5m. **Other major cities** Tangshan 1.9m; Luancheng 1.8m; Baoding 1.2m; Handan 1.2m; Zhangjiakou 1.0m.

Peoples 👪

Han Chinese 96%, speaking Putonghua. Manchu 3%. Hui 0.7%. Mongol 0.2%.

Religion

Secularism and traditional Chinese religions. Muslim 1.5%. Christian 8.8%: House churches 2.7%, TSPM 0.5% Catholic Patriotic Association 1.8%, Roman Catholic 3.8%.

1 **Hebei continues in its reputation** for being one of the most rigidly policed provinces in China. Christians have suffered unrelenting and harsh persecution over the past three decades as a result, yet their growth to such a size (nearly six million) brings them increasing resilience and even influence with local government officials. Pray for both grace and greater freedom for the Christians in this strategic province.

2 **Hebei is the heart of Catholicism in China** with a large proportion of Catholics. Many remain loyal to the Vatican. They have suffered severely, since they do not submit to state control, but they also continue to grow. Pray for a healthy and helpful relationship between the state-church mechanisms (CPA, TSPM) and their unregistered counterparts.

Heilongjiang Province

Geography 🌐

Area 463,600 sq km. China's most-northerly province, bordering Russia. One of the three provinces of former Manchuria. Huge natural resources, but many "rust belt" industries.
Population 39,377,000; 85 people/sq km.
Capital Harbin 4.3m. **Other major cities** Qiqihar 1.6m; Daqing 1.5m; Jixi 1.0m; Yichun 1.0m; Zhaodong 1.0m.

Peoples 👪

Han Chinese 94.6%. Manchu 3.0%. Korean 1.2%. Mongolian 0.5%. Hui 0.4%. Daur 0.1%. Xibe 0.03%. Other 0.1%. There are between 35 and 47 indigenous ethnic minorities of small populations.

Religion

Shamanism and Buddhism are prevalent among the indigenous peoples. Muslim 0.5%. Christian 10.5%: House churches 7.2%, TSPM 3.0%, all Catholics 0.3%.

1 **There is significant freedom to practice the Christian faith** and great creativity and vision on the part of churches to share the good news and build the Church. Praise God that churches in Heilongjiang are known throughout China for their dynamism and growth.

2 **A great harvest has been gathered and is still coming** in this fertile province. Rapid growth is occurring in house churches and the TSPM, in rural and urban areas. Church growth came late to Heilongjiang, but has been dramatic – with the Christian population doubling every 10 years. Pray for their deepening faith, greater knowledge of Scripture and continued multiplication of their numbers.

3 **Most of the small indigenous Mongolian and Altaic peoples** are shamanistic. Many are resentful of the Chinese "takeover" of their homelands. They are being caught up in the harvest that is coming as a result of the move of God. Among the Daur, Christians number at least 1,000 and growing. Pray for missionaries to commit their lives to reaching these peoples in sensitive and appropriate ways. Most peoples, such as the Hezhen, Bogol, Khakas, Kyakala, Olot and Saman, total only about 15,000 people.

Henan Province

Geography 🌐

Area 167,000 sq km. North-central China on the fickle Yellow River, prone to flooding and course changes with frequent loss of life.
Population 96,737,000; 579 people/sq km. China's most populous province by residency.
Capital Zhengzhou 3.0m. **Other major cities** Shangqiu 1.9m; Xinyang 1.7m; Luoyang 1.5m; Anyang 1.1m; Pingdingshan 1.0m; Xinxiang 1.0m.

Peoples 👪

Han Chinese 99%, speaking Henan dialects of Mandarin or Jin. Hui 1%.

Religion 🙏

Muslim 1%. Christian 18.3%: House churches 9.8%, TSPM 5.9%, all Catholics 0.6%, marginal groups 2%.

1 **Henan province has endured much suffering.** Frequent floods blight the landscape. Mao's misguided policies disastrously allowed eight million Henanese to die of famine. Up to 70% of the population are peasant farmers eking out a living. Widespread poverty caused tens of thousands to contract HIV; unscrupulous dealers offered cash for bought blood, extracted using infected needles. Additionally, selective abortion, abandonment and infanticide have yielded a massive gender imbalance – 140 male children under 5 for every 100 females. Pray for policies that will allow Henan to develop. Pray that the especially vulnerable groups – female babies and the unborn, HIV victims and poor farmers – might be protected, supported and sustained.

2 **Henan was declared an "Atheistic Zone" in the 1960s,** but since then has been the engine room of church growth in China. Fangcheng county is referred to as the "Jesus Nest"! Church growth has been spectacular. Revival began during the Cultural Revolution with mass conversions, miracles and vision for evangelizing China. Some counties in Henan today are reported to be a large majority Christian. It comfortably has the largest TSPM and house church populations, but growth is beginning to slow and churches are consolidating. Henan, taken as a separate country, would have the world's seventh-highest number of evangelicals. Outreach from Henan churches is one of the great stories of the expansion of Christianity. Church-planting teams (often young women) fanned out over China, followed by discipling teachers. Praise God for this massive and nation-changing growth.

3 **There are many needs in the Church and challenges facing believers:**

a) Persecution continues to be prevalent and often severe. Pray for perseverance and endurance, especially for house church leaders who are especially targeted.

b) Pseudo-Christian cults are many and active in Henan, more so than in any other province. Cults such as Eastern Lightning use false teachings, kidnapping, brainwashing and the structures and methods of criminal societies to prey upon members of house church networks. These occur more easily here due to limited biblical knowledge among believers, lack of solid teaching and prevalent poverty and human need.

c) The primarily rural church networks need to figure out how to deal with the major trend of migration/urbanization as well as the need for a transition of leadership from the faithful founders of their movements to a younger generation. Pray for wisdom and grace for all involved.

Hubei Province

Geography

Area 187,500 sq km. Astride the Yangtze River, a province of many lakes and much agriculture. Wuhan, the capital, is a traditional centre of education.
Population 58,637,000; 313 people/sq km.
Capital Wuhan 7.7m. **Other major cities** Tianmen 1.8m; Xiantao 1.6m; Xiangfan 1.4m; Jingmen 1.1m; Jingzhou 1.0m.

Peoples

Han Chinese 96.0%, speaking Putonghua and some southwestern Mandarin dialects. Minorities 4.0%. Tujia 3.3% (1.94m); Miao 0.6% (340,000); Hui 0.1% (65,000); Dong 0.1% (50,000).

Religion

Muslim 0.2%. Christian 4.7%: House churches 3.0%, TSPM 1.2%, all Catholics 0.5%.

C

1. **The registered Church grew considerably** before 1949, but since then has not matched the growth of many other areas. Authorities maintain a tight control, especially over the cities, so registered churches are relatively few. In the capital, Wuhan, each main TSPM church must serve 10,000 members. Pray for a shattering of the political, ideological and spiritual chains that bind the people.

2. **House churches have grown significantly** in many parts of the province – much of this the result of compassionate ministry to flood victims. But growth has come at a cost; persecution is often high, and many (if not most) leaders have been arrested and imprisoned. A disproportionate number of church members are women. Pray for the churches to continue to grow, to disciple well their rapidly increasing numbers and to see more men come into faith.

3. **The ethnic minorities of the province are largely unreached.** Among the polytheistic, animist and ancestor-worshipping Tujia, Enshi Miao and Northern Dong, as among the Muslim Hui, Christians make up less than 1% and usually closer to 0.1% of their populations. Pray for their evangelization.

Hunan Province

Geography

Area 187,500 sq km. Central China.
Population 65,322,000; 348 people/sq km.
Capital Changsha 2.4m. **Other major city** Hengyang 1.1m; Yueyang 1.1m; Yongzhou 1.0m; Zhuzhou 1.0m.

Peoples

According to the latest census, there are 41 ethnic groups in Hunan. Han Chinese 93.8%, Putonghua and Xiang are widely spoken. Miao/Hmong 2.4%. Gao-Xong(2) 1.25m; Hmu 290,000. Tai 1.4%. Dong(2) 950,000. Yao-Mien 0.4%. Iu Mien 216,000; Wunai 12,000. Others 0.5%. Zhuang, Uyghur, Hui, many small ethnic groups. Tibetan/Himalayan 1.5%. Tujia 890,000; Bai 100,000; Mozhihei 7,000.

Religion

Atheism/Maoism still strong among Han. Most minorities are animists or polytheists. Muslim 0.1%. Christian 4.0%: House churches 2.4%, TSPM 1.2%, all Catholics 0.4%.

1. **Hunan province is traditionally closed,** conservative and isolated, usually by choice. Hunan, Mao's birthplace, is historically hostile to foreigners and was one of the provinces that eagerly adopted the Cultural Revolution. Hunan possibly has China's most spiritually hard Han Chinese populations. Pray for spiritual breakthrough in this resistant province.

2. **The Church was traditionally very small** but has started to grow rapidly in the last generation. This is apparent in the fact that almost all believers are younger people and first-generation Christians. Almost all churches in the area are growing, but so are cults and Confucianism. The True Jesus Church is strong here. There is a great need for trained leaders;

in 2009, TSPM had only 65 ordained leaders for 1,200 congregations. There are also around 40,000 house churches; these have leadership and discipleship needs of their own. In rural areas, congregations are overwhelmingly made up of women. Pray for further growth among all generations, both genders and all areas – peoples in the more remote western mountains are hardly touched by the gospel. Pray also for the establishment of effective training structures.

3 The less evangelized:

C

a) *Changsha,* the capital, is where Mao converted to communism – and where Hudson Taylor died and is buried. Its people were notoriously closed to foreign influences such as Christianity. It has perhaps 50,000 Christians out of a metropolitan area population of over six million, most growth resulting from house church evangelists from other parts of China. Rural areas of Hunan have proven much more responsive.

b) *The Tujia* are one of the larger peoples in the world without a written language, and therefore, none of the Bible. About 2.0% of Tujia are Christian. The majority are animists with particular reverence for white tigers.

c) *Other peoples.* There are no known believers among the Wunai and Mozhihei. The Iu Mien, Dong and Hmu have tiny minorities of Christians, while the small Uyghur and Hui enclaves also have no known believers or outreach. The Ghao-Xong are marginally reached with 5,000 Catholics.

Inner Mongolia Autonomous Region (Nei Mongol)

Geography 🌐

Area 1,177,500 sq km. A grassland and desert region bordering Mongolia and Russia. The western point is 3,500 km from its northeastern point.
Population 24,689,000; 21 people/sq km.
Capital Hohhat 1.6m. **Other major city** Baotou 1.9m.

Peoples 👤👤👤

Han Chinese 70.9%, speaking Putonghua. Mongolian 17%. 5 peoples; largest are Mongolian 16.2%; Buryat 0.5%; Khalkha 0.3%. Manchu 2.0%. Hui 1.0%. Turkic-Altaic 0.2%. Evenki(2), Oroqen. Other 0.1%. Korean.

Religion

Most Mongolians are Lamaistic Buddhists but many of the smaller minorities are Shamanists. Christian 9.5%: House churches 5.1%, TSPM 1.1%, Roman Catholic 2.1%, CPA 1.1%.

---

1 Inner Mongolia is experiencing a boom in economic development (especially the energy industry) and, inevitably, in the mass immigration of Han Chinese. The region has sustained China's highest annual GDP increase for five years running. The recently arrived millions of Han also brought the gospel to Inner Mongolia on a much greater scale than ever before.

2 Mongolians are now a minority in their own land, and their culture is imperilled, due to massive Han Chinese immigration in recent decades. Yet there are more Mongolians here – over four million – than in independent Mongolia to the north. Hundreds of thousands have been forcibly resettled from their ancestral pastures. Mongolians are much less evangelized than the Han majority, but they are very open to the gospel, probably exceeding 40,000 believers – a number that is growing rapidly. Pray for:

a) *The binding of spiritual powers* that blind Mongolians to the truth. Their religious practices include aspects of shamanism, ancestor worship, totemism and magic, combined with Lamaistic Buddhism of a variety similar to that practiced by Tibetans. In all cases, the spirit world is very real and profoundly powerful and influential.

b) *More workers.* Praise God for the increase of mission-minded believers from neighbouring Mongolia, from the Han majority and even from further afield. Yet more workers are still needed.

c) *The recently translated Old and New Testaments* in three different scripts and two different translations. Praise God for this great achievement! Some Scripture is also available in audio format. Pray that sufficient copies would be available and well used for witness and discipleship.

*d) **Worship music,*** which has been developed in the Mongolian language and style.

*e) **FEBC broadcasts*** in Mongolian on shortwave and FM radio.

3 **House churches have multiplied across the region like wildfire,** but almost all are Han groups. Christians are now increasingly reaching out to non–Han groups across the region. Catholics also have a notable presence here. Continuing repression of churches in many districts requires that they keep a low profile. Cult groups prey on the rapid growth and lack of teaching in house churches; in some areas, 80% of house churches have been taken over by the Eastern Lightning cult. Pray for continued growth as well as the availability of solid biblical teaching for all. Pray for believers to know the truth that sets them free, and pray that they would not be taken in by a counterfeit gospel.

4 **Among the traditionally nomadic Evenki and Oroqen peoples** along the Russian border is very little evangelical witness and only a small number of Christians. Most practice a mix of shamanism, animism and Lamaistic Buddhism. Pray for them to be reached with the good news of Jesus.

Jiangsu Province

Geography 🌐

Area 102,600 sq km. Relatively prosperous; fertile coastal province west of Shanghai.
Population 77,764,000; 758 people/sq km. China's highest population density province.
Capital Nanjing 4.5m. **Other major cities** Wuxi 2.7m; Suzhou 2.4m; Changzhou 2.1m; Xuzhou 2.1m; Xinghua 1.8m; Huaian 1.4m; Nantong 1.4m; Suqian 1.4m; Yancheng 1.3m; Yangzhou 1.1m; Zenjiang 1.0m.

Peoples 👪

Han Chinese, speaking Mandarin. Small numbers of Hui and Manchu.

Religion 🙏

Muslim 0.2%. Christian 9.2%: House churches 3.6%, TSPM 4.2%, all Catholics 1.4%.

---

1 **Church growth has been spectacular since 1980,** with over three million associated with TSPM churches – the greatest church growth of any province except Henan. The burgeoning house churches account for approaching three million more. However, the Church cannot rest comfortably. The government still routinely cracks down hard on unregistered congregations, and cults are very active in this region. The Lingling cult began in Jiangsu. The increasing wealth in this area can also be a snare to immature Christians. Pray for God to preserve, purify and build His people in this already blessed province.

2 **Nanjing is a key city for Christianity in China.** The national seminary for the TSPM is here, as is the Amity Press, China's biggest printer and the source of 50 million Bibles and NTs so far, with millions more published every year. Its sister organization, Amity Foundation, has a ministry involved in community development, medical care, rural education and social welfare. It also majors on promoting church involvement in social service, a crucial step in the maturation and development of Christianity in China.

Jiangxi Province

Geography

Area 164,800 sq km. South-central China.
Population 44,691,000; 271 people/sq km.
Capital Nanchang 2.7m. **Other major city** Pingxiang 1.0m.

Peoples

Han Chinese 99%, speaking Mandarin, Gan and Hakka. Other 1%, including Hui and Zhuang.

Religion

Christian 5.6%: House churches 2.9%, TSPM 1.6%, all Catholics 1.1%.

1. **The Communist Long March began here** – a march that ended with political triumph for that ideology, but much pain and trouble for China. Jiangxi still possesses much Communist heritage, and it suffers from weak and often corrupt leaders, who institute policies that frequently spark massive protests and even riots by disgruntled farmers and peasants. The province remains mostly poor, especially in contrast to its very wealthy neighbouring provinces to the east. Pray for the release of this province from all that opposes God.

2. **Christians are a lower proportion in Jiangxi** than nationally, but numbers are growing substantially, especially among the house church networks. The Church is multiplying in many areas, but other parts of the province are relatively underevangelized.

Jilin Province

Geography

Area 187,000 sq km. Part of former Manchuria, bordering on North Korea and Siberia.
Population 28,046,000; 150 people/sq km.
Capital Chang-chun 3.6m. **Other major cities** Jilin 1.9m; Fuyu 1.1m.

Peoples

Han Chinese 90.3%, speaking Mandarin. Korean 4.6%. Manchu 3.9%. Mongolian 0.7%. Hui 0.5%.

Religion

Many Koreans practice a mix of Buddhism and Shamanism. Muslim 0.6%. Christian 7.6%: House churches 5.0%, TSPM 1.6%, all Catholics 1.0%.

1. **The Church is relatively strong** with many registered and unregistered congregations. Jilin is home to two-thirds of China's ethnic Koreans. Koreans are a large minority of Jilin's Christians. Nearly a third of the 2.4 million Koreans in Liaoning, Jilin and Heilongjiang Provinces are Christian. Praise God for this.

2. **The large cities,** Changchun and Jilin City, have a much lower percentage of Christians. Pray for churches to be multiplied in urban areas, especially as increasing numbers of rural people migrate to cities.

3. **The Chinese Korean Church** has a special and strategic role to play for North Korea. Hundreds of thousands have fled that repressed land in the past decade, the vast majority crossing over into NE China. Christians play a dangerous role in sheltering and hiding these refugees who are hunted by both North Korean security forces and Chinese police; the punishment for sheltering or aiding such escapees is severe and exceeded only by the penalty meted out to the North Koreans if they are caught. China's Korean believers will also play a massive part in whatever national rebuilding occurs should North Korea's regime crumble.

4. **The recent rise of pseudo-Christian cults** in Jilin is a concern. Groups such as the Eastern Lightning specifically target house churches to steal away believers. Even pastors and church leaders have been led astray by these groups.

Liaoning Province

Population 43,991,000; 291 people/sq km.
Capital Shenyang 5.2m. **Other major cities**
Dalian 3.3m; Anshan 1.7m; Fushun 1.4m.

Geography 🌐

Area 151,000 sq km. Southernmost of the three provinces of Manchuria, bordering on the Yellow Sea and North Korea. Heavily industrialized – much of it is state-controlled, but moving toward privatization – and agriculturally fertile.

Peoples 👪

Han Chinese 85.6%, speaking Mandarin. Manchu 13.1%. Mongol 1.7%. Hui 0.7%. Korean 0.6%. Xibe 0.3%.

Religion 🙏

Muslim 0.8%. Christian 7.0%: House churches 4.6%, TSPM 1.4%, all Catholics 1.0%.

C

1 **Liaoning was the northern heart of modern China's industrialization,** then of its decline, with much unemployment. It is now making a comeback – thanks to a combination of industry, technology, agriculture, growing foreign investment and the port of Dalian – though advances are far from those made in the southern and eastern coastal provinces. Shenyang and other cities attract many economic migrants from the wider region. Pray that wise policies will rebuild this region and afford gainful employment for the millions who were laid off in years past.

2 **The Church has grown remarkably,** with house churches more than doubling in the last 10 years, building on a pre-revolution foundation of Presbyterian mission activity. A high proportion, perhaps 20%, of Christians in the province are Korean. Both locals and foreigners, especially Koreans, are active in ministry and church planting. Pray for greater levels of discipleship and continued evangelistic fervour for believers.

3 **Liaoning's border with North Korea** makes it a highly significant place spiritually. North Korean refugees attempt to escape from that tragic land; around 30,000 each year make it into China. Both North Korea and China are cracking down hard on escapees and any who assist or shelter them. North Koreans who become Christians through the ministry of believers in China are treated especially brutally – either labour camps or execution. Most who make it across are women; many of these sadly end up trafficked by unscrupulous opportunists into an equally nightmarish existence as domestic or sexual slaves. Pray that those who escape from North Korea might find freedom, safety and the light of the gospel in China.

4 **The Manchu** conquered and ruled China from 1644 to 1911, but lost their culture in the process. They are the second-largest minority group in China. Of the 13.3 million Manchu, the majority live in the three provinces of former Manchuria but are also scattered across China. Most are largely assimilated into Chinese society, but a few retain their culture, their shamanist religion and their language. Praise God for a significant response to the gospel recently, both in Manchu congregations and those integrated into Han-majority churches.

Ningxia Hui Autonomous Region

Population 6,221,000; 94 people/sq km.
Capital Yinchuan 911,000.

Peoples 👪

Han Chinese 65.1%, speaking Mandarin. Hui 34.5%. Manchu 0.4%.

Religion 🙏

Muslim 34%. Christian 4.0%: House churches 1.9%, TSPM 1.2%, all Catholics 0.9%.

Geography 🌐

Area 66,400 sq km. Arid steppe with a fertile strip along the Yellow River in north China.

1 **The Hui are officially China's third-largest minority group** (officially 13.2 million but possibly more). They are found in every province of China, and only a minority of two million live in Ningxia, their Autonomous Region. They are descendants of a mix of Persian and Arab Muslim traders, Mongolians and Chinese. They strongly retain their culture and religion and speak their own brand of Mandarin, but they also speak the local dialect of wherever they live. After 30 years of mission outreach before 1951, very few had become believers. There is renewed interest in reaching them. Points for prayer:

a) *Praise God for what He is doing among the Hui.* While there are still fewer than 1,000 believers, there are now a handful of fellowships and congregations where a few years ago there were none. Interest and focus – from both Han Chinese and expatriate believers – are also growing to reach the Hui for Christ. Pray for a growing harvest among the Hui.

b) *The Hui are almost entirely Muslim* (and 80% Sunni). There are some episodes of bloody enmity as the presence of a Chinese majority generates among the Hui attitudes of suspicion and mistrust of the Han. Outreach by Han Chinese therefore requires great sensitivity and humility. Some Hui are vulnerable to further Islamization and possibly even radicalization by foreign Islamist elements.

c) *Hui identity is deeply tied to Muslim identity.* According to government definitions, to be Hui is to be Muslim; technically, one cannot be both Hui and Christian. Most Hui who become Christian assimilate into Chinese churches and lose their Hui identity. Pray that there might be a movement to Christ that allows Hui to follow Jesus and retain their socio-cultural distinctives. The Bible and other Christian resources are being adapted to Hui terminology; pray for the completion of these projects and their widespread use.

2 **There is a significant turning to Christianity** in the north, along the Yellow River where many Han immigrants live. Christian ministry to the poor has yielded great response among farmers and working-class people. Pray for the formation of churches where the many new believers can be led in discipleship and study of the Bible.

Qinghai Province

Geography 🌍

Area 721,000 sq km. A huge, alpine and desert province in West China on the Tibetan Plateau. There are six Tibetan Autonomous Prefectures in Qinghai; Tibetans are a large majority in four of them.
Population 5,644,000; 8 people/sq km.
Capital Xining 1.3m.

Peoples 👪

Han Chinese 54.7%. Tibetan-Himalayan 20.9%. 9 peoples – largest are Amdo(3) 13.0%; Golog 2.9%; Khampa Tibetan 2.4%; Sogwo Arig 0.7%. Hui 15.7%. Mongolian 6.7%. 4 peoples – Tu 3.9%; Oirat 1.8%; Mongour 0.9%; Bonan 0.1%. Turkic-Altaic 2.0%. 2 peoples – Salar 1.8%; Kazakh 0.2%.

Religion 🔥

Buddhist >25%. Muslim 17.0%. Christian 5.0%: House churches 3.8%, TSPM 0.9%, all Catholics 0.3%.

---

1 **The 2010 earthquake in Yushu Prefecture** flattened many thousands of homes and other buildings, injured tens of thousands and killed thousands more – officially, 2,200 were killed, but grassroots sources estimate 10,000 to 20,000. This predominantly Tibetan area has seen admirable rescue and relief efforts from the Chinese government and military as well as from NGOs assisting with the needs of those affected. Pray that the Tibetan Buddhist people of Yushu – very fatalistic in their worldview – might encounter the love of Christ, and that through this disaster, life might come to them.

2 **This desolate region is dotted with dozens of labour and prison camps;** previous estimates placed these camps as having 10% of Qinghai's overall population. Many thousands of prisoners have endured great hardship there – including many believers. Pray for all prisoners of conscience, that their faith in God might grow and bless those around them.

3 **In the 1940s there were only a few hundred Christians,** mainly in Xining, but in the last 20 years growth has been quite remarkable. Today there are over 280,000 Christians. Most of this growth is among the Han Chinese, and a significant amount through migration. Praise God for this rapid growth. Pray also that the Han Christians might gain passion and vision for the unevangelized peoples among whom they live.

4 The unreached. Qinghai is a unique geographical region where the Tibetan, Han, Mongol, Hui and Turkic worlds meet. Qinghai has the highest percentage ethnic-minority population of any full province in China.

a) The Tibetan peoples remain strongly entrenched in Lamaistic Buddhism. Living conditions are harsh, and they traditionally depend on large herds of yak. China's central-government policy of "development" and forced resettlement threatens their traditional way of life. Most Tibetans are strongly bound by powers and principalities of the high places of the Tibetan plateau and religion. There are now a handful of isolated believers, but, despite great amounts of intercession and attention, no breakthrough has yet occurred.

b) The Tu, Oirat and Mongour are Lamaistic Buddhists with only a handful of known believers. They are isolated from existing outreach.

c) The Muslim Hui in Xining are numerous and there are a handful of Christians among them. Han Christians are beginning to reach out to them.

d) The Muslim Salar have a few dozen believers, but the Bonan remain completely unreached.

Shaanxi Province

Geography 🌏
Area 195,800 sq km in north central China.
Population 38,470,000; 196 people/sq km.
Capital Xi'an 4.7m. Once the capital of China in the T'ang dynasty. Famous for the buried terra-cotta army. **Other major cities** Yulin 1.2m; Xianyang 1.0m.

Peoples 👪
Han Chinese 99.5%, speaking Putonghua. Hui 0.5%.

Religion 🙇
Muslim 0.5%. Christian 9.4%: House churches 4.8%, TSPM 2.4%, Catholics 2.2%.

---

1 Shaanxi is the birthplace of Christianity in China. The Nestorians built their first church in Xi'an in 635, but terrible persecution wiped out this witness. Pray that the 21st Century may be one of triumph for the Church.

2 This was the endpoint of the Long March, which resulted in the triumph of Communism in China. Poverty remains widespread today, and the ministry of Christians to those so afflicted has yielded much fruit.

3 The Church has grown rapidly and dramatically, especially in the last 20 years – from 30,000 Christians in 1949 to an estimated 3.6 million in 2010. Lack of biblical teaching and trained leaders makes the Church vulnerable to heresy; the Disciples is a cult started in Shaanxi. Pray for spiritual growth, health and unity for Shaanxi Christians.

4 There are over one million students in Xi'an. Pray for effective student ministry in this key city. Pray also for effective programmes that help those students who come to Christ integrate into churches upon graduation. Far too many come to faith as students but are then lost to the Church as they enter the working world.

Shandong Province

Geography 🌏

Area 153,300 sq km. Northern coastal province on the Shandong Peninsula, which extends into the Yellow Sea.
Population 95,882,000; 625 people/sq km. China's third most populous province.

Capital Jinan 3.2m. **Other major cities** Qingdao 3.3m; Zibo 2.5m; Weifang 1.7m; Yantai 1.5m; Xintai 1.5m; Heze 1.4m; Linyi 1.4m; Jining 1.3m; Linqing 1.2m; Zaozhuang 1.2m.

Peoples 👪

Han Chinese 99%, speaking Putonghua. Other 1%. Hui, Manchu.

Religion

Muslim 0.5%. Christian 5.1%: House churches 2.5%, TSPM 1.7%, Catholics 0.9%.

1 **This peninsular province is one of China's richest** due to strong traditions in industry and manufacturing and solid investment from the proximate South Korea and Japan. Pray that its economic stability and connections to the wider world might be the means by which the gospel spreads within Shandong and to the rest of China.

2 **Shandong was the birthplace and home of Confucius,** whose philosophy and writings deeply moulded Chinese culture, even to this day. Pray that the Chinese may be freed from the social demands that hinder many from commitment to Christ.

3 **Tai'an is near Taishan, China's most "holy" mountain** according to Daoist and Confucian traditions. This is a major spiritual stronghold up on which prayer should be focused.

4 **The Jesus Family,** a remarkable form of communal Christianity, began in this province. They were influential in the start of the house church movement, into which they were subsequently integrated. Pray for the spiritual health of all forms of indigenous Christianity and for the centrality of Scripture in their life and teaching. Persecution, cults and lack of trained leaders are all threats to this.

Shanghai Municipality

Geography 🌏

Area 6,200 sq km. China's largest and wealthiest city (after Hong Kong) and an industrial hub for the country, with a large international seaport.
Population 19,500,000; 3,145 people/sq km.

Peoples 👪

Han Chinese 97.5%: indigenes speak Shanghainese, a dialect of Wu Chinese and mutually unintelligible with Putonghua, which is also widely spoken by younger generations and outsiders. Other 2.5%.

Religion

Muslim 0.4%. Christian 11.0%: House churches 5.1%, TSPM 2.3%, all Catholics 3.6%.

1 **Shanghai is China's largest city** (and the largest city proper in the world), a financial and trading powerhouse and the nation's largest port. Materialism and even naked greed characterize much of the drive behind the city's growth. Pray that the great wealth fuelling Shanghai's rise might be used for redemptive purposes; pray also that those coming to Shanghai from the far-flung parts of China might be reached with the gospel.

2 **Shanghai traditionally had a diverse religious heritage and Church life,** but these were all but destroyed in the Cultural Revolution. Today, as a cosmopolitan urban centre, it has a varied religious landscape and a dynamic church scene. This includes many Catholics, TSPM churches (close to 200 official congregations) and hundreds, even thousands, of unregistered house churches and training programmes. Shanghai is a strong centre for the Local Church, which emerged from the ministry and teachings of Watchman Nee. Professionals, academics and students swell the ranks of the churches. Pray for the many Christians here to be profound witnesses in this massive, multi-faith city.

3 **This municipality also hosts China's largest expatriate population,** which includes large communities of Westerners, Koreans and especially Taiwanese and other overseas Chinese. There are many active Christians among them and much Christian activity by and for them. Pray for a positive interaction, when it is beneficial to do so, between national and foreign believers.

4 **Other demographic groups.** Shanghai is a magnet for between 4.8 and 5.8 million migrant workers. These come from all over China but especially from neighbouring provinces. Shanghai also has more than three million residents over 60 years of age – 22% of its population. This group, the generation of the Cultural Revolution, needs specific and focused outreach. Pray for ministry to both Shanghai's aging natives and its immigrating outsiders.

Shanxi Province

Geography 🌏
Area 157,100 sq km. Northeast China, west of Beijing. Not to be confused with neighbouring Shaanxi.
Population 34,762,000; 221 people/sq km.

Capital Taiyuan 3.2m. **Other major city** Datong 1.3m.

Peoples 👪
Han Chinese 99.7%, speaking Jin and Zhongyuan dialects of Mandarin. Other 0.3%. Hui, Mongol, Manchu.

Religion 🙏
Muslim 0.2%. Christian 8.6%: House churches 4.8%, TSPM 1.5%, Catholics 2.3%.

1 **Shanxi is China's industrial heart,** still pumping but weakened and diseased. Heavy industry and many factories have wrought a harsh toll on the now-polluted landscape. Widespread problems – health and disease, harsh working conditions for factory employees and especially miners, the arid climate, geographic isolation and relative poverty – combine to spread a sense of hopelessness and desperation. Pray for hope, expressed ultimately in the new and eternal life found in Jesus.

2 **The government maintains strict control** over the TSPM Church here, and house churches are persecuted in waves. This heritage of persecution is longstanding; during the Boxer Rebellion in 1900, thousands of Chinese (and 200 expatriates) were martyred for their faith. The religious freedom that does exist actually causes great anxiety, since new crackdowns can come at any time and without warning.

3 **The Church in Shanxi** is one of the fastest growing in China, possibly because of these two aforementioned issues. The TSPM, the house churches and even Catholics are growing; many thousands of new believers come into the fold every year. Praise God and pray for continued growth of both numbers and maturity.

4 **The region has several spiritual strongholds.** Mount Wutai is a holy mountain for Buddhism, Mount Hengshan is one of five Daoist holy mountains in China and Dazhai was set forth as a Maoist holy place during the Cultural Revolution. Pray for God Almighty to demonstrate His sovereignty and build His Kingdom in Shanxi.

Sichuan Province

Geography 🌐

Area 487,000 sq km. A large, fertile and resource-rich province on the Yangtze River ringed by high mountains. The "panda province".

Population 88,150,000; 181 people/sq km.

Capital Chengdu 4.7m. **Other major cities** Nanchong 2.7m; Suining 1.5m; Leshan 1.2m; Mianyang 1.0m.

Peoples 👥

Han Chinese 93.8%, most speaking southwestern dialects of Mandarin. Tibetan-Himalayan 5.4%. 44 peoples – largest are Nosu/Yi(8) 2.7%; Eastern Khampa 1.4%; Qiang(12) 0.4%; Jiarong(5) 0.3%; Suodi 0.3%; Rtahu Amdo 0.1%; Ergong 0.07%; Chrame 0.05%; Mosuo 0.03%. Miao-Hmong 0.8%: Miao (Enchi and Chuan).

Religion 📿

Lamaistic Buddhist 4.5% among Tibetans, Jiarong, Mosuo, Chrame. Animist, polytheist among Nosu, Qiang, Miao. Christian 3.2%: House churches 1.2%, TSPM 0.5%, Roman Catholics 1.0%, CPA 0.5%.

1 **The devastating 2008 Wenchuan earthquake** not far from Chengdu took 70,000 lives, injured 375,000 and left at least 4.8 million (some claim up to 11 million) homeless, with many other buildings destroyed or damaged. Many lost all they possessed; it will take years to recover. Yet the tragedy offered Christians the chance to demonstrate the love and power of Jesus to those who were suffering. Thousands came to know Christ through compassionate ministry offered by believers. Just as crucially, TSPM and house church Christians worked together in unprecedented ways. Pray for continued reconstruction – without the shortcuts and corruption that caused many poorly built structures to easily collapse in 2008. Pray also for Christians to build effectively on this platform of cooperation.

2 **Sichuan has the lowest Christian percentage** of the Han-majority provinces. The Catholics arrived in 1696, and LMS and CIM in 1868/81. But even with recent significant growth among Catholics and in house churches, no major breakthrough has been seen. Pray that the spiritual mountains that ring this province might be breached and millions turn to Christ.

3 **Chengdu,** with 4.3 million people in its city proper and 11 million in its larger conurbation, is a key city for the whole of western China. In addition to the growing TSPM churches in the city, there are over 130,000 believers in the house church networks. The gospel is making great headway in this city. There are many ethnic-minority groups, especially Tibetans. Pray for this needy city and those seeking to reach it.

4 **Ethnic minorities indigenous to Sichuan** total 5.5 million in 44 indigenous peoples, but 33 are unevangelized. Praise God that the gospel is beginning to reach these groups; in several instances during the last few years, the very first converts came to Jesus. Intercede for:

a) *The major groups with no or negligible witness;* the Qiang cluster of peoples, the Tibetan groups, Suodi, Mosuo, Enshi Miao, others. Many of these peoples, though related, speak mutually unintelligible languages.

b) *The Nosu* are a particular challenge. They are a proud people who once dominated their area and enslaved the Han Chinese. They were finally subdued by the central government only in 1953. They are known for their violence, war-making, intimidation and polytheism. The JESUS film has had some impact, but only the Shengzha Nosu are greater than 1% Christian. Pray for this spiritual stronghold to be breached.

c) *The small Christian groups* among these peoples to become strong, effective witnesses.

d) *Ethnic minorities in Yunnan and elsewhere* with large Christian communities to become missionaries to these peoples.

e) *The Han Chinese believers who move to the minority areas as witnesses.* They possess great zeal, but need wisdom and patience to learn cross-cultural skills. Pray for them to invest sufficient time in learning the language and culture of their host peoples. Pray also for them to retain focus on these unreached minorities and not be distracted by the ministry needs of other Han Chinese.

f) **Bible translators.** The Bible is available for the Khampa and Amdo Tibetans, and there are portions of Scripture for the Chuan Miao and Shengzha Nosu, but no other group has anything of God's Word.

Tianjin Municipality

Geography

Area 11,300 sq km. The port city of Beijing.
Population 12,450,000; 1,100 people/sq km.

Peoples 👫👫

Han Chinese 97.2%, speaking Tianjin dialect of Mandarin. Hui 1.9%. Manchu 0.6%. Other 0.3%.

Religion

Muslim 2.0%. Christian 3.8%: House churches 0.9%, TSPM 0.6%, Catholics 2.3%.

C

1 **Tianjin, as a major international port,** should be a vibrant and dynamic city with a strong economy, but quirks of history, poor city planning, an economic slowdown and the decrease of export shipping have stunted its development. Despite this, there are a wide range of Chinese ethnicities and foreign nationalities present along with the vision and potential to be a world-class port city with a thriving economy. Pray that such growth and openness to the region as a seaport would also bring the strong presence of the good news.

2 **The Church** is almost as tightly controlled in Tianjin as in nearby Beijing, but church growth has been more limited. Catholics have fared better. Church leaders tend to be quite aged, and an injection of younger leadership is needed. Pray for an easing of the harsh restrictions, for more church growth and for a new generation of committed, trained leaders.

Tibet – Xizang Autonomous Region

Geography

Area 1,221,600 sq km. High, barren Tibetan plateau north of the Himalaya Mountains, much of which is uninhabited and includes Mount Qomolangma (Everest); often called the "Roof of the World". The Tibet Autonomous Region (TAR) is less than half of the area of historic Tibet. Six of the world's great rivers have their source in Tibet.
Population 2,894,000; 2 people/sq km.
Capital Lhasa 154,000.

Peoples 👫👫

Han Chinese 20%, from large-scale immigration and a large military presence. Tibetan–Himalayan 80%. 24 peoples – largest are Central (Lhasa) 25.6%; Gtsang 20.6%; Western Khampa 7.1%; Monba(2) 1.7%; Deng(2) 0.7%; Groma 0.7%; Lhoba 0.4%.

Religion

Lamaistic Buddhist 80%. Two factions: Yellow Hat and Red Hat. Interwoven with the pre-Buddhist Bon religion. Muslim 0.2%. Christian 0.3%: 8,000 largely Catholic in southeastern corner of Tibet; 1,300 house church followers.

1 **Tibet is a contentious international issue.** It lost its short-lived independence as a theocratic Buddhist state in 1950 when China re-invaded the land. China's central government has systematically sought to destroy the culture, religions and ethnic identity of the Tibetan people. Resistance to the occupiers has resulted in frequent revolts and unrest. Over 6,000 monasteries have been destroyed, over one million people may have lost their lives and a further 100,000 may have been forced into exile, including the spiritual and political leader of Tibetans, the Dalai Lama. His spiritual influence is global and extends far beyond Tibetan Buddhism. But he is now in his 70s; his advocacy for Tibetan freedom cannot last forever. Once he is gone, many reckon Tibet's cause will suffer a fatal blow. Pray for a just and peaceful settlement for all concerned.

2 **Tibetan Buddhism permeates society** and has a powerful hold on the people. It incorporates many elements of the pre-Buddhist Bon religion, which still exists in its own right as well. Bon has powerful demonic and occult influences and spirit appeasement. The high places of the Tibetan plateau are known to be a spiritual stronghold highly resistant to the gospel. In TAR, there are still 1,789 monasteries and 46,000 Buddhist monks. Pray that present sufferings may be God's means for bringing spiritual freedom to Tibetans.

3 **After centuries of failed attempts and limited fruit,** there may be just over 1,000 evangelical and 2,000 Catholic Christians among the five million ethnic Tibetans in the world. There are a handful of underground fellowships in Lhasa, some scattered believers elsewhere in the TAR and some small groups elsewhere in China. Although there are believers among the larger Tibetan peoples (Central Tibetan, Amdo, Kham), many less populous peoples have no believers at all. Although few in number, fearful and under great pressure to fall back into their old ways, Tibetan Christians are growing and emerging as a viable Church with their own leaders and patterns of worship and fellowship. Pray for this fledgling Church.

4 **Christian materials in Tibetan languages and dialects** are limited, but growing. The Tibetan Storytelling Project summarizes the story of salvation using traditional Tibetan art (thangka paintings), songs, choreography and rhythmic speech. It and the Hope DVD are available in the Central Tibetan dialect with more translations planned. Scriptures are available in some Tibetan languages, but further translation work is definitely needed. **GRN** has produced audio materials in several Tibetan languages, the JESUS film is available and Christian radio programmes are broadcast every day (**FEBC** and others). Pray that through all these means, many more Tibetans would hear and respond to the good news.

5 **Political sensitivity and tensions** in Tibet make entry and travel in the country difficult for both Chinese and foreign Christians who desire to share the love of Jesus there. Pray for open doors and freedom to proclaim the gospel. China's economic development of the region has improved access and transport but is also accused of cultural genocide against Tibetans. Personal witness is more achievable in the surrounding provinces of Gansu, Qinghai and Sichuan. More than 150,000 Tibetans live in exile in Nepal, India and the West, where they are more accessible.

6 **There are growing numbers of Han Chinese in Tibet;** official sources state less than 5%; Tibetan exiles claim that more than 50% of people in TAR are Han. Pray for the planting of house fellowships among them – some have been started. Lhasa is now a Han Chinese-majority city. As economic development continues, more and more Han will pour into the TAR. Pray that among them will be many believers committed to reaching Tibetans for Christ.

Xinjiang Uyghur Autonomous Region

Geography

Area 1,646,900 sq km. Ringed with mountains surrounding the Taklamakan Desert in northwest China.
Population 21,115,000; 13 people/sq km. Most live at desert oases or in the mountains.
Capital Urumqi 2.4m.

Peoples

The sheer scale of Han migration into Xinjiang and politicization of Uyghur independence mean that accurate numbers for both Uyghurs and Han Chinese are impossible to obtain.

Turkic 56.8%: 14 peoples – largest are Uyghur(7) 48.6%; Kazakh 7.2%; Kyrgyz 0.9%; Uzbek 0.08%. Han Chinese 36.8%, rapidly increasing through immigration; most living in cities; Urumqi is over 95% Han. Hui 4.4%. Manchu 0.1%. Mongol 1.4%. Torgut 1.1%; Western Xibe 0.3%; Tuva 0.02%. Other 0.4%. Tajik(2) 0.3%; Russian 0.05%.

Religion

Muslim 61.4%, the Turkic peoples, Tajik and Hui. Lamaistic Buddhist 1.4%, Mongols. Christian 4.1%: House churches 3.2%, TSPM 0.7%, all Catholics 0.2%.

1 **Xinjiang has long been one of China's most troubled regions.** It is the homeland of the Uyghur peoples – possibly numbering up to 11 million in China. In the last few years, riots, insurrections, separatist rhetoric, revisionist history and harsh government crackdowns have increased. There are numerous reasons for the strife:

a) *Xinjiang possesses rich natural resources and a strategic location.* China's hunger for raw materials and its unswerving commitment to its own territorial integrity have generated a state-endorsed massive immigration of Han Chinese into Xinjiang.

b) *Such large-scale incursions* – not just into larger cities but also into the fertile oases that form the basis of Uyghur territory and history – threaten the long-term existential viability of Uyghur identity and culture.

c) *A reactionary trend* that drives many Uyghurs into a deeper and frequently more radical expression of Islam, fuelled by external Islamist influences.

d) *Beijing's inflexibility toward compromise solutions* that actually allow for some real autonomy for Uyghurs – in contrast to the strict implementation of state control – makes a sad irony of the moniker "Autonomous Region". Thousands, mostly Uyghurs, have lost their lives or been imprisoned amid the ruthless implementation of centralized policies and the repression of separatist sentiment.

e) *Centuries-old animosity* between Uyghurs and Han.

2 **Almost all the indigenous peoples are Muslim.** The highly charged political and religious atmosphere, the removal of expatriate Christian workers from most of the region and the general lack of vision by Han Chinese to evangelize these peoples mean that the vast bulk of Xinjiang's indigenous peoples are untouched by the gospel. Reaching them will be difficult (but not impossible!), requiring perseverance, cultural sensitivity and great faith. Pray for an awakening among Christians in China and those globally to the great spiritual needs of Xinjiang's unevangelized peoples.

3 **The 850,000 Christians in Xinjiang,** almost all Han Chinese, are culturally isolated from the indigenous population, but have experienced significant growth nonetheless. Pray that they may have a vision for and understanding of witnessing to Muslims. Many live in the capital, Urumqi. Among the non-Chinese are a few hundred known Christians; their numbers are growing, but they are subjected to harsh repression from the state and social and family pressures to return to Islam. The government takes a hard line against Christian ministry in Xinjiang (on the pretext that it might provoke Muslim anger), and expats find it very difficult to minister at all.

4 **There was once a thriving Church among the Uyghur people** – Nestorian Christianity was present as early as the 6th Century and peaked in the 13th Century. There were also believers and some churches among the Uyghur in the 1930s, but during violent persecution the churches were destroyed and believers killed or scattered. There are now 200 to 300 Uyghur believers in Xinjiang, and another 500 in neighbouring Kazakhstan. Praise God for the completion and distribution of the NT, Genesis and Exodus. Work on the OT – vital for reaching Muslims – is proceeding. The JESUS film, Christian audio recordings, gospel songs, Christian radio (**TWR**) and other resources now exist in the Uyghur language. Pray for the strengthening and growth of the small Uyghur house churches in Xinjiang.

5 **Other ethnicities in Xinjiang** also see the beginnings of a Church being formed among them. Kazakhs especially, but also Hui, Kyrgyz and others are finding life in Jesus.

Yunnan Province

Geography 🌐

Area 436,200 sq km. In China's mountainous southwest.
Population 46,174,000; 106 people/sq km.
Capital Kunming 3.1m.

Peoples 👪

Han Chinese 65.4%, speaking several southwestern Mandarin dialects and Putonghua.
Tibetan–Himalayan 25.5%. 11.6m in 154 peoples.
Main people clusters:
  West China/Yi 17.0%. Bai 4.3%; Nasu(4) 2.3%; Nisu(3) 2.2%; Laluo 1.7%; Luolupo 1.6%; Lahu 1.3%; Naxi 0.7%; Lipo 0.6%; Poluo 0.6%; Sani 0.3%; Lami 0.3%. Dozens of smaller peoples.
Hani 4.2%. 8 peoples. Hani 1.6%; Akha 0.5%; Baihong 0.5%; Haoni 0.35%; Kado 0.35%; Biyo 0.35%; Woni 0.3%; Lami 0.25%.
Nosu 1.9%. 4 peoples.
Lisu 1.9%.
Tibetan 0.4%. Deqen and Zhongdian.
Tai 5.2%. 23 peoples. Largest: Tai(6) 3.3%; Giay 0.7%; Hongjin Tai 0.4%; Huayao Tai 0.2%.
Hmong 2.4%. 8 peoples. Hmong(6) 1.8%; Kim Mun 0.5%.
Mon-Khmer 1.4%. 4 peoples. Wa 0.8%; Bulang 0.2%; Kawa 0.2%; Klawa 0.15%.
Other 0.1%.

Religion 🙏

Buddhist, animist, polytheist and ancestor worship. Muslim 1.7%. Christian 7.2%: House churches 3.1%, TSPM 2.6%, Roman Catholic 1.0%, CPA 0.5%.

1 **Yunnan is, ethnically, China's most complex province.** There are over 200 different ethno–linguistic peoples, but possibly up to 400 groups regard themselves as distinct peoples. There were famous and dramatic workings of the Holy Spirit among some of the tribal groups earlier last century, especially among the Lisu, Hmong, Wa, Jingpo and Nu. The Eastern Lipo, Hani, Maru, Ayi, Eastern Nasu, Naluo, Lawa, Lashi and Nu peoples also have a large proportion of their population who are Christian, but out of hundreds of peoples, this is only a humble beginning. Although the Church thrives in a few ethnic groups, the mountainous terrain, vast numbers of cultures and languages, ancient hostilities and spiritual bondage all hinder the spread of the gospel. Pray that many more peoples may experience similar spiritual breakthroughs.

2 **Yunnan's indigenous ethnic minorities** – numbering 16 million in at least 208 ethno–linguistic peoples – are an immense challenge for the Church in China and the world. Pray for Christians to be raised up who will intercede on their behalf, raise awareness of their plight and go to them as spiritually effective and culturally astute missionaries.

a) *Ninety-five peoples have no known Christians,* and a further four are less than 1% Christian. Many of these groups are small in number, geographically isolated and with unique languages and cultures. Most of these groups believe in some combination of animism, ancestor worship, polytheism and Buddhism.

b) *Pray for indigenous believers* to reach out to related ethnic groups still unreached; pray also for missionaries from elsewhere in China and beyond to reach these unreached of Yunnan. The poverty of local believers and difficulties in travel slow any attempts at evangelism.

3 **The Han Chinese Christians** have experienced notable church growth in the last 10 years, among both Catholics and Protestants, registered and unregistered. Yet the percentage of Han Chinese in Yunnan who are Christian is still only at the national average. Pray for the growth of the Church among them, and pray for an awakening to the spiritual needs of the ethnic minorities among whom they live.

4 Special issues needing prayer:

a) *A combination of social evils plagues many peoples in Yunnan.* The proximity to the Golden Triangle countries of Thailand, Myanmar and Laos, as well as to Vietnam, means that drug trafficking and human trafficking for the sex trade are constant threats. Widespread drug abuse as well as prostitution/sexual exploitation have led to Yunnan possessing China's highest prevalence of HIV/AIDS. The opening of the area to trade, tourism and transport combined with the region's endemic poverty accelerate these destructive patterns. Pray that the government, NGOs and morally concerned people among Yunnan's indigenous groups might be able to put an end to these evils. Praise God that some Christian peoples, such as the Lisu, have demonstrated the harmony and wholesomeness of communities who follow Jesus.

b) **Bible translation is a massive unmet need.** The Bible is available for four languages, the NT in a further four and work is in progress in another six languages. The great majority of languages have nothing; a large number of these have in fact no written system at all. Many languages have a high degree of mutual intelligibility with another language, so good surveys are necessary to ascertain translation needs. Pray for this vital ministry to be expanded in Yunnan.

c) **Christian materials in minority languages are essential.** FEBC broadcasts several in different languages. The JESUS film is available in a few, and **GRN** and other audio ministries are producing Christian content in more and more languages. Pray for maximal impact of these ministries, made all the more important by the lack of written Scripture, the low literacy rates and the oral nature of many of these cultures.

Zhejiang Province

Geography 🌐

Area 101,800 sq km. Prosperous coastal province south of Shanghai.
Population 51,294,000; 504 people/sq km.
Capital Hangzhou 3.9m. **Other major cities** Wenzhou 2.7m; Ningbo 2.2m; Taizhou 1.3m; Jiaxing 1.0m.

Peoples 👪

Han Chinese 99.2%, mostly speaking several Wu dialects and Putonghua. Others 0.8%. She 0.4%; Hui.

Religion

Secularism and traditional Chinese religions. Muslim 0.3%. Christian 19.5%: House churches 9.0%, TSPM 5.8%, all Catholics 4.7%.

1 **Traditionally one of China's wealthiest and most stable provinces,** Zhejiang's powerful economic growth since the 1980s can be attributed to the fact that 90% of businesses are privately owned. Zheijiang's entrepreneurs were investing overseas even before it was legal in China to do so! Its wealth is also more evenly spread than in most provinces; pray that Zhejiang's success might spur on other provinces toward greater private enterprise, more financial equality and less corruption.

2 **Zhejiang province enjoys China's highest proportion of Christians.** At 19.5%, it almost certainly possesses more born-again believers than any European country. Wenzhou Prefecture is nearly 30% Christian. Yongjia county and Xiaoshan district both hover around 50% Christian! Praise God for this amazing growth in the Church – TSPM, Catholics and especially house churches enjoy sustained increases in numbers and maturity.

3 **Zhejiang's Christians have done much to evangelize** other parts of China as well as the two million migrant labourers who work here. Many wealthy Christian entrepreneurs use their business skills to reach the rest of China, travelling around on business and setting up fellowships (and businesses) as they go. These "boss Christians" use their business acumen and their companies as a means to spread the good news. Other Christians are likewise generous in supporting the vision of China's evangelization. Pray for this vision to grow.

4 **The government continues to exert pressure** on non-TSPM congregations, destroying hundreds of unregistered church buildings each year in a drive to eliminate religious expressions operating with no state approval. But a new breed of Church arises in Zhejiang, one that raises or restores church structures and registers publicly, but does not adhere to the state/TSPM restrictions. Government crackdowns on these sites have in turn caused tensions and even riots. But this new expression of Christian faith is bold and confident, legally savvy as to their rights and will not be intimidated. It may even point the way forward to China's Christian future.

Hong Kong

China, Hong Kong

Special Administrative Region of China

Asia

Geography

Area 1,092 sq km. A mountainous peninsula and 230 islands on the coast of Guangdong Province.

Population		Ann Gr	Density
2010	7,069,378	0.54%	6,474/sq km
2020	7,701,346	0.81%	7,053/sq km
2030	8,185,181	0.54%	7,496/sq km

One of the most densely populated areas in the world. The north of Hong Kong Island and Kowloon are extremely dense with the rest of the New Territories and other islands being scattered with small numbers of people.
Capital None. **Urbanites** 100%. **Pop under 15 yrs** 12%. **Life expectancy** 82.2 yrs.

Peoples

Chinese 95.2%. Cantonese 88.7%; other Chinese groups (including Hakka, Chaochow, Fujianese, other smaller groups) 6.5%.
Other 4.8%. Filipino 2.1%; Indonesian 1.4%; South Asian 0.6%; Caucasian 0.3%; Japanese 0.2%.
Literacy 93.5%. **Official languages** Chinese and English (about 38% speak English); Cantonese is the established local dialect, but Putonghua (Mandarin) is increasingly common and influential.

Economy

Rapid growth through free markets, low taxes and non-interference by the state make Hong Kong one of the world's richest cities and largest economies. Consistently ranked as the world's most free economy. International trade (as one of world's busiest container ports),

finance and industry are all mainstays. Hong Kong's finance fuels much of China's rapid economic growth and is now inexorably tied to China's economic fortunes. A large and widening gap between the richest elite and the poorest class.
HDI Rank 24th/182. **Public debt** 13.9% of GDP. **Income/person** $30,726 (65% of USA).

Politics

The British wrested Hong Kong from China in the infamous Opium Wars (1840-58), through the 1842 Treaty of Nanking. The PRC resumed control in 1997, but its constitutional document, the Hong Kong Basic Law, guarantees the existing legal, political and economic structures for 50 years. While it does not possess 100% of democratic freedoms, it remains one of the most open and free societies in Asia. China is responsible for defence and foreign policy under the "One Country, Two Systems" policy.

Religion

Religious freedom in a secular state is guaranteed by the Hong Kong Basic Law for all the many expressions of religious faith.

Religions	Pop %	Population	Ann Gr
Chinese	59.57	4,211,228	-0.2%
Non-religious	21.92	1,549,608	2.8%
Christian	12.41	877,310	0.2%
Other	3.80	268,636	0.5%
Muslim	1.23	86,953	1.9%
Hindu	0.53	37,468	5.3%
Buddhist	0.40	28,278	0.5%
Sikh	0.13	9,190	6.0%
Jewish	0.01	707	0.5%

Christians	Denoms	Pop %	Affiliates	Ann Gr
Protestant	61	5.60	396,000	1.0%
Independent	39	1.43	101,000	2.4%
Anglican	1	0.37	26,000	1.6%
Catholic	1	4.54	321,000	-1.4%
Orthodox	1	<0.01	<1,000	8.3%
Marginal	5	0.47	33,000	0.7%

Churches	MegaBloc	Congs	Members	Affiliates
Catholic Church	C	51	189,941	321,000
HK Baptist Conv	P	150	68,500	93,845
HK Council, Ch of Christ	P	44	33,000	43,890
Ang Ch (Sheng Kung Hui)	A	45	17,931	26,000
Evang Free Church	P	51	13,000	26,000
CMA	P	68	26,000	24,200
Latter-day Saints (Mormon)	M	33	12,815	22,939
Ev Luth Church of HK	P	55	11,469	16,400
China Rhenish Ch (HK)	P	18	2,662	14,000
Chinese Methodist Ch	P	26	8,084	13,500
Assemblies of God Assoc	P	34	8,467	12,700
Ling Liang WW Ev Miss	I	16	8,400	12,600
CNEC Churches	I	21	6,300	10,521
Pentecostal Holiness Ch	P	15	6,833	10,250

Jehovah's Witnesses	M	54	4,800	9,600
Other denominations[93]		929	129,818	220,234
Total Christians[108]		**1,610**	**548,020**	**877,679**

TransBloc	Pop %	Population	Ann Gr
Evangelicals			
Evangelicals	6.1	434,079	1.4%
Renewalists			
Charismatics	1.7	122,333	2.4%
Pentecostals	0.8	53,887	1.0%

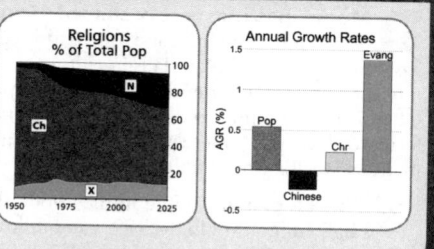

C

Answers to Prayer

1 **The rightful return of Hong Kong to China** has seen most freedoms retained in this Special Administrative Region. Continued religious liberty is praiseworthy as is the opportunity for appropriate Christian testimony by Christians in Hong Kong (HK) to much of the rest of China.

2 **Hong Kong's Kingdom impact,** regionally and globally, far outweighs its small size. It continues to be the source of many missionaries as well as a hub for financing ministry, outreach, discipling, media and literature ministries to the Chinese-speaking world in particular.

3 **Church unity** has seen marked improvements over the bitter divides of the past. GCOWE in 1995, the handover in 1997, the unifying efforts of the Hong Kong Christian Council, the Chinese Christian Church Union and events such as the March for Jesus and latterly the Global Day of Prayer have seen conservatives and charismatics reconciled through forgiveness and prayer. In each of Hong Kong's districts, pastors' networks help to foster united prayer and action.

Challenges for Prayer

1 **The future of Hong Kong's freedoms is uncertain.** Some aspire to full representative democracy; others foresee increasing state control over politics, the press and jurisprudence. The Chief Executive and all others in leadership must balance satisfying Beijing with satisfying their own people in Hong Kong. Pray for wisdom, discernment and courage to take the right path.

2 **Hong Kong's role within China** can potentially be a powerfully redemptive one – financially, socially, culturally and spiritually. There is incredible opportunity to influence the PRC, still taking shape as a 21st Century nation, with the gospel that impacts every area of life. Alternatively, HK could acquiesce to being a mere financial spearhead for the Chinese economic juggernaut, gaining the world but losing its soul. Christians need to play a key role within this framework. Pray for committed and astute individuals and ministries to help shape a biblical worldview for this great nation.

3 **The religious context of Hong Kong is unique,** dominated by a melange of Buddhism, Daoism, Confucianism and Chinese folk religion practiced by the majority. There are over 700 temples and monasteries, not to mention the countless shrines dedicated to various powers and for various purposes. Many other residents follow no religion. Most other faiths are present but largely practiced by immigrant populations. The resulting spiritual mosaic makes for the opportunity to openly share Jesus, but it also reflects very real spiritual powers opposed to Christ's lordship.

4 **The Christian community** has a disproportionately influential role in serving society. Although only 10% of the population, the Church runs the majority of schools and social organizations and 25% of hospitals. Many elderly, poor, foreigners and others in need of assistance are blessed by such efforts. So far, the potential threat of state interference or limitation has not materialized. Pray that the Church may continue to be salt and light in this way and to boldly continue this leavening, transforming role in society.

⑤ Money has inexorably shaped Hong Kong's past. The outstanding port has drawn the wealth of nations, and as a British colony, Hong Kong became very wealthy. Sadly, this has generated a very materialistic culture that can sap the spiritual vitality of Christians, a significant problem in the churches. But positively, the wealth is used by the well-resourced Christian community to do many good works – among the needy of Hong Kong, for the suffering of East and Southeast Asia and for ministry to the whole world. Pray that Hong Kong's material wealth would find its proper place – at the feet of the Lord Jesus.

⑥ Church growth, rapid in the 1960s, slowed in the 1980s and again in the 21st Century. High emigration in the 1990s and following (19% of Christians) was offset by new believers coming into the Church. Hong Kong's high pressure, competitive environment regarding living space, work hours and education as well as many uncertainties about the future often make people open to the gospel. Fastest growing are large churches and megachurches that incorporate a cell group structure.

⑦ Many challenges confront the Hong Kong Church:

a) *The continuing need for renewal and revival.* Only half of Protestants regularly attend church. Many high-profile crusades have drawn much attention but little lasting fruit. The Church Renewal Movement works toward cultivating spiritual change and social impact by the churches.

b) *The lack of several key resources* – such as capable workers, funds for the many projects and opportunities and, notably, physical space in which to hold services and do ministry (real estate is very expensive and hard to come by in crowded HK) – creates considerable challenges to growth. Because of the real estate problem, many congregations meet in smaller numbers and in improvised spaces.

c) *The elements of prayer and intercession* are increasingly recognized as essentials for ministry. Training in these areas and establishing houses of prayer are occurring not just in Hong Kong itself but also further out into the region.

⑧ Christian leadership is in short supply, with only two-thirds of congregations having a pastor. Emigration contributes substantially to this, so that a much younger and less-experienced generation of leaders is forced to emerge. Pray for these:

a) *The 35 Bible colleges,* with more than 1,200 students, have shaped the outlook of many thousands of former students now pastoring, ministering or in the laity.

b) *Key seminaries,* such as the Alliance Bible Seminary, the Baptist Theological Seminary and the China Graduate School of Theology.

⑨ Commitment to missions is high, with around 60% of congregations consistently engaged in or supporting mission activity. Pray for:

a) *Wisdom in serving the burgeoning Church in the PRC.* Many congregations, ministries, colleges and seminaries long to facilitate further growth, maturation and training of the mainland Church, which already dwarfs Hong Kong's Church in size but not in history or resources. Many Hong Kong churches and ministries believe that their role is to support the massive missions movement emerging from mainland China.

b) *The Hong Kong Association of Christian Missions* is a focal coordinating point for 30 agencies, 15 denominations and many congregations that are channelling over 400 missionaries overseas.

c) *The foreign mission body* in Hong Kong has significantly reduced as HK and PRC Churches mature and take on a greater ministry load and as organizations relocate their regional offices away from Hong Kong. But many expats remain here in a host of roles – from church planting to media to PRC-focused work.

⑩ The CCCOWE (Chinese Coordinating Committee on World Evangelization) plays a vital role in linking together Christians in the 40 million Chinese diaspora for fellowship and outreach to less evangelized Chinese communities. Its headquarters is in Hong Kong. Pray for the effective mobilization of Chinese wealth and manpower for world evangelization.

11 There are many spiritually needy segments of society. Pray for the following groups:

a) The working class and poor underclass. Their lot has generally improved but many still live in desperate and crowded situations without any real hope, material or spiritual. **OMF** and others do grassroots evangelism among the working class, and many ministries work among the most destitute (work made famous by Jackie Pullinger's *Chasing the Dragon*).

b) Immigrants from mainland China, 150 more every day. Their living conditions can be appalling, and they face much discrimination. They are disillusioned, have trouble adjusting and are probably the most responsive segment of society. A number of churches and missions seek to alleviate immigrants' physical needs and meet their spiritual needs (WVI, **OMF**, ECF, **OM**, Mission to New Arrivals). Additionally, around 10,000 mainlanders arrive daily as commuting workers or tourists. This provides an excellent opportunity to share the gospel.

c) The Southeast Asian population, mostly Filipino and Indonesian domestic workers. They are frequently poorly treated and subjected to undignified working conditions and inhumane treatment. Many are believers, but others are very lonely and in need of Christ.

d) The South Asian population, a legacy of British rule. Most are traders (Sindhi, Punjabi, Gujarati), in the security industry (Nepali Gurkhas) or in menial jobs (Pakistanis).

e) The Muslims, who are largely Hui Chinese, Pakistani, Malay, Indonesian and Middle Easterner.

12 Student and youth ministries are strong and growing. **CCCI**, HKFES(**IFES**), the Navigators and others are very active, each with dozens of staff on most campuses. Newer and more radically oriented ministries exist, such that Hong Kong has one of the world's most dynamic and creative youth ministry scenes; Campus Church Network and Breakthrough are two good examples of this. Many denominations also focus on youth ministry and training, and the 225% increase in young people attending church from 1999 to 2004 is an indicator that such approaches bear fruit. Pray for this to continue, to deepen and to be exported beyond the shores of Hong Kong.

13 Hong Kong is a vital nerve centre for media. Through networks such as the Association of Christian Publishers, more than 30 Christian publishers (double the number from 2001) and 70 Christian bookstores exist just among Protestants. Groups such as Christian Communications Ltd, **AOI** and many others facilitate writing, printing and distributing millions of Bibles, books, tracts and other printed matter. The Bible Society plays a key role as well; a new Chinese-language Bible translation was completed in 2010. Hong Kong is a key location for studios preparing radio programmes (**FEBC**, FEBA, **TWR**, others). There are also half a dozen Christian media agencies broadcasting Christian TV, not to mention the many cutting-edge film, music and new media ministries in this very modern, tech-savvy and creative city. Pray for these skills and gifts to make an impact on Hong Kong, but also to be felt on a wider, even global, scale.

Guangdong
Zhujiang Kou
Hong Kong
Macau

Macau

South China Sea

China, Macau

Special Administrative Region of China

Asia

Geography

Area 29.2 sq km. A tiny peninsula and two islands 64 km west of Hong Kong on the coast of Guangdong Province of China.

Population		Ann Gr	Density
2010	547,591	2.35%	32,211/sq km
2020	587,727	0.67%	34,572/sq km
2030	611,192	0.28%	35,952/sq km

The Macau government estimates faster growth than the above UN estimates. One of the most densely populated areas on earth.

Capital Macau 548,000. **Urbanites** 100%. **Pop under 15 yrs** 13%. **Life expectancy** 79.9 yrs.

Peoples

Chinese 93.6%. Mainly Cantonese; 3.2% Mandarin speakers. About half of all Chinese in Macau were born outside of Macau.
Macanese (Eurasian) 2.4%.
Other 4.0%. European; Filipino; other Southeast Asian (Indonesia, Vietnam, Myanmar).
Literacy 94.5%. **Official languages** Chinese and Portuguese. The majority (86%) speak Cantonese, but Mandarin is also widely spoken.

Economy

One of the richest cities in the world in the 16th and 17th Centuries. The economy is dominated by gambling and tourism, both fuelled by visitors from mainland China, but both also highly vulnerable to the rise and fall of the mainland economic boom. The government receives a hefty chunk of the massive casino income; private wealth is concentrated in the

hands of a few, and with huge amounts of cash changing hands, the challenge of corruption is ever-present. Protests against the sleaze and corruption, or rather its unequally distributed benefits, are increasingly frequent and violent. Macau is also an important gateway for China's special economic zones such as the adjoining Zhuhai.

Politics

Rented by the Portuguese in 1557. Became a Portuguese Colony in 1887; considered a Chinese Territory under Portuguese administration since 1974. Macau reverted to Chinese rule as a Special Administrative Region in 1999, with a high degree of economic and political autonomy. It was both Europe's first and last colonial possession in Asia.

Religion

Freedom of religion is guaranteed by law.

Religions	Pop %	Population	Ann Gr
Chinese	62.01	339,561	2.6%
Buddhist	17.10	93,638	2.8%
Non-religious	14.94	81,810	1.4%
Christian	5.35	29,296	0.7%
Baha'i	0.50	2,738	7.0%
Muslim	0.10	548	9.9%

Christians	Denoms	Pop %	Affiliates	Ann Gr
Protestant	32	1.61	9,000	3.4%
Independent	10	0.22	1,000	2.7%
Anglican	1	0.09	500	7.4%
Catholic	1	3.14	17,000	-1.0%
Marginal	2	0.29	2,000	2.7%

Churches	MegaBloc	Congs	Members	Affiliates
Catholic Church	C	8	10,178	17,200
Macau Evang Church	P	14	1,400	3,500
Latter-day Saints (Mormon)	M	2	500	1,300
Baptist Church	P	6	400	800
Seventh-day Adventist	P	1	235	588
Other denominations	[40]	103	3,284	5,871
Total Christians	**[46]**	**134**	**15,902**	**29,259**

TransBloc	Pop %	Population	Ann Gr
Evangelicals			
Evangelicals	1.6	8,527	3.2%
Renewalists			
Charismatics	0.5	2,829	3.3%
Pentecostals	0.2	855	3.7%

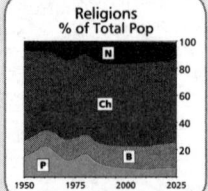

Religions % of Total Pop

Annual Growth Rates

Answers to Prayer

1 **There is increasing growth and unity** in the Church. Although not blessed with the long legacy of a strong Church, as in Hong Kong, or the spectacular growth of the mainland, numbers in both Chinese- and foreign-speaking congregations are growing. The Union of Christian Evangelical Churches in Macau sees the various evangelical groups draw together more than ever before in recent years.

Challenges for Prayer

1 **Macau has the dubious distinction** of being the first Christian territory in Asia to become non-Christian. In 1600, 95% of Macau's population were Catholic. By 2010, this had reduced to about 3.1%, a monumental decline. Protestant churches, while growing, have always been small. The number of Protestant churches grew from 33 in 1986 to more than 70 Chinese-speaking churches and more than 20 in other languages. Pray for believing Christians to win back this territory for the Saviour.

2 **Macau is one of the least-discipled Chinese communities** in the world. The major hindrances to evangelism and breakthrough are the strength of the gambling industry, the social cohesion of Chinese culture, Buddhist/Daoist beliefs and fear of offending A-Ma, the local god after which the city was named. The Church is small, weakened by emigration and a high turnover of leadership. Pray for local leaders to be raised up who will help the Church survive and grow and be a blessing to China and the world. The Macau Bible Institute was the first theological school; there are several other practical ministry training programmes in place as well.

3 **Macau's reputation as a "City of Sin"** is well founded; gambling revenues here surpass even those of Las Vegas and are still growing. The government regulates the industry, and local owners control a majority share with large foreign investors also present; the historic association with Triad influence is much less than in the past. Pray about the following:

a) *Materialism and greed* are the harvests reaped from this seed. Such an environment strangles spirituality as testified to by tiny churches but burgeoning casinos, the cathedrals of mammon.

b) *Gambling is a religion* that takes much and gives little. Addiction and desperation are epidemics taking on a massive scale. The Church has largely failed to minister to gambling addicts, but groups such as the Macau Evangelical Church, Industrial Evangelical Fellowship and Horizon Christian Fellowship are beginning to address this.

c) *Prostitution and substance abuse* are natural parasites of the gambling industry. Most sex workers are trafficked in, often against their will, from the mainland or other Southeast Asian countries. Rahab Ministries reaches out to mainland women involved in prostitution in Macau. Pray for this ministry and for more such groups to reach out to these at-risk people.

d) *Lucrative salaries in casinos* encourage young people and Christians to seek employment there at the expense of university education or involvement in church or the community. Pray for viable work alternatives to the gambling industry.

4 **Macau was the starting point of Protestant missions to China.** There, the first Chinese convert was baptised, the first Chinese Bible translated and Robert Morrison, the first Protestant missionary to the Chinese, was buried. There is praiseworthy freedom to enter as missionaries, but residency permits are increasingly hard to obtain (for immigration and not religious reasons). The lion's share is from Hong Kong, with many other nationalities present as well. Workers are engaged in evangelism, church planting and discipleship as well as community work and compassionate ministry to drug addicts, the homeless and others. Teaching English is an effective and much-desired way to build relationships and share the good news. Pray for their effectiveness in this crowded and pressurized city.

5 **Other strategic ministry issues** include:

a) *The rising cost of real estate* in this densely populated city-state is pricing small and poorly resourced congregations out of their rented spaces. Pray for financial provisions as well as creative solutions to this problem.

b) Ministry to tourists from mainland China, since Macau enjoys religious freedom. Distribution of gospel media in various formats is the main expression for this. Southern Cross (**IMB**) and China Tourist Ministry are two groups engaged in such evangelism.

c) Ministry to those working in the service industry. Huge numbers work in the hotels, restaurants and casinos; a large number are from the mainland. Some ministries (such as the Baptists) focus on reaching this large population with the gospel.

d) Support ministries. Macau has increasing access to Christian radio and TV via Christian broadcasts from Hong Kong stations and connectivity to the outside world in Chinese (especially from Taiwan), English and Portuguese. There is also good availability of printed, audio and video resources. There are four Christian bookshops. Christian worship bands from abroad have an especially positive impact on young people.

6 **Less-reached minorities:**

a) Casino workers are a crucial subsection of society, well paid, but isolated from the gospel. All casino dealers must be Macau natives; they number at least 50,000. Casino Workers Outreach Ministry was recently started to address this need.

b) Indonesians and Vietnamese, mostly engaged in domestic labour, are particularly vulnerable to exploitation. There is little outreach specifically to them.

c) The Macanese (mixed Portuguese-Cantonese) are often Catholic, but usually very nominal. There is one evangelical church among them, but they are largely neglected by evangelical agencies and churches.

Republic of China, Taiwan

Asia

Geography

Area 36,000 sq km. A mountainous island 160 km east of mainland China, together with the Penghu archipelago and the islands of Matsu and Kinmen close to the mainland. One of the world's most densely populated countries.

Population		Ann Gr	Density
2010	23,561,660	0.58%	654/sq km
2020	24,437,503	0.29%	679/sq km
2030	24,677,625	0.03%	685/sq km

Two million refugees from mainland China arrived 1945-1950.
Capital Taipei 2,633,153. **Other major cities** Kaohsiung 1.6 million; Taizhong 1.3mill. **Urbanites** 81%. **Pop under 15 yrs** 17.6%. **Life expectancy** 78.5 yrs.

Peoples

Chinese 96.2%. Speaking three major languages.
  Taiwanese (Hoklo, Minnan) 66.2%. Settled in Taiwan 300 years ago.
  Hakka 15.0%. Settled in Taiwan 200 years ago.
  Mainland Chinese 15.0%. Refugees from mainland China 1945-50. Almost entirely urban.
Austronesian mountain peoples 1.7%. 14 recognized tribes, 11 unrecognized. The largest: Amis(2) 0.7%; Paiwan 0.3%; Tayal 0.2%; Bunun 0.2%; Sediq (Taroko) 0.15%; Pyuma; Drukai; Tsou.
Other 2.1%. Indonesian 0.5%; Thai 0.4%; Filipino 0.4%; Vietnamese 0.4%; other Asians; Westerners.
Literacy 97.5%. **Official language and language of education** Mandarin. Hoklo and Hakka are widely spoken. **All languages 28. Indigenous languages 22.**

Economy

Rapid industrialization and economic growth to become one of the world's most dynamic export-oriented economies, focusing particularly on high-tech goods. Surprisingly close economic ties to mainland China, its primary export market.
Public debt 29.4% GDP. **Income/person** $16,988 (36% of USA).

Politics ⚔

Under Japanese rule 1895-1945, then granted to the Nationalist Government of China. After the fall of mainland China to the Communists in 1949, Taiwan became the refuge of the Nationalist Chinese government, which claimed to represent all of China. This led to international diplomatic isolation and internal political polarization in Taiwan. It was effectively a mainlander-dominated, one-party republic until the 1987 elections. It is now a multiparty democracy. More and more people think of themselves as Taiwanese first and Chinese second or not at all. However, recent rapid economic (on the mainland) and political (in Taiwan) changes may herald a new future direction. For all the military-political sabre-rattling, the two states are economically and culturally closer than ever.

Religion 🙏

Secular state with freedom of religion. The great majority of the population follow the unique Chinese blend of Buddhism, Daoism and Taiwan folk religion. A more unadulterated Buddhism has grown markedly in influence and numbers.

Religions	Pop %	Population	Ann Gr
Chinese	60.74	14,311,352	-0.2%
Buddhist	28.80	6,785,758	2.0%
Christian	5.82	1,371,289	1.4%
Non-religious	2.31	544,274	1.5%
Other	1.90	447,672	2.1%
Muslim	0.35	82,466	0.6%
Baha'i	0.05	11,781	5.2%
Ethnoreligionist	0.03	7,068	0.6%

Christians Denoms		Pop %	Affiliates	Ann Gr
Protestant	82	1.79	423,000	0.6%
Independent	53	2.04	480,000	3.1%

Anglican	1	0.01	2,000	-0.8%
Catholic	1	1.25	295,000	-0.5%
Marginal	2	0.31	74,000	3.7%
Unaffiliated		0.42	99,000	0.4%

Churches	MegaBloc	Congs	Members	Affiliates
Catholic Church	C	475	162,088	295,000
Presby Ch in Taiwan	P	1,208	92,017	219,000
Independent Chs	I	575	69,048	145,000
Little Flock	I	209	67,582	123,000
True Jesus Church	I	556	63,986	91,500
Latter-day Saints (Mormon)	M	115	34,545	53,200
Bread of Life Chr Ch	I	73	25,000	49,500
Chinese Baptist Conv	P	232	26,720	33,400
Taiwan Holiness Ch	P	83	13,343	26,800
Jehovah's Witnesses	M	99	7,200	20,880
Taiwan Lutheran Ch	P	51	8,650	17,300
Local Church, The	I	23	6,595	12,125
Seventh-day Adventist	P	55	5,750	10,638
Other denominations[107]		1,156	97,419	176,236
Total Christians[139]		**4,910**	**679,943**	**1,273,579**

TransBloc	Pop %	Population	Ann Gr
Evangelicals			
Evangelicals	2.8	648,506	2.2%
Renewalists			
Charismatics	1.3	303,732	0.9%
Pentecostals	0.6	141,892	2.7%

Missionaries from Taiwan

P,I,A 280 long-term in 29 agencies; also Bread of Life church has planted 150 churches outside Taiwan.

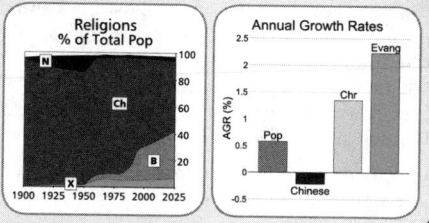

Answers to Prayer

1 **A new era of Christian growth** is underway after a long stagnation of several decades. Much more than in the past, this growth encompasses megachurches and house churches, charismatic and conservative, and spans ethnic, language and class barriers. In recent years, many churches have had a greater emphasis on prayer, personal evangelism and community outreach.

2 **Church growth among migrant workers** in the last 15 years has been quite remarkable. Among Filipinos, Thais, Indonesians, Vietnamese and others, many are coming to faith in Jesus. This is happening through collaboration between Taiwanese and expat ministries, which is itself praiseworthy for the unity and cooperation demonstrated.

Challenges for Prayer

1 **Taiwan's controversial and ambiguous political status** – as a de facto independent state, yet a de jure renegade province of China – generates frequent tension, domestically and internationally. Claiming independence would almost certainly bring a hostile, even military response from China. Domestically, the focus is therefore on improving socio-economic conditions. Pray for wisdom for leaders and that peaceful and mutually beneficial relations might be established for the long term. Recent trade agreements between the two nations offer positive signs.

2 **A history of alleged deep-seated corruption** in the political realm has persisted through much of the Kuomintang's (Chinese Nationalist Party) rule and has extended to other parties as well. Now, connections to gangsters and "black gold" (corrupt money) have been replaced with high-profile public campaigns against corruption. Pray that such campaigns would be allowed to be fully successful; pray for openness and honesty to characterize the present and future leaders of Taiwan.

3 **Taiwan remains a stronghold of Buddhism and Taiwanese folk religion.** Over 90% of Taiwanese see themselves somewhere in the spectrum of Buddhism, Confucianism, Daoism and Taiwanese folk religion. Many adherents mix Buddhist ideas with a folk religion worldview, seemingly unconcerned by the contradictions.

a) *"Purer" Buddhism is growing steadily* in influence, most evident at universities and among educated professionals; at the grassroots level, Buddhism faces the same challenges Christians faced in overcoming thousands of years of traditional Chinese folk religions. The largest of the Buddhist organizations has millions of adherents and uses its influence to build temples and monasteries overseas and spread Buddhism throughout the world.

b) *Folk religions are ubiquitous* and underlie most of Taiwanese society. These believe in a host of gods arranged in a heavenly hierarchy similar in structure to the ancient Chinese court. Entrenched ancestor worship and occult practices such as consulting spirit mediums, fortune telling and offerings to ghosts are all essential parts of this animistic and informal set of practices and beliefs.

4 **Taiwan is politically open but spiritually closed.** Visitors from mainland China often comment on the spiritual darkness and the hardness of people's hearts in Taiwan. Ministry in Taiwan is difficult and fruit is hard won. Taiwan is still the only major Han Chinese population in the world where a significant spiritual breakthrough has not occurred. Only recently has Christianity started growing again after decades of stagnation; Christianity's percentage of the population in 1965 (5.6%) was only surpassed in 2008. The major challenges to be faced by the Church are the following:

a) *Spiritual opposition to the gospel* is very real. Powerful opposition from non-Christian religions makes breaking away from one's past to embrace Christianity a real challenge.

b) *Unity must be cultivated.* There are frequent prayer events and evangelistic meetings to foster unity, but much more work must be done. A biblical view of the body of Christ must be cultivated.

c) *Materialism* is one of the greatest barriers to the good news in today's Taiwan. Many people are very focused on their career, on their children's education and on how to live the most affluent life possible. There is very little time left for spiritual nourishment or ministry. Ask God to pour out His Spirit to create a true hunger for Him.

d) *Low levels of commitment and sanctification.* Only a minority of converts become disciples deeply engaged in the life of the local congregation and active in ministry; nominalism is a problem and the dropout rate significant. Vices such as gambling and the sex industry, which sadly permeate much of Taiwanese society, are constant temptations.

e) *Lack of pastors and full-time workers* – a long-standing problem that requires either the calling of more workers or the mobilization of the laity, or both.

f) *The disparity in the distribution of Christians.* The majority of Christians are found in bigger cities among Mandarin speakers (or Mainlanders). There are far fewer churches in rural areas and among Taiwanese- and Hakka-speaking peoples. Minority groups, both indigenous and immigrant, are either strongly Christianized or very unreached.

5 **The lack of pastors** remains a long-term need. Rural congregations tend to suffer the most. Growing numbers of professionals are actually moving into full-time ministry. There are over 33 seminaries and Bible schools, some with international acclaim such as the China Evangelical Seminary, as well as a number of TEE programmes. There is a nation-wide push to train another 1,000 pastors and church leaders. Pray for a new generation of Christian leaders who are biblically grounded, culturally savvy, humble in character and spiritually empowered.

6 **Youth and university students** are generally more open to the gospel. The key to reaching this group of over one million people is dynamic and relevant outreach. The Presbyterians sponsor 60 Christian study groups in universities and churches. Campus Evangelical Fellowship (**IFES**) has an outreach to students, with 40 full-time staff workers ministering also in secondary schools. **CCCI** has a large campus ministry. Student ministries are training local churches for this kind of ministry; pray for churches to mobilize toward this vision. Pray for these young hearts to grow in maturity as they dedicate their lives for Christ.

7 **A decline in numbers of missionaries** working in Taiwan has become evident in the last 20 years – more marked than any other country in Asia. This is not due to a finished task, but rather to attrition and the attraction and fruitfulness of other locations. The door is wide open for missionaries to enter and serve in many capacities; it is especially ideal for those looking to do full-time mission work rather than tentmaking. Cults such as the Mormons seize this openness by sending huge numbers of missionaries; how can biblical Christians allow it to be ignored? Pray that this window of opportunity might be fully exploited by evangelical missions. Largest agencies include **YWAM, AoG, OMF, SEND**, TE, **OMS**, Free Methodist.

8 **Missions vision from Taiwan** suffered with its diplomatic isolation, but is increasing again. Many churches, however, are more willing to give money than their best people. Many churches and agencies envision Taiwan as a gospel carrier to neighbouring mainland China and to Asia generally. The Chinese Christian Evangelical Association networks and strengthens church growth and global missions.

9 **Less evangelized people groups:**

a) The Taiwanese working class is linguistically (Hoklo/Hokkien) and culturally separated from the majority of evangelical churches, which use Mandarin. Economic and social changes in recent years have made life difficult for them. This group comprises 60% of the population, but a mere 0.5% are Christian. They are becoming increasingly responsive to the gospel. **OMF, IMB** and TIEF are committed to reaching this group.

b) The Hakka communities are only 0.35% evangelical, having been resolute to retain their own language, culture and religion. Pray for organizations that reach specifically to them (Hakka Evangelical Association, **SEND**, Presbyterians and others). Resources available in the Hakka language include the Bible, audio (**GRN** and radio) and video (the JESUS film).

c) The Muslim community is largely Hui. More than 60,000 Hui live in Taiwan, which may be one of the larger people groups in the world without a known Christian fellowship group. Indonesians make up most of the rest of the Islamic community; it is possible that there are significantly more Indonesians in Taiwan than the official figure of 130,000. There are six mosques throughout Taiwan, with the most notable being the Taipei Grand Mosque. Some ministry to Indonesians has proved fruitful, but very little is being done for the Hui.

d) The Penghu Islanders number 93,000. Church planting efforts have regressed, since the majority of churches have closed. Most Islanders are fisher folk and highly superstitious. The Islands and local marine life have suffered massive environmental damage of late; pray for these people to find Christ again in their current precarious existence.

e) Foreign brides are a rapidly growing population. One in seven marriages has a partner from another country. There are around 320,000 migrant foreign brides, mostly from mainland China and Vietnam. Many of them are non-Christian and barely evangelized. Taiwan Expatriates Caring Committee partners with national Churches to minister to them. Pray for a greater mobilization of outreach and mission from Taiwanese churches to these groups.

10 **The indigenous, Austronesian peoples** of Taiwan live in the mountainous west and in some cities. They comprise 25 tribes that account for a mere 1.7% of Taiwan's population. They are around 80% Christian, due to mission work by Presbyterians. But other groups, including sects, are increasingly common, as is nominalism and a lack of the Scriptures and biblical teaching. As with many other aboriginal populations, Taiwan's indigenous peoples struggle to preserve their traditional life in the face of massive social change and family breakdown, alcoholism and urban migration. Activated Ministries and others continue to minister; **AoG** has a Bible Institute that runs short courses to equip lay leaders and bivocational ministers.

⑪ Support ministries for prayer:

a) *Christian literature.* Much is now being published of both local and foreign origin. The Bible Society offers Scriptures in nine languages. The *Book of Hope* has been distributed to over 500,000 in public schools.

b) *Electronic resources* – such as Scripture on mobile phones, the Bible in MP3 format and several Christian websites – are all vital tools for reaching the tech-savvy Taiwanese.

c) *Visual media.* Christian agencies produce ever-more-professional material. Good TV and ORTV are on the leading edge of Christian broadcasting, producing and broadcasting excellent gospel material for the whole Chinese-speaking world.

Colombia

Republic of Colombia

Latin America

Geography 🌍

Area 1,141,748 sq km. Northwest corner of South America. The fourth-largest country on the continent. Mountains in west; plains, forests and jungles in east.

Population		Ann Gr	Density
2010	46,300,196	1.47%	41/sq km
2020	52,278,350	1.15%	46/sq km
2030	57,264,259	0.84%	50/sq km

Capital Santa Fé de Bogotá 8,499,820. **Other major cities** Medellín 3.6 million; Cali 2.4mill; Barranquilla 1.9m; Bucaramanga 1.1m. **Urbanites** 75.1%. **Pop under 15 yrs** 29%. **Life expectancy** 72.7 yrs.

Peoples 👪

Spanish-speaking 97.5%. Estimated composition: Mestizo (Eurindian) 57.6%; white 20%; mulatto (European and black) 14%; African-Colombian 4%; Zombo (Afro-Indian) 1.9%.

Indigenous Amerindian 1.6%. (50% of pop in 1850). 94 recognized groups speaking 300 dialects. Only the Guajiro and Paez number over 100,000; some groups are less than 200 people.
Other 0.9%. Jamaican 0.5%; European, Asian, Middle Eastern.
Literacy 72.7%. **Official language** Spanish. **All languages** 83. **Indigenous languages** 80. **Languages with Scriptures** 1Bi 41NT 52por 23w.i.p.

Economy 🖥

Rich in resources; Colombia's main export earner is manufactured goods, and its main employer is agriculture. Oil, coal and cocaine are the main export commodities. Colombia supplies 90% of the US's cocaine, which, as an extremely lucrative cash crop, is tempting to farmers; drug trade is often controlled by guerrilla groups or private armies of drug lords. Economic reforms have curbed inflation and brought the debt under control. A very wide gap between rich and poor.
HDI Rank 77th/182. **Public debt** 42.6% of GDP. **Income/person** $4,989 (11% of USA).

Politics ❌

Independent of Spain in 1819 and a separate state in 1831. Polarization contributed to 170 years of partisan politics, dictatorships and civil wars. Many turned to support a variety of violent Marxist guerrilla groups. Some aligned themselves with drug cartels, who have their own terror groups, leading to a pandemic of assassinations and kidnappings. Right-wing paramilitary groups, formed to combat the guerrillas, have waged terror wars of their own. Recent political stability has seen levels of violence and kidnappings decrease and the economy improve as the government took a hard line on terrorism and the paramilitaries.

Some would argue that human rights have suffered, but the country has moved toward stability. The peace process, initiated in 2004, has seen significant numbers of fighters from all sides demobilize. Strong, albeit at times controversial, leadership during President Uribe's two terms has been followed up in 2010 with the former Minister of Defence becoming the new president.

Religion

After years of persecuting and discriminating against religious minorities, the Roman Catholic Church's privileged position was ended in the 1991 constitution, which accords greater freedom to ethnic and religious minorities.

Religions	Pop %	Population	Ann Gr
Christian	94.42	43,716,645	1.4%
Ethnoreligionist	2.90	1,342,706	2.9%
Non-religious	2.40	1,111,205	2.3%
Baha'i	0.16	74,080	1.5%
Muslim	0.07	32,410	4.6%
Hindu	0.02	9,260	1.5%
Jewish	0.01	4,630	1.5%
Chinese	0.01	4,630	1.5%
Buddhist	0.01	4,630	1.5%

Christians Denoms		Pop %	Affiliates	Ann Gr
Protestant	88	3.32	1,539,000	4.8%
Independent	79	4.47	2,069,000	6.1%
Anglican	1	0.02	8,000	5.9%
Catholic	1	82.05	37,989,000	1.0%
Orthodox	1	0.03	12,000	5.9%
Marginal	6	1.21	559,000	- 1.7%
Unaffiliated		3.77	1,746,000	-0.2%
Doubly affiliated		*-0.45*	*-210,000*	*0.0%*

No accurate survey of churches has been done for many years. Some statistics below are estimates.

Churches	MegaBloc	Congs	Members	Affiliates
Catholic Church	C	2,540	20,100,165	37,989,311
United Pentecostal Ch	I	2,107	168,531	482,000
Seventh-day Adventist	P	1,229	295,000	413,000
Jehovah's Witnesses	M	2,194	158,000	395,000
NT House Churches	I	2,833	85,000	195,000
Int Charismatic Mission	I	40	61,667	185,000
Latter-day Saints	M	274	95,749	159,900
Assemblies of God	P	430	43,000	150,000
Foursquare Gospel Ch	P	306	42,904	130,000
Avivamiento	I	6	46,000	115,000
Assoc, Interamerican Chs	P	235	31,667	95,000
Christian Crusade Ch	P	225	27,000	72,900
Caribbean Assoc, Ev Chs	P	823	41,143	72,000
Pan-American Mission	I	126	12,600	63,000
Colombian Baptist Conv	P	160	19,000	57,000
Other denominations[161]		11,523	730,875	1,601,845
Doubly affiliated				*-210,000*
Total Christians[176]		**25,051**	**21,958,301**	**41,965,956**

TransBloc	Pop %	Population	Ann Gr
Evangelicals			
Evangelicals	7.5	3,460,847	6.0%
Renewalists			
Charismatics	18.1	8,377,362	4.6%
Pentecostals	3.9	1,807,500	5.7%

Missionaries from Colombia

P,I,A 297 (216 long-term) in 40 agencies: in Colombia 84, elsewhere in South America 24, Europe 88, Africa 16.

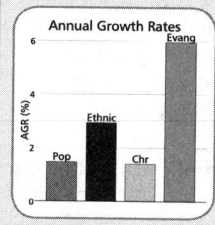

Annual Growth Rates

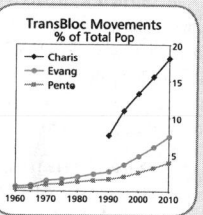

TransBloc Movements % of Total Pop

Answers to Prayer

1 **Colombia is moving toward stability and order.** Murder, kidnapping and crime rates show significant decreases in recent years with crackdowns on violent groups on both sides of the political spectrum. Thousands of guerrillas and paramilitaries are demobilizing due to government amnesty. Problems still abound and Colombia is far from peaceful, but clear progress in the last several years is an encouragement to most.

2 **The Church continues to grow,** even out of Colombia's history of crime, lawlessness, terror and murder. From a tiny minority in 1960 (0.6% of the population), evangelicals have grown to 7.5%, and charismatics now number an estimated 18% of the population. Such growth is all the more wonderful considering that Christians have often been targets of drug cartels, guerrillas, paramilitaries and others. The greatest denominational growth has been within indigenous Colombian churches which have sprung up locally.

3 **The success story of Bellavista Prison,** a maximum-security prison in Medellin that was often called "hell on earth", is an inspiration. Through prayer and bold Christian witness, the prison has seen a remarkable turning of hardened criminals to Christ and the end of rampant murderousness. Many inmates are now believers, and there is regular prayer, fasting, evangelism and even a Christian radio station. A Bible Institute has formed in the prison, training inmates to minister in prison and after release.

Challenges for Prayer

C

1 **Colombia remains volatile and dangerous,** although a strong government has stabilized the nation in recent years. Levels of violence, kidnapping and assassination are still abnormally high. Leftist guerrillas and right-wing paramilitaries both seem to have abandoned ideological agendas and have effectively become gangs profiting from cocaine and kidnapping. Political or religious leaders who oppose such groups are targeted. Cocaine production has actually grown despite the government's efforts to reduce it. Crop destruction has driven the rebels and coca growers into national parks and ecological reserves where they are destroying much of Colombia's rich ecosystem and biodiversity. Pray for a government that will be strong in opposing violence and wise and just in moving the nation forward. A number of key government figures have been exposed as having ties to paramilitary groups. This is a revelation that will ultimately prove healthy for transparency and accountability, but will shake many people's trust in the government in a land where faith in state institutions is already weak.

2 **The upheaval from political and drug-related violence** has had a terrible human cost. Tens of thousands have died, producing many orphans and widows. Colombia has the world's second-highest number of internally displaced people (three million). These *desplazados* are pushed from rural into urban areas, where there is little work or shelter, but much exploitation. Former guerrillas and paramilitaries who have disarmed under amnesty conditions find themselves ill-equipped to re-enter civilian life. Three million more Colombians who have fled the country exist largely in conditions of poverty and a precarious immigration status. Pray for all who suffer from loss, that the Lord might meet their needs and that they might find in their Creator hope and restoration.

3 **Satan's hold on Colombia** must be broken by prayer. Christ's lordship must be proclaimed over the spirits of violence, revenge, lawlessness and corruption as well as the occult practices that have brought the nation so low. The web of drug barons, guerrillas, paramilitaries, corrupt politicians and occult groups generates great violence against the saints through intimidation, property destruction, murder and assassination. Every year, dozens of pastors and priests are killed.

4 **The Roman Catholic Church** has seen its role and influence greatly decrease since the 1991 constitution ensured the religious freedom of other groups. The great increase of evangelicals has been at the expense of Catholicism, especially among the poor. The majority of Catholics are strongly traditional, but widely nominal; only 25% practice their faith. There is a very strong charismatic element among those who are active in the Church. Many of the faithful have opposed violence and structural sin – and paid dearly for such commitment. Pray for renewal within Catholicism that awakens and purifies the Church.

5 **Evangelical growth has been significant.** In 1933, there were only 15,000 evangelicals. In 2010, they numbered 3.5 million. Some claim numbers as high as five million. Local, citywide and national evangelistic outreaches have resulted in large increases in numbers of congregations and believers. Some churches have grown 1,000-fold over the last two decades! *Amanacer Colombia* is a vision seeking to see 18,000 more evangelical churches planted. Pray for solutions in:

a) The challenge of violence. The work of evangelicals among the poor and disenfranchised is a good testimony to all and the engine for church growth. Ministry to the suffering directs people away from violent alternatives. The conversion of guerrillas and paramilitaries to Christ leads them to quit the fighting, which in turn makes the churches a target. As a result, many pastors have been assassinated or have left the country.

b) The challenge of leadership intensifies with the growth of churches and with pastors being murdered or fleeing. There are more than 20 theological training institutions, most of them packed with students, but they are desperate for qualified teachers. The role of TEE is crucial, with CIPEP coordinating such training for over 3,500 every year.

c) **The challenge of unity.** The diversity of Colombia's churches can become a stumbling block or a strength, depending on how well they work together. The prayer nights in Cali and Medellin, attracting more than 45,000 people each, are examples of Church unity. CEDE-COL, the Evangelical Confederation of Colombia, links over 50 evangelical denominations and coordinates interchurch action. A formal statement by CEDECOL members against violence and outlining a peace process will raise the profile of the Church, encouraging cooperation but making evangelicals more of a target than ever.

6 **Missionaries are targets** for the enemies of the gospel, both physical and spiritual. They live under constant threats of kidnapping, murder and extortion. Many areas miss out on vital ministry, since workers are forced to withdraw. Pray for courage and faithfulness for both native and expatriate missionaries. The complex scene of denominational and church-mission relations requires patience, humility and grace. Major mission agencies: **YWAM, CB**/**CMML**, **AoG, NTM, ABWE, AI, LAM**.

7 **Colombian missionary vision is growing.** Several Amerindian peoples are closed to foreigners, but Colombians are increasingly reaching them. The large majority of Colombian missionaries serve short term within their own country. A small but growing number of Colombians have gone to other lands, but church support is limited. Pray for the ongoing ministries of **COMIBAM** as well as *Centro Cristiano de Misiones Mundiales* in inspiring Christians to be involved in mission.

8 **Unreached peoples.** Pray specifically for:

a) **The thousands of gamines, or street urchins,** in the cities. Bogotá has one of the highest numbers of street children of any Latin America city. **YWAM, LAM,** Tearfund and several new local ministries provide food, shelter and preparation for a life off the streets.

b) **The wealthier classes** are small in number but control most of the economy. White rather than mestizo, they are overwhelmingly Catholic (although often very nominal) and generally isolated from evangelicals, who focus on the poor. Their wealth and ties to the circles of political and ecclesiastical power make them objects of resentment.

c) **The Muslim community** numbers around 35,000 of Syrian, Lebanese or Palestinian background.

d) **Student and youth work** is slow and hard. The history on campuses of Marxist ideology and then post-modern individualism hinders interest in serving others and seeking God. With more than half of the population under age 25, reaching the younger generation is crucial. Campus and youth ministries and even youth-oriented prayer movements such as Tribal Generation are all growing. Pray for their work to be creative, passionate and fruitful.

9 **Amerindians have been oppressed** and subject to discrimination in the past, and their rich contributions to Colombian culture and society are disregarded. The 1991 constitution granted wide autonomy and support to the 94 recognized indigenous peoples. But they are still largely poor, undereducated and most vulnerable to the violent conflict and ecological exploitation occurring in Colombia's rural areas. Response to the gospel is varied, with some powerful people movements to Christ and other groups remaining unreached. Pray for:

a) **Strong, viable, well-led churches** that are culturally rooted and able to cope with drug traffickers and modernization. Legislation on autonomy for indigenous groups is, in some areas, being misinterpreted as the right to force Amerindian Christians to revert to their traditional religious beliefs. This brings pressure and persecution to some indigenous Christians, but it also causes believers from different tribal groups to band together in mutual support in a way that could never have happened before.

b) **Church-planting ministries** of **NTM**, South American Mission, **CMA** and increasingly Mestizo Colombian missionaries sent to their own countrymen.

c) **Bible translation.** Today, 37 languages are still without a NT and 25 have no Scripture at all; **WBT** and **NTM** are working on several projects. Some Bible translators have been kidnapped or killed, which in turn has caused translation teams to move to cities – away from the people whose language they are working with – or out of the country altogether. This causes the work to slow or even be abandoned. Pray for breakthroughs in this area.

d) **Amerindian peoples,** closed or inaccessible thus far. This number is reducing as Mestizo and Amerindian Colombian missionaries strive to reach every tribe; only around 15 remain unevangelized. The small populations of these groups make them difficult to find and to build trust with. Pray for these unique and precious groups to find the culture-transforming and preserving gospel before they disappear forever.

10 Support ministries:

a) Literature is still underutilized but increasingly vital for evangelism and for teaching believers. **CLC** has six bookstores, a wholesale outlet, a wide distribution network for literature and a growing productivity as a publisher of locally-produced Spanish titles. The Colombian Bible Society works with various organizations to distribute Christian literature among the poorest and children, and it has overseen large-scale distributions of hundreds of thousands of pieces of literature. One such example is the simple and effective *Book of Hope*.

b) Christian radio. Evangelicals have little access to national radio, but local Christian FM broadcasts are popping up. Evangelical broadcasters, including **HCJB**, **TWR** and Christian Vision, broadcast 667 hours per week in Spanish.

c) Audio and video resources reach many who do not or cannot read. FCBH is a programme with widespread use. **GRN** has audio material in 62 languages. The JESUS film is available in Spanish and nine other languages, including Colombian Sign Language, (the deaf are the nation's largest unreached group). A large proportion of Colombians have seen this film.

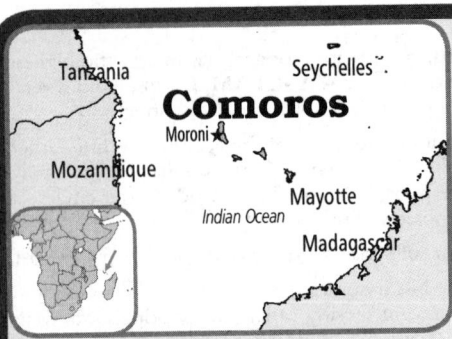

Comoros

The Union of the Comoros

Africa

Geography 🌍

Area 1,862 sq km. Three volcanic islands between Madagascar and Mozambique, all densely populated and resource-poor. Mayotte, which voted in 2009 to integrate fully with France, is claimed by Comoros.

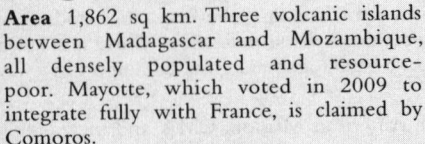

Population		Ann Gr	Density
2010	691,351	2.32%	371/sq km
2020	838,310	1.80%	450/sq km
2030	975,284	1.47%	524/sq km

Capital Moroni 49,800. **Urbanites** 28.2%. **Pop under 15 yrs** 38%. **Life expectancy** 64.9 yrs.

Peoples 👪

Comorian 97.6%. Mixed Arab, African and Malagasy ancestry, part of Swahili-Bantu people cluster.
Minorities 2.4%. Makua, Malagasy, Réunionese, French, Arab.
Literacy 56.2%. **Official languages** Arabic, French, Comorian (a mix of Swahili and Arabic).
All languages 7. **Indigenous languages** 6.
Languages with Scriptures 3Bi 1por.

Economy 🗺️

Underdeveloped, poor and overpopulated, Comoros is one of Africa's poorest countries. The major exports – perfumes and spices (vanilla, cloves) – are highly subject to fluctuating market prices. Despite the majority working in agriculture, the nation is still dependent on food aid and rice imports. High rate of economic emigration and high dependence on remittances from Comorians abroad.
HDI Rank 139th/182. **Public debt** 89.2% of GDP. **Income/person** $816 (2% of USA).

Politics ⚔️

A one-party state until 1990, when a multiparty democratic government was instituted. There have been over 20 coups and attempted coups since independence, some involving foreign mercenaries and French military intervention. The two smaller islands, Moheli and Anjouan, constantly agitate for autonomy or independence. A new constitution in 2001 granted each island greater autonomy, but has not prevented rebellions, secession attempts and further intervention from the African Union.

Religion

Religions	Pop %	Population	Ann Gr
Muslim	98.84	683,331	2.3%
Christian	0.93	6,410	2.3%
Non-religious	0.14	968	-1.6%
Hindu	0.09	622	2.3%

Christians Denoms		Pop %	Affiliates	Ann Gr
Protestant	4	0.21	1,000	3.0%
Independent	3	0.08	1,000	3.4%
Catholic	1	0.64	4,000	1.9%
Marginal	1	<0.01	500	5.7%

Churches	MegaBloc	Congs	Members	Affiliates
Catholic Church	C	5	2,558	4,400
Malagasy Protestant Ch	P	6	465	930
Assemblies of God	P	3	277	360
Indig Comorian believers	I	3	126	180
Jehovah's Witnesses	M	1	16	33
Other denominations[4]		5	255	510
Total Christians[9]		**23**	**3,697**	**6,413**

TransBloc	Pop %	Population	Ann Gr
Evangelicals			
Evangelicals	0.2	1,276	3.9%
Renewalists			
Charismatics	0.2	1,323	4.3%
Pentecostals	0.1	360	4.4%

Annual Growth Rates

TransBloc Movements % of Total Pop

Challenges for Prayer

1 **The vast majority of the population are Muslim.** They were almost completely unevangelized before 1973. Islamic fundamentalism is on the rise. However, most are involved in occult practices through witchcraft, curses and spirit possession. Many young people – disillusioned with life in this society that offers so little hope – attempt to find solace in drugs, sex or the opportunity to leave the islands. Pray that they might have opportunities to hear the gospel of life that offers hope to all.

2 **There are severe restrictions on Christians.** Evangelism is forbidden, and those who convert to Christianity can expect severe reprisals from the community and from their own family. Harassment and persecution have risen in frequency and intensity in recent years. Pray for courage for those choosing to follow Jesus, and wisdom for all who must walk out their faith in this hostile atmosphere.

3 **Comorian believers are gradually increasing in number,** although the majority of believers are Réunionese, Malagasy and French. Each Comorian believer faces a difficult path fraught with likely opposition, and yet the body of Christ grows. Pray that leaders may be raised up for the increasing groups gathering for fellowship, and pray for the people and resources to train and disciple them. Response to the gospel is greater on Anjouan than on the other islands.

4 **The quiet witness of Christian medical and veterinary workers** in the Republic and on Mayotte has won credit and public honour as well as opportunities to share the Lord Jesus with the people. Pray for continued and increased opportunities for witness and that such may bear fruit.

5 **Christian resources.** The JESUS film is available in Shimaore and Shingazidja. The NT is available in Shimaore, and portions are available in Shingazidja. Radio has been effective in introducing Comorians to Christ and discipling them, although programmes are not yet available in Comorian. Pray that all these tools will be a blessing to Comorians, and pray for two more film translations that are needed but not yet started.

Congo-DRC
Democratic Republic of Congo (Formerly Zaire)
Africa

Geography

Area 2,345,410 sq km. Congo contains most of the Congo River system and much of the vast Central African rainforest.

Population		Ann Gr	Density
2010	67,827,495	2.80%	29/sq km
2020	87,639,982	2.51%	37/sq km
2030	108,593,509	2.05%	46/sq km

Large areas are sparsely populated.
Capital Kinshasa 8.75million **Other major cities** Kolwezi 1.6mill; Lubumbashi 1.5m; Mbuji-Mayi 1.5m. **Urbanites** 35.2%. **Pop under 15 yrs** 47%. **Life expectancy** 47.6 yrs.

Peoples

Nearly 250 ethno-linguistic groups and numerous sub-groups; linguists claim 214 languages in the country. An uncountable number of refugees and displaced peoples have moved back and forth between the DRC, Rwanda, Burundi, Uganda, Sudan and Tanzania in the last 20 years.
Bantu 80.2%. 161 ethnic groups in centre and south. Largest: Tuba Kongo 11.2%; Luba-Lulua 10.8%; Lingala 4.2%; Luba-Bambo 3.9%; Mongo 3.2%; Ekonda 3.1%; Songye 2.6%; Lower Kongo 2.3%; Nande 2.3%; Tetela 1.9%; Ngala 1.5%; Lega 1.4%; Yaka 1.4%; Chokwe 1.3%; Yombe 1.3%; Tabwa 1.2%; Pende 1.1%; San Salvador Kongo 1.1%; Sanga 1.1%; Havu 1.0%.
Sudanic 9.8%. 34 peoples. Largest: Zande 2.2%; Mangbetu 2.0%; Lendu 1.6%.
Adamawa–Ubangi 4.3%. 17 peoples. Largest: Ngbaka 2.1%; Ngombe 0.7%.
Nilotic 1.5%. 4 peoples in northeast. Largest: Alur 1.4%.
Pygmy 1.5%. 12 peoples scattered throughout the country's forested regions.

Other 0.5%. Westerners, South Asians, Arabs, others.
Literacy 89.8% (officially). Greatly reduced by the collapse of the education system. **Official language** French. **Trade languages** Lingala/Bangala in north and northwest, Swahili in east and south, Tshiluba in centre and Kikongo/Tuba in west. **All languages** 217. **Indigenous languages** 215. **Languages with Scriptures** 30Bi 20NT 56por 29w.i.p.

Economy

Immense economic possibilities from diamonds, mineral resources and agriculture. Rich and diverse flora and fauna. The Congo River alone has the hydro-electric potential to power the entire continent. A corrupt and venal elite, poor administrative structures, nearly non-existent infrastructure and frequent war and strife reduced the nation to one of the world's poorest. Profitable agricultural plantations have reverted to forest, transport systems hardly function and the vast majority live without electricity, plumbing and educational or medical services. Former President Mobutu's personal plundering of the nation was followed by civil strife and continued hyperinflation. Anything resembling a nationwide economic or political infrastructure is destroyed or paralyzed, with devastating effects on the population.
HDI Rank 176th/182. **Public debt** 138% of GDP. **Income/person** $185 (<0.5% of USA).

Politics

For centuries, Congo has suffered the depredations of Arab slavers, Western exploitation and, in recent years, exploitation by Africans. A Belgian colony for 60 years, the precipitate granting of independence to an unprepared people led to years of violence, anarchy and secessionist wars, culminating in Mobutu's military coup in 1965. His Western-supported dictatorship suppressed opposition and oversaw staggering levels of corruption. The Great Lakes War in Rwanda and Burundi spilled over into eastern Congo and the Tutsi/Banyamulenge area. This in turn led to Laurent Kabila coming to power in 1997 with Rwandan and Ugandan support; his rule was erratic and autocratic. Further war resulted from invasions by Uganda and Rwanda, requiring intervention and aid from Angola, Zimbabwe and Namibia as well as a UN peacekeeping mission. Kabila was assassinated in 2001 and his son, Joseph, appointed in his place. By 2003, all foreign forces had officially withdrawn. In 2006, the country had its first free elections with a turnout of more than 70%. Although contested, Joseph Kabila won after a runoff and has set about trying to rebuild what is effectively a failed state. Rebel militias (*mai-mais*) in the east (both Hutu and Tutsi) from neighbouring Rwanda still operate with relative impunity. The conflict in Congo has yielded more deaths than any since WWII.

Religion

In 1972, President Mobutu decreed that only six organized religions were permitted to operate and own property: Catholic, one Protestant Church (ECC), Kimbanguist Church, Orthodox, Muslim and Jewish. Traditional African religious beliefs are ubiquitous, but usually syncretized with Christianity rather than practiced outright. The authenticity programme of the government between 1971 and 1978 placed controls and limitations on Christian institutions and activities. Economic disasters and war have forced change, and from 1980 onward there has been religious freedom – this has resulted in the proliferation of new churches and sects. Many social, health and education services are now maintained by Christian groups in lieu of a functioning government.

Churches	MegaBloc	Congs	Members	Affiliates
Catholic Church	C	1,130	19,709,302	33,900,000
Kimbanguist Church	I	19,521	4,880,240	8,150,000
ECC-Presbyterian	P	1,857	1,058,559	2,350,000
New Apostolic Ch	I	2,654	796,296	2,150,000
ECC-United Methodist	P	5,967	716,000	1,432,000
ECC-Baptist-River	P	1,262	694,118	1,180,000
Seventh-day Adventist	P	1,680	452,500	905,000
ECC-Chs of Pentecost	P	1,507	339,130	780,000
Jehovah's Witnesses	M	3,270	159,770	695,000
ECC-Baptist-West	P	630	466,667	686,000
ECC-Disciples of Christ	P	1,540	354,211	673,000
ECC-Ev Free Ch (Ubangi)	P	1,025	198,502	530,000
Anglican Church	A	1,406	154,655	515,000
ECC-CECCA(WEC)	P	2,558	133,032	395,000
Ch of God Prophecy	P	408	142,322	380,000
ECC-Zaire (Congo)Ev	P	347	125,095	329,000
Other denominations[328]		29,834	3,684,804	8,986,499
Doubly affiliated				-1,540,000
Total Christians[344]		**76,596**	**34,065,203**	**62,496,815**

TransBloc	Pop %	Population	Ann Gr
Evangelicals			
Evangelicals	18.7	12,689,720	3.7%
Renewalists			
Charismatics	25.8	17,515,897	3.3%
Pentecostals	6.3	4,249,600	3.9%

Religions	Pop %	Population	Ann Gr
Christian	92.15	62,503,037	2.7%
Ethnoreligionist	5.10	3,459,202	4.1%
Muslim	1.90	1,288,722	5.1%
Baha'i	0.38	257,744	1.8%
Non-religious	0.32	217,048	4.1%
Hindu	0.15	101,741	4.2%

Christians	Denoms	Pop %	Affiliates	Ann Gr
Protestant	72	22.39	15,183,000	3.4%
Independent	266	20.19	13,695,000	3.2%
Anglican	1	0.76	515,000	3.2%
Catholic	1	49.98	33,900,000	2.8%
Orthodox	2	0.04	25,000	4.7%
Marginal	2	1.06	718,000	5.2%
Doubly affiliated		-2.27	-1,540,000	0.0%

Missionaries from Congo (DRC)

P,I,A 445 (350 long-term) in more than 40 agencies: 44 international.

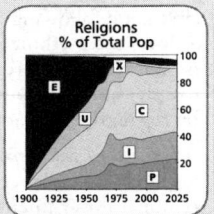

Religions % of Total Pop

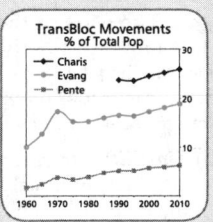

TransBloc Movements % of Total Pop

Answers to Prayer

1 **The turning to Christ** in the 20th Century has been massive. The number of Christians grew from 1.4% of the population in 1900 to over 90% professing Christianity today. Though much of this would be nominal, there have been revivals in some areas before and after independence. Evangelicals have increased 10-fold since 1960.

2 **The Church's social impact has grown,** since it has emerged as the only viable national structure to endure in the general social, political and economic collapse of the country. Despite the destruction of countless churches and ministry buildings, only the Church has plugged the gap left by a failed state in terms of caring for the many needs in this broken land. In the much-needed area of peacemaking and reconciliation, Christians and churches lead the way for a new start to a land that desperately needs one.

3 **Praise for the many prepared to pay the price** for this harvest. Thousands of Christians and hundreds of Catholic and Protestant missionaries were martyred in the Simba Rebellion of 1964. Many others died in the conflicts from 1991 until today, some specifically as martyrs for their faith and refusal to compromise. Their example gives strength to others, and their sacrifice is the foundation for future harvests.

4 **The long-despised and neglected Pygmy people have turned to Christ** in large numbers, through loving witness and culturally relevant ministry. The burgeoning Pygmy Church is finding new strength to resist the predations of slavers, substance abuse and a destructive self-image in their remote jungle regions, yet many who come to Christ remain in a nominal faith. There is real openness but a need to develop disciple-making skills.

C Challenges for Prayer

1 **The evils of Congo's tragic history** must be overcome through repentance and reconciliation.

a) *Arabs and Belgium's King Leopold II enslaved and looted* the country in the 19th Century. The latter's private empire in Congo probably halved the population, leading to the deaths of 10 million people in 30 years before the Belgian government took over in 1908.

b) *Belgian colonial rule* and international mining companies exploited Congo's resources but neglected the people – most of the improvements came through extensive Protestant and Catholic efforts.

c) *Interventions by foreign powers* and, latterly, African countries often with selfish motives. The West's propping up of Mobutu's corrupt regime is, in large part, the cause of the present chaos.

d) *Inter-ethnic hostility* during the 1990s led to warfare, killings and many fleeing for their lives in Shaba in the south and the Great Lakes in the east and northeast. Hutu and Tutsi ethnic militias, of both Congolese and foreign origin, still roam the Great Lakes region, terrorizing the populace and perpetuating violence, destruction and terror.

The evils of the past need to be admitted, repented of and put right for the Congo to have a viable future. Some Christian groups in Belgium have offered identificational repentance for the predations of their country, a positive development.

2 **The wars of the 1990s** and following embroiled the military forces of seven nations and provoked the rise of local inter-ethnic conflicts and warlords. None of these forces and factions had Congo's best interests at heart. Most foreign forces have withdrawn, although Rwandan troops often cross the border to pursue rebels. Many militias are still at large, and the ravages of war must still be repaired. Pray earnestly for:

a) *Hostilities to cease and peace to take hold.* Now, only the eastern Kivu and northeastern areas remain unstable with regular violence, a patchwork of rebel forces and militias. Pray for international bodies, regional governments and the woefully inadequate DRC army and police to act with justice, decisiveness, wisdom and authority in making and keeping peace. The UN peacekeeping force (MONUSCO) is large but impossibly overstretched in its new remit to help rebuild Congo.

b) *Illegal forces to be disarmed and disbanded.* Most militias have devolved into little more than personal armies of dangerous warlords, wreaking terror upon an innocent and helpless populace far from the safety of government or international forces. Included among these are the Lord's Resistance Army (from Uganda) and countless groups in the provinces of Kivu, Maniema and Orientale, including PARECO, CNDP, FDLR, FNI, Simba, Mai-Mai Simba, Mai-Ami Kapopo, Mai-Mai Yakutumba, others. Providing jobs and even basic needs as incentives for these desperate men to lay down their arms is a great challenge. Pray for these men to be convicted and disillusioned with this life and for those continuing to perpetrate such violence to be stopped. Pray for past and present warlords and war criminals to be stopped and brought to justice.

c) *The return of the 1.7 million displaced people to their homes.* Around 1.3 million people in the east of the country alone have been uprooted. Life in refugee camps is miserable and uncertain. Those interned are vulnerable to militia attacks, disease and sexual predation, and they live with little or no resources for anything beyond mere survival.

d) *The cessation of war crimes and exploitation of the conflict.* Untold horrors have been committed against many thousands of innocents. Rape is routinely used as a weapon of fear, as are mutilation and torture. Stealing cattle – the portable wealth of many tribes – is a normal activity for militias, as is illicit mining of diamonds and other resources to be sold to unscrupulous foreign buyers. Pray for an end to such evils.

3 **The Democratic Republic of Congo is a failed state** by any measure of the term. The lands under this name have no centralized government, no connectedness between the vast and far-flung regions, almost no functioning infrastructure and no single language or culture to unite its many diverse peoples. More than five million people have lost their lives through war, violence, starvation and the virtual collapse of the health system. Pray for:

a) *The will to re-establish a single nation.* Many of the players in this tragic game do not want to see such a thing emerge. A shattered nation leaves resources more easily exploited, wars more easily conducted and influence more easily exerted, especially by the militia groups. The international community has not demonstrated the ability to rebuild Congo, and the nation itself has not proved its capability to stand on its own.

b) *The formation of an effective national government* that can establish centralized authority with honesty, justice and respectful concern for the interests of the governed – a miracle if it does occur. Sadly, the 2010 elections – which had promised the first properly elected government in decades – appear to have been deeply flawed. Bitter recriminations and violence are possible, even likely. Pray for a peaceful solution to this serious issue.

c) *Economic recovery* and wise use of finances to pay government officials, the military and police, teachers and medical workers. Job creation is one of the government's top five priorities. Without this, corruption as a way of life cannot end.

d) *The rebuilding of a ruined infrastructure,* including health and education. Transport links will unite the country and weaken the militias; healthcare will save many lives and provide hope; education will be the foundation for future development.

4 **The powerful spiritual evil** that presides over much of the land manifests in many ways, beyond mere civil wars, killing, tribalism, greed and corruption. Systematic rape, unspeakable mutilation and brutality, cannibalism, witchcraft and occult practices are evil enough. Practicing them against children as well as accusing tens of thousands of children of witchcraft (often as a pretext for abuse and abandonment) defies comprehension. That these horrors are so endemic in a land with over 90% professing Christians is baffling, heart-rending and a call to spiritual warfare. Cry out for God to deliver this land, binding the spirits that exercise such wicked control over the suffering people.

5 **The Christian Church** is an essential entity for rebuilding the DRC. It remains the only viable national social structure to survive and retain some credibility. Its role in rebuilding the nation is crucial. Most hospitals, clinics and schools now operate with Christian initiative. The Catholics admirably invest much into these institutions. Pray for Christian leaders of spiritual maturity and moral integrity to be raised up for ministry both in the Church and in society. Many leaders compromised and lowered their standards during the manipulative dictatorship of Mobutu and the chaos of the 1990s.

6 **The Church of Christ in Congo (ECC)** was a conglomeration forced by government edict in 1970, which artificially bonded conservative Protestants, Pentecostals/charismatics and syncretistic African Initiated Churches, sixty-five denominations in all. Most evangelical leaders are now in favour of their membership in the ECC. Positive benefits include a reduction of tribalism in the Church, a reduction of unnecessary competition, rationalized administration and increased cooperation in training schemes and media. But today, restructuring, change and renewal are imperative in order to face the daunting challenges that exist. Pray for:

a) *Nominal Christians to find new life in Christ.* Nominalism is a major problem. Large numbers have no clear grasp of repentance and faith in Christ nor of salvation by grace and not works. Much nominalism is due to inadequate preaching of the gospel, satisfaction with a superficial response and failure to follow up with those touched by the preaching. There is a notable lack of biblical knowledge in most churches; pray that the Bible would be read, used and applied in churches in the DRC.

b) *"Revival churches",* which are growing rapidly. Their spiritual liveliness and strong faith are positive, but many lack biblical teaching and are often led by charlatans who use their pastoral position for personal gain rather than to serve the faithful. Prosperity theology runs strong through these churches and draws in many with its promises of wealth for a population in desperate economic straits.

c) *Syncretism, witchcraft and false teachings to be rooted out* of the Church. Animistic thought patterns, occult influences and fear of witchcraft are major problems present in the underlying culture, polluting the faith of millions. Such continued spiritual ties oppress Christians and stymie their spiritual growth. Many are falsely accused and subject to cruel "exorcism" rituals. The JWs with glossy literature and cheap Bibles are making rapid inroads into the country.

d) *Biblical leadership patterns.* The cultural tendency toward centralized leadership has sometimes harmed local congregational life and initiative. It has stimulated hierarchical structures and has increased power seeking, pride of position and misuse of funds. It has compromised the Church's prophetic role. Changes must come, but not at the expense of unity, fellowship and cooperation.

7 **Pray for vision for the future.** The DRC needs a complete re-evangelization. Colonial comity agreements and formation of the ECC served well in earlier eras, but they imposed rigid geographical boundaries on any outreach activity. This left many areas devoid of an evangelical witness and hindered cross-cultural outreach. There is great freedom to minister the gospel in many ways, but lack of vision, resources and stability hampers potential outreach. The work of the Holy Spirit in some areas has led to increased love for God's Word, prayer movements, mobilization of youth and a new indigenous hymnody. Pray for:

a) *New initiatives in research.* After radical change prompted by the past chaos, destruction and displacement, a nationwide survey is desperately needed to reveal the state of the Church and the needs of the nation. Before strategies can be developed and implemented, the real situation in this vast, populous and complex nation must be understood. Pray for a team of capable researchers, supported by the national Churches, to undertake this daunting task.

b) *New starts in evangelism and church work.* The trauma experienced in the DRC betrays the failure of discipleship. But out of the ashes, new models of ministry – holistic in approach, community-based, discipleship-focused and sustainable in nature – can be developed. Pray that this opportunity for fresh ministry might be seized by believers, both indigenous and expatriate.

8 **Leadership training** at every level is a priority that is more important than ever.

a) *Lay leadership was neglected* for years, and TEE programmes were few and localized. Even these were often forced to shut down due to upheaval and lack of resources. Pray for re-establishment of TEE, a vital model due to Congo's sheer size and poverty. Training courses are often held by churches for lay leaders, many of whom are then sent out as church planters to unchurched villages. Bible Training Centre for Pastors and Evangelism Resources are two such lay training ministries. Pray for these visions to be implemented throughout the country.

b) *Bible schools once abounded,* but some were closed due to the conflicts. Pray that all might reopen and acquire the resources, staff and students they need. There are large numbers of primary local-language and trade-language Bible schools and a smaller number of French ones. They often function with scant resources (books are rare and precious). Pray that spiritual material and teaching content may be constantly improved.

c) *Higher-level institutions,* both seminaries and Christian universities, need prayer. Some important ones are *Institut Supérieur de Théologie in Kinshasa*, Shalom University in Bunia and several denominational schools all under the umbrella of the *Association des Institutions d'Enseignement Théologique en Afrique Central.* These are strategic for shaping a new generation of well-educated pastors and leaders. Pray that such evangelical institutions may mature theologically and stand firmly for the truth of the gospel in the face of doctrinal challenges. Pray too for imaginative and appropriate means to maintain themselves financially.

9 **Sectors of society** in particular need of the gospel:

a) *Rural villages.* The upheavals of the last 15 years mean that an entirely new wave of church planting in rural areas is needed. Thousands of congregations were uprooted and the buildings destroyed or seized by militias – and so the churches must be restored. Villages having a resident Protestant pastor were reduced from 50% in 1960 to 15% in 1985, provoking a re-evaluation of church planting, but by the mid-1990s it had mostly fizzled out. The Portable Bible Schools movement has been crucial, training 30,000 lay church planters for church planting in the 60,000 pastor-less villages.

b) **Young people.** Children under age 16 constitute 50% of the country's population. Sexual promiscuity, AIDS and enforced service in militias are all huge challenges with no easy answers. Ministries to youth are limited by lack of funds, skills, training and vision. Pray for:

i *University students, who face great trials.* Corruption in the system makes bribery and sexual favours sadly common; a lack of funds can also force students into these situations. Christians are ministering by providing vocational training to enable students to earn their own money and by exposing these wicked practices to the media and government. **CCCI** in particular has an extensive ministry, with over 700 staff members and volunteers.

ii *Street children,* who have increased greatly in numbers. Orphaned by AIDS or wars, by broken homes and by accusations of witchcraft, they number 250,000. Every Child Ministries and many others try to offer these children Jesus' love, hope and a safe place to sleep, live and learn. Another 11,000 are estimated to still be serving as child soldiers with various militia groups.

c) **The Kimbanguist Church** is one of the largest indigenous African bodies, with eight million followers. This body with Puritan morality and millenarian urgency has gained a measure of international recognition, and some within have moved to a more biblical faith. However, there remain significant problems in their theology and practice at a popular level, where Kimbangu, the founder, is revered as the Holy Spirit or seen as a visible image of God, while his descendant Kiangani is known as the Christ. The Kimbanguists these days are split into two main factions, apparently divided over how far along the path of this idolatry the Church should move. Pray for the enlightenment of this large denomination through biblical truth, and pray for wisdom for those called to minister to them.

d) **Diseases claim the lives of millions.** Most of these losses are preventable. Over 400 children die every day in the DRC, half from malaria. Official figures suggest 1.4 million people are HIV positive. The likely figure is far higher because of huge movements of refugees, warring armies, lack of medical facilities and widespread sexual promiscuity and rape. Over one million children have lost one or both parents to AIDS. Tuberculosis is also on the rise. Pray that churches may rise to the challenge of living and preaching biblical morality before and in marriage and may give appropriate help to the victims.

e) **The female victims of rape** – and there are millions due to years of upheaval, conflict and war – are at high risk of contracting HIV from their tormentors. These women face not only the tragic consequences of infection and other physical damage, but also personal trauma, ostracism and rejection from their communities.

f) **The vast swamplands** northeast of Kinshasa, which are sparsely populated and under-evangelized. Many other similar pockets of neglect exist. Pray for more concerted research in locating these areas and for church planting to be initiated.

g) **The Swahili-speaking Muslim communities** in eastern towns, Kinshasa and along the eastern border see little Christian outreach. There are considerable missionary efforts, however, by Muslims to spread Islam and wildly divergent claims as to their actual numbers. Grace Ministries International reaches out to Muslims, but the Congolese Church has not been equipped to do the same.

10 **The Pygmy peoples**, long despised and exploited by the Bantu majority, are becoming very responsive to the good news after long resistance and suspicion. They have been enslaved, poorly compensated for hard labour and even hunted, killed and eaten by militia fighters for the alleged magical properties of their flesh. Ministries such as *Mission Evangélique du Pygmée en Afrique*, the Covenant Church, Baptists and Presbyterians (as well as others) defend these Baka peoples and help to evangelize and disciple them. Justice and advocacy as well as literacy training, oral teaching and church planting are all much needed. Pray for the maturing of this movement, provision of adequate, spiritual leadership and emergence of a truly indigenous Pygmy Church.

11 **Missionary involvement** is reduced to a mere fraction of what it once was, due to war, instability and the breakdown of communications and government. Due to fruitful past ministry, most agencies are highly integrated into their daughter indigenous movements and churches. But the staggering needs and the lack of workers mean that the DRC has openings for expatriate Christian ministers on a greater scale than any other African nation – church planting, discipleship, development and holistic ministry, Bible and leadership training and specialized areas such as media, translation and medical work. Pray for:

a) *A new surge of workers* from around the world to live out the gospel in Congo and to meet the many needs – spiritual, physical, emotional, psychological – of the population. Just to replace the hundreds of workers who left in the last 15 years is a great challenge, but would still not be enough.

b) *Wise deployment* and the most effective use of their gifts.

c) *Harmonious and effective partnering* between nationals and expatriates.

d) *Safety.* While the worst of the violence is over, the DRC is still dangerous in many areas, as much for foreign workers as anyone else. Disease, isolation and spiritual darkness add to the challenges missionaries will face.

e) *Development of the right strategies* for mission agencies, with particular emphasis on moving the Church toward maturity and concern for the unreached. Major mission agencies with commitment of personnel are: **MAF**, International Ministries, Central African Missions, **AIM**, **WEC**, **AoG**.

12 **Christian help ministries** will be essential for the foreseeable future due to the destruction of recent years. The government nationalization of hospitals and schools in the 1970s was a disaster. Churches and missions work hard to maintain and restore them, but the demands in funding and personnel are staggering. Pray specifically for:

a) *Health Services.* A large number of major and smaller hospitals – too many to list – are run by networks such as Interchurch Medical Assistance (an association of 12 Protestant agencies) and agencies or churches such as Baptists, Adventists, Community of Disciples of Christ, **WEC** and others. Intercommunity/mission hospitals, such as *Centre Médical Evangélique* at Nyankunde in the northeast, are both a good testimony and an essential ministry. Expatriate personnel are in constant demand.

b) *The school system* suffers, with plummeting enrollment, negligible financing, lack of educational resources and a shortage of good teachers. Poverty and lack of opportunity constrain many families from sending their children to school. It is a minor miracle that the education system continues to function at all. Thank God for the educational ministries of the Catholic Church and increasingly Protestant churches, without which an entire generation may have gone without education. Around five million children still go without schooling today. Pray that churches and missions may use the immense opportunities for the gospel in the desperately needy education system.

c) *Transportation.* The breakdown in surface transportation adds to the strategic importance of the seven agencies with aviation programmes (the largest of which is **MAF**, with eight aircraft in the DRC). Pray for safety in flying over trackless forests and swamps, provision of fuel, finance and personnel.

13 **Christian media ministry,** crippled by Congo's woes, is beginning to be set back on course. Pray for the resumption or growth of:

a) *Bible translation* – still a major unfinished task. The profusion of 215 languages led to an emphasis on trade-language evangelism, which limited gospel penetration and stunted the development of indigenous Christian lifestyles, music and worship. There are 94 languages in need of translation programmes by Congolese and/or expatriate believers and another 29 with works in progress. The majority of these are being done by **WBT** with ECC churches.

b) *Christian literature, publishing and distribution.* There is a famine of contextually appropriate and helpful literature, even in trade languages. Distribution and poverty are enormous problems. **EHC** has had a wide impact – six million pieces of evangelistic literature have been given away and 1,850 fellowships established as a result. The Bible Society distributes over 100,000 Bibles a year, but most areas suffer a severe lack of God's Word; most people have never owned a Bible.

c) *Audio resources* are extremely important due to many dialects, the oral cultures and low literacy among many peoples. **GRN** has Scripture and teaching available in 274 languages and dialects.

d) **The JESUS film** has been viewed by much of the population in many areas. It is available in 47 languages, with several more in production. Pray for gifted translators for the many languages and dialects as yet untranslated.

e) **Christian radio's** importance has never been greater; radio ministry has great potential. Christian radio, including locally run FM stations, is setting up all over the country, frequently with the help of **HCJB**. Small-scale transmitters empower and inform local communities, and they enable Christian radio to be locally run and flavoured.

Congo
Republic of Congo (Brazzaville)
Africa

Geography

Area 342,000 sq km. West of Democratic Republic of Congo (Congo-Zaire), with which it is often confused. Around 60% of the country is covered with tropical rainforest, which is declining from deforestation. Grasslands and bush in the central and southwest, forest in the north.

Population		Ann Gr	Density
2010	3,758,678	1.93%	11/sq km
2020	4,699,083	2.15%	14/sq km
2030	5,478,797	1.47%	16/sq km

Capital Brazzaville 1,323,311. **Other major city** Pointe Noire 656,000. **Urbanites** 62.1%. **Pop under 15 yrs** 41%. **Life expectancy** 53.5 yrs.

Peoples

Nearly 80 ethnic groups, not to be confused with the differently structured language groupings found in the country.
Bantu 91.7%. Over 55 peoples and sub-groups. Largest: Kituba 18.8%; Kongo 16.7%; Teke(10) 12.7%; Yombe 11.5%; Mbosi 3.6%; Sundi 3.4%; Lingala 3.0%; Lari 3%; Kunyi 2.6%.
Pygmy 1.3%. 5 groups: Bayaka 0.7%; Monzombo 0.3%.
Adamawa-Ubangi 6.5%. 7 peoples: Ngbaka Ma'bo 3.1%; Sango 2.2%.

Other 0.5%. Central, West and North African, European, Asian.
Literacy 84.7%. **Official language** French. **Trade languages** Lingala, Munukutuba (Kongo Creole). **All languages** 66. **Indigenous languages** 62. **Languages with Scriptures** 6Bi 7NT 13por 16w.i.p.

Economy

Huge undeveloped potential due to limited transportation. Rich oil and mineral deposits, extensive rainforests and agricultural potential. An over-dependence on oil, a top-heavy government and civil sectors, corruption and seven years of civil unrest and war make transitioning away from socialist structures (especially in agriculture) slow and difficult. About 50% of the population live below the poverty line, making less than $1/day. **HDI Rank** 136th/182. **Public debt** 165% of GDP. **Income/person** $2,952 (6% of USA).

Politics

Independent from France in 1960. A Marxist-Leninist People's Republic 1968-1991. Constitutional reform and elections in 1992 led to the ousting of President Sassou-Nguesso. This led to civil conflict and war and his ultimate return to power in 1997. The capital and much of the south were severely damaged during conflicts in 1997 and 1998-99. Congo is now a constitutional republic, with Sassou-Nguesso still in power as elected president.

Religion

During the Marxist period, youth were heavily indoctrinated against religion, 18 denominations were banned and some missions expelled. All restrictions were removed and freedom of religion declared in 1992.

Religions	Pop %	Population	Ann Gr
Christian	89.72	3,372,286	1.9%
Ethnoreligionist	5.20	195,451	0.8%
Non-religious	2.80	105,243	4.3%
Muslim	1.58	59,387	3.0%
Baha'i	0.60	22,552	2.3%
Other	0.10	3,759	1.9%

Christians	Denoms	Pop %	Affiliates	Ann Gr
Protestant	9	11.31	425,000	2.0%
Independent	53	14.51	546,000	1.9%

Catholic	1	61.48	2,311,000	2.2%	**TransBloc**	**Pop %**	**Population**	**Ann Gr**
Orthodox	1	0.01	500	2.6%	**Evangelicals**			
Marginal	2	0.66	25,000	4.5%	Evangelicals	15.9	598,234	2.4%
Unaffiliated		1.80	66,000	-7.6%	**Renewalists**			
					Charismatics	16.2	610,688	3.2%

Churches	MegaBloc	Congs	Members	Affiliates			
					Pentecostals	3.0	111,000	2.8%
Catholic Church	C	446	1,343,605	2,311,000
Evangelical Ch of C	P	2,492	149,500	351,325
Kimbanguist Church	I	618	114,371	191,000
Assem of God, Pentecost	I	613	36,800	92,000
New Apostolic Ch	I	171	34,118	58,000
Bougist	I	114	22,800	57,000
Char Ch of Brazzaville	I	49	15,720	39,300
Salvation Army	P	85	19,000	24,950
Jehovah's Witnesses	M	165	6,600	19,800
Evang Ch of C (Likouala)	P	46	5,017	15,200
Ch of God (Cleveland)	P	38	7,500	13,800
Evang Chr Community	I	18	6,000	12,000
Other denominations[54]		221	58,517	121,300
Total Christians[66]		**5,076**	**1,819,548**	**3,306,675**

Religions % of Total Pop

TransBloc Movements % of Total Pop — Charis, Evang, Pente

Challenges for Prayer

1 **The Congo is a land of past troubles, but future potential.** Two decades of Communism have been followed by a sham of a democracy, with the past dictator reinstated as president after provoking a civil war that devastated the land, killed thousands and displaced over 300,000. Congo is a land rich with natural resources, but the majority of the population live in or very near to poverty level. Pray for benign government, for wise economic policies and for justice to prevail in society.

2 **The Church needs revival and restoration.** Congo has been Christianized – superficially, at least – but never truly converted. The majority of the population are Christian, but some sources claim that up to 50% are actually animists. What is undeniable is that for a vast number, Christianity is a thin veneer over traditional African religion. The upheaval of the 1990s was a major setback for many ministries. Pray for a new move of the Spirit, greater than the revival that blazed through the region more than 50 years ago. Churches need to be swept clear of flawed worldviews and false beliefs, and instead filled with the Spirit's power and led by biblical truth.

3 **Church life is a complex mix of physical need and spiritual diversity.** Catholics, African Initiated Churches, mainline Protestants, Western cults, conservative evangelicals and Pentecostal/charismatics all vie for the faith of the people. Thankfully, relations are improving among denominations with strong evangelical values. But poverty and instability not only interrupt and undermine long-term ministry, but they also cause many Christian leaders to leave for other lands. Pray for a greater commitment to biblical unity and for long-term stability in which to build stronger leadership and ministry.

4 **Training for Christian leaders** is a point for concern. Pray for full restoration of this strategic ministry. UWM has a four-year residential school and a TEE programme. The Salvation Army runs a Bible college. **CMA** has a Bible school in Brazzaville and a facility in Pointe-Noire that includes a Bible school and TEE centre. The Evangelical Church of the Congo has a Seminary and Bible Institute; the Haggai Institute is active in training leaders as is **MANI**. Beyond theology, biblical leadership and management principles also need to be instilled.

5 **Young people** were denied ministry during the Marxist days, and in subsequent years, few churches developed ministries to children or youth. Religious meetings are still prohibited on university campuses. The student movement *Groupe Biblique Universitaire et Scolaire du Congo* (GBUSC) has three full-time staff and three volunteers who serve 120 students.

GBUSC also runs mission camps and gives away large numbers of the Gospels to young people. Pray for a flowering of youth and children's ministries in this nation where 41% of the population are under age 15.

6 **Mission work** thrived until 1968, when nearly all expatriates were expelled. Some returned in the 1990s, but the civil war further complicated full resumption of their work. There is great scope for Christian workers willing to help churches restart abandoned ministries, to address poverty, health and education issues and to once more tackle evangelization of all the country. The largest missions are the Swedish and Norwegian Mission Covenant Church, working with the Evangelical Church, **CMA**, Salvation Army, Global Outreach Mission and UWM. A small Congo missions vision is being re-launched, and there are now about 30 missionaries – 10 serving in other lands.

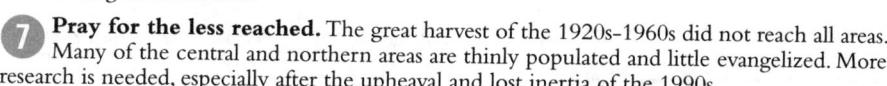

7 **Pray for the less reached.** The great harvest of the 1920s-1960s did not reach all areas. Many of the central and northern areas are thinly populated and little evangelized. More research is needed, especially after the upheaval and lost inertia of the 1990s.

a) ***Parts of the large group of Teke*** peoples in the centre and north are unreached. **CMA** focuses on reaching the Teke.

b) ***The Pygmy tribes*** are semi-nomadic jungle groups and the original inhabitants of the region. They are difficult to reach. Their numbers are unknown and could be anywhere from 40,000 to 60,000. The Bayaka are the largest group and account for half of this total. UWM and several Congolese national church associations work with the Bayaka in Congo. ACATBA/SIL's work in the CAR needs to be adapted for the Yaka dialects spoken in Congo.

c) ***Other peoples*** are believed to be unreached, but there is little information to clarify this. Some of the least evangelized groups include Muslim traders living in urban centres and Europeans living and working in Congo. In addition to the Bayaka, the Baka, Twa and Bongo peoples are also in need of sensitive and appropriate ministry.

8 **Christian resources:**

a) ***Bible translation*** is an ongoing challenge. The Bible is available in nine languages. Six more languages have a NT and another 10 have some portions completed. There are 13 active translation projects. The completion of the NT in Kituba was a significant milestone; pray for its widespread use and for the completion of the OT translation. SIL has significant input and seeks to involve and train many more Congolese in Bible translation. Pray also that churches might catch the vision for mother-tongue Scripture use.

b) ***The JESUS film*** is available in 12 languages.

c) ***Radio.*** A **CMA** station recently launched in the coastal city of Pointe-Noire. This supplements the shortwave and local Christian radio available, until now, only in Brazzaville. Online radio and other resources, mainly in French, are abundant for the few who have reliable Internet access.

Cook Islands

Tokelau · Kiribati
Samoa · Cook Islands · French Polynesia
Tonga · ★Alofi
Niue · Avarua ★
South Pacific Ocean · Adamstown ★ Pitcairn

Cook Islands

The Cook Islands
Pacific

The Cook Islands, Niue, Tokelau and Pitcairn are all officially, or unofficially in the case of the last, related to New Zealand. None are independent. All have seen a large part of their population move to New Zealand or Australia.

Geography

Area 236 sq km. Over 100 coral atolls and volcanic islands 3,500 km northeast of New Zealand, 15 of which are inhabited.

Population		Ann Gr	Density
2010	19,933	0.87%	84/sq km
2020	21,005	0.51%	89/sq km
2030	21,987	0.50%	93/sq km

Capital Avarua 15,000. **Urbanites** 75.3%. **Pop under 15 yrs** 29%.

Peoples

Polynesian 89.2%. Including Rarotongan (Cook Island Maori) 66.4%.
Euronesian 5.7%.
European 4.5%.
Other 0.6%.
Official languages English, Cook Island Maori.
All languages 6. **Indigenous languages** 5.
Languages with Scripture 2Bi 3w.i.p.

Economy

Tourism, selling fishing rights, agriculture and offshore banking.

Politics

Self-governing parliamentary democracy in free association with New Zealand.

Religion

Religions	Pop %	Population	Ann Gr
Christian	96.20	19,176	0.7%
Non-religious	3.00	598	7.3%
Baha'i	0.80	159	0.9%

Christians Denoms		Pop %	Affiliates	Ann Gr
Protestant	4	55.41	11,000	-0.3%
Independent	6	2.06	<1,000	2.9%
Anglican	1	0.50	<1,000	0.0%
Catholic	1	16.56	3,000	-0.6%
Marginal	2	13.04	3,000	2.1%
Unaffiliated		8.60	2,000	14.9%

Churches	MegaBloc	Congs	Members	Affiliates
Cook Islands Chr Ch	P	83	3,720	9,300
Catholic Church	C	16	1,650	3,300
Latter-day Saints (Mormon)	M	5	1,228	2,050
Seventh-day Adventist	P	13	710	900
Assemblies of God	P	10	385	800
Jehovah's Witnesses	M	2	175	550
Other denominations[8]		7	287	555
Total Christians[14]		**136**	**8,155**	**17,455**

TransBloc	Pop %	Population	Ann Gr
Evangelicals			
Evangelicals	12.6	2,517	1.4%
Renewalists			
Charismatics	6.8	1,348	1.9%
Pentecostals	4.0	800	1.7%

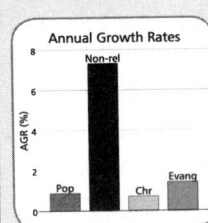

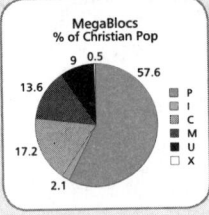

Niue

Geography

Area 258 sq km. The world's largest coral island.

Population		Ann Gr	Density
2010	1,438	-2.64%	6/sq km
2020	1,171	-1.50%	5/sq km
2030	1,081	0.09%	4/sq km

Capital Alofi 615. There are possibly 10 times as many Niueans living overseas, mostly in New Zealand. **Urbanites** 37.5%. **Pop under 15 yrs** 25%.

Peoples

Polynesian 90%. Niueans.
Other 10%. Samoans, Tongans, Europeans.
Literacy 99%. **Official languages** Niuean, English. **All languages** 3. **Languages with Scriptures** 2Bi 1w.i.p.

Economy

Aid, remittances from Niueans abroad, Internet earnings, fishing, agriculture and a growing tourist industry.

Politics

Self governing democracy in free association with New Zealand.

Religion

Religions	Pop %	Population	Ann Gr
Christian	94.90	1,365	-2.6%
Non-religious	4.10	59	-4.0%
Baha'i	1.00	14	-4.5%

Christians Denoms		Pop %	Affiliates	Ann Gr
Protestant	2	60.15	1,000	-3.2%
Independent	2	5.56	<100	-4.4%
Anglican	1	2.78	<100	0.0%
Catholic	1	5.56	<100	-1.2%
Marginal	2	20.17	<300	-1.0%

Churches	MegaBloc	Congs	Members	Affiliates
Niue Chr Church	P	14	212	850
Latter-day Saints (Mormon)	M	3	95	210
Catholic Church	C	1	36	80
Jehovah's Witnesses	M	1	30	80
Other Independents	I	1	35	60
Other denominations[3]		3	28	75
Total Christians[8]		**23**	**436**	**1,355**

TransBloc	Pop %	Population	Ann Gr
Evangelicals			
Evangelicals	8.0	115	-4.1%
Renewalists			
Charismatics	7.4	106	-3.9%

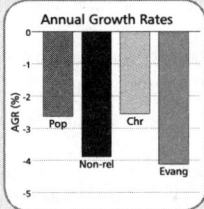
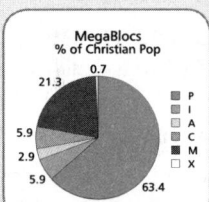

Pitcairn Islands

Pitcairn is one of the smallest (47 sq km and 47 people) and most isolated territories in the world. It is a British overseas territory (formerly a colony), but is administered from New Zealand. It is famous for its settlement in 1790 by mutineers from the British ship, the *Bounty*. The costs of maintaining human presence on the islands have long been underwritten by the UK, but this may not be the case for much longer. All are Seventh-day Adventists. A sex abuse scandal in 2004 rocked the islands' tiny community.

Population		Ann Gr	Density
2010	50	0.00%	1.1/sq km
2020	55	1.52%	1.2/sq km
2030	53	-0.37%	1.1/sq km

Tokelau

Geography

Area 12 sq km. Three infertile coral atolls 480 km north of Samoa.

Population		Ann Gr	Density
2010	1,206	-0.12%	100/sq km
2020	1,202	0.17%	100/sq km
2030	1,208	-0.05%	101/sq km

Pop under 15 yrs 35%.

Peoples

Polynesian 98%.
Other 2%. Another 5,000 Tokelauans live abroad, mostly in New Zealand.
Literacy 99%. **Official language** Tokelauan (close to Samoan). **Languages with Scripture** 1Bi 1por.

Economy

Dependent on aid, remittances from Tokelauans abroad and sale of postage stamps.

Politics

An external territory of New Zealand with increasing autonomy and self-administration.

Religion

Religions	Pop %	Population	Ann Gr
Christian	100.00	1,206	-0.1%

Christians Denoms		Pop %	Affiliates	Ann Gr
Protestant	2	65.92	1,000	-0.1%
Catholic	1	31.51	<400	-1.0%
Marginal	1	1.41	<100	5.5%
Unaffiliated		1.20	<100	0.0%

Churches	MegaBloc	Congs	Members	Affiliates
Congregational Church	P	5	314	785
Catholic Church	C	2	190	380
Other denominations[2]		2	15	27
Total Christians[4]		**9**	**519**	**1,192**

TransBloc	Pop %	Population	Ann Gr
Evangelicals			
Evangelicals	3.4	41	-0.1%
Renewalists			
Charismatics	1.2	15	-1.0%

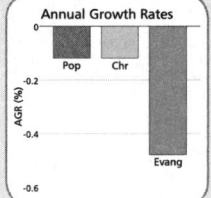

Annual Growth Rates

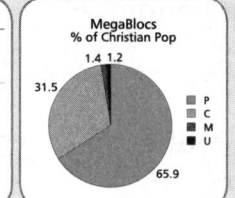

MegaBlocs % of Christian Pop

Answers to Prayer

1 **Niue has effectively shut down its offshore banking industry,** since it was becoming a money-laundering haven. Praise God for the commitment to root out evil practices. Pray for just and wholesome ways to earn a living – for islanders who already suffer from a lack of resources.

2 **The Gospels were translated into Tokelau** in 2005. Pray that this Scripture in their heart language may impact their walk with God.

Challenges for Prayer

1 **The strong Christian legacy** of over 150 years – bordering on theocracy on some islands – is fading rapidly. Increasing numbers are nominal or even non-religious, and Mormons and Jehovah's Witnesses are the fastest growing groups. Pray for reversal of these trends and for new life to come to the mainline Churches.

2 **Many smaller islands have no known evangelical witness.** There are evangelicals in several Pentecostal and Independent churches and small groups within the older churches. **YWAM**'s new base in Rarotonga could be instrumental in rejuvenating the churches of the Cook Islands and beyond. Pray for an outpouring that would see older churches revived, new churches planted and every island with the presence of active believers.

3 **Migration to New Zealand for employment** creates another means of bringing new life into the islands. Around 90% of Niueans, 75% of Tokelauans and over 67% of Cook Islanders now live in New Zealand. Pray for those who remain, that despair and decline would not take hold, but that there would instead be a renaissance of Island culture. Pray for the Island churches in Auckland and other New Zealand cities, for new life there and for those finding it to bring it back to their homelands.

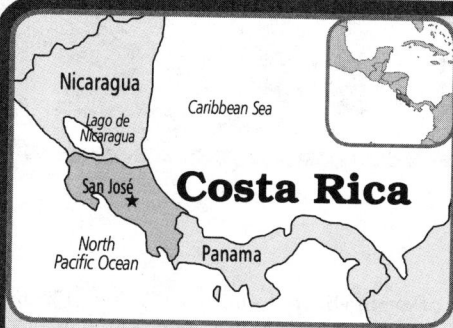

Politics

Independent of Spain in 1821. A long history of a stable, multiparty democratic government. Costa Rica has exercised a stabilizing influence in the conflicts of surrounding lands.

Religion

Roman Catholicism is the official state religion and all limitations on the free exercise of other religions are illegal, but in practice other religions are not yet equal before the law.

Costa Rica

Republic of Costa Rica

Latin America

Geography

Area 51,100 sq km. Agriculturally and ecologically rich land that straddles the Central American isthmus.

Population		Ann Gr	Density
2010	4,639,827	1.40%	91/sq km
2020	5,249,816	1.16%	103/sq km
2030	5,761,733	0.86%	113/sq km

Capital San José 1,460,864. **Urbanites** 64.3%. **Pop under 15 yrs** 26%. **Life expectancy** 78.7 yrs.

Peoples

Spanish-speaking 93.9%. Costa Rican 76.9%; Mestizo 9.4%; other Latin American 7.6%.
Amerindian 1.1%. Five small groups as well as detribalized Amerindians.
Other 5.0%. Jamaican/Creole 1.3%; Chinese 0.8%.
Refugees 500,000–700,000 Nicaraguan refugees and migrant labourers.
Literacy 95.8%. **Official language** Spanish. English and Mekitelyu spoken on Caribbean coast. **All languages** 13. **Indigenous languages** 10. **Languages with Scriptures** 2Bi 1NT 3por 3w.i.p.

Economy

Traditionally dependent on agriculture. Recent growth in the tech sector and a boom in tourism (especially eco-tourism) have gone a long way in relieving a depressed economy. Inflation and the deficit are very high, and 20% still live in deep poverty. A leading country for ecological conservation.
HDI Rank 54th/182. **Public debt** 42% of GDP. **Income/person** $6,544 (14% of USA).

Religions	Pop %	Population	Ann Gr
Christian	93.94	4,358,653	1.3%
Non-religious	4.17	193,481	4.4%
Ethnoreligionist	0.80	37,119	0.9%
Chinese	0.53	24,591	2.6%
Baha'i	0.28	12,992	1.4%
Other	0.13	6,032	6.9%
Buddhist	0.10	4,640	1.4%
Jewish	0.05	2,320	-2.2%

Christians	Denoms	Pop %	Affiliates	Ann Gr
Protestant	68	12.49	579,000	4.1%
Independent	67	4.62	214,000	3.3%
Anglican	1	0.02	1,000	-1.7%
Catholic	1	73.28	3,400,000	1.2%
Marginal	14	2.44	113,000	2.1%
Unaffiliated		3.73	173,000	-5.5%
Doubly affiliated		-2.64	-122,000	0.0%

Churches	MegaBloc	Congs	Members	Affiliates
Catholic Church	C	225	1,798,942	3,400,000
Assemblies of God	P	621	99,301	142,000
Seventh-day Adventist	P	200	56,000	127,120
Jehovah's Witnesses	M	300	24,300	51,030
Ch of God (Cleveland)	P	400	28,300	50,657
Latter-day Saints (Mormon)	M	85	25,374	37,300
Foursquare Gospel Ch	P	145	11,800	24,780
Assoc of Bible Chs	P	194	12,250	24,500
Pente Holiness Ch	P	87	9,160	21,800
Evang Assoc of C Am	P	115	5,400	15,444
Methodist Ch (UMC)	P	457	10,500	14,200
Other denominations[140]		2,687	193,497	399,197
Doubly affiliated				-122,500
Total Christians[151]		**5,516**	**2,274,824**	**4,185,528**

TransBloc	Pop %	Population	Ann Gr
Evangelicals			
Evangelicals	14.8	688,771	3.7%
Renewalists			
Charismatics	22.0	1,018,635	4.1%
Pentecostals	9.6	443,682	4.2%

Missionaries from Costa Rica
P,I,A 129 (84 long-term) in 14 agencies: to
Africa 22, South America 19, Middle East 17.

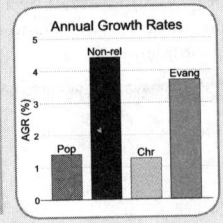

Annual Growth Rates

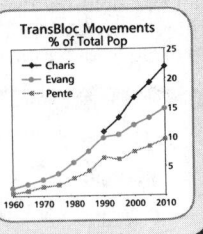

TransBloc Movements
% of Total Pop

Answers to Prayer

1 **The sustained and large-scale growth of evangelicals** from 2.5% in 1970 to 15% in 2010. Some reckon as many as 25% to be of evangelical persuasion, but these higher numbers cannot be substantiated by denominational statistics. One of Latin America's most effective mission advances was established on this foundation.

Challenges for Prayer

1 **Evangelical churches lose almost as many as they gather.** Many unattached evangelicals and many more "ex-evangelicals" have returned to the Catholic Church, turned to sects or given up on religion altogether. The following causes need to be addressed in prayer:

a) *A failure to disciple converts.* Most Costa Rican churches are good at reaching out and winning "converts", but they fail in raising them in godly lifestyles and biblical knowledge. When times get difficult, spiritually stunted Christians either fall away or migrate to a different church.

b) *Pastors are under-resourced,* usually surviving on minimal incomes and without strong teams to help in their work. This generally leads to a failure to provide solid pastoral care for struggling believers, which in turn leads to members drifting away.

c) *Rivalry and divisions* among and within denominations and congregations disillusion many. Pray for a spirit of unity and love to prevail.

d) *Rigid legalism* and failure to enculturate the gospel forced alien forms of faith and culture onto Costa Rican Christianity. Pray for dynamic, relevant and culturally appropriate ministries and churches to spring forth.

2 **The Roman Catholic Church** is deeply impacted by charismatic renewal. Many have come to a living, personal faith in Christ, which has strengthened the Catholic Church (higher mass attendance, more indigenous seminarians and priests). Although 73% of the nation is Catholic, this percent declines every year, and most Catholics are quite nominal in their faith. From the charismatic renewal, many left the Catholic Church for evangelical churches; however, large and increasing numbers of "post-evangelicals" have returned to the familiarity and structure of Catholicism. Pray for both charismatics who stayed in the Catholic Church and those who have returned – may their faith bring further renewal to the mainstream of Catholicism.

3 **These are signs of progress:**

a) *Increased cooperative efforts for outreach and mission,* despite lingering hesitations on the part of some evangelicals. The Costa Rican Evangelical Alliance, representing the majority of denominations, initiated the programme "Costa Rica Century XXI" to promote the development of churches at every level. Pray for a cutting edge to this vision, and for the leaders of this ambitious programme.

b) *Some of the best training options in Latin America.* There are 26 Bible schools and seminaries and a very extensive and effective TEE programme (SEAN). Two of the most influential are UNELA (Evangelical University of the Americas) and UBILA (Latin American Biblical University); both train Christians to minister effectively to all segments of society – be it through church work, missions or marketplace ministry. There are plenty of training opportunities; pray that Costa Ricans would use them to raise the bar for leadership and to strengthen the Church.

4 **Ethnic minorities:**

a) Amerindian tribes are small in number, but each is culturally unique and special to God. Most are nominally Catholic or animist. There is, however, an active indigenous Church among the Cabécar, and evangelical missionary input to the Boruca, Bribri, Guaymi and Maleku. The Bribri have a NT – after nearly 100 years of translation work! Pray that these peoples might see truly indigenous biblical churches planted and thriving, and using their mother tongues.

b) The Chinese population is increasing rapidly, with many Chinese immigrating from Taiwan and mainland China. Some have become Catholic, and there are now some growing evangelical fellowships. The Chinese Christian Mission started a work among them in 1985. Pray that workers would be raised up from both Costa Rica and the global Chinese diaspora to reach these people.

c) The Mekitelyu African Caribbean community on the Caribbean coast is nominally Protestant, but few people have a vital, life-affecting faith in Christ. Pray for revival within these churches and for the more dynamic Costa Rican churches to reach out to these people.

d) Asian immigrants are relatively small in number but increasing. They are mainly Arab, Iranian and South Asian, and are Muslim as well as Hindu.

e) English speakers may number more than 100,000 and are usually affluent and unconnected to any local church. Pray for ministry geared specifically toward them.

5 **Ministry to young people** is essential, given that two-thirds of Costa Ricans are under age 30. As with many other nations, alcoholism, drug addiction, violence and immorality plague this generation. Christian student and youth ministry has been weak in the past, but vision is growing and ministry increasing. ECU(**IFES**) in 17 universities and 17 colleges, Alfa y Omega (**CCCI**), Maranatha (a Pentecostal student work) and others are very active. On the "Street of Bitterness", located near the national university, there exist both many social problems and sustained outreach.

6 **Missions.** The largest agencies are **YWAM**, **LAM**, **AoG**, **RG**, IT, **ABWE**, **CCCI**. The country's stability makes it an ideal base for many regional and global ministries. Pray for cooperation and close fellowship among agencies – efforts are too often duplicated. In many agencies, North Americans' dominance of personnel, money and culture can diminish both diversity and the opportunity for local expressions.

7 **National ministries and missions are beginning to blossom** as the Costa Rican Church matures and as foreign missions hand over control to nationals. These most often take shape as holistic ministries aimed at helping the poor, the sick, the broken and children at risk. Some exciting partnerships are forming. One example is Christ for the City, whose work has resulted in short-term mission teams sent abroad as well as ministry to the most needy at home.

8 **Christian help ministries:**

a) Radio and TV. There are six Christian radio stations, one TV channel and five Internet radio sites; other secular stations air Christian programmes. Pray for quality programming that will reach into the hearts of the lost and build up believers.

b) The Bible Society. Demand for Scriptures is strong and growing. Works in reaching students and Nicaraguan immigrants are especially fruitful.

c) The Spanish Language Institute, where many missionaries learn Spanish. Pray for staff and missionary students.

trade language in the north and Abidjan. **All languages** 93. **Indigenous languages** 77. **Languages with Scriptures** 5Bi 29NT 33por 16w.i.p.

Côte d'Ivoire

Republic of Côte d'Ivoire

Africa

Geography

Area 322,463 sq km. On the west African coast between Ghana and Liberia. Rainforest in the south and savannah/highlands in the north.

Population		Ann Gr	Density
2010	21,570,746	2.31%	67/sq km
2020	26,954,068	2.17%	84/sq km
2030	32,550,662	1.82%	101/sq km

There has been a large influx of migrants from surrounding lands over the last few decades, especially Burkina Faso and Mali, interrupted only by the civil strife in 2002-2004. **Capital** Yamoussoukro 885,267. **Other major city** Abidjan 4.1 million. **Urbanites** 50.1%. **Pop under 15 yrs** 41%. **Life expectancy** 56.8 yrs.

Peoples

The large and undocumented population of migrants from Burkina Faso, Mali and other surrounding countries means that all figures are estimates.

Guinean/Akan 31.7%. 21 groups: Baule 15.8%; the dominant people today. Anyi 4.4%; Attie 2.7%; Anyin/Morofo 1.7%; Akan 1.5%; Abe 1.2%.
Gur 24.6%. 21 groups: Mossi 12.0%; Senufo(7) 9.2%; Kulango 1.0%.
Malinke(3) 18.7%. 11 groups: Maninka(4) 10.5%; Bambara 4.9%; Jula/Dioula 1.4%.
Mande 10.0%. 11 groups: Dan 5.9%; Gouro 2.4%.
Kru 9.1%. 28 groups: Bete(3) 3.2%; Guere 1.8%; Dida(2) 1.2%; Wobe 1.1%.
Other Africans 4.9%. Fulani(2) 2.1%.
Other 0.9%. Arab, French, German.
Literacy 48.1%. **Official language** French, used by a high proportion of the population. Jula is the most widespread indigenous language, used as a

Economy

One of the world's largest producers of cocoa, coffee and palm oil – all subject to global market changes in price. Nearly 70% of the population depend on agriculture and related activity, despite government attempts to diversify the economy. Oil and gas production now garner more income than cocoa. The post-independence economic boom attracted massive immigration of job-seekers from surrounding lands, which in turn led to numerous problems. Political woes, from a coup in December 1999 to the conflicts of 2002-2007, drove the economy downward as infrastructures failed and foreign investment disappeared. **HDI Rank** 163th/182. **Public debt** 66.4% of GDP. **Income/person** $1,132 (2% of USA).

Politics

Independent from France in 1960. Formerly a one-party presidential government under Houphouet-Boigny, who died in 1993. His elected successor was deposed and fled the country during a coup at Christmas 1999. The military-led transitional government oversaw blatantly rigged elections in 2000. Protests forced in a new president – Laurent Gbagbo. After a failed coup in 2002, the nation was subject to an armed rebellion by disaffected northerners who claimed discrimination against them in the political sphere. A peace agreement signed in 2003 saw the fighting (which claimed thousands of lives) calm, with sporadic outbreaks until 2007. A new agreement in that year saw the former rebel leader come onboard as prime minister and militias on both sides begin to be decommissioned, disarmed and integrated into the armed forces. Elections to replace the president have been postponed several times and are years overdue; corruption is alleged to be rife within the corridors of power. Conflict and division in the country are along north-south lines that reflect, to a large degree, ethnic differences, with southern Christian and animist political interest groups attempting to shut out the northern Muslims from power. Tensions will not relax for some time, but Ivoirian stability is essential to the entire region, already one of the world's poorest and most strife-torn.

Religion

Religious freedom, although the conflicts of 2002-2007 drove out many missionaries and saw an increasing religious demarcation of Muslim north and non-Muslim south. The government remains receptive to mission activity and development. Traditional religions are generally stronger in the centre and west. Both Islam and Christianity are highly syncretized with African traditional beliefs, making these three religions difficult to precisely enumerate.

Religions	Pop %	Population	Ann Gr
Muslim	41.80	9,016,572	3.2%
Christian	33.64	7,256,399	2.9%
Ethnoreligionist	24.09	5,196,393	0.2%
Non-religious	0.27	58,241	3.1%
Baha'i	0.13	28,042	2.3%
Buddhist	0.05	10,785	2.3%
Hindu	0.02	4,314	2.3%

Christians Denoms		Pop %	Affiliates	Ann Gr
Protestant	47	11.29	2,436,000	2.2%
Independent	150	5.40	1,164,000	2.0%
Catholic	1	15.90	3,430,000	3.8%
Orthodox	4	0.18	38,000	2.9%
Marginal	2	0.18	38,000	4.3%
Unaffiliated		0.69	149,000	-2.9%

Churches	MegaBloc	Congs	Members	Affiliates
Catholic Church	C	325	1,994,186	3,430,000
Assemblies of God	P	535	525,000	815,000
United Methodist Ch	P	853	677,355	800,000
Christian & Miss Alliance	P	1,600	320,000	408,000
Eglise Harriste	I	773	67,987	206,000
Works & Mission Bapt	I	1,850	92,500	185,000

Ashes of Purification	I	190	94,910	158,500
Les Eglises "Reveille"	I	643	65,818	98,727
Evang Alliance (WEC)	P	506	48,031	84,054
UEESO-MICI	P	64	15,351	79,000
Apostolic Pente Mission	I	702	42,143	59,000
Into Africa Project	P	433	22,917	55,000
Seventh-day Adventist	P	52	14,500	47,850
Baptist Convention	P	149	22,400	33,600
Jehovah's Witnesses	M	195	8,600	24,596
Assoc of Ev Bapt Chs	P	400	8,000	20,000
Other denominations[175]		2,814	272,275	601,839
Total Christians[204]		**12,084**	**4,291,973**	**7,106,166**

TransBloc	Pop %	Population	Ann Gr
Evangelicals			
Evangelicals	10.5	2,256,431	3.0%
Renewalists			
Charismatics	8.9	1,924,968	3.5%
Pentecostals	5.6	1,208,829	3.1%

Religions % of Total Pop

MegaBlocs % of Christian Pop

Answers to Prayer

1 **The establishment of a peace agreement** after years of effective civil war and uneasy ceasefires. While all the issues that generated the troubles are not resolved, the return of stability to the country is a point for praise, since economic activity, education, development and rebuilding can now resume – and since the north is once again much more accessible for Christian ministry.

2 **Continued growth in evangelical churches,** despite the upheavals of the 2002-2007 conflicts. In Abidjan alone, there are probably more than 3,000 churches, most of them relatively new and independent.

3 **The further consolidation of Christian unity** – this comes in large part through the work of Transformation Africa/Global Day of Prayer, through *Radio Fréquence Vie* (the only national Protestant radio station), and through the work of interdenominational ministries such as The Bible Society, **CCCI** and GBU/**IFES**, the Christian publisher CPE, **SIM**'s Pastors' Book Set project and the *Africa Bible Commentary*.

Challenges for Prayer

1 **The country has been essentially divided** between Muslim north and multi-faith but predominantly Christian south. Although peace is established and the nation is moving forward, the loss of life, of infrastructure and of confidence in Côte d'Ivoire's fundamental unity will leave scars on the nation's psyche. Pray for political leaders who are visionary, non-partisan, free of corruption and able to boldly take the nation forward and past this unfortunate episode in Côte d'Ivoire's history. Pray also for a satisfactory solution to the remaining challenge – how to handle the millions of immigrants from neighbouring countries, a problem at the core of the conflict of 2002-2007.

2 **The Catholic Church** has made a deep impact through an extensive educational system. Catholics are a large minority in the south and among the upper and middle classes as a result. Nominalism is common in the Catholic and Methodist denominations, two of the country's largest. But there are significant numbers of genuine believers in both as well as a vibrant charismatic movement.

3 **Animism is still strong in Côte d'Ivoire,** despite apparent numerical decline. Although evangelical congregations outnumber sacred fetish groves for the first time in the nation's history, animism's power remains unbroken and penetrates deep into the worldview and practices of both Christians and Muslims. Many believers are affected by the power of African traditional religion, especially through fetish charms and ancestor worship, compromising both their witness and their own life in Christ. Pray that all who have not fully left behind this past might be completely delivered by the power of Jesus. Pray that believers might withstand temptation to revert to old practices of animism.

4 **Pray for evangelicals and their ministry** in Côte d'Ivoire. Partnerships and teamwork are on the rise, but more progress needs to be made if the growth enjoyed in the 1990s is to be repeated, if the country is to be effectively evangelized and if the Church is to be discipled.

a) *Protestant and evangelical networks.* The Evangelical Federation of Côte d'Ivoire, despite being nearly 50 years old, has little to show for its efforts. Several new networks have formed as a result, including one specifically for Christians in media. Pray for leadership that knows how to make cooperative ventures work and to bring them to pass.

b) *National strategy for evangelization.* Côte d'Ivoire has a long way to go before the task is even close to being finished. **MANI** (Movement for African National Initiatives) and **CAPRO** are both engaged in research of the nation's people groups in order to stimulate greater mission and church planting endeavours. Both are committed to reaching the unreached by mobilizing the national Church to send missionaries – a grassroots and indigenous movement. Côte d'Ivoire has also played a major role in church and mission consultations for all of Francophone West Africa.

5 **Knowledge and understanding of the Bible are low,** partly a result of rapid church growth, but also from a cultural lack of regular Bible reading. This naturally affects the maturation and discipleship of believers and whole churches. Many churches endorse prosperity teachings, and ministry can at times focus more upon miracles and healings rather than on the One who is their source or on the study of His Word. However, theological education is growing, both full-time (seminaries, colleges and institutes) and part-time (modular and TEE courses). Nearly every denomination has at least one Bible training institute. The quality of these varies greatly; pray for a greater level of partnership in theological education.

6 **Evangelical agencies had a late and slow start** compared to other West African lands. **CMA** arrived in 1930 and focused on the Baule in the centre of the country. *Mission Biblique* began in 1927 among the Yacouba and Guéré in the southwest, later joined by **UFM**, and **WEC** began in 1934 among the Gouro and Gban (Gagou). **AoG**, though starting only in the 1950s, now has churches all over the country, surpassing all the other denominations in terms of growth and outreach. The number of mission personnel shrank drastically due to the outbreak of violence in 2002 and has not recovered to former levels. This has in turn cast greater responsibility onto the indigenous church, but foreign missionaries are still welcomed and needed in most aspects of ministry. Evangelism, church planting and Bible translation ministries only scratch the surface of possibilities.

7 **There are now several African mission agencies;** some are denominational. They work mainly in Côte d'Ivoire but increasingly beyond, targeting the remaining unreached peoples of West Africa and the world. Main areas for prayer:

a) *Missionary training.* **CAPRO** has a missions training institute in Abidjan to serve Francophone West Africa. It is the first such institute for this region. The great challenge is to prepare missionaries for Muslim outreach. A consortium of Methodists, the UEESO and the General Conference Baptists are developing a missionary training school. Pray for these endeavours, and pray that such schools would produce excellent Ivoirian missionaries for the harvest field.

b) *Sending.* Congregations are usually supportive of indigenous missionaries, but leadership can at times feel threatened, and economic strain can limit financial support. Many missionaries live by faith on very little income. Pray that God might supply all of their needs and that their churches might support them in every possible way.

8 **Peoples that are unevangelized** and without a major church planting breakthrough abound, especially in the north. The perception that Côte d'Ivoire is reached, because of the popularity of Christianity and presence of missionaries in the south, is a false notion that delays the gospel reaching millions in the north.

a) The Mande and Malinke people clusters of the northwest. The Malinke especially are strongly Muslim and mostly unreached. They include the Jula (CMFI and WorldVenture), Koro (Baptists), Mahou (Norwegian Lutherans), Maninka(3) (**SIM, IMB**), Ngan, Wassulu, Worodougou (**CAPRO, UEESO, WEC, SIM**), Jeri Kuo and Ngan. None is more than 1% evangelical, and yet these clusters account for 20% of the country's population.

b) The Gur people cluster of the north and northeast. Most practice African traditional religions, and none of the following is more than 1% evangelical: Lobi (**CAPRO**, Free Will Baptists), Koulango/Bouna (**CAPRO**, Free Will Baptists), Senoufo(5) (WorldVenture), Nafanra, Khisa and Karaboro.

c) Other, primarily foreign African peoples. These include the Soninke, Fulani(2), Hausa, Bozo and Wolof, all of whom have immigrated at some past point from other West African countries.

9 **The large influx of foreigners** rapidly reversed with the outbreak of war. They are returning now, but precisely how many have done so is unknown. While their presence in Côte d'Ivoire is the source of much strife, it is also a timely evangelistic opportunity to reach them when they are separated from close tribal ties. Around 70% of the foreign population is Muslim. At their peak, foreigners made up nearly 30% of the country's total population, but half of that 30% had lived in Côte d'Ivoire for at least one generation.

10 **Islam spread and grew rapidly during the 20th Century,** from 5% in 1900 to near 41.8% today. Tribal groups in the north and pockets of tribes all over the country are becoming Muslim. Urban concentrations of Muslims are high as are conversion rates among new immigrants to the cities. Sadly, many southern Ivoirian Christians have aligned themselves with the president and his political agenda, and have thereby undermined their potential for genuine witness to northerners; foreign Christian witness may be the most effective way to reach the north. Pray that Christians may be zealous to win non-Muslims while they can and to show humility and love for them. Pray for the healing of the north-south ethnic divide created by politicians, which is making outreach to Muslims even harder than before.

11 Demographic sectors of society needing the gospel:

a) Abidjan's exploding population has doubled in the last 15 years to five million in the metropolitan area, making it the third largest city in the Francophone world. It is the strategic key for evangelization of Côte d'Ivoire, Mali and Burkina Faso. All people groups of these latter two lands have a significant community in the city, but most are neglected by the Church. Over 2.5 million Muslims, roughly half of the city, are scarcely touched with the gospel. Missionaries from **CAPRO, SIM, CMA** and the Baptists are a mere drop in the bucket of church planting needs. Many new congregations are started every month, but these focus on already-Christian peoples.

b) AIDS is a major problem in the country, although HIV prevalence rates have gone down to 4.7% of the population – still nearly one million people. The large majority of those HIV-positive are women. Both the government and many Christian ministries (CMFI, REMAR, Church of God) are doing good work in terms of awareness, education and care for those infected.

c) Young people are responsive, and wherever churches minister specifically to them, there is fruit – denominations are increasingly introducing student ministry to their work. Liberty to teach Scripture in public schools is an exciting but under-used opportunity through lack of qualified personnel. SU makes a vital contribution in school evangelism and discipleship. The **IFES** Francophone Africa headquarters is in Abidjan, and there are strong GBU/**IFES** groups present. **CCCI** is also well established, with 30 full-time staff, reaching students in several cities.

12 **Christian literature.** Pray for the bookstores and depots of various missions, including The Bible Society, *Maison de la Bible*, **CLC**, CDM and others. Pray for the inter-mission/ church Evangelical Publication Centre (CPE) and other publishers, that they might find the means to print books locally at a suitable quality. Currently, many books are printed in Asia or elsewhere. Well-intentioned efforts by outside ministries to sell their literature at subsidized prices keep African authors from publishing more relevant Christian works – because they cannot compete with these lower-priced books. Also needing prayer: lack of qualified staff (especially French-speaking), financial pressures and lack of good distribution outlets and marketing strategies.

13 **Bible translation** is one of the most pressing and demanding ministries for Christian workers. A considerable number of national and expatriate workers are involved in 28 translation projects, many being among the superficially Christianized people of the south. SIL's contribution is especially significant. Three OTs and six NTs were completed between 2000–2009, including the completion of the Jula Bible. Pray also for:

a) Distribution of Scripture. Pray for a wider distribution of Bibles and NTs already translated. Relative poverty and a negative attitude toward reading, especially in one's tribal language rather than in French, are challenges that must be addressed.

b) Literacy projects are vital to make full use of translated Scripture. Pray for SIL, UBS, other missions and local churches endeavouring to bring the gift of reading to Ivoirians.

c) Audio Scriptures are even more important to the many peoples who are oral learners in this land. SIL is focusing on audio formats for Scripture, and **GRN** produces Scripture and Christian teaching in 65 of Côte d'Ivoire's languages.

14 **Christian media:**

a) Publishing and literature took a serious blow in the civil conflicts, as stocks were looted, buildings damaged, foreign partners fled the country and economic upheaval decimated business. United Bible Society, **CLC**, CPE (Evangelical Publication Centre) and *Maison de la Bible* were all affected. Pray for these ministries to be restored to the functionality and influence they had before the war. Pray also for the impact of the *Africa Bible Commentary* (Langham) and the **SIM** Pastors' Booksets projects.

b) Radio. Radio Fréquence Vie broadcasts in French and Jula. **SIM**'s plan is to eventually turn it over to the national Church. Five other cities have relay stations to further broadcast the programmes in French, Jula, Baule, Abidji, Bété, Senufo, Mahouka and other languages. Methodists also recently started their own station. The Evangelical Radio Association in Côte d'Ivoire represents several stations, as Christians seek to utilize this most popular form of media. **TWR** and others produce radio programmes in studios in Abidjan, which are broadcast throughout West Africa and to the whole world. Much radio ministry is funded by private donors, since churches have been slow on the uptake to support this strategic ministry.

c) PEMA, the film studio for the Association of Evangelicals in Africa, based in Abidjan, produces culturally relevant programmes on video for transmission by national television stations across West Africa. Topics such as HIV/AIDS, family life and other relevant social issues get a sound biblical treatment in these programmes.

d) The JESUS film is in use in 12 languages, with another two dubbing projects underway. Praise God for the completion of the film in Jula.

e) Christian music writing and recording continues to be influential in Côte d'Ivoire and indeed from here to the rest of West Africa. Many quality albums and songs have been recorded and produced here. Pray that the messages of the songs remain biblically sound and that the lifestyle of the artists reflects the message.

and Serb peoples. Their mutual hatred dominated the politics of the former Yugoslavia and was one cause of the Balkan wars of the 1990s, wherein Croatia lost and subsequently regained much land. The transition from nationalist politics to liberal democracy continues; entry into the EU is anticipated by the end of 2010.

Religion

Freedom of religion in a secular state, but Catholicism enjoys an unofficial favoured status. Many leaders in the Catholic Church are at the forefront of reconciliation and justice issues.

Croatia
Republic of Croatia
Europe

Geography

Area 56,438 sq km. Crescent-shaped country between the Danube River and Adriatic Sea. The land is almost bisected by Bosnia.

Population		Ann Gr	Density
2010	4,409,659	-0.15%	78/sq km
2020	4,317,710	-0.24%	77/sq km
2030	4,179,634	-0.35%	74/sq km

Capital Zagreb 687,000. **Urbanites** 57.8%. **Pop under 15 yrs** 15%. **Life expectancy** 76 yrs.

Peoples

Slavic 93.4%. Croat 87.5%; Serb 4.5%; Bosnian 0.5%; Slovene 0.3%.
Other European 1.3%. Hungarian 0.4%; Albanian 0.3%; Friulian 0.2%.
Other 5.3%. Romani(4) 2.3%; about 2.9% unclassified/unknown.
Literacy 98.1%. **Official language** Croatian – closely related to Serbian but written in Latin rather than Cyrillic script. **All languages** 22. **Indigenous languages** 7. **Languages with Scriptures** 3Bi 1por.

Economy

Long-term Communist mismanagement and the war with Serbia undermined a previously solid economy. Recovery is still in process, with relatively high unemployment and low wages. A resurgent tourist sector and the privatization of state industries have helped Croatia begin to turn the corner and develop over the last decade. **HDI Rank** 45th/182. **Unemployment** 12.7%. **Public debt** 42.7% of GDP. **Income/person** $15,634 (33% of USA).

Politics

Over 1,600 years of Great Power rivalries lie behind the division between the related Croat

Religions	Pop %	Population	Ann Gr
Christian	91.96	4,055,122	-0.2%
Non-religious	6.01	265,021	0.5%
Muslim	1.90	83,784	-0.2%
Jewish	0.10	4,410	-0.2%
Hindu	0.02	882	-0.2%
Buddhist	0.01	441	0.0%

Christians Denoms		Pop %	Affiliates	Ann Gr
Protestant	25	0.52	23,000	-0.2%
Independent	3	0.25	11,000	0.1%
Catholic	2	87.54	3,860,000	-0.2%
Orthodox	1	5.90	260,000	0.2%
Marginal	2	0.30	13,000	1.1%
Doubly affiliated		-2.55	-112,000	0.0%

Churches	MegaBloc	Congs	Members	Affiliates
Catholic Church	C	1,600	2,655,172	3,850,000
Serbian Orthodox Ch	O	47	179,310	260,000
Jehovah's Witnesses	M	103	6,400	12,544
Eastern Rite Catholic	C	30	5,556	10,000
Seventh-day Adventist	P	82	3,000	4,620
Evangelical Ch (Pente)	P	60	2,400	4,000
Baptist Church	P	56	2,100	3,570
Ev Ch of Croatia (Luth)	P	9	1,550	3,100
Reformed Christian Ch	P	21	1,800	3,100
Other denominations[24]		69	7,976	13,755
Doubly affiliated				-112,000
Total Christians[33]		2,077	2,865,264	4,054,689

TransBloc	Pop %	Population	Ann Gr
Evangelicals			
Evangelicals	0.4	19,359	0.6%
Renewalists			
Charismatics	0.4	18,846	3.0%
Pentecostals	0.2	6,628	2.2%

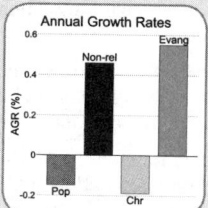

Annual Growth Rates

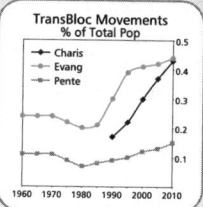

TransBloc Movements % of Total Pop

Challenges for Prayer

1 **The profound impact of historic and recent hatred** among Croat, Serb and Bosnian could continue to hamper the affected nations for generations to come. The iron bond shackling ethnicity to religion also hampers progress and stifles spiritual breakthrough. Many suffer continued psychological and emotional trauma as a result of the upheavals, and little has been done to address this. It is an area where churches might have a great impact. Pray for true reconciliation and for the religious and ethnic bondages to be broken – these can only happen through the power of Christ.

2 **The Catholic Church** is highly influential in Croatia. About 15% of Catholics regularly attend mass – a high proportion for Europe. Some Catholic leaders are at the forefront of the reconciliation movement and some cooperate with evangelicals. There is a small but active charismatic movement within the Catholic Church, but a significant shortage of young men joining the priesthood. Pray that all Croatians would move beyond empty rituals to a living relationship with Jesus.

3 **Evangelicals are one of the few groups that straddle the ethnic divide.** Many Bosnians, Croats and Serbs have been won to Christ and brought into fellowship together. The churches' and missions' care and love for those who suffered in the war won much credit for the gospel. Pray that evangelicals would continue to demonstrate the boundary-breaking, universal love of God.

4 **Believing churches are spreading.** Though still relatively small in size and number, new fellowships are popping up around the country, but several areas require urgent prayer:

a) *Continued growth.* Planting churches is high on the priority list of almost all groups working among the unreached. Baptist, Pentecostal and Independent groups partner with foreign groups (Baptists, **ECM**, **GEM**, **SEND**, Pioneers, UWM, **AoG**, others) to establish vibrant new faith communities across the nation. Pray for creative and strong local expressions of the body of Christ.

b) *Unity.* Cooperation and partnership across denominational lines are essential in this land with a history of division. Evangelicals recognize the power of unity and the testimony it gives, but the enemy is in opposition. Pray for God's people to win through as they draw together.

c) *Leadership.* Many evangelical pastors have no formal theological education and are often bi-vocational. As new churches outgrow the number of trained leaders, training new pastors and church leaders becomes a great challenge. Pray for effective, relevant and affordable training.

d) *Theological education.* The Evangelical Theological Seminary in Osijek, an international, interdenominational school, is greatly impacting much of Central and Eastern Europe. Many fruitful ministries have been birthed out of it. Pray for the continued spiritual fruitfulness and theological health of faculty, students and graduates. Baptists, Pentecostals and Church of Christ also run Bible schools.

e) *Prayer movements* are springing up as the recognition spreads that Croatia will be transformed only through persistent, prevailing intercession.

5 **The less reached.** Historically, minority groups were the main force among Protestants/ Independents, but this is changing. There are still peoples and areas with very little evangelical presence:

a) *Croatians.* Novi Zagreb is a region of the capital with one-eighth of Croatia's population – but as of 2007, it had no evangelical church. The Istrian Penninsula, the Dalmatian coast and Zagorje in the north are all frontiers for witnessing believers to move into.

b) *Romani.* These peoples are neglected by evangelicals, but prove very responsive to the gospel, especially the young people. Pray for culturally appropriate churches to emerge among the Romani.

c) *Other minorities.* Albanians, Slovenes, Italians, Germans and others who have little exposure to or interaction with the good news.

Specialist ministries for prayer:

a) *Young people.* High unemployment, little confidence in the future, functional godlessness and widespread drug use (80% of teens) show that hope is in short supply. Creative outreach and authentic love will see a response if believers are willing to stick it out. There is a strong focus by evangelicals on ministering to drug addicts.

b) *Students.* There is a witness among the 25,000 tertiary students through STEP(**IFES**) and **CCCI**. More staff and volunteers are needed to reach this searching generation.

c) *Other sectors of society include families and business professionals.* With both of these groups, **CCCI** is pioneering helpful means of sharing the gospel and having a positive redemptive effect on society in general.

d) *Bibles.* The Croatian Bible is available in print, online and in audio format, and an easy-to-read NT has recently been published. There is also a children's version. Pray for widespread distribution and impact of God's Word into many lives.

e) *Christian publishing.* Izvori Publishing House of the Evangelical Church publishes literature and three Christian magazines. Increasing numbers of Christian books, especially on discipleship, are being translated into Croatian. Pray that useful Christian resources will be developed to help disciple believers and to reach unbelievers.

f) Christian media. Radio has wide coverage – more than 30 hours per week in Croatian (IBRA, **TWR**) across all bandwidths. Internet radio in Croatian is another new and developing ministry. *Izvori-Vjere* radio ministry is broadcasting on over 52 stations in Croatia and Bosnia. Christian TV in Croatian is also available to more than 60% of the population via eight regional stations.

C

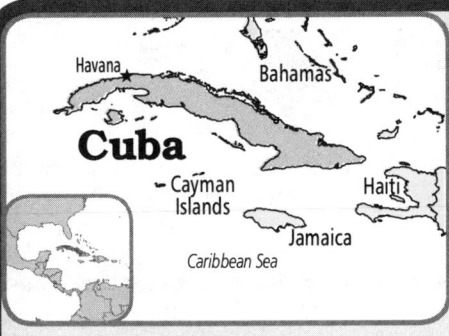

Havana
Bahamas
Cuba
Cayman Islands
Haiti
Jamaica
Caribbean Sea

Cuba
Republic of Cuba
Caribbean

Geography

Area 110,861 sq km. The largest island in the Caribbean.

Population		Ann Gr	Density
2010	11,204,351	0.02%	101/sq km
2020	11,193,470	-0.04%	101/sq km
2030	11,019,440	-0.23%	99/sq km

Capital Havana 2,130,000. **Urbanites** 76%. **Pop under 15 yrs** 18%. **Life expectancy** 78.5 yrs.

Peoples

Hispanic 98%. White Hispanic 62%; Mulatto & Mestizo 25%; Black 11%. Racial lines are extremely blurred; most likely the black population is higher than given.
Asian 1%. Primarily Chinese, also South Asian.
Other 1%. Haitian, Russian, Palestinian.
Literacy 99.8%. **Official language** Spanish.
All languages 4. **Indigenous languages** 2.
Languages with Scriptures 1Bi.

Economy

Sugar production, along with the rest of the economy, collapsed with the Soviet meltdown as aid and subsidies dried up. The US trade embargo, devastating hurricanes, repressive centralized socialist planning, corruption and poor productivity hamper progress. Lack of many essentials (including food) still affects the country, yet there is a high standard in literacy, education and health. Tourism is becoming more and more economically important.
HDI Rank 51st/182. **Public debt** 35% of GDP. **Income/person** $2,300 (5% of USA).

Politics

Independent from Spain in 1898. Castro's revolution brought Communism to power in 1959, replacing a corrupt and venal regime. After decades of exporting revolution to Latin America and Africa, Cuba remains among the last protagonists of Communism. An ailing Fidel Castro passed along power to his brother, Raúl Castro (now

President), in 2008. Subsequent economic reform has not been accompanied by civil or political change; political opposition remains illegal despite increasing dissident activity, prompting emigration and pervasive hopelessness.

Religion

Strict control of all church activities and repression of religious freedom in earlier years of Communist rule, but since 1990 the degree of pressure has lessened. A secular rather than atheist state, discrimination against Christians is illegal. But discrimination and harassment continue as growing churches are often perceived as a threat to regime stability. The Cuban Council of Churches is the Protestant umbrella body sanctioned by the regime. It endorses an expression of faith more in keeping with the revolutionary ideals of the regime, including liberation theology.

Religion	Pop %	Population	Ann Gr
Christian	56.53	6,333,820	0.8%
Non-religious	25.01	2,802,208	-1.9%
Ethnoreligionist	18.00	2,016,783	0.6%
Hindu	0.14	15,686	1.5%
Chinese	0.14	15,686	0.0%
Other	0.14	15,645	0.0%
Buddhist	0.04	4,482	-4.4%

Christians	Denoms	Pop %	Affiliates	Ann Gr
Protestant	43	5.66	634,000	4.3%
Independent	14	1.83	205,000	4.2%
Anglican	1	0.12	14,000	7.0%
Catholic	1	48.37	5,420,000	0.5%
Orthodox	1	0.08	10,000	3.5%
Marginal	1	1.16	130,000	0.9%
Unaffiliated		1.5	168,000	-0.6%
Doubly affiliated		-2.19	-245,000	0.0%

Churches	MegaBloc	Congs	Members	Affiliates
Catholic Ch	C	808	3,474,359	5,420,000
Assemblies of God	P	4,500	110,000	169,000
Jehovah's Witnesses	M	2,906	93,000	130,200
Bapt Conv of E Cuba	P	2,300	36,452	113,000
Evang Pentecostal Ch	I	306	55,000	110,000
Methodist Ch of C	P	533	16,000	60,000
Bapt Conv of W Cuba	P	1,118	19,000	45,600
Los Pinos Nuevos	P	250	27,000	45,090
Christian Pentecostal Ch	I	600	18,000	45,000
Seventh-day Adventist	P	262	25,100	33,000
Presbyterian Reformed	P	270	8,100	19,550
Pentecostal Holiness Ch	P	257	18,000	19,000
Ch of God (Cleveland)	P	65	4,100	14,637
Episcopal Church	A	54	4,895	14,000
Open Bible Standard Ch	P	226	7,000	14,000
Other denominations[46]		2,098	80,215	120,017
Doubly affiliated				-245,000
Total Christians[61]		**16,553**	**3,996,221**	**6,167,094**

TransBloc	Pop %	Population	Ann Gr
Evangelicals			
Evangelicals	8.8	980,553	3.5%
Renewalists			
Charismatics	7.1	798,836	3.8%
Pentecostals	3.5	395,488	3.8%

Religions % of Total Pop

TransBloc Movements % of Total Pop

Answers to Prayer

1 **The Church has continued to multiply at impressive rates.** Growth from the 1990s continues and, while slowing, remains strong. Praise God for a dynamic and expanding Church.

2 **Opposition and hostility toward the Church has refined it,** causing believers to depend radically upon God, strengthening their prayer life (individually and corporately) and encouraging unity of the Body of Christ.

3 **Numerical growth is accompanied by increased maturity and confidence.** Although Christian resources are hard to come by for churches not aligned with the government, the Church in general is beginning to minister in innovative and bold ways, and members see no conflict between their "Cuban-ness" and their faith.

Challenges for Prayer

1 **Cuba faces a difficult future.** Pray for the following needs:

a) Political. This last bastion of Communism in the West defies fundamental change through the continued influence of Fidel Castro, his President brother, Raúl Castro, and "old guard" Party leadership. Pray for their salvation and for wise leadership that governs in the best interests of its people.

b) Economic. The current model is simply unsustainable in the long term, despite substantive assistance from Venezuela, China and Bolivia. While the Castro family sits on a personal fortune, endemic poverty has led to a thriving black market where crime, drugs and prostitution (including sex tourism) are widespread. Black and mulatto Cubans suffer greater deprivation with fewer opportunities than whites. Only Haiti and the Dominican Republic are poorer in the Caribbean region. Pray for sensible reforms and economic freedom, and that structural sins might be overcome by good.

c) Demographic. Cuba has a top-heavy population, with large and increasing numbers of aged dependent on too few in the younger generation for support. This demographic time bomb will place further stress on an already fragile economy.

d) Ideological. The wounds inflicted by Marxism need healing. More than 500,000 have been imprisoned for ideological reasons and over one million have become ideological or economic refugees, many in Florida, USA. Both the USA and Cuba have used refugees as a weapon of war. Pray that forgiveness might abound among all Cubans, and that relations might improve between Cuba and the wider world.

2 **Catholicism was the default religion** before the revolution. Although the majority still confess Catholicism, huge swathes of the church are rife with syncretism; it is often hard to tell where Catholicism ends and Afro-Cuban Spiritism begins. The statistics do not (and can not) reflect the depth of influence Spiritism possesses. Less than 10% frequent mass. Priests and nuns are less than half their pre-revolutionary numbers. However, the Catholic Church is experiencing something of a comeback after several very difficult decades. True believers are few but growing in number. Pray for the Catholic Church, that it might be purified, revived and established as a place where millions will find Jesus.

3 **Evangelical churches were devastated by waves of emigration** to the USA as well as by persecution. Recovery has taken a long time, but the Church is now a force to be reckoned with. Protestants alone more than doubled between 1995 and 2010. Many new believers are young people. Charismatic/Pentecostal groups in particular report spectacular (albeit statistically dubious) growth. Pray that this dynamic faith community would be a light to the nation and have a powerful transforming effect on Cuba; the potential for positive impact is great.

4 **Persecution of Christians,** more severe in the past, continues in the form of harassment and discrimination including occasional imprisonment of leaders. A seven-year sentence handed down to an evangelical pastor was the harshest thus far. Following Jesus remains a sacrificial choice while the regime fears the Church as a social movement like that which undermined Communism in Eastern Europe and China. Pray for continued courage and perseverance for suffering believers.

a) The government has tried to strangle Christian growth by making it nearly impossible economically to build new churches; the resulting house church movement has proved even more fruitful!

b) Disunity plagues the Cuban Church. While government attempts to reign in the house churches yielded some greater unity across groups, cross-denominational cooperation and ministry remain difficult. Historical infiltration by informers yielded more stringent membership and baptism criteria, in turn generating more committed and mature members; however, it has simultaneously produced a destructive climate of distrust and suspicion.

5 **Leadership for the churches** remains an urgent need. Many fled or were expelled following the revolution. Praise God for those who stood firm and were trained in the school of suffering; many are weary from long years of service and need fresh vision. Cuba has a dozen evangelical and two Catholic Bible schools or seminaries. Student numbers are limited by government interference and a lack of both material and human resources. TEE programmes, itinerant and visiting intensive training modules and hand-couriered laptops crammed with Bible resources are creative ways of addressing this challenge. Pray for a multiplication of visionary leadership for the churches that enables them to cope with the growth and change.

6 **The less reached:**

a) *Spiritism* has been actively supported by the government as "cultural". African Caribbean religions under a thin veneer of Catholicism have a greater following than the 18% attributed to Spiritism. There may be more than three million devotees of *Santería* and other cults which resemble Haitian voodoo; "*Santería* tourism" grows as increasing numbers come on pilgrimage to Cuba. Pray that Christians may exercise love, understanding and spiritual power to see many delivered from this satanic bondage.

b) *The Indians, Chinese and Palestinians* have been largely assimilated into the Hispanic majority, but still retain much of their old culture. Little is being done to specifically reach them.

7 **Foreign missions are largely restricted** to tactful support and occasional visits from outside the country. A few workers remain in low-profile teaching ministry; others visit to train church leaders in all aspects of ministry. The government blacklisted dozens of foreign organizations, one way of denying precious resources to the national Church. Pray that wise input from abroad will serve Cuba in an effective way.

8 **There are over one million Cuban refugees** (legal and illegal) living in the USA, mainly from the white middle and upper classes and predominantly Catholic. Pray that they will not be victims of the temptations offered by the "free" society they sought so desperately. Pray that the Cuban diaspora might also find Christ and have a redemptive influence on their nation of origin. Pray that their faith might shape their views and approaches to their home country.

9 **Christian help ministries** for prayer:

a) *Bible distribution* – the need remains urgent as church growth outstrips supply. Over one million copies of the Scriptures have been printed in-country on the Cuban Bible Society press, and many thousands are imported every year. A new easy-to-read Spanish Bible will help make the gospel more accessible to many, but it is still difficult for many Christians to get a Bible. The need for the state-appointed Council of Churches to approve Bible translations limits options and prevents good translations from being available.

b) *Christian literature* has been extremely hard to acquire for years and is an intense need. As the church and its leaders grow, more materials are needed. More can now be imported, but permission for local printing is difficult to obtain. Pray that the wide range of Spanish-language resources would make its way into Cuba.

c) *Christian radio* remains an untapped potential. Although a cumulative 878 hours per week are broadcast, almost all of it is over shortwave, which is very hard to receive as shortwave radios are illegal in Cuba. Some FM Christian radio can be picked up from other Caribbean islands. Local Christian broadcasting is still not permitted.

d) *Music* is a core aspect of Cuban culture and identity. Raising up and training Christian musicians and worship leaders is hugely strategic. Some prominent musicians have become believers, increasing Cuba's exposure to the good news.

Cyprus

Europe

The country is divided as a result of Turkey's 1974 invasion and occupation of the north. The Greek and Turk populations are separated: the north calling itself the Turkish Republic of Northern Cyprus (TRNC) and the south claiming the whole island as the Republic of Cyprus (ROC). The ROC is internationally recognized as the legal government of the whole island; only Turkey recognizes the TRNC. Some statistics below apply to the whole island and some to the two entities, necessitated by an absence of unified data.

Geography

Area 9,251 sq km. Strategic island in northeast Mediterranean Sea. ROC in the south is 64% of the island, TRNC in the north is 36%.

Population		Ann Gr	Density
2010	879,723	1.02%	95/sq km
2020	970,100	0.97%	105/sq km
2030	1,052,680	0.76%	114/sq km

Capital Lefkosia (Nicosia) 243,000. **Urbanites** 70.3%. **Pop under 15 yrs** 19%. **Life expectancy** 79.6 yrs.

Peoples

Literacy 96.8%. **Official language** Greek. **All languages** 6. **Indigenous languages** 4. **Languages with Scriptures** 3Bi.

Economy

HDI Rank 32nd/182. **Public debt** 49% of GDP. **Income/person** $32,745 (69% of USA).

Religion

The Christians are almost all in ROC and Muslims in TRNC. There is freedom of religion in both ROC and TRNC, but proselytism by minority groups is carefully monitored.

Religions	Pop %	Population	Ann Gr
Christian	72.42	637,095	0.9%
Muslim	23.67	208,230	1.2%
Non-religious	3.60	31,670	2.8%
Hindu	0.15	1,320	5.6%
Buddhist	0.07	616	13.0%
Chinese	0.04	352	16.1%
Sikh	0.03	264	9.6%
Jewish	0.02	176	1.0%

Christians	Denoms	Pop %	Affiliates	Ann Gr
Protestant	21	0.48	4,000	3.6%
Independent	15	0.25	2,000	5.2%
Anglican	1	0.33	3,000	-1.3%
Catholic	3	1.59	14,000	1.5%
Orthodox	6	66.31	583,000	0.9%
Marginal	3	0.46	4,000	1.1%
Unaffiliated		3.00	26,000	-2.2%

Churches	MegaBloc	Congs	Members	Affiliates
Orthodox Church	O	292	204,643	573,000
Catholic Church	C	8	7,143	14,000
Armenian Apos Ch	O	3	5,604	10,200
Jehovah's Witnesses	M	17	1,520	3,800
Anglican Church	A	6	1,160	2,900
Charismatic fellowships	I	23	1,167	1,750
Protestant groups	P	12	700	1,400
Greek Evangelical Ch	P	4	420	798
Other denominations[15]		37	1,597	2,871
Total Christians[49]		**402**	**223,954**	**610,719**

TransBloc	Pop %	Population	Ann Gr
Evangelicals			
Evangelicals	0.8	6,616	3.5%
Renewalists			
Charismatics	0.6	4,947	4.2%
Pentecostals	0.2	1,630	5.1%

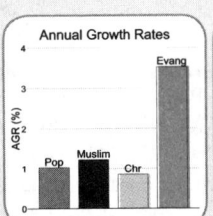

Annual Growth Rates

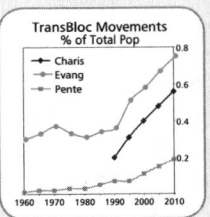

TransBloc Movements
% of Total Pop

Republic of Cyprus

Geography 🌍

Area 5,896 sq km. The southern, less-fertile two-thirds of the island. **Capital** (divided) Lefkosia (Nicosia) 219,200. **Pop under 15 yrs** 21.4%. **Life expectancy** 79.2 yrs.

Peoples 👪

Cypriot 92.0%. Greek Cypriot 91.8%.
Foreign 8.0%. Arab 3.4%; British/American 1.6%; Russian, Filipino, Sri Lankan, others.
Literacy 97%. **Official languages** Greek, Turkish; English widely used.

Economy 📊

Crippled by Turkey's seizure of the north and by a third of the population being made refugees. Rapid recovery and development of light industry and tourism. One-sixth of the world's merchant ships are registered in Cyprus.

Politics ☒

Ruled by 11 foreign empires over three millennia. Independent from Britain in 1960. The 1974 abortive coup (supported by Greece) and subsequent Turkish invasion partitioned the island. As a result, 230,000 people became refugees. All efforts to achieve a settlement have foundered due to Turkey's desire to maintain influence, the mistrust between the communities and the intransigence of the politicians. Cyprus joined the EU in 2004. Membership and EU laws apply to the whole island, but are suspended for the north.

Religion 🙏

Christians 94.4%; Non-religious 4.5%; Muslim 0.7%; Other religions 0.4%.

Challenges for Prayer

1 **The 50-year conflict between the two communities,** fuelled by the involvement of foreign powers, has gone on too long. Political intransigence by a few hampers the reunification seemingly favoured by the majority. Pray that old grievances and bitterness might be overcome by forgiveness. Pray that external meddling would stop and that Cypriots might move forward into a unified future. Since 2004, Cypriot and EU citizens have been free to cross the dividing line. A greater degree of interaction between the communities has shown that, for most, it is possible to live together in peace.

2 **The Orthodox Church** is a crucial focal point for Greek Cypriot culture and identity. The challenge lies in encountering the gospel amid the ethnic–cultural–political traditions. Cyprus is very religious for an EU country, but church attendance is largely practiced by rural folk and the older generation. Pray for the Holy Spirit to draw religious Cypriots into a living relationship with Christ and for renewal within the Orthodox Church. The Orthodox Church has taken to distributing NTs in the public schools; pray that this might bear much fruit among the students.

3 **Evangelical churches among Greeks are few.** Negative prejudice is easing, but still holds many back. Pray that the unease of Cypriots with evangelicals may be removed and that significant church growth may begin. Few workers and ministries focus on the majority – **YWAM** is one ministry that does.

4 **Ethnic minority evangelicals have grown rapidly** among the English-speaking, Russian, Filipino, Sri Lankan and Iranian communities. Pray for their active and effective witness to their own communities and to the indigenous population. Several ministries work in this area.

5 **The Logos bookstore (CLC)** is a vital centre for books, tracts and BCCs. Logos is also the core of a range of Christian education ministries that are a boost to the evangelical witness. Pray for its effectiveness and that of The Bridge Christian bookshop.

6 **Cyprus is a major base for Christian organizations** ministering to the surrounding Middle Eastern states. Most expatriate Christian workers are involved in these rather than in local outreach. Pray specifically for:

a) A number of missions that have headquarters or regional centres in Cyprus (**MECO, CCCI, YWAM**, Interserve, others).

b) Christian literature in Arabic, Greek and other languages that is both printed and stocked for distribution throughout the region. The Bible Society has distributed many Greek NTs throughout the ROC.

c) SAT-7, which is based in Cyprus. This key, innovative, Christian satellite TV ministry is hugely influential, with a wide audience and good response, and is impacting the whole of the Arab world with its daily programmes.

d) Christian radio programmes broadcast over Cyprus in Greek, English and most of the immigrant languages, amounting to over 35 hours per week. No Christian radio is yet available in Turkish.

7 **The two large British military bases.** Pray for the ministry of Mission to Military Garrisons, working with the 3,000 British military personnel and their families. Pray also that a clear witness may be given by Christian service personnel to the Cypriots. Pray also for opportunities to share the gospel with the multinational UN peace-keeping force.

8 **There is proportionately a very large population of foreign workers** – legal and illegal – from Asia, Africa, the Middle East and Eastern Europe. Many are believers; many others are open to the gospel. Pray for effective outreach to all of these groups in Cyprus's newly cosmopolitan society.

Turkish Republic of Northern Cyprus

Geography

Area 3,355 sq km. The northern third and 55% of the coastline of the island. **Population** 205,800. Augmented significantly by Turkish immigrants/colonists, offset by Turkish Cypriot emigration. **Capital** (divided) Lefkosa (Nikosia) 49,200.

Peoples

Turkish Cypriot/Turkish 98.6%.

Other 1.4%.
Official language Turkish.

Economy

A lower standard of living than the south due to diplomatic and economic isolation. Heavily dependent on Turkish subsidies and trade. High unemployment.

Politics

A democratic government set up after the 1974 partition, but diplomatic isolation followed the declaration of the separate state of TRNC in 1983, which Turkey alone recognizes and acts as its only lifeline. The pull of EU access and employment is proving irresistible to many, as thousands take Republic of Cyprus passports.

Religion

A secular republic with two established religions – Islam (99%) and Christianity (0.4%).

Challenges for Prayer

1 **Almost the entire population is Muslim,** but also quite secularized. Pray that the historic, ethnic and cultural prejudices against Christianity would not prevent spiritual openness.

2 **The slow move toward political reunification** presents new opportunities for Turkish Cypriots. Pray that what unfolds in the politico-economic sphere also brings chances to encounter the true gospel.

3 **Small numbers of Turkish Cypriots have become believers.** Pray for numerical and spiritual growth. Pray for protection, wisdom and fruitfulness for those seeking to share Christ with those in the north.

C

Germany · Poland · Prague · Czech Republic · Slovakia · Austria · Hungary

Czech Republic

Europe

Geography

Area 78,864 sq km. Landlocked central European state.

Population		Ann Gr	Density
2010	10,410,786	0.42%	132/sq km
2020	10,568,487	0.11%	134/sq km
2030	10,519,764	-0.10%	133/sq km

Capital Prague 1,162,393. **Urbanites** 73.5%. **Pop under 15 yrs** 14%. **Life expectancy** 76.4 yrs.

Peoples

Slavic 96.1%. Czech 93.2%; Slovak 1.9%; Polish 0.5%.
Romani 2.9%. Difficult to precisely enumerate.
Other 1.0%. German 0.5%; Hungarian 0.2%; Chinese 0.1%.
Literacy 99%. **Official language** Czech. **All languages** 20. **Indigenous languages** 10. **Languages with Scriptures** 5Bi 1NT 3por 1w.i.p.

Economy

One of the most developed economies in central Europe, with a strong tradition of industry and manufacturing. Unemployment is higher among the older population, but is generally low. Tourism is a vital and increasing economic sector. Pension and healthcare reforms are significant economic issues in an aging population.
HDI Rank 36th/182. **Public debt** 26.8% of GDP. **Income/person** $20,760 (44% of USA).

Politics

The bloodless "velvet revolution" against Communist rule in 1989 was followed by rapid democratization and the "velvet divorce" from Slovakia in 1993. Multiparty presidential democracy and EU member since 2004.

Religion

A long and turbulent religious history. Believers suffered, especially under the Communist regime. Subsequent freedom sees a significant falling away and fading of religious influence in Czech society – although it has not been a particularly religious society for hundreds of years.

Religions	Pop %	Population	Ann Gr
Non–Religious	71.41	7,434,342	1.6%
Christian	25.92	2,698,476	-2.9%
Other	2.50	260,270	5.0%
Muslim	0.13	13,534	5.8%
Baha'i	0.02	2,082	0.4%
Jewish	0.01	1,041	0.4%
Buddhist	0.01	1,041	0.4%

Christians	Denoms	Pop %	Affiliates	Ann Gr
Protestant	21	1.88	195,000	-1.9%
Independent	12	0.88	92,000	-1.3%
Anglican	1	<0.01	125	2.6%
Catholic	2	20.16	2,098,000	-2.3%
Orthodox	1	0.38	40,000	-1.0%
Marginal	8	0.33	34,000	-0.1%
Unaffiliated		2.30	239,000	-9.0%

Churches	MegaBloc	Congs	Members	Affiliates
Catholic Church	C	1,371	1,645,669	2,090,000
Ev Ch of Czech Brethren	P	260	77,692	101,000
Hussite Church	I	150	52,448	75,000
Orthodox Church	O	30	20,000	40,000
Silesian Ev Ch (Luth)	P	33	23,000	36,000
Jehovah's Witnesses	M	215	16,500	26,400
Slovak Ev Ch (Luth)(SL)	P	14	10,140	14,500
Free Evangelical Ch	P	67	5,500	9,850
Christian Fellowships	I	46	4,500	9,000
Seventh-day Adventist	P	140	7,400	9,000
Uniate Catholic Ch	C	9	5,971	8,300
Christian Brethren	P	65	2,600	7,050
Apostolic Ch (Pente)	P	42	3,400	6,800
Baptist Union	P	37	2,200	3,500
Other denominations[31]		182	12,081	22,985
Total Christians[45]		**2,661**	**1,889,101**	**2,459,385**

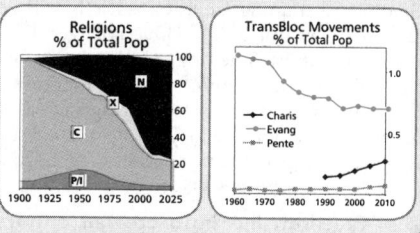

TransBloc	Pop %	Population	Ann Gr
Evangelicals			
Evangelicals	0.7	72,853	0.3%
Renewalists			
Charismatics	0.3	27,968	3.8%
Pentecostals	0.1	6,895	3.1%

Missionaries from Czech Republic
P,I,A 28 in 6 agencies to 9 countries.

Answers to Prayer

1 **New expressions of Christianity are springing up** and connecting with the younger generation. Dynamic church planting, paired with creative ministry (teaching English, business-as-mission), sees fruit.

2 **Czech churches now send missionaries** to several countries in Europe and around the world. This is an answer to prayer and will hopefully also generate spiritual vitality on the home front.

Challenges for Prayer

1 **Freedom for Czechs has too often translated into a "free-for-all".** A generally successful shift to a market economy is positive for the country, but it places economic stress on too many of the most vulnerable. The moral vacuum that has emerged sees hedonistic materialism assume primacy; crime, sexual immorality, substance abuse as well as depression and suicide are more prevalent today than in Communist times. Atheism rose from 40% in 1991 to 60% in 2001 (and 71% non-religious in 2010), but apparently this does not preclude widespread use of horoscopes and a fuzzy mishmash of spiritual ideas. Pray for this existential and spiritual heaviness over the Czech Republic; pray that serious soul-searching may take place and that a shift in the spiritual atmosphere might occur.

2 **The Catholic Church** is in what could almost be described as freefall. Despite outnumbering all other confessions nearly 6 to 1, its influence is waning quickly. The openness of the 1990s was a window of opportunity that was passed up. Instead of offering a living faith, traditionalism ("religion for grannies") and a failure to act decisively relegated Catholicism to a minor role in society – a strong contrast to neighbouring Slovakia and Poland. Increasing adaptation and renewal movements may not be enough to save Catholicism from declining further, since both laity and priesthood are generally quite old.

3 **Czech Protestants must both reclaim their heritage and demonstrate new life.** Since the defeat of the Bohemians by Catholic forces in 1620, Protestants have suffered in one way or another. There is now freedom but also spiritual decline; the remarkable legacy of both John Hus and then the Moravians is under threat (and has been so for some time). Pray for evangelicals – the traditional but shrinking Protestant denominations and the smaller, younger groups such as Baptists, Pentecostals and others. Determined, deliberate and loving outreach and evangelism are necessities, as is the prayer that must precede them.

4 **New expressions of Christian faith.** Czech antipathy toward institutions weighs heavily against established denominations, but the grassroots church-planting movement (spearheaded by the Czech EA) is seeing much greater openness to alternate forms of Christian fellowship. Small congregations, house churches and cell groups all fare better than top-heavy structures. The growth of charismatic elements in many denominations coincides with this, since a more experiential faith appeals to many Czechs. An effective approach appears to be consistently applying principles of discipleship in a more organic context rather than maintaining more Western-style structures oriented toward large events.

5 **Christian leadership development is a key to growth.** For many years, little training was permitted, especially in biblical theology. But now the nation enjoys several excellent theological training facilities in the best Protestant traditions – Baptist, Reformed, Pentecostal and interdenominational Bible colleges. The Evangelical Theological Seminary and the International Baptist Theological Seminary, both in Prague, wield positive biblical influence throughout central Europe. TEE programmes are also vital for training capable leaders across the country, since church planting increases the number of small congregations. Pray for all forms of theological education to shape knowledgeable, relevant, Christ-like leaders. Pray also that leadership formation, extending beyond the academic classroom, may create authentic spiritual communities where such learning is applied in the lives of the Czech people.

6 **Freedom has both created opportunities and taken the edge off the church;** greater division and spiritual error are threats. Marginal sects are very active in proselytism. Rejecting the hard path of unity and partnership to do one's own thing is easier than ever. Pray that the many expatriate workers would serve Czech churches in positive and fruitful ways (as most already do!) rather than build rival kingdoms. The Evangelical Alliance coordinates member churches toward common goals. Pray for the indigenous Church as it matures into a sending Church. The Christian Mission Society (KMS) is vital in coordinating home and foreign mission.

7 **There are new ministry challenges** in the new Czech Republic. With many younger people leaving to work in other lands and a low birthrate, the population is increasingly aged. This requires new and specific approaches to ministry. Likewise, increasing numbers of immigrants are coming into the country – especially Russian speakers and East and Southeast Asians. These groups also need loving and focused outreach tailored to their needs and communities.

8 **Special ministries** can potentially touch almost every aspect of society:

a) *Young people* ask questions unanswered by traditional religion. SU (primary schools), **IFES/** VBH (groups in several universities) and Youth Outreach, an indigenous ministry, focus on the younger generation. Also, teaching English and summer camps (speaking Czech, German and English) impact young people. Pray for enthusiastic workers and much fruit.

b) *Christian literature* is increasing in distribution and scope. The Bible Society sells large numbers of Bibles and NTs and has opened its first permanent Bible House. *Navrat Domu*, *Nova Nadeje* and other publishing houses increasingly produce Christian materials in Czech; discipleship and apologetic materials are important, as is development of Czech Christian authors. The Bible in Czech is available (text and audio) on the Internet. A new Czech Bible translation in everyday modern language (called Bible21) was completed in 2009 and became a national bestseller that year. The vision is to see one million copies distributed in coming years. Pray for the fulfilment of this ambitious vision.

c) *Christian radio and TV programmes* are going from strength to strength. There is now a Czech Christian TV station (*TV Noe*); Christian programmes are increasingly aired on state television. Pray for continued growth and funding. **TWR** (transmitting globally and locally), **HCJB** Global (via Internet) and Radio 7 all provide excellent programming in Czech and other languages. The JESUS film has been translated into these languages as well and has enjoyed a wide viewership.

Quotes on Prayer

The man who mobilizes the Christian church to pray will make the greatest contribution to world evangelization in history.
Andrew Murray

You do not test the resources of God until you attempt the impossible.
F.B. Meyer

A man is what he is on his knees - nothing more and nothing less.
Robert Murray McCheyne

It is well said that "asking is the rule of the kingdom." It is a rule that will never be altered in anybody's case. If the royal and divine Son of God cannot be exempted from the rule of asking that He may have, you and I cannot expect the rule to be relaxed in our favour.
C.H. Spurgeon

In no other way can the believer become as fully involved with God's work, especially the work of world evangelism, as in intercessory prayer.
Dick Eastman

Prayer succeeds when all else fails. Prayer has won great victories and has rescued, with notable triumph, God's saints when every other hope is gone.
E.M. Bounds

Prayer is not overcoming God's reluctance, but laying hold of His willingness.
Variously attributed

Prayer does not fit us for the greater work; prayer is the greater work.
Oswald Chambers

Every great movement of God can be traced to a kneeling figure.
D.L. Moody

Prayer is weakness leaning on omnipotence.
W.S. Bowd

Beware in your prayers, above everything else, of limiting God, not only by unbelief, but by fancying that you know what He can do. Expect unexpected things 'above all that we ask or think'.
Andrew Murray

Intercession is truly universal work for the Christian. No place is closed to intercessory prayer. No continent – no nation – no organization – no city – no office. There is no power on earth that can keep intercession out.
Richard Halverson

There has never been a spiritual awakening in any country or locality that did not begin in united prayer.
A.T. Pierson

Denmark

The Kingdom of Denmark

Europe

Geography

Area 43,092 sq km. The most southerly of the Scandinavian countries. See separate entries for Faeroe Islands and Greenland, which are autonomous regions of Denmark.

Population		Ann Gr	Density
2010	5,481,283	0.24%	127/sq km
2020	5,556,556	0.12%	129/sq km
2030	5,615,545	0.09%	130/sq km

Capital Copenhagen 1,185,654. **Urbanites** 87.2%. **Pop under 15 yrs** 18%. **Life expectancy** 78.2 yrs.

Peoples

Danish citizens 92.2%. Danish 91.2%; Faeroese 0.9%; Greenlander 0.1%.
Foreign 7.8%. European 3.3%; Middle Eastern and Asian 4.4%; African 0.1%.
Literacy 99%. **Official Language** Danish. **All Languages** 13. **Indigenous languages** 7. **Languages with Scriptures** 6Bi 1w.i.p.

Economy

Strong economy founded on a large service sector, environmental innovation, agriculture/fishing and light industry. Social security system requires high taxes.
HDI Rank 16th/182. **Public debt** 33.5% of GDP. **Income/person** $62,097 (131% of USA).

Politics

Stable parliamentary democracy with a constitutional monarchy. A cautious member of the EU, also frequently asserts its independence.

Religion

There is complete religious freedom, though the Lutheran Church is recognized as the national church and is supported out of a state-levied church tax.

Religions	Pop %	Population	Ann Gr
Christian	85.29	4,674,986	-0.2%
Non-religious	9.81	537,714	2.6%
Muslim	4.10	224,733	4.1%
Buddhist	0.40	21,925	4.2%
Hindu	0.21	11,511	3.4%
Jewish	0.10	5,481	-1.7%
Chinese	0.05	2,741	4.8%
Baha'i	0.04	2,193	0.2%

Christians Denoms		Pop %	Affiliates	Ann Gr
Protestant	39	81.31	4,457,000	-0.1%
Independent	18	0.03	2,000	3.5%
Anglican	1	0.05	3,000	-2.8%
Catholic	1	0.66	36,000	0.7%
Orthodox	2	0.01	1,000	3.8%
Marginal	12	0.43	23,000	-0.8%
Unaffiliated		2.80	153,000	-3.1%

Churches	MegaBloc	Congs	Members	Affiliates
Lutheran Church	P	2,030	880,000	4,400,000
Catholic Church	C	66	20,111	36,200
Jehovah's Witnesses	M	200	14,000	16,800
Pente Movement in D	P	57	5,250	9,188
Baptist Union	P	49	4,960	7,936
Latter-day Saints (Mormon)	M	23	2,756	4,300
Apostolic Church	P	45	2,048	3,420
Danish Covenant Ch	P	21	2,075	3,299
Seventh-day Adventist	P	42	2,470	3,211
Other denominations[64]		229	16,364	37,376
Total Christians[73]		**2,762**	**950,034**	**4,521,730**

TransBloc	Pop %	Population	Ann Gr
Evangelicals			
Evangelicals	3.5	193,344	0.2%
Renewalists			
Charismatics	1.5	84,255	3.0%
Pentecostals	0.4	20,508	2.4%

Missionaries from Denmark
P,I,A 511 international (204 long-term) in more than 40 agencies; also 7,033 volunteers in Denmark.

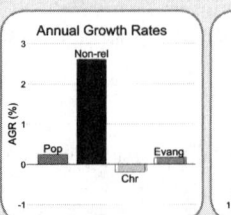

Answers to Prayer

1 **There is some encouraging progress on the spiritual scene,** including a marked increase in spiritual openness among Danes. The number who believe in a personal God, while still low (33%), has notably increased in recent years. New churches are being planted, new ministries are being founded and unity among believers is increasing. Groups include Pray for Denmark and Intercessors for Denmark.

Challenges for Prayer

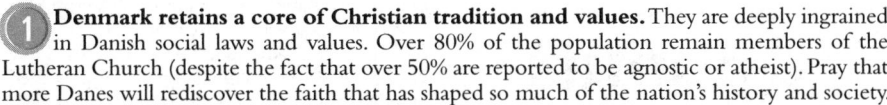

1 **Denmark retains a core of Christian tradition and values.** They are deeply ingrained in Danish social laws and values. Over 80% of the population remain members of the Lutheran Church (despite the fact that over 50% are reported to be agnostic or atheist). Pray that more Danes will rediscover the faith that has shaped so much of the nation's history and society.

2 **Much of the Lutheran Church** is experienced by ordinary Danes as ritualistic and dead, and the fresh winds of the Holy Spirit must blow through this institution. Church attendance is around 2%. There are a number of organizations promoting renewal or revival in the state Church – *Indre Mission, Luthersk Mission, Evangelisk Luthersk Mission, Oase* and *Nyt Liv*. Free churches, Lutheran and otherwise, contribute greatly to the spiritual life of the nation. Pray for wisdom for all who seek to transform the Church and make it relevant to secular Danes.

3 **Old non-missional theologies are devastating for the Church,** since they fail to equip the Church in effective discipleship and mission in a secular realm. Pray for theological and missional renewal in all seminaries and Bible schools that will encourage a vibrant missions vision. Pray also for leaders to be raised up who are able to communicate Christ with the Danish postmodern youth culture.

4 **There is a shortfall of pastors,** especially for Free Churches of all types. Even with a number of fresh and new ministries and church planting efforts, many evangelical congregations, especially those without a pastor, are in stagnation or even decline. Pray for the provision of capable, godly leaders and for the revitalization of these evangelical congregations.

5 **Quest for spirituality.** Much of the obvious growth in spirituality in recent years has not led Danes to Christian faith and the Church. Pray that their spiritual search will lead more Danes to genuine Christian belief. Pray also that the Church will become effective and creative in reaching out to seekers.

6 **The notion of overseas missions is changing.** New generations seek new and more meaningful ways to be involved in mission internationally. Pray that attempts in tentmaking ministry will become fruitful, and pray that mission among the many migrants in Denmark will gain momentum.

7 **Immigrants to Denmark** have proved to be both a harvest force and a harvest field.

a) Christian immigrants. Guest workers and refugees may prove to be a significant force for spiritual and mission renewal in Denmark, since many of these migrants are Christian. Over 150 new churches of migrants have been established over the last few years, and it is estimated that one-third of people in church on a given Sunday attend a foreign-run congregation. Pray that Danish Christians will receive this new missionary gift – and that this young Christian migrant community will be effective in its mission in Denmark.

b) Unevangelized immigrants. Tens of thousands of Turks, Arabs, Pakistanis, Iranians, Chinese and others have recently settled in Denmark. Many of them are open to the gospel but have never heard it. Pray for ministries to reach out with cultural sensitivity and in effective ways – and to plant churches that can incorporate these minority groups.

c) Islamic relations. The infamous "cartoon riots" of 2006 revealed a nation dealing with crucial issues of free speech, religious fault lines and intercommunity relations. At the time, Muslims numbered only 4% of the population, but they receive 40% of the social welfare. Their integration into society and the workforce is a major challenge. This in turn has shifted the nation from having one of Europe's most liberal immigration policies to having one of its toughest. Pray for Danes and others to display uncompromising Christian love to Muslims in Denmark.

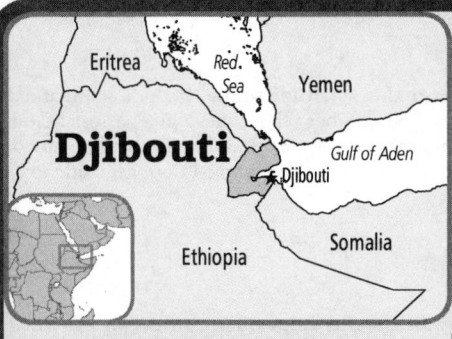

Djibouti
Republic of Djibouti
Africa

Geography

Area 23,200 sq km. A hot, dry, desert enclave between Ethiopia, Eritrea and Somalia, with possibly the hottest average temperatures of any country on earth.

Population		Ann Gr	Density
2010	879,053	1.78%	38/sq km
2020	1,027,401	1.52%	44/sq km
2030	1,192,219	1.42%	51/sq km

Capital Djibouti 577,000. **Urbanites** 88.1%. **Pop under 15 yrs** 36%. **Life expectancy** 55.1 yrs.

Peoples

Somali 61%. In three major clans in southern half of the country: Issa (half of Djibouti's Somali population); Gadaboursi; Issaq.

Afar(Danakil) 28%. In northern half.

Arab 8%. Yemeni, Omani, Saudi.

Other 3%. French 2.2%; several other nationalities, including other African.

This breakdown is only an estimate; it does not account for the Ethiopian and Eritrean refugees and the very fluid Somali population, including a refugee camp population.

Literacy 72.2%. **Official languages** French and Arabic. **Trade languages** Somali, Afar. **All languages** 10. **Indigenous languages** 5. **Languages with Scriptures** 3Bi 1NT 1por.

Economy

Lack of water, arable land and natural resources makes the country's viability dependent on French aid and the large French and American military bases. The US base is a huge source of income and employment for Djibouti. The deepwater ports of Djibouti, the rail link to landlocked Ethiopia (85% of port activity involves trade with Ethiopia) and Djibouti's status as a free trade zone are its only major economic assets. Development is occurring, but the cost of living is rising.

Unemployment rates of 50-80% combine with high levels of *qat* consumption to seriously stunt the potential of the workforce.

HDI Rank 155th/182. **Public debt** 47.5% of GDP. **Income/person** $1,252 (3% of USA).

Politics

The French took control of the area in 1884 because of its strategic location, but the boundaries straddled a centuries-old conflict zone between Afars and Somalis. Independent since 1977 as a multiparty republic, it is dominated by Somali Issas. Civil war raged between them in 1991-94; peace accords were finally signed by all in 2001. Only French and American military presence prevented Djibouti from embroilment in regional conflicts between Eritrea, Ethiopia and Somalia. Shari'a law was replaced in 2002 by a Family Court.

Religion

Islam is the religion of the state and of almost every native, but there is considerable religious freedom for foreigners. Proselytism is not technically illegal, but is discouraged; even interest in conversion brings risk of intense persecution. The following tables do not include the large US military base in the country.

Religions	Pop %	Population	Ann Gr
Muslim	97.03	852,945	1.8%
Christian	1.75	15,383	0.2%
Non-religious	1.20	10,549	1.8%
Hindu	0.02	176	-6.2%

Christians Denoms		Pop %	Affiliates	Ann Gr
Protestant	4	0.09	1,000	1.9%
Independent	6	0.05	<500	4.8%
Catholic	1	0.80	7,000	0.0%
Orthodox	2	0.81	7,000	-0.1%

Churches	MegaBloc	Congs	Members	Affiliates
Catholic Church	C	5	3,846	7,000
Ethiopian Orth Ch	O	1	3,500	7,000
Ethiopian Protestants	P	6	300	600
Other foreign churches	I	5	125	250
French Protestant Ch	P	1	100	200
Other denominations[2]		5	165	340
Total Christians[13]		**23**	**8,036**	**15,390**

TransBloc	Pop %	Population	Ann Gr
Evangelicals			
Evangelicals	0.1	1,207	3.4%
Renewalists			
Charismatics	<0.1	674	3.1%

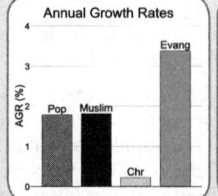

Challenges for Prayer

1 **Djibouti, Africa's third-smallest state, is a haven of calm** in a stormy region. Western military presence, due to the strategic location, helps foster a climate of relative peace, safety and freedom. Pray that these present freedoms may not be eroded by the politics of the Horn of Africa nor by the Islamist voice that seeks to shape Djibouti according to its own set of values.

2 **Serious social and economic problems** continue to plague Djiboutians, notably widespread famine, extreme unemployment and the rising urban issues of human trafficking, prostitution and drug abuse. The French Protestant, Roman Catholic and Ethiopian Orthodox Churches represent the only active Christian witness recognized by the government. They sponsor various social projects, including work among refugees and the poor. Seventh-day Adventists run both an eye clinic and a dental-care clinic. Pray for effective cooperation and unity among Christians. Pray for fruitful ministry amid abject poverty and human suffering.

3 **Mission work is a challenge** in this hot, dry, but often humid land, and working conditions are extreme. Physical and spiritual oppression, economic disparity, ethnic tensions and a paucity of believers lead easily to discouragement and worker attrition. Pray for the present ministries in education, public health, literature, Bible translation, literacy and youth work – opportunities to witness abound in these. Pray that contacts lead to disciples for Jesus. Pray for God to send long-term workers, especially from nearby countries and people groups. Pray for unprecedented spiritual breakthroughs, long-awaited but as yet unseen. There is notable interest in Christianity from a small but increasing number of locals.

4 **Several evangelical fellowships exist among the immigrant groups** flooding Djibouti in recent years – from Ethiopia, Madagascar, Congo-DRC, the Philippines, Eritrea and other places. Many of these congregations share a strong spiritual burden to reach the Somali and Afar peoples. Pray that they may be relevant and effective in their witness. Pray that their own reconciliation and unity made possible in Christ might be a witness to the divided and hostile peoples of Djibouti.

5 **The few Somali and Afar believers** are often isolated and suffer many pressures from relatives. Their families may ostracize, beat or even kill them for deserting Islam. Pray that they might stand firm in their commitment to follow Jesus. There are many disruptive forces such as tribalism and jealousy that create division among the believers and make them reluctant to meet together. Pray for a new bond of unity. Many of the believers are jobless, and some are illiterate – pray for effective use of literacy and vocational training programmes. Small groups of local believers are gathering for fellowship. Pray for effective use of the Scriptures in these meetings and for the Holy Spirit to work in each life. Pray that God will raise up strong Christian leaders from among and for the Somali and Afar believers.

6 **Pray for the peoples of Djibouti:**

a) **The Afars'** main territories are in Ethiopia and Eritrea, where there is little witness at present. In Djibouti, the primarily nomadic Afar are increasingly urbanized due to economic pressures. There is no known church among them.

b) **The Somalis** are a small branch of the larger populations in Somalia and Ethiopia. The Somalis in Djibouti are a key for the evangelization of their kinsmen across the border.

c) **Arabs, both local and Yemeni,** need a specific approach directed to their spiritual needs. There is no work among them, despite possibly being more accessible here than in Yemen.

d) **The ethnic minorities.** As a strategic port city, Djibouti attracts foreigners from many lands. Most of these – French, Greek, Pakistani, Senegalese, Indian and others – have little exposure to vibrant Christian witness.

7 **Christian support ministries:**

a) **Bible translation and distribution.** The Afar NT is published, as are parts of the nearly completed OT. There is a key project to record both Afar Scripture songs and the entire NT on tape – a vital means of communicating God's Word in a largely illiterate population. Praise God for the recent printing of a newly revised Somali Bible.

b) **Audio resources.** **GRN** has Scripture and Christian recordings available in Somali, Afar and Arabic as well as most of the expat languages. Pray for their wide distribution.

c) **Radio broadcasts** by FEBA and **TWR** lead the way in radio ministry, broadcasting into Djibouti with 7.5 hours per week in both Afar and Somali. There are also broadcasts in Amharic, Arabic and Tigrina.

d) **The JESUS film** is available in Somali, Afar and Arabic. Pray for Spirit-inspired fruit wherever it is shown.

e) **Innovative outreach using Internet technology and fine arts** is in development. Pray for guidance as believers make use of resources and talents available to them.

D

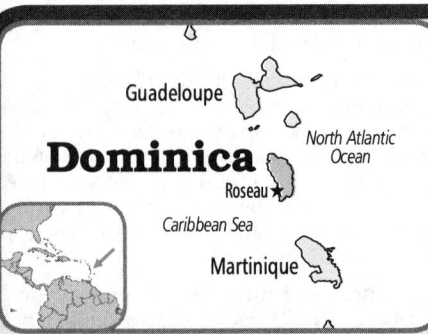

Guadeloupe

Dominica

North Atlantic Ocean

Roseau ★

Caribbean Sea

Martinique

Dominica

Commonwealth of Dominica

Caribbean

Geography

Area 750 sq km. A hurricane-prone, rugged, mountainous island between the French islands of Guadeloupe and Martinique; ruled by France until 1759, which has determined much of its religious and cultural development.

Population		Ann Gr	Density
2010	66,515	-0.28%	89/sq km
2020	67,107	0.11%	89/sq km
2030	68,644	0.13%	92/sq km

A very high emigration rate to USA, Canada and UK. There are more expatriate Dominicans than indigenous. **Capital** Roseau 14,300. **Urbanites** 74.6%. **Pop under 15 yrs** 30%. **Life expectancy** 75.6 yrs.

Peoples

African Caribbean 94.9%. Descended from slaves brought by the French and English. About 6% are of mixed race.
Amerindian 3.6%. Caribs 3,000; the descendants of the original inhabitants, but considerably intermarried with the African Caribbean people.
Other 1.5%. Small populations of Europeans, Asians and Middle Easterners.

Literacy 88%. **Official language** English, but as many as 80% speak a French Creole. **All languages** 3. **Languages with Scriptures** 1Bi 1NT 1por.

Economy

Highly dependent on banana exports, which makes the economy vulnerable to price fluctuations and violent weather. Eco-tourism in Dominica's beautiful interior is increasing, but limited infrastructure is a challenge. Development of offshore finance makes Dominica a target for money launderers.
HDI Rank 73rd/182. **Public debt** 74.6% of GDP. **Income/person** $5,082 (11% of USA).

Politics

Dominica had the British Caribbean's first Black-majority government for a period in the 19th Century. Independent in 1978 as a democratic republic.

Religion

Religions	Pop %	Population	Ann Gr
Christian	91.75	61,028	-0.4%
Non-religious	3.20	2,128	4.8%
Ethnoreligionist	2.70	1,796	-0.3%
Baha'i	1.75	1,164	-0.1%
Muslim	0.20	133	-0.3%
Hindu	0.20	133	-0.3%
Chinese	0.20	133	-0.3%

Christians	Denoms	Pop %	Affiliates	Ann Gr
Protestant	12	22.85	15,000	1.5%
Independent	12	5.11	3,000	3.2%
Anglican	1	0.60	<1,000	0.0%
Catholic	1	60.14	40,000	-1.1%
Marginal	1	1.35	1,000	0.5%
Unaffiliated		2.50	2,000	-12.9%
Doubly affiliated		*-0.75*	*-500*	*0.0%*

Churches	MegaBloc	Congs	Members	Affiliates
Catholic Church	C	30	21,164	40,000
Seventh-day Adventist	P	23	4,545	6,500
Methodist Church	P	5	1,300	2,210
Ch of God of Prophecy	P	8	660	1,650
Christian Union	P	16	900	1,350
Gospel Mission Chs	I	20	800	1,280

Jehovah's Witnesses	M	8	360	900
Other denominations[19]		68	3,319	6,007
Doubly affiliated				-500
Total Christians[28]		**178**	**33,048**	**59,397**

TransBloc	Pop %	Population	Ann Gr
Evangelicals			
Evangelicals	16.8	11,146	1.8%
Renewalists			
Charismatics	9.4	6,285	2.7%
Pentecostals	5.9	3,912	2.7%

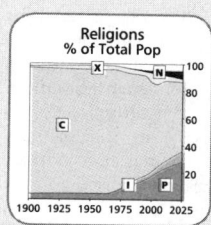

Religions
% of Total Pop

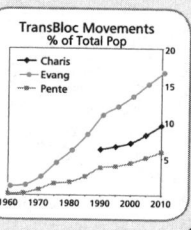

TransBloc Movements
% of Total Pop

D

Challenges for Prayer

1 **Practicing Catholics have substantially decreased** in recent years, indicating a high degree of nominalism. Pray for those who still adhere to Catholicism and those who have disaffiliated themselves, that the Holy Spirit might speak to their hearts about the reality of the gospel.

2 **Evangelical Christians have increased** from 2% in 1970 to nearly 17% in 2010. The Association of Evangelicals is providing good leadership. Pray for continued growth in the gospel witness.

3 **Due to Dominica's economic vulnerability,** many pastors must take a second job to support themselves. Pastoral "burn-out" is a resultant problem. The island's relative isolation is also a challenge for fresh spiritual input and leadership.

4 **The Carib Indians** live on an isolated reservation on the northeast coast of Dominica. They are among the last indigenous peoples in the Caribbean to survive the arrival of colonialism and subsequent waves of immigrants. Most are nominally Christian, but only a small number actively follow Christ. Pray that these socially deprived people may find their true identity and fulfilment in Him.

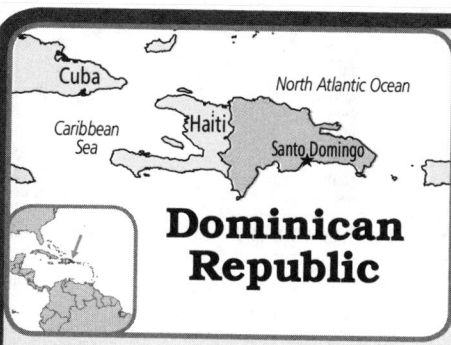

Dominican Republic

Caribbean

Geography 🌍

Area 48,443 sq km. The eastern two-thirds of the island of Hispaniola, shared with Haiti.

Population		Ann Gr	Density
2010	10,225,482	1.41%	211/sq km
2020	11,450,700	1.05%	236/sq km
2030	12,430,548	0.75%	257/sq km

Capital Santo Domingo 2,180,150. **Urbanites** 70.5%. **Pop under 15 yrs** 32%. **Life expectancy** 72.4 yrs.

Peoples 👥

Dominican 87.5%. Mestizo 64.1%; white Dominican 14.7%; black Dominican 8.6%.

Haitian 10.2%. Speaking French Creole; a minority are Dominican-born – most are undocumented, illegal migrant labourers.

Other 2.3%. Spanish 0.8%; US citizen 0.7%; Jamaican 0.3%; Chinese 0.3%.

Literacy 87.7%. **Official language** Spanish. **All languages** 8. **Indigenous languages** 4. **Languages with Scriptures** 3Bi.

Economy

Growth in the early 1970s was replaced by decline from mismanagement, corruption and bloated ineffective government. In 2004, robust policies saw marked and continued improvement. Tourism has replaced agricultural exports (sugarcane, coffee, tobacco) as the primary revenue source, followed by remittances from abroad. Very large gap between the rich and the large numbers of poor.

HDI Rank 90th/182. **Public debt** 37.4% of GDP. **Income/person** $4,992 (11% of USA).

Politics

Independence achieved four times – twice from Spain (1821/65), once from Haiti (1844) and once from the USA (1924)! Thirty years of repressive dictatorship ended in 1961. Subsequent democratic governments, although usually manipulative and corrupt, have overseen a slow move toward more fair and representative democracy. The poor and the oppressed Haitian underclass remain largely disenfranchised.

Religion

Catholicism is unofficially the state religion based on a concordat with the Vatican. The Catholic Church jealously guards its privileged status. Full freedom of religion in basic rights for non-Catholics.

Religions	Pop %	Population	Ann Gr
Christian	94.35	9,647,742	1.3%
Non-religious	3.20	327,215	4.9%
Ethnoreligionist	2.23	228,028	2.0%
Muslim	0.11	11,248	5.6%
Baha'i	0.08	8,180	4.2%
Buddhist	0.02	2,045	1.4%
Jewish	0.01	1,023	1.4%

Christians	Denoms	Pop %	Affiliates	Ann Gr
Protestant	32	7.11	727,000	2.7%
Independent	37	1.93	197,000	3.6%
Anglican	1	0.04	5,000	0.4%
Catholic	1	82.44	8,430,000	1.0%
Marginal	2	1.75	179,000	3.3%
Unaffiliated		1.42	145,000	11.3%
Doubly affiliated		-0.34	-35,000	0.0%

Churches	MegaBloc	Congs	Members	Affiliates
Catholic Church	C	320	4,390,625	8,430,000
Seventh-day Adventist	P	1,424	168,000	223,000
Ch of God (Cleveland)	P	700	65,000	162,500
Latter-day Saints (Mormon)	M	301	60,294	102,500
Ch of God of Prophecy	P	471	33,000	94,380
Jehovah's Witnesses	M	378	29,400	76,440
Assemblies of God	P	527	48,000	74,000
Defenders of the Faith	I	42	8,900	24,920
Ch of the Nazarene	P	170	11,150	24,753
Free Methodist Ch	P	175	7,500	20,500
Christian Assem of God	I	145	11,600	19,372
Misión Principe de Paz	I	91	8,200	18,614
Christian Reformed Ch	P	230	3,400	17,000
Christian Bible Ch	P	67	6,700	16,750
Christian Brethren	P	180	7,500	15,000
Salvation Army	P	44	4,370	12,498
Dominican Evang Ch	P	88	4,130	9,500
Other denominations[56]		7,479	91,417	196,010
Doubly affiliated				-35,000
Total Christians[73]		**12,832**	**4,959,186**	**9,502,737**

TransBloc	Pop %	Population	Ann Gr
Evangelicals			
Evangelicals	9.1	931,234	2.8%
Renewalists			
Charismatics	12.9	1,322,536	4.1%
Pentecostals	4.5	457,201	3.1%

Missionaries from Dominican Republic
P,I,A 32 (15 long-term) in 7 agencies: to the Caribbean 14, Middle East 6.

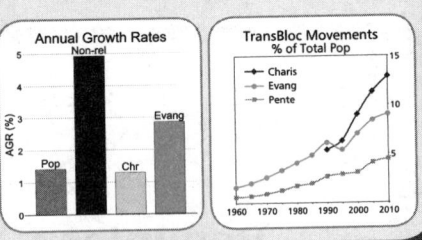

Challenges for Prayer

1 **Columbus' declared affection for this island** and subsequent European colonization have yielded 500 years of turmoil. Foreign disease and the Spanish destroyed the one million indigenous Arawak Taino people. Sugar cane crops soon became massive plantations, which then required the importation of slaves. Both European colonial powers and Dominican governments have ruthlessly exploited the land and the people – this can be seen in the massive gap between a small wealthy elite and the poor majority. Pray for justice – economic and political – something missing from most of the Dominican Republic's history.

2 **Catholicism has held sway** since the arrival of the Spanish and their "converted" slaves. Unfortunately, nearly half of those who call themselves Catholic are not active in their faith. Up to 25% of those claimed by the Catholic Church declare themselves to have no religion. Many who are active practice a dangerous blend of Christianity and Afro-Spiritism, influenced by Cuban *santeria* and Haitian voodoo. The influence of the Catholic Church was such that, in the past, becoming a Protestant meant disapproval and ostracism. Pray for widespread renewal and awakening among Catholics to the power of Scripture and the Holy Spirit. Thank God for the faithful who continue to follow Jesus within Catholicism.

3 **Evangelical growth continues** – with numbers more than doubling from 1990 to 2010. The Pentecostal/charismatic churches claim large increases in numbers; the ministries of Brethren, Baptists and many others are effective in their holistic and empowering approach. Pray that the dynamism and ambition of the former groups might be wedded to the hands-on transforming ministry of the latter, so that growth might be in number and in quality. Many are open to the gospel when presented simply and in love.

4 **The major challenges confronting Christians** are:

D

a) *Religious liberty.* Outright persecution is rare, but those outside the religious majority are often faced with bureaucratic antipathy and low-level hostility. Pray for complete freedom in ministry and of public religious life.

b) *Retention of those converted.* There has been growth in many denominations, especially Pentecostal/charismatic groups, but only a small proportion of those who respond through evangelism become participating members of a local congregation.

c) *Development of biblical ethics* for Christian involvement in a society where corruption, violent crime and promiscuity are alarmingly widespread.

d) *Cultivation of a missions vision.* There are increasing numbers of Dominican missionaries. The Assemblies of God in DR is becoming a missionary-sending force. A few ministries are trying to develop a Dominican missions movement.

5 **Church resources are a constant battle.** Evangelicals generally work out of a context of poverty, which usually cultivates a receiving-only attitude and a relationship of dependency on foreign organizations. Many current and potential spiritual leaders leave the country for the economic improvements of life in the USA or Puerto Rico. Pray for endurance, provision and faithfulness to those called to minister, especially those serving in the poorer, rural areas. Pray that the 15 or so Bible schools and the National Evangelical University may provide spiritual, mature and stable leaders for the future.

6 **Foreign missions** are generally welcomed, but wisdom is required for them to have maximum impact. The most fruitful and effective ministries are holistic, combining evangelism with development and education. Children at risk and the disabled are areas where ministry is fruitful. Some agencies serving in DR: Kids Alive, **BIM**, **AoG**, **YWAM**, **IMB**.

7 **The large Haitian underclass** proves to be a scapegoat and a challenge, but a responsive mission field. Haitians are immigrants, or descendants of immigrants, who are usually despised by Hispanics and forced to work as manual labourers in unjust and harsh conditions. They bring many of Haiti's problems with them and face discrimination from Dominicans – even from Christians. As Haiti continues to stagnate, the situation will only increase and intensify. Pray for the growing Haitian churches in DR (Christian Reformed, Baptist, Nazarene, others). Pray for the Dominican Church to take up this challenge with faith and good grace.

8 **The less evangelized for prayer:**

a) *The unchurched majority* are nominally Christian, but occultism is pervasive and strong. As many as 4,000 villages have no evangelical witness.

b) *The middle and upper classes* have relatively fewer evangelicals. **CMA** and Foursquare Missions have majored on reaching them. The potential influence and impact of these classes are great.

c) *Youth.* There are 37 universities and colleges with more than 200,000 students, but the need to work to pay for tuition and the lack of job prospects and purpose in life cripple initiative. Pray for ADEE(**IFES**) and **CCCI**, who have fewer than 1,000 students in their groups. Pray for staff/student workers and for their ministries of proclaiming the gospel and training leaders.

d) *The Chinese,* who have only two congregations of believers among them. The **IMB** has a work among them.

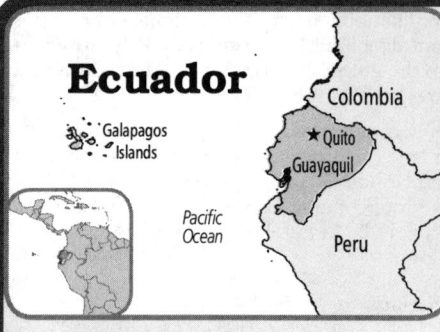

Ecuador

Republic of Ecuador

Latin America

Geography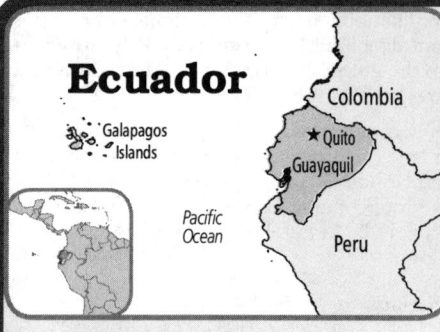

Area 269,178 sq km. Amazon jungle in the east, high Andean Sierra in the centre, fertile coastal plain on Pacific Coast. Also the Galapagos Islands, 1,000 km to the west.

Population		Ann Gr	Density
2010	13,774,909	1.07%	51/sq km
2020	15,375,550	1.05%	57/sq km
2030	16,678,751	0.74%	62/sq km

Capital Quito 1,845,804. **Other major city** Guayaquil 2.7 million. **Urbanites** 66.9%. **Pop under 15 yrs** 31%. **Life expectancy** 75 yrs.

Peoples

Spanish-speaking 56.4%. Non-Amerindian; much racial mixing: Ecuadorian 50.1%; Afro-Ecuadorian 5.2%; Zambo 1.1%.
Amerindian 40.8%.
   Quichua (Quechua in surrounding nations) 40.5%. Quichua Mestizo 24.5%. Ten other groups, the largest: Chimborazo 10%; Otavalo 4.3%; Canari 1.0%; Tena 0.5%.
   Other Amerindians 0.5%. 10 small groups, some numbering in the mere hundreds.
Other 2.8%. English-speaking 1.5%; German-speaking 0.7%; Middle Easterners; East Asians.
Literacy 91%. **Official language** Spanish. **All languages** 25. **Indigenous languages** 23. **Languages with Scriptures** 3Bi 13NT 14por 3w.i.p.

Economy

The main export commodities are oil, flowers, shrimp and bananas; Ecuador is the world's largest exporter of bananas. Oil exploitation enriches a small minority (and the foreign oil companies), but Amerindian groups and the environment endure great loss with no compensation. Since the banking system collapsed in 1999 and the country defaulted on its debts, there has been encouraging economic growth. Poverty is still rife and economic disparity massive.
HDI Rank 80th/182. **Public debt** 25.1% of GDP. **Income/person** $3,928 (8% of USA).

Politics

Independent from Spain in 1830. Political stability has been rare; presidents rarely last even 18 months in the job. The broadening democracy brings some political voice to the long-oppressed Quichua. The need for constitutional reform and political house-cleaning is evident, and Ecuador sees itself aligning with the increasingly assertive leftist governments in other parts of South America.

Religion

The culture is strongly moulded by Catholicism; though there is freedom of religion, rural populations are not so receptive to change.

Religions	Pop %	Population	Ann Gr
Christian	94.45	13,010,402	1.0%
Non-religious	4.85	668,083	3.0%
Ethnoreligionist	0.36	49,590	0.0%
Chinese	0.16	22,040	1.1%
Baha'i	0.14	19,285	1.1%
Muslim	0.03	4,132	9.6%
Jewish	0.01	1,377	1.1%

Christians Denoms		Pop %	Affiliates	Ann Gr
Protestant	49	6.05	834,000	4.1%
Independent	82	2.44	335,000	6.1%
Anglican	1	0.02	2,000	2.1%
Catholic	1	80.58	11,100,000	0.6%
Orthodox	1	0.02	2,000	2.2%
Marginal	2	3.11	428,000	3.6%
Unaffiliated		3.30	457,000	-4.1%
Doubly affiliated		*-1.09*	*-150,000*	*0.0%*

Churches	MegaBloc	Congs	Members	Affiliates
Catholic Church	C	2,440	6,098,901	11,100,000
Assoc of Indian Ev	P	1,200	120,000	240,000
Jehovah's Witnesses	M	820	72,000	230,000
Latter-day Saints (Mormon)	M	400	122,981	198,000
Independent churches	I	400	77,477	172,000
Assemblies of God	P	1,161	65,000	130,000
Ch of God (Cleveland)	P	175	38,000	95,000
Seventh-day Adventist	P	117	49,102	82,000
Foursquare Evang Ch	P	520	61,000	80,520
Baptist Convention	P	255	24,000	36,000
CMA	P	88	12,963	35,000
Other denominations[78]		2,524	130,586	303,724
Doubly affiliated				*-150,000*
Total Christians[136]		**10,100**	**6,872,010**	**12,552,244**

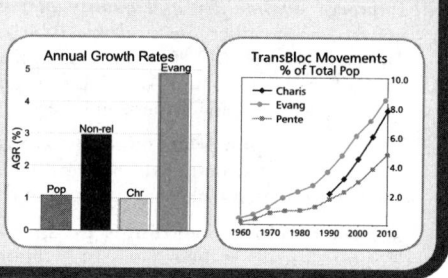

TransBloc	Pop %	Population	Ann Gr
Evangelicals			
Evangelicals	8.5	1,170,089	4.9%
Renewalists			
Charismatics	7.8	1,070,313	6.4%
Pentecostals	4.8	657,141	5.8%

Missionaries from Ecuador
P,I,A 162 (106 long-term) in 19 agencies: to Ecuador 41, Europe 87.

Answers to Prayer

E

1 **The impact of the gospel on sections of the Quichua** is a modern–day miracle. In 1967, there were only 120 believers among 3 million people; now, there are some areas with over 50% evangelicals. Most notable is the 100-year ministry of **Avant**, with approximately 240,000 linked with the churches planted through them.

2 **The steady growth of evangelicals.** Ecuador had Latin America's lowest percentage of evangelicals in 1960, but this has increased from 17,000 seventy-fold to 1.2 million in 2010. Most growth is in the rapidly growing cities and among the Quichua. Evangelical churches in Ecuador may not have the size of Brazilian churches or the proportion of Central America's, but they are growing in number, in size, in maturity and in social impact, particularly in the last 10 years.

3 **HCJB Radio,** launched in 1931, was the first of the great Christian mission radio broadcasters. Today, this ministry is known around the world, and both Ecuador and the world are blessed as a result.

Challenges for Prayer

1 **The country's greatest need may be stable government.** The seemingly endless carousel of presidents and finance ministers further undermines progress. Leadership needs the courage and stickability to tackle economic injustice, social problems and the deep-seated corruption which favours an entrenched elite.

2 **The Catholic Church** sees its privileged position erode, even as evangelical and marginal groups rapidly increase. There are sporadic, local incidents of mob violence, burning of churches and intimidation against evangelicals. Pray for continued freedom of religion, harmony among denominations and an increase in spiritual life among Catholics. There is a modest but growing charismatic movement in the Catholic Church in Ecuador.

3 **Evangelical numbers are large enough to significantly impact society.** The potential is great, but many in-house issues need resolution. Many churches exist independently, with no accountability or authority structure. Pray for the following:

a) Vision and growth to continue – some churches have lost their evangelistic zeal. Mega-churches are springing up in urban areas, but not all are concerned with continued evangelism of the unreached.

b) Unity within the great variety of churches. Issues of denomination, class, culture and personality often lead to division and parochial attitudes. For the Church to exercise a rightful impact on Ecuadorian life, these divisions must be overcome. The Evangelical Confraternity (COMEC) is a network linking most evangelicals in vision and in speaking out on issues of social concern.

c) Cultural sensitivity and integration of Quichua and Lowland Indians into the national Church scene. Amerindians compose the lion's share of evangelicals, but much of the power and influence falls within the Spanish-speaking evangelical population. Pray that both groups would fellowship and cooperate without losing their respective cultural distinctiveness.

d) Improved availability and quality of pastoral training. False teachings and evangelical nominalism are otherwise inevitable. Bible schools and seminaries are increasing. The Quichua Training Institute (**MTW**) is just one of many institutions supported by outside groups such as **OMS**, Foursquare and **AoG**. TEE programmes and In Service Training are demonstrably effective at developing leaders, and they are affordable and flexible.

e) Effective and appropriate ministry to children and young people. Poverty and child labour are particularly widespread, so ministry must be of a holistic nature and relevant to this generation, which makes up the bulk of the population.

4 **False teachings seemingly prosper** as marginal sects and Catholic syncretism rapidly spread, usually at the expense of traditional Catholics or evangelicals. Pray for the error of these groups to be made known; pray for ministers and laity to be equipped to address them with truth and love.

5 **Pioneer work among the small jungle tribes** attracted worldwide attention in 1956 when one **MAF**, one Avant and three Brethren missionaries were killed by the primitive Waorani (Auca). Nearly all of these tribes now have churches and the Scriptures through the work of various missionary groups. Pray for:

a) The maturing of the jungle churches to cope with modernity and the onslaught of the Spanish and Quichua cultures. While many profess to be Christian, practicing believers are in fact much fewer.

b) The efforts by Amerindian believers to preserve their lands and promote their spiritual development. FEINE (Ecuadorian Federation of Evangelical Indians) is a key body to this end.

c) Relationships with the outside world. Anti-missionary propaganda from humanistic anthropologists, leftist agitators, traders, jungle exploiters and even well-meaning but ignorant Christians all threaten or delay the effective flowering of the gospel among these unique peoples.

6 **Bible translation and distribution.** Ecuador was one of the first countries entered by **WBT**. They were involved in 12 NT translation projects before they were obliged to withdraw. Pray for completion of translation programmes in progress. Pray for the effective use of the Bibles and NTs now available; some Ecuadorians still copy the Bible by hand, verse-by-verse. The Bible Society has a pivotal role in promoting and distributing the Scriptures in this nation.

7 **Missions vision is young but growing.** The number of Ecuadorians serving in cross-cultural mission grew from 10 in 1996 to over 100 in 2005. This number continues to increase as churches catch the vision. Congregations are learning the commitment and cost involved. Foreign groups such as **OM** and **SIM** and national bodies such as AMEE (Evangelical Missionary Association of Ecuador) serve the Church through mobilization.

8 **Missions.** The largest groups are **HCJB**, **MAF**, **AoG**, **CB**/CMML, **AV**, **OMS**, **IT**. Many opportunities remain for missionary recruits in supportive ministries, church planting and pioneer work in the groups mentioned below. Pray for good church-mission relationships. The ever-present danger of administrative and financial paternalism threatens to impose Western patterns and stifle Ecuadorian initiatives.

9 **The less-evangelized:**

a) The slum-dwellers of Quito and Guayaquil. Over 60% of the latter's population are extremely poor, and many live in slums built on a polluted marsh. Few Christian workers have a vision for these deprived people.

b) The upper and middle classes are relatively unresponsive (**CMA, OMS** and others).

c) University and school students. Over eight agencies are involved in campus ministries among the 250,000 students (on more than 300 campuses), including **CCCI**, CECE (**IFES**), **YFC, LAM** and four denominational groups. There is still much room for growth.

d) The Afro-Ecuadorian people are only 0.03% evangelical. Although there are many Catholics among them, Spiritism is the true spiritual power at work in their midst. Pray for a breakthrough among this unique group.

e) **The 28,000 people living on the distant and barren Galapagos Islands** now have a growing ministry in their midst through MVI. The islands host many eco-tourists who, through Darwin's legacy, are often hostile to biblical Christianity.

f) **Loja province** is isolated from mainstream Ecuadorian life and is only 0.1% evangelical. Operation Esperanza is a multi-agency effort to see fruit in this region through prayer, radio, evangelism and holistic ministry (**SIM, OMS, WV**). Good Shepherd Radio broadcasts the gospel to many isolated villages otherwise difficult to access.

⑩ Christian media.

a) **Radio.** There are over 1,200 hours per week of Christian broadcasts in 12 languages thanks to **HCJB**, *Radio Biblica Cristiana*, Christian Vision and others. **HCJB** also has an extensive range of supportive ministries – including follow-up, education, pastoral training and medicine (two teaching hospitals and clinics). Pray also for the one Shuar and two Quichua Christian radio stations, under local leadership but started by Avant, broadcasting to these indigenous groups. There are eight full-time radio stations in all; pray for lasting fruit.

E

b) **TV** is a burgeoning ministry in Ecuador. Channels include *Asoma Visión*, *Enlace Ecuador* and *Unsión Television Network*. Pray for programming that not only blesses, but also teaches, encourages and disciples.

c) **The JESUS film** in Spanish is widely aired on TV as well as projected as a film. It is also available in Chimborazo and Shuar. Pray for the several hundred teachers trained to use the CrossRoads curriculum, "Life at the CrossRoads", showing the JESUS film.

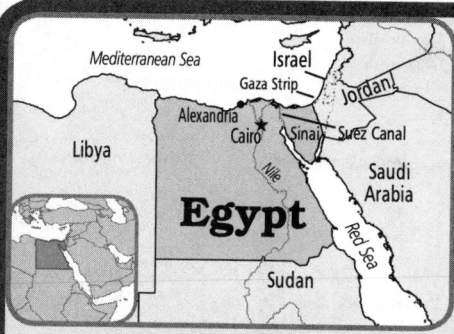

Egypt
Arab Republic of Egypt
Africa

Geography 🌍

Area 997,739 sq km. Mostly desert; only 3% is arable land – along the banks and delta of the Nile River and around the Western Desert oases.

Population		Ann Gr	Density
2010	84,474,427	1.83%	85/sq km
2020	98,637,781	1.45%	99/sq km
2030	110,907,127	1.11%	111/sq km

Fertile areas average nearly 2,000/sq km.
Capital Cairo 11,001,378. **Other major city** Alexandria 4.4 million. **Urbanites** 42.8%. **Pop under 15 yrs** 32%. **Life expectancy** 69.9 yrs.

Peoples 👪

Arab 92.1%. Egyptian, speaking Arabic, but claimed by some to be descendants of the ancient Coptic-speaking people of biblical times. Egyptian Arab 84.3%; Sudanese 5.4%; Bedouin 1.2%.
Berber 2.0%. Mostly Arabic-speaking.
Gypsy(Dom) 1.4%. Most now Arabic-speaking. Halebi 1.2%; Ghagar 0.3%.
Nubians 1.1%. Arabic-speaking 1.6%; Nobiin 0.3%; Kenusi-Dongola 0.2%.
Other 0.8%. Westerners 0.6%; others.
Refugees 2.4%. Black Sudanese may number more than 2m. Also Ethiopians, Palestinians, Eritreans, Somalis, others.
Literacy 71.4% (functional literacy is below 50%). **Official language** Arabic. **All languages** 27. **Indigenous languages** 11. **Languages with Scriptures** 2Bi 1NT 3por.

Economy 🏭

Egypt's wealth has traditionally been in agriculture, which still employs about one-third of the population. Already limited arable land continues to be lost to expanding cities. The past few years have seen significant economic growth in many areas due to rapid privatization. But a large proportion of Egyptians live in poverty – most blame institutionalized corruption, a bloated public sector and recent economic advances that fail to trickle down to the masses. These recently resulted in some unprecedented labour unrest in state-run industries. Main sources of income: natural gas and some oil, textiles, tourism, Suez Canal dues and remittances from expatriate Egyptians.

HDI Rank 123rd/182. **Public debt** 86.5% of GDP. **Income/person** $2,162 (5% of USA).

Politics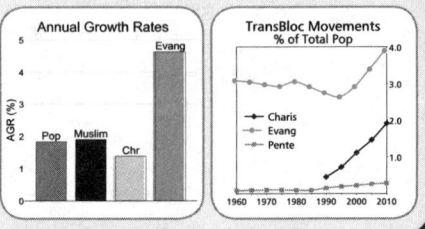

Egypt has enjoyed years of relative stability under President Mubarak, whose rule has been secular and highly pragmatic. Islamist groups have grown greatly in strength in the last 20 years, despite harsh (and costly) suppression from the government. Transition to greater levels of democracy was undermined when, in 2006, the Muslim Brotherhood gained 20% of the elected parliament. They ran as independents, since religious parties were banned from running, but the government limited their number of seats and has since imprisoned a number of them. With such an uncertain future, many Egyptians are disillusioned with the political process.

Religion

Islam is the state religion; until recently the large Christian minority were left in relative peace. The last 10 years, however, have seen higher levels of communal violence. The rise of Islamism caused Islamist violence and terror against Christians, combined with police collusion and the government failing to intervene. Investigations into incidents of religious violence are rarely properly conducted. Several high-profile cases relating to religious freedom have recently come to the Supreme Court; the outcome of these will shape Egypt's religious policies and attitudes profoundly.

Religions	Pop %	Population	Ann Gr
Muslim	86.67	73,213,986	1.9%
Christian	12.83	10,838,069	1.4%
Non-religious	0.50	422,372	1.8%

Christians Denoms		Pop %	Affiliates	Ann Gr
Protestant	18	0.75	634,000	1.4%
Independent	16	0.10	85,000	3.8%
Anglican	1	<0.01	4,000	3.9%
Catholic	7	0.39	332,000	2.1%
Orthodox	7	11.59	9,787,000	1.3%
Marginal	6	<0.01	2,000	3.3%

Churches	MegaBloc	Congs	Members	Affiliates
Coptic Orthodox Ch★	O	1,531	4,900,000	9,410,000
Evangelical Ch of E	P	350	55,833	335,000
Catholic Church	C	216	193,023	332,000
Greek Orthodox Ch	O	181	23,478	270,000
Assemblies of God	P	130	34,000	195,000
Armenian Orthodox Ch	O	34	68,182	105,000
Free Methodist Church	P	105	21,000	44,000
Chr Brethren (Exclusive)	P	283	17,000	27,500
Pentecostal Ch of God	P	81	3,900	9,750
Other denominations[40]		660	79,083	116,088
Total Christians[55]		**3,571**	**5,395,499**	**10,844,338**

★Copts are numbered by some as low as 7 million; Copts themselves claim over 12 million.

TransBloc	Pop %	Population	Ann Gr
Evangelicals			
Evangelicals	3.9	3,282,646	4.6%
Renewalists			
Charismatics	1.9	1,611,264	7.4%
Pentecostals	0.3	235,853	3.1%

Annual Growth Rates

TransBloc Movements % of Total Pop

Answers to Prayer

1 **The Church has endured nearly 2,000 years of discrimination and persecution** yet retains its spiritual vitality and strength. The name "The Church of the Martyrs" has been earned. The last 20 years have seen an intensification of suffering, but there is a lot of life in all branches of the Church.

2 **Large-scale Bible distribution** and creative ways to maintain a public presence make The Bible Society a highly strategic ministry. Scripture is more accessible than ever, especially to young people, and Christians and the Christian message have greater exposure in the media.

3 **The innovative use of electronic media** through websites, chat rooms, satellite TV and mobile phone downloads has opened a way for millions of Muslims to hear the gospel clearly, in safer environments for true seekers. Signs indicate a very widespread response.

4 **A prayer and renewal movement** has burst onto the scene in recent years with many thousands from all the major churches participating, even to the top level of church leadership. This cultivates unity, spiritual vitality and vision for outreach in Egypt and beyond.

Challenges for Prayer

1 **For over 1,000 years, Egypt was a majority-Christian country,** even after the Arab Muslim conquest in AD 640. Egypt gave to the Christian world some of its greatest theologians and the monastic movement. Egyptian Christians may be more clearly linked to the original Egyptian civilization that pre-dates the coming of Islam. Some efforts have been made to minimize Egypt's great Christian heritage, to downplay the size of the Church and to marginalize its contribution to society. But the Church survives. Pray for recognition of its history and role within Egypt and for an even greater role in the future.

2 **The government is in a precarious position,** between the Muslim Brotherhood, the silent majority, minority groups, strident anti-government bloggers and international pressure on some issues. It seems to lack the willpower to root out corruption; failure to address this and the issue of police violence only strengthen the hands of the Islamists and critics. Water issues are becoming very serious and, combined with population growth, intensify both poverty and unemployment. Pray that corruption would be rooted out, justice done and fair laws passed and then carried out in the interests of the people.

E

3 **Egypt is arguably the intellectual centre of Sunni Islam,** and Islamist groups such as The Brotherhood have grown greatly as they push for a more Islamic state. Their slogan (now "illegal"), "Islam is the solution", will never actually be tested unless they attain power. The stridency and harshness of some of their teachings and actions cause many to question this, yet they are also generous providers of social welfare. Pray that their leaders, their members and those disillusioned with conflict might discover the Light of the World.

4 **The Coptic Church** is by far the largest body of Christians in the Middle East and is a strategic key for the evangelization of the region. Pray for:

a) Church leaders, especially the Coptic Pope. Wisdom, grace and confidence are needed in handling the Muslim authorities, Islamist persecution and the questioning world. A close walk with God is essential to be both a bridge between communities and an example to their flock.

b) A spiritual awakening Church-wide in the midst of mounting pressures and communal tensions. Many Copts are very nominal. The responses to Muslim agitation need to be humble and loving but strong, and only those walking in faith are capable of this.

c) The biblically based renewal movement in the Coptic Church, which has steadily gained momentum since 1930. It strongly emphasizes Bible study and personal faith, and many are fervent witnesses for the Lord. Monasticism sees a rejuvenation as well. Pray for the growth and effectiveness of this movement of the Spirit.

d) Christians are numerous in business, the professions and health services, but overall the Coptic influence within Egypt is much less than their large numbers warrant. Pray that Copts might have a positive and transforming effect in the nation, just as Joseph did millennia ago.

5 **The Protestant churches sprang out** of the Orthodox Church, but did not significantly grow for a long while. However, since 1973, a renewal movement and a new generation of bold leaders are spurring growth. Young people are numerous and active in these churches, and several Pentecostal and evangelical denominations see notable increases. Many churches have extensive social and medical programmes to help the very poor and the disabled.

6 **Persecution of Christians has steadily intensified** in the last 20 years. Harassment, discrimination on individual and communal levels and financial incentives for Christians to adopt Islam are all used to break the morale of Christians. Some areas, such as Upper Egypt, face more intense pressure than others. In most cases, the attacks that occur are carried out by vigilante Islamist groups – but often with the tacit acceptance of local security forces. Identity cards stating religion can be a huge challenge for believers from Muslim backgrounds, who tend to be on the receiving end of persecution more frequently than Copts. Pray for:

a) Christians to stand firm in their faith and live exemplary lives before their oppressors and in the face of police mistreatment. A number have died or suffered incarceration and torture in prison, usually on false charges.

b) Christians who waver. Estimates indicate that several thousand annually are coerced or enticed to become Muslim. Significant numbers of Christian girls fall in love with or are enticed by Muslim males, often leading to the girl eventually converting to Islam. In a growing minority of cases, violent abduction and forced conversion occurs. Pray for strength for all to keep the faith through every circumstance.

c) *Government response to persecution and violence.* Government forces usually respond to attacks too late or not at all. This lack of decisive action by police emboldens Islamists, and the violence enables the state to enact draconian security measures. Pray for a government that will act with fairness to protect all of its communities from violence.

7 **Muslim-background believers are increasing in number** and include a number of high-profile, former Muslim religious leaders. Conversion is not illegal, but some are imprisoned for "despising Islam" or under false pretexts; others have fled for their lives. It is thus far impossible for Muslim converts to change their identity cards and register as Christians. The numbers are not certain, but are indisputably on an unprecedentedly high level. Egyptian religious authorities claim that up to one million Muslims in Egypt have become believers in recent years. This is most likely exaggerated fear-mongering, but brings to light the more modest but nonetheless notable thousands who have recently come to Christ from a Muslim background.

8 **Training for pastoral and missionary service** is a great need. Many evangelical churches have no trained pastor. As the Church grows and faces great trials, solid leadership is essential. Pray also for the growing numbers in theological training at the Coptic Evangelical Church Seminary (which had 120 students preparing for the ministry in 2007), as well as the **AoG** and the Free Methodist Bible schools.

9 **Unreached peoples.** Most Muslims have never heard a Christian personally share the gospel. Pray that Christians may take opportunities to witness by their words and Christ-like lives. Specific prayer targets:

a) *The urban population* – many are uprooted peasants in slums. One thousand people a day migrate to Cairo; a high proportion are nominally Christian.

b) *The Nubians of Upper Egypt.* For centuries a Christian kingdom, but eventually under pressure, Nubians became Muslim in the 17th Century. Today there are only a handful of Christians. Only a minority still speak the two main Nubian dialects, but they are culturally distinct. Many are poor, their ancestral lands flooded as a result of the Aswan dam. Pray for a rediscovery of their Christian roots, and for many to come to Christ.

c) *The Bedouin,* proud desert nomads and descendants of the first Arabs in the region. Beset by poverty and unemployment, their traditional tribal way of life is under threat. Increasingly drawn toward radical Islam, there are very few Christians among them.

d) *The Berbers* in ancient Siwa and other western oases. A culture apart from Arabs, their Islam is rife with folk magic.

e) *The Beja,* a non-Arab group settled along the Nile River and Red Sea for 4,000 years. Traditionally nomadic, they are slowly being forced into sedentary existence. Folk Islam and fear of djinn characterize their faith.

f) *Dom Gypsies,* cousins to the Romani of Europe, exist almost invisibly, taking casual labour to sustain their existence. Heavily marginalized, they are only very nominally Muslim, practicing magic and superstition. Those few who become believers are often ostracized from both Dom and general Egyptian society.

10 **The Southern Sudanese,** having fled to Egypt in their millions from the long civil war in Sudan, find themselves again under fire. Forced removal, using lethal violence, and angry protests have recently occurred. Most live in poverty, refugees on the fringes of society. Many are Christians. Pray for the spiritual health of these displaced, suffering people. There is already some Christian and social ministry to them (Episcopal Church, **CMS**, **OM**, Tearfund).

11 **The Egyptian Church's vision for outreach is growing,** but still in a very youthful stage in this modern era, though the Copts have an ancient legacy of sending out workers. Egyptian Christian workers have many advantages over non-Arabs in the Muslim world. Pray that the millions of Egyptian Christians in the West and Middle East may catch the vision to support such a thrust. Pray for:

a) *Egyptian tentmakers in every Arab nation.* Egyptians work and are respected throughout the Arab world, an ideal opportunity for Egyptian Christians to have an impact in the region.

b) New initiatives focused on effective ways of reaching the majority population.

c) The development and implementation of training courses focused on ministry within Egypt and beyond.

12 **Openings for low-profile ministry** by professional, qualified expatriates are now more numerous than for many years. Pray for qualified and experienced labourers to partner with the Egyptian Church, which is taking up the challenges of compassionate ministry on the home front. Some examples of fruitful ministry:

a) Visiting and encouraging struggling churches and providing training for leaders (Open Doors).

b) Empowerment programmes and holistic ministry that includes micro-enterprise, ministry to women and assisting Christian schools and hospitals, especially with the disabled. **MECO**, Pioneers and **AWM** are a few of the expatriate agencies at work; there is much more being done by indigenous groups.

c) Drug addicts number around 500,000. Related problems of crime and AIDS also need addressing. The Freedom Project and other local ministries focus on helping these broken, needy people.

E

13 **Christian media** is the most potent means of witness to the majority of Egyptians. Pray for:

a) Scripture distribution, which has increased in the last 10 years. The Bible Society's effective marketing every year at the Cairo International Bookfair sees great success, with video and audio cassettes being especially popular. Special distribution for youth and children is very fruitful. The Society regularly comes up with creative ways to get Scripture into the hands of Egyptians and continues to enjoy high visibility.

b) Widely distributed Christian literature. There are over 30 Christian bookstores. The need is for more local Christian authors to write evangelistic and teaching materials. Pray also for production of evangelistic tools to be used by Christians in approaching their neighbours, which will help to break down Islamic misconceptions about the gospel.

c) The JESUS film in Arabic is widely seen on DVD and satellite TV. Pray for its wider distribution and availability.

d) Satellite TV. SAT-7 broadcasts 24/7, beaming high-quality Arabic programmes on both its adult and children's channels. A large, loyal audience is building among Christians and non-Christians. Over the years, another seven stations have joined the effort, and many of them are very effective, such as *Al Hayat*, The Miracle Channel and two Coptic channels (*Aghapy* and Coptic TV).

e) Christian radio. This is a potent tool. Pray for the various Arabic-language studios where programmes are prepared, and for Christian broadcasters and listeners. There are over 40 hours of shortwave programming weekly by FEBA, **HCJB**, **TWR** (also using medium wave), IBRA, the AWR and others, as well as Internet and digital radio.

f) The Internet is an extremely effective means of impacting Egyptians. Several high-profile Coptic apologists (such as Father Zakaria) and former Muslims with websites are causing many to turn to Christ with their powerful testimonies and arguments for the gospel.

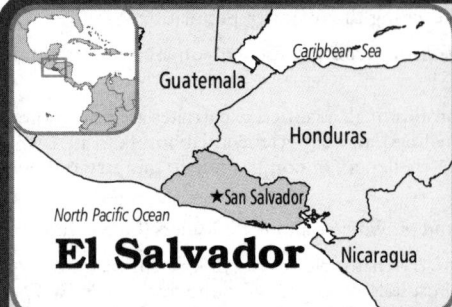

E El Salvador

Republic of El Salvador

Latin America

Geography

Area 21,041 sq km on the Pacific Coast of Central America. The smallest and most-densely populated Spanish-speaking mainland state in the Americas. Sub-tropical and susceptible to earthquakes.

Population		Ann Gr	Density
2010	6,194,126	0.44%	294/sq km
2020	6,617,741	0.73%	315/sq km
2030	7,176,865	0.80%	341/sq km

Capital San Salvador 1,565,202. **Urbanites** 61.3%. **Pop under 15 yrs** 32%. **Life expectancy** 71.3 yrs.

Peoples

Hispanic 90.1%. Ladino (Mestizo).
Amerindian 9.5%. Part-Indian 4.5%; Pipil (Aztec) 4.0%; Lenca 0.8%.
Other 0.4%.
Over 30% of Salvadoreans live outside the country due to economic migrations.
Literacy 80.6%. **Official language** Spanish. **All languages** 7. **Indigenous languages** 5. **Languages with Scriptures** 2Bi.

Economy

Centuries of exploitation of the majority, followed by years of devastating civil war, have held back development of this impoverished nation. There was subsequent improvement between 1991 and 2005, halving the number of those living in poverty. Coffee and light industry are the main economic activities, the service sector employs the majority and remittances from Salvadoreans working abroad are a very significant boost to many.
HDI Rank 106th/182. **Public debt** 44.7% of GDP. **Income/person** $3,824 (8% of USA).

Politics

Independent from Spain in 1821 as part of a united Central America, and then as a separate nation in 1838. All power remained in the hands of wealthy plantation owners allied with the military. A long series of corrupt dictatorships and gross inequalities between the rich and poor provoked an armed leftist insurrection in 1981. Over 75,000 were killed in fighting, in crossfire or by death squads. The ending of the fighting, revulsion over human rights abuses and international pressure forced through a peace accord in 1992. The democratic government is more established, with the main leftist party having won 2009 elections after four successive right-wing governments.

Religion

The constitution recognizes the legal status of the Catholic Church, but there is freedom of religion for other denominations and faiths. The Catholic Church vocally opposed oppression and human rights abuses during the war, and several high-profile clergy were murdered as a result. Other clergy sympathized with and even aided the leftist militias.

Religions	Pop %	Population	Ann Gr
Christian	94.63	5,861,501	0.4%
Non-religious	4.90	303,512	0.9%
Baha'i	0.40	24,777	0.4%
Muslim	0.03	1,858	0.4%
Buddhist	0.03	1,858	0.4%
Jewish	0.01	619	0.4%

Christians Denoms		Pop %	Affiliates	Ann Gr
Protestant	45	26.83	1,662,000	4.5%
Independent	21	10.79	669,000	3.6%
Anglican	1	0.10	6,000	8.5%
Catholic	1	65.06	4,030,000	-1.1%
Marginal	2	3.04	188,000	1.7%
Doubly affiliated		-11.19	-693,000	0.0%

Churches	MegaBloc	Congs	Members	Affiliates
Catholic Church	C	325	2,214,286	4,030,000
Assemblies of God	P	1,560	139,000	315,000
Elim Church	P	71	142,857	200,000
Prince of Peace	I	514	90,000	198,000
Seventh-day Adventist	P	610	102,000	170,340
Apostolic Ch (A&P)	I	500	75,000	166,500
Baptist Convention	P	230	69,000	153,180
Ch of God (Cleveland)	P	440	45,000	112,500
Latter-day Saints (Mormon)	M	160	70,280	100,500
United Pentecostal Ch	P	300	40,000	100,000
Jehovah's Witnesses	M	580	35,000	87,500
Luth Salvadoran Synod	P	140	9,664	69,000
Central American Ch	P	160	24,000	53,280
Other denominations[57]		3,358	351,125	798,682
Doubly affiliated				-693,120
Total Christians[70]		**8,948**	**3,407,212**	**5,861,362**

TransBloc	Pop %	Population	Ann Gr
Evangelicals			
Evangelicals	31.6	1,960,405	4.5%
Renewalists			
Charismatics	30.6	1,892,450	4.6%
Pentecostals	23.5	1,455,776	4.8%

Missionaries from El Salvador
P,I,A 165 long-term.

Answers to Prayer

1 **The consolidation of peace, stability and democracy** since 1992 is an answer to prayer, after the intense suffering of civil war. Elections and economics now replace death squads and assassinations.

2 **The astonishing increase of evangelicals** during the war has continued, albeit at a slower rate. Evangelicals were but 2.3% of the population in 1960, leaping to 32% in 2010. Some of Latin America's largest megachurches are found in El Salvador.

Challenges for Prayer

1 **Recovery from the social and psychological wounds** of centuries of oppression and 12 years of civil war is a priority. The web of violence, hate, suspicion, atrocities and murder will take time to unravel. At the height of the war, 20% of the population fled the country, and the USA poured in $6 billion to shore up the government. Overall, more than 75,000 were killed. Pray for repentance, reconciliation and a fair society based on respect for human rights.

2 **Rapid social and demographic shifts** are changing the face of the country and require prayer and action. Most notable among them are the following:

a) The 3.3 million Salvadoreans living abroad, many in the USA. Their remittances sent home keep many out of poverty, yet they have spiritual needs of their own. Many are working illegally and are vulnerable to exploitation. Their absence has also triggered social shifts back home.

b) The new urban population. In one generation, El Salvador has gone from a predominantly agrarian, rural society to one in which 60% live in cities. This flow to the cities generates new challenges regarding infrastructure, crime and poverty.

c) The large numbers of youth involved with the powerful *maras.* These gangs have attracted up to 70% of young men, partially orphaned by absent fathers. The Church finds that reaching the 15-30 age bracket is particularly difficult with its current methods. New methods must be adopted or an unchurched generation will quickly emerge in El Salvador.

d) The massive megachurches, such as Elim and *Tabernáculo Bíblico Bautista,* both of which have grown from almost nothing to over 100,000 affiliates in their wider networks. With significant financial and political clout, these cell-based churches have the opportunity to powerfully and positively influence society.

3 **The growth of Evangelicals in the midst of travail has been a modern-day miracle,** but now the need is for consolidation of the work. There is a growing number of ex-evangelicals that underscores this need. The 1990s saw bold goals set for church planting; although those goals were not met, as many as 9,000 churches were planted. This fervour has subsided of late, even though more evangelical congregations are needed in the country. Pray for effective discipling and motivation of believers for service, witness and missions. Pray also for increased unity and vision for outreach so that this nation might belong to Jesus — *El Salvador* is Spanish for 'the Saviour'.

4 **Leadership for churches must be multiplied.** The war, lack of finance and insufficient staff crippled what training was available. Pray for the Bible schools, seminaries and TEE programmes. Pray for the provision of all material needs for staff and students in this time of economic stress. This ministry needs more missionary input. Many mission agencies are heavily committed to health, social betterment and educational ministries.

5 **Missions vision has grown.** The ministries of COMISAL (the national expression of **COMIBAM**) and of indigenous missions – such as MIES, AMIGA, EDEHM, COMIFAD, ADN, TRES, ATN and **AoG** Missions – are expressions of El Salvador's missions vision. These are in addition to international mission groups such as **OM** and **YWAM**/JUCUM. An estimated 165 missionaries are serving in other lands. Pray that mission involvement might increase and be fruitful.

6 **Sections of society of special challenge:**

a) *The Amerindian population* retain many of their cultural values and traits, even though they have largely lost their languages. Their treatment in the 20th Century has been horrific. Pray for effective ministries to begin and for culturally sensitive church planting among them.

b) *The 115,000 university students.* MUC(**IFES**) has 35 student groups, reaching most universities and colleges. **CCCI** also works in El Salvador. Training leaders is the greatest challenge.

7 **The impact of Christian institutions and media** is wide-ranging and ever-increasing. There are three Christian universities, around 80 Christian schools, five TV stations and 30 radio stations. Those leading these ministries can enrich themselves if they seek to do so, or they can have a real Kingdom impact on society. Pray for the latter.

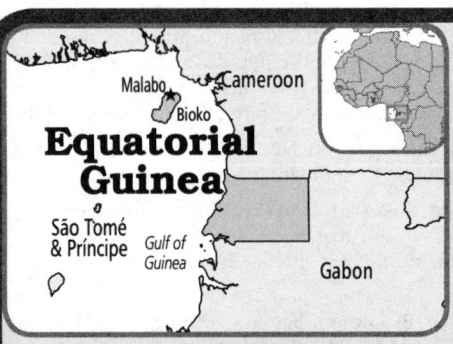

Equatorial Guinea

Republic of Equatorial Guinea

Africa

Geography 🌍

Area 28,051 sq km. A small enclave, Rio Muni, on the African mainland and several islands in the Gulf of Guinea, including Bioko (2,000 sq km) and Pegalu (Annobon, 10 sq km).

Population		Ann Gr	Density
2010	693,385	2.64%	25/sq km
2020	875,242	2.32%	31/sq km
2030	1,066,881	1.90%	38/sq km

Capital Malabo 131,000. **Urbanites** 39.7%. **Pop under 15 yrs** 41%. **Life expectancy** 49.9 yrs.

Peoples 👪

Bantu 77.3%. Nine groups.
Mainland Fang 57.2%, politically dominant; Seke 2.5%; Ngumba 3.4%; Batangan 2.0%; Ngumbi 1.0%.
Islands Bubi 10.3%.
Other African 19.5%. Yoruba 8.3%; Igbo 4.2%; Eurafrican 2.5%; Hausa 2.1%; Fernandino Creole 1.2%.
Others 3.2%. Spanish.
Literacy 84.2%. **Official languages** Spanish and French. **All languages** 14. **Languages with Scriptures** 3Bi 2NT 6por 2w.i.p.

Economy 🏠

Prosperous until independence; subsequent mismanagement brought the nation to economic ruin by 1979. Discovery of massive offshore petroleum deposits in 1995 transformed the economy; the nation now has one of the world's highest per capita incomes. Oil revenues – precise figures are a state secret – enabled the rapid transformation of the capital; the development of rural areas from this income is on a much more modest level. A small minority of foreign investors and local elite have been greatly enriched, but the majority continue to live in poverty. Corruption is a major problem.

E

HDI **Rank** 118th/182. **Public debt** 0.9% of GDP. **Income/person** $14,941 (31% of USA).

Politics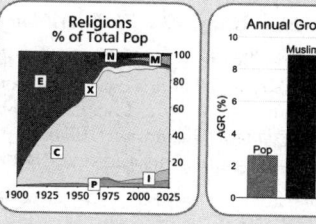

Independence from Spain in 1968. A coup in 1969 brought Macias Nguema to power. With Soviet bloc assistance, this atheist dictator turned his country into a slave-labour camp. A military coup in 1979 saw Nguema's nephew Obiang rise to the position of president. The multiparty system introduced in 1991 still needs to see greater freedom for opposition political parties. Despite a history as one of the worst human rights abusers in Africa, praiseworthy progress is being made in political reform, education and the country's infrastructure. The uncertainty of succession in political leadership, combined with the great oil wealth and a weak democratic tradition, make stability essential for the future.

Religion

In colonial times, almost the entire population were baptized as Catholics. The savage persecution of the 1970s, with the repression of religions, is now followed by limited but increasing religious freedom.

Religions	Pop %	Population	Ann Gr
Christian	90.00	624,047	2.5%
Muslim	3.90	27,042	8.9%
Ethnoreligionist	3.10	21,495	1.4%
Non-religious	2.60	18,028	1.1%
Baha'i	0.40	2,774	3.2%

Christians	Denoms	Pop %	Affiliates	Ann Gr
Protestant	10	3.35	23,000	3.6%
Independent	24	3.96	27,000	4.9%
Catholic	1	80.33	557,000	2.4%
Marginal	2	0.60	4,000	2.9%
Unaffiliated		1.80	12,000	-3.0%

Churches	MegaBloc	Congs	Members	Affiliates
Catholic Church	C	141	373,826	557,000
New Apostolic Ch	I	20	5,090	8,500
Council of Ev Chs	P	91	4,541	8,400
Other Indigenous chs	I	91	3,650	7,300
Assemblies of God	P	41	820	4,100
Seventh-day Adventist	P	22	2,550	3,800
Betania	I	20	980	2,450
Crusade Chs [WEC]	P	47	880	2,200
Other denominations[15]		235	8,702	18,138
Total Christians[37]		**708**	**401,039**	**611,888**

TransBloc	Pop %	Population	Ann Gr
Evangelicals			
Evangelicals	4.4	30,442	5.3%
Renewalists			
Charismatics	6.3	44,019	4.0%
Pentecostals	2.0	13,872	5.7%

E

Challenges for Prayer

1 **The unusual politico-economic situation** of Equatorial Guinea betrays a massive gap between the haves and have-nots. Pray for the following issues:

a) Economic justice. Millions of dollars of oil money enrich a minority, as Western oil companies happily collude with a regime possessing a less-than-stellar human rights record in order to obtain their own profits. Spending on infrastructure (especially in the capital) is increasing, but very little trickles down to the masses. A battle with corruption and an historic governmental unfamiliarity with how to steward such wealth mean prayer for wisdom is needed.

b) The oil boom brings in foreigners, most drawn by wealth, and includes an influx of evangelical Christians and Muslims. Pray that foreign companies might do business in a way that benefits the local people. Pray that expat believers might be moved to engage with the spiritual and physical needs of the nation.

c) Political freedoms. In over 30 years, the country has had only two rulers. Opposition parties do not have the freedom to operate that a multiparty democracy should offer. Freedom of the press is limited. Some progress is being made, however.

2 **The vast majority are Roman Catholic,** the highest percentage of any African nation. But beneath the surface of the imposed colonial religion lies the reality that animistic beliefs and practices were never abandoned. Pray that the 85% who claim Christianity – without having been born again – might hear and respond to the true gospel of Jesus Christ.

3 **An encouraging increase in religious freedom** has occurred alongside a number of newer, growing Pentecostal, charismatic and evangelical denominations (**AoG**, Deeper Life, several indigenous denominations). Pray for purity of life and fervency of evangelism in the churches despite the prevailing poverty, corruption and despair. The government has actually been quite positive about the potential role of the Church and missions in developing society, a much-needed foil to the oil-oriented multinational corporations.

4 **Training leaders and discipling believers** are strategic and growing ministries. Three training institutions exist (Reformed, **WEC**, **AoG**) along with TEE programmes. **YWAM** runs short-term Discipleship Training Schools. Pray that graduates may be used of the Spirit to evangelize the nation and disciple believers. Pray for greater opportunities for laity to grow in their faith; the move from a nominal Catholic/animist worldview to a biblical one is a significant transition.

5 **Missionaries have increased in number,** including growing numbers from West and Central Africa, but they need wisdom in the convoluted socio-political situation. Several delicate and difficult situations in relating to indigenous leadership have occurred in recent years. Pray for grace and humility on the part of both expats and nationals. The main agencies are: EqGuiMsn, **YWAM**, **AoG**, **WEC**.

6 **The large majority of peoples are predominantly Catholic,** with strong strains of animism. Pray especially for:

a) The Fang, who are the majority people and politically dominant. They are only around 2–3% evangelical.

b) The Hausa, numbering around 12,000. Originating from Nigeria and staunchly Muslim, they are only 0.1% Christian.

c) The Ngumba, Benga and Fa D'Ambu peoples, all less than 1% evangelical.

7 **The Bible Society and AoG distribute Scriptures,** but importing and distributing networks are a challenge. Seven indigenous languages have Scriptures. However, most of these translations are archaic. The Fang NT is being translated by Outreach International/ *Asociacion Cristiana de Traducciones Biblicas*; pray for its completion. **CLC** runs a bookshop in Bata, and there are numerous audio and video resources in Fang and other languages.

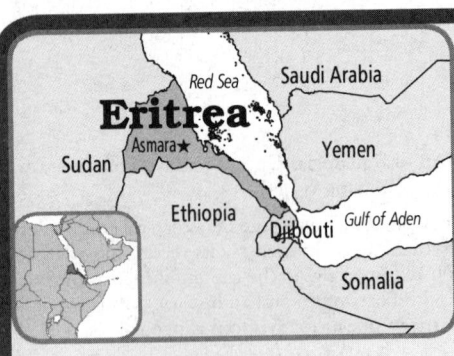

Population		Ann Gr	Density
2010	5,223,994	3.15%	43/sq km
2020	6,718,974	2.26%	55/sq km
2030	8,085,605	1.78%	67/sq km

Capital Asmara 683,000. **Urbanites** 21.6%. **Pop under 15 yrs** 42%. **Life expectancy** 59.2 yrs.

Peoples

Horn of Africa Peoples 87.1%.
  Semitic 72.5%. Tigrinya 44.9%; Tigre 24.3%; Belin 2.3%.
  Afar 9.2%. Saho 4.9%; Afar 4.3%.
  Other 5.4%. Beja 4.0%; Somali 1.4%.
Nilotic 5.1%. Kunama 2.9%; Nara 2.2%.
Arab 7.8%. 5 groups. Yemeni Arab 2.0%; Sudanese Arab 1.8%.
Literacy 56.7%. **Official language** Tigrinya. Tigre, Arabic and English (especially for secondary and tertiary education) also widely used. **All languages** 18. **Indigenous languages** 12. **Languages with Scriptures** 6Bi 2NT 4por.

Eritrea

State of Eritrea

Africa

Geography

Area 121,100 sq km. Arid, temperate highland plateau and a strategic desert plain along the busy Red Sea Coast shipping lanes.

Economy

Traditionally based on subsistence agriculture in a land where such is increasingly unfeasible due to war, drought, land destruction and degradation;

food production amounts to a fraction of what is needed to feed the population. Government possession of nearly all land and enterprise has accelerated the exodus of most of the highly educated and skilled professionals. Over 50% of the population live on less than $1US/day; around 30% of the GDP comes from diaspora remittances. Some development of infrastructure and of the mining industry are among the few positives.
HDI Rank 165th/182. **Public debt** 58.4% of GDP. **Income/person** $295 (1% of USA).

Politics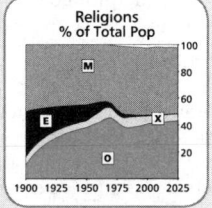

Italian colony 1890-1941. UN-arranged federation with Ethiopia in 1952. In 1963 the federation was terminated, and Eritrea became a province of Ethiopia. A guerrilla war for Eritrean independence led by Eritrean Peoples Liberation Front (EPLF) began in 1961 and culminated in 1991. The EPLF assumed control from then until 1993, when Eritreans voted for independence in a UN-sponsored referendum. Development of the country was seriously disrupted by the 1998-2000 border war with Ethiopia. A single president since 1993 who has espoused Marxist ideology, postponed elections several times, clamped down hard on freedoms and placed such restrictions on the UN and foreign NGOs that they left the country. Somewhat of an international pariah.

Religion

Recognition of four religious groups: Sunni Islam, Eritrean Orthodox, Roman Catholic and Lutheran. All other religious groups have been persecuted with increasing intensity since 2002, and even these officially recognized groups must endure government appointments and interference.

Religions	Pop %	Population	Ann Gr
Muslim	50.26	2,625,579	3.1%
Christian	47.31	2,471,472	3.3%
Non-religious	1.87	97,689	1.3%
Ethnoreligionist	0.56	29,254	-1.4%

Christians Denoms		Pop %	Affiliates	Ann Gr
Protestant	20	1.39	73,000	3.2%
Independent	6	0.31	16,000	9.9%
Catholic	2	3.43	179,000	2.7%
Orthodox	4	41.87	2,187,000	3.5%
Marginal	1	0.01	1,000	-8.6%
Unaffiliated		0.30	16,000	-12.4%

Churches	MegaBloc	Congs	Members	Affiliates
Eritrean Orthodox Ch	O	1,530	1,289,941	2,180,000
Catholic Latin&Coptic	C	139	104,070	179,000
Evang Luth Ch of E	P	98	14,336	41,000
Seventh-day Adventist	P	5	560	1,400
Other denominations[26]		196	21,606	54,325
Total Christians[33]		**1,968**	**1,430,513**	**2,455,725**

TransBloc	Pop %	Population	Ann Gr
Evangelicals			
Evangelicals	2.1	111,400	4.6%
Renewalists			
Charismatics	1.2	63,318	6.8%
Pentecostals	0.2	10,900	3.9%

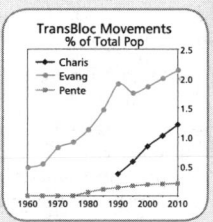

Religions % of Total Pop

TransBloc Movements % of Total Pop

Answers to Prayer

1 **The growth of the Church in Eritrea is strong,** despite steadily intensifying government oppression. Persecution and restraints on personal freedoms test believers sorely. But the closure of most denominations and ministries has prompted the flowering of a hard-pressed but growing house church movement. There are growing renewal movements in the mainline churches: *Medhaniel Alem* (Orthodox) and *Tebadasso* (Catholic). Many in prison or en route to refugee camps in another country have received the gospel of Jesus Christ in their time of trial, including some from the less-reached people groups of Eritrea.

Challenges for Prayer

1 **Peace and national stability remain out of reach** for Eritrea, in and out of conflict with neighbouring countries for decades, most notably with Ethiopia. Pray for:

a) *The establishment of peace with Ethiopia.* Unresolved border disputes have led to mounting tensions and failed UN peacekeeping missions. Pray for humility, willingness to compromise on the parts of the leaders, just and wise actions by the international community and an end to the hostilities that neither country can afford.

b) National economic recovery and progress are virtually impossible, since the majority of the workforce are conscripted to military service for an indefinite period. Facing mandatory military careers, many young people flee Eritrea, seeking a brighter future elsewhere, an action that can bring reprisals against family members left behind.

c) Adequate food and resources. The ongoing threat of war, international relations and severe drought leave millions of Eritreans dependent on foreign assistance for food, whether through relatives abroad or the promise of humanitarian aid often not received. Many face extreme poverty with no relief in sight.

2 **Religious freedom remains a major issue.** A 2002 government ruling banned all religious groups from meeting together and practicing their faith without official recognition, and it granted recognition only to Sunni Islam, Eritrean Orthodox, Roman Catholic and Evangelical Lutheran groups. The effects of this on all Eritreans are significant, especially so on Christians within non-approved groups. Some posit this as a reaction against the evangelical growth within the Orthodox Church and during the long war with Ethiopia. Pray for government acceptance of religious groups and for restoration of basic human rights and religious freedom to all Eritreans.

3 **The Christian Church faces terrible ongoing persecution,** both outside the recognized churches and, to some degree, within. Many leaders and lay members are in prison, and more are under house arrest; the government has seized many church assets. Christians are largely Orthodox, mostly from among the Tigrinya, with some from among the Kunama, Bilen or other peoples. Evangelicals are fewer, but are present to varying degrees within most denominations. Christians of all denominations have been refined and drawn together in fellowship through recent decades due to war, drought and government oppression. But the intense suffering of the Church in Eritrea is one of the untold stories of the past decade – a story of tragedy and ultimately, we pray, great spiritual harvest. Pray that Christians may remain fervent for Jesus amid hardship and make a significant impact on their nation and beyond.

4 **Evangelicals are growing despite severe persecution.** Being officially banned, these groups now operate in underground networks based in homes. Around 20 or more networks are known, but numbers are impossible to ascertain. Pray for these issues:

a) Imprisonment and torture are reality. Key evangelical leaders were imprisoned following the ban on their churches. Since then, arrests have included pastors, prominent evangelicals in society and, more recently, those known to practice their faith. Prison conditions are harsh – beatings and agonizing torture techniques cripple many and even lead to death in some cases. Some estimate that over 3,000 Christians are currently in prison. Pray for those in prison, that they may be strengthened and enabled to endure suffering while radiating grace. Pray also for their families, who often find themselves bereft of not only loved ones but usually of the income earner as well.

b) Leadership for the churches. With so many pastors, leaders and evangelists now living outside the country or in prisons, the Church moves forward under new leadership, often young men or new believers, some who encountered Jesus in prison. Pray for them to be full of God's wisdom as they learn to lead and grow.

c) Ongoing evangelistic outreach. Amid such hardship, the Church has grown rapidly, often most among those fleeing the country, those living in camps in Ethiopia and elsewhere, those in prison and those living abroad. Witnessing Christians, though violently opposed by the authorities, have spread far and wide. Still, many villages and towns remain unimpacted by the gospel. Pray for continued commitment of believers to preach Christ whatever the cost and without compromise.

d) Harvest among the Eritrean diaspora, both in the wider region in Africa and globally. Many suffer by proxy with their brethren back in Eritrea, but significant numbers of Eritreans outside the country are encountering the Lord Jesus in profound ways. Pray for this to continue and to multiply.

5 **Missionaries, as such, are no longer welcome in Eritrea.** Since 2002, almost all foreign aid workers, Christian or otherwise, have been expelled or forced to leave. Much work has largely been suspended or terminated as a result. The few that remain, along with the national workers, keep well under the radar and are confined in their activities. Pray for open doors for workers to return to Eritrea; pray that those who do have access will move quickly, taking advantage of every opportunity to demonstrate God's love.

6 **Pray for the less reached,** specifically for:

a) ***The Tigre,*** mostly Muslim, and one of only a few Eritrean or Ethiopian Semitic peoples who are not Orthodox. They are related to the Tigrinya, but culturally distant from them. The Bible is available, but there are few Christians.

b) ***The Jabarti*** – a Muslim minority among the Tigrinya. Pray that the unrest might create opportunities for Tigrinya Christians to engage this related but previously distant group.

c) ***The Afar and related Saho peoples,*** largely nomadic pastoralists in the southeast with few Christians.

d) ***The Beja and Nara peoples*** of the northwest with no known witness. Many are nomadic.

e) ***The Arab Rashaida,*** who migrated from Saudi Arabia in the 19th Century. Recent work among these peoples has been reported, but there are still no known churches.

7 **Christian support ministries** have grown even more vital in recent years, since more conventional work has been shut down or suspended.

a) ***Students*** still in Eritrea remain fervent in evangelizing and discipling their peers, and large numbers continue to come to faith. Many recent evangelical movements were started or fuelled by students committed to Jesus.

b) ***Radio and satellite TV*** provide programming for Christians in Tigrinya and English, though some work has shut down in recent years, including an evangelistic work among the Tigre and Beja peoples. Christian radio is being broadcast into Eritrea from neighbouring countries. Pray for the gospel to go forth through these channels; shortwave radio Bible studies reach even into the military camps.

c) ***Other resources*** include the JESUS film (six languages), **GRN** audio Scriptures/teachings (in eight languages) and a series of tracts as well as a Bible Correspondence Course developed by FFM. Pray for widespread and effective use of these; pray also for development of more materials that will bless Christians and more tools for use in reaching others.

E

Population		Ann Gr	Density
2010	1,339,459	-0.11%	30/sq km
2020	1,332,507	-0.07%	29/sq km
2030	1,301,132	-0.30%	29/sq km

Capital Tallinn 399,000. **Urbanites** 69.5%. **Pop under 15 yrs** 15%. **Life expectancy** 72.9 yrs.

Peoples 👪

Finno-Ugric 69.8%. Estonian 68.6%; Finnish 0.8%.
Slavic 29.2%. Russian 25.7%; Ukrainian 2.1%; Belarussian 1.2%.
Other 1.2%. Tatar, Jews, others.
Literacy 99%. **Official language** Estonian; Russian is still common. **All languages** 18. **Indigenous languages** 2. **Languages with Scriptures** 1Bi 1NT 1por.

Estonia

Republic of Estonia

Europe

Geography 🌍

Area 45,215 sq km. Northernmost of the three Baltic states. Separated from Finland to the north by the Gulf of Finland.

Economy 🏭

Movement to a capitalist free market society and joining the EU has attracted foreign investment and sustained significant economic growth. One of the most successful of the post-Soviet economies.
HDI Rank 40th/182. **Public debt** 4.8% of GDP. **Income/person** $17,532 (37% of USA).

Politics

Long dominated by surrounding nations. Independent 1918-1940. The Soviet invasion in 1940 and subsequent deportation and murder of many Estonians caused deep resentment against Russia. Became independent as a multiparty democracy by 1991. 2004 entry to the EU and NATO reflects increasing Western orientation.

Religion

Severe persecution of all faiths under the Soviet occupation 1940-1988. No state religion, and freedom of religion since independence.

Religions	Pop %	Population	Ann Gr
Non-religious	54.00	723,308	1.0%
Christian	45.30	606,775	-1.4%
Ethnoreligionist	0.20	2,679	5.8%
Muslim	0.20	2,679	-0.1%
Jewish	0.15	2,009	-3.7%
Buddhist	0.08	1,072	9.7%
Other	0.07	938	6.8%

Christians	Denoms	Pop %	Affiliates	Ann Gr
Protestant	13	14.85	199,000	0.4%
Independent	39	1.04	14,000	2.9%
Anglican	1	0.03	<400	3.1%
Catholic	1	0.38	5,000	0.4%
Orthodox	5	14.67	196,000	-0.8%
Marginal	2	0.53	7,000	-0.2%
Unaffiliated		13.54	185,000	-4.4%

Churches	MegaBloc	Congs	Members	Affiliates
Lutheran Church	P	165	46,000	177,000
Orthodox Church	O	29	66,387	158,000
Estonian Orthodox	O	55	12,571	22,000
Old Believers	O	11	5,500	16,500
Ev Chr/Baptist Union	P	81	5,900	9,440
Jehovah's Witnesses	M	42	3,750	6,375
Catholic Church	C	7	1,821	5,100
Christian Pente Ch	P	38	2,556	4,600
Evang Char congs	I	13	1,450	2,422
Other denominations[50]		117	13,106	20,461
Total Christians[61]		**558**	**159,041**	**421,898**

TransBloc	Pop %	Population	Ann Gr
Evangelicals			
Evangelicals	4.9	65,726	0.5%
Renewalists			
Charismatics	1.9	25,956	1.8%
Pentecostals	0.6	7,930	1.2%

Missionaries from Estonia

P,I,A 22 long-term international in 12 agencies; 6 serving among the deaf in Southern Europe.

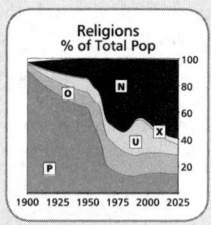

Religions % of Total Pop

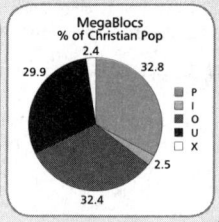

MegaBlocs % of Christian Pop

Challenges for Prayer

1 **Estonia is a former-Soviet success story,** as the small nation transitions to a more Western economy and political structure. However, poverty is not vanquished, and materialism's influence grows. There is a crisis of values, recognized even by the media and the state, as secularism and pluralism tighten their grip. Pray for righteousness and biblical values to be modelled by a wise and upright government.

2 **Religious freedom is an open door to Christian ministry** but also to theological error. Many marginal Christian sects are increasing in number and influence – Mormons have more missionaries in Estonia than any Christian agency has there. While actual practitioners are few, a recent poll showed 11% of Estonians expressed warmest feelings toward pre-Christian pagan religions. Pray for the truth and light of Christ to be established in this new marketplace of religious options.

3 **Despite a Protestant heritage, genuine faith in Estonia is rare.** Many have limited Christian belief, but very few follow Jesus in any meaningful way. Most of the population need to be re-evangelized. Young people have little to equip them against the predations of post-Christian values, since the traditional Christian confessions are weak and in decline. Pray for a new vision for evangelism and revival to reawaken the nominal majority.

4 **Unity in the Church is a potentially powerful witness** to a cynical population. The Estonian Evangelical Alliance seeks to foster unity in diversity among many denominations through fellowship and prayer events. Pray that all of Christ's faithful would demonstrate Christ's love for one another.

5 **Christian education and formation remain essential.** Preparing believers, both clergy and laity, for effective Christian living becomes more important as Estonia changes. Lutheran, Baptist, Methodist and Pentecostal seminaries or Bible schools all train pastors and lay Christians. Module-based correspondence courses are proving helpful in preparing believers in biblical faith and in an effective Christian life and witness.

6 **Ministry to minorities.** Specific outreach is needed for the large Russian population, with whom reconciliation is still a point for prayer. Pray also for the gospel to be shared with the Tatar Muslims, the Jews and the growing minority groups in Estonia.

7 **Student ministry continues to grow.** There is work in five universities with a view to expand further. Pray for outreach to the 50,000 university students; training Christians to ably share their faith is a need.

8 **Christian media.** Radio, television and printed media are all growing ministries. Radio 7 broadcasts the gospel over four frequencies.

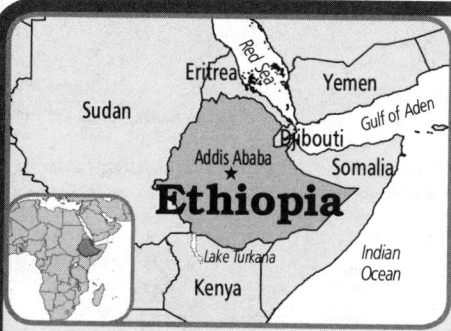

Ethiopia
Federal Democratic Republic of Ethiopia
Africa

Geography

Area 1,106,000 sq km. Fertile, mountain plateau surrounded by the drought-prone lowlands and deserts of the Red Sea coast; borders on Eritrea, Somalia, Kenya and Sudan. Landlocked since the secession of Eritrea.

Population		Ann Gr	Density
2010	84,975,606	2.62%	77/sq km
2020	107,964,331	2.33%	98/sq km
2030	131,560,907	1.89%	119/sq km

Capital Addis Ababa 2,929,626. **Urbanites** 17.6%. **Pop under 15 yrs** 44%. **Life expectancy** 54.7 yrs.

Peoples

The first three major categories consist of the Horn of Africa peoples – 97.8% of Ethiopia's population.
Semitic/Ethiopian 41.5%. 18 peoples including: Amhara 31.3%; Tigrinya 5.6%; Gurage(3) 1.7%; Silti 1.5%.

Cushitic 41.6%. Three main sub-groups:
Oromo 34.6%. 12 peoples. Hararghe 7.5%; Tulama 7.5%; Wallega 5.6%; Macha 5.4%; Selale 4.2%; Arsi 2.8%.
Somali 5.3%. 3 groups, large numbers shifting across border due to civil strife in Somalia.
Afar 1.7%. 3 groups.
Omotic 14.7%. 49 peoples in south and southwest; Sadama 3.1%; Wolaita 2.1%; Hadiyya 1.6%; Gamo 1.2%; Gedeo 1.1%; Kafa 1.0%; Kambata 1.0%.
Nilotic 1.0%. 19 peoples.
Other 1.2%. Other sub-Saharan African, Arab, Western, Asian.

Literacy 35.9%. **Official language** Amharic; majority of the population are able to speak it; English widely taught. Regional languages are very important. **All languages** 88. **Indigenous languages** 85. **Languages with Scriptures** 7Bi 17NT 19por 34w.i.p.

Economy

Heavily based on agriculture (50% of GNP), which in turn depends on unreliable weather and on exhausted land from 3,000 years of cultivation. The main export is coffee, which is believed to have originated in Ethiopia. Decades of underdevelopment due to war, famine and changing political systems. Increasingly frequent droughts and tensions with Eritrea and Somalia slow economic development. Chronic malnutrition of millions, but systemic dependence on foreign aid and food undermines the work ethic and local agriculture.
HDI Rank 171st/182. **Public debt** 32% of GDP. **Income/person** $333 (1% of USA).

Politics

One of the oldest nations known, with a long written history. Africa's oldest independent nation. Amhara-dominated Empire 1896-1974, with Italian occupation 1936-41. The revolution of 1974 overthrew the Emperor Haile Selassie and imposed Marxism on the country. Regional uprisings together with severe droughts and man-aided famines ultimately led to the collapse of Mengistu's Marxist regime in 1991. The Tigray-led democratic government federalized the country with a devolution of power to 10 regions, largely ethnically defined. The costly 1998-2000 war with Eritrea drained but unified the nation. The third successive election success in 2005 of Prime Minister Meles was bitterly contested and alleged to be fraudulent. Somalia's civil strife sees Ethiopia embroiled against the Islamist forces there.

Religion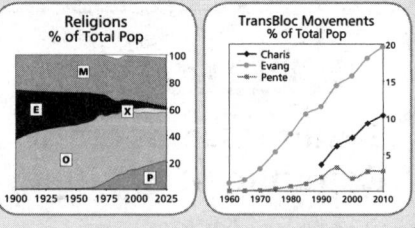

North Ethiopia was one of the first Christian nations – from the 4th Century. The Ethiopian Orthodox Church was the state church from 1270 until the 1974 revolution. The Marxist regime persecuted Christians, especially evangelicals, with many churches destroyed and congregations scattered. Since 1991, there has been freedom for worship and witness. Increasingly active and ambitious Islamist groups threaten the delicate balance of religious powers, even as Orthodox, Catholic and evangelical groups make overtures to one another and begin to work together.

Religions	Pop %	Population	Ann Gr
Christian	60.68	51,563,198	2.7%
Muslim	34.10	28,976,682	2.9%
Ethnoreligionist	3.70	3,144,097	-1.8%
Non-religious	1.50	1,274,634	6.4%
Baha'i	0.02	16,995	2.6%

Christians Denoms		Pop %	Affiliates	Ann Gr
Protestant	33	17.54	14,904,000	4.4%
Independent	24	1.66	1,412,000	2.6%
Anglican	1	<0.01	1,000	0.0%
Catholic	3	0.72	610,000	2.7%
Orthodox	3	39.52	33,584,000	1.9%
Marginal	2	0.03	28,000	4.6%
Unaffiliated		1.21	1,028,000	0.8%

Churches	MegaBloc	Congs	Members	Affiliates
Ethiopian Orthodox	O	20,620	19,869,822	33,580,000
Kale Heywet, KHC	P	7,714	3,250,000	6,500,000
Mekane Yesus, EECMY	P	10,158	1,371,382	5,279,822
Apostolic Church	I	1,293	388,000	970,000
Full Gospel,Mulu Wengel	P	1,317	329,200	823,000
Cath (Coptic & Roman)	C	555	360,947	610,000
Pentecostal Holiness	P	289	285,643	571,286
Heywet Birhane (AoG)	P	1,060	265,000	530,000
Meserete Kristos Ch	P	390	190,419	318,000
Seventh-day Adventist	P	451	158,000	237,000
Birhane Wengel Ch	P	290	58,086	176,000
Misgana Church	I	337	62,083	149,000
Sefer Genet (FFM)	P	436	65,455	144,000
Chs of Christ	P	618	61,800	93,936
Other denominations[51]		2,378	227,731	556,198
Total Christians[67]		**46,800**	**26,943,568**	**50,538,242**

TransBloc	Pop %	Population	Ann Gr
Evangelicals			
Evangelicals	19.6	16,657,376	4.3%
Renewalists			
Charismatics	10.3	8,787,079	5.0%
Pentecostals	2.7	2,286,612	3.0%

Answers to Prayer

1 **Sustained and remarkable growth of evangelical numbers** over the years is praiseworthy. Since the deposition of Haile Selassie in 1974, evangelicals have grown from 5% to 20%, a near-tenfold increase. The greatest growth has been in the last 20 years, and there are many signs that growth will continue, since outward vision and courageous evangelism continue.

2 **Unity among believers, forged through suffering, continues.** The Italian occupation (1936-1941) and Marxist period (1974–1990) saw harsh persecution. Many were martyred, but millions were won to Christ. Evangelical churches in Ethiopia suffered together then and are working together now. Bold and dynamic plans for church planting and evangelism among the less evangelized are being implemented.

3 **The Bible is increasingly distributed and read;** demand far outstrips supply. New translation projects are springing up amid several of the many languages. Access to the Bible in the Orthodox Church has brought tens of thousands into living faith in Christ. Increasingly, Orthodox churches are seeing the Spirit move, and they are relating more amicably with other Christian groups, including Catholics and evangelicals.

4 **There has been increased political stability,** economic growth and job opportunities in the past few years on a scale not seen for decades.

Challenges for Prayer

1 **The nation continues to be torn** with social, political and economic crises:

a) *Hostilities with neighbours Eritrea and Somalia* cripple efforts to revive and modernize the country. The Eritrean war was immensely costly in money and lives for no real gain. Embroilment in the civil conflict in Somalia could become a huge expense.

b) *Ethnic fragmentation remains a possibility.* Regionalization brings greater autonomy to the major ethnic groups – Amhara, Tigrinya, Oromo, Somali and Afar. Some scenarios could see federal power break down and tribalism increase.

c) *Corruption has increased with economic growth.* The country's resources are accumulating in the hands of a few. This is creating a widening gap between the multitudinous poor and the rich elite and is generating increasing resentment. Crime and corruption are becoming significant concerns for the nation.

2 **Poverty defines the lasting images of Ethiopia,** from the famines of the 1980s until now. Marxist mismanagement and droughts made Ethiopia dependent on hundreds of thousands of tonnes of food aid every year. This dependency continues, unbalancing the domestic economy and undermining local agriculture, and yet tens of thousands die annually of malnutrition. The careless application of aid can do more harm than good. Pray for better harvests, wise economic governance and outside assistance rightly applied.

3 **The Ethiopian Orthodox Church** is enduring a time of immense change. Centuries of isolation from the rest of the Christian world – as a Christian island in a sea of Islam – helped form its unique culture, theology and traditions.

a) *It had to adjust to losing political privilege under Communism,* which has only been partially restored since 1990. Syncretism and superstitions are widespread among millions of the more nominal Orthodox.

b) *The rapid spread of the use of Scriptures* and the growth of Protestant denominations led to millions of defections and the emergence of strong evangelical and charismatic networks within the Orthodox Church. Orthodoxy is learning to find common ground with evangelicals while retaining its own unique character.

c) *Pray for a deep work of the Holy Spirit* to revitalize this ancient Church, its biblical heritage and its spiritual legacy.

4 **Massive growth in Protestant and Independent churches** creates a great expectation for further harvest. Pray for:

a) *Revival and growth to be sustained* and for divisions and carnality to be avoided.

b) *Effective means for generating income to support Kingdom workers,* to develop the needed structures and facilities and to fund social programmes that are essential in the prevailing conditions of deep poverty. The Church must minister as the poor to the poor; pray for creative solutions to the challenges this brings.

c) *Continued unity and cooperation among leaders,* qualities forged through past suffering. Relationships among denominations seem stronger than the divisions that occur within denominations; pray against the dividing influences of the enemy and human pride. Pray especially for the Evangelical Churches Fellowship (ECFE), which represents the majority of evangelicals in the country.

d) *Missions vision* was birthed out of suffering during the Marxist regime and the withdrawal of Western agencies during that time. Through ECFE, a long-term strategy for evangelizing Ethiopia has emerged, one that includes intercession, focus on unevangelized peoples and church mobilization – only 3% of evangelical churches are regarded as being "mission-mobilized". The vision entails planting, cross-culturally, thousands more churches in all regions of Ethiopia and even sending to the Horn of Africa and South Asia.

5 **Leadership training** is identified as a major reason that the churches' potential is unfulfilled. The majority of church leaders have one year or less of training. Leadership is not meeting the demands (neither in numbers nor in quality) placed on it by such rapid church growth. Pray for the following:

a) *Post-graduate training* at the Ethiopian Graduate School of Theology in Addis Ababa. Pray for the provision of theologians and teachers who are godly and steeped in the Scriptures. Pray for provision for students who wish to pursue studies.

b) *Degree-level training* – the Evangelical Theological College (KHC and **SIM**), Mekane Yesu Theological Seminary, Meserete Kristos College, the Pentecostal Bible College, Berhane Wongel Theological College, Trinity College and St. Paul's (both Orthodox).

c) *The numerous Bible schools* across the country run by denominations, such as the 127 Amharic Bible schools (KHC) and Mekane Yesu with many more.

d) *The network of evening and short-term Bible schools and TEE programmes* around the country where many thousands of local leaders and evangelists are trained. The Berhan Media Ministry runs a widespread Bible Correspondence Course. Bible Training Centres for Pastors trains nearly 1,500 students as part of a TEE programme. Poverty and long distances make these programmes all the more essential.

6 **The less evangelized.** ECFE and **DAWN** cooperated on studies that established the need for further mission research, and identified 30 unevangelized peoples accounting for 25 million people, mostly away from the centre of the nation. There are Ethiopians working among all of these:

a) *The largely Muslim Somali, Harari and Afar regions* in the east. Many thousands of Somalis have crossed into Ethiopia, fleeing the violence at home. Ethiopian ethnic Somalis number 4.5 million and are one of Africa's least reached peoples. The number of Christians is growing, but ministry to these people comes at great risk and personal cost to those sharing.

b) *Many sections of Oromia,* especially in the east and south, are strongly Muslim and increasingly assertive within the federal framework. A number of agencies, foreign and national, reach out despite some hostility toward Christianity. Intertribal Oromi warfare has disrupted much work but gives opportunity to show compassion.

c) *The many peoples of the southwest,* bordering on Sudan, are isolated and smaller in numbers; some are nomadic. Nearly all are now engaged by evangelists and missionaries. Pray for healthy churches to be planted through pioneering work among the Aari, Bench, Bodi (5,000), Bumi (40,000), Hamer-Banna, Daasenach, Dime (15,000), Ebore (5,000), Karo (5,000), Me'en, Mali (39,000), Mursi (5,000), Tarra (15,000), Tsamai (20,000) and Wata (5,000).

7 **Islam is becoming a greater challenge.** Ethiopia has remained a bastion of Christianity, withstanding Islamic advances for centuries. Muslims now target this nation for Islamization – educational, employment and financial inducements are offered, a massive mosque-building programme is underway and thousands of wells are being drilled. Violent – even murderous – reactions against evangelical outreach create a climate of religious tension and fear, but this same violence causes many other Muslims to consider Jesus. Those committed to reaching Muslims for Christ demonstrate that, while costly, it is possible. From only a few hundred believers 10 years ago, there are now tens of thousands of believers from a Muslim background.

8 **Young people** make up the majority of Ethiopia's population – 70% are under the age of 30. Yet, far too little ministry is focused on reaching and discipling them. Among students, EVASUE(**IFES**) and **CCCI** see incredible growth and fruitfulness despite frequent opposition. Pray for children to be able to be schooled and to find employment as they finish. Pray also that church and parachurch ministries would make discipling the next generation a top priority.

9 **AIDS is a major scourge** of the nation; Ethiopia has the world's fifth-highest number of people with HIV/AIDS. About one million have already died of the disease, and another two million have HIV. Over one million have been orphaned by AIDS-related deaths. Many ministries are meeting this call for love and mercy. From local churches (such as KHC and Lutherans) to foreign agencies (**SIM**, Food for the Hungry) to other ministries (The Bible Society), Christians are working in education, prevention, counselling, home care and orphan ministry.

10 **Foreign mission workers** will never regain their pre-Marxist-revolution numbers or influence, but their role today is different. Lutheran and Pentecostal missions from the four Nordic nations have a long tradition of faithful service, as does **SIM**. The growing and maturing Church needs co-labourers and partners in areas such as training, Bible translation, reaching the last remaining unevangelized groups and especially in holistic ministry – health, agriculture, education and community development. The largest agencies are: **SIM**, Norwegian Lutheran Mission, Swedish Pentecostal Mission, Word for the World.

11 **Bible translation remains a major challenge.** Up to 88% of congregations use local languages in their meetings, so Bible translation is a must. There are 35 translation projects in progress; this represents nearly half of all living languages. Another 17 languages have translation needs that are currently unaddressed. Many groups are involved with projects: **WBT**, Mekane Yesu Church, KHC, **SIM**, The Bible Society and Word for the World. Pray for wisdom in knowing which projects are priorities, and pray for more nationals to become involved in them. A hugely ambitious Bible distribution programme by The Bible Society needs finance and prayer.

12 **Christian help ministries.**

F

a) Literature. Improved literacy and swelling populations create millions of new readers. Reading materials are increasing in various languages, and opportunities for "evangelism through literacy" are growing. Pray especially for good resources in minority languages, for youth-oriented literature and for widespread distribution in a country where poverty and poor infrastructure present many challenges.

b) Audio Scripture. This alternate format for presenting gospel material is vital and very much in demand in Ethiopia's oral society. **GRN** has 73 languages on offer, Faith Comes By Hearing has a successful audio programme and hundreds of "Bible Listening Groups" have sprung up, even among the Orthodox.

c) Radio. Religious broadcasting from within the country is prohibited. But there are about 77 hours per week of shortwave broadcasts – in Amharic, Tigrina, Oromo, Somali, Afar – by **TWR**, FEBA and Adventist World Radio. Pray for more foreign radio broadcasts aimed at Ethiopians and for the future opening of Ethiopia to local Christian radio.

North Atlantic Ocean
Torshavn
Norwegian Sea

Faeroe Islands

Shetland Islands
(United Kingdom)

Faeroe Islands

Europe

Geography

Area 1,399 sq km. Archipelago of 18 rugged islands between Iceland and Scotland, 16 of which are inhabited.

Population		Ann Gr	Density
2010	50,152	0.63%	36/sq km
2020	53,293	0.61%	38/sq km
2030	56,078	0.45%	40/sq km

Capital Torshavn 20,300. **Urbanites** 40.3%. **Pop under 15 yrs** 22.4%. **Life expectancy** 79.3 yrs.

Peoples 👤👤👤

Faeroese 97%.
Danish 2.6%.
Other 0.4%.
Literacy 99%. **Official languages** Faeroese, which is of the Scandinavian family; Danish. Both have Bibles.

Economy

The fishing industry (along with fish farming) accounts for 50% of the GDP and for almost all exports. There remains hope, although dwindling, of exploitable oil reserves, which would help diversify the economy.

Politics X

A self-governing region of Denmark. The parliamentary democracy is usually represented by coalition governments, and since it is not part of the EU, all trade is governed by special treaties.

Religion

Complete freedom of religion, although the Lutheran Church is recognized as the national church and is supported by a state-levied tax.

Religions	Pop %	Population	Ann Gr
Christian	90.59	45,433	0.5%
Non-religious	9.28	4,654	1.8%
Other	0.08	40	10.6%
Baha'i	0.05	25	0.6%

Christians	Denoms	Pop %	Affiliates	Ann Gr
Protestant	8	87.58	44,000	0.4%
Independent	1	0.96	<500	1.8%
Catholic	1	0.34	<200	2.5%
Marginal	1	0.31	<200	2.9%
Unaffiliated		1.40	1,000	0.0%

Churches	MegaBloc	Congs	Members	Affiliates
Lutheran Church	P	56	24,286	37,400
Christian Brethren	P	30	3,160	4,930
Pentecostal Church	P	8	680	1,047
House churches	I	10	287	480
Other denominations[7]		11	533	872
Total Christians[11]		**115**	**28,946**	**44,729**

TransBloc	Pop %	Population	Ann Gr
Evangelicals			
Evangelicals	28.8	14,430	2.0%
Renewalists			
Charismatics	5.2	2,632	2.3%
Pentecostals	2.1	1,047	1.5%

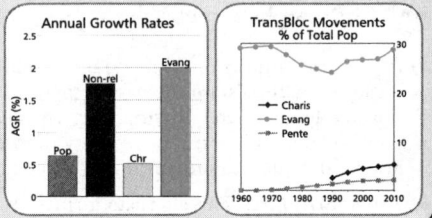

Challenges for Prayer

1 **Wisdom in government is needed** as large numbers of Islanders hope for a more independent future. Pray that God would give the leaders wisdom to oversee increasing autonomy from Denmark. Also pray that God would give them courage to make strong decisions in managing the shrinking fishing industry and the still-speculative oil industry – both having great environmental and social repercussions.

2 **The Faeroese need revival.** From the Lutheran Church (with many nominals as well as a solid evangelical contingent) to the Pentecostals and charismatics, local Christian leaders all agree that these islands are starting to see a fresh move of the Holy Spirit. The Lutheran Church has declined, but its recent independence from Danish Lutheranism sees an emerging evangelicalism, such as the growing Pietist Home Mission with 35 prayer houses and up to 5,000 affiliates. Pray for the Spirit to make the Faeroes truly Christian – and not just in name only.

3 **Evangelicals are many,** 29% of the population, in contrast to the mother country of Denmark. In particular, the Brethren churches make a significant impact as missionaries, both at home and abroad. The Faeroe Islands send a proportionately large number of missionaries – around 100 in more than 20 countries; pray that this may continue. Pray for the Spirit to continue impacting the Church in the Faeroe Islands; pray that Christians will be wise in engaging the postmodern and secular attitudes that increasingly challenge the primacy of the Bible and Christian tradition.

4 **Christian resources are plentiful** for this small population – two Bible translations (and one modern paraphrased NT being prepared), Christian Radio (Radio Lindin), Iktus Christian TV, online Bible in Faeroese, a Christian magazine and two bookstores. Pray that these may together have a strong impact on discipling the islands.

Falkland Islands

South Atlantic Ocean

Tierra del Fuego
Staten Is.
Argentina

Stanley

Falkland Islands

Latin America

Geography

Area 12,173 sq km. Consists of over 740 islands – 2 are inhabited year-round. South Georgia and the South Sandwich Islands also fall under the remit of the governor, despite having no permanent population. The Falklands are 600 km east of Patagonia in Argentina.

Population		Ann Gr	Density
2010	3,038	0.41%	0/sq km
2020	3,100	0.14%	0/sq km
2030	3,084	-0.10%	0/sq km

This does not include around 1,000 military personnel stationed on the islands.
Capital Stanley 2,200. **Urbanites** 73.6%. **Pop under 15 yrs** 16%.

Peoples

British 95%.
Other 5%.
Literacy 99%. **Official language** English.

Economy

Fishing is a mainstay of the economy, supplemented by sheep farming, tourism and the British military presence. There is no unemployment; future exploitation of offshore oil reserves could herald further income.

Politics

Self-governing British Overseas Territory. Argentinean claims on the islands as the Islas Malvinas led to the 1982 conflict. The 2009 constitution makes the islands virtually self-sufficient and self-governing (apart from the issue of defence) and reflects the mindset of the Islanders.

Religion

Freedom of religion.

Religions	Pop %	Population	Ann Gr
Christian	65.20	1,981	-0.2%
Non-religious	33.50	1,018	1.7%
Other	0.90	27	-1.7%
Baha'i	0.40	12	0.4%

Christians Denoms		Pop %	Affiliates	Ann Gr
Protestant	5	4.71	<1,000	-2.6%
Anglican	1	26.50	1,000	-0.6%
Catholic	1	18.50	1,000	-0.5%
Marginal	1	0.26	<1,000	0.0%
Unaffiliated		15.20	<1,000	0.0%

Churches	MegaBloc	Congs	Members	Affiliates
Ch of England in F	A	1	35	805
Catholic Church	C	2	225	562
United Free Church	P	1	25	100
Other denominations[5]		3	35	51
Total Christians[8]		**7**	**320**	**1,518**

TransBloc	Pop %	Population	Ann Gr
Evangelicals			
Evangelicals	10.8	329	-0.1%
Renewalists			
Charismatics	3.0	91	2.1%

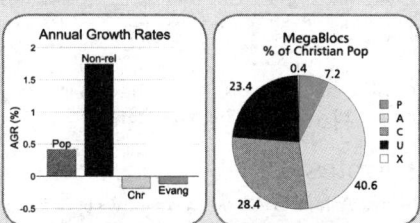

Annual Growth Rates — AGR (%): Non-rel, Pop, Chr, Evang

MegaBlocs % of Christian Pop: 0.4, 7.2, 23.4, 40.6, 28.4 — P, A, C, U, X

F

Challenges for Prayer

1 **The issues of sovereignty and autonomy** are keys to understanding the Falkland Islands' history and mentality. The political wrangling between the UK and Argentina, which culminated in the 1982 conflict, does not adequately reflect the Islanders' overwhelming desire for self-governance; the 2009 constitution does. Pray for wise and fair agreements and for understanding among all three parties for the sake of the diplomatic and economic life of the whole region. Pray also for Christians working and praying for reconciliation of all involved.

2 **There are only three significant denominations** among the Islanders (Anglican, Roman Catholic and Tabernacle United Free Church). Most of the population are very nominal in what faith they may have. Pray for a renewal of faith in all three of these groups. Pray for believers in their witness to fellow Islanders and to fishermen, oilmen and tourists of different nationalities who stop off in the islands.

3 **The British forces** based on these windswept but spectacular islands enjoy the support of the local populace, but are far from home. Pray for the work of chaplains ministering to them as well as the Oasis coffee shop, an outreach ministry on the military base itself. Pray for believers in the forces as they witness to their comrades.

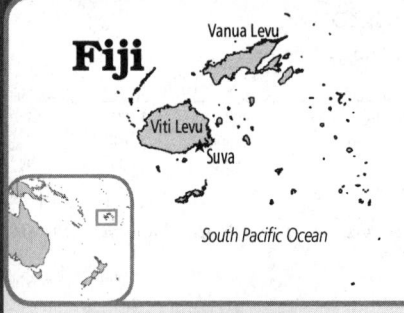

Fiji
Vanua Levu
Viti Levu
Suva
South Pacific Ocean

Fiji

Sovereign Democratic Republic of Fiji

Pacific

Geography

Area 18,274 sq km. Two larger and 110 smaller inhabited islands, both volcanic and coralline.

Population		Ann Gr	Density
2010	854,098	0.62%	47/sq km
2020	887,759	0.31%	49/sq km
2030	918,474	0.29%	50/sq km

Capital Suva 176,000. **Urbanites** 53.4%. **Pop under 15 yrs** 31%. **Life expectancy** 68.7 yrs.

Peoples

South Asian 36.7%. Mainly descendants of indentured labour imported by the British between 1879 and 1916; also subsequent Gujarati and Sikh immigrants. Hindi 20.8%; Bihari 2.4%; Gujarati 2.2%; Bengali 2.1%; Tamil 7.4%.
Fijian 52.0%. Speaking six related main languages and 30 dialects, Melanesian and Polynesian elements. Includes mixed Euro-Fijians.
Other 11.3%. Vanuatan 6.4%; Caucasian 1.4%; Rotuman (on Rotuman Island) 1.2%; Solomons 0.8%; many other immigrants from other Pacific islands; Chinese 0.7%.
Literacy 92.9%. **Official language** English; Hindustani and Bau Fijian commonly used. **All languages** 21. **Indigenous languages** 10. **Languages with Scriptures** 4Bi 1por 3w.i.p.

Economy

One of the Pacific's most well developed economies, based largely on tourism and sugar. Consistent budget and trade deficits mean that Fiji is one of the world's largest per capita recipients of aid. The Indian community dominates nearly all commercial activities but lacks long-term security, with almost all land rights denied them. This has in turn caused significant emigration, a brain-drain the country can ill afford.
HDI Rank 108th/182. **Public debt** 8.4% of GDP. **Income/person** $4,094 (9% of USA).

Politics

British rule 1874-1970. Post-independence calm, inter-racial balance and relative harmony are consistently disrupted by military coups. In 1987 and 2000, Fijian ethnic interests were at the heart of the coups, in undermining the elected governments with strong Indian elements. The coup in 2006 occurred on the pretext of stopping corruption and endemic racism, but was more likely retribution for the clemency extended to previous coup plotters as well as prevention of ethnic Fijian interests from establishing themselves again. In every case, the coups have been universally condemned by the global community and resulted in expulsion/ suspension from the Commonwealth as well as sanctions. Sadly, such actions seem not to prevent further coups, and the ones suffering most from such actions are the poor of all races.

Religion

Religious freedom exists, but there are accusations that much of the political machinery favours Christianity against minority religions and that it tightly aligns with Methodism in particular.

Religions	Pop %	Population	Ann Gr
Christian	65.05	555,591	1.2%
Hindu	27.81	237,525	-0.3%
Muslim	5.70	48,684	-0.4%
Non-religious	0.60	5,125	-2.4%
Sikh	0.53	4,527	0.3%

Baha'i	0.28	2,391	-0.1%	Anglican Church	A	57	4,255	6,850
Chinese	0.02	171	0.6%	Other denominations[24]		222	12,056	23,965
Jewish	0.01	85	0.6%	*Doubly affiliated Pentecostals*				*-14,250*
				Doubly affiliated				*-42,750*

Christians Denoms		Pop %	Affiliates	Ann Gr
Protestant	14	45.91	392,000	0.6%
Independent	16	10.59	90,000	3.3%
Anglican	1	0.80	7,000	0.4%
Catholic	1	11.59	99,000	1.6%
Marginal	3	2.83	24,000	2.2%
Doubly affiliated		*-6.67*	*-57,000*	*0.0%*

Total Christians[35]		2,790	285,612	555,595

TransBloc	Pop %	Population	Ann Gr
Evangelicals			
Evangelicals	25.2	215,408	2.1%
Renewalists			
Charismatics	17.5	149,723	2.7%
Pentecostals	8.2	70,350	1.7%

Churches	MegaBloc	Congs	Members	Affiliates
Methodist Church	P	1,134	56,703	258,000
Catholic Church	C	47	51,563	99,000
Assemblies of God	P	650	65,000	69,500
Chr Mission Fellowship	I	161	32,222	58,000
Seventh-day Adventist	P	250	27,000	41,580
Latter-day Saints (Mormon)	M	55	8,939	16,000
Apostles GOF Int	I	40	8,500	12,500
United Pentecostal Ch	P	67	10,000	10,500
Chr Outreach Centre	I	70	6,294	9,000
Jehovah's Witnesses	M	37	3,080	7,700

Religions % of Total Pop

TransBloc Movements % of Total Pop

Challenges for Prayer

1 **British colonial greed left a long-term legacy** of rival ethnicities and segregation in Fiji:

a) Indigenous Fijians have long resented imported Indian indentured labourers, from 1870 onward. At times, Fijians were a minority in their own country. This challenge has resulted in a positive restoring of many traditional Fijian ways, but also a negative protectionist bias in politics and land issues.

b) The Indian communities work hard to build up what they have and yet feel little security in a nation where they cannot own land and where systemic racism undermines their efforts. Their treatment by the British and then by Fijians discredits the gospel in the eyes of most Indians. Pray for a spirit of repentance and reconciliation and for a society marked by freedom and equality.

2 **Fiji's social and political problems are many.** Alcoholism and broken homes are major social ills that need to be addressed nationwide. But greater still is a political issue – there have been four coups in the last two decades; every time the country seems about to turn the corner, another coup disrupts and destabilizes progress. Pray that righteousness and justice might be established and the rule of law and democratically elected governments observed.

3 **The Methodist Church has been the de facto state church** in Fiji for 150 years as well as the faith of the majority of ethnic Fijians. It has also been tightly aligned with the nation's political structures – to the detriment of the gospel. Methodism's past failure to adequately condemn the endemic racism and racially motivated coups has prompted splits within the Church. A lack of spiritual vitality has spurred a large-scale exodus to newer denominations. But there has also been change in recent years as issues of renewal and reconciliation have come to the fore. Pray for new life and right priorities for this highly influential denomination.

4 **New churches with spiritual dynamism and evangelistic vision** have surged in growth in the last decade; Pentecostal groups are the most notable among these. Also within the Methodist, Anglican and Catholic churches are strong evangelical/charismatic movements. There are many claims of great revival in Fiji, and there is undeniable fruit of God at work in remarkable ways, as individuals, communities and even the environment see transformation. Some specific areas that warrant prayer:

a) Unity. The Association of Christian Churches of Fiji was formed after the 2000 coup to establish unity and reconciliation. It is composed of mostly evangelical Protestant churches and has a great impact. The more ecumenical Fiji Council of Churches also works toward the same goal. The Evangelical Fellowship of Fiji exists to unite evangelicals.

b) Leadership training for the many churches. There is a wealth of options as the Methodists, **AoG**, Baptists, Nazarenes, Catholics and others offer training programmes and degrees. In addition, the interdenominational Pacific Theological College offers degrees up to doctoral level. World Harvest Institute (Christian Mission Fellowship), South Pacific Missionary Training Centre and Fiji College of Theology and Evangelism focus on training for mission and evangelism.

c) Mission vision. Fiji was once a hotbed of mission-sending throughout the Pacific. This legacy is being revived as **YWAM**, **WEC** and **CMF** have been prominent in channeling Fijians to mission fields around the world. The Deep Sea Canoe Mission seeks to foster a missions vision. Pray for existing missions and for a greater future of Fijian missionary investment.

5 **Less-reached peoples.** The Indians of Fiji form the largest non-Christian community in the Pacific. As few as 3% of them claim to be Christian. The greatest challenges for Indian-majority churches are developing (and retaining) mature and experienced leaders and integrating with the rest of the body of Christ. For specific prayer:

a) Hindus remain mostly unevangelized. The number of converts to Christianity is accelerating. **AoG** in particular but also Methodists, Baptists and Pentecostals have seen fruit from this ministry. Multi-racial congregations are springing up among them. **Pioneers** also has church planting ministries committed to reaching Indians. Pray for real disciples and not mere surface converts; pray also for more culturally appropriate outreach to this people. The minority of Indo-Fijians who are Christians are taking initiative in reaching their own people.

b) Sikhs and Punjabis retain more of their culture and language, but there is little specific outreach to them. Many are emigrating to Antipodean or Western countries.

c) Gujaratis in particular have remained unevangelized among all Fiji's South Asian origin peoples. They have largely retained their caste structures. There are only a few believers from among this group, and no specifically focused outreach to them has ever been made.

d) The Muslim community is tightly knit, very resistant to the gospel and increasingly Islamized via Saudi and Pakistani influence. Little is being done to reach them; the few converts to Christ suffer from considerable persecution and from the churches' failure to integrate them. Several Fijian villages have become Muslim. An increasing awareness, regionally and globally, of this people – the Pacific Islands' largest unreached group – has generated a groundswell of attention and prayer; locally, this is translating into encouraging signs of spiritual interest and response from the Muslim community.

6 **Christian help ministries** in Fiji have a Pacific-wide impact. Pray for:

a) Christian literature. The Bible Society of the South Pacific is based in Fiji. Pray for translation work, printing and distribution of God's Word throughout the Pacific. Translation and revision work in Fijian and Fiji Hindi are both needed, since good Christian material is lacking in these two languages. Thank God for progress of the NT in Fijian Hindi. **CLC** has recently opened three Christian bookshops.

b) Ministry to young people. Fiji has serious sociological problems among its youth, yet there is a responsiveness that needs to be met. Pray for those specifically ministering to young people in Fiji and the Pacific – **CEF**, **YFC**, SU and **YWAM** among youth, and Pacific Students for Christ (**IFES**) and **CCCI** among students. The University of the Pacific in Fiji has students from every island territory and is strategic for impacting many islands which have much nominal Christianity.

c) The more remote communities are much less reached and resourced by the Church. **YWAM**'s Mobile Ministry seeks to reach these communities by ship and by truck, sharing the gospel and providing medical and dental care.

d) Media ministry. Fiji has Christian TV and radio stations run from within the country. Pray that they might be fruitful in reaching and discipling many. Radio programmes and the JESUS film are available in all the major languages of Fiji.

Finland

Republic of Finland

Europe

Geography

Area 338,145 sq km. This northern country is 70% forest, 10% lake, 8% arable land.

Population		Ann Gr	Density
2010	5,345,826	0.38%	16/sq km
2020	5,495,753	0.24%	16/sq km
2030	5,543,810	0.04%	16/sq km

Capital Helsinki 1,116,608. **Urbanites** 63.9%.
Pop under 15yrs 17%. **Life expectancy** 79.5 yrs.

Peoples

Finno-Ugric 97.6%. Finns 97.6%, of which 5.5% are Swedish-speaking, largely in SW and on Åland Islands in the Gulf of Bothnia; Saami(3) 0.05%.
Other European 0.9%. Russian 0.5%.
Other 1.5%. Immigrant groups, mainly from Middle East and East Asia.
Literacy 100%. **Official languages** Finnish, Swedish, Saami, sign language. **All languages** 23.
Indigenous languages 12. **Languages with Scriptures** 4Bi 1NT 6por 4w.i.p.

Economy

Specialized and primarily high-tech, export-oriented economy, supported by the traditional economy based largely on wood products. Solid economic growth since the late 1990s, but unemployment (especially of minorities) remains a concern.
HDI Rank 12th/182. **Public debt** 33.7% of GDP. **Income/person** $51,588 (109% of USA).

Politics

Ruled by Sweden for 700 years, then by Russia for a further 100. Independent in 1917. A stable multiparty democracy. Member of EU.

Religion

Freedom of religion, but Evangelical Lutheran and Finnish (Greek) Orthodox Churches are recognized as national churches.

Religions	Pop %	Population	Ann Gr
Christian	83.75	4,477,129	0.0%
Non-religious	15.54	830,741	2.4%
Muslim	0.56	29,937	5.8%
Other	0.11	5,880	2.3%
Jewish	0.02	1,069	0.4%
Hindu	0.01	535	0.4%
Baha'i	0.01	535	0.4%

Christians Denoms		Pop %	Affiliates	Ann Gr
Protestant	34	83.25	4,450,000	-0.2%
Independent	11	0.03	2,000	2.6%
Anglican	1	<0.01	<200	-1.0%
Catholic	1	0.18	10,000	3.5%
Orthodox	3	1.11	60,000	0.6%
Marginal	8	0.56	30,000	-1.4%
Doubly affiliated		*-1.38*	*-74,000*	*0.0%*

Churches	MegaBloc	Congs	Members	Affiliates
Evang Lutheran Ch	P	1,348	1,685,547	4,315,000
Finnish Pentecostal Ch	P	223	52,000	96,200
Greek Orth (Finnish)	O	127	39,860	57,000
Jehovah's Witnesses	M	300	17,500	24,500
Evangelical Free Ch	P	102	14,800	19,240
Catholic Church	C	15	6,643	9,500
Seventh-day Adventist	P	70	3,800	5,054
Latter-day Saints (Mormon)	M	30	2,849	4,530
Free Russian Orthodox	O	3	1,840	2,300
Pentecostal Friends	P	1	120	200
Other denominations[47]		275	11,614	18,033
Doubly affiliated				*-73,800*
Total Christians[58]		**2,494**	**1,836,573**	**4,477,757**

TransBloc	Pop %	Population	Ann Gr
Evangelicals			
Evangelicals	12.1	648,682	-0.1%
Renewalists			
Charismatics	6.2	331,145	0.1%
Pentecostals	1.9	100,796	0.5%

Missionaries from Finland
P,I,A 908 long-term in about 70 countries; 8 serving cross-culturally in Finland.

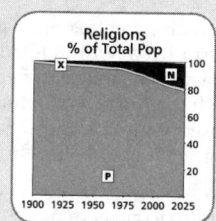

Religions
% of Total Pop

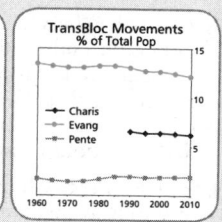

TransBloc Movements
% of Total Pop

Answers to Prayer

1 **Finland's strong Christian tradition and geographical location** give it a strategic role in reaching the many peoples in the former Soviet Union. Of particular importance is the impact of ministry-oriented Finnish believers on the Finno-Ugric peoples of Russia's interior, their distant ethnic cousins.

2 **The nation is one of the most affluent and peaceful on earth.** It consistently ranks at or near the top of the table in global surveys that measure civil liberties, education, peace, income, stability and environmental issues. While this is a point for thanksgiving, pray also that this would be a platform for generous giving and committed ministry and outreach.

3 **The legacy of missionary sending remains strong,** even as the Church faces the challenge of stagnation and decline. Finns and their churches are effective at sending out missionaries, especially to the unevangelized world.

F Challenges for Prayer

1 **Humanism, secularism and materialism have strangleholds** on most Finns. While the majority (90%) look favourably upon the Church's social work, only 8% of Finns attend any kind of religious service monthly or more, and only 3% of Lutherans attend weekly. Spirituality has more or less become privatized. Christians may number 84% of the population, but society is effectively a secular one. The last revival occurred during the 1960s. Interest in spiritual things offers some hope, but Islam and fringe religious movements are currently the fastest growing. Pray for a spiritual breakthrough that will cause people to seek the Lord.

2 **The Lutheran Church retains a stronger evangelical tradition** than most state churches, partly a heritage of the revival movements of the past that have influenced its spirituality. The large majority still claim affiliation with Lutheranism, but much of it is a nominal or social attachment. Only around 12% of Lutherans would be regarded as evangelical. The wider Lutheran Church faces several challenges:

a) Liberalism. To a large degree, the teachings and direction of the Church are shifting from traditional biblical values to a much broader morality. This is the source of much controversy, since the prophetic role of the Church in society is blunted.

b) Independent and lay movements within the national Church framework. There are many such groups, a large number from a revivalist background. It is in these that most committed Lutherans find their fellowship and platform for evangelism. They may face increasing restrictions in their evangelical preaching and teaching from a liberal Lutheran hierarchy, but these groups are a very important element of Finland's spiritual life. Pray for their continued freedom to function and lead in many aspects of spiritual life.

c) Younger leadership. Increasingly, aging church populations find themselves out of touch with a younger generation. A more vibrant spirituality must replace traditional religious and cultural forms. Sadly, a growing number of younger, more evangelical Lutherans are frozen out of leadership positions precisely because their faith is too dynamic! Pray that these vibrant younger evangelicals might not lose heart, and pray that God will open doors for them to have a great revitalizing effect on the national Church.

d) Future tensions. As with many mainline groups elsewhere, a major fault line is appearing in Finnish Lutheranism between the liberal element and a more evangelical, conservative element. How this plays out, and who is perceived as causing the conclusive schism, will profoundly shape both the Lutheran Church and Finnish perceptions of Christianity. Some of the more conservative groups and fellowships have already split off and formed new denominations along what they believe to be more biblically faithful teaching.

3 **The Free Churches,** both Pentecostal and non-Pentecostal, are relatively small but spiritually vigorous; charismatic renewal has had a marked impact. These churches are not growing, but they are holding their own in a wide context of decline. These groups are enjoying a greater unity than in years past. Pray for this to continue, for cooperation in evangelism and missions among these various bodies, and between the Free Churches and Lutherans.

4 **A new paradigm for the Church is required** if it is to grow in Finland. An ultra-modern country such as Finland probably needs some structural reformation in the Church and some new expressions of faith. This is particularly true for the next generation, who are less traditional and more pragmatic about Christian spirituality. Specific issues:

a) The many rootless believers who "church-hop" and lack commitment to one fellowship. And many disillusioned believers with genuine faith don't engage in any fellowship at all. Pray that the Spirit would convict them to integrate more fully into His body.

b) The widespread growth of house groups. Some of these groups are planted by Lutheran revival movements, some by other denominations and some are independent of churches altogether. Pray for ways for these groups to integrate themselves into the larger faith scene and to have a profound spiritual impact on the unchurched.

5 **Ministry to young people** is still valuable. A high proportion of Finnish young people attend confirmation camps; this is an opportunity for them to come to a living faith in Christ. Pray for believing and godly camp leaders. Pray for the student ministries of the Evangelical Lutheran Student Mission (**IFES**, in 15 of 20 university cities), LEAF and **CCCI**. Interest and responsiveness are not problems in Finland: good follow-up and discipleship are.

6 **The heritage of sending missionaries is under threat.** The strength of mission sending has largely been through parachurch agencies or independent movements within the larger Lutheran framework. The churches need to catch a missions vision and become more involved in the sending process, rather than relying totally on agencies. But an over-centralization of mission-sending structures, under the rubric of the Lutheran Church, could drastically stunt missions as it could effectively isolate mission sending from the congregations altogether. The disconnectedness of many Finns from local churches doesn't help the situation. Specific mission-mobilizing events have helped bring together different agencies and raise the profile of missions. Pray for more workers as well as more supporters.

7 **Particularly needy sectors of society** include:

a) Immigrant minority groups. Although Finland has one of Europe's lower immigration rates, there are still many minority groups to reach. The number of foreign university students is growing; many of these are from other faiths. Very few churches are actively reaching out to unreached immigrant groups. Pray that foreigners in Finland might have the chance to encounter Jesus in a real and attractive way. Praise God that, at the same time, much of the immigrant population is from a Christian background bringing a vibrant church life to their newfound host country.

b) Indigenous minorities are small in number but unique in culture. The Saami people of Lapland are Europe's last truly nomadic people group, and number over 100,000 across the Nordic countries. They are nominally Lutheran, but with an underlying animistic worldview. Pray for the ministries working with them. Pray also for a flourishing of culturally relevant expressions of Christian faith in their midst.

c) Men's ministry is a real need in Finland. Discipling men is difficult in a highly passive and private culture. Pray for ministries that will be able to call Finns into relationships that involve pastoring, mentoring and accountability.

France

Republic of France
Europe

Geography 🌍

Area 543,965 sq km. The largest country in Western Europe.

Population		Ann Gr	Density
2010	62,636,580	0.53%	115/sq km
2020	64,930,944	0.32%	119/sq km
2030	66,473,807	0.21%	122/sq km

Capital Paris 10,485,263. **Other major cities** Marseille 1.5 mill; Lyon 1.5m; Lille 1.0m; Nice 977,202; Toulouse 912,115. **Urbanites** 77.8%. **Pop under 15yrs** 18%. **Life expectancy** 81 yrs.

Peoples 👪

Indigenous and immigrant ethnic-minority figures are approximate due to naturalization, assimilation, illegal immigration and a lack of official statistics.

European 83.5%.
  French 69.5%. Regional identities have faded with increased movement of people within France and standardization of modern French.
  Germanic 5.1%. Alsatian 2.6%; Fleming 1.3%; German 1.0%.
  Other European 8.9%. Italian 1.7%; Basque 1.4%; Portuguese 1.4%; Slav(6) 1.4%; Spaniard 1.1%; Armenian 0.7%; Catalonian 0.5%.
North African/Middle Eastern 9.2%. Berber (Kabyle, Shawiya, Riff, others) 5.6%; North African Arab 2.0%; Levant Arab 0.6%; many other Middle Eastern/West Asian peoples.
African/Caribbean 4.0%. Representing every francophone nation, most West and Central African ethnic groups and French Caribbean ethnicities.
Asian 2.0%. Vietnamese 0.9%; Chinese 0.4%; Lao/Hmong 0.2%.
Other 1.3%. Jews 0.8%; Romani(4) 0.4%.
Literacy 99%. **Official language** French. Regional languages in decline. French is the first language of 136 million people worldwide. **All languages** 62. **Indigenous languages** 23. **Languages with Scriptures** 10Bi 3NT 11por 2w.i.p.

Economy 📊

The sixth-largest economy in the world. A solid base in agriculture and industry as well as the world's foremost tourist destination, leading to a strong service industry. Socialized economic policies provide good public service (such as health care), infrastructure and a highly trained professional workforce, but they have created a system prone to bureaucracy and strikes. Some sectors were hit hard by the economic downturn of 2008-2009. Systemic resistance to reform, coupled with fear of impending decline, paralyzes decisive action to improve the economy. Yet, this same conservatism guarded against even greater financial damage in 2008-09. Some of the immigrant/minority communities form a restive and, at times, violent economic underclass.
HDI Rank 8th/182. **Public debt** 68.1% of GDP. **Income/person** $46,037 (97% of USA).

Politics ❌

Democratic republic with a strong presidency/executive balanced by parliament. Left-right polarization of major parties. Traditionally centralized, but devolving toward regions and departments. A core member of the EU, trying to clarify its role in global politics while addressing serious challenges internally that have emerged from unassimilated minorities/immigrants.

Religion ⛪

Before the 1789 Revolution, a long history of severe persecution of dissenters and reformers; now a resolutely secular state with freedom of religion. Anti-sectarian legislation was passed in 2000, and obvious religious apparel is banned for those working in public services and education. Traditionally dominant Catholicism has been in decline for decades, while atheism and other faith groups grow. The government currently forbids collecting data on individuals' religious faith, so all statistics are estimates.

Religions	Pop %	Population	Ann Gr
Christian	61.14	38,296,005	-0.6%
Non-religious	26.03	16,304,302	2.4%
Muslim	10.50	6,576,841	2.8%
Buddhist	0.97	607,575	1.8%
Jewish	0.94	588,784	-0.9%
Other	0.40	250,546	0.5%
Baha'i	0.02	12,527	0.5%

Christians Denoms		Pop %	Affiliates	Ann Gr
Protestant	100	1.91	1,193,000	1.1%
Independent	31	0.14	86,000	3.7%
Anglican	1	0.03	18,000	-1.1%
Catholic	3	57.58	36,068,000	-0.7%
Orthodox	12	1.05	660,000	1.1%
Marginal	16	0.56	350,000	0.1%
Doubly affiliated		-0.13	-80,000	0.0%

Churches	MegaBloc	Congs	Members	Affiliates
Catholic Church	C	32,200	10,457,500	41,830,000
Reformed Church	P	479	50,000	300,000
Armenian Apos, W Eu	O	118	118,000	295,000
Assemblies of God	P	920	65,714	230,000
Jehovah's Witnesses	M	1,540	135,000	211,000
Ch of Augsburg (Luth)	P	315	119,760	200,000
Orthodox Church	O	23	6,000	133,000
Gypsy Evang Mission	P	191	34,535	115,000
Russian Orthodox Chs	O	108	53,947	82,000
Greek Orthodox Ch	O	43	55,639	74,000
Evang Lutheran Ch	P	47	4,000	40,000
Ref Ch, Alsace&Lorraine	P	52	2,400	36,000
Full Gospel Federation	P	86	16,000	26,720
Brethren Assem (Darby)	P	104	12,500	24,500
Seventh-day Adventist	P	130	12,500	13,400
Eglises d'Expressions Afr	P	38	5,909	13,000
Indep Reformed Ch	P	37	2,500	13,000
Eglise Prot Evangelique	P	6	5,300	6,625
Other denominations[141]		3,006	298,831	532,324
Disaffiliated				-5,800,000
Doubly affiliated				-80,000
Total Christians[163]		**39,443**	**11,456,035**	**38,295,569**

TransBloc	Pop %	Population	Ann Gr
Evangelicals			
Evangelicals	1.0	603,192	2.4%
Renewalists			
Charismatics	1.0	633,830	2.8%
Pentecostals	0.7	417,182	2.7%

Other studies identify a smaller number of evangelicals in France, but differences in definitions and methodology can account for the discrepancy.

Religions % of Total Pop

Annual Growth Rates

F

Answers to Prayer

1 **Evangelical Christianity has grown** over the last 50 years despite the systemic secularization of society, religious indifference and decline in church involvement. In 1960, evangelicals in France numbered 180,000; by 1990, they had reached nearly 400,000, and in 2010, they were 600,000. Evangelicals meet in over 2,500 fellowships with dozens more forming every year.

2 **An encouraging growth of unity among evangelicals** has emerged in recent years out of a history of division and lack of cooperation. Through the French Evangelical Alliance, the French Evangelical Federation and the larger Pentecostal and charismatic unions, the National Council of French Evangelicals (CNEF) was initiated in 2001. It has since grown and now represents most of the 43 church unions of all denominations as the voice for evangelical Protestants in France.

Challenges for Prayer

1 **France as a politico–economic entity is at a crossroads.** Amid a brave fight against globalization, radical reforms are urgently needed in industry and in state economic structures. France, like many European nations with an aging population, must face the inevitable and unsustainable pressure on the pension system and retirement age. Painful decisions that are right for the country must be made despite opposition. Coupled with this is the increasing tension between traditional French identity and the growing, restive immigrant community; the model of integration in which France has taken pride no longer appears to function. The majority of French are content individually but place little confidence in the collective future of the Republic; too many centrifugal social forces are at play.

2 **Major spiritual strongholds** hinder acceptance of the gospel:

a) France's religious history is stained with violence – the bloody wars of religion in the 16th Century which claimed 200,000 lives, the brutal persecutions of the Huguenots in the 17th Century and the French Revolution in 1789-1801. Starting with the Reformation and then Counter-Reformation, France moved through the Enlightenment to philosophically culminate in modern-day atheistic existentialism and a materialist view of life.

b) *The widespread involvement with occult practices.* There are more people earning a living in occult practices than there are registered doctors, and 10 times more than evangelical pastors and missionaries. The spiritual vacuum created by aggressive secularism has been filled with witchcraft and esotericism, since most French have no meaningful contact with dynamic Christian faith.

3 **The accelerating decline of religious faith** since the 18th Century has seen France's Catholic and mainline Protestant legacies plummet in recent years, even as atheism has grown. Hostility toward organized religion as well as the privatization of spirituality mean that regular attendance in any church is below 8%. Some surveys show that over 30% of French people are non-religious. Most French have a profound ignorance of, or indifference to, the gospel, many having never meaningfully encountered it. Yet, the relativism of postmodernity has generated acute emptiness and existential angst; as many have noted, this in turn has created a spiritual hunger that has grown rapidly in recent years. Pray that such hunger might overcome the suspicion toward religion. Pray that Christians would be prepared to patiently and relationally share Jesus with those who seek.

4 **The Catholic Church has lost much of its influence** in society, a process accelerating since the 1980s. In 2005, only 150 men in France completed training for the priesthood. Recent polls suggest as few as 51% of French self-identify as Catholic – but this still constitutes a majority of the population. Tensions exist among conservative traditionalists, liberals, modernists, radicals and charismatics; the traditionalists (opposed to the "liberalizing" Vatican II changes) and charismatics are the most vigorous wings of the Church today. Such rapid decline has removed from Catholicism much of the meaningless ritual and paternalism and has taught humility. The Alpha Course is widely used in Catholic parishes. Pray for these changes to bring gospel light and life to French Catholicism.

5 **Protestants were accepted** at the Reformation, and at one stage some estimate that up to 25% of the French population had embraced the new teaching. But persecution (from the mid-16th Century until the late 18th Century), humanism and nominalism (in the last 200 years) have reduced this to 1.9% in 2010. Protestantism – though widely respected – is spiritually compromised by liberal theology, universalism and the acceptance of contradictory doctrinal and ethical views. Protestants are more numerous in Alsace and the south, but nominalism and decline are common. Yet there are staunch evangelical believers in most Reformed and Lutheran congregations. Pray for restoration to the faith and commitment shown by their martyr forebears.

6 **Evangelical Christians are few** (1.0% across all confessions), split between many denominations and confessions. They demonstrate high levels of commitment and are a younger population than France's average. Growth is steady, and a new congregation is planted almost every week. Pentecostals and charismatics are the fastest growing. This is all in the face of strong secularizing trends in public life. Pray for:

a) *The public perception of evangelicals.* To most French people, the evangelical message is still seen as an alien ideology of immigrant groups and of the American right wing rather than an indigenous expression of spirituality. This bias has led to discrimination and difficulties in dealing with local authorities. Pray for transparency and good conduct by evangelicals that will demonstrate the positive impact on society their faith can have.

b) *Unity among true believers* has made great strides in recent years. Most evangelicals can be found in member churches of the CNEF or the *Fédération Protestante*. Further cooperation is being planned, at times involving believing Catholics as well. Pray especially for a deepening of unity between the various immigrant churches and French indigenous congregations.

c) *The fast-growing minority churches,* especially Africans, Antilleans and Gypsies. More than 250 ethnic churches exist just in the greater Paris area, and more pop up every month. The passion and faith of these groups bring new verve to evangelicalism, but they suffer a negative bias from local government and media, which is generally but not always unearned. These minority churches tend to attract the poorest and most vulnerable of society, which is both an answer to and a challenge for prayer. Pastors tend to have little training or accountability. Pray for strengthening of the recent alliances formed for African churches (CEAF and ECOC) and for Caribbean churches (UEEHAC).

d) *Physical and human resources are a key to church growth* in France. Having a visible building gives the Church credibility. But pioneer churches have to face two challenges simultaneously: hiring a pastor and finding a building. Pray for God to provide solutions to these formidable challenges.

e) *Vision for outreach.* The deep malaise and emptiness of secular postmodernity create a hunger for truth and for those who live it out. French evangelicals are coming out of their shell to rediscover evangelism anew. The CNEF has picked up the vision started by France Mission to plant one church for every 10,000 people. France remains difficult ground for church planting; pray for the grace, endurance and faith needed to establish the 4,200 fellowships remaining to meet this goal.

7 **The unreached sectors of French society** are many, such as:

a) *The nearly 50 million French people* who have no real link with a Christian church.

b) *Many urban areas,* where evangelical presence is proportionately low. Inner-city Paris, Nantes, Nancy and other cities need many more congregations planted.

c) *Of the 37,000 communes, around 35,000 have no evangelical church.* Many rural communes are quite traditional and resistant to change. More than 300 towns and cities of over 10,000 people have no evangelical presence.

d) *The Loire Valley and Brittany, Picardy and Centre regions* are particularly lacking in evangelical congregations.

e) *The Basques* in the southwest are virtually without an evangelical witness in their language; they are suspicious of outside influences and allegedly quite disinterested in spiritual things.

f) *The island of Corsica,* birthplace of Napoleon, is quite closed to outside influences. In the population of 290,000, there are perhaps 300 evangelical believers.

8 **The unreached minorities.** France has integrated several waves of immigrants in the past two centuries, but it has not always been easy. Recent difficulties with integrating immigrant communities have led to tightened policies, a climate of fear and insecurity and increasing frustration for both sides. Pray about the following:

a) *The French Jewish community* ranks third in the world in size, following the USA and Israel. There are between 580,000 and 700,000 French Jews – 320,000 in Paris alone and a further 100,000 in Marseille. Of the total Jewish population, 77% never attend a synagogue service. There are about 600 Messianic Jews in France – 95% of these are integrated into evangelical churches. The other 5% are affiliated with the three known Messianic assemblies. Fewer than 20 workers in six missions labour among Jewish people in France (MT, CWI, **JFJ**, CPM and the French TMPI). A number of French Jews are leaving as a result of increasing anti-Semitism, perpetrated by some Muslims and the far-right-wing movements.

b) *North Africans* are almost entirely Muslim, few having ever heard the gospel. The majority live in large, low-cost housing areas in larger cities; antagonism between them and the French majority – coupled with unemployment, discrimination and hopeless frustration among youth – make for a ticking time bomb. Pray for churches and agencies seeking to break down barriers through friendship evangelism, radio, film, BCCs and literature. Believers of Muslim backgrounds do enjoy good relations with other evangelicals, a good testimony to Muslims and atheists alike. Agencies involved: **AWM, CCCI, WEC, IMB** and **OM**.

c) *The Berbers* form a large minority among the North Africans and possibly make up the majority of Algerians. Kabyle believers are increasing in number, although not on the scale of growth happening among their brethren in Algeria. Christian videos, audio resources, radio programmes and literature in Kabyle are being developed.

d) *Black Africans* have come in large numbers from Francophone Africa as students, refugees and work-seekers. There is great imbalance in Christian presence and ministry among them, with vibrant churches full of Central Africans while the West African Bambara, Wolof, Malinke, Soninke and others languish with few Christians and little outreach.

e) *The large number of Indo-Chinese refugees* of the 1970s and '80s from France's former colonies retain a mostly insular existence. There are over 82 Asian evangelical churches, including 33 Chinese, 17 Korean, 11 Hmong and 9 Vietnamese. There is a definite shortfall of pastors and full-time workers for these people who remain unreached. COCM (Chinese) and **CMA** (Southeast Asians) are two groups ministering among Asians.

9 **Islam is now the second religion of France.** Growth is largely through immigration and a higher birth rate, but there are an estimated 150,000 French converts to Islam, mostly via marriage. Pray for the following issues:

a) *There are deep divisions within French Islam,* primarily between fundamentalists and secularists. Over 70% of Muslims in France are of Maghrebian origin, but many mosques are financed by hard-line groups from other countries.

b) *Assimilation of Muslims into French society* is a huge concern for a republic founded on secularism and integration. A large percentage of Muslims live in poor urban contexts, forming an increasingly dissatisfied underclass that is conflicted about its own identity. Rates of crime, unemployment and under-education are all higher in French Muslim communities.

c) *Christian ministry to Muslims.* Fear and ignorance prevent Christians from reaching out; there are only around 100 full-time Christian workers doing so. Despite this, reports suggest that up to 15,000 Muslims are converts to Christianity, one-third of those becoming Protestant.

10 **There are around 10 evangelical Bible schools and seminaries,** both denominational and interdenominational, with around 250 students. Notable among the latter are *Institut Biblique de Nogent* and Vaux Evangelical Seminary. There are also denominational seminaries for Baptists, Pentecostals/**AoG** and the Aix-en-Provence Seminary for Reformed Church students. The Geneva Bible Institute in Switzerland also attracts many French students. Pray for:

a) *Full-time workers* to be called to ministry in France. Most evangelical congregations cannot support a pastor, creating the need for bivocational ministry. Most of the few pioneer church planters are expats. The lack of support, both financial and cultural, for full-time Christian ministers yields a shortage of believers willing to undergo full-time training for ministry, which in turn puts pressure on training institutions.

b) *A deep work of the Holy Spirit* to equip those trained with the theological understanding and spiritual maturity to make an impact for eternity. There is a serious lack of basic Bible knowledge in France generally, although there is growing interest among evangelicals for short-term and modular training.

c) *The blessing of the whole Francophone world* through French and foreign students who graduate. A high proportion of students are from other lands, with great potential to impact all French-speaking peoples.

11 **French evangelicals have sent out around 400 missionaries,** about half of those to other lands. General missions interest in Protestant churches is low and support small. The largest agencies are **YWAM, AoG, WEC, SIM, OM.** Pray for French churches to see beyond the significant challenges in their own country and gain a vision for world evangelization. Pray also for the impact of the French edition of *Operation World*, entitled *Flashes sur le Monde*.

12 **Mission agencies, both French and foreign,** play a vital role in evangelism and church planting. There are not enough full-time French Christian workers to begin to meet the need. Adapting to French culture and communicating the gospel in this context are difficult. Foreign cultural baggage must be left behind, and authentically French forms of witness and fellowship adopted. Fruit is hard-won, discouragements many and the missionary dropout-rate high. Larger mission agencies working in France include France Mission Trust, **CB**/CMML/ EoS, Baptists, **ECM, AWM, WT, TEAM, CW, GEM, AV, WEC, WH, OM,** others. Pray for good identification with French culture, perseverance, effectiveness, adequate provision of financial support and spiritual power.

13 **Youth ministries** are vital in a nation suffering a crisis among young people. A generation has grown up with a crisis of identity, with young people longing for meaning, purpose and belonging. The steep rise in violent crime among youth, high rates of youth unemployment (23%, and up to 40% among ethnic minorities) and Europe's highest rate of youth suicide point to a deep malaise. Once believers, young people are often strongly committed to spiritual community. But they need deep and lasting discipleship to instil a Kingdom worldview, replacing the permissive amoral relativism they are used to.

a) *Children's ministry* – AEE/**CEF** ministers through Good News Clubs, Holiday Bible Clubs and camps. From their Paris base, French literature for children is exported around the world.

b) ***Young people*** are receptive to the gospel, having experienced the emptiness of secularism in their parents' generation. Many groups specialize in this ministry – **YFC, YWAM, CCCI,** Young Life, **TEAM** and *Jeunesse de l'Action Biblique* are but a few. Camps and youth clubs are the main locus of ministry: Teen Challenge among drug addicts, SU through publishing and the Internet. Pray for many young people to be saved and integrated into good evangelical churches – the latter step usually being much harder than the former!

c) ***Youth networks and movements*** are emerging to encourage and connect French Christian youth. Some examples of groups and events are *Mission Radicale*, ON AIR, Alive-3 and Teen Street. Pray for this fire to spread and grow and to have a national impact among young people, saved and unsaved.

d) ***There are over two million students in tertiary education*** in hundreds of universities and *grandes écoles*. Of these, 270,000 are foreign students (the world's third-highest number), so ministry to these students has global implications! Witness in this highly secular and post-Christian environment can be difficult. Evangelical ministry has been slow to develop, but now there are 85 GBU(**IFES**) groups. **CCCI**, Navigators and Crossworld also have campus ministries, as does the French-originated *Foyer Evangélique Universitaire* (FEU). Students are more open than ever, especially foreign ones.

F

14 Christian Help Ministries for prayer:

a) ***The Bible is alien to most French people*** – less than 10% own a Bible and 80% have never even handled one. Yet, Bible sales are at an all-time high, spurred by the spiritual hunger evident among many and the availability of inexpensive ($2) Bibles in supermarkets and secular bookstores. Study Bibles are proving popular as well. The French Bible Society, Geneva Bible Society and Biblica all contribute to printing, sale and distribution of hundreds of thousands of copies every year.

b) ***Literature*** is a valuable tool for evangelism and discipleship. Literature campaigns by CMM (**EHC**) are useful to sow the seed widely. **AoG** and Baptists publish Christian magazines and books nationally to add to the many titles translated from English. Pray for Christian book-stores (more than 80), of which 13 are run by **CLC**.

c) ***Radio and TV ministry*** are important in this media-rich nation. Pray that Christians may cooperate to make effective use of these media. **TWR** broadcasts by satellite, AM and short-wave. Local expressions such as the *Radio Evangile* ministry and the station Radio Colombe/PHARE FM (as well as others) utilize web radio and audio downloads as well as conventional Christian radio. There is at least one Christian TV station in France as well, but marginalization sees evangelicals arrive late to this scene.

d) ***Internet resources abound*** in French. Savvy and media-rich sites such as topchretien.com, unpoissondansle.net and vi7vi.com offer evangelistic, apologetic and discipleship materials.

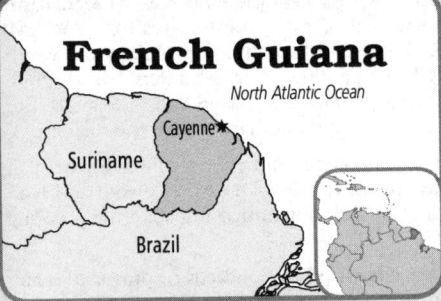

French Guiana

North Atlantic Ocean

Cayenne ★

Suriname

Brazil

French Guiana

Department of French Guiana

Latin America

Geography

Area 86,504 sq km. Sparsely inhabited jungle territory in northeast South America. Great diversity of flora and fauna with over 400,000 species known.

Population		Ann Gr	Density
2010	231,313	2.75%	3/sq km
2020	291,714	2.25%	3/sq km
2030	353,963	1.85%	4/sq km

Capital Cayenne 63,900. **Urbanites** 76.4%. **Pop under 15 yrs** 34%. **Life expectancy** 77.4 yrs.

Peoples

African Caribbean 62%. Franco-Guyanese Creole 45.3%; Haitian 9.1%; Surinamese Creole 6.1%; Afro-Guyanese 1.5%.
European 15.1%. Mainly French or French-background.
Asian 12.2%. Chinese (Hakka) 5%; Indian 4%; Laotian Hmong 1.5%; Javanese 1.0%; Syrian/Lebanese 0.5%.
South American 5.5%. Brazilian 5.0%.
Afro–American Maroon 3.2%. Saramaccan 2.0%; Aukan 1.1%.
Amerindian 2.0%. Six groups.
Official language French. Guianese French Creole widely spoken. **All languages** 15. **Indigenous languages** 12. **Languages with Scriptures** 2Bi 5NT 5por 1w.i.p.

Economy

Partially developed coastal strip, and undeveloped jungle hinterland. Heavily subsidized by France as a *département*. The Guyanese Space Centre at Kourou (a launch facility for the European Space Agency) is the major source of income and brings rapid development. Main exports – gold, shrimp, fish and forest products. Tourism is a potential growth industry. **Unemployment** 20.6%.

Politics

French Overseas Department. For years, infamous as a French penal colony. There is little incentive for independence, due to the high subsidies paid by France/the EU, but pockets with a nationalistic desire for independence do exist.

Religion

Freedom of religion, but secular in outlook.

Religions	Pop %	Population	Ann Gr
Christian	91.25	211,073	2.8%
Non-religious	2.65	6,130	4.0%
Ethnoreligionist	2.10	4,858	0.9%
Muslim	1.80	4,164	5.2%
Sikh	0.90	2,082	2.8%
Chinese	0.90	2,082	0.6%
Baha'i	0.40	925	-1.7%

Christians	Denoms	Pop %	Affiliates	Ann Gr
Protestant	19	5.77	13,000	3.4%
Independent	3	1.01	2,000	2.9%
Anglican	1	0.04	<300	0.0%
Catholic	1	75.66	175,000	3.1%
Marginal	2	1.86	4,000	2.3%
Unaffiliated		6.91	16,000	-3.4%

Churches	MegaBloc	Congs	Members	Affiliates
Catholic Church	C	30	92,593	175,000
Jehovah's Witnesses	M	37	2,000	4,000
Seventh-day Adventist	P	12	2,420	3,388
Assemblies of God	P	30	980	2,300
Baptist Federation	P	6	550	1,340
Ch of the Nazarene	P	3	780	1,100
Evang Reformed Ch	P	8	525	1,050
Christian Brethren	P	13	500	910
Full Gospel Church	P	6	400	600
Salvation Army	P	3	350	600
Other denominations[14]		31	2,684	4,770
Total Christians[26]		**179**	**103,782**	**195,058**

TransBloc	Pop %	Population	Ann Gr
Evangelicals			
Evangelicals	4.5	10,361	3.5%
Renewalists			
Charismatics	5.3	12,161	4.8%
Pentecostals	1.9	4,360	3.7%

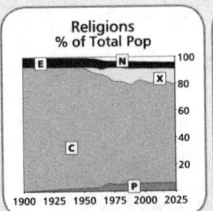

Religions
% of Total Pop

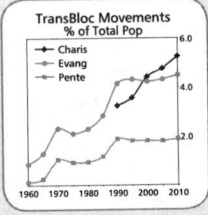

TransBloc Movements
% of Total Pop
Charis / Evang / Pente

Answers to Prayer

1 **The growth of evangelicals has been steady** if not spectacular in the last 20 years. This is true for many minority groups but also among the Creole, previously considered to have few believers. Pentecostal churches and independent house churches have especially flourished, but the latter often need theological guidance and accountability of practice.

2 **Give praise for the opening of work** among several Amerindian groups, with several churches planted among the Caribs/Galibi in particular. Brethren workers from Suriname, Full Gospel ministers along the coast, Baptists and Nazarene among Haitians and Brazilian Christians in the interior are all making progress.

Challenges for Prayer

1 **A new image of French Guiana is emerging,** one that moves past the penal colony image to embrace rich multiculturalism and economic and touristic development, but also French secularism and many moral challenges. Several socio-economic challenges are particularly notable for prayer.

a) ***The relationship to France,*** as with the other overseas departments, is troubled. The standard of living is significantly less than in France itself, but higher than in most neighbouring countries. Unemployment is high, especially among young people, which leads, in turn, to disillusionment and unrest. The availability of French satellite TV has brought widespread exposure to graphic pornography and placed further strain on the already delicate moral fabric of French Guiana.

b) ***Environmental degradation*** combines with illegal immigration and people trafficking through gold mining and the workers needed for that industry. Brazilians in particular are caught up in this clandestine, often illegal but impossible to police, industry.

c) ***Family issues,*** observed in high rates of illegitimate births and of single-parent families, combine with eroding moral standards to increase pressure on society.

2 **The most responsive peoples** are Haitians, Antilleans, Hmong, Amerindian tribal peoples, Brazilians and the interior bush tribes (Maroons). It is among these groups that the Pentecostals, Baptists, **CMA**, Nazarenes and Brethren are growing. Pray for a cooperative spirit among evangelicals and for continued unifying influence of the Suriname Bible Society, especially among ministers.

3 **The least reached peoples** include:

a) ***French Guianese Creole youth,*** large in number due to high birthrates and immigration. They are bombarded with the modern gospel of secular materialism, but with little recourse to acquire its riches. **IFES**/*Union des Groupes Bibliques Universitaires* (UBGU) has groups on the campuses of the one public university.

b) ***The Amerindian tribes*** – pray especially for the animist Wayana (1,100), Wayampi (700) and Emerillon (500), least evangelized of all the tribes. **GRN** has audio resources for each of these groups, and the JESUS film is available in Wayampi.

c) ***The largely animistic Maroon tribes*** (Aukan, Boni and Saramaccan) who live in the interior. Tribal Christians from Suriname work among them.

d) ***The Chinese*** who control much of the small-scale market economy. Just one congregation is known among them.

e) ***The French and European communities*** linked with the space programme – few are active Christians.

4 **Scripture availability is limited.** Biblica is developing the Gospels in Guyanese French Creole. Faith Comes By Hearing audio-recorded the NT in several Surinamese languages that are also used in French Guiana. Pray for their effective and fruitful use.

French Polynesia

Territory of French Polynesia

Pacific

Geography

Area 3,521 sq km. Five island archipelagos and 118 islands – (Society, Tuamotu, Marquesas, Austral and Gambier) in south–central Pacific. Tahiti, the largest island at 1,042 sq km, is where over 70% live.

Population	Ann Gr	Density
2010	272,394	1.30%	77/sq km
2020	304,378	1.03%	86/sq km
2030	328,548	0.68%	93/sq km

Capital Papeete 134,000. **Urbanites** 51.4%. **Pop under 15 yrs** 26%. **Life expectancy** 75.5 yrs.

Peoples

Polynesian 61.9%. Speaking 10 distinct languages, largest: Tahitian, Tuamotuan, Tubuaian, Marquesan(2), Mangarevan.
Mixed race 16.5%. Polynesian, European, Chinese.
Chinese 10.9%. Mainly traders.
European 10.7%. Administrators, military, others.
Literacy 99%. **Official languages** French and Tahitian. **All languages** 11. **Indigenous languages** 9. **Languages with Scriptures** 3Bi 1NT 3por 4w.i.p.

Economy

Heavily dependent on French aid and military spending, but the income has not benefited all. Tourism, pearls and agriculture make up the rest of the economy. The suspension, then end, of nuclear testing has had a significant effect on the economy.
Public debt 13.22% of GDP. **Income/person** $17,290 (38% of USA). **Unemployment** 12% (unofficially much higher).

Politics

French colony in 1880. Overseas Territory in 1957–2003. Since then, an overseas territory of France, with a high degree of autonomy and its own president. The controversial use of Mururoa Atoll for testing nuclear weapons provoked international opposition and fuelled the Tahitian independence movement.

Religion

There is complete religious freedom, but society is increasingly materialistic and secular.

Religions	Pop %	Population	Ann Gr
Christian	92.25	251,283	1.3%
Non-religious	5.00	13,620	1.3%
Chinese	2.10	5,720	2.3%
Ethnoreligionist	0.30	817	1.3%
Baha'i	0.25	681	5.9%
Jewish	0.10	272	3.5%

Christians	Denoms	Pop %	Affiliates	Ann Gr
Protestant	4	41.92	114,000	0.5%
Independent	12	0.78	2,000	2.0%
Catholic	1	36.34	99,000	1.0%
Marginal	3	13.00	35,000	-0.1%
Unaffiliated		11.20	31,000	3.6%
Doubly affiliated		*-11.01*	*-30,000*	*0.0%*

Churches	MegaBloc	Congs	Members	Affiliates
Catholic Church	C	88	47,143	99,000
Ma'ohi Protestant Ch	P	82	32,000	90,500
Latter-day Saints (Mormon)	M	80	12,422	20,000
Seventh-day Adventist	P	45	5,500	17,600
Sanito (Ref Mormon)	M	48	4,800	9,600
Jehovah's Witnesses	M	30	2,231	5,800
Assem of God (French)	P	9	1,796	3,000
Other Reformed chs	I	11	500	1,150
Other charismatic	I	6	529	900
Other denominations[3]		27	2,538	3,170
Doubly affiliated				*-30,000*
Total Christians[20]		**426**	**109,459**	**220,720**

TransBloc	Pop %	Population	Ann Gr
Evangelicals			
Evangelicals	7.2	19,712	2.6%
Renewalists			
Charismatics	13.9	37,779	2.9%
Pentecostals	2.3	6,130	3.2%

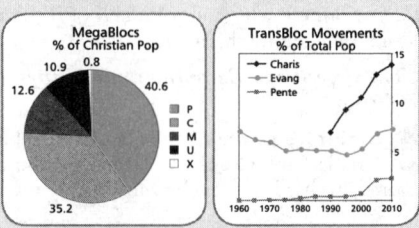

MegaBlocs % of Christian Pop — 10.9, 0.8, 40.6, 12.6, 35.2 — P C M U X

TransBloc Movements % of Total Pop — Charis, Evang, Pente — 1960 1970 1980 1990 2000 2010

Challenges for Prayer

1 **Tahiti is a paradise lost.** Formerly a strongly Christian nation that sent missionaries all over the Pacific, Tahiti is now being debased by increasing vice and immorality as well as serious challenges to traditional values and ways of life. There is spiritual openness, but it seems to be shouted down by materialism. No longer do Tahitian missionaries leave for other lands as they once did.

2 **Those with a vital personal faith are now rare.** As a result, there is a reversion to the bondage of pagan occultism and a multiplication of syncretistic and foreign sects, especially two forms of Mormonism. Pray for a spiritual revolution to take place among the many nominal Catholic and Protestant Christians.

3 **The LMS-planted Ma'ohi Church has declined.** Once the Church of the majority of Islanders, liberal theology is now predominant and evangelicals are few. Splits and defections have reduced its percentage and influence, and some well-publicized cases involving misuse of funds damaged the Church's reputation further. Pray for a moving of the Spirit of God to bring this Church back to its first love, as in the early 19th Century. There are some signs of life with the greater inclusion of young people and women.

4 **The Catholic Church,** originally supported by the French colonial powers against the British LMS, is now the largest denomination. Through the 1980s and 1990s, strong charismatic renewal brought significant growth but also controversy, as intellectuals saw this as a reemergence of tribal pagan influence. Today, 25-30% of Catholics are involved in the renewal movement; the rest are mostly non-practicing and very nominal.

5 **The evangelical witness is very small,** consisting of Pentecostal and charismatic churches and a few splinter groups from the Ma'ohi Church. Evangelical agencies found elsewhere in the Anglophone Pacific have neglected Francophone territories. In contrast, two varieties of Mormonism have thrived in these islands for over 150 years. Evangelicals are increasing slowly, but greater cooperation is required – an Evangelical Fellowship/Alliance is needed. Pentecostals run a Bible school and radio station.

6 **The less-evangelized** – almost all adhere to some form of Christianity, but many are without a clear gospel witness:

a) *The outer island groups* are largely Catholic with little evangelical presence. The Marquesans, Mangarevans and Tuamotuans cannot easily understand the related Tahitian language, and have little of the Bible in their own languages.

b) *Significant emigration* from the outer islands to Tahiti gives opportunities for Islanders to encounter Jesus in Papeete, but those who move are too often lost to the Church.

c) *The Chinese* have a few Protestants, Catholics and Chinese ethnoreligionists, but most Chinese are effectively secular.

d) *The French community* lives a life apart, having minimal contact with any Church.

e) *The Jewish community,* newly arrived and in need of their Messiah.

F

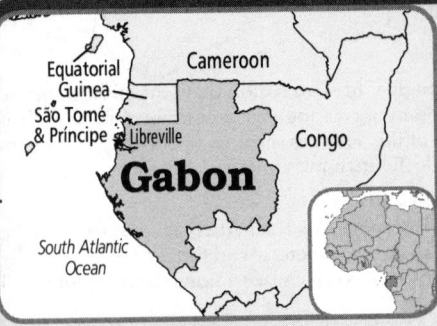

Equatorial Guinea
Cameroon
São Tomé & Príncipe
Libreville
Congo
Gabon
South Atlantic Ocean

Gabon

Gabonese Republic

Africa

Geography

Area 267,667 sq km. Coastal, Central African state on the equator, two-thirds being dense tropical rainforest and 10% being nature reserves.

Population		Ann Gr	Density
2010	1,501,266	1.86%	6/sq km
2020	1,779,155	1.66%	7/sq km
2030	2,044,308	1.31%	8/sq km

Capital Libreville 633,000. **Urbanites** 86%. **Pop under 15 yrs** 36%. **Life expectancy** 60.1 yrs.

Peoples

Bantu 94.1%. Major groupings:

Central-Congo(8) 51.5%, in the northern half of Gabon. Fang 41.41%; Mbede 3.7%; Kota 2.7%; Wumbvu 1.5%.

Northwest(30) 41.8%, in Gabon's southwest. Punu 9.7%; Njebi 8.4%; Myene 3.7%; Eshira 3.1%; Western Teke 2.7%; Sangu 1.6%; Mitsogo 1.6%; Lumbu 1.5%.

Other African 5.2%. Baka/Pygmy native people as well as immigrants from neighbouring countries and West Africa, drawn by economic opportunities. Some place this number over 10%, but reliable statistics do not yet exist.

Other 0.7%. European, Arab.

Literacy 84%. **Official Language** French. **All languages** 43 **Indigenous languages** 42. **Languages with Scriptures** 3Bi 4NT 10por.

Economy

One of Africa's wealthier countries; rich in natural resources, Gabon imports food and exports oil, wood and minerals. The majority are still involved with agricultural work and do not directly benefit from most of the wealth. The inexorable depletion of oil reserves, mineral deposits and old-growth timber make wise investment in the present all the more vital.

HDI Rank 103rd/182. **Public debt** 24.7% of GDP. **Income/person** $12,500 (25% of USA).

Politics

The president, with four decades of stable rule under his belt, was the world's longest-ruling politician. He installed a multiparty democracy, but the last several elections have suffered allegations of vote rigging to favour the incumbent party. In 2009, the president passed away and his adopted son (who had been Minister of Defense for 10 years) won the Presidential election.

Religion

Freedom of religion. The Catholic Church has been dominant, but its influence is waning. Traditional beliefs remain strong, with many syncretistic groups. The former president became Muslim in 1973, his son and successor is likewise, and apparently more devout. Islam is rapidly growing in Gabon.

Religions	Pop %	Population	Ann Gr
Christian	79.35	1,191,255	1.4%
Muslim	10.40	156,132	4.6%
Ethnoreligionist	7.76	116,498	2.1%
Non-religious	2.40	36,030	4.6%
Baha'i	0.09	1,351	1.9%

Animism's influence in both Christianity and Islam extends far beyond its statistical presence.

Christians Denoms		Pop %	Affiliates	Ann Gr
Protestant	14	15.67	235,000	2.2%
Independent	22	17.55	264,000	1.5%
Catholic	1	40.63	610,000	-0.2%
Marginal	6	1.33	20,000	1.8%
Unaffiliated		5.77	87,000	4.4%
Doubly affiliated		*-1.60*	*-24,000*	*0.0%*

Churches	MegaBloc	Congs	Members	Affiliates
Catholic Church	C	36	401,316	610,000
Evangelical Ch of G	P	143	52,333	157,000
Eglise de Banzie	I	1,438	90,625	145,000
Bethany	I	53	10,511	35,000
CMA (EACMG)	P	357	25,000	35,000
Pentecostal Ch of AoG	P	66	8,600	21,500
Nazareth	I	26	4,696	10,800
Jehovah's Witnesses	M	37	3,900	10,400
Seventh-day Adventist	P	67	3,700	8,100
Other denominations[34]		394	43,751	71,811
Total Christians[43]		**2,617**	**644,432**	**1,104,611**

TransBloc	Pop %	Population	Ann Gr
Evangelicals			
Evangelicals	12.7	190,552	2.8%
Renewalists			
Charismatics	12.5	187,351	3.1%
Pentecostals	6.7	101,302	3.0%

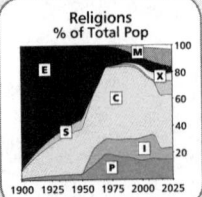

Religions % of Total Pop

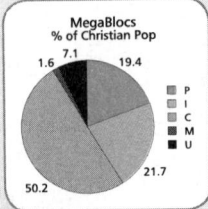

MegaBlocs % of Christian Pop

1.6 7.1 19.4

50.2 21.7

P I C M U

Answers to Prayer

1 **Evangelical growth in Gabon has been steady** and sustained. Through the **CMA**, the Pentecostals and newer indigenous African churches, evangelicals increased from 2.3% in 1960 to 12.7% in 2010. The Church is also maturing, as indicated by increasing numbers of prayer events – yearlong prayer chains, all night prayer gatherings, weekend prayer retreats and such.

2 **Peoples of the interior** – long unreached and even previously out of bounds for evangelical missionaries – are opening to the gospel. Research in the late 1990s identified the unengaged and least-reached peoples, and Christians are beginning to plant churches among them. Included in these are the Baka people, Gabon's earliest inhabitants, who are proving quite responsive to outreach.

Challenges for Prayer

1 **Despite Gabon being wealthy in resources,** many Gabonese continue to dwell in poverty. This is largely due to decades of neglecting the nation's infrastructure and to prevalent corruption that prevents the country's wealth from trickling down to all. Women and children are vulnerable to poverty through lack of education and social mores; exploitation and trafficking of children are particularly evil situations. Pray for righteousness to prevail over those seeking to gain profit at the expense of others.

2 **Spiritist beliefs and practices** (such as Bwiti syncretism) are widely observed and deeply pervasive in much of Catholicism, other Christian groups and Islam. This continues to cause many to fall back on fetishes, hallucinogenic drugs, ancestral spirits and dependence on the medicine men who have held them in bondage for generations. Secret societies are common; many government elite, police officers and members of the army participate in often-bloody nighttime rituals including witchcraft and black magic. Christians who refuse to participate in these "harmless clubs" can be refused academic or professional advancement.

3 **Muslim numbers continue to grow,** initially by immigration of Hausa, Fulani and other West African Muslims, and more recently by conversions among Gabonese men. The former president's conversion to Islam played a huge role in this, and his son/successor is likely to continue favouring Islamic evangelism, which often involves financial inducements. West African Muslim immigrants, who make up much of the merchant class, and the Arab influence in the oil industry have shaped the country. Despite plans to do so, the Church has not yet effectively started evangelizing Muslims.

4 **The Catholic Church** wielded great influence in the colonial era but has seen its power steadily wane since then. The majority of the population were baptized Catholic, but a large number still follow the old animist ways. The Catholic Church's growth peaked decades ago, with steady losses in recent years to Islam, other churches and sects. Pray that the many nominal Christians may see and embrace the pure gospel. Some charismatic prayer cells are multiplying and growing.

5 **The first major Protestant denomination** was the fruit of French missionary work. But the legacy of liberal theology is a stagnant, nominal, daughter Church, with leadership more concerned with social issues than with evangelism. Ask God's Spirit to revive this Church and make it again a force for evangelism.

6 **The evangelical Church sees encouraging progress** but faces challenges on many levels:

a) ***The need remains for solid, indigenous church leaders.*** Prosperity teaching and spurious philosophy potentially plague Gabon as much as any other African country. Gabonese Christians require teaching and pastoring in order to mature, but the first step is to train national pastors and leaders for this. Opportunities for trainers and openings for students exist in the five Bible schools in Libreville.

b) ***Evangelical churches are committed to evangelizing the whole country.*** The vision is that by 2025 evangelicals will be 20% of the country's population, and every Gabonese person will have had the chance to hear the gospel. The **CMA**-planted churches have a World Missions

Centre and a Prayer Chapel for the nations and are beginning to send workers to other countries. Bethany churches have been sending missionaries for years. Pray for all evangelical churches to catch the same vision that the leaders share.

c) *Prosperity teaching* is a foreign element that has made rapid inroads into the Gabonese Church. In a poverty-stricken country, such promises of health and wealth are met with great hope, but generally only the pastor sees any prosperity. Pray for responsible teaching that gives Gabonese believers true hope and enables them to find responsible and biblical ways out of poverty.

d) *Missionary sending* is a new concept for Gabonese churches, but is beginning to grow. The Gabonese **CMA** has sent and is supporting three families as foreign missionaries to other African countries. Pray that these firstfruits of sending might herald a greater harvest.

7 **Less-reached peoples:**

a) *The east region* was long closed to evangelicals, and the northeast was the least evangelized and least developed. Born-again Christians are very few among the many pockets of peoples – notably Yongho, Wandji, Sanghu, Tsogo, Duma, Ngom, Kaningi, Bubi and Minduumo. But these areas, now open, are seeing churches planted and people reached, although much work remains.

b) *The Fang* are the dominant people (41% of the population) and largely Protestant or Catholic. They are a profoundly religious people, but most of their fervency is dissipated in syncretistic ancestral worship.

c) *The Baka/Babinga,* often called Pygmies, live in the virgin forest. They have been exploited and mistreated by other peoples, despite their unique culture and gentle nature. The **CMA** and Deeper Life work among them and see much responsiveness and many conversions. There are at least 10 Baka congregations, with a number of other Baka joining churches of other ethnic groups.

8 **Support ministries:**

a) *Bible translation* may be needed in 22 languages. **CMA** works on the Yinzebi OT, but generally the Gabonese prefer to use the French translation of the Bible.

b) *The JESUS film* in French is shown widely and is available in five other languages. It has been a key tool for opening ministry to unreached peoples, and it continues to be received enthusiastically.

c) **GRN** has recordings in 25 languages and dialects.

d) *Both national radio and TV* are wide-open avenues for evangelism and Bible teaching, but are neglected. *Radio Evangile Gabon* is one of five Christian FM stations that reach Libreville; ways are being sought to extend coverage to the interior. There is also a Christian TV station on air.

e) *Bongolo Hospital* is a strategic ministry. In addition to the basic medical services offered, HIV/AIDS treatment is an increasing emphasis. Over 1,700 people every year are coming to Christ through the hospital's work. Air Cavalry supports the hospital through aviation ministry. Pray for continued grace and that all who visit would receive healing of body and soul.

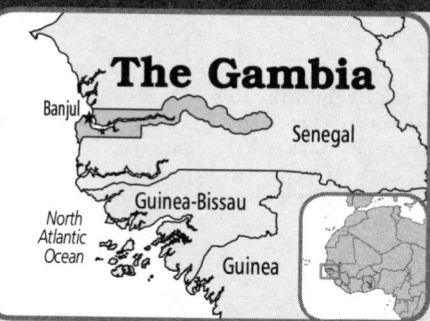

The Gambia

Republic of The Gambia

Africa

Geography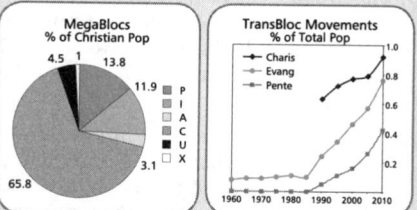

Area 10,689 sq km. A narrow, 400-km-long riverine enclave that virtually divides Senegal's Casamance from the rest of the country.

Population		Ann Gr	Density
2010	1,750,732	2.78%	164/sq km
2020	2,227,413	2.33%	208/sq km
2030	2,736,133	2.00%	256/sq km

Capital Banjul 455,000. **Urbanites** 58.1%. Half the population lives in the greater Banjul area. **Pop under 15 yrs** 42%. **Life expectancy** 55.7 yrs.

Peoples

Over 25 ethnic groups that are very intermingled. **Malinke** 42.5%. Mandinka (Mandingo) 40.5%. **Atlantic** 5.9%. Serere-Sine 2.0%; Balanta 2.0%; Manjaco 1.7%. **Jola** 4.7%. Three groups, mostly Jola-Fonyi. **Wolof** 12.6%. **Fulani/Fula** 17.3%. **Soninke/Serahule** 9.9%. **Other sub-Saharan African** 10.1%. **Other** 1.7%. Maure 1.5%. **Literacy** 38%. **Official language** English. **Trade languages** Mandinka, Wolof. **All languages** 23. **Indigenous languages** 10. **Languages with Scriptures** 2Bi 3NT 7por.

Economy

Subsistence agriculture and dependence on groundnut cultivation, tourism, foreign aid and the "grey economy" over the porous border with Senegal. Remittances from Gambians overseas are a large economic boost. Possible oil and gas reserves. **HDI Rank** 168th/182. **Public debt** 114% of GDP. **Income/person** $497 (1% of USA).

Politics

Independent from Britain in 1965. Senegalese intervention to quell the 1981 coup resulted in abortive efforts to create a Senegambian confederacy, which finally collapsed in 1989. A bloodless coup in 1994 ushered in a military government that in turn became a civilian government through multiparty elections, despite tight state controls over political and media activity.

Religion

Relative religious freedom, with easy-going tolerance among communities despite the large Muslim majority.

Religions	Pop %	Population	Ann Gr
Muslim	89.49	1,566,730	2.8%
Ethnoreligionist	5.60	98,041	1.4%
Christian	4.48	78,433	3.6%
Baha'i	0.35	6,128	0.1%
Non-religious	0.07	1,226	15.0%
Buddhist	0.01	175	2.8%

Christians Denoms		Pop %	Affiliates	Ann Gr
Protestant	52	0.58	10,000	4.8%
Independent	15	0.71	13,000	6.2%
Anglican	1	0.13	2,000	4.7%
Catholic	1	2.77	48,000	3.2%
Marginal	1	0.04	1,000	5.9%
Unaffiliated		0.25	4,000	-4.4%

Churches	MegaBloc	Congs	Members	Affiliates
Catholic Church	C	48	24,250	48,500
Anglican Church	A	17	759	2,300
Lutheran churches	P	13	1,000	2,000
Methodist Church	P	5	1,099	2,000
Seventh-day Adventist	P	5	1,180	1,653
Church of Pentecost	I	23	958	1,150
Assemblies of God	P	4	490	980
Winners Chapel	I	3	700	1,000
Deeper Life Church	I	10	300	650
Evang Ch of Gambia	P	9	150	484
Other denominations[57]		206	7,264	12,284
Total Christians[67]		**347**	**38,731**	**74,056**

TransBloc	Pop %	Population	Ann Gr
Evangelicals			
Evangelicals	0.8	13,351	8.9%
Renewalists			
Charismatics	0.9	16,099	6.0%
Pentecostals	0.4	7,350	13.0%

MegaBlocs
% of Christian Pop

4.5 1 13.8

11.9

P
I
A
C
U
X

3.1

65.8

TransBloc Movements
% of Total Pop

Charis
Evang
Pente

1960 1970 1980 1990 2000 2010

G

Answers to Prayer

1 **The degree of religious freedom and relatively amicable relationships** between Islam and Christianity in the Gambia are noteworthy. There is greater openness than in most Muslim countries, although much of the freedom may be from a lack of ambition by the Gambian Church to do more direct outreach to Muslims. Even so, pray that the relative harmony and freedom in the religious sphere might enable the good news to impact this nation to a much greater degree.

Challenges for Prayer

1 **Islam is dominant,** but the traditional Gambian expression is a gentler version rather than the more strident edition from Libya and Saudi Arabia seeking to exert influence over the education and economic systems and the political process. Most Christian work and presence have been near the coast, with few involved in reaching out to the Muslim majority, especially those living upriver. Pray for continued ability to minister to all peoples and for Christians to take advantage of the religious freedom to share and demonstrate the gospel to all parts and all peoples of the Gambia.

2 **Missionary work was pioneered** by Anglicans and Methodists and mostly confined to the Aku (Creole-speaking descendants of freed slaves in Banjul). Nominalism is a challenge in most denominations, although the ministries of the above and of the Mennonites have had a valuable impact in development, education and medical work, especially among the Jola and Manjako. Many newer ministries from Nigeria, Sierra Leone, Ghana, Liberia and Cameroon have recently started. These have greatly added to the harvest force and the vitality of church and mission efforts. In all cases, the nominal Christian population receives much more spiritual attention than the unreached Muslim majority. Pray for effective ministry of expatriate Christian groups in demonstrating the good news. Pray also for nominal Christians to discover a genuine life in Jesus.

3 **The Gambian evangelical Church is small,** and committed believers are few. Active Christians are usually overstretched in their ministries; the need is great for discipleship and leadership training. Many pastors work in the Greater Banjul area, but few feel called to go into the hinterland, where there is less development and few amenities; financial support is difficult to maintain for those who are willing. Pray for Gambians to have a vision to reach their own people; pray for wisdom in knowing how to support those who do move into more isolated areas. Pray that the indigenous Church might be set free by the Holy Spirit from the restraints of fear and lack of confidence; pray that Christians might minister powerfully and effectively to their fellow Gambians.

4 **Ministries concentrating on the non-Christian majority are few. WEC** and the ECG Church have planted congregations of believers from Muslim backgrounds. The House of Wisdom specifically trains these MBBs in spiritual development and self-sustainability. Pray for new believers from Muslim backgrounds to become strong in their faith and able to witness to their extended families; pray also for more Gambian Christians to gain a burden for reaching their compatriots with the gospel. Pray that those reaching out already might be wise, effective and fruitful in their labours.

5 **Unreached peoples in the Gambia:**

a) Mandinka. Ninety-five percent of all Mandinkas are Muslim, believing in a mixture of Islam and traditional customs. Due to tremendous social and family pressures, few Mandinkas leave Islam. Those who have converted to Christianity are viewed as traitors to their families and their heritage. The entire NT and two-thirds of the OT are available in Roman-scripted Mandinka.

b) Fulani. Largely sedentary in the Gambia despite traditional associations with nomadic pastoralism, the Fulani are considered to be custodians of Islam in West Africa. There is some response to Christian witness in the region from the Fula, but their unique culture requires a different expression of church from the sedentary majority.

G

c) Jola. The majority of Jolas are from an animistic background and are beholden to the spirit powers they revere. Jolas in Gambia are increasingly being Islamized, with a small number of Christians. Only some Scripture portions are available in their language. Pray for more Jolas to come to freedom in Christ, and pray for effectiveness in the medical, translation and church planting ministries in their areas (**WEC, IMB**).

d) Wolof, Serahule, and Serer – all more prevalent in neighbouring Senegal, all very much unevangelized and with little outreach or mission directed toward them. There are probably fewer than 10 known Christians among the 180,000 Serahule of Gambia. Medical work has opened doors in some villages. Pray for more groups of believers to be formed who can withstand the pressure from family and society to return to Islam.

6 **Young people** have flocked to Banjul and are increasingly subject to Western culture at the expense of their traditional values. Ministries include GAMFES(**IFES**), with several groups meeting, SU and **YFC**. The first **YWAM** DTS took place in 2008. Pray that God would raise up a new generation of Christian young people who will lead their peers into a lifestyle of godliness. Most youth work is in the capital and outlying areas, though **WEC** also has ministry inland.

7 **Pray for specialized Christian ministries:**

a) Prison evangelism is particularly fruitful. Pray both for conversions and for integration of converts into their communities and churches upon their release.

b) Bible translation continues for Mandinka and Jola Fonyi. None of the indigenous Gambian languages has a full translation of the Bible; pray for an accurate assessment of the needs and for wide distribution of existing portions and NTs. The Mandinka Bible and Jola NT should be ready in 2011.

c) The JESUS film has been shown all over the country in seven languages. Pray for the ongoing dubbing into new languages and the fruitful use of this key resource.

d) Christian radio. Chronological Bible teaching, The Way of Righteousness, is recorded in Mandinka, Wolof, Fula, Jola-Fonyi and Hassaniya and is broadcast on national radio. **CMF** has a radio ministry in Manjako focused on evangelism and discipleship. A number of African-originated churches also have radio ministry in English. Pray for more broadcasts in local languages.

e) Christian TV programmes. Abiding Word Ministries, the Gambia Christian Council, the Network of Biblical Storytellers and others have gained wide acceptance for the gospel through their much-appreciated weekly TV programmes. Pray for lasting fruit.

f) GRN offers gospel material on tape in 16 language groups of the Gambia.

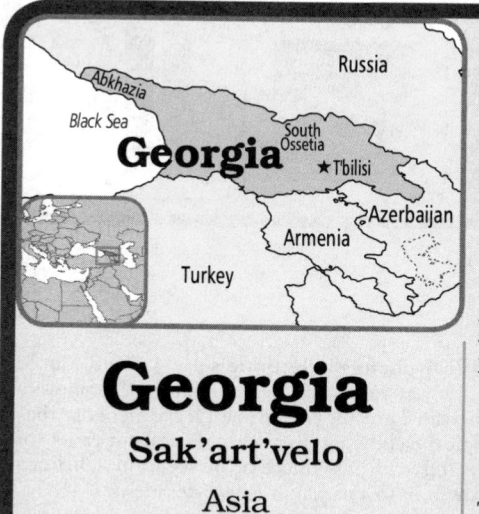

Georgia

Sak'art'velo

Asia

Geography

Area 69,700 sq km. Black Sea state between the Caucasus Mountains and Turkey. Moderate climate with good natural resources and soil.

Population		Ann Gr	Density
2010	4,219,191	-1.12%	61/sq km
2020	3,982,461	-0.50%	57/sq km
2030	3,779,025	-0.57%	54/sq km

Capital T'bilisi 1,120,126. **Urbanites** 52.9%. **Pop under 15 yrs** 17%. **Life expectancy** 71.6 yrs.

Peoples

Eurasian 92.0%.
  Caucasus 81.7%. Georgian 69.9%; Mingrelian 9.1%; Abkhazian 1.9%.
  Armenian 5.4%.
  Slavic 1.9%. Russian 1.5%.
  Other 3.0%. Pontic Greek 2.5%.
Turkic 6.4%. Azerbaijani 6.2%.

Iranian–Median 1.2%. Ossetian 0.8%.
Other 0.4%. Assyrian, Jews.
Literacy 100%. **Official language** Georgian.
All languages 25. **Indigenous languages** 13.
Languages with Scriptures 3Bi 2NT 3por 2w.i.p.

Economy

Productive soil and good climate for fruit, tea, cotton, wine and tourism, but the industry and service sectors match agriculture as a percentage of the GDP. Tax reform, anti-corruption measures and some privatizations have won Georgia international favour; much progress has been made since the 2003 "rose revolution". Potential for hydro-electric power remains promising as does the possible exploitation of Georgia's strategic location along an old Silk Road route for European-Asian transit of goods, oil and gas.
HDI Rank 89th/182. **Public debt** 38.2% of GDP. **Income/person** $2,924 (6% of USA).

Politics

Independent since 1991 after centuries of domination by surrounding empires. Stability was consolidated by 1995, but a dictatorial president failed to bring further progress, prompting the "rose revolution" in 2003, followed by new elections in 2004. Significant democratic progress since then. Georgia's great challenge is the existence of two breakaway regions, Abkhazia and South Ossetia, supported and recognized by Russia. The Ossetians and Abkhazians have de facto independence. Attempts by Georgia to exercise greater control over South Ossetia drew in Russian military interference in 2008; Russia remains present in significant force as a "peacekeeping" measure. The dynamics of Georgia's relationships with its breakaway regions and with Russia will shape Georgia's future profoundly.

Religion

Over the centuries, the Georgian Orthodox Church was the one stable factor preserving Georgian culture and nationalism. Georgia and neighbouring Armenia are surrounded by Muslim ethnic groups; many are small and part of Russia. Despite Orthodox agitation, religious freedom is improving for non-Orthodox groups, especially since changes to the laws in 2005.

Religions	Pop %	Population	Ann Gr
Christian	78.67	3,319,238	-1.2%
Muslim	11.30	476,769	-1.8%
Non-religious	9.58	404,198	0.0%
Jewish	0.25	10,548	-2.6%
Other	0.20	8,438	3.4%

Christians Denoms		Pop %	Affiliates	Ann Gr
Protestant	6	0.52	22,000	0.2%
Independent	22	0.29	12,000	0.7%
Catholic	2	0.95	40,000	0.0%
Orthodox	12	76.13	3,212,000	-1.2%
Marginal	1	0.78	33,000	0.8%

Churches	MegaBloc	Congs	Members	Affiliates
Georgian Orthodox	O	486	1,214,583	2,915,000
Armenian Apostolic Ch	O	18	45,000	225,000
Russian Orthodox	O	15	29,720	42,500
Jehovah's Witnesses	M	186	17,500	32,700
Cath Ch – Latin Rite	C	7	14,286	22,000
Cath Ch – Eastern Rite	C	12	11,688	18,000
Evang Baptist Ch	P	72	4,896	14,400
Greek Orthodox Ch	O	14	6,750	13,500
Ukrainian Orthodox	O	2	3,846	5,500
Syrian Orthodox	O	3	3,234	5,400
Pentecostal (AoG)	P	110	3,100	5,000
Other denominations[32]		158	14,193	20,132
Total Christians[43]		**1,083**	**1,364,796**	**3,319,132**

TransBloc	Pop %	Population	Ann Gr
Evangelicals			
Evangelicals	1.5	65,247	-0.6%
Renewalists			
Charismatics	0.4	14,952	-0.4%
Pentecostals	0.3	12,280	-1.0%

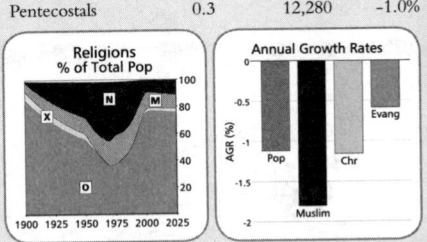

Religions % of Total Pop

Annual Growth Rates

Answers to Prayer

1 **Positive social, economic and political changes continue** since 1991. Reduced corruption and democratic reform pave the way for a more peaceful future. Openness to spirituality and Christianity in particular has increased greatly. The former Department of Atheism at the national university is now a theological faculty, and legal changes make it easier for non-Orthodox faiths to operate more freely and with less threat of persecution. Christian groups of all expressions have experienced growth in this nation in recent decades.

Challenges for Prayer

1 **Georgia's independence,** gained with such hope, is soured by a series of inter-ethnic wars aided and abetted by Russian efforts to undermine and control the country. Following the Rose Revolution, economic and political progress started in 2004 and helped lift the country out of some of its woes. Much of this progress was reversed in the August War of 2008, when Russian troops briefly occupied much of the country. Pray for an end to Russian belligerence, for peace to be established and for the economic situation to once again stabilize and make progress.

2 **Inter-ethnic conflicts** of the past decade within the autonomous regions have displaced nearly a quarter of a million people from home and village. Many now live in camps or makeshift accommodation in and around the capital, Tbilisi. Humanitarian needs are great, with adequate food, water, heat in winter and medical supplies in high demand. Unemployment for these people is very high, and emotional and spiritual needs are vast. Pray for the effective witness of various church and agency personnel working among these struggling families; pray for provision of physical needs.

3 **The Georgian Orthodox Church's** history stretches back to AD 150; it can be regarded as the world's second-oldest Christian nation. Communist repression, infiltration and subversion brought both martyrdom and compromise. Since Communism's collapse and Georgian independence, many have returned to the Church of their ancestors. Some minority groups converted as well. For most Georgians, this is mostly an expression of nationalism and cultural identity, not a living spiritual faith. Pray for access to the Word of God, and that through it many may find the Truth of the gospel. Pray also for renewal among Orthodox clergy; some small beginnings of this are occurring.

G

4 **The small Protestant Church struggled** under Communism and, since independence, at the hands of some factions of the Orthodox Church. Evangelical ministries have been repressed, their work maligned as sectarian. They have had problems acquiring buildings and the permits necessary to hold meetings. There have been incidents of meetings being broken up, sometimes violently, and materials confiscated. Some legal changes in 2005 offer hope of greater freedom of religious expression. Pray for a relationship of mutual respect and understanding between the Orthodox and other churches; pray that Protestant and Independent churches and believers might conduct themselves in Christ-like ways, even amid hostility.

5 **Evangelicals** are effectively comprised of Baptists and Pentecostal/charismatic groups, but more and more congregations from both streams wish to remain independent of denominational affiliation. Evangelicals are not growing, but they are at least shrinking slower than the overall population. There has been some creative development in contextualized evangelical worship and practice and in work among Christian young people. The following need prayer:

a) Poverty. Village unemployment/underemployment is nearly 100%. Few congregations have the resources to support pastors and often have dilapidated church buildings. High-profile outreach and ministry are not feasible, especially when expensive foreign ministry models require dependence on foreign funds. Pray for creative ideas for church meetings and outreach, and pray for God's provision in the daily needs of pastors and church members living in poverty.

b) Unity. The small but deeply divided evangelical community has taken significant steps toward unity and collaboration. Evangelical leaders across several denominations and ministries met in fellowship, committing to defend biblical values and to promote religious freedom within Georgia. Well-intentioned but ignorant foreign "help" for churches and increased influence of prosperity theology among many Pentecostals are causing further theological differences, even amid deliberate efforts to fellowship and work together. Pray for a greater willingness among all churches to put aside their own plans and to work together for the benefit of the Kingdom of Jesus Christ.

c) Cultural irrelevance among youth. Young Georgians have lost interest in the Church, with a majority leaving during teenage years. Youth groups have grown in some cases where intentional efforts were made to reach out to young people in creative and relevant ways and where youth were empowered to lead. Pray for churches to thoughtfully share the gospel with young people in relevant ways.

6 **Pray for the spiritual need of ethnic minorities.** Georgian believers are best placed to reach ethnic minorities, but they need a greater desire to train, send and support workers to do this. There is a little outreach to Muslims; some Baptists are receiving training to reach out to them. Pray for these believers to gain a burden for ethnic peoples, including the following:

a) Abkhazians – mostly Orthodox and with a sizeable Muslim minority, they tend to reflect a worldview and practice that is more ethnoreligionist and pagan in its outlook. They live in their own breakaway region in the northwest; effective outreach would require cultural insight as well as spiritual breakthrough.

b) Jews. There is no known witness to them. They face a rising tide of anti-Semitism in a country that has historically been for them a haven.

c) The Kish live mostly in and near the Pankisi Gorge and are closely related to Chechens. Many live in poverty. They are mostly Sunni Muslim, but with some Christian and pagan influences among them.

d) The Mingrelians number around 400,000; while many are Orthodox in name, the large majority are non-religious.

e) The Svaneti people live in the mountainous west in remote villages, a dangerous area of Georgia often plagued by Chechen rebels. The Svaneti are largely untouched by the gospel; those who are Orthodox have little knowledge of their own faith. One Pentecostal couple works among this unreached people.

f) Azerbaijanis, who are Muslim. There is at least one Azeri congregation, and the Bible is available in their language, as is the JESUS film.

7 **Christian help ministries for prayer** include:

a) Literature distribution. The Bible Society, **OM**, BIEM and the Fellowship Tract League produce or distribute tracts and Christian literature in Georgian.

b) The Georgian Bible, in use until a few years ago, was an ancient translation. The two recent translations (1990s) are the standard Bibles today, but due to their popularity, there is a great need to print more. A children's Bible is also available. The Bible Society projects are a welcome success in inter-confessional ministry; they also produce a Bible magazine and run a Bible shop. Their desire to distribute Scriptures in Abkhazia and South Ossetia has often been disrupted by the conflicts and instability there.

c) Christian radio programmes in Georgian are another need. There is a wealth of radio broadcasting in Russian from abroad, but solid Christian content in local languages is sorely lacking.

d) The JESUS film and related resources have been completed in Georgian, Russian, Ossetian and Mingrellian (the first ever film in this language!). Svan and Abkhazian productions are held up due to the conflict; pray for the completion of these translations. The JESUS film, combined with other discipleship tools, has proven to be very effective.

G

Germany
Federal Republic of Germany
Europe

Geography 🌍

Area 357,042 sq km. Strategically placed in the centre of Europe and of the expanding EU.

Population		Ann Gr	Density
2010	82,056,775	-0.09%	230/sq km
2020	80,422,308	-0.23%	225/sq km
2030	77,854,102	-0.36%	218/sq km

Large influx of ethnic German and other immigrants from Eastern Europe and Central Asia in 1989/1991 and thereafter no longer offsets general population decline.

Capital Berlin 3,449,540. **Other major cities** Rhein–Ruhr 6.7 millon; Stuttgart 2.7mill; Hamburg 1.8m; München (Munich) 1.3m; Bielefeld 1.3m; Hannover 1.3m; Nurnberg 1.2m; Aachen 1.0m; Koln 1.0m. **Urbanites** 73.8%. **Pop under 15 yrs** 14%. **Life expectancy** 79.8 yrs.

Peoples 👪

Germanic 88.3%. There are a number of regional dialects of German (complete with different regional identities), but these do not constitute fundamental or distinct ethnicities.

Other European 5.9%. Slavic(12) 2.6%; Italian 1.0%; Greek 0.7%; many European minorities.

All Other 5.8%. Turk 3.0%; Gypsy/Romani(5) 0.6%; more than 30 others.

Recent studies indicate that up to 19% of those residing in Germany have a "migration background" – whether from German communities elsewhere or from other ethnicities altogether. 33% of children under age five are from this migration background.

Literacy almost 100%. **Official language** German. There are over 95 million German-speakers worldwide. **All languages** 69. **Indigenous languages** 27. **Languages with Scriptures** 8Bi 4NT 13por 1w.i.p.

Economy 📈

Dramatic post-WWII recovery to become one of the world's strongest economies. One of the world's largest industrial producers, with a massive trade surplus built on the back of a solid export base. In the 1990s, incorporating the crippled East German structure led to high social security costs, while rigid labour laws hampered progress as did low-cost production in neighbouring and competing Central European economies. Economic and social reforms introduced post-2004 have the efficient economic machine running once again. Unemployment remains a concern (3 million), especially in the east, but Germany remains Europe's strongest economy.

HDI Rank 22nd/182. **Public debt** 66% of GDP. **Income/person** $44,729 (94% of USA).

Politics ☒

The collapse of Hitler's Reich in 1945 was followed by 40 years of partition between the democratic and market-economy Federal Republic (FRG) and the Socialist "Democratic" Republic (GDR). The collapse of Communism at the end of the 1980s led to a rapid reunification of the two states in 1990, in reality a takeover by the FRG, which proved socially and economically painful to all. Germany is a very stable and strong democracy, is a core member of the EU and plays a central role in European affairs. Only now, as the post-war generation takes over leadership, is Germany asserting itself once again in an active international role.

Religion ⛪

Religious freedom guaranteed in the constitution. The Catholic and Lutheran Churches are established churches but not formally state churches as such. They collaborate with the government in religious education, media and such and benefit from state-levied taxation on their behalf. The high Christian numbers below are often those only nominally affiliated and who have not opted out of this taxation system. There is increased awareness of other religious options but also increasing suspicion of much of organized religion. Post-9/11, there is a great public interest in the Christian way as an alternative and counterbalance to Islam. Evangelicals are much more prominent than ever before in media and politics.

Religions	Pop %	Population	Ann Gr
Christian	64.25	52,721,478	-0.9%
Non-religious	30.51	25,035,522	1.4%
Muslim	4.40	3,610,498	1.8%
Buddhist	0.27	221,553	4.1%
Jewish	0.25	205,142	-0.1%
Other	0.18	147,702	2.3%

G

Hindu	0.09	73,851	5.1%
Sikh	0.03	24,617	-0.1%
Baha'i	0.02	16,411	-0.1%

Christians Denoms		Pop %	Affiliates	Ann Gr
Protestant	153	31.55	25,891,000	-0.3%
Independent	70	0.80	654,000	0.3%
Anglican	1	0.04	29,000	0.0%
Catholic	1	30.63	25,130,000	-0.9%
Orthodox	19	1.87	1,537,000	2.1%
Marginal	42	0.50	407,000	-0.5%
Unaffiliated		0.03	25,000	-53.5%
Doubly affiliated		-1.17	-960,000	0.0%

Churches	MegaBloc	Congs	Members	Affiliates
Catholic Church	C	15,450	19,632,813	25,130,000
Prot Ch in G	P	16,250	19,312,500	24,720,000
Greek Orthodox Ch	O	62	341,259	488,000
New Apostolic Church	I	2,449	244,898	360,000
Romanian Orthodox	O	120	80,000	320,000
Free Baptist Chs (fSU)	P	310	155,000	310,000
Serbian Orthodox Ch	O	65	142,500	285,000
Jehovah's Witnesses	M	2,225	160,588	273,000
Russ Orth, D Moscow	O	43	122,378	175,000
Fell, Ev Free (Bapt/Bre)	P	855	107,000	128,000
Bulgarian Church	O	15	44,118	75,000
Assoc of Free Pente Chs	P	750	45,000	70,500
Syrian Orthodox Ch	O	12	24,800	62,000
Methodist Church	P	585	34,731	58,000
Evangelical Free Ch	P	400	35,000	56,000
Christian Brethren	P	272	31,928	53,000

Gypsy Evang Movement	I	188	23,500	47,000
Seventh-day Adventist	P	585	36,000	40,000
Latter-day Saints (Mormon)	M	180	17,568	39,000
Armenian Apos Ch	O	6	17,500	35,000
Indep Lutheran Ch	I	280	24,476	35,000
Other denominations[259]		4,180	512,284	888,719
Doubly affiliated				-960,000
Total Christians[286]		**45,282**	**41,145,841**	**52,688,219**

TransBloc	Pop %	Population	Ann Gr
Evangelicals			
Evangelicals	2.1	1,740,880	0.9%
Renewalists			
Charismatics	1.1	864,848	2.0%
Pentecostals	0.3	244,279	3.0%

Missionaries from Germany
P,I,A 3,719 (3,144 long-term) from over 165 agencies: in Germany 463, Brazil 248, Kenya 153, Russia 114, Tanzania 110.

Religions % of Total Pop

Annual Growth Rates

Answers to Prayer

1 **Expressions of grassroots spirituality are springing up** around the country. House churches, youth movements, multicultural congregations, increasing Christian publications and Bible versions in German, new streams of worship and the like demonstrate there is vibrant spiritual life beyond declining organized religion. This in itself is appealing to unbelievers put off by traditional religious structures but with spiritual questions.

2 **The decline of Christianity has drawn believers together.** Prayer movements are forming and spreading as are city- and region-wide unity initiatives among churches, a revitalized spirituality and an openness to a new way of "doing faith".

3 **Evangelism, outreach and mission are being rediscovered** in Germany. From the dynamic, media-driven outreach of *ProChrist/JesusHouse* all the way to increasing missional values in the mainline churches, there is a growing confidence in the gospel in many circles that is being expressed in outward demonstrations of faith.

Challenges for Prayer

1 **Germany's wealth, influence and strategic location** in the EU and Europe could be of inestimable value for the Kingdom of God. For this, a strong, courageous leadership based on Christian values is needed – a fact recognized by many in the nation. Sadly, the past decade witnessed significant erosion of the ethical platform on which such leaders need to stand. Pray for God to raise up leaders who will hold fast to righteousness and strong moral values despite opposition and temptation to compromise.

2 **The 1989 unification of the country remains a burden,** although now more spiritually and psychologically than economically. The eastern part of the country remains a poor sibling, characterized by high unemployment, economic malaise, continued emigration, social and spiritual emptiness and growing racism directed toward immigrant minorities moving in. This is due to the historic lack of knowledge of the good news and despite the government's very costly regeneration efforts. Pray for new life – economic, social and spiritual – to come to this depressed region.

3 **The nation's spiritual health is failing.** Humanism and destructive criticism of the Bible in the 19th Century enfeebled churches and opened the way to compromise and to pagan Nazi tyranny in the 20th. Post-war dynamics accelerated the secularization and de-Christianization of society. Symptoms of this sickness are:

a) *The marginalization of Christianity.* The Church is widely perceived as irrelevant, and open hostility to anything Christian is increasing.

b) *The rise of false religious teachings.* New Age, the occult, Satanism and other religions, including new expressions of pre-Christian paganism, are increasing.

c) *Mental illnesses* are occurring in record numbers, including clinical depression. Suicide is the second-largest killer of 15-29 year olds. Gruesome crimes and killings are also on the rise as many lack a moral foundation to their worldview.

4 **The exodus from organized Christianity** continues into the 21st Century, yet at a slower rate than in the 1990s. West Germany was 97% Christian in 1960, but Germany is now 63% Christian, a percentage that declines with each passing year. In northeastern Germany, possibly only 0.5% are evangelicals. Church attendance is down across the board, falling to near 11% for Catholics, 4% for Lutherans. Thousands are formally disaffiliating in order to avoid the church tax of 8-9% of their income tax, and many churches are closing. Churches seem paralyzed, having lost much of their identity, purpose and income. Germany needs another reformation as deep and lasting as the one sparked by Luther nearly 500 years ago. Some would argue that a more radical revolution, fuelled by altogether new structures, such as house churches, is needed.

5 **The EKD is a federation** of 23 Lutheran, Reformed and United Protestant regional/ national churches, but it suffers deep divisions on many levels. The more evangelical/ conservative groups and congregations are concentrated in Württemberg, Siegerland and south Saxony. Steadily declining attendance – and therefore income – translates into not only low morale for congregations, but also increasingly empty and crumbling physical structures. Many of the Lutheran clergy do not even believe in life after death; it is often difficult for born-again ministers in the EKD to openly minister in their own churches! Since 2001, the need for evangelization is recognized, and new church-development concepts enjoy popularity; without a return to genuine faith in the Bible, however, new concepts and programmes will never replace the need for renewal.

6 **The Free Churches have a higher proportion of evangelicals,** but they constitute only 1% of Germany's population. Many denominations are stagnant or in decline, but others are growing, including charismatic fellowships. Many of these churches are effectively marginalized in the wider society and have minimal genuine impact outside of their traditional constituencies. Pray for vision that will enable these more conservative groups to break forth into dynamic new expressions of faith that both rejuvenate the faithful and draw in those open to Jesus.

7 **German evangelicals** are holding their own as the broader decline in the mainline churches is offset by the growth of some evangelical groups. Over 1,000 churches have been planted in the last 15 years, but this is clearly not enough. Notable trends include:

a) *The EKD continues to decline,* with an overall loss of numbers, although evangelicals are beginning to return. Despite this, the Pietist movement continues to be an influential force within the EKD (especially in Württemberg in the south and in rural areas), numbering hundreds of thousands.

b) *The Evangelical Alliance is a vital network* for over 1.2 million evangelicals in all denominations and hundreds of missions. It exists as a focal point for prayer, theological reflection, cooperative projects, social action, evangelism and mission.

c) *The influx of ethnic Germans* from Central Asia and Eastern Europe over the last 30 years has led to a large increase of Mennonite and Baptist congregations catering for their spiritual health. There are over 4,000 such congregations with more than 350,000 associated with them. Though increasingly missions-minded, they are often culturally isolated from the mainstream of evangelicals.

d) *The increasing number of immigrant churches* is also a point of encouragement. While many German churches decline, congregations are springing up among African, Asian and Latino populations. Pray that their dynamism and spiritual fervour might have an impact beyond their own languages and ethnic groups.

8 **Unity is a great challenge facing believers.** Besides the Protestant-Catholic and liberal-conservative divides, there is also long-standing suspicion between conservative evangelical and Pentecostal/charismatic groups. The increasing marginalization of Christians has helped weaken denominational boundaries. But both sides cooperating on the international level – such as in the Lausanne Movement and the **WEA** – has influenced Germany, and nationwide evangelistic campaigns such as ProChrist/JesusHouse have brought them together in action. Pray for genuine unity within diversity rather than insistence on uniformity, and pray that recent progress in cooperation may continue and expand.

9 **Theological education** was a major cause of decline in the national Protestant Church, because the unchallenged monopoly of state-endorsed academic training and the continued influence of higher criticism undermined confidence in God's Word. For decades, liberal, neo-orthodox and other non-biblical theologians monopolized the degree-granting universities for the EKD, and evangelicals were marginalized. This is now changing as several strong evangelicals hold positions at prominent state faculties. Pray for more professors who openly proclaim the Truth in these institutions, and pray for greater numbers of evangelical students in what used to be spiritual morgues. Pray also for the many other Bible colleges, seminaries and training institutions that retain a closer adherence to biblical truth; pray that effective and practical ministry training might occur. Changes in European education policies now mean that evangelical institutions can get academic accreditation from the government; several have already done so.

10 **Missionary vision has never been outstanding,** although German evangelicals have proportionately been solid missionary senders. The total number of Protestant missionaries has grown considerably in the last 30 years; this is due to the growth of evangelical missions – which today makes up more than 90% of the total Protestant mission force – while ecumenical missions reduced their sending of personnel. Pray for a further increase in mission-sending vision. Pray also for the Association of Evangelical Missions (AEM), with more than 90 members, representing 3,700 missionaries – a catalytic and vital stimulant for training, promoting and sending missionaries. In 1998, the Association of Pentecostal and Charismatic Missions was formed; today it has 43 agencies and 400 missionaries. Both of these groups have grown significantly in recent years. Several unique missions are the **DMG** (German Missionary Fellowship) with 338 missionaries serving with 102 international missions and the *Vereinigte Deutsche Missionshilfe* (**VDM**) with 210 missionaries, but with no foreign fields of their own. Other significant German missions include *Liebenzeller Mission, Christoffel-Blindenmission,* **OM**, *Wiedenest, Allianz-Mission, Christliche Fachkräfte Int,* **WBT**, *Diguna,* **WEC**, *Logos, Kontaktmission.*

11 **Ministry to young people** is vital for a fading Church. The large majority of active Christians are over age 50, and only about 2% of the nation's youth call upon Jesus as their Saviour. There is a new openness to Jesus as the spiritual immunization of quasi-Christianity fades. Pray for the following ministries:

a) *Large-scale outreach events and programmes* – such as *Christival*, JesusHouse, TeenStreet and others – give a sense of excitement and belonging to many young people, while impart-ing good teaching and exhortation. Hundreds of thousands in Germany and beyond are impacted.

b) *Campus ministries.* SMD(**IFES**) has about 70 groups in universities and 800 groups in secondary schools. **CCCI**/Agape with 120 staff is involved in a host of ministry activities. Navigators also minister through university witness. These ministries reaching students are more crucial than ever.

c) **Wort und Wissen** is a significant ministry that prepares students for university life by giv-ing them a good Christian foundation.

d) *CEF(KEB)* has 45 staff workers committed to children's ministry. They have about 200 Good News Clubs, and they run an effective telephone ministry for children in many cities. They also offer a well-accepted correspondence course and a unique website for children. Scripture Union (BLB) also reaches out to children.

12 **Much of the German population is effectively unreached.** Five centuries after the Reformation finds the land of Luther a spiritual wasteland in many parts. German churches as well as increasing numbers of mission agencies attempt to spread the light and plant new churches in the areas of greatest need:

a) *Those in the east* must first overcome three generations of imposed atheism before the Church can flourish. About 80% are effectively unevangelized, and 65% are agnostic or atheist. Eastern Germany remains, for the most part, both economically and spiritually unregenerated. But there is a solid, core group of believers standing firm for Christ.

b) *Whole areas of western Germany,* while superficially Christianized over a thousand years ago, have never really been evangelized. Despite the influence of the Reformation and the Pietist revival movement, many are almost devoid of a live evangelical witness – the northern plains, Bavaria and the Eifel area are examples.

c) *Many cities have become extremely secular* and spiritually needy. Pray especially for Berlin, where 65% have no link with a church and only 3% regularly attend. Together for Berlin is a network promoting unity and cooperation among churches.

d) *The churchless towns of Germany.* A significant proportion of Germany's towns (of more than 5,000 population) do not have an evangelical church. Many new congregations have been planted by independent groups and the Free Church denominations; pray for these small congregations to have a growing impact.

13 **Foreigners.** The rising tide of immigrants, guest workers, international students and refugees since 1989 has been a challenge to German government and society. In many inner cities, migrants are the majority population. Many are illegally in the country and connected to sophisticated criminal networks. While some are vibrant Christians, most have never heard the gospel. A violent and bitter reaction against this inflow, especially in the east, causes many foreigners to resent their mishandling. Pray also for:

a) *The exciting increase of diaspora churches.* Among many foreign peoples – Asian, African, Latin American and European – there is great openness and rapid church growth. Pray for this window of opportunity to be seized, and for immigrant churches to, in turn, reach out cross-culturally to their hosts and neighbours.

b) *The AMIN* (*Arbeitskreis für Migration und Integration*) is a fellowship of mission groups seeking to evangelize through a wide variety of ethnic ministries. A number of local congregations also seek to reach these groups.

c) *Greater involvement in outreach to immigrants* by German Christians. Some congregations are notable exceptions to this, but in the main, most mission outreach is by foreign missionaries in Germany. The Church's response to this opportunity and challenge could determine the future health and size of Christianity in Germany.

d) *International students in Germany,* numbering nearly 250,000, comprise the world's fourth-largest total, after the USA, UK and France. SMD, YMCA, campus ministry groups and increasing numbers of local congregations are focusing on this strategic ministry. "*Der Weg*" is an easy-language, German Christian broadsheet that is effective among students learning German and among the millions of German-language students in Eastern Europe and Eurasia.

e) *Muslim* numbers have grown – mostly through immigration and latterly through high birth rates – to 3.6 million from over 40 nations. Many of them live in ethnic ghettoes with only minimal integration into German society. An estimated 4,000 to 5,000 Muslims come to faith in Christ annually, but 1,000 or more ethnic Germans convert to Islam every year. There are over 2,200 mosques or prayer houses, and Islamic organizations are intensifying their activities.

f) *Least-reached peoples for prayer:*

i *Turks,* together with Kurds, number 2.5 million. More than a dozen agencies seek to reach them (including *Orientdienst*, **WEC**, **OM**, **WV**). The number of Turkish believers is rising, but so is the level of dedication to Islam among Turks in Germany. Lack of integration,

G

joblessness, resentment and honour killings are sadly common themes, even among third-generation German Turks. There are many resources, especially on the Internet, in Turkish for believers and seekers.

ii Kurds – as many as 1 million. A group of agencies is seeking to reach them, with increasing response. Scripture, radio programmes and Christian literature in Kurdish are all being developed.

iii Iranians – 100,000, with several Christian groups and localized outreach attempts.

iv North African Arabs and Berbers – 300,000 and with little outreach.

v Bosniaks (Bosnian Muslims) – numbering 285,000 with little outreach.

vi Jews suffered severely in the Holocaust – 564,000 in 1925 became 27,000 in 1945. With immigration, their numbers have rapidly increased since the 1990s. They now number up to 200,000, mostly from the fSU, and perhaps 2,000 have come to faith in Messiah Jesus. Jews for Jesus and others minister to them.

14 Christian media for prayer:

G

a) Christian literature and publishing has grown enormously over the past decades. Many have been blessed, and literature plays a major part in evangelical growth and consolidation. The German language enjoys more theological publications than any language after English. Pray for the impact of more than 150 evangelical magazines.

b) Christian radio and TV. Pray for:

i The German partner of **TWR***, Evangelium-rundfunk (ERF Medien),* makes an impressive impact on the German-speaking world, with a daily listenership of 200,000 (and 4 million who listen less frequently) on satellite, cable and medium wave. They also produce programmes in 20 other languages for broadcast in Germany and beyond.

ii The many broadcast hours in German across all radio bands, catering to different tastes and generations.

iii The increased programming available in other languages. Pray for many listeners and a good response.

c) Christian TV is increasing. The two key stations are *Bibel-TV* and *ERF Medien*; both run Christian programming 24 hours/day. Additionally Media Vision e.V. and a Coptic Christian channel are just two examples of recent developments, in addition to the annual ProChrist event broadcast over satellite.

d) Internet evangelism has developed greatly in the last few years, with many excellent sites with resources for both believers and seekers (Jesus.de, Gottkenne.com, others). ERF-online also has a website for children.

e) ProChrist and its youth version, JesusHouse, are Christian transdenominational outreaches linked by satellite transmission, held in alternating years, connecting hundreds of sites in Europe. It is based on a main event in one city transmitted live via satellite to 1,000 local broadcast sites in Germany and around Europe, which allows for local mobilization and participation. Pray for great fruitfulness for this high-profile, professional outreach.

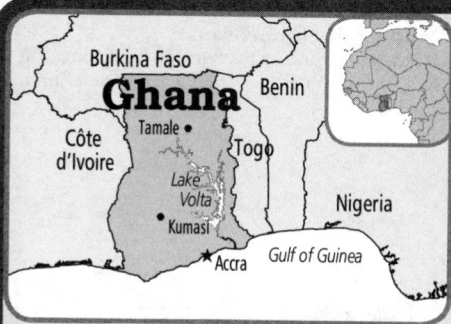

all are subject to external factors and fluctuations. A new lake and hydro-electric project on the western border are being developed. Foreign aid accounts for 10% of GDP. A fertile and once-prosperous land with rich natural resources, Ghana now struggles with poverty – 79% of the population earn less than $2US/day. Once-rich tropical forests have been over-logged, and soil degradation and unreliable rainfall impoverish northern farmers and fuel migration. But a stable political context and good infrastructure hold promise for greater improvement.

HDI Rank 152nd/182. **Public debt** 53.8% of GDP. **Income/person** $739 (2% of USA).

Ghana

Republic of Ghana

Africa

Geography ⊕

Area 238,533 sq km. Grasslands in north, farmland and forest in south. Centre dominated by the 520-km-long Lake Volta, Africa's largest man–made lake.

Population		Ann Gr	Density
2010	24,332,755	2.11%	102/sq km
2020	29,567,415	1.89%	124/sq km
2030	34,883,758	1.59%	146/sq km

Around 70% of the population live in the southern regions. **Capital** Accra 2,341,882. **Other main cities** Kumasi 1.8 million; Tamale 361,000. **Urbanites** 51.5%. **Pop under 15 yrs** 38%. **Life expectancy** 56.5 yrs.

Peoples ††††

About 100 ethnic groups.
Guinean/Kwa 69.2%. Five major groupings in centre and south.
  Akan 40.9%. 10 groups, largest: Ashanti 14.2%; Fante 11.3%; Abrong 5.2%; Akyem 2.9%; Akuapim 2.6%; Kwawu 2.0%; Wassa 1.5%.
  Ewe 11.1%. In southeast.
  Ga-Adangme 7.3%. Dangme 3.9%; Ga 2.9%.
  Guang(13) 3.6%. Gonja 1.1%; Awutu 0.8%.
Gur 25.6%. 29 peoples in 3 major sub-groups in the north. Larger groups: Southern Dagaaba 4.9%; Dagbamba 3.6%; Frafra 3.6%; Konkomba 2.4%; Kusasi 2.0%; Mossi 1.5%; Mamprusi 1.1%.
Yoruba 1.6%.
Other 3.6%. Bissa 0.8%; other African, Westerner, Asian.
Literacy 54.1%. **Official language** English. **All languages** 84. **Indigenous languages** 79. **Languages with Scriptures** 12Bi 28NT 35por 28w.i.p.

Economy ⊠

Agricultural products (especially cocoa and timber), gold and tourism are the main revenue sources, but

Politics ☒

Independent from Britain in 1957. Nkrumah's "socialist" experiment was a disaster. There have been five military regimes since Nkrumah's overthrow in 1966, but since Rawlings' presidency in 1992, the stable transition to multiparty democracy prevails, with several elections praised as open and orderly. Ghana plays a positive regional and continental role in diplomacy and peacekeeping.

Religion ⚵

Secular state with religious freedom since 1992. Traditionally peaceful relations among Christians, Muslims and ethno-religionists seem to now hang in the balance with aggressive outreach by Muslims. Widespread overlaps of religious practices and beliefs, and contradictory claims of numbers of faithful, make exact measurement of affiliates impossible.

Religions	Pop %	Population	Ann Gr
Christian	63.40	15,426,967	2.2%
Muslim	23.79	5,788,762	3.6%
Ethnoreligionist	12.50	3,041,594	-0.9%
Non-religious	0.21	51,099	5.3%
Baha'i	0.10	24,333	2.1%

Christians Denoms		Pop %	Affiliates	Ann Gr
Protestant	60	25.74	6,264,000	3.9%
Independent	161	22.15	5,389,000	3.7%
Anglican	1	1.25	305,000	2.1%
Catholic	1	12.04	2,930,000	1.8%
Marginal	12	1.56	379,000	3.8%
Unaffiliated		0.66	161,000	-30.2

Churches	MegaBloc	Congs	Members	Affiliates
Catholic Church	C	2,000	1,550,000	2,930,000
Church of Pentecost	I	13,300	1,094,595	1,620,000
Methodist Church	P	3,100	1,246,154	1,620,000
Assemblies of God	P	2,150	746,354	1,433,000
Presbyterian Ch of G	P	2,250	451,667	1,355,000
Seventh-day Adventist	P	1,161	375,000	768,750
New Apostolic Ch	I	1,272	254,444	458,000
Anglican Church	A	598	152,500	305,000
Apostolic Church	P	2,043	194,085	291,128
Ch of the 12 Apostles	I	570	114,000	285,000
Jehovah's Witnesses	M	1,477	96,000	259,200
Afr Faith Tab Ch	I	1,420	162,400	203,000

Musama Disco Ch	I	1,564	86,000	172,000
Afr Meth Episcopal Zion	I	421	105,333	158,000
Divine Healers Church	I	950	47,000	142,410
Apostles Revelation	I	570	68,500	137,000
Ghana Baptist Conv	P	617	74,000	123,580
Evang Presbyterian Ch	P	273	39,000	118,170
Ch of Christ, Spiritual	I	323	92,000	115,000
Churches of Christ	P	330	42,273	93,000
Deeper Life Bible Ch	I	781	39,048	82,000
Other denominations[214]		11,478	1,501,724	2,598,011
Total Christians[235]		**48,648**	**8,532,342**	**15,267,249**

TransBloc	Pop %	Population	Ann Gr
Evangelicals			
Evangelicals	24.2	5,879,102	4.5%
Renewalists			
Charismatics	23.1	5,611,790	4.2%
Pentecostals	19.9	4,839,867	4.4%

Missionaries from Ghana

P,I,A An estimated 2,000; one denomination has 70 mission fields; one Charismatic church has 50 fields.

Religions % of Total Pop

TransBloc Movements % of Total Pop

G Answers to Prayer

1 **The relative stability of Ghana,** while not perfect, stands in contrast to the fortunes of its many troubled regional neighbours. Ghana is an example of how a multi-ethnic and multi-faith nation in West Africa can remain largely at peace. Praise God for this and pray that peace might continue to set deeper roots.

2 **Ghana enjoys both a rich Christian tradition** and the emergence of many new churches. Many of the traditional denominations such as Methodist, Presbyterian and Anglican have a vibrant spiritual life, while African Independent Churches (AICs) also grow quickly.

3 **Evangelism among the unreached,** especially the northern peoples (in the north, and northern migrants in the south), is increasing as indigenous churches adopt the challenge of the unevangelized in their midst and send missionaries of their own. The Ghana Evangelism Committee was instrumental in catalyzing this movement.

4 **The continued surge to translate Scripture** into written and audio formats is a powerful driving force behind recent church growth and discipleship. Only five languages had the Bible in 1965; now the majority of Ghanaians have at least the New Testament in their mother tongue. The work of Ghana Institute of Linguistics Literacy and Bible Translation (GILLBT) and UBS is crucial to this. Every language in Ghana still needing a Bible translation has a work in progress! Hundreds of churches have been planted largely due to people's response to newly translated Scriptures in their language.

Challenges for Prayer

1 **The rocky first decades after independence** finally gave way to sustained democratic rule in the 1990s. The solid education system and sensible constitution, both designed to be pan-ethnic, played strong roles in that process. While avoiding large-scale civil war and genocide, Ghana has still been witness to violence along both political and ethnic lines; no country is safe from human sinfulness. Some 47% of Ghana's college-educated citizens live abroad, hampering Ghana's development and prosperity. Pray that those in government might rule with righteousness and wisdom, seeking guidance from God and not from human philosophies or the spirits.

2 **Christianity has long been established in the south.** About 63% of Ghanaians call themselves Christian, but many have only a tenuous link to a church, and attendance figures rarely top 10%. African traditional worldviews and practices too often lie beneath a veneer of Christianity; this dual spirituality is the greatest challenge to the Church in Ghana. The formality and foreignness of many older churches have stimulated rapid growth among some AICs and charismatic churches, which instead offer excitement, involvement and healing, but not always salvation by faith. Pray that the true gospel may shine into the hearts of those who call themselves Christian but who are not born from above. Pray for a decisive break from all fetishism and occult bondages, and that true liberty in Jesus is found.

3 **Pray for a Christian vision for the nation.** Although statistically Ghana enjoys a strong Christian presence, reality presents a much more significant challenge. The GEC conference in 1989 not only set ambitious evangelistic goals, but it also offered great insight into the real evangelistic status of Ghana. These are continuing prayer challenges:

a) The 1.7 million who call themselves Christian but have no link to a church.

b) The millions of Christians who may attend church but whose worldview and values more reflect traditional animist beliefs than biblical truth.

c) Church planting throughout the nation, but especially in the north. There is significant impetus through the GEC and National Church Survey of 2007-08. Thousands of villages in Ghana remain unchurched. A third NCS is due out in 2010.

4 **Mature Christian leaders remain at a premium.** As churches multiply, biblical faith is challenged and doctrines become confused. Compared with some other countries, however, Ghana is blessed by the number of training institutions. Among the many schools are Christian Service University College in Kumasi started by **WEC**, Maranatha University College (**SIM**), Ghana Christian University College and Good News Theological College & Seminary. There are over 30 other accredited denominational and interdenominational Bible schools as well as a range of TEE and lay training programmes run by different denominations and agencies, including a growing number in the AICs.

5 **The missions vision of the Ghanaian Church has grown,** as have agencies and workers. The commitment of southerners to sacrificially reach out to northerners is increasing. There are a number of significant movements worthy of prayer:

a) Missions training is given by several organizations and institutes – CSC and Maranatha as well as Africa Christian Mission, Ghana Evangelical Missionary Institute and GlobeServe Ghana.

b) Christian Outreach Fellowship, with more than 50 missionaries working among Ghana's least-reached peoples. Torchbearers (12 missionaries) and others are also good examples for Ghanaian indigenous missions.

c) The Church of Pentecost has sent church planters to many countries in West Africa and in Europe, especially to the Ghanaian/African diaspora there.

6 **Young people** remain key in the efforts to bring revival to Ghana. Over 40% of the population are under age 15, but specific efforts to reach them are insufficient, despite their spiritual openness. This is particularly the case outside the major cities. In the villages, Islam and African traditional religions tend to hold sway. Pray for the impact of SU in secondary schools; GHAFES(**IFES**) (10 workers), Navigators and **CCCI** in universities and colleges; and **CEF** among young children. Pray for the conversion and discipleship of a new generation of Christians who will make an impact in the religious, cultural, political and economic life of Ghana.

7 **Missionary personnel are still needed** to serve as Bible teachers and trainers, Bible translators, in support roles and even as pioneer evangelists. A key area for prayer is for healthy, helpful partnerships between indigenous church leaders and missionaries. Pray for missions serving the Lord in this land; the largest are: Mercy Ships, **SIM**, Pioneers, **WEC** and **GMS**.

8 **Islam has set out to conquer Ghana** and is making serious headway. The number of Muslims has grown significantly through birthrates, immigration and conversion (especially Muslim men marrying non-Muslim women). Now, the majority of Muslims live in the seven non-Muslim southern regions. Mosques are springing up everywhere, and Islam is becoming a dominant force in the political scene. Education is one area of Islamic attention: founding Islamic educational institutions in Ghana and offering scholarships for promising young Ghanaians to study abroad in Muslim countries. In Muslim areas, religious tension and persecution of non-Muslims are increasing. Despite this, significant numbers of Muslims, including imams, are finding Christ as their Saviour. Pray for loving witness by believers and for the Holy Spirit to win many more Muslims to Jesus.

9 **The less-evangelized peoples of Ghana** remain quite receptive to the good news. Both Ghanaian and expatriate workers are needed for the harvest. In most, less than 2% are Christian of any variety, though few have no Christians. Churches are usually small, and leaders generally have only the most basic training. Pray for:

a) The Gur people cluster, who live mostly in the north. Among the more populous of these 29 northern peoples, only the Wala have a large Christian minority, and only the Mossi have a significant evangelical population at 12.5%.

  i *The traditional peoples* are a complex medley of small population groups that are often scarcely touched by the gospel. ECG/**WEC** is planting churches in this area; response is growing among the Birifor and Konkomba. Pray for greater church growth among the Sisaala (**SIM**), Kasena, Mamprusi, Bulsa (**SIM**) and Frafra (**SIM, AoG, WEC**). Response is slow among the Bimoba, Kusasi and Tampulma (**AoG** and Lutheran). Several smaller groups still have no expatriate or Ghanaian missionaries reaching them.

  ii *Muslim peoples* are traditionally much more resistant to the gospel. These include the Dagbamba (**AoG, SIM, IMB, WEC**) with 1% Christian, the Wala (Baptist Mid-Missions), the Kotokoli and Fulani. There is a new openness among the Dagomba in the **SIM** areas, with new churches being planted.

b) The Guinean/Kwa people cluster, some of whom have been minimally impacted by the gospel. Among them are the Muslim peoples: the dominant Gonja (3% Christian, **WEC**), Anufo (2% Christian), and the animist Chumburung (8% Christian) and Gikyode (4% Christian). These peoples live in the northern or Volta regions of Ghana.

c) Two Mande peoples, the Bissa and the Ligbi.

d) Immigrant peoples, most strongly Islamic in culture. These would include the highly influential Hausa people, whose culture shapes much of West African Islam, as well as the Yoruba, Mandinka and Bissa peoples.

10 **Less-evangelized sectors of society:**

a) The cities have grown by absorbing many ethnic groups. The more than one million northerners in southern cities easily turn to Islam; Christians are now mobilizing to share the gospel with them. Some churches of northerners exist in the south, but they are few and not evangelistic in nature. Pray that both Ghanaian and expatriate workers may be used of God to increase the number of northern-language congregations in the southern cities – this work needs to be deliberately cross-cultural.

b) Trokosi (girls enslaved by fetish priests) number as many as 20,000, mostly in the Ewe and Dangme peoples, as a part of traditional religious practice. It was made illegal in 1998. Several ministries to trokosi women see great responsiveness to the freedom offered in Christ (Every Child, International Needs). Great courage and faith are required to openly oppose this practice, since fetish priests wield significant spiritual power.

c) Street children number over 30,000 (possibly that many in Accra alone). A host of ministries work with these needy children, who usually are abandoned or orphaned.

11 **Christian help ministries for prayer:**

a) Bible translation has made great strides over the last 30 years; GILLBT/**WBT** and The Bible Society are presently working on 34 language projects. Already 20 languages have a NT due to GILLBT's work.

b) Literacy programmes have often been too slow, too late and too limited to make good use of newly translated Scriptures. Pray for many literacy programmes now underway, that they may inspire both young and old with zeal for reading. Pray also for:

  i *Use of audio cassettes* in 67 languages where literacy is low. **GRN** has a wide range of languages and programmes for precisely this. Audio material such as Faith Comes By Hearing is vital for the many oral cultures of Ghana.

  ii *The Bible League's* church-planting literacy project, successfully used to help plant churches in some areas.

c) Literature. Pray for the importation and distribution of Bibles (Ghana Bible Society with UBS) and of Christian literature, by agencies such as Book Aid in the UK and the indigenous Challenge Enterprises/**SIM**, which handles the great majority of all Christian literature in Ghana. Christian bookstores in Ghana number a mere 15. Africa Christian Press publishes a range of Christian books for Africa-wide distribution. Problems are enormous in running an economically viable, indigenous publishing ministry. Bible Correspondence Courses have been most successful (**SIM**, GU/**AoG**).

d) Christian films are used with great effect. The five mobile "cinevans" of Challenge Enterprises/**SIM** have a total audience of over 1.5 million annually. The JESUS film is in use in 34 languages with four more in progress; it is a key to the annual Church Planting Project, coordinated by the GEC. Book of Hope's *The GodMan* is another film with widespread exposure.

e) Other media. Radio, TV and websites are all areas where Ghana's indigenous churches and ministries are beginning to flourish in their ability to both evangelize non-Christians and encourage and disciple believers.

Gibraltar

British Overseas Territory of Gibraltar

Europe

Geography 🌍

Area 6.5 sq km. A strategically located rocky peninsula on the south coast of Spain.

Population		Ann Gr	Density
2010	31,073	0.23%	5,179/sq km
2020	31,582	0.13%	5,264/sq km
2030	31,439	-0.11%	5,240/sq km

Capital Gibraltar 31,000. **Urbanites** 100%. **Pop under 15 yrs** 18%.

Peoples 👪

Gibraltarian 66.0%. Italian, Maltese, British, Jewish, Spanish and Portuguese descent.

Other 34.0%. British 12.9%; Spanish 9.4%; Moroccan 8.56% (with many more as temporary workers); Jewish 2.0%; South Asian 1.1%.

Official languages English and Spanish. **All languages** 3. **Languages with Scriptures** 2Bi.

Economy 📈

Previously largely dependent on a British dockyard and military presence; now a self-sufficient economy balanced between shipping, offshore finance and tourism.

Politics ❎

A British overseas territory after its capture in 1704 (and an important military base until 1991); the 2007 constitution reflects the autonomy and right of self-determination for Gibraltar. The local population steadfastly and overwhelmingly resist Spanish pleas, pressures and blockades to restore the Rock (Gibraltar) to Spain. Most issues are being resolved through tripartite talks involving Gibraltar, UK and Spain.

Religion 🔑

There is full religious freedom.

Religions	Pop %	Population	Ann Gr
Christian	84.80	26,350	0.1%
Muslim	8.90	2,765	0.7%
Non-religious	3.20	994	3.0%
Jewish	2.00	621	0.2%
Hindu	1.10	342	0.2%

Christians Denoms		Pop %	Affiliates	Ann Gr
Protestant	7	1.29	<1,000	1.5%
Independent	4	1.18	<1,000	1.8%
Anglican	1	6.53	2,000	0.2%
Catholic	1	74.66	23,000	0.5%
Marginal	3	0.77	<1,000	-1.6%
Unaffiliated		0.40	<1,000	0.0%

Churches	MegaBloc	Congs	Members	Affiliates
Catholic Church	C	6	14,410	23,200
Church of England	A	3	914	2,030
Charismatic congs	I	3	130	208
Jehovah's Witnesses	M	1	90	180

Filadelfia	I	1	100	160
Other denominations[9]		10	288	460
Total Christians[16]		**24**	**15,932**	**26,238**

TransBloc	Pop %	Population	Ann Gr
Evangelicals			
Evangelicals	2.9	903	1.7%
Renewalists			
Charismatics	3.0	943	1.0%
Pentecostals	0.5	160	2.1%

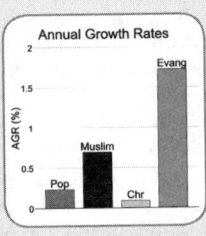

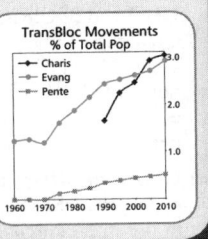

Challenges for Prayer

1 **Most of the population are Catholic,** but there are other mainline denominations (Anglican, Presbyterian and Methodist) as well as a growing number of evangelicals/ charismatics. From four evangelical congregations in 2000, there are now 10. Ministry by these latter groups to the Gibraltarian majority can be difficult due to Catholic predomination. Every home has received at least some Christian literature; the Christian bookshop sells many Bibles. There is a need for unity among believers of these different and diverse small groups, most of which came into being out of the mainline denominations. Pray for further evangelical growth and for revival among the mainline majority churches.

2 **Gibraltar is well placed for outreach** – there are many tourists (especially Spaniards coming for duty-free goods), several thousand Moroccan guest workers as well as a Jewish and a Hindu community. The lack of churches for both southern Spain and North Africa makes Gibraltar a key position for regional outreach. Pray that local congregations would gain a passion for outreach.

3 **Muslims working in or visiting Gibraltar** are very open to receive Christian material and to hear about Jesus; pray that this opportunity might be utilized sensitively but decisively. Pray for effective methods of reaching them and for more workers for this rare opportunity.

islands in the Ionian, Aegean and Mediterranean Seas. The islands constitute 20% of the land area.

Population		Ann Gr	Density
2010	11,183,393	0.22%	85/sq km
2020	11,283,784	0.04%	86/sq km
2030	11,234,382	-0.07%	85/sq km

Capital Athens 3,257,213. **Other major city** Thessaloniki 837,000. **Urbanites** 61.4%. **Pop under 15 yrs** 14%. **Life expectancy** 79.1 yrs.

Greece

Hellenic Republic

Europe

Geography 🌍

Area 131,957 sq km. Southernmost part of Balkan Peninsula in southeast Europe and 150 inhabited

Peoples 👪

Rapid and largely undocumented immigrant movements mean that all numbers are estimates. **Greek** 85.9%. The descendants of the ancient Greeks whose civilization so enriched the world. Includes: Pontic Greeks 1.8%.
Other European peoples 8.5%. Albanian 4.0%; 'Slavomacedonian' 1.8%.
Others 5.4%. Turkish- and Bulgarian-speaking minorities 1.4%; Gypsy/Romani 0.8%; Filipino 0.6%; Arab(4) 0.4%.
Literacy 91%. **Official language** Greek. **All languages** 24. **Indigenous languages** 14. **Languages with Scriptures** 5Bi 3NT 3por.

Economy

EU membership now seems a millstone around Greece's neck. A combination of factors has propelled the economy downward from being potentially dangerous to being outright disastrous. Impossible debts and deficits, increasing unrest and no easy solutions all point toward a troubled financial future for Greece – and the entire EU – no matter what the outcome of the crisis. Tourism, agricultural products and industry are all important. Greece has the largest fleet of merchant ships in the EU.

HDI Rank 25th/182. **Public debt** 97.4% of GDP. **Income/person** $32,105 (68% of USA).

Politics

Nearly four centuries of Turkish rule ended with independence in 1827. The last 100 years have been punctuated by a civil war, two military dictatorships and tensions with neighboring Turkey over the political status of the Cyprus and Aegean borders. Historically hostile relations with Turkey have warmed in recent years due to mutual assistance after earthquakes in both countries. Large-scale immigration from the Balkans and Middle East/Asia is unsettling the ethnic/religious status quo. Greece is a republic with a parliamentary democracy.

Religion

Historically protected by the state, the Orthodox Church is deeply linked to Greek identity. Rapidly increasing minority faiths (mostly through immigration) and corruption scandals in the Orthodox Church have loosened its grip as many call for a separation of church and state.

Religions	Pop %	Population	Ann Gr
Christian	91.46	10,228,331	0.0%
Muslim	5.80	648,637	2.8%
Non-religious	2.70	301,952	4.4%
Ethnoreligionist	0.02	2,237	0.2%
Jewish	0.02	2,237	-7.6%

Christians Denoms		Pop %	Affiliates	Ann Gr
Protestant	19	0.36	40,000	1.6%
Independent	27	0.05	5,000	2.2%
Anglican	1	0.03	4,000	0.5%
Catholic	4	1.48	165,000	6.1%
Orthodox	7	91.84	10,271,000	0.2%
Marginal	2	0.42	47,000	0.8%
Doubly affiliated		*-2.73*	*-305,000*	*0.0%*

Churches	MegaBloc	Congs	Members	Affiliates
Ch of Greece (Orth)	O	29,700	8,564,103	10,020,000
Authentic Old Cal Orth	O	178	105,000	210,000
Catholic Church	C	134	120,438	165,000
Jehovah's Witnesses	M	390	30,500	47,000
Free Apos of Pentecost	P	180	9,000	18,000
Greek Evangelical Ch	P	34	2,640	6,600
Free Evang Chs of G	P	60	2,400	4,900
Foursquare Gospel Ch	P	11	1,688	2,600
Other denominations[49]		205	32,281	58,916
Doubly affiliated				*-305,000*
Total Christians[60]		**30,892**	**8,868,050**	**10,228,016**

TransBloc	Pop %	Population	Ann Gr
Evangelicals			
Evangelicals	0.4	41,376	1.6%
Renewalists			
Charismatics	0.3	30,824	2.2%
Pentecostals	0.2	26,221	1.7%

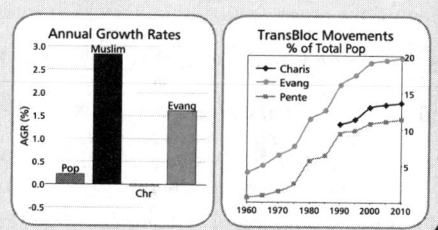

Answers to Prayer

1 **Increased openness,** if only on a legal level, as Greece comes to terms with the existence of large minorities in their midst and as the EU insists on increased religious liberties.

2 **Greece and Turkey's relations,** while still delicate, continue to improve after centuries of hostility. This helps reduce tensions in this volatile region and offers possible solutions to other problems such as the reunification of Cyprus.

Challenges for Prayer

1 **Greece's economic and social travails of the past few years** have caused much uncertainty, upheaval and disruption. The massive deficit and debt, the crisis of the Euro and the threat of financial meltdown regardless of what actions are taken cause fingers of blame to point in all directions. Protests and riots are increasingly common and frequently violent. Regardless of how low the Greek economy must sink until it hits rock-bottom, it has amounted to a genuine shaking of the nation's foundations. Pray that such shaking might drive the nation to cry out to God rather than to trust in the obviously flawed financial solutions offered by economists and politicians.

2 Greece was the first European country to be evangelized (Acts 16:10), but Christianity is now mostly a cultural expression. Less than 3% of the population regularly attend church. Evangelical churches represent less than 0.5% of the population, including all non-Greek evangelicals. The Macedonian call to evangelize is just as valid today.

3 The Orthodox Church was a rallying point for Greece during the long Ottoman and then German occupations. Orthodoxy became a deep part of Greek identity and contributed to an attitude of xenophobia. Other expressions of Christianity are seen as a threat. Renewal within the Orthodox framework tends to mean anti-heresy movements and increased monasticism. Most Greeks are ignorant of the gospel message and are unreceptive to any non-Orthodox witness. Points for prayer:

a) Spiritual renewal and reformation are needed within the Greek Orthodox Church. Pray for the archbishop, the bishops and priests to be led by the Word of God and the Holy Spirit and to in turn lead the people of Greece into a life-changing encounter with the living God.

b) The relationship between Orthodox and Protestant communities has been characterized by rivalry, mistrust and hostility. Pray that members and leaders in both might recognize the true enemy and work together to build God's Kingdom.

c) There are growing calls from within the Orthodox community for the re-evangelization of the Greek people. Thank God for the recognition that there is spiritual work to be done; pray that this may lead to greater collaboration between Orthodox and evangelical churches.

4 Religious minorities have in the past been persecuted by the Greek government and frowned upon socially by the majority. But in recent years things have improved, although discrimination occasionally occurs due to ignorance or fanaticism. While Muslims and Jews enjoy official recognition, Catholics and Protestants often face difficulties in getting the same recognition. In such cases, proselytism tends to be the stumbling block – any groups perceived as attempting to woo Greeks away from Orthodoxy will face opposition. Pray that such discrimination might end and, in turn, that evangelicals might see the effectiveness of working toward the re-evangelization of Greeks in appropriate ways and through the right channels.

5 Ethnic Greek evangelicals are few. Please pray for:

a) Courage to witness in a society where the extreme majority claim to be Christian yet do not have a living faith and relationship with Jesus. Greek society is not just secular and post-Christian, but is subject to a faith that is syncretistic – the amalgamation of Christianity, inherited superstition, atheism, paganism and such.

b) Wisdom in outreach and witness. Greek Protestants acknowledge that proselytism is unnecessary, but that evangelism is. Greeks are more likely to experience new life in Christ through a revitalization of the Orthodox Church than through Protestants drawing Greeks away from their Orthodox background. Pray for ways that allow evangelicals to urgently communicate the need for salvation while respecting the great legacy and heritage of Orthodoxy.

c) Unity in the Spirit. Unfortunately, divisions still exist even among the various Protestant denominations; division can compromise the message they preach. The Pan-Hellenic Evangelical Alliance works as a mouthpiece for all evangelicals and challenges illegal discrimination. Pray for all believing churches to join together and for the Evangelical Alliance to represent them with wisdom and clarity.

6 Evangelism and discipleship remain the real needs in reaching Greece. Short-term ministries (AMG, Hellenic Ministries, **OM**, **WEC** and others) spread the gospel to many, but to have a lasting impact, a longer-term presence is needed. Pray that national churches might develop in the areas of prayer, outreach and church planting. The 2004 Olympics saw the awakening of greater vision for outreach and the completion of some excellent facilities for this purpose, such as the AMG Cosmovision Center. New, non-threatening forms of outreach are being developed that are more engaging and acceptable to a society wary of evangelism. Many of these involve community development service by young people, sports and activities; beyond the gospel being shared, the desired outcome is strengthened families and communities.

7 **Theological training still needs improving.** There are two training institutes, the Greek Bible Institute (**GEM**) and the **AoG** college. A seminary to provide advanced training is a real need.

8 **Many Greeks have never clearly heard the gospel.** More specifically, pray for:

a) *The 150 islands.* Most of the Dodecanese, the Cyclades, the Ionian Islands and others are without evangelical congregations. The believers who are there find themselves spiritually isolated. Hellenic Ministries uses its yacht *The Morning Star* in short-term outreaches to evangelize these isolated communities.

b) *University students.* **CCCI** and **IFES** have strong works among students in Thessaloniki and Athens, but most of the 300,000 students in tertiary education have little exposure to the gospel.

c) *Albanians* number at least 500,000, many of whom are in Greece illegally. Involvement in smuggling and criminal activities results in stigmatization and high incarceration rates. Pray for Greeks and others to reach out in Christian love to this, Greece's largest ethnic minority.

d) *Immigrant communities.* Many thousands of immigrants and asylum-seekers pour into Greece every year from Iraq, Afghanistan, Pakistan, Iran and other places. After a long history of emigration, Greece must recognize that more than 10% of those in the country are foreigners – many from unevangelized nations. The fastest growing churches are the immigrant churches – Russians, Romanians, Filipinos, Africans, Afghans, Iraqis and Pakistanis. Helping Hands (HH) is one ministry that combines compassion with evangelism; many refugees and immigrants have encountered the risen Lord through such outreach. Pray for more churches to get involved in this fruitful ministry.

e) *Indigenous ethnic minorities in the north.* Centuries-old Balkan conflicts have left these groups less-reached than most groups in Greece. Pray for effective outreach to the Albanians and to the Muslim Turks, Romani (Gypsies) and Bulgarian-speaking Pomaks.

f) *The 200,000 drug addicts.* Philemon Center, Kerameas, Pan-Hellenic Mercy Mission, Betel, Reto and others have a year-round ministry to them.

g) *Ministry to the 10,000 prostitutes* is bearing some fruit. Among ministries working in this area are Lost Coin (International Teams), United World Mission, *Nea Zoh* (New Life), *Porta Zohs* (Door of Life). Most women are trafficked in from other countries.

9 **Foreign missions** have not found Greece to be an easy field because of strong nationalism, visa restrictions and the high degree of cultural adaptation required. A general lack of responsiveness (or outright hostility) means that calling must be certain to endure long-term. Major Western mission agencies include **GEM**, **IT**, **CB**/CMML, AMG. Greece's EU membership facilitates the residence of missionaries from other member states, an opportunity not yet fully utilized. Pray for more workers and greater fruit from their faithful labour.

10 **The Greek missionary movement is very small;** only a handful of Greeks serve cross-culturally abroad. But increasing mission interest among a younger generation of believers and growing awareness of the unreached within Greece indicate that Greece might soon become much more of a sending nation than it is today. Greece's position near the Arab, Turkic, Balkan and Slavic worlds makes it highly strategic.

11 **Literature has proven to be a useful tool** in the past, but greater variety would be a blessing. Pray for the seed-sowing work of the Greek Bible Society and the Gideons in disseminating the Scriptures and SU in producing Bible reading aids. AMG founded the publishing house *O Logos* and operates five Christian bookstores around the nation; other publishing ministries include *Pergamos* and *Anogeion*.

12 **Christian Radio and TV.** Some evangelistic programmes have been aired, including the JESUS film. The legalization of private radio stations will allow both Pentecostals and evangelicals to start FM stations once permits are actually given. **TWR** broadcasts by satellite and on secular stations. Pray for the best use of these media and for effective impact.

13 **The large Greek diaspora** totals nearly 7 million of Greek background in 108 countries: USA 3.0 million; Australia 800,000; Germany 400,000; Canada 220,000; Britain 200,000; South Africa 120,000; Russia 100,000. It is both an opportunity for evangelism (especially through the many evangelical Greek churches in USA, Australia, Canada and others) and a good source of Christian workers for Greece itself.

Greenland

Kalallit Nunaat

North America

Geography 🌐

Area 2,175,600 sq km. Land area is 85% glacial ice cap. The world's largest island and with the lowest population density of any country.

Population	Ann Gr	Density
2010	57,291	0.04%	0.03/sq km
2020	57,130	-0.08%	0.03/sq km
2030	54,962	-0.50%	0.03/sq km

Capital Nuuk 15,200. **Urbanites** 84.2%. **Pop under 15 yrs** 24%. **Life expectancy** 70 yrs.

Peoples 👪

Greenland Inuit 88%.
Danes 8.0%.
Other 4.0%.
Literacy 100%. **Official Languages** Inuktitut (Greenlandic), which has three distinct dialects; Danish. **All languages** 2. **Languages with Scriptures** 2Bi.

Economy 🗺️

Based primarily on fishing with substantial support from the Danish government.
Public Debt 2.4% of GDP. **Income/person** $38,747 (85% of USA).

Politics ☒

Overseas administrative division of Denmark with internal self-government since 1979. Increasing autonomy since 2009.

Religion

Freedom of religion since 1953, before which the Lutheran Church was the state church.

Religions	Pop %	Population	Ann Gr
Christian	96.56	55,320	0.0%
Non-religious	2.10	1,203	2.1%
Ethnoreligionist	1.05	602	-1.8%
Baha'i	0.29	166	0.7%

Christians Denoms		Pop %	Affiliates	Ann Gr
Protestant	7	64.59	37,000	-0.3%
Independent	1	0.10	<100	1.1%
Catholic	1	0.23	<200	2.1%
Marginal	1	0.45	<300	-1.1%
Unaffiliated		31.19	18,000	0.0%

Churches	MegaBloc	Congs	Members	Affiliates
Lutheran Church	P	63	26,667	36,000
New Life Church	P	11	290	580
Jehovah's Witnesses	M	8	140	260
Catholic Church	C	1	80	133
Christian Brethren	P	2	50	120
Evangelical (NTM)	P	3	44	75
Other denominations[4]		5	189	285
Total Christians[10]		**93**	**27,460**	**37,453**

TransBloc	Pop %	Population	Ann Gr
Evangelicals			
Evangelicals	4.7	2,664	8.4%
Renewalists			
Charismatics	3.8	2,205	8.1%
Pentecostals	1.0	580	6.7%

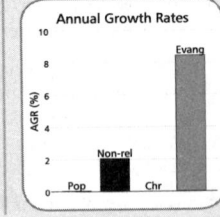

Annual Growth Rates

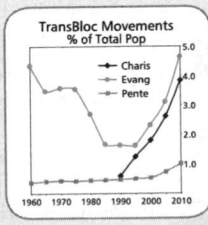

TransBloc Movements % of Total Pop

Challenges for Prayer

1 **Greenland has been Christianized, but not converted.** Nearly every settlement has its Lutheran church building – but too many lack real spiritual life. Pray for renewal and new life for Dane and Greenlander alike. The tightly knit communities of Greenland could easily be impacted powerfully by a move of God.

2 **The culture of Greenland,** so finely tuned to the inhospitable environment, is devastated by modernity. The dire results are widespread immorality and sexual abuse, alcoholism, mental illness and suicide. Deep emotional and spiritual healing are necessary for many to move beyond their pain and hurt. Thankfully, some indigenous believers, missionaries and short-term workers minister in counselling, healing and deliverance and see wonderful fruit as increasing numbers are transformed by the work of the Holy Spirit. Many of those working in Greenland, including many indigenous people, are newly empowered to minister as a result. Pray for this to continue and for those receiving help to get plugged into communities of faith.

3 **Evangelical witness is quite recent.** In 1984, there were only about 20 born-again believers. Now, a growing evangelical movement in several denominations exists – mostly within the New Life Church/Pentecostal framework, although Brethren and **NTM** churches also exist. Travel conditions are extremely harsh, and communities along the coasts isolated; those outside the larger settlements have very little chance to hear the gospel. Thank God for airstrips now built in several remote towns, opening these places for ministry.

4 **Indigenous believers and forms of church are growing.** With input from faithful Caucasian missionaries and indigenous Christian leaders, the Greenlandic Church is expressing itself in ways that are culturally compelling as well as biblical. Pray that the unique worldview and culture of the Inuit people might be made complete in Christ.

5 **Special ministries:**

a) A new and more contemporary version of the Bible in Greenlandic was released in 2001 – pray that many will read it and be changed.

b) The JESUS film was translated into the Greenlandic language through a collaboration of **YWAM**, the Pentecostal Church and **CCCI**; it has received widespread distribution, impacting many.

c) Training for leaders and counsellors. With such widespread brokenness and responsiveness, more Greenlandic Christians must be equipped to minister effectively. Recently, INO established a leadership training school for local believers, for the equipping of the national Church.

G

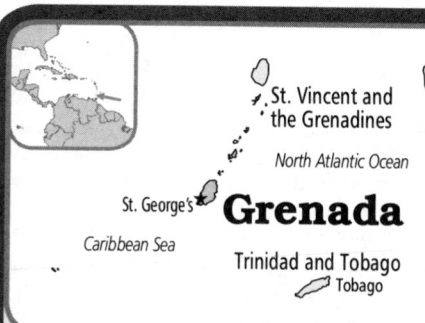

St. Vincent and the Grenadines

North Atlantic Ocean

St. George's **Grenada**

Caribbean Sea

Trinidad and Tobago
Tobago

Grenada
Caribbean

Geography 🌐

Area 345 sq km. One larger island north of Trinidad and some of the Grenadine islets south of St Vincent. The most southerly of the Windward Islands in the West Indies.

Population		Ann Gr	Density
2010	104,342	0.36%	302/sq km
2020	108,393	0.34%	314/sq km
2030	108,327	-0.13%	314/sq km

Capital St. George's 40,800. **Urbanites** 31.0%. **Pop under 15 yrs** 28%. **Life expectancy** 75.3 yrs.

Peoples 👪

African Caribbean 93.1%. Predominantly African with a mix of East Indian, Caucasian and some Carib/Arawak.

East Indian 3.6%.
Euro–American/Other 3.3%.
Literacy 95%, functional literacy much lower.
Official language English, but a distinct Grenadian dialect thereof is much more common.
All languages 3. **Languages with Scriptures** 1Bi 1NT 1por.

Economy 🗺️

Major economic activities are tourism (especially cruise ships) and agriculture (spices, cocoa, bananas). One of the fastest-growing economies in the Caribbean; poverty is nonetheless widespread and a major cause of urbanization and emigration. Recent hurricanes greatly damaged the infrastructure and economy. **HDI Rank** 74th/182. **Public debt** 67.8% of GDP. **Income/person** $6,587 (14% of USA). **Unemployment** 15%.

Politics ❌

French rule 1650-1783, when ceded to Britain. Independent in 1974 as a parliamentary monarchy. Independence has proved stormy – with eccentric leaders, radical revolutions and two increasingly socialist coups. Having started with good intentions for the poor, the coups devolved into greater repression; the last provoked the request for US intervention in 1983 and restoration of democratic government. A stable constitutional monarchy with a parliamentary democratic form of government since 1983.

Religion

There is complete freedom of religion.

Religions	Pop %	Population	Ann Gr
Christian	93.70	97,768	0.2%
Non-religious	3.50	3,652	4.2%
Ethnoreligionist	1.60	1,669	3.1%
Hindu	0.70	730	0.4%
Muslim	0.35	365	2.2%
Baha'i	0.15	157	0.4%

Christians	Denoms	Pop %	Affiliates	Ann Gr
Protestant	23	29.31	31,000	1.0%
Independent	4	4.48	5,000	1.0%
Anglican	1	13.61	14,000	0.3%
Catholic	1	53.72	56,000	0.0%
Marginal	5	2.03	2,000	1.0%
Doubly affiliated		-9.49	-10,000	0.0%

Churches	MegaBloc	Congs	Members	Affiliates
Catholic Church	C	20	30,797	56,050
Seventh-day Adventist	P	130	13,000	14,600
Anglican Church	A	25	4,965	14,200
Pentecostal Assemblies	P	23	1,814	3,030
Methodist Church	P	14	1,385	2,520
NT Ch of God	P	17	1,500	2,280
Jehovah's Witnesses	M	9	586	1,320
Presbyterian Church	P	6	660	1,188
Christian Brethren	P	8	682	1,160
Foursquare Gospel Ch	P	11	846	1,100
Open Bible Standard Ch	P	7	630	1,052
Other denominations[23]		84	4,637	9,125
Doubly affiliated				-9,900
Total Christians[34]		**354**	**61,502**	**97,765**

TransBloc	Pop %	Population	Ann Gr
Evangelicals			
Evangelicals	19.6	20,447	0.7%
Renewalists			
Charismatics	13.6	14,163	0.7%
Pentecostals	11.4	11,862	0.9%

Religions % of Total Pop

TransBloc Movements % of Total Pop

Challenges to Prayer

1 **The devastation of hurricanes** in 2004 and 2005 is still felt. Although fewer than 40 were killed, 90% of the nation's buildings were destroyed, and the agriculture and tourism sectors were virtually annihilated. Both sectors have been rebuilt, but the nation is deeply in debt as a result. Pray for ways to recover from this debt and to protect from such scale of damage in the future; and, above all, pray for a dependence on God rather than on material things.

2 **The Grenadian diaspora is large,** numbering possibly twice as many as those living in the country. The weak economy is the major cause of emigration, exacerbating the challenges of urbanization and a listless, dissatisfied younger generation.

3 **Christianity in Grenada** accounts for the vast majority, but most are nominally Catholic because of the earlier French legacy. However, several mainline, conservative and emerging denominations enjoy a healthy existence. Points for prayer include:

a) Unity among denominations. The mainline denominations enjoy strong connections through the Conference of Churches of Grenada. Evangelicals are taking steps toward greater unity and cooperation through a recently formed Evangelical Alliance. Pray that such unity would be genuine and effective rather than superficial.

b) Moral and family decline, even in evangelical congregations. Sexual promiscuity and teen pregnancies are widespread; around 45% of households are led by women, with men absent (often abroad in search of employment).

c) Lack of vision in churches. There is very little missionary vision or evangelistic impetus, although there are signs of improvement in this area.

d) Support ministries. There are two Christian bookstores, one in St. George's run by the Berean Bible Churches, and an independent one in Grand Anse. Radio ministry includes Good News FM broadcast from Grenada and Harbour Light, a Christian radio station that broadcasts on AM and FM to Grenada and the Windward Islands. Churches consider the six Christian and church-run schools to be important ministries.

Guadeloupe

Department of Guadeloupe

Caribbean

Geography 🌐

Area 1,780 sq km. One larger pair of islands and three smaller islands: Marie Galante, Les Saintes, La Désirade.

Population		Ann Gr	Density
2010	467,182	0.51%	262/sq km
2020	483,814	0.31%	272/sq km
2030	491,843	0.11%	276/sq km

Capital Basse-Terre 13,100. **Urbanites** 98.4%. **Pop under 15 yrs** 22%. **Life expectancy** 79.1 yrs.

Peoples 👪

African descent 71%.
South Asian descent 15%. Mostly Tamil.
Creole 2%.
Other Caribbean 3%. Haitian, Dominican, others.
Arab 2%. Lebanese/Syrian.
European 7%. Mostly French.
Literacy 90%. **Official language** French. The French Creole is widely spoken. **All languages** 4. **Languages with Scriptures** 3Bi 1w.i.p.

Economy 🗺️

Agriculture, services and tourism are sustained by large subsidies from Europe. The standard of living is heavily dependent on imports. There is widespread unemployment, especially among youth. Both the standard of living and the cost of living are higher than many Caribbean islands. Though Guadeloupe is a French *département*, 2009 was marked by protests and riots over Guadeloupe's standard of living, which is notably lower than that in France.

Politics ❌

French colony since 1635. Overseas Department of France since 1946. This status allows access to public funds from France and the EU, creating low motivation for more autonomy and greater demands for French subsidization.

Religion 🙏

Religious freedom, but with a strong secularist tendency.

Religions	Pop %	Population	Ann Gr
Christian	94.09	439,572	0.4%
Non-religious	4.61	21,537	3.5%
Muslim	0.50	2,336	0.5%
Hindu	0.50	2,336	0.5%
Baha'i	0.30	1,402	-5.1%

Christians Denoms		Pop %	Affiliates	Ann Gr
Protestant	12	7.29	34,000	1.4%
Independent	5	0.54	3,000	2.9%
Catholic	1	85.04	397,000	0.1%
Marginal	2	4.00	19,000	2.9%
Doubly affiliated		*-2.78*	*-13,000*	*0.0%*

Churches	MegaBloc	Congs	Members	Affiliates
Catholic Church	C	52	210,000	397,300
Jehovah's Witnesses	M	135	9,000	17,200
Seventh-day Adventist	P	61	12,700	15,700
Evangelical Ch (WT)	P	27	3,500	9,000
Assemblies of God	P	16	1,400	3,500
Ch of God (Cleveland)	P	11	1,250	1,700
Baptist Convention	P	13	750	1,200
Evang Reformed Ch	P	14	719	1,200
Ch of the Nazarene	P	5	720	900
Other denominations[11]		38	2,353	4,915
Doubly affiliated				*-13,000*
Total Christians[20]		**372**	**242,392**	**439,615**

TransBloc	Pop %	Population	Ann Gr
Evangelicals			
Evangelicals	4.3	20,273	1.3%
Renewalists			
Charismatics	8.6	40,080	1.5%
Pentecostals	1.4	6,630	1.2%

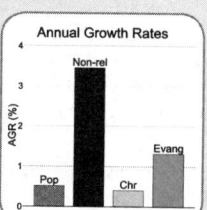

Annual Growth Rates

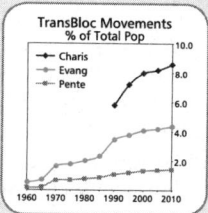

TransBloc Movements
% of Total Pop

Challenges for Prayer

1 **The protests, strike and riots of 2009** were the largest in Guadeloupe's history and pointed to deep dissatisfaction with its relationship to France. Many feel like second-class citizens in a cul-de-sac of poverty, resentful of the continued colonial dynamic with France and its rich white scions living on the islands. Though a settlement was based around increased wages for tens of thousands, the deeper issues of autonomy and identity will continue to simmer. Pray for wisdom for both France and Guadeloupe's leaders to handle these issues in peaceful ways that bring genuine long-term benefit to the people.

2 **The grim legacy of slavery** has left its mark in the endemic economic disparity and in the lack of meaningful marriage relationships. Over 40% of households have only one parent; 90% of these are led by the mother. Racial tension and class envy are other marks left by slavery's long history. Pray that the gospel may transform and uplift this society.

3 **Christianity, especially Catholicism, is a cultural veneer for most.** The rapid growth of sects and evangelical groups highlights the spiritual emptiness. Occultism and magic are widespread influences. Pray for the Holy Spirit to convict of sin and bring many to true repentance.

4 **Evangelicals hardly existed before 1946,** but through the work of World Team, Southern Baptists and **AoG**, a strong network of churches has sprung up, supplemented by several other recent denominational arrivals. Many evangelical groups practice strict, even legalistic, codes of conduct in order to avoid moral compromise and occult influence. Pray for a greater degree of unity, collaboration and a profound understanding of the freedom to be found in Christ.

5 **Areas and peoples less reached with the gospel:**

a) *The outlying islands are less evangelized* – Marie Galante, Les Saintes and La Désirade. **WT**/Evangelical Church work on these islands. But island communities are closely knit, making it difficult for believers to break with tradition.

b) *Those of Asian descent* – most are Tamil in background, but also Chinese and Arab. Most Tamils are nominally Catholic, while retaining many of their Hindu beliefs. There is at least one Chinese congregation.

c) *Haitian immigrants* are proving quite responsive to the gospel through the ministry of the Evangelical Baptist Mission.

d) *The metropolitan French* are largely from France; they are mostly in military or civil service. Few show any spiritual interest.

6 **Leadership training** for the growing churches is provided locally through the Evangelical Church's TEE programme with 250 students and through the **YWAM** DTS. Pray that national Christian workers may be called for service at home and to the Francophone lands around the world.

7 **Specialist Christian ministries** for prayer:

a) *Young people.* The GBU(**IFES**), with a strong evangelistic and missionary focus, is very active in the schools and university, where secular-humanist values are propagated. **YWAM** works with young people, **WT** and **CEF** with children. **CEF** runs Good News Clubs, trains workers to evangelize children and has a weekly radio broadcast and correspondence course for children.

b) *Literature.* **CLC** runs a bookstore on Guadeloupe. The Gideons and The Bible Society distribute Bibles and Christian literature.

c) *Broadcasting.* *Radio Souffle de Vie* is a Christian FM station running 24/7. There are other Christian broadcasts from outside Guadeloupe available on radio, television and, of course, via the Internet.

North Pacific Ocean

Northern Marianas

Agana **Guam**

Guam

US Territory of Guam

Pacific

Geography

Area 541 sq km. Most southerly and largest island of the Marianas Archipelago; 6,000 km west of Hawaii. Also included here (but not as part of Guam itself) are the three tiny US Territories of Johnston Island (2.8 sq km; 1,300 km from Hawaii), Midway Island (5.2 sq km; 2,350 km) and Wake Island (6.5 sq km; 3,700 km).

Population		Ann Gr	Density
2010	179,893	1.31%	333/sq km
2020	201,438	1.09%	372/sq km
2030	220,312	0.82%	407/sq km

There are estimated to be a further 26,000 illegal immigrants. Also included here: Johnston Island, population 1,700; Midway 13; Wake 300.
Capital Agana 155,000. **Urbanites** 93.2%. **Pop under 15 yrs** 28%. **Life expectancy** 78.6 yrs.

Peoples

Micronesian 49.2%. Chamorro 45.8%; other Islanders 3.3%, mainly Chuukese.
Asian 37.9%. Filipino 31.1%; Korean 3.6%; Japanese 1.7%; Chinese 1.4%.
Caucasian 12.9%. Mostly US citizens.
Literacy virtually 100%. **Official languages** English and Chamorro. **All languages** 8. **Indigenous languages** 2. **Languages with Scriptures** 1Bi 1por 1w.i.p.

Economy

One-third of the island is used for US military bases. More than a third of Guamanians are employed by the government or military, a number set to dramatically increase as the US marine base in Okinawa relocates to Guam in 2014. Tourism, a growing industry, is the largest component of the economy. 25% of the local populace is dependent on welfare assistance.
Income/person $22,661 (50% of continental USA).

Politics

Spanish rule 1565-1898. A self-governing, unincorporated US Territory since then. Guamanians are US citizens.

Religion

Religions	Pop %	Population	Ann Gr
Christian	96.69	173,939	1.3%
Buddhist	1.40	2,519	-0.1%
Baha'i	0.74	1,331	1.0%
Chinese	0.45	810	6.5%
Non-religious	0.40	720	-3.1%
Ethnoreligionist	0.32	576	-0.5%

Christians Denoms		Pop %	Affiliates	Ann Gr
Protestant	33	14.64	26,000	0.4%
Independent	9	1.28	2,000	2.8%
Anglican	1	0.61	1,000	1.3%
Catholic	1	76.71	138,000	1.0%
Marginal	2	1.47	3,000	0.5%
Unaffiliated		1.98	3,500	32.0%

Churches	MegaBloc	Congs	Members	Affiliates
Catholic Church	C	31	78,857	138,000
Seventh-day Adventist	P	6	2,100	4,200
Assemblies of God	P	8	1,400	2,200
Korean Presbyterians	P	35	1,250	2,125
Latter-day Saints (Mormon)	M	2	958	1,600
Episcopal Church	A	3	730	1,095
Jehovah's Witnesses	M	7	630	1,052
Independent Baptists	P	3	600	1,002
General Baptist Mission	P	4	300	670
Baptist Conv (IMB)	P	2	250	625
Other denominations[34]		105	8,490	17,813
Total Christians[46]		**206**	**95,565**	**170,382**

TransBloc	Pop %	Population	Ann Gr
Evangelicals			
Evangelicals	14.2	25,621	0.6%
Renewalists			
Charismatics	11.9	21,322	1.6%
Pentecostals	5.4	9,751	-0.7%

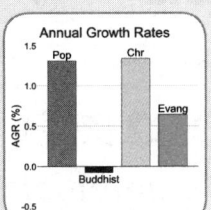

Annual Growth Rates

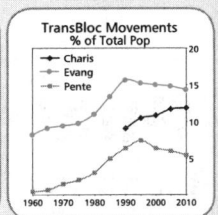

TransBloc Movements
% of Total Pop

Challenges for Prayer

1 **Guam is the hub of Micronesia,** and as such, the population is multicultural and diverse. There is spiritual and church growth among many of the immigrant communities, including the Chinese, Koreans and Filipinos. Micronesian groups have dozens of churches, although their more isolated villages and their tribal culture present an evangelistic challenge. The continued influence of cultural and animistic traditions holds back their discipleship. Also, with such ethnic and denominational variety, unity is an important issue and a need for prayer.

2 **The influx of US culture,** with all of its pros and cons, has irrevocably shaped Guam. There is an increasing presence of wealth and tourism, but also gambling, substance abuse and prostitution/sex trafficking. With the American military presence increasing on the island, these issues will only intensify in the future. Pray for biblical righteousness to shape Guam's society and public life.

3 **The indigenous Chamorro** have a long history of oppression and, more recently, disorientation with the influx of US culture. The majority are nominally Catholic and historically resistant to the gospel. Chamorro worldview is also rooted in animistic traditions. Pray for the emergence of a true Chamorro Christian witness and culture.

4 **Expatriate missionary work** focuses on church planting among indigenous and immigrant peoples, Bible teaching and development. Major missions are SdA, Korean Presbyterians, **LM**, CoG(Anderson), **CoN**, Elim Fellowship. There are three Bible colleges, the main one being Pacific Islands University with about 100 students on site. Practical ministries include addiction recovery centres and vocational training for individuals with disabilities.

5 **Missionary outreach from Guam is beginning to occur.** The churches have the capacity and desire to send missionaries to the Pacific nations, and the increasing influx of tourists from Japan, Korea and elsewhere makes for witnessing opportunities right at home.

6 **The Prison Fellowship of Guam** has a ministry to prisoners that is also penetrating the indigenous population in a small but significant way. It has fostered a cooperative unity among evangelical churches (with 85 volunteers), which is sadly lacking elsewhere. Pray for resources to teach and train converts who remain in prison.

7 **Christian radio. TWR's** transmitting station in Guam broadcasts radio programmes to China, Cambodia and several other nations. Pray for more workers for this ministry.

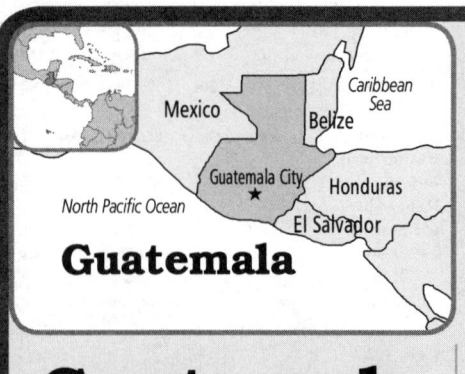

Guatemala

Guatemala

Republic of Guatemala

Latin America

Geography

Area 108,889 sq km. A land of mountains, volcanoes and lakes. Mexico's southern neighbour.

Population		Ann Gr	Density
2010	14,376,881	2.50%	132/sq km
2020	18,091,326	2.20%	166/sq km
2030	21,692,293	1.71%	199/sq km

Capital Guatemala City 1,104,072. **Urbanites** 49.5%. **Pop under 15 yrs** 42%. **Life expectancy** 70.1 yrs.

Peoples

Spanish-speaking Ladinos 53.0%. Mixed European and Indian.

Amerindian 44.7%.

　Maya 36.3%. 31 ethnic groups. Largest: Quiche(8) 22.7%; Mam(6) 5.3%; Kekchi 3.9%; Kanjobal(2) 1.2%; Pocomchi(2) 0.9%; Pocomam(3) 0.5%.

　Other Central America indigenous 8.4%. 21 groups. Cakchiquel(11) 5.0%.

Other 2.3%. Korean, Chinese, Arab, Garifuna, Western, other.

Literacy 69.1%. Much lower in practice. **Official language** Spanish; 23 recognized Amerindian languages. **All languages and dialects** 42-52. **Languages with Scriptures** 6Bi 27NT 37por 21w.i.p.

Economy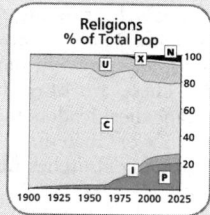

Agriculture provides 23% of the country's GDP but provides 75% of its exports and half of the nation's jobs – mainly coffee, sugar and bananas. Major inequity in income and living standards as the majority still live in poverty; indigenous peoples are particularly oppressed. Since the 1996 peace accord, economic growth and living standards have improved. Leaving ruin in their wake, frequent hurricanes have been major setbacks. A major transshipment point for the drug trade; 70% of the cocaine bound for the USA passes through Guatemala.
HDI Rank 122nd/182. **Public debt** 25.7% of GDP. **Income/person** $2,850 (6% of USA).

Politics

Independent from Spain in 1821, and from the Federation of Central American States in 1838, but controlled by a few plantation owners through a series of dictatorships and military governments. The poor, particularly the Mayans, suffered years of indignity and deprivation, which exploded in 1960 into 36 years of guerrilla war, with around 200,000 deaths, mainly at the hands of the US-armed military. The human rights record during those years was appalling, with over 40,000 "disappearances", widespread torture and displacement of 1 million internal and 250,000 international refugees. The 1996 peace agreement ended warfare and allowed the country to move forward. Elections in 2007 saw a centre-left party win on a platform that emphasized national unity and opportunities for Mayan peoples.

Religion

Official separation of church and state for over 100 years has given great freedom for evangelicals and increased their influence at the expense of the previously dominant Catholic Church. A significant proportion of Catholics are basically syncretized Christo-pagans, with their traditional Mayan gods becoming Catholic "saints". Syncretism is also a challenge for evangelicals, especially those of Amerindian background.

Religions	Pop %	Population	Ann Gr
Christian	96.12	13,819,058	2.4%
Non-religious	3.50	503,191	5.7%
Ethnoreligionist	0.30	43,131	-3.2%
Buddhist	0.05	7,188	2.5%
Chinese	0.02	2,875	2.5%
Muslim	0.01	1,438	2.5%

Christians	Denoms	Pop %	Affiliates	Ann Gr
Protestant	42	19.23	2,765,000	3.0%
Independent	28	6.57	945,000	3.3%
Anglican	1	0.02	2,000	2.6%
Catholic	1	55.19	7,935,000	2.0%
Marginal	3	2.06	296,000	3.4%
Unaffiliated		15.07	2,167,000	-0.5%
Doubly affiliated		*-2.03*	*-292,000*	*0.0%*

Churches	MegaBloc	Congs	Members	Affiliates
Catholic Church	C	285	4,289,189	7,935,000
Assemblies of God	P	2,720	133,127	430,000
Ch of God, Full Gospel	P	1,900	210,000	378,000
Evang Ch, C Amer	P	2,414	140,000	280,000
Latter-day Saints (Mormon)	M	687	127,027	235,000
Prince of Peace Evang	P	1,900	135,000	229,500
Seventh-day Adventist	P	477	120,787	215,000
Ch of the Nazarene	P	580	76,500	153,000
Elim Christian Mission	P	1,314	92,000	138,000
Christian Brethren	P	920	58,000	121,800
Baptist Convention	P	350	43,000	99,000
Lluvias de Gracia	I	179	42,000	84,000
Calvary Christian Min	P	288	23,000	46,000
Ev Miss, Holy Spirit	I	267	24,000	40,080
Voice of God Ev Assoc	I	333	20,000	40,000
Other denominations[60]		10,281	680,285	1,518,647
Doubly affiliated				*-291,900*
Total Christians[75]		**24,895**	**6,213,915**	**11,651,127**

TransBloc	Pop %	Population	Ann Gr
Evangelicals			
Evangelicals	24.4	3,514,428	3.2%
Renewalists			
Charismatics	18.5	2,659,311	3.7%
Pentecostals	14.8	2,123,430	3.0%

Missionaries from Guatemala
P,I,A 161 (103 long-term) in 29 agencies: in Guatemala 21, elsewhere in Central America and Mexico 41, Middle East 20, Europe 19.

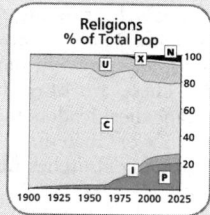

Religions % of Total Pop

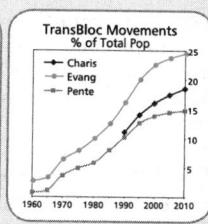

TransBloc Movements % of Total Pop

Answers to Prayer

1 **Growth among evangelicals** (and charismatics) was sustained over several decades to reach a peak of 24.4% of the population. Some see this growth continuing, but those more sober-minded point to an impending evangelical decline. Contributing factors to this growth are the devastating 1976 earthquake, the violence and pain of war, the effective witness of believers and the large, dedicated force of missionaries.

2 **The authorities' appreciation for and cooperation with evangelicals and committed Catholics** contributing toward solutions of social problems such as street children, substance abuse, homelessness and illiteracy.

3 **The rightful placement of justice** for the Mayan peoples on the social agenda, after centuries of dispossession, exploitation and oppression. Both the government and the churches are beginning to address a litany of wrongdoings.

Challenges for Prayer

G

1 **Sins of the past must be recognized,** repented of and reparations made. Most notably this includes the terrible mistreatment of the indigenous population and a generation of war with atrocities on both sides. The part played by the USA in arming the oppressors and turning a blind eye to human rights abuses has only been partially acknowledged. There must also be a recognition of the multicultural character of the country. Progress is being made in these areas. Pray especially for evangelical leaders from both Mayan and Spanish-speaking communities as they work toward the healing of the nation.

2 **Violence is a present-day plague** caused by the upheaval and ruin of the last few decades. Murder is common, and life is cheap. Guatemala has the highest murder rate in all Latin America. The causes: *maras* (youth gangs), drug traffickers, organized crime and "social cleansing" – a.k.a. death squads. Government forces can do little to tackle these issues, and private armed guards outnumber police two to one. Pray for a binding of the spirit of murder and for the peace of Christ to prevail.

3 **The Catholic Church has declined** in influence and number. Defection to evangelicalism or to the revived Mayan spirituality is massive. Efforts by the Church to limit the impact of the large, charismatic renewal movement have only further hastened the decline, with many Catholic charismatics leaving to start new churches or to join evangelical denominations. Pray for new life to permeate the Church, and that charismatics may be rooted in Scripture rather than in subjective experience.

4 **Widespread evangelism occurs by many means** – city crusades, nationwide efforts, 148 Christian schools and institutes, two Christian television channels, more than 50 local Christian radio stations, numerous Christian magazines and newspapers as well as the fervent personal witness of individual Christians. Pray that the fruit may be retained, the believers matured and the new generation won for Christ. Shallow professions of faith and an increased rate of backsliding are becoming common as evangelicals become more "popular". Nominal evangelicalism is a new challenge facing the churches.

5 **The strength and growth of evangelicals are not yet fully reflected** in their social impact and spiritual depth. There are now as many as 25,000 congregations of evangelical persuasion. A number of rapidly growing megachurches have recently emerged to ascend to great size and influence. These are often based on cell models and prosperity theology. Pray that unity among evangelical leaders might continue to improve and be maintained, an aim of the Evangelical Alliance of Guatemala, which represents the vast majority of evangelicals. Pray that these quickly-growing churches might reach out to address the many needs in the wider community.

6 **The future of evangelicalism is uncertain.** While there has been great growth since the 1960s, especially among Pentecostals, much of this growth is superficial, impressive only in number. Discipleship is sorely lacking as a deep value in most evangelical churches. Syncretism is nearly as common in many evangelical churches – particularly among Amerindians – as it is in

Catholicism. If serious efforts are not made to build disciples on a solid biblical foundation, the next couple of decades will see stagnation and possibly a disastrous decline in evangelicalism. Some claim this decline has been occurring for over 10 years, obscured only by strong growth in a few churches and zealous over-reporting in most others. Pray that this crucial issue of turning converts into disciples might be rightly addressed by evangelicals as the key to Guatemala's spiritual future.

7 **Leadership training** is a key issue, but a solid foundation has been laid. There are six seminaries, including SETECA (Central American Theological Seminary), founded by **CAMI** and now under Guatemalan leadership. It has 1,000 students from 18 countries, and 2,000 graduates serving worldwide. There are many Bible schools (including 27 of **AoG**) and over six TEE programmes. TEE was pioneered here by Presbyterians in the 1960s and is now used worldwide. Pray especially for effective ways to train leaders of poorer rural churches. Pray also that pastors and leaders would demonstrate Christ-like humility and graciousness and rise above petty divisions, pride and carnality.

8 **Mayan culture is enjoying a renaissance** after the rediscovery of their ancient civilization. For some, this is a resurrection of the old, long-submerged Mayan religion, but to others, it is a blossoming of indigenous Christianity aided by the many new translations of the Bible in indigenous languages. There are church-planting movements among many groups, most notably the Kekchi (Baptists and Mennonites). **CAMI, CoN** and Mennonites also work among Mayan peoples. There has been outreach to every tribe. Pray for these churches to become mature, effectively led and a vital contribution to the Church in the nation.

9 **Bible translation.** SIL made a significant contribution to 38 Amerindian peoples in overseeing NT translations for many of them. National believers now carry the torch for most or all of the dozen remaining translation projects. Pray for the successful completion and effective use of these translations.

10 **The less-reached:**

a) Amerindian peoples with fewer active believers – the Chorti, Pocomchi, Ixil and Jacaltec show less response to the gospel, yet there are active, growing churches and ministries among them.

b) Garifuna (Black Carib), who are descendants of Africans and Carib Amerindians. The JESUS film has been dubbed in their language, and the whole Bible was completed in their language in 2002.

c) Asians, including the Chinese. Only a few small fellowships of believers are known for this rapidly growing population. The numbers of Koreans and Arabs are also growing.

d) Young people and students are a massive harvest field; 72% of the population are under 30 years old. Both **CCCI** (four groups) and **GEU/IFES** (seven groups) have campus ministries and evangelistic outreach – but there are over 100 colleges in the capital city alone.

11 **Children at risk.** The majority of children between ages six and 18 live in extreme poverty, with large numbers orphaned or from broken homes. Non-existent social support structures drive them to child labour or toward drugs, gangs or the sex industry. Around 15,000 children live on the streets. Many documented cases exist of death squads murdering these unwanted "nuisances". A number of local and international ministries seek to help them; pray for real solutions to these desperate needs.

12 **The Guatemalan missionary movement** began in 1982 with a vision for the world. In 1984, the *Agencia Misionera Evangélica* (AME) was founded, and since then, other missions have been launched. There are at least three missionary training centres. CONEM (the National Commission of Mission to the World) coordinates the national missions effort. A missions conference for pastors put on by national mission organizations is a new development; pray for its effectiveness in helping church leaders catch a vision for missions.

13 **Foreign missions** have lavished attention on the land. The pioneer missionaries' battle of faith sowed today's harvest. Special note must be made of the Presbyterians, **AoG**, ICFG, **CAMI**, Brethren and Nazarene pioneers. Though much foreign input is being phased out, there are still key areas where mission input is important.

a) **The JESUS film,** available in 13 languages, has been widely used by many churches. Please pray for progress in the translation and production of the JESUS film in the remaining languages of smaller, isolated people groups who currently have little or no access to Scripture in their mother tongue.

b) **Christian TV/Radio programmes** are widely available on many national and local radio stations – there are literally dozens of stations. **HCJB** moved its TV operations to Guatemala and cooperates with a local Christian station to broadcast to Guatemala and globally. Radio Cultural TGN is one of a few broadcasting in several indigenous languages. However, a number of Christian radio stations are being forced to shut down due to pressure from secular radio on the government.

c) **Audio recordings** are vital for the many illiterates. **GRN** has gospel resources in 47 languages. Scripture tapes produced by SIL and others are a key contribution to teaching. Pocket-sized digital audio players packed with Scripture and Christian teaching are proving effective; translating the materials into indigenous languages is the next challenge.

G

Mikifore 0.1%.
Mande–Fu 9.2%. Kpelle 4.7%; Toma 2.0%; Kono 1.3%; Mano 1.0%.
Other 2.3%. Refugees: Liberian/Sierra Leonean, other smaller groups; European, Lebanese, others.
Literacy 41%. **Official language** French. **Major vernacular languages** Fulbe, Malinke, Susu, Kissi, Guerze and Toma. **All languages** 38. **Indigenous languages** 34. **Languages with Scriptures** 1Bi 10NT 12por 10w.i.p.

Economy

Guinea's huge mineral deposits, along with fertile and plentiful land and water, offer potential riches. Inept and corrupt governance have reduced it to subsistence and poverty, leading to occasional riots and demonstrations.
HDI Rank 170th/182. **Public debt** 88% of GDP. **Income/person** $439 (1% of USA).

Guinea

Republic of Guinea

Africa

Geography

Area 245,857 sq km on Africa's west coast, between Guinea-Bissau and Sierra Leone.

Population		Ann Gr	Density
2010	10,323,755	2.29%	42/sq km
2020	13,467,039	2.60%	55/sq km
2030	16,896,954	2.20%	69/sq km

Capital Conakry 11,653,495. **Urbanites** 35.4%. **Pop under 15 yrs** 43%. **Life expectancy** 57.3 yrs.

Peoples

About 40 ethnic groups.
West Atlantic 45.8%. Fulbe(3) 39.2%; Kissi 4.4%; Wassoulounke 1.0%; Baga(5) 0.5%; Landoma 0.2%; Konyagui 0.1%; Bassari 0.1%.
Mande 42.7%. Malinke 25.1%; Susu 11.1%; Konyanke 2.0%; Yalunka 0.9%; Kuranko 0.9%; Sankaran 0.8%; Manya 0.6%; Lele 0.4%; Mandéni 0.3%; Jakanke 0.3%;

Politics

French colony until independence in 1958. President Touré led the country into a Marxist experiment that virtually destroyed it. This regime was swept away in a military coup in 1984. The succeeding president led the country for 24 years. His passing was followed by a military junta seizing control; then the head of the junta was shot by an aide. Regional powers, including Burkina Faso's leader, stepped in to help the remaining junta members accept a transition to a civilian government, which culminated in democratic elections in 2010.

Religion

There is relative freedom for Christian witness and missionary activity. In recent years, intolerance by Muslims has increased in certain areas.

Religions	Pop %	Population	Ann Gr
Muslim	88.33	9,118,973	2.5%
Ethnoreligionist	6.90	712,339	-0.9%
Christian	4.47	461,472	3.4%
Non-religious	0.30	30,971	6.1%

Christians Denoms		Pop %	Affiliates	Ann Gr
Protestant	18	0.63	65,000	1.1%
Independent	9	0.16	17,000	0.9%
Anglican	1	0.01	1,000	-0.8%
Catholic	1	1.84	190,000	2.1%
Marginal	1	0.03	3,000	0.7%
Unaffiliated		1.80	186,000	3.7%

Churches	MegaBloc	Congs	Members	Affiliates
Catholic Church	C	50	110,465	190,000
Evang Protestant Ch	P	900	7,714	54,000
New Apostolic Church	I	25	2,000	6,000
Shekinah	I	70	1,720	4,300
Jehovah's Witnesses	M	31	1,240	3,100
Church of Pentecost	I	46	2,083	3,000
Assemblies of God	P	39	1,083	2,600
Pente Assem of Canada	P	30	1,136	2,500
Seventh-day Adventist	P	6	750	1,875
Anglican Church	A	8	481	1,300
LCMS	P	49	394	1,300
Bethel	I	9	429	1,200
Other denominations[18]		70	2,360	4,695
Total Christians[30]		**1,330**	**131,855**	**275,870**

TransBloc	Pop %	Population	Ann Gr
Evangelicals			
Evangelicals	0.7	74,526	1.5%
Renewalists			
Charismatics	0.5	46,914	2.9%
Pentecostals	0.1	15,030	3.7%

Religions % of Total Pop

TransBloc Movements % of Total Pop

Answers to Prayer

1 **Praise God for the major improvements** in the country since 1984:

a) Relatively stable for 20 years. Guinea has much room for improvement, but nevertheless has been a place of refuge for other nationalities fleeing strife and war in their own countries.

b) Religious freedom, a reaction against the Marxist-Muslim years of terror, which made Muslims more receptive to Christianity. This liberty is being progressively eroded, however, especially in major towns outside the forest region.

c) The presence of more than 20 evangelical missions and evangelism intensifying to the unreached. Out of more than 40 people groups, only a handful still have no church planting effort, and almost all of them number less than 10,000. The increase in work among Muslim peoples is particularly encouraging.

2 **The vision for missions deepens.** Guinea's foreign mission groups show an incredible level of unity, strategic coordination and quality of research. There is also an indigenous mission movement, which is still quite small and young but showing many encouraging signs. Mission training courses are held for Guinean believers, and mission mobilization congresses are planned for pastors and Christian students. A few Guineans already serve cross-culturally.

Challenges for Prayer

1 **The Christian population is still a small minority** and concentrated in Conakry and the southeast forests. It is overwhelmingly Kissi, Kpelle and Toma in composition. The Evangelical Protestant Church (EPEG) – primarily affiliated with the **CMA** and MPA – has long been the largest Protestant group. Pray that their influence might be toward Spirit-led godliness, outward focus and genuine unity. Over 37 peoples are still unreached; pray for their evangelization.

2 **The Church suffered serious numerical setbacks** in the late 1990s and early 2000s. Some established denominations shrank significantly, and evangelism and church planting slowed – probably largely due to nominal Christians falling away. Pray for believers who will persevere, and pray against the enemy who seeks to destroy these young or weak Christians before they can grow.

3 **Leadership training for pastors and laymen is a great need.** Guinea has three Bible schools, two run by EPEG/**CMA** and one by **AoG**. Six leadership training schools for laymen are run by the EPEC for the Kissi, Toma and Kpelle churches. PAoC and EPEG/**CMA**/ MPA both run TEE programmes. Despite all of this, there is still an overall lack of leaders in most areas, which delays church growth and evangelization. Pastors and leaders also need to be trained as mission mobilizers; pray for more godly leaders to be raised up and trained.

4 **Guinea remains largely unreached.** Despite increased missionary activity, most peoples remain a pioneer challenge. Muslims have strong animistic elements, and the three dominant peoples are all Muslim. Pray for the courage and boldness of those who follow Christ, and for families and groups to turn to Christ; it is very difficult for isolated individuals to maintain their walk of faith. While the number of converts from these groups is a steady trickle, much prayer is required before a major breakthrough is seen. If these peoples could see breakthrough, the entire nation would be transformed:

a) Malinke. **SIM** in Guinea focuses primarily on the Malinke; the past radio ministry needs to be revived. **SIM** facilitated the composing and recording of worship music written and performed by Malinkes. **CMA**, EPEG and Lutherans also have an outreach to the Malinke. There are now a few Malinke churches with Malinke leaders. Pray for effective new strategies and greater responsiveness to the gospel.

b) Fulbe, or Futa Jalon, are strongly Muslim and known as the custodians of Islam throughout West Africa. There is a partnership of missions attempting to reach the Fulbe with the gospel. Through the work of **CRWM, CMA, CAPRO, WEC, IMB, AoG** and the Swiss AME/ *Mission Philafricaine*, there is a small but growing number of believers. It is hard for new believers to break free from Islam's societal and spiritual bonds. Radio broadcasts, audio resources, the recently completed New Testament, development projects and mission workers all help to reach the Fulbe. Pray for a culturally appropriate way to share faith in Jesus with the traditionally nomadic Fulbe.

c) Susu. Apart from the eight rather nominal Anglican congregations on offshore islands and in Conakry, there are a few believers through the witness of **CMA, CAPRO, WEC**, Open Bible Standard Mission, the Nigerian Shekinah Mission, PBT, **NTM** and the **IMB**. There are three small Susu churches in and around Conakry, and also Susu believers in the southern interior and near the Guinea-Bissau border. The New Testament has just been translated and audio Scripture recorded; pray for their effective distribution.

d) Young people's ministry is vital in Guinea, since 43% of the population are under age 15. **CCCI, YWAM** and **IFES** all have ministry in the country. **IFES** has campus ministry in 20 of 33 cities, but consolidation of these newly formed groups is essential. **CAPRO** runs a youth centre in Conakry and **CMA**/MPA in Télimélé, with encouraging response. Sports ministry (particularly football) is proving very fruitful as well. Pray for the Spirit to draw these younger Guineans to Christ.

e) The forest region of Guinea especially needs intercession. Scores of thousands of refugees from Liberia and Sierra Leone remain. They are mostly Mandingo and often restive ex-rebels. Their Islamic aggression and belligerent presence create great tension with the native Kpelle, among whom there are many Christians. Some perceive this as a potential powder keg waiting to explode and destabilize the whole region.

f) Missions. Since 1981, EPEG/**CMA** have welcomed new evangelical agencies. Most work in close cooperation as members of the *Association des Eglises et Missions Evangéliques en Guinée* (AEMEG). Pray for close fellowship among mission agencies and with national churches. Guinea is a hard land requiring genuine pioneer missionaries; pray for strength, health and perseverance for all brave enough to answer God's call. Pray for still more missionaries, especially to the Muslim groups. Also pray for national believers to become more mobilized for mission; the Guinean Church must engage in outreach. Major missions are **NTM, CMA**, MPA (AME), PBT, **IMB, SIM, CRWM**.

5 **Help ministries:**

a) Cassette ministry is important in this multi-lingual land. **GRN** has recordings in 36 languages; some languages need to be re-recorded. **CRWM** has recordings in Pular for the influential Fulbe language, PBT and MERN for Susu and **SIM** for Malinke.

b) **_Literature_** is a challenge. There are three Christian bookstores, but literacy training is needed to make use of both Christian literature and the Bible. The reading room concept is fruitfully implemented by **CMA**, **IMB**, MERN, **SIM**, MPA, **CAPRO** and CFI as a neutral location where both converts and seekers can study, learn and fellowship.

c) **_Bible translation_** will remain a major missionary task for years to come. Twenty-three languages may need translation teams. Translation or revision work is in progress in 10 languages. AEMEG has identified Bible translation as a key strategy for Guinea and plans for redoubled efforts.

d) **_The JESUS film_** also has great potential in evangelizing Guinea. Perhaps half of the country has seen the film; it has been translated into eight languages and is in production for more. Pray for a lasting impact through this film.

e) **_Radio._** A collaborative project has resulted in an NGO starting up a community radio station out of a Christian ethos. Its programmes have become very popular. Pray for God's protection over this station and that it might be increasingly effective and its work fruitful.

G

Fulbe (2 groups) 21.7%. Fulakunda 16.6%.
Malinke (5 groups) 11.9%. Mandinka 9.9%.
Crioulo 11.9%.
Other 1%. Other African groups, European, Arab, Chinese. This number may be much higher.
Literacy 39.6%. **Official language** Portuguese.
National language Portuguese Creole, spoken by as much as half the population. **All languages** 25. **Indigenous languages** 21. **Languages with Scriptures** 5Bi 6NT 5por 7w.i.p.

Economy

Little developed in colonial times. Devastated by the long war of independence, by subsequent socialist policies and conflict and by both civil war and clashes with Senegalese Casamance rebels. One of the world's poorest countries, it relies mainly on cash crops of cashew nuts, but also on fish, hardwood and other agricultural products. Massive foreign debt. It is a major transshipment point of cocaine from Colombia to Europe, a most dangerous development given the gripping poverty, poor enforcement and lucrative nature of the drug trade.
HDI Rank 173rd/182. **Public debt** 327% of GDP. **Income/person** $264 (1% of USA).

Politics

Independent of Portugal in 1974. One-party revolutionary government until 1994, when multiparty elections took place. In 1998, another uprising led to a civil war, resolved in 2000 with a new government elected. After a bloodless coup in 2004, yet another president was elected in 2005, but he was murdered in 2009 – apparently as a reprisal for the killing of the armed forces leader mere hours before. Subsequent elections were postponed, but results finally saw the new president take office in 2009.

Guinea-Bissau

Republic of Guinea-Bissau

Africa

Geography

Area 36,125 sq km. Coastal state wedged between Senegal and Guinea, including the Bijagos archipelago.

Population		Ann Gr	Density
2010	1,647,380	2.27%	46/sq km
2020	2,064,988	2.24%	57/sq km
2030	2,536,229	2.01%	70/sq km

Capital Bissau 309,000. **Urbanites** 30%. **Population under 15 yrs** 43%. **Life expectancy** 47.5 yrs.

Peoples

Over 27 ethnic groups. Major people clusters:
Atlantic (17 groups) 53.5%. Balanta 22.9%; Manjaco 11.0%; Papel 8.0%; Mankanya 2.8%; Biafada 2.8%; Bijago 1.9%; Jola/Felupe 1.5%.

Religion

Under Portuguese rule, the Catholic Church functioned almost as an arm of the colonial government, and evangelicals were forbidden or discriminated against. Since independence, the measure of freedom for Christian activities has steadily increased. Until 1990, only one Protestant mission (WEC) was allowed in the country, but since then, several more have entered. Freedom of religion exists for all groups. Syncretism of Islam and Catholicism with African traditional religions is such that accurate figures are difficult to obtain.

Religions	Pop %	Population	Ann Gr
Muslim	52.05	857,461	3.2%
Ethnoreligionist	35.10	578,230	1.3%
Christian	10.90	179,564	1.1%
Non-religious	1.95	32,124	3.9%

Christians Denoms		Pop %	Affiliates	Ann Gr
Protestant	5	1.43	24,000	5.6%
Independent	16	0.24	4,000	9.9%
Catholic	1	7.92	130,000	0.4%
Marginal	2	0.07	1,000	2.3%
Unaffiliated		1.24	20,000	-2.8%

Churches	MegaBloc	Congs	Members	Affiliates
Catholic Church	C	63	78,144	130,500
Evang Ch of G-B	P	160	12,500	20,000
Seventh-day Adventist	P	2	1,175	2,350
Church of Pentecost	I	19	868	1,250
Assemblies of God	P	7	258	850
Other denominations[19]		61	1,908	4,333
Total Christians[24]		**312**	**94,853**	**159,283**

TransBloc	Pop %	Population	Ann Gr
Evangelicals			
Evangelicals	1.6	27,118	6.2%
Renewalists			
Charismatics	0.9	15,469	5.1%
Pentecostals	0.3	4,850	8.5%

Religions % of Total Pop

Annual Growth Rates

Answers to Prayer

1 **Praise the Lord for continued receptivity to the gospel** and for religious freedom, a contrast to many other countries in the region. Evangelicals assisted with humanitarian needs during the civil war and worked with Catholics and Muslims in the political reconciliation efforts. The Evangelical Church of Guinea-Bissau is therefore viewed with a good deal of respect by the government and has garnered freedom to operate as a result. Pray that the Church might continue to lead in showing practical love and compassion and in encouraging peace and reconciliation.

Challenges for Prayer

1 **Poverty, political unrest and violent conflict** combine to grind down the population of this land. There is some limited potential in untapped natural resources, but the opportunity for genuine progress and development seems distant. The influence of narcotics shipments has great potential to corrupt police, army and government figures, and enslave otherwise impoverished people. The short but strife-filled political history of Guinea-Bissau points to the need for stability, forgiveness and true peacemakers. Pray that God might raise up righteous leaders to lead their people.

2 **Church leadership is solid, mature and indigenous,** with increasingly well-organized training programmes for general discipleship and for pastoral training. The Bible Institute of the Evangelical Church is key to this process, with evening Bible classes and sponsorship of promising pastors to study in Brazil. But poorer and more remote rural congregations are much less appealing to workers and are therefore neglected. Those who do minister rurally must often care for several congregations at once. Pray for the vision of the evangelical Church to be fulfilled, and for trained, passionate national workers to go to the remote and unreached parts of Guinea-Bissau and to the entire region.

3 **There is an increasing number of missionaries** in the country, mostly Latin American and Asian, but notably fewer Westerners. The largest agencies are **WEC,**

YWAM and Kairos (Brazil). Many new groups are arriving, including some theologically marginal bodies. Some set up denominations near existing churches rather than going to needy and unreached areas. The majority do not stay long term, and many are sent by their supporting churches without real accountability or support. Pray for missionaries to cooperate across organizational lines and with the national Church; pray also that a greater emphasis might be given to working among the unevangelized.

4 **The less-reached groups** for whom prayer is needed:

a) *The Muslim Fula/Fulbe and Mandinka.* Both are large, dominant groups in many West African countries with a rich history and much influence. They are largely responsible for bringing Islam to Guinea-Bissau; may they instead become responsible for spreading the good news. The Fula are increasingly responsive to the gospel, and in a few locations, groups of believers are forming. The Mandinkas are more resistant but have some individual believers in the cities.

b) *Smaller-population peoples of mixed Muslim and animist beliefs.* The Biafada, Nalu, Masoanke, Jahanka, Jola-Fonyi, Soninke, Susu and Badyara have had very little, if any, work concentrated on them using their language and culture. Pray for ministry among them, and that fruit might be forthcoming.

c) *Traditional-religion peoples* are much more evangelized than the Muslim peoples. Praise God that there are Christians from almost all of these groups. These include the Balanta, Papel, Bijago, Manjaco, Mancanha, Jola-Felupe and Bayote. Pray also for the gospel to reach the other smaller, and often overlooked, peoples.

G

5 **Scripture and literature** are areas of great need and great potential. Poverty and low literacy make this a challenge, but the spiritual need and pressure from other faiths make this ministry essential.

a) *Bible translation.* The Bible in Creole is a great success. Almost all churches use it, and it is already on a fourth printing. NTs are available in Papel, Bijago, Fula and Mandinka and soon in Balanta, though not used nearly as much. SIL/ALEM, The Bible Society, The Seed Company, KIMON and the national Church all partner for further translation and literacy work as well as training.

b) *Christian books* have low circulation, few readers and high costs, and there are only two Christian bookshops in the country. Pray for the development of helpful written material to equip the saints. Pray for the Church to gain a vision for Christian literature.

c) *Literacy* must be enhanced to maximize the benefits of new material being printed. Pray for the educational infrastructure – including many primary schools for locals set up and run by the national Church and mission agencies – and for literacy courses for adults to have a great effect that generates a hunger for reading material and in turn leads people to Scripture. Greater coordination is needed for the local education provided by Protestant churches, which is currently a fragmented scene, including how these many groups are represented before the government's Ministry of Education.

6 Media ministry:

a) *Christian radio.* A programme is broadcast every week on national radio. Pray for the producers to be able to improve its quality and for continued permission to broadcast. Pray for the new Christian radio station in the Bafata area; it broadcasts in several languages. Many towns have local radio stations, and most give time to local pastors for weekly programmes.

b) *Audio resources,* including cassettes, have great potential in a largely oral society. The Creole NT is available on cassette, and **GRN** has recordings in 28 languages and dialects. The Proclaimer and Megavoice are two solid-state audio players with Scripture and Bible storying. Pray that all these resources be used well.

c) *The JESUS film,* now available in 14 languages, is used widely in evangelism. Availability of the film in tribal languages is limited; praise God for the development of a DVD that includes tribal languages, Creole and Portuguese. Pray for its greater availability and for lasting fruit that yields notable church growth.

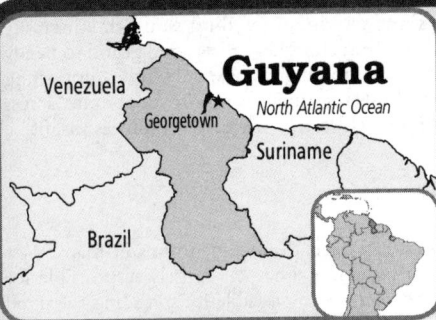

Guyana

Cooperative Republic of Guyana

South America

Geography 🌐

Area 215,000 sq km. On the north coast of South America. A developed coastal strip with under-developed, forested interior.

Population		Ann Gr	Density
2010	761,442	-0.06%	4/sq km
2020	745,024	-0.25%	3/sq km
2030	713,778	-0.52%	3/sq km

About 90% live on the coast.
Capital Georgetown 132,000. **Urbanites** 28.5%.
Pop under 15 yrs 30%. **Life expectancy** 66.5 yrs.

Peoples 👪

Colonial importation of labour for the sugar industry created the current racial diversity and political tension.
South Asian 42.5%. Predominantly rural farmers from the Indian sub-continent. Declining through emigration.
African 29.7%. Dominant in government, civil service and in urban areas.
Mixed 16.5%. Primarily Eurafrican, but some Asian and Amerindian also.
Amerindian 8.9%. The majority live in the sparsely inhabited interior. Main groups:
  Arawak 3.2%. Arawak; Wapishana.
  Carib 2.9%. Largest: Macushi, Patamona, Akawaio, Carib.
  Detribalized Amerindian 2.0%.
  Other 0.9%.
Other 2.4%. Portuguese, Chinese, British.
Literacy 96.5%. **Official languages** English; Creole used by 90% of the population. **All languages** 19. **Indigenous languages** 16. **Languages with Scriptures** 2Bi 5NT 9por 4w.i.p.

Economy 📈

Mainstays are gold, sugar, rice, forest products and minerals. A 20-year Marxist economic experiment impoverished the country despite its economic potential. Living standards fell, foreign investment dried up and many of the better-educated are still leaving the country. A gradual improvement since 1992, but severe flooding in 2005 caused $415 million of damage.
HDI Rank 114th/182. **Public debt** 157% of GDP. **Income/person** $1,509 (3% of USA).

Politics 🗳

Dutch rule 1750-1814; British rule until independence in 1966. Both main political parties were previously Marxist in orientation but remain bitterly divided along racial lines (Indo-Guyanese versus Afro-Guyanese). Racial tension continues. Venezuela to the west and Suriname to the east both lay claim to large parts of Guyana.

Religion 🙏

Atheism promoted until 1985, with considerable tension between the government and the main churches. A secular state with full religious freedom since then.

Religions	Pop %	Population	Ann Gr
Christian	52.68	401,128	0.0%
Hindu	30.30	230,717	0.5%
Muslim	9.40	71,576	0.2%
Non-religious	4.00	30,458	2.6%
Ethnoreligionist	3.00	22,843	-0.7%
Baha'i	0.40	3,046	-0.1%
Buddhist	0.22	1,675	-0.1%

Christians	Denoms	Pop %	Affiliates	Ann Gr
Protestant	40	24.20	184,000	1.2%
Independent	29	11.06	84,000	1.4%
Anglican	1	8.41	64,000	-0.6%
Catholic	1	11.95	91,000	0.2%
Orthodox	1	1.00	8,000	-0.8%
Marginal	9	1.53	12,000	3.0%
Doubly affiliated		-5.47	-42,000	0.0%

Churches	MegaBloc	Congs	Members	Affiliates
Catholic Church	C	40	48,148	91,000
Seventh-day Adventist	P	150	48,000	70,000
Anglican Church	A	123	16,000	64,000
Full Gospel Fellowship	I	160	12,800	48,000
Assemblies of God	P	78	12,000	24,000
NT Church of God	P	70	11,000	19,000
Lutheran Church	P	42	4,200	10,500
Methodist Ch (MCCA)	P	40	3,200	8,200
Ethiopian Orthodox	O	28	5,000	7,600
Jehovah's Witnesses	M	38	2,700	7,560
Wesleyan Church	P	37	3,105	5,900
Ch of the Nazarene	P	48	3,200	4,750
Other denominations[69]		667	43,548	82,216
Doubly affiliated Pentecostals				-15,000
Doubly affiliated				-26,650
Total Christians[81]		**1,521**	**212,901**	**401,076**

TransBloc	Pop %	Population	Ann Gr
Evangelicals			
Evangelicals	19.8	150,993	1.0%
Renewalists			
Charismatics	15.5	117,729	1.3%
Pentecostals	14.0	106,965	1.3%

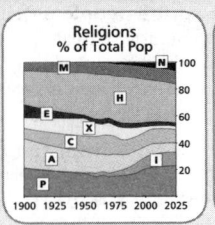

Religions % of Total Pop

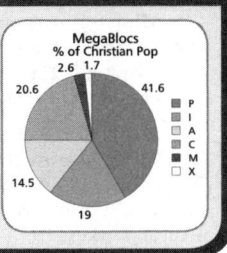

MegaBlocs % of Christian Pop

Answers to Prayer

1 **Complete religious freedom** since the waning of atheistic rhetoric in the 1980s.

2 **Continued responsiveness to the gospel** among most ethnic groups in the country.

3 **Christian unity is getting stronger** in this diverse and often divided country, providing a testimony to the nation and a drawing point for those considering the gospel.

Challenges for Prayer

1 **Guyana seems to exist precariously on many levels.** It is constantly under threat from persistent claims on its land by Venezuela and Suriname. The political sphere is defined along racial lines. The economy is vulnerable to the climate, as the disastrous floods of 2005 attest. Large-scale emigration has denuded the country of much of its population, including many of the most gifted. Pray that an enduring hope might come to Guyana, most expressly through the transformation that only the gospel can enact.

2 **There is a vital, vibrant, growing evangelical witness,** and evangelicals are found in all levels of society. Pentecostal, charismatic ("clap-hand") and evangelical denominations and fellowships continue to grow despite negative population growth. Churches are still largely divided along racial lines, but the multiracial congregations that do exist are some of the few ethnic bridges in the country. The cross-denominational work of the Guyanese Evangelical Fellowship is vital in this area. Pray for all believers to demonstrate the power of the gospel in their unity, in their words and in holy living.

3 **Most Afro-Guyanese and mixed-race Guyanese are Christian,** but nominalism is widespread, stable two-parent families rare (a legacy of the time of slavery) and syncretistic and deviant beliefs common. Obeah Spiritism and witchcraft, Rastafarianism and foreign sects as well as the racist Nation of Islam are influential here. Pray for the true and uncorrupted gospel to radically impact these communities.

4 **The Indo-Guyanese population is mostly Hindu,** but with large and equally sized Muslim and Christian communities. Pray for:

a) The many Hindu rural communities and for their evangelization.

b) The large numbers of Muslims – increasingly influenced by Islamist rhetoric. Some have been won to Christ out of this context, but Guyanese Muslims remain the least reached group in the nation.

5 **The Amerindian peoples are largely Christianized** and predominantly Catholic, but significant numbers are also becoming Pentecostals through the ministry of **AoG**, Church of God and the Full Gospel Fellowship. **UFM**'s work in the south among the Waiwai, Macushi and Wapishana has resulted in a growing, missionary-minded Church. Pray for the development of indigenous Christian leadership and mature churches that can retain their cultural identity and still survive the impact of modernity.

6 **Ministry among young people** is vital because family life, further education, employment and the future in general are great challenges. Most evangelical denominations have work among youth. **IFES** has an extensive ministry with 12 full-time staff and more than 200 groups at primary, secondary and tertiary levels where they reach over 12,000 students every week. Praise God for many decisions to follow Jesus; pray for effective discipleship.

7 **Medical ministry is both important and fruitful.** With limited medical facilities and widespread AIDS (Guyana has the second highest prevalence in the Caribbean region) and malaria, Guyana is in need of better medical care. The loving testimony of Christian medical workers from many groups, including **YWAM** and Operation Guyana, opens many doors for the gospel to be shared.

8 **Christian missions have had a deep and positive impact on society.** Missions are free to work in every capacity. The majority are involved in church planting, Bible translation, leadership training and development. Major missions: Adventist World Aviation, **CC**, **ELCA**, Global Outreach International.

9 **Christian literature and Bible translation** are all the more important given the relative dearth of Christian radio and TV in the vernacular of the vast majority. Functional literacy remains significantly lower than the official literacy rate.

H

Other 0.3%.
Literacy 51.9%. Functional literacy may be as low as 20%. **Official language** French (10% speak it). **Common languages** Haitian Creole, English and Spanish increasingly used as a second language. **Languages with Scripture** 2Bi 1w.i.p.

Haiti
Republic of Haiti
Caribbean

Geography

Area 27,400 sq km. Western third of the island of Hispaniola; shared with the Dominican Republic.

Population		Ann Gr	Density
2010	10,188,175	1.60%	372/sq km
2020	11,722,392	1.36%	428/sq km
2030	13,195,567	1.13%	482/sq km

One of the most-densely populated countries in the Americas. Hundreds of thousands of Haitians have fled/emigrated. These figures do not reflect the loss of life from the January 2010 earthquake and subsequent emigration. **Capital** Port-au-Prince 2,143,458. **Urbanites** 49.6%. **Pop under 15 yrs** 36%. **Life expectancy** 61 yrs.

Peoples

African Caribbean 94.3%.
Mulatto (Eurafrican) 5.4%.

Economy

The poorest state in the Western Hemisphere, aggravated by overpopulation, deforestation (only 2% of original forests remain), soil erosion, pollution and hurricanes. Around 75% live on less than $2/day, and two-thirds are under- or unemployed. Political instability and violence prevent proper aid distribution and long-term investment. The 2010 earthquake devastated much of what little economic infrastructure did exist. After this disaster, it will take billions of dollars and many years of stability, coupled with sustained redevelopment, to see any long-term economic progress. Major sources of income include remittances from expatriate Haitians and, now, aid, relief and development funds earmarked for earthquake recovery.
HDI Rank 149th/182. **Public debt** 33% of GDP. **Income/person** $790 (2% of USA). **Unemployment** 32.7%.

Politics

A slave revolt against the French in 1804 created the first black republic in the world. Haiti was made to pay for its freedom with steep reparations to France and economic/diplomatic isolation by the European and American imperial powers, crippling the nation in its early years. Since then, it has had a troubled history of bloodshed and dictatorships. The deposing of the Duvaliers in 1986 ended a particularly brutal dictatorship. A succession of coups and military governments since, including

US-led intervention in 1994, have done little to instill stability, but the longer-term presence of the UN has assisted. Haiti annually appears at or near the top of the corruption index; crime is rife, and 25% of the already-under-strength police force are in the pockets of drug lords and gangs. The earthquake and the devastation it caused to the physical infrastructure, the psyche of the people and the loss of life, combined with the massive influx of international aid and assistance, may profoundly reshape how politics are done in Haiti.

Religion

The Roman Catholic Church's role as the state church ended in 1987. An estimated 75% of Christians are also actively involved in voodoo, a development of West African Spiritism and witchcraft. But religious sentiment is strong, and almost all Haitians primarily identify themselves as Christian. There is freedom of religion.

Religions	Pop %	Population	Ann Gr
Christian	95.12	9,690,992	1.6%
Ethnoreligionist	2.78	283,231	2.7%
Non-religious	1.95	198,669	2.7%
Baha'i	0.10	10,188	1.6%
Muslim	0.05	5,094	6.2%

Christians	Denoms	Pop %	Affiliates	Ann Gr
Protestant	32	15.37	1,566,000	1.9%
Independent	236	3.37	344,000	3.4%
Anglican	1	1.21	123,000	1.4%
Catholic	1	69.31	7,062,000	0.9%
Marginal	2	0.49	50,000	2.6%
Unaffiliated		15.90	1,617,000	-0.6%
Doubly affiliated		*-10.50*	*-1,070,000*	*0.0%*

Churches	MegaBloc	Congs	Members	Affiliates
Catholic Church	C	247	4,105,523	7,061,500
Seventh-day Adventist	P	420	325,185	439,000
Ch of the Nazarene	P	523	100,000	167,000
Baptist Convention	P	96	85,000	139,500
Ch of God (Cleveland)	P	395	70,556	127,000
Episcopal Church	A	430	36,937	123,000
Ev Bapt Ch of S Haiti	P	487	37,954	115,000
Conservative Bapt Miss	P	348	17,750	76,400
Assemblies of God	P	278	45,000	67,500
Evang Baptist Union	P	160	40,000	60,000
Ch of God of Prophecy	P	415	29,500	59,000
Ch of God in Christ	I	150	23,000	57,500
United Pentecostal Ch	P	629	38,976	49,500
Chr Methodist Episc Ch	I	215	28,000	46,760
Other denominations[258]		4,510	261,532	555,106
Doubly affiliated				*-1,070,000*
Total Christians[272]		**9,303**	**5,244,913**	**8,073,766**

TransBloc	Pop %	Population	Ann Gr
Evangelicals			
Evangelicals	16.0	1,633,193	2.2%
Renewalists			
Charismatics	8.1	821,505	3.6%
Pentecostals	5.1	515,150	2.9%

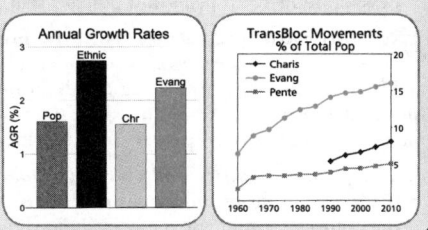

Answers to Prayer

1 **The spiritual response to the tragedy of the 2010 earthquake** was an almost universal outpouring of prayer, repentance and calling upon God for mercy and deliverance. Out of the disaster, God appears to be doing something radical and new among the people of Haiti. Reports abound that the three days of prayer and fasting called for by the president – replacing February 2010's Mardi Gras – were attended by over one million people.

2 **Evangelical Christians have steadily grown in number** over the decades, through evangelism, love in action and by openly standing against voodooism and the spiritual forces behind it. Vision Haiti (HAVIDEC), a concerted prayer movement that includes many denominations and organizations, is determined to see deliverance for Haiti through prayer. The power of the gospel over the spiritual forces of evil has been clearly demonstrated in several instances.

3 **Church-mission relations have improved greatly** in the last decade; both expat and indigenous believers, working together for common goals, have yielded not only better relationships but also greater fruitfulness.

Challenges for Prayer

1   **The earthquake of 2010 was a disaster on many levels.** But it also offers hope out of tragedy. It is believed that 230,000 lost their lives, 300,000 were injured and over one million were rendered homeless. Hundreds of thousands of homes and buildings were also destroyed, including some major government buildings. Aid arrived from around the world, but coordination was difficult in the aftermath of the earthquake, and assistance will be needed for a long time to come. For a host of reasons, Haiti struggled as a nation from its very inception. This shattering disaster could be an opportunity to reshape not just the physical infrastructure of the nation, but the cultural, economic, political and societal infrastructures as well. Some points to cover in prayer include:

a) The rebuilding efforts will take years. Haiti's infrastructure was never good, and Port-au-Prince's was especially weak due to rapid urbanization from poorer rural areas. Countless homes will need to be rebuilt or restored; the sheer scale of money and manpower needed is staggering for the Western Hemisphere's poorest nation. Pray for the best long-term development for the city and nation, rather than quick fixes. Pray for generous assistance from wealthier neighbours and nations and agencies from further abroad.

b) The human suffering was immense in the immediate aftermath and will continue for years. The shared emotional trauma of the events, the massive loss of life and the long-term injuries will all leave major scars on the Haitian population. Healing from such hurts needs time, care and the love of God.

c) Haiti was a financial and social mess even before the earthquake. Repairing all the damage, however, will not create a healthy economy. Haiti must rebuild beyond its previous state and develop long-term plans and policies that are shaped with wisdom and justice.

2   **Haiti must find release from the bondages of its past.** The Spanish genocide against the indigenous Arawaks, and the cruel slavery instituted and maintained by the Spanish and then the French, form a tragic background. The tyrannies, cruelties and use of voodoo as a means of control have fostered a spirit of fear that permeates every level of society. More recent interventions by foreign powers have not banished the endemic problems. Pray that:

a) The powerful spirits underlying voodooism might be bound in the name of Jesus. Pray that the ubiquitous influence and enduring legacy of voodoo might be made subordinate to the authority of Christ – especially in the lives of Christians.

b) Haitians who call themselves Christian might experience the transforming nature of a personal relationship with Christ. Only through the regeneration and power of the Holy Spirit will the heritage of voodoo be overcome.

c) This nation might enjoy stability, safety and sustained development by removing the systemic evils holding it back and by instilling biblical values and practices on every level of society.

3   **Haiti needs godly leaders** who will prioritize the good of the nation and address its massive problems. Two centuries of misrule, tyranny and recent flawed democratic attempts have brought hopelessness and despair. Corruption is rampant, and robberies and kidnappings commonplace. The economic plight of most Haitians deepens each year, exacerbated by the events of 2010. Many seek to escape, some physically by fleeing the country in unsafe and leaky boats, others emotionally through taking drugs. Pray that men and women may be raised up who will reverse these trends and establish justice, righteousness and long-term stability.

4   **The spiritual outpouring of faith in God in the aftermath of the earthquake** also shook the nation and moved the entire world. When the president called for three days of prayer and fasting during Mardi Gras – traditionally a time of partying and excess – no one expected one million people to turn out. Throughout the country, churches were filled to overflowing and services were held amid rubble and in the ruined streets. Pray that this spiritual shaking would not merely be an expression of grief, fear and desperation, but would shape itself into an unprecedented turning to God that redefines the spiritual life of Haiti. Numerous traditions allege that Haiti was dedicated to Satan through its voodoo past; pray that today it might be known as a nation wholly dedicated to the Lord Jesus.

5   **Haitians overwhelmingly identify themselves as "Christian",** but many if not most Catholics have also dabbled in voodoo (although many others actively oppose it). Haiti is often referred to as "90% Catholic and 100% Voodoo". The credibility and impact of the Catholic Church are sorely compromised. Pray for renewal, reformation and the cleansing work of the Holy Spirit to sweep through this massive and influential denomination.

6 **The steady growth of Protestant churches** is no surprise – no other faith offers the spiritual hope and practical help available to evangelicals. Yet there are areas for prayer:

a) *The rural poor are the most responsive.* Illiteracy, marginalization in society and lack of adequate teaching have all reduced the Church's potential impact. But evangelicals are doing a great job of addressing these challenges via radio, children's education and pastoral and lay training.

b) *Denominational fragmentation* on issues of personality, charismatic growth and liberation theology confuse and divide Christians. The Protestant Federation and the Council of Evangelical Churches give Protestants a platform for speaking with one voice to the government and for cooperating in social, evangelistic and prayer initiatives.

c) *Spiritual opposition.* Recently, those who practice voodoo have been more outspoken, especially through the media, about their animosity toward Protestants. Pray for spiritual purity and for the love and power of Christ to shine through believers.

7 **Leadership training is too limited** because of the poverty of churches. A rigid traditionalism of imported theologies and systems is widespread. Many pastors have little training; some are barely literate. Pray for the 20 or so Bible schools/seminaries and the many TEE programmes that seek to meet the need. Pray for Haitian leaders to be men of faith and spiritual authority, who are not diverted by material inducements. Pray for resources in Creole that will foster lay training and leadership development.

8 **Desperate physical and social needs** attract a wide range of Christian community development agencies, such as WVI, Tearfund, World Concern, the Mennonites and many others. Sensitivity and wisdom are needed to preserve the indigeneity, integrity and independence of the churches and their leaders and to not create further dependency. Pressing needs must be addressed regarding ecology, agriculture, healthcare, AIDS, education and children at risk. Pray that every expression of Christian concern might have long-term redemptive impact and draw people to the Saviour.

9 **Particularly needy or strategic groups:**

a) *The Mulatto elite* are wealthy, French-oriented and isolated from the majority. Few realize their need for a personal faith. The wealthiest 15% of Haiti's population control 90% of its resources; active Christians who wield such influence could make a great difference in the nation.

b) *The youth.* Poverty, unemployment, illiteracy and constant turmoil that disrupts the education system all make for a difficult context for Haitian youth. Guns and gangs are the paths many take to cope. Too few churches have active programmes designed for young people. GBEUH(**IFES**) has three full-time staff and around 25 student groups; **CCCI** and Navigators are also active.

c) *Refugees.* The Haitian diaspora numbers in the millions – in the USA, Cuba, Bahamas and elsewhere. Their destitution and need make them spiritually receptive. A number of missions (**WT, OMS, CoN** and others) seek to minister to them. Aiding or harbouring Haitian illegal refugees in other Caribbean nations can bring legal consequences, creating a dilemma for those seeking to show compassion. Pray for more workers called to reach the Haitian diaspora.

d) *The restaveks* (from the Creole – "stay-withs") are effectively child slaves, numbering 300,000 to 400,000 – or 10% of all children in Haiti. They are easily available to be bought or sold. They are usually orphans, runaways or poor rural children whose parents can't afford to care for them. These children labour endlessly; they have no education and no health care. Pray for God to raise up people and organizations dedicated to showing compassion and love to the *restaveks*.

10 **Missions plays a valuable supportive role to the national Church.** Upheavals and violence have forced most missionaries out of the country at one time or another; many never return. Pray for these servants of the Lord, for their testimony and service, and that they may contribute to the maturing of the Haitian Church. The larger missions are: **CCCI, OMS, CW, MAF, YWAM.**

H

11 **Christian Ministries:**

a) ***Bibles and Christian literature*** are in short supply; there is a clear need for more Scripture and discipleship material. The Creole Bible has a significant impact on the understanding and application of God's Word. The Bible Society, the Bible League and others distribute what they can. Pray also for effective literacy programmes to be maintained.

b) ***Christian radio*** is possibly the most effective tool for reaching and discipling Haitians. A high proportion of the population listens to *Radio Lumière's* five stations in the south and centre – Evangelical Baptist Church of South Haiti (**WT**) and 4VEH (**OMS**) in the north. **TWR** and others broadcast over 2,000 hours weekly. Radio 4VEH also streams over the Internet, reaching the Haitian diaspora. Vandalism against radio towers and relays is a real challenge.

H

Holy See (Vatican City State)

Mediterranean Sea — Italy — Rome

Holy See
Vatican City State
Europe

Geography 🌍

Area 0.5 sq km. The world's smallest state; an enclave in the heart of the city of Rome, the last remaining vestige of the once-considerable papal domains in central Italy.

Population		Ann Gr	Density
2010	785	0.05%	1,570/sq km
2020	785	0.00%	1,570/sq km
2030	765	-0.29%	1,530/sq km

Almost entirely comprised of members of the global Catholic hierarchy.

Economy 📈

Financed by contributions from Roman Catholic dioceses around the world, from tourism, from sales of mementos, coins and stamps and from interest earned on its sizeable investments and real estate portfolio.

Politics ☒

The Pope is the head of state as well as leader of the world's Catholics, advised and elected by the College of Cardinals.

Religion 🙏

Religions	Pop %	Population	Ann Gr
Christian	100.00	785	0.1%

Christians Denoms		Pop %	Affiliates	Ann Gr
Catholic	1	100.00	1,000	0.1%

TransBloc	Pop %	Population	Ann Gr
Evangelicals			
Evangelicals	2.5	20	4.6%
Renewalists			
Charismatics	15.0	118	3.0%

Challenges for Prayer

1 **The Pope is head of the single largest religious body on earth** and of a state that is the outcome of a long history and of a unique conception of what the role of the Church in the world should be. He exercises an enormous influence within and beyond the Roman Catholic Church. Pray for the right man to fill the post for the right time, and pray for the redemptive use of the Vatican's formidable politico-religious influence.

2 **The Roman Catholic Church** is going through a time of turmoil and change. There are many doctrines and positions that divide this increasingly diverse body – ecumenism, the celibacy of the priesthood, the position of women, homosexuality and issues of AIDS and contraception. Pray for the essence of the gospel to be recaptured and for unbiblical forms and practices to be excised from the Church.

3 **The loss of credibility** through numerous scandals, aggressive papal doctrinal positions and sustained decline in vocations (of priests, monks and nuns) will force many changes on Catholicism; pray for wisdom in adapting the Church to 21st Century realities.

4 **Pray for spiritual renewal.** Catholic charismatic renewal has an impact far beyond the 235 countries and 120 million involved. Pray for them to be a bridge to believers in other denominations and to not be absorbed or rendered ineffective by the system. A large proportion of the Catholic missionary force is charismatic. At the same time, the Roman Catholic Church is expanding in many spiritual directions – theological conservatism, charismatic renewal, Marian devotion, folk religious practices and others. Pray for nominal Catholics – many millions strong – to experience the radical conversion and cultural transformation that their pontiff insists is essential to faith.

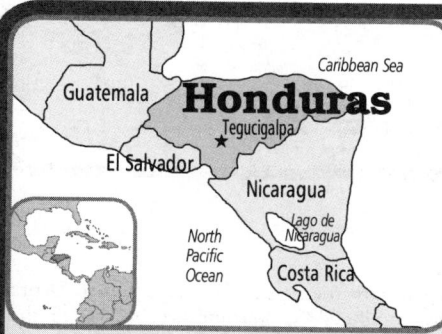

Honduras

Republic of Honduras

Latin America

Geography 🌐

Area 112,088 sq km. A mountainous land with rain forests and fertile coastal plains on the Caribbean and Pacific coasts.

Population		Ann Gr	Density
2010	7,615,584	2.01%	68/sq km
2020	9,136,431	1.73%	82/sq km
2030	10,491,748	1.28%	94/sq km

Capital Tegucigalpa 1,027,976. **Urbanites** 48.8%. **Pop under 15 yrs** 37%. **Life expectancy** 72 yrs.

Peoples 👪

Spanish-culture 89.0%. Mestizo (Ladino) 85.0%; Afro-American 2.0%; White 2.0%.
Amerindians 7.9%. Seven peoples whose languages are rapidly disappearing. Largest: Detribalized (mainly Lenca origin) 4.0%; Lenca 1.4%; Garifuna (Black Carib) 1.8%; Miskitu 0.5%.
Other 3.1%. Arab (Palestinian) 0.8%; Jamaican 0.5%; various other ethnicities.

Literacy 80%. **Official language** Spanish. **Other language** English on the northern coast. **All languages** 13. **Indigenous languages** 10. **Languages with Scriptures** 5Bi 2NT 1por 1w.i.p.

Economy 🗺️

One of the Western hemisphere's poorest countries, with most wealth in the hands of a very small minority. Widespread unemployment, low wages, the devastation of Hurricane Mitch in 1998 and limited development weigh in to make life difficult for the majority, with most of the population below the poverty line. Agriculture, services, tourism and remittances account for most of the economic activity.
HDI Rank 112th/182. **Public debt** 20.4% of GDP. **Income/person** $1,826 (4% of USA). **Unemployment** 27.9%.

Politics ⚔️

Independent from Spain in 1821, but 134 revolutions and revolts by 1932. Military rule for much of the 20th Century. Democratic civilian government since 1984 has been hampered by the power and autonomy of the military and by US meddling in the region in the 1980s. Stamping out government corruption, creating jobs and tackling crime will be challenges for any elected leader for years to come.

Religion 🙏

The Roman Catholic Church is officially recognized, but there is separation of Church and state with religious freedom.

Religions	Pop %	Population	Ann Gr
Christian	96.64	7,359,700	2.0%
Non-religious	1.90	144,696	5.6%
Ethnoreligionist	0.80	60,925	-0.4%

					Other denominations[67]	5,621	259,721	642,263
Baha'i	0.45	34,270	2.0%		*Doubly affiliated*			*-861,000*
Muslim	0.18	13,708	3.2%		**Total Christians[130]**	**15,047**	**3,998,892**	**7,358,816**
Buddhist	0.03	2,285	2.0%					

Christians	Denoms	Pop %	Affiliates	Ann Gr
Protestant	58	19.37	1,475,000	3.9%
Independent	62	5.98	455,000	5.1%
Anglican	1	0.11	8,000	2.7%
Catholic	1	79.77	6,075,000	1.0%
Orthodox	3	0.07	5,000	-0.4%
Marginal	5	2.66	203,000	3.4%
Doubly affiliated		*-11.32*	*-861,000*	*0.0%*

TransBloc	Pop %	Population	Ann Gr
Evangelicals			
Evangelicals	23.0	1,751,873	4.4%
Renewalists			
Charismatics	15.0	1,142,177	5.1%
Pentecostals	14.2	1,078,804	4.6%

Churches	MegaBloc	Congs	Members	Affiliates
Catholic Church	C	930	3,164,062	6,075,000
Indig Pente/Charis Chs	I	2,185	78,671	225,000
Foursquare Gospel Ch	P	325	77,000	215,600
Seventh-day Adventist	P	450	90,000	198,000
Ch of God (Cleveland)	P	1,968	61,000	184,830
Latter-day Saints (Mormon)	M	394	80,838	135,000
Assemblies of God	P	888	35,500	119,000
Principé de Paz	I	486	34,000	113,220
Christian Brethren	P	462	42,000	105,000
Central American Ch	P	800	24,000	82,800
Jehovah's Witnesses	M	298	19,100	63,603
World Gospel Mission	P	240	33,000	61,500

Missionaries from Honduras
P,I,A 116 (79 long-term) in 22 agencies: to elsewhere in Central America/Mexico 35, Europe 25, North America 22.

Religions % of Total Pop

TransBloc Movements % of Total Pop

Answers to Prayer

1 **Five decades of evangelical growth** began with the successful Evangelism in Depth programme of 1963. In 1960, evangelicals numbered 32,000 and were 1.7% of the population. They are now 1,750,000 and 23.0%, and growth shows little sign of stopping. Some polls show that up to 36% of the population identify with evangelical beliefs.

2 **The indigenous peoples of the eastern rainforests.** The Miskitu, Garifuna, Sumo and Tol have won significant concessions to preserve their endangered habitat and cultures in the face of economic predation of their environment. Formerly a voiceless, legally disadvantaged underclass, these concessions enable them to protect, preserve and develop their traditional culture.

Challenges for Prayer

1 **The government faces an uphill battle** in establishing true stability and order. A young nation, Honduras' colonial past and military rule for most of its independence mean that democratic structures and mentalities must be nurtured. Corruption within the government, preferential treatment of the rich minority and prevalent poverty make the nation vulnerable to structures of sin. Pray for righteousness and for wise and resolute governance.

2 **Socio-economic problems are widespread** and deeply entrenched. At the root of most problems lies endemic and lasting poverty, affecting up to 80% of the population. Pray for these issues:

a) Children at risk. More than half of Honduras' population are children, the majority living in poverty. Destitution drives them to desperate measures.

  i Illegal emigration. Thousands of children attempt to cross to the USA to find family members working there. Usually, they end up incarcerated in Guatemala or Mexico – in terrible conditions.

  ii Pepenadores, or garbage dump children, are more prevalent in Honduras than in any nation in the Americas.

  iii Street children, numbering in the thousands, are often exterminated as a nuisance by ruthless groups in the name of social cleansing.

iv Vice and crime. Many of the above groups and others get swept up by organized crime and exploited as gang members and sex workers.

*b) **Powerful gangs** known as maras* are made up mostly of youth, but have massive influence and power in Honduran society. They are becoming more violent and ruthless and are linking up with drug cartels using Honduras as a transshipment point. The government is waging an increasingly intense war against these groups for whom kidnapping, extortion and assault are the main activities.

*c) **AIDS has decimated the population.*** Honduras is home to 60% of Central America's AIDS cases. Poverty, ignorance, a widespread sex industry, a macho culture and the Catholic stance against contraception all contribute to its rapid growth. Pray for moral courage and an educational shift among Hondurans to halt the spread of AIDS.

*d) **The devastation of Hurricane Mitch*** continues to blight Honduras. Many towns, villages and churches were virtually destroyed. The needs after 10 years are to re-establish both infrastructure and self-sustaining industries. Pray for all involved (World Relief, Tearfund, WVI, Lutheran World Relief, others).

3 **Catholicism's influence is rapidly declining.** In some polls, the 80% affiliation rate is reportedly as low as 47%. The greatest factors contributing to this decline include the lack of indigenous personnel, widespread nominalism, the influence of animism/paganism within the Church and large-scale migration to evangelical churches. Only about 20% of Catholics are actively involved in the Church. There is considerable agreement between Catholics and evangelicals on communal and social issues. Pray for a Holy Spirit-driven revival to sweep through the Catholic Church; the impact of this could still transform Honduran society.

4 **The growing number and influence of evangelicals** is praiseworthy, as is the greatly increasing number and size of many congregations. *La Cosecha* ("The Harvest") is a Foursquare church with a weekly attendance of 20,000, despite being founded only 20 years ago. Sadly, much of the progress among evangelicals in Honduras is undermined by their fragmentation into countless denominations and the resulting jealousies and isolationism. In part, this is due to the imported divisions and rivalries brought in by missionaries. Pray for the *Confraternidad Evangélica* (founded in 1987), which represents 90% of evangelicals in the country. It works to cultivate fellowship and cooperation across denominations.

5 **Leadership training** becomes ever more vital as the number of congregations continues to grow. Many seminaries and Bible schools face difficulties (costs, staffing, cooperation), enhancing the importance of networks of TEE programmes run by various denominations. Pray that the trainers might impart biblical knowledge and be models for spiritual ministry.

6 **Amerindian peoples** have partially assimilated into Spanish culture. Among the Lenca, **WGM** and **CAMI** are working to great effect. The peoples of the eastern forests (Miskitu, Garifuna, Sumo and Tol) retain more of their cultural identity. In recent years many have come to Christ. MOPAWI (*Mosquitia Pawisa*), an indigenous body founded on Christian principles, is dedicated to development of local cultures, to community projects and to advocacy of full equality under the law. Baptists, Christian Fellowship Mission, Miskito Missions and others work among the very poor but responsive peoples. Pray for healthy development of churches among them and for all forms of exploitation to end.

7 **Missions vision has grown significantly** in the past decade. There are now several mission agencies, both denominational and interdenominational, that train and send cross-cultural workers. Some examples: **YWAM**, *Puerto al Mundo*, Baptists, *El Cordero* and the Council of Evangelical Churches. Pray for the whole Honduran Church to gain a greater vision for outreach and mission.

8 **Foreign mission agencies can still play a key role** in training and development, specialized ministries and in holistic projects, for which there are many openings. Pray for humble sensitivity and for a legacy of raising up and empowering Honduran leadership and initiatives. The largest agencies are: **CCCI**, **WGM**, **CAMI**, **CB**/CMML, CCCC, **BIM**.

9 **Specialist Christian ministries.** Pray for:

*a) **Student outreach by both CCCI and IFES.*** With a burgeoning young population, many churches are also taking up ministry to children and students.

b) Christian literature. Hosanna and Vida's bookstores are important resources for Christian growth.

c) Radio. National radio gives time to several evangelical churches, and there are 41 local evangelical radio stations (such as HRVC, *Stereo Luz* and *Cosecha*) and two TV channels as well as Internet radio.

Hungary
Republic of Hungary
Europe

Geography

Area 93,030 sq km. A landlocked, central European state on the River Danube.

Population		Ann Gr	Density
2010	9,973,141	-0.21%	107/sq km
2020	9,766,105	-0.22%	105/sq km
2030	9,509,025	-0.29%	102/sq km

Capital Budapest 1,706,177. **Urbanites** 68.3%. **Pop under 15 yrs** 15%. **Life expectancy** 73.3 yrs.

Peoples

Magyar (Hungarian) 86.8%. Over a third of all Hungarians live in other lands: Romania 1.8 million; USA 1.4mill; Slovakia 600,000; Serbia 300,000; Ukraine 200,000; many in other nations.
Minorities 13.2%. Romani (Gypsy) 7.7; Slavic(9) 1.8%; German 1.2%; Jews 1.0%; Romanian 1.0%.
Literacy 99%. **Official language** Hungarian. **All languages** 17. **Indigenous languages** 9. **Languages with Scriptures** 6Bi 1NT 1por.

Economy

Traditionally rich agricultural land. Hungary has negotiated a successful, albeit difficult, transition from a socialist economy to a market economy. The older generation struggles in some ways to adjust – from a system that cared for their needs to one in which they, mostly, must look after themselves. Hungary enjoys a strong share of foreign investment into Central Europe. Economic difficulties, compounded by the financial crisis of 2008-2009, have required reform and austerity measures.
HDI Rank 43rd/182. **Public debt** 67.7% of GDP. **Income/person** $15,523 (33% of USA).

Politics

Hungary lost 60% of its land area at the breakup of the Austro-Hungarian Empire in 1918, leaving large Hungarian minorities in surrounding lands. After WWII, the Soviets imposed Communism, only leaving in 1991. The Hungarian uprising against Communism in 1956 brought terrible revenge from the Soviets; 80,000 were killed, wounded or deported, and 200,000 fled to the West. Hungary was the first Communist bloc state to abandon Marxism and institute a multiparty democracy (1990) although most of the leaders were the same ones as under Communism. Corruption and unpopular policies kept any party from gaining conclusive control of parliament, until 2009, when a centre-right party gained the two-thirds majority needed to change the legal system, the constitution, etc. There has been recent growth of far-right parties. Part of NATO and the EU.

Religion

In 1600, Hungary was 90% Protestant. Many reverted to Catholicism during the Counter Reformation and the periods of discrimination that followed. The Communists enforced strict controls on all Christians from 1948-1988, through discrimination, intimidation and infiltration. In 2000, Hungary celebrated 1,000 years since its conversion to Christianity. Freedom of religion since 1990.

Religions	Pop %	Population	Ann Gr
Christian	87.99	8,775,367	-0.5%
Non-religious	10.90	1,087,072	1.9%
Jewish	0.91	90,756	-0.2%
Muslim	0.16	15,957	4.0%
Buddhist	0.04	3,989	5.7%

Christians Denoms		Pop %	Affiliates	Ann Gr
Protestant	16	23.73	2,367,000	-0.7%
Independent	26	1.09	109,000	2.7%
Catholic	1	59.56	5,940,000	-0.4%
Orthodox	4	1.07	107,000	0.6%
Marginal	5	0.77	77,000	7.1%
Unaffiliated		1.77	177,000	-3.9%

Churches	MegaBloc	Congs	Members	Affiliates
Catholic Church	C	2,330	4,466,165	5,940,000
Reformed Church	P	1,250	506,250	2,025,000

H

					Missionaries from Hungary
Evang Lutheran Ch	P	320	72,500	290,000	P,I,A 60 (45 long-term; 20 cross-cultural) in 3
Romanian Orthodox	O	22	52,632	80,000	agencies: in Hungary 40, among the Romani 5,
Faith Church	I	70	31,000	62,000	Central Asia 9, Romania 2.
Jehovah's Witnesses	M	265	23,700	46,200	
Baptist Church	P	333	11,500	19,850	
Seventh-day Adventist	P	119	5,950	11,900	
Fell of Ev Pentecostals	I	146	4,730	10,500	
Other denominations[43]		711	65,981	113,391	
Total Christians[52]		**5,566**	**5,240,408**	**8,598,841**	

TransBloc	Pop %	Population	Ann Gr
Evangelicals			
Evangelicals	2.8	282,181	0.9%
Renewalists			
Charismatics	2.4	238,107	2.9%
Pentecostals	0.2	17,430	0.1%

Missionaries from Hungary
P,I,A 60 (45 long-term; 20 cross-cultural) in 3 agencies: in Hungary 40, among the Romani 5, Central Asia 9, Romania 2.

Answers to Prayer

1 **The small, but historically rich, evangelical movement** is growing in size, maturity, diversity and confidence. Many types of ministries are springing up around the nation, and the vision exists to see an evangelical church planted in every city, town and village in Hungary.

2 **Unity across denominations** is experiencing much-needed growth, as churches come together to pray, worship and minister. There are also many prayer ministries that represent the different flavours of Christian faith – Budapest Prayer Wall, National Prayer Network and 168-hour Intercessory Prayer Chain are examples of these.

Challenges for Prayer

1 **Disillusion, dissatisfaction and upheaval** against the government and economy in particular often characterize life in Hungary. The 1956 uprising and widespread demonstrations in 2006 and following demonstrate the desire for a better state of affairs. Political scandal has brought much disappointment and skepticism. Pray for elected officials, that they would look past political point-scoring, root out the widespread corruption and labour toward improving life for the whole nation.

2 **Hungarians have lost contact with the gospel,** despite enjoying a rich theological history. They seek answers in many places: materialism, hedonism, alcohol and, increasingly, false religion. Postmodern mentalities predominate. In recent years, public spiritual life is characterized by an alarming rise in occult activity and eastern mysticism, including pagan witchcraft, ancient Magyar shamanism and Tibetan Buddhism. Most common is a pick-and-choose spirituality that is effectively non-religious, with some personal sentiment. Pray for all falsehoods and empty philosophies to be exposed as such and for Christ to be exalted as the truth in this historically Christian nation. Pray that Hungarians might see the truth of the gospel and the freedom it brings through Jesus.

3 **The openness of the post-Communist 1990s has passed.** It is now increasingly difficult to openly witness – restrictions forbid teachers, doctors and such from sharing their faith in the workplace. The Church failed to respond adequately to the window of opportunity that is now largely closed. Christianity, while present and active, does not quite have the impact it should on society, politics, ethics, education and the economy. Pray for a new revival in the Church – following on those from 1939 and 1946-50 – that gives birth to a new spirit of witness and activism.

4 **The Church's impact in Hungary is uneven and inadequate.** Some parts of the country are much more alive than others. Within the major denominations, including Catholic and Reformed, are vibrant charismatic and renewal movements. Independent and emerging churches are growing, but trust and unity need to be built between these and the traditional churches. In all groups, positive holiness and spiritual maturity are real needs. In Budapest, believers are blessed with many churches, but they often church-hop rather than commit to one congregation. Apathy and worldliness, as in so many lands, are challenges, even for evangelicals. Pray for unity, trust and cooperation to flourish among churches, and for the Holy Spirit to bring revival and renewal to all expressions of God's family.

5 **There remains a great need for evangelism,** despite the increasing amount and types of outreach and public ministry. Christians need to acquire confidence in the power of the gospel and its effectiveness when shared in the right way and in the Spirit. The number of nominal Christians is high, and millions of people have only cursory contact with the good news. There is still resistance to the gospel in much of Hungary. Pray for Spirit-led, creative forms of witness and for wisdom in how, when and where to reach out. Thank God for increasing levels of collaboration in outreach among churches and denominations.

6 **There is a deficit of Christian leadership** in Hungary. Pray for the following:

a) Leaders with high morals and fresh vision. Many evangelistic challenges are unmet, many eyes scrutinize the conduct of Christian leaders and many leaders are cautious because of the past. Pray for God's anointing and inspiration for those in leadership.

b) The release and empowerment of lay leaders. Most pastors are overworked and spread too thin, and there is a shortage of young pastors, both in active ministry and in training to join the ministry. There is a strong Reformed Elders Association. Lay-training movements are on the rise in most denominations. Pray that the Church might mature in its giving in order to support nationals involved in local and foreign Christian work.

c) Leadership training. Hungary is a Central European hub for theological education. There are four Christian universities providing education in theology, humanities and law, with several thousand students enrolled. There is an increasing focus on missions and evangelism. Pray also for the Protestant Institute for Mission Studies, the Pentecostal Theological College, Calvary Chapel Bible College and for teaching seminars run by New Hope International and others. Central European Theological Academy and Word of Life are two of several English-language theological institutions. TEE/BEE is increasingly used, especially to train laity. Pray for the younger generation to commit itself to the work of the Lord, and for the Lord to provide for those who take on full-time training.

7 **Young people** remain one of the most receptive groups to loving and culturally relevant witness. Pray especially for:

a) Teaching of religious knowledge in schools, in the several hundred Christian schools and in public schools that invite this input. Increasingly, restrictions prevent teachers and evangelists from sharing the gospel in the public school context. Pray for freedom to witness in schools and for gifted people who focus on this ministry.

b) Children's and youth programmes in churches. Since Hungary opened up, denominational and parachurch youth associations, such as YMCA, Awana, **CEF**, *Dunamisz* and others, have grown in scale and impact. Large-scale youth conventions are proving attractive. Foreign mission groups contribute much in this area of ministry.

c) University students, who are open to most spiritual influences, both healthy and unhealthy. Nationally led international ministries such as **CCCI**, MEKDsz(**IFES**) and **YFC** continue to grow in size and impact. But with over 200,000 university and college students in Hungary, the majority have no contact with a Christian group.

d) Summer outreach programmes – by many Hungarian churches and by *Barnabas Csoport*, The Bible League and **OM** – train scores of young people from various denominations to participate in evangelism and follow-up work.

8 **The less-reached:**

a) The Jews. Before the Holocaust, there were 800,000. Now their numbers are 90,000 – which is still Eastern Europe's largest concentration of Jews outside of Russia. There are several Messianic Jewish communities. Pray for a reconciliation between Christians and Jews.

b) **The Romani** (Gypsy) community, Hungary's largest minority and most certainly its most socially and economically disadvantaged. This group has not seen the same spiritual breakthrough as have the Romani in Spain, France and Romania, but several new Protestant and charismatic fellowships are among them. Also, a number of agencies are attempting to meet their social and spiritual needs and, increasingly, ethnic Hungarians are gaining a burden to show the love of Christ to this needy people in both spiritual and practical ways.

c) **The homeless** – who are concentrated in Budapest and number as many as 30,000 – face very difficult living conditions. Pray for the ministries of churches and missions that seek to reach out to them; pray for the establishment of Christian facilities that can care for them and demonstrate the gospel in real ways.

d) **The many immigrant peoples** who make Hungary their home. These include mostly the various Slavic peoples, Chinese and others. Most have a better chance to encounter the gospel in Hungary than in their own nation.

e) **Hungarians abroad.** Concerns remain about discrimination against Hungarian ethnic minorities in Serb-controlled Vojvodina, Romanian Transylvania and southern Slovakia – all remnants of Greater Hungary. Pray for reconciliation between these minorities and the various national majorities, and pray for Hungarian Christians to reach out to their own who live abroad.

9 **Expatriate missions increased numerically** in the 1990s, but have since levelled off. Pray for sensitivity and a true servant attitude in seeking to help the Hungarian Church. The main ministries required of expatriates are leadership training and mentoring, equipping the laity and imparting missionary vision. The need is still very real for long-term workers who will learn the language and culture. The Hungarian missions movement is still in its infancy, but the great promise is beginning to be realized – a Missions Expo recently attracted 20,000 people. The largest agencies are: **CCCI**, **YWAM**, **RG**, **ABWE**, Greater Grace World Outreach.

10 **Christian help ministries:**

a) **Scripture distribution.** The Hungarian Bible Society was revitalized in 1989. Pray for its ministry in distributing the Bible. A revised New Translation of the Bible in 1990 marked the 400th anniversary of the original Hungarian version.

b) **Christian literature is in demand.** Many new Christian publishing companies have been founded. The need continues for Christian books, written in Hungarian, that communicate the gospel to non-Christians in today's language and idioms. Balanced books, written in Hungarian, for the spiritual growth of believers are also needed. **CLC** has two bookstores in Hungary. The Hungarian Literature Mission is a major source of evangelistic materials.

c) **Christian media.** In addition to many broadcast hours a week in Hungarian by **TWR**, opportunities are increasing for local Christian programmes on TV and radio. Hungarian Gospel Radio Foundation and the Reformed and Lutheran Churches have their own radio programmes. **IT** has a music-recording studio to serve Central Europe. The Internet and a host of Christian websites offer another means for discipling believers and reaching out to non-Christians.

Iceland

Norwegian Sea

Greenland

Reykjavik

Faeroe Islands

Norway

North Atlantic Ocean

United Kingdom

Iceland
Republic of Iceland
Europe

Geography

Area 103,000 sq km. A volcanic island in the North Atlantic; mountainous, largely barren with many large glaciers.

Population		Ann Gr	Density
2010	329,279	2.17%	3/sq km
2020	370,487	0.97%	4/sq km
2030	391,989	0.44%	4/sq km

Capital Reykjavik 202,000. **Urbanites** 92.3%. **Pop under 15 yrs** 21%. **Life expectancy** 81.7 yrs.

Peoples

Icelandic 91.7%.
Other 8.3% (mostly European but increasingly otherwise). Danish 1.2%; Swedish 0.6%; Polish 0.6%.
Literacy 100%. **Official language** Icelandic. **All languages** 2. **Languages with Scriptures** 1Bi.

Economy

One of the world's highest living standards. Fishing and limited agriculture are being supplanted by tourism, hydroelectric-energy plants and aluminum-smelting projects. A fast-growing finance sector infamously triggered a financial crisis and banking collapse in 2008-2009; consequences of the financial crisis have already seen the demise of one government. Energy plants and aluminum factories are controversial, given Iceland's unique and fragile environment.
HDI Rank 3rd/182. **Public debt** 56.5% of GDP.
Income/person $53,058 (112% of USA).

Politics

The world's oldest parliament, established in 930.

Under Norwegian and Danish rule 1262-1944. Parliamentary republic and a member of NATO. Not part of the EU.

Religion

The Lutheran Church is still recognized as the state church, but there is religious freedom.

Religions	Pop %	Population	Ann Gr
Christian	90.60	298,327	1.2%
Non-religious	8.33	27,429	18.2%
Other	0.60	1,976	4.0%
Buddhist	0.27	889	5.5%
Muslim	0.11	362	8.9%
Baha'i	0.09	296	0.0%

Christians Denoms		Pop %	Affiliates	Ann Gr
Protestant	19	83.57	275,000	0.4%
Independent	2	0.46	2,000	2.0%
Catholic	1	2.52	8,000	5.2%
Orthodox	2	0.11	<500	3.1%
Marginal	2	0.27	<1,000	0.8%
Unaffiliated		3.67	12,000	32.0%

Churches	MegaBloc	Congs	Members	Affiliates
Lutheran Church	P	275	177,273	253,500
Lutheran Free Chs	P	4	11,958	17,100
Catholic Church	C	5	5,929	8,300
Pentecostal Church	P	8	1,518	2,270
Charismatic churches	P	4	528	900
Pentecostal Fellowship	I	4	553	800
Seventh-day Adventist	P	7	525	760
The Way Chr Fell	I	1	438	700
Jehovah's Witnesses	M	9	358	680
Other denominations[11]		209	882	1,190
Total Christians[26]		**526**	**199,962**	**286,200**

TransBloc	Pop %	Population	Ann Gr
Evangelicals			
Evangelicals	3.8	12,641	2.6%
Renewalists			
Charismatics	2.0	6,700	3.1%
Pentecostals	1.2	4,005	4.0%

Missionaries from Iceland
P,I,A 8 (6 long-term) in one organized agency, and denominational efforts: to Ethiopia 4, Kenya 2.

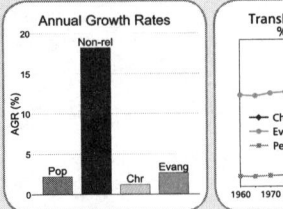

Annual Growth Rates

Non-rel

Pop   Chr   Evang

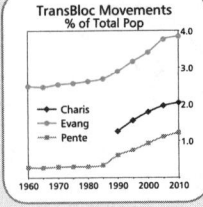

TransBloc Movements % of Total Pop

Charis
Evang
Pente

1960 1970 1980 1990 2000 2010

Challenges for Prayer

1 **Traditional Icelandic life can be considered under threat.** High-profile disputes divide opinion between conservationists wanting to preserve the environment and industrialists wanting to cash in on the resources. Although the total number of immigrants is not massive, Iceland's relatively small population has seen possibly the largest migration rate in Europe, bringing other faiths and cultures into a traditionally guarded society. Pray for wisdom for leaders and the people in dealing with these new challenges.

2 **The majority of Icelanders are Christian, but only nominally so.** Biblical Christianity and a lifestyle of following Christ are alien concepts to most. Some of the more isolated areas are spiritual wastelands, with almost no active Christianity at all. Ask the Lord to break into Icelandic society and orchestrate a revival that touches every person and aspect of life.

3 **The Lutheran and the smaller, but similar, Free Churches** are suffering the same challenges as much of Europe – declining and aging congregations, low attendance and a general lack of spiritual vitality. There is, of course, a segment of Lutherans who faithfully follow Jesus; pray that their numbers might multiply. And, there is actually a surfeit of young trainees – so much so that churches may "export" them to serve in Lutheran or Anglican congregations abroad! Pray for a surge of new life in the congregations and the leadership. Pray also for the theological faculty where all pastors are trained.

4 **Evangelical believers are not many** (3.8%), but their numbers are growing. In particular, Lutheran Free Churches, Pentecostals and charismatic churches are increasing and displaying admirable unity and cooperation. The Pentecostal Church, together with World Horizons, runs a short-term discipleship ministry, and the ex-**YWAM** training centre is now a residential Christian training community. Several congregations use the Alpha Course to good effect. Pray that the living faith and unity of evangelicals might open the hearts of many to the good news.

5 **The Bible Society** launched in 2000 a new Bible translation, which was well received. The 2007 release of *The 100-Minute Bible* in Icelandic resulted in many acquiring Bibles. Pray that many would come back into contact with the transforming Word of God.

6 **Christian Radio.** Radio Lindin, which can reach about 90% of the population, remains on air and is a blessing to believers. And it has been used to bring some unbelievers to faith. It is also available via the Internet.

I

India

Republic of India

Asia

Geography

Area 3,166,000 sq km. A further 121,000 sq km of Kashmir – a contested area – is administered by Pakistan and China. Geographically and politically, India dominates South Asia and the Indian Ocean. There are 28 Union States and 7 Union Territories.

Population		Ann Gr	Density
2010	1,214,464,312	1.44%	384/sq km
2020	1,367,224,576	1.10%	432/sq km
2030	1,484,597,882	0.73%	469/sq km

Capital Delhi 22,156,810. **Next largest city** Mumbai (Bombay) 20,040,868. **Other cities** 45 cities of over 1 million people; 459 of over 100,000. **Urbanites** 30.1%. **Pop under 15 yrs** 31%. **Life expectancy** 63.4 yrs.

Peoples

India's ancient, complex and often historically inscrutable past; its racial, ethnic, religious and linguistic diversity; and the caste system all make detailed population analysis exceedingly difficult.

Ethnicities

The most ethnically diverse nation on earth, with over 2,500 distinct people groups. Community and identity are based on caste as much as on race and language. The greatest shift in India's ethnic history remains the Indo-Aryan migration into the subcontinent over 3,000 years ago. Differing schools of thought label this mass people movement as conquest, absorption or both. Regardless, many of the original inhabitants (tribal peoples) and Dravidian peoples were forced to endure centuries of subjugation. The following list is based on Omid/JPL data and covers only the largest groups by Affinity Bloc and people cluster. Treatment of India is unique on this issue, since caste is often a major factor in determining people group identity.

South Asian Peoples 97.7%.

Hindi 37.0%. 297 groups. Brahmin 4.9%; Yadava 4.8%; Chamar 4.3%; Rajput 3.5%; Kurmi 1.5%; Teli 1.5%; Kumhar 1.2%; Dhobi Hindu 1.0%; Nai 0.9%; Mali 0.8%; Lohar 0.8%; Kahar 0.6%; Pasi Hindu 0.6%; Sonar 0.6%; Lodha 0.5%; Gadaria Hindu 0.5%; Badhai Hindu 0.5%; Bhoi Hindu 0.5%; Kachhi Hindu 0.5%; Dosadh Hindu 0.5%; Bhangi Hindu 0.4%; Mina 0.4%.

Bengali 14.25%. 162 groups. Shaikh 6.6%; Mahishya 0.9%; Kayastha 0.7%; Koiri 0.6%; Namasudra Hindu 0.4%; Rajbansi 0.4%.

Telugu 5.4%. 135 groups. Kapu 1.4%; Viswakarma 0.7%; Madiga 0.6%; Mala 0.5%.

Marathi-Konkani 5.3%. 110 groups. Mahratta 2.4%; Mahar Hindu 0.7%; Mau Buddh 0.7%.

Rajasthan 5.3%. 110 groups. Bania 2.2%; Gujar 0.6%; Bania Agarwal 0.4%.

Tamil 4.6%. 89 groups. Vanniyan 1.0%; Adi Dravida 0.8%; Nadar 0.4%.

Gujarati 4.1%. 127 groups. Kunbi 1.4%; Koli 1.0%; Mahratta Kunbi 0.6%.

Kannada 3.1%. 162 groups. Lingayat 0.6%; Vakkaliga 0.5%.

Malayali 3.1%. 97 groups. Mappila 0.8%; Nair 0.6%; Ilavan 0.6%; Syrian Christian 0.3%.

Urdu Muslim 3.1%. 142 groups. Ansari 0.8%; Sayyid 0.6%.

Jat 2.8%. 104 groups. Jat Hindu 1.3%; Jat Sikh 1.0%.

Munda-Santal 1.4%. 11 groups. Santal 0.7%; Munda 0.3%.

Punjabi 1.4%. 120 groups.

Oriya 1.4%. 284 groups.

Gond 1.4%. 6 groups. Gond 1.2%.

Bhil 1.3%. 4 groups. Bhil 1.2%.

Gypsy 0.6%. 8 groups. Banjara Hindu 0.5%.

Kashmiri 0.6%. 42 groups. Kashmiri Muslim 0.5%.

Assamese 0.4%. 21 groups.

Oraon 0.4%. 1 group.

Tibetan/Himalayan Peoples 1.1%. 252 groups. Almost all in north and northeast.

Iranian-Median 0.9%. Northern Pashtun 0.9%; 4 other groups.

Others 0.3%. Southeast Asian, Eurasian/European, Turkic, Chinese, Arab, Jews.

Languages

Indo-Aryan 76%. Main languages, mainly north and central India. Hindi, Bengali, Marathi, Urdu, Gujarati, Rajasthani/Mawari, Bhojpuri, Oriya, Punjabi, Magahi, Chhattisgarhi, Assamese, Maithili, others.
Dravidian 21.6%. 83 languages, mainly south India. Telugu, Tamil, Kannada, Malayalam, Oraon, others.
Austro-Asiatic 1.2%. 32 main languages, scattered over central, south and northeast India. Mundari, Ho, Khasi, Juray, others.
Sino-Tibetan 1.0%. 157 main languages. Bodo, Meitei, Garo, Miri, Mizo, Karbi, Kuki-Chin, others.
Other 0.2%. Arabic, others.
Literacy 67% (55% for females, 77% for males). Functional literacy is lower. **Official languages** Constitutionally there are 22 official languages. The official language is Hindi (spoken by 40% of the population). English is a subsidiary official language. **All languages** 456, including 18 with more than 10 million speakers. The SIL Ethnologue lists 438 living languages. **Languages with Scriptures** 70Bi 120NT 89por 136 w.i.p.

Language	Pop 2010	Dialects	People groups
Hindi	489.6m		297
Bengali	96.7m	15	159
Telugu	85.8m	9	355
Marathi	83.4m	42	170
Tamil	70.5m	20	247
Urdu	59.8m	6	163
Gujarati	53.5m	15	199
Kannada	44.0m	20	174
Rajasthani★	41.8m	20	>130
Bhojpuri★	38.4m	10	42
Malayalam	38.4m	17	129
Oriya	38.3m	10	200
Punjabi	33.8m	10	85
Magahi★	16.2m	3	30
Chhattisgarhi★	15.4m	12	66
Assamese	15.3m	5	38
Maithili	14.1m	8	42
Bhili/Bhilodi	11.1m	16	6
Haryanvi★	9.3m	5	44
Santali	7.5m	6	1
Kanauji★	7.0m	3	
Kashmiri	6.4m	17	47
Nepali	3.3m	3	24
Gondi	3.1m	8	11
Sindhi	2.9m	9	9
Konkani	2.9m	14	55
Dogri	2.6m	7	55

★There is debate as to whether these are dialects of Hindi or languages in their own right. There are 29 languages with over 1 million speakers in India.

Caste

The caste system reflects ancient social and occupational hierarchies, but its origins are disputed and unclear. Ancient Indo-Aryan traditions, Hindu religious texts and beliefs, Indian social structures, the British Empire and even modernization and globalization today have shaped how the caste system impacts life in India. Today, the four major divisions are: Forward Castes, Other Backward Castes, Dalit/Bahujan/ Scheduled Castes and Scheduled Tribes. Around 4,700 castes and 25,000 subcastes (or *jatis*) function as clearly defined, hierarchically arranged, endogamous hereditary groups. These have been the foundation of Indian social order for centuries. This system impacts life much more profoundly in rural areas than in cities, where educational, economic and social mobility increasingly blurs caste lines. Discrimination based on caste is constitutionally illegal, and the government has affirmative action policies in place to help the groups previously most disadvantaged by the system. But caste-based discrimination persists throughout much of India.

Economy 📈

Traditionally an agricultural economy, but because of market-economy policies adopted in 1991, India has rapidly transitioned to become more financially diverse. Industry and especially services are taking the lead in the 21st Century. India is a nuclear power, has a space industry and is increasingly a world leader in the IT sector. Its booming economy is one of the success stories of the last decade and will significantly impact the global economy for the foreseeable future.

The rapid growth of the new rich is outdone only by the increase in the middle class, which now possibly numbers around 350 million. Yet, the rural poor and impoverished urban slum-dwellers still number in the hundreds of millions. For those at the bottom of the heap, India's economic boom is meaningless.

The inadequate infrastructure – for travel, power and sanitation in particular – must be addressed if growth is to be sustained long-term. Corruption, inefficiency and prejudice remain further obstacles to overcome for economic improvements to be made to all of Indian society. Nearly 40% of the population live below the poverty line, and 40% of children are underweight.

India's widespread use of English gives the country a major advantage as its economy opens to the world.

HDI Rank 134th/182. **Public debt** 56.4% of GDP. **Income/person** $1,017 (2% of USA).

Politics 🗺

Independent from Britain in 1947. The world's largest functioning democracy. The RSS and the VHP (Hindu extreme nationalist movements) grew in strength and influence, and as a result, the Hindu nationalist BJP party gained political power in the 1990s. Since then, a coalition government led by the Congress Party (INC) has won two elections. The current administration emphasizes economic growth and social progress on issues including caste and freedom of religion. As a result, significant progress has been made in terms of equality for all groups in India, but millennia of oppression will take some time to overturn. Long-standing tensions with Pakistan continue, especially over the issue of Kashmir.

Religion 🙏

India's constitution provides full religious freedom of worship and witness for all religions. The rise of Hindutva extremism resulted in a hate campaign against Muslims in the early 1990s and against Christians in the late 1990s as followers of "foreign" religions. Due to mass-conversion movements by Dalit groups away from Hinduism, and to evangelistic activities by Christian groups, issues of conversion and anti-conversion laws are of high importance and sensitivity. Persecution levels range widely, usually depending on the strength of Hindutva groups from one state to the next.

Religions	Pop %	Population	Ann Gr
Hindu	74.33	902,711,323	1.2%
Muslim	14.20	172,453,932	2.0%
Christian★	5.84	71,011,000	3.7%
Sikh	1.86	22,589,036	1.3%
Ethnoreligionist	1.35	16,395,268	1.0%
Buddhist	0.82	9,958,607	2.7%
Non-religious	0.48	5,829,429	2.8%
Other	0.47	5,707,982	1.0%
Baha'i	0.15	1,821,696	0.1%

★For many reasons, the most recent census (2001) significantly underenumerated Christians at 2.34%. Christian researchers in India indicate much higher results, even up to 9%. New 2011 census results are expected before 2013.

Christians Denoms		Pop %	Affiliates	Ann Gr
Protestant	319	2.13	25,924,000	4.2%
Independent	860	1.44	17,442,000	4.8%
Anglican	1	0.02	270,000	2.1%
Catholic	3	1.55	18,790,000	1.9%
Orthodox	10	0.18	2,236,000	1.1%
Marginal	15	0.02	221,000	1.9%
Unaffiliated		0.80	9,725,000	3.7%
Doubly affiliated		-0.20	-2,429,000	

Churches	MegaBloc	Congs	Members	Affiliates
Catholic Church	C	6,681	8,016,760	14,350,000
Ch of S India (CSI)	P	15,300	2,056,338	4,380,000
Syro-Malabaresi Cath	C	723	1,879,524	3,947,000
Seventh-day Adventist	P	3,819	1,470,364	2,747,769
Oriental Orth	O	1,660	1,191,617	1,990,000
United Evang Luth Chs	P	12,974	1,167,665	1,950,000
Believers Church	P	9,000	1,500,000	1,800,000
Ch of N India (CNI)	P	4,500	824,176	1,500,000
Presby Ch of I	P	2,456	585,970	1,394,609
Methodist Ch in I	P	723	575,000	1,150,000
Mar Thoma Syrian Ch	P	1,171	626,347	1,046,000
Samavesam of Telugu	P	1,407	633,333	950,000
Assemblies of God	I	3,427	367,841	835,000
Orissa Bapt Evang	P	3,865	405,000	745,000

					TransBloc	Pop %	Population	Ann Gr
Nagaland Bapt Ch	P	1,400	484,174	726,261	**Evangelicals**			
New Life Fellowship	I	3,899	206,667	620,000	Evangelicals	2.2	26,290,283	3.9%
Garo Baptist Conv	P	2,407	242,402	600,000	**Renewalists**			
Churches of Christ	P	6,400	224,000	560,000	Charismatics	1.6	19,636,544	3.6%
Syro-Malankaresi Cath	C	588	294,118	500,000	Pentecostals	0.4	5,219,760	0.4%
Indian Nat Evang Fell	I	4,262	262,368	472,262				
Brethren Assem	P	1,929	135,000	449,550				
Evang Ch of India	P	2,494	176,986	442,465				
Ch of God (Cleveland)	P	2,020	285,000	430,000				
Christ Groups	I	9,749	243,713	407,000				
Menn Savodara Sangam	P	1,040	130,000	395,000				
Indian Evang Team	I	5,140	205,600	385,500				
Salvation Army	P	4,062	224,368	374,695				
Manipur Bapt Conv	P	1,284	173,320	363,972				
FMPB	I	2,118	180,000	360,000				
Nagaland Chr Revival	I	1,195	161,364	355,000				
Manna Full Gospel	P	1,605	144,444	325,000				
India Gospel League	I	6,900	192,814	322,000				
Assem Jehovah Shammah	I	910	95,000	310,000				
Good Shepherd	P	3,000	150,000	300,000				
Filadelfia Fellowship	I	1,400	210,000	295,000				
Other denominations [1,131]		125,383	7,351,708	13,507,111				
Total Christians [1,208]		**256,891**	**33,072,981**	**61,286,194**				

Missionaries from India

P,I,A 82,950 long-term in more than 200 agencies; nearly all serving cross-culturally in India.

Annual Growth Rates — AGR (%): Pop, Hindu, Chr, Evang

MegaBlocs % of Christian Pop — P, I, C, O, U, X: 19.9, 0.6, 35, 18, 23.7, 2.7

I Answers to Prayer

1 **The restoration of political centrism** – following the election defeat of a Hinduistic government with extremist tendencies – has returned a measure of religious freedom and has overseen economic growth and the addressing of injustices inherent to the caste system. Burgeoning numbers of indigenous NGOs, policy changes meant to uplift those in (or beneath) the lowest strata of the caste system and even legal changes all point toward a society looking to be more modern, pluralistic and humane.

2 **Action on the plight of the Dalits/Bahujans/Scheduled Castes and Scheduled Tribes,** who together amount to over 25% of the population. This comes after literally millennia of oppression, justified by the caste system and by Hinduism. The UN, the Indian government and international NGOs have all taken action to address this situation. Most notably, the Indian and the global Church have begun work to establish human rights, education, health, employment and salvation of the Dalits. Encouraging change is occurring at an admirable pace, although so much remains to be done.

3 **Christianity's positive contribution to Indian society** is best known from William Carey's incredible legacy. But it is also the result of Catholic work and, more recently, of evangelical awareness of effective holistic ministry. The work of Christians in education and health and in challenging social ills brings goodwill, makes the appeal of Christianity more effective and makes it more difficult to stir up anti-Christian sentiment.

4 **Praise for continued freedom for Indian Christians** to proclaim the gospel, despite efforts from certain communal and political forces to limit this freedom through legislation, intimidation and persecution.

5 **Persecution of Christians** – especially in Orissa, Karnataka and Gujarat – has not only refined the Church and drawn it together, but it has also caused the Church to re-evaluate its methods and priorities in evangelism and ministry. Persecution has exposed the hateful agenda of extremist religious groups and made Christians more aware of their constitutional rights.

6 **Missions, church planting and research initiatives** in India have grown far beyond the humble beginnings in the 1960s, which were largely controlled by foreign groups. Today, over 1,000 Indian mission agencies and church-based initiatives have sent out over

100,000 church planters, evangelists and social workers – many of them cross-culturally – and have planted tens of thousands of Christ-following congregations. Considerable thought and practice are now shaping an Indian Church and society that can follow Christ and live out the gospel in a contextualized fashion.

7 **The increased response** of previously resistant peoples and regions. This is most notable in Uttar Pradesh, but also in many other states in north and central India, particularly among lower-caste Hindus and tribal peoples. Other groups of peoples from other religions and social groups are increasingly open to the good news.

Challenges for Prayer

1 **Political, economic and social challenges to the country** place a great burden upon India's government. Much positive progress has been made in many areas; to consolidate and build on such progress, prayer is called for. Pray for India's leaders, that they might:

a) Continue to uphold the constitution by maintaining religious freedom and protecting religious and ethnic minorities. Religious freedom and affirmative action provisions in the constitution have recently come under threat. Some state governments have a poor record for abuse of human rights and discrimination against Christians, Muslims and Dalits; several states have passed anti-conversion laws that, among other things, deny state benefits to low-caste people who become Christian.

b) Uproot corruption in all levels of government – from national to state levels and right down to the local level. Mass media is a powerful means of exposing corruption, and the Right to Information Act forces government staff to be more accountable. With 100 of the 543 members of Parliament having criminal cases pending against them in 2010, clearly the system needs transparency. Pray for courage and resoluteness to stay the course when allowing a culture of corruption to persist is a much easier and safer option.

c) Tackle the serious ills of society with greater commitment and effectiveness – reduce malnutrition, which affects 40% of the population; improve the national infrastructure; deal with widespread use of child labour, bonded labour and female infanticide; tackle the rapid spread of AIDS and serious environmental degradation.

d) Address the growing threat of Maoist/Naxalite insurgency. The stretch of rural India from Nepal down to Andra Pradesh is known as the Red Corridor. These movements threaten stability and security, both locally and regionally. They also threaten the healthy growth of the Church through Naxalite infiltration of Christian communities and the general disruption caused by violence.

e) Manage the economic situation with wisdom. India has the world's highest number of poor, the fourth-most millionaires and the greatest disparity between rich and poor. Millions enter the workforce every year; millions of jobs must be created to sustain them. Amid a growing economy and a growing middle class, ways to reduce poverty must also be found.

f) Wisely address increasing threats to stability, including terrorism, tensions with neighbouring countries, and Hindu nationalist groups and their targets: Christians, Muslims and Naxalites/Communists.

2 **The "New India"** is a youthful, ambitious, cosmopolitan and modern entity, where differences of religion, caste and gender mean less and less. It is increasingly urban and tech-savvy. The India of call centres, cricket, Bollywood, *bhangra* and globally connected Indian culture is exposed to and open to new ideas and ways of living, including Christianity. The most significant influence in this context is materialism – as capable of entrapping Hindus as any other group. This younger generation – 70% of India is under age 35, and 31% under age 15 – will shape India's future. As such, they are a hugely strategic group to reach for Jesus; completely new and different missiological strategies must be undertaken to communicate and model the gospel to them. Indian churches and missions are now focusing on this issue; initial success thus far is very modest.

3 **India has more human need than any other nation** – largely by virtue of its massive population, but also due to many areas of suffering that must be addressed through considered action and sustained prayer.

a) ***Poverty affects hundreds of millions,*** often as utter destitution that is far below any arbitrary income level mathematically calculated by international bodies. Recent economic liberalization and initiatives to assist the poorest communities will help India move further in the right direction to significantly reduce poverty.

> i *Poverty is predominantly rural, despite increasing urbanization.* While the growing urban slums of large cities such as Mumbai and Kolkata are well publicized and contain around 75 million people, India remains predominantly a rural nation, and it is in the villages where most of the poor live.

> ii *Caste issues are closely tied to poverty.* Most of India's poorest are from the Dalit/Bahujan/ Scheduled Castes and Scheduled Tribes, many of them surviving as landless farm labourers. Their landlessness and lack of guaranteed income often lead to debt slavery, which is passed down through generations. Pray for these peoples – may they see God's justice and love demonstrated to them.

> iii *There is a complex relationship between poverty and overpopulation.* Children are seen by many as future guarantors of assistance and income – the more, the better. India's population issues and poverty issues need to be tackled in tandem.

b) ***Health concerns*** affect huge swathes of India's population. Around 40% of children under age three suffer from malnutrition, since inadequate sanitation and lack of clean water multiply the waterborne diseases that impact mostly children and the poor. In India, an estimated 900,000 people per year die as a result of drinking unclean water or breathing polluted air. The health sector is overstretched, under-resourced and prone to corruption. India has the world's third-largest HIV-positive population and accounts for one-third of the world's tuberculosis cases. Excellent healthcare and medical training were two of Christianity's finest contributions to India; these are under threat due to Christian emigration/brain drain. Pray that this important legacy might be preserved.

c) ***Women and children*** suffer disproportionately.

> i *Children in crisis* – no country can rival India's staggering need. Of India's 400 million children under 15 years old, possibly up to 35 million are orphans. Eleven million are abandoned (90% girls); three million live on the street. There are 20 million child labourers (including many instances of bond slavery to pay family debts) – some estimates claim 50 million. Up to two-thirds of children suffer physical abuse, and one-half some kind of sexual harassment or abuse. Over 1.2 million children are involved in prostitution; many of them are Nepali or Bangladeshi.

> ii *Women and girls.* Lower literacy and education rates, the dowry tradition, widespread domestic abuse and the evil tradition of temple prostitution all cry out for action. Society's preference for boys, combined with the illegal application of ultrasound technology, leads to selective abortion of girls and to female infanticide. A female population deficit of 35 million – and growing – compared to the male population demonstrates the severity of the situation.

Pray that these desperate needs may be addressed through loving Christian ministries and state structures. Pray that attitudes and practices in society, especially toward those most vulnerable, might be changed to reflect God's care for women and children.

4 Hinduism is the world's third-largest religious system. Hinduism, most broadly understood, is a civilizational dynamic incorporating every aspect of life, embracing those who live in or identify with India and its culture. As a religion, it is a pluralistic network of religious beliefs and systems ranging from the philosophical (self-realization), to Vedic-influenced rituals, to popular expression (idols), to village Hinduism (animism, occultism). It absorbs elements of any religion it encounters and is widely regarded as an inclusive religion, one of tolerance and peace. Its global influence is significant through movements such as yoga, Hare Krishna/ISKCON, New Age, Art of Living and others. Many concepts of Hinduism have become part of 21st Century postmodern culture – yoga, gurus, karma, dharma, reincarnation and transcendental meditation. How can we pray?

a) ***Hinduism has strong cultural appeal,*** yet in their search for fulfilment and purpose, Hindus still long for true communion with the Creator. Pray that Christians (considered as "Western") may demonstrate, in authentic Indian cultural expressions, true spirituality and the transformation Christ brings.

b) ***The Hindu caste system*** remains a major issue. It has been only partly addressed through constitutional equality, the legal ban on discrimination and affirmative action favouring the underprivileged in education and government jobs. The rising demands by Dalits for their constitutional rights and for a share in the land and wealth of the country, and by tribals for protection of their ancestral lands and ways, are often met by obstruction, intimidation and repression. Pray that:

i *The government may wisely handle the realities of casteism* and the impoverishment of a large percentage of the population. This includes dealing firmly with violence against Dalit and tribal communities and applying affirmative action to all Dalits, irrespective of their religion.

ii *The Christian response may be both biblical and Christlike,* ministering to all oppressed people while rooting out casteism within its own ranks. About 80% of all Christians are of Dalit or tribal communities, and the average Hindu associates Christianity with the underclasses of their society.

iii *The churches.* Pray that in their outreach they may be sensitive to the caste networks and facilitate people movements to Christ, and that in their fellowship they may work toward elimination of the dividing walls of society. Many churches are themselves guilty of caste-based discrimination.

c) ***Hindutva extremism*** casts a baleful shadow over India. Militant Hindus of the RSS, Bajrang Dal, Durga Bahini, Shiv Sena, VHP and Sangh Parivar have infiltrated their members into every influential part of society, gaining a notable measure of political power and patronage. They are attempting to promote revisionist histories, to institutionalize discrimination against religious and ethnic minorities and to control the media. The Hindutva ideology of "India is Hindu only" is used to justify intimidation and violence against Muslims and Christians, stigmatizing them as "foreign" faiths. Pray that:

i *Communal violence* might end, and its instigators repent and find Christ.

ii *Christians and Christian leaders might be united* and courageous in the face of widespread and localized persecution. Attacks number over 1,000 a year. They are sporadic and concentrated in BJP-ruled states.

iii *The "re-conversion" programme of Hindu extremists might not succeed* and that threatened Christians may stand firm in Christ whatever the cost.

iv *Christians may show the love* and forgiveness of Christ to their persecutors.

5 **The Church in India** is highly diverse, has a long legacy and is, at the same time, vital and growing, and nominal and declining. Much of Indian Christianity is the result of people movements over the past 300 years, punctuated by local revivals. In many denominations, it remains in Western forms. Liberal theology, universalism and growing nominalism in the Church have dried up the spirit of outreach to the millions of non-Christians. Many congregations have no first-generation believers from a non-Christian background. Disputes over personalities, power and property have led to many divisions, court cases, widespread disillusionment and continuous loss of young people to materialism. At the same time, steady streams of Christians transfer from these groups to newer, more dynamic Independent churches. Pray that present pressures and the work of the Holy Spirit might bring new life to traditional forms of Christianity.

a) ***The Orthodox Churches*** are the oldest expressions of Christianity in India, tracing their heritage back to the tradition of the Apostle Thomas, who reputedly ministered and was martyred here in the 1st Century. Orthodox Christians number in their millions, and many denominations of other confessions are also heavily influenced by the Thomist tradition. These groups are rooted strongly in Kerala and southwest India.

b) ***Catholics*** represent the largest single body of Christians in India with nearly 20 million affiliates. They are known for their charitable work – most notably Mother Teresa's legacy among the poorest of the poor and the more than 5,000 Catholic-run health-care facilities, comprising more than 20% of India's total.

c) ***The need for change in the Church*** is urgent and has never been greater. Pray for:

i *Unity.* The National United Christian Forum brings together the Catholic Bishops' Forum, the National Council of Churches and the Evangelical Fellowship. The All India Christian Council serves Christians of all denominations, with over 5,000 agencies, NGOs, denominations and

I

institutions working for human rights, social justice, religious freedom and protection of minorities. A spirit of divisiveness characterized the past; now, unity is greater than ever before, in part due to hostility from external forces. Pray for unity to mature and to endure. Greater cooperation and accountability are needed between local churches and sending agencies.

ii *Indigenization of Church culture, structure and expression* – for too long, churches have relied on foreign cultural forms.

iii *Greater reliance on an Indian model of cell/house churches* rather than on Western-style modes and places of worship.

iv *Effective discipling* – through coordinated, collaborative efforts – of the many being impacted by any one of the multiple methods of evangelism. Many new believers come to faith through large rallies, healings or miracles, but opportunities are few for Christian instruction to strengthen and sustain them in their faith.

v *More relevance in impacting the mainstream of national life.* The Church is seen as linked to the marginalized, deprived sections of society. Business, politics, arts, culture and the middle and upper classes – all shapers of Indian society – have not yet been impacted by the gospel.

6 **Bible-believing churches and groups are growing** to a degree that far exceeds what is reflected in official figures, but it is hard to reliably enumerate the scale of growth. Current reality on the ground, however, is but a fraction of the goals expressed by the Church and by mobilization movements such as Vision 2020. Some of the many factors related to this growth are:

a) *A multiplicity of dynamic, newer Pentecostal and charismatic fellowships.* These have sprung up and spread to every area of India.

b) *The number of evangelical denominations has increased* and congregations multiplied. Several key networks link many denominations – Evangelical Fellowship of India (links over 224 denominations and agencies), Pentecostal Fellowship of India (links all major Pentecostal denominations) and Baptist Evangelical Alliance, to name a few. These are used of God to mature, stabilize and mobilize believers through prayer, conventions, pastors' retreats, and coordination of training, literature production, missions and outreach.

c) *The charismatic movement* in the Catholic Church began in 1972 and has spread to nearly every Catholic congregation. It has had a profound impact, brought many to new life and stimulated outreach; an estimated 10% of Catholics in India are charismatic in their faith.

d) *The Yesu Darbar,* a gathering of Jesus followers in North India numbering in the tens of thousands, models biblical worship and fellowship patterns in an Indian context. There are literally millions of followers of Jesus (*Yesu Bhaktas*), secret believers and unbaptized Christians outside of established denominational structures. Pray for effective discipling of this growing group.

e) *Many networks interceding for the evangelization* of the country have flourished, involving millions of Christians. Literally hundreds of new and often massive prayer movements and groups, many driven by women and even children, are behind much Kingdom growth in India.

f) *Millions have become more open to the message of Christ* through literature, widely broadcast radio and TV programmes and extensively used Christian videos, films and cassettes. Indian-produced Christian media is vital to effectively reach Indians with the gospel.

7 **Training Christian workers is an important need** that is immediately urgent and essential in the long term. The life and health of the Church depend on the proper development of pastors, teachers, evangelists and missionaries. In churches, poor discipling and lack of teaching and modelling of biblical life and leadership are problems. India's strong philosophical tradition and religious, cultural and ethnic diversity make adequate training crucial, but most workers are sent out with very little specific preparation for their ministry context. There are over 100,000 full-time workers in India; about half are pastoring local churches. There is, on average, one trained pastor for every six congregations. Pray for:

a) *Degree-level seminaries,* which now number over 100; praise God for the multiplication of these! There are three accrediting agencies – Senate of Serampore College, Asia Theological Association and Indian Institute of Missiology. Many of these seminaries are theologically evangelical. The number of seminary graduates opting for missionary service, however, is decreasing. Pray for an increasing stream of well-trained, spiritually passionate workers with a burden for effective ministry in their nation.

b) Bible schools number over 1,000 and are doubling in number every 10 years. Evangelical institutions are full. Bible schools are moving from merely teaching theology to giving practical skills for ministry, particularly for church planting.

c) Training centres for indigenous workers play a significant role. Set up largely for church planters, these number over 100 (**FMPB, IEM, OM**, ICRM, **GEMS**, Missions India, Seva Bharat, Operation Agape, others). **GFA** has set up 55 such centres, with 7,000 currently receiving training.

d) New, creative ways for multiplying leaders must be developed. The need is greater than what residential institutions can produce, and 90% of pastors lack access to adequate theological training. Also, residential institutions must move beyond a Western maintenance model that has minimal impact on the non-Christian majority. Thankfully, there is a growing stream of non-formal education that is looking at how to address this challenge.

e) Training Christians – those outside of the traditional roles of pastor, evangelist and missionary – to be effective witnesses and ministers is essential. The Indian Church must learn to have a greater impact in the workplace, especially in the newer areas of IT, business and such.

f) The house/cell church movement is rapidly spreading in many parts of the country, with estimates of up to 100,000 such gatherings. These movements are proving culturally appropriate, affordable, biblically authentic and very effective.

g) The South Asia Bible Commentary will be a boon to potentially hundreds of thousands of pastors, lay leaders and students.

8 **The growth of Indian cross-cultural outreach agencies** – in number, size and maturity – is remarkable and has occurred despite increasingly intense opposition in many cases. In 1973, there were 420 missionaries. In 2009, India Missions Association (**IMA**) alone represented over 235 organizations and 40,000 missionaries. Encouraging progress has also been made in upgrading training, improving the quality of ministry, planning strategically, setting goals, initializing research and partnering with others. Pray for:

a) Indian mission-agency networking structures. These play a key role in furthering cooperation, setting goals and facilitating fellowship. **IMA** is the main one, along with National Prayer and Church Transformation Initiative, UP Network, BORN, CONS and others.

b) An increase in effective research. Numerous agencies research India's harvest fields and harvest force. The OMID database, **IMA** and several associated members gathered data on each state, city, language, people group and even Pincode zone of India. Never before has there been such clarity about the unfinished task! Pray for ongoing research initiatives, which need to move from quantitative data to missiological strategy. Pray also for the effectiveness of the research in helping churches to visualize and fulfil the Great Commission.

c) The Asian Theological Association–India and the Indian Institute of Missiology, which accredit, facilitate and network mission-training schools. There are over 150 such schools; almost all started since 1980. **IET** started 27 of these.

d) The mission agencies themselves, for their leadership to be strategic, for provision of pastoral care and support to their workers, for fruitfulness in ministry and for spiritual unity. Newer, emerging missions are approaching the size and impact of older, established agencies.

e) Indian missionaries serving in other lands number over 500. Living costs for them are much higher and support is difficult to raise, given the immense need within India itself. Pray for provision of all of their needs. Reverse mission is becoming more common – such as Mizo Christians sending missionaries to the Welsh, who evangelized them in the 19th Century.

f) OM graduates. OM's impact through implanting a missions vision is vast. The Association of OM Graduates links together 40,000 full-time Christian workers. Many of these lead some of the most effective agencies in India today.

g) A widening of ministry to other needy sections of the population. Hitherto, half the cross-cultural missionaries worked among tribal groups, and many of the rest among the downtrodden, marginalized or needy sections of the population. Few today work among the urban middle class and the higher castes. This needs to change, but most workers feel inadequately prepared for such challenges.

h) *Better and closer relationships between local churches and mission agencies.* Many mission agencies are supported by multi-congregational, informal prayer networks. Because greater accountability is needed between field workers and sending churches, mobilizing churches for more involvement is an increasing need. Publications by **IMA** and Mission Educational Books help churches gain mission awareness.

i) *Expatriates serving in India* now number only 1,000. Visas are increasingly difficult to arrange; student, business and medical visas are the best way forward, when done with authentic engagement in those disciplines. Some specialized roles could be filled by expatriates, for example in support of existing Indian ministries pioneering in sections of the population not easily reached by indigenous workers. International advocates are needed to adopt people groups and areas and to raise prayer support.

9 **Ministry among the Dalits** is one of the defining issues for the 21st Century Church, despite being a very complex one. The centuries-long oppression of these peoples is being made right, and Christians are at the forefront of such efforts. While the opportunity remains to reach up to 300 million with the gospel through compassionate ministry, Dalit issues extend beyond evangelism into human rights, development, education, economic empowerment and community transformation. Specific points for prayer:

a) *The Church,* which is itself comprised mostly of people from Scheduled Castes and Scheduled Tribes, has a rare opportunity to demonstrate the love of Christ unhindered by caste, race, language and economic status. Initial enthusiasm for this cause could easily wane if it is treated as opportunistic capitalization rather than as biblical compassion and justice. For the gospel to be seen as valid, Dalits must be treated as equals in the Church.

b) *Dalits are a highly diverse grouping* of many races, languages and all major religions, and they have sociological and economic hierarchies even among themselves. Any ministry to Dalits must take into account the unique status and context of each group.

c) *The Dalit Freedom Network,* the primary advocate for this challenge among Christians, addresses issues related to Dalit rights and their freedom.

10 **India has more unreached individuals** than any other nation. Christians in India are very unequally spread – the south and northeast have a much higher proportion of Christians than the more populated north and west. Thirteen states in North India are less than 1% Christian. Pray that the Church worldwide might rise to this task. Pray for:

a) *The North India Ganges plains,* with their teeming millions, in the Hindi-speaking heartland. The states through which the Ganges flows (Himachal Pradesh, Uttarakhand, Uttar Pradesh, Bihar and West Bengal) combine to account for 382 million people. None of these states is more than 1% Christian, according to census data. There is, however, more church growth than ever in the north, from megachurches of 7,000 to networks of tens of thousands of house churches. A vision exists for 1 million churches planted in the north in the next 10 years.

b) *The great cities,* with rapid growth and a mix of great wealth and abject poverty. Chennai, Mumbai and even Hyderabad with significant Christian populations exist in contrast to Kolkata, Delhi, Varanasi, Lucknow and others where Christian witness is very small. Increasing urbanization sees millions drawn from rural areas into urban areas annually, often with little by way of resources and connections. As a result, India's slum-dwelling population now exceeds 70 million.

11 **The world's least-evangelized peoples are concentrated in India.** Of 159 people groups of over 1 million people, 133 are unreached. Hundreds more groups of fewer than 1 million are unreached. Also, 953 ethnic groups have populations greater than 10,000; of these, 205 have no church and little to no outreach from Christians. They can be found in every state, although they tend to be more concentrated in the north. A few of the most significant peoples for prayer:

a) *The Brahmin* are the priestly caste, which is the highest caste in the Hindu world. They number over 50 million, but perhaps only 18,000 follow Jesus. They are the most influential group in India, but few focused efforts to reach them have been made.

b) *Forward Castes* – the Rajput (43.0m), Mahratta (29.0m), Hindu Jat (16.0m), Mahishya (10.6m), Kayastha (8.1m), Nair (7.5m), Agarwal/Bania (5.0m), Arora (3.9m), Bhumihar (3.0m), Vellalan (2.5m), Hindu Khatri (2.1m) and others. Several others are considered

Forward Castes in some states but Backward in others. Forward Castes have very negative views of Christians – that they are Dalits, simple and cowardly, and they reject Hindu culture for Western colonial ideas. There remains little effective ministry among the Forward Castes. These people groups will need a different and a sensitive, loving approach and adequate preparation of workers if the barriers to faith in Christ are to be breached.

c) *Backward Caste peoples* represent anywhere from 27% to 52% of India's population, depending on definition and source. The most numerous include the Yadava (59.0m), Kurmi (17.9m), Teli (17.9m), Kunbi (16.6m), Kapu (15.9m), Nai (11.5m), Pashtun (11.3m), Mappila (9.6m), Lingayat (9.5m), Kairi (7.7m), Sonar (7.4m), Gujar (6.6m), Vakkaliga (6.3m) and literally thousands more. Of the groups listed above, all are less than 0.1% Christian, most less than 0.01% Christian.

d) *Scheduled Castes/Dalits* have responded more to the gospel, some in large numbers. But the Dhobi (12.6m), Mahar (9.1m), Pasi (7.5m), Namasudra (5.1m), Rajbansi (5.0m), Bagdi (3.6m) and Pod (3.2m) are all less than 0.1% Christian.

e) *Numerous Scheduled Tribes* are still unevangelized or underevangelized. After years of ministry, the Bhil (14.5m) and Gond (14.1m) have numerous churches among them, yet both are only around 1% Christian. The Koli (12.1m) are only 0.3% Christian.

f) *There are 485 people groups* with populations of over 10,000 that are unreached and unengaged, almost three quarters of the world's 639 people groups that come under this category.

12 Specific communities requiring specialized ministry include:

a) *The increasingly affluent 350 million of the middle classes* have little meaningful contact with Christianity. They are key sectors of society in the 21st Century.

b) *Students* number over 11.5 million in 320 universities and 23,000 colleges. The large majority of these will graduate but be considered unemployable due to the competitiveness of industry and inadequate quality of education. Pray for the ministries of **YFC**, ICCC, Inter Collegiate Prayer Fellowship (ICPF) and Union of Evangelical Students of India (UESI/**IFES**). UESI alone has 15,000 student members and 7,000 graduates. Pray for their clear, vibrant witness to the thousands of non-Christian students. Pray for their growth and integration into local churches.

c) *Young people* – the statistics present a staggering need for this population of 400 million under 15 years old. Only 15% reach high school, and functional literacy is around 30%. Around 40% live below the poverty line. Many live in a moral and spiritual vacuum. Most churches lack the resources and know-how to minister to them. **YFC**, **OM**, Blessing Youth Ministry, **CEF**, SU, **CCCI** and others reach out to some.

d) *Leprosy sufferers,* of which there are 150,000 new cases every year. Leprosy originated in India. It still possesses the majority of the world's cases, and there are over 1,000 leper colonies in India. Christian agencies work with them, in particular TLM (18 leprosy hospitals and around 100 projects).

e) *The blind.* As many as 15 million people in India are blind (and another 50 million visually impaired) – this is nearly 40% of the world's total. Of these cases, 70% would be preventable were there sufficient doctors and optometrists. Braille is an under-utilized tool. Agencies with ministry to blind people are Mission to the Blind, India Fellowship for Visually Handicapped and Torch Trust for the Blind. Compass Braille is an agency specializing in producing Braille Scriptures in Indian languages by means of computer. Christian audio resources such as Megavoice, Proclaimer and others are vital for reaching and discipling India's blind people.

13 Minority religious communities. India has the world's largest populations of Sikhs, Zoroastrians, Jains and Baha'is. Pray for these groups:

a) *Muslims* officially number 160 million (14.2% of India's population), making India the third-largest Muslim country in the world. Most likely, they number significantly higher than 14.2%. Muslims ruled much of India for over 600 years but are now a pressured minority. Seventy million speak Urdu/Dekkani, and 90 million speak other languages. Muslims in India are concentrated in Uttar Pradesh, West Bengal and Bihar, and are among the least-evangelized peoples in the world, despite being some of the most populous and accessible.

Among Indian and global Christians, interest and concern are rising for India's Muslims, and growing numbers of agencies are committing to ministry among them.

b) ***The Sikh community*** worldwide numbers around 23 million. But there is little understanding of Sikhism among Christians to enable dialogue and bring them to knowledge of Christ. Today, a significant and growing number of Sikhs follow Jesus, both secretly and openly, in India and in Canada.

c) ***Buddhist Tibetans*** number about 100,000, the large majority of whom are refugees from Tibet. Only a few dozen believers are known. Dharamsala in Himachal Pradesh is the present headquarters of the Dalai Lama. Pray for him and his followers.

d) ***The 6 million Jains and 70,000 Parsees,*** with their wealth, isolation and unique religions, are extremely hard to reach, yet they are very influential in society, industry and business.

14 **Christian media and help ministries** play key roles in reaching hundreds of millions who have negligible interaction with Christians or churches. For prayer:

a) ***The Bible Society*** has had a long and remarkable ministry in India – its 200-year anniversary is in 2011. It has played a key role in distributing over 30 million portions of Scripture or Bibles annually. Other organizations also supply and distribute Scriptures, such as World Home Bible League, Bibles for the World, Biblica and Bharatiya Bible League. India Bible League does excellent work in effective Bible distribution and simple discipleship via their Project Philip.

b) ***Bible translation*** is a major challenge.

 i India has 456 languages; 429 of those are spoken by more than 1,000 people. At present, the full Bible is available in only 70 languages and the NT in 120. Translation is underway in another 136 languages. A new effort as great as that of William Carey's 200 years ago must occur. At the current rate of project completion, it will take until the end of this century to see all of India's languages covered. But a partnership of agencies is establishing a translation-training centre that will drastically increase the projected rate of completion.

 ii Indian missions have identified 154 languages that still need Bible translation. Of these, seven have more than 1 million speakers and 21 have more than 100,000.

 iii United Bible Society has 86 projects in hand.

 iv Various Indian agencies are involved in Scripture translation projects – Indian Bible Translators, **IEM**, **IET**, **FMPB**, NIEA, **GFA**, ORBIT, NLCI and Wycliffe India.

 v Wycliffe India provides training in linguistics for many agencies and helps to monitor progress in dozens of projects.

 vi Modern, culturally appropriate translations are needed in Urdu and many other languages.

c) ***Literature distribution.*** Writing, publishing and distributing Christian literature are major factors in evangelism, especially by groups such as **OM**, **EHC**, **GFA**, Operation Agape and SGM. **EHC** alone has produced 500 million pieces of Christian literature for India.

d) ***Christian publishing and bookstores.*** Encouragingly, books written by indigenous authors and published locally are increasing. But publishers must still contend with a relative lack of titles by Indians for Indians and with prohibitive costs in making books available for the poor. **OM** Books/Biblica is now the largest literature-distribution agency in Asia, with more than 30 branches within India. Pray for Gospel Literature Service in Mumbai (publishing books, tracts and such) and Evangelical Literature Service (**CLC**) with headquarters in Chennai (17 stores and 350 book titles in print). **GFA** Bible Society is one of the largest producers of literature in India, annually distributing 50 million pieces. Christian Booksellers Association was formed in 2000.

e) ***Bible Correspondence Courses,*** sent out from over 70 centres, have proved fruitful.

f) ***Audio resources,*** such as Talking Bibles, are strategically vital, since over half the population are functionally illiterate. **GRN**, as part of Project India, has recordings in over 400 languages and dialects and seeks to record into another 800. Faith Comes By Hearing/Hosanna, World Cassette Outreach and The Bible Society have large programmes for making audio-Scriptures available in all possible languages.

g) Christian medical work remains crucial to Christian witness, but is declining as the government increases its capacity for healthcare. Christian Medical Association and Catholic Health Association share oversight of over 700 hospitals. Emmanuel Hospitals Association has responsibility for 23 hospitals and 30 community-health programmes in North India. The high proportion of Christians in healthcare and nursing in particular is a positive testimony; pray that physical healing and spiritual new life might be found through these workers and the many Christian health care facilities they serve.

h) Christian films and videos are important:

i *Dayasagar* (also known as *Karunamaiyudu* and other names), an Indian feature-length film on Jesus, is available in 21 main languages of India; tens of millions have seen this film. Over 300 film teams from several different organizations show this film all over the country, to powerful effect. Showings number up to 2,000 a month and viewers of these up to 3 million a year.

ii *The JESUS film* is available in 110 languages. Pray that the hundreds of partners using this film will have success as they plant new churches across India.

i) Radio and TV are increasingly important media as millions more Indians tune in each year. Christian broadcasting has won an enormous following among Christians and non-Christians alike. Pray for:

i *Programme producers* – there is great need to generate quality programmes and to find talented, committed, native speakers. Some agencies involved: India Gospel Outreach, HBI, **GFA**, **WEC**-Radio Worldwide, BBI.

ii *Broadcasters.* The major agencies – **TWR**, FEBA and **FEBC** – broadcast between them 770 hours per week in over 100 languages on both shortwave and medium wave frequencies, and increasingly on national and local radio.

iii *The massive growth in satellite and cable TV use* means that TV is replacing radio. Foreign-based TV ministries are beamed into the country, and others have operations in India (such as CBN). Praise God also for the several Indian indigenous 24-hour Christian TV channels initiated in the last 5-10 years. Most of them are still regional. Pray that more Christian ministries may adapt and make use of the possibilities of this medium.

iv *Internet evangelism* is poised to become possibly the most significant media ministry in the country as India continues to accelerate in its technological revolution and maintain its place as one of the world's leaders in IT. The number of active Internet users was 1.4 million in 1999, 45 million in 2009. Engaging and effective Christian content and sites for both evangelism and discipleship, in many languages, are needed now and even more for the future.

15 The Indian diaspora now numbers nearly 30 million and is spread across 130 countries. Large numbers have emigrated to the Americas: USA (2.2m, where they have built over 500 Hindu temples), Canada (1.0m), Trinidad (500,000), Suriname (150,000); others to Europe: UK (1.5m), France (290,000); many to Africa: South Africa (920,000), Mauritius (870,000); to the Pacific: Fiji (310,000), Australia (225,000); to Asia: Nepal (5.5m), Malaysia (2.1m), Myanmar (2.5m), Sri Lanka (1.5m), Singapore (400,000); and to the Middle East: Saudi Arabia (1.4m), UAE (1.4m), Kuwait (560,000), Oman (385,000). They are influential in their adopted lands, especially in business, technology and culture. They are likewise a great influence on their relations and communities back in India. Many are open to the gospel – especially first-generation immigrants – and in some countries, there has been significant outreach and response (South Africa, USA, Canada, Mauritius, Middle East). Outreach by Indian missions to diaspora communities is overdue, as is the envisioning of diaspora Christians to reach out to India.

I

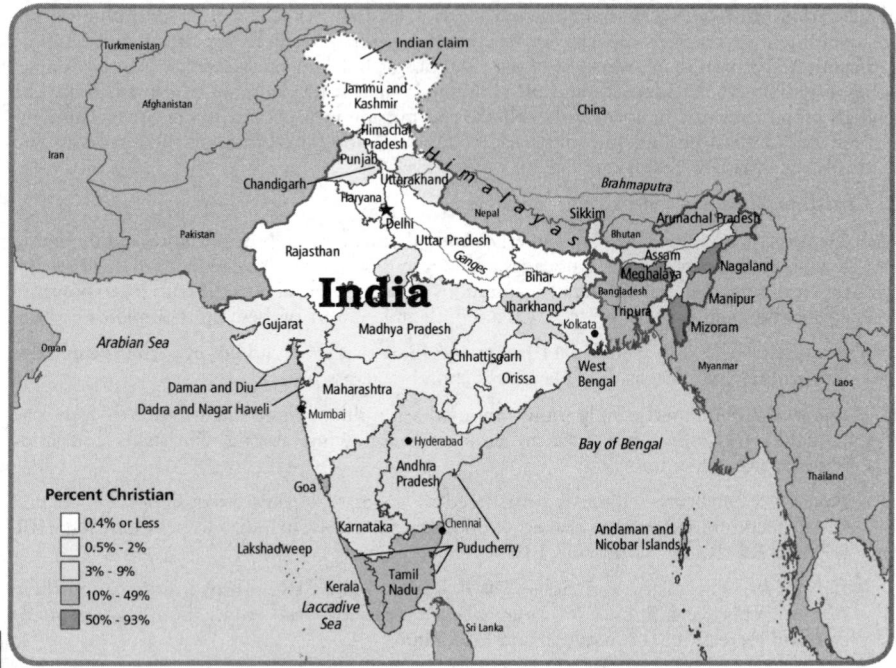

Percent Christian

- ☐ 0.4% or Less
- ☐ 0.5% - 2%
- ☐ 3% - 9%
- ☐ 10% - 49%
- ☐ 50% - 93%

States of India

Most of these states are far larger than the majority of nations covered in this book, yet limitations of space allow only a brief description of each here. Most specifics about ministries and agencies have been restricted for security reasons. Many of the Indian agencies already mentioned are active in outreaches and ministries alluded to below. Religion figures for each state are taken from the most recent census data; the spiritual reality on the ground in most states would suggest significantly more Christians than census figures indicate. For this reason we have also included the 2010 Christian percentages (in parentheses) from the WCD. Only the 10 largest people groups per state are listed, with the people cluster to which they belong in parentheses.

Andhra Pradesh

Geography 🌐

Area 277,000 sq km. India's fifth-largest state, in the southeast.
Population 87,202,366; 325 people/sq km.
Capital Hyderabad 4.0m. **Other major cities** Visakhapatanam 1.6m; Vijayawada 1.2m.

Peoples 👪

People groups 556. Ten largest: Kapu (Telugu, 16.4% of state pop); Yadava (Hindi, 8.9%); Madiga (Telugu, 7.9%); Shaikh (Bengali, 6.3%); Mala (Telugu, 6.2%); Dhobi (Hindi, 4.3%); Brahmin (Hindi, 4.3%); Bania (Rajasthan, 3.7%); Viswakarma (Telugu, 3.1%); Banjara Hindu (Gypsy, 2.8%).
Languages 28. Telugu 88.5%; Urdu 8.6%; Tamil 1.1%; Hindi 0.6%.

Religion ⛪

Hindu 89.0%; Muslim 9.2%; Christian 1.6% (3.0%); Other 0.2%.

① The number of Christians is a contentious issue. Official census information reflects a decline, from 4.2% in 1971 to 1.6% in 2001 – the most notable decline of all Indian states. However, church leaders (and Hindutva agitators) claim documentable numbers of Christians at

9% or even higher, the result of strong church growth from missions and evangelism. Nominalism remains an issue in many churches.

② **The conversion (and re-conversion) of Dalits on a large scale** – significant efforts exist to win them to Christ as well as to re-convert them to Hinduism.

③ **Hyderabad is a key city for Christian ministry.** Nearly 200 Christian organizations have bases in this very modern, fast-growing and well-connected hub city. It is a centre for mission administration, research and strategy. Pray that these agencies will prosper and grow and have great spiritual impact on the state and the entire nation.

④ **Hyderabad is also the key centre for Islam in South India.** Nearly 40% of the city is Muslim; it is the hub of the 14 million South Indian Deccani Muslims. Islam in the state grew from 8.2% in 1971 to 9.2% in 2001. Very little is done to reach out to them, despite the presence of many Christians.

⑤ **Gospel outreach continues** with numerous people coming to Christ. There are churches in every district, and tribal groups especially are being reached. Many Indian mission agencies are active throughout the state. The challenges:

a) *The evangelization of the influential Forward Castes.*

b) *Three districts and 107 subdistricts* are less than 0.1% Christian.

c) *16 people groups* of over 100,000 people each are unreached and unengaged. These include the Telaga, Balija, Shaikh and Nai.

d) *Large-scale immigration* from all over India to the modern, fast-growing city of Hyderabad means that many people and groups can potentially be reached in one place.

e) *The Hindu-pilgrimage site Tirupathi* draws millions from around India and beyond every year, presenting an opportunity to reach out to many.

I

Arunachal Pradesh

Geography 🌐

Area 83,000 sq km. Mountainous, northeastern frontier state bordering Bhutan, China (Tibet) and Myanmar.
Population 1,273,337; 16 people/sq km.
Capital Itanagar.

Peoples 👪

People groups 303. Ten largest: Nissi (Adi, 8.8% of state pop); Adi Gallong (Adi, 6.0%); Wancho (Kuki-Chin-Naga, 4.4%); Bangni (Adi, 3.9%); Monpa (South Himalaya, 3.8%); Ahom (Assamese, 3.7%); Tagin (Adi, 3.4%); Adi Minyong (Adi, 3.0%); Tanu (South Himalaya, 3.0%); Adi (Adi, 2.9%).
Languages 32, but possibly as many as 50. One of Asia's highest concentrations of languages and dialects. Most are of the Tibeto-Burman family.

Religion 📿

Hindu 34.6%; Ethnic religions 30.7%; Buddhist 13.0%; Christian 18.7% (25.0%); Muslim 1.9%.

① **The Church has grown dramatically,** from 0.8% of the population in 1971 to 19% today. Indian missionaries from Nagaland and northeast India did much of the pioneer work. Baptists are the largest Christian group here; they, as well as others, continue to increase. There are numerous churches among the Nissi, Wancho, Adi, Nocte and Tangsa. Praise God for this, but pray for greater cooperation among them.

② **Conversion usually brings opposition.** Early Christian converts often suffered persecution in this Himalayan area. Legal safeguards are in place to preserve the local animist tribal religions, such as *Donyi-Polo*, from heavy-handed proselytism and Hinduization; Arunachal Pradesh is one of India's states with a firmly ensconced anti-conversion law. Pray that Christians wishing to win others to Jesus may do so in bold but gentle and appropriate ways.

③ **The unfinished task** – Arunachal Christians have the vision that every people in the state are reached. Some prayer targets:

a) **Buddhist peoples of the west** (Monga, Khampti) adjoining Bhutan have little opportunity to hear the gospel. There are few churches and believers; those leaving Tibetan Buddhism usually face rejection and persecution.

b) **Animist peoples** – the Tagin, Adi Minyong, Miri, Tanu and Galong.

c) **Seven regions** are less than 0.1% Christian.

Assam

Geography 🌍

Area 78,400 sq km. Noted for tropical forests (60% of state) and the Brahmaputra River. Main exports: tea, oil and forest products.
Population 31,758,087; 401 people/sq km. Large-scale immigration from Bangladesh.
Capital Dispur. **Major city** Guwahati 1.1m.

Peoples 👫👤

People groups 357. Ten largest: Shaikh (Bengali, 21.7% of state pop); Assamese Muslim (Assamese, 8.6%); Garo Bodo (Garo-Tripuri, 6.1%); Brahmin (Hindi, 5.0%); Munda (Munda-Santal, 4.5%); Bania (Rajasthan, 3.8%); Santal (Munda-Santal, 2.9%); Ahom (Assamese, 2.9%); Kaibartta (Bengali, 2.5%); Namasudra Hindu (Bengali, 2.4%).
Languages 53. Assamese, Bodo, Bengali all hold official status; many others.

Religion 🕌

Hindu 65.0%; Muslim 30.9%; Christian 3.7% (7.0%); Buddhist 0.2%; Other 0.2%.

I

1 **Assam remains the major spiritual challenge in northeast India.** After two centuries of Christian work, professing Christians are a small and marginalized minority. Pray for a reversal of this trend and for revival, vision and impact on society to characterize the many lukewarm traditional congregations. Major denominations are Baptist (4), Lutheran (2), CNI and Catholic.

2 **An evangelical witness** has been present for over 100 years, yet it is confined to a few Baptist associations, some newer Independent and charismatic groups and to Indian (mainly Mizo and Naga) mission agencies. These groups are effective in reaching some of the tribal peoples, but thus far there has been little interest in reaching Hindus or Muslims.

3 **The history of violence and conflict** is largely due to the co-existence of many different peoples and religions. Continued immigration of Bengali speakers from Bangladesh is a major source of resentment and tension as is the migration of Hindi speakers from elsewhere in India. Ethnic rebels and violent separatist groups still operate, ostensibly to create an independent Assamese homeland. Any Christian witness must be done with sensitivity to this. Inter-ethnic and interdenominational Christian unity would be a powerful witness, but it is rarely displayed.

4 **The less evangelized** for whom prayer is needed:

a) **The Assamese-speaking peoples** are mostly Hindu and include some of the least evangelized major Hindu people clusters in India. Several groups – such as Brahmin, Bania, Kaibartta, Namasudra, Mahishya and Kayastha – number over 500,000 but have no known Christian groups and little to no witness.

b) **Bengali-speaking Shaikhs** are largely Muslim and comprise about 80% of all Indian Muslims. Many have immigrated from poor, overpopulated Bangladesh, with considerable hostility generated among Assamese. Muslims are a majority in six of Assam's 23 districts. There is virtually no Christian witness to or among the 9.7 million Muslims, and only a few Bengali Christians are known.

c) **Assam tea-estate workers** number in the millions. Nearly 70% of Assam's workforce is tied to agriculture. Many are migrant Santal, Munda, Kharia, Orang or other tribal minorities from other states. They are open to the gospel, but few are there to share it.

d) **Evangelization of the tribal peoples is incomplete.** The Miri, Rajbansi, Deori and Kachari are all less than 1% Christian.

e) **One district and 25 subdistricts** are less than 0.1% Christian, and there are 11 unreached, unengaged people groups larger than 100,000.

Bihar

Geography 🌐

Area 94,163 sq km. Ganges alluvial plain.
Population 99,556,918; 805 people/sq km.
Largely agricultural and 90% rural.
Capital Patna 2.3m.

Peoples 👪

People groups 377. Ten largest: Yadava (Hindi, 14.1% of state pop); Shaikh (Bengali, 10.3%); Brahmin (Hindi, 7.0%); Koiri (Bengali, 5.1%); Chamar (Hindi, 4.7%); Dosadh Hindu (Hindi, 4.6%); Rajput (Hindi, 4.6%); Kurmi (Hindi, 3.7%); Teli (Hindi, 2.7%); Musahar Hindu (Hindi, 2.5%).
Languages 21, but with many dialects. Bihari dialects (Bhojpuri, Maithili, Magahi), Hindi, Urdu, tribal languages, Bengali.

Religion ⛪

Hindu 83.2%; Muslim 16.5%; Christian 0.1% (0.3%). Both Buddhism and Jainism began in Bihar, but few adherents remain today.

1 **India's poorest state** and second highest for population density, Bihar is a byword for deprivation and misery. It ranks highest on every index related to corruption for India's states. The recent separation of timber- and mineral-rich Jharkhand Province exacerbates the already significant economic challenges. The gripping poverty is exceeded only by the lack of development and progress and by the contrast to Bihar's more glorious past. Bihar is where Buddhism and Jainism began, the seat of the great Mauryan and Gupta Empires was located and was at the forefront of India's modern struggle for independence. Its recent political history is marked by incompetence, corruption, division and communal tensions. Pray that the liberating, saving, restoring gospel of Christ might find the suffering millions of Bihar.

2 **Long known as "the graveyard of missions"**, Bihar presents many obstacles to evangelization. Beside deep poverty sits widespread illiteracy, lack of resources in local languages (Bihari languages were for decades wrongly regarded as mere dialects of Hindi), strong spiritual opposition and persecution of religious minorities by the Hindu majority. The inhospitable environment, where malaria and disease are rife, spells very real danger to the lives of Christian workers. There is little collaboration among Christians and almost no Christian voice in public life. Pray that the Lord might demonstrate his powerful passion and love for Biharis through an unprecedented surge of ministry to these needy peoples.

3 **The first fruits of spiritual harvest are now ripe.** The number of those coming to Christ is increasing, more than doubling the census figures for Christians (but still a mere drop in the ocean of humanity in Bihar). Those sharing the gospel perceive a greater spiritual openness. Pray for continued acceleration of this praiseworthy trend and for implementation of effective means of discipleship for the tens of thousands of new Christians. Previously, they came from Scheduled Castes and Scheduled Tribes. This change has resulted in no small part from:

a) *The massive investment of personnel by Indian missions.* There are over 4,000 Indian missionaries in Bihar. **GEMS** (Gospel Echoing Missionary Society) has over 2,000 missionaries, and BORN (Bihar Outreach Network) has 300. **FMPB**, *Vishwa Vani*, **GFA**, Emmanuel Christian Fellowship Centre, **OM**, India Missions, NIEA, **AoG**, **YWAM**, Operation Agape and others supplement this number.

b) *Excellent research and analysis* that highlight people groups, castes, languages, religions and needs. Vision 2020 is setting ambitious goals for ministry and church planting in Bihar.

c) *A focus on prayer,* church planting and holistic outreach (including medical facilities), schools, children's homes, community healthcare projects and vocational training.

4 **Bihar is one of the least-evangelized mega-populations in the world.** There are 24 districts (accounting for 57 million people) that are less than 0.03% Christian.

a) *The 16.5 million Forward Caste Hindus* have increasing exposure to the gospel, but little response. Christianity is associated with untouchables, tribals and foreigners. Only a few thousand call themselves Christian.

b) *The 16.5 million Muslims* are unreached and gradually increasing as a percentage of the population. They are among the poorest and the least-reached people in the world. Some are reaching out to them, but only a very small number have become followers of Christ. As a community, they are insecure and frequently subject to Hindu mob violence.

I

c) **The 15.5 million Dalits** are increasingly being reached and are responding to the gospel, but still only a small percentage (>2%) are Christian. People movements earlier in the 20th Century fizzled out. Pray that these abused, despised, illiterate peoples in grinding poverty might find liberty in Christ.

d) *Outreach challenges:*

  i *Bihar is 90% rural,* one of the world's highest rates. Outreach and church planting must focus on towns and villages, with sensitivity to the close-knit community dynamics therein.

  ii *Bihar is a young population,* with as high as 60% of the population under 25 years old.

  iii *Unreached peoples.* There are 22 groups of over 100,000 that are unreached and as yet unengaged. Among the largest unevangelized peoples in Bihar are the Yadava (11.7m), Shaikh (8.5m), Brahmin (5.8m), Koiri (4.2m), Chamar (3.9m), Dosadh (3.9m) and Rajput (3.8m).

Chhattisgarh

Geography

Area 135,200 sq km. Statehood in 2000 when separated from Madhya Pradesh.
Population 25,091,107; 182 people/sq km.
Capital Raipur 942,555. **Other major city** Durg-Bhilai Nagar 1.1m.

Peoples

People groups 450. Ten largest: Gond (Gond, 18.5% of state pop); Teli (Hindi, 9.3%); Chamar (Hindi, 8.6%); Yadava (Hindi, 8.0%); Kawar (Hindi, 3.9%); Oraon Kurux (Oraon, 3.2%); Panika (Hindi, 3.2%); Halba (Marathi-Konkani, 3.2%); Bhoi Hindu (Hindi, 3.1%); Kurmi (Hindi, 3.1%).
Languages 98 languages and dialects. Most peoples speak various forms and dialects of Chhattisgarhi, a branch of Eastern Hindi.

Religion

Hindu 94.7%; Muslim 2.0%; Christian 1.9% (2.5%); Other 1.5%.

1 **Chhattisgarh is a young state** with a high concentration of resources – and conflict. Pray for God's purposes to be fulfilled in the following areas:

a) *Development.* Chhattisgarh is high in potential but trailing in development. It has excellent economic prospects due to its mineral deposits, extensive forests and fertile river plains for cultivating rice. But it is undereducated (20% literacy), highly rural (80%) and massively underdeveloped with regard to infrastructure and industry. Pray for the wise, responsible and equitable development of this young state for the benefit of all.

b) *Politics.* This is a volatile area. Naxalites (Maoist rebels) are highly active in the forests and jungles, and the extreme Hinduist BJP is very strong in this state that boasts one of the highest Hindu-population ratios in India. BJP legislates and violently agitates against conversion activity.

2 **The Christian Church has always been small here,** never more than 2% officially, but growth is starting to occur. It is difficult going, however, fraught with much opposition – politically, culturally and spiritually. Violent reaction to Christian outreach is common, and persecution of Christians is also intense in Chhattisgarh's neighbouring states. Low literacy rates and poverty make evangelistic films, personal evangelism and holistic ministry most effective. House churches are the most appropriate means of fellowship; growth of these is accelerating.

3 **Chhattisgarh is known as the "Home of the Tribals",** with Dalits making up a large proportion of the population as well. Tribal peoples are generally poor, undereducated, highly superstitious and religious, and deeply engaged in the world of spirits, witch doctors and sorcery. BJP's neglect of tribals and Dalits is matched only by their reaction when Christians attempt to minister to them. Pray that the liberating light of the gospel might shine into every one of the many tribal groups here. The Gond tribe is the state's largest people; over 30 agencies now seek to reach out to them with the gospel.

Delhi

Geography 🌐

Area 1,483 sq km. The National Capital Territory.

Population 22,157,000; 11,059 people/sq km. India's capital city and centre of power, wealth and industry. A trendsetting city with significant communities from nearly every ethnic and caste group in India.

Peoples 👪

People groups 589. Ten largest: Jat Hindu (Jat, 10.9% of state pop); Shaikh (Bengali, 8.9%); Brahmin (Hindi, 7.2%); Chamar (Hindi, 7.1%); Rajput (Hindi, 6.5%); Arora Hindu (Hindi, 6.3%); Khatri Hindu (Hindi, 3.9%); Bhangi Hindu (Hindi, 3.4%); Bania (Rajasthan, 3.4%); Gujar (Rajasthan, 2.7%).

Religion ✍

Hindu 82.0%; Muslim 11.7%; Sikh 4.0%; Jain 1.1%; Christian 0.9% (1.8%).

1 **Delhi's role as capital** and centre of power and finance makes it a huge influence over the entire nation. Many nationwide Christian organizations make their headquarters here. Major Christian growth in Delhi, or even revival of the Church already there, would in turn affect the rest of India. Pray for the government based in Delhi; the world's largest democracy faces many obstacles from within and without. Pray that leaders may have wisdom, even-handedness, humility, uprightness and openness to God.

2 **Delhi's massive population growth** – spurred by immigration and rapid urbanization – has fuelled a serious crisis. The large majority of new arrivals end up living in illegal squatter colonies that grow into slums, most lacking water, electricity, sewage and legal status. Slums are often polluted and crime-ridden, and politicians usually exploit squatters' desperation as a means to garner votes by promising development or to legalize illegal settlements. Another 10 million are expected to swell the population by 2021. Urban planning, both long- and short-term, is crippled by inefficiency, corruption and constant change; the threat of major disruption and civil disorder over the severe lack of housing is very real. Pray that in this turmoil many might seek after the Lord Jesus Christ. Pray also that Christians might be moved to share and demonstrate the gospel in these slums; there are now over 3,000 of them in Delhi alone.

3 **Christians officially number over 130,000,** but the informal number is as high as 400,000. There are over 3,000 churches, trebling the number in 1999. Many of these Christians are migrants; most do not regularly attend church. Pray for revival, new life and effective outreach by those who claim to be followers of Christ. Vision 2020 hopes to establish another 1,500 congregations for 1.5 million new Christians by 2020.

4 **Specific outreach challenges for prayer:**

a) ***The millions of slum–dwellers*** need far more input from holistic ministry and discipling programmes. They are responsive to practical demonstrations of Christ's love. Mode of Deliverance Mission and **GFA** have successful ministries among them.

b) ***Ethnic communities*** among whom churches are being planted – Muslim and Hindu Bengali (2.4m), Nepali, others. Churches are growing among the Balmiki, Sindhi, Punjabi, Burmese and middle–class Hindi, and a significant breakthrough has occurred among Ansari Muslims. **IET** has planted dozens of churches in 10 people groups.

I

Goa

Geography

Area 3,700 sq km. Portuguese colony 1510–1961. Full statehood in 1987.
Population 1,727,494; 432 people/sq km.

Peoples

People groups 290. Ten largest: Goan Catholic (Marathi-Konkani, 24.8% of state pop); Kunbi (Gujarati, 13.1%); Mahratta (Marathi-Konkani, 10.8%); Brahmin (Hindi, 6.6%); Shaikh (Bengali, 4.8%); Halwakki Wakkal (Kannada, 3.1%); Bania (Rajasthan, 2.1%); Bhansala (Marathi-Konkani, 2.0%); Sonar (Hindi, 1.7%); Giddikki (Marathi-Konkani, 1.6%).

Religion

Hindu 65.8%; Christian 26.7% (41.5%), almost entirely Catholic; Muslim 6.8%; Other 0.2%.

1 **Goa is a beautiful, bio-diverse area** that attracts many tourists from India and the world each year. But with this come structures of sin, such as drug trafficking and child prostitution. Pray for a government that will act decisively to end these evils; pray for those caught up in them to be delivered into new life.

2 **Traditional Catholicism** is the legacy of Portuguese rule. Hindu beliefs and customs are interwoven with Christianity. New life in Christ and a clear understanding of biblical Christianity are great needs; pray for both. There is a significant Catholic charismatic presence, but Protestants are only around 1,300 in number and churches are very few.

3 **Workers able to communicate in Konkani** (the language of most Christians and many others) are a great need. Labourers to reach nominal Catholics, Hindus or Muslims are few but growing (**GFA**, Mustard Seed Ministries). Praise God for the recent completion of a new Konkani Bible – after 18 years of translation work. Other literature is needed to supplement this, for both evangelism and for discipling nominal Christians.

Gujarat

Geography

Area 196,000 sq km. Coastal state adjoining Pakistan. Desert in NW, fertile in SW; wealth through oil, industry and agriculture.
Population 59,855,330; 305 people/sq km.
Capital Gandhinagar 235,000. **Other major cities** Ahmedabad 5.7m; Surat 4.2m; Vadodara 1.9m; Rajkot 1.4m.

Peoples

People groups 631. Ten largest: Koli (Gujarati, 13.4% of state pop); Kunbi (Gujarati, 13.3%); Mahratta Kunbi (Gujarati, 7.3%); Bhil (Bhil, 6.6%); Rajput (Hindi, 4.3%); Bania (Rajasthan, 4.0%); Brahmin (Hindi, 3.6%); Mahyavanshi (Gujarati, 3.1%); Shaikh (Bengali, 2.9%); Dhangar (Gujarati, 2.5%).
Languages 17. Gujarati 90.0%; several other languages. Hindi often used as a second language.

Religion

Hindu 89.1%; Muslim 9.1%; Jain 1.0%; Christian 0.6% (1.2%).

1 **Gujarat remains a focal point for religious tensions and persecution.** Hindu extremist groups, with the support of the local BJP government, the police and the administration, have pursued a long-term strategy of intimidation, slander and harassment of Muslims and Christians in Dalit and tribal groups. An anti-conversion law was passed in 2003 that makes evangelism and church planting very difficult to do legally, but no such constraints are placed on aggressive Hinduization of tribal Christian groups such as the Dang. Pray for a government that will promote intercommunal harmony and true freedom of religion. Gujarat was Gandhi's birthplace – may the peace and tolerance he promoted become reality here.

2 **The Christian Church** is predominantly Catholic, Church of North India and Methodist. Many other smaller evangelical denominations are also present, including recently planted indigenous churches. The oppressive religious context has prevented outreach, sapped spiritual vitality, fomented division and, in some sections, seen the Church compromise with Hinduism.

Yet persecution has also often triggered new life and revival. Pray for the Holy Spirit to do a powerful new work in the churches of Gujarat.

3 **There is significant church growth in five districts.** The impact of the Methodist Church, the Salvation Army and new Indian missionary efforts among tribals contrasts the earlier decline in the state, with rapid church growth in the southeastern Dangs district. Many Bhil, Kukna, Gamit, Chaudhri, Garasia, Koli, Dhodia and others have come to Christ, slightly increasing the percentage of Christians in the state. Pray that this turning to God may continue unchecked by external opposition or internal failures.

4 **The unreached** – while some tribal peoples are responding to the gospel, much need remains. There are nine districts and 128 subdistricts that are less than 0.1% Christian. There are also 19 peoples, each with populations over 100,000, who are unreached and as yet unengaged by Christian ministry. Pray for labourers to:

a) *Saurashtra,* the western peninsula reaching in to the Arabian Sea, with 12 million people including over 1 million Jains; only 0.07% are Christian. This area was the worst affected by the 2001 earthquake.

b) *Muslims,* who number 5.4 million and are the largest and least-reached segment of the population. There are 76 distinct people groups among them – mostly in the west, north and in Ahmadabad and Baruch districts in the east.

c) *Unreached caste groups.* Dalit groups – Bhangi, Nadia and Pasi – are urbanized and becoming responsive, with over 3% Christian.

d) *The 20 tribal peoples* with little outreach – the larger being Bhil, Dubia, Dhodia and Rathawa.

e) *Parsees* – they are an ancient community of well-educated, wealthy people of Persian origin who follow the Zoroastrian religion. There are only a few dozen known believers in the whole world among the 4.5 million Parsees. Pray for the beginnings of ministry among them and for the translation of the Bible into their language.

f) *The Jain religion* – an ancient Indian religion with a strong emphasis on moral purity and non-violence. Gujarat has over 700,000 Jains of India's total of 5 million. Ahmadabad is a major Jain centre with over 100 temples. Jains are often wealthy and control much trade and industry in the state. Little has ever been done to evangelize them.

5 **Large Gujarati communities** have grown up in east and central Africa and in Britain. Most have become wealthy traders but, although surrounded by Christians, there has been little success in evangelism.

Haryana

Geography 🌐

Area 44,200 sq km. Between Delhi and Punjab in India's northwest.
Population 25,224,807; 566 people/sq km.
Capital Chandigarh 1.0m (shared with Punjab and is a Union Territory). **Other major city** Faridabad 1.5m.

Peoples 👪

People groups 375. Ten largest: Jat Hindu (Jat, 15.9% of state pop); Chamar (Hindi, 9.9%); Arora Hindu (Hindi, 7.8%); Rajput (Hindi, 7.2%); Brahmin (Hindi, 7.1%); Chuhra (Punjabi, 3.8%); Bania (Rajasthan, 3.3%); Jat Sikh (Jat, 3.1%); Shaikh (Bengali, 3.0%); Teli (Hindi, 2.9%).
Languages Haryanvi and Hindi dominate; also Punjabi 6.0%; Urdu 2.0%.

Religion 🙏

Hindu 88.2%; Sikh 5.5%; Muslim 5.8%; Jain 0.3%; Christian 0.1% (0.3%).

1 **Haryana is one of India's least-evangelized states.** Only 32,000 identify themselves as Christian. There were only 650 churches and prayer cells, occupying less than one-half of the state's 449 Pincode areas. The Church is weak, small and routinely under threat from Hinduists. With the economic advancement Haryana enjoys, there is a large influx of peoples from other states, bringing in peoples both evangelized and unevangelized.

2 **The unreached** – 6,000 villages have no Christian witness or outreach. Also, 10 peoples of populations over 100,000 each have no church and no ministry among them. Jats number over 4 million in Haryana, but there are fewer than 20 known Christians among them. There are very few known Christians among the 1.7 million Brahmins and the 750,000 Shaikhs. This state has the second-largest Sikh population and is actually seeing a significant number come into the Kingdom; pray that this might be increased and spill over to Sikhs elsewhere.

3 **Christian ministry.** Increasing numbers of Indian agencies work in this state, including Haryana Mission, Haryana Harvest Network, **GFA**, **CCCI**, Operation Agape, **FMPB**, RSP, **OM** and Indian Inland Mission. There are now 15 Christian training institutions in Haryana – pray for the equipping and sustenance of many new workers. Pray also for the unreached Muslims and Jains. There are a few Bible portions translated into the local language, Haryanvi.

Himachal Pradesh

Geography 🌐

Area 55,700 sq km. Mountainous Himalayan state, bordering Kashmir and Tibet.
Population 6,950,298; 129 people/sq km.
Capital Shimla 430,000.

Peoples 👪

People groups 358. Ten largest: Rajput (Hindi, 29.7% of state pop); Brahmin (Hindi, 10.2%); Koli (Gujarati, 7.9%); Chamar (Hindi, 7.2%); Arora Hindu (Hindi, 4.7%); Rathia Hindu (Hindi, 4.7%); Ghirath Hindu (Gypsy, 4.1%); Lohar (Hindi, 2.8%); Julaha (Hindi, 2.5%); Gaddi (Urdu Muslim, 1.8%).
Languages 35. Hindi – most actually speak Pahari, a group of languages close to Punjabi. Also Punjabi, Mahasui, Kangri, Gojri, Mandeali and a host of other Tibeto-Burmese tongues.

Religion ⛪

Hindu 95.4%; Muslim 2.0%; Buddhist 1.3%; Sikh 1.2%; Christian 0.1% (0.2%).

I

1 **Himachal Pradesh** had long been India's least-evangelized state, although this may no longer be the case. Called the "land of the gods", Himachal Pradesh is a centre for Hindu pilgrimages. Every mountain is named after a god, and there is much devotion to idols. Pray that many may be freed from bondages and find liberty in Jesus.

2 **There has been significant growth in the Church.** From a few thousand Christians in years past, there are now reportedly 600 congregations as well as numerous house groups meeting to worship Jesus. This is a result of the committed witness of Christian workers sent by Indian agencies to preach the gospel. Pray for the ongoing ministry of Operation Agape, FMPB, **IEM**, **GFA**, North India Community Outreach (NICO) and others. There are now over 380 Christian workers and three training schools that equip and train church planters (run by Beracah Ministries, **GFA**, ECI). Pray for the multiplication of believers and churches and for the fellowship and collaboration of all groups engaged in gospel work.

3 **Persecution and anti-conversion legislation** are reactions of Hindutva groups and the government to Christian preaching. Some Christians have been forcibly converted back to Hinduism. Laws passed in 2007 make evangelism increasingly difficult. Pray for the freedom to share the gospel and for boldness for Christians to share, whatever the cost.

4 **The challenges of the unreached.** Every people group is, at best, marginally evangelized. Of the 115 people groups, only 15 have congregations of believers. Pray specifically for:

a) The Kangra Valley. The Kangri NT portion is being translated. God's Story video is available in the Kangri language. The Ghirath are the largest unreached people group in this region.

b) The Kullu valley. There are now several congregations (**IEM**). Portions of the NT are being translated into Kullu.

c) Unevangelized districts. Bilaspur, Una and Hamipur are the least evangelized.

d) Lahul-Spiti district is largely culturally Tibetan. Over 5,000 Tibetan refugees have settled in Dharamsala, the Dalai Lama's headquarters. Much international aid flows into efforts to retain

Tibetan identity, culture and language, which are now being lost in Tibet. Pray for the gospel to reach the 100,000 Tibetan refugees in India; Tibetan Buddhism is immensely resistant to spiritual breakthrough. SEANET-India is engaged in reaching Buddhists. There are a precious handful of Lahuli/Bhotia believers.

Jammu & Kashmir

Geography 🌏

Area 222,000 sq km. The disputed state has been dismembered – Pakistan seizing 83,000 sq km in 1947, and China taking 38,000 sq km of Himalayan Ladakh in 1950. India, Pakistan and China each claim territory currently controlled by others. **Population** 13,121,738; 54 people/sq km. **Capitals** Srinagar 1.2m; Jammu 450,000.

Peoples 👪

People groups 329. Ten largest: Kashmiri Muslim (Kashmiri, 55.1% of state pop); Rajput (Hindi, 8.0%); Brahmin (Hindi, 6.5%); Gujjar (Rajasthan, 5.6%); Megh Hindu (Rajasthan, 2.9%); Jat Hindu (Jat, 2.2%); Chamar (Hindi, 1.9%); Rajput Muslim (Urdu Muslim, 1.6%); Dom Hindu (Oriya, 1.5%); Jat Sikh (Jat, 1.4%). **Languages** 15. Urdu, Kashmiri, Dogri are official languages.

Religion 🙏

Muslim 67.0%; Hindu 29.6%; Sikh 2.0%; Buddhist 1.1%; Christian 0.2% (0.3%).

① **The Jammu and Kashmir state, an integral part of India, has endured tragic suffering and strife,** dating back centuries, most particularly since the partition of India in 1947 when Pakistan and India contested the possession of Kashmir. Hindu rulers of a predominantly Muslim princely state opted to join India, creating India's only Muslim-majority state. Broken down further, the Kashmir Valley region has a 97% Muslim majority, the Jammu region has a 66% Hindu majority and in Ladakh region, 46% are Buddhist. The troubles take many forms:

a) *Tensions between countries,* at times, have come to a head in outright conflict. Kashmir is a thorn in the side of relations between India and Pakistan. Pakistan has gone to war (directly or by proxy) over this divided state four times. The competing claims seem at an impasse. But issues of Kashmir's long-term governance, its degree of autonomy and its very identity must be resolved for lasting peace to take hold. Pray for calm heads and for the will to work out a peaceful solution by all parties.

b) *Islamic militancy* grew out of the call to "liberate" Kashmir from Indian rule (and create a Muslim state or join Pakistan). Their war against the state to achieve this end not only cost over 40,000 lives, but it also displaced over 800,000 people, crippled the region's economy and drove a wedge between the two nations. The intensity of the insurgency has decreased of late, but the threat remains. Pray that those who use terror and violence would be thwarted and that wisdom, statesmanship and justice would prevail.

② **Christians in Kashmir have always been few,** but this is changing. In 1990, there were only 12,000 Christians, mostly low-caste or immigrant peoples. In 2000, there were over 20,000. Since then, numbers have more than doubled again. As a result of outreach, entire villages are coming to faith as a whole. Many are weary of the enmity, bloodshed and upheaval and find peace, hope and life in Christ. Most workers in Jammu are with **GFA**, Operation Agape, HEM(KEF) and several independent indigenous ministries; ministry in the Kashmir Valley is fraught with risk, but there is fruitfulness among both Muslims and Hindus.

③ **Persecution is a common reaction** to rapid Christian growth. Angry and even violent responses from families and communities can see converts ostracized and even kicked out of homes or villages. Missionaries can also be on the receiving end of violent opposition, particularly when they are not sensitive in their means of evangelism. Pray for wise and sensitive witness by Christian workers and for the protection and preservation of new believers.

④ **Unreached peoples.** Almost all peoples in Jammu and Kashmir are unreached. Pray for the following:

a) **Kashmiri Muslims** have become more militant in their Islam. A number of smaller Muslim peoples are unreached, such as the Gujjars as well as the Makhmi, Purig-Pa and Balti peoples (all Tibeto-Burmese Muslim groups). Increasing numbers are coming to faith, from fewer than 100 in 2001 to more than 1,000 in 2010. Those who become believers face many dangers. Several agencies work among them; Bible correspondence courses see very positive responses. Pray that Islamist extremism may cause Muslims to seek an alternative way – and find it in Jesus.

b) **Tibetan Buddhists** (Ladakhi/Mangrik, Mon and other small groups) in the mountainous east and northeast have been only marginally evangelized. The Moravians have a small work with two churches, a school and only 200 Ladakhi believers. There are perhaps 10 believers from among the other Tibetan Buddhist and animist groups of Ladakh district. The JESUS film is now being used in the area.

c) **The high-caste Brahmin Pandits** of Kashmir were 1 million in 1900, but since the 1940s, Muslim hostility, terror and violence have reduced them to 50,000 today and only 3,000 in their Kashmir Valley home area. Between 300,000 and 500,000 have been displaced in recent years alone. There are very few known Christians among this group.

5 **Christian radio** – there are broadcasts several times a week in Kashmiri, Gujjari, Ladakhi and several other languages specific to the region (**GFA**, **TWR**, FEBA).

Jharkhand

Geography 🌏

Area 75,000 sq km. Hilly, forested region in east. Formed from southern Bihar in 2000.
Population 31,844,037; 424 people/sq km.
Capital Ranchi 1.1m. **Other major cities** Jhamshedpur 1.4m; Dhanbad 1.3m.

Peoples 👪

People groups 415. Ten largest: Santal (Munda-Santal, 9.7% of state pop); Shaikh (Bengali, 9.2%); Yadava (Hindi, 8.0%); Kurmi (Hindi, 7.0%); Ho (Munda-Santal, 6.0%); Oraon Kurux (Oraon, 5.4%); Munda (Munda-Santal, 4.3%); Teli (Hindi, 3.8%); Ansari (Urdu Muslim, 3.4%); Chamar (Hindi, 3.0%).
Languages Official: Hindi, Santhali. Oriya, Khota and Bengali also common.

Religion 🙏

Hindu 68.6%; Muslim 13.8%; Ethno-tribal religion (Sarna) 13.0%; Christian 4.1% (6.0%).

1 **Jharkhand,** the "Land of Forests and Hills", is one of India's youngest states. It is 78% rural, generally poor and undereducated, but it has great potential due to rich natural resources in the rocky hills and dense forests. It suffers the inevitable growing pains of a new state. Pray for its healthy development – 80% of the population are farmers, and it contains some of India's poorest people.

2 **The 32 tribal (Adivasi) peoples** in Jharkhand amount to nearly one-third of the state's population. Scheduled Castes are another 12%. Jharkhand's history is littered with tribal uprisings, particularly against the excesses of British colonialism; separatist sentiments among many tribal groups continue today. The actions of the Naxalite Maoist movement add further fuel to the fire. Sporadic but frequent violence affects many, including Christian workers attempting to bring the gospel to Hindu and animist tribal groups. Pray with regard to:

a) **Christian ministry to tribal peoples.** They are very diverse and often isolated and divided. There is actually much mission and ministry to tribal groups – German Lutherans (Gossner Evangelical), **OM**, **GFA**, **FMPB**, *Vishwa Vani*, **GEMS**, **AoG** and International Living Mission are just a few. Some tribal groups are up to 30% Christian (Oraon, Munda, Kharia); others are barely touched by the gospel (Kol, Bedia, Chero, other small groups). Pray that all tribal groups might have the opportunity to encounter the love of Christ.

b) **Negative reactions to evangelism** are common and often violent by animists and Hindu tribals. Such rejection to evangelism is expected and is frequently orchestrated by militant Hindu groups, but it is on occasion exacerbated by evangelists' lack of sensitivity. Pray for contextualized outreach that takes into account the unique nature of each of these peoples as well as their practical needs.

3 **Other unevangelized peoples** include Shaikh Muslims (3.0m), Yadava (2.5m), Kurmi (2.1m) and Teli peoples. In Jharkhand, none of these groups has a congregation of believers. Pray for their rapid and effective evangelization.

Karnataka

Geography 🌏

Area 192,000 sq km. Southwestern coastal state.
Population 60,906,894; 325 people/sq km.
Capital Bangalore 7.2m.

Peoples 👨‍👩‍👧

People groups 744 (162 from Kannada people cluster). Ten largest: Lingayat (Kannada, 10.2% of state pop); Vakkaliga (Kannada, 9.4%); Shaikh (Bengali, 7.2%); Adi Karnataka (Kannada, 6.0%); Kuruba (Kannada, 5.2%); Brahmin (Hindi, 3.9%); Bedar Hindu (Telugu, 3.5%); Naikda (Kannada, 3.2%); Mahratta (Marathi-Konkani, 3.0%); Holer (Kannada, 2.5%).

Languages 19. Kannada 65%, along with 20 dialects; also Urdu 10%, Telugu 8%, Tamil 5%, Marathi 4%, Tulu 3%.

Religion 🙏

Hindu 83.9%; Muslim 12.2%; Christian 1.9% (4.0%); Jain 0.8%; Buddhist 0.7%.

1 **Karnataka** is South India's most spiritually needy state. Beyond the growing (and increasingly expensive) cities, rural areas are largely gripped by poverty. Christian communities tend to be dormant, inward-looking and culturally isolated – the wealthier multi-language churches of Bangalore and the south (CSI), and the more Catholic coastal districts. Pray for a breakdown of all barriers to witness and the gospel. Hinduists are intensifying their campaigns to pass an anti-conversion law. There are now over 1,000 attacks each year by Hindu militants against Christians, in part due to the positive response that evangelism receives in some quarters. However, this also strengthens the faith and resolve of Karnataka churches.

I

2 **Bangalore** is the centre of India's rapidly growing IT and software industries and the fastest-growing city in India. It is also home to over 800 Christian ministry headquarters – Indian missions (**IEM**, Quiet Corner); international agencies (The Bible Society, Language Recordings India/**GRN**, SGM, **OM**, **EHC**, Asia Graduate School of Theology, International Correspondence School of **AoG**, India Bible League, FEBA, others); and theological institutions. Pray that these ministries might be great blessings to Bangalore and to all India.

3 **Bangalore's Christian community** was mostly middle and upper class in the past, but now many lower castes and slums dwellers are becoming believers, especially through the ministries of charismatic churches. Yet despite being 8% of the population, Christians have thus far failed to make any major impact on Bangalore. Christians here must not leave God's work to full-time missionaries from elsewhere; pray for a revival of the churches and for their mobilization to allow all Karnataka to hear the good news. Pray also for increased unity in churches – across languages, castes and denominations.

4 **The less evangelized** – the majority of Karnataka's peoples are unreached.

a) ***Praise God for a breakthrough among the Lingayats.*** They are predominantly in the north, prominent in society and politics and very devoted to a particular expression of Hindu belief. Numbering between six and 12 million, they have seen many thousands won to the Lord, forming hundreds of fellowships. This has been done almost entirely by Lingayat Christians witnessing into their own communities. Pray for strengthening of this movement and that it might grow, deepen and even spill into other groups.

b) ***The Banjara,*** a Gypsy people, are also responding. Despite challenges, there are now over 55,000 Banjara believers (out of 20 million Banjara nationally).

c) ***The Devadasi*** are girls from untouchable castes who are forced into temple prostitution. There are over 50,000 in the state.

d) ***The 70,000*** street children living among the 1 million in Bangalore's 700 slums.

e) ***The 79 peoples who remain unreached and unengaged.*** These include Idiga (2.0m), Bhovi (1.2m) and Bant (1.0m) peoples.

Kerala

Geography 🌍

Area 39,000 sq km. India's most southwesterly state.
Population 36,324,062; 964 people/sq km.
Capital Trivandrum 1.0m. **Other major cities**
Cochin 1.6m; Calicut 1.0m.

Peoples 👪

People groups 408. Ten largest: Mappila (Malayali, 23.9% of state pop); Nair (Malayali, 16.0%); Ilavan (Malayali, 11.9%); Syrian Christian (Malayali, 9.5%); Malabar Catholic (Malayali, 6.6%); Nadar (Tamil, 4.7%); Pulayan Hindu (Malayali, 3.7%); Viswakarma (Telugu, 3.0%); Brahmin (Hindi, 1.9%); Paraiyan (Tamil, 1.2%).
Languages Malayali (Malayalam) 96%; Tamil 2.3%.

Religion 🙏

Hindu 56.2%; Muslim 24.7%; Christian 19.0% (35.5%).

1 **Syrian Christians,** with links to the Syrian Jacobite Church, are descendants of those traditionally believed to have been evangelized by the apostle Thomas. They form the majority of Kerala's Christians and are members of Orthodox, Catholic and Protestant denominations. They have high social, political and economic status but have become little more than a caste within Hindu society, though a small number have broken out to become vital witnesses to those of other cultures. They are faced with the twin challenges of nominalism in their own ranks and of the increasing allure of dynamic, younger, Independent churches appearing all across Kerala. Pray for God to instigate renewal that will bring new life and passion to these ancient confessions.

2 **Kerala has a diverse Christian scene.** A multitude of ministries and denominations are based in or operate in this state, which comfortably has more Christians than any other state in India. The longstanding investment of Christians into the educational system has rendered Kerala the most literate and well-educated state in India as well as the most favourable for the status of women. Protestants include mainline, Brethren and Pentecostal groups, as well as burgeoning numbers of fast-growing Independent groups, usually from a charismatic background. There is notable tension between traditional mainline groups and emerging groups; theology, style of worship, caste-related issues and style of evangelism are all areas of significant differences. Pray for unity and sensitivity among churches, their shared commitment to have a good testimony to society and for God's Kingdom to be placed ahead of their own interests.

3 **Unreached peoples.** Many Kerala churches continue to grow in missions interest. However, social barriers are very high; many believers need to be liberated from the spirit of caste, both to evangelize other social groups and to welcome converts as brethren.

a) *Of the 35 small tribal groups,* only three or four have significant Christian groups and 10 others have a handful of believers. Most are Hindu, animist or demon worshippers. Only seven tribal groups have populations of over 10,000, and several face the threat of extinction. Kerala Christians must gain a vision to reach them – praise God for the few that have.

b) *The Malabar Muslims, or Mappila,* are numerous in the north of Kerala and number nearly nine million. Ministries of a few agencies have led to several thousand known conversions and groups of believers, but resistance to the gospel is high and new Christians suffer much. Pray for those involved in this arduous and costly ministry.

c) *In the higher castes and 41 Dalit groups of Hindus,* an increasing number are seeing people movements to Christ. The humble and egalitarian nature of Pentecostalism has generated significant response. Yet, despite growing numbers of Dalits in the churches, their presence in ministry and leadership is still lacking. Pray that all Dalit groups might be reached with the liberating gospel, but pray also that Christians would fully integrate them, as equals in Christ, into every level of the Church.

4 **Christian media** does much to generate missions interest, and TV and radio programmes to the wider population generate a wide response. **GFA** and some of the newer Pentecostal/charismatic groups are especially active in this area.

Madhya Pradesh

Geography 🌐

Area 297,000 sq km. Poor and underdeveloped central state.
Population 73,512,931; 240 people/sq km.
Capital Bhopal 1.8m. **Other major cities** Indore 2.2m; Jabalpur 1.4m; Gwalior 1.1m.

Peoples 👪

People groups 660. 46 Scheduled tribes. Ten largest: Rajput (Hindi, 8.2% of state pop); Chamar (Hindi, 7.7%); Gond (Gond, 7.5%); Bhil (Bhil, 7.2%); Brahmin (Hindi, 5.7%); Yadava (Hindi, 3.5%); Kachhi Hindu (Hindi, 3.4%); Shaikh (Bengali, 2.9%); Kurmi (Hindi, 2.8%); Bania (Rajasthan, 2.7%).
Languages Hindi dominates (80%), including dialects/variants; also Gondi, Bhil, Marathi, Urdu.

Religion 🙏

Hindu 91.1% (most Dalit and tribal groups are actually animists); Muslim 6.4%; Jain 0.9%; Christian 0.3% (2.2%); Other 1.2%.

1 **This state was one of the last to open up for missions,** with slow response to the gospel until recently. It is strongly Hindu with stern laws limiting conversions to Christianity. The largest denominations are Catholic, Church of North India, Lutheran and Mennonite Churches, and most are Dalit or tribal in origin. Pray for the end of opposition to the gospel in high places and for the frustration of extremist Hindu efforts to "reconvert" Christians – thousands of tribal peoples have been forced to renounce Christianity. The whole state remains a pioneer mission field, but growth in both outreach and response are increasing.

2 **Christian numbers declined** in census statistics, from 0.92% in 1981 to 0.3% in 1991, but this refers only to the established mainline groups and does not take into account the accelerating grassroots growth occurring, especially through house church networks. A statewide saturation, church-planting network has seen thousands of groups planted in the last 20 years; there are now more than 4,000. The vision of the Madhya Pradesh Harvest network is to place workers in every Pincode – more than half now have some Christian workers. Rather than pick from each other's flocks, mainline denominations instead agreed to cooperate. Pray that unity might increase and be the platform for outreach and effective ministry to this spiritually needy state.

3 **The challenge of the unreached** – pray for the many needs of this state and for the timely and effective sharing of the gospel to each people group and in each area.

a) The tribal peoples in Madhya Pradesh, larger in number than anywhere else in the world, represent around 30% of India's tribal population. They are a majority in the southern four districts, especially Bastar. There is now a burgeoning house church movement in many tribes through the labours of various agencies; the Oraon are now largely Christian. However, all represent a tough pioneer challenge. Most practice a Hindu-influenced animism. Witchcraft, Saktism (worship of female energy) and Saivism (worship of Shiva) abound.

b) The 12.4 million Gond are the largest tribe in India, and number around five million in Madhya Pradesh alone. In this state, only 0.4% are Christian. Over 30 mission agencies minister to them, and churches are multiplying despite local and statewide opposition.

c) The 11.9 million Bhil are India's second-largest tribe. In Madhya Pradesh, they also number five million and are 0.6% Christian. As Hindus with animistic influence, they remain responsive to what outreach has come their way.

d) Bhopal, the state capital of MP, was the scene of the world's worst-ever industrial accident, claiming 25,000 lives and poisoning the land for years to come. Tensions between Hindus and the large Muslim minority, high rates of poverty, illiteracy and crime in the 300-plus slums ringing the city and vulnerability of these same slums to flooding and disaster make Bhopal an area of concern. Christian work among the needy and those affected by the disaster has borne fruit and goodwill.

I

Maharashtra

Geography🌍

Area 308,000 sq km. India's most urbanized and industrialized state.
Population 113,426,742; 371 people/sq km.
Capital Mumbai (Bombay) 20.0m; India's commercial, economic and industrial heart.
Other major cities Pune 5.0m; Nagpur 2.6m; Nashik 1.6m; Aurangabad 1.2m; Solapur 1.1m.

Peoples 👪

People groups 735. Ten largest: Mahratta (Marathi–Konkani, 22.5% of state pop); Mahar Hindu (Marathi–Konkani, 6.8%); Shaikh (Bengali, 6.1%); Nau Buddh (Marathi–Konkani, 6.0%); Kunbi (Gujarati, 5.7%); Brahmin (Hindi, 3.9%); Bania (Rajasthan, 3.0%); Mali (Hindi, 2.5%); Mahratta Kunbi (Gujarati, 2.4%); Matang (Marathi–Konkani, 2.2%).
Languages Marathi 68.9%; Hindi 11.0%; Urdu 7.1%; Gujarati 2.4%; Kannada 2.4%; Tamil 1.3%; Telugu 1.3%.

Religion 🛐

Hindu 80.4%; Muslim 10.6%; Buddhist 6.0%; Jain 1.3%; Christian 1.1% (2%); Other 0.4%.

---

1 **Maharashtra's name means "state of large territory"**, and it is huge – in land area, in population and in influence – often playing the lead role in the nation's political, economic and cultural destiny. Despite Maharashtra being one of the most diverse states, ethnically and religiously, Hindutva agendas often control or influence the government. This has meant intercommunal tensions through discrimination against Muslims, Buddhists and Christians. Re-conversion efforts are increasing, especially for tribal and Dalit peoples who become Christian. Pray that the state government may be impartial.

2 **Mumbai** is the economic and cultural powerhouse of India, home of the stock exchange and the hugely influential film industry, Bollywood. It is also a city in great need of prayer.

a) *Mumbai's huge economy* pulls in migrants from most of India, resulting in a massive influx of people, most of whom end up in slums. This results in great diversity, but also tension and desperation. It is host to India's largest slum (Dharavi, with over one million people and 16,500 people per square mile population density); in fact, 60% of Mumbai's population live in slums.

b) *Human need and suffering in Mumbai are great.* There are 200,000 victims of the sex trade, over 100,000 street children and nearly 300,000 AIDS cases. The slums especially are rife with crime, pollution, disease, poverty, unemployment and, too often, hopelessness.

c) *Mumbai has the second-highest Christian population* of India's megacities, but the Christian percentage has actually gone down in recent years from 5% to 4%. There are many Catholics and a growing number of Protestant denominations and churches. Pray that Christians may be salt and light in their city. New Life Fellowship has won many non-Christians through a house church/cell model and Scripture distribution. They have now planted 4,200 cell churches and have a vision to plant a church in every village of the state.

3 **The Christian Church needs prayer.** Christians are few in smaller cities and rural areas. Maharashtra did not experience the same scale of mass people movements to Christ in the past as did other states. Pray for:

a) *The established denominations and ministries.* Many churches struggle with nominalism; church attendance is barely 50%. Infighting and legal squabbles have crippled ministry and undermined witness. Much good work done by missions was undone by their inability to raise up a second generation of leaders who would take the baton. Now, many of these ministries face the twin spectres of irrelevance and financial insolvency.

b) *Outreach and growth.* Since the early 1980s, new waves of outreach have turned the tide; Love Maharashtra, New Life Fellowship, the CONS saturation church–planting vision and a multiplication of agencies and workers have reached many new peoples, districts and villages. Pray that revival, growth and outreach may become normal parts of church life.

c) *The new challenges that come with new growth.* Lack of sensitivity and over-aggression in evangelism and church planting have often and unnecessarily led to backlashes from alarmed Hindus. Church growth is not always accompanied by follow-up of solid teaching and discipleship, and error creeps into fellowships. Divisions between local Marathi Christian leaders and missionaries from South India can occur when both sides fail to practice humility and grace.

d) *Persecution is increasingly common* as the Church continues to grow; this is partly inevitable and partly avoidable when wise outreach practices and good missiology are adopted at grassroots level. Christianity is accused of offending traditional, orthodox practices and beliefs, while the powerful influences of materialism and the modern values of Bollywood remain relatively free of such rigorous criticism.

4 **Unreached areas and peoples.** At least 73 peoples remain unreached and unengaged. Pray for the 175 or more Indian agencies and churches reaching out. A few merit special mention: Maharashtra Village Ministries, **IEM**, **GFA**, **FMPB**, *Navajeevan Dhara*, **OM**, Love Maharashtra. There are 40,000 unreached villages in Maharashtra.

a) *Many Hindu caste groups* and the Mahar (many of whom became Buddhist in the 20th Century) have little opportunity to hear the gospel; major church growth and revival are blocked by caste barriers. There are very few Christians among them.

b) *Muslims* number 12 million in the state, including 2 million in Mumbai. There is a lack of outreach, of workers, of awareness of their needs and of Scripture in their languages and dialects.

c) *Tribal groups,* such as Gond, Bhil, Korku and Kolam and many other smaller groups, are responding to the gospel. While the presence of Christian ministry has increased, so has opposition. Many people groups are still without viable congregations.

d) *The 1.5 million Jains and 150,000 Parsees* in their wealthy, cocooned religious communities remain unevangelized.

Manipur

Geography 🌐

Area 22,300 sq km. On eastern border with Myanmar.
Population 2,787,547; 121 people/sq km. Full Indian statehood only in 1972.
Capital Imphal 250,000.

Peoples 👪

People groups 191. Ten largest: Manipuri Meitei (Kuki-Chin-Naga, 50.0% of state pop); Shaikh (Bengali, 6.2%); Tangkhul (Kuki-Chin-Naga, 6.0%); Thado (Kuki-Chin-Naga, 5.8%); Hmar (Kuki-Chin-Naga, 4.3%); Kabui (Kuki-Chin-Naga, 3.5%); Paite Christian (Kuki-Chin-Naga, 2.8%); Illemei (Kuki-Chin-Naga, 2.4%); Assamese Muslim (Assamese, 2.2%); Christian unspecified (Tamil, 1.8%).

Official languages Manipuri (Meeteilon) and English.

Religion 🙏

Hindu 46.0%; Christian 34.0% (41.8%); Muslim 8.8%; Other 11.2%.

I

1 **Manipur has been constantly disrupted** in recent decades by several separatist insurgency movements, all with different and often competing agendas. They usually target non-indigenous peoples as well as Christians, both being easy scapegoats. This violence has claimed over 1,000 lives, has stymied access to and ministry in Manipur and has hindered development of the region. Pray that those taking up arms for their many causes would instead find peace and unity in Christ.

2 **Many problems apart from separatism beset Manipur.** Unemployment is over 30%, and the only "good" employment is in government jobs, which are bought through bribes. There is almost zero private investment, and immigrant peoples dominate what little economy there is. Manipur's proximity to the Golden Triangle exposes it to high occurrences of human and drug trafficking and to HIV/AIDS. There is much corruption, little infrastructure and poor leadership. Pray for hope to come to Manipur, ideally through the loving ministry of Christians and through social and economic transformation that the gospel can bring.

3 **Nearly all the Naga, Kuki and Chin** peoples became Christian in the 20th Century. Baptists (21 denominations) and Presbyterians predominate, along with Catholics and increasingly Pentecostals. Nominalism is widespread, and sadly, intertribal warfare (especially Naga-Kuki, Kuki-Zomi) has plagued the state for decades. These ethnic conflicts severely compromise witness and hamper outreach by Christians to Muslims and Hindus. Pray for full reconciliation, ethnic harmony and humble, sanctified cooperation among all who claim to follow Christ. Hundreds of Manipur missionaries serve cross-culturally today.

4 **Specific important groups:**

a) *The Meitei,* Manipur's largest people, have been Hindu for three centuries but are experiencing a revival of their traditional religion, Sanamahi. There are also around 200,000 Meitei Muslims. Most Meitei still disdain Christianity as a religion only for tribal peoples. There are 10-15,000 Christians, mostly Baptist and Presbyterian, but a real breakthrough is yet to come. The Bible and the JESUS film are available for them.

b) *Bengali-speaking Muslims and other immigrant groups* are largely unreached. They are resented by the indigenes and are often targets for violence and separatist sentiment.

Meghalaya

Geography 🌐

Area 22,700 sq km. Mountainous state on Bangladesh's northern border. It has the world's highest rainfall – 12 metres annually.
Population 2,690,986; 121 people/sq km.
Capital Shillong 305,000.

Peoples 👥

People groups 193. Ten largest: Khasi (Mon-Khmer, 50.4% of state pop); Garo (Garo-Tripuri, 30.3%); Shaikh (Bengali, 3.8%); Hajang (Bengali, 3.4%); Rabha (Tibetan, 1.4%); Tiwa (Assamese, 1.3%); Rajbansi (Bengali, 1.0%); Magar (South Himalaya, 0.8%); Chhetri (Nepali-Pahari, 0.6%); Brahmin (Hindi, 0.5%).

Religion

Christian 70.3% (76.0%); Hindu 13.3%; Muslim 4.3%; Ethnoreligionist/Other 11.8%.

1 **Meghalaya is a Christian-majority state;** most of the tribals who make up the majority became Christian in the 19th and early 20th Centuries. Churches are numerous – Khasi Presbyterians, Garo Baptists and many growing Catholic and charismatic congregations. Traditionalism has been a problem, but in the 21st Century, revivals and renewal are breathing new life and dynamism into many, many churches. Pray that this move of the Holy Spirit might spread, deepen and have a lasting impact on the lives and lifestyles of Christians. Pray also for unity among churches.

2 **Challenges for the Church:**

a) *Attempts to revive ancient traditional religions* are occurring alongside intensifying Hindutva policies. These spell trouble from both sides for Christians from Scheduled Tribes, who make up the majority of the state's population.

b) *The younger generation* are drifting away from the Church, nominalism is a concern and drug and alcohol abuse are widespread and well-documented problems.

c) *Issues of poverty* and the widening gap between rich and poor; the local economy is monopolized by a few. Pray for integrity and righteousness in governmental and economic spheres.

d) *Churches suffer from lack of pastoral care* and lack of strong biblical teaching, especially in rural areas, since most pastors are based in cities. Pray that God will raise up pastors and evangelists with a heart for evangelism and mission.

3 **Specific groups** that need focused prayer and ministry:

a) *Some smaller tribes.* The Hajong, Rabha Koch and Mikir are still entrenched in animistic ways. The Hindu and Muslim minorities are little touched by the gospel, and their numbers are increasing by immigration from Bangladesh and from other states.

b) **Shillong** has the highest concentration of non-Christians, with half the population Hindu, Muslim, animist and others. At the same time, revival recently impacted the 150-plus churches in the city.

c) **Students** from across NE India are concentrated in Shillong due to the education opportunities there. Pray for them to be impacted by the gospel and even to become part of the harvest force to reach the rest of India and beyond.

Mizoram

Geography

Area 21,100 sq km. Almost an enclave between Bangladesh and Myanmar.
Population 1,039,892; 50 people/sq km.
Capital Aizawl 270,000.

Peoples

People groups 133. Ten largest: Mizo (Mizo-Lushai, 38.2% of state pop); Chakma (Garo-Tripuri, 9.6%); Poi (Mizo-Lushai, 6.2%); Hmar (Kuki-Chin-Naga, 3.5%); Ralte (Kuki-Chin-Naga, 3.4%); Pawi (Kuki-Chin-Naga, 3.1%); Chin Mara (Kuki-Chin-Naga, 2.8%); Kuki other (Kuki-Chin-Naga, 2.7%); Paite Christian (Kuki-Chin-Naga, 2.1%); Mizo Fanai (Mizo-Lushai, 1.6%).

Religion

Christian 87.0% (89.6%); Buddhist 7.9%; Hindu 3.6%; Muslim 1.1%.

1 **Mizoram has one of the largest Christian populations by proportion** of any state in the world. Most Christians are Presbyterian, Pentecostal or Baptist, but there are now over 100 denominations and groups. Awakenings and revivals in recent years have dynamized the Church and helped transform society. Mizoram remains one of the most literate, well-educated and egalitarian states in India. Mizo missionaries in India and beyond number over 2,300 – one of the highest sending statistics in the world.

2 **The challenges** to be tackled by Christians:

a) **Divisions within denominations** and inter-ethnic tensions are a discredit to the unity expected of believers. Pray for a new outpouring of the Spirit that will join believers together and remove man-made divisions.

b) **The increase of false teachings,** sects, cults and even devil worship, particularly among the younger generation.

c) **Serious societal problems** – increased corruption, youth delinquency, abuse of drugs and alcohol. Proximity to the Golden Triangle raises the threat of drug abuse and HIV/AIDS.

d) **Several less-reached peoples**, such as the mostly Buddhist Chakma and the increasing numbers of immigrant peoples, need to receive loving witness from Mizo Christians.

Nagaland

Geography

Area 16,600 sq km. Mountainous state bordering on Assam, Arunachal Pradesh and Myanmar.
Population 2,320,657; 142 people/sq km.
Capital Kohima 92,000.

Peoples

People groups 176. Ten largest: Sema (Kuki-Chin-Naga, 12.2% of state pop); Ao (Kuki-Chin-Naga, 12.1%); Konyak (Kuki-Chin-Naga, 11.7%); Lotha (Kuki-Chin-Naga, 7.9%); Angami (Kuki-Chin-Naga, 7.6%); Chakhesang (Kuki-Chin-Naga, 6.5%); Kahha Phom (Kuki-Chin-Naga, 5.9%); Sangtam (Kuki-Chin-Naga, 4.7%); Christian unspecified (Tamil, 3.7%); Yimchungra (Kuki-Chin-Naga, 3.1%).

Religion

Christian 90.0% (93.1%); Hindu 7.7%; Muslim 1.8%.

1 **Nagaland is unique,** with the highest percentage of Baptists of any state in the world (between 65% and 80%). Revivals in 1956, 1966 and 1972 brought new life, fervour and a surge of evangelistic and missions outreach, and thousands of Nagas have served the Lord in other parts of India and beyond. Praise God for what He has already done among the 20 Naga tribes.

2 **Church growth has not necessarily brought radical change** to all Christians' lives or worldviews; a number of factors blunt Christian witness.

a) *Tribal feuds,* with each other and against other groups, as well as the long fight for Naga independence reveal that many have been Christianized without being truly changed. The Naga insurgency has been the main catalyst for most of NE India's other independence-related conflicts. Pray that a spirit of reconciliation and forgiveness might replace the politics of hate and violence that have kept the Nagas oppressed for many years.

b) *Fragmentation of denominations* has created 20 Baptist groups and countless newer, Independent churches. A true sense of Christian unity is lacking. Pray that the Nagaland for Christ movement might draw churches together.

c) *Generations of creeping nominalism* have rendered many churches spiritually dead and allowed in liberal teaching and even financial corruption. Pray for another revival to sweep the cobwebs out of the Church, which runs the risk of losing a younger generation to materialism, immorality and substance abuse.

3 **Christian training and sending** – few Christian areas in the world have such a high density of theological colleges; there are at least 19. Pray for more students who will become effective pastors, social workers, church planters and missionaries. A vision exists to see 10,000 Naga missionaries sent out from this most Christian state in India.

4 **Pray for further Bible translation.** The many highly educated theologians have ensured that the two million Nagas (in 20 tribes with 36 languages and 124 dialects) are well served with Bible translations. Bibles or NTs exist in nearly 30 languages, with work progressing in 10 more.

Orissa

Geography

Area 155,700 sq km. Eastern coastal state prone to severe cyclones.
Population 42,337,396; 279 people/sq km.
Capital Bhubaneswar 765,000. The Bhubaneswar-Cuttack urban agglomeration is around 2 million.

Peoples

People groups 799. Ten largest: Yadava (Hindi, 8.4% of state pop); Mahishya (Bengali, 5.4%); Brahmin (Hindi, 5.1%); Kui Khond (Gond, 3.9%); Gauda (Oriya, 3.7%); Pan (Oriya, 3.5%); Khandait (Bengali, 3.4%); Teli (Hindi, 3.0%); Gond (Gond, 2.4%); Santal (Munda-Santal, 2.2%).
Languages Oriya 83.0%; Hindi 2.4%; Telugu 2.1%; Santal 2.1%; Kui 2.0%.

Religion

Hindu 94.4% (many animistic tribal peoples included); Christian 2.4% (2.0%); Muslim 2.1%; Other 1.1%.

1 **Persecution of Christians** remains more intense in Orissa than anywhere else in India. Hindu extremist violence is equalled only in Gujarat. After a prominent Hindu swami was murdered in 2008 (most likely by Maoist guerillas), Hindus responded by venting their wrath against Christians – a soft target. Over 120 Christians were murdered, hundreds of churches destroyed and around 52,000 Christians displaced from their homes. Harsh anti-conversion regulations have done little to placate Hindu extremists. In many districts, some threat remains for Christians to either reconvert to Hinduism, leave their village or face death. Pray that the right to freedom of belief as laid out in the Constitution might prevail in Orissa and that no amount of intimidation or violence would overcome it. The persecution has no perceptible end in sight; pray therefore that churches might grow in unity and in their ability to withstand persecution. Pray for peace and harmony where possible, and pray for suffering believers and communities to wisely use the law and available legal aid to protect themselves from unduly harsh treatment.

2 **Church growth has multiplied** despite great opposition. The census numbers Christians as 2.4% in Orissa, but some groups (both Christian and Hindutva) claim 28% or more. This is certainly an exaggeration, but it is nevertheless indicative of both rapid Christian growth and alarmed reaction. Most Christians in Orissa are tribal and Dalit peoples; these are by far the most responsive to outreach. Pray for the many Indian agencies seeking to augment this growth. Pray that caste discrimination, particularly prevalent in Orissa, might end – Christians suffer acutely from it.

3 **Tribal peoples of Orissa** (and in adjoining Jharkhand and Chhattisgarh) have responded enthusiastically to Christian witness. The Oraon, Kharia, Munda, Savara, Kisan, Khond and Kol have significant numbers of Christians. Their illiteracy, economic deprivation and political marginalization are the main reasons for their responsiveness – and for the shackles on further Christian growth. Numerous denominations and agencies work among them. Ministry training schools and shared missions vision among agencies has resulted in tribal Christians ministering cross-culturally, and not just to their own people.

4 **The unfinished challenge** – of the 799 peoples present in Orissa, 709 register on the census as having zero Christians.

a) The Forward Castes, such as Brahmin and Korono, have never been reached out to on a large scale with the claims of Christ. Some are seeking to minister to them; pray for the multiplication of Christian *satsangs* that are an effective expression of fellowship among them.

b) The tribals. Of the 62 groups, 20 are less than 0.1% Christian, and 42 are less than 1%. Pray specifically for a breakthrough among the Bhathudi, Bhuiya, Bhumiji, Gond, Kolho, Paraja, Santal, Siyal and Koya.

c) The rural population constitutes 85% of Orissa. Outreach, church planting and discipleship must take this into account, along with the isolation, traditions and close community ties that are intrinsic elements of rural life.

5 **Christian media.** A new Oriya Bible was published in 1998, yet low literacy hampers its usefulness; the large majority of women, Scheduled Tribes and Dalits cannot read. Pray also for the effective use of audio Scripture, Christian radio and Christian TV programmes.

Punjab

Geography

Area 50,400 sq km. Northwestern India; one of the most fertile agricultural regions in the world.
Population 28,216,088; 571 people/sq km.
Capital Chandigarh is shared as a capital with Haryana. Largest cities: Ludhiana 1.8m; Amritsar 1.3m.

Peoples

People groups 407. Ten largest: Jat Sikh (Jat, 32.4% of state pop); Mazhabi (Punjabi, 8.7%); Chamar (Hindi, 6.9%); Chuhra (Punjabi, 4.4%); Ad Dharmi (Punjabi, 4.4%); Jat Hindu (Jat, 3.2%); Tarkhan Sikh (Punjabi, 3.2%); Mahtam Sikh (Punjabi, 2.2%); Saini Sikh (Punjabi, 2.1%); Rajput Sikh (Punjabi, 1.7%).
Languages Official: Punjabi. A small minority speak Hindi.

Religion

Sikh 59.9%; Hindu 36.9%; Christian 1.2% (2.2%); Muslim 1.6%; Other 0.4%.

1 **Punjab is the home state of the Sikhs** and the only state where they are in the majority. Their famed Golden Temple is in Amritsar. A violent guerrilla war waged by Sikh extremists seeking independence led to up to 100,000 deaths, including that of Prime Minister Indira Gandhi, and caused much economic disruption over a decade from 1980. Praise God that peace came in 1992. Since then, there has been rapid and remarkable economic progress, with many thriving industries and a strong, developed infrastructure. Though tensions still exist, there is also healing of intercommunal wounds and unprecedented openness for the gospel.

2 **The Sikh religion** with its unique doctrines and culture has spread to many parts of India and beyond. There are up to 25 million Sikhs in the world. Little specific Christian study of and dialogue with Sikhs has ever been undertaken. The Mazbahi, Jat, Ramdasias and Rai – all castes of Sikhs – are more responsive to the gospel. A number of agencies and indigenous churches are now reaching out. Praise God for the several Christian leaders from the Sikh community now actively professing and proclaiming the good news in Punjab and abroad.

3 **Most of the Christian community** originated in the 19th Century from mass movements of depressed Chamar and Chuhra castes. Christians were underprivileged, generally nominal, discouraged and in decline. In the last 20 years, there has been a wave of outreach by many agencies and churches. The number of churches has grown and church attendance tripled. In the last decade, there has also been encouraging growth in local, indigenous Christian leaders ministering in Punjab. There are now over 100 denominations. GSCC and Operation Agape are two of several significant agencies planting churches. Praise God for His moving in Punjab; pray for a revived, effective and dynamic Church. Two main Bible colleges in Punjab (Punjab Bible College and Agape Institute of Leadership Development) offer degree courses, and over a dozen smaller Bible schools offer short-term courses.

4 **The vision of planting churches** in all of Punjab's villages and urban areas is shared by a growing number of churches and ministries. Some points for prayer:

a) Peoples. There are 14 peoples who are unreached and unengaged. Another 14 are unreached, but with some work at least started among them somewhere in India. Pray that every people may be impacted by the gospel with churches planted and leaders raised up.

b) Districts. Two districts – Mansa and Sangrur – are less than 0.1% Christian, along with 38 subdistricts less than 0.1% Christian.

5 **The Ludhiana Christian Medical College and Hospital** has had a worldwide reputation for Christian care and witness for many decades. Pray for this witness to be maintained and to be fruitful.

Rajasthan

Geography 🌍

Area 342,000 sq km. An arid state bordering Pakistan. India's largest state in area.
Population 68,591,484. 194 people/sq km.
Capital Jaipur 3.1m. **Other major city** Jodhpur 1.1m.

Peoples 👪

People groups 489. Ten largest: Rajput (Hindi, 8.5% of state pop); Jat Hindu (Jat, 7.6%); Bania (Rajasthan, 7.6%); Brahmin (Hindi, 6.5%); Mina (Hindi, 6.3%); Bhil (Bhil, 5.2%); Chamar (Hindi, 5.0%); Shaikh (Bengali, 4.4%); Gujar (Rajasthan, 4.1%); Megh Hindu (Rajasthan, 3.1%).

Languages Hindi is the official state language, but Rajasthani (and its five principal dialects) is the mother tongue of many.

Religion 🕊

Hindu 88.8%; Muslim 8.5%; Sikh 1.4%; Jain 1.2%; Christian 0.1% (0.4%).

1 **Christians are still a minority within a minority,** most being from Dalit and tribal groups. However, there has been rapid growth in the Church, particularly in the south and among the Bhil tribe. Some inside sources claim as many as 300,000 believers – five times more than census figures. Most of these are believers who have discovered Jesus in the last 10 years. Praise God for such growth!

2 **Harassment of the small Christian community** is increasing due to pressure by the BJP upon the state government. An anti-conversion bill passed in 2008 makes things even more difficult. Hindu extremists have targeted Christian ministries – including hospitals and orphanages – with such ruthlessness that even secular groups and sympathetic moderate Hindus are protesting against such treatment. Pray that all such attempts to destroy God's people would result in greater church growth. Pray that the hatred of extremists and the loving humility of Christians would draw many more into the Kingdom.

3 **Ministry in Rajasthan is multiplying** despite persecution. Now, 165 organizations and churches work in the state. Indigenous ministries, such as Emmanuel Mission International, Native Missionary Movement and many others, are effectively reaching the needy, the lowly and those previously unevangelized. Rajasthan Bible Institute and Filadelfia Bible College train church planters and missionaries at a higher education level, and they themselves are also substantially engaged in outreach.

4 **Unreached peoples:**

a) Tribal groups such as Bhil Gametia, Bhil Kataria, Bhil Meena, Damor, Garasia, Mina, Bairwa, Chamar, Dholi, Meghval/Mehar and many other smaller groups are responding to the gospel, but progress is slow.

b) The Meo are Muslim but heavily influenced by Hindu culture and beliefs. There are very few, if any, Christians among them.

c) Higher castes, especially Rajputs (who originated from Rajasthan) and Jats, show almost negligible response to the gospel. The large majority are Hindu, but some are Jain or Muslim.

d) Jaipur, the capital, with 3.2 million people (over six million in the metro region), has around 22,000 Christians. Originally, most were migrants from South India, but today increasing numbers of local believers are present. Agape Fellowship and Assemblies of God work among the Meena and Bairwa living in Jaipur.

5 **Other ministries worthy of prayer:**

a) EHC has blanketed every home with Christian literature twice. Currently on the third round, they are seeing greatly increased responsiveness.

b) Evangelistic efforts among the many tourists who travel to Rajasthan, India's most popular tourist destination. Approximately 1.5 million foreign and 25 million domestic tourists visit Rajasthan every year.

c) The major Rajasthani languages, such as Marwari (6.5m), Bhili (1.2m) and Wagri (10.5m), have no portions of the Bible translated and no Christian literature available. Pray also for the initiatives to develop ethno-linguistic music and oral resources to equip the growing churches among various people groups.

I

Sikkim

Geography

Area 7,100 sq km. Himalayan state sandwiched between Nepal and Bhutan, and for years a buffer state between Tibet (China) and India. Annexed by India in 1975.
Population 630,302; 90 people/sq km. India's least-populous state.
Capital Gangtok 50,000. Only 11% urban population.

Peoples

People groups 88. Ten largest: Khambu (Bengali, 16.7% of state pop); Bhotia Buddhist (Tibetan, 14.6%); Khas (Nepali-Pahari, 11.1%); Brahmin (Hindi, 10.2%); Tamang (Nepali-Pahari, 8.3%); Lepcha (South Himalaya, 7.4%); Magar (South Himalaya, 5.1%); Newah (Nepali-Pahari, 4.7%); Kami (Nepali-Pahari, 3.6%); Monpa Limbu (South Himalaya, 2.7%).
Languages 11 official languages. Nepali is now the lingua franca.

Religion

Hindu 60.9%; Buddhist 28.1%; Christian 6.7% (7.5%); Muslim 1.4%; Other 2.6%.

1 **Sikkim has enjoyed significant religious freedom in recent years,** a contrast from a history of persecution. Christians are taking advantage of this open window, but they are not alone. Muslims and Maoists are also very active in proselytism, so much so that, combined with growing immigration, the rapid religious demographic change is of great concern to many in the state. Pray for social and political harmony as well as wise leadership to handle the rapid changes.

Pray that existing freedom might continue and that Christians might use the opportunity – while it exists – to share the good news of Jesus.

2 **The Church in Sikkim** consists mostly of Lepcha people, first reached in the 19th Century. It is growing rapidly, from 7,000 people in 1981 to 53,000 in 2002, and significantly more in 2010. Evangelical Presbyterians are the main denomination, but the Church of North India, Pentecostals, Baptists and Independent groups also minister. Praise God for dozens of new congregations established annually in what was traditionally a Buddhist stronghold – and for the inclusion of former Buddhist monks and religious leaders among the numbers of those saved.

3 **Specific vision in Sikkim** touches on several areas. Pray for development of a shared vision and strategy by churches for the effective evangelization of Sikkim.

a) Leadership development is a key ministry. **GFA**, Sikkim Bible Institute, House of Revival and Evangelical Presbyterians as well as others focus on training and raising up pastors and leaders for the many leaderless new congregations constantly forming. This coincides with the formation of local mission agencies such as the Evangelical Mission (Presbyterians).

b) Outreach from Sikkim to neighbouring nations. Nestled in the lower range of the Himalayas, Sikkim is linked to Bhutan, Nepal and Tibet – a highly strategic location. Pray that Sikkim will bring light to its neighbours and within India as well.

4 **Pray for these strategic peoples:**

a) The Lepcha people, original inhabitants of the land and traditionally strongly Buddhist. A significant minority of Lepcha have been most responsive to the gospel; they constitute the largest group of Christians in Sikkim. They will be key in reaching other Himalayan peoples.

b) The Nepali, Sikkim's largest group, are mostly Hindu. They are recent arrivals to Sikkim.

c) The various Buddhist peoples, including Bhotia (Sikkimese), Sherpa and Tibetan peoples. A number of agencies are reaching them. It is notoriously difficult to see spiritual breakthrough among Himalayan Buddhist peoples, but it is not impossible, as the Lepcha have shown. Pray for God to work powerfully among all these peoples.

Tamil Nadu

Geography 🌐

Area 130,000 sq km. India's most southeasterly state and close to Sri Lanka. Historically agricultural but also India's most industrialized and urban state.
Population 70,453,739; 567 people/sq km.
Capital Chennai (formerly Madras) 7.5m. **Other major city** Coimbatore 1.8m; Madurai 1.4m.

Peoples 👪

People groups 510. Ten largest: Vanniyan (Tamil, 14.5% of state pop); Adi Dravida (Tamil, 11.5%); Pallan (Tamil, 4.6%); Yadava (Hindi, 4.2%); Maravan (Tamil, 4.2%); Viswakarma (Telugu, 3.9%); Paraiyan (Tamil, 3.7%); Nadar (Tamil, 3.7%); Tamil (Tamil, 3.3%); Brahmin (Hindi, 3.2%).

Languages Official: Tamil, used by 85% of the population. English widely used, also Telugu, Kannada.

Religion 🙏

Hindu 88.1%; Christian 6.1% (19.0%); Muslim 5.6%; Other 0.2%.

1 **The ebb and flow of religion and politics** affect the Church and mission. An anti-conversion law was passed in 2002 but was later repealed as Hindutva-aligned parties were defeated in elections. Despite this change, many Tamil Christians fear the social disruption large-scale conversions will cause. Hindu extremism continues to press in upon the growing Church, especially regarding Dalits, who are increasingly being won to Christ. The political and judicial arenas remain fragmented, unduly influenced by celebrities and highly prone to corruption. Pray for religious freedom to be preserved and for a society to be developed that ensures justice and fairness for all its peoples.

2 **Christians continue to grow,** and at rates greater than official statistics would imply. Pentecostal and charismatic groups are increasing especially rapidly. Chennai in particular enjoys a significant Christian presence. The large majority of this outreach and growth occurs among Dalit and tribal peoples. Pray for:

a) **Tamil Nadu's brilliant legacy** of establishing Christian ministries and sending missionaries. Many Christian organizations throughout India have been founded by Tamils. Pray that mission vision and outreach may continue to be important parts of Tamil Nadu Christianity.

b) **Christian training and leadership.** Tamil Nadu has many training opportunities available, from Bible schools to less formal systems, including short-term courses. Pray for the effective training of pastors, lay leaders and missionaries.

c) **The complications of money.**

  i *Sponsorship and assistance from outside sources* can affect decision making, values and motivation. "Successful" ministries will see greater income for both ministry and minister. Pray that those in Kingdom service might not be swayed by such influences.

  ii *The reservation system* gives greater chances of education, employment and social benefits to Dalits and tribals who remain in – or reconvert back to – Hinduism. Choosing to follow Christ therefore has serious implications for Dalits, especially if Christians fail to provide assistance and opportunities for these generally impoverished people.

3 **The less evangelized.** Despite the large Christian presence and numerous agencies, large segments of the population remain unreached:

a) **Northern and western districts** have far fewer Christians than the coastal areas, where churches are much stronger.

b) **Higher caste groups** have very little outreach directed toward them. These upper and middle class peoples are highly influential but barely touched by the gospel. Brahmins and Yadavas (known locally as Idayan or Konar) have little motivation for becoming Christian, a faith associated with foreigners and untouchables.

c) **Tamil-speaking Muslims,** as well as the large numbers of Shaikh and Sayyid Muslims, have very few Christians and even fewer Christian workers.

4 **Specific outreach challenges and opportunities:**

a) **Ministries focused on reaching and discipling youths and children** are increasing. This includes work among orphans, street kids and other children at risk.

b) **Students.** UESI(**IFES**) has more than 300 cell groups in the state, led by 28 staff. They see many of their graduates become leaders in churches and missionary movements.

c) **Tentmaking ministries,** business-as-mission and English teaching to communicate the good news are all areas of growth and great potential.

d) **New media outreach.** Tamil Nadu has India's highest number of business enterprises and is the most urban state, so Internet, TV and similar media are proving important and effective.

I

Tripura

Geography

Area 10,500 sq km. Almost an enclave within eastern Bangladesh.
Population 372,451; 362 people/sq km. Ongoing inflow of Bengalis.
Capital Argatala 400,000.

Peoples

People groups 284. More than half of groups are less than 200 in population. Includes 19 major tribal groups. Bengali illegal immigration makes accurate statistics difficult to render. They are now a majority. Ten largest: Tipera (Garo–Tripuri, 17.3% of state pop); Kayastha (Bengali, 7.9%); Shaikh (Bengali, 7.8%); Jogi Hindu (Bengali, 7.6%); Namasudra Hindu (Bengali, 5.9%); Brahmin (Hindi, 4.4%); Tuikuk (Garo–Tripuri, 3.8%); Mahishya (Bengali, 3.2%); Chakma (Garo–Tripuri, 2.8%); Bania (Rajasthan, 2.7%).

Religion

Hindu 85.6% – including Tripuri animists as "Hindu"; Muslim 8.0% (Bengali); Buddhist 3.1%; Christian 3.2% (5.5%).

1. **Indigenous peoples** are now a minority in their own state. Massive Bengali immigration has occurred over the last 60 years, and Bengalis have taken political and economic control. Indigenes, who were 85% of the population at the time of annexation, have been reduced to less than 28% of the state's population in 2010. This was done at the encouragement of the national government to suppress potential independence movements. Violent backlash by separatist Tripuris (including guerrilla and terrorist activities) has been met in kind by Bengali militant groups. Tripuris are under-represented in the political sphere, economically disadvantaged and increasingly forced off their traditional tribal lands. Through this, increasing openness to the gospel is now apparent. All tribal peoples have at least some Christians. Tribals account for 95% of Christians, while non-tribals represent 97% of the unreached. Pray that the tensions and insecurity might draw many more to turn to the gospel.

2. **Christians have been persecuted** by animists and by extremist Hindu groups. Of late, there have been attacks as well as false propaganda against the Church, accusing it of collusion with rebel groups. Pray that Christians might walk blamelessly in a region of strife and resentment and continue to express and demonstrate the love and grace of Christ, even to their accusers and persecutors.

3. **Church-related issues needing prayer:**

a) *New mission groups* appearing on the scene have generated some division in churches; such missions need to operate with sensitivity and humility. Pray for greater Christian unity and better coordination of Kingdom work within the state.

b) *TBCU Baptist Church* represents 80% of Tripura's Christians. Pray for revival and its equipping to win Tripura for Christ. Christian tribals are poor and have few resources. Pray for the emergence of young and motivated leaders from within Tripura's peoples.

c) *Tripura Prayer Network* leads a new movement solely dedicated to pray for revival and for transformation of the land. Pray that TBCU's stated commitment to establish prayer groups in every district will yield a rich harvest for the Lord.

4. **The less evangelized** are a huge challenge, especially in a context where tribal and ethnic enmity is so rife. Pray for:

a) *The Bengali-speaking majority* of 2.5-2.7 million who are largely unreached. Most are Hindu, having left Muslim Bangladesh and found a welcome of sorts in Hindu-majority India. They are beginning to respond to the gospel. Young, educated Bengalis are the most open. Pray for a breakthrough, with a house-church movement just beginning to take shape.

b) *The Buddhist Chakma* (50,000) who fled from Muslim Bangladesh. Some are starting to respond to the gospel; others are very resentful at the enticements Christian missionaries are accused of using.

c) *The tribal peoples* have been most responsive to ministry and comprise almost all the state's Christians. The non-Christian majority of them adhere to a unique local blend of animism and Hinduism, applying Hindu identities to their old gods. Pray that the remainder might be reached for Jesus. The largest of these groups are the Tripura, Riang, Jamatia, Chakma and Halam.

Uttar Pradesh

Geography 🌐

Area 242,000 sq km. India's strategic heartland in the Ganges Valley, yet poor and underdeveloped. **Population** 202,557,152; 811 people/sq km. India's most-populous state. If independent, would be the world's fifth-most populous country.

Capital Lucknow 2.9m. **Other major cities** Kanpur 3.4m; Agra 1.7m; Ghaziabad 1.5m; Meerut 1.5m; Varanasi 1.4m; Allahabad 1.3m.

Peoples 👪

People groups 613. Ten largest: Chamar (Hindi, 12.3% of state pop); Yadava (Hindi, 7.1%); Brahmin (Hindi, 6.6%); Rajput (Hindi, 5.6%); Shaikh (Bengali, 5.3%); Kurmi (Hindi, 3.5%); Pasi Hindu (Hindi, 3.3%); Bania (Rajasthan, 2.5%); Pashtun Northern (Pashtun, 2.5%); Ansari (Urdu Muslim, 2.3%).
Languages Hindi 89%, a complex of related

languages and dialects (Hindi, Bhojpuri, Awadhi, Braj, Bundeli, Charwali, Kumaoni, others); Urdu 10%; Punjabi 0.4%.	**Religion**
	Hindu 80.6%; Muslim 18.5%; Sikh 0.4%; Buddhist 0.2%; Christian 0.1% (0.3%); Jain 0.1%.

1 **Uttar Pradesh is the home of Hinduism,** and it has a long historical connection to Buddhism and Jainism – but it has given no home to the gospel. Millions of Hindu pilgrims visit Varanasi, the holy city of Hinduism on the Ganges River, but few find the Living Water that only Jesus can give. Pray that there might be a major mobilization of prayer for this key state and that God may send the workers who will turn the tide for the gospel.

2 **The scale of human need and suffering is immense.** Cities are crowded and polluted. Rural areas have no amenities, little infrastructure or power, and a severe shortage of health care facilities. Water-borne diseases are widespread. The large majority of the world's polio cases occur in Uttar Pradesh. The majority of children are undernourished. In the political arena, poor governance, corruption and short-term mentalities combine to stunt progress. Pray that the gospel might be made manifest in easing suffering and righting wrongs.

3 **The Christian Church** is still a tiny minority community of officially only 0.1% of the population (although in reality the number may be double that). Most come from the Chamar and Dom groups – both are Dalits. The Chamar are Uttar Pradesh's largest people group, numbering as many as 24 million. They are despised as untouchables. There are reports of accelerating church growth, especially among Dalit peoples. The widespread presence of persecution, intimidation and "reconversion" campaigns spreads fear and limits growth – and betrays the oppressive beliefs of the perpetrators. Persecution also serves to refine the Church and to remove unnecessary alien associations for true followers of Jesus – much Christianity in Uttar Pradesh has been dressed in inappropriate foreign trappings. Pray for the preservation and growth of the Church. Pray also that indigenous and local expressions of faith in Jesus might flourish and spread.

I

4 **Give praise for the growing awareness of and focus on Uttar Pradesh** and the great needs therein among a multiplying number of churches, mission agencies and prayer networks, both national and expat. As more ministries and denominations begin to establish a presence in UP, pray for effective and Christ-honouring cooperation and partnerships.

5 **The awesome immensity of the unfinished task** should drive us to prayer.

a) The unevangelized. Were Uttar Pradesh its own country, it would have the third-largest unevangelized population in the world. There are 191 people groups that are unengaged and unreached. According to the most recent census, 579 of 613 people groups had no Christians at all. This single state of India probably represents the most intense concentration of unevangelized people and groups in the world, and thereby the greatest mission challenge.

b) The Brahmin, Rajput and Ahir together number 22 million in Uttar Pradesh. They and other high castes despise Christianity because of its links with Dalits. The Church offers little to those in such privileged positions; pray for them to become acutely aware of their need for the salvation that comes through Jesus alone.

c) Muslims are a large minority of over 35 million. Most are from the Shaikh, Pashtun and Ansari groups. There is a history of religious violence between them and the Hindu majority, exacerbated by Hindu extremist mobs and Muslim extremist bombers. Growing numbers of Christian agencies seek to reach Muslims. Some humble first fruits have emerged, but results are yet meagre.

d) Students represent a great opportunity and challenge. UESI(**IFES**) has over 40 student groups for the 32 universities and 2,000-plus colleges. Pray for the multiplication of these groups and of the 10 full-time workers. The roles of GSCC and Allahabad Christian University in developing student ministry are significant.

Uttarakhand

Geography 🌐

Area 54,000 sq km. On the south slopes of the Himalayas.
Population 10,077,402; 185 people/sq km.
Capital Dehradun 550,000.

Peoples 👪

People groups 446. Ten largest: Rajput (Hindi, 31.9% of state pop); Brahmin (Hindi, 15.4%); Silpkar Hindu (Nepali-Pahari, 9.6%); Chamar (Hindi, 5.1%); Shaikh (Bengali, 3.5%); Bania (Rajasthan, 1.6%); Teli Muslim (Urdu Muslim, 1.5%); Jat Sikh (Jat, 1.4%); Ansari (Urdu Muslim, 1.4%); Kahar (Hindi, 1.3%).
Languages Official: Hindi, Kumaoni, Garhwali, Sanskrit.

Religion 🙏

Hindu 85.0%; Muslim 11.9%; Sikh 2.5%; Christian 0.3% (0.6%); Buddhist 0.1%; Jain 0.1%.

1 Freedom for Uttarakhand is only recent. Its struggle for statehood and separation from Uttar Pradesh was finally won in 2000. This upland region has two divisions – hilly Kumaon and mountainous Garhwal. The people of both identify themselves as *Pahari* (mountain people) and speak their own Indo-Aryan languages as well as Hindi. There is good potential for development, but also great need for it, especially in the hills and mountains. Pray for good governance that can bring cooperation between these two regions and languages. Pray that further freedom might be found not in statehood, but in knowing Christ.

2 Many barriers stand between the people of Uttarakhand and the flourishing of the gospel. Pray that the Lord of hosts might break down the following barriers between the people of this state and Himself:

a) *Religion and culture.* Hindus are 85% of the population. Uttarakhand is home to some of Hinduism's most holy pilgrimage sites – Haridwar (host of the Kumbh Mela), Badrinath, Kedarnath and others attract millions of pilgrims each year. A holy Sikh shrine also attracts many visitors. The people of Uttarakhand claim to be guardians of the gods' land and are therefore very resistant to the gospel. Pray that both the native peoples and the pilgrims who come seeking release from the cycle of suffering will find it in Jesus.

b) *Spiritual forces.* This region is known for mixing animism with Hinduism, especially in Gahrwal. Occult practices and magic abound among these people, with their ardent belief in the power of spirits.

c) *Caste.* Uttarakhand's population is largely upper caste, dominated by Rajput (70%) and Brahmin (20%). Christians who minister here must be fluent in Hindi and local languages and able to present the gospel in enlightened, more intellectual ways; methods used to reach oppressed Dalits and tribals will probably accomplish very little.

3 Christians officially number fewer than 35,000 out of a population of 10 million, although this is almost certainly an underestimation.

a) *Churches are represented* by a wide range of denominations, none of them very large. Methodists are the most numerous. A small but growing house church movement has made inroads in recent years. Pray for further church growth. Pray for sensitive, effective, well-supported evangelistic ministry that will draw many more to Jesus.

b) *Theological education.* Dehradun is a strong centre for Christian activity. Pray for these three theological institutions – Presbyterian Theological Seminary (PTS), Doon Bible College (DBC) and New Theological College (NTC). There are a number of smaller Bible schools, some working in English, some in Hindi. Pray for their vision of training Christian workers equipped to reach North India.

4 Specific groups in Uttarakhand presenting a mission challenge:

a) *Students* number 140,000 in 11 universities and 230 colleges. UESI(**IFES**) has groups in 10 cities of Uttarakhand.

b) *Tribal peoples* make up a small but significant minority and tend to be more responsive to the good news. The largest are Tharu, Jannsari, Buksa and Bhutia. State restrictions against foreigners contacting these groups will set responsibility at the feet of national missionaries.

c) *Muslims,* numbering 1.2 million, are largely from Shaikh, Teli, Ansari, Rajput and Hajam peoples.

West Bengal

Geography 🌐

Area 88,800 sq km. Bordering on Bangladesh (once East Bengal), from the Himalayan foothills of Darjeeling to the Bay of Bengal.
Population 93,239,044; 1,066 people/sq km. There are millions of undocumentable immigrants from Bangladesh.
Capital Kolkata (Calcutta) 5.1m, metro area up to 15.6m. **Other major city** Asansol 1.4m.

Peoples 👪

People groups 634. Ten largest: Shaikh (Bengali, 22.6% of state pop); Mahishya (Bengali, 7.6%); Yadava (Hindi, 5.0%); Brahmin (Hindi, 4.7%); Rajbansi (Bengali, 4.4%); Namasudra Hindu (Bengali, 4.1%); Bagdi (Bengali, 3.7%); Kayastha (Bengali, 3.3%); Santal (Munda-Santal, 3.2%); Pod (Bengali, 2.8%).
Languages Official: Bengali. Hindi and English also widespread. Nepali, Santali and others are used in specific regions.

Religion 🙏

Hindu 72.5%; Muslim 25.2%; Christian 0.6% (1.2%); Buddhist 0.3%; Other 1.3%.

1 **The Bengalis** number 250 million, with communities found throughout the world. The 67 million Bengalis living in West Bengal are the large majority of the state's 82million people. Globally, they are the world's largest unreached ethnic group. William Carey's pioneer work 200 years ago was among Bengalis. Carey and his successors achieved much in Bible translation and in social and economic transformation, but these achievements are now past glories; little of that legacy remains. The barriers: pride of culture, demonic powers, a spirit of independence, little adaptation of the Christian gospel to local culture and, in recent years, obstruction from the long-reigning Marxist state government. Pray for the removal of every barrier to Bengalis believing in Jesus.

2 **Christians are less than 1% of the population,** numbering 610,000 based on census figures. Nominalism remains a problem in many churches. Of Christians, 90% come from poor and marginalized communities. But hope is growing:

a) *Prayer has yielded an increased response* with significant key conversions and a new vision in some denominations to plant congregations where there are none.

b) *The number of denominations and agencies at work* is approaching 200. Some have grown very rapidly. National Fellowship, a mission that started in 1989, now has over 700 workers and volunteers. A rising number of these agencies focus on unreached areas and peoples in West Bengal.

c) *Praise God for a new colloquial Bengali Bible translation* and for the growth of Christian radio in the region.

3 **Kolkata,** once India's capital and leading city, has continued to decline since 1954 due to political instability, violent clashes because of a strong Marxist movement and economic stagnation from failure to modernize. Some growth has occurred since 2000, thanks largely to a burgeoning IT industry. The city faces huge challenges in terms of poverty, congestion and pollution; many of its population live in squalid slums. Kolkata is dedicated to and named after Kali, the Hindu goddess of destruction.

a) *There are over 150,000 Christians* in the city, but only a minority are Bengali-speaking. Pray for a multiplication of congregations alive in the Spirit.

b) *Non-Bengali immigrants* are 45% of the population. Bihari, Marwari and Oriya make up around half of these. There is little if any Christian presence or witness among them. Oriya has a Bible translation, Bhojpuri a NT, Marwari just a few portions – other Christian resources are scarce. Pray for workers and churches for each of the immigrant communities crowded into Kolkata.

c) *Street dwellers,* estimated at up to one million. At a conservative estimate, there are 100,000 street children; a number of missions work among them.

4 **The least evangelized.** The majority of West Bengal's peoples are unevangelized. There are 67 people groups that are both unreached and unengaged, 27 of them over 100,000 in population.

a) Muslims make up the vast majority of the Bengali people cluster. In West Bengal, the Shaikh number nearly 20 million. Other Muslim peoples include Pathan, Sayyid, Ansari, Kalu and Malik.

b) Hindus. There are 20 Hindu people groups each with over one million population in this state alone. Mahishya, Brahmin, Yadava, Rajbangsi, Namasudra and Bagdi each number over three million.

c) Tribal peoples, often neglected but usually responsive to the gospel. Most significant among them are Santal, Oraon, Munda and Bhumij peoples. The first three already have sizeable Christian minorities.

The Seven Union Territories

Specific mention is made here of two of the more unique Union Territories.

The other five are similar to the state of which they are enclaves: The National Capital Territory of Delhi (12.5m); Chandigarh (capital of Punjab and Haryana, 1,127,964); Dadra and Nagar Haveli (Gujarat 278,012); Daman and Diu (Gujarat 199,489) and Puducherry (Tamil Nadu 1,139,637).

---

1 **Andaman and Nicobar Islands** have 436,118 inhabitants on 38 islands in the Bay of Bengal. Over 20% of the population are Christian; over 90% of the indigenous Nicobarese are Christian. The unreached include the four isolated negrito peoples of the Andamans – only 450 people, but all mission work is forbidden among them. **GFA**, The Bible Society and others now seek to reach these and other communities. In both sets of islands, there are just over 300 people groups – nearly all are in need of outreach. Hindus comprise 69% and Muslims 8% of the population. The coasts and lower-lying islands were devastated by the 2004 tsunami.

2 **Lakshadweep** is made up of twelve coral atolls and 36 islands in the Arabian Sea. Its 32 sq kms are home to over 73,217 people. Over 98% of the population are devotedly Muslim; the rest are Hindu and Christian immigrants from the mainland. No long-term ministry to these Malayali-speaking Muslims has ever been permitted or openly attempted.

Indonesia

Republic of Indonesia

Asia

Geography 🌐

Area 1,919,317 sq km. The Republic's 17,500 islands (6,000 inhabited) stretch over 9.5 million sq km of the Indian/Pacific Oceans, with 33 provinces, 5 of which have special status. Includes the world's second-largest rain forest and vast coral reefs.

Population		Ann Gr	Density
2010	232,516,771	1.19%	121/sq km
2020	254,217,770	0.81%	132/sq km
2030	271,485,076	0.62%	141/sq km

The world's fourth most populous nation. Population density varies from Java's 1,100 people/sq km to West Papua's 6/sq km.

Capital Jakarta 9,210,000. **Other major cities** Surabaya 2.5 million; Bandung 2.4mill; Medan 2.1m; Semarang 1.3m; Makassar 1.3m; Palembang 1.2m; Tegal 1.1m; Bogor 1.0m. **Urbanites** 53.7%. **Pop under 15 yrs** 27%. **Life expectancy** 70.5 yrs.

Peoples 👪

Diverse population with over 750 distinct peoples. Politico-religious agendas mean that many non-Muslim minorities will be undercounted.
Indo–Malay 94.3%. Javanese(6) 25.5%; Sunda 13.1%; Indonesian 11.0%; Madura 6.3%; Batak(6) 3.8%; Minangkabau 2.4%; Banjar 2.5%; Bali 1.7%; Bugis 1.8%;

Aceh 1.7%; Malay 1.7%; Betawi 1.4%; Makassar 1.1%; Sasak 1.1%; Deli 0.9%; Riau 0.9%.

Chinese 3.9%. Increasingly integrated into the Indonesian majority. Less than 20% consistently use Chinese dialects. Scattered throughout the nation. Mainly urban.

Pacific Island peoples 0.6%. 258 peoples in New Guinea cluster, in West Timor, Alor, Halmahera and Papua.

Other 1.2%. Arab, Indian, European, US citizen, mixed race.

Literacy 89%. **Official language** Indonesian (Bahasa Indonesia). Its increasing use is unifying the nation and lessening the importance of smaller languages to the younger generation. **All languages** 722; 18 spoken by more than 1 million speakers; 247 spoken in Papua. **Languages with Scriptures** 29Bi 64NT 125por 150w.i.p.

Economy 📈

Growing and diverse economy based on natural gas, forest products, agriculture and textiles, with large reserves of many minerals. The service industry is the largest employer. Steady economic improvement of 30 years was significantly reduced by the Asian economic crisis of the late 1990s and to a lesser degree by the global economic crisis of the late 2000s. Recovery and further growth are hampered by political and religious instability, endemic corruption and the need for economic reform. Close to one-sixth of the population lives below the poverty line, and close to half survive on less than US$2/day. Much wealth (and disparity) in burgeoning urban areas. Environmental damage is immense, with widespread deforestation in Sumatra, Kalimantan and elsewhere. With further reform, stability and sharp leadership, Indonesia has immense economic potential. But the wrong combination of conditions could spell economic meltdown.

HDI Rank 111th/182. **Public debt** 29.3% of GDP. **Income/person** $2,239 (5% of USA).

Politics 🗡

Colonial rule by Portuguese (1511-1605), Dutch (1605-1942, 1945-49), British (1807-15) and Japanese (1942-45). The influential nationalist leader Sukarno declared independence in 1945 and was appointed president. Sukarno ruled for 20 years until deposed by General Suharto after the abortive Communist coup in 1965. President Suharto sought to bring economic growth while crushing political dissent. The 1997 economic crisis led to Suharto's downfall, following large demonstrations against the corruption and nepotism of the regime. The difficult process of restructuring and transitioning to an elected government has borne fruit with largely peaceful and successful elections in 2004 and 2009, with the voting public opting for a secular-nationalist government. The president sits over the People's Consultative Assembly, consisting of an elected House of Representatives and a smaller Regional Representative's Council. The government's stated priorities are boosting the economy, creating more jobs and stamping out corruption. The greatest threats facing Indonesia, the world's third-largest democracy, are possible interference and disruption by the previously politically involved military and the various Islamist groups throughout the country. These – combined with Indonesia's poor human rights record, religious tensions and mass relocation programmes due to overpopulation – generate tensions that could potentially boil into major violence.

Religion 🛐

Monotheism and communal peace are bases for the stated government ideology of *Pancasila*. Only six religions are officially recognized: Islam, Hinduism, Buddhism, Confucianism, Catholicism and Protestantism. Islam's strength and influence in numbers and power allow it to exert itself on the religious scene, giving itself preferential treatment and limiting Christian activities and public presence. Such power also enables the use of violence, mass demonstrations and threats to achieve its socio-political goals.

Religions	Pop %	Population	Ann Gr
Muslim	80.31	186,734,219	1.2%
Christian	15.85	36,853,908	1.6%
Hindu	1.30	3,022,718	0.6%
Ethnoreligionist	1.20	2,790,201	-3.2%
Chinese	0.90	2,092,651	1.2%
Buddhist	0.40	930,067	-1.2%
Non-religious	0.04	93,007	7.2%

Religious figures, official and unofficial, often differ widely. Muslims are officially 86%, but actually significantly less. Indonesian Muslims are split into three groups: "high identity and high practice" observant Muslims, "high identity but low practice" more nominal Muslims and "low identity and low practice" Muslims. Many in this latter group, though officially regarded as Muslim in census figures, are influenced by the Javanese mystical traditions of Kejawan/Kebatinan, which predate Islam, or they are animists who (to a greater or lesser extent) accept some of the outward aspects of Islam. Islam is strongest in Sumatra, Java and many coastal areas in the east of the country.

Animism is not officially recognized by the government but is strong among some peoples in Papua, Sumba and inland Sumatra, Kalimantan and Sulawesi, among others. Folk Islam, followed by many Indonesians, is strongly influenced by animism. Nationwide, it is a dominant spiritual force, though under siege from stricter Islamic forces.

Also, discriminatory policies cause many Chinese (Buddhists and Confucians), Hindus and Christians to remain circumspect in official polls regarding their faith.

Christians Denoms		Pop %	Affiliates	Ann Gr
Protestant	243	10.17	23,651,000	2.3%
Independent	10	0.65	1,507,000	3.1%
Anglican	1	<0.01	4,000	0.6%

Catholic	1	3.04	7,058,000	1.9%
Orthodox	1	<0.01	<1,000	3.6%
Marginal	10	0.12	283,000	1.8%
Unaffiliated		1.87	4,348,000	-3.7%

Churches	MegaBloc	Congs	Members	Affiliates
Catholic Church	C	6,925	3,878,022	7,058,000
HKPB-Batak (Luth)	P	3,300	1,950,000	3,900,000
GBI-Bethel (CoG)	P	5,652	1,130,435	2,600,000
GPI-PCdI (Pente)	P	12,700	2,081,500	2,500,000
GMIT-W Timor (Ref)	P	1,904	373,200	933,000
Assoc, Chr Foundations	I	1,875	375,000	843,750
GBI-Jakarta (Ref)	P	4,004	360,360	800,000
GMIM-Minahasa (Ref)	P	856	308,000	770,000
GKI-I-J (Ref)	P	1,364	300,000	660,000
GPIB-W Indon (Ref)	P	271	249,049	655,000
GPM-Maluku (Ref)	P	871	426,573	610,000
GIdI (Evangelical)	P	1,250	90,000	450,000
Toraja Church (Ref)	P	913	283,000	450,000
GKII (CMA)	P	1,920	202,450	385,000
HKI-Sumatra (Luth)	P	744	133,840	352,000
Pentecostal Ch of God	P	208	156,000	346,320
Seventh-day Adventist	P	1,546	201,000	335,670
BNKP-Nias (Luth)	P	573	149,099	331,000
GBKP-Karo Batak (Ref)	P	778	126,000	315,000
Assemblies of God	P	1,300	164,865	305,000
Bethel Tabernacle	I	807	121,000	302,500
GKPI-N Sumatra (Luth)	P	1,053	200,000	298,000
GKE-Kalimantan (Ref)	P	1,032	103,200	258,000
GKJ-Java (Ref)	P	750	142,515	238,000
GKPS-Simalungun (Luth)	P	545	103,604	230,000
GMI (Methodist)	P	804	112,500	225,000
GPI (Pentecostal)	P	400	85,000	223,550
GMIST-Sanghir-T (Ref)	P	352	70,492	215,000
GKS-Sumba (Ref)	P	399	79,848	210,000
GKST-Sulawesi (Ref)	P	138	65,000	195,000
GBIS (Full Gospel)	P	766	114,970	192,000
Other denominations[235]		17,378	2,533,967	5,315,966
Total Christians[266]		**73,378**	**16,670,489**	**32,502,756**

TransBloc	Pop %	Population	Ann Gr
Evangelicals			
Evangelicals	5.6	13,010,751	2.8%
Renewalists			
Charismatics	4.4	10,283,549	3.3%
Pentecostals	3.9	9,005,800	3.1%

Missionaries from Indonesia

P,I,A Estimated 3,000 long-term missionaries in about 30 agencies: 2,800 serving cross-culturally in Indonesia; 200 serving in 22 other countries.

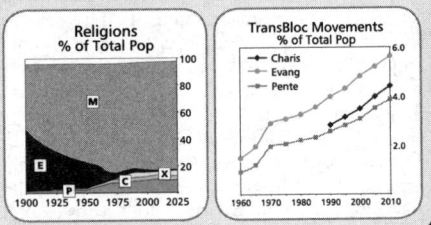

Answers to Prayer

1 **Praise God for the sustained growth** of the Church over the last 50 years. During this period, evangelicals have grown from 1.3 million (1.4% of the population) to 13 million (5.6%). Several of the following have a long–lasting legacy.

a) **Great people movements to Christ** have occurred in many animistic peoples, among three of the eight Java sub-groups and among Indonesians of Chinese descent. Over 50% of the latter are now Christian.

b) **The lives and vibrant witness of committed Christians** have made an impact on a society influenced by the power of the occult and have offered many the path to freedom.

c) **The government mandate** that all citizens adhere to one of six recognized religions impels many animists to consider the claims of the gospel.

d) **The development and use of Indonesian as the national language** make sharing the gospel across geographic and ethnic boundaries easier in many areas of the country.

2 **More recent developments** in political, religious and Church scenes are causes for thanksgiving, even if not immediately obvious points for praise. These include:

a) **The transition to true democracy,** although still in a fragile state. The more moderate government has blunted the harsh excesses of the military and of theocratic Islamists. Democracy allows moderates and Christians to have a voice and to help shape Indonesia's future, without fear of reprisal.

b) **The increasing openness of moderate Muslims** repelled by the harsh extremism of Islamists. The strict legalism of Islam also makes Christianity more attractive to animists.

c) **High levels of persecution** have caused great suffering, but also greater unity among Christians and greater dependence on God.

d) *The development of national structures* that serve and build the Indonesian Church. These include the Indonesian Peoples Network (IPN), a burgeoning national prayer network, plus international networks having an impact in Indonesia through research, intercession and mission.

Challenges for Prayer

1 **Indonesia's vast diversity** is both its strength and its peril. With 17,500 islands strewn across nearly 10 million sq km of ocean, 33 provinces, 722 languages, even more ethnic groups, myriad religious expressions and deeply divided political agendas, holding this nation together is a monumental task. Pray for political strength for the maturing democracy to stay balanced between national unity and regional identity. Pray also for the government to act with righteousness in honouring all peoples and communities; Indonesia's history, especially recently, is characterized by discrimination, exploitation and favouritism.

2 **The fledgling democratic government** faces a daunting task. Its first years were marked by powerlessness in the face of extremist demands from strident Islamists and manipulation by the powerful former regime and military. Positive signs see moderation and democracy taking root and displacing the old culture of extremism, corruption, cronyism and nepotism. There is a long way to go, however, to see political, economic and social renewal. Pray that the president, vice-president and the People's Consultative Assembly may be courageous, decisive and fair in bringing betterment to the whole nation.

3 **The mass displacement of people** within, and out from, Indonesia is massive and has many causes.

a) *The Transmigration Scheme* was one of the world's largest planned resettlements of people ever organized. Vast areas of virgin territory in Sumatra, Kalimantan, Sulawesi and Papua were opened for migrants from overpopulated Java and Bali. Over eight million were relocated. These new settlements have been difficult for the newcomers and have caused notable violent clashes between migrants and locals. Yet, among these migrants, there is an openness to the gospel.

b) *Natural disasters* – earthquakes, tsunamis and flooding – since 2001 have killed close to 200,000 and rendered millions homeless or displaced. Sumatra is the hardest hit. Indonesia lies in a geologically volatile region, which, combined with high populations and poor infrastructure, make future tragedies inevitable. Pray that Christians, both national and expatriate, may use these disasters as opportunities to demonstrate the compassion of Christ.

c) *Victims of communal violence and religious persecution,* most notably Christians from Maluku and central Sulawesi. They total more than 500,000 and must deal with profound personal loss, bitter trauma and the loss of their ancestral homelands.

d) *Migrant workers* from Indonesia to other nations, numbering 400,000 legal migrants and many more illegal ones. While there are highly educated and skilled migrants among them, many workers provide mostly unskilled domestic labour; they number over 80% female. Though their remittances garner for them the title of "foreign-exchange heroines", they often are paid poorly and are subject to abuse. Their lonely and often difficult situations open them up to loving witness by Christians.

4 **A spiritual conflict rages for Indonesia.** Ancient and strong occult powers seek to oppose the influence of the gospel, while modern Muslim stratagems seek to eliminate Christianity and remove the presence of the good news. Pray specifically for the binding of these powers and for continued growth of the Church in the midst of intense opposition and growing persecution.

5 **The creeping Islamization of Indonesia** is eroding religious freedom and the long-prevailing communal tolerance. Islam itself is remarkably varied – the *santri* puritanical Islam; the *abangan*, a more Sufist interpretation heavily influenced by pre-Islamic Javanese mysticism; the Islam of modern secular-moderate Muslims. However, it is generally the more conservative, aggressive, fundamentalist groups that continue to grow in power, partly by intimidating other Muslims into acquiescence. There are many reasons to pray:

a) *The Islamist vision* of an Indonesia without Christians generates pressure and persecution, often yielding violence, destruction and atrocities. This is manifest through:

i Domination by presence. Massive mosque-building programmes – paid for through petro-dollars – introduce a Muslim presence on every corner of the nation and are usually associated with the more radical, aggressive splinters of Islamic practice. Transmigration programmes deliberately relocate Muslims into traditionally non-Muslim areas. This is ostensibly due to overpopulation, but demonstrably includes religious colonization.

ii Domination by eradication. The aim is the complete elimination of Christianity in the country. An orchestrated Islamic jihad against Christians destroyed thousands of churches in the last decade, and some areas with large Christian populations (such as parts of Maluku) are subject to attacks. A Christian presence has been eradicated from whole towns and regions, with great loss of life and property.

Pray that these plans might be frustrated and come to ruin, that what some intend for evil God may turn out for good. Pray for their own religious hatred and violence to discredit Muslim extremism and cause many persecutors to become believers.

b) *The more than 45 million abangan Muslims* and even greater numbers of moderate and nominal Muslims are often victims of extremist intimidation. Tens of thousands of *abangan* (still influenced by pre-Islamic animism and Hinduism) have been killed over the years by Malay- and Arab-influenced *santri*. Pray for many Muslims to grow disillusioned with the violence and oppression – so that they may seek a true relationship with God through Christ.

c) *The secular government and national leaders* require great courage to actually oppose the excesses of the Islamist agenda. Pray that they would intervene to stop religious violence when it occurs; pray that they would be strong enough to withstand and even to limit the influence extremists exert over the country.

d) *The courts, legal systems and constitution* still guarantee religious freedom and offer the foundation for a stable, diverse society. Shari'a-inspired laws are being passed in more and more communities and even in entire provinces. This imposition of such religious apartheid spells disaster for non-Muslims.

e) *The Christian response* to Islamic aggression is as crucial as the aggression itself. Pray for Christians to respond with tact and love, but also firmness, and in all ways to commend the gospel. Pray that fear of witnessing might be replaced by courage to share about Jesus. Pray also for heartfelt repentance among all Christians for the ways they have damaged their witness by attitudes and actions of enmity and reprisals toward Muslims.

6 The challenges within the Church are no less serious than those outside it. While praising God for Christian growth, pray also for the overcoming of these weaknesses:

a) *Nominalism* has blighted the Church in areas that have been Christian for centuries: Manado in North Sulawesi, North Sumatra, West Timor and Maluku. Many denominations are spiritually lifeless and riddled with carnality, internal politics, divisions and active practice of indigenous occultism. These bodies need renewal and revival with many having a true conversion experience.

b) *The failure of discipleship.* For those seeking the Lord and for new believers, there are too few teachers and disciplers. Many traditional Churches have little idea how to adequately disciple those in their midst. Rapid growth of newer Pentecostal and charismatic churches often outpaces the capacity of leadership to put in place good discipleship principles. The availability of Scripture and teaching in a language ordinary people understand will make a huge difference in the area of discipleship.

c) *Theological error in the Church.* Beyond forms and structures that encourage nominalism, inadequate teaching has led to a multiplicity of errors, to syncretistic Christianity loaded with occultism and animistic thought patterns and to controversy over "prosperity" theology.

d) *Foreign expressions of Christianity* for an Indonesian context. What may work for Christians in the West or in Singapore might not be ideal in all of Indonesia. Large mega-churches are springing up in Jakarta, as are outside forms and styles of church and worship. These have the potential to strengthen or to hinder the Church's growth in Indonesia. Pray for wisdom for Indonesia's Christians, that they might adopt what is both biblical and most useful for their own context, and leave that which is not.

e) *New believers from a Muslim background* often face rejection and persecution (including violence and occasionally martyrdom) for following Jesus. They can also find it difficult to fit into the existing Christian culture and church structure they encounter. Pray for households to come to Christ as a unit and to find healthy expressions of faith within their communities and cultures.

7 The need for mature, spiritual church leaders has never been greater. The importance of developing pastors is heightened by rapidly multiplying Pentecostal/charismatic churches. The pastor plays a significant role in Reformed and Lutheran traditions from the Netherlands and Germany. The ability to train and equip quality leaders, however, is far outstripped by the need for them. Pray for:

a) *The development of effective lay leadership.* Only 40% of congregations in the Communion of Churches in Indonesia (PGI) have a pastor. Trained lay leadership is therefore essential.

b) *Continuing training and discipleship* for church leaders in general and pastors in particular. Many pastors have been serving faithfully despite inadequate preparation; many need training (or re-training), new zeal and, in some cases, to be born of the Spirit for the first time.

c) *Theological education and training* are vital needs. Pray for these:

   i *The Bible schools* that focus on training pastors for ministry. These are usually less academic, focused on effectively teaching and discipling pastors. Many of these are evangelical and often provide pastors for rural congregations.

   ii *The more than 100 degree-level seminaries* and 22 Christian universities, the majority of which are not evangelical. Pray for an increase in the number of evangelical faculty members and pastors in the large and influential regional Lutheran and Reformed seminaries and universities especially.

   iii *The 11 evangelical seminaries* relating to the Asian Theological Association as well as those in PASTI and PESRATPIM – evangelical and Pentecostal associations, respectively. All are bulging with students and potential. Pray for an outflow of life through graduates to old and new churches and to the mission fields of Indonesia and beyond.

   iv *A notable example of how academic and practical trainings combine successfully* is ETSI, whose graduates claim to have planted over 6,000 churches since 1979, almost all among predominantly Muslim peoples. ETSI has 33 satellite campuses. They focus on academics and require each student to minister in a village and plant a church before graduation.

d) *The spiritual quality and commitment* of current pastors and spiritual leaders to be high. This is even more vital than discipling and recruiting new pastors and spiritual leaders. Pray especially that current developing leaders might have a willingness to go to the harder areas of the country for Jesus' sake.

8 A vision for the evangelization of Indonesia grows even as the opposition increases, joining ecumenical, Pentecostal and evangelical Protestants in a common vision. Nearly 100 million people can be regarded as unevangelized. From 1996 onward, national and regional consultations have focused on unreached Indonesian peoples. Excellent research by the Indonesian Peoples' Network continues, and Indonesian ministries placing workers among these peoples have significantly increased. Pray for the attainment of these visions:

a) *A viable witnessing church* for every people group in the country. In Indonesia, there are 128 people groups larger than 10,000 people with a Christian population of under 1% – these account for 60% of the country's population. About 30 of these have no known believers or full-time workers. Another 200 or more unreached people groups have less than 10,000 people. Pray that the Indonesian Church may take the lead as expatriate workers partner with them.

b) *A church in every village.* The vision of many is to see at least one church planted in each of Indonesia's 76,000 villages within one generation. Over 45,000 villages still lack a single church.

c) *A unified Indonesian prayer movement* with a prayer group in every neighbourhood, linked into prayer networks in every city and province. This is quickly becoming a reality as God blesses the burgeoning national prayer network, formed in 1990 and now spread to over 450 cities.

9 Pray for the development of a missionary vision. The history and background of Indonesian Christianity are unique. Indonesians are able to make a significant contribution to world evangelization. Pray for:

a) **Churches to be gripped by the challenge** of hundreds of unreached peoples in their own country and in other lands of Asia and Africa. The financial and human resources are there. Denominations will need to work together on an unprecedented level.

b) **The sending out of Christians** – individuals, teams and communities – as migrants to unevangelized areas with a vision for church planting. Christians need to be set free from tribalism, denominationalism and local loyalties, and learn to be sensitive to the subtleties of ministering cross-culturally.

c) **Indonesian missionary agencies** are increasing in number. Most are involved in evangelistic and church-planting ministries within Indonesia, and a few have workers outside the country. Also, some Indonesians serve with international missions (**YWAM, WEC, OM**, Navigators and others).

d) **Training and strategy issues** are vital for such a vision to be accomplished. Changing the mindset of ordinary Christians – and theological students in particular – to become more missional is crucial. Vocational training that will allow believers to meaningfully contribute to unreached communities in sensitive and hostile areas is also needed.

10 **Young people** represent an untapped potential for both harvest field and harvest force. Around one-third of the population are under 18 years of age. Pray for:

a) **Students in universities.** They number 3.5 million in over 2,300 higher education institutions. A number of specialized agencies have extensive ministry on campuses (Navigators, **IFES, CCCI** and others). The **IFES**-linked student movement PERKANTAS has groups in over 50 cities. Islamic universities are rapidly growing in number and in influence. A significant minority of Indonesians study overseas, many in open nations – pray that they may be reached in other lands. Others are attracted by scholarships to study in Saudi Arabia.

b) **School children.** Forty percent of kids never make it to middle school. Children at Risk, Compassion International, Child Evangelism Fellowship, Awana, and Kids' EE as well as denominations such as **CMA** work together to bring the gospel to the children of Indonesia. Many are at risk. Nearly three million are child labourers, often in dangerous jobs and, every year, thousands of others are trafficked for more nefarious purposes.

11 **The work of missions has been blessed of God** despite the obstacles of geography, bureaucracy and the spirit world. Stand with these brothers and sisters in the battle for:

a) **Visas,** which are very difficult for foreign missionaries to get. Only those who work among animists or in theological education are able to acquire visas. Pray for doors to open for those whom God is calling to this nation.

b) **Innovative ministry alternatives** for those seeking to live a committed Christian life and witness in Indonesia – as business professionals, teachers, students, in aid and relief and such. Pray for effective cooperation among those focused on incarnating the gospel among unreached peoples.

c) **Missionaries serving in animistic areas** of West Kalimantan, Papua and Maluku where young churches are developing to maturity. Church/mission relationships must be covered in prayer.

d) **The great lack of missionaries** in Sumatra, Nusa Tenggara Barat and Sulawesi needs to be filled. Pray that no island may remain unserved by national or international gospel workers.

e) **The wide variety of international mission organizations** working in Indonesia. Major ministries include teaching, theological training, assisting in training Indonesian missionaries, working for relief and development and supporting Indonesian media ministries such as literature and radio. Pray for more Asian missionaries to come to Indonesia.

12 **Supportive ministries:**

a) **Bible translation.** The Bible Society, Wycliffe and other groups are involved in 150 translation projects across the country. The rapid reduction in expatriate visas has severely hampered the progress on many translations. Pray for their speedy completion. Pray also for the Indonesian Bible translation agency, *Kartidaya*, and for the calling and training of many Indonesian translators. Despite the increasing use of Indonesian, this nation is one of the major unmet Bible-translation challenges in the world today, having 414 languages with definite or possible needs. The prevalence of an oral culture among many of Indonesia's peoples means that Bible storying is important and in need of further development.

b) *Literature.* There is an insatiable appetite for good Christian literature, but too little is widely available at a price people can afford. Numerous Indonesian organizations and international missions have extensive printing and publishing ministries. Most are primarily focused on providing books and other resources for Christians and churches. Some are focused on outreach and evangelistic follow-up. Pray for the provision of literature to meet the need, especially literature written by Indonesians and more appropriate for the local context. An Indonesian New Testament, using religious terminology with which the majority of Indonesians are familiar, is proving very helpful in opening doors of understanding and in discipling new believers.

c) *Missionary flying.* This is a boon to Christian workers in this huge, rugged island nation, but it is costly and dangerous. Indonesia is **MAF**'s greatest global effort with 22 aircraft, including floatplanes, serving isolated villages. Missionary work in some areas of Kalimantan, Sulawesi and Papua would be nearly impossible without it. **WT**, HeliMission, Adventist Aviation and others also have flying programmes. Pray for the staff and for the safety of the planes.

d) *The JESUS film* is completed in 38 languages. Pray for wisdom to decide which of the hundreds of smaller remaining languages should be translated, as well as for qualified translators. Pray that small groups of new believers will form as a result of viewing the film.

e) *Practical ministries.* In the last few years, programmes for community development, health, education and relief have grown. These all provide opportunities for sharing the gospel. Agencies include WVI, Christian Reformed World Relief, AMG, **YWAM**, Tearfund and many others.

f) *Christian radio.* With dense rainforests separating rural communities and a shortage of pastors, radio is an imperative method for reaching and discipling Indonesians. Up to 50% of the population listen to religious programmes at least once a week. Praise God for the work of **TWR**, whose programmes are broadcast over 121 stations, AM and FM. **FEBC** trains hundreds of new broadcasters to share the good news and reaches out to those in emergency situations.

g) *Audio ministry.* Over 518 languages and dialects are now recorded; the goal of **GRN** is 560. The widespread use of Indonesian makes many insensitive to the need for the gospel in the heart language of the people. Languages with audio Scriptures: 20Bi 38NT 77por. Pray for more helpers to get the recordings into the hands of those who need to hear the gospel in their heart language.

h) *New media.* With a young population and burgeoning modernization and urbanization, effective use of media such as the Internet, TV and mobile phones is essential for Kingdom purposes.

The Islands of Indonesia

Each major island or island archipelago is so unique and complex that some of the more significant are handled separately – from west to east.

Sumatra

Geography 🌐

Area 473,000 sq km. The world's sixth-largest island. A vast potential storehouse of minerals and agricultural produce, but much is untamed jungle, swamp and volcanic mountains, often with poor soil and poorer surface communications. Irresponsible exploitation of natural resources is causing serious environmental damage.

Population 48,812,000 in 10 provinces: Bengkulu; Jambi; Lampung; Riau; Riau Islands; Bangka-Belitung; North, South and West Sumatra; and the special autonomous district of Aceh. 103 people/sq km.

Peoples 👪

Major indigenous peoples: Aceh, Batak, Minangkabau, Lampung-Komering and many Melayu (Malay) sub-groups such as Deli, Riau, Jambi and Palembang, plus many others. There are also many Javanese, Chinese and other peoples who are not indigenous.

Religion 📖

Official figures (2005): Muslim 87%; Christian 10% (Protestant 9%, Catholic 1%); Buddhist 2%; Hindu 1%.

1 **Sumatra is prone to natural disasters,** since it lies in a geologically volatile area. The earthquake and tsunami in 2004 killed over 200,000 – mostly in Aceh – and rendered 500,000 people homeless. Further tragedies are inevitable. Meanwhile, ruthless logging threatens the environment, the traditional lifestyles of many peoples and a large number of critically endangered species. Pray that wise government will curtail the destruction occurring in the name of greed and that responsible planning will minimize loss of life in future earthquakes and floods.

2 **Sumatra is the largest unevangelized island on earth.** Most of its largest people groups are staunchly Muslim; many others practice folk Islam. If it were a nation, only nine other nations would have more unreached peoples. There are many spiritual strongholds to be broken.

Of its 49 unreached peoples, at least 29 have no indigenous church and eight still have no known gospel workers. Most Muslims have had little or no exposure to the person of Jesus, and most peoples have never had a long-term gospel presence in their midst. Some have access to a NT, the JESUS film, Christian radio, audio ministry or even local witness, but many have none of these.

3 **Christianity is strong among formerly animist peoples,** the only areas where the Dutch colonial administration allowed mission work. These are:

a) *The Batak-Nias people cluster* consisting of 13 peoples and totalling 9.4 million, the vast majority of them in Sumatra. The Bataks (Toba, Dairi, Karo and Simalungun) are all 70% or more Christian. Most of the Angkola and Mandailing are Muslim with only a small minority of Christians. The Batak are a dynamic and successful people who have migrated all over Indonesia, yet their ethnic pride and strong adherence to old customs combine with frequent enmity with Sumatran Muslim peoples to hinder Bataks' effectiveness as cross-cultural witnesses. The Nias and Mentawai live on islands off Sumatra's west coast. Lutherans are by far the largest denomination, but sadly, nominalism prevails and animistic and occultic practices are widespread.

b) *The Chinese* are in most cities, but in Medan, capital of North Sumatra, Chinese are up to 20% of the population and operate 60% of the businesses. There are Buddhists, Confucians, even Hindus as well as many Christians. Significant ministry still occurs among the Chinese. Pray that these Christians may experience revival and break out of their ethnic cocoons to become effective witnesses to the non-Christian peoples around them.

4 **Pray for the unreached:**

a) *The 3.5 million Aceh people* are very strongly Muslim and have been influential in spreading Islam to other Indonesian peoples. Unrest and violence associated with an independence movement plagued the province for over 300 years. A peace treaty was signed in 2005, with Aceh made into a special territory having significant autonomy. The devastation of the 2004 tsunami drew many Christian aid and relief organizations to the area. The differing approaches of agencies for demonstrating God's love while offering assistance caused some problems with the strict Muslims; some encouraging fruit has come from these efforts. The Aceh NT was published in 1992.

b) *The smaller people groups of northern Sumatra.* Simeulue Island is 100% Muslim. It was hard hit by the tsunami, but aid has brought roads, an airport, a hospital, new homes and dissatisfaction with a subsistence lifestyle. The Gayo are folk-Islamic and grow coffee high in the mountains. The folk-Islamic Tamiang have no known believers. The Mandailing are proud to have almost no Christians among their group, while the Angkola group is 3-5% Christian.

c) *The Minangkabau-Rejang people cluster.* The 8.1 million matrilineal Minangkabau of West Sumatra are well educated, widely travelled and successful – as well as being devoted Muslims. There may be 500-1000 believers at most. The 350,000 Rejang and the 300,000 Kerinci practice folk Islam, with magic having great influence. They have little to no Christian resources in their languages, and believers between them number less than 200.

d) *The Malay-related peoples of Eastern and Southern Sumatra,* including the Deli (2.1m), Melayu Riau (2.1m) and Jambi (1m). There are several dozen believers among the first two groups, but these have almost all moved away from their communities or distanced themselves culturally. The Jambi are among Indonesia's least-evangelized people with only a handful of Christians, all of whom live outside the Jambi region.

e) *The Muslim peoples of Central and South Sumatra* are all without a congregation of believers, despite increasing outreach. There are a handful of believers among the Batin, Bengkulu, Enim and Lembak, but none at all among the Kaur, Lematang, Ogan and Semendo.

f) *The peoples of Lampung in the south.* The indigenous peoples are resentful of newcomers from Java. No churches are known among the indigenous Lampung Peminggir (500,000), Komering (450,000), Lampung Abung (180,000) or Lampung Pubian (100,000). There are churches among the many Java transmigrants in the area, and some ministry among these groups. Translation of the Bible into Lampung is underway.

Java

Peoples 👪

Major peoples: Javanese, Sundanese, Madurese.

Geography 🌐

Area 132,200 sq km. Fertile, volcanic soil. Several active volcanoes.
Population 136,800,000; 59% of Indonesia's population. 1,034 people/sq km. Economically, culturally and politically dominant in Indonesia.

Religion 🙏

Muslim more than 90%; Christian more than 5% (Protestant two-thirds, Catholic one-third); Buddhist 0.8%; Hindu 0.2%.

1 **Praise God for the longstanding receptivity** to the gospel of the Javanese people and Indonesians of Chinese descent. In spite of economic woes, socio-political upheaval, military oppression and religious persecution, the Church on Java continues to grow. Nearly 50% of the Chinese-descent Indonesians and about 5% of Javanese profess to be Christian – ranging greatly depending on which Javanese subgroup. Pray that such growth might not be stymied, but rather would continue to flourish in its difficult but fruitful conditions.

2 **Java's historic religious diversity and tolerance** face many threats. The pluralism and tolerance of Indonesia's past seem a fading memory. *Santri* Muslims are more aggressive and confrontational, not just against other religions, but against the less orthodox variants of Islam as well. Persecution takes shape most commonly in obstructionist laws that prevent Christians from building, and – with alarming acceleration – that cause the destruction of churches and Christian property. Pray that persecution will purify and grow the Church, and that the strident harshness of *santri* will impel many to consider the person of Jesus.

3 **Christians of many traditions are drawing together** as never before, uniting in prayer, worship, mutual support and information sharing throughout Java. Loving action by Christians continues to draw many Muslims to Christ, even amid persecution and destruction of church buildings. This is a time of harvest! The Christian response to needs in the aftermath of recent floods and earthquakes has been a powerful testimony. Likewise, the deliberate transformational approach of focusing ministry on the marginalized and most needy – orphans, lepers, AIDS victims, the mentally unstable and those in squatter communities in "unclean" cemeteries – has a powerful effect. Pray for greater momentum in reaching out to the much less evangelized in small towns and rural villages.

4 **Jakarta and the other urban centres** of Surabaya, Bandung and Semarang are key cities for the evangelization of Indonesia. Almost every ethnic group has a presence in Jakarta. Many Ambonese/Maluku, Minahasa, Batak, Dayak, Toraja and Timor Christians migrated to Jakarta, often displaced by economic pressures or even persecution. Jakarta is now over 13% Christian, with diverse expressions of Christian faith and practice. As with Jakarta's massive wealth and influence in the economic realm, a spiritual movement here is impacting the whole country. Megachurch structures, some seating 10,000, are going up in Jakarta. Some consider these to be foreign and unnecessarily provocative; others argue that they can provide their own security and that they symbolize the determination and boldness of the Church. A grassroots cell church movement is also multiplying and maturing. Pray that God might use the dynamic Christian presence in Jakarta to impact all of Indonesia.

5 **The major unreached people groups,** however, are traditionally resistant and usually neglected:

a) *The Javanese ethnic sub-groups* of 2% Christian or less include: Banten (570,000), concentrated in the northwestern part of the island; Banyumasan (5.8m), located along the south central coast; Osing (490,000), living on the extreme eastern tip; Pasisir Kulon (3.4m) and Pasisir Lor (23.3m), populating the north central coastline. All of these are staunchly Muslim, with very small numbers of believers, despite the significant response to the gospel of millions of Javanese Christians in the other three Javanese sub-groups.

b) *The 34 million Sunda live in West Java.* They profess Islam but are highly influenced by underlying animism and traditional Sunda beliefs. They are one of the largest unevangelized groups in the world, with only 0.08% Christian. Christian Sunda number about 25,000, but some are nominal and culturally isolated from the Muslim majority. There is a dearth of workers, of suitable literature and of radio programme airtime. Interest in the gospel is increasing, and contextualized methods that respect the culture see some success. But Islamic missionaries also work among them, to "purify" nominal Muslims and make them faithful to a stricter observance. Pray for a breakthrough that sees a church planting movement among the Sundanese.

*c) **The Madura are concentrated in East Java,*** but have been transmigrated elsewhere, often with violent repercussions. In the province of East Java, Madura peoples live both on Java and on two smaller adjacent islands just to the north: Madura and Bawean. They are comprised of the main group of Madurese (7m), the Bawean (86,000), the Kangean (110,000) and the Pendalungan (7.5m) – the latter being the offspring of Java-Madura intermarriages since 1671. Staunchly Muslim but also influenced by magic, they have a reputation for anger and violence. Pray that Christians may overcome their fear and antagonism to embody Christ's love to them.

*d) **The Java Tengger people*** living on the slopes of Mount Bromo in East Java continue to resist Islamic inroads. Instead, they are experiencing a Hindu resurgence through cooperative efforts with Balinese Hindu religious workers. However, several Tengger Christian groups have emerged in the area. And over the last 25 years, a Tengger Church and leadership have developed; pray for their long-term viability.

Bali

Geography 🌍
Area 5,633 sq km. Fertile, volcanic soil. Several active volcanoes.
Population 3,555,000; 630 people/sq km.

Peoples 👪
Major peoples: Bali.

Religion 🙏
Hindu 90%; Muslim 7%; Christian 1.5%; Buddhist/Chinese/Other 1.5%.

I

---

1 **A unique blend of Hinduism dominates** the spiritual landscape of Bali. There are 49,000 Hindu temples on Bali. Protestant churches number over 100, Catholic churches 35. City churches tend to be less than 50% Balinese. With strong aspects of occult, magic and Spiritism running through the island and its people, Bali needs the liberating power of the gospel. One million Balinese people live on the neighbouring islands of Sumatra, Sulawesi and Lombok; these Balinese migrants tend to be more open to the gospel.

2 **Balinese Christians are few.** The cost of discipleship is high, and converts to Christ often face ostracism, persecution and financial loss – even the loss of inheritance and land ownership rights – when they break with their family and community's way of life. Pray for the witness of Christians, which has great impact in leading others to make a decision.

3 **The Balinese Bible** was published in 1990. Its use is limited because most do not understand its "high caste" language. The JESUS film is also in this language, as are audio recordings of the NT and The Jesus Story. Pray for effective communication of God's Word to all Bali's peoples. Both **TWR** and **FEBC** broadcast to Bali.

4 **The unique culture of Bali,** combined with the island's beauty, attracts millions of tourists. These foreigners can bring the gospel, godless hedonism, material wealth to uplift the island's economy or any number of other influences. Pray that the intermingling of foreigners and Balinese might serve to make both groups aware of their need for the gospel.

West Lesser Sunda Islands (Nusa Tenggara Barat)

Geography 🌐
Area 20,177 sq km. The islands of Lombok and Sumbawa. **Population** 4,520,000; 225 people/sq km.

Peoples 👪
Major peoples: Sasak, Sumbawa, Bima.

Religion 🙏
Muslim 96%; Hindu 3%; Buddhist 0.7%; Christian 0.2% (Protestant 0.1%, Catholic 0.1%).

1 **These staunchly Muslim island peoples** are some of the least evangelized in Indonesia and are among the least developed. The 22,000 Protestants are mainly immigrant peoples in the towns (Javanese, Timorese, Chinese Indonesians).

2 **Unreached peoples include:**

a) The Hindu Bali people – more than 100,000 on Lombok and probably more open to the gospel than on their home island.

b) The three major indigenous people groups remain largely unevangelized amidst ongoing efforts to reach them for the past 20 or more years, although greater responsiveness is also reported. They are: Muslim Sasak (2.75m) on Lombok, and Bima (650,000) and Sumbawa (400,000) on Sumbawa Island. There are less than 200 known believers among the Sasak, less than 100 among the Bima and less than 20 among the Sumbawa. All three groups are strongly Muslim but still adhere to animistic beliefs. Several second- and third-generation house fellowships have formed among the Bima and Sumbawa.

3 **Two small churches,** founded by **CMA** in the 1940s in the area of Bima, have approximately 100 believers but struggle to survive, since many young people convert to Islam in order to get married.

4 **Scriptures are being translated** into the Sasak, Bima and Sumbawa languages. **FEBC** broadcasts 3.5 hours per week in Sasak. The JESUS film is available in Sasak and Bima.

East Lesser Sunda Islands (Nusa Tenggara Timor)

Geography 🌐
Area 47,876 sq km. The islands of Sumba, Flores, Lomblin, Alor and West Timor. **Population** 4,455,000; 93 people/sq km.

Peoples 👪
Major peoples: Timor, Manggarai, Solar, Lio, Rote, Sikka, Sumba.

Religion 🙏
Christian 90% (Catholic 57%, Protestant 33%); Muslim 8%; Hindu 1%; Traditional ethnic 1%.

1 **Flores is 80% Catholic** but steeped in pagan and idolatrous rituals sometimes involving snake worship. Born-again Christians are very few and largely Timorese. No language of Flores has Scripture. The Manggarai (660,000) – around half are Muslim and half are animist – are the largest group in the Flores-Sumba-Alor people cluster. Pray for spiritual breakthrough for the Manggarai and others to encounter the power and love of Jesus.

2 **Sumba, an island long known for its animism** and resistance to the gospel, saw a movement of the Spirit in the late 1980s, with Protestants doubling from 75,000 to 160,000 in five years. Pray that this movement may impact all seven language groups on the island; nearly one-third are still animists while many Christians, both Reformed and Catholic, are nominal.

③ West Timor:

a) *A great outpouring of the Spirit* in 1965-68 resulted in renewal within the Church and thousands of conversions. About 20% of Timorese were converted; the vast majority stayed with their faith through the decades, despite the changes those decades brought.

b) *The wide-scale killing and destruction* that followed East Timor's (Timor Leste) vote to become independent of Indonesia resulted in a number of refugee camps holding thousands of people in West Timor. Today, the remaining camps are populated by ex-militia and their families who cannot go back to Timor Leste. Hundreds of these families are involved in prayer and Bible study groups. Pray that this development would grow and impact many more lives.

c) *Sabu people on Sabu Island and West Timor* (130,000) are predominantly professing Christians. A significant minority still practice animism; Sabu is a spiritual battleground. There is great hunger for the limited Scriptures available in the local language.

d) *The Ambenu Timor and Belu Tetun in West Timor* are largely Catholic. Most are nominal, but God is at work among a notable minority of believers.

④ **The lack of Scriptures** for the languages of the two Lesser Sunda Provinces is a major reason for the lack of progress of the gospel. Only a handful of the 65 languages have a NT, but The Seed Company is participating with national translation teams in 20 different translation projects. A facility for training and translation work is a felt need. The increasing availability of Scripture in indigenous languages is generating a revolution in the life of Christians here. Pray for the completion of the projects and the widespread use of the finished translations, bringing long-term spiritual transformation to the different language groups.

Kalimantan

West, Central, East and South Kalimantan. 24 people/sq km.

Geography 🌐
Area 539,000 sq km. The Indonesian three-quarters of the island of Borneo, shared with Malaysia and Brunei. An island of tropical rain forest and rivers, but few roads.
Population 12,774,000 in four provinces –

Peoples 👪
Major peoples: Banjar, Dayak, Javanese.

Religion 🙏
Muslim 73%; Christian 21%; Hindu 2%; Buddhist 2.5%; Traditional ethnic 1.5%.

---

① **The indigenous peoples of Kalimantan** number 2.8 million in the Borneo-Kalimantan and Barito people clusters, comprised mostly of Dayak peoples. They represent 65 peoples and many more sub-groups and speak a range of nearly 80 languages and numerous dialects. Although many retain their animist beliefs and some have converted to Islam, Christians are a majority in many groups and a sizeable minority in most. Church growth remains high but often without a clear break from the spirit world.

a) *The CMA work in East Kalimantan* resulted in a strong Church among the 10 or more Kenyah and Kayan peoples as well as outreach to other ethnic groups as far as South Kalimantan.

b) *In Central Kalimantan,* many of the Ngaju and Ma'anyan are linked with the Reformed Church, founded through the work of the Rhenish and Basel Missions.

c) *West Kalimantan* has been a major field for **CMA**, WorldVenture and World Outreach. Others such as **WEC** and World Team have handed extensive work over to the national Church and to indigenous missions (such as YPPII), which are thriving in their own right. Some Dayak sub-groups have been more difficult to win, and many of the Dayaks who profess Christianity need a more personal encounter with Jesus.

② **Leadership training is a definite need** as the Church grows, but illiteracy, poverty, geographic isolation and lack of indigenous Scriptures have all slowed development. There are a number of Bible schools. Pray for churches to mature and have a vision for outreach; pray also for expressions of Christian faith to be culturally resonant and appropriate.

3 **The unreached** – although Kalimantan has many Christian peoples, dozens of groups remain largely untouched by the gospel.

a) *The large Kalimantan Malay people cluster* of 4.5 million is dominated by the Banjar, at 3.5 million and one of Indonesia's least-evangelized peoples. They live along the eastern and southern coasts and up the rivers; they devotedly practice Islam with strong animistic elements. Increasing numbers of individuals, churches and groups have begun to pray for and reach out to them. Converts are few, and almost all those who follow Christ have to live as secret believers. Pray for entire families to come to Christ and to be able to remain as witnesses in their communities.

b) *Transmigrants* number over one million. These are Javanese (nominally Muslim), Balinese (Hindu), Bugis and Madurese (strongly Muslim). They live in transmigrant settlements and oil-boom towns in the east. Only among the Javanese are there growing churches, but they have little vision for outreach to other groups. In the late 1990s, Dayak resentment of the high-handedness of Madurese transmigrants in West Kalimantan boiled into violence, with hundreds massacred and thousands displaced. Pray that local nominal Christians may overcome their anger – as well as cultural and religious barriers – to reach out in love to transmigrant groups.

c) *Animist peoples of the interior* present a challenge. They are predominantly of Dayak origin. The least reached of these are the Barito cluster, including the Bakumpai, Siang and Ampunang. The complexities of reaching such isolated tribal groups are immense and living conditions difficult. Medical and educational work and ministry with orphans are all potentially fruitful. Praise God for **MAF**'s valuable aviation ministry that allows access to these areas. Pray for more pioneers willing to reach out to these hard-to-access but receptive peoples.

d) *The Chinese-descent Indonesians,* 20% of the population in West Kalimantan, prove less responsive to the gospel than elsewhere, though many are nominally Christian. Pray for the witness of Chinese Christians and for churches on the coast, in Pontianak and up the Kapuas River.

I

Sulawesi

Geography 🌏

Area 191,800 sq km. A large, orchid-shaped mountainous island, stretching 1,300 km from north to south. Also many satellite islands. Formerly called Celebes.
Population 16,850,000 in six provinces – Central, West, North, South, Southeast Sulawesi and Gorontalo. 88 people/sq km.

Peoples 👪

Major peoples: Bugis, Makassar, Mongondow, Gorontalo, Toraja.

Religion 🙏

Muslim 75%; Christian 20% (Protestant 17.5%, Catholic 2.5%); Traditional ethnic 3%; Hindu 1.5%; Buddhist 0.25%.

1 **Sulawesi, the world's eleventh-largest island,** is a patchwork of more than 110 ethnic groups and of varied responses to the missionary religions of Islam and Christianity. Generally, nearly all the coastal peoples are Muslim. Christians are a majority in the northeast and in the central highlands. The main Christian ethnic groups are:

a) *The Minahasa-Sangir people cluster* (15 peoples, 2.3m), the largest of which is the Mongondow (1.25m). They have been mostly Protestant for over 300 years. They are among the wealthiest and best-educated peoples of Indonesia and have the highest percentage of Christians. Pray that they might not become lackadaisical in the Christian faith they have held for so long.

b) *The Toraja people cluster* (20 peoples, 1.7m) mostly adhere to one of the four Reformed Churches. They need more training in living the Christian life and freedom from the traditional fears of their past. Pray for personal experiences with Christ.

All these peoples need revival. Pray that they would guard against the ingress of cults, of Islamization and of shallow, nominal Christianity. Pray also that God might use them to reach other Muslim and animist peoples in Indonesia and in neighbouring Philippines.

2 **Less-reached peoples are many,** but there are small Christian minorities in most of the larger groups. Pray specifically for:

a) The Bugis (5m) and related Makassar (2.1m) of South Sulawesi, with colonies all around the coast. Trading is their major occupation. By Indonesian standards, Islam is more orthodox among them. There are a few thousand Christians among these groups, the Makassar being one of the few significant orthodox Muslim groups responding in any numbers to the gospel.

b) The Muslim Gorontalo (more than 1m), a cluster of five Muslim-animist peoples scattered around the north, and the Bungku-Bajau cluster in the southeast. There are some small churches indigenous to these peoples, but response is slow and many areas remain untouched.

3 **Bible translation is an enormous unfinished task.** Many years have been invested in research, in surveys and now in 18 translation projects in this linguistically complex region. Pray that nothing may hinder the publication of these Scriptures; several non-Christian people groups express longing for Scriptures in their language. There are definitely more than 20 and possibly up to 100 languages with Bible translation needs. Pray for fruitful partnership between expatriate and Indonesian translation workers, and pray for the timely completion of many Scripture translations.

4 **Violent confrontations between Muslims and Christians** in the 1990s and 2000s resulted in the deaths of over 1,000 people and in violent episodes flaring up years later. Christians feel unfairly treated, victimized and disproportionately punished. Pray for a Christ-like response. Pray also for church planting and Bible translation works to push on regardless of such considerations.

Maluku

I

Geography

Area 77,871 sq km. A medley of over 1,000 small islands scattered over Indonesia's eastern seas. Two provinces: Maluku, North Maluku. **Population** 2,244,000; 29 people/sq km.

Peoples 👪

113 indigenous peoples.

Religion 👤

Muslim 70%; Christian 29.5% (Protestant 25.7%, Catholic 3.8%); Hindu 0.2%; Buddhist 0.1%; Other 0.7%.

1 **The terrible violence and ethnic cleansing** of 1999-2000 left these provinces scarred and changed forever. Growing ethnic, political and religious tensions between communities in Maluku were compounded by outside agents with wicked agendas. This eventually boiled into violence and warfare that became characterized as religiously motivated. Escalating cycles of retribution resulted in over 400 churches and many mosques being destroyed. Thousands of Islamist jihad fighters were recruited, armed and sent to Maluku to wipe out Christianity from the islands; complicit rogue army units, sent to stop the fighting, aided them. Large parts of the Christian population on the islands of Ambon, Seram, Ternate, Tidore, parts of Halmahera and others were forced to flee. As a result, over 500,000 became refugees and over 20,000 were killed. With the conflict now over and peace restored, nearly all groups are working toward peace. Pray that these efforts and attitudes might prosper and continue; some *jihadis* remain in Seram, Buru and elsewhere.

2 **The Maluku Protestant Church,** founded in 1605, is Asia's oldest Protestant denomination. Nominalism has compromised the witness of the Church, while the proportion of Muslims has grown through immigration, conversion of Maluku peoples and most notably the enforced flight of Christians to other regions. Other denominations entered Maluku and see modest growth, despite the upheaval and persecution of recent years. The arrangement of separate villages for Christians and Muslims allows peace to prosper somewhat, but believers know this is not a long-term solution for effective witness and outreach. Pray for healing for the many who suffered great trauma and loss. Pray also for their ability to lovingly witness to their Muslim neighbours, even to their former persecutors.

3 The less evangelized include:

a) Muslim peoples, including the Fordate, Geser-Gorom, Ternate, Tidore, Tulehu and numerous other smaller people groups.

b) Many island communities in South and Southeast Maluku are nominally Christian, but little evidence of faith remains. Pray for effective means of reaching them.

4 Bible translation is a challenge. The government has done much to encourage the use of the national language – a blessing for communication and evangelism. But 117 languages remain in active use in Maluku; only four have a NT, even though many of these peoples are "Christian". Translation teams are involved in 34 languages, and 64 more have definite translation needs. Pray for the continuation of translation work, which, along with other ministries, is disrupted by violence.

[West] Papua (Irian Jaya)

Geography

Area 422,000 sq km. Formerly Irian Jaya. The western half of the world's second-largest island, New Guinea (see Papua New Guinea for the eastern half). The island, known for its wild beauty, has some of the most inhospitable terrain on earth. **Population** 2,504,000; 6 people/sq km.

Peoples

238 indigenous Melanesian peoples; only the Dani of the central highlands and the Ekagi of the west-central highlands have populations over 100,000. 274 languages are spoken.

Politics

In modern times was ruled by the Netherlands until 1963, when annexed by Indonesia. Controversially split into two provinces by the national government, both with Special Autonomy status. Location of significant conflict with transmigrant Muslim groups.

Religion

Christian 68% (Protestant 51%, Catholic 17%); Muslim 26%; Traditional ethnic 5%; Other 1%.

---

1 Praise God for people movements of the last 100 years and more that have seen the majority of the 275 tribes come to Christ. Over 90% of the indigenous population are officially reckoned as Christian. Agencies labouring faithfully in these remote and challenging environments to see long-term fruit include: Pioneers, **CMA**, **WT**, **UFM**/CrossWorld, Global Interaction, **TEAM** and others.

2 The untold catastrophes of ecology and demography threaten West Papua's stability, viability and very future. Pray against:

a) The large-scale ethnic displacement happening to the indigenous peoples. The national government is facilitating the mass migration of Javanese Muslims to this more spacious region to ease the population pressure in Java and to Islamize this most Christian of Indonesia's provinces. The army has committed heavy-handed violence against the indigenous Papuans, mostly in remote areas. The Javanese immigrants often regard the indigenous Melanesian Christians with contempt; this can be seen in the economic and employment disparity between the two groups. Pray for this oppression to end. Pray that the plight of the West Papuan peoples might be made known to the world so that other governments and international bodies might force this injustice to end.

b) The over-exploitation of precious natural resources. Corrupt forces conspire to harvest huge stretches of pristine old-growth forests, taking the profits for themselves; the provincial government and native peoples rarely benefit at all. The greed of China and the West for such wood only fuels the predation. Pray that unsustainable logging would be ended and that profits for sustainable logging would go to the people who have occupied the land for centuries.

3 Strong, Bible-centred, maturely led Papuan churches are the great need as modernization, education and the outside world impact these isolated cultures. Christians must face up to the challenges of tribalism, syncretism, separatist politics and discrimination by the increasingly dominant Javanese Muslims. All these require wisdom, courage and profound faith.

4 **Missionary numbers are on the increase again** – both expatriate and indigenous Indonesians and Papuans. Most work in towns and coastal areas and serve in a wide range of ministries. More are needed who can pioneer unreached rural areas and transmigrant communities. Other pioneer areas have opened up as well in recent years.

5 **Christian aviation is essential** in this land with few roads. **MAF** has 22 planes here. WT-*Tariku*, *Yajasi* (a SIL-JAARS partner) and Helimission also have flying programmes in some of the most rigorous conditions in the world. Pray for safety; there have been bad accidents. Pray for more to be called to this ministry and for its funding. Flying costs can be high, but inland economies often depend on this.

6 **The less reached,** numbering 100 peoples – virtually all the ethnic groups have at least been located and contacted. Many of them number a mere few hundred people. Those still requiring pioneer evangelism and church planting include:

a) Small peoples east of Cenderawasih Bay, on New Guinea's "shoulder".

b) Peoples in the northern foothills of the eastern highlands.

c) Peoples in the southern foothills of the main range of mountains bisecting the island.

d) The Baliem Dani of the highlands, who have not been as responsive as the rest of the Western Dani.

e) The Mai Brat-speaking Ayamaru in the northwest, the largest of the unreached indigenes, with around 30,000 people.

7 **The transmigrants** continue to arrive (5,000 every week from Java alone), to multiply and to dominate. They have often gained land and privileges at the expense of the indigenous Papuans and care little for the injustices suffered by the people onto whose land they are moving. Transmigrants already dominate the few urban centres. Pray that God may call some Christians to boldly and lovingly bring the gospel to these people, who themselves are in a new and foreign land. The Free Papua Movement has introduced uncertainty and threats of violence against these transmigrants as well.

8 **Bible translation** for the many small language groups is an immense task. There are 31 languages with a NT, 27 with Bible portions finished, and 2 with complete Bibles. There are 40 works in progress, with a need for 120 others. Pray for:

a) The completion, publication and effective use of the NTs being translated or printed. **WBT**, The Seed Company and others are hard at work on these.

b) Cooperation between churches and agencies to have portions of Scripture translated into every vernacular still used as a primary language.

c) Mother-tongue speakers with the skills, gifts, spiritual insight and motivation to tackle the arduous task of translation.

d) The use of audio resources for Scriptures and Christian messages. For most oral cultures, there is great value in providing Scripture and evangelistic and discipleship material in audio format in the heart languages of the people. **GRN** has recordings in over 200 languages.

I

Iran

Islamic Republic of Iran

Asia

Geography

Area 1,648,196 sq km. Situated between the Caspian Sea to the north and the Persian Gulf and Gulf of Oman to the south. A central desert ringed by mountains.

Population		Ann Gr	Density
2010	75,077,547	1.19%	46/sq km
2020	83,740,317	1.06%	51/sq km
2030	89,935,691	0.63%	55/sq km

Capital Tehran 7,241,000. **Other major cities** Mashhad 2.7 million; Esfahan 1.7mill; Karaj 1.6m; Tabriz 1.5m; Shiraz 1.3m; Ahvaz 1.1m; Qom 1.0m. **Urbanites** 69.5%. **Pop under 15 yrs** 24%. Life expectancy 71.2 yrs.

Peoples 👪

Approximately 100 ethnic groups, but dominated in population by Persians and Azerbaijanis.
Iranian–Median 67.9%.
  Persian 52.4%. Persian 40.9%; Mazanderani 5.5%; Gilaki 5.5%; 22 other small groups.
  Luri-Bakhtiari 6.6%. Luri(2) 3.5%; Bakhtiari 1.5%; Laki 1.5%.
  Kurd 1.5%.
  Baloch 1.5%.
  Other Iranian-Median peoples 1.5%. Including Aimaq, Parsee, Pashtun, Tajik, Talysh.
Turkic 25.9%.
  Azerbaijani 22.2%. Azerbaijani 18.0%; Qashqai 2.3%; Khorasani Turk 1.1%; 11 other groups.
  Other Turkic peoples 3.7%. Turkmen 3.1%; 5 others.
Arab 2.3%. Iranian Arab 1.8%; 3 others.
South Asian 2.3%. Domari (Gypsy) 2.0%.
Other 0.5%. Armenian, Georgian, Jew, West European, East Asian.
Literacy 82.4%. **Official language** Persian (Farsi; Dari and Tajik are major dialects); almost all Iranians speak some form of Persian as a mother tongue or second language.

All languages 79. **Languages with Scriptures** 4Bi 6NT 7por.

Economy 🏭

Great wealth in oil and natural gas, which supply 80% of export earnings. Inefficiencies in the industry and infrastructure undermine profitability. Only 20% of the economy is in the private sector. Corruption and political-religious belligerence put off many potential foreign investors. Recent reforms (or at least attempts at such) aimed at income redistribution and job creation have not rendered sufficient change. Rapid urbanization and earlier rapid population growth created millions of jobless, young urbanites – unemployment recently peaked at 28%. Iran's strategic location – between East and West, between the Caspian Sea and the Persian Gulf – could help generate greater future economic growth.
HDI Rank 88th/182. **Public debt** 19.4% of GDP. **Income/person** $4,600 (10% of USA, in 1982 it was 18%).

Politics ⚔

The Shah was deposed in the Shi'ite Muslim Revolution, and a theocratic Islamic Republic declared in 1979. Invasion by Saddam Hussein's Iraq in 1980 consolidated the rule of the Ayatollahs. Hardship caused by the war led to a more pragmatic approach in the 1990s, which culminated in a decisive victory for Reformists in the 1997 presidential election. But Supreme Leader Ayatollah Khamanei ensured the Reformists were thwarted; their resulting inability to effect change led to the election in 2005 of hard-liner Mahmoud Ahmadinejad. His promises to improve the lot of the poor and to reinstate the original values of the revolution generally failed and led to expectation of his defeat in the 2009 election. His unexpected victory sparked massive anti-government demonstrations of an intensity, scale and longevity that surprised many. The government's response was ruthless, with thousands arrested and some sentenced to death. The opposition retreated, but still exists. Iran's determination to develop nuclear power and strong belief in this right unites almost all Iranians, but creates fear in the rest of the world despite assurances that such ambitions are for energy purposes only. The mishandling of this issue by the West could have disastrous consequences for the whole region.

Religion ☪

Shi'a Islam is the state religion, and 89% of Iranians follow this. Sunni Islam is respected and largely followed by the Turkmen, Kurd and Baloch populations. The Iranian attitude toward religion can seem contradictory – heavy-handed but laid back, very chaste in public but much less so in private. The courts have the right to impose the death sentence on male apostates and life imprisonment for female apostates. Historic religious minorities such as Jews, Zorastrians and Assyrian and Armenian Christians are recognized by the constitution, but the Baha'i are not. Effectively, Iran is a religious dictatorship where little of consequence can occur without the approval of the Mullahs.

Churches	MegaBloc	Congs	Members	Affiliates
Armenian Orthodox	O	200	150,000	200,000
Indigenous believers	I	1,000	65,868	110,000
Assyrian Ch of the East	O	65	15,000	30,000
Catholic Church	C	57	16,484	30,000
Assemblies of God	P	3	2,000	5,500
Evang Ch (Presbyterian)	P	14	1,703	3,100
Russian Orthodox	O	10	1,316	2,000
Other denominations[23]		25	1,773	4,297
Total Christians[31]		**1,374**	**254,144**	**384,897**

Religions	Pop %	Population	Ann Gr
Muslim	98.64	74,054,491	1.2%
Christian	0.51	384,897	5.1%
Baha'i	0.40	300,310	-1.2%
Non-religious	0.28	210,217	7.2%
Other	0.15	112,616	4.1%
Jewish	0.02	15,016	-1.2%

TransBloc	Pop %	Population	Ann Gr
Evangelicals			
Evangelicals	0.2	117,678	19.6%
Renewalists			
Charismatics	0.1	64,330	18.6%
Pentecostals	<0.1	5,500	6.1%

Christians Denoms		Pop %	Affiliates	Ann Gr
Protestant	21	0.02	12,000	4.3%
Independent	1	0.15	110,000	22.4%
Anglican	1	<0.01	<1,000	5.6%
Catholic	1	0.04	30,000	4.6%
Orthodox	4	0.31	232,000	-0.2%
Marginal	3	<0.01	<1,000	-0.4%

Annual Growth Rates

TransBloc Movements % of Total Pop

Answers to Prayer

1 **Disillusionment with the Islamic Revolution** still grows and spreads. Thirty years of war, economic hardship, a strict authoritarian government and lack of freedom yield widespread disappointment, especially among the younger generation. Iranians' sense of disconnectedness with their rulers – and even with their national religion – makes them exceptionally open to the gospel. The long and respectable history of Christianity in Persia, the Church's noble suffering under persecution and the natural bridges between Shi'ism and Christianity make for unprecedented opportunities for church growth. There is a great hunger for the good news and for authentic spirituality.

2 **Massive numbers have recently been coming to Jesus.** From only 500 Muslim-background believers in 1979, conservative estimates now suggest over 100,000 MBBs in Iran, a number rapidly increasing. Some, more optimistic, place this number as high as a million. Never since the 7th Century has the Church in Persia grown so fast as post-1979, and the most recent years are the most fruitful. In a country able to apply the death sentence for apostasy, this underground church multiplication is a remarkable move of the Holy Spirit. Signs and wonders, dreams and visions seem to abound.

3 **Ministry to Iranians has grown exponentially,** both inside Iran and abroad. Christian satellite-TV broadcasts and Christian websites in Persian languages are having an unprecedented impact and reach even to remote villages with the gospel. The increasing availability of Scripture – brought mostly by hand-couriers – is also very significant, as is the emphasis on training national Christians to share the good news and lead house groups. All of these fuel and sustain the remarkable growth of the Church in Iran.

Challenges for Prayer

1 **The many promises of the Islamic Revolution,** made over 30 years ago, have yet to materialize. The peace and prosperity that strict adherence to Islam was supposed to deliver have never materialized. Instead, a legacy of bloodshed, cruelty, injustice, extremism and economic deprivation discredits the conservative religious leaders and the narrow brand of Islam they promote. Repression, corruption, injustice and human rights abuses are frequent; religious leadership controls the police, army and judicial system. Strong allegations of fraud in the 2009 elections sparked widespread and continued protests, an indication of the frustration felt by millions. Pray that corruption and repression might end and a government that provides true justice and safety for all be established.

2 **Iran's political, economic and social situations are fragile** and mystify many outside observers. It is an ancient, noble and proud civilization, but one that in the modern era seems set on irritating allies and provoking everyone else. The ruling elite are as pragmatic as they are unpopular.

a) Politically, Iran has a strong regional foreign policy, seeing itself as a regional superpower. This fuels a volatile attitude toward the West and Israel, accusations of financing of terrorist groups, and expansion into the power vacuum left by the conquest of Iraq. Such actions could be attributed to the fact that, for most of the last 1,500 years, Iran has been dominated by foreign powers. It also points, at least in part, to attempts to prepare the way for the *Madhi*, the future Imam who, according to Shi'ism, will establish Islam as the global religion and will defeat the Antichrist.

b) Financial prospects do not inspire much hope, despite vast oil and gas deposits and long-stated rhetoric about empowering the poor. Steady inflation and squandered oil wealth combine with aborted or failed economic reforms to instill low confidence in the future. Unemployment rises to over 30% for those under age 30. An estimated 13 million Iranians live below the poverty line.

c) Social breakdown is evident as never before. The widespread and illegal underground party-circuit flouts Islamic values. Around 200,000 of Iran's best-educated young people emigrate every year, and 36% of Iranians aged 15-29 expressed an intention to do the same. There are nearly five million drug addicts (Iran has the highest rate of opium addiction in the world), 200,000 street children and a very large number of prostitutes. Pray that those facing pressure and hopelessness might find release and hope in Christ; there is greater openness than ever to the gospel and a great need for Christian ministry to these groups of desperate people.

Pray that Iranians' aspirations for greatness, prosperity, freedom, and even righteousness might be expressed honourably and ultimately in reverence for and worship of Jesus.

3 **Religious persecution** of certain minorities has intensified since 2005. This is particularly aimed at the Baha'i (a religion that originated in Iran but not recognized as a valid religious group), at Sufi Muslims and at Christians, especially believers from a Muslim background. According to the state, only Armenians and Assyrians can be Christian – ethnic Persians are by definition Muslim, and therefore ethnic Persian Christians are by definition apostates. This makes almost all Christian activity illegal, especially when it occurs in Persian languages – from evangelism to Bible training to publishing Scripture and Christian books. Yet the regime's harsh treatment of Christians only further fuels the flames of church growth. Pray that the body of Christ might continue to multiply and mature despite persecution.

4 **The majority of the wider Christian community** are Christian Armenians with a smaller number of Assyrians and Chaldeans. They are cultural and linguistic islands isolated in a Muslim sea. While they live in relative peace, their fear of persecution and of job and educational discrimination, as well as their desire to offer their families a more stable and promising future, drive many to emigrate, denuding Iran of the richness of communities that predate Islam by centuries. Pray for a work of the Holy Spirit in these often-nominal churches, that Jesus might shine through their lives and that they might have a burden for their Muslim neighbours.

5 **Evangelical churches** before the revolution were generally small and struggling, and they contained very few Muslim-background believers. The traumatic changes and suffering that followed the revolution gave churches a brief period of renewal, outreach, literature distribution and many conversions. Barriers among denominations broke down. The hostility of the regime toward evangelicals caused much greater interest in Christianity among Persians – Presbyterians and Assemblies of God, especially, grew as a result. Intimidation, infiltration and martyrdom of several church leaders, and pressure from the government to not welcome Muslims into services, have caused many churches to adopt house church models. Most churches that meet publicly now tow the government line and do not overtly evangelize Muslims. Pray for:

a) *Adequate income for Christians* who face poverty both from general economic decline and from religious discrimination in the workplace. Emigration is a solution for pressured Christians, but their vital witness in needy Iran is then lost. Pray that believers may break through this economic pressure and resist the temptation to leave.

b) *Courage and fortitude* such that their persecutors are won for Christ. While Armenians and Assyrians are discriminated against, Muslim-background believers are actively persecuted. Pray also for greater freedom for churches to minister, as they long to do.

c) *Protection and deliverance for all MBBs.* The large majority meet secretly in small house groups. There is always a danger that such meetings could be discovered and those involved punished, especially the leaders. A decentralized cell structure and the use of techniques honed by the underground party-circuit help house groups avoid detection and arrest.

d) *Churches outside of Tehran* often face more intimidation as fundamentalist forces exercise more control in less-urban areas. Many towns and villages lack any churches at all. However, this is changing due to the increasing influence of the Internet and satellite TV as well as the enthusiasm of young Iranian Christians to evangelize their countrymen. House church movements are spreading throughout the country.

6 **The Iranian Diaspora** is around four million. Most have found refuge in the USA, Canada, Western Europe, Turkey, Gulf States and other lands – where they can be evangelized. Western countries are making it harder for Iranians to immigrate. Pray for:

a) *Diaspora churches.* There are probably about 800 Persian-speaking Iranian churches and house fellowships, totalling around 200,000 people. Unity is frequently a challenge. Yet these diaspora Christians are highly active and generous regarding ministry into Iran and among other Iranians abroad; their contribution in this regard is crucial.

b) *Ministries reaching out to the diaspora,* providing not only evangelism tools and outreach but also church planting, discipleship and leadership training, so that Iranians living abroad will be reached and hopefully then reach other Iranians. Christian refugees fleeing from persecution are also assisted. Many diaspora Christians visit Iran and powerfully minister to their countrymen. Significant ministries include Elam Ministries, 222 Ministries, Persian World Outreach, Iran Alive Ministries and Iranian Christians International.

7 **Young people are particularly responsive to the gospel.** With nearly two-thirds of the population under age 30, with disillusionment at an all-time high and with frustrated desires for freedom, there is a unique window of opportunity to impact this generation with the liberating good news about Jesus. Political, economic and social frustrations are often expressed in resentment against the regime and in increasing hedonism and materialism. Pray that the unmet longings of their hearts might be fulfilled as they meet Christ. Already, much of the underground church is made up of this younger generation.

8 **Leadership training and development** are absolutely vital if the burgeoning Church in Iran is to continue to grow and mature. The countless house churches need to see capable leaders trained, and these leaders in turn must be taught to train others as Iranian fellowships keep multiplying. Much training of Iranian Christian workers occurs abroad. Elam Ministries operates residential courses in the region and in Europe; much of their material has been filmed for wider distribution. There are growing numbers studying via correspondence courses, with one online Bible college in Persian having over 500 students. Short-term training courses are happening in several regions as well. Other Iranians study in English-language programmes. Pray for the development and distribution of programmes that will cultivate many passionate, capable and well-trained leaders for the underground Church in Iran.

9 **Missions are not free to minister** in the land, but some tentmaking opportunities arise and tourism is actively encouraged. Pray for the door to Iran to open in God's perfect timing. Millions remain unevangelized. Pray also for agencies around the world to pray, plan and network together with Iranian believers in preparation for that day.

10 **The spiritual needs of religious minorities:**

a) *The Zoroastrians or Parsees* follow an ancient Persian monotheistic religion, founded 1,000 years before Christ. Many of them fled before Islam in the 7th Century and settled in Gujarat, India. There are between 35,000 and 100,000 Parsees in Iran. There are many bridges between Christianity and Zoroastrianism, so they are potentially a very responsive people; pray for loving and insightful ministry that will reach them with the gospel.

b) **The Baha'i,** whose religion has spread worldwide since the 19th Century, are persecuted severely in Iran. They are regarded by Muslims as a heretical sect for their belief that their founder, Baha'u'llah, is a prophet after Mohammed. The government seeks to drive them from Iran through mistreatment, intimidation, prejudice in education and employment, and destruction of sacred Baha'i sites. Very little Christian love and witness has been shared with the 300,000 Baha'i in Iran or among the five million worldwide. Pray that in their desperation they may find refuge in the Lord Jesus.

c) **The Persian-speaking Jews** are descendants of those exiled to Babylon 2,700 years ago. Due to pressure and harassment, their numbers are declining through emigration. A number have become active, witnessing Christians.

11 **Less-evangelized peoples.** Iran contains some of the largest unreached, unengaged peoples in the world. Dozens of peoples have no known believers among them, but the multiplication of churches and Christian resources in Persian and other languages is seeing that change. Some organizations are committed to seeing church planting movements among every people in Iran. Pray specifically for:

a) **The nomadic and semi-nomadic Luri and Bakhtiari and the Turkic Qashqai,** largely unreached peoples who live in the Zagros Mountains. There are only a few dozen known believers from these groups. Their mobile lifestyle makes church planting among them a challenge. Scripture, Christian radio and the JESUS film exist in some of their languages and dialects. The use of Farsi as a trade language also gives them access to further Christian resources. Persian Christians are beginning to reach out to these peoples. Pray that the small groups of believers and seekers from these groups, meeting both inside Iran and abroad, might grow and multiply.

b) **The various Kurdish peoples** of northwest and northeast Iran. They continue to face economic hardship and political and cultural suppression from the regime (which they usually oppose). Most are Sunni Muslims. There are some Christian resources in the dialects of the Kurdish language. Pray that the increasing numbers of Kurds in Iraq who are coming to faith in Jesus might, in turn, influence their kin in Iran.

c) **The Turkic Azeri and Turkmen** in the north are closely related, but have scarcely had any positive contact with Christianity. Azeris form the largest minority group within Iran; their population is usually underestimated. It is listed here as 13.5m, but could conceivably be double that. Praise God for the completion and distribution of the Azeri NT, Psalms and Proverbs, while the OT is nearing completion – pray that the availability of Scripture in their heart language might spur many to read and be transformed. The traditionally nomadic Turkmen live in a geographically isolated area, but there are the beginnings of a church among this people.

d) **The peoples of the southeast** – the Baloch and Brahui. The Baloch are restive and unhappy with Iranian rule; hostilities and lawlessness appear to be increasing. There are only a handful of believers, but Christian resources such as radio and the JESUS film are increasing in number.

e) **The Gypsy communities** include the Domari and the sub-groups Ghorbati and Mawari. They number 1.3 million people. Their low social status and semi-nomadic nature keep them relatively unknown in Iran. There are no Christian workers dedicated to reaching them.

12 **Christian help ministries** are an important component in reaching Iranians and providing resources for the burgeoning Iranian Church. Many media ministries and resources have emerged in recent years.

a) **Bibles** are in very short supply and very high demand – 10 million Bibles would be readily received. It is illegal to print and distribute the Scriptures, yet they continue to slip into the country. Several ministries, especially Elam Ministries and Open Doors, focus on increasing the availability of Scripture to Iranians. There are three translations of the Bible in Persian, with another version due out in 2012. Pray for innovative and effective ways of distributing God's Word and for a deep impact to be made through it. Pray also for translation teams to be raised up for the other languages that have a need for Scripture translation.

b) *Christian literature,* when available, is much sought after, but many more publications are needed, especially in Persian. Elam, 222 Ministries, Sohrab Books, Persian World Outreach, Iranian Christians International and others are involved in production and distribution. Pray also that the Lord will raise up more indigenous writers to produce Christian material to meet the accelerating demand from the Iranian Church. Pray that God will continue to open new avenues for distribution. Pray specifically for the development of children's materials – a glaring need with 15 million Iranians aged 15 or younger.

c) *Radio* remains a valuable ministry. Millions listen despite government restrictions, and thousands of response e-mails and letters are received. Voice of Christ Media Ministries, **TWR** and others prepare daily programmes in Persian and Azeri and broadcast them on satellite, shortwave and medium wave.

d) *Other media* include Christian and worship music (very popular with the younger generation, in particular) and film, including the raft of materials associated with the JESUS film. Pray for these to have a great impact.

13 **TV ministry is an area of huge growth for reaching Iranians.** Many ministries pour resources and efforts into developing videos for evangelism and Christian teaching. Possibly 20 million illegal satellite dishes are used to access television broadcasts. Stations such as **SAT-7** Pars, Nejat TV, MOHABAT TV, and producers such as Iran Alive Ministries, 222 Ministries, Elam Ministries and others reach millions through this popular medium. Live worship broadcasts with music and teaching prove especially effective. Pray also for the development of Christian video programming and materials for youth and children, who constitute such a large swathe of Iran's population.

14 **The Internet** is another powerful tool for the evangelization of Iran, enormously popular among young people in particular. It is the ideal medium for a host of materials – readings, audio and video – in Persian. Many ministries are developing resources, from evangelistic sites to Christian news, to teaching materials to worship music in the main languages of Iran. Just a few examples – Farsi Christian News Network, Kalameh, Farsinet, Iranian Christian Broadcasting, Online Kelisa, Farsipraise Ministries, PWO and many others. Around 23 million Iranians have access to the Internet. Iran is the world's third-largest blogging community, but the regime is very active in shutting down sites that pose perceived threats to the status quo. Over 40 million have mobile phones – another potential but unexploited means of transmitting the good news. Pray for the vast potential of the Internet to be realized for reaching Iran with the good news and for building up the body of Christ.

I

Iraq
Republic of Iraq
Asia

Geography 🌍

Area 438,317 sq km. Fertile plains of the Tigris and Euphrates Rivers; high mountains to the north and Syrian desert in southwest. Site of the ancient Sumerian, Assyrian and Babylonian Empires.

Population		Ann Gr	Density
2010	31,466,698	2.19%	72/sq km
2020	40,227,611	2.31%	92/sq km
2030	48,909,281	1.82%	112/sq km

Capital Baghdad 5,891,000. **Other major cities** Mosul 1.5 million; Irbil (Kurdish Autonomous Region – KAR) 1.0mill; Basra 923,000. **Urbanites** 66.4%. **Pop under 15 yrs** 41%. **Life expectancy** 67.8 yrs.

Peoples 👪

The Sunni Arab minority long dominated other ethnic groups; for political gain, all claim higher statistics for their own group.

Arab 74.3%. Iraqi Arab 64.8%; Najdi Bedouin 4.4%; Egyptian Arab 1.2%.

Iranian–Median 22.0%. 10 groups, largest: Northern Kurd 9.8%; Southern Kurd 7.8%; Central Kurd 1.6%; Persian 1.1%.

Turkic 2.5%. In centre and north. Turkmen (Iraqi Turks speaking a form of Azeri, different from the Central Asian Turkmen people group). May be larger, many claimed by Kurds.

Other 1.2%. Other Middle East peoples, Western, Asian.
Literacy 40.4%. **Official languages** Arabic; Kurdish in the KAR. **All languages** 26.
Languages with Scriptures 4Bi 3NT 3por.

Economy

Oil-based economy – since Genesis 11! Profits were spent during Saddam's rule on building a war machine. War with Iran halted economic development. The two Gulf Wars and 13 years of UN sanctions further devastated the economy and impoverished ordinary people. Iraq has the world's third-largest known oil reserves. Control and distribution of that wealth are key issues that will dominate the politics of the next few years. Rebuilding the national infrastructure after five decades of tyranny and war will take many years. This is made much more difficult by rampant corruption in government, the seemingly irreconcilable armed factions and instability. Unemployment is high (18–30%), and the population young (83% under 40 yrs).
Income/person $3,007 (6% of USA).

Politics

Created as a political entity by the victorious Allies after WWI. Faisal was installed by the British as king in 1923. Independent as a monarchy in 1932. Faisal II was overthrown in a revolution in 1958. The Baathist military regime became a dictatorship under Saddam Hussein. A massive military machine was built up; it was used to protect the dictatorship, to repress Kurds and Shi'as, to launch a war against Iran (1980-88) and then to invade Kuwait in 1990. UN forces defeated Iraq and imposed sanctions until 2003. The subsequent US invasion in 2003 was prompted by Iraq allegedly possessing weapons of mass destruction (which never materialized). Western occupiers ousted Hussein and set out to create a new government and rebuild the economy (on terms favourable to Western oil interests), but were hampered by intense attacks by Islamist insurgents. The country was governed by Shi'a political parties after the 2005 election, but the 2010 election was narrowly won by a secular, Sunni-backed alliance of political groups. Although a representative and constitutional democracy, politics can often align along ethnic-religious lines. The lethal mix of longstanding divisions and rivalries (Shi'a-Sunni and Arab-

Kurd) combined with Islamist terrorism, in the end, make the country difficult to govern peacefully.

Religion

Pan-Arab socialism rather than Islam was the ideology of the Baathist regime. Under Saddam, Shi'a Muslims were persecuted and Christians tolerated. Since 2003, Islamist groups have stepped up persecution of religious minorities, causing mass emigration of the ancient Christian confessions, whose presence in Iraq pre-dates the Arabs by centuries. The new constitution states that no law can be passed that contravenes Islam, so guarantees of religious freedom are not particularly trustworthy. Registration of new churches is particularly difficult.

Religions	Pop %	Population	Ann Gr
Muslim	95.91	30,179,710	2.3%
Other	1.90	597,867	-0.8%
Christian	1.59	500,320	-2.4%
Non-religious	0.60	188,800	8.2%

Christians Denoms		Pop %	Affiliates	Ann Gr
Protestant	12	0.04	12,000	-6.1%
Independent	8	0.13	42,000	7.1%
Anglican	1	0.01	4,000	32.7%
Catholic	1	1.18	370,000	-2.2%
Orthodox	8	0.23	72,000	-6.9%
Marginal	1	<0.01	<1,000	1.9%

Churches	MegaBloc	Congs	Members	Affiliates
Catholic Church	C	80	200,000	370,000
Assyrian Ch of the East	O	45	22,527	41,000
Armenian Apos Ch	O	7	6,593	12,000
Syriac Orthodox Ch	O	14	7,186	12,000
Arab Evangelical chs	P	60	3,153	7,000
Anglican Church	A	1	2,846	3,700
Other denominations[24]		63	8,903	55,630
Total Christians[31]		**270**	**251,208**	**500,310**

TransBloc	Pop %	Population	Ann Gr
Evangelicals			
Evangelicals	0.2	53,371	3.4%
Renewalists			
Charismatics	0.1	45,275	4.6%
Pentecostals	<0.1	1,450	-14.1%

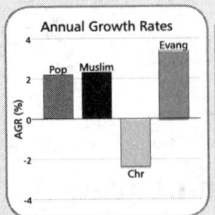

Annual Growth Rates

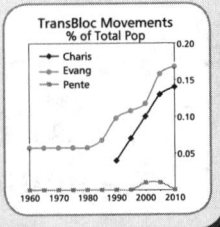

TransBloc Movements
% of Total Pop

Answers to Prayer

1 **The establishment of a representative government,** consolidation of stability, reduction of sectarian violence and the end of a brutal dictatorship responsible for the deaths of millions are points for praise. Growing pains and strife are inevitable, but there is also hope for the emergence of a stable, self-governed Iraq. Reforms in politics, the economy, education, healthcare and welfare offer signs of progress.

2 **The emergence of Iraqi Arab evangelicals** in recent years is an answer to prayer. During Hussein's rule, there were a few hundred; now there are an estimated 53,000 in the country. Many of them come from Muslim backgrounds but have encountered Christ through evangelical witness, gospel radio and especially through dreams and visions of Jesus. They are obvious targets for persecution.

3 **A Kurdish Church is now a reality.** With the increased autonomy of the Kurdish region – including religious freedom – an exciting and significant movement of people to Christ is occurring.

Challenges for Prayer

1 **Iraq's future remains uncertain.** Saddam Hussein's dictatorship was removed, but a host of problems still plagues the country. Pray for:

a) *The establishment of a national government* that fairly balances the conflicting expectations of the various religious and ethnic communities, and provides an environment that promotes accountability to the people, economic growth and religious freedom. Without these, the future is bleak. Anarchy, civil war, fragmentation of the country and further suffering for the people – especially Christians – could follow. Pray therefore for anointed national leaders who can act with wisdom, courage and integrity.

b) *Healing after decades of suffering.* Nearly every person bears some scars of traumatic experiences – from Hussein's cruelty, from the US-led invasions or from the sectarian violence that has followed. Only the gospel can provide a full solution; pray that this may be freely proclaimed.

c) *The elimination of corruption.* Iraq is ranked as one of the world's most corrupt nations. This has significantly held back the nation from repairing damage and achieving development.

d) *The suffering the Iraqi people have endured.* The number of lives lost as a result of invasions, insurgencies and deprivation may be as high as 600,000, with nearly two million people displaced. More than half of the population live in poverty.

   i *Women* suffer forced marriage, abduction, honour killing, violence and rape, used as a threat and weapon against them. They have almost no recourse to legal protection, and the religious establishment does little or nothing to protect them.

   ii *Children* live in a context of instability and uncertainty. Many do not attend school, less than half have access to safe drinking water and some even face malnourishment. Hundreds of thousands face life as refugees in neighbouring, and often unwelcoming, countries.

2 **Many deep divisions** run like fault lines through Iraqi society – Kurds against Arabs, Shi'as against Sunnis, Muslims against religious minorities, secular Baathists against Islamist groups. These groups jostle for the power and money that could be wrested from Iraq's uncertain future. These divisions run deep; they cripple the future hope of Iraq and cannot be erased over-night – probably not even in one generation. Only the power of the gospel is potent enough; pray that somehow, against all odds, the good news might break through, and Iraq might be transformed by God's love and justice.

3 **Monumental political changes have occurred since 1991.** The Kurds have been grateful to the USA since it liberated their homelands in northern Iraq that year. For the rest of Iraq, Saddam's harsh rule came to an end in 2003. But the US invasion was the perfect platform for Islamist insurgents to unleash terror against the erstwhile occupiers, government forces and other perceived collaborators in an orgy of violence. Rival Shi'a and Sunni factions turned on each other with murderous, even suicidal, intent. Through all this, ordinary people suffered intimidation, kidnappings and bombings. With the withdrawal of Western forces, the responsibility of maintaining and building peace lies with the Iraqis themselves. Signs are promising that they possess the will and the ability to build a stable society. Pray not just for the absence of terror but also for the palpable presence and influence of the Prince of Peace.

④ Pray for true freedom of religion and from persecution. Islamists vociferously demand exclusive rights for Muslims with full implementation of shari'a law. Christians of all confessions, Yazidis, Mandeans and even heterodox Muslim groups face "protection tax", kidnapping and paying ransom, destruction of their property, rape and murder. The government and police are not yet strong enough or inclined enough to offer substantial protection. Muslim leaders – both Shi'a and Sunni – are increasingly progressive, conciliatory and unity-oriented, but extremist groups have their own agenda and continue attempts to sow terror and destabilize the country. Pray that Christians might persevere in this difficult situation; pray also for their protection and preservation.

⑤ The Christian community has lived an unbroken existence in Iraq since the 1st Century, but this legacy is at risk of disappearing. The majority are Assyrians and descendants of the Nestorian, or Ancient Church of the East, centred in Nineveh and Mosul. The Nestorian Church was one of the greatest missionary denominations of history, winning 6% of all of Asia's population 1,000 years ago. Today, it is reduced through persecution, harassment and compromise to less than two million in the world. Christians in Iraq, the victims of sustained persecution and even genocide, are now only half of what they numbered in the 1990s. Most have fled persecution to Syria or Jordan, others to the West. Few are likely to ever return. Two-thirds of Baghdad's churches are closed or destroyed. Pray for the preservation of Iraq's biblical heritage, and for the restoration and rejuvenation of this most historic of Churches.

⑥ The Church is characterized by fragmentation – denominationally, ethnically and politically, despite the great opposition all Christians face. The majority are in the Catholic-linked Chaldean Church, but others are part of the Assyrian Church of the East, Syriac Orthodox, Armenian Apostolic, Protestant denominations or even a Muslim-background believers' network. Some in the historic denominations are being impacted by revival; others resent and oppose what they perceive to be aggressive proselytism and a money-spinning focus of the newer Protestant groups. Outreach to the Muslim majority remains a terrifying prospect to most, although compassionate ministry by some Christians to all in need sees many Muslims profoundly touched. Pray for unity among believers, with a Christ-centred front that responds to hatred and persecution with boldness, forgiveness and love.

⑦ Evangelicals are growing at an unprecedented rate. Many are coming from Muslim and even extremist backgrounds, touched by the peace, love and hope Christ offers. They are Arab and Kurd, in the north and south, within Iraq and scattered abroad. However, they come nowhere near offsetting the loss endured by Christianity as a result of the flight of the ancient confessions from Iraq. Pray for these believers, for their witness to non-Christians and for their faith to endure despite many difficulties.

⑧ Leadership for the churches is an increasingly desperate need. Many good leaders have fled the country; many others are dead, specifically targeted by Islamists. Some Iraqis are in training in Jordan, Lebanon and even in Iraq itself. Much of the pastoring and discipling is handled by Christian widows of slain leaders; pray for their equipping and enabling. With a young population and many Muslims coming to faith, leaders gifted in discipleship and teaching are crucial. Pray for the return of leaders who have fled, for the development of new leaders and for protection of all who shepherd God's people in Iraq.

⑨ All peoples are unevangelized except Assyrian and Armenian minority groups. Pray for:

a) *The Shi'a Arabs of Basra and the south.* The exceptional brutality of the Sunni Baathist government brought death to many and devastation to their land and communities. As the majority population, they now control the government and military as well as possess powerful militia groups. There is very little direct witness to them.

b) *Sunni Arabs* gained the most from the former dictatorship, but, as they see their influence eclipsed, Sunni extremist groups remain a violent threat. Politically minded Sunnis are amenable to power-sharing agreements. Few have heard the gospel.

c) **The Madan or Marsh Arabs** probably descended from the ancient Sumerians. An oppressive, even genocidal, government policy toward them reduced their population from 450,000 in the 1950s to a maximum of 90,000 today. Perhaps only 20,000 remain in the marshlands, reduced to 15% of their original size. Restoration of the marshes is now occurring, but the younger generation remain rooted in the cities, not in their traditional marsh homelands. There are no known Christians and no sustained outreach specifically to them.

d) **The Bedouin** number 1.4 million and remain thoroughly unevangelized. Their poverty, marginalization and semi-nomadic lifestyle make them difficult to reach. They have no churches, no outreach to them and only a handful of believers.

e) **Turkmen,** an Azeri-speaking Turkic group, are Iraq's third-largest ethnicity, concentrated in the north. They identify with Turkey and harbour their own dreams of autonomy in a region of Iraq controlled by Kurds. Their number may be anywhere from 500,000 to two million. Split between Shi'a and Sunni Islam, they may have several thousand Catholics in their number but remain largely unreached.

f) **The Yazidi** are a syncretistic offshoot of both Zoroastrianism and Sufi Islam. They originated from India centuries ago and have a unique religion, venerating the "peacock angel", identified by Muslims as Lucifer. This has resulted in centuries of persecution, most intensely since 2003. There are a small number of believers, but they have faced stiff persecution from Muslims and their own leaders.

g) **The smaller Domari (Gypsy) and Mandean populations.** Both peoples are looked down upon. There are few, if any, believers in their midst.

10 **The Kurdish Autonomous Region** possesses significant autonomy but many of its own problems as well. Dominated by Kurds, it possesses restive minorities (Turkmen, Arabs, Assyrians) as well as strong antipathy to neighbouring Turkey. The Kurds have fought long for an independent state; Iraqi Arab reprisals have been particularly cruel, and broken Western promises embittering. The KAR's degree of autonomy remains a sensitive issue, nationally and regionally. Pray for the following:

I

a) **Kurdish desires for freedom and security** are being realized, at least in Iraq, but neighbours with large Kurdish populations see this as a possible threat to stability. Control over the highly contested and oil-rich city of Kirkuk is a particularly hot issue. The Kurdish desire for sovereignty is probably the primary, long-term destabilizing issue for Iraq. The "trigger line", where Arab and Kurdish areas of control meet, is the most violent place in Iraq, and the historic Christian populations are caught in the middle.

b) **Economic improvement** to a region traditionally fraught with poverty. Initially NGOs lent much assistance. Now, the KAR is exporting oil via Turkey. However, the two most powerful (and rival) Kurdish clans have enriched themselves in the post-1991 and post-2003 power plays, much to the disgust of many other Kurds. Most of Iraq's Kurds were displaced by Saddam's genocidal intentions; their return en masse strains the KAR's ability to care for them.

c) **The Church** is officially tolerated in the KAR more than the rest of Iraq, with the Kurdish government even encouraging the work of Christian NGOs and the building of churches. Nonetheless, non-Kurdish ethnic minorities, such as the 45,000 Assyrian Christians, suffer growing marginalization at the hands of the increasingly dominant Kurds.

d) **The number of Kurdish believers** continues to grow – praise God. Even for Kurds, leaving Islam can have dangerous consequences, but many are coming to faith and have a passion for winning others as well. The Church is still young and small, and it faces not only growing pains from within but also pressures from without. Pray also for positive interface between Western Christian NGOs and the Kurdish people, both Christian and non-Christian.

11 Christian support ministries:

a) **The Bible Society** has been actively involved in Iraq since 1985, importing and printing many Scriptures and NTs. The recent translation of the Bible into Kurdish is one significant boost; almost all languages in Iraq have at least some Scripture. Most recently, the NT has been completed in Sorani Kurdish, and the Bahdini Kurdish NT was near completion in 2010.

b) **Christian literature** is in great demand. Much is imported. There is a growing need and hunger for commentaries, study books and Bibles. Pray that the increasing Scripture distribution would continue and would bear much fruit; more than one million Bibles in Arabic alone have been sent into Iraq. The development of Christian literature in Arabic is well advanced; pray for more materials to be developed in the different dialects of Kurdish.

c) **The JESUS film** is available in 11 languages and is widely seen on TV and extensively distributed in video format. Pray for its impact in the homes and hearts of Iraqis.

d) **Christian satellite TV and radio** are huge influences in Iraq. Millions watch **SAT-7** programmes as well as three other Arabic Christian channels. **TWR**, FEBA and IBRA broadcast radio (mostly via shortwave) into Iraq in Arabic, Sorani Kurdish and a few other languages. The KAR has a local Christian radio station. Pray that the good news might reach further using these media; pray also that these tools would be helpful in building up and discipling.

Ireland
Republic of Ireland
Europe

Geography

Area 70,285 sq km. Comprises 80% of the island of Ireland. Northern Ireland is a constituent part of the United Kingdom.

Population		Ann Gr	Density
2010	4,589,002	1.85%	65/sq km
2020	5,145,254	1.04%	73/sq km
2030	5,573,182	0.75%	79/sq km

Millions of Irish have emigrated throughout the English-speaking world, especially to the USA and the UK.
Capital Dublin 1,098,636. **Urbanites** 62%. **Pop under 15 yrs** 21%. **Life expectancy** 79.7 yrs.

Peoples

Anglo–Celtic 91.2%. Irish 88.2%; British 3.0%.
Other 9.8%. Polish 2.3%; African 0.9%; Asian 1.5%; North American 0.5%; increasing numbers of other immigrant groups, including Eastern European, Latino, Asian, African. Many of these groups are very difficult to enumerate due to their unofficial status and transient nature.
Literacy 99%. **Official languages** Irish, English. Irish spoken as a first language by less than 4% of the population; 40% of the Irish population can speak Irish. There are no monolingual Irish speakers. **All languages** 5. **Languages with Scripture** 2Bi 1NT 1por.

Economy

High-tech industry and services replaced dairy farming and tourism as most important. EU membership in 1973; an economic boom since the 1990s has transformed the country, with one of Europe's most successful growth rates. The juxtaposition of the growth boom ending, of house prices dropping and of the financial crisis of 2008–09 caused the economy to significantly contract. But for some, a very uneven spread of the new affluence makes life more difficult.
HDI Rank 5th/182. **Public debt** 44.2% of GDP. **Income/person** $60,510 (128% of USA).

Politics

Ireland was under British rule for over 700 years. In 1921, Ireland was partitioned between the 26 counties that were Catholic and Celtic, and the 6 counties in Northern Ireland that were predominantly Protestant Scots Anglo-Saxon. The south became independent in 1922 and then a parliamentary republic in 1949. The violence and strife of the past continues to fade as Ireland's political scene has moved from being a parochial backwater on the edge of Europe to a dynamic force in the EU. The last generation has borne witness to remarkable progress and change in the political sphere.

Religion

There is freedom of religion. The Catholic Church has no official link with the state. Though it had a massive influence over everyday life in the past, this influence is waning rapidly.

Religions	Pop %	Population	Ann Gr
Christian	91.72	4,209,033	1.4%
Non-religious	7.26	333,162	8.5%

Muslim	0.87	39,924	6.4%
Hindu	0.09	4,130	10.5%
Jewish	0.04	1,836	1.9%
Chinese	0.01	459	1.9%
Buddhist	0.01	459	1.9%

Christians Denoms		Pop %	Affiliates	Ann Gr
Protestant	36	0.91	42,000	2.2%
Independent	17	0.34	16,000	5.1%
Anglican	1	2.20	101,000	1.2%
Catholic	1	81.72	3,750,000	0.6%
Orthodox	3	0.60	28,000	6.7%
Marginal	7	0.30	14,000	1.5%
Unaffiliated		5.58	256,000	17.2%

Churches	MegaBloc	Congs	Members	Affiliates
Catholic Church	C	1,616	2,586,207	3,750,000
Ch of Ireland	A	563	53,492	101,100
Orthodox Church	O	23	13,800	27,600
Presbyterian Ch in I	P	91	7,712	12,030
Methodist Church	P	65	6,908	10,500
Jehovah's Witnesses	M	113	5,700	10,374
Independent churches	I	85	4,945	9,000
Redeemed Chr Ch	I	72	2,160	4,320
Lutheran Church	P	7	2,406	3,200

Latter-day Saints (Mormon)	M	15	2,021	2,850
Assemblies of God	P	18	1,265	2,150
Christian Brethren	P	19	1,330	1,902
Ch of God (Cleveland)	P	8	1,520	1,900
New Churches	I	28	1,100	1,837
Other denominations[39]		153	7,495	13,298
Total Christians[65]		**2,868**	**2,696,541**	**3,950,161**

TransBloc	Pop %	Population	Ann Gr
Evangelicals			
Evangelicals	1.5	71,080	3.3%
Renewalists			
Charismatics	1.2	56,110	4.6%
Pentecostals	0.2	10,380	5.1%

Religions % of Total Pop (1900–2025)

Annual Growth Rates

Answers to Prayer

1 **The move of the Holy Spirit** in the last decades changed Ireland from rigid Catholicism to a spiritually dynamic land where new fellowships are rapidly forming. Many of these are Pentecostal or charismatic in orientation, and a large number are either formed of immigrants or are multi-ethnic in composition. These immigrant groups bring new life and passion to the traditional denominations, which were previously in decline.

2 **Effective inter-governmental cooperation,** beginning in the late 1990s, strengthened hope for lasting peace and for democratic solutions to Northern Ireland's problems. Although not all issues are definitively resolved, the change on the island is quite remarkable and a true answer to prayer.

Challenges for Prayer

1 **Transformation has rapidly overtaken Ireland,** led by the economic boost of EU membership, heavy foreign investment in a well-educated, English-speaking workforce, and increased contact with Europe and the world. But this new affluence has benefitted only some, and many were left downcast from the effects of the recession. This shift has also radically affected immigration/demographics, spirituality and culture. Pray that amid the change, the nation's leadership might also focus on protecting the vulnerable, providing for the needy and building a lasting infrastructure and legacy that will be a blessing to all.

2 **Ireland's ancient Celtic Church** strongly shaped society 1,500 years ago through its dynamic and holistic spirituality. Then followed centuries of suffering, oppression, violence and bloodshed at the hands of the Vikings and the British. Sadly, the long conflict has, in the eyes of the world, been portrayed as religious in origin. Pray that:

a) **Irish society might be made whole.** Progress is made on this front with violence reduced and formerly opposing parties now cooperating on certain issues. The political future of Northern Ireland remains a sensitive issue, but healing, reconciliation and forgiveness can occur nevertheless.

b) **All Christians might work toward shared Kingdom-goals.** Encouraging signs are apparent; the bipolar nature of Irish Christianity (Catholic versus Protestant) is an increasingly outdated understanding of Irish spirituality, as outside groups arrive and post-denominational churches arise.

3 **The Catholic Church** was, for centuries, the preserver and defender of the Irish. Catalyzed by secularism, the rapid onset of modernity and a series of high-profile scandals and cover-ups in the priesthood, the nation is rapidly losing the deep Catholic sensibilities that once tied it together. Once an exporter of trained priests, the Catholic Church today ordains few. Weekly church attendance, once 85% nationally, is now less than 50%, and as low as 5% in parts of Dublin – and there are more non-religious Irish than ever before. Despite this, there is a vibrant charismatic renewal movement within the Catholic Church and unprecedented collaboration with other expressions of the Christian faith. Pray for the Irish nation to rediscover its ancient heritage of deep and profound faith in Christ.

4 **The sex abuse scandals that rocked the Catholic Church** devastated the nation's confidence in what was once a deeply trusted institution. Possibly the only things more damaging than this tragic and sinful abuse are the cover-ups and collusion that occurred after these incidents came to the knowledge of Church leaders. Ireland's Catholic faith was already on a downward trajectory; these scandals may have thrust it into a death spiral. Pray that true repentance, forgiveness and, where possible, restoration might occur on the part of those involved, and that this may lead to purification and redemption of Catholicism in Ireland.

5 **Immigration sees a "new Ireland" emerge,** complete with radical change in ethnic, cultural and spiritual spheres. The pastoral Celtic image of days past has given way to a context where 90% of population growth is from immigration, and where foreign religions and denominations thrive. Ireland willingly adopts these new arrivals, who in turn bring cultural diversity and spiritual passion. Pray for those who do not know Christ or who come from other religious backgrounds, that Ireland may be the land where they meet the Saviour.

6 **Evangelicals are experiencing sustained growth,** especially among charismatic and Pentecostal groups. The immigration surge contributes to this, with around one-third of evangelicals coming from non–Irish ethnicities. Pray for:

a) *Unity amid the new diversity.* The recently formed Evangelical Alliance in Ireland will be a major help in this area, drawing believers together from across denominational (and racial) lines. Anglicans (Church of Ireland), traditional Protestants and newer immigrant or multi-ethnic Independent and/or charismatic fellowships can all benefit from shared vision and cooperation.

b) *Continued growth.* Ireland still has the lowest percentage of evangelicals of any English-speaking nation, but they have shifted from a huddled and marginalized minority to a confident and dynamic movement. Some Christian leaders speak of a 20/20 vision, wherein 20% of Ireland's population has a personal relationship with Christ by the year 2020.

c) *Good Bible-trained leadership* to be raised up. The Irish Bible Institute launched in 2000 as a merger of two Bible colleges and subsequently merged with the Global University-based ministry of the **AoG**.

d) *The further development of holistic ministry* by evangelicals. This already includes helping the unemployed find work, assisting those suffering with AIDS and reaching out to the urban poor, especially children. Urban Soul and Serve the City focus on blessing neighbours through community service and acts of kindness. Pray that evangelicals might be salt and light in their communities and demonstrate the whole gospel by word and by deed.

7 **Pray for young people.** Ireland has a young population by European standards, with 21% under age 15. Their spiritual need is underlined by the rapid increase of serious social issues: alcoholism, suicide, broken families, alternative lifestyles and post-Christian attitudes. Many are open to the gospel when it is presented and expressed in a new way. Ministry in schools and Christian camps is run by Scripture Union, **CEF** (67 full-time workers), the Faith Mission, **IFES** and others. Ireland also hosts increasing numbers of international students. Pray for many young people to have life-changing encounters with Christ.

8 Significant ministry challenges:

a) *The older generation,* many of whom are entrenched in rigid traditional mentalities about religion, faith and culture. Many are rural and Irish-speaking. Relational, patient interaction is required to have an impact on them. The Irish Evangelistic Band was formed in 1936 to reach such people.

b) ***Muslim numbers*** are increasing faster than evangelicals. They are an ethnically diverse immigrant population, poised to continue rapid growth. Pray for Irish believers to reach out to them in friendship and Christian love.

c) ***Travellers (Gypsies),*** numbering 25,000 and growing, have been in Ireland for centuries, and they spread from here to elsewhere. They tend to be poor, illiterate and with the lowest life expectancy of any group in Ireland. Little has been done specifically to reach them.

9 **Missionaries now work** in all 26 counties, but they are mostly focused on the Dublin area. **GEM** is instrumental in leadership training and church planting, with 16 full-time workers. Other significant missions include **AoG**, **OM**, **TEAM**, **IMB**, **UFM** and Christian Associates. Pray for their ability to minister ably, for new congregations to be planted and for long-term investment in indigenous churches and leaders.

10 **Ireland has a long tradition of sending missionaries,** from the *peregrini* of the early Celtic Church onward. But now the number of Catholic missionaries is rapidly declining as is the number of traditional Protestant missionaries, though to a lesser degree. The new churches recognize the need for reaching the unevangelized in their midst and in the wider world. Pray for the release, training and funding of more Irish missionaries and leaders by evangelical churches and fellowships.

Israel

State of Israel

Asia

Geography 🌐

Area 20,700 sq km. A further 7,540 sq km of the West Bank, Gaza and the Golan Heights have been controlled by Israel since 1967.

Population		Ann Gr	Density
2010	7,285,033	1.71%	352/sq km
2020	8,306,679	1.21%	401/sq km
2030	9,219,268	1.01%	445/sq km

The Palestinian Authority, although under Israel administration, is treated separately.

Capital Jerusalem 783,000; but not recognized internationally. **Other major cities** Tel Aviv 3.3 million; Haifa 1.0mill. **Urbanites** 91.7%. **Pop under 15 yrs** 28%. **Life expectancy** 80.7 yrs.

Peoples 👪

Jews 75.5%. 28 groups. Israeli Jew 23.1%; Russian Jew 13.6%; Romanian Jew 5.6%; Polish Jew 5.5%; Eastern Yiddish Jew 4.7%; Maghrebi 4.4%; Spanish Jew (Ladino) 2.7%; Yahudic 2.3%; Beta Israel/Falasha (Ethiopian) 1.8%; Hungarian Jew 1.3%; Dzhidi 1.2%; German Jew 1.2%; French Jew 1.1%; Yemeni Jew 1.0%; Bukharic Jew 1.0%.

Arabs 20.4%. Israeli Arab/Palestinian 16.5%; Druze 1.8%; Bedouin 1.3%.

Other 4.1%. European, African, Chinese, Thai, Filipino, North and South American. The numbers are probably significantly larger.

Literacy 96.9%. **Official languages** Hebrew, Arabic. Numerous immigrant languages from all over the world are spoken. **All languages** 48. **Indigenous languages** 33. **Languages with Scriptures** 12Bi 1NT 6por.

Economy 📈

Modern, sophisticated industrial state. Well developed high-tech, bio-tech, chemical and agricultural sectors. Many start-up companies. Brakes on further growth, however, include the high burden of defence expenditure due to security issues, the cost of absorbing new immigrants and the growing crisis of lack of water (despite extensive desalination and reuse). Israel lacks natural resources and needs to import petroleum, coal, grains and military hardware. Large gas and oil deposits under the Mediterranean could significantly alter Israel's energy status.

HDI Rank 27th/182. **Public debt** 76.8% of GDP. **Income/person** $28,409 (60% of USA). **Unemployment** 8.2%.

Politics ⚔️

The founding of Israel in 1948 ended 1,900 years of exile for the Jews. Six wars with surrounding states in 1948, 1956, 1967, 1973, 1982-85, 2006 plus the Gaza War in 2009 have kept the country on a war footing. Repeated military engagement in Lebanon, the rising pressure of Palestinian civil unrest, the *intifada*, acts of terrorism by Islamist groups (Hamas, Hezbollah, others) and the increased threat from Iran have sapped Israeli stamina. Israeli society remains deeply divided on the peace process, the future of Jewish settlements in the Disputed Territories and the future of Jerusalem and of the Golan Heights. The four-way division of political parties (left, right, far right religious, Arab) means that coalitions generally must be formed – giving disproportionate influence to the ultra-orthodox Jewish *Haredi* minority. Repeated efforts by the UN, USA and others to facilitate a peace deal have met with only limited success. Divisions internally (in Israel and in the Palestinian Authority) as well as fundamentally irreconcilable and deeply held convictions on both sides make long-term solutions very difficult to envision.

Religion

All religions are free to minister within their own communities. Jews who follow Messiah Jesus, however, have in the past been denied legal standing as a religious body and faced difficulties obtaining premises for fellowship. This changed in 2009, enabling Messianic congregations to register as houses of prayer and religious entities. Reform and Conservative Jews are often marginalized by ultra-Orthodox influence, which applies constant pressure to limit freedom of religion through anti-conversion laws and persecution of Messianic Jews.

Religions	Pop %	Population	Ann Gr
Jewish	75.40	5,492,915	1.5%
Muslim	16.70	1,216,601	2.5%
Non-religious	3.81	277,560	3.3%
Christian	2.04	148,615	0.5%
Other	1.90	138,416	2.3%
Baha'i	0.15	10,928	1.7%

The Jewish population is approximately 25% Orthodox, 20% secular and the rest somewhere in the middle.

Christians	Denoms	Pop %	Affiliates	Ann Gr
Protestant	43	0.18	13,000	5.9%
Independent	25	0.24	17,000	5.3%
Anglican	1	0.02	2,000	0.0%
Catholic	3	0.99	72,000	-0.6%
Orthodox	7	0.57	42,000	-0.8%
Marginal	2	0.04	3,000	3.6%

Churches	MegaBloc	Congs	Members	Affiliates
Catholic Ch (5 rites)	C	80	42,604	72,000
Greek Orthodox Ch	O	11	23,750	38,000
Messianic Assemblies	I	160	6,000	12,000
Assoc of Baptist Chs	P	20	800	3,000
Baptist Conv Israel	P	30	1,500	3,000
Jehovah's Witnesses	M	21	1,480	2,960
Assemblies of God	P	15	1,150	1,500
Episcopal Church	A	3	833	1,500
Seventh-day Adventist	P	44	800	1,200
Coptic Orthodox Ch	O	2	639	1,150
Other denominations[65]		1245	6,565	12,400
Total Christians[81]		**510**	**86,121**	**148,710**

TransBloc	Pop %	Population	Ann Gr
Evangelicals			
Evangelicals	0.4	31,045	5.6%
Renewalists			
Charismatics	0.3	22,472	4.9%
Pentecostals	<0.1	3,080	4.5%

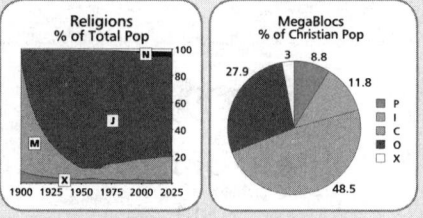

Religions % of Total Pop

MegaBlocs % of Christian Pop

Answers to Prayer

1 **Within Israel, interest in the gospel is increasing,** notably among Jews, and especially in the last few years. The hard shells that surround Israelis are beginning to crack open to the gospel. The numbers of Messianic Jews are rising rapidly, now up to 12,000 or possibly even higher. Some of these even come from a *Haredi* background. Messianic Jews are becoming a recognized part of Israeli society, but greater growth has intensified persecution.

2 **Globally, there is a significant response to the gospel** among the 14.5 million Jews. Even the more conservative estimates indicate an unprecedented response, and some of the more optimistic claims exceed 100,000 said to be linked with Messianic congregations. Most of these believers are in North America as well as Russia, Ukraine and the UK. A much larger number have integrated into mainstream Christian churches.

Challenges for Prayer

1 **The return of Jews to Israel** was a watershed period in Jewish history; it is finally likely that Israel is the nation with the world's largest population of Jews. Many see this as a fulfilment of prophecy (Ezekiel 20:32-34, 36:16-24). The majority returned to their ancient land in unbelief, but a movement to Messiah Jesus is occurring mostly among returnees from Eastern Europe, Russia and Ethiopia. Pray for the nation's spiritual restoration (Romans 11:25-31). There is currently an increased intensity in Israel's spiritual life. Many thousands of Jews are turning to God, fervently praying and turning to Scripture.

2 **Israeli-Arab conflict in the Holy Land** moved to a new level over a century ago, intensifying since 1948. Resolution is elusive due to competing claims and agendas. Both sides lay claim to the land, and all human efforts to resolve this conflict have failed. Pray that both sides will find true reconciliation and genuine Shalom through Jesus the Messiah.

a) The threat of violence and war from outside persists. Between the 2005 withdrawal of settlers and soldiers from Gaza and the controversial 2009 invasion, over 3,500 rockets were fired into Israel from Gaza. Hezbollah's growing strength, Al Qaeda's threats and Iran's increasingly strident rhetoric all point to potential trouble on the horizon.

b) The as-yet-unfinished security barrier is planned to effectively separate Palestinian and Jewish areas, making movement and access very difficult and exacerbating tensions. Pray that it would not unduly restrict free movement of Palestinian citizens of Israel. Pray that Jesus, who destroyed the wall of separation of hostility between God and man, might also bring reconciliation between Israeli Jew and Palestinian Arab.

3 **The Jewish mindset toward Christianity,** often characterized by animosity and part of a long and painful history, is a barrier to be overcome. "Christian" nations are seen to be destroyers of the Jewish nation whether by persecution (as in the Holocaust) or by proselytization. Pray that the gospel may be understood as a fulfilment of their Jewish heritage, and pray that a widespread turning to their Messiah might come. Those who oppose the gospel are more active than ever; pray also that all attempts to restrict religious freedom and to deny the Jewish identity of Messianic believers may ultimately cause even more Jews to come to faith.

I

4 **The Christian Church in Israel is fragmented,** although soundings of unity are beginning. It is comprised of about 80% Arabs, 12% expatriates (Egyptian, Ethiopian, Greek, Russian, Armenian, Italian, others) and 8% Jews. There are Catholics (five rites), Orthodox (nine traditions) and Protestants/Independents (over 20 denominations, many individual congregations and over 100 mission agencies). Pray for spiritual unity that transcends history, ethnic conflict, national origins, eschatology and secondary areas of theology.

5 **Followers of Jesus in Israel** are likewise a mix of Messianic Jews, foreign believers and Arab-Israeli Christians. All three groups have grown recently – especially Messianic and expatriate believers – the result of both immigration and conversion. There are over 120 Hebrew-speaking gatherings. Russian-speaking congregations are the next-largest number (as many as 50), followed by eight Amharic-speaking (Ethiopian) congregations and a smattering of fellowships in various European languages. Israeli-born Messianic Jews are around 1,000. Pray for:

a) Boldness in witness and perseverance of faith despite difficulties and opposition. The *Haredi* regard evangelicals as subversive and a threat to Judaism, and therefore malign and occasionally harass them. Tolerance of Christians and Messianic Jews is high, but proselytism is increasingly opposed, especially by the ultra-Orthodox.

b) Full legal rights of immigration and social acceptance in the face of national, social and family pressures. Israeli law states that national identity and religious identity of Jews are one; secular Jews can become citizens, but Christian Jews cannot.

c) Clarity of teaching and understanding about their Jewishness – there needs to be a cultural identity without compromising New Testament truth. There are now Bible training colleges in Tel Aviv, Jerusalem, Haifa and Nazareth for the formation of capable leaders.

d) Arab evangelicals are more numerous in Protestant and Independent denominations – but total fewer than 4,000. Of these, only a few dozen are Muslim-background believers. The number of those coming to faith is growing at an encouraging rate, but they emigrate to the West just as rapidly.

6 **Unity between Messianic Jews and Arab Christians.** A quiet revolution in relationships between Jewish and Arab believers is beginning in the Holy Land. The recently formed Convention of Evangelical Churches in Israel (and an equivalent organization in the Palestinian Authority) is a major step forward. Jewish and Arab believers cooperate in ministry through the National Evangelism Committee. Their joint outreach efforts into Muslim areas are well received. Many other grassroots initiatives, often unreported, see these two groups of believers, from very different backgrounds, blazing a trail of reconciliation and friendship that is an example to the rest of the region. But some others question or are even opposed to such developments. Pray that there might be grace among all who call upon Jesus/Yeshua/Isa to love, support and bear with one another.

7 **Major outreach challenges:**

a) The ultra-Orthodox Haredi are only 10% of the population, but they see themselves as the preservers of true Jewishness in Israel. They maintain a policy of political engagement with cultural detachment. More than 50% live below the poverty line. Strong religious legalism makes them quite difficult to reach. Pray that many more of these modern Pharisees may become like Nicodemus, a process that is already happening.

b) Jews from the former Soviet Union and Poland are now the largest component of the population. They have changed Israel and are more receptive than most groups to the gospel, already comprising the majority of Messianic Jews. Many still need to be evangelized.

c) The Ethiopian Jews (Beta Israel) have become a disillusioned, largely impoverished urban underclass since their immigration to Israel a decade ago. They number around 120,000; among them are fewer than 2,000 Messianic believers.

d) The Arabs. Over 90% are Muslim, yet they also comprise the majority of Christians in the Holy Land. They are being slowly squeezed out by a combination of Israeli discrimination, Islamist persecution and international ignorance and apathy toward their plight.

e) The Druze community (120,000) in Israel as well as in the West Bank and the Golan Heights. They are very closed to outsiders, but a movement to Jesus is beginning and accelerating. Opposition from within the Druze community toward Druze followers of Jesus will be intense.

f) Guest workers. Since the Palestinian workforce was reduced for security reasons, a number of Romanian, Chinese, Filipino, Ghanaian and Nigerian workers took their place, and, more recently, Sudanese refugees have come in through Egypt. The Israeli government is cracking down on illegal workers, but there are a substantial number of Christians among them.

g) Young people and children. They face security threats and an uncertain future, irreligious attitudes, New Age concepts and many cults and deviant groups seeking to win the hearts of the younger generation of Israelis. The children of poorer immigrants face intense disadvantages, both economically and educationally.

8 **The Protestant missionary force** is impossible to enumerate, due to security concerns and the presence of so many who enter as tentmakers. It certainly exceeds 1,000. At times the hardness of the ground and unfulfilled visions can lead to disillusionment, but Israeli society is generally quite open. Many are searching for real solutions to the uncertainty, conflicts and suffering. Years of sowing seeds and breaking down long-held prejudices against Christianity are now bearing fruit. Foreign Christians must work to encourage and support the growing local congregations and ministries who are increasingly reaching out. Literature ministry is another area of fruitful contribution. The Ministry of the Interior often makes visas difficult to obtain or renew for Christian workers.

9 **Jews of the dispersion** (those outside Israel) are declining in numbers through a lower birth rate, emigration to Israel, mixed marriages, secularism and conversions to other religions. There are now an estimated eight million Jews outside of Israel. The largest concentrations are in the USA (5.3m), former USSR (1m), France (500,000), Canada (370,000), Britain (280,000), Germany (200,000) and Argentina (180,000). There are 1.6 million Jews just in New York. In the USA, there is much openness, elsewhere less so. More workers are needed in places such as France. Pray for the ministry of **JFJ** (216 workers globally), CPM (161), MT, CWI, CMJ, Caspari Center and others; their work involves long hours of patient, loving ministry to individuals and families. Pray for a greater sensitivity on the part of Gentile churches toward problems of Jewish survival and for the Jewish remnant within the Church.

a) Christian literature and Scripture are of great importance in spreading the gospel due to the multiplicity of languages – Jews have returned to Israel from scores of nations. In addition to humanitarian work, The Bible Society distributes over 110,000 Bibles, NTs and Scripture portions annually. **OM** is also highly involved in literature distribution. *HaGefen Publishing* and *Keren Ahvah Meshihit* are both publishers that translate and produce literature into Modern Hebrew, including children's and digital media. Pray for Christian publishing houses and for increased production of Christian literature and Scripture in Hebrew, Russian, Arabic, Amharic and other languages. There are four Messianic Jewish periodicals, some having a readership beyond the Messianic Jewish community. Many homes have a NT. Pray for the fruitfulness of God's Word in the land of Israel.

b) Student work has grown, but the need for ministry to teenagers and young adults is still keenly felt. The **IFES**-linked student movement Fellowship of Christian Students in Israel has 10 groups with 150 students. Hearts to Serve is another ministry for students; both focus on reconciliation between Israeli and Palestinian students.

c) Films on the life of Jesus. The JESUS film is completed in 10 languages (Hebrew, Yiddish, Russian, Romanian, Modern Standard Arabic, English, Polish, Hungarian, Amharic and Adygey). Other Christian films are also having an impact. Pray for widespread distribution, and pray for effective follow up to inquiries generated by such films.

d) Radio. **TWR**, FEBA, IBRA and *Netivyah* together broadcast many hours in Hebrew, Russian, Arabic and other languages by radio and Internet.

e) Websites with material, resources and discussions about the nature of Jesus as Messiah are available in many languages. The Internet is widely and heavily used in Israel and has massive ministry potential. Pray that the Spirit may draw seekers to these sites.

I

Italy

Italian Republic

Europe

Geography 🌍

Area 301,000 sq km. A long, mountainous peninsula that dominates the central Mediterranean Sea. Also two large islands, Sardinia and Sicily.

Population		Ann Gr	Density
2010	60,097,564	0.49%	199/sq km
2020	60,408,428	-0.06%	201/sq km
2030	59,549,396	-0.16%	198/sq km

Capital Rome 3,362,252. **Other major cities** Milano 3.0million; Napoli 2.3mill; Torino 1.7m. **Urbanites** 68.4%. **Pop under 15 yrs** 14%. **Life expectancy** 81.1 yrs.

Peoples 👪

Italian 93.4%. Deep cultural and historical differences between the north and south and with a wide variety of regional cultures and dialects. Main groups/dialects: Italian 38.0%; Lombard 15.2%; Neapolitan/Calabrian 12.6%; Sicilian 8.3%; Piedmontese 5.4%; Venetian 3.8%; Emilian 3.5%; Ligurian 3.3%; Sardinian(5) 2.7%; Friulian 1.1%.

European 3.8%. Includes Albanian(2) 0.4%; French(4) 0.8%; Austrian 0.4%; German 0.4%; Greek 0.3%. A number of these groups have been resident for centuries.

Other 2.8%. Arab(3) 1.0%; Filipino 0.3%; Chinese 0.3%; African; many others increasing in number and diversity.

Literacy 98.5%. **Official language** Italian, but vigorous use of nine regional languages akin to Italian. **All languages** 42. **Indigenous languages** 33. **Languages with Scriptures** 8Bi 4NT 19por 1w.i.p.

Economy 🏭

Highly industrialized, Italy is the world's seventh-largest economy and known for quality manufactured goods. A notable contrast exists between the affluent north and the south, where economic modernization has been limited and

where unemployment is widespread and higher. Corruption, organized crime and weak law-enforcing state mechanisms are common and discourage investment and expansion in many sectors. The world's third-largest debt.
HDI Rank 18th/182. **Public debt** 105.8% of GDP. **Income/person** $38,996 (82% of USA).

Politics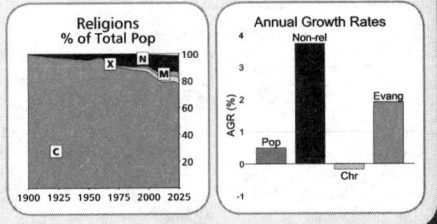

United as a single state in 1870. Republican democracy since 1946. Known for its precarious political life, Italy has thus far had 62 governments (including reshuffles and elected coalitions) since WWII, though with an underlying social stability. Member of the EU. Some improvements have occurred since the early 1990s, when the Italian political scenario underwent a seismic shift with the "Clean Hands" operation, which exposed corruption and the influence of organized crime at the highest levels of politics and big business.

Religion

Roman Catholicism ceased to be the state religion in 1984. All religions have equal freedom before the law, but not in practice.

Religions	Pop %	Population	Ann Gr
Christian	82.38	49,508,373	-0.2%
Non-religious	14.13	8,491,786	3.7%
Muslim	2.60	1,562,537	4.9%
Buddhist	0.43	258,420	8.0%
Hindu	0.26	156,254	5.9%
Sikh	0.13	78,127	5.9%
Jewish	0.06	36,059	0.5%
Baha'i	0.01	6,010	0.5%

Christians	Denoms	Pop %	Affiliates	Ann Gr
Protestant	112	0.63	376,000	0.3%
Independent	21	0.44	262,000	4.0%
Anglican	1	0.02	10,000	-0.2%
Catholic	20	84.37	50,703,000	-0.1%
Orthodox	9	1.74	1,045,000	1.7%
Marginal	4	0.77	463,000	0.8%
Doubly affiliated		-5.59	-3,357,000	0.0%

Churches	MegaBloc	Congs	Members	Affiliates
Catholic Church	C	25,480	38,097,744	50,670,000
Romanian Orthodox	O	33	265,000	530,000
Jehovah's Witnesses	M	3,090	243,000	432,000
Ukrainian Orthodox	O	7	140,000	210,000
Assem of God in Italy	P	1,200	127,820	170,000
Greek Orthodox Ch	O	10	62,500	125,000
Pente Chs Federation	I	380	31,000	62,000
Int Evangelical Ch	I	210	18,250	36,500
Albanian Orthodox Ch	O	4	17,647	30,000
Evang Chr Breth Ch	P	272	17,610	28,000
Waldensian & Meth Ch	P	151	15,597	24,800
Latter-day Saints (Mormon)	M	120	13,772	23,000
Pente Chr Congs	I	55	10,000	17,000
Other denominations[154]		2,034	245,054	500,597
Doubly affiliated				-3,357,000
Total Christians[167]		**33,046**	**39,304,994**	**49,501,897**

TransBloc	Pop %	Population	Ann Gr
Evangelicals			
Evangelicals	1.1	632,714	1.9%
Renewalists			
Charismatics	3.3	2,010,192	2.9%
Pentecostals	0.7	449,500	1.8%

Answers to Prayer

1 **Increasing acceptance of diversity** within the Church bears witness to a gradual change from the decades, even centuries, of division within Protestantism. There is a growing sense of grace and acceptance of appropriate theological differences. Widespread division, legalism, fragmentation and distrust stunted the potential impact of evangelicals, but respect and even cooperation are starting to develop.

2 **Global awareness has grown with rising immigration.** The impact is two-fold: the presence of vibrant congregations of Eastern Europeans, Romanians, Africans, Asians and Latinos is a great encouragement to the Church in Italy, and the presence of large numbers of unevangelized peoples reminds native Italians of the need for outreach and mission at home and abroad.

Challenges for Prayer

1 **This great and gifted nation has contributed much to the world** – legal systems (Roman law), language (Latin), culture (Renaissance, art, music) and innovation (fashion, cars). Christianity flourished here, but soon became a formalized state religion. Italy was virtually untouched by the Protestant Reformation and has never seen widespread biblical revival. The majority of Italians remain culturally Catholic but increasingly cynical about the Church. Pray for the removal of the multiple barriers that limit understanding of the gospel.

2 **Organized crime networks** have infiltrated every level of society. Their criminal activities have influence even in local and federal governments, despite the state's attempts to reduce their power. Their income, largely from drugs and extortion/protection rackets, is such that only the government has a higher financial turnover. The Sicilian mafia and Neapolitan *camorra* are more well known but now less powerful than the Calabrian *'Ndrangheta*. Pray for those courageous enough to oppose this parasitic system draining the Italian economy. Pray for Christians to live out Kingdom values and morals when faced with difficult decisions. Pray for a transformation of Italian government, law enforcement and economy.

3 **The Roman Catholic Church** continues to show signs of crisis. Studies suggest that, at most, 15% (but as low as 3%) of Italians faithfully practice Catholicism. The north is largely secular; in the south, a mix of religious Catholicism and folk superstition prevails. Yet at the same time, the Catholic Church is active and outgoing – it embodies Italian identity amid a fragmented political system and high immigration, as well as taking a strong stand against the onset of secularization and greater relativism. However, the numbers of attending faithful and of new priests are rapidly declining. Hoped-for renewal from the Catholic charismatic movement, while welcomed, is limited. Pray for the millions of Italians either locked in dead traditions or disillusioned by organized religion altogether; may they discover the living Christ.

I

4 **Indifference to the gospel** has typified Italy for ages. Secular materialism ensnares many. Satanism is growing in various areas, Turin being one of the global centres of its activities. Occultism continues to be alarmingly widespread – there are more than 150,000 practicing soothsayers, prognosticators and healers, in contrast to around 50,000 Catholic priests! Eastern and esoteric spirituality are increasingly popular. Italians are more liable to dabble in an occult, New Age or pagan practice than to read the Bible. Those who do pray will often pray to Padre Pio (37%) or Saint Anthony (21%) rather than to Jesus (less than 10%). Cults are active; Jehovah's Witnesses number more in Italy than all its Protestants combined.

5 **Protestantism has an 800-year history in Italy.** The world's oldest Protestant denomination, the Waldensian Church, developed in northwest Italy, but for centuries was subjected to terrible persecution. Italian Catholic bishops officially apologized for this in 1997. The Waldensian Church – now part of a federation with, among others, Methodists and the mainline Baptist Union – is openly dominated by liberal theology. The broader Protestant witness is weak and divided, polarized and fragmented. Traditional Pentecostalism is strong, particularly in the south. The fast-growing and diverse charismatic churches are increasingly numerous, dynamic and holistic in their outreach. The relationship between Pentecostals/charismatics and conservatives, deeply opposed in the past, shows small and encouraging signs of progress. Strategic church planting is rare; bitter splits are still more common. Many congregations are small, insular and resistant to change and to mission. Larger congregations at times battle with superficiality, the need for discipleship and the challenge of nominalism among second- and third-generation believers. Pray for revival that breaks down barriers of individualism, mistrust and doctrinal extremes, and leads to fellowship and cooperative outreach.

6 **Signs of hope for the Church.** Many challenges and difficulties remain, and progress is invariably painfully slow. Some encouraging glimmers of hope, however, need to be earnestly prayed for:

a) Cooperation among churches. Division and polarization have been the legacies of Protestantism, but things are beginning to change. Several different church networks are beginning to foster trust, respect and even collaboration across the denominational divide. The Evangelical Alliance works to this end, as do various network initiatives.

b) Evangelism and outreach. Relational evangelism is an effective approach, as are the cell groups and house churches that often result. These and other new expressions of fellowship are increasingly popular. Also, groups such as Christ Is the Answer, Italy for Christ, the Brethren and some Pentecostals continue with larger-scale, event-based evangelism. Christian TV has an impact, but largely by promoting prosperity teachings.

c) **Missions vision is still in its infancy.** The churches in Italy are supporting holistic projects (Compassion, AMEN, *Missione Evangelica contro la Lebbra, Missione Possibile*, to name a few) and developing short-term sending (**OM, NTM, WEC, YWAM**, GLO). Few Italians, however, are involved in long-term career missions whether in Italy or beyond. Italian Ministries is committed to facilitate a vision for mission and has also developed a mission agency option for interested Italians. Denominational initiatives continue. International mission groups (among these: **OM, YWAM, NTM**) operate in Italy and seek to facilitate Italians' involvement in mission. Encouraging developments among youth bring hope for the future; "9.37" is one such group.

d) **Immigration of believers into Italy** – particularly from Eastern Europe and Africa but also from Latin America and Philippines – infuses new vitality and openness into the churches, and it opens Italians' eyes to the needs on their doorstep and abroad. It is now conceivable that the majority of evangelicals in Italy are no longer ethnic Italians. Pray that this new reality might spur indigenous churches to greater faith, cooperation and good works.

7 The challenge of Christian leadership in Italy remains urgent, since a lack of mature, qualified and gifted leaders persists. Academic and pastoral training are needs, but finance, time and lack of vision limit opportunities. Authentic servant leadership must be demonstrated, since authoritarian structures, power struggles and dependence on programmes rather than on pastoral discipling are unfortunately common. Thankfully, increasingly diverse options are available:

a) **Full-time training institutions.** IBEI and IBI(**AoG**) offer academic degrees through residential programmes. A newly established Pentecostal faculty in the Naples area offers accredited theological degrees. There are a few shorter, residential programmes (**YWAM/** *Gioventu in Missione*).

b) **Modular programmes** are growing quickly, especially helpful for bivocational pastors and lay leaders. Among others are *Accademia Teologica Italiana* (Aurora Mission) and *Istituto di Formazione Evangelica e Documentazione*. Local training initiatives are also increasingly popular.

Pray that the various means of training would bolster pastoral leadership across the nation and, in turn, uplift and disciple the whole Church to entirely new levels of maturity.

8 The least reached sectors of the population:

a) **More than 70% of Italy's 8,101 comuni** (communities ranging from small village to large city) are without an established Bible-believing congregation.

b) **Many areas of Italy lack a strong indigenous evangelical presence** (specifically: Abruzzo, Friuli, Liguria, Marche, Molise, Trentino, Umbria, Valle d'Aosta and Veneto). Immigration and some very modest church growth are slowly improving the situation.

c) **Sardinia,** a Mediterranean island with limited autonomy, has 1.67 million people and its own language and culture. Sardinia has only about 30 evangelical churches and a few Christian workers. There has been radio outreach for some years. Suspicion of outsiders, fear, vendettas, the occult and the activities of JWs all make any evangelistic outreach difficult.

d) **The 1,850,000 students** in 94 universities remain a needy and crucial mission field. GBU(**IFES**) has nearly 30 groups with around 300 students and aims to eventually have 50. Agape(**CCCI**), Great Commission in northern Italy and a growing number of local congregations focus on students as well. In Milan alone, there are more than 175,000 students with little outreach being done – **CW** is one of a handful working in this context. Also, there are increasing opportunities to reach international students in Italy.

e) **The estimated 500,000 drug addicts** have high rates of HIV infection and crime. Cocaine and sniffing solvents are the fastest-growing problems, affecting young people in particular. Evangelicals are only beginning to meet the challenge (Betel in 5 centres; Teen Challenge 2; **AoG** 2).

9 Unreached minorities:

a) Ancient minority groups are clustered in different parts of Italy, but most have even less gospel light than the main Italian majority. These include Albanians, several minorities in the northeast, and Greeks and Croatians in the south. Most have largely integrated with Italian life and culture.

b) Muslims. Their numbers have grown rapidly through legal and illegal immigration to nearly 1.5 million, 70% of whom are North African. Most of the Muslim population are concentrated in cities of the north. META is involved in reaching them and mobilizing the churches to do the same.

c) Romani (Gypsies). Many have recently flooded into Italy, becoming the latest immigration challenge for Italian authorities. While their treatment by authorities is sometimes poor and harsh, as are their living conditions, a high proportion are involved in illegal activities. Pray for outreach to this group, since they have shown great responsiveness to the gospel in other Western European nations.

d) Illegal immigration is a major challenge on many fronts. Italy functions as a gateway into the EU, and many people brave the dangerous sea crossing in overcrowded boats to get there, some dying along the way. This desperation fuels and funds organized crime in Italy and abroad and drains the resources of the government. Increased xenophobia in some parts is another side effect. Pray for illegal immigrants who find themselves in Italy; may they discover spiritual freedom and richness in Jesus Christ.

10 **The need for expatriate workers** has not diminished, but it has changed. Helping the existing Italian Church mature, expand and reach out, as partners and with a servant attitude, is now needed. Attrition is traditionally high here, often due to inadequate preparation, entrenched opposition and relatively low fruitfulness. Some significant groups (and a number of expatriates) in the country are **CB**/CMML/EoS, **TEAM**, **Avant**, *Missions-gesellschaft*, Campus Missions International. Italian Ministries is a field-based mission, started in 1998, that has a positive impact in further enabling foreign workers.

11 **Literature and Bible distribution** have not had a wide impact due to Italians' reluctance to read. There are about 15 Christian bookshops, including **CLC** with nine bookstores and The Bible Society with Italy's largest Bible and literature centre. Pray for the growing number of Italian publishing houses – ADI Media (**AoG**), Alfa & Omega (Reformed publishers), GBU and *Passaggio*, among others. Pray also for the spread of the newly published Bible dictionary (GBU) and theological dictionary (by IFED). Pray for a hunger for God's Word, for a desire for wholesome Christian literature and that quality material that leads people to Christ would be found in the more than 1,000 Catholic bookshops. The Gideons are active throughout Italy in distributing Scripture. Italy For Christ has spearheaded the distribution of over 600,000 NTs in schools as well as many copies of the evangelistic *Book of Hope*.

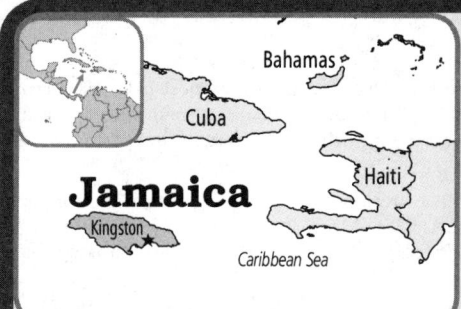

Jamaica

Kingston ★

Caribbean Sea

Jamaica

Caribbean

Geography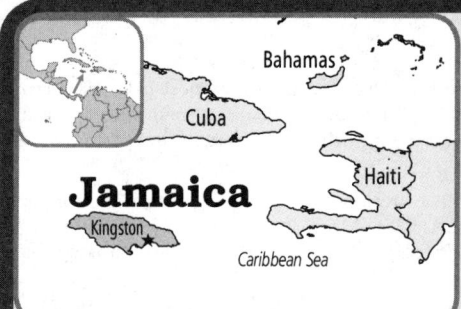

Area 10,991 sq km. The 3rd largest island in the Caribbean after Cuba and Hispaniola. Mostly mountainous with only 17% arable land.

Population		Ann Gr	Density
2010	2,729,909	0.46%	248/sq km
2020	2,834,321	0.34%	258/sq km
2030	2,873,362	0.05%	261/sq km

Jamaicans have emigrated in large numbers (more than 2 million) to North America, UK, and increasingly elsewhere. 80% of Jamaicans with higher education live abroad.
Capital Kingston 582,000. **Urbanites** 53.7%. **Pop under 15 yrs** 29%. **Life expectancy** 71.7 yrs.

Peoples

African Caribbean 96.0%. Jamaican 93.7%; Haitian 2.0%.
Asian/Afro-Asian 3.0%. East Indian 1.7%; Chinese 1.2%.
Euro–American 1.0%. British 0.4%; American 0.3%.
Literacy 87.6%. **Official language** English; 97% of the population speak Jamaican Creole. **All languages** 7. **Indigenous languages** 3. **Languages with Scriptures** 1Bi 1w.i.p.

Economy

Tourism, remittances, the mining of bauxite, and agriculture are the main revenue sources. High debt servicing, frequent hurricane damage and rising crime rates can be added to the normal financial challenges of underemployment, inflation and foreign competition. Servicing the large public debt takes up much of the GDP.
HDI Rank 100th/182. **Public debt** 116.3% of the GDP. **Income/person** $5,199 (11% of USA).

Politics

Originally inhabited by the Taino Indians. Spanish "discovery" and rule from 1494 followed by British rule from 1655 until independence in 1962, when Jamaica became a parliamentary democracy. Notable political stability has not always translated into the social, criminal or economic spheres. Gang rivalries and warfare for "turf", illicit drug dealing, alignment of political parties and the dubious dealings in granting construction contracts all blend in an unsavoury mix to allow for a rise in crime, corruption and violence.

Religion

Freedom of religion.

Religions	Pop %	Population	Ann Gr
Christian	82.91	2,263,368	0.4%
Ethnoreligionist	10.20	278,451	0.7%
Non–religious	4.65	126,941	1.1%
Other	0.90	24,569	2.9%
Hindu	0.65	17,744	2.1%
Muslim	0.30	8,190	4.2%
Baha'i	0.20	5,460	0.5%
Chinese	0.18	4,914	2.9%
Jewish	0.01	273	–2.5%

Christians	Denoms	Pop %	Affiliates	Ann Gr
Protestant	53	36.05	984,000	0.8%
Independent	106	10.20	279,000	1.2%
Anglican	1	3.66	100,000	–0.2%
Catholic	1	4.25	116,000	0.2%
Orthodox	1	0.10	3,000	–0.6%
Marginal	9	1.95	53,000	3.6%
Unaffiliated		26.70	729,000	–1.1%

Churches	MegaBloc	Congs	Members	Affiliates
Seventh-day Adventist	P	600	210,000	265,000
NT Church of God	P	800	75,000	165,000
Catholic Church	C	93	67,442	116,000
Jamaica Baptist Union	P	315	38,000	108,680
Anglican Church	A	266	50,000	100,000
Ch of God of Prophecy	P	300	28,000	70,000
NT Church of Christ	I	158	31,500	69,930
Ch of God (Anderson)	P	106	5,000	50,000
United Church	P	200	17,500	47,000
Methodist Church	P	170	17,400	44,000
Jehovah's Witnesses	M	205	16,538	43,000
United Pentecostal Ch	P	240	26,000	39,000
Revival Zion	I	318	17,500	30,625
Apostolic Church	P	36	9,000	27,270
Moravian Church	P	55	6,300	25,000
Other denominations[156]		1,942	170,842	334,238
Total Christians[171]		**5,804**	**786,022**	**1,534,743**

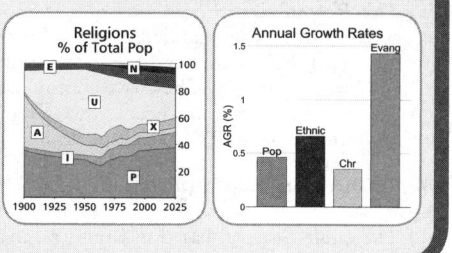

TransBloc	Pop %	Population	Ann Gr
Evangelicals			
Evangelicals	28.0	764,733	1.4%
Renewalists			
Charismatics	20.7	564,541	1.8%
Pentecostals	15.9	433,675	1.6%

Missionaries from Jamaica
P,I,A Approximately 100 in 18 agencies from 26 countries.

Answers to Prayer

1 **Jamaica has a wonderful Christian heritage.** Praise God that many leadership positions have transitioned from foreign workers to national leaders, enabling the Jamaican Church to come into its own.

2 **This nation has a rich but little-known mission sending history.** Praise God for those rediscovering this spiritual legacy and remobilizing Jamaica to once again become a sending powerhouse. Increasing numbers of mission agencies are operating branches out of Jamaica.

Challenges for Prayer

1 **The country finds itself in the midst of moral and social collapse.** Powerful South American drug cartels, using Jamaica as a transshipment point for cocaine destined for the USA, wield great influence. This fuels violence, putting Jamaica fourth globally for murders per capita. Rape and domestic abuse are widespread. As part of an anti-corruption drive, the government has invited greater participation from churches. Pray that government and church leaders may reject compromise. Pray for courage, moral integrity and determination to turn the country back to God. The National Leadership Prayer Breakfast brings church leaders together with leaders in politics, business and the security forces to address and pray for these issues.

2 **Jamaican Christianity needs reformation and renewal.** It enjoys one of the world's highest number of churches per square mile, but the majority of self-proclaimed Christians in Jamaica neither attend church nor lead a Christian life. Networks – such as the Jamaica Council of Churches, the Jamaica Association of Evangelicals and the Jamaica Pentecostal Union as well as many ministers' fraternals – seek to address and combat the political and social ills while working for unity and true Christian faith and practice in the Church.

3 **With the most evangelicals and the best-resourced churches** in the Caribbean, Jamaica can and should be a spiritual leader in the region for evangelism and mission, training and unity. Pray that the 15 Bible schools and seminaries in Jamaica as well as the Keswick teaching conferences, which serve the whole Caribbean, may be powerhouses of biblical theology, practice and vision.

4 **Young people.** OAC has reached over one million in its 20-plus years of evangelistic outreach to school assemblies. **CCCI** has a presence on both university campuses in the capital. **CEF** ministers through Bible clubs, camps and devotions in schools. **IFES** and SU have a combined ministry (SCFSU), producing Bible reading materials and witnessing in over 200 schools and 20 tertiary institutions. Pray for effective evangelism and discipling of young people that will prepare them to cope with the many challenges of life.

5 **The less evangelized** who need prayer:

a) The very poor have little exposure to the gospel except by radio. There is a large underclass, including the pseudo-orphaned "barrel children", among whom mostly Catholic and Anglican ministries work. These gospel-neglected people have little by way of moral foundations; pray for the whole gospel to touch their lives and communities.

b) The Rastafarians began as a protest movement that mixed Christian beliefs with Black consciousness ideas and deified the Ethiopian Emperor Haile Selasse I. They are well known for their reggae music and use of *ganja* (marijuana), as well as for their non-violent "peace and love" philosophy. They have considerable influence in Jamaica and have spread to Europe and North America. In recent years, a few prominent Rastafarians have professed Christ as Saviour and become active evangelicals.

6 **Christian help ministries** – many serving the whole Caribbean.

a) The Bible Society, based in Kingston, channels Scriptures to most of the mini-states of the region. The Society has a strong vision of making Scripture accessible to young people in particular.

b) Christian bookstores. Source of Light Ministries operates six Christian bookstores in Kingston and runs the region's largest Bible Correspondence Course. **CLC** has a notable ministry through three bookstores.

c) Christian broadcasting. Radio is broadcast in English by **TWR** (from within Jamaica) and by others from outside, totaling 77 hours per week. In the country itself, there is also a religious radio (LOVE FM) and TV station.

d) The Student Christian Fellowship and Scripture Union (SCF/SU), as well as Jamaica Youth for Christ and Jamaica Child Evangelism Fellowship, do valuable work among the younger generation. Many outstanding Christian leaders serving globally or in Jamaica are products of these ministries.

Japan
Nihon
Asia

Geography 🌐

Area 377,801 sq km. A 3,000 km arc of four large islands (Honshu, Hokkaido, Shikoku, Kyushu) and 3,000 small islands in NW Pacific. Mountainous; only 13% can be cultivated.

Population		Ann Gr	Density
2010	126,995,411	-0.07%	336/sq km
2020	123,664,363	-0.34%	327/sq km
2030	117,423,894	-0.56%	311/sq km

Capital Tokyo-Yokohama 36,669,000. **Major cities** Osaka–Kobe 11.4million; Nagoya 3.3mill; Fukuoka 2.8m; Sapporo 2.7m; Sendai 2.4m; Hiroshima 2.1m; Kyoto 1.8m. **Urbanites** 66.8%.

Pop under 15 yrs 13%. **Life expectancy** 82.7 yrs.

Peoples 🧍🧍🧍

Indigenous 98.5%.

Japanese 98.5%. Sub-groups: Ryukyuan 0.8%; South American Japanese returnees 0.2%.

Ainu 0.02%. The aboriginal inhabitants who have largely lost their original languages and largely been assimilated into Japanese culture. Officially numbering just over 25,000, unofficial estimates range up to 200,000.

Foreign 1.5%. Korean 0.5%; Chinese 0.3%; Filipino 0.3%; other Asian, Western.

Illegal immigrants. Possibly 1 million Pakistani, Iranian, Bangladeshi, Filipino, Thai, Malaysian, others.

Literacy 100%. **Official language** Japanese. **All languages** 16 (including 11 Okinawan-Ryukyuan dialects). **Languages with Scriptures** 2Bi 1NT 2por 1w.i.p.

Economy 📈

One of the world's most powerful export-oriented economies despite lack of natural resources and oil. High savings and low interest rates stimulated a massive capital investment boom based on high property values. This property bubble burst in 1989, leading to recession and a debt crisis. What followed is known as "The Lost Decade", characterized by zero growth and higher unemployment as Japan struggled to bail out its failing banking sector. However, Japan's enormous trade surplus with the world continued. The 2008-09 worldwide recession led to Japan's first trade deficits in many years as well as its highest post–war unemployment rate (5%). Public debt is close to 200% of GDP, but private savings levels are still extremely high, protecting many individuals from the poor economic performance. The low birth rate and aging population are major societal and economic concerns for the future.

HDI Rank 10th/182. **Public debt** 172% of GDP. **Income/person** \$38,457 (81% of USA).

Politics 𝕏

Constitutional monarchy with a parliamentary democracy. Years of stability and economic expansion since WWII turned Japan into an economic superpower. Rising nationalism and willingness to exert political power in the Pacific cause unease among neighbours. Numerous scandals, corruption and factional politics discredit the present political system and delay the implementation of reforms. In the general election of 2009, the Democratic Party of Japan (DPJ) defeated the Liberal Democrat Party (LDP), which had been in power almost continuously since WWII.

Religion 🙏

Freedom of religion is guaranteed to all by the constitution. Over 70% of Japanese claim no personal religion, but the majority follow the demands of idolatrous and ancestor-venerating Buddhism, and rituals of polytheistic Shintoism. Historically, Japanese identity is deeply tied to Shintoism, and formal disassociation from this connection is extremely difficult in a land where conformity rules. Many also follow some of the hundreds of newer religious movements that are off-shoots or interpretations of these. The main ones: *Sokka Gakkai* (10m), *Risshokosekai* (5.5m), *Seicho no Ie* (3.7m). Therefore, figures in the table below cannot adequately show the multiple religious loyalties of the Japanese, which could be described as New Religions 24%, Buddhist 85%, Shinto 90%!

Religions	Pop %	Population	Ann Gr
Buddhist	69.59	88,376,107	-0.1%
Other	23.70	30,097,912	-0.2%
Non-religious	5.00	6,349,771	1.2%
Christian	1.54	1,955,729	-0.2%
Muslim	0.15	190,493	1.3%
Baha'i	0.02	25,399	-0.1%

Christians Denoms		Pop %	Affiliates	Ann Gr
Protestant	155	0.44	555,000	-1.1%
Independent	37	0.25	317,000	0.9%
Anglican	1	0.04	57,000	0.0%
Catholic	1	0.40	513,000	0.2%
Orthodox	2	0.03	32,000	1.5%
Marginal	8	0.38	484,000	-0.3%

Churches	MegaBloc	Congs	Members	Affiliates
Catholic Church	C	1,095	358,741	513,000
Jehovah's Witnesses	M	3,180	212,000	354,040
United Ch of Christ	P	1,730	130,769	187,000
Spirit of Jesus Church	I	624	74,850	125,000
Latter-day Saints (Mormon)	M	300	99,600	124,500
Holy Catholic Ch	A	316	28,450	56,900
Independent churches	I	751	33,786	47,300
Baptist Convention	P	335	16,875	35,100
Assemblies of God	P	215	22,800	31,000
Evang Lutheran Ch	P	160	7,267	22,020
Seventh-day Adventist	P	119	15,300	17,150
Japan Holiness Ch	P	168	5,400	13,500
J Gospel Ch of Christ	P	228	9,600	12,960
Presby Ch of Christ	P	125	5,485	12,450
Immanuel General Miss	P	123	7,029	12,300
Christian Brethren	P	165	8,500	11,200
Korean-speaking chs	P	139	6,950	10,425
English-speaking chs	P	189	6,667	10,000
Reformed Ch in Japan	P	154	5,297	9,800
J Chr Allliance (TEAM)	P	190	6,704	9,050
Holy Ecclesia of Jesus	I	112	6,885	8,400
Baptist Union	P	70	4,420	7,028
Other denominations[159]		5,087	217,646	328,747
Total Christians[204]		**15,575**	**1,291,021**	**1,958,870**

TransBloc	Pop %	Population	Ann Gr
Evangelicals			
Evangelicals	0.5	596,498	-0.4%
Renewalists			
Charismatics	0.3	374,431	1.1%
Pentecostals	0.2	256,679	0.8%

Missionaries from Japan
P,I,A Estimated 300 serving outside Japan.

Religions % of Total Pop

MegaBlocs % of Christian Pop

Answers to Prayer

1 **Uncertainty about the future has prompted spiritual searching.** This is partly in response to many economic and social changes that threaten the status quo in Japan. The constant threats of a major earthquake, of economic decline, the widening generation gap and the feeling of social isolation (*hikikomori*) that so many suffer provoke widespread soul-searching.

2 **Give praise for increasing openness to Christianity.** As Japan increasingly engages with the outside world, as Christian work doggedly presses on and as Japanese society itself changes, more people are opening to the gospel. A recent poll indicates that 3% of Japanese identify themselves as "Christian" (not all would truly be so, but it is indicative of changing mentalities), and 10% see Christianity as a viable religious option for themselves. Many believe Japanese society is poised for an unprecedented awakening to the gospel.

3 **Creativity and cultural insight in ministry** are reshaping the way church and mission are being done. Many new initiatives seek to connect with the heart of Japanese mentality and culture. After centuries of outreach from a predominantly Western outlook and extremely modest church growth, new approaches are welcome and even overdue.

Challenges for Prayer

1 **Japan is a nation facing many crises** and is a culture with no apparent direction. Accompanying this drifting is its lack of hope or confidence in the future. Pray for the following issues, all profoundly felt by Japanese society:

a) A lack of a moral centre. Japan's own leaders called it "a superpower without a moral compass". This is most notable among young people, who struggle with particular challenges such as social phobia or social anxiety (*Hikikomori*), a suicide epidemic (over 30,000/year), bullying and teenage prostitution. High rates of suicide in other age groups and divorce also reflect this challenge.

b) Political leadership is characterized more by factional dynamics with self-seeking parties than by nation builders. The legacy of WWII hangs over and holds back the government in many ways. A recent, rapid succession of prime ministers has relatively paralyzed urgently needed reforms to address economic and birth rate issues.

c) Major economic transitions. The world's third-largest economy, rocked by recessions in recent years, stands at a crossroads. The job-for-life salarymen are becoming outdated, and the younger generation is uninterested in the type of lifelong commitment that forged Japan into an economic giant. Lack of natural resources, increasingly competitive high-tech markets and demographic changes make for an uncertain economic future. The inability (or unwillingness) of many of the younger generation, even well-educated ones, to get full-time career jobs is another recent phenomenon.

d) The percentage of the aged in Japan's population is rapidly increasing (faster than any other nation), with one of the world's lowest birth rates and highest life expectancies. By 2055, half of Japanese will be pensioners – an unprecedented demographic situation and a monumental economic challenge. Caring for the elderly already accounts for the majority of the health budget.

e) Crime rates have significantly increased in recent years. Japan used to be one of the world's safest places, but the recent influx of foreign criminal elements, the influence of the yakuza mafia, the rapid growth of random, meaningless violent crime and the unpreparedness of the state and police to counter these changes combine to cause many Japanese to feel stressed and no longer safe.

2 **Spiritual openness is mitigated by hindrances to the gospel.** There are several ways in which the eyes of the Japanese are blinded to the good news:

a) The spiritual powers and principalities that exercise authority in Japan have never been decisively challenged. The powers associated with idolatry in temples and ancestor worship in homes prevail, even in modernistic, "non-religious" Japan. Japanese Christians face notable social and family pressures to conform to Shinto practices, particularly at the New Year and during funerals. Additionally, too many Christians are either ignorant or in denial of the very real spiritual battle.

b) The Bible is alien to the worldview of the Japanese – the concept of a Creator God is foreign to most. Strong pressure to conform to the norm causes many new believers to compromise or eventually fall away. The shame/honour mentality held by many Japanese is a different paradigm from that of most missionaries to Japan. Christians new and old must be discipled to have their entire worldview transformed.

c) *The persistent influence of nationalistic Shintoism,* which is hostile to anything 'un-Japanese' and compromises Christians involved with it. Pray for Christians to stand firm in Jesus against this pervasive spiritual force.

d) *Socio-economic life.* The sincere, polite, hardworking Japanese are too busy to give heed to the gospel. Materialism, very much on the rise, dominates the ambitions of most younger people. Only 10% believe in the existence of a personal God; only 50% have ever even desired help from God or gods.

e) *New religions.* The Japan-based Buddhist lay movement *Sokka Gakkai* has grown to include 10 million affiliates. Scores of new religions are started each year – many based on the occult, worship of extraterrestrial aliens and so on. Their excesses, mind-control and brainwashing are well documented in the national media. Pray for the removal of a spirit of delusion. The 1995 gas attack on the Tokyo subway by the *Aum Shinrikyo* sect reaffirmed to many the danger of deviating from traditional Shinto sensibilities.

3 **The Church in Japan** experienced growth between 1945 and 1960, but both Catholic and Protestant percentages have increased only marginally since then, with conversions only just exceeding backslidings. It is believed that half of those baptized in Japan leave their churches within two or three years. The decisive breakthrough has yet to come, so pray for:

a) *The United Church* – a union of all Protestant churches formed under duress during WWII. Almost all compromised with Shinto and emperor worship, losing their spiritual vitality. After the war, many groups pulled out to form their own denominations. The United Church, and subsequently many other denominations, issued statements repenting of their participation in war and idol worship during the war. The ethos of repentence is widely held by Japanese Christians, and many believe that a truly national-level repentance for this sad episode is a key for spiritual breakthrough.

b) *The growing evangelical witness.* In 1950, evangelicals were 40% of Protestants and Independents; in 2010, they measured 67%. The Japan Evangelical Association (JEA) is one major coordinating body for the many denominations.

J

c) *Quasi-Christian groups* such as Jehovah's Witnesses and Mormons have grown far faster than evangelicals or Catholics and are the largest and most visible "Christian" presence in many areas, numbering nearly as many as Protestants or Catholics. There are several agencies committed to helping JWs to faith in Christ, but overall, there is little ministry devoted to pointing these people toward biblical faith.

4 Specific challenges facing the Church:

a) *Christianity is still regarded as an outside, Western religion* rather than a universal faith with the capacity to be truly Japanese. This is despite 500 years of Christian presence in Japan. This also allows for confusion between various Western cultural imports and genuinely Christian expressions of the good news.

b) *The minority complex.* Christians are a tiny minority in a society where consensus and conformity are important. Too few families come to faith, and too many individuals feel exposed. Pray for the Church to reach the size of critical mass and native character that will give it social credence and acceptability.

c) *Unity is lacking in a Church* that numbers only 1.5% of the population. Literally hundreds of denominations and groups exist along very fragmented lines. Such organizational and theological divides and lack of nationwide cooperation hamper progress and increase attrition rates. The United Church and the JEA have started enjoying much improved relations.

d) *A new way of doing church needs to be discovered.* Too often traditions and forms of worship have authority nearly equal to the Bible itself. Nonessential forms of the Church must be adapted to look less like the introduced Western culture of years past and more like 21st-century Japan. House churches are another way of reaching Japanese who are uncomfortable with being part of traditional churches.

e) *The strong Confucian tradition in Japan* has admirably created a society with high ethical standards; the need for the Church to maintain these standards as a minimum can often lead congregations into legalism.

f) Non–active membership and backsliding. Church attendance is low; less than half of church members regularly attend. Often, Christians are influenced by the Buddhist/Shinto religions, which have no regular attendance requirements, and they carry this thinking into Christian activities. Although evangelicals number up to 0.5% of the population, regular Protestant church attendance may be less than half of that.

g) Too few viable, active congregations. At least 70% of all churches have an average attendance of less than 30. Too much is expected of the pastor. Pray for pastors willing to activate lay people to engage in persistent, innovative outreach to non–Christians. Most churches will not have even one baptism in any given year!

h) The lack of men in churches. The drive for success and desire to satisfy the demands of employers make it hard for men to openly identify with and become active in a church. On average, women attenders outnumber men 7 to 1.

5 **The impact of the Japanese Church** on the nation is inadequate. The Church must turn from its insular, bunker mentality to engage with society. The government is not adequately solving the social ills confronting Japan; the transforming power of Christ, as expressed through a revived Church, is an answer not being adequately offered. There is, however, a new emphasis on evangelism in many churches and a willingness to try new paradigms of ministry. Pray for Christianity to have a massive and redemptive impact on the nation.

6 **Bible training** for Christian workers is vitally needed and provided by 125 denominational and interdenominational seminaries and Bible schools. Pray for a new generation of pastors; 70% are over age 50. Leadership transition can be difficult and sensitive in a society that so reveres the elderly. Particularly notable are Asian Access's Japan Growth Institute (where 1% of Japan's pastors have been trained – but that 1% accounts for 90% of church growth in the country) and JEMA's Church Planting Institute. A number of theological institutions are also doing admirable work. Financial constraints are one of the biggest challenges facing students/ pastors; pray for provision.

7 **The missions vision of Japanese Christians is noteworthy.** There are up to 300 Japanese serving in 34 lands around the world. However, churches generally have little vision for missions and little understanding of the challenges facing cross-cultural missionaries. Mission training programmes for prospective Japanese missionaries are increasing, both in Japanese and in English. The Japanese Overseas Missions Association has a membership of over 20 Japanese agencies.

8 **Mission to Japan** – Japan is the largest unevangelized nation that is completely open to missionaries. Yet, due to spiritual, socio-cultural, linguistic and financial difficulties, becoming an effective minister of the gospel is a long, hard process of adaptation.

a) Cooperation among mission agencies has been limited in the past and, while improved, still needs greater unity today. JEMA is a coordinating body for 46 mission organizations, representing over 1,100 missionaries. Most are involved in church planting and evangelism, but real church growth is elusive. Pray for strategic insight, for the anointing of the Spirit and for fruitful collaboration. The profusion of agencies and nationalities defies listing here. Largest missions: **OMF**, **TEAM**, Pac Rim/**IMB**, **SEND**, JCCC(**CCCI**), **MTW**), **BIM**, Asian Access, Every Nation, UMC, **WEC**, **AoG** USA, Mission to Unreached Peoples and Navigators.

b) Opportunities for missionary service are many, the most needful being evangelism, teaching, and planting and serving churches. Many missionaries are involved with existing congregations, assisting them to become reproductive through church planting and discipleship training. Teaching English is a wide-open door for tentmakers, with hundreds if not thousands of positions available. Long-term missionaries are the greater need because of the years needed to acquire the language and understand the culture.

c) The growing contribution of Korean missionaries is remarkable in light of historic animosities; they need special prayer cover to adapt well and have effective ministries.

d) Japanese returnees who became believers overseas are a hugely strategic group. Over a million Japanese live abroad; their numbers are greatest in the USA, Brazil and China. Every year, over 1,600 return home having encountered Jesus, many with a missional burden for their homeland. Japanese who return home having become Christians abroad struggle to integrate into the native church scene. Japanese Christian Fellowship Network, Japan Christian Link, Reaching Japanese for Christ, Friends International UK and several other ministries focus on this challenge. Pray for good coordination between ministries reaching Japanese abroad and those helping returnees to reintegrate into Japanese life. Pray for returning Christians to have a major impact on church life.

9 **The less-evangelized areas and peoples of Japan:**

a) There are 24 cities in Japan with no church at all, including Akabira, Utashinai, Obanazawa, Mino, Motosu, Inabe, Akitakata, Matsuura, Kamiamakusa and Kaseda. Of the 1,020 towns and villages, 595 have no church. Pray for a church planting movement that will penetrate these unreached areas.

b) Numerous rural areas are scarcely touched with the gospel. The Japanese Church has little vision for reaching out to the many towns with minimal or no Christian presence.

c) The ruling elite have been minimally influenced by the gospel. Pray for the emperor and royal family, cocooned in tradition and committed, by their position, to Shintoism. Pray for politicians and businessmen, those in control of finance and industry who have such global impact. There are some ministries aimed at them; the most dynamic among these is the VIP Club.

d) Koreans are descendants of those forcibly taken to Japan between 1903 and 1945. They are generally poorly treated and are classified as resident aliens – even into their third and fourth generations. The Korean community is sharply divided in their allegiance to either North or South Korea. South Korean missionaries have planted over 500 churches among them, but the percentage of Christians is lower than that of South Korea.

e) Chinese, who number 25,000, but perhaps twice that when including illegal immigrants. There are about 30 Chinese churches only, with fewer than 2,000 believers. Japan probably has the least-evangelized Chinese population of almost any nation. **OMF** and **AoG** are just two of the agencies focused on them.

f) The Ainu, ethnically unrelated to the Japanese, first settled in north Japan. They number as few as 25,000, and their heritage is at risk of extinction. The number of Ainu believers (if any) is unknown, and specific outreach is necessary.

g) Exploited women and their exploiters. The yakuza criminal network has actively imported 200,000 foreign women to become sex-slaves, usually through debt bondage. There are an estimated 100,000 Thai and also many Filipina women involved. Sex crimes against children are rapidly rising; Japanese men remain a significant source of the demand for prostitution of women and children across East and Southeast Asia. Child pornography is another polluting and exploitative evil that must be brought down through prayer and action. Pray for this evil system to be halted and for these tragically exploited women and children to be liberated at every level.

h) Muslims have increased through legal and illegal immigration of Bangladeshis, Malays, Iranians, Pakistanis and others. Some Japanese have become Muslim, largely through marriage. Little is being done to reach them.

10 **Young people** are becoming a "rare" breed due to Japan's low birth rate. The bonds that once held Japanese society together have rapidly dissolved, and the youngest generation are the most obvious casualties. Fully 85% of Japanese teens wonder why they exist at all, and 11% wish they had never been born. Those aged 18 to 23 are the most open to the gospel; the previously mentioned troubles that Japanese youth face explain their openness, but few actually become active believers. Student witness is one of the most strategic for the future of the Church. There are more than 3 million tertiary students in over 1,200 campuses. KGK (**IFES**) works on 250 of these. **CCCI** has 90 missionaries and 47 national staff, Navigators has 65 workers. **YWAM** and **AoG** are also involved in student ministry.

11 **The greying of Japan** is a serious demographic challenge, now and in the future. But it also makes for a greater opportunity to share Jesus, as many search for spiritual peace. Christian nursing homes and hospices will be strategic; pray for more to be opened. Christian care workers are also going to be in high demand, creating a clear tentmaking/mission opportunity for believers from other nations, such as the Philippines.

12 **Christian literature.** In no other country of the world is literature more appropriate for evangelism. A highly literate, reading, commuting society offers an excellent market for publishing and distributing high-quality Christian literature. Pray for:

a) *More Christian writers* of evangelistic and apologetic literature who can communicate with non-Christian enquirers.

b) *Scripture distribution.* The Gideons and The Bible Society cooperate to distribute nearly 2 million Bibles and NTs each year – another 1 million are sold. A new translation of the Bible in 2003 has been a blessing to this effort. Despite a significant minority of Japanese owning Scriptures, understanding this alien message is a challenge for most.

c) *Manga* (graphic novels) accounts for a third of all published books and magazines in Japan. *The Manga Bible*, the *Manga Messiah* and other Christian manga publications – including "The Gospel Edition" manga comic book, which prints 2 million copies per year – are therefore crucially important in reaching the Japanese.

d) *Christian bookstores* number over 100, with several large networks, including Word of Life (14 stores) and **CLC** (9 stores), websites and a bookmobile ministry.

e) *Evangelistic literature.* New Life League may be the largest producer of literature in Asia, producing 15 million pieces of literature annually for Japan, Asia and Eastern Europe. **EHC** has distributed nearly 200 million tracts over the years.

f) *Word of Life Press Ministries* (Swedish Alliance Mission) is Japan's largest non-profit publisher, with 190 Japanese Christian staff. Its 12 semi-independent divisions publish Bibles, books, music, videos, cassettes, CDs, computer software, Christian education materials, church supplies, two monthly magazines, a quarterly journal for pastors, tracts, gifts, cards and a weekly newspaper. It has a vital role in evangelicalism in Japan.

13 **Christian media** are very valuable in technologically astute Japan. Pray for these:

a) *The Internet* has opened many new streams of media. There are many sites for Japanese, from teaching and discipling of believers to apologetics and pre-evangelism. Congregations' websites are one major way that seekers find local churches.

b) *Arts,* both traditional and modern, are important to this sophisticated culture. Christians in the Arts Network encourages, connects and mobilizes artistic endeavours in the Church.

c) *Video and film.* Redemptive Films is a studio producing much-needed Christian films, and is a part of Christians in the Arts Network. The JESUS film is available in many formats. Pray for the distribution drive every Christmas.

d) *Christian TV and radio* are widely available for the tech-savvy Japanese. Light of the World, Harvest Time and Calvary Chapel Hours are three well-known programmes with millions of viewers. There are many ministries broadcasting or producing programmes for radio (shortwave, medium wave, FM and Internet radio). These include, but are not limited to, **FEBC**, **TEAM**, **TWR**, **HCJB**, Japan Mission, Lutheran Hour, Bible Broadcasting Network and BBI/Friendship Radio.

e) *Christian music,* particularly Black Gospel choirs, has an enthusiastic following in Japan. Many non-Christian Japanese sing in Black Gospel choirs; Hallelujah Gospel Family is a growing network of 35 gospel choirs with over 600 members – over 80% are non-Christian. Christmas music is also a popular contact point for the gospel in mainstream Japanese society.

Jordan

Hashemite Kingdom of Jordan

Asia

Geography 🌍

Area 89,206 sq km. Lies on the eastern bank of the Jordan River. Agriculture and population are concentrated near the river. Most of the country is desert.

Population		Ann Gr	Density
2010	6,472,392	3.06%	73/sq km
2020	7,518,599	1.56%	84/sq km
2030	8,616,498	1.27%	97/sq km

Capital Amman 1,105,402. **Urbanites** 78.5%. **Pop under 15 yrs** 35%. **Life expectancy** 72.4 yrs.

Peoples 👪

With mass relocation of Palestinians, Kuwaitis and Iraqis in the past decades, no precise figures exist.
Arab 95.4%. Palestinian 33.2%; East Bank Jordanian 31.3%; Iraqi 13.8%; Bedouin 4.0%.
Jordanian minorities 2.2%. Adygei (Circassian) 1.6%; Armenian, Kurd, Turkmen, Chechen.
Non-Jordanian 2.4%. Assyrian, Greek, Western, Pakistani, others.
Literacy 91.1%. **Official language** Arabic. **All languages** 16. **Indigenous languages** 10. **Languages with Scriptures** 2Bi 2NT 4por.

Economy 📈

The geopolitics of the last 60 years have seriously hindered economic development, making poverty and unemployment significant issues. Main income sources: tourism, phosphates, agricultural products. Jordan has no oil and little water. Broad economic reforms by King Abdullah since 1999.
HDI Rank 96th/182. **Public debt** 62.2% of GDP. **Income/person** $3,626 (8% of USA). **Unemployment** 14.5%.

Politics ⊠

Part of the Turkish Empire until 1918. Independent from Britain in 1946. Constitutional monarchy with King Abdullah having executive powers. Turmoil in the Middle East profoundly affects life, due to loss of land, massive influx of refugees and economic disruption. Jordan relinquished its claim to the West Bank area, but Palestinians are the largest group in the nation. A moderate Arab nation and a Western ally; suicide bombers in 2005 again brought to light Jordan's precarious position.

Religion 🤲

Islam (Sunni) is the state religion, but the constitution prohibits discrimination and promotes the free exercise of religious belief and worship. The Church has a visible public presence and relative freedom, but there is some pressure on evangelical churches.

Religions	Pop %	Population	Ann Gr
Muslim	96.47	6,243,917	3.1%
Christian	2.24	144,982	0.4%
Non-religious	1.00	64,724	3.1%
Other	0.28	18,123	3.1%
Baha'i	0.01	647	3.1%

Christians	Denoms	Pop %	Affiliates	Ann Gr
Protestant	16	0.23	15,000	3.2%
Independent	2	0.09	6,000	6.7%
Anglican	1	0.06	4,000	-0.5%
Catholic	3	0.40	26,000	-3.5%
Orthodox	4	1.46	94,000	0.8%
Marginal	1	<0.01	<300	2.3%

Churches	MegaBloc	Congs	Members	Affiliates
Greek Orthodox Ch	O	26	40,223	72,000
Catholic Church	C	60	14,857	26,000
Armenian Orthodox	O	2	9,581	16,000
Syrian Orthodox Ch	O	1	840	4,200
Evang Lutheran Ch	P	6	2,395	4,000
Episcopal Church	A	11	2,275	3,800
Jordan Baptist Conv	P	25	1,500	2,500
Coptic Church	O	2	1,150	2,300
Assemblies of God	P	10	1,200	1,950
Iraqi Evangelical chs	I	10	1,000	1,800
Other denominations[15]		53	6,784	10,218
Total Christians[27]		**206**	**81,805**	**144,768**

TransBloc	Pop %	Population	Ann Gr
Evangelicals			
Evangelicals	0.3	19,116	3.3%
Renewalists			
Charismatics	0.1	8,328	4.0%
Pentecostals	<0.1	2,250	1.1%

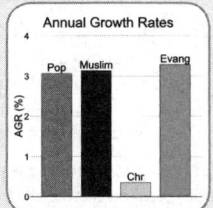

Annual Growth Rates

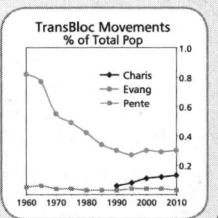

TransBloc Movements % of Total Pop

Challenges for Prayer

1 **King Abdullah's rule began with promise and hope.** But war in Iraq and the resulting turmoil have placed great pressure on the nation. Over a million immigrants fleeing from the two wars in Iraq have intensified Jordan's economic and political stresses. Half of them still remain. The tourist industry is a bright spot, but Islamist suicide bombings in 2005 demonstrated Jordan's fragility. Rising tensions between moderate and Islamist sentiments portend further difficulties. Pray for the peace of this land and for the king and government.

2 **Christians are a community under pressure.** Since Jordan's independence, lower birth rates and high emigration rates have contributed to the Church's numerical decline. Additionally, a huge influx of Muslim refugees and the rise of politicized Islam place increasing pressure on Christians, especially evangelicals. From 1980-2010, Jordan's Christian population dropped from 6.5% to 2.2% of the population. Yet, Christians are found in all walks of life, including in Parliament, and often in positions of influence. Christianity needs to be seen as an important component of Jordanian society and history. Pray that Christians may be salt and light in Jordanian society and find ways to witness to nominal Christians as well as non-Christians.

3 **The evangelical Church is experiencing encouraging growth,** doubling from 1995 to 2010. Believers meet at more than 50 churches and many more house groups. Most new believers are from the nominal Christian community, but recently more and more Muslims are coming to faith, possibly hundreds every year. This causes some increased pressure on churches from the authorities. Relationships between traditional and evangelical churches and believers from a Muslim background are cautious, but improving. A newly formed evangelical synod balances the diversity of denominations in a small evangelical population. In fact, churches work together rather well. Pray that all in Jordan who call on Christ might cooperate together to make Him known.

4 **The steady loss of leadership potential** through emigration is a drain on the body of believers. There is a great shortage of both lay leaders and full-time trained ministers. But, through several agencies and TEE courses, more Arab leaders are being trained for service in Jordan or in the wider Arab world. The work of Jordan Evangelical Theological Seminary is strategic in this regard. Pray for its continued impact in education and leadership development. Youth work, Christian bookstores and Christian camp ministries have been fruitful in recent years. Pray for more Jordanian believers to be called to full-time work.

5 **Religious freedom could be a casualty** amid rising religious tensions. This nation is a centre for many Christian activities and ministries, and much Christian work in the Middle East would suffer were a setback to occur in Jordan. A number of converts find life difficult – pressure comes from family, work and society. Emigration is often seen as an obvious and safe option. Pray for the freedom to proclaim the gospel and for followers of Jesus to be able to remain in Jordan.

6 **Ministry opportunities for foreign Christians are under threat,** but remain important. A crackdown on Islamist extremism resulted in some Christian ministries being shut down and visas denied. Several agencies are involved in a wide range of activities, usually supporting and enhancing the national Church and meeting humanitarian needs. Jordan also hosts a language school wherein many learn Arabic for their service in the Arab world. Pray that these expatriates' lives may commend the Lord Jesus and gain witness opportunities. Pray that the well-placed Jordanian Church might experience growth in its mission vision.

7 **The unreached comprise the vast majority of Jordan's population.** Upheaval in Iraq and the lethal violence of Islamism open many hearts to examine Isa al-Masih. Pray that every Jordanian may have opportunity to hear the gospel. Pray especially for:

a) *The Muslim majority.* Many have still not heard the clear gospel. Pray for a sensitive witness to Muslims. Several successful methods include literature, media ministry, friendship evangelism, development programmes, home meetings and camps. Pray for the protection of converts amid persecution. Pray also that the growing number of Muslim-background believers might have the legal right to convert from Islam.

b) *The millions of Palestinians,* who are a majority in Jordan. Many are the second or third generation after those removed from their traditional homeland. Some integrate into

Jordanian life; others suffer from disillusionment, bitterness and frustration which only the Man of Calvary can heal.

c) *Iraqi refugees.* During and after the two Gulf Wars, around one million Iraqis fled to Jordan. Years later, nearly half of these are unable or unwilling to return home. Christian work among them (Jordan Evangelical Committee for Relief and Development, **CMA**, WVI, Tearfund) elicits a very good response. Equally, Jordanian churches have effective and wide-spread ministry to these people. Though the welcome that Jordan extended to these refugees is strained, Iraqi Christians nonetheless benefit from training and resources available to them in Jordan. Pray that churches may be granted permission to provide education to refugees; this is a ministry on their hearts.

d) *The 300,000 Bedouin.* Many are still nomadic; others (*fellahin*) are settled and more easily reached. Believers are very few, but there is some ministry among them. Pray for more specific outreach to these, the "true" Arabs.

e) *Dom Gypsies* are a hidden, poor and marginalized people. Cousins of the European Romani Gypsies, the Dom Gypsies have a great need for holistic ministry and for Scripture (especially in audio format) in their language.

f) *People of many nationalities* present in Jordan. Saudi and Gulf Arabs visit for the summer. Many nationalities come to work. Adygei, Druze and Chechens form proud minorities. Pray that they all may encounter the gospel while in Jordan.

8 **Outreach** to the majority community, and development of house churches, remain unaccomplished goals. Perhaps only 10% of churches have any meaningful interaction with Muslims. Pray that believers may catch a vision for sharing Christ and for developing house groups; both are keys for the expansion of the Church.

9 **Media ministry.** Jordan's circumstances enhance the importance of radio, TV, videos, films and literature. Arabic radio (49 hours per week) from FEBA, IBRA and **TWR** has a significant effect. Satellite TV has a large impact – **SAT-7**, *Al Hayat*, The Miracle Channel and others are making great strides in Arabic-language Christian TV. The JESUS film is available in Adygey, Colloquial Egyptian and Standard Arabic. Pray for long-term fruit.

10 **Literature in Arabic** is widely available, with increasingly diverse materials offered. There are three Christian bookstores in Amman. They are the focal point of a successful Bible and Christian literature ministry in which The Bible Society and others are actively involved. From these literature centres, much material is sent to Iraq and to other Arab nations.

K

Geography

Area 2,717,300 sq km. World's ninth-largest country. Dominating Central Asia and trade routes between east and west. Much of the country is semi-desert.

Population		Ann Gr	Density
2010	15,753,460	0.73%	6/sq km
2020	16,726,108	0.53%	6/sq km
2030	17,243,600	0.25%	6/sq km

Capital Astana 658,000. **Other major city** Almaty 1.4 million. The real population is higher than the official government figure. **Urbanites** 58.5%. **Pop under 15 yrs** 24%. **Life expectancy** 64.9 yrs.

Peoples

Diverse population with 76 peoples. The Kazakh diaspora is approximately 3.5 million. Since 1991, there has been a massive emigration of Europeans and an influx of Kazakhs. Increasing industry heralds large numbers of economic migrants.

Kazakhstan

Republic of Kazakhstan

Asia

Turkic 63.0%. Kazakh 56.2%; Uzbek 2.2%; Tatar(2) 1.7%; Uyghur 1.4%; Turkish(3) 0.5%; Azeri 0.5%.
European 35.9%.
  Slavic 31.7%. Russian 27.2%; Ukrainian 3.5%; Belarusian 0.8%; Polish 0.2%.
  Other 4.2%. German 2.4%; Kurdish 0.2%; Chechen 0.2%; Tajik 0.2%.
All others 1.1%. Korean 0.7%; Dungan 0.3%.
Literacy 99.5%. **Official language** Kazakh. **All languages** 43. **Indigenous languages** 8. **Languages with Scriptures** 8Bi 2NT 4por.

Economy

Enormous oil and mineral reserves have lubricated an unwieldy, reluctant change to a market economy. One of the world's fastest-growing economies. A minority profit handsomely from the country's economic growth, while the majority suffer from poverty and the nation's well-documented ecological disasters (salt and toxic waste, radiation, pollution). **HDI Rank** 82nd/182. **Public debt** 8.6% of GDP. **Income/person** $8,719 (18% of USA).

Politics

Declared independence after collapse of the USSR in 1991. Although a multiparty democracy, the only president since 1991 has continued his authoritarian rule and presided over recognizably tainted elections. Increased Kazakh influence in all aspects of state activity is being pursued.

Religion

Under Communism all religion was suppressed. Today, only the traditionally recognized groups can operate freely. Increased Islamist agitation has caused the government to continually consider increasingly oppressive religion laws. These laws subsequently have an effect on the newer and more active Christian denominations and can be used to limit, restrict and even persecute Christians.

Religions	Pop %	Population	Ann Gr
Muslim	53.68	8,456,457	1.2%
Non-religious	33.94	5,346,724	0.8%
Christian	12.15	1,914,045	-1.5%
Buddhist	0.15	23,630	-4.9%
Ethnoreligionist	0.03	4,726	0.7%
Jewish	0.03	4,726	-4.9%
Other	0.02	3,151	15.7%

Christians	Denoms	Pop %	Affiliates	Ann Gr
Protestant	48	0.83	131,000	2.4%
Independent	8	0.11	17,000	5.6%
Catholic	2	0.88	138,000	-7.6%
Orthodox	14	9.82	1,547,000	-1.4%
Marginal	7	0.28	44,000	2.7%
Unaffiliated		0.20	36,000	2.4%

Churches	MegaBloc	Congs	Members	Affiliates
Russian Orthodox	O	206	825,175	1,180,000
Ukrainian Orthodox	O	95	190,625	305,000
Catholic Church	C	42	83,916	120,000
Jehovah's Witnesses	M	154	15,357	43,000
Ev Chr & Baptist chs	P	315	11,000	27,500
Lutheran Church	P	65	11,976	20,000
Pentecostal groups	P	156	7,800	19,500
Presbyterian Church	P	274	7,400	18,500
Ukrainian Greek Cath	C	2	12,587	18,000
Old Believers	O	10	10,490	15,000
Methodist Churches	P	28	6,944	12,500
Unregistered Baptists	P	45	2,000	7,500
Other denominations[49]		392	53,297	90,159
Total Christians[79]		**1,784**	**1,238,567**	**1,876,659**

TransBloc	Pop %	Population	Ann Gr
Evangelicals			
Evangelicals	0.7	104,511	3.5%
Renewalists			
Charismatics	0.3	54,270	5.8%
Pentecostals	0.2	29,360	6.6%

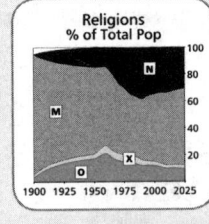

Religions % of Total Pop

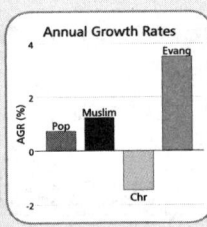

Annual Growth Rates

Answers to Prayer

1 **The Kazakh Church continues to grow in number and stature.** From virtually no Kazakh believers in 1990, there were about 15,000 in 2010! They meet in over 100 Kazakh-speaking congregations. Two-thirds of the country's *raions* (districts) have a Christian witness. Pray for further growth (the growth rate is slowing) and maturation. Kazakhs are taking on greater leadership in churches and reaching out cross-culturally in significant numbers.

2 **Partnerships and alliances have emerged** that cross both ethnic and denominational lines, resulting in greater cooperation in evangelism and combined meetings. There are also a large number of mixed churches, where ethnicities formerly at odds with one another find oneness in Christ.

Challenges for Prayer

1 **Economic boom times** from the bounteous natural resources are starting to transform Kazakhstan, as new buildings spring up and industries grow. While there are many public works going on, a few privileged elite are becoming incredibly rich, while most are being bypassed by this wealth, especially in rural areas. With new money comes increasing corruption, materialism and a strong urban pull. Pray that Kazakhstan will have a government with the best interest of all its citizens in mind and that it will use the newfound wealth on works that benefit all. Pray that the failures of secular materialism might not be repeated in Kazakhstan as in the West.

2 **The revival of Kazakh identity.** The government's deliberate policy on this issue sees a notable increase in both the use of the Kazakh language and a renaissance of Kazakh traditional culture. Despite having a very diverse population, social cohesion is quite good – pray for continued stability. Pray also that a healthy appreciation of cultural minorities might strengthen and not undermine the nation.

3 **"To be a Kazakh is to be a Muslim"** – but theirs is a folk Islam strongly influenced by shamanistic practices. Other Muslim countries (Saudi Arabia, Iran, Turkey, Pakistan) invest huge amounts of money to send Muslim missionaries – some are effective even in converting Russians to Islam. The number of registered mosques grew from 46 in 1989 to 1,282 in 2002 (quite apart from many unregistered ones). Traditional Islam is on the rise, even trendy in some sectors, despite the government actively opposing radical Islam. Orthodox Christianity is perceived as the religion of Russians, and evangelicals are often regarded as dangerous sects. Pray for this misconception to be broken; pray for freedom from historic spiritual bondages and prejudices.

4 **Russians and Ukrainians** – from the early 1990s onward – have emigrated back to their ancestral homeland in large numbers. Most who remain are non-religious or Orthodox with German Catholics and Lutherans as well. The Orthodox Church increasingly aligns itself with Muslims, seeking to cement its own religious status at the expense of newer religious groups. Pray for renewal among the Orthodox. Many Russians are impacted by the fast-growing evangelical/charismatic/Pentecostal churches, much more so than Kazakhs.

5 **Unreached minorities.** Kazakhstan's cultural and religious diversity provides many opportunities for evangelizing Central Asian peoples. A number of Uzbeks and Uyghurs in Kazakhstan are turning to Christ – and beginning to take the gospel back to their own people! Christianity is still largely an urban phenomenon, but the churches and missions (Baptists, Korean groups, some Western agencies) are recruiting for village ministry. Pray that the gospel might be shared, in the listeners' language, in the many towns and villages of this sprawling land.

K

6 **The Christian population** in Kazakhstan is slowly shifting from an ethnic European majority toward an Asian one. Korean churches have grown, as have most charismatic, Pentecostal and some Baptist groups among Central Asian ethnicities. The challenges are manifold:

a) Training is vital. There were a healthy number of Bible colleges and seminaries as well as discipleship schools; all have had to shut down due to changes in the law, and none have been allowed to re-register. TEE and distance learning have potential, if churches are willing to invest in the concept. Appropriate models of training that can be implemented on a wider level are essential as budding leaders need mentors and spiritual fathers. Pray for programmes that develop informed, well-trained, godly leaders.

b) Culturally helpful forms of following Jesus communally. Spirit-led expressions of Kazakh, as well as multicultural, worship, prayer, discipleship and teaching are necessary for the Church to go to the next level. Only 26% of believers are men; clearly some cultural preconceptions need to be shifted.

c) Persecution is increasing. Harassment from authorities, from strident Muslims and from unbelieving family members makes life difficult, especially for converts outside the two main cities. Unconstitutional laws on registering churches are complicated by obstructionism for those who try to register and heavy fines for those who don't.

d) The level of unity and partnership is encouraging. The Evangelical Alliance of Kazakhstan is at a growing stage but has great potential to draw the many groups together. Pray that in the face of increasing opposition and growing theological diversity, believers may stay united.

e) Kazakhstan is becoming a sending nation, a distant dream only 15 years ago. Several mission-training institutes in Kazakhstan had been supported by a number of indigenous, Russian, Western and Korean groups and agencies until their recent closure. Kazakhs (including ethnic minorities) are a strategic key to reaching Central Asia and the Muslim world. Pray for this very young mission movement to grow and spread.

7 **The expatriate Christian community is very diverse.** Many speak Kazakh and are committed to long-term work in Kazakhstan. Russians, Americans, Koreans, Germans and many other nationalities all enrich the ministry in their own way. Pray for humility as they serve the indigenous Church. Thank God for the coordinating work of the Kazakh Partnership. There are many needs – reaching the unreached, training, discipling, tentmaking as well as business-as-mission and work focused on material needs. The government can be suspicious of and hostile to the presence of missionaries – pray for the doors to remain open to minister. The threat of intimidation, expulsion and even violence exists, even if it is not common.

8 **Christian mercy ministries.** There is widespread dysfunction and brokenness in many Kazakh families. Alcoholism and drug addiction are widespread; heroin is as easy to obtain as alcohol. Family breakdown and widespread corruption exacerbate the suffering of many. Pray for Christians to have a powerful transforming effect on society as they demonstrate Christ's love. There are increasing numbers of ministries focusing on these needs. One of the most remarkable is Mission Agape, a live-in programme where addicts are discipled and trained – over 100 have become missionaries and church planters.

9 **Christian media ministries** for prayer:

a) Literature. A number of denominations and organizations produce literature in Kazakh and Russian, ranging from children's books to apologetic materials. The range of topics and of target audiences is still very limited; resources for young people need to be developed. Most publications have been translated from other languages. Encouragement and help for local writers, publishers and distributors are needed to stimulate indigenous literature production. Distribution is also a challenge. Pray for God's protection and blessing from conception to distribution.

b) Bibles. There is a great demand for Bibles, both among the Kazakhs and the Russians. Thousands of Bibles and portions have been distributed, but only a fraction of them in Kazakh. The NT in Kazakh is now complete (and available on cassette); the Kazakh OT is nearly complete. Also recently completed is *God's Blessed Way*, a Russian-language Bible that is culturally sensitive to Central Asian Muslims. Pray for wide and wise distribution of all biblical materials, and pray for ongoing translation projects.

c) The Alpha Course is having a significant impact. Alpha coordinators have bold visions for both church planting and leadership development.

d) The JESUS film is available in Kazakh, Russian, Ukrainian, Uyghur and several other languages. A large proportion of the population have seen the film.

e) Radio. Praise God for the establishment of two local Christian radio stations! These will allow the good news to be disseminated much more easily to populations in the largest cities. Only five hours a week are broadcast in Kazakh from abroad. There are also Christian broadcasts in other languages beamed in from abroad, although Russian predominates. Pray for increasing numbers of quality Kazakh programmes and for development of media ministries by the people of Kazakhstan for their own.

Kenya

Republic of Kenya

Africa

Geography

Area 582,646 sq km. Most people live in the fertile plateaus of the south and west. Much of the north and east is desert. Only 8.9% of the land is cultivable.

Population		Ann Gr	Density
2010	40,862,900	2.67%	70/sq km
2020	52,033,545	2.30%	89/sq km
2030	63,198,912	1.88%	108/sq km

Capital Nairobi 3,523,349. **Other major cities** Mombasa 1.0 million; Nakuru 332,000. **Urbanites** 22.2%. **Pop under 15 yrs** 43%. **Life expectancy** 53.6 yrs.

Peoples

108 ethno-linguistic groups.
Bantu 66.0%. 38 peoples, largest: Kikuyu 19.0%; Luyha(3) 11.6%; Kamba 10.6%; Gusii 6.6%; Meru 5.5%; Giriama 2.1%; Bukusu 1.8%; Embu(2) 0.9%.
Nilotic 29.8%. 21 peoples, largest: Luo 13.1%; Kalenjin 4.1%; Kipsigis 3.1%; Nandi 1.7%; Maasai 1.6%; Turkana 1.2%; Pokot 1.0%.
Cushitic 2.7%. 13 peoples, largest: Somali(3) 1.4%; Garreh 0.4%; Boran 0.3%.
Khoisan 0.1%. 7 peoples.
South Asian 0.3%. Gujarati 0.2%.
Other 1.1%. Swahili 0.6%; Arab 0.2%; British 0.2%.
Literacy 73.6%. **Official languages** English, Swahili. **All languages** 74. **Indigenous languages** 69. **Languages with Scriptures** 16Bi 13NT 20por 13w.i.p.

Economy

Predominantly agriculture, light industries and a major tourist industry. Post-independence stability aided good growth until 1976, but debt, recession and mismanagement have eroded this. The venal elite have siphoned massive amounts of wealth – Kenya is infamous for its rampant corruption. Infrastructure development is essential. Drought, floods and famines have laid waste large areas, causing food prices to rise and devastating the livestock population.
HDI Rank 147th/182. **Public debt** 60% of GDP. **Income/person** $838 (2% of USA).

Politics

Independent from Britain in 1963. President Moi's Kipsigis-favouring government subverted opposition and marginalized the major ethnic groups (Kikuyu, Luo and Luyha), but passed on a legacy of stability – vital for this turbulent region. Now a multiparty state, many of Kenya's political battles are over a promised but overdue new constitution, rampant corruption and improvement of education and the economy. A controversial election in 2007 was followed by two months of violence and ethnic conflict, which only ended through the establishment of a coalition government; it will be a challenge for the two major political opponents to work well together.

Religion

Full freedom of religion – although tensions are emerging due to regional instability, strong proselytism and disagreements regarding issues of religious jurisprudence in the constitution.

Religions	Pop %	Population	Ann Gr
Christian	82.61	33,757,346	3.0%
Muslim	8.32	3,399,289	3.7%
Ethnoreligionist	7.21	2,946,215	-1.3%
Baha'i	0.98	400,456	2.3%
Hindu	0.41	167,538	1.7%
Non-religious	0.23	93,985	5.6%
Other	0.19	77,640	1.6%
Sikh	0.05	20,431	-1.0%

Figures are estimates – no comprehensive survey has been taken for decades.

Christians Denoms		Pop %	Affiliates	Ann Gr
Protestant	164	32.57	13,310,000	3.2%
Independent	306	24.20	9,887,000	2.7%
Anglican	1	8.86	3,620,000	1.3%
Catholic	1	21.54	8,800,000	1.9%
Orthodox	3	0.84	345,000	2.0%
Marginal	19	0.36	149,000	5.4%
Doubly affiliated		-5.76	-2,354,000	0.0%

Churches	MegaBloc	Congs	Members	Affiliates
Catholic Church	C	730	4,656,085	8,800,000
Anglican Church	A	3,850	2,207,317	3,620,000
Africa Inland Churches	P	4,200	1,480,000	2,400,000
Presbyterian Church	P	1,800	1,287,425	2,150,000
Afr Indep Pente Ch	I	1,160	580,000	1,450,000
Seventh-day Adventist	P	3,800	650,000	1,300,000
New Apostolic Church	I	2,133	426,667	1,280,000
Assemblies of God	P	3,200	250,000	1,150,000
Baptist Convention	P	3,250	800,000	1,150,000

K

					TransBloc	Pop %	Population	Ann Gr
Methodist Church	P	2,200	420,000	1,050,000	**Evangelicals**			
Pentecostal Assemblies	P	2,462	320,000	960,000	Evangelicals	48.9	19,991,743	3.4%
Episcopal Ch of Afr	I	816	244,800	612,000	**Renewalists**			
Full Gospel Church	P	3,929	275,000	550,000	Charismatics	39.5	16,138,921	4.7%
Afr Brotherhood Ch	I	2,162	216,216	480,000	Pentecostals	18.6	7,615,088	3.3%
Salvation Army	P	1,300	142,400	356,000				
Pente Evang Fell (Elim)	P	2,692	175,000	350,000				
Ch of Christ in Africa	I	1,619	161,905	340,000				
African Gospel Ch	P	1,941	165,000	330,000				
African Orthodox Ch	O	307	132,000	330,000				
Free Pente Fell in K	P	450	112,500	270,000				
Afr Israel Ch Nineveh	I	576	98,000	245,000				
Other denominations[473]		33,070	3,236,521	6,938,046				
Doubly affiliated				-2,353,700				
Total Christians[493]		**77,647**	**18,036,836**	**33,757,346**				

Religions % of Total Pop

TransBloc Movements % of Total Pop — Charis, Evang, Pente

Answers to Prayer

1 **Kenya remains a regional and continental hub** for Christian mission, theological education and church ministry. The troubles in the region make this reality all the more strategic.

2 **Kenya has a massive evangelical presence.** Nearly 50% of the population identify themselves as such (from 17% in 1960), and they come not just from Protestant but also Independent, Anglican and Catholic backgrounds. Pentecostal churches in particular show explosive growth at nearly triple the country's rate of population growth.

3 **Missions from Kenya are moving** from mere vision to reality. Within Kenya, the Finish the Task movement is mobilizing the Church for saturation church planting and for reaching every unreached people in the nation. Kenyans are also increasingly moving out to minister the gospel in other nations.

Challenges for Prayer

1 **Kenya's long-term stability** cannot be taken for granted. Droughts in the north caused the deaths of 80% of the livestock, and the decrease of pasturelands causes violent clashes among various ethnic groups claiming the resources. Fragile ecosystems, overdue land reform, widening gaps between rich and poor, increasingly scarce water, rapidly expanding urban slums and burgeoning populations of street children/AIDS orphans all point to future tensions. Many of these issues were components of the ethnic violence and political crisis of 2007-08. Pray for peace, for wise governance and for practical solutions that can be implemented effectively.

2 **Corruption is rampant and systemic** – this in a country whose population is 82% "Christian"! Task forces are targeting corruption, but it is so entrenched that terrorists and international drug traffickers use Kenya as a key hub. Corruption within the state mechanisms themselves must be cleaned up before anything else can be. A just and honest government that will uplift the poor and punish the wicked is vital for Kenya to move forward.

3 **Political issues increasingly impact the churches.** Examples are intimidation of the press, human rights abuses, ethnic discrimination and, above all, the controversial points in the new constitution. Christianity is increasingly politicized as many churches seek to transform Kenyan politics with new parties and fresh vision. Pray that all Christians might unite in opposing wrong and in upholding policies that honour God. Pray for gifted, holy and accountable believers to be appointed to positions of influence in the nation.

4 **Waves of church growth and renewal** have impacted the nation deeply. The East African Revival (1948-1960) made a deep and lasting impression on the Anglican, Presbyterian and Methodist Churches. This revival was quenched by legalism, divisions, materialism and personality clashes. More recent growth in evangelical/Pentecostal churches (both international and indigenous) is massive. One of the largest groups is the Africa Inland Church, birthed from the missionary input of **AIM**. Charismatic renewal beyond Pentecostal churches is remarkable – this movement has impacted 33% of Catholics and 25% of Anglicans.

5 **Long-term and rapid growth in churches** has brought significant challenges:

a) *Nominalism is a major issue,* even among evangelicals/Pentecostals. Attendance nationally is only 7%, less than one-tenth of all Christians. Establishing effective means of discipleship is a huge need as increasing numbers associate themselves with the Church, yet with no true spiritual growth in their lives.

b) *The recent explosion of Independent churches.* These churches are able to grow and multiply rapidly, but many are single congregations with minimal or no accountability. This presents dangers in financial and theological integrity; many adopt syncretistic practices or unbiblical beliefs and practices. Pray for their integration into biblical faith and church networks.

c) *Tribalism,* "kingdom building" and multiplied denominations cause divisions. Pray for biblical unity that transcends culture and personalities.

d) *The need for trained leaders* for the more than 80,000 congregations gives cause for concern. Over 70 institutions train Christian workers for ministry. All major denominations have training centres. The Nairobi Evangelical Graduate School of Theology (300 students, including a PhD level), the Pan African Christian University and Daystar University serve all of Anglophone Africa. Yet these academic programmes are insufficient to address the sheer numbers needing to be trained. TEE programmes abound, but pray for grassroots training programmes, such as Langham Preachers Seminars, that aim to ground leaders in the Word and to help them lead and plant truly biblical, truly African churches.

6 **Missions vision has significantly altered** Kenya's church scene. A large and increasing number of Kenyans are serving cross-culturally within Kenya or abroad, with agencies such as Horn of Africa Mission, but the potential is so much greater. For prayer:

a) *The clarion call to see a church accessible* to every person, community and people group in Kenya was championed by Vision 2010, but results of this nationwide initiative are not yet known. Churches are very unevenly distributed throughout Kenya.

b) *Finish the Task/Afriserve* has been making the Church aware of the least reached within Kenya since the late 1990s. It continues to raise awareness, prayer and workers for completing the effective evangelization of Kenya.

c) *The African Centre for Missions* (ACM), opened in 2000, mobilizes for cross-cultural missions by training trainers, missionaries and mission pastors. ACM is a collaboration of several major denominations, the **AEA** and others.

d) *For churches, denominations, Bible schools and seminaries* to make the Great Commission a key part of their spiritual DNA. Kenya has the capacity to send many more missionaries, especially to the needy Horn of Africa region.

7 **Foreign missions have seen great fruit** in Kenya, but their role is changing. Since Kenyans are clearly capable of leading national ministries, expats focus more on partnering with nationals in pioneer outreach, Bible teaching and service ministries. Many agencies have supportive, global or regional ministries in Kenya – hence the large missionary population. Some major agencies: **AIM, AoG, IMB,** *Diguna,* **WGM, BBF, CC/CC, DMG, FIDA.**

8 **Major sectors of the population** needing specialized ministry:

a) *Young people.* The majority of Kenyans are children, so children and youth ministries are of utmost importance. **CEF** has more than 40 full-time workers committed to children's ministry. SU has a great impact on primary and secondary students. FOCUS(**IFES**) operates in over 40 universities and colleges. FOCUS disciples, trains and mobilizes students and graduates for ministry, having sent 15 abroad as missionaries. Over 1,000 university students recently committed themselves to missions.

b) *HIV/AIDS sufferers* – around 500 pass away every day due to AIDS, despite the halting of the infection rate. Much of the very public campaign to reduce infection rates is built on a

K

platform of fidelity and abstinence. The Anglican Church recently apologized to all who suffer from AIDS for previously shunning those with HIV. Pray that Christians may lead in ministry in this area; pray also for those who suffer and for the hundreds of thousands of orphans left behind.

c) **The large numbers of city slum dwellers,** including over 100,000 street children or orphaned householders. Several ministries work among them; pray for ways to minister to all aspects of these children's lives.

9 **Islam is an increasing challenge.** The coast and the NW have been Muslim for centuries. Islam is still a relatively small minority, but it is growing in size and ambition. Muslims seek to Islamize the regions where they are prevalent, to implement shari'a law, to increase their presence in civil services and the government and to convert non-Muslims through financial inducements. Christian-Muslim tension is at an unprecedented level, and violent outbreaks are increasingly common. Although there are many converts from Islam to Christianity, they are subject to harassment, persecution and violence. Pray for peace between the communities, for those ministering to Muslims and for truth-seekers to find the Messiah.

10 **Less-evangelized peoples** – 4-5% of Kenya's population are least-reached or unreached peoples. In the last 15 years, major progress has been made in reaching the unevangelized. Nearly every group has been adopted or targeted by Kenyan and foreign Christian groups, and FTT has identified the least reached. Pray for:

a) **The largely pastoral, animistic peoples** of the north and west, who are increasingly responding to the gospel – the Turkana (15% Christian), Pokot (15%), Endo (15%), Sabaot (2%), Rendille (0.2%), Samburu (0.5%), Daasenach (0.9%) – through the ministry of AIC/**AIM**, Anglicans and many others. Thank God, and pray for well-led, culturally appropriate churches to be established. The well-known Maasai are now 25% Christian.

b) **The Muslim Oromo-related peoples** of the northeast – the Borana and related Njemps (Chamus), also the Garreh-Ajuran, Orma, Malakote and Munyoyaya. There are churches among only the Njemps (1.5% Christian, but already sending evangelists to other peoples) and the Borana (less than 1% Christian).

c) **The Khoisan** (Bushmen-related) peoples, which include the Boni, Dahalo and Dorobo (8 subgroups). These small, spread-out peoples are largely hunter-gatherers and adhere mainly to traditional religions.

d) **The Mijikenda peoples** of the coastal hills. The beliefs of the Giriama, Duruma, Chonyi and Pokomo(2) are mixed traditional and Muslim, but they also have a large minority of Christians. The Digo, Segeju and Bajun are almost entirely Muslim. Pray for those seeking to reach them.

e) **The coastal Swahili and Arab populations,** which are strongly Muslim and largely unreached. They tend to be quite resistant to outreach. Some Kenyan churches now minister to these groups; pray for a testimony of truth, power and love.

f) **The Somali** in the northeast and in cities. Instability in Somalia has driven tens of thousands of these people into Kenya, bringing their strife with them but also making them more accessible to the gospel. Numerous Christian workers (AIC/**AIM**, **SIM**, **CBIM**, Baptists, Sheepfold Ministries and Mennonites) are reaching the Somali in Kenya, especially through holistic ministry. Somali Christians number perhaps a few hundred.

g) **The Asian community** is Muslim, Hindu, Jain, Parsee and Sikh. They are prominent in trading and private industries, but feel insecure amid Kenya's struggling economy. **AIM**, **Christar** and Sheepfold Ministries work among them. ASCKEN (Asian-African Concern Kenya) is a partnership of Asian, African and international ministries seeking to reach all of East Africa's Asian population. Several churches have been planted, but, in general, African churches have not yet picked up the missional challenge of Kenya's Asians.

11 **Bibles and Bible translation.** Most languages have Scripture portions, and 16 indigenous languages have the whole Bible. Pray for the invaluable work of The Bible Society (UBS) and of SIL and the related, but indigenous, work of Bible Translation & Literacy. Together they handle most of the translation, printing and distribution of Scripture, as well as the demanding task of increasing literacy to maximize the impact of the translated Word.

(12) Support ministries:

a) *Aid programmes* – through many agencies such as Tearfund, WVI, Food for the Hungry and others – have become more vital as drought and famine intensify. Pray for those involved in this difficult ministry that opens hearts to receive the love of Christ.

b) *MAF* (with 79 staff and 7 aircraft) serves the region from its base in Nairobi, flying to many parts of East Africa and northeast Congo-DRC. This ministry enables much Christian work in the poorest and most remote regions that would otherwise be impossible. All aspects of ministry are supported – humanitarian, evangelism, biblical teaching and others. **AIM**-Air also has an extensive flying programme in the region.

c) *GRN* has recordings available in 75 languages.

d) *The JESUS film* is widely shown and is in 30 languages with a further two in process.

e) *Christian broadcast media.* Many Christian programmes are aired on radio and TV networks both nationally (Pentecostals) and from abroad (FEBA, IBRA, **TWR**). Broadcasts in English and Swahili dominate programming, but programmes in about 15 other languages are also available.

(13) **Nairobi is a strategic hub for ministry** in Africa and beyond. Many international Christian organizations have continental offices based here. The Ecumenical AACC (All Africa Conference of Churches), the **AEA** (Association of Evangelicals of Africa) and PACLA are a few of these. **AEA** plays a key role in promoting evangelical unity and ministries in theology, training, literature and fellowship. Pray for this key work and its extension throughout Africa.

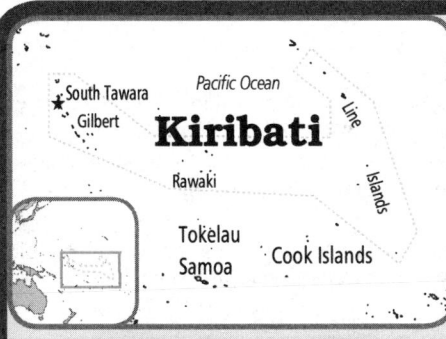

Literacy 94%. **Official language** English, but I-Kiribati is more widely spoken. **All languages** 3. **Indigenous languages** 2. **Languages with Scripture** 2Bi 1w.i.p.

Economy

Dependent on copra, fish, foreign aid and remittances sent from I-Kiribati abroad. Large distances between islands and few natural resources make improvements difficult to achieve. **Public debt** 11.3% of GDP. **Income/person** $1,372 (3% of USA).

Politics

Independent from Britain in 1979 as a democratic republic.

Kiribati

Republic of Kiribati
Pacific

Geography

Area 849 sq km. Three archipelagos – Gilbert, Rawaki (Phoenix) and Line, with 33 coral atolls (23 inhabited) scattered across 2,000,000 sq km of the Pacific Ocean.

Population		Ann Gr	Density
2010	99,547	1.59%	117/sq km
2020	115,185	1.44%	136/sq km
2030	130,503	1.18%	154/sq km

Capital Tarawa 43,700. **Urbanites** 44%. **Pop under 15 yrs** 36%. **Life expectancy** 62.5 yrs.

Peoples

I-Kiribati 98.9%.
Other 1.1%. Mixed, Tuvaluan, European.

Religion

Religions	Pop %	Population	Ann Gr
Christian	98.50	98,054	1.6%
Baha'i	1.00	995	3.8%
Non-religious	0.50	498	6.2%

Christians	Denoms	Pop %	Affiliates	Ann Gr
Protestant	5	40.94	41,000	1.5%
Independent	2	1.20	1,000	3.8%
Anglican	1	0.15	<1,000	0.0%
Catholic	1	55.35	55,000	1.0%
Marginal	2	11.32	11,000	4.3%
Doubly affiliated		-10.45	-10,000	0.0%

Churches	MegaBloc	Congs	Members	Affiliates
Catholic Church	C	24	29,784	55,100
Kiribati Protestant Ch	P	135	15,322	35,700
Latter-day Saints (Mormon)	M	33	6,587	11,000

K

Assemblies of God	P	18	1,200	1,950
Seventh-day Adventist	P	13	1,175	1,680
Other denominations[6]		41	1,663	3,030
Doubly affiliated				-10,400
Total Christians[11]		**264**	**55,731**	**98,060**

TransBloc	Pop %	Population	Ann Gr
Evangelicals			
Evangelicals	7.2	7,157	3.1%
Renewalists			
Charismatics	6.0	5,955	3.4%
Pentecostals	4.3	4,250	3.9%

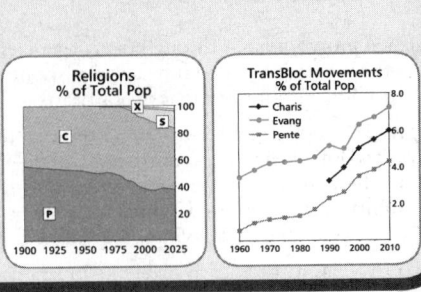

Challenges for Prayer

1 **The once-strong Congregational Church** (Kiribati Protestant) is in slow decline and losing members to other groups. The theological college in Tarawa is not evangelical. Pray for a return to the Bible. Nominalism and syncretism with traditional spiritist practices are all too common.

2 **Evangelical Christians are increasing,** mainly through Pentecostals. **AoG** and Church of God both have Bible colleges. Growth is too often followed by decline, since foreign financial windfalls and occasional healings seem to be the main attractions rather than biblical preaching and transformed lives.

3 **The more needy:**

a) *I-Kiribati* migrate for work on Nauru and as seafarers on foreign ships. Their remittances are a key part of the economy, but many return home with AIDS or drug problems.

b) *Young people.* Overpopulation and unemployment combined with increasing alcohol abuse create a difficult environment in which to grow up. Pray for a revival among young people, for wholesome lives with godly purpose.

c) *The entire nation faces eradication* if sea levels rise. Pray that this possible impending disaster would remind residents that our eternal home is in heaven and that they would live with this in mind.

K

Korea, North

Democratic People's Republic of Korea

Asia

Geography

Area 122,370 sq km. The larger part of the Korean peninsula, with a more rigorous climate than in the south. About 70% of the land area is mountainous.

Population		Ann Gr	Density
2010	23,990,703	0.39%	196/sq km
2020	24,802,254	0.33%	203/sq km
2030	25,301,254	0.14%	207/sq km

Capital Pyongyang 2,741,000. **Other major city** Namp'o 1.1 million. **Urbanites** 63.4%. **Pop under 15 yrs** 22%. **Life expectancy** 67.1 yrs.

Peoples

Korean 99.8%.
Chinese 0.2%.
Literacy 95%. **Language** Korean. **Languages with Scriptures** 1Bi.

Economy 📈

Probably the most centralized and most isolated economy in the world. It is in rapid decline due to costly attempts to become a nuclear power, high military expenditure and falling agricultural yield. Profits from a worldwide network of illicit drugs, cigarettes, counterfeit money and gambling establishments are drying up as neighbouring countries and the US tighten the net. The black market continues to grow rapidly. The world's number one seller of missiles. Heavily dependent on aid. Some joint development projects with China and, especially, South Korea create tension between economic necessity and isolationist ideology. Chronic food shortages and widespread malnutrition force some limited economic reform.
Public debt 81.6% of GDP. **Income/person** $6,410 (14% of USA).

Politics 🗡

Occupied by Japan 1910–45. On Russian insistence, Korea was partitioned after WWII. A Communist regime was installed in 1948. North Korea invaded the South in 1950, and civil war dragged on until 1953. The fortified border between the Koreas is one of the most impenetrable in the world, watched by a huge military force. North Korea continues to drag concessions from its neighbours by the threat of further nuclear development and military sabre rattling. The dictator, "Dear Leader" Kim Jong-il, presides over one of the most repressive regimes in the world and is completely dedicated to the ideology of *Juche*, literally, "self-reliance". As Juche becomes increasingly untenable and deluded, the regime appears ever more vulnerable. Kim's age and poor health, the relative uncertainty of succession, a strong cadre of military generals and a clearly untenable economic system mean that sudden change could occur at short notice.

Religion 👥

The only acceptable religion is Cheondogyo, or "Kim Il-Sung-ism", the cult of the deceased leader, inextricably tied to *Juche* ideology. All other religions are harshly repressed. Hundreds of thousands of Christians have died because of persecution, and today, up to 100,000 are in prisons or work camps. The true number of Christians is unknown, so all figures given are estimates.

Religions	Pop %	Population	Ann Gr
Non-religious	69.30	16,625,557	0.4%
Ethnoreligionist	15.50	3,718,559	0.4%
Other	13.20	3,166,073	0.1%
Christian	1.48	355,762	5.2%
Buddhist	0.40	95,963	-4.0%

Christians	Denoms	Pop %	Affiliates	Ann Gr
Protestant	2	0.04	10,000	1.0%
Independent	55	1.27	305,000	6.1%
Catholic	1	0.17	40,000	0.0%

Churches	MegaBloc	Congs	Members	Affiliates
Secret believers	I	n/a	n/a	300,000
Catholic Association	C	1	27,972	40,000
Korean Christian Fed	P	1	8,400	10,500
Other denominations[7]		27	1,150	5,300
Total Christians[59]		**29**	**37,522**	**355,800**

TransBloc	Pop %	Population	Ann Gr
Evangelicals			
Evangelicals	1.0	246,400	6.0%
Renewalists			
Charismatics	0.5	121,500	6.6%

Annual Growth Rates

TransBloc Movements % of Total Pop

K

Challenges for Prayer

1 **The "Hermit Kingdom" is a repressive nightmare,** where the populace are kept ignorant of the outside world and forcibly indoctrinated into the bizarre doctrines and policies of the "Dear Leader". He has over 70 bronze statues (total value over $1 billion) – and literally tens of thousands of other monuments, towers and figures – of his father Kim Il-Sung, the Father in the twisted Cheondogyo trinity of Father, Son and Juche spirit. The nuclear threat of this rogue nation is only surpassed by the nation's great suffering and deprivation. Pray for the leader and his cadre, that the Holy Spirit might bring them to repentance and belief.

2 **North Korea's economy and environment** are in states of disaster, the former propped up only by illicit money-spinner ventures outside the country and by Chinese and South Korean generosity, which ebbs and flows with ever-shifting North Korean politics. Yet the cost of continually propping up North Korea will eventually tally up to more than the cost of rebuilding a crumbling nation after a regime change. Pray for a watershed moment in God's timing that will bring thorough change, freedom and complete transformation to this land.

3 **Food shortages are often severe.** With only 15% arable land, low yield from medieval agricultural practices and regular floods caused by massive deforestation, more than three million have starved since 1994. Pray for:

a) *Starving North Koreans,* forced to desperate measures to feed their families. This may include theft, foraging for edible grass and plants, hazarding the dangerous passage to China or even black market cannibalistic activity. Pray that, in some form, food might arrive to sustain their lives without their resorting to crime or sin.

b) *Aid agencies,* many of them Christian, have been able to offer food but never with permission to share the gospel. Pray that this food might get to the population – much is diverted to Mr. Kim's inner circle and the military. Pray for wisdom on the part of foreign governments and NGOs in handling this tragic and delicate situation.

4 **The Church in North Korea** was the birthplace of Korean revival – Pyongyang was known as the "Jerusalem of the East". But most Christians fled to the south during the Korean War or were martyred and their churches destroyed. Very little is known about today's underground Church, only that it has survived and is growing amid great suffering and danger. There are four propaganda "show" churches in the capital, but up to 100,000 Christians are interned in labour camps. Possessing the Bible, saying "God" or "Jesus" and meeting as believers are all punishable by death. Pray for North Korean believers, that they persevere in what is probably the most difficult country in which to be a Christian.

5 **Access to ministry in North Korea** is greater than commonly perceived. Foreign NGOs, both Korean and Western, are on site through aid and development projects. Strict limitations on ministry are in place, but the very presence of believers and the testimony of loving generosity can make a difference in many lives. There are possibly hundreds of Christians in North Korea in this capacity.

6 **Present ministry opportunities:**

a) *Radio.* Many South Korean Christian broadcasts as well as **TWR** and **FEBC** reach far into North Korea, but most radios are pre-tuned to government stations. Smuggled radios pre-tuned to gospel frequencies and Chinese tuneable radios are making their way into the country.

b) *Bibles, the Gospels and tracts* are smuggled into the country by various means as well as floated in via balloons from South Korea. Smugglers are liable to be executed if caught, but the rarity of Scriptures makes them extremely precious to believers. A North Korean dialect version of the Bible is being prepared.

c) *Korean Christians from China* and elsewhere who are able to visit and gain opportunities to witness. Korea is open to Chinese businessmen, and their easy access to the country could be strategic for the gospel.

d) *Prayer networks for North Korea* have multiplied in recent years, too many to list, and most have an Internet presence. Many thousands of believers are forming an unbroken chain of intercession for this nation.

7 **North Korean refugees in China** number in the region of 300,000. It is highly risky to attempt escape – capture means imprisonment and likely torture or death. Pray for:

a) *Chinese authorities,* who are caught between international pressure against such inhumane repatriation of North Korean refugees and awkward loyalty to North Korea. North Korean agents in China will go so far as to pose as pastors, build fake churches to entice Korean refugees and then capture them.

b) *The 200,000 ethnic Korean Christians* living in neighbouring Chinese provinces. Many try to shelter North Korean refugees and share the gospel with them, but they are punished if caught harbouring refugees.

c) *Korean refugees* in China, who must live in hiding and are hunted by Chinese and North Korean agents. Some estimate that between 70% and 90% of women refugees end up as slave-wives or sold into the sex trade. Many refugees find Jesus through the kindness of Christians who help them. Some make it to South Korea via other nations, but find it very difficult to adjust to life there. Other converted North Korean escapees return home to take back the gospel at extreme risk to their own lives.

8 **Reunification of North and South** is a wish and a prayer for most Koreans on both sides of the demilitarized zone, but on very different terms. South Korean Christians praying for unification might need to first look at unity among themselves before being truly prepared for any such prayers to be answered. If or when the two nations become one, at worst, it could be on the back of a terribly damaging war and, at best, it would require massive external assistance to relieve a failed state.

Korea, South

Republic of Korea

Asia

Geography 🌍

Area 99,067 sq km. Southern half of Korean peninsula. Forested mountain ranges; 22% arable.

Population		Ann.Gr.	Density
2010	48,500,717	0.39%	490/sq km
2020	49,474,990	0.13%	499/sq km
2030	49,146,236	-0.14%	496/sq km

Capital Seoul 9,773,000. **Other major cities** Pusan 3.4 million; Inchon 2.6mill; Taegu 2.5m; Taejon 1.5m; Kwangju 1.5m; Changwon-Masan 1.3m; Suwon 1.1m; Ulsan 1.1m. **Urbanites** 81.9%. **Pop under 15 yrs** 17%. **Life expectancy** 79.2 yrs.

Peoples 👪

One of the world's most ethnically homogeneous nations.
Korean 97.8%. An ancient and cultured nation.
Other 2.2%. A mix of Western, Chinese, Japanese and many South and Southeast Asians. Of the approximately 1 million foreigners, nearly one-half reside for work purposes and one-fourth are illegal immigrants.
Literacy 100%. **Official language** Korean.
All languages 4. **Indigenous languages** 2.
Languages with Scripture 2Bi 1por.

Economy 📈

Transformed from a poor, devastated nation in 1953 into the eleventh-largest economy in the world by rapid industrialization and modernization. A wide range of sophisticated, export-oriented industries, driven by the powerful *chaebol* conglomerates. The Asian financial crisis of 1997-99 exposed several weaknesses in the Korean system, but liberalization helped the economy push on. Few natural resources and high dependence on exports make Korea financially vulnerable, but a highly educated workforce and technological innovation mitigate this.
HDI Rank 26th/182. **Public debt** 24.4% of GDP. **Income/person** $19,136 (40% of USA).

Politics 🗡

A millennia-old history of frequent invasions and interference from surrounding nations. The Japanese occupation (1910-1945), the foreign-engineered division of Korea (1945-48) and the devastating Korean War (1950-53) have moulded the attitudes and politics of Koreans. Strong military-civilian governments held power from 1950 until 1987, when public unrest led to constitutional change and a more open, multiparty democracy. The first civilian president in 32 years was elected in 1992. The disastrous state of North Korea seems to make either conflict or unification inevitable.

Religion 🙏

Complete religious freedom. Published numbers range widely due to uncertain boundaries between religious heritage and actual belief and practice.

Religions	Pop %	Population	Ann Gr
Non-religious*	30.98	15,025,522	0.9%
Christian	30.95	15,010,972	0.4%
Buddhist	23.70	11,494,670	0.5%
Ethnoreligionist	7.00	3,395,050	-1.0%
Other	4.30	2,085,531	0.9%
Chinese	2.70	1,309,519	-2.4%
Muslim	0.29	140,652	3.4%
Baha'i	0.08	38,801	3.1%

*Many Koreans have no formal religious ties but do have a connection to Confucian values and teachings.

Christians Denoms		Pop %	Affiliates	Ann Gr
Protestant	180	34.48	16,723,000	0.3%
Independent	19	0.86	416,000	1.6%
Anglican	1	0.10	50,000	0.2%
Catholic	1	9.18	4,450,000	0.3%
Marginal	69	2.98	1,446,000	1.2%
Doubly affiliated		-16.65	-8,075,000	0.0%

K

The huge number of doubly affiliated can be attributed to countless denominational schisms, inconsistent enumeration mechanisms in churches and widespread failure to account for dual and transferred memberships, especially within Protestant bodies. The actual number of Protestants may be near half of what is claimed in official denominational reports.

Churches	MegaBloc	Congs	Members	Affiliates
Catholic Church	C	1,243	2,486,034	4,450,000
Presby-HapDong	P	11,112	1,164,990	2,912,476
Presby-Tong Hap	P	7,671	1,343,406	2,686,812
Korean Methodist Ch	P	5,443	762,019	1,585,000
Korea Assembly of God	P	2,800	948,000	1,185,000
Korea Baptist Conv	P	2,785	801,437	931,000
Presby-HapDong Jeong	P	3,004	262,606	866,599
Korea Holiness Evang	P	1,011	374,000	748,000
Jesus Korean Holiness	P	2,758	112,852	564,260
Presby-Ko Shin	P	1,689	197,520	474,047
Presby-Ki Jang	P	1,291	148,458	337,000
Presby-HapDong BoSu	P	877	140,000	242,000
Seventh-day Adventist	P	695	206,000	238,960
Presby-Gae Hyuk	P	3,163	129,928	220,877
Presby-Ye Jang Hap Bo	P	179	114,706	195,000
Jesus Assembly of God	I	1,008	69,620	174,051
Presby-HapDong Jung	P	1,012	53,333	160,000
Other denominations[242]		19,449	2,497,582	5,113,947

Doubly affiliated Pentecostals		-350,000
Doubly affiliated		-7,725,369
Total Christians[270]	67,190 11,812,491	15,010,660

TransBloc	Pop %	Population	Ann Gr
Evangelicals			
Evangelicals	16.8	8,164,977	0.7%
Renewalists			
Charismatics	4.3	2,103,888	2.5%
Pentecostals	2.7	1,311,424	0.6%

Missionaries from South Korea

P,I,A 21,500 Korean missionaries in about 175 countries with about 200 mission agencies: 97% international, 95% cross-cultural, 95% long-term. Many Korean missionaries are sent by indigenous denominational groups but serve with international agencies, resulting in some duplication.

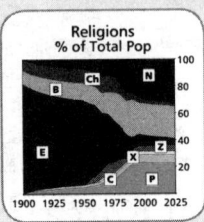

Religions
% of Total Pop

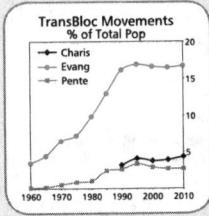

TransBloc Movements
% of Total Pop

Answers to Prayer

K

1 **Praise God for the unique Korean Church.** It was founded on sound indigenous principles, blessed with a succession of revivals, refined by persecution and is now one of the foremost Churches in the world for missions vision. It has one of the highest proportions of evangelicals in Asia. Korea's Church presence is highly visible; Korean society has been impacted on many levels by it, and a number of high-profile leaders of politics and industry are Christian. From the first Protestant church planted in 1884, South Korea now has possibly 50,000 Protestant congregations.

2 **Commitment to sustained, sacrificial and passionate prayer,** both corporately and individually, characterizes much of the Korean Protestant Church. With early morning and evening prayer meetings every day and all night, prayer concerts on weekends and prayer mountains (retreat centres), the commitment of Korean Christians to prayer is remarkable; the fruit of these prayers will never be fully known this side of heaven.

3 **Korean Christianity is one of superlatives.** Six of the ten largest churches in the world are in Korea as are some of the world's largest theological colleges, baptismal services and evangelistic and Christian gatherings in history. Praise God, not for the size of these events, but for the growth and strength that they reflect.

4 **Korea's missionary-sending movement** has expanded to make it the second-largest foreign-mission-sending nation on earth. Over 20,000 workers have been sent out from South Korea. Even greater numbers are targeted for the longer term.

Challenges for Prayer

1 **Society and culture in Korea** saw great change in the last generation. Pray for the following issues:

a) *Economic growth has been remarkable* in the last 50 years. But the global success of some Korean brands has exposed corruption in politics and industry. The economy is highly dependent on exports, and inequity between rich and poor is accelerating. Pray for wisdom for leaders and justice for those most vulnerable.

b) Moral foundations appear to be eroding. This traditionally conservative society must face increasing materialism, a growing generation gap, greatly increased suicide rates, Internet addiction and, as with most developed nations, a rapidly rising sex industry, a vanity-driven cosmetic surgery industry and decreased sensitivity to violence in the media.

c) Traditional religious faiths increasingly co-exist with Christianity and modern-day agnosticism. A spectrum of Buddhism, Confucianism, Korean shamanism and New Religions (usually a blend of Christianity, Buddhism and Eastern mysticism) accounts for most of the population, although the majority do not faithfully practice. In recent years, however, there has been an awakening of religious sentiment among non-Protestant faiths, which has happened to coincide with a relative decline in Protestant growth.

2 **The looming spectre of North Korea** must not be ignored. With Seoul only 30 miles from the demilitarized zone, any conflict would immediately affect millions. More likely than an invasion is the collapse of North Korea's state structure, bringing with it massive humanitarian needs and a huge challenge to the South. Pray that political and Christian leaders may be ready for such an occasion and make wise decisions for the healing of all Korea. Mission to the North is almost impossible, but many in the South prepare and pray for reunification and for the opportunity to share the gospel. **OMS/KEHC** is pursuing ministry among North Korean refugees as a first step. Other initiatives include the Open Doors prayer campaign, CCK's Save North Korea campaign and initiatives by **OMF**, the Methodists and others.

3 **The Korean Church has major spiritual challenges** to face if its credibility before the world and effectiveness in ministry are to be at their maximum:

a) Stagnation and saturation. Numerical growth in the Church has all but stopped despite continued evangelism and prayer. Exaggerated membership claims and double counting are common enough that up to 45% of all "claimed" Christians might be counted by two or more groups. This is especially true of the younger generation, which some claim is drifting away from genuine Christian faith and practice.

b) Spiritual pride, including the belief in some circles that success and prosperity are indicators of God's favour. There is often a pride in statistical growth and impressive organizations and buildings, along with exaggerated claims made. It is a constant temptation for Christian leaders to seek success, wealth and academic degrees more than to lift up the Cross, and to attribute God's blessings to their own hard work or brilliance.

K

c) Divisions and schisms sadly typify the Korean Protestant scene. At the end of the Japanese occupation, there was only one Presbyterian denomination; now there are over 100 and growing. While some splits were actually healthy, domineering leadership patterns and personality clashes have been at the root of much division; Jesus' prayer for the unity of His disciples needs more attention. Yet some work has been done to address this: 2009 was A Year of Prayer for Unity, adopted by Catholics and Protestants alike. Pray for humility, reconciliation and a new spirit of cooperation to be evident in every part of the Church.

d) Patterns of leadership. Leadership is sometimes too authoritarian. The elevated status of pastors hinders biblical servant-leadership, promotes division and personality cults and stunts discipleship, since too many depend more on pastoral guidance than on celebrating the priesthood of all believers.

e) Church structures are not always conducive to practical holiness or effective discipleship. Christians have at times condoned low ethical standards, bribery and corrupt practices, and they have not addressed the wrongs in wider society. Megachurches can gravitate against effective discipleship and integration of new believers into the body of Christ, which in turn causes "church hopping". With many new Christians from Buddhist/Confucian backgrounds, solid teaching and discipleship are essential.

f) Lack of transformational impact on society. The large, influential and affluent Church has not yet fulfilled its capacity to have a transforming effect on the social problems affecting Korea today. Poverty, corruption, moral drift and unreached segments of society in particular could be more directly addressed. Christians would have remarkable potential to shape society were the churches mobilized to act in concert.

4 **Theological training in Korea** is unique; the nation enjoys an amazingly high number and ratio of workers with pastoral training and theological education. There may be 300 theological institutions in Korea. In addition to the 15,000 or more students in the top Presbyterian seminaries, there are, throughout the English-speaking world, thousands more Koreans studying for Christian ministry. For many who graduate, there are few openings in city congregations – yet the poorer rural congregations and mission agencies have many opportunities to serve. Pray that a new generation of trained Christian workers would seize these humble opportunities with joy and fervour.

5 **Young people** are at a critical juncture in Korea. Increased affluence and a low birth rate have created a coddled generation that feels greater pressure than ever to meet extremely high expectations.

a) There is a notable cooling of spiritual fervour in the younger generation. The Church will have to work hard to retain any of the hard-fought gains of the last several years as the siren call of the world becomes ever stronger. Some state that Christianity is actually declining among young people. Pray for a new awakening that will particularly impact young people.

b) Student ministry remains crucial to disciple young Christians and to share the gospel with non-believers. Pray for more workers among university students. Korea has the world's highest proportion of adults with post-secondary education (83%). There are 3.6 million students in 408 universities. Several agencies have large numbers of workers involved: UBF, **CCCI**, **Navs**, **IFES**/IVCF, SFC, Joy Mission, **YWAM** and others.

6 **The missions vision of the Korean Church** continues, remarkably, to grow and mature. Over 170 agencies are sending Korean missionaries cross-culturally. The larger Korean agencies are: Global Mission Society, University Bible Fellowship, **PC(T-hap)**, **KMCBM**, Korean **AoG**, **KBC**, InterCP, Paul Mission, Tyrannus International Mission, Korean Evangelical Holiness Church, GMF, GP.

a) Mobilization of young people for missions keeps gaining momentum. God has used Korean young people to spearhead the missions movement in other Asian nations. Mission Korea is a coalition of 24 mission agencies and 11 campus ministries working together for the common goal of mobilizing young Korean adults and college students for world mission; they hold a nationwide conference every two years, attracting over 5,000 young people. Pray that these young people may be at the forefront of missions – by going, praying or giving.

b) A number of new and effective missionary training and orientation programmes have been developed. Some of the many training institutions are: The Center for World Mission (Presbyterian TongHap), Global Missionary Training Center (interdenominational), Kosin MTI, the Missionary Training Institute (Presbyterian HapDong), the Missionary Training Center (Korean Evangelical Holiness Church) and the Global Professionals' Training Institute (for tentmakers). Pray for effective preparation of Korean missionary trainees, most of whom already have a theology degree or pastoral training.

c) Korean missionaries serving overseas need prayer. The rapid increase in their numbers generates several great needs, most notably member care and collaboration with other missionaries and agencies. The latter issue requires humility and cultural flexibility for Koreans coming from a very homogenous cultural framework.

d) Field strategy must be re-evaluated. What works in Korea does not necessarily work elsewhere, and cultural sensitivity is essential for missions to be effective abroad; Koreans, like other nationalities, can be insensitive to the local context. The kidnapping episodes in Iraq (2004) and Afghanistan (2007) prompted a lot of criticism from the secular media, resulting in much-needed soul searching, reflection and re-evaluation about how Koreans minister abroad.

7 **The less-evangelized** groups that need special approaches in ministry:

a) Shamanism is resurgent, though few openly claim to be followers of this ancient Korean religion. It is estimated that there are more than 300,000 shamans and 300 shamanistic temples within one hour of Seoul. Many Koreans still consult shamans and fortune tellers.

b) Korean Muslims. These are growing in number as a result of Islamic missionary efforts among Koreans working in the Middle East. There are about 35,000 to 40,000 Korean

Muslims as well as over 100,000 illegal migrant workers; the significant majority are in Seoul. There are eight mosques in Korea. There is only a small amount of outreach to them and a lack of sufficient experience and knowledge on how to reach them.

c) *The 250,000-plus illegal migrants,* often working in appalling conditions and for long hours. Bangladesh claims the largest share, but China, Vietnam, Nepal, Indonesia, Philippines and Mongolia also weigh in. A number of local churches provide a much-needed and welcome haven of love and assistance to these, in contrast to the coldness they face from Korean society in general.

d) *New religionists.* There are as many as 300 new religions in South Korea, drawing upon traditional beliefs, Christianity and Buddhism. Chondokyo, with over one million adherents, is a mix of Buddhist, Confucian, shamanistic, Taoist and Catholic practice and belief. New religions are often a reaction to "Western Christianity" in Korean society.

8 **Pray for the Korean diaspora.** Waves of emigration and extensive business ventures have multiplied Korean communities around the world to an excess of 6 million, many in the USA. Around 70% of diaspora Koreans were reported to be Christian – many become believers shortly after arriving in their newly adopted land. Their own role in supporting and sending missionaries is formidable. Recently, KODIMNET (Korean Diaspora Missions Network) and the World Korean Diaspora Forum (including Korean Research Institute for Diaspora) were established to support the Korean diaspora's contribution to cross-cultural missions.

9 **Missions to Korea** has a valuable servant role in giving fresh perspectives to biblical teaching, personal holiness and student work. Specialist agencies such as **FEBC** (150 expat workers, broadcasting 24/7 via radio and Internet to China, Russia, Japan and the Koreas) and **CCCI** (827) serve in reaching out as well as in mobilizing for mission. A number of mission agencies have made a major impact in church planting, including several Presbyterian agencies, Baptists, SdA and **OMS**.

10 **Christian literature** has been a key ingredient to growth. The Bible in Korean has gone through several translations and has become a treasured part of the culture. The Korean Bible Society prints over 2 million Korean Bibles/NTs annually in Korean and even greater numbers for other countries and languages. Additionally, there are six other major Bible production companies. Christian publishers are likewise producing increasingly diverse and helpful books; more than 150 different publishers are part of the Korea Christian Publication Association. Pray that these ministries might have a powerful impact in getting the Word of God into non-Christian hands and helpful in shaping a biblical worldview among Christians.

11 **Digital media and the gospel.** South Korea is at the leading edge of the digital revolution, with higher levels of technology consumption and connectivity than anywhere else. A number of churches and ministries work to provide top-quality content in the form of media-rich Internet sites, downloadable materials and live TV. The Christian Global Network is a satellite TV station targeting diaspora Korean Christians. Evangelism by mobile phone is already happening in Korea.

Iraq

Iran

Kuwait

Kuwait · Persian · Gulf

Saudi Arabia

Kuwait
State of Kuwait
Asia

Geography

Area 17,818 sq km. An oil-rich wedge of desert between Iraq and Saudi Arabia at the northwest end of the Arabian Gulf.

Population		Ann Gr	Density
2010	3,050,744	2.47%	171/sq km
2020	3,690,110	1.78%	207/sq km
2030	4,272,555	1.39%	240/sq km

The fluctuating expatriate community dramatically affects the size and composition of the population.
Capital Kuwait City 2,305,404. **Urbanites** 98.4%. **Pop under 15 yrs** 23%. **Life expectancy** 77.5 yrs.

Peoples

Arab 61%.
  Kuwaiti 35%.
  Foreign Arab 22% (Egyptian, Syrian, Lebanese, Palestinian).
  Bidoon 4%. Stateless Arab refugees.
Others 39%. South Asian, Filipino, Iranian, Western, Chinese, others.
Literacy 93.3%. **Official language** Arabic. **All languages** 7. **Indigenous languages** 3. **Languages with Scriptures** 1Bi 1por.

Economy

Previously a poor Arab backwater, Kuwait's oil (10% of the world's reserves) has enriched it immeasurably. The Iraqi invasion and Gulf War in 1990-91 wrought destruction, but the oil industry has recovered and accounts for 95% of export revenues. Total reliance on oil and foreign labour.
HDI Rank 31st/182. **Public debt** 7.6% of GDP.
Income/person $45,920 (97% of USA).

Politics

Former British protectorate; became independent in 1961. Constitutional monarchy and parliamentary democracy with the Sheikh and his family exercising quasi-autocratic control. Stuttering democratic progress since 1986; only recently granted women's suffrage. Key Western ally in the region.

Religion

Sunni Islam is the state religion with a large Shi'a minority. Immigrant religious minorities are permitted some worship facilities. Religious tolerance in Kuwait is significantly higher than in most of the region. Proselytizing Muslims is forbidden, and much of jurisprudence is influenced by shari'a.

Religions	Pop %	Population	Ann Gr
Muslim	81.64	2,490,627	1.9%
Christian★	13.79	420,698	5.7%
Hindu	3.30	100,675	4.4%
Buddhist	0.65	19,830	8.0%
Non-religious	0.60	18,304	0.9%
Baha'i	0.02	610	2.5%

★The vast bulk of Christians in Kuwait are expatriates.

Christians	Denoms	Pop %	Affiliates	Ann Gr
Protestant	26	0.91	28,000	6.2%
Independent	19	0.42	13,000	6.8%
Anglican	4	0.04	1,000	13.2%
Catholic	8	9.24	282,000	6.6%
Orthodox	5	3.08	94,000	3.0%
Marginal	1	<0.01	<500	4.8%
Unaffiliated		0.10	3,000	0.0%

Churches	MegaBloc	Congs	Members	Affiliates
Catholic Church	C	20	183,333	220,000
Coptic Orthodox Ch	O	7	41,053	78,000
Other Catholic	C	10	40,000	60,000
National Evang Ch	P	3	7,983	19,000
Independent churches	I	53	5,278	9,500
Syrian Orthodox	O	5	4,037	6,500
Greek Orthodox	O	3	3,205	5,000
Melkite Greek Cath	C	1	1,111	2,000
Other denominations[34]		63	10,919	18,000
Total Christians[63]		**165**	**296,919**	**418,000**

TransBloc	Pop %	Population	Ann Gr
Evangelicals			
Evangelicals	1.5	46,391	7.3%
Renewalists			
Charismatics	0.9	26,720	7.8%
Pentecostals	0.2	7,070	5.7%

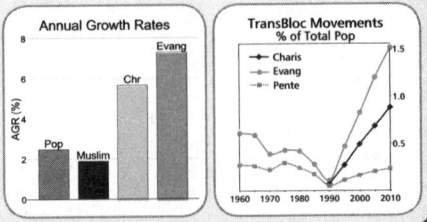

Annual Growth Rates

TransBloc Movements % of Total Pop

Answers to Prayer

1 **The underground Kuwaiti Church** is gaining strength, numbers and maturity, and more converted Kuwaitis are making themselves known publicly. These latter believers are gathering for worship, teaching and prayer with boldness and open witness. While those who openly identify themselves as Christian are still a small minority, both this group and the much larger underground are growing rapidly.

2 **Satellite television** is probably the most powerful tool in reaching not only Kuwait but also the entire Gulf region. Several full-time Arabic-language channels offer a wide array of programmes focused on evangelism and discipleship. There are signs of great response from seeking Muslims. *Al Shifaa* (Healing), the Miracle Channel, *Al Hayat*, **SAT-7**, a Lebanese Maronite channel and more are having an impact and need prayer and support.

Challenges for Prayer

1 **Kuwait's material wealth** has answered few problems. The government is divided between modernists and traditionalists. Islamist activity is increasing. Young people are frustrated and very bored. Materialism still holds powerful sway, since many have no greater vision about how to use their wealth for good. Pray that Kuwaiti leaders and people might embrace the Saviour.

2 **Expatriate ethnic minorities.** Part of Kuwait's tolerance for other faiths is based on the reality that foreigners comprise most of the workforce. Few expatriates are permanent residents – most are men on short-term work contracts who must leave their families back home. Poor and unfair treatment of these labourers is all too common; this, combined with loneliness, opens many to sensitive Christian witness.

a) Arab groups. Palestinians were the largest group in the past, but Palestine's support for Iraq in the Gulf War resulted in discrimination against Palestinians and expulsion of many. Egyptians make up for the decrease in Palestinian numbers, as do Lebanese, Iraqis and many other Arab groups. There are many nominal Christians among them all – and many opportunities to minister the love of Christ.

b) The Bidoon (literally "without") are stateless Arabs originally from the Kuwait region, but now adrift in the Middle East. They are present in Kuwait in significant numbers. They have no known believers and almost no ministry to them.

c) Asians. South Asians and Filipinos predominate, but there are also many Indonesians, Chinese and Koreans. They are largely contract laborers or domestic servants. A large number of Kuwaiti families leave much of the child raising to the maids and nannies who are often committed believers. Increasing numbers live and work in difficult circumstances, since they are considered beneath Arabs and there are no official channels handling the mistreatment and abuse that regularly occurs. Fortunately, the situation is beginning to improve through changes to the law. Pray for God to encourage the many believers and, through them, break into the lives of those from other faiths. Precisely because of their humble occupations, many of these Asians have amazing access to the homes and lives of Kuwaitis.

3 **Expatriate Christians** have a good reputation thanks to a hundred years of medical mission history. The churches have been allowed to grow, but evangelism of Muslims is illegal; pray for greater freedom or shrewder boldness in this regard. Pray that the rich diversity of congregations would be united in making the Kingdom of God manifest, rather than merely tending to their own interests. The pastors must lead the way in this regard. Kuwait's Catholics, Orthodox, Anglicans and Protestants have formed the Fellowship of Christian Churches in Kuwait, for the purposes of working together to play a larger role in society and having a greater voice and impact therein. Advocacy on behalf of the poor and disadvantaged is a strong point of the Church's presence in Kuwait. Pray also that indigenous Kuwaiti believers might be given the chance to increasingly take the lead in ministering the gospel to the peoples of Kuwait.

4 **Further growth is hampered** by the fact that meetings are permitted only on a handful of compounds; each of these is then used many times by many congregations through the week. The majority of congregations are of South Indian or Filipino composition. The National Evangelical Church compound hosts 60 congregations, representing 25,000 people. The most significant grievance by Kuwaitis regarding churches is that their informal meetings (that is, of those who do have compounds) cause too much traffic and noise. While sharing physical resources and compound space has encouraged greater fellowship and cooperation among churches, pray nevertheless that the government might release more land to the churches so that they might continue to increase. This has occurred already for the Coptic Church.

5 **Kuwaiti Arabs are increasingly exposed to Christians** via travel, business contacts and studying abroad. This is particularly so for students; Kuwaiti students abroad are being reached so effectively that many families are now sending their children to study in Egypt, UAE, etc. in order to protect them from Christian witness. Pray that Christians might take advantage of these opportunities to share and demonstrate the good news and that it might fall on open hearts prepared by the Holy Spirit. Pray also for those Kuwaitis who hear and want to respond; cultural and familial pressures prevent many from following Christ.

6 **Christian literature** is a strategic ministry with considerable freedom. UBS, a private book importer (Book House), and the Catholic-run Bible Resource Centre contribute to making Scriptures available in Kuwait. Pray that Christians might make the best use of these services and that the Word of God might make its way into the hands of all who are open. Pray that permission might be granted to open a Christian bookshop in the capital city.

7 **Other Christian media** are valuable, both for evangelism and for discipling and training. Pray for:

a) *Radio broadcasts* – 105 hours per week in several languages (42 hours per week in Arabic), mostly by FEBA, IBRA, **TWR** and AWR. Pray for more programmes on FM and satellite, instead of shortwave and medium wave. Pray also for wide audiences and lasting responses.

b) *Christian audio and video materials.* Pray for effective distribution and follow-through. The JESUS film on video has been widely and quietly disseminated.

c) *Kuwait's Christian website* (www.prayforkuwait.com) is becoming an effective tool in reaching Kuwaitis with the good news, in discipling Kuwait believers and in communicating the spiritual needs of Kuwait to the rest of the world.

K

Kyrgyzstan

Kyrgyz Republic

Asia

Geography

Area 198,500 sq km. Central Asian state in Tien Shan mountain range bordering on China, Kazakhstan, Tajikistan and Uzbekistan. Most land area is mountainous.

Population		Ann Gr	Density
2010	5,550,239	1.23%	28/sq km
2020	6,159,279	0.94%	31/sq km
2030	6,543,486	0.51%	33/sq km

Capital Bishkek 863,650. **Other major city** Osh 231,000. **Urbanites** 36.6%. **Pop under 15 yrs** 29%. **Life expectancy** 67.6 yrs.

Peoples

Great ethnic diversity relative to its population.
Turkic 82.8%. Kyrgyz 64.8%; Uzbek 13.6%; Uyghur 1.0%; Tatar 0.9%; Kazakh 0.9%; Turk 0.7%.
European 14.4%.
  Slavic 13.5%. Rapid decrease from 24.3% in 1989 through emigration. Russian 12.4%; Ukrainian 1.0%.
  Other 0.9%. German 0.4%.
East Asian 1.6%. Dungan (Chinese Muslim) 1.1%; Korean 0.4%.
Other 1.2%. Tajik 0.9%.
Literacy 98.7%. **Official languages** Kyrgyz, Russian. **All languages** 32. **Indigenous languages** 3. **Languages with Scriptures** 2Bi 1NT 2por.

Economy

A predominantly agricultural country; still poor, but with potential in mining, hydro-electricity and tourism. Geography (very mountainous and isolated from major trade routes/partners) and the prevalence of corruption make economic development difficult. The previous government was notoriously corrupt. By contrast, the new government has stated good economic intentions, but the fruit of these intentions remains to be seen. Widespread poverty and unemployment have caused up to 500,000 to seek work abroad, mostly in Russia and Kazakhstan.

HDI Rank 120th/182. **Public debt** 84.5% of GDP. **Income/person** $951 (2% of USA).

Politics

Independent of the USSR in 1991. Was the first Central Asian republic to replace its post-Soviet regime, on the back of populist demonstrations in 2005 (the "Tulip Revolution"). The subsequent democratic government was troubled by the same accusations of corruption, ineptitude and heavy-handedness. Economic hardship, criminal influence over the economy and growing power of Islamic militants in the Fergana Valley in the south generate further uncertainty over the nation's political future. Riots in 2010 – orchestrated by the political opposition protesting corruption (especially in the 2009 election) and increased living costs – spread and escalated to a countrywide level. They ultimately led to the flight of the President and the swearing in of a new, provisional President in July 2010. These changes also heralded the creation of Central Asia's first parliamentary democracy. However, in June 2010, terrible violence occurred in the south of the country, mainly in two cities. Much of the violence was ethnically based (Kyrgyz and Uzbek). While the majority of those who suffered were ethnic Uzbeks, there is no evidence that a majority of Kyrgyz were involved in the violence. Most people of all ethnicities in the south fled from the troubles and simply wanted peace. There are also claims that the violence was initiated by anti-government and/or criminal drug interests.

Religion

The state has remained secular despite some pressure from Muslim and Orthodox groups for exclusive status. There has been a steady increase in restrictions on, and government scrutiny of, all religious practice, particularly since July 2007. Extremist Islamic movements are perceived by the government to be a threat, and a 2005 law against extremism was passed, as well as a new law on religious activity in January 2009. Christians, Muslims and other religious groups have all suffered in different ways under the past governments, although most persecution has been grassroots and not always "official". There is some hope that the religious laws may change under the new government, as they have restored much freedom of the press, but there are not yet any changes to the religious law.

Religions	Pop %	Population	Ann Gr
Muslim	88.73	4,924,727	1.8%
Non-religious	5.30	294,163	-4.0%
Christian	5.27	292,498	-1.2%
Buddhist	0.42	23,311	3.3%
Ethnoreligionist	0.20	11,100	1.2%
Jewish	0.05	2,775	-2.4%
Baha'i	0.03	1,665	9.8%

Christians Denoms		Pop %	Affiliates	Ann Gr
Protestant	27	0.44	24,000	0.5%
Independent	16	0.38	21,000	6.8%
Catholic	1	0.01	1,000	8.5%
Orthodox	9	4.34	241,000	-2.0%
Marginal	1	0.08	5,000	5.6%

Churches	MegaBloc	Congs	Members	Affiliates
Russian Orthodox	O	45	139,610	215,000
Ukrainian Orthodox	O	10	10,000	20,000
Ch of Jesus Christ	I	40	10,000	15,000
Pentecostal churches	P	35	4,000	8,200
Baptist churches	P	49	3,100	5,270
Jehovah's Witnesses	M	45	2,556	4,600
Lutheran Church	P	17	1,650	2,475
Seventh-day Adventist	P	28	1,000	2,400
Korean Methodist	P	8	861	1,550
Other denominations[32]		120	9,449	17,347
Total Christians[54]		**397**	**182,226**	**291,842**

TransBloc	Pop %	Population	Ann Gr
Evangelicals			
Evangelicals	0.7	40,152	4.3%
Renewalists			
Charismatics	0.6	30,885	5.7%
Pentecostals	0.4	23,200	5.2%

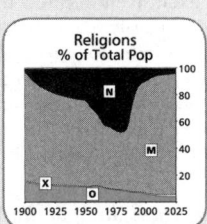

Religions % of Total Pop

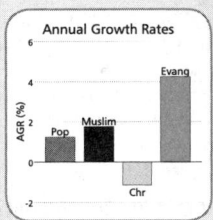

Annual Growth Rates

K

Answers to Prayer

1 **The Church grew impressively** in the first years after the nation's rebirth. It has since slowed in numbers but is maturing. Despite the laws, Kyrgyzstan still has more religious freedom than many neighbouring countries. Bible translation and resources (literature, electronic, radio and TV) have all been developed, though there is room for further growth.

Challenges for Prayer

1 **The government needs courage,** resources and even miracles to right the economy and society in general. The regimes subsequent to Communism have thus far only brought about greater corruption, crime and poverty; frequent demonstrations point to widespread disillusionment, and the 2010 protests and coup were a most poignant illustration of this. The swiftness and intensity with which such fierce violence broke out points to deeper-lying ethnic, political and communal tensions in the country. Hope and optimism for the future are scant, even though some positive foundations have been laid. Pray for a just and righteous government that will oversee the genuine transformation of the Kyrgyz nation.

2 **The people of Kyrgyzstan** continue to have the chance to hear of the Lord Jesus Christ. Pray that the harvest may continue and increase. Pray down the barriers to a people movement.

a) History. For centuries, foreigners have ruled the Kyrgyz and imposed their foreign religions – since the 8th Century foreign armies of various nations brought Islam; Russians in the 19th Century brought Orthodoxy and then imposed Communism in the 20th. Christianity is sadly associated with the occupiers who slaughtered many of the Kyrgyz people's ancestors and also with the West (and its wars in Afghanistan and Iraq).

b) A resurgent Islam. The vast majority of Kyrgyz are culturally Muslim, but practice and understanding of Islam are low. Northern Kyrgyz are more Russian-influenced, but southerners are more traditional and Islamic. Muslim missionaries (200 registered, many more unregistered) from several nations seek to strengthen and purify Islam. Around 2,000 mosques and prayer rooms were built between 2000 and 2005, mostly funded by foreign money. The close association of Kyrgyz cultural identity and Islam makes becoming a Christian a difficult decision; the same holds true for other Central Asian peoples.

c) Shamanism and ancestor worship are significant forces beneath the façade of Islam. Fear of the "evil eye", use of amulets, the occult and demonization are widespread. Shamans still wield great influence.

d) Kyrgyz nationalism has grown as Russian influence declined, although the Russian language serves as the vehicle of social intercourse among the 80 people groups of the country in all spheres of life. Most minorities do not speak Kyrgyz. The conflict between Kyrgyz and Uzbek in southern Kyrgyzstan in June 2010 demonstrated that all is not well in this post-Soviet multicultural society. It desperately needs healthy new ideas to fill the vacuum left by communism.

3 **Christianity** was exclusively limited to the non-indigenous communities before 1990, primarily Orthodox (mainly Slavs) and Protestant Germans. Large-scale emigration since the late 1980s has reduced Orthodoxy to a fraction of its previous population. Baptists, Pentecostals and Adventists face the struggle against decline through emigration. Newer post-1990 denominations have grown, with an increasing Kyrgyz component. The most notable growth is in charismatic churches, particularly the multicultural Church of Jesus Christ. The heady growth of the decade after independence, however, has all but halted and, in some cases, has reversed. Pray for:

a) Further growth and multiplication of churches. There were only 45 Protestant congregations in 1990; 20 years later that number is closing in on 300 and does not include illegal house churches. Pray that the fire and passion of the initial years will not give way to lukewarmness or false doctrines.

b) The maturing and growth of Kyrgyz-speaking congregations. From being a tiny minority in the Church, Kyrgyz believers are now a significant proportion of the nation's Christians.

Effective Kyrgyz Christian leaders have come to the fore, and more services are being held in Kyrgyz. There is a growing missionary concern for their own people, for other Central Asian peoples and beyond. An inter-church mission society has been formed, and several churches have sent out workers to surrounding countries

c) **Preparing leaders** is vital as the Church multiplies, matures and becomes more indigenous. While some Bible schools continue to operate, some have closed. TEE courses and training, locally run, are highly valuable. Discipleship-training courses are also being offered.

d) **Wisdom in outreach.** Culturally relevant and appropriate means need to be found and used. Muslims and Orthodox will often react strongly against perceived proselytism. Many Kyrgyz are held back from faith by fear of alienation from families, fear of not being given a proper burial and by negative propaganda.

e) **Unity among Christians.** Cooperation/collaboration of denominations and ethnicities is vital for the sake of both effectiveness and a good testimony to all in this nation where racism is evident. The wide gulf between the Orthodox and non-Orthodox continues to be a problem.

4 **Expatriate Christians** number several hundred from Asia, the Americas and Europe. Most are tentmakers and need to minister with discretion. Missionaries need to work with the goal of developing the local church so that it is strong and has a healthy relationship with the global body of Christ. Good relationships between national and expatriate believers is also a key; several informal networks focus on unity and strategy for all believers working for God's Kingdom in Kyrgyzstan.

5 **Persecution** is partly the consequence of church growth and evangelism in a Muslim land. The government is taking a harder line toward any religious expression which it feels may cause social or political instability, and this includes evangelicals. Registration is commonly denied to churches, and expatriate work permits are limited. Beyond growing government hostility, resurgent Islamism targets evangelicals with intimidation, property destruction and physical violence. Scaremongering by Muslims, claiming astronomical and untrue growth in the churches, helps little. Pray for believers to stand firm and demonstrate the power and love of Christ.

6 **The economic situation affects all.** The poor, the elderly and the disabled suffer the most. Pray that local Christians might find gainful, legal employment; micro-enterprises are making a difference in this area. There is a large-scale movement of people from rural to urban areas in order to find work, creating a growing underclass of slum dwellers in Bishkek. Large numbers leave Kyrgyzstan to find work in Kazakhstan and Russia. High rates of alcoholism, corruption, international drug trafficking, gambling, prostitution and unemployment are all huge challenges; pray that believers can address these and have a transformational effect on society and the economy.

7 **The less evangelized** for prayer:

a) **The rural and semi-nomadic pastoralist Kyrgyz** who usually live in more remote villages. Few have heard of Christ, and the majority of the nation's unreached live in rural areas.

b) **The Fergana Valley** in the south is shared with Tajikistan and Uzbekistan. The Tajik and large Uzbek minorities (770,000 combined) are mostly unreached. This is where Islamic insurgents flow in across the borders and where Islam is more strident. The few successful church plants here are meeting significant opposition.

c) **The Dungan** are descendants of Chinese Muslim refugees who speak Chinese but use a Cyrillic alphabet. In 2000, a significant multi-agency effort to reach them began.

d) **The many smaller ethnicities** blanketing the country who have little to no specific outreach: Tatars, Chinese, Uyghur, Jews and many others.

8 **Christian support ministries** are varied. There are many possibilities in literature and electronic media, but the greatest potential for positive impact might be medical, community development and business ministries. Pray specifically for:

a) **Bible translation, publishing and distribution.** The NT was first published in 1992, the same time as a Kyrgyz version of the Qur'an. In 2000, Beam of Hope published a translation of both the Old and New Testaments. This is widely used by Kyrgyz Christians. IBT, UBS and Linguaserve, together, produced an improved and more readable NT in 2006. Work has started on a revision of the Old Testament.

*b) **Christian literature*** is a great challenge. There are three main Christian publishers as well as a key bookstore in Bishkek. Little Christian literature is available in Kyrgyz, and evangelistic, apologetic and teaching materials are needed. Pray for economic self-sufficiency, for Christian publishers, for increased numbers of indigenous authors and for a greater variety of titles for this ministry.

*c) **The JESUS film*** is widely viewed on TV and in film showings in Russian and in Kyrgyz. It is also available in many other minority languages. God's Story is also available in Kyrgyz.

*d) **Christian radio.** **TWR*** airs programmes in Kyrgyz, in other Central Asian languages and in Russian, which most people understand.

Quotes on Mission

The history of missions is the history of answered prayer.
Samuel Zwemer

If Jesus be God and died for me, then no sacrifice can be too great for me to make for him.
C. T. Studd

The Spirit of Christ is the Spirit of Missions, and the nearer we get to Him the more intensely missionary we must become.
Henry Martyn

He is no fool who gives what he cannot keep to gain what he cannot lose.
Jim Eliot

All God's giants are weak men who did great things for God because they reckoned that God was with them.
Hudson Taylor

If a commission by an earthly king is considered an honour, how can a commission by a Heavenly King be considered a sacrifice?
David Livingstone

If God has called you to be a missionary, don't stoop to be a king.
Jordan Groom

As long as there are millions destitute of the Word of God and knowledge of Jesus Christ, it will be impossible for me to devote time and energy to those who have both.
J.L. Ewen

The Great Commission is not an option to be considered; it is a command to be obeyed.
Hudson Taylor

The weakness of much current mission work is that we betray the sense that what is yet to be done is greater than what Christ has already done. The world's gravest need is less than Christ's great victory.
P.T. Forsyth

Expect great things from God. Attempt great things for God.
William Carey

Do not pray for easy lives; pray to be stronger men. Do not pray for tasks equal to your powers; pray for powers equal to your tasks. Then, the doing of your work shall be no miracle, but you shall be a miracle.
Bishop Phillips Brooks

I have but one passion – it is He, it is He alone. The world is the field, and the field is the world; and henceforth that country shall be my home where I can be most used in winning souls for Christ.
Count Nikolaus Ludwig Von Zinzendorf

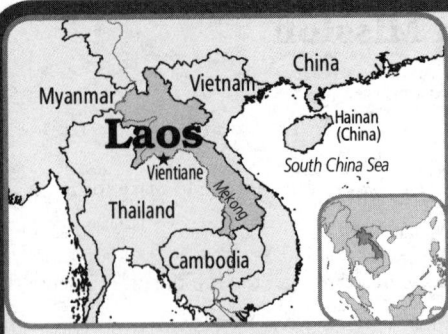

poor infrastructures, corruption and a very low economic baseline as a starting point. Other formidable obstacles include rapid deforestation and increases in illegal trafficking (persons and narcotics) and drug use.

HDI Rank 133rd/182. **Public debt** 144% of GDP. **Income/person** $859 (2% of USA).

Politics

Independent from France in 1954. Lao and Vietnamese communist forces were in complete control by 1975. Anti-government guerrilla activity in the northwest has recently waned. The Communist Party is still in full political control despite economic liberalization. Dissent is suppressed and freedoms are limited.

Religion

Communist persecution of Christians was especially harsh between 1975 and 1978. Restrictions eased afterward, but churches and Christians are still watched and targeted. Buddhism has regained much of its old influence, but is heavily syncretized with animism. Persecution tends to happen in cycles and is expressed on a local or regional level as much as on a national scale. In all cases, though, it can be intense and ruthless toward the Church.

Religions	Pop %	Population	Ann Gr
Buddhist	57.29	3,687,238	1.8%
Ethnoreligionist	34.70	2,233,324	1.7%
Non-religious	4.20	270,316	0.9%
Christian	3.38	217,540	5.7%
Chinese	0.30	19,308	-3.9%
Muslim	0.10	6,436	6.5%
Baha'i	0.03	1,931	10.4%

Christians Denoms		Pop %	Affiliates	Ann Gr
Protestant	9	2.26	145,000	6.9%
Independent	1	0.44	28,000	5.9%
Catholic	1	0.67	43,000	2.0%
Marginal	5	0.01	1,000	11.8%

Churches	MegaBloc	Congs	Members	Affiliates
Lao Evangelical Church	P	700	56,000	140,000
Catholic Church	C	119	25,000	43,000
Indigenous House Chs	I	233	7,000	28,000
Assemblies of God	P	5	90	1,800
United Pentecostal Ch	P	15	600	1,500
Seventh-day Adventist	P	3	667	1,400
Marginal Groups	M	12	350	700
Other denominations[4]		4	300	500
Total Christians[16]		**1,091**	**90,007**	**216,900**

Laos

Lao People's Democratic Republic

Asia

Geography

Area 236,800 sq km. Narrow, landlocked country mainly between Thailand and Vietnam. Mountainous and 55% forested.

Population		Ann Gr	Density
2010	6,436,093	1.82%	27/sq km
2020	7,650,708	1.71%	32/sq km
2030	8,853,949	1.37%	37/sq km

Capital Vientiane 831,472. **Urbanites** 33.2%. **Pop under 15 yrs** 38%. **Life expectancy** 64.6 yrs.

Peoples

A complex mix of 143 groups, compounded by government classifications based on altitude of home environment.

Lao-Tai 59.2%. Lao 43.8%; Tai(15) 4.3%; Phutai 2.9%; Lu 2.6%; Phuan 2.0%.

Mon-Khmer 28.1%. Khmu(6) 10.9%; So 2.1%; Katang 2.0; Bru 1.3%; Kui/Suei 1.0%.

Hmong-Mien 4.0%. Hmong Njua (Blue Miao) 2.9%; Hmong Daw (White Miao) 1.1%; Mien 0.4%.

Tibetan-Himalayan 2.7%. Akha(12) 1.3%; Phunoi 0.7%.

Other 5.3%. Vietnamese 1.6%; Chinese 1.5%. **Literacy** 68.7%. **Official language** Lao. **All languages** 89, also many dialects. **Indigenous languages** 84. **Languages with Scriptures** 5Bi 5NT 13por.

Economy

Subsistence agricultural economy accounts for 80% of employment. The Vietnam War and its aftermath combined to make Laos the poor relation of Southeast Asia. The Communist regime is opening up the country for investment and private enterprise, and economic growth is encouraging. Offsetting this development are

L

TransBloc	Pop %	Population	Ann Gr
Evangelicals			
Evangelicals	2.6	170,215	6.8%
Renewalists			
Charismatics	0.8	53,535	10.1%
Pentecostals	0.1	3,300	3.7%

Answers to Prayer

1 **Rapid church growth,** despite restrictions and persecution. Almost all of the evangelism (and the churches that result) is led by indigenous Laotians. Growth is happening among several different peoples, in rural and urban areas, and throughout the country.

Challenges for Prayer

1 **Much of Laos remains unevangelized.** The remarkable growth of the church is still dwarfed by the size of the task remaining. Most peoples remain unreached, and the gospel has not easily crossed ethnic barriers. Buddhism and tribal religions are often blended together and prevail throughout; compare 5,000 temples to the 250 church buildings. Pray for the gospel light to shine throughout Laos and to draw many to Christ.

2 **The suffering Church** has recognized that persecution is one factor in its growth – persecution keeps them praying and relying on God. The situation has improved very slightly; but at the local and village levels, Christians still find themselves to be targets. Persistent social pressure and the prevention of building new church buildings are two primary opposition strategies. Persecution takes personal forms as well, with strong spiritual opposition compounding family and social pressures to continue practicing traditions. Pray for:

a) **Perseverance and grace** for those who must endure, especially those singled out by persecutors. Property has been seized, and ministers arrested and even killed.

b) **Increased openness to evangelism,** church planting and building – not illegal, yet still obstructed by the government. Much growth, by necessity, takes place "underground" in house groups, since the more formal congregations are watched and must be cautious. Pray for continued boldness to share the gospel.

c) **Discipleship, teaching and biblical literacy** for all who respond to Christ. Pray that believers will grow strong in faith and not fall away. Pray also that they become salt and light in their own society, and in a way that is truly Lao.

d) **A cross-cultural missions vision** in the church to reach the many ethnic minorities.

3 **The Lao Evangelical Church** is one of two recognized Protestant bodies (along with the SDA) wherein several groups have been forced by the government to amalgamate. It is the largest and most influential Church, and where most of the Christian growth has occurred. Pray for the LEC, in particular the pastors, that they might demonstrate unity, genuine love and humility; pray for wisdom to handle the growth and to deal with the situations in both established congregations and house churches. As the primary state-approved Christian body, the LEC itself struggles with issues of accountability, transparency in finances, and healthy relationships with smaller and newer denominations. Pray that God might expose any wrongdoing among church leaders and raise up faithful, humble and authentic servant leaders in the LEC.

4 **Leaders for the churches.** Over 90% of all trained leaders left Laos in 1975. Most congregations do not have a trained pastor, even as church growth increases the urgency of the need. The LEC now has a Bible school training programme, complemented by a Catholic seminary and an increasing role for TEE and module-based training. Just as pressing is the need to develop reproducible training for lay leaders, in particular for the house church movements which, due to their unregistered nature, often lack the structures and resources for solid training.

5 **There are many needs** that Christian workers could help address, but missionaries are forbidden. Some believers are serving the nation through aid and development, bomb removal (dropped by the USA during the Vietnam War), business training and English teaching. Asian believers (from neighbouring China and Thailand as well as the Philippines and South Korea) have a major role to play. Pray that the foreign workers and churches would serve the Laotian people in the best possible way.

6 **Unreached peoples.** The sheer ethnic diversity is one of the greatest barriers to effective evangelization of the whole country. Pray for:

a) **The Lao.** The nation's dominant people are described as gentle and peace loving. But anti-Christian bias in government and society, strong family pressure to conform and the passive nature of Lao culture are major obstacles to faith. There has been major growth among the Lao (>40,000 Christians), and they are key in bringing the gospel to the rest of Laos.

b) **The Tai tribes,** speaking 15 languages. They are mostly unevangelized and have almost no resources in their dialects; but their close affinity to the Lao, linguistically and ethnically, affords them some opportunities to discover the good news.

c) **The mountain-dwelling Hmong** are known for having resisted, sometimes violently, communism and government control. Most Hmong Christians fled Laos in 1975. Although the proportion of Christians is lower among them, the Hmong are the most responsive peoples in the country and significant numbers are coming to faith.

d) **The northern peoples.** Many have responded to the gospel in China and Thailand. Political conditions have never allowed missionary work; pray that this will change.

e) **The many small southern tribes** received the gospel for the first time between 1957 and 1963, but war prevented the planting of churches among most of them. They are deeply enmeshed in the fear of spirits; pray that they find freedom through Jesus.

7 **Christian help ministries.**

a) **Media ministries** are very fruitful, including literature, cassettes, radio and resources on video, CD and DVD. The government's obstruction of both importing and producing materials nationally is a great need for prayer. Pray also for indigenous artists to write and perform Christian songs, and to develop effective evangelism and discipleship tools using stories, drama, music and other creative expressions of truth.

b) **Bible and literature distribution.** The UBS and the Bible League distribute Bibles. AsiaLink is an agency deeply committed to literature ministry for Laotians. Hundreds of thousands of pieces of literature were hand carried into Laos. Pray for the free and widespread distribution of all Christian literature; pray also for the safety of those who carry in Christian materials.

c) **Bible translation.** The local linguistic situation is highly complex. Several groups are looking into ways to address this challenge. There are 31 languages with a definite need for translation teams and possibly a further 26 languages will need them. Praise God that the Mien Bible has now been printed. Pray for the effective use of all available tools in speeding up the process of making God's Word available.

d) **GRN** has prepared audio messages in 91 languages and dialects of Laos. This is a vital ministry in a nation where literacy is relatively low.

e) **Christian radio.** FEBC and others broadcast 71 hours weekly in indigenous languages, including Lao, Hmong, Khmu, Tai, Akha, Lahu and Mien. Radio has great potential.

f) **Christian media.** The JESUS film is available in Lao, Khmu, Hmong(2), Mien, Akha, Vietnamese and Chinese and is being produced in several more languages. The God's Story Project materials are also available in Lao.

Latvia

Republic of Latvia

Europe

Geography

Area 64,610 sq km. A fertile plain with 3,000 lakes; indented by the Gulf of Riga. The central of the three Baltic republics.

Population		Ann Gr	Density
2010	2,240,265	-0.46%	35/sq km
2020	2,152,631	-0.41%	33/sq km
2030	2,049,164	-0.50%	32/sq km

Capital Riga 707,000. **Urbanites** 68.2%. **Pop under 15 years** 14%. **Life expectancy** 72.3 yrs.

Peoples

European 98.7%.
  Baltic 59.1%. Latvian 57.7%; Lithuanian 1.4%.
  Slavic 38.9%. Russian 29.6%; Belarusian 4.1%; Ukrainian 2.9%; Polish 2.4%.
  Other 0.7%.
All other 1.3%.
Literacy 99.7%. **Official language** Latvian (Lettish). **All languages** 13. **Indigenous languages** 5. **Languages with Scriptures** 2Bi 3NT 3por.

Economy

A robust but vulnerable economy. Poorest EU nation, but fastest economic growth in the EU for several years running. Also has highest inflation in EU, a dangerously high external debt and trade deficit. A lack of natural resources has forced Latvia to develop – faster than other former Soviet states – an industrialized economy and a liberalized, privatized market economy. But the growing gap between rich and poor is a major issue.
HDI Rank 48th/182. **Public debt** 19.5% of GDP. **Income/person** $14,964 (32% of USA).

Politics

Has been ruled by the Germans, Danes, Poles, Swedes and Russians since the Middle Ages. Its brief independence from Russia (1917–1940) was ended by Stalin's re-conquest. Stalin liquidated a fifth of the population, deported many more and forcibly settled Russians in their place. This history still influences modern politics as the large Russian minority struggles to find its place and role in modern Latvia. Independent in 1991 as a multiparty democracy. Joined NATO and the EU in 2004.

Religion

Long and deep pagan roots; among the last European peoples to be Christianized (13th Century). Latvians were early supporters of Luther, and much of the population converted to Lutheranism. The churches were harshly persecuted under both the Nazis and the Communists. Religious freedom in 1988 caused a burst of re-affiliation that has since mostly petered out. Freedom for all forms of religious expression.

Religions	Pop %	Population	Ann Gr
Christian	60.00	1,344,159	-0.2%
Non-religious	38.44	861,158	-0.9%
Other	0.90	20,162	0.7%
Muslim	0.42	9,409	0.5%
Jewish	0.24	5,377	-3.5%

Christians Denoms		Pop %	Affiliates	Ann Gr
Protestant	16	21.81	489,000	-0.3%
Independent	15	4.27	96,000	0.7%
Catholic	1	18.08	405,000	-1.2%
Orthodox	6	15.46	346,000	0.9%
Marginal	2	0.28	6,000	3.1%
Unaffiliated		0.10	2,000	0.0%

Churches	MegaBloc	Congs	Members	Affiliates
Lutheran Church	P	303	300,000	450,000
Catholic Church	C	273	242,515	405,000
Latvian Orthodox	O	122	194,805	300,000
Old Believers	I	69	33,750	67,500
Ukrainian Orthodox	O	59	23,529	40,000
Baptist Church	P	88	6,800	13,600
Message of Hope	I	3	5,455	12,000
New Generation Min	I	4	4,091	9,000
Seventh-day Adventist	P	60	4,100	7,380
Pentecostal Churches	P	23	3,500	6,300
Other Protestant	P	50	3,333	6,000
Jehovah's Witnesses	M	28	2,500	5,000
Other denominations[28]		105	14,001	25,943
Total Christians[40]		**1,137**	**835,046**	**1,341,723**

L

TransBloc	Pop %	Population	Ann Gr
Evangelicals			
Evangelicals	7.0	157,351	1.2%
Renewalists			
Charismatics	3.2	71,431	3.5%
Pentecostals	0.4	8,748	0.8%

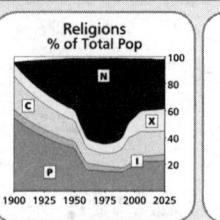

Religions
% of Total Pop

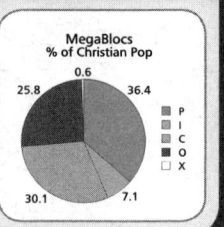

MegaBlocs
% of Christian Pop

Challenges for Prayer

1 **The general social climate** has changed since independence. The Soviet departure left a moral vacuum, which many negative influences rushed to fill. EU money has also brought EU-style social problems. Alcohol, drugs, a rapidly growing sex trade, high abortion rates, the world's fourth highest suicide rate and notable corruption in government all indicate that something is not right. Despite economic growth there is a prevalent attitude of spiritual apathy, even of hopelessness. Pray for society to awaken to this challenge and to build a nation characterized by hope and righteousness.

2 **Christianity is characterized mostly by nominalism**, since the excitement of the 1990s has yielded to a lethargic status quo. Although 60% belong to a Christian confession, only a small minority actually practice their faith. The Lutheran, Catholic and Orthodox churches dominate the religious scene; and while they are trusted, social institutions need an injection of spiritual dynamism and renewal. The spread of cults, both Christian and pagan, is a challenge to Christianity. Pray for a new move of the Spirit in the mainline churches; there are certainly many signs of life already. Pray for the many nominal Christians to become true believers.

3 **Unprecedented unity in the churches** was caused in part by challenges to biblical morality in society. The aggressive lobbying by homosexual and anti-family agendas in particular elicited joint statements and coordinated activism by the churches. But more important are the prayer and worship summits attended by the leaders of almost every denomination and confession – these meetings are the foundation for revival in Latvia. Pray that this unity might reverse the moral tide in Latvia, and that the laity might emulate their leaders to worship and work together for the Kingdom.

4 **Missions vision** in Latvia is still in its infancy, but is demonstrating impressive diversity and determination. Pray that this spark might grow into a flame to take the life-changing gospel to the less-reached in Latvia and beyond. Pray also for groups such as Bridge Builders International, the Latvian Evangelical Alliance and its CP-21 vision, which seeks to work with indigenous churches to plant new churches and reach every Latvian. Peoples of special note for prayer are:

a) Rural populations. They have far fewer opportunities to encounter the living Christ. Pray for renewal in their mainline congregations and for more teams such as **YWAM** that will evangelize in villages.

b) The Russian minority – mostly non-religious or Orthodox. Pray for increasing reconciliation and partnerships between believing Latvians and ethnic Russians – a painful legacy is still not entirely resolved.

c) The 7,000 Jews in Latvia, very resistant to the gospel and increasingly subjected to anti-Semitism. Pray for a loving and patient Christian witness to them.

5 **Ministry to young people** is strategic – this includes campus, youth and children's ministries as well as summer camps. **IFES** and Agape (**CCCI**) are having an impact on Latvian and, increasingly, international students. **CEF** is reaching up to 40,000 primary students every week through religious instruction in school. SU, **YWAM**, Latvian Christian Mission and others hold summer camps/events and minister to youth from Latvia and indeed all Eastern Europe. Pray for more workers with the vision to reach young people. Pray that this generation might be reached before they lapse into the irreligion or atheism of their forebears.

a) Scripture. A new NT in Latvian was released in 2007 and work on the OT continues. Pray for widespread distribution of Scripture in Latvia. The Bible Society uses its ecumenical platform to cooperate with many denominations.

b) Radio ministry is very well resourced and still growing. Examples are:

i Lutheran Hour and other Christian programmes, broadcasting on national and local radio as well as live broadcasts of services on TV. Lutheran Hour also broadcasts discipleship programmes and has a Bible Correspondence Course.

ii Russian Christian radio (**FEBC** and World Harvest Radio) runs 24/7.

iii Latvian Christian Radio has had broadcasts 24/7 in Latvian since 1993.

c) TV. The Lutheran Church broadcasts a series of services, Christian films and talk shows. Pray for more Latvian Christian television programmes that will profoundly communicate Jesus.

d) Internet evangelism is proving a very cost-effective and creative medium for sharing the good news. Pray for the websites and forums in Latvian to have a great impact.

i The Latvian Bible is available in its entirety online.

ii Internet radio (QBS) is focused on reaching an unchurched generation.

Lebanon
Republic of Lebanon
Asia

Geography

Area 10,230 sq km. A fertile, mountainous state in the East Mediterranean. Rests between Israel and Syria. The site of ancient Phoenicia.

Population		Ann Gr	Density
2010	4,254,583	0.83%	416/sq km
2020	4,586,655	0.72%	448/sq km
2030	4,858,343	0.51%	475/sq km

During the civil war, up to 900,000 emigrated with up to 300,000 more since the war's end. No official census has been taken since the 1930s.

Capital Beirut 1,936,990. **Urbanites** 87.2%. **Pop under 15 yrs** 25%. **Life expectancy** 71.9 yrs.

Peoples

Arabs 93.5%.
  Lebanese 66.4%.
  Other Arab 27.1%. Palestinian 12.2%; Druze 7.7%; Syrian 1.6%; Egyptian 1.6%.
Other 6.5%. Armenian 4.5%; Kurd 1.7%.
Literacy 86.5%. **Official language** Arabic; French and English are widely used. **All languages** 9. **Indigenous languages** 6. **Languages with Scriptures** 4Bi 1NT 2por.

Economy

Lebanon was the commercial hub of the Middle East until the civil war reduced Beirut to rubble and ruined its profitable trading, banking and tourist industries. Recovery began in 1992 but was reversed by Israel's war in 2006, including the bombing of part of Beirut and widespread infrastructure destruction. Incredible staying power as a commercial centre despite the constant upheaval, but tourism has not boomed as hoped. Many question the long-term economic viability of such a strife-torn and debt-ridden nation.
HDI Rank 83rd/182. **Public debt** 160% of GDP. **Income/person** $7,708 (16% of USA).

Politics

French-mandated territory in 1919; independent in 1943 as a republic, with its constitution based on a delicate balance related to the size of the 18 recognized religious communities. Changing Muslim-Christian demographics and the influx of 300,000 Palestinian refugees between 1948 and 1976 upset the status quo, precipitating the 1975-1990 civil war. Israel

L

occupied parts of southern Lebanon 1982–2003. Shi'a, Sunni, Druze and Christian militias fought bitterly with each other. The Syrian army imposed a measure of peace in 1990 and opened the way for the Taif agreement of 1990/91 and a new Lebanese government. Syrian military presence and control ended in 2006 as a result of massive protests after the assassination of Prime Minister Rafiq al-Hariri. Israel invaded again in 2006 after Hezbollah provocation, wreaking widespread destruction. The country seems in constant political turmoil, with influence and interference by Syria, Iran and Saudi Arabia.

Religion

Freedom of religion; the only Arab state that is not officially Muslim. The Shi'a are about 37% of the population and Sunni 22%. There are 18 recognized religious communities: four Muslim, one Druze, one Jewish and 12 Christian. All figures used here are estimates. The last reliable census including religion was in 1932, when Christians were 53.7% of the population. Deep communal and religious divisions manifest themselves politically. Shi'as are the fastest growing, and only the poorly integrated Palestinians are more under-represented in the political sphere. Lebanon's religious demographics are out of sync with Parliamentary representation, which serves to heighten problems. The Church's greatest challenge is the large-scale emigration of Christians.

Religions	Pop %	Population	Ann Gr
Muslim	58.96	2,508,502	0.7%
Christian	31.97	1,360,190	0.7%
Other	7.00	297,821	1.7%
Non-religious	2.05	87,219	3.5%
Baha'i	0.02	851	0.8%

Christians Denoms		Pop %	Affiliates	Ann Gr
Protestant	22	0.35	15,000	-0.1%
Independent	8	0.23	10,000	5.2%
Anglican	1	<0.01	<1,000	-1.1%
Catholic	6	23.90	1,017,000	0.9%
Orthodox	7	7.32	312,000	-0.2%
Marginal	5	0.17	7,000	0.2%

Churches	MegaBloc	Congs	Members	Affiliates
Maronite Patriarchate	C	970	457,792	705,000
Melchite Cath Patriarchate	C	334	150,270	278,000
Greek Orthodox Church	O	273	108,380	194,000
Armenian Apostolic Ch	O	196	58,659	105,000
Chaldean Catholic	C	5	5,587	10,000
Latin-rite Catholic	C	5	5,028	9,000
Syrian Cath Patriarchate	C	3	4,358	7,800
Armenian Cath Patriarchate	C	9	3,911	7,000
Syrian Orthodox Ch	O	4	4,132	6,900
Jehovah's Witnesses	M	62	3,018	6,700
Church of the East	O	2	2,371	4,150
Baptist Convention	P	30	2,100	3,200
National Evang Union	P	3	1,099	2,000
Other denominations[36]		176	11,174	21,735
Total Christians[49]		**2,072**	**817,879**	**1,360,485**

TransBloc	Pop %	Population	Ann Gr
Evangelicals			
Evangelicals	0.5	21,410	2.1%
Renewalists			
Charismatics	0.5	22,932	4.1%
Pentecostals	<0.1	650	1.4%

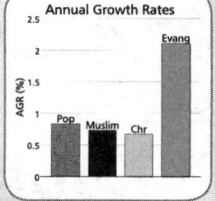

Answers to Prayer

1 **Openness to spiritual things** and a growing number of converts from other religious communities continue. Praise God for the grace shown by Christians to those uprooted by the 2006 Israeli invasion. Evangelicals are showing vision and commitment to loving outreach.

2 **Lebanon remains the only land** in the Middle East where all are legally free to change their religious affiliation. Believers from most other Arab countries can more freely come to Lebanon for Christian training. Pray for this religious freedom to be maintained.

Challenges for Prayer

1 **Lebanon's tragic history** over the last 70 years, with communal wars, foreign interventions and hostage-taking. With adequate political stability, Lebanon has demonstrated great resilience and potential to rebuild. Pray specifically for:

a) ***The government and its leaders.*** There is a lot of disillusionment with the traditional political elite. Pray for a government that rules for the common good, balancing traditional values and demographic realities.

b) ***Full political freedom*** to be gained and religious freedom protected. Lebanon, for all its troubles, remains unique in the Middle East for its freedom.

c) ***The healing of deep hurts*** in communities, families and individuals. Over 80% of the population were displaced at one time or another during the wars. All have lost loved ones; many lost homes and jobs.

d) ***A spirit of forgiveness.*** All have suffered and there are countless opportunities for bitterness and hatred. Pray that the Holy Spirit might do His work of reconciliation.

e) ***The rebuilding of the South*** after multiple wars and occupations. Many unexploded munitions from 2006 make rebuilding dangerous.

2 **The entire nation has been deeply traumatized,** especially Christians. Many despair of any future in Lebanon and have emigrated en masse for economic and security reasons. The Christian percentage has dropped from 62% in 1970 to 32% in 2010. Pray that many may come to personal faith in and deep commitment to the Lord Jesus. Though most Christians would leave if they had the chance, pray for many to choose to stay and remain salt and light in Lebanon.

3 **The wide variety of Orthodox and Catholic Churches** have a long history of struggling to survive. In the midst of traditionalism, deadness and politicization, there are significant renewal movements, notably in the Maronite and Eastern Orthodox Churches. Church attendance remains high. The Middle East Council of Churches draws together mainline groups. Pray for new life to infuse these ancient communities and for key religious leaders to personally experience new life.

4 **The Protestant Church has struggled to find acceptance,** and the many small denominations communicate a message of fragmentation and divisiveness. Conversions have barely replaced losses through emigration. Pray for the ministry of Protestant groups – with a number of new converts from non-Christian backgrounds – that they might grow in number and missions vision. Pray for new growth among mainline Protestants as well. Pray for further fellowship and cooperation to develop among evangelicals. In the 2006 crisis, churches worked together to assist refugees fleeing the war in the South. The Supreme Council represents Protestants in the national framework.

5 **Trained leadership** in evangelical churches is a precious resource. The decline in foreign missionaries and the emigration of national leaders has left many congregations without effective pastoral care. Despite this, Lebanon has a good number of evangelical Bible schools – the Arab Baptist Theological Seminary, Mediterranean Bible College (Church of God), Christian Alliance Institute of Theology (**CMA**), and the Near East School of Theology (Presbyterian in origin). These colleges equip many Arab students from outside of Lebanon. Pray for staff members, the supply of needs and for more students. Pray that increasing cooperation among these colleges would result in significant advances for the Kingdom.

6 **Lebanon has long been a key centre for Christian ministries** to the whole Middle East. So much of this was interrupted, but is regaining momentum once more with stronger indigenous leadership. Pray that Lebanese believers might regain a vision for others and for other lands – the war has caused too many to become insular. Pray specifically for these ministries:

a) ***The Bible Society*** distributes many Bibles within Lebanon and to surrounding nations. It is growing to meet the increased demand for Bibles and NTs in all communities. The Society has opened some new centres in busy shopping areas. Many in Orthodox and Catholic churches are reading and studying the Scriptures. The Society is one of the few ministries that has good relationships with all confessions.

b) ***Christian schools and orphanages.*** These are much appreciated, having had a long and fruitful ministry, and have gained in credibility from 1990 onward. Many children from all communities hear the gospel and some come to Christ (LES – Lebanon Evangelical School, Baptists, **MECO**, and others). Many Lebanese political and societal leaders have attended an evangelical school.

c) **Young people and students,** who often struggle with hopelessness as well as frustration with lack of progress and job opportunities. Many feel as if they have been given up on; many are active for real change in Lebanon. Pray for relevant and effective ministry to young people of all faiths – they are the future of Lebanon. Drop-in centres and camps are particularly effective. Most youth are responsive to genuine Christian love, yet more needs to be done (**YFC**, *Grain du Blé*, **YWAM**, Focus on the Family, **IFES**, **CCCI**, local churches).

d) **Christian literature production** is too often disrupted by civil upheavals. Much of this ministry has been transferred to Cyprus, Europe and elsewhere. Pray for Clarion Publishing House (LES), **OM**, Middle East Lutheran Ministry, the Baptist Publishing Center and others who publish and distribute literature for Lebanon and the Arab world.

e) **Radio.** FEBA, IBRA, **TWR** and others broadcast 56 hours/week in Arabic and more in Armenian and English. There are also several local FM stations that broadcast Christian programmes, and Arabic Christian radio is widely available through the Internet.

f) **Christian TV.** Television is the primary source of information and entertainment. There are a number of local Christian TV stations. Satellite television channels, including but not limited to **SAT-7**, have had a deep impact. Programmes are also re-broadcast by the Catholic TV station *Télélumière*. **SAT-7**'s main studios for the Middle East are now in Beirut.

7 **Expatriate Christian workers** still have a role to play in Lebanon. Pray for more to be called and enabled to identify with and serve the Church and all Lebanese. There are many areas where the love of Christ may be demonstrated – reconstruction, work with young people, drug rehabilitation as well as discipleship and church development ministries (**CMA**, **MECO**, **AoG**, **BMS**, **IMB**, WVI, **WEC**, **YWAM**, **OM** and others).

8 **The unreached.** Conversion to Christ, although legal, is nonetheless very costly to those from other backgrounds. Despite this, the number of those coming to Jesus is significantly increasing. So pray for:

a) **The Shi'a Muslims** are the fastest growing population and increasingly influential. They live mainly in the south, in the Bekaa Valley and in southern Beirut. The Hezbollah party is supported by Iran. Pray that more might discover the emptiness of a religion without Christ, as ever-growing numbers have done!

b) **The Sunni** are mainly in the northeast, and in the cities of Beirut, Tripoli and Sidon.

c) **The Druze** and their well-organized, close-knit community. Their heartland is the mountain area east of Beirut. They have a secretive religion that came out of Islam; only 20% are fully initiated into it. A multi-agency partnership is seeing several hundred come to Christ. Most Druze believers remain incognito, but others form a growing church or take their new faith back to Syria with them.

d) **The Palestinians.** Their story is full of tragedy, poverty and disenfranchisement. No full peace or harmony is possible without a lasting solution to their situation, especially for those in refugee camps. There are Christians among them, some evangelical, but the majority are Muslim and unreached. Differences among radical Islamist minority groups have brought suffering onto the majority, such as the conflict in the Nahr al-Bared refugee camp.

e) **The poor and disadvantaged.** The majority of the very poor are Muslim. The blind, deaf and disabled are often neglected by society in general, but doors are open for Christians to minister to them. Pray for more Christians and agencies to demonstrate care and love to these needy people.

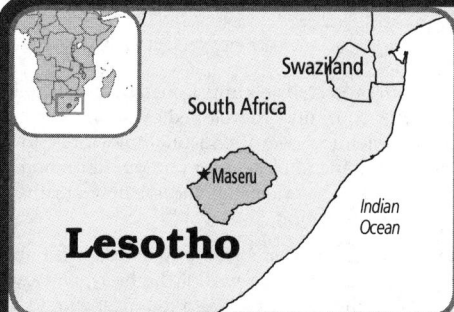

South Africa

Swaziland

★Maseru

Indian
Ocean

Lesotho

Lesotho

Kingdom of Lesotho

Africa

Geography

Area 30,355 sq km. A mountainous country completely surrounded by South Africa. Only 10% is arable.

Population		Ann Gr	Density
2010	2,084,182	0.88%	69/sq km
2020	2,244,475	0.69%	74/sq km
2030	2,358,881	0.45%	78/sq km

It is the only country in the world with its entire area above 1,000 metres in altitude.
Capital Maseru 228,000. **Urbanites** 26.9%. **Pop under 15 yrs** 39%. **Life expectancy** 44.9 yrs.

Peoples

Bantu 99.4%. Basotho 81.0%; Zulu up to 15.0%; Phuti 2.4%; Xhosa 1.1%.
Other 0.6%. European, Asian.
Literacy 81.4%. **Official languages** Sesotho, English. **All languages** 6. **Indigenous languages** 5. **Languages with Scriptures** 5Bi.

Economy

The mountainous topography, limited transport and communication infrastructures, and lack of agricultural land have kept the country poor and have hastened soil erosion. Half of the population live below the poverty line and unemployment can often reach as high as 45%. Poor soil quality and drought have meant that Lesotho cannot feed itself, even though the large majority engage in some subsistence farming. Sources of income include hydroelectricity, the textile industry, diamond mining and remittances from labourers working abroad, mostly in South Africa. AIDS has also had a devastating economic effect. Highly dependent on South Africa for trade.
HDI Rank 156th/182. **Public debt** 58.2% of GDP. **Income/person** $660 (1% of USA).

Politics

A British protectorate in 1865. Independence in 1966, but a geographical hostage due to its size and isolation as an enclave within South Africa. Now a constitutional monarchy with a mostly ceremonial kingship and a prime minister leading a multiparty parliament. After years of instability, dictatorship and political polarization resulting in South African Development Community (SADC) intervention, the young democracy is showing signs of stability and maturity.

Religion

Freedom of religion.

Religions	Pop %	Population	Ann Gr
Christian	89.31	1,861,383	0.9%
Ethnoreligionist	9.50	197,997	0.5%
Baha'i	0.80	16,673	-1.5%
Non-religious	0.25	5,210	11.7%
Hindu	0.10	2,084	0.9%
Muslim	0.04	834	0.9%

Christians	Denoms	Pop %	Affiliates	Ann Gr
Protestant	26	18.27	381,000	1.4%
Independent	225	13.40	279,000	1.5%
Anglican	1	5.37	112,000	0.4%
Catholic	1	47.64	993,000	0.5%
Marginal	1	0.41	8,000	3.0%
Unaffiliated		4.20	88,000	2.2%

Churches	MegaBloc	Congs	Members	Affiliates
Catholic Church	C	514	616,770	993,000
Lesotho Evang Ch	P	600	86,901	272,000
Other Indigenous	I	858	128,743	215,000
Anglican Church	A	438	67,066	112,000
Assemblies of God	P	50	21,078	43,000
Zion Christian Church	I	45	7,083	17,000
Zion Foundation Ch	I	67	5,708	13,700
African Meth Epis Ch	I	47	7,000	12,500
Dutch Ref Ch in Afr	P	15	3,900	10,300
Methodist Church	P	10	5,000	10,000
Jehovah's Witnesses	M	70	3,400	8,500
Seventh-day Adventist	P	33	5,600	8,400
Mahon Mission	P	32	3,900	7,800
Full Gospel Ch of God	P	50	2,720	6,800
Other denominations[31]		342	18,677	43,524
Total Christians[254]		**3,171**	**983,546**	**1,773,524**

TransBloc	Pop %	Population	Ann Gr
Evangelicals			
Evangelicals	12.1	253,040	2.7%
Renewalists			
Charismatics	16.9	351,997	3.0%
Pentecostals	3.6	75,719	3.4%

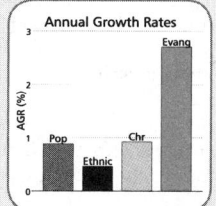

Annual Growth Rates

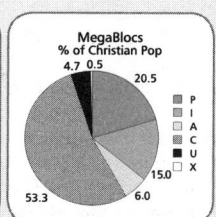

MegaBlocs
% of Christian Pop

L

Challenges for Prayer

1 **Lesotho faces a tough future.** The nation is both protected and imprisoned by its isolated geographical location. Dwindling agricultural returns, an underdeveloped economy, widespread HIV/AIDS, urbanization, family breakdown, endemic poverty and unemployment for much of the population, and limited access to water all combine to place great burdens upon both the people and the government of Lesotho. Pray for wisdom in leadership and for new, creative and sustainable ways to improve the quality of life of the population.

2 **AIDS** is the greatest challenge facing Lesotho. It has devastated the population with an HIV infection rate of 23.2% (now stabilizing, but among the world's highest), already leaving 100,000 orphans. The 20-40 age group, so vital to the economy, is also the most afflicted. A host of agencies, missions and church ministries are answering this challenge in many ways (education, prevention, care). But the risk of reductionism is present as spiritual ministry to needy souls is at times taken over by the overarching spectre of HIV. Pray for a balanced ministry approach that brings life to the whole person.

3 **The Basotho** were Christianized generations ago, but most were never fully converted. The social pressure against becoming *bapholosoa*, or born again, is wielded by traditional religious forces, mainline churches and family members alike. All the factors have reduced the mainstream church to maintaining the religious status quo with marginal redemptive impact on society. Pray for the Holy Spirit to sweep out impurities from the churches and bring new life. There are two issues of particular importance:

a) Traditionalism and nominalism are common in the Catholic Church and in the Lesotho Evangelical Church. The latter is the fruit of the great pioneering work by French missionaries of the Paris Evangelical Missionary Society.

b) Many AIC churches compromise with African traditional religious practices and beliefs. Sometimes this is due to a lack of biblical teaching; sometimes it is a deliberate syncretization. Practices like *balimo* (ancestor worship), curses and charms, and the Sephiri (a secret society involving African traditional magic rites) are all an affront to the holiness of God and the purity of the gospel.

4 **Newer evangelical/renewalist groups** and agencies continue to see growth (**AIM**, **YWAM**, **IMB**, various South African groups). Special items for prayer:

a) Bible teaching. A strategic need, since most evangelical pastors lack experience and training. There are five residential Bible colleges/seminaries, as well as further TEE programmes, the Bible Training Centre for Pastors and the missions-specific ECMTC (Operation UP).

b) Theological purity. Several foreign African groups have entered Lesotho preaching a gospel that includes excessive or incorrect emphases on prosperity, healings and other issues. Pray for discernment for the leaders of Lesotho's churches to know what is right and biblical and appropriate for their own context.

c) Unity in the churches. There are many evangelical, charismatic and Pentecostal groups for such a small country, but no central body through which they can relate together. Pray for a spirit of humility and cooperation.

5 **The mountain population of 600,000** are among the poorest and most vulnerable. Nominally Christian, they have little contact with the life-giving gospel. Lesotho's churches are beginning to wake up to this challenge. Operation UP, an indigenous agency, is committed to reaching every family in the mountains and planting 50 evangelical churches in the next five years. Other agencies include **AIM**, Joy to the World, **YWAM**, Fill the Gap Ministries, the Full Gospel Church and Global Evangelism Ministries. Many villages are accessible only on horseback, others by **MAF** plane. Pray for fruitful and sustainable ministry that yields thriving churches.

6 **Christian support ministries:**

a) **MAF** has a unique and vital role in this land of high mountains and few roads. **MAF** planes operate on 26 landing strips with 17 full-time workers and 6 aircraft. They provide support for Christian workers and a fly-in doctor service. Pray for these pilots, their families/support teams and for their safety.

b) Youth work. Scripture Union is active in sharing God's Word with young people, especially through school groups.

c) Christian literature in Sesotho (the mother tongue for most) is in short supply. Operation UP and others are working on addressing this shortage by translating materials from English.

d) Christian radio has had a strong and positive impact in the lowlands. Harvest FM, Catholic Radio, *Jesu ke Karabo FM*, Mo-African FM and KEL Radio. These stations are instrumental in reaching even non-churchgoers. Pray that they will be used for spiritual rather than political purposes. **TWR** broadcasts daily in English.

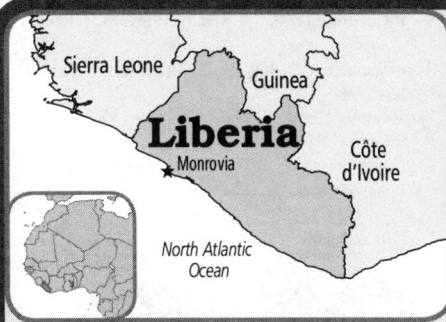

Sierra Leone
Guinea
Liberia
Côte d'Ivoire
Monrovia
North Atlantic Ocean

Liberia

Republic of Liberia

Africa

Geography 🌍

Area 99,067 sq km. Heavily forested coastal state adjoining Sierra Leone, Guinea and Côte d'Ivoire.

Population		Ann Gr	Density
2010	4,101,767	4.23%	41/sq km
2020	5,252,580	2.40%	53/sq km
2030	6,470,182	2.01%	65/sq km

In the 1990s, 250,000 were killed and over 1 million became refugees abroad. The majority have returned.

Capital Monrovia 827,465. **Urbanites** 61.5%. **Pop under 15 yrs** 43%. **Life expectancy** 57.9 yrs.

Peoples 👪

Sub-Saharan African 93.8%. 16 major indigenous ethnic groups divided into three language families.

Mande/Malinke 48.7%. Nine groups, largest: Kpelle 19.2%; Mano 7.1%; Dan 7.0%; Loma 5.5%; Vai 3.5%; Gbandi 2.6%; Mandingo 1.8%; Maninke 1.2%.

Kru 35.1%. 19 groups, largest: Bassa 13.7%; Kru (Klao) 7.2%; Grebo(7) 7.0%; Krahn(3) 5.1%.

Atlantic/Guinean 10.0%. Kissi 4.6%; Gola 3.5%; Akan(2) 1.7%.

Other 6.2%. Americo-Liberian (returned American blacks) 2.5%; Kongo (returned Caribbean freed slaves) 2.5%; Caucasian, Lebanese, and others.

Literacy 51.9%. **Official language** English. **All languages** 31. **Languages with Scriptures** 2Bi 13NT 15por 12w.i.p.

Economy 📈

Well watered; abundant natural resources of rubber, iron, diamonds, timber and others. Maritime registry of ships is the second largest revenue source. Made destitute by decades of institutionalized corruption by an elite (up to 1980) and ensuing civil wars and chaos (1989-2003). Much of the capital, the road system and most of the buildings have been destroyed, and much farmland has reverted to forest. Foreign investment and aid are helping to rebuild the shattered economy; but large debt and the devastated infrastructure will slow recovery, even with an upright government. Poverty is rife; joblessness is as high as 75%, and the majority survive on less than $1US/day.
HDI Rank 169th/182. **Public debt** 239% of GDP. **Income/person** $216 (<0.5% of USA).

Politics ⚔️

In 1847 Liberia became Black Africa's first independent state, created as a colony for freed American slaves. Liberian-American dominance ended in the coup of 1980. The military government grew increasingly unstable. Massive corruption and repression of the Mano and Gio peoples provoked the 1989 rebellion led by Charles Taylor. The war engulfed the country in an orgy of intertribal killings and three armies contending for power. The West African States' (ECOWAS) military intervention proved a disaster, prolonging the civil war until 1996 and resulting in Taylor gaining power. Taylor's excesses led to a second civil war in 1999. Further ECOWAS and US presence and pressure eventually led to Taylor's resignation and exile from Liberia. Peaceful elections in 2005 saw the appointment of Ellen Johnson Sirleaf, Africa's first elected female leader. With Taylor on trial for war crimes, a Truth and Reconciliation Commission has been set up to address past atrocities and crimes.

L

Religion ⚜

Liberia was founded as a Christian state, but with no state church. Freedom of religion continues in theory, but in practice, occult secret societies exercise significant influence. Religious and denominational figures are mostly estimates due to the massive population upheaval from the wars.

Religions	Pop %	Population	Ann Gr
Ethnoreligionist	42.50	1,743,251	2.9%
Christian	41.43	1,699,362	4.9%
Muslim	15.50	635,774	6.4%
Other	0.30	12,305	6.5%
Baha'i	0.27	11,075	2.8%

Christians Denoms		Pop %	Affiliates	Ann Gr
Protestant	44	18.28	750,000	4.1%
Independent	126	9.73	399,000	4.5%
Anglican	1	0.95	39,000	4.7%
Catholic	1	4.92	202,000	4.1%
Marginal	2	0.48	20,000	7.3%
Unaffiliated		7.1	290,000	4.2%

Churches	MegaBloc	Congs	Members	Affiliates
Catholic Church	C	125	125,466	202,000
United Methodist Ch	P	436	130,769	170,000
Baptist Convention	P	270	72,000	138,000
Lutheran Churches	P	278	44,500	89,000

Assemblies of God	P	485	29,075	66,000
Ch of the Lord (Aladura)	I	173	20,800	52,000
Seventh-day Adventist	P	42	22,500	45,000
Afr Chr Fell Int (ACFI)	I	230	21,000	42,000
Episcopal Church	A	107	25,325	39,000
Pente Assem of the World	P	125	15,600	39,000
United Pentecostal Ch	P	138	19,461	32,500
United Lib Inland Ch	P	67	10,000	28,000
African Meth Epis Ch	I	155	11,588	27,000
Bethel World Outreach	I	125	12,500	25,000
Other denominations[157]		2,669	208,691	415,031
Total Christians[174]		**5,425**	**769,275**	**1,409,531**

TransBloc	Pop %	Population	Ann Gr
Evangelicals			
Evangelicals	14.6	600,533	4.6%
Renewalists			
Charismatics	12.5	511,331	5.2%
Pentecostals	7.7	317,573	5.0%

Religions
% of Total Pop

MegaBlocs
% of Christian Pop

Answers to Prayer

L

① **Peace and stability** seem to have arrived for the longer term. The resignation of Taylor, his exile and trial, and the appointment of Africa's first elected female leader – combined with the return of hundreds of thousands of refugees and acceleration of Liberia's reconstruction – generate a forward-looking atmosphere of hope, despite urgent and obvious challenges.

② **Christian ministry is once again thriving,** having been almost completely disrupted for years. Most denominations and missions are not content to merely plant churches, but are active in holistic ministry to the deep physical and spiritual scars of this recovering land.

Challenges for Prayer

① **Rebuilding after two civil wars** is Liberia's greatest challenge. The country was devastated and the people traumatized. War was a blight that also poisoned Sierra Leone and Guinea. Its roots fed on deep ethnic hatreds, greed and corruption, lust for power and Christians' failure to have a redemptive effect on society, all giving Satan opportunity. Pray specifically for:

a) ***The president and government.*** Elections have given legitimacy to the current regime, but wisdom and forward thinking are essential. A culture of graft, patronage and corruption must be overturned. The task force against corruption must achieve – and be seen to achieve – results. Pray for uprightness and justice to characterize Liberia's leaders.

b) ***Economic recovery.*** Almost the entire nation needed rebuilding as of 2005. Already deeply in debt, Liberia must manage its considerable natural resources shrewdly, responsibly, and in its own best interests, not those of foreign speculators. Poverty still affects the majority of the population; unemployment grips the nation.

c) Reconciliation among the ethnic groups involved in fighting, atrocities and massacres – especially the Mandingo and Krahn on one side and the Mano and Gio on the other. Several agencies are doing reconciliation and peacebuilding work.

d) Healing of the terrible physical, psychological and spiritual wounds of war – 65% of the population were uprooted. Almost the entire population are either victims or perpetrators of harsh crimes, some unspeakably cruel.

② The testimony and impact of the Church, compromised in the past, must be regained in power and purity. African traditional beliefs, tribal secret societies, fetishism and Freemasonry pervasively influenced every confession of Christianity in Liberia. These resulted in a lack of holiness and spiritual power and the enemy's insidious influence in the Church. Lack of compassion and care for the most vulnerable was another problem. However, the situation is thankfully changing and the Church is becoming an instrument of healing and restoration. Ministries (both African and foreign) are free to operate once again. Biblical teaching and modelling is happening, which will help excise what is rotten and build up that which is good. Pray for the Holy Spirit to purify, renew and build up the body of Christ.

③ Obstacles facing the Church include the following:

a) Repair of church buildings and reactivation of closed institutions – including schools, Bible colleges, hospitals and other facilities. Looting and destruction spared a few; many people are working to restore those that were lost.

b) Lack of biblical teaching. The church is often characterized by scriptural ignorance and materialism. As chaos seized the nation, established churches dissolved. A number of syncretistic African independent churches have increased in recent years. The majority of congregations and pastors are open to sensitive teaching and instruction. CenterPoint International Foundation, Development Associates International and Christian Education Foundation of Liberia are a few of the agencies at work in this capacity.

c) Leadership development is a great need; trained spiritual leaders are few. Many leaders had to flee or were killed; most Bible training was brought to a halt. Some refugees who studied theology in the West or elsewhere in Africa are returning with wider vision. Bible schools and seminaries are opening and rebuilding – the Baptist Seminary, Africa Bible College University, the ACFI Christian College, Liberia International Christian College (ULIC), and a Lutheran training centre among them. Trauma counselling must be an integral part of training for Christian leaders and pastors. Pray for the raising up of a new generation of leaders who preach the whole gospel without compromise, competitiveness or jealousies.

④ The physical needs in Liberia are many – poverty, illiteracy and under-education, HIV/AIDS, public health and sanitation, agricultural reclamation, vocational training. Pray for wisdom and effectiveness for WVI, World Relief, Tearfund and many others seeking to enable Liberians to rebuild their society.

⑤ Islam's expansion was previously tied to specific regimes or tribes, but today it attempts to operate in broader and more sophisticated realms. The Muslim Mandingo first profited and then suffered badly from their ties to the Doe regime and their part in precipitating the war; ethno-religious violence between Mandingos and other groups still flares up. Up to 1,000 mosques were destroyed or damaged from 1989-2003. Today, foreign-given Islamic money is used to restore these mosques and to propagate Muslim beliefs; Liberia remains a major target for African Islam. Significant numbers of Muslims in Monrovia are non-Liberian. Pray for the winning of many Muslims to Christ.

⑥ Ministry to young people and children is possibly the most strategic issue in Liberia. Nearly half of the nation is under 15 years old. This whole generation has been deeply traumatized and robbed of its family life, its chance for normality, its very innocence. Over 50,000 children were killed in the fighting. Pray for churches and agencies seeking to minister in this difficult context. The restoration of normative family life is a crucial challenge for prayer. Cry out to God for:

a) Former child soldiers. The 15,000 who survived have little chance of a normal life. Memories of the atrocities they witnessed, endured and committed haunt them. Over 30% have already attempted suicide at least once. As terrible as their past experiences were, the prejudice and stigma they face in post-war Liberia is nearly as bad.

b) *Thousands of fatherless children* of West African peacekeeping forces. Thousands more children were fathered by rebels or soldiers; they will grow up never knowing their fathers. Most of these are children of rape. They face a stigma that will be hard to overcome, while usually living in abject poverty.

c) *Victims of sexual abuse.* During the war, thousands of girls were taken by military troops or rebels to serve as maids, porters and, ultimately, as sexual slaves. Even in the post-war era, girls are being sexually used by peacekeepers, aid workers, teachers and others in positions of power. Pray that the initiatives taken by the government and NGOs to stop and to prevent such abuses would be effective.

d) *Students.* Not a single Liberian child was spared from the disruption and destruction war visited upon the education system. Following years of civil unrest, a strong ministry has been reintroduced among university students, who are living out the gospel among their friends. The Liberia Fellowship of Evangelical Students (LIFES) has 4 groups with 250 students. Pray for the ministry of SU, **YFC**, **YWAM** and the churches to children and young people.

7 **Less-reached peoples** – despite considerable exposure to the gospel, many of Liberia's indigenous peoples remain followers of African traditional religions and Islam. Progress is being made, but there is still much work to be done. Pray for:

a) *Muslim groups.* The Vai (**CRWM**) in the west, Gola in the north and the Manya/Mandingo (**SIM**) and Maninka of the northern borders are largely Muslim with few active Christians. Recent ministry by Muslim-background believers is seeing dramatic and increasing fruit, as are the holistic Community Health Evangelism programmes. Liberia is one of the few places where Muslims can be openly reached with the gospel and are responsive when they see it demonstrated.

b) *Peoples of animistic faith* who live in the forests of the interior. Victorious gospel encounters must occur among the Mande peoples of the north (Kpelle, Mano, Dan, Loma, Gbandi), some south-central peoples from the Kru cluster (Western Krahn, Sapo, Southern Kissi) and the Southern Kissi in the far north. All have a small or even sizeable Christian minority, but the power of fetishism among these peoples is great. To see a harvest, spiritual warfare and break-through must occur, and they must continue if the church is to remain free from the spiritually polluting clutches of the enemy.

8 **The task of evangelization and mission** must fall to Liberians and other Africans. Foreign missionaries had a long, hard, uphill struggle to plant churches in the interior; but disease, language diversity, entrenched fetishism and the disruption of war all hampered the work and eventually drove out all expat workers. Few have returned. Pray for those with a burden to return; pray for wisdom to know how they can best serve in rebuilding the nation, and best help the Liberian church complete the evangelization of every people. National mission leadership is making progress in missions advocacy among churches and in researching the nation's current status in terms of evangelization.

9 **Christian help ministries** are essential in this land of great spiritual hunger, great spiritual needs, but few material resources:

a) *Bible translation* and distribution ministries were gravely disrupted. The Bible Society and Lutheran Bible Translators projects have recommenced; 12 projects are active but another four languages have definite Bible translation needs. The completion in 2005 of the Bassa Bible (Liberia's second largest indigenous language) was a major achievement.

b) *Christian literature.* Many pastors and Christians have lost all they owned, and there is a great lack of Bibles, New Testaments and Christian literature, and few available bookstores. **EHC** continues nationwide literature distribution; recent focus was on the Mandingo people. Literacy is also a huge challenge in this country where almost a whole generation never had a proper chance to learn to read.

c) *The JESUS film* has been viewed by the majority of the population and continues to have a converting impact on Muslims. It is available in 13 languages; six more are in production.

d) *GRN audio recordings* are being used in 67 languages and dialects. These are essential for low-literacy contexts and oral learners. **GRN** has a Liberian base from which it has conducted nationwide outreaches and distribution. This base is well positioned to produce many more Christian recordings for evangelism, discipleship and training.

e) Christian radio. **SIM**'s Radio ELWA might still be Africa's best known station, despite being evacuated four times and destroyed twice during the wars. ELWA has been resurrected, with eight hours daily in English and with broadcasts in nine Liberian languages, and plans for three more. Other local stations include Worship FM and a station by the Christian Education Foundation of Liberia as well as a station planned by the **AoG** and United Methodist Church. Praise God for the message that goes out. Pray for the provision of funds for these ministries and for the production of excellent content that will both reach and bless the entire nation.

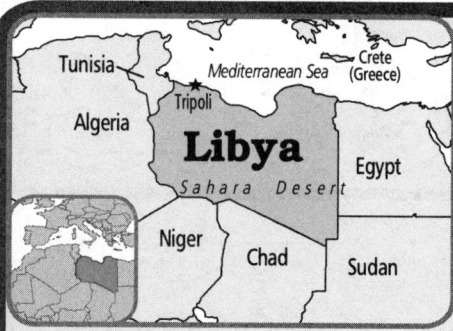

Libya

Socialist People's Libyan Arab Jamahiriya

Africa

Geography 🌐

Area 1,775,500 sq km. Mostly Saharan desert; only a coastal Mediterranean strip, 2% of its land area, is arable.

Population		Ann Gr	Density
2010	6,545,619	2.02%	4/sq km
2020	7,698,742	1.47%	4/sq km
2030	8,518,558	0.90%	5/sq km

Capital Tripoli 1,107,556. **Other major city** Banghazi 1.3 million. **Urbanites** 77.9%. **Pop under 15 yrs** 30%. **Life expectancy** 73.8 yrs.

Peoples 👪

Population data remains a difficult issue, since undocumented foreign migrants compose a sizeable but indeterminate percentage of Libya's population (possibly up to 25%). All figures are estimates.

Arab and related 95.9%.

> **Arab** 76.4%. Libyan Arab 30.1%; Cyrenaican Arab 27%; Egyptian 7.7%.
> **Berber** 5.8%. About half are Arabized, assimiliation makes measuring Berber peoples difficult. 8 groups, largest: Nafusah; Jalo; Zuwarah; Jofrah; Ghadames.
> **Bedouin** 13.7%. Sanusi 9.0%; Fezzan 3.2%.

Others 4.1%. Many labourers from surrounding lands. Predominantly Punjabi, Italian, Serbian, Gypsy, Croatian,

Sinhalese. Many thousands of undocumented sub-Saharan Africans in transit to Europe are not included here.

Literacy 85.4%. **Official language** Arabic. **All languages** 32. **Indigenous languages** 9. **Languages with Scriptures** 1Bi 1por.

Economy 📈

Transformed by discovery of oil in 1959. Oil accounts for 95% of export income, but little of this wealth trickles down to the masses. US-led sanctions significantly damaged the economy; with sanctions now lifted, the economy is accelerating. Attracting foreign investment, reducing a high rate of unemployment and increasing productivity through privatization are the main challenges.

HDI Rank 55th/182. **Public debt** 55% of GDP. **Income/person** $14,479 (31% of USA).

Politics 🗡

Ruled by Italy 1911-1943. Full independence in 1951 as a monarchy. The military coup of 1969 led to a revolutionary republic under the leadership of Muammar Qaddafi. He has shifted from Islamic revolution to Arab nationalism to a more moderate stance in recent years, although the police and military still play a prominent role. Relationship with the EU is crucial to Libya, since it is inundated with migrants seeking illegal entry into Europe.

Religion ⛪

Sunni Islam is the state religion, and the government endorses a moderate form of Islam. Radical Islamist ideology is seen as a threat. Evangelism of Libyan citizens is illegal, but Christians are generally left alone unless families ask the state to intervene. All faiths are free to worship in their own homes; meetings of more than six people are illegal, though this law is not often enforced. Figures below are approximations.

Religions	Pop %	Population	Ann Gr
Muslim	97.02	6,350,560	2.0%
Christian	2.64	172,804	2.8%
Non-religious	0.30	19,637	5.8%
Buddhist	0.03	1,964	2.0%
Hindu	0.01	655	2.0%

L

Christians	Denoms	Pop %	Affiliates	Ann Gr
Protestant	10	0.14	9,000	2.8%
Independent	4	0.01	1,000	7.6%
Catholic	1	1.22	80,000	1.3%
Orthodox	4	1.19	78,000	4.3%
Unaffiliated		<0.01	3,000	8.5%

Churches	MegaBloc	Congs	Members	Affiliates
Catholic Church	C	6	44,444	80,000
Coptic Orthodox Ch	O	5	27,200	68,000
Coptic Evangelical Ch	P	2	2,700	6,750
Greek Orthodox Ch	O	2	871	2,900
Other Protestant groups	P	7	1,050	1,438
Other denominations[12]		16	6,057	9,164
Total Christians[21]		**38**	**82,322**	**168,252**

TransBloc	Pop %	Population	Ann Gr
Evangelicals			
Evangelicals	0.3	19,662	5.2%
Renewalists			
Charismatics	0.2	10,951	10.4%

These numbers consist almost exclusively of expatriates living in or in transit through Libya.

MegaBlocs % of Christian Pop
1.5 0.4 5.3
45.8 47.0
P C O U X

TransBloc Movements % of Total Pop
Charis
Evang
1960 1970 1980 1990 2000 2010

Answers to Prayer

1 **The spiritual climate in Libya has changed significantly.** God is doing a new work in this land (a response to the sustained and specific intercession of past years?). There is notable spiritual hunger among Libyans, but not enough Bibles for those seeking them. Increasing numbers of Libyans are coming to Christ (though still only a few), and expatriate Christians now enjoy greater spiritual liberty than in the past. Praise God for these developments and pray that they would continue.

Challenges for Prayer

1 **Libya's long isolation is ending.** Sanctions have ended, foreign investment and trade are increasing and the government is becoming more moderate. Libyan nationals have distinguished themselves as gracious and friendly; pray that they might be open to the gospel as it is shared sensitively. Pray also for Libya's future; its ruler will not live forever, and whoever succeeds him could shape the nation profoundly.

2 **Large numbers of migrants pass into Libya,** mostly from sub-Saharan Africa, looking for economic opportunities. Some find work in Libya, most are trying to get into Europe. Migration drains Libya's coffers and human resources and often ends in disillusionment or even tragedy for those braving the deserts and seas to find a new life. Pray that these tens or even hundreds of thousands would find salvation and not just earthly treasures. A significant portion are believers; pray that they might have a powerful spiritual impact on Libyans and fellow migrants.

3 **The Christian community is growing,** but is mostly foreign. Catholic and Orthodox groups dominate numerically, but Protestants and Independent groups are more active in faith and practice. The need for pastoral care is felt across almost all denominations. Pray for renewal in the churches; the opportunity is great for nominals to meet Christ, and for believers to impact others with the gospel.

4 **Libyan believers are increasing in numbers and faith** and enjoy surprising freedom as a Christian community, but they still face many obstacles to fellowship, including fear of infiltrators. Libyans remain off-limits for evangelism, and approaches to them are risky for all involved. Continued state surveillance and family/social pressures are strong disincentives. Pray for greater religious freedom so that more might hear the gospel and be able to follow Jesus openly. Pray also for Libyan believers to stand firm in their faith and to find spiritually edifying relationships – including suitable marriage partners in a society where marriage is typically arranged with extended family.

L

a) Broadcasting. Radio and satellite television provide two of the very few ways to evangelize Libyans. Three different shortwave-radio stations broadcast programmes to Libya: IBRA (over Radio Moscow), **HCJB** and Adventist World Radio, but only 4.5 hours/week are in Arabic. The widespread use of satellite dishes (in the majority of households) enables **SAT-7** and other Christian satellite-television broadcasts to reach into homes. Pray for creative and effective programmes with the means to disciple responsive listeners, and pray for protection for those who respond.

b) Scripture. There is a great need for Bibles; there are far too few to go around. There are many materials in standard Arabic, but no Scriptures and almost no audio or video resources in Libyan Arabic. Pray that work on this may start so Libyans can read or hear the gospel in their heart language.

c) Internet. Access, though strictly censored in Libya, is becoming more available and open. Pray that Libyans may be drawn to Christian websites and attracted to the gospel. Many Christian-focused websites in Arabic are having a profound impact.

d) The visit of the OM ship built bridges between the global Christian community and Libya as well as provided much-needed books and literature for the Libyan public. Pray for further opportunities to connect Libya and her people to the wider Christian world.

Liechtenstein
Principality of Liechtenstein
Europe

Geography 🌐

Area 160 sq km. Mountainous enclave on the Rhine between Switzerland and Austria. One of two doubly landlocked countries.

Population		Ann Gr	Density
2010	36,190	0.84%	226/sq km
2020	38,940	0.72%	243/sq km
2030	41,500	0.60%	259/sq km

Capital Vaduz 5,200. **Urbanites** 14.2%. **Pop under 15 yrs** 17%. **Life expectancy** 81 yrs.

Peoples 👪

Germanic 91.4%. Liechtensteiner 66.1%; Swiss 12.1%; Austrian 5.8%; Walser 4.2%; German 3.3%.
Other 8.6%. Turkish 4.5%; Italian 3.8%; and others.
Literacy 100%. **Official language** German, but the common tongue is Alemmanic, a divergent dialect of Standard German. **All languages** 4. **Indigenous languages** 3. **Languages with Scriptures** 1Bi 1NT 1por.

Economy 🏭

Wealthy through diversifying its industrial economy and promoting free enterprise, including manufacturing, banking and tourism. Nearly 30% of state revenue comes from "letterbox" companies registered in Liechtenstein (attracted by low tax) but operating elsewhere. Lax financial controls have been responsible for money laundering scandals, and Liechtenstein takes great pains to not be seen as a blacklisted tax haven by the OECD.
HDI Rank 19th/182. **Public debt** none. **Income/person** $100,845 (221% of USA).

Politics ☒

A constitutional principality in customs and monetary union with Switzerland. A 2003 referendum gave the prince sweeping political powers.

Religion 🙏

Freedom of religion is guaranteed. The Catholic Church has traditionally been the state church, but disestablishment and religious equality is inevitable.

L

Religions	Pop %	Population	Ann Gr
Christian	79.16	28,648	0.1%
Non-religious	13.86	5,016	4.0%
Muslim	6.70	2,425	3.4%
Buddhist	0.15	54	3.8%
Jewish	0.13	47	0.8%

TransBloc	Pop %	Population	Ann Gr
Evangelicals			
Evangelicals	0.5	186	1.3%
Renewalists			
Charismatics	1.1	398	1.0%
Pentecostals	0.2	71	3.4%

Christians Denoms		Pop %	Affiliates	Ann Gr
Protestant	4	8.65	3,000	2.0%
Independent	4	0.22	<100	5.9%
Catholic	1	69.36	25,000	-0.1%
Orthodox	5	0.75	<300	2.0%
Marginal	1	0.18	<100	-1.5%

Churches	MegaBloc	Congs	Members	Affiliates
Catholic Church	C	10	19,015	25,100
Free Evangelical Ch	P	2	1,200	1,850
Evang Lutheran Ch	P	4	909	1,200
Orthodox Church	O	1	208	270
Other denominations[7]		8	156	225
Total Christians[15]		**25**	**21,488**	**28,645**

Religions % of Total Pop

Annual Growth Rates

Challenges for Prayer

Liechtenstein has changed from a feudal backwater in the 1930s to a sophisticated and affluent modern state. The last remaining vestige of the Holy Roman Empire; the prince's family has always been Catholic and the vast majority of native citizens are likewise, albeit most only nominally. Expatriates represent several Christian confessions, but non-religion and Islam are growing rapidly. Few in this country have ever been confronted with the necessity of a personal faith in Christ. Pray that, as the immigrant population increases, encounters with the gospel might likewise multiply.

The first and only evangelical fellowship of believers was started in 1985 after an evangelistic campaign launched by British, Norwegian and Swiss believers. The evangelical population, mostly expatriates, is now slowly increasing. Campus for Christ had a part-time presence hosting evangelistic breakfasts. Some members of the extended royal family profess personal faith in Christ, with links to the Catholic charismatic renewal movement.

Lithuania
Republic of Lithuania
Europe

Geography

Area 65,301 sq km. The southernmost of the three Baltic states. Flat, arable land with many forests and lakes.

Population	Ann Gr	Density
2010	3,255,324	-0.96%	50/sq km
2020	3,058,404	-0.55%	47/sq km
2030	2,908,516	-0.52%	45/sq km

Capital Vilnius 541,000. **Urbanites** 67.2%. **Pop under 15 yrs** 15%. **Life expectancy** 71.8 yrs.

Peoples

Baltic 83.6%. Lithuanian 83.5%.
Slavic 14.8%. Polish 6.7%; Russian 6.3%; Belarusian 1.2%; Ukrainian 0.6%.
Other 1.6%. Jews, Tatars, other Europeans, Asians.
Literacy 99.6%. **Official language** Lithuanian.
All languages 12. **Indigenous languages** 4.
Languages with Scriptures 1Bi 2NT 3por.

Economy

An industrial and agricultural economy that has progressed significantly since inclusion in the European Union. Significant emigration into more affluent EU countries, however, has had a detrimental effect.
HDI Rank 46th/182. **Public debt** 29.3% of GDP. **Income/person** $14,086 (30% of USA).

Politics

A parliamentary democracy. In the 14th Century was a powerful duchy controlling much of West Russia, Belarus and Ukraine. Later, a joint state with Poland, until annexation by Russia at the end of the 18th Century. Gained independence in 1918. Occupied by the Soviets 1940-1990; independent again in 1990. A member of the EU, and swiftly orienting to the West.

Religion

The last European nation to be Christianized. Because of strong Polish influence, Catholicism was politically dominant until the Soviet occupation, when all faiths were repressed. Religious freedom, but preference shown to Catholics and other traditional groups. Evangelical and other new religious groups have faced some opposition and negative bias.

Religions	Pop %	Population	Ann Gr
Christian	85.36	2,778,745	-1.1%
Non-religious	14.20	462,256	0.1%
Jewish	0.16	5,209	-3.3%
Muslim	0.14	4,557	2.1%
Ethnoreligionist	0.12	3,906	2.7%
Other	0.02	651	-1.0%

Christians Denoms		Pop %	Affiliates	Ann Gr
Protestant	11	0.95	31,000	-2.0%
Independent	13	1.51	49,000	-2.1%
Catholic	1	73.11	2,380,000	-0.6%
Orthodox	2	4.85	158,000	-1.5%
Marginal	2	0.21	7,000	5.6%
Unaffiliated		4.70	154,000	-6.5%

Churches	MegaBloc	Congs	Members	Affiliates
Roman Catholic Ch	C	606	1,425,150	2,380,000
Russian Orthodox	O	63	100,649	155,000
Old Believers	I	20	8,750	35,000
Lutheran Ch	P	55	7,200	18,000
Jehovah's Witnesses	M	24	3,333	6,000
New Apostolic Church	I	27	2,727	6,000
Reformed Ch in L	P	9	1,200	6,000
Word of Faith	I	36	1,500	2,600
Pentecostal Union	P	26	1,333	2,000
Seventh-day Adventist	P	21	900	1,800
Baptist Union	P	8	500	750
Other denominations[18]		64	6,588	10,610
Total Christians[29]		959	1,559,830	2,623,760

TransBloc	Pop %	Population	Ann Gr
Evangelicals			
Evangelicals	1.1	35,894	2.7%
Renewalists			
Charismatics	1.1	37,171	5.1%
Pentecostals	0.1	2,150	3.1%

Missionaries from Lithuania
P,I,A 10 (long-term).

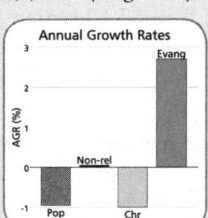

Annual Growth Rates

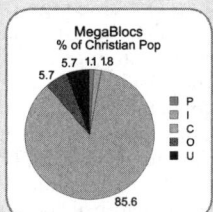

MegaBlocs % of Christian Pop

L

Answers to Prayer

1 **Religious freedom in the post-Soviet era** has seen many dynamic new Christian groups emerge, injecting new life into the nation's spirituality. Unity between different Christian groups and denominations is very good, especially for a former Soviet state.

Challenges for Prayer

1 **Freedom has brought progress.** Doors for the gospel remain open, and evangelical positions can have a hearing in society. However, with freedom came many dangers – increased materialism, hedonism and nihilism. Substance abuse, suicide and, most sinister, trafficking women for prostitution in the West all disintegrate the nation's foundations. Often, the most gifted leave Lithuania for more lucrative positions elsewhere. Economic growth must be paired with real social and spiritual transformation; pray that God would bring massive societal change through His people.

2 **Catholicism retains a crucial role** in Lithuanian society, but has not fully emerged from old ways of thinking to embrace its potential for godly influence in society. Pray that the Catholic Church uses its significant influence to draw people to Christ. Only one-sixth of Catholics attend church weekly. Fellowship with and acceptance of other Christian groups must be improved. Several Franciscan, charismatic and evangelical-style networks in the Church bring young leadership, new thinking and fresh spirituality; pray for their further growth.

3 **The other confessions of Christianity** also face many challenges:

a) Traditional groups (Lutheran, Reformed and Orthodox) are struggling just to maintain their numbers, as are most denominations. The Orthodox are almost exclusively ethnic Russians; other traditional groups are mostly Lithuanian. Lutherans desire to see their Pietistic heritage renewed. Pray for new life in these historic groups.

b) Baptists, Pentecostals and Adventists, the more established of the evangelicals in Lithuania, have struggles of their own. Retained traditions, which saw them through the Soviet era, must be balanced with the spiritual and organizational needs of a new era. Pray for new spiritual impetus for these faithful groups.

c) Newer Pentecostal and charismatic churches grew quickly in the last decade through dynamic spirituality combined with active outreach and ministry. Growth looks set to continue; but against this backdrop, quality discipleship of new believers is key. Pray also for these churches to become genuinely indigenous, not just carbon copies of popular Western expressions of the Church.

d) All believers. Some low-level prejudice against new religious groups exists, and there is still a widespread perception that evangelicals are a sect. Leaders and congregations must gain a greater understanding of their own evangelical faith before they can assert it in a broader context. The rapid growth of the early '90s has passed, and pastors are kept busy with pastoral responsibilities. Pray for God to raise up those gifted in evangelism.

e) Evangelical unity. There is still no Evangelical Alliance in Lithuania. Increased cooperation and demonstrable unity are essential if evangelicals are to have a greater impact on the nation.

4 **The shortage of trained Christian leaders** is a result of rapid growth in the newer churches and difficulty in establishing denominations. Religious freedom has also yielded an increase of cults and theological error. Solid biblical foundations must be established, but leaders trained abroad too frequently do not return. Catholics have four seminaries and three faculties in universities; Lutherans have one. The Pentecostals founded a pastoral, mission-oriented training institute, Vilnius College; the Baptist Union has a training institute (NEBIM). The non-denominational Evangelical Bible Institute (EBI) is in the process of accrediting a bachelor of theology degree. LCC International University is an inter-denominational and inter-confessional institution with a vision to train future leaders with a Christian worldview. Pray that these institutions might raise up godly, well-educated and visionary leaders for the nation.

⑤ **Expatriate missions.** About 30 missionaries minister long-term in the country, plus around 35 Western faculty and staff of the Lithuania Christian College. **YWAM** has a team serving alongside local parishes, working with families, youth, orphanages, summer camps and humanitarian aid distribution. Pray for more missionaries to serve in this land; there are still many opportunities for foreigners called of God to have a Kingdom influence here.

⑥ **Specialized ministries** need prayer. These include:

a) Radio. **TWR** broadcasts 30 minutes/day. More radio programmes in Lithuanian are needed. Good News Center was formed by a wide range of Protestant denominations to facilitate spreading the gospel by radio in Lithuania.

b) Internet. The widespread use of Russian and English give Lithuanians good access to Christian resources. Some churches or unions have excellent websites. Pray for the full potential of the Internet to be utilized with the younger generation.

c) Christian literature. A growing but still very small ministry. Two modern Lithuanian versions of the Bible and over 100 Christian books are published in Lithuanian. Word of Faith produces a bi-monthly newspaper. Good books are desperately needed; The Bible Society serves well, but also struggles. Pray for the seven Christian publishing organizations and their vital role in building up Christians and spreading the Christian worldview into society.

d) Student ministries. LKSB(**IFES**) operates in four cities at eight universities. **CCCI** began ministry work in 1993. SU camps have been running since 1997. Summer camps are popular and highly strategic for evangelizing and discipling young people.

Luxembourg

Grand Duchy of Luxembourg

Europe

Geography 🌐

Area 2,586 sq km. The smallest of the Benelux, or Low Countries.

Population		Ann Gr	Density
2010	491,772	1.17%	190/sq km
2020	549,839	1.12%	213/sq km
2030	614,500	1.11%	238/sq km

Capital Luxembourg 91,200. **Urbanites** 82.2%. **Pop under 15 yrs** 18%. **Life expectancy** 79.4 yrs.

Peoples 👪

Luxembourgers 57.4%. The lowest percentage of indigenous population of any European country.
Expatriates 42.6%. Mostly other Europeans. Portuguese 16.2%; French 5.3%; Italian 3.8%.
Literacy 100%. **Official language** French, used in official communication. German dominates education and the newspapers. *Lëtzebuergesch* (of Franco-Mosellan origin) is the national language; English learning is compulsory in schools. **All languages** 6. **Indigenous languages** 3. **Languages with Scriptures** 2Bi 1por.

Economy 📈

Highly industrialized and diversified economy, with a highly educated, multilingual workforce and excellent infrastructure. Banking and finance are dominant economic elements, and the country is attractive for its low taxes. Has the 2nd highest GDP per capita in the world, despite recent downturns.
HDI Rank 11th/182. **Public debt** 10.2% of GDP. **Income/person** $113,044 (238% of USA).

Politics 🗡

Parliamentary democracy with a constitutional monarch, in economic union with Belgium and Netherlands. A member of EU, and headquarters of many EU institutions. The only sovereign Grand Duchy in the world, although the Grand Duke's powers were recently reduced to a virtually nominal status after disputes with parliament over euthanasia.

Religion

Freedom of religion. Catholicism still predominates but other religions as well as atheism have grown rapidly of late. The major confessions have established conventions and thereby financial support.

Religions	Pop %	Population	Ann Gr
Christian	81.63	401,433	0.4%
Non-religious	15.77	77,552	5.0%
Muslim	1.90	9,344	6.1%
Baha'i	0.30	1,475	1.2%
Other	0.20	984	7.2%
Jewish	0.20	984	1.2%

Christians	Denoms	Pop %	Affiliates	Ann Gr
Protestant	18	1.96	10,000	1.9%
Independent	9	0.19	1,000	2.8%
Anglican	1	0.12	1,000	1.8%
Catholic	1	79.31	390,000	0.1%
Orthodox	4	1.02	5,000	6.2%
Marginal	3	1.10	5,000	1.6%
Doubly affiliated		-2.07	-10,000	0.0%

Churches	MegaBloc	Congs	Members	Affiliates
Catholic Church	C	279	307,087	390,000
Orthodox Churches	O	4	3,759	5,000
Prot Ref Ch of Lux	P	4	250	3,500
Jehovah's Witnesses	M	33	2,000	3,400
Danish Evang Luth Ch	P	2	1,562	2,500
Prot Ch of Grand Duchy	P	5	1,000	1,300
German-speaking Prot Ch	P	2	570	855
Other denominations[26]		42	3,458	5,026
Doubly affiliated				-10,200
Total Christians[36]		371	319,686	401,381

TransBloc	Pop %	Population	Ann Gr
Evangelicals			
Evangelicals	0.5	2,554	4.6%
Renewalists			
Charismatics	0.8	4,020	2.3%
Pentecostals	0.1	510	9.2%

Annual Growth Rates

TransBloc Movements
% of Total Pop

Challenges for Prayer

L

1 **Luxembourg's strong Catholic heritage** remains, but is slowly dwindling. Sea changes in Catholicism have had little impact here, and while the majority profess Catholicism, only a small percent regularly attend mass or practice their faith. A melange of secularism, materialism and a fuzzy personalized spirituality all weigh in heavily in shaping the prevalent worldview of this highly affluent Grand Duchy. Veneration of Mary plays a great role in cultural tradition and ritual. It is tradition more than conviction that keeps Luxembourg Catholic. Pray that people discover the power of the living Christ.

2 **The growth of other faiths** presents a challenge to traditional faith. Islam, Orthodoxy, Jehovah's Witnesses, and Eastern mysticism and the multiplication of Protestant and Independent groups have transformed this small nation into a melting pot of religious expression. Pray that believers in the Lord Jesus might seek and make use of chances to share the gospel, and help shape the nation according to biblical principles.

3 **Evangelicals are a small minority,** and a high proportion of them are foreigners (although almost all congregations have at least some indigenes). In the 23 evangelical churches, worship is conducted in nine different languages, and only a minority have full-time pastors. There is still a great need for more Bible teaching, more Christ-centered churches and more workers to labour in these churches. Evangelicals face several other challenges:

a) *A negative bias* on the part of government and society, with the stigma of "cults". This bias makes state recognition, public perception and the renting of buildings difficult for evangelicals.

b) *Unity* has been a major challenge. While there are still obstacles to seeing real spiritual unity (as opposed to the papery ecumenical variety), genuine progress is being made as the different churches begin to trust one another and to pray and worship together on occasion – great Kingdom potential exists as a result. Pray that old hurts will be overcome and restored relationships achieved.

c) Outreach is limited. Door-to-door and street evangelism is frowned upon by society and the government; gentle and creative methods are much more likely to be effective. Believers are slowly learning how to reach out and are beginning to gain more experience and interest.

④ Foreigners comprise both some of the staunchest believers and some of the least reached. The majority of expatriates are present for employment, business or EU affairs (with day commuters, Luxembourg becomes over 50% foreign!), and show little interest in spiritual things. Others, such as Muslim immigrants from the Balkans, adhere to other faiths. Pray for the vision and strategy for reaching each group, and for receptive hearts.

⑤ The Lëtzebuergesch language is spoken by many as their heart language. Most are fluent in French or German (or both), but to have the Bible in Lëtzebuergesch could be helpful to opening many hearts to the good news. Various versions of the NT are in progress. Pray that they might be completed in a timely manner and with the highest standards of Bible translation principles. There is one solitary Christian bookstore in the country, but others in neighbouring countries are readily accessible.

Macedonia

Republic of Macedonia

Europe

Geography 🌍

Area 25,713 sq km. Landlocked state surrounded by Serbia/Kosovo, Bulgaria, Greece and Albania.

Population		Ann Gr	Density
2010	2,043,360	0.08%	79/sq km
2020	2,045,824	0.00%	80/sq km
2030	2,016,164	-0.20%	78/sq km

Capital Skopje 524,000. **Urbanites** 67.9%. **Pop under 15 yrs** 18%. **Life expectancy** 74.1 yrs.

Peoples 👪

Ethnic populations are a politicized issue, and despite census data, are difficult to enumerate accurately.
Slavic 64.9%. Macedonian 61.6%; Bosnian 0.9%; Serb 1.6%.
Albanian 25.2%.
Other 9.9% Romani(2) 5.2%; Turk 3.9%; Other 0.8%.
Literacy 96.1%. **Official language** Macedonian, one of the southern Slavic languages. **All languages** 10. **Languages with Scriptures** 3Bi 3NT 4por 1w.i.p.

Economy 🏭

One of the poorest regions of former Yugoslavia. Mostly reliant on agriculture and an increasingly obsolete industrial sector. High unemployment and low standard of living have spurred a significant exodus, especially of the young and talented, to the EU, North America and even New Zealand.
HDI Rank 72nd/182. **Public debt** 20.8% of GDP. **Income/person** $4,657 (10% of USA).

Politics ☒

Macedonia, having been contested throughout history by many powers, still endures claims by neighbouring powers. A multiparty democracy. Macedonia has endured some tensions due to the unrest associated with the Albanian population of the region (in Albania, Kosovo, etc). But the most notable political issue is Macedonia's candidacy for the EU and NATO. In both cases, Greece holds veto power and blocks Macedonia from joining over its insistence on using the name "Republic of Macedonia". Greece resents the use of such a term due to possible territorial aspirations for a Greater Macedonia which would encompass the part of Greece also named Macedonia as well as parts of several other countries in the region.

Religion ⛪

The dominant Macedonian Orthodox Church actually emerged from the Serbian Orthodox Church, and tensions persist over this issue. Although there is some discrimination against newer religious groups (in particular, regarding building permissions), the religious communities are leading the way in the area of reconciliation and dialogue. The most recent religion law was passed mostly in order to prevent the Serbian Orthodox Church from gaining legal status.

M

Religions	Pop %	Population	Ann Gr
Christian	65.50	1,338,401	0.1%
Muslim	31.00	633,442	1.1%
Non-religious	3.49	71,313	-6.7%
Jewish	0.01	204	0.1%

Christians Denoms		Pop %	Affiliates	Ann Gr
Protestant	7	0.26	5,000	2.7%
Independent	5	0.04	1,000	4.9%
Anglican	1	0.01	<200	0.0%
Catholic	2	0.98	20,000	0.0%
Orthodox	7	64.10	1,310,000	0.1%
Marginal	1	0.11	2,000	-0.9%

Churches	MegaBloc	Congs	Members	Affiliates
Macedonian Orth Ch	O	1,150	850,340	1,250,000
Other Orthodox	O	21	40,382	61,800
Catholic Church	C	26	12,903	20,000
Methodist Ch	P	15	567	1,700
Evangelical Ch (Pente)	P	8	1,056	1,500
Seventh-day Adventist	P	19	750	1,155
Other denominations[11]		47	2,051	4,260
Total Christians[23]		**1,286**	**908,049**	**1,338,415**

TransBloc	Pop %	Population	Ann Gr
Evangelicals			
Evangelicals	0.2	4,270	3.2%
Renewalists			
Charismatics	0.1	3,010	3.8%
Pentecostals	0.1	2,090	3.9%

Missionaries from Macedonia
P,I,A 10 (long-term).

Religions % of Total Pop

Annual Growth Rates

Answers to Prayer

1 **The evangelical church in Macedonia is one of the fastest growing** in Europe and displays growing unity across its theological breadth. Churches are ambitious in their outreach and church planting goals, and they minister across ethnic and national boundaries to share the gospel with their neighbours, a remarkable feat given the Balkanization of the region.

Challenges for Prayer

M

1 **Macedonia's ethnic composition** dominates its political and social existence, where segregation is more prevalent than harmony. The large (and growing) Albanian minority feel more connected with their own kind in Albania and Kosovo than with the other ethnicities of Macedonia. Greece, Bulgaria and Serbia also have agendas for Macedonia. Economic difficulties cause significant emigration and urban pull; many of the 2,000 villages are dwindling or disappearing altogether. Pray for wisdom for the government, and pray that the divided communities might find ways to build their nation together.

2 **The Macedonian Orthodox Church** claims to represent almost two-thirds of the population, but more than 1,000 churches remain largely empty, and most Macedonians are secular and unreligious in practice. The Macedonian government effectively endorsed this Church's hegemony by imprisoning the local bishop of the Serbian Orthodox Church, from which the Macedonian Orthodox illegitimately split. The Orthodox Church sometimes opposes new religious expressions such as evangelicalism, but dialogue is increasing. Pray for new life to touch this Church and all those who belong to it.

3 **The evangelical witness is small, but growing.** Almost every Protestant/Independent expression of faith is active and increasing. Even so, there are fewer than 100 evangelical congregations. Pray for the many challenges of and opportunities for the Church:

a) Opposition. The label of "cult" persists, but is slowly fading for evangelicals. Obstructive tactics by the government often hold back the church from building the facilities needed to host the growing congregations. Pray for favour from the government and a humble attitude from the Church.

b) *Unity.* Expressions of oneness in Christ are increasing, including pastors' prayer summits and networks, citywide worship events, and even websites focused on the issue. Pray that believers might press into true unity and that Christians' love for one another might attract many to Christ.

c) *Church planting, evangelism and mission.* Macedonian believers "punch above their weight" in terms of outward-focused ministry. Many congregations look to reproduce and so deliberately move into cities and neighbourhoods previously unevangelized. House churches are a great part of this focus. Pray for a grassroots movement that sees the numbers of Macedonian believers rapidly multiply. Indigenous groups such as Macedonian Mission to the Balkans (reaching all ethnicities in the southern regions of the former Yugoslavia) are impacting Macedonia as well as neighbouring countries.

d) *Training and discipleship.* The first (non-Orthodox) theological school in the country is being planned – Macedonia Bible Seminary is aiming to open by autumn 2010. In the meantime, ministries such as **SEND**, **YWAM** and SGA all focus on raising up mature and biblically literate believers. Generally, multiple small congregations increase the need for leaders, yet are a better structure in which to disciple Christians.

4 **The ethnic minorities are numerous,** and all are in need of ministry.

a) *Albanians* represent 25% of Macedonia's population, and their numbers are rapidly increasing through birth rates and immigration. Greater tensions between Albanians – with their demands for increasing political influence – and the majority of Macedonians seem inevitable, but neither group desires the upheaval suffered in neighbouring Kosovo. Almost all Macedonian Albanians are unevangelized Muslims, but there is an openness to loving witness. Thus far, there are no groups of Christians from a Macedonian Albanian background.

b) *The Romani population* is chronically poor, oppressed, uneducated, unemployed and captive to a blend of Islam and folk superstitions. Sutka, near Skopje, is home to many of Macedonia's 80,000 Romani and is one of the largest Romani communities in the world. **YWAM**, Pioneers, the Methodists, Pentecostals and Baptists are all seeing fruit among the Romani.

c) *The Turkish community* lives mainly in eastern Macedonia. There are a handful of believers, but no evangelical church among them. A few groups are now engaged in outreach to them.

5 **Foreign missions** find Macedonia to be one of Europe's neediest lands, responsive yet difficult. Worldshare, **IMB**, Pioneers, Frontiers, **AoG**, **CMA**, the Nazarenes and Partners International actively conduct ministry alongside indigenous ministry organizations. Pray also for the ministry of Exodus/**IFES**; many new converts are young people.

6 **Media and literature** are important ministries in Macedonia.

a) *The Bible Society* oversees the distribution of two new Macedonian translations of the Bible – one translation by a partnership of SGA, IVP and a local translation team, the other a collaboration between Orthodox and Protestants. The Gideons are the largest distributors of Scripture, giving out many NTs. The Bible League distributes Bibles and other literature, and conducts seminars for local churches.

b) *A Christian Cultural Centre* in Skopje includes a Christian bookstore (SGA), although only a few books have been translated into Macedonian. Pray for more Christian material to be developed and distributed in Macedonian, especially material chosen or written by Macedonian believers – **PI** and Exodus(**IFES**) have a vision for this. Revelation Bookshop has published 40 titles in Macedonian.

c) *Broadcasting.* **TWR** Serbia broadcasts 30 minutes/week in Macedonian and Smile/Evangelical Church Negotina broadcasts locally. There is a great need for good Christian radio and TV programmes and broadcasting in Macedonian and Albanian.

d) *The JESUS film* has been widely viewed on television and film. It is available in Albanian, Macedonian, Romani and Turkish.

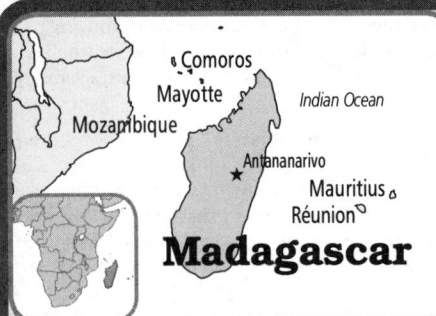

Comoros
Mayotte
Mozambique
Indian Ocean
Antananarivo
Mauritius
Réunion
Madagascar

Madagascar
Republic of Madagascar
Africa

Geography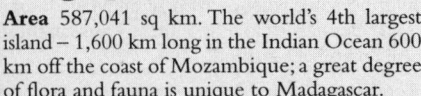

Area 587,041 sq km. The world's 4th largest island – 1,600 km long in the Indian Ocean 600 km off the coast of Mozambique; a great degree of flora and fauna is unique to Madagascar.

Population		Ann Gr	Density
2010	20,146,442	2.72%	34/sq km
2020	25,686,510	2.37%	44/sq km
2030	31,528,452	1.97%	54/sq km

Capital Antananarivo 1,879,013. **Urbanites** 30.2%. **Pop under 15 yrs** 43%. **Life expectancy** 59.9 yrs.

Peoples

Malagasy 97.5%. 38 peoples of mixed African, Indonesian and Arab origin, speaking numerous regional forms of an Indonesian-related language.
Other 2.5%. French 0.5%; Réunionese 0.4%; Gujarati 0.3%; Chinese 0.3%; Arab 0.2%.
Literacy 70.6%. In decline; functional literacy much lower. **Official languages** Official Malagasy, French and English (though not widely used). **All languages** 20. **Indigenous languages** 17. **Languages with Scriptures** 3Bi 1NT 4por.

Economy

Agriculture, fishing and forestry were traditionally the primary means of living for most people, but slash-and-burn farming has destroyed vast areas of forest and caused serious erosion. The service sector is now very important to the country. Was recently listed as the world's 11th poorest nation; much of the population live in poverty. Frequent cyclones, lack of clean water and sanitation, and a lack of infrastructure and foreign investment all limit progress. A slow economic recovery has been underway for nearly 10 years, fuelled by improved education,

transport infrastructure and a boom in mining and eco-tourism. Continuing political instability threatens to undermine any progress made.
HDI Rank 145th/182. **Public debt** 85% of GDP. **Income/person** $468 (1% of USA).

Politics

The highland Merina people gained control of the whole island in the 19th Century, a fact still resented by the lowlander peoples. Annexed by France in 1896; independent in 1960. A coup in 1972 led to a failed experiment with Marxism. Popular protest and demands for change were violently suppressed before constitutional change was conceded and multiparty elections granted in 1993. In 2002 the former Marxist ruler was ousted by the newly-elected president after months of massive demonstrations and military confrontation. The president targeted corruption and aimed to stimulate economic growth and reduce poverty while centralizing executive powers, a move viewed suspiciously by some. His tenure ended when an early 2009 military-backed takeover saw the capital's mayor proclaim himself president. This was followed by months of political upheaval, a failed power-sharing agreement and broad international condemnation from within Africa as well as globally. Corruption has long been a major problem.

Religion

There is officially religious freedom. The power of the old Malagasy folk religion remains pervasive. The four mainline churches have great influence. The government and traditional churches are suspicious of the emergence of younger, more charismatic groups.

Religions	Pop %	Population	Ann Gr
Christian	53.53	10,784,390	3.0%
Ethnoreligionist	37.65	7,585,135	2.0%
Muslim	8.00	1,611,715	4.3%
Non-religious	0.24	48,351	4.5%
Other	0.23	46,337	3.6%
Hindu	0.15	30,220	4.2%
Chinese	0.10	20,146	2.7%
Baha'i	0.10	20,146	2.7%

Christians	Denoms	Pop %	Affiliates	Ann Gr
Protestant	40	31.52	6,350,000	2.2%
Independent	101	5.97	1,203,000	4.4%
Anglican	1	1.86	375,000	2.6%
Catholic	1	23.13	4,660,000	2.1%
Orthodox	1	0.10	20,000	4.6%
Marginal	2	0.25	51,000	7.9%
Unaffiliated		0.30	60,000	-5.8%
Doubly affiliated		-9.60	-1,935,000	0.0%

M

Churches	MegaBloc	Congs	Members	Affiliates
Catholic Church	C	320	2,560,440	4,660,000
Lutheran Church	P	15,962	830,000	3,320,000
Church of JC - FJKM	P	4,062	731,092	2,610,000
Episcopal Church	A	1,349	134,892	375,000
New Protestant Church	I	556	100,000	350,000
Seventh-day Adventist	P	430	113,000	161,590
METM	I	420	71,000	142,000
Tranozozoro Atranobiriky	I	153	67,500	135,000
Assemblies of God	I	420	51,471	105,000
Jesus Saves Pente Ch	P	194	38,739	86,000
United Pentecostal Ch	P	640	68,908	82,000
Jehovah's Witnesses	M	351	23,500	47,000
Eglise du Reveil	I	837	19,250	38,500
Rhema	I	118	11,833	35,500
FAAKRI	I	102	10,167	30,500
Bible Baptist Churches	I	60	15,000	25,000
CEIM	P	65	10,000	18,000
Other denominations[129]		2,262	196,265	438,100
Doubly affiliated				-1,935,000
Total Christians[146]		**28,301**	**5,053,057**	**10,724,190**

TransBloc	Pop %	Population	Ann Gr
Evangelicals			
Evangelicals	11.5	2,310,539	3.5%
Renewalists			
Charismatics	4.1	821,180	6.2%
Pentecostals	2.1	425,500	5.9%

Religions % of Total Pop

MegaBlocs % of Christian Pop

Answers to Prayer

1 **Church growth continues** in the midst of political and environmental crises. The most notable increases are of charismatic and neo-Pentecostal groups, who have also endured some opposition. The Holy Spirit is moving among students, young people and laypersons, causing the multiplication of small congregations and house groups.

Challenges for Prayer

1 **Madagascar is locked in a battle with poverty**, even though it is often called the "8th continent" and is rich in ecology, ethnicity and history. The majority live on an average of less than $1US/day and survive by subsistence agriculture. The common slash-and-burn technique is destroying the rainforest cover as well as many unique plant and animal species. About 80% of the original rainforest cover has already been lost. Repeatedly, cyclones further hamper development and destroy property. Pray for appropriate and sustainable development that lifts people out of poverty, and for a long-term approach to this complex challenge.

2 **Political troubles and conflict plague this land.** Many thought political freedom had arrived with the conclusive defeat of Marxist rhetoric and the ending of civil strife in 2002. The victor of the 2002 and 2006 presidential elections was concerned for the poor but criticized for his autocratic style. He was forced to resign in 2009 after his rival, the capital's mayor, orchestrated street demonstrations and the necessary military backing to seize the presidency. Widespread political condemnation of this move from most of the EU, the African Union and the UN, demonstrates Madagascar's continued democratic fragility and vulnerability to military intervention. Pray for leadership that will serve the people with humility and transparency, not seeking power for its own ends.

3 **The Protestant Churches** have a glorious history of faith despite their persecution by heathen rulers and harassment by the French Catholic colonial authorities. It grew from 5,000 in 1861 to one million in 1900. There have been significant revival movements within the larger churches in 1895, 1941, 1948, and during the 1980s. Springing from the revivals, movements of indigenous lay "shepherds" are operating within the mainline churches. Their emphasis on healing and exorcism – which relate strongly to the spiritist mentality – has led to conversions and full churches in some areas. Pray that this movement might continue to grow and be rooted in Scripture.

4 **The old beliefs still prevail in many ways,** despite the growth and spread of Christianity. Compromise with the old beliefs, veneration of ancestral spirits, and witchcraft is widespread among those who claim to be Christian. A Christian veneer often prevails, but many have little understanding of the biblical message of salvation. Many churches appear to be spiritually dead and in numerical decline, particularly in mainline denominations. Revival as well as biblical teaching and leadership are urgently needed. Pray for a new move of the Holy Spirit to reawaken these churches that have such a strong legacy.

5 **The Church is highly divided.** Most growth is in the charismatic denominations – by transfer growth and some conversion. Opposition to these newer groups – coming from traditional denominations and the government – has on occasion even reached hostility. Churches split to form new denominations with alarming regularity, too often based on personal feuds between leaders. Promises of prosperity lure the poor away from their previous congregations. Pray for greater unity among leaders and churches, and that pride and jealousy might give way to humility and Kingdom consciousness.

6 **Discipleship and biblical training** are the greatest needs of churches. For both the burgeoning but untrained newer churches and the frequently compromised/syncretized older ones, a knowledge of God's Word and a biblical worldview are essential. Pray for:

a) Lay discipleship and instruction. There is little by way of structured training or teaching for ordinary believers. Pray for new grassroots movements that are accessible and relevant to all Christians and that can be multiplied and reproduced throughout the country.

b) Formal theological training is a great need, since most pastors are undertrained. There are more than 20 seminaries and Bible colleges run by every denomination of note, but the level of instruction and study resources (especially books) are limited. Bible Training Centers for Pastors (BTCP) runs a two-year training course. Some institutions are subject to theological compromise. Pray for the generation of resources to equip these places, and pray for more teachers with both academic and spiritual credentials.

7 **Young people** are the key to the future of this rapidly growing population. Among the many groups working with young people (from children to university students) are UGBM(**IFES**), **CEF**, SU, **YFC** and **YWAM**. Thousands are ministered to every week through various programmes, groups and camps. Cities are greatly impacted, but rural areas have been neglected. Pray for the further development of Sunday School and catechism programmes.

8 **Less-reached areas and peoples:**

a) The northern and southern extremities of the island host the least evangelized of the Malagasy peoples. Animism prevails with strong Muslim influence in the north and northwest, and 80% of the south is still non-Christian. Inaccessibility is the greatest challenge, and missionaries have thus far failed to penetrate these regions effectively. Malagasy evangelists travel for days to reach such villages – pray for health, bicycles, finances and faith for them.

b) Malagasy ethnic religion dominates among the Sakalava in the west, Tsimihety in the north, Tandroy and Tanosy in the south as well as the Betsimisaraka, Antesaka, Antemoro and Tanala. These are just the larger groups. Shaman healers and witchcraft abound, and demonic oppression is common. Some mission organizations are actively targeting these areas: NMS, **AIM**, **IMB**, the Anglicans and others. Pray for the love and power of Christ to be demonstrated to these people groups.

c) Muslims are growing in numbers among Sakalava groups on the west coast, the Antemoro in the east and the Antankarana in the north. Extensive Islamization efforts abound; mosque building, radio broadcasts and offers of education are gathering momentum. Folk Islam is the norm. Pray that these peoples are not abandoned to Islam by the Church. Specific outreach to Muslims, though very limited, is proving fruitful; pray for more. The Lutheran Church has a vigorous outreach through the Shalom programme, and **AIM** has started a ministry among the Sakalava and Bara.

d) Ethnic minorities. Pray for the Muslim Comorians, Gujaratis and Arabs, with few known believers among them.

9 **The Protestant mission force** remains smaller than the formidable needs and challenges. Most urgent is the need for more pioneer workers to go to areas where health and living

M

conditions are difficult. Long-term commitment to and love for the people, their language and their culture is needed; short-term outreaches abound but their lasting impact has yet to be established. Trainers and teachers are still needed. The endemic poverty means that there are plentiful opportunities in aid, development, vocational training, education and health. Many expatriates are committed to ministry with and for existing indigenous denominations in these capacities. Largest mission agencies: **AIM**, Norwegian Mission, **AoG**, **CCCI**, Loving Concern International. Two indigenous Christian associations (AMEN in Fianarantsoa and CEMI in Tulear) seek to address the overwhelming social problems from a Christian worldview. The Lutherans and FJKM do excellent work in health care and education.

10 **Christian support ministries.** Pray for increased impact of the following:

a) Aviation ministry. Because much of the land is inaccessible, the ministry of **MAF** and Helimission is very strategic in flying workers and supplies to the places of greatest need. MedAir and several secular aid agencies benefit from these organizations.

b) Bible translation. The Protestant Malagasy Bible has been available since 1836. A revised modern version, using more current Official Malagasy, has been produced by various collaborating denominations. Currently, only the official Merina dialect has the Bible; translation work is ongoing in 10 different Malagasy languages. The Bible Society (UBS) has a widely recognized ministry and a vigorous distribution programme, but lack of foreign exchange limits importation and printing of the Scriptures. *The Children's Bible* is also a popular resource as is the Bible on mobile phone; a high proportion of Malagasy use mobile phones routinely.

c) Christian literature is in short supply. There are few good spiritual books in Malagasy. The Lutherans and Catholics have printing presses, but they badly need modernizing. Quality Christian material that speaks to the Malagasy mindset is also needed.

d) Audio Scriptures are vital in a country where literacy is below 50% and functionally as low as 30%, which makes all the more valuable resources such as FCBH and audio teaching in 13 languages on offer through **GRN**, GNM and UBS.

e) Christian radio. Christian programmes such as those by UBS and SU are regularly aired on national and many local FM stations in the larger urban centres, but organization and consistent quality programmes remain a need. Avotra, a local ministry, has a radio station in Nosy-Be with good local impact. **HCJB** has helped to set up a number of the FM stations in different parts of the island. Both **TWR** and the Adventists broadcast in Plateau Malagasy. Most crucial is providing isolated rural peoples with radios and radio transmissions that reach them; the cities are well covered already.

f) The JESUS film is now available in seven languages, the result of recent translation work. Five more are in progress. Pray for its effective use.

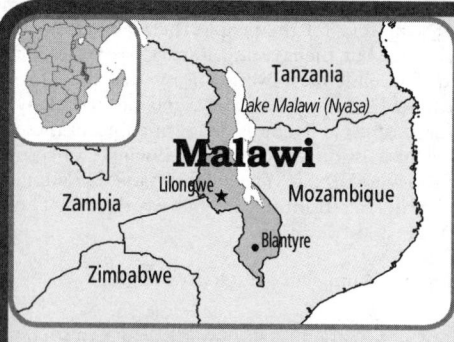

Malawi

Republic of Malawi

Africa

Geography

Area 118,484 sq km. Central African state extending along Lake Malawi and its outflow river, the Shire. A landlocked nation whose southern half is virtually an enclave within Mozambique.

Population		Ann Gr	Density
2010	15,691,784	2.82%	132/sq km
2020	20,536,979	2.67%	173/sq km
2030	25,896,558	2.23%	219/sq km

Capital Lilongwe 864,608. **Other major city** Blantyre 856,000. **Urbanites** 19.8%. **Pop under 15 years** 46%. **Life expectancy** 52 yrs.

Peoples

Bantu peoples 97.2%. 22 peoples divided roughly into northern, central and southern groups.

Chewa–Sena(7) 70.4%. Chewa 46.9%; Southern Nyanja 11.6%; Tumbuka 8.0%; Sena 2.3%; Tonga 1.4%. **Yawo**(3) 12.3%. Yawo 8.5%; Lomwe 2.1%; Kokola 1.7%.

Ngoni(2) 7.8%.

Central-Tanzania(6) 4.8%. Ngonde 3.0%.

Other 2.8%. South Asians 0.7%; many migrant peoples from Central and East Africa en route to South Africa.

Literacy 64.1%. **Official languages** Chichewa and English. **All languages** 24. **Indigenous languages** 16. **Languages with Scriptures** 8Bi 1NT 1por 3w.i.p.

Economy

A densely populated country with little development, cycles of drought/heavy rainfall, soil exhaustion (especially from tobacco growing) and widespread AIDS. Heavily dependent on agriculture, and therefore vulnerable to both global markets and local weather. Foreign aid props up the economy but pushes Malawi deeper into external debt – although much of it has recently been cancelled. Many live in poverty, but the economy has been growing in recent years. High unemployment drives many Malawians to work in other lands. **HDI Rank** 160th/182. **Public debt** 49% of GDP. **Income/person** $313 (1% of USA).

Politics

Independent from Britain in 1964. Dr. Hastings Banda ruled for 30 years as a colourful but ruthless dictator. Economic stability was gained at the expense of political freedom. Internal and international pressure against increasing corruption led to multiparty elections in 1994. The elected National Assembly is led by a separately elected president. Recent general elections were peaceful and fair; for the first time, voting was aligned in terms of issues rather than ethnoregional loyalties.

Religion

Freedom of religion exists; the various confessions of Christianity and Islam as well as smaller faiths co-exist peacefully.

Religions	Pop %	Population	Ann Gr
Christian	76.00	11,925,756	3.0%
Muslim	16.90	2,651,911	3.2%
Ethnoreligionist	6.50	1,019,966	0.5%
Non-religious	0.20	31,384	5.0%
Hindu	0.20	31,384	2.8%
Baha'i	0.20	31,384	2.8%

Christians	Denoms	Pop %	Affiliates	Ann Gr
Protestant	62	29.47	4,625,000	2.4%
Independent	331	6.83	1,072,000	3.1%
Anglican	1	1.78	280,000	1.9%
Catholic	1	23.06	3,618,000	2.0%
Orthodox	1	<0.01	1,000	0.0%
Marginal	1	1.03	162,000	4.0%
Unaffiliated		13.80	2,170,000	3.1%

Churches	MegaBloc	Congs	Members	Affiliates
Catholic Church	C	165	1,884,375	3,618,000
Ch of Central Afr Presby	P	467	700,800	1,752,000
Assemblies of God	P	2.500	553,191	780,000
Seventh-day Adventist	P	1,212	272,642	445,000
Other Afr Indep Chs	I	2,890	173,423	385,000
Anglican Church	A	425	112,000	280,000
Baptist Convention	P	1,500	112,500	225,000
Zambezi Evang Ch	P	630	100,455	221,000
Jehovah's Witnesses	M	1,210	81,000	162,000
Zion Churches	I	1,212	72,727	160,000
African Baptist Assembly	P	811	60,800	152,000
Charismatic Chs	I	200	60,000	92,400
Churches of Christ	P	1,500	40,000	92,000
Luth Ch of Christ Afr	P	260	44,667	67,000
Living Waters	I	193	29,000	58,000
Chr Chs/Chs of Christ	P	55	32,934	55,000
Ch of the Nazarene	P	266	24,490	48,000

M

United Pentecostal Ch	P	430	20,000	45,000
Africa Evangelical Ch	P	135	12,941	44,000
Apostolic Faith Mission	P	230	18,300	40,626
United Evang Ch	P	132	13,201	40,000
Other denominations[59]		6,167	421,912	995,185
Total Christians[397]		**22,590**	**4,841,358**	**9,757,211**

TransBloc	Pop %	Population	Ann Gr
Evangelicals			
Evangelicals	19.6	3,069,243	2.9%
Renewalists			
Charismatics	12.5	1,968,034	3.8%
Pentecostals	7.9	1,241,668	3.6%

Religions % of Total Pop

TransBloc Movements % of Total Pop

Answers to Prayer

1 **Malawi remains a stable and peaceful land** in a region plagued by wars, civil strife and violent politics. This reflects the peaceful and mostly rural nature of the people – despite intensifying pressure from population growth, AIDS and large-scale movements of peoples into, out of and through Malawi. The multiparty democracy is in good health, having a president with a background in economics and a tough anti-corruption stance. Praise God for the peace that allows Christian ministry and national development to continue unhindered.

2 **Malawi continues to be a rich spiritual scene** with steady evangelical growth. Years of outreach (**AE, DM**, Global Field Evangelism, CFAN evangelistic campaigns), youth ministry (SU, SCOM/**IFES**), New Life For All programmes in the churches, house meetings and prayer movements have all contributed. Evangelical presence is widespread in mainline, conservative and African Initiated Churches (AIC). The gospel has penetrated nearly every section of society, and some places have seen local revivals. While charismatic growth in Malawi is less explosive than in other parts of Africa, there is a solid if unspectacular increase in biblical faith across the board, which is in itself a more praiseworthy trend.

Challenges for Prayer

M

1 **Malawi faces serious challenges in the future,** such as the combination of poverty, high population growth and increasing pressure on agricultural land. High levels of national debt, AIDS and unemployment, when added to the aforementioned economic factors, produce challenges that will require wisdom, long-term planning and proactive policies by the government. The grip of poverty hampers development not only in the financial sense but also in terms of education, AIDS prevention, family life and even effective ministry and discipleship. Pray for leaders in Malawi, most of whom are church members, to act with wisdom, humility and long-term planning on biblical principles.

2 **The increasing activity of Islam** is a significant issue in Malawi. Over 80% of the Yao are Muslim, and make up the largest block of Muslims in Malawi. The Qu'ran has been translated into Chichewa. A Quranic movement (Sukuti) is trying to replace the prevalent Qaddiriya folk Islam with a more scriptural version of the faith. Malawi has a great influx of funds via the Africa Muslim Agency. These extend Islam's influence through primary education, scholarships for tertiary students to go to Muslim nations, aid distribution, drilling wells, medical aid, mosque building and many other means. Although the impact of these has thus far been quite limited, pray for awareness and training for the equipping of Christians to meet this challenge. Pray also for a persistent, loving witness to Muslims throughout Malawi.

3 **AIDS has been a terrible scourge.** Life expectancy was reduced at one point to age 43, and over 1 million are infected with HIV. AIDS is the leading cause of death for those aged 20 to 49 years. The 15- to 24-year olds are most affected; within this group, females account for more than twice as many cases as males. There are over 500,000 AIDS orphans. Pray also for the "Why Wait" programme, which in the fight against HIV/AIDS educates teachers and others on the blessings of abstinence before marriage. Anti-retro viral treatments are available and effective, but the social stigma remains. Pray that churches might be better equipped and envisioned to face AIDS with effective ministries; SU and SCOM/**IFES** work among students and teachers in this area.

4 **The CCAP (Church of Central Africa, Presbyterian)** is the largest Protestant denomination and the direct fruit of the vision of 19th Century explorer David Livingstone. It is a union of the churches planted by the South African Dutch Reformed Church, the Church of Scotland and the Free Church of Scotland. Pray for revival as nominalism and the influence of African traditional religion are commonplace, yet there are also many strong evangelical leaders and congregations. Pray for unity within this diverse denomination, and for many to come to genuine faith within the framework of the CCAP.

5 **The major issues to be tackled** by the churches are:

a) Maintaining effective ministry in the midst of deep poverty and the growing AIDS crisis.

b) Effective and appropriate theological education. There are 17 Protestant and four Roman Catholic seminaries and Bible schools. Pray for the CCAP theological faculty at Zomba to take a more strongly evangelical stand. Pray for many to be called into the ministry. Pray for the further establishment of pastoral training programmes among the fast-growing Pentecostal and charismatic churches.

c) Training for pastors and workers, because the traditional model of theological education cannot produce leaders fast enough to meet the needs of the rapidly growing Church. Poor rural churches are especially needy – few can afford to train or support workers. TEE courses are run from Zomba by TEEM (TEE of Malawi). In-service training for pastors is available through various means.

d) Financial provision for theological students and pastors in training, since poverty is the primary factor hampering theological education. Pray for provision via funding and partnerships. Pray also for new models of training that can accommodate the many poor and already overstretched pastors.

e) Unity. Pray for more cooperation among the Evangelical Association of Malawi (EAM), the more mainline Christian Council (CCM) and the charismatic churches.

6 **Student ministries flourish** (Life Ministries/**CCCI**, SCOM/**IFES**, SU, Chi Alpha), with over 500 SCOM student groups, involving 30,000 young people. **CCCI** moves beyond the campus to partner with churches in discipleship and evangelism training. Students are spiritually open, but not just to the gospel. Pray for a lasting impact from student ministries – that lifelong disciples be formed and the entire nation transformed.

7 **The least evangelized.** Pray that both Malawian and expatriate workers may effectively share the love of Christ with:

a) The Yawo, mostly Muslim, remain the biggest missional challenge in Malawi. Currently, outreach attempts are made by a partnership of evangelical missions – **SIM**, Brethren in Christ, **AoG**, Frontiers, Australian and South African Baptists, FEBA, **CAPRO**, Deeper Life and others – but few have come to Christ. Bible translation, audio resources and radio broadcasts are all being developed, and a Yawo church is coming to life!

b) The various tribes that still practice traditional ethnic religion. All of these have some Christians among them, but usually a smaller minority. They include the Southern Nyanja (11.6% of the population), the Kokola (1.7%), Nyungwe (0.1%) and a few smaller groups.

c) The Asian peoples, including Gujaratis, Kachis and Tamils. Only sporadic attempts are made to evangelize these predominantly Hindu and Muslim peoples.

8 **Expatriate missionaries** primarily support existing denominations and agencies in training, outreach and Christian institutions. Pray for genuine partnerships between foreigners and Malawians that result in fruitful ministries. The largest agencies: **SIM**, **IMB**, NGK, Liebenzell Mission, **PAoC**.

Christian help ministries for prayer:

a) *Bible translation.* Completing the whole Bible in Lomwe and Chilambya is the next major challenge. The Yawo Bible will be finished in 2011. Several minority languages are without a NT and may need translations.

b) *The Bible Society.* There are great demands for Scripture for local use and for the refugee community – but limited funds to meet them. Many rural Christians have no Bibles. The Bible in audio format is a fast developing ministry; Scriptures and/or teaching already exist in 26 languages (Bible Society, **GRN**, **TWR**).

c) *Literature* is much sought after, but expensive. Pray for an adequate supply of quality reading material for the literate, growing, but poor Church. The bulk of available literature includes secondhand Christian books in English and some locally published material.

d) *Christian radio.* The national broadcasting network regularly airs Christian programmes. Local channel All Nations Radio covers half of the districts in the country. **TWR** now broadcasts 24/7 from Lilongwe along with six other private local Christian stations, including the African Bible College and FEBA.

Malay 41.8%. Peninsular Malay 26.0%; Orang Pantai Timur 8.2%; Orang Negeri 3.3%; Indonesian 2.9%. Predominantly rural, but dominating politics, civil service, armed forces and police.
Tribal peoples 16.6%. Borneo-Kalimantan (91 peoples) 7.6%; Banjar(2) 4.7%; Filipino(10) 3.1%. A majority in Sarawak, and largest segment of Sabah's population.
Chinese 31.0%. 12 peoples. Hokkien 7.0%; Hakka 6.3%; Cantonese 5.1%; Teochew 3.7%; Mandarin 3.6%. Influential in commerce and business.
South Asian 9.4%. Tamil 6.6%; Nepali 0.8%. Mainly urban or poor estate workers. Almost all in PM.
Southeast Asia 0.8%. 10 peoples.
Other 0.4%. Western, Arab, Iranian and others.
Literacy 88.7%. **Official language** Malay (Bahasa Malay). **All languages** 145. **Indigenous languages** 137. **Languages with Scriptures** 16Bi 10NT 24por.

Malaysia

Asia

Geography

Area 330,434 sq km. Two distinct parts: Peninsular (West) Malaysia on the Kra peninsula of mainland Asia (PM), and East Malaysia (EM) consisting of the territories of Sarawak and Sabah on the northern third of the island of Borneo. Well-watered, tropical rainforest.

Population		Ann Gr	Density
2010	27,913,990	1.72%	84/sq km
2020	32,016,875	1.28%	97/sq km
2030	35,275,495	0.88%	107/sq km

PM 79.2%; Sabah 12.0%; Sarawak 8.8%.
Capital Kuala Lumpur 1,519,166. **Other major cities** Penang 1.4 million; Klang 1.1mill. **Urbanites** 72.2%. Chinese and Indians are largely urban. **Pop under 15 yrs** 30%. **Life expectancy** 74.1 yrs.

Peoples

The Malay population is increasing at the expense of the Chinese and Indian populations.
Bumiputeras (indigenous peoples) 58.4%. 141 peoples.

Economy

Export-based nation producing rubber, palm oil, petroleum and forest and agricultural products as well as, increasingly, hi-tech manufacturing. Large-scale industrialization and increased exploitation of natural resources has rapidly boosted the economy. Government-enforced programmes since 1971 include positive discrimination in order to uplift the Malay and indigenous populations' economic status to a level closer to the Chinese and Indian groups who have dominated the economy since before independence. A new wave of immigrants from poorer Asian countries, attracted by the wealth, continues to increase.
HDI Rank 66th/182. **Public debt** 40% of GDP.
Income/person $8,118 (17% of USA).

Politics

Independent from Britain in 1957 as the Federation of Malaya. In 1963, Sabah and Sarawak

M

joined to form Malaysia, a federation of 13 states with a constitutional monarchy. Recent years have been dominated by the efforts of the politically powerful Malays to extend their influence over the non-Malay half of the population in educational, economic and religious life, enriching and empowering themselves, while many normal Malays are left behind. The ruling party has recently lost its majority to a broad coalition of Chinese, liberal and Islamist parties. Political Islam, both in the ruling party as well Islamist opposition groups, threatens to further polarize the country on both religious and ethnic lines.

Religion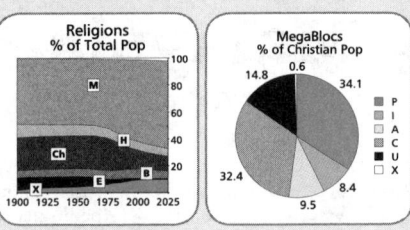

Sunni Islam is the official religion. Despite constitutional freedoms, discriminatory legislation and actions against minorities seem to be creeping in. Shari'a law, applicable for Muslims only, actually supercedes constitutional law on many issues, a portentous issue in a country with a strong and agitating Islamist movement. Proselytism of Muslims is illegal, but considerable effort and lawmaking is exercised to induce tribal peoples and other minorities to become Muslim.

Religions	Pop %	Population	Ann Gr
Muslim	62.61	17,476,949	2.0%
Chinese	12.70	3,545,077	0.6%
Christian	9.43	2,632,289	1.9%
Buddhist	6.50	1,814,409	1.1%
Hindu	6.20	1,730,667	1.4%
Non-religious	1.30	362,882	5.2%
Ethnoreligionist	0.90	251,226	-2.3%
Baha'i	0.30	83,742	-0.2%
Sikh	0.06	16,748	-1.4%

Christians	Denoms	Pop %	Affiliates	Ann Gr
Protestant	47	3.22	898,000	1.6%
Independent	18	0.79	220,000	2.8%
Anglican	1	0.90	250,000	2.6%
Catholic	1	3.06	855,000	1.8%
Orthodox	1	0.01	2,000	-1.8%
Marginal	7	0.05	13,000	4.3%
Unaffiliated		1.40	391,000	0.0%

Churches	MegaBloc	Congs	Members	Affiliates
Catholic Church	C	168	452,381	855,000
Methodist Church	P	382	109,871	303,984
Anglican Church	A	274	145,349	250,000
Evang Ch of Borneo SIB	P	1,090	110,000	242,000
Independent Churches	I	601	84,118	143,000
Seventh-day Adventist	P	343	51,500	64,000
Basel Christian Church	P	179	30,440	55,400
Assemblies of God	P	325	34,097	53,486
Malaysia Baptist Conv	P	184	18,750	37,500
Protestant Ch of Sabah	P	302	17,964	30,000
Full Gospel Assembly	I	62	12,500	25,000
Presbyterian Church	P	100	7,000	14,500
Christian Brethren	P	150	6,750	13,500
CNEC Churches	P	102	4,600	11,500
True Jesus Church	I	36	7,200	11,448
Other denominations[51]		905	66,703	127,868
Total Christians[75]		5,203	1,159,223	2,238,186

TransBloc	Pop %	Population	Ann Gr
Evangelicals			
Evangelicals	4.3	1,207,985	2.9%
Renewalists			
Charismatics	2.3	653,369	2.8%
Pentecostals	0.5	141,261	3.8%

Missionaries from Malaysia
P,I,A 430 (380 long-term), 180 international.

Answers to Prayer

1 **Greater accountability in the political sphere** as a strong coalition opposition brings balance to Parliament. Amid significant corruption and abuses of power comes a growing hope for and expectation of genuine justice, political transparency and less discrimination against all minority groups.

2 **The maturation of the Church.** Growth is steady if not spectacular, but churches are increasingly engaging in the social and political spheres. They are increasingly savvy about how to operate as a vibrant and outward-focused faith in an Islamic nation.

3 **Christians are networking and cooperating** as never before, across confessional, denominational and even racial lines. National-level networks for churches, for evangelicals, for prayer and for mission agencies are all growing in strength and effectiveness.

Challenges for Prayer

1 **Malaysian society faces a troubled and contested future** as fault lines appear.

a) *Malays,* the largest, most dominant and most quickly growing population, are divided among themselves on a number of levels. Pray for changes in these realms:

  i *Economic.* The ruling party's affirmative action of the last 40 years has enriched a minority of Malays, while increasing the gap between the connected elite and the poorer majority. Such discrimination and favouritism now hobbles economic progress as well as foreign investment.

  ii *Political.* The ruling party, UNMO, faces an opposition coalition comprised of moderates, liberals, Chinese ethnic parties and even Islamists. This indicates the level of disillusion with the government. The next election will demonstrate if the coalition's recent strong showing is based on large-scale change or is just a protest vote against UNMO. Appeasing both the minorities and conservative Muslims, while holding the country together, is a difficult balancing act.

  iii *Religious.* Powerful and vocal Islamist agendas are resulting in passing legislations on state and federal levels that effectively introduce sharia law for Malays and deepen the divide between Islamic radicals and moderates/liberals. Many rural Malays practice a folk Islam influenced by pre-Islamic Hindu and Buddhist elements as well as animist practices; they will inevitably be pushed into adopting a "purer" version of Islam.

b) *Minority groups* feel frustrated with discrimination and corruption as well as with changes to civil and religious liberties. Some seek legal and political solutions, but others plan for a future outside Malaysia – a potentially tragic loss of diversity and economic clout for a land that has long prided itself on both.

2 **Islam is gaining ground** in both numbers and socio-political power. Although many, including large numbers of Malays, are opposed to shari'a, the creeping changes in Malaysian public, religious and legal affairs are cause for concern and for prayer.

a) *Islam itself is a battleground.* With over 100 radical Islamist groups, there is never-ending agitation for sharia and the subjugation of all Malaysia to a much stricter version of Islam. Pray against the imposition of a harsh, aggressive Islam, which would bode ill for moderates, for minorities and for any Christian ministry.

b) *Apostasy laws* make conversion from Islam illegal in all but one state, with many states meting out harsh punishment for such offenses. It is nigh impossible for a Muslim (and therefore, by definition, for all Malays) to legally change their religion. Pray that federal constitutional rights might be upheld in courts. Pray for discretion and courage for all Muslims who choose to follow Christ.

c) *Proselytizing Muslims* is technically not illegal in federal law, but it is illegal in the more powerful state law in 10 of 13 states. Punishment includes a prison sentence and caning. Malays are increasingly isolated from the gospel, both socially and legally; pray for opportunities for them to encounter Jesus. Pray also for wisdom and fearlessness for Christians seeking to share the good news with Muslims.

3 **Religious freedom for all faiths** is constitutionally guaranteed despite changes that threaten this. Pray especially that the Christian community may continue to possess the liberty to practice, profess and propagate their faith amid the discrimination and intimidation arising from the process of Islamization currently occurring.

4 **The Christian community** faces many challenges beyond the external issues of religious freedom and evangelizing Muslims. Pray for:

a) *Unity among Christians.* They face social ills, injustices and growing discrimination against ethnic and religious minorities. The Christian Federation of Malaysia represents evangelicals, Catholics and mainline denominations before the government. The National Evangelical Christian Fellowship (NECF) consists of evangelical churches and organizations focused on building unity, prayer, ministry and mission. The NECF assists evangelicals in

M

transforming the nation by promoting economic sufficiency, justice/advocacy and national righteousness.

b) Godly leadership within the Christian community. Pray for godly leaders who are prepared, at considerable cost, to lead their churches by nurturing and empowering members to live godly lives – in the discipline of prayer and the task of evangelism – as they manifest witness to the concerns and needs of every sphere of society.

c) Lack of Christian workers. Many smaller churches have no trained pastor, even with a healthy number of Bible colleges, seminaries and church-training programmes. Too few respond to God's call to service because of family expectations, materialism, a lack of role models and the perception that years of theological training are required.

d) Marginalization creates anxiety, a ghetto mentality and the desire to withdraw from being the witnesses Christians should be. Emigration rates of professionals and Bible school graduates are high.

5 **Since Malay became the official national language,** Christians have been confronted with a series of challenges. Pray for improvements in:

a) The need for Christian literature in the Malay language. Writers are few and the market is still small, yet the younger generation is educated in this medium. There are numerous Christian bookstores, including online ones, and an active Bible Society.

b) Restrictions on the use of the Malay language Bible and other Christian books. These were banned when the government deemed their contents to be detrimental to public peace. One main issue is the use of the word Allah for God in such material. After forcing Malaysians to use Malay as a common language, the government now fears that such use in Christian literature and services will induce Malays to become Christian. Pray for Christian publishers and ministries to be strong and shrewd in defending their legal rights over this issue.

c) The language used in church services. Many churches, especially Catholic and the SIB, have congregations that use Bahasa Malaysia. Implementing an official and national language could be a positive development; pray that freedom to use the language in its entirety, by all faith communities, would reflect the multi-faith and multi-cultural make-up of the nation.

6 **Ministry to young people** is crucial as the generation gap widens and many churches consist predominantly of older people. The temptations to young people – criminal activity, gambling, substance abuse, sexual immorality – are more pronounced than ever and are part of the reason for the resurgence of fundamentalist Islam. Many Indian, Chinese, East Malaysians and immigrants are finding Jesus through agencies such as **YFC**, **CCCI**, Navigators, SU, FES(**IFES**) and others working in schools and universities. Pray for these ministries and their focus on discipling Christian young people to stand against the many influences that draw them away from their Saviour.

7 **Expatriate Christian workers** have declined in numbers due to visa restrictions. Their presence is still valued, and various ministries depend on their input. Pray for the issue of necessary visas and extensions; long-term presence is possible for those with adequate funds. Pray also for effective ministry within the limitations that exist.

8 **The missions vision** of the Church in Malaysia continues to increase. There are over 30 agencies invested in the harvest. The NECF as a national body trains local congregations and denominations to send out qualified workers. The Malaysian Centre for Global Missions also works to this end. Major agencies include Interserve, **WBT**, **OMF**, **OM**, STAMP/Strategic Missions Program, Methodists and **YWAM**. Many independent churches send workers directly as well; these are nearly impossible to enumerate.

9 **The immigrant and foreign labourer population** has swelled to over two million – probably significantly more with illegals included. They come from Indonesia, Philippines, Nepal, Bangladesh, Myanmar, Vietnam, India and elsewhere. This includes some of the world's least-evangelized peoples such as Acehnese and Miningkabau. Most work for very low wages in difficult, often back-breaking, labour. They are mostly Muslim but with some Hindus and Buddhists as well. The Malaysian Church has a wonderful opportunity to reach many unevangelized groups who are right on their doorstep. Pray that Christians might have the vision and the courage to reach out and seize this opportunity.

Peninsular Malaysia

Geography 🌐
Area 132,000 sq km. 40% of Malaysia; the south-easternmost point of mainland Asia.
Population 22,289,000.

Peoples 👪
Malay 64%.
Chinese 27%.
Indian 8%.
Orang Asli (the original indigenous peoples) 1%. Largest: Semai 42,000; Jakun 22,000; Temuan 19,000; Temier 18,000.

Religion 🔥
Muslim 64%; Chinese religions/Buddhist 24.6%; Hindu 7.5%; Christian 2.8%; Other 1.1%.

Challenges for Prayer

1 **The Church is small, but growing.** Only 3% of Peninsular Malaysia (PM) is Christian. PM has 80% of Malaysia's population but only 25% of its Christians. Christianity, however, is growing among all non-Muslim ethnic groups; about 10% of the Orang Asli, 10% of Chinese and 8% of Indians are Christian. Still, the continual external pressures from Islam at every level and from non-Christian families undermine progress. Pray for continued church growth, but also for a deep work of the Holy Spirit in preserving, building up and emboldening believers to thrive amid the pressure.

2 **The relentless pressure from Islamist circles** has manifested in court decisions related to religion, apostasy and conversion. Decisions reflect fear by the judiciary and weakening of the civil courts' constitutional power. Pray that the government might uphold the religious rights of all citizens. Pray also for the thwarting of radical Islamist elements seeking to oppress all other expressions of religion.

3 **Church practices must adapt to changing realities.** Cell groups are thriving, especially among the Bumiputeras (both Malay and non-Malay). Using Bahasa Malaysia in church services can also introduce complications because of certain laws. The lure of materialism and worldly lifestyles tempts many young urban Christians of all ethnic groups; meanwhile, traditional congregations are increasingly aged. Effective discipleship and community must be developed. Pray for wisdom for church leaders and for renewal that sees churches full and relevant.

4 **Pray for the less-evangelized.** The Malaysian Church has the resources and the understanding of the local scene in PM to reach the less-reached, but it also needs the courage and commitment. Pray especially for:

a) The Malays, regarded by the government as Muslim by definition. The legal and social barriers are high, but it is possible for Christians to share their faith. There are some Malay believers in house groups and multi-ethnic churches, but there are no viable public congregations of ethnic Malays. Malays can be reached more easily abroad and in nearby Singapore. By dint of both population and religion, the Malay people are one of the world's largest unreached groups.

b) The Chinese. Although there is a significant minority of Christians, specific areas need prayer. Materialism and traditional religions are strong. Churches are growing, but mostly among the urban, middle-class, English-speaking Chinese. Those speaking primarily Hainanese, Hakka and Teochew have much less Christian presence. Rural and small-town Chinese are patchily evangelized, and only half of the 450 Chinese villages have a church.

c) The Orang Asli number less than 200,000 despite being the original inhabitants of the Malaysian peninsula.

   i *They are subject to both exploitation and Islamization.* The Malay-dominated government regards them as Muslims, even though most are animist. They are generally not interested in education, technology or development and are therefore very vulnerable to exploitation.

M

The forests in which they traditionally live are being logged out or reserved for recreation/wilderness.

ii *There are no churches or believers in 8 of the 19 groups.* Only the Semai and Mah Meri have any of the Bible in their language. The Orang Asli have three Bible training centres; the Semai and other West Malaysians work among other Orang Asli groups. JEKOA is an indigenous church comprised of Orang Asli people; along with SIB and others, they focus on seeing a church planting movement born among the indigenous peoples of Peninsular Malaysia. Pray that an indigenous and appropriate expression of the gospel might take root among them.

d) *Indians.* Indian Malaysians sadly comprise a disproportionately high number of the country's poor and, occasionally, deliquents. There are many Tamil Christians, but few among the estate labourers. Other Indian ethnic minorities are less reached, the Punjabis (mostly Sikh) and Telugus in particular. Indian Muslims number nearly 60,000; there has been no specific outreach to them. The Tamil Bible Institute (AsEF) is training Christian workers to reach Indian communities with the gospel.

e) *The socially marginalized.* Drug addiction is a major problem, especially among the Malay youth. Once addicted or convicted, they are generally rejected by family and end up in a life of crime. Crime rates, in particular among youth, are at alarming levels, as are divorce rates. Pray for effective Christian ministry to all who suffer from these serious threats to healthy society.

Sabah
(Formerly North Borneo)

Geography 🌍

Area 74,000 sq km. Rich in natural resources.
Population 3,150,000. Probably higher due to rapid population growth augmented by many immigrants from the Philippines and Indonesia.

Peoples 👪

All figures approximate.
Indigenous peoples 45.2%. Of 38 peoples, the largest: Kadazan-Dusun(18) 18.1%; Murut(11) 3.3%; Bajau 2.5%.
Other Malaysian 29.6%. Malay 11.5%; Chinese 13.2%; others 4.8%.
Migrant peoples 25.1%. The real number is likely to be much higher, but is impossible to document. Mostly Indonesian and Filipino (especially Tausugg).

Religion 🕌

Muslim 63%; Christian 29%; Buddhist/Chinese 7%; Other 1%.

M

Challenges for Prayer

1 **Government, on both the state and federal levels,** has enriched itself while overseeing the nation's poorest state (26% are below the poverty line). The rich natural resources are plundered, but locals have not benefitted. Racial discrimination, exploitation of immigrants, corruption and higher levels of crime (including drug trafficking and piracy) blight this beautiful region. Pray for leadership that is honest, impartial, just and committed to stewarding the environment and governing the people with wisdom and righteousness.

2 **Rapid church growth is taking place** among the Chinese, Kadazan-Dusun, Tagal and Murut peoples through the work of the Basel Mission, Anglicans and SIB. The SIB has over 500 congregations in Sabah. The charismatic movement deeply affects nearly every denomination. Over one-third of Chinese and the majority of indigenous peoples are now Christian. Nominalism, the drift to the cities of tribal peoples and a serious lack of full-time workers are unresolved problems for churches. Pray for greater unity and cooperation, social engagement and evangelism, and pray against apathy and undue influence from political interests. The Sabah Council of Churches seeks to serve and catalyze the church on all these issues. The great difficulty for expatriate mission and ministry makes it necessary for local Christians to evangelize the unreached in Sabah, if this work is to be done.

3 **Peoples needing prayer.**

a) The Muslim peoples are almost untouched. Pray for specific outreach to:

  i *The Filipino-related peoples,* many of whom are refugees from the strife resulting from Muslim agitation in Mindanao, Philippines.

  ii *The Indonesians,* most being illegal immigrants from Sulawesi and Java. Little is being done to reach them.

  iii *The local Malay* and Muslim tribal peoples, notably the Bisaya and Bajau.

b) Indigenous (Bumiputera) groups are neglected in many ways.

  i *Some groups are still only partially evangelized,* though there have been large people movements among them. Few languages have the NT. There are Bible translation needs in 12 languages but virtually no foreign personnel left; nationals must pick up the slack.

  ii *These rural, tribal peoples* suffer the most intense levels of poverty, unemployment and lack of education. The government fails to invest its significant income from Sabah's natural resources into assisting non-Malay Bumiputeras. Claims that Muslim immigrants receive greater favour and help than the Christian and animist tribals are common.

Sarawak

Geography 🌐

Area 124,500 sq km. Forested, but subject to over-exploitation.
Population 2,475,000.

Peoples 👪

All figures approximate.

Indigenous 48.2%. Over 46 groups, largest: Iban (Sea Dayak) 30.5%; Bidayuh/Dayak 10%; Melanau 2.2%; Orang Ulu – Kedayan, Kayan(3), Kenyah(5), Punan 5.5%.
Malay 22.2%.
Other Malaysian 25.9%. Chinese 25.5%.
Other immigrants 3.7%.

Religion

Christian 42%; Muslim 32%; Buddhist/Chinese 14%; Traditional ethnic 5%; Other/unknown 8%.

Challenges for Prayer

1 **Sarawak enjoys spiritual blessing** with 70 years of God moving. The SIB has nearly 300 congregations, over five Bible schools, a work among over 10 peoples – many unreached – and vigorous outreach to rural areas. The SIB focuses on the north, the Anglicans the south, and the Methodists the centre with over 600 preaching points among the Iban and work among urban Chinese Malaysians. The majority of Iban are Christians and nearly half the Chinese now profess Christianity, though a significant number are more nominal in their faith.

2 **Poverty, neglect and exploitation** explain the wide disparity between the haves and have nots. The tribal peoples comprise almost all of the indigenous poor, especially in the remote rural areas. They have been failed by a rapacious and discriminatory government, self-serving local officials and even by unmoved churches. They enjoy very few opportunities for improvement in education, employment or healthcare. Pray for good governance on both the state and grassroots levels; pray also for Christians to become more mobilized to assist their disadvantaged brethren and to reach out in love to those more needy than themselves.

3 **The Church faces trials on many fronts.** Materialism is a strong pull in urban areas; pressure from Muslims is strong in rural areas. The underlying animism and traditional beliefs of the Iban people and other former headhunters, as well as their geographic isolation, make ministry and discipleship painstakingly difficult. The many Chinese churches suffer mixed fortunes, some thriving and some struggling. Pray for churches to overcome these trials; pray also for greater relevance, passion for the lost and unity across denominational and ethnic boundaries. Pray also for increased partnership with and support from the more well-established and well-resourced churches on the Peninsula.

4 **Growth is held back** by lack of workers, especially in rural areas. Nearly half the SIB congregations have no pastor. There are 21 languages needing Bible translation. Pray for the calling of more pastors and Christian workers to this needy but responsive province.

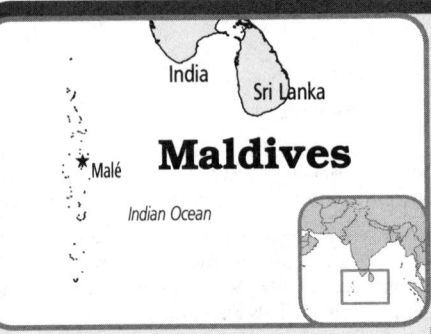

India
Sri Lanka
*Malé **Maldives**
Indian Ocean

Maldives
Republic of Maldives
Asia

Geography

Area 298 sq km. 1,200 coral islands in 20 administrative groups, 600 km southwest of Sri Lanka in the Indian Ocean. Only 202 islands are inhabited. These have an average size of less than 1 sq km. Average elevation is one metre.

Population		Ann Gr	Density
2010	313,920	1.43%	1,053/sq km
2020	361,689	1.39%	1,214/sq km
2030	402,807	0.96%	1,352/sq km

Population figures for the Maldives section generally do not include non-Maldivians.
Capital Malé 126,000. **Urbanites** 40.5%. **Pop under 15 yrs** 28%. **Life expectancy** 71.1 yrs.

Peoples

Indigenous 80%. Maldivians of South Asian Dravidian origin.
Foreign 20%. Indian, Sri Lankan, Pakistani, Bangladeshi and some Westerners, almost entirely in temporary employment. In reality, foreign worker population possibly exceeds 80,000.
Literacy 97.2%. **Official language** Dhivehi of Sanskrit origin. **All languages** 2. **Languages with Scriptures** 1 w.i.p.

Economy

Tourism and fishing dominate the economy. Lack of fertile soil and fresh water and the high population density keep most people at subsistence level. The 2004 tsunami damaged significant agricultural and tourism infrastructure, while the worldwide economic downturn has hampered tourism significantly.
HDI Rank 95th/182. **Public debt** 32.9% of GDP. **Income/person** $3,654 (8% of USA).

Politics

The nominal British protectorate was terminated in 1965. A non-party republic since 1968. An autocracy since 1978, ruled by one president who has cultivated a very poor human rights record. An independent judiciary has recently been established. Significant pro-reform demonstrations, international pressure and desire to portray itself as a developing republic all pulled the Maldives toward multiparty democracy, which was realized in the 2008 presidential election. The opposition's victory brought some limited freedoms – but not in the religious sphere.

Religion

Islam is the only recognized religion. The open practice of all other religions is forbidden. Sunni Islam is strongly promoted for national unity and preservation of the government's power, but a more fundamentalist brand of Islam has rapidly grown in size and influence in recent years. Almost all adherents of other religions are foreigners.

Religions	Pop %	Population	Ann Gr
Muslim	99.04	310,906	1.4%
Buddhist	0.40	1,256	0.5%
Hindu	0.35	1,099	2.6%
Christian	0.17	534	4.0%
Non-religious	0.04	126	1.4%

Christians	Denoms	Pop %	Affiliates	Ann Gr
Protestant	1	0.06	<200	4.6%
Independent	1	0.02	<100	3.7%
Catholic	1	0.09	<300	3.9%

TransBloc	Pop %	Population	Ann Gr
Evangelicals			
Evangelicals	0.1	235	4.3%
Renewalists			
Charismatics	<0.1	99	6.1%

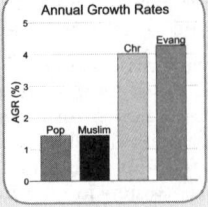

Annual Growth Rates

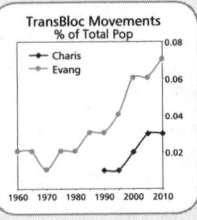

TransBloc Movements
% of Total Pop

M

Challenges for Prayer

1 **The fragile ecosystem of the Maldives** is threatened by rising sea levels that could flood and destroy. Coral mining and rises in sea temperatures have killed much of the coral that is the foundation of these islands. The 2004 tsunami and the 2008-2009 economic downturn demonstrated how fleeting life on these islands could be; pray that this would cause many to seek eternal assurance obtainable only through Christ.

2 **Behind the facade of island paradise lies a darker reality.** Freedom of expression and belief is strongly curtailed by powerful societal and regulatory forces. One of the highest divorce rates in the world, rising crime and gang activity, abuse of children and endemic drug use among teens (possibly up to 70%) indicate that all is not well. Beyond Islamic beliefs lies a widespread adherence to pre-Islamic occult practices called *fanditha*. Pray for the light of the gospel to shine into the lives of Maldivians. Pray against strongholds of pride, fear, duplicity and sensuality.

3 **The desire to honour human rights and increase freedoms** has been expressed by the current government, but freedom of religion is highly unpopular and violent opposition to it has been promised. Grassroots religion has shifted in a decidedly Islamist and Arabized direction, losing its indigenous Maldivian roots. Pray for the future of the people of the Maldives, torn between oppressive religion and empty freedoms.

4 **The Maldivians are still among the least evangelized** on earth. Neither mission work nor Christian literature has ever been allowed. Paradoxically, the government denies the existence of Christianity among Maldivians while arresting those who do believe. The perception of Christianity is so bad (largely due to Western media and tourist immorality) that political opponents use the term "Christian" to slander one another. Pray for the true name and nature of Jesus to be made known in this nation. Pray that the state's contradictions and heavy-handedness toward Christianity would generate great curiosity.

5 **Persecution of believers is intense.** Any Maldivian practicing Christianity can expect mockery, ostracism, incarceration and even torture. Pray for those who believe – for their protection, their courage in the face of great trials and for opportunities to grow in and spread their faith. On numerous occasions expatriate believers have been expelled, especially for sharing their faith.

6 **Other means of witness** – pray for lasting fruit through:

a) *Witness to Maldivians in other lands.* Many travel outside the Maldives as sailors or students, some to seek medical care or for other reasons. Also, there are Maldivian communities in Sri Lankan, Indian and Malaysian cities.

b) *The Scriptures* being translated into Dhivehi. Remarkably, a translation of the Gospels was completed and subsequently lost or destroyed in 1811! Only the Gospel of Luke and Acts are currently available. Pray for the progress of translation efforts and for ways people can freely access the Word in their heart language. Pray also for ways to import Scriptures and Christian literature – totally illegal at the moment.

c) *Christian video and audio messages* and web pages in Dhivehi are available on the Internet – for those clever or persistent enough to find their way past the government's blockages.

7 **Minicoy** is part of the Indian-ruled Lakshadweep Islands to the north of the Maldives, but its population is ethnically Maldivian. Pray for an open door for the gospel.

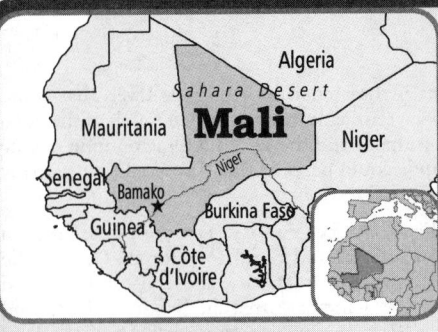

Mali

Republic of Mali

Africa

Geography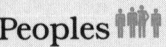

Area 1,240,192 sq km. Landlocked state. Dry southern grasslands merge into the Sahara Desert. The Niger River runs through the southern part of the country.

Population		Ann Gr	Density
2010	13,323,104	2.40%	11/sq km
2020	16,767,115	2.26%	14/sq km
2030	20,466,789	1.93%	17/sq km

Capital Bamako 1,698,520. **Urbanites** 33.3%. **Pop under 15 yrs** 44%. **Life expectancy** 48.1 yrs.

Peoples 👪

Sub-Saharan African peoples 89.4%. 55 peoples. Major people clusters:

Malinke–Bambara 30.2%. Bambara 28.9%.

Gur 17.4%. 23 peoples. Senoufo(4) 10.0%; Dogon(15) 5.4%; Bobo (Bomu/Bwa) 1.4%.

Soninke 12.5%. Soninke 8.1%; Bozo(4) 4.4%.

Malinke 10.2%. 9 peoples. Kita 6.9%; Khasonke 1.4%; Maninka 1.2%.

Fulbe 9.7%. Maasina Fulani 7.0%; 4 other groups.

Songhai 7.2%. Songhai(3) 6.5%; Idaksahak 0.7%.

Other Sub-Saharan Africans 2.2%.

Arab/Berber 10.5%. Tuareg (speaking two Tamacheq languages and including Bella, the former slaves of the Tuareg) 5.1%; Arab 5.4% including Moor 3.0%.

Other 0.1%. Mostly French.

Literacy 19%. **Official language** French. **Trade languages** Bambara, Fulbe, Songhai. **All languages** 60. **Indigenous languages** 56. **Languages with Scriptures** 4Bi 10NT 20por 17w.i.p.

Economy 🗺

One of the world's poorest nations. Subsistence farming and fishing occupies 80% of the population; drought, locust plagues and desertification frequently devastate the land. The exports of gold and cotton are highly vulnerable to market fluctuations.

HDI Rank 178th/182. **Public debt** 72.5% of GDP. **Income/person** $657 (1% of USA).

Politics ☒

The modern successor to the great Malian empire of AD 1230-1400. Independent from France in 1960. Popular protests ousted a military dictatorship in 1991. Elections and a multiparty democracy have since endured. Tuareg unrest in the northeast sees frequent outbreaks of violence, usually settled by government concessions over autonomy or poverty reduction. But restive Moors in the north and Al-Qaeda add to the trouble, augmented even further by rapidly growing drug cartels using the desert as a transshipment point for drugs from South America into Europe.

Religion 🔥

A secular state with freedom of religion despite the large Muslim majority. Islam is strongest in the north and centre. The traditionally animist peoples, such as Dogon, Bobo and Senufo, are now largely Muslim; the window of opportunity to reach them before their Islamization is now all but closed.

Religions	Pop %	Population	Ann Gr
Muslim	87.38	11,641,728	2.6%
Ethnoreligionist	9.88	1,316,323	0.8%
Christian	2.64	351,730	2.5%
Non-religious	0.10	13,323	2.4%

Christians Denoms		Pop %	Affiliates	Ann Gr
Protestant	17	0.70	93,000	2.5%
Independent	8	0.01	1,000	5.1%
Catholic	1	1.92	256,000	2.4%
Marginal	1	0.01	1,000	1.5%

Churches	MegaBloc	Congs	Members	Affiliates
Catholic Church	C	45	143,017	256,000
Evang Protestant Ch	P	260	22,000	43,000
CMA	P	360	9,875	39,500
Assemblies of God	P	67	1,107	3,100
Seventh-day Adventist	P	4	1,650	2,250
Alliance Mission	P	24	486	1,020
Jehovah's Witnesses	M	11	275	880
Church of Pentecost	I	13	583	670
Norwegian Prot Mission	P	18	264	660
Evang Baptist Mission	P	8	242	460
Other denominations[15]		116	1,662	3,521
Total Christians[27]		**926**	**181,161**	**351,061**

TransBloc	Pop %	Population	Ann Gr
Evangelicals			
Evangelicals	0.7	93,630	2.5%
Renewalists			
Charismatics	0.2	29,347	6.2%
Pentecostals	<0.1	4,120	2.7%

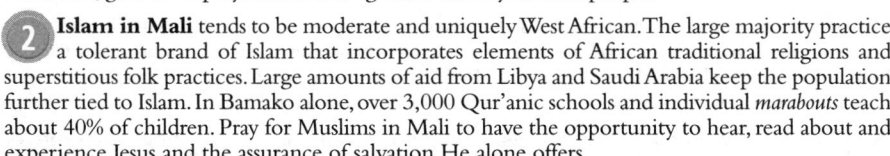

Religions % of Total Pop

TransBloc Movements % of Total Pop — Charis, Evang, Pente

Answers to Prayer

1 **The continuing stability,** in the midst of poverty, is a reason for praise. Mali stands as a role model of democracy and stability in a sea of troubled nations, free from the coups, civil wars and shady politics of its neighbours. It remains secular despite strong pressure from neighbouring countries to become an Islamic state.

2 **The consolidation of the gospel** is an answer to prayer:

a) The Church is taking root in a number of the cultures and peoples of Mali as believers persevere and second-generation Christians emerge.

b) A diversity of ministry sees church planting, development work and all types of holistic approaches bear fruit. Most missions combine outreach with works of compassion, since both are clearly needed.

c) Partnerships have formed for all Protestant ministries in Mali – *Association des Groupements d'Églises et Missions Protestantes Évangéliques au Mali* (AGEMPEM) – and for the evangelization of seven of the largest or most strategic peoples in Mali or West Africa generally: the Bozo, Fulbe, Malinke, Soninke and Tuareg.

Challenges for Prayer

1 **Mali's socio-economic quandary is sobering.** It is one of the poorest nations on earth, with people making on average $1.5US/day. Cotton growing employs one-third of the population but is highly vulnerable to world market fluctuations and competing growers elsewhere. Functional literacy is low and secondary school enrolment is under 20%. About one-fifth of children will not survive to the age of five, and of those who do, one-third will be malnourished. Two-thirds of the land area is desert or semi-desert, and the threat of desertification is ever present. Pray that Mali's leaders have wisdom and insight in knowing how to provide health, education, gainful employment and long-term stability to their people.

2 **Islam in Mali** tends to be moderate and uniquely West African. The large majority practice a tolerant brand of Islam that incorporates elements of African traditional religions and superstitious folk practices. Large amounts of aid from Libya and Saudi Arabia keep the population further tied to Islam. In Bamako alone, over 3,000 Qur'anic schools and individual *marabouts* teach about 40% of children. Pray for Muslims in Mali to have the opportunity to hear, read about and experience Jesus and the assurance of salvation He alone offers.

3 **The number of Christians has not increased by enough** to even keep pace with Mali's rapid population growth – evangelicals fell from 0.91% of the population in 1990 to 0.69% in 2010. Most growth is biological, and many who make decisions for Christ return to their former religion. This could be addressed with better follow-up through evangelism activities, discipleship programmes, pastoral training and Bible schools, but lack of funds to train for and support such ventures is a real problem. There are nearly 700 evangelical congregations, but most of them are not actively engaged in evangelism and outreach, despite many in Mali being spiritually open. Pray for boldness, passion and a burden for the unsaved to awaken in the churches and for a new wave of evangelism such as happened in the 1980s.

4 **Opportunities abound for a positive impact** by caring Christians. Pray for the many agencies actively involved in the following: church planting and evangelism (Avant, **CAPRO**, World Venture); relief; local development to conserve soil, vegetation and water (**CRWM**, Norwegian Lutherans); education (UWM); digging wells; and medical outreach (**CMA**, *Allianz Mission*). All of these groups minister in more than just one way, and many others work in Mali as well. The door is open to serve in Mali; ask God to send more workers for the harvest.

5 **Missions have multiplied** and few areas of the country are untargeted, but breakthrough has not yet been seen. Mali is still a pioneer missions country, with two-thirds of the population unevangelized. For years there were only four Protestant missions – Avant, **CMA**, and then UWM and Evangelical Baptists. Only in the more receptive Avant and **CMA** areas have strong churches emerged. There are now over 40 agencies from all continents, comprising several hundred workers. But the trickle of responses has not yet become a flood. More and more African and even Malian ministries work here; pray for them to collaborate with foreign missions and to have a galvanizing effect on the national churches.

6 **Bamako, the capital** and only major city in the country, has 60 small churches and over 100 expatriate missionaries, but only a minority are involved in urban church planting. Many suburbs are still without a meaningful witness, even as the city rapidly grows and spreads. The churches struggle with limited facilities and with expanding what facilities do exist. A prominent, visible Christianity – with actual buildings as symbols of growth and presence – would be an answer to prayer; a dynamic, growing movement of people to Christ irrespective of physical infrastructure would be even greater!

7 **Of the 60 indigenous ethnic groups,** only five are more than 1% evangelical – the Bambara (1.1%), Bobo (2.9%), Dogon (3.5%) and Senufo (1%). All peoples are in desperate need of the good news; 35 of them are categorized as unreached. Pray also for the smaller (therefore often neglected) groups of 25,000 people or less with no or few known believers (Wolof, Fulbe Jeeri, Kagoro, Banka, Yalunka, Jahanka, Humburi-Senni, Pana, Tiemacewe). Ask God to reveal the right approach so that they might be reached with the gospel. Pray for a decisive breakthrough among all peoples.

8 **There are a few strategic peoples** among whom pioneer work has been established, but for which prayer is requested:

a) The Bambara are a key people for the evangelization of the country. Many agencies work among them, and most denominations include some Bambara speakers. There are small victories in evangelism but no major breakthroughs. Pray for the spiritual and numerical growth of the church among this strategic people.

b) The Fulbe (mostly Fulbe Maasina), who are often semi-nomadic, reside throughout the country but are concentrated in central Mali. Several groups of believers are discipled by workers from nine different agencies, including the Norwegian Lutherans, **CRWM**, Pioneers and the Eglise Protestante. Some solid foundations are laid for a more significant spiritual breakthrough among these peoples.

c) The Northern peoples are more strongly Muslim, yet hard pioneering work has resulted in some congregations and believers among the Tamacheq/Tuareg and Songhai.

  i *Work among the desert-dwelling, semi-nomadic Tamacheq* is often disrupted by frequent insurrections, but upheaval, desertification and urbanization create opportunities for the gospel. The Idaksahak, a distinct Muslim people living among the Tamacheq, appear responsive. There are now congregations of Tamacheq believers and a NT.

  ii *The Songhai,* once rulers of an empire, practice folk Islam with strong elements of sorcery. There is Baptist work among them, and the JESUS film and portions of Scripture – especially in audio format – are proving effective.

d) The Dogon, including 15 sub-groups, are known for their traditional religion with rich mythology, songs and masks. But many looking for alternatives now turn to Islam. The Dogon are more evangelized than most groups in Mali through the **CMA**, and they have a relative wealth of Christian resources (NT, the JESUS film, audio resources, holistic ministry projects); this unprecedented opportunity for the gospel must not be missed.

e) The Soninke group, including the four Bozo fishermen peoples, has very few Christians but are engaged by teams from many different missions. The Soninke presence across much of

West Africa makes them strategic. A spiritual breakthrough amid all the ministry in Mali could easily spill into several other countries.

9 **Christian specialist and support ministries** for prayer:

a) Bible translation. Translation work is in progress for 18 languages. Nine languages have definite translation needs; another four have probable needs. Only eight Malian languages have a NT and only one has the entire Bible. Bible translation is a key ministry that must involve all confessions. Pray for effective partnership among SIL, the Malian Bible Society and all the churches and missions working with each people group in Mali.

b) Literacy projects to raise Mali's low literacy rates are essential if Bible translations are to be useful. UBS (Alpha Project), World Vision and a host of others have projects that will help spread the Word and uplift the people.

c) Oral learning projects are much more in keeping with the strong oral traditions of Mali. One-story (**IMB**) and Listening to the World (UBS) are two initiatives that train believers to share stories from Scripture in a style that connects with Malians.

d) Media ministry is crucial in a culture where functional literacy could be as low as 15%.

　i *Audio resources.* With such low literacy rates, cassettes, digital audio Scriptures and stories are greatly appreciated and highly effective. **GRN** has made recordings in 43 dialects and languages. FCBH, The God's Story Project, and The Story of Jesus are all Christian audio resources available in several languages.

　ii *Christian programmes on Radio Mali* have a wide audience. The 42 FM stations run under the auspices of the ACCM/Christian Association of Communication in Mali (but run by several different missions and churches) cover Bamako and six other states. Most of these stations broadcast many hours a day and in several languages: French, Bamanankan (Bambara), Pulaar (Fulani), Songhai, Tamacheq and others. IBRA, FEBA and **TWR** also broadcast in shortwave into Mali.

　iii *TV* is another crucial medium with high-perceived value but only one national station. Pray for the biblical TV programmes produced by ACCM (70 minutes per week) to have great impact; pray also for provision of funds for production and broadcast expenses.

　iv *The JESUS film* is a major instrument for opening whole areas and peoples for church planting. It is available in 17 languages. Pray for the effective use of this precious resource and for many to respond as they see and hear the gospel in their heart language.

e) Student ministry. GBEEM(**IFES**) began in Mali in 1980 and has 330 students in over 20 groups. **YWAM** also works among young people and students from six different locations.

f) Bible training and correspondence courses are beginning to be used, and TEE classes are helping to train Christian leaders. New seminaries and training centres are popping up, including Bethel Bible Institute, Global Mission Institute and, vitally, FATMES (*Faculté de Théologie et de Missiologie Evangélique au Sahel*).

g) Christian education is a potent tool to bless a country in need of educational development and to make clear the gospel to students and families alike. There are dozens of schools run by Christians.

Catholic commitment tends to socially isolate other faiths.

Religions	Pop %	Population	Ann Gr
Christian	96.82	396,961	0.3%
Non-religious	1.90	7,790	1.5%
Muslim	1.20	4,920	4.1%
Other	0.08	328	0.4%

Christians	Denoms	Pop %	Affiliates	Ann Gr
Protestant	9	0.35	1,000	4.0%
Anglican	1	0.24	1,000	-0.6%
Catholic	1	91.46	375,000	0.4%
Marginal	2	0.30	1,000	2.0%
Unaffiliated		4.50	18,000	-2.1%

Churches	MegaBloc	Congs	Members	Affiliates
Catholic Church	C	80	234,375	375,000
Jehovah's Witnesses	M	8	600	1,050
Church of England	A	1	216	970
Int Pente Holiness	P	1	80	100
Latter-day Saints (Mormon)	M	1	95	180
Evangelical Baptist	P	5	93	130
Bible Baptist Church	P	2	74	125
Other denominations[5]		11	550	1,071
Total Christians[13]		**109**	**236,093**	**378,626**

TransBloc	Pop %	Population	Ann Gr
Evangelicals			
Evangelicals	1.3	5,245	2.3%
Renewalists			
Charismatics	4.2	17,333	2.3%
Pentecostals	0.1	236	-12.6%

The majority of charismatics and even evangelicals are found within the Catholic renewal movements in Malta.

Malta

Republic of Malta

Europe

Geography

Area 316 sq km. Three small but strategic islands in the central Mediterranean. Dry limestone hills with no rivers.

Population		Ann Gr	Density
2010	409,999	0.37%	1,297/sq km
2020	422,300	0.26%	1,336/sq km
2030	426,887	0.05%	1,351/sq km

Capital Valetta 200,000. **Urbanites** 94.7%. **Pop under 15 yrs** 16%. **Life expectancy** 79.6 yrs.

Peoples

Maltese 93.0%. Descendants of Phoenicians, Greeks, Romans, Arabs, Normans and others.
Other 7.0%. British, Italian, plus increasing numbers of immigrants from Africa and Asia/Middle East.
Literacy 87.9%. **Official languages** Maltese, English. Maltese is a unique blend of Arabic, Latin and Punic. **All languages** 4. **Languages with Scriptures** 2Bi.

Economy

Based primarily on tourism, light industry, shipping (building, repairing, registering and as a container port), I.T. and financial services.
HDI Rank 38th/182. **Public debt** 16.7% of GDP. **Income/person** $20,281 (43% of USA).

Politics

Independent from Britain in 1964. Parliamentary republic since 1974. Malta entered into the EU in 2004 and the Eurozone in 2008.

Religion

Roman Catholicism is the state church according to the constitution. Freedom of religion is also guaranteed therein. Widespread

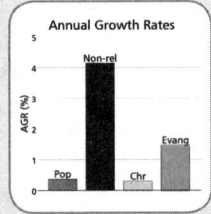

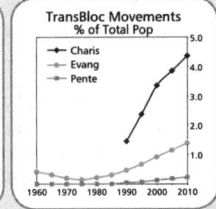

M

Challenges for Prayer

1 **Malta was the first nation in Europe to embrace Christianity,** after the Apostle Paul's shipwreck on the island. From the Phoenicians in 1000 BC onward, many powers seized the islands (including the Romans, Arabs, Normans, Ottomans, French and British), but the Maltese have retained their identity throughout. This identity has long been staunchly Christian. Pray that Malta's enduring Christian identity might be truly appreciated and lived out by its people.

2 **The most religious nation in Europe,** Malta has deeply Catholic sensibilities. The majority regularly attend mass and over 80% feel that their religion is important to them. However, not many Maltese enjoy a personal walk with the living Lord Jesus. Pray that their strong religious tradition may serve as a door into and not a barrier against greater commitment to the Kingdom.

3 **Catholic charismatic groups** are widespread and have had a significant impact; many wonderful believers have emerged as a result. Both the Alpha Course and the JESUS film have been key parts of this movement. Pray for a deeper and wider move of the Holy Spirit through the more than 65 groups. Pray for wisdom for the leaders to know how to have maximum impact while retaining biblical faithfulness.

4 **Protestant evangelical witness** did not exist until after independence in 1964 – British rulers did not permit it. Praise God for steady, albeit slow, growth since then. There are around 500 evangelicals in the 10-14 Protestant congregations and house churches in Malta. Pray for:

a) *The Baptist and Pentecostal groups* and their increasing outreach to the Maltese and to tourists. Official opposition to Protestant activities is a thing of the past, but social pressures on seekers and new converts can be intense. For most, to be Maltese is to be Catholic. Pray for multitudes to come to living faith in Christ.

b) *The older, English-speaking mainline denominations,* which have long catered to the needs of the expatriate community. There is much nominalism and little effective outreach to the indigenous population.

5 **Many Maltese have emigrated to other lands,** such as Australia, Britain, Italy and Canada, where some have come to the Lord. Although the Maltese diaspora still outnumbers the Maltese population, increasing numbers are returning to their homeland. Pray that those returning would include active, witnessing followers of Christ.

6 **Immigration presents a massive challenge.** The numbers attempting to enter Europe (2,000 per year and increasing) could potentially overwhelm the small population of Malta. Policing its waters as well as housing and providing for such immigrants are a significant strain on Malta's limited resources. Its proximity to North Africa – a launching point for immigrants from a host of nationalities – makes it all the more vulnerable. Maltese demonstrate general antipathy to those who exploit its accessibility. Most immigrants want to move from Malta; living in a detention centre is more akin to prison than the freedom they sought. Pray for Maltese to demonstrate compassion and Christian love; pray that many of these immigrants might discover the living Christ.

M

7 **Malta's proximity to North Africa** means not only significant challenges (such as immigration) but also great opportunities for meaningful exchange. Pray for a positive and godly witness to nations such as Libya and Tunisia.

8 **Christian support ministries** for prayer:

a) *The Trinitarian Bible Society* published the first one-volume Bible in Maltese in 1980; a Catholic version was published in 1985 by the Maltese Bible Society. The Gideons widely distribute Maltese, Arabic and English NTs in hotels, schools and institutions. Pray that many may read the Word with inner enlightenment and outward change.

b) *Christian literature* in Maltese is limited in quantity and variety. Pray for an increase in both evangelical titles and in those gifted in writing or translation. Pray for an effective publishing and distribution structure to be established.

c) **The JESUS film,** now dubbed into Maltese – the first full-length film ever to have this.

d) **Christian radio.** Christian Light Radio broadcasts 24 hours/day by FM in Malta and via the Internet in both English and Maltese. Pure Gold Radio (an evangelical station) started broadcasting in 2010.

e) **Outreach to seafarers** on the many cruise and container ships that pass through Malta is a potential new ministry that could impact thousands per week.

f) **Adopting a Maltese village for prayer** is a strategy that Ministries for Malta uses to connect churches globally to spiritual needs locally.

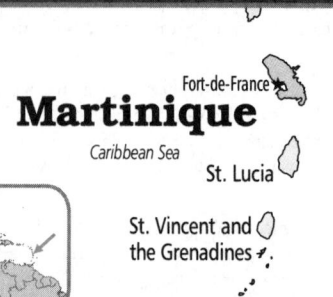

Martinique
Department of
Martinique
Caribbean

Geography

Area 1,091 sq km. A volcanic island in the eastern Caribbean Sea. The most northerly of the Windward Islands, and 100 km south of its sister island, Guadeloupe.

Population		Ann Gr	Density
2010	406,001	0.39%	372/sq km
2020	415,147	0.19%	381/sq km
2030	417,596	0.00%	383/sq km

Capital Fort-de-France 88,900. **Urbanites** 89.1%. **Pop under 15 yrs** 20%. **Life expectancy** 79.4 yrs.

Peoples

African Caribbean (black and mixed Creole) 94%. Increasing number of Haitians, Dominicans and others.
French 3.3%. Including local land-owning Beke.
Asian 2.7%. Mainly Tamil 1.9%; also Chinese, Vietnamese, Syrian.
Literacy 43.6%. **Official language** French. Créole Martiniquais is widely spoken. **All languages** 3. **Languages with Scriptures** 1Bi.

Economy

Based on tourism and, to a lesser degree, sugar, bananas, petroleum and rum. Heavily dependent on French aid and on imports paid for by French subsidies. Higher standard of and cost of living than most Antillean islands.
Public debt 3.7% of GDP. **Income/person** $13,160 (29% of USA). **Unemployment** 32.5%.

Politics

A French possession since 1635. An overseas department of France since 1946. The landowning Martinique French still control much of the economy, more so than in Guadeloupe. Nationalist sentiment occasionally flares, but is tempered by the high economic dependence on France. Protests and riots in Guadeloupe in 2009 spilled into Martinique, protestors demanding higher wages and lower prices.

Religion

There is freedom of religion.

Religions	Pop %	Population	Ann Gr
Christian	95.80	388,949	0.4%
Non-religious	2.40	9,744	1.3%
Muslim	0.65	2,639	2.0%
Baha'i	0.50	2,030	0.4%
Other	0.35	1,421	3.5%
Hindu	0.30	1,218	0.4%

Christians Denoms		Pop %	Affiliates	Ann Gr
Protestant	12	10.60	43,000	1.3%
Independent	6	0.39	2,000	4.2%
Catholic	1	84.98	345,000	-0.2%
Marginal	1	2.32	9,000	2.2%
Doubly affiliated		-2.49	-10,000	0.0%

Churches	MegaBloc	Congs	Members	Affiliates
Catholic Church	C	50	197,143	345,000
Seventh-day Adventist	P	61	15,200	23,408
Jehovah's Witnesses	M	58	4,700	9,400
Assemblies of God	P	31	3,100	6,200
Evang Mission of Mart	P	26	4,161	5,950
Ch of God (Cleveland)	P	9	594	1,700
Christian Brethren	P	17	600	1,002
Other denominations[13]		71	3,185	5,915
Doubly affiliated				-10,100
Total Christians[20]		**323**	**228,683**	**388,475**

TransBloc	Pop %	Population	Ann Gr
Evangelicals			
Evangelicals	6.1	24,861	1.6%
Renewalists			
Charismatics	3.0	12,255	3.0%
Pentecostals	2.0	8,290	3.9%

Annual Growth Rates

TransBloc Movements
% of Total Pop
Charis
Evang
Pente

Challenges for Prayer

1 **Martinique can be a dangerous place to live.** It periodically suffers major volcanic eruptions and earthquakes – in 1902, Mt. Pelée erupted, killing 30,000. Tropical storms and misuse of pesticides are more recent blights upon the population. But spiritual apathy is the most dangerous element that grips much of the population. Pray that they may see their basic instability and be shaken out of their carelessness about the things of God.

2 **The legacy of slavery remains strong in Martinique,** as with its sister department, Guadeloupe. The white minority controls a disproportionate amount of the economy and land, while many Creole find themselves increasingly hard-pressed due to high costs of living. The protests and riots of 2009 show deep needs for reconciliation and for society to be built on equity and justice – and that there are those who would manipulate such events to empower themselves.

3 **Pray for the churches.** There is an evangelical presence through the Assemblies of God, *Mission Chrétienne Evangélique, Eglise de Dieu,* Baptists, Nazarenes and among some Adventists. Many Christians come from dysfunctional or single-parent families and from a background of immorality and drug abuse. Pray for churches to be grounded in the Word, and for young people to be called into full-time service.

4 **As many as 40% of all Guadeloupans and Martiniquans live in France,** where they are known as Antilleans. They comprise a large minority in many Parisian evangelical churches. Pray for the witness of these believers. **WT** works among Antilleans in the Paris area.

5 **Christian resources,** including:

a) Literature. **CLC** operates a well-used bookstore that sells and lends books and tapes. Over 3,000 French Bibles are sold annually through the store. Pray that more local churches may see the value of Christian literature for spiritual growth and for evangelism.

b) Audio/Radio. **GRN** has recordings in Martinique Creole as well as French. *Radio Evangile Martinique* broadcasts in FM; their content is 70% locally produced and a result of collaboration between several evangelical denominations. *Radio Saint-Louis* is another Christian station also based in Martinique.

M

Mauritania

Islamic Republic
of Mauritania

Africa

Geography

Area 1,030,700 sq km. Entirely desert apart from the north bank of the Senegal River on its southern border.

Population		Ann Gr	Density
2010	3,365,675	2.43%	3/sq km
2020	4,091,379	1.86%	4/sq km
2030	4,791,136	1.52%	5/sq km

In 1970, 70% were nomadic, but drought and urbanization have reduced this to less than 20% today. **Capital** Nouakchott 729,000. **Urbanites** 41.4%. **Pop under 15 yrs** 40%. **Life expectancy** 56.6 yrs.

Peoples

Reliable statistics are hard to come by, since ethnicity involves caste as well as economic and political issues. Many prefer to simply divide the population into equal thirds – White Moor, Black Moor, Sub-Saharan African.
Arab (Hassaniya-speaking) up to 70%. Black Moors (Haratine) 40%, descended in part from slaves of the White Moors. White Moors (Bidan) of Arab and Berber origin 30%. White Moors have dominated in power since before independence.
Sub-Saharan African 28.8%. Fulbe/Tukulor (Pulaar); Wolof; Soninke; Bambara. Most are settled farmers in the south with important concentrations in Nouakchott and certain regional capitals.
Other 1.2%. West Africans, French, other expatriates.
Literacy 51.2%. **Official language** Arabic; the Hassaniya dialect is used as the vernacular for two-thirds of the population. French is the language of government and commerce. **All languages** 8. **Languages with Scriptures** 1Bi 3NT 3w.i.p.

Economy

One of the world's poorest countries. Continuing drought in the 1970s and 1980s devastated the country and led to rapid urbanization. Subsistence farming and animal herding are the main sources of employment; the main exports are fish, iron ore and, recently, oil (offshore production since 2006). Corruption is still a significant factor in the economy at all levels. Two issues dominate political debate – the alleged persistence of slavery in the interior and the interethnic tensions between Sub-Saharan African and Moor.
HDI Rank 154th/182. **Public debt** 170.6% of GDP. **Income/person** $1,042 (2% of USA).

Politics

Independent from France in 1960, followed by a long succession of military coups that were a continuation of rivalry among Moorish tribes. The military junta transformed itself into a multiparty democracy in 1992, but was ousted by a bloodless coup in 2005. The restoration of a civilian government came after the 2007 elections. Another coup took place in 2008, and then further presidential elections were held in 2009, re-establishing civilian government.

Religion

Officially an Islamic Republic, with a combination of several legal traditions including shari'a law. The Constitution officially states that Islam is the religion of the people and the state. Moderate Sunni Islam permeated by folk magic is practiced by the vast majority. There is tremendous social pressure against anyone converting to another faith.

Religions	Pop %	Population	Ann Gr
Muslim	99.75	3,357,261	2.4%
Christian	0.25	8,414	2.4%

Christians Denoms		Pop %	Affiliates	Ann Gr
Protestant	4	0.02	1,000	3.2%
Independent	4	0.06	2,000	7.4%
Anglican	1	0.03	1,000	4.1%
Catholic	1	0.14	5,000	0.4%
Marginal	1	<0.01	<100	11.8%

Most of the Christians are expatriates.

Churches	MegaBloc	Congs	Members	Affiliates
Catholic Church	C	5	2,570	4,600
Other Afr Chr groups	I	7	400	1,600
Anglican Church	A	1	611	1,100
Evangelical fellowships	P	7	266	380
Other denominations[4]		6	548	640
Total Christians[11]		**26**	**4,395**	**8,320**

M

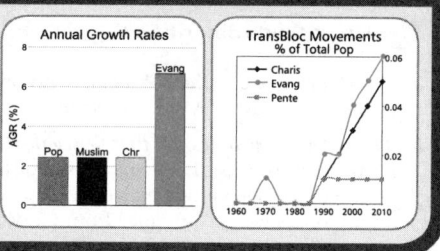

TransBloc	Pop %	Population	Ann Gr
Evangelicals			
Evangelicals	0.1	2,081	6.7%
Renewalists			
Charismatics	0.1	1,778	7.9%
Pentecostals	<0.1	170	2.5%

Challenges for Prayer

1 **Islam has been entrenched for 1,000 years** with little challenge. Many are the barriers to change – laws hindering proclamation of the gospel, powerful social resistance to change, an historic reluctance to engage with the outside world, geographical isolation, low literacy and minimal exposure to Christians and Christian media. Pray for greater spiritual openness and hunger for God. World Vision, Caritas, the Lutherans and others are working in development as well as with issues such as AIDS, human rights and environmental protection.

2 **Mauritania is one of the world's neediest countries.** One-third of children face chronic malnourishment, and many families struggle to afford basic necessities. Widespread divorce also causes social difficulties. Desertification threatens the remaining arable land, which amounts to perhaps only 1% of the total land area. The discovery of oil and new mineral reserves could either bring wealth to the country or increase corruption and the divide between rich and poor. Pray for political stability and wisdom for the government to enable revenues from Mauritania's natural resources to benefit the poor.

3 **Political issues are historical and highly charged,** although the elected government is widely seen as progressing forward. Despite slavery being illegal, allegations of slavery persist, and thousands are thought to live in such circumstances. Interethnic and intertribal tensions remain from past violence over the White Moor-dominated government seizing Black African lands and livestock. Pray for justice for all who have been oppressed.

4 **Expatriate Christians in Mauritania are few.** Most are from various West African countries working at menial jobs, although some work as professionals. Others work in diplomatic services, development and commerce. Expatriate Protestants are petitioning the government for legal protection from sporadic police harassment in certain precincts. Expatriates suspected of proselytizing Mauritanians are subject to harassment, interrogation, brief imprisonment, expulsion and even murder. The murder of a foreign Christian by Islamic terrorists in 2009, as well as extremist activities, have led to many expatriate believers leaving the country. Pray that the lives of Christians might clearly demonstrate the love of Jesus. Pray also that the Lord might grant them wisdom, protection and make them powerful witnesses for His name.

5 **All Mauritanian peoples remain essentially unreached,** and the vast majority have yet to hear the good news of God's grace through faith in Jesus. There are only a small number of Mauritanian believers worldwide, although the exact number is unknown. Believers in Mauritania have at times been imprisoned, beaten for their faith, or have endured ostracism by family or tribe. Pray for godly indigenous leadership to develop. Pray for increasing freedom of religion, both socially and legally. Pray for seekers to encounter Jesus, and that any who follow Him might be courageous in the faith. Also pray that God might minister to believers despite the lack of fellowship.

6 **Mauritanians in other lands are an opportunity.** Mauritanians reside in many countries in West Africa as well as in France, Spain and the USA. There is some work among them in Senegal. Pray that these scattered people may be evangelized and that Mauritanian believers, wherever they may be, might increase.

7 **Unreached minorities**. Pray for:

a) *The Haratine or Black Moors,* who are Moors by culture and language as well as the former slave class of Moorish society.

b) *The African peoples of the Senegal River Valley,* including the Pulaar (Tukulor and Fulakunda), Soninke, Bambara and Wolof. Some of these peoples have suffered much persecution, yet many previously exiled are now returning to their homeland. Their persecution and dispersion, as well as assistance from Christian agencies, have opened them for the gospel.

c) *The nomads of the desert,* descended from Berber and Arab Bedouin tribes, are even less accessible for evangelization due to their nomadic ways.

8 **Sub-Saharan African refugees** are increasingly using Mauritania as an illegal transit point to Europe (Canary Islands). Each year, tens of thousands make the attempt in unsafe boats, and over a thousand of those die in the attempt. Pray that those seeking riches in the West might somehow find Christ.

9 **Other ministries.** Pray for:

a) *Bible translation.* Outside Mauritania, efforts are underway to translate the Bible into Hassaniya Arabic. The Pulaar NT exists and work on the OT is progressing; work is being done in Soninke as well. Low literacy and a prevalent oral culture pose a challenge.

b) *The JESUS film* exists in all the local languages. It has had the most success among minorities in urban areas.

c) *Radio and satellite TV broadcasts* in the local dialects are still in the experimental stage; prayer is needed for the development of biblical content. There are some radio programmes in Pulaar and Bambara. While awaiting the production of local material, much good could be done by broadcasting quality programming already available in French and modern standard Arabic; but for technical and geographical reasons, those available in North Africa do not usually reach Mauritania. The main radio and TV stations have no Christian content.

d) *The Internet* is more widely available in the main districts of Nouakchott and the regional capitals, and is one way for Mauritanians to access the good news.

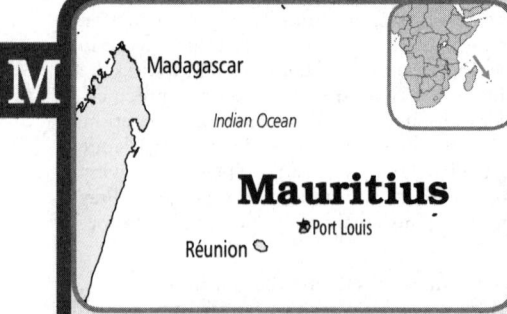

M

Madagascar

Indian Ocean

Mauritius

🔴 Port Louis

Réunion ○

Mauritius

Republic of Mauritius

Africa

Geography 🌍

Area 2,040 sq km. One larger and three smaller islands east of Madagascar in the western Indian Ocean. One of these, Rodrigues Island, is 500 km to the east of the others. Mauritius also claims the Chagos archipelago, including Diego Garcia, which comprise the British Indian Ocean Territory.

Population		Ann Gr	Density
2010	1,294,569	0.70%	635/sq km
2020	1,369,990	0.52%	672/sq km
2030	1,417,642	0.28%	695/sq km

Capital Port Louis 150,000. **Urbanites** 42.6%. **Pop under 15 yrs** 23%. **Life expectancy** 72.9 yrs.

Peoples 👪

All peoples immigrated with permanent settlements from the 18th Century onward.
Indo–Mauritian 66%. Bhojpuri 46%; Tamil 6%; Hindi 5%; Urdu 4%; others.
Creole 28%. Mixed African and European.
Chinese 3%. Majority are Hakka.
European 3%. Largely French, controlling sugar plantations and big business.
Literacy 85.1%. **Official language** English. **All languages** 13. **Indigenous languages** 6. **Languages with Scriptures** 4Bi 1NT 2por 1w.i.p.

Economy 📈

The once-dominant sugar and textile industries are losing their clout due to global markets and are being eclipsed by successful diversification and industrialization. Tourism, offshore banking and the use of Mauritius as a tax haven have become the main revenue generators. One of the more balanced and successful African economies.
HDI Rank 81st/182. **Public debt** 56.5% of GDP. **Income/person** $6,872 (14% of USA).

Politics ☒

A French colony between 1715 and 1810, and then British until independence in 1968. Following the racial war of 1968, the only African parliamentary democracy to have uninterrupted stability since 1969. Party politics are dominated by ethnic and religious divisions. The Hindu Indian bloc is in the majority, but increasingly forced to work with other groups in coalition.

Religion 🙏

Freedom of religion, but with a tendency to favour Indianization and, by implication, Hinduism. Mission work and Christian witness are allowed, but proselytism is looked on unfavourably in this multi-faith society.

Religions	Pop %	Population	Ann Gr
Hindu	48.60	629,161	0.4%
Christian	32.71	423,454	1.2%
Muslim	17.02	220,336	0.8%
Non-religious	0.42	5,437	1.2%
Baha'i	0.40	5,178	-3.7%
Chinese	0.33	4,272	1.3%
Buddhist	0.32	4,143	-0.5%
Sikh	0.20	2,589	0.7%

Christians	Denoms	Pop %	Affiliates	Ann Gr
Protestant	11	8.37	108,000	2.4%
Independent	21	1.92	25,000	6.9%
Anglican	1	0.39	5,000	-2.9%
Catholic	2	21.53	279,000	0.0%
Marginal	3	0.35	4,000	1.4%

Churches	MegaBloc	Congs	Members	Affiliates
Catholic Church	C	49	150,406	278,251
Assemblies of God	P	140	50,000	85,000
Ch of God (Cleveland)	P	43	9,667	14,500
Seventh-day Adventist	P	38	3,779	5,500
Anglican Church	A	17	3,247	5,000
Jehovah's Witnesses	M	29	1,850	4,120
Christian Church	I	7	1,500	2,700
Voice of Deliverance Ch	I	31	1,227	2,700
Presby Ch of Mauritius	P	5	1,100	1,463
Evang Ch of Mauritius	P	5	500	850
Other denominations[28]		118	9,764	21,405
Total Christians[38]		**482**	**233,040**	**421,489**

TransBloc	Pop %	Population	Ann Gr
Evangelicals			
Evangelicals	10.1	130,801	3.1%
Renewalists			
Charismatics	14.1	182,087	3.2%
Pentecostals	7.9	102,590	2.3%

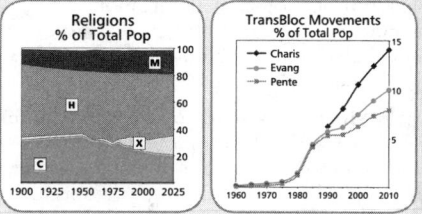

Religions % of Total Pop — TransBloc Movements % of Total Pop

M

Challenges for Prayer

1 **This complex multi-ethnic and multi-religious society** makes evangelism a challenge; pray for great wisdom and discernment among Christians. The Hinduization of government and culture, as well as strong ancestral and ethnic ties, make it difficult for Indians to become believers. However, large numbers of Hindus are coming to Jesus through the bold witness of evangelical/Pentecostal churches.

2 **Most older churches face slow decline** and are nominal in faith. Roman Catholics are seeing Hindu beliefs and practices make their way into churches in some places. But the charismatic movement is making a big impact on Catholics, with many coming to personal faith in Christ. Many of those impacted formed their own independent groups. The Roman Catholic Church is experiencing a move back to Bible reading, and now runs several active ministries on the island. Pray for a greater spread of this spiritual vitality among traditional churches in Mauritius.

3 **Among evangelicals, growth is most rapid** within the charismatic groups. Other evangelicals and independent house groups experience modest growth, but not without opposition. Subtle discrimination when applying for official permits – and more open hostility when sharing the gospel – are common. Proselytizers are painted as imperialistic and intolerant in this atmosphere of hyper-ecumenism. The Church has suffered from internal division, but the 1995 formation of a Fellowship of Christian Churches in Mauritius (FCCM) was a significant step forward, drawing together a wide range of churches and ministries. A similar group serves Pentecostals specifically. Pray for unity among Christians to deepen, to inform ministry and strategy, and to shape a positive testimony to non-believers.

4 **Training leaders is of prime importance.** The **AoG** School of Ministry offers multi-level programmes ranging from correspondence to degree-level courses. TEE is utilized by most denominations and there are several correspondence schools, one being the Emmaus BCC. To train clergy and laity, the Anglican Church opened the Training Centre for Ministries and Community Development in Curepipe. The most exciting development is the rebirth of the Mauritian Bible Training Institute, an evangelical Bible school started with input from **SIM**, which now enjoys a partnership with Vose Seminary in Australia. Praise the Lord for the development of Bible training, but also pray that Mauritius might receive more teachers of the Word who are well-trained models of godliness.

5 **Ministry to young people** is met with encouraging openness. While they are less bound by ethnic loyalties, many are held back from open commitment by family pressures or liberal church leaders. The challenges they face have intensified in recent years: violent crime, sexual immorality and an erosion of traditional values. Intravenous drug use is second highest in the world; some ministries have opened work to help drug users. Opportunities are limited for ministry in schools and campuses (the university is non-residential), but **YFC**, **YWAM**, **IFES**, **CCCI**, SU and **CEF** reach students and children by creative means. Praise God for government recognition of these ministries, and pray for their fruitfulness.

6 **Rodrigues Islanders,** numbering around 38,000, are largely Creole, largely Catholic, and tend to be poor and isolated. There is a small presence of other faiths (Hindu and Muslim) and other denominations (Anglican, Pentecostal, SdA) on this semi-autonomous island. Christians are active in education with five schools under their care, but faith tends to be nominal, blending biblical teachings with ungodly traditional beliefs. Pray for God's Spirit to work anew among the Creole.

7 **Missionary work in Mauritius** is limited due to the difficulty in obtaining long-term visas and lack of appropriately trained personnel. Valuable ministry could be done if expats and locals work together in effective partnerships. Missionaries sent from Mauritius are few due to isolation and lack of missions vision in local churches. Five Mauritians are serving overseas, four with **WEC**. Pray that Mauritian believers and congregations may become more active in supporting world evangelization.

8 **Specific unreached minorities.** Pray for:

a) **Muslims.** While the Muslim population has become more visible, the number of believers from a Muslim background remains quite small compared to their population size, and only a handful of Christians actively reach out to them. An appropriate and specific outreach is needed.

b) **Speakers of major Indian languages,** Bhojpuri, Hindi and Urdu, all representing large unreached groups in India. The JESUS film and literature distribution are used to reach them.

c) **The Chinese community.** Most Chinese have become Catholic, and a number of those are impacted by the charismatic renewal. Evangelical believers number over 700 in six congregations. Pray for the combined barriers of spiritual powers and the drive for wealth – keeping many from a full commitment to Christ – to be removed.

d) **The Chagos Islanders** were evacuated to Mauritius from the British Indian Ocean Territories 1,700 km to the northeast in 1966-70. For the last 10 years, they have been forced to go through courts of law to uphold their right of abode in their homeland, the Chagos Archipelago. Law courts repeatedly affirm their right to return; the government repeatedly quashes the rulings. They live in very difficult conditions with high rates of poverty and unemployment. Almost all are Catholic. Pray for their return and resettlement, and for continued opportunities for these 8,000 Chagossians to hear and respond to the gospel. *Mo Pense Toi* ("I Think and Care about You") is a Bible-based NGO seeking to bring the Chagossian community relief, comfort and hope through holistic application of the gospel.

9 Help ministries needing prayer:

a) *The Bible Society* has a vital role in distributing Scriptures in all the island territories of the Indian Ocean – Seychelles, Réunion, Comoros and others. Over 200,000 Scripture portions, NTs and Bibles are distributed each year. A modern Creole NT is being put together.

b) *Christian bookshops* grew from two in 1990 to eleven in 2009. Despite this, Christian literature is not getting into the hands of unbelievers. Pray for the provision and distribution of appropriate Christian literature.

c) *Scripture Union* distributes daily Bible-reading materials and coordinates various short-term outreaches and ministries on a national level.

d) *Christian radio broadcasts.* Catholics, Anglicans, Baptists and SdA are all allotted time on the government station. Private stations are not allowed to broadcast religious programmes. FEBA and **TWR** beam programmes in French and English on shortwave.

e) *The JESUS film* is now available in almost all spoken languages in Mauritius – French, Creole, English, Hindi, Bhojpuri, Marathi, Tamil, Telegu, Urdu, Hakka, Mandarin, Cantonese, Malagasy, as well as a children's version in Creole.

f) *Internet resources* are in great need, since Mauritius boasts the highest connectivity rate per inhabitant in Africa. Pray for developments in this area, particularly to address the paucity of online resources in Mauritian Creole.

Mayotte
Overseas Department of Mayotte
Africa

Geography

Area 373 sq km. One larger island, Grande Terre, and one smaller, Petite Terre.

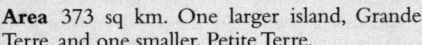

Population		Ann Gr	Density
2010	199,065	2.67%	534/sq km
2020	250,252	2.23%	671/sq km
2030	302,108	1.77%	810/sq km

The French government estimates the population as already exceeding 200,000, significantly higher than UN population figures used here.

Capital Mamoudzou 62,000. **Urbanites** 50.1%. **Pop under 15 yrs** 39%. **Life expectancy** 61.8 yrs.

Peoples

Maore 90%. Indigenes of Mayotte, speaking Shimaore (65%) or Shibushi (35%).
Other 10%. Includes a mix of Malagasy, Creole, Bantu immigrants (from Rwanda and Mozambique), French and Arabs. Illegal immigrants account for up to 30% of Mayotte's present population.
Literacy 32-58%. **Official languages** French; Shimaore (a Bantu language) is spoken by 80%, Shibushi (a Malagasy language) by 30%. **All languages** 4. **Languages with Scriptures** 2Bi 1NT 1por.

Economy

More prosperous than the rest of the region, through the military base and French aid, but this aid has dramatically reduced local initiative and entrepreneurship. Agriculture (in the form of subsistence farming) has declined greatly. Almost everything is imported from abroad, making the cost of living very high. Over-population and illegal immigration from other islands hinder progress.

Politics

Ceded by Madagascar in 1843 to France with the Comoros Islands, Mayotte voted in 1974 and 1976 to forgo independence as part of Comoros and remain with France. Comoros continues to assert sovereignty, but Mayotte voted to become a French Departmental Collectivity in 2000, and in 2009 to become a French overseas department – which qualifies it for EU funding – to the consternation of both Comoros and the UN.

M

Religion 🙏

Almost all Maores are Sunni Muslim, but mosque attendance is low. Almost all Christians are non-indigenous and from other Francophone countries.

Religions	Pop %	Population	Ann Gr
Muslim	97.86	194,805	2.7%
Christian	1.64	3,265	2.3%
Non-religious	0.50	995	3.5%

Christians Denoms		Pop %	Affiliates	Ann Gr
Protestant	3	0.11	<300	3.0%
Catholic	1	1.26	2,000	2.4%
Marginal	1	0.07	<200	-0.7%
Unaffiliated		0.20	<500	0.0%

Churches	MegaBloc	Congs	Members	Affiliates
Catholic Church	C	2	1,497	2,500
Protestant Churches	P	3	110	220
Jehovah's Witnesses	M	2	80	144
Total Christians[5]		**7**	**1,687**	**2,864**

TransBloc	Pop %	Population	Ann Gr
Evangelicals			
Evangelicals	0.1	236	4.0%
Renewalists			
Charismatics	0.2	365	5.2%

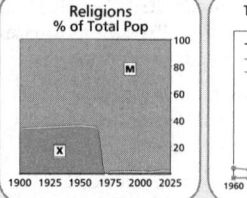

Religions % of Total Pop

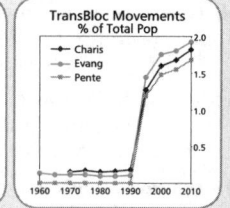

TransBloc Movements % of Total Pop

Challenges for Prayer

1 **Pray for the Muslim majority.** The indigenous people of Mayotte are 99.9% Muslim. Although there is religious freedom and direct, open-air evangelism is permitted (and practiced by the **AoG**), response has been very slow and most converts have returned to Islam. Maore folk Islam is heavily shaped by magic and cults practicing spirit possession. Despite this, a spirit of complacency rests upon the people, exacerbated greatly by the increased economic assistance from France and the EU. Pray for a spiritual breakthrough. The name Mayotte means "place of death"; pray that it may become a place of spiritual life in Christ.

2 **There is some very small responsiveness to the good news,** generally expressed as curiosity more than receptivity. Students and youth, impacted by French/Western social influences, demonstrate the greatest openness. Children who have demonstrated responsiveness to the gospel have been known to be punished for such interest or even taken to live elsewhere in the islands. Illegal immigrants from the Comoran island of Anjouan are also surprisingly responsive. Pray for a harvest among these groups.

3 **The three evangelical churches in Mayotte** need a greater degree of unity and cooperation, although there are signs of improvement in these areas. Pray for an approach to evangelism that is culturally appropriate yet effective, and pray for a great emphasis on discipling converts.

4 **Pray for more labourers to be called to Mayotte** for long-term ministry, especially Francophone Africans. Those already here do a great job in a difficult field. Pray for encouragement and unity and for an increase in their number and their fruitfulness. A mission team is in place, working among the Shimaore, and one is being prepared to work among Shibushi speakers.

5 **Support ministries for prayer:**

a) Bible translation. The NT is available in Shimaore and OT translation is in progress. There is no Scripture whatsoever in Shibushi. **AIM** workers also run a literacy programme to encourage reading of the Shimaore NT; pray for more students.

b) Radio. There are two main gospel broadcasts from local FM stations – an open door for witness to the whole territory.

c) Other media. The JESUS film and Good News Media materials have been dubbed into Shimaore. Pray for their strategic use.

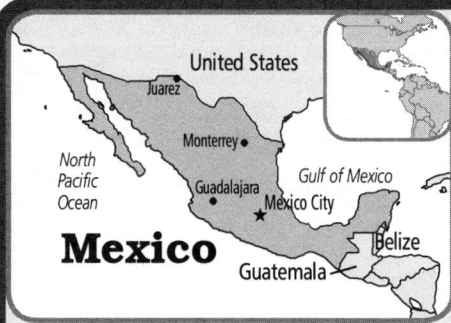

United States
Juarez
Monterrey
North
Pacific
Ocean
Guadalajara
Gulf of Mexico
Mexico City
Mexico
Belize
Guatemala

Mexico

United Mexican States

Latin America

Geography 🌍

Area 1,958,201 sq km. Latin America's third largest country. Wide range of topography and rainfall ranging from arid northern plateau, central volcanic plateau and the southern mountains and rain forests. Only 10% of the country is arable.

Population		Ann Gr	Density
2010	110,645,154	0.99%	57/sq km
2020	119,682,457	0.71%	61/sq km
2030	126,457,343	0.50%	65/sq km

Capital Mexico City 19,460,212. **Other major cities** Guadalajara 4.4 million; Monterrey 3.9mill; Puebla 2.3m; Tijuana 1.7m; León 1.6m; Toluca 1.6m; Juarez 1.4m; Torreón 1.2m; Tuxtla Gutiérrez 1m; San Luis Potosí 1m; Querétaro 1m; Mérida 1m. **Urbanites** 77.8%. **Pop under 15 yrs** 29%. **Life expectancy** 76 yrs.

Peoples 👪

The spectrum from Euro–American whites to Mestizo to Amerindian is impossible to clearly demarcate.
Mestizo 65.1%. Mexican(Amerindian)/Spanish mestizo.
Euro–American 13.6%. Largely of Spanish origin; with some other European stock.
Amerindian 19.3%.
 Detribalized Amerindian 9.9%.
 Amerindian-speaking 9.4%. Indigenous peoples officially recognized by the government. Major groupings: Nahuatl (Aztec, 39) 2.0%; Maya(26) 1.8%; Zapoteco(101) 1.0%; Otomi(111) 0.7%; Mixteco(60) 0.6%; Mixe(12) 0.2%; others(38) 0.9%.
Other 2.0%. Arabs 0.8%; US citizens 0.4%; Russian 0.3%; other Europeans and Asians.
Literacy 91.6%. Functional literacy is much lower. **Official language** Spanish; the world's largest Spanish-speaking nation. **All languages** 297. **Languages with Scriptures** 11Bi 116NT 160por 84w.i.p.

Economy 📈

Free market economy fuelled by oil, industry, manufactured goods, tourism and agriculture. NAFTA (North American Free Trade Agreement) and 12 other FTAs have opened foreign trade to unprecedented levels. Reforms have occurred, but more are needed to modernize the economy and free it from the grip of elite, archaic land-tenure systems and institutionalized corruption. Infrastructure needs further development. Income and wealth distribution is highly inequitable. More than 50% of the workforce labours in the informal economy. The poverty-stricken lower third of the population has yet to feel much benefit. The insidious evil of the drug trade refuses to go away and is a more urgent issue than ever; much of the northern border region is under the control of well-armed and organized cartels.
HDI Rank 53rd/182. **Public debt** 35.8% of GDP. **Income/person** $10,200 (22% of USA).

Politics 🗳

The sophisticated Aztec Empire in central Mexico was destroyed by the Spanish and smallpox in the early 16th Century. Independent from Spain in 1821. Much of its northern territories were lost to the US in the 19th Century. The 1910-17 Revolution resulted in a one-party federal democracy with power centralized in the president and the Institutional Revolutionary Party (PRI). PRI dominance was maintained by various means (some illicit) until 2000, with the election of an opposition candidate as president. Several strong parties now contest for leadership in the federal republic. There is a history of small guerrilla movements in the south that promote land and culture rights for the native Mexican population (Amerindians).

Religion 🙏

Secular state with freedom of conscience and practice of religion. The 130-year break between the Mexican government and the Vatican ended with official relations being restored and many restrictions ended in 1992. Constitutional changes in 1992 also granted fairer treatment for religious minorities, but persecution of non-Catholics persists in some areas.

Religions	Pop %	Population	Ann Gr
Christian	95.03	105,143,877	1.0%
Non-religious	3.60	3,983,226	1.6%
Ethnoreligionist	1.20	1,327,742	-3.4%
Buddhist	0.10	110,645	3.1%
Jewish	0.04	44,258	1.0%
Baha'i	0.03	33,194	1.0%
Muslim	<0.01	2,213	1.0%

A large proportion of the Amerindian population, though baptized as Catholic, still adhere to their pre-Conquest religions in practice.

M

Christians	Denoms	Pop %	Affiliates	Ann Gr
Protestant	290	7.39	8,172,000	3.9%
Independent	21	2.43	2,689,000	3.1%
Anglican	1	0.03	28,000	2.3%
Catholic	1	87.62	96,945,000	0.8%
Orthodox	3	0.03	38,000	-1.0%
Marginal	52	2.61	2,889,000	2.2%
Unaffiliated		1.22	1,348,000	2.9%
Doubly affiliated		-6.29	-6,965,000	0.0%

Churches	MegaBloc	Congs	Members	Affiliates
Catholic Church	C	5,829	51,293,783	96,945,250
Jehovah's Witnesses	M	12,900	730,000	1,735,000
National Presby Ch	P	4,800	624,000	1,450,000
Latter-day Saints (Mormon)	M	2,446	562,500	1,125,000
Assemblies of God	P	7,400	444,000	1,110,000
Union of Indep Evang Chs	I	1,500	450,000	970,000
Seventh-day Adventist	P	2,670	650,000	845,000
Methodist Church	P	400	55,000	330,000
Indep Evangelical Chs	P	1,409	155,000	310,000
Ch of God (Cleveland)	P	1,643	189,000	283,500
Apos Ch of Faith in JC	I	1,400	150,000	280,000
Ch of God in Repub of M	I	1,167	140,000	280,000
National Baptist Conv	P	1,700	136,000	272,000
Indep Pente Movement	I	3,833	115,000	209,300
Revival Churches	I	358	71,500	143,000
National Chr Ch of AoG	I	1,556	70,000	140,000

Centres of Faith,Hope&Love	I	350	65,000	130,000
Spiritual Chr Evang Ch	P	362	62,500	106,250
Other denominations[350]		35,861	2,183,061	4,096,827
Doubly affiliated				-6,965,000

Total Christians[368]		87,584	58,146,344	103,796,127

TransBloc	Pop %	Population	Ann Gr
Evangelicals			
Evangelicals	8.3	9,166,346	3.8%
Renewalists			
Charismatics	11.9	13,157,806	4.1%
Pentecostals	5.1	5,637,825	4.7%

Missionaries from Mexico

P,I,A 1,139 (794 long-term) in 52 agencies: in Mexico 395, North America 428, Europe 127, Middle East 59.

Annual Growth Rates

TransBloc Movements % of Total Pop

Answers to Prayer

1 **There is a steady growth of evangelicals,** who were only 2.1% (800,000) in 1960, but are now over 8% and numbering over nine million. If anything, such growth appears to be accelerating, not slowing.

2 **Increasing freedom for ministry continues,** a contrast from the oppressive Catholic monopoly of decades past. Even the government – municipal, state and national levels – is more open to evangelical work as a counter to the seemingly unsolvable problems of gangs, drug trafficking, kidnappings and violence.

3 **The missions movement is beginning to blossom** and play a greater role globally. The numbers of missionaries sent out from Mexico, mission agencies, training institutions and mobilizing events have mushroomed in recent years.

Challenges for Prayer

1 **Mexico is a growing nation** that is still discovering its own identity. Meso–American origins, Hispanic history and a dynamic but turbulent relationship with its neighbours all shape Mexico profoundly. This search often manifests itself through religious identity (both animist and Catholic) and the inevitable accompanying anti-Protestant sentiment. Pray that Mexicans, both indigenous and mestizo, might find their ultimate identity and destiny in the love of Christ and the purposes of God.

2 **Many socio-economic challenges face Mexico.** The state recognizes the difficulty of traditional solutions and increasingly invites Christians and churches to show initiative and partnership in meeting the many human needs. Pray for:

a) *The poor,* both the impoverished rural poor and the exploited slum-dwellers. While the president's top-priority goal is to reduce poverty, the gap between rich and poor in Mexico is the widest of all OECD nations. Fully 60% of Mexico's population struggle with poverty.

b) *The marginalized native Amerindians.* They officially number 9.4% of the population, but many more are partly or mostly Amerindian without such official status. They tend to face greater poverty, lack education and live in areas with the most upheaval. Radical political expression has also contributed to unrest. There is significant response to as well as opposition to evangelical ministry in those regions.

c) *Corruption in politics and the police.* The advent of multiparty politics unseated the increasingly corrupt PRI, but the problem remains in all levels of government. Corruption in government has seen millions embezzled, and corruption in the police forces allows for greater growth in organized crime.

d) *The massive drug trade* and gang violence that accompanies it. Drug trafficking is big business in Mexico – thanks to both the USA's insatiable habit and Mexico's own growing troubles. Sadly, this structure of sin brings huge amounts of money into Mexico's economy, so the desire to halt it is less than the cost and effort to do so.

   i The 500,000-plus addicts, whose number has grown rapidly due to increasing availability of cheap drugs. Mexico is poorly positioned to cope with the number of addicts in terms of prevention, treatment and ministry to those afflicted.

   ii The wealthy, powerful cartels that control it are ruthless. Most of their violence is directed toward each other, but police, armed forces, journalists and helpless citizens also die at their hands. Pray for a way to reach out to the cartel leaders and members.

   iii The government and police face great difficulties in combating the drug trade and those who run it. Informers and corruption undermine the effort, and fear of the heavily armed gangs prevents decisive action. Pray for courage and wisdom in dealing with these great challenges.

3 **The relationship with the USA** shapes Mexico inexorably. Despite resentment on both sides, the reality is that the countries need each other. Pray for:

a) *Political–economic cooperation.* The economies of both nations could benefit from truly fair trade and movement of goods and services. Pray for equitable relations and for justice to prevail in all dealings between the nations.

b) *Collaborative law enforcement* is necessary to thwart the drug cartels as well as human trafficking. There is no love lost, but only cooperation and trust will overcome the wickedness that seeks to prosper on both sides of the border.

c) *Immigration and labour issues.* Migrant Mexican labour in California and other US border states has long been a feature of national life. They number nearly 13 million and are overwhelmingly male and predominantly young. There are many implications to their presence:

   i Those trying to enter the USA number more than one million each year, hundreds of them dying in the attempt. They are also a huge drain on US coffers via the costs of border protection.

   ii Those left behind. Millions in Mexico depend on earnings made by relatives who successfully find work in the USA. Downturns in the US economy impact Mexico deeply. Some towns in Mexico have almost no able-bodied men, as all have left for America.

   iii Those already in the USA. Many work demanding jobs for long hours and little pay. Some US states' economies would collapse without the informal economy driven by Mexican migrants. Many Mexicans also find Jesus while away from home, since there are many opportunities for them to hear the gospel. Pray for ministry in Spanish by **CAMI**, Avant and many denominational workers in these areas.

4 **For 300 years the Catholic Church dominated Mexico.** Recent times have seen it stripped of much of its privilege and power, while retaining a high degree of cultural influence. Catholicism in Mexico is very diverse in expression, from liberation theologians to charismatics to conservatives to syncretistic "popular Catholicism". There is encouraging growth in Christ-centred renewal within the Catholic Church, but frequently the figureheads of such movements leave to start their own independent megachurches. The Alpha course is having a positive impact within Catholicism. Most Mexicans are culturally Catholic but not practising; only 10% are regular churchgoers. Many others blend elements of Amerindian spiritism, including gods and goddesses, into folk Catholicism. Pray for renewal to spread and

M

deepen by the Holy Spirit's power, and for the polluting influences of ancient gods and the spirit-world to be broken among those with Christo-pagan beliefs and practices.

5 **Evangelicals have grown,** even amid some opposition in certain areas. Growth is in both international denominations and in vigorous newer indigenous movements. Pray that the momentum might be maintained. The highest concentrations of evangelicals are in large cities, in northern states bordering the USA and in southern states where there is a higher proportion of Amerindian peoples. Returnees from the USA are influential in bringing evangelical Christianity back with them. Many Mexicans seek a spirituality beyond what they see as empty religious traditions; both evangelicals and charismatic Catholics benefit from this searching. Pray for this growth to be sustained in both numbers and spiritual depth.

6 **The specific challenges for evangelicals** are substantial, but indicate a wealth of opportunity more than an overwhelming threat.

a) *Unity.* The Evangelical Fraternity of Mexico (CONEMEX) works to strengthen unity, deal with the government and sponsor important events. A Pentecostal fellowship also exists to bring together the millions of Pentecostals. There needs to be a more effective strategic partnership among mission agencies. Large-scale events such as the March for Jesus/March of Glory as well as nationwide prayer movements are drawing believers together, but much more could be done.

b) *Discipleship and biblical commitment* are great needs, since many families are split by brokenness or geography. Many are first generation believers and have only a very superficial understanding of their faith. Commitment needs to extend to giving – few pastors and missionaries are adequately supported and therefore must work bivocationally to survive. This especially affects poorer churches in rural areas and urban slums.

c) *Leadership training* is the key to the future health of the Church. There are well over 100 Protestant Bible schools and seminaries training thousands of future leaders at all levels, from indigenous primary-level language to degree-awarding schools, as well as numerous TEE programmes. Pray that spiritual depth, evangelistic vision and sound teaching may be imparted to the students. Doctrinal shallowness, error and moral and personal relationship breakdowns impair the growth of the Church. Pray also for the provision of godly pastors for poor rural and urban slum congregations; most prospective pastors seek a more "successful" placement.

d) *Development of a missions vision.* Sending of missionaries by the Mexican Church has developed rapidly, but awareness of "people group thinking" needs to grow in the churches. An increasing number of congregations send and support missionaries. COMIMEX provides a nationwide umbrella linking most agencies, national and international, and involved denominations. COMIMEX operates through 13 departments (focusing on issues such as mobilization, prayer and member care) and three networks (churches, sending structures and training institutions). Significant international agencies have been birthed in Mexico, such as PMI, with its involvement in the Muslim world. There may be as many as 1,200 Mexican evangelical missionaries with over 50 agencies. The majority of them serve abroad, with increasing numbers in the 10/40 Window.

e) *The evangelical approach to money and finance* needs wisdom, maturity and balance. Many Protestants, and Mexicans in general, have only recently begun to emerge from poverty. The traditional humble material possessions of Mexican evangelicals now combine with recent economic growth, the influence of US-style prosperity gospel and the very public salvation of a number of high profile and successful Mexican businessmen and media figures. Pray for a release of finances into Kingdom work; pray also for the right biblical perspective on how to handle issues of money.

7 **Persecution of evangelicals** occurs in certain parts of Mexico. In general, acceptance of Protestants is higher in recent years as their profile increases. But in the southern states, particularly Chiapas, Oaxaca and Guerrero, believers face prejudice, harassment, evictions and church and property damage. This mostly occurs due to believers' refusal to participate in community religious events that involve traditional Christo-pagan practices. Pray that the believers may demonstrate the meekness and love of their Saviour when maltreated. Pray also for full implementation of religious freedom at both national and local levels.

8 **Ministry to young people** is vital. Around one-third of Mexicans are aged 15 or younger. Due to its focus on youth ministry, the evangelical faith has made great inroads among young people in Mexico. This staggering challenge is being only partially met.

a) University students number over 2.5 million in nearly 10,000 campus locations. Outreach is yielding exciting results. Pray for the wide-ranging ministries of **CCCI** (on campuses and among churches). **IFES**-linked student movement *Compañerismo Estudiantil A C* (Compa) has 170 groups in 50 universities with 1,500 students served by seven full-time and 11 part-time staff and 16 volunteers. A number of Mexican-originated movements are also rapidly growing.

b) Young people. Although evangelical churches appeal to the younger generation, too few churches target them; most programmes use the approaches of previous generations. Pray for creative and cutting-edge ministry to today's youth.

c) Street children, especially in Mexico City. There may be up to 800,000 homeless or street children. They sleep in whatever shelter they can find and desperately need love and help.

d) Child labourers. As many as 11 million Mexicans under the age of 15 work. The income may be crucial to their poverty-stricken families, but many of these children drop out of school in order to work.

9 **Foreign missionaries' roles** have changed significantly. Their presence is still needed in facilitating Bible translations, mobilizing Mexicans for mission, children and youth work, theological education and leadership development. The majority are US citizens, so they need sensitivity and tact in their cultural adaptation in order to overcome perceptions arising from their origin and wealth. Pray that their ministries may assist the Church to be what God desires.

10 **Sections of the population and peoples** with few committed Christians:

a) The Rosary Belt, a region in central Mexico consisting of Zacatecas, Jalisco, Aguascalientes, Guanajuato, Colima, Michoacán and Querétaro. This region is often called the 10/40 Window of the Americas by Latino evangelicals. Spanish colonial and religious influence is very strong here. None of these states numbers over 2% evangelical, and Querétaro is only 0.25% evangelical.

b) Indian peoples are largely Catholic in name but pagan in practice. Most of the old pantheon of gods and spirits have Catholic names; others retain their original identities. According to research by COMIMEX, of 298 people groups, 15 are without a viable Christian witness, 98 have a church that still needs help from the outside to finish preaching the gospel in their group and a further five are inadequately researched. The complex syncretism, traditional isolation and linguistic diversity make these groups difficult to effectively evangelize. Vital discipleship and church planting ministries must be expanded to build on the impressive Scripture translation programme of SIL. Some of the least evangelized include peoples from the Náhuatl (3), Zapoteco (4), Mixteco (2), Popoloca, Chatino, Huichole and Mixe groups of peoples.

c) The wealthy elite. There is a strong atheist-agnostic current among them reinforced by an education system designed to dilute the influence of the Church. The large gap in income, lifestyle and even physical security between these elite and the rest of society means that generally they remain aloof from Christian growth. High-profile evangelical ministries have attracted some; pray for others to also show interest in spiritual things.

11 **Mexico City** is still a major challenge, as the cultural, financial and political powerhouse of the nation. The metropolitan area is one of the world's largest urban agglomerations, but Mexico City proper is losing residents to the suburban areas and other regions. It has one of the higher percentages of Protestants (over 7%), but church participation is generally lower in this city where secular influences are strong. Pray for:

a) The hundreds of neighbourhoods without an evangelical congregation; especially needy are the upper-class areas.

b) The slum-dwellers. About 80% of the millions in the capital are poor, living in desperate economic conditions, often amid great squalor. Christian ministry to them is fraught with difficulty and challenge. Few are prepared to commit themselves to it.

c) The million Indians representing nearly every language of Mexico. Very little is being done to cater for their spiritual needs.

d) Marginal sects are rapidly growing through aggressive proselytism. The Mormons add over 1,000 members a month just from Mexico City alone and are already the second-largest Mormon population in the world, after the USA.

12 **Bible translation and distribution.** Despite centuries of social and cultural pressure, use of indigenous languages is vigorous and varied. The many dialects illustrate translation and language needs beyond the ordinary. Pray for:

a) Translation. Since 1936, Bible translation work has been remarkable, with programmes among 190 languages and NTs completed in 120. Currently SIL is involved in 84 translation projects. Research shows that 11 languages still have a definite need for a full translation, and a further 20 exist where a more limited project would meet the need. Pray for the achievement of the current NT and Bible translation goals by the Mexican Bible Society, New Tribes, SIL and others. There are many requests for help with NT revisions and adaptations. Pray for UNTI (the Union of Indigenous Bible Translators) as they seek to find and support local, trained personnel to help with these needs. A great need is for strong partnerships among those who promote Scripture use and literacy. Pray for translation agencies to have continued good relations with federal and state government agencies.

b) Printing and distribution. The Bible Society plays an important role in producing and distributing Spanish and indigenous Scriptures in Mexico and the whole region, as does the Bible League. Pray that the dissemination and reading of the Scriptures may transform individuals, congregations and the nation.

13 **Christian media** is a vital and growing cluster of ministries with great potential. Pray for these:

a) Christian literature, a ministry growing in size and influence as the evangelical population grows. Pray for more Mexican evangelical writers and publishers. Milamex is a key ministry that publishes several evangelical periodicals such as the seminal Prisma magazine. Pray for a literate, well-taught and well-equipped Church to be the result.

b) Christian broadcasting was long denied to evangelicals in Mexico. As a result, hundreds of hours/week are beamed into the country from the USA, Guatemala and elsewhere. Doors are only now opening for Christian radio and TV from within the country. Much more could be done if resources – people, skills and finances – were available. Pray for a release of such and for the Holy Spirit to gift key believers for Kingdom media impact.

c) The JESUS film has been extensively used as a film and on TV. The film is in use in 66 Mexican languages and is being prepared in a further three. Pray for progress in the translation and production in the remaining languages of the smaller, isolated people groups with little or no access to Scripture in their mother tongue.

d) Cassette recordings. GRN has messages available in 390 languages and dialects. It is a vital tool in the complex linguistic situation, where dialects and sub-dialects do not require or cannot justify their own Bible translation. Pray for recordists, for new recordings and wide distribution, and for eternal fruit. Audio Scripture Ministries has recorded NTs in 37 languages, most in Oaxaca.

Micronesia

Pacific

The former US-administered UN Trust Territory is retained here as a single entity because of the small populations and commonalities among the four constituent States.

Geography

Area 1,950 sq km. The 2,000 islands of the Caroline, Marshall and Mariana archipelagos lie in 7 million sq km of the North Pacific. Only 100 are inhabited.

Politics

For centuries, a strategic global pawn. Ruled by Spain 1710-1897, Germany 1897-1914, and Japan 1914-1945 before the USA took over the administration as a UN Trust Territory. Four separate republics in free association with the USA have emerged since 1978.

Religion

During Spanish rule, all islanders were forcibly Catholicized, but the underlying pre-Christian customs and animistic religion remain influential. In each republic there is, theoretically, freedom of religion, but some islands show hostility to variant newer denominations and religions.

Federated States of Micronesia

Geography

Area 702 sq km. Over 600 coralline islands in four main groups: Chuuk, Pohnpei, Yap and Kosrae.

Population		Ann Gr	Density
2010	111,101	0.31%	158/sq km
2020	117,533	0.65%	167/sq km
2030	125,276	0.56%	178/sq km

Capital Palikir 6,227 (UN). **Urbanites** 22.7%. **Pop under 15 yrs** 37%. **Life expectancy** 68.4 yrs.

Peoples

Micronesian 91.7%. Trukese 28.6%; Ponapean 19.2%; Chamorro 10.5%; Kosraean 7.7%; Yapese 6.4%; Mortlockese 4.5%; Ulithian 2.4%; Carolinian 2.2%; Pingilapese 1.6%; Woleaian 1.3%.

Other 8.3%. US citizens 4.0%; English-speaking Micronesians 1.9%; Filipinos 0.9%.

Literacy 92.4%. **Official language** English. **All languages** 19. **Languages with Scriptures** 4Bi 5NT 2por 4w.i.p.

Economy

Predominantly subsistence farming and fishing. Over 90% of government income is from US aid.
Public debt 32.8% of GDP. **Income/person** $2,090 (6% of USA).

Politics

A federal republic with four constituent states. Independence in 1991, but in free association with the USA, the latter administering defence and foreign policy.

Religion

Separation of church and state, with religious freedom. Yap is predominantly Catholic; Pohnpei, Chuuk and Kosrae predominantly Protestant.

Religions	Pop %	Population	Ann Gr
Christian	96.65	107,379	0.5%
Ethnoreligionist	1.40	1,555	-8.8%
Non-religious	0.85	944	1.5%
Chinese	0.60	667	-1.3%
Baha'i	0.50	556	0.3%

Christians Denoms		Pop %	Affiliates	Ann Gr
Protestant	11	49.00	54,000	0.1%
Independent	5	0.68	1,000	4.6%
Catholic	1	52.56	58,000	0.2%
Marginal	2	4.09	5,000	2.1%
Doubly affiliated	1	-9.68	-11,000	0.0%

M

Churches	MegaBloc	Congs	Members	Affiliates
Catholic Church	C	31	33,953	58,400
Liebenzell Church	P	162	9,700	19,400
United Ch of Pohnpei	P	20	6,000	13,200
Protestant Ch of Chuuk	P	20	6,050	12,100
Latter-day Saints	M	19	2,341	3,910
United Ch of Kosrae	P	8	1,900	3,800
Seventh-day Adventist	P	7	1,460	1,750
Assemblies of God	P	14	985	1,300
United Pentecostal Ch	P	8	525	1,050
Other denominations[10]		35	1,374	3,225
Doubly affiliated				-10,750
Total Christians[20]		**324**	**64,288**	**107,385**

TransBloc	Pop %	Population	Ann Gr
Evangelicals			
Evangelicals	24.3	27,006	0.9%
Renewalists			
Charismatics	4.2	4,656	3.8%
Pentecostals	2.8	3,100	3.2%

Religions % of Total Pop

MegaBlocs % of Christian Pop

3.8 0.6
46.1
49.4

Challenges for Prayer

1 **Biblical Christianity faces challenges on three fronts.** On one front are the traditional cultural elements such as the use of magic and of sakau, the herbal drink used as a communal narcotic. Another front is the pull of Western consumerism encouraged by US aid and the temptation to migrate to the USA. Finally, Mormon missionaries are highly active in Micronesia. All three require a response of wisdom and faith. Pray for a revelation of the power and love of Jesus to the peoples of FSM.

2 **A large proportion of the population is Protestant,** the result of a century of ministry by US Congregationals and the German Liebenzell Mission, but nominalism and cronyism in leadership are widespread. Pray for revival among these long-standing groups. Pray also for the newer, fast-growing Pentecostal groups – negotiating the tension between traditional Micronesian culture and biblical practice is not straightforward.

3 **Pray for Bible translation and distribution.** The whole Bible exists only in Chuuk and Pohnpein; the others have only the NT at best. This, combined with a non-literary culture, holds back the spiritual development of the largely Christian population and opens them to error and the predation of cults. Pray for the development of reading programmes and oral resources based on Scripture that would dynamically impact the population.

4 **Ministry from Micronesia.** There are two Bible colleges, the Pacific International University and a small **AoG**-run school. The Pacific Missionary Aviation/Pacific Mission Fellowship includes mission aviation, Sea Haven (a medical ship operating exclusively in Micronesia), an orphanage, an FM radio station and several congregations. Pray that the impact of these ministries will continue to grow.

Marshall Islands

Republic of the Marshall Islands

Geography

Area 181 sq km. There are 34 atolls with 1,156 islands, spread over nearly 2 million sq km of Pacific.

Population		Ann Gr	Density
2010	63,398	2.25%	350/sq km
2020	74,877	1.48%	414/sq km
2030	82,630	0.89%	457/sq km

High density on Majuro. Many islands are sparsely inhabited.
Capital Majuro 30,400. **Urbanites** 71.8%. **Pop under 15 yrs** 42%. **Life expectancy** 70.3 yrs.

Peoples

Micronesian 89.2%. Marshallese (two dialects).
Other 10.8%. Pacific Islanders 5.8; USA 5%.
Literacy 92%. **Official languages** Marshallese

and English. **All languages** 2. **Languages with Scriptures** 2Bi.

Economy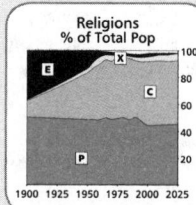

US aid is 61.3% of the Marshall Islands' annual budget, which undermines the potential for agriculture, fisheries and tourism. Urbanization has destroyed traditional subsistence farming and forced almost all food to be imported. High unemployment.
Public debt 10% of GDP. **Income/person** $3,070 (7% of USA).

Politics

An independent republic since 1986, in free association with the USA.

Religion

Freedom of religion; different denominations run an extensive schooling system.

Religions	Pop %	Population	Ann Gr
Christian	97.10	61,559	2.2%
Baha'i	1.90	1,205	3.4%
Non-religious	0.70	444	4.8%
Ethnoreligionist	0.30	190	-3.5%

Christians Denoms		Pop %	Affiliates	Ann Gr
Protestant	6	91.50	58,000	1.4%
Independent	7	3.92	2,000	3.1%

Catholic	1	6.94	4,000	0.7%
Marginal	2	7.65	5,000	1.5%
Doubly affiliated		*-12.92*	*-8,000*	*0.0%*

Churches	MegaBloc	Congs	Members	Affiliates
United Ch of Christ	P	92	8,800	30,800
Assemblies of God	P	72	11,300	22,600
Catholic Church	C	5	2,558	4,400
Latter-day Saints (Mormon)	M	13	2,605	4,350
United Pentecostal Ch	P	83	2,071	2,900
Ref Congregational Ch	I	5	575	1,150
Other denominations[10]		27	1,577	3,545
Doubly affiliated				*-8,190*
Total Christians[16]		**297**	**29,486**	**61,555**

TransBloc	Pop %	Population	Ann Gr
Evangelicals			
Evangelicals	44.5	28,212	3.0%
Renewalists			
Charismatics	37.3	23,645	2.1%
Pentecostals	34.7	22,000	2.0%

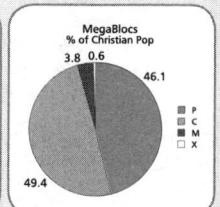

Challenges for Prayer

1 **The traumatic history** of occupation, exploitation and war, as well as the impact of US nuclear bomb testing, have all had a devastating effect on the Marshallese. Traditional values of land, family and community – the roots of society – are being undermined. Over-urbanization, unemployment, substance abuse, sexual immorality and a high birth rate threaten the Marshallese way of life. Many inhabitants suffer the effects of nuclear radiation, including genetic disorders and high rates of cancer. Pray for leaders who will govern wisely and bravely, for economic dependency to be broken, and for the positive aspects of Marshallese traditional culture to be restored and upheld.

2 **The great majority of Marshallese are Protestant** and nearly half are evangelical. The churches have great influence at every level in society, but often fail to create mature disciples. The United Church of Christ, which was the de facto state Church, is losing in numbers and spirituality. The Assemblies of God have grown rapidly and generated several splinter denominations in the process.

3 **The need for godly leadership** in the churches is great. Theological training is limited to a very small United Church college and the **AoG**-run Calvary Bible Institute. Pray for the effectiveness of these institutions in equipping God's people, as groups such as Mormons, Jehovah's Witnesses, Baha'is and others actively proselytize.

Northern Marianas

Commonwealth of the Northern Mariana Islands

Geography

Area 477 sq km. A chain of 14 volcanic and coralline islands 650 km north of Guam. The southernmost islands, Saipan, Tinian and Rota, are the largest and most important economically.

Population		Ann Gr	Density
2010	88,409	1.97%	185/sq km
2020	103,539	1.54%	217/sq km
2030	118,983	1.36%	249/sq km

There are over 20,000 legal migrant workers and their families in the country at any one time. There are also many illegals.
Capital Saipan 80,700. **Urbanites** 91.3%. **Pop under 15 yrs** 26%. **Life expectancy** 71.4 yrs.

Peoples

Pacific Islanders 45.8%. Chamorro 27.2%; Carolinian 6.8%; Tanapag 5.6%; Palauan 4.0%. The Chamorro are also indigenous to nearby Guam.
Asians 49.2%. Mostly on contract, few long-term, many illegal immigrants. Filipino 30.8%; Chinese 8.5%; Korean 7.5%; Japanese 2.7%.
Other 4.0%. US Americans.
Literacy 100% (indigenous). **Official language** English. Chamorro widely spoken, also some Carolinian. **All languages** 7. **Indigenous languages** 4. **Languages with Scriptures** 1Bi 1por 1w.i.p.

Economy

Tourism, especially from Japan, and garment manufacturing (using migrant labourers) are the main industries, both subject to the whims of markets and economic changes. Substantial US aid is another main source of national income. More prosperous than the other three Micronesian States.

Income/person $13,350 (29% of USA) – including migrant labour.

Politics

A self-governing Commonwealth Territory of the USA since 1977. The population were granted US citizenship in 1990.

Religion

Freedom of religion.

Religions	Pop %	Population	Ann Gr
Christian	85.20	75,324	1.7%
Chinese	5.80	5,128	0.9%
Buddhist	5.50	4,862	4.8%
Non-religious	3.00	2,652	5.8%
Baha'i	0.50	442	3.7%

Christians Denoms		Pop %	Affiliates	Ann Gr
Protestant	12	15.28	14,000	2.7%
Independent	2	2.85	3,000	4.4%
Catholic	1	57.69	51,000	-0.4%
Marginal	2	1.50	1,000	0.0%
Unaffiliated		7.90	7,000	28.5%

Churches	MegaBloc	Congs	Members	Affiliates
Catholic Church	C	9	28,333	51,000
Korean Churches	P	16	2,096	3,500
Filipino Baptist Chs	P	4	1,916	3,200
United Ch of Christ	P	12	1,250	2,250
Iglesia ni Kristo	I	2	1,188	1,900
Palau Evangelical Ch	P	2	465	930
General Baptist Church	P	7	405	900
Assemblies of God	P	3	386	850
Latter-day Saints (Mormon)	M	1	449	750
Other denominations[8]		20	1,485	3,078
Total Christians[17]		**76**	**37,973**	**68,358**

TransBloc	Pop %	Population	Ann Gr
Evangelicals			
Evangelicals	12.7	11,260	3.2%
Renewalists			
Charismatics	9.3	8,216	5.4%
Pentecostals	2.0	1,780	1.7%

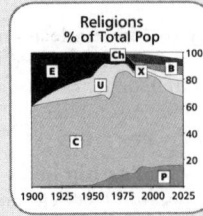

Religions % of Total Pop

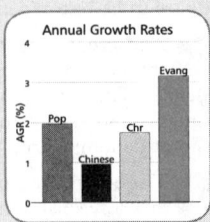

Annual Growth Rates

M

Challenges for Prayer

1 **The indigenous Chamorro majority** were baptized as Catholics, but their deeper beliefs and worldview betray an underlying animist outlook. Pray that the light of the gospel may shine on this people. Although Catholicism's influence is waning, evangelical outreach is only recent. Pray for the ministry of the numerous Bible-believing churches from various denominations and from the **YWAM** base in Saipan.

2 **The Asian population is diverse.** There are over 20 Asian congregations – Korean, Filipino and Chinese; most are growing and have vigorous outreach to their compatriots. Opportunity abounds to reach especially the Japanese and Chinese (both from Mainland China and Taiwan); several thousand migrant Chinese factory workers have been won to Christ over the years. Many Japanese also come to the island as tourists and to visit the Shinto shrines.

3 **Existence can be simultaneously precarious and dull** because of the fickle garment and tourist industries, heavy dependence on US aid and geographical isolation. This drives some into the arms of faith, but others into immorality. Prostitution is common and most youth are sexually active. Pray for renewal that would give meaning and focus to the young and old alike.

4 **Christian media ministries** for prayer:

a) Bible translation. Pray for the completion of the Chamorro NT and for translation to commence in the two Carolinian languages. Little or no progress has been made recently.

b) Radio. **FEBC** has two broadcast services from Saipan – internationally on short-wave to Russia, Central Asia, China and South East Asia (98 hrs/wk) and a local service to the islands in five languages. Pray for deep and lasting impact. Pray for spiritual and physical protection of both workers and valuable facilities; Saipan is in an area prone to typhoons.

Palau

Republic of Palau

Geography

Area 488 sq km. Sixteen inhabited volcanic and coralline islands.

Population		Ann Gr	Density
2010	20,531	0.40%	42/sq km
2020	22,197	1.07%	45/sq km
2030	24,505	0.91%	50/sq km

Capital Ngerulmud 570. **Urbanites** 82.7%. **Pop under 15 yrs** 21%. **Life expectancy** 70 yrs.

Peoples

Micronesian 81.4%. Three languages: Palauan 76.0%; Sonsorol 5.4%.
Other 18.5%. Filipino 15.6%; Chinese 1.5%; US citizens 1.0%.
Literacy 99%. **Official language** Palauan; English used widely. **All languages** 4. **Languages with Scriptures** 1Bi 1NT 1por 1w.i.p.

Economy

Subsistence agriculture, fishing and some tourism. The government is the main employer and relies heavily on US aid.
Public Debt 13.9% of GDP. **Income/person** $8,093 (18% of USA).

Politics

The Compact of Free Association with the USA, signed in 1982, was implemented only after repeated and violently contested referenda failed to ratify the new constitution.

Religion

Religions	Pop %	Population	Ann Gr
Christian	95.90	19,701	0.4%
Non-religious	2.40	493	1.7%
Chinese	1.05	216	-0.5%
Baha'i	0.65	134	-1.1%

Christians Denoms		Pop %	Affiliates	Ann Gr
Protestant	3	25.56	5,000	0.5%
Independent	6	3.45	1,000	5.4%
Catholic	1	42.45	9,000	0.5%
Marginal	3	11.24	2,000	0.3%
Unaffiliated		13.2	3,000	0.0%

Churches	MegaBloc	Congs	Members	Affiliates
Catholic Church	C	17	3,488	8,720
Koror Evangelical Ch	P	24	1,925	3,850
Modekngei	M	0	640	1,600
Seventh-day Adventist	P	0	820	1,050
Latter-day Saints (Mormon)	M	1	138	460
Assemblies of God	P	2	185	350
Jehovah's Witnesses	M	1	100	250
Other denominations[6]		9	365	709
Total Christians[13]		**54**	**7,661**	**16,989**

M

TransBloc	Pop %	Population	Ann Gr
Evangelicals			
Evangelicals	23.9	4,905	1.4%
Renewalists			
Charismatics	5.8	1,198	4.7%
Pentecostals	1.7	350	2.1%

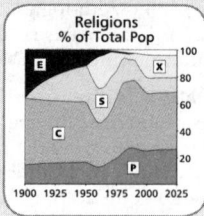

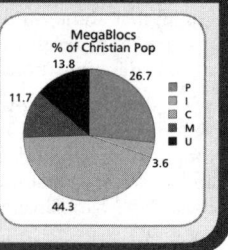

Challenges for Prayer

1 **Christianity is generally professed,** but nominalism is widespread, the most ardent Catholics being the Filipinos. Many older people are followers of the *Modekngei* movement, a religion unique to Palau that is a mixture of Christianity and magic; materialism and pluralism are the greater threats to the younger generation. Pray for the revival of the Koror Evangelical Church – the fruit of the work of the Liebenzell Mission. The **AoG** have a small but growing work.

2 **Hindrances to the gospel** need to be removed. Closed cultures and strong traditionalism make many villages and outlying islands unwilling for change. The debilitating effects of US aid, material comforts and enormous consumption of beer make discipleship and commitment rare. Only the NT is available in Palauan (and nothing in Sonorol or Tobian), so theological depth is lacking. Outreach to smaller unevangelized island communities is complicated by their geographic isolation.

3 **Missionary vision** for less-evangelized Micronesian islands and beyond is being stimulated by the **YWAM** base in Palau. **YWAM** is also having an impact on the campus of the only college in Palau.

4 **Palau is curiously being used** as a new place of settlement for Uyghur ex-detainees of Guantanamo and for Burmese political refugees. May these and other immigrants find not only a new home but a new life in Christ as well.

M

Moldova

Moldova
Republic of Moldova
Europe

Geography 🌐

Area 33,700 sq km. Landlocked republic between the Ukraine and Romania.

Population		Ann Gr	Density
2010	3,575,574	–1.00%	106/sq km
2020	3,378,426	–0.49%	100/sq km
2030	3,182,495	–0.67%	94/sq km

Capital Chisinau 656,000. **Urbanites** 41.2%. **Pop under 15 yrs** 17%. **Life expectancy** 68.3 yrs.

Peoples 👪

European 93.4%. Widespread intermarriage and mixing.
  Latin 76.0%. Moldavian 73.8%; Romanian 2.2%.
  Slavic 17.0%. Ukrainian 8.5%; Russian 6.0%; Bulgarian 1.9%.
  Other 0.3%. German, Armenian, other European.
Turkic 4.0%. Gagauz 3.4%.
All other 2.6%. Romani, Jews, others.
Literacy 99.1%. **Official language** Moldovan Romanian. **All languages** 13. **Indigenous languages** 5. **Languages with Scriptures** 2Bi 2NT 2por 1w.i.p.

Economy 🗺️

Rich agricultural land with unfulfilled potential. Europe's poorest nation due to persistent and unresolved political problems, lack of industry and trade, economic dependence on Russia and lingering effects of communism. **HDI Rank** 117th/182. **Public debt** 22.3% of GDP. **Income/person** $1,693 (4% of USA).

Politics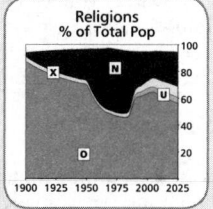

Most of Moldova's political grief is descended from the USSR's policy of hacking up and reassigning regions across ethnic and cultural lines. The largely autonomous Transnistria region of Moldova has, with Russian backing, effectively seceded from the rest of Moldova and is a haven for organized crime and smuggling. The Gagauz region in the southwest operates with autonomy. The Communist party won the 2009 elections, but these were contested as fraudulent, and a subsequent election saw an opposition coalition take power.

Religion

The Orthodox Church regained strong political influence and uses it against those it regards as threats – unregistered Protestants, Muslims and rival Orthodox groups. Schism in the Orthodox Church between Russian and Romanian patriarchates further divides the country's religious population. Some degree of religious freedom exists, since the government stalls on further legislation of freedom.

Religions	Pop %	Population	Ann Gr
Christian	73.36	2,623,041	-1.5%
Non-religious	21.56	770,894	0.8%
Muslim	4.95	176,991	-0.4%
Jewish	0.13	4,648	-20.9%

Christians	Denoms	Pop %	Affiliates	Ann Gr
Protestant	13	3.86	138,000	2.4%
Independent	20	0.53	19,000	14.5%
Catholic	2	2.04	73,000	-0.3%
Orthodox	9	61.74	2,208,000	-2.0%
Marginal	2	1.21	43,000	1.0%
Unaffiliated		3.98	142,000	1.6%

Churches	MegaBloc	Congs	Members	Affiliates
Moldovan Orthodox Ch	O	860	682,517	976,000
Russian Orthodox	O	270	447,552	640,000
Metro Ch of Bessarabia	O	55	358,741	513,000
Catholic Church	C	35	43,000	73,000
Bulgarian Orthodox	O	17	38,000	58,000
Baptist Union	P	500	23,000	57,000
Jehovah's Witnesses	M	270	19,000	43,000
Seventh-day Adventist	P	170	13,000	32,500
Pentecostal Churches	P	240	13,500	32,000
Old Believers	O	22	9,091	14,000
Charismatic Churches	I	30	4,000	8,000
Other denominations[18]		194	15,878	34,187
Total Christians[46]		**2,663**	**1,667,279**	**2,480,687**

TransBloc	Pop %	Population	Ann Gr
Evangelicals			
Evangelicals	3.7	132,471	3.2%
Renewalists			
Charismatics	1.7	60,141	4.8%
Pentecostals	0.9	32,250	2.7%

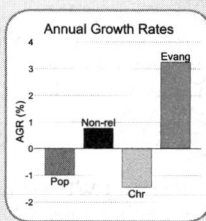

M

Answers to Prayer

1 **Moldova remains very fertile ground** for the gospel, and believing churches continue to grow and multiply. There is a sense of increasing momentum as the gospel permeates deeper into Moldova through evangelism and church planting.

Challenges for Prayer

1 **The nation cannot move forward** until several major issues find resolution. Transnistria remains a de facto separate state and undermines stability and progress for the rest of Moldova. Unemployment and alcohol abuse are widespread problems. The depressed economy forces up to 25% of Moldovans to seek work abroad, often at the risk of exploitation – Moldova is the source for the largest numbers of young women lured abroad into human trafficking rings. Pray for a government that will wisely and effectively address these devastating and costly challenges.

2 **The influence of the Orthodox Church** makes evangelical work difficult. Preaching and planting churches in traditionally Orthodox villages is especially opposed, frequently with violence. Bureaucratic antipathy to any non-Orthodox work means that building and registering churches is a difficult process; houses are usually converted to make new evangelical buildings. Yet there is also life in the Orthodox Church, especially through Agape, a ministry of The Lord's Army. Pray that the Holy Spirit would deepen the spiritual life of many from the Orthodox faith.

3 **Evangelical Christians** have multiplied greatly in spite of many challenges. Materially lacking, their spiritual vitality and determination yield much fruit. Still, poverty has forced many pastors and up to 20,000 evangelicals to leave Moldova in recent years. Pray that God might provide the church's material needs – employment, buildings, discipleship materials, training resources. Agape and the Salvation Army are particularly active in assisting the poor. Praise God that unity among denominations is increasing.

4 **Leadership training and discipleship** are still the greatest needs – most acutely for pastors and student leaders. SGA runs the strategic Moldovan Mission School; many pastors and church planters in northern Moldova are graduates. Both Baptists and Pentecostals have theological schools, there is an independent evangelical Bible School in the capital and the Brethren and **OM** are involved in Bible teaching. Pray for all these programmes to raise up godly, mature leaders. Pray for the provision of resources for both students and schools.

5 **The less reached** for prayer:

a) The Gagauz, who are Turkish but Orthodox Christians. Among them are some evangelicals, who have a vision to reach Muslims both in Moldova and in Eurasia.

b) The Muslim minorities. Increasing numbers of Turkic Muslims (>20,000) face antipathy from the Orthodox majority, but the Gagauz and Moldovans (Romanian Missionary Society) are sharing the gospel with them.

c) The Gypsy population is large and has very few evangelical Christians.

6 **Mission vision** among Moldovans is rapidly growing, but training and support are serious obstacles requiring prayer. **OM** and the European Baptist Federation are just two of the groups dedicated to finding innovative ways to train, send and support economically-limited Moldovans through partnerships with other Christians. Pray for a release of resources to support those called by God to serve in Moldova and abroad.

7 **Christian help ministries** for prayer:

a) Radio. **TWR** broadcasts out from Moldova to many Eastern European countries. Moldovans can tune in to 19.5 hours/week in eight languages. Also, a local Christian radio ministry, Micul Samaratan, has 12 stations; they enjoy a fruitful ministry and widespread response.

b) The JESUS film, which is available in Romanian, Ukrainian, Russian and Bulgarian, and has been widely viewed.

c) Short-term missions. Many Western groups send short-term teams, ostensibly to serve the church there through erecting church buildings, teaching and assisting local congregations and ministries. Pray that these guests will serve humbly, affirm national leaders and allow for an authentic Moldovan expression of God's Kingdom.

d) Summer camps and outreach programmes engaged in sports ministry. Nearly every church is actively involved in this work each summer.

Italy

France

Monaco

Monaco

Mediterranean Sea

Monaco
Principality of Monaco
Europe

Geography 🌍

Area 2 sq km. The second smallest state in the world. On France's south coast.

Population		Ann Gr	Density
2010	32,904	0.28%	16,452/sq km
2020	33,806	0.27%	16,903/sq km
2030	35,370	0.27%	17,685/sq km

Capital Monaco 32,900. **Urbanites** 100%. **Pop under 15 yrs** 13%. **Life expectancy** 79.1 yrs.

Peoples 👪

Monégasque 21.5%. Speaking Ligurian and French.
French 28%.
Italian 19%.
Other 31.5%. British, Swiss, Belgian, German, many others. Numerous French and Italian daily commuter workers.
Literacy 100%. **Official language** French. **All languages** 3. **Languages with Scriptures** 1Bi 2por.

Economy 📈

A byword for a very high standard of living. Most revenue is from tourism, but Monaco also serves as a tax haven and gambling destination. Allegations persist of suspicious fiscal activities in the country.
Income/person $35,000 (77% of USA).

Politics ⚔️

A constitutional monarchy. The prince, of the house of Grimaldi since 1297, shares his power with the National Council, which is elected.

Religion 🕌

Roman Catholicism is the state religion, but there is freedom of religion, though proselytism is strongly discouraged and frowned upon.

Religions	Pop %	Population	Ann Gr
Christian	84.78	27,896	-0.1%
Non-religious	11.42	3,758	2.9%
Jewish	2.90	954	1.7%
Muslim	0.70	230	3.4%
Other	0.20	66	0.3%

Christians Denoms		Pop %	Affiliates	Ann Gr
Protestant	1	1.98	1,000	-0.9%
Independent	2	0.27	<100	3.7%
Anglican	1	0.87	<300	-1.0%
Catholic	1	81.30	27,000	-0.1%
Orthodox	2	0.36	<200	1.8%

Churches	MegaBloc	Congs	Members	Affiliates
Catholic Church	C	9	19,815	26,750
Ref Church of Monaco	P	1	130	650
Anglican Church	A	1	130	285
Orthodox Church	O	1	72	120
Monaco Chr Fellowship	I	1	59	90
Total Christians[7]		**13**	**20,206**	**27,895**

TransBloc	Pop %	Population	Ann Gr
Evangelicals			
Evangelicals	1.2	379	2.8%
Renewalists			
Charismatics	1.2	403	2.1%

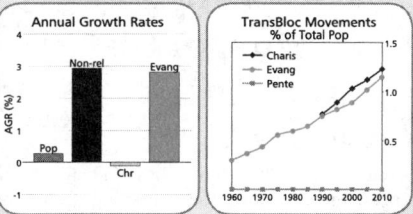

Annual Growth Rates

TransBloc Movements % of Total Pop

M

Answer to Prayer

1 **Praise God** that, for the first time, there is a small group of Monégasque evangelical believers.

Challenges for Prayer

1 **Monaco is culturally Catholic,** but the real culture is one of materialistic hedonism. It is very difficult to foster interest in spiritual things in such an environment. Pray that many would see the ultimate emptiness of such a lifestyle and seek the fullness of life Christ offers.

2 **The expatriate community** is 78.5% of the population. Apart from the prevalent Catholic Church, three congregations serve the expatriate community – Anglican, French Reformed and the strongly evangelical, bilingual Monaco Christian Fellowship. Pray that committed believers in all three might impact the whole of society.

3 **Evangelicals are so few** that their impact is limited, especially in the hard spiritual ground that is Monaco. But the great numbers of nationalities (more than 160) in Monaco, and the highly transitory nature of many expats there, represent a good opportunity to reach the nations from this small principality. Pray for culturally appropriate witness in a context where evangelism is regarded as socially unacceptable.

4 **Christian radio. TWR** broadcasts from Monaco have had a wide audience for years (using transmitters there – **TWR** has no staff in Monaco). Powerful medium- and short-wave transmitters broadcast in 10 European and four North African languages. Pray for spiritual impact on the materialistic and indifferent cultures of Europe and the much more spiritually responsive ones in North Africa.

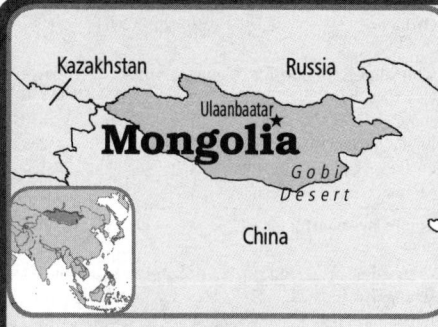

Mongolia
Mongol Uls

Asia

Geography

Area 1,565,000 sq km. Grassland, forests in north, three major mountain ranges and the great Gobi Desert in the east and south. Subject to climatic extremes.

Population		Ann Gr	Density
2010	2,701,117	1.16%	2/sq km
2020	3,002,051	1.01%	2/sq km
2030	3,236,104	0.64%	2/sq km

Approximately 33% are nomadic pastoralists.
Capital Ulaanbaatar (Ulan Bator) 965,961. **Urbanites** 57.5%. **Pop under 15 yrs** 26%. **Life expectancy** 66.2 yrs.

Peoples

Mongolian 90.9%. Seven distinct dialects. Khalkha 67.0%; Kalmyk-Oirat 7.0%; Northern Mongol 5.0%;

Durbet 2.9%; Buryat 2.7%.
Turkic 6.6%. Kazakh 5.3%; Tuvan 1.2% in far west.
Other 2.5%. Chinese 1.5%.
Literacy 97.8%. **Official language** Khalkha Mongolian. **All languages** 15. **Indigenous languages** 13. **Languages with Scriptures** 4Bi 4NT 4w.i.p.

Economy

A traditionally pastoral and agricultural economy, but mining secures the highest proportion of foreign exchange. The livestock (especially cashmere) and tourism trades are growing earners. Severe winters brought great losses of livestock, which impoverished many and forced thousands to move to the cities seeking work. Changing from a USSR-dependent, central economy to a market economy has been difficult. A minority have become rich, but many are in greater difficulty than before. Large-scale emigration is occurring as many thousands of Mongolians seek employment abroad.
HDI Rank 115th/182. **Public debt** 4.24% of GDP. **Income/person** $1,975 (4% of USA).

Politics

Unified as a nation in 1206, which, under Genghis Khan, became the greatest land empire ever known, stretching from China and Korea to Central Europe. Under foreign domination between 1368 and 1911. Autonomous from Chinese and Manchu domination in 1911. A Russian-supported revolution in 1921 installed a Marxist revolutionary government. A multi-party democracy was instituted in 1990. Protests over corruption and failure to help the poor plague the current government.

Religion

Buddhism, Shamanism and Islam are recognized as Mongolia's main religions, but certain religious freedoms are granted to all people. There are some restrictions on foreign religious workers, but Mongolia is effectively one of the most open countries in Asia, with limited government interference in Christian work.

Religions	Pop %	Population	Ann Gr
Buddhist	35.30	953,494	4.0%
Ethnoreligionist	32.40	875,162	1.4%
Non-religious	26.48	715,256	-2.6%
Muslim	4.10	110,746	1.4%
Christian	1.72	46,459	7.5%

All figures are estimates, since no national survey has been done, and distinctions between Buddhism and shamanism are blurred.

Christians Denoms		Pop %	Affiliates	Ann Gr
Protestant	15	0.29	8,000	5.8%
Independent	47	0.98	27,000	8.7%
Catholic	1	0.03	1,000	3.1%
Orthodox	4	0.03	1,000	1.8%
Marginal	3	0.39	10,000	7.6%

Churches	MegaBloc	Congs	Members	Affiliates
Mongolian indig groups	I	195	5,800	17,800
Latter-day Saints	M	29	4,550	9,100
Charismatic groups	I	38	3,846	7,500
Assemblies of God	P	10	1,825	2,870
Assembly Hall Chs	I	23	492	1,230
Other denominations[21]		66	3,933	8,090
Total Christians[70]		**361**	**20,446**	**46,590**

TransBloc	Pop %	Population	Ann Gr
Evangelicals			
Evangelicals	1.2	33,496	7.9%
Renewalists			
Charismatics	0.8	22,106	9.0%
Pentecostals	0.1	2,870	4.1%

Missionaries from Mongolia
P,I,A 20 cross-cultural; 5 international.

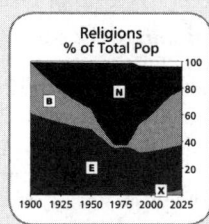

Religions % of Total Pop

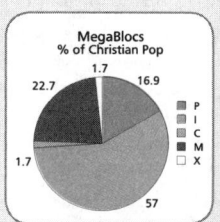

MegaBlocs % of Christian Pop

Answers to Prayer

1 **In 1989 there may have been only four Mongolian Christians.** By 2000, there was an estimated community of 8,000 to 10,000. Today, there are over 40,000 believers in hundreds of churches and groups, meeting in most parts of the country.

2 **The Mongolian Church is maturing rapidly,** often out of necessity. Less than one generation old, it already sends missionaries to unreached areas of Mongolia and beyond, running many national ministries originally founded by missionaries and developing a culturally appropriate worship canon.

Challenges for Prayer

1 **The difficult economic situation,** a major challenge for the government, deeply affects every aspect of life – employment, education, children's welfare and others. The very feasibility of traditional nomadic pastoralism is under threat. "Insider capitalism" yields great wealth for a few but gripping poverty for many others. Failing to address this adequately has already caused the collapse of one government. Pray that the leaders of Mongolia might rule with fairness and wisdom.

2 **Mongolia's traditional religions,** Lamaistic Buddhism and shamanism, have experienced resurgence since independence. Buddhism numerically dominates, but most do not understand it well. Deeper in the Mongolian psyche are beliefs in shamanism, traditional ethnic superstitions and even occult practices. Increasing numbers of Mongolians, especially younger ones, are consulting shamans for help with health, finance and relationship issues. Pray that Mongolians might find complete liberation and have transformed lives through following the Lord Jesus Christ.

3 **Christianity in Mongolia** is a reality for the first time in modern history. There are now close to 200 churches in the capital as well as believers, if only in tiny groups, in every one of Mongolia's provincial centres. Yet there are challenges:

a) Many are interested in Christianity, but their reasons are mixed. In the past, a significant attraction was the chance of employment by missionaries/NGOs. Today, some who come into the church drift away or never become disciples. Pray for effective discipleship and Christ-like living among believers. Only a few of the larger churches have become financially autonomous from foreign sponsors.

b) Christianity must shed its foreign-ness, becoming truly Mongolian and still biblically centred. Many missionaries enter with inadequate cross-cultural preparation. Pray for a better contextualization of biblical truths to fit Mongolian culture.

c) Age-imbalanced congregations are usually comprised of many young adults and students, but far fewer of the older generation, especially older men. Children tend not to be brought to church. Pray for a harvest among all ages and generations.

d) Rural churches have very little support or teaching due to a lack of finances and their distance from the capital, where most of the training and resources exist. An effective nomadic church concept has yet to be established.

e) The need for spiritual unity. The Mongolian Evangelical Alliance (MEA) seeks to bring together all Mongolian churches for fellowship, growth and a united front in representing Christians to the government. Pray for vision, leadership and real oneness to come out of the MEA.

4 **Developing Mongolian church leaders** is a strategic need and the key to strengthening the Church. Good training is central to this – most churches, especially rural ones, desperately need biblically astute leaders and teachers. There are eight Bible colleges, mainly denominational in character. The largest is the interdenominational Union Bible Theological College, which focuses on training church leaders. There are also other Bible training centres, run by local churches and missions. Given the country's vast size and rapid church growth, developing a TEE programme that serves the far-flung congregations is possibly the Mongolian Church's greatest need. Pray for the right models of leadership and appropriate support structures to develop, from high-level academic study to informal training of laity.

5 **The expatriate Christian workforce** has a significant role to play. Many, as members of NGOs, focus on aid and development. Missionaries are now shifting from evangelism and discipleship to helping train and serve the Mongolian church to rightly assume those roles. Joint Christian Services (a network of nearly 15 Western-based agencies) and another umbrella group of Korean agencies are striving to coordinate work, along with the MEA and other Christian groups. Most work is based in Ulaanbaatar, but increasingly is moving into rural areas – pray for this to continue. Pray especially for unity among agencies, long-term commitment, willingness to truly learn and adapt to Mongolian culture and close, humble relationships of trust with Mongolian leaders. Pray also that openness in Mongolia continues so that Christian ministry can carry on.

6 **Economic difficulties have led to widespread social upheaval**, exploitation and the breakdown of traditional values. Crime, alcoholism and prostitution are tragically common. Homelessness can still be a problem in the cities. Most agencies are involved in some kind of health, relief, education or literature programme; these are opportunities to demonstrate Christ's compassionate love. Pray for maximum long-term benefit to the people and the emerging Church.

7 **The less evangelized** for prayer:

a) Nomads find their traditional life increasingly difficult to maintain. Pray for culturally sensitive holistic ministries that demonstrate the gospel to them.

b) Kazakhs are a majority in the far-western province of Bayan-Olgiy. Most are Muslim, but a few are Christian. Some Christians work among them, and Muslim missionaries seek to re-Islamize these people.

c) Ethnic minorities. The Chinese and Russian communities have a few believers, with at least one church for each group. Little to no specific outreach is directed toward the Kalmyk, Tuvan and Evenki peoples.

d) Students. **CCCI**, **IFES**, UBF (Korean student campus churches) and others work to reach students through camps, seminars and student discipleship groups. Mongolian leadership is emerging through this ministry, but the process of taking young adults from initial interest to mature disciples requires patience and faith.

8 **Specific Christian support ministries** for prayer:

a) Bible translation is a very important issue. One main translation is used by most churches and is currently being revised. A couple of other translations exist, one using a different set of religious vocabulary. Pray for increased use of Scripture by Mongolians and for the Holy Spirit to teach, grow and guide many through God's Word. Braille Bibles and audio Scriptures are available for those unable to read.

b) The JESUS film, available in most indigenous languages, is widely used on television and film screenings around the country. Many have been moved by it.

c) **MAF** flies as Blue Sky Aviation. Mongolia's vastness and need for evangelism, training and humanitarian work makes this a strategically important venture.

d) Christian radio and television. FEBC operates a Christian radio station in the capital – Wind FM provides a vital service, but needs greater range to reach the rural population. Programming includes news, music and Christian teaching. Eagle TV is a Christian-owned terrestrial station that has a much-loved news programme and is airing Christian programmes that share the gospel through drama, teaching and testimonies.

Montenegro

Republic of Montenegro

Europe

Geography

Area 14,026 sq km. A coastal Adriatic state. Small, but mountainous and picturesque.

Population		Ann Gr	Density
2010	625,516	0.03%	45/sq km
2020	631,002	0.14%	46/sq km
2030	633,958	0.02%	46/sq km

Capital Podgorica 144,000. **Urbanites** 59.5%. **Pop under 15 yrs** 19%. **Life expectancy** 74 yrs.

Peoples

The narrow distinction between Montenegrins and Serbs and the politicized element of ethnicity makes it difficult to ascertain precise figures.
Slavic 92.8%. Montenegrin 46.7%; Serb 34.6%; Bosniak 8.4%; Croat 1.2%; Slovak 1.0%.
Albanian 5.6%.
Romani 0.7%. Probably significantly higher.
Other 0.9%. Central and Western Europeans, Arabs.
Literacy 97.3%. **Official language** Ijekavian dialect of Serbian, one of the southern Slavonic languages. **All languages** 6. **Languages with Scriptures** 4Bi 1NT 1por.

Economy

Montenegro's economy suffered from war and sanctions in the 1990s, since it was tied to Serbia as part of Yugoslavia. Adopting the Euro and making the economy investment-friendly has helped. A beautiful coastline hosts Europe's fastest growing tourist industry.
HDI Rank 65th/182. **Public debt** 38% of GDP.
Income/person $4,904 (11% of USA).

Politics

Recognized as a state as early as 1077, Montenegro became part of the Kingdom of Yugoslavia in 1918. A controversial and flawed referendum retained ties to Serbia in 1992. Perceived by many as the lesser partner, Montenegro successfully separated following a

M

referendum in 2006. A multiparty parliamentary democracy.

Religion 🙏

Historically, the Orthodox Church has had a strong influence – a theocratic principality ruled from 1516 to 1852. Religious freedom, but few would consider changing faiths. A feud between the predominant Serbian Orthodox and the breakaway Montenegrin Orthodox Church dominates the religious scene.

Churches	MegaBloc	Congs	Members	Affiliates
Serbian Orthodox	O	587	234,667	352,000
Other Orthodox	O	12	37,333	56,000
Montenegrin Orthodox	O	55	18,182	40,000
Catholic Church	C	13	21,000	33,000
Seventh-day Adventist	P	3	250	450
Jehovah's Witnesses	M	5	158	300
Pentecostal Church	P	2	50	80
Brethren Church	P	1	35	58
Reformation Church	P	2	35	58
Total Christians[14]		**680**	**311,710**	**481,946**

Religions	Pop %	Population	Ann Gr
Christian	77.05	481,960	-0.3%
Muslim	15.00	93,827	-0.2%
Non-religious	7.79	48,728	4.5%
Other	0.12	751	3.7%
Buddhist	0.03	188	8.5%
Jewish	0.01	63	0.0%

Christians Denoms		Pop %	Affiliates	Ann Gr
Protestant	4	0.10	1,000	3.6%
Catholic	1	5.28	33,000	1.9%
Orthodox	8	71.62	448,000	-0.5%
Marginal	1	0.05	<500	3.7%

TransBloc	Pop %	Population	Ann Gr
Evangelicals			
Evangelicals	<0.1	286	5.2%
Renewalists			
Charismatics	0.1	414	3.3%
Pentecostals	<0.1	80	9.9%

Annual Growth Rates

TransBloc Movements % of Total Pop

Challenges for Prayer

1 **Independence has brought optimism and hope.** Montenegro is a small country but has great potential. If it can avoid the enmity between ethnic/religious communities that plagues most of the Balkans, there is much to look forward to. However, economic development (mostly through a burgeoning tourist industry and the aim of joining the EU) brings neither peace nor salvation, and less upright elements of society will now see the nation as a ripe new target for their vice. Pray for Montenegro to be a just, peaceful and corruption-free nation which enjoys ethnic harmony. Pray that people will seek the truth in the midst of their new-found nationhood.

2 **The Orthodox Church** is characterized by an almost farcical drama of claims, counter-claims and mutual anathematizations as the Montenegrin Orthodox Church seeks to establish itself in place of the Serbian Orthodox Church. Before the 20th Century the Montenegrin Orthodox Church existed as an autocephalous group. Pray that instead of squabbling over rights and property, Orthodox leaders would demonstrate Christlike leadership to a population whose faith is, for the most part, nominal. Pray for new spiritual life to come to the nation's Orthodox community (75% of the population).

3 **The evangelical community is tiny,** but multiplying. The Pentecostals, Baptists and Brethren have active growing churches. Evangelicals increased five-fold between 2000 and 2005, but they still only number 0.03% of the population. Evangelical congregations, while only a handful, have a vision for sharing the gospel; pray for continued church growth. Pray for steadfast witness in the face of opposition, for unity among denominations and for fruitful ministry.

4 **Most ethnic minorities** have little to no meaningful interaction with the good news. Pray for sensitive and loving outreach to:

a) *Bosniaks,* who may number up to 11% of the population and will be almost exclusively Muslim. Their extreme hostility toward Christians is justified, given the atrocities in the Balkans during the 1990s.

b) Albanians, among whom there are no evangelical churches or groups of believers.

c) The Romani, officially only 0.5% of the population but likely significantly more. As in other Balkan nations, they are poorer, often despised and are proving more open to the gospel than most ethnic groups.

5 **Foreign missions** are only just discovering Montenegro. There are workers from Pioneers, Baptists, Finnish Pentecostals and other groups. Pray that a fruitful and mutually edifying partnership can arise among the growing local churches and the foreign workers.

Montserrat

British Overseas Territory of Montserrat

Caribbean

Geography 🌍

Area 102 sq km, since increased by lava flows from Mt. Soufrière, which erupted 1995-2003. One of the Leeward Islands in the Caribbean.

Population		Ann Gr	Density
2010	5,962	1.16%	58/sq km
2020	6,441	0.66%	63/sq km
2030	6,756	0.43%	66/sq km

Over 80% of the population evacuated in 1995/7 to Antigua, Guadeloupe, UK and elsewhere. Only a fraction have since returned; many never will. Only the northern one-third of the island is habitable.
Capital Brades 850. **Pop under 15 yrs** 19%.

Peoples 👫

African Caribbean 97%.
Euro-American 2%.
Other 1%.
Official language English. **All languages** 2.
Languages with Scripture 1Bi.

Economy 📈

Post-eruption Montserrat faces a serious challenge in reestablishing itself.

Politics 🗳

Dependent territory of the UK. Without British assistance, the island probably would not have been reestablished.

Religion 🙏

All figures are estimates because of the upheaval in population.

Religions	Pop %	Population	Ann Gr
Christian	95.30	5,682	1.1%
Non-religious	2.70	161	1.9%
Baha'i	2.00	119	1.2%

Christians Denoms		Pop %	Affiliates	Ann Gr
Protestant	6	38.41	2,000	1.2%
Independent	2	3.35	<200	3.3%
Anglican	1	26.84	2,000	0.3%
Catholic	1	18.45	1,000	1.9%
Marginal	1	0.35	<100	0.0%
Unaffiliated		7.90	<500	0.0%

Churches	MegaBloc	Congs	Members	Affiliates
Anglican Church	A	3	800	1,600
Catholic Church	C	2	683	1,100
Seventh-day Adventist	P	2	524	750
Methodist Church	P	2	275	550
Pentecostal Assemblies	P	2	200	350
Ch of God of Prophecy	P	4	132	220
Other denominations[5]		7	336	641
Total Christians[11]		**22**	**2,950**	**5,211**

TransBloc	Pop %	Population	Ann Gr
Evangelicals			
Evangelicals	23.4	1,394	2.6%
Renewalists			
Charismatics	14.1	842	3.7%
Pentecostals	12.9	770	4.0%

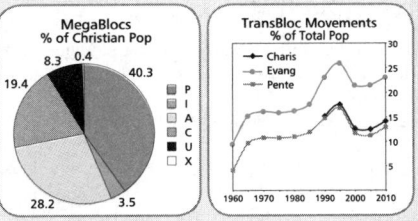

Challenges for Prayer

1 **The massive devastation** caused by the volcanic eruptions in the late 1990s nearly destroyed Montserrat as a habitable island. It will never completely recover. Pray for a new start, with Christ placed at the centre of island life rather than nominal Christianity, which largely prevailed in the past.

2 **Church life was severely disrupted.** Pray for effective rebuilding of congregations, community life, property and outreach.

Morocco

Kingdom of Morocco

Africa

Geography

Area 458,730 sq km. Northwest corner of Africa. Fertile coastal areas in the north, Atlas mountains inland and Sahara Desert to the south and southeast. A further 252,000 sq km of former Spanish Sahara claimed and occupied by Morocco since 1975.

Population		Ann Gr	Density
2010	32,777,808	1.25%	71/sq km
2020	36,784,700	1.10%	80/sq km
2030	39,934,409	0.73%	87/sq km

Capital Rabat. **Other major cities** Rabat/Salé 1.8 million; Casablanca 3.3mill; Fèz 1.1m; Marrakech 928,000. **Urbanites** 56.7%. **Pop under 15 yrs** 28%. **Life expectancy** 71 yrs.

Peoples

The indigenous Berbers were gradually conquered and subdued by the Muslim Arabs after AD 684.
Arabic 57.7%. Moroccan Arab 47.8%; Jebala 4.4%; Black Maure 2.1%.
Berber 41.4%. Many dialects: Arabized Berber 12.9%; Tashilhayt (known also as Ishilhayn, S. Shilha, Souss) 9.4%; Imazighen (Tamazight) 7.9%; Rif (Tarifit) 5.1%.
Other 0.9%. French 0.3%.
Literacy Officially 53.5%, lower in practice.

Official language Arabic. Berber is used in many homes. French widely used; English increasing. **All languages** 10. **Languages with Scriptures** 2Bi 1NT 4por.

Economy

Tourism, agriculture, textiles and phosphate mining are important foreign exchange earners. Morocco and Western Sahara have 70% of the world's phosphate reserves. Great gap between wealthy few and large numbers of poor, but a growing middle class. Unemployment is officially around 11% but in reality is much higher, especially for young people. To keep pace with population growth, 400,000 jobs must be created annually. Millions of Moroccans seek work elsewhere – especially in Europe – and send remittances home. This foreign income contributes more to the Moroccan economy than any internal industry apart from tourism.
HDI Rank 130th/182. **Public debt** 55.6% of GDP. **Income/person** $2,827 (6% of USA).

Politics

Independent in 1956 from French and Spanish rule. A limited democracy with an executive monarchy under King Hassan until his death in 1999. His successor, King Mohammed VI, instituted liberalizing changes, but shifted to a much more repressive stance in 2010. A growing Islamist presence opposes these changes, and terrorist bombings in 2003 showed the threat radical Islam poses to Morocco's stability. Since then it has vied with a sophisticated materialistic Islam for prevalence in the political sphere. Since the "Green March" of 1975, Morocco has occupied Western Sahara, but the subsequent warfare with the Polisario and the postponed UN referendum have left this issue unresolved.

Religion

Sunni Islam is the state religion; the existence of Christians and Jews is tolerated, but the existence of an indigenous Moroccan Church is not accepted by the government. The opposing influences of prosperous, hi-tech Middle Eastern Islam and hard-line radical Islam both exert considerable pressure. It is legal both to talk about Christ and to invite friends home

M

for discussion, but authorities carefully monitor all known Christian activity. In 2010, a large number of expatriate Christians were deported and institutions with a Christian ethos closed. Local Christians are harassed and intimidated by police informers; some Christians have been imprisoned, accused of proselytizing. The media stir up public prejudice against the gospel.

Churches	MegaBloc	Congs	Members	Affiliates
Catholic Church	C	32	12,849	23,000
Indigenous believers	I	30	500	2,000
Evang Reformed Ch	P	6	140	1,600
Other denominations[19]		66	1,626	3,324
Total Christians[24]		**134**	**15,115**	**29,924**

TransBloc	Pop %	Population	Ann Gr
Evangelicals			
Evangelicals	<0.01	4,774	4.6%
Renewalists			
Charismatics	<0.01	3,378	5.1%
Pentecostals	<0.01	40	4.6%

Religions	Pop %	Population	Ann Gr
Muslim	99.88	32,738,475	1.3%
Christian	0.09	29,000	1.3%
Jewish	0.02	6,556	-6.6%
Non-religious	0.01	3,278	1.3%

Around 90% of the Christians are not Moroccan in origin.

Missionaries from Morocco
P,I,A estimated 10, most in Morocco.

Christians Denoms		Pop %	Affiliates	Ann Gr
Protestant	14	0.01	4,000	4.7%
Independent	3	0.01	2,000	3.3%
Anglican	1	<0.01	<200	-4.4%
Catholic	1	0.07	23,000	0.0%
Orthodox	4	<0.01	1,000	-1.2%
Marginal	1	<0.01	<200	1.5%

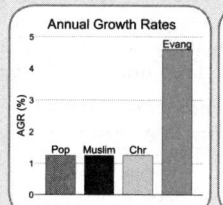

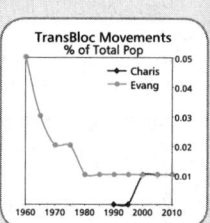

Answers to Prayer

1 **A Moroccan Church is emerging** and accelerating in growth and maturity. While figures differ significantly, national Christian leaders estimate that there are about 2,000 Moroccan Christians in 20 to 30 small fellowships.

Challenges for Prayer

1 **Islam was introduced by invading Arab armies** in the 7th Century. The once strong North African, and largely Berber, Church was erased. Pride in Morocco's glorious past as a centre of Islamic civilization and learning, and deeply rooted prejudice against Christianity, remain barriers to the acceptance of the gospel. Only a small percentage of the population has been clearly presented with the gospel. Pray that this nation may become open for the good news.

2 **Stability and relative openness** make Morocco one of the West's most favoured Arab nations. Yet a troubled past and uncertain future make for challenges. Economic growth is essential to care for and give hope to the burgeoning young population, and the deeply sensitive and controversial issue of Western Sahara continues to stand between Morocco and better foreign relations. Pray for wisdom for the government, that policies and planning might establish justice, fairness and openness.

3 **Moroccan Islam** faces serious division as the country increasingly polarizes between Islamists and moderates. The suppression of Christian activity is meant to forestall sectarian conflict desired by extremists in other African Muslim countries. The intensifying difficulties reflect the deepening fault line; most citizens are troubled by the implications and do not wish for religious violence. Islamism finds a fertile recruiting ground especially but not exclusively among the poor and frustrated young population. Pray for peace throughout the nation, and pray that those seeking to commit violence be stymied. Pray for the country's leaders; may they navigate these troubled waters with wisdom and good decision-making.

4 **The indigenous Church emerged** into the nation's awareness, thanks to a media that reports obviously inflated numbers of converts to Christianity. The mostly negative press nonetheless serves to make Moroccans aware that some of their countrymen left Islam to follow Christ. There are many prayer needs for this national Church:

a) *Fellowship and unity* are essential in a Church that meets almost entirely in homes, and where many believers have little to no fellowship. There is a strong and growing informal network of indigenous Christians throughout the country; pray this network extends as believers travel to visit family groups and individuals, often isolated. Pray that no divisions upset this.

b) *Strength and perseverance* for those under pressure from family, police or religious authorities. Intensified persecution and media attention have created opportunities for witness for those bold enough to take a stand. Pray that the community of believers might grow amid such persecution as it did in the years of the early Church, through faith, witness, mutual support and encouragement.

c) *Discipleship of believers* is always difficult in a context of persecution, isolation and fear. This is intensified here by lack of Scripture and teaching materials, low levels of literacy and a shortage of established mature leaders. Pray that believers might increasingly engage with Scripture, focus on Christ, understand their faith and welcome newcomers.

d) *Leadership development and training* are needed. Pray for programmes that will reliably reproduce solid leaders. Pray that there may be God-given, Spirit-gifted leadership for every group of believers.

e) *Christians' practical needs.* Believers often have difficulty finding jobs, education and spouses. Christian families are integral to building solid house churches.

f) *Official recognition by the government* of the legitimate existence of Moroccan believers and their identity as genuine Moroccans.

5 **Specific unreached minority peoples.** Pray for:

a) *The Berber peoples.* Many were nominally Christian until Arabic Islam came; Islam among Berbers is laced with folk magic (especially in rural areas) but devout nevertheless. Currently, there is a revival of traditional language and culture. There are some believers in each of the three major Berber peoples, but nothing like the significant response among Berbers in neighbouring Algeria. Rapid and loving Christian response to a 2004 earthquake in the north generated greater openness and responsiveness to the gospel. Pray that there may soon be groups meeting together using the indigenous languages in each of the three regions.

b) *The Maghreb Jews* once numbered more than 250,000 and enjoyed a rich cultural identity. Most emigrated to Israel in 1948. Today only a few thousand remain in Morocco. There is no known outreach to them at this time.

c) *The nomadic desert tribes* of the south and east, who have little contact with the gospel.

d) *Rural Moroccan Arabs,* while part of the majority people group, are particularly unreached and isolated from the gospel. Few ministries even attempt to reach them.

6 **Missionary work,** as such, is not openly permitted, but Christian workers are able to take up various types of employment, share their faith and encourage believers. Many live in the country in order to share and live out the love of Jesus. Pray especially for the following issues:

a) *A recent crackdown on expatriate Christian workers* has seen over 100 expelled on very short notice, and their ministries all but disintegrated. In some cases, these ministries were clearly meeting social needs. The crackdown appears to be orchestrated at a very high national level and seriously endangers the continuation of foreign Christian work. Pray that the door would remain open for as long as God desires and for as long as the national Church needs in order to be raised up to finish the task in Morocco.

b) *Relationships with nationals.* The government is attempting to drive a wedge between expatriate and indigenous believers. Expatriate Christians can endanger nationals as much as serve them if wisdom is not exercised. Pray for a good balance in how and how much foreign believers interact with indigenous Christians.

*c) **Serving the needy.*** There remain some holistic ministries open to foreign Christian involvement – working with the stigmatized and disabled, assisting the destitute, building the economy through business and development links. Much discretion and patience is required until a greater freedom for the gospel is achieved.

*d) **Sub-Saharan Africans and Asians*** by the thousands seek entry to Europe. They are often subject to exploitation by traffickers and harsh treatment by the Moroccan government. Some reside there as students. Many are already Christian and have formed vibrant fellowships; many others are coming to faith through the ministry of other Christians in Morocco. Pray for their positive witness to Muslims.

7 **Bible and Christian literature ministries.** For prayer:

*a) **Arabic Bibles*** can be imported only in small quantities and Berber Scriptures not at all. Distribution is discreet. Pray for believers to acquire the discipline of reading the Word every day. Recordings are effective for the illiterate; pray that they would listen daily. Arabic and Berber Scriptures are available on the Internet.

*b) **Bible translation*** continues in the three main Berber languages in both Arabic and Berber scripts as well as in Moroccan Arabic. Pray for the translators and their work. Work is underway to record and distribute Scripture and other Christian materials in the Berber languages. The NT in Tashilhayt is available in MP3 format, loadable onto mobile phones.

*c) **BCCs in combination with Christian broadcasting*** have been influential in the past, but with the coming of satellite TV fewer people now listen to foreign radio stations. Nevertheless, BCC materials still have much to offer at all academic and spiritual levels. Pray especially that leaders may benefit from Arabic-language Bible College courses available on the Internet.

*d) **Various media agencies.*** Most are based in Europe. They are working to write, print and distribute Arabic and Berber materials for North Africa.

*e) **Operation Transit*** distributes annually tens of thousands of packages containing evangelistic materials to North Africans crossing from Europe to Africa and back for summer vacation. Pray for these materials to be read and considered, and pray for fruit from this sowing.

8 **Christian electronic media ministries** are making a potent impact.

*a) **Satellite TV*** has spread rapidly and is very popular in both urban and rural areas. *Al-Hayat*, SAT-7, and Miracle are all having an impact on millions. Pray for the production of programmes that are culturally sensitive and biblically sound. Pray for good reception of programmes and for impact on the lives and worldview of Moroccans.

M

*b) **Christian radio*** has a role in outreach and in linking scattered believers. Seminars in radio and music ministry enable national believers to develop high-quality programmes. There are broadcasts 33 hours/week in Arabic and a total of 18 hours per week in the three Berber languages.

*c) **The JESUS film, God's Story, and other DVDs*** are distributed in Arabic and the three major Berber languages. There is a need, however, for wider distribution.

*d) **Audio recordings.*** Great effort is being made to record the Scriptures and other Christian resources, such as indigenous worship music and discipleship materials, into audio formats. Pray for recordings to be increased in number and variety, and for further development of indigenous Christian music, songs, poetry and theology. Where people are not habitual readers, the role of audio resources is vital.

*e) **The Internet*** is an increasingly effective medium for the gospel. Many young people access sites that host serious theological discussions between Muslims and Christians. Some are coming to faith. Pray that they may be integrated into local fellowships. The Internet also connects people worldwide who are praying for Morocco.

9 **Moroccans migrate in large numbers** to search for employment, many illegally and dangerously. There are significant numbers of Moroccans in Europe: in France (approx. 1.1 million); Spain, including Ceuta and Melilla (397,000 and probably an equal number illegally); the Netherlands (315,000); Belgium (215,000); Germany (99,000); and Britain (50,000). Others reside in the Spanish North African enclave cities of Ceuta and Melilla. Pray for the various agencies seeking to reach them in these lands – some include Avant, **AWM**, Frontiers, **YWAM**, **OM**, PMI and **WEC**.

Western Sahara

Geography ⊕

Area 252,000 sq km. Almost entirely desert, but has huge phosphate deposits, one of the world's richest sea fishing areas and possibly large oil reserves beneath its territorial waters.
Population An estimated 400,000.
Capital El Aaiun 221,000. **Urbanites** 81.8%.
Pop under 15 yrs 29%.

Peoples 🧍🧍🧍

Arab-Berber Moroccan "settlers" 200,000; Saharawi indigenous 75,000; a further 270,000 refugees in four main camps near Tindouf, Algeria. There are also up to 130,000 Moroccan military personnel.

Economy 🗺️

Great potential for development due to natural resources; lack of water hinders this. The Moroccan occupation is costly and limits outside investment. At the same time, it has contributed to massive development of the region in the last 30 years.

Politics 🗡️

Ruled by Spain until 1975 and then occupied by Morocco. Sixteen years of Polisario-Moroccan warfare ensued. A UN-brokered cease-fire of 1991 has not yielded the promised referendum on the future status of the area. Morocco is fully intent on holding on to it despite some international pressure to release it. The occupied territory (70% of total) is protected by a Moroccan-built earthen wall; the other 30% is under Polisario control (who are themselves backed by Algeria). The Saharawi Arab Democratic Republic is recognized by more than 75 governments.

Religion 🔥

Almost 100% Muslim.

Challenges for Prayer

M

1 **Pray for a peaceful and fair resolution** to decades of costly conflict.

a) Morocco's determination to remain is strengthened by their value as an Arab ally to France and the USA, and will only be entrenched by the likelihood of oil reserves offshore. The cause of the Polisario is remarkably enduring and strong. Pray for justice, for an equitable solution, and for the Saharawi people to be able to return to their homeland.

b) Where there are believers, God is breaking down enmity between those in opposition politically. Pray for the Church to model the reconciliation available in Christ, turning hearts away from attachment to futile political ambitions and toward a zeal for Jesus.

2 **There are only a handful of Christians** among this entire people, but we see a new day of growth and witness among the Saharawi through low-key mission work and national believers. There are openings for ministry to refugees through relief and development, and difficult political and living conditions lead to considerable openness. The JESUS film is available and the Hassaniya NT is in preparation. Pray for those who are, and could be, serving among them.

Mozambique
Republic of Mozambique
Africa

Geography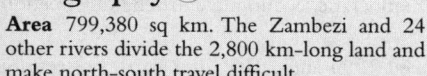

Area 799,380 sq km. The Zambezi and 24 other rivers divide the 2,800 km-long land and make north-south travel difficult.

Population		Ann Gr	Density
2010	23,405,670	2.35%	29/sq km
2020	28,545,405	1.92%	36/sq km
2030	33,893,821	1.68%	42/sq km

Civil war and natural disasters have rendered demographic research nearly impossible, with millions displaced in the 1990s and well over a million dying from war, famine, floods and AIDS between 1990 and 2010.
Capital Maputo 1,654,700. **Other major cities** Matola 793,000; Beira 787,000; Nampula 601,000. **Urbanites** 38.4%. **Pop under 15 yrs** 44%. **Life expectancy** 47.8 yrs.

Peoples 👪

Bantu peoples 97.6%.
  Northern peoples 63.0%. Makhuwa(5) 37.8%; Lomwe 7.4%; Chuwabo 5.7%; Nyanja 2.2%; Marenje 2.1%; Makonde(2) 1.8%; Yao 1.4%; Lolo 1.0%.
  Central peoples 15.5%. Sena 8.3%; Shona (Zezuru, Ndau, Tewe, Manyika, Tawara) 4.8%; Nyungwe 1.4%.
  Southern peoples 19.1%. Tsonga(2) 10.2%; Tswa 3.7%; Chopi 2.9%; Ronga 2.2%.
Other 2.4%. Portuguese Mestizo 1.6%.
Literacy 46.5% (official); 20% (functional). **Official language** Portuguese, understood by less than 30%. **All languages** 53. **Indigenous languages** 43. **Languages with Scriptures** 11Bi 8NT 13por 14w.i.p.

Economy 📈

One of the world's poorest countries – the result of centuries of colonial predation, the disastrous results of Marxist economic theories and 30 years of intense guerrilla warfare. Climatic extremes of flooding and drought further impoverish the population, of whom up to 80% are subsistence farmers. Fertile agricultural land and large mineral wealth are under-utilized. Travel infrastructure is very poor, but improving. Heavily dependent on foreign aid and crippled by foreign debt. Since peace in 1995, there have been notable improvements, offset by further natural disasters. **HDI Rank** 172nd/182. **Public debt** 21.4% of GDP. **Income/person** $477 (1% of USA).

Politics 🗳

A Portuguese colony for 470 years. Independent in 1975 as a Marxist-Leninist state, after a long and bitter war for independence. The Renamo resistance movement opposed the Marxist Frelimo and an exceptionally brutal war ensued, devastating the countryside. The war and international pressure encouraged the Frelimo government to renounce Marxism in 1988 and to institute a multiparty democracy and a market economy in 1990. A peace accord in 1992 was fully implemented in 1995. The formerly warring entities of Frelimo and Renamo now dominate parliamentary seats.

Religion 🔌

Government policy between 1975 and 1982 was the exclusive propagation of Marxism and relentless attempts to root out Christianity. Since 1994, there has been religious freedom.

Religions	Pop %	Population	Ann Gr
Christian	46.48	10,878,955	2.6%
Ethnoreligionist	32.08	7,508,539	2.0%
Muslim	18.60	4,353,455	2.6%
Non-religious	2.80	655,359	2.4%
Hindu	0.04	9,362	2.4%

Christians	Denoms	Pop %	Affiliates	Ann Gr
Protestant	50	10.90	2,550,000	5.1%
Independent	508	19.03	4,453,000	2.4%
Anglican	1	0.52	122,000	2.1%
Catholic	1	20.59	4,820,000	2.2%
Orthodox	1	<0.01	1,000	-1.7%
Marginal	1	0.51	119,000	1.2%
Unaffiliated		1.68	393,000	-5.5%
Doubly affiliated		-6.75	-1,580,000	0.0%

Churches	MegaBloc	Congs	Members	Affiliates
Catholic Church	C	350	2,939,024	4,820,000
Zion/AICs	I	5,583	1,675,000	3,350,000
Evang AoG	P	1,444	345,000	900,000
Other Independent	I	576	230,435	530,000
Assemblies of God, Afr	I	490	122,378	350,000
Seventh-day Adventist	P	1,000	200,000	334,000
United Baptist Church	P	1,700	135,000	330,000
Presbyterian Church	P	805	53,648	125,000
Anglican Church	A	251	42,657	122,000
Jehovah's Witnesses	M	1,150	35,207	119,000
Ch of the Nazarene	P	1,300	92,000	115,000

M

					TransBloc	Pop %	Population	Ann Gr
Ref Ch in Moz	P	450	48,000	105,000	**Evangelicals**			
Baptist Convention	P	539	38,288	85,000	Evangelicals	11.1	2,606,512	5.4%
United Methodist Ch	P	289	56,429	79,000	**Renewalists**			
Ch of God (Anderson)	P	500	37,500	75,000	Charismatics	11.7	2,748,905	4.8%
New Alliance (Brethren)	I	120	18,500	46,250	Pentecostals	6.1	1,423,260	6.6%
Int Assemblies of God	P	262	21,000	42,000				
Apostolic Faith Mission	P	158	19,000	38,000				
Free Methodist Ch	P	240	20,000	27,000				
Full Gospel Ch of God	P	74	9,000	25,740				
Other denominations[43]		3,581	202,243	447,325				
Doubly affiliated				-1,580,000				
Total Christians[562]		**20,862**	**6,340,309**	**10,485,315**				

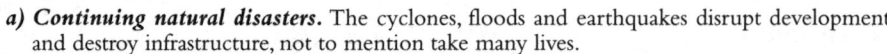

Religions % of Total Pop

MegaBlocs % of Christian Pop — 3.2 1.9 20.5 38.7 35.8 — P I C U X

Answers to Prayer

1 **The country has enjoyed peace** since 1992 after 30 years of war, and the politicians have genuinely endeavoured to maintain and build on this peace. The government has performed admirably in advancing the nation's democratic, economic and religious freedom status.

2 **Amazing growth in the Church** between 1990 and 2010. After harsh persecution under the Marxist-oriented regime, the Christian faith spread rapidly, tripling from 1985 to 2010. After being highly unevangelized, Mozambique now sees many from all faiths and regions beginning to follow Christ.

Challenges for Prayer

1 **Mozambique's brokenness continues.** After being shattered by colonialism and civil war, natural disasters and debt burdens, Mozambique remains one of the world's poorest nations. Personal brokenness also persists as many have been traumatized by the violence and deprivation. Turn these major challenges into prayer:

a) *Continuing natural disasters.* The cyclones, floods and earthquakes disrupt development and destroy infrastructure, not to mention take many lives.

b) *Dependency.* Heavy reliance on aid and a high public debt combine with existing poverty to make economic growth a challenge. Many struggle from day to day just to survive, but progress is being made.

c) *Disease.* Life expectancy averages only 48 years, to a large degree because of disease and extremely basic medical facilities for most. Pray for effective, practical programmes that assist those who need it most.

i *AIDS* is a major challenge, with 16% of the adult population HIV-positive. The faith communities and government have united with a national action plan. Pray that a reversal, as in some other African countries, might occur.

ii *Malaria* is an even greater bane, with a much higher prevalence – over 5 million cases a year – taking many lives and sapping the health of those who survive.

iii *Other medical issues* such as diarrhoea and tuberculosis become even more lethal amidst intense poverty and especially when combined with the above two diseases.

2 **Mozambique enjoys religious freedom** for the first time in its history. Catholicism dominated under the Portuguese. Then, under Marxism, all Christians suffered. Missionaries were expelled, Christian leaders intimidated and imprisoned. Many churches were destroyed during this period. Many people died for their faith, but growth came as a result of their sacrifice. Pray that this freedom might continue and that true Christian faith and love might be expressed throughout society.

3 **Spiritual responsiveness** is one result of the suffering and deprivation endured. Congregations of indigenous Christians mushroomed all across the country. Evangelicals were 3.5% of the population in 1975 and grew to 12% by 2005. Natural disasters in 2000/01 and 2006/07 stimulated much Christian assistance, and churches were planted in refugee camps. Isolation, due to past anti-Christian governments and poverty, means that much of Mozambican church practice is genuinely indigenous. But massive growth also presents proportionally huge challenges: ignorance of biblical teaching and standards, syncretism and legalism. Fortunately, the church is also characterized by an eagerness to learn. Pray for growth in maturity and truth that matches growth in numbers – without forsaking cultural authenticity.

4 **Training church leadership** is an urgent priority, probably the most strategic spiritual issue in the country. As many as 80% of pastors/church leaders have little or no formal training, with a large number, possibly even the majority, functionally illiterate. Funds and facilities for formal theological education are lacking. Pray that the effective formation of biblically literate, godly leaders would match the ever-increasing needs of the church. Pray for:

a) *Literacy and orality.* Degree programmes and biblical resources are worthless if they cannot be utilized. Pray for literacy projects to have a great impact across the nation in order to unlock the resources in print. Pray also for the development of projects that build biblical knowledge among oral learners, who constitute the majority of the population.

b) *Seminaries and Bible colleges* are increasing in number. Evangelical institutions number 20 and counting. In addition to several interdenominational groups (**AIM**, **OMS**), the Baptists, Reformed Church, Nazarenes and Pentecostal Assemblies of Canada also operate schools. Most of these are concentrated in the south; pray for more opportunities in the neglected north. PROFORTE is an umbrella network of theological institutions in the north, founded in 2004, and it now has five member colleges.

c) *Non-formal training* – shorter discipleship-oriented training with **OM**, **YWAM**, World Outreach, *Afrika Wa Yesu* and others – has proven effective. Bible Training Centre for Pastors has 350 students in its two-year course in Mozambique.

d) *Theological Education by Extension* is absolutely crucial when travel is difficult, money tight and existing schools already stretched. TEE, mobile training and correspondence courses are spreading throughout the country (**PAoC**, **AIM**, **SIM**, Baptist, Nazarenes, Emmaus Bible School of the Brethren). Radio is a natural medium for this concept and **TWR** is building on its already substantial work in this area.

5 **Unreached peoples** are still more concentrated in Mozambique than anywhere else in southern Africa. But this is rapidly changing, since many are responding to outreach. Most existing outreach is through Mozambican missionaries and pastors. Challenges for prayer include:

a) *The Makhuwa.* Mostly Catholic-animistic (interior), Muslim (coastal) or a mix thereof, these six northern peoples represent nearly 40% of Mozambique's population. There is a remarkable ingathering of Makhuwa into the Kingdom as a result of preaching, aid and miracles. Iris Ministries, Churches of Christ/Christian Churches, **AIM**, **IMB**, **NTM** and others work among them. Pray for the many thousands of new believers to become solid disciples in biblical churches.

b) *The Yao* of Niassa Province, along the shores of Lake Malawi, are 96% Muslim. Only about 2% are Christian of any kind (mainly Anglican, Catholic and Assemblies of God, African). Many Christian resources are available (**GRN**, the JESUS film, radio, literature) and several groups work among them.

c) *Other northern/coastal Muslim peoples,* Islamized centuries ago by Swahili traders (Mwani, Koti, Makwe, Swahili, Ngoni, Makua-Mwinika). These may be the least responsive of Mozambique's peoples. Bible translation is in progress for Mwani, Koti, Ngoni and Makwe. **NTM** started work among Makua-Mwinika in Zambezia province.

  i *Mwani* believers are very few, despite **AIM** ministry, Scripture portions, oral chronological stories, the JESUS film and **GRN** recordings being available.

ii **The Koti** are staunchly Muslim, but there is a very encouraging breakthrough among them, with perhaps 20 churches and 1,200 believers. The True Way movement remains focused on this group, despite greater responsiveness from neighbouring groups.

iii **The Muslim Ngoni** expelled all priests after independence, and have had no exposure to the gospel since. The few remaining believers left the area due to social pressure.

iv **The Makwe** live in the extreme north of Mozambique and are one of the forgotten peoples in remote places.

d) The animistic peoples of the Zambezi valley, especially the Sena, Tawara, Nyungwe, Lolo, Kokola, Manyawa, Marenje and Takwane. The Church among the Sena people is growing quickly in most areas.

6 **Expatriate missionaries** have a vital but sensitive role to play, particularly among the unevangelized. There is a great need for missionaries in this open and spiritually responsive country. Pray especially for these issues:

a) Hard conditions such as travel difficulties, widespread disease, hot and humid weather, poor infrastructure, very active spiritual powers. A real calling is necessary in order to persevere. Workers must be willing to sacrifice and suffer as the national Church has done for decades.

b) Relationships between missions and churches are often very fragile. Foreigners must learn to serve and truly partner with the national church where it exists; the spectre of colonialism must be avoided. Tribal languages must be learned, since only a minority understand Portuguese.

c) Churches too often see foreign agencies as a cash cow to finance their every need. Money, being so scarce, can be a hugely divisive and destructive issue that needs to be handled with wisdom.

The greatest needs are for all levels of leadership training, initiating youth and children's work, aid/relief, medical programmes and grassroots business development. Major mission agencies: *Nederduitse Gereformeerde*, **NTM**, **SIM**, **YWAM**, CCCC, **IMB**, *Convenção Das Igrejas*.

7 **Bible translation and distribution.** The Bible Society has a bookshop and depots, but ministry is limited by a lack of Bibles, funds, distribution means and low literacy. Audio Scriptures (Faith Comes By Hearing) are increasingly available. Bible Society translation projects are underway in Ronga, Bitonga, Chopi, Lomwe, Mozambique Shangana and Makhuwa of Nampula. SIL projects in progress are Sena, Nyungwe, Takwane, Koti, Mwani, Makhuwa of Cabo Delgado, Makonde and Ngoni. Chuwabo translation started in 2009 as a joint SIL-Bible Society project. **NTM** started Bible translation in Lolo. Further work in Bible translation and use is possibly needed in Ndau and Tawara. Pray for the 17 translation projects in progress.

M **8** **Christian help ministries** for prayer:

a) Literature ministry is hampered by the same problems that hamper Bible distribution, plus, there is a lack of materials in most languages. Those who can read are desperate for literature, which is very hard to obtain. **CLC** has a bookstore in Maputo. FIEL (Faithful Publishers) has one in Nampula. There is significant potential to import second-hand Christian books from Brazil. Agencies outside the country have done much to send in good evangelistic literature but need to branch out beyond Portuguese.

b) Radio is used of God in church planting and teaching. Both **TWR** and FEBA have studios in Mozambique, and there are more than 10 Christian stations around the country. Several hours per day, programmes in Portuguese and nine other indigenous languages are broadcast on FM, medium and shortwave.

c) The JESUS film is widely used among refugees and in some areas in Mozambique. The film is translated into nineteen languages in Mozambique; pray for these translations to be fully utilized to reach many.

d) Audio Scripture is a highly effective means of propagating the gospel. **GRN** has Christian audio materials in 27 languages and dialects. SIL produces audio Scriptures from translated portions.

e) Development programmes by Christian agencies are welcomed by the government; these are great in scope of blessing, but the needs are enormous and great discernment is required.

In addition to the relief efforts that traditional missions and denominations are engaged in, more specialist groups such as WVI, World Relief, Food for the Hungry, Mennonite Central Committee and others supply basic needs to many. **MAF** (based in Nampula) and others have several planes involved in these programmes, but flying conditions are tricky. Pray that the love of Christ will be evident in all of this and that it will serve to strengthen and extend the church.

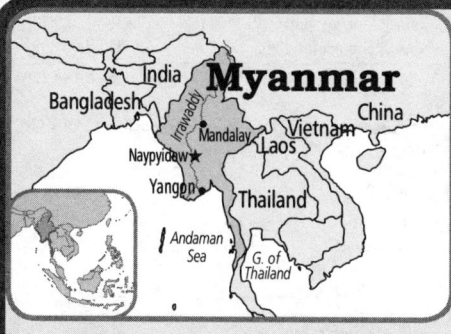

Myanmar
Union of Myanmar
Asia

Geography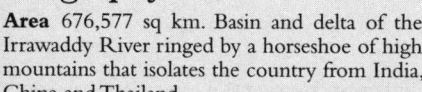

Area 676,577 sq km. Basin and delta of the Irrawaddy River ringed by a horseshoe of high mountains that isolates the country from India, China and Thailand.

Population		Ann Gr	Density
2010	50,495,672	0.87%	75/sq km
2020	55,496,711	0.89%	82/sq km
2030	59,352,944	0.61%	88/sq km

Capital Naypyidaw 1,024,062. **Other major cities** Yangon 4.3 million; Mandalay 1.0mill. **Urbanites** 33.9%. **Pop under 15 yrs** 27%. **Life expectancy** 61.2 yrs.

Peoples

Very diverse ethnically. There are eight major national races and (officially) 135 sub-groups and tribes. There are many more smaller tribes and language groups. Official figures deliberately underestimate minority ethnic populations, and there are no reliable census figures since 1931.

Tibetan–Himalayan 78.7%.
  Burmese (Bama) 62.8%. Burmese 55.8%; Rakhine 7.2%; 4 other peoples.
  Karen 9.4%. 24 peoples including S'gaw 3.6%; Eastern Pwo 2.2%; Black Karen 1.6%.
  Kuki–Chin 2.5%. 39 peoples. Chin(19) 1.8%.
  Miri–Kachin 2.4%. Kachin 1.9%.
Southeast Asian 14.8%. Shan 8.5%; Mon-Khmer(14) 4.5%; Palaung(4) 1.4%.
South Asian 4.2%. Rohingya 1.9%.
Other 2.3%. Chinese(4) 2.0%.

Literacy 89.7%. **Official language** Burmese. **All languages** 116. **Languages with Scriptures** 26Bi 15NT 24por. Another 135 languages or dialects with no Scripture.

Economy

Richly blessed with teak forests, fertile soil for agriculture, precious gems and minerals, and offshore oil and gas deposits, but most people live in poverty or at subsistence levels. The military junta has both pillaged and stunted the economy so that the former "rice bowl of Asia" sees two-thirds of its children malnourished and the majority survive on less than $1/day. Amphetamines replaced opium as the illicit drug of choice. Inflation, political isolation and the devastation of cyclone Nargis in 2008 combine to intensify the pressure on an already impoverished populace.
HDI Rank 138th/182. **Public debt** 4.5% of GDP. **Income/person** $446 (1% of USA).

Politics

Independent in 1948, after being part of India under the British Empire and occupied by Japan during WWII. Unfulfilled promises of autonomy for the ethnic regions prompted armed separatist movements, which persist to this day. The military dictator of 25 years faced popular demonstrations in 1988-89. After the 1990 elections were swept by the opposition, the military arrested the opposition leader, Aung San Suu Kyi, and ignored the election results. She has spent most of her time since then as a detainee of the regime. The secretive military junta, the "State Peace and Development Council", has used its position to imprison opponents, implement forced labour, commit genocide against restive minorities and generally repress all expressions of dissent. The crackdown on 2007 protests and the relocation of the capital to Naypyidaw further isolated the junta from the population. A member of ASEAN. A new constitution was written by the regime and endorsed in a rigged referendum in 2008; elections are planned for 2010.

Religion

The regime recognized the special status of Buddhism in Myanmar. Freedom of religion exists, at least according to the constitution, and Christianity and Islam are strong among several minority groups. The combination of ethnic,

M

political and religious differences along with violent opposition means that some Christian minorities suffer greatly at the hands of the military.

Religions	Pop %	Population	Ann Gr
Buddhist	80.04	40,416,736	0.6%
Christian	8.98	4,534,511	2.7%
Muslim	7.20	3,635,688	2.0%
Chinese	2.30	1,161,400	2.7%
Ethnoreligionist	0.63	318,123	-1.2%
Hindu	0.45	227,231	0.0%
Non-religious	0.40	201,983	0.9%

Numbers for minority religions are certainly larger than what government figures state.

Christians	Denoms	Pop %	Affiliates	Ann Gr
Protestant	32	4.52	2,285,000	1.6%
Independent	55	2.29	1,156,000	4.6%
Anglican	1	0.13	64,000	0.6%
Catholic	1	1.33	672,000	2.2%
Marginal	1	0.03	13,000	3.8%
Unaffiliated		0.68	343,000	5.5%

Churches	MegaBloc	Congs	Members	Affiliates
Myanmar Bapt Conv	P	4,530	1,142,000	1,720,000
Catholic Church	C	334	417,391	672,000
Lisu Christian Church	I	967	58,000	145,000
Churches of Christ	P	1,769	92,000	138,000
Assemblies of God	P	1,251	43,634	100,358
Myan Gospel Outreach	I	500	37,500	75,000
Ch of Province of Myan	A	132	31,323	63,899
Believers Church	I	600	30,000	60,000
Evang Believers Conf	I	357	20,000	44,000
Evang Baptist Church	I	243	17,000	37,740
Mara Christian Church	P	92	18,500	37,000
Seventh-day Adventist	P	227	27,231	35,400
Presby Ch of Myanmar	P	246	17,448	29,791
Other denominations[77]		5,506	535,551	1,031,091
Total Christians[90]		**16,754**	**2,487,578**	**4,189,279**

TransBloc	Pop %	Population	Ann Gr
Evangelicals			
Evangelicals	5.0	2,517,184	2.5%
Renewalists			
Charismatics	1.4	724,391	3.8%
Pentecostals	0.5	267,766	3.6%

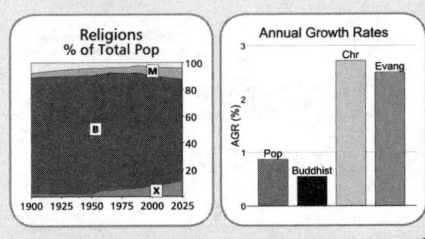

Religions % of Total Pop

Annual Growth Rates

Answers to Prayer

1 **The continued growth of the church** amid great suffering and repression is an answer to prayer. While the majority of believers still come from certain ethnic minorities, there is an increasing response from the Buddhist majority, particularly monks. Momentum in evangelism is building as an indigenous missions movement begins to flourish.

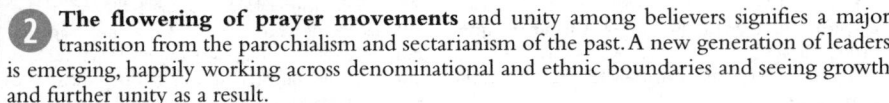

2 **The flowering of prayer movements** and unity among believers signifies a major transition from the parochialism and sectarianism of the past. A new generation of leaders is emerging, happily working across denominational and ethnic boundaries and seeing growth and further unity as a result.

3 **Praise God for the refining of the Church,** made possible by the desperation of persecution, poverty and isolation. Liberal groups have drawn closer to biblical truth, and lax believers are driven toward a more dynamic life of faith. Myanmar is a classic example of how suffering, while lamentable, serves to accomplish God's purposes for His people.

Challenges for Prayer

1 **The military junta** has redefined the term "ruthless". Their self-serving policies of isolation impoverished an otherwise wealthy land and made it an international pariah. The violent crackdown on protests led by Buddhist monks in 2007 drove a wedge between those who control power and those who hold moral authority in this deeply spiritual nation. The population is increasingly disillusioned with the regime to the point of being openly critical. UN resolutions addressing the junta's actions were blocked by China and Russia, and ASEAN's influence is negligible. Pray for intervention that will bring justice; pray also for repentance of those who use their power in wicked ways.

2 **A policy of systematic violence** against certain minorities yields a harvest of destroyed villages, rape, torture, uprooted populations and international condemnation. Great suffering is inflicted upon such peoples as the Karen, Chin, Shan, Mon and Wa with the Karen and Chin particularly sought out due to their Christian faith and separatist militias. Myanmar is a deeply fractured nation on a political, ecclesiological and especially ethnic level. Pray for seemingly impossible ethnic harmony, effective federalism and peace.

3 **The suffering and poverty** of the Burmese is an increasing challenge in the light of:

a) ***The devastation of cyclone Nargis.*** When it ripped through the country in May 2008, around 140,000 people lost their lives from the storm itself and the disease and deprivation that followed. About $10 billion (US) in damage was done. The destruction was exacerbated by the government's slow response, the regime's refusal to allow foreign aid groups to enter affected areas with relief and aid, and corruption which saw the best of the aid siphoned off to the army.

b) ***A downward-spiralling economy.*** The currency is devaluing, food and fuel prices are rising quickly and people live from hand to mouth with little to spare – 10% are chronically malnourished. This is mostly due to government corruption and mismanagement. Such a precarious existence makes people even more vulnerable.

4 **The military regime seeks to destroy Christianity** (which it calls "the C-virus"), yet faith keeps spreading. Christians are generally kept out of positions of power and influence. Military campaigns against Christian minorities are well publicized, and over 3,000 Christian villages have been burned out in the last 10 years. Churches are not given permission to register and are thereby considered illegal and subject to harassment. The expulsion of foreign Christian workers in 1966 left a young church to cope on its own with little mature leadership or infrastructure. Adversity, persecution and isolation have helped shape a resilient, enduring faith.

5 **The Church faces many challenges** in Myanmar. Pray about these issues:

a) ***Limitations on the freedom to function*** as the Church, since many restrictions exist. Authorities generally disallow new church buildings from being constructed. The importation of Christian literature is severely limited. In many cases Christians are pressured or forced to convert to Buddhism.

b) ***Nominalism and revival are simultaneous dynamics.*** Several generations after the arrival of Christianity through Adoniram Judson and others, it is to some more a tradition with irrelevant forms than a living faith. In some circles, Western humanism erodes the Bible's authority. But at the same time, many mainline and traditional denominations find themselves in the midst of revival and renewal, which is happening across previously entrenched denominational lines.

M

c) ***Most Christians are from minority groups*** that are embroiled in military actions against the central government. Pray that this may not cause bitterness, hatred of other peoples, compromise of their faith or blunting of a missions vision. Isolation, poverty and lack of training hamper the ability of these groups to be a witness, but this is changing.

d) ***Reconciliation and unity*** among Christians is a crucial issue. There were many causes of division – ethnic, political, passivism or military activism, and doctrinal. Strong centralized control under one authoritarian church/denominational leader along with parochialism kept Christians apart and growth limited. Pray for:

i *The forces of spiritual unity.* The burgeoning prayer movement, those impacted by renewal and the emerging generation of leaders are joining to stand as one.

ii *The organizational bodies fostering fellowship.* Pray that the Myanmar Council of Churches (MCC), the Myanmar Evangelical Christian Fellowship (MECF) and the Myanmar Biblical Christian Fellowship (MBCF) may effectively promote Christian unity.

iii *Cultural leadership patterns* combining with imported sectarianism from abroad. The need to start one's own denomination, the foreign money available for ministry and the sectarian principles imbued upon nationals who studied abroad is a dangerous cocktail. Pray for wisdom for national leaders in learning to deal with these challenges.

6 **Theological education** is of vital importance; this is reflected by the rapid multiplication of training institutes in the last 10 years – from 90 in 2000 to over 200 in 2009. Many are very small, with scant resources or materials and poorly trained instructors. Women account for nearly 50% of the students. The threat of liberal theology existing in the previous generation has profoundly reversed in most cases, but is still present in a few mainline denominations. Pray specifically for:

a) *The more notable institutions,* including the Myanmar Evangelical Graduate School of Theology (MEGST) and the Association for Theological Education in Myanmar (ATEM, tied to MCC). A new consortium for undergraduate establishments has great potential but is still in developmental stages.

b) *Training and mission mobilizing* in short, intensive courses. These are proving effective for bivocational workers and lay Christians.

c) *The right balance* of biblical truth, evangelism training and strong missiological preparation for interacting with and ministering to the Buddhist worldview, which is so different from Christianity. One methodology developed by a former Buddhist monk is seeing remarkable response.

d) *The retention of leaders.* Far too many attend seminary in order to learn English, seen as a ticket out of the country. Others study abroad but don't return to the challenging life of ministering in Myanmar. Praise God for the establishment of Masters degree programmes at MEGST which enable aspiring ministry leaders to get equipped and remain in Myanmar.

e) *Theological Education by Extension* (TEE) is an essential tool for multiplying trained leaders for the fast-growing Church. This concept is working well in both traditional churches and in the Buddhist-background believers' movement.

7 **Buddhism is strongly entrenched** among the Burmese majority as well as the Shan, the Rakhine and the Mon, and has deep influence among more animistic peoples. Burmese Buddhism incorporates much pre-Buddhist spiritism, occult beliefs, astrology and superstition, and devotion is strong. Most children are educated in monasteries, so the influence of Buddhist thought is pervasive. The Church must learn to understand and address the Buddhist mindset as well as minister in spiritual power if it is to see a harvest among this majority. But positive signs are there including a growing openness to Jesus, especially among the 700,000 monks. Many study the gospel and listen to Christian radio. Reportedly, thousands have quietly become believers; no doubt many more would also believe were there not such powerful cultural, social and spiritual constraints against leaving Buddhism. The government crackdown against the monks' political demonstration reduced their influence to a degree.

M **8** **The least evangelized peoples.** There are still many millions of unreached, and the need for bold but sensitive outreach and church planting persists. There is a young but encouraging movement to Christ that expresses the gospel in a framework sensible to Buddhists. It began among the Rakhine and moved to Burmese and Karen Buddhists. Pray for:

a) *The Bama* (Burmese) peoples, staunchly Buddhist (only 0.1% Christian). It is not easy for tribal believers to witness to them due to years of mistrust; nor is it easy for the politically dominant Bama to receive the gospel from them without prejudice. Pray for conversions among this staunchly Buddhist people.

b) *The Shan* are related to the Thai and live in the Golden Triangle area. Despite being primarily Buddhist, they suffered much in the wars with the military regime. Only 0.9% are Christian, and few have Bibles. The new Shan Bible translation was published in 2003.

c) *Other Buddhist minorities* have few Christians – Arakanese/Rakhine (0.1%), the Palaung (0.2%), Mon (0.9%), Lu (0.2%), Yangbye (0.5%) and several smaller groups.

d) *The dozens of animistic peoples,* many of whom are proving responsive to loving outreach. Pray for the emergence of vital church planting movements among all of them.

e) *The Chinese* number over one million, but only about 2.5% are Christian. Long holding significant influence in Myanmar, a recent and massive influx of Chinese over the Yunnan border has caused resentment. The recent arrivals are less evangelized than Burmese-born Chinese. Mandalay is over one-third Chinese.

f) *The Rohingya* of Arakan, Muslim descendants of Arabs, Moors, Moghuls and Bengalis who settled in Arakan 1,000 years ago. They are one of the most neglected and unwanted peoples on earth. They are denied citizenship and face numerous restrictions in their basic rights. Many have fled to neighbouring Bangladesh or emigrated illegally to other countries. There is little outreach to them. Pray for the few scattered believers.

g) The nine Hindu peoples were long neglected. In 1928 the first church was planted among them, but they still are only around 1% Christian.

9 **Pray for the vast number of refugees/IDPs.** In Thailand alone there are over two million Burmese (mainly for economic rather than political reasons), and more in Malaysia, Singapore and Western nations. Another one million are internally displaced, mostly from Christian areas. Both within Myanmar and among the diaspora there is increasing ministry and spiritual fruit, with many Burmese churches being planted. But many remain without the gospel, uprooted and far from home.

10 **The missionary vision of the Myanmar Church** continues to grow and mature. A number of nationals serve the Lord cross-culturally. There are many Bible schools in Yangon, accounting for at least 1,000 students; most of these include mission as a key part of the curriculum. Pray for a willingness to serve in the rural villages and not just the cities, for genuine love across deep ethnic divides, and for good training so that the indigenous church is well equipped to evangelize the nation.

11 **Christian support ministries** are coming into their own. The maturing of indigenous missions and the country's desperate plight create many new opportunities to demonstrate Christ's compassion. Prayer needs include:

a) The aftermath of cyclone Nargis, while tragic, created an open door for the practical ministry of providing food, water, clothing, shelter and other basic necessities as well as meeting the deeper economic, spiritual and psychological needs of the survivors. The response by many Christians and the openness of many Buddhists led to the cyclone being referred to as "the blessed storm". Since foreign agencies are banned or heavily restricted in operating locally, indigenous ministries and international partnerships are rising to the challenge.

b) AIDS victims. Myanmar has one of the most severe AIDS crises in the region, with about 1.5% of the population infected, sadly much of it in the "Christian" areas. Inadequate prevention measures by the government, combined with large-scale prostitution (often involuntarily trafficked rural girls), destroy the lives of many. ATEM, Tearfund and the Presbyterians are a few of the key groups working to prevent the further spread of HIV and to minister to those impacted by this disease.

c) Drug addicts. Intravenous drug use is widespread (given the proximity to the Golden Triangle Area) and, unsurprisingly, closely linked to HIV/AIDS. The Myanmar Young Crusaders is one of several groups with effective ministry seeing the lives of addicts transformed through Christ's power.

d) Children at risk are a populous group (more than 750,000), given the civil conflicts and the destruction by Nargis. Increasing numbers of local churches and missions run orphanages or work with street children, usually on quite a small and local scale. Pray for financial provision for these grassroots ministries, for the freedom to operate and for the children to meet Jesus in these difficult circumstances.

12 **Media resources** for the church. Pray for:

a) Bibles and Christian literature are in desperately short supply due to import and printing restrictions. More Christian bookshops are opening in the cities (The Evangelical Literature Centre, **CLC**, others), but they are far from enough to meet the need. Too much unhelpful Christian literature from abroad only complicates matters. Pray for more culturally appropriate, well-translated, biblically faithful writings and that God would raise up Burmese writers to meet this need.

b) Bible translation is a major challenge. There are teams working on 16 NT or whole-Bible translations, but dozens more are needed. Most work needs to be done by Myanmar translators. Pray for evangelical translators to be raised up to continue existing programmes and to finish these strategic and long-term projects.

c) Christian radio is very effective due to its mobility and privacy, with broadcasting in 35 languages. Major radio agencies and their broadcasting languages include **FEBC** (28 languages, including Bama/Burmese, totalling 76 hours/week) and **TWR** (Burmese, Karen, 11 hours/week). Also broadcasting are Adventist World Radio, Gospel for Asia and Radio Veritas Asia. Several others broadcast primarily in English. Pray for the production of programmes and the provision of equipment.

d) **GRN** has made recordings available in 127 languages, but importation and distribution problems have thus far limited their impact. Pray for this potentially massive ministry.

e) **The JESUS film** has been widely shown in film and on television and is available in 42 languages.

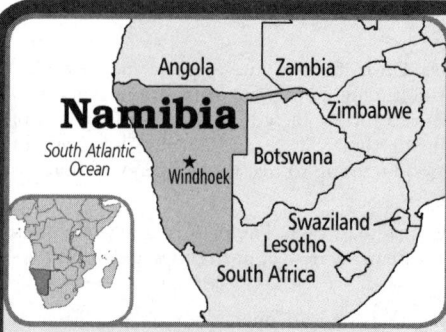

Namibia

Republic of Namibia

Africa

Geography 🌍

Area 823,144 sq km. Predominantly arid, semi-desert; the driest African land south of the equator.

Population		Ann Gr	Density
2010	2,212,037	1.94%	3/sq km
2020	2,614,338	1.62%	3/sq km
2030	2,993,057	1.27%	4/sq km

Most people live on the central plateau and the better-watered northern border regions adjoining Angola.
Capital Windhoek 354,000. **Urbanites** 38%. **Pop under 15 yrs** 37%. **Life expectancy** 60.4 yrs.

Peoples 👪

Five major groupings and 28 languages.
Bantu 69.8%. Dominated by Ovambo grouping of peoples in the north. Ovambo 43% (Ndonga 22.8%; Kwanyama 14.0%; Ngangela 3.5%; Kwambi 1.5%); Kwangali 7.9%; Herero 7.6%; Lozi 2.3%; Chickwahane 1.5%.
Khoisan 8.9%. Khoi and San are separate groups. Nama (4.8%) is the largest Khoi group.
European 8.5%. Afrikaner 7.3%.
Mixed Race 12.8%. Afrikaans-speaking. Coloured 9.0%; "Baster" 1.1%.
Literacy 85.0%. **Official language** English, though few speak it; most speak Afrikaans. **All languages** 37. **Indigenous languages** 28. **Languages with Scriptures** 9Bi 4NT 6por.

Economy 📈

Mining diamonds, uranium and many other minerals, cattle ranching, fishing and increasingly tourism are important. Many still live in deep poverty.
HDI Rank 128th/182. **Public debt** 20% of GDP. **Income/person** $4,278 (9% of USA), but a large gap between rich and poor.

Politics 🗳

A German colony from 1883-1915. Ruled by South Africa 1915-1990. Independence gained in 1990 after a long, costly war that severely disrupted the social and economic fabric of the country. The major party, SWAPO, renounced Marxism and espoused multiparty democracy. The longstanding president handed over power to a protégé in 2005. A member of the British Commonwealth.

Religion ⛪

Secular state with freedom of religion.

Religions	Pop %	Population	Ann Gr
Christian	91.44	2,022,687	1.7%
Ethnoreligionist	4.52	99,984	9.4%
Non-religious	4.00	88,481	1.9%
Jewish	0.04	885	-2.5%

Christians	Denoms	Pop %	Affiliates	Ann Gr
Protestant	41	60.64	1,341,000	1.2%
Independent	128	11.59	256,000	2.6%
Anglican	1	5.20	115,000	1.3%
Catholic	1	17.86	395,000	1.4%
Marginal	2	0.19	4,000	4.2%
Unaffiliated		3.30	73,000	0.0%
Doubly affiliated		*-7.32*	*-162,000*	*0.0%*

Churches	MegaBloc	Congs	Members	Affiliates
Evang Luth Church	P	330	264,000	660,000
Catholic Church	C	103	236,527	395,000
Ev Luth Ch in Rep of N	P	70	158,333	380,000
Anglican Church	A	177	23,000	115,000
Evang Ref Ch in Afr	P	119	37,107	59,000
Uniting Ref Ch of SA	P	140	28,750	57,500
Protestant Unity Ch	I	225	22,455	37,500
Seventh-day Adventist	P	65	18,000	32,000
Full Gospel Ch of God	P	105	12,800	25,600
Ovamboland Anglican Ch	I	75	11,261	25,000

N

Dutch Reformed Ch	P	47	16,300	24,600
Rhenish Ch in Namibia	P	14	9,600	19,200
Evangelical Bible Ch	P	18	6,700	13,400
AoG (Back to God)	I	63	6,930	12,474
African Meth Epis Ch	I	44	3,498	10,600
Other denominations[157]		1,165	131,811	244,969
Doubly affiliated				*-162,000*
Total Christians[173]		**2,760**	**987,072**	**1,949,843**

TransBloc	Pop %	Population	Ann Gr
Evangelicals			
Evangelicals	12.2	270,326	2.2%
Renewalists			
Charismatics	6.8	150,207	4.7%
Pentecostals	2.9	63,224	4.4%

Religions % of Total Pop

TransBloc Movements % of Total Pop — Charis, Evang, Pente

Answers to Prayer

1 **Stability and some economic progress** marked the post-independence 1990s, despite the fears of many of ethnic strife and economic collapse. The scars of the colonial and apartheid past are gradually healing. There was much united prayer by Christians at the time. There is a significant national prayer movement.

Challenges for Prayer

1 **Namibia is a stable country** rich in natural resources, but there is significant risk of strife and collapse if able governance and communal harmony do not prevail. Pray that the nation's leaders would address the issues of poverty, land ownership and AIDS with wisdom and determination.

2 **German and Finnish Lutheran and then Anglican missionaries** gave birth to large denominations in the 19th Century. Liberal theology and syncretistic Afro-Spiritism eroded that spiritual heritage, and now many self-styled Christians are either nominal or incorporate unbiblical practices into their faith. Reformation is greatly needed, but first there needs to be an opening of hearts to the Spirit. Pray for a biblical faith to be restored throughout Namibia's many churches.

3 **New life in the churches** has come recently through new mission activity by **SIM/AIM, YWAM** as well as Reformed, Baptist and Pentecostal groups, particularly to under-reached areas and peoples. Charismatic fellowships – both independent and within many denominations, including the mainline groups – bring new life and fervour. Several strategic groups formed to see Namibia transformed for Christ, the Evangelical Fellowship most notable among these. Pray for all to hear the gospel once again and many to turn back to Christ, and pray for unity and cooperation among all groups seeking to uplift Christ in this nation.

N

4 **Spiritual leaders.** Pray for current and future pastors and leaders to be trained and formed to God's standards. Crucial to biblical formation are Namibia Evangelical Theological Seminary in Windhoek (**SIM/AIM**, NGK), the Namibia Ministry Training Institute (Pentecostal) and **YWAM**'s training bases. TEE plays an important role, especially in the north, through the NETS distance education programme. Pray also that the mainline training institutes would capture a love and respect for God's Word.

5 **Major social issues loom ominously** over Namibia's future. Averting disaster requires appropriate government action, but more so a mobilization of the Church.

a) Poverty. A dangerous gap separates the rich and poor. Over 35% are unemployed. Ovamboland in the north is most acutely affected. Migration to the cities to find work creates shantytowns.

b) AIDS. Namibia has the fourth highest infection rate in the world. This prevalence (25% of adults and young people) and ineffective government programmes create a major crisis as life expectancy plummets. The Caprivi Strip records a staggering 43% adult infection rate. SU addresses this through their Aid for AIDS progamme, and many churches and missions are finally making this tragedy a ministry priority.

c) Reconciliation. Namibia's colonial past under German and then South African rule, the legacy of apartheid and the Cold War-fuelled fighting and terrorism before independence have left many scars. Some good progress is being made in the area of reconciliation; pray that in Christ both perpetrators and victims might find forgiveness and peace.

6 **Missions are experiencing a time of growth** as the need to re-reach many peoples in Namibia becomes apparent. Pray that they would minister in the power of the gospel, but also with sensitivity. Major missions are: **AIM, YWAM, AoG, SIM**.

7 **The less-evangelized peoples.** Pray for:

a) The San (Bushmen) cluster of peoples – much romanticized but in reality a suffering people. Their traditional way of life is threatened by cattle ranching, mining and conservation efforts, not to mention the havoc wrought by sedentary vices. The NGK and Pentecostal Assemblies work among them, yet the San have barely been touched by the gospel; their animistic faith and semi-nomadic lifestyle require a very special kind of outreach.

b) The peoples of the Kavango and Caprivi Strip in the northeast – the Mbukushu, Wayeyi, Gckiruku and Fwe. Many are animists. **AIM/SIM** planted several churches among them. A number of Adventists are among them as well.

c) The Himba (5,000) and Dhimba (15,000) are offshoots of the Herero people in the barren northeast and in southwest Angola. Nearly all are animist, though a few are Lutheran and Reformed Christians. Bible translation into Dhimba is nearly completed, along with Scripture songs in traditional Dhimba forms.

8 **Christian help ministries.** Pray for these:

a) Bible translation. All the major languages have full Bibles. The Namibia Bible Society and Lutheran Bible Translators are involved in revisions of several of these, including Dhimba, Damara/Nama, Ju/'huoan and Kwanayama. A Bible in the Hands of Every Namibian is a major project for the Society.

b) Christian literature for local languages and away from main centres is scarce. The Bible Society's mobile Bible shop, a specially equipped van with literature and media resources, is a big boost to getting materials into the hands of Namibians. SU and **YWAM** have bookstores.

c) The JESUS film soundtrack has been prepared by Media for Christ in several Namibian languages with more in preparation. Pray for lasting results from the showing of this film.

d) Christian radio. Radio teaching on national networks has a wonderful impact in strengthening biblical faith in the nation (especially within mainline churches) as well as in effectively reaching resistant peoples. Evangelical presence in mainstream radio and TV is decreasing, but Media for Christ runs a station with many other effective, related ministries. Pray for continued impact on the nation through Christian media.

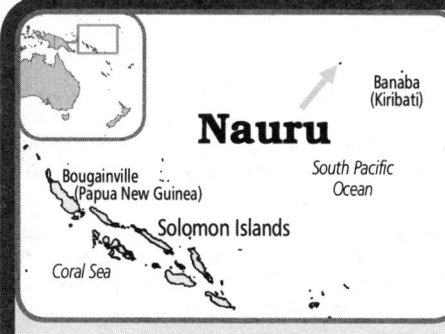

Nauru

Banaba (Kiribati)

South Pacific Ocean

Bougainville (Papua New Guinea)

Solomon Islands

Coral Sea

Nauru
Republic of Nauru
Pacific

Geography

Area 21 sq km. A raised coral atoll ringed with sandy beaches, with a central plateau of phosphates from fossilized bird droppings; 300 km west of Banaba, Kiribati.

Population		Ann Gr	Density
2010	10,254	0.28%	488/sq km
2020	10,812	0.45%	515/sq km
2030	11,070	0.16%	527/sq km

Capital None, but administrative centre in Yaren. **Urbanites** 100%. **Pop under 15 yrs** 36%. **Life expectancy** 62.8 yrs.

Peoples

Micronesian 73.4%. Nauruan 59.5%; I-Kiribati 11.6%.
Other 26.6%. Chinese 15.2%; Caucasian 7.2%; Tuvaluan 3.6%.
Literacy 97%. **Official languages** Nauruan, English. **All languages** 9. **Indigenous languages** 3. **Languages with Scriptures** 2Bi.

Economy

Its once-booming economy has collapsed, since phosphate mining now produces only a fraction of its former output and offshore banking has been stopped. Accommodating Australia's offshore asylum-seekers has also ceased. The country is deeply in debt from overspending during the boom, with the only income sources – some mining and sale of fishing rights – horribly inadequate to cover costs.

Politics

German rule 1888-1914. UN trusteeship administered by Australia and Britain until independence in 1968. Nauruans resisted invitations to resettle elsewhere in 1964. Became a UN member in 1999. The world's smallest republic.

Religion

Freedom of religion.

Religions	Pop %	Population	Ann Gr
Christian	91.50	9,382	0.3%
Non-religious	5.30	543	1.5%
Chinese	3.20	328	-1.5%

Christians Denoms		Pop %	Affiliates	Ann Gr
Protestant	9	57.35	6,000	0.4%
Anglican	1	2.93	<300	-1.3%
Catholic	1	29.06	3,000	0.2%
Marginal	2	1.39	<200	0.7%
Unaffiliated		0.80	<100	0.0%

Churches	MegaBloc	Congs	Members	Affiliates
Congregational Ch	P	16	1,625	3,900
Catholic Church	C	1	1,733	2,980
Nauru Independent Ch	P	2	283	650
Anglican Church	A	3	135	300
Other denominations[9]		12	624	1,474
Total Christians[13]		**34**	**4,400**	**9,304**

TransBloc	Pop %	Population	Ann Gr
Evangelicals			
Evangelicals	12.1	1,245	2.3%
Renewalists			
Charismatics	10.8	1,110	2.4%
Pentecostals	7.9	810	2.4%

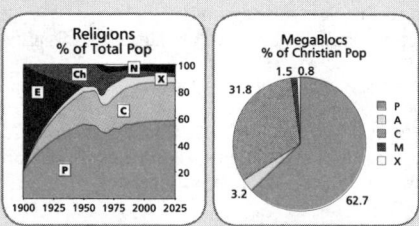

Religions % of Total Pop

MegaBlocs % of Christian Pop

N

Answers to Prayer

1. **Offshore banking on the Internet** has been shut down, having been revealed as a front for the money-laundering activities of Russian criminals. It was a courageous move, forfeiting the flow of money through the country – an amount approaching tens of billions of dollars per year. Pray that God may reward the prioritizing of righteousness over riches.

Challenges for Prayer

1 **Economic meltdown has struck this tiny nation.** After years of boom, Nauru has gone bust. The mining industry is a shadow of its former self, and the two other major income sources have also dried up. Almost all food must be imported, and freshwater supplies are insufficient. Half of the indigenous population has diabetes; 90% are overweight and unemployed. Pray for sustainable economic solutions that will provide livelihoods for those making the island their home.

2 **Spiritual awareness grows** as the economy shrinks. Materialism's decline is faith's gain. Church life is reawakening and evangelical numbers are growing. The Nauru Independent Church is the largest evangelical group, but there are believers in the other denominations as well. The JESUS film has been seen by almost the entire population.

Bengali 7.9%. 49 groups. Shaikh 3.0%; Koiri 1.1%.
Newar 5.5%.
Rajasthan 1.2%. 24 groups.
Urdu Muslim 0.9%. 51 groups.
Other South Asian 1.1%.
Tibetan–Himalayan 21.5%. 38 peoples mainly in north and west.
South Himalayan peoples 20.7%. 19 groups. Magar 7.2%; Tamang 5.6%; Rai 2.8%; Gurung 2.4%; Limbu 1.7%; Sherpa/Bhotia 0.7%.
Tibetan peoples 0.9%. 17 peoples.
Other 0.5%. Other Asian and Western ethnicities.
Literacy 48.6%. **Official language** Nepali. **All languages** 127. **Languages with Scriptures** 8Bi 17NT 20por.

Nepal
Federal Democratic Republic of Nepal
Asia

Geography

Area 147,181 sq km. A mountainous Himalayan state between China (Tibet) and India. It contains 8 of the 10 highest mountain peaks in the world.

Population		Ann Gr	Density
2010	29,852,682	1.86%	203/sq km
2020	35,268,659	1.65%	240/sq km
2030	40,646,415	1.34%	276/sq km

Capital Kathmandu 1,037,073. The city doubled in size during the 1990s. **Urbanites** 18%. **Pop under 15 yrs** 37%. **Life expectancy** 66.3 yrs.

Peoples

As many as 100 ethnic groups, consisting of over 300 peoples, sub-groups and castes. Caste is often as important a distinction as ethnicity in this strongly Hindu culture.
South Asian 78.0%. 285 peoples/castes. Mainly in south and east.
Hindi 36.1%. 84 groups. Brahman 13.3%; Tharu 6.7%; Yadava 4.0%; Teli 1.3%; Chamar 1.2%.
Nepali–Pahari 25.3%. 35 groups. Chhetri 15.8%; Kami 4.0%; Darjee 1.7%; Thakuri 1.5%; Sarki 1.4%.

Economy

One of the world's poorest countries, with around one-third of the people living below the poverty line, on less than $1US/day. Subsistence agriculture occupies up to 90% of the population and accounts for 38% of GDP. Geographical isolation, difficult terrain, poor infrastructure destroyed or damaged by Maoist conflict, rapid deforestation, environmental damage and susceptibility to natural disasters all weigh against development. Recovery will be difficult so long as current political instability remains. Despite the difficult situation, Nepal has made notable progress in the last 50 years since it was effectively an isolated medieval kingdom. Great potential for hydroelectric power and tourism. **HDI Rank** 144th/182. **Public debt** 50% of GDP. **Income/person** $444 (1% of USA).

Politics

The ancient and hereditary monarchy ended in 2008 as Nepal became a multiparty constitutional republic. Never ruled by colonial powers, Nepal's political isolation from the outside world ended in 1951. In 1962, the king assumed executive power in a government system with no political parties. The 1990s and 2000s were characterized by painful and disruptive civil unrest provoked mostly by Maoist rebels. A Maoist-dominated government took office in 2008 after two years of wrangling with other parties, but the Prime

Minister resigned in 2010. The government remains insolvent, and constitutional reform has been delayed further. The integration of the 20,000-strong Maoist army into the national army is a very complicated and sensitive issue. Also, many groups – such as the Dalits, Madheshis (in the lowland Terai) and the indigenous Tibetan-Himalayan groups comprising the Nepal Federation of Indigenous Nationalities – have grievances with their exclusion from the political process. Addressing the issues of impoverished rural communities and resisting perceived "foreign interference" dominates political rhetoric.

Religion

Once the world's only Hindu Kingdom, Nepal is now officially a secular democracy. Foreign religious NGOs can operate freely as long as they do not proselytize. Hindu fundamentalism has increased in recent years.

Religions	Pop %	Population	Ann Gr
Hindu	75.01	22,392,497	1.7%
Buddhist	16.00	4,776,429	1.9%
Muslim	4.40	1,313,518	4.8%
Christian	2.85	850,801	5.3%
Other	0.90	268,674	-1.4%
Non-religious	0.75	223,895	6.5%
Sikh	0.06	17,912	1.9%
Baha'i	0.03	8,956	1.9%

The boundary between Hinduism and Buddhism is often difficult to distinguish.

Christians	Denoms	Pop %	Affiliates	Ann Gr
Protestant	23	0.44	132,000	5.1%
Independent	63	2.41	721,000	5.3%
Catholic	1	0.02	7,000	2.0%
Marginal	6	0.02	5,000	6.1%
Doubly affiliated		*-0.04*	*-13,000*	*0.0%*

Churches	MegaBloc	Congs	Members	Affiliates
Indep Nepali groups	I	2,000	124,000	198,400
House church networks	I	1,200	60,000	108,000
Christ groups (EHC)	I	3,367	50,500	101,000
Nat Chs Fell of N (NCFN)	I	380	33,182	73,000
Assemblies of God	P	382	12,613	42,000
Calvary Churches	I	480	15,833	38,000
Believers Church	I	330	13,200	33,000
Evang Chr Fell of N	I	180	12,917	31,000
Other India-related chs	I	243	12,174	28,000
Agape Fellowship	I	60	9,600	24,000
Nepal Bapt Chr Council	P	115	14,000	24,000
Evang Alliance Ch of N	I	60	7,500	18,750
Emmanuel Church Assoc	I	66	8,000	14,400
Assemblies (El Shaddai)	I	77	6,500	13,000
Bethel Church	I	47	5,200	13,000
Other denominations[34]		793	53,362	91,819
Total Christians[93]		**9,780**	**438,581**	**851,369**

TransBloc	Pop %	Population	Ann Gr
Evangelicals			
Evangelicals	2.8	837,596	5.3%
Renewalists			
Charismatics	2.0	608,197	5.2%
Pentecostals	0.6	169,866	4.7%

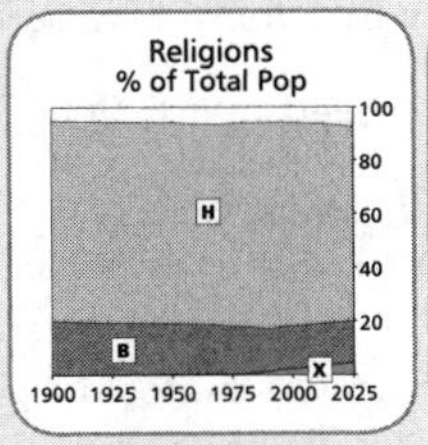

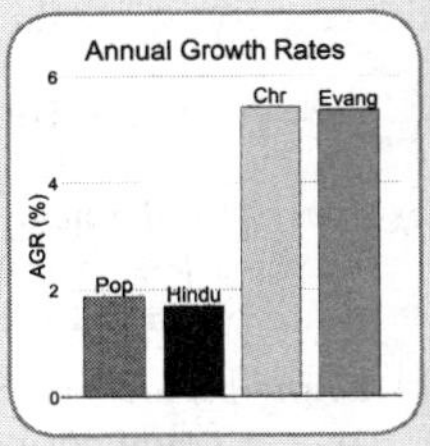

Answers to Prayer

1 **A new Nepal began in 2008** with the absolute power of the Hindu monarchy yielding to pro-democracy protests. Sweeping political change, begun in the 1950s, has climaxed in the last couple of years. This is an answer to the specific prayers of almost all Christians in Nepal who have interceded for their nation, and it paves the way for new freedoms and opportunities for Christian ministry.

2 **Sustained church growth over decades** and through many trials gives Nepali Christianity a strong foundation. The first church was formed in 1952 with 29 Christians. At the height of persecution in 1990, there were 200,000 believers. In 2010 there are as many as 850,000 Christ-followers in nearly 10,000 groups. This was achieved by willingness to suffer for the gospel, profound prayerfulness and a Nepali-driven long-term commitment to evangelism and church planting. Now, new social and transformational ministries are growing on the back of this foundation.

3 **There is a church planted** in every one of the 75 districts of Nepal, and there are at least some believers in almost every people and caste group.

4 **Praise God for increased unity** within Christianity and for greater cooperation between Christianity and other faiths. The Nepal Christian Society was formed in 1996 as a coordinating fellowship for Evangelicals, the National Council of Churches of Nepal in 1999 for social and national development and Christian Efforts for Peace, Justice, and Reconciliation (CEPJAR) was formed in 2003. CEPJAR later joined a multi-faith peacebuilding process with representatives of all other faiths.

Challenges for Prayer

1 **Nepal enjoys a window of opportunity** with the new government and new constitution, but positive strides must be made quickly before disillusionment or entrenchment occurs. With deep divisions still affecting society – various religious groups, deeply opposed political parties – real progress must be made if the new government is to have a true chance of success. The Maoist former rebels, still listed in some other nations as a terrorist organization, hold the keys to the finely balanced government. Pray for wisdom, courage and grace on the part of Nepal's leaders, and that they might put personal or party differences aside and work together to fight the immense economic problems still gripping the country.

2 **The many human rights abuses** that occurred during the conflict have not been righted. Justice has not been administered for the bereaved of the 13,000 killed during the conflict – many of them extra-judicially. Not one person has been prosecuted, and the Maoist leadership – now holding Nepal's reigns of power – would suffer greatly were their excesses and evil deeds brought to light. Unless justice is done and seen to be done, violence will continue to be justified as a means to a political end. Pray for justice and righteousness to be upheld in this country where they have for so long been withheld.

3 **Socio-economic needs** remain a huge challenge in this beautiful but troubled land.

a) ***Poverty and unemployment*** keep Nepal from progressing. Fully 47% are underemployed (working less than 40% of their available working hours). Pray for creative and sustainable means of gainful employment.

b) ***Young people*** comprise two-thirds of Nepal's population, which is one of the world's youngest and fastest growing. Most live in rural areas, deprived of education and opportunity. Illiteracy is widespread. Young people are vulnerable to economic exploitation, sex trafficking, drug abuse, HIV/AIDS and radicalization (political or religious). Pray for changes here that offer young people hope and a future.

c) ***Despite becoming a secular democracy,*** Nepal's social structures remain dominated by Hinduism. This perpetuates the caste system, which oppresses many, most notably Dalits who make up as much as 14% of the population. Caste discrimination is technically illegal but ubiquitous nonetheless. Converts from Hinduism to Christ usually become outcastes as well. Pray for the shattering of this unjust system.

4 **Freedom of religion is guaranteed by law,** but only in limited measures. Non-Hindus cannot proselytize. If they do, they risk fines, imprisonment and, in the case of expatriates, expulsion. Despite this law, the Church in Nepal grows because of courageous evangelism. Hindu fundamentalists as well as Maoists often single out Christians; their non-violent nature and connections to the West make them soft targets. Pray for perseverance for believers, that neither laws of man nor threats of violence deter them from sharing the gospel.

5 **The Church in Nepal continues to flourish** amid pressure as a remarkable indigenous movement; the large majority of Nepali Christians worship and fellowship in thoroughly indigenous structures and networks. The Church is growing in numbers, diversity and maturity, but prayer is still needed regarding:

a) ***The public image of Christianity*** in Nepal is as a foreign, mostly Western, intrusion that undermines traditional culture and society and appeals only to lower castes. Despite this, Nepal's Christians are, with increasing confidence, defending their rights and building a fully Nepali, fully Christian identity. Pray for discernment, courage and faithfulness for those seeking to overturn two generations of negative opinion.

b) ***Denominationalism.*** Many foreign-based denominations as well as indigenous networks of churches are established. Pray that the Church may be kept from division and error. Pray specifically for the Nepal Christian Society (NCS) as it seeks to provide a forum for prayer, sharing, unity and cooperative ministries.

c) ***Persecution*** remains, though less acute than in the past. It can come from the religious majority but also socially from within families and communities. Pray for grace and perseverance for believers, and that Christians may be accepted and appreciated for their contribution to the country's well being. Pray also for the efforts of NCS and others seeking to secure the legal and religious rights of Christians regarding arbitrary arrests, evangelism, property, discrimination and other maltreatments.

d) ***Partnership between Nepali churches and foreign agencies.*** As the Nepali Church matures, it increasingly takes stake in ministry and mission to its own country. Foreign input, especially through finance, often generates tension or dependency and continues to be an issue. But the national Church is flourishing, and indigenous Christian NGOs are mushrooming around the country.

6 **The next generation of Nepali Christians** must build on the good foundation laid by their elders. Pray for:

a) ***Effective transfer of leadership*** to a second generation. Along with this challenge is the task of properly discipling both new believers and the large number of second-generation Christians.

b) ***Leadership training*** is possibly the most urgent need in the Church. For years, no formal training was available. Now, there are over 15 Bible colleges and seminaries. Many churches and agencies offer short-term and modular training courses. The majority are linked with the Association of Theological Educators, Nepal. **GFA** has three centres from which 100 Nepali evangelist-missionaries graduate annually. DAI just started Nepal's first accredited Masters in Christian Leadership. The Institute for TEE in Nepal has over 3,000 students in half of Nepal's districts. Despite these developments, there is a huge training shortfall. As the Church grows, the need for leadership-training structures and models becomes increasingly desperate. Pray for a multiplication of feasible, effective methods of ministry training.

c) ***Provision of pastors*** amid gripping poverty is a constant challenge. Since Nepal was never colonized by foreign powers and the Church is mostly outside of international fraternal structures, external financial support can be very low, and the temptation to extract income from foreign donors is great. Pray that leaders would learn to function as tentmakers, and that congregations would learn to support their pastors as much as they are able.

d) ***Holistic ministry.*** The Church stands at the crux of spiritual and physical needs and is well positioned to minister to both. The time has come for the Church to engage with the many needs in Nepali society. Pray for a paradigm shift in which Christians include social transformation as a key part of evangelization. Nepali Christian NGOs increasingly address holistic needs.

N

7 **Christian ministry must address a host of challenges** under the government's watchful eye. High unemployment, illiteracy, low levels of development, environmental degradation and dependence on foreign aid are all being addressed by Christians. Pray for practical, sustainable and innovative ways to address the following issues:

a) ***Child labour.*** An estimated 2.6 million children work as child labourers; 70% of them are forced to work 10-hour days or longer. The government seeks to eliminate by 2014 the worst forms of child labour, such as mining and rag picking. Pray for the success of this programme. Education and subsequent development are impossible until Nepal gets children out of the workplace and into school.

b) ***Trafficking of Nepali girls*** for the Indian, Middle Eastern and domestic sex trade. There are up to 300,000 girls in India alone (mainly in Mumbai), where they are terribly abused; possibly 90% of returnees are HIV-positive. AIDS has rapidly spread through the rest of society as a result, and there is no coherent national plan for AIDS prevention. Poor and lower-caste girls are the primary targets of this evil trade, and usually as unwilling victims. Nepali Christians reach and rescue some of these unfortunates in Nepal and in Mumbai.

c) ***Health and disease.*** Over 20% of hospitals and clinics, and nearly all of leprosy-control work, are Christian-run (TLM, United Mission to Nepal, International Nepal Fellowship, others).

Nepal suffers high rates of infant mortality and of deaths during childbirth. Community health is vital; over 80% of diseases are caused by a lack of basic sanitation, and 60% of the 50,000 child deaths each year are caused by malnutrition.

8 **Pray for the less reached;** around 55% of the population are unevangelized, and a staggering 309 peoples/castes are unreached. Pray for:

a) *The influential high-caste Hill Brahmin and Chhetri* (Rajput). They represent 30.9% of the population and play a dominant role in shaping modern Nepal. While those in Nepal are more responsive than those in India, pride, fear and longstanding spiritual investments in Hinduism keep most in bondage, unable to openly proclaim Christ as Lord.

b) *The Awadhi and Bhojpuri speakers and Maithili of the Tarai lowlands* on the Indian border. Few have heard the gospel, and even fewer have responded. The Tharu are more animist than Hindu; many small churches are springing up among them.

c) *The Mountain peoples,* almost entirely Tibetan-related. Most are lamaistic Buddhists living in isolated mountain communities, such as the Loba people of Mustang. Most groups are small in number, and Christians are few. Among the famous Sherpa of the Everest region, where there is not a single church, there are perhaps 50 believers. Climbing for Christ seeks to reach them with the gospel.

d) *Tibetan refugees* – long unreached, with no legal status and numbering 20,000. There is now a steady trickle seeking the Lord and a handful of congregations among them. Evangelistic International Ministries focuses on them.

e) *The increased number of Muslims.* Most are Bengali, Kashmiri or Urdu-speaking farmers and unskilled labourers. Eastern Mennonite Missions seeks to develop a network to share Christ with them.

f) *University students.* Over 150,000 students are in higher education – in three universities on 150 campuses. **YWAM**'s seven bases include Kathmandu Centre with 65 on staff. The **IFES**-linked student movement, University Christian Students Fellowship of Nepal (NBCBS), has 62 groups with 2,100 students served by 10 workers. Campus Crusade for Christ is also highly active with 18 campus ministry teams.

9 **Holistic ministry by foreign agencies** powerfully demonstrates the love of Christ in practical and spiritual ways. The restrictive conditions for entry require authenticity and integrity by these NGOs. Their supportive role is invaluable – in hospitals, dispensaries, leprosy treatment, agriculture, education and assisting society's most vulnerable. The United Mission to Nepal is the largest body, representing 24 agencies from 15 countries. The International Nepal Fellowship has 31 expatriate workers as well as over 300 Nepali staff, mainly in the west of Nepal. India also contributes largely to Christian work, with at least 12 Indian evangelical agencies with **GFA** the largest. Pray for vision, wisdom and humble faithful service for all working in Nepal.

N

10 **The Nepali diaspora** is officially two million, but the number of Nepalis illegally working abroad (by choice and increasingly by compulsion) may exceed 10 million. Nearly every family in Nepal has at least one member working away from home. Most go to India, but Nepalis can be found in over 100 nations. Nepalis abroad are more open to the gospel than are those at home. Numerous churches are established among Nepali migrants, even in restricted-access nations. Pray that creative ways might be found to share the good news with these scattered peoples.

a) *In India, Sikkim state is 75% Nepali,* and Darjeeling district in West Bengal is 60% Nepali. Nepali churches in India, some established since the early 1900s, have sent their first missionaries to Nepal; pray for growth, release from stagnation and greater involvement in cross-cultural outreach.

b) *Many Nepalis serve as Gurkha soldiers* in the British, Brunei and Indian armies. Others serve as security guards throughout Asia. Becoming a Gurkha is a great honour and a way to financial security for oneself and one's family; competition is fierce. There are some Christian groups working among these soldiers. Pray for effective outreach to them.

c) *Other Asian nations.* The Persian Gulf nations host 87% of official Nepali migrant workers. Women working here are particularly vulnerable to exploitation and unfair treatment. Pray for outreach to them; they can easily get lost in the crowd of migrant labourers in the Gulf. Malaysia has seen rapid Christian growth among Nepali migrant workers, with more than 50 Nepali congregations now operating there.

11 **Other help ministries** for which prayer is requested:

a) Bible translation. William Carey first translated the NT into Nepali in 1821. Eight of Nepal's 80 languages have a complete translation; an estimated 44 have further translation needs, but low literacy hampers the effectiveness of all translations. Pray for the translation teams. Pray also for literacy programmes that will uplift the populace in so many ways, in addition to Bible reading.

b) The Bible Society registered officially, after years of difficulties in the area. They published a Simple Nepali Bible and the OT in Tibetan. Pray for effective networking with other distribution channels such as The Bible League, Gideons and others.

c) Christian literature can now be freely printed and distributed without censorship. Import difficulties have encouraged local publishing and distribution. Pray for The Bible Society bookshop in Kathmandu and for **OM** and **GFA** publishing house and literature distribution teams. **EHC** has reached 270,000 homes with over a half million pieces of literature, matching the distribution numbers of the Gideons. Good News Publishers and Derek Prince Ministries have also translated and distributed large numbers of books. Pray that these growing ministries might have a long-lasting effect on Nepal's evangelization and discipling.

d) Audio Bibles are popular for the millions of non-readers. **GRN** produced recordings in over 100 of the known 145 languages and dialects of Nepal, to enthusiastic response. FCBH and the Audio Bible are two such audio resources having an impact among Nepalis.

e) Bible correspondence courses remain a key but under-resourced means of reaching people. More than 290,000 Nepalis have enrolled in a course designed for people from a Hindu background. Much of this is organized by Nepal Gospel Outreach Center (NGOC) and Institute for TEE in Nepal. Many churches have been planted as a result of conversions to Christ from these courses.

f) Christian radio. **GFA** Radio broadcasts the gospel in over 12 languages on stations across the country, including the government's Radio Nepal. **TWR**, FEBA and AWR broadcast in several languages as well, and Women of Hope broadcasts several hours a week. Reception, publicity and availability of radios are obvious challenges in this mountainous and poor nation.

g) Christian films. The Indian-produced film *Daya Sagar* on the life of Jesus is popular among non-Christians. Probodh Group made several Christian films that have powerfully touched the lives of many. Several other Christian film-production ministries are growing in ministry and output capacity. The JESUS film has been widely used, and about 25% of the population have viewed it. It is now available in 19 languages. Pray for the safety of the teams deployed in the mountain regions to shows these films and share the gospel.

N

North Sea
Germany
Netherlands
The Hague ★Amsterdam
Rotterdam
Belgium

Netherlands

Kingdom of the Netherlands

Europe

Geography

Area 41,785 sq km. Northwestern Europe occupying the Rhine delta; over 20% is below sea level.

Population		Ann Gr	Density
2010	16,653,346	0.41%	399/sq km
2020	17,142,910	0.27%	410/sq km
2030	17,498,329	0.17%	419/sq km

Capital Amsterdam (administrative capital) 1,048,914; The Hague (seat of government) 474,000. **Other major city** Rotterdam 1 million (Europe's busiest seaport). **Urbanites** 82.9%. **Pop under 15 yrs** 18%. **Life expectancy** 79.8 yrs.

Peoples

European 89.2%. Dutch 78.2%; Frisian 5.1%; Groningers 3.7%. Many other European nationalities.
Asian 8.3%. Arab(6) 1.5%; Indonesian(4) 1.4%; Turkish 1.4%; many others.
Caribbean 2.1%. Suriname Creole 1.5%; Antillean 0.6%.
African 0.4%.
Literacy 99%. **Official languages** Dutch (Nederlands), Frisian. Many also speak English. **All languages** 38. **Indigenous languages** 15. **Languages with Scriptures** 3Bi 2NT 8por 1w.i.p.

Economy

Strong industrial, agricultural and trading economy. One of the world's leading exporting nations. Member of the EU. Unemployment is low, and a generous social security system supports a large number who are registered as unable to work.
HDI Rank 6th/182. **Public debt** 58.2% of GDP. **Income/person** $52,500 (111% of USA).

Politics

Protestant-led revolt against Spain established Dutch independence in 1568 and dynamized the country to become one of the world's great commercial nations. Stable, democratic, constitutional monarchy.

Religion

There is freedom of religion – but also freedom for almost any lifestyle! Anti-discrimination legislation increasingly threatens Christian liberties and absolutes in the name of tolerance, and fear to speak out stifles the truth.

Religions	Pop %	Population	Ann Gr
Non-religious	46.86	7,803,758	1.4%
Christian	46.55	7,752,133	-0.8%
Muslim	5.50	915,934	2.3%
Hindu	0.35	58,287	1.0%
Other	0.30	49,960	4.1%
Buddhist	0.22	36,637	1.4%
Jewish	0.18	29,976	-0.7%
Baha'i	0.04	6,661	0.4%

Christians	Denoms	Pop %	Affiliates	Ann Gr
Protestant	68	17.35	2,890,000	0.7%
Independent	105	0.97	161,000	2.0%
Anglican	1	0.22	37,000	2.5%
Catholic	1	25.70	4,280,000	-1.6%
Orthodox	9	0.17	28,000	5.2%
Marginal	39	0.44	74,000	-0.6%
Unaffiliated		1.70	283,000	-4.2%

Churches	MegaBloc	Congs	Members	Affiliates
Catholic Church	C	1,425	2,993,007	4,280,000
Prot Ch in the N (PKN)	P	1,790	873,016	2,200,000
Reformed Ch (Liberated)	P	278	64,953	124,710
Reformed Chs in N&NA	P	162	53,400	106,800
Chr Reformed Ch (CGK)	P	167	36,650	73,300
Restored Reformed Ch	P	95	27,500	55,000
Jehovah's Witnesses	M	395	30,059	50,800
Ch of England	A	19	15,542	37,300
Neth Ref Chs (NGK)	P	88	18,415	30,200
Orthodox Churches	O	40	19,860	28,400
Assem of God (VPE)	P	177	9,615	25,000
Moluccan Indonesian	P	56	10,000	25,000
Reformed Chs in Neth	P	53	10,875	21,750
Moravian Church	P	26	13,986	20,000
Baptist Union	P	85	10,700	17,600
Other denominations[182]		2,576	218,785	374,629
Total Christians[223]		**7,432**	**4,406,363**	**7,470,489**

TransBloc	Pop %	Population	Ann Gr
Evangelicals			
Evangelicals	4.3	716,883	0.6%
Renewalists			
Charismatics	1.8	301,688	0.7%
Pentecostals	1.1	189,242	1.0%

N

Missionaries from Netherlands
P,I,A estimated 4,000 (2,000 long-term) in more than 90 agencies and 20 denominations.

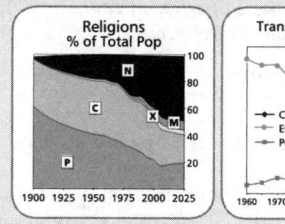

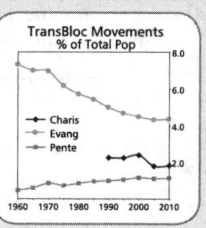

Challenges for Prayer

1 The Netherlands has two major claims to fame:

a) A glorious history as a Christian nation – its fight for religious freedom, ministry to refugees and Jews, and a record of extensive involvement in missions to other lands.

b) A decadent present as a secular society that has turned its back on its past. The number of Christians in this generation is dramatically declining, and today's openly permissive society renounces its heritage. There are few restrictions on drugs, deviant lifestyles, prostitution, homosexuality and abortion. The Netherlands is the first country to legalize euthanasia and is a world leader in promoting post-Christian, secular and New Age worldviews and values. Pray for a revival that restores the nation spiritually. Pray that the government may also be influenced for good.

2 The tolerance for which the Dutch are famous is strained in Europe's most crowded country as cultural and religious tensions multiply. It would appear that this vaunted tolerance was largely indifference. The once-liberal immigration policies are now tightening, religious expression and missionary work are often curtailed, and many Muslim communities fail to integrate into Dutch life and society and face increasing antipathy. Pray for this crisis to induce serious soul-searching that would cause many Dutch to rediscover their Christian roots and many believers to reach out with the good news to these groups.

3 Christianity in the Netherlands seems to have hit rock bottom. Less than 20% attend church with any regularity – the lowest figure in centuries. Possibly 65% of Dutch claim no affiliation with a church. Half of the nation's church buildings have been destroyed or converted for other purposes, such as bars and mosques. The Church has effectively withdrawn from engaging society in the public sphere. But many think that hedonism and secular materialism's emptiness are becoming apparent, and that church decline is slowing and even reversing. Pray for this opportunity to be seized by astute believers to regain momentum for church growth and spread the leaven of the Kingdom.

4 The Roman Catholic Church is rapidly decreasing – from 41% in 1975 to 26% (other reports claim 18%) in 2010 – and every year has fewer priests and missionaries. Weekly attendance is reportedly as low as 300,000 on any given Sunday, and the aged composition of the faithful points toward further decline. However, there is also clear growth in the charismatic and evangelical groups within Dutch Catholicism, and a proliferation of Alpha Courses.

5 The historic Protestant churches also suffer calamitous losses, from 60% of the population in 1900 to 18% in 2010. By 2015, over half their membership will be over age 65, in both the many Calvinist denominations and in most of the Free Churches. Pray for:

a) Spiritual renewal and dynamism to replace empty traditions, structural rigidity and increasingly irrelevant theological disputes in some Christian traditions.

b) A recommitment to Scripture and biblical holiness, instead of free-thinking liberalism and tolerant pluralism.

c) A prophetic message to society that contains authority and appeals to young people and addresses the tide of secularism, materialism, rampant immorality, false spiritualities and hopeless nihilism.

d) *Concern for the salvation of souls* in a church climate defined by apathy, lack of spiritual confidence and greater ecclesiastical concern for dialogue than for evangelism.

e) *A new generation of leaders* possessed by spiritual passion, theological depth, cultural relevance and winsome holiness.

6 **There are signs of hope** amid the decline. Pray for:

a) *Growth* in the number and strength of many independent churches, and continued vitality among charismatic Pentecostal Christians. Pray that spiritual depth, lasting discipleship and effective outreach might be strengthened. There are new international churches and small congregations being planted which demonstrate the openness of some hearts to receive the good news.

b) *Immigrant churches* bring diversity, vitality and a new sense of hope to the Netherlands. Pray for the effective integration of these 700,000 immigrant Christians into Dutch church life. Pray also that they might have dynamic partnerships with indigenous congregations and a burden for cross-cultural church outreach to their host nationality and to other immigrant groups.

c) *The Gereformeerde Bond and Evangelisch Werkverband* are growing evangelical expressions in the PKN (Protestant National Church) with over 500 pastors involved. These movements are increasingly respected and instrumental in sending missionaries, fostering unity and planting new churches using new models.

d) *Unity within evangelicalism* sees progress, but remains a challenge. The *Evangelische Omroep* and the Evangelical Alliance are important in this regard. Evangelicals come from a very wide spectrum and are often fragmented and isolated. SKIN is an interdenominational network bringing together the growing number and diversity of migrant churches. Pray for spiritual unity that draws denominations, institutions, agencies and ethnic groups into a single vision for reaching the nation and the world, and for their willingness to financially support this with generosity.

7 **Young people's ministry** is difficult due to their indifference and perception that Christianity is at best irrelevant and at worst an intolerant threat to postmodern liberties. Pray for:

a) *Family ministry,* as the basic spiritual social unit. Studies indicate that Dutch children have the best welfare in Europe, in such an open and tolerant society. But this means little if they are lost or in spiritual bondage. Pray for the impartation of faith from the parents' and grandparents' generation to the young people of the Netherlands.

b) *Ministry to young people* requires media savviness, immediate relevance and, above all, authenticity. Many local churches and parachurch ministries reach out to youth through the Internet, sports, music and arts, coffee houses and personal evangelism. Pray for **YWAM, YFC, OM** and many others engaged in these vital activities. National-level youth conferences such as *EO-Jongerendag, Opwekking,* XNoizz, Soul Survivor and Heart Cry have a great impact on the spiritual life of the younger generation.

c) *University students* who live in a high-pressure ideological battle zone, where it is hard to stand for Jesus. **IFES** (40 groups), Navigators (15 groups) and Agape minister on many campuses.

8 **Dutch missions** no longer have the numbers or influence they once had, but there are positive signs and modest growth. The EMA has grown to a membership of approximately 120 agencies with around 1,250 missionaries serving abroad. The influx of immigrants has awakened many churches to the reality and need of the unevangelized world. Many Dutch missionaries are involved in Bible translation as well as in aid and development programmes. Up to 2,000 more Dutch are involved in mission-related activities outside of traditional mission structures. Pray for an increase of workers for the harvest field and greater mission awareness and support from the churches.

9 **Most people have little meaningful contact** with the good news. No longer a highly Christianized nation, few today really understand the gospel and only a small minority have a meaningful link with authentic Christianity. Open and relational approaches

N

such as the Alpha Course (over 150,000 participants thus far) prove effective. Pray specifically for:

a) **The highly secularized and international cities.** Only 1-3% of Amsterdam attends church; of those, the majority are migrants. The vast majority of natives and many immigrants are unchurched. Nearly half of Amsterdam's population are immigrants. Other large cities in the Netherlands face similar challenges and opportunities. Pray for the outreach efforts of the small minority of lively churches. Pray also for **YWAM**, Agape, **OM**, IZB, Serve the City and other Dutch ministries seeking to make an urban impact. Churches are increasingly taking initiative in urban ministry.

b) **Migrant ethnic minorities** are increasing in numbers and diversity. By 2050, it is predicted that one-third of the whole country will be immigrants. Many form an urban underclass, unassimilated and with high unemployment, involved with drugs and crime. They also constitute the least-evangelized peoples of the country. Pray that there may be spiritually effective and vigorous outreach to every culture.

c) **Muslim** numbers are still increasing, as the many mega-mosque projects around the country demonstrate. But this growth is overwhelmingly through immigration (which is being reined in) and birthrate (which is falling) and hardly on a scale that will threaten atheism or Christianity. The Muslim community is troubled, seeing a backlash from a suspicious Dutch majority, facing a violent faction within its midst and struggling with spiritual apathy and even apostasy (to atheism and Christianity) among many. Now is an opportune time to reach out in friendship with the love and power of Christ.

  i *Specialized efforts and committed friendship* are needed to reach Muslims. Pray for those seeking to minister to them, such as *Gave, Evangelie & Moslims*, **OM** and others. However, these ministries tend to focus only on refugees, who represent just 30% of the Netherlands' Muslims. Pray for outreach that is sensitive and appropriate.

  ii *There is a steady trickle of Muslims* believing in Christ; pray that the trickle becomes a stream and then a torrent. Pray for these believers to be integrated into groups of likeminded disciples with whom they can walk the walk of faith in Jesus. Pray also for their safety; there are risks, even in Europe, associated with conversion from Islam.

  iii *Turks* (230,000) and Kurds (55,000), among whom are now several groups of believers.

  iv *Moroccans* (270,000), the majority being Berber Rif and Shilha rather than Arab.

  v *Smaller Muslim peoples,* who, in their frequent status as asylum seekers, often receive much outreach. These include Indonesians, Tunisians, Iraqis, Somalis, Iranians, Afghans, Arabs, Farsi-speakers and others.

d) **Chinese,** numbering over 100,000, many of whom are Buddhist. There are over 25 churches among them. COCM, **CMA** and EMSI work among the Chinese. Pray for outreach to the smaller number of Vietnamese and Thai.

e) **Hindus** – mainly Suriname Asians (**Christar**) and Sri Lankan Tamils.

10 Christian media ministries:

a) **The Bible,** found in over two-thirds of Dutch homes, is usually neglected. New translations into Dutch in 2004 (Netherlands Bible Society) and 2008 (Biblica) as well as one in plain Dutch planned for 2014 have recently made the Bible more accessible and high-profile. Pray for these editions to penetrate the lives and minds of many Dutch, and pray for the ministries devoted to promoting God's Word.

b) **Christian broadcasting.** Much Christian programming is available on TV, radio and the Internet. *Evangelische Omroep* (EO) has had a remarkable ministry for 40 years and is one of the largest Christian broadcasting companies in the country, including a large young people's club. Strict regulations make overt gospel programming difficult. Some other good initiatives in the broadcasting field are also emerging, including *Groot Nieuws Radio* and Family7.

N

Netherlands Antilles map

Netherlands Antilles

St. Martin
Saba
St. Eustatius
Curaçao
Bonaire
Willemstad
Caribbean Sea
Venezuela

Netherlands Antilles

Caribbean

Geography

Area 800 sq km. Two larger, barren islands, Curaçao and Bonaire off the coast of Venezuela, as well as three islands in the Leeward Islands 800 km to the northeast – St Eustatius, Saba and the Dutch half of St Martin (St Maarten). In 1986, Aruba withdrew from the Netherlands Antilles as an autonomous territory of the Netherlands.

Population	Ann Gr	Density
2010	200,726	1.49%	251/sq km
2020	209,708	0.25%	262/sq km
2030	209,269	-0.11%	262/sq km

Curacao 68.5%; St Maarten 22%; Bonaire 7.6%; St Eustatius 0.8%; Saba 0.6%.
Capital Willemstad 126,000. **Urbanites** 93.2%. **Pop under 15 yrs** 21%. **Life expectancy** 76.1 yrs.

Peoples

Caribbean Peoples 89.6%.
  African Caribbean/Creole 76.3%. A blend of African, Amerindian, Dutch, Surinamer and Latin American origin. Also immigrants from other Caribbean islands, especially Dominican Republic, Haiti, English-speaking Antilles.
Foreign 10.4%. Dutch 5.8%; Latin American (Colombian, Venezuelan) 2.0%; Jewish 1.3%; US citizen 0.8%.
Literacy 96.9%. **Official language** Dutch. **Common languages** Papiamento predominates, but use of English is widespread. **All languages** 7. **Indigenous languages** 4. **Languages with Scripture** 3Bi 1w.i.p.

Economy

Well developed for the Caribbean, mainstays are tourism, petroleum refining and offshore finance. **Public debt** 14.5% of GDP. **Income/person** $16,146 (35% of USA).

Politics

Integral part of Kingdom of the Netherlands with domestic autonomy for each island and parliamentary democratic government. In 2006, it was agreed that Curaçao and St Maarten would become separately autonomous as per Aruba, and the remaining islands would be directly incorporated into Dutch rule.

Religion

Complete freedom of religion.

Religions	Pop %	Population	Ann Gr
Christian	91.58	183,825	1.2%
Non-religious	5.90	11,843	7.1%
Jewish	1.30	2,609	1.5%
Hindu	0.66	1,325	1.5%
Muslim	0.33	662	2.1%
Chinese	0.15	301	-2.2%
Buddhist	0.05	100	1.5%
Baha'i	0.03	60	1.5%

Christians	Denoms	Pop %	Affiliates	Ann Gr
Protestant	28	10.96	22,000	1.3%
Independent	24	2.20	4,000	2.8%
Anglican	1	1.00	2,000	0.0%
Catholic	1	74.23	149,000	1.3%
Marginal	2	2.79	6,000	1.8%
Unaffiliated		4.40	9,000	0.0%
Doubly affiliated		*-4.00*	*-8,000*	*0.0%*

Churches	MegaBloc	Congs	Members	Affiliates
Catholic Church	C	25	88,166	149,000
Seventh-day Adventist	P	31	2,143	5,100
Jehovah's Witnesses	M	21	1,643	4,700
United Protestant Ch	P	3	1,800	3,200
Assemblies of God	P	8	912	2,680
Baptist Convention	P	24	1,497	2,500
Methodist Church	P	3	1,100	2,442
Evangelical Church	P	31	940	2,350
Other Pentecostal	I	18	1,100	2,200
Anglican Church	A	1	699	2,000
Other charismatic	I	16	950	1,900
Other denominations[25]		40	2,707	4,936
Doubly affiliated				*-8,030*
Total Christians[56]		**221**	**103,657**	**174,978**

TransBloc	Pop %	Population	Ann Gr
Evangelicals			
Evangelicals	7.7	15,427	2.1%
Renewalists			
Charismatics	6.1	12,178	3.4%
Pentecostals	3.0	6,080	3.2%

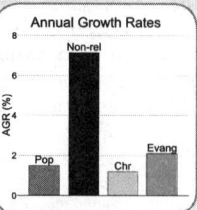

Annual Growth Rates

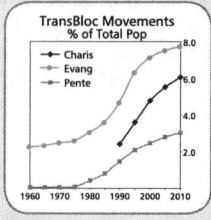

TransBloc Movements
% of Total Pop

Challenges for Prayer

1 **Freedom for the gospel** has not resulted in a great harvest. Nominalism, superstition and growing marginal sects show how few understand the message of salvation. Catholics are the majority on all islands but St Eustatius, which is predominantly Protestant. Pray that the large majority who call themselves Christian might discover a dynamic relationship with the living Saviour.

2 **Evangelical witness progresses slowly** but steadily. A vital, growing Church on every island is a target for prayer. Pentecostal/charismatic (often single-congregation denominations) and Baptist groups are the fastest growing and most outreach-oriented.

3 **The Papiamento Bible** was published in 1997 (**TEAM**) (Dutch and English are available as well). Pray for impact on the majority of the population who use it. Pray also for literacy programmes and more Christian literature in the language. There is a Christian bookstore on Curaçao. Biblical literacy will go a great distance in discipling and renewing the Christian population.

4 **Christian radio** is a very strategic ministry. Pray for these areas:

a) *Local programmes in Papiamento* (7 hours/week), Dutch and English are on FM, medium wave and shortwave. **TWR**, from its powerful station on Bonaire and by satellite, broadcasts to Latin America and the world in Spanish and English.

b) *The Caribbean Gospel Network* brings Christian programming to the whole region through culturally and regionally appropriate news, music and Bible teaching. Pray for fruit and effective follow-up.

c) *The* **TWR** *missionary community* of expatriate workers on Bonaire and local workers who maintain the radio ministry, touching millions of lives worldwide but often unaware of how great their impact is.

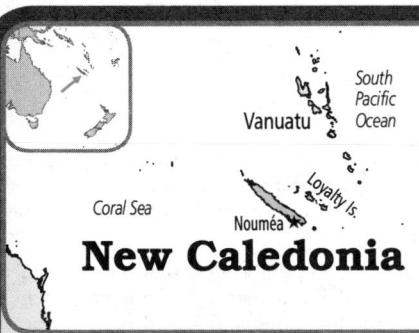

New Caledonia

New Caledonia

Territory of New Caledonia and Dependencies
Pacific

Geography 🌏

Area 18,734 sq km. One large 400 km-long island, the Loyalty Islands, and other smaller coral islands 1,400 km northeast of Australia.

Population		Ann Gr	Density
2010	253,743	1.56%	14/sq km
2020	288,298	1.22%	15/sq km
2030	318,432	0.93%	17/sq km

Capital Nouméa 146,000. **Urbanites** 57.4%. **Pop under 15 yrs** 26%. **Life expectancy** 75.2 yrs.

Peoples 👪

Melanesian 45.9%. Indigenous (Kanak), 32 groups, 35.1%; mixed race 10.8%.
Polynesian 16.2%. Wallisian/East Uvean 9.8%; Tahitian 2.9%; Futunan 2.1%.
Caucasian 31.5%. French 26.9% (of which 75% are Caldoche locals and 25% civil servants from France); Italian 3.3%.
Asian 6.4%. Javanese 4.6%; Vietnamese 1.6%.
Literacy 91%. **Official language** French. **All languages** 41. **Languages with Scriptures** 6Bi 1NT 4por 5w.i.p.

Economy 🏭

Possesses rich mineral deposits, especially nickel (possibly 40% of the world's reserves), which dominate the economy. Some service industry, but also relies on subsidies from France.
Income/person $27,387 (60% of USA). **Unemployment** 6.4%.

N

Politics 🏴

French colony in 1883; overseas territory of France since 1946. Exploitation of, and discrimination against, the indigenous peoples provoked an independence movement that led to violence in 1985. Agreement was reached for three regional governments in 1988, leading to a referendum on independence in 1998. This resulted in an agreement for 20 years of local autonomy with partnership between the indigenous Melanesians and immigrant peoples.

Religion 🙏

Freedom of religion in an increasingly secularized society. The large majority, especially non-Melanesians, have almost no meaningful contact with a church.

Religions	Pop %	Population	Ann Gr
Christian	80.65	204,644	1.5%
Non-religious	15.05	38,188	2.0%
Muslim	3.50	8,881	1.6%
Buddhist	0.50	1,269	1.6%
Baha'i	0.30	761	1.6%

Christians	Denoms	Pop %	Affiliates	Ann Gr
Protestant	3	14.46	37,000	1.4%
Independent	5	2.52	6,000	4.3%
Anglican	1	0.10	<300	2.6%

Catholic	1	51.08	130,000	1.7%
Marginal	3	3.58	9,000	-0.4%
Unaffiliated		8.90	23,000	-0.9%

Churches	MegaBloc	Congs	Members	Affiliates
Catholic Church	C	38	62,308	129,600
Evang Chs of NC & LI	P	195	7,402	32,200
Jehovah's Witnesses	M	24	2,664	6,500
Assemblies of God	P	59	3,800	3,700
Latter-day Saints	M	9	844	2,110
Free Evangelical Ch	I	74	400	1,300
Seventh-day Adventist	P	5	425	800
Other denominations[6]		60	3,410	6,620
Total Christians[13]		**459**	**80,828**	**182,030**

TransBloc	Pop %	Population	Ann Gr
Evangelicals			
Evangelicals	7.0	17,649	3.7%
Renewalists			
Charismatics	5.4	13,654	4.7%
Pentecostals	1.5	3,700	1.1%

Religions % of Total Pop

Annual Growth Rates

Challenges for Prayer

1 **The indigenous Melanesian Kanaks** were marginalized by the French during the repressive colonial period. The 1998 accord attempts to bring them into full equality in the economic, legal and political life of the nation while respecting their unique culture. Pray that this transition may be healing, peaceful and fair.

N

2 **The inequality in society** is illustrated not only economically but also by lifestyle. Sadly, too many Kanaks and immigrants from Wallis and Futuna struggle with poor living conditions, substance abuse and domestic violence. Pray for ministry that will help lift these addictions and replace them with a full and vibrant life in Christ.

3 **Most Kanaks are Christianized** and most villages have a church, but the gospel is often confused with Western culture. Animist practices usually underlie a Christian veneer. Pray for pastors to discern between tradition and the pure gospel, and that a truly biblical, truly Kanak church may continue to grow and demonstrate the power of Jesus over the evil one.

4 **Many older churches are spiritually stagnant.** Most Caledoche (descendants of former French prisoners and settlers) are culturally Catholic but lack genuine faith. Pray for:

a) Spiritual awakening among Catholics. Most are Caledoche and only nominally religious.

b) Unity and reconciliation among Christians wounded by division. The Free Evangelical Church is divided between the more liberal and the more charismatic and evangelical believers.

c) House groups and independent churches with signs of dynamic spiritual life to mature and expand as a vital part of New Caledonian Christianity.

d) *The interdenominational Bible school* to be soundly established and to grow.

e) *Club Biblique Street,* an interdenominational Christian children's club (**YWAM**-connected), to evangelize and disciple both churched and unchurched children.

5 **Less reached peoples:**

a) *The 11,000 Muslims* of Javanese or Arab descent retain their religion but not their languages. Little has been done to reach them.

b) *Polynesian Islanders* have kept both their culture and their language. There are a few evangelical believers among the traditionally Catholic Wallisians and Futunans.

c) *The Caledoche* live mostly in or near Nouméa. The **AoG** continue to work with them, but they are fairly closed to outside influence and few are evangelical believers.

d) *The Metropolitan French* (bureaucrats or business people) usually stay only a few years. Very few are involved with a church.

6 **Bible translation** is still a challenge as Melanesian languages are now used in the schools. There are five works in progress, and up to 20 other languages need further attention. Pray for the ongoing work and for the calling and equipping of new translation teams. Praise God for the completion of Bibles in Futunan and Wallisian and of the NT in Paici.

New Zealand

Auckland
Tasman Sea
Wellington
South Pacific Ocean

New Zealand

Aotearoa

Pacific

Geography 🌏

Area 267,515 sq km. Two mountainous main islands 1,600 km southeast of Australia.

Population		Ann Gr	Density
2010	4,303,457	0.92%	16/sq km
2020	4,669,002	0.78%	17/sq km
2030	4,971,630	0.58%	19/sq km

Capital Wellington 395,000. **Other major city** Auckland 1.4 million. About 30% of the population live in the Auckland area. **Urbanites** 86.8%. **Pop under 15 yrs** 20%. **Life expectancy** 80.1 yrs.

Peoples 👪

European 73.1%. 29 groups. Over 75% of this group are from British roots, but other Europeans increasing.
Pacific Islanders 20.0%. Maori 13.4%; Samoan

3.0%; Cook Is 1.3%; Tongan 1.0%.
Asian 6.3%. Chinese(4) 2.8%; Indo-Pakistani 1.7%.
Other 0.6%.
Literacy 99%. **Official languages** English, Maori. Samoan widely spoken. **All languages** 22.
Indigenous languages 4. **Languages with Scriptures** 3Bi 1w.i.p.

Economy 📈

Economy heavily based on tourism, export of agricultural and forest products and, increasingly, a range of technological and software-based innovations. Reform in the 1980s and 1990s was painful but effective in propelling the economy forward. The loss of workforce and knowledge to emigration is sufficient to affect the economy; with 16% of all Kiwis living overseas, only Ireland has a higher percent of its population living abroad.
HDI Rank 20th/182. **Public debt** 24.4% of GDP. **Income/person** $30,030 (63% of USA).

Politics 🗳

The Treaty of Waitangi, between the Maori and the British in 1840, granted the latter the right to settle in exchange for guarantees of Maori land and natural resources. This treaty was repeatedly dishonoured, causing much pain for the Maoris, much legal debate and spiritual concern as well. Independent of Britain in 1907. A stable parliamentary democracy with the British Monarch as official head of state. Regarded as one of the least corrupt nations, if not the least corrupt, in the world.

Religion ⛪

Freedom of religion. No established church.

N

Religions	Pop %	Population	Ann Gr
Christian	53.20	2,289,439	-0.8%
Non-religious	40.92	1,760,975	3.1%
Hindu	2.02	86,930	3.9%
Buddhist	1.45	62,400	1.6%
Muslim	1.23	52,933	5.2%
Other	0.60	25,821	4.7%
Sikh	0.31	13,341	7.1%
Jewish	0.16	6,886	-1.4%
Baha'i	0.06	2,582	-2.1%
Chinese	0.05	2,152	5.5%

Jehovah's Witnesses	M	180	12,146	20,891
Ringatu	M	70	10,509	17,550
Orthodox Churches	O	19	11,136	16,926
Christian Brethren	P	202	10,496	16,164
Seventh-day Adventist	P	80	11,630	15,468
New Life Church	I	139	6,966	11,633
Elim Pentecostal Ch	P	52	7,343	10,500
Salvation Army	P	93	3,312	10,368
Other denominations[82]		1,278	98,036	180,611
Total Christians[106]		**4,778**	**779,729**	**2,057,852**

Christians Denoms		Pop %	Affiliates	Ann Gr
Protestant	67	17.46	751,000	-0.7%
Independent	15	3.12	134,000	2.6%
Anglican	1	12.20	525,000	-1.1%
Catholic	1	12.35	532,000	0.9%
Orthodox	6	0.39	17,000	5.0%
Marginal	16	2.29	99,000	1.7%
Unaffiliated		5.40	232,000	-7.4%

TransBloc	Pop %	Population	Ann Gr
Evangelicals			
Evangelicals	18.2	784,015	0.5%
Renewalists			
Charismatics	9.4	405,485	3.1%
Pentecostals	1.9	83,023	1.8%

Churches	MegaBloc	Congs	Members	Affiliates
Catholic Church	C	368	356,785	531,609
Anglican Church	A	584	73,529	525,000
Presbyterian Church	P	707	42,406	353,241
Methodist Church	P	168	18,507	123,441
Baptist Union	P	185	21,590	61,746
Latter-day Saints	M	122	36,744	54,749
Ratana Church	I	156	31,231	52,155
Cong Chr Ch of Samoa	P	132	11,200	28,000
Assemblies of God	P	243	16,163	27,800

Missionaries from New Zealand
P,I,A 1,250 in 128 agencies, with over 1,000 overseas to 150 countries.

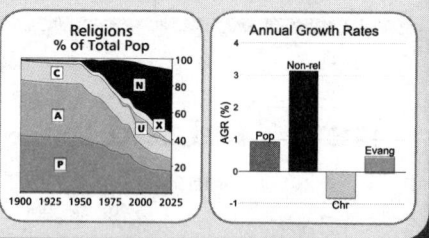

Answers to Prayer

1 **The Holy Spirit has moved in many denominations** since the 1960s. A host of new charismatic and Pentecostal groups emerged, and the large mainline denominations became more evangelical. There is a wealth of dynamic new churches, and strength remains in many of the traditional churches as well. The predicted decline and disappearance of Christianity from New Zealand is very premature indeed.

2 **New Zealand as a sending nation** consistently commissions a higher ratio of its church members as missionaries than the vast majority of countries. Nevertheless, the ambitious shared vision of Missions Interlink and many churches is to achieve, in time, a sending rate of 1 missionary per 1,000 committed believers, amounting to 3,000 workers – more than double the number being sent currently!

Challenges for Prayer

1 **The increasing presence of other religious and spiritual options** presents a challenge for Christians. The influx of immigrants from other faith backgrounds is an opportunity for Kiwis to share the gospel cross-culturally. More pressing, though, is the permeation of society with New Age spirituality. Its individualistic, non-structural, nature-attuned character appeals to many who are disillusioned with Christianity. Pray for ways for the gospel to be shared in an engaging and relevant manner; Jesus is still attractive to many who are turned off by organized religion.

2 **Kiwi society is increasingly post-Christian and secular.** Other religions are far less a threat to the Church than basic unbelief. The last 20 years have seen significant proportional decline among Anglicans, Presbyterians, Methodists and, to a lesser extent, Catholics. Those claiming to be non-religious increased from 1.1% in 1951 to 40.9% in 2010; at current rates of change, Christianity will cease to be the majority religion before 2020. Church attendance is also in decline. About 14% attend weekly; 40% of Kiwis attended church in the past but no longer do so. Pray for:

a) *A further outpouring of the Spirit* to renew those in churches and to draw in again those who have left. 24/7 prayer rooms and other prayer groups are multiplying throughout the country, indicating that God is indeed stirring the Church.

b) *Effective training and discipleship tools* that enable all Christians, ministers and laity to connect meaningfully with the unchurched. New bridges to non-believers need to be built.

c) *New expressions of church* that are dynamic, relational, relevant and culturally appropriate to both the Pakeha (Caucasian) majority and the many minorities.

d) *Wisdom for the Church* as it comes under increasing pressure from the government to cooperate with other religions.

3 **Christian division is a threat.** There are tensions in many denominations over a variety of issues, and cooperation among denominations has declined. Some tension exists among Pentecostal churches. The activity of some churches in politics is criticized by others. New Zealand Christian Network (formerly Vision Network) is a national body linking denominations and agencies that represent the majority of New Zealand's Christians. Pray God's wisdom for this group in what is a vital ministry for the health of the Church and its testimony to non-believers.

4 **Young people** are deeply affected by the strong secular emphasis of the state education system, and relatively few are active Christians. Pray for the ministry of SU in secondary schools; TSCF (**IFES**) and Tandem Ministries (**CCCI**) in universities are important. The Churches Education Commission is the national body aiming to share God's love with all schoolchildren. TSCF has a specific ministry to the increasing numbers of international students. A popular Christian music festival, Parachute, has a large following. In a nation of sports lovers, there are some fine Christian sportsmen and women and active ministry by groups like Athletes in Action. Despite increasing biblical illiteracy and spiritual apathy, many young people are spiritually open, and a youth church movement is gaining traction. Effective new ways of introducing them to Jesus are required.

5 **The continuing Maori cultural revival** and the rapidly increasing Maori population move Maori interests higher on the agenda. The state is still coming to grips with its obligations to the Maori. Cultural dislocation in the past was a main cause of social problems such as high unemployment, relative poverty, crime, domestic violence and youth gangs. Syncretistic sects such as Ringatu and Ratana as well as the Mormons have gained large followings. Very few attend evangelical churches. Pray that Maori may find their full cultural blossoming in embracing the fullness of the gospel, and pray for a new generation of Maori evangelical leaders to emerge.

6 **New Zealand's cultural diversification** continues apace as the nation's prosperity, stability and freedoms attract immigrants. But natural increase now outstrips immigration as the largest cause of population growth (much is attributed to higher birthrates in minority populations). Challenges remain to meaningfully employ and to integrate some of these groups into the broader society. Two-thirds of Asian migrants live in Auckland, where they comprise 20% of the population. Increasing numbers of churches reach out to new immigrants with English-language classes and other practical assistance, which creates significant opportunities. Pray for these groups:

a) *Polynesians immigrate to NZ* to seek employment. Large communities of Samoans, Tongans and Islanders from the NZ-administered Cook, Tokelau and Niue Islands live in the cities. Auckland has the largest Polynesian population of any city in the world. Many live in poorer areas of South Auckland where poverty and lack of employment are common and crime is high. But increasing numbers enter higher-profile professions such as sports, the media and the arts. Christian roots are common, but the younger generation is increasingly non-Christian.

b) *Chinese immigrants* have a long history in New Zealand. Immigration has recently increased, with mainland Chinese swelling the numbers of those from Hong Kong and Taiwan. Chinese churches and congregations with a significant Chinese membership are multiplying. Pray that they may be challenged to daring discipleship and missions.

c) *Indians* in increasing numbers immigrate from Fiji, India, Malaysia, South Africa and elsewhere. There are a number of Indian Christians and some outreach, but a lack of Indian Christian leadership.

d) *Other Asian groups,* including refugees/migrants from Southeast Asia (growing in number), and the Japanese community, are predominantly Buddhist. Attempts are made to reach them, and there are some Japanese congregations.

e) *The 7,000 Jews* have some Messianic believers and ministry to them (CWI and others).

f) *Muslims* are a small but fast-growing community from different parts of the world. They are assertive in establishing their own congregations – there are now around a dozen mosques in Auckland alone. There is definite need for outreach from Christians; little has been done to date.

g) *South Africans and Koreans* are two growing minorities with many churches already established. Pray for their integration into the wider Christian community; they have great potential for outreach and mission.

7 **Specialized Christian ministries:**

a) *Radio Rhema* has wide coverage and listenership throughout the country (10% of the population tune in at least weekly). Programmes are also produced for young people (Life FM). Besides Rhema's three radio networks across the country, they also broadcast nonstop as a Christian cable TV station.

b) *Alpha Courses* grew phenomenally across the country with over 1,000 churches involved. Courses such as Alpha and Christianity Explored are proving fruitful.

c) *Prison ministries* are active in many prisons. Many prisoners have been converted. Pray for them in the difficulties they face following their release.

Most live on the Pacific coast and adjacent highlands. Central America's second-most sparsely populated state. **Capital** Managua 943,626. **Urbanites** 57.3%. **Pop under 15 yrs** 35%. **Life expectancy** 72.7 yrs.

Peoples

Latino 84.0%. Mestizo 67.5%; White Latino 16.5%.
Afro–Nicaraguan 8.7%. On the Caribbean coast, speaking Creole English.
Amerindian 5.9%. Miskito 3.6% (many Spanish-speaking); Matagalpa 0.7%; Monimbo 0.3%; Sumo; Subtiaba.
Other 1.4%. Middle Eastern 0.8%; Chinese 0.2%; Romani 0.2%; European.
Literacy 76.7%. **Official language** Spanish. English-speaking communities on east coast. **All languages** 7. **Languages with Scriptures** 4Bi 1por 1w.i.p.

Nicaragua

Republic of Nicaragua

Latin America

Geography

Area 127,849 sq km. The largest of the Central American republics. Central mountainous area between Pacific and Caribbean coasts.

Population		Ann Gr	Density
2010	5,822,265	1.31%	46/sq km
2020	6,681,798	1.30%	52/sq km
2030	7,387,209	0.92%	58/sq km

Economy

Many minerals, fertile soil and low population make the country potentially wealthy. One of the poorer states in the Americas due to nearly two centuries of dictatorships, civil wars and natural calamities. Sandinista Marxist economic policies and US meddling in the 1980s led to hyper-inflation and economic collapse. Since 1991 there has been encouraging progress because of a more balanced approach. A mixed economy. Heavily dependent on remittances from Nicaraguans working abroad. Illegal logging of rainforest hardwood is an increasing problem.

HDI Rank 124th/182. **Unemployment** 5.2%. **Public debt** 74.8% of GDP. **Income/person** $1,028 (2% of USA).

Politics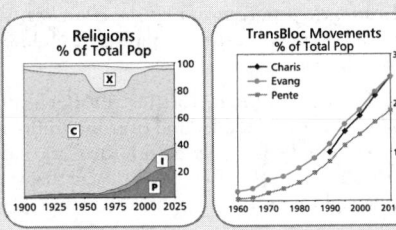

Independent republic since 1838. The corrupt Somoza dictatorship ended in 1979 after a bitter civil war. The Sandinista government introduced Marxist ideology and economics, but was violently opposed by US-sponsored "Contras" from surrounding lands. This influence and conflict coupled with economic failure helped the right wing win elections in the 1990s. The new millennium sees the ascension of the Sandinistas to elected government once more, with a "post-Marxist" left-wing platform. Left-right cooperation may be a sign of either genuine progress or corrupt collusion.

Religion

A secular state with complete religious freedom since 1990.

Religions	Pop %	Population	Ann Gr
Christian	97.32	5,666,228	1.4%
Non-religious	1.70	98,979	-2.9%
Ethnoreligionist	0.80	46,578	-3.1%
Chinese	0.06	3,493	9.9%
Baha'i	0.05	2,911	5.9%
Buddhist	0.04	2,329	7.3%
Muslim	0.03	1,747	1.3%

Christians Denoms		Pop %	Affiliates	Ann Gr
Protestant	39	21.25	1,237,231	4.5%
Independent	75	11.76	685,000	7.0%
Anglican	1	0.19	11,000	2.6%
Catholic	1	69.39	4,040,000	0.5%
Marginal	2	2.39	139,000	4.8%
Doubly affiliated		-7.65	-446,000	0.0%

Churches	MegaBloc	Congs	Members	Affiliates
Catholic Church	C	365	2,137,566	4,040,000
Assemblies of God	P	910	260,000	425,000
Seventh-day Adventist	P	160	63,871	99,000
Moravian Church	P	209	24,300	91,500
Ch of God (Cleveland)	P	510	36,100	90,000
Chr Apos Min Centre	I	50	50,000	90,000
National Bap Conv	P	271	36,000	79,200
Apos Ch of Faith in JC	I	312	25,000	77,500
Jehovah's Witnesses	M	475	24,700	70,000
Latter-day Saints (Mormon)	M	138	36,508	69,000
Pente Ch of God Mission	P	305	16,800	58,000
Good Samaritan Bapt Ch	P	265	20,000	56,000
Ch of God of Prophecy	P	410	21,300	50,000
Christian Assemblies	P	125	13,333	40,000
Christian Pente Ch	P	159	12,500	35,000
Assoc of Chs of Christ	P	118	15,000	21,750
Ch of the Nazarene	P	207	11,400	20,000
Other denominations[101]		4,889	268,112	699,756
Doubly affiliated				-445,500
Total Christians[118]		**9,878**	**3,072,490**	**5,666,206**

TransBloc	Pop %	Population	Ann Gr
Evangelicals			
Evangelicals	29.8	1,732,307	5.5%
Renewalists			
Charismatics	29.5	1,716,159	6.1%
Pentecostals	19.7	1,149,250	5.0%

Missionaries from Nicaragua
P,I,A 13 in 3 agencies: to Africa 5.

Religions
% of Total Pop

TransBloc Movements
% of Total Pop

N

Answers to Prayer

1 **God has used various means** to bring about a remarkable turning to Himself, many involving suffering:

a) *Natural disasters* such as volcanic eruptions, earthquakes and hurricanes shocked many into considering issues of life and eternity.

b) *The massive upheavals* of war, conflict and political polarization forced many to turn to the compassion of Christians and hope in Christ.

c) *Extensive evangelism* by mass crusades, "Evangelism in Depth" programmes and local church outreaches all added to the number of believers.

2 **Evangelical growth** is high and sustained amid the upheaval. Evangelicals grew from 2.2% in 1960 to 29.8% in 2010. This is more than a 40-fold numeric increase in 50 years, with no signs of such growth abating.

Challenges for Prayer

1 **Nicaragua's divided past** still influences the present. The traumatic events of 1979-1998 divided politics (left- and right-wing), communities (the Hispanic-Mestizo west and Creole-Amerindian east), trade unions, churches and families. The situation is changing, but there is still lingering distrust along these fault lines that needs to be overcome.

2 **Poverty is a deep-seated issue** that is both the cause and the result of many political troubles. After years of civil war, Hurricane Mitch further devastated the nation's economy and infrastructure. Economic wisdom and long-term development are needed. Many economic uplift programmes have been launched by CEPAD (The Evangelical Committee for Relief and Development), **AoG** and others. This longstanding state of poverty also shapes the spirituality of Nicaragua, with both liberation theology and prosperity theology playing major roles.

3 **Rapid evangelical growth** in an impoverished and dysfunctional society creates both challenges and opportunities. Pray about the following:

a) *The deep trauma suffered by many* who are now turning to the churches – bereavement, family break-ups, material loss and other traumas.

b) *Division among and even within churches* on liberation theology, the work of the Holy Spirit and interpersonal conflicts. The Evangelical Alliance of Nicaragua (FAENIC) represents 62 denominations and is crucial in forging a healthy national Christian presence.

c) *The emergence of US-style megachurches* with their dynamism and confidence. Nicaragua needs culturally appropriate churches that serve the people and do not just mimic foreign models.

d) *Economic programmes by the churches.* With widespread poverty, churches are ministering to the most destitute (such as street children) and developing ways to assist their most needy members.

4 **Involvement in politics.** Evangelicals – a quarter of the population – are beginning to wield considerable (and overdue) influence in the public sphere. Many in the government are becoming believers, and both the Catholic Church and some evangelical megachurches have significant political muscle to flex. Pray that believers might have the wisdom and determination to be a righteous influence on the nation.

N **5** **Ministry challenges** for the Church:

a) *Revival for the English/Creole and Miskito churches* in the Caribbean eastern provinces. Many are Moravian, Anglican or Catholic and are often traditional and syncretistic. The Miskito in particular suffered severely at the hands of the Sandinistas.

b) *Those devastated by the civil war.* Ex-Sandinistas and Contras often find that, while the conflict has passed, their suffering and loss remain. They need those who can minister love and spiritual healing to them after the bitter war, with its many atrocities meted out to opponents and innocent civilians alike.

c) *The Hispanicized Indians.* These are nominally Catholic, and few active evangelical congregations exist among them.

d) *The Garifuna* are still largely animist, but there are some churches among them. The NT is being translated.

e) *Immigrant groups* are increasing, particularly Westerners looking to develop the economy and Chinese. There are no churches among this latter group.

6 **Young people** have grown up in a country ravaged by war and disaster and distorted by political ideologies. Stable families are rare. Not many churches are equipped or committed to meet their needs, despite the fact that 75% of the population is under age 30. CECNIC(**IFES**) has 22 groups in the universities where, along with **YWAM** and **CCCI**, they are active in evangelism and mission trips. There are even three evangelical universities; pray for a redemptive and transforming impact on society.

7 **Missions vision is still in an early stage.** There are a number of national agencies, linked by *Movimiento Misionero Transcultural Nicaraguense* (MMTN). This is driving a greater movement not only toward mission sending but toward unity in the churches involved as well. Pray that MMTN might be used of God to bring churches together and to ignite a strong missionary-sending movement.

8 **The expatriate missionary force** has changed in its numbers and direction. The major tasks for missionaries are Bible teaching, leadership training and helping Nicaraguans launch holistic ministries that address spiritual, financial and social needs. The largest agencies are **AoG, YWAM, BBF, ABWE.**

9 **Christian support ministries** for prayer:

a) Christian radio and TV. There is one Christian TV station and 10 radio stations.

b) The Bible Society has done much in enabling the translation and distribution of the new Sumo and Miskito Bibles. The Bible League and **GRN** also provide gospel literature and recordings in several languages.

c) Development projects for urban and rural communities by means of credit and training that contributes to socio-economic and spiritual growth. These projects are a key aspect in empowering Nicaraguans to move their nation forward toward stability and prosperity.

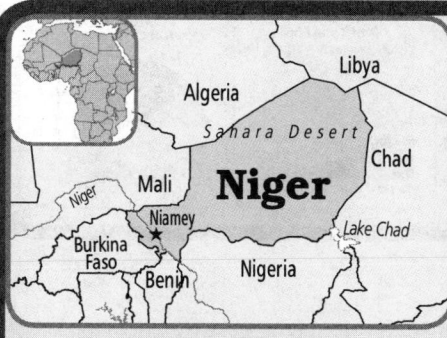

Niger
Republic of Niger
Africa

Geography 🌐

Area 1,186,408 sq km. Sahara desert in centre and north. Only the southwest and a narrow strip along the Nigerian border in the south are savannah grasslands.

Population		Ann Gr	Density
2010	15,891,482	3.94%	13/sq km
2020	22,946,657	3.68%	19/sq km
2030	32,562,695	3.52%	27/sq km

Capital Niamey 1,047,686. **Urbanites** 16.7%. **Pop under 15 yrs** 50%. **Life expectancy** 50.8 yrs.

Peoples 👪

Sub-Saharan African 89.4%.
> **Hausa** 43.2%. Adarawa 39.1%; Mauri 3.3%; Kawar 0.8%.
> **Songhai** 29.3%. 5 groups. Zarma (Djerma) 23.9%; Koryaboro 4.6%.
> **Fulbe (Fulani)** 10.4%. The more settled Sokoto 4.1%; the largely nomadic Wodaabe/Bororo 3.3% and Western Fulani 3.0%.
> **Kanuri-Saharan** 4.8%. 8 peoples. Manga 2.6%; Yerwa 0.8%.
> **Gur** 1.2%. Mossi 0.9%.
> **Other Africans** 0.5%. Nigerians, Togolese, others.

Arab World 10.4%.
> **Arab** 1.4%. Arabized Berber 1.2%; Moors, Lebanese, Shuwa nomads.
> **Tuareg/Tamacheq** 9.0%. Six ethnic groups. Tahoua Tamacheq 4.4%; Arabized Tamacheq 2.0%; Air Tamacheq 1.7%.

Other 0.2%. French, others.

Literacy 28.7%. **Official language** French. Language of wider communication is Hausa. **All languages** 21. **Languages with Scriptures** 3Bi 4NT 9por 8w.i.p.

Economy 🗺️

One of the world's poorest nations and right near the bottom of the Human Development Index. Most people barely survive on subsistence agriculture and livestock. Droughts and locust plagues further devastate the already fragile economy. Possession of some of the world's largest uranium deposits should bring

N

investment if the uranium market improves. Very dependent on aid and IMF loans.
HDI Rank 182nd/182. **Public debt** 67.9% of GDP. **Income/person** \$391 (1% of USA).

Politics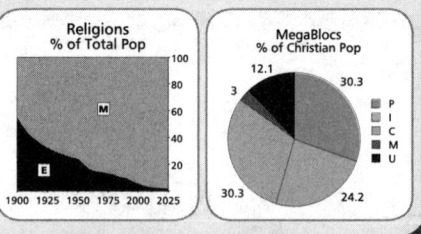

For centuries the Tuareg dominated much of the Sahel. French colonial rule 1921-1960. Military regimes with a number of coups. A brief period of democratic rule, 1993-96, presaged the democratic government formed in 1999. Yet another military coup in 2010 ousted the former president who had forced a change in the constitution, allowing himself to stay in power longer. There has been intermittent Tuareg insurgency in the north for some years.

Religion

A non-confessional state with considerable freedom of religion and few restrictions on mission work. Tensions between Muslims and Christians have escalated due to the situation in Nigeria, the rise of fundamentalist Muslim groups in Niger and the less-than sensitive approaches of some Pentecostal groups.

Christians	Denoms	Pop %	Affiliates	Ann Gr
Protestant	17	0.10	16,000	3.2%
Independent	19	0.08	13,000	1.4%
Catholic	1	0.10	16,000	0.0%
Marginal	1	0.01	1,000	0.9%
Unaffiliated		<0.01	6,000	3.7%

Churches	MegaBloc	Congs	Members	Affiliates
Catholic Church	C	16	8,466	16,000
Evangelical Ch (EERN)	P	100	1,200	6,000
Assemblies of God	P	30	1,738	3,650
Un of Ev Prot (UEEPN)	P	40	1,375	3,300
Jehovah's Witnesses	M	6	343	1,200
Abundant Life Church	I	30	575	1,150
Ev Chr Assem (ACEN)	I	12	408	1,020
Un of Bapt Chs (UEEB)	P	4	350	700
Other denominations[30]		89	7,945	13,625
Total Christians[38]		**327**	**22,400**	**46,645**

TransBloc	Pop %	Population	Ann Gr
Evangelicals			
Evangelicals	0.1	21,541	3.7%
Renewalists			
Charismatics	0.1	16,639	2.4%
Pentecostals	0.03	4,985	6.2%

Religions	Pop %	Population	Ann Gr
Muslim	97.14	15,436,986	4.2%
Ethnoreligionist	2.50	397,287	-2.8%
Christian	0.33	52,442	2.1%
Baha'i	0.03	4,767	3.9%

Religions % of Total Pop
1900 1925 1950 1975 2000 2025

MegaBlocs % of Christian Pop
12.1
3
30.3
30.3
24.2
P I C M U

Answers to Prayer

N

1 **The establishment of groups of believers** among most of the peoples of Niger, including the Wodaabe/Bororo, Manga Kanuri, Zarma, Tuareg/Tamacheq, Songhai and others.

2 **Many churches have been planted** through the impact of humanitarian help by Christians in education, well-digging, agricultural development, leprosy control and health services.

3 **The Alliance of Evangelical Churches and Missions of Niger (AMEEN)** continues to develop as a united, visionary and cross-denominational organization.

Challenges for Prayer

1 **This Muslim land is open for the gospel,** and there is encouraging spiritual openness among its peoples. Still, Islam is pervasive, and groups with strict and aggressive interpretations of it are on the increase. Pray that the land may remain open for Christian mission, and that every social, religious and spiritual barrier to the knowledge of the Lord may be removed. The spiritual effects of folk Islam and demonic oppression are major hindrances to people coming to Christ.

2 **Christianity is growing,** but more slowly than the population overall; the same applies for evangelicals, who remain a tiny minority. People are coming into the Kingdom in a trickle; pray for the trickle to turn into a torrent. Positively, many previously unreached people groups now have their first believers, and pastors, who converted from Islam themselves, lead the majority of congregations. But social and cultural pressure to remain in or revert to Islam prevents many, who would otherwise do so, from following Christ. Pray for a critical mass of open, practicing Christians that begins larger people movements to Christ.

3 **Issues facing the church:**

a) Many believers are isolated, often illiterate and rarely have systematic Bible teaching available. Pray for literacy programmes as well as oral methods of learning scriptural truths and becoming disciples. Pray for groups to form, even if only very small, for the sake of those who need fellowship with other Christians.

b) Unity is needed. Despite the small size of the Church, a number of denominations have split. Pray for greater unity, especially through the work of AMEEN.

c) Leadership training. The EERN and UPEEN denominations run two middle-level Bible schools. Also, **SIM** and its five church partners operate a higher-level Bible school (ESPRiT) in Niamey. Many small Bible training schools and modular/TEE schools are run by different denominations, such as *Institute Biblique Baptist de Soir.* Pray for effective ways to train more leaders and to further train those currently in pastoral work.

d) Educational needs provide an opportunity for Christians to make a huge difference in Niger. The government cannot afford to educate all children, so many – especially girls – receive no schooling at all. Agencies such as **SIM,** Tearfund and World Horizons, as well as denominations such as EERN, open and run schools that offer valuable education for primary-aged children and open doors for demonstrating the gospel. Pray for material and human resources to properly seize this opportunity.

4 **This pioneer land** still needs missionaries for all parts of the country. Loving ministry by Christian missionaries – working through aid, development, health and education – has won credibility for the gospel and increased interest and response from both Muslims and animists. Pray for more labourers. There is a growing contribution to missions by Nigeria and Brazil. Pray for sensitivity in helping small, young churches and their leaders to maturity.

5 **Some of the least-reached peoples** of Niger are particularly strategic for prayer:

a) The Tuareg/Tamacheq, once rich, are now impoverished and resentful due to drought, famine, changing trade patterns and political changes. Holistic outreach and selfless ministry by workers from **SIM,** the Baptists, JEMED/**YWAM,** Sahara Desert Mission, Tearfund and others has seen the advent of several groups of believers. **SIM** and SIL workers are translating the Scriptures; the Tamacheq NT was published in 1991. Tuareg customs and their unique alphabet hint at a possible once-Christian heritage.

N

b) The Zarma are Muslim but strongly influenced by traditional practices. Only a few hundred believers are known. Evangelical Baptist missionaries laboured long to produce a complete Bible translation and to plant several congregations.

c) The five Kanuri peoples have a 1,000-year-long history of Islam. Though considered resistant to the gospel, they prove receptive to sensitive witness. Manga Christians have grown to a few congregations. They pray for their families and villages to believe, as natural social units, but also for the sake of security in the face of persecution. While Manga has only a few Scripture portions, Yerwa Kanuri has a complete NT and the JESUS film. Further translation as well as oral Scripture resources are vital, and some are in preparation (**SIM,** SIL).

d) The Fulbe (Fulani), both the settled Sokoto and nomadic Wodaabe/Bororo Fulbe of the west and the less Islamized, nomadic Fulbe across the whole country. **SIM** has 10 workers committed to the Fulbe. The Wodaabe Church continues to grow, from 60 in 1991 to over 1,000 today. **IMB,** AFM and others work among the increasingly responsive Fulani peoples in Niger.

e) The Songhai, a riverine people who once ruled an empire, have very few Christians among them, as few as 0.2%. **SIM, IMB** and some Brazilian workers reach out to the Songhai, a difficult task to a strongly Muslim people who regard converts as traitors.

*f) **The Tubu peoples** in the east. SIL is working on a translation for the Dazaga language, and several national workers minister among them.

*g) **Arab peoples,** including not only Arabized Berbers but also Moors and Libyans. **SIM** is preparing workers to reach out to them.

6 **Young people** are the most open and responsive, yet not enough has been done to reach this key sector of the nation. The fragile politico–economic situation often causes the universities to be closed, disrupting student ministries. GBU(**IFES**) operates groups in the university in Niamey and works in high schools in two other cities. The Navigators and **CCCI** also have ministries, and **SIM** runs an evangelistic student centre near the University of Niamey. Pray for a deep and lasting impact through campus ministries.

7 **Pray for the specialist Christian ministries** in Niger, including:

*a) **Aid and development projects** for one of the world's poorest countries should ideally uplift and then empower the people. Samaritan's Purse, Impacting Niger, World Vision, Lutheran World Relief and many others try to invest wisely into the lives of the people by providing for their needs. Pray that such ministry by Christians would demonstrate the love of God and make an eternal difference in the lives of those impacted.

*b) **Medical ministry** is very effective in this deprived nation. **SIM** runs the Galmi hospital, and TLM runs the **SIM**-founded Danja hospital, which has the national referral centre for leprosy as well as an ophthalmic centre.

*c) **The many prostitutes in the capital** are the focus of a significant outreach by **CAPRO**. The problem of prostitution in southern Niger intensifies as shari'a law is enforced in northern Nigeria, but a lack of funds and personnel threatens this crucial ministry.

8 **Media–oriented ministries** include:

*a) **Bible translation and distribution.** SIL and **SIM** workers commit to translation programmes in Tamacheq-Tawellemmet, Kanuri-Manga, Kanuri-Tumari, Fulbe (Fulfulde), Wodaabe and Tubu-Daza; there are active projects in eight different languages.

*b) **Christian literature.** Poverty and illiteracy are severe limitations. Literacy programmes must be a key aspect of development programmes, both Christian and secular. There are just two Christian bookstores in the country.

*c) **Radio** is a recent development in Christian ministry. EBM produces Christian programmes for the national radio station and a commercial station. A Christian FM station, *Radio Espoire*, launched in Niamey in 2004 and includes spiritually and socially redemptive programming in several languages. Words of Hope is involved in programme development and training.

*d) **The audio–media ministry** is inadequately funded and exploited. **GRN** has prepared messages in 36 languages/dialects of Niger. Solid-state audio and cassettes are vital in the contexts of poverty and nomadism.

*e) **The JESUS film** is now available in 11 languages.

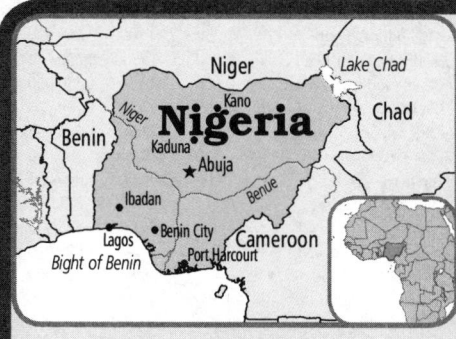

Ijaw 1.8%. 10 peoples. South-central coasts.
Adamawa–Ubangi 1.2%. 41 peoples, mostly in the east.
Other Sub-Saharan African 1.7%.
Other 0.4%. Arab, Western, Chinese, others.
Literacy 69.1%. **Official language** English. Hausa is widely used in the north and middle belt, Yoruba in the southwest, Igbo in the southeast and Pidgin English all over the south. **All languages** 521; 96% of the population use 21 major languages. **Languages with Scriptures** 22Bi 60NT 98por.

Nigeria
Federal Republic of Nigeria
Africa

Geography

Area 923,768 sq km. Mangrove and tropical rain forests in the south, savannah and grasslands in the north. The country is drained by the Niger-Benue river systems.

Population		Ann Gr	Density
2010	158,258,917	2.35%	171/sq km
2020	193,252,473	1.90%	209/sq km
2030	226,650,634	1.53%	245/sq km

Africa's most populous nation.
Capital Abuja 1,995,187. **Other major cities** Lagos 10.6 million; Kano 3.4mill; Ibadan 2.8m; Kaduna 1.6m; Benin City 1.3m; Port Harcourt 1.1m; Ogbomosho 1.0m. **Urbanites** 49.8%. **Pop under 15 yrs** 43%. **Life expectancy** 47.7yrs.

Peoples

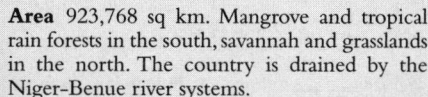

Over 520 ethnic groups. The triangular rivalry among the Hausa/Fulani, Yoruba and Igbo has dominated Nigerian politics since independence and continues to do so.
Sub-Saharan African 99.6%.
Yoruba 22.8%. 8 peoples, including Oyo Yoruba 18.6%. Mostly in south and southwest.
Benue 17.8%. 255 peoples. Ibibio 3.0%; Tiv 2.5%; Ebira 1.1%; Anaang 1.0%. Many small people groups in east-central (Benue state) and southeast.
Hausa 16.0%. 3 peoples, including Ajawa Hausa 15.6%. Mainly in centre and north.
Igbo 14.9%. 10 peoples, including Igbo 13.2%. Mainly in southeast.
Fulani 10.4%. 5 peoples, mostly in north. Toroobe 4.8%; Haabe/Bauchi 1.7%; Sokoto 1.7%; Mboboro 1.5%; Adamawa 0.8%.
Chadic 4.5%. 104 peoples, most of which are small in number. East and northeast of country.
Kanuri 4.0%. 4 peoples. Far northeast.
Guinean 2.5%. 31 peoples, including Edo 0.9%.
Nupe 2.0%. 9 peoples. Central belt to the west.

Economy

Fertile agricultural land, extensive mineral resources and vast oil reserves. Highly dependent on income from export of crude oil and gas – such income accounts for 95% of foreign exchange earnings. But much revenue has been lost through capital flight by multinationals, squandered on prestige projects, embezzled by a series of corrupt rulers and wasted through inability to harvest and refine all that is drilled. "Bunkering" (illegal siphoning by local militia and gangs) and other disruptions from disgruntled locals, who see no benefit from the untold oil wealth, often bring production to a standstill, threatening the entire nation's economy. Corruption is a massive evil in the country, ubiquitous at every level of society. Repayment of external debt is nearly done, heralding a potential increase in economic progress. Despite reforms, central commercial banks remain fragile and need stabilizing. Infrastructure is often sagging. The majority still live below the poverty line.
HDI Rank 158th/182. **Public debt** 13.4% of GDP. **Income/person** $1,401 (3% of USA).

Politics

Independent from Britain as a federation in 1960. Component states now number 36 with a federal capital area. Vast differences between the feudal, predominantly Muslim north and the more developed, largely Christian south – plus, the rivalry among the Yoruba, Hausa and Igbo – constantly generate tension. Muslim machinations to extend politico-economic control are the main causes for the turbulent post-independence history of tension, violence, coups and civil war. Obasanjo, a Christian, was elected president in 1999 following a long period of (Muslim) military dictatorship. He served two terms and then oversaw the elections that led to the installation of Umaru Yar'Adua, a Muslim, as president with Goodluck Jonathan, a Christian, as his vice president. After a long illness, Yar'Adua died and Jonathan became president. President Jonathan has many challenges facing his government – achieving a permanent resolution to strife in the Niger Delta, restoring peace to the troubled Plateau State, fighting corruption and establishing a truly independent Electoral Commission to

N

oversee free and fair elections in 2011. The danger of national fragmentation along tribal or religious lines is never far away.

Religion

Nigeria is constitutionally a secular state with freedom of religion. But the northern ruling elite give preferential treatment to Muslims and discriminate against Christians. Little has been done to stem the growth of violent Islamist groups or to stop persecution of Christians in the north, resulting in hundreds of churches burned and many Christians killed. Since 1999, Muslim state leaders have imposed shari'a law in nine northern states and parts of four others.

NOTE: Claims and counter-claims by Muslims, Christians and individual denominations are impossible to verify and are often inflated. Estimates for Muslims vary between 30% and 55%, and for Christians between 40% and 65%. Eight states appear to be overwhelmingly Muslim, 18 are overwhelmingly Christian and 10 are split around 50% of each.

Religions	Pop %	Population	Ann Gr
Christian	51.26	81,123,521	2.7%
Muslim	45.12	71,406,423	2.7%
Ethnoreligionist	3.31	5,238,370	-4.8%
Non-religious	0.30	474,777	2.4%
Other	0.01	15,826	2.4%

Actual practice of traditional religions may be as high as 10% of the population; percentages of both Muslim and Christian would therefore correspondingly decrease.

Christians	Denoms	Pop %	Affiliates	Ann Gr
Protestant	524	21.91	34,671,000	3.7%
Independent	3,915	15.16	23,992,000	2.7%
Anglican	1	12.61	19,950,000	3.3%
Catholic	1	12.08	19,118,000	1.3%
Orthodox	3	<0.01	6,000	1.9%
Marginal	23	0.95	1,502,000	3.9%
Doubly affiliated		-11.45	-18,121,000	0.0%

Churches	MegaBloc	Congs	Members	Affiliates
Anglican Church	A	7,600	5,000,000	19,950,000
Catholic Church	C	1,976	8,892,166	19,118,157
Baptist Convention	P	10,000	3,000,000	6,500,000
Evang Ch Winning All	P	10,949	3,000,000	6,000,000
Apostolic Church	P	5,500	2,027,027	4,500,000
Celestial Ch of Christ	I	2,029	912,941	3,880,000
Ch of Christ in Nigeria	P	3,000	1,340,000	3,350,000
Cherubim & Seraphim	I	12,708	1,525,000	3,050,000
Assemblies of God	P	10,700	1,156,000	2,890,000
Christ Apostolic Ch	I	7,000	1,050,000	2,625,000
Methodist Church	P	2,250	900,000	2,250,000
Redeemed Chr Ch	I	6,300	1,013,514	2,250,000
Ch of God Mission Int	I	6,600	732,000	1,830,000
Ch of the Lord (Aladura)	I	1,469	587,459	1,780,000
Luth Ch of Christ in N	P	2,400	387,789	1,745,050
Evang Reformed Ch	P	310	485,000	1,700,000
Presbyterian Church	P	1,000	500,000	1,000,000
Jehovah's Witnesses	M	5,417	325,000	877,500
Deeper Life Bible Ch	I	11,300	500,000	825,000
Gospel Faith Mission	I	2,500	250,000	625,000
Living Faith Ministries	I	472	235,849	625,000
Charis Fellowship Int	I	2,500	300,000	600,000
Ch of the Bre (EYN)	P	450	180,000	540,000
United Methodist	P	157	375,940	500,000
Foursquare Gospel	P	1,992	162,389	470,000
Holy Spirit Ministries	M	850	255,000	460,000
Seventh-day Adventist	P	840	285,000	395,000
Chr Reformed Ch	P	457	142,276	350,000
Reformed Ch of Christ	P	187	140,476	295,000
United Evang Ch	P	1,000	178,125	285,000
Syn Ch, All Nations	I	6	93,333	280,000
Christ Chosen Ch of God	I	750	90,000	225,000
Christian Brethren	P	514	90,000	180,000
Other denominations[4,430]	26,465	3,353,192	7,207,323	
Doubly affiliated				18,121,000
Total Christians[4,467]	**147,648**	**39,465,476**	**81,119,127**	

TransBloc	Pop %	Population	Ann Gr
Evangelicals			
Evangelicals	30.8	48,806,250	3.4%
Renewalists			
Charismatics	19.4	30,662,342	3.1%
Pentecostals	8.0	12,737,941	2.6%

Missionaries from Nigeria

P,I,A 8,944 (6,644 long-term), most cross-cultural, most in Nigeria, but also in 56 other countries.

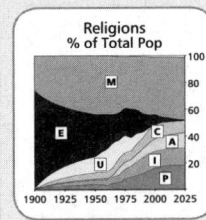

Religions % of Total Pop

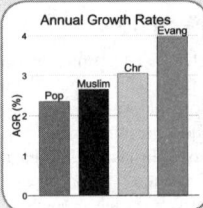

Annual Growth Rates

Answers to Prayer

1 **The successful transition from one civilian government to another** is a first for Nigeria. Attempts to strengthen the national banks and economy and to combat corruption have met with some success. The promise of further development assistance for the aggrieved oil-rich states has also helped establish a measure of peace. Praise God that despite many threats, Nigeria's national stability seems to be consolidating.

(2) Nigeria's prayer movement is one of the world's strongest, stimulated by political stresses, by Muslim persecution of Christians and by a genuine desire for revival and evangelization. Some of the largest prayer meetings in history have been in Nigeria (an estimated 3 million in Lagos). Positive political developments and church growth can be attributed in large part to these movements.

(3) The dynamic growth of the Church continues to be impressively solid. This has been among Anglicans, Methodists, Presbyterians, Baptists, evangelical groups such as ECWA (Evangelical Churches Winning All/**SIM**) and TEKAN with interdenominational roots (**SIM**, Pioneers, others) and Pentecostal and charismatic denominations (both indigenous and international). A few specifics:

a) The Church of Nigeria (Anglican) has grown from 900,000 in 1960 to perhaps nearly 20 million in 2010. They are a bulwark for evangelicals and conservatives in the global Anglican community.

b) SIM's work, which started with such cost a century ago, has resulted in a dynamic Church, ECWA, with 6,000 churches and six million people.

c) The Apostolic Church, birthed out of the 1904-05 Welsh revival, has six million affiliates globally; 4.5 million of them are in Nigeria.

d) Deeper Life Bible Church began as a campus Bible study in 1973 and has grown to nearly one million affiliates in Nigeria and many more globally.

e) Redeemed Christian Church of God started in 1952 as a single, local congregation and has grown to over three million affiliates worldwide, with a presence in over 130 countries. It is the fastest-growing denomination in Nigeria.

f) Evangelicals have grown from 2.1 million in 1960 (5.7%) to 49 million in 2010 (30.8%).

(4) Missions vision was birthed in the 1970s through revival among university students. This vision has blossomed into a movement accounting for over 5,000 Nigerian missionaries at home and abroad, helping lead the way for Africa-wide mission mobilization.

Challenges for Prayer

(1) Nigeria's unity has survived, almost miraculously, despite countless threats. The cumulative effects of ancient tribal rivalries, Muslim conquests, British colonial policy in which the north and south were handled differently, the bitter Biafra war of 1967-70 and heightened religious tensions have left deep scars. Pray for healing and reconciliation; pray also for leadership that will serve to reconcile and unite rather than to embitter and divide.

N

(2) The challenges facing the government are myriad and urgent – extremist Muslim agitation in the north, armed militias in the disgruntled and oil-rich southeast, pervasive corruption, a self-serving network of bureaucratic elite, emigration/brain drain, widespread poverty and an apparently disintegrating sense of national identity. These are challenges enough for any established government, never mind a fledgling democracy. Pray for the right balance between caution and decisiveness in addressing such threats, and between prudence and ambition in economic development and in combating poverty.

(3) The scale of corruption in Nigeria is staggering. It is widely regarded as one of the world's most corrupt societies and is infamous for e-mail scams, international crime and drug-running.

a) Graft, bribery and embezzlement are commonplace at every level of society. Since the 1960s, over $400 billion has been lost through corruption, almost all to the very people entrusted with the nation's stewardship. Politicians, bankers, police, military, even religious leaders have all been found guilty. Corruption is not even discouraged by either a strong Christian presence or shari'a law; it appears to be more deep-seated than both of these.

b) Capital flight. Much of Nigeria's vast wealth has been siphoned out of the country through various illicit and corrupt means by multinational companies operating in Nigeria.

c) **The impact of corruption on Nigeria** is devastating and crippling. It pulls others into the grasping free-for-all, it undermines those who attempt good governance, it inspires the imposition of shari'a, it disarms the effectiveness of Christians caught in its grip, it leaves the nation's reputation in tatters and it generates such disillusionment that violent and extreme reactions appear to be the only ones that work.

Pray that God may raise up many more who fear Him and have the moral integrity and courage to tackle the rottenness manifest in society.

4 **The introduction of shari'a law** in northern Muslim states is a direct challenge to the federal government. It is an open door to human rights abuses and the further infiltration of Nigeria by extremists. It is a danger to national stability and a threat to Christian ministry in those states so affected. Pray for the intrinsic cruelty and injustices of shari'a to be exposed and for those seeking moral order and social righteousness to find it in the practice of biblical principles under the authority of Christ.

5 **Church growth has been massive and remains so.** Nigeria has a large majority of West Africa's evangelicals. But such growth is not without its own dangers. Pray against:

a) A failure of discipleship: the emphasis on evangelism and soul winning without adequate follow-up and balanced biblical teaching. Africa's – and Nigeria's – greatest spiritual challenge is not Islam, not corruption, not even the need for missions, but discipleship. If the Nigerian Church were truly discipled and brought to maturity in Christ, it would be an unstoppable force.

b) Unbalanced prosperity theology and chasing after dubious miracles cheapen the good news. Numerous doctrinal distortions, greed masquerading as biblical prosperity, spiritual charlatanism and unethical fundraising not only exchange the truth for lies, but they also inoculate millions against the real message of the gospel. Pentecostal groups are especially prone to these excesses.

c) Second-generation nominalism in both traditional and younger churches is a big problem. Double standards are widespread, and immorality, membership in secret societies and compromise with the world bring strife and disrepute to the gospel.

d) Syncretistic Christianity. Many newer indigenous groups have a desire for God but also much admixture of unbiblical worldviews and practices. Many are open to greater gospel light but are often isolated from, or shunned by, the more orthodox churches. They are increasingly benefitting from access to solid evangelical seminaries and sound theological literature.

e) Enthusiastic and aggressive but uninformed approaches to African spirituality. This is often and most sadly expressed in witch hunters, who identify and accuse children of being witches or being possessed by demons and then administer harsh, even fatal, "cures". Pray that biblical truth and practice might prevail over superstition.

f) Division and disunity. There are several major networks of churches in Nigeria. The Christian Association of Nigeria (CAN) is the umbrella body for five major Christian blocks – the Catholic Secretariat of Nigeria (CSN); Christian Council of Nigeria (CCN); ECWA/TEKAN (Protestant mainline); PFN/CPFN (Pentecostals); and the Organization of African Instituted Churches (OAIC). Praise God for their vital contribution to national Christian life and unity. Some megachurches and newer denominations do not bother to integrate into the wider Christian scene. Pray that leaders and in turn believers might look past the denominational and tribal rivalries that may exist to focus on their underlying and more profound unity in Christ.

6 **Christian leaders** are under great stress in today's Nigeria, including spiritual opposition, political pressure and financial temptations. Those in the north also face very real dangers from Muslim extremists. Many have ministries with wider African or even global impact. Pray for:

a) Integrity and unity in leadership. There is frequently a gap between what is preached and what is perceived to be practiced by Christian leaders. Especially among the newer, fast-growing churches, prayer is needed for:

   i Unity. The fragmented nature of the Church is not so much about personal ambition and personal conflicts as it is about denominational or tribal differences. If leaders cannot work together, then neither will their followers.

ii Honesty. A profusion of competing denominations and sects has emerged, many of them claiming inflated numbers to increase the prestige of their leaders.

iii Personal holiness. Extravagant lifestyles and oily showmanship usurp spiritual depth and biblical preaching as indicators of anointing. Instances of corruption, theft, embezzlement and sexual immorality are tragically frequent.

iv Accountability is often absent; the "big man" dynamic plays into the same materialism, pride and carnality that cripple Nigeria politically and economically.

Pray that humility, simplicity and holiness might become the watchwords of the Nigerian Church.

b) *The multiplication of leaders* who are Spirit-led, well versed in the Scriptures, skilled in disciple-making and steeped in the knowledge of God and the power of prayer.

c) *The hundreds of seminaries, colleges, Bible schools and training programmes* in Nigeria, as well as the many TEE courses. The rush of many theological institutions to affiliate to Nigerian universities has produced neither the academic excellence nor the genuine spirituality that the churches so badly need. Several of Nigeria's leading seminaries are strengthened by pursuing the standards of ACTEA (Accrediting Council for Theological Education in Africa). Though demand for places is high from their own constituent churches, evangelical seminaries are able to offer significant help in the training of pastors for African Initiated Churches.

d) *Servant-leaders and mentors to be raised up.* One-man ministries, dictatorial leadership, empire-building and unwillingness to entrust responsibility to the upcoming generation are common weaknesses. The generation gap between older and younger pastors is often large and a source of resentment, since the older leaders cling to their power and influence rather than passing the torch.

e) *Expatriate ministries, seeking high-profile campaigns* that are not necessarily needed or welcomed by established Nigerian leadership networks, can always find other nationals through whom to run their events. This fosters further division and is symptomatic of the Church's inability to stand as one.

7 **Nationwide interdenominational movements,** more than in most nations, have made a deep impact on specific sections of the community. Of note:

a) *Secondary schools.* SU operates mainly in the south, while its partner organization FCS (Fellowship of Christian Students) operates in 20 northern states. They have had a huge influence in discipling and training Christian young people. There is considerable opposition and trials in the three northern regions, often including bloody violent attacks, yet a great harvest is being won. Pray that Christian teachers, advisors and student leaders may be encouraged and strengthened.

b) *Universities and colleges.* NIFES (Nigeria Fellowship of Evangelical Students), the largest member movement of **IFES**, has over 35,000 members on 300 campuses, with their largest groups in the central and southern parts of the country. FCS is stronger in the central and northern regions, having also mobilized outreach into schools and colleges, winning many to Christ. There are now many other church-based campus fellowship groups associated with some of the larger denominations. Christian students face many challenges – temptations to immorality and unethical paths to success, false teaching from "Christian" sects and pressure from Muslims. Christian witness has been divided in recent years by unhealthy competition from many other campus fellowships.

c) *Peace House,* a non-denominational revival and retreat ministry, plays a significant role in encouraging the spiritual life within many professional groups, including pastors. The longstanding ministry of the Full Gospel Businessmen's Fellowship supplements this strategic work.

8 **The scale of persecution of Christians by Muslims** has accelerated in Nigeria's northern states and as far south as the central plateau. It has caused the death of thousands, including pastors, and the destruction of hundreds, even thousands, of churches. It has united Christians and driven them to the Lord in prayer, but it also threatens the very fabric of Nigerian society and statehood. Pray for:

N

a) *An understanding of the causes* of this complex situation. Muslims fear a loss of power, influence and land as the Church grows and as democracy spreads. Tribal and political rivalries contribute to the tension. Jihadist influences foment pre-planned violence and use the flimsiest pretexts to invoke riots. Not least, the evil one seeks to kill, steal and destroy, from both Christians and Muslims.

b) *Restoration and recovery* for those who have suffered loss, bereavement and rape. Both Nigerian churches and international agencies are providing new homes, clothing, food and essentials, but inner healing cannot be so easily procured.

c) *Forgiveness* for persecutors and deliverance from a spirit of revenge.

d) *The Christian Association of Nigeria* and its ministry of representing Nigeria's 88 million Christians in five major blocs to the local and federal authorities.

e) *Decisive actions by the authorities.* Not enough is done to prevent and discourage the outbreak of violence by Muslims – many feel the police and/or military are compromised. Justice is rarely seen to be done, and compensation for the loss and destruction is often promised but almost never delivered.

f) *The exposure of the violent and hateful nature of extremist groups.* Christians suffer a series of attacks, often pre-planned and well coordinated, and even attempts to force them to convert to Islam under threat of death. This has led to several courageously dying as martyrs. In a number of situations, Christians are unable to trust the protection of government security forces or police to prevent attacks from invading militants.

g) *The conversion of Muslims,* both of persecutors and of those appalled by the behaviour of their co-religionists. Many of these have been won to Christ over recent years, which is part of the reason for the attacks.

h) *The best possible response by Christians.* Until now, forbearance has been mistaken for weakness. The large majority of Christians endure such predations without retaliation. But at times of provocation, pastors struggle to prevent their members, especially nominal members, from taking vengeance. Many Christians are involved in peacemaking and pray for a supernatural love of enemies that no force can defeat.

9 **Ministry challenges among specific population segments include:**

a) *Young people and schools.* Legally, religious education should be given to all in schools. This is a great opportunity to engender religious understanding and explain the gospel, but Christian religious education teachers are limited in number and resources. With help from the International Institute for Christian Studies, government sponsored in-service training and manuals are giving fresh impetus. **CEF** reaches children and offers training seminars for Christian teachers and parents. CEM, an indigenous agency, has a significant Christian camping ministry. Sports ministries are also increasing in popularity and effectiveness.

b) *Development ministries for the rural poor.* Poverty has prompted many Nigerian churches to establish departments of health and rural development, many recognized by the government as development agencies. Most notably, RURCON and its local subsidiary, CRUDAN, provide consultation and training. Pray for effective holism in ministry by the Church.

c) *HIV and AIDS.* Official estimates state that 2.7 million carry the virus. The actual figure may be double that. An estimated two million children are orphaned by AIDS. Many groups are making use of awareness resources available through Africa Christian Textbooks (ACTS). The Government has adopted biblically based materials developed by the Faith Based AIDS Awareness Initiative for AIDS to help with education and prevention in schools and colleges of education. FCS, SU, Tearfund, ACET, NIFES, **CAPRO**, ECWA, Baptist and Methodist churches all offer AIDS awareness programmes, but much progress is needed to fight the stigma associated with HIV and to care for those already infected.

10 **Specific religious communities needing prayer and attention** are many; Nigeria's religious context is highly complex and varied beyond the obvious domination of the Christian-Muslim dynamic. The major blocs are:

a) *Muslims.* Many are more open to the gospel despite – or even because of – Nigeria's religious tensions. Tens, and possibly hundreds, of thousands have come to Christ. But many face death threats, discrimination and ostracism. Powerful Christian literature for Muslims and effective outreach methods are increasingly available. One important ministry is caring for converts from Islam; beyond discipleship, they often need shelter and employment in an area away from their home due to threats against their lives. There are many expressions of Islam in Nigeria, including the majority Sunni and Shi'ite, Sufi and militant, and the hostility between some of these groups is evident.

b) Practitioners of African traditional religion. While they number officially only around 3%, they more likely number around 8%; even beyond this, their practices and beliefs penetrate deeply into some forms of both Islam and Christianity. Paganism has not so much disappeared as gone underground, often seething beneath the surface of Christian nominalism. Many of Nigeria's remaining smaller unreached-people groups are animist; they are responsive to the good news, yet are being rapidly Islamized. Pray for urgent Christian outreach to them while the door remains open.

c) African indigenous "spiritual" churches have multiplied – especially those related to the Aladura, Cherubim and Seraphim Church and Christ Apostolic Church. Some are highly syncretistic; others maintain varying degrees of biblical orthodoxy. Pray that their leadership may be rightly helped by other Christians, with biblical theology and practices adopted.

11 **Pray for Nigeria's unreached.** Research from the last 20 years reveals that 168 peoples are inadequately reached due to lack of resident workers, indigenous churches, Bible translation and such. Of these, 26 remain unengaged by Christian outreach. Notable among these are the Bole, Ganagana, Gera, Lala and West Marghi. Several others have no known Christians. Other strategic groups include the increasingly open Fulani (15m) and the highly resistant Kanuri (6m). Pray that those agencies and churches that have adopted them for ministry may carry that commitment through to a successful conclusion.

12 **Missions vision.** Nigeria is one of the leading missionary-sending countries of the developing world. Pray for:

a) Nationwide mission networks. The Movement for African National Initiatives (**MANI**), Nigeria Evangelical Missions Association (NEMA) and Agape Missions and Evangelical Network (AMEN) all play huge roles in pushing forward the mission impetus started at the 1974 Lausanne Congress on World Evangelization and at the Nigeria Congress on Evangelization in 1975. This impetus is encapsulated with the Back to Jerusalem movement along with Vision 50:15, which has the goal of mobilizing 50,000 Nigerians for missions in the next 15 years. Currently, 5,300 long-term Nigerian missionaries are under the NEMA umbrella, representing 115 agencies. Around half serve cross-culturally within Nigeria; the other half serve outside the country.

b) Denominational agencies with a strong missions programme. The Evangelical Missionary Society of ECWA has by far the largest number of cross-cultural missionaries (1,600 in 2009). Deeper Life Bible Church and Living Faith Ministries have sent missionaries to over 40 nations. The former has planted over 3,000 churches outside of Nigeria. **AoG**, Baptists, Churches of Christ in Nigeria (TEKAN) and others also have strong missionary-sending programmes. Pray that other denominations may catch the vision.

c) Interdenominational agencies have multiplied – **CAPRO**, Christian Missionary Foundation (**CMF**), Missionary Crusaders Ministries (MCM), Evangelical Missionary Society (EMS), Great Commission Movement (GCM), Soul Harvesters, Full Stature Mission and growing numbers of others. Pray for their increase and for the Nigerian Church – usually so centered on congregational life – to support their ministries.

d) Missionary training and support. There are now 50 missions-training institutions in Nigeria, an answer to prayer. Congregations still need to understand the vital roles they play in supporting and sending Nigerian missionaries into the field. Pray for Nigerian support agencies that seek to address this problem and to act as a bridge between churches and missionaries on the field. About 2,000 Nigerian missionaries serve in other lands, mainly in West Africa; they face difficulties in receiving funds to provide for their material needs and educate their children.

e) Research on the unreached – by ECWA, **CAPRO**, **AoG** and the Nigerian Baptist Convention – focuses the attention of churches and agencies. All of Nigeria's 168 least-reached peoples have been adopted for prayer and outreach. The Searchlight Project, run by the National Research Working Group, is undertaking vital research on the Nigerian harvest force and on the least reached and is developing strategies, training and collaborative ministry.

13 **Expatriate missionaries** have steadily declined in numbers, as the large and mature Nigerian Church takes over the ministries of expats. Yet, 3,500 cross-cultural workers still serve in Nigeria (many of them being Nigerian or African). Pray for harmonious cooperation between foreign and indigenous agencies and churches. Key ministries for expatriates include Bible teaching, leadership training, a wide range of supportive and aid ministries and training Nigerian missionaries. Pray for the safety, health and effectiveness of the missionary force – each of these factors is even more a spiritual battleground in today's Nigeria. Some of the larger agencies are: **WBT, SIM, CRWM, IMB**, Mission Africa.

14 **Literature is vital** for the maturation of the Church, especially in the areas of discipleship, Bible studies and theology. These are avidly sought after, but in short supply. The number of bookstores is very few, given the number of Christians. Pray for:

a) Nigerian authors. Many megachurch pastors write copiously, but the topics are the same – prosperity, success and overcoming. Pray for those who are interested in writing on a wide range of issues, and in a culturally and contextually relevant way, but lack the means and publishing resources. Pray for the new publisher, Africa Christian Textbooks (ACTS), working in partnership with other African publishers and Langham Literature to help African authors. ACTS has a growing list of titles designed for Nigerian leaders wrestling with Africa's issues.

b) Publishing. Due to mismanagement, several older Christian publishers are no longer functioning. Some new organizations such as Evangel have grown but tend to concentrate on reprinting foreign books. Denominational publishing is also low. But Oasis International, the Joint Sunday School Project and ACTS produce new materials useful for pastoral training and spiritual growth.

c) Distribution. Although there are well over 300 Christian bookstores in Nigeria, the range of books in stock is severely limited in the search for profitability. Denominational bookshops such as Challenge Bookshops have been declining for some time. Most growing bookshops are in the hands of private entrepreneurs. Christian Booksellers Association of Nigeria is a force for good. Major distribution agencies are Oasis, ACTS, Edysyl and others.

15 **Media plays a greater role than ever,** communicating not just information but also theology and style of worship, particularly for the burgeoning Pentecostal and charismatic ministries. Pray for:

a) Bible translation. Nigeria possesses the third-highest translation needs remaining of any country. With The Bible Society of Nigeria and Nigeria Bible Translation Trust at the forefront, the many Bible translation organizations are making great progress toward meeting the needs of more than 500 different languages in the country. Currently, there are 21 full Bibles, 61 New Testaments and more than 70 languages with Scripture portions and works in progress. This still leaves more than 300 languages with possible translation needs. A Bible translation degree programme has been developed at the Theological College of Northern Nigeria, the first in the country, and the first graduates from the programme are committing themselves to meeting this huge remaining translation need.

b) Christian radio. Nigeria has one of the world's highest proportions and numbers of short-wave radio listeners. Even more have access to FM. Christians use both local and international radio broadcasts. With Nigeria's low rural literacy level and strong oral storytelling culture, radio is vital for evangelism and discipleship. Pray for all unreasonable restrictions to be lifted for local radio. Many unevangelized groups can receive Christian radio broadcasts in their own language. The Broadcasting Organization of Nigeria (BON) is known to play a restrictive role on Christian broadcasts on national stations as well as in setting up Christian radio stations. This calls for prayer.

c) Audio resources. **GRN** has recordings in 573 languages/dialects and innovative cassette and record playback machines for ease of use. Sometimes a **GRN** recording is the only gospel witness to an unconverted ethnic group. Pray for recordings in 127 northern languages yet untackled. The Iseko, Izon, Vute, Yekhee, Kanuri and even Yoruba-language families need more.

d) Christian TV. Television is used by many Christian groups. Pentecostal groups in particular exploit this medium to expand their ministries. Solid Bible teaching as well as creative and diverse programming are great needs. NLFA, ELWA, Baptist Media and Muryar Bishara all have studios.

e) Movies and films. The JESUS film is extensively used in 70 languages. Another 70 are in production. Mount Zion Faith Ministries started their studio in 1999 and have already produced 24 films on DVD and seven TV series, which have been shown on 74 Nigerian TV stations. ECWA and Baptists have also produced films; pray these tools may be used effectively.

f) The Internet is being utilized by many groups of all Christian expressions. For those with Internet access, a wealth of sermons, Bible study resources, streaming programmes and such are readily available.

The States of Nigeria

Three main regions emerged as a result of colonial policy. The British retained the pre-colonial, Hausa-Fulani Muslim feudal rulers of the North and allowed them to extend their rule over the peoples of the Middle Belt, few of whom were Muslim at that time. The South developed a more Western system of government. Between 1967 and 1995, the number of states increased from 12 to 36, plus a Federal Capital Territory. These states are clustered in six geo-political zones: SE, SS, SW, NC, NE and NW, but here they are grouped broadly in the three major regions of Nigeria.

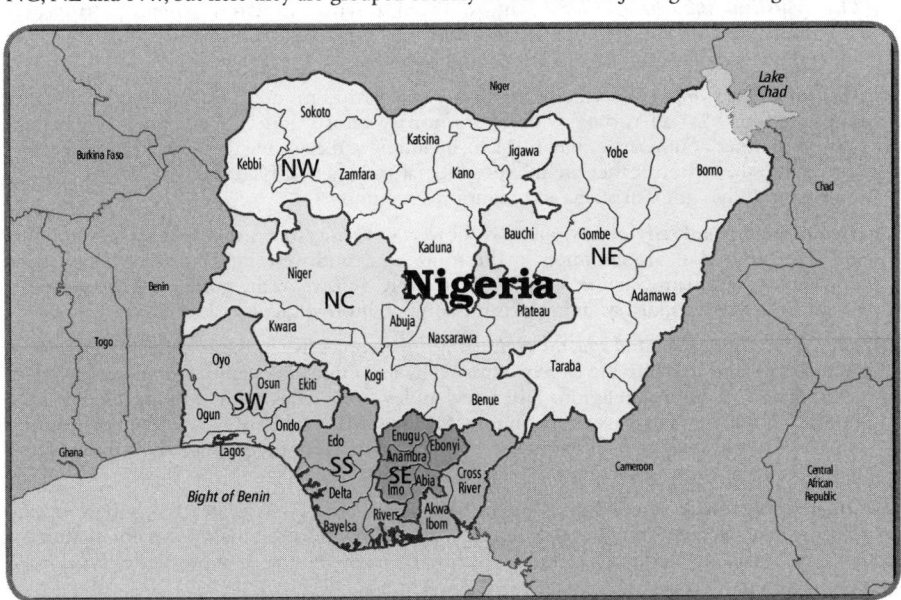

The Southern Zones

SS
Area 84,587 sq km. Six states: Akwa Ibom, Bayelsa, Cross River, Delta, Edo, Rivers.
Population 21,000,000.
Major peoples Ijaw, Isekiri, Isoko, Urhobo, Ibibio, Efik.

SE
Area 29,525 sq km. Five states: Abia, Anambra, Ebonyi, Enugu, Imo.
Population 16,400,000.
Major peoples Igbo.

SW
Area 78,771 sq km. Six states: Ekiti, Lagos, Ogun, Ondo, Osun, Oyo.
Population 27,600,000.
Major peoples Yoruba.

1 **Critical issues:**

a) ***Christian–Muslim relations*** continue to sour. The imposition of shari'a law and subsequent violence against Christians in the northern states generate resentment and even backlashes against Muslim minorities in southern cities. Pray for Christian values to prevail.

b) ***The oil industry*** has polluted the pristine agricultural land of millions, but only an elite (or corrupt) few have benefited. In this environmental disaster, natural gas is wasted, the land is degraded and the sea polluted. After many years of increasingly violent protests and struggles, both the federal government and oil companies have recognized these issues. In 2009, oil companies paid their first reparations and compensation settlement (with the Ogoni people); the government granted amnesty to activists and promised $1 billion in development aid. Pray monies will be spent justly and prudently for the benefit of all and that peace will result.

2 **The SW was pioneered** by Anglicans, Methodists and Southern Baptists, and the SS and SE by Presbyterians, Catholics, Qua Iboe (Mission Africa) and others. Christians are in the great majority. Pentecostal churches are the predominant influence and the fastest growing – ranging from small groups meeting in homes to megachurches. Rural areas lack dedicated pastors because of the relative poverty. Pray for sacrificial concern among Christians for the less-reached and less-privileged areas. Pray that revival might make the Christians into true disciples of Jesus.

3 **The less-reached peoples and areas include:**

a) ***The Muslim suburbs*** (*sabongari*) in southern towns and cities where Northerners congregate. Very little prayer or outreach is directed to these difficult areas, despite their being much more accessible for witness and loving ministry.

b) ***Muslim groups among Southern peoples.*** Yoruba Muslims are influential and constitute over one-fourth of all Yoruba. Muslim missionary efforts and enticements have brought pockets of other Southern peoples to Islam, including some among the Igbo. Pray for specific outreach to these groups; they are the most liberal and open of Nigeria's Muslims, coexisting more peacefully with Christians and traditional religionists.

c) ***African traditional religionists,*** such as followers of Orisha spirituality, Ogun (iron and war) and Osun (the seas), are common in the south and southwest, intermingling beliefs with Christianity and Islam. Such religionists often are responsive to the gospel and the power of Christ, but excising idolatry and spiritism is a much more difficult task.

d) ***The Niger Delta (SS) and coastal regions.*** Many peoples live in these virtually inaccessible swampy, riverine areas that are largely bypassed by missions. Christianity is often just a veneer over African traditional religion. Just a few miles from cities with thriving churches lie unreached villages awash with paganism. **CMS**, **CMF** and **AoG** have church-planting ministries in the area; local churches need to be convinced of their own responsibility – and ability – to reach out to these needy places.

e) ***Other needy areas:*** the Benin border (SW) and Cross River state (SS), where ethnic religions and secret societies are strong (ECWA/**SIM**). Edo state is known for significant levels of "sexual networking", including furnishing many thousands of prostitutes for Europe and Italy in particular.

N

The Central Zone

NC and Federal Capital Territory

Area 266,617 sq km. Seven states: Abuja, Benue, Niger, Kogi, Kwara, Nasarawa, Plateau.
Population 20,600,000.
Major peoples No dominant group, but a medley of over 230 languages, most using Hausa as a trade language. Largest: Edo, Esan, Gbari, Idoma, Igala, Igbirra, Nupe, Tiv.

1 There has been dramatic church growth over the last 50 years. Major denominations are ECWA, Anglican, Baptist, the TEKAN family of churches and, more recently, various Pentecostal and charismatic churches. Pray for the spiritual growth of believers and for true conversion of the younger generation – evangelical nominalism is a major problem. Pray for revival and a vision for cross-cultural outreach.

2 Muslim missionary activity has intensified in the region. Considerable efforts are made to win over followers of ethnic religions and backsliding Christians. Pray that these attempts may actually result in many coming to Christ. Pray that Christians may overcome historic hatreds and personal fears for the sake of courageous witnessing to Muslims in love.

3 The occurrences of religious violence and persecution in this region, especially Plateau state and its capital, Jos, have been prominent in the last decade (see main section, point 8). It is the fault line between Christian- and Muslim-dominated Nigeria. British colonial arrangements placed Muslim rulers over Christian populations; most recently, this has seen the imposition of shari'a on Christian-majority areas as well as the overturning of Muslim rule via democratic elections. Jos is a centre of Christian ministry; Jos itself and many believers therein have suffered as a result of much destruction and chaos. Pray for boldness and faithfulness in the midst of pressures and for a Christlike response to opposition.

4 Less-reached peoples. There are still 50-60 peoples in the region among whom outreach (and response) is limited. Two main areas of particular need:

a) Plateau state. Many peoples have turned to the Lord, but some are more resistant, such as the predominantly traditionalist Goemai (375,000), Kofyar (145,000) and Mada (140,000).

b) Along the Niger River and Benin border are numerous unreached and partially reached peoples. Pray for the Nupe cluster of peoples, some nominally Christian with most practicing folk Islam. Only a handful of Christian workers are attempting to reach them (UMCA, **CMF**, **CAPRO**, **CRWM**, LCCN, EMS-ECWA). The Benue cluster has many peoples (255); a few are still largely unevangelized.

The Northern Zones

NE
Area 272,395 sq km. Six states: Adamawa, Bauchi, Borno, Gombe, Katsina, Taraba, Yobe.

Population 22,800,000.
Major peoples Kanuri, Fulani, Bachama.

NW
Area 191,873 sq km. Six states: Jigawa, Kaduna, Kano, Kebbi, Sokoto, Zamfara.
Population 30,000,000.
Major peoples Hausa, Fulani.

N

1 Critical issues:

a) The imposition of shari'a law in nine northern states and portions of four others has precipitated a constitutional crisis and directly challenged the federal government. Pray for a wise defusing of this explosive situation.

b) Shari'a law is accompanied by restrictions on church buildings, the banning of Christian religious education in state schools, communal violence, destruction of many churches and loss of life – mostly of Christians, who are automatically degraded to second-class citizens. Pray that Christians may respond with love, wisdom, peace and spiritual authority; pray they will be able to freely exercise their constitutional right to testify about Christ.

c) Persecution is often so severe that many Christian workers have fled the region. In some areas, many churches and even entire denominations have been burned out. Rebuilding often happens – occasionally multiple times – at great expense to the congregation and without compensation or assurances that attacks won't happen again. Pray for great faith and endurance for those Christians suffering such loss.

2 The gospel has made progress since independence despite considerable opposition from Muslims. Many smaller non-Muslim peoples and an increasing number of

Muslim–majority peoples are responding to the gospel. Believers from a Muslim background are often driven either underground or out of their home area. As a result, an underground network of believers is developing, as are Christian ministries focused on sheltering and discipling converts. Pray for the protection and growth of this accelerating movement.

③ There is a great need for Nigerian missionaries to ensure that the costly gains in church growth are not lost. The Nigerian Church is burdened for this area and knowledgeable because of the good research done. Pray for the sending of workers, from the scores of denominations and churches who will be well prepared and effective in such a hostile, dangerous environment.

④ Pray for the unreached peoples.

a) **The Fulani (Fulbe)** are a strategic people across Africa and sub-Saharan Africa's largest unreached-people cluster. Their origins are in Senegal, but their greatest numbers are in Nigeria, where 16 million of the 32 million Fulani live. They form both the strongly Muslim ruling class (Sokoto/Toroobe) and the nominally Muslim nomadic cattle grazers over much of Nigeria and the Sahel. Over 90% of Nigerian Fulani are Muslim, but an increasing number are responding to the gospel. Recently, the Nigerian and global Church caught the vision for the evangelization of the Fulani, and partnerships were formed for mobilization, strategy and coordination of ministry. Effectively reaching nomadic pastoralists is a particular challenge. If the gospel gripped this group, all of West Africa would be affected! Many of the urban Fulani speak only Hausa and must be reached through this language.

b) **The Hausa** are known as predominantly Muslim, but a number actually follow traditional religions. Among these are the Maguzawa, a people with their own distinctive culture who retain the pre-Islamic, traditional Hausa religion. An exciting turning to Christ is happening among them. The Isawa, a Hausa Muslim fringe group that gives high honour to Jesus, are also responding to the gospel. Christian resources in Hausa are widely available. Pray for large numbers of Hausa to be won for Christ; this is happening on an increasingly larger scale.

c) **The Kanuri of Borno state** are proudly Muslim and have been so for 1,000 years. They doubt that other peoples can even practice Islam properly. There are few believers among the 5.2 million Kanuri, even after years of witness by TEKAN-Pioneers, **CMF**, **CAPRO** and 22 other Nigerian missions. There is only one Kanuri church, but now the NT is published and the JESUS film and other resources are available.

d) **The Gwoza Hills** (Adamawa and Borno). The area is hotly contested spiritually, with some peoples turning from paganism – more to Christianity than to Islam. Over 23 peoples live in the area. Pray for those in the heart of this battle, such as the Guduf (30,000), Dughwede (20,000) and Marakam (4,000).

e) **The mountain regions in the east** along the Cameroon border in Taraba and Adamawa states. This is the home of numerous peoples, some scarcely affected by the modern world and deeply trapped in the fearful world of spirits and ancestors. Over 50 peoples live in the area, many unreached. Pray especially for pioneer ongoing outreach to the seven tribes of the Mumuye (625,000, 50% or more of whom follow African traditional religions), the Chamba (150,000) and Bata (150,000).

Norway
Kingdom of Norway
Europe

Geography 🌐

Area 323,878 sq km. A long, mountainous fjord-indented land. One of the four Scandinavian countries. Also included are the Arctic dependencies of Jan Mayen and Svalbard (Spitzbergen) Islands – 62,000 sq km.

Population	Ann Gr	Density
2010	4,855,315	0.93%	15/sq km
2020	5,200,079	0.64%	16/sq km
2030	5,518,034	0.57%	17/sq km

A further 2,400 on Svalbard (Russians 70%; Norwegians 30%).

Capital Oslo 888,435. **Urbanites** 77.6%. **Pop under 15 yrs** 19%. **Life expectancy** 80.5 yrs.

Peoples 👪

Indigenous 92.6%. Norwegian 92.0%; Sami (Lapp, 5 groups) 0.5%; Romani (Gypsy) 0.1%.
Foreign-origin 7.4%.
  European 3.0%. Swedish 0.5%; Danish 0.4%; Bosnian 0.3%; Serbian 0.3.
  Asian 3.6%. Pakistani 0.6%; Iraqi 0.4%; Vietnamese 0.4%; Turk 0.3%; Iranian 0.3%; Tamil 0.3%; Punjabi 0.3%.
  African 0.6%. Somali 0.3%.
Literacy 99%. **Official language** Norwegian (Bokmal and Nynorsk). **All languages** 20. **Indigenous languages** 10. **Languages with Scriptures** 2Bi 2NT 1por 1w.i.p.

Economy 📋

Strong and wealthy industrial state with high earnings from oil, mining, fishing, forest products and high-tech industries.
HDI Rank 1st/182. **Public debt** 55.7% of GDP.
Income/person $94,387 (199% of USA).

Politics ❌

Independent from Sweden in 1905 as a parliamentary monarchy. Not a member of the EU, but participates in the EEC.

Religion 🙏

The Lutheran Church (or Church of Norway) is the official state church, but there is complete freedom for other denominations and religions.

Religions	Pop %	Population	Ann Gr
Christian	91.08	4,422,221	0.7%
Non-religious	6.10	296,174	3.0%
Muslim	1.90	92,251	5.8%
Other	0.70	33,987	4.1%
Buddhist	0.15	7,283	0.9%
Jewish	0.04	1,942	0.9%
Baha'i	0.03	1,457	0.9%

Christians Denoms		Pop %	Affiliates	Ann Gr
Protestant	23	85.80	4,166,000	0.5%
Independent	39	1.66	81,000	3.8%
Anglican	1	0.02	1,000	-1.6%
Catholic	1	1.09	53,000	2.7%
Orthodox	4	0.15	7,000	8.3%
Marginal	6	0.40	19,000	-0.4%
Unaffiliated		7.00	341,000	1.3%
Doubly Affiliated		*-5.07*	*-246,000*	*0.0%*

Churches	MegaBloc	Congs	Members	Affiliates
Lutheran Church	P	1,418	2,977,778	4,020,000
Catholic Church	C	61	39,259	53,000
Pentecostal Movement	P	210	30,195	46,500
Evangelical Luth Free Ch	P	82	8,217	23,500
Mission Covenant Ch	P	84	9,100	18,200
Jehovah's Witnesses	M	170	7,747	14,100
Methodist Church	P	39	4,936	11,500
Free Evang Assemblies	P	70	6,871	10,100
Baptist Church	P	65	4,545	10,000
Salvation Army	P	28	6,169	9,500
Orthodox Church	O	5	1,440	7,200
Other denominations[60]		486	54,812	103,468
Doubly affiliated				*-246,000*
Total Christians[74]		**2,718**	**3,151,069**	**4,081,068**

TransBloc	Pop %	Population	Ann Gr
Evangelicals			
Evangelicals	8.4	409,731	1.0%
Renewalists			
Charismatics	4.4	211,616	2.9%
Pentecostals	1.8	86,456	2.4%

Missionaries from Norway
P,I,A 1,060 (610 long-term), all international, nearly all cross-cultural.

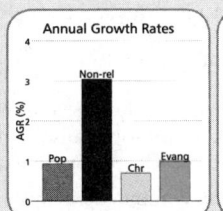

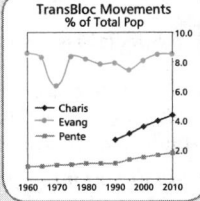

Answers to Prayer

1 **The state church of Norway,** Lutheranism, is a rarity in that many of its leaders are soundly evangelical and stand firm on many theological and moral issues. Praise God for this positive influence in the Church and nation.

2 **Norway has strong mission-sending traditions** and lively mission vision today. Pentecostals and independent mission organizations within the Lutheran Church are the core of this sending tradition. Norway remains proportionally one of the top sending nations, even while again focusing on the renewed need for home missions. But a new wave of younger missionaries is called for.

Challenges for Prayer

1 **Norway has a powerful spiritual heritage.** The influence of Pietism, prayer and revival movements within Lutheranism over the past 200 years is still strong. About 90% of Norwegians are church members, but it can no longer be taken for granted that they are believers. Less than 10% of young people are committed Christians, and only 4% of the nation attend church on any given Sunday. More than half doubt or don't believe in the existence of God. Pray for the roots of Norway's rich Christian past to be reestablished.

2 **The Lutheran Church,** while a pillar of society and the most evangelical of all state churches in Europe, faces challenges nonetheless. It has, in the past, seen revivals, prayer and mission houses and many mission and volunteer agencies formed. But today it faces the same pluralistic challenge as other European societies as well as an internal battle over homosexuality. Pray for new revival and for a deep commitment to biblical faith and practice.

3 **The formation of independent mission organizations** within and without the Lutheran Church is bringing high levels of member-commitment to congregational life and to missions. These groups blend Lutheran heritage with informal Pietist-rooted evangelicalism. The hubs of these movements are found in mission houses – informal nodes of worship, prayer and community where the lay organizations were founded. Almost the entire foreign missionary effort of the Church of Norway, and a considerable amount of domestic evangelistic work, are carried out by these organizations; the Norwegian Missionary Society, Norwegian Lutheran Mission, Normisjon and others are part of this movement. Pray for their continued role and impact in a changing society.

4 **The (non-state) Free Churches** also strongly contribute to Norwegian church life, although they too struggle to retain members. Pentecostal and charismatic churches are the largest, with the Mission Covenant Church, Methodists, Baptists and others also present. Pray for these groups to likewise contribute to rejuvenating the spiritual life of the nation.

5 **Church planting is a real need** in a society where church membership is high but actual belief and attendance are low. **DAWN** is catalytic in this respect, and many denominations are getting behind the vision; even missions traditionally focused on foreign fields see the need on the home front. Between 1996 and 2005, more than 250 new congregations were planted. The challenge is two-fold: to disciple the many nominal Christians and to reach the increasing numbers of non-Christians in Norway. Pray for many new groups of committed believers to be formed.

6 **Young people's ministry** continues to be spearheaded by new charismatic youth movements, such as Jesus Revolution as well as the older **IFES** movement. The younger generation is much less committed to Christianity and more open to other ideas. Pray that these ministries would have a powerful and lasting impact on lives.

7 Special issues for prayer.

a) **The 25,000 Sami** traditionally live in the far north and are culturally and linguistically very different from sedentary Norwegians. Some are still reindeer herders. Most are nominally Lutheran, but committed Christians are relatively few.

b) **Immigrant minorities** continue to increase rapidly. Norway's high quality of life draws many to this northern land from around the globe. A number are Muslims; Islam is now the second-largest religious group after Lutherans. But a greater number of migrants are vibrant Christians, forming dynamic new congregations that are beginning to have an impact on Norwegian church life.

i *Muslims* from Pakistan, Iran, Somalia, Turkey. Significant numbers do not practice their faith. Some 75% live in the Oslo area; a few are responsive to the gospel, but a specific strategy is called for.

ii *Asians.* Of special need are the Sri Lankan Tamils, Vietnamese, Punjabi and Chinese.

iii *Immigrants from former communist nations* – Bosnia, Serbia, Albania, Poland, Russia.

c) **Oslo and the surrounding area** have a lower number of evangelical Christians, but over half the population live in these areas. Norwegians of a non-Christian persuasion are concentrated here. The majority of adherents to other religions also reside in and around Oslo. Some of the newer Pentecostal and charismatic churches are seeing many born again and set free from alcohol and drugs. To see Norway truly transformed, Oslo must be the focal point of church planting and ministry.

Oman

Sultanate of Oman

Asia

Geography

Area 309,500 sq km. A mountainous land on the southeast coast of Arabia and the strategic tip of the Musandam Peninsula that dominates the entrance to the Arabian/Persian Gulf.

Population		Ann Gr	Density
2010	2,905,114	2.10%	10/sq km
2020	3,495,132	1.79%	12/sq km
2030	4,048,408	1.37%	13/sq km

Capital Muscat 650,000. **Urbanites** 71.7%. **Pop under 15 yrs** 32%. **Life expectancy** 75.5 yrs.

Peoples

Approximately 25% of the official population is expatriate, comprising the majority of the workforce.
Arab 66.8%. Omani 42.7%; Gulf Arab 15.1%; Dhofari 2.5%; Mahra 1.8%; Egyptian 1.5%.
Iranian-Median 16.6%. Baloch 13.4%; Persian 2.6%.
South Asian 14.3%. Malayali 4.4%; Bengali 4.0%; Punjabi 2.0%; Urdu 1.4%.

Other 2.4%. Filipino 1.8%, African, European, North American.
Literacy 74.4%. **Official language** Arabic. **All languages** 21. **Indigenous languages** 16. **Languages with Scriptures** 2Bi 1NT 2por.

Economy

Oil production is the primary source of revenue, followed by agriculture, fishing and light industry. Tourism is increasing. Oil wealth has been distributed wisely for the improvement of living standards, but its declining production requires economic diversification. High proportion of workforce from South Asia.
HDI Rank 56th/182. **Public debt** 56% of GDP. **Income/person** $21,646 (46% of USA).

Politics

An isolated feudal monarchy until 1970; a benevolent absolute monarchy since then, when the then Sultan was ousted by his son. No political parties permitted, but a high degree of personal freedom and political stability for the region. Universal suffrage to elect the Consultative Assembly.

Religion

Islam is the state religion; the Ibadi sect predominates. Churches and church activities for the expatriate communities are permitted, but proselytizing Muslims is forbidden. Since his reign began in 1970, the Sultan has consistently opposed extremist strains of Islam.

Religions	Pop %	Population	Ann Gr
Muslim	88.72	2,577,417	1.9%
Hindu	6.80	197,548	3.7%
Christian	2.76	80,181	2.9%
Buddhist	0.65	18,883	3.8%
Sikh	0.55	15,978	6.3%
Baha'i	0.30	8,715	2.1%
Non-religious	0.22	6,391	3.1%

O

Christians Denoms		Pop %	Affiliates	Ann Gr
Protestant	17	0.42	12,000	5.3%
Independent	7	0.19	5,000	6.7%
Anglican	1	0.16	5,000	2.8%
Catholic	1	1.10	32,000	1.3%
Orthodox	3	0.59	17,000	5.5%
Unaffiliated		0.30	9,000	-2.1%

TransBloc	Pop %	Population	Ann Gr
Evangelicals			
Evangelicals	0.8	23,986	5.9%
Renewalists			
Charismatics	0.4	12,790	5.9%
Pentecostals	0.2	5,820	5.9%

Churches	MegaBloc	Congs	Members	Affiliates
Catholic Church	C	22	20,513	32,000
Orthodox Church	O	64	12,782	17,000
Anglican Church	A	4	1,704	4,600
Filipino Chr Fellowship	I	20	2,000	3,000
Pentecostal Fellowship	P	14	1,350	2,700
Indian/Pakistani Chs	P	22	1,300	2,600
Mar Thoma Syrian Ch	P	9	1,087	2,500
Arab Charismatic groups	I	32	1,600	2,400
Other denominations[10]		90	2,513	4,494
Total Christians[29]		**277**	**44,849**	**71,294**

Annual Growth Rates

MegaBlocs % of Christian Pop

Answers to Prayer

1 **Praise God that Oman** enjoys a reasonably open and liberal society compared to neighbours in the region. All residents are free to practice their faith, and the government has generously given land for places of worship to be built.

2 **Christians are growing in number.** The large majority of converts actually come from expatriate workers and usually from non-Muslim backgrounds, but Omanis are also coming to faith in Christ.

Challenges for Prayer

1 **Oman has been transformed** since 1970 into a relatively progressive and open society. Oil wealth, although declining, allowed for a much greater level of education and economic diversification. Pray for spiritual openness as well, that the gospel might have a powerful impact on all levels and peoples in Oman.

2 **The unreached.** The entire Muslim majority remains a big challenge. Proselytism of Muslims is illegal, and the few Omanis who have come to faith face huge pressure to return to Islam. There are no known churches among the semi-nomadic Mahra or Jibbali of Dhofar, the Baluch of the eastern coasts, the rural population or the Swahili speakers.

3 **Almost the entire Christian population is expatriate.** There are four centres where Christians of over 30 denominations or languages meet and where services in many languages are held. There are no restrictions on evangelism among expatriates, and there is a steady stream of conversions among Asians in both the newer and more traditional churches. Churches are very active, conducting home groups, TEE and Alpha Courses. Pray for the Christians to live godly lives that clearly display Christ to their unbelieving neighbours, both expatriate and Omani.

4 **Christian professionals and workers.** The door remains open for Kingdom workers to share the gospel effectively through words, actions and lifestyles that honour Jesus. The Reformed Church in America has had a good witness here since 1890, when Samuel Zwemer, the famous missionary to Muslims, began his work in Oman. Its hospital, clinics and missionary workers have been incorporated into the government health service. Christians also have a strong presence in the education and business sectors. Pray that more workers would be willing to serve here. Pray also that, despite obvious limitations, mission-minded Christians might be fruitful and effective in planting, watering and reaping a spiritual harvest.

5 Other means of witness.

a) *The Bible Society* has a good ministry in distributing the Scriptures in many languages to the expatriate communities. There are four Bible Resource Centres, one in each Christian Resource Centre of Oman. The Bible Society also partners with **CEF** and other Middle Eastern-based ministries to reach children with the good news contained in Scripture.

b) *Christian radio broadcasts* in Arabic are clearly heard from FEBA, **TWR**, IBRA and Adventist World Radio. They broadcast 108 hours/week, in Arabic (57 hours/week) as well as English and several Asian languages. There is a sizeable audience, and some have come to the Lord as a result. **SAT-7** makes a significant impact through satellite television broadcasts.

c) *More than 2,000 Omanis study abroad.* Pray for effective witness to them.

d) *The Internet* is used widely and is an evangelistic medium of great potential. Pray that this may prove a good way to reach and disciple a new generation of Omanis.

e) *The mobile phone* is everywhere and has great potential for rapidly and discreetly spreading the gospel in video, audio and text formats.

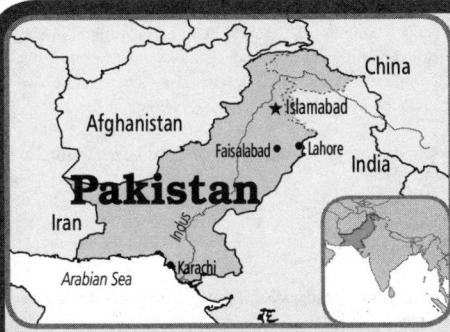

Pakistan

Islamic Republic of Pakistan

Asia

Geography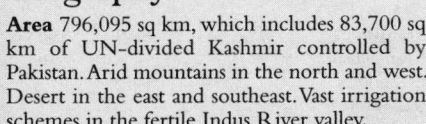

Area 796,095 sq km, which includes 83,700 sq km of UN-divided Kashmir controlled by Pakistan. Arid mountains in the north and west. Desert in the east and southeast. Vast irrigation schemes in the fertile Indus River valley.

Population		Ann Gr	Density
2010	184,753,300	2.19%	232/sq km
2020	226,186,778	1.94%	284/sq km
2030	265,689,904	1.53%	334/sq km

Currently home to approximately 1.3 million refugees from Afghanistan. A few million migrant workers are in the Persian Gulf, Arab Peninsula and elsewhere. There is a lack of recent published national data on the economy and population.

Capital Islamabad 855,648. **Other major cities** Karachi 13.1 million (urban agglomeration up to 18 million); Lahore 7.1mill; Faisalabad 2.8m; Rawalpindi 2.0m; Multan 1.7m; Gujranwala 1.7m; Hyderabad 1.6m; Peshawar 1.4m. **Urbanites** 37%. **Population under 15 yrs** 37%. **Life expectancy** 66 yrs.

Peoples

Pakistan's ethnic population and the groups enumerated below must be understood in the context of ethnicity, language and caste – a far more complex arrangement than in most nations. People cluster and people group affiliations remain under review, and the group names can be misleading if one assumes they are informed only by geographical or linguistic factors.

South Asian 81.4%.
> **Urdu Muslim** 30.5%. 103 groups. Rajput Muslim 8.6%; Arain Muslim 5.3%; Sayyid 3.2%; Ansari 2.3%; Kumhar Muslim 2.0%; Mochi 1.9%; Teli Muslim 1.5%; Machhi Muslim 1.3%; Lohar Muslim 1.1%; Mirasi Muslim 1.0%.
> **Jat** 16.0%. 3 groups.
> **Sindhi** 12.8%. 32 groups. Sindhi Sama 1.2%.
> **Punjabi** 7.6%. 65 groups. Awan Muslims 2.9%; Tarkhan Muslim 1.6%; Mussali 1.4%.
> **Bengali** 6.8%. Shaikh 6.0%; Hajam 0.8%.
> **Rajasthani** 3.7%. 19 groups. Gujar Muslim 2.4%; Gujjars 1.3%.
> **Kashmiri** 1.3%. 22 groups.
> **Brahui** 1.2%.
> **Other people clusters** 2.1%. Including many smaller Hindi and Gujarati peoples.

Indo-Iranian 18.1%.
> **Pashtun** 13.6%. Many undocumented Afghan refugees and immigrants swell this number further.
> **Baloch** 4.4%. 6 groups.

Other 0.5%. Turkic, Tibetan, Arab, Parsi, Eurasian peoples.

Literacy Officially 56%, but a more realistic estimate is 25-45%, depending on socio-economic and religious group. **Official language** English is the official government language, Urdu is the national language and becoming widely understood by most Pakistanis. **All languages** 77. **Languages with Scriptures** 6Bi 9NT 14por.

Economy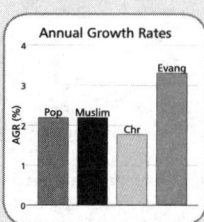

Agriculture, light industry and the service sector dominate. High inflation, huge budget deficits and widespread corruption are all crippling factors in economic development. Severe shortages of electricity and gas disrupt normal life and reduce the effectiveness of industry. Poverty affects much of the population, especially in rural areas. Around 20% live below the poverty line. Much of the GDP is spent on the military and security. The fight against radical Islamist groups is a huge drain economically, and huge debts or bankruptcy will only serve the Islamists further. This issue, combined with poverty and unemployment, creates dissatisfaction and resentment against the government and foreign influences. Rapid population growth, limited land and water and a crumbling infrastructure are other factors that must be addressed. The devastation of the August 2010 floods not only wrought immediate havoc, but caused damage to development and infrastructure that will take years to fully recover from.

HDI Rank 141st/182. **Public debt** 51% of GDP. **Income/person** $1,022 (2% of USA).

Politics

Muslim politicians lobbied for a separate state, resulting in the partition of British-ruled India at independence in 1947. Pakistan's subsequent history includes four conflicts with India, the loss of East Pakistan (which became Bangladesh), the destabilizing effects of decades of war in Afghanistan and almost constant political upheaval. A series of governments have each been as corrupt as their predecessors. Most recently, politics is increasingly polarized between modern secularists and an Islamist extremist minority that has close ties with the Taliban in Afghanistan. After leading a military coup in 1999, General Musharraf brought a semblance of order during a time of Islamist-generated upheaval. He eventually stepped down from the presidency in 2008 under threat of impeachment, replaced by the civilian widower of former Prime Minister Benazir Bhutto, whose party led a civilian coalition government. The unavoidable problems with Afghanistan, an awkward dynamic with America and the West and continued tensions with India (especially over disputed Kashmir) dominate foreign relations.

Religion

An Islamic republic with a Sunni majority. Previous governments pursued Islamization of the legal system, taxation and public life as well as discrimination against all religious minorities, despite widespread popular misgivings. Despite its contravention of the constitution, shari'a law is increasingly applied – even to Christians and Hindus – especially in areas where Islamist groups have control or influence. This gives numerous opportunities to oppress Shi'a and Ahmaddiya Muslims, Hindus and Christians. There is a notable degree of religious freedom promised to minorities by law, but in practice, non-Muslims and non-Sunnis must practice their faith cautiously and under varying degrees of threat from Islamists.

Religions	Pop %	Population	Ann Gr
Muslim	95.80	176,993,661	2.2%
Christian	2.45	4,526,456	1.8%
Hindu	1.60	2,956,053	2.2%
Baha'i	0.05	92,377	2.2%
Sikh	0.03	55,426	2.2%
Other	0.03	55,426	2.2%
Non-religious	0.02	36,951	17.4%
Ethnoreligionist	0.02	36,951	2.2%

Shi'a Muslims constitute 15-20% of the Muslim population. The Ahmaddiya are a deviant sect of Islam that is not considered Muslim by the state. However, they are also included in the Muslim percentages here.

Christians Denoms		Pop %	Affiliates	Ann Gr
Protestant	25	1.39	2,567,000	1.5%
Independent	37	0.35	643,000	2.7%
Catholic	1	0.71	1,320,000	2.1%
Marginal	1	<0.01	4,000	2.5%

Churches	MegaBloc	Congs	Members	Affiliates
Church of Pakistan	P	1,980	920,000	1,430,000
Catholic Church	C	121	713,514	1,320,000
Presbyterian Ch of Pak	P	340	72,564	484,000
Associated Ref Pres Ch	P	288	43,165	180,000
United Pentecostal Ch	P	2,411	33,750	135,000
Salvation Army	P	150	57,485	96,000
Full Gospel Assemblies	P	83	19,814	64,000
Pakistan Gospel Assem	I	3,000	30,000	60,000
Bethany Chs (Brethren)	P	148	13,333	44,000
National Methodist Ch	P	17	9,500	27,170
Other denominations[54]		3,147	432,808	693,467
Total Christians[64]		**11,685**	**2,345,933**	**4,533,637**

TransBloc	Pop %	Population	Ann Gr
Evangelicals			
Evangelicals	0.6	1,140,589	3.3%
Renewalists			
Charismatics	0.4	793,882	3.8%
Pentecostals	0.2	300,570	5.0%

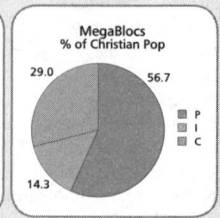

Annual Growth Rates

MegaBlocs % of Christian Pop

Answers to Prayer

1 **Prayer movements within Pakistan** – and for Pakistan from abroad – have quickly multiplied and grown. Thousands intercede for breaking events, emerging needs and long-standing challenges. A troubled land such as Pakistan surely stands in need of prayer.

Challenges for Prayer

1 **Pakistan's government alternates** between inept civilian parties crippled by infighting and corruption, and autocratic military dictatorships. Economic and social development is then hindered, while too much power and wealth lies in the hands of a few elite. The country is under stress from fundamentalist forces in Pakistan's west and neighbouring Afghanistan as well as in the Punjab. Tensions with India and long-standing troubles in Kashmir, a region driven by religious and political divisions, also threaten stability. Pray that Pakistan would be freed from spirits of lawlessness and violence that continue to bleed the nation. Pray for the raising of leaders of integrity and a government that will be effective in moving the nation forward and uplifting those who most need their protection and assistance. That Pakistan persists as a nation at all is a testament to the amazing resilience and flexibility of its people.

2 **The 2010 monsoon floods** wrought devastation from north to south as a gorging Indus River swept away homes, farmland and even entire villages. At least 1,500 people were killed, hundreds of thousands left homeless and an estimated 20 million affected by disease or lack of basic resources. Pray for Christians – those from Pakistan and those bringing aid from outside – to demonstrate the love of Jesus in meeting both the short-term and long-term needs created by this disaster. Pray also that God might use this tragedy to open new doors for the gospel into these regions, among the least reached in the world.

3 **Fundamentalist Islam,** driven by the Taliban, is upheld by a minority, but impacts the whole nation. It has escalated violence against religious minorities (including Shi'a Muslims), shattered social cohesion and divided the country. It also disables economic development and keeps millions in poverty through the disruption it causes and the values it endorses. Of particular note for prayer:

a) *The violence and war* conducted by insurgents, especially in the scenic northwestern Swat Valley, emptied hundreds of villages, towns and schools, cost thousands of lives and disrupted the lives of millions. The militants' success gave them temporary control over the region and forced concessions by the government, which has largely wrested control back.

b) *The imposition of shari'a in the northwest* – a result of government compromise with the militants – spells woe for many, epecially non-Muslims. It also invites further aggression from the militants, since such tactics previously yielded significant gains and concessions.

c) *The proliferation of madrasas* (estimated at 20,000 in number) – religious schools that in shari'a-controlled areas usually offer little education beyond memorizing the Quran and pushing the brand of Islam favoured by the militants. These schools, located throughout Pakistan, exist in part due to the lack of quality state-run schools and the expense of private ones, and they produce a new generation of recruits for the militant cause.

d) *The status of women under such militant values* is miserable. They endure almost no freedoms or rights, minimal education and widespread domestic abuse; social structures and cultural mores make it extremely hard to evangelize them.

Pray that the true nature of such an expression of Islam might be exposed for all to see, and thereby rendered powerless. Pray for safety for those most at risk under the rule of shari'a. Pray for the government to have insight in how to deal with this force that appears impossible to root out.

4 **Discrimination and persecution against religious minorities** take many forms and are directed not only against Christians but also against Hindus, Ahmaddiyas and Shi'a Muslims. The list of wrongs perpetrated makes for very sobering reading.

a) *Institutionalized discrimination against minorities* has increased since the government started pursuing a policy of Islamization in the 1980s. This affects government posts, employ-

P

ment and education opportunities, and much of public life. It also entrenches the lower status of minorities and prevents their social and economic advancement. Financial and social inducements to convert to Islam also present a problem to non-Muslims, who are generally poorer and have fewer career and education opportunities.

b) **The notorious blasphemy law** imposes the death penalty on anyone who defames Mohammed, and life in prison for anyone who defiles a Quran. Extremists routinely use the law – as a pretext for underlying personal motives of revenge or envy – to falsely accuse innocents and stir up enough religious frenzy to generate mob justice. Half of those charged under the blasphemy law have been Muslim.

c) **Persecution and violence** are reality for many Christians and for others. Frequently, churches are vandalized or destroyed and people are beaten, murdered, abducted, raped or forced to convert. Police are usually either cowed by or complicit with the fanatics and mobs, and reparation or justice is often not attained.

d) **An atmosphere of intimidation and fear** pervades the lives of Christians and other minorities. Although sharing the gospel is legal, few Christians try to do so with Muslims due to fear of violent repercussions. Christians' prevailing negative attitudes towards Muslims must also be overcome.

Pray that religious freedom might be maintained, both in law and in practice. Pray that those seeking to abuse Pakistan's laws to foment terror and hate might themselves be subject to justice. Pray that Christians might always be prepared to share about Jesus, and to repay prejudice with forgiveness and violence with love.

5 **The Church continues to grow** despite many obstacles. In effect, most Christians exist as second-class citizens, coming from poor backgrounds and classes. Pray for:

a) **Revival.** Poverty, illiteracy and lack of teaching have hastened corruption, carnality and lowering spiritual standards. Substance abuse occurs frequently enough among Christians to be a terrible testimony to Muslims. There are pockets of real devotion (perhaps 10% are reckoned to be committed, vivid believers), but the large majority of the Church is nominal or immature.

b) **Spiritual leadership in churches.** Leadership struggles, court cases, factions and divisions are far too common. Many minister for the financial gain to be had. Pray for the raising up of humble, committed leaders with a passion to serve the Church.

c) **Unity.** Recent intensified persecution and violence serve to bring somewhat more unity among Christians, but much further progress is needed. The National Council of Churches and the Pakistan Evangelical Alliance aim to draw Christians together and foster united prayer and collaborative ministry.

d) **Finances.** Most Christians are from poor backgrounds, and material support from the outside world appears to be decreasing. Secure compounds for churches, Bible schools and other Christian facilities are now necessary for higher security measures, which are financially costly or downright unaffordable. Much of Christian-used infrastructure is in disrepair with few resources just to maintain, let alone increase, buildings. Pray for creative solutions to this long-term issue.

e) **Relationship to the state.** Despite discrimination and often outright hostility from the government, most Pakistani Christians love their nation and wish it to prosper. Believers are considering demonstrable ways they can be both Christian and Pakistani. Pray for a healthy dynamic between state and Church, and that Christians might be a blessing to their land.

f) **Education** is an area in which Christians could potentially have great strategic impact on Pakistan. In the past, schools run by Christians helped shape many of the country's top leaders. But many Christians who receive quality higher education leave Pakistan for better opportunities abroad. Pray that more might stay as redemptive influences in Pakistan.

6 **Leadership training** is a hugely critical need for the Church. Pray for educational and training institutions, for an increase in students, for wise and godly leadership, for sufficient qualified faculty and for adequate financial resources. Give thanks for the new generation of emerging Pakistani leaders, and pray that a higher proportion of them may be able to serve in national churches without needing the support of foreign agencies.

a) *Residential training centres.* There are 12 Protestant and six Catholic theological colleges and Bible schools, most significantly Gujranwala Theological Seminary, United Bible Training Centre, Full Gospel Assembly (FGA) Bible College, Zarephath Bible Institute and St. Thomas' Theological College.

b) *Church-based training centres.* Most denominations also use TEE courses from the Open Theological Seminary in Lahore which has 3,000 students in more than 200 centres taking accredited courses up to the bachelor of theology level.

c) *Bible Correspondence courses.* The Pakistan Bible Correspondence Institute operates out of five cities, with around 3,300 enrolled. It also sends out large numbers of NTs and copies of the JESUS film. Enrolment for these courses has declined of late; pray for a resurgence in student numbers. The vast majority of Muslim-background believers have taken a BCC as part of their spiritual pilgrimage.

7 **Outreach by Pakistani Christians** is an issue needing major change. Few Muslims have ever come to Christ because the existing Church emerged from the lowest rungs of society – mainly Hindu Dalits of the Punjab and Hindu tribal peoples of the Sindh. Huge cultural boundaries exist between the Muslim majority and the Christian minority. Little has been done to reach Muslims or even Hindus. Many factors conspire to make Christians fearful, introspective and silent, yet despite the negatives, there is a considerable degree of freedom to openly share the gospel for those with the boldness and faith. **OM** teams challenge many believers to become involved in outreach. Pray for Christians to be impassioned and equipped to share their faith and to answer the claims and questions of Muslims. Signs of an awakening in this area are appearing, and a small but growing number of indigenous believers are starting to reach out cross-culturally.

8 **Believers from a Muslim background** are in a unique and challenging situation. Islam, particularly under shari'a, has grave or deadly punishments for apostates. Yet increasing numbers of Muslims are coming to faith in Jesus, often through media such as literature, radio, TV as well as dreams and visions and the witness of Pakistani Christians. Some are ex-militants. Churches, comprised mostly of Hindu-background and lower caste believers, do not know how to integrate and disciple these people, and so the large majority of them revert to Islam, turn to atheism or retreat to private faith. Some networks of Muslim-background believers are emerging for mutual spiritual support and discipleship. Pray for such networks to spread and fellowships to form for these believers so that they do not easily fall away. Ask the Lord to raise up leaders for these believers, and for their protection. Pray that any such movement will develop solid disciples with hearts to reach other Muslims.

9 **Pakistan lies at the very heart of the unevangelized world.** Over 350 peoples and castes can be regarded as unevangelized. Many of these have no churches, no Christians, no missionaries and no witness. Pakistan is the world's second-largest concentration of unengaged, unevangelized peoples and the world's second largest Muslim population. Few countries, if any, present a greater challenge for missions. Pray for the calling of more intercessors, advocates and missionaries for these people in such hard places:

a) *The Punjabi majority* on the Indus plain. Few of these highly populous Muslim groups have been reached. There are some fellowships among them as well as growing numbers of secret believers.

b) *The Pashtuns* of the North-West Frontier with Afghanistan are famed as combative, clannish and fundamentalist, comprising the majority of the Taliban. They control the lucrative drug and weapon trades in Pakistan and Afghanistan. Over two million live in Karachi. There are only two known Pushtu-speaking fellowships, but a response to the gospel is beginning. A handful of expatriate workers and agencies are committed to ministry among them, but those who learn the language come under intense spiritual attack. Some claim the Pashtun heartland is one of the most spiritually oppressive places on earth.

c) *The Seraiki-speaking peoples* have thus far been largely ignored by Christian work, with very few Christian resources available to them. Largely rural, they number 14 million, divided among 200 peoples speaking Seraiki as either their primary or secondary language.

d) *The Sindhi peoples* are among the poorest and least-evangelized people groups in the world. There are only a couple hundred known believers from a Muslim background and no truly Sindhi congregation among these groups which number up to 25 million people. FEBA, **TWR** and **GFA** broadcast in Sindhi as well as other languages. **WV** runs a hospital that meets many health needs, especially for women. An International Sindhi Partnership links churches and agencies interested in the Sindhi. Signs of the Holy Spirit's working among the Sindhi are becoming evident.

e) **The Baloch and the Brahui.** Some 75% of the world's ten million Baloch live in Pakistan. They are notoriously difficult to reach – Balochistan is geographically inhospitable, poor and very hard to access for expatriates, but some Baloch are very responsive to the gospel. Over one million live and work in Karachi. Only a few hundred Baloch and Brahui believers are known globally with reports of increasing numbers coming to faith, but the vast majority of them remain untouched by the gospel.

f) **The Mohajirs** are Urdu-speaking peoples who are native to India. They are highly urbanized and make up nearly half of Karachi's population. They are financially more prosperous than most groups and are quite accessible, yet there is only one fellowship and only one church-planting team trying to reach as many as 10 million Mohajirs.

g) **The peoples of the far north.** Over 27 smaller people groups live in the mountain valleys of Kashmir, Kohistan, Swat, Dir, Chitral, Gilgit and the Hunza. The Kalash are largely animist but are increasingly becoming Muslim. All the other peoples are Muslim – Sunni, Shi'a and Ismaili. Pray especially for the Burusha of the Hunza, the Tibetan-related Balti, the Khowari of Chitral, the Shina, the Kohistani and Turbvali as well as the numerous smaller groups. There are only a few Christians and a handful of fellowships among these peoples.

h) **Karachi** is a chaotic city with a huge population (double the official population figures), inter-ethnic conflicts, kidnappings, violent crimes and widespread drug addiction. Karachi has six peoples of over one million population (Pashtun, Sindhi, Baloch, Punjabi, Bengali and Urdu-speaking Mohajirs) and nine more over 100,000. Only three have a dedicated team of missionaries focused on reaching them. **CMS** and others have a ministry to some of the two million addicted to drugs or at risk. Karachi is the business and economic centre, the locus of ethnic interaction and an easier place for foreigners to work. As such, it is the strategic key to reaching and influencing Pakistan with the gospel.

i) **Afghan refugees.** Between 1–1.8 million immigrants remain in Pakistan's north, most of whom are there to stay. Most are Dari- and Pushtu-speaking, but there are also many Uzbek, Tajik and other groups. Many are moving from refugee camps into the cities. For years, Christian groups have faithfully offered aid and assistance, often at great risk to themselves. As a result, there are a number of Afghan believers in Karachi and Islamabad. Pray for dedicated Christians, both foreign workers and nationals, to reach Afghans in Pakistan's cities.

j) **The Ahmadiyya** are a missionary-minded Muslim sect, largely driven underground in Pakistan by persecution. Viewed as heretics by other Muslims, they are one of the most intensely persecuted religious groups in Pakistan. Few of the four million Ahmaddiya in Pakistan or the 10 million worldwide have ever come to Christ, but their sufferings are making them more open for the good news. Currently no groups are focused on reaching them.

10 **Young people** are a major subject for prayer, since 37% of the population are under age 15 and 50% are under 24. School enrolment is low (only 40% in state schools), but thankfully rising as child-labour rates decline. Pray about these issues:

a) **Rural youth,** two-thirds of Pakistan's young people, must deal with poverty and the perpetuation of medieval practices – such as child labour, bonded labour (often lasting multiple generations) and forced marriages (often of children to repay debts). They usually have little chance of advancement in life and little opportunity to hear the gospel.

b) **Young urbanites** face endemic corruption in both education and employment practices as well as disillusionment with politics and the system in general. The future holds grave danger if these issues are not addressed; eager recruiters for militant groups easily prey on such youth.

c) **Drug addiction is a massive challenge.** Studies indicate up to seven million chronic drug abusers, many of whom are university students or from the educated class.

d) **Ministry specifically to young people** is rare but gaining momentum. Good work is being done by SU, **OM**, Church Foundation Seminars and the Christian Youth Development Organization. PFES(**IFES**) has 70 groups with 1,000 students in 10 cities. **CCCI** has 74 national staff operating in 20 cities. Discipling and training Christian young people for future impact, leadership and mission are strategic investments of ministry. Pray for the development of more resources specifically for them.

11 **Christian missions have worked** in Pakistan since 1833. Presbyterian, Anglican, Methodist, Catholic and, later, Salvation Army missionaries pioneered the work. Other missions, predominantly evangelical, entered Pakistan around the time of independence. There is a great need for workers in this country of immense challenges.

a) ***Pray for many more labourers,*** especially among Muslims in the east and south of Pakistan. Post-9/11, a large number of missionaries left Pakistan and never returned. This left an overwhelming void of workers, especially among the roughly 128 million Muslims in Punjab and Sindh Provinces. Pray for greater awareness of this need. Pray that God might place a burden for Pakistan on the hearts of many. Pioneer workers among unevangelized peoples is the greatest need, but it requires a real calling, a profound faith and a long-term commitment.

b) ***Expatriate workers*** continue to minister in Pakistan. One can still get a missionary visa in this otherwise closed country, but entering is getting more difficult. Opportunities to serve abound in medical, educational and equipping ministries within established and legally recognized organizations. There are, of course, other creative-access ministry possibilities. The work of mission hospitals continues to have significant impact. Most expatriates still work with established churches and Hindu minorities, but that is changing. While numbers of Western workers are significantly down, others – Asians in particular – more than compensate for that decline. Pray for doors to remain open to Pakistan, and pray for protection and fruitfulness of mission work, especially that which is focused on the Muslim majority.

12 **Pakistanis have emigrated all over the world** in recent years – especially to the Middle East, North America, Britain and Australia. The Pakistani diaspora is around seven million strong. Very few of them have come to Christ, and Christians have generally done little to reach out to them. Praise God for accelerating efforts to reach the one million living in Britain and the more than two million Pakistanis living as labourers in the Arab Gulf region. Even so, more workers and more coordination are needed for this increasingly promising and fruitful, yet sensitive and at times dangerous, ministry.

13 **Christian media ministry.** In all of the following cases, developing resources that are relevant and contextualized for the prevalent Muslim culture is crucial and will be a blessing to the growing number of Muslim-background believers.

a) ***Bible translation*** is a big challenge with only seven of Pakistan's 70 languages having a NT or Bible. Translation teams are working on 16 languages; three more need extensive revision; eight have definite translation needs and six more need further research. Many existing translations are old, outdated or not in use. Modern Urdu and Sindhi translations are a point for praise; the same need exists for Punjabi and Seraiki in particular. An Urdu translation that incorporates terminology more appropriate for Muslim Urdu speakers is also needed. Pray for expatriates and nationals to be called and equipped for translation work.

b) ***Literature production.*** The interdenominational MIK Christian Publishing House was pioneered by Brethren missionaries. Here, a wide range of Christian literature, including SGM publications, is translated, edited and published. Other publishing and translation ministries are adding to the catalogue of Christian books available, particularly in Urdu.

c) ***Literature distribution.*** The Bible Society has a vital Bible printing, translating and distribution network. **OM** teams and, increasingly, national ministries such as Potohar Fellowship are distributing more printed gospel materials. More new material is needed for the contemporary Muslim public.

d) ***Audio recordings.*** **GRN** has recordings to distribute in 98 languages and dialects. Pakistan Christian Recording Ministries (Urdu, Punjabi and Seraiki), Good News Studios/**TEAM** (Urdu and Hindko) and IBRA (Pashto) are also producing Bible, evangelistic and teaching materials. Audio cassettes and CDs have a potentially huge impact in a Muslim country such as Pakistan.

e) ***Radio*** is, for millions, the only way to hear the good news. The need remains for mature, trained Christians to produce more programmes. Several radio ministries are broadcasting into Pakistan, including **GFA**, IBRA, **HCJB**, **TWR**, FEBA and AWR. The government monopoly of medium-wave radio means that shortwave is widely used and listened to. Pray for more workers, more languages, more programmes, more broadcast hours and more who listen and respond. FEBA broadcasts 2.5 hours per day in Urdu, Punjabi, Pushtu, Sindhi,

Siraiki, Hindko, Balti and Chitrali. **TWR** broadcasts in Urdu and Pushtu. IBRA broadcasts five hours of Pushtu per week.

*f) **Video material.*** **TEAM** is producing a raft of Christian video materials, and some indigenous organizations are moving into this ministry as well. The JESUS film (and Magdalena, the version focused on reaching women) has been translated into 22 languages of Pakistan. Projection teams show these in local communities; pray for their protection and for receptiveness to the gospel.

*g) **Cable television*** is a newer medium increasingly being used by the national church. Christian radio stations are illegal, but Christian TV channels and programmes are allowed. Pakistan Christian Network, Jesus Christ Television and Gospel Broadcasting Network are three such examples with potential viewerships of millions. Pray that such channels would effectively minister to Christians and be a helpful witness to Muslim viewers in explaining and demonstrating the gospel.

*h) **Internet sites.*** Areas of Internet Christian outreach and support have great potential: online evangelistic sites, discipleship and teaching materials, apologetics for answering Islam and even Bible translations. Online chat facilities would allow Christians to interact with seekers when security and safety are issues. Computers and mobile phones, especially in cities, allow more people access to these gospel materials and have the potential to reach many more in the future. Internet accessibility also allows the truth about Christianity and the Bible to be told and potentially brings transparency to social, economic and political issues where deceit once ruled. However, false teachings and anti-Christian propaganda also proliferate through this same medium.

 Pakistan's regions are widely diverse, and each presents unique challenges. Pakistani history and culture, the centralized government and the pervasive influence of Islam make for a national identity, but a few regionally specific comments are warranted. Pray for each of these regions, that Jesus might be made known more widely, more deeply and more quickly.

*a) **Punjab,*** the densely populated fertile plains of the Indus and tributaries. Although the location of the majority of Pakistan's Christians (primarily nominal), this region has a higher number of unreached individuals per Christian worker than any place in the world. A conservative, but more Sufi-influenced than fundamentalist, brand of Islam predominates. Lahore, Pakistan's most culturally influential city, is in this region. With nine million people in the Lahore area, this city is 95% Muslim and contains communities of all major people groups in Pakistan.

*b) **Khyber-Pakhtunkhwa*** (formerly North-West Frontier Province) and FATA (Federally Administrated Tribal Areas) are the mountainous regions bordering Afghanistan. Fundamentalist Islam and the Taliban are strong here, and shari'a is implemented in much of this area dominated by Pashtun tribal groups. It remains chaotic and dangerous, for Christians and Christian workers in particular.

*c) **Azad Kashmir,*** the Pakistani-administered part of the highly contested Kashmir region. Apart from the strained relations with India as a result of contentious claims over this region, Kashmir is a place of great need. Earthquakes in 2005 and 2007 took over 150,000 lives and rendered millions homeless. The aid and relief given by Christian groups had a very positive impact among the Muslims of this mountainous area. Some continue to minister here.

*d) **Balochistan*** is an arid and unfertile region that is very poor and underdeveloped with a sparse population. It is dominated by the staunchly Muslim Baloch. There are very few Christian workers in this region, but the smallest beginnings of some people movements exist.

*e) **Sindh*** is the very arid, even desertified, and very poor region of the south. Sufism saturates the area. The Sindh is where most Hindu tribal groups (and most Hindu-background believers) are, and home to a young, indigenous church. The Muslim population is much less resistant here than in other areas; a growing number of Muslim-background believers exists among them. It is also home to Karachi, Pakistan's largest, most dynamic and ethnically diverse city, which could be considered a region unto itself.

Palestine
The Palestine Authority
Asia

Geography 🌍

Area 6,243 sq km comprising two separate parts – the West Bank and the Gaza Strip. The Palestine Authority controls the main towns and scattered enclaves. Jewish settler enclaves and Israeli military authorities control the rest.

Population	Ann Gr	Density
2010	4,409,392	3.23%	747/sq km
2020	5,806,284	2.67%	984/sq km
2030	7,320,305	2.24%	1,241/sq km

All Palestinians number over 10 million globally. This includes 2.2 to 3.0 million in Jordan, over 1 million in Israel and a large number elsewhere in the Middle East and the West.
Capital Jerusalem (claimed); Ramallah 27,000 (administrative). **Other major city** Gaza 576,000.
Urbanites 72.1%. **Pop under 15 yrs** 45%. **Life expectancy** 73.3 yrs.

Peoples 👪

Arabs 92.3%. Almost all Palestinian Arabs, with small numbers of other Arab peoples.
Jews 6.3%.
Other 1.4%. Westerners, Gypsy.
Literacy 91.9%. **Official language** Arabic.
All languages 6. **Indigenous languages** 4.
Languages with Scripture 1Bi 1por.

Economy 🗺️

Israel's control of access points has undermined industry and caused foreign investment to fall by 95%. Restricting travel and access to water and power supplies exacerbates this. Much economic activity is limited to small family businesses. Limitations on Palestinian labour in Israel helped to reduce living standards and raised unemployment as high as 30%. Palestine's less-than-efficient administration offers few economic solutions thus far.
HDI Rank 110th/182. **Income/person** $1,500 (3.3% of USA).

Politics 🗡️

The loss of most of their land in 1948 and the conquest of the remainder by Israel in 1967 dominate the lives of Palestinians. International efforts to achieve a compromise settlement of the bitter confrontations between Israelis and Palestinians have only a small chance of overcoming the deadly stalemate. The Palestinian Authority is being allowed to extend its jurisdiction to increasingly more towns and rural areas, but Israel's presence still looms large. The Palestinian National Authority was appointed as an administrative body in both the West Bank and Gaza. After winning a large majority in the Palestinian Parliament in 2007 and defeating rival Palestinian party Fatah in a series of violent clashes, Hamas now governs the Gaza portion of the Palestinian Territories. The struggle continues.

Religion 🤲

Israeli occupation and Islamist persecution squeeze out the dwindling Christian minority.

Religions	Pop %	Population	Ann Gr
Muslim	87.69	3,866,596	3.3%
Jewish	8.50	374,798	2.5%
Other	2.20	97,007	4.2%
Christian	1.61	70,991	0.2%

Christians Denoms		Pop %	Affiliates	Ann Gr
Protestant	9	0.06	3,000	-0.9%
Independent	4	0.04	2,000	1.4%
Anglican	1	0.01	<1,000	-1.9%
Catholic	5	0.39	17,000	-2.2%
Orthodox	8	0.90	40,000	0.7%
Marginal	1	0.01	1,000	1.1%
Unaffiliated		0.20	9,000	0.0%

Churches	MegaBloc	Congs	Members	Affiliates
Greek Orthodox Ch	O	15	22,188	35,500
Catholic Church	C	18	9,444	17,000
Ancient Ch of the East	O	5	1,176	2,000
Coptic Orthodox Ch	O	5	528	950
Seventh-day Adventist	P	1	9	20
Other denominations[19]		68	4,159	6,603
Total Christians[28]		**112**	**37,504**	**62,073**

TransBloc	Pop %	Population	Ann Gr
Evangelicals			
Evangelicals	0.1	4,116	0.0%
Renewalists			
Charismatics	0.1	5,505	0.6%
Pentecostals	<0.1	995	0.6%

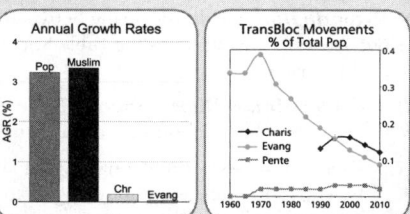

P

Challenges for Prayer

1 **Pray for God's purposes to be fulfilled** in the following areas:

a) A just settlement of the land issue and the future of both Jewish settlements in the Palestinian areas and Palestinians in Israel itself. Both sides feel strong legitimate claims to the land, but their respective national aspirations are mutually exclusive.

b) The improvement of living conditions. Estimates are that 70% of Gaza lives in deep poverty and 80% are dependent upon external aid. Widespread unemployment and Israel's imposition of economic controls prevent the majority from working their way out of poverty.

c) A fair apportionment of the water resources. Palestine has access to only 17% of the available water resources, with the remainder used by settlers, by Israel or sold back to Palestine. Only 28% of Gaza has regular access to clean water.

d) The political leadership of Palestine and Israel. The Palestinian National Authority is an elected quasi-government which all know has no real power to govern. Pray for a means by which legitimate and effective leadership might govern Palestine.

e) The future of Jerusalem, claimed by both Israelis and Palestinians, each as their exclusive capital.

Pray not only for the peace of the land, but that both Jewish Israeli and Palestinian Arab meet the Prince of Peace. It is through Him alone that any meaningful reconciliation will come.

2 **Palestinian Christians** find themselves attacked or betrayed from all sides. They are regarded as Arab Palestinians by Israel and as Western collaborators by extremist Muslims, and they are generally ignored or abandoned by the global Church. Yet they trace their roots back to pre-Islamic times. Their numbers in Palestine itself have declined at an accelerating rate, largely due to emigration. The pull to leave is strong, with a vastly greater quality of life available elsewhere, and with increasing pressures from Israel on one side and Islamists on the other. Pray that those who remain might continue to stay strong in both their Christian faith and in their commitment to live out the gospel in very difficult conditions. Pray that they might also know God's protection.

3 **Arab evangelicals** number several thousand in 30 churches, most on the West Bank. They feel isolated and rejected by Jews, Arabs, traditional Christians and even Western evangelicals. The formation and operations of the Council of Local Evangelical Churches in the Holy Land are very positive developments. The loss of leadership through emigration is very damaging. Bethlehem Bible College plays a key role in training new leaders but faces many challenges. Pray for this ministry, and pray for courage, endurance and a spirit of love for evangelicals in Palestine. Pray especially for believers from a Muslim background to stay strong and to grow in their new faith.

4 **Areas of special challenge** for ministry:

a) Poverty and hopelessness are looming spectres in the life of almost every Palestinian family. Few of them have the opportunity to hear and see the gospel of life demonstrated in action.

b) The rise of Islamic extremism in this most fertile of recruiting grounds. The influence of certain politicized Islamic forces, combined with the aforementioned hopelessness, added to the perception that no one – especially not in the West – cares about Palestine, all contribute to make violent radicalism a very real threat.

c) Reconciliation work, especially between Arab Christians and Messianic Jews, is a long road but a worthy investment. The Bible Society, Open Doors and Musalaha among others work in this capacity.

d) The Palestinian Bible Society's Bible Shop in Gaza remains closed since 2008. Pray that the Lord will bring about the changes necessary to re-open the bookshop.

5 **Palestinian exiles** make up 61% of all Palestinians. While Israel's harshness toward them was not admirable, neighbouring Arab lands were grudging and unhappy hosts. Palestinians in exile have mostly lived for generations in refugee camps (breeding grounds for extremism) and still face the spectre of poverty and uncertainty. Their possible return to the Holy Land remains a hugely divisive issue, since sheer numbers would threaten to swamp Israel's population. Pray for a solution that offers justice and righteousness to these unwanted people. Pray also for Christians to demonstrate love and concern for them in effective ways.

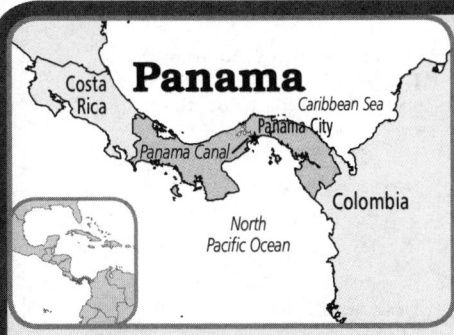

Panama Canal sees 4% of the world's trade pass through its length, and a plan to expand the facility is approved and underway. With one of the most developed infrastructures in Latin America, Panama's prospects are good. But there is a great level of inequity, since most wealth is concentrated in the hands of a few and 40% live in poverty. A porous border with Colombia means that drug cartels wield considerable influence.
HDI Rank 60th/182. **Public debt** 45% of GDP. **Income/person** $6,784 (14% of USA).

Panama

Republic of Panama

Latin America

Geography 🌍

Area 77,082 sq km. The narrowest point of the Central American isthmus, and bisected by the Panama Canal.

Population		Ann Gr	Density
2010	3,508,475	1.66%	46/sq km
2020	4,026,687	1.31%	52/sq km
2030	4,487,696	1.02%	58/sq km

Over half the population live close to the Canal.
Capital Panama City 1,378,470. **Urbanites** 74.8%. **Pop under 15 yrs** 29%. **Life expectancy** 75.5 yrs.

Peoples 👪

Considerable racial intermingling, but a fairly stratified society.
Spanish-speaking 66.6%. Latino (Mestizo) 56.8%; Panamanian Caucasian 8.8%.
Amerindian 10.9%. Speaking 12 languages: Guaymi(2) 5.1%; part-Indian 3.0%; Kuna(2) 1.9%.
Caribbean 9.37%. Creole-speaking Jamaicans.
Asian 6.5%. East Indian 4.0%; Chinese(3) 1.5%; Arab(3) 0.6%.
European/American 6.6%. American 4.0%; French 1.0%; Spaniard 1.0%.
Literacy 91%. **Official language** Spanish. **All languages** 18. **Indigenous languages** 14. **Languages with Scriptures** 3Bi 6NT 9por 4w.i.p.

Economy 🗺️

Due to its key geographic location, Panama's economy is service-based, heavily weighted toward banking, commerce and tourism. The

Politics ❌

Republic with a constitutional democracy. With US backing, Panama seceded from Colombia in 1903 and promptly signed a treaty with the US, allowing for the construction of a canal and US sovereignty over a strip of land on either side of the structure (the Panama Canal Zone). The USA Army Corps of Engineers built the Panama Canal between 1904 and 1914. On 7 September 1977, the transfer of the canal to Panama was formalized and was accomplished by the end of 1999. Three consecutive peaceful elections point to political stability.

Religion 🔥

Secular state with religious freedom, but also recognition of Catholicism as the religion of the majority.

Religions	Pop %	Population	Ann Gr
Christian	90.54	3,176,573	1.4%
Non-religious	4.30	150,864	5.9%
Ethnoreligionist	1.17	41,049	1.1%
Other	1.10	38,593	3.6%
Baha'i	1.05	36,839	2.7%
Buddhist	0.80	28,068	2.4%
Muslim	0.70	24,559	3.2%
Jewish	0.15	5,263	0.4%
Chinese	0.15	5,263	0.4%
Hindu	0.03	1,053	1.7%
Sikh	0.01	351	1.7%

Christians Denoms		Pop %	Affiliates	Ann Gr
Protestant	36	13.85	486,000	3.4%
Independent	46	7.28	256,000	6.2%
Anglican	1	0.74	26,000	1.2%
Catholic	1	66.70	2,340,000	0.3%
Orthodox	1	0.04	1,000	0.9%
Marginal	2	2.65	93,000	3.7%
Doubly affiliated		*-0.70*	*-25,000*	*0.0%*

P

Churches	MegaBloc	Congs	Members	Affiliates
Catholic Church	C	192	1,307,263	2,340,000
Foursquare Gospel Ch	P	660	63,000	126,000
Assemblies of God	P	395	44,681	105,000
Seventh-day Adventist	P	235	51,497	86,000
Ch of God (Cleveland)	P	140	15,000	49,950
Latter-day Saints	M	121	25,397	48,000
Jehovah's Witnesses	M	250	13,514	45,000
Episcopal Church	A	17	4,000	26,000
Churches of Christ	P	260	8,700	21,750
Baptist Convention	P	120	8,100	20,250
New Tribes Mission	P	46	5,700	14,250
Other denominations[76]		1,231	110,183	319,511
Doubly affiliated				*-24,560*
Total Christians[87]		**3,634**	**1,657,035**	**3,078,711**

TransBloc	Pop %	Population	Ann Gr
Evangelicals			
Evangelicals	19.3	676,573	4.5%
Renewalists			
Charismatics	17.8	624,301	5.4%
Pentecostals	15.0	525,391	5.1%

Missionaries from Panama

P,I,A 94 (77 long-term) in 13 agencies: to Panama 26, Europe 13, South America 12.

Religions % of Total Pop

TransBloc Movements % of Total Pop

Answers to Prayer

1 **Political and religious freedoms** continue to take root. Since the days of military dictatorship, there is a liberal democracy and spiritual openness for Christians to minister in Panama.

2 **Continued spiritual interest and responsiveness.** Evangelicals have grown from less than 5% of the population in 1970 to nearly 20% in 2010. Their presence is needed in a nation with many challenges before it.

Challenges for Prayer

1 **Panama is a nation of great diversity and great potential.** Because of its strategic location and the Canal, Panama is a melting pot of many races. The country's motto is "Panama, Bridge to the World, Heart of the Universe". Pray that this unique nation may bless the world.

2 **Panama's strategic location and stability** also attract many other forces to the area. Proximity to Colombia and the prevalence of offshore finance mean that drug cartels and other undesirables are strongly present and using much of the economy to launder money. Pray for a government that will root out corruption and oppose wickedness.

3 **The Church's impact** is significantly less than its size. Nominalism is widespread in both the Catholic Church and in many English-speaking churches. Catholicism has lost much impetus to the more dynamic evangelicals, JWs, Mormons and Muslims. The Church lacks the strength to turn this trend around and is further compromised by many of its members dallying with the false teachings of New Age, astrology and psychics. Pray for the intervention of the Holy Spirit.

4 **Evangelicals,** despite much growth, face major obstacles and challenges:

a) *Spiritual unity and vision.* Despite some progress in recent years, too often local churches are more concerned about their own "success" than about working together to transform the nation. Pray for the churches to grow in unity and for the work of the Panamanian Evangelical Alliance to this end.

b) *Traditional morality* is under siege. Divorce, illegitimate children, domestic violence, immorality and drug use are common. This is partly due to Christians' failure to provide a biblical model and example of godly living. Pray for the conviction of sin and for solid discipleship that shows people how to live.

c) *Inadequate impact on society.* Evangelicals are strong in number, but have barely begun to engage the wider needs of Panama. Pray for an informed Church that will bring the gospel into the spheres of politics, culture and the marketplace.

d) *Effective ministry to young people.* For many, local church structures and ministry do not connect with them. There is an increasing problem with young people forming gangs and taking drugs. Pray for dynamic and relevant ministries to young people. The Bible Society is having an impact in schools through Bible classes and distribution.

e) *Theological training* that encourages holiness of life and spirituality. There are now nearly 35 Bible schools (20 within **AoG** alone) and seminaries, as well as four TEE programmes. Pray for more Panamanians to be called into full-time service. Godly, mature leadership is needed to energize the Church and to combat widespread proselytism by marginal sects and Islam.

5 **Amerindians** respond positively to the gospel; there are churches in all tribal groups, many of them active and thriving. The goal of **NTM** and Avant is to phase out their work as indigenous churches grow and mature. Pray that other ministries might follow suit and allow the flourishing of indigenous leadership and indigenous expressions of Christian faith. There is a NT in each language, except two which have works in progress; pray for their completion.

6 **Missionary vision.** Panama is developing into a sending nation. There are over 94 Panamanians serving cross-culturally, a number bound to increase. A number of agencies work to mobilize the Church into world missions (**YWAM, AoG**, Baptists, others). The network PAAM ("Panamanians Reaching the World") is at the vital core of the movement and brings together dozens of ministries and denominations. The main obstacles to greater mission sending are lack of unity, lack of vision and lack of training.

7 **The less-reached sections of the population.** Pray for:

a) *The upper-middle classes.* They are under-represented in the churches, but a number of lively charismatic fellowships have started in recent years. There are now many professional and business people who follow Christ.

b) *The Chinese.* Most still speak Hakka (60%) and Cantonese, with many traditional Chinese religionists and some nominal Catholics among them. Allegedly, the Chinese population in Panama has spiralled upward to 300,000, most of them recently arrived illegal immigrants. There are only 11 congregations among them (none of them speaking Hakka) and a mere handful of workers. Pray for more workers and fruit in this rapidly growing community.

c) *The South Asians,* who are largely Gujarati-speaking. Most are Muslims, some Hindus, and others Sikh. There is no known specific outreach to them.

d) *The 9,000 Jews.* There is a Panamanian Christian outreach to them called Messianic Association "Remnant of Israel". Most Jews are Orthodox and hard to reach.

P

8 **University students** are a key challenge, since 65% of the population are under age 35. There are 120,000 students in 65 tertiary institutions. Campus ministries include Minamundo or CEC (**LAM, IFES**) as well as the work of Campus Crusade, but the number of groups is few. Pray for greater growth of both evangelism and discipleship among tertiary students.

9 **Foreign missionaries.** The majority of the mission force is North American. The Panama-Colombia border continues to be a problem area of violence as Colombian guerrillas and drug cartels increase their activities. This endangers both the indigenous peoples and expatriate workers. The largest agencies: **YWAM, NTM, AoG, BBF**, Free Will Baptists.

10 **Christian help ministries** for prayer:

a) *Literature* – distributed by The Bible Society and a dozen bookstores (one **CLC**). Literature ministry is limited by a lack of literacy and a non-reading culture. **GRN** has audio Scripture in 14 languages.

b) *The JESUS film* is widely shown in seven main languages, including Guaymi and Kuna.

*c) **Radio and television*** are the media with the most impact and the most potential. There are three Christian TV stations and 16 radio stations; HOXO, affiliated with **HCJB** Ecuador, broadcasts 24/7. Pentecostal groups are the fastest-growing groups in broadcasting, including **AoG** and Hosana Apostolic Community.

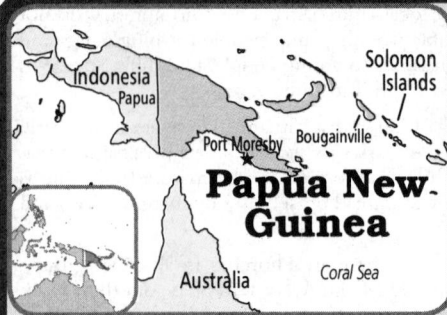

Papua New Guinea

Independent State of Papua New Guinea

Pacific

Geography

Area 462,840 sq km. Eastern half of New Guinea, the second largest island in the world, and many smaller islands in the north and east together make up the nation of Papua New Guinea (PNG). A land of high mountains, dense forests, lowland swamps, coral islands, torrential rainfall, many rivers and great biodiversity.

Population		Ann Gr	Density
2010	6,888,387	2.40%	15/sq km
2020	8,468,136	1.98%	18/sq km
2030	10,057,925	1.66%	22/sq km

Capital Port Moresby 321,000. **Urbanites** 13%. **Pop under 15 yrs** 40%. **Life expectancy** 60.7 yrs.

Peoples

About 1,000 peoples speaking approximately 830 languages, 20% of the world's total. Ethnically and linguistically the world's most complex nation whose cultures have been moulded by geography, successive immigrations, sorcery, fear and warfare, and more recently from outside by colonialism, Christian mission and modernity.

Melanesian 98.2%. Numerous ethnic groups, over half of which number less than 2,000 in population. Enga 5.2%; Melpa 3.3%; Huli 1.9%; Kuman 1.9%; Papuan 1.8%; Kamano 1.7%; Golin 1.6%; Sinasina 1.6%; Tolai 1.5%; Ambulas 1.1%; North Waghi 1.1%; Benabena 1.0%; Kapau 1.0%.

Other 1.8%. Chinese, Caucasian, Polynesian, East and Southeast Asian, West Papuan refugees.
Literacy 57.3%. **Official language** English, Tok Pisin (Melanesian/English Creole) and Motu. **All languages** 830. **Languages with Scriptures** 12Bi 210NT 289por 260w.i.p.

Economy

Traditional subsistence agricultural/fishing economy supplemented by cash crops (tea, coffee and copra). Exploitation of natural resources – oil, gas, minerals and timber – is increasing rapidly. Many problems (land compensation claims, rugged terrain, declining infrastructure, greedy multinational corporations, violent upheavals) complicate wise stewarding of the land's rich resources. Heavily dependent on trade (and aid) from Australia. High urban unemployment; 70% of the population lives with very few resources. **HDI Rank** 148th/182. **Public debt** 32% of GDP. **Income/person** $1,306 (3% of USA).

Politics

The north coast and island provinces (historically called German New Guinea) were under German control until WWI, and the south (called British New Guinea) under British rule until 1901. The latter then came under Australian rule as Papua. Australia administered the Territory of Papua and New Guinea until independence in 1975 when Papua New Guinea became a state within the British Commonwealth. The nation is governed by a democratic parliamentary system. The 1988-98 uprising of Bougainville proved costly at every level, but peace is being maintained with the island now effectively autonomous.

Religion

Freedom of religion. Almost the entire population has some link to a Christian denomination, but the old ethnic, predominantly animistic religions remain a powerful underlying influence.

Religions	Pop %	Population	Ann Gr
Christian	95.84	6,601,830	2.4%
Ethnoreligionist	3.50	241,094	3.6%
Non-religious	0.30	20,665	2.4%
Baha'i	0.25	17,221	2.4%
Buddhist	0.05	3,444	-1.3%
Muslim	0.04	2,755	8.5%
Chinese	0.02	1,378	-5.6%

Over 95% self-identify as Christian, but nominalism, false teaching and various cults in the Church – combined with the pervasive influence of animism in many peoples – lead to a false assumption that PNG is thoroughly Christianized.

Christians	Denoms	Pop %	Affiliates	Ann Gr
Protestant	58	52.65	3,627,000	1.6%
Independent	44	5.89	406,000	3.0%
Anglican	1	2.46	170,000	0.2%
Catholic	1	26.49	1,825,000	1.6%
Marginal	47	2.38	164,000	2.2%
Unaffiliated		12.40	856,000	2.4%
Doubly affiliated		*-6.45*	*-444,000*	*0.0%*

Churches	MegaBloc	Congs	Members	Affiliates
Catholic Church	C	2,454	1,079,882	1,825,000
United Church	P	4,998	649,701	1,085,000
Evang Luth Ch of PNG	P	3,340	557,143	858,000
Assemblies of God	P	925	165,000	480,000
Seventh-day Adventist	P	968	268,000	348,400
Anglican Church	A	565	67,800	169,500
Gutnius Lutheran Ch	P	1,069	84,444	152,000
Chr Revival Crusade	I	527	58,000	104,400
Foursquare Gospel Ch	P	1,250	77,000	103,000
Bethel Pentecostal Tab	I	297	44,500	89,000
Evangelical Ch of PNG	P	252	29,000	81,500
Evang Brotherhood Ch	P	820	24,600	69,000
Baptist Union (W Highl)	P	316	34,737	66,000

Revival Centre	I	44	17,500	49,000
United Pentecostal Ch	P	130	44,286	46,500
Apostolic Church	P	265	30,000	45,000
Indigenous Chs (NTM)	P	243	22,300	42,370
Ch of the Nazarene	P	540	15,700	26,700
Evang Bible Mission	P	580	14,500	24,650
Apostolic Christian Ch	P	71	6,050	24,200
Christian Brethren	P	118	10,000	20,000
Other denominations[130]		2,660	231,083	482,131
Doubly affiliated				*-444,000*

Total Christians[151]	22,432	3,531,226	5,747,351

TransBloc	Pop %	Population	Ann Gr
Evangelicals			
Evangelicals	25.7	1,773,348	3.1%
Renewalists			
Charismatics	18.1	1,247,283	3.6%
Pentecostals	13.3	914,144	3.4%

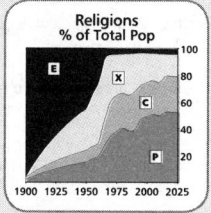

Religions % of Total Pop

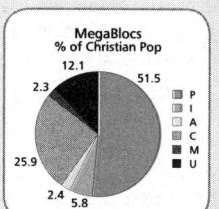

MegaBlocs % of Christian Pop

Answers to Prayer

1 **Increased Christian influence in Parliament,** a result of recent elections. While most members of Parliament confess Christianity, every indication reveals less than half are actively practicing; still, the prayer and pastoral presence is encouraging.

2 **Bible translation has seen great progress in recent years,** especially with increased involvement of nationals in the process as translators and assistants. Over 200 projects are in progress and several new NTs are completed every year!

3 **A growing mission vision among the PNG churches.** Although economically poorer and often less educated than their expatriate counterparts, believers are full of faith, accustomed to hardship and well aware of the wide cross-cultural contexts and spiritual warfare that come with mission work.

P

Challenges for Prayer

1 **The nation faces many crises** just to prevent meltdown, never mind to oversee progress. Some groups and governments involved with PNG see an impending failed state and social chaos. Corruption is endemic and hampering progress. Pray for a government that will act with courage and foresight, moral integrity and wisdom.

a) ***The sheer ethnic diversity*** and geographic isolation of most groups make attempts to mould a single national PNG identity monumentally complex. Tribal fighting and revenge killings have been ongoing for millennia. Pray for a means to establish both a peace that surpasses the mere absence of violence and an identity that transcends immediate ethnic ties.

b) ***Economic development*** is an uphill struggle. The vast wealth of natural resources is hard to access, and is plundered by rapacious foreign companies and their local collaborators, a rich elite. The majority of citizens (>75%) survive through subsistence farming. Corruption dissipates the bulk of foreign aid and a significant amount of the national expenditure meant to help locals.

c) **Accelerating urbanization** intensifies pressure on the job market, public utilities and health care, ethnic relations and social stability. Violent crime in cities is rising. Traditional structures of village life are not present in urban squatter camps, hence the accompanying social decay.

2 **The last 130 years of great mission success in PNG** started along the coast, moved inland, reaching finally to the Highlands and almost every people. Some have seen mass movements to Christ. Over 95% of all peoples now claim to be Christian. Praise God for the presence of a living, vibrant Church today. But a deeper level of discipleship is lacking in many places, sometimes resulting in disillusionment and a turning back to ungodly traditions, drunkenness, gambling, "cargo cults" or other syncretistic groups. Revivals have come (East and West Sepik, New Britain, North Solomons and Highlands areas); more are needed to see lasting change.

3 **AIDS is an impending scourge** with HIV infections increasing at an alarming rate, approaching a pandemic comparable to that of sub-Saharan Africa. Lack of awareness is a major challenge: mostly spread through sexual immorality, HIV is often attributed to all kinds of causes, some superstitious. TSCF(**IFES**), Anglicans (Anglicare) and Baptists are just three ministries educating on causes of AIDS, removing the associated stigma and cultivating biblical lifestyles so as to eradicate the infection.

4 **Witchcraft and sorcery are on the rise again.** "Witch hunts" are becoming more common wherein those suspected of black magic are tortured into a confession and killed. This gruesome trend is in part a reflection of the spiritually-attuned culture, but also a reaction to the rapid increase in AIDS. Pray for an end to occult activities and related violence; the existence of such problems in a 96% Christian nation illustrates both the failure of and challenges to the Church.

5 **There are many challenges** facing the churches:

a) **Effective discipling** is the most urgent and prevalent need. Nominalism, syncretism and pollution of Christianity with spiritism and the occult are sadly widespread. Culturally appropriate ways of building biblical faith, character, lifestyle and worldview must be developed; pray for creative, insightful groups to achieve this.

b) **Failure to engage with Scripture.** Lack of Scripture translations and widespread functional illiteracy generate both spiritual stuntedness and vulnerability to nominalism or theological error. Pray for more Bible and discipleship material specifically developed for oral learners.

c) **The Wantok ("one talk") system is one of mutual sharing** – important in a society of subsistence hunting and farming. Yet the communal, trans-generational sense of obligation and mutuality can not only hinder economic progress but also restrain those who wish to press on in their Christian walk.

d) **Continued divisiveness based on ethnicity.** Strong tribal ties, ancient animosities and diversity of languages persist. These barriers hinder fellowship and the flow of spiritual blessing.

e) **Denominational division** is less now than in the past, but unity and cooperation are far from achieved. The PNG Council of Churches draws together mainline denominations; the Evangelical Alliance does the same for most Protestant and many independent groups. They see good progress at the leadership level. Pray for divisions to be broken down, particularly on the local congregational level.

f) **Attempts to Islamize PNG** are underway and will be an increasing challenge to the Church. Pray for adequate preparation and equipping that will enable Christians to wisely face such encroachment.

6 **Leadership training** is a top priority. Churches and missions run many small Bible schools, and there are a few denominational theological colleges. The Christian Leaders' Training College (CLTC) – with 120 full-time students, a community of 500 from all over PNG and the Solomon Islands, and an international faculty – trains leaders for churches. Churches are recognizing TEE as a valuable training tool for marginally-literate, rural pastors and church workers who received minimal grounding in the faith. Pray for:

a) **Men and women called of God** to full-time Christian work. Highly paid jobs lure those with good education. Primitive, isolated conditions of rural areas dissuade many from service, leaving believers there without good teaching or leadership.

b) **Bible teachers and pastors** who can impart a love of God's Word in a way that both applies to the local culture and helps shape the spiritual life of the nation.

c) **Specialized training programmes.** CLTC (Centres in Port Moresby and Lae) prepares leaders for urban ministries; increasing urbanization makes this a strategic ministry. Goroka Baptist Bible College (run by **ABWE**) prepares Christians for ministry work in the church and in schools as teachers and administrators.

d) **TEE programmes** serving PNG and the Pacific, run mainly by CLTC and the Evangelical Brotherhood Church with enormous influence. Over 1,000 students enrol annually. Pray for more and better-trained staff and for financial provision; inflation and increased postage and air freight costs hamper rural students' ability to enrol. Pray for more TEE programmes in Tok Pisin, developed by Melanesians with good theological education and an understanding of local spiritual needs.

7 **The vision of sending missionaries is growing.** For 30 years the Church sent out small numbers of cross-cultural workers, many through **OM** and **YWAM**. The mid-'80s formation of the indigenous PNG Missionary Association stimulated mission awareness, sending workers primarily to Indonesia. Newer indigenous agencies such as PNG World Missions and denominational groups now send to a variety of fields. Drawing on the vision and model of the Deep Sea Canoe movement (missionary movement of Pacific Islanders), CLTC runs an annual mobilizing conference (Launch Out). **NTM** is instrumental in training and sending nationals to serve cross-culturally at home and abroad, and CLTC offers a missions course. Papua (the Indonesian side of the island) is an area of particular interest, as PNG nationals potentially have a crucial role in helping Papuans withstand increasing Islamization. The vision for a burst of missions from PNG to the unreached world is rising.

8 **A land with a rich legacy of missionary success and sacrifice,** PNG's large missionary presence is mostly focused on health, education, development, translation, teaching, discipling, leadership training and support work. The larger mission agencies are: **WBT, NTM**, Swiss Evangelical Brotherhood Mission, Pioneer Bible Translators, CCCC, **LM, ABWE, MAF**, Pioneers. Pray for:

a) **The gospel to take a more New Guinean shape.** Christianity must become more relevant to nationals if it is to have the leavening effect society desperately needs.

b) **Those building up the existing church.** Discipleship and leadership training are crucial tasks and the main challenges facing Christianity in PNG.

c) **Those involved in health, education and community development programmes.** The pressures facing PNG society need addressing in a brave but loving way.

9 **Aircraft of missionary organizations** are an essential lifeline for churches and missions. Many areas are only accessible by air and therefore highly dependent on such ministry. Flying conditions are among the worst in the world with thick forests, high mountains, dense clouds and treacherous weather. Understaffing often reduces the number of flights. Pray for the flying staff of **MAF** (36 expat and 120 national workers with 14 planes), of SIL/JAARS (six planes and two helicopters), **NTM** (three planes and one helicopter), and all who service these aircraft and travel in them.

10 **The younger generation** hangs in the balance. Modernity/postmodernity, globalization and social crises could see generations of Christian heritage all but wiped out unless young people are properly discipled. Unemployment and the snare of gangs are two of the biggest challenges. SU has good ministry in high schools. TSCF(**IFES**) has 66 groups comprising 10,000 tertiary student members. **YWAM** has valuable input in youth training and mobilizing for evangelism and missions. Camps (especially at Easter) are very significant for youth ministry.

11 **Translation and literacy programmes** and appropriate Christian literature are fundamental for acculturating the gospel. SIL, **NTM**, PNG Bible Translation Association, The Bible Society, Pioneer Bible Translators and other indigenous groups participate in over 260 translation projects; about 210 languages have a NT, but only 12 or so have a complete Bible. Translation teams are needed for 160 languages and possibly for a further 250. Pray for

P

translators, for means of making the arduous task faster and more accurate and for indigenous translators/language assistants. Pray also for literacy training – the written, translated Word of God is of little help if no one is reading it. Good use of storytelling and oral forms of Scripture can also have great impact.

12 **Christian help ministries** for prayer:

a) *Christian Radio Missionary Fellowship* (CRMF), with 19 staff, serves churches and missions by providing two-way radio contact for those in isolated areas.

b) *Local radio* is a vital tool for PNG. Isolation and illiteracy make radio both a link to the outside world and a medium for learning. A number of stations operate nationally or regionally. Radio Light collects and records indigenous Christian music, a particularly effective means of evangelism and teaching.

c) *Christian audio resources* – including cassettes, CDs, DVDs and MP3s - are effective tools for evangelism and teaching, especially for large numbers of rural illiterates, many of whom speak only the language of their own ethnic group. Language Recordings (**GRN**) has produced materials in 650 languages and dialects.

d) *Christian literature.* There are five main publishing groups: Christian Books Melanesia (Brethren), Evangelical Brotherhood Church (Swiss Brethren, with five bookshops), Kristen Press (Lutheran), the interdenominational Melanesian Institute and The Bible Society. Most towns have Christian bookstores; **CLC** has two stores and a mail order ministry. Christian songbooks and Bible memory books prove effective for learning biblical truth.

Bougainville

Geography

Area 9,300 sq km. The most northerly of the Solomon Islands but arbitrarily linked to PNG in colonial times.
Population 230,000. About 20,000 lost their lives in the fighting of the 1990s. Thousands more became refugees.

Peoples

Approximately 25 Melanesian and Polynesian peoples.

Economy

A copper mine was the primary source of income (and of tension with PNG) until its closure in 1989. Bougainville now survives largely through subsistence farming; reopening the mine is possible if political stability improves. Highly dependent on Australian aid and development.

Politics

Local opposition to incorporation in PNG (at 1975 independence) led eventually to war for independence in 1988. After intense fighting, a cease-fire was finalized in 1998. In 2001 a peace deal was signed, in 2004 a constitution drafted, and provincial elections held in 2005. Effectively autonomous, a referendum will be held post-2015 regarding complete independence.

Religion

Almost entirely Christian. Roman Catholics 83%, United Church 8%, Adventists, Pentecostals and indigenous marginal sects. Many are nominal with much syncretism.

Challenges for Prayer

1 **Pray for long-term peace** after decades of bitterness and hatred between the PNG government and the Bougainville islanders. There is still a need for forgiveness and reconciliation. The slow move towards independence is being handled cautiously, but reopening the copper mine could reopen old wounds as well.

2 **The island's economy and social structures are depressed.** The civil war damaged or destroyed most of the already few services there before. There is little by way of education and healthcare, and most people exist in subsistence mode. Pray for the Church to work in partnership with the government in envisioning a new Bougainville, providing a pastoral and prophetic voice.

3 The spiritual need of Bougainville is much greater than in PNG, as the evangelical presence is quite small. Pray for revival throughout the Bougainville Church, and for leaders to develop vision and initiatives reflective of Christ's mission.

a) Overall church membership is decreasing, though Pentecostal churches such as Foursquare (21 congregations) are growing and beginning mission work in neighbouring Solomon Islands. Syncretism and nominalism abound. Pray for sound teaching and discipleship that matures believers and for effective outreach across denominations that bears lasting fruit.

b) Genuine faith in Christ needs reviving. During the Bougainville civil war many people flocked to churches professing faith in Christ, only to fall away once the war ended. Pray for wisdom as believers strive after unity, understanding and respect for one another in these days of restoration.

Paraguay
Republic of Paraguay
Latin America

Geography

Area 406,752 sq km. Landlocked nation between Brazil, Argentina and Bolivia. The Paraguay River divides the more fertile and developed east from the scrub forests, marshes and ranches of the sparsely populated Gran Chaco.

Population		Ann Gr	Density
2010	6,459,727	1.81%	16/sq km
2020	7,532,572	1.46%	19/sq km
2030	8,482,617	1.11%	21/sq km

Capital Asuncion 2,029,666. **Urbanites** 61.5%. **Pop under 15 yrs** 34%. **Life expectancy** 71.7 yrs.

Peoples

One of the most homogenous populations of South America.
Spanish/Guaraní-speaking 90%. Of mixed Spanish and Guaraní descent. About 8% speak only Guaraní.
Amerindian peoples 1.9%. Mainly in the sparsely populated Chaco. 21 groups, all very small populations.
Immigrant minorities 8.1%. German 3.1%; Spanish 1.9%; Mennonite 1.2%; several other immigrant populations, European and East Asian.

Literacy Officially 90%, functionally perhaps half of that. **Official languages** Spanish, Guaraní. The latter is understood by almost 90% of the population. **All languages** 27. **Indigenous languages** 20. **Languages with Scriptures** 9Bi 3NT 7por 6w.i.p.

Economy

Few natural resources besides agriculture and vast hydro-electric potential. Landlocked status, lack of mineral resources and endemic corruption hinder development. Inequitable land distribution (1% of the population owns 77% of the land) creates widespread poverty and a subclass of landless peasant farmers. A burgeoning contraband/black market.
HDI Rank 101st/182. **Public debt** 19.9% of GDP. **Income/person** $2,601 (5% of USA). **Unemployment** 11.1%.

Politics

Independent from Spain in 1811. Devastating wars with surrounding nations from 1864–70 and 1932–35. Corrupt military dictatorship 1954–89. Since then, economic and democratic reforms slowly reintegrate Paraguay into the world's political and trade networks. The most recently elected president is a Catholic former priest who ran as an independent on a platform of fighting endemic corruption; he defeated the Colorado party, which had effectively been in power since 1954.

Religion

Complete separation of Church and State and equality before the law of all religious bodies was declared in 1992, but the Catholic Church still wields far-reaching political and social influence.

Religions	Pop %	Population	Ann Gr
Christian	96.30	6,220,717	1.8%
Non-religious	1.65	106,585	5.2%
Ethnoreligionist	1.62	104,648	0.8%
Buddhist	0.19	12,273	0.8%
Baha'i	0.12	7,752	3.6%
Muslim	0.06	3,876	5.6%

P

Chinese	0.03	1,938	1.8%
Jewish	0.03	1,938	-3.9%

Christians	Denoms	Pop %	Affiliates	Ann Gr
Protestant	64	5.05	326,000	2.5%
Independent	27	4.62	299,000	2.7%
Anglican	1	0.33	21,000	2.6%
Catholic	1	86.00	5,555,000	1.2%
Orthodox	3	0.19	12,000	2.6%
Marginal	2	1.30	84,000	4.3%
Unaffiliated		0.80	52,000	0.4%
Doubly affiliated		*-2.00*	*-129,000*	*0.0%*

Churches	MegaBloc	Congs	Members	Affiliates
Catholic Church	C	370	2,777,700	5,555,400
El Pueblo de Dios	I	276	55,143	193,000
Latter-day Saints (Mormon)	M	175	34,921	66,000
Mennonite groups	P	108	20,000	61,000
Assemblies of God	P	86	19,200	59,500
Chilean Pentecostal Ch	I	286	14,286	30,000
Congregation of Paraguay	I	282	14,100	28,200
Seventh-day Adventist	P	52	14,300	25,740
Anglican Church	A	40	8,540	21,350
Ch of God (Cleveland)	P	182	8,300	20,750
Baptist Convention	P	100	7,680	19,200
Jehovah's Witnesses	M	130	10,600	17,702
Evang Miss AoG	P	47	8,413	17,500
Other Independent	I	75	6,000	15,000

Other Pentecostal	P	120	6,000	15,000
Grace and Glory Ch	P	83	7,500	15,000
Other denominations[50]		1,046	59,715	137,375
Doubly affiliated				*-129,000*
Total Christians[98]		**3,458**	**3,072,398**	**6,168,717**

TransBloc	Pop %	Population	Ann Gr
Evangelicals			
Evangelicals	6.1	393,263	3.1%
Renewalists			
Charismatics	4.5	291,462	3.9%
Pentecostals	3.5	227,498	3.8%

Missionaries from Paraguay

P,I,A 79 (51 long-term) in 21 agencies: in Paraguay 27, Asia 10, itinerant 9, Europe 7.

Annual Growth Rates

TransBloc Movements % of Total Pop

Challenges for Prayer

1 **Paraguay still suffers from the effects** of two centuries of devastating wars and bad government. The nation's progress has been hindered by the failure of its leaders to govern, through corruption or outright folly. Thankfully, there are politicians on the scene today who seem to be dedicated to changing that. Pray for them, that they might establish a legacy of uprightness and wisdom for the sake of Paraguay's suffering people.

2 **The Roman Catholic Church** has long dominated the spiritual and political life of Paraguay. Although it admirably opposes corruption and immorality, there is also much superstitious traditionalism, strong devotion to Mary and occult-related bondage to many pre-Christian deities and customs. These practices keep millions from liberty in the Lord Jesus and must be broken by prayer. The Church often actively opposes the work of evangelicals. Paraguay has never had a true spiritual awakening, and few of the Catholic Spanish-Guaraní majority have a living relationship with Christ.

3 **A large proportion of Paraguay's believers** are from immigrant backgrounds: German-speaking (Mennonites and Lutherans), Brazilian (Pentecostals), Ukrainian (Baptists and Pentecostals) and Korean (Presbyterians). These immigrant communities are sometimes inward-looking and isolated from mainstream national life. But there is a growing awareness of their responsibility to reach out with the gospel; Mennonites actively work with indigenous peoples in the Chaco, and Koreans are involved in outreach also. Pray for a spiritual awakening and great mission vision in the immigrant churches.

4 **Evangelical church growth continues,** particularly within the churches with Pentecostal/charismatic tendencies. Most of these groups entered Paraguay from Brazil, Chile and Argentina. While zealous, there is much room for growth in fellowship with other Christian groups, in attitudes toward wealth and in leadership models. Pray for a balanced faith that submits to both the Word and the Spirit.

5 **Christian leaders increasingly collaborate** on projects and visions that are greater in scope and scale than any one denomination can manage alone. The great needs for prayer are:

a) **Leadership development** is an essential ministry. For those from Protestant, Anglican and Independent confessions, several Bible Colleges, a few seminaries and an Evangelical University provide training. More pastors (and therefore students) are needed as well as qualified long-term theological instructors. Pray also for the TEE programmes, which are extremely vital for the isolated and the poor.

b) **Unity in the church** must come from the top down. An association of pastors works to promote united strategies for the country's evangelization and to assist pastors of small or isolated rural churches.

c) **The impartation of a missionary vision to the Church.** The formation of a National Committee for Missions (CONAMI) moved things forward. Now pray that local churches might take up the challenge of the unreached and needy within Paraguay and beyond. The shift from a receiving mentality to a giving mentality has to happen.

6 **Work among the indigenous minority peoples** remains fruitful. Many have become Christians through the work of SAMS (now merged with **CMS**) among the Enxet, Sanapaná, and Angaite; the Mennonites/Light to the Indians among the Lengua, Chulupí and Guaraní; and **NTM** with the Aché, Angaité, Ayoré, Manjui, Pai Tavytera and Sanapaná. **NTM** looks to expand its work to another eight tribal groups, all small in numbers but great in salvific potential. Various development projects, education, Scripture translations and training help many new churches become viable and self-sufficient. Quality leadership is as crucial to these churches as it is to the majority people. Pray for the gospel to take root deeply in these unique cultures.

7 **Missionaries are still very much needed,** and there are opportunities for those who can serve the Paraguayan brethren and strengthen national leadership. The main ministries needing personnel are church planting, leadership training, holistic mission and education. Rural areas are responsive to aid and development; healthcare, vocational/business/IT training and agricultural development are all areas of need. The largest agencies are: **NTM**, *Deutsche Indianer Pionier*, **AoG**, **CMS**, **SIM**, **CCCI**.

8 **Education** is an area where believers can have a great impact. Many school-aged children are forced by poverty to work instead of studying, and there is a nationwide underinvestment in the educational infrastructure. Developing schools, training teachers and raising educational and literacy rates among children are keys to seeing Paraguay transformed. **CMS**, **LAM**, **BMS** and several other missions are involved in this crucial ministry.

9 Christian help ministries:

a) **The Bible Society.** Scripture distribution is widespread but blunted by limited functional literacy, particularly among rural people and the Amerindians.

b) **Bible translation.** The Guaraní Bible was completed in 1996. A number of indigenous translation projects are underway. Pray for the safe completion of these long-term but vital projects and accompanying literacy programmes.

c) **GRN** has made recordings in 17 languages or dialects. Pray for their wise and widespread use.

d) **Radio** is an effective and growing medium for the gospel. **HCJB**, **TWR**, Christian Voice, Nuevo Mu and others broadcast in every bandwidth. *Radio Obedira* is a full-time Christian FM station. **SIM**, Lutheran Hour and World Mission Broadcast produce programmes, broadcast through secular affiliates. Radio is a great tool for evangelization, discipleship and training, given Paraguay's relative poverty and lower literacy in some areas.

e) **The JESUS film** is used in German, Guaraní(2), Plautdietsch and Spanish. Pray for the completion of versions in the smaller indigenous languages.

Galapagos
Colombia
Ecuador
Peru
Amazon
Brazil
Marañon
Andes
Ucayali
Lima
Bolivia
South Pacific
Ocean
Chile

Peru
Republic of Peru
Latin America

Geography

Area 1,285,216 sq km. Three main zones – dry coastal plain in the west where most of the cities and industry are located, high Andean plateau which is more agricultural, and Amazon jungle in the east.

Population		Ann Gr	Density
2010	29,496,120	1.17%	23/sq km
2020	32,880,637	1.06%	26/sq km
2030	36,005,627	0.84%	28/sq km

Capital Lima. **Other major cities** Lima/Callao 8.9 million; Arequipa 789,000; Trujillo 714,000; Iquitos 385,000. **Urbanites** 72%. **Pop under 15 yrs** 30%. **Life expectancy** 73 yrs.

Peoples

The mixing of ethnicity, cultures and languages makes a clear breakdown difficult.
Amerindian 50.4%.
　Highland peoples 49.4%. Quechua(33 groups) 46.8%, including Detribalized Quechua 26.0%; Cuzco 7.3%; Ayacucho 3.6%; Ancash(6) 3.5%; Aymara(4) 4.3%.
　Lowland peoples 1.0%. 51 peoples, including 19 Amazonian groups.
Latino/Hispanic 46.3%. Mestizo 32.0%; White Peruvian 13.5%; Afro-Peruvian(3) 0.7%.
Other 3.3%. Chinese 2.9%; Japanese 0.3%.
Literacy 87.9%. **Official languages** Spanish, Quechua. **All languages** 93. Spanish-speakers 80.3%. Most Amerindians are Spanish-speaking or bilingual; 16.5% of the total population speak Quechua. **Languages with Scripture** 5Bi 44NT 56por 23w.i.p.

Economy

Fishing, mining, and increasingly, agriculture (especially coffee) and tourism, are mainstays of an economy which saw strong growth from 2000. There is untapped potential to improve, but corruption, a flawed tax structure, military spending and vast economic inequalities hold Peru back. Over 50% live in poverty with nearly 20% in extreme poverty. There are no quick fixes; long-term stable growth and addressing aforementioned problems are the way forward. Cocaine production and ruthless oil exploitation in the Amazon basin remain serious issues as well.
HDI Rank 78th/182. **Public debt** 24% of GDP. **Income/person** $4,448 (9% of USA).

Politics

Fully independent from Spain in 1824. A long history of dictatorships and repressive military rule. Democratic government between 1980 and 1991 failed to reform the inequalities in society and deal with the corrupt judiciary and police. Two violent, extremist and Maoist terrorist movements brought the country to its knees in 15 years of guerrilla warfare. Around 70,000 perished through the terrorism or the equally cruel military reaction. Repairs to infrastructure will take large amounts of time and money. President Fujimori dealt strongly with terror and the economy, but is now imprisoned for murderous abuse of power. Future governments must act wisely with regard to poverty, corruption, ecology and continued instability in neighbouring lands.

Religion

Religious freedom is guaranteed in the 1978 constitution, but the Catholic Church as the officially recognized state church receives some degree of preferential treatment. This status was used in the past to discriminate against non-Catholics in taxes, property, education and politics.

Religions	Pop %	Population	Ann Gr
Christian	95.45	28,154,047	1.2%
Non-religious	2.78	819,992	0.7%
Ethnoreligionist	1.35	398,198	2.4%
Buddhist	0.20	58,992	1.2%
Chinese	0.10	29,496	1.2%
Baha'i	0.10	29,496	1.2%
Jewish	0.02	5,899	16.2%

It is estimated that 25% of Peruvians are Christo-pagan, influenced by animism and witchcraft as much as Christianity.

Christians Denoms		Pop %	Affiliates	Ann Gr
Protestant	61	8.26	2,437,000	2.9%
Independent	98	5.81	1,714,000	4.7%
Anglican	1	0.01	2,000	-1.1%
Catholic	1	81.71	24,100,000	0.5%
Marginal	4	3.98	1,175,000	2.9%
Unaffiliated		0.12	35,000	-3.1%
Doubly affiliated		-4.44	-1,310,000	0.0%

P

Churches	MegaBloc	Congs	Members	Affiliates
Catholic Church	C	2,648	13,241,758	24,100,000
Seventh-day Adventist	P	1,477	650,000	800,000
Latter-day Saints (Mormon)	M	1,159	266,484	485,000
Indigenous Pentecostal	I	2,252	135,135	450,000
IEP-Evang Ch of Peru	P	2,567	128,333	385,000
Independent Churches	I	1,500	140,000	350,000
Jehovah's Witnesses	M	1,150	105,105	350,000
Israelite Ch of New Cov	M	1,700	170,000	340,000
Assemblies of God	P	2,450	158,683	265,000
CMA	P	510	53,000	183,000
Ch of the Nazarene	P	920	55,959	133,000
Evang Pente Ch of JC	I	1,020	52,000	130,000
Evang Pentecostal Ch	I	1,049	41,958	120,000
Evang Miss Movement	I	290	57,500	115,000
FAIENAP-NatvAm Chs	I	525	45,652	105,000
Union of Bapt, S Peru	P	263	24,800	62,000
Assoc of Indep Pente	I	240	25,000	60,000
Ch of God of Prophecy	P	598	22,727	50,000
Indep Baptist Church	P	400	20,000	50,000
World Miss Movement	I	290	25,000	50,000
Other denominations[98]		7,426	352,492	844,318
Doubly affiliated				-1,310,000
Total Christians[165]		**30,434**	**15,771,586**	**28,117,318**

TransBloc	Pop %	Population	Ann Gr
Evangelicals			
Evangelicals	11.6	3,427,351	4.2%
Renewalists			
Charismatics	9.1	2,680,191	4.5%
Pentecostals	4.8	1,422,010	4.1%

Missionaries from Peru

P,I,A 523 (318 long-term) in 20 agencies: in Peru 360, elsewhere in South America 49, Europe 29, Asia 15.

Religions % of Total Pop

TransBloc Movements % of Total Pop

Answers to Prayer

1 **Notable socio-political progress and economic growth** after many lean and difficult years have accompanied the crippling of Maoist terror groups in Peru and the bringing to justice of abusive and corrupt politicians from previous regimes. For a nation subject to so much suffering, these are welcome and praiseworthy developments.

2 **The emergence of evangelicals** as a force to be reckoned with. From less than 1% in the 1960s to more than 10% in 2010, Peruvian believers are now significant in both number and influence. More and more they engage in social and political issues, recognized by the state as a force for positive change and involved in bringing the fullness of the gospel to all peoples in Peru and beyond.

3 **The remarkable flowering of Christianity** among many indigenous peoples, especially the Quechua and Amazonian groups. The exceptional Bible translation and literacy work of SIL and others played a significant part in this.

Challenges for Prayer

P

1 **Peru remains a nation facing urgent challenges.** Among them are:

a) Political stability. A stable government, able to implement just and strong policies, is needed after decades of dictatorships, corruption and threats to the nation's security (such as the Shining Path terrorists).

b) Economic progress. Peru has greatly improved in the past decade, but vast economic disparity and widespread poverty still hamper the nation. Further increases to the GDP and income are little improvement if they do not assist the neediest segments of society.

c) Social change. Many still suffer in the aftermath of the leftist terror groups and the death squads. Amerindian minority groups face gross racial injustice, and rapid urbanization has created a new underclass of poor migrants from rural areas. Pray for justice and righteousness for the downtrodden and oppressed.

2 **The complex and ruthless matters of foreign exploitation,** manifested via oil, mining and cocaine in particular. With oil and mining, foreign companies willingly endanger pristine environments, threatening the very existence of vulnerable peoples for grotesque profit. With cocaine, foreign demand for an illicit drug in turn drags poor farmers into cultivating the coca leaf for profit. Collateral damage from drug wars and attempts to eradicate the crop, as well as massive amounts of drug money laundered through the country, create a complex situation with no easy solution. Pray for structures of sin to be cast down, for evil to be exposed and for a godly solution to be found.

3 **The Catholic Church faces a crisis** following a large loss of membership to evangelicals, foreign sects, atheism and revived Andean paganism. Catholics who remain are polarized between the traditionalists and those who espouse liberation theology. The majority of clergy are foreign. Only 5% of Catholics are regular in church attendance; many are syncretistic Christo-pagans. Charismatic movements (such as the Christian Life Movement) have had widespread impact, but those touched often formed autonomous groups or joined evangelical churches. Pray for many to come to the light and liberty of the biblical gospel.

4 **Evangelical churches have grown dramatically** since the first evangelical congregation began a century ago. Evangelicals multiplied 40-fold, from 78,000 in 1960 to 3.4 million in 2010. Some estimate their number at over four million. The greatest growth came in the worst times of violence and social breakdown, as both the leftists and the army each regarded evangelicals as being on the other side. Over 750 evangelical leaders were martyred and some sentenced to imprisonment on trumped-up charges. Growth has been notable in the **CMA**, IEP(**SIM**-Latin Link), **CoN** and **AoG** but more so among the myriad indigenous Pentecostal groups. After peace came, growth slowed. Pray for a new and deeper work of the Holy Spirit to reignite the Church.

5 **Recognition of evangelicals** as a genuine religious presence and social force has accompanying expectations and challenges. Pray for:

a) Unity. Evangelicals have become a significant source of leadership, stability, social aid and hope since 1980. There are sharp divisions within and between some denominations, and with recent "success" has also come pride. Countless congregations are springing up with little or no wider accountability or fellowship. Pray for a national body that will ably bring together all the diverse groups of believers.

b) The deeper issue of discipleship. All the euphoria and self-congratulation at growth will be for naught if believers slide into nominalism, remain immature or are picked off by cults. Churches must make discipleship, accountability and quality teaching priorities; implementation will require both great commitment and resource availability.

c) The prophetic role of the church in society. Serious and widespread social ills should be actively opposed, especially as believers' political and social influence grows. A poor record in this area and unwise political allegiances have compromised the reputation of evangelicals.

d) Ministry to the poor. Political and economic upheaval, climate change and urbanization add pressure to years of entrenched poverty. Many Christian ministries (WVI, Food for the Hungry, Compassion International, Agape Network, Tearfund) have contributed to programmes for both rural and urban slum areas.

6 **The Quechua and Aymara peoples,** descendants of the Incas, are emerging from centuries of oppression, cultural deprivation, grinding poverty and isolation. Quechua was recognized as an official language in 1975. The Quechua Church is flourishing as Christianity at last becomes indigenized in Scriptures, structures, worship and music. Whole villages are turning to Christ. Pray for:

a) Millions of mountain Quechua and Aymara still bound by superstitions of pagan and "Christian" origin. Massive urbanization has seen many drift into the cities; pray for ministry to both urban and rural populations.

b) Bible translation has been a major factor in the Quechuan renaissance and church growth. The Cuzco and Ayacucho languages have the whole Bible. The NT in Huaylas, Lambayeque, Caquinte, Wana, Urarina and Asheninka have all been completed in recent years (UBS, SIL, IEP, **IMB**); several more translations are underway. Pray for the teams at work and for widespread use of these new resources.

c) *The full reconciliation* between Quechua- and Spanish-speakers at the foot of the cross, and the full integration of all ethnic groups into national Christian life.

7 **The Lowland Amerindians** have responded to the ministry of SAMS, Swiss Mission and others. Lately, Amerindian missionaries have become active in reaching their own and related tribes. The three Lowland provinces of the upper Amazon still have the highest percentage of evangelical believers in the country. A network of Amerindian churches is developing and growing (FAIENAP) among 17 peoples. The problems they face are huge – ecological insensitivity of oil, mining and logging companies, terrorism, drug trafficking and their very extinction as a people. Pray for ministries to these peoples, for the training programmes among them and for translation projects underway. SIL, using mainly local workers, is focused on making the NT and much of the OT available for the majority of groups.

8 **A lack of trained leaders** is so acute that both future growth and current discipleship are threatened. The absence of solid biblical theology amongst pastors is apparent in the churches as doctrinal confusion, false teaching and the influence of marginal sects grow. A culture of autocratic leadership style hampers not only the congregation but the potential impact of pastors themselves. A new paradigm of leadership formation is essential. Pray for:

a) *Academic training.* There are over 10 seminaries, some of which are strategic for all Latin America. At least 20 other Bible schools also prepare workers for ministry. Poverty and lack of finances seriously limit the number who can receive such training.

b) *TEE is a valuable alternative,* but is hampered by lack of teaching personnel and materials. **SIM** missionaries are involved with 700 TEE students. *Segadores* trains rural pastors and potential missionaries. But even this form of learning excludes the majority, who are not literate and tend to learn better orally.

c) *The raising up of humble and godly role-model pastors* who walk with Jesus and lead by example. Their mentoring role could have a greater effect than all the academic courses combined.

d) *Sunday school teachers and youth leaders.* The majority of congregations provide no special teaching or programmes for young people, a deficiency that must be rectified.

9 **Foreign missions** have passed through difficult times, especially missions from the USA (over half of the missionary force in Peru); anti-US bias, accusations of espionage, occasional lack of cultural sensitivity, active hostility of anthropologists regarding Amerindian groups and widespread activities of Mormons and JWs have not helped. The majority of missionary effort is rightly directed to pioneer work in the eastern jungle, Bible translation, leadership training and the developing of holistic ministry. Some larger agencies are: **CB**/CMML, **ABWE**, **SIM**, **MTW**, **BMM**, **VDM**.

10 **Challenge areas** for ministry:

a) *Lima is Latin America's fifth-largest city.* Almost two-thirds of the population live in slums ringing the city where abject poverty, unemployment and malnutrition are rife. Evangelization of the sprawling slums of Lima and nurture of churches in that difficult environment are a challenge, although Pentecostal groups, SAMS and Latin Link (**LL**) are seeing real progress. Praise God for the remarkable church growth in Lima through the work of foreign missions as well as many new Peruvian churches and ministries.

b) *Less reached Amerindian tribal peoples.* There are still a number of unreached peoples (at least 12) with populations often only a few hundred per group. Wariness of outsiders and inaccessibility make reaching them extremely sensitive work that must be undertaken with great wisdom and patience.

c) *The business/professional and upper classes* are traditionally staunchly Catholic and rather isolated from most existing evangelical witness. This is changing with the work of **SIM** and the influence of the emerging charismatic megachurches.

d) *Ethnic minorities.* The 9,000 Gypsies are coming to Christ in significant numbers. The nearly 900,000 Chinese have only a few established evangelical churches, and the Japanese population (declining in number) needs more of a witness.

e) Street children have multiplied in number, especially in certain areas of Lima. Poverty, social breakdown and war led to many being abused, exploited and forced to work long hours for a pittance. SU and others are working in their midst.

11 **Student ministry** is a necessary investment for any bright future in Peru. The next generation of leaders in society and the Church are being formed, but the 900,000 students have a lower proportion of evangelicals among them than possibly any other major section of the population. Pray for the ministries of AGEUP(**IFES**) and **CCCI** as well as **SIM**; their handful of workers are inadequate to effectively impact the 50 universities and hundreds of other higher educational institutions.

12 **Peruvian missions interest** is growing but is still punching below its weight. Indigenous mission agencies have multiplied – such as AMEN (*Asociación Misionera Evangélica a las Naciónes*), ATOCRI and IMA (*Impacto Mundial de Avivamento*) – and a wide number of Western agencies have begun sending Peruvians. The large majority still serve in Peru itself, albeit often cross-culturally. There is a post-graduate faculty of Mission at CEMAA in Lima as well as a growing number of mission training programmes run by numerous groups. Pray for continued growth in the Peruvian mission sending movement.

13 **Christian media.**

a) Radio has a wide audience, both the local *Radio del Pacífico* (**TEAM**) in Lima and the large international stations of **HCJB** and **TWR**, with thousands of hours of broadcasting per week in Spanish and 360 hours/week in Quechua and Aymara dialects. Satellite and Internet radio are catching on, and small local stations run by newer charismatic and Pentecostal churches are multiplying.

b) Christian programmes on local secular channels are proving important for reaching many, including those living in well-guarded high-rise apartments.

c) The JESUS film is in use in seven languages. Pray for progress in translating and producing it in the remaining languages among smaller, isolated people groups that currently have little or no access to Scripture in their mother tongue.

d) Christian literature. **CLC** has a bookstore and mobile ministry. **SIM** has launched a large mini-library project for pastors. **EHC**, The Bible Society and the Baptists are all mass-distributing literature.

e) Audio resource providers have made recordings available in 60 of Peru's languages and dialects. **WBT**, FCBH and other groups have helped translate and record many of these.

P

Philippines

Republic of the Philippines

Asia

Geography 🌏

Area 300,000 sq km. 80 provinces; 7,250 islands, of which over 700 are inhabited, 11 of which contain the vast bulk of the population. The largest are Luzon (116,000 sq km) in the north and Mindanao (102,000 sq km) in the south. Over 75% mountains; prone to devastating typhoons.

Population		Ann Gr	Density
2010	93,616,853	1.83%	312/sq km
2020	109,682,980	1.52%	366/sq km
2030	124,383,926	1.18%	415/sq km

Capital Manila. **Other major cities** Manila/Quezon City 11.6 million; Davao 1.5mill; Cebu 860,000. **Urbanites** 66.4%. **Pop under 15 yrs** 34%. **Life expectancy** 71.6 yrs.

Peoples 👤👤👤

Malayo-Indonesian Filipinos 98.1%.
  Major peoples 83.4%. Tagalog 16.6%; Visayan/Cebuano 24.0%; Ilocano 11.4%; Hiligaynon 9.6%; Bicol 4.2%; Waray 4.1%; Mestizo 3.1%; Pampangan 2.3%; Pangasinese 1.4%.

Tribal peoples 9.6%. 132 peoples in the more inaccessible mountain areas. Albay/Bicolano 2.7%; Ibanag 0.8%; Kinaray-A 0.6%.

Muslim majority peoples 5.0%. 14 peoples, the largest (in Mindanao): Maranao 1.3%; Magindanao 1.3%. On the islands southwest of Mindanao: Tausug 1.2%.

Chinese 1.7%. Min Nan 1.1%; Filipino-Chinese 0.5%. Urban, extensive involvement in commerce and industry.

Other 0.2%. US Americans, Arab, Japanese, Korean, South Asian, Europeans, others.

Literacy 92.6%. **Official languages** Filipino (based on Tagalog), English. **All languages** 181. **Languages with Scriptures** 17Bi 68NT 90por 54w.i.p.

Economy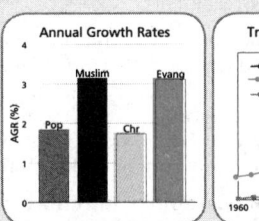

A mixed agricultural and industrial economy. High population growth, widespread corruption, protectionism, social and political unrest and a series of natural disasters have played havoc with the economy, perpetuating widespread poverty and unemployment. Massive gaps between rich and poor continue. Problems with ineffective governments, high crime levels and a lack of foreign investment hamper progress. Remittances from Filipinos working abroad are a crucial source of income as are, increasingly, electronics exports, tourism and business process outsourcing. Over 30% live below the poverty line.

HDI Rate 105th/182. **Public debt** 56.9% of GDP. **Income/person** $1,845 (4% of USA).

Politics

A Spanish colony from 1565 to 1898, hence the Catholic majority and many Spanish customs. Ruled by the USA until independence in 1946. Martial law imposed in 1971 to combat Communist subversion; the country became virtually a one-party republic. Political manipulation, mismanagement and abuse of civil liberties stimulated antipathy to the Marcos regime and led to its downfall in 1986. Estrada's rule met a similar fate in 2001. Arroyo's subsequent regime faced similar pressure for alleged corruption and legal issues. No government has adequately addressed the need for implementing land reform, for taming military excesses, for limiting the elite's power and for ending the Muslim secessionist and Marxist guerrilla wars. A proposal to reform government from American-style Republic to a parliamentary democracy is being considered. A member of ASEAN.

Religion

Freedom of religion. The Catholic Church wields enormous influence, but emerging independent and Protestant groups exert increasing influence on social and political issues as well. The Muslim minority in Mindanao seeks to set up an independent Islamic state in the south.

Religions	Pop %	Population	Ann Gr
Christian	92.25	86,361,547	1.7%
Muslim	5.65	5,289,352	3.1%
Non-religious	1.10	1,029,785	4.9%
Ethnoreligionist	0.55	514,893	0.1%
Baha'i	0.25	234,042	1.8%
Buddhist	0.10	93,617	1.8%
Chinese	0.10	93,617	1.8%

Christians Denoms		Pop %	Affiliates	Ann Gr
Protestant	102	6.20	5,803,000	1.6%
Independent	345	7.09	6,636,000	1.9%
Anglican	1	0.14	135,000	1.6%
Catholic	1	76.86	71,950,000	1.6%
Marginal	43	5.40	5,055,000	2.1%
Unaffiliated		0.80	711,000	16.1%
Doubly affiliated		*-4.20*	*-3,930,000*	*0.0%*

Churches	MegaBloc	Congs	Members	Affiliates
Catholic Church	C	3,140	38,891,892	71,950,000
Iglesia ni Cristo	M	5,000	1,422,156	2,375,000
Phil Indep Ch (Aglipayan)	I	693	1,038,961	1,600,000
Jesus is Lord Church	I	1,420	568,182	1,250,000
United Ch of Christ	P	4,082	510,256	995,000
United Methodist Ch	P	1,350	370,879	675,000
Latter-day Saints (Mormon)	M	1,668	467,133	668,000
Jesus Miracle Crusade	I	1,275	382,353	650,000
Seventh-day Adventist	P	4,330	457,143	640,000
Assemblies of God	P	3,928	188,852	576,000
Chr & Miss Alliance	P	2,744	284,431	475,000
Jehovah's Witnesses	M	3,220	168,000	436,800
Conv of P Bapt Chs	P	1,000	136,364	300,000
Chr Ch/Ch of Christ	P	1,585	130,000	260,000
United Pentecostal Ch	P	5,303	185,606	245,000
Phil Bapt Conv (IMB)	P	2,106	99,000	219,780
New Apostolic Church	I	1,350	135,000	216,000
Foursquare Gospel	P	1,684	83,832	140,000
Ch of God (Cleveland)	P	530	75,000	135,000
Episcopal Church	A	535	45,000	135,000
Other denominations[470]		30,662	3,014,585	5,636,977
Doubly affiliated				*-3,930,000*
Total Christians[492]		**77,605**	**48,654,625**	**85,648,557**

TransBloc	Pop %	Population	Ann Gr
Evangelicals			
Evangelicals	12.3	11,558,344	3.1%
Renewalists			
Charismatics	21.7	20,359,064	5.1%
Pentecostals	2.6	2,388,833	0.6%

Missionaries from Philippines
P,I,A Estimated 4,500 long-term.

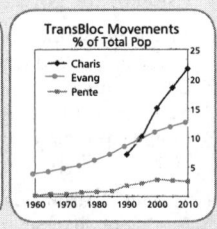

Annual Growth Rates

TransBloc Movements % of Total Pop

P

Answers to Prayer

1 **The continued growth of nearly all evangelical denominations,** most marked among the indigenous Pentecostal denominations, but almost all evangelical denominations are growing significantly faster than the national growth rates. Church planting rates have slowed since the surge of the 1980s, but many large and megachurches have sprung up, and the sophistication and diversity of ministry within evangelical churches have come along significantly.

2 **Increased spiritual unity.** The Philippine Council of Evangelical Churches (PCEC) establishes warm fellowship and cooperates in developing common goals for ministry among 68 denominations, 150 independent congregations and 170 mission agencies and parachurch groups. Philippines for Jesus (PFJ) is a network of Pentecostal and charismatic groups. The National Council of Churches in the Philippines (NCCP) covers more mainline groups. Many local and regional Ministerial Fellowships are established as well. Pray that this unity continues and strengthens, and that it extends across broader confessional lines.

3 **The Philippines have emerged as a missionary-sending force.** Through the mobilizing and coordinating impact of the Philippine Missions Association (PMA), the Philippines already supports well over 3,000 cross-cultural workers. Even more significant is the role of the PMA in training and enabling the more than 500,000 Filipino evangelicals employed abroad to see themselves as Kingdom ambassadors.

Challenges for Prayer

1 **Philippines' great economic and political potential** is not yet realized despite a wealth of natural resources, deeply democratic sentiment and a well-educated population. Failures by successive governments to deal with serious economic and social issues hold back development, accelerate unsustainable urbanization and keep half the population in poverty. Pray specifically for:

a) *A government that actively pursues justice and righteousness.* Increasingly, committed Christians take major posts of leadership; pray that they may decisively influence the nation for good. Pray for the Fellowship of Christians in Government, which promotes biblical standards in state structures and among Christian public servants.

b) *The end of corruption and graft,* which has robbed the country of $48 billion in the last 20 years. A flawed political system helps maintain endemic greed and cronyism and keeps the country's elite in power and wealth. The fact that the Philippines is Asia's most Christianized nation – yet is the fourth most corrupt – is scandalous.

c) *Recovery from the tropical storms of 2009.* A series of storms battered the country, displacing millions of people, killing over 1,000 and causing hundreds of millions of dollars in damages. The aftermath revealed the need for change in a number of areas: government that mishandles disaster relief and assigned relief funds, deforestation that leads to flooding and landslides, and poverty that leads to illegal shantytowns forming in high-risk areas. There are no easy solutions, but many pressing problems.

d) *Much needed reform to land ownership issues.* Most farmers are landless. Changes would hugely improve the lot of the tens of millions of poor. Reform laws passed in 1988 are not implemented; continued injustices produce frustration and violence and perpetuate poverty for millions of farmers. Long-term investment into health, education and other basic infrastructures is also greatly needed, but requires commitment, huge sums and long-term vision by the government.

e) *Peace in Mindanao* among the marginalized, resentful Muslim (Moro) population, the government and the local "Christian" majority. Islamist factions, such as the Moro Islamic Liberation Front, will not compromise. They claim four provinces, two with Muslim minorities, for an Islamic state. Pray for a fair, workable solution that ends the cycle of military presence, violence, kidnappings and suffering. Pray also that centuries of perceived "Christian" oppression might end with freedom and respect for the gospel.

2 **The Roman Catholic Church** sees much change in the Philippines and within itself as society changes and the religious scene diversifies. Some of the major issues:

*a) **Coping with the loss of its position** of privilege and with the decreasing proportion of population affiliated with Catholicism. Some seek to preserve the status of Catholicism in politics and society; others work to oppose threatening movements (such as nominalism, Protestant and Independent groups). Pray for new life to course through the Church and its leadership, institutions and parishes. Over 2,000 Filipino Catholic missionaries serve in other lands.*

*b) **Large numbers of Catholics** are more influenced by animism and witchcraft than by Christianity. In some parts of the islands, Catholicism is a thin veneer over long-held indigenous superstitions. They need exposure to the biblical gospel.*

*c) **The charismatic networks** have large numbers and spiritual fervour. Recent surveys indicate that anywhere from 15 to 30% of Catholics identify themselves as charismatic. El Shaddai claims eight million members. Couples for Christ (and now Singles for Christ), Ligaya Ng Panginoon, FAMILIA Community and Bukas Loob Sa Diyos add up to millions more. Within these movements are many committed evangelicals, but also some extra-biblical superstitions and beliefs. Pray for God's grace upon these dynamic and influential communities.*

3 **Church growth among Protestants and Independents continues,** but not at the rate of the 1980s and '90s. The impetus provided by **DAWN** was an invaluable part of that increase. Growth now occurs in three main ways: smaller congregations plant daughter and granddaughter churches, attendance increases in the megachurches and – unfortunately – churches split. Still, much work remains. Of the Philippines' 42,000 *barangays* (its smallest government/administrative unit), 23,000 have no evangelical church, and these 23,000 contain 30 million people. Pray for new drive and passion in the vision for and commitment to church planting.

4 **Spiritual vitality does not always equate to biblical truth.** Philippines is awash with sects and cults that blend Christian ideas with all manner of false teachings. Some of these are schisms from Catholicism, some are independent groups that sprang from Protestant contexts, some are effectively neo-pagan religions with a Christian veneer. Most feature highly controlling and manipulative leadership and teachings. Pray for all lies to be exposed, and pray for effective Christian apologetics and ministry to the millions caught within these groups.

5 **Many new challenges confront evangelicals,** often in significant contrast to the typical Catholic hostility and poverty of earlier generations. Pray for the spiritual health of the Church and the right way to address:

*a) **The unabating fragmentation of churches.** There are now over 2,000 registered religious denominations, not including the hundreds of unregistered cults and sects. Diversity itself is not a problem, since there are many strong umbrella networks for churches. Too often, the divisions reflect schisms, broken fellowship or unhealthy and authoritarian leadership patterns.*

*b) **The lack of discipleship and solid biblical teaching** for new believers and new congregations. Frequently, the results are lack of fellowship with other groups, erroneous beliefs, a syncretistic worldview and superficiality.*

*c) **Spiritual complacency and second-generation nominalism.** Growing in maturity and depth needs to take priority over mere numbers. The "arrival" of evangelicals as a force in the Philippines must not spawn apathy. Pray for new vision and for a new direction from God for setting biblical priorities and goals.*

*d) **Poverty in many congregations,** especially rural ones. Churches often take one of two extremes – either unhealthy health-and-wealth teachings or equally destructive dependence on foreign funds and sponsorships. Pray that Filipinos in stronger financial positions might assist their less-well-off brethren. Pray that Christian organizations find and implement sustainable ways to empower and uplift the poor in churches. Pray also for loving sensitivity to this on the part of foreign workers and donors seeking to help.*

6 **Leadership development** is a priority. Praise God for many Filipino leaders with national and international influence. Yet, even the more than 100 seminaries and Bible colleges and numerous TEE courses have not kept pace with the need. Splits and schisms – often led by those with minimal training and little accountability – have led to doctrinal distortions and moral failures. Many see formal training as an unaffordable luxury or an unnecessary distraction. Graduates are often reluctant to serve in needier rural areas; many emigrate to the USA. Thousands of rural congregations languish without adequate leadership; thousands of pastors struggle to survive on the meagre offerings of their congregations. Pray for such institutions as the Alliance Bible Seminary (**CMA**), Philippine Baptist Theological Seminary (**IMB**), ATS, FEBIAS (**SEND**), APTS in Baguio (**AoG**), and IGSL (**CCCI**). TOPIC plays a key role in equipping Christian leaders in the Philippines. Pray that God may continue to raise up godly, committed leaders.

7 **The Filipino Church** is now a significant missionary-sending Church. With over 50,000 evangelical congregations and a widespread diaspora, the potential is great. Filipino cultural flexibility, resilience in difficult environments, good education, language skills (including use of English) and positive foreign relations all weigh heavily in favour of Filipino missionaries. Pray for:

a) *The Philippine Missions Association.* The PMA is a coordinating body for most of the mission agencies based in the country. Pray for effective national and international networking to maximize the impact of this movement, crucial to world evangelization.

b) *Growth of this vision,* that it be embraced by local churches – with all the supportive implications. The PMA seeks to raise up 25,000 mission-supporting congregations by the end of 2010.

c) *Major Filipino sending agencies:* CAMCOP(**CMA**), Free Believers in Christ, Philippines Missionary Fellowship, Tribes and Nations Outreach, RCMH, Hosanna, Christ to the Orient, **AoG**, Asian Center for Mission, FIFCOP, Church of God, Philippine Frontline Ministries, Victory World Mission, Church of the Foursquare Gospel. There are also significant numbers of Filipinos serving with international mission agencies: **CCCI**, SdA, **YWAM**, **OM**, AEF, **WV**, International Teams, **OMF**.

d) *The PMA goal* of sending out 5,000 cross-cultural missionaries. About 3,300 are already on the field. They also seek to raise up 2,000 mobilizers, 200,000 Filipino tentmakers and 500,000 mission intercessors; pray for the fulfilment of these ambitious and faith-filled goals.

e) *Missionary training.* Praise God for programmes such as Asian Center for Missions (ACM) in eight locations, Great Commission Missionary Training Center, School of Frontier Missions and Cross-Train, where many Filipinos prepare for missionary service. Pray for the further development of these programmes; such preparation will be essential if the above mobilization goals are to be met.

8 **Expatriate missionaries** see their role changing rapidly as the Philippine Church matures. Praise God for all achieved! However, much remains unfinished, and outside assistance is welcome. Pray for wisdom for expatriate Christians in finding the most appropriate roles for this time, for wise input from Filipino Christian leaders and for fruitful partnerships between expats and nationals. The largest mission agencies: **WBT**, **AoG**, **NTM**, **GMS**, PCT-hap, **OMF**, **AI**, **KBC**, **KMCBM**, **YWAM**.

9 **Metro Manila is a mega-city** of 11 million, with the Greater Manila area totalling up to 20 million. It faces enormous challenges, but God is working greatly here. As many as 15% of the population are linked to an evangelical church, but a big proportion come from outside Metro Manila. Pray specifically for:

a) *The poor.* Modern ministry to the urban poor was pioneered in Manila. One-third of the NCR live in 1,000 or more slums and squatter communities – the kind devastated by the storms of 2009. Of these, nearly 50% still have no evangelical church. Many slums are built on the city's dumps, since over 4,000 tons of garbage are produced in Greater Manila every day. Many living in these areas are very receptive to the gospel, but most evangelical churches are in the more affluent areas.

b) *Those who minister to the poor.* Many cooperative efforts linking national and international agencies and churches have sprung up, such as the National Coalition for Urban Transformation (NCUT) which links denominations to facilitate urban improvement. The Alliance of Christian Transformational Agencies and Mission Ministries Philippines are interagency networks aiming at innovative ministries for the poor. Special mention must be made of the ministries of **AI**, Servants to Asia's Urban Poor and **IT**. Pray for discernment for effective ministry, for eternal fruit and for viable churches that impact the city.

c) *The rich.* Manila is home to those who control most of the nation's wealth. Possibly over 75% of the GDP lies under the thumb of the elite who congregate in Greater Manila's wealthiest neighbourhoods. They are isolated from the gripping poverty of millions of their neighbours. But they have the potential to transform not only Manila but also the entire nation. Pray for the gospel to impact these wealthy elite and for them to use their formidable resources to build God's Kingdom in the Philippines.

10 **Special ministry challenges:**

a) Students, over 2.5 million in 1,800 tertiary colleges and universities. Many agencies are involved: **CCCI** with vision for Christian movements on 125 campuses nationwide, IVCF(**IFES**) with 42 staff in ministry on 125 campus chapters, Navigators, **AoG** and others. There are also many locally initiated student ministries such as Student Missionary Outreach and Student Movement for Christ International. Pray for effective evangelical cooperation, multiplication of conversions and the development of a nationwide student missions movement.

b) Children. More than half of the population are under age 20. **CEF** has over 120 workers with ministry for school children in 55 areas. However, 24% of school-aged children are unable to attend school; most either work or have no local school. There are 75,000 street kids in Manila alone. Action International, International Teams and World Vision are just three of dozens of ministries focused on children.

c) Sex trade workers. Up to 100,000 children and 400,000 women are involved, many of them trafficked to other countries. The sex industry is apparently the fourth largest source of income. Pray for all involved (**YWAM**, Jubilee Action and others) in rescuing, rehabilitating and discipling these tragic victims of sin.

11 **The major export of the Philippines is people.** Filipinos are rich in skills but work opportunities are few, even for university graduates. Over 8.1 million live abroad. Of those, over four million work in Asia, the Middle East and Europe, often as nurses, engineers, seamen, domestic servants, nannies and menial workers. Many go to difficult and "closed" countries to be witnesses for Christ, and some suffer much for the gospel. Pray that all Christians may shine for Him. Pray that the unconverted may hear the gospel; especially pray for the 245,000 Filipino seamen scattered around the world (the largest number from any nation).

12 **Pray for the less-reached peoples and areas.** Great progress has been made in reaching out to isolated tribal peoples all over the islands, so much so that of the 17 remaining indigenous and unreached peoples, only two of them practice mainly tribal religions. The rest are Muslim. Pray for the Church to be stirred up in loving concern for Muslims and led into wise ways of reaching them.

a) Mindanao has a healthy number of evangelicals, but growth slowed recently and revival is needed. Continued violence between government forces and Muslim rebels, and deep resentment of the Magindanaw, Maranao and Iranun, are all major obstacles to witness. Christian concern for them increased, and now over 200 (mainly Filipinos) work among them, often in highly dangerous situations. Increasing numbers have been won to Christ and over 100 house churches planted. Pray for these believers who face great pressures. **OMF**, **SEND**, **TEAM**, **SIM** and others have ministry to them.

b) The Sulu Islands, between Mindanao and Borneo, are the home of the Muslim Tausug, Sama(3), Sinama and Yakan peoples. There is a significant breakthrough among the Sama Bajau Sea Gypsies who moved to urban areas of the region. They now take the gospel back to their home areas.

c) Palawan – a long, isolated island – is rapidly developing, with many new Tagalog and Muslim immigrants. Through the ministry of **NTM**, these have responded: the indigenous Palawano groups, three Tagbanwa groups and plains Cuyunon. Much Bible translation work is completed, and churches are planted. The remaining challenge is to see more spiritual fruit among these: the superficially Muslim Molbog on Balabac and surrounding islands, the Batak, Brooke's Point Palawano and Sama Mapun on Cagayan Island. Recent response and growth among the Molbog and Batak are encouraging. Praise God for some beginnings among these peoples.

d) Luzon. Praise God for church growth in the north-central mountainous area, where many of its peoples – the Ifugao, Bontok, Kankanay, Kalinga and Isnag – see the beginnings of people movements from animism to Christ. The Bicol region remains the neediest, with Albay Camarines Norte and Catanduanes provinces having the lowest evangelical percentages. Many

P

small, semi–nomadic, hunter–gatherer Dumagat (Agat, Alta, Arta, Ayta, other) peoples live on the typhoon–lashed, rugged north and northeast coastal mountains of Luzon. Few are Christian, and the task of church planting is complex. **NTM** makes a large investment of personnel among these peoples.

e) Visayas is in some ways the most needy region of the country. Christianity is widespread, but too often very nominal. The islands of Samar, Cebu and Leyte all see growth but remain well below the national average for evangelical presence. Widespread poverty often combines with a lack of hope to create a toxic socio-economic climate.

13 Ethnic minorities:

a) The Chinese number nearly a million. Most are wealthy targets of much crime and kidnapping. Many are Catholic, but only 2-3% are evangelical Christians. Some of the Philippines' oldest Protestant churches are Chinese in makeup. The challenge of reaching out to both the younger generation of Chinese-Filipinos and the newly arrived Chinese from the mainland needs prayer.

b) South Asians. Among the Punjabis, many are Sikh (21,000); others are Muslim and Hindu. Among the 12,000 Sri Lankans are both Tamil and Sinhalese. Pray for spiritual breakthroughs among them, and that the few believers may multiply. Pray for the few Christian workers trying to reach them (**Christar**).

14 Christian support ministries for prayer:

a) The Philippine Bible Society. The PBS(UBS) is extensively involved in translation, production and promotion of the Bible. Millions of Bibles, NTs and portions are distributed every year. Pray for the Bible to make a deep and lasting impact on lives.

b) Bible translation has been and continues to be a major ministry of a number of agencies. Of special mention are SIL and **WBT**'s affiliate organization, The Translators Association of the Philippines. By 2010, 25 Bibles and 67 NTs were completed. There are another 54 active projects and 14 more with translation needs.

c) Literature is extensively used by Christians. Nearly 50 denominational and non-denominational literature agencies print, publish and distribute. Pray for the work started by **OMF** (publishing house and network of more than 50 bookstores), **CMA**, **CLC** and others. There are more than 100 Christian bookstores in the country. The use of Bible comic books is effective in reaching youth.

d) The ministries of EHC and the Bible League have significant impact. **EHC** has distributed more than 54 million gospel booklets through the country. The Bible League has sent out over 8.5 million Bible Correspondence Courses and provided Bibles for discipling, leading to many conversions and hundreds of new churches.

e) GRN has prepared messages in 137 of the nation's languages.

f) Christian radio. FEBC and **TWR** between them broadcast over 2,000 hours of programming a week in 20 languages for the Philippines. This is in addition to the many local Christian radio stations, both Catholic and Protestant/Independent. Pray for the effectiveness of these broadcasts in reaching unbelievers and in helping disciple believers. Pray also for the fruitfulness of outgoing shortwave broadcasts to Asian countries and regions more difficult to access – especially China, Siberia, Indochina and Myanmar.

g) Christian television. Christians make widespread use of radio and TV, including the charismatic networks within the Catholic Church. Few countries have more extensive Christian television coverage. A Pentecostal TV Channel, Zoë Broadcasting (Jesus is Lord Church), is one of the more prominent evangelical channels in operation full-time.

h) The JESUS film, available in 36 languages, has been seen by around 75% of the population. In a recent initiative, all of the country's 122,000 police officers received a copy of the film on DVD.

i) Internet usage is growing rapidly in the Philippines, and many ministries and churches extensively exploit this medium to spread their message. From online communities to webstreaming TV to podcast sermons to Bible studies, the dynamic and technologically savvy Filipino Church is making a powerful redeeming impact via the web.

Poland
Republic of Poland
Europe

Geography

Area 312,683 sq km. Central European plain with Baltic coastline.

Population		Ann Gr	Density
2010	38,038,094	-0.08%	122/sq km
2020	37,496,737	-0.15%	120/sq km
2030	36,186,569	-0.42%	116/sq km

Capital Warsaw 1,712,264. **Other major cities** Katowice 2.9 million; Lodz 765,000; Kraków 756,000; Wroclaw 629,000. **Urbanites** 61.2%. **Pop under 15 yrs** 15%. **Life expectancy** 75.5 yrs.

Peoples

Overwhelmingly Polish in composition. Minority population size is uncertain due to an historic suppression of Ukrainian and Belarusian identity; also, in the latest census, twice as many declined to answer the ethnicity question as gave an answer other than "Polish".
Slavic 98.8%. Polish 96.7%; Belarusian 0.15%-1.6%; Ukrainian 0.1%-2.1%; Silesian; Kashubian; Slovak; Russian; others.
Other 1.2%. German, Armenian, Romani(4), Greek, others.
Literacy 99.7%. **Official language** Polish. **All languages** 20. **Indigenous languages** 14. **Languages with Scriptures** 5Bi 3NT 5por.

Economy

Historically an agricultural economy until Communist rule added heavy industry. Steady liberalization and several phases of reform since 1990 now see significant growth. Even so, challenges include an exodus of young workers and skilled labour combined with unemployment for many remaining. The economic crisis of 2008-2009 saw increasing numbers return back to Poland.

HDI Rank 20th/182. **Unemployment** 10.3%. **Public debt** 45.2% of GDP. **Income/person** $13,846 (29% of USA).

Politics

Poland gained a national identity in the 10th Century and united with Lithuania in 1569. It has been weakened, divided and occupied by many nations since then. One quarter of the population died in World War II. Communist rule was imposed in 1945, but poverty and labour turmoil led to the Solidarity Movement protests and a multiparty democracy in 1989. Poland joined the EU in 2004 and continues to see political progress. The Polish president and other senior leaders were killed in an air crash in April 2010, a tragic event for a country already familiar with tragedy.

Religion

All religions have equal rights before the law, but the Roman Catholic Church exercises its traditional pride of place in Polish society. Its role since 1989 in attempting to shape a state based on Catholic principles and theology causes some disillusionment. Evangelicals tend to be categorized by the more established denominations as sectarian, although less so than in the past.

Religions	Pop %	Population	Ann Gr
Christian	89.63	34,093,544	-0.4%
Non-religious	10.13	3,853,259	3.4%
Muslim	0.10	38,038	2.0%
Other	0.10	38,038	-0.1%
Buddhist	0.02	7,608	-0.1%
Jewish	0.01	3,804	-0.1%
Hindu	0.01	3,804	-0.1%

Christians	Denoms	Pop %	Affiliates	Ann Gr
Protestant	36	0.44	169,000	0.5%
Independent	15	0.17	63,000	-1.1%
Catholic	2	85.69	32,595,000	-0.6%
Orthodox	8	1.44	547,000	-0.9%
Marginal	13	0.58	219,000	0.4%
Unaffiliated		1.31	498,000	20.3%

Churches	MegaBloc	Congs	Members	Affiliates
Catholic Church	C	9,900	21,394,737	32,520,000
Orthodox Church	O	273	300,000	480,000
Jehovah's Witnesses	M	1,830	125,150	209,000
Cath Ch Eastern Rite	C	23	37,500	75,000
Evang Ch, Augsburg	P	270	59,600	74,500
Pente Ch of Poland	P	117	12,389	22,300
Old Cath Mariavite Ch	I	51	13,789	22,200
Polish Nat Catholic Ch	I	46	9,153	17,300
Seventh-day Adventist	P	117	4,482	9,725
Old Ritual Ch (priestless)	O	7	4,311	7,200
Polish Baptist Union	P	81	4,312	6,900
Churches of Christ	P	38	3,802	6,350
Other denominations[62]		929	74,477	142,430
Total Christians[74]		**13,682**	**22,043,702**	**33,592,905**

TransBloc	Pop %	Population	Ann Gr
Evangelicals			
Evangelicals	0.3	95,416	1.5%
Renewalists			
Charismatics	0.6	218,204	0.0%
Pentecostals	0.1	42,450	2.1%

Challenges for Prayer

1 **The materialist dream of wealth** post-independence proves elusive and hollow for most. Violence, immorality and the loss of a moral compass haunt the younger generation in particular, and much of the rural population remains mired in unemployment and poverty. Praise God for the stability, progress and freedom that allow the good news to be preached. Pray that the Polish quest for material advancement might be subordinated to their search for God.

2 **The Catholic Church** was long the guardian of Polish culture and nationalism in the face of Russian imperialism and Soviet communism. It performed this role admirably, to the point where it is difficult to separate Catholic identity from Polish statehood. Poland is one of the most religious states in Europe.

a) *The Catholic Church's popularity decreases* with every attempt to control or influence Polish politics and society. Also, the ties Poles feel to Catholicism decrease each passing year since the death of the Polish Pope John Paul II. Regular mass attendance dropped from 58% in 1989 to 28% in 2008. Despite increasing disillusionment with organized Catholicism and decreasing influence of faith in their daily lives, the vast majority of Poles consider themselves Catholic, most still committed to their faith.

b) *Polish Catholicism* is particularly noted for its devotion to Mary. Polish Catholics believe Mary to be the spiritual queen of Poland, co-redemptrix and intercessor between humanity and Jesus. The shrine of the Black Madonna in Czestochowa is the most important of the more than 500 shrines in Poland. Pray for appropriate honouring, but against the undue worship, of Mary. Pray that biblical teachings and values might be retained and enhanced, and Jesus rightly placed at the heart of the Catholic Church.

c) *Renewal in the Catholic Church* has a significant legacy, both among leaders and laity. Poland is rare in that applications for the priesthood are rising; it currently has about 6,000 priests serving in other countries. Movements such as Oasis/Light of Life had much influence in the 1980s when many came to personal faith in Christ as a result of Bible study groups. Pray for all Catholics to find spiritual vitality and new life in the person of Jesus.

3 **Evangelical Christians** have always been a very small minority, but some positive development is evident. Unfortunately, the growth immediately following Communism's fall was replaced by relative stagnation in the new millennium.

a) *Evangelical unity is progressing well* from the divisions of years past, but genuine cooperation is still new territory for most churches. The Polish Evangelical Alliance now represents over 90% of evangelicals. Pray for the ministry of the Polish Ecumenical Council which brings together many Christian groups outside of the Roman Catholic Church. Pray that the Holy Spirit may bring reconciliation, fellowship and unity of vision in Jesus' name.

b) *The multiplication of foreign sects and religions* brings confusion. Jehovah's Witnesses outnumber evangelicals two to one. Pagan, Wicca and especially New Age groups steadily gain followers, with many practitioners comfortably combining these with Catholicism. Pray for the defeat of every ideological assault on biblical truth and a demonstration of the power and lordship of Jesus Christ.

c) *The large Polish diaspora* consists of millions who live and work elsewhere in Europe, particularly in the UK (peaking at up to one million). Of these, a large number are exposed to the gospel in a new way and in a more open environment. Pray for their responsiveness and for host cultures to take the opportunity to reach out to them.

4 **Bible training** for church leaders, a much-needed ministry, developed quickly but has recently fallen off the pace. There are about 25 Protestant institutions ranging from seminary level to part-time or correspondence Bible schools. The current shortfall in students could spell trouble for several of these schools as well as intensify the current lack of evangelical leadership. Well-trained, experienced pastors are in short supply, and many who complete their studies leave Poland for other lands. Pray for a new surge of students and for biblical faithfulness, spiritual power and missions vision to be hallmarks of graduates' ministry.

5 **There is a great need for witness in Poland,** with 90% of municipalities having no evangelical church. There are more evangelicals in Saudi Arabia than in Poland. Most Poles are resistant to the gospel due to either their cultural Catholicism or their spiritual apathy. *Proecclesia*, Proem Ministries, *RealnaNadzieja.pl* and Life and Mission Ministry are among the local evangelistic ministries, supplemented by SGA, **ECM** (Project Poland), International Messengers and the Baptists. There is certainly a need and an open door for missionaries to come and serve alongside the national church. Pray for evangelicals to rise to this great challenge and catch a vision for the salvation of their countrymen as well as of their European neighbours.

6 **The younger generation** are caught up in the secular materialism that has rapidly emerged in Poland, although many are spiritually responsive. CCC, with almost 100 full-time staff, works in several major cities. The **IFES**-linked student movement has 30 groups with 330 students served by six full-time staff and 20 volunteers. SU and **CEF** focus their ministries on younger students and children. Summer camps are a major ministry for nearly all evangelical denominations and agencies. Pray that Polish youth and children might have plentiful opportunities to meet the living Christ.

7 **The evangelical missionary movement** from Poland is tiny, even for the small evangelical population. Poles are potentially excellent missionaries, especially to the former Soviet Union, but a dearth of full-time Christian workers domestically and a relative lack of resources can be obstacles. Biblical Mission Association is a rare Polish agency devoted to training and sending cross-cultural missionaries. Pray for the flowering of a healthy and large sending movement from Poland.

8 **Christian tools and resources** now abound. Pray for the following areas:

a) *The Bible is important in Poland,* and The Bible Society plays a vital role in printing and distribution in Poland and surrounding lands. There are already two Bibles and two NTs, but another two translations are in progress.

b) *Literature ministry* continues to grow. Christian commentaries and books are translated into Polish and printed in increasing numbers. Publishing houses are increasing in number and diversity: Areopag, Logos, Koinonia, *Dobry Skarbiec* and Credo are the more notable ones. **CLC** has three Christian bookstores and an online shop. Pray that these burgeoning ministries might remain financially viable while blessing many with God's Word.

c) *Teaching English (TEFL)* is a wonderful opportunity to serve as a bridge to the gospel; young people are especially keen to learn. Many agencies and churches utilize this opportunity.

d) *Christian media,* such as radio, television and the Internet, now have a wealth of material available in Polish. There are over 50 hours/week of broadcasts into the country as well as local Christian stations and broadcasts such as Voice of the Gospel. Increasingly, audio and video material for evangelism, apologetics and discipleship are available online.

P

Portugal
Portuguese Republic
Europe

Geography 🌐

Area 92,389 sq km occupying 15% of the Iberian Peninsula, which is shared with Spain. Also, the Atlantic islands of the Azores (2,247 sq km, nine islands) and Madeira (794 sq km, two islands).

Population		Ann Gr	Density
2010	10,732,357	0.35%	116/sq km
2020	10,767,052	-0.04%	117/sq km
2030	10,619,704	-0.16%	115/sq km

Capital Lisbon 2,823,965. **Other major city** Porto 1.3 million. **Urbanites** 60.7%. **Pop under 15 yrs** 15%. **Life expectancy** 78.6 yrs.

Peoples 👪

Portuguese 91.3%. Over 1.8 million live and work in other European countries.

Indigenous minorities 1.1%. Romani (Gypsy, 3) 0.8%; Galician 0.1%; Mirandese 0.1%.

Europeans 1.7%. Spanish 0.4%; Ukrainian 0.3%; French 0.2%; Italian 0.2%; rapidly increasing Eastern European population.

Other 5.9%. Brazilian 1.8%; Angolan 0.8%; Caboverdian 0.8%; East Asian 0.9%; Mozambican 0.2%.

Literacy 93.8%. **Official language** Portuguese. **All languages** 9. **Languages with Scriptures** 2Bi 2NT 3por.

Economy 📈

Impoverished by years of dictatorship and colonial wars. Living standards and economic growth improved following its 1986 entry into the EU, but has decelerated since 2001. Portugal is positioned below the top-ranked European economies and has difficulty competing for investment with the lower economies of Asia and Eastern/Central Europe. Tourism, manufacturing and services are major components of the GDP.

HDI Rank 34th/182. **Public debt** 66.4% of GDP. **Income/person** $23,041 (49% of USA).

Politics 🗳

Independent kingdom from 1143. A republic in 1910. The 1974 revolution ended 48 years of dictatorship whereupon a parliamentary democracy was instituted. All Portugal's African colonies (Mozambique, Angola, Guinea-Bissau, São Tomé & Príncipe, Cape Verde) were hastily granted independence in 1975. Membership in the EU brought stability and strengthened democracy.

Religion ⛪

Freedom of religion since 1974, but with the Roman Catholic Church retaining some privileges.

Religions	Pop %	Population	Ann Gr
Christian	94.40	10,131,345	0.3%
Non-religious	5.14	551,643	2.0%
Muslim	0.32	34,344	2.4%
Hindu	0.08	8,586	0.4%
Other	0.03	3,220	0.4%
Buddhist	0.02	2,146	0.4%
Jewish	0.01	1,073	0.4%

Christians	Denoms	Pop %	Affiliates	Ann Gr
Protestant	48	1.25	134,000	0.5%
Independent	28	2.19	235,000	1.5%
Anglican	1	0.04	4,000	2.7%
Catholic	1	89.64	9,620,000	0.3%
Orthodox	5	0.75	80,000	5.9%
Marginal	2	1.23	132,000	1.5%
Doubly affiliated		*-0.70*	*-75,000*	*0.0%*

Churches	MegaBloc	Congs	Members	Affiliates
Catholic Church	C	4,325	6,822,695	9,620,000
UCKG	I	48	52,000	130,000
Jehovah's Witnesses	M	700	53,254	90,000
Assemblies of God	P	530	45,000	80,000
Manna Christian Ch	I	90	20,000	50,000
Latter-day Saints	M	95	21,000	42,000
Seventh-day Adventist	P	97	8,700	20,000
Other denominations[78]		968	91,103	172,660
Doubly affiliated				*-75,000*
Total Christians[85]		**6,853**	**7,113,752**	**10,129,660**

TransBloc	Pop %	Population	Ann Gr
Evangelicals			
Evangelicals	3.0	318,868	1.1%
Renewalists			
Charismatics	2.8	302,672	1.2%
Pentecostals	2.7	288,994	1.0%

Missionaries from Portugal
P,I,A 94 (74 long-term) in 29 agencies: in Africa 53, South America 25, Europe 12.

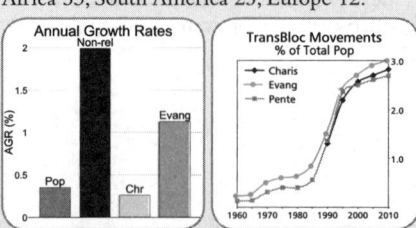

Challenges for Prayer

1 **Religious and political freedoms** gained in 1975 have transformed the nation, but high religious affiliation and freedom does not translate into genuine faith. This is reflected in the challenges of materialism, individualism and increasing substance abuse. The religious freedom gained is taken advantage of by Jehovah's Witnesses, Mormons and New Age philosophies. Pray for the truth about Jesus to be made known by wise Christian leaders of all confessions.

2 **The Roman Catholic Church** is strongly traditional and retains much influence, but it is in need of renewal. The north is more loyal to Catholicism, but in the centre and south, religion is becoming irrelevant to the secularized majority. In some southern areas, less than 3% attend mass, despite efforts of several congregations to reach young people and young families. Pray for the Holy Spirit to work so that many are freed from traditionalism and encounter the Scriptures and the Saviour in a meaningful way.

3 **Evangelical growth remains encouraging** but is also hampered by certain challenges:

a) *Serious divisions.* Many denominations suffered acrimonious splits, especially some Pentecostal denominations. Some recent progress has been made to overcome these; pray for churches to major on the core elements of the faith and extend grace in the minor distinctives.

b) *The need for a united vision.* The Portuguese Evangelical Alliance (EA) continues to grow in impact, a necessary development. Pray for wisdom, vision and courage for its leaders and members, since the EA plays a key role.

c) *The need for passion for the lost.* The Portuguese Church has a unique role to play because of the widespread use of the language. Most churches could easily increase involvement in evangelism and in mission. Some churches and missions are active in sending. A new national sending agency (MEVIC) recently began.

d) *Church planting.* Many more churches are needed. **DAWN**, together with the EA, targets a goal of 4,000 evangelical churches by 2015. Several groups adopted cell-church models but face the difficulty that, for many Portuguese, a physical structure communicates religious legitimacy. Pray for continued church growth, for affordable and appropriate meeting places and for leaders for these future churches.

4 **Many congregations lack full-time workers** with adequate theological depth and spiritual maturity; church growth exacerbates this problem. These institutions are therefore highly strategic: Assemblies of God, Portuguese Bible Institute (**GEM**, **ECM**), Presbyterian, Baptist and Brazilian-founded Bethel Bible Institutes. TEE programmes and *Núcleo*, a widely used Bible correspondence course, are also strategic. Pray that these may contribute to meeting the ministry needs of the churches.

5 **There remain pioneer challenges,** despite recent church growth. Pray for:

a) *The seven northern and northeastern provinces,* which are strongly traditional Catholic; relatively few evangelical churches exist. Brethren, Baptists, **AoG**, **GEM**, **TEAM**, **ECM**, *Missão Antioquia* and several other missions all have church-planting programmes in the area.

b) *The four provinces in the south* that are poorer and much less religious. Attendance at mass is very low, and evangelical churches are few.

c) *The 316 counties,* 44 of which still have no evangelical congregation. This is praiseworthy progress from the 69 in 2000 that lacked a church. The Evangelical Alliance set a target to plant a church in every county by 2015 through its member churches and organizations. Pray for this goal to be met and surpassed.

d) *Madeira Island* (270,000), which has fewer than 20 small evangelical churches, and the Azores (250,000), with a further 26, most being Assemblies of God and Baptist.

e) *Ethnic minorities.* Large numbers of immigrants continue to flow into Portugal. The earlier waves of Portuguese-speaking West Africans and Brazilians are joined by Chinese, Macanese and Eastern Europeans – especially Ukrainians, who now comprise Portugal's second-largest community. Many of these are unevangelized but open to the gospel; pray for the churches (both Portuguese and foreign) to gain a vision to reach them.

6 **Young people** are often spiritually neglected.

a) Drug abuse is a growing problem – over 50% have experimented with drugs. Teen Challenge, Betel-Spain as well as **TEAM** and **ECM** have ministries rehabilitating and discipling addicts.

b) Student work is still in a pioneer stage. GBUP(**IFES**) has a ministry in eight universities and some high schools. **CCCI** (Agape) and Navigators also have ministries on several campuses.

c) SU and **CEF** have ministries among school children.

d) Sports are a useful form of outreach. Agape (Athletes in Action) and **YWAM** (Athletes for Christ) both minister in this way.

7 **Expatriate missions** find Portugal a difficult but promising field. Growth is hard-won but steady; much comes not from ethnic Portuguese but from immigrant groups. Quality workers are still very much needed for evangelism, church planting, Bible training and music. A wide array of expatriate agencies work in Portugal. Brazilians represent a particularly large portion of expatriate missionaries and agencies; pray for them to be sensitive to the unique culture of Portugal.

8 **Christian media ministries:**

a) The Bible Society has a growing national and international ministry in producing and distributing Bibles and Bible portions. In a nominally Christian country, the potential of this ministry is huge.

b) Núcleo has a vital coordinating ministry for the body of Christ in research, publishing, printing tracts and distributing cassettes and films.

c) Ten Christian bookstores, one run by **CLC**.

d) CEDO, a gospel broadsheet ministry of **WEC**, sends out 140,000 copies in Portuguese four times a year to 60 countries around the world.

e) Christian radio is widely used. Local FM and medium-wave stations are used by various denominations and agencies to broadcast 35 hours/week, half of which is in Portuguese. The Evangelical Alliance produces two TV programmes weekly. The Catholics have a TV station.

f) The Internet is an area for evangelistic ministry that needs to be taken up by Christians having the right skills.

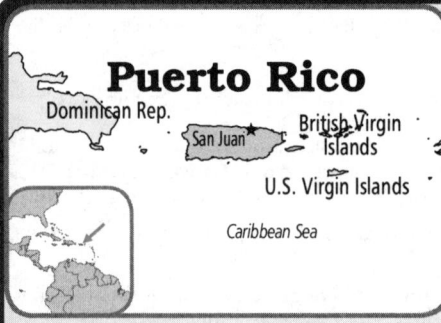

Puerto Rico

Puerto Rico
Commonwealth of Puerto Rico
Caribbean

Geography

Area 9,104 sq km. Greater Antilles, between Dominican Republic and the Virgin Islands.

Population		Ann Gr	Density
2010	3,998,010	0.43%	439/sq km
2020	4,134,563	0.29%	454/sq km
2030	4,195,467	0.09%	461/sq km

Puerto Ricans in the USA now number 3 million.
Capital San Juan. **Other major city** San Juan/Caguas/Guaynabo 2.7 million. Two-thirds of the population live in the metropolitan area. **Urbanites** 97.6%. **Pop under 15 yrs** 20%. **Life expectancy** 78.5 yrs.

Peoples

Latino–American 70.6%. Hispanic Puerto Ricans 70.4%. 98.7% of the population is Latino in orientation, language and culture.
African Caribbean 25.9%. African-Puerto Rican 15.5%; Mixed Puerto Rican 10.3%.
Other 3.5%. US citizen 2.3%.

Literacy 94%. **Official languages** Spanish, English. **All languages** 13. **Indigenous languages** 3. **Languages with Scriptures** 2Bi.

Economy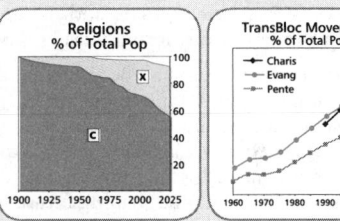

Mountainous and densely populated with few natural resources. A free market economy with manufacturing, trade and tourism the largest sources of income. One of the highest per capita incomes in the Caribbean, but also one of the highest costs of living. Un- or under-employment is a serious issue, the main stimulus to the historic and large-scale emigration. **Public debt** 49.5% of GDP. **Income/person** $21,845 (48% of USA).

Politics

A Spanish colony for 400 years. Related to the USA after the Spanish–American war of 1898. US president is chief of state, but Puerto Rico is administered by an elected governor.

Religion

Religions	Pop %	Population	Ann Gr
Christian	95.28	3,809,304	0.1%
Non-religious	3.82	152,724	13.2%
Ethnoreligionist	0.70	27,986	0.4%
Hindu	0.10	3,998	0.4%
Jewish	0.06	2,399	-2.6%
Muslim	0.03	1,199	0.4%
Buddhist	0.01	400	0.4%

Christians	Denoms	Pop %	Affiliates	Ann Gr
Protestant	44	12.18	487,000	1.1%
Independent	55	12.91	516,000	2.8%
Anglican	1	0.30	12,000	-0.3%
Catholic	1	67.16	2,685,000	-0.8%
Orthodox	3	0.03	1,000	0.5%
Marginal	8	2.76	111,000	-0.1%
Unaffiliated		2.35	94,000	-1.2%
Doubly affiliated		-2.41	-96,000	0.0%

Churches	MegaBloc	Congs	Members	Affiliates
Catholic Church	C	1,230	1,534,286	2,685,000
Other Pentecostal	I	2,484	223,602	360,000
Pentecostal Ch of God	P	592	82,000	123,000
Baptist Convention	P	110	37,500	75,000
Jehovah's Witnesses	M	315	24,100	68,926
Seventh-day Adventist	P	147	17,800	44,500
Defenders of the Faith	I	210	21,200	38,160
Assemblies of God	P	326	22,100	30,000
United Methodist Ch	P	25	10,000	27,000
Ch of God (Cleveland)	P	260	19,500	25,935
Disciples of Christ	P	107	11,700	19,539
Latter-day Saints	M	44	13,636	19,500
Chr & Miss Alliance	P	72	7,700	19,250
Boriquén Presby Synod	P	75	10,100	18,382
Other denominations[69]		1,417	127,647	257,396
Doubly affiliated				-96,352
Total Christians[112]		**7,414**	**2,162,871**	**3,715,236**

TransBloc	Pop %	Population	Ann Gr
Evangelicals			
Evangelicals	25.2	1,007,520	2.2%
Renewalists			
Charismatics	24.7	988,024	2.2%
Pentecostals	16.4	654,575	2.1%

Missionaries from Puerto Rico
P,I,A 176 (116 long-term) in 26 agencies: elsewhere in the Caribbean 47, Europe 34, North America 20, Mexico/Central America 17.

Religions % of Total Pop

TransBloc Movements % of Total Pop

Challenges for Prayer

1 **The issue of Puerto Rico's political identity** divided the nation in the past. Independence, US statehood or the current arrangement of commonwealth are all options, but most people now seem content with the status quo. Many are concerned with the increasing Americanization of government. The biggest problem may be, however, the high levels of corruption that plague local government. Pray for wise governance that works for the best interests of the islands' inhabitants.

2 **Puerto Rico is traditionally Catholic,** but evangelicals have grown steadily from 0.1% in 1900 to 25.2 % in 2010, with some claiming even higher. A strong majority of evangelicals are renewalist in theology. A host of small indigenous groups, mostly neo–Pentecostal and charismatic, accounts for the majority of denominations and churches, and this is where most growth is currently happening. There is also a large charismatic movement in the Catholic Church, which is otherwise in marked decline. Sadly, the churches make little impact on the many social needs of the nation.

3 **Societal problems cry out for Christian involvement.** The incidence of substance abuse, disease, corruption, crime and poverty are some of the highest in the Americas. This being so in a land that is 97% Christian and 25% evangelical is an affront to the gospel. Specific prayer needs are:

a) Poverty. Over 45% of the population live below the poverty line. It is significantly poorer than the poorest US state of Mississippi, and half of the island relies on food aid (in the form of food stamps).

b) Education. Only 11% have a college degree, while 62% fail to complete secondary school – the highest dropout rate in the USA. These low education levels are profoundly linked to unemployment, poverty and crime issues.

c) Home life. An astonishing 61% poverty rate for households headed by females. Given the widespread family breakdown on the island, this accounts for a large portion of the population; many youths grow up deprived of material security as well as a father figure and male role model.

d) Health and substance abuse. Puerto Rico endures some of the highest rates of HIV/AIDS, drug addiction and alcoholism of any US state or territory.

4 **The spiritual ministry of the Church.**

a) Discipleship ministry is much needed. Most of the new and growing Puerto Rican churches and pastors are not connected with international ministries, but are impacted by **COMIBAM** events or training conferences in the USA. However, the fragmented denominational scene gravitates against rapid changes in church life. Pray for effective grassroots movements that will meaningfully transform the lives of ordinary believers.

b) Missions vision is on the rise, but still needs nurture after decades of uninvolvement. Spain is a field of particular interest. Puerto Ricans serve in indigenous movements such as AMIES-**WEC** and international missions such as **YWAM**, **OM** and **WBT**. But most promising is the increasing presence and influence of mission boards in local denominations. Pray for effective training and support of new mission ventures. RECOMI(**COMIBAM**) networks the various agencies and organizations, facilitating their efforts and providing a shared platform for furthering world evangelization.

c) Student ministry is proving both fruitful and vital. ABU(**IFES**) has a growing work on the bigger campuses but is limited by lack of funds and personnel. However, indigenous student movements across almost all campuses (called "confras") are backed by the *Asociación Cristiana Interuniversitaria*. Many of Puerto Rico's current evangelical church leaders were strongly influenced by this movement. Pray for these ministries to reach all remaining campuses and to continue shaping future leaders.

d) Media ministry flourished with the explosion of renewalist churches. There are many Christian media ministries (10 Christian TV channels, many local radio stations, Internet sites and others). These hard-hitting new programmes offer practical and relevant answers to questions of faith and life. One notable ministry is the Bible Correspondence School of the Caribbean, now with 23,000 students in 62 nations.

P

5 **Puerto Ricans number nearly as many in the mainland USA** as in their own land. Urbanization and unemployment in Puerto Rico crowd the cities and fuel emigration but leave rural areas fairly empty. But the traditional stereotype of a US Puerto Rican – that of a ghetto-dweller in New York City – paints an incomplete picture. There are now pockets in Florida, New England, Chicago and elsewhere, and they span the entire economic spectrum. Pray for those ministering to Puerto Ricans living in the USA.

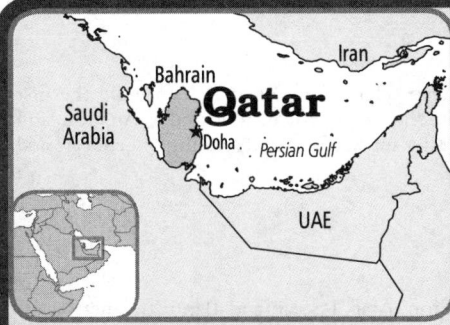

Qatar
State of Qatar
Asia

Geography

Area 11,400 sq km. Arabian peninsular state that is almost entirely desert.

Population		Ann Gr	Density
2010	1,508,322	11.24%	132/sq km
2020	1,740,077	1.32%	153/sq km
2030	1,951,333	1.09%	171/sq km

Capital Doha 457,000. **Urbanites** 95.8%. **Pop under 15 yrs** 16%. **Life expectancy** 75.5 yrs.

Peoples

The expatriate community makes up about 65% of the population and is very difficult to accurately enumerate due to their transient and often undocumented presence. Many Qatari citizens are of foreign extraction.

Arab 58.3%. Qatari 22.1%; other Arab (Palestine, Lebanon, Syria, and others) 36.3%.
South Asian 10.9%. Indian, Pakistani, Sri Lankan. Some sources claim up to 35%.
Persian 16.1%.
Filipino 4.4%.
Bantu 7.7%.
Other 2.6%. Caucasian 2.0%.
Literacy 89%. **Official language** Arabic. **All languages** 6. **Indigenous languages** 3. **Languages with Scriptures** 2Bi.

Economy

Petroleum products are 85% of exports. Qatar has some of the world's largest gas reserves. Oil wealth is used to diversify the economy which continues to grow rapidly. Most Qataris live in great wealth, but Asians constitute an economic lower class.
HDI Rank 33rd/182. **Public debt** 5.1% of GDP. **Income/person** $93,204 (196% of USA).

Politics

Part of the Turkish–Ottoman Empire until 1918. Under British protection until independence in 1971. The current Emir ousted his father in a bloodless coup in 1995. His foreign and domestic policies reflect a remarkably open and progressive attitude.

Religion

The strict Wahhabi form of Sunni Islam is the state religion. Proselytism of Muslims is forbidden, but expatriate Christians are allowed to practice their faith.

Religions	Pop %	Population	Ann Gr
Muslim	88.39	1,333,206	12.0%
Christian	5.91	89,142	2.2%
Hindu	2.70	40,725	13.0%
Buddhist	1.90	28,658	12.5%
Non-religious	0.55	8,296	12.5%
Other	0.35	5,279	8.3%
Baha'i	0.20	3,017	11.2%

Christians Denoms		Pop %	Affiliates	Ann Gr
Protestant	20	0.79	12,000	2.7%
Independent	5	0.21	3,000	5.1%
Anglican	1	0.53	8,000	2.7%
Catholic	3	3.98	60,000	1.8%
Orthodox	3	0.23	4,000	1.8%
Marginal	5	0.17	2,000	4.6%

Churches	MegaBloc	Congs	Members	Affiliates
Catholic Church	C	1	33,333	60,000
Anglican Church	A	3	2,000	8,000
Pentecostal groups	P	0	3,500	7,000
All Orthodox	O	7	2,096	3,500
All Independent chs	I	7	2,000	3,200
Other Protestant	P	40	1,600	3,200
Marginal groups	M	4	1,562	2,500
Other denominations[4]		29	884	1,730
Total Christians[37]		**91**	**46,975**	**89,130**

TransBloc	Pop %	Population	Ann Gr
Evangelicals			
Evangelicals	1.0	14,552	3.3%
Renewalists			
Charismatics	1.0	15,128	4.1%
Pentecostals	0.5	7,000	3.1%

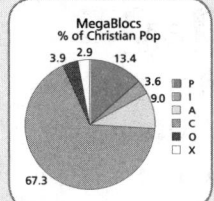

MegaBlocs % of Christian Pop
3.9 2.9 13.4 / 3.6 / 9.0 / 67.3
P I A C O X

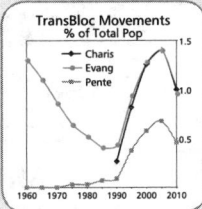

TransBloc Movements % of Total Pop
- Charis
- Evang
- Pente
1960 1970 1980 1990 2000 2010

Answer to Prayer

1 **Qatar's Christian communities** have been offered land on which to build the first churches in Qatar since Islam's arrival. A Catholic facility will be followed by Anglican and Protestant buildings. Pray that this will enable greater unity, effective discipling of believers and sensitive sharing of faith.

Challenges for Prayer

1 **Qatari believers number but a few.** From Arab, Persian and Bantu (former slaves) extraction, Qataris are almost without exception Muslim. Pray that a Qatari church would be birthed and that Qataris at home and abroad would hear about Jesus.

2 **Expatriates are drawn from many nations** by the high earnings in Qatar, but Christians are limited by strict anti-proselytism laws. Pray for the employment opportunities (from manual labour up to executive positions) to be filled by Christians who would be an intentional Kingdom presence in Qatar.

3 **Christians' ability to meet together** is limited by government policy and by the high cost and difficulty of renting facilities capable of hosting larger groups. There are not yet opportunities for the large Asian fellowships and those congregations committed to outreach and evangelism to have their own places of worship.

4 **Christian impact on society.** Pray that the many groups of believers among Filipinos, Westerners, Lebanese, Indians, Pakistanis and others may bear fruitful witness to their own communities. Pray also that there might be opportunities to share with non-Christians of all people groups in the country.

5 **Media ministry.** No anti-proselytism laws can prevent the airwaves and Internet from influencing Qatar. Pray that gospel radio (FEBA, IBRA and others), TV (Al Hayat, **SAT-7** and others) and Christian websites might penetrate the homes and hearts of those living in Qatar. The programmes of Father Zakaria make a great impact in Qatar and throughout the Arab world. Many Arabic language sites, chat rooms and programmes seem to have a powerful effect.

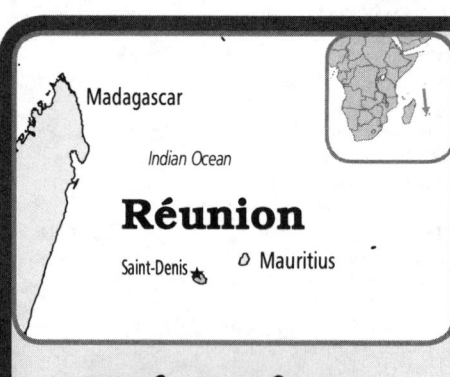

Réunion

Department of Réunion

Africa

Geography

Area 2,512 sq km. Rugged, mountainous volcanic Indian Ocean island 700 km east of

Madagascar. The largest of the Mascarene Islands, which include Mauritius.

Population		Ann Gr	Density
2010	837,094	1.32%	333/sq km
2020	931,473	1.00%	371/sq km
2030	1,009,297	0.74%	402/sq km

Capital Saint-Denis 143,000. **Urbanites** 94.0%. **Pop under 15 yrs** 26%. **Life expectancy** 76.2 yrs.

Peoples ♂♀♂

Réunion's population is very mixed; these numbers indicate more of a heritage than distinct ethnicities.

African Creole 50%. Afro-Malagasy or Cafres, often descended from slaves.

South Asian 24%. Tamil, Gujarati, Urdu, Panjabi.

White Creole 13%. Descended from the first European settlers.

European 6%. French and Réunionese; also military personnel.

Chinese 3.5%. Cantonese, Hakka, Mandarin.

African 3.5%. Recent immigration from Comoros, Mayotte, Madagascar.

Literacy 88.9%. **Official language** French. **Common language** French Creole, spoken by

over 85%, which is replacing minority languages.
All languages 9. **Indigenous languages** 3.
Languages with Scripture 2Bi.

Economy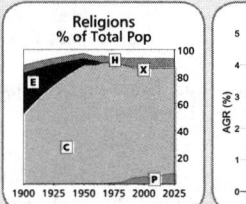

Economy based on agriculture and tourism. Sugar, rum, vanilla, pineapple and light industry provide some export earnings. Heavily dependent upon French/EU subsidies and aid as well as income from the military bases. High rates of unemployment and emigration.
Income/person $8,880 (13.7% of USA).

Politics

Uninhabited until French settlement in 1642. Overseas department of France since 1946. The level of dependency on France means there is little incentive to seek greater autonomy. Protests in 2009 against the high cost of living and a politico-economic system that allegedly perpetuates poverty and dependence and favours the wealthy.

Religion

Catholicism is culturally dominant. French legislation allows for religious freedom and both discourages dangerous sectarian groups and causes complications for smaller denominations.

Religions	Pop %	Population	Ann Gr
Christian	86.96	727,373	1.3%
Hindu	6.42	53,700	1.0%
Muslim	4.05	33,876	1.7%
Non-religious	2.49	20,827	0.3%
Baha'i	0.08	669	1.3%

Christians Denoms		Pop %	Affiliates	Ann Gr
Protestant	10	5.97	50,000	4.0%
Independent	4	0.10	1,000	3.7%
Catholic	1	80.10	670,000	1.1%
Marginal	2	0.79	7,000	2.1%

Churches	MegaBloc	Congs	Members	Affiliates
Catholic Church	C	80	374,302	670,000
Assemblies of God	P	44	25,000	42,500
Jehovah's Witnesses	M	32	2,920	5,840
Seventh-day Adventist	P	17	1,420	3,220
Evangelical Church	P	10	600	1,020
Reformed Church	P	3	625	1,010
Other denominations[11]		42	2,364	3,823
Total Christians[17]		**228**	**407,231**	**727,413**

TransBloc	Pop %	Population	Ann Gr
Evangelicals			
Evangelicals	5.9	49,112	4.1%
Renewalists			
Charismatics	7.7	64,412	3.4%
Pentecostals	5.2	43,380	4.5%

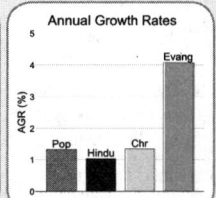

Answers to Prayer

1 **Praise God for dramatic growth** since 1966, when the French Assemblies of God (locally called *Mission Salut et Guérison*) arrived and then after 1970, when AEF/**SIM** missionaries began work here. Many churches have helped people to be freed from occult bondage. The March for Jesus previously and now **MANI** have contributed to a greater networking of Reformed, charismatic and evangelical congregations. Pray for growth in grace, numbers and spiritual understanding in these young and enthusiastic churches.

R

Challenges for Prayer

1 **The dark legacy of slavery,** abolished in 1848, still overshadows the present. The Creole population are descendants of those slaves. Poverty (over half the population), unemployment (25-33%), alcoholism, dysfunctional families and high illegitimacy marginalize this large underclass. A deep work of healing and laying to rest the legacy of the past is far from complete. Pray for the entire population to come to terms with the past, possible only through faith in Christ.

2 **Although Catholicism is the professed religion** of 80% of the population, many Catholics are either very nominal, highly syncretized or both. The Malabar religion – a synthesis of Hinduism and African witchcraft – is practiced by many. Religious beliefs have mixed and blended as much as the Creole people have, such that "Creole Christianity" incorporates Catholicism, other religions, superstitions and the occult. Yet in the Catholic Church there is a vigorous charismatic element and an evangelically oriented house church movement. Pray for those who call themselves Christian but do not know the delivering power of Christ in their lives.

3 **Mature leadership** for the young, growing churches is a priority. Most leadership training is informal or must be pursued outside the territory. As with the territory's economic dependence on France, the churches are often dependent on outside help. Pray for recent moves toward developing the local church leadership as well as establishing both spiritual and financial autonomy.

4 **Young people** need prayer:

a) Christians in the churches. Pray that they have high standards of holy living and that spiritual leaders for the future might be raised up.

b) The disadvantaged. The gap is widening between the disadvantaged and the sophisticated, educated youth (also clearly along racial lines), hence the protests/riots in 2009. There are many challenges to reaching them effectively.

c) YWAM has a good ministry in motivating youth for evangelism and missions. **CEF** has a significant ministry to children through camps and Good News Clubs.

5 **Christian media.** Pray for impact through:

a) Christian literature and Bible distribution. There is only one Christian bookstore, which is in the south of the island (the capital is in the north). Nevertheless, much literature has been distributed around the island.

b) Radio. Private radio stations are run by the Catholics, SdA and **AoG**. There is an encouraging response to FEBA's daily broadcasts in French from Seychelles.

c) Media. The JESUS film has been shown around the island several times. **GRN** audio resources are available in eight languages. Online material in Creole is very limited, although French and Tamil have many Christian resources for the few who have regular online access.

Population		Ann Gr	Density
2010	21,190,154	-0.41%	89/sq km
2020	20,379,656	-0.40%	86/sq km
2030	19,488,596	-0.48%	82/sq km

Capital Bucharest 1,934,433. **Urbanites** 54.6%. **Pop under 15 yrs** 15%. **Life expectancy** 72.5 yrs.

Peoples 👤👤👤

Romanian 86.5%. A Latin people descended from Romans settled in Dacia.
Hungarian 6.6%. Primarily found in Transylvania.
Romani (Gypsy) 3.8%. This percent reflects a population of 800,000; actual numbers could be over 2 million.
Slav 1.4%. 9 peoples.
Turkic 0.8%. Rumelian Turks 0.7%.
Other 0.9%.
Literacy 97.3%. **Official language** Romanian. **All languages** 23. **Indigenous languages** 15. **Languages with Scriptures** 8Bi 4NT 5por 2w.i.p.

Romania

Europe

Geography 🌍

Area 238,391 sq km. Balkan state on the lower Danube River, a mix of mountains, hills and plains.

R

Economy

A land rich in agriculture, minerals and oil, but became more industrialized during Communism. Foreign investment is increasing as economic restructuring accelerates; Romania hopes to adopt the Euro by 2014. Romania now struggles with employment issues, especially in the service sector, since many people of working age emigrate to work elsewhere in Europe and increasing numbers of rural people abandon their farms.

HDI Rank 63rd/182. **Public debt** 14.7% of GDP. **Income/person** $9,310 (20% of USA).

Politics

An independent country from 1859, followed by a Communist coup in 1947 with Russian support. Suffered under one of the Communist bloc's most oppressive and cruel regimes. The Revolution of 1989-90 overthrew that regime and introduced a parliamentary government. Economic and political gradualism characterized the 1990s, but the 21st Century sees positive progress with 2007 entry into the EU. A high-profile, anti-corruption campaign smoothed Romania's EU acceptance, but corruption and political power struggles continue to impede progress. Anti-minority nationalism persists against Hungarians and Gypsies.

Religion

Oppressive persecution was commonplace under Communism. Now, Romania is officially a secular state, but is dominated by the Orthodox Church, which replaced the government as the primary vehicle of religious discrimination. A 2006 law made it much more difficult to register denominations or charities and could be used to limit proselytism.

Religion	Pop %	Population	Ann Gr
Christian	96.96	20,545,973	-0.2%
Non-religious	2.39	506,445	-8.7%
Muslim	0.58	122,903	-1.1%
Other	0.04	8,476	5.5%
Jewish	0.03	6,357	-0.4%

Christians	Denoms	Pop %	Affiliates	Ann Gr
Protestant	24	6.64	1,406,000	0.3%
Independent	21	0.82	173,000	2.0%
Anglican	1	<0.01	<1,000	1.3%
Catholic	2	5.28	1,118,000	-0.9%
Orthodox	9	87.14	18,464,000	-0.4%
Marginal	3	0.80	169,000	0.8%
Doubly affiliated		-3.72	-789,000	0.0%

Churches	MegaBloc	Congs	Members	Affiliates
Romanian Orthodox	O	12,400	12,629,371	18,060,000
Roman Catholic	C	1,080	676,619	940,500
Reformed Ch of Rom	P	890	451,299	695,000
Pente Apos Ch of God	P	2,700	210,180	351,000
The Lord's Army	O	300	150,000	300,000
Greek Catholic	C	60	106,587	178,000
Romanian Bapt Union	P	1,770	67,714	118,500
Seventh-day Adventist	P	582	72,143	101,000
Jehovah's Witnesses	M	550	41,905	88,000
Unitarian Chs in Rom	M	172	15,600	78,000
Gypsy Evang Movement	I	483	29,000	58,000
Christian Brethren	P	870	22,550	45,100
Ukrainian Orthodox	O	23	30,075	40,000
Other denominations[41]		1,750	172,516	278,877
Doubly affiliated				-789,000
Total Christians[60]		**23,630**	**14,675,559**	**20,542,977**

The Romanian government officially recognizes 19 denominations; many more groups function as associations, a recognized but lesser status.

TransBloc	Pop %	Population	Ann Gr
Evangelicals			
Evangelicals	5.4	1,149,647	2.3%
Renewalists			
Charismatics	2.9	620,168	2.7%
Pentecostals	2.1	438,527	2.9%

Missionaries from Romania

P,I,A 230 international (130 long-term) in more than 12 agencies, to about 50 countries: many in India, China, Turkey, Peru, Romania, Moldova, Albania and Mozambique.

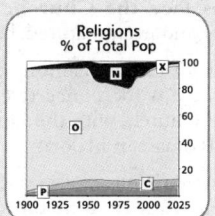

Religions % of Total Pop

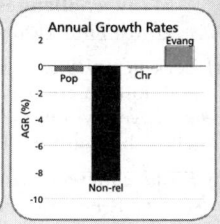

Annual Growth Rates

Answers to Prayer

1 **Romania has a large and growing evangelical population,** Europe's fourth largest. This is despite an overall decline in population. In fact, evangelicals are the only growing major religious group. Romania is considered one of the more spiritually receptive European nations.

2 **A sustained church planting movement** has existed since the fall of Communism. There are nearly 6,000 evangelical congregations in Romania, a number that is steadily increasing. There is also a long-term strategy to see churches planted in every remaining unreached town and village.

Challenges for Prayer

1 **A legacy of brokenness endures** from the days of Ceausescu's regime, a moral vacuum being filled with every kind of social evil. Substance abuse, prostitution, pornography, human trafficking and challenges to child welfare are widespread. Romania has one of the highest abortion rates in the world, with three or more abortions for every child born. Poverty is still common, with widespread unemployment and economic instability, caused to a large degree by rampant and entrenched corruption. Divisions in government reduce its effectiveness; major strides forward are needed in its legal, education and health care systems as well as police and local administrations. Pray for leadership that has the wisdom to chart the right path and the integrity to implement the right policies.

2 **Romania is one of the world's most Christian nations by percentage,** yet this is hard to perceive in society. A worldview shaped by atheistic Communism persists. Nominalism, legalism, hypocrisy and slander of other denominations are problems in all confessions, and such antagonism does not glorify Christ nor edify the Church. Folk religious practices and the occult permeate beyond rural superstitions even into the practice of some clergy. Very little practical ministry is being done to address community needs; the Church neglects many poor people. Pray for a breakthrough of love, holiness, discipleship and prayer in all denominations.

3 **The Orthodox Church dominates** society with 87% of the population affiliated. Cultural pressure to remain Orthodox, however nominal, persists. For many, this affiliation is inherited rather than reflective of a deeply held personal faith. Some Orthodox priests frequently oppose, sometimes violently, evangelical outreach. Yet within this ancient confession there is life and potential for great good. Pray for renewal from within and for the Holy Spirit to awaken those whose faith lies dead or dormant.

4 **The Lord's Army is a remarkable renewal movement** within the Orthodox Church with about 300,000 converted affiliates and many more sympathizers. Severely persecuted in the past, it is more accepted today. There are two expressions of one movement – one a branch of Orthodoxy, and the other a more independent movement linked to the Evangelical Alliance. Pray that these believers may act as leaven in the wider Orthodox Church with its large nominal membership. Pray also that the Lord's Army might inspire and foster similar movements in other Orthodox nations.

5 **Many challenges face the Church.** Since the fall of Communism, the Church has grown numerically and even matured, but there remains a long way to go.

a) *Lack of unity* is a major problem among denominations and within congregations. There is almost no cooperative work, concerted prayer or unified public voice. Ethnic divisions exist even within the Church, with the Hungarian and Romani minorities rarely enjoying fellowship with the Romanian majority.

b) *Blind adherence to tradition* creates a Christian ghetto out of touch with the wider society. It becomes increasingly difficult to connect to non-Christians and young people in particular. Pray that churches find a balance between genuine holiness and cultural relevance.

c) *Materialism imported from the West* has a toxic effect on spirituality.

  i *The deep spirituality of long-suffering churches is damaged.* Materialism is now a prevalent attitude, especially among the younger generation who aspire to a Western lifestyle at the cost of spiritual vitality.

  ii *An unhealthy dependence on outside money* was created as a result of generous but ill-advised material assistance. This stunts the local church in many ways, it introduces potential divisions locally and it introduces difficulty in ministry partnerships as well as dangers of manipulation and questionable motives.

6 **Leadership development** in churches is a great need. The average pastor supervises multiple churches. Most new churches lack a pastor, and many pastors lack training. Active congregations with effective programmes will emerge from well-trained leaders.

a) *Bible schools and seminaries* have been launched by many denominations, many focused on pastoral training and leadership development. Yet these places of learning are not enough to fill the needs of the churches. Pray that the schools might be able to train increasing numbers of students who are biblically astute, spiritually on fire and ready to lead.

b) *Entrust* (formerly BEE - Bible Education by Extension) was pioneered in Romania and spread to many Communist Bloc countries. Pray for the hundreds of evangelical leaders studying part-time in BEE and other TEE courses. Now, an advanced course is also part of the programme.

7 **Church planting** is still a vital ministry. Over 100 new churches are planted each year, but many more are needed. A consortium of mission agencies works across evangelical denominational boundaries to facilitate reaching the 19 cities and 9,500 villages (43% of all villages) without a single evangelical church. Many more congregations are still needed in the cities. There is notable resistance to non-Orthodox expressions of Christianity in most villages, and rising costs and rapid cultural change make for urban challenges. Pray for this vision to become a widespread movement, owned by the national church and effective at planting churches in every city, town and village.

8 **Foreign missionary deployment** was rapid and profuse in the immediate post-Communist years. Amid much that was good and worthwhile, some workers went in with little tact and less wisdom, causing almost as much harm as help. There is still a great need for expatriate missions in training, church planting and meeting the many social needs. Pray that expatriate Christians called to serve may show sensitivity, humility, true partnership and an ability to learn from, and work alongside, Romanian Christians. Many Western (and Korean, African and Latin American) groups now work in partnership with Romanian agencies and churches. Among the largest sending agencies are ReachGlobal(**RG**), **IMB**, **GEM**, **ABWE**, OCI, AoG. Increasingly, ministries started by expats are being handed over to national direction and leadership.

9 **The younger generation** is a poignant image of the brokenness of Romania. Yet young people, especially in urban areas, are the segment of the population most responsive to the gospel. There are several significant prayer needs:

a) *Stories of the hundreds of thousands of orphans* and abandoned children in the 1990s broke the hearts of many. While this is still a great need, churches and missions do an increasingly good job caring for these young people. Working among them are the Baptists, Samaritans Purse, SGA, WVI and many other expatriate and national agencies. EU policies helped limit the unscrupulous use of adoption as a means of profit for some, but these actions also make it difficult for those doing effective ministry with orphaned and at-risk children.

b) *The relevance of Christianity to youth* is a challenge – this is more an issue of church culture and tradition than openness. Churched youth are often dedicated and effective in ministry. Unfortunately, most church programmes are not attractive to unbelieving young people. Pray for effective programmes and pastors who are willing and able to mobilize the youth into ministry, an area of ministry surprisingly lacking until now.

c) *Students and their discipleship.* CCCI, OSCER/**IFES**, Romanian Missionary Society (RMS), **YFC**, **CEF**, and the SdA all actively work with children and young people. Christian camps (RMS, Life 2 Romania) are a very fruitful ministry.

R

10 **Romanians as a mission force** are a new and quickly expanding dynamic. At least ten indigenous sending agencies have emerged since 2000, and training programmes are multiplying. Members of Partners in Mission, most notably **OC**, were instrumental in shaping these changes. Romanians can easily access fields that Westerners cannot, and agencies are interested in Romanians serving with them. Limiting factors are the lack of financial support/sponsorship and the lagging missions vision in many churches. Pray for the removal of every barrier to the full flowering of an indigenous missions movement.

11 **The Romanian diaspora in Europe** can be regarded as both crisis and opportunity. Looking for a better life, between 10 and 20% of Romanians have left the country since 1990, a trend accelerated by EU entry in 2007. Combined with urbanization, this damages social structures and many families and churches. The exodus of the younger generation and the brain-drain of intellectuals and professionals will have a serious effect on the nation as will the trend of parents leaving their children with grandparents while they move abroad. But, on the positive side, many dynamic evangelical churches have been planted throughout Western Europe as a result. Pray that these churches might reach out beyond Romanians to the spiritually needy nations that host them. Pray also for more Romanian Christians to stay or to return in order to build up and transform their own nation.

12 **Evangelical churches are not evenly spread** throughout the nation. Pray for the following:

a) The southeast regions. On average, the 15 counties in the northwest have many times more evangelicals than the 27 counties in the southeast. There are 7,000 villages in the southeast without an evangelical church. Pray that believers might be burdened for these less-reached areas and bring the light of the gospel to them.

b) Ethnic groups that are less evangelical include Hungarians, Russians/Lipovens and Serbs – all a significantly lower proportion than ethnic Romanians.

c) The Muslim community is not large, but it is in need of Christian witness. Most are Turks, Tatar or immigrants. Very little is done to reach them, although there have been some commendable initiatives in recent years.

d) The Romani (Gypsy) community, notoriously difficult to count, but numbering between 500,000 and 2.5 million. Although they are proportionately more evangelical than majority Romanians, they remain a needy people. They suffer discrimination and isolation, with much lower standards of living, education, health care and employment. Government programmes raise these standards and integrate them into society, but deep-seated prejudice must be overcome. Hundreds of thousands flee Romania only to meet harsh treatment in other European countries. But they are also the most spiritually responsive ethnicity to the gospel. Increasingly, Christian Romani now have bold vision to reach their own people.

13 **Christian media ministries.**

a) Literature. Pray for the Christian publishing houses and for the distribution networks to establish a viable, indigenously funded literature ministry. Pray that more locally written material might become available. Few pastors have a theological library. Pray that the recent inter-confessional NT will be a blessing and a useful tool for all Bible-minded Christians.

b) Broadcasting. Radio ministry continues to develop despite difficulties with permission and licences. It is a powerful tool in Romania. RMS and **HCJB** collaborate with the EA on the Voice of the Gospel radio network, which includes eight FM stations, all uplinked to satellite. Pray for both local commercial Christian stations and transmissions from abroad. Alfa Omega TV and Credo are interdenominational stations available on cable, satellite and the Internet with immense potential impact in evangelism, discipleship and promoting Christian values.

Ural-Siberian 6.8%. 37 peoples. Tatar(5) 3.9%; Bashkort 1.2%; Chuvash 1.1%; Yakut 0.3%; Tuva(3) 0.2%.
Kazakh 0.5%. 3 peoples.
Other 0.7%. 9 peoples. Azerbaijani 0.4%.
Other 1.4%. 29 peoples. Ossetian 0.4%; Buryat 0.3%; Jews(4) 0.2%. East Asians, Southeast Asians, Iranian-Medians, others.
Literacy 99.4%. **Official language** Russian; local languages in autonomous republics. **All languages** 135. **Indigenous languages** 100. **Languages with Scriptures** 6Bi 19NT 47por 21w.i.p.

Russia
Russian Federation
Europe

Geography

Area 17,075,400 sq km. The world's largest country, extending across 9 time zones between the Baltic and the Pacific. The Russian Federation is composed of 83 administrative districts, including 46 oblasts (provinces), 21 republics, 9 territories, 4 autonomous okrugs, 1 autonomous oblast and 2 federal cities.

Population		Ann Gr	Density
2010	140,366,561	-0.39%	8/sq km
2020	135,405,523	-0.38%	8/sq km
2030	128,864,354	-0.53%	7.5/sq km

Massive decline – an estimated loss of 30 million between 2000 and 2050 is likely. A further 25 million Russians live in 15 other fSU states. Siberia has one of the lowest population densities in the world.

Capital Moscow 10,549,892. **Other major cities** St. Petersburg 4.6 million; Novosibirsk 1.4mill; Ekaterinburg 1.3m; Nizhny Novgorod 1.3m; Samara 1.1m; Omsk 1.1m; Kazan 1.1m; Chelyabinsk 1.1m; Ufa 1.0m; Rostov-na-Donu 1.0m; Volgograd 977,000. **Urbanites** 72.8%. **Pop under 15 yrs** 15%. **Life expectancy** 66.2 yrs.

Peoples 🏃🏃🏃

Great diversity made more complex by migrations, intense efforts to Russify minorities and continued large-scale immigration of fSU peoples into the present Russian Federation.
Eurasian peoples 90.6%. 82 peoples.
Slavic(9) 83.2%. Russian 80.5%; Ukrainian 2.1%; Belarusian 0.6%.
Caucasus 3.8%. 34 peoples. Chechen 1.0%; Avar 0.5%; Cherkess (Kabardian, Adyghe, Cherkess) 0.5%; Dargwa 0.4%; Kumyk 0.3%; Ingush 0.3%; Lezghi 0.3%.
Finno-Ugric 2.0%. 24 peoples. Udmurt 0.4%; Mari 0.4%; Mordvin(2) 0.5%; Komi(3) 0.3%.
Other 1.5%. 15 peoples. Armenian 0.8%; German 0.4%.
Turkic–Altaic 8.0%. 49 peoples.

Economy

Vast natural resources including gas, oil, timber and minerals as well as huge amounts of arable land offer great economic power and potential. Sheer size, geographic isolation and few decent seaports have historically limited advancement. Marxist centralized politics and infrastructure prevented efficient exploitation of these resources for the people's benefit, but did allow for large-scale plundering. Oligarchs, Russia's homemade billionaires, at an opportune moment seized control of what had been state industries, thus concentrating most of the economy in the hands of a few men. Centralized forces under a strong president, a revamped manufacturing sector and high oil prices turned around the economic disaster of the 1990s to a stronger performing decade from 2000 to 2010, but government rhetoric makes it difficult to obtain accurate figures. What is undeniable is that Russia's poor and unemployed number in the millions, and the economy remains very dependent on oil and gas exports. A huge budget deficit, endemic corruption and bribery, a crumbling and aged infrastructure, limited foreign investment, low productivity (both industrially and agriculturally) and, most alarmingly, rapid demographic decline – all present a challenging future for Russia.
HDI Rank 71st/182. **Public debt** 6.5% of GDP. **Income/person** $11,807 (25% of USA).

Politics 🗡

Russia has known little but autocracy or tyranny since it became a country in the 8th Century. Imperialist Russia collapsed in 1917, shortly before the Bolshevik Communist revolution. Russia dominated the USSR from its founding in 1922, and the Communist leadership exploited ordinary Russian people as well as the many ethnic groups and satellite states it seized or controlled. A multiparty federal democracy was instituted in 1990. The subsequent decade was a tense tug of war between various forces in Moscow as well as the restive republics and regions. Putin's appointment in 1999 (and election in 2000) restored strong central authority, which in many ways echoed the Soviet era of state control.

R

In 2008, Putin "stepped down" to become prime minister as his protégé (many would say puppet), Medvedev, became president. Xenophobic nationalism and erosion of basic freedoms remain very real threats. Freedom of the press and media is limited; all television stations are government controlled or strongly self-censored. Relationships with the West, Ukraine, Belarus and emerging Asian superpowers are crucial but are often characterized by belligerence. Upheaval in Dagestan and Ingushetia point toward a possible full civil war – on the scale of Chechnya – in the not too distant future.

Religion

The Church in Russia has suffered some of the most severe and sustained persecution of any nation in recent history. Deaths in the Gulag (prison camps) between 1920 and 1990 are reckoned at 20 million; many prisoners were Christian. Up to 200,000 Christian leaders were martyred. Of the 100,000 church-owned buildings in 1920 (mainly Orthodox), almost none, by 1940, were in use by Christians; they had been seized or destroyed. Structures and ministries were emasculated or manipulated, leadership was cowed into compliance and compromise, Christians and their children were discriminated against and millions were consigned to years of imprisonment, exile or psychiatric "treatment". Today, freedom of religion is written into the constitution, as is the equality of all religions before the law and the separation of church and state. In reality, this is not the case. Orthodoxy's 1,000-year history as part of the culture of Russia gives the Church enormous political influence. The 1997 federal religion law – focused on issues of registration and operation of religious congregations – can override local laws, impose restrictions on and discriminate against minority religions. The legislation's complexity and ambiguity makes the religion law a tool for arbitrary application against newer religious groups and especially foreign-based ones.

Religions	Pop %	Population	Ann Gr
Christian	66.90	93,905,229	0.0%
Non-religious	19.15	26,880,196	-2.4%
Muslim	12.50	17,545,820	0.9%
Buddhist	0.71	996,603	-0.1%
Ethnoreligionist	0.40	561,466	-0.4%
Jewish	0.20	280,733	-4.7%
Other	0.10	140,367	-5.5%
Hindu	0.03	42,110	-0.4%
Baha'i	0.01	14,037	-0.4%

Christians	Denoms	Pop %	Affiliates	Ann Gr
Protestant	74	1.24	1,747,000	1.9%
Independent	13	0.80	1,129,000	-1.5%
Anglican	1	<0.01	4,000	1.2%
Catholic	1	0.56	783,000	-0.2%
Orthodox	22	64.02	89,860,000	0.0%
Marginal	12	0.28	395,000	0.6%

Churches	MegaBloc	Congs	Members	Affiliates
Russian Orthodox	O	12,300	56,493,506	87,000,000
Ukrainian Orthodox	O	222	886,667	1,330,000
Old Believers	I	260	668,085	942,000
Armenian Apos Ch	O	63	544,910	910,000
Catholic Church	C	51	508,442	783,000
R United Un of Pente	P	2,400	396,000	594,000
True Orthodox Chs	O	4,901	264,667	397,000
Un of Pente Chr	P	1,600	207,647	353,000
Jehovah's Witnesses	M	1,047	157,000	290,000
Lutheran Church	P	141	143,713	240,000
Un of Chrs of Ev Faith	P	400	60,000	180,000
Un of Ev Chr Baptists	P	1,750	80,000	110,400
Assoc Chr Chs (ACCR)	I	490	58,800	105,840
Other denominations[85]		3,395	432,944	682,073
Total Christians[123]		**29,020**	**60,902,381**	**93,917,313**

TransBloc	Pop %	Population	Ann Gr
Evangelicals			
Evangelicals	1.2	1,636,627	2.3%
Renewalists			
Charismatics	1.0	1,416,220	2.7%
Pentecostals	0.9	1,211,027	2.9%

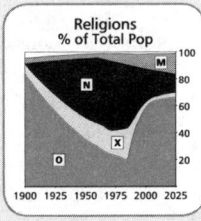

Religions
% of Total Pop

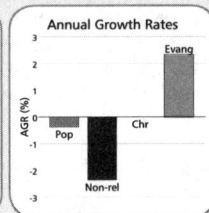

Annual Growth Rates

Answers to Prayer

1 **The fall of the Iron Curtain** opened Eastern Europe and Central Asia to unprecedented access to the good news – opportunities for evangelism, church planting, re-establishing a Christian infrastructure, many partnering networks, theological education and Bible translation and distribution. Churches more than doubled in number and in size, and those identifying themselves as non-religious or atheist dropped by more than half from pre-1991.

R

2 **Evangelicals are moving forward,** from being a hunted minority to a recognized part of the religious landscape of Russia. Many of the larger denominations and networks now number in the hundreds of thousands of affiliates. Their experience and maturity allow them to weather both foreign Western and domestic government agendas and have even placed evangelicals in councils in the Kremlin.

3 **Ambitious and faith-filled church planting vision** in many current evangelical networks is a far cry from the insular survival mode of Communist-era Christianity.

4 **Many hitherto totally unreached peoples** – Muslim, superficially Orthodox, pagan and Buddhist – have the opportunity to hear the gospel for the first time, and many churches are being planted.

Challenges for Prayer

1 **Russia is a proud nation with a great legacy,** but it remains a mystery and a contradiction. Some see a bleak future, others a resurgent Russia. Some regard the last decade or two as an economic disaster; others see growth and strength. For centuries, it was systematically plundered by those who held sway, from the Tsars to the Communists to the oligarchs. Most Russians still see a grim outlook. For the nostalgic older generation, the stability of life under the Communists is preferred; for the younger generation, modern life offers little real hope. Pray especially for the following long-term cultural issues:

a) Demographics reveal a civilization caught in a deadly decline. Russia's population drops by over 500,000 each year. Such a rapid numerical decline spells certain doom for populations unable to reverse the trend. Russia's birthrate is among the lowest in the world; even generous incentives to produce children are not effective. Conversely, Russia's abortion rate remains one of the world's highest. Figures indicate more abortions than live births, with an alarmingly high number also resulting in the mother's death.

b) Health issues are spiralling to crisis level. Health care is inefficient, underfunded and costly, making it inaccessible to many – just when it is most urgently needed:

   i *The alcoholism rate in Russia is one of the world's highest.* Increased incidences of disease, homicide and suicide can in large part be attributed to the low prices and wide availability of cheap, illegal and often poisonous vodka; Russia sells over 2 billion litres each year.

   ii *Drug addiction controls the lives of as many as 2.5 million people.* The government claimed at one point that 8% of teens used drugs daily. The increased prevalence of hard drugs has led to mafia involvement and control. Ministry to drug addicts is a fruitful area for Christians – and a necessary one.

   iii *Russia has Europe's highest and fastest-rising rate of HIV/AIDS.* This, combined with tuberculosis, raises mortality rates and drastically reduces life expectancy. HIV claims mostly young people, further robbing Russia of its future.

c) Russian nationalism and its outworkings. Strong nationalistic sentiment has existed for centuries, from religious Orthodox Russia to the Soviet era to the modern day. But complex 21st Century trends seem to be leading to irrevocable troubles.

   i *Racist nationalism is increasing.* Nazi-style expressions are growing more popular among Russian Slavs as an expression of identity and "patriotism". This has led to more powerful, far-right political groups, but also to thuggery against visible minorities and immigrants. Such racist attacks increased by 30% in 2008 alone, forcing the president to take measures to address this issue.

   ii *Nationalism in foreign policy* and Russification internally, reasserted under Putin's leadership, often led to belligerence, particularly in Chechnya and other Caucasus regions. Pray for good relations with foreign powers and with minority republics within the Russian Federations.

d) Minority groups from within the former Soviet Union face exploitation and rejection by the very ones who colonized them through Russian imperialism and then Communism. Millions of Central Asian immigrants work in Russian cities, most of them undocumented and uncounted in census figures. The great irony is that without these workers, the Russian

R

economy would violently contract; and without massive-scale immigration in the future, Russia may become a pale shadow of its former self.

2 **The government faces many daunting tasks,** present and future. Lift up to the Lord the many threats facing Russia.

a) ***Pray for political wisdom.*** Russia is prone to authoritarian rule and admits that in the current climate good governance is more important than democracy and personal freedoms. Current and forecasted troubles would further erode freedoms and entrench a centralized power. Pray for the balancing of strong government with democratic accountability and respect of basic freedoms.

b) ***Economic stability is threatened*** by hopelessly inadequate infrastructures – both physical and legal/financial – including disappearing investment, a huge budget deficit and dwindling cash reserves. The struggles of millions with poverty and general hopelessness raises to alarming heights crime, drug abuse, alcoholism, family breakdown and suicide. Yet, vast natural resources and potential for greater output hold much promise. Pray for wise fiscal policies and for the long-term vision and strength to follow through on them.

c) ***Corruption must be rooted out.*** The power of oligarchs is being reined in, but criminal networks remain highly influential at home and abroad. They cripple honest business initiative and subvert the bureaucracy. There is no chance of change for the better without confronting these dark forces, a war that will require immense resolve and courage.

3 **The current religious climate of Russia is mixed,** both spiritually open and closed at the same time. Orthodoxy is culturally strong yet spiritually weak in the lives of most of its followers. Millions call themselves Russian Orthodox without actually believing in God. Current gloom has not led to high degrees of spirituality, and the surge of religious activity in the 1990s has all but stalled. Cults and sects, both Eastern and Western, and belief in the paranormal are common. Pray that the Russian peoples' hearts will be hungry for and open to promptings of the Holy Spirit and the gospel of Christ.

4 **The Russian Orthodox Church** (ROC) survived Communism and remains the one major symbol of Russian identity. It regards itself as the preserver of Christian civilization handed down from Rome and Byzantium. Its liturgy and teachings continue to mould Russian culture. The number of openly professing Orthodox increased from 30 million in 1985 to 87 million in 2010 (up to 100 million in some sources). The Church is using every possible means to regain its exclusive spiritual dominance lost nearly a century ago. Pray for:

a) ***An emphasis on the many positive elements*** of this ancient confession – foremost among them are the beauty and greatness of God, the mystery of Christ and His resurrection. Protestants can learn much from Orthodox theology.

b) ***An end to the ROC's intolerance,*** which is instead increasing thus far in the 21st Century. The ROC's claims – as the one true apostolic Church and that all other Christian expressions are invalid or sectarian – stimulates repression and bigotry. Inflexibility and heavy-handedness often characterize the ROC's relationship with other groups and even with its own constituents. The ROC is complicit in the laws passed and implemented that discriminate against other Christian groups.

c) ***True spiritual life.*** The ROC claims to speak for all Russians, and the majority of ethnic Russians confess some sort of affiliation, but only 6-10% are actively involved. Factors contributing to this lack of involvement include Church leaders cozying up to and collaborating with the state, poor education of church leaders, lack of unity (both within the ROC and without) and sincerity, and neglect of the younger generation's unique spiritual needs. Pray for leadership that will address all these issues in a biblical manner.

d) ***Renewal movements within the ROC.*** Traditionalists are the more powerful but are increasingly out of touch, clinging to a Slavonic Church liturgy which few understand, and grasping for political power. The reformers are often marginalized but are more Bible-focused, open for change and tolerant. Pray that future leaders may come from this more spiritual movement.

5 **The windows of opportunity for open ministry** and religious freedom appear to be closing. The excesses and insensitivities of Western ministries in the 1990s, the new vigour of Russian nationalism and the retrenched influence of the Orthodox Church have combined to see laws passed that can be (and are being) used to slowly squeeze out foreign agencies and workers and to discriminate against other faiths. Russian evangelicals claim these complex laws (registering congregations and organizations, building codes) are being used capriciously – or even systematically – to make life as difficult as possible for them. Laws requiring educational licences to conduct instruction are being misused to stop Bible teaching on the academic and even the informal level. Pray that such prejudice will only serve to strengthen the resolve and dependence on God for all who suffer. Pray that those who seek to thwart God's work will instead see it prosper and grow.

6 **Evangelicals in Russia are in a time of both growth and pressure.** Times have changed from the euphoria of the 1990s; in places such as St. Petersburg, non-Orthodox church attendance plateaued and may even be declining. The Church is settling in for the long haul as a small but significant minority. Much prayer is needed for:

a) *Growth, which has occurred, but not consistently.* Evangelicals have trebled since 1991, a feat all the more impressive given overall population decline. Some large charismatic mega-churches that started in the 1990s now have more than 4,000 in attendance; other congregations remain stuck in Communist-era survival mode. Since 1991, the number of congregations for some Christian networks has multiplied 30-fold. Pray for sustainable, balanced growth that matches quality with quantity.

b) *Evangelical culture.* With aggressive ingress in the 1990s, Western evangelists were often culturally insensitive and imported forms and styles harmful to shaping a mature Russian evangelicalism. Some groups remain unregistered; others prefer to cooperate with and even influence the government. Some reject Western forms of worship and practice; others take what they like and leave the rest. Some are traditionalist and conservative, others ambitiously progressive and modern. Pray that Church leaders might have the wisdom to guide Russia's evangelicals into becoming truly Russian, while remaining truly biblical.

c) *Church unity,* deliberately targeted by Communists in the past and even by the government and Orthodox Church today. Tensions remain between Baptists and renewalists, and between old-school Pentecostals and newer charismatics. While church networks – such as RUECB (Baptist), OTsKhVE (classical Pentecostal), ROSKyVeP and SKhVEP (Pentecostal/charismatic) and ACCR (charismatic) – join many thousands of congregations among them, there is still no effective national-level body drawing together all Russian evangelicals. Pray for a Russian Evangelical Alliance, for the regional interdenominational committees and for the National Prayer Breakfast, all of which can play key roles in uniting believers.

d) *The decline of the more-traditional Protestant groups,* which had been rapid, especially since 1991. Many of the evangelical population under Communism were ethnically German – now most Mennonites, many Lutherans and Baptists have emigrated to Germany. These more historic denominations held more respect from the Orthodox establishment, but their potential impact as a bridge disintegrated along with their plummeting numbers. Pray that those who remain would regain a heart for the Russian nation and its people and work toward the salvation thereof.

7 **Christian leaders,** who are few in number, must rise to many great challenges. Lack of training in the past, need for funding today and loss of many pastors and educators through emigration contribute to this lack of leaders. The role of foreigners will be highly limited; solutions must come from within Russia. Pray for these needs:

a) *Biblical leadership patterns need to be instilled.* Authoritarian leadership styles, a legacy of Russia's past, sadly shape how most Russian pastors operate today. This is particularly difficult because women make up the large majority of churchgoers, men have a much lower life-expectancy and too few pastors have an extensive theological education. Christian Women in Partnership is a joint venture that prepares women to be effective in ministry.

b) *Discipleship patterns are sorely inadequate.* Many churches across all evangelical groups are filled with younger folk. But most of these come from non-Christian backgrounds and need grounding in Scripture and a Christian worldview. Systematic Bible study and expository preaching are rare. Cell-based Bible study groups are one key solution; pray for their multiplication.

c) *Theological education is crucial.* Hundreds of theological institutions have formed since 1991, from discipleship schools up to seminaries. Pray for the Euro-Asian Accreditation Association that seeks to ensure high standards in the more academic institutions. Theological education needs to be indigenized and to address the issues relevant to Russia's unique situation.

d) TEE is an equally important training tool. SEAN (Study by Extension for All Nations) has a very extensive nationwide TEE programme under the guidance of the Open Russian Theological Academy. To assist the thousands of pastors and preachers with minimal theological education, many denominational and interdenominational networks are embracing SEAN. Bible Education by Extension (BEE) and Emmaus Bible College and others have TEE courses used throughout the country.

8 **Pray for a vision for outreach.** Many churches, especially newer groups, have ambitious goals for evangelism and church planting – locally, regionally and nationally. Pray that this new spirit of faith and expectancy will result in great fruit from the effective proclamation and demonstration of the gospel. Pray for:

a) Church planting. Thousands more churches need to be planted; 90% of Russians still have no meaningful link to any kind of church – Orthodox, Protestant or otherwise. There is one Protestant church for every 18,000 people in Russia, and 42 of Russia's 125 largest cities had no evangelical church as of 2009. The NT Church of Perm – which meets in what was once Lenin's Palace of Culture – planted 300 daughter churches from 1991 to 2009 and aimed to plant 100 more in 2009 alone. The goal of Russian Baptists, together with SGA, is to see a Bible-preaching church accessible to each of Russia's 100,000 communities.

b) A vision for social transformation and activism. Newer churches and younger people in particular are engaging with many needs of society – ministry to the poor, to widows and orphans, to those in prison, to those with HIV/AIDS and to drug addicts. Such ministry is also winning evangelicals a better name with the government and opening doors for collaboration with the Orthodox Church. Pray for the passion, the funding and the people to be sufficient in order to see a powerful gospel impact in this way.

c) An indigenous, trans-denominational network to emerge. Most of the larger groups have an admirable desire to plant new congregations; getting them to work together would be a true answer to prayer. There needs to be initiative and funding for research and publicity as well as envisioning for Russian believers.

d) Missions mobilization. For years, Russian culture and language dominated while those of ethnic minorities were suppressed. Nearly 20% of the population are non-Russian and speak 100 languages. Pray for a mission vision in the Russian Church, and for the ability to bridge the cultural and social barriers Russian missionaries face; the legacy of imperialistic Tsars, Russian Orthodoxy and Communists puts them at a disadvantage. Ukrainians are more active than Russians in cross-cultural outreach in Russia. Pray for the launching of many more Russian mission agencies.

9 **Expatriate ministry in Russia** did not earn a good name for itself with the enthusiastic but often ill-judged activities in the years immediately following the collapse of the Soviet Union. Some estimate over 1,500 missions and church-based agencies launched into ministry with little coordination. Insensitivities, short-termism, importation of foreign cultural forms and ecclesiastical empire-building offset much of the good that was achieved. Since then, the government is squeezing out foreign mission presence through legal changes and visa regulations. It is difficult, but not impossible, to maintain a long-term presence as a Christian worker. Foreign believers can still have a strategic impact through short-term visits to teach, train and help set up locally run ministries. Pray for missionaries and agencies to model networking and cooperative fellowship as well as to humbly assist the national Church to fulfil its own purpose. Pray also for the international partnerships focused on the major ethnic minorities for Bible translation, outreach and other ministry.

10 **Nationwide ministry challenges** in special need of prayer include:

a) The uneven growth of evangelicals. Moscow and St. Petersburg hold only 10% of the population but command a much greater share of mission activity, ministry and resources. This is to the neglect of the smaller and more remote cities and towns.

b) Students and young people. Hopelessness prevails in the attitude of most of Putin's generation, who grew up in a context of rapid change, widespread corruption, plummeting health and creeping despair. Over 3.5 million study in 50 universities and over 850 higher-education institutes. Various international student agencies work with networks of Christian groups on campuses, despite regulations limiting their activities. Pray for ministry to young people that impacts them on intellectual, emotional and spiritual levels; CCX(**IFES**), **CCCI**, **YFC** as well as increasing student ministry from Russian churches – these reach out to students and young people.

c) **Children.** There are more than 800,000 orphans in Russia; many more live in broken families. There are over one million street children (some claim many more). These are at high risk of abuse. Many turn to extreme violence and crime. The CoMission for Children at Risk is a network of 218 groups involved in ministry to children; pray that their ministry and that of local Russian congregations would reach many.

d) **Prisoners.** Over 825,000 are incarcerated, one of the world's highest rates of imprisonment. TB, AIDS and drug addiction each claim tens of thousands of lives. Pray for more ministries to reach this most needy – and responsive – group.

e) **New religionists.** Some claim massive followings, despite often intense persecution. Their false teachings not only inoculate Russians against the truth but can also raise the ire of the Orthodox Church and government against all foreign groups. Scientology is found all over the Russian Federation. The JWs now claim 290,000. Theosophy, esoterism, parapsychology, the occult, shamanism and others exert influence over many. Pray that Christians may be trained and armed with the Word of God to combat these false beliefs and to win those ensnared. The Center for Apologetics Research helps pastors and churches with training and literature.

11 **Unreached peoples.** There are 78 ethnic minorities considered unreached, totalling over 13 million in population. (See the different ethnic republics below.) Most expatriates and even Russian ministries focus on reaching ethnic Russians. Moscow operates as the centre of the former Soviet world, and nearly every ethnicity from the fSU can be found there. Most of these ethnicities are more accessible and open away from their home location and cultural setting. Pray for effective partnering and viable strategies to plant churches among them.

a) **Muslims** number over 17 million and account for the majority of non-Russians in the Russian Federation. Their growth and the ethnic-Russian decline could make Muslims a majority in Russia by the end of the 21st Century. The largest groups are Tatars (5.5 million) and Bashkirs (1.6 million), but there are also many Central Asians and peoples of the Caucasus. Undocumented and often illegal, millions of Central Asians live as temporary workers in Russia. Pray for openness to the gospel on the part of Muslims, and a loving and sensitive passion for their salvation on the part of Christians in Russia.

　　i　*Radicalization of Islam.* While only around 20% (at most) of Muslims faithfully practice Islam, the radicalization of Muslims in Russia accelerated due to the Chechen war and foreign Islamist influences. Russian military belligerence in the south and the equation of Christianity to Russian imperialism make witness to these peoples difficult for practical, cultural and spiritual reasons.

　　ii　*Conversions to Christianity.* Some reports claim up to two million Muslims converting to Orthodoxy. This is seen as a reaction of horrified Muslims to terrorist atrocities, such as the Beslan massacre, and consists of mostly nominal Muslims in the Caucasus region. Protestant missionary effort is limited but sees fruit among the peoples of the Caucasus.

b) **Several widely dispersed peoples** need prayer:

　　i　*The Jews* once numbered over two million, but are now reduced to one-eighth of this. Emigration to Israel continues, but there are important concentrations in European Russian cities. Significant numbers – over 10,000 – have come to Christ, and a large proportion of Messianic Jews in Israel are of recent Russian or Ukrainian origin. However, pockets of Georgian, Tat and Hill Jews in the Caucasus region are still unreached. The Jewish Autonomous Oblast in Far East Russia only has a few thousand Jews remaining, but there is outreach to them.

　　ii　*The Romani (Gypsy)* live scattered over European Russia with many in the Urals; they are significantly Christianized but also heavily marginalized. Some areas see an awakening and churches planted. About 5% of Russian Gypsies are evangelical.

R

iii The Chinese number over 50,000 in Moscow alone and over one million nationally, including temporary migrant workers in Siberia and the Russian Far East. They are largely unevangelized, though a few dozen small churches exist. Russian attitudes toward Chinese are poor, but Chinese in China and abroad have a growing heart to reach these unappreciated workers who are essential to Asiatic Russia's economy.

c) **The 16.5 million Russians of the "near abroad".** The collapse of the USSR left many as ethnic minorities in the 15 new states formed, where they are often resented. Their status and future are far from secure. Nearly 20 million Russians emigrated back to the Russian Federation in the last 25 years – often with few possessions. Pray that many among them might be receptive to the gospel and in turn gain a burden for the non-Christian peoples among whom they lived.

12 **Christian support ministries** for prayer include:

a) **Bible distribution.** The Bible Society of Russia (BSR), reestablished in 1992, works to ensure that all people can read the Scripture in a language they understand. It prints one million books annually, most of these being Bibles or other forms of Scripture, which are distributed from their four centres.

b) **Bible translation** is an ongoing challenge. IBT, started in Sweden in 1973, is the main agency working on translation into the minority languages in the fSU. They oversee around 100 translation projects, publishing several new translations of the Bible or NT each year. The transforming effect of Scripture in the languages of minority groups is often astonishing. Pray for the personnel, for competent native language speakers, for finances and for the freedom to complete this daunting task.

c) **Christian literature.** There are now several Christian publishers – MIRT and Triad are two large ones. Printing, distribution and sales are immense challenges due to Russia's size and economic crisis. Narnia Centre produces titles focused on children and young people. Pray for effective cooperation in literature strategies.

d) **MAF–USA** entered Russia in 1992 and from its base in Moscow developed an unusual service – logistics, warehousing of Christian materials for 70 organizations, Internet/IT services for Christian organizations and distance learning. They are now moving into mission aviation in Siberia. This was possible only after finding Russian nationals to act as pilots; foreigners are not allowed to fly as pilots in Russia.

e) **The JESUS film** has been extensively shown on TV, film and video. It is available in 31 languages.

f) **Christian radio** played an honoured role in evangelism and encouragement of Christians during Communist rule. But today, less than 1% of cities in Russia have a local Christian radio station. New Life Radio, Christian Radio for Russia and Radio Theos are examples of Russians taking the lead in providing Christian media. IIR/TV, **FEBC**, **TWR**, IBRA, WCB and World Harvest Radio are all foreign-based ministries broadcasting into Russia in 17 languages. A wealth of Christian radio for the languages of Russia is available via satellite and the Internet. Pray that those whose hearts are open might find these broadcasts.

R Geo-ethnic Regions of the Russian Federation

The Russian Federation is a complex patchwork of republics, oblasts, territories and okrugs varying in size, population, ethnic background and religious affiliation. European Russian ethnicity and language have long dominated the country, and, since the 1990s, Orthodox Christianity has become equated with being "Russian". But now, minority ethnic languages, cultures and religion are once more on the rise, particularly in the North Caucasus. In some areas, Christianity is seen as part of a Russian oppression that inflicted great harm on entire minority populations. Sharing the gospel in this context is not easy. Pray for a revelation of God's love to reach into hearts and minds, and for forgiveness and reconciliation through Jesus to become a reality to all, no matter their background or ethnicity.

The following sections are divided by federal districts. For space reasons, however, only the regions highlighted on the map in the darker blue colour are specifically addressed in the text. Those included are of special interest due to their spiritual needs or unique ethnic groups. Please turn the facts that follow into prayers for the salvation of many unreached in these regions and for the building up of the body of Christ.

Southern Federal District

Including Dagestan 2,580,000; Chechnya 1,100,000; Kabardino-Balkaria 900,000; North Ossetia-Alania 705,000; Ingushetia 465,000; Adygea 445,000; Karachay-Cherkessia 435,000.

1 **The North Caucasus region** lies between the Black and Caspian Seas. There are seven republics and a medley of 50 to 60 ethnic groups of Caucasus, Turkic and Iranian origin. These restive peoples have long resented Russian domination. The Chechen wars of the 1990s and related terrorist incidents destabilized the whole region. These regions are not only the least stable but also the poorest, with the highest unemployment and the highest birthrates as well as widespread corruption. Pray for wisdom, restraint and moderation to replace present extremes and rhetoric, and for a fair political solution – especially in Chechnya, Dagestan, Ingushetia, Abkhazia and South Ossetia.

R

2 **Islam predominates** in all the indigenous peoples except the Ossetians, a majority of whom are nominal Orthodox. Islamists, both local and foreign, work to radicalize Islam in this region and to subvert the complex ethnic, political, economic and religious factors of the North Caucasus conflicts into a jihad defined solely along religious lines. Pray that Islamist plans may be thwarted and the whole region experience peace, progress and religious freedom.

3 **The North Caucasus peoples** remain some of the least reached on earth, and they live in Europe's least-evangelized region. Most of the 50 or so ethnic groups have little by way of Scripture in their languages or churches among their peoples. Thankfully, this is changing.

Groups of believers are springing up through the faithful work of Christians from the Russian Federation and beyond. An interagency partnership works to bring blessing in Christ to this region; pray for this partnership. Pray also for IBT and its work of Bible translation in 25 languages of the area.

4 **Dagestan** is more than 90% Muslim and home to 34 ethnic groups. The largest indigenous groups: Avar 30%; Dargin 16%; Kumyk 14%; Lezgin 13%; Lak 5%; Tabassaran 4%. It is the poorest republic in the RF and has 50% unemployment. The nearby Chechen War deeply destabilized the republic. Ancient enmities among the larger indigenous ethnic groups deepen the strife. Extremist Muslim groups are violently bent on forming an Islamic republic and displacing the Sufist traditions of the indigenous Muslims. Kidnapping, intimidation and violence occur frequently. Christian work can be dangerous. The number of believers from among the 34 indigenous peoples is few, but growing. Hosanna Church in the capital and its daughter churches have Muslim-background believers as members. Association for Spiritual Renewal (ASR)/Russian Ministries runs School Without Walls to train Christian leaders. IBT works in the major languages of Dagestan; an Avar NT and Lezgin Children's Bible were recently completed. Tabassaran is one of the world's most complex languages.

5 **Chechnya** has long resisted Russian rule. The wars of the 1990s between the Russian military and Chechen rebels ended only in 2009 with Russian withdrawal and a pro-Moscow president installed. The conflicts were part of a wider strategy to form an Islamic Caucasus state (self-titled as Nokhchiyn). The 1.4 million Chechen are almost entirely Muslim, and many have been radicalized by international Islamists. The nation endured great devastation (and rebuilding), and Christian presence is largely eliminated or expelled, but a Baptist presence remains in Grozny. Most Christian organizations withdrew to work among refugees in North Ossetia and Ingushetia (Salvation Army, Russian Ministries, World Concern, WVI). Hatred of Russians (and thereby all Christians) and ruthless Islamist groups make ministry extremely sensitive work. Pray that out of this suffering might emerge a Chechen Church; there are now as many as 100 Chechen believers throughout Russia.

6 **Kabardino–Balkaria** is essentially comprised of two ethnic enclaves, the Kabardins (55% Caucasian) and the Balkars (12% Turkic); both are mostly Muslim. There is significant rivalry and tension between them. Russians make up most of the remaining population. Islamist militants (both Chechens and locals) clash with government forces here, although it is much more peaceful than neighbouring republics. The Karbards and Balkars were once Christian but converted to Islam in the 15th Century. ASR, New Way Mission, Light in the East and other groups (both Russian and expat) have ministry here; a revised NT was published by IBT in 2007 and there are several dozen believers among the two namesake peoples of this republic.

7 **North Ossetia–Alania** is the only majority Christian republic of the Caucasus region. The Ossetians account for two-thirds of the population here; they are perhaps 20% Muslim and the rest Orthodox, with a small Protestant minority from several denominations. The Beslan tragedy of 2004 was perpetrated by Chechen militants. It prompted a renewal of Christian sentiments in many Ossetians, but also prompted angry and violent reactions against the Ingush, their ancient neighbours and enemies, by others. Many ministries are active in this republic; the Ossetian Church and Scriptures owe much to the pioneering work of the German mission Light in the East and the Swedish IBT.

8 **Ingushetia** is one of Russia's smallest and poorest republics, dominated demographically by Ingush (77%) and Chechen (20%) peoples. The Ingush identify strongly with the Chechens, and many joined them in fighting against Russia. Ingushetia suffers increasing chaos due to the escalating conflict between militants and Russian special forces. There are at most a handful of Ingush believers, a few Ingush Scripture portions and some ministry by ASR and WVI.

9 **Adygea** is dominated by Russians (63%), while the Adyghe, part of the Cherkess peoples, make up only 25%. The Adyghe, with their Kabard and Cherkess brothers, were split in the 1920s by Soviet imposition of false borders. Light in the East and **CMA** have planted numerous churches in this region. Only one uses Adyghe for services; the rest are in Russian with Adyghe in attendance. IBT has translated the NT, Psalms and other OT portions into Adyghe.

10 **Karachay–Cherkessia** is made up of 39% Karachay, 32% Russian and 12% Cherkess. The Turkic Karachay are closely related to the Balkars, the Caucasian Cherkess to the Kabards and Adyghe. Ethnic rivalries between the two likewise dominate life in this republic. There is a small minority of Christians (mostly Russian and mostly nominal), but very little ministry to the Muslim peoples resident here.

11 **Kalmykia** lies northwest of the Caspian Sea. There is rapid desertification and impoverishment due to local corruption and mismanagement. Kalmyks are 53% of the republic's population. They are Europe's only Buddhist people, practicing a Tibetan Buddhism strongly influenced by Mongolian shamanism. This revival of Buddhism has attracted ire against Kalmyk Christian believers, labelling them as cultural traitors. Light of the Gospel pioneered church planting; other missions followed, most notably **CMA**. There are now a handful of Kalmyk churches with Kalmyk pastors. East Asian missionaries to these people are very effective due to their native Buddhist context. The NT in the Kalmyk language and common script has been available since 2002.

<table>
<tr><td>

Northwestern Federal District

</td><td>

Including Komi Republic 1,010,000. Also Kaliningrad Oblast 950,000; Nenets Autonomous Okrug 40,000.

</td></tr>
</table>

1 **In the Republic of Karelia,** 74% of the population are Russian; only 10% are Karelian. The Karelian people consist of three groups: the Olonets Karelians, the North Karelians and Tver Karelians. Literature is published in the first two of these languages. The Orthodox, Lutherans and others minister to the Karelians. Praise God for publication of the NT, the Psalms and Children's Bible in the Karelian Olonets dialect and of the NT and Children's Bible in Veps, a related language. NT translation of the North Karelian dialect is nearing completion.

2 **Komi** in the north is a mineral-rich area, attracting Russian industry. The Finno-Ugric Komi number 26% of the population. By religion, most Komis are Orthodox; however, many became atheist as a result of the Soviet era. Komi Christian Evangelical Church ministers to the Komi people. Its original pastor laboured in secret for years to translate the Bible into Komi. The closely related Komi-Permyak, who live mainly in Perm Krai, are mostly Orthodox but with some evangelicals. Komi peoples in smaller numbers live in neighbouring districts. The Komis received the NT in 2008, and the Komi-Permyaks expect the NT in the near future.

3 **Kaliningrad Oblast** is a small exclave on the Baltic coast, separated from Russia by Lithuania. As part of Russia, it remains 81% Russian and over 90% Slavic, but isolated. Pray for this most-western part of Russia to enjoy the richness of the gospel as has been traditionally experienced by other Baltic countries.

4 **The Nenets Autonomous Okrug** is named for the indigenous Nenets people, who make up nearly 20% of the population here. The Arctic-dwelling Finno-Ugric Nenets are animist, with a small minority of Christians. A Bible translation is in progress as is fruitful ministry here by several agencies, but their lack of cooperation undermines effectiveness and breeds confusion.

R

<table>
<tr><td>

Volga Federal District

Including Bashkortostan 4,100,000; Tatarstan 3,800,000; Udmurtia 1,600,000; Chuvashia 1,300,000; Mordovia 890,000; Mari-El 725,000. The indigenous peoples of three republics

</td><td>

(Bashkortostan, Chuvashiya and Tatarstan) are Turkic and descendants of the ancient Bolgar peoples. The other three republics are basically Finno-Ugric. The Chuvash, Udmurt, Mari and Mordvin are Orthodox, but among the Chuvash, Udmurt and Mari some syncretism appears as Orthodox and animism blended together. The Tatar and Bashkort (Bashkir) are largely Muslim.

</td></tr>
</table>

1 **Tatarstan** has abundant resources – minerals and farmland. It has a high degree of political and religious autonomy.

a) The Tatar have long been Muslim and are Russia's largest Muslim people (5.5 million) and Europe's second largest. They are more numerous in neighbouring regions of Russia and Central Asia than in Tatarstan itself. The majority are nominal or secular; only 10% faithfully practice Islam. Only 10% of Tatars are nominally Orthodox. For most, to be Tatar is to be Muslim. Since 1991, Islam has advanced from a handful of mosques to over 1,200 and an Islamic university.

b) The number of evangelical churches and groups is now possibly over 100. Most are Russian-speaking, but Tatar believers are increasing. Persecution from government, Muslim and Orthodox circles brings about closer fellowship among evangelicals historically divided by language and theology. Pray especially for Tatar believers to be protected.

c) Christian ministry. The NT was completed in 2001, and the OT is nearly complete. A Children's Bible in Tatar is also published, and, increasingly, Christian books in Tatar are being published. The Eurasian Missionary College trains workers for the hinterlands of Russia and Central Asia.

2 **Bashkortostan** is home of the Bashkort (Bashkir), a Turkic people related to the Tatar. They are 30% of this republic and number another 600,000 in neighbouring regions and countries.

a) The Bashkirs became Muslim in the 13th Century, but the old paganism/folk religion remains strongly entrenched. Pray for binding of the powers that hold them.

b) There were nearly 50 congregations of evangelicals by 2010 – up from only one in 1991. But Bashkir-speaking congregations number only a handful. Registration of churches is very difficult, and the authorities are obstructive. There is response among university students. Pray for planting and growth of mature Bashkir churches; Baptists in particular have a vision for a church planting movement among Bashkirs.

c) The Bashkir OT is underway, with the NT recently completed. UBS assist nationals in this project, made difficult by lack of adequate theological vocabulary in Bashkir.

3 **The Udmurt,** a Finno-Ugric people, are 31% of the population of Udmurtia, where the large majority live. Their numbers are declining. The Udmurt are mainly Orthodox, but paganism is also found especially among the Udmurts living in Tatarstan and Bashkortostan. However, evangelical churches are multiplying rapidly as they offer life to many who struggle with hopelessness, alcoholism and other problems. The NT and Children's Bible are available in Udmurt; the OT is being translated. Most evangelical congregations are made up of Russians or mixed Russians and Udmurts. Pray for opportunities for Udmurts to worship, pray and study in their own language and culture.

4 **Chuvashia** consists of 68% Chuvash people, who are nominally Orthodox with pagan origins, but effectively secular. Another 700,000 live elsewhere in Russia. There are a few Chuvash-speaking evangelical churches, but most use Russian. A new Children's Bible and NT in Chuvash are having an impact.

5 **Mordovia** includes the Mordvins (both Erzya and Moksha languages), who are 32% of this republic and actually number twice as many as a diaspora in the regions neighbouring Mordovia. These Finno-Ugric peoples were forced into Orthodoxy but retain some pre-Christian elements in their beliefs. There are some evangelicals, but they are mostly mixed into Russian churches rather than having their own congregations; pray for more Mordovian evangelical churches. The NT and Children's Bible are published in Erzya, and parts of each in Moksha. The Erzya OT translation is underway. Pray for wide distribution and impact of these Scriptures.

6 **Mari El** is the traditional home of the Mari people, who account for 43% of this republic's population. Another 300,000 live farther afield. Most retain their pre-Christian shamanist-animist beliefs, although around one-third are Christian. Mari nationalism is expressed through attempted revivals of Mari culture and religion, often met with opposition by the government. Teams of Estonian Christians, their ethnic cousins, minister among them with some results. Pray for the 40 or so struggling evangelical churches in the region. The Mari NT was completed in 2007, and the OT translation is in progress.

R

Urals Federal District

Including Tyumen Oblast 3,250,000 – which incorporates Khanty Mansi Autonomous Okrug 1,500,000 and Yamalo Nenets Autonomous Okrug 500,000.

1 **The Urals** are a vast area, rich in minerals and resources. They are populated mostly by Russians and Ukrainians but include significant numbers of most of the least-evangelized peoples of the Russian Federation including Bashkirs, Tatars, Chuvash, Udmurt, Mari and Mordvinians. Pray for Christians to gain a burden for these peoples living outside of their ancestral homelands.

2 **Khanty-Mansi and Yamalo-Nenets Autonomous Okrugs** are home to the Khanty, Mansi, Nenets and even some Komi peoples. (Nenets are mentioned in Nenets Autonomous Okrug.) The Khanty and Mansi peoples are small in number, a tiny minority even in their own lands. They are northern Finno-Ugric peoples whose very existence is endangered by small numbers and threatened hunter-gatherer lifestyle. They retain most of their traditional animist beliefs, despite a veneer of imposed Russian Orthodoxy. They are open to the gospel as long as it is not linked to the Russian culture that treated them cruelly in the past. Recently, many Khantys have become believers. In both Khanty and Mansi, some portions of the NT exist.

Siberian Federal District

Including Republics: Buryatiya 980,000; Khakassia 540,000; Tuva 305,000; Altay 200,000.

1 **The Buryat people** live north of Mongolia, around Lake Baikal which contains 20% of the world's fresh water. Half of Russia's 450,000 Buryats live here, with the rest in the immediate neighbouring regions. They are the largest indigenous ethnic group in Siberia. Lamaistic Buddhism and shamanism have revived considerably since 1990. An abortive attempt at evangelizing the Buryat by the LMS from England (1817-1830) was ended by Buddhist and Orthodox opposition. Since 1990, a partnership of 26 agencies has worked for their evangelization. A revival among Buryats prompted efforts to translate the Bible; 20 OT books are translated and the NT is nearly completed. Increasing numbers of believers are coming into the Church, often as a result of the passionate ministry of Buryat, Russian and expat believers. There is also local radio (**FEBC**) and TEE (ORTA) ministry.

2 **Khakassia** to the northwest of Tuva is only 13% Khakass. The Khakass (80,000 globally) are Turkic animist-shamanists with close ties to neighbouring Tuvan and Altai peoples. There are only two known Khakass churches, with just over 100 believers. New Life Mission works among them, and IBT recently completed the Khakass NT. Pray that this small people group might be evangelized.

R

3 **Tuva** lies northwest of Mongolia. The Tuvans (240,000) are one of only two Turkic peoples in the world to have embraced Buddhism (in this case, a Lamaistic version highly influenced by shamanism). They suffered severely under Communist rule and remain today a people with one of Russia's highest rates of poverty, unemployment and crime. They are renowned for their unique khomeii singing with two voices. There were no believers in 1990; today there are a few thousand (Pentecostal, New Life Mission, InterAct). Spiritual warfare saw a significant breakthrough in response from Tuvans. The NT was completed in 2002 (IBT) with the OT translation well underway and the Children's Bible in Tuvin completed as well. Discipleship is crucial for the many new Tuvan believers.

4 **The Altay Republic** is located where Russia, Mongolia, China and Kazakhstan meet. The formerly nomadic Altat people (34% of the population) are mostly shamanistic. The Altay region is highly important to both shamanism, Buddhism and even New Age religions; significant spiritual opposition to the gospel is common, fuelled by renewed vigour in both "black" and "white" shamanism in particular. Pray for the power and love of Jesus to break through to those opposing the gospel. Evangelical numbers are growing; there are some Altay evangelical churches with Altay pastors as well as an Altay NT (book and audio) and a growing hymnody of Altay worship songs.

# Far Eastern Federal District	Including Sakha Republic 935,000; Primorsky Krai 2,000,000; Chukotka Autonomous Okrug 50,000. The climate is harsh and living conditions extreme. Most of the indigenous peoples are of hunting, gathering and reindeer-herding cultures. The Russian communities work mostly in the oil industry or mining and live in the towns.

1 **Sakha** has a high degree of autonomy and is potentially wealthy with gold, diamonds, other minerals, oil and gas. Russians are 40% of the population; Sakha (also known as Yakut) are nearly 50%. The Sakha are a Turkic people, Christianized by the Orthodox Church, but with strong animist roots. Evangelical work was pioneered by Light in the East. InterAct and other agencies have joined them. In 1987, there were 30 Sakha believers, but now there are over 500, and they actively evangelize their own people. The NT in Sakha was completed in 2004 (IBT), **GRN** produced audio resources in Sakha, and Christian music in the unique Sakha style is flourishing.

2 **Primorsky Krai** is predominantly Russian in population, but occupies a strategic location. Its capital, Vladivostok, is the terminus of the Trans-Siberian Railway and the port for Russia's Pacific fleet. It hosts a large Armenian community as well as over 100,000 Muslims from Russia's minority peoples. Significantly, it is also connected directly to China and to North Korea by railways. Pray this strategic position is used to reach its unevangelized residents and neighbours.

3 **Chukotka** is home to the Inuit-related Chukchi (15,000). A number of Chukchi have come to Christ through Alaskan Inuit evangelists as well as through faithful Russian and American missionaries.

4 **The indigenous peoples** of the Russian Far East are small in population but unique. Spread across several federal subjects, they include the Evens (closely related to the Evenki of Siberia), Nanai, Koryak, Yupik and other even smaller groups. Indigenous, Russian, Korean and Western workers focus significant ministry on them. There are also significant numbers of Koreans (including North Koreans), Japanese and Jews, many being reached with the good news.

R **5** **Chinese** are numerous, and numbers are increasing in both the Russian Far East and in Siberia. Russian visa laws prevent many from permanently settling, so most are present as temporary workers or small business owners. However, the rapid decline of Russia's population, the vast number of landless Chinese in China, the huge amount of empty land and the possibility of global warming allowing more productive agriculture could potentially see millions – if not tens of millions – of Chinese making their way into Russia. Such possibilities would inevitably lead to tensions and conflicts, but could also rejuvenate the Russian economy and population – and even bring new life to the non-religious Chinese and/or the Russian Orthodox Church. Evangelicals already work among Chinese in these regions, planting churches and training Chinese leaders for them.

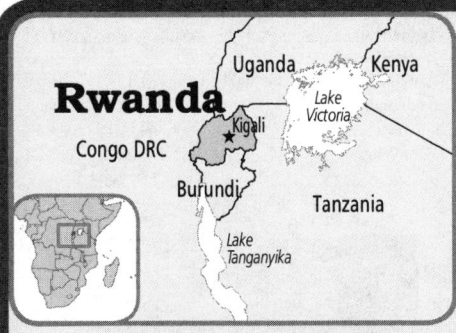

Rwanda

Republic of Rwanda

Africa

Geography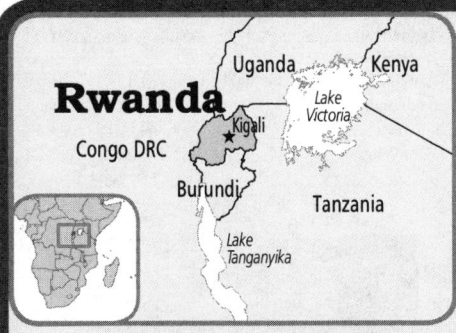

Area 26,338 sq km. A fertile, mountainous country similar to its southern neighbour, Burundi.

Population		Ann Gr	Density
2010	10,277,212	2.71%	390/sq km
2020	13,233,373	2.42%	502/sq km
2030	16,104,452	1.87%	611/sq km

A massive 23% population loss in 1994-95 through massacres, genocide (nearly 1 million) and flight of refugees (over 1 million). Most of the latter have returned. **Capital** Kigali 939,425. **Urbanites** 18.9%. **Pop under 15 yrs** 42%. **Life expectancy** 49.7 yrs.

Peoples

Rwanda abolished ethnicity as a means of identification due to ethnically motivated genocides in the past. Now, according to government policy, everyone is only Rwandan, and using the terms Hutu and Tutsi to refer to ethnicity is no longer allowed; the following are estimates.
Bantu 97.7%. 6 peoples, including those formerly regarded as Hutu and Tutsi.
Other 2.3%. Including Twa (Pygmy) 1.6%; Asian, Arab and Western peoples.
Literacy 64%. **Official languages** French, English, Kinyarwanda. The entire population speaks Kinyarwanda. **All languages** 5. **Indigenous languages** 3. **Languages with Scriptures** 3Bi.

Economy

Fertile agricultural land with few other natural resources. Coffee, tea and aid still dominate as income sources, although the government plans to wean the nation off the foreign aid, upon which it is so dependent, by developing Kigali into an economic and information-tech hub for East Africa. Over-population and distance from the sea inhibit development. The terrible events of 1994-95 decimated the economy; restoring, restructuring and privatizing the economy have been the emphases of the last decade. Rapid urbanization also sees a rise in unemployment and, as a result, crime. Most people survive on subsistence farming on tiny parcels of land.
HDI Rank 167th/182. **Public debt** 71% of GDP. **Income/person** $465 (1% of USA).

Politics

Rwanda was a feudal Tutsi monarchy, which continued through German colonial occupation (1899-1916) and Belgian Mandate (1916-1962). A Hutu revolt overthrew the Tutsi government in 1959 with many Tutsi killed or driven into exile. A Tutsi invasion from Uganda in 1990 led to conflict, many deaths and the displacement of thousands of people. Hutu extremists seized power in 1994 and began the genocide of the Tutsi minority and Hutu moderates. In 100 days, 800,000 perished. The more disciplined Tutsi-led forces gained control, and over a million Hutu fled to surrounding lands. Hutu and Tutsi rebels and militias remain at large in Congo, a thorn in both countries' sides. The government made massive strides in excising ethnicity from politics and society, making the country safe and rebuilding infrastructure. The current parliament is more than 50% female, the world's highest rate. Political dissent is currently met with little tolerance. Rwanda, a former Belgian colony, joined the British Commonwealth and enjoys improving relations with France.

Religion

There is full freedom of religion.

Religions	Pop %	Population	Ann Gr
Christian	89.12	9,159,051	2.7%
Muslim	5.20	534,415	4.8%
Ethnoreligionist	3.80	390,534	2.2%
Non-religious	1.70	174,713	-1.5%
Baha'i	0.18	18,499	0.6%

Christians Denoms		Pop %	Affiliates	Ann Gr
Protestant	30	24.68	2,537,000	2.6%
Independent	22	1.46	150,000	7.2%
Anglican	1	9.73	1,000,000	1.9%
Catholic	1	45.25	4,650,000	2.4%
Orthodox	1	0.02	2,000	0.7%
Marginal	1	0.54	55,000	6.6%
Unaffiliated		7.44	765,000	2.4%

Churches	MegaBloc	Congs	Members	Affiliates
Catholic Church	C	1,597	2,554,945	4,650,000
Anglican Church	A	450	300,300	1,000,000
Seventh-day Adventist	P	1,500	450,000	620,000
Pentecostal Church	P	3,526	264,423	550,000
Baptist Union	P	120	265,000	477,000
Presbyterian Church	P	86	130,000	281,000

R

					TransBloc	Pop %	Population	Ann Gr
Free Methodist Church	P	135	100,000	130,500	**Evangelicals**			
Assoc of Baptist Chs	P	189	45,000	112,000	Evangelicals	26.9	2,761,140	3.0%
United Methodist Ch	P	127	30,000	66,000	**Renewalists**			
Jehovah's Witnesses	M	400	16,400	55,000	Charismatics	13.3	1,364,984	4.6%
Comm of Chr Chs in Af	P	149	21,850	43,700	Pentecostals	6.7	689,300	5.1%
Assemblies of God	P	170	14,500	43,500				
Lutheran Ch of Rwanda	P	55	18,261	42,000				
Church of the Nazarene	P	145	21,000	38,000				
Other denominations[42]		1,447	139,051	284,980				
Total Christians[56]		**10,096**	**4,371,300**	**8,393,680**				

Religions % of Total Pop

TransBloc Movements % of Total Pop

Answers to Prayer

1 **Rwanda has made great progress** in many areas since the tragic events of 1994-95.

a) *The nation's infrastructure* was brutalized during the conflicts. Political stability since 2000 allows for rebuilding and developing roads, buildings, government services, water and sanitation, education and communications systems.

b) *Financial recovery* is encouraging, with Rwanda one of the fastest-growing economies in Africa. The mainstays of national income – tea and coffee – have seen their high quality and significant output restored. Eco-tourism is a burgeoning industry. The stated goal of the nation to cease its dependence on foreign aid is a sign of confidence in further growth, but many hurdles remain.

c) *The presence of women in leadership.* Over half the elected parliament are female, surely a sign of progress, especially since men were the primary perpetrators in the genocides and women mostly victims.

d) *Give praise for the commitment to reconcile and peace-build,* to move on from the terrible past and toward a brighter future. The very fact that efforts are being made in a land with centuries of endemic ethnic tension, is cause for praise. Also encouraging is the fact that churches are at the forefront of the movement.

2 **Evangelicals emerged** from the ashes to grow rapidly post-1994. Today, they are present in great numbers in political leadership, education and health and nation-building. While the spike of Protestant/Independent growth has plateaued, the consolidation of evangelicals as a force in society is to be lauded.

R Challenges for Prayer

1 **Recovery from the 1994 genocide** that claimed up to one million lives is difficult, but it displays the people's remarkable resilience and willingness to forgive and move forward despite great pain and loss. Pray for:

a) *Proper healing for those affected.* Deep, deep wounds remain, which cannot be fixed by superficial measures. Pray for the continuation of long-term programmes for counseling, rehabilitation and reconciliation. The Church has played and must continue to play a key role in the healing process; there is a great need for more ministries that focus on this.

b) *Rwanda's post-ethnic identity.* Banning ethnic identification (Hutu, Tutsi and others) is regarded by many as a positive move. People are said to be Rwandans and only Rwandans. This may help dissolve ethnic divisions, but it may also allow current inequity in the balance of power to continue unopposed. Pray that all such inequity based on ethnicity might end.

c) **The process of justice.** Only 27 have been convicted in the International Criminal Tribunal. The normal judicial system could not cope with the burden, so the government initiated *gacaca*, community-based courts, to try lesser offenders. When done properly, *gacaca* allowed justice to be done and to be seen to be done. But a number of cases were poorly handled; pray that the Lord might bring justice and heal the wounds of those who did not receive fair treatment.

d) **The release of prisoners,** since the prisons can neither hold such large numbers nor afford the cost. The eventual reintegration of the 125,000-plus people originally imprisoned – many guilty of terrible crimes – will be a true test of Rwanda's progress. Over half are no longer incarcerated. Some have not been tried. Some tried were found not guilty, some granted amnesty, others found guilty and served their sentence. Most releases trigger at least some outrage by past victims. Pray for true forgiveness as well as true repentance.

2 **Rwanda's longer-term future** must eventually move past the events of the 1990s. A development programme called Vision 2020 intends to transform Rwanda's economy, infrastructure and values. Other challenges loom large on the horizon, most notably:

a) **Political stability** is achieved, yet greater freedoms could still be achieved. Political leadership is strong, but a healthy political opposition movement and a more independent press could make Rwanda even stronger. The government is very sympathetic toward Christianity, but is not without its critics, especially in the areas of freedom of expression, human rights and foreign policy toward the DRC. Righteousness exalts a nation; pray for such a dynamic to characterize Rwanda.

b) **The military–political conundrum of relationships** among Rwanda, Burundi, Congo-DRC and Uganda remains a challenge. With the activities of rebels and militias, relationships are often strained and rise and fall regularly. Pray for patience, understanding and cooperation to work together for justice and to root out those who would destabilize the region.

c) **Rapid population growth and limited land** promise to intensify the issue hidden at the root of the massacres. The traditional habit of parcelling out inherited land to all offspring created tiny parcels of farmland insufficient to even feed a family. Jealousy and greed were behind countless local episodes of murder and theft during the dark days of 1994-95. The terrible loss of life depopulated much land, but this same issue will inevitably resurface – Rwanda is already Africa's most densely populated country. Pray that wise solutions might be found to this deep-seated and long-term problem.

3 **The religious scene of Rwanda** has been reshaped by the 1990s. A country in which 80% call themselves Christian, yet allowed and perpetrated such atrocities, might have been Christianized, but it clearly was not converted. Pray for:

a) **The Catholic Church,** which lost much credibility by failing to adequately oppose evil and speak against the ethnic hatred that led to the massacres. Many righteous Catholics, including priests and nuns, laid down their lives to protect others. But others failed to intervene or even connived with the perpetrators. As a result, many defected away from Catholicism out of disillusion. Pray that such nominalism and compromise might never happen again and that genuine renewal will transform the Catholic Church; signs that Catholics are seeking renewal are encouraging.

b) **Evangelicals** grew rapidly in the aftermath due to very active evangelism, aid programmes, ministry to the hurt and traumatized and a message of hope for all regardless of tribe. The East African Revival of the 1930s began in Rwanda. Pray for a new revival to break out, one that places tribalism and revenge at the foot of the cross and is characterized by repentance and reconciliation. Some evangelical groups seem concerned only with numerical growth rather than discipleship and transformation.

c) **Muslims** also increased significantly in the last 15 years – unsurprisingly for similar reasons as evangelicals. Aggressive mosque building, aid and education programmes, a universal message that transcends ethnicity as well as the moral high ground for playing a less active role in the genocide have seen Muslim numbers increase to possibly over 5% of the population, although this number is disputed. There is negligible Christian outreach to Muslims, and churches have little idea how to do so; pray for a loving witness by believers.

R

4 **Thousands of spiritual leaders** were murdered or fled and have not been replaced. The remaining often despair of being able to cope with the desperate physical, social, psychological and spiritual damage done. Less than 10% of evangelical pastors have any formal theological training. Several theological colleges have a born-again presence, including the Rwanda Institute of Evangelical Theology (the encouraging result of the merger of two colleges), an Anglican college and a Pentecostal college. All face challenges. Some pastors train and study in Uganda or Kenya. A number of other programmes, including TEE and modular training, are also being utilized. Poverty often prevents pastors from getting the training they need and long for. There is a dearth of good Bible study aids, and the government's decision to rapidly transition from French to English as the language of education will impact training for some years. Pray that God may raise up godly men and women fitted for Rwanda's hour of need. Pray also for financial provision for both students and schools.

5 **Children and young people** were deeply scarred by the events of the 1990s, but they are now the young adults and future leaders of Rwanda. They carry a painful legacy and difficult burdens no young people should have to bear. Pray for:

a) Ministry to university students. Most GBU(**IFES**) Bible study leaders lost their lives, but a new generation of workers is being raised up. **CCCI** also ministers in the universities and many colleges. Pray for more workers and resources for the task.

b) Young people's ministries, such as Scripture Union, AEE/Rwanda(**AE**), **YWAM**, **YFC**, Moucecore, Solace Ministries and Christ for the Nations Ministries, which work across denominations. Bible reading programmes, prayer groups, youth camps, alternate education programmes, AIDS awareness as well as assisting orphans, street kids and child heads-of-households are all aspects of current work.

c) Orphans from genocide, war and AIDS may number up to 900,000 – 30% of all Rwandan children. There are over 30,000 child-led households caring for 100,000. They are the most vulnerable to exploitation. Pray for:

i *Counselling* for those who witnessed or suffered traumatic experiences and for those who must live without parents. Their numbers are vast, their pain is deep and the church is still learning how to offer such ministry.

ii *Social networks* – such as the extended families of these children – to offer love, mercy and kindness to them, treating them as their own. Pray also for friends for these orphans; 74% say they have none, and 40% feel life is meaningless.

iii *The children of genocide perpetrators.* Pray for the breaking of any ties that might carry on the legacy of guilt and violence; pray for freedom in Christ and a new identity.

iv *Models of family and community,* which these children have not experienced. Pray for churches, ministries and relations to teach and show them how to live as part of a family, a community and a society in a manner that glorifies God.

6 **Missionary presence continues to increase.** There is also a growing host of NGOs helping with development work. Government policy has been instrumental in assisting the increase of evangelical missionaries, as has the establishment of a Christian international school in Kigali (KICS). Notable agencies include the Churches of Christ, **CMS**, **AoG**, Baptist groups, Evangelical Friends, WVI, Compassion, **AIM**, IJM, **WV**, Rwanda Partners and the well-publicized PEACE plan of Saddleback Church. Conditions can be emotionally harrowing, especially when engaging those most affected by genocide and by AIDS. The need is still great for counselling and reconciliation ministries, discipleship and church work, education, health, income generation and much more. Pray that ministry might empower Rwandans rather than create dependency; pray also that the many programmes and workers might reach beyond Kigali and into the villages and rural areas.

7 **Ministry challenges** that need intercession:

a) HIV/AIDS is a massive challenge in Rwanda. The prevalence rate is as high as 10% for 14-49 year-olds, and 33% for pregnant women, a ticking time bomb to rob Rwanda of its next generation. SU, Mothers' Union, Christian Aid (UK), WorldRelief, WVI, AEE, Solace and many denominational ministries work in prevention and care. Rwanda is often touted as a success story in the battle against AIDS, but much remains to be done. Pray for:

i *Education and prevention programmes* to reduce this blight. People's knowledge about the disease is still lacking.

ii *Care for those who already have AIDS,* whether to prolong an active life or to ease the passing of those seriously ill.

iii *Removal of the stigma surrounding HIV/AIDS* so that those afflicted do not suffer discrimination and can therefore contribute to rebuilding the nation.

b) **The Pygmy Twa** are a small ethnic group who live in rural, often primitive, conditions. Many are potters and farmers, since their traditional hunter-gatherer jungle lifestyle is under threat from deforestation and unjust eviction from forest reserves. They suffered acutely during the genocide as innocent victims of the Hutu-Tutsi violence. They are generally poorer and less educated, and are often exploited by others. The percentage of believers among the Twa is lower than other groups. Pray for Rwandan churches and expat missions to minister to this unique but vulnerable group in a humble, sensitive and loving way.

c) **Women at risk.** Many were widowed by the genocide; others are effectively widowed as their husbands still languish in prison. Between 100,000 and 250,000 were raped, a systematic use of terror that left nearly half of the victims HIV-positive, psychologically traumatized and socially stigmatized. Females tend to have less education and less opportunity for work; as a result, many have fallen into or been forced into prostitution. Pray for more ministries to work with these women; **CCCI**, Rwanda Partners, Mothers' Union, AEE, Solace and others are already doing so.

d) **A lack of discipleship and biblical teaching.** Many call themselves Christian but lack a depth of understanding of their faith. The prosperity gospel is beginning to extend its influence in Rwanda; churches need trained leaders and laity who can respond to such problematic issues. Teaching programmes such as the Alpha Course can go a long way in building up the body of Christ, which is at risk of adopting an "evangelical nominalism". Pray for evangelicals in Rwanda to become mature in Christ, biblically sound and a transforming influence in their nation.

8 **Christian support ministries:**

a) **Bible and Christian literature** distribution offers words of hope to those who suffer. The Bible Society published a modern translation in Kinyarwanda, which is more accessible to those with limited literacy. Poverty and illiteracy limit the impact of literature, so African Enterprise, The Bible Society and others work to increase literacy through programmes as well.

b) **Audio resources** are therefore vital. **GRN** recordings are available in all the major languages, and Faith Comes By Hearing distributes solid-state audio players packed with Scripture and Christian teaching.

c) **Christian radio.** A number of Christian radio stations operate locally. These are supplemented by **TWR** broadcasts in Kinyarwanda, with programmes designed to minister to the specific needs of this nation. AWR also ministers in this way.

d) **The JESUS film** has been viewed by over half of the population.

R

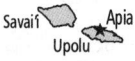

Samoa

Savai'i · Apia
Upolu · American Samoa

South Pacific Ocean

· Tonga

Samoa

Independent State of Samoa

Pacific

Geography

Area 2,831 sq km. Two large volcanic islands, Savai'i and Upolu, and seven small islands covered by lush tropical rainforest.

Population		Ann Gr	Density
2010	178,943	0.00%	63/sq km
2020	183,903	0.30%	65/sq km
2030	191,354	0.39%	68/sq km

Over 200,000 Samoans live in American Samoa, USA, New Zealand and Australia.
Capital Apia 36,100. **Urbanites** 23.4%. **Pop under 15 yrs** 39%. **Life expectancy** 71.4 yrs.

Peoples

Indigenous Polynesian 99%. Samoan 89%; Euronesian (mixed) 10%.
Other 1%. Other Polynesian, European, Chinese.
Literacy 99%. **Official languages** Samoan, English. **All languages** 2. **Languages with Scriptures** 2Bi.

Economy

Growing population, limited and decreasing resources and the communal land system strain the economy. Large-scale emigration and remittances mitigate the strain. Moving away from agriculture toward a service economy focused on tourism. The 2009 earthquake and tsunami caused 150 deaths, destroyed several villages and damaged much infrastructure – causing a significant economic setback.
HDI Rank 94th/182. **Public debt** 55% of GDP.
Income/person $2,608 (5% of USA).

Politics

German rule 1900-1914; thereafter, New Zealand UN trusteeship until independence in 1962. First Pacific island nation to win post-colonial independence.

Religion

Constitutional freedom of religion is occasionally contravened by intimidation on the local level.

Religions	Pop %	Population	Ann Gr
Christian	96.60	172,859	0.0%
Baha'i	1.90	3,400	0.0%
Non-religious	1.50	2,684	2.9%

Christians Denoms		Pop %	Affiliates	Ann Gr
Protestant	16	57.53	103,000	-0.7%
Independent	6	4.55	8,000	1.9%
Anglican	1	0.21	<400	0.8%
Catholic	1	18.72	34,000	-0.4%
Marginal	6	19.03	34,000	3.6%
Doubly affiliated		*-3.44*	*-6,000*	*0.0%*

Churches	MegaBloc	Congs	Members	Affiliates
Congregational Chr Ch	P	194	13,584	52,300
Catholic Church	C	29	16,750	33,500
Latter Day Saints	M	75	22,378	32,000
Methodist Church	P	98	9,500	23,700
Assemblies of God	P	54	6,532	14,500
Seventh-day Adventist	P	30	5,600	7,250
Worship Centre	I	4	1,120	2,800
Samoan Full Gospel Ch	I	55	1,100	2,200
Cong Ch of Jesus Christ	I	10	1,000	2,000
Jehovah's Witnesses	M	10	440	1,570
Other denominations[20]		84	3,807	1,050
Total Christians[30]		**643**	**81,811**	**172,870**

TransBloc	Pop %	Population	Ann Gr
Evangelicals			
Evangelicals	18.0	32,263	0.7%
Renewalists			
Charismatics	13.8	24,766	1.7%
Pentecostals	12.4	22,150	1.5%

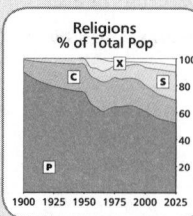

Religions
% of Total Pop

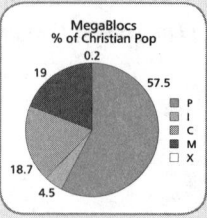

MegaBlocs
% of Christian Pop

Challenges for Prayer

1 **Samoans have been Christian** for over a century, and every village has at least one church. But the traditional class structure and pre-Christian cultural standards were not necessarily transformed by the gospel. Much of the Church suffers from nominalism, and rivalry among denominations does not generate a good spiritual atmosphere. Pride and politics influence church life too much, and the financial demands on a poorer population are heavy. These, coupled with the modern challenges of domestic strife and imported moral vice, make for a society in need of prayer.

2 **Mormonism** is a point of contention; it is growing quickly, but the numbers they claim and the census results are hugely divergent. Mormons receive and send more missionaries to/from Samoa than any other denomination. Pray for all seeking to win Mormons to Jesus and to enlighten Samoan Christians of Mormonism's errors. Pray for renewal and revival within churches that will safeguard against further Mormon growth.

3 **The growth of evangelicals** is encouraging – through renewal movements in mainline churches as well as through newer groups, especially Pentecostals/charismatics. This growth parallels a major decline in traditional denominations. Pentecostals/charismatics and other evangelical agencies, such as Youth for Christ, are met with opposition, particularly from some mainline denominations. Pray for harmony between the newer and the more traditional branches of the Church.

4 **Unity among evangelicals** needs developing. Pray that the Samoan Evangelical Alliance, formed in 1991, may be a means to overcome the prevailing nominalism, to underscore personal commitment to Christ and to further the cause of the gospel. In a small constituency, the spirit of competition is too easily manifest. Pray that the birth of Graceland Broadcasting Network (90% Trinity Broadcasting Network content, 10% local content) might be a bridge between evangelical groups.

5 **Samoan missionaries** played a major role in evangelizing the Pacific in the last century. Today, most Samoans who serve outside of Samoa are pastoring the many Samoan migrant congregations abroad. An exception to this is the contingent of around 50 Samoan **YWAM**ers serving around the world. Pray for them, and pray for their ongoing influence on their home churches,

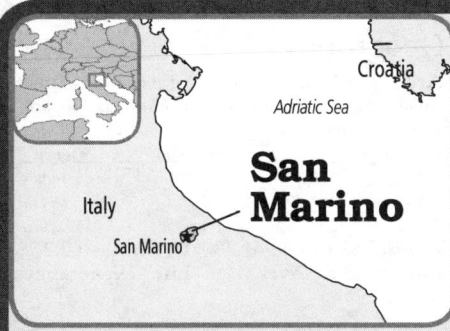

Population		Ann Gr	Density
2010	31,537	0.84%	517/sq km
2020	32,914	0.29%	540/sq km
2030	33,407	0.11%	548/sq km

Capital San Marino 4,400. **Urbanites** 94.3%. **Pop under 15 yrs** 15%. **Life expectancy** 82.4 yrs.

Peoples

Sammarinese 92%.
Italian 6%.
Other 2%.
Literacy 99%. **Official language** Italian. **All languages** 2. **Languages with Scriptures** 1Bi.

San Marino
Most Serene Republic of San Marino
Europe
Geography

Area 61 sq km. A city state in north central Italy near Rimini.

Politics

Independent republic since AD 301. In customs union with Italy. Main foreign exchange earners are tourism (3.3 million visitors annually) and the banking industry. Has a two-tiered parliamentary structure – a larger Council and a smaller Congress.

Public Debt 6% of GDP. **Income/person** $29,360 (64% of USA).

Religion

No official religion, though the vast majority are baptized Catholic.

Religions	Pop %	Population	Ann Gr
Christian	88.79	28,002	0.8%
Non-religious	10.41	3,283	1.7%
Baha'i	0.70	221	0.8%
Other	0.10	32	0.8%

Christians Denoms		Pop %	Affiliates	Ann Gr
Protestant	1	0.05	<20	2.9%
Catholic	1	88.00	28,000	0.7%
Marginal	1	0.74	<250	1.6%

Churches	MegaBloc	Congs	Members	Affiliates
Catholic Church	C	12	18,258	27,752
Jehovah's Witnesses	M	2	195	234
Waldensian Church	P	1	9	15
Total Christians[3]		**15**	**18,462**	**28,001**

TransBloc	Pop %	Population	Ann Gr
Evangelicals			
Evangelicals	<0.1	4	5.6%
Renewalists			
Charismatics	1.8	555	0.7%

Religions % of Total Pop

TransBloc Movements % of Total Pop
- Charis
- Evang

Challenges for Prayer

1 **The Sammarinese are Catholic by tradition and culture,** but most give only lip service to the Church and are very materialistic. Increasing numbers reject their religious heritage altogether, with smaller numbers of JWs, a small group of Baha'i, a few Waldensians and a scattering of people from other faith backgrounds. Pray that they may have a life-changing encounter with the Lord Jesus Christ.

2 **San Marino proclaims itself "Ancient Land of Liberty".** There is freedom to worship, but evangelism hardly exists. In the past, outreach by evangelicals resulted in jailing or expulsion from the country. As a result, no churches or ministries currently evangelize in San Marino.

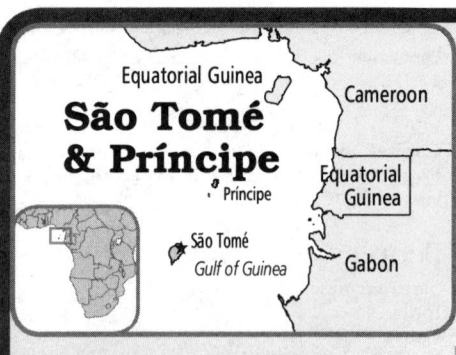

Equatorial Guinea

Cameroon

São Tomé & Príncipe

Príncipe

Equatorial Guinea

São Tomé

Gulf of Guinea

Gabon

S

São Tomé & Príncipe

Democratic Republic of São Tomé and Príncipe

Africa

Geography

Area 1,001 sq km. Two larger and several smaller islands in the Gulf of Guinea, 200 km west of Gabon.

Population		Ann Gr	Density
2010	165,397	1.62%	165/sq km
2020	197,499	1.89%	197/sq km
2030	233,680	1.63%	233/sq km

Capital São Tomé 61,400. **Urbanites** 62.2%. **Pop under 15yrs** 41%. **Life expectancy** 65.4 yrs.

Peoples

Mestiços/Forros 76%. Descendents of Portuguese colonists and African slaves.

Other groups 24%. Caboverdian Mestiço, Angolar (descendants of Angolan slaves), Portuguese, Prinicipense, Fang from Equatorial Guinea, Chinese and other foreign groups, including contract labourers from Cape Verde, Angola and Mozambique.

Literacy 83.1% (much lower in practice). **Official language** Portuguese and three Creole dialects. **All languages** 5. **Languages with Scriptures** 1Bi.

Economy

Agriculturally based (subsistence and plantation). Cocoa accounts for 95% of exports, which makes the country vulnerable to market fluctuations. Oil speculation in the Gulf of Guinea holds forth great economic potential. Economic reform and privatization are aimed at reducing the significant debt and spurring growth.
HDI Rank 131st/182. **Public debt** 615% of GDP. **Income/person** $1,094 (2% of USA).

Politics

Settled by the Portuguese in 1493, and became a plantation colony and major slave transhipment centre. Independent from Portugal in 1975 as a Marxist republic. A multiparty democracy was instituted in January 1991.

Religion

Secular state with freedom of religion.

Religions	Pop %	Population	Ann Gr
Christian	87.55	144,805	2.2%
Ethnoreligionist	7.45	12,322	-4.9%
Muslim	3.50	5,789	4.8%
Non-religious	1.40	2,316	2.4%
Baha'i	0.10	165	1.6%

Christians	Denoms	Pop %	Affiliates	Ann Gr
Protestant	9	4.18	7,000	4.2%
Independent	11	9.12	15,000	2.3%
Catholic	1	73.16	121,000	2.0%
Marginal	1	1.09	2,000	5.9%

Churches	MegaBloc	Congs	Members	Affiliates
Catholic Church	C	14	73,780	121,000
New Apostolic Church	I	23	4,667	11,200
Seventh-day Adventist	P	12	1,530	3,825
Charismatic groups	I	15	760	1,900
Jehovah's Witnesses	M	9	720	1,800
Assemblies of God	P	8	700	1,750
Other denominations[10]		46	1,713	3,333
Total Christians[22]		**127**	**83,870**	**144,808**

TransBloc	Pop %	Population	Ann Gr
Evangelicals			
Evangelicals	4.2	7,010	6.5%
Renewalists			
Charismatics	11.0	18,194	2.6%
Pentecostals	2.7	4,484	7.0%

Religions % of Total Pop

TransBloc Movements % of Total Pop

Challenges for Prayer

1 **The majority of the population are Catholic,** but practice is usually mixed with deep-seated African spiritist beliefs. Appeasing spirits and ancestors is often of greater importance than honouring God. Pray for the Holy Spirit to move through the Catholic Church, bringing renewal. Pray for the sovereignty of Jesus to be clearly demonstrated amid syncretized Catholicism and the growth of Islam and marginal sects.

2 **Evangelicals are free to minister** and do see significant growth. There are close links with several Portuguese and Brazilian groups, such as the Assemblies of God, the Nazarenes, Deeper Life (Nigeria), **YWAM** and several others. Pray that their missionaries might have a great impact on these islands. Pray for the development of locally led, culturally relevant congregations with effectively trained Christian leaders. Pray also for local support of national workers and for the launching of an interdenominational training centre.

3 **Less-reached sections of the population** are the Príncipe islanders, the Angolares (rural fisherfolk) and the *serviçais* (contract labourers), with each group having its own distinct Creole dialect. Pray for outreach to and salvation for these groups.

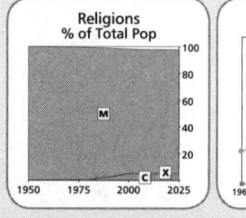

Saudi Arabia

Kingdom of
Saudi Arabia

Asia

Geography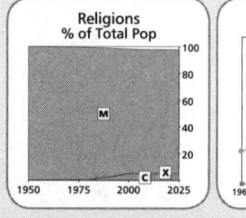

Area 2,240,000 sq km. The main portion of the Arabian Peninsula; almost entirely desert, but contains 25% of the world's known oil reserves.

Population		Ann Gr	Density
2010	26,245,969	2.14%	12/sq km
2020	31,607,829	1.78%	14/sq km
2030	36,545,034	1.35%	16/sq km

Capital Riyadh 4,847,840. **Other major cities** Jiddah 3.2 million; Mecca 1.5mill; Medina 1.1m. **Urbanites** 82%. **Pop under 15 yrs** 32%. **Life expectancy** 72.7 yrs.

Peoples

With a sizeable and inadequately documented expatriate presence, all figures are estimates.
Arab 80.4%.
  Saudi Arab 73.0%.
  Foreign Arab 7.4%. Egyptian 2.8%; Yemeni 1.9%; Palestinian 1.2%; Lebanese 0.6%.
Asian 17.4%. Indian 5.2%; Pakistani 3.3%; Filipino 3.7%; Bangladeshi 3.7%; Iranian 0.5%.
African 1.5%. Somali, Arab-African, Nigerian.
Other 0.7%. Westerners.
Literacy 83%. **Official language** Arabic. **All languages** 20. **Indigenous languages** 5. **Languages with Scriptures** 1Bi.

Economy

Enormous oil wealth produces 75-90% of government revenue and is the foundation of the economy and infrastructure, while also being used to export Islam globally. Massive reliance on the foreign labour force and the looming financial burden of a burgeoning younger generation will require greater financial austerity and economic diversification. Unemployment among Saudis is high, between 20-40%, largely due to Saudis' disdain for certain types of jobs.

HDI Rank 59th/182. **Public debt** 18.9% of GDP. **Income/person** $18,855 (40% of USA).

Politics

An absolute monarchy and a semi-feudal state tightly controlled by the large royal family. An advisory council is elected by eligible Saudi males. Increasing external and internal pressure to liberalize the country is offset by fear of a hard-line Islamist backlash.

Religion

An Islamic state committed to the role of custodian of Islam and its holiest sites. Most Saudis are Wahhabi Sunnis; Shi'ites make up to 8% and are discriminated against. People of faiths other than Islam can live in Saudi Arabia, but they may neither practice their religion openly nor gather privately. All non-Muslim figures are estimates.

Religions	Pop %	Population	Ann Gr
Muslim	92.41	24,253,900	2.1%
Christian	5.43	1,425,156	2.6%
Hindu	0.78	204,719	4.4%
Non-religious	0.66	173,223	2.8%
Buddhist	0.42	110,233	3.1%
Other	0.30	82,993	4.5%

Christians Denoms		Pop %	Affiliates	Ann Gr
Protestant	23	0.23	60,000	3.2%
Independent	30	0.15	40,000	4.6%
Anglican	1	0.01	2,000	1.4%
Catholic	3	4.67	1,225,000	2.4%
Orthodox	4	0.29	75,000	4.6%
Marginal	4	0.05	13,000	3.4%
Unaffiliated		0.03	8,000	0.0%

Churches	MegaBloc	Congs	Members	Affiliates
Catholic Church	C	0	856,643	1,225,000
Orthodox Churches	O	0	52,448	75,000
Protestant groups	P	54	10,800	54,000
Independent groups	I	0	25,000	40,000
Other denominations[8]		116	11,796	21,130
Total Christians[65]		**170**	**956,687**	**1,415,130**

TransBloc	Pop %	Population	Ann Gr
Evangelicals			
Evangelicals	0.3	88,620	4.3%
Renewalists			
Charismatics	0.3	70,848	6.6%
Pentecostals	<0.1	1,880	7.6%

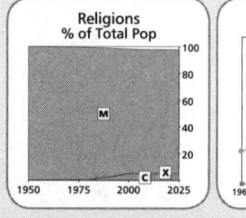

Religions
% of Total Pop

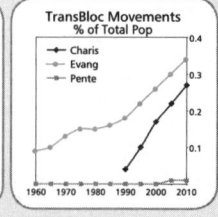

TransBloc Movements
% of Total Pop

Challenges for Prayer

1 **Saudi Arabia is the birthplace and stronghold of Islam.** From Mecca, Islam holds sway over billions and permeates many cultures. Pray that the Lord would shake this centre of spiritual influence and make His Lordship known. If a spiritual breakthrough glorifying Jesus Christ would happen here, it would transform Islam and those subject to it.

2 **All Muslims must pray toward Mecca five times daily.** Yearly, over two million make the *Hajj*, or pilgrimage, to Mecca, required of all Muslims once as one of the five pillars of Islam. This is the culmination of many people's religious life. Pray that many, as they go seeking God, might encounter the living Christ. Praise God that He is revealing Himself to increasing numbers of *hajis* through dreams and visions.

3 **Saudi Arabia's record on religious freedom and human rights** is notorious and probably the world's worst. Abuses occur through a corrupt judicial system and through aggressive and ubiquitous religious police *(mutaween)* who operate with minimal accountability and the government's acquiescence. Christian and secular international bodies promoting equality and freedom of conscience regularly condemn Saudi practices. Pray for a greater recognition of human rights and religious freedom.

4 **The nation faces great stresses.** Under increasing pressure, the aging leadership must walk the impossible path between those pushing for liberalization and those demanding stricter Islamization. The following challenges need prayer:

a) Economic. Over-reliance on oil exports and foreign labour has taken its toll – the growing gap between rich and poor, and widespread unemployment and discontent among the spoiled younger generation, often push them into the arms of extremism. The Saudi-ization of the economy results in more difficult conditions for expats as well as pressure to create hundreds of thousands of new and acceptable jobs for Saudis. Spiraling personal debt and the need for personal "connections" to secure a desirable job add to the financial stress for many.

b) Social. Strict Islamic laws keep the nation in a stranglehold. The most controversial and contradictory issue is that of women's rights. Driving, voting, working, even going out are prohibited or severely restricted for women. Despite harsh societal restrictions, alcohol and drug abuse, sexual immorality and HIV/AIDS are hidden but real problems.

c) Military. Although the government can point to several successes, the battle between the military and Islamist terrorists intensifies with each year. The presence of Western military forces rankles many.

5 **Massive Islamic missionary efforts** are coordinated by the Muslim World League in Mecca. Every year, billions of oil dollars are spent around the world to propagate Islam – especially the virulent Wahhabist brand native to Saudi Arabia. Investments to expand Islam include giving aid to sympathetic countries, building mosques, sending missionaries, distributing literature and, more recently, funding Western academic institutions with the condition that a centre for Islamic studies must be built. Islamic materials promoting hatred of non-Muslims are shipped to the West. The Saudi government, while denying to Christians the liberty to share their faith, demands this liberty for Muslims living elsewhere. Some of the world's largest printing presses are in Saudi, churning out 30 million Qur'ans annually for worldwide distribution.

6 **Saudis who come to faith in Christ** face the death penalty if discovered; executions are definitely known to occur. Despite this, increasing numbers are secretly seeking and finding Jesus, and there are believers in every Saudi city. Pray for believers to persevere and even to multiply. Pray for a miracle – the legalization of Christianity for Saudis; pray that Saudi believers may be able to meet together in safety and have access to God's Word. Also pray that believers might find believing spouses.

7 **Life is difficult for expatriates.** The benefits of money made from working here are offset by stifling social restrictions, often cruel working environments, endemic racism and a total lack of personal and religious freedom. Many of these foreigners have little access to the gospel, although there are sizeable numbers of Christians among them. Pray for a witness to flourish among all foreign workers – and that many might come to Jesus while in the land of Mohammed.

S

8 **Christian expatriates live under strict surveillance;** even meeting in homes as a group of believers is forbidden. Those caught can be subjected to humiliating beatings, imprisonment, expulsion and even execution. This is particularly so for Asian Christians who are often the most effective witnesses and whose governments have the least international influence. Sadly, most Christians are nominal and few practice faithfully, although many more would join them were the risks not so great. Pray for encouragement, strength, wisdom and courage for the believing community. There are few opportunities to meaningfully interact with Saudis, and very few expatriates speak Arabic. Pray that other Arabs might gain a burden to reach Saudis.

9 **Witnessing by other means:**

a) *Saudis abroad.* Students, businessmen and tourists visit the West and other more open Arab states, where they can be reached. Most prefer to travel during the hot season and the month of fasting!

b) *Christian radio.* **HCJB**, IBRA and others broadcast in Arabic and in several languages of expat communities. Many listen secretly, yielding isolated converts in some regions.

c) *Christian literature and video materials* are banned, including the Bible – and are therefore in great demand. Scriptures in different formats and films such as the JESUS film and *The Passion of the Christ* do a brisk business on the black market.

d) *Satellite television.* About 90% of homes have satellite television, an indication of the hunger for what the outside world offers. In this environment, Christian television such as **SAT-7**, The Bible Channel, *al-Hayat,* the Miracle Channel and numerous other Christian Arabic- and English-language channels can be used tremendously to bring Saudis to Jesus.

e) *The Internet* is accessible to the majority of the population, but the government blocks and monitors traffic. Pray that those in the country would be able to access the many evangelistic, discipling and discussion sites on the web.

Senegal
Republic of Senegal
Africa

Geography 🌍

Area 196,722 sq km. Mainland Africa's most westerly state – arid, with few natural resources.

Population		Ann Gr	Density
2010	12,860,717	2.66%	65/sq km
2020	16,196,985	2.20%	82/sq km
2030	19,541,446	1.81%	99/sq km

The majority of the population live on the southern coast and around the capital.

Capital Dakar 2,862,879. **Urbanites** 42.9%. **Pop under 15 yrs** 44%. **Life expectancy** 55.4 yrs.

Peoples 👪

Over 56 ethnic groups in three main linguistic families; only the largest are listed.
West-Atlantic 57.5%.
  Wolof(2) 38.3%. Wolof 36.9%; Lebu 1.4%.
  Jola(13) 4.6%. Jola-Fonyi 3.5%.
  Atlantic(15) 14.6%. Serer-Sine 10.7%; Balanta 1.0%.
Fulbe (Fulani, Pulaar) (4) 24.9%. Fulakunda 12.1%; Tukulor 7.1%; Fulbe Jeeri 4.6%; Futa Jalon 1.2%.
Malinke(6) 9.8%. Mandinka 5.5%; Malinke 3.4%.
Other African(8) 4.6%. Soninke 2.1%.
Arab-Berber(5) 1.8%.
Other 1.4%. French, other Europeans and Asians.
Literacy 39.3%. **Official language** French. Language of wider communication, Wolof; spoken as a first language by around 40% of the population. **All languages** 46. **Indigenous languages** 37. **Languages with Scriptures** 3Bi 7NT 16por 17w.i.p.

Economy 🗺️

Subsistence agricultural economy. Main exports are peanuts and phosphates. Poverty and high unemployment prompt many attempts to illegally migrate to Europe. Remittances sent home to Senegal from

S

abroad are a key part of the economy, as is foreign aid. Much of its external debt has been slashed by the IMF.
HDI Rank 166th/182. **Public debt** 21.4% of GDP. **Income/person** $1,066 (2% of USA).

Politics 🗵

Independent from France in 1960. A multiparty democracy, with a commendable peaceful transfer of power to the former opposition in 2000. Separatist conflict in the southwest Casamance province caused disruption and distress, but rebels and the government signed peace accords in 2004.

Religion 🙏

A secular state with freedom of religion, despite the large Muslim majority. The three Muslim Sufi brotherhoods – the Mouride, Tidjani and Qadiri – have great influence in political and economic life.

Religions	Pop %	Population	Ann Gr
Muslim	91.05	11,709,683	2.7%
Christian	6.42	825,658	3.0%
Ethnoreligionist	2.22	285,508	1.0%
Baha'i	0.20	25,721	2.7%
Non-religious	0.10	12,861	7.3%
Buddhist	0.01	1,286	2.7%

Christians Denoms		Pop %	Affiliates	Ann Gr
Protestant	23	0.14	18,000	5.5%
Independent	10	0.23	29,000	3.5%
Catholic	1	6.03	775,000	2.9%
Marginal	1	0.02	3,000	3.1%

Churches	MegaBloc	Congs	Members	Affiliates
Catholic Church	C	143	450,581	775,000
New Apostolic Church	I	233	7,000	17,500
Church of Pentecost	I	35	2,970	4,900
Lutheran Ch (Finnish)	P	62	2,635	4,400
Mission Inter-Senegal	I	34	740	3,700
Presbyterian Church	P	50	1,500	3,000
Assemblies of God	P	58	798	2,850
Other denominations[28]		188	5,999	13,347
Total Christians[35]		**803**	**472,223**	**824,697**

TransBloc	Pop %	Population	Ann Gr
Evangelicals			
Evangelicals	0.2	25,792	6.1%
Renewalists			
Charismatics	0.3	44,094	4.2%
Pentecostals	0.1	7,914	5.7%

Religions % of Total Pop

Annual Growth Rates

Challenges for Prayer

1 **Spiritually, Senegal is both open and closed.** The nation enjoys religious freedom and is remarkably tolerant toward other faiths – a point of pride for Senegalese, perhaps because so few Muslims have ever come to Christ. Despite a longstanding Christian presence and outreach, a spiritual heaviness covers the land. Allegiance to religious leaders renewed in each generation prevents any significant people movement to Christ. Virtually all Wolof, Fulbe and Mande peoples remain Muslim. Pray for the spiritual breakthrough for which so many wait.

2 **Islam dominates religious life,** growing from about 45% of the population in 1900 to over 90% by 1960. The Muslim Sufi brotherhoods are well organized, wealthy and politically powerful; over 85% of all Muslims belong to one of them. The Mouride Brotherhood is virtually a state within a state, based in their capital, Touba. But aggressive Islamist groups funded by Saudi Arabia and Libya are making inroads and threaten the tolerant status quo. Pray that religious tyranny might be thwarted, and that God may use all forces to draw people to Himself.

3 **The Casamance region** in the south has been troubled for many years by groups who are, at times, separatists, but often mere bandits. The Casamance is separated from most of Senegal by geography (separated by Gambia), ethnic composition (Jola-dominated as opposed to Wolof) and even religion (significantly more animist and Christian sentiment in the south). Pray for long-term stability and peace as well as for sustained Christian ministry – these are often disrupted by sporadic violence.

4 **The largest Christian communities** are among the Serer, Jola, Bassari and Cape Verdean peoples. Most are nominally Catholic and from a non-Muslim background. Their influence is disproportionately great through their input into health services and education.

S

Their lifestyle, however, often brings no credit to the cause of Christ, for few know real freedom in Jesus and victory over the powers of darkness. Sadly, Muslims often refer to Christians as "those who drink" rather than those who follow Christ.

5 **Evangelical believers are few.** Their growth rate is slow, and only among the Serer (FLM, **AoG**), Bassari (**AoG**), Balanta (**WEC, AoG, NTM**) and Jola (**WEC, IMB, CAPRO**) has there been any significant church planting. But members of the fledgling Church are growing confident about their identity in Christ and as evangelicals in Senegal. Pray that the Church will take hold of its identity in Christ and powerfully demonstrate its outworking to the nation.

6 **Christian training** is increasingly available for leaders and grass-roots members. Only around 120 nationals serve as pastors or in home missions, but this number is growing. *Institut de Théologie Évangélique du Senegal* (ITES) is a cooperative effort of **WV**, UWM, **MTW**, Brethren and two local churches. There are a few other Bible schools, **YWAM** runs a six-month discipleship course and the West African Theological Institute (WATI) provides modular pastoral training – just three of several training expressions available. Pray for God to use these to raise up increasing numbers of dynamic and well-prepared evangelists, pastors and Christian leaders.

7 **Mission activity in Senegal** is changing significantly. Increasingly, workers and agencies arrive from Latin America and Africa to join the work of older and established missions such as **NTM, WEC, YWAM, SIM**, UWM, **IMB** and Finnish Lutherans. In 1936, **WEC** entered the Casamance among the Fulbe, in the 1950s among the Jola and Balanta and later the predominantly Muslim Senegal River Valley in the north. Today, over 50 church planting missions serve under the *Fraternité Évangélique du Senegal*. SIL is an important presence, providing help in literacy, linguistic research and Bible translation in many language groups. Mission Inter-Senegal, a national mission organization, trains Senegalese evangelists and church planters to reach their own nation. Pray that many would answer the mission call and take advantage of the open doors of this increasingly Muslim nation.

8 **Dakar, the capital,** is the most strategic location for evangelizing the entire country. It hosts over 25% of the nation's population as well as representatives of every ethnic group. From 15 evangelical groups meeting in 1990, there are over 60 today. But while Dakar itself is blessed with many congregations, the outlying areas have only a few small churches – for the nearly three million dwelling there. Dakar is the mission base for most agencies, but only a few missionaries are actually committed to church planting there. Pray for this city to become a source of gospel light for the whole country.

9 **Young people.** Of Senegal's population, 55% are under age 20. Many of these are children in crisis; ministry among them is growing – drop-in centres, vocational training and others. The younger generation, often less committed to "formal religion", are thereby more open to the gospel. An increasing number of ministries are focusing on reaching young people. Pray especially for:

a) *Students.* The small GBUSS/**IFES** group in Dakar is fervent; many of its members are non-Senegalese, but nationals are an increasing proportion. Lack of employment opportunities, poor economic conditions, political instability and no real hope for the future are disincentives for this growing section of the population. Pray that the God of the Bible could be that source of hope for young people with so much potential. Language clubs are opportunities to reach out to students. Pray for many such clubs to start and grow.

b) *The 100,000* **Talibés** (literally, "a person in need of something" and often known as "tin-can boys") are children sent from their homes – due to poverty and religious sentiment – to live and study the Qur'an with religious *marabouts*. The *marabouts* in turn send the boys to beg in the streets for food and money. These *talibé* live in tight quarters and are often neglected and in poor health. Pray for an increase in the work of **WEC, IMB, CMA** and others working with them. Pray also for God to raise up more ministry to the 30,000 street children in Dakar alone and 400,000 children at risk generally.

10 **Unreached peoples.** Pray for strong churches to be planted among the:

a) *Wolof* and the Lebu sub-group, resolutely Muslim despite much and varied outreach from the **AoG**, **WV**, **IMB**, Brethren, **WEC**, **SIM**, Mennonites and others; results are meagre.

Though only around 100 believers and the beginnings of a few congregations exist, a change is occurring. A raft of Christian resources, including the NT in Wolof, audio Scripture, the JESUS film, Christian radio, Wolof worship music and more, along with increased workers – both expat and national – give more opportunities than ever for the Wolof to know Jesus. Pray for the underlying Spiritism that binds many to be broken, and for the birth of an indigenous Wolof Church.

b) Fulbe – including the Fulakunda, Tukulor and Fulba Jeeri – largely a pastoral people. Many are nomadic, which presents a great missiological challenge to those seeking to plant churches. Almost all are at least nominally Muslim, and the Tukulour consider themselves the progenitors and defenders of Islam in Senegal. The Lutherans work among the northern Fulbe. **WEC** works in the Casamance, where there are two small congregations. The Tukulor NT was published in 1998 and the Fulakunda NT in 2000. Partnerships to reach these peoples are emerging, and the number of believers, while still tiny, is increasing.

c) Jola, speaking 13 major dialects and languages – only five of them have any Scripture at all. Islam is more prevalent in the north of their area, but all are bound by fetishism. There are now more than 15 Jola-led congregations and fellowships (**WEC**, **CAPRO**, **IMB** and others). The Jola Kasa NT was published in 2009.

d) Maures. All are Muslim, with only a few known believers. The majority live in inaccessible Mauritania, though many can be reached in the Senegal River Valley. There are weekly broadcasts of Scripture readings on several radio programmes in the Hassaniya language.

e) Malinke peoples, mostly in the south, include the Mandinka, Maninka, Jahanka, Kassonke and Yalunka. Almost all are Muslim with folk practices; the *marabouts* are highly influential among these peoples. Several mission agencies work among them; the NT, the JESUS film and many audio and written gospel materials exist for the Malinke.

f) Other significant peoples who number among the largest and least evangelized include the Soninke (Pioneers, **WEC**, Korean Methodists), Serer-Safi, Manjaco (**NTM**) and Susu. **NTM** also works among many of the smaller tribes in the south, several of whom are animistic or nominally Muslim.

g) Illegal emigrants, while not strictly a people, are a group worthy of prayer. Every year, thousands attempt the dangerous sea voyage to the Canary Islands in hope of finding work and a new life in Europe. Some die at sea or are repatriated; those who make it often find a hard and lonely life. Numbers are dropping due to increased vigilance by Spanish and other naval forces. Pray for compassionate ministry to those in Spain and that, in their new situation, they would be open to the gospel.

11 **Bible translation.** Much has been achieved in the last 25 years. At least seven long-awaited NTs are published, namely Wolof, Serer, Mandinka, Tukulor, Fulakunda, Jola Kasa and Bassari. Work is underway on 17 other translations, with several teams being led by Senegalese. Pray especially for work on several Jola languages (**WEC**, **WBT**). The Wolof OT is being translated. Just as vital is the work in literacy training – translations without readers are useless. Pray for the Scripture translation teams, and for widespread distribution of and response to the Scriptures.

12 **Specialist Christian ministries** for prayer:

a) Literature. Several agencies seek to publish and distribute affordable French Christian literature (SU, Lutherans, SBIS and others). Reading rooms are a helpful means of outreach to young urban Senegalese. Pray for meaningful conversations with enquirers. Pray for the publication and distribution of effective Christian literature.

b) Audio resources, in a predominantly oral culture, are extremely useful. **GRN** has recordings available in 36 language groupings. Scripture on tape is particularly effective for the Wolof and Serer.

c) The JESUS film is widely used in 12 languages with three more in progress.

d) Christian radio programmes can be broadcast on national and local stations. Pray that churches and missions make full use of this medium (**IMB**, **WEC**, Brethren). FEBA, **TWR** and IBRA broadcast three hours per week in Wolof and Pulaar (Fula).

Serbia

Republic of Serbia

Europe

(All statistics include Kosovo unless otherwise stated.)

Geography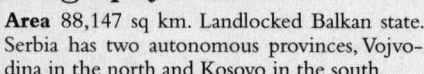

Area 88,147 sq km. Landlocked Balkan state. Serbia has two autonomous provinces, Vojvodina in the north and Kosovo in the south.

Population		Ann Gr	Density
2010	7,771,633	-0.22%	76/sq km
2020	7,686,436	-0.12%	75/sq km
2030	7,561,877	-0.17%	74/sq km

Capital Belgrade 1,117,200. Belgrade has been destroyed and rebuilt 40 times in its history. **Urbanites** 52.4%. **Pop under 15 yrs** 18%. **Life expectancy** 73.9 yrs.

Peoples

(Does not include Kosovo.)
Slavic 89.6%. Serb 82.9%; Bosnian 1.8%; Croat 0.9%; Montenegrin 0.9%; Slovak 0.8%.
Other 10.4%. Hungarian 3.9%; Romani(3) 2.0%; Albanian 0.8%; Romanian 0.5%.
Official language Serbian. **All languages** 21. **Indigenous languages** 14. **Languages with Scriptures** 6Bi 1NT 2por 3w.i.p.

Economy

Poorly served by 45 years of Communism. The breakup of the larger Yugoslav entity in 1991 and ensuing Balkan wars led to UN trade sanctions and NATO military intervention. The economy has grown rapidly since Milosevic was deposed, but as of 2009 had not yet surpassed the 1990 GDP levels.
HDI Rank 67th/182. **Public debt** 37% of GDP. **Income/person** $6,782 (14% of USA).

Politics

Since its defeat to the Turks in Kosovo in 1389, Serbia has rarely been an independent nation, ruled by the Ottomans and then by Austria-Hungary. Ethnic nationalism in the region helped trigger WWI and provoke genocidal civil war during WWII. Pan-Yugoslavian Communism imposed by Tito in 1945 suppressed ethnic hatred between Serb and Croat, and Serb and Albanian. Tito's death in 1980, however, exposed the nation's festering wounds, and Yugoslavia began to unravel. Secessions followed in 1991 and war broke out in 1992. Serbia fought with Croatia and Bosnia in order to link Serbian enclaves in Bosnia and Croatia to the Serbian Republic. (Tito deliberately drew borders to create such destabilizing minorities in each republic, fostering dependence on the central state mechanism.) The nationalism and greed of President Milosevic and his cohorts were major contributory factors to the violence and "ethnic cleansing" that brought the world's condemnation. Repression of Albanians in the Kosovo region led to NATO's military intervention in 1999 followed by UN governance. After popular protests, Milosevic was ousted in 2000 and relationships with the world began to normalize. A parliamentary democracy.

Religion

Strong links between ethnicity and religion have exacerbated tensions in the Balkans for centuries. Constitutionally, there is freedom of religion, but with preferential treatment accorded to the Orthodox Church. A controversial religion law makes registration and activity by non-traditional religious groups very difficult. Frequent occurrences of sectarian-motivated violence and arson against non-Serbian Orthodox.

Religions	Pop %	Population	Ann Gr
Christian	80.37	6,246,061	-0.3%
Muslim	16.10	1,251,233	0.2%
Non-religious	3.51	272,784	0.3%
Jewish	0.02	1,554	-0.2%

Christians Denoms		Pop %	Affiliates	Ann Gr
Protestant	59	1.42	110,000	0.1%
Independent	18	0.24	19,000	4.8%
Anglican	1	<0.01	<200	0.0%
Catholic	2	5.00	388,000	-1.0%
Orthodox	6	73.72	5,729,000	-0.3%
Marginal	1	0.08	6,000	-0.3%

Churches	MegaBloc	Congs	Members	Affiliates
Serbian Orthodox	O	1,907	3,910,345	5,670,000
Roman Catholic	C	165	256,552	372,000
Romanian Orthodox	O	24	23,500	47,000
Slovak Ev Chr Ch (Luth)	P	57	31,469	45,000
Reformed Church of S	P	20	6,680	16,700
Catholic (Byzantine)	C	9	4,459	16,500
Evang Ch (Pente)	P	96	8,000	11,000
Seventh-day Adventist	P	175	7,500	9,300
Gypsy Evang Movement	I	17	2,560	6,400
Jehovah's Witnesses	M	44	3,920	5,958
CoN Community	P	3	1,880	4,700

Evang Ch in S (Luth)	P	8	2,250	4,500
Baptist Union	P	55	2,200	4,000
Church of the Spirit	I	6	1,000	2,000
Other denominations[70]		200	16,526	31,071
Total Christians[87]		**2,765**	**4,278,841**	**6,246,129**

TransBloc	Pop %	Population	Ann Gr
Evangelicals			
Evangelicals	0.6	45,580	1.8%
Renewalists			
Charismatics	0.4	30,233	1.9%
Pentecostals	0.3	21,370	1.5%

Religions % of Total Pop

Annual Growth Rates

Challenges for Prayer

1 **Serbia is a nation with a public relations problem.** It sees itself as defender of Europe and the Christian faith against Muslim aggression, as misunderstood and betrayed by the rest of Christendom and as victim of a propaganda war. Conversely, much of the world perceives Serbia as a war-mongering, hyper-nationalist power guilty of ethnic cleansing and atrocities, and as a perpetrator of ethnoreligious hatred. Both views have some justification. A long history of victimization by other nations (Turks, Austrians, Germans, Croats and others) has left a legacy of bitterness. Pray for the healing and redemptive transformation of Serbian identity; a mighty work of God is necessary for this to happen.

2 **The Balkan Wars** left a range of unresolved issues: the devastated economy, a fragile democracy, and poor relations with neighbouring countries and treatment of minority groups (including in Kosovo). Resolutions must be found, but a stubborn government and entrenched ethnocentrism in the main faith groups (Orthodoxy, Islam and Catholicism) make political and religious structures part of the problem. Pray that the tiny evangelical community – the only body that has retained multi-cultural fellowships – might prove a catalyst for good.

3 **The Serbian Orthodox Church** seeks to regain great influence over national life – it has suppressed other Orthodox churches serving ethnic minorities (Romanians, Macedonians and Montenegrins) and pushed for a harsh and self-serving religion law that entrenches mono-ethnic religious groups. Pray for new life within this ancient Church, and that it may turn its back on totalitarian instincts and support true religious freedom.

4 **Protestantism has a long history** among Hungarian and Slovak minorities in Vojvodina but little impact on Serbs and Albanians. Perhaps half of the believers in Serbia are actually ethnic Serbs. Protestants number 110,000, but much nominalism exists in Lutheran and Reformed congregations. Pray for revival that frees churches from empty tradition and enables their effective witness.

5 **Evangelical believers in Serbia** face many difficulties. For new religious groups – such as most evangelicals – the new religion law makes operating very difficult. Non-Serbian Orthodox buildings are increasingly attacked. Evangelicals are often viewed as a sect, even as traitors, by any mono-religious ethnicity. Despite this, newer churches are growing and engaging in many forms of ministry. Crucial issues for prayer include:

a) Leadership training is limited, and poverty hinders the flow of people into ministry. There are now two Bible schools, the Belgrade Bible School (Brethren and Baptist) and the newer Novi Sad Theological College. Also, Project Timothy serves all evangelical churches in leadership and church development.

b) Cooperation in outreach and church planting. Unity is essential amid the divisions in Serbia, especially given the relatively small number of evangelicals.

6 **Outreach challenges.** Pray specifically for:

a) Compassionate ministry to war refugees from the former Yugoslavia – millions were uprooted and became refugees or internally displaced. Few have returned to their original homes due to further balkanization of ethnic groups. Inevitably, trauma and disillusionment will open hearts to sensitive Christian ministry. Many organizations, indigenous and foreign (Bread of Life, Eurovangelism, MCC), share Jesus' love through practical aid – and they see responsiveness.

b) *Young people* are the most responsive, having seen the destruction wrought by their parents' generation.

   i *Children.* **CEF** and others actively reach out to children and train national Christians to do the same.

   ii *Students.* EUS(**IFES**) has groups on most campuses in Belgrade, Nis and Novi Sad. There is a vision to extend ministry to other areas for student witness. Camps, conferences and seminars train and equip Christians to share the good news effectively. Alpha and Omega is the publishing arm of EUS.

   iii *Addicts.* A growing trend. Through shelters and Christ-centred rehabilitation, Teen Challenge Serbia ministers to young men and women suffering from drug abuse.

7 **Christian mission agencies** find it hard to establish long-term ministry. Pray that openings may increase and long-term workers be called; pray that every part of the country be reached. Significant agencies involved are **ECM**, **GEM** and **IMB**.

8 **Many Serbians moved,** as war or economic refugees, to other parts of Europe, North America and Australia. Pray for effective outreach to Serbs and others in Germany, Austria, Switzerland, Sweden, France and elsewhere; far too often they carry their troubles with them to other lands.

9 **The Romani people** are very responsive to the gospel. Their total population is unknown but may number as many as 200,000. Romani denominations, such as the Protestant Evangelical Church, have the fastest growing churches in Serbia and enjoy a cultural expression that resonates strongly with the Romani people. Their spiritual growth is matched only by their material needs – they are uniformly the poorest ethnic group. Pray for lasting fruit in these churches and for evangelization of the entire Romani people.

10 **Christian media ministries:**

a) *The Alpha Course* is a new means of reaching people in Serbia. Pray that it might have the same impact here as elsewhere in the world.

b) *Christian radio ministries.* **TWR** Serbia broadcasts locally-produced programmes in Serbian (5 hours/week) as well as in Macedonian, Bosnian and Romani languages. Studios for further production of Romani and Serbian programmes are valuable resources. Romani-language Christian programming airs on five FM stations, with more planned for the future.

c) *Internet radio* (**TWR**) and Serb-language websites serve not just Serbia but also the whole Serbian diaspora.

KOSOVO

Europe

Geography

Area 10,912 sq km. A rugged mountainous region in the central Balkans with a continental climate.

Population		Ann Gr	Density
2010	2,084,224	0.84%	191/sq km
2020	2,096,100	0.02%	192/sq km
2030	2,082,100	-0.09%	191/sq km

Capital Pristina 183,000.

Peoples

Albanian 88%.
Serb 7%. As many as 250,000 ethnic Serbs (12% of Kosovo's population).

Other 5%. Bosniak 1.9%; Romani 1.7%; Turk 1.0%.
Official languages Albanian, Serbian, English.

Economy

One of the weakest economies in Europe. Even during the Yugoslav era, Kosovo depended on external subsidies from other Yugoslav republics. Sanctions, poor policies, damage from military conflict, weak trade links, organized crime and corruption all make growth quite difficult. About 50% of the economy is derived from foreign aid and remittances from Kosovars abroad.

Politics

Officially a province of Serbia, Kosovo is in reality still occupied by NATO forces and administered by the UN – a result of rebellion by the Kosovo Liberation Army (KLA), an ethnic

S

Albanian guerrilla army fighting against Serbian rule. Both sides committed atrocities, but the KLA morphed into a police force and its leader into the province's leader. Although demographically dominated by Albanians, Kosovo will not be willingly granted independence by Serbia, largely because of Serbia's defeat by the Turks in Kosovo in 1389 and because Kosovo is the cradle of Serb culture. High-level talks sponsored by the UN are unfruitful in the face of Serb intransigence, but independence would simply create an extremely fragile and vulnerable state.

Religion

Ethnicity and religion are closely tied; Muslim Kosovars deeply resent the Christianity of their Serb occupiers of the last five centuries. Religious violence damaged many sites (almost exclusively Christian), and NATO forces are dispatched to protect them.

Religious populations (estimated): Muslim 80%; Christian 10% (Orthodox 6%; Catholic 4%; Protestant 0.1%); Non-religious 10%.

Challenges for Prayer

1 Kosovo's future is uncertain and gloomy. Ancient enmity between Serbs and ethnic Albanians in Kosovo precipitated the crisis of 1998-1999. Peace remains fragile, and the restoration of this region is a distant hope. Pray that communal hatreds might be resolved and lasting peace, not dependent on foreign military forces, be established; the process surrounding independence is a highly charged issue.

2 Restoration is hardly the right word to describe the needs of a region depressed and underdeveloped even before the war. The economy is actually shrinking, unemployment is at 70%, internal politics are divided and organized crime/smuggling syndicates are the main beneficiaries of this chaos. Pray for a growing economy that provides stability and honest gainful employment. Pray for the suppression of those exploiting the difficulties for personal gain.

3 The Kosovar Albanian population is mostly Muslim, but there are some Christians. Many Kosovars are quite nominally Muslim, but extremism is on the rise. Large financial injections from Saudi Arabia and Iran come with strings attached that pull Kosovo toward more radical forms of Islam. While hundreds of mosques have been erected using this money, hundreds of Christian sites have been damaged or destroyed by angry mobs. Pray that religious hatred might be quelled, and that Muslims would see beyond ethno-religious hatred to Jesus, to whom they are precious.

4 The evangelical Church is very small but growing. From around 80 believers at the outbreak of war in 1998, there are now over 2,000, mostly young men and teens (often, girls are forced to keep their faith secret). Churches mushroomed with the foreign humanitarian presence, but several have since closed; there are now about 35 evangelical churches, and they are quite evangelistic in their outlook. The formation of an evangelical alliance (Evangelical Movement of Kosovo) and the recognition of evangelicals as one of Kosovo's five faith communities are both answers to prayer. Pray for unity among believers and continued growth in numbers and spiritual maturity.

5 Ministries in Kosovo find work difficult, but fruitful. **OM, BMS, CMA, ECM,** the Brethren and several others are active. Work with children and young adults sees a lot of response. Discipleship and leadership development are crucial works in Kosovo. More male workers are needed. Pray that expatriate groups would retain the freedom to work in this predominantly Muslim land, and that they might use opportunities wisely and well.

S

Seychelles

Republic of Seychelles

Africa

Politics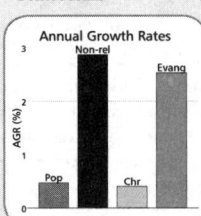

French colony 1756–1814, then British-ruled until independence in 1976. The coup of 1977 resulted in a one-party socialist government. The end of the Cold War and resulting foreign aid finally brought about a multiparty election in 1992, wherein the dictator became the president. Recent political troubles and demonstrations plague his successor, elected in 2006.

Religion

Religious freedom, and good relationships among the various groups.

Religions	Pop %	Population	Ann Gr
Christian	96.09	81,292	0.4%
Non-religious	2.70	2,284	2.9%
Hindu	0.46	389	0.0%
Baha'i	0.32	271	1.8%
Muslim	0.22	186	2.4%
Buddhist	0.21	178	1.5%

Christians	Denoms	Pop %	Affiliates	Ann Gr
Protestant	5	3.31	3,000	2.6%
Independent	4	0.67	1,000	9.3%
Anglican	1	6.32	5,000	0.1%
Catholic	1	84.99	72,000	0.5%
Marginal	1	0.69	1,000	3.4%
Unaffiliated		0.11	<200	

Churches	MegaBloc	Congs	Members	Affiliates
Catholic Church	C	17	42,544	71,900
Anglican Church	A	11	2,034	5,350
Seventh-day Adventist	P	15	539	900
Evangelical Church	P	2	539	830
Pentecostal Church	P	4	457	800
Jehovah's Witnesses	M	4	290	580
Other churches	I	7	250	500
Other denominations[3]		6	115	342
Total Christians[12]		**66**	**46,768**	**81,202**

TransBloc	Pop %	Population	Ann Gr
Evangelicals			
Evangelicals	5.9	4,959	2.5%
Renewalists			
Charismatics	6.5	5,534	3.2%
Pentecostals	1.2	1,000	3.3%

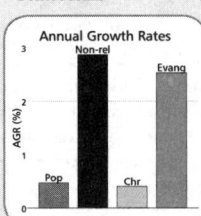

Annual Growth Rates

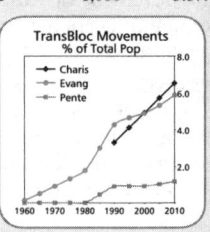

TransBloc Movements
% of Total Pop

Geography

Area 453 sq km. A group of 92 granite and coral islands spread across 400,000 sq km of the Indian Ocean; 1,600 km east of Kenya.

Population		Ann Gr	Density
2010	84,600	0.47%	187/sq km
2020	88,707	0.65%	196/sq km
2030	93,272	0.46%	206/sq km

Capital Victoria 26,400. **Urbanites** 55.3%. **Pop under 15 yrs** 24%. **Life expectancy** 72.3 yrs.

Peoples

Creole 94.7%. Predominantly of African, European and some Asian origin.
Asian 1.1%. Chinese, Hindi, Gujarati, Tamil.
African 0.3%. Réunionese, Swahili.
European 3.9%. British, French.
Literacy 92%. **Official languages** French, English and Seselwa (a French Creole). **All languages** 3, but 90% use Seselwa as their first language. **Languages with Scriptures** 2Bi 1NT 1por.

Economy

Tourism and fishing are foundations of the economy. Quite stable and wealthy for an African country, but unsustainably high levels of public debt and a freeze on currency export undermine this.
HDI Rank 57th/182. **Public debt** 74.2% of GDP. **Income/person** $9,640 (20% of USA).

S

Challenges for Prayer

1 **The vast majority of Seychellois claim to be Christian,** but evidence of true spiritual transformation seems outweighed by superstition and nominalism. *Gris-gris*, a voodoo-like African spiritism based on black magic and herbalism, permeates the lives of Christians.

Despite the disapproval of religious leaders, most Seychellois remain happy to mix religion into this dangerous cocktail. Pray that the Holy Spirit may bring new life evidenced by repentance and sustained fruit.

2 **Relationships among churches** are generally positive, but there is in some areas a lack of unity. The process of translating the Bible into Seselwa is helping relationships. Pray for renewal across all denominations, rather than mere opportunities for cooperation.

3 **Evangelical vision is growing.** Despite being small in number (only 2,000 regularly attend an evangelical church), evangelicals in Seychelles have a large vision. All evangelical groups share the goal of saturation church planting throughout the country. Pray for this vision to have a powerful and positive impact on the spiritual life of the nation.

4 **Less reached peoples:**

a) The outer and less-populated islands are isolated and have had little challenge to make a personal commitment to Christ.

b) The small Buddhist, Hindu and Muslim communities need loving outreach from believers who demonstrate the true gospel.

5 **The vernacular of Seselwa has a translated NT,** but the shelves are empty – financial troubles and the inability to exchange local currency means a shortfall of NTs and all Christian literature. There is an OT translation team in place. Pray for a solution that enables Seychellois to have access to Scripture and materials, and that these will have an impact on their spiritual life.

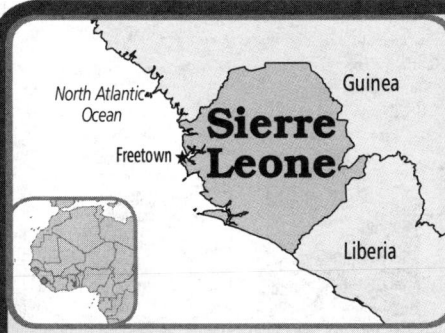

Sierra Leone

Republic of
Sierra Leone

Africa

Geography

Area 71,740 sq km. Small coastal state between Guinea and Liberia.

Population		Ann Gr	Density
2010	5,835,664	2.70%	81/sq km
2020	7,317,803	2.22%	102/sq km
2030	8,943,117	1.97%	125/sq km

Capital Freetown 900,847. **Urbanites** 38.4%.
Pop under 15 yrs 43%. **Life expectancy** 47.3 yrs.

Peoples

Atlantic(11) 38.4%. Temne 23.8%; Limba 5.9%; Sherbro 3.4%; Kissi 3.0%.
Mande(4) 32.1%. Mende 24.6%; Kono 4.2%; Loko 2.9%.
Krio (Creole) 11.4%. Descendants of released slaves and detribalized urbanites.
Malinke(3) 8.3%. Kuranko 5.5%; Mandingo 2.2%.
Fulbe(2) 4.8%. Fula Jalon 3.7%; Krio Fulani 1.0%.
Susu 3.2%.
Other 1.8%. Other Africans, South Asians, Westerners, Lebanese.
Literacy 39%. **Official language** English.
Trade language Krio (Creole), spoken by 10% of the population as first language and 90% as second. **All languages** 26. **Languages with Scriptures** 2Bi 14NT 15por 4w.i.p.

Economy

Rich in natural resources – diamonds, gold, titanium, iron ore, cocoa, coffee, fish and others. The descent into anarchy caused the economy to collapse, and Sierra Leone became possibly the most desperate country on earth. Since 2002, order has slowly taken hold, but huge infusions of outside aid are needed to prop up the state. If its greatest obstacles – corruption and the need to rebuild its entire infrastructure – can be overcome, the country can become a prosperous one. The vast wealth of the diamond fields was contested by rebels and mercenaries during the conflict, but restored order has greatly decreased smuggling and increased legitimate diamond exports, offering much needed income into state

S

coffers. Poverty is still widespread, and unemployment can run as high as 80%. Two-thirds of the population engage in subsistence agriculture. **HDI Rank** 180th/182. **Public debt** 156% of GDP. **Income/person** $332 (1% of USA).

Politics 🗡

Founded as a home for freed slaves in 1797. Independent from Britain in 1961. The violence of the Liberian civil war in 1990 spilled over and triggered government collapse. A series of military coups and guerrilla wars (spearheaded by the AFRC and RUF in particular) ensued over efforts to control the lucrative diamond fields in the southeast part of the country. Sierra Leone ceased to function as a viable state, and anarchy reigned in much of the country. Involvement by Nigeria/ECOMOG, the Organization of African States (OAS) and the UN proved ineffective. Intervention by the British military eventually defeated the rebel forces. Since 2002, democracy has prevailed with several successful and peaceful elections. Government priorities have moved from peacebuilding – disarming former rebels and establishing the Truth and Reconciliation Commission – to combating corruption, poverty and joblessness.

Religion ⛪

Freedom of religion. Islam steadily increases in influence, but the power of ethnic religions, the occult, secret societies and Freemasonry permeates the practice of both Islam and Christianity.

Religions	Pop %	Population	Ann Gr
Muslim	63.00	3,676,468	4.1%
Ethnoreligionist	23.31	1,360,293	-0.8%
Christian	13.15	769,390	3.1%
Non-religious	0.50	29,178	7.4%
Hindu	0.04	2,334	2.7%

Some reports from credible sources put Christianity as high as 30%, but this number is impossible to substantiate.

Christians	Denoms	Pop %	Affiliates	Ann Gr
Protestant	29	5.94	347,000	3.8%
Independent	60	2.80	163,000	2.2%
Anglican	1	0.44	26,000	0.5%
Catholic	1	3.68	215,000	2.9%
Orthodox	1	0.01	1,000	11.8%
Marginal	2	0.28	16,000	6.7%

Churches	MegaBloc	Congs	Members	Affiliates
Catholic Church	C	1,488	125,000	215,000
United Methodist Ch	P	529	119,048	125,000
Methodist Church of SL	P	335	23,110	39,750
Wesleyan Church of SL	P	276	12,141	38,000
Seventh-day Adventist	P	55	19,500	27,885
Anglican Church	A	53	13,333	25,600
Baptist Convention	P	125	10,500	22,000
United Bre in Christ	P	105	11,000	22,000
Assemblies of God	P	130	8,000	16,800
National Pentecostal Ch	I	30	8,982	15,000
Evang Lutheran Ch	P	53	3,422	9,000
Other denominations[83]		1,327	108,556	213,473
Total Christians[94]		**4,506**	**462,592**	**769,508**

TransBloc	Pop %	Population	Ann Gr
Evangelicals			
Evangelicals	3.9	229,366	4.0%
Renewalists			
Charismatics	3.9	226,366	3.0%
Pentecostals	1.6	91,138	4.0%

Religions % of Total Pop

MegaBlocs % of Christian Pop

Answers to Prayer

1 **The nation is moving forward** from its tragic recent history. The successful election of a new government can now build on the peace restored in the last few years. The presence of British military and then UN peacekeepers helped end the conflict and move Sierra Leone into a new era. Thank God for the end of 11 years of madness that claimed up to 100,000 lives, maimed many thousands and scarred most of the population in one way or another.

2 **Christian ministries are actively involved** in rebuilding the country. Most organizations are engaged in holistic ministry to meet the spiritual, physical and psychological/emotional needs of the people. This approach is most appropriate and sees notable fruit on all levels.

Challenges for Prayer

1 **The end of the conflict does not guarantee wholeness** for Sierra Leone. Many threats to peace remain, corruption being the greatest – a significant minority of diamond mining still occurs illegally. Food security is another major issue. The Truth and Reconciliation

Commission enables many ex-combatants to reintegrate into their communities; this is a point for praise. Yet, the conditions that led them to fight in the first place persist today. Peace prevails but is still fragile. Most people long for safety, stability, food, work and honesty from those in power. Pray that these expectations might be met and give no cause for further violence.

2 **Sierra Leone remains a land of suffering.** The people are still mired in desperate poverty, most surviving on less than a dollar a day. It has ranked as the world's poorest country for most of the last 10 years. With the highest infant and maternal mortality rates in the world and widespread disease (malaria, HIV, others), life expectancy is age 47 and not rising. Much work remains to ease the suffering of these who have already endured so much. Pray for more attention from the worldwide community – especially from Christians – to address these needs.

3 **Secret societies and their occult influence** shape the country profoundly. This spiritual evil lies behind the greed and cruelty of Sierra Leone's darkest times, and is now at the heart of spiritual and social opposition to education, anti-corruption measures and the empowerment of women. Many Christians compromised their spiritual purity, resulting in the disempowerment of the Church. Pray that these dark powers may be bound and the influence of secret societies broken. Pray that Christians will live lives of faith, depending on Jesus alone for provision, protection and power.

4 **Sierra Leone was the first West African country to be evangelized.** The first Protestant Church started in Freetown, among freed slaves, in 1785. Yet after over 200 years of effort, only 13% of the country claim to be Christian. Very few historic denominations have grown significantly in the last 40 years or made a lasting impact on the country. The newer, more dynamic groups tend to be spiritually shallow and overly focused on prosperity teaching and miracles. Pray for churches that balance the Word and the Spirit, for hearts of unity and prayer and for a deep desire to reach out in loving witness to the non-Christian majority.

5 **Effective Christian ministry is crucial** for a Church and a nation with many pressing needs. Rebuilding and restoring people, congregations, buildings and organizations will require great commitment, wisdom and generosity. Pray for:

a) *The Evangelical Fellowship of Sierra Leone,* a focal point for cooperation, vision and ministry for many agencies and denominations. Its goals are to unite, mobilize and strengthen the Church, to be a public voice for evangelicals and to provide humanitarian services for those in need.

b) *Few churches are equipped to minister* to present humanitarian needs. Pray for the Holy Spirit to gift and empower many to minister in this area and to enable victims to become effective disciples. Pray also for humanitarian aid agencies that seek to alleviate suffering (WVI, Tearfund, World Relief and many others). Pray for effective partnerships among local churches and the many Christian NGOs doing excellent work in the country.

c) *Ministering to casualties of war.* Churches must be places of compassion, forgiveness and healing for the many who endured – or committed – atrocities. These include many orphans, those forced to become child soldiers or slaves of rebels, victims of amputation, mutilation or rape, those suffering mental trauma from their experiences and those who perpetrated such acts. Such ministry is very demanding and draining but also rewarding and essential. Pray for NGOs involved in this work; pray also for churches to gain vision and training for such ministry.

6 **The lack of spiritual and biblically trained leadership** is critical; disruption from the conflict crippled theological education. Seminaries and colleges are run by Catholics, Anglicans and Methodists (Sierra Leone Theological College), Wesleyans and Baptists (The Evangelical College of Theology), **AoG**, Nazarenes and others such as the Travelling Bible School (**UFM**) and Bible Training Centers for Pastors. Many pastors lack even a secondary school education, let alone formalized theological degrees. Beyond theology, pastors need to be equipped in counselling, spiritual warfare and ministry to the poor and disabled. Finances and even educational resources are in short supply. Pray for the provision of staff, students, books, facilities and operation expenses for this most strategic of needs.

7 **Young people's ministry** has never been more crucial and needs to be expanded. SU and **YFC** impact the more educated. SLEFES(**IFES**) has 34 groups with over 3,500 students served by nine full-time staff. Pray that Christian graduates may decisively impact the nation. Beyond student ministry, many children remain in difficult situations. Rainbows of Hope and other ministries work with youth prisons, children of prostitutes, disabled children and other groups of children at risk.

8 **The fallout from the conflict remains** – the human suffering of survivors. Pray for the following groups:

a) *Those with emotional and psychological trauma* from their experiences. This could include the majority of the population, but especially those who suffered rape. Proper trauma counselling and Christian love can see these wounds healed, but much remains to be done in ministry and especially in training people to minister to these needs.

b) *Victims of mutilation and maiming.* Sierra Leone's conflict was particularly noted for amputation of hands, arms and feet – for no reason other than pure cruelty and evil. Those who survived such treatment need loving acceptance and integration into normal society as well as vocational training for future employment.

c) *Former child soldiers.* Over 10,000 fought in the conflict, enduring as well as inflicting much suffering. The stigma associated with this role makes their reintegration very difficult. As they grow into men, they remain troubled and troublesome, knowing no life other than one of crime and violence. Pray for ministries that will reach out to these and provide opportunities for them to live whole and wholesome lives.

9 **The challenge of the unfinished task.** The pride and attitude of superiority shown by the Krio "Christian" population, and the continued growth of Islam, have limited church growth in the tribal hinterland. Most outreach is to animists, even though Muslims have shown responsiveness to the good news. Pray for:

a) *The Muslim peoples.* During the 20th Century, Islam grew from 10% to over 60% of the population. Islam's recent increase in influence is in part thanks to UN peacekeeping forces. Troops from Bangladesh, Pakistan and India erected mosques wherever they were stationed. Other Muslim countries sent missionaries to further Islamize the nation. Islam and Christianity enjoyed peaceful relations until now. Pray that Christian witness to Muslims might be clear and bold, but be done with sensitivity and humility. The Fula Jalon, Krio Fulani, Mandingo, Susu, Temne–Banta, Vai and Yalunka are the least reached, but this is being addressed by a number of agencies working with these groups in neighbouring countries.

b) *The more animistic groups* are more easily won to Christ, but are rapidly being Islamized as well. Christians must show more urgency in reaching them. The Bom, Kuranko, Loko, Northern Kissi and Sherbro are all 5% Christian or less.

10 **Expatriate missions** have ministered for two centuries, but Sierra Leone remains a pioneer field. Much work, wiped out in the conflict, has to be restarted, almost from scratch. Pray for the right ministry strategies for the current context, and for excellent partnering relationships among local Christians and churches. Many workers are needed for rehabilitative and holistic ministries, leadership training and Bible translation. Major foreign agencies involved in ministry include **CCCI**, **GRN**, Lutheran Bible Translators, **UFM**, **AoG** and Methodist and Wesleyan groups. Also, Mercy Ships regularly visit Sierra Leone, providing medical and surgical care as well as partnering with local churches in outreach ministry.

11 **Christian support ministries:**

a) *Bible translation* is a continuing need. Work is underway for four languages, mainly through Lutheran Bible Translators. The Kuranko Bible and Kono NT were recently completed after many disruptions and delays.

b) *Audio resources* are vital for this oral culture that also suffers from low literacy rates. **GRN** has audio resources in 26 languages and dialects. Scripture portions and teachings are also available on specialized, handheld audio devices in Krio, Mende, Kuranko, Themne and other major languages.

c) *Christian radio* is a heavily used and widely trusted source of news and information. Two local Christian FM stations (Believers Broadcasting Network and Radio Trinity) supplement the many hours of shortwave broadcasts from further afield. Although English dominates these broadcasts, programmes in numerous tribal languages also exist.

d) *Christian literature.* **CLC** has two well-used bookstores in Freetown and one in Bo. Pray for the ministry of the written page; such resources are much needed and very valuable in these times of poverty and church growth with so many young Christians. The distribution work of **EHC** and The Bible Society is therefore vital. The EMA-**CLC** Book Aid project of importing second-hand Christian books is a spiritual lifeline.

e) Film and video. The JESUS film is used in 13 languages with a further two in preparation. It has been seen by almost the entire population.

Singapore
Republic of Singapore
Asia

Geography

Area 699 sq km. One larger and 54 smaller islands off the southern tip of Peninsular Malaysia; strategically located for communications and trade. Singapore is Asia's cleanest and greenest city.

Population		Ann Gr	Density
2010	4,836,691	2.54%	7,776/sq km
2020	5,219,377	0.63%	8,391/sq km
2030	5,460,110	0.36%	8,778/sq km

Capital Singapore 4,836,691. **Urbanites** 100%. **Pop under 15 yrs** 16%. **Life expectancy** 80.2 yrs.

Peoples

Multi-racial and multi-lingual society, with 95 racial groups residing in the country. Lower Chinese percentage due to lower birthrates and high immigration of other ethnicities.

Chinese 74.2%. Language origin: Hokkien 20%; Teochew 10%; Cantonese 10%; Hakka 3.5%; Hainanese 3.5%; others.
Malay 13.6%. 11 peoples. Malay 12.9%; Filipino 1.8%; Indonesian 1.1%.
Indian/South Asian 9.2%. 12 peoples. Tamil 4.1%.
Other 3.2%. Thai 1.1%; British 1.0%; Eurasian 1.0%; many Asian ethnicities.
Literacy 100%. **Official languages** Mandarin (Chinese), English, Malay, Tamil Indian. English is the primary language for education. **All languages** 31. **Indigenous languages** 21. **Languages with Scriptures** 16Bi 2NT 2por.

Economy

Post-independence growth to become one of the world's most efficient trading and financial centres. Among the wealthiest countries per capita and with one of the highest standards of living. Heavily export-dependent and increasingly dependent on the employment of foreign nationals in many industries. **HDI Rank** 23rd/182. **Public debt** 99.2% of GDP. **Income/person** $38,972 (82% of USA).

Politics

British rule 1824-1959. Autonomy 1959-63. Part of the Malaysian Federation 1963-65. Independent as a parliamentary democracy in 1965. The strong, paternalistic government of Prime Minister Lee Kuan Yew and his successors (including his son and current prime minister) provides direction and stability for spectacular and sustained economic growth. In return for such stability and affluence, most have accepted the strong influence of government policies and the limitation of certain freedoms.

Religion

Freedom of religion, but the goal of preserving ethnic and religious harmony resulted in legislation against action or speech that would threaten such harmony.

Religions	Pop %	Population	Ann Gr
Buddhist	40.30	1,949,186	1.9%
Non-religious	18.06	873,506	4.2%
Christian	16.04	775,805	3.9%
Muslim	13.90	672,300	1.8%
Chinese	7.00	338,568	0.6%
Hindu	4.10	198,304	2.8%
Sikh	0.50	24,183	2.5%
Baha'i	0.10	4,837	2.5%

Christians	Denoms	Pop %	Affiliates	Ann Gr
Protestant	73	4.58	222,000	2.1%
Independent	91	2.99	145,000	4.7%
Anglican	1	1.12	54,000	2.5%
Catholic	1	3.62	175,000	1.6%
Orthodox	7	0.06	3,000	1.1%
Marginal	12	0.15	7,000	1.4%
Unaffiliated		3.52	170,000	7.2%

Churches	MegaBloc	Congs	Members	Affiliates
Catholic Church	C	31	122,378	175,000
Anglican Church	A	26	21,720	54,300
Methodist Church	P	38	36,253	52,500
Assemblies of God	P	48	24,500	36,500
City Harvest	I	13	12,250	25,600
New Creation Church	I	1	7,200	19,000
Bible Presbyterian	P	31	8,400	18,648

S

Faith Community Bapt	I	10	10,062	16,100
Christian Brethren	P	22	7,250	14,500
Presbyterian Church	P	42	7,967	14,500
Baptist Convention	P	35	7,143	10,000
Other denominations[173]		631	101,748	169,384
Total Christians[185]		**928**	**366,871**	**606,032**

Missionaries from Singapore
P,I,A 693 international, long-term.

TransBloc	Pop %	Population	Ann Gr
Evangelicals			
Evangelicals	7.8	377,398	3.2%
Renewalists			
Charismatics	5.2	250,841	4.2%
Pentecostals	1.1	51,635	2.9%

Religions
% of Total Pop

MegaBlocs
% of Christian Pop

Answers to Prayer

1 **The growth of the Church in Singapore** has been steady and sustained since 1970. Evangelicals in particular increased 20-fold from 1960 to 2010; 1 out of 13 people in Singapore is now evangelical. Independent and charismatic churches represent nearly half of all new churches, and some of them now attract over 20,000 in weekly attendance. Additionally, the mainline churches such as Anglicans, Methodists and Presbyterians have very strong evangelical components and continue to grow.

2 **The responsiveness of the educated continues to be a strong trend.** The perception of Christianity as a progressive belief system, coupled with the positive influence of mission schools and effective campus ministries, draw many of Singapore's educated to the faith. Nearly one-third of English-speaking Chinese university graduates are Christian. As a result, believers have a strong impact on Singaporean society, with great potential for tentmaking missionary service.

3 **Unity among Christians** has moved forward significantly. Denominational reconciliation and cooperation is demonstrated through an impressive host of initiatives. Notable examples are Love Singapore, the Global Day of Prayer, National Day of Thanksgiving, GoForth National Mission Conference, Together in Transformation, the National Prayer Alliance, the National Council of Churches in Singapore and the Evangelical Fellowship of Singapore.

4 **Singapore is now a strategic hub for mission activity** and mission sending. Many regard it as the Antioch of Asia. It is a centre of mission administration and sends out hundreds of long-term missionaries and tentmakers. Every year, mission organizations and local churches mobilize several thousands of believers on short-term mission trips. Many of these are disaster relief and medical missions, drawing on the expertise and training of many Singaporeans.

Challenges for Prayer

1 **Singaporean society** is built on dedicated labour, discipline and self-reliance. These engender stability, good governance and a corruption-resistant culture, but also an emphasis on performance and wealth. Materialism has noticeably increased. Much of Singapore's affluence is now dependent on imported labour from poorer countries; entire sectors of the nation's economy would collapse without it. Pray for justice and fair treatment for all those from abroad; despite good legal safeguards, exploitation does exist. Pray that churches might become more active in assisting those at risk. Pray also that the admirable strengths of Singapore might not in themselves become idols.

2 **The increase of the Church's size and impact** brings challenges. Pray for the following concerns:

a) *Coping with affluence.* There is the threat that believers mistake riches for spirituality and trade discipleship for wealth management. Many young Christians become inactive once they marry and become enmeshed in the materialistic "rat race" for the "five Cs": career, cash, car, club and condo.

S

b) *Spiritual pride* is a constant temptation for such an influential, affluent Church. The same traits of sophistication and success that draw much of cosmopolitan Singapore to Christianity could be the very things that cripple and undermine it. The poor and working classes (heartlanders) are significantly under-reached and marginalized. Pray for urgent correction to this imbalance. Pray for transformed lives inside and out – for humility, continued brokenness and greater dependence on God.

c) *Fear of control and intimidation* in a closely governed and multi-religious society. Legislation against overt proselytism exists, but the only force preventing effective outreach is the Church's own unfounded fears. Pray that Christians would know how to maintain inter-religious harmony without compromising on evangelism.

3 **Strategic issues facing the Church include:**

a) *The family under threat.* Singapore's birthrate is one of Asia's lowest. Many young couples rule out having children to pursue careers instead. The government now offers incentives that promote marriage and family. The challenge is great for Christians to maintain balance of their work, family and church life.

b) *Increasing social concerns* include broken marriages, family violence, elderly poor, dysfunctional youth, depression, issues of sexuality, drug abuse and gambling addiction. The number and types of social-welfare initiatives that minister to the hurting have significantly increased. Pray for more to be done, especially through the local church with its ready pool of volunteers.

c) *Effective Bible and leadership training* for prospective pastors and missionaries. Excellent theological training opportunities abound, such as Singapore Bible College, Trinity Theological College, Theological Centre for Asia, East Asian Theological Seminary, Biblical Graduate School of Theology, Asia Theological Centre for Evangelism and Missions and Chin Lien Bible Seminary. Specific mission-preparation institutions include **YWAM**, Asian Cross-Cultural Training Institute, Discipleship Training Centre, Antioch Missions and Bethany International University. The Haggai Institute provides short-term courses for pastors/Christian workers from around the world, especially Asia and Africa. Many churches run their own theological training programmes. There is, however, an increasing need to balance academic learning with practical training for ministry in the 21st Century. Pray for new initiatives to fill this gap. Pray that continued educational excellence might produce many outstanding pastors, missionaries and theologians for Singapore and for the world.

d) *Young people* remain the most responsive segment of the population. Among undergraduates, about 35% are involved with student ministry of some kind: FES(**IFES**), **CCCI** and Navigators groups, or the growing ministries of some megachurches. But spiritual vitality appears to be cooling as young people face many challenges, such as the high demands of studying and, increasingly, worldly pleasures. Many churches struggle to remain relevant to Singapore's fast-changing youth culture. Pray for the discipling of a new generation with ministry that is relevant, fresh and full of spiritual power.

4 **Singapore's capacity as a mission-sending nation** has grown in leaps and bounds. The Singapore Centre for Global Missions (formerly SCEM) played a catalytic role in unifying and mobilizing the Singaporean mission enterprise. The Fellowship of Missional Organizations of Singapore (FOMOS), an association of several agencies and para-church groups, and the triennial GoForth National Mission Conference also have a notable impact. Many churches have active mission programmes; one outstanding example is Victory Family Centre, which has sent over a thousand short-term missionaries and planted hundreds of churches in 80 nations. Singaporean missionaries serving abroad increased from 140 in 1988 to an estimated 693 in 2010. As many as half of all congregations send missionaries directly to the field. Many others serve with international mission agencies such as **OMF, OM, CCCI, YWAM, WEC**. Pray specifically for:

a) *Strategic impact.* While a formidable number of Singaporeans go on short-term mission trips, usually through their local church, the greater need is for qualified, long-term workers. Singapore retains great potential to train, support and send many outstanding long-term workers into the unevangelized world, but the possibility also exists to reduce their impact to mere "mission tourism" and sponsorship.

b) ***Strong relationships between churches and sending agencies.*** Churches sending missionaries directly can have even greater impact if input from and cooperation with mission agencies can grow. This is thankfully occurring as churches realize the challenges of long-term mission.

5 **Pray for Singapore's less-reached peoples.** The nation is a magnet for people from many unevangelized lands. Over 100 nations are represented in Singapore's population of 1.25 million foreigners. The majority are transient workers engaged in lower end jobs. A tremendous opportunity exists to reach them with the good news.

a) ***The Malay population*** number over 500,000 and are considered Muslim by birth, but there are a growing number of believers in Jesus. The Religious Harmony Act requires great wisdom and sensitivity when sharing Jesus with Muslims, as it seeks to prevent remarks being made or printed which could cause religious enmity. Pray that churches will receive a passion and burden to minister to them. Along with Malays, there are 150,000 Indonesians including the Bugis, Riau and Madurese peoples. Pray that churches gain a passion and burden to reach them.

b) ***The Indian population,*** numbering nearly 400,000, is mostly Tamil by origin. They are predominantly Hindu (over 50%), and about 25% are Muslim. There are a number of lively congregations among Hindu groups of South Asian origin but very little outreach to Muslim groups such as the Gujarati, Sindhi, Hindi and Bengali-speaking communities of North Indian origin. Pray for effective outreach to these groups. There are also growing numbers of Sri Lankans, Bangladeshis and Pakistanis arriving as professionals, students and transient workers in manual labour.

c) ***The Mainland Chinese*** population has grown rapidly to now number over 200,000 (some estimates are much higher). They may locate in Singapore as professionals, students or migrant workers. Some are Christian, but the majority remain unevangelized. A number of churches hold Sunday services especially for Mainland Chinese peoples. They also minister through Bible studies, English language classes and free health screenings. Singapore's ethnic Chinese churches have no excuse not to effectively reach out to these responsive people.

d) ***Migrant workers.*** Numbers have greatly increased, constituting at least 33% of Singapore's workforce, and it is a sensitive issue in Singaporean society. They include large numbers of Indonesians, Filipinos, Burmese, Bangladeshis, Thais, Sri Lankans and Vietnamese. There is ministry to all of these groups; pray for the right strategies, for effective follow-up and for integration of converts into local churches and home groups. Particularly needy for outreach are the Burmese (less than 2% Christian in Singapore), Bangladeshis and Sri Lankans.

6 **Singapore is a strategic centre** for regional and global Christian mission due to its infrastructure, stability, location and strong Christian population. Most expatriate missionaries based in Singapore are involved in international ministry. Several organizations have their headquarters in Singapore – **OMF**, **WBT**, **WEC** and others. Dozens of others maintain bases there – notably UBS, SU, Navigators, **IMB**, TLM, **OM**, **SIM**, **YWAM** and others. Pray that Singapore will be a blessing to the least-evangelized nations and peoples around it and a servant leader that facilitates the emerging missions movement from other Asian nations.

7 **The many Christian support ministries** with national or international impact through involvement in:

a) ***Literature.*** There are nearly 100 Christian bookstores and at least 10 publishers of books, magazines and tracts.

b) ***Radio.*** **FEBC** and **TWR** have offices here, and a host of local Christian radio stations, including Internet radio, cater to diverse interests.

c) ***Internet ministry*** abounds, with tech-savvy Christians creating evangelistic and discipleship tools. Most churches have well-developed websites for their members. The dark side of Singapore's connectivity is a widespread Internet vice – addiction to online gaming is rapidly growing, even among Christians. Pray for the fruitful kingdom use of this particularly potent form of media.

Slovakia

Slovak Republic

Europe

Geography

Area 49,035 sq km. Landlocked central European state, ranging from fertile Danube shores to the Tatra Mountains.

Population		Ann Gr	Density
2010	5,411,640	0.10%	110/sq km
2020	5,441,569	0.02%	111/sq km
2030	5,347,906	-0.24%	109/sq km

Capital Bratislava 428,000. **Urbanites** 56.8%. **Pop under 15 yrs** 15%. **Life expectancy** 74.6 yrs.

Peoples

Slavic 79.7%. Slovak 77.8%; Czech 1.1%; Ruthnian 0.3%; Ukrainian 0.3%.
Other 20.3%. Hungarian 10.7%; Romani (Gypsy) 9.3%.
Literacy 99.6%. **Official language** Slovak. **All languages** 13. **Indigenous languages** 10. **Languages with Scriptures** 9Bi 1NT 2por.

Economy

Determined policy changes make Slovakia the poster child of post-Communist economic reform. Increasing privatization and foreign investment boost the economy, although unemployment is a problem, especially among the older generation. One of the strongest-growing economies in the EU, but significant regional disparity in wealth and employment persists.
HDI Rank 42nd/182. **Public debt** 28.7% of GDP. **Income/person** $17,646 (37% of USA).

Politics

Part of Czechoslovakia until Slovakia's separation from the Czech Republic in 1993. Multiparty republic, characterized by a wide spectrum of parties, from reinvented Communists to increasing nationalist political expressions. Admittance to the EU and NATO in 2004. Reform of state administrative sectors lags far behind economic reform, creating significant infrastructure problems.

Religion

Constitutional freedom of religion, generally respected by the government.

Religions	Pop %	Population	Ann Gr
Christian	93.34	5,051,225	0.0%
Non-religious	6.53	353,380	1.1%
Other	0.05	2,706	4.7%
Jewish	0.05	2,706	-3.5%
Muslim	0.03	1,623	8.6%

Christians Denoms		Pop %	Affiliates	Ann Gr
Protestant	18	9.38	508,000	0.0%
Independent	4	0.14	8,000	3.5%
Catholic	2	79.75	4,316,000	0.7%
Orthodox	1	1.10	60,000	1.6%
Marginal	2	0.47	26,000	2.1%
Unaffiliated		2.50	135,000	-13.6%

Churches	MegaBloc	Congs	Members	Affiliates
Catholic Church	C	1,075	2,546,875	4,075,000
Evang Ch, Augsburg	P	176	176,190	370,000
Greek Catholic Ch	C	115	172,143	241,000
Reformed Church	P	719	87,692	114,000
Orthodox Church	O	159	39,667	59,500
Jehovah's Witnesses	M	214	13,492	25,500
Apostolic (AoG)	P	27	2,250	7,200
Ev Ch of the Brethren	P	37	1,636	3,600
Baptist Union	P	23	1,933	3,480
Other denominations[18]		129	8,550	16,916
Total Christians[27]		**2,674**	**3,050,428**	**4,916,196**

TransBloc	Pop %	Population	Ann Gr
Evangelicals			
Evangelicals	1.2	67,163	1.9%
Renewalists			
Charismatics	0.7	40,079	3.4%
Pentecostals	0.1	7,276	3.4%

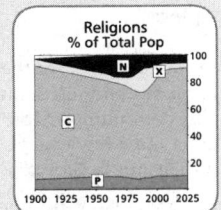

Religions % of Total Pop

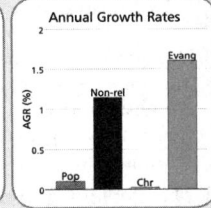

Annual Growth Rates

S

Challenges for Prayer

1 **Slovakia is a nation in the midst of significant change.** Economic reforms and EU membership both created as well as solved problems. Increasing wealth (for some) is accompanied by the new influences of materialism and moral relativism. Depression and suicide rates are among the highest in Europe; pray that many might seek for hope and truth, and find these in Christ.

2 **Slovakia enjoys a strong Christian heritage,** but Catholic, Lutheran and Reformed churches, while many, suffer from widespread nominalism and low attendance. However, renewal movements are growing in these churches, especially among Lutherans as they focus on young people and small groups (Family Fellowships). Pray that these movements would expand and increase. Pray that the strong foundation of Christianity in Slovakia would be brought to vibrant life by a new move of the Holy Spirit.

3 **Evangelical denominations are few and small.** The growth of recent years has slowed, but there is a new desire to reach out and be more active in church planting. The difficulty in registering as a religious organization complicates church life for smaller denominations. To recapture vitality, each congregation must understand what being the Church actually means. Pray for the quality of spiritual life and for fervour in evangelical churches. Another huge challenge to the Church is the growth of Jehovah's Witnesses – their attendance outstrips that of Protestant evangelicals.

4 **Vision for the future must be recaptured.** Previous church planting initiatives have waned, but there are new ideas via the Slovak Evangelical Alliance, Natural Church Development and others. Discipleship, evangelism and church multiplication – on the grassroots level – are essential for the gospel to reach the entire nation. Many desire to see churches in every city and town, but to achieve this, thousands of new congregations must be planted. Pray for this ambitious desire to be achieved.

5 **Appropriate training for both leaders and believers** is essential. The Slovak Evangelical Alliance's programme that trains laity for church planting has now graduated over 140 people. The collaboratively-run Bible school and seminary in Banska Bystrica (KETM) is crucial for preparing pastors, evangelists, Christian teachers for schools and such, but wisdom regarding accreditation is needed. Shorter training programmes are run by SIET, the Baptists and a number of others. Pray that the cumulative effect of these programmes would be a new generation of well-trained, godly leaders.

6 **Creative ministry** is manifesting itself in many ways, particularly through partnerships between local visionaries and foreign ministries. SIET, IN Network, Integra Ventures and many others move the transforming gospel into the marketplace, into popular and youth culture, into prisons and addiction centres. Pray for even greater vision and fruitfulness for these expressions of grace.

7 **Foreign mission presence** has plateaued. Several agencies with missionaries work in Slovakia (International Messengers, **CCCI**, **MTW**, **ABWE**), but more workers could be utilized for both evangelism/church planting and training. The Apostolic Church now sends Slovak missionaries cross-culturally. Pray that mission agencies and local churches cooperate to the best effect, with joy and humility. Ask the Lord to burden Slovaks for world evangelization.

8 **Less-reached peoples:**

S

*a) **Hungarians*** make up more than 10% of the population. Tensions persist over minority rights and language use; pray for fair and just solutions. A Hungarian-specific political party enjoys strong support from this community. Most Hungarians are Catholic, but with a number of Reformed congregations and a few evangelical groups. Pray that Hungarian Christians may be mobilized to reach their kin in Slovakia.

*b) **The Romani*** (Gypsies) are usually misunderstood and marginalized and suffer from low education and a high level of poverty – but they are the most responsive people to the gospel in all Central and Eastern Europe. Persistent efforts to reach them overcame resistance and now see encouraging responsiveness. Pray for those reaching out to them, for love that will overcome all barriers and stereotypes.

9 Special ministries:

a) ***Youth work*** remains an exciting area with diverse activities and ministries. SIET is a network of national youth organizations with an excellent record for cooperation among denominations, including Lutherans, and a strong focus on training. Josiah Venture is central to this vital network. Pray that God may raise up a new generation of holy, faith-filled believers through these movements. Pray for **IFES** and **CCCI** as they minister to tertiary-level students.

b) ***Christian resources.*** Through *Porta Libri*, Slovak evangelical literature is multiplying (although many more books exist in closely related Czech), and Christian bookstores abound. Pray for more of the right books to be translated or written in Slovak. The Bible and other materials in Slovak are also available on the Internet and in audio format. Pray that many would make use of these available materials.

c) ***Radio.*** Radio 7 broadcasts in collaboration with **TWR** Czech, airing 24 hours daily in the Czech and Slovak languages. Programmes are available via Internet, satellite and medium wave. There is still a real need for materials to be written and broadcast in the Romani languages.

Slovenia

Republic of Slovenia

Europe

Geography

Area 20,256 sq km. Alpine state adjoining Italy, Hungary, Croatia and Austria.

Population		Ann Gr	Density
2010	2,024,912	0.24%	100/sq km
2020	2,053,200	0.09%	101/sq km
2030	2,036,889	-0.13%	101/sq km

Capital Ljubljana 260,000. **Urbanites** 48%. **Pop under 15 yrs** 14%. **Life expectancy** 78.2 yrs.

Peoples

Slavic 94.5%. Slovene 90.2%; Serbo-Croatian 3.0%; Bosniak 1.5%.
Other 5.5%. German/Austrian 2.3%; Hungarian 0.5%; Italian(3) 0.6%.
Literacy 99.7%. **Official languages** Slovene, Hungarian, Italian. **All languages** 10. **Indigenous languages** 4.

Economy

The most prosperous of the former Yugoslav republics. The transition to a market economy was difficult but quite successful. Good infrastructure, an educated workforce and an important location between Western Europe and the Balkans. Has adopted the Euro as currency and moved from borrower to donor status with the World Bank.
HDI Rank 29th/182. **Public debt** 23% of GDP. **Income/person** $27,149 (57% of USA).

Politics

Dominated for centuries by Austria. Part of Yugoslav Federation in 1918 until independence in 1991. Masterfully negotiated from being part of Yugoslavia into the EU (2004), and with a minimum of violence and upheaval. The first former Communist country to hold presidency of the EU (2008). A parliamentary democracy with a coalition government.

Religion

Freedom of religion, with a traditional Catholic culture that is rapidly giving way to secularism.

Religions	Pop %	Population	Ann Gr
Christian	54.18	1,097,097	0.0%
Non-religious	43.79	886,709	0.5%
Muslim	1.95	39,486	2.4%
Other	0.04	810	6.2%
Baha'i	0.02	405	0.2%
Jewish	0.01	202	0.2%
Buddhist	0.01	202	0.2%

Christians Denoms		Pop %	Affiliates	Ann Gr
Protestant	6	1.07	22,000	-0.7%
Independent	5	0.06	1,000	-1.4%
Catholic	1	44.20	895,000	-0.7%
Orthodox	3	2.00	40,000	-0.7%
Marginal	2	0.15	3,000	0.8%
Unaffiliated		7.88	160,000	8.8%

S

Churches	MegaBloc	Congs	Members	Affiliates
Catholic Church	C	945	557,241	895,000
Orthodox Churches	O	5	25,312	40,500
Lutheran Church	P	31	7,720	19,300
Jehovah's Witnesses	M	28	1,920	2,570
Old Catholic Ch	I	2	475	950
Pentecostal Church	P	13	569	950
Seventh-day Adventist	P	13	530	775
Baptist Church	P	8	165	248
Other denominations[6]		12	497	799
Total Christians[18]		**1,063**	**594,829**	**961,492**

TransBloc	Pop %	Population	Ann Gr
Evangelicals			
Evangelicals	0.1	1,822	-0.2%
Renewalists			
Charismatics	0.1	2,370	0.5%
Pentecostals	<0.1	950	-1.4%

Religions % of Total Pop

Annual Growth Rates

Challenges for Prayer

1 **A long history of Catholic tradition is under threat.** The three main Christian groups (Catholic, Orthodox, Lutheran) are lacking in spiritual vitality. They are rapidly declining into irrelevance while agnosticism, New Age and different forms of Eastern religious beliefs are increasing, as is general spiritual apathy, even among those who notionally believe in God. Pray for an awakening in the mainline churches that draws the many nominal Christians into personal faith in Christ.

2 **Evangelicals are few, underfunded and divided.** There is an evangelical presence in only 28 out of 210 municipalities, so church planting teams are clearly needed. The tiny evangelical population often reflects the divisive culture of the South Slavs – pray for unity and the formation of an Evangelical Alliance. Of the few dozen fellowships, almost none are self-funding; most pastors rely on secular employment or external financial support, and there is little teaching in churches on stewardship and giving. Pray for Slovene believers to rise to the challenge of personal evangelism, to support their own pastors and even to send missionaries.

3 **Vital Christian resources are in short supply.** With the dearth of local fellowships, availability of quality materials in Slovene is vital for both discipleship and evangelism. Pray for:

a) *Christian literature.* Very few Christian books have been capably translated into this difficult language. Pray for more quality materials to be translated, and for Slovene authors to be raised up.

b) *The Slovenian Bible Society,* as it works on newer and more accurate modern translations. Pray also for insight on how to engage the general population with the Bible.

c) *The new, modern translation* of the works of Primoz Trubar, the Slovene Protestant reformer who wrote the first books in Slovene (a language he helped to synthesize). He is highly regarded, although few have read his works. Pray that the Catechism and others of his books may lead many to a right understanding of God.

d) *More means of engaging Slovenes with the gospel.* EHC has blanketed the nation in the past with Christian literature. There is a definite need for other media, including radio, Christian bookshops, Christian magazines, newspapers and the like. Visions of Christian coffee shops, radio stations and Slovene Christian websites abound; pray for these dreams to become reality.

4 **Slovenia has had a Protestant witness** since the Reformation, but there are still very few evangelical churches. Even these few lack teaching and leadership training, although two informal Bible training schools operate with help from outside professors. Pray for the following ministries:

a) *Church planting.* A number of ministries work in Slovenia. Pray for faithfulness, fruitfulness and sensitivity on their part.

S

b) **Student work.** **IFES**, **CCCI** and the Nazarenes are pioneering student witness in Ljubljana and elsewhere. Josiah Venture works with middle school and high school students in a variety of denominations and churches. **CEF** is training more Slovene leadership for its outreach to children through clubs and camps.

c) **Radio.** Catholic radio is broadly listened to, and some local churches have programmes on local radio, but there is no regular national evangelical presence on radio or TV, except for a 15-minute **TWR** shortwave broadcast.

Literacy 76.6%. One of the lowest literacy rates in the Pacific Islands. **Official language** English. **Trade language** Solomons Pijin, spoken by more than half the population. **All languages** 71. Up to 120, if distinct dialects are included. **Languages with Scriptures** 3Bi 19NT 21por 28w.i.p.

Solomon Islands

Pacific

Geography

Area 27,556 sq km. Six of the seven major volcanic islands of the Solomon Islands, also numerous smaller coral atolls. The seventh, Bougainville Island, is part of Papua New Guinea. The major island and island groups are Guadalcanal, Choiseul, New Georgia, Santa Isabel, Malaita, Makira/San Cristobal, Gela, Santa Cruz and the Russells.

Population		Ann Gr	Density
2010	535,699	2.49%	19/sq km
2020	661,675	2.03%	24/sq km
2030	787,957	1.68%	29/sq km

Capital Honiara 75,000 on Guadalcanal Island. **Urbanites** 18.6%. **Pop under 15 yrs** 39%. **Life expectancy** 65.8 yrs.

Peoples

Over 76 ethno-linguistic peoples.
Melanesian 90.2%. Speaking 60 languages, largest: Kwara'ae 6.9%; Solomoni Creole 6.3%; Areare 4.6%; Ndai/Lau 4.4%; Tasemboko 3.5%; Kwaio 3.4%; To'ambaita 3.2%; Talise 3.2%; Ghari 3.1%; Nggela 3.1%; Vanuatan 2.2%; Neo-Melanesian Papuan 1.4%.
Polynesian 4.2%. Speaking 4 languages – mostly on outlying coral atolls.
Micronesian 1.2%. I-Kiribati, also known as Gilbertese.
Other 4.6%. Euronesian 3.4%; Han Chinese 0.7%.

Economy

The large majority of the population depend on subsistence agriculture and fishing. Rich mineral resources are largely undeveloped, although two goldmines are on their way to being opened. Fishing and forestry, the main export earners, are subject to over-exploitation by overseas interests. Political upheaval from 1998 to 2003 led to civil war, which killed many, displaced up to 30,000 and seriously hampered the economy. **HDI Rank** 135th/182. **Public debt** 55% of GDP. **Income/person** $1,228 (3% of USA).

Politics

Independent from Britain in 1978 as a parliamentary democracy with recognition of the British monarchy. Little actual sense of nationhood; ethnicity predominates in defining identity. Ethnic tensions between peoples of Guadalcanal and large numbers of immigrants from Malaita erupted in violence in 1998, resulting in a Malaitan-led coup in 2000 with a virtual collapse of effective government. Elections were held in 2001, but tensions resurfaced, and an Australian-led international military and police force (RAMSI) intervened in 2003 to disarm the ethnic militias. The country has free elections and a free press, but instability in party loyalties makes stable government a challenge. Corruption is a major problem, largely due to the influence of overseas interests that use money to further their own ends.

Religion

Freedom of religion, but with a strongly Christian emphasis.

Religions	Pop %	Population	Ann Gr
Christian	95.80	513,200	2.4%
Other	2.50	13,392	7.2%
Ethnoreligionist	1.10	5,893	0.7%
Baha'i	0.60	3,214	6.3%

S

Christians	Denoms	Pop %	Affiliates	Ann Gr
Protestant	12	39.50	212,000	1.5%
Independent	10	5.07	27,000	2.0%
Anglican	2	33.79	181,000	1.5%
Catholic	1	19.60	105,000	2.9%
Marginal	2	1.17	6,000	1.2%
Unaffiliated		2.46	13,000	13.2%
Doubly affiliated		*-5.79*	*-31,000*	*0.0%*

Churches	MegaBloc	Congs	Members	Affiliates
Anglican Ch, Melanesia	A	1,182	70,909	156,000
Catholic Church	C	47	61,047	105,000
South Sea Evang Ch	P	650	59,756	98,000
Seventh-day Adventist	P	246	32,695	54,600
United Ch in SI	P	248	24,762	52,000
Episcopal Church	A	189	11,364	25,000
Chr Fellowship Ch	I	47	5,694	10,250
Jehovah's Witnesses	M	46	2,000	6,050
Chr Outreach Centre	I	35	2,075	4,150
Wesleyan Methodist Ch	I	14	1,500	3,000
Assemblies of God	P	24	891	2,700

Ch, Living Word	I	7	1,050	2,100
Other denominations[14]		92	5,531	12,160
Doubly affiliated				*-31,000*
Total Christians[28]		**2,827**	**279,274**	**500,010**

TransBloc	Pop %	Population	Ann Gr
Evangelicals			
Evangelicals	33.3	178,587	2.9%
Renewalists			
Charismatics	16.4	88,115	4.4%
Pentecostals	4.0	21,480	1.1%

Religions % of Total Pop

MegaBlocs % of Christian Pop

Answers to Prayer

1 **The Solomons have a history of revivals** – in the South Sea Evangelical Churches in 1935 and 1970, then in nearly all denominations after 1982. In the 1980s and 1990s, new charismatic networks and churches emerged in another wave of spiritual life. Evangelical and charismatic believers grew in number across almost all denominations.

2 **Christian ministry** during and since the civil conflict has been a good testimony. Peacekeeping efforts by all churches, including the Melanesian Brotherhood (resulting in the martyrdom of seven of these Anglican brothers), and counselling to those traumatized have been much-needed blessings to the nation. The government, at the Church's request, initiated a Truth and Reconciliation Commission – the Church has a great role to play in the issue of reconciliation.

Challenges for Prayer

1 **The civil war of 1998-2003** paralyzed the nation on a number of levels and left many thousands uprooted and in need of practical help and spiritual counselling. Though outside intervention imposed peace and disarmed the ethnic militias, a deeper malaise in the nation remains. Pray for the effectiveness of the Truth and Reconciliation Commission, the Winds of Change movement for fairer elections and political processes and the continued ministry of Women for Peace. Pray for true forgiveness and reconciliation that come only through repentance. Without these, the nation can never really progress.

2 **Ethnic diversity and fragmentation** as well as geography render the Solomons a patchwork of tribes and political groups rather than a unified nation. This hinders not just national identity but also Christian ministry. Myriad languages and cultures necessitate a specific approach for each small tribal group, with resources and translation required. Neo-tribalism is expressed through denominationalism. Pray that Christianity might take root in each group in a relevant way, one that can help overcome division. Pray that God might knit these many islands and tribes together in the gospel.

3 **Nominalism is a problem** even though the Islands are overwhelmingly Christian. The Church has sometimes stagnated; a proper enculturation of the gospel would go a long way in overcoming this. The Baha'i, Jehovah's Witnesses and Unification Church prospered formerly; two different Islamic groups are now making inroads. Counterfeit Christian movements and quasi-Christian cults have also grown, and the old animistic worldview persists in some areas. Many Christians, even committed believers, drift from one group to the next, since most groups compete for members. The revivals of the past are in the past, and a new awakening is needed; pray for the Spirit to reinvigorate the many churches that possess such a strong spiritual heritage.

4 **Training of pastors and leaders** is a strategic need for church growth both in numbers and in maturity. Pray for the several Bible schools and denominational seminaries of traditional churches, evangelical groups and newer charismatic churches. TEE programmes (especially ones developed in Fiji) and preaching seminars (run by the Langham Partnership) show great growth and impact. Hundreds are being trained and are in turn training and discipling whole congregations, with valuable input from Papua New Guinea, where such programmes have had similar impact. The South Sea Evangelical Church, in particular, is experiencing a burst of vitality as a result.

5 **Local and grassroots ministries** are coming into their own as expatriate ministries decline. A number of areas need special attention. Ministry to young people is vital, due to rapid population growth and the many young nominal Christians who need discipleship. SU, **CEF**, **YWAM**, **CCCI** and others focus on work among youth. Other local agencies such as the Christian Care Centre (Anglicans), Haven in the Storm and Bible Way Centre minister to women and young people affected by recent upheavals. Prison ministry is also bearing much fruit, with especially high enrolment in Bible correspondence courses.

6 **Christian support ministries** for prayer:

*a) **Bible translation.*** Praiseworthy progress has been made, but many needs remain – only three languages have the whole Bible. The Bible in Solomons Pijin (the most widely used language) was completed in 2008. The NT was recently completed in Wala, Bughotu and Natugu. National believers are taking the initiative, and this long-underestimated ministry now receives the attention it deserves. Pray for the 19 translation projects shared by **WBT**, UBS and local believers; 28 more languages may still need translations. Pray also for the Solomon Islands Translation Advisory Group (SITAG), which coordinates Bible translation and for the Solomon Islands Bible Translation and Literacy Partnership (SIBTLP), the fellowship of Solomon Islander translators.

*b) **GRN has gospel messages in 88 languages and dialects**,* a crucial resource in a nation with so many small language groups and low literacy levels. Faith Comes By Hearing distributes audio NTs in Pijin to rural communities.

*c) **"Gud Nius Redio"*** (Pijin for Good News Radio) broadcasts in FM from the capital. It is the nation's first Christian radio station, started through the help of UCB and **HCJB**.

*d) **Christian hospitals and clinics*** are significant for the country, which has one of the highest incidences of malaria in the world.

*e) **Education*** is one area where Christian ministries can have a positive impact, especially for girls, who tend to leave school early. The government invited churches to take over schools, and the SSEC and United Church have been active in this. New Hope International developed a programme to assist churches in making truly Christian schools. This is already bearing fruit in the lives of teachers and communities.

*f) **Missions.*** SWIM (Short Workshops In Mission) facilitates overseas short-term mission teams through its centre in Honiara. A number of others serve overseas long-term.

Solomon Islands | October 28

Somalia

Soomaaliya

Africa

Geography

Area 637,000 sq km. The mostly arid Horn of Africa east of Ethiopia and Kenya.

Population		Ann Gr	Density
2010	9,358,602	2.30%	15/sq km
2020	12,246,171	2.68%	19/sq km
2030	15,743,903	2.49%	25/sq km

These population figures are estimates; no reliable source of population data exists.

Capital Mogadishu 1,500,000; Somaliland: Hargeisa 324,000; Puntland: Garoowe. **Urbanites** 37.4%. **Pop under 15 yrs** 45%. **Life expectancy** 49.7 yrs.

Peoples

Somali 94.7%. Complex hierarchy of clans based on paternal descent.

Northern Somali 74.4%. Four major clan families: Dir, Daarood, Hawiye, Isxaaq. Numerous clans and subclans, largely semi-nomadic.

Southern Somali 20.4%. One major clan: Rahanwein, consisting of Digil (mostly farmers) 3.3% and Mirifle (pastoralists) 20%.

Other 5.3%. Arab(3) 1.4%; Ethiopian 1.1%; Afar 0.9%; Oromo 0.6%; Bantu 0.5%.

Literacy 19.2%. **Official languages** Somali, Arabic (few speak it). **All languages** 15. **Languages with Scriptures** 5Bi 1NT 1por.

Economy

Subsistence pastoral economy – two-thirds of Somalis are livestock herders; overgrazing and desertification are problems. Some agriculture in south and northwest. The economy, never very strong, was devastated by the predations of warlords and the ruin of civil wars. The narcotic leaf qat drains the economy and the desire of many Somali men to work. Millions are dependent on aid and remittances from relatives abroad.

Public debt 75.9% of GDP. **Income/person** $282 (<0.5% of USA).

Politics

United as a single country in 1960, soon after the British (in the north) and the Italians (in the south) granted independence to their respective fiefs. Cold War rivalries provided Somalia with ample weapons – first from the USSR, then from the USA – for disastrous wars against Ethiopia and for clan fighting. These brought the country to destitution. Civil war in 1991 toppled the dictatorship, but no viable alternative emerged, with 14 failed governments in 14 years. Clan warfare with warlords vying for power caused the nation to slide further into destitution. In late 2000, a transitional national government formed; the Islamist group Union of Islamic Courts also emerged as a national power. The government is supported by Ethiopia and other democratic nations, the Union of Islamic Courts (UIC) supported by Islamic powers and jihadists. These two have fought several times over Mogadishu, uprooting hundreds of thousands. Somaliland in the northwest declared its independence from Somalia in 1991 but remains unrecognized internationally, despite being a de facto separate nation. Puntland in the northeast set up its own autonomous government.

Religion

Sunni Islam is the official religion. Islamists (UIC) gained religious primacy and political power, and seek to enforce order through shari'a law. A small but significant number of Ethiopian Orthodox remain in Somalia. The murder of Christians and especially converts from Islam to Christianity is increasingly common.

Religions	Pop %	Population	Ann Gr
Muslim	99.67	9,327,719	2.3%
Christian	0.33	30,883	-1.1%

Christians Denoms		Pop %	Affiliates	Ann Gr
Protestant	2	0.01	1,000	2.7%
Independent	2	0.04	4,000	9.5%
Anglican	1	<0.01	<1,000	-3.2%
Catholic	1	<0.01	<1,000	5.4%
Orthodox	2	0.28	26,000	-2.2%

Churches	MegaBloc	Congs	Members	Affiliates
Ethiopian Orthodox	O	n/a	10,400	26,000
Other denominations[6]		14	2,277	4,833
Total Christians[8]		**14**	**12,677**	**30,833**

S

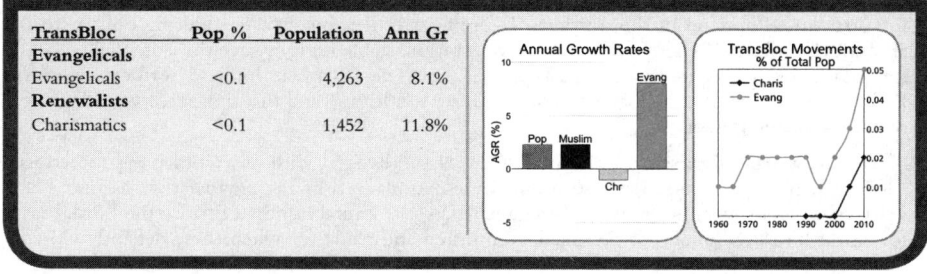

Answers to Prayer

1 **An infant Somali Church** is emerging amid great tribulation. Somali Christians are despised and heavily persecuted, even martyred, but are also growing in faith and in vision. Burdened for their country, they are leading more boldly and will clearly not just disappear. Those in power admit that Somalis are no longer 100% Muslim but more stridently insist that all Somalis remain Muslim.

Challenges for Prayer

1 **Africa's most failed state** continues to struggle for stability. More than 20 years after the start of war, violence and anarchy still reign. Several attempts to restore law and order failed – the "transitional" federal government (TFG) still does not control most of the country or even most of Mogadishu. Strong clan structures have thus far undermined rather than strengthened attempts at governing the south. Al Shabaab and other fundamentalist factions control significant amounts of territory, even driving the TFG from its former stronghold. Pray that all Somalis would support the government and that its authority would be established throughout the country. Pray that future rulers might learn from the past, govern the nation for the good of the people, respect human rights and grant true religious freedom.

2 **The role of Islam** is a troubled one. Radical Islamists contribute to the present troubles. Many jihadists flood into Somalia, eager to fight against the government. The Islamic courts have restored order in their spheres of influence, but by the most ruthless means, imposing strict shari'a on all. Pray that Islamist plans will be thwarted and a new religious tyranny prevented.

3 **The economic, social and physical health** of the nation is terrible, the result of years of war and neglect. More than 750,000 people are internally displaced, and 500,000 died as a result of the fighting. Warfare/upheaval and a particularly strict form of Islam make outside assistance very difficult to give. Pray for:

a) *Order and stability.* Chaos has created a haven for smugglers, bandits, pirates and terrorists, only fueling the problems. Such danger and an oppressive interpretation of Islam also prevent aid and workers from assisting anyone.

b) *Structures of sin* allow great wrongs to persist. Most women suffer female genital mutilation. Many women have been raped, many divorced and left by their husbands and many children have been smuggled out of Somalia and into exploitation or abandonment.

c) *Medical need.* Somalia has the lowest health budget of any nation, and the highest infant mortality rate – nearly 12% of all children die as infants. Droughts and warfare-induced famines render huge numbers dependent on food aid.

d) *Wise administration of aid.* Access is difficult and opportunities limited; violent reactions to perceived "Christian" aid occur. Pray for protection and effective ministry for aid workers, many of whom are Christians.

4 **Somaliland and Puntland.** Somaliland in the northwest declared itself an independent republic in 1991. In great contrast to the chaos of the south, it has remained stable as a de facto separate state – thanks largely to clan structures left intact by the British and to a stronger infrastructure. Puntland in the northeast has self-governed since 1998, suffering only a small amount of civil strife. These two much safer and more stable regions have the potential to help restore the south. Despite the stability, there are almost no Christians in these northern regions. Pray that the peace of Somaliland would permeate southward, and that this peace would create openings for the gospel.

5 **The work of missions,** always dangerous and hedged with restrictions, was forced to cease in 1972 when their institutions were nationalized by the new Marxist regime. The work of different missions between 1897 and 1974 saw several hundred turn to the Lord. Pray for workers to the Somalis to be called, committed and ready for when these defiantly closed doors open.

6 **The Somali Church** was driven underground in 1991 when the dictatorial regime of Mohamed Siyad Barre fell in a popular uprising. Most of the several hundred Somali believers went underground or fled the anarchy, taking refuge abroad. There are possibly about 4,000 Somali Christians in Somalia and twice that in the diaspora. Some meet in secret, but others follow Jesus in isolation. Pray for protection as well as discipleship and fellowship opportunities. Even as targeted persecution of believers escalates, so does the boldness of the church. But increasing numbers of believers are paying for their faith with their very lives. Pray for perseverance for Christians in this most difficult situation. Pray for Somali Christian families to be raised up – the great majority of Christians are men.

7 **A negative prejudice against Christianity** must be overcome if the community of faith is ever to make a greater breakthrough. These issues include:

a) *False notions of Christianity.* Pray that the association of Christianity with Western decadence, European colonialism and Ethiopian interference would be broken.

b) *Practical demonstrations of Christ's love* through aid and mercy ministry must be done in the right manner. Pray that refugees and recipients of help from Christians would be touched and would respond.

c) *Nomadic pastoralism* and the tightly bound clan structures of Somali society are perceived to be incompatible with Christianity; 60-70% of Somalis are at least semi-nomadic and 95% are tied into clans.

8 **The Somali diaspora** numbers about six million. Ethiopia (4.2m), Yemen (900,000), Kenya (500,000) and Djibouti (300,000) host the largest numbers. A large proportion of refugees are often marginalized in their host countries. A further 1.4 million are internally displaced within Somalia. A number of mission agencies seek to reach Somalis in various countries. Pray that these ministries may have a powerful impact on Somalis and that viable Somali churches may be planted; responsiveness is greater outside of Somalia.

9 **Christian specialist ministries:**

a) *The Somali Bible* was first published in 1977; a recent revision is currently on sale in the USA and Kenya. Distribution can occur only outside of Somalia. Pray for the wide dissemination of the Scriptures.

b) *Bible translation* for the Maay Somali (Rahanwein clan), whose language is somewhat divergent, is in progress.

c) *Christian radio* is a vital evangelistic and pre-evangelistic tool for reaching Somalis from outside the country. Pray for the work of Somali Voice of New Life (CNC-**SIM**), Voice of the Path of Peace and broadcasts of FEBA, **TWR**, IBRA and Adventist World Radio. It is a constant struggle to maintain, and a challenge to expand, this service.

d) *Other formats of Christian material* for Somalis include audio resources from **GRN** and Bible Voice, websites such as Somali Christian Ministries and Bible Correspondence courses (CNC).

South Atlantic Ocean — **South Africa** — Cape Town — Indian Ocean

Zimbabwe, Botswana, Mozambique, Namibia, Johannesburg, Pretoria, Lesotho, Swaziland

South Africa

Republic of South Africa

Africa

Geography

Area 1,218,363 sq km. A republic with nine provinces at the southernmost point of Africa. Relatively well watered in the east; arid with increasing desertification toward the west coast.

Population		Ann Gr	Density
2010	50,492,408	0.99%	41/sq km
2020	52,671,375	0.38%	43/sq km
2030	54,726,243	0.35%	45/sq km

Estimates for immigrants and asylum seekers from other African countries, especially Zimbabwe, range up to several million.

Capital Cape Town (legislative) 3,404,807. Pretoria (administrative) 1,428,987. Bloemfontein (judicial) 443,000. **Other major cities** Johannesburg 3.7 million; Ekurhuleni 3.2mill; Durban 2.9m; Port Elizabeth/Uitenhage 1.7m; Vereeniging 1.1m. Large townships and the numbers of migrants living in urban shantytowns swell these numbers, but are impossible to accurately enumerate. **Urbanites** 61.7%. **Pop under 15 yrs** 31%. **Life expectancy** 51.5 yrs.

Peoples

Black African 79.1%.

Nguni 46.4% in 5 groups: Zulu 23.7%; Xhosa 18.6%; Swazi 2.6%; Ndebele 1.5%.

Sotho-Tswana 24.3% in 3 groups: Tswana(11) 5.1%; Sotho(2) 9.1%; Pedi (N. Sotho) 7.5%.

Other 8.4%. Tsonga 4.5%; Venda 2.3%; Shona 0.7%; Khoisan 0.02%.

White/Caucasian 8.9%. Declining through emigration and lower birth rates. Afrikaner 4.6%; English-speaking 1.9%; Portuguese 1.2%; German 0.7%.

Coloured (mixed race) 8.9%. 90% live in the Northern and Western Cape. Cape Malays are considered part of this community.

Asian 2.8%. Over 75% in KwaZulu Natal. South Asians 2.4%; Chinese, Arab.

Other 0.3%.

Literacy 82.4%, but lower in practice. **Languages** 11 – all the major ethnic languages. English and Afrikaans are the main languages in higher education. **All languages** 40. **Indigenous languages** 24. **Languages with Scriptures** 16Bi 1NT 1por.

Economy

The richest and most industrialized country in Africa, with a strong agricultural base and some of the world's largest deposits of non-petroleum minerals – especially gold, platinum and chrome. Well diversified, industrial economy, with finance and tourism increasingly important. A vast gap exists between rich and poor. High unemployment (officially 27%, in reality much higher), with one-third of the population living below $2(US)/day. Land redistribution (from white farmers to blacks) is a significant and sensitive issue. This and affirmative action are regarded as either damaging the free economy or necessarily redressing the injustices of apartheid. Significant brain drain as many professionals, especially whites (some claim up to half of the white population), leave the country. Corruption and the impact of AIDS also undermine economic progress; dangerously high crime rates also reflect these problems.

HDI Rank 129th/182. **Public debt** 31.6% of GDP. **Income/person** $5,685 (12% of USA) – but big disparity between wealthy and poor. **Unemployment** 26.7% (may be much higher).

Politics

The Union of South Africa was formed in 1910. A white-minority parliamentary republic was created in 1961. The infamous "apartheid" system politically and economically marginalized non-whites and brought untold pain and suffering to the majority. A worsening economic climate, increasing political isolation, a deteriorating security situation and the ending of the Cold War all triggered rapid changes in the 1980s. The final laws undergirding apartheid were repealed in 1991, and the country's first free national democratic elections took place in 1994. Nelson Mandela's government worked hard to set up a free, non-racial government and constitution, and it initiated the long healing process with commendable successes. His successors, Mbeki and then Zuma, have not been as successful in seeing these changes through. Much disillusionment has set in due to the slow rate of change, limited economic growth and increasing crime and corruption.

Religion

Freedom of religion. The emphasis on pluralism and diversity has given high profile to ethnic African religions, Islam, Hinduism, humanism and the interfaith movement, somewhat at the expense of the large Christian majority.

S

Religions	Pop %	Population	Ann Gr
Christian	75.24	37,990,488	0.9%
Ethnoreligionist	13.50	6,816,475	-0.1%
Non-religious	7.73	3,903,063	3.6%
Muslim	1.73	873,519	2.8%
Hindu	1.20	605,909	0.7%
Baha'i	0.42	212,068	-0.4%
Jewish	0.15	75,739	-0.3%
Buddhist/Chinese	0.03	15,148	1.0%

Christians Denoms		Pop %	Affiliates	Ann Gr
Protestant	191	15.21	7,681,000	-0.2%
Independent	543	39.82	20,107,000	1.9%
Anglican	2	2.81	1,420,000	-1.2%
Catholic	1	6.04	3,050,000	-0.3%
Orthodox	4	0.10	48,000	0.1%
Marginal	12	0.66	335,000	3.7%
Unaffiliated		10.60	5,352,000	-0.6%

Churches	MegaBloc	Congs	Members	Affiliates
Apostolic Faith Mission	I	2,500	1,800,000	3,100,000
Catholic Church	C	762	1,906,250	3,050,000
Methodist Church	P	4,100	700,000	1,750,000
Ang Ch, Southern Afr	A	1,563	337,662	1,300,000
Uniting Ref Ch, SA	P	650	688,889	1,240,000
Assemblies of God	I	2,050	864,000	1,080,000
Dutch Ref Ch (NGK)	P	855	658,537	1,080,000
12 Apostles Ch in Christ	I	3,737	411,111	740,000
Full Gospel Ch of God	P	1,523	342,767	545,000
Ev Luth Ch in SA	P	1,635	305,389	510,000
New Apostolic Ch	I	1,572	292,163	438,245
Presbyterian Ch of Afr	I	268	88,571	310,000
Nazarite Baptist Ch	I	376	139,000	278,000
Bantu Beth Ch of Zion	I	357	117,727	259,000
United Cong Church	P	1,310	175,510	258,000
Jehovah's Witnesses	M	1,750	91,000	245,000
Afr Catholic Church	I	82	131,737	220,000
Seventh-day Adventist	P	840	91,000	185,000
Uniting Presby Ch, SA	P	288	72,000	180,000
Pente Protestant Ch	P	650	104,000	160,160
African Meth Epis Ch	I	459	82,703	153,000
Dutch Ref Ch (NHK)	P	302	105,002	133,544
Ch of England in SA	A	146	38,339	120,000
Members in Christ Ch	P	220	48,500	107,670
Baptist Union of SA	P	538	42,000	105,000
Other denominations[683]		23,817	6,667,345	15,093,834
Total Christians[4,353]		**52,350**	**16,301,202**	**32,641,453**

TransBloc	Pop %	Population	Ann Gr
Evangelicals			
Evangelicals	21.1	10,649,521	2.2%
Renewalists			
Charismatics	24.4	12,302,817	2.8%
Pentecostals	12.4	6,241,878	3.8%

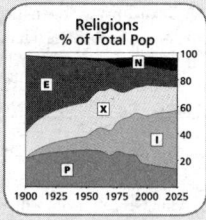

Religions
% of Total Pop

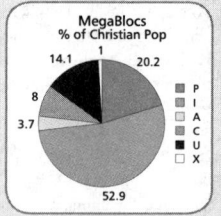

MegaBlocs
% of Christian Pop

Answers to Prayer

1 **Prayer initiatives** started in South Africa have gone on to impact the entire world. The Global Day of Prayer started in Cape Town and is now observed in every country in the world by hundreds of millions of Christians. Groups such as Transformation Africa and Jericho Walls also have profound spiritual influences far beyond South Africa. The Mighty Men weekend conferences impacted the hundreds of thousands who attended with a muscular and uncompromised gospel message.

2 **The continuing, expanding mission involvement** and global vision of South Africans are encouraging. Innovative strategies for sending and supporting are underway, and work is growing from among all races and denominational types. Most evangelical congregations have some involvement in mission work in other countries, especially in central and southern Africa.

3 **The multiplication of Christian ministries** helping the disadvantaged is a remarkable testimony, even as the numbers of these unfortunates continue to increase. There are profoundly touching and effective ministries to victims of rape, crime and AIDS, to those in prison, to slum-dwellers and the unemployed and to the poorest of the poor.

4 **South Africa's functioning democracy,** which has continued now through four general elections, allows the population a say in determining the country's future and sets a positive example for the rest of Africa that such models are sustainable and practicable.

Challenges for Prayer

1 **Government and leadership** are challenges for the future. Finding another unifying figure such as Mandela, with his benign statesmanship, would be a miracle in itself. But lesser subsequent presidents have in turn seen the ruling ANC party lose its two-thirds majority in parliament, which could itself be another step toward a more progressive democracy. Corruption, cronyism and demagoguery are widespread, but greater transparency and a more mature democracy and free press are helping to address this. Many fear what may happen once Mandela's presence no longer restrains more radical actions. Pray for all in leadership, that justice, wisdom, righteousness and economic betterment for all may be their priorities and their legacy. There are many committed Christians at every level of society.

2 **The legacy of apartheid** continues to impact the nation. Despite progress in some areas, inequalities and injustices of the past continue to shape the future. Pray especially for:

a) Reconciliation among all races. This applies not just to black-white dynamics, but also to coloured and Indian peoples as well as to relationships among various black ethnicities. The "rainbow nation" must still deal with contempt, mistrust and deep-seated hurts and fears among peoples of this diverse but troubled land. Pray that the Church might lead the way by living out the truth of oneness in Christ Jesus.

b) Poverty and economic inequality. Land redistribution and affirmative action in employment are contentious intiatives that seek to assist the previously disadvantaged, but they come at a cost to the efficient running of the economy. Extremes of wealth and poverty persist. The black majority itself includes a wealthy elite and a poor majority, but the middle class is growing. Pray for economic measures that might uplift those most needing assistance without crippling the effective running of the economy.

c) Rape and violent crime rates are alarmingly high. The proliferation of illegal firearms, poverty, desperation and lack of justice fuels hopelessness and anarchy. Pray for those working for justice and for people's safety – especially pray for the beleaguered police force. Pray for Christian ministries working with children at risk, jobless young people, prisoners and the police force. Pray that the spirit of violence – both physical and sexual – might be bound under the authority of Christ.

3 **AIDS remains a scourge** of the population. The HIV-occurrence rate is dropping, but the impact of AIDS is already devastating and yet to be fully felt – on the economy, demography and in ministry. There are around 500,000 new infections every year and nearly two million AIDS orphans. About 14% of the population are infected (some sources say more), but some regions or groups are much higher (infection rates of women aged 20-34 are at more than 40%). Nearly half of those with HIV have access to anti-retrovirals, but half of those with HIV also have tuberculosis, greatly increasing mortality rates. Pray that Christians might be used of God to care for the victims, the orphans and the bereaved. In Christ, there is a meaningful message of eternal hope, plus the spiritual power and moral foundation to mitigate the impact of AIDS. There are dozens of Christian agencies and NGOs, as well as many churches, active in this field.

4 **Biblical Christianity** continues to be strong and influential.

a) Evangelism outreaches, ministries to social concerns and prayer networks have all multiplied. A great variety of Christian agencies minister to needy sections of society.

b) Pentecostal denominations flourish among all communities, growing from 400,000 affiliates in 1960 to 6.3 million in 2010. Growth since 1995 has been especially pronounced and has incorporated an enterpreneurial approach to ministry and outreach. Notable ministries are the various **AoG** groups, Apostolic Faith Mission, Full Gospel Church of God and others.

c) Charismatic numbers have rapidly multiplied among all groups – to now one-fourth of the population. Networks draw together many such churches under apostolic leadership from across all regions and races in South Africa. There is much good to be said about the robustness of these movements.

d) Mainline denominations have, in part, been transformed by new vision, structures and outreach. The cell church movement has significant impact. The NGK has many megachurches, much increase in mission output and renewal in many congregations.

e) **The massive growth of African Initiated Churches** to 33% of the African population. Most of these in South Africa originate from the Zion Christian Churches. There are as many as 4,500 groups (many being of one congregation only), which range from evangelical/Pentecostal to highly syncretistic to barely recognizable as Christian. The work of *KwaSizabantu Mission* is particularly commendable and effective in rooting a dynamic Christian faith deeply among the Zulu people.

5 **Christianity faces many challenges** – not least is the question of how a nation that is 75% Christian can be crippled by poverty, violence, crime, AIDS and racial strife. Yet, believers are at the forefront of addressing all of these issues in many ways. Pray for:

a) **A prophetic voice for the Church** in a society that no longer holds to moral absolutes, and where the post-Christian worldview has centre stage in the media and has pushed through legalization of abortion, gay marriage, pornography, prostitution and gambling. Groups such as The Evangelical Alliance, Christian Action and Christians for Truth mobilize believers to oppose legislation that contravenes biblical standards and to reinforce positive laws.

b) **Transformational ministry.** South Africa needs the Church to step even further into radical engagement with all the ills besetting society. The life-changing power of the gospel can bring about change that no government policy ever will, but Christians must make the sacrifices, take the risks and live out Christ's love in the hard places. The temptation to withdraw to a safe, comfortable, but unengaged existence is ever-present.

c) **Unfinished church planting.** To effectively reach and then disciple the millions of unchurched (but usually nominally Christian) South Africans, an estimated 30,000 further congregations are needed.

d) **Deep reconciliation.** Since evangelicals were slow to denounce apartheid, divisions and unfinished business remain. A number of denominations have gone through painful periods in dealing with the past. The Evangelical Alliance of South Africa now offers a context for churches to work out healing and develop unity. More work is required for real trust, understanding and cooperation to fully develop across cultural barriers. Pray that the whole Church may put the sad conflicts of the past to rest and demonstrate the powerful reality of unity in Jesus.

e) **Revival,** particularly in mainline denominations. While there is much spiritual life, there also is much traditionalism, nominalism and "churchianity" in the Dutch Reformed family of churches, Anglicans, Methodists and others.

6 **Training of Christian leaders** is a strategically vital but multi-faceted task:

a) **There are 28 theological, degree-awarding university faculties and seminaries,** and many more Bible colleges with around 5,000 full-time residential and 8,000 distance-learning students. Funding theological education is a challenge for churches, students and the institutions themselves, leading to a decline in numbers. Many of the larger, newer churches prefer to run their own Bible training programmes.

b) **TEE and modular training** are cost-effective, contextually sensitive alternatives, and they offer training even to pre-tertiary level. Over 20,000 are involved with TEE studies in South Africa, including over 3,000 at TEE College (jointly supported by nine denominations), where programmes up to a Bachelor of Theology degree are available in five of the national languages. Live School is another example of flexible training made available to those who otherwise have no training opportunities.

c) **The numerous African Independent Churches** (AICs) are often pastored by those with little education. Many of these churches can be highly syncretistic and are more influenced by African customs and worldviews than by biblical truth. Suspicious of Western motives for involvement, many AICs instruct self-sufficiently through on-the-job apprenticeships. But appropriate and sensitively applied teaching is increasingly welcomed. Increasing numbers of Christian educators provide this crucial ministry; African Enterprise and **SIM**, along with others, enjoy unprecedented opportunities in this area. Pray that this extraordinary and significant movement may retain the best of African culture yet become more biblical and accountable to the wider body of Christ.

7 **Ministry challenges** for the Church in South Africa:

a) Urban dwellers. The enforced rural poverty among Africans in the apartheid era transformed into continued poverty in shantytowns, squatter camps, slums and townships, where conditions range from poor to terrible. Over 60% of South Africans are urban dwellers, a figure set to rise by 2020 to as high as 75%. The financial fortune spent by the government – trying to improve the quality of life for the millions living in these squatter settlements – has made only a small impact thus far. The majority are unemployed; many are unemployable. Pray for:

i *Churches, believers and their witness* in a society full of social stress, where tribal and family authority has broken down, and where criminal, ethnic and political violence is commonplace. Pray for their protection, and pray that they might be given grace to stand for Jesus and be lights for Him in these very difficult places.

ii *Evangelistic outreach* through churches and agencies (**AoG**, African Enterprise, Dorothea Mission, Africa for Christ Evangelistic Association and others). The major new challenge is evangelization of squatter settlements, leading to church planting. Much is being done locally, and church growth in these settlements is rapid.

b) Young people and children. One-third of the population are under age 15, and 70% are under 35. Youth ministry is vital for South Africa's future spiritual health.

i *There are dozens of agencies* with specific ministry to young people. The great challenge is meeting the needs of the many poor; they are without opportunities and education and are both vulnerable to and a fertile recruiting area for violence and crime. There are over 10,000 child prostitutes, as young as 10 years old, in an industry that is flourishing in South Africa.

ii *School-aged children* are ministered to by over 25 major agencies – SU with 125 full-time staff, **CEF** with 27 full-time workers and 300 volunteers and many others. There are 28,000 schools in South Africa. The big growth area is coping with rapidly increasing numbers of AIDS orphans and victims of sexual abuse.

iii *University students.* SCO(**IFES**) ministers through 50 campus groups, involving over 3,500 students, and through over 2,500 high school groups. **CCCI** has more than 50 full-time workers, mostly in campus ministry. His People/Every Nation has a dynamic work on many campuses as well.

c) Mine workers are drawn from all over rural South Africa and surrounding nations, especially Lesotho. Many men live separated from their families for long periods of time. At any one time, 400,000 workers live on large mine compounds of Free State, Gauteng and Northern Provinces. HIV and tuberculosis rates are very high for mine workers. Various missions and agencies seek to minister to them.

8 **Immigrants,** legal and illegal, have streamed over South Africa's borders, especially from Zimbabwe, Congo-DRC, Mozambique, Angola, Somalia, Rwanda, Burundi and Nigeria. Their peak numbers are estimated at five million (although some claim it is as high as 18 million), but many of these use South Africa only as a jumping-off point to other destinations. A pitiful 100,000 are recognized as refugees or asylum seekers. Zimbabweans alone exceed one million (and may be more than three times that), most of them having fled Mugabe's cruel regime and the chaos there. Anti-immigration sentiment subsequently rose, with dozens of riots and episodes of murderous violence against those seeking refuge. The sad irony is that this violence is perpetrated by blacks against blacks. Pray for the nation to recognize that as a main African power, economically and politically, it has a responsibilty to assist those in great need. Pray for ministries of compassion to those from other lands seeking food, jobs or simply safety. Pray for the evangelism and discipleship of these millions.

9 **Ethnic and religious groups** for specific prayer focus:

a) Muslims are less than 2% of the population, but they exercise an influence far greater than their numbers. Very few Muslims have ever openly become followers of the Lord Jesus. Pray for groups of believers from Muslim backgrounds to emerge. Pray for ministries among:

i *Cape Malays* (260,000 Muslims), who live mainly around Cape Town and are part of the Afrikaans-speaking coloured community. They are descendents of criminals, political prisoners and slaves brought by the Dutch to the Cape centuries ago. They cling strongly to their religion and culture. A cooperative fellowship of agencies seeks to witness and disciple them (Life Challenge Africa/**SIM**, **WEC** and others). There is some fruit, but pressures on these believers can be intense.

ii *Asians* (300,000 Muslims), mainly in the Durban area of KwaZulu-Natal. Most are of Gujarati, Urdu or other Indian ethnic groups. About 27% of the South Asian community are Muslim. Ministry among them is low key and fruit hand picked. Full Gospel churches, Baptists, **SIM** and Jesus to the Muslims are all involved in this outreach.

iii *Black Africans.* Over 100,000 Africans have become Muslim in recent years. Islam is one of the fastest-growing religious movements in South Africa. The appeal of Islam's holistic outlook, emphasis on charity and demand for a pure lifestyle – albeit legalistic – is an indictment of Chistianity's failure of discipleship.

b) Hindus are 50% of the Asian population. With a steady flow of Hindu people coming to Christ, now 19% of the Asian population is Christian. Still, many need the freedom found only in Christ. Demonization is a major problem. The work of Jivannadi Mission, Full Gospel Church of God, Apostolic Faith Mission, NGK, AEF/**SIM**, Church of England in South Africa and Baptists is fruitful, with some large and lively churches. The great potential for these believers to go out as missionaries is beginning to be realized.

c) East Asians. The Chinese are of three types – long-term residents, immigrants from Taiwan in the 1980s and the present legal and illegal immigrants from mainland China. There is a significant Vietnamese community as well. A number of churches and missions (**SIM** included) have ministry among these groups. Mainlanders are the most responsive to ministry at this time.

d) The Portuguese and Greek communities are largely Catholic or Orthodox. There are some Portuguese evangelical congregations, but Greeks are more neglected.

e) The Jews live largely in Gauteng and in Cape Town. They are mostly Orthodox in religious practice. There is a small but growing number of Messianic Jews as well as believers of Jewish background who have assimilated into Christian churches. Jews for Jesus and CWI work in South Africa to reach Jews for the Messiah.

10 **Mission vision** continues to be strong as the nation sends out a disproportionately high number of missionaries. South Africa's commitment in the past was notable, with internationally known agencies such as AEF (now **SIM**), Healthcare Christian Fellowship International (HCFI) with its worldwide ministry to and through medical workers, Africa Evangelistic Band, Dorothea Mission, the NGK and more recently African Enterprise. Local AFM and many charismatic churches have new mission initiatives. **OM** and **YWAM** have done much in training and sending out young people into ministry. Pray for:

a) Mission mobilizing and involvement. The World Evangelization Network of South Africa (WENSA) is a network of mission networks, each focused on a different aspect of the Great Commission. This hub of missions vision is vital for the nation's outreach, both internally and internationally. As local congregations increasingly engage directly in mission, mission agencies must adapt to this new reality.

b) South African missionaries around the world. There are most likely around 2,000 South Africans serving abroad in missions, and nearly as many serving within South Africa (500 of them cross-culturally). Support remains a challenge due to economic limitations and many ministry needs domestically, especially for missionaries from the Coloured, Asian and African communities; new and relevant ways of doing mission need to be sought to draw these population groups into cross-cultural mission.

c) The emergence of missionary outreach from the Black churches, still waiting to flourish. There is great potential, but obstacles for its realization are enormous, and the relatively few missionaries from this community have a hard task convincing church leadership of the validity of missions, let alone raising missionary support. The Mission Mobilizers Network (part of WENSA) has a burden for this to happen.

11 **Expatriate missions.** Mission work began among indigenous peoples in 1738. Nearly every major denomination in Europe and North America has played a part in their evangelization. Despite tragic mistakes, heroic efforts yielded much fruit. The missionary force reduces in number as mature churches emerge, and most existing ministries work in church development, leadership training, youth ministry, literature and radio ministries. Pray for fruitful ministries for them in times of great challenge.

⑫ Christian help ministries. The scope and scale of specialized Christian ministries are impressive. The giving needed to sustain them is prodigious! Pray specifically for:

a) Bible production and distribution. Nearly every language has the entire Bible. The Bible Society sells or distributes over 1.4 million Scriptures annually, of which over half are full Bibles. Pray for increased reading of the Scriptures and for lasting, formative impact on lives. Southern Ndebele is the only official language without a full Bible; pray for the OT to be completed as soon as possible.

b) Christian literature is abundantly available, with 40 Christian publishers and over 200 Christian bookstores.

c) Audio resources are also vital. **GRN** has recordings in 24 languages; the full NT is available in audio format for the larger languages.

d) Broadcasting is widely used and has a large following. Pray specifically for:

  i *Local FM radio stations,* such as Radio Pulpit and Radio Khwezi, which broadcast successfully in most of the primary urban centres and in some rural areas. Pray that more groups will apply for licences, particularly in secondary towns. There are opportunities for interdenominational Christian groups to begin broadcasting with assistance from the Association of Christian Broadcasters (which covers all of southern Africa and represents over 75 members).

  ii *The effectiveness of Christian programming,* available nationally on radio and television (TBN and God-channel) via satellite. **TWR** also broadcasts into South Africa on short-wave radio from Swaziland and to the rest of Africa from Johannesburg.

  iii *Organizations* such as Africa by Radio and Radio Africa Network, as well as international broadcasters such as CVC, **TWR** and FEBA who help establish small Christian FM stations throughout Africa from their offices in South Africa.

  iv *Application for licence.* Christian stations are under constant pressure from government authorities to become interfaith or community stations rather than specifically Christian. It is very difficult to get a licence as a Christian station; pray for a breakthrough in this situation.

e) Mobile phone users. Pray for strategies to reach the millions of people in South Africa who have cell-phone connectivity, but no access to satellite reception or computers.

f) New media resources, such as the Internet and digital video, are utilized effectively by groups in South Africa such as Media Village (**YWAM**), with national and international impact.

g) MAF has a base in South Africa. With two aircraft and 13 staff, they assist in reaching isolated peoples in nearby countries, especially in Mozambique.

S

Spain

Kingdom of Spain

Europe

Geography 🌍

Area 504,783 sq km. The major part of the Iberian peninsula and Balearic Islands in the Mediterranean. Also included are the Canary Islands off northwest Africa and the enclaves of Ceuta and Melilla on the North African coast.

Population	Ann Gr	Density
2010	45,450,497	1.02%	90/sq km
2020	48,701,629	0.57%	96/sq km
2030	49,915,060	0.21%	99/sq km

Capital Madrid 5,851,288. **Other major cities** Barcelona 5.1 million; Valencia 814,000; Sevilla 773,000; Zaragoza 694,000. **Urbanites** 77.4%. **Pop under 15 yrs** 15%. **Life expectancy** 80.7 yrs.

Peoples 👪

An estimated 5.6m immigrants live in Spain, including 3m non-registered people, mainly from North Africa and Latin America.

European 91.7%.

  Spanish 85.4%. Major groups: Castilian 53.2%; Catalan 17.0%; Galician 7.3%; Aragonese 4.4%; Extremaduran 2.5%; Asturian 1.1%.

  Basque 2.5%. Estimates vary on the Basque population and on how many speak Euskera as a primary language.

  Other European 3.7%. British 1.7%; Romanian 1.1%; many others.

Latin American 3.9%. Ecuadorean 1.0%; Colombian 0.6%; every other Latino nationality.

Arab World 1.9%. Moroccan 1.5%.

Gypsy/Romani 1.4%. Known locally as Gitanos, also with a wide range of population estimates.

Others 1.2%. Sub-Saharan Africans and Asians.

Literacy 97.7%. **Official languages** Catalán, Galician and Basque are official languages in the respective autonomous regions. Castilian (Spanish) is the only official language for all the Spanish territory. Spanish is the first language of over 340 million people; the world's third most widely used language. **All languages** 21. **Indigenous languages** 14. **Languages with Scriptures** 4Bi 1NT 3por 4w.i.p.

Economy 📈

The world's mightiest economic power in the 16th Century, followed by three centuries of decline and economic stagnation until entry into the EU in 1986. This helped transform the country into a modern economic power with rapidly rising living standards. Main sources of income are tourism, industry and agriculture. The recession, which began in 2008, and bursting of the housing bubble slowed economic growth significantly. One of Europe's higher unemployment rates. **HDI Rank** 15th/182. **Public debt** 40.7% of GDP. **Income/person** $35,117 (74% of USA).

Politics ⚔

Spain's tumultuous past moulds the present. The Muslim Moorish occupation lasted 700 years, ending in 1492. The worldwide Spanish empire lasted for three centuries. The 19th and 20th Centuries were marked by instability, civil wars and dictatorships; the most recent one, under General Franco, lasted from 1939 to 1975. Constitutional monarchy with an effective multiparty democracy. Wide powers have been given to 17 autonomous communities and to the two autonomous cities of Ceuta and Melilla as a means of preserving national unity. The Basque ETA terrorist campaign for full Basque independence has plagued Spain and divided the Basque community since 1961.

Religion 🙏

During Franco's dictatorship, Catholicism was the state religion. Non-Catholics, especially evangelicals, were subject to discrimination and even persecution. The 1978 constitution guaranteed equality of rights for all ideologies and religions, though Catholicism remains under special consideration from the State. The "cooperation agreements" with the government signed in 1992 for evangelicals, Muslims and Jews are a step forward. Spain is fast moving from a traditional Catholic society to a secular-dominated, multicultural, multireligious one.

Religions	Pop %	Population	Ann Gr
Christian	77.13	35,055,968	0.1%
Non-religious	19.47	8,849,212	4.7%
Muslim	2.40	1,090,812	4.8%
Jewish	0.70	318,153	2.2%
Other	0.10	45,450	1.0%
Hindu	0.10	45,450	1.0%
Buddhist	0.10	45,450	1.0%

Christians	Denoms	Pop %	Affiliates	Ann Gr
Protestant	114	0.84	383,000	3.0%
Independent	39	0.24	108,000	5.3%
Anglican	1	0.17	76,000	4.8%
Catholic	2	74.83	34,010,000	-0.2%
Orthodox	14	1.24	562,000	19.9%
Marginal	8	0.48	220,000	0.8%
Doubly affiliated		*-0.67*	*-305,000*	*0.0%*

Churches	MegaBloc	Congs	Members	Affiliates
Catholic Church	C	23,000	9,664,935	37,210,000
Other Orthodox groups	O	70	350,000	560,000
Filadelfia Evang Ch	P	725	101,750	203,500
Jehovah's Witnesses	M	700	113,000	161,000
Anglican Church	A	17	15,200	76,000
Latter-day Saints	M	125	31,818	45,500
Assemblies of God	P	220	13,622	25,200
Christian Brethren	P	180	9,200	19,596
Assemblies of Brethren	P	145	10,389	18,700
Seventh-day Adventist	P	120	14,000	14,500
Baptist Union	P	88	9,680	12,100
Other denominations[161]		1,261	120,555	208,824
Disaffiliated				*-3,200,000*
Doubly affiliated				*-305,000*
Total Christians[178]		**26,651**	**10,454,149**	**35,049,920**

TransBloc	Pop %	Population	Ann Gr
Evangelicals			
Evangelicals	1.0	461,998	3.4%
Renewalists			
Charismatics	1.1	481,675	3.3%
Pentecostals	0.7	311,989	3.4%

Missionaries from Spain
P,I,A 915 (512 long-term) in 28 agencies: elsewhere in Europe 243, South America 216, Mexico/Central America 133, Africa 119.

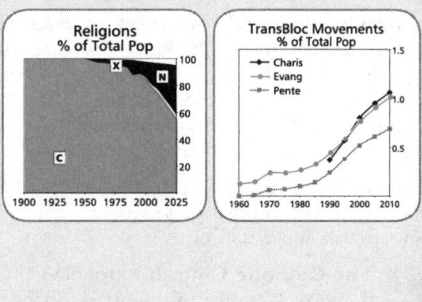

Answers to Prayer

1 **Spain's transformation since 1978 is astonishing,** from dictatorship to liberty, poverty to wealth, isolation to integration into Europe and religious discrimination to religious liberty. Spain has had only two brief periods of religious freedom, 1868-1875 and 1931-1939, before the new Constitution passed in 1978. Thank God for more than 30 years of liberty, and pray that Spain's believers would take full advantage of it.

2 **Evangelical growth has followed this freedom,** largely because of immigration. Most evangelicals in Spain are immigrants. Latin American, Romanian and African believers flood into Spain, bringing their dynamic faith in Jesus with them. Their arrival swelled the number of evangelicals from under 40,000 (0.1%) in 1960 to over 450,000 (1%), meeting in nearly 3,000 churches in 2010. Praise God for a truly diverse and multicultural expression of Christianity that offers Spaniards some new options for belief in Jesus.

3 **The "Filadelphia" movement** among Spain's Romani (Gypsies) since 1966 is a point for praise. The Filadelfia movement is the largest evangelical body in the country, with more than 200,000 people associated with it.

Challenges for Prayer

1 **Spain's modern transformation** is not all positive. Secular materialism brought religious freedom and economic advancement, but it has also struck a crushing blow to traditional foundations of society and created a spiritual vacuum that is being filled with many dangerous elements.

a) Morality, and values in general, have suffered. Decadent behaviours and hedonistic lifestyles, combined with increased material possessions, cause greater degrees of depression, addiction, debt and lost direction. The younger generation rejects the idea of absolute truth. Pray that Christianity might still be able to provide a moral compass and demonstrate moral authority.

b) Spiritual confusion. False beliefs are quickly multiplying – a natural consequence of the rapidly formed vacuum left by departure from religious faith. Spaniards flirting with occult practices is common. New Age deceptions abound. Marginal cults such as Jehovah's Witnesses and Mormons have a large presence, augmented now by the arrival of new foreign sects and other religions.

c) **Drugs are a blight** on Spain, one of the world's heaviest users of cocaine, heroin and marijuana. Around two million take drugs, most of them young people. Cocaine dominates the drug trade, but heroin wreaks particular havoc on the health of users. As yet, there are no signs of drug abuse or addiction abating.

d) **Gambling addiction** remains a problem for the nation as well. It is estimated that 15% of net household income is spent on betting, possibly one of the highest proportions of any nation in the world. Bookmakers and gambling companies press in harder on the lucrative Spanish market, well aware of the breadth of addiction.

e) **Sexual ethics and behaviours are a battleground,** since immorality, prostitution and abortion are common. Children are sexualized at ever younger ages, while an "anything goes" mentality characterizes young people especially. The Spanish have all but stopped having children – they have one of the lowest fertility rates in the world, lower still if excluding immigrant families. All of these will have devastating future consequences in terms of disease, social attitudes and demographic pressure.

Pray for Spain to wake up to the lies that have blinded it to the truth of the gospel. Pray for social renewal, and that those working for the salvation of the Spanish might be endowed with love, power and wisdom.

2 **The Catholic Church** is troubled, finding itself in crisis. From being regarded as one of the most Catholic of countries, Spain is fast becoming one of the most irreligious. The challenges include:

a) **The legacy of a tarnished past.** The Inquisition casts a dark shadow across history. In the 16th Century, thousands of suspected apostates were tortured or killed and hundreds of thousands of Jews, Muslims and Protestants forced to convert or flee the country. This weapon of repression was then used throughout the Americas against the indigenous population. The Church was also tainted by association with the Franco dictatorship. Pray that this stain on the Spanish nation may be fully repented of and renounced, and that the shame on Christianity would be diminished.

b) **The loss of authority in the present day.** There is widespread mistrust of the institution of the Church, which often finds itself pitted against the current liberal government on issues of morality, sexuality and the sanctity of life. Most Spaniards feel caught in the middle. Less than 17% regularly attend mass. For most younger people, the rituals and feasts of Catholicism hold little to no religious or spiritual meaning. Pray for a renewal in Catholicism that breathes new life and relevance into the Church.

c) **The bleak future.** Only 14% of young people describe themselves as religious, and less than half identify themselves as Catholic at all. The numbers enrolling in the priesthood or in training are drying up. Within one generation, Spain may no longer be a majority-Catholic country. Pray that the pendulum, swinging as it is toward rampant secularism, may be reversed and the Spanish nation drawn back to God.

3 **Evangelical numbers have grown,** but not as fast or in the ways hoped for. Many evangelical churches are concentrated in Catalonia (especially Barcelona), along the east coast, in Andalucía and in the areas around Madrid. Pray for:

a) **Revival.** Spain has never experienced a national outpouring of the Holy Spirit in revival, and, as secular attitudes predominate, the general spiritual atmosphere is drier than ever.

b) **Greater cooperation among denominations.** Unity is actually a positive point overall, but deliberate collaboration is scarce. FEREDE, the Federation of Spanish Evangelical Religious Entities, is a key network hub for evangelical denominations, giving focus in ministry and speaking for evangelicals to the government. The Evangelical Alliance of Spain has promoted unity among evangelicals for more than 130 years.

4 **The perception of evangelicals** in Spain still needs to improve, as does the culture and forms that too many evangelicals tend to use. Pray for:

a) **Evangelical churches to lose their "foreign-ness".** While many of the older evangelical churches were planted by Spanish workers, many newer congregations imported Anglo-Saxon

S

dynamics and structures. Many evangelicals are Gypsies, Latin Americans, Eastern Europeans, Africans and other foreigners who bring their own idiosyncrasies and styles with them.

b) *Perceptions of Christianity by Spaniards.* The media can be quite hostile. Pray for the effectiveness of the few opportunities that exist in national and regional media to project a positive image. Evangelical church culture can isolate congregations from relevance in modern-day society.

c) *Discrimination still exists,* even if outright persecution has faded. Preferential treatment of Catholics and restrictions on other religious groups have seen some congregations shut down by local authorities over issues of permits and licences.

5 **Leadership training.** Few churches can afford to pay for a full-time pastor, let alone a team of them. As a result, churches must use bivocational pastors or be entrusted to full-time foreign missionaries, who end up pastoring instead of church planting. There are at least 15 seminaries and Bible schools. IBSTE(**GEM**), UEBE Seminary, GU and CSTAD (all **AoG**), SEFOVAN(WorldLink), *Seminario Teológico Al-Ándalus*, CEIBI and SEUT (collaborative effort) are just a few of the notable seminaries. The Brethren have four Bible schools. The *Escuela Evangélica de Teología* runs a rapidly growing online seminary. Some newer, larger churches provide in-house leadership and theological training. TEE is a significant need. Pray that these schools would be filled with young Spanish future leaders, shaped by solid instruction in the Word of God.

6 **There is a considerable increase in missionaries** and agencies since 1978, probably numbering over 1,000 today. But some areas remain largely unreached. Proliferation of agencies and lack of coordination are issues for concern. Pray for:

a) *Christian workers* to be called to less-evangelized areas, such as Castilla Leon, parts of Andalucía, Extremadura, the northern provinces of Galicia, Asturias, Cantabria and the Basque country.

b) *Missionaries* to be able to integrate fully into Spanish culture and life. Challenges adapting and integrating persist.

c) *Latin Americans* are present in great numbers. Careful and conservative estimates state that 48% (others suggest up to 80%) of all new churches are planted by Latinos – missionaries, tentmakers and economic migrants. This claim is contested by others, but there is no denying the massive missional impact of Latinos upon Spain.

Some larger missions are **AoG**, **WEC**, **YWAM**, **CB**, **ECM**, **OM**, **TEAM**, **GEM**, **ABWE**, **OMS** and **WH**.

7 **The evangelistic challenges facing Spain** are enormous, including:

a) *Unreached cities.* There is no evangelical church in 345 cities and towns of over 5,000 people. Many smaller towns, villages and districts have no witness whatsoever. Of 8,112 municipalities, only around 650 have an evangelical church.

b) *Of the 17 regions,* Galicia and Asturias are less than 0.2% evangelical, and Extremadura and Navarre are less than 0.1%.

c) *Of the 50 provinces,* Soria and Avila have less than one evangelical for every 1,000 people, and 28 provinces have less than 1,000 members of evangelical churches.

d) *While religious liberty exists on paper,* difficulties and discrimination are still widespread for evangelicals, especially for obtaining licences to broadcast and to open new churches.

e) *Evangelical congregations* are small and dependent on foreign resources, with poor facilities in less than ideal locations. Pray for wisdom in knowing how to be more effective in outreach and balanced in testimony.

8 **The Canary Islands** form an archipelago of seven larger islands off Africa's northwest coast. Among the two million inhabitants, at least 10,000 are evangelical – most live on the two larger islands and over half belong to Assemblies of God. Evangelicals may be stronger in the Canaries than in most of Spain; with strong churches among both nationals and immigrants. Even so, more ministry is needed on the smaller islands of Lanzarote, Fuerteventura, Gomera, La Palma and El Hierro, and more teaching is needed for the scattered groups of believers. Illegal immigrants from Morocco, Senegal and other parts of Africa are a challenge to the government, but an opportunity for Christian ministry.

9 **Ceuta and Melilla** (70,000 each) are two city enclaves on Morocco's north coast. Approximately half of the population are Muslim, half speaking Cherja, a Berber language. There are four evangelical churches in Ceuta and seven in Melilla. Betel, REMAR and The Bible Society have ministries in both enclaves. Pray for these cities to be effective means of bringing the gospel to North Africa.

10 **Vision for the future** has been limited but is now coalescing. Pray for effective, culturally appropriate methods of outreach and for nationwide evangelistic strategies to be developed. Pray for the vision to mature. Pray also for the growth and development of Spanish mission agencies. Decision Spain and *Evangelismo a Fondo* are indigenous Christian groups researching the cities that are without testimony in Spain, and PUEDES is a new entity focusing on research in order to formulate a national plan for evangelism. These groups and the Conference for the Evangelization of Spain work to coordinate evangelism and mission efforts in Spain.

11 **Mission sending.** Spaniards have had a miniscule legacy of sending missionaries, largely because of a tiny evangelical population focused mostly on its own nation. But now, more than 20 Protestant groups send out missionaries, including REMAR, RETO, Betel, **AoG**, Foursquare, Open Bible, **CMA**, Brethren, Baptists and others.

12 **Key groups for outreach.** Pray for these:

a) The Basques are an ancient and proud people without a single Euskera-speaking Protestant church. The Basque ETA movement terrorizes and polarizes society in the Basque region. There are fewer than 100 evangelical churches in the four provinces where Basques live (Guipúzcoa, Vizcaya, Alava and Navarra) and all of these are Spanish-speaking. The few Basque-speaking evangelicals there find it difficult to worship or witness in their own language. Only now are Christian resources in Euskera appearing. The differing dialects in an already difficult language complicate the task. Pray for those involved in ministry, including **AoG, YWAM, WEC** and **OM**. Pray that centuries-old suspicions and fears, and the reserve of the Basque people, may be broken down.

b) Muslims may number over two million and are growing rapidly. The Moors ruled much of Spain for 700 years, and Muslims long to win back what they lost. The vast majority are immigrants from Morocco, but from many other African nations as well. South Spain is a key base area for many agencies committed to evangelizing Muslims in North Africa and in Spain; very few have been won to Christ. Pray for the Malaga Media Centre and the Ibero-American Institute of Islamic Studies (PMI). Pray for Muslim hearts to be opened and for believers in Spain to reach out in love.

c) Chinese numbers have increased to over 100,000. COCM, **CMA** and **OMF** work among them. There are now over 30 churches among the Chinese, who still number only 2% Christian.

d) Drug addiction is a blight on Spain (see point 1c), which has one of Europe's highest rates of heroin and cocaine addiction. This in turn is a major contributing factor in the AIDS epidemic and the crime rate. In their centres across the country, RETO, REMAR and Betel (**WEC**-related) successfully rehabilitate drug addicts. RETO has 80 rehabilitation centres and ministers in 25 countries. REMAR has communities in 175 Spanish towns and works in 58 countries. Betel ministers in 80 urban areas and has planted churches in 21 countries. Over 100,000 former addicts have been set free, and many of them won to Christ through these vital ministries.

e) Young people need the gospel, having given themselves over to postmodern materialism and hedonism. They distrust organized religion. Their lifestyle is based on experience. Ministry to them must be highly relational and authentic. The **IFES**-linked student movement, *Federación de Grupos Bíblicos Universitarios de España*, has 35 university groups with 400 students – a tiny drop in the bucket of over one million students. Alongside GBU(**IFES**), AGAPE(**CCCI**) also works among students in several universities. *Contra Corriente*, an indigenous Spanish ministry to young people and students, possibly has the greatest impact. A growing number of alternative and underground ministries among young people are proving effective.

f) The elderly and retirees. This is a growing segment of the population, both among Spaniards and immigrants which will only get larger in the future. Some ministries are already proving quite effective in outreach to this generation; Doukonia is one such example.

S

13 **Pray for the effectiveness of these Christian help ministries:**

a) Bible translation. New versions are being produced in regional languages and in dialects of Spain. A conversational Spanish Bible, an Aragonese NT as well as Bibles in Euskera (Basque), Galego (Galicia), Asturian, Catalan and Romani are examples. Pray that many will read and be impacted by these translations.

b) Christian literature is a major factor in church growth, although literature work is expensive and bookstores hard to finance. Pray for Christian bookstores; **CLC** has six centres and a distribution network serving evangelical bookstores throughout Spain. Pray for more Christian authors who can write from a truly Spanish perspective.

c) Pocket Testament League impacts Spain through literature, well-publicized research and promotion of missionary vision.

d) Christian radio. Evangelicals run over 90 radio stations. However, licensing for evangelical radio remains a problem, while Catholics easily obtain AM, FM and TV licensing.

e) Christian TV. There are now around 30 small evangelical TV stations, all without a licence but tolerated by the state. Evangelical programmes on public TV maintain an evangelical presence in the secular and mainstream media.

f) Internet. There are countless evangelical websites in Spanish. *Protestante Digital* is Spain's leading evangelical news agency. *Solidaria* is a Castilian TV channel on the Internet and satellite, run by REMAR. Pray for the growing number of Internet radio stations in Spanish.

g) Christian camps are a ministry through which many youth in Spain come to Christ. Some 37 evangelical camps do wonderful work in evangelism, discipleship and leadership training. Pray for their continued impact and effectiveness in breaking down negative preconceptions of evangelicals and in winning many to Jesus.

Sri Lanka

Democratic Socialist Republic of Sri Lanka

Asia

Geography 🌍

Area 65,610 sq km. Large island 80 km southeast of India.

Population		Ann Gr	Density
2010	20,409,946	0.88%	311/sq km
2020	21,713,430	0.51%	331/sq km
2030	22,194,370	0.15%	338/sq km

Capital Colombo (administrative) 683,000; Sri Jayewardenepura Kotte (legislative) 123,000. **Other major city** Jaffna 174,000. **Urbanites** 15%. **Pop under 15 yrs** 24%. **Life expectancy** 74 yrs.

Peoples 👪

Sinhala 75.9%. One of few Buddhist people clusters with castes.
Tamil 14.3%. Declining through war and flight from the country; massive displacement makes precise enumeration impossible.
> **Lanka Tamil** 9.4%. Resident for over 1,000 years in Jaffna in the north and on the east coast.
> **Estate Tamil** 4.9%. Descendants of migrant workers arriving in 19th and 20th Centuries and working mainly on highland tea plantations.

Sri Lankan Moor 8.3%. Of Arab-Tamil descent.
Other South Asians 1.5%. Sri Lankan Malay (of Indonesian descent) 0.3%; Burgher (of Eurasian descent) 0.2%. 25 other groups.
Literacy 90%. **Official languages** Sinhala and Tamil, with English as the link language. **All languages** 7. **Languages with Scriptures** 3Bi 1NT 1por.

Economy 🏭

Textiles, tea and tourism are major sources of income. The largest source is the remittances sent home by the many who take work abroad, especially in the Gulf region. The civil war slowed and distorted what could have been a healthy economy. Much of the national infrastructure is damaged, but tourism and foreign investment (especially from China) are rising quickly now that the war is over. The country's financial burden of so many unemployed, displaced peoples is a major economic drain.

HDI Rank 102nd/182. **Public debt** 77% of GDP. **Income/person** $1,972 (4% of USA).

Politics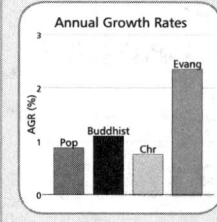

After 450 years of successive colonial administrations by the Portuguese, Dutch and British, independence was gained in 1948 as a parliamentary democracy. Attempts to Sinhalize national life in 1956 and the attendant discrimination against ethnic and religious minorities provoked increasing communal violence and efforts by extremists to fight for an independent Tamil state in the north and east. A bitter civil war raged on and off from 1983 until 2009. All efforts to settle the conflict failed, as the Tamil LTTE built a formidable guerrilla army and both sides remained intransigent. The 2009 military campaign to destroy the LTTE was successful, but displaced between 350,000-500,000 and drew criticism from human rights groups. Subsequent differences between the re-elected president and the general who was the architect of the campaign caused some unrest. A political solution to the Tamil issue is still needed, because although the LTTE was crushed, the social grievances that led to the uprising remain, and a strong Tamil diaspora continues to agitate for greater autonomy for Tamils in Sri Lanka.

Religion

Buddhism is the national religion and, as such, is protected and promoted. Freedom of religion is assured by law. Anti-conversion initiatives and sporadic violence against Christians occur as a result of some extreme Buddhist groups. Christianity is often perceived as foreign and evangelism as an unethical inducement to conversion.

Religions	Pop %	Population	Ann Gr
Buddhist	70.02	14,291,044	1.0%
Hindu	12.80	2,612,473	-0.6%
Muslim	8.52	1,738,927	1.7%
Christian	8.38	1,710,353	0.8%
Non-religious	0.20	40,820	0.9%
Baha'i	0.07	14,287	-1.8%
Sikh	0.01	2,041	0.9%

Christians Denoms		Pop %	Affiliates	Ann Gr
Protestant	24	0.77	156,000	1.6%
Independent	43	0.68	138,000	2.7%
Anglican	1	0.16	33,000	-4.2%
Catholic	1	6.92	1,412,000	0.7%
Marginal	2	0.05	10,000	1.7%
Doubly affiliated		*-0.20*	*-40,000*	*5.2%*

Churches	MegaBloc	Congs	Members	Affiliates
Catholic Church	C	410	788,827	1,412,000
Assemblies of God	P	179	25,000	48,000
Anglican Church	A	146	13,586	33,150
Methodist Church	P	134	17,425	29,100
Foursquare Gospel	P	551	13,769	17,900
Believers Church	I	100	12,000	17,000
Gethsemane Prayer Centre	I	50	10,000	17,000
Calvary Church	I	50	7,031	11,250
Fellowship of Free Chs	I	32	5,500	11,000
Ch of South India	P	38	4,500	10,800
Jehovah's Witnesses	M	84	4,600	8,020
Other denominations[60]		1,342	79,652	137,633
Doubly affiliated				*-42,500*
Total Christians[71]		**3,116**	**981,890**	**1,710,353**

TransBloc	Pop %	Population	Ann Gr
Evangelicals			
Evangelicals	1.2	242,965	2.3%
Renewalists			
Charismatics	1.6	320,751	3.2%
Pentecostals	0.9	179,205	2.6%

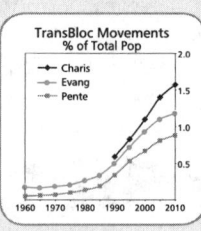

Annual Growth Rates

TransBloc Movements % of Total Pop

Answers to Prayer

1 **The end of the civil war** came amid much violence and probably human rights violations; but effectively removing the threat of the Tamil Tigers can potentially spell a new era for Sri Lanka, one that will involve safety, stability and the free and open movement of the gospel of Jesus Christ. A sense of peace and freedom of movement now prevails.

2 **The anti-conversion bill** was not brought to pass, not so much defeated as deferred. Its implementation would bring difficulties for a number of minorities, but especially for evangelicals seeking to share the good news. Praise God that it has not yet become reality; pray that it may never become so.

3 **The emergence of Sri Lankan churches and denominations** planted and led by Sri Lankan Christians is a point for praise. The establishment and growth of these groups – that make a point of not being tied to any Western funding agency – go a long way in establishing Christianity as a valid indigenous expression of faith.

4 **Evangelical growth continues to be strong.** From 0.2% of the population in 1960, evangelicals were 1.2% in 2010 – a 13-fold population increase! That largely indigenous workers drive such growth makes it remarkable; that growth comes amid upheaval, civil war and militant opposition makes it worthy of thanks to God.

Challenges for Prayer

1 **Sri Lanka has suffered much in the past generation.** From the constant threat of the Sinhala-Tamil conflict to the tsunami of 2004 to the civil war's bloody conclusion in 2009, over 100,000 people have lost their lives, over 900,000 (mostly Tamils) emigrated or fled and over one million are displaced. Points for prayer:

a) A resolution of the long-term conflict between Tamils and Sinhalese. Defeating the LTTE as a force means little if enmity, resentment and rebellion are still brewing. Key players are the Sri Lankan government, the former LTTE core members, the Sri Lankan Tamil diaspora and even India and China. Power sharing may be the only way to long-term peace. A new constitution is being considered, one to resolve ethnic antipathy and return the nation to a more secular status with no religious favouritism. Pray that wise heads may prevail, and that peace, reconciliation and freedom for religious minorities might take precedence over ethnocentrism, prejudice and pride.

b) A government that will work toward transparency, justice and the fair representation of all communities and their civil, economic and religious rights. Corruption and nepotism are too common. Post-2009, courageous decisions have been and will need to be made to oversee the healthy stewardship and development of this nation.

c) The handling of immense human needs in the aftermath of the civil war. Former LTTE fighters need to be reintegrated into society, the many injured and maimed government soldiers must be rehabilitated and given new vocations, orphans and widows must be cared for and half a million who were displaced need to be returned to their homes to rebuild their lives.

d) The fight against the many growing social ills:

i *The plight of children* – malnutrition, selective abortion/female infanticide or abandonment, abuse (including sexual abuse) and child prostitution (including sex tourism) are evils that are sadly making names for themselves in Sri Lanka.

ii *Sri Lankans working abroad,* especially in the Middle East and Gulf regions, are vulnerable to abuse and exploitation, especially since most of them are female domestic helpers. There are up to 700,000 such women willing to endure the risk in order to earn enough to send remittances home. Their absence is often very difficult on the children they leave behind.

iii *Threats to traditional Sri Lankan culture* include alcoholism, suicide, casual violence and rape.

2 **Tolerance and non-violence** have historically been watchwords of Sri Lanka. For centuries, it was a Buddhist kingdom that welcomed refugees from India fleeing persecution – Hindus, Muslims and Christians. However, this multi-religious, multi-ethnic country now sees religious extremism and persecution rising. Pray for:

a) The disarming of the spiritual powers and principalities that heavily influence a very religious society. Beneath the layers of Buddhism and Hinduism lie an ancient cocktail of spirits, gods and demons.

b) The exposure of Buddhist extremism as a hateful aberration. This has taken shape as a very ethnocentric Sinhalese response to Tamil intransigence and to waves of Christian "proselytism". But it has also been used to polarize society, to unduly influence politics and the military, and to marginalize and suppress ethnic and religious minorities. Pray that such extremism might create disillusionment and generate interest in the gospel.

3 **Traditional mainline Churches** have declined from 21% of the population in 1722 to 7% in 2010. The causes – nominalism, theological liberalism, insufficient outreach and lack of indigeneity. Aggressive Buddhist proselytism and emigration of Tamil Christians steadily whittle away their flocks. Praise God for growing evangelical movements in most of the Protestant denominations today. Pray for renewal that will correct the above shortcomings and see God shape a purified, biblically sound indigenous Church with a focus on extending the love and truth of Christ in word and deed to all of Sri Lanka.

4 **The growth of evangelicals** is both quantitative and qualitative, but it has a long way to go before maturity and fullness. Numbers continue to surge upward, and Sri Lanka sees the emergence of maturing, faith-filled congregations. This relatively small Christian community produces an impressive number of top-quality, global Christian leaders, thinkers and writers. Pray also for:

a) *Increased unity.* The Church as a whole is divided – between Tamil and Sinhalese, between Catholic and Protestant, between mainline and evangelical, even between older Pentecostal and newer neo-Pentecostal. These divisions offer a poor testimony, give ammunition for opponents of Christianity and hinder progress in evangelization. Pray for the vital work of the National Christian Evangelical Alliance, the National Christian Council and the National Christian Fellowship of Sri Lanka, the last of which is the network for many of the Sri Lankan indigenous denominations. There are also a significant number of regional pastoral fellowships. Relying on foreign denominational structures and finance can also cause divisions.

b) *The potential of the Church* as a channel for reconciliation. Ultimately, no other national structure can meaningfully bring together the bitterly divided ethnic communities with their various castes and political expressions except a flourishing biblical Christianity. Pray that the universal love of God and authority of Christ might catalyze both Church and Sri Lankan society toward reconciliation.

c) *Theological education,* an area where evangelicals make a notable contribution. Lanka Bible College (LBC), Colombo Theological Seminary (CTS) and Assemblies of God Bible College, as well as Bible schools of Foursquare, GFA, Baldaeus Theological College and others train Christian leaders and ministers. LBC runs a degree programme to train teachers of Christianity in schools. A number of agencies run extension and TEE courses. Pray that the education received might equip students to capably minister with spiritual power, biblical truth and a critical ability to understand and address the cultural contexts of both the Church and the prevalent Buddhist mindset.

5 **Evangelism and church growth are priorities,** but also present are many sober and serious challenges that need a major shift:

a) *The fixation with rapid growth* has led to prioritizing winning converts rather than making disciples, to attracting crowds with promises of miracles rather than with Christ-like character, to filling seats instead of meeting needs, to a lack of accountability and to unhealthy competitiveness.

b) *The need for workers* pushes undertrained and immature Christians into roles for which they are not prepared. It also allows unsuitable people to assume positions of ministry and church leadership on the false assumption that secular success equates to spiritual anointing.

c) *The disunity and lack of a centralized strategy* can create an environment where splinters, duplicated efforts, competition and unscrupulous sheep-stealing occur.

d) *Dependence on outside funding* in some ministries can lead to exaggerated reporting of converts, and it displaces accountability from national leadership to foreign backers. It also gives ammunition to accusations of both Western religious-cultural imperialism and, in the case of Tamil churches, harbouring and financing terrorism.

e) *The failure to root Christian practice* in authentic Sri Lankan forms hampers church growth, the process of discipleship and the acceptance of Christianity by society at large. Pray for inspired, thoughtful, biblical ways that Sri Lankan Christians can fellowship, worship and witness.

6 **Christian presence in Sri Lanka is patchy and uneven,** but this is changing rapidly. Most Christians are concentrated in the urban areas of Colombo and Jaffna and on the northwest coast. However, recent evangelism sees Christian witness extending into every administrative division of Sri Lanka. Many trained workers emigrate, and few are willing to work in the less-privileged areas. There are many new Christians from the Buddhist and Hindu communities. Pray for ministers who are willing to serve in the humble and challenging – but responsive and open – rural environments.

7 **Persecution comes in waves and is sporadic,** but it is intense when it occurs. Over 250 churches have been destroyed or damaged in recent years. This persecution is a double-edged sword; it threatens believers, but also fuels church growth and spiritual passion. Its causes are multiple – the hatred of the enemy for God's people, the extremist agendas of some Buddhist and Hindu groups, the historic association of Christianity with foreign oppressors and the inappropriate, insensitive methods adopted by some evangelists and church planters.

a) Christian response. Pray that, as far as possible, Christians might be without fault in the way they conduct ministry, in their financial dealings and in the winsomeness of their attitudes. Pray that loving humility and compassion, rather than arrogant triumphalism, might characterize Christian witness.

b) Enduring persecution. Pray for believers to equip themselves to endure by being rooted in the Word of God, and to see that such persecution is a badge of honour, not of defeat and shame. Pray for a spirit of forgiveness among all who suffer for the name of Christ.

8 **Missionary work** seems headed in opposite directions:

a) Mission by expatriates has all but ended due to restriction of visas; tentmaking jobs are just about the only means for foreigners to do Kingdom work. Pray for a change – there are enough needs to which outsiders can still meaningfully contribute.

b) Sri Lanka's mission-sending movement is on the rise. The first interdenominational mission agency in Sri Lanka was recently formed. The focus is on sending workers to countries in South and Western Asia; several have already been sent out to different people groups. Pray for these workers and for those presently in training for future cross-cultural ministry. Pray also that their sending churches might wholeheartedly support them in their calling and work. Notable for home missions are *Kithu Sevana*, Margaya Fellowship, Gospel Ministries, Lanka Village Ministries (LBC Alumni) as well as denominational missions.

9 **Special ministry challenges:**

a) The Lanka Tamil community, once relatively prosperous but now undone and scattered by the violence perpetrated by the LTTE and the Sri Lankan military. The diaspora is over 700,000 strong; pray for the many churches among them to be forces for the evangelization of Sri Lanka, rather than agitators pushing for an independent Tamil state.

b) The Estate Tamils have long been a despised, poverty-stricken and marginalized community, but growing numbers are turning to Christ. A significant amount of outreach is directed toward them by the Free Churches Fellowship, **AoG** and the Smyrna Church.

c) Young people. Ministry to young people in Sri Lanka is a growing area, but still needs more attention. Many congregations have no resources for ministry to youth and children. Pray for:

  i *The groundbreaking and holistic ministries among urban youth* of **YFC** and **CCCI**.

  ii *The work of FOCUS(IFES) among students* in half of the country's universities. **CCCI** has an effective evangelistic ministry among students.

d) The villages still present a challenge. There remain 25,000 villages without a church. Many are devoid of any witness. The ravaged villages of the north and east are particularly needy. Ministries are recognizing the need for specialized training and strategy for rural ministry.

e) Compassionate ministry to victims of the tsunami's destruction, the civil war and general poverty. There must be a clear separation of physical assistance and gospel outreach in a society highly sensitized to issues of proselytism, Western money and buying converts. Many local ministries operate aid programmes independently of their outreach work; pray for wisdom for and response to both.

10 **Unreached peoples of Sri Lanka:**

a) The Moors are generally traders, bureaucrats and farmers. Until recently there were few converts out of Islam, but now a few hundred are responding to the sensitive witness of Christians.

b) The Malays are syncretistic Muslims and are potentially more open. Pray for a specific ministry to them.

c) The self-named "Kaffirs" are descendents of African slaves brought by the Portuguese to work on plantations; they adhere variously to all of Sri Lanka's religions.

d) Other unreached social groups – the educated Buddhists, the coastal-belt fishing communities and the Tamil and Sinhala militants, who continue to polarize the country.

e) Tribal groups – the Rodhiya (7,000), Ahikuntikas (Gypsies, 2,000) and Sri Lanka's original inhabitants, the Veddah (2,000). Kithu Sevana Ministries has a work among the Rodhiya.

11 **Christian media ministries:**

a) Literature is in great demand. Literacy is high, but affordable quality literature that is culturally relevant is lacking. The main publishers – Margaya Fellowship, Pragna Publishers, The Bible Society, Gospel Ministries, **YFC**, Lanka Bible College and Colombo Theological Seminary (theological books and study materials), SGM (Scripture portions) – have produced much, but there are too few points of distribution. Pre-evangelistic materials are needed, especially for Buddhists. New Life Literature has a printing press, which is much used for printing gospel literature and the Gideons New Testaments in Sinhalese and Tamil. **EHC** has been involved in a nationwide gospel-literature distribution programme several times. **CLC** has recently established three Christian bookstores with a growing distribution ministry.

b) The JESUS film has been extensively shown. Weekly, national TV broadcasts the Indian production "Jesus Calls" in three languages. Other Christian television content is increasingly available.

c) Radio. Sri Lanka is thinly covered by international broadcasters – FEBA, **HCJB**, **GFA**, **TWR**, Christian Vision and AWR all beam shortwave to Sri Lanka, but only a small proportion of it is in Sinhalese or Tamil. However, BBI locally broadcasts nearly 30 programmes a week in Sinhalese and Tamil. **TWR** broadcasts from Sri Lanka on medium wave to South Asia, with 77 weekly programmes in 24 different languages.

Anguilla

St. Martin

St. Maarten (Netherlands Antilles)

Gustavia

St Barthélemy

Saba (Netherlands Antilles)

Caribbean Sea

St Barthélemy

Collectivity of St Barthélemy

Caribbean

Geography

Area 21 sq km. One main island and several small islets in the Leeward Islands.

Population	Ann Gr	Density
2010	9,300	2.06%	443/sq km

Capital Gustavia 3,000 (est).

Peoples

Large majority of French Caucasians with smaller numbers of Americans, Portuguese, Brazilians, Swedes and French West Indies Creole. **Literacy** 100%. **Languages** French (specifically a Norman dialect), English. **Languages with Scripture** 2Bi.

Economy

High-end tourism and luxury duty-free items, mostly bought by wealthy American and French visitors. The island is a remote playground for moneyed jetsetters. Tourism and the related service and construction industries provide the mainstays of employment. All food and most fresh water must be imported, yielding a very high cost of living.

Politics

An overseas collectivity of France, having been a part of Guadeloupe until 2007. Was Sweden's only Caribbean colony, from 1784 to 1878.

Religion

Freedom of religion.

Religions	Pop %	Population	Ann Gr
Christian	61.00	5,673	1.4%
Non-religious	35.00	3,255	3.3%
Other	4.00	372	2.1%

Christians Denoms		Pop %	Affiliates	Ann Gr
Protestant	1	2.15	200	3.3%
Anglican	1	2.15	200	2.1%
Catholic	1	52.37	5,000	1.6%
Marginal	1	0.32	<50	3.7%
Unaffiliated		4.0	<400	0.0%

Churches	MegaBloc	Congs	Members	Affiliates
Roman Catholic	C	3	2,706	4,870
Episcopal Church	A	1	91	200
Pentecostal Church	P	1	111	200
Jehovah's Witnesses	M	1	18	30
Total Christians[4]		**6**	**2,926**	**5,300**

TransBloc	Pop %	Population	Ann Gr
Evangelicals			
Evangelicals	2.3	210	3.2%
Renewalists			
Charismatics	3.8	350	2.6%
Pentecostals	2.2	200	3.3%

Annual Growth Rates

Non-rel   Evang

Pop

Chr

AGR (%)

MegaBlocs
% of Christian Pop

6.6 0.5 3.5 3.5

85.9

P
A
C
U
X

S

Challenges for Prayer

1 **This island caters to the uber-rich,** trading on its sophistication and isolation for its exclusivity. There is little interest in spiritual things. Pray that amid the boutiques, cafés and villas there might awaken a hunger for spiritual reality and the opportunity to know God. Pray also that the few churches on the island might minister meaningfully into this unique context.

St Helena

Jamestown

South Atlantic Ocean

St Helena
British Overseas Territory of St Helena
Africa

Geography

Area 412 sq km. St Helena (122 sq km), 2,000 km west of Angola in the south Atlantic. Two dependencies: Ascension Island (90 sq km), 600 km to the northwest, and Tristan da Cunha (100 sq km), 1,200 km to the south. Also several uninhabited islands.

Population		Ann Gr	Density
2010	4,406	-1.34%	11/sq km
2020	4,408	0.66%	11/sq km
2030	4,612	0.38%	11/sq km

St. Helena 75%; Ascension 20%; Tristan 5% of population.
Capital Jamestown 680. **Urbanites** 39.7%.

Peoples

St Helenan 99%. Predominantly British, but also Chinese, African, Malay.
Expatriate 1.0%. Also, a transient population of British and American military and some civilian contractors on the islands, particularly on the Ascension airbase.
Literacy 99%. **Official language** English. **All languages** 1. **Languages with Scriptures** 1Bi.

Economy

Weak economy; almost all revenue is support from the UK. Isolation and the lack of an airport undermines potential for tourism. About

25% of St Helena's population have recently emigrated to the Falklands and the UK, looking for jobs.

Politics

British overseas territory; people have the right to full UK citizenship.

Religion

Full religious freedom.

Religions	Pop %	Population	Ann Gr
Christian	94.70	4,172	-1.6%
Non-religious	5.10	225	3.6%
Baha'i	0.20	9	1.3%

Christians Denoms		Pop %	Affiliates	Ann Gr
Protestant	3	7.04	<400	-1.2%
Independent	2	2.95	<200	-3.7%
Anglican	1	87.38	4,000	-1.3%
Catholic	1	2.04	<100	-2.1%
Marginal	1	4.99	<300	-4.0%
Doubly affiliated		-9.69	-427	0.0%

Churches	MegaBloc	Congs	Members	Affiliates
Anglican Church	A	12	2,962	3,850
Jehovah's Witnesses	M	3	120	220
Baptist Church	P	1	58	115
Seventh-day Adventist	P	1	75	100
Salvation Army	P	1	62	95
Catholic Church	C	3	58	90
Other denominations[2]		2	80	130
Doubly affiliated				-427
Total Christians[8]		**23**	**3,415**	**4,173**

TransBloc	Pop %	Population	Ann Gr
Evangelicals			
Evangelicals	8.8	389	0.5%
Renewalists			
Charismatics	3.0	131	-3.7%
Pentecostals	1.8	80	-2.8%

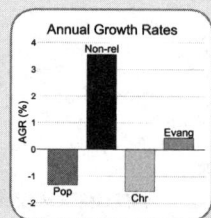

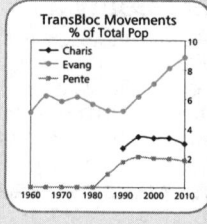

Challenges for Prayer

1 **Emigration from St Helena** increases as jobs become scarcer. Much of the employment occurs on the communications and military bases of Ascension and the Falkland Islands. Pray for an effective witness to those working on these bases. Also, pray for those leaving to find work elsewhere; failure to approve building an airport deflated many hopes for St Helena's development.

2 **The Christian heritage of St Helena** is strong but islanders' committed to faith are decreasing. Most Christians are nominal, and church attendance continues to decline. A critical mass of evangelicals on the islands is needed to generate spiritual momentum. Pray for Baptists and the Salvation Army, where most evangelicals can be found, and for the Anglican Church – the largest group, but spiritually dormant.

3 **The isolation of the islands** makes vibrant ministry and church life a huge challenge. Connection to the outside world and to Christian resources is limited. The small and more transient populations of Ascension and Tristan have even less evangelical presence and ministry, if any.

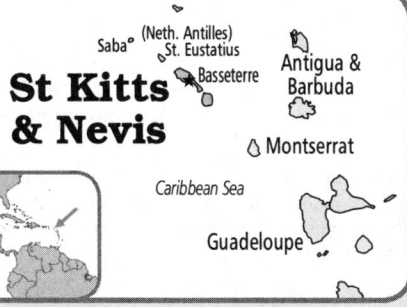

St Kitts & Nevis

Saba° (Neth. Antilles)
St. Eustatius
Basseterre
Antigua & Barbuda
Montserrat
Caribbean Sea
Guadeloupe

St Kitts and Nevis

Federation of St Kitts and Nevis

Caribbean

Geography

Area 269 sq km. Two volcanic islands in the Caribbean Leeward Islands. St Kitts 176 sq km; Nevis 93 sq km.

Population		Ann Gr	Density
2010	52,368	1.28%	195/sq km
2020	58,676	1.08%	218/sq km
2030	63,693	0.74%	237/sq km

Capital Basseterre 13,000. **Urbanites** 43%. **Pop under 15 yrs** 31%. **Life expectancy** 72.2 yrs.

Peoples

African Caribbean 97%. Black 86%; Mixed background 11%.
South Asian 1%.
European background 2%.
Literacy 97.8%. **Language** English. **All languages** 2. **Languages with Scriptures** 1Bi.

Economy

Nevis was once the richest Caribbean island, producing 85% of the British Empire's sugar.

The collapse of the world sugar price shut down this industry completely. Tourism is now the primary industry, with offshore finance growing quickly.
HDI Rank 62nd/182. **Public debt** 78.5% of GDP. **Income/person** $10,310 (22% of USA).

Politics

Independent from Britain in 1983 as a federal parliamentary democracy. Nevis has internal self-rule.

Religion

Complete religious freedom.

Religions	Pop %	Population	Ann Gr
Christian	92.95	48,676	1.1%
Non-religious	5.70	2,985	3.6%
Other	0.90	471	5.0%
Baha'i	0.45	236	2.2%

Christians	Denoms	Pop %	Affiliates	Ann Gr
Protestant	26	42.51	22,000	0.4%
Independent	6	3.25	2,000	1.2%
Anglican	1	20.62	11,000	1.2%
Catholic	1	7.64	4,000	1.6%
Orthodox	1	0.19	100	2.1%
Marginal	7	2.12	1,000	0.2%
Unaffiliated		16.60	9,000	2.4%

Churches	MegaBloc	Congs	Members	Affiliates
Anglican Church	A	11	5,400	10,800
Methodist Church	P	24	4,500	9,000
Catholic Church	C	10	2,857	4,000
Moravian Church	P	4	800	2,450
Seventh-day Adventist	P	9	1,438	2,300
Ch of God Prophecy	P	22	1,167	2,100
Wesleyan Church	P	18	817	1,470
Ch of God (Cleveland)	P	10	900	1,440
Baptist Convention	P	9	886	1,240
Ch of God (Anderson)	P	6	350	560
Christian Brethren	P	9	320	512
Other denominations[31]		29	2,031	4,102
Total Christians[42]		**161**	**21,466**	**39,974**

TransBloc	Pop %	Population	Ann Gr
Evangelicals			
Evangelicals	21.7	11,390	1.5%
Renewalists			
Charismatics	11.8	6,184	3.0%
Pentecostals	7.8	4,100	3.2%

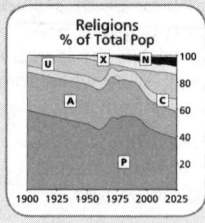

Religions
% of Total Pop

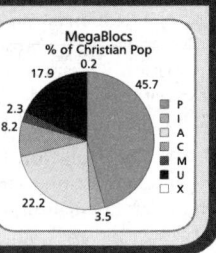

MegaBlocs
% of Christian Pop

Challenges for Prayer

1 **The shift in economy,** from sugar to tourism and offshore finance, has borne unwanted fruit in attracting, along with the money, undesirable elements. Pray for personal and social righteousness to combat this trend.

2 **There is no lack of churches** or other ministries on these islands, but their impact is limited. Pray for the Holy Spirit to revive, empower and embolden believers for Kingdom effectiveness. Pray especially for ministries that draw together the diverse denominations, such as the Evangelical Association and Youth Impact Ministries.

3 **Women lead 45% of households.** Teenage mothers account for 19% of the total number of live births nationally. Pray that God might work to restore the strength of family life in this nation.

Martinique

Caribbean Sea

Castries

St Lucia

St. Vincent and the Grenadines

Barbados

St Lucia

State of St Lucia

Caribbean

Geography 🌍

Area 617 sq km. Windward Islands between Martinique and St Vincent. One of the most beautiful islands in the Caribbean.

Population		Ann Gr	Density
2010	173,942	1.04%	282/sq km
2020	190,333	0.86%	308/sq km
2030	203,758	0.62%	330/sq km

Capital Castries 15,600. **Urbanites** 28%. **Pop under 15 yrs** 26%. **Life Expectancy** 73.6 yrs.

Peoples 👪

African Caribbean 90%.
Mixed race 6%.
South Asian 3.2%.
Euro–American 0.8%.
Literacy 90.1%. **Official language** English, but 80% speak French Creole (Kweyol). **All languages** 2. **Languages with Scriptures** 1Bi 1NT 1por.

Economy 🗺

Tourism is important and becoming more so. Agriculture, offshore finance and manufacturing make St Lucia one of the most diverse and stable economies in the Caribbean.
HDI Rank 69th/182. **Public debt** 32.4% of GDP. **Income/person** $5,806 (12% of USA).

Politics ☒

Contested by French and British, changing hands 14 times, but British since 1814. Independent from Britain in 1979. A stable parliamentary democracy.

Religion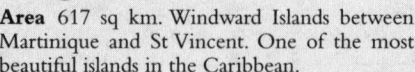

Religions	Pop %	Population	Ann Gr
Christian	95.08	165,384	1.0%
Ethnoreligionist	1.80	3,131	2.2%

Non-religious	1.10	1,913	5.2%	Ch of God (Cleveland)	P	24	1,615	2,100
Hindu	0.97	1,687	1.9%	Other denominations[34]		121	7,494	14,174
Muslim	0.50	870	1.0%	*Doubly affiliated*				*-10,380*
Other	0.35	609	4.2%	**Total Christians[43]**		**291**	**77,027**	**132,554**
Baha'i	0.20	348	1.0%					

Christians	Denoms	Pop %	Affiliates	Ann Gr
Protestant	27	20.85	36,000	2.2%
Independent	9	2.07	4,000	6.7%
Anglican	1	1.87	3,000	-0.1%
Catholic	1	55.77	97,000	-0.7%
Marginal	5	1.61	3,000	1.8%
Unaffiliated		18.90	33,000	4.1%
Doubly affiliated		*-5.97*	*-10,000*	*0.0%*

TransBloc	Pop %	Population	Ann Gr
Evangelicals			
Evangelicals	14.5	25,303	3.2%
Renewalists			
Charismatics	8.2	14,250	4.3%
Pentecostals	8.1	14,020	4.3%

Churches	MegaBloc	Congs	Members	Affiliates
Catholic Church	C	21	51,323	97,000
Seventh-day Adventist	P	64	9,581	16,000
Pentecostal Assemblies	P	30	2,994	5,000
Anglican Church	A	2	1,630	3,260
Apostolic Faith Ch	P	6	1,240	3,100
Baptist Churches	P	23	1,150	2,300

Annual Growth Rates

MegaBlocs % of Christian Pop

Challenges for Prayer

1 **The veneer of religion** without true faith is a widespread problem – the more historic churches are in significant decline. Living Christianity decreasingly influences much of society, as increasing materialism undermines spiritual life. A staggering 86% of all children are born out of wedlock and 45% of all households are led by women. Pray for genuine renewal in the churches and for the spiritual and moral transformation of society.

2 **Evangelically oriented churches** have multiplied – as have divisions. Pray for true unity amid the increasing diversity so that churches can offer a united front for the gospel's sake. The Fellowship of Gospel Preaching Churches is working to develop that unity in practical terms.

3 **The majority of St Lucians** speak a French Creole. The NT, recently translated into Creole, is being used for literacy projects. **CLC** has a Christian bookstore in Castries. Pray for the Word of God to be acquired, read and applied in the lives of St Lucians.

4 **Other ministries. IFES** works in secondary schools with plans to expand. Pray that Bible-believing Christians may influence every level of society for good and for God.

S

Caribbean Sea | Ânguilla

St Martin Marigot

St. Maarten (Netherlands Antilles)

Saint Barthélemy

Saba (Netherlands Antilles)

St Martin

Collectivity of St Martin

Caribbean

Geography

Area 53 sq km. Shares an island with Saint Maarten – which is part of the Netherlands – as well as several neighbouring islets. Part of the Leeward Islands in the Caribbean.

Population		Ann Gr	Density
2010	38,250	1.64%	722/sq km

Capital Marigot 5,700 (est).

Peoples

Majority comprised of French Caucasians, with smaller numbers of Dutch, French West Indies Creole, East Indian, Guadeloupans, Haitians and others. **Literacy** 100%. **Official language** French. **Other languages** English, Dutch, Creole, Papiamento.

Economy

Tourism, mostly of the high-end variety from USA and France, dominates the economy and accounts for 85% of employment. Reported to have the highest per capita income in the Caribbean. Almost all food, energy and manufactured goods must be imported. There is free movement between the Dutch and French sides of the island, which strengthens the economies of both.

S

Politics

An overseas collectivity of France, having been a part of Guadeloupe until 2007. As part of France, it comprises the most westerly point of the EU and is the world's smallest island shared by two countries. The election of the president of the Territorial Council descended into farce after five presidents in two years.

Religion

Freedom of religion.

Religions	Pop %	Population	Ann Gr
Christian	83.85	32,073	1.2%
Non-religious	15.30	5,852	3.8%
Other	0.85	325	5.7%

Christians	Denoms	Pop %	Affiliates	Ann Gr
Protestant	11	3.37	1,000	3.7%
Anglican	1	0.46	<200	1.8%
Catholic	1	76.47	29,000	1.6%
Marginal	1	0.39	<200	2.9%
Unaffiliated		3.16	1,000	-12.9%

Churches	MegaBloc	Congs	Members	Affiliates
Catholic Church	C	3	16,250	29,250
Nazarene Church	P	2	190	380
Anglican Church	A	1	97	175
Baptist Church	P	1	75	150
Jehovah's Witnesses	M	2	75	150
Methodist Church	P	1	60	120
Other denominations[8]		7	324	640
Total Christians[14]		**17**	**17,071**	**30,865**

TransBloc	Pop %	Population	Ann Gr
Evangelicals			
Evangelicals	2.5	972	4.3%
Renewalists			
Charismatics	0.7	258	5.1%

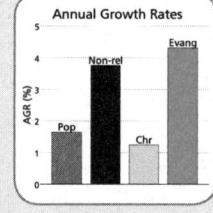

Annual Growth Rates

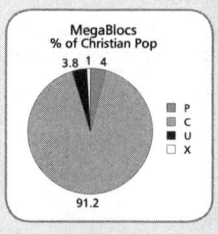

MegaBlocs % of Christian Pop

Challenges for Prayer

1 **The tropical location** and French liberality combine to make this a playground for the most wealthy. Exclusive hotels, clothing-optional beaches, designer-clothing boutiques and cafés typify the island's culture. There is little room for or interest in a life of service to Christ. Pray that in the midst of this elegant but hedonistic paradise, people might gain a hunger for an eternal heaven.

2 **A variety of churches** serves the French, American and Caribbean populations. Many provide church services for holidaymakers as well as locals. Pray for unity and cooperation among the diverse denominations in this place where spiritual apathy is a much greater rival than other denominations.

3 **The St Martin United Ministerial Foundation** seeks to provide a platform for united action among evangelical Christian leaders on both the French and Dutch sides of the island. Pray that God might use this fledging organization to powerfully impact this small island.

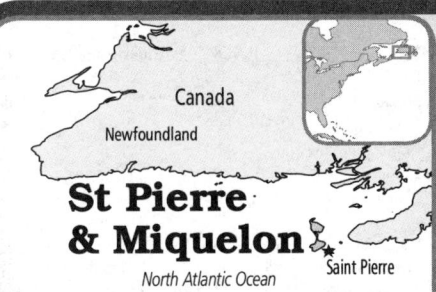

Canada
Newfoundland
St Pierre·
& Miquelon
North Atlantic Ocean Saint Pierre

St Pierre & Miquelon

Territorial Collectivity of St Pierre and Miquelon

North America

Geography

Area 242 sq km. An island group at the mouth of Canada's Gulf of St Lawrence, 25 km south of Newfoundland.

Population		Ann Gr	Density
2010	6,044	-0.34%	25/sq km
2020	6,046	0.00%	25/sq km
2030	6,040	0.00%	25/sq km

Capital St Pierre 5,400. **Urbanites** 90.6%.

Peoples

French of predominantly Breton and Basque origin. **Literacy** 99%. **Official language** French. **All languages** 3. **Languages with Scriptures** 2Bi.

Economy

Collapse of the cod-fishing industry makes the islands heavily dependent on French economic aid.

Politics

An overseas territorial collectivity of France, the last vestige of France's once-vast North American possessions.

Religion

Freedom of religion.

Religions	Pop %	Population	Ann Gr
Christian	96.94	5,859	-0.6%
Non-religious	3.06	185	9.6%

Christians Denoms		Pop %	Affiliates	Ann Gr
Protestant	2	0.17	<50	0.0%
Catholic	1	96.46	6,000	-0.6%
Marginal	1	0.31	<50	-1.0%

Churches	MegaBloc	Congs	Members	Affiliates
Catholic Church	C	2	3,667	5,830
Jehovah's Witnesses	M	1	8	19
Other denominations[2]		1	5	10
Total Christians[4]		4	3,680	5,859

TransBloc	Pop %	Population	Ann Gr
Evangelicals			
Evangelicals	<0.1	3	0.0%
Renewalists			
Charismatics	0.5	31	3.7%

S

Challenges for Prayer

1 **These isolated islands and their people** have long been Catholic. Traditions are strong and change has come slowly, despite the economic downturn when the fishing industry all but disappeared. Pray for people to find hope in a living relationship with Christ.

2 **There are no longer any evangelical groups.** The Baptists and **AoG** have both withdrawn from this hard field. While there may be a few private believers, there is no longer a formal evangelical or even Protestant presence in the islands.

St Vincent
and the Grenadines

Kingstown

Caribbean Sea

Grenada

St Vincent

St Vincent and the Grenadines

Caribbean

Geography

Area 389 sq km. Windward Islands; located between St Lucia and Grenada. One larger island and a chain of 16 smaller islands and islets to the south.

Population		Ann Gr	Density
2010	109,284	0.10%	281/sq km
2020	110,278	0.14%	283/sq km
2030	112,623	0.23%	290/sq km

Capital Kingstown 28,500. **Urbanites** 47.8%.
Pop under 15 yrs 27%. **Life expectancy** 71.4 yrs.

Peoples

African Caribbean 66%.
Mixed race 19%.
East Indian 6%.
Carib 2%. With much African intermarriage.
Euro-American 4%. Many Portuguese.
Other 3%.
Literacy 88.1%. **Languages** English (official), Vincentian Creole. **All languages** 3. **Languages with Scriptures** 1Bi 1w.i.p.

Economy

Economic reliance on a single crop, the banana, is being alleviated somewhat by growth in tourism. Poverty is common due to chronic underemployment and unemployment (15%, but 39% amongst those under 25 years old). Illegal cultivation of marijuana in the island's interior is occurring as a result.
HDI Rank 91st/182. **Public debt** 48% of GDP.
Income/person $5,615 (12% of USA).

Politics

Independent from Britain as a parliamentary democracy in 1979. A member of the Commonwealth.

Religion

Complete freedom of religion.

Religions	Pop %	Population	Ann Gr
Christian	90.10	98,465	-0.1%
Hindu	3.80	4,153	1.8%
Non-religious	2.60	2,841	2.6%
Ethnoreligionist	2.00	2,186	0.1%
Muslim	1.20	1,311	1.9%
Baha'i	0.30	328	0.1%

Christians	Denoms	Pop %	Affiliates	Ann Gr
Protestant	37	65.15	71,000	1.3%
Independent	5	14.50	16,000	0.8%
Anglican	1	17.29	19,000	-0.5%
Catholic	1	6.77	7,000	-2.0%
Marginal	2	0.98	1,000	0.8%
Unaffiliated		2.50	3,000	-12.9%
Doubly affiliated		*-17.11*	*-19,000*	*0.0%*

Churches	MegaBloc	Congs	Members	Affiliates
Anglican Church	A	22	3,780	18,900
Seventh-day Adventist	P	38	13,650	16,700
Methodist Churches	P	42	6,350	15,240
Spiritual Baptist	I	26	6,571	13,800
Pente Assoc of W Indies	P	16	2,229	7,800
Catholic Church	C	65	3,915	7,400
Ch of God (Cleveland)	P	20	2,200	4,884
Evang Ch of W Indies	P	29	1,750	3,850
Christian Brethren	P	19	1,904	3,180
Foursquare Gospel Ch	P	7	2,530	3,162
Baptist Church	P	17	1,500	2,505
Other denominations[30]		87	10,016	16,997
Doubly affiliated				*-18,700*
Total Christians[46]		**388**	**56,395**	**95,718**

TransBloc	Pop %	Population	Ann Gr
Evangelicals			
Evangelicals	39.1	42,720	1.3%
Renewalists			
Charismatics	25.1	27,439	1.3%
Pentecostals	23.1	25,250	1.7%

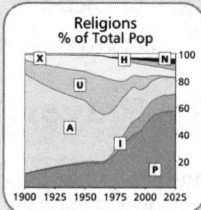

Religions % of Total Pop

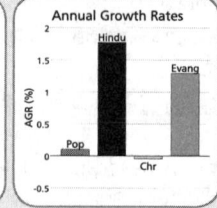

Annual Growth Rates

S

Answers to Prayer

1 **Through the ministries of the Evangelical Association,** cooperation among the various evangelical churches remains strong. A cross-denomination prayer movement recently started as well.

Challenges for Prayer

1 **St Vincent is a religious country,** but most are not related to God through a personal faith in Jesus Christ. There is a crisis of holiness, lack of spiritual fruit and growing apathy, especially regarding missions. Pray for revival and for restoration of a biblically-based, Spirit-led Church.

2 **The need continues for biblical leadership** and training in churches, although it is being addressed by programmes such as Bible school extensions and BCCs (PAWI, Church of God, BCM).

3 **The smaller Grenadine Islands** suffer a lack of churches due to their more isolated nature. Groups such as the Methodists, Pentecostals and Baptists seek to plant more churches in the Grenadines.

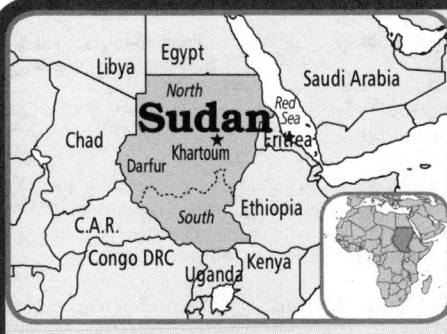

Sudan
Republic of Sudan
Africa

Geography

Area 2,503,890 sq km. Africa's largest country. Desert in the north, merging into grasslands and mountains in the centre and tropical bush in the south. Straddling the Nile Rivers. Nuba Mountains in the centre.

Population		Ann Gr	Density
2010	43,192,438	2.22%	17/sq km
2020	52,308,944	1.85%	21/sq km
2030	60,994,832	1.48%	24/sq km

Any population figures available are either very rough estimates or results of a census many feel is fundamentally flawed and even manipulated. Over 2 million deaths through war, genocide and famine since 1983, and as many as 7 million displaced. Most of the southern population was affected by the north-south conflict. Great loss of life and displacement of people have also occurred in Darfur, in inter-tribal conflict in the south and in the LRA activities in the far south.

Capital Khartoum 5,172,283. The three-city metropolis of Khartoum, Omdurman and Khartoum North is surrounded by millions living in shantytowns. **Urbanites** Officially 45.2%. **Pop under 15 yrs** 39%. **Life expectancy** 57.9 yrs.

Peoples

Over 597 ethnic groups and subgroups – one of Africa's most diverse populations.

Arab World 58.3%. Predominantly in the north. The Arab population has intermingled with numerous indigenous peoples and is not regarded as "pure Arab" by some other Arab nations. Many distinct peoples of the north and centre have become Arabized. Nearly half of Sudan's blacks consider themselves to be Arab. Specific categories (with overlap):

Sudanese Arab 52.7%. 44 peoples. Sudanese Arab 20.7%; Gaaliin 6.5%; Guhayna 3.9%; Shaikia 1.9%; Gawamaa 1.9%; Kawahia 1.9%; Bederia 1.8%; Dar Hamid 1.5%; Hasania 1.4%; Rufaa 1.1%.
Shuwa Arab 2.3%. 5 peoples. Messiria (Baggara) 1.2%.
Other Arab 3.3%. Egyptian 1.3%; Hamar 0.9%; 4 others.
Horn of Africa-Cushitic 7.6%. 9 peoples. Beja/Bedawi 6.8%.
Sub-Saharan African 33.8%. Largely in the centre and south. More than 150 groups.
Nilotic 17.6%. 53 peoples. Largest: Dinka(6) 6.2%; Nuer 3.6%; Bari 1.2%; Shilluk 0.9%.
Ouaddai-Fur 4.2%. 14 peoples. Fur 2.3%.
Sudanic 2.8%. 22 peoples. Zande 1.6%.
Nuba Mountain peoples 2.8%. 48 peoples; most are small in number.
Kanuri-Saharan 2.5%. 7 peoples.

S

Adamawa-Ubnagi 0.4%. Cluster of 13 peoples with small populations.

Other Sub-Saharan 3.6%. 14 peoples. Hausa 1.5%.

Other peoples 0.3%. Europeans, Asians, Jews.

Literacy 59%, but much lower in practice. **Official languages** Arabic and English. **All languages** 134. **Languages with Scriptures** 11Bi 23NT 35por.

Economy

Rich in agricultural and mineral resources. One of the world's fastest-growing economies, centred on Khartoum, but many Sudanese remain mired in poverty. Economic dynamics in north, centre and south differ greatly. Rapid increase of crude oil production as well as great potential in hydro-electrics and mineral exploitation. Years of widespread economic mismanagement, civil war, diplomatic isolation and famine have held back economic progress, particularly devastating to the embattled south. Currently shifting from socialist to market economic practices. Agriculture still employs the largest segment of the population and accounts for 37% of the GDP. Sudan's main trade partners are, perhaps unsurprisingly, China and Saudi Arabia, but also Indonesia and Malaysia. **HDI Rank** 150th/182. **Public debt** 100% of GDP. **Income/person** $1,522 (3% of USA).

Politics

Joint Egyptian and British control from 1899 to independence in 1956. Civil war began even before independence due to conflict between the Islamized, Arabized north and the non-Arab, Black African south, with bitter fighting from 1955-72. After 12 years of uneasy peace, fighting broke out again in 1983. An extremist Islamist coup in 1989 led to increased fighting between Muslims and southerners (led by the Sudan People's Liberation Army – SPLA) in the Nuba Mountains and the southern provinces. The Comprehensive Peace Agreement (CPA) officially ended the fighting in 2005, granting limited autonomy to the south and a referendum for independence scheduled for 2011. Oil profits are to be split between north and south, and there is one vice-president from each region. The government and its sponsored militia groups then fought against other Muslim groups in the Blue Nile region along the Ethiopian and Eritrean borders from the 1990s and in Darfur shortly thereafter. The Eastern Front signed a peace and power-sharing treaty with the government. In Darfur in the west, government policies have displaced millions, seen over 300,000 dead and elicited widespread international condemnation along with charges of war crimes against Sudan's president from the International Criminal Court. Since independence, aggressive Arabization and Islamization have provoked violent resistance from many quarters, which in turn elicited responses of greater discrimination, war and genocide by the government and military against its own people. Accused of harbouring international terrorists, Sudan typically endures hostile relations with most, if not all, of its neighbours.

Religion

A Sunni Muslim majority, but primarily among the Sudanese Arabs in the north. Sufi religious orders are strong – especially Ansar, followers of the famous Mahdi. The constitution offers some religious freedoms, but in practice, those freedoms are arbitrarily abused. The Naivasha Agreement established some protections for non-Muslims in the north (although apostasy is legally punishable by death) and it clarified that Islamic law does not apply in the south. But attempts to impose Islamic law – in contravention of several previous peace agreements – generate a hostile religious context and a cause of civil war. Despite the military's systematic destruction of churches, hospitals and schools in the south and the Nuba Mountains, there is considerable freedom to minister.

Religions	Pop %	Population	Ann Gr
Muslim	61.38	26,511,518	1.6%
Christian	26.11	11,277,546	4.8%
Ethnoreligionist	11.10	4,794,361	0.1%
Non-religious	1.40	604,694	3.8%
Other	0.01	4,319	2.2%

Many contend that the Muslim population has dropped to as low as 55%, and African traditional religionists to well below 10%; losses offset by growth among Christians and non-religious. All religious data are estimates.

Christians Denoms		Pop %	Affiliates	Ann Gr
Protestant	23	3.90	1,685,000	5.6%
Independent	28	0.51	220,000	5.7%
Anglican	3	10.42	4,500,000	6.7%
Catholic	1	10.72	4,630,000	2.9%
Orthodox	5	0.54	233,000	2.1%
Marginal	1	0.02	7,000	7.9%

Churches	MegaBloc	Congs	Members	Affiliates
Catholic Church	C	1,380	2,691,860	4,630,000
Episcopal Ch of S	A	4,505	1,351,351	4,500,000
Presbyterian Ch of S	P	500	400,000	1,000,000
Sudanese Ch of Christ	P	156	25,000	250,000
Coptic Orthodox Ch	O	40	80,000	200,000
Africa Inland Church	P	267	23,988	160,000
Sudan Pentecostal Ch	I	395	34,286	120,000
Sudan Interior Ch	P	704	63,333	95,000
Ch of the Nazarene	P	548	6,304	35,124
Ethiopian Orth Ch	O	41	12,273	27,000
Seventh-day Adventist	P	51	18,000	27,000
Evangelical Presbyterian	P	188	13,174	22,000
Trinity Presby Ch of S	I	358	8,955	19,700
Evangelical Free Ch of S	P	80	4,800	12,000
Other denominations[40]		690	71,881	179,621
Total Christians[61]		**9,903**	**4,805,205**	**11,277,445**

S

TransBloc	Pop %	Population	Ann Gr
Evangelicals			
Evangelicals	14.7	6,336,018	6.4%
Renewalists			
Charismatics	6.8	2,931,473	8.8%
Pentecostals	0.3	131,439	5.6%

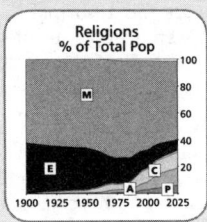

Religions
% of Total Pop

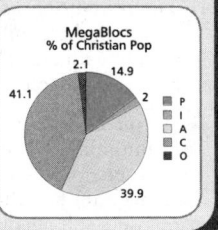

MegaBlocs
% of Christian Pop

Answers to Prayer

1 **The Comprehensive Peace Agreement** (CPA), signed in 2005, has held since then and allowed the war-torn south to attempt rebuilding some semblance of infrastructure and stability. A heavy presence of northern military and militias remains in the south, as do widely held questions of how long the peace will last. But peace, however tenuous, and the opportunity to plan and build for the future continue for now.

2 **The prolonged conflict and war** caused Christians to scatter throughout the country and beyond. This resulted in churches being planted in places and among peoples who were previously unreached. Now, many of those won to Christ while displaced are returning to their home areas with the goal of starting new fellowships.

3 **The massive growth of Christianity,** especially among central and southern peoples, is a point for praise. Christian numbers, 1.6 million in 1980, now exceed 11 million. Southern peoples may be as much as 80% Christian – remarkable growth amid terrible violence, warfare, persecution and even genocide. One such example is the spiritual transformation of the Dinka Bor people from animist to Christian.

4 **The planting of churches** in previously unreached areas and peoples. The crisis in Darfur, while tragic, has also seen the entry of Christian relief work along with the gospel. Sudanese Christians are church planting in Darfur, and the peoples of Darfur who fled elsewhere are encountering the gospel in their new locations.

Challenges for Prayer

1 **Sudan has known only war** for its entire modern history. Violence is rife throughout Sudan, which is regarded as one of the world's least stable nations. The belligerent government/military waged war against restive populations in the south, west and east at massive human and economic cost to its own citizens. With such religious, ethnic and linguistic diversity added to civil conflicts and hostile relations with neighbours, peace is nearly impossible. Pray for sweeping change at the highest levels and throughout the land – for repentance, restitution and rebuilding of communal life.

2 **Darfur is a 21st Century byword for tragedy.** Low-level conflict began in the 1970s, but in 2003 fighting escalated between rebel groups and the government-sponsored Janjawid militia. The people of Darfur are Black African Muslims, the Janjawid are Arabized Sudanese. Many consider the atrocities of Darfur to be racially motivated genocide. Massacres, rapes, mutilations and destruction of villages, food and water supplies are signatures of this systematic, government-sponsored campaign. The conflict – and refugees – spilled over into Chad as well, even leading to Chad's declaration of war against Sudan (ended in 2007). Pray for:

a) *A complete end to the violence* and upheaval in Darfur that has cost over 300,000 lives and displaced over 2.5 million people. Even a peace agreement in 2006 did not stop further predation by militias.

b) *The execution of justice* upon all those guilty of atrocities, from militias and rebels to top government and military figures. Pray for courage and determination from international bodies to bring the perpetrators to justice, and for foreign nations to act with moral uprightness rather than out of greed for cheap oil.

S

c) The restoration of peace and a normal functioning of life. Most NGOs trying to aid those caught in the conflict were forced out of the region. Pray that they might be able to return to help with aid and development. Pray that international assistance does not dry up simply because the violence ends.

③ South Sudan has officially been at peace since the CPA of 2005, when significant autonomy was established. During the 21-year civil war, 1.5 to 2 million people, mostly southerners, lost their lives, 5 million were internally displaced and a further 500,000 (and probably far more) fled the country to escape genocide by the Islamist, Arabized north. There are many issues still needing prayer:

a) The peace agreement is desperately fragile in many areas. It is often not observed by northern troops who displaced tens of thousands, destroyed most of the homes in the region and are colonizing the area with northerners in anticipation of the 2011 vote. The northern armed groups' predations may provoke a unilateral breakaway by the south, which in turn would inevitably lead to war, chaos and further destruction. Pray that peace might prevail and that those perpetuating violence and disorder may be stopped. Pray also that the bombed-out infrastructure might be rebuilt without the threat of further destruction.

b) The 2011 referendum on independence will determine south Sudan's future. No one knows the implications of a vote one way or another, but independence would spell many trials in forming a young nation. There would be at least one possibly hostile, resentful neighbour, since most of Sudan's oil reserves are in the south. Were independence chosen, pray that upheaval and violence would be minimal and that wise, righteous leaders might emerge to move the fledgling nation forward. The oil-rich Abeyi and Nuba mountain regions have also suffered heavily at the hands of the military and militias; Abeyi will also hold a referendum about whether to join the North or South in 2011.

c) The remarkable church growth of the last 20 years occurred mostly in the south, in a context of war and destruction. The faith of the southern Sudanese amid persecution and suffering is remarkable, but cannot be presumed for the next generation. Pray that neither the peace agreement nor possible independence might blunt the keen edge of their faith. Pray that the Church might play a central and redemptive role in shaping the future of the south.

④ The persistence of slavery in Sudan is a serious issue, again made prominent in the 1990s during the civil war. Almost all slaves are from the south and the Nuba Mountains. Northern militias are the main perpetrators, but inter-tribal raiders and even the SPLA also take captives for enforced labour. Their lot – whether slaves, abductees or POWs – is misery. In the north alone, an estimated 40,000 to 100,000 (or more) southerners are now held as chattel. The controversial buying back of slaves by Western NGOs frees some and raises awareness, but probably exacerbates the problem. Pray that all such wrongs may end, and pray that world leaders may prevail upon all involved to end this wickedness. Shari'a law in the north and the impunity with which northern militias act help perpetuate this barbarism.

⑤ Sudan's leaders, as much as they are able, have aggressively imposed Islamic shari'a on the rest of the country and boasted of their role as leaders of the Islamic Revolution in Africa. In fact, an Arab minority used religion as a tool to consolidate power and to justify killing, stealing and destroying in the south, despite its legal autonomy. There was once a strong Christian presence in northern Sudan, and for nearly a millennium the majority of the population were Christian. Muslims invaded and defeated the Christians at the end of the 13th Century and gradually Islamized the area by the 15th Century. Pray that plans to uproot, wipe out or convert Christian populations in Sudan may fail spectacularly.

⑥ Persecution of the Church, persisting over most of the last 60 years, has been most intense since 1985. Deliberate attempts to eliminate a viable Christian presence are extreme and include bombing of Sunday church services, destruction of churches, hospitals, schools, mission bases and Christian villages, massacres and mutilation, and murder of pastors and leaders. Persecution is especially severe in the Nuba Mountains. Whole areas have been laid waste and lands seized and given to Arabized northerners. Pray that Christians may bear good witness to their persecutors in these sufferings and become spiritually strong as a result. Pray also that the sufferings of Christians might become widely known and that peace, justice and religious freedom may be firmly established.

7 **The Church is growing** amid suffering and persecution – incredibly so. Catholics, Anglicans, Presbyterians, Church of Christ in Sudan (**Pioneers**) and African Inland Church (**AIM**) see remarkable turnings to Christ.

a) *The faith and optimism of Christians* is an inspiration. Their churches, bombed out multiple times, keep getting rebuilt. Long-term planning for church planting, mission, education and others continues. Some of the persecutors have even been won to faith in Christ.

b) *People movements* have broken down barriers of customs and languages to bring many to Christ from hitherto unreached peoples, such as the Nuer, Mabaan, Uduk, Dinka, Moru, Toposa, Acholi and some of the Nuba tribes. Pray that Christians may demonstrate love and concern for others that transcends ethnic and racial divisions – these persist even among Christianized groups in the south.

8 **The pressing needs of the Church** include:

a) *Unity* that transcends tribal boundaries and denominational lines. Great church growth into a relative vacuum – spiritually and politically – has resulted in power struggles. Working to consolidate the unity that was strong during the peak of persecution is crucial. The Sudan Council of Churches and the Cush Consultation (expat and indigenous ministries) all work toward this end. Pray that ethnic and denominational considerations as well as the lure of power might be placed at the foot of the cross.

b) *Discipling, teaching and strengthening* the millions of believers who have come into the Church. Many were drawn to Christianity as an expression of opposition to Islam. Nominalism and tribalism still retain a hold over large numbers. Most new believers have an animist background and do not fully understand the gospel beyond the most basic elements. The Church stands at risk of widespread syncretism. Pray for churches to raise new believers to a maturity that enables them to stand in the face of persecution and not be overwhelmed by Islam, or instead not be seduced by worldliness or idols. Growing secularism adds new challenges for the Church.

c) *Recovery.* Many churches, villages and towns in the south have been destroyed and rebuilt several times. Education and health services have scarcely functioned for two decades. Various ministries are required to build a stable future:

   i *Physical infrastructure and needs.* Christians, assisted by the global Church, could lead the way in restoring devastated schools, hospitals and other services crucial to society. Transparency in using funds given for building projects is also essential; the temptation to impoverished pastors is great, since lack of organizational skills and experience in handling such sizeable funds is widespread.

   ii *Basic human needs* such as food, medicine and agricultural supplies are still scarce, but generosity must be wed to wisdom in distributing these. Health care and doctors are extremely sparse. Many agencies risked much to bring help to Christians during the war. Of special note is the work of Open Doors, Voice of the Martyrs, Frontline Fellowship, Samaritan's Purse and WVI. Numerous indigenous NGOs are also springing up. Pray for a wise and appropriate approach to material assistance for Sudan.

   iii *Spiritual and emotional healing* is essential; every family in the south has been traumatized in one way or another. Training in counselling, reconciliation and peacemaking is needed.

9 **Sudanese Christian leaders** have achieved so much against great odds. Many even lost their lives in serving Jesus. Few have opportunity for formal theological education. The sheer number of young converts overwhelms the number of trained pastors. There are many points for prayer:

a) *Theological training institutions.* Trained pastors are a great need due to rapid church growth. All major denominations have Bible colleges and/or seminaries; altogether there are around 50 in the country. Large numbers of Sudanese also undertake theological studies abroad. Besides solid biblical teaching and discipleship methods, pastors and Christian leaders need to acquire skills in AIDS ministry, conflict resolution, trauma counselling and reconciliation ministry. Pray for the provision of facilities, staff and students adequate to shape the future of Sudanese Christianity.

S

b) _Informal training programmes_ are essential; there are simply not enough formal institutions to meet the need for pastors, evangelists, disciplers, lay leaders and other workers. The larger denominations and some mission organizations are developing programmes to this end. Training emerging young leaders to be biblically sound while retaining their spiritual zeal requires a discerning touch.

c) _Income for pastors._ Due to the economic situation, congregations usually cannot support their own pastors. This often means vocational training for Christian leaders and ministers, so they can earn their own living in a context where poverty and joblessness are already common.

⑩ Ministry challenges for the Church:

a) _Muslim majority._ The population in the north is largely Sunni Muslim, though among them are 200,000 or more Coptic Christians and up to four million southerners displaced by war.

  i _Increasing numbers of Muslims_ are turning to Jesus, in some cases, even entire villages. They are often disillusioned by Islam and attracted to Jesus. The openness among many is remarkable, and believers from Muslim backgrounds number in the tens of thousands. But millions remain virtually unreached by the gospel.

  ii _Southern Sudanese Christians' attitudes_ toward Muslims need prayer. Most are willing to forgive the Arabized Muslims who devastated their land and committed atrocities. But loving them enough to reach out in witness and trusting them as Christian brothers is, for many, understandably a step too far. Pray that the Holy Spirit might work in the hearts of those who struggle in this area.

b) _Khartoum_ is a booming conurbation of approximately seven million inhabitants, including the vast shantytowns on the outskirts, which consist mostly of displaced Nuba Mountain, Darfurian and southerner populations. Poverty and deprivation are widespread, and Christians are often subjected to harassment, destruction of church buildings and discriminatory taxes and laws. Khartoum actually has a higher Christian presence than any other northern city, but remains dominated by Islam.

c) _The Nuba Mountain peoples,_ an island of mostly Christian peoples in a sea of Islam, suffered harshly under the government's heavy hand. Whole tribes have turned to Christ (Episcopal Church, Sudanese Church of Christ); a few others have become Muslim. There are still a number of unreached groups among the 79 peoples here. Most of the population fled during the military's genocidal campaign, but many are now returning, despite the continued threat of renewed persecution.

d) _The SPLA,_ the southern (and formerly rebel) army, bravely resisted the predations of the north, but are guilty of atrocities themselves. Groups such as Frontline Fellowship and Far Reach Ministries train chaplains for this army. Many thousands of soldiers in this army have become Christians through the work of these chaplains. Pray for the maturing and growth of this movement.

e) _Children and young people._ Nearly half of Sudan's population are under age 18; almost all have grown up in a context of suffering and trauma. Pray for:

  i _Education._ An entire generation has almost no schooling, with potentially disastrous future implications. The education sector is being rebuilt. Training teachers is a great need (9,000 needed in the south alone), but getting kids into school is just as important. **CMS** helps Christians with an "Under Tree School" programme. Hope for the Future and Aid to the Church in Need are two of many agencies providing Sudanese Christian children with education. Only 22% of children are enrolled in school – partly due to compulsory fees introduced in 1999 – and only 1% of girls in Sudan finish school. ACES, the Association of Christian Educators in Sudan, is a united Christian voice on issues of education.

  ii _Child soldiers._ There are possibly as many as 9,000 still in Sudan. Many were forced to serve in the SPLA, the cultic Lord's Resistance Army or as pro-government militias. Since the war ended in the south, most are now in Darfur.

  iii _Street children_ – over 70,000 just in the northern part alone. Orphaned street kids in the war-battered south are uncounted. Almost all of Khartoum's more than 30,000 street kids were born elsewhere and are nearly all boys. Pray for Christian ministry to these vulnerable children. Operation Mercy, SOS Children, Kids Alive International and Living Water work with children at risk, but many more such ministries are needed.

11 **Less-evangelized peoples** are many in the west, east and north of Sudan. Also, some peoples in the Nuba Mountains and in the south are still largely unreached. Pray especially for these:

a) **Darfur Province** was Christian a millennium ago. Though one of the least-evangelized areas in the world, there are now handfuls of believers in many of the peoples of this region. The Daju, Fur, Masalit, Midob, Tama/Kimr and Zaghawa all number among the least-reached peoples in Africa. Pray for outreach to them in this most difficult of areas. Tearfund, Operation Blessing and the major denominations in Sudan minister through relief and aid; pray that the love of Christ might also be shared.

b) **The Beja** on the Red Sea Coast were famed as the "Fuzzie Wuzzies". They were once Christian, but now practice folk Islam. There is limited ministry among them. Only a few Christians are known.

c) **The Nubians** of the Nile valley – an ancient people with great kingdoms – were Christian for 1,000 years. Relentless Muslim pressure led to their Islamization 600 years ago. There are only a handful of believers today. Several Christian agencies have ministry to them.

d) **The nomadic and semi-nomadic Baggara** tribes in the central belt of the country are numerous, but few have had much exposure to the gospel, and little is done to reach them. They speak three to four major Arabic dialects, but many are of non-Arab origin.

12 **Missionary activity** is seeing a dichotomy in its fortunes. Pray for these:

a) **Ministry in the north.** The government expelled 13 NGOs in 2009, drastically reducing not only the number of those working but also the capacity to deliver aid. Agencies are allowed to operate in the north but find working under the government's thumb very difficult. Many indigenous ministries, especially connected to the churches, work in and around Khartoum, but they focus mostly on Christians. Outreach to unevangelized peoples is quite limited.

b) **Burgeoning activity in the south,** especially since the CPA in 2005. Many ministries work in south Sudan but retain offices in Kenya. Besides notable expat-originated missions – such as **CMS**, **SIM**, **AIM**, **Pioneers**, Tearfund, Open Doors, Frontline Fellowship and others – there are also cross-organizational groups such as ACROSS and Sudan Partners, which collaborate to develop the indigenous church's capacity to do mission and ministry.

c) **African missionaries to Sudan,** increasing in number and stature. Nigeria, Ethiopia, Kenya and other nations send workers and entire teams to work with both Christians and the unreached.

d) **The calling and preparation** of indigenous and expatriate workers to evangelize the many peoples of the north who have never heard the gospel. Presbyterians and Baptists have recently seen a burst of missions vision and desire for collaborative ministry.

13 **Christian help ministries:**

a) **The Bible Society** has done much to supervise translation work and to distribute Scriptures from its Khartoum depot. It has an ambitious goal of distributing 10 million Scriptures in seven years, due to high demand from the many new believers.

b) **Bible translation** is still a major need. Of 114 languages, only 10 have the whole Bible in print (the Nuer Bible was recently completed). Twelve have translation work in progress, and another 21 still have translation needs. Pray for the many Sudanese Christians planning for, or actually translating, the Scriptures. Expatriates seek to help, encourage and train for the task. Pray for the rapid completion of these NTs and Bibles despite the many obstacles.

c) **Christian literature** is in short supply in most areas. Pray for all involved in bringing Scriptures, hymnals and other materials into the country (Frontline Fellowship, Open Doors and others). Christian book fairs in Khartoum draw many, both Christian and Muslim, and distribute countless pieces of literature. Pray that the great hunger for Christian and educational reading materials might be met.

d) **The JESUS film** is extensively used in the 21 languages translated so far. A large proportion of the population has seen it, with great response.

S

e) **Christian radio** is a rapidly growing ministry, especially local FM stations. ACROSS and many other Christian agencies have radio ministry. Sudan Christian Media Network serves countrywide, facilitating work in radio, audio, video and other media.

f) **GRN** has recordings in 129 languages and dialects. Wind-up and solar audio and MP3 players are very useful tools in much of the country with no electricity.

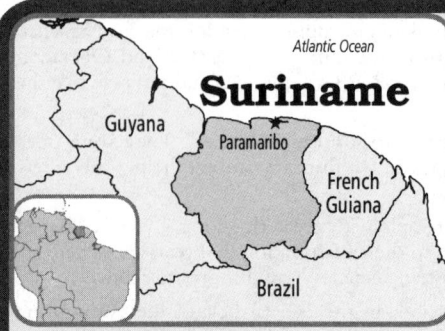

Atlantic Ocean

Suriname

Guyana
Paramaribo

French Guiana

Brazil

Suriname

Republic of Suriname

Latin America

Geography

Area 163,820 sq km. Northeast coast of South America, between Guyana and French Guiana.

Population		Ann Gr	Density
2010	524,345	0.97%	3/sq km
2020	567,766	0.74%	3/sq km
2030	602,436	0.54%	4/sq km

Many Surinamers migrated to the Netherlands around the time of independence.
Capital Paramaribo 263,000. **Urbanites** 75.6%. **Pop under 15 yrs** 29%. **Life expectancy** 68.8 yrs.

Peoples

Startling ethnic diversity, a legacy of colonial importation of indentured labour.
Asians 46.7%. East Indian (mostly originating from Bihar) 29%; Indonesian (mainly Javanese) 15%; Chinese(2) 2.7%.
Surinamese Creole 19%
Maroon 16%. 5 groups.
Mixed-race 11.3%.
Amerindian 4%. Seven ethnic groups.
Other 3%. Dutch; Lebanese; Portuguese.
Literacy 88%. **Official language** Dutch. **Trade language** Sranan Tongo (a Dutch Creole). **All languages** 20. **Indigenous languages** 16. **Languages with Scriptures** 3Bi 8NT 9por 2w.i.p.

Economy

Bauxite, oil, timber, marine and agricultural products and growing eco-tourism are the main sources of revenue. Post-independence economic decline has been replaced by modest growth. Remittances from emigrant Surinamers still supplement many incomes. Porous borders allow illegal gold extractions and drug transshipments to multiply.
HDI Rank 97th/182. **Public debt** 25.7% of GDP. **Income/person** $5,504 (12% of USA).

Politics

Independent from the Netherlands in 1975. A socialist military government ruled from 1980 to 1987; the former dictator still influences politics despite being convicted in the Netherlands of drug trafficking. A succession of coups, uprisings and abortive elections followed. An internationally supervised election in 1991 and an agreement in 1994 with rebels restored the country to democratic government and peace. Racial diversity makes for parties shaped along ethnic lines, which usually leads to awkward and ineffective coalitions.

Religion

Full freedom for the diverse religious groups.

Religions	Pop %	Population	Ann Gr
Christian	49.57	259,918	1.0%
Hindu	22.80	119,551	0.7%
Muslim	16.90	88,614	0.4%
Non-religious	5.50	28,839	3.3%
Ethnoreligionist	4.20	22,022	2.0%
Baha'i	0.70	3,670	-0.4%
Chinese	0.18	944	1.0%
Jewish	0.15	787	1.0%

Christians Denoms		Pop %	Affiliates	Ann Gr
Protestant	47	21.02	110,000	3.3%
Independent	24	2.47	13,000	3.1%
Anglican	1	0.03	<200	-5.6%
Catholic	1	20.60	108,000	0.4%
Marginal	2	1.37	7,000	3.8%
Unaffiliated		4.08	21,000	-1.0%

Churches	MegaBloc	Congs	Members	Affiliates
Catholic Church	C	30	35,000	108,000
Moravian Church	P	60	22,222	40,000
Full Gospel Churches	P	92	8,187	14,681
Gospel Center Suri	P	55	8,024	13,400
Jehovah's Witnesses	M	47	2,450	6,125
Seventh-day Adventist	P	18	3,700	5,200
God's Bazuin	P	52	2,994	5,000
Evang Lutheran Ch	P	5	2,198	4,000

S

					TransBloc	Pop %	Population	Ann Gr
Reformed Church	P	3	2,123	3,800	**Evangelicals**			
Baptisten Unie	P	17	1,700	3,774	Evangelicals	13.8	72,235	6.3%
Indep Faith Mission	P	20	1,850	3,090	**Renewalists**			
Faith & Love Ministries	P	6	1,500	2,505	Charismatics	11.5	60,133	7.1%
Bribi Ministries	I	14	893	2,500	Pentecostals	9.7	50,642	7.9%
Foundation Chr Ch	P	12	650	1,086				
Other denominations[56]		117	7,779	15,328				
Total Christians[75]		**548**	**101,270**	**228,489**				

Religions % of Total Pop

MegaBlocs % of Christian Pop
12.1 · 0.1 · 2.8 · 38.6 · 41.6 · 5
P I C M U X

Answers to Prayer

1 **The Church among the Maroon peoples has grown** since the 1960s, bringing up to 60% of the distinctive Maroon population to faith in Christ in the Surinamese interior. Praise God that faithful sowing of the gospel by **WT, IMB**, local churches and others has already borne substantial fruit. The government's apology to victims of a 1980s massacre of Maroons was a step toward a wider reconciliation within the nation.

2 **Churches among the southern tribal Amerindians** have embraced the Great Commission and now send missionaries to unevangelized tribes and villages in French Guiana, Brazil and other parts of Suriname.

3 **Movements uniting Christians in prayer and action** have grown in number as the Surinamese Church grows in strength and stability. There are networks for Christian women, an organization (Man Mit'Man) to unite men in having a godly influence on family and society, youth movements, prayer movements and others. Partnerships emerge across denominational and agency lines for purposes of strategy, mission and reconciliation.

Challenges for Prayer

1 **Suriname's post-independence existence** faces challenges old and new. While more stable than in the troubled years of coups and dictatorships, the nation remains largely compartmentalized by race and religion – polarizations that cripple political and social development. The sudden and seemingly unstoppable rise of a criminal economy through drug trafficking and gold smuggling requires both wise and concerted action. Pray for the emergence of godly leaders and for a spiritual awakening in this young nation.

2 **Nearly half the population profess to be Christian,** but many have little understanding of their faith, and Christian belief is often mixed with spiritism. In the larger Catholic and Moravian denominations, growth has been incremental, but recent Pentecostal and charismatic growth has been rapid. Pray for new life and dynamism to replace traditionalism and syncretism practised by many. Pray for increasing trans-denominational cooperation to continue in Bible-related ministries and outreach to every ethnic group in Suriname.

3 **Christian leaders** across all denominations face challenges within both the Church and society.

a) Church growth necessitates leaders to emerge, from all cultural backgrounds, who possess strong biblical faith and solid ability to minister into Suriname's unique context. Pray for the right individuals and families to step forward and lead faithfully.

b) Three interdenominational Bible institutes now provide training in-country for Surinamese pastors and workers, obviating the need to study abroad. Several denominational Bible

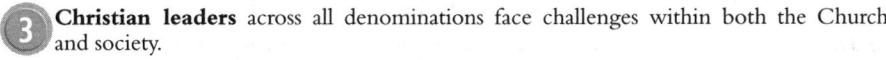

schools and informal Bible and leadership training programmes serve the church. Pray that these will effectively shape well-trained and well-equipped Christian leaders.

c) *Christian leaders must re-lay biblical foundations* and standards in this nation that lost its way morally and ethically in the confusion following independence. Pray that Christian leaders seek greater unity in the body of Christ and hunger after the Word of God in order to powerfully impart it to their congregations.

4 **Most of the six Amerindian peoples** are now at least nominally Christian. **WT** sees people movements among the Wayana, Akurio and Trio. The coastal Carib and Arawak are more needy. Some Amerindian churches are growing in faith and actively engaging in cross-cultural mission. Others struggle, reverting to sinful indigenous customs or outside secular and materialist pressures. Pray for stability, maturity and indigeneity to be maintained in tribal churches. Pray that Wayana and Trio missionaries rapidly learn and adapt, and pray for the cross-cultural workers among the Amerindians.

5 **Foreign missionaries** have perhaps decreased in Suriname in the last decade, though the number of Surinamese missionaries and Christian workers increased. Many international organizations have affiliates or branches run by Surinamese staff (**MAF**, **YWAM**, others), while others work in close partnership with local churches. Pray for effective collaboration in discipling and training new leaders, in Bible translation and use, and in outreach to the less-evangelized peoples.

6 **Less-reached peoples.** Pray for these:

a) *The Javanese* are predominantly Muslim, but nominally so. New generations of Javanese Christians, across denominations, rise to the challenge of reaching their own people. **CMA** and **IMB** now facilitate church planting training and mobilize churches to reach the Javanese. The Suriname Javanese NT was published in 2000, and plans are underway to translate the OT.

b) *The Indian community* is only now beginning to respond to the gospel. **WT**, in partnership with SKS (a Hindustani organization), seeks to see a church within walking distance of every Hindustani. But local congregations are slow on the uptake regarding outreach to this long-neglected group; pray for this partnership to spark greater zeal for ministry among them. Currently, there is no work or witness among Muslims within the Hindustani. Pray that the barriers of prejudice and misunderstanding be removed and the spiritual powers preventing their evangelization be rendered helpless.

c) *Chinese churches* are growing and actively joining other local churches and missions to plant more churches among Chinese in the region. **CMA** and the Moravians are involved in this outreach to the Chinese, who come mostly from the southern coastal provinces of China.

7 **Specialist Christian ministries** for prayer:

a) *The Suriname Bible Society* (UBS) plays a key role in not only Bible translation and distribution but also in production of media resources that address social and family issues. Bible distribution has increased since independence. With SIL Suriname, the SBS provides literacy training, while **CCCI** and others offer access to the JESUS film.

b) *Bible translation* continues through the Suriname Bible Society and other local and foreign agencies. At least five translation projects are underway or planned for the future.

c) *Student ministry.* JSSM(**IFES**) has three university groups and eight high school groups, totalling 200 students. **CCCI** also ministers in schools using their Crossroads programme. Multi-cultural pluralism in Suriname is a threat to Christian young people; many are unable to understand or defend the uniqueness of Christ.

d) *The JESUS film* has been extensively used to draw many to Christ. It is now in the heart language of several Maroon tribes, as well as in the Suriname Javanese, Chinese and in Sranan Tongo, the Creole trade language. Follow-up teams are crucial to long-term success.

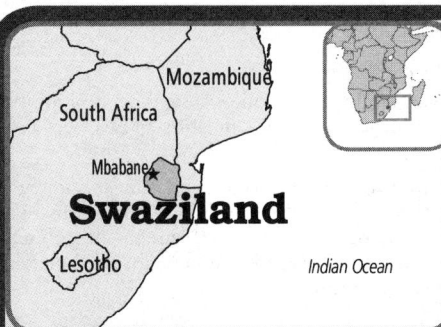

Swaziland

of the monarchy in this poor country is a highly charged issue.

Religion

Religions	Pop %	Population	Ann Gr
Christian	84.68	1,017,772	1.6%
Ethnoreligionist	12.20	146,632	-0.4%
Non-religious	1.50	18,029	3.5%
Muslim	1.00	12,019	1.8%
Baha'i	0.48	5,769	0.9%
Hindu	0.14	1,683	1.3%

Christians Denoms		Pop %	Affiliates	Ann Gr
Protestant	32	9.64	116,000	0.6%
Independent	86	49.01	589,000	-0.4%
Anglican	1	0.88	11,000	-0.7%
Catholic	1	4.74	57,000	0.7%
Marginal	2	0.61	7,000	1.6%
Unaffiliated		19.80	238,000	7.2%

Churches	MegaBloc	Congs	Members	Affiliates
All Indigenous AICs	I	4,200	210,000	525,000
Catholic Church	C	105	31,319	57,000
Ch of the Nazarene	P	152	10,500	28,350
AoG (Back to Life)	I	70	10,000	20,000
Methodist Church	P	95	9,444	17,000
Evangelical Ch of S	P	130	5,856	13,000
Anglican Church	A	80	5,300	10,600
Free Evang Assembly	I	75	4,500	9,000
Kukhanyokuaha Ch	I	26	4,400	8,800
Seventh-day Adventist	P	13	4,600	7,820
Africa Evangelical Ch	P	61	3,000	7,500
Jehovah's Witnesses	M	66	2,203	6,300
Ch of Christ (non-inst)	P	41	3,250	5,428
Full Gospel Ch (Clev)	P	13	1,850	4,700
Evangelical Lutheran	P	11	2,200	4,400
United Pentecostal Ch	P	35	2,932	3,900
Ch of God of Prophecy	P	32	1,900	3,800
Swedish Free Church	P	16	2,333	3,500
Other denominations[34]		360	20,881	43,805
Total Christians[122]		**5,581**	**336,468**	**779,903**

TransBloc	Pop %	Population	Ann Gr
Evangelicals			
Evangelicals	25.1	301,801	0.2%
Renewalists			
Charismatics	45.9	551,458	0.8%
Pentecostals	4.5	54,304	1.9%

Swaziland

Kingdom of Swaziland

Africa

Geography

Area 17,364 sq km. Small, landlocked enclave between Mozambique and South Africa.

Population		Ann Gr	Density
2010	1,201,904	1.34%	69/sq km
2020	1,376,154	1.35%	79/sq km
2030	1,524,445	0.93%	88/sq km

Capital Mbabane 74,500. **Other major city** Manzini 87,000. **Urbanites** 25.5%. **Pop under 15** 39%. **Life expectancy** 45.3 yrs.

Peoples

Bantu 96.6%.
   Nguni 91.9%. Swati (Swazi) 82.3%; Zulu 9.6%.
   Other 4%. Tsonga 2.3%; Mozambican groups.
Other 3.4%. Afrikaner 1.4%; Mixed 1.0%.
Literacy 79.2%. **Official languages** siSwati, English. **All languages** 8. **Indigenous languages** 5. **Languages with Scriptures** 5Bi.

Economy

Mostly pastoral and agricultural, but also some mineral production and manufacturing. Main exports: sugar, citrus fruit, wood pulp. Fertile land is vulnerable to soil depletion, drought and flood. Large majority of trade is with South Africa. The prevalence of AIDS seriously affects the economy.
HDI Rank 142nd/182. **Public debt** 18% of GDP. **Income/person** $2,778 (6% of USA).

Politics

A British protectorate 1899–1968. A strong monarchy with democratic government based on a much-disputed constitution. The constitution, signed in 2005, was the nation's first and finally allows political parties. The comparatively obscene and ostentatious wealth

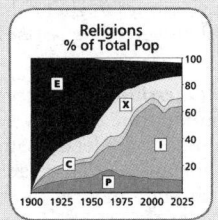

Religions
% of Total Pop

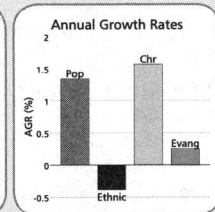

Annual Growth Rates

Answers to Prayer

1 **Faithfully sowing the gospel for 160 years** has led to a strong evangelical community, comprising 25% of the population. Swaziland has a solid core population of believers and regular church attenders.

2 **The Swaziland Evangelism Task** (SET) continues to offer vision and ministry strategy to churches in order to effectively saturate the nation with the gospel. Despite obvious differences, the three main councils of Churches – Council of Swazi Churches (mainline), Swaziland Conference of Churches (evangelicals) and League of African Independent Churches – have some fellowship and share direction on areas of commonality.

Challenges for Prayer

1 **The impact of HIV/AIDS** cannot be overstated – it has devastated the population. Life expectancy plummeted to age 32 in 2008 (according to some reports), and 26% of adults (up to 40% in other reports) are HIV-positive. Sixty-one percent of all deaths could be attributed to HIV/AIDS. The pandemic has denuded society of a young adult workforce, and many households are orphaned and led by the oldest sibling. All talk about ministry and evangelism is irrelevant if this issue is not addressed. Pray for:

a) *Treatment of those afflicted.* Anti-retrovirals are available for free, but there is a severe shortage of adequate care facilities. Widespread poverty exacerbates the suffering.

b) *Sexual morality must be restored.* Until purity and fidelity are practiced as a social norm, this scourge will never be defeated. Polygamy and a lack of holiness among Christians contribute to the problem. Pray for marriages and families to function as God intended; that in itself will be a great victory against AIDS.

c) *Christian response.* Genuine Christian love, demonstrated in practical and gracious ways, has the potential to win many to the Lord. No church trying to be relevant can afford to ignore the physical, emotional and spiritual needs of AIDS sufferers. Training pastors to address this challenge is a strategic key.

2 **The Church** faces many challenges:

a) *Nominalism is widespread.* Far too many Christians live no differently from their unbelieving compatriots. Pray for God's Spirit to bring revival. Many churches, even traditional evangelical groups, are stagnating and losing their young people.

b) *Traditional practices* adopted uncritically lead to syncretism, but outright rejection of them leads to legalism and irrelevance. Pray for the wisdom and grace to practise a culturally relevant but biblical Christianity. Men especially need to be drawn into the Church – the large majority of the faithful are female.

c) *The African Independent Churches* claim more than half the population. Their beliefs range from an evangelical theological position to a high degree of compromise with polygamy, witchcraft, ancestor veneration and appeasement sacrifices. The large "Zionist" movement strongly emphasizes both pentecostal gifts and traditional African spiritual customs. Pray that these groups might be shaped by Scripture and directed by the Holy Spirit. Pray also for increased interaction between Zion and evangelical churches; this will teach and benefit both groups.

d) *Quality Christian leadership* is in short supply and sporadic in quality. Most pastors are unpaid and limited in the time they can contribute to the ministry. Few congregations are trained to share the gospel confidently with either traditionalists or intellectuals, and so have little impact on the unchurched. There are seven Bible schools or seminaries in Swaziland, and TEE is available through most of the major denominations. Pray for Swazi pastors and lay Christians to make use of the training resources in the country.

e) *Youth ministry.* The young people of Swaziland have little opportunity to be young due to poverty, unemployment and the AIDS devastation. Pray for churches to minister meaningfully to young people, both evangelizing and discipling effectively. Pray also for godly models and mentors for them.

3 **Vision for the future.** Pray for:

a) ***Growth is evident*** in the **CoN**, **AoG**, CoGoP and more recently in Deeper Life Bible Church from Nigeria, Rhema Church from South Africa and the indigenous Christian Family Centre, International Tabernacle and Faith Christian Fellowship. Most Christian and even evangelical denominations are in decline due to spiritual stagnation and AIDS deaths.

b) ***The SET vision*** from 1995 is to double the number of churches in Swaziland by 2015 and increase the average congregation size from 52 to 74.

4 **Protestant foreign workers.** Most are evangelical; the largest agencies are **AoG**, **CoN**, **CCCI**, University Bible Fellowship. The majority are heavily committed to institutional programmes and to radio ministry, and only a minority are in direct church development or AIDS-related work. Pray that expatriate and national Christians would work together to effectively serve the nation and build the Church.

5 **Christian media ministries** to pray for:

a) ***The Bible in Swati.*** It is available in a recent translation, and Christian bookstores exist, such as ones run by **CLC** and the Nazarenes.

b) ***National Christian radio.*** The SCC Media Centre produces 18 hours of Christian programming weekly for broadcasting on national radio.

c) ***International Christian radio.*** **TWR** Swaziland has three shortwave and one medium wave as well as one FM transmitter, reaching a potential 700 million people in 58 languages in Africa and southwest Asia. Pray for provision of programming in each language – especially in languages with few believers – and in areas of unrest.

Sweden

Kingdom of Sweden

Europe

Geography 🌍

Area 449,964 sq km. The largest of the Scandinavian countries, a land of mountains and forests. Only 10% of the land is cultivated.

Population		Ann Gr	Density
2010	9,293,026	0.49%	21/sq km
2020	9,713,109	0.45%	22/sq km
2030	10,075,918	0.32%	22/sq km

Capital Stockholm 1,285,387. **Other major cities** Göteborg 854,000; Malmö 250,000. **Urbanites** 84.7%. **Pop under 15 yrs** 17%. **Life expectancy** 80.8 yrs.

Peoples 👪

European 94.7%.
  Scandinavian 87.5%. Swedish 86.5%; also Norwegian, Danish, others.
  Finno–Ugric 3.1%. Finnish 1.9%; Saami(6) 1.0%.
  Slavic 2.6%. Serb 0.6%; Polish 0.5%; Bosniak 0.5%.
Other 5.3%. A diverse mix of nearly 200 immigrant nationalities.
  Arab(6) 1.8%. Iraqi Arab 1.0%.
  Other Asian(44) 2.4%. Iranian 0.6%; Turkish 0.4%.
  All others 1.1%. Chilean 0.3%; Somalian 0.2%.
Literacy 99%. **Official language** Swedish, with five official minority languages. **All languages** 30. **Indigenous languages** 12. **Languages with Scriptures** 4Bi 2NT 5por 4w.i.p.

Economy 🗺

Highly developed, mixed economy focused mainly on export-oriented industry and information technology. An extensive social welfare system that requires high taxation, but provides one of the best standards of living in the world. **HDI Rank** 7th/182. **Public debt** 36.7% of GDP. **Income/person** $52,181 (110% of USA).

S

Politics

Parliamentary government with a limited constitutional monarchy. Nearly 200 years of neutrality, and the last 70 years of almost uninterrupted social democracy as a welfare state has moulded Swedish society. An EU member, but declined membership in NATO and the Eurozone.

Religion

Complete freedom of religion. The Church of Sweden (Lutheran) was the State Church until 2000. It still has an important role because of its size and history, although increasing numbers are disaffiliating. Sweden is becoming more and more a secular state and is systematically marginalizing religious views in the public sphere.

Religions	Pop %	Population	Ann Gr
Christian	57.20	5,314,682	-0.7%
Non-religious	38.35	3,564,925	2.1%
Muslim	3.61	335,358	3.6%
Buddhist	0.31	28,808	4.9%
Other	0.22	20,445	1.4%
Jewish	0.17	15,798	-0.7%
Hindu	0.13	12,081	3.9%
Baha'i	0.01	929	0.5%

Christians	Denoms	Pop %	Affiliates	Ann Gr
Protestant	40	61.93	5,755,000	-0.6%
Independent	9	0.42	39,000	-1.0%
Anglican	1	0.03	3,000	0.7%
Catholic	1	1.39	129,000	-2.2%
Orthodox	14	1.28	119,000	1.2%
Marginal	8	0.53	49,000	-0.9%
Doubly affiliated		-8.39	-780,000	0.0%

Churches	MegaBloc	Congs	Members	Affiliates
Ch of Sweden (Luth)	P	1,470	5,734,475	6,967,498
Catholic Church	C	52	100,781	129,000
Swedish Miss Cov Ch	P	610	58,636	129,000
Pentecostal Movement	P	475	83,202	117,000
InterAct	P	382	30,800	52,976
Swedish Evang Mission	P	390	15,700	45,500
Syrian Orthodox Ch	O	55	27,273	42,000
Finnish Lutheran Ch	P	16	15,600	39,000
Church of Norway	P	40	28,148	38,000
Jehovah's Witnesses	M	305	21,500	36,980
Nat Ch of Denmark	P	339	20,359	34,000
Serbian Orthodox Ch	O	10	13,500	27,000
Baptist Union	P	220	16,700	23,500
Swedish Alliance Mission	P	184	13,100	23,335
Other denominations[58]		620	91,641	170,329
Disaffiliated				-1,780,000
Doubly affiliated				-780,700
Total Christians[73]		**5,168**	**6,271,415**	**5,314,418**

Many Swedes have membership in both the former State Church and in other denominations or fellowships.

TransBloc	Pop %	Population	Ann Gr
Evangelicals			
Evangelicals	6.9	642,248	-0.6%
Renewalists			
Charismatics	2.2	208,781	-0.3%
Pentecostals	1.5	141,489	-0.8%

Missionaries from Sweden
P,I,A 1,145 (873 long-term) in 24 agencies.

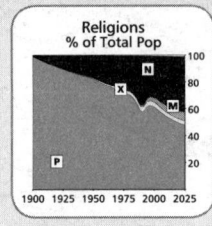

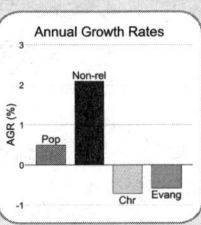

Answers to Prayer

1 **Increased unity among evangelicals** is a praiseworthy outworking of the continued decline of state-sponsored Christendom and a sign of God's Spirit at work. Evangelical groups from across the theological and denominational spectrums increasingly work, pray and worship together as they see themselves as a minority in a secular society. Each year at Pentecost, around 20,000 from around the country gather in Stockholm for "Jesus Manifestation".

Challenges for Prayer

1 **Sweden has a rich Christian history,** with a legacy of revivals (especially in the 19th Century), a vigorous Free Church movement and great commitment to missions. Gustavus Adolphus finalized the establishment of Sweden as a Lutheran nation and fought in Europe to preserve the fledgling Protestant movement. But the 20th and 21st Centuries have been characterized by advancing secularism and moral decline. Pray for a national spiritual awakening and for the re-evangelization of Sweden.

② **The Church of Sweden** is no longer the State Church. Its size, political influence and social impact are large, but on the wane. Liberal theology and practice dominate the Church, from endorsing same-sex marriage to universalism and rejecting the divine authority of Scripture. Politicians (often without any clear faith in Jesus) are frequently chosen to sit on parish councils. Unsurprisingly, the Church is in numerical decline and attendance is between 1-2% of membership. On the local level, there are a number of evangelical congregations, pastors and members, but the national structures are dominated by a liberal agenda. Pray for God to shake and refine this Church. Movements such as Taizé, Oasis and Pilgrimage are having a positive and inspirational influence on the Lutheran Church.

③ **The spiritual decline of Sweden** is apparent on many levels. Only 23% of people believe in a personal God. Nearly every religious group faces dropping numbers of members and attendees. The number of active Christian youth and of missionaries sent from Sweden drastically declined in the last 30 years. Society, especially the younger generation, is so effectively secularized that any discussion of the gospel must involve a painstaking amount of pre-evangelism. Materialism, hedonism and individualism are among the most cherished of values, and adherence to absolute values or truth is regarded as "intolerance". Pray for a new awakening for this spiritually struggling nation; recent signs are that young people are moving back toward more traditional values.

④ **A secular, postmodern worldview** dominates society. It is difficult to express a biblical faith in public or in the academic sphere without deprecation and opposition. Good apologetics and sharp Christian thinking are required to win back this lost ground; helpfully, a number of scientists and academics have recently "come out" as believers. Pray for God to raise up outstanding Christian speakers and thinkers who can establish the legitimacy and indeed the superiority of a classical biblical worldview in the marketplace of ideas.

⑤ **There are positive signs among evangelicals.** Pray for these to grow:

a) The continued presence of evangelicals in Lutheranism (for example, the Swedish Evangelical Mission), in low/Free churches and in the charismatic/Pentecostal movement as well as numerous evangelicals outside of church structures altogether. The diversity of expression and very real unity within evangelical circles demonstrate that evangelicalism is still a living and dynamic presence in Sweden.

b) Increasing social engagement by most denominations. There is growing unity among churches and denominations increasingly have strategic church planting projects. Churches are increasingly involved in diaconal ministry to help people with problems such as alcoholism, sexual abuse and unemployment. The Swedish Evangelical Alliance is a growing movement with a public voice and clear standpoint for biblical faith.

c) CREDO, the IFES-linked student ministry, has grown through some innovative outreaches; there are groups on 80 university campuses and in 50 secondary schools. Over 1,000 participate in camps and conferences annually. New Generation began in 2002 and has grown through innovative ministry to number around 500 groups in secondary schools.

d) The Alpha Course movement continues to grow, with over 500 courses run annually. Other similar courses appropriate to a more secularized, younger generation are also effective.

⑥ **Theological training is a key prayer target.** Theology and religious science are taught in 20 state universities and colleges. Many pastors are trained there, but these have been influenced by the humanism and liberalism of the prevalent university climate. There is now a slight shift back to more biblical Christian faith. The Johannelund Seminary is associated with the Swedish Evangelical Mission; many graduates become Lutheran pastors. There are also seminaries and Bible colleges run by InterAct, Swedish Mission Covenant Church/Baptist Union/Methodist Church, Word of Life, Pentecostals and the Swedish Alliance. There are also many short-term Bible courses offered by most denominations. Additionally, there are independent Bible schools that run mostly one-year courses. **YWAM** trains young people on their five bases in Sweden, and **OM** has also done much to motivate young people for evangelism and missionary service. Sweden desperately needs pastors, teachers and leaders who are well trained in the Word, culturally aware and not compromised by the prevalent mindset in Swedish society and the majority Church.

7 **Missionary outreach from Sweden,** traditionally strong, has declined markedly in recent years across several mission agencies. The Swedish Mission Council serves 36 organizations in coordinating and encouraging mission. A number of agencies and national churches (including World of Life and Light in the East) train workers for ministry among the unreached. The Institute of Bible Translation in Stockholm carries the vision of publishing the Bible in every non-Slavic language of Russia and the CIS; pray for its strategic work. Pray also for a new wave of missions vision and workers to come out of Sweden and out of Scandinavia generally.

8 **Ministry challenges** in Sweden:

a) *Youth.* This youngest generation can be accurately described as post-Christian; most are thoroughly secularized and ignorant of biblical truth. The aging population and overall spiritual malaise contribute to a general decline in youth ministries, but a new spiritual curiosity is starting to build. Culturally relevant youth-focused ministry is as vital as ever.

b) *The indigenous Saami peoples* (20,000-25,000 in Sweden) of Lapland in the north speak four languages, and at least some of them retain their traditional culture. Most are at least nominally Lutheran. Mission Covenant Church, **ECM** and the Lutherans have fruitful ministry among them. Translating the Bible and publishing Christian materials in Saami is a slow and expensive process; praise God for the NT completed in two Saami languages. Pray that there might be an authentic Saami expression of the Church.

c) *European immigrants* from former Communist nations are one of the faster-growing groups. Influx has made Orthodoxy the fastest-growing Christian megabloc. Pray for genuine Christian witness and ministry to the spiritually needy Bosniaks, Serbs, Poles, Russians and others.

d) *Muslims* have grown from a handful in 1960 to around 330,000 in 2010. They are primarily from Iraq, Iran, Turkey, Bosnia and Somalia.

   i *Integration is a major problem.* Large swathes of these populations never learn Swedish or successfully enter employment, potentially creating a Muslim underclass. In Stockholm and Malmö, some Muslim neighbourhoods are deliberately non-integrative and can be unsafe for outsiders to enter.

   ii *Nominalism and secularism* are challenges for Muslims as well as for Christians, since a large number of the younger generation stray from the faith of their fathers. The response to European liberalism can often be a dangerous reactionary fundamentalism.

   iii *There are very few workers* focused on these largely unevangelized groups. Pray for more awareness, more workers and more resources for this challenging task.

e) *East and South Asian peoples,* of nearly 35 nationalities, number from 6 to 15,000, depending on the group. Their small numbers make them difficult to discover and reach. COCM works among the Chinese in Sweden and has at least six churches.

Switzerland

Swiss Confederation

Europe

Geography

Area 41,293 sq km. Mountainous land; 25.7% agriculturally unproductive. The Swiss Alps are one of the greatest tourist attractions in the world.

Population		Ann Gr	Density
2010	7,594,561	0.41%	184/sq km
2020	7,878,558	0.37%	191/sq km
2030	8,148,004	0.32%	197/sq km

Capital Bern (admin) 347,000. Lausanne (judicial) 122,000. **Other major cities** Zürich 1.1 million; Geneva 186,000; Basel 173,000. **Urbanites** 73.6%. **Pop under 15 yrs** 15%. **Life expectancy** 81.7 yrs.

Peoples

European 96.5%. Swiss German 62.1%; Franco-Swiss 18.9%; Italian (3 groups, including Italians and Italian-speaking Swiss "Ticino") 5.4%; Serbo-Croat-Bosniak 4.9%; German 1.6%; Albanian 1.3%; Portuguese 1.2%; Spanish 1.2%.
Other 3.5%. Turk 0.8%; Kurd 0.5%; several other small groups.
More than 22% of the people living in Switzerland are foreign-born, one of the highest rates in Europe.
Literacy 99%. **Official languages** German, French, Italian, Romansh. **All languages** 26. **Indigenous languages** 12. **Languages with Scriptures** 5Bi 1NT 4por.

Economy

A very wealthy industrial state with an educated and skilled workforce; highly dependent on trade. Exports play a large role for both high-tech and more traditional commodities. Tourism and banking are also important foreign exchange earners. The EU is the largest trading partner. Living costs are high.
HDI Rank 9th/182. **Public debt** 40% of GDP. **Income/person** $68,433 (144% of USA) – one of the world's highest.

Politics

Confederation founded in 1291, and federal state in 1848. Federal democratic government, with the constituent 20 cantons and 6 half-cantons retaining a high degree of autonomy. With its strong policy of non-involvement in world politics and strict neutrality, Switzerland, only by a narrow margin, voted to join the UN in 2002. Direct democracy is practised more in Switzerland than in almost any place on earth, with referenda determining many important laws and policies.

Religion

The federal constitution guarantees religious freedom, but relationships between cantonal governments and the churches are decided locally. Post-Reformation confrontations between Catholics and Protestants helped determine the majority religion of each canton, but this identity is fading in many cantons.

Religions	Pop %	Population	Ann Gr
Christian	75.76	5,753,639	-0.3%
Non-religious	14.82	1,125,514	3.4%
Muslim	6.05	459,471	2.3%
Other	2.00	151,891	1.4%
Hindu	0.56	42,530	3.6%
Buddhist	0.48	36,454	4.1%
Jewish	0.23	17,467	-0.4%
Baha'i	0.10	7,595	0.4%

Christians	Denoms	Pop %	Affiliates	Ann Gr
Protestant	98	31.95	2,426,000	-0.6%
Independent	120	1.47	112,000	1.8%
Anglican	1	0.18	14,000	0.3%
Catholic	2	38.29	2,908,000	-0.3%
Orthodox	11	2.08	158,000	1.0%
Marginal	31	1.09	82,000	0.9%
Unaffiliated		0.70	53,000	4.3%

Churches	MegaBloc	Congs	Members	Affiliates
Catholic Church	C	1,500	1,453,500	2,907,000
Fed of Swiss Prot Chs	P	750	1,250,000	2,250,000
Serbian Orthodox	O	7	35,000	70,000
New Apostolic Church	I	225	22,867	34,300
Jehovah's Witnesses	M	280	18,200	32,578
Swiss Pfingstmission	P	70	10,200	24,500
Fell of Pente Free Chs	P	307	11,648	21,200
Exclusive Brethren	P	199	7,973	17,700
Fell of Free Ev Congs	P	92	7,368	14,000
Methodist Church	P	140	7,000	14,000
St Chrischona Pilgrim	P	105	8,000	14,000
Anglican Church	A	14	9,857	13,800
Old Catholic Church	I	24	6,853	9,800
Latter-day Saints (Mormon)	M	44	5,490	7,850
International Chr Fell	I	15	3,600	7,200
The Apostolic Church	P	30	4,410	6,615
Un of Free Miss Congs	P	58	4,615	6,600
Evangelical Fell (EGW)	P	42	4,500	6,435
Charismatic Luth Ch	I	60	3,000	6,000
Other denominations[204]		1,354	147,742	236,659
Total Christians[263]		**5,316**	**3,021,823**	**5,700,237**

S

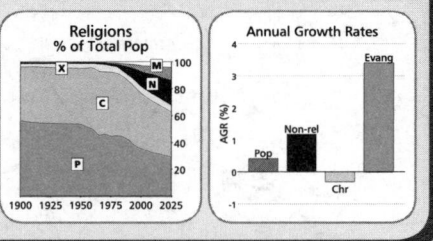

TransBloc	Pop %	Population	Ann Gr
Evangelicals			
Evangelicals	4.4	336,275	1.2%
Renewalists			
Charismatics	4.1	314,030	2.6%
Pentecostals	0.9	67,958	1.7%

Missionaries from Switzerland
P,I,A 2,183 (1,712 long-term), 95% international.

Answers to Prayer

1 **Unity is increasing among churches** of different backgrounds for the purpose of jointly proclaiming Christ. These include traditional evangelical, charismatic and rapidly growing immigrant churches.

2 **The spreading public presence of the gospel** is a result of creative outreach and ministry. Examples can be found in TV, radio, Internet, newspapers, seminars and conference events; praise God for the use of both new and traditional media for sharing the good news.

3 **Continued Swiss commitment** to world evangelization, despite the relatively small community of evangelicals, is a real blessing.

Challenges for Prayer

1 **This exceptional nation now struggles** with the same social and spiritual malaise shared by its neighbours, despite its traditional policy of neutrality and its relative isolation. Spiritual decline is mirrored by political apathy – in this direct democracy, election/referendum turnout is now 40%, down from 80% a century ago. Low birthrates and a rapidly growing aged population pressure the pension system and require high levels of immigration, in itself a huge social issue. Over 22% of the population are foreigners, many from Muslim backgrounds. Integration of these groups is often a problem, as is the reactionary presence of far-right political groups. Yet, tensions such as the Minaret referendum in 2009 cause many to consider again Switzerland's Christian heritage. Pray for wisdom for leaders who must attempt to preserve Swiss identity while guiding the country forward.

2 **The great reformers,** Calvin and Zwingli, expounded the truths of Scripture in this land, but few today have any interest or understanding of real Christianity. Wealth, comfort, indifference and a vague religiosity are the norm. The younger generation explores eastern religions and the occult as much as Christianity. Many baptized as children retain no real link with a church, and enrolled membership of Protestants and Catholics dropped from over 90% to 70% in the last 30 years. Pray that the Swiss may find the true way in Jesus Christ and that the nation might be stirred again by the Holy Spirit.

3 **Stagnation and decline have sapped the Church.** In the Catholic Church, lack of clergy is reaching crisis proportions, and the spreading liberal theology undermines the faith of many Catholic and Reformed congregations. Yet changes are afoot. Modest growth continues in Free churches, an active movement for renewal lives in Reformed churches and Catholics are returning to a more conservative and traditional faith. Pray that:

a) *Men and women of God in leadership and in congregations* may be used to bring renewal to the State Churches and revival to the entire Swiss nation.

b) *The high level of unity* in prayer and vision among evangelical leaders within the Evangelical Alliance and the Federation of Free Churches – across denominations – may be protected and grow in depth and witness.

c) *Congregational outreach* may increase through personal evangelism, home Bible studies and cell/house church planting. Pray that true believers in State and Free Churches may be more effectively motivated and activated for outreach.

S

4 **Renewed vision for evangelicals** is bubbling up. The Swiss Evangelical Alliance, Free Churches and other agencies are working on a renewed vision for the evangelization of Switzerland. Most Christian non-profit groups have united as a more audible voice within society regarding religious freedom, evangelism and mission, aid and social responsibility, environmental issues, media, youth and others. While church planting remains an important goal, they see renewal and Christian testimony within society as equally important. Pray for increasing numbers of congregations as well as for renewal of many existing ones. Pray for newer groups, such as the International Christian Fellowship (ICF) and the house church movement, that are reaching people outside of traditional church structures.

5 **In the Catholic cantons,** predominantly in the south and centre of the country, the small evangelical witness is growing; centuries-old prejudices and religious polarizations are breaking down. Pray that many may find a personal relationship with Jesus and come to assurance of salvation, and that a living fellowship of believers may come into being in every community.

6 **Young people** are drifting away from Christianity, despite 60-80% of them being interested in God and religious matters. There is both great threat and great opportunity in the current spiritual climate among young people in Switzerland. Pray for:

a) Youth-oriented churches and church services such as ICF and the God-network, which are deliberately progressive, especially in using music and media to reach those disinterested in traditional church. They are active in many Swiss cities.

b) Outreach through agencies such as **OM, YWAM,** KingsKids, *Bund Evangelischer Schweizer Jungscharen* (BESJ) and YMCA-*Jungschar.*

c) Specific ministries to young people such as SU, **CEF** and other children's ministries.

d) Student ministry. For too many students, life is meaningless and without purpose, leading to self-destructive lifestyles. **CCCI** ministers widely. **IFES** works with both Francophone groups (GBU) and German-speaking groups (VBG).

7 **Bible training** is provided by a number of institutions. From them, graduates have gone all over the world in Christian service. Pray for:

a) German-speaking seminaries: STH Basel, TDS Aarau, TSC St. Chrischona, TS Bienenberg, SBT Beatenberg, IGW and ISTL.

b) French-speaking Bible schools: Institut Biblique Emmaus, Institut Biblique de Genève, IBETO (Pentecostal) and **YWAM.**

Pray that these may retain their spiritual cutting edge and become a means of blessing and revival in Switzerland. Pray also that these institutions might be flexible and relevant for today's generation, and that many might be called and equipped for service through them.

8 The *Arbeitsgemeinschaft Evangelischer Missionen* (AEM), formed in 1972, strengthens and coordinates missionary vision and outreach, especially in the Free Churches. There are 45 member agencies, representing nearly 1,500 long-term missionaries. The *Fédération des Missions Evangéliques Francophones* (FMEF) has the same vision for the French-speaking Protestant churches in Switzerland, France and Belgium. Mission21, *Échange et Mission*(**DM**) and other groups connected to the Evangelical Alliance serve in similar capacities. Pray for greater awareness and sense of responsibility in Swiss churches for world evangelization, and of support for the commendably large missionary force.

9 **Less-evangelized peoples** include:

a) Cantons. The German-speaking cantons of Luzern, Zug, Schwyz, Unterwalden and Uri, the largely Francophone Valais and Fribourg and the Italian-speaking Ticino are culturally Catholic with few evangelical groups, although there is increased openness in several Catholic cantons.

b) The more than 100 foreign nationalities. Switzerland has the highest proportion of foreign residents of any major state in Europe. The major cities are becoming internationalized – Geneva is 45% non-Swiss! A number of agencies and churches are committed to ministry among them. Most are linked to *Arbeitsgemeinschaft für interkulturell Zusammenarbeit* (AgiK). Some of these minorities are highly unevangelized. Others, such as Latinos and Africans with over 200 congregations, are actually contributing to outreach in Switzerland.

S

c) ***Religious minorities.*** Not long ago, almost every person in Switzerland would have been either Catholic or Protestant. Today, around one in seven considers himself non-religious. Muslims account for as much as 6%, with many other religions appearing and growing rapidly. Swiss society and indeed most Swiss Christians are ill equipped to handle these changes in religious population. Pray for clear and loving outreach to these new faith communities.

10 **The use of media** for outreach is widespread and sophisticated. Several outreach initiatives have the potential of a large audience in society: *Fenster zum Sonntag* (ERF, Alphavision) averages nearly 100,000 TV viewers weekly, *4telstunde für Jesus* (Evangelical Alliance) is printed one to three times annually with 500,000 to 1,000,000 copies per issue, www.jesus.ch (livenet) and the radio station Lifechannel (ERF) reach tens of thousands daily. Pray for these and other innovative methods of reaching the unchurched; pray also for open hearts and changed lives.

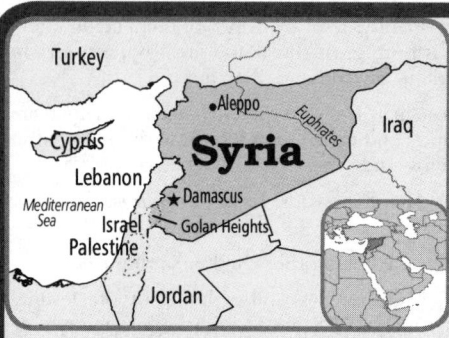

Syria

Syrian Arab Republic

Asia

Geography 🌐

Area 185,180 sq km. Fertile plain on Mediterranean coast; 60% desert in centre and east but crossed by the Euphrates River.

Population		Ann Gr	Density
2010	22,505,091	3.31%	122/sq km
2020	26,475,482	1.57%	143/sq km
2030	30,559,849	1.34%	165/sq km

As many as 1.8 million Iraqi refugees, many of them Christian, have swelled the population, but are not accounted for in any ethnic or religious estimates.
Capital Damascus 2,597,093. **Other major cities** Aleppo 3.0 million; Hims 1.0mill. **Urbanites** 54.9%. **Pop under 15 yrs** 35%. **Life expectancy** 74.1 yrs.

Peoples 👪

Arab 90.3%. Syrian Arab 67.0%; Alawi 7.9%; Bedouin 7.1%; Palestinian 3.1%; Druze 2.2%.
Other 9.7%. Kurd 6.7%; Dom Gypsy 1.6%; Armenian 0.9%; Turk/Turkmen 0.9%.
Literacy 82.9%. **Official language** Arabic. **All languages** 22. **Indigenous languages** 16. **Languages with Scriptures** 3Bi 3NT 4por.

Economy 📈

Agriculture, oil and tourism are important. Relatively poor economic performance, largely due to high military spending, widespread corruption and a powerful insider's network of businesses. Some economic progress due to partnership with Iran, Venezuela, and the arrival of many Iraqis along with UN relief money. Economic reforms are promised, but slow in arriving. Unemployment is very high among young people.
HDI Rank 107th/182. **Public debt** 25.4% of GDP. **Income/person** $2,768 (6% of USA).

Politics ❎

An ancient civilization. Damascus is known as the oldest continuously inhabited city in the world. In the modern era, independent from France in 1946. Continuous upheavals until the 1970 coup. Internal stability under an Alawite-minority, military-civilian socialist government. Political expression is very limited. Since 1973, Syria has been deeply involved in Lebanon's affairs, initially with the UN and Arab League's approval. It escalated to the point of military occupation and allegedly orchestrating assassinations of high-level Lebanese officials. Significant international pressure and Middle East destabilization forced Syria to moderate its foreign policies.

Religion 🕌

Since independence from France, Syria has been a secular state, with Islam recognized as the religion of the majority. Other minorities are accorded rights and privileges, with a measure of religious freedom.

Religions	Pop %	Population	Ann Gr
Muslim	90.00	20,254,582	3.3%
Christian	6.34	1,426,823	5.5%
Other (Druze, others)	2.25	506,365	2.9%
Non-religious	1.40	315,071	-0.6%
Baha'i	0.01	2,251	3.3%

Christians Denoms		Pop %	Affiliates	Ann Gr
Protestant	17	0.14	31,000	0.2%
Independent	1	0.04	8,000	11.2%

S

Anglican	1	0.02	6,000	4.1%
Catholic	6	3.11	700,000	9.2%
Orthodox	6	3.02	679,000	2.4%
Marginal	6	0.01	1,000	2.4%

Significant increases in some groups due to massive Christian immigration from Iraq.

Churches	MegaBloc	Congs	Members	Affiliates
Catholic Church	C	489	391,061	700,000
Greek Orthodox Ch	O	161	145,251	260,000
Syrian Orthodox Ch	O	54	108,939	195,000
Armenian Apos Ch	O	27	82,418	150,000
Assyrian Ch of the East	O	38	38,462	70,000
Union of Ev Armen Chs	P	11	7,418	13,500
Nat Ev Synod of L & S	P	37	3,600	6,012
Anglican Church	A	7	3,293	5,500
Nat Ev Alliance Ch	P	15	650	1,100
Other denominations[17]		106	8,529	25,522
Total Christians[31]		**945**	**789,621**	**1,426,634**

TransBloc	Pop %	Population	Ann Gr
Evangelicals			
Evangelicals	0.1	23,663	4.2%
Renewalists			
Charismatics	<0.1	8,585	7.4%
Pentecostals	<0.1	350	5.3%

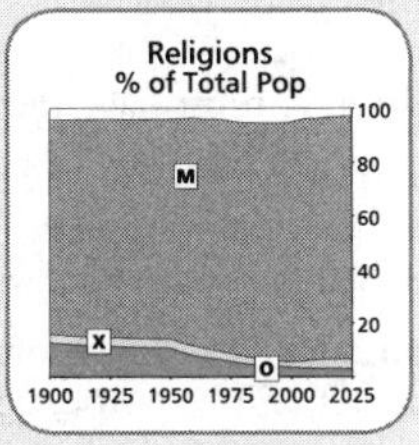

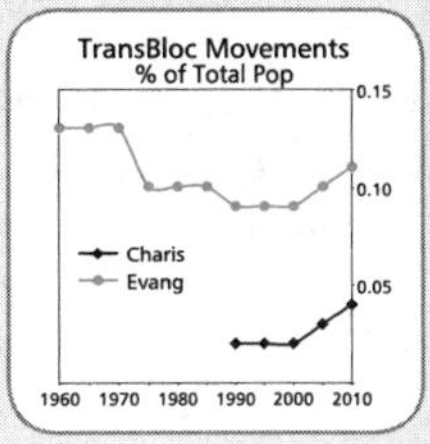

Challenges for Prayer

1 **Syria's role in the Middle East** has been a troubled one in recent decades. But a new and younger president, economic difficulties, nervous minorities and, above all, shifting political fault lines in the region put Syria's own stability at risk. Lasting peace in the Middle East cannot be achieved without Syrian participation in any solution. Pray that God might somehow use this nation to bring peace to the area.

2 **Changes within the country** point to a potentially dangerous future. The Iraq situation created possibly 1.8 million refugees to add to the 600,000 Palestinians in Syria. They are now beginning to move onward, either to Western countries or back to Iraq. Traditionally moderate Sunni Islam is shifting toward more fundamentalist expressions just as the exploding youthful population find themselves jobless and without prospects. Water issues grow more significant in the region. Pray for God to use the uncertainty to draw people to seek the truth more urgently.

3 **Syrian Christian minorities** enjoy freedom and stability, possibly unparalleled through the Middle East. The Orthodox and Catholic churches existed since before Islam and endure still with many godly members. The majority are Arab, but there is also a large Armenian community. Christians are concentrated in the cities, but finding housing and employment is increasingly challenging due to discrimination. Their proportion steadily declines through continual emigration. Pray against this trend. Thank God for their longstanding presence and the wise leadership of the Christian communities, and pray that these communities might flower again. Pray for renewal in these ancient traditions.

4 **The Protestant presence is small** but growing. Most Protestant converts come from Orthodox and Catholic backgrounds. There is an evangelical presence in most cities, but rarely in smaller towns. Growth can only occur if more leaders (ordained and lay) receive theological and leadership training; the signs are that many are willing. TEE is very helpful in this area – pray for more TEE tutors. Pray that all believers might gain a deep desire to grow in godliness and outreach.

5 **Syria's Antiochan Church** was instrumental in initiating mission to the Gentiles (Acts 13). Today, Christians must exercise caution and wisdom in relating to the state and to Muslims. Evangelicals in particular must discern how to effectively share Christ without proselytizing. Biblical training and a loving attitude toward Muslims are essential. Pray that believers might rediscover the zeal and faith of the NT Church of Antioch.

6 **New believers from other backgrounds** are increasing in number. Longstanding religious, cultural and spiritual barriers must be overcome. For those who do cross over to

Christ, pray for perseverance in persecution, acceptance into fellowship by other believers and growth to maturity. Churches are increasingly willing to reach out. Some positive results are occurring, such as Bible correspondence courses, prison ministry and student outreach. The uprooted thousands who came from Iraq seeking shelter and compassion are particularly responsive.

7 **Unreached peoples** to pray for:

a) *The Sunni Arab majority,* most have never heard the gospel.

b) *The Alawites* are a minority but also the group that produces the presidents. They are very influential in the army and government. They are an offshoot of Islam whose beliefs differ much from orthodox Islamic faith, with some potential spiritual bridges to Christianity.

c) *The Druze* in the south are a secretive offshoot of Islam. Though hard to reach in the past, there is increasing contact and response, with a few small groups of believers.

d) *The Kurds* of the north and northwest are more receptive than most Arabs. Due to the politically sensitive nature of the Kurdish issue, it is generally difficult to engage them. Some are Orthodox Christian, others Yezidis and Shi'a, but most are Sunni Muslim.

e) *The Bedouin, Circassian, Turkmen and Gypsy minorities* are mostly unreached. There are now some Christians among the Bedouin and Gypsy peoples, and there is hope of more.

8 **Foreign Christian workers** are allowed to minister within the Christian community, but only under the capable leadership of the national church. The door is more open than ever for those with a servant mentality, with several strategic opportunities. Pray for the ministry of Christian professionals, especially other Arabs, living in the country. These tentmakers play a vital role in developing Syria professionally as well as spiritually; pray for them. The presence of Christian workers in Syria is a fragile and precarious thing; pray for great wisdom and discretion for them and for openness on the part of the government.

9 **Christian media.** Pray for these:

a) *Literature* is freely available, and the two Bible Society bookrooms sell Bibles and other Christian materials. This organization is well known through the annual book fair, since it is the only one working with all branches of the church. Pray for the powerful impact of God's Word on all who read it.

b) *Radio.* Many Muslims listen to Christian radio. FEBA, IBRA and **TWR** broadcast many hours per week in Arabic and other languages. Syrian Kurds receive programmes broadcast for Turkish and Iraqi Kurds.

c) *Television.* Al Hayat, The Miracle Channel, **SAT-7** and others have a vital ministry in beaming Christian TV programmes to those with satellite dishes. A Syrian-based telephone counselling centre run by Life Agape has come out of this. However, most Syrians cannot receive these channels - the satellite transmitting them also transmits Western channels with questionable content. Pray for a solution to this so that devout Syrians with good morals might be able to receive Christian channels while successfully avoiding immoral programming.

d) *Other media.* The JESUS film is widely circulated in eight Syrian languages. A film about the life of the apostle Paul – produced by Syrians, in Syria - is watched by many Muslims. Arab-language Christian materials (literature, cassette and electronic media) are growing in number and quality, increasingly produced by Arab Christians. Pray for many non-Christians to follow Jesus as a result.

S

Tajikistan

Republic of Tajikistan

Asia

Geography

Area 143,100 sq km. Bordering on Afghanistan, China, Uzbekistan and Kyrgyzstan. The Pamir and Tien-Shan Mountains are 93% of the surface area.

Population	Ann Gr	Density
2010	7,074,845	1.60%	49/sq km
2020	8,446,497	1.71%	59/sq km
2030	9,618,020	1.17%	67/sq km

Capital Dushanbe 716,000. **Urbanites** 26.5%.
Pop under 15 yrs 37%. **Life expectancy** 66.4 yrs.

Peoples

Civil war in the 1990s caused the exodus of the majority of non-indigenous peoples and the great loss of ethnic diversity.
Iranian-Median 69.7%. Tajik 65.9%; Shughni 1.4%; Persian 0.8%; Guhjali 0.4%; Pashtun 0.4%.
Turkic 26.5%. Uzbek 22.8%; Kyrgyz 1.4%; Tatar 1.4%; Turkmen 0.4%.
Eurasian 2.7%. Russian 2.1%; Ukrainian 0.3%.
Other 1.1%. Korean 0.3%.
Literacy 99.5%. **Official language** Tajik.
All languages 33. **Indigenous languages** 12.
Languages with Scriptures 2Bi 1por.

Economy

Significant untapped mineral and hydro-electric potential. The Soviet collapse and ensuing civil war sorely damaged the economic infrastructure, causing the country to rank the poorest of the former–USSR states. Racketeers and those in the drug trade prosper, while most of the population live in poverty. Still dependent on external aid for development.
HDI Rank 127th/182. **Public debt** 74.7% of GDP. **Income/person** $795 (2% of USA).

Politics

The northern portion of the Persian Empire until the 12th Century. Russian colonial rule from the mid-19th Century. In 1929, Stalin defined Central Asian republics' borders to deliberately create large ethnic minorities in each to discourage ethnically motivated insurgency against Moscow. After the Soviet collapse, civil war broke out with various regional warlords fighting for power until 1997. Secular national forces prevailed and continue to shape political and religious policy. Elections in 2000 and 2006 (although flawed) point the way forward.

Religion

Religious freedom is guaranteed by the constitution, but fear of radical Islam prompts the government's attempts to control all religious expression and to pass draconian religious laws. Sunni majority, with small Shia and Ismaili minorities.

Religions	Pop %	Population	Ann Gr
Muslim	93.93	6,645,402	1.9%
Non-religious	5.00	353,742	-3.0%
Christian	1.04	73,578	-2.2%
Other	0.02	1,415	18.4%
Baha'i	0.01	707	1.6%

Christians Denoms		Pop %	Affiliates	Ann Gr
Protestant	6	0.11	8,000	4.1%
Independent	3	0.01	1,000	14.9%
Catholic	1	0.01	1,000	-12.9%
Orthodox	7	0.90	63,000	-2.7%
Marginal	1	0.01	1,000	3.1%

Churches	MegaBloc	Congs	Members	Affiliates
Russian Orthodox	O	12	34,965	50,000
Korean Pentecostal	P	14	691	2,300
Pentecostal Church	P	14	700	1,750
Seventh-day Adventist	P	12	900	1,350
Baptist Church	P	20	500	1,000
Catholic Church	C	1	599	1,000
Jehovah's Witnesses	M	5	350	931
Other Christian groups	I	53	533	800
Lutheran Church	P	2	479	800
Evangelical Union	P	16	400	600
Other denominations[6]		5	8,701	13,050
Total Christians[18]		**154**	**48,818**	**73,581**

TransBloc	Pop %	Population	Ann Gr
Evangelicals			
Evangelicals	0.1	6,952	6.9%
Renewalists			
Charismatics	0.1	4,748	8.4%
Pentecostals	0.1	4,050	8.0%

The vast majority of these are ethnic Slavs and Germans as well as expatriates.

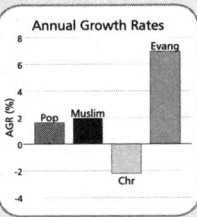

Annual Growth Rates

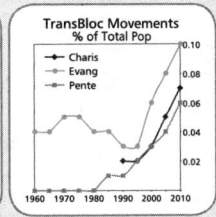

TransBloc Movements % of Total Pop

Answers to Prayer

1 **The birth of a Tajik Church,** although a slow and painstaking process, is now reality. The Church among Tajiks is small, only a thousand, but growing.

2 **Marked improvement in stability** and security since the end of the civil war allows for effective ministry.

Challenges for Prayer

1 **The civil war** left an indelible mark on the nation, which is still recovering more than 10 years later. Hardship is widespread, with 83% of the population under the poverty line. The most vulnerable segments of society particularly at risk are prisoners, elderly, widows and orphans.

2 **The Christian population** has been massively reduced by emigration. It was and remains largely Russian Orthodox. The civil war and its aftermath drove out the majority; most of the remainder are cultural/nominal Christians with little desire to share the gospel with indigenous peoples. Pray that such a vision might be awakened. While multi-ethnic congregations exist in a few cities, the bulk of the rural majority remains unreached. Pray also for contextually sensitive outreach efforts and for church structures that will reproduce in rural areas.

3 **Although Islam is the religion of 94%** of the population, only a small fraction practice "pure" Islam. Most are more influenced by folk superstitions and Zoroastrian beliefs. Mosques sprouted up everywhere in the years following independence, but now the government places severe restrictions on mosque building. Tajikistan's proximity to Iran and Afghanistan makes it vulnerable to Islamism. Pray for extremism to be restrained, and that Muslims might have unprecedented opportunities to discover Christ.

4 **Freedom of religion exists,** but barely. The government, to prevent the growth of extremism in Islam, introduced many restrictions that place a stranglehold on Christian ministry. Religious teaching, publishing and proselytism is made very difficult if not illegal. Registering churches is also very difficult. Pray for the gospel to spread and Christians to find ways to teach and minister despite these harsh restrictions.

5 **Expatriate involvement.** Tajikistan, with its great social and spiritual needs, is ripe for Christian ministry done sensitively and appropriately. Relief and development are much-needed and fruitful ministries, as are education and business training. Young people, prisoners, drug addicts and women in difficult situations are particularly responsive. Pray for the calling and entry of more long-term personnel. Pray for ethnically related Iranian Christians to become witnesses; they could play a unique role in winning Tajiks to Jesus.

6 **Tajiks number 13 million in Central Asia.** For nearly a thousand years, there was no significant outreach to Tajiks. Now, in addition to more than 1,000 believers in Tajikistan, there are a greater number of Tajik believers in Afghanistan as well as some in Pakistan and Uzbekistan. Pray for further growth, and pray for the establishment of a truly indigenous Tajik Church – this is beginning to happen as Tajik church leaders emerge. Pray especially for unity in this young expression of Christ's body.

7 **Emigration is a major social challenge.** As many as one million Tajik men are working abroad, mostly in Russia. This is a huge proportion of the population and especially of the male population of working age. Entire villages are denuded of the younger generation. One additional difficulty this creates is the constant drain on church leadership; many Christians move away for financial reasons. Pray for job creation within Tajikistan generally and, in particular, for churches to be able to hold onto their leaders.

8 **Specific unreached groups.** Pray for indigenous peoples with little opportunity to hear the gospel:

a) *Tajiks, especially non-Russified rural Tajiks,* comprise the largest unevangelized segment of the population. They have also been among the least responsive to what little outreach they have encountered.

b) Uzbeks. Uzbeks are the largest minority in Tajikistan, with an approximate population of 1.7 million. Though there are a number of Uzbek believers in Tajikistan today, there are almost no Uzbek churches. Pray for the establishment of Uzbek churches that can effectively reach out to their own people in a culturally appropriate way.

c) The mountain peoples of the Pamirs in the east. There are no known churches in the Pamirs. In that region live six Muslim peoples of the Ismaili sect – the Ishkashimi, Roshani, Bartangi, Shughni, Wakhi and Yazgulyam – who have never been reached.

d) The many other ethnicities in Tajikistan; very few have specific Christian outreach.

9 **Christian media ministries.**

a) The whole Bible in Tajik exists; work on a much-needed simplified translation is underway with the Gospels already available. **GRN** has materials in seven languages. Importing Bibles and Christian literature is extremely difficult; pray for the effective entry and distribution of the good news in printed form.

b) Video. A number of Christian videos and DVDs, including the JESUS film, are available in most languages spoken in Tajikistan. Such material is in high demand in several languages.

c) Christian radio. **TWR** broadcasts in Tajik for 90 minutes per week. Various agencies broadcast in Uzbek 2.5 hours per week. There are many programs in Farsi that can be understood and in many minority languages; pray for more to listen to these life-changing words.

d) Satellite TV. Many Farsi and Russian religious programs are available by satellite and watched by many in Tajikistan.

e) Internet. A few websites share the gospel in Tajik, such as www.isoimaseh.com and www.dardidil.com.

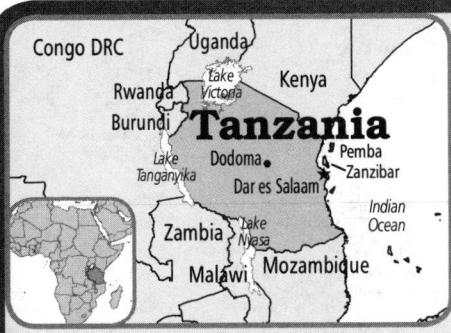

Tanzania
Republic of Tanzania
Africa

Geography 🌍

Area 945,037 sq km. Comprising mainland Tanganyika and the offshore islands of Zanzibar and Pemba (2,460 sq km).

Population		Ann Gr	Density
2010	45,039,573	2.92%	48/sq km
2020	59,602,598	2.72%	63/sq km
2030	75,497,972	2.30%	80/sq km

Capitals Dodoma 210,000 (official); Dar-es-Salaam 3,349,134 (de facto). **Urbanites** 26.4%. **Pop under 15 yrs** 45%. **Life expectancy** 55 yrs.

Peoples 👪

More than 150 indigenous ethnic groups. Widespread promotion and use of Swahili has obscured some tribal divisions.

Bantu peoples 86.3%. 121 groups, largest: Sukuma 11.6%; Gogo 4.6%; Haya 4.5%; Nyamwezi 3.7%; Ha 3.1%; Makonde 3.0%; Hehe 2.6%; Nyakyusa 2.6%; Luguru 1.9%; Shambala 1.9%; Turu 1.9%; Bena 1.8%; Iramba 1.6%; Chagga 1.62%; Pare 1.6%; Mwera 1.4%; Makhuwa 1.4%; Yao 1.4%.
Swahili 7.8%. 7 groups: Swahili-Pemba 2.0%; Zaramo 1.7%; Shirazi 1.5%.
Nilotic 2.2%. 8 groups: Maasai(3) 1.3%.
Cushitic 1.7%. 7 groups: Iraqw 1.4%.
Khoisan 0.3%. 7 groups: the San/Bushmen original inhabitants of Africa.
Other 1.7%. South Asian (predominantly Gujarati), Arab, Chinese.
Refugees. Mainly Burundi and Rwanda Hutu. Also Somalis, Congolese, others.
Literacy 69%. **Official languages** Swahili, English; 2% speak only Swahili and no local African language. **All languages** 127. **Languages with Scriptures** 9Bi 15NT 32por 43w.i.p.

Economy 📊

One of the world's poorest nations wherein an agricultural subsistence economy dominates. Earlier disastrous efforts to socialize the economy still weigh heavily on the nation through debt-

T

servicing costs and expensive but ineffective infrastructure. Health and education sectors require massive investments. Continues to attract aid and investment due to its stability and dedicated leaders. Great potential through mineral deposits and a huge tourist industry.
HDI Rank 151st/182. **Public debt** 23.2% of GDP. **Income/person** $520 (1% of USA).

Politics 🗡

Tanganyika gained independence from Britain in 1961, Zanzibar in 1963. The two countries united as a one-party federal socialist republic in 1964, although Zanzibar retained a considerable degree of autonomy. The one-party system ended in 1992, and a multiparty democracy was instituted. For 50 years, Tanzania has remained stable in a troubled region. Zanzibar remains a troubled region, both internally and in its links to the mainland.

Religion 🕊

There is religious freedom; all major faiths have the ability to share and propagate their faith. Religious harmony is remarkably high given the size and activism of Christian and Muslim communities.

Religions	Pop %	Population	Ann Gr
Christian	54.07	24,352,897	3.7%
Muslim	31.20	14,052,347	2.9%
Ethnoreligionist	12.97	5,841,633	-0.1%
Hindu	0.90	405,356	2.9%
Baha'i	0.43	193,670	3.4%
Non-religious	0.40	180,158	9.0%
Sikh	0.03	13,512	2.9%

Christians	Denoms	Pop %	Affiliates	Ann Gr
Protestant	48	17.43	7,849,000	2.1%
Independent	44	2.22	1,001,000	3.0%
Anglican	1	7.33	3,300,000	2.2%
Catholic	1	27.10	12,207,000	3.1%
Orthodox	1	0.06	28,000	0.7%

Marginal	2	0.09	39,000	4.2%
Unaffiliated		4.20	1,878,000	24.9%
Doubly affiliated		-4.33	-1,950,000	0.0%

Churches	MegaBloc	Congs	Members	Affiliates
Catholic Church	C	860	6,598,297	12,206,850
Evang Lutheran Ch	P	2,720	1,360,000	3,400,000
Anglican Church	A	2,705	1,352,459	3,300,000
Baptist Convention	P	3,704	500,000	910,000
Pentecostal Chs Assoc	P	2,933	440,000	880,000
New Apostolic Ch	I	1,725	345,000	690,000
Africa Inland Church	P	1,750	196,667	590,000
Moravian Church	P	412	267,647	455,000
Seventh-day Adventist	P	1,760	342,105	455,000
Assemblies of God	P	1,300	260,870	420,000
Ch of God (Cleveland)	P	573	67,000	154,100
Mennonite Church	P	290	58,000	133,400
Pente Evang Fellowship	P	450	45,000	90,000
Pentecostal Holiness	P	140	40,000	80,000
Pente Assem of God	P	924	23,102	70,000
Full Gospel Bible Fell	I	39	23,200	58,000
Ch of God (Anderson)	P	360	21,600	43,200
Jehovah's Witnesses	M	580	16,000	38,000
Foursquare Gospel Ch	P	250	15,500	31,000
Other denominations[77]		2,736	183,512	419,351
Doubly affiliated				-1,950,000
Total Christians[97]		**26,211**	**12,155,959**	**22,473,901**

TransBloc	Pop %	Population	Ann Gr
Evangelicals			
Evangelicals	17.9	8,042,731	2.4%
Renewalists			
Charismatics	11.5	5,173,548	4.3%
Pentecostals	4.3	1,926,760	2.8%

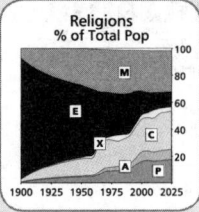
Religions % of Total Pop

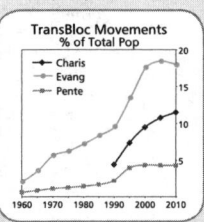
TransBloc Movements % of Total Pop

Answers to Prayer

1 **Tanzania remains an "island of peace"** amid many troubled nations. This not only allows positive inter-communal relations but also allows Tanzania to shelter over a million refugees who have fled from violence in their own lands and to function as an operation base for much regional ministry.

2 **The continued growth of evangelicals** within mainline churches (Lutheran, Anglican) as well as the growth of Pentecostal denominations have seen the evangelical population increase from 2.4 million (9.2%) in 1990 to 8 million (17.9%) in 2010.

3 **The strong church planting movement** in Tanzania has, since the 1980s, birthed new agencies within the country and a greater level of partnership between nationals and expatriate missionaries. There is a strong focus on planting new churches and reaching the remaining unevangelized peoples of Tanzania, with much fruit evident in recent years among animist and Muslim populations.

Challenges for Prayer

1   **The delicate inter-communal balance** and religious stability of the country cannot be taken for granted. The Muslim community is increasingly polarized between moderates and Islamists, the latter pressing for political influence and the establishment of separate Islamist courts. Witchcraft is widespread and permeates both Christianity and Islam. Spiritual super-stitions and outright occultism incur great financial expense and often result in sexual abuse or even death for the victims of such practices. Pray that the government may be ruthless in uprooting evil and wise in fostering communal harmony and religious freedom.

2   **Widespread and systemic poverty** is both a challenge and an opportunity. Many areas require development assistance – schools, universities, hospitals, roads, drinking water and agriculture. Half of all secondary schools are privately funded. Rapid urbanization and endemic corruption intensify the problems. Holistic ministry is necessary and a wonderful way to bring transformation to all levels of Tanzanian life. Most foreign Christian agencies at work in Tanzania already minister in this capacity; pray for more projects to be started and to be finished effectively.

3   **Growth in the mainline Churches** has been good but sporadic. Renewal movements in Lutheran, Anglican and Catholic churches bring life to traditional congregations; most of the bishops are evangelical. Some problems that limit further growth in numbers and spirituality are:

a) *Extensive areas where churches have stagnated* and where many potentially open villages remain unreached. The need is great for more evangelists and church planters.

b) *African worship patterns,* choirs and collections combined with Western cultural forms have taken priority over biblical teaching.

c) *Swahili* is used in fully 96% of church services even though it is not the heart language of the majority. Pray for the development of songs, teaching and resources in the first languages of all Tanzania's peoples.

d) *AIDS* continues to spread and affect many. It has now afflicted over 1.7 million (8.8% of the population) and orphaned over one million children. Tanzania's social fabric and economic structure are deeply affected. There are several initiatives led by religious and church communities for prevention, counselling and care. Pray for these programmes to be followed through and to have a powerful positive impact.

4   **The Pentecostal movement** has flourished in the last 20 years and is the fastest growing segment of Christianity. Although the origins of many of these groups are foreign, good use of outreach tools combined with spiritual fervency have seen Pentecostalism grow and take root in Tanzanian culture. Pray for continued growth, increased maturity and unity between Pentecostals and other evangelicals – essential if the church is to impact Muslims and animists in the nation.

5   **Tanzania's Christian population,** though numerous, needs discipleship. More than half of Tanzanians might be "Christian", but church attendance runs around 8%. Many see lack of biblical knowledge as the greatest challenge for the Church. As immature Christians are discipled, lifestyles and worldviews will change, and this in turn will impact the social, economic and political life of the nation.

6   **Leadership development** and theological training must become top priorities in churches. There is a critical lack of trained, mature leaders, and many pastors must care for 10 or more congregations, often miles apart.

a) *Theological schools.* Facilities and funding are dwarfed by the need. Pray for the many Bible schools, colleges and seminaries as well as the Christian universities run by Catholics, Anglicans and Lutherans. Many need upgrading to higher standards to prepare leaders for an increasingly literate population.

b) *Short-term and modular training courses,* TEE, Bible Training Centre for Pastors and cassette Bible schools are all vital for training local leaders, given the size and poverty of the country. Every denomination of note has institutions and programmes for furthering these modes of training.

c) **Pray for those already in leadership** positions to have opportunities for personal development and further training amid their demanding ministries. Pray for the release of resources to fund these many programmes.

7 **National initiatives for reaching the country** took root in the 1990s and 2000s with research and mobilizing initiatives focusing on the unevangelized.

a) **Excellent research on Tanzania's ethnic groups,** through Pioneer Bible Translators and others, established the need. Thirty-five peoples are estimated to be less than 5% Christian – many of these are still unreached and with very few known believers.

b) **National church planting strategies** have been used by God to unite churches for evangelism. Remaining Task Mission has undertaken extensive research and sets ambitious goals for national churches to plant enough new churches to represent 1 church for every 1,000 urban, and every 500 rural, Tanzanians – 40,000 villages and towns are still without a single church. Any national strategy must take into account that 75% of Tanzania's population is rural.

c) **Indigenous missions** have been formed to address these challenges. With minor assistance from expatriate agencies, exciting new ministries, such as Horn of Africa Mission and Christian Mission Fellowship, train and send Tanzanians as cross-cultural church planting missionaries. Hundreds of pastors and church planters are already trained and sent, even as the movement grows.

8 **Tanzania's young population** makes ministry to youth and children essential. Religious education in schools is an open door that requires trained instructors; Christian teachers can and do have a big impact. Scripture Union's Aid for AIDS programme educates and encourages young people toward pure lifestyles. TAFES(**IFES**) groups operate on 37 university and college campuses. Many students are being converted, including Muslims.

9 **The unfinished task in Tanzania.** Great growth among Christians must not obscure the real needs. Peoples of the coast, Zanzibar and some southern provinces are largely or almost entirely Muslim. Although conversions among Muslims have increased, the majority are still unreached. Pray specifically for:

a) **Zanzibar,** which is famous for its spices but infamous as an Arab base for its centuries-long African slave trade.

   i **On the two main islands,** Zanzibar and Pemba, live three of the original Swahili peoples. Almost all are Muslim, though there are a few believers. Radical Islam is dividing the islands' population, spreading fear and violence – and causing many to seek Jesus. The oppressive religious environment prevents many others from seeking.

   ii **Areas of special need.** Zanzibar Town, Mafia Island, the east coast and the small Tumbatu Island are spiritual strongholds and oppression is intense.

   iii **Christians have increased in number,** boldness and unity despite persecution. There are more than 60 congregations, mostly Pentecostal, on the islands. Pray for their continued perseverance and loving witness.

b) **The Muslim peoples** of coastal regions live under the curse of the historic slave trade. They are among the least evangelized of Tanzania's peoples. Their numbers have rapidly grown in recent years; their increased influence also presents a challenge to Christians. The most urgent challenges: the Digo (**AIM**), Zigula, Somali in the northeast, Rufiji, Ngendereko and Zaramo (**CoGWM**) in the central east and Machinga, Mwera and Ngindo in the southeast. Pray that Christians from other ethnic groups among them may be used of God to bless them with the gospel.

c) **The Inland peoples. AIM**/AIC have small church plants among the largely animist Datooga and Barabaig. They also have started work among the Rangi, who are mostly Muslim. Continue to pray for the Muslim Chasi/Alagwa and Kami, among whom there is no work yet started, and the animist Nilamba.

d) **The peoples on the Mozambique border.** The Brethren see some fruit among the Makonde and Yao. The Makhuwa are also in need of a breakthrough.

e) **The South Asian community** speaks a range of Indian languages, predominantly Gujarati, but Hindi and Punjabi speakers are also present. Most are Hindu or Muslim, with few Christians. **AIM** is looking at possibilities for ministry among them.

10 **Missionaries** continue to play a strategically vital role, even as they are increasingly replaced by capable national workers. They serve in a wide range of ministries in outreach, church support, training and specialist ministries. Major mission agencies are **IMB**, **YWAM**, **AIM**, *Missionshaus Bibelschule*, Swedish Pentecostal Church, Danish Lutheran Church.

11 **Christian support ministries:**

a) *Bible translation* is an urgent need finally being addressed. Widespread use of Swahili masked the need for further translations. Still, 51 languages have no Scripture at all and a further 32 have only portions. Several agencies focus on translation: The Bible Society, Pioneer Bible Translators and Word for the World among them. Pray for more translation teams, including Tanzanians and foreigners, for projects to be finished quickly and well, and for the necessary literacy programmes to accompany the translations.

b) *Christian literature* is vital for an increasingly literate nation, yet poverty and supply difficulties hamper printing and distribution on the necessary scale. Pray for more Tanzanians with the gifts and calling to write appropriate Christian articles and books. Pray also for the Central Tanganyika Press (Anglican), Inland Press (AIC), *Kanisa la Biblia Publishers* (Bible commentaries and theological books), the extensive publishing and printing ministry of the Pentecostal Churches Association and for effective distribution of their products. SU, The Bible Society, AIC and **CLC** have thriving Christian bookstores. The Gideons are active in placing NTs in schools.

c) *Missionary aviation* is still an essential service to churches, missions and humanitarian agencies because of the lack of good roads and the size of the country. **MAF**'s biggest operation is in Tanzania – 8 aircraft, 3 bases with 77 staff. They transport Christian workers and maintain medical programmes and fruitful outreach to the Maasai, Iraqw and Barabaig. Evangelism and showing the JESUS film at airstrips is one evangelistic spin-off! **AIM** operates a floatplane on Lake Victoria to facilitate a much-needed community health/evangelism programme.

d) *Christian radio* is widespread. Lutherans, Pentecostals/IBRA and **TWR** have recording studios. IBRA (four FM stations) has a daily audience of millions in Swahili, with a significant response. **TWR** broadcasts from Swaziland and Tanzania in English, Swahili, Makhuwa and Yao. FEBA and Adventist Radio also broadcast in a few languages. SIL has started programmes in some regions using Swahili and local languages. Pray for lasting fruit in lives to result. Christian TV is also increasing, including global satellite content and local Christian programmes.

e) *The JESUS film* is widely used in 18 languages. The film is extensively used in evangelism among the unreached with great response.

f) *GRN* has recordings in 88 languages and dialects. Cassettes are widely used for evangelism, Scripture reading and teaching. Lack of non–Swahili literature and significant illiteracy make these audio resources all the more important.

T

Thailand

Myanmar · Laos · China
Chiang Mai
South China Sea
Bangkok · Vietnam
Andaman Sea · Cambodia
Malaysia

Thailand

Kingdom of Thailand

Asia

Geography

Area 513,115 sq km. A fertile and well-watered land bordering on Myanmar, Laos, Cambodia and Malaysia.

Population		Ann Gr	Density
2010	68,139,238	0.66%	133/sq km
2020	71,443,041	0.43%	139/sq km
2030	73,462,037	0.23%	143/sq km

Capital Bangkok. **Other major city** Bangkok/Thonburi conurbation 7.0 million. **Urbanites** 34%. **Pop under 15 yrs** 22%. **Life expectancy** 68.7 yrs.

Peoples

Southeast Asian 81.0%.

Thai 78.4%. Four main peoples: Central 31.3%; Isan (Lao-Thai) 26.5%; Northern 10.6%; Southern 9.2%.

Mon-Khmer 1.2%. 25 peoples. Largest: Kui 0.5%.

Tai 0.9%. 16 peoples.

Other Southeast Asian 0.5%. Vietnamese, Miao/Hmong, Lao, Shan, Cham, others.

East Asian 10.8%. Chinese (7) 10.6%. Most are now Thai-speaking; some sources claim up to 17% Chinese.

Malay 6.1%. 8 peoples. Most in the far south. Pattani Malay 5.0%; Malay 1.0%.

Tibeto-Burman 1.2%. 17 peoples, largest: Karen(8) 0.9%.

Other 0.9%. South Asian; Western; other.

These numbers do not account for the more than 1 million Burmese migrants who come from many ethnicities.

Literacy 92.6%. **Official language** Thai. **All languages** 85. **Indigenous languages** 74. **Languages with Scriptures** 16Bi 9NT 19por.

Economy

Free market principles, foreign investment, fertile agricultural land and recent industrialization have led to strong exports – textiles, shrimp, sugar, rubber, jewellery and electronics. Thailand is also the world's largest exporter of rice. Rapid economic growth in the 1980s and '90s was halted by a crash in the late 1990s. Subsequent investment-driven growth was hampered again by the economic crisis of 2008-09. Tourism is a major aspect of the economy; there is also an endemic economy of vice, in particular the sex trade and drug trafficking.

HDI Rank 87th/182. **Public debt** 37.9% of GDP. **Income/person** $4,116 (9% of USA).

Politics

A kingdom since the 13th Century, and never ruled by a Western power. A constitutional monarchy; the popular king – the world's longest-reigning monarch – plays a strong, unifying and stabilizing role. The powerful army dominated politics and commercial life for 60 years; widespread corruption ensued, which persists to a degree today. A military coup ousted the prime minister in 2006. Elections in 2007 saw his party re-elected at the head of a coalition. Opposition groups demonstrating en masse and counter-demonstrations escalated in 2008. The courts then dissolved the ruling coalition on charges of electoral fraud, after which a new coalition was formed, led by the main opposition group, the People's Alliance for Democracy. In 2010, the Red Shirts political pressure group, loyal to the People's Power Party (which was deposed in 2008), initiated sustained protests that took over key areas of central Bangkok, paralyzing much of the city. The main protest sites were eventually seized by the army and police, but disruption is far from over. The Thai political scene is deeply divided; some regard civil war as a worst-case scenario. Additionally, violent insurgency among Muslims in the south at times destabilizes that region.

Religion

Freedom of religion is guaranteed in the constitution, which was modified in 1998 to loosen ties between the state and Buddhism and increase harmony among religious communities. All new religious groups must come under one of the government-recognized umbrella networks in order to be legally recognized.

Religions	Pop %	Population	Ann Gr
Buddhist	85.32	58,136,398	0.5%
Muslim	7.90	5,383,000	2.3%
Non-religious	2.40	1,635,342	2.0%
Chinese	1.80	1,226,506	-0.4%
Ethnoreligionist	1.20	817,671	-0.9%
Christian	1.10	749,532	2.8%
Other	0.10	68,139	0.7%
Hindu	0.10	68,139	0.7%
Baha'i	0.08	54,511	0.7%

Christians	Denoms	Pop %	Affiliates	Ann Gr
Protestant	55	0.48	330,000	3.5%
Independent	29	0.08	54,000	4.3%
Anglican	1	<0.01	1,000	3.9%
Catholic	1	0.50	341,000	2.0%
Orthodox	4	<0.01	2,000	9.0%
Marginal	2	0.04	25,000	3.7%

Churches	MegaBloc	Congs	Members	Affiliates
Catholic Church	C	454	256,541	341,200
Ch of Christ (CCT)★	P	1,095	76,648	139,500
Karen Baptist Conv	P	416	27,040	33,800
Hope of God Int	I	496	17,365	29,000
Latter-day Saints	M	81	9,730	18,000
Associated Chs (OMF)	P	318	11,143	15,600
Lahu Bapt Conv of T	P	66	5,320	13,300
Thai Bapt Chs Assoc	P	94	7,156	11,020
Christian Fell (AoG)	P	72	5,000	8,350
Full Gospel Chs in T	P	135	6,750	8,100
Gospel Ch of T (CMA)	P	140	4,790	8,000
Other denominations[81]		1,727	75,167	124,540
Total Christians[92]		**5,094**	**502,650**	**750,410**

★The Karen and Lahu Baptist Conventions are part of the CCT, but are counted here separately.

TransBloc	Pop %	Population	Ann Gr
Evangelicals			
Evangelicals	0.5	307,305	3.6%
Renewalists			
Charismatics	0.2	105,102	4.1%
Pentecostals	0.1	70,590	4.1%

Missionaries from Thailand

P,I,A Estimated 468 long-term, nearly all in Thailand.

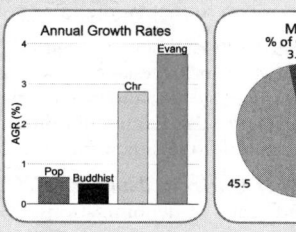

Annual Growth Rates — AGR (%); Pop, Buddhist, Chr, Evang

MegaBlocs % of Christian Pop — 3.6, 43.6, 7.3, 45.5 — P, I, C, M

Answers to Prayer

1 **The Church in Thailand is growing.** Numeric increases have always been modest at best, but of late, they are proportionately more rapid. There is a perception of greater interest in the gospel by many in Thailand. Many church and mission leaders feel Thailand is poised for its greatest – or first – breakthrough of church growth. Already, 65% of ethnic Thai church members are first-generation believers.

2 **Emerging indigenous leadership** is making up for years of shortfall in this area; they now have ambitious goals for reaching the whole country. The Thailand Evangelism and Church Growth Committee has bold plans to reach every one of Thailand's 80,000 villages and neighbourhoods with the gospel through intercession, outreach and the wise use of sound research.

3 **Missiological maturity** has come in leaps and bounds. Foreign expressions of Christianity dominated the church scene for too long, but increased understanding of and sensitivity to Buddhist worldviews and Thai culture are shaping more effective missionaries and national workers.

Challenges for Prayer

1 **Thailand has been an island** of stability and freedom in a troubled region, but "The Land of Smiles" is also awash with difficulties. Pray for these pressing issues and for the wise leadership and reform needed to address them:

a) **The political upheaval** of 2006-2008 revealed deep fault lines among various political parties, the military and the royalty. Protests brought the country to a standstill.

b) **The violent insurgency** in the southern areas near Malaysia has claimed thousands of lives. It is a result of some discrimination against the predominantly Malay Muslim minority and the radicalization of the same.

c) **Tensions with other neighbours,** including disputes with Cambodia and more notably Myanmar, from which over a million have fled disaster and persecution into Thailand.

T

d) *Structures of sin and vice* continue to prosper, despite increasing efforts to combat them. Corruption allows unscrupulous men – in business, politics, the military and police – to enrich themselves while oppressing others. The moral blights of the sex trade, drug networks, crime syndicates and ecological degradation will remain as long as they are profitable and tolerated. Pray for the breaking of these structures of sin by God's power.

2 **Thailand means "Land of the Free"** because it successfully retained its freedom when surrounding countries were colonized by Western powers. Yet the land is held captive in a complex web of Buddhism, traditional culture, spirit appeasement and even occult practices, with a social cohesiveness out of which few have dared to come. The Buddha is the object of people's adoration, but the spirit world is deeply ensconced in Thailand. Phra Sayam Devadhiraj, the venerated guardian spirit that protects the land, has a golden idol in the capital's Grand Palace. For many Thai, their nationality and religious identity are inextricably linked. Pray for spiritual breakthrough so that, in the Lord Jesus, the Thai may be free indeed.

3 **Church growth** has been less than spectacular. After four centuries of Catholic work and nearly 200 years of Protestant work, Thai Christians hover around 1% of the population. Catholicism's percentage has increased little in 50 years. Protestant growth has been very modest despite many missionaries and programmes. Nearly half of Protestants are from tribal groups, which amount to less than 5% of the country's population. Pray for:

a) *The Church of Christ in Thailand (CCT),* the largest Protestant, ecumenical network. It hosts a broad range of denominations, from mainline to conservative. Pray for renewal to come to this group; some of the member bodies have stagnated and need a new burst of spiritual life.

b) *The Evangelical Fellowship of Thailand.* This links more than 120 mission organizations, 55 church associations and seven Christian institutions. It is regarded as the "home" for many of Thailand's evangelicals (along with CCT). Pray for unity, effective collaboration and accelerating growth.

c) *High standards in church life.* The tolerant and relaxed nature of Thai culture can gravitate against holiness in churches. Pastors must lead by personal example, but they also need to squarely face up to syncretism and the high rate of backsliding in churches. Lifestyles of prayer, Scripture reading, witness and ministry must be cultivated.

d) *Church growth and evangelism* in Thailand are taking on new dimensions. Driven increasingly by a confident national leadership, Vision 2010/Love Thailand/TEC has the goal of seeing all of Thailand, including the country's 80,000 villages, reached with the gospel. This sweeping vision includes the formation of a national prayer network, leadership development, extensive research and community-development ministry in addition to evangelism.

e) *The less-reached areas.* The large majority of Thailand's churches are small (30-50 members) and are concentrated in Bangkok and the northwest. Over 6,000 of the 7,415 sub-districts have no church. In the southern and northeastern (Isaan) regions, more than 90% of the sub-districts are without a church.

4 **A truly indigenous expression** of Thai Christianity must be developed. In a recent survey of Thai non-Christians, 89% said the Christian message was unintelligible. The gospel has never adequately shed its Western trappings and become contextualized, which is vital for it to do in a Buddhist culture with deeply divergent worldviews. Pray for Thai music, hymnody, art forms, worship patterns, architecture, and styles of leadership, Bible study and witness to be encouraged and developed under the Holy Spirit's guidance. This will not only make church more relevant to non-Christians, but it will also give believers new spiritual insight and grounding.

5 **The historic lack of Thai leadership** in the churches is part of the slow growth, the failures of rural churches and the lack of vision, but this is rapidly changing. Over 1,500 recently gathered for training with the Thailand Evangelism Committee (TEC). About 20 Bible schools and seminaries and 17 TEE centres operate in the country. Pray for the Bangkok Bible College (**CMA** and **OMF**), Phayao Bible Training Centre (**OMF**) and the many Bible colleges tied to specific denominations or churches. There are also a number of less-formalized training programmes such as **YWAM**'s courses. Pray for the shaping of Christian leaders who demonstrate vision, integrity and wisdom and who assist in the flowering of a truly Thai Church.

6 **Missions** have considerable freedom for ministry despite a quota system that somewhat restricts the number of visas issued. Major involvement in the past was institutional; medical work and schools played an important role in winning the first converts and planting the first churches in many parts of the land. Major emphases now are evangelism, church planting, Bible teaching, English teaching and compassionate ministry to vulnerable segments of society. Pray for:

a) *The calling, entry and preparation* of new workers to this exacting field. There are many opportunities for both long- and short-term workers in all parts of the country. Keys to their effectiveness are adequate training in the highly cross-cultural nature of their work and grounding in biblical teaching on spiritual warfare.

b) *Effective partnership with Thai believers* in strategic outreach; expatriates are learning to relinquish leadership of joint efforts to indigenous workers.

c) *The major agencies.* **OMF** works in five fields (110 workers among Thai throughout the country and around 60 more among tribals in the north and Muslims in the south). Other major agencies: **YWAM, CCCI**, PCKH, **NTM, AoG, CC/CC** and MUP.

7 **The extensive sex trade,** focused in Bangkok, Pattaya, Phuket and Hat Yai, is profoundly embedded in Thai society. Millions derive income from this "industry". Estimates – none of which can be verified – range up to 2.8 million who engage in sex work. Some claim 10% of all tourist money is spent on the sex industry. Pray for:

a) *The girls involved* (and the much smaller numbers of men). They are usually from poor, rural backgrounds and mostly from Isaan/the northeast, from ethnic minorities or from neighbouring countries, especially Myanmar. They are often sold into the sex trade by family members needing money or fewer mouths to feed. Their introduction into the trade can be brutal. Leaving can be nearly impossible due to "debts" owed to traffickers. Many others enter willingly, seeking an income higher than any other job would offer or the prospect of a rich foreign boyfriend or husband. All are at high risk of mistreatment and disease; all are in need of the redemption and unconditional love that Christ offers.

b) *Those who profit from the trade.* Those who exploit others for their own gain must be brought to task. Pray for corrupt police and officials, the traffickers, the Chinese-Thai mafia, owners of the establishments where the trade occurs, relatives who sell the girls into indentured sexual servitude. Pray for moral conviction to fall upon them. Pray for this wicked flesh trade to be brought to an end.

c) *The users.* Westerners and East Asians in their hundreds of thousands arrive in the country specifically or in part for sex tourism. Thai men who pay for sex outnumber both of these groups by far. Pray for blind eyes to be opened, and pray for the freedom these men also need from this vile practice.

d) *The government,* which officially states opposition to sex tourism, but does very little to discourage it. Billions are tied up in the trade, and there is little willpower in the government to disperse the tangled web of the sex trade and the billions it generates, directly and indirectly.

e) *Agencies seeking to minister* to those caught in the trade. Ministries such as Rahab and Nightlight work with prostitutes, providing care, counselling and vocational training for those wanting out. Many other groups work in anti-trafficking. It is a valuable and honourable battle, but a difficult one that cannot ultimately be won solely by "rescuing" girls or closing individual brothels.

8 **Particularly needy groups of people** include:

a) *Children in crisis.* Over one million children are estimated to be child labourers in Thailand. This includes 40,000 or even more sold into the sex trade as minors. Many are from minority or foreign backgrounds. All forms of labour usually entail backbreaking hours, minimal pay and subjection to all kinds of abuse and ill treatment. There are tens of thousands of homeless street children. Pray for all involved in reaching out to these tragic little ones.

b) *HIV/AIDS sufferers.* Thailand's infection rate is Asia's highest by far, with around 700,000 officially carrying the virus. The true figure could be double this. While the spread is being arrested by vigorous government actions, the combination of the ubiquitous trades in sex and drugs keeps new infection rates high. Churches must wake up to this crisis and minister love and life to the suffering and the bereaved.

*c) **Students*** are responsive to the gospel, but they also demonstrate openness to many harmful influences. **YFC**, TCS(**IFES**), **CCCI** and an indigenous movement called *Yuwakrit* see conversions and growth of groups on campuses. Evangelism and camps/retreats often receive enthusiastic spiritual response, but the large majority of the 1.3 million students remain unevangelized. Backsliding is a prominent challenge. Christian hostels for students, run by six agencies, prove valuable for discipling students.

*d) **Buddhist monks*** number over 300,000 and enjoy a highly regarded position of honour in Thailand. The monastic institution, however, has been troubled by some high-profile scandals and is targeted by Islamist insurgents in the south. Pray for Christian outreach to them – many are true seekers and open to the gospel.

*e) **Refugees.*** Thailand has long served as a haven for those fleeing upheaval in neighbouring countries. The most notable and needy are the 1.2 million refugees from Myanmar. Many are from persecuted minorities such as the Karen, Chin and Shan. Most are present illegally. These refugees face harsh exploitation, from dangerous manual labour to sex slavery. Pray for groups to reach out with compassionate, holistic ministry to these desperate peoples.

9 **Of the 5.3 million Muslims,** almost 80% are Malay speakers residing in the south. There are also Thai-speaking Muslims in most Thai provinces and 600,000 in Bangkok alone. Since 2004, the three provinces bordering Malaysia have experienced political tension, unrest and almost daily killings linked to Muslim insurgency. This is the only major Muslim population in Southeast Asia open for evangelism, yet after years of hard work, there are only a few small indigenous worshipping communities of former Muslims. The radicalization of Islam is affecting Thai Muslims and complicating outreach, and many seekers are held back by community pressures. Pray for local believers and for different agencies involved in outreach to Muslims in Thailand. Pray also for the Jawi Malay NT and Scripture portions and for a new BCC in Thai and Malay, all developed for Thai Muslims.

10 **The tribal peoples,** largely marginalized, are responding in significant numbers. This follows years of hard work by Baptists and **WEC** among the Karen, and by **OMF** among eight tribes in the north. The younger work of **NTM** in 12 tribes around the country is seeing results in tribal churches planted. Many workers are needed to win and disciple tribal peoples. Pray for:

*a) **The multiplying but scattered congregations*** among the northern Hmong, Lahu, Lisu, Akha and Karen peoples. Nominalism is a real problem in many churches. The Buddhist Shan and Taoist/animist Yao are less responsive.

*b) **The Kui, Khmu and Khmer peoples*** in the east who are unreached. **CMA** works in the area, but the number of workers is insufficient. The Khmer and Khmu are proving highly responsive to the work of **CMA** and the Mennonites.

*c) **The Golden Triangle.*** Opium poppies are a lucrative cash crop for most of the northern tribes. Cultivation is an acute temptation for Christians and a formidable barrier to repentance for non-believers. The narcotics trade breeds insecurity and violence. Pray for believers and missionaries in sensitive areas.

*d) **Training for tribal Christians.*** The ministry of Chang Rai Bible Seminary (founded by **AOI**), and several other Bible schools, has yielded native-planted churches among many ethnic minorities, not just in Thailand but also throughout the region.

11 **Chinese-Thai Christians are a significant minority** in the Church, especially at the leadership level. The dynamism and financial clout of this community, if fully activated, could be a significant force for evangelization. As it stands, it is often deeply embedded in many of the structures of sin – prostitution, gambling and drugs. The Chinese-Thai community has in the last few generations increasingly intermingled and assimilated into wider Thai culture. Pray for more Chinese-Thai Christians to be called into serving in and supporting full-time ministry.

12 **Christian help ministries** are well developed in Thailand and bearing fruit.

*a) **Bible translation*** is still a major target for prayer. Work is in progress in several languages – main agencies being Thailand Bible Society, Biblica, SIL, **NTM** and **OMF**. Of 29 languages without Scriptures, 10 definitely need translation programmes. Of the four versions of the Thai Bible in circulation, a new version from 2007 is an effective study version.

*b) **Christian radio*** remains very effective. Many Thai stations daily air Christian programmes. **FEBC**, Full Gospel Radio (The Way) and The Voice of Peace Studio prepare a wide range of programmes. Response is gratifying – from both Buddhists and Muslims – from **FEBC** programmes broadcast over 27 different Thai stations.

*c) **Christian literature*** is increasing. Over 1,000 Thai books have been published. Several Christian publishers (such as **CLC**, **OMF** [Kanok], **CMA** and Mittam) play crucial roles in providing appropriate materials for both evangelism and teaching. There are more than 20 Christian bookstores in the land, three of which are run by **CLC**. Interest is high in **FEBC**'s Bible Correspondence Courses. **EHC** has distributed over 20 million pieces of gospel literature.

*d) **The JESUS film,*** in 25 languages, has been viewed by millions.

*e) **Audio resources*** for unevangelized mission fields were pioneered in Thailand. The Voice of Peace Studio pioneered the use of evangelistic and teaching cassettes; now they digitally record Christian materials for the same purposes. **GRN** has materials in 79 languages and a key base in Chiang Mai.

*f) **Digital resources.*** **MAF** created a digital library of over 4,000 resources in Thai – an invaluable and portable collection of materials for Christian workers and pastors. These materials for evangelism, discipleship and leadership development are also available on the Internet.

Timor Leste

East Timor

Asia

Geography

Area 14,874 sq km. Eastern half of Timor and the Ocussi-Ambenu enclave in Indonesian West Timor and Atauro Island.

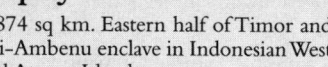

Population		Ann Gr	Density
2010	1,171,163	3.38%	79/sq km
2020	1,617,517	3.15%	109/sq km
2030	2,124,649	2.60%	143/sq km

Havoc wrought from 1999 to 2001 displaced up to 100,000 to West Timor.
Capital Dili 174,000. **Urbanites** 28.1%. **Pop under 15 yrs** 45%. **Life expectancy** 60.7 yrs.

Peoples

Timorese 95.9%. Largest peoples: Mambai 13.7%; Tetum(2) 11.5%; Makasai 9.7%; Tokode 8.7%; Galoli 8.6%; Kemak 8.6%; Bunak 8.2%.
Indonesian/Javanese 3.5%.
Other 0.6%.
Literacy 58.6%. **Official languages** Portuguese (13.5% understand), Tetum (and its dialects) is understood by 91%. Bahasa Indonesia is also common, understood by 43%. **All languages** 19. **Languages with Scriptures** 1Bi 3por 2w.i.p.

Economy

Ignored by the Portuguese, much developed by the Indonesian military but more as a source for enriching the elite, then destroyed in vengeance after the vote for independence in 1999. The new nation faces major rebuilding. Potential in agriculture, sandalwood and minerals, but massive oil and gas deposits shared with Australia will be major sources of revenue for the future. Meanwhile, the majority live in poverty.
HDI Rank 162nd/182. **Income/person** $469 (1% of USA).

Politics

Portuguese rule from 1511 to 1974. This was followed by civil war, Indonesian invasion and suppression, famines, lack of health facilities and economic distress. Indonesia's occupation was independently adjudged to have directly caused 100,000 deaths. Its occupation and Timorese resistance made a mockery of claims that inte-

T

gration of East Timor into Indonesia was voluntary. International pressure led to a referendum on independence in 1999. Armed militia supported by the army systematically looted and destroyed 75% of the country's infrastructure and economy before the UN intervened. Finally achieving independence in 2002, Timor has been blighted by internal strife and outbreaks of violence between various factions, most notably in 2006. It will take decades for Timor to be restored to the place where it can stand on its own.

Religion

One of only two Asian nations with a Catholic majority. Catholicism was the state religion and the religion of the elite until 1975. Some prejudice against Protestants and Muslims is reported.

Religions	Pop %	Population	Ann Gr
Christian	87.39	1,023,479	4.1%
Ethnoreligionist	10.81	126,603	1.5%
Muslim	1.10	12,883	-17.6%
Hindu	0.50	5,856	31.5%
Buddhist	0.10	1,171	0.0%
Chinese	0.10	1,171	-4.7%

Christians Denoms		Pop %	Affiliates	Ann Gr
Protestant	4	3.64	43,000	2.9%
Independent	2	0.19	2,000	8.0%
Catholic	1	81.50	954,000	3.7%
Marginal	1	0.02	<1,000	6.8%

Churches	MegaBloc	Congs	Members	Affiliates
Catholic Church	C	72	575,529	978,400
IPTL - Ref Ch of T	P	60	14,118	24,000
Assemblies of God	P	90	15,000	18,500
Other denominations[5]		14	1,269	2,610
Total Christians[8]		**236**	**606,149**	**1,023,860**

TransBloc	Pop %	Population	Ann Gr
Evangelicals			
Evangelicals	2.3	27,119	3.6%
Renewalists			
Charismatics	2.6	30,519	4.1%
Pentecostals	1.8	20,700	2.3%

Religions % of Total Pop

TransBloc Movements % of Total Pop

Challenges for Prayer

1 **Timor's traumatic birth left deep scars.** The vindictive destruction and forcible removal of many Timorese by the departing Indonesian military and its Timorese militia allies left a legacy of hatred and trauma that will take decades to heal. Internal tensions – between Eastern and Western, disaffected armed gangs and rival political factions – cause violence and unrest to persist, despite the presence of international (mostly Australian and some Portuguese) peacekeepers. Pray for peace for Timor, that grievances might be laid to rest and that reconciliation might begin to take root.

2 **Timor appears caught in a descending spiral** of poverty, poor health and illiteracy. It is the poor who suffer most from the violence and destruction wrought by various factions. With a shattered infrastructure and ill-equipped public servants, the nation needs transformation in all spheres of life. Major investments are needed in education, job creation, health care and training of leadership. The oil and gas fields of the Timor Sea will hopefully bring the finances required; pray that Australia will be fair and generous in sharing the revenues, and that the income will be justly and wisely invested into projects that benefit the whole population and not just enrich a few.

3 **The Catholic Church** grew rapidly as a visible symbol of national resistance to Indonesians, but traditional Spiritism remains, permeating Christianity and rebounding as a religion in its own right. Catholic agencies serve at the forefront of the mercy ministries so desperately needed in Timor. Protestants are viewed with suspicion as originating from Indonesia. Pray for Christians to renounce all vestiges of animism; pray also for greater unity and cooperation between Catholics and Protestants.

4 **Protestant churches** emerged only recently and their growth is modest. The **AoG**, working here since the 1960s, has grown on Atauro Island and in Dili. The Reformed IPTL (GKTT) was started by Indonesian immigrants, and many Timorese joined, but rarely with true conversion. Nominalism and lack of understanding of the gospel characterize the majority. There is great need for biblically trained and spiritually active pastors. Pray that evangelical churches may be planted among every people and in every area of Timor. Pray for true unity among national church leaders.

Specific ministry challenges:

a) Timor's peoples remain mostly ignorant of the gospel; none can be considered adequately evangelized. Specific outreach to each of the 19 indigenous peoples is needed. Pray for pioneer church planters who will risk all to see the Kingdom of God established here.

b) Children and young people – most are traumatized and many have lost everything, including parents. Droves roam the streets, often forming dangerous gangs. Pray for effective holistic and discipleship ministries to be established. **WEC** (The Esperanza Project), **YWAM**-Arms, the Nazarene Center, JMM (*Projeto Vida Mais*) and JAMI (*Centro Shalom*) focus on ministering in this capacity. JUVEPE has a Child at Risk Program that provides support for abused kids, especially for teenage girls.

c) Holistic ministry is the best option for Timor, since needs are both physical and emotional. Christians must share the whole gospel for Timorese to respond. Christian Vision (UK/Brazil) and Transformation Alliance (Singapore) are two ministries seeking to impact every village with practical and spiritual assistance.

d) Christian resources are almost non-existent. A Catholic translation of the NT is available in Tetum and a Wycliffe-coordinated NT project is underway, but 13 languages have no Scripture whatsoever. The JESUS film is now in Tetum as well as in Portuguese and Indonesian. Christian Vision's radio station – Radio Voz FM 89.5 – broadcasts in Portuguese, Tetum, Indonesian and English.

5 **Foreign missions.** Many NGOs assist with Timor's great needs, but instability yields constant disruptions and evacuations. Significant missions include Christian Vision, Transformation Alliance, **YWAM**, **WEC** and Church of the Nazarene. Pray for:

a) Effective strategies that assist with physical needs, counselling and reconciliation. The government's current emphasis on human development, especially education, opens a door for professionals in these fields to serve. **YWAM**, JUVEPE and AME opened nursery and/or primary schools; a Filipino school offers language and computer classes. **MAF** gives aviation support for remote areas. Tentmakers have opportunity to work with the government as lawyers or as educators in universities and national schools.

b) Long-term involvement that models biblical faith and trains and empowers Timorese Christians to finish the task is another great need. Pray for healthy partnership between expatriate workers and national church leaders.

T

Burkina Faso

Benin

Togo

Ghana

Nigeria

Lomé
Gulf of Guinea

Togo
Togolese Republic
Africa

Geography

Area 56,785 sq km. The Atlantic coastline is only 56 km long, but the land stretches 540 km northward to the Sahel; wedged between Ghana and Benin.

Population		Ann Gr	Density
2010	6,780,030	2.50%	119/sq km
2020	8,444,829	2.11%	149/sq km
2030	10,114,908	1.73%	178/sq km

Capital Lomé 1,667,016. **Urbanites** 43.4%. **Pop under 15 yrs** 40%. **Life expectancy** 62.2 yrs.

Peoples

Over 57 ethnic groups in 2 major language families.
Guinean 47.4%. 22 peoples. Mainly in the southern half of Togo, largest: Ewe 21.2%; Wachi 9.0%; Mina 4.9%; Adja 2.6%; Akposo 2.7%; Anufo (Chakossi) 1.0%; Akebu 1.0%.
Gur 45.5%. 21 peoples. Mainly in the north, largest: Kabiye (Kabré) 15.7%; Kotokoli (Tem) 5.0%; Moba (Bimoba) 4.7%; Nawdm (Losso) 3.6%; Lama (Lamba) 2.9%; Ntcham 4.4%; Gurma 3.0%; Konkomba 1.2%.
Other Sub-Saharan African 6.5%. Yoruba(3) 4.4%; Fulani 1.2%.
Foreign 0.6%. Lebanese, French, others.
Literacy 53%. **Official language** French. Only two indigenous languages used in education system: Ewe/Mina and Kabiye. **All languages** 43. **Indigenous languages** 39. **Languages with Scriptures** 5Bi 11NT 15por 12w.i.p.

Economy

Agriculture dominates the economy, with coffee and cocoa the main cash crops. The country is self-sufficient in basic foodstuffs. Commerce, especially via the port at Lomé, as well as phosphate and cement exports, supplement agricultural income. A lack of fiscal discipline in past years slowed the flow of aid and investment, and living standards have dropped significantly since the early 1990s.
HDI Rank 159th/182. **Public debt** 89.6% of GDP. **Income/person** $436 (1% of USA).

Politics

German colony 1884-1914. Independent from France in 1960. One-party, military-civilian regime since 1967. Political parties legalized in 1991, and a democratic constitution introduced in 1992. The president's death in 2005 (after 38 years in power) led to a military coup, which installed his son as president. Bloody protests at this move and at allegedly rigged elections in 2005 (won by the incumbent) saw over 500 killed and 40,000 flee the country, with widespread international condemnation. The 2007 legislative elections saw the ruling party establish a majority. Presidential elections in 2010 will demonstrate how much democratic progress has been made in Togo. The more populous Guinean peoples of the south rankle at political-military domination by the central-northern Gur.

Religion

A period of intense anti-Christian rhetoric in the 1970s cooled to official indifference. In 1978, 20 religious groups were banned; only Muslims, Catholics and five Protestant churches were legally permitted to function. In 1990, nearly all restrictions were lifted, with considerable religious freedom since.

Religions	Pop %	Population	Ann Gr
Christian	45.38	3,076,778	3.0%
Ethnoreligionist	36.87	2,499,797	1.5%
Muslim	17.50	1,186,505	3.3%
Non-religious	0.25	16,950	2.5%

Christians	Denoms	Pop %	Affiliates	Ann Gr
Protestant	28	13.92	944,000	3.7%
Independent	58	4.21	286,000	5.0%
Catholic	1	25.29	1,715,000	2.8%
Marginal	1	0.76	52,000	2.3%
Unaffiliated		1.20	81,000	-5.8%

Churches	MegaBloc	Congs	Members	Affiliates
Catholic Church	C	314	942,308	1,715,000
Evang Presbyterian	P	630	93,525	390,000
Fed of Evang Chr Chs	P	1,020	114,344	279,000
Baptist Convention	P	750	42,000	81,000
Pente Holiness Ch	P	950	28,199	62,038
Methodist Church	P	193	29,000	58,000
Jehovah's Witnesses	M	255	17,600	51,500
Deeper Life Bible Ch	I	38	9,583	23,000
Seventh-day Adventist	P	42	12,400	20,708
Church of Pentecost	I	264	9,700	14,400
Other denominations[78]		2,778	170,486	301,269
Total Christians[88]		**7,234**	**1,469,145**	**2,995,915**

TransBloc	Pop %	Population	Ann Gr
Evangelicals			
Evangelicals	10.7	722,952	4.7%
Renewalists			
Charismatics	10.6	721,787	4.3%
Pentecostals	6.0	405,588	3.5%

Religions
% of Total Pop

TransBloc Movements
% of Total Pop

Answers to Prayer

1 **Christianity,** particularly evangelical and Pentecostal, has grown rapidly since 1990. Evangelicals increased sevenfold from 1990 to 2010, growing from 2.7% to 10.7%. Praise God for the multiplication of Pentecostal and charismatic movements, fuelled by the Holy Spirit and largely driven by West African pastors and evangelists.

Challenges for Prayer

1 **Political injustices continue.** The illegal appointment (by the army) of the former president's son, the series of rigged elections and the political system tweaked to serve the ruling party all perpetuate resentment and bitterness between southern and central people clusters. Pray for leaders to emerge who fear God, respect the constitution and serve the people justly. In raising up such leaders, pray that God breaks down walls of enmity between the Guinean and Gur people clusters.

2 **The economic situation** remains precarious. With little foreign investment and few natural resources, poverty is widespread and people are vulnerable to exploitation. Such poverty makes prostitution common and drives many orphans and unwanted children into the arms of human traffickers. Rich Muslim businesses entice young Christians to work there and eventually convert to Islam. Pray for Christians, locally and internationally, to stand firm despite such problems and to invest in creating ethical employment for the people of Togo.

3 **The Church in Togo** stagnated between 1960 and 1990. Long-established groups – Catholic, Evangelical Presbyterian Church and Methodist – grew slowly and remained confined to particular ethnicities. From 1980, newer evangelical groups began to grow – **AoG**, Baptist and Missouri Synod Lutheran. Many new denominations from outside Togo commenced work in the 1990s, and all denominations grew rapidly. The influx of many Pentecostal groups from Nigeria, Ghana, Benin and Burkina Faso augments the growth sparked by Western mission agencies. False shepherds and unbalanced prosperity teachings are also increasing as the true Church grows. Pray that strong, indigenous congregations and denominations with solid teaching, biblical worldviews and visionary leadership be established.

4 **Leadership development** is a great need for the young and quickly growing body of Christ in Togo. The **AoG** has trained pastors for only half its congregations. Training facilities in Togo are now increasing in number. Baptist (WABAST) and **AoG** (WAAST) graduate theological schools serve students from all West Africa, and most denominations have colleges or institutes. TEE and lay-training programmes are also increasing. Pray for training and education programmes for full-time ministers and lay people to be effective; pray that they may be formative in raising up leaders for churches in Togo.

5 **Unity in the Togolese Church** has made progress, under the auspices of reaching every home and planting a church in every village in the country. But there is a long way to go. Barriers of mistrust and denominationalism must be broken down, and the recently arrived churches must be willing to work with each other and with the more established churches. Pray that this vision might unify the Church and call all believers to action.

6 **The strongly entrenched powers of darkness** have scarcely been challenged through intercessory prayer and confrontation with the power of the gospel. The two major forces to be tackled:

a) The idolatry and strong secret societies of the Ewe, Fon and other tribes that intensely oppose the gospel. The majority of the population, including many Christians, still participate in animistic and voodoo rituals; some of these are outright evil. Believers cannot grow in their faith without a clean break from the works of darkness.

b) The growing strength of Islam. Muslims dominate commerce and education. Islamization is in full swing as generous subsidies from oil-rich Muslim countries fuel the building of many mosques, schools and charity projects. Throughout Togo, the stream of conversions to Islam is steady, yet few Christian workers focus on Muslim evangelism among the 13 Muslim peoples or within the high concentrations of Muslims in urban areas.

7 **The less-evangelized peoples** of Togo. Togo and Benin have long had the highest percentage of unevangelized traditionalists in Africa. The major challenges:

a) The 13 majority-Muslim peoples – the Kotokoli (**SIM**, Baptists, hundreds of believers), Anufo (**YWAM**, **ABWE**, a few believers), Akaselem (**AoG**, handful of believers), Ditammari, Bariba, Bago, Dagomba, Bissa, Akpe as well as the more dispersed Arabs, Hausa, Yoruba, Kambole and Fulbe (Baptists).

b) The northern traditional animistic peoples – the Moba, Bassari, Nawdm (**AoG**, Baptists, Deeper Life), Gurma, Lama, Gangam, Karaboro, Mossi (**AoG**), Logba and Waama. Pray for these pioneering efforts to see breakthroughs for the gospel.

c) The southern traditional animistic peoples – the Watchi, Adja, Akebu, Adele, Anyanga and Kpessi.

Ghanaian and Benin believers of the same language groups could best reach many of these peoples.

8 **Ministries to young people and children** developed rapidly in the greater freedoms post-1992.

a) Schools and the university are fertile ground for secularism and Islam, but also for Christian witness. **CCCI** and GBUST(**IFES**) have campus ministries with a growing number of students involved. The latter had 49 groups in 2009. SU has a good ministry in schools as well as camps, family ministry and AIDS education. Pray for the development of mature believers and groups.

b) Churches are generally ill equipped to address the needs of children and young people. Over half of the population are under age 19, so a change must happen if the Christian growth of the current generation is to continue into the next. Pray for more workers with vision and gifting to help change this situation.

c) The illegal trade in child labourers who are "exported" to urban areas or to other lands, often for the sex industry, still flourishes. These unprotected children – usually from poor rural contexts and often orphans – number over 300,000. Pray for an end to this evil.

9 **Evangelical mission agencies** are shockingly few for an open, responsive, needy country with so many unreached. The opportunities are many – church planting, evangelism, discipling, leadership training, education, aid/development, holistic ministry and many more. The largest missions are GGWO, **ABWE**, **CAPRO**, **CC**, **CMF**. Pray for more workers in this rare harvest opportunity.

10 **Bible translation** remains a major ministry challenge. The whole Bible is completed in Kabiye, one of two indigenous languages used in schools. Four languages have definite Bible translation needs. Work in 12 languages is in progress, much of it by **WBT** workers. Training national translation workers is now one of the greatest priorities for Bible translation.

11 **Christian media ministries** for prayer are:

a) Christian literature is in great demand and cheap to produce. Pray for the ministry of The Bible Society as well as the **CLC** and **ABWE** bookshops in distributing Scripture. **ABWE**, **WBT** and others undertake literacy projects, which enable such resources to actually be used.

b) *Audio resources* are vital in this low–literacy nation. **GRN** produced materials in 55 languages, including the FCBH series. Audio Scripture Ministries trains nationals to produce Christian audio resources such as music and teaching.

c) **EHC** distributes hundreds of thousands of pieces of literature as well as ministers through primary health care to the communities they reach.

d) *Christian radio and TV.* Local stations broadcast Christian programmes; there is also one well-acclaimed Christian radio station in Lomé. Christian television channels include *Television la Solution* and TV Zion. African Christian Television produces programmes for broadcast on the national channels. The JESUS film is shown extensively in film and on TV and is available in 18 languages.

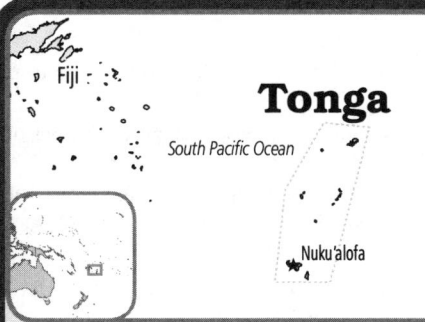

Tonga

South Pacific Ocean

Nuku'alofa

Tonga
Kingdom of Tonga
Pacific

Geography

Area 747 sq km. Archipelago of 171 coral and volcanic islands, 36 being inhabited, 600 km east of Fiji.

Population		Ann Gr	Density
2010	104,260	0.46%	140/sq km
2020	108,351	0.65%	145/sq km
2030	115,487	0.65%	155/sq km

Capital Nuku'alofa 24,300. **Urbanites** 25.3%. The Tongan diaspora (New Zealand, Australia, USA) is as numerous as the population of Tonga itself. **Pop under 15 yrs** 37%. **Life expectancy** 71.7 yrs.

Peoples

Tongan 98.2%. Speaking three related languages.
Other 1.8%. Includes mixed race, Caucasian, Chinese, other Polynesian.
Literacy 100%. **Official language** Tongan. **All languages** 3. **Languages with Scriptures** 2Bi 2w.i.p.

Economy

Remittances are the largest source of income, followed by tourism. Subsistence agriculture continues. The value of imports is five times larger than exports.

HDI Rank 99th/182. **Public debt** 47.7% of GDP. **Income/person** $2,510 (5% of USA).

Politics

British Protected State 1900–1970. Constitutional monarchy with the king and nobles having predominant influence. A growing movement toward democracy since 1990 and with the death of the king in 2006, but political demonstrations indicate that the pace is too slow for many pro-reformers. The first elected prime minister assumed responsibilities in 2006.

Religion

Though avowedly Christian, there is freedom for all religions. The Free Wesleyan Church enjoys a privileged position, with the king as titular head.

Religions	Pop %	Population	Ann Gr
Christian	95.76	99,839	0.4%
Baha'i	3.50	3,649	2.3%
Non-religious	0.40	417	-1.9%
Chinese	0.20	209	6.4%
Buddhist	0.11	115	0.5%
Hindu	0.03	31	9.0%

Christians Denoms		Pop %	Affiliates	Ann Gr
Protestant	8	42.62	44,000	-0.8%
Independent	10	11.37	12,000	0.3%
Anglican	1	1.58	2,000	1.9%
Catholic	1	15.35	16,000	0.3%
Marginal	2	52.53	55,000	0.8%
Doubly affiliated		-27.72	-29,000	0.0%

The high doubly affiliated figure is largely due to Mormon claims for those who retain membership in other denominations.

Churches	MegaBloc	Congs	Members	Affiliates
Latter-day Saints	M	220	21,800	54,500
Free Wesleyan Church	P	138	8,263	29,500
Catholic Church	C	13	9,302	16,000
Free Church of Tonga	P	76	6,993	10,000
Ch of Tonga	I	33	3,323	5,550
Tokailolo Fellowship	I	10	1,500	3,000
Assemblies of God	P	60	1,850	2,500
Other denominations[15]		83	4,421	7,648
Doubly affiliated				-28,900
Total Christians[22]		**633**	**57,452**	**99,798**

T

TransBloc	Pop %	Population	Ann Gr
Evangelicals			
Evangelicals	15.5	16,110	0.4%
Renewalists			
Charismatics	12.0	12,537	3.2%
Pentecostals	5.5	5,720	1.1%

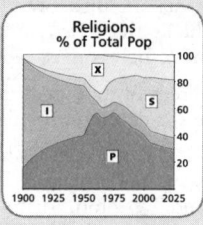

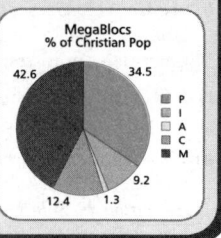

Answers to Prayer

1 **A strong Christian presence** and influence in daily life means that nearly all Tongans have access to the gospel.

2 **The Jesus March and Global Day of Prayer** continue to be annual proclamations of Christ's lordship.

3 **Tonga sends significant numbers of missionaries** from both Catholic and Protestant traditions, despite its relative poverty and isolation. Much more can be done; **YWAM** and other evangelical groups are working toward this.

Challenges for Prayer

1 **Tonga's rich Christian heritage** is a blessing, but has reached the point of oversaturation. The proliferation of denominations generates competition among churches, as newer groups entice believers away. Isolation and the difficult economic situation complicate issues further. Pray that Tongan Christians would seek ways to contribute to the Kingdom of God rather than seeking the church that benefits them the most.

2 **The past century** has been one of spiritual decline. There is a long and sad history of bitter schisms within Methodism. Politics and Church are inextricable; even the newer denominations' apolitical stance assumes acceptance of the status quo. Pray for a true spirit of unity among all believers and churches, and pray for leaders who will exemplify unity with gracious and humble spirits.

3 **Tonga** has the world's highest national percentage of Mormons, but possibly the majority of those claimed by Mormons would not consider themselves such. The country's largest employers are Mormons; many financial perks are on offer for those considering the switch. Pray for the error of this sect to be exposed as such, and for many to find freedom in Christ.

4 **The Tongan diaspora** is now larger than the population of Tonga itself. Many lose their faith in their host nations, others retain it only loosely as a cultural identity. Pray that Tongans abroad might also recapture the dynamic faith of their forefathers and the vision to take the gospel to the world.

5 **Specialized ministries.** Pray for the lasting impact of:

a) Youth ministries. **YFC**, SU, **CCCI** and **YWAM** work among young people, who are a high proportion of the Tongan population.

b) Christian TV. Praise God that much TV available in Tonga is Christian.

c) Christian literature. The Bible Society and SU distribute Bibles and other Christian materials widely.

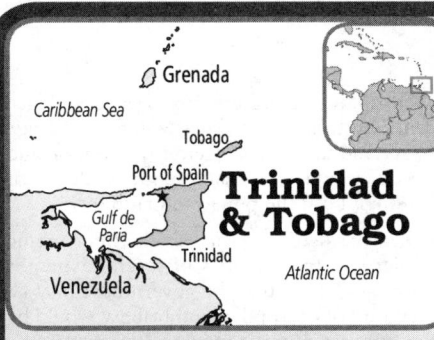

Trinidad & Tobago

Republic of Trinidad and Tobago

Caribbean

Geography 🌐

Area 5,124 sq km. Two islands off the coast of Venezuela.

Population		Ann Gr	Density
2010	1,343,725	0.38%	262/sq km
2020	1,383,641	0.23%	270/sq km
2030	1,381,863	-0.09%	270/sq km

Capital Port of Spain 59,000. **Urbanites** 13.9%.
Pop under 15 yrs 21%. **Life expectancy** 69.2 yrs.

Peoples 👪

Indo-Trinidadian 40.0%.
African origin 37.5%.
Mixed ethnicity 20.5%.
Euro-Trinidadian 0.6%.
Other 1.4%. Chinese 0.3%; Lebanese 0.1%.
Literacy 77.4%. **Official language** English.
All languages 7. **Languages with Scriptures** 2Bi 2NT 2w.i.p.

Economy 🏠

Oil and gas are very important, providing half of export earnings. Low inflation, trade surpluses and a growing tourist sector, added to a strong industrial base, make for the strongest Caribbean economy. A strong anti-corruption drive is present but needs definitive results. Growing troubles with drugs as the nation becomes a major transshipping site.
HDI Rank 64th/182. **Public debt** 26.6% of GDP. **Income/person** $19,870 (42% of USA).

Politics 🗳

Independent of Britain in 1962 as a parliamentary democracy. Prolonged economic recession in the 1980s provoked political and ethnic tensions, culminating in an abortive coup by militant black Muslims in 1990. The elected government has flip-flopped between Afro-Trinidadian and Indo-Trinidadian since then. Tensions persist and politics generally polarize racially between these two main groups. Bribery is common.

Religion 🙏

There is religious freedom for all.

Religions	Pop %	Population	Ann Gr
Christian	65.59	881,349	0.5%
Hindu	21.60	290,245	0.0%
Muslim	5.80	77,936	0.4%
Non-religious	3.59	48,240	0.8%
Other	0.82	11,019	0.9%
Baha'i	0.75	10,078	-0.1%
Sikh	0.72	9,675	-0.4%
Ethnoreligionist	0.40	5,375	0.4%
Chinese	0.36	4,837	-0.7%
Buddhist	0.27	3,628	-0.3%
Jewish	0.10	1,344	0.4%

Christians	Denoms	Pop %	Affiliates	Ann Gr
Protestant	57	24.03	323,000	2.3%
Independent	37	12.40	167,000	3.4%
Anglican	1	6.18	83,000	-1.8%
Catholic	1	21.95	295,000	-2.1%
Orthodox	3	0.59	8,000	0.8%
Marginal	10	2.36	32,000	1.7%
Doubly affiliated		*-1.92*	*-26,000*	*0.0%*

Churches	MegaBloc	Congs	Members	Affiliates
Catholic Church	C	50	168,571	295,000
Spiritual Baptists	I	510	35,714	100,000
Anglican Church	A	83	33,200	83,000
Pentecostal Assemblies	P	106	10,000	65,000
Seventh-day Adventist	P	152	38,235	65,000
Presbyterian Church	P	100	13,986	40,000
Open Bible Standard	P	86	16,000	24,000
Ch of God (Cleveland)	P	82	9,300	23,250
Foursquare Gospel Ch	P	45	13,800	22,080
Jehovah's Witnesses	M	108	9,000	19,980
Baptist Convention	P	63	6,000	12,000
Methodist Church	P	26	4,100	10,250
Assoc of Evang Bap	P	13	1,000	2,380
Other denominations[93]		921	77,017	145,184
Doubly affiliated Pentecostals				*-13,000*
Doubly affiliated				*-12,800*
Total Christians[109]		**2,345**	**428,423**	**881,324**

TransBloc	Pop %	Population	Ann Gr
Evangelicals			
Evangelicals	20.2	271,568	3.4%
Renewalists			
Charismatics	22.9	307,299	4.0%
Pentecostals	13.2	177,052	4.4%

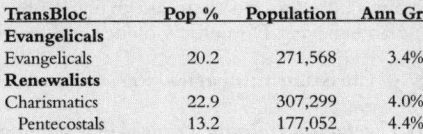

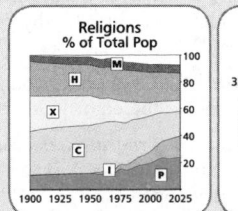

Religions
% of Total Pop

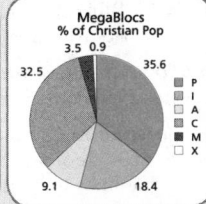

MegaBlocs
% of Christian Pop

T

Challenges for Prayer

1 **Many social challenges** face Trinidad & Tobago. Increasing crime and gang violence associated with the illicit drug trade are worsened by endemic weaknesses in the policing/ justice system. Alcoholism, kidnapping, armed robbery and theft are dangerously common and a high percentage of children are born out of wedlock and to teenage mothers. Pray that righteous and effective solutions might be found through both the public and faith sectors.

2 **The nation's racial diversity** could also be considered a racial divide. Inter-ethnic harmony is hindered by racially aligned politics and the activities of several extremist minorities among Muslims, Hindus and some "Christians". Pray that the government may be impartial and fair to all ethnic groups and that the culture of corruption and bribery would be exposed and eliminated. The Church is one of the only structures connected to every community, and therefore has enormous but unrealized potential to bridge the racial divide. Pray that churches would be instruments of reconciliation and demonstrate that all are one in Christ.

3 **Christianity is professed by nearly two-thirds** of the population, but true disciples faithful to God's Word are not so common. Many Christians are nominal; many others are polluted with witchcraft, Afro-Spiritist beliefs and Hinduism-influenced worldviews. Family life and morals within the Christian sphere often do not demonstrate the lordship of Christ. Greater theological training – for leaders as well as laity – is needed and a discipleship mentality must be fostered. Thank God for the minority who do live to please God, and pray that purity and passion might be restored across all denominations.

4 **The Christian Church** is very fragmented among traditional denominations that are rapidly declining, newer evangelical groups and a constantly multiplying swarm of single congregations (mostly charismatic/Pentecostal). There is little cohesion in common spiritual goals, outreach or missions involvement; national vision and purpose are needed. Pray for revival to enliven and empower the Church. Pray for the work of the T&T Council of Evangelical Churches. Pray that the desire for unity in the body of Christ might overcome the still-pervasive divisions.

5 **Christian impact on students** remains widespread. Many believers engage in this ministry through several groups (**YFC**, **CEF** and **IFES**). Some of those impacted go on to work cross-culturally. Pray for youth of all races; the nation has a high proportion of young people. Deliberately discipling children and youth in the churches is a vitally important ministry that has come nowhere near fulfilling its potential. The freedom to minister the gospel in schools must be utilized to a greater degree.

6 **Cross-cultural vision** is quite small but growing. The nation needs to move from a receiving mentality to a sending mentality. Pray for greater awareness of local and world needs, and for effective training to be given in cross-cultural outreach. A handful of Trinidadians work overseas as missionaries; pray for more. **YWAM** and **WBT** recently opened centres on Trinidad. These two groups as well as **OM** are active in mobilizing and sending workers abroad.

7 **The South Asian community,** largely originating from North India, is the largest non-Christian group in the Caribbean. Many Hindus and some Muslims have turned to Christ, and over 20% of the population are Christian today. The Presbyterians, **WT** and **TEAM** planted strong churches, and there are many Pentecostal and charismatic congregations with largely Indian believers. Domestic violence and female suicide are factors needing prayer and ministry.

8 **Christian ministries.** Pray for these:

a) Theological training is crucial in a nation with many churches but few disciples. Pentecostals, Open Bible Churches, Baptists, Presbyterians and several others maintain colleges and seminaries to this end.

b) Christian literature. **CLC** operates four bookstores, which are widely appreciated and extensively used. Pray for the eight workers.

c) Christian radio and TV programmes broadcast locally on the national network. There are also many shortwave programmes in several languages. Pray for locally relevant materials and programmes to be developed.

Tunisia
Republic of Tunisia
Africa

Geography 🌐

Area 154,530 sq km. Mountainous and agricultural in the north, Sahara desert in the south. The site of notable civilizations: Carthaginian, Berber Christian and Arab Islamic.

Population		Ann Gr	Density
2010	10,373,957	0.98%	67/sq km
2020	11,366,244	0.87%	74/sq km
2030	12,126,846	0.55%	78/sq km

Capital Tunis 766,750. **Other major city** Sfax 300,000. **Urbanites** 67.3%. **Pop under 15 yrs** 23%. **Life expectancy** 73.8 yrs.

Peoples 👪

Arab 97.8%. Mixed Berber, Arab, African and European descents make it difficult to ascertain actual ethnic division. A small number from other Arab countries.
Berber 1.9%.
Other 0.3%. French, Italian, Jewish.
Literacy 74.3%. **Official language** Arabic. French widely used but declining as English increases. **All languages** 10. **Indigenous languages** 6. **Languages with Scriptures** 2Bi 2por.

Economy 🗺️

Impressive stability and development given limited natural resources and a large trade deficit. Tourism, textiles, olive oil and phosphates are the major foreign currency earners as the service industry increases.
HDI Rank 98th/182. **Public debt** 48.4% of GDP. **Income/person** $3,955 (8% of USA). **Unemployment** 14.1%.

Politics 🗳️

Independent from France in 1956. A republic with a strong presidential government and a virtual single-party state. Repression of a rising fundamentalist Muslim movement has been severe, with frequent serious human rights abuses. Multi-party elections were held in 2004, where the president received 94% of the vote.

Religion 🙏

Islam is the state religion. The government strongly maintains a secular tone; only a minority actively practice their faith, although this appears to be growing. Politicized Islam, which has been on the rise, is met with little tolerance by the state. Not favourable to any form of Christian proselytism, but tolerance shown to foreign religious minorities, and increasingly to native Christians.

Religions	Pop %	Population	Ann Gr
Muslim	99.37	10,317,975	1.0%
Non-religious	0.30	31,122	9.5%
Christian	0.22	22,785	1.0%
Jewish	0.02	2,075	1.0%

Christians	Denoms	Pop %	Affiliates	Ann Gr
Protestant	6	0.01	<1,000	6.8%
Independent	1	<0.01	400	5.9%
Anglican	1	<0.01	<400	8.5%
Catholic	1	0.20	21,000	1.0%
Orthodox	2	<0.01	<300	0.7%
Marginal	1	<0.01	<50	0.0%

Churches	MegaBloc	Congs	Members	Affiliates
Catholic Church	C	14	12,209	21,000
Indigenous believers	I	4	200	400
Anglican Church	A	5	200	375
Reformed Church	P	8	150	188
Other denominations[8]		9	406	662
Total Christians[12]		**40**	**13,165**	**22,625**

The vast majority of Christians are non-Tunisians.

TransBloc	Pop %	Population	Ann Gr
Evangelicals			
Evangelicals	<0.1	1,154	4.7%
Renewalists			
Charismatics	<0.1	852	7.2%
Pentecostals	<0.1	36	4.4%

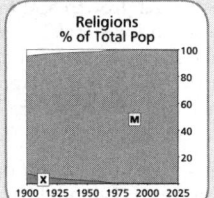

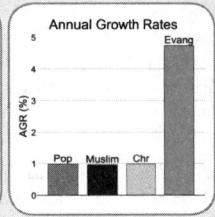

T

Challenges for Prayer

1 **In earlier centuries** the Christian Church was widespread, producing such leaders as Tertullian and Cyprian. Schism, heresy, failures to put roots deep into the local culture and to translate the Bible into local languages, foreign invasions and finally Islam brought about its demise. There are about 500 committed indigenous believers today, but only one-third of those meet together regularly for worship. Pray that a living, growing Church might become a reality again in this land.

2 **Islam is experiencing a new vitality** in Tunisia, which has not been particularly renowned for its religious commitment. In the years since 9/11 and subsequent events in the political-religious sphere, many Tunisians have become more fervent in their Islamic faith. This is reflected in their choice of clothing as well as mosque attendance. Although the government strives against politicized Islam, the general trend in the Arab world at large and locally, and the lack of future prospects for the younger generation, are pulling society toward greater Islamization.

3 **Tunisia is one of the most progressive** and open societies in the Arab world. However, the economic transformation is not as widespread as many feel it should be. The rapid change to a social, demographic and economic existence resembling Tunisia's European neighbours (more than its African ones) is offset by the greater influences of Islam and a pan-Arab media in terms of Tunisia's collective identity. Pray that the advancement of both materialism and the practice of Islam might actually serve to illuminate a deeper need in people's hearts.

4 **Change is evident** after a century of missionary involvement that produced little fruit. Pray that continued intercession might break through the centuries-old barriers to the gospel. There are more open doors and opportunities to share than ever before. Pray for Christians, foreign and national, to take advantage of these opportunities. The necessity of learning Arabic is a barrier to many non-Tunisian Christians.

5 **The government still prohibits indigenous churches** from owning their own property and having their own bank accounts. Pray for the government to officially recognize the Tunisian Church. Pray for the return of buildings and land that were previously taken by the state; may these provide space for the Tunisian Christians to establish their own places of worship.

6 **New believers have increased** and new church groups have come into being over the past few years. Pray for their continued growth and discipleship. Unity is an issue that is currently in need of much prayer. The Church is still a tiny proportion of the total population. Pray for lasting commitment to Jesus, since few Tunisian believers have stood in the faith for more than 10 years. Among the increasing numbers of new believers, pray for safety, encouragement, and effective discipleship and integration into the body. Pray that Tunisian believers might overcome their fear of sharing their faith. There are also probably significant numbers of isolated and hidden believers – pray for opportunities for their spiritual growth and fellowship.

7 **Leadership is gradually developing** for the groups of national believers, but prayer is needed for their spiritual growth and for more leaders. As in many other countries with nascent churches, the relationship between national and expatriate Christians can benefit from prayer; praise God for the shared vision that does exist for reaching the rest of Tunisia. Practical holiness and accountability need to be demonstrated. Pray that anointed and tolerant leaders may be raised up for this time, and that the right means for their spiritual and pastoral growth might be developed.

8 **The Christian population** is predominantly nominal, expatriate and Catholic, and is only a fraction of its pre-independence size. There are two functioning Protestant denominations – Anglican and French Reformed. The relocation of a large international development organization to Tunis has resulted in Sunday church attendance in most churches tripling. Pray that these expat Christians, mostly Africans, would find opportunities to relate to their Tunisian neighbours. Pray also for compassion and a persevering, servant spirit in situations that require sensitivity and wisdom.

9 **Expatriate workers** are quite numerous for the small Christian churches, but nowhere near adequate for reaching the millions of unevangelized. Pray for more to be raised up, especially believers from Arabic-speaking countries, to serve in many capacities. There are ample opportunities in the areas of teaching, development and healthcare/therapy.

10 **Specific unreached areas and peoples:**

a) Young people are disillusioned with the existing situation, and many are negative about their own land; many are completely apathetic about spiritual things. There is currently a demographic bubble of youth with a limited window of opportunity (10 years or so) to reach them while they are still open to new ideas.

b) Women have more freedom here than in some other Muslim countries, as reflected by their participation in politics and the work force and excelling in academic and economic sectors. But the issues of divorce and domestic violence remain. Women are still hard to reach with the gospel due to persisting cultural and traditional restrictions.

c) The southern part of the country is a spiritual desert. Sfax, Gabes and Gafsa are needy cities. There are a few witnesses in this region, but many more are needed.

d) The Berber communities maintain some of their distinctives even though they have largely lost their languages and are now considered a very small group. Their ancestors were Christian. The island of Djerba with 65,000 people, mostly Berber, is a specific challenge with its unique culture and very few known Christians. There are also two Jewish settlements.

e) Kairouan is seen by some as the fourth-most holy city in Islam – many go there for blessings, healing and help. Pray that in their heartfelt search they might find Jesus.

11 **Reaching Tunisians** by other means.

a) Miracles, Hayat and Arab Vision regularly broadcast Christian programmes into Tunisia.

b) Scripture translation into the Tunisian dialect of Arabic is in progress, an important task if the gospel is to be clearly heard and understood by all Tunisians. Pray for Tunisian attitudes about their own language, which many view as inferior to modern Arabic.

c) Some Christian literature is now sold openly, but is not widely available. Pray that the Bible and Christian books might become more widely distributed through bookshops, and that Christian literature be made available throughout the land.

d) Satellite TV and radio broadcasts are highly effective in reaching Tunisians. There are many programmes in Arabic, and they can reach to the most isolated and private corners of the country.

e) The JESUS film is available in two translations – Standard Arabic and Tunisian Arabic. Pray for the wide dissemination of this film and the development of a wider ministry of Christian cassettes and videos in Tunisian Arabic. *The Passion of the Christ* is also in wide circulation.

f) More than 6.5 million tourists visit Tunisia each year, including those from other Arab states. Music festivals often feature gospel choirs from abroad. Pray for a ministry to Muslim tourists and also for sensitive sharing opportunities for Christians who come as tourists.

T

Turkey

Republic of Turkey

Asia

Geography

Area 779,452 sq km. Straddles two continents; 3% in Europe (Thrace), 97% in Asia (Anatolia). Also controls the Bosphorus Strait and the Dardanelles, vital sea links between the Black Sea and the Mediterranean. Its strategic position has made the area of prime importance throughout history.

Population		Ann Gr	Density
2010	75,705,147	1.24%	97/sq km
2020	83,873,140	0.96%	108/sq km
2030	90,375,144	0.68%	116/sq km

Capital Ankara 3,906,044. **Other major cities** Istanbul 10.5 million; Izmir 2.7mill; Bursa 1.6m; Adana 1.4m; Gaziantep 1.1m. **Urbanites** 69.6%. **Pop under 15 yrs** 27%. **Life expectancy** 71.7 yrs.

Peoples

Turkic peoples 71.8%. A Central Asian people that conquered and largely absorbed the indigenous peoples of the land from the 11th Century onward. Though ethnically diverse, Turks have a fairly homogeneous culture. Sub-groups: Azeri 0.7%, living in the east; Koruk (Gagauz) 0.5%.

Iranian–Median 21.1% (Kurds constitute possibly as much as 20%). An Indo-Iranian people with concentrations in east and southeast Anatolia. Many Kurds use Turkish as their primary language. Other Iranian language groups: Kurmanji 10.8%; Zaza(3) 1.8%.

Arab 2.5%. In south Anatolia, adjoining Syria.

Eurasian peoples 2.8%. Cherkess (Adyghe) 0.8%; Pomak 0.4%; Bulgarian 0.4%. Small numbers of several European peoples. Rapid decline through emigration. There were 1.75m Armenians and 1.5m Greeks in Turkey in 1900.

Other 1.8%. Jews, East Asians, South Asians, Africans, South Americans.

Literacy 88.3%. **Official language** Turkish. **All languages** 45. **Indigenous languages** 34. **Languages with Scriptures** 10Bi 7NT 12por.

Economy

A mix of traditional agriculture, modernizing industry and commerce, and a strong tourism sector. Agriculture still employs more than one-third of the workforce. Continued development of both the Tigris and Euphrates river basins in the east. Economic reforms in the 1990s and 2000s and a growing private sector yielded a great deal of growth, though somewhat undermined by high inflation. Turkey has the world's 16th largest economy, but is marked by high trade deficits and rising unemployment. It is simultaneously one of Europe's poorer nations and the richest, most developed of the six Turkic nations in West and Central Asia. The push to fully join the EU persists, although friction between EU-demanded reforms and Turkish intransigence on certain issues continues to slow the process.

HDI Rank 79th/182. **Public debt** 40% of GDP. **Income/person** $10,479 (22% of USA).

Politics

The Turkish Ottoman Empire once stretched across North Africa, Arabia, Western Asia and Southeast Europe. Its demise and final fragmentation in World War I led to revolution, the birth of modern Turkey and the formation of a republic in 1923 by the much revered Atatürk. Periods of social disorder and military rule were followed by a return to democratic government in 1983, but with the military retaining considerable influence. Turkey is a member of NATO, but in dispute with fellow NATO member Greece, largely regarding full recognition of Cyprus. The long, bitter strife with Kurdish separatists caused 30,000 deaths and the ravaging of the southeast, but since 1999 its intensity has considerably reduced. Legal reforms in 2002-2003 significantly improved the lot of Kurds in Turkey. Economic links with Europe, cultural links with Central Asia and proximity to traditional conflict areas of Iraq, the Balkans and the Caucasus enhance Turkey's strategic importance. This unique situation positions Turkey as a potentially excellent diplomatic mediator among the region's various powers.

Religion

Turkey's Ottoman Empire was for centuries the guardian of all the holy places of Islam and its chief protagonist. Since the sweeping reforms of the 1920s, Turkey has officially been a secular state. There is, however, a fault line between Islamists and secularists. Constitutional guarantee of religious freedom has not been fully upheld. Recent death threats and murders of Christians highlight the present reality and severity of persecution and the likelihood of more to come. The EU ruling against including religion on Turkish identity cards may help prevent discrimination against Christians.

Religions	Pop %	Population	Ann Gr
Muslim	96.64	73,159,940	1.2%
Non-religious	3.10	2,346,860	3.3%
Christian	0.21	163,140	-1.4%
Other	0.03	22,712	1.2%
Jewish	0.02	16,655	-4.2%

Sunni Muslims 70-80%, Alevi 15-25% (amongst Turks, Kurds, Zaza). Shi'a among Azeri and Iranians. There are also Yezidis among the Kurds.

Christians Denoms		Pop %	Affiliates	Ann Gr
Protestant	15	0.02	13,000	1.0%
Independent	2	0.01	4,000	1.1%
Anglican	1	<0.01	2,000	-1.0%
Catholic	2	0.06	46,000	1.6%
Orthodox	12	0.12	94,000	-2.3%
Marginal	2	<0.01	4,000	2.0%

Churches	MegaBloc	Congs	Members	Affiliates
Armenian Orthodox	O	24	33,000	55,000
Catholic Church	C	69	18,563	31,000
Bulgarian Orthodox	O	5	7,500	15,000
Foreign Protestants	P	32	3,497	10,000
Ancient Ch of the East	O	5	2,100	4,200
Turkish indigenous chs	I	42	2,517	3,600
Jehovah's Witnesses	M	31	2,030	3,390
Other denominations[21]		105	23,109	40,950
Total Christians[34]		**313**	**92,316**	**163,140**

TransBloc	Pop %	Population	Ann Gr
Evangelicals			
Evangelicals	<0.1	7,267	1.2%
Renewalists			
Charismatics	<0.1	7,005	0.6%
Pentecostals	<0.1	228	3.7%

Close to 4,000 nationals are part of the overlapping evangelical and charismatic movements. The large majority of these are ethnic Turks and Kurds from a Muslim background plus a few ethnic Assyrian and Armenian evangelicals; the other evangelicals are expatriates living in Turkey. Growth rates for various Christian groups (ethnic Turks, all nationals, expats, etc) differ, often significantly.

Missionaries from Turkey
P,I,A 24 (14 long-term); 10 short-termers serving among Turks in Germany, Romania, Bulgaria, France.

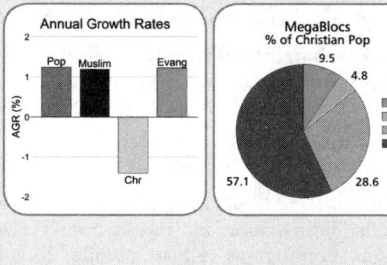

Answers to Prayer

1 **The opening of Turkey** to EU influence and its own developing role as a regional diplomatic force. Both invite increased possibilities for sharing the gospel in Turkey.

2 **Give praise for the slow but steady growth** of Turkish evangelical Christianity. Turkish and Kurdish believers probably numbered around 10 in 1960. This number rose to around 4,000 by 2010. While growth is not as rapid as many hoped for or expected, a sense of consolidation and maturation distinguishes the Church today.

Challenges for Prayer

1 **Turkey is a nation torn in different directions.** Straddling Europe and Asia, neither Middle Eastern nor Western, Turkish society is secular yet Muslim. Critical to shaping the nation's future are several issues that must be addressed. Pray for leaders who will act justly and wisely, focused on the welfare of all who call Turkey home. Pray for:

a) *The rivalry between secular Turkish nationalism and Islamism.* Legality of the *hijab* (Islamic headscarf) has been a flashpoint for this division. While the constitution, judiciary and military are secular and notionally meant to uphold religious freedom, secular Turks can be as anti-Western, anti-minority and anti-Christian as any hardline Islamists. Wahhabist influences help to fuel fundamentalist Islam, while hardline nationalism is also strong and rising. Pray that Turkey might steer a moderate path between these twin dangers.

b) *The issue of membership in the European Union.* Some strive to introduce necessary reforms for greater integration with Europe (especially on human rights, religious freedom and Kurdish, Armenian and Cypriot issues). Others aim towards leadership of a Turkic bloc of nations and an increased role in the Middle East. The tension between introducing modernity and retaining traditional roots is difficult to resolve.

c) Challenges facing the political realm. The role of the military within the state needs adjusting to allow for democratic functioning of the civil government. Recent moves toward multi-cultural and multi-religious democratization have ushered this challenge to the fore, with the resulting national identity crisis provoking a notably reactionary response. A power struggle rages between the secularists and pro-Islamic/freedoms groups. Serious failings in human rights must be addressed, and likewise for the Kurdish issue which has cost the lives of thousands of soldiers and civilians.

2 **Turkey's transformation** from guardian of Christendom to unevangelized nation has been almost comprehensive. For over 1,000 years the region was a bastion of Christendom, but it later became a strong propagator of Islam. The Christian population has declined from 22% to 0.21% since 1900. Only 0.008% of people in Turkey are evangelical; many are ethnic Turks and Kurds, but others are expatriate or from historically Christian minorities. Few of the 73 million Muslims have ever truly heard the gospel. Turkey's location along the ancient Silk Road routes connected it deeply to Islam for centuries; pray that it might also be used as a bridge between Europe and Asia for the transmission of a revitalized Christianity.

3 **The barriers of intense prejudice, mistrust and dislike of Christianity** can appear insurmountable, as a deep resistance toward Christian influences persists and even grows. Pray for the following negative elements to be broken down:

a) Historical. Turkey's long association with Islam and more than a millennium of bitter wars with "Christian" Europe make conversion appear almost an act of treason.

b) Cultural and legal. To be a Turk is to be a Muslim, even if only nominally so. Family pressure, police intimidation and threats from Turkish nationalists and Muslim extremists keep many from coming to Christ, while forcing others to remain secret believers. It is illegal to "insult Turkishness", a law with hazy definitions and therefore subject to abuse. A few Christian converts from Islam now involved in evangelism have been legally tried for such "crimes".

c) Fixed attitudes. Among the general public, a deep-seated resistance to all things Christian makes any form of witnessing difficult. Pray for radical change in public attitudes and in press coverage of Christians.

d) Biased understandings and deliberate disinformation. Evangelical Christians are associated with the Crusades, the Inquisition, marginal cults such as the JWs, imperialistic policies and the moral compromises of Western nations. Sensational articles in the press and biased television programmes spread untruths about Christians, further inflaming public opinion. Muslim misconceptions about Christian life and teaching present another major barrier.

e) The historical legacy of harsh suppression of the Armenian minority. Turbulence and political instability during the collapse of the Ottoman Empire before and during World War I brought about widespread violence, including the massacre and deportation of the majority of Armenians. Millions of Armenians suffered and perished during that time. Pray that the cloud of prejudice and darkness might be lifted and that many might find joy and peace in the forgiveness offered by the Lord Jesus. Turkey's handling of the historicity of these events continually affects its image and relations abroad.

4 **The ancient churches** survived until the beginning of the 20th Century, but have since been nearly wiped out by massacres (Armenians), severe persecution (Assyrians) and emigration (Greeks, etc). Pray for the remnant that survives – for a re-kindling of faith and a work of the Holy Spirit. Numbers have been reduced to an estimated 130,000 across 12 different traditions.

5 **A Church amongst Turks** has at last become a visible reality, but it still only constitutes 0.005% of the population. Pray for:

a) Renewed church growth. The increases of the 1990s and early 2000s slowed in the face of spiritual, legal and cultural opposition. While this has caused an increase of prayer and focus on discipleship, the evangelism and church planting impetus of the past generation must be kept alive.

b) *The Association of Protestant Churches of Turkey* (TeK), founded in 1989. This body links most evangelical fellowships and leaders and provides them with advocacy and support, increasingly important in this time of heightened pressure.

c) *Strong relationships within churches.* Close family ties and the security this confers often make family rejection after conversion traumatic. Pray for fellowships that have had to become surrogate families. Backsliding is common, compromise in marrying non-Christians frequent and relationship breakdowns between believers disheartening. Pray also for families to see and accept a new life in Christ as something good and separate from simply conversion to a foreign religion.

d) *Indigenous yet biblical faith expressions.* Doctrinal extremes, legalism, personality clashes and disunity are all potential stumbling blocks. Denominationalism has not been an issue but could become so. Pray that Turkish leaders may be discerning and wise in developing sound relationships bolstered by both wholesome biblical applications and structures designed for holistic, reproducible growth.

6 **Persecution and hostility are on the rise.** Several events in recent years highlight the increasingly strident and violent nature of both Turkish nationalism and radical Islam in their opposition to the people of God. The murder of a Catholic priest in 2006 and the grisly torture and murders of one expat and two Turkish Christians in Malatya in 2007 illustrate this. The Malatya case points to powerful nationalist elements in the state, including the security forces (army and police). The two murdered Turks were the first Turkish converts from Islam to be martyred in the modern Turkish Church. The Church anticipates they will not be the last. Pray for:

a) *Courage amid persecution.* Social ostracism, harassment by security forces, arbitrary arrests, and disruptions of church services on spurious pretexts all occur, bringing some insecurity, fear and uncertainty. Outright violence and murder form another level of persecution Christians must endure. Pray for protection and for boldness, and pray against a spirit of fear. Greater growth will inevitably lead to greater opposition; pray that such opposition in turn leads to greater growth!

b) *Perseverance.* Emigration is often a way to escape persecution, find a good paying job or find a foreign marriage partner. Backsliding into Islam or merely fading into obscurity by distancing oneself from Christian community are other avoidance options. Pray for local believers to persist in following Jesus, whatever the cost.

c) *The legal standing of Christians,* both as a whole and as individual congregations. Preparation for EU entry brought promises to liberalize laws restricting non-Islamic religions, yet believers continue to face endless obstructions. Congregations can now be legal entities as associations and while they can theoretically gain permission to build churches, such applications are often unfairly blocked or saddled with requirements most congregations cannot afford. Renting space often results in frequently getting evicted by worried landlords. Prejudices in state or religious educational instruction and materials can also incite harassment. TeK works proactively to encourage religious freedom.

7 Developing the future church:

a) *Leadership development and Bible training.* Various in-church or TEE programmes exist. Current nationwide efforts in Bible training are *Hasat, Filipus,* Martin Bucher Institute, and *Donat.*

b) *Reaching the younger generation* is vital but difficult. Over 60% of the population is under 28 years old. It is illegal for adults to proselytize those under 18, but there is nothing stopping youths from evangelizing their peers. Camp ministries have been effective; one called *Kucak* has been active for 20 years. Pray especially for Christian youth – second-generation Turkish Christians need to have their own experience with Jesus if they are to stand firm.

8 **The Kurdish situation** is a long-standing challenge. Kurds can be found throughout Turkey – numbering as many as 15 million – but make up the majority population in 16 provinces of the east and southeast. Though widespread use in public remains uncommon, the Kurdish language is now recognized. The government is seeking to resolve Kurdish discrimination, but this is a complex issue involving challenges such as poverty and high unemployment in the east. Pray for:

a) A complete end to hostilities between the army and Kurdish separatists, and a fair resolution of the causal issues. Over 30,000 have been killed, thousands of villages razed and millions displaced and impoverished. Discrimination and desperation often drive Kurds into illegal and violent organizations such as the Kurdistan Workers' Party.

b) Cultural rehabilitation of the Kurds. Vigorous suppression of their culture and language has moderated. Kurdish newspapers are now allowed and the JESUS film in two dialects of Kurmanji has been legalized.

c) The Muslim Alevi (with roots in Shi'ism), some of whom are Kurds and Zaza. They are 15-25% of Turkey's population. Nominal Islamic practice, high respect for Jesus and shared identity as a pressurized minority create unique witness opportunities. New literature and music cassettes are being developed specifically for them.

d) The emergence of a Kurdish expression of the Church. In mixed areas, most Kurds integrate into Turkish fellowships, in itself an answer to prayer. Pray for all those seeking openings for reaching them – for the effective use of the JESUS film and other Kurdish literature. The Bible in Kurmanji was completed recently; pray for its widespread use.

9 **Other specific unreached peoples** and areas abound. Pray for:

a) A living, growing fellowship of believers in each of the 81 provinces; most if not all have believers, but the majority still have no fellowship groups. The Black Sea coast (with many Laz) and the central Anatolian plateau are spiritually hard places. The turbulent eastern Anatolian provinces (largely Kurdish) are also in need of prayer.

b) University students. There are 1.9 million students in 118 universities and over 1,000 colleges, but there is very little specific campus ministry apart from a few major cities. Pray for the students who have come to the Lord and are now meeting together.

c) Children are difficult to reach due to laws prohibiting proselytism of minors. The problem of homeless children is growing, especially in Istanbul which has over 30,000 street kids. A children's Bible and other resources are available in Turkish.

d) The ethnic Muslim minorities. The largest of these are the Azeri, Gagauz, Crimean Tatar and Karakalpak. Also included are peoples from the Central Asian republics. The gospel is starting to reach some of these latter groups. Many minorities are isolated, living in their own communities, so connecting with them can be difficult.

e) Refugees. Many Iranians fled the violence and Islamic extremism of the 1979 Revolution. Over 620,000 remain in Turkey – many in Istanbul – while others moved on to Western countries. These refugees and *emigrés* are proving quite open to the gospel. Several groups of believers have formed, but such groups tend to be transitory, comprised of people on the move. Increasing numbers of African and Asian refugees use Turkey as a stepping stone to Europe. They face many hardships and enjoy few rights. A great need exists for ministry among them.

f) The Arab minority is a mix between primarily Levant Arabs near the Syrian border and Iraqi refugees in the southeast. A number of them are Christian, but the majority are Muslim.

g) The Romani peoples (numbering between 500,000-1,000,000) live in poverty, surviving by seasonal labour and collecting recyclable materials. There is some openness to the gospel among them, and in recent years increasing numbers have been coming to the Lord.

10 **The work of evangelization** began in 1821, but was soon directed to the more receptive non-Muslim minorities in hopes of reaching the majority through them. The 1970s and 1980s were very difficult for Christian workers, but in the 1990s, more encouraging results began to occur. Increased opposition since 2006 has slowed church growth. Pray for:

a) Those who are called, equipped and gifted for tentmaking ministries in this land where sharing the gospel must be done with tact and sensitivity, but also with boldness and clarity. Business as mission is a growing area, but faces challenges with visas, taxes and unethical business competition. Being a Christian worker in Turkey is not an easy ministry, despite its rewards. Pray for each worker to have a good testimony that glorifies Christ and shows love and respect for the people of Turkey.

b) Opportunities for ministry that expose the whole country to the gospel. Most Christian expatriates engage in teaching, study, business or enter on tourist visas. Few have ever lived in eastern Anatolia, the Black Sea coast or the interior provinces – these are some of the spiritually hardest places for Christians to live and minister. Pray that Christ-like lives of service and love may help break down long-held barriers to the gospel.

c) **More than 50 agencies,** with around 1,350 expatriates from over 20 countries, share a specific burden and calling to bring blessing to the Turkish people. Pray for the continuance of fruitful cooperation among them.

d) **Advocacy networks** promote the evangelistic challenge of Turkey and connect churches and organizations to this goal. They also engage in research, leadership development and prayer mobilization, and include International Turkey Network and SILAS Ministries.

11 **Other means of witness** are bearing fruit and need prayerful support. Relational evangelism remains the most effective – and widespread – way of reaching out to this highly social culture. This can be supplemented by:

a) **Bible translation.** Two Turkish NT translations published in 1988/89 were well received. A new translation of the Bible – *Kutsal Kitap*, completed in 2001 – has been widely appreciated and distributed, as has a study Bible based on this translation launched in 2010. Over 500,000 Turkish NTs have been distributed throughout the country.

b) **Bible correspondence courses** are effective at reaching seekers in a discreet fashion.

c) **Christian bookstores** around the country. While providing a good opportunity for all to browse and purchase Bibles and Christian material, such shops are subject to fear of vandalism, violence and media opposition.

d) **Christian literature.** Several Turkish Christian publishing houses produce Bibles, magazines and hundreds of book titles. Literature is often well received, but distributors are sometimes threatened by extremists. There is a great need for Turkish Christian authors.

e) **Christian radio.** Easing of regulatory controls opened the way for a number of Christian radio stations run locally on FM, 24 hours a day. International broadcasters also have significant input. **TWR**, partnering with IBRA, broadcasts 15 hours per week.

f) **Two TV channels** (*Kanal Hayat* and Turk 7) on satellite are potentially reaching millions with the gospel, both in Turkey and in neighbouring countries, including Europe. Response is encouraging. Follow-up correspondence courses tie into the programmes on these channels.

g) **Internet evangelism** is another effective means of reaching people, through Christian websites in Turkish, the online Turkish NT, as well as chat rooms. Pre-evangelism, apologetics and even discipleship can be conducted virtually and with anonymity from any location.

h) **Telephone and Internet ministry.** Telephone hotlines and online chat rooms, running in multiple cities and staffed by Turkish believers, receive many enquiries seeking prayer and guidance and requesting NTs.

12 **Ministry to Turks** outside Turkey include:

a) **The millions of Turks and Kurds** in Western Europe. The diaspora of Turks – all approximate numbers – in Germany (2.8m), France (400,000), Netherlands (350,000), UK (300,000), Austria (200,000), Belgium (150,000), Switzerland (80,000) and Sweden (40,000) are far more accessible to Christian workers but are also often more closed to the gospel. There is also a work among the 150,000 Turks in Australia. A number of churches and international agencies seek to evangelize them, but local hostility to migrant workers impedes this outreach. Organizations working outside of Turkey are **OM**, **WEC**, Frontiers, Turkish World Outreach and *Orientdienst*. There are possibly hundreds of born-again Turks as a result of these ministries, but more Turks still come to Jesus inside Turkey than outside. Pray for the multiplication of Turkish and Kurdish Christian groups in these areas and for them to make an impact on their homelands.

b) **Turks in the Balkans.** Opportunities for ministry exist among Turkish minorities in Bulgaria (>750,000), Greece (140,000), Macedonia (80,000), Serbia (50,000), and Romania (45,000). Little, if any, specific outreach is directed toward many of these minorities. Given the historical enmity between Turks and most Balkan peoples, ministry to Turkish Muslims in Orthodox-majority European countries may fall to expatriate workers, but a loving witness by born-again Balkan peoples would be a powerful testimony.

Turkmenistan

Asia

Geography

Area 488,100 sq km. Two populated strips of irrigated land on its northern and southern borders, separated by the barren Kara-Kum Desert. Only 1% of the country is irrigated, arable land; 80% is desert.

Population		Ann Gr	Density
2010	5,176,502	1.34%	11/sq km
2020	5,816,404	1.09%	12/sq km
2030	6,275,908	0.66%	13/sq km

Capital Ashgabat 651,000. **Urbanites** 49.5%. **Pop under 15 yrs** 30%. **Life expectancy** 64.6 yrs.

Peoples

Numerous but declining ethnic minorities from all over the former USSR, since most are emigrating.

Turkic 94.5%. Turkmen 82.1%; Uzbek 9.4%; Kazakh 1.0%; Tatar 1.0%; Azerbaijani 1.0%.
Eurasian 3.0%. Russian 2.2%; Armenian 0.5%; Lezgian 0.3%.
Iranian–Median 2.2%. Baluch 1.9%.
Other 0.3%.
Literacy 98.8%. **Official language** Turkmen using Latin script as in Turkey since 1994; previously Cyrillic script. **All languages** 9. **Indigenous languages** 4. **Languages with Scriptures** 2Bi 7por.

Economy

Famed for its carpets, horses, camels and desert, but oil and gas production are the major sources of wealth – it has some of the largest unexploited gas and oil fields in the world. Cotton is also a source of income and employment. The country is dangerously dependent on water from the Amu Darya River, which is already over-exploited and polluted. The nation is limited by its geographical position, landlocked and surrounded by the politically sensitive Caucasus and the nations of Iran, Afghanistan and Russia – oil and gas pipelines must run for thousands of kilometres. The massive economic potential of gas deposits has thus far been spent by the former dictator, mostly on prestige projects and monuments to himself rather than the betterment of the people. Rural areas are especially deprived in contrast to the gleaming capital.
HDI Rank 109th/182. **Public debt** 32% of GDP. **Income/person** $3,606 (8% of USA).

Politics

Nomadic tribal past; only united as a country under Russian Tsarist rule in 1881. A Soviet Republic until independence in 1992. The former Communist leader Saparmurat Niyazov transformed himself into a nationalist dictator, controlling the army, police, the justice system, the economy and the press. His death in 2006 heralded the potential for great change, since his appointed successor demonstrates signs of moving toward a more open and less repressive system.

Religion

Constitutionally, there is freedom of religion. In practice this is limited to Sunni Islam or Russian Orthodoxy – all other forms of Islam or minority religions are subject to severe repression and harassment. Unregistered religious gatherings – of any size or kind – are strictly forbidden.

Religions	Pop %	Population	Ann Gr
Muslim	96.16	4,977,724	2.3%
Non-religious	2.00	103,530	-18.7%
Christian	1.83	94,730	-2.1%
Jewish	0.01	518	1.3%

Christians Denoms		Pop %	Affiliates	Ann Gr
Protestant	5	0.02	<2,000	-1.1%
Independent	5	0.02	<2,000	5.8%
Catholic	1	0.01	<1000	0.0%
Orthodox	3	1.64	85,000	-2.5%
Marginal	1	0.14	7,000	3.1%
Unaffiliated		0.01	<1,000	0.0%

Churches	MegaBloc	Congs	Members	Affiliates
Russian Orthodox	O	4	40,000	66,000
Armenian Apostolic Ch	O	1	6,000	10,000
Other Orthodox	O	3	6,000	9,000
Jehovah's Witnesses	M	21	2,102	7,000
Independent churches	I	30	500	800
Pentecostal churches	P	5	180	400
Other denominations[6]		16	751	1,348
Total Christians[15]		**80**	**55,533**	**94,548**

TransBloc	Pop %	Population	Ann Gr
Evangelicals			
Evangelicals	<0.1	1,718	2.1%
Renewalists			
Charismatics	<0.1	1,100	1.1%
Pentecostals	<0.1	400	-4.4%

Religions % of Total Pop (1900 1925 1950 1975 2000 2025)

Annual Growth Rates — AGR (%)

Answers to Prayer

1 **The demise of the man** who built himself up as a god-king, wrote his own "Holy Book" and named himself Turkmenbashi, "the father of all Turkmen", brings what is hopefully the beginning of transformation. It is still early to pass judgment, but there is a greater sense of hope about openness and positive change from the repressive personality cult of the past.

2 **The atmosphere of the country** is experiencing positive change. Turkmen citizens can travel abroad and within the country much more easily. Two Protestant churches have recently been allowed to officially register and meet publicly.

Challenges for Prayer

1 **The new government and leadership** face difficult decisions about continuing Niyazov's legacy, about domestic policies and about the awkward relationships with Russia (its main buyer of gas), Iran, Afghanistan and China. Pray for godly wisdom for the new leader, for a departure from oppressive policies of the past and for the respect of constitutionally guaranteed human rights and religious freedoms.

2 **Ethnic Turkmen Christians** are few but have increased since independence, from one or two people to as many as 1,000. Most Christians are Russian, Ukrainian or Armenian; among them are a thousand or so evangelical believers. Persecution has brought growth, greater unity and a strong spirituality, and the Church continues to grow despite the constant threats. Pray for these believers to stand firm in their faith and to win others to Christ.

3 **Hostility** against any non-Orthodox Christian activity or even presence has persisted for over 10 years. Almost every foreign Christian has been expelled. Several national pastors have been exiled, beaten, heavily fined or imprisoned. Congregations continue to be intimidated and forbidden to meet. Registration is a difficult, near-impossible process, and when it does occur, it only subjects the church to greater surveillance. Pray for a softening of the attitude of the authorities, for courage for Christians in the country to stand firm and for Christians outside to pray and speak up against these hostile actions.

4 **Expatriate Christians** concerned for Turkmenistan continue to pray from a distance, mobilize and prepare for the day when the country is open again. Pray for openings for humanitarian organizations to operate and bless the people in ways both practical and spiritual. Expatriate Christians found to be doing religious training are expelled. Pray for the small handful of foreign Christians still in Turkmenistan – that they might be delivered from harassment by secret police, that they might be able to continue to work in the country and that they might soon be joined by an increasing number of Christian workers.

5 **Witness by other means:**

a) *The Turkmen NT* was published in 1994, but requires editing and revision. Work continues on completing the OT. Pray for this work to be completed quickly; pray also for its importation, distribution and impact on readers. There are also a number of Christian book titles available in Turkmen.

T

b) *Christian radio programmes* commenced in Turkmen in 2001. Pray for all involved in producing and airing these programmes. Thank God for Christian broadcasts in Russian on satellite TV, and pray for Turkmen-language Christian TV broadcasts to begin soon.

c) *The JESUS film*, video and audio tapes are available in Turkmen, and it has been occasionally shown on national TV. Pray for the lasting impact of this film and other Christian audio and video resources – may they have a powerful impact and be widely spread throughout the country.

6 **The diaspora.** The Turkmen people live in many surrounding lands: Iran (2m), Afghanistan (1m), Iraq (340,000), Uzbekistan (175,000), Syria (130,000), Russia (50,000) and Tajikistan (27,000). There are now Christians (Turkmen and foreign) working in evangelism and church planting among these people in Iraq and Afghanistan. Pray for the fruitfulness of these ministries. Pray for similar work among the almost completely unevangelized Turkmen in the other countries mentioned.

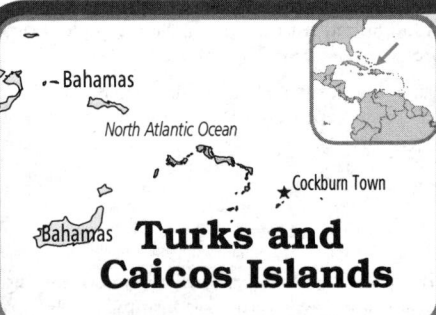

Turks & Caicos Islands

Caribbean

Geography 🌏

Area 500 sq km. An archipelago of 30 coral islands at the southeastern end of the Bahamas.

Population		Ann Gr	Density
2010	32,990	1.56%	66/sq km
2020	36,416	0.84%	73/sq km
2030	38,858	0.61%	78/sq km

Capital Grand Turk (Cockburn Town) 6,300. **Urbanites** 93.3%. **Pop under 15 yrs** 29%. **Life expectancy** 75 yrs.

Peoples 👪

African Caribbean 90%. Includes a large and undocumented Haitian population.
Euro-American 10%.
Literacy 87%. **Official language** English. **All languages** 2.

Economy 📈
Tourism, offshore financial services and fishing are the main sources of income. The islands have an unfortunate history of being used by those involved with the drug trade and money laundering.
Income/person $11,500 (36.6% of USA).

Politics ❌
A territory of the UK with considerable local autonomy until 2009, when direct rule was imposed due to systemic corruption in the government. Issues related to the drug trade still significantly affect the islands' administration.

Religion 🙏
Complete freedom of religion. Catholic numbers are possibly significantly larger than indicated due to the presence of Haitian immigrants.

Religions	Pop %	Population	Ann Gr
Christian	90.35	29,806	1.5%
Non-religious	6.65	2,194	1.8%
Ethnoreligionist	3.00	990	3.0%

Christians	Denoms	Pop %	Affiliates	Ann Gr
Protestant	10	39.81	13,000	1.6%
Independent	3	6.06	2,000	3.9%
Anglican	1	6.97	2,000	-1.2%
Catholic	1	4.00	1,000	-2.9%
Marginal	1	1.51	<500	2.1%
Unaffiliated		32.00	10,500	1.9%

Churches	MegaBloc	Congs	Members	Affiliates
Baptist Union	P	12	1,700	5,100
Seventh-day Adventist	P	9	1,400	2,338
Anglican Church	A	8	852	2,300
NT Ch of God (Clev)	P	5	750	1,665
Methodist Church	P	7	800	1,600
Catholic Church	C	3	923	1,320
Ch of God of Prophecy	P	11	367	1,230
Other denominations[9]		18	1,856	3,699
Total Christians[16]		**73**	**8,648**	**19,252**

TransBloc	Pop %	Population	Ann Gr
Evangelicals			
Evangelicals	32.4	10,686	2.1%
Renewalists			
Charismatics	16.9	5,563	3.4%
Pentecostals	14.8	4,895	3.7%

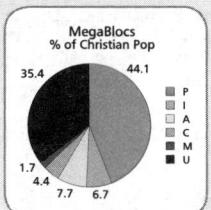

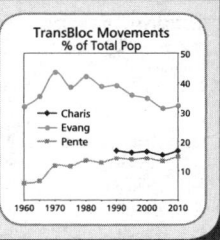

Challenges for Prayer

1 **Christian values in society** are challenged by offshore finance with its frequent money laundering, by tourism with its increasing licentiousness and by illegal drug trafficking. Pray that churches might address these through holy living and genuine faith.

2 **The inflow of immigrants** – most are illegal and from Haiti. They are poised to outnumber natives, or "Belongers". Pray that believers might meet these newcomers with biblical love and share with them the gospel.

3 **Poverty is an issue** – 25% live below the poverty line, despite a growing economy. Pray that God might open new opportunities for the economically disadvantaged and that any social and economic advancement would be for the betterment of the whole population.

South Pacific
Ocean

Funafuti

Tuvalu

Tuvalu

State of Tuvalu

Pacific

Geography

Area 24 sq km. Nine low, coral atolls in the central Pacific, eight of which are inhabited.

Population		Ann Gr	Density
2010	9,970	0.42%	415/sq km
2020	10,432	0.49%	435/sq km
2030	10,889	0.38%	454/sq km

Capital Funafuti 5,100. **Urbanites** 50.4%. **Pop under 15 yrs** 32%. **Life expectancy** 68.7 yrs.

Peoples

Pacific 98.2%. Tuvaluan 92.6%; Mixed 4.0%; I-Kiribati 1.6%.
Other 1.8%. European 0.9%.
Literacy 95%. **Official languages** Tuvalu, English. **All languages** 2. **Languages with Scriptures** 2Bi.

Economy

Beyond subsistence farming, the main income sources are fisheries licence fees, Internet hosting (with the "tv" domain suffix) and remittances from Tuvaluans abroad, particularly seafarers. **Public debt** 23% of GDP. **Income/person** $2,240 (5% of USA).

Politics

Independent from Britain in 1978 as a parliamentary monarchy. Once known as the Ellice Islands.

Religion

Strongly Protestant; other religions were not granted freedom until 1964.

Religions	Pop %	Population	Ann Gr
Christian	97.71	9,742	0.4%
Non-religious	1.19	119	1.7%
Baha'i	1.10	110	1.4%

Christians Denoms		Pop %	Affiliates	Ann Gr
Protestant	7	94.60	9,000	0.4%
Catholic	1	1.00	<100	-1.9%
Marginal	1	2.11	<300	1.0%

Churches	MegaBloc	Congs	Members	Affiliates
Tuvalu Church	P	14	3,538	8,845
Assemblies of God	P	3	195	300
Jehovah's Witnesses	M	3	55	210
Other churches	P	6	112	180
Seventh-day Adventist	P	1	75	107
Catholic Church	C	1	60	100
Total Christians[9]		**28**	**4,035**	**9,742**

TransBloc	Pop %	Population	Ann Gr
Evangelicals			
Evangelicals	17.8	1,773	3.7%
Renewalists			
Charismatics	3.4	336	6.1%
Pentecostals	3.0	300	6.4%

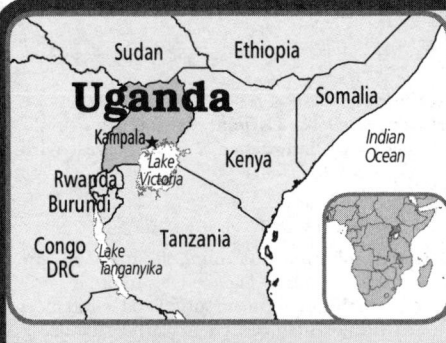

Challenges for Prayer

1 **Tuvalu faces an uncertain future.** Very limited resources, possible rising sea levels and modern/global external influences make this traditional culture fragile, both environmentally and socially. Pray that wisdom would prevail in preserving Tuvalu as a nation and culture, and that the long-standing presence of the Church would play a major role in this.

2 **Tuvalu was first evangelized** by Cook Island missionaries and then the LMS. The Congregational Church (Tuvalu Christian Church) is effectively the established church, but decline has set in on the back of nominalism. Newer works such as the more dynamic **AoG** see significant progress. Pray for renewal and biblical faith for all who identify themselves as Christians.

Uganda

Republic of Uganda

Africa

The numbers of those who perished from Amin's dictatorship, civil wars, famines and tribal killings are unknown, but estimates vary from 800,000 to 2 million. AIDS has significantly impacted the rate of population growth. **Capital** Kampala 1,597,916. **Urbanites** 13.3%. **Pop under 15 yrs** 49%. **Life expectancy** 51.9 yrs.

Peoples

Over 60 ethnic groups; four major divisions.
Bantu 65.6%. 28 peoples. Ganda 12.8%; Nkole 8.6%; Chiga 7.6%; Soga 7.5%; Gisu 4.3%; Tooro 2.6%; Fumbira 2.5%.
Nilotic 24.1%. 16 peoples. Teso(2) 5.7%; Lango 5.4%; Acholi 4.3%; Alur 2.1%.
Sudanic 6.8%. 10 peoples. Lugbara(2) 4.7%.
Other 3.5%. Other Africans, South Asians, Westerners.
Literacy 68%. **Official languages** English, Swahili. **All languages** 45. **Languages with Scriptures** 18Bi 9NT 16por 13w.i.p.

Economy

Fertile – with good soil, regular rainfall and three growing seasons. Agriculture accounts for 80% of the work force. The healthy economy of the 1960s was crippled in 1972 by the expulsion of the Asian business community, and then virtually destroyed by tyranny and wars. The slow, steady improvement made since 1992 was undermined by the conflict in the north and

Geography

Area 241,551 sq km. Much of the land is fertile and well watered. The climate is temperate in the highlands. Long known as the "Pearl of Africa".

Population		Ann Gr	Density
2010	33,796,461	3.32%	140/sq km
2020	46,319,320	3.13%	192/sq km
2030	60,818,796	2.63%	252/sq km

west and by the ravages of AIDS and disease. Debt relief allows for longer-term development, but poverty remains widespread.
HDI Rank 157th/182. **Public debt** 18.8% of GDP. **Income/person** $455 (1% of USA).

Politics

Independent from Britain in 1962. An attempt to balance power between southern Bantu kingdoms and northern Nilotic peoples ended in 1967, when the northerner Milton Obote took control. Anarchy increased until Idi Amin seized power in 1971. The unhinged dictatorship of Amin brutalized the country as the army pillaged and murdered with impunity. Amin's invasion of northwest Tanzania in 1978 provoked Tanzanian and Ugandan exiled troops to depose Amin's regime, restoring Obote to power. Continued intertribal warfare and government incompetence racked the country. Yoweri Museveni gained power in 1986 and has gradually brought peace and stability over the last two decades. A "no-party" democracy was constituted out of expediency. A multiparty system was introduced in 2005 in a vote that also demolished the two-term limit of the presidency and allowed Museveni to stand for a third elected term. The Rwanda-Burundi wars, subsequent Central African War and the terrorism of the Lord's Resistance Army have involved Uganda in military adventures in Congo, Sudan and Rwanda.

Religion

Under previous regimes of governance there were restrictions and intense persecution of Christians. There is now freedom of religion.

Religions	Pop %	Population	Ann Gr
Christian	84.74	28,639,121	3.4%
Muslim	11.49	3,883,213	3.6%
Ethnoreligionist	2.65	895,606	-1.4%
Non-religious	0.47	158,843	4.2%
Hindu	0.35	118,288	3.9%
Baha'i	0.30	101,389	3.3%

Christians	Denom	Pop %	Affiliates	Ann Gr
Protestant	141	6.60	2,231,000	5.5%
Independent	291	3.28	1,109,000	3.8%
Anglican	1	36.10	12,200,000	3.2%
Catholic	1	39.35	13,300,000	3.5%
Orthodox	2	0.08	28,000	0.7%
Marginal	2	0.07	25,000	4.7%
Doubly affiliated		*-0.74*	*-253,500*	*0.0%*

Churches	MegaBloc	Congs	Members	Affiliates
Catholic Church	C	585	7,600,000	13,300,000
Ch of Uganda (Ang)	A	14,600	5,126,050	12,200,000
Pente AoG	P	7,214	202,000	505,000
Ch of God (Cleveland)	P	675	135,000	449,550
New Apostolic Ch	I	888	177,500	355,000
Indig Pente/charis	I	3,242	162,088	295,000
Seventh-day Adventist	P	1,135	185,000	265,000
Ch of the Redeemed	P	930	93,000	186,000
Ch of God (Anderson)	P	480	80,000	176,000
Charismatic Ch of U	I	193	77,143	162,000
Baptist Church	P	1,975	79,000	150,100
Full Gospel	P	1,200	34,848	115,000
Elim Pentecostal Fell	P	1,125	63,000	113,400
Deliverance Church	P	200	39,000	78,000
Miracle Center	I	18	33,500	67,000
Christian Life Church	I	15	20,000	40,000
Other denominations	[422]	2,089	216,057	435,652
Doubly affiliated				*-253,500*
Total Christians[438]		**36,564**	**14,323,186**	**28,639,202**

TransBloc	Pop %	Population	Ann Gr
Evangelicals			
Evangelicals	37.0	12,507,182	3.7%
Renewalists			
Charismatics	19.0	6,436,315	6.4%
Pentecostals	5.7	1,934,650	5.2%

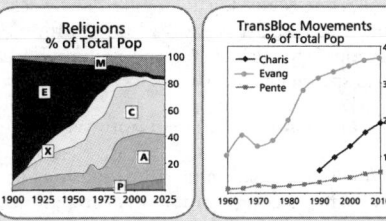

Religions % of Total Pop

TransBloc Movements % of Total Pop

Answers to Prayer

1 **Revival and growth** from 1986 onward – widespread prayer movements, strong evangelical presence in the Church of Uganda and renewal movements in the Catholic Church. These make Uganda one of the most truly Christian nations in the world, with church attendance high and public prayer common, even in government and judicial buildings.

2 **Pentecostal and charismatic growth** in the last 20 years is remarkable. The fastest-growing churches in Uganda are almost all from this background – from megachurches of 15,000 to house and storefront churches. The spiritual fervour and expectation see transformational effects – in Kampala, crime rates have fallen and it is estimated that more than half the population attend evangelically oriented services.

U

Challenges for Prayer

① **Uganda has worked hard to recover** from the devastation of the Amin and Obote years and has made great strides to this effect. Pray for peace both regionally (Congo-DRC, Kenya, Sudan, Horn of Africa) and internally (Lord's Resistance Army). Pray that the government might exercise its authority with even-handed honesty and a true concern for its own people.

② **Uganda's battle with AIDS** massively reduced cases, from 25% in 1992 to below 10% in 2001. The government and churches bravely and successfully worked to achieve this reduction, largely on a platform of abstinence and fidelity but moving toward encouraging condom use. A debate now rages over the validity of these reduced percentages and a resurgence of HIV cases; some allege infection rates are rising. Pray that all ground gained in this battle might be consolidated by right belief and right lifestyles. Even with the progress made, millions still suffer or are bereaved. Churches and agencies are doing much in AIDS support and education (Christian AIDS Network, ACET, **CMS**, **YWAM**, SU – Aid for AIDS) and in care for orphans (Watoto Childcare, **PAoC**/Pentecostal Assemblies).

③ **The Lord's Resistance Army** (LRA) spreads terror and has committed countless atrocities, having evolved over 20 years into little better than an occult-powered militia group. Its predation displaced nearly two million people and has taken more than 120,000 lives. Pray for:

a) **The dissolution of the LRA.** Pray for the Lord to demonstrate His sovereignty in this desperate situation. Many remain in the LRA out of fear. Pray also for peace and for reconciliation in northern Uganda.

b) **The 800,000 displaced people,** forced to live in camps amid difficult conditions. The camps were perfect breeding grounds for AIDS, poverty, corruption and the breakdown of moral values. Pray for peaceful resettlement of the Internally Displaced Peoples (IDPs) in the north.

c) **Children** are the most vulnerable victims of this tragedy. Thousands were abducted for use as child soldiers or sex slaves. Tens of thousands, fearing abduction, journey every night from their villages to the safety of larger towns – known globally as the "Gulu walk". Pray for the preservation and protection of the innocent. Pray for the reintegration of former child soldiers into their families and communities, a huge task requiring a great degree of trust and reconciliation.

d) **The many Christian NGOs** and ministries working among the victims of this immense suffering. Many Ugandans are deeply scarred psychologically, maimed physically and in great need spiritually. World Vision, Tearfund, MedAir, **MAF**, Samaritan's Purse and many other groups offer aid, shelter, counselling, education and vocational training as well as Bible studies and spiritual ministry.

④ **The Church** has seen both wonderful breakthroughs and immense obstacles:

a) **Unity.** There are numerous divisions in the Church, and the proliferation of independent and single-congregation denominations makes true unity a massive challenge. Pray for reconciliation and fellowship among Protestant and Catholic, charismatic and non-charismatic, denominational and independent.

b) **Superficial Christianity.** The majority of Ugandans identify themselves as Christian, but materialistic attitudes, polygamous practices and non-biblical worldviews – all affecting lifestyle – are common. For many, being "Christian" simply means not being Muslim. Pray for renewal that would turn nominal Christians into disciples.

c) **Syncretistic practices** and false teachings are multiplying even as the Church grows. The lack of biblical and Christian literature in local languages plays a part in this. The prosperity gospel is spreading rapidly. Many of the fastest growing groups have the fewest ordained pastors, the lowest training standards and the fewest accountability structures. The National Fellowship of Born Again Churches plays a crucial role in this area. The Africa Centre for Apologetics Research works to address the challenge of syncretism and cults. Pray that the Holy Spirit might lead Christians into all truth and that all falsehood might be cast aside.

d) **Training leaders for the Church.** Solid biblical formation for pastors is a key issue – training that is affordable, relevant and empowering. There are numerous Pentecostal Bible schools and a Baptist Seminary. **YWAM** provides short-term training, and Uganda Christian University serves strategically to educate professionals using a Christian worldview. Pray for the preparation of spiritual, godly leaders.

5 **Major ministry challenges** for the Ugandan Church:

a) ***Young people's ministry*** is fundamental to rebuilding the country in the wake of AIDS and the LRA devastation. Pray for the extensive ministry of SU in schools and for FOCUS(**IFES**) and Life Ministry (**CCCI**) on university/tertiary campuses; evangelism, discipleship and training are the main ministries. Pray also for effective youth programmes in churches.

b) ***Children in crisis.*** Numbing poverty deprives many children – including up to two million orphans – of care, finances for education and hope. Pray especially for street children, who are most numerous in Kampala (**AIM**, Viva, others), and for children in the north.

6 **Missions vision** in the Ugandan Church. A large, strong church that has endured suffering, combined with Uganda's geographical position next to several needy nations, make mission potential enormous. But this potential is still largely untapped due to lack of awareness and structures. Few Ugandan cross-cultural ministries exist; UEMA (Uganda Evangelical Missions Agency), African Initiative for Mission Service, Here Is Life and Life Ministries Uganda (**CCCI**) are notable ministries raising the profile of cross-cultural mission sending. Pray for many Ugandans to be called, trained and sent. Kampala Evangelical School of Theology, Africa Bible University, Reformed Theological College, Uganda Christian University and other theological colleges have missions degree programmes.

7 **Expatriate workers** are appreciated. Social, economic and educational needs make for many ministry opportunities. In today's climate, close fellowship and effective partnership between expatriates and Ugandans is essential. Areas of greatest potential service include reconstruction, development, counselling, Bible and vocational training, youth and children's ministry. Some of the larger missions include **IMB**, **AIM**, GGWO, **BIM**, **YWAM**, **GMS**.

8 **The growing challenges of other religions.**

a) ***Muslim*** numbers and influence are quickly growing. Politicized Islam is increasingly common in the Islamic population, and Arab states have poured large sums of money into education and Islamic infrastructure. Muslims are a minority in many peoples, but the Kakwa, Aringa and Madi peoples in the northwest and the Soga in the southeast have significant numbers of Muslims. Relatively little has been done to sensitively reach out specifically to Muslims. Converts are few and have been persecuted.

b) ***Animistic tribal religious practices,*** previously in decline, may be increasing as well as infiltrating and polluting Christian faith and practice. In some dioceses, the number of pagan shrines is double that of church buildings.

9 **Christian support ministries:**

a) ***The Bible Society*** has done much to promote new Bible translations and to publish Bibles, but sales are less than what they were in the 1980s. All Christian literature ministries are similarly crippled, but The Bible Society, Gideons and others distribute several hundred thousand Bibles and NTs every year. Thirteen languages remain without God's Word and a further 18 have only part of the Bible. SIL is assisting in this ministry task. Pray for the provision of Scriptures to all, in their own language.

b) ***Audio Scriptures*** and teaching are vital due to poverty, illiteracy, the widespread oral culture and unstable conditions.

c) ***MAF's*** flying programme has blessed many – their planes enable ministries to serve churches, refugees, health and vaccination programs, development work and many others. **MAF's** work focuses on the least developed, most vulnerable and insecure regions such as the northeast.

d) ***The JESUS film*** is available online in at least 40 languages. Pray for Life Ministry, COTN and other teams showing the film around the country.

e) ***Christian radio and TV programmes*** air on the national network and are growing in impact and influence. Evangelical presence is felt through seven FM radio stations and two TV stations, although such influence is more significant in Kampala than in the countryside. Pray for effective programming and lasting fruit.

Ukraine

Europe

Geography

Area 603,700 sq km. A flat, fertile, forested plain with few natural boundaries.

Population		Ann Gr	Density
2010	45,433,415	-0.65%	75/sq km
2020	42,945,414	-0.56%	71/sq km
2030	40,188,380	-0.70%	67/sq km

Capital Kyiv (Kiev) 2,804,781. **Other major cities** Kharkov 1.5 million; Dnepropetrovsk 1mill; Odessa 1m; Donetsk 965,000. **Urbanites** 68%. **Pop under 15 yrs** 14%. **Life expectancy** 68.2 yrs.

Peoples

Intermingling of Ukrainians and Russians blurs ethnic divisions.
Eurasian 97.1%.
  Slavic 95.2%. Ukrainian 72.1%; Russian 13.2%; Polish 2.3%; Ruthene 1.1%; Belarusian 0.9%.
  Other 1.9%. Moldavian/Romanian 0.9%; Hungarian 0.4%.
Turkic/Altaic 1.0%. Crimean Tatar 0.7%.
Other 1.9%. Gypsy(4) 1.5%; Jew 0.3%.
Literacy 99.4%. **Official language** Ukrainian, but Russian widely spoken. **All languages** 42. **Indigenous languages** 13. **Languages with Scripture** 4Bi 3NT 5por 2w.i.p.

Economy

Rich in mineral deposits (especially coal and iron ore) and highly arable land; Ukraine has great economic potential. A sustained post-independence economic plummet was reversed by several years of growth, but many Ukrainians hover on the edge of poverty. Transition to a market economy, while holding hope for a brighter future, has thus far been blighted by corruption, cronyism and uneven progress (cities grow while smaller towns wither and fade). Dependent upon Russia's oil and gas.
HDI Rank 85th/182. **Public debt** 10% of GDP. **Income/person** $3,910 (8% of USA).

Politics

Ukraine was dominated and fought over for centuries by a succession of powers. Although political freedom came to all with independence in 1991, a small but powerful cadre vastly enriched and entrenched itself. The country has since been deeply divided between those wanting to reassert links with Russia and those looking westward for the future. The "Orange Revolution" in 2005 won Ukrainians national dignity, press freedoms and open political mechanisms, but infighting and rivalries have crippled progress with 2010 election results again revealing the underlying impasse. Promises of rooting out corruption have borne little fruit as it is deeply embedded.

Religion

The Church was severely persecuted under Communism. Freedom of religion since 1990, but some prejudice remains against non-traditional groups.

Religions	Pop %	Population	Ann Gr
Christian	79.01	35,896,941	-0.7%
Non-religious	19.48	8,850,429	0.4%
Muslim	1.05	477,051	2.5%
Jewish	0.30	136,300	-6.2%
Other	0.14	63,607	2.5%
Ethnoreligionist	0.02	9,087	-0.7%

Christians Denoms		Pop %	Affiliates	Ann Gr
Protestant	43	3.76	1,708,000	2.2%
Independent	17	2.02	919,000	1.9%
Catholic	2	10.14	4,607,000	-0.7%
Orthodox	7	61.15	27,781,000	-1.0%
Marginal	2	0.72	326,000	2.1%
Unaffiliated		1.8	818,000	0.6%
Doubly affiliated		*-0.58*	*-261,000*	*0.0%*

Churches	MegaBloc	Congs	Members	Affiliates
Ukr Orth Ch (Moscow)	O	11,300	15,931,034	23,100,000
Ukr Orth Ch (Kiev)	O	3,550	2,758,621	4,000,000
Eastern-rite Catholics	C	3,470	2,692,308	3,850,000
Latin-rite Catholic	C	920	491,558	757,000
Autocephalous Orth	O	1,150	414,935	639,000
Ev Chr & Baptists	I	2,517	151,000	452,000
Old Believers Ch	I	51	248,503	415,000
Evang Pente Union	P	1,309	144,000	374,400
Jehovah's Witnesses	M	1,000	150,000	310,000
Other Orthodox	I	81	181,818	260,000
Unregistered Pente	P	565	65,000	195,000
Ch of God of Prophecy	P	54	73,810	155,000
Seventh-day Adventist	P	218	65,300	141,000
Reformed Church	P	108	19,000	130,000
Other charismatic chs	I	450	62,874	105,000
Embassy of God	I	280	50,000	105,000
Indep Pente Union	P	280	37,000	99,900
Other denominations[32]		965	132,750	250,578
Doubly affiliated				*-261,300*
Total Christians[70]		**28,268**	**23,669,511**	**35,077,578**

U

TransBloc	Pop %	Population	Ann Gr
Evangelicals			
Evangelicals	3.8	1,737,245	3.1%
Renewalists			
Charismatics	2.6	1,164,047	3.8%
Pentecostals	1.9	842,370	2.5%

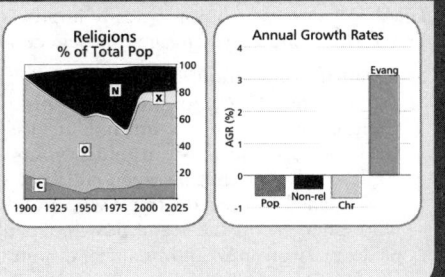

Missionaries from Ukraine
P,I,A 2,849 (1,599 long-term), with the largest number serving in Russia, then Ukraine; many also in Central Asia.

Answers to Prayer

1 **Thank God for the rich Christian heritage** of Ukraine. This was the "Bible Belt" of the Soviet sphere, and churches here suffered greatly until independence. Faithful perseverance is now bearing fruit as the Church comes of age and increasingly impacts society across all spheres. There is today a spiritual ambition and vision previously not present in Ukraine.

2 **Sustained growth of evangelicals.** Newer charismatic groups have grown in particular. Many churches were begun by foreigners, notably Africans, but increasingly a fruit of the Ukrainian soil in which they were planted. One recent successful house church movement has seen great growth both in Ukraine and neighbouring countries by focusing on relational outreach, lay leadership and reproducing churches.

3 **Praise God for the emergence** of dynamic and visionary Ukrainian mission agencies who minister both at home and throughout the former Soviet Union. Ukraine is the Antioch of the Slavic world.

Challenges for Prayer

1 **Communism fell two decades ago,** but its effects are still deeply felt. The market economy has actually driven many to poverty while lining the pockets of the elite. Corruption reaches to the highest levels while pensioners, teachers, doctors and other state employees struggle economically. The moral vacuum of post-Communist freedom led to rapidly increasing rates of alcoholism and AIDS. Pray for righteousness, justice and compassion to shine forth into this situation.

2 **The Orange Revolution** displayed both the incredible potential and the predictable humanity of Ukraine. After non-violent mass demonstrations forced new elections and greater freedoms, many felt Ukraine was on the road to widespread transformation. Sadly, much remains unchanged. Opposing political leaders undermined one another, and the nation remains intrinsically divided between East and West. Pray for this fault line to be repaired by genuine healing and reconciliation.

3 **Ukraine is a key nation,** a bridge between East and West, Orthodox and Catholic. Slavic Christianity was born in Kyiv 1,000 years ago. Most Ukrainians are part of the Ukrainian Orthodox Church, but it is torn by factions loyal to competing patriarchs in Kyiv and Moscow. The Autocephalous Orthodox Church condemns both for compliance with the Communists, but is itself beset with schisms. The Greek or Uniate Catholic Church, which follows the Orthodox liturgy and structure but accepts the leadership of the Pope, is also large. There is much competition for limited resources, reacquired buildings and dwindling populations. Superstition and superficiality are widespread, but those with a love for God and the Scriptures remain faithful. Pray that spiritual life and renewal, rather than power-politics, may govern structures and relationships within these large Christian bodies.

4 **Ukraine has a strong Christian legacy,** and evangelicals emerged stronger and more numerous from 130 years of sustained persecution in which millions of Christians were killed. Freedom of religion is vastly improved but not yet enshrined in both law and practice. Pray for the Church to engage this new context with boldness. There are several challenges:

a) Reconciliation and unity. Ukrainian religious life is marred by strife among and inside all major groups. Competing schisms within Orthodoxy in particular, but also factions within Catholicism and Protestantism, blunt the effectiveness of religious faith. The Communist era is over, but scars of intimidation and betrayal need further healing – all three major confessions were split between collaborators and resisters. Pray for right responses to those who yielded to pressure, those who stood firm but often remain inflexible today, and those who emerged on the scene post-independence. Often divisions are the result of personal pride, unforgiveness and financial disputes rather than theological differences alone.

b) The emergence of the newer churches is a great blessing, though it has upset the balance of the religious establishment. Dynamism, Western style and African leadership have ruffled some feathers amongst more traditional groups. Pray for sensitivity and gracious attitudes for all, and for ways to maximize both the spiritual fervour of newer groups and the remarkable spiritual heritage of more traditional ones.

c) Growth is somewhat limited by current needs for training, infrastructure, adequate facilities and active input from lay Christians. Opportunities for holistic and compassionate ministries abound, and to miss this open door would be a shame. Pray for a mentality of abundance and generosity that provides for the material needs of church growth without too much recourse to foreign funds, which can bring their own complications.

5 **Leadership training** is probably the primary church need in Ukraine. Twenty years of sustained growth created thousands of new congregations requiring leadership formation. There are dozens of seminaries, Bible schools and institutes, the capacities of which must grow to meet current and future demands. Western agencies contribute helpfully in this area, including SGA, **GEM**, Calvary Chapel Mission, Baptist and Pentecostal groups and others. Pray for them to serve professionally and humbly. Ask for God's provision for good academic resources and textbooks, for building projects and also funding for student scholarships.

6 **Expatriate agencies.** Light in the East, SGA, **SEND**, **IMB** and others faithfully served the persecuted church before 1989 and continue to do so today. More have flocked to the country since then, but all too often with insensitivity to local cultural and financial issues. There is still a place for long-term workers willing to learn the language and culture, most particularly in Bible teaching, leadership training and facilitating/assisting Ukrainians in setting up their own ministries and missions.

7 **Indigenous agencies.** A blossoming of agencies followed independence with Ukrainians now working in outreach (evangelism, literature, media), with children (in summer camps and schools), and especially in humanitarian work (with prisoners, hospitals, orphanages and soup kitchens). Pentecostals/charismatics and Baptists minister both within Ukraine and without, sending missionaries to other former Soviet states. Pray for the burgeoning Ukrainian missionary movement – for further growth, provision and fruitful partnership with Western and other agencies.

8 **Outreach challenges:**

a) Students. CCX(**IFES**), **CCCI**, the **Navigators** and others have active campus ministries and student groups are multiplying. CCX groups meet in 16 different cities, and most student missions have a mix of expatriate and national workers. Youth work (**YFC** and many others) and summer camps (often held in former Communist Youth facilities) have proved fruitful. Pray for continued responsiveness from students; there are allegedly 300,000 students in Kyiv alone.

b) Children at risk. There are tens of thousands of street children, over 100,000 living in orphanages and many others in precarious living situations. Many of these suffer health complications from Chernobyl. The majority of orphans will become involved in drugs, crime or prostitution unless they can be lovingly reached by Christians. The CoMission for Children at Risk brings together dozens of ministries dedicated to doing just that.

c) Crimea – a region in contrast to the rest of Ukraine. Communist beliefs and a strong Russian connection persist here, and churches have not grown as much as in other parts of the country. More than 250,000 previously exiled Crimean Tatars have been welcomed as well. The vast majority are Muslim (although often nominally) and are being sought by Muslim missionaries from Turkey and the Arab world. Significant numbers of Christians are specifically reaching out to them with substantial fruit (Russian Ministries/River of Joy, Crimean Tatar Partnership, **YWAM**). The increasing number of Tatar believers are noted for their fiery faith.

d) ***Ukrainian Jews.*** Many have emigrated to Israel and the West, and the population continues to plummet by 7% annually. Chosen People Ministries has planted several Messianic synagogues, and a Messianic Bible school has been formed. Ukraine's Jews are among the most responsive in the world to the gospel.

e) ***Foreign immigrants, often students*** - most are from the Middle East and Asia. Many are lonely and subject to hostile or racist attitudes from xenophobic elements in Ukraine. A large number are very open to the gospel, and Ukraine's evangelistically-minded churches are reaping a harvest.

f) ***Cults remain a serious issue.*** From Jehovah's Witnesses to Hare Krishna to indigenous pagan groups such as RUNVira and the Perunists, churches must realize there are other groups at work in Ukraine. In 2010, the Mormons dedicated their first full temple in the former Soviet Union. Pray for the apologetics and research centres whose goal is to promote greater discernment among Christians and encourage outreach to cult followers.

9 **Christian media ministries:**

a) ***Bible ministries.*** The Ukrainian Bible Society (UBS) restarted in 1991. A need for biblical truth and the restoration of moral values in society have drawn together partners from across the confessional spectrum – Orthodox, Catholic and Protestant. The ministry has grown greatly in the past decade and now distributes hundreds of thousands of copies of Scripture every year. More could be done with the provision of further finances; pray for their release.

b) ***Literature,*** a great need since most Christian literature was destroyed during the Communist occupation. Russian literature is plentiful, but it is a struggle to get good materials published in Ukrainian. **EHC** has distributed over six million pieces of literature through Ukrainian churches. UBS/FCBH, Bible League, Mission Without Borders and others all work to get the printed Word of God into the hands of Ukrainians, especially children and students.

c) ***Radio and television*** are open for Christian programmes. **FEBC** and **TWR** broadcast several hours a week in Ukrainian and Russian with good response. **HCJB** has partnered with CMAssociates to set up recording and radio studios, and has been instrumental in founding Radio Emmanuel, a local Christian station. CBN has a major television network based in Kyiv, and some of the newer, larger churches are developing their own television programmes.

d) ***The JESUS film*** is shown in seven major languages in Ukraine – pray for more workers to show the film at Family Festivals throughout the country.

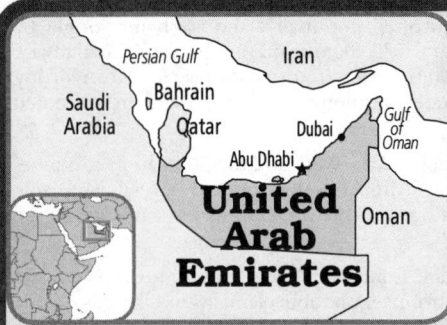

only Fujairah and Umm al Qaiwain do not have oil reserves. Weaning itself from overdependence on increasingly restive migrant labourers is a major challenge. Overinvestment – particularly in Dubai – created massive debts almost the size of the GDP.
HDI Rank 35th/182. **Public Debt** 40.7% of GDP. **Income/person** $55,028 (116% of USA).

Politics 𝕏

The British-protected Trucial States became an independent confederation of monarchies in 1971. The first tentative steps toward a very limited democracy are occurring. The Sheikh of Abu Dhabi is president of the Supreme Council, which rules the country. While there are federal laws applying to the whole country, each emirate also has its own regulations.

Religion

Islam is the state religion, with a Sunni majority and a small Shi'a minority. Admirably high levels of religious freedom for an Arab state, but proselytism is still illegal. Religious figures are estimates.

Religions	Pop %	Population	Ann Gr
Muslim	67.65	3,184,493	3.2%
Hindu	15.50	729,633	1.8%
Christian	8.55	402,475	2.3%
Buddhist	3.70	174,170	1.8%
Other	2.40	112,975	1.2%
Non-religious	1.60	75,317	5.6%
Baha'i	0.60	28,244	4.7%

This population includes expatriates and nationals. Almost all natives of UAE are Muslim.

Christians Denoms		Pop %	Affiliates	Ann Gr
Protestant	30	0.69	32,000	3.6%
Independent	12	0.36	17,000	9.2%
Anglican	1	0.26	12,000	1.5%
Catholic	1	4.82	227,000	1.8%
Orthodox	7	2.22	104,000	1.7%
Unaffiliated		0.20	9,000	5.2%

Churches	MegaBloc	Congs	Members	Affiliates
Catholic Church	C	13	158,741	227,000
All Orthodox	O	11	19,900	99,500
All Other Protestant	P	14	4,054	13,500
Anglican Church	A	12	3,664	12,200
Indian Pente Ch of God	P	124	7,444	9,900
Independent groups	I	20	4,900	9,800
Kings Revival Intl Ch	I	31	3,889	7,000
Other denominations[5]		227	8,397	14,010
Total Christians[51]		**452**	**210,989**	**392,910**

United Arab Emirates

Asia

Geography

Area 77,700 sq km of desert and mountains on the Arabian Gulf and the Gulf of Oman. Seven emirates: Abu Dhabi, Dubai, Sharjah, Ras al Khaimah, Ajman, Umm al Qaiwain and Fujairah.

Population		Ann Gr	Density
2010	4,707,307	2.86%	61/sq km
2020	5,659,742	1.73%	73/sq km
2030	6,555,490	1.42%	84/sq km

Capital Abu Dhabi 685,000. **Other major city** Dubai 1.6 million. **Urbanites** 78%. **Pop under 15 yrs** 19%. **Life expectancy** 77.3 yrs.

Peoples

All figures are estimates. The massive presence of expatriate workers – often illegal – makes accurate figures difficult to obtain. If anything, the non-Arab population is much higher than reported.
Arab 56.0%. Gulf Arab 24.1%; Other Arab 31.9%. Gulf Bedouin, Egyptian, Omani, Saudi.
South Asian 23.2%. Indian, Pakistani, Bangladeshi, Sri Lankan.
Other 20.8%. Filipino, Iranian, European, East Asian.
Literacy 88.7%. **Official language** Arabic. **All languages** 36. **Indigenous languages** 7. **Languages with Scriptures** 3Bi 1por 1w.i.p.

Economy

Astonishing transformation in one generation from poor Arab backwater to playground of the ultra-rich. Mind-boggling spending on development, funded by oil wealth, in order to diversify the economy into commercial, IT, industrial and entertainment spheres. Abu Dhabi and Dubai are the wealthiest emirates;

TransBloc	Pop %	Population	Ann Gr
Evangelicals			
Evangelicals	1.3	60,774	5.5%
Renewalists			
Charismatics	1.0	45,896	6.5%
Pentecostals	0.1	4,700	5.5%

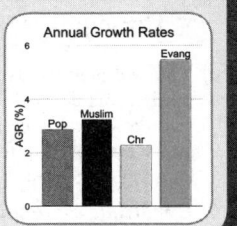

Answers to Prayer

1 **The religious freedom enjoyed** by all major faith groups is notable. Ruling families have loaned some land and allowed building of compounds for several confessions of Christianity as well as for Hindus and Sikhs. Praise God for this freedom, and pray that these facilities would not become Christian ghettos but rather launching pads for ministry.

2 **Increased numbers of people** coming to Christ from other backgrounds. This is shifting from a trickle to a flow as more and more Arabs, South Asians, East Asians and others meet Jesus in a personal way. Some ministers are overwhelmed by responses to the gospel – praise God for such a challenge!

Challenges for Prayer

1 **Radical changes in the last generation** created a culture crisis in the UAE. Traditionalists and progressives face off over many issues such as the role of women and democracy. The younger generation hangs in the balance, but will their Islamic heritage merely be replaced by selfish materialism? Pray that new opportunities will yield a spiritual hunger for the truth and not just the trappings of a wealthy lifestyle.

2 **Expatriate Christians** have opportunities for discreet sharing as the nation becomes more open and international. However, arrests, imprisonment and deportation still occur for those who evangelize or distribute Christian literature unwisely. Pray that believers would demonstrate Christ in their words and deeds with discernment and confidence. Pray for the English, Arabic, Urdu, Filipino and Indian language worship groups and congregations in their worship and witness.

3 **Christian ministries:**

a) ***Large numbers of foreign labourers*** have a much greater opportunity to hear the gospel in the UAE. Their disillusionment with poor employment conditions opens many to hear the good news. Some expatriate Christians have a vision for evangelising within their own ethnic group and beyond, but training is required.

b) ***Domestic labourers,*** in particular, have unique access and witness to their Gulf Arab employers, despite frequently enduring difficult conditions. Pray that their humble witness might lead many to Jesus.

c) ***There are several TEE*** and broadcast media programmes aimed at training leaders – pray for this vital work.

d) ***Strategic prayer networks*** focused on the UAE and Gulf region play a crucial role in preparing the ground for a spiritual harvest.

e) ***Student ministries*** and **IFES** in particular are allowed to establish official campus fellowships in a number of universities, including frequent Muslim-Christian dialogue events.

4 **Medical ministry** through a Christian hospital and clinics. These have operated since the "old days" in the 1960s, especially in poorer areas, and have sown many spiritual seeds as well as engendered goodwill from the government with faithful service. Pray for continued useful ministry, for provision of finances and qualified staff, and for visible fruit.

U

5 **The unreached:**

a) ***The indigenous Arab population.*** Both urban educated and rural illiterate (including the semi-nomadic Bedouin) have limited meaningful access to the gospel. The Arab believing population is increasing, however, though not without significant risk to their livelihood and safety. Discipleship for these believers and opportunities for fellowship are great needs. Arabic language BCCs and teaching via broadcast media are valuable resources.

b) ***Expatriate communities.*** Iranian (Persian, Baluch), Pakistani/Afghan (Punjabi, Pushtun and Baluch), Bengali, Somali and Sudanese communities all have few if any believers. Pray for them to somehow receive the good news.

6 **Media available for outreach.** There is a definite interest in and hunger for Christian media resources. Where public proclamation is extremely difficult, these means are easily accessed in private. Pray that many might come to accept Jesus as Saviour and grow as disciples, despite the obvious lack of church structures for these private believers.

a) ***Radio and television.*** FEBA and IBRA contribute 57 hours per week of radio broadcasts from abroad, in Arabic. Another 64 hours per week are broadcast in several other languages. Satellite television programs (on the *Al Hayat*, Miracle and **SAT-7** channels) disciple, teach and witness in Arabic. Pray that many would see and hear this life-changing material.

b) ***The JESUS film*** is translated into most of the languages present in the emirates, including Arabic. The God's Story Project is also available in many of the languages present in the UAE.

c) ***Christian literature*** distribution is limited in that it must be done discreetly. Pray for the opportunity to open a Christian reading room or library that would give all in the UAE the chance to interact with Scripture and other Christian materials.

d) ***The Internet.*** A myriad of websites powerfully share the gospel in Arabic and other languages. Pray that many in this increasingly high-tech country would find the truth online. Pray also that restrictions on accessing sites with Christian materials and Christian-Muslim dialogue might be lifted.

United Kingdom

United Kingdom of
Great Britain and
Northern Ireland

Europe

Geography 🌍

Area 244,110 sq km. Two main islands: Britain and the northeast of Ireland. A union of four countries: England 103,400 sq km, Scotland 78,800 sq km, Wales 20,800 sq km, Northern Ireland 14,100 sq km. Also three small autonomous states that are dependencies of the British Crown: Isle of Man 588 sq km (in the Irish Sea); Channel Islands 194 sq km (Guernsey, Jersey).

Population		Ann Gr	Density
2010	62,129,818	0.54%	255/sq km
2020	65,321,580	0.49%	268/sq km
2030	68,187,438	0.40%	279/sq km

England 83.8%. Scotland 8.4% (~60,000 speaking Gaelic). Wales 4.9% (~740,000 speaking Welsh). Northern Ireland 2.9%.

Capital London 8,631,325. Other major cities included in constituent country section. **Urbanites** 90.1%. **Pop under 15 yrs** 17%. **Life expectancy** 79.3 yrs.

Peoples 👪

Anglo-Saxon/Celtic 85.2%. English 69.2%; Scots 9.3%; Irish(2) 4.1%; Welsh 1.8%; Cornish 0.8%.
Asian 6.3%. Largest groups: Urdu-speaking 1.5%; Punjabi 1.1%; Hindi 0.7%; Chinese(4) 0.7%; Bengali 0.5%;

Gujarati 0.5%; Filipino 0.4%; Tamil 0.3%.
European 3.3%. Polish 0.7%; Greek (includes Greek Cypriot) 0.6%; German 0.3%; Italian 0.3%.
Middle Eastern/West Asian 1.9%. Arab(10) 0.6%; Jews 0.5%; Pashtun(2) 0.3%; Turk (includes Turkish Cypriot) 0.2%.
African Caribbean 1.4%. Caribbean origin; majority British-born.
African 0.8%. Nigerian, Somali, Ghanaian, others.
Other 1.1%. Romani/Gypsy/Irish Travellers(6) 0.5%; North American 0.4%.
Literacy 99%. **Official language** English; in Wales both English and Welsh. English is the primary language of 400 million in the world, as well as the major language of international communication for over 1.4 billion. **All languages** 15 indigenous; over 200 immigrant languages. **Languages with Scriptures** 5Bi 3NT 3por 2w.i.p. There have been more translations of the Scriptures into English than into any other language.

Economy

The world's first industrialized economy – now primarily a post-industrial service economy and highly dependent on financial and business services. The post-WWII decline through poor management, low investment, labour unrest and high levels of public ownership was reversed from the mid-1980s to the late 2000s. One of the hardest hit by the 2008-2009 economic crisis (the impact of which will be felt for some time to come), but still the world's fifth-largest economy. Unemployment was 2.5m in 2010. Resistant to entry into Euro monetary system. **HDI Rank** 21st/182. **Public debt** 52% of GDP. **Income/person** $43,734 (92% of USA).

Politics

Parliamentary, constitutional monarchy. The UK was formed in 1801 as a Union of Great Britain and Ireland. Southern Ireland formally seceded from the Union in 1921. The British Empire, once covering one-fourth of the world, has become 60 independent states, most being members of the British Commonwealth. Since 1945, the transition from a world power to a European state linked to its own continent has not been easy, but close ties to both the USA and the EU continue. The UK remains a political, military and cultural power with disproportionate influence globally. The centuries-long conflict between the Irish and British (over sovereignty of Northern Ireland) is largely resolved on a political level, but not necessarily in the hearts of the people involved. The smaller constituent members of the UK – Scotland, Wales and Northern Ireland – enjoy a great degree of autonomy due to the devolution process of the last 10-15 years.

Religion

A Christian nation for centuries, religious freedom still exists, although nominalism, pluralism and hostility to overt religiosity in the general public and the media increasingly threaten religious expression. The Church of England (Anglican) is recognized as the Established Church in England, and the Church of Scotland (Presbyterian) in Scotland. The Sovereign is recognized as the titular head of the Church of England. Disestablishment of the Church is increasingly advocated.

Religions	Pop %	Population	Ann Gr
Christian	59.66	37,066,649	-0.8%
Non-religious	34.49	21,428,574	2.8%
Muslim	3.20	1,988,154	2.2%
Hindu	0.94	584,020	1.4%
Sikh	0.63	391,418	1.5%
Jewish	0.40	248,519	-0.4%
Buddhist	0.34	211,241	3.1%
Other	0.22	136,686	2.5%
Chinese	0.10	62,130	0.5%
Baha'i	0.02	12,426	0.5%

The percentage of those self-identifying as Christian ranges significantly depending on the source.

Christians	Denoms	Pop %	Affiliates	Ann Gr
Protestant	194	6.91	4,293,000	-1.1%
Independent	279	1.36	845,000	1.8%
Anglican	4	36.23	22,509,000	-0.8%
Catholic	6	8.61	5,350,000	-0.3%
Orthodox	20	1.06	660,000	0.5%
Marginal	54	0.89	552,000	-0.6%
Unaffiliated		6.81	4,231,000	0.3%
Doubly affiliated		*-2.25*	*-1,400,000*	*0.0%*

Churches	MegaBloc	Congs	Members	Affiliates
Church of England	A	16,100	1,200,000	21,900,000
Catholic Church	C	4,550	2,409,910	5,350,000
Church of Scotland	P	1,480	500,000	1,100,000
Methodist Ch of GB	P	5,500	260,000	780,000
Baptist Union of GB	P	2,000	139,000	545,000
Other New Churches	I	1,105	95,000	285,000
Presby Ch in Ireland	P	400	197,000	280,000
Church in Wales (Ang)	A	1,420	68,657	274,600
Church of Ireland	A	430	120,000	265,000
Jehovah's Witnesses	M	1,520	130,000	255,000
Greek Orthodox	O	110	141,176	240,000
Latter-day Saints	M	340	115,584	178,000
Assemblies of God	P	650	74,500	149,000
Elim Pentecostal Ch	P	500	55,000	138,000
Luth Council of GB	P	170	59,000	118,000
Christian Brethren	P	1,000	43,000	105,000
United Reformed Ch	P	1,600	62,893	100,000
Salvation Army	P	680	43,000	60,000
Other denominations[340]		12,607	1,218,188	2,110,125
Disaffiliated				*-1,400,000*
Total Christians[387]		**52,162**	**6,931,908**	**32,832,725**

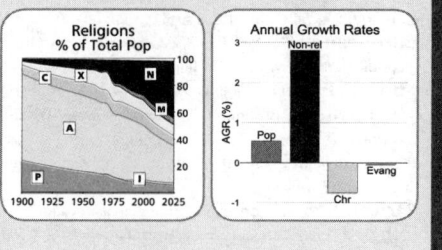

TransBloc	Pop %	Population	Ann Gr
Evangelicals			
Evangelicals★	8.8	5,490,134	0.0%
Renewalists			
Charismatics	4.7	2,902,227	1.0%
Pentecostals	1.0	635,071	1.3%

★This figure is an indication of belief rather than of practice; about one-third of this number attend church regularly.

Missionaries from UK
P,I,A 6,405 long-term; 5,726 international.

United Kingdom – General

Answers to Prayer

1 **The UK's contribution** to global Christianity has been significant for centuries. From Wycliffe and Tyndale up to today – with the Alpha Course, 24-7prayer and a host of evangelical writers, theologians and worship leaders – the UK continues to offer blessing to the nations of the world.

2 **The Church is growing** among many ethnic minorities. Part of this is through widespread immigration from strongly Christian nations such as Nigeria and Brazil, whose Christians bring with them much-needed vitality and spiritual confidence in the gospel. Part is through considerable conversion growth among Africans, Chinese, Polish, "Travellers" (Romani/ Gypsy) and even modest growth among South Asians and others. Multi-ethnic churches are sprouting up and seeing new converts to Christ from among largely unevangelized peoples.

Challenges for Prayer

1 **Britain needs to discover a sense of purpose** and direction for the 21st Century. Its sense of nationhood and core identity has increasingly diminished since the end of the British Empire and plays itself out in the context of:

a) *Foreign policy,* which remains globally engaging. As a permanent UN Security Council member and head of the Commonwealth, and because of its special relationship with the USA, Britain's involvement with the wider world remains extensive in both diplomatic and military contexts. Pray for this influence and power to be wielded for the sake of what is just and right, when needed and called for.

b) *Integration with the EU* remains a political hot potato. The loss of autonomy to the Byzantine politics of the EU sits poorly with many in the UK, but greater integration appears inevitable. Balancing maximum participation in the EU with maximum retention of autonomy seems an impossible compromise.

c) *Devolution of the UK into federalism.* This will grant greater autonomy to Scotland, Wales and Northern Ireland, but at significant financial and political costs. Britain and "Britishness" will suffer at the hands of buoyant national identities and agendas.

2 **The sense that all is not well** pervades the country. "Broken Britain" is the catchphrase of the tabloid news. The "freedoms" of the 1960s led to social disaster and hastened spiritual decline. Many are discouraged about the future and cynical about the seeming impotence of politicians to deal with the malaise; this trait is exacerbated by the media. Violent crime, alcohol and drug abuse, sexually transmitted diseases, immorality, prostitution, illegitimacy and abortion rates, gambling addiction and personal debt levels are not just alarmingly high, but in some cases are tacitly encouraged by misled government policies. Conservatives point to breakdown of the family and traditional morality as primary causes. The simultaneous decline of Christian values in society over this same period is hardly a coincidence. Without a radical change, disaster looms. Pray for national repentance and restoration to the spiritual vigour that once made Britain's Christians a blessing to the world. Many Christians are praying for revival.

3 **Immigration** remains a massive challenge, but is also an utter necessity and an unavoidable reality. The seat of British Empire now draws many from the far reaches of its former domains – and beyond. There are an estimated 600,000 to 900,000 illegal immigrants in the UK. Fully 70% of net population growth in the next 25 years is anticipated to be from immigration; in some boroughs and towns more babies are born to immigrants than to citizens. Pray with an eye toward:

a) ***A core identity and purpose for Britain.*** Without a cultural centre or core set of values around which to build a multi-cultural society, disintegration and division will triumph. Pray for Britain to regain a sense of what makes it Britain; pray that these values would celebrate and reflect what God rejoices in.

b) ***Integration.*** Unwillingness or inability to adjust to life in the UK and lack of support and welcome for many immigrants all contribute to the creation of ethnic ghettoes.

c) ***Criminal and terrorist threats.*** Immigrants tend to suffer lower rates of employment and education, and higher rates of poverty and crime. They are much more vulnerable to exploitation by human traffickers, crime lords and religious fanatics. The number of people who enter the UK with the intention of criminal or terrorist activity is of course unknown, but it is far too many nonetheless. Pray for all who intend to exploit, disrupt or destroy to be thwarted by the authorities.

d) ***Christian and mission impact.*** Immigration, a trend reviled by reactionaries, also brings great blessing to these shores. Christian immigrants have staved off even greater declines in mainline churches and brought new life to many recent movements. "Reverse mission" is an undeniable trend, with around 1,500 Christian missionaries coming into the UK from the Americas, Africa and Asia. Immigration has also brought many unevangelized peoples right onto the doorstep of gospel-oriented churches. Thank God for these twin blessings; pray that both might be fully utilized to see new churches planted, new peoples reached and Jesus glorified.

4 **Multi-cultural pluralism** has replaced Judeo-Christian tradition as the foundation of society. Minority religions, particularly Islam, receive notable attention and government support – in education, legislation and freedoms – yet they still feel discriminated against. Astrology, New Age, the occult and old-world paganism (Druid/Wicca) are popular, with a massive increase of literature and websites promoting their ends. The UK itself is now a mission field. Praise God for religious freedom; pray for it to be retained; pray that it does not prompt further turning against, or away from, the Christian faith that shaped the UK so profoundly for the better.

5 **A national awakening** is needed. There has been one in virtually every century of the last 800 years – the last was in 1859-69. The steep decline of organized Christianity in the UK is almost unparalleled in Europe – especially among Methodists, Anglicans, United Reformed, Brethren and other Protestant denominations. Pray that Christians might grow passionate for God's honour, burdened to pray for revival and free from deadening negativism and materialism that pervade the churches.

6 **Christianity is increasingly marginalized** by a hostile media and public mood. Christian morality and belief in the uniqueness of Jesus are labelled "intolerant". Government regulations make it increasingly difficult to minister in the public arena. Many believe serious persecution is not far off. Pray that believers may recognize and address the decline of Christianity in the public sphere. Pray that they may recover confidence in the gospel and boldness and passion to share it – lovingly and unapologetically – with the majority who have little concept of its content.

7 **The Church of England** is deeply mired in crisis. It is the "mother" Church for the world's 81.6 million Anglicans. Anglicanism, the umbrella under which Anglo-Catholics, liberals and evangelicals uncomfortably co-exist, lacks unity and even basic fellowship over some fundamental theological issues. Fragmentation is evident over issues such as ordination of women and homosexuals, endorsement of same-sex unions, ecumenism and disestablishment. Globally, the rapid growth of non-Western evangelicals within the Church of England (particularly in the Fellowship of Confessing Anglicans) and the continued decline of the predominantly Western liberal wing further set these two ends of the Anglican spectrum resolutely against each other. Nationally, the Church lies trapped between being socially marginalized and being resented for its position of privilege as the state religion. Evangelicalism is a growing force and gaining centre stage in the Church of England. It accounts for 34% of UK's Anglicans and 50% of the UK's evangelicals, but less than 10% of all Anglicans regularly attend services. The charismatic movement also contributes to extensive renewal within the Church. Pray that Church leadership might regain a prophetic role and speak, in unity and with clear biblical authority, to a nation that is morally and spiritually adrift.

8 **There are signs of hope** – water these tender plants with prayer:

a) ***Traumatic social change*** and the devastating consequences of family breakdown, drifting identity, violence and fear for the future bring a new openness to consider spiritual solutions.

b) ***Renewal movements.*** Many pastors and congregations experienced charismatic renewal between the 1960s and 1990s, giving rise to a new family of churches. The New Churches grew fast and became significant spiritual forces in the nation and enlivened worship across the denominational spectrum. Their growth has since slowed. Nationwide, these changes have been stimulated by major transdenominational gatherings such as Spring Harvest, Soul Survivor, Greenbelt, New Wine and New Word Alive. But even these events are increasingly compartmentalized by sub-culture and theological persuasion.

c) ***New younger-generation movements*** are emerging with new approaches – culturally appropriate worship styles, prayer movements and outreach efforts. Notable groups – including 24-7Prayer, The Message Trust, Soul Survivor, Tribal Generation, NGM and many others – are springing up in different parts of the country.

d) ***The Alpha Course*** and Christianity Explored have spread across the country to nearly every denomination and around the world as hugely effective outreach programmes. These user-friendly introductory courses explain Christianity in a relaxed and informal environment. About 8,450 congregations used the Alpha Courses in 2008, with over 2.5 million individuals having completed one in the UK alone.

e) ***Evangelical generosity.*** Studies have shown that evangelical churchgoers give nine times as much to charity as do average Britons, even in the midst of the financial crisis.

9 **Evangelical Christianity** is no longer growing. Without immigration of evangelicals (from Africa in particular), decline would be pronounced. The prominent challenges are:

a) ***To maintain and increase unity*** in fellowship and vision. The Evangelical Alliance does much to encourage this and gives credibility to evangelicals in national life. The EA represents 74 denominations and 725 agencies and is a focal point for its 1.5 million constituents.

b) ***The widespread loss of confidence*** and certainty in the veracity of the gospel, in the uniqueness of Jesus and in models for church life and outreach. These are simultaneous with increasingly assertive and confident atheism and Islam. Initiatives for reformation, renewal and national outreach have been attempted since the 1990s, but few have had significant or lasting impact. Christians need to learn why they can be confident in their own faith and the truth thereof.

c) ***Cynicism*** about the Church's future and lack of spiritual ambition cripple enthusiasm for missions locally and overseas. Pray for restoration of vision and faith in God's ability to change Britain once again.

10 **Christian leadership** is under intense pressure – from increasingly demanding church members, from increasingly intense scrutiny by the public and from the lack of effective Bible teachers and expositors. Pray for effective discipling and training of new leaders; previous failure to develop a younger generation of leaders is now costing the Church dearly. There are 105 residential theological colleges offering 8,600 places of study. Pray that these may impart not only theological education, but also spirituality and world vision.

11 **Young people** are a source of great concern. Some studies claim greater spiritual openness, but others point to a largely negative view of religion and to ignorance or complete disinterest in even the concepts of sin and salvation. Despite greater than ever freedoms, unhappiness, suicide, self-harm and mental health problems have reached alarming levels. The UK "leads" Europe in most of the following categories: teenage sexual activity, sexually transmitted diseases, teen pregnancy, abortion, binge drinking, drug abuse, violent crime and non-participation in either school or the workplace. Poverty intensifies the problems and reduces the solutions for an increasingly desperate underclass. The breakdown of the traditional family unit and high levels of family dysfunction contribute greatly to this huge challenge. Pray for:

a) *Religious education (RE) teachers in schools.* By law, RE is a core subject. It is increasingly popular, but there is a shortage of well-trained teachers. And, religious education has shifted from instruction in the Christian faith to a relativistic comparative-religions class. Pray for Christians involved in this ministry and for meaningful ways of making the message of the gospel come alive.

b) *Effective discipling of young people.* Sunday school is a fading institution, and viable alternative models are lacking, even as "Millennials" demonstrate low commitment levels as a generational trait. Meanwhile, millions of children and youth are virtually untouched by the gospel; because of Christians' failure to adequately reach out and minister to young people, much of an entire generation is lost to the Church. Half of evangelical congregations have no specific children's ministry; the rate is probably even less for non-evangelical churches. Unsurprisingly, churches with vibrant youth/children's programmes tend to be growing churches.

c) *Youth movements.* Urban Saints, Scripture Union and **YFC** have long had significant impact, especially in secondary schools, few of which have live, outgoing witness from staff or student groups. Newer movements and conferences such as Soul Survivor, NewDay and Audacious are innovative and effective.

d) *Missions vision.* Few young people have much exposure to a vision for evangelism and missions. **OM**, World Horizons, **YWAM** and The Message Trust, along with several others, seek to redress this.

12 **Students in higher education** are exposed to great pressures. A largely godless, consumeristic and hedonistic younger generation is being formed by the secular system. Less than 2% of students are actively involved in church. Pray especially for a life of consistent and loving witness by Christian students; they are the ones best equipped to reach their own peers. Pray for:

a) *The Christian Union groups* among students, especially the more than two million in colleges and universities. Their growth and diversity are encouraging, the main ones being Agapé (**CCCI**), Navigators, Fusion and UCCF(**IFES**). The oldest and most widespread is the work of UCCF, with over 10,000 students involved in Christian Unions. Pray for mature, stable leadership and for effective support and advice from the 70 full-time workers and more than 60 volunteers. Pray also for solutions to the increasing challenge of maintaining a witness on campuses, which are ever more biased against Christianity.

b) *Overseas students.* There are about 400,000 international students in the UK – 80,000 from China alone – plus many thousands in English-language schools. Outreach to them is varied but too limited, and many return home without hearing the gospel. Friends International, UCCF(**IFES**), Navigators, COCM and others have ministry to them.

13 **Britain's contribution to world evangelization** and the Protestant missions movement in the last 220 years is unique, but interest is waning as the Church weakens. Fewer than one in six Protestant churches has missionaries serving on the field. Widespread misconceptions are that the job is largely completed or that efforts should be concentrated on Britain's needs. Pray these for the Church:

a) *A strengthened conviction* that all peoples need to hear the saving story of Jesus and enjoy the transformation only the gospel can bring. When churches lose the belief that souls can be lost for eternity, mission and evangelism suffer.

b) *A renewed commitment* by local congregations to participate in world evangelization, to pray out their members to areas of greatest need and to adequately care for those who go.

c) *An increase in recruitment* for missions; pray that the growth in short-term involvement may lead to increased long-term mission commitment and support.

d) *The coordinating role of Global Connections* (EMA) in promoting vision and cooperation among mission agencies and in local churches for world evangelization.

14 **The growing ethnic-minority populations** form a significant part of UK urban life. Some cities have large minority populations; in some areas, specific ethnic-minority communities form the largest single group. Active Christians number a higher proportion of some communities – such as African Caribbean, African and East Asian – than in the indigenous population. Others come from countries where the gospel is little known and entry of missionaries is impeded. Cultural distance, racial discrimination and even open hostility antagonize many minorities against what is falsely perceived to be "Christianity". Pray for:

a) *Local congregations* in multi-ethnic areas to open their doors, homes and hearts to this mission field on their doorsteps, and to find wise, loving and effective ways to make friendships, meet needs and win some for the Lord.

b) *More cross-cultural workers*, some called to train churches and others to minister to specific ethnic groups. Unique ministries already involved include South Asian Concern, **OM** (Turning Point and LifeHope) and missionaries linked with Interserve (Urban Vision), **ECM**, **MECO**, Crosslinks, **Christar**, **WEC**, World Harvest Mission, International Teams, ReachAcross, Naujavan and **CMS**, as well as some non-Western mission agencies.

c) *Better coordination of efforts* and research. Many ethnic-minority communities are completely unreached due to lack of information or awareness of their locations, populations and needs. The recently formed South Asian Evangelical Alliance (as part of the EA of the UK) provides such a forum for the UK's South Asian Christians; sadly, the African & Caribbean EA recently suspended its operations indefinitely.

d) *Outreach* that is bold and confident, but sensitive and culturally appropriate. Those from other religions face many issues and obstacles to accepting the gospel, including pressures from family and community and threats of rejection or violence. Pray that Christians will help those from ethnic-minority communities to follow Christ within their own cultural context as much as is possible.

e) *Effective use of resources.* **WEC**'s "SOON" broadsheet ministry reaches many, in English, French, Swahili, Portuguese and Pulaar. Kitab is an important Christian resource centre specializing in literature and resources on Islam and related issues. South Asian Concern's website is valuable for seekers from a South Asian background.

15 **Specific ethnic minority groups** that need intercession:

a) *South Asians,* the largest minority grouping, number over three million. They are too commonly ghettoized into ethnic enclaves. Growing numbers are coming to Christ from the Hindu and Sikh communities, but few from among Muslims; about 4% of all South Asians are Christian. The greatest needs are among the Kashmiri/Mirpuri Pakistani, Bangladeshi, Punjabi, Gujarati and Pathan communities.

b) *Caribbean and African peoples* – 17% of the population are church-going, a rate triple the national average. There are over 200 denominations; these churches were previously somewhat isolated from the evangelical mainstream, but multi-cultural churches are increasing. Competition for worshippers, however, can be an unhealthy factor in the way some of these churches relate. The needs for prayer are significant; poverty and undereducation are far higher for these peoples than for the general population. Half the families from a black or mixed background are single-parent families. The 100,000 Somalis are one of the UK's (and the world's) least-evangelized groups; thus far, little is being done to reach them.

c) *Middle Eastern and North African peoples.* Outreach is largely localized and sporadic. Many wealthy Arabs come to the UK as tourists, businessmen or students; some have come to faith. There are several Christian fellowships for Arabs and a few for Turks, Kurds and Iranians. The latter are quite responsive to the gospel (Elam Ministries, Interserve). Yemenis, Moroccans and Algerians are more recent arrivals and are largely unreached.

d) *The Chinese,* approaching 500,000 in number, came from Hong Kong and Vietnam in the past, but today most come from Mainland China as students and for business. Many thousands are trafficked or enter illegally into the country; most of these are subject to cruel working conditions. Chinese Overseas Christian Mission (COCM) has successful church planting and student ministries, as do **OMF** and **OM**. There are over 100 Chinese churches, and about 5% of Chinese are Christian.

e) ***The Jewish community*** is slowly eroding due to secularism (80% have no religious commitment to Judaism) and assimilation (through cultural and marital dilution). The proportion of strict Orthodox Jews is increasing due to higher birth rates. Many of the Jewish followers of Jesus, between 3,500 and 6,000, integrate into Gentile churches, though there are also possibly 20 fellowships of Messianic Jews. Pray for Church's Ministry Among Jewish People, Messianic Testimony, Christian Witness to Israel and the newer ministries, Jews for Jesus and Chosen People Ministries. Such ministries face opposition from the increasingly influential and strict Orthodox Jews, from liberal Christians and from an anti-proselytizing society in general.

16 **Muslims** now number two million and possibly more, with a high growth rate due to immigration and births. Those of Pakistani origin are the largest group; Bangladesh, India, the Middle East, Somalia and North Africa also contribute large numbers. Large-scale illegal immigration, Islamic terrorism, little effort to assimilate into British society and rapidly growing influence of strident militant Islam all create a wary and even fearful majority. These, coupled with harsh anti-terrorism measures, drive alienated Muslims into more radical forms of Islam, creating a vicious circle. The number of mosques has increased nearly five-fold in 20 years; hardline Islamic sects control half of these. Muslims see the conversion of England to Islam as a key strategy for winning the West. London is now a hub for Islam, especially for extremist organizations. Pray for the breakdown of cultural and social barriers on both sides and for opportunities to share the gospel.

17 **Christian media ministries** include:

a) ***Christian literature and Bibles.*** Few nations have available such an extensive range of Christian and evangelical literature as well as Bible versions. The Gideons International has distributed over 37 million NTs and Bibles in its 60 years of ministry in the UK. There are over 400 Christian bookstores and over 100 Christian publishers, although these ministries are suffering a downturn of late. The Bible Societies – with ministries of Bible translation, publication and distribution in Britain and around the world – also have a wide range of catalytic ministries to stimulate Christian growth. BookAid has a remarkable ministry exporting one million donated surplus and second-hand Christian books annually to poorer countries. Pray for these ministries and for Christians to become more avid readers.

b) ***Christian broadcasting.*** Christians are free to own and run national-level Christian radio and TV stations. Christian radio will increase, since local licences are now granted. Premier Radio has national coverage via FM and satellite and is the most accessible of Christian broadcasting ministries. Pray for wisdom and balance in the face of opportunities. Many Christians are active in secular broadcasting as well as in religious programming on national radio and TV – millions view "Songs of Praise" every week on TV and online. Pray for positive impact in an environment often hostile to outspoken Christian faith.

c) ***New media,*** such as myriad Christian Internet sites, digital content for mobile phones and even electronic/online congregations all provide further opportunities for a tech-savvy and church-wary generation. Pray for effectiveness; pray also for those impacted by such media to plug into means for them to be discipled.

England

Geography 🌐
Area 130,400 sq km.

Population 51,460,000; 395 people/sq km.
Capital London 8,631,325. **Other major cities** Manchester 2.3 million; West Midlands/Birmingham 2.3mill; West Yorkshire 1.5m; Tyneside 891,000; Liverpool 819,000; Nottingham 666,000; Sheffield 647,000.

1 **England is the most secular** of the four countries that comprise the UK. The steady decline in belief and church attendance is of deep concern. Only 6% of people regularly attend church; those who do attend rarely engage with the unbelieving majority. Notional Christianity is giving way to atheism as the main barrier to true faith; the trappings of inherited cultural forms of Christianity are being discarded. This presents both a great challenge and a new opportunity for a fresh start to the re-evangelization of England. Pray that the Holy Spirit may break into lives and bring a sense of the reality of God and the truth of the gospel.

2 **London** is one of the world's hub cities for finance, travel, politics, culture and such. The spiritual life of London also has global impact. As the destination of a high proportion of the inflow of migrants over the last 50 years, London has a strong claim to be the world's most international city. Pray for these:

a) Church life in London, in many senses, is rich and vibrant. The percentage of Londoners (especially 20- and 30-somethings) who attend church is higher than the national average. London's churches are on average twice as large, more diverse and more engaged in outreach and projects of many kinds. London offers a host of vibrant church options – large Pentecostal churches (especially among Africans), flagship churches (such as Kensington Temple, Holy Trinity Brompton, All Souls and Hillsong), charismatic networks with large numbers of smaller congregations (Pioneer, Ichthus, New Frontiers) and even house church networks. Even so, in London, the majority are unchurched, other religions are assertive and growing and churches would be in notable decline were it not for London's many church-going immigrants.

b) Ethnic minorities, increasingly, are becoming the majority in many boroughs. In London, over 50 nationalities have communities of over 10,000 people, and every nationality in the world is represented in some number. Nearly 60% of church-goers in London are ethnic minorities. These provide incredible opportunities for witness and evangelism of otherwise unreached people groups.

3 **England's inner cities** are in threat of becoming physical and spiritual wastelands, riddled with drugs and crime. Dying congregations, closed churches and churches converted into Muslim mosques, Hindu temples or Sikh *gurdwaras* are commonplace. Most white evangelicals moved to comfortable, middle-class suburbs and towns a generation ago. Whites trapped in inner-city poverty and joblessness usually have fewer prospects than even their ethnic-minority neighbours. Pray that God may raise up an army of workers with effective ways of meeting the many needs of these impoverished and often troubled areas. Ministries such as The Message Trust (in Manchester) and Street Pastors (in many cities) are brilliant examples of what can be done.

Northern Ireland

Geography 🌍

Area 14,100 sq km.
Population 1,775,000; 126 people/sq km.
Capital Belfast 737,000.

Politics 🗙

The problems of Northern Ireland today are a continuation of the centuries-old tension between the Celtic Irish and Anglo-Saxon Scots-English. It is partly a historical coincidence that the former are Catholic and the latter largely Protestant. The partitioning of Ireland between the 26 counties of the South and the 6 counties of Ulster in the north did not solve the problem, since a notable minority of Catholic Irish in Ulster agitated for union with the south. Their civil rights campaign in the late 1960s degenerated into civil violence waged by extremist IRA and "Loyalist" factions. The impact on social, economic and political life in the Province and the UK was large, resulting in over 3,600 deaths. The 1998 political agreement led to a cease-fire, Ireland-wide consultative structures and a power-sharing government in Belfast. The peace that has remained largely intact since then significantly benefits the economy.

1 **Peace has prevailed in Northern Ireland** since the 1998 Good Friday Agreement and especially since a power-sharing agreement in 2007. Only a small number of dissidents persist, but through them, the threat of violence remains. Greater risks to long-term peace are the mistrust and resentment that can remain in people's hearts. Pray for repentance and forgiveness of past transgressions and crimes and for reconciliation between communities. Pray for those who work to uphold the peace, especially politicians and police.

2 **Segregation and sectarianism remain,** despite the prevalent peace. Separate confessions, separate churches, separate schools, separated communities keep Ulster a divided land. Pray that both Catholics and Protestants may take initiative in instigating reconciliation. Northern Ireland's history has long been used as an example of religion's destructive influence; pray that it may become a testimony of faith's power to heal and restore.

3 **Church attendance is in decline,** even though it remains higher in Northern Ireland than in the rest of the UK. The frequency of attendance is dropping, even as the number rises of those who claim to be non-religious. As elsewhere in the West, materialism and hedonism grip the hearts and souls of many. However, within a 50 km radius of Belfast is one of the highest concentrations of evangelical churches in the world, and most Protestant congregations remain stoutly evangelical. Pray that the emptiness of the "new paganism" might be exposed and that churches would be able to offer a dynamic alternative full of life and relevance.

4 **The missionary burden** of Northern Ireland's churches is higher than elsewhere in the UK. Pray that this generosity in giving of money and personnel for world evangelization may continue!

Scotland

Geography 🌍

Area 78,800 sq km.
Population 5,169,000; 66 people/sq km.
Capital Edinburgh 482,000. **Other major cities** Glasgow 1.2 million; Aberdeen 201,000.

Politics 🗡

After nearly 300 years of representation only in London, Scotland re-established its own parliament in 1998. A strong minority (and a slim majority in some polls) continue to press for full independence within the EU.

1 **Scotland faces a potent cocktail of social ills.** Nearly half of all children are born out of wedlock. Alcohol and drug abuse are high. The country has the inauspicious title of the worst-performing Western European nation, based on economy, employment, health and education. Increasingly, Christian groups are engaging these problems; pray that the transforming impact of the gospel may be evident through loving witness and ministry.

2 **Revivals in past centuries,** localized revivals of the northeast coast in 1925 and Lewis in the Hebrides in the 1950s – as well as notable missionaries such as David Livingstone, Robert Moffatt, Mary Slessor and Eric Liddell – brought blessing to Scotland and the world. May new revivals and a new wave of God's servants make a great impact on this land; 27.5% of Scots claimed no religion in the last census.

3 **The Church of Scotland** is Presbyterian in structure and is the established church. Membership is in steep decline – half of what it was 50 years ago – and attendance a tiny fraction of membership. There is a shortage of clergy; many current clergy are out of touch with the needs of their congregations. Nominalism is widespread, liberal theology still dominant and Freemasonry influential. Still, there are stirrings of new life through those evangelicals who remain. Pray for the Church of Scotland to return to its biblical roots and to the radical but biblically grounded faith of its early martyrs.

4 **Church growth** is evident among the non-institutional groups – Pentecostals, Baptists, Brethren and the Salvation Army. Pray for the effective re-evangelization of Scotland. The Aberdeen area has the highest percentage of non-church-goers.

Wales

Geography 🌍

Area 20,800 sq km.
Population 2,990,000; 144 people/sq km.

Capital Cardiff 346,000. **Other major city** Swansea 268,000.

Politics 🗡

Wales has had a national assembly since 1998, but for the nationalists, this falls far short of their dream of Welsh independence.

U

1 **Economic changes** have had a profound impact on the nation. The decline of the coal and slate industries led to much depopulation and depression in industrialized areas. These, coupled with the acceptance of a social gospel, have led to empty chapels and a spiritually hardened population. Pray for those church leaders and fellowships with a clear vision to witness and serve faithfully, many of them in hard and unreceptive areas.

2 **Wales is known** as the land of revivals and the land of song. From early in the 18th Century, Wales experienced a consistent series of revivals, the last of these occurring in 1904. Since then, decline in church attendance and closure of churches in Wales have been higher than in any other part of the UK. Although many congregations remain, most are small churches of 25 people or less. National weekly attendance of religious services is 7% and only 3.5% among under-30s. In recent years, though, pockets of growth have appeared, especially within evangelical congregations that both proclaim the gospel and demonstrate it through community involvement. Pray that revival may come again and that the entire country will again sing the praises of Jesus.

3 **Wales struggles** to preserve its own language and culture. About 22% of the population speak Welsh, and Welsh-language education is flourishing. With ageing congregations, however, the decline in Welsh-speaking churches is dramatic. Pray that the Holy Spirit might breathe upon the Welsh culture and revive congregations to again be a blessing to the world.

Isle of Man

Geography 🌏
Area 588 sq km.
Population 80,000; 136 people/sq km.
Capital Douglas 26,000. **Pop under 15 yrs** 17%.

Politics ☒
The Isle of Man is a self-governing, British Crown dependency. It is governed by Tynwald, arguably the world's oldest continuous parliament. However, it relies upon the UK for defence and foreign relations.

1 **The Isle of Man has a long Christian tradition,** but just as in the UK, nominalism is rife and non-religion is growing. Pray that the Church will continue to strive to bring people back into the fold and that the Isle of Man might see an awakening.

Channel Islands

Geography 🌏
Area 194 sq km.
Population 150,000; 773 people/sq km.
Capital Jersey: St Helier 28,310; Guernsey: St

Peter Port 16,488 (UN data). **Pop under 15 yrs** 16%.

Politics ☒
The Channel Islands are an archipelago of British Crown dependencies, divided into the two separately administered bailiwicks, Jersey and Guernsey; the Bailiwick of Guernsey includes the islands of Guernsey, Alderney, Herm and Sark. Though not part of the UK, both bailiwicks rely on Britain for defence and international representation.

1 **Guernsey and especially Jersey rely upon the financial sector** for their economic growth, leading to accusations they are used as tax havens. Relative prosperity and an emphasis on material wealth have inevitably blunted the spiritual life of the islands; pray for an awakening.

2 **The island of Sark** was the last feudal state in Europe. In 2008, they held their first democratic elections, which led to a great deal of controversy and to the closing of many businesses. Though all businesses reopened within a few weeks, the economy was negatively impacted, and the political situation remains somewhat uncertain. Pray that the island will be able to build a just government while continuing to protect its delicate ecosystem.

U

South Asian 0.7%. 25 peoples.
Southeast Asian 0.7%. 22 peoples.
North American Indigenous 0.6%. 126 peoples, 550 recognized tribes.
Other 1.1%. Including African, Turkic, Iranian-Median, Tibetan-Himalayan, Pacific Islander, Malay affinity blocs.
Literacy 99% (functional literacy 85%). Official language English. The growing Spanish-speaking Hispanic population is 11.2% of the population and numbers 34 million. All indigenous languages 176, of which 77 are close to extinction. Numerous languages and dialects still used by immigrants from all continents. About 13% of the population use a language other than English in the home. Indigenous languages with Scriptures 17Bi 26NT 61por 12w.i.p.

United States of America

North America

Geography 🌐

Area 9,529,063 sq km. The world's third-largest nation in area and population.

Population		Ann Gr	Density
2010	317,641,087	0.97%	33/sq km
2020	346,153,494	0.82%	36/sq km
2030	369,981,139	0.62%	39/sq km

Immigration rates are high, with an estimated 11.2 million undocumented immigrants and 1 million legally naturalized annually. The only industrialized nation with large projected-population increases, largely due to immigration. **Capital** Washington, DC 4,459,904. **Other major conurbations** New York 19.4 million; Los Angeles 12.8mill; Chicago 9.2m; Miami/Fort Lauderdale 5.7m; Philadelphia 5.6m; Dallas/Fort Worth 5.0m; Atlanta 4.7m; Houston 4.6m; Boston 4.6m; Detroit 4.2m; and 32 other conurbations over 1m. **Urbanites** 82%. **Pop under 15 yrs** 20%. **Life expectancy** 79.1 yrs.

Peoples 👪

A nation of immigrants, with the greatest ethnic-origin diversity of any nation in history. Thirty-one ethnicities have a population over 1 million in the USA.
US Caucasian 58.1%. The result of a melting pot of many peoples.
Latin-Caribbean American 14.7%. 25 peoples. US Hispanics 9.5%; Creole 1.5%; Mestizo 1.4%; Puerto Rican 0.8%.
African-American 12.2%. 8 groups.
Eurasian 6.6%. 63 peoples. Irish 1.0%.
Jews 1.8%. 7 groups.
East Asian 1.6%. Korean 0.7%; Chinese(7) 0.7%.
Arab 1.4%. Lebanese Arab 1.0%; 17 others.
Malay 1.1%. Filipino 1.0%; 8 others.

Economy 📈

Still the world's largest and most diverse economy, driven by technology, industry, natural resources, agriculture and services. Yet most gains in household income since 1975 have gone to the most wealthy 20%, increasing the gap between rich and poor. The 2008-2009 recession has to a large degree also caused many other economies to suffer. The world's largest importer; the world's largest debtor, for both public and private debt, both external and internal. The USA accounts for 25% of the world's GDP and up to 50% of the world's military spending. The world's most entrepreneurial economy and society.
HDI Rank 13th/182. **Public debt** 60.2% of GDP. **Income/person** $47,440.

Politics 🗳

Independent from Britain in 1776 as a federal republic. The number of states increased from the original 13 to 50 as the nation expanded westward across the continent and the Pacific Ocean. The strong democratic tradition, emphasis on private initiative and civil liberties have helped to make the nation a world leader. Checks and balances built into the political system limit abuse of power but can also stymie meaningful political progress. The USA emerged from WWII as the leading industrial and military power in the world, but for 40 years was in Cold War confrontation with the USSR. Post-Cold War and post-9/11 realities see the emergence of a complex, multi-polar world order of new alliances in which the USA no longer has the same dominance. The threat of terrorism at home and abroad has seen US forces increasingly engaged overseas, a foreign policy that generates significant backlash from some parts of the world.

Religion 🙏

Freedom of religion is written into the constitution. The principle of separation of church and state, intended to protect both, is misused by

U

liberal and anti-Christian minorities to attempt to remove the public exercise of religion, while some on the far right continue to advocate something resembling a Christian theocracy.

Religions	Pop %	Population	Ann Gr
Christian	77.62	246,553,012	0.5%
Non-religious	16.50	52,410,779	3.3%
Jewish	1.65	5,241,078	-0.8%
Muslim	1.63	5,177,550	1.9%
Other/New Religions	0.77	2,445,836	6.1%
Buddhist/Chinese	0.75	2,382,308	2.6%
Ethnoreligionist	0.46	1,461,149	2.3%
Hindu	0.42	1,334,093	2.0%
Baha'i	0.11	349,405	-3.8%
Sikh	0.09	285,877	3.4%

Christians	Denoms	Pop %	Affiliates	Ann Gr
Protestant	748	27.51	87,389,000	0.0%
Independent	223	7.81	24,803,000	1.5%
Anglican	2	0.65	2,068,000	-0.6%
Catholic	61	21.19	67,298,000	0.8%
Orthodox	75	1.67	5,307,000	0.8%
Marginal	361	3.64	11,577,000	0.6%
Unaffiliated		17.47	55,492,000	-0.6%
Doubly affiliated		-2.35	-7,450,000	0.0%

Churches	MegaBloc	Congs	Members	Affiliates
Catholic Church	C	28,223	46,286,208	67,115,001
Southern Baptist Conv	P	45,000	16,228,438	20,750,000
Nat Baptist Conv, USA	P	31,000	9,254,237	10,920,000
United Methodist Ch	P	33,332	6,283,190	7,853,987
Latter-day Saints	M	12,433	4,177,651	5,974,041
Evang Luth Ch in Amer	P	9,870	3,484,126	4,633,887
Nat Bapt Conv of Amer	P	12,400	3,442,623	4,200,000
Ch of God in Christ	P	15,330	1,244,745	4,145,000
Jehovah's Witnesses	M	13,100	1,114,009	2,930,000
Assemblies of God	P	12,400	1,685,873	2,899,702
Presbyterian Ch (USA)	P	12,644	2,275,962	2,844,952
Full Gospel Networks	P	8,300	1,647,059	2,800,000
African Meth Epis Ch	I	8,423	1,895,105	2,710,000
LCMS	P	5,325	1,757,405	2,337,349
Prog Nat Bapt Conv	P	1,100	1,909,836	2,330,000
Episcopal Ch in USA	A	6,750	1,231,911	2,057,292
Amer Bapt Chs, USA	P	4,912	1,331,127	1,705,000
Pente Assem of World	I	1,800	1,231,343	1,650,000
Chs of Christ (Non-ins)	P	13,000	1,058,442	1,630,000
United House of Prayer	I	150	1,000,000	1,600,000
Greek Orth, N&S Am	O	580	1,200,000	1,500,000
Afr Meth Epis Zion Ch	I	2,703	1,000,000	1,400,000
Chr Chs/Chs of Christ	P	5,260	860,714	1,205,000
Orthodox Ch in Am	O	660	804,196	1,150,000
Seventh-day Adventist	P	4,700	860,150	1,144,000
Baptist Bible Fell Int	P	2,424	678,788	1,120,000
United Ch of Christ	P	4,043	889,353	1,111,691
Ch of God (Cleveland)	P	6,590	765,835	1,072,169
Chr Meth Episcopal	I	3,700	520,958	870,000
Ch of the Nazarene	P	5,070	550,000	825,000
United Pente Ch	P	4,400	540,000	810,000
Other denoms[3,409]		209,656	19,658,266	33,238,194
Doubly affiliated				7,450,000
Total Christians[3,483]		**525,278**	**136,867,550**	**191,082,265**

Several independent polls and surveys indicate around 78% of Americans self-identifying as Christian. The sum of population affiliated to all churches only comes to 60%. There are many thousands of congregations that are independent from any formal denominational ties.

TransBloc	Pop %	Population	Ann Gr
Evangelicals			
Evangelicals	28.9	91,764,554	0.8%
Renewalists			
Charismatics	19.8	62,764,236	2.4%
Pentecostals	6.8	21,682,183	1.1%

Numbers reflect those affiliated to some form of organized Christianity. Some polls indicate evangelical identification as high as 35% and up to 36% for charismatic identification. Such figures cannot be substantiated from denominational data – there is a vast difference between identification in surveys/polls and documented affiliation, itself a telling insight into American religious dynamics.

Missionaries from USA
P,I,A 93,500 long-term: 50,000 in USA. International: 700 agencies sending to 211 countries.

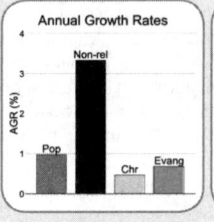

Annual Growth Rates

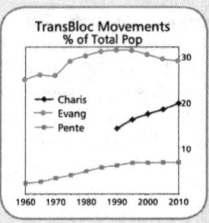

TransBloc Movements % of Total Pop

Answers to Prayer

1 **A rich legacy of Christian history** has profoundly shaped the USA. From the nation's early days through today, no other country has been so strongly influenced by biblical Christianity. The national percentage of evangelicals lies at 28.9%, and is spread throughout all major ethnic groups and strata of society.

U

2 **Give praise for the emergence of new expressions** of Christian and evangelical faith that take seriously both spirituality and holistic ministry and that are based on authentic practice of faith, worship and engagement of the community. They tend to possess a greater commitment to social action and justice. They are not defined by political partisanship or denominational barriers. There are growing pains, but these movements offer a fresh new take on Christian life in a culture that needs such authenticity.

③ The continued rise of the newer charismatic and Pentecostal movements, across the spectrum of Christian megablocs and denominations, from less than 10% of the population in 1970 to nearly 20% in 2010. Pentecostal/charismatic groups make up most of the growing Christian denominations in the USA, and charismatic ministries have an impact far beyond their immediate sphere. New networks and movements of churches and Christians align together based around renewal and revival rather than on denominationalism. Millions in both historic and newer denominations have had their faith rejuvenated; many of these would not identify themselves as "evangelical", but they possess a living and profound faith.

④ Prayer networks, movements and resources keep growing. Although too many to mention, some of the more notable ones are The Mission America Coalition, International House of Prayer, the National Pastors' Prayer Network, See You At The Pole, Lydia Fellowship and Seek God for the City. 24/7 prayer initiatives are springing up in many different places and among different Christian traditions.

⑤ The growth and maturation of minority churches. Dynamic, confident and active, these black, Hispanic and Asian churches play their part not just in ministering to their own people but also in reaching entire communities and helping shape American Christianity. Of particular praiseworthiness are the powerful missionary-sending movements among Asian-American churches and the birth of the same among black and Latino churches.

⑥ The nationwide impact of parachurch movements.

a) Countless ministries combat the evils of society and minister to those broken by these evils – drug abuse, promiscuity and pornography, crime, abortion and abuse. Christian opposition to these ills is often unfairly caricatured in the media, twisting the image of both Christianity and of the USA. But believers are at the forefront of the battle against poverty and structures of sin. Pray for the multiplicity of networks and bodies that have sprung up, that they may be effective in both loving those who are hurting and opposing structures of sin.

b) Movements that impact the wider world, including the work of Billy Graham, probably *the* evangelical of the 20th Century, who preached to live audiences totalling over 200 million. Graham's great support for conferences promoting world evangelization helped spark such strategic movements as the Lausanne Congress on World Evangelization in 1974. The AD2000 and Beyond movement also saw unprecedented attention and commitment to church planting and evangelism among the unreached. In the 21st Century, a multiplicity of movements and initiatives from the USA have had a wonderful impact on the global Church and the wider mission movement.

c) Renewal among Catholics – around one-fourth of US Catholics are charismatic, a figure that rises to 50% for Hispanic US Catholics. Catholics are an influential force in America, but they face a rapidly changing religious context within US Catholicism and without.

Challenges for Prayer

① The 21st Century sees a different role for a different America. The end of the Cold War, the aftermath of 9/11 and subsequent invasions of Afghanistan and Iraq, and the emergence (or re-emergence) of other nations spell the end of the USA as the world's only superpower. The moral authority of the USA was undermined by its response to 9/11, its economic primacy is increasingly questionable and its diplomatic authority, while still immense, is now one of several global leaders. There is much to pray for:

a) Domestic politics saw a definitive change as President Obama replaced President Bush. Both claim to be Christian believers; each has been highly divisive in his own way; these illustrate the intractable nature and interminable polarity of US politics more than anything else. Pray that politicians and the populace might overcome some fundamental differences and work together to see justice, fairness and righteousness exalted in the nation.

b) The world's perception of America plummeted as it exerted its military and economic powers unilaterally in questionable ways. Yet the USA still has a vital, even God-ordained, part to play in the theatre of nations – provider of stability and aid, peacekeeper, proponent of democracy, military/economic superpower and still a world leader in almost every area that matters. Pray that this solemn role might be fulfilled from a platform of selflessness and service to humanity.

2 **America's massive cultural and social influence** makes it the world's greatest force for good and its greatest purveyor of sin. The generosity of aid and development, the defence of human rights and opposition to tyranny, the many breakthroughs in technology and media, the great levellers of education, information and capitalism have all made the world a better place. These are in contrast to the insensitive cultural imperialism, selfish individualism, unbridled corporate greed and exportation of immorality (such as pornography, casual violence and shallow materialism) that are foisted upon the world. America's appetite for illicit drugs and massive consumption of fossil fuels cause wars abroad, prop up corrupt regimes and inflict suffering on indigenous peoples of other lands. Pray that God might shape this nation to be a greater force for good and destroy the structures of sin that pollute much of the world.

3 **America's Christian legacy** is undeniable and foundational to its identity. The Pilgrim Fathers were determined to establish a land in which they were free to exercise their Christian faith. On that foundation developed one of the largest and most dynamic Christian movements in history. In the USA are 17.6% of the Protestants in the world, 16.8% of the evangelicals and still a significant proportion of all the world's foreign missionaries. Christian values incubated in American society shaped modern democracy, human rights and economic development. Furthermore, generosity, evangelistic vitality and ability to dream big are major factors in the surge of gospel progress. Pray that these may be maintained.

4 **The spiritual heritage of the USA is being attacked** by an unholy alliance of human- ist, atheist, New Age and homosexual agendas. They exploit their influence in the media to disparage Christians and dismantle all they can of anything Christian in public life. They exploit constitutionally-provided free speech while denying the same right to the Christian viewpoint. Freedom of religion is becoming freedom from religion. The concept of "tolerance" is abused to silence truth and promote anti-Christian values. Pray that Christians in America – still a sizeable majority – would be able to speak the truth in love and retain both their Christian legacy and the free speech enabled by it. While this will involve many battles, legal and ideological, pray that these would be conducted with Christlike attitudes and conduct.

5 **The religious canvas of American life** is being repainted before our eyes. This happens both in the wider framework and within the Church.

a) *The introduction and growth of world religions* accelerate through immigration. Post- modernity and permissiveness encourage every expression of spirituality imaginable, healthy and unhealthy. Since 1990, there has been a pronounced decline in the overt affiliation to organized Christianity. This loss is not to other religions or new religious movements so much as a rejection of all organized religion – the non-religious bloc nearly doubled from 9% in 1990 to 16.5% in 2010. Almost all of the largest Protestant denominations declined as a proportion to the total population from 2000 to 2010.

b) *Shifts within Christianity itself* have transformed the landscape. While most denominations struggle to even maintain their numbers, post-denominational movements thrive. These are expressed mostly through megachurches and their networks and satellite churches, and through the burgeoning house church/simple church movement, both of which account for millions of believers. Pray that the Church might recognize these shifts and call out to God to revitalize and revive, equipping the Church to once more transmit the truth and power of the gospel to the entire nation.

6 **The American Church needs** *revival* – not the slick mass evangelism and theatrics associated with the word, but true revival with conviction of sin, repentance and an outpouring of the Holy Spirit. More often than not, the public face of Christianity turns people away from Jesus rather than drawing them to Him. The gospel is often little more than a self-help philosophy. Thank God for the pockets where revival is happening; pray that it may spread. These are some of the prayer challenges for the 21st Century Church:

a) *Notional Christianity* illustrates a failure of discipleship. If all of the US's self-proclaimed believers were to actually practice their faith, the transformation in society would be incredible. Instead, a pick-and-choose spirituality and inconsistent application of Jesus' teachings yield a disconnect between how Christians live and what the Bible instructs.

b) Syncretism is as common in America as anywhere. In the US's version, biblical Christianity is mixed with hyper-individualism, consumeristic materialism, moral relativism and national pride, creating a dangerous strain of faith that justifies selfishness, immorality and hubris. Pray for the ability to distinguish between what is scriptural and what is cultural.

c) The need for biblical holiness in a time when Christians display little difference from non-Christians in values and lifestyle – this applies to divorce, sexual morality and attitudes toward finance. Image supersedes character in appraising giftedness. The succession of high-profile failures of Christian leaders in the Church and in politics undermines the gospel. Spiritual outpourings in Florida have blessed millions, but left just as many hurt, confused and disillusioned due to lack of holiness and discernment by Christian leaders. Pray that Christians may recapture the sense of being set apart, and then repent of carnality and change their ways of thinking and living.

d) Spiritual unity. The Church in the USA is conditioned to accept divisions and schisms. Churches split and split again on issues both weighty and petty. Homosexuality, gender roles, universalism, Bible versions, spiritual gifts, eschatology, prosperity theology, creation/evolution and countless other issues serve to divide believers – while issues of world evangelization are sidelined. Pray for an earnest seeking after God's priorities, and pray that, through love and grace, a sensitive and balanced handling of difficult areas might be found.

e) Church life, worship and leadership demand, in many instances, a revolutionary shift toward organic expressions of fellowship and away from showy spirituality. Pastors are often required to function as CEOs more than as shepherds. Worship and preaching can become performances rather than fellowship. Many disillusioned Christians opt for emerging church expressions or for house church movements or they simply practice their faith alone. Pray for the development of both the laity and the ordained such that those so gifted might serve God's people effectively; pray that church culture might become a pathway rather than an obstacle to seeing the body of Christ built up to full maturity.

f) Leadership training possibilities abound. The variety and number of theological training possibilities defies full analysis! In the USA and Canada, there are over 2,000 recognized institutions that award theological degrees. These institutions graduate 30,000-50,000 students each year, most of whom desire to impact the nation or the world with a Christ-centric worldview. The Association for Bible Higher Education includes 200 accredited evangelical colleges; the Association of Theological Schools, 250. Pray that training would shape biblically-minded leaders who include the Great Commission and prayer as core elements of their ministry. Pray also for flexibility and innovation in leadership training, fitted for the times in which we live.

7 **Christian interaction with society** must be re-examined; believers are not making the impact they should. God is birthing many collaborative citywide movements that seek to make a Kingdom impact through unity, prayer and ministry. Issues to cover in prayer are these:

a) Christians must engage even more deeply with public life. The American Church has a rich history of biblical activism; withdrawal today from wider society to form a Christian subculture is not the solution. The school system, the prison system, the health care system, the welfare system, the entire political system – all of these need committed believers striving for the best for the nation and its neediest people. A spectrum of evangelical groups work for social change, including the National Association of Evangelicals, Mission America Coalition, Sojourners, WVI, Prison Fellowship, Christian Community Development Association, Evangelicals for Social Action and many others. Pray for balance, wisdom and long-term involvement of Christians as salt and light in society.

b) Evangelical Christianity's image is associated – wrongly – with white, middle-class, right-wing sensibilities, and evangelicals are caught up in strident, resource-sapping "culture wars" over justifiably important issues. Yet, the evangelical community does not adequately demonstrate God's compassion for the poor, the homeless, for widows and orphans, for immigrants and for society's most vulnerable. Praise God that emerging ministries are redressing the balance – addressing very real human needs as Scripture clearly commands while affirming biblical views on sexuality and the sanctity of life.

8 **This generation of young people** is both the most privileged and the most damaged. Humanistic and New Age philosophies, spiritual confusion, moral relativism, broken families, sexual permissiveness, drug and alcohol abuse, mindless violence, widespread acceptance of the occult and callous self-absorption combine to reap a bitter harvest. Most young people, even Christian ones, do not understand the meaning of following Christ. Two-thirds believe that all religions ultimately pray to the same God. Organizations such as **OM**, **YWAM**, **CCCI**, Teen Challenge and others instill the truth into teens and make a great impact on the world. God is also raising a new generation of movements for this century – pray for YouthQuake Live, Teen Mania, The Call, International House of Prayer and others. Without a decisive work of God's Spirit, this generation could be America's most broken.

9 **Student ministries continue to play a vital role.** Movements such as InterVarsity Christian Fellowship (**IFES**), Navigators, **CCCI**, Campus Outreach, Chi Alpha, Campus America, Campus Church Net, SVM2 and others combine to generate effective outreach, discipleship and prayer on campuses. The large Urbana conferences of InterVarsity, The Traveling Team and other ministries challenge many students with the needs of a lost world. The ministries of Navigators and **CCCI** have diversified into a wide range of activities in the USA and around the world. The Passion conferences profoundly impact the lives of many thousands of students every year. It is in their college years that the largest percentage of Christians fall away; yet, student movements have been at the heart of almost every revival and missions movement in America's history.

10 **The 38-million-strong African-American community** suffered immensely due to its origins in slavery and to subsequent racial discrimination. The civil rights movement and the election of the first black president have achieved great change in attitudes and awareness, but for many the cycle of unemployment, poverty, family instability and crime is unbroken. Pray for:

a) *Young people at risk.* Over half of inner-city black males fail to complete secondary school. Many are in prison or in gangs. Poverty, drugs and violence are rampant. Murder is the major cause of death for inner-city, African-American males ages 15 to 34. Pray for an expression of Christian faith that enables these men to leave their shackles and find meaning, belonging and fulfilment in Christ.

b) *African-American Muslims,* whose numbers have rapidly grown up to two million – most of these from a Christian background. Sunnis account for the largest proportion; some small but vocal minorities belong to Black nationalist groups and to the Nation of Islam organization. Most were drawn to Islam as a result of failings in the Church. Pray for effective and loving outreach to them.

c) *Black churches.* More than any other race in the USA, African-Americans are likely to be Christian. Many of the largest and most vigorous evangelical churches are Black, but they are often isolated from mainstream evangelical Christianity and from meaningful involvement in missions. Pray for a unity of believers that transcends ethnicity. Pray for a new move of the Spirit of God in these churches.

d) *Community impact.* African-American churches have always had a strong redemptive influence in their communities. This is increasing as congregations now join to effect deliberate and strategic transformation in the neediest areas.

11 **Hispanics are now the US's largest minority.** Predominantly from Mexico, they have immigrated in huge numbers, not always legally. Around 68% are Catholic, but 23% of Hispanics are Protestant or Independent, and this number is growing rapidly. Fully 40% of Hispanic evangelicals in the USA converted from Catholicism, largely due to evangelical services being oriented toward their language, culture and personal needs. Nearly half of Hispanic Catholics identify with the charismatic movement. All these factors combine to make Hispanics a powerful religious bloc with a living, dynamic faith. As immigrants, many struggle with poverty and the breakup of traditional family structures – 50% of Hispanic children are born out of wedlock. Pray for the effective discipleship of the nearly 50 million Hispanics in the USA; many of them eventually return to their homelands as highly effective missionaries.

12 **Native Americans,** also called American Indians, have suffered intensely through centuries of encounters with white people. Before European contact, Native Americans numbered at least 20 million; by 1890, only 250,000 remained – most perished through diseases brought by Europeans. Through ruthless colonization and a long string of treaties and promises made and broken by whites, the natives lost almost all their lands, identity, heritage, culture and self-respect. Forced resettlement onto arid, fruitless lands helped create a dependency on the federal government. Today, hopelessness, poverty, disease, alcoholism, suicide, abuse and unem-

U

ployment are common. Indigenous culture is being revived and demands for reparation are meeting with success. Pray for these:

a) **The flourishing of Christianity among Native Americans.** The failure by missions to enculturate the gospel, the imposition of European religious forms, the paternalistic and often cruel treatment of natives by the missions and the collusion of missionaries with the federal government all undermined the potential impact of the gospel. Today, perhaps only 5% of Native Americans are born again. Culturally appropriate ministry, development of indigenous forms of Christian worship and attention to the important processes of healing and deliverance are yielding fruit. Native Americans are realizing that they can be both Christian and Native American.

b) **The full reconciliation of native and immigrant peoples.** This goes far beyond apologies and financial reparations for wrongs done generations ago. True repentance by white Americans and true forgiveness by American Indians, when genuine, are usually precursors to great spiritual breakthrough.

c) **Bible translation** has regained importance as local languages are revived. Over 50 languages (and many more dialects) are in common use, and SIL and others have teams working in 27.

d) **An indigenous movement of the gospel** that will complete the evangelization of all 550 recognized tribes. God is raising up native American ministries to reach their own; Wiconi International, Eagles' Wings Ministry, Indian Life Ministries and The Native American Resource Network are just a few. First Nations Monday is a multifaceted prayer network for and by the US's indigenous peoples.

e) **The indigenous peoples of Alaska** have retained their identity, but their subsistence lifestyle places them at odds with the modern world and with the degradation of their environment. Today, many evangelical missions – such as **SEND**, Interact Ministries, Avant, Evangelical Covenant Church and Arctic Barnabas – work effectively in partnership, a sharp contrast to the demarcations of a century ago. The rigours of wilderness isolation, marked by vast distances accessible only by aircraft, and a harsh Arctic environment complicate the effective engagement of the unreached. No decisive people movement to Christ has yet occurred among the aboriginal peoples of Alaska.

13 **Ethnic minority churches** are the growing edge of US evangelicalism today. This is predominantly an urban phenomenon, but 10% of US counties now have racial and ethnic minorities as the majority. Points for prayer:

a) **Asian Church growth is pronounced.** Dynamic networks of congregations are springing up among the 7,000-plus Asian churches. Korean churches number 4,000. Chinese in the USA have over 1,000 churches and are experiencing rapid church growth. There are even more Filipino congregations (America's second-largest immigrant nationality after Mexico). There has also been church growth among Arabs, South Asians, Vietnamese and Iranians. Pray that such growth might continue – of any ethnicity, Asians in the USA retain the lowest rate of Christian affiliation.

b) **The cultural balance of these churches.** The greatest challenge is finding a way to integrate first-generation immigrants with second- and third-generation younger people. The integrity of the original culture and the appeal of mainstream US culture often conflict, even in church life. Pray for the provision of wise and forward-looking leaders. Pray for the calling of many to Kingdom service; cultural pressures often make the choice for full-time ministry a very difficult one.

c) **Effective strategies and cooperation between Anglo-American and ethnic-minority churches and agencies** to ensure these minorities are discipled in what is a highly fragmented ministry. In 2005, nearly 60% of **IMB** church plants were among ethnic minorities; 35% of all **AoG** churches are among ethnic minorities; **CMA**, CoG (Cleveland) and many others, especially Pentecostal and charismatic groups, focus on reaching minority communities.

d) **Growth of missions vision** is occurring most dramatically among Asian-American churches, Koreans in particular. Korean-Americans have the highest proportional sending rates of any ethnicity in the USA. The beginnings of similar mission movements are now seen among Chinese-Americans, Hispanics and African-Americans. One development with massive implications is mobilizing immigrant Christians as missionaries to their country and people of origin.

14 **The less-reached.** The sheer scale of outreach and the saturation of Christian media mean that very few are without ready access to the gospel, but many groups do need further specific attention for witness and intercession. Although the annual number of immigrants and refugees are fewer since 9/11, minority communities are still large in size and diversity.

a) ***Immigrants are more numerous and diverse*** in the USA than anywhere else on earth. In the USA, 31 ethnicities have populations of over one million. Mexico, China, Philippines, India, Colombia, Haiti, Cuba and Vietnam top the list of US immigrants. Millions come from countries where missionary access is very limited and where the majority are unreached. Their presence in the USA is the perfect opportunity to impact these less-reached peoples with the love and power of Christ – pray that churches will wake up to and seize this opportunity.

b) ***International students*** number nearly 700,000 and come from nearly every country in the world; well over half are from Asia. The largest numbers are from India (103,000), China (99,000), South Korea (75,000), Canada (30,000), Japan (30,000) and Taiwan (28,000). For many, this is their first opportunity to encounter the gospel. Most will return to leadership positions in their home nations after study. Their responsiveness to loving Christian ministry is remarkable, and is increasing with time. The Association of Christian Ministries to Internationals is an umbrella body linking ministries such as **ISI** (with 163 staff), InterVarsity(**IFES**), **CCCI**, Navigators and others. Pray for conversions and for discipling ministries that will enable these students to be effective witnesses when they return home.

c) ***The 5.2 million Jews*** are an influential minority, although proportionately in decline. Outside of Israel itself, the USA has the largest concentration of Jews in the world. In both Miami and New York, 9-10% of the population is estimated to be Jewish. Their growing receptivity and response to the gospel have been evident since 1970, and more Jews are being won to Christ in the USA than anywhere else since New Testament times. There are estimated to be up to 250,000 Messianic Jews. Many have integrated into Christian churches, but there are over 300 Messianic synagogues in the USA where Jewish customs and culture are preserved under Yeshua the Messiah. Nearly 50 agencies focus on reaching Jews with the good news; Jews for Jesus is one of the most dynamic of these.

d) ***Muslim numbers have steadily increased*** through immigration and conversion of African-Americans (especially in large urban areas). Still, two-thirds of Muslims in the USA are foreign-born. Estimated populations range from 1.3-7 million, meeting in more than 1,200 mosques. Although many more integrate into mainstream US life than their co-religionists in Europe, Muslims in America are also vulnerable to indoctrination by Wahhabist and other extremist interpretations that tend to control and fund many of the mosques and Islamic centres.

   i *Arabs.* Many are Muslim, but two-thirds are Christian. The small minority of Islamists among them have gained notoriety for the community.

   ii *Iranians* may now number up to 1.5 million. Around 5-10% are Christian, a large proportion of them by conversion. Disillusionment with Islam and with Iranian politics causes many to be open to Jesus. There are now around 40 Iranian Christian fellowships.

   iii *Somalis, Afghans, Bosnians* and others all have significant refugee communities.

   iv *The prison population, especially among African-Americans,* sees a rapid growth of Islam among prisoners. Up to 20% of the US prison population are now Muslim, and 80% of men who "find faith" are converts to Islam.

e) ***South Asians*** are one of the more affluent and well-educated ethnic communities in the USA. Most migrate for opportunities in business, technology, medicine or education. Nearly all are Muslim, Hindu or Sikh and come from sections of Indian society least exposed to the gospel; few are Christian. They number 5.5 million. Christian outreach to them is increasing.

f) ***The cults*** pose a challenge. Most function under the guise of Christianity but are full of false and extra-biblical teaching. Mormons and Jehovah's Witnesses are the most aggressive proselytizers of these, and the fastest growing. Scientology does not even purport to be Christian but wields great influence, especially among celebrities. The popularization of the occult and the supernatural among youth culture and the media leads many astray as well. In all of these cases, well-informed and specific engagement must occur in order to draw them to Jesus – who is the way, the truth and the life.

g) **The US prison population** is very large, with 2.3 million in jail. It is the world's largest prison population and nearly the highest incarceration rate. One-third of the prison population are African-American. There are over 2 million drug-related arrests annually, with 500,000 in prison and another 1.5 million on probation or parole due to drug-related offences. Pray for ministries such as Prison Fellowship International that seek to minister to them, win them to Christ, care for their families and rehabilitate them back into society.

15 **US Christians have pioneered and generously supported missions** on a massive scale for more than a century. The number, variety and commitment of US missionaries and agencies have impacted every nation on earth. Major umbrella bodies for evangelical mission agencies are The Mission Exchange and CrossGlobal Link. The US Center for World Mission remains hugely influential through its publications, including the "Perspectives" course, *Mission Frontiers* magazine and the William Carey Library. Caleb Resources and ACMC (Advancing Churches in Missions Commitment), both now part of Pioneers, have acted as catalysts for missions mobilization since 1975. The largest denominational agencies: **IMB, AoG, ABWE, BIM, CC/CC, BMM**. The largest interdenominational agencies: **YWAM, WBT, CCCI, Pioneers, NTM, SIM**. Pray for:

a) **Local churches** to make the Great Commission central to their church life. Only a decreasing fraction do so – a small minority of evangelical churches were carrying the great bulk of the task of supporting 43,500 foreign missionaries in 2010.

b) **Effective partnerships between local churches and mission agencies**. For this, churches need to recognize the experience and knowledge of mission agencies, and agencies need to adapt their way of operating. Many churches send missionaries directly to the field – not always a strategic success.

c) **Viable long-term strategies** that impact the least-evangelized peoples and places. The large majority – possibly 80% – of US missionaries work among majority-Christian peoples, while many unevangelized peoples still languish without the good news. The huge growth in short-term missions, while positive in some respects, can also be to the detriment of long-term impact and fruit. Pray that the fervour and enthusiasm of those who go on mission trips would be channelled into long-term commitment.

16 **Christian media ministries.** In the media-conscious, media-savvy USA, the right usage of such tools can be highly effective, but poor or irresponsible application can alienate. With such a profusion, only a brief mention for prayer is made here; pray for:

a) **Christian literature**. It remains a huge industry not just for US readership but for the global readership as well. Large numbers of Christian bookshops have disappeared, replaced by online sales and the religion sections of secular bookstores. This in turn has spurred the creation of church bookshops, serving a specific congregation. Pray that Christian literature produced and read would be of the highest quality, offering solid teaching and compelling stories for believers and non-believers alike.

b) **Radio and TV ministries** have developed dramatically since 1961. The National Religious Broadcasters (NRB) represents the interests of more than 1,400 Christian radio, TV and Internet broadcasters and associated ministries, which produce 75% of all religious programmes in the United States. There are about 2,400 Christian radio stations (more than double the number in 2001) and over 100 full-power Christian TV stations in the USA. Pray for:

i *Wise and sensitive use of these powerful media*. The distorted teaching and fraudulent, immoral lifestyles of certain televangelists give a bad name to those who minister authentically and with accountability to the body of Christ. Sadly, some high-profile figures continue to preach a distorted gospel and maintain questionable lifestyles and consumption patterns. In doing so, they inoculate many against the real truth.

ii *Wise stewardship in the use of funds* and for God's provision; such ministries are very expensive to maintain.

iii *Programming that uplifts the Lord Jesus* and includes strong biblical truth and culturally relevant, effective communication – rather than a focus on personalities, products or organizations.

iv Unity among Christian broadcasters and communicators and an "open door" from the Lord to extend the message of Jesus Christ into the entire world, especially to nations that have traditionally been closed to the gospel.

c) **Use of the Internet and digital media.** The past generation is remarkably transformed by the advent of the Internet, the Web and the ubiquitous availability of digital content. Sadly, these advances are often driven by wicked agendas such as pornography, gambling, pirating and callow celebrity worship. But the Internet is also a powerful tool for the gospel, penetrating into otherwise inaccessible places, connecting believers remotely and providing myriad resources for evangelism, discipleship, apologetics, fellowship, worship and Bible study. Pray for churches, missions and parachurch ministries to make full and wise use of new media for maximum impact on the media-hungry generations of today and tomorrow.

Uruguay
Oriental Republic of Uruguay
South America

Geography

Area 176,215 sq km. Located between Brazil and Argentina on the east bank of the River Plate estuary.

Population		Ann Gr	Density
2010	3,372,222	0.28%	19/sq km
2020	3,492,966	0.37%	20/sq km
2030	3,588,153	0.24%	20/sq km

Capital Montevideo 1,634,809. **Urbanites** 92.5%. **Pop under 15 yrs** 23%. **Life expectancy** 76.1 yrs.

Peoples

The Charrua Amerindians, the indigenous people, were destroyed after the arrival of Spanish settlers.
Latin American 90.6%. Uruguayan White 86.9%; Afro-Uruguayan 1.8%; Argentinean White 0.9%.
European 8.7%. 18 peoples. Italian 2.6%; Galician 1.2%; Spaniard 0.9%; German 0.9%.
Other 0.7%. Mostly Arab and Asian.
Literacy 97.7%. **Official language** Spanish. **All languages** 12. **Indigenous languages** 2. **Languages with Scriptures** 1Bi.

Economy

A relatively high standard of living for Latin America, but with a costly, extensive welfare system. Recent necessary financial restructuring includes privatization, inflation reduction and debt servicing. An economy with little industry and vulnerable to swings in the larger economies of neighbouring Argentina and Brazil. Generous water supplies and potential mineral resources offer possible future growth.
HDI Rank 50th/182. **Public debt** 59.8% of GDP. **Income/person** $9,654 (20% of USA). **Unemployment** 9.2%.

Politics

Independent from Spain in 1828. Apart from a military regime between 1973 and 1985, a long and largely unbroken tradition of democracy and civil liberties has prevailed. After many years of right-wing governments, a broad leftist coalition was elected in 2004 and again in 2009.

Religion

Separation of church and state in 1918, with no legal preference given to any religion. The most secular state in South America.

Religions	Pop %	Population	Ann Gr
Christian	64.69	2,181,490	0.4%
Non-religious	27.41	924,326	-0.4%
Ethnoreligionist	6.30	212,450	1.6%
Jewish	0.80	26,978	-1.2%
Other	0.60	20,233	4.0%
Muslim	0.10	3,372	4.9%
Baha'i	0.10	3,372	0.3%

Christians	Denoms	Pop %	Affiliates	Ann Gr
Protestant	38	3.68	124,000	2.6%
Independent	40	4.70	159,000	3.7%
Anglican	1	0.04	1,000	0.7%
Catholic	2	54.86	1,850,000	0.1%
Orthodox	6	1.01	34,000	0.6%
Marginal	7	3.81	128,000	2.6%
Doubly affiliated		-3.41	-115,000	0.0%

U

Churches	MegaBloc	Congs	Members	Affiliates	TransBloc	Pop %	Population	Ann Gr
Catholic Church	C	199	1,532,374	2,130,000	**Evangelicals**			
Latter-day Saints (Mormon)	M	182	62,000	93,000	Evangelicals	6.2	210,267	3.2%
Other Pentecostal	I	293	13,200	33,000	**Renewalists**			
Other Independent	I	364	14,545	32,000	Charismatics	5.9	198,398	3.0%
New Apostolic Church	I	140	21,050	28,000	Pentecostals	3.6	119,895	2.9%
Jehovah's Witnesses	M	139	11,159	26,000				
Christ Is the Answer Tab	I	33	8,000	17,600	**Missionaries from Uruguay**			
Seventh-day Adventist	P	50	7,000	14,000	**P,I,A** 31 (14 long-term) in 7 agencies: else-			
Ch of God (Cleveland)	P	74	5,200	13,000	where in South America 14, Europe 7.			
AoG (USA)	P	101	6,000	12,000				
Baptist Convention	P	60	5,000	11,000				
Waldensian Church	P	23	3,846	11,000				
Assem of God (Finland)	P	82	3,300	8,250				
Mision Vida	I	15	3,700	8,140				
Lord Is My Shepherd	I	35	1,750	4,375				
Other denominations[54]		687	64,332	124,237				
Disaffiliated				-280,000				
Doubly affiliated				-115,000				
Total Christians[94]		**2,477**	**1,762,406**	**2,170,602**				

Religions % of Total Pop

Annual Growth Rates

Answers to Prayer

1 **Spirituality is increasing.** A high degree of secularization persists, but many thousands of non-religious and nominal Christians are discovering in the postmodern era a spiritual dimension that has been missing from their lives, and churches are growing as a result.

2 **Evangelicals' growth** is rapidly accelerating. The last 20 years have witnessed significant growth in a country previously very resistant to the gospel. The Evangelical Alliance's efforts to double the number of congregations between 1998 and 2005 were completed – also doubling the number of believers in the process!

Challenges for Prayer

1 **Uruguayan society** has been characterized by secularism and hope in man for over 100 years. The Catholic Church espoused liberation theology and failed to attend to the spiritual needs of Uruguayans. Catholicism may lay claim to 55% of the population, but only 2.3% attend Mass. Most Catholics are, in practice, non-religious. Such godlessness has in turn led to some of the highest rates of depression, suicide, abortion and divorce in Latin America. Pray for the Lord, through His Church, to radically transform Uruguayan society for His glory.

2 **Lack of knowledge of God** gives opening to a spirit of error. Afro-Brazilian Spiritism is the fastest growing religion in Uruguay. The largest non-Catholic religious bodies are cults and sects of questionable orthodoxy. While 81% believe in God, most adhere to a "do-it-yourself" spirituality influenced by New Age thinking. Pray for all religious deceptions to be exposed and the demonic powers behind them defeated.

3 **Evangelical churches** struggled to make an impact on Uruguayan society in the 20th Century, garnering only meagre fruit in converts. However, since the late 1990s, growth of evangelicals, especially Pentecostal groups, has rapidly increased. Pray for a continuing harvest, and that the thousands of new believers might be discipled and pastored effectively.

4 **The recent awakening** generates many challenges. Evangelical Alliance churches work together on an unprecedented scale to fulfill the **DAWN**(*Amanecer*) goals. Pray also for the hugely strategic ministries of the 20 or so seminaries or Bible schools; doubling the number of congregations creates a demand for godly, well-trained pastors. Some schools have been negatively impacted in the past by liberal theology.

5 **Expatriate workers** are still needed, even though the Uruguayan Church has come into its own. Those who would serve and resource the burgeoning local churches would be valued. Larger missions: **SIM**, **AoG**, **BWM**, **BMW**. Church planters from other Latin American countries are having success; pray that they, too, would be sensitive to Uruguay's unique culture and people.

6 **Missions vision** is still limited, but interest is growing. At least two Uruguayan mission agencies send workers (*Avance* and *Desafio Mundial*). There are active international sending bodies such as **OM**, **YWAM**, Baptists and **AoG**. Pray for the growth in Uruguay to mature into a vibrant missionary-sending movement.

7 The less-reached:

a) *The Jews* are concentrated in Montevideo. JAMI has a small witness among them. There is some openness to the gospel.

b) *The Chinese and Japanese communities.* There is very little ministry.

c) *The Palestinians* living in several border towns. *Desafio Mundial* focuses on them.

d) *The upper middle-class* living along Montevideo's coast are probably the largest unevangelized group in the country; in their relative affluence, they are isolated from the gospel.

e) *The poor* are a growing segment of society, even as the middle-class shrinks. Many children are born into poverty. Slums are popping up around the urban areas. **CMS** runs a shelter for the homeless in Montevideo. Pray that the many new churches would mobilize to reach this needy group.

8 Christian support ministries.

a) *Literature* is a vital Christian ministry in this highly literate land. **CLC** has a ministry through its bookstore and a countrywide bookmobile ministry. **IMB** and The Bible Society have an extensive literature and Bible distribution ministry. Pray that the written Word may make a lasting impact.

b) *Radio and TV.* With the rise of community radio, evangelical radio is rapidly multiplying. More than 100 local congregations started radio ministries, but the passing of a new community radio law means these will need to obtain licences or stop broadcasting. The Evangelical Armenian Church has a TV ministry that is also having some impact in Uruguay.

Uzbekistan

Republic of Uzbekistan

Asia

Geography

Area 447,400 sq km. Fertile, irrigated mountain valleys in the east, notably the Ferghana Valley. Desert and Aral Sea in the west.

Population		Ann Gr	Density
2010	27,794,296	1.10%	62/sq km
2020	31,185,201	1.15%	70/sq km
2030	33,932,590	0.73%	76/sq km

Capital Tashkent 2,209,647. **Urbanites** 36.9%.
Pop under 15 yrs 29%. **Life expectancy** 67.6 yrs.

Peoples

Turkic 89.9%. 15 peoples. Uzbek 78.4% (some are actually ethnic Tajik); Kazakh 4.1%; Tatar(4) 3.0%. Karakalpak 1.8%; Kyrgyz 0.6%; Turkmen 0.6%.
Iranian-Median 5.4%. 7 peoples. Tajik 4.8%.
Eurasian 3.1%. 33 peoples. Russian 2.5%; Ukrainian 0.2%.
Other 1.6%. Korean 0.9%.
Literacy 99.3%. **Official language** Uzbek.
All languages 39. **Indigenous languages** 8.
Languages with Scriptures 1Bi 4NT 6por.

Economy

Self-sufficient with export capacity in both oil and natural gas, and with significant mineral deposits. A fragile water supply is a strategic issue in this heavily agriculturalist society. The world's fifth-largest cotton producer, but irrigation is costly. Close economic ties to Russia; economic stagnation brought about by corruption. Most struggle to make ends meet. Many young men move to Russia looking for work. Uzbekistan is a main transshipment nation for the drug trade from Afghanistan to Russia and on to Europe.
HDI Rank 119th/182. **Public debt** 10.4% of GDP. **Income/person** $1,027 (2% of USA).

Politics

Samarkand was the 14th Century capital of Tamerlane's vast Mongol/Turkic Empire. Russian colonial rule 1865-1917. Independent as a democratic republic in 1991. A multiparty republic in name only. Tokens of ethnic and Islamic culture were adopted as cover for a policy of no change. Torture of dissidents; the massacre of hundreds of protestors in 2005 brought worldwide attention and condemnation; the autocratic dictator is in control as firmly as in Communist times. Close political ties to Russia. Uzbekistan retains a strategic position in Central Asia.

Religion

A secular state promoting a moderate, tightly controlled form of Islam. The growing Islamist movement is handled with venom by the state. Christians are third-party victims of this struggle. Believers among non-Muslim minorities have more freedom. Ethnic Uzbek Christians receive particularly harsh treatment. Proselytizing of Muslims is illegal.

Religions	Pop %	Population	Ann Gr
Muslim	84.93	23,605,696	1.3%
Non-religious	13.80	3,835,613	0.1%
Christian	0.75	208,457	-1.6%
Ethnoreligionist	0.20	55,589	1.1%
Buddhist	0.16	44,471	-0.1%
Jewish	0.16	44,471	-1.3%

Most Christians are of ethnic minorities – mainly Russian and Korean. Large-scale Russian emigration explains the negative overall growth rate of Christianity.

Christians	Denoms	Pop %	Affiliates	Ann Gr
Protestant	31	0.28	79,000	2.5%
Independent	3	0.10	26,000	8.7%
Catholic	3	0.01	2,000	-7.8%
Orthodox	7	0.30	82,000	-7.6%
Marginal	1	0.01	4,000	4.6%
Unaffiliated		0.05	7,000	0.0%

Churches	MegaBloc	Congs	Members	Affiliates
Russian Orthodox	O	260	51,948	80,000
Pentecostal groups	P	217	6,500	21,645
Charismatic groups	I	162	5,333	16,000
Full Gospel Church	P	150	6,000	15,000
Korean Presbyterian	P	32	4,400	9,680
Baptist Union	P	28	2,500	5,000
Lutheran Church	P	4	3,333	5,000
Other denominations[35]		156	16,014	30,680
Total Christians[45]		**1,009**	**96,028**	**203,005**

TransBloc	Pop %	Population	Ann Gr
Evangelicals			
Evangelicals	0.3	84,957	4.4%
Renewalists			
Charismatics	0.2	64,480	5.9%
Pentecostals	0.1	38,245	4.8%

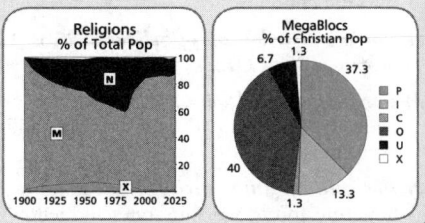

Challenges for Prayer

1 **Uzbekistan** is an arena of competing value systems. The term Uzbek means "master of himself", but many seek to enslave the Uzbeks with their ideologies: warmed-over communism, radical Islamism (especially in the fertile Ferghana valley) and occult-tainted folk Islam. Pray that Uzbeks might find freedom by serving the Lord their Creator and true Master.

2 **Uzbekistan is the strategic key** to Central Asia, hence the intensifying struggle between the post-Soviet regime and the Islamist movements. The government's "iron fist" policy is not deterring thousands of jobless young men from joining these movements. But much of the population is torn between these two and tired of the poverty, corruption and failure to progress. Pray for genuine change, reform and leadership that demonstrates uprightness and governs for the sake of the people. Pray that in the midst of the struggle, many may find true peace that only Jesus can give.

U

3 **Tashkent is the Islamic capital** of Central Asia in terms of both numbers and influence. Islam is more a part of the Uzbek cultural identity than it is a faithfully practiced religion; folk/occult practices are deeply tied into the beliefs of mostly the rural Uzbeks. Since a burst of Islamic activity soon after independence, the government has reined in most Islamic missionaries and mosque-buildings and tightly controls and monitors all Islamic activity.

4 **Transplanted minorities** predominate the Christian population. Most are emigrating in large numbers. The Orthodox population is only 10% of what it was in the 1980s. Evangelical Christianity, especially Pentecostals/charismatics, is growing among those remaining. Pray for:

a) *Freedom for ministry.* Minorities who keep to themselves are not specifically targeted, but the government is harsh on any who attempt to reach Uzbeks or other non-Muslim peoples. Yet the Russians and Koreans have considerable freedom to evangelize their own people, and are doing so.

b) *The bridging of the cultural divides* of Uzbeks, Russians and Koreans. Their differences, histories, past insensitivities and fears for the future all make cross-cultural outreach difficult. Pray that Russian and Korean Christians might have a heart for outreach to Uzbeks in culturally sensitive ways.

c) *Unity.* Mistrust and rivalry characterized past relations among groups, but widespread persecution has drawn together most Christians. Pray for humility, teachability and reconciliation among Christian leaders.

5 **Uzbek believers** continue to increase despite great opposition. The prospect of retribution from three sides – the government, local Muslim leaders and the community (family and neighbours) – has not halted growth. There are now probably more than 10,000 Uzbek believers, where there were possibly none only a generation ago. But much prayer is still needed:

a) *For the discipling and mentoring* of new believers. No one knows how many isolated individuals and clusters exist, but there are far more than those affiliated with officially recognized churches. Many fall away when difficulties intensify; pray that Christians might be integrated quickly into home groups or fellowships where they can grow. Many others find their witness curtailed by fear; pray for boldness for them.

b) *For local believers* who are accused of being cultural/religious traitors and "rice Christians". Pray for gentleness and humility as well as right motives for all those who seek to integrate into the churches.

c) *For the distribution of believers.* Most Uzbek Christians live in Tashkent and other cities, despite 63% of Uzbeks living in rural areas.

d) *For indigenous leadership* to be raised up. Bible training for this infant Church is urgently needed, as is spiritual maturity and godliness. Fast-growing churches need quality leaders even more urgently.

e) *For cultural authenticity.* Ask the Lord to raise up culturally appropriate Uzbek Christian literature, music, worship styles and fellowship structures. There are Uzbek ministry-training courses, led and taught completely by Uzbeks. These things are beginning to emerge, with significant fruit as a result.

6 **Uzbekistan's government** relentlessly persecutes the Church. Dynamic and evangelism-oriented churches, especially Uzbek churches, are particularly targeted. Uzbek Christian leaders have extensive files on them compiled by the 14 different government agencies that monitor religious activity. Persecution tactics include: public humiliation, property seizure, book and Bible-burning, expulsion of Christian students, dismissal of Christian employees, arrests (followed by beating and torture) under the flimsiest of pretexts and massive fines for first offences (up to 50 times the annual salary). The near impossibility of legally registering has birthed a mobile and fast-growing house church movement. A well-networked union of house churches helps to create stability and support amid the persecution. Pray for Christians who are under pressure to betray fellow believers to the authorities. Pray too for those persecuted and in prison, that God may give them strength and boldness.

7 **Expatriate Christians** serving the Lord in Uzbekistan have almost all been expelled and foreign agencies shut down – a mixed blessing as it forces the indigenous Church to unite, mature and stand firm. Pray that those whom the Lord has called to minister to Uzbeks might find ways and places to serve them and win them to Christ.

8 **The unreached.** Only a small fraction of the Muslim majority have ever had the opportunity to hear the gospel. Almost every Muslim people group is less than 0.1% Christian. Pray specifically for the:

a) *Karakalpaks,* who live south of the Aral Sea and are more Russified Sunni Muslims with strong Sufi influence. Nukus, the regional capital, is witnessing unprecedented church growth, despite persecution being most intense in this area. A few thousand have come into the Kingdom in recent years. Since the government shut every non-Orthodox church, almost all growth is through underground house churches. Uzbeks in the region are also coming to Christ. Pray for the Church here to stand fast and to keep growing and for the completion of the Bible in Karakalpak.

b) *Tajiks* comprise a majority in both Samarkand and Bukhara. There are few believers among them. Iranian-Median rather than Turkic, they are discriminated against by the government. Pray that their suffering might draw them to Christ.

9 **Christian media ministries.**

a) *Bible translation and distribution* are ongoing tasks. Pray for the translation of the OT and a more understandable revision of the NT in Uzbek. Pray for the government-recognized Uzbek Bible Society, that it may play a key role in distributing the Bible and printing additional Christian literature. It is allowed to exist, but is heavily restricted in terms of importing or printing Christian materials. Scriptures are not legally for sale anywhere else in the country.

b) *Christian literature* in Uzbek is desperately needed, but its production or importation is virtually banned by the government. Pray for mother-tongue writers, poets and hymnologists to be raised up and their works printed and distributed.

c) *Christian radio* is a mixed situation: nearly 200 hours per week, but mostly in Russian and English. There is a little radio (two hours per week by IBRA, **TWR** and **FEBC**) in Uzbek, also some in Tajik, Kazakh, Kyrgyz. Access to medium and shortwave radios is sparse; as a result, so is response. Pray for effective ways to communicate the good news by this medium.

d) *Video resources.* The JESUS film is available in Uzbek, Tajik, Kazakh, Russian and most other languages spoken here. Increasing numbers of Christian films and media resources are available. Pray for their circulation and use. Pray for the creation of video resources that will help evangelize the younger generation.

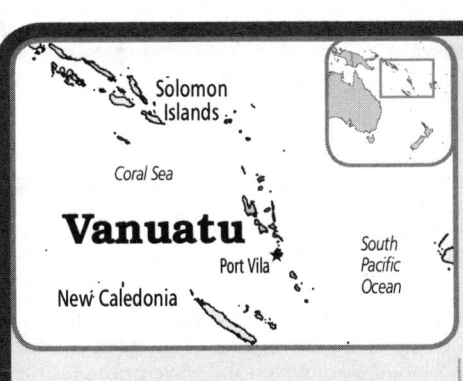

Vanuatu
Republic of Vanuatu
Pacific

Geography 🌍

Area 12,190 sq km. Twelve larger and 70 smaller islands, southeast of the Solomon Islands in the southwest Pacific. Formerly New Hebrides.

Population		Ann Gr	Density
2010	245,786	2.58%	20/sq km
2020	307,463	2.15%	25/sq km
2030	369,245	1.76%	30/sq km

Capital Vila 45,500 on Efate Island. **Urbanites** 25.6%. **Pop under 15 yrs** 39%. **Life expectancy** 69.9 yrs.

Peoples 👤👤👤

Ni-Vanuatu 91.9%. 104 groups. Detribalized Melanesian 13.9%; Lenakel 4.6%; Hano 4.5%; Bislama 3.9%; Paama 3.7%; West Ambae 3.6%; Apma 3.6%; East Ambae 3.3%; Uripiv-Atchin 3.2%.
Other Pacific Islanders 4.0%. 9 groups, including 6 Polynesian. Mele-Fila 1.8%.

V

Others 4.0%. Westerners and Asians. New Caledonian French 1.1%; French 1.1%.
Literacy 74%. **Official languages** Bislama (Pidgin English), English, French. **All languages** At least 108, but more than 60 are spoken by less than 1,000 people. **Languages with Scriptures** 6Bi 11NT 39por 30w.i.p.

Economy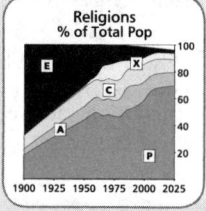

Highly dependent on agriculture and tourism (to volcanoes and pristine beaches); both are vulnerable to weather and climate changes. Many are abandoning food crops for kava roots, a cash crop for export. Lacking the natural resources of Melanesia, the marine resources of Micronesia and the remittances of Polynesia, Vanuatu is the third poorest nation in the Pacific. **HDI Rank** 126th/182. **Public debt** 28% of GDP. **Income/person** $2,442 (5% of USA).

Politics

Anglo–French influence since 1887. NaGriamel nationalistic independence movement formed in 1960; independence achieved in 1980 under Father Walter Lini, a church leader. Political factionalism led to riots and mutinies 1997–2004, but stability since then, with a notable government commitment to zero corruption. Parliamentary system with president and prime minister. British Commonwealth member.

Religion

There is religious freedom.

Religions	Pop %	Population	Ann Gr
Christian	94.08	231,235	2.9%
Ethnoreligionist	3.40	8,357	-5.8%
Baha'i	1.80	4,424	7.9%
Non-religious	0.50	1,229	2.6%
Buddhist	0.17	418	6.6%
Muslim	0.05	123	13.6%

Christians Denoms		Pop %	Affiliates	Ann Gr
Protestant	10	73.49	181,000	2.4%
Independent	5	1.86	5,000	3.1%
Anglican	1	12.06	30,000	0.8%
Catholic	1	11.88	29,000	0.8%
Marginal	8	3.39	8,000	1.2%
Doubly affiliated		-8.58	-21,000	0.0%

Churches	MegaBloc	Congs	Members	Affiliates
Presbyterian Church	P	550	41,500	69,000
Assemblies of God	P	220	24,479	47,000
Seventh-day Adventist	P	64	18,400	33,000
Ch of Melanesia	A	197	20,734	29,650
Catholic Church	C	63	16,977	29,200
Churches of Christ	P	100	3,500	7,000
Foursquare Gospel Ch	P	185	4,062	6,500
Apostolic Church	P	50	2,250	4,500
Latter-day Saints	M	21	2,462	3,521
Other denominations[16]		150	11,561	22,993
Doubly affiliated				-21,100
Total Christians[25]		**1,600**	**145,925**	**231,264**

TransBloc	Pop %	Population	Ann Gr
Evangelicals			
Evangelicals	45.9	112,874	3.1%
Renewalists			
Charismatics	29.1	71,477	3.6%
Pentecostals	24.7	60,750	2.7%

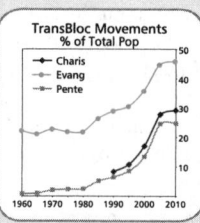

Religions % of Total Pop

TransBloc Movements % of Total Pop

Answers to Prayer

1 **Thousands have turned to Christ,** coming out of the "John Frum" cargo cults, despite these groups forbidding contact with Christians and the gospel. (These cults emerged from WWII and a belief that loads of supplies on ships and planes would come from "John from" America.) Recent work by Presbyterians, the JESUS film and **WBT** sees a new wave of over 7,000 positive responses to the good news.

2 **The rededication of Vanuatu to the Lord** occurred May 14, 2006 at the 400th anniversary of naming the South Pacific Islands the "Great Southlands of the Holy Spirit". Thousands participated in acts of repentance, celebration, communion and prayer, including the President, First Lady and other government figures.

Challenges for Prayer

1 **Vanuatu's motto is "In God We Stand".** Pray that leaders of this complex little nation may be examples in doing so. Committed Christians played a major role in attaining independence, and they continue to help lead the country – not least is the President himself.

2 **The Protestant Church** is numerically strong. Presbyterians are the largest group, but AoG and other Pentecostal/charismatic groups claim rapid growth. Most of them are represented in the Vanuatu Christian Council. Revival has occurred on some islands and in several denominations, but not in all places; some islands are spiritually stagnant. Church-planting mission is still needed for a few superficially evangelized peoples. Pray for the training of future leaders in the seven Bible colleges/schools. Pray that pastors and group leaders would lead with guidance from both the Word and Spirit.

3 **The spiritual challenges** for Christians:

a) Small pockets of traditional ethnic religion remain on Tanna, Aniwa, Santo, Vao and other islands. Many still follow *kastom* (custom) and strict taboos. Cargo cults persist, though declining significantly in number.

b) Culture and the gospel. Different churches have come to different conclusions on how much traditional culture is appropriate to retain, with extremes on both sides. Pray that ni-Vanuatu believers would be guided rightly in what parts of *kastom* can be redeemed and what parts must be set aside.

c) The increasing influx of other faiths. Mormon numbers have grown quickly because of missionary activity. Baha'i numbers are likewise growing rapidly. Muslims are active and offer free Islamic schooling in Fiji to students. Pray for the truth to be made manifest and for ni-Vanuatu to hold fast to the life they found in Christ.

d) Pray for a deeper grasp of the Christian faith in Vanuatu. Most of those drawn into other religions or cults lack an adequate understanding of the Bible, which safeguards them against such false teachings.

4 **Christian media:**

a) Bible translation. Vernacular literacy and training for ni-Vanuatu are major ongoing tasks. At least 30 languages have active translation or revision projects, and another 49 have such needs; UBS and **WBT** are involved with most of these.

b) Audio Scriptures are essential in a country with low literacy rates. **GRN** have recordings in 53 languages, and the Megavoice audio player is used to transmit some recent translations, such as the 2008 NT translation in North Tanna.

c) The JESUS film is widely shown in several languages.

d) Radio. Vanuatu Christian Radio broadcasts 24 hours a day.

Venezuela
Bolivarian Republic of Venezuela
Latin America

Geography

Area 912,050 sq km. About 80% of the population live along the Caribbean coastal belt in the north; the centre and south are grasslands and tropical forest.

Population		Ann Gr	Density
2010	29,043,555	1.68%	32/sq km
2020	33,412,159	1.32%	37/sq km
2030	37,144,702	0.98%	41/sq km

Capital Caracas 3,089,964. **Other major cities** Maracaibo 2.2 million; Valencia 1.8mill; Barquisimeto 1.2m; Maracay 1.0m. **Urbanites** 94%. **Pop under 15 yrs** 30%. **Life expectancy** 73.6 yrs.

Peoples

Hispanic 96.5%. Mixed Spanish, indigenous and African background and includes Colombians, Cubans and others. No census has been taken that classified the population according to ethnicity. Roughly 66% Mestizo, 20% European, 10% African.
Other groups 2.7%. From many different ethnicities: European, Middle Eastern, Asian.
Amerindians 1.8%. 30 peoples including Guajiro, Yanomami, Warrau, Piaroa.
Literacy 93%. **Official language** Spanish. **All languages** 47. **Indigenous languages** 40. **Languages with Scriptures** 1Bi 17NT 24por 9w.i.p.

Economy

The world's fourth-largest producer of oil, with massive reserves and great economic potential. About 33% of the GDP and 80% of export earnings come from oil. A formerly strong middle class was reduced by falling oil prices, but the recent boom has enriched only a small minority. Despite massive fuel exports, the nation struggles with energy shortages. High economic growth is accompanied by high inflation and unemployment. Massive investment in social structures should benefit the poor in the long run. **HDI Rank** 58th/182. **Public debt** 13.8% of GDP. **Income/person** $11,388 (24% of USA). **Unemployment** 9.4%.

Politics

Independent from Spain as part of Gran Colombia in 1821, and a separate state in 1830. A succession of revolutions and harsh dictatorships ended in 1958. Stable democracy for decades until economic stress and disillusionment with corrupt government provoked a number of civilian riots and political coup attempts, which finally succeeded in 1998 under the leadership of Chavez, a former army colonel. Since then, government has been consolidated to further empower the authoritarian president – and his "21st Century socialism" – who aligns himself with Cuba, Iran and other states opposed to the USA. There is strong opposition to Chavez as demonstrated by mass protests and failed coup attempts; his leadership is dynamic and determined, favours the poor, but is also increasingly mercurial and at times with elements of belligerence and even paranoia.

Religion

Religious freedom is still guaranteed in the constitution. The Catholic Church regained official recognition in 1964 after years of strained church-state relations, but its influence is under threat due to criticism by the president and growth among evangelicals.

Religions	Pop %	Population	Ann Gr
Christian	84.54	24,553,421	0.8%
Non-religious	12.17	3,534,601	9.2%
Other	1.42	412,418	2.0%
Ethnoreligionist	0.70	203,305	-1.0%
Baha'i	0.47	136,505	3.5%
Muslim	0.40	116,174	3.3%
Jewish	0.10	29,044	-2.0%
Chinese	0.10	29,044	1.7%
Buddhist	0.10	29,044	1.7%

Christians	Denoms	Pop %	Affiliates	Ann Gr
Protestant	58	5.45	1,583,000	3.1%
Independent	107	6.74	1,957,000	3.3%
Anglican	1	<0.01	1,000	0.0%
Catholic	2	71.16	20,668,000	-0.5%
Orthodox	6	0.12	34,000	2.6%
Marginal	5	1.75	507,000	3.4%
Unaffiliated		10.51	3,052,000	9.0%
Doubly affiliated		-11.19	-3,250,000	0.0%

Churches	MegaBloc	Congs	Members	Affiliates
Catholic Church	C	1,843	14,703,297	26,760,000
Assemblies of God	P	890	224,670	510,000
Seventh-day Adventist	P	567	152,000	380,000

Jehovah's Witnesses	M	1,350	105,000	315,000
Light of the World	I	4,000	140,000	280,000
Latter-day Saints	M	376	86,500	173,000
Kingdom of God (UCKG)	I	94	47,000	126,900
United Pentecostal Ch	P	2,119	93,220	110,000
God Is Love	I	86	30,000	72,000
FIELPV	I	248	31,000	68,200
Indig Ven Ch of Apure	I	603	30,150	60,300
Baptist Convention	P	480	20,979	60,000
Ch of the Cross	P	45	17,718	59,000
Assoc of Ev Chs	P	500	16,000	57,120
Fed of Emmanuel Pente	I	276	23,500	56,400
Christian Congregation	I	133	15,916	53,000
OVICE (TEAM)	P	329	27,000	45,090
Iglesia Pente Las Acacias	I	7	11,000	31,460
Other denominations[159]		7,247	710,248	1,631,600
Disaffiliated				-6,100,000
Doubly affiliated				-3,250,000
Total Christians[179]		**21,193**	**16,485,198**	**21,499,070**

TransBloc	Pop %	Population	Ann Gr
Evangelicals			
Evangelicals	10.8	3,147,421	3.2%
Renewalists			
Charismatics	10.0	2,892,920	3.5%
Pentecostals	6.3	1,839,034	3.1%

Missionaries from Venezuela

P,I,A 236 (180 long-term) in 22 agencies: to Venezuela 91, Europe 29, Middle East 25, Asia 23.

Annual Growth Rates

TransBloc Movements % of Total Pop

Answers to Prayer

1 **The increasing size and influence of evangelicals.** Not only is numerical growth continuing at a modest but stable rate, but evangelicals are beginning to be recognized as a legitimate expression of the Church and as key players in social and political scenes.

2 **Believers are not content to rest on their laurels.** In 2002, a goal was set to plant 25,000 churches and fellowships by the year 2015; many feel this is achievable. Beyond basic evangelism, churches are also starting new ministries that impact social and communal ministry and mission vision. Research by *Amanecer* (**DAWN**) along with many evangelical groups is resulting in improved awareness of the needs of each region.

Challenges for Prayer

1 **Venezuela is a volatile and divided nation.** The economy is deeply dependent on the price of oil, and the political scene is polarized between the president's supporters and his detractors. Increasingly strident anti-Western posturing offsets widespread investments in social and economic programmes for the poor. Pray for the wisdom to administer the nation wisely, to implement sensible policies that strengthen the nation and to strive for peace domestically and abroad.

2 **On a social level, Venezuela is struggling.** Poverty is still widespread and may be growing, and relative living standards are dropping (60% of urbanites live in slums). Power is concentrated in the hands of an ever-shrinking cadre, and the nation is regarded as the second most corrupt in Latin America after Haiti. Venezuela is increasingly used as a transshipment point for trafficking primarily drugs but also people. The promised utopia of "21st Century socialism" is not taking root, at least not as quickly as hoped. Pray that amid significant economic change and political turmoil, the neediest in society would be cared for and communities would be strengthened.

3 **The religious climate of the country** reveals a spiritual battleground:

a) Venezuela is not the Catholic bastion that it seems. The majority of Catholics are nominal – only 10% attend mass – making Venezuela one of the least-churchgoing nations in Latin America. A secular, materialist mindset prevails in public life. Its privileged position is eroding, and literally millions are opting for evangelicalism or no religion at all.

b) Spiritism is dangerously strong. The majority of Venezuela's "Christians" have to some degree dabbled with Spiritism. There are thousands of occult and spiritist shops where witch doctors and their ilk are frequented by rich and poor alike. The animist cult of Maria Lionza is one formalized expression of this, attracting up to half a million devotees.

c) All manner of spiritual forces draw Venezuelans away from Christ. New Age spirituality is increasing, especially among the educated and rich. Satanists actively seek to destroy the Church. Caracas is the site of Latin America's largest mosque. Jehovah's Witnesses and Mormons claim large numbers and are still growing. Pray that the powers blinding Venezuelans to the truth might be bound, and that the exalted Christ might be revealed to all, drawing many to faith in Him.

4 **Venezuela's evangelical breakthrough** was later (1980s) and less dramatic than in other Latin nations, but has remained stable. Early Protestant growth was slow, but some indigenous churches (especially those linked with the work of the **AoG** and the Brazilian neo-Pentecostal groups) are growing at 10% a year or higher. Evangelicals are also active in the political and social arenas, trying to impact the nation positively. The poor are particularly responsive to evangelical ministry.

5 **Challenges facing the churches.** The need is for:

a) Commitment to discipleship. Confronted with poverty, political activism and outright spiritual warfare, believers need to make wise choices. A life of true discipleship is not easy, and full-time ministry is even more of a challenge.

b) Unity is essential for further growth and for the power to stand up to opposition. Cooperation is higher than ever before through the work of the Evangelical Council of Venezuela (representing 150 Christian groups), *Amanacer/***DAWN** and others.

c) Theological orthodoxy. Spiritual error has crept into many churches through prosperity teaching, legalism or unbiblical practices instituted by misguided leaders.

d) Missions vision is spreading within the churches, and interest is growing, especially among younger people. But the challenge of sending workers to Latin America and beyond is significant. Foursquare, **YWAM**, **AoG**, *Horizontes* and Kairos have mission-training schools (the latter two of Brazilian origin). Pray for the Lord to prosper this young but accelerating missions movement.

6 **Leadership training** is crucial for sustaining church growth and preserving biblical doctrine. There are two main seminaries, a Baptist seminary and the Evangelical Seminary of Caracas, which serves both mainline and Pentecostal churches. A host of denominations run Bible institutes and schools. Even more vital are modular and correspondence training courses and in-service training programmes, increasingly available to people who lack the time or income to study full-time. Church planter training also occurs on a modular level through *Amanecer* and DCPI.

7 **Ministry to 30 Amerindian tribal peoples** by evangelicals has met opposition from anthropologists, leftist politicians, the government and some Catholic priests. The work of **NTM** and **MAF** was effectively ended by government decree in 2005. The indigenous peoples themselves have not been consulted much in this process, but illegal gold prospecting and expanding cattle ranching threaten their lands and their health. Pray for:

a) The opportunity for every Amerindian people to hear the gospel – few still live in their traditional ways that some would "protect".

b) Churches to reach the few remaining unevangelized tribes. Venezuelans of **AoG** and ADIEL (Evangelical Free Church) have well-established tribal works; other Venezuelans are taking up this challenge in places where expats have been forced out.

c) The continued ingathering of the Guajiro, Maquiritare, Yanomami, Panare, Motilone and others into culturally appropriate churches. Most of the larger tribes have significant and growing churches.

d) Bible translation work continues in 11 languages. There are still 14 language groups with no Scripture. Pray for God's Word to transform these peoples and equip them to survive the inevitable encroachment of Venezuelan culture and all the trappings of civilization.

8 **Mission work by evangelicals** is difficult. Obtaining visas for religious purposes is often a battle in faith; the government increasingly refuses applications and the process is slowing. The government's hostility toward Western groups can at times be compounded by Catholic hesitations regarding evangelicals. Expats are now all but prohibited from evangelizing Amerindian groups. But there is a great need for more missionaries for urban church planting and Bible teaching ministries. Pray for good relationships between expatriates and national workers, and for open doors for those called to serve here. The largest missions: **CLC**, **BIM**, CCCC, **AoG**, TE, Church Resource Ministries.

9 **The needier sections** of society:

a) ***The upper and middle classes*** are under-evangelized but influenced by other religious groups. A number of missions and churches are concentrating efforts to reach these important groups.

b) ***Cities.*** Caracas, the capital, is one of the least-reached areas. Over one million live in the ranchos (slums), and gangs or drug barons control entire areas – but there are fewer than 300 churches in the city. Churches and missions are mobilizing to reach the cities in this most urbanized of Latin American countries.

c) ***Students, young people and children*** need more focused outreach. Fewer than 20 Christian student groups (**CCCI**, MUEVE/**IFES**) exist for 100 universities, despite over 40 years of campus ministry. Many children live in poverty and have little opportunity to encounter the genuine gospel. More needs to be done to evangelize and disciple this key sector of society.

d) ***Prisoners*** live with severe overcrowding, inhumane conditions, frequent violence, torture of detainees, lengthy pre-trial detention and seemingly untouchable criminals operating within the government, police and armed forces. VOCEP and others share Christ in these dangerous places, and significant numbers are coming to faith. Pray for the safety of believing prisoners, for their spiritual growth and for their integration into society and the Church upon release.

10 **The unreached minorities:**

a) ***The growing Arab community*** (more than 130,000) has become prominent in commerce. Most are Lebanese and Syrian. Many are Orthodox and Maronite Catholics, but most are Shi'a and Sunni Muslims. No direct effort to evangelize them has been made, although some ministries (**WEC**) have a vision for outreach. There are also growing numbers of Iranians and Turks.

b) ***The Chinese*** are mostly Cantonese and are growing in number. There are several congregations of believers for the 50,000-strong community. Several missions have a ministry among them (Mennonites, **CMA** and **WEC**).

c) ***Western immigrant groups,*** such as Italians, Portuguese and Spanish, have almost no evangelical believers or outreach focused on them. There is one Messianic Jewish assembly.

11 **Christian literature** is in higher demand, but economic conditions affect production and distribution costs. **TEAM** and the Baptists founded publishing houses that are now run by Venezuelans. There remains a pressing need for Christian literature written by national and Latino authors as opposed to works translated from English. **CLC** has a growing wholesale and retail distribution network with six centres. The Bible Societies are working hard to get Scriptures into the more remote and tribal areas. Already, they distribute over one million Bibles, NTs or portions thereof annually.

12 **Media.** Christian radio is a strategic ministry. There are over 10 local evangelical radio stations, and **TWR**, **HCJB** and others broadcast in shortwave around 550 hours per week in Spanish. Some of their material is being used on secular stations as well. Venezuelans are starting commercial Christian FM, AM and TV stations. **GRN** has audio Scripture in 24 Venezuelan languages. Pray for all these resources to be well supported, full of powerful content and free to continue their work without interference.

Vietnam

Socialist Republic
of Vietnam

Asia

Geography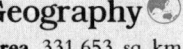

Area 331,653 sq km. Long, narrow country occupying the entire eastern and southern coastline of Indochina.

Population		Ann Gr	Density
2010	89,028,741	1.15%	268/sq km
2020	98,011,415	0.92%	296/sq km
2030	105,446,593	0.66%	318/sq km

Capital Hanoi 2,814,417. **Other major cities** Ho Chi Minh City 6.2 million; Hai-phong 2.0 mill. **Urbanites** 28.8%. **Pop under 15 yrs** 26%. **Life expectancy** 74.3 yrs.

Peoples 👪

Vietnamese 84.0%. Predominantly coastal people; large cultural differences between northern and southern Vietnamese.
Mon-Khmer 4.3%. 53 ethno-linguistic peoples. Largest: Muong 1.5%; Khmer (Cambodian) 1.4%.
Zhuang 3.0%. Tai Tho 1.9%; Highland Nung 1.1%.
Thai-Dai 1.9%. 17 ethno-linguistic peoples.
Hmong/Miao 1.5%. 8 peoples. Hmong Daw/White Meo 1.0%.
Cham 1.1%. 9 peoples.
Other Southeast Asian peoples 1.4%.
Chinese 2.6%.
All others 0.2%. Westerners, other Asians.
Literacy 90.3%. **Official language** Vietnamese. **All indigenous languages** 106. **Languages with Scriptures** 7Bi 9NT 25por.

Economy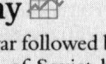

Decades of war followed by Marxist economics, then the loss of Soviet-bloc financial backing which left the economy in complete shambles. Reforms begun in 1986 have modernized the economy, tamed inflation somewhat and seen the emergence of a young middle class. Joining ASEAN Free Trade Area and WTO has also made a significant difference. There remains a large gap between urbanites and the rural poor. Poverty reduction, job creation and foreign investment remain economic priorities. Vietnam is the world's 2nd largest rice exporter, and seafood product exports are likewise crucial. **HDI Rank** 116th/182. **Public debt** 48.8% of GDP. **Income/person** $1,042 (2% of USA).

Politics ⚔

Vietnam gained independence from France in 1954, an event followed by three decades of war until re-unification of the North and South under the Communist Party in 1975. The Communist Party retains supreme control of all state policy and activity; the government and military are the other major powers, both tied closely to the party. Strong authoritarian rule brooks no dissent, especially not from minorities, ethnic or religious. As a result human rights violations continue despite some improvements. Economic growth and increasing materialism present great challenges to the Marxist-Leninist ideals of the Party.

Religion 🙏

The constitutional guarantee of freedom of religion is greatly diminished by a vast Bureau of Religious Affairs and Religion Police bureaucracies. For Protestants, new regulations in 2004 and 2005 ostensibly provided improvement through a regime for church registration. They also outlawed forced renunciations of faith, although some cases still occur. Registration is still denied to most churches in Vietnam. Those who do have it report a change in problems rather than significantly more freedom. Unregistered churches and ethnic minority Christians still suffer harassment, discrimination and sometimes outright persecution.

Religions	Pop %	Population	Ann Gr
Buddhist	52.48	46,722,283	0.8%
Non-religious	23.30	20,743,697	1.8%
Christian	9.43	8,395,410	2.3%
Ethnoreligionist	7.85	6,988,756	0.9%
Other	5.40	4,807,552	0.8%
Chinese	1.00	890,287	0.2%
Baha'i	0.39	347,212	0.6%
Muslim	0.08	71,223	1.2%
Hindu	0.07	62,320	1.2%

Christians Denoms		Pop %	Affiliates	Ann Gr
Protestant	14	1.28	1,141,000	2.3%
Independent	94	0.72	639,000	3.4%
Anglican	1	<0.01	4,000	1.1%
Catholic	1	7.69	6,845,000	2.3%
Marginal	2	0.02	20,000	2.6%
Doubly affiliated		-0.28	-250,000	0.0%

V

Churches	MegaBloc	Congs	Members	Affiliates	TransBloc	Pop %	Population	Ann Gr
Catholic Church	C	2,615	4,444,805	6,845,000	**Evangelicals**			
EVCN (2)	P	928	219,937	695,000	Evangelicals	1.8	1,576,889	2.6%
Hmong churches	P	1,450	103,704	280,000	**Renewalists**			
House ch movement	I	1,600	100,000	250,000	Charismatics	0.8	736,929	4.5%
VN Chr Mission Ch	I	1,141	57,057	190,000	Pentecostals	0.1	93,214	5.5%
Chr Fellowship Ch	I	139	11,111	30,000				
Seventh-day Adventist	P	24	13,000	21,710				
Bapt Chs of V (BCV)	P	450	6,993	20,000				
Mennonite Ch of V	P	133	6,000	15,600				
Presbyterian Church	P	103	9,000	12,600				
Other denominations[37]		2,666	149,768	289,714				
Doubly affiliated				*-250,000*				
Total Christians[125]		**11,249**	**5,121,375**	**8,399,624**				

Significant overlap exists between the ECVN, the House church movement, the Hmong and Montagnard church networks and the many foreign denominations claiming affiliates in Vietnam. The doubly affiliated category attempts to account for the fuzzy lines between these groups.

Religions % of Total Pop

Annual Growth Rates

Answers to Prayer

1 **A growing, witnessing Church** is emerging from years of persecution. Catholic and Protestant, new expression and old, a significant turning to God is occurring in different places, in both registered and unregistered churches, and among different people groups. The Vietnamese diaspora is also seeing many become believers. These converts then bring the gospel back to Vietnam with them. There are three main groups where church growth is occurring:

a) Among the mountain tribal peoples of central and southern Vietnam. Praise God for preservation and growth – by some estimates as great as nine-fold increase in just over thirty years! This occurred despite cruel persecution on the part of the government.

b) Among the Hmong and other minority peoples of Northern Vietnam. The 1990s saw the Church grow rapidly among the Hmong from no believers in 1988 to estimates of up to 400,000 just two decades later, catalyzed by **FEBC** radio broadcasting. House church movements among Northern peoples have spread.

c) Among the ethnic Vietnamese (Kinh) themselves. Although much more modest among this group, clear church growth is happening, in the formally recognized Evangelical Church of Vietnam [which actually consists of two separate organizations, one in the north EVCN(N) and one in the south EVCN(S)], in other, smaller but registered denominations and in the unregistered church networks as well. A Christmas gathering and service in Ho Chi Minh City in 2009 attracted 40,000 people.

2 **Increased numbers of Bibles** in Vietnamese and major tribal languages are printed and released with permission from the government. This is a great need, as the Church has spread rapidly and has a shortage of Bibles in the heart languages of Vietnam's peoples. Many Christian books and study materials have recently been published, some by the government's own publishing company.

Challenges for Prayer

1 **One of the few Communist nations** in the 21st Century, Vietnam faces new challenges. Repression of all types of freedom continues, but at the same time, social ills are on the rise. Drug addiction, AIDS, prostitution and exploitation of children are all too common. The land has seen great violence. Division and mistrust have been effective tools in the enemy's hands in recent generations. Pray that the ideological and moral darkness over this nation might be banished by the light of the gospel.

V

2   **The deepest spiritual allegiance** in Vietnam is not to Communism, nor to the amalgam of Buddhism, Taoism and Confucianism traditionally practiced by Vietnamese. It is the veneration and worship of ancestors that runs deepest and across most religious practices. Its impact is usually underestimated. Christians face hard questions in dealing with this issue biblically. Pray for the gospel to be wisely contextualized into this reality even while generational bonds that run counter to Christ are broken.

3   **The country is increasingly opening up** as economic progress continues. Most of the population was born after the Vietnam War and are more interested in capital gain and the outside world than Communist propaganda. They are proving responsive to the gospel – for reasons good and bad. At the same time, newfound prosperity has opened the door to rampant materialism and other competing ideologies. Pray that the Truth might be clearly and effectively proclaimed, particularly among the growing masses of young professionals.

4   **All open Protestant missionary work** ceased in 1975. **CMA** had laboured for 64 years (for 50 years as the only Protestant mission). Other agencies arrived in the 1950s, notably **WEC**, **IMB**, and UWM. In 1974 there were 280 missionaries in South Vietnam from about 20 organizations. Those years of sowing are today reaping an abundant harvest. Current economic development gives opportunity for Christians in business as well as for English teachers. Christian NGOs who propose legitimate aid projects are increasingly invited to work here. Literally hundreds of organizations from both Asia and the West now claim some kind of work in Vietnam. Many of these organizations work in deliberate partnership together. Pray that Vietnam may become fully open to Christian workers, and that many committed and prepared workers may respond.

5   **Suffering and persecution** has characterized the story of Christianity in Vietnam, as well as great faith and perseverance. The situation since 2005 has seen some marked improvement, yet government harassment, duplicity, discrimination and outright persecution continues to affect Catholics and Protestants today. Praise God that, through it all, the Church has persevered and grown. Pray for:

a) Those in prison for their faith. There are still hundreds of Christians, almost all Montagnards and including some Christian leaders, in prison. They were convicted in sham trials for anti-government activity. Most have endured imprisonment in grim conditions. Pray for them – many prisoners have come to faith through such witness. Pray also for the families of those imprisoned, that all their needs might be met.

b) Registration of churches. Beyond the two EVCN groups, seven additional denominations have been granted official registration – a governmental requirement for operation in Vietnam – yet most remain unregistered. Registration remains a difficult and divisive issue for the Church. Registered churches battle government pressure to compromise and conform to strict regulations. Unregistered churches are harassed by the police, with meetings sometimes still broken up and leaders detained and questioned. There are tensions among church leaders in both groups. Open evangelism and itinerant ministry is forbidden and contact with foreign Christians restricted. Yet the courage and tenacity of these believers under pressure rarely fails, and growth continues. Pray for a solution to this issue that best unifies and builds the Church of Vietnam.

c) Meeting places. Appropriate locations for church meetings are difficult to find. Even registered churches find permits to build difficult to acquire. Unregistered churches likewise struggle to find venues for large celebration meetings. In the past, the government seized many church properties. The EVCN(S) is still contesting the confiscation of more than 250 properties.

d) The ethnic minority churches, including the Hmong and the Montagnard Ede, Jarai, Koho, Mnong, Stieng and others. They have suffered particularly savage persecution, especially in the past – churches razed, congregations scattered, Christians killed. Yet people movements to Christ are still reported. Maintaining adequate fellowship is hard where meetings are illegal and few of their languages have Scriptures. This lack has led to schisms and false teaching in some areas.

6   **The rapid growth of evangelicals** – ninefold growth from 1975-2010 – is cause for praise, but it also generates some challenges of its own. Some of these threaten to undermine and divide much of what has been accomplished. Pray about:

a) ***Unity.*** While in one sense, the persecution has drawn Christians together, the somewhat chaotic situation also serves to divide. The house church movement has at least 70 different streams. The early house church groups split off from the ECVN(S), the largest Protestant group, historically connected with the **CMA**. The government often plays these groups against one another. Pray for the essential unity of the Church and that the enemy might not drive a wedge between believers.

b) ***Expatriate influence.*** A small number of foreign denominations and ministries, keen to be associated with God's workings in Vietnam, are effectively buying the affiliation of Vietnamese congregations. This introduces imported divisions, materialistic motivations and dependency. It is in deep contrast to the autonomous and indigenous expressions of Christian faith that have been normative until recently. The desire to be able to proclaim large "growth" numbers by expat groups is as problematic as the willingness of nationals to sell their affiliation to multiple buyers. Pray for integrity and accountability to be practiced by all. Pray for unbiblical agendas to be broken and God's glory to be paramount.

7 **Leaders' development and theological training** are the most urgent needs of the Vietnamese church. As numbers increase, so does the potential for false teaching and error. Opportunities for training are still highly restricted and piecemeal. The Catholics have reopened several seminaries, all monitored by the government. The only legal Protestant training institute is run exclusively for the ECVN(S). Some other registered churches are allowed to train their pastors on a case by case basis. There are informal study programmes and unofficial Bible schools in Hanoi, Ho Chi Minh City, Danang and elsewhere, but a standardized curriculum would be a boon. Expatriates often quietly enter the country to do leadership seminars and modular training, but their low profile limits the impact. Beyond theology, training in other leadership skills such as management, finance, accounting and vocational training is crucial. Many pastors are already responsible for multiple congregations and have no time or money for full-time training. Pray for creative, sustainable and effective means of developing a new generation of Christian leaders.

8 **The Vietnamese Diaspora** has two elements: those who fled the Communists, mostly in the 1970s, and those who more recently travelled abroad as guest workers in other Asian countries. Over three million live around the globe, where they are more accessible to ministry. Hundreds of thousands (including many from minority ethnic groups) are labouring abroad as migrant workers and have encountered the gospel in Malaysia, South Korea or other transit points, often through the evangelistic work of Vietnamese living abroad. Many overseas Vietnamese are returning to their homeland with a spiritual burden for their country; pray for fruitful and sensitive ministry to flourish as a result.

9 **Pray for the less–reached.** Present church growth is not evenly distributed – two-thirds of evangelicals are from the ethnic minority groups which comprise at most 13% of the overall population. Many other groups remain scarcely touched by the gospel, but over 12 groups have seen churches planted in the last 10 years where there were previously no believers at all. These include:

a) ***The northern Vietnamese.*** As a result of the longer Communist presence, they are much less evangelized than their southern brethren, but God is at work, and there is accelerating church growth in the north.

b) ***The Muslim Cham and Buddhist Khmer*** of the Mekong Delta – only a handful have believed. There has been a greater response amongst these peoples in neighbouring Cambodia, but small beginnings have been made in Vietnam also.

c) ***The northern minority peoples.*** Most are animist or Buddhist, many without any known believers. Christian radio is a key ministry, but only some have programmes in their language. The majority of the newly reached peoples are found in the mountainous northwest region.

d) ***The Cao Dai and Hoa Hao religionists*** strongly resisted Communism. Together they may number as many as six million, but these religions are not growing. Pray that Christians might familiarize themselves with these unique beliefs and cultures and reach the Cao Dai and Hoa Hao with the gospel.

e) ***Communist party members,*** government officials and military personnel. These are the three pillars of Vietnamese society, but Christians are sorely under-represented in all of them.

10 Christian literature and media:

a) **Bible translation** is an ongoing task. Many ethnic minorities lack the Word in their languages – 37 have a definite translation need. An easy-to-read Vietnamese Bible was published in 2008. Pray for the resources and people to complete the demanding task of translating those languages without God's word.

b) **Vietnamese Bibles** were finally printed legally and locally in the 1990s. Since 1990, Bible Societies have partnered with Vietnamese churches to print 700,000 Bibles and two million New Testaments, yet a large need remains. Hundreds of thousands of Scripture portions and Bible tracts have also been printed. Praise God for the recent government-endorsed printing of the Bible in four minority languages.

c) **Christian audio–visual media.** The JESUS film and video is available in 16 languages. **GRN** has prepared recordings in over 65 of the languages of Vietnam. Pray that these recordings, as well as players, may be circulated throughout the country.

d) **Christian radio programmes** of **FEBC** have been remarkable in their scope and impact. Their ministry has been the catalyst for massive people movements among the Hmong and other northern groups. Vital for evangelizing more isolated groups and for discipling believers, Christian broadcasts are widely heard despite difficulties and government attempts to jam the signal. **FEBC** broadcasts in 23 different languages of Vietnam, and **TWR** broadcasts into the north of the country as well.

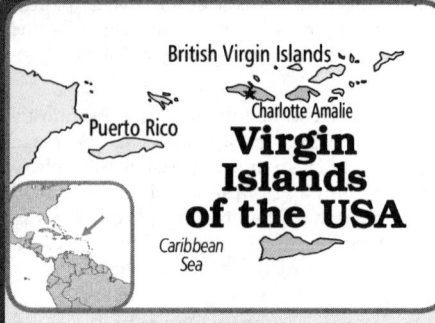

Virgin Islands of the USA

Caribbean

Geography🌐

Area 352 sq km. In the Leeward Islands, lying between Puerto Rico and British Virgin Islands. Three larger and 50 smaller islands.

Population		Ann Gr	Density
2010	109,326	–0.07%	311/sq km
2020	105,751	–0.41%	300/sq km
2030	98,553	–0.82%	280/sq km

Rapid growth in the 1970s and 1980s through immigration from other Caribbean islands, but decline since then.

Capital Charlotte Amalie 53,200. **Urbanites** 94.4%. **Pop under 15 yrs** 21%. **Life expectancy** 78.9 yrs.

Peoples 👪

Caribbean 74%.
  Virgin Islanders 45%.
  Other Caribbean 29%.
Others 26%. American 13%; Puerto Rican 6%; Other (European, Asian) 7%.
Literacy 90-95%. **Official language** English, but Spanish widely spoken. **All languages** 5. **Indigenous languages** 2. **Languages with Scriptures** 1w.i.p.

Economy 🏠

Tourism is the mainstay of the economy, with over 2 million visitors a year. A growing industry base, with one of the largest oil refineries in the world. Thousands of poor immigrants have bolstered the workforce but created tensions in society as well.
Public debt 37.3% of GDP. **Income/person** $27,300 (60% of USA).

Politics 🗡

Danish colony until 1917, when purchased by the USA. A self-governing unincorporated US territory.

Religion 🔥

Freedom of religion as in USA.

Religions	Pop %	Population	Ann Gr
Christian	94.95	103,805	-0.2%
Non-religious	3.50	3,826	2.4%
Baha'i	0.70	765	1.4%
Hindu	0.45	492	2.3%
Jewish	0.30	328	-0.1%
Muslim	0.10	109	2.1%

Christians	Denoms	Pop %	Affiliates	Ann Gr
Protestant	37	31.52	34,000	0.2%
Independent	26	12.95	14,000	0.9%
Anglican	1	10.06	11,000	-2.5%
Catholic	1	26.98	30,000	-0.3%
Orthodox	1	0.32	<500	1.5%
Marginal	7	2.21	2,000	1.0%
Unaffiliated		19.1	21,000	1.0%
Doubly affiliated		*-8.23*	*-9,000*	*0.0%*

Churches	MegaBloc	Congs	Members	Affiliates
Catholic Church	C	6	16,857	29,500
Seventh-day Adventist	P	13	8,000	11,200
Episcopal Church	A	7	5,500	11,000
Methodist Church	P	7	1,700	3,400
Independent Baptist	P	6	2,100	2,800
Assemblies of God	P	7	1,600	2,672
Moravian Church	P	7	1,400	2,660
Lutheran Church	P	7	1,350	2,160
Baptist General Conf	P	14	1,200	2,050
Ch of God of Prophecy	P	7	1,000	2,000
Ch of God (Cleveland)	P	7	820	1,700
Jehovah's Witnesses	M	8	560	1,400
Other denominations[61]		145	11,327	10,343
Total Christians[73]		**241**	**53,414**	**82,885**

TransBloc	Pop %	Population	Ann Gr
Evangelicals			
Evangelicals	23.8	26,055	0.3%
Renewalists			
Charismatics	16.5	18,058	0.9%
Pentecostals	9.6	10,472	1.1%

Annual Growth Rates

MegaBlocs % of Christian Pop

Challenges for Prayer

1 **Tourism and the influx of wealth** affect society profoundly, corroding its moral fabric. Pray that the gospel might impact society, personal lifestyles and family life.

2 **The Christian Church** has become very nominal, lacking in vitality and vision. The Moravians had a glorious past, but they and all churches need revival. The Catholic Church increases through immigration of Puerto Ricans and through charismatic renewal. Some evangelical groups have grown; the great need is revival.

3 **Specific outreach** is needed for the many tourists, the Hispanic immigrants, the Rasta-farians and those involved in the morally questionable aspects of island life. Pray that local churches and their leaders may work together in evangelism and in vision for the future.

Wallis and Futuna Islands

Mata-Utu

Wallis

South Pacific Ocean

Futuna

Wallis and Futuna

Territory of Wallis and Futuna Islands

Pacific

Geography

Area 274 sq km. Three volcanic tropical island groups 300 km west of Samoa.

Population		Ann Gr	Density
2010	15,446	0.70%	56/sq km
2020	16,516	0.63%	60/sq km
2030	17,048	0.21%	62/sq km

A further 16,000 work in New Caledonia.
Capital Mata-Utu 1,100. **Pop under 15 yrs** 30%.

Peoples

Polynesian 99%. Wallisian (East Uvean) 67%; Futunan 32%.
Other 1%. French.
Literacy 50%. **Languages** French, Uvean, Futunan. **Languages with Scriptures** 2Bi 1por 1w.i.p.

Economy

Heavily subsidized by France. Also revenue from fishing rights, export of labour and coconuts.

Politics

An overseas territory of France until 2003; now an overseas collectivity of France (possessing its own statutory laws).

Religion

Roman Catholicism is the only recognized religion. Most of the population are church-going.

Religions	Pop %	Population	Ann Gr
Christian	99.00	15,292	0.7%
Non-religious	0.50	77	2.9%
Baha'i	0.50	77	0.7%

Christians	Denoms	Pop %	Affiliates	Ann Gr
Protestant	2	0.98	<200	6.5%
Catholic	1	96.47	15,000	0.5%
Marginal	1	1.55	<300	9.6%

Churches	MegaBloc	Congs	Members	Affiliates
Catholic Church	C	5	8,514	14,900
Jehovah's Witnesses	M	4	120	240
Futuna Evangelical Ch	P	1	48	80
Pentecostal	P	2	48	72
Total Christians[4]		12	8,730	15,292

TransBloc	Pop %	Population	Ann Gr
Evangelicals			
Evangelicals	1.0	152	6.5%
Renewalists			
Charismatics	0.5	80	8.6%
Pentecostals	0.5	72	8.5%

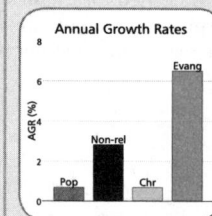

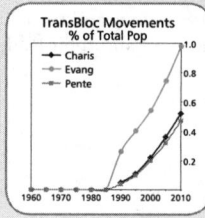

Answers to Prayer

1 **Evangelical numbers are increasing** through the missionary efforts of Pentecostals from New Caledonia. *Action Missionaire Calédonienne* has sent several New Caledonian missionaries to Wallis and Futuna, yielding dozens of new believers. Pray for a greater growth of this wonderful development – Pacific Islanders reaching cross–culturally to other Pacific Islanders.

Challenges for Prayer

1 **The Catholic Church** and Polynesian culture and social structures are so interwoven that adherence to Christianity is often more outward than through a living, personal faith. Pray for firsthand faith for these two island peoples.

2 **More Wallisian and Futunans** live in New Caledonia than live in their own home islands. Seeking work, many find themselves caught in a spiral of substance abuse instead. Pray for those in New Caledonia to find freedom in Christ and to, in turn, bring blessing back to their homeland.

3 **Christian resources are scarce.** The Bible was recently completed in Futunan, but Wallisian/Uvean only has portions. Beyond the Bible, there are no Christian resources of note in either language, so believers must understand French to read or listen to Christian material.

Yemen
Republic of Yemen
Asia

Geography

Area 531,869 sq km. Mountainous south and southwestern portion of the Arabian Peninsula and the Indian Ocean island of Socotra.

Population		Ann Gr	Density
2010	24,255,928	2.90%	46/sq km
2020	31,634,843	2.60%	59/sq km
2030	39,350,052	2.08%	74/sq km

Capital Sana'a 2,342,043. **Urbanites** 31.8%. **Pop under 15 yrs** 44%. **Life expectancy** 62.5 yrs.

Peoples

Arab 97%. Over 1,700 clans and tribes. Also: Socotri 0.25%; Mahri 0.35%.
Immigrant and refugee communities 2.6%.
Somali 2%; Ethiopian 0.5%.
Other 0.4%.
Literacy 54%. Only 30% for women. **Official language** Arabic. **All languages** 14. **Indigenous languages** 10. **Languages with Scriptures** 1por.

Economy

Poorest country in the Arab world. Oil-poor, but oil still provides 75% of foreign earnings.

Remittances from Yemenis working in Saudi and the West provide another source of foreign earnings. High unemployment; 75% make their living through agriculture (especially qat) and herding. Dwindling oil and water supplies pose enormous challenges in a country with rapid population growth.
HDI Rank 140th/182. **Public debt** 28.1% of GDP. **Income/person** $1,171 (2% of USA).

Politics

A turbulent history of wars and conquests. The north was part of the Ottoman Empire until 1918, and then an isolated feudal theocracy until the 1962 Egyptian-engineered republican revolution. Aden (the south) was ruled by Britain until independence in 1967. The two countries united in 1990 with the north as the dominant partner. A southern secessionist revolt in 1994 led to a northern victory. There is a long-established presidential government with a measure of democracy, but the current political situation is fragile. A low intensity internal war grows in influence, while voices of the south clamour to secede from the north.

Religion

Islam is the official religion, and the legal system is based on shari'a law. Sunni Islam is 66% (in centre and south), Zaidi Shi'a is 34% (in north), Ismaili is 0.9%. Islam is very conservative in Yemen, and there is very little religious freedom, although expatriates are free to practice without proselytizing.

Religions	Pop %	Population	Ann Gr
Muslim	99.92	24,236,523	2.9%
Christian	0.08	19,405	2.9%

Christians	Denoms	Pop %	Affiliates	Ann Gr
Protestant	6	<0.01	1,000	1.4%
Independent	5	0.01	3,000	5.7%
Anglican	3	<0.01	<400	3.1%
Catholic	1	0.04	8,000	1.2%
Orthodox	2	0.03	7,000	4.0%

Y

Churches	MegaBloc	Congs	Members	Affiliates
Catholic Church	C	5	1,700	8,500
Orthodox groups	O	5	2,333	7,000
Ethiopian groups	I	10	1,000	1,400
Indigenous believers	I	n/a	n/a	1,125
Other denominations[9]		9	709	1,390
Total Christians[17]		**29**	**5,742**	**19,415**

TransBloc	Pop %	Population	Ann Gr
Evangelicals			
Evangelicals	<0.1	4,275	5.1%
Renewalists			
Charismatics	<0.1	3,530	7.0%

Annual Growth Rates — AGR (%): Pop, Muslim, Chr, Evang

MegaBlocs % of Christian Pop: 37.5, 12.5, 50 — I, C, O

Answers to Prayer

1 **Increasing numbers have encountered Jesus.** Despite difficult circumstances – opposition from culture, religion and families – increasing numbers are finding life in Christ. Through radio broadcasts, Bible distribution, tactful faith sharing and the Lord's use of dreams and visions, God is drawing more and more people to Himself. At this point, they meet secretly and only in small groups. Praise God for the growing number of followers of Jesus who are learning how to honour their culture and family while still being faithful to the Lord. Fewer seek to emigrate as they understand that they can be faithful followers without travelling to the West.

Challenges for Prayer

1 **Yemen has suffered** almost unending conflict over the last four decades – three civil wars, conflict with neighbouring states, the effects of the Gulf War, Somalia's collapse into anarchy, the Ethiopian/Eritrean war and tribal skirmishes. Tensions between Shi'a and Sunni Muslims make Yemen ripe for sectarian violence, to the point of insurgencies or even outright civil war. The treasured right of Yemenis to bear arms fuels tribal rivalries, while kidnapping, crime and sabotage are common forms of protest and fundraising. There are between three and four firearms for each person in the country. Pray for a fair and just government that will bring about national unity and peace.

2 **Yemen's future stability is fragile** due to religious and political tensions, rapidly dwindling resources and one of the world's highest birthrates. It is estimated that by 2017, Yemen will cease earning income from its oil reserves and the capital will run out of viable water supplies. Sana'a is the world's fastest-growing capital city, with 7% annual growth. Pray for new means and methods for this nation to care for the very survival of its economy and people. Foreign involvement due to the political, religious and economic situation is almost inevitable; pray that outside powers act in a responsible and wise manner.

3 **Yemen was once famous for frankincense, myrrh and coffee,** but now growing the mild narcotic qat dominates agriculture. Over 80% of the adult population chew it, nearly 40% of the national economy is involved in qat farming and 55% of all water usage is devoted to its production. An estimated 20 million working hours a day are spent chewing it. The negative effects are immense on productivity and social and family life. Attempts to alleviate poor health care, low levels of education and economic underdevelopment are all undermined by widespread corruption.

4 **Christianity once had a strong presence,** but was almost completely wiped out by the 7th Century Muslim conquest. According to tradition, Shem founded the city of Sana'a, and the Queen of Sheba reigned in Yemen and sought wisdom from Solomon three millennia ago. May the modern people of Sheba seek after the wisdom from God as promised in Isaiah 60:6.

5 **Openly believing in Jesus is dangerous for Yemenis** – shari'a law, culture and family expectations are all factors in this. Pray for greater freedom for believers to encourage others to follow Christ and to be agents of cultural transformation. Pray for the transformation of their families, for it is from them that the worst persecution comes.

6 **Most Christians are expatriates.** Many are Ethiopian refugees, among whom are several thriving evangelical congregations. Others are Westerners, South and East Asians and other Arabs in secular jobs. No church buildings are yet allowed in the north. Pray that expatriate believers may maintain their spiritual growth amid discouragement, sickness, isolation and constant threats to their presence in the land.

7 **Opportunities for expatriates to serve God are varied** – business, education, health and development programmes. Hospitals and clinics run by expatriate Christians are much-needed blessings for the Yemeni people. There are many needs in Yemen, and faithful, loving service plants many seeds, as the various agencies attest. Pray for more believers who are willing to live and serve sacrificially and lovingly in this difficult land.

8 **Yemen is one of the world's least evangelized countries,** with one of the youngest and fastest-growing populations. Pray for salvation to come to:

a) *The northern tribes,* including the people of Sana'a, the capital, and the peoples of the northern mountains and northeastern deserts. A number are semi-nomadic.

b) *The southern Yemenis,* the key cities being Aden, Taiz and Ibb.

c) *The Tihama Arabs* of the coastal plains. Many Gulf War returnees were settled in this region. The key city is Hodeida.

d) *The Hadhramaut,* including the historic areas of Shibam and Tarem as well as the port city of Mukalla.

e) *The Mahri* along the Omani border are a fishing people and very isolated from the modernity that is seeping into the rest of Yemen.

f) *The Socotra islanders,* who were nominally Christian until the 17th Century. There are no known Christians on this isolated Indian Ocean island, and even humanitarian work is very limited and difficult to do.

g) *Yemeni women* – their lot is harsh and their opportunities for education and a life outside the home are limited. How will they hear about Jesus and learn to live for Him?

h) *Children.* High fertility rates generate large families, which in turn can create a host of poorly supervised children left generally to their own devices, especially if the parents chew qat. The education system is very limited and focused largely on Islamics. Many children are at risk of abduction by organized gangs (from a neighbouring country) for indoctrination into extremism and even more macabre exploitation.

i) *The South Asians* – many are traders and artisans in Aden. Most are Muslim; some are Hindu or Catholic Christians. Pray also for the 300 or so remaining Yemeni Jews.

j) *The Somalis* – many are Yemeni residents and others refugees. Their numbers could possibly exceed 500,000. A few have come to faith, but most remain unevangelized.

9 **Christian media** for prayer:

a) *Bible translation and distribution* – there is need for Socotri and Mahri Bibles. Low literacy rates hamper effectiveness and call for audio Scripture portions in local dialects. Distribution is difficult but possible; many desire an opportunity to read and listen to the Bible.

b) *Video.* The JESUS film is available in Arabic and Somali, but opportunities to show or distribute the video are limited. Audio cassettes of Christian music, Scriptures and teaching are available.

c) *Christian Radio.* Broadcasts by FEBA, IBRA and **TWR** in Arabic (standard and Yemeni) are clearly received (50 hours per week). Many are regular listeners, and this has raised interest levels. Pray for further response. Pray for the satellite that transmits Arabic Christian channels (such as Life Channel, Miracle Channel, Al Shefa and **SAT-7**) to become available in Yemen; it is currently nearly impossible to receive this signal.

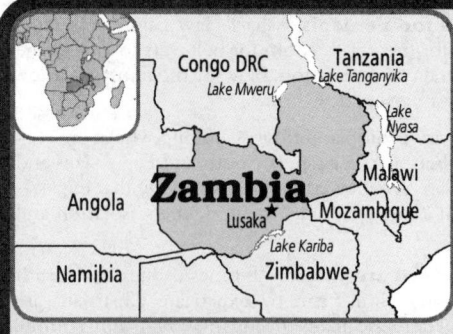

Congo DRC
Lake Mweru
Tanzania
Lake Tanganyika
Lake Nyasa
Angola
Zambia
Lusaka ★
Malawi
Mozambique
Lake Kariba
Namibia
Zimbabwe

Zambia

Republic of Zambia

Africa

Geography 🌍

Area 752,614 sq km. Landlocked central/southern African country; largely savannah grasslands with forested areas.

Population		Ann Gr	Density
2010	13,257,269	2.46%	18/sq km
2020	16,915,933	2.46%	22/sq km
2030	20,889,077	2.03%	28/sq km

Half of the population live within reach of the Congo-Zimbabwe railway that runs through the country.
Capital Lusaka 1,450,759. **Other major cities** Ndola 487,000; Kitwe 473,000. **Urbanites** 35.7%. **Pop under 15 yrs** 46%. **Life expectancy** 44.5 yrs.

Peoples 👪

80 ethnic groups.
Bantu 97.8%. Including Bemba 30.0%; Tonga(5) 11.8%; Nyanja 10.7%; Lozi 5.7%; Nsenga 3.4%; Nyiha 3.6%; Tumbuka 2.5%; Kaonde 2.3%; Lunda 2.1%; Lala 2.0%; Lamba 1.9%; Luvale 1.9%; Namwanga 1.5%; Lenje 1.4%; Mbunda 1.4%; Ngoni 1.2%; Bisa 1.0%.
Khoisan (Bushmen) 0.5%. 4 groups in the west, large majority are Mashi tribe.
Foreign-origin 1.7%. Afrikaner, British, Chinese, South Asian (mainly Gujarati).
These numbers do not include the many refugees, including 40,000 Angolans, 60,000 Congolese, many Burundian and Rwandan refugees and probably hundreds of thousands of Zimbabweans. **Literacy** 67.9%, but lower in practice and declining. **Official language** English. **Trade languages** Bemba and Nyanja spoken by large segments of the population. **All languages** 72 including dialects. **Languages with Scriptures** 18Bi 9NT 10por 9w.i.p.

Economy 📈

Copper mining and refining have long been the major sources of foreign exchange, but subject to the whims of global markets. The global fall of copper prices, lack of access to seaports, mismanagement and corruption, harsh World Bank impositions regarding debt repayments and AIDS combined to drive Zambia's economy downward – such that 86% live below the poverty threshold. Agriculture employs a significant amount of the working population. The recent contributions of "exiled" Zimbabwean farmers significantly increased Zambia's agricultural output and economy generally. A number of mines have opened or re-opened of late, which significantly assists the economy. With an anti-corruption campaign, valuable (but highly controversial) investment from China and India and many natural resources, Zambia has great economic potential.
HDI Rank 164th/182. **Public debt** 29.5 % of GDP. **Income/person** $1,248 (3% of USA).

Politics ✖

Independent from Britain in 1964. Single-party state under President Kaunda's leadership until 1991. Growing corruption, economic collapse and a revulsion against a single-party regime prompted multiparty elections in which Chiluba was elected. The two subsequent elected presidents promised to continue the goals of economic development and to stamp out corruption, but too little progress has been seen.

Religion 🙏

Kaunda's socialist humanism was government policy. Chiluba, as an active Christian, declared Zambia a Christian country in 1991, but with full religious freedom for all faiths. This was written into the constitution in 1996.

Religions	Pop %	Population	Ann Gr
Christian	86.95	11,527,195	2.6%
Ethnoreligionist	10.80	1,431,785	1.4%
Muslim	1.35	178,973	4.9%
Baha'i	0.40	53,029	2.5%
Non-religious	0.34	45,075	4.4%
Hindu	0.16	21,212	3.8%

Christians Denoms		Pop %	Affiliates	Ann Gr
Protestant	51	38.67	5,127,000	2.8%
Independent	101	14.05	1,862,000	2.7%
Anglican	2	1.03	137,000	2.9%
Catholic	1	28.59	3,790,000	2.1%
Orthodox	4	0.06	8,000	1.4%
Marginal	8	4.20	556,000	2.0%
Unaffiliated		9.10	1,206,000	-1.0%
Doubly affiliated		*-8.75*	*-1,160,000*	*0.0%*

Churches	MegaBloc	Congs	Members	Affiliates
Catholic Church	C	299	1,994,737	3,790,000
New Apostolic Ch	I	4,620	993,333	1,490,000
United Church	P	1,280	823,353	1,375,000
Seventh-day Adventist	P	1,960	684,615	890,000

					TransBloc	Pop %	Population	Ann Gr
Pente Assem of God	P	450	453,333	680,000	**Evangelicals**			
Reformed Ch in Z	P	152	249,580	594,000	Evangelicals	25.7	3,406,297	3.2%
Jehovah's Witnesses	M	2,220	129,697	428,000	**Renewalists**			
Full Gospel Ch of God	P	630	207,500	415,000	Charismatics	25.8	3,413,874	3.4%
Christian Brethren	P	1,300	103,571	145,000	Pentecostals	10.7	1,420,901	3.1%
Anglican Church	A	472	54,000	135,000				
Baptist Union of CA	P	480	55,000	115,500				
Baptist Convention	P	1,150	46,000	115,000				
Ch of Christ (Non-ins)	P	1,450	77,600	97,000				
Ch of God (Anderson)	P	475	37,800	94,500				
Evang Ch in Zambia	P	1,250	75,455	83,000				
African Meth Epis Ch	I	479	40,750	81,500				
Pente Holiness Ch	P	728	36,563	69,469				
Other denominations[150]		3,796	439,305	882,739				
Doubly affiliated				*-1,160,000*				
Total Christians[167]		**23,191**	**6,502,192**	**10,320,708**				

Religions % of Total Pop

MegaBlocs % of Christian Pop

Answers to Prayer

1 **Christianity continues to be widely accepted,** even in public institutions and the media. Influential Christians such as past presidents have further increased evangelical Christianity's profile. Freedom of all religions is practiced, and the opportunity to minister as believers to the many challenges Zambia faces means an open door for Christian work. Evangelicals were 3.8% in 1960, 8% in 1980, 25.7% in 2010.

2 **New holistic ministries** are springing up, initiated both from abroad and from within the nation. The human needs in Zambia are formidable – 17th from the bottom in the UN Human Development Index – but creative grassroots projects and agencies are beginning to meet these needs. Praise God for ambitious, faith-filled people working for transformation on both small and grand scales.

Challenges for Prayer

1 **The declaration of Zambia** as a Christian nation in 1991 was encouraging, but the outworking is sorely lacking. Ex-President Chiluba, an outspoken believer, was accused (and cleared in court) of embezzlement, and his successor Mwanawasa, who actively rooted out such corruption, died suddenly and unexpectedly. While Zambia remains an island of stability and peace surrounded by countries rocked by war and strife, national transformation along biblical lines is conspicuous by its absence. Pray that the dedication of Zambia to Christ would be reflected by the dedication of its leaders and its Christians to see a land blessed by and honouring God.

2 **Poverty and its many causes** need to be tackled wisely but aggressively. Consider the following: up to 86% of the population are below the poverty line; agriculture and copper mining, which employ the large majority of the population, are dependent on erratic weather and markets. Between 33% and 50% of children are malnourished; 40% of the people do not have access to clean water or adequate sanitation. Illiteracy in rural areas is 90%. Current economic growth cannot offset the high birthrate or AIDS prevalence. All of these challenges are beginning to be met by a great host of agencies working in development, healthcare, education, vocational training, microfinance and other areas. Pray for wise policy-making, responsible borrowing by the state and for long-term sustainable investing and ministry that will uplift the nation to greater development. Pray for the right balance between external assistance and homegrown solutions.

3 **The "brain drain"** of many of Africa's brightest and best to richer nations impacts Zambia deeply. While Zambian doctors, lawyers, businessmen, professionals and pastors set up shop in South Africa, Europe and North America, their home nation cries out for precisely the skills and resources they have to offer. Pray for conviction to return to be blessings and the ideal missionaries to their country.

Z

4 **Growth among Protestant and Independent churches** is encouraging. Growing Pentecostal churches are matched by evangelical and renewalist growth in mainline churches such as the United Church. Yet there are dangers:

a) Superficiality and lack of biblical understanding and teaching. Too few know the Word of God or how to live a Christian life. Good teachers and trained pastors are greatly needed.

b) Imported forms and structures of worship cause a disconnect between African culture and the gospel, but syncretism with indigenous beliefs and practices that are not biblical is no improvement. The flourishing of truly African but also truly biblical expressions of Christian lifestyle, theology and worship patterns is essential; praise God that this is already happening.

5 **Churches still vary widely** in spiritual quality and vigour. Pray for:

a) The many thriving evangelical congregations in the northwest. This area has a high concentration of evangelical believers, largely as a result of the ministry of the Brethren/CMML, **SIM** and Baptists. There is still a need for spiritual depth and learning, but enthusiasm is high for ministry and mission.

b) The fruitful work of the Brethren in Christ and Churches of Christ among the Tonga peoples in the south; health care and pastoral training are two key emphases in this area.

c) The Reformed Church among the Nyanja peoples in the east, which is theologically evangelical, large in number and still growing.

d) The Lozi and southwestern peoples and the Bemba and northern peoples, who traditionally have few evangelical congregations. Many have become nominally Christian or have been swept into sectarian or syncretistic indigenous churches. Pray for churches to be planted in these spiritually needy areas. HeartCry, Africa Outreach Ministries and Baptists are church planting among these peoples and among Bemba-speaking peoples in the north, where there is an exciting growth of evangelical congregations.

6 **The Evangelical Fellowship of Zambia (EFZ)** is a network of over 200 denominations, churches, missions and parachurch organizations and an important focal point of fellowship and cooperative efforts. It has spearheaded efforts to address the challenges of AIDS, poverty and long-term food security, and works to imbue churches with holistic vision. Pray that the EFZ might be anointed and effective in this crucial work.

7 **Zambia is a major destination** and thoroughfare for people. Instability in nations surrounding Zambia has sent hundreds of thousands of refugees fleeing into Zambia, especially from Zimbabwe of late. Also, Zambia is vulnerable to traffickers of both child labourers and sex workers. Thank God for a recently passed law specifically criminalizing human trafficking; pray for its effective implementation. Pray that Zambia might be the location where many uprooted people find succour and discover the Living God.

8 **The AIDS crisis** overwhelms the health services, the economy (as many trained professionals succumb to the disease), the pastoral work of churches (over 100,000 AIDS-related deaths per year) and family life. Pray specifically for:

a) Those working to reduce AIDS. All major denominations have adopted pragmatic policies to combat the spread of the disease and to assist those infected. Many have specific ministries devoted solely to AIDS issues such as Jesus Cares Ministries, Advocates for Change and SU's Aid for AIDS programmes.

b) Attitudes toward AIDS have changed. A lot of the stigma, superstition and bad information are now replaced with compassion in action. Infection rates have reduced from 20% to 15% in 10 years, with much greater reductions in specific segments of the population.

c) The military, police and copper mine workers have some of the highest rates of infection. These groups tend to frequent sex workers through whom AIDS is passed and who most likely have the highest infection rate of all.

d) Children. Zambia has 710,000 orphans, mostly due to AIDS; nearly 20% of all children are suffering the loss of their parents. Over 90,000 live on the streets. Almost 75% of Zambian households care for a relative orphaned by AIDS.

Z

9 **Leadership training** is an urgent need, the natural outworking of sustained church growth. This is a massive priority in a land where nominalism and syncretism are common. The EFZ has sponsored the Theological College of Central Africa in Ndola – the first evangelical, degree-awarding theological institution in Central Africa. There are many more colleges and Bible schools, representing every major denominational expression. Pray for spiritually and educationally qualified leaders to be prepared through these institutions. TEE is widely used and increasing in scope, scale and effectiveness. In-service and modular trainings for both the ordained and laity are essential, especially since most church planting is actually done by lay workers.

10 **Young people.** SU has a significant impact in secondary schools, with large, lively groups in most of them. Many missionaries and Zambian believers teach the Scriptures in government schools. ZAFES(**IFES**) has four staff and groups in every post-secondary institution in Zambia. The ministry of **CEF** leads thousands of children to Christ each year.

11 **Missions.** There is an open door for ministry, although few are unevangelized.

a) Receiving. The emphasis is rightly on partnering with Zambians, training them for leadership and service and developing holistic ministries that are sustainable and useful. The largest are: **CB**/CMML, **SIM**, **IMB**, **LM**.

b) Sending. The Zambian Church's interest in missions has grown in the last 10 years, in large part due to the GLO Centre and ProChristo/**OM**. Hundreds now serve cross-culturally within Zambia and to neighbouring nations, almost all of which are much less evangelized and even more in need of practical assistance. The Brethren/CMML alone has sent out 150 workers within Zambia, into the region and even to India and the UK. Pray for these first fruits to represent a much greater harvest.

12 **The less reached** – there are still unevangelized pockets and a few peoples who have received much less ministry than the majority.

a) The many smaller groups of peoples in the southwest are minimally reached – the Subiya, the four Khoisan groups, others.

b) The urban satellite towns of Lusaka, the Copperbelt and Kabwe are spiritually needy. Many are squalid shanty settlements, rife with poverty, AIDS and little hope. Pray for the work of Dorothea Mission, World Outreach Team Action and others in evangelizing these areas.

c) The Indian Gujarati community is both Hindu and Muslim, but few are Christian. South African **SIM**, Pentecostal Assemblies of God and Asian missionaries from Tanzania work among them.

13 **Other faiths** present a challenge to biblical Christianity. These include:

a) Witchcraft and sorcery, based on animism, strongly affect the lives and worldview of many Christians. They rarely are expressed as a separate religion but often overlap with and pollute Christian belief. Widespread superstitions and occult practices hamper spiritual growth, compromise believers and leave the door open for the enemy to work ill in peoples' lives. Pray that Christians might cast off all ties to the spirits and live pure and holy lives that depend on God alone for spiritual empowerment and blessing.

b) Islam is aggressively targeting Zambia, especially in the east, and is growing twice as fast as Christianity here. Muslims take advantage of the freedom of religion to propagate Islam, and they make liberal use of funds from oil rich Muslim nations to entice Christians. Mosque building, free education and material inducements are effective in this poor country. Pray for powerful outreach to Muslims. Few Zambian Christians are equipped for this.

c) Jehovah's Witnesses are already numerous and very active in outreach, particularly in the east. Their literature floods the nation, while Christian ministries cannot afford to print and distribute the truth.

14 **Christian specialist ministries:**

a) Bible translation and distribution. The Bible Society has a key role in a number of translation projects. Pray for wisdom to know which languages need Bible translation most urgently.

Z

b) **Christian literature.** The quantity, range and local applicability of available literature are limited. Lack of learning and biblical knowledge makes literacy and Christian material for pastors and laity alike crucial for faith in Zambia.

c) **The Pastor's Book Set Programme** (**SIM**/EFZ) has provided a collection of study aids, including the *African Bible Commentary*, to about 7,000 pastors. Each set is worth around $1,000 and is a huge blessing to pastors who could not otherwise afford such valuable study, preaching and teaching tools.

d) **Christian radio and television ministries** have expanded rapidly. There is a wide availability of both TV and radio programmes, but many are of little help for the real-life context of the average Zambian. There are too many frothy Western shows whose performance techniques are copied by local preachers.

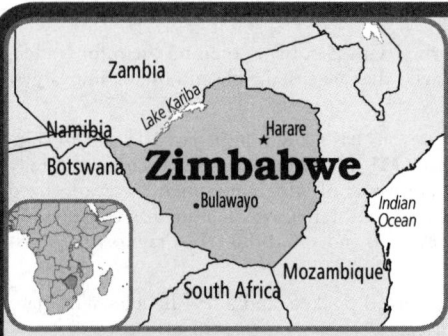

Zimbabwe
Republic of Zimbabwe
Africa

Geography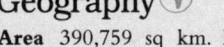

Area 390,759 sq km. Landlocked state in southern Africa.

Population		Ann Gr	Density
2010	12,644,041	0.27%	32/sq km
2020	15,571,017	2.11%	40/sq km
2030	17,917,471	1.32%	46/sq km

These UN-projected figures fail to account for the massive emigration that has followed the economic and social meltdown of Zimbabwe, or for the extensive scourge of disease. Estimates suggest 25–50% of the population has fled the country, mostly to neighbouring African states, even if only until things improve.

Capital Harare 1,631,594. **Other major city** Bulawayo 756,000. **Urbanites** 38%. **Pop under 15 yrs** 40%. **Life expectancy** 43.4 yrs.

Peoples

Over 42 peoples.
Bantu peoples 97.8%.
  Shona 68.2%. 9 major peoples. Central 23.0%; Karanga 15.4%; Zezuru 13.2%; Manyika 6.8%.
  Nguni 14.0%. Ndebele 12.2%, 3 other peoples.
  Chewa-Sena 8.2%. Nyanja 5.2%, 6 other peoples.

Other 7.4%. Sotho-Tswana(5) 3.3%; Venda 1.1%; Tonga 1.1%; Tswa 1.3%.
Other African 0.6%.
Other 1.6%. European, South Asian, East Asian, Coloured.
Literacy 90%. **Official language** English. **Trade languages** Shona spoken widely, Ndebele in the West. **All languages** 22. **Indigenous languages** 19. **Languages with Scriptures** 11Bi 4NT 5por 2w.i.p.

Economy

An unmitigated economic disaster despite rich agricultural land and mineral deposits. Mismanagement, corruption, the devastation of disease, costly military adventurism in the Congo and the land redistribution programme which seized white-owned farms – a crucial economic pillar – plunged the nation into an economic death spiral. Hyperinflation (at one point calculated at 230 million percent) and mass unemployment (over 90%) ensued, prompting effective abandonment of the Zimbabwean dollar and the use in business of the US dollar, the rand and the Botswanan pula. Direct foreign investment and tourism have plummeted. Education and health systems were paralyzed by the economic freefall.
Public debt 266% of GDP. **Income/person** $268 (1% of USA).

Politics

In 1965 the white minority declared Rhodesian independence from Britain. This led to intense guerrilla warfare and eventually independence as Zimbabwe in 1980. Effectively a one-party state and dictatorship until 2008, presided over by Mugabe's ZANU-PF. Elections in 2000, 2002, 2005 and especially 2008 were widely deemed rife with fraud and intimidation and accompanied by threat, violence and destruction of property. A power sharing agreement with opposition party (and likely 2008 election winners) MDC saw Tsvangirai (a former trade union leader) become Prime Minister with Mugabe retaining the Presidency. This inclusive government has in fact brought progress to the country since 2008.

The desperate socio-economic situation, Mugabe's age and the influence of ZANU-PF's Joint Operations Command make for an uncertain future.

Religion

Freedom of religion exists but has been seriously compromised by political interference in church affairs, political appointments of ecclesiastical positions and state disruptions of Christian events and ministry on political grounds.

Religions	Pop %	Population	Ann Gr
Christian	77.99	9,861,088	1.1%
Ethnoreligionist	19.20	2,427,656	-2.8%
Non-religious	1.40	177,017	1.8%
Muslim	1.10	139,084	1.2%
Baha'i	0.20	25,288	0.3%
Hindu	0.08	10,115	-2.1%
Jewish	0.02	2,529	-12.7%
Buddhist	0.01	1,264	0.3%

Christians Denoms		Pop %	Affiliates	Ann Gr
Protestant	51	22.62	2,860,000	2.1%
Independent	102	44.75	5,659,000	1.6%
Anglican	1	2.90	367,000	1.0%
Catholic	1	9.66	1,222,000	1.2%
Orthodox	1	0.04	5,000	0.0%
Marginal	12	1.35	171,000	1.9%
Unaffiliated		3.50	439,000	-6.7%
Doubly affiliated		*-6.80*	*-860,000*	*0.0%*

Churches	MegaBloc	Congs	Members	Affiliates
Zim Assem of God, Afr	I	5,625	1,125,000	2,250,000
Catholic Church	C	216	646,561	1,222,000
Afr Apos Ch J Marange	I	343	412,000	1,030,000
Seventh-day Adventist	P	1,417	598,000	897,000
Zion Apostolic Chs	I	1,483	445,000	890,000
Zion Christian Church	I	2,181	261,667	785,000
Apostolic Faith Mission	P	2,973	148,649	495,000
Anglican Church	A	1,468	146,800	367,000
Baptist Convention	P	335	119,500	239,000
Methodist Church (UK)	P	1,643	115,000	230,000
Evang Lutheran Church	P	300	72,072	160,000
United Methodist (US)	P	1,210	98,000	129,000
Reformed Church in Z	P	211	42,400	106,000
AoG - Back to God	I	297	49,000	98,000
Jehovah's Witnesses	M	960	39,640	88,000
Other denominations[151]		5,027	669,842	1,297,228
Doubly affiliated				*-859,800*
Total Christians[168]		**25,689**	**4,989,131**	**9,423,428**

TransBloc	Pop %	Population	Ann Gr
Evangelicals			
Evangelicals	30.9	3,910,631	2.2%
Renewalists			
Charismatics	47.6	6,017,974	1.7%
Pentecostals	24.5	3,098,067	2.5%

Religions % of Total Pop

TransBloc Movements % of Total Pop

Answers to Prayer

1 **The Church has grown in numbers and passion** amidst great trials, even as the country disintegrates all around. The state failed the population, and while many find refuge in spirituality and faith, churches also work hard to meet the many desperate physical and social needs they encounter.

2 **Target 2010** is the follow-up to the successful saturation church planting vision (Target 2000) which saw 10,000 new churches planted. Target 2010 aims to address realities facing today's Church: leadership development, community transformation, prayer and mission mobilization, research, sustainable church planting and healthy church growth. Meeting such lofty goals amid such deprivation will take great commitment and faith across the evangelical spectrum.

Challenges for Prayer

1 **Zimbabwe's desperate situation** would be farcical were it not so tragic. Suffering has reached unprecedented levels; intransigent misrule and deluded finger-pointing have prevented solution finding. State-endorsed violence and even murder and frequent human rights violations target members of non-ZANU-PF parties, the media and social activists. Pray for Zimbabwe's leadership, that God might bring humility and a servant attitude or else put leaders in place who will govern for the sake of the people and for the restoration of the nation.

Z

2 **Urgent human needs abound.** A web of inter-related disasters combined to create a state of emergency. Pray especially for:

a) The economy. Hyperinflation and economic meltdown have driven millions into gripping poverty from which there seems no escape.

   i Hyperinflation reached ridiculous proportions, possibly up to one billion percent per year with the printing of $500 trillion notes. The government knocked 16 zeros off the currency; Zimbabwean money is regarded as worthless and people demand payment in South African or US currency. The taming of inflation is essential to building up the economy.

   ii Unemployment reached 90%, and those few employed rarely get paid in a useful currency. Negligible recourse to meaningful or gainful work not only impoverishes a nation but destroys its morale as well.

b) The education system, once among the best in Africa, has ground to a halt. Enrolment plummeted from a once admirable 92.5%, as few can afford the $4/term school fee. Entire terms are cancelled as schools and universities shut down altogether. The paralyzation of education robs Zimbabwe of its future.

c) Health care is also in meltdown. Power failures, lack of supplies and inability to pay workers leave hospitals inoperable. Even basic health care is under siege, now provided by NGOs more than by the state. The 2008 cholera epidemic prompted the government to declare a state of emergency, though it continues to lack resources to prevent further spread. Over 100,000 may have been infected.

3 **The calamitous land redistribution** changed Zimbabwe from being a food exporter to being food-import dependent. Before independence, white settlers built agricultural output, employing and housing up to two million people. The Mugabe-endorsed seizure of 5,500 white-owned farms allowed over 100,000 "war veterans" to settle over 10 million hectares. This process descended into anarchy and wrought devastation as squatters now camp on once fertile farmland. Not only does the nation rely on international aid to feed itself, but over two-thirds of the wildlife has been killed since 2000, mostly for food. Land reform is needed; pray that it might be equitable, wise and beneficial to the country's longer term future. Pray for the rule of law and for justice to prevail for all involved.

4 **The AIDS pandemic** in Zimbabwe is one of the world's worst cases. A combination of inadequate government action, lack of healthcare, traditional (and modern) practices that exacerbate spread and the failure to address the stigma result in great suffering. Thankfully, prevalence rates have apparently declined to around 14%, but over 2,000 are still dying per week and there are around one million AIDS orphans. Pray for:

a) A radical change in hearts and attitudes to sex and to AIDS itself. Figures indicate this is beginning as NGOs and churches lead the way in education and awareness. With the collapse of medical services, current prevalence rates are difficult if not impossible to assess.

b) Effective and specific programmes to address the issue. Pray that all churches might face up to the moral, spiritual and economic implications of the pandemic for their ministry, and that pastors would lead the way in endorsing helpful initiatives, holy and transparent lifestyles and loving compassion for those afflicted.

5 **Demographic upheaval** is the disaster hidden in plain sight. Remember:

a) The exodus of literally countless millions from Zimbabwe to neighbouring African nations and beyond. This "brain drain" includes much of academia, the business community, opposition politicians and spiritual leaders. Their emigration, even temporary, is a serious loss to Zimbabwe. Pray for the swift and safe return and reconciliation of these people to help rebuild a nation on its knees. Pray for strength of community among the Zimbabwean Church in diaspora, currently dissipated, and for unity befitting their role in reconstruction.

b) The millions of deaths, past and future, due to AIDS. Massive numbers of deaths and plummeting life expectancy (from over 60 down to near 40 years) robs the nation of trained professionals and leaders and steals from the productive working life of millions. Pray for wise, forward thinking that will enable the nation to cope with the inevitable loss.

6 **As the Church has grown, so have the challenges.** Pray for:

a) The relationship with the government. The Church must be a prophetic voice engaged in the politico-economic life of the nation. Any such engagement has brought heavy-handed reprisals from the government including the intimidation and harassment of pastors and the destruction of certain church buildings. Some denominations have compromised their testimony by blindly endorsing Mugabe; others have spoken against government policies and suffered for it. The Zimbabwe Christian Alliance and the Save Zimbabwe Campaign are examples of churches engaging in the political process to catalyze change.

b) Social action. With much of the country in decay, it is increasingly falling to churches to feed the hungry, care for orphans, protect the vulnerable and heal the sick. With assistance from ministries based in South Africa and around the globe, Zimbabwe's churches are doing this, but they could benefit from further mobilization, training and, of course, financial resources.

c) Theological training and education – crucial as the church grows but threatened by widespread instability and want. There are at least 23 Bible colleges and seminaries, but the real growth is in modular training and TEE. Positions for study exist here and in broader university religious study programmes as well, but funding in the present economic environment is scarce to non-existent. Pray for effective teaching and discipling of those called to serve the Lord.

d) Spiritual unity. Divisions and splits still occur, especially within Apostolic and charismatic groups. The gap separating evangelicals, mainliners and African Independent Churches (AICs) makes collaborative efforts difficult at a time when a unified mission of the Church is greatly needed. The Evangelical Fellowship of Zimbabwe links over 121 denominations and 20 organizations, and *Fambidzano*/EFZIM links AICs for fellowship and theological instruction. The Zimbabwe Council of Churches (ZCC), Zimbabwe Catholic Bishops Conference (ZCBC), National Pastors' Conference and Ministers Fraternal all hold influence and therefore opportunity.

e) The purity of the Church is often compromised by traditional African practices that are incompatible with the gospel, often by outright witchcraft and occult activities. The growth of AICs is commendable for cultural relevance but not at the expense of theological orthodoxy. Pray for churches to find truly Zimbabwean expressions of biblical faith rooted firmly in God's Word.

7 **Young people** have watched idealistic visions fade to empty slogans and oppressive misrule. They constitute a huge swathe of the population, but have little reason to hope for improvement to their difficult lot. Pray for the ministries of:

a) Fellowship of Christian Unions – FOCUS(**IFES**) has 50 groups with 5,000 students served by five full-time and one part-time staff. In the midst of societal dysfunction the students continue to declare the gospel and help where they can to serve the practical needs of the people.

b) Scripture Union has had a decisive impact on the educated via its work in secondary schools. They impart life skills to younger students, work with orphans and children at risk and provide HIV/AIDS education. Camp ministry has been especially fruitful. Pray for more Christian teachers to nurture this work in their spare time.

c) African Enterprise impacts about 50,000 people and hundreds of churches per year with its youth-oriented Foxfire ministries. This ministry, going since 1980, has spiritually shaped many of the nation's top Christian leaders.

8 **Pray for the less-evangelized.** Zimbabwe has been extensively evangelized, but areas of need remain:

a) The rural areas, often neglected for church planting and for sending qualified workers. Pray more will be called to this humble but vital task. Pray also for evangelistic outreaches and suitable literature distribution specifically to these areas.

b) The burgeoning cities, swollen with hundreds of thousands of rural migrants looking for non-existant jobs. Squatter settlements are multiplying and crime is on the increase. Outreach to the unemployed is a major challenge.

Z

c) Less-reached peoples. There are some congregations in every indigenous people, but relatively few among the Tonga, Nambya and Dombe of the Hwange-Kariba area in the northwest (where the **AoG** have made a significant impact), the Kunda in the northeast and the Tswa in the southeast.

d) Muslims. They are a small minority but wield disproportionate influence on the country through foreign aid "with strings", mosque-building and scholarships in Muslim universities. Most are Yao from Malawi, some are South Asian immigrants and a few are indigenous Shona-speakers. Little Christian outreach has been made to win them and churches are ill-equipped to do so.

9 **The expatriate mission force** has steadily declined due to government obstruction and the growing maturity of the indigenous church. There is still a wide range of ministries where input is helpful. **MAF** serves Zimbabwe from South Africa, as do many other missions. Major agencies are **CCCI**, **TEAM**, Dorothea Mission.

10 **Christian media** is needed now more than ever amid Zimbabwe's troubled existence.

a) Scripture distribution. The Bible Society continues to print and distribute Scripture in these difficult times when demand is great. Significant developments include modern translations of the Bible in Ndebele and Shona as well as translations in Ndau (by **SIM**/UBS), including an audio version in Shona.

b) Audio-visual tools are extremely valuable. Good News Media and **GRN** combined to produce gospel materials in 65 languages and dialects. CAVA (Christian Audio Visual Action) produces literature and audio-video which focus on evangelism and discipleship to peoples with primarily oral traditions. They remain the only major publisher of literature in Shona.

c) Radio programmes are broadcast on the national networks (FEBA), but less frequently due to government increase in charges for air time. Internationally, **TWR** Swaziland broadcasts into Zimbabwe in English, Shona, Ndebele and Ndau.

d) The JESUS film has been extensively used in 16 languages and dialects for church planting, especially in rural areas where it has yielded much fruit.

Global Facts and Figures

This section of maps, charts and lists communicates a host of issues pertinent to world evangelization. They are more than sets of data. They indicate the ebb and flow of population, mission and church growth. They point to the rise and fall of societies. They visually and statistically encapsulate the task remaining for the fulfillment of the Great Commission. In this capacity, we hope that some of this content will spur the reader on to prayers of faith and further sustain intercession for the nations and peoples of the world.

Population Growth

Population growth occurs by immigration and childbirth. The countries with the greatest growth include both of these factors. Countries with the most pronounced decline usually have to face the twin spectres of very low childbirth and significant and sustained emigration (and frequently a low life expectancy as well).

Countries with the Highest Population Growth Rate (AGR)			Countries with the Lowest Population Growth Rate (AGR)		
Rank	Country	Ann Gr	Rank	Country	Ann Gr
1	Qatar	11.2%	1	Georgia	-1.1%
2	Liberia	4.2%	2	Moldova	-1.0%
3	Niger	3.9%	3	Lithuania	-1.0%
4	Afghanistan	3.5%	4	Ukraine	-0.6%
5	Burkina Faso	3.4%	5	Bulgaria	-0.6%
6	Timor Leste	3.4%	6	Belarus	-0.5%
7	Uganda	3.3%	7	Latvia	-0.5%
8	Syria	3.3%	8	Romania	-0.4%
9	Palestine	3.2%	9	Russia	-0.4%
10	Benin	3.2%	10	Dominica	-0.3%
11	Eritrea	3.2%	11	Serbia	-0.2%
12	Jordan	3.1%	12	Hungary	-0.2%
13	Tanzania	2.9%	13	Croatia	-0.2%
14	Burundi	2.9%	14	Bosnia	-0.1%
15	Yemen	2.9%	15	Estonia	-0.1%
16	United Arab Emirates	2.9%	16	Germany	-0.1%
17	Malawi	2.8%	17	Poland	-0.1%
18	Chad	2.8%	18	Japan	-0.1%
19	Congo, Republic of	2.8%	19	Virgin Is of the US	-0.1%
20	Gambia	2.8%	20	Guyana	-0.1%
21	French Guiana	2.7%	21	Samoa	0.0%
22	Madagascar	2.7%	22	Cuba	0.0%
23	Angola	2.7%	23	Montenegro	0.0%
24	Rwanda	2.7%	24	Greenland	0.0%
25	Sierra Leone	2.7%	25	Macedonia	0.1%

Countries by Population

Within this list of the most populous countries you will find included a number of the provinces of China and states of India as if they were independent nations. This is done to indicate the enormous population size of many of these sub-national regions.

Rank	Country	Population	Rank	Country	Population
1	China, PRC	1,330,584,783	22	United Kingdom	62,129,818
2	India	1,214,464,312		*Karnataka*	*60,906,894*
3	USA	317,641,087	23	Italy	60,097,564
4	Indonesia	232,516,771		*Gujarat*	*59,855,330*
	Uttar Pradesh	*202,557,152*		*Hubei*	*58,637,000*
5	Brazil	195,423,252		*Zhejiang*	*51,294,000*
6	Pakistan	184,753,300	24	Myanmar	50,495,672
7	Bangladesh	164,425,491	25	South Africa	50,492,408
8	Nigeria	158,258,917		*Guangxi Zhuang*	*48,605,300*
9	Russia	140,366,561	26	Korea, South	48,500,717
10	Japan	126,995,411	27	Colombia	46,300,196
	Maharashtra	*113,426,742*		*Yunnan*	*46,174,000*
11	Mexico	110,645,154	28	Spain	45,450,497
	Bihar	*99,556,918*	29	Ukraine	45,433,415
	Henan	*96,737,000*	30	Tanzania	45,039,573
	Guangdong	*96,376,000*		*Jiangxi*	*44,691,000*
	Shandong	*95,882,000*		*Liaoning*	*43,991,000*
12	Philippines	93,616,853	31	Sudan	43,192,438
	West Bengal	*93,239,044*		*Orissa*	*42,337,396*
13	Vietnam	89,028,741	32	Kenya	40,862,900
	Sichuan	*88,150,000*	33	Argentina	40,665,732
	Andhra Pradesh	*87,202,366*		*Heilongjiang*	*39,377,000*
14	Ethiopia	84,975,606		*Guizhou*	*38,697,000*
15	Egypt	84,474,427		*Shaanxi*	*38,470,000*
16	Germany	82,056,775	34	Poland	38,038,094
	Jiangsu	*77,764,000*		*Kerala*	*36,324,062*
17	Turkey	75,705,147	35	Algeria	35,422,589
18	Iran	75,077,547		*Shanxi*	*34,762,000*
	Madhya Pradesh	*73,512,931*		*Fujian*	*34,300,000*
	Hebei	*71,049,000*	36	Canada	33,889,747
	Tamil Nadu	*70,453,739*	37	Uganda	33,796,461
	Rajasthan	*68,591,484*	38	Morocco	32,777,808
19	Thailand	68,139,238		*Jharkhand*	*31,844,037*
20	Congo-DRC	67,827,495		*Assam*	*31,758,087*
	Hunan	*65,322,000*	39	Iraq	31,466,698
	Anhui	*62,933,000*	40	Nepal	29,852,682
21	France	62,636,580			

Population Growth

Population growth, measured over decades, tells a much greater story than when measured over the course of only one year. It can indicate societal success or failure for a host of different reasons. Although a number of these countries are smaller in population, the percent increase (or decrease) communicates significant issues regardless – issues crucial to the survival of those countries.

Rank	Countries with the Greatest Growth (1960-2010) Country	Pop Growth	Rank	Countries with the Least Growth (1960-2010) Country	Pop Growth
1	United Arab Emirates	5,116.8%	1	Niue	-70.0%
2	Qatar	3,251.8%	2	Pitcairn Islands	-65.5%
3	Kuwait	997.5%	3	Montserrat	-50.7%
4	Djibouti	935.8%	4	Christmas Island	-36.0%
5	Northern Mariana Islands	784.3%	5	Tokelau Islands	-35.2%
6	Mayotte	730.6%	6	Holy See	-13.4%
7	Jordan	622.3%	7	Saint Helena	-7.0%
8	French Guiana	612.3%	8	Bulgaria	-4.7%
9	Cayman Islands	565.4%	9	Hungary	-0.1%
10	Andorra	548.0%	10	Georgia	1.4%
11	Saudi Arabia	544.1%	11	Saint Kitts & Nevis	2.3%
12	Côte d'Ivoire	526.2%	12	Latvia	5.6%
13	Turks & Caicos Islands	476.3%	13	Ukraine	6.2%
14	Gambia, The	450.8%	14	Croatia	9.0%
15	Bahrain	417.0%	15	Czech Republic	9.1%
16	Oman	413.9%	16	Cook Islands	9.2%
17	Kenya	404.2%	17	Estonia	10.2%
18	Uganda	397.9%	18	Barbados	11.2%
19	Brunei	397.6%	19	Cocos (Keeling) Islands	11.7%
20	Niger	390.2%	20	Dominica	12.4%

Rank	Countries with the Greatest Projected Growth (2010-2050) Country	Pop Growth	Rank	Countries with the Greatest Projected Decline (2010-2050) Country	Pop Growth
1	Niger	266.3%	1	Virgin Is of the US	-31.4%
2	Timor Leste	174.7%	2	Bulgaria	-28.1%
3	Uganda	170.1%	3	Guyana	-26.7%
4	Afghanistan	153.9%	4	Belarus	-24.1%
5	Somalia	151.3%	5	Moldova	-23.5%
6	Burkina Faso	150.7%	6	Ukraine	-22.9%
7	Tanzania	143.0%	7	Georgia	-22.6%
8	Chad	141.4%	8	Lithuania	-20.8%
9	Benin	138.6%	9	Bosnia	-20.0%
10	Malawi	133.1%	10	Japan	-20.0%
11	Palestine	132.8%	11	Romania	-18.5%
12	Guinea	132.2%	12	Russia	-17.3%
13	Angola	122.5%	13	Latvia	-17.2%
14	Yemen	121.3%	14	Poland	-15.8%
15	Zambia	118.4%	15	Germany	-14.1%
16	Congo, Republic of	117.5%	16	Croatia	-13.3%
17	Guinea-Bissau	115.8%	17	Cuba	-13.2%
18	Liberia	115.5%	18	Greenland	-12.9%
19	Gambia	114.9%	19	Hungary	-10.4%
20	Rwanda	114.9%	20	Slovakia	-9.1%

World's Largest Cities

Rank	City or Conurbation	Population	Rank	City or Conurbation	Population
1	Tokyo/Yokohama	36,668,510	26	Shenzhen	9,005,283
2	Delhi	22,156,810	27	Lima/Callao	8,940,555
3	São Paulo	20,262,493	28	Guangzhou	8,883,865
4	Mumbai	20,040,868	29	Kinshasa	8,753,869
5	Mexico City	19,460,212	30	London	8,631,325
6	New York	19,425,069	31	Bogota	8,499,820
7	Shanghai	16,575,110	32	Tianjin	7,884,473
8	Kolkata	15,552,080	33	Wuhan	7,681,099
9	Dhaka	14,648,354	34	Chennai	7,546,954
10	Karachi	13,124,793	35	Tehran	7,241,004
11	Buenos Aires	13,074,389	36	Bangalore	7,217,570
12	Los Angeles	12,762,091	37	Lahore	7,131,864
13	Beijing	12,385,263	38	Hong Kong	7,069,378
14	Rio de Janeiro	11,949,619	39	Bangkok/Thonburi	6,976,471
15	Manila/Quezon City	11,628,288	40	Hyderabad	6,750,650
16	Osaka/Kobe	11,337,016	41	Rhein/Ruhr	6,708,000
17	Cairo	11,001,378	42	Ho Chi Minh	6,167,090
18	Lagos	10,577,672	43	Santiago	5,951,554
19	Moscow	10,549,892	44	Baghdad	5,890,677
20	Istanbul	10,524,625	45	Belo Horizonte	5,852,358
21	Paris	10,485,263	46	Madrid	5,851,288
22	Seoul	9,772,717	47	Miami/Fort Lauderdale	5,749,900
23	Chongqing	9,401,170	48	Ahmadabad	5,717,173
24	Jakarta	9,210,211	49	Philadelphia	5,625,504
25	Chicago	9,203,838	50	Toronto	5,449,456

Urbanization is an inevitable trend of 21st-Century life and even human existence. This is clearly articulated in the Bible. Mankind's story begins in a garden (Genesis 2:8), but ends in a megacity (Revelation 21-22). However, it was only as recently as 2009 that the world's population became 50% urban. Today, cities are increasingly the centre of human activity and growth. In much of the world this growth occurs largely through migration to informal settlements on the fringes of cities proper – in slums, squatter camps, shantytowns, *barrios* and *favelas*. Most of these offer little by way of safety, sanitation and electricity or employment and education opportunities; poverty, exploitation and desperation abound. Ministry possibilities are almost endless. Remember, though, that while urban ministry is crucial and will become increasingly so, 49% of humanity remains in a rural context. Let Christians not ignore the needs of the world's 3.4 billion rural dwellers.

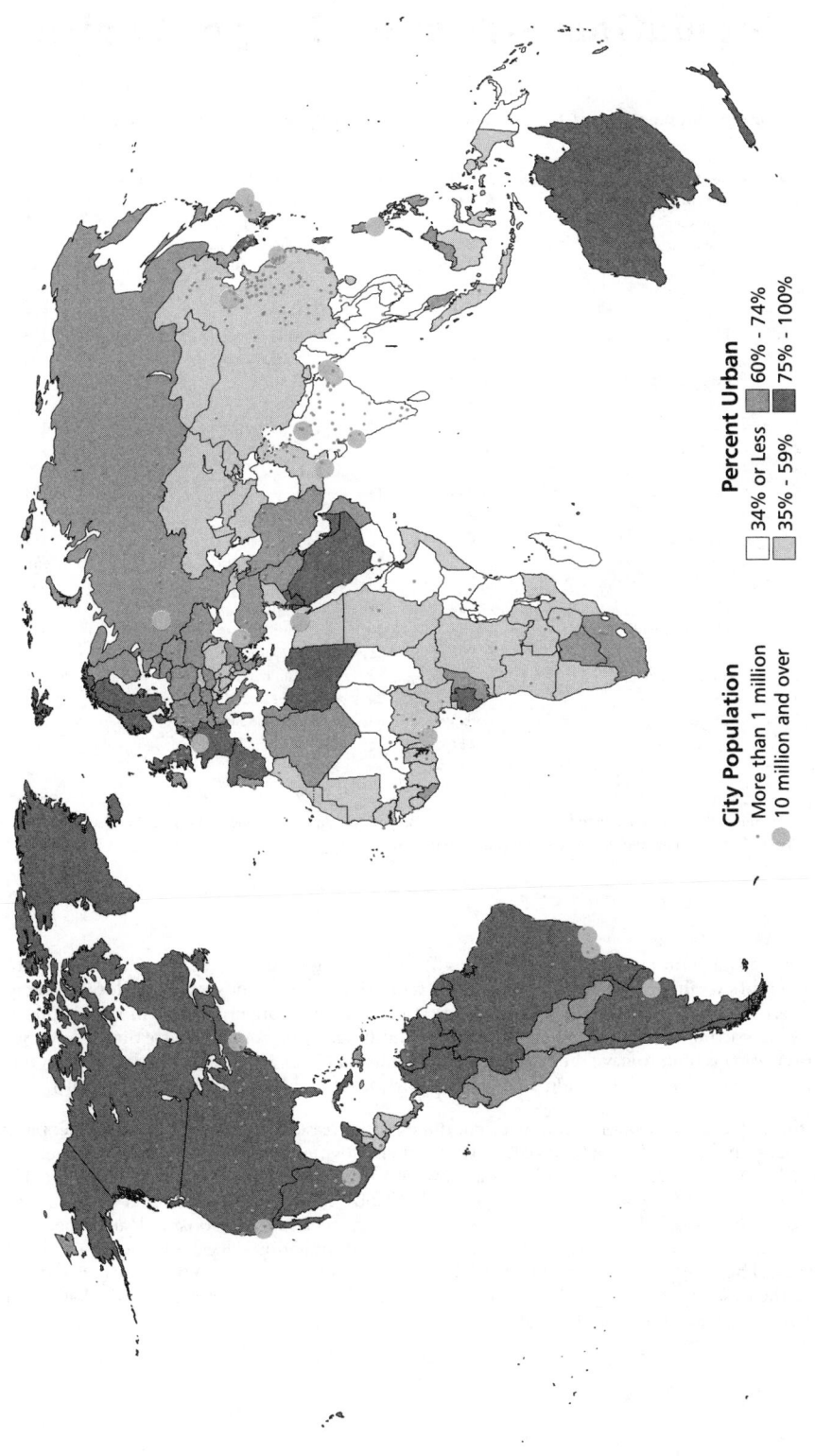

City Population

. More than 1 million

● 10 million and over

Percent Urban

- 34% or Less
- 35% - 59%
- 60% - 74%
- 75% - 100%

Appendix 1: Global Facts & Figures   905

Population, Age and GDP per Capita

Countries with the Highest GDP per Capita			Countries with the Lowest GDP per Capita*		
Rank	Country	GDP/capita (USD)	Rank	Country	GDP/capita (USD)
1	Luxembourg	113,044	1	Burundi	138
2	Norway	94,387	2	Congo-DRC	185
3	Qatar	93,204	3	Liberia	216
4	Switzerland	68,433	4	Guinea-Bissau	264
5	Denmark	62,097	5	Zimbabwe	268
6	Ireland	60,510	6	Eritrea	295
7	United Arab Emirates	55,028	7	Malawi	313
8	Iceland	53,058	8	Sierra Leone	332
9	Netherlands	52,500	9	Ethiopia	333
10	Sweden	52,181	10	Niger	391
11	Finland	51,588	11	Afghanistan	416
12	Austria	50,039	12	Togo	436
13	USA	47,440	13	Guinea	439
14	Belgium	47,289	14	Nepal	444
15	Australia	46,824	15	Myanmar	446
16	France	46,037	16	Uganda	455
17	Kuwait	45,920	17	Central African Republic	459
18	Canada	45,085	18	Rwanda	465
19	Germany	44,729	19	Madagascar	468
20	United Kingdom	43,734	20	Timor Leste	469
21	Italy	38,996	21	Mozambique	477
22	Singapore	38,972	22	Gambia, The	497
23	Japan	38,457	23	Tanzania	520
24	Brunei	37,053	24	Bangladesh	521
25	Spain	35,117	25	Burkina Faso	578

*Bear in mind that for some countries experiencing great political and economic instability, data (even reasonable estimates) are inaccessible, and therefore not included in this list.

An undeniable connection exists between affluence, average population age and fertility rates. The world's wealthiest populations are almost without exception those with the lowest average number of children per family and the highest median age. Longer periods in education, the delay in starting families and smaller desired family sizes all contribute to this. Conversely, poorer nations tend to have much higher fertility rates, a larger average family size, and younger populations (by virtue of having a greater proportion of children and shorter life spans).

As the population of poorer countries continues to increase, so will the number of people in competition for already-scarce resources, land and employment. In affluent countries, population growth is low, or even in decline, with a growing proportion of society at retirement age. This creates a demand for younger workers from other lands. These factors, combined with the large income gap between the world's richest and poorest, now fuel migration on a scale unprecedented in human history. As these trends continue, the levels of migration – legal and illegal – will only increase. This reality will profoundly shape Christian ministry to poorer countries, which also tend to be the least evangelized. Further, it confirms that ministry to migrant populations will continue as a growing area of need and opportunity.

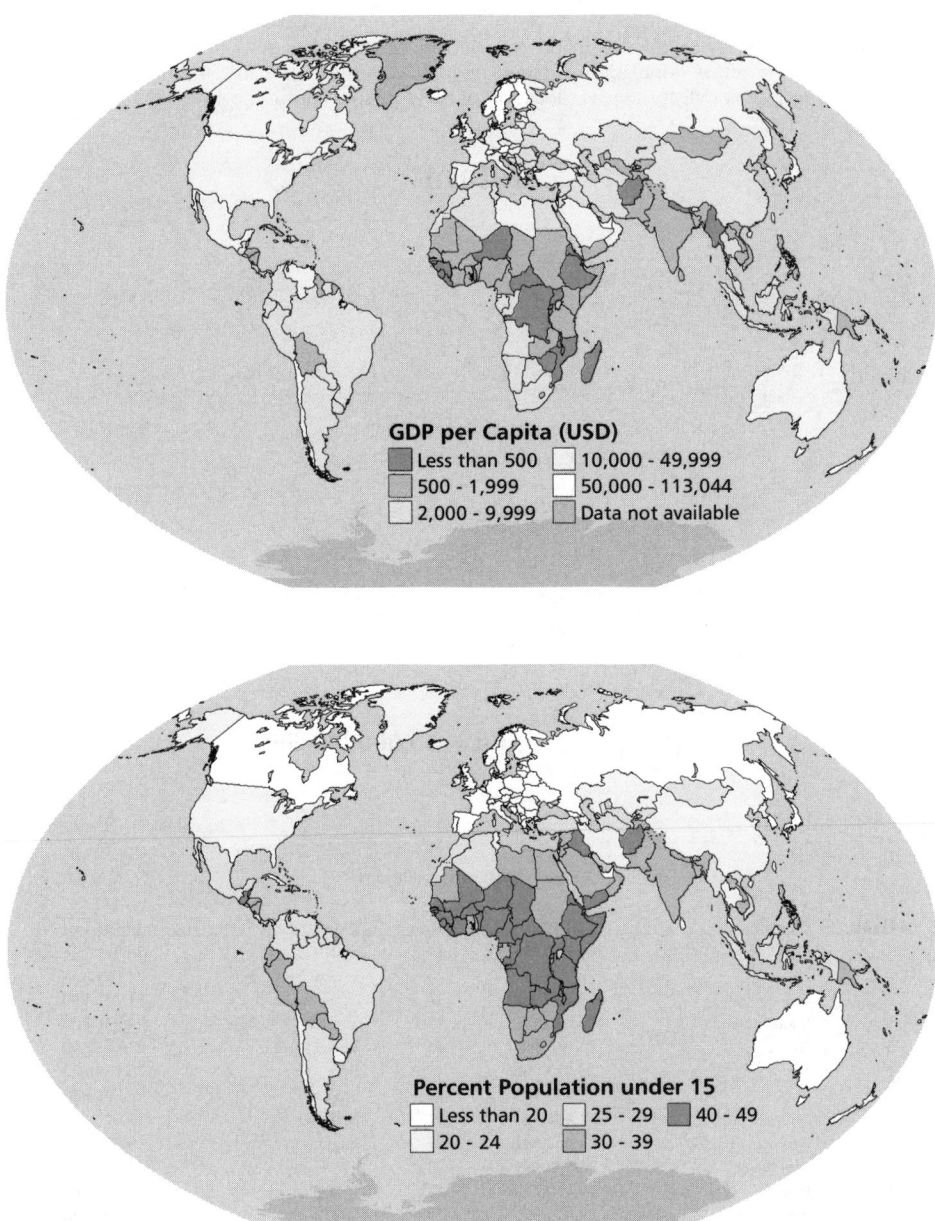

Appendix 1: Global Facts & Figures   907

Population of the World's Major Religions

The following maps show the dispersion of various religious populations. Please note that dots are representative of the population of countries and regions rather than religious groups, and so do not in all cases reflect the exact location of these people within the country.

Islam

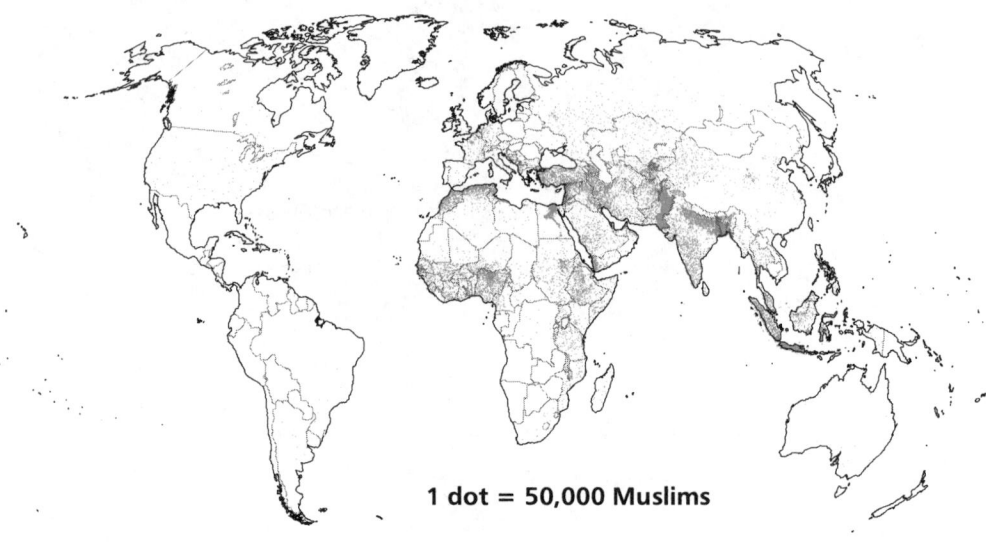

1 dot = 50,000 Muslims

Largest Muslim Populations

Rank	Country	Muslims	Rank	Country	Muslims
1	Indonesia	186,734,219	14	Sudan	26,511,518
2	Pakistan	176,993,661	15	China, PRC	24,881,935
3	India	172,453,932	16	Saudi Arabia	24,253,900
4	Bangladesh	146,355,130	17	Yemen	24,236,523
5	Iran	74,048,985	18	Uzbekistan	23,605,696
6	Egypt	73,213,986	19	Syria	20,254,582
7	Turkey	73,159,940	20	Russia	17,545,820
8	Nigeria	71,406,423	21	Malaysia	17,476,949
9	Algeria	34,462,637	22	Niger	15,436,986
10	Morocco	32,738,475	23	Tanzania	14,052,347
11	Iraq	30,179,710	24	Senegal	11,709,683
12	Afghanistan	29,074,395	25	Mali	11,641,728
13	Ethiopia	28,976,682			

Hinduism

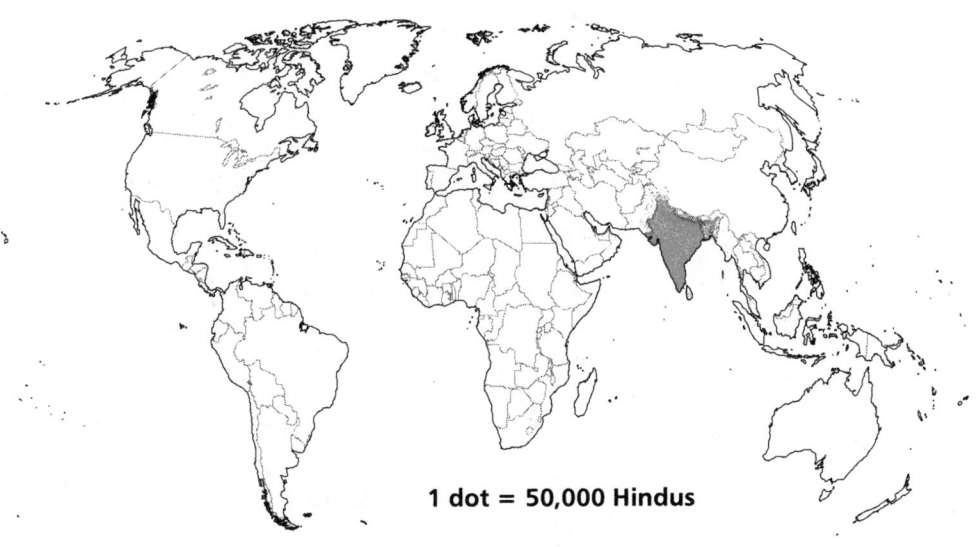

1 dot = 50,000 Hindus

Largest Hindu Populations

Rank	Country	Hindus	Rank	Country	Hindus
1	India	902,711,323	14	Canada	338,897
2	Nepal	22,389,512	15	Trinidad & Tobago	290,245
3	Bangladesh	14,962,720	16	Fiji	237,525
4	Indonesia	3,022,718	17	Guyana	230,717
5	Pakistan	2,956,053	18	Myanmar	227,231
6	Sri Lanka	2,612,473	19	Saudi Arabia	204,719
7	Malaysia	1,730,667	20	Australia	204,320
8	USA	1,334,093	21	Singapore	198,304
9	United Arab Emirates	729,633	22	Oman	197,548
10	Mauritius	629,161	23	Kenya	167,538
11	South Africa	605,909	24	Bhutan	158,913
12	United Kingdom	584,020	25	Italy	156,254
13	Tanzania	405,356			

Buddhism

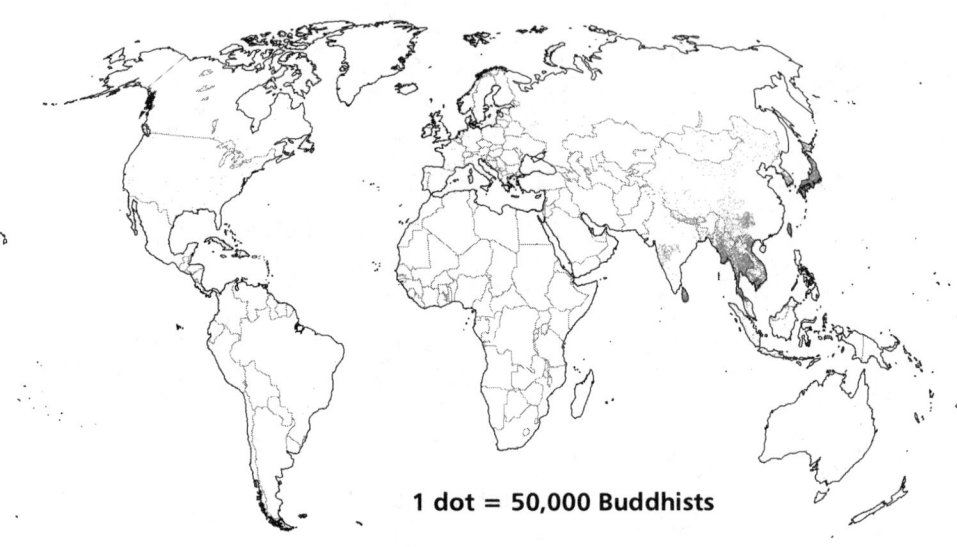

1 dot = 50,000 Buddhists

Largest Buddhist Populations

Rank	Country	Buddhists	Rank	Country	Buddhists
1	China, PRC	166,323,098	14	Singapore	1,949,186
2	Japan	88,376,107	15	Malaysia	1,814,409
3	Thailand	58,136,398	16	Russia	996,603
4	Vietnam	46,722,283	17	Bangladesh	986,553
5	Myanmar	40,416,736	18	Mongolia	953,494
6	Sri Lanka	14,209,404	19	Indonesia	930,067
7	Cambodia	12,545,264	20	France	607,575
8	Korea, South	10,621,657	21	Australia	559,192
9	India	9,958,607	22	Bhutan	528,246
10	China, Taiwan	6,785,758	23	Brazil	508,100
11	Nepal	4,776,429	24	Canada	372,787
12	Laos	3,687,238	25	Italy	258,420
13	USA	2,287,016			

Non-religious

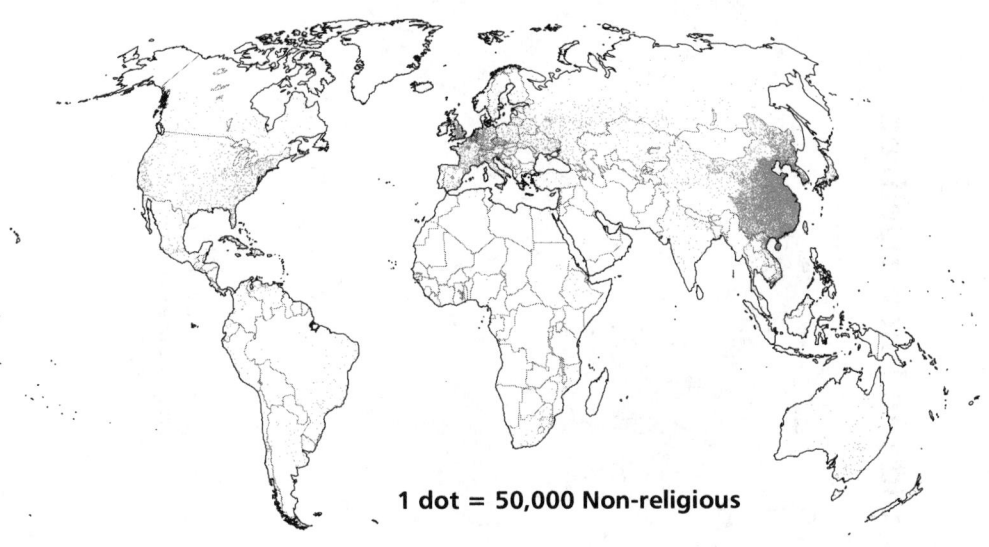

1 dot = 50,000 Non-religious

Largest Non-religious Populations

Rank	Country	Non-religious	Rank	Country	Non-religious
1	China, PRC	590,247,410	14	Czech Republic	7,434,342
2	USA	52,410,779	15	Canada	6,469,553
3	Russia	26,880,196	16	Japan	6,349,771
4	Germany	25,035,522	17	India	5,829,429
5	United Kingdom	21,428,574	18	Kazakhstan	5,346,724
6	Vietnam	20,743,697	19	Australia	4,996,165
7	Korea, North	16,654,346	20	Brazil	4,377,481
8	France	16,304,302	21	Mexico	3,983,226
9	Korea, South	14,962,471	22	South Africa	3,903,063
10	Ukraine	8,850,429	23	Poland	3,853,259
11	Spain	8,849,212	24	Uzbekistan	3,835,613
12	Italy	8,491,786	25	Venezuela	3,534,601
13	Netherlands	7,803,758			

Christians and the Unevangelized

Blue dots represent Christians
Grey dots represent Unevangelized
1 dot = 50,000 people

Largest Christian Populations

Rank	Country	Christians	Rank	Country	Christians
1	USA	246,553,012	14	France	38,296,005
2	Brazil	178,616,852	15	South Africa	37,990,488
3	China, PRC	105,382,315	16	United Kingdom	37,066,649
4	Mexico	105,143,877	17	Indonesia	36,853,908
5	Russia	93,905,229	18	Argentina	36,843,153
6	Philippines	86,361,547	19	Ukraine	35,896,941
7	Nigeria	81,123,521	20	Spain	35,055,968
8	India	76,997,037	21	Poland	34,093,544
9	Congo-DRC	60,854,829	22	Kenya	33,805,877
10	Germany	52,721,478	23	Uganda	28,639,121
11	Ethiopia	51,563,198	24	Peru	28,154,047
12	Italy	49,508,373	25	Venezuela	24,553,421
13	Colombia	43,716,645			

Countries with the Highest Christian Population (% Total Pop)* / Countries with the Lowest Christian Population (% Total Pop)

Rank	Country	% Christian	Rank	Country	% Christian
1	Nicaragua	97.67	1	Afghanistan	0.05
2	Romania	96.96	2	Yemen	0.08
3	Malta	96.82	3	Morocco	0.09
4	Guam	96.69	4	Maldives	0.17
5	Micronesia	96.65	5	Tunisia	0.21
6	Honduras	96.64	6	Turkey	0.21
7	Samoa	96.60	7	Mauritania	0.25
8	Paraguay	96.30	8	Algeria	0.28
9	Guatemala	96.12	9	Niger	0.33
10	Papua New Guinea	95.84	10	Somalia	0.33
11	Martinique	95.80	11	Iran	0.52
12	Solomon Islands	95.80	12	Bangladesh	0.66
13	Tonga	95.76	13	Uzbekistan	0.75
14	Peru	95.45	14	Comoros	0.93
15	Puerto Rico	95.28	15	Tajikistan	1.04
16	Haiti	95.12	16	Thailand	1.10
17	Saint Lucia	95.08	17	Korea, North	1.48
18	Mexico	95.03	18	Japan	1.54
19	US Virgin Islands	94.95	19	Iraq	1.59
20	Barbados	94.94	20	Palestine	1.61
21	Bahamas, The	94.65	21	Mayotte	1.64
22	El Salvador	94.63	22	Mongolia	1.72
23	Cape Verde Islands	94.56	23	Djibouti	1.75
24	Ecuador	94.45	24	Turkmenistan	1.83
25	Armenia	94.43	25	Israel	2.04

*This list was generated from countries with a total population greater than 100,000, as very small population size – when comparing percentages – can be misleading. Furthermore, the list generated from all states and territories for which OW has data produces a list topped largely by entities of very small population, not necessarily countries in their own right.

World Evangelical Population

Rank	Country	% Evangelical
	Countries with the Highest % of Evangelicals (% Total Pop)	
1	Kenya	48.92
2	Vanuatu	45.92
3	Marshall Islands	44.50
4	Saint Vincent	39.09
5	Uganda	37.01
6	Bahamas, The	35.92
7	Barbados	34.15
8	Solomon Islands	33.34
9	Turks & Caicos Islands	32.39
10	Central African Republic	32.25
11	El Salvador	31.65
12	Zimbabwe	30.93
13	Nigeria	30.84
14	Nicaragua	29.75
15	USA	28.89
16	Faeroe Islands	28.77
17	Jamaica	28.01
18	British Virgin Islands	27.30
19	Burundi	27.04
20	Rwanda	26.87
21	Brazil	26.27
22	Papua New Guinea	25.74
23	Zambia	25.69
24	Fiji	25.22
25	Puerto Rico	25.20
26	Swaziland	25.11
27	Guatemala	24.44
28	Micronesia	24.31
29	Bermuda	24.29
30	Ghana	24.16
31	Palau	23.89
32	US Virgin Islands	23.83
33	Montserrat	23.38
34	Honduras	23.00
35	Norfolk Island	22.72

Rank	Country	% Evangelical
	Countries with the Lowest % of Evangelicals (% Total Pop)	
1	Turkey	0.01
2	Tunisia	0.01
3	San Marino	0.01
4	Morocco	0.01
5	Yemen	0.02
6	Afghanistan	0.03
7	Turkmenistan	0.03
8	Somalia	0.05
9	Montenegro	0.05
10	Saint Pierre & Miquelon	0.05
11	Bosnia	0.06
12	Mauritania	0.06
13	Maldives	0.07
14	Slovenia	0.09
15	Palestine	0.09
16	Tajikistan	0.10
17	Syria	0.11
18	Mayotte	0.12
19	Niger	0.14
20	Djibouti	0.14
21	Iran	0.16
22	Iraq	0.17
23	Comoros	0.18
24	Senegal	0.20
25	Azerbaijan	0.21
26	Macedonia	0.21
27	Algeria	0.24
28	Poland	0.25
29	Jordan	0.30
30	Libya	0.30
31	Uzbekistan	0.31
32	Saudi Arabia	0.34
33	Andorra	0.36
34	Greece	0.37
35	Bangladesh	0.39

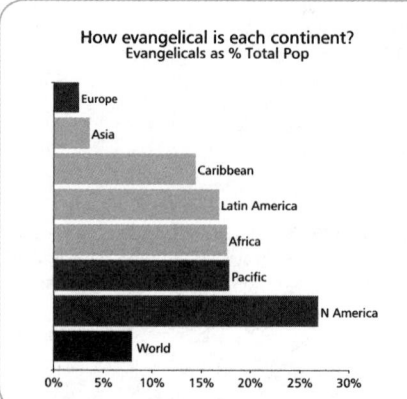

How evangelical is each continent?
Evangelicals as % Total Pop

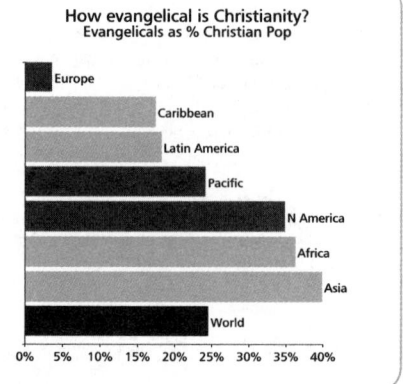

How evangelical is Christianity?
Evangelicals as % Christian Pop

The blue bars represent Majority World regions.

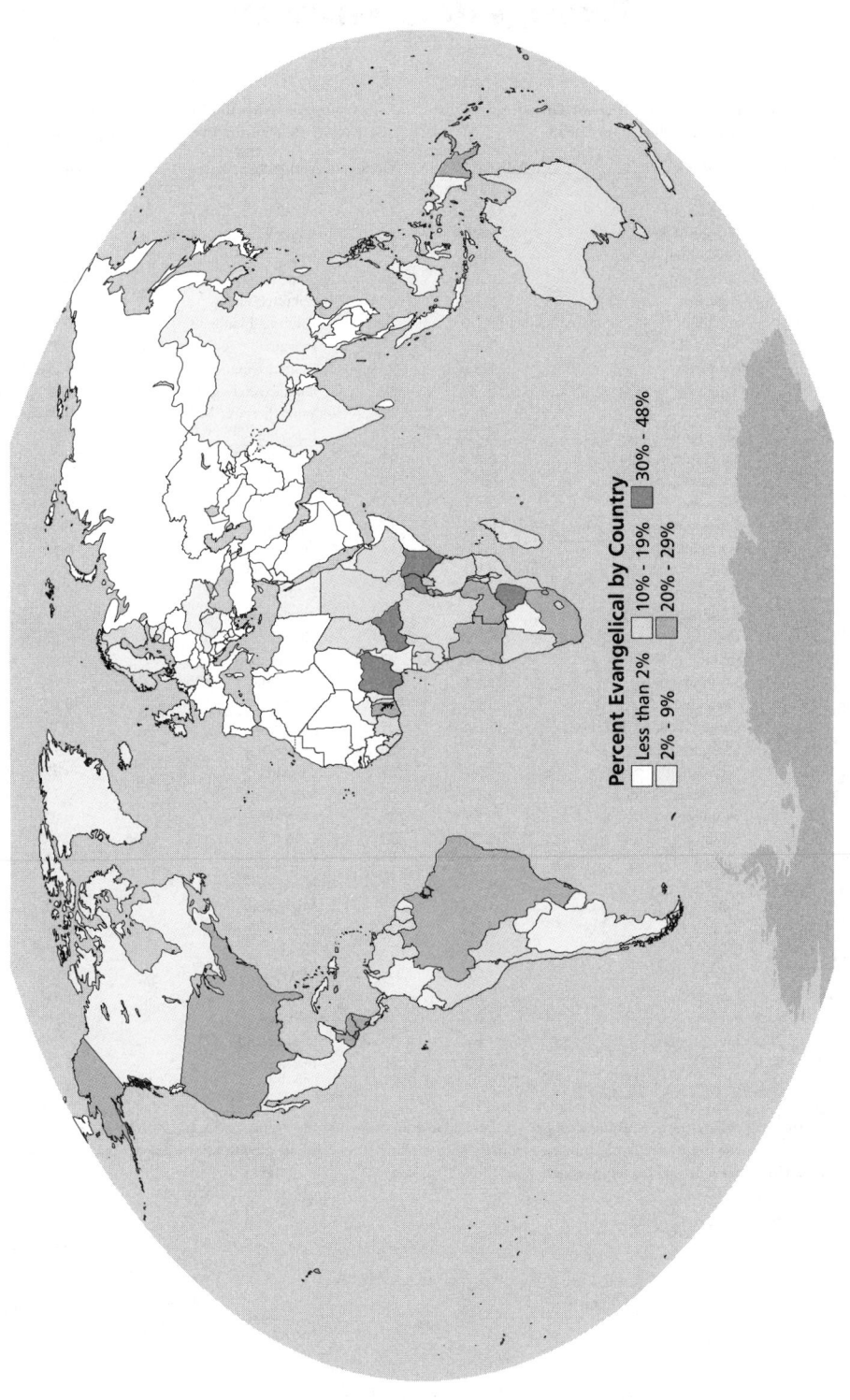

Percent Evangelical by Country

- Less than 2%
- 2% - 9%
- 10% - 19%
- 20% - 29%
- 30% - 48%

Evangelical Growth

	Countries with the Fastest Growing Evangelical Population			Countries with the Slowest Growing (or Fastest Declining) Evangelical Population	
Rank	**Country**	**Ann Gr***	**Rank**	**Country**	**Ann Gr**
1	Iran	19.6%	1	Niue	-4.1%
2	Afghanistan	16.7%	2	Sweden	-0.6%
3	Gambia, The	8.9%	3	Georgia	-0.6%
4	Cambodia	8.8%	4	Japan	-0.4%
5	Greenland	8.4%	5	Slovenia	-0.2%
6	Algeria	8.1%	6	Tokelau Islands	-0.1%
7	Somalia	8.1%	7	Falkland Islands	-0.1%
8	Mongolia	7.9%	8	Finland	-0.1%
9	Kuwait	7.3%	9	United Kingdom	0.0%
10	Tajikistan	6.9%	10	Cocos (Keeling) Islands	0.0%
11	Laos	6.8%	11	Saint Pierre & Miquelon	0.0%
12	Mauritania	6.7%	12	Palestine	0.0%
13	São Tomé & Príncipe	6.5%	13	Denmark	0.2%
14	Sudan	6.4%	14	Swaziland	0.2%
15	Suriname	6.3%	15	Czech Republic	0.3%
16	Guinea-Bissau	6.2%	16	US Virgin Islands	0.3%
17	Senegal	6.1%	17	Tonga	0.4%
18	Korea, North	6.0%	18	Saint Helena	0.5%
19	Colombia	6.0%	19	Estonia	0.5%
20	Andorra	5.9%	20	New Zealand	0.5%
21	Oman	5.9%	21	Croatia	0.5%
22	Israel	5.6%	22	Netherlands	0.6%
23	San Marino	5.6%	23	Bermuda	0.6%
24	Nicaragua	5.5%	24	Guam	0.6%
25	United Arab Emirates	5.5%	25	Bulgaria	0.7%
26	Mozambique	5.4%	26	Korea, South	0.7%
27	Nepal	5.3%	27	Grenada	0.7%
28	Equatorial Guinea	5.3%	28	Samoa	0.7%
29	Montenegro	5.2%	29	Barbados	0.8%
30	Libya	5.2%	30	USA	0.8%
31	Yemen	5.1%	31	Canada	0.8%
32	Ecuador	4.9%	32	Hungary	0.8%
33	Belize	4.8%	33	Micronesia	0.9%
34	Tunisia	4.7%	34	Germany	0.9%
35	Togo	4.7%	35	Guyana	1.0%
36	Egypt	4.6%	36	Norway	1.0%
37	Liberia	4.6%	37	Australia	1.1%
38	Albania	4.6%	38	Portugal	1.1%
39	Luxembourg	4.6%	39	Switzerland	1.2%
40	Bolivia	4.6%	40	Botswana	1.2%

*For many of these countries, evangelical growth rates appear high because the evangelical population base is so small to begin with, borne out by the fact that many countries with the highest evangelical growth rates are also found on p914 in the list Countries with the Lowest % of Evangelicals (% Total Pop).

Christian Population
by World and Regions

World

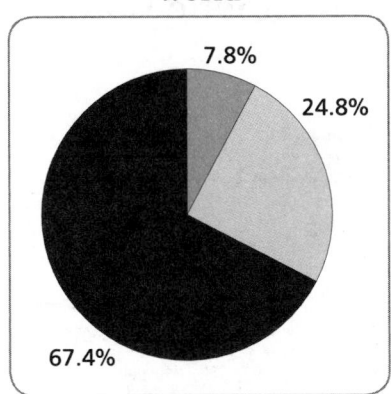

7.8%

24.8%

67.4%

Africa

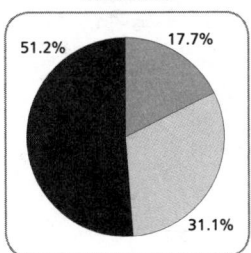

51.2% 17.7%

31.1%

Asia

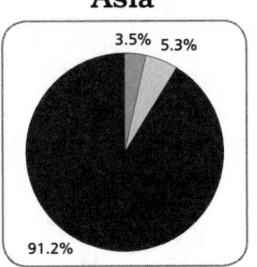

3.5% 5.3%

91.2%

Caribbean

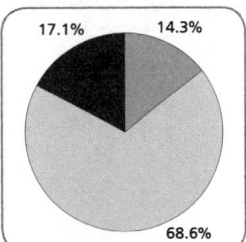

17.1% 14.3%

68.6%

Europe

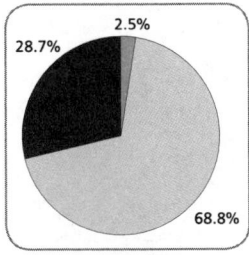

2.5%

28.7%

68.8%

Latin America

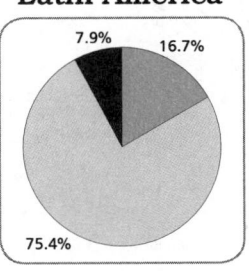

7.9% 16.7%

75.4%

North America

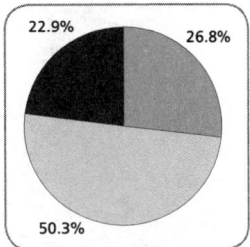

22.9% 26.8%

50.3%

Pacific

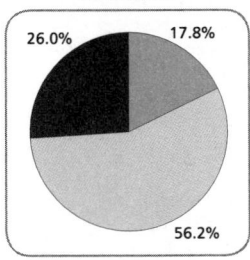

26.0% 17.8%

56.2%

Evangelicals

All other Christians

Non-Christians

Unreached Peoples

Geopolitical Boundaries in Contrast to Ethnolinguistic Boundaries

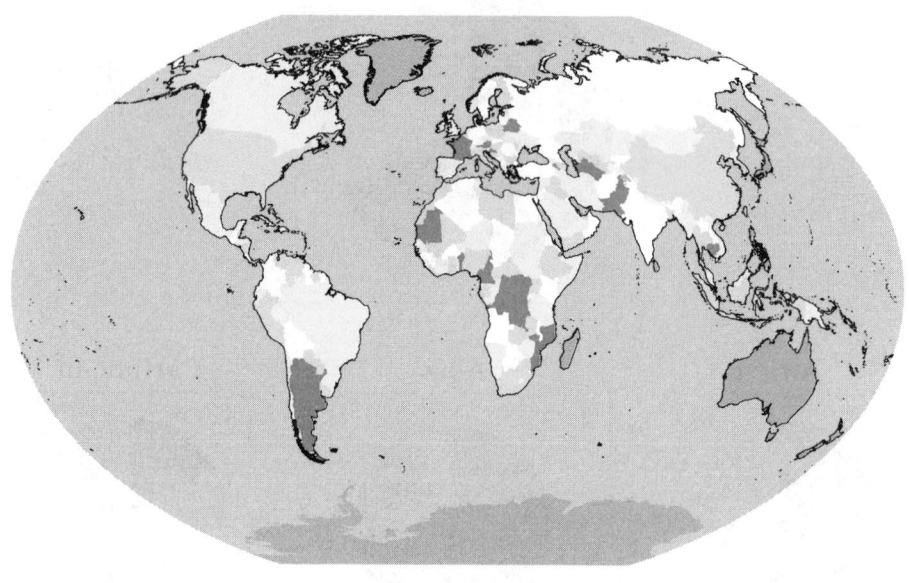

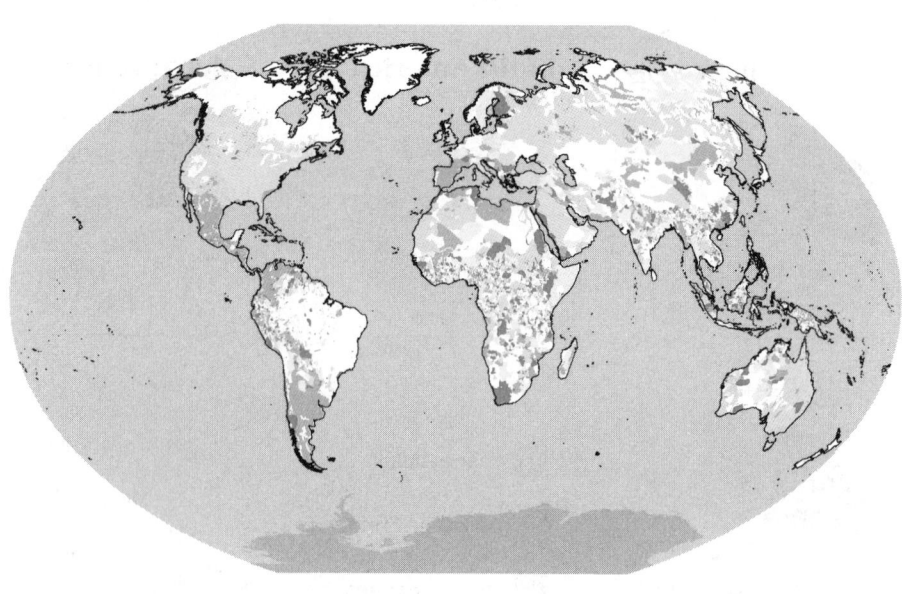

The maps on the facing page highlight the difference between a geopolitical concept of nation and the biblical concept of *ethne* (translated from Greek to English as "nation"). The complexity of countries is vastly greater than the simple straight lines drawn on a map. In fact, many country boundaries were "drawn" by foreign imperial powers with complete disregard for the geography of the land and affinity of the peoples therein, the most infamous example being that of the Berlin Conference of 1884-5. Colours in these maps only indicate boundaries and do not represent any values.

The bottom map indicates the scale of the task of contextualized evangelism, church planting, disciple-making and Bible translation. Pray for all those seeking to minister the gospel and see the church established across such cultural and ethnolinguistic boundaries; it takes a special gift and calling to commit to such efforts as a long-term ministry.

Each polygon on the bottom map represents a unique people, with its own language, worldview, values and culture. Note the particularly complex ethnic patchwork in much of Africa, in South and Southeast Asia and Papua New Guinea. On the list below, note that the top five countries for numbers of unreached peoples all have contiguous borders with one other. Twelve of the top 16 countries form a single contiguous cluster.

Countries with the Highest Number of Unreached Peoples

Rank	Country	Unreached Peoples	Rank	Country	Unreached Peoples
1	India	2,223	21	Kazakhstan	41
2	China, PRC	427	22	Israel	40
3	Pakistan	374	23	Turkey	38
4	Bangladesh	353	24	Mali	37
5	Nepal	325	25	Uzbekistan	37
6	Indonesia	200	26	Algeria	35
7	Sudan	138	27	Kenya	35
8	Laos	134	28	Côte d'Ivoire	34
9	Iran	93	29	Tanzania	33
10	Russia	77	30	France	33
11	Thailand	75	31	Bhutan	32
12	Chad	72	32	Cambodia	30
13	Afghanistan	71	33	Guinea	29
14	Nigeria	67	34	Burkina Faso	28
15	Sri Lanka	64	35	Libya	28
16	Vietnam	63	36	Niger	28
17	USA	59	37	United Kingdom	28
18	Brazil	58	38	Senegal	27
19	Malaysia	56	39	Kyrgyzstan	27
20	Myanmar	51	40	Tajikistan	27

Appendix 1: Global Facts & Figures

Largest Unreached People Groups

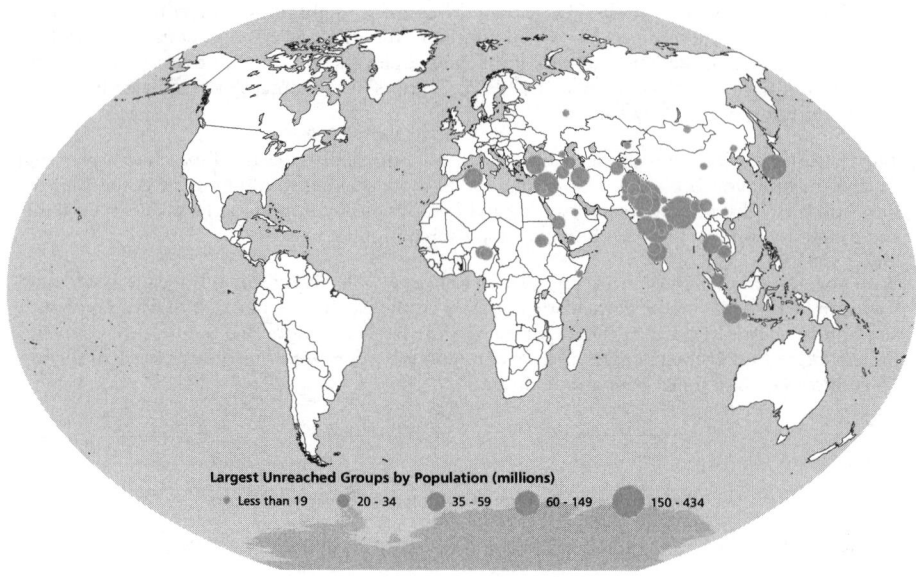

Largest Unreached Groups by Population (millions)

Less than 19 — 20 - 34 — 35 - 59 — 60 - 149 — 150 - 434

No country is comprised of only one people group. Some have thousands of diverse groups — India alone has 2,533 people groups. Some countries are divided among a handful of significant minorities. Other countries have one majority people that dominates the population (and usually the political and economic structures as well). The above map points out the size and location of the largest unreached peoples.

Pray for healthy relations among peoples; often rivalry, tension and outright hostility characterize their interactions. These dynamics can date back centuries and profoundly shape entire countries and regions. Yet the gospel has been shown to powerfully overcome such enmity once it has a foothold in cultures. Pray for national leaders as they deal with the challenge of diversity, hopefully with wisdom and justice. Pray for Christian leaders as they seek to bring the gospel to every people group, neglecting none. Pray for Christians from differing ethnic backgrounds to be shining examples of the peace and reconciliation that come only through Jesus.

People Group Diversity in Contrast to Prevalence of Largest People Group

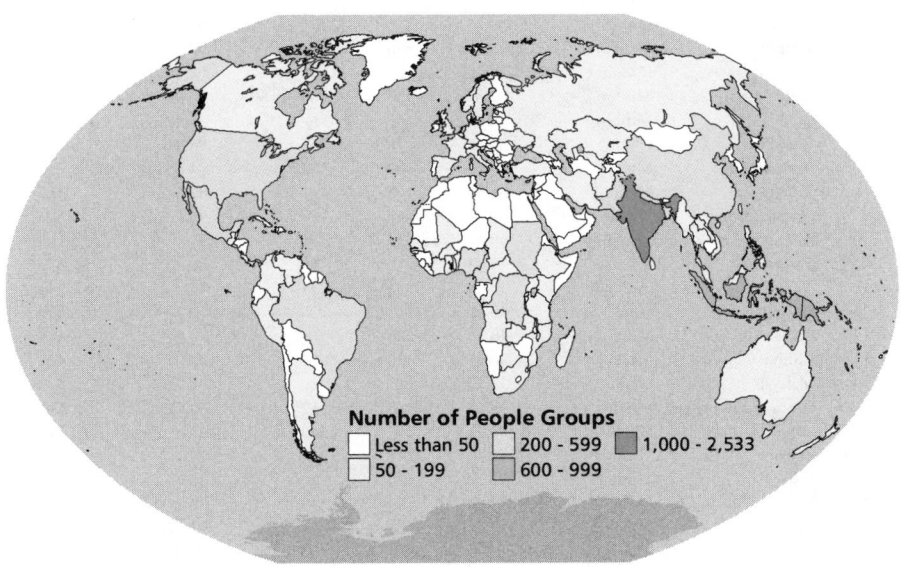

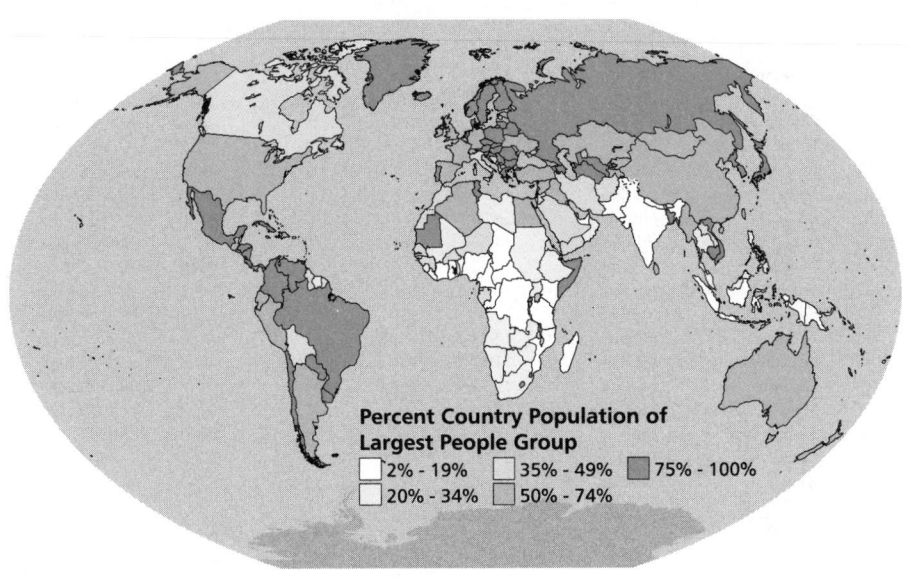

Largest Unreached People Clusters

Rank	People Cluster	Main Religions	Pop (mill)	Peoples All	UP	% Unreached	Main Region
1	Hindi	Hindu	434.46	586	529	90.3	S Asia
2	Bengali	Muslim	325.29	395	385	97.5	S Asia
3	Japanese	Buddhist	128.78	57	39	68.4	E Asia
4	Urdu Muslim	Muslim	103.87	358	358	100.0	S Asia
5	Jat	Muslim	68.84	166	164	98.8	S Asia
6	Rajasthan	Hindu	68.42	178	177	99.4	S Asia
7	Arab, Levant	Muslim	65.40	129	32	24.8	Middle East
8	Telugu	Hindu	61.55	164	147	89.6	S Asia
9	Marathi-Konkani	Hindu	59.77	140	129	92.1	S Asia
10	Arab, Maghreb	Muslim	59.41	35	34	97.1	N Africa
11	Turkic	Muslim	58.04	58	50	86.2	W Asia
12	Thai	Buddhist	55.08	33	31	93.9	SE Asia
13	Gujarati	Hindu	50.20	212	205	96.7	S Asia
14	Persian	Muslim	48.26	88	65	73.9	W Asia
15	Pashtun	Muslim	46.51	26	26	100.0	S Asia
16	Malayali	Hindu	36.10	115	82	71.3	S Asia
17	Sunda-Betawi of Java	Muslim	35.63	3	2	66.7	SE Asia
18	Kannada	Hindu	34.91	164	160	97.6	S Asia
19	Punjabi	Muslim	33.70	241	230	95.4	S Asia
20	Hausa	Muslim	33.28	20	20	100.0	W Africa
21	Fulani / Fulbe	Muslim	32.64	50	49	98.0	W Africa
22	Burmese	Buddhist	32.46	26	24	92.3	SE Asia
23	Kurd	Muslim	29.86	53	53	100.0	W Asia
24	Arab, Arabian	Muslim	29.37	93	66	71.0	Middle East
25	Azerbaijani	Muslim	29.21	36	36	100.0	W Asia
26	Uzbek	Muslim	27.17	20	20	100.0	C Asia
27	Mon-Khmer	Buddhist	25.96	223	161	72.2	SE Asia
28	Malay	Muslim	24.82	82	44	53.7	SE Asia
29	Arab, Sudan	Muslim	23.46	44	43	97.7	N Africa
30	West China / Lolo	Ethnoreligionist	21.24	170	127	74.7	E Asia/SE Asia
31	Zhuang	Ethnoreligionist	18.92	29	26	89.7	E Asia/SE Asia
32	Chinese-Hui	Muslim	18.54	18	17	94.4	East Asia
33	Bedouin, Arabian	Muslim	17.37	15	15	100.0	Middle East
34	Oriya	Hindu	16.13	313	302	96.5	S Asia
35	Somali	Muslim	15.96	29	28	96.6	Horn of Africa
36	Gond	Hindu	15.88	11	8	72.7	S Asia
37	Uyghur	Muslim	15.61	24	24	100.0	E Asia/C Asia
38	Madura of Java	Muslim	14.90	5	4	80.0	SE Asia
39	Bhil	Hindu	14.65	8	8	100.0	S Asia
40	Jews	Ethnoreligionist	14.55	181	176	97.2	Middle East
41	Manchu	Non-religious	13.42	4	4	100.0	E Asia
42	Other South Asian	Hindu	13.41	161	134	83.2	S Asia
43	Kazakh	Muslim	12.93	34	33	97.1	C Asia
44	Nepali-Pahari	Hindu	12.87	85	77	90.6	S Asia
45	Ural-Siberian	Muslim	11.67	104	57	54.8	E Europe
46	Caucasus	Muslim	11.32	157	122	77.7	W Asia/E Europe
47	Miao / Hmong	Ethnoreligionist	11.23	69	47	68.1	SE Asia
48	Arab, Yemeni	Muslim	11.18	16	16	100.0	Middle East
49	Mongolian	Buddhist	11.09	49	43	87.8	E Asia
50	Baloch	Muslim	10.44	22	22	100.0	S Asia

Further Prayer Information

The information in *Operation World* gives a general overview of the world and the growth of the Kingdom of the Lord Jesus Christ, but for more effective and specific prayer, make use of other material containing more detailed and updated information. To enable this, many agency names/abbreviations are displayed in bold type throughout this book. Our prayer is that you make use of the contact details of these agencies and publishers of printed and electronic information. Every Christian with a heart for the evangelization of the world ought to subscribe to several publications. Many missionaries and intercessors recall their younger years spent with noses eagerly buried in tales of exploration and adventure, reading missionary prayer letters from far-off fields or poring through copies of *National Geographic*. We enthusiastically encourage subscribing to, or bookmarking in your web browser, a selection of the following links.

These lists are by no means comprehensive! They represent but a few of our own favourites and those we rely on for information, inspiration and news. There are far too many publications and websites to even attempt an extensive list in this book (URLs occasionally change). However, check the OW website (www.operationworld.org) for a more frequently updated set of links to valuable resources on prayer and mission.

a) Prayer Networks

The multiplication of prayer movements and networks since the mid-1990s is one of the biggest points for praise in the worldwide Church! The global prayer movement is gathering momentum as never before, springing up in many regions of the world and focusing on ever-more diverse places, peoples and issues. Intercessors all over the world connect with each other, thanks to modern communications technology. You can be one of them.

Visit the websites that follow to connect with other people with a heart for prayer and mission. This is only a selection of those globally focused prayer networks known to us. There are more we know of and most likely many we do not – especially those based in the Majority World. Countless networks focus on specific peoples, issues, themes, countries, regions, cities, and even neighbourhoods; naturally, too many to include here.

Global

24-7 Prayer
www.24-7prayer.com
An international, interdenominational movement of prayer, mission and justice now in over 100 nations.

International Prayer Connect
www.ipcprayer.org
A network of networks, connecting prayer movements globally. Free video and written resources for mobilizing prayer for adults, youth and children.

Ethnê
www.ethne.net/prayer
Prayer networks for the world's least reached peoples.

Intercessors Network
www.intercessors.wordpress.com
Excellent prayer and mission-focused news from around the world.

Jericho Walls International Prayer Network
www.jwipn.com
Mobilizing the global Church as a house of prayer for all nations.

International House of Prayer
www.ihop.org
24-hour intercessory worship and prayer.

Every Home for Christ
www.ehc.org
School of Prayer, prayer groups and resources.

Prayer Central
www.prayercentral.net
Offering tools and equipping intercessors.

Prayer Guard
www.prayerguard.net
Set up or connect to a prayer network for any missionary or unreached people.

Prayer Planet
www.prayerplanet.net
Online prayer network with customizable prayer groups and themes.

Global Prayer Connection
www.globalprayerconnection.com
Connecting people to form prayer groups and pray online for any local, national or global issue.

Wycliffe International Prayer Focus
www.wycliffe.net
Weekly prayer and praise updates from around the world.

National Pastors' Prayer Network
www.nppn.org
Encouraging citywide pastoral prayer groups; articles on prayer.

Intercessory Prayer Ministry International
www.goipmi.com
US and worldwide prayer networking and information.

Generals International
www.generals.org
Reformation Prayer Network (RPN), spiritual warfare, prophetic words.

Lydia Fellowship International
www.lydiafellowshipinternational.org
Women's prayer network, with regional and local branches.

Thematic

4/14 Window Global Initiative
www.4to14window.com/newsletter
Raising awareness of the 4-14 age group.

Bibleless Peoples Prayer Project
www.bit.ly/mH6SB
Focused prayer on language groups still waiting for God's Word.

Viva Network
www.viva.org
Prayer for children at risk.

b) Prayer Resources

Here follows a brief list of publications wholly or mostly given to providing resources for prayer. This list is regularly updated on the Operation World website.

Intercession Tools and Resources

Awaken the Watchmen 24-7 Prayer
www.global24-7.org
Resources for establishing 24-7 prayer watches.

Waymakers
www.waymakers.org
Guides for prayerwalking, praying for your city and other practical prayer matters.

Global Day of Prayer
www.globaldayofprayer.com
A 10-day and 90-day prayer guide for the days before and after the GDOP.

Harvest Prayer Ministries
www.harvestprayer.com
Equipping the local church to become a house of prayer for the nations.

Intercessors Arise International
www.intercessorsarise.org
Training and resources to develop mission-oriented intercession.

Children in Prayer
www.childreninprayer.org
Various resources useful to start or maintain a CiP ministry in your church or city.

Children's Prayer Network
www.kidspray.org.au
Mobilizing and networking praying groups of children.

Kids Prayer Network
www.kidsprayer.com
Resource for praying kids and for teaching kids to pray.

Global or Peoples Focus

Global Prayer Digest
www.globalprayerdigest.org
Monthly prayer guides for unreached peoples.

Window International Network
www.win1040.com
Praying through the 10/40 Window.

Joshua Project
www.joshuaproject.net
Worldwide people group information, including people-of-the-day for prayer.

Joel News International
www.joelnews.org
Worldwide news on Kingdom breakthroughs and prayer needs.

Etnopedia
www.en.etnopedia.org
Editable website on the peoples of the world from a Christian perspective.

Peoples around the World
www.imb.org/main/aroundtheworld.asp
Prayer information for the world's peoples by affinity blocs.

AFM People Profiles
www.afm-us.org
People group profiles for prayer, by Anglican Frontier Missions.

SIM People Group Profiles
www.sim.org/index.php/category/people-groups
People group profiles for prominent African groups.

Prayercast
www.prayercast.com
Content- and media-rich country profiles for prayer.

Regions, Themes and Issues

Asia Harvest
www.asiaharvest.org/pages/profiles/profiles.html
Newsletter option, people group profiles for Asian countries.

30 Days Hindu Prayer Focus
www.30daysprayer.com/hindu
Praying for the Hindu world in 30 short sections.

South Asian Peoples
www.go2southasia.org/resource/printables
Downloadable prayer guides for religious blocs and issues of South Asia.

Southeast Asian peoples
www.seasianpeoples.org
Links to prayer resources for the countries and some people groups in this region.

Prayer for Southeast Asia
www.seapc.info
Prayer info on Southeast Asian nations with no dedicated website; specific prayer points sent in by e-mail.

OMF Resources: Peoples of the Buddhist World
www.omf.org/omf/buddhism/pray
Resources for praying for the Buddhist world.

FFM Prayer Bulletin
www.f-f-m.org.uk; www.ffmna.org
Emphasis on Muslims.

Praying through the Arabian Peninsula
www.pray-ap.info
Broad source of information and resources for prayer for this region.

Cry Out Now: Syria, Lebanon, Jordan, Iraq
www.cryoutnow.org
Prayer resources for the Fertile Crescent.

Turkish World Outreach
www.two-fot.org
News and prayer information for Turks and ministry to Turkic peoples.

Pray for Europe
www.prayeurope.com
Prayer information for European countries.

Prayer Alert
www.prayer-alert.net
Mobilizing prayer for and across the British Isles and Ireland.

Jewish Prayer Guide
www.zioninstitute.net
Prayer guide in praying for Jews and for peace in Jerusalem.

West Africa
www.gowestafrica.org/pray
Prayer requests and people group profiles for West African peoples.

Purposeful Africa
www.purposefulafrica.org/blog/category/country-profiles-and-prayer-guides
Prayer profiles for countries of West Africa and Africa-related issues.

Australia Prayer Network
www.ausprayernet.org.au
A resource to those called to pray for Australia and the world.

Campus America
www.campusamerica.org
Raising up prayer on every college campus in the USA.

Luke 18 Project
www.luke18project.com
Planting and fuelling prayer furnaces on every campus.

Hollywood Prayer Network
www.hollywoodprayernetwork.org
Mobilizing prayer for the globally influential entertainment industry.

Country Focus

There are countless websites that request prayer for specific countries. The sites below are a few that are well maintained with good content.

Pray for China
www.prayforchina.com

Pray for Denmark
www.prayfordenmarkblog.blogspot.com

Pray for France
www.prayforfrance.org

Iran 30
www.iran30.org

40 Days of Prayer and Fasting for Iran
www.prayforiran.org

IraqPrayer
www.iraqprayer.org

Japan Prayer Network
www.japanprayernetwork.com

Light for Libya
www.lightforlibya.org

Malaysia Prayer Net
www.prayer.net.my

PrayMalta
www.praymalta.net

Arise Shine Morocco
www.ariseshinemorocco.org

Global Day of Prayer for Burma (Myanmar)
www.prayforburma.org

Days of Prayer for Nepal
www.prayerfornepal.org/40-days-global-prayer

North Korea
www.omf.org/omf/uk/asia/countries_omf_centres/korea/north_korea_prayer_blog

Love Singapore
www.lovesingapore.org.sg

Somalia and Somalis Worldwide
www.prayforsomalia.org

Prayer for Thailand
www.blessthailand.net

Global Day of Prayer for Tibet and Tibetans
prayer@caf-international.net

Love Timor Leste
www.loveeasttimor.com

Revive Tunisia
www.revivetunisia.com

Day of Prayer for Turkey
www.prayforturkey.com

Intercessors for America
www.ifapray.org

National Day of Prayer (US)
www.nationaldayofprayer.org

c) Special Global Days for Prayer

March

Women's World Day of Prayer
www.worlddayofprayer.net

IPMI 2010 Twenty-One Days Fast
www.goipmi.com/main.asp?_p=62

Day of Prayer and Fasting for World Evangelization
bit.ly/aXyOgl

Pentecost Sunday

Global Day of Prayer
www.globaldayofprayer.com

September

International Day of Prayer for Peace
www.overcomingviolence.org/about-dov/international-day-of-prayer-for-peace.html

October

International Day of Prayer for the Peace of Jerusalem
www.daytopray.com

November

International Day of Prayer for the Persecuted Church
www.idop.org

Ramadan

30 Days of Prayer for the Muslim World
www.30-days.net

Further Mission Information

a) International Missional Networks

The following major interdenominational or inter-mission networks are important sources for information, networking, cooperation and mission. Many offer information for prayer, and all provide ways to learn more about, and get more involved in, world mission. This is not a comprehensive list; we simply point praying Christians toward certain major centres and resources.

Global

LCWE   **The Lausanne Movement**
www.lausanne.org
A worldwide movement that mobilizes evangelical leaders to collaborate for world evangelization. Formerly the Lausanne Committee for World Evangelization.

WEA   **World Evangelical Alliance**
www.worldevangelicals.org
The major body of global evangelical unity and cooperation.

–   **Ethnê to Ethnê**
www.ethne.net
A global network focused on the least-reached people groups of the world.

–   **Transform World**
www.transform–world.net
A global movement fostering cooperative ministry to address all areas of need in society.

AERDO   **Association of Evangelical Relief & Development Organizations**
www.aerdo.net
A network of agencies and a catalyst for learning, collaborating and building Christ-centred unity around the shared vision of eliminating poverty.

–   **Call2All**
www.call2all.org
A partnership of mission agencies, denominations and organizations working toward the fulfilment of the Great Commission in this generation, with a core group of key US agencies; sponsors a series of large congresses.

DAWN   **Dawn Ministries**
www.dawnministries.org
Encourages and helps national cooperative initiatives in saturation church planting.

–   **Faith2Share**
www.faith2share.net
An international network of Christian mission agencies that, together, strengthen indigenous movements of the mission of God.

IMTN   **International Missionary Training Network**
www.theimtn.org/tiki–index.php
A WEA network developing best practices for missionary training.

–   **Integral Alliance**
www.integralalliance.org

A global alliance of Christian relief and development agencies, working together to present a more effective response to poverty worldwide.

– **Micah Network**
www.micahnetwork.org
A group of over 330 Christian relief, development and justice organizations from 81 countries.

LPI **Langham Partnership International**
www.langhampartnership.org
International network working alongside church leaders globally, especially Majority World, planting national movements for biblical preaching, providing and creating evangelical literature, and funding faculty development in theological education.

NPN **Nomadic Peoples Network**
www.nomadicpeoples.net
Giving attention to the many nomadic peoples of the world and the unique means required to bring Christ to them.

RHP **Refugee Highway Partnership**
www.refugeehighway.net
A network of individuals and ministries engaged in reaching out to people along the many phases of internal and international displacement.

TEENET **Theological Education by Extension Network**
www.teenet.net
A global network of persons engaged in contextual, community-based and open theological education, helping the indigenous Church through formats such as Distance Education, Theological Education by Extension, and Diversified Learning.

TOPIC **Trainers of Pastors International Coalition**
www.topic.us
International network equipping pastors to lead churches, especially in regions where formalized training is lacking.

– **VisionSynergy**
www.visionsynergy.net
Developing strategic international Christian networks focused on high-impact opportunities for world evangelization.

– **Viva Network**
www.viva.org
A global network of ministries working with children at risk.

WEA-MC **World Evangelical Alliance – Mission Commission**
www.worldevangelicals.org/commissions/mc
A global network of national and regional mission association leaders.

By Continent or Region

Africa

AEA **Association of Evangelicals of Africa**
www.aeafrica.org

AFMIN **Africa Ministries Network**
www.afmin.org

MANI **Movement for African National Initiatives**
www.maniafrica.com

Asia

AEA   **Asia Evangelical Alliance**
www.asiaevangelicals.org

AMA   **Asia Missions Association**
www.asiamissions.net

SEALink   **Southeast Asia Unreached Peoples Network**
Related to the Ethnê movement

Caribbean

EAC   **Evangelical Association of the Caribbean**
www.caribbeanevangelical.org

Europe

EEA   **European Evangelical Alliance**
www.europeanea.org

–   **Hope for Europe**
www.hfe.org
A network of networks working together toward spiritual, social and cultural transformation.

–   **Mission-Net (European Youth Mission Congress and Movement)**
www.mission-net.org

Latin America

COMIBAM   *Cooperación Misionara Iberoamericana*
www.comibam.org

FIDE   **Latin American Evangelical Fellowship**
www.worldevangelicals.org/members/fide.htm

North America

COMHINA   *Cooperacion Misionera de los Hispanos de Norteamerica*
comhina.org/cms

–   **Cross Global Link**
www.crossgloballink.org
A fellowship of mission agencies. Historically most members were interdenominational missions.

EMS   **Evangelical Missiological Society**
www.emsweb.org

–   **The Mission Exchange**
www.themissionexchange.org
A fellowship of mission agencies. Historically most members were denominational missions.

Pacific

SPEA   **South Pacific Evangelical Alliance**
www.worldevangelicals.org/members/efsp.htm

By Country

Argentina

RMM   *Red Misiones Mundiales*
www.mm-comibam.org
COMIBAM Argentina.

Australia

AEA   **Australian Evangelical Alliance**
www.ea.org.au

–   **Missions Interlink**
www.missionsinterlink.org.au

Austria

AEA   **Austrian Evangelical Alliance**
www.evangelischeallianz.at

–   *Allianz Evangelikaler Missionen-Osterreich*
www.evangelischeallianz.at/links.html

Belgium

AEFB   *Alliance Evangélique Francophone de Belgique*
French-speaking alliance.

EAV   *Evangelische Alliantie Vlaanderen*
www.alliantie.org
Flemish-speaking alliance.

Brazil

AMTB   *Associação de Missões Transculturais Brasileiras*
www.amtb.org.br

Canada

EFC   **Evangelical Fellowship of Canada**
www.evangelicalfellowship.ca

Chile

CMI   *Cooperación Misionera Iberoamericana Chile*
www.comibamchile.cl
COMIBAM Chile.

China: Hong Kong

CCCOWE   **Chinese Coordination Centre of World Evangelism**
www.cccowe.org

HKACM   **Hong Kong Association of Christian Missions**
www.hkacm.org.hk

China: Taiwan

CCEA **Global Mission Center, Chinese Christian Evangelistic Association**
www.ccea.org.tw/missionworld

TMF **Taiwan Missionary Fellowship**
www.tmf.org.tw

Colombia

CCMM *Centro Colombiano de Misiones Mundiales*
www.comibam.org/catalogo2006/Esp/consulta-2006/Col/comibam.
htm
COMIBAM Colombia.

Costa Rica

FEDEMEC *Federación Misionera Evangélica Costarricense*
www.fedemec.org

Denmark

– **Danish Evangelical Alliance**
www.evangeliskalliance.dk

DMR **Danish Mission Council**
www.dmr.org

Egypt

– **The Fellowship of the Evangelicals in Egypt**
www.rabtaeg.org

Estonia

– **Evangelism and Missions Workgroup, Estonian Evangelical Alliance**
www.misjon.ee

Finland

FMC **Finnish Mission Council**
www.lahetysneuvosto.fi

MESK **Finnish Evangelical Alliance**
www.mesk.net

France

AEF *l'Alliance Evangélique Française*
www.alliance-evangelique.org

FMEF *Fédération de Missions Evangéliques Francophones*
www.fmef.over-blog.org

Germany

AEM *Arbeitsgemeinschaft Evangelikaler Missionen*
www.aem.de

| EAD | *Die Evangelische Allianz in Deutschland* |
| | www.ead.de |

Ghana

| GEMA | **Ghana Evangelical Missions Association** |
| | www.ghanaglobal.org/GEMA |

Guatemala

CONEM	*Cooperación Nacional Evangélica de Misiones*
	www.comibam.org/equipo.htm
	COMIBAM Guatemala.

Hungary

| – | **Hungarian Evangelical Alliance-Mission Commission** |
| | www.aliansz.hu |

Iceland

| IMS | **Icelandic Mission Society** |
| | www.sik.is |

India

| AICC | **All India Christian Council** |
| | www.indianchristians.in |

CONS	**HBI Ministries/Council on National Service**
	www.hbionline.org/cons.asp
	A plan toward a church for every 1,000 people in India, connected to the Hindustan Bible Institute.

| EFI | **Evangelical Fellowship of India** |
| | www.efionline.org |

| IMA | **India Missions Association** |
| | www.imaindia.org |

Indonesia

| – | **Bless Indonesia** |
| | *National organization working with associations and churches to bless the least reached peoples of this country.* |

| IPN | **Indonesia People Network** |
| | *A cooperative, multi-organization, multi-denomination initiative to reach the unreached peoples of Indonesia.* |

PGLII	*Persekutuan Gereja – Gereja dan Lembaga – Lembaga Injili Indonesia*
	www.pglii.org
	Indonesian Evangelical Alliance

Ireland

| EAI | **Evangelical Alliance Ireland** |
| | www.evangelical.ie |

| IMAP | **Ireland Mission Agencies Partnership** |
| | www.imap.ie |

Israel

| UCCI | **United Christian Council in Israel** |
| | www.ucci.net |

Japan

| JEMA | **Japan Evangelical Missionary Association** |
| | www.jema.org |

| JOMA | **Japan Overseas Mission Association** |
| | www.joma.mydns.jp |

Korea, South

| CCK | **The Christian Council of Korea** |
| | www.cck.or.kr |

| KNCC | **National Council of Churches in Korea** |
| | www.kncc.or.kr |

| KRIM | **Korea Research Institute for Missions** |
| | www.krim.org |

KWMA	**Korean World Mission Association**
	www.kwma.org
	KWMA was established in 1992 for cooperation and partnership among Korean major denominations, churches and mission organizations.

Malaysia

| NECF | **National Evangelical Christian Fellowship** |
| | www.necf.org.my |

| MCGM | **Malaysian Center for Global Ministry** |
| | www.mcgm.net.my |

Mexico

| COMIMEX | *Cooperación Misionera de México* |
| | www.comimex.org |

Mongolia

JCS	**Joint Christian Services International**
	www.jcsintl.org
	A consortium of Christian organizations serving in Mongolia since 1993.

Nepal

| – | **Himalayan Mission** |
| | www.himalayanmission.com |

| INF | **International Nepal Fellowship** |
| | www.inf.org |

Netherlands

EA   *Evangelische Alliante*
                www.eanl.nl

EZA   *Evangelische Zendingsalliantie*
                www.eza.nl

New Zealand

–   **Missions Interlink**
                www.missions.org.nz

Nigeria

AESA   **Association of Evangelicals in Nigeria**
                www.nigeriaef.org
                Uniting evangelicals in Africa for holistic ministries that make a difference.

NEF   **Nigeria Evangelical Fellowship**
                www.aeafrica.org/membership/fullmembership.htm

NEMA   **Nigeria Evangelical Mission Association**
                www.nematoday.org

Norway

NORME   **Norwegian Council for Mission and Evangelism**
                www.norme.no

Philippines

ACM   **Asian Center for Missions**
                www.acmnet.org

PCEC   **Philippine Council of Evangelical Churches**
                www.pceconline.org

PMA   **Philippines Mission Association**
                www.cybermissions.org/pma
                A partnership of evangelical mission agencies, local churches, denominational missions commissions and cross-cultural missions training organizations.

Portugal

AEP   *Aliança Evangélica Portuguesa* – **Mission Commission**
                www.portalevangelico.pt

Puerto Rico

RECOMI   *Red de Cooperación Misionera de Puerto Rico*
                www.recomi.org

Singapore

EFOS   **Evangelical Fellowship of Singapore**
                www.efosingapore.org

SCGM	Singapore Centre for Global Missions
	www.scgm.org.sg

South Africa

TEASA	The Evangelical Alliance of South Africa
	www.teasa.org.za
WENSA	World Evangelisation Network of South Africa
	www.wensa.org.za

Spain

AEE	*Alianza Evangélica Espanola*
	www.aeesp.net

Sri Lanka

NCEASL	National Christian Evangelical Alliance of Sri Lanka
	www.nceasl.org/NCEASL/missions/home.php

Sweden

SEA	Evangelical Alliance Sweden
	www.sea.nu
SMC	Swedish Mission Council
	www.missioncouncil.se

Switzerland

AEM	*Arbeitsgemeinschaft Evangelischer Missionen*
	www.aem.ch
SEA	*Schweizerische Évangélische Allianz*
	Alliance Evangelique Suisse
	www.each.ch

Thailand

EFT	Evangelical Fellowship of Thailand
	www.eft.or.th

United Kingdom

EA	Evangelical Alliance
	www.eauk.org
GC	Global Connections
	www.globalconnections.co.uk

United States

AIMS	Accelerating International Missions Strategies
	www.aims.org
	A mission association mainly serving Pentecostal and charismatic churches and ministries.

b) Mission Agencies

This is by no means a comprehensive analysis of the world's thousands of mission agencies. The listing below is merely a sampling of 112 of the largest and/or more influential mission organizations at work in the world. Obviously, the list is biased toward Western agencies, but some effort has been made to include significant sending organizations from the Majority World as well. The listing works as follows:

OW CODE   **Mission Agency Name**
website
International HQ (italicized) and other major sending bases
Number of workers and fields, including numbers of workers in largest fields.

ABWE   **Association of Baptists for World Evangelism**
www.abwe.org
USA, Canada
1,053 workers in 61 fields; USA(135), Brazil(91), S Africa(52), Togo(47)

AE   **African Enterprise**
www.africanenterprise.org
South Africa, N America(2), Europe(3), Australia
10 teams in 8 African countries

AEFI   **Asia Evangelistic Fellowship**
www.aefi.org.au
Australia, Singapore, Canada, USA
200 workers in South Asia region

AI   **Action International Ministries**
www.actionintl.org
USA, Canada, Europe
362 workers in 24 countries; Philippines(91), USA(68), Brazil(32), Zambia(19)

AIM   **AIM International**
www.aimint.org
UK, USA, Australia, Brazil, Canada, Netherlands, S Africa
615 workers in over 20 countries; Kenya(210), USA(147), Tanzania(43)

AM   **Antioch Mission (Brazil)**
www.missaoantioquia.com
95 workers in 21 countries; Brazil(20), Bolivia(17), Burkina Faso(8), UK(7)

AoG   **Assemblies of God**
www.worldmissions.ag.org
USA, Australia, Brazil, NZ, UK
2,355 workers in 153 countries and regions; Mexico(79), S Africa(73), India(61), Philippines(60), Kenya(42), other Asian countries(264)

AOI   **Asian Outreach International**
www.asianoutreach.org
HK, Australia, Canada, NZ, Singapore, UK, USA, Asia
670 workers throughout Asia

AV   **Avant Ministries (formerly GMU)**
www.avantministries.org
USA, Canada
269 workers in 24 countries; Spain(42), Bolivia(28), Italy(25), Ecuador(23), Brazil(19)

AWM   **Arab World Ministries**
www.awm.org/i
UK, Canada, Europe
(USA branch merged with Pioneers; *OW 2010* includes AWM workers separately) 419 workers, mainly in Arab-speaking world and Europe

BBF   **Baptist Bible Fellowship International**
www.bbfimissions.com
USA
710 workers in 79 countries; UK(55), Philippines(46), Kenya(34), Brazil(32), Australia(28), Argentina(17)

BCB   **Baptist Convention of Brazil**
www.jmm.org.br
Brazil
153 workers in 26 countries; Spain(14), Portugal(10), Mozambique(7)

BGC/CW   **Baptist General Conference Board / Converge Worldwide**
www.scene3.org
USA
84 workers in 12 countries; Philippines(17), Cameroon(16), Brazil(13), Mexico(11)

BI   **Bethany International**
www.bethanyinternational.org
USA, Singapore
145 workers in 22 countries; Brazil(15), Mexico(10)

BIM   **Baptist International Missions**
www.bimi.org
USA
755 workers in 78 countries; Japan(68), Mexico(55), Brazil(48), Uganda(36), Philippines(35)

BMM   **Baptist Mid-Missions**
www.bmm.org
USA, Canada
521 workers in 50 countries; Brazil(139), USA(48), France(29), Zambia(15)

BMS   **BMS World Mission**
www.bmsworldmission.org
UK
183 workers in 33 countries; UK(26), Nepal(25), Brazil(11), Uganda(10)

BMW   **Biblical Ministries Worldwide**
www.biblicalministries.org
USA
191 workers in 29 countries; UK(22), Germany(16), S Africa(12), Ecuador(10)

BWM   **Baptist World Mission**
www.baptistworldmission.org
USA
683 workers in 68 countries; Brazil(46), Nepal(35), Rep Congo(33), SE Asia(30), France(24)

C	**Crosslinks**

Crosslinks
www.crosslinks.org
UK
113 workers in 22 countries; UK(24), S Africa(18), Tanzania(9), Uganda(6)

CC/CC **Christian Churches/Churches of Christ (USA)**
USA
629 workers in 69 countries; Brazil(103), UK(52), Mexico(38), Japan(36), Germany(28), Kenya(22)

Christar **Christar International (formerly IMI)**
www.christar.org
USA, Canada
338 workers; USA(40), majority in Asian countries

CAMI **CAM International**
www.caminternational.org
USA, Canada
210 workers in 11 countries; Mexico(80), Guatemala(48), Honduras(26), Spain(16)

CAPRO **Calvary Ministries (CAPRO)**
www.capromissions.org
Nigeria
609 workers (from around 20 countries) in 31 countries; largest fields: Nigeria, Togo, Côte d'Ivoire, Kenya, Sudan

CB **Christian Brethren Assemblies**
Also **Echoes of Service** (UK) and **Christian Mission in Many Lands** (CMML, Australia)
www.echoes.org.uk, www.cmmlusa.org
UK, USA, Australia, Canada, NZ
Christian Brethren Missions: 836 workers in 74 countries; Mexico(62), France(33), Zambia(25), Bolivia(25), Peru(22), Ireland(14), Spain(11)
CMML: 609 workers in 62 countries; Mexico(56), Zambia(49), France(31), Peru(29), Ireland(27), Bolivia(25), Spain(2)
Echoes of Service: 315 workers in 39 countries; France(47), Zambia(35), Italy(22), Ireland(20), Spain(11), Bolivia(8), Peru(4), Mexico(3)

CBIM **Canadian Baptist International Ministries**
www.cbmin.org
Canada
73 workers in 12 countries; Canada(33), Kenya(10)

CCCI **Campus Crusade for Christ International**
www.ccci.org
USA, Australia, Canada, S Africa, UK
9,913 workers in 128 countries; USA(6,469), S Korea(847), E Asia(462), Singapore(131), Thailand(120)

CEF **Child Evangelism Fellowship**
www.cefonline.com
USA, Canada, Korea
403 workers in 89 countries; USA(140), UK(14), Zambia(13), Japan(8), Brazil(6), Philippines(6), Suriname(6)

CLC **CLC International**
www.clc.org.uk/clcinternational
UK, Australia, N America, Europe
626 workers in 56 countries; UK(58), India(47), France(44), Colombia(41), Chile(34), Japan(24)

Appendix 3: Further Mission Information   941

CMA   **Christian & Missionary Alliance**
www.cmalliance.org
USA, Canada, HK, Peru, Philippines
586 workers in 39 countries and regions; Japan(50), Indonesia(30),
Canada(28), Mexico(20), Peru(16)

CMF   **Christian Missionary Foundation**
fmcfondation.ifrance.com/eng_index.html
Nigeria, Côte d'Ivoire
400-plus workers in West African countries

CMS   **Church Mission Society**
www.cms-uk.org
UK, Ireland, Australia
354 workers in 50 countries; UK(69), Uganda(29), Paraguay(18), Kenya(16),
Chile(13), Tanzania(12)

CoGWM   **Church of God World Missions**
www.cogwm.org
USA
320 workers in 72 countries; Philippines(20), Albania(21), Germany(14),
UK(12), Ecuador(10)

CoN   **Church of the Nazarene**
www.nazareneworldmission.org
USA, UK
423 workers in 95 countries; Argentina(23), PNG(20), Philippines(17),
S Africa(17), Guatemala(14), Kenya(12)

CRWM   **Christian Reformed World Missions**
www.crcna.org/pages/crwm.cfm
USA, Canada
129 workers in 22 countries; Nigeria(22), USA(20), Mexico(16), Guinea(13),
Japan(12)

CW   **Crossworld (formerly UFM)**
www.crossworld.org
USA, Canada
353 workers in 38 countries; Brazil(45), USA(38), Canada(27), France(27),
Italy(17), Haiti(16)

DM   **Dorothea Mission**
www.dorothea.org.za
S Africa, UK
58 workers in 6 countries; S Africa(18), Zimbabwe(16), Mozambique(8),
Malawi(6)

DMG   ***Deutsche Missionsgemeinschaft* (German Missionary Fellowship)**
www.dmgint.de
Germany
352 workers in 81 countries; Brazil(24), Germany(23), Kenya(19), Austria(18),
Russia(17)

ECM   **European Christian Mission**
www.ecmbritain.org
UK, Australia, Canada, Ireland, Germany, Netherlands, USA
175 workers in 20 countries; Spain(34), France(20), Portugal(19), Austria(15),
Italy(12), Albania(8)

EHC   **Every Home for Christ**
www.ehc.org

USA, Australia, Canada, Europe, UK, S Africa
At work in 96 nations

ELCA   **Evangelical Lutheran Church in America**
www.elca.org
USA
196 workers in 39 countries; USA(44), Japan(29), Tanzania(21), Senegal(12), Cameroon(10)

F   **Frontiers**
www.frontiers.org
UK, Europe(7), Americas(7), Asia(3), Africa(1)
950 workers in 52 countries/regions; Asia(245), Africa(245), M East(206), W Asia(155)

FEBC   **Far East Broadcasting Company**
www.febc.org
USA, Australia, NZ, Korea
198 workers in 10 countries; Korea(145), Canada(25)

FH   **Food for the Hungry**
www.fh.org
USA, Canada, S Korea, Sweden, Switzerland, UK
964 workers in 72 countries; Philippines(69), Thailand(27), from S Korea (359 worldwide)

FIDA   **Finnish International Development Agency**
www.fidadevelopment.fi
Finland
411 workers in 37 countries; Asia(133), Europe(93), Africa(71)

FMI   **Foursquare Missions International**
www.fmi.foursquare.org
USA
137 workers in 147 countries

FMPB   **Friends Missionary Prayer Band**
www.fmpb-vlk.tk
India
886 workers in South Asia

FMWM   **Free Methodist World Missions**
www.fmwm.org
USA
114 workers in 82 countries

GCMT   **Great Commission Movement Trust**
India
1,045 full-time workers, of which 209 cross cultural; based in Gujarat

GEM   **Greater Europe Mission**
www.gemission.org
USA, Canada
296 workers in 27 countries; Germany(90), France(28), Romania(16), Austria(14), Netherlands(14)

GEMS   **Gospel Echoing Missionary Society**
www.gemsbihar.org
India
2,205 workers, mostly in northern India, but some in neighbouring South Asian countries

Appendix 3: Further Mission Information   943

GFA	**Gospel for Asia**
	www.gfa.org
	USA, Canada, Germany, UK
	9,550 workers in 9 countries of South and East Asia

GI	**Global Interaction (formerly ABMS)**
	www.globalinteraction.org.au
	Australia
	180 workers, mostly in Asia

GMS	**Global Mission Society – Presbyterian Church (Hapdong)**
	www.gms.kr
	Korea
	1,991 workers in 100 countries; Asia(1,264), Africa(210), Europe(174), L America(139)

GRN	**Global Recordings Network**
	www.globalrecordings.net
	USA, bases worldwide in Africa, Americas, Asia, Europe, Pacific
	362 workers in 67 countries; USA(35), India(17), Nigeria(15), Liberia(12), Mexico(11)

HCJB	**HCJB Global**
	www.hcjb.org
	USA, Australia, Canada, UK
	271 workers in 22 countries; USA(89), Ecuador(87), Singapore(14), Australia(8), Spain(8), Czech Republic(6)

I	**Interserve**
	www.interserve.org.uk
	UK, Australia, Canada, Korea, Netherlands, NZ, USA
	1,006 workers in 45 countries/regions; mainly Asia and M East

IA	**InterAct – *Evangeliska Frikyrkan***
	Formerly InterAct – *Nygybbet-Kristen samverkan*
	www.efk.se
	Sweden
	73 workers in 23 countries; Asia and M East(36), Europe(14), Africa(12)

IEM	**India Evangelical Mission**
	www.indiaevangelical.org
	India
	463 workers throughout India

IET	**Indian Evangelical Team**
	www.ietmissions.org
	India
	2,093 workers of which 465 serve cross-culturally; largely in India with a few workers in Bhutan and Nepal

IFES	**International Fellowship of Evangelical Students**
	www.ifesworld.org
	UK, Australia, Canada, Europe, N America, and all regions around the world
	104 workers in 51 countries

IMB	**International Mission Board (formerly SBC)**
	www.imb.org
	USA, Canada
	5,110 workers, in all regions of the world, especially Asia and Africa

ISI   **International Students Incorporated**
www.isionline.org
USA
183 workers, 180 in USA working cross-culturally with international students

IT   **International Teams**
www.iteams.org
USA, Australia, Canada, UK
299 workers in 26 countries; USA(85), Austria(30), Ecuador(18), Costa Rica(17), France(16)

JFJ   **Jews for Jesus**
www.jewsforjesus.org
USA, UK
213 workers; USA(203)

KBC   **Korea Baptist Convention**
www.fmb.or.kr
Korea
635 workers in 53 countries; Asia(462), Europe(75), L America(19)

KMCBM   **Korea Methodist Church Board of Missions**
www.kmc.co.kr
Korea
962 workers in 72 countries; Philippines(80), Japan(41), Malaysia(37), Thailand(28), other Asia(434), Africa(82), L America(35)

LAM   **Latin America Mission**
www.lam.org
USA, Canada
169 workers in 15 countries; Costa Rica(38), Mexico(37), USA(19), Colombia(13), Brazil(11)

LCMS   **Lutheran Church Missouri Synod**
www.lcms.org
USA
93 workers in 18 countries; USA(34), China, Taiwan(9), Puerto Rico(8), Japan(7)

LL   **Latin Link**
www.latinlink.org
UK
110 workers in 13 countries; Peru(20), Bolivia(18), Brazil(18), Argentina(13), Ecuador(12)

LM   **Liebenzell Mission**
www.liebenzell.org
Germany, USA, Canada, Netherlands
279 workers in 27 countries; Japan(32), Zambia(30), PNG(28), Micronesia(23)

MAF   **Mission Aviation Fellowship**
www.maf.org
USA, Australia, Canada, Europe, NZ, UK
753 workers in 35 countries; N America(337), Asia(136), Africa(106), L America(72)

MECO   **Middle East Christian Outreach**
www.aboutmeco.org
UK, Australia, Canada, NZ, S Africa, USA
117 workers in 9 M East countries

Appendix 3: Further Mission Information   945

MS   **Mercy Ships**
www.mercyships.org
USA, Australia, Canada, Germany, Korea, NZ, S Africa, UK
589 cross-cultural workers in 6 countries; Liberia(367), Ghana(113), Sierra Leone(106)

MTW   **Mission to the World**
www.mtw.org
USA
539 workers in 56 countries; USA(69), Mexico(40), UK(31), Japan(29), Peru(26), Ukraine(25)

N, Navs   **Navigators**
www.navigators.org
USA, Australia, Canada, Korea, NZ, Singapore, UK
4,647 workers (1,265 cross-cultural), in 108 countries

NMMI   **Native Missionary Movement India**
www.nmmindia.org
India
1,012 full-time workers of which 77 cross-cultural; based in Rajasthan, but working in 14 states

NTM   **New Tribes Mission**
www.ntm.org
USA, Australia, Canada, Netherlands
2,467 workers in 26 countries; Brazil(493), Indonesia(469), PNG(459), Philippines(230), Venezuela(124), Mexico(80), Thailand(68)

OC   **OC International**
www.onechallenge.org
USA, UK
400 workers in 25 countries; USA(110), Asia(106), Brazil(39), Romania(18), S Africa(15)

OD   **Open Doors**
www.od.org
UK, Australia, Brazil, Canada, Netherlands, S Korea, NZ, USA

OM   **Operation Mobilisation**
www.om.org
UK, Australia, Canada, Finland, Germany, India, Korea, NZ, Singapore, S Africa, USA
6,332 workers in 87 countries/regions/ministries; Asia(2,881), Europe(928), M East(445), Ships(441), Africa(392), Central Asia(265), L America(160)

OMF   **OMF International**
www.omf.org
Singapore, Australia, Canada, Korea, NZ, UK, USA
1,557 workers in 22 countries of Asia

OMS   **OMS International**
www.omsinternational.org
USA, Australia, Canada, NZ, S Africa, UK
423 workers in 30 countries; USA(119), L America(90), Asia(60), Europe(45)

P   **Pioneers**
www.pioneers.org
USA, Asia, Australia, Canada, Europe, UK
1,166 workers in 5 regions of the world

PAoC **Pentecostal Assemblies of Canada**
www.paoc.org
Canada
137 workers in 27 countries; Canada(46), Malawi(12), Mozambique(8)

PC(T-hap) **Presbyterian Church (Tonghap)**
www.pckwm.org
Korea
1,144 workers in 83 countries; Asia(667), Europe(136), L America(122),
Africa(77), Pacific(29)

PCUSA **Presbyterian Ch (USA)**
www.pcusa.org/worldmission
USA
374 workers in 4 regions of the world; Asia(89), L America(88), Africa(82),
Europe(37), unspecified(78)

PI **Partners International**
www.partnersintl.org
USA, Australia, Canada, NZ, UK
65 workers in Asia and N America

RA **ReachAcross (formerly RSTI)**
www.reachacross.net
UK, Australia, Canada, Germany, NZ, Switzerland, USA
51 workers in six 10/40 Window countries

RG **ReachGlobal – EFCA**
www.efca.org/reachglobal
USA, Canada
461 workers in 40 countries; USA(101), Europe(148), Asia(118),
L America(55), Africa(28)

SA **Salvation Army**
www.salvationarmy.org
UK, Australia, Canada, NZ, USA
245 workers in 48 countries; Europe(67), Africa(66), L America(33)

SAT-7 **SAT-7**
www.sat7.org
Cyprus, Europe, N America, UK
138 workers in media ministry to the Arab-speaking world

SEND **SEND International**
www.send.org
USA, Canada, Europe
560 workers in 19 countries; Europe(214), Asia(183), N America(163)

SIM **SIM International**
www.sim.org
USA, Australia, Brazil, Canada, E Asia, Europe, Korea, Sthn Africa, UK
1,600 workers in 51 countries; USA(233), Ethiopia(78), Niger(77),
Nigeria(74), Bolivia(58), Kenya(31), S Africa(25), Ghana(21), Paraguay(18)

SMB **Synod Mission Board**
India
1,826 workers; strong emphasis on training women for ministry and social
development areas

Appendix 3: Further Mission Information   947

SPM   **Swedish Pentecostal Movement**
www.pingst.se
Sweden
332 workers in 63 countries; Thailand(33), Bulgaria(24), Tanzania(18), Argentina(11)

TEAM   **The Evangelical Alliance Mission**
www.teamworld.org
USA, Canada
672 workers in 45 countries; Asia(306), Europe(144), Africa(43), L America(43)

TEAR   **TearFund**
www.tearfund.org
UK
48 long-term workers in 29 countries; larger numbers of short-term workers assist in projects at any one time

TPM   **The Paul Mission**
www.bauri.org
Korea
328 workers in 84 countries; Philippines(21), Japan(19), W Asia(12), other Asia(106)

TWR   **Trans World Radio**
www.twr.org
USA, Canada, Singapore, S Africa, UK
140 workers in 11 countries; USA(51), S Africa(21), Austria(16), Singapore(11)

UFM   **UFM Worldwide**
www.ufm.org.uk
UK
95 workers in 22 countries; Brazil(25), UK(16), PNG(8), France(6)

VDM   *Vereinigte Deutsche Missionshilfe*
(United German Mission Aid Association)
www.vdm.org
Germany
217 workers in 40 countries; Peru(30), Germany(18), Spain(16), Brazil(14), S Africa(14), Paraguay(11)

VV   *Vishwa Vani*
www.vishwavaniweb.com
India
2,123 workers in 25 states of India

WBT   **Wycliffe Bible Translators**
www.wycliffe.org
USA, Australia, Canada, NZ, S Africa, UK
5,021 workers in 50 countries; Asia(1,181), Africa(1,066), L America(706), PNG(510), USA(407), Canada(261), Philippines(245), Europe(204), Australia(103)

WEC   **WEC International**
www.wec-int.org.uk
UK, Australia, Brazil, Canada, HK, Korea, NZ, Singapore, S Africa, USA
1,819 workers in 80 countries; Asia(150), Brazil(65), Spain(43), S Africa(34), Thailand(34)

WGM	**World Gospel Mission**
	www.wgm.org
	USA, Canada
	256 workers in 15 countries; USA(82), Kenya(46), Bolivia(37), Mexico(12)

WH	**World Horizons International**
	www.worldhorizons.org
	Spain, Brazil, France, UK, USA
	381 workers in 31 countries; Europe(158), N Africa(57), Asia(46), other Africa(23)

WT	**World Team**
	www.worldteam.org
	USA, Australia, Canada
	324 workers in 30 countries; USA(52), Cambodia(29), PNG(23), Cameroon(19), France(17)

WV	**WorldVenture (formerly CBI)**
	www.worldventure.com
	USA
	463 workers in 61 countries; Asia(89), Philippines(33), Senegal(30), Brazil(22), Uganda(19), Spain(15)

YFC	**Youth for Christ International**
	www.yfc.net
	USA, Australia, Canada, Singapore, UK
	159 workers in 20 countries; Thailand(40), Guinea-Bissau(30), USA(16), Germany(9)

YFGC	**Yoido Full Gospel Church (Korea)**
	www.yfgc.fgtv.com, www.english.fgtv.com
	Korea
	552 workers in 54 countries; Japan(206), other Asia(130), Australia(52), NZ(28), Germany(26), Brazil(10), Kenya(10)

YWAM	**Youth With A Mission**
	www.ywam.org
	USA, Africa, Asia, Australia, Europe, Korea, NZ, Pacific, UK
	Over 5,000 long-term, cross-cultural workers in 154 countries; several thousand more short-term workers

c) The World's Missionary Force

Nearly every country is a missionary-sending country. What used to happen "from the West to the rest" is now an extensive and expanding global activity. Missionary vision is alive even in those countries where the Church is young, small or under persecution. When praying for those many places in the world that need more missionaries, pray with an awareness that the answer may come from east, west, north or south, from a neighbouring culture or one on the other side of the world.

For purposes of *Operation World,* the term *missionary* is defined as meeting the following criteria:

Self-identification as a missionary and serving in the ministry context out of a deliberate sense of spiritual calling and Kingdom purpose.

Commissioning and recognition as a missionary by home church and sending agency.

Term of service of at least two years.

Serving Christ outside of their home context – this usually but not exclusively implies serving abroad/outside their home region, and across cultural boundaries.

When not cross-cultural, work is occurring in an unevangelized context where the Church has not been established.

The statistics below are limited to long-term missionaries (serving longer than two years) and to Protestant, Independent and Anglican missionaries, but are not limited to international or cross-cultural workers. Due to security issues (especially post-9/11) and other complications, we are only able to compile and publish statistics on selected countries. Countless hours and e-mails, letters and phone calls have gone into this effort, knowing that 21st Century realities will significantly limit our knowledge of the harvest force. Most agencies, for both security and cultural reasons, are no longer willing or able to share the size, location and composition of their field teams. This is a frustration to us, but not a problem to the Lord of the Harvest!

The list below is incomplete but still instructive. Thanks largely to the **COMIBAM** movement, reliable statistics are available from many Latin-American countries. Africa is much more under-represented – not because the countries of Africa are not sending missionaries, but because these emerging movements tend to be more diverse, more decentralized, and less well monitored than elsewhere; therefore, accurate numbers are simply not available. Also note that although many of the numbers are from 2010, many also are from other years in the late 2000s, since counts of this kind usually are done only periodically.

Our lost and hurting world and the growing population therein need more missionaries than ever. The total number of unevangelized people actually increases every year! Please pray for each country's missionary force and for the emergence, strength, health and growth of the national mission movement of every country, including those not listed below.

Select Missionary-sending Countries

Country	Missionaries	Country	Missionaries
Algeria	12	Iceland	6
Argentina	350	Japan	300
Austria	82	Lithuania	10
Bolivia	71	Macedonia	10
Central African Republic	99	Malaysia	380
Chile	149	Mongolia	20
China, Taiwan	280	Morocco	10
Colombia	216	Nicaragua	6
Congo-DRC	350	Panama	77
Costa Rica	84	Paraguay	51
Denmark	204	Peru	318
Dominican Republic	15	Portugal	74
Ecuador	106	Puerto Rico	116
El Salvador	165	Romania	130
Estonia	22	Thailand	468
Guatemala	103	Turkey	14
Honduras	79	Uruguay	14
Hungary	45	Venezuela	180

Country	Missionaries	Country	Missionaries
China, PRC	100,000	Netherlands	2,000
USA	93,500	Brazil	1,976
India	82,950	Switzerland	1,712
Korea, South	19,950	Ukraine	1,599
Nigeria	6,644	New Zealand	1,200
United Kingdom	6,405	Finland	908
Canada	5,200	Sweden	873
Philippines	4,500	Mexico	794
Australia	3,193	Singapore	693
Germany	3,144	Norway	610
Indonesia	3,000	Spain	512
Ghana	2,000	Bangladesh	500

The gospel of Jesus Christ spreads by many paths across boundaries of communities, countries, peoples and languages. Missionaries are central and vital to this and will continue to be in the future, but they are not alone. The numbers above are only a count of a certain kind of Christian worker; they do not represent the total of any country's contribution to evangelization, mission or international witness. As you pray for missionaries, pray also for the important international ministries of tentmakers, Christian professionals and business people, international students, migrants, broadcasters, Internet evangelists and others.

Worthy of special mention are diaspora witnesses. Due to economic difficulty and unemployment, more than eight million citizens of the Philippines have been scattered to live and work in 211 countries. Of those, 700,000 are evangelical Christians, and of those an estimated 50,000 are active in evangelism and church planting, with the result that many hundreds of churches have been planted in scores of countries – including in many of the countries most inaccessible to Christian witness. Beyond this one example, diaspora witness is a huge and rapidly growing reality from many Asian, African and other countries, done in the spirit of Acts 8:4, "Those who had been scattered preached the word wherever they went" (NIV). Join with Filipino Christian leaders in praying for one million such diaspora witnesses from their country. Pray also for these other goals: for one million such witnesses from the Korean diaspora, and two million from the Indian diaspora.

d) Major Mission Journals, Periodicals or Resources

The following are widely known general mission publications of various media: print, online or by e-mail. Most mission agencies publish their own newsletters, magazines or periodicals; for those, contact the organizations directly.

Brigada Today
www.brigada.org
A lively and eclectic e-mail newsletter packed with practical ideas, resources and opportunities for missionaries and mission-active Christians.

Connections
www.weaconnections.com
A thrice-annual magazine of the World Evangelical Alliance Mission Commission; articles from a group of international mission leaders.

Dharma Deepika
www.dharmadeepika.org
A South Asian, inter-disciplinary journal of missiological research and reflection.

Evangelical Missions Quarterly
www.emisdirect.com
A professional and practical journal out of the USA, from and for missionaries, mission leaders and local church mission leaders.

GlobalMissiology.org
www.globalmissiology.org
A thoroughly international, web-based mission journal with a wide range of contributions, operating in eight languages.

International Bulletin of Missionary Research
www.internationalbulletin.org
A quarterly journal, from the Overseas Ministries Study Center in the USA, with extensive analysis of Christianity and mission across the globe and a distinctive emphasis on mission history.

International Journal of Frontier Missiology
www.ijfm.org
An evangelical journal focused on mission to the least-evangelized peoples; thus, for example, including many articles on mission to the Muslim world.

Lausanne World Pulse
www.lausanneworldpulse.com
A web-based monthly magazine with mission and evangelism news briefs and themed articles; from the Lausanne Movement and the Billy Graham Center (Wheaton College).

Missiology
www.asmweb.org/missiology.htm
Quarterly journal of the American Missiological Society, which includes Conciliar, Evangelical, Catholic, Pentecostal and Orthodox scholars.

Missionalia
www.missionalia.org.za
Thrice-annual journal of the Southern Africa Missiological Society, with articles, book reviews and abstracts from a wide range of mission publications.

Mission Frontiers
www.missionfrontiers.org
A bi-monthly magazine with a very large global distribution, dedicated to "A Church for Every People", from the US Center for World Mission.

Missions Catalyst
www.missionscatalyst.net
A weekly electronic digest of missions news and resources for inspiration and to encourage involvement.

Perspectives on the World Christian Movement
Global Perspectives Family of Resources
www.perspectives.org, www.perspectivesfamily.org
A course that has mobilized tens of thousands to engagement in God's work around the world through prayer and service. Courses offered in several languages in over 10 countries. Related mission study courses of varied length and level available through the Perspectives Family website.

Abbreviations and Acronyms

Abbreviations and Symbols (General)

~	approximately
<	less than
>	greater than
$	US dollar
#	number
/	per with numbers (2%/year); with text (his/her)
%	percentage
Abbrev	abbreviation
AD	in the year of our Lord (anno Domini)
Afr	Africa, African
AGR, Ann Gr	annual growth rate
App	Appendix (in this book)
Bi	Bibles
C	Central
E	East
eg	for example (exempli gratia)
esp	especially
et al	and others (et alia)
etc	and so forth (et cetera)
Fr	French
HQ	headquarters
hrs/wk	hours per week
ie	that is (id est)
Is	Islands
IT	information technology
km	kilometre
LA	Los Angeles, California (USA)
m, mill	million
misc	miscellaneous
N	North
NE	Northeast
NJ	New Jersey (USA)
NW	Northwest
NY	New York, New York (USA)
n/a	not applicable
Neth	Netherlands
pop	population
por	Scripture portion
S	South
SE	Southeast
SS	South-south
SW	Southwest
sq km	square kilometre/s
TB	tuberculosis
TV	television
W	West
w.i.p.	work/s in process (Bible translation)
yrs	years

2	doubly affiliated Christians	Int	International
A, Ang	Anglican/s	J	Jews
A&P	Apostoles y Profetas (El Salvador)	JC	Jesus Christ
Af, Afr	Africa, African	LatAm	Latin America
AGR, Ann Gr	annual growth rate	LCMS	Lutheran Church, Missouri Synod
Am, Amer	America, American	Luth	Lutheran
AME	African Methodist Episcopal Church	M	Marginal (for MegaBloc chart), Muslim (for Religion chart)
AoG	Assemblies of God	Menn	Mennonite
Apos, Ap	Apostolic	Meth	Methodist
As	Asia	Metro	Metropolitan
Assem	Assemblies	Min	Ministry, Ministries
Assoc	Association	Miss	Missionary or Mission
B	Buddhists	N, Non-rel	Non-religious
Bapt	Baptist	Nat	National
Beth	Bethlehem	NatvAm	Native American
Bre	Brethren	NGK	*Nederduitse Gereformeerde Kerk* (Dutch Reformed Church, South Africa)
C, Cath	Catholic/s		
C Amer	Central America		
Cal	calendar	NHK	*Nederduits Hervormde Kerk* (Dutch Reformed Church, South Africa)
CC/CC	Christian Churches/Churches of Christ		
Ch	Church; Chinese (Religions charts only)	Non-Chr	Non-Christian
		Non-ins	Non-instrumental
Char	charismatic/s	NT	New Testament
Chr	Christian	O, Orth	Orthodox
Chs	churches	P, Prot	Protestant/s
CoG	Church of God	Pa	Pacific
CoGoP	Church of God of Prophecy	PCUSA	Presbyterian Church, USA
CoN	Church of the Nazarene	Pente	Pentecostal/s
Conf	Conference	Pop	Population
Cong	Congregational	Presby	Presbyterian
Congs	congregations	Prog	Progressive
Conv	Convention	Ref	Reformed
Cov	Covenant	Rel	Religion/s
Denoms	denominations	Repub	Republic
E	Ethnic traditional	S	Christian marginal sects (usually M, except in Religion graph)
EECMY	Ethiopian Evangelical Church *Mekane Yesus*		
		SdA	Seventh-day Adventist
ELCA	Evangelical Lutheran Church in America	Syn	Synagogue
		Tab	Tabernacle
Epis	Episcopal	U	Unaffiliated Christians
Eu	Europe	Un	Union
Ev, Evang	Evangelical/s	Unev	unevangelized
Fell	Fellowship	Univ	Universal
H	Hindus	UP	Unreached Peoples
I	Independent, indigenous (in MegaBloc chart/table)	WW	Worldwide
		X	Christians (generic)
Indep	Independent/s	Z	Other, various combined groups
Indig	indigenous		

Note: At times, a country name is abbreviated to its first letter in the table of denomination names.

ACET	AIDS Care Education and Training	EA	Evangelical Alliance
ACMC	Advancing Churches in Missions Commitment	EBM	Evangelical Baptist Missions
		ECF	ECF International (Evangelize China Fellowship Incorporated)
AfAsLA	Africa, Asia and Latin America		
AFM	Anglican Frontier Missions	ECOWAS	Economic Community of West African States
AGR	Annual Growth Rate		
AICs	African Independent Churches (or African Initiated Churches)	ECWA	Evangelical Church of West Africa
		EEC	European Economic Community
AIDS	Acquired Immune Deficiency Syndrome	ESL	English as a Second Language
		ESV	English Standard Version (of the Bible)
AMAA	Armenian Missionary Association of America		
		EU	European Union
AMG	AMG International (Advancing the Ministries of the Gospel)	FCBH	Faith Comes By Hearing
		FEBA	FEBA (radio ministry)
AMI	*Alliance Missionnaire Internationale* (Swiss agency)	FFM	Fellowship of Faith for Muslims
		FLM	Finnish Lutheran Mission
ASEAN	Association of Southeast Asian Nations	FM	frequency modulation (radio)
		fSU	former Soviet Union
AWR	Adventist World Radio	FTT	Finishing the Task
BBI	Back to the Bible International	GDOP	Global Day of Prayer
BCC/s	Bible correspondence course/s	GDP	Gross Domestic Product (excluding imports and exports)
BCM	Bible Centred Ministries International		
		GLO	Gospel Literature Outreach
BEM	Belgian Evangelical Mission	GMI	Global Mapping International
BIEM	Baptist International Evangelistic Ministries	GNP	Gross National Product (including imports and exports)
BIOT	British Indian Ocean Territories	GU	Global University (formerly ICI and Berean)
BTCP	Bible Training Centers for Pastors		
BTJ	Back to Jerusalem movement	HDI	Human Development Index
CAN	*Comunidad Andina* (Andean Community of Nations)	HIV	Human Immunodeficiency Virus
		HK	Hong Kong
CAR	Central African Republic	HM	Hellenic Ministries
CARICOM	Caribbean Community	IBRA	International Broadcasting Association
CBA	Christian Booksellers Association		
CBN	Christian Broadcasting Network	IBT	Institute for Bible Translation
CCL	Christian Communications, Ltd (Hong Kong)	ICFG	International Church of the Foursquare Gospel
CFAN	Christ for all Nations	ICRM	Indian Christian Revival Movement
CFI	Christian Friends of Israel	IDPs	Internally-displaced peoples
CIA	Central Intelligence Agency (of the US government)	IHOP	International House of Prayer
		IJM	International Justice Mission
CIM	China Inland Mission (now OMF)	IMF	International Monetary Fund
CiP	Children in Prayer	IPC	International Prayer Connect
CIS	Commonwealth of Independent States	IVCF	InterVarsity Christian Fellowship
		JAARS	JAARS (from Jungle Aviation And Radio Service)
COCM	Chinese Overseas Christian Mission		
CMJ	The Church's Ministry Among Jewish People	JFJ	Jews for Jesus
		JP/JPL	Joshua Project/List
CORD	Christian Outreach Relief & Development	JW/JWs	Jehovah's Witness/es
		KAR	Kurdish Autonomous Region (Iraq)
CPA	Catholic Patriotic Association (China)	KIMON	*Kinderhulp Mondiaal* (Dutch agency)
CPM	Chosen People Ministries	LBT	Lutheran Bible Translators
CWI	Christian Witness to Israel	LCMS	Lutheran Church, Missouri Synod
DAI	Development Associates International	LHM	Lutheran Hour Ministries
		LMS	London Missionary Society
DRC	Democratic Republic of Congo (Congo-DRC)	MBB/s	Muslim-background believer/s
		MCC	Mennonite Central Committee
DTS	Discipleship Training School	ME, M East	Middle East

Mercosur	Mercado Común del Sur/Sul (Southern Common Market)		SFC	Students for Christ
MERN	Mission Évangélique Réformée Néerlandaise (Dutch Reformed Church mission, Guinea)		SGA	Slavic Gospel Association
			SGM	SGM Lifewords (Scripture Gift Mission)
MK/s	Missionary kid/s (children raised in a missionary family)		SIL	SIL International (was Summer Institute of Linguistics)
MT	Messianic Testimony		SU	Scripture Union
MVI	Missionary Ventures International		TAR	Tibet Autonomous Region
NAFTA	North American Free Trade Agreement		TBN	Trinity Broadcasting Network
			TE	Team Expansion
NASB	New American Standard Version (of the Bible)		TEE	Theological Education by Extension
			TESOL	Teaching English to Speakers of Other Languages
NATO	North Atlantic Treaty Organization		TSPM/CCC	Three Self Patriotic Movement/ China Christian Council (China)
NCR	National Capital Region			
NGO/s	non-governmental organization/s		TLM	The Leprosy Mission
NIV	New International Version (of the Bible)		UAE	United Arab Emirates
			UBF	University Bible Fellowship
NT	New Testament		UBS	United Bible Societies
NZ	New Zealand		UCB	United Christian Broadcasters International
OAC	Open Air Campaigners International			
			UCKG	Universal Church of the Kingdom of God
OECD	Organization for Economic Cooperation and Development			
			UK	United Kingdom of Great Britain and Northern Ireland
OT	Old Testament			
OW	Operation World		UMC	United Methodist Church
PBT	Pioneer Bible Translators		UN	United Nations
PCKH	Presbyterian Church in Korea (Hapdong)		US, USA	United States of America
			USD	United States Dollar/s ($)
PMI	Pueblos Musulmanes Internacional		USSR	Union of Soviet Socialist Republics
PNG	Papua New Guinea		USCWM	US Center for World Mission
POW	Prisoner of War		UWM	United World Mission
PRC	People's Republic of China		WCB	World Christian Broadcasting
REMAR	Remar Charity (Rehabilitation of people on the margins of society)		WCC	World Council of Churches
			WCD	World Christian Database
RETO	Rehabilitacion de Toxicomanos (Rehabilitation of Drug Dependents)		WCE	World Christian Encyclopedia
			WOI	World Outreach International
			WTO	World Trade Organization
SAM	South American Mission (formerly South American Indian Mission)		WVI	World Vision International
			WWI, WWII	World War I, World War II
			YMCA	Young Men's Christian Association
SEAN	SEAN International (from Study by Extension to All Nations)			

Note: Mission and Prayer Networks, Association and Agencies included in Appendices 2 and 3 are not included on this list

Definitions

10/40 Window The area of the world between latitudes 10° and 40° north of the equator, covering North Africa, the Middle East and Asia. This window contains most of the world's areas of greatest physical and spiritual need, most of the world's least-reached peoples and most of the governments that actively oppose Christianity.

adherent A follower of a particular religion, church or philosophy. This is a broad category based on self-identification rather than a qualitative category of practice and devotion. It includes professing and affiliated adults and their children (practising and non-practising) who may reside in a given area or country. It refers to those who, if not under coercion, would claim to have a religion even if their adherence is only nominal.

adult members Adult church members (aged over 12 or over 18 years depending on the denomination) who are communicants or full members. Adult members are given in the Members statistical column in the denominations table.

affiliated Christians All who are considered as belonging to organized churches. This includes full members, their children and other participants of the faith community. These figures represent the whole Christian community or inclusive membership. Affiliated Christians are given in the Affiliates statistical column of the denominations table as well as in the Pop % and Affiliates (a rounded, total number) statistical columns of the MegaBloc table.

Affinity Bloc A major grouping of peoples who share a broad range of affinities such as geography, culture, language, history. Examples include Arab, Turkic, Malay. There are 15 Affinity Blocs in the world.

Ahmaddiya An Islamic revivalist movement that originated in Pakistan, but has now spread to Africa and other continents. It is not considered truly Islamic by orthodox Muslims.

Alpha Course Informal gatherings – in homes, churches, cafés and a host of other venues – for introducing the gospel to non-Christians. Started in the UK but spread to many countries in the past 15 years. Has proven to be effective in most cultural contexts.

animism Belief that inanimate objects are inhabited by spirits, which must be appeased/placated to avert harm.

born-again believers Those who by grace and through faith in the atoning work of Christ have been regenerated by the Holy Spirit. However, in common usage it often includes those who claim an evangelical conversion experience. The latter is numerable; the former is not.

cargo cults Melanesian Pacific syncretistic religious movements that sprang up during WWII, synthesizing ethnic beliefs and Western materialism.

charismatics Those who testify to a renewing experience of the Holy Spirit and present exercise of the gifts of the Spirit such as glossalalia, healing, prophecy and miracles. The charismatic renewal, or "Second Wave" Pentecostalism, has generally remained within mainline denominations. A further "Third Wave" renewal movement occurred with many characteristics of the Second Wave, but with less open identification with formal Pentecostalism or the charismatic movement. Second and Third Wave charismatics are counted as a single entity in this book. In our global survey of denominations, we have assessed percentages of affiliated charismatic Christians for each of the 37,500 denominations in the world from 1990-2010. The assessment largely excludes those no longer actively associated with charismatic renewal.

Christian Anyone who professes to be Christian. The term embraces all traditions and confessions of Christianity. It is no indicator of the degree of commitment or theological orthodoxy. The primary emphasis utilized is that of recognizing self-identification as well as accepting the Scriptural principles illustrated in Matt 10:32 and Romans 10:9.

Church (upper case C) A particular denomination or the universal, invisible Church at a national or worldwide level.

church (lower case c) A local fellowship of believers. The word is commonly used to mean a church building or church service, but here this usage has largely been avoided. The starting of churches is termed **church planting**.

creative-access nation A country that limits or forbids the entry of Christian missionaries and for which alternative legal means of entry are required to enable Christians to witness for Christ.

cross-cultural missionaries Full-time Christian workers sent by their churches to work among peoples of a different culture, either cross-culturally within their own nations or abroad.

denomination Any association or network of local congregations linked together, formally or informally, within any given country. Note that international denominations are counted multiple times according to the number of countries in which they have an established presence.

disaffiliated Christians Those who have repudiated their church membership. Appears in both the denominations and the MegaBloc tables as a negative figure and in italics. This generally occurs only in contexts of large state churches where secularization is strong and where the difference between state church figures and actual self-identification is significant.

doubly affiliated Christians Those with links with two or more denominations at the same time and are claimed as affiliated by both. This appears as an italicized, negative figure in both the denominations and the MegaBloc tables.

ethnic religions A generic term covering a range of informal religions based on ethnicity – ancestor worship, animism, fetishism, shamanism, spiritism and such.

ethnocultural A people with commonalities of culture, history, customs and a self-identity that may be a sub-division of, or transcend, language or ethnicity, eg caste groups in India.

ethnolinguistic people An ethnic or racial group speaking its own language. A people distinguished by its self-identity with traditions of common descent, history, customs and language. In this book, a transnational people is counted multiple times according to the number of countries where it has maintained its own ethnolinguistic identity and culture.

ethnoreligionist This is a collective term for adherents of faiths that are usually specifically confined to a particular ethnic group rather than being open or universal. It encompasses (but is not limited to) animists, ancestor-worshippers, polytheists, spirit-worshippers, shamanists, folk religionists, pantheists, cargo cults, tribal messianic movements and other such expressions of religious belief.

evangelicals All who emphasize and adhere to all four of the following:

The Lord Jesus Christ as the sole source of salvation through faith in Him, as validated by His crucifixion and resurrection.

Personal faith and conversion with regeneration by the Holy Spirit.

Recognition of the inspired Word of God as the ultimate basis and authority for faith and Christian living.

Commitment to biblical witness, evangelism and mission that brings others to faith in Christ.

Evangelicals are largely Protestant, Independent or Anglican, but some are Catholic or Orthodox. It is one of the TransBloc movements in this book.

This definition is very close but not identical to the definition introduced in David Bebbington's *Evangelicalism in Modern Britain: A History from the 1730s to the 1980s* as the Bebbington Quadrilateral, which offered crucicentrism, conversionism, biblicism and activism as the four qualities of evangelicalism.

The definition of evangelicals and the statistics relating to them are so fundamental to the contents of this book that it is important for the reader to understand the implications. It enables a measurement of the size and spectacular numerical growth of evangelical Christians over the past few decades.

Evangelicals are enumerated in OW as:

> All affiliated Christians (church members, their children, other participants of the faith community) of denominations that are definitively evangelical in theology as explained above.

> The proportion of the affiliated Christians in other denominations (that are not wholly evangelical in theology) who would hold evangelical views, whether Western in origin or otherwise.

This is a theological and not an experiential definition. It does not mean that all evangelicals as defined above are actually born-again. In many nations, only 10-40% of evangelicals so defined may have had a valid conversion and regularly attend church services. However, it does show how many people align themselves with churches where the gospel is being proclaimed as such.

evangelism The activity of Christians spreading the gospel.

evangelization The process of proclaiming the gospel and seeing the outworking of such proclamation.

evangelized The state of having had the gospel communicated and offered in such a way that the hearer becomes aware of the claims of Christ and the need to obey and follow Him. Possibly 1.7-1.9 billion people in 2010 fall within this category.

evangelized non-Christian world Non-Christians who have been, or are likely to have been, exposed to the gospel. The equivalent of World B.

fetishist One who attributes magical powers to inanimate objects and depends on amulets, charms or other objects for protection or aggression. Mainly found in Africa and the Americas.

First Wave charismatics Members of classical Pentecostal denominations.

foreign missionaries Full-time Christian workers serving in a country other than their own, sent and commissioned by a church or mission organization to propagate the gospel.

Global North The countries of Europe and North America as well as Australia and New Zealand. This is in contrast to the Global South.

Global South The countries of Latin America and the Caribbean, Africa, Asia and most of the Pacific. This North/South dichotomy has been increasingly popularized since the late 1990s, but is synonymous with (and as equally imperfect as) the West/non-West dichotomy.

gurdwara A Sikh place of worship.

Great Commission The final series of commands of the Lord Jesus Christ before His Ascension – for His followers to evangelize, baptize, disciple and teach all the peoples of the world.

harvest force The entire body of Christians potentially or actively engaged in Great Commission activity.

Appendix 5: Definitions

home missionaries (or **domestic missionaries**) Full-time Christian workers serving as missionaries (usually cross-culturally) in their own country, sent and commissioned by a church or mission organization to propagate the gospel.

Independents One of the six major Christian MegaBlocs used in this book. This category includes many of the more recent breakaways from denominations in other MegaBlocs, indigenous denominations not started by foreign missionaries and post-denominational networks.

Least Reached people See definition of unreached people.

Liberation theology Christian theology redefined on the basis of sociological and often Marxist presuppositions of oppression, thereby motivating the poor to claim equal participation in society.

Majority World The countries of Latin America, Africa and Asia. This is the term preferred in *OW* over non-West and Global South.

Marginal One of the six Christian MegaBlocs as defined in this book, comprising marginal or fringe Christian groups. See definition of marginal groups.

marginal groups A general term used in this book to describe all semi-Christian or fringe groups, sects and cults that accept certain Christian features and parts of the Scriptures, together with supplementary revelations claimed to be divine. Most claim that they alone have the "truth". Many readers may understandably question the validity of including these groups as Christian. However, we consistently classify a person's religion according to his or her self-assessment. All of these groups claim allegiance to Christ even if their theological understanding of His person, deity, atoning work or resurrection may be defective.

MegaBloc One of the six major groupings of Christian denominations as used in this book. Frequently abbreviated as follows: Protestant–P, Independent–I, Anglican–A, Catholic–C, Orthodox–O, Marginal–M. The categories Unaffiliated, Disaffiliated and Doubly affiliated are not MegaBlocs in themselves, but together with the six MegaBlocs make up the sum total of Christian adherents.

missionary One who is sent with a message. This word of Latin derivation has the same basic meaning as the wider use of the term "apostle" in the New Testament. Christian missionaries are commissioned by a local church to evangelize, plant churches and disciple people, away from their home area and often among people of a different race, culture or language. Modern usage varies widely with strong regional preferences:

> The stricter North American usage – all sent to evangelize, plant churches or minister outside their homelands.

> The wider European and Latin American usage – all sent to evangelize, plant churches or minister cross-culturally, whether in other lands or in their homelands.

> The even broader African and Asian usage, which is closer to the biblical concept indicated above and which encompasses all those sent to evangelize, plant churches and minister away from their home areas, whether cross-culturally or not and whether in their own countries or abroad. However, such breadth in the use of missionary makes it difficult for the researcher to specify the cultural or geographical distance a Christian worker must cover in order to be properly categorized as a missionary (as contrasted with an evangelist). It is especially helpful in such a case to be able to identify the subdivision of missionaries working within their own or a near culture.

OW generally seeks to synthesize differing perspectives in dividing all missionaries of each country and region into the three categories of foreign, cross-cultural and home/domestic. Most, but not all, foreign missionaries are cross-cultural, for some are actually working within expatriate communities of their own culture. Our own usage/methodology is explained further in Appendix 3 Further Mission Information on p930.

non-Western world The countries of Latin America, Africa and Asia. Previously, it was common to use Third World or Two-Thirds World to describe these countries. These terms are now obsolete, since the collapse of the Communist Second World. Synonymous with Global South and Majority World.

Pentecostals Those affiliated to specifically Pentecostal denominations committed to a Pentecostal theology, usually including a post-conversion experience of a baptism in the Spirit, present exercise of the gifts of the Spirit and speaking in tongues.

people cluster A grouping of ethnolinguistic peoples with commonalities of a shared identity, language, culture, history and often a common name. Usually transnational.

people group A significantly large sociological grouping of individuals who perceive themselves to have a common affinity. From the viewpoint of evangelization, this is the largest possible group within which the gospel can be spread without encountering barriers of understanding or acceptance. There are basically three types:

Ethnolinguistic people group, which defines a person's identity and primary loyalty according to language and/or ethnicity. This is the category emphasized in this book. We have generally reserved the word "people" rather than **people group** for this type. Cross-cultural church-planting teams of missionaries are needed for peoples in this category. According to the Joshua Project, there are 10,340, if national boundaries are ignored, or 16,350 if the same people are counted separately for each country.

Sociological people group – a grouping defined by its long-term relation to the rest of society, such as by migration or traditional occupation or class, but not having a self-contained culture or identity as an ethnic group. In most cases, local church outreach is required – either to plant daughter churches or to incorporate converts into multi-social congregations. There are probably hundreds of thousands of such people groups.

Incidental people groups – casual associations of individuals that may be temporary and are usually the result of circumstances rather than personal choice. Examples of such groups are high-rise flat dwellers, drug addicts, occupational groupings, commuters and such. These groupings present unique problems and opportunities for evangelism, but only at times is it appropriate for specific churches to be planted for the sole benefit of such groups.

people movement A movement of a large number of non-Christians of a particular people into the Church. This is frequently a group decision. It presents a wonderful opportunity to win and disciple many for the Lord by leading them into a personal faith in the Lord Jesus Christ. Failure to do so can soon lead to nominalism or syncretism.

polytheism Belief in many gods.

post-charismatics Those once involved but no longer engaged in charismatic movements. This is not necessarily a theological decision or a rejection of the Holy Spirit's active presence in believers' lives so much as a disillusion with the charismatic church sub-culture and excess that occurred, especially in the West in the 1990s and 2000s.

professing A claim of allegiance to a religious belief – whether known to, or listed in the records of, an organized religion. In many countries, professing Christians number more than affiliated Christians. Where the difference is significant, a figure for unaffiliated Christians is added to the MegaBloc table in the country section. Professing = (affiliated + unaffiliated) − (doubly affiliated + disaffiliated).

reached/unreached A term widely used today to describe people groups and areas that have or have not responded to the preaching of the gospel. Use of the term has been continued in this book despite the faultiness of the terminology. Strictly, it should be a measure of the *exposure* of a people group to the gospel, not a measure of the *response*.

renewal A quickening or enlivening of personal commitment to Christ in the churches. Charismatic renewal in the historic denominations is an example. See definition of charismatics above.

Renewalists A term increasingly used to describe Christians who adhere to either Pentecostal or charismatic theology and practice.

restricted-access nations States that limit or prevent Christian ministry by expatriates as missionaries. Alternatively they are called creative-access nations, where expatriates must seek secular avenues of entry – business, medical work, teaching, as house servants or other means. Most countries in this category have been Communist or Muslim, but today are predominantly Muslim.

revival The restoring to life of believers and churches that have previously experienced the regenerating power of the Holy Spirit but have become cold, worldly and ineffective. Often wrongly used of evangelistic campaigns, revival really signifies a sovereign act of God as an answer to prayer in bringing about a spiritual awakening and outpouring of the Holy Spirit on His people.

Second Wave charismatics Christians who have experienced renewal within mainline non-Pentecostal denominations.

shamanism Traditional ethnic religious belief centred on a hierarchy of healers and soothsayers. A term used primarily in Asia.

shari'a The Islamic body of law based on the Qur'an and tradition (*hadith*).

Shi'a Muslims Followers of Ali, the cousin of Mohammed. The second-largest branch of Islam. Strong in Iran, Central and South Asia.

short-term worker (STW) A missionary serving for a period of six months to two years.

Sufi A practitioner of Sufism, which focuses on the esoteric, ecstatic, mystical and internal aspects of Islam.

Sunni Muslims Followers of the main branch of Islam.

syncretism The attempt to synthesize elements of different religious systems into a single body of belief and practice. Baha'i, for instance, is a synthesis of Islamic, Christian and other religious tenets. Some African Indigenous Churches have sought to synthesize elements of Christianity with pre-Christian traditional beliefs.

Third Wave charismatics Christians in newer charismatic denominations or post-denominational networks.

Traditional ethnic A generic term used to describe all the informal and ethnic religions in a country.

TransBloc movement A term used to cover evangelicals, charismatics and Pentecostals in this book. Each of these is found in some or most of the six Christian megablocs.

unaffiliated Christians Those who profess to be Christian but are not associated with any formal church denomination or group.

unevangelized Those who have had no adequate opportunity to hear the gospel or respond to it.

Universalism The belief that ultimately all people will be saved irrespective of religious belief or lack of it while on earth. The underlying premises are that many have an implicit awareness of a supernatural being to which they respond by doing good to others and that a loving God could not consign people to eternal punishment for sin – non-biblical teaching rejected by most evangelicals.

unreached people An ethnolinguistic people among whom there is no viable indigenous community of believing Christians with adequate numbers and resources to evangelize their own people without outside (cross-cultural) assistance. At times, the terms Least Reached People, Hidden People or frontier people group are used.

Wahhabi A conservative, fundamentalist Muslim sect. Largely in Saudi Arabia, the Gulf States and Central Asia.

Western World The countries of Europe, North America, Australia and New Zealand.

World A Nations and peoples in the least evangelized world. Those nations and peoples that are less than 50% evangelized as defined in the *World Christian Encyclopedia* and World Christian Database.

World B Nations and peoples in the evangelized non-Christian world. Defined as those nations and peoples that are more than 50% evangelized, but less than 60% Christian (including all major Christian groups).

World C Nations and peoples in the Christian world. Defined as those nations and peoples that are more than 60% professing Christian. This includes all nominal and affiliated Christians of all ecclesiological traditions and not only Protestants.

Yezidi A syncretistic religion in Iraq, Turkey and the Caucasus based on Zoroastrian, Jewish, Nestorian, Christian and Muslim beliefs. Largely among Kurds.

Appendix 5: Definitions

Operation World Database

The bulk of the OW database is being made available with the publication of the book. The electronic version of *Operation World* will give more details about its contents.

Development of the Database

We developed the database in 1984 in preparation for the 1986 edition of *Operation World*. A major contributory factor was the publication of the *World Christian Encyclopedia* (WCE) in 1982. This volume, together with a wide-ranging search for denominational and religious data, enabled us to compile tables for denominations, religions and countries. We have updated these tables for each five-year period since 1960.

In 1990, we added a fourth set of tables on mission agencies, covering mission details, sending bases and fields.

We have not developed our own tables for peoples or languages, but instead have relied upon and amended materials from the Ethnologue, the Joshua Project and, to a lesser degree, the WCE database. The input of OW (and Patrick Johnstone in particular) into these resources has been considerable.

The OW database contains the following:

1 Denominations Approximately 38,000 denominations are covered (about 7,360 records for individual denominations and an additional 725 records, each referring to undocumented denominations we have further grouped together). This contains nearly 1.4 million discrete pieces of information! The period covered is 1960–2010.

2 Religions with 4,350 records covering 18 major religions and MegaBlocs, for the period 1900–2025.

3 Missions with information on 3,250 agencies and 5,000 bases of ministry.

4 Countries with geographic, economic and social information from multiple sources.

The development of the programming was ably done by Kathy Lannon of Global Mapping International for the 1986 edition, followed by Marko Jauhiainen for the 1993 edition and rewritten by Maurice Manktelow in Delphi software for the 2001 edition. The 2010 edition was produced using Access, with the invaluable guidance and assistance of Maurice Manktelow, supplemented by Richard Heck (denominational database) and Chris Maynard (data extraction for chart production).

Methodology of the Database

The statistics in *Operation World* are an important supportive framework for the main thrust of the book. Because we see the statistics as part of our accountability to God and to our readers, we follow a number of fundamental principles:

1 **Verifiable data.** All information is sourced. Much has had to be by extrapolation, interpolation and derivation in religions and denominations. Where this has been done, it is clearly indicated. Where data provided has proved inconsistent or has been adjusted to fit new population estimates, the source is modified by a following "★" or "%". For this reason, we are happy to publish the information. We hope that data in areas where we have had to make estimates in the past will be replaced by reliable and accurate research!

2 **The 100% rule.** All data components must add up to the whole – all peoples in a country must equal the population of the country, all denominations must add up to the total of affiliated Christians, and so on. We have therefore had to devise mechanisms for adding missing data or for subtracting over-counted or doubly counted populations. For instance:

a) *Many Chinese and Japanese* follow both Buddhism and their ethnic religion, such as Taoism or Shintoism.

b) *Many Latin Americans* were baptized as Catholics but are now active Pentecostals. The Catholic Church still counts these as Catholic.

3 **Making all statistics compatible** so that realistic totals may be derived. For example:

a) *Denominational data* is often incompatible – some denominations define "members" as active adult baptized members, others as the whole Christian community or affiliates. Sometimes a denomination changes its definition from one year to the next. We therefore use a ratio system to relate congregation size, adult membership affiliates and, where known, attendance figures. The ratios are derived uniquely for each denomination based on past statistics, growth patterns, family sizes, age structures and so on. All these ratios are accessible to the user of the electronic version.

b) *Mission data.* Many agencies now decline to publish their worker data, at least by country of service. Often the best we can convince them to share is a global total or continental totals. Therefore, worker data is not included on a country-by-country basis.

c) *Religions data* is often distorted by power and politics – over-counting of Hindus in India, inflated statistics for Muslims in Nigeria, Malaysia, Indonesia and other places, Catholic claims based on past history rather than present realities in Latin America and Europe and so on. We have had to modify some statistics to adhere to our 100% rule, but always do so in the hope of being as close to reality as possible.

4 **Major focus on the evangelical/charismatic streams of Christianity,** from which come the majority of this book's users. Objective statistics are few. We therefore make percentage estimates for each denomination based on:

a) *Firm local data or estimates.*

b) *The theological position of the denomination.* All denominations considered theologically conservative evangelical were entered as 100% evangelical (see **evangelicals** in Appendix 5 Definitions). All denominations considered charismatic or Pentecostal were entered as 100% charismatic.

c) *General developments within pluralistic denominations,* such as the (Presbyterian) Church of Scotland becoming more evangelical and the African Methodist Episcopal Church becoming more charismatic. Evangelical percentages were entered for 1960-2010 and charismatic percentages for 1990-2010, taking into account what we could know regarding shifts within each group during these periods.

5 **Compatibility with the World Christian Database** (WCD) and *Atlas of Global Christianity*. There are only two extant global statistical surveys of Christianity – the WCD/Atlas and OW. Many readers may never see a copy of the WCD, but we felt it important to point out the issues noted below. Over the years, the authors of these two projects have sought to collaborate as far as possible in sharing information, standardizing categories, agreeing on definitions and converging in key concepts. The two projects serve very different readerships and have different goals. Over all, the high degree of similarity in the global and continental summaries (or the consistency of the factor of difference) despite methodological differences, is a gratifying relief!

a) *The convergences*

   i *Both volumes use the UN continental divisions.* So, totals for continents are comparable.

ii *Both volumes use the UN world population figures* issued in 2008.

iii *The six MegaBlocs of Christianity* were hammered out in much discussion as we wrestled to cope with post-denominationalism and the growing phenomenon of independent groups within Christianity. This led us to readjust some of our MegaBloc and denomination codes to align with the WCD.

iv *Sharing of data and information* from both OW and WCD research was extensive between 1990 and 1998, and between 2005 and 2009. The respective pressures of publication and the project phases focusing on denominational research are reflected by these specific years of data sharing.

b) **The divergences**

i *The Christian MegaBlocs* – WCD and OW use slightly different criteria in assigning post-1945 denominations to the "I" category. OW is more cautious. As a result, Protestants especially – but all other blocs as well – tend to be more numerous, and Independents fewer, than in the WCD.

ii *Denominational data.* Having relationships to different networks and sources, OW and the WCD often inform each other in areas where the other is less strong. Broadly speaking, mainline denominations and Catholic and Anglican groups tend to be more closely linked to the WCD, evangelical and charismatic groups to OW.

iii *Definition of evangelical.* This is, perhaps, the most significant difference between WCD and OW. OW largely continues using the same definition for evangelicals and the same methodology as in past editions. The WCD uses a radically different measure of evangelicals (related to historic denominations with links to the Reformation) and of Great Commission Christians in all MegaBlocs. OW's evangelicals are theologically defined and in size, fall between the WCD's narrower evangelicals and much broader Great Commission Christians.

iv *Handling of charismatic renewal.* At best, any figures are reasonable estimates for most denominations. We are more cautious in OW and tend to use figures for active participants.

6 **To give enhanced value with the publication of the electronic version.** The volume of information is so large that even this 1000-page book can do no more than present a summary for data and information. The electronic version contains much more information. Thus this book has:

a) **Limited listings** of denominations and agencies.

b) **Limited inclusion of charts, maps and other visual resources.** Restrictions of space and colour mean that many further materials are available electronically than are in the book.

c) **No Special Ministries section**, as in past versions. This will be included on the OW website and, in the electronic version.

d) **No sources given.**

e) **Inability to manipulate the data.**

We trust that the electronic version will be a good stimulus for further research and development.

Statistical Sources

A complete bibliography is impossible to provide here! Only some of the more significant sources can be given.

a) Primary Sources

Personal correspondence. For the production of this edition we sent out or received approaching 100,000 e-mails, faxes, personal letters and questionnaires seeking information and to check data and text. We aim to achieve a healthy balance of internal and external perspectives – nationals and expatriates. This is not always achievable, for a host of reasons.

Personal conversations around the world in many providential times of fellowship with key informants, in person, by telephone and by skype.

Numerous surveys and documents as well as circulars and reports produced by individuals and mission agencies. Much of the more significant information gathered has been collated in chronologically-ordered country or subject files – both paper and electronic – located at the OW offices in the UK. They provide a wealth of information much greater than could ever be included between the covers of *Operation World*.

Wide-ranging Internet searches. The revolution of information technology, even from the late 1990s to 2010, has radically altered research and communication. What once took weeks of patient reading, letter-writing and physically researching in libraries can now be achieved in seconds or minutes through Internet search engines, e-mails and phone and skype calls. Despite all this, much information for which we search is not available, simply because adequate research has never been done.

b) Secondary Sources

1 **General** (includes Area, Population, Literacy, Development and Economic data, other).

Britannica Book of the Year, 2007-2009. Published by Encyclopædia Britannica. USA.

Human Development Report. Published by the United Nations Development Programme. Retrieved from hdr.undp.org, 2009. USA.

International Monetary Fund: Data & Statistics. Retrieved from www.imf.org/external/data.htm, 2009-2010. USA.

National censuses, where available.

United Nations Statistics Division. Retrieved from unstats.un.org/unsd/default.htm, 2004-2010. USA.

The World Bank: Data & Research. Retrieved from econ.worldbank.org, 2009-2010. USA.

World Christian Database. Published by Brill. Retrieved from www.worldchristiandatabase.
org, 2005-2010. USA.

The World Factbook. Published by the Central Intelligence Agency. Retrieved from www.cia.
gov, 2004-2010. USA.

2 Religions

Britannica Book of the Year, 2007-2009. Published by Encyclopædia Britannica. USA.

National censuses, where available.

Personal communications with and information sent from Todd Johnson and Peter Crossing,
extracted from their work on the World Christian Database.

World Christian Database. Published by Brill. Retrieved from www.worldchristiandatabase.
org, 2005-2010. USA.

World Christian Encyclopedia. Edited by David B Barrett and Todd M Johnson. Published by
Oxford University Press, 1982, 2001. USA.

3 Peoples and languages

Ethnologue: Languages of the World. Published by SIL International. Retrieved from www.
ethnologue.com, 2004-2010. USA.

Joshua Project database. A ministry of the US Center for World Mission. Retrieved from www.
joshuaproject.net, 2004-2010. USA.

The Omid database. A comprehensive database of traditional castes and tribes of South Asian
countries, compiled in South Asia.

World Christian Database. Published by Brill. Retrieved from www.worldchristiandatabase.
org, 2005-2010. USA.

4 Statistics for specific items

a) Languages and Bible translation

Ethnologue: Languages of the World. Published by SIL International. Retrieved from www.
ethnologue.com, 2004-2010. USA.

Personal correspondence with SIL data experts, such as Ted Bergman and Roger Hanggi,
who assisted with the extraction of valuable data for use in *Operation World.*

b) Denominations

Denominational statistics, handbooks and responses to questionnaires.

National surveys, handbooks and other references from numerous countries.

World Christian Database. Published by Brill. Retrieved from www.worldchristiandata-
base.org, 2005-2010. USA.

c) Missions

Mission Handbook: US and Canadian Protestant Ministries Overseas. Edited by Linda J Weber and
Dotsey Welliver. Published by EMIS, 2000, 2007-2009. USA.

Mission journals and publications.

National surveys. In a number of countries, we had to conduct a national survey by post
because no such survey had been carried out in recent years.

Questionnaires were sent to many hundreds of mission agencies. For those listed in Appendix 3, this was done multiple times between 2004–2010.

UK Christian Handbook. Edited by Heather Wraight. Published by Christian Research, 2004/05, 2007/08. UK.

Other *Operation World* Related Resources

OPERATION WORLD

Operation World: Prayer Map gives you a window into a world in need of prayer. This full-colour 24" by 36" wall map is an effective tool to engage everyone in your home, office, church, classroom or residence hall with the global challenge. The map highlights Operation World data globally and provides unique call-out maps that help you to pray.

Published by GMI (www.gmi.org).

Available from www.operationworld.org

Operation World: Enhanced eBook – Personal CD-ROM Edition is a prayer, research and mobilization tool providing the complete content of *Operation World* (text, tables, charts and maps) as a full-colour PDF. This easy-to-use Enhanced eBook is perfect for using *Operation World* on the go, searching for specific content, and much more.

Published by GMI (www.gmi.org).

Available from www.operationworld.org

Operation World: Enhanced eBook – Professional DVD-ROM Edition is a prayer, research and mobilization platform including all features and content of the Personal CD-ROM. In addition, gain access to *Operation World* content not published in the book:

• Extended global, country, religion, and denominational data tables.

• Multimedia and other presentation resources.

• Additional maps and full-colour graphs for each country.

Ideal for teaching on global evangelization, leading others in prayer for the nations, or engaging in mission research.

Published by GMI (www.gmi.org)

Available from www.operationworld.org

Operation World: Children's Prayer Atlas – link your child to a global prayer movement for kids of every nation! Children learn and pray their way through the world's physically and spiritually diverse regions with these colourful maps and graphs, vivid photographs, curious facts, true stories about kids, and essential points for prayer – all drawn from the wealth of *Operation World* knowledge and its global network of collaborators. An ideal prayer tool for children in your church, Christian school, home school, mission organization or family – and sure to delight adults, too!

Updates on Publisher and release date available from www.operationworld.org

The Future of the Worldwide Church is an expansive overview and unprecedented analysis of the changes in Global Christianity. With unparalleled knowledge and experience, Patrick Johnstone explores the implications of the continuing expansion of the Church, extrapolates previous research on evangelicalism forward to the year 2050 and identifies significant trends and their likely impact on Christian ministry. This volume, in a book/CD-ROM combination, is packed with interpretive maps, charts and timelines and will provide inspiration and tools for strategy and mobilization.

For foreign language editions of *Operation World*, and for updates on future products, please visit the Operation World website at www.operationworld.org.

Frequently Asked Questions (FAQs)

Across the years, we have received regular queries from our readers. We pass these questions and our answers on to you, hoping the information provided will prove useful. Note that *Operation World* is abbreviated throughout as *OW*.

For questions regarding abbreviations found in the text, please see Appendix 4 Abbreviations and Acronyms on p953.

For questions regarding the charts found in the book, please see Explanation of the Statistics and Abbreviations on pviii.

For questions regarding the use of specific terms in the text, please see Appendix 5 Definitions on p957.

Operation World – the Book

Where can I obtain another copy of *OW*?

OW is available in all its formats via our website (www.operationworld.org) or in a variety of retail stores. Support your local Christian bookstore if you have one!

Besides English, is *OW* available in other languages? How can I get a copy of *OW* in another language?

Previous editions of *OW* – or portions thereof – have been translated into 12 languages. Plans are currently in place to translate this edition into Korean, German, Portuguese, Spanish, Chinese, French and Arabic. For information on these translation projects, or to obtain a copy of *OW* in one of these languages, please visit the *OW* website, where links to these translations' publishers will be maintained.

I wish to translate *OW* into another language. Whom do I contact?

We are eager for *OW* to make its way to the hands of intercessors around the world in a language they can understand, and therefore we welcome those willing to undertake the significant task of translation. To begin the process, please contact Pieter Kwant at www.piquanteditions.com.

I wish to share or distribute some of the information in *OW* with my prayer group/ in a presentation/on my website. Is that okay?

We are eager for this information to be shared, that prayers might increase! We also adhere to international laws governing the copyright of published material. Please consult the guidelines found on the copyright page of this book. If you have questions or would like further clarification please contact the publisher.

I have found in the text what I believe to be an error, or information that needs to be updated. How do I submit corrected or new information for use in a future edition?

Together, the OW team and publisher work earnestly to present a resource as accurate as we are able to make it. Regrettably, it is all but impossible to produce a manuscript of such volume and complexity without inaccuracies or mistakes. You'll find a page on the OW website for submitting corrections and updates (as well as disagreements!). If you disagree with our conclusions, please feel free to voice your opinion, but please, first carefully read Appendix 5 Definitions and Appendix 6 Operation World Database before doing so!

When will material be updated next?

A collection of OW team members will remain after the publication of this 2010 edition, all committed to work on related *OW* products and to look toward publication of the next *OW*, should the Lord see fit to provide for such.

Since how we present, consume and interact with information changes at every turn in the 21st Century, we will also look at ways to accelerate the laboriously long publication cycle of *OW*.

Operation World – the Information

Where does OW find the information included?

For a detailed description of source material, please see Appendix 7 Statistical Sources, p967.

Why do you count as "Christian" groups that many evangelicals consider questionable, even heretical?

This is perhaps the most commonly asked question, particularly, why *OW* includes Mormons and Jehovah's Witnesses as Christian denominations. The answer, while perhaps not satisfying, is relatively simple – sociological research typically relies on self-identification as a means of determining inclusion in a group. In other words, if a group claims an allegiance to Christ, *OW* counts them statistically as Christian. If an individual claims affiliation with a particular denomination, *OW* counts them as part of that group. This approach to research is not atypical. Matthew 10:32 and Romans 10:9 are good Scriptures to refer to on this issue.

This means that from a research perspective, the label Christian is not an indicator of theological orthodoxy but of affiliation with a particular tradition or confession of Christianity. Were we to adhere to the theological persuasions of some Christians, no group except their own would be included as truly Christian.

Does this mean OW is unconcerned with theological orthodoxy? Or with biblical teachings?

Not at all! *OW* takes a clear position with regard to Jesus and the Bible, as communicated in The Ethos of *Operation World* (see pi) and throughout the text. The measure for theological orthodoxy in *OW* figures comes not with the label *Christian,* but with the label *evangelical.* This label is based on adherence to four foundational beliefs (see **evangelicals** in Appendix 5 Definitions, p957). Therefore, to ascertain the number of people in a country who adhere to these beliefs, please reference figures related to evangelicals for that country.

For more information, and a more detailed explanation of methodology, please see Appendix 6 Operation World Database. Also, see definitions for both **Christian** and **evangelicals** in Appendix 5 Definitions.

Why, in the Religion section, do I see two different totals for Christians in the same country?

There are two places where Christians are reported in the Religion section of each country – first in the Religions table (given as a Pop %, and as a total Population), then again in the denominations table (given as number of Affiliates for each denomination). The difference is usually a tiny fraction of the total and attributable to rounding performed in calculations. Specifically, in the Religion table, the number of Christians (Population) is calculated by taking the assigned percentage from the 2010 population figure (Pop %), while the Affiliates number in the denominations table is calculated by summing the number of Affiliates given for every denomination for which *OW* collected data.

Whom do you count as a missionary?

In the past decade, the task of determining the number of "missionaries" has become increasingly complex, perhaps more so than any other in *OW*. For more information regarding this question and an explanation of *OW* methodology, see Appendix 3 Further Mission Information. Also, see the definition for *missionary* in Appendix 5 Definitions.

Why are some of the prayer points highlighted?

An additional grey circle around the blue number circle indicates prayer points of special significance. While all points included are vital for prayer, the author believes some to be particularly strategic, needing focused intercession or essential keys to open the door to Kingdom breakthrough and advancement within that country.

Occasionally, this book seems to portray a strong Western bias. Is that true?

OW strongly desires to represent the global Church as experienced by evangelicals of many cultures, regions and Christian confessions. However, the author and many within the team are Western evangelical Christians and cannot extract themselves entirely from either their heritage or the society within which they currently reside. In some cases, this offers a unique strength and vantage point helpful to the global Church. In others it presents a limitation, though one impossible to overcome. To address this potential weakness, representatives of each country – at our initiative – review drafts of their country; we welcome their perspectives, outside of our own, which must be considered.

Why does it take so long to produce a new edition of *OW*?

This edition contains articles on 242 states and territories; each article contains, among many things, information on the denominations present. Acquiring this breadth of data in and of itself requires years of information gathering, researching, praying, networking and more. Once gathered, the data are analyzed and prayer points written; then they are reviewed by contacts made through the research-gathering process. This current edition was completely updated and revised, requiring additional time.

Why is this book so long? Are all these statistics really necessary in a prayer handbook?

Because *OW* is used for many purposes – from an individual's devotional prayer, to prayer conferences, to mission research – the breadth of information is in fact necessary. To gain the informed, global and – we believe – authoritative perspective given in *OW*, substantial research to discover the facts is utterly necessary. From William Carey's *Enquiry* of 1792 to *Operation World* today, God has worked mightily across the centuries through statistics and maps, using them to propel men and women of faith and devotion to the places on earth with the fewest numbers of Christians and mission workers.

Operation World – the Electronic Version and Other Resources

What other formats of *OW* are available?

In addition to the book, the information from this edition is also available in CD/DVD format. Also, we plan to make it available by subscription on our website. The electronic format will go beyond the information printed in this book to include all information in our databases we have available and are able to publish.

What about *OW* apps for my audio player, smart phone or electronic reader?

We plan to explore and develop a variety of *OW* resources for today's new media and tools, including smart phone versions, a version for electronic readers and other media possibilities. Check out the OW website for news on the development of these and other apps.

Will you ever offer an online version that is updated in real time?

We hope to make increasingly greater use of the Internet for distribution of *OW* information, and we hope you find our current website – built around this edition – more user-friendly and content-rich than the previous. There are, however, myriad factors involved in synchronizing the many data streams that shape *OW* information – population, denominational affiliates, religious adherents, polls and censuses and more. Changes to any record in a country, a denomination, or a religion have a cascading effect that alters countless other records and undermines the integrity of our data. Any attempt to feature a "live" and up-to-the-minute version, is not only impossible, but disingenuous.

Why not just put all of *OW* on the web for free?

Unless someone underwrites all the expenses involved in producing *OW*, we must charge in order to recoup the costs of production. All royalties are seeded into a trust fund used to offset the day-to-day operational expenses of this project, to finance production costs of future editions and to assist in publishing other language editions. Remember, all team members are volunteers who receive no personal income from *OW* royalties; they instead trust the Lord to meet their needs, as do missionaries serving in other fields. Other projects of similar scope are either several times more expensive or, if free, are funded by large organizations with multi-million dollar budgets.

Operation World – the Team and Project

How many people work on the team compiling an edition of *OW*?

Team size has fluctuated from one solitary worker to a full house of over ten people. Most team members live and work in the UK, though some work at a distance (either within the UK or elsewhere). The team has, until most recently, been based around production of *OW* the book, and once the book was produced, team members moved on to other pursuits. However, God has recently built a core team of workers committed beyond book publication, which allows us to develop other resources and plan forward for the future ministry of *OW*.

I would like to help work on *OW* – how do I get involved?

Many different skills sets are needed on the OW team and for other projects we engage in. These include, but are not limited to, database development, geographic information systems, web design and development and media/communications. But there are many lesser technical roles as well. You could get involved in two ways:

Volunteer to help short-term. At times, we are able to welcome volunteer help for various tasks or projects, ranging from four weeks to one year.

Long-term service. *OW* has become an ongoing ministry, where the book is but one expression of a larger vision to inform and inspire mission and intercession. OW remains a ministry of WEC, an international mission agency, and most of us serve on the OW team as trained and supported WEC missionaries.

How can I make a donation to the ministry of OW?

To make a charitable contribution to this ministry, contact the WEC office in your country or visit the Operation World website (www.operationworld.org).

What happened to Patrick Johnstone?

Patrick handed leadership of the team and ministry of OW to Jason Mandryk in 2004 in order to focus on other projects and ministry. His role related to *OW* since 2004 has been to support, advise and encourage – from a distance! The fruit of his labours can be seen in the brilliant new book *The Future of the Worldwide Church* (see Appendix 8 Other *Operation World* Related Resources on p970).

Special Matters for Prayer

Leaders of the World's Nations

Political changes in the world occur so rapidly that the names of leaders have generally not been included in the text for individual countries. Yet these leaders need prayer, as the Scriptures exhort us (1 Samuel 12:23, 1 Timothy 2:1-4).

The following websites provide up-to-date lists of leaders, information on government and titular rulers, cabinet members and regional leaders:

http://rulers.org Lists heads of state and heads of government for all countries and territories.

https://www.cia.gov/library/publications/world-leaders-1 Maintained by the CIA (USA).

As pressures on world leaders increase, so do the uncertainties and dangers in the 21st Century. The ones who lead us need special prayer. Pray specifically for:

1 **Good and just rulers to be raised up.** In many instances in history, God has used rulers, whether believers or not, to accomplish His purposes on Earth, for example Cyrus in the Persian Empire. Neither the collapse of Communism nor the spread of democratic governmental systems has ended tyrannies, autocratic power-seekers or corrupt, greedy dictators. Pray that those who are unfit to rule their lands may repent and change (as did Nebuchadnezzar) – or be removed (as were Pharaoh and Belshazzar).

2 **Those who face major crises.** The challenges facing 21st-Century leaders are of an altogether different nature from those of even 50 years ago. As the world becomes more interconnected, crises of many kinds – economic, political, ecological, demographic, military and others – trouble our nations with accelerating frequency. Pray for courage to make right decisions, however unpopular. Compromise of ideals and failure to take decisive action in order to maintain popularity or power are ever-present temptations.

3 **Those who give just and godly leadership, many of whom are committed Christians.** The scrutiny under which many leaders work, combined with the complexity of the challenges before them, make leadership an all-but-impossible task. Leaders make difficult decisions for a majority who may not share their faith. Pray that they may continually stand firm for what is good, moral and just for the nations they rule. Also pray that they neither give way to pressure from those who wish to gain advantage for vested interests, nor push to relax laws that forbid what the Bible clearly names as sin.

4 **Christians to actively promote justice,** righteousness, honest government and wise rule for the good of all in their homelands. In too many cultures, Christians either opt out of the political process, allowing wrong people to rule by default, or they compromise, becoming part of the problem.

Operation World

Response to the previous six editions of *Operation World* has been encouraging. Many faithfully pray through the book, and we regularly receive e-mails and letters that testify of God's guidance for ministry or call to missionary work through *Operation World*. This alone makes the monumental effort behind each edition worthwhile! Areas and peoples, hitherto unevangelized, have been prayed open, entered and churches planted.

We estimate that well over two million copies of all earlier editions have been distributed – over 80% in English, but also in Korean, German, Portuguese, Chinese, Spanish, French, Russian, Czech and others. We are grateful and humbled by reports that these have had a major input in developing a world missions vision in the non-Western world.

Challenges for Prayer

1 **The seventh edition of *Operation World*.** Including all languages and formats, this edition will likely have the widest distribution ever, but the publication world – at least that of *OW* – is still dominated by the English language and the print format. Pray that plans might be realized to get the book into the hands of praying Christians who have not previously encountered *OW*.

2 **Other language editions of *Operation World*.** Plans are underway to translate and publish *OW* in 10 or more languages, including some into which *OW* has not yet been translated. Pray that these editions may be used of God to give a missions vision to growing churches around the world and to further enhance the developing global missions movement, especially in Latin America, Africa and Asia.

3 **The electronic edition of *Operation World*,** both on CD/DVD and on the OW website. The possibilities of electronic media are exciting – to enhance and enrich *OW* content and to keep it more frequently updated and more collaborative – but these require great resources, time and skills.

4 **The Children's Prayer Atlas,** a project already underway. This is a new expression of the same spirit that created *You Can Change the World*, *You Too Can Change the World* and *Window on the World*. Pray that *The Children's Prayer Atlas* might have the same impact as the previous resources, serving to challenge and stimulate children to pray for the world. Pray that, as a result, many might be called of God to serve as missionaries when the time is right. Pray that all these resources may put missions and prayer rightly at the heart of Sunday school curricula the world over!

5 **An easy-English edition.** There are tens of millions of praying Christians for whom English is a second language; an easier-to-understand English version would be a blessing for them, especially for those whose first language does not have a translation of *OW*. Pray for opportunities to get *OW*'s content into countries and languages with economic struggles and lower literacy rates; we are working on solutions to this challenge.

6 **Any future editions of *Operation World*.** The changing way that information is consumed and interacted with, the increasing rate of change in most nations, the higher level of security and confidentiality for most frontier mission situations, the birth and growth of many excellent research and information services in the Church and the changing expectations and demands of a global praying Church mean that Operation World must continually re-examine its role and purpose. If God is leading us to retain our core focus, to adapt slightly, to change radically, or to shut the shop altogether, may we be open to His leading.

7 **The army of helpers and informants around the world** who have contributed to all previous volumes. Pray that their ministries might be blessed, for trust to be built between them and a future *Operation World* team and that the vital flow of information will continue, making future editions possible. It is easy for differences of culture, language, organization, operation, personality and even theology to create occasion for broken fellowship; we constantly pray the Lord's grace over all our dealings and communications.

The Lord's Return

The last prayer in the Bible is "Come, Lord Jesus" (Revelation 22:20). Peter tells us that we should be "waiting for and hastening the coming of the day of God" (2 Peter 3:12 ESV). How better can we do it than by praying for the fulfilment of Genesis 12:3, Revelation 7:9-10 and Matthew 24:14? Pray for:

1 **The speediest possible evangelization of the world,** of every unreached people group, area, city and nation.

2 **The Great Commission to be restored to its rightful centrality** in the ministry of the Church worldwide.

3 **Your part in achieving this.** What is God's will for *your* life? In the coming year, are you willing to do whatever He commands regarding the needs of the world? Is it possible God is calling *you* to a specific ministry in praying, supporting or going to the ends of the earth for your Master?

4 **Your local church's part.** Pray that your fellowship may grow in missionary zeal and commitment in the coming year.